The Story
and Its Writer

NINTH EDITION

THE STORY
AND ITS WRITER

An Introduction to Short Fiction

Ann Charters

University of Connecticut

BEDFORD/ST. MARTIN'S
BOSTON • NEW YORK

For Bedford / St. Martin's
Senior Executive Editor: Stephen A. Scipione
Assistant Director of Development: Maura Shea
Publishing Services Manager: Andrea Cava
Senior Production Supervisor: Dennis J. Conroy
Associate Editor: Sherry Mooney
Project Management: Cenveo Publisher Services
Senior Art Director: Anna Palchik
Text Design: Lisa Buckley Design
Cover Design: Donna Lee Dennison
Cover Art: The Laundromat, by Adrian Tomine
Composition: Cenveo Publisher Services
Printing and Binding: Quad/Graphics

Manufactured in the United States of America.

0   9   8   7
e   d   c   b

For information, write: Bedford / St. Martin's, 75 Arlington Street, Boston, MA 02116 (617-399-4000)

ISBN 978-1-319-12518-9

Acknowledgments

PREFACE

A true work of fiction is a wonderfully simple thing — so simple that most
so-called serious writers avoid trying it, feeling they ought to do something
more important and ingenious, never guessing how incredibly difficult it is.
A true work of fiction does all of the following things, and does them elegantly,
efficiently: it creates a vivid and continuous dream in the reader's mind; it is
implicitly philosophical; it fulfills or at least deals with all of the expectations it
sets up; and it strikes us, in the end, not simply as a thing done but as a shining
performance.

> — John Gardner, "What Writers Do"

If John Gardner's description summarizes what writers of fiction do, then this
anthology was created to enable readers of short fiction to experience their
"shining performance" as elegantly and efficiently as possible. *The Story and
Its Writer* grew out of my desire to teach from an anthology filled as much
as possible with writer talk about short stories. After years of dissatisfaction
using textbooks filled with too much editor talk, I realized the books available
tended to be of two types: textbooks with a limited number of stories and a
cumbersome, often prescriptive, amount of editorial material; or large anthologies with many stories but very little discussion by anyone about matters sure
to be perplexing to students. The first type made the editor the authority; the
second type imposed that role on the teacher. In neither case were the storytellers — those best qualified to speak about fiction — given space to express
their authority about their craft. *The Story and Its Writer* redresses these
imbalances, and its success over eight editions confirms the appeal and usefulness of its premise.

Those looking for good fiction will find it in abundance in *The Story and
Its Writer*: 138 stories in this edition, arranged alphabetically by author. The
stories range from classic tales by Nathaniel Hawthorne and Edgar Allan Poe
through modern masterpieces by Flannery O'Connor and William Faulkner
to contemporary selections from the work of writers such as Jhumpa Lahiri,
Junot Díaz, David Foster Wallace, and of graphic storytellers like Alison
Bechdel and Art Spiegelman. The sheer number and variety of stories offer
plenty of choice and teaching flexibility.

The most distinctive feature of *The Story and Its Writer* is the "Commentaries" section that immediately follows the anthology of stories. These
commentaries — ninety-one in this edition — justify the title of the book. In

most of the commentaries, writers discuss their stories and the stories of fellow writers that appear in the anthology, and more generally remark on the form of the story and the vocation of the storyteller. I also include a sampling of commentaries by literary critics about stories in the anthology, representing different critical perspectives, in the expectation that students will learn something about deploying such tactics in their own reading and writing. Other commentaries are included because they provide the reader with important biographical and historical contexts that illuminate an author or a story. Finally, thirty-five of these commentaries are collected in illustrated "Casebooks" that take an in-depth look at particular writers, including Raymond Carver and Flannery O'Connor, as well as three stories, graphic storytelling, and magical realism. I, and the many instructors who have used the earlier editions, find these commentaries to be just the ingredient to stimulate class discussion and give rise to lively writing.

My own editorial instruction is designed to support students without getting in the way of their reading. Most of it is packed at the back of the book, to be consulted when appropriate, if appropriate. It includes a chapter on the history of the short story, an outline of the elements of fiction, an extensive section on writing about fiction, a glossary of more than one hundred literary terms, a chronological listing of authors and stories, and a thematic index of stories and commentaries. The stories themselves appear with substantial biographical headnotes, but with no other apparatus that might constrain a student's response — no interpretive introductions, no directive questions or assignments.

Those interested in additional editor talk may want to examine the comprehensive instructor's manual, *Resources for Teaching The Story and Its Writer* (described on page vii).

New to This Edition

The ninth edition of *The Story and Its Writer* features forty-two new works, and its representation of women writers, multicultural writers, international writers, and especially contemporary writers is stronger than ever. In recent years, graphic narratives have been embraced by the mainstream, on college campuses, and continue to be vital in this new edition. Students will find graphic stories, including Nora Krug's recent work "Kamikaze," sprinkled throughout the anthology, with ample support to make comparisons between the techniques of traditional forms of fiction and those of a more visually oriented age. Also new to this edition is an emphasis on the literary genre of magical realism. With important and engaging stories by Isabel Allende, Jorge Luis Borges, Alejo Carpentier, Julio Cortázar, Gabriel García Márquez, and others we offer students the opportunity to delve deeply into this ground-breaking and distinctly Latin American genre. An all-new casebook on magical realism completes the exploration, offering a historical overview, contextual images, and commentaries by magical realist writers and those influenced by them. In addition to new stories and commentaries, we have expanded our coverage of close reading in the appendix on Reading Short Stories, and added a Thematic Index to the Stories and Guide to the Commentaries.

Compact Edition and New Compact PDF-Style e-Book

The Story and Its Writer is also available in a Compact Ninth Edition containing eighty stories and fifty-one commentaries. It includes casebooks on Raymond Carver and Flannery O'Connor's fiction, and the genre of magical realism. The shorter edition retains all of the longer book's editorial features for those who want a smaller, less expensive anthology. For the first time, we are offering the compact edition in print or e-Book to Go formats. The e-Book to Go version is a PDF-style e-book that matches the print book page to page, and can be downloaded to your laptop, iPad, tablet, or other device.

Student and Instructor Resources for *The Story and Its Writer*

The Story and Its Writer doesn't stop with a book. Online, you'll find both free and affordable premium resources to help you teach the course and your students to get even more out of it. To learn more about or order any of the products below, contact your Bedford/St. Martin's sales representative, e-mail sales support (sales_support@bfwpub.com), or visit the Web site at **bedfordstmartins.com/chartersstory/catalog**.

- *Resources for Teaching The Story and Its Writer* This manual includes discussions of each story, questions and writing assignments for students, suggested readings, a thematic index of the stories, a guide to the commentaries, and a listing of short stories on film and video. For the PDF version, go to **bedfordstmartins.com/chartersstory/catalog**. To order the print edition, use ISBN 978-1-4576-8396-1.
- *VideoCentral: Literature* This Bedford/St. Martin's production created with writer and teacher Peter Berkow is a growing collection of video interviews with today's writers, talking about their craft. Your students can hear from Ha Jin on how he uses humor and tension in his writing, T. C. Boyle on how he uses language and style, and Anne Rice on how she advances plot through dialogue. For a list of authors and topics and a sample video, visit **bedfordstmartins.com/videolit**. *VideoCentral: Literature* can be packaged free with new student editions of the book. An activation code is required. To order *VideoCentral: Literature* with the print book, use ISBN 978-1-4576-8753-2.
- *Re:Writing for Literature,* **bedfordstmartins.com/rewriting lit** Free and open resources for students on avoiding plagiarism, citing sources, and much more.
- **Literary Reprints** Titles in the Case Studies in Contemporary Criticism series, Bedford Cultural Edition series, and the Bedford College Edition

series can be shrink-wrapped with *The Story and Its Writer* for instructors who want to teach longer works in conjunction with the anthology.

- **TradeUp**   A way to add value and choice to your students' learning experiences. Package their Bedford/St. Martin's textbook with one of a thousand titles from Macmillan publishers at a discount of 50 percent off the publishers' regular price. For more information, go to **bedfordstmartins .com/tradeup**.

Acknowledgments

I wish to acknowledge the help of many people in the preparation and revision of the anthology and the instructor's manual. I want to thank William Sheidley of the University of Southern Colorado, whose insightful commentaries on many stories that appear in *The Story and Its Writer* can be found in the instructor's manual. Thanks also to past and present graduate students whose work helped shape the manual from edition to edition: Martha Ramsey, Robert Gaspar, Dennis Lazor, Maureen Grogan, Patricia Vincent, and Ning Yu. My colleagues in the English Department at the University of Connecticut — Lee Jacobus, Scott Bradfield, Compton Rees, William Curtin, Milton Stern, Jack Davis, Jack Manning, Michael Meyer, Francelia Butler, and Feenie Ziner — generously contributed suggestions and advice. I am grateful to Herbert Lederer, emeritus professor of German at the University of Connecticut, for serving as an experienced and knowledgeable consultant for the translation of the Kafka stories into American English, and to Kurt Fendt of MIT for double-checking the translations and offering good advice. The staff at the Homer Babbidge Library, especially Leanne Pander, Pamela Skinner, David McChesney, Carol Abramson, and David Garnes, gave unflagging assistance. Students in my short story classes diligently drafted the sample essays illustrating the various ways to write about stories. Charles Flynn of the Rockefeller Library and Emily Medeiros and Clare Durst of the Dean of the College Office at Brown University were also particularly helpful.

In addition, professors who used the previous editions of the anthology and generously took time to share their ideas about it include Steven Almquist, Spring Hill College; Kathaleen Amende, Alabama State University; Eleni Anastasiou, University of Pittsburgh; Noreen Bider, Vanier College; Nathan Breen, College of Lake County; James Brown, California State University at San Bernardino; Gene Browning, Austin Community College; Keith Carver, Western Michigan University; Erica Ciccarone, Borough of Manhattan Community College; Susan Dalton, Alamance Community College; Laura Eidam, Purdue University; James Freeman, Bucks County Community College; Jonathan Gagas, Temple University; Sheryl Gifford, Florida Atlantic University; Rachel Golland, St. Thomas Aquinas College; Elaine Harrington, University of Vermont; Graley Herren, Xavier University; Thomas Hitchner, Orange Coast College; Martina Holliday, Butler County Community College; Bernard Kaplan, University of Delaware; Kathleen Kenney, Lakes Region Community College; Nathanael Myers, Weber State University; William Nedrow,

Triton College; Andrea Nolan, Old Dominion University; Joe O'Connell, Austin Community College; Esther Otwell, Tarleton State University; Jennifer Read, Capilano University; Frederick Redman, Florida Atlantic University; Mauricio Rodriguez, El Paso Community College; Becky Rudd, Citrus College; Melanie Trost, Tiffin University; Steven Werkmeister, Johnson County Community College; Ryan Wilcox, University of Massachusetts Lowell; and Dominika Wrozynski, Florida State University. I thank them for their help and encouragement, which made the task of revising *The Story and Its Writer* a challenging and enjoyable one.

In preparing the ninth edition of *The Story and Its Writer*, I am grateful to senior executive editor Steve Scipione and assistant director of development Maura Shea, who offered expert advice throughout development. Others at Bedford/St. Martin's who helped with this edition include Denise Wydra and Karen Henry for their ideas and direction; associate editor Sherry Mooney for her thorough and invaluable research; text permissions editor Virginia Creeden and art permissions editor Sarah D'Stair; and especially my conscientious production editors, Janette Krauss and Andrea Cava. In the English Department of the University of Connecticut, I am grateful to Professors Tom Roberts, Margaret Higgonet, Patrick Hogan, and Lisa Sanchez, and graduate student A. Robin Hoffman. Last, but by no means least, I particularly want to thank my husband, Samuel Charters, my daughters, Mallay and Nora, and my friends Jennifer Hartig, Mel and Bob Chatain, Suzie Staubach, Jenny Schuessler, Rolf Lunden, Rosetta Reitz, Marsha Kramer, and Glenn Occhiogrosso for sharing their ideas about short fiction during the preparation of this and earlier editions of the anthology.

Ann Charters
Storrs, Connecticut

CONTENTS

Part Two: Commentaries   1381

Part Three: Casebooks 1539

Part Four: Appendices 1665

The Story
and Its Writer

THE STORY
AND ITS WRITER

Read literature for the pleasure of it, Ernest Hemingway once told an interviewer, adding, "Whatever else you find will be the measure of what you brought to the reading." The stories in this anthology represent a range of great short fiction written by authors from all over the world. I hope you will find them a pleasure to read. We all have different personalities and come from different backgrounds, but we all look forward to being entertained when we turn to a story.

Reading short fiction attentively and imaginatively promises further pleasure — the enjoyment of how the storyteller uses language to create that miracle called a work of art. This way of reading brings us closer to understanding the achievement of the stories in this anthology and their writers. Literature is invention, and storytellers are inventors, whether they appear in the guise of entertainers, teachers, or enchanters. The authors whose stories are collected here are experts at invention. They delight us most completely when we apprehend the genius of their art by studying how they select the details and shape the patterns of their fiction.

What Is a Short Story?

The literary form *short story* is usually defined as a brief fictional prose narrative, most often involving one unified episode. Early in the nineteenth century the American writer Edgar Allan Poe was one of the first to attempt an analysis of the short story's aesthetic properties. He stressed *unity* of effect as the story's most characteristic feature. Since the flood of events we experience in life is rarely unified by a single impression, in a sense all fiction — whether short story, long story, or novel — is "lies." Paradoxically, however, the measure of success for all fiction is how *true* it is to our emotions, how accurately it reflects the life we all live.

The short story is a concentrated form, dependent for its success on feeling and suggestion. When readers understand the ways an author uses language to create a fictional world, the story's unity has an even greater impact. Then every detail of the narrative adds to our enjoyment of its final impression. Writers of short stories must forgo the comprehensiveness of the novel, but they often gain a striking compression by using language with the force of poetry. Like poets, short story writers can impress upon us the unity of their vision of life by focusing on a single effect.

The range and quality of the writer's mind are the only limitations on a story's shape. Authors create narratives using different elements of fiction. Among their most important resources are *plot,* the sequence of related events composing the narrative, and *characters,* the persons who play their parts in the narrative. The author's choice of *setting,* the place and time in which the action occurs, helps to give the story verisimilitude. The *point of view* establishes a consistent perspective on the characters and their actions as the narrative unfolds. The author's literary *style,* the way he or she uses the multifarious resources of language, also shapes the expression of a story. Finally, the author is guided by his or her perception of *theme,* the unifying idea suggesting the values of the writer that brings to life all the other elements of fiction.

Without human understanding, experience is "the worst kind of emptiness," wrote the short story author Eudora Welty in her essay "Words into Fiction." All stories embody a personal vision when the elements of plot, character, setting, point of view, style, and theme are set in motion by the writer's perception of the mystery and magic of everyday life. Authors of fiction are free to invent and shape experience to the fullest extent of their imaginations.

Human understanding is not the exclusive privilege of the writer, of course. It functions in the reader too. Fiction created by the imagination of the writer for the imagination of the reader is an illusion come full circle. If the story is well told, our imaginations will be involved in it. If the story is a success, our imaginations will be ignited.

For most readers, the basic appeal of storytelling lies in the unity of the narrative pattern, suggesting connections and coherence in experience. When writers go beyond this appeal and ignite our imaginations, they do so by touching us intellectually and emotionally through language. Using the elements of fiction, they enchant us by evoking our thoughts and feelings about the mysteries of human experience. Then we catch a glimpse of what life is like from its reflection in the story.

Reading Short Stories

The meaning of the story (its truth, vision, or reflection of the world) is, in part, a result of the reader's response to it. As Hemingway said, read literature for the pleasure it brings. Anything else *you* must bring to the reading. A story becomes more meaningful when you read actively, relating the author's personal vision embodied in the form and content of the narrative to your own experience of life and the questions you ask of it.

What is the best way to read a short story? The writer Vladimir Nabokov once suggested that the ideal reader should develop "a combination of the artistic and the scientific [temperament]. The enthusiastic artist alone is apt to be too subjective in his attitude towards a book, and so a scientific coolness of judgment will temper the intuitive heat." Read a story the first time for pleasure; bring out your "scientific coolness" when you study it the second time.

The first time you read a story, you may find yourself concerned primarily with *arriving* at the end of the narrative, seeing how the author resolves the plot. The second time, however, you can focus on *getting there,* seeing how the author invents and shapes the narrative by using the elements of fiction. Study each story closely. As the novelist John Gardner understood,

> For most readers, complete emotional grasp of a good piece of fiction does not come automatically. The chief reason is that the inexperienced reader often takes too much of the story for granted. He fails to be pleased by excellent touches in characterization because he accepts uncritically all characterization, competent or incompetent, wherever he finds it; and he fails to empathize with characters because he has missed characterization and thus does not know how the characters feel. He fails to recognize a convincing or interesting action or plot because, like a child in front of a television set, he is interested in any action whatsoever, or worse, because he is hoping to encounter some *other* action. He fails to recognize an inter-esting and effectively used setting because he mistakes fiction for fact and thus assumes that the setting could not be other than it is. And he fails to recognize an interesting exploration of theme because he has never noticed that fiction concerns itself with values. In the beginning, the reader must study stories closely and open-mindedly and must discipline himself to catch emotional qualities whether or not the story seems at first glance to deserve such study.

Ideally, you should keep a little aloof, a little detached when reading the second time. Cherish the details of the story's pattern. Enjoy the pleasure of beginning to understand its magic by taking notes on your response to the author's use of the different elements of fiction.

The best way to give short stories a chance to enchant you is to sit down, preferably with a dictionary at your side, and grant them your full attention. Then read them carefully straight through from beginning to end. Try to avoid what the author William Gass described in "On Reading to Oneself" as "the sullenness of inattention, the annoying static of distraction." Concentrate so that the words of the story can live within you. Understand, as Gass recog-nized, that the words of a writer in a story move only as the reader moves them: "It is like cycling, reading is. Can you feel the air, the pure passage of the spirit past the exposed skin?"

Unless you give the stories your complete attention, the magic of their artistry will never have the chance to make you care about them. As readers we can participate in the creative process of storytelling. The critic Alexandra Schwartz analyzed the intimacy between "the real mind" of the reader and "the invented mind" of the fictional characters. She found that our close attention to the text enables us "to be entirely incorporated into their way of taking mea-sure of the world, to become so guided by their consciousness that it comes to feel, strangely, inadvertently, without warning, nearly as familiar" as our own. She believed that our total absorption in a story is "why anyone bothers to read fiction at all: to be made to see differently, to find ourselves, if only for a moment, going through the world as someone else." Perhaps the storyteller T.C. Boyle defined the reader's task most succinctly when he said, "My job is to put you in the situation. Your job is to experience it."

How This Book Is Organized

The Story and Its Writer is organized in four parts. In the first the stories themselves appear, introduced by headnotes about the authors that highlight their personal and intellectual backgrounds and their intentions as writers of short fiction. The date preceding each story is the year it was published. To make it easier for you to find particular stories, they are presented alphabetically by their authors' names. The table of contents has a listing of stories and the related commentaries, stories, and casebooks found within this book.

The second part, the commentaries, gathers statements by authors about their practice and theory of writing short fiction, including discussion of the meanings of some individual stories. Different critical approaches to stimulate your responses to the stories are also included here.

The third part consists of casebooks grouping several commentaries on important writers and stories: Raymond Carver, Flannery O'Connor, James Baldwin's "Sonny's Blues," Charlotte Perkins Gilman's "The Yellow Wallpaper," and Joyce Carol Oates's "Where Are You Going, Where Have You Been?" This part concludes with a casebook on magical realism focusing on the work of writers such as Jorge Luis Borges, Alejo Carpentier, and Julio Cortázar and one on graphic storytelling — that is, narration through cartoons and images — focusing on the work of Alison Bechdel, Marjane Satrapi, and Joe Sacco.

The fourth part of the anthology presents an appendix on reading short stories, an analysis of the elements of fiction, a brief history of the short story, an explanation of various ways to write papers about short stories, a concise discussion of literary theory and critical perspectives, a glossary of important literary terms, a thematic index, and a chronological listing of the authors and the stories.

PART ONE

STORIES

Chinua Achebe

Chinua Achebe (1930–2013) was born and grew up in Ogidi in eastern Nigeria, the son of devout Christian parents. He recalled that in his childhood "the bounties of the Christian God were not to be taken lightly—education, paid jobs, and many other advantages that nobody in his right senses could underrate." As a member of the Ibo tribe, his first language was Igbo, which he said was "spoken with such eloquence by the old men of the village"; he learned English at the age of eight. After graduating from the University College of Ibadan, Achebe began a career in radio. In 1966 he resigned as director of external broadcasting in Nigeria and joined the Biafran Ministry of Information to help raise funds for his compatriots in the upheaval of the Biafran War. When Nigeria was put under military rule, he left the country to teach. While on the faculty of the University of Massachusetts, Amherst, he gave a controversial chancellor's lecture titled "Racism in Conrad's 'Heart of Darkness,'" which was later published in his collection of essays *Hopes and Impediments* (1988).

Achebe said he began to think about becoming a writer after reading "some appalling novels about Africa" written by European authors. These made him decide, while still a student, "that the story we had to tell could not be told for us by anyone else no matter how gifted or well-intentioned." As the writer Chimamanda Ngozi Adichie realized, he "began to understand the enormous power that stories had, and how much this power was shaped by how they were told." Achebe won acclaim with his first novel, *Things Fall Apart* (1958), a brilliant depiction of the decay of an African state under the impact of Europe. It was the first part of *The African Trilogy: Things Fall Apart; No Longer at Ease; Arrow of God,* completed in 2010. Some other books include his short story collection *Girls at War* (1973) and his novel *Anthills of the Savannah* (1988). A paraplegic after an automobile accident in 1990, Achebe lived in the United States and published an essay collection, *Home and Exile*, in 2000. In 2007 he was awarded the Man Booker International Prize.

The story "Civil Peace" dramatizes Achebe's awareness of catastrophic disturbances in the lives of ordinary people in war-torn Nigeria. He believed that Africans have always lived in what he called "the crossroads of cultures."

> We still do today, but when I was a boy one could see and sense the peculiar quality and atmosphere of it more clearly. I am not talking about all that rubbish we hear of the spiritual void and mental stresses that Africans are supposed to have, or the evil forces and irrational passions prowling through Africa's heart of darkness. We know the racist mystique behind a lot of that stuff.... What I do remember is a fascination for the ritual and the life on the other arm of the crossroads.

RELATED COMMENTARY
Chinua Achebe, "An Image of Africa: Racism in Conrad's 'Heart of Darkness,'"
page 1385.

Civil Peace

1971

JONATHAN IWEGBU COUNTED himself extraordinarily lucky. "Happy survival!" meant so much more to him than just a current fashion of greeting old friends in the first hazy days of peace. It went deep to his heart. He had come out of the war with five inestimable blessings — his head, his wife Maria's head, and the heads of three out of their four children. As a bonus he also had his old bicycle — a miracle too but naturally not to be compared to the safety of five human heads.

The bicycle had a little history of its own. One day at the height of the war it was commandeered "for urgent military action." Hard as its loss would have been to him he would still have let it go without a thought had he not had some doubts about the genuineness of the officer. It wasn't his disreputable rags, nor the toes peeping out of one blue and one brown canvas shoes, nor yet the two stars of his rank done obviously in a hurry in Biro, that troubled Jonathan; many good and heroic soldiers looked the same or worse. It was rather a certain lack of grip and firmness in his manner. So Jonathan, suspecting he might be amenable to influence, rummaged in his raffia bag and produced the two pounds with which he had been going to buy firewood which his wife, Maria, retailed to camp officials for extra stock-fish and corn meal, and got his bicycle back. That night he buried it in the little clearing in the bush where the dead of the camp, including his own youngest son, were buried. When he dug it up again a year later after the surrender all it needed was a little palm-oil greasing. "Nothing puzzles God," he said in wonder.

He put it to immediate use as a taxi and accumulated a small pile of Biafran money ferrying camp officials and their families across the four-mile stretch to the nearest tarred road. His standard charge per trip was six pounds and those who had the money were only glad to be rid of some of it in this way. At the end of a fortnight he had made a small fortune of one hundred and fifteen pounds.

Then he made the journey to Enugu and found another miracle waiting for him. It was unbelievable. He rubbed his eyes and looked again and it was still standing there before him. But, needless to say, even that monumental blessing must be accounted also totally inferior to the five heads in the family. This newest miracle was his little house in Ogui Overside. Indeed nothing puzzles God! Only two houses away a huge concrete edifice some wealthy contractor had put up just before the war was a mountain of rubble. And here was Jonathan's little zinc house of no regrets built with mud blocks quite intact! Of course the doors and windows were missing and five sheets off the roof. But what was that? And anyhow he had returned to Enugu early enough to pick up bits of old zinc and wood and soggy sheets of cardboard lying around the neighbourhood before thousands more came out of their forest holes looking for the same things. He got a destitute carpenter with one old hammer, a blunt plane, and a few bent and rusty nails in his tool bag to turn this assortment of wood, paper, and metal into door and window shutters for five Nigerian shillings or fifty Biafran pounds. He paid the pounds, and moved in with his overjoyed family carrying five heads on their shoulders.

His children picked mangoes near the military cemetery and sold them to soldiers' wives for a few pennies — real pennies this time — and his wife started making breakfast akara balls for neighbours in a hurry to start life again. With his family earnings he took his bicycle to the villages around and bought fresh palm-wine which he mixed generously in his rooms with the water which had recently started running again in the public tap down the road, and opened up a bar for soldiers and other lucky people with good money.

At first he went daily, then every other day, and finally once a week, to the offices of the Coal Corporation where he used to be a miner, to find out what was what. The only thing he did find out in the end was that that little house of his was even a greater blessing than he had thought. Some of his fellow ex-miners who had nowhere to return at the end of the day's waiting just slept outside the doors of the offices and cooked what meal they could scrounge together in Bournvita tins. As the weeks lengthened and still nobody could say what was what Jonathan discontinued his weekly visits altogether and faced his palm-wine bar.

But nothing puzzles God. Came the day of the windfall when after five days of endless scuffles in queues and counter-queues in the sun outside the Treasury he had twenty pounds counted into his palms as ex-gratia award for the rebel money he had turned in. It was like Christmas for him and for many others like him when the payments began. They called it (since few could manage its proper official name) *egg-rasher.*

As soon as the pound notes were placed in his palm Jonathan simply closed it tight over them and buried fist and money inside his trouser pocket. He had to be extra careful because he had seen a man a couple of days earlier collapse into near-madness in an instant before that oceanic crowd because no sooner had he got his twenty pounds than some heartless ruffian picked it off him. Though it was not right that a man in such an extremity of agony should be blamed yet many in the queues that day were able to remark quietly on the victim's carelessness, especially after he pulled out the innards of his pocket and revealed a hole in it big enough to pass a thief's head. But of course he had insisted that the money had been in the other pocket, pulling it out too to show its comparative wholeness. So one had to be careful.

Jonathan soon transferred the money to his left hand and pocket so as to leave his right free for shaking hands should the need arise, though by fixing his gaze at such an elevation as to miss all approaching human faces he made sure that the need did not arise, until he got home.

He was normally a heavy sleeper but that night he heard all the neighbourhood noises die down one after another. Even the night watchman who knocked the hour on some metal somewhere in the distance had fallen silent after knocking one o'clock. That must have been the last thought in Jonathan's mind before he was finally carried away himself. He couldn't have been gone for long, though, when he was violently awakened again.

"Who is knocking?" whispered his wife lying beside him on the floor.

"I don't know," he whispered back breathlessly.

The second time the knocking came it was so loud and imperious that the rickety old door could have fallen down.

"Who is knocking?" he asked then, his voice parched and trembling.

"Na tief-man and him people," came the cool reply. "Make you hopen de door." This was followed by the heaviest knocking of all.

Maria was the first to raise the alarm, then he followed and all their children.

"Police-o! Thieves-o! Neighbours-o! Police-o! We are lost! We are dead! Neighbours, are you asleep? Wake up! Police-o!"

This went on for a long time and then stopped suddenly. Perhaps they had scared the thief away. There was total silence. But only for a short while.

"You done finish?" asked the voice outside. "Make we help you small. Oya, everybody!"

"Police-o! Tief-man-o! Neighbours-o! we done loss-o! Police-o! . . ."

There were at least five other voices besides the leader's.

Jonathan and his family were now completely paralysed by terror. Maria and the children sobbed inaudibly like lost souls. Jonathan groaned continuously.

The silence that followed the thieves' alarm vibrated horribly. Jonathan all but begged their leader to speak again and be done with it.

"My frien," said he at long last, "we don try our best for call dem but I tink say dem all done sleep-o . . . So wetin we go do now? Sometaim you wan call soja? Or you wan make we call dem for you? Soja better pass police. No be so?"

"Na so!" replied his men. Jonathan thought he heard even more voices now than before and groaned heavily. His legs were sagging under him and his throat felt like sandpaper.

"My frien, why you no de talk again. I de ask you say you wan make we call soja?"

"No."

"Awrighto. Now make we talk business. We no be bad tief. We no like for make trouble. Trouble done finish. War done finish and all the katakata wey de for inside. No Civil War again. This time na Civil Peace. No be so?"

"Na so!" answered the horrible chorus.

"What do you want from me? I am a poor man. Everything I had went with this war. Why do you come to me? You know people who have money. We . . . "

"Awright! We know say you no get plenty money. But we sef no get even anini. So derefore make you open dis window and give us one hundred pound and we go commot. Orderwise we de come for inside now to show you guitar-boy like dis . . . "

A volley of automatic fire rang through the sky. Maria and the children began to weep aloud again.

"Ah, missisi de cry again. No need for dat. We done talk say we na good tief. We just take our small money and go nwayorly. No molest. Abi we de molest?"

"At all!" sang the chorus.

"My friends," began Jonathan hoarsely. "I hear what you say and I thank you. If I had one hundred pounds . . . "

"Lookia my frien, no be play we come play for your house. If we make mistake and step for inside you no go like am-o. So derefore . . . "

"To God who made me; if you come inside and find one hundred pounds, take it and shoot me and shoot my wife and children. I swear to God. The only money I have in this life is this twenty pounds *egg-rasher* they gave me today . . . "

"OK. Time de go. Make you open dis window and bring the twenty pound. We go manage am like dat."

There were now loud murmurs of dissent among the chorus: "Na lie de man de lie; e get plenty money . . . Make we go inside and search properly well . . . Wetin be twenty pound? . . . "

"Shurrup!" rang the leader's voice like a lone shot in the sky and silenced the murmuring at once. "Are you dere? Bring the money quick!"

"I am coming," said Jonathan fumbling in the darkness with the key of the small wooden box he kept by his side on the mat.

At the first sign of light as neighbours and others assembled to commiserate with him he was already strapping his five-gallon demijohn to his bicycle carrier and his wife, sweating in the open fire, was turning over akara balls in a wide clay bowl of boiling oil. In the corner his eldest son was rinsing out dregs of yesterday's palm-wine from old beer bottles.

"I count it as nothing," he told his sympathizers, his eyes on the rope he was tying. "What is *egg-rasher*? Did I depend on it last week? Or is it greater than other things that went with the war? I say, let *egg-rasher* perish in the flames! Let it go where everything else has gone. Nothing puzzles God."

Sherman Alexie

Sherman Alexie (b. 1966) was born in Spokane, Washington. A registered member of the Spokane tribe through his mother, he attended grammar school on the Spokane reservation in Wellpinit, Washington. At Washington State University he found an anthology of Indian poetry in his first college literature class and discovered that women were paying more attention to him. "All these years I thought basketball would do it," he says humorously. "I should have been writing poems all along." After Alexie took a creative writing course with Alex Kuo, he began to publish in magazines such as *The Beloit Poetry Journal, The Journal of Ethnic Studies, New York Quarterly, Ploughshares*, and *Zyzzyva*. In 1991 he was awarded a poetry fellowship from the Washington State Arts Commission; the following year he received a poetry fellowship from the National Endowment for the Arts.

In 1992 Alexie published his first two books, *I Would Steal Horses* and *The Business of Fancydancing: Stories and Poems*. Several more titles followed in rapid order, including *The Lone Ranger and Tonto Fistfight in Heaven* (1993), which received a PEN/Hemingway Award for best first book of fiction. Alexie also won the American Book Award for his novel *Reservation Blues* (1995), in which he imagined what would happen if the legendary bluesman Robert Johnson were resurrected on the Spokane Indian Reservation. His film *Smoke Signals* won prizes at the Sundance Film Festival. In 2007 he was awarded the Western Literature Association's Distinguished Achievement Award.

Alexie has stated, "I am a Spokane/Coeur d'Alene Indian from Wellpinit, Washington, where I live on the Spokane Indian Reservation. Everything I do now, writing and otherwise, has its origin in that." His short fiction, like "The Lone Ranger and Tonto Fistfight in Heaven," reflects his use of the icons of popular culture—radio and television programs, 7-Eleven stores, the neon promise of advertising—to facilitate a rapid crossover between storyteller and reader. As the critic Susan B. Brill has noticed, "Little ever changes in the lives of Alexie's characters. Commodity food, alcoholism, and desperation are constants in the stories." *Ten Little Indians* (2003), *War Dances* (2009), and *Blasphemy: New and Selected Stories* (2012), are other story collections.

RELATED COMMENTARY
Sherman Alexie, "Superman and Me," page 1390.

The Lone Ranger and Tonto Fistfight in Heaven

1993

TOO HOT TO SLEEP so I walked down to the Third Avenue 7-11 for a Creamsicle and the company of a graveyard-shift cashier. I know that game. I worked graveyard for a Seattle 7-11 and got robbed once too often. The last time the bastard locked me in the cooler. He even took my money and basketball shoes.

The graveyard-shift worker in the Third Avenue 7-11 looked like they all do. Acne scars and a bad haircut, work pants that showed off his white socks, and those cheap black shoes that have no support. My arches still ache from my year at the Seattle 7-11.

"Hello," he asked when I walked into his store. "How you doing?"

I gave him a half-wave as I headed back to the freezer. He looked me over so he could describe me to the police later. I knew the look. One of my old girl-friends said I started to look at her that way, too. She left me not long after that. No, I left her and don't blame her for anything. That's how it happened. When one person starts to look at another like a criminal, then the love is over. It's logical.

"I don't trust you," she said to me. "You get too angry."

She was white and I lived with her in Seattle. Some nights we fought so bad that I would just get in my car and drive all night, only stop to fill up on gas. In fact, I worked the graveyard shift to spend as much time away from her as possible. But I learned all about Seattle that way, driving its back ways and dirty alleys.

Sometimes, though, I would forget where I was and get lost. I'd drive for hours, searching for something familiar. Seems like I'd spent my whole life that way, looking for anything I recognized. Once, I ended up in a nice residential neighborhood and somebody must have been worried because the police showed up and pulled me over.

"What are you doing out here?" the police officer asked me as he looked over my license and registration.

"I'm lost."

"Well, where are you supposed to be?" he asked me, and I knew there were plenty of places I wanted to be, but none where I was supposed to be.

"I got in a fight with my girlfriend," I said. "I was just driving around, blowing off steam, you know?"

"Well, you should be more careful where you drive," the officer said. "You're making people nervous. You don't fit the profile of the neighborhood."

I wanted to tell him that I didn't really fit the profile of the country but I knew it would just get me into trouble.

"Can I help you?" the 7-11 clerk asked me loudly, searching for some response that would reassure him that I wasn't an armed robber. He knew this dark skin and long, black hair of mine was dangerous. I had potential.

"Just getting a Creamsicle," I said after a long interval. It was a sick twist to pull on the guy, but it was late and I was bored. I grabbed my Creamsicle and walked back to the counter slowly, scanned the aisles for effect. I wanted to whistle low and menacingly but I never learned to whistle.

"Pretty hot out tonight?" he asked, that old rhetorical weather bullshit question designed to put us both at ease.

"Hot enough to make you go crazy," I said and smiled. He swallowed hard like a white man does in those situations. I looked him over. Same old green, red, and white 7-11 jacket and thick glasses. But he wasn't ugly, just misplaced and marked by loneliness. If he wasn't working there that night, he'd be at home alone, flipping through channels and wishing he could afford HBO or Showtime.

"Will this be all?" he asked me, in that company effort to make me do some impulse shopping. Like adding a clause onto a treaty. *We'll take Washington and Oregon, and you get six pine trees and a brand-new Chrysler Cordoba.* I knew how to make and break promises.

"No," I said and paused. "Give me a Cherry Slushie, too."

"What size?" he asked, relieved.

"Large," I said, and he turned his back to me to make the drink. He realized his mistake but it was too late. He stiffened, ready for the gunshot or the blow behind the ear. When it didn't come, he turned back to me.

"I'm sorry," he said. "What size did you say?"

"Small," I said and changed the story.

"But I thought you said large."

"If you knew I wanted a large, then why did you ask me again?" I asked him and laughed. He looked at me, couldn't decide if I was giving him serious shit or just goofing. There was something about him I liked, even if it was three in the morning and he was white.

"Hey," I said. "Forget the Slushie. What I want to know is if you know all the words to the theme from 'The Brady Bunch'?"

He looked at me, confused at first, then laughed.

"Shit," he said. "I was hoping you weren't crazy. You were scaring me."

"Well, I'm going to get crazy if you don't know the words."

He laughed loudly then, told me to take the Creamsicle for free. He was the graveyard-shift manager and those little demonstrations of power tickled him. All seventy-five cents of it. I knew how much everything cost.

"Thanks," I said to him and walked out the door. I took my time walking home, let the heat of the night melt the Creamsicle all over my hand. At three in the morning I could act just as young as I wanted to act. There was no one around to ask me to grow up.

In Seattle, I broke lamps. She and I would argue and I'd break a lamp, just pick it up and throw it down. At first she'd buy replacement lamps, expensive and beautiful. But after a while she'd buy lamps from Goodwill or garage sales. Then she just gave up the idea entirely and we'd argue in the dark.

"You're just like your brother," she'd yell. "Drunk all the time and stupid."

"My brother don't drink that much."

She and I never tried to hurt each other physically. I did love her, after all, and she loved me. But those arguments were just as damaging as a fist. Words can be like that, you know? Whenever I get into arguments now, I remember her and I also remember Muhammad Ali. He knew the power of his fists but, more importantly, he knew the power of his words, too. Even though he only had an IQ of 80 or so, Ali was a genius. And she was a genius, too. She knew exactly what to say to cause me the most pain.

But don't get me wrong. I walked through that relationship with an executioner's hood. Or more appropriately, with war paint and sharp arrows. She was a kindergarten teacher and I continually insulted her for that.

"Hey, schoolmarm," I asked. "Did your kids teach you anything new today?"

And I always had crazy dreams. I always have had them, but it seemed they became nightmares more often in Seattle.

In one dream, she was a missionary's wife and I was a minor war chief. We fell in love and tried to keep it secret. But the missionary caught us fucking in the barn and shot me. As I lay dying, my tribe learned of the shooting and attacked the whites all across the reservation. I died and my soul drifted above the reservation.

Disembodied, I could see everything that was happening. Whites killing Indians and Indians killing whites. At first it was small, just my tribe and the few whites who lived there. But my dream grew, intensified. Other tribes arrived on horseback to continue the slaughter of whites, and the United States Cavalry rode into battle.

The most vivid image of that dream stays with me. Three mounted soldiers played polo with a dead Indian woman's head. When I first dreamed it, I thought it was just a product of my anger and imagination. But since then, I've read similar accounts of that kind of evil in the old West. Even more terrifying, though, is the fact that those kinds of brutal things are happening today in places like El Salvador.

All I know for sure, though, is that I woke from that dream in terror, packed up all my possessions, and left Seattle in the middle of the night.

"I love you," she said as I left her. "And don't ever come back."

I drove through the night, over the Cascades, down into the plains of central Washington, and back home to the Spokane Indian Reservation.

When I finished the Creamsicle that the 7-11 clerk gave me, I held the wooden stick up into the air and shouted out very loudly. A couple lights flashed on in windows and a police car cruised by me a few minutes later. I waved to the men in blue and they waved back accidentally. When I got home it was still too hot to sleep so I picked up a week-old newspaper from the floor and read.

There was another civil war, another terrorist bomb exploded, and one more plane crashed and all aboard were presumed dead. The crime rate was rising in every city with populations larger than 100,000, and a farmer in Iowa shot his banker after foreclosure on his 1,000 acres.

A kid from Spokane won the local spelling bee by spelling the word *rhinoceros*.

When I got back to the reservation, my family wasn't surprised to see me. They'd been expecting me back since the day I left for Seattle. There's an old Indian poet who said that Indians can reside in the city, but they can never live there. That's as close to truth as any of us can get.

Mostly I watched television. For weeks I flipped through channels, searched for answers in the game shows and soap operas. My mother would circle the want ads in red and hand the paper to me.

"What are you going to do with the rest of your life?" she asked.

"Don't know," I said, and normally, for almost any other Indian in the country, that would have been a perfectly fine answer. But I was special, a former college student, a smart kid. I was one of those Indians who was supposed to make it, to rise above the rest of the reservation like a fucking eagle or something. I was the new kind of warrior.

For a few months I didn't even look at the want ads my mother circled, just left the newspaper where she had set it down. After a while, though, I got tired of television and started to play basketball again. I'd been a good player in high school, nearly great, and almost played at the college I attended for a couple years. But I'd been too out of shape from drinking and sadness to ever be good again. Still, I liked the way the ball felt in my hands and the way my feet felt inside my shoes.

At first I just shot baskets by myself. It was selfish, and I also wanted to learn the game again before I played against anybody else. Since I had been good before and embarrassed fellow tribal members, I knew they would want to take revenge on me. Forget about the cowboys versus Indians business. The most intense competition on any reservation is Indians versus Indians.

But on the night I was ready to play for real, there was this white guy at the gym, playing with all the Indians.

"Who is that?" I asked Jimmy Seyler.

"He's the new BIA[1] chief's kid."

"Can he play?"

"Oh, yeah."

And he could play. He played Indian ball, fast and loose, better than all the Indians there.

"How long's he been playing here?" I asked.

"Long enough."

I stretched my muscles, and everybody watched me. All these Indians watched one of their old and dusty heroes. Even though I had played most of my ball at the white high school I went to, I was still all Indian, you know? I was Indian when it counted, and this BIA kid needed to be beaten by an Indian, any Indian.

I jumped into the game and played well for a little while. It felt good. I hit a few shots, grabbed a rebound or two, played enough defense to keep the other team honest. Then that white kid took over the game. He was too good. Later, he'd play college ball back East and would nearly make the Knicks team a couple years on. But we didn't know any of that would happen. We just knew he was better that day and every other day.

The next morning I woke up tired and hungry, so I grabbed the want ads, found a job I wanted, and drove to Spokane to get it. I've been working at

---

[1] Bureau of Indian Affairs.

the high school exchange program ever since, typing and answering phones. Sometimes I wonder if the people on the other end of the line know that I'm Indian and if their voices would change if they did know.

One day I picked up the phone and it was her, calling from Seattle.

"I got your number from your mom," she said. "I'm glad you're working."

"Yeah, nothing like a regular paycheck."

"Are you drinking?"

"No, I've been on the wagon for almost a year."

"Good."

The connection was good. I could hear her breathing in the spaces between our words. How do you talk to the real person whose ghost has haunted you? How do you tell the difference between the two?

"Listen," I said. "I'm sorry for everything."

"Me, too."

"What's going to happen to us?" I asked her and wished I had the answer for myself.

"I don't know," she said. "I want to change the world."

These days, living alone in Spokane, I wish I lived closer to the river, to the falls where ghosts of salmon jump. I wish I could sleep. I put down my paper or book and turn off all the lights, lie quietly in the dark. It may take hours, even years, for me to sleep again. There's nothing surprising or disappointing in that.

I know how all my dreams end anyway.

Isabel Allende

Isabel Allende (b. 1942) was born in Peru, the daughter of a Chilean diplomat. After her parents' divorce, she spent her childhood in her maternal grandparents' household; she was especially close to her grandmother, a believer in the occult. When Allende's mother remarried another diplomat, Isabel left Chile to live during her adolescence in Bolivia, the Middle East, and Europe. She began her career by working as a journalist in Chile, writing articles for a radical women's magazine and eventually creating her own television program. In 1970 her father's first cousin Dr. Salvador Allende Gossens became the first Marxist-Leninist to be freely elected as president of Chile. Three years later he was assassinated by Augusto Pinochet Ugarte, who instituted a repressive military dictatorship backed by the United States until 1990. Allende and her family fled to Venezuela; she felt that "my life had been cut into pieces, and that I had to start over again."

In 1981, after the death of her grandparents, Allende began to write her first work of long fiction. This was the internationally acclaimed novel *The House of the Spirits* (1982), a chronicle of several generations of an imaginary family in Chile based on her memories of her own family. She has said that "in Latin America, we value dreams, passions, obsessions, emotions, and all that which is very important to our lives has a place in literature—our sense of family, our sense of religion, of superstition too. . . . Fantastic things happen every day in Latin America—it's not that we make them up," as she shows in her story "An Act of Vengeance."

Allende followed the success of her first book with several novels, including *Of Love and Shadows* (1986), *Eva Luna* (1988), *Daughter of Fortune* (2000), and *Maya's Notebook* (2011). "An Act of Vengeance" is from her volume of short stories, *The Stories of Eva Luna* (1991). *The Sum of Our Days* (2008) is a recent memoir.

RELATED CASEBOOK

See Casebook on Magical Realism, pages 1627–1646, including Jorge Luis Borges, "Borges and I," page 1631; Alejo Carpentier, "On the Marvelous Real in America," page 1633 and "The Baroque and the Marvelous Real," page 1635; Luis Leal, "Magical Realism in Spanish American Literature," page 1637; William Gass, "The First Seven Pages of the Boom," page 1639; Ursula K. Le Guin, "The Kind of Fiction Most Characteristic of Our Times," page 1641; Mario Vargas Llosa, "The Prose Style of Jorge Luis Borges and Gabriel García Márquez," page 1645.

An Act of Vengeance

1990 / Translated by E. D. Carter Jr.

ON THAT GLORIOUS NOONDAY when Dulce Rosa Orellano was crowned with the jasmines of Carnival Queen, the mothers of the other candidates murmured that it was unfair for her to win just because she was the only daughter of the most powerful man in the entire province, Senator Anselmo Orellano. They admitted that the girl was charming and that she played the piano and danced like no other, but there were other competitors for the prize who were far more beautiful. They saw her standing on the platform in her organdy dress and with her crown of flowers, and as she waved at the crowd they cursed her through their clenched teeth. For that reason, some of them were overjoyed some months later when misfortune entered the Orellano's house sowing such a crop of death that thirty years were required to reap it.

On the night of the queen's election, a dance was held in the Santa Teresa Town Hall, and young men from the remotest villages came to meet Dulce Rosa. She was so happy and danced with such grace that many failed to perceive that she was not the most beautiful, and when they returned to where they had come from they all declared that they had never before seen a face like hers. Thus she acquired an unmerited reputation for beauty and later testimony was never able to prove to the contrary. The exaggerated descriptions of her translucent skin and her diaphanous eyes were passed from mouth to mouth, and each individual added something to them from his own imagination. Poets from distant cities composed sonnets to a hypothetical maiden whose name was Dulce Rosa.

Rumors of the beauty who was flourishing in Senator Orellano's house also reached the ears of Tadeo Céspedes, who never dreamed he would be able to meet her, since during all his twenty-five years he had neither had time to learn poetry nor to look at women. He was concerned only with the Civil War. Ever since he had begun to shave he had had a weapon in his hands, and he had lived for a long time amidst the sound of exploding gunpowder. He had forgotten his mother's kisses and even the songs of mass. He did not always have reason to go into battle, because during several periods of truce there were no adversaries within reach of his guerrilla band. But even in times of forced peace he lived like a corsair. He was a man habituated to violence. He crossed the country in every direction, fighting visible enemies when he found them, and battling shadows when he was forced to invent them. He would have continued in the same way if his party had not won the presidential election. Overnight he went from a clandestine existence to wielding power, and all pretext for continuing the rebellion had ended for him.

Tadeo Céspedes's final mission was the punitive expedition against Santa Teresa. With a hundred and twenty men he entered the town under cover of darkness to teach everyone a lesson and eliminate the leaders of the opposition. They shot out the windows in the public buildings, destroyed the church door, and rode their horses right up to the main altar, crushing Father Clemente when he tried to block their way. They burned the trees that the Ladies' Club had planted in the square; amidst all the clamor of battle, they continued at a gallop toward Senator Orellano's house which rose up proudly on top of the hill.

After having locked his daughter in the room at the farthest corner of the patio and turned the dogs loose, the Senator waited for Tadeo Céspedes at the head of a dozen loyal servants. At that moment he regretted, as he had so many other times in his life, not having had male descendants who could help him to take up arms and defend the honor of his house. He felt very old, but he did not have time to think about it, because he had spied on the hillside the terrible flash of a hundred and twenty torches that terrorized the night as they advanced. He distributed the last of the ammunition in silence. Everything had been said, and each of them knew that before morning he would be required to die like a man at his battle station.

"The last man alive will take the key to the room where my daughter is hidden and carry out his duty," said the Senator as he heard the first shots.

All the men had been present when Dulce Rosa was born and had held her on their knees when she was barely able to walk; they had told her ghost stories on winter afternoons; they had listened to her play the piano and they had applauded in tears on the day of her coronation as Carnival Queen. Her father could die in peace, because the girl would never fall alive into the hands of Tadeo Céspedes. The one thing that never crossed Senator Orellano's mind was that, in spite of his recklessness in battle, he would be the last to die. He saw his friends fall one by one and finally realized that it was useless to continue resisting. He had a bullet in his stomach and his vision was blurred. He was barely able to distinguish the shadows that were climbing the high walls surrounding his property, but he still had the presence of mind to drag himself to the third patio. The dogs recognized his scent despite the sweat, blood, and sadness that covered him and moved aside to let him pass. He inserted the key in the lock and through the mist that covered his eyes saw Dulce Rosa waiting for him. The girl was wearing the same organdy dress that she had worn for the Carnival and had adorned her hair with the flowers from the crown.

"It's time, my child," he said, cocking his revolver as a puddle of blood spread about his feet.

"Don't kill me, father," she replied in a firm voice. "Let me live so that I can avenge us both."

Senator Anselmo Orellano looked into his daughter's fifteen-year-old face and imagined what Tadeo Céspedes would do to her, but he saw great strength in Dulce Rosa's transparent eyes, and he knew that she would survive to punish his executioner. The girl sat down on the bed and he took his place at her side, pointing his revolver at the door.

When the uproar from the dying dogs had faded, the bar across the door was shattered, the bolt flew off, and the first group of men burst into the room. The Senator managed to fire six shots before losing consciousness. Tadeo Céspedes thought he was dreaming when he saw an angel crowned in jasmines holding a dying old man in her arms. But he did not possess sufficient pity to look for a second time, since he was drunk with violence and enervated by hours of combat.

"The woman is mine," he said, before any of his men could put his hands on her.

A leaden Friday dawned, tinged with the glare from the fire. The silence was thick upon the hill. The final moans had faded when Dulce Rosa was able to stand and walk to the fountain in the garden. The previous day it had been surrounded by magnolias, and now it was nothing but a tumultuous pool amidst the debris. After having removed the few strips of organdy that were all that remained of her dress, she stood nude before what had been the fountain. She submerged herself in the cold water. The sun rose behind the birches, and the girl watched the water turn red as she washed away the blood that flowed from between her legs along with that of her father which had dried in her hair. Once she was clean, calm, and without tears, she returned to the ruined house to look for something to cover herself. Picking up a linen sheet, she went outside to bring back the Senator's remains. They had tied him behind a horse and dragged him up and down the hillside until little remained but a pitiable mound of rags. But guided by love, the daughter was able to recognize him without hesitation. She wrapped him in the sheet and sat down by his side to watch the dawn grow into day. That is how her neighbors from Santa Teresa found her when they finally dared to climb up to the Orellano villa. They helped Dulce Rosa to bury her dead and to extinguish the vestiges of the fire. They begged her to go and live with her godmother in another town where no one knew her story, but she refused. Then they formed crews to rebuild the house and gave her six ferocious dogs to protect her.

From the moment they had carried her father away, still alive, and Tadeo Céspedes had closed the door behind them and unbuckled his leather belt, Dulce Rosa lived for revenge. In the thirty years that followed, that thought kept her awake at night and filled her days, but it did not completely obliterate her laughter nor dry up her good disposition. Her reputation for beauty increased as troubadors went everywhere proclaiming her imaginary enchantments until she became a living legend. She arose every morning at four o'clock to oversee the farm and household chores, roam her property on horseback, buy and sell, haggling like a Syrian, breed livestock, and cultivate the magnolias and jasmines in her garden. In the afternoon she would remove her trousers, her boots, and her weapons, and put on the lovely dresses which had come from the capital in aromatic trunks. At nightfall visitors would begin to arrive and would find her playing the piano while the servants prepared trays of sweets and glasses of orgeat. Many people asked themselves how it was possible that the girl had not ended up in a straitjacket in a sanitarium or as a novitiate with the Carmelite nuns. Nevertheless, since there were frequent parties at the Orellano villa, with the passage of time people stopped talking about the tragedy and erased the murdered Senator from their memories. Some gentlemen who possessed both fame and fortune managed to overcome the repugnance they felt because of the rape and, attracted by Dulce Rosa's beauty and sensitivity, proposed marriage. She rejected them all, for her only mission on Earth was vengeance.

Tadeo Céspedes was also unable to get that night out of his mind. The hangover from all the killing and the euphoria from the rape left him as he was on his way to the capital a few hours later to report the results of his punitive expedition. It was then that he remembered the child in a party dress and crowned with jasmines, who endured him in silence in that dark room where the air was impregnated with the odor of gunpowder. He saw her once again in the final scene, lying on the floor, barely covered by her reddened rags, sunk in the compassionate embrace of unconsciousness, and he continued to see her that way every night of his life just as he fell asleep. Peace, the exercise of government, and the use of power turned him into a settled, hard-working man. With the passage of time, memories of the Civil War faded away and the people began to call him Don Tadeo. He bought a ranch on the other side of the mountains, devoted himself to administering justice, and ended up as mayor. If it had not been for Dulce Rosa Orellano's tireless phantom, perhaps he might have attained a certain degree of happiness. But in all the women who crossed his path, he saw the face of the Carnival Queen. And even worse, the songs by popular poets, often containing verses that mentioned her name, would not permit him to expel her from his heart. The young woman's image grew within him, occupying him completely, until one day he could stand it no longer. He was at the head of a long banquet table celebrating his fifty-fifth birthday, surrounded by friends and colleagues, when he thought he saw in the tablecloth a child lying naked among jasmine blossoms, and understood that the nightmare would not leave him in peace even after his death. He struck the table with his fist, causing the dishes to shake, and asked for his hat and cane.

"Where are you going, Don Tadeo?" asked the Prefect.

"To repair some ancient damage," he said as he left without taking leave of anyone.

It was not necessary for him to search for her, because he always knew that she would be found in the same house where her misfortune had occurred, and it was in that direction that he pointed his car. By then good highways had been built and distances seemed shorter. The scenery had changed during the decades that had passed, but as he rounded the last curve by the hill, the villa appeared just as he remembered it before his troops had taken it in the attack. There were the solid walls made of river rock that he had destroyed with dynamite charges, there the ancient wooden coffers he had set afire, there the trees where he had hung the bodies of the Senator's men, there the patio where he had slaughtered the dogs. He stopped his vehicle a hundred meters from the door and dared not continue because he felt his heart exploding inside his chest. He was going to turn around and go back to where he came from, when a figure surrounded by the halo of her skirt appeared in the yard. He closed his eyes, hoping with all his might that she would not recognize him. In the soft twilight, he perceived that Dulce Rosa Orellano was advancing toward him, floating along the garden paths. He noted her hair, her candid face, the harmony of her gestures, the swirl of her dress, and he thought he was suspended in a dream that had lasted for thirty years.

"You've finally come, Tadeo Céspedes," she said as she looked at him, not allowing herself to be deceived by his mayor's suit or his gentlemanly gray hair, because he still had the same pirate's hands.

"You've pursued me endlessly. In my whole life I've never been able to love anyone but you," he murmured, his voice choked with shame.

Dulce Rosa gave a satisfied sigh. At last her time had come. But she looked into his eyes and failed to discover a single trace of the executioner, only fresh tears. She searched her heart for the hatred she had cultivated throughout those thirty years, but was incapable of finding it. She evoked the instant that she had asked her father to make his sacrifice and let her live so that she could carry out her duty; she relived the embrace of the man whom she had cursed so many times, and remembered the early morning when she had wrapped some tragic remains in a linen sheet. She went over her perfect plan of vengeance, but did not feel the expected happiness; instead she felt its opposite, a profound melancholy. Tadeo Céspedes delicately took her hand and kissed the palm, wetting it with his tears. Then she understood with horror that by thinking about him every moment, and savoring his punishment in advance, her feelings had become reversed and she had fallen in love with him.

During the following days both of them opened the floodgates of repressed love and, for the first time since their cruel fate was decided, opened themselves to receive the other's proximity. They strolled through the gardens talking about themselves and omitting nothing, even that fatal night which had twisted the direction of their lives. As evening fell, she played the piano and he smoked, listening to her until he felt his bones go soft and the happiness envelop him like a blanket and obliterate the nightmares of the past. After dinner he went to Santa Teresa where no one still remembered the ancient tale of horror. He took a room in the best hotel and from there organized his wedding. He wanted a party with fanfare, extravagance, and noise, one in which the entire town would participate. He discovered love at an age when other men have already lost their illusions, and that returned to him his youthful vigor. He wanted to surround Dulce Rosa with affection and beauty, to give her everything that money could buy, to see if he could compensate in his later years for the evil he had done as a young man. At times panic possessed him. He searched her face for the smallest sign of rancor, but he saw only the light of shared love and that gave him back his confidence. Thus a month of happiness passed.

Two days before the wedding, when they were already setting up the tables for the party in the garden, slaughtering the birds and pigs for the feast, and cutting the flowers to decorate the house, Dulce Rosa Orellano tried on her wedding dress. She saw herself reflected in the mirror, just as she had on the day of her coronation as Carnival Queen, and realized that she could no longer continue to deceive her own heart. She knew that she could not carry out the vengeance she had planned because she loved the killer, but she was also unable to quiet the Senator's ghost. She dismissed the seamstress, took the scissors, and went to the room on the third patio which had remained unoccupied during all that time.

Tadeo Céspedes searched for her everywhere, calling out to her desperately. The barking of the dogs led him to the other side of the house. With the help of the gardeners he broke down the barred door and entered the room where thirty years before he had seen an angel crowned with jasmines. He found Dulce Rosa Orellano just as he had seen her in his dreams every night of his existence, lying motionless in the same bloody organdy dress. He realized that in order to pay for his guilt he would have to live until he was ninety with the memory of the only woman his soul could ever love.

Sherwood Anderson

Sherwood Anderson (1876–1941) was born the son of a jack-of-all-trades father in Camden, Ohio. He did not publish his first book until he was over forty years old, after working for many years as a newsboy, farm laborer, stable boy, factory hand, and advertising copywriter. Dissatisfied with the commercial spirit of the advertising business, Anderson made friends with writers in Chicago and began to publish his own poetry and fiction. The poet Carl Sandburg encouraged him, but Anderson's literary style was most influenced by *Three Lives* (1909), an experimental book of stories by the expatriate American writer Gertrude Stein, which he felt revolutionized the language of narrative.

In 1916 Anderson published his first novel, *Windy McPherson's Son*. He followed it with another novel and a volume of poetry, but he did not receive wide recognition until 1919, with the book *Winesburg, Ohio*. This was a collection of related stories, including "Hands," about life in a small town that explored the devastating consequences of the repressive conventions of a provincial society. It was followed by other important collections of stories: *The Triumph of the Egg* (1921), *Horses and Men* (1923), and *Death in the Woods and Other Stories* (1933). In his time Anderson was a strong influence on Ernest Hemingway, William Faulkner, Richard Wright, and John Steinbeck. In 1941, the editor Martha Foley described this influence:

> Sherwood Anderson set out on new paths at a time when the American short story seemed doomed to a formula-ridden, conventionalized, mechanized, and commercialized concept. When *Winesburg, Ohio* appeared in 1919 it was intensely influential on writers who either had lost heart or had not yet found their way. His vision was his own; his characters were people into whose hearts and minds he seemed intuitively to peer; his prose was simple, deceptively simple, sensuous, rich, and evocative.

As literary critics have observed, the characteristic tone of Anderson's short fiction is melancholy reminiscence. Anderson's importance in our literature is suggested by Richard Wright's acknowledgment that Anderson's stories made him think that through the powers of fiction, "America could be shaped nearer to the hearts of those who lived in it."

RELATED COMMENTARY
Sherwood Anderson, "Form, Not Plot, in the Short Story," page 1394.

Hands

1919

UPON THE HALF DECAYED VERANDA of a small frame house that stood near the edge of a ravine near the town of Winesburg, Ohio, a fat little old man walked nervously up and down. Across a long field that had been seeded for clover but that had produced only a dense crop of yellow mustard weeds, he could see the public highway along which went a wagon filled with berry pickers returning from the fields. The berry pickers, youths and maidens, laughed and shouted boisterously. A boy clad in a blue shirt leaped from the wagon and attempted to drag after him one of the maidens who screamed and protested shrilly. The feet of the boy in the road kicked up a cloud of dust that floated across the face of the departing sun. Over the long field came a thin girlish voice. "Oh, you Wing Biddlebaum, comb your hair, it's falling into your eyes," commanded the voice to the man, who was bald and whose nervous little hands fiddled about the bare white forehead as though arranging a mass of tangled locks.

Wing Biddlebaum, forever frightened and beset by a ghostly band of doubts, did not think of himself as in any way a part of the life of the town where he had lived for twenty years. Among all the people of Winesburg but one had come close to him. With George Willard, son of Tom Willard, the proprietor of the new Willard House, he had formed something like a friendship. George Willard was the reporter on the *Winesburg Eagle* and sometimes in the evenings he walked out along the highway to Wing Biddlebaum's house. Now as the old man walked up and down on the veranda, his hands moving nervously about, he was hoping that George Willard would come and spend the evening with him. After the wagon containing the berry pickers had passed, he went across the field through the tall mustard weeds and climbing a rail fence peered anxiously along the road to the town. For a moment he stood thus, rubbing his hands together and looking up and down the road, and then, fear overcoming him, ran back to walk again upon the porch of his own house.

In the presence of George Willard, Wing Biddlebaum, who for twenty years had been the town mystery, lost something of his timidity, and his shadowy personality, submerged in a sea of doubts, came forth to look at the world. With the young reporter at his side, he ventured in the light of day into Main Street or strode up and down on the rickety front porch of his own house, talking excitedly. The voice that had been low and trembling became shrill and loud. The bent figure straightened. With a kind of wriggle, like a fish returned to the brook by the fisherman, Biddlebaum the silent began to talk, striving to put into words the ideas that had been accumulated by his mind during long years of silence.

Wing Biddlebaum talked much with his hands. The slender expressive fingers, forever active, forever striving to conceal themselves in his pockets or behind his back, came forth and became the piston rods of his machinery of expression.

The story of Wing Biddlebaum is a story of hands. Their restless activity, like unto the beating of the wings of an imprisoned bird, had given him his name. Some obscure poet of the town had thought of it. The hands alarmed their owner. He wanted to keep them hidden away and looked with amazement at the quiet inexpressive hands of other men who worked beside him in the fields, or passed, driving sleepy teams on country roads.

When he talked to George Willard, Wing Biddlebaum closed his fists and beat with them upon a table or on the walls of his house. The action made him more comfortable. If the desire to talk came to him when the two were walking in the fields, he sought out a stump or the top board of a fence and with his hands pounding busily talked with renewed ease.

The story of Wing Biddlebaum's hands is worth a book itself. Sympathetically set forth it would tap many strange, beautiful qualities in obscure men. It is a job for a poet. In Winesburg the hands had attracted attention merely because of their activity. With them Wing Biddlebaum had picked as high as a hundred and forty quarts of strawberries in a day. They became his distinguishing feature, the source of his fame. Also they made more grotesque an already grotesque and elusive individuality. Winesburg was proud of the hands of Wing Biddlebaum in the same spirit in which it was proud of Banker White's new stone house and Wesley Moyer's bay stallion, Tony Tip, that had won the two-fifteen trot at the fall races in Cleveland.

As for George Willard, he had many times wanted to ask about the hands. At times an almost overwhelming curiosity had taken hold of him. He felt that there must be a reason for their strange activity and their inclination to keep hidden away and only a growing respect for Wing Biddlebaum kept him from blurting out the questions that were often in his mind.

Once he had been on the point of asking. The two were walking in the fields on a summer afternoon and had stopped to sit upon a grassy bank. All afternoon Wing Biddlebaum had talked as one inspired. By a fence he had stopped and beating like a giant woodpecker upon the top board had shouted at George Willard, condemning his tendency to be too much influenced by the people about him. "You are destroying yourself," he cried.

"You have the inclination to be alone and to dream and you are afraid of dreams. You want to be like others in town here. You hear them talk and you try to imitate them."

On the grassy bank Wing Biddlebaum had tried again to drive his point home. His voice became soft and reminiscent, and with a sigh of contentment he launched into a long rambling talk, speaking as one lost in a dream.

Out of the dream Wing Biddlebaum made a picture for George Willard. In the picture men lived again in a kind of pastoral golden age. Across a green open country came clean-limbed young men, some afoot, some mounted upon horses. In crowds the young men came to gather about the feet of an old man who sat beneath a tree in a tiny garden and who talked to them.

Wing Biddlebaum became wholly inspired. For once he forgot the hands. Slowly they stole forth and lay upon George Willard's shoulders. Something new and bold came into the voice that talked. "You must try to forget all you have learned," said the old man. "You must begin to dream. From this time on you must shut your ears to the roaring of the voices."

Pausing in his speech, Wing Biddlebaum looked long and earnestly at George Willard. His eyes glowed. Again he raised the hands to caress the boy and then a look of horror swept over his face.

With a convulsive movement of his body, Wing Biddlebaum sprang to his feet and thrust his hands deep into his trousers pockets. Tears came to his eyes. "I must be getting along home. I can talk no more with you," he said nervously.

Without looking back, the old man had hurried down the hillside and across a meadow, leaving George Willard perplexed and frightened upon the grassy slope. With a shiver of dread the boy arose and went along the road toward town. "I'll not ask him about his hands," he thought, touched by the memory of the terror he had seen in the man's eyes. "There's something wrong, but I don't want to know what it is. His hands have something to do with his fear of me and of everyone."

And George Willard was right. Let us look briefly into the story of the hands. Perhaps our talking of them will arouse the poet who will tell the hidden wonder story of the influence for which the hands were but fluttering pennants of promise.

In his youth Wing Biddlebaum had been a school teacher in a town in Pennsylvania. He was not then known as Wing Biddlebaum, but went by the less euphonic name of Adolph Myers. As Adolph Myers he was much loved by the boys of his school.

Adolph Myers was meant by nature to be a rare teacher of youth. He was one of those rare, little-understood men who rule by a power so gentle that it passes as a lovable weakness. In their feeling for the boys under their charge such men are not unlike the finer sort of women in their love of men.

And yet that is but crudely stated. It needs the poet there. With the boys of his school, Adolph Myers had walked in the evening or had sat talking until dusk upon the schoolhouse steps lost in a kind of dream. Here and there went his hands, caressing the shoulders of the boys, playing about the tousled heads. As he talked his voice became soft and musical. There was a caress in that also. In a way the voice and the hands, the stroking of the shoulders and the touching of the hair was a part of the schoolmaster's effort to carry a dream into the young minds. By the caress that was in his fingers he expressed himself. He was one of those men in whom the force that creates life is diffused, not centralized. Under the caress of his hands doubt and disbelief went out of the minds of the boys and they began also to dream.

And then the tragedy. A half-witted boy of the school became enamored of the young master. In his bed at night he imagined unspeakable things and in the morning went forth to tell his dreams as facts. Strange, hideous accusations fell from his loose-hung lips. Through the Pennsylvania town went a shiver. Hidden, shadowy doubts that had been in men's minds concerning Adolph Myers were galvanized into beliefs.

The tragedy did not linger. Trembling lads were jerked out of bed and questioned. "He put his arms about me," said one. "His fingers were always playing in my hair," said another.

One afternoon a man of the town, Henry Bradford, who kept a saloon, came to the schoolhouse door. Calling Adolph Myers into the school yard he began to beat him with his fists. As his hard knuckles beat down into the frightened face of the schoolmaster, his wrath became more and more terrible. Screaming with dismay, the children ran here and there like disturbed insects. "I'll teach you to put your hands on my boy, you beast," roared the saloon keeper, who, tired of beating the master, had begun to kick him about the yard.

Adolph Myers was driven from the Pennsylvania town in the night. With lanterns in their hands a dozen men came to the door of the house where he lived alone and commanded that he dress and come forth. It was raining and one of the men had a rope in his hands. They had intended to hang the schoolmaster, but something in his figure, so small, white, and pitiful, touched their hearts and they let him escape. As he ran away into the darkness they repented of their weakness and ran after him, swearing and throwing sticks and great balls of soft mud at the figure that screamed and ran faster and faster into the darkness.

For twenty years Adolph Myers had lived alone in Winesburg. He was but forty but looked sixty-five. The name Biddlebaum he got from a box of goods seen at a freight station as he hurried through an eastern Ohio town. He had an aunt in Winesburg, a black-toothed old woman who raised chickens, and with her he lived until she died. He had been ill for a year after the experience in Pennsylvania, and after his recovery worked as a day laborer in the fields, going timidly about and striving to conceal his hands. Although he did not understand what had happened he felt that the hands must be to blame. Again and again the fathers of the boys had talked of the hands. "Keep your hands to yourself," the saloon keeper had roared, dancing with fury in the schoolhouse yard.

Upon the veranda of his house by the ravine, Wing Biddlebaum continued to walk up and down until the sun had disappeared and the road beyond the field was lost in the grey shadows. Going into his house he cut slices of bread and spread honey upon them. When the rumble of the evening train that took away the express cars loaded with the day's harvest of berries had passed and restored the silence of the summer night, he went again to walk upon the veranda. In the darkness he could not see the hands and they became quiet. Although he still hungered for the presence of the boy, who was the medium through which he expressed his love of man, the hunger became again a part of his loneliness and his waiting. Lighting a lamp, Wing Biddlebaum washed the few dishes soiled by his simple meal and, setting up a folding cot by the screen door that led to the porch, prepared to undress for the night. A few stray white bread crumbs lay on the cleanly washed floor by the table; putting the lamp upon a low stool he began to pick up the crumbs, carrying them to his mouth one by one with unbelievable rapidity. In the dense blotch of light beneath the table, the kneeling figure looked like a priest engaged in some service of his church. The nervous expressive fingers, flashing in and out of the light, might well have been mistaken for the fingers of the devotee going swiftly through decade after decade of his rosary.

Margaret Atwood

Margaret Atwood (b. 1939) is a Canadian writer of poetry and fiction. Born in Ottawa, Ontario, she spent the first eleven years of her life in the sparsely settled "bush" country of northern Ontario and Quebec, where her father, an entomologist, did research. She remembers her early start as a writer:

> I did not spend a full year in school until I was in Grade Eight. I began to write at the age of five—poems, "novels," comic books, and plays—but I had no thought of being a professional writer until I was sixteen. I entered Victoria College, University of Toronto, when I was seventeen and graduated in 1961. I won a Woodrow Wilson Fellowship to Harvard, where I studied Victorian Literature, and spent the next ten years in one place after another: Boston, Montreal, Edmonton, Toronto, Vancouver, England, and Italy, alternately teaching and writing.

Atwood's first poem was published when she was nineteen. To date she has published numerous collections of short stories, several novels—including the best-sellers *Surfacing* (1972), *The Handmaid's Tale* (1986), *Cat's Eye* (1989), *The Robber Bride* (1993), *Alias Grace* (1996), *The Blind Assassin* (2000; Man Booker Prize), and *The Year of the Flood* (2009)—and more than fifteen books of poetry. She was encouraged to write as a young woman because Canadians of her generation felt a strong need to develop a national literature. In 2011 she published *In Other Worlds: SF and the Human Imagination.*

Atwood has compared writing stories to telling riddles and jokes, all three requiring "the same mystifying buildup, the same surprising twist, the same impeccable sense of timing." She took pleasure in writing "Happy Endings," but she was puzzled by the form the story took:

> When I wrote "Happy Endings"—the year was, I think, 1982, and I was writing a number of short fictions then—I did not know what sort of creature it was. It was not a poem, a short story, or a prose poem. It was not quite a condensation, a commentary, a questionnaire, and it missed being a parable, a proverb, a paradox. It was a mutation. Writing it gave me a sense of furtive glee, like scribbling anonymously on a wall with no one looking.
>
> This summer I saw a white frog. It would not have been startling if I didn't know that this species of frog is normally green. This is the way such a mutant literary form unsettles us. We know what is expected in a given arrangement of words; we know what is supposed to come next. And then it doesn't.
>
> It was a little disappointing to learn that other people had a name for such aberrations [metafiction], and had already made up rules.

RELATED COMMENTARY
Margaret Atwood, "Reading Blind," page 1397.

Happy Endings

1983

JOHN AND MARY meet.
What happens next?
If you want a happy ending, try A.

A

John and Mary fall in love and get married. They both have worthwhile and remunerative jobs which they find stimulating and challenging. They buy a charming house. Real estate values go up. Eventually, when they can afford live-in help, they have two children, to whom they are devoted. The children turn out well. John and Mary have a stimulating and challenging sex life and worthwhile friends. They go on fun vacations together. They retire. They both have hobbies which they find stimulating and challenging. Eventually they die. This is the end of the story.

B

Mary falls in love with John but John doesn't fall in love with Mary. He merely uses her body for selfish pleasure and ego gratification of a tepid kind. He comes to her apartment twice a week and she cooks him dinner, you'll notice that he doesn't even consider her worth the price of a dinner out, and after he's eaten the dinner he fucks her and after that he falls asleep, while she does the dishes so he won't think she's untidy, having all those dirty dishes lying around, and puts on fresh lipstick so she'll look good when he wakes up, but when he wakes up he doesn't even notice, he puts on his socks and his shorts and his pants and his shirt and his tie and his shoes, the reverse order from the one in which he took them off. He doesn't take off Mary's clothes, she takes them off herself, she acts as if she's dying for it every time, not because she likes sex exactly, she doesn't, but she wants John to think she does because if they do it often enough surely he'll get used to her, he'll come to depend on her and they will get married, but John goes out the door with hardly so much as a good-night and three days later he turns up at six o'clock and they do the whole thing over again.

Mary gets run-down. Crying is bad for your face, everyone knows that and so does Mary but she can't stop. People at work notice. Her friends tell her John is a rat, a pig, a dog, he isn't good enough for her, but she can't believe it. Inside John, she thinks, is another John, who is much nicer. This other John will emerge like a butterfly from a cocoon, a Jack from a box, a pit from a prune, if the first John is only squeezed enough.

One evening John complains about the food. He has never complained about the food before. Mary is hurt.

Her friends tell her they've seen him in a restaurant with another woman, whose name is Madge. It's not even Madge that finally gets to Mary: it's the restaurant. John has never taken Mary to a restaurant. Mary collects all the

32

sleeping pills and aspirins she can find, and takes them and a half a bottle of sherry. You can see what kind of a woman she is by the fact that it's not even whiskey. She leaves a note for John. She hopes he'll discover her and get her to the hospital in time and repent and then they can get married, but this fails to happen and she dies.

John marries Madge and everything continues as in A.

C

John, who is an older man, falls in love with Mary, and Mary, who is only twenty-two, feels sorry for him because he's worried about his hair falling out. She sleeps with him even though she's not in love with him. She met him at work. She's in love with someone called James, who is twenty-two also and not yet ready to settle down.

John on the contrary settled down long ago: this is what is bothering him. John has a steady, respectable job and is getting ahead in his field, but Mary isn't impressed by him, she's impressed by James, who has a motorcycle and a fabulous record collection. But James is often away on his motorcycle, being free. Freedom isn't the same for girls, so in the meantime Mary spends Thursday evenings with John. Thursdays are the only days John can get away.

John is married to a woman called Madge and they have two children, a charming house which they bought just before the real estate values went up, and hobbies which they find stimulating and challenging, when they have the time. John tells Mary how important she is to him, but of course he can't leave his wife because a commitment is a commitment. He goes on about this more than is necessary and Mary finds it boring, but older men can keep it up longer so on the whole she has a fairly good time.

One day James breezes in on his motorcycle with some top-grade California hybrid and James and Mary get higher than you'd believe possible and they climb into bed. Everything becomes very underwater, but along comes John, who has a key to Mary's apartment. He finds them stoned and entwined. He's hardly in any position to be jealous, considering Madge, but nevertheless he's overcome with despair. Finally he's middle-aged, in two years he'll be bald as an egg and he can't stand it. He purchases a handgun, saying he needs it for target practice — this is the thin part of the plot, but it can be dealt with later — and shoots the two of them and himself.

Madge, after a suitable period of mourning, marries an understanding man called Fred and everything continues as in A, but under different names.

D

Fred and Madge have no problems. They get along exceptionally well and are good at working out any little difficulties that may arise. But their charming house is by the seashore and one day a giant tidal wave approaches. Real estate values go down. The rest of the story is about what caused the tidal wave and how they escape from it. They do, though thousands drown, but Fred and Madge are virtuous and lucky. Finally on high ground they clasp each other, wet and dripping and grateful, and continue as in A.

E

Yes, but Fred has a bad heart. The rest of the story is about how kind and understanding they both are until Fred dies. Then Madge devotes herself to charity work until the end of A. If you like, it can be "Madge," "cancer," "guilty and confused," and "bird watching."

F

If you think this is all too bourgeois, make John a revolutionary and Mary a counterespionage agent and see how far that gets you. Remember, this is Canada. You'll still end up with A, though in between you may get a lustful brawling saga of passionate involvement, a chronicle of our times, sort of.

You'll have to face it, the endings are the same however you slice it. Don't be deluded by any other endings, they're all fake, either deliberately fake, with malicious intent to deceive, or just motivated by excessive optimism if not by downright sentimentality.

The only authentic ending is the one provided here:

John and Mary die. John and Mary die. John and Mary die.

So much for endings. Beginnings are always more fun. True connoisseurs, however, are known to favor the stretch in between, since it's the hardest to do anything with.

That's about all that can be said for plots, which anyway are just one thing after another, a what and a what and a what.

Now try How and Why.

Isaac Babel

Isaac Babel (1894–1940) was born in the Moldavanka district of Odessa, Russia. When he was a boy, his grandmother told him, "You must know everything." His father, a Jewish businessman, made him study Yiddish, the Bible, and the Talmud, but the young Babel's favorite subject was French literature. By the time he was fifteen he was writing stories in French, "à la Maupassant," and his later story "Guy de Maupassant" (1932) is a tribute to the influence of this writer. In 1915 Babel moved to Saint Petersburg and tried unsuccessfully to publish his stories. His only encouragement came from the Russian writer Maxim Gorky, who advised him to get more life experience: "Go to the people." For six years Babel took Gorky at his word. He became a soldier on the Romanian Front in World War I, worked as a press correspondent attached to the Soviet Cavalry, and found other jobs as a reporter and a printer during the chaotic period of civil war that followed the Russian Revolution of 1917. In 1924 he began to publish his stories in *Left*, a Soviet avant-garde literary magazine devoted to revolution in politics and the arts. A year later he published his first collection of tales, *The Story of My Dove-Cote*, and in 1925 his best work appeared—*Red Cavalry*, thirty-four sketches depicting scenes of bravery and suffering during the Polish campaign of 1920, when Babel was with the Soviet Cavalry.

Babel's literary style has been called "as terse as algebra," but its lyricism is also unmistakable. He juxtaposed poetic and natural details in his descriptions, often stressing the sensual and the grotesque, as in "My First Goose." Critics have noted that these tactics are Babel's way of catching us off-guard and breaking down our defenses so that we will be more receptive to his main theme as a writer—the complex relation between our illusions about life and the truth of life. The eyeglasses of the Jewish intellectual who narrates the story represent Babel's commitment to see everything clearly. The Soviet memoirist Nadezhda Mandelstam recalled that "Everything about Babel gave an impression of all-consuming curiosity. . . . particularly his eyes. It is not often that one sees such undisguised curiosity in the eyes of a grownup."

Babel revised his stories several times before he was satisfied. When his books first appeared, he was hailed in the Soviet Union as a master prose stylist, but during Stalin's purges in the 1930s he was attacked for his ideological shortcomings. In 1937 he told his Soviet critics, who asked him why he published so little, that he could manage only short things. "Let me put it this way: the point is that Tolstoy was able to describe what happened to him minute by minute, he remembered it all, whereas I, evidently, only have it in me to describe the most interesting five minutes I've experienced in twenty-four hours." The tone of Babel's reply is joking, but underneath is a sense of his bitterness and frustration. He also wrote, "No steel can pierce the human heart so chillingly as a period at the right moment," a pun on Stalin's name as "the man of steel." Babel's brave affirmation of individuality was unacceptable to the Soviet authorities. In May 1939 he was arrested and disappeared into Lubyanka Prison in Moscow. On January 26, 1940, he was executed by a firing squad in the basement of the prison and his body was buried in a communal grave.

RELATED STORIES
Etgar Keret, "Not Human Beings," page 752; Frank O'Connor, "Guests of the Nation," page 1044.

RELATED COMMENTARY
Cynthia Ozick, Isaac Babel: "Let Me Finish," page 1500.

My First Goose

1925 / Translated by Walter Morison

SAVITSKY, COMMANDER OF THE VI DIVISION, rose when he saw me, and I wondered at the beauty of his giant's body. He rose, the purple of his riding-breeches and the crimson of his little tilted cap and the decorations stuck on his chest cleaving the hut as a standard cleaves the sky. A smell of scent and sickly sweet freshness of soap emanated from him. His long legs were like girls sheathed to the neck in shining riding-boots.

He smiled at me, struck his riding whip on the table, and drew toward him an order that the Chief of Staff had just finished dictating. It was an order for Ivan Chesnokov to advance on Chugunov-Dobryvodka with the regiment entrusted to him, to make contact with the enemy and destroy the same.

"For which destruction," the Commander began to write, smearing the whole sheet, "I make this same Chesnokov entirely responsible, up to and including the supreme penalty, and will if necessary strike him down on the spot; which you, Chesnokov, who have been working with me at the front for some months now, cannot doubt."

The Commander signed the order with a flourish, tossed it to his orderlies and turned upon me grey eyes that danced with merriment.

I handed him a paper with my appointment to the Staff of the Division.

"Put it down in the Order of the Day," said the Commander. "Put him down for every satisfaction save the front one. Can you read and write?"

"Yes, I can read and write," I replied, envying the flower and iron of that youthfulness. "I graduated in law from St. Petersburg University."

"Oh, are you one of those grinds?" he laughed. "Specs on your nose, too! What a nasty little object! They've sent you along without making any inquiries; and this is a hot place for specs. Think you'll get on with us?"

"I'll get on all right," I answered, and went off to the village with the quartermaster to find a billet for the night.

The quartermaster carried my trunk on his shoulder. Before us stretched the village street. The dying sun, round and yellow as a pumpkin, was giving up its roseate ghost to the skies.

We went up to a hut painted over with garlands. The quartermaster stopped, and said suddenly, with a guilty smile:

"Nuisance with specs. Can't do anything to stop it, either. Not a life for the brainy type here. But you go and mess up a lady, and a good lady too, and you'll have the boys patting you on the back."

He hesitated, my little trunk on his shoulder; then he came quite close to me, only to dart away again despairingly and run to the nearest yard. Cossacks were sitting there, shaving one another.

"Here, you soldiers," said the quartermaster, setting my little trunk down on the ground. "Comrade Savitsky's orders are that you're to take this chap in your billets, so no nonsense about it, because the chap's been through a lot in the learning line."

The quartermaster, purple in the face, left us without looking back. I raised my hand to my cap and saluted the Cossacks. A lad with long straight flaxen hair and the handsome face of the Ryazan Cossacks went over to my little trunk and tossed it out at the gate. Then he turned his back on me and with remarkable skill emitted a series of shameful noises.

"To your guns — number double-zero!" an older Cossack shouted at him, and burst out laughing. "Running fire!"

His guileless art exhausted, the lad made off. Then, crawling over the ground, I began to gather together the manuscripts and tattered garments that had fallen out of the trunk. I gathered them up and carried them to the other end of the yard. Near the hut, on a brick stove, stood a cauldron in which pork was cooking. The steam that rose from it was like the far-off smoke of home in the village, and it mingled hunger with desperate loneliness in my head. Then I covered my little broken trunk with hay, turning it into a pillow, and lay down on the ground to read in *Pravda* Lenin's speech at the Second Congress of the Comintern. The sun fell upon me from behind the toothed hillocks, the Cossacks trod on my feet, the lad made fun of me untiringly, the beloved lines came toward me along a thorny path and could not reach me. Then I put aside the paper and went out to the landlady, who was spinning on the porch.

"Landlady," I said, "I've got to eat."

The old woman raised to me the diffused whites of her purblind eyes and lowered them again.

"Comrade," she said, after a pause, "what with all this going on, I want to go and hang myself."

"Christ!" I muttered, and pushed the old woman in the chest with my fist. "You don't suppose I'm going to go into explanations with you, do you?"

And turning around I saw somebody's sword lying within reach. A severe-looking goose was waddling about the yard, inoffensively preening its feathers. I overtook it and pressed it to the ground. Its head cracked beneath my boot, cracked and emptied itself. The white neck lay stretched out in the dung, the wings twitched.

"Christ!" I said, digging into the goose with my sword. "Go and cook it for me, landlady."

Her blind eyes and glasses glistening, the old woman picked up the slaughtered bird, wrapped it in her apron, and started to bear it off toward the kitchen.

"Comrade," she said to me, after a while, "I want to go and hang myself."
And she closed the door behind her.

The Cossacks in the yard were already sitting around their cauldron. They sat
motionless, stiff as heathen priests at a sacrifice, and had not looked at the goose.

"The lad's all right," one of them said, winking and scooping up the cabbage
soup with his spoon.

The Cossacks commenced their supper with all the elegance and restraint
of peasants who respect one another. And I wiped the sword with sand, went
out at the gate, and came in again, depressed. Already the moon hung above
the yard like a cheap earring.

"Hey, you," suddenly said Surovkov, an older Cossack. "Sit down and feed
with us till your goose is done."

He produced a spare spoon from his boot and handed it to me. We supped
up the cabbage soup they had made, and ate the pork.

"What's in the newspaper?" asked the flaxen-haired lad, making room
for me.

"Lenin writes in the paper," I said, pulling out *Pravda*. "Lenin writes that
there's a shortage of everything."

And loudly, like a triumphant man hard of hearing, I read Lenin's speech
out to the Cossacks.

Evening wrapped about me the quickening moisture of its twilight sheets;
evening laid a mother's hand upon my burning forehead. I read on and
rejoiced, spying out exultingly the secret curve of Lenin's straight line.

"Truth tickles everyone's nostrils," said Surovkov, when I had come to the
end. "The question is, how's it to be pulled from the heap. But he goes and
strikes at it straight off like a hen pecking at a grain!"

This remark about Lenin was made by Surovkov, platoon commander of
the Staff Squadron; after which we lay down to sleep in the hayloft. We slept, all
six of us, beneath a wooden roof that let in the stars, warming one another, our
legs intermingled. I dreamed: and in my dreams saw women. But my heart,
stained with bloodshed, grated and brimmed over.

James Baldwin

James Baldwin (1924–1987) was born the son of a clergyman in Harlem, where he attended Public School 24, Frederick Douglass Junior High School, and DeWitt Clinton High School. While still a high school student he preached at the Fireside Pentecostal Assembly, but when he was seventeen he renounced the ministry. Two years later, living in Greenwich Village, he met who encouraged him to be a writer and helped him win a Eugene Saxton Fellowship. Soon afterward Baldwin moved to France, as had, to escape the stifling racial oppression he found in the United States. Although France was his more or less permanent residence until his death from cancer nearly forty years later, Baldwin regarded himself as a "commuter" rather than an expatriate:

> Only white Americans can consider themselves to be expatriates. Once I
> found myself on the other side of the ocean, I could see where I came from
> very clearly, and I could see that I carried myself, which is my home, with me.
> You can never escape that. I am the grandson of a slave, and I am a writer. I
> must deal with both.

Baldwin began his career by publishing novels and short stories. In 1953 *Go Tell It on the Mountain*, his first novel, was highly acclaimed. It was based on his childhood in Harlem and his fear of his tyrannical father. Baldwin's frank depiction of homosexuality in the novels *Giovanni's Room* (1956) and *Another Country* (1962) drew criticism, but during the civil rights movement a few years later, he established himself as a brilliant essayist. In his lifetime Baldwin published several collections of essays, three more novels, and a book of five short stories, *Going to Meet the Man* (1965).

"Sonny's Blues," from that collection, is one of Baldwin's strongest psychological dramatizations of the frustrations of African American life in our time. Like Wright's autobiographical books, Baldwin's work is an inspiration to young writers struggling to express their experience of racism. The African writer Chinua Achebe said that "as long as injustice exists . . . the words of James Baldwin will be there to bear witness and to inspire and elevate the struggle for human freedom."

RELATED CASEBOOK
See Casebook on James Baldwin's "Sonny's Blues," pages 1543–1555, including James Baldwin, "Autobiographical Notes," page 1544; Keith E. Byerman, "Words and Music: Narrative Ambiguity in 'Sonny's Blues,'" page 1548; Kenneth A. McClane, "'Sonny's Blues' Saved My Life," page 1553.

Sonny's Blues

1957

I READ ABOUT IT in the paper, in the subway, on my way to work. I read it, and I couldn't believe it, and I read it again. Then perhaps I just stared at it, at the newsprint spelling out his name, spelling out the story. I stared at it in the swinging lights of the subway car, and in the faces and bodies of the people, and in my own face, trapped in the darkness which roared outside.

It was not to be believed and I kept telling myself that, as I walked from the subway station to the high school. And at the same time I couldn't doubt it. I was scared, scared for Sonny. He became real to me again. A great block of ice got settled in my belly and kept melting there slowly all day long, while I taught my classes algebra. It was a special kind of ice. It kept melting, sending trickles of ice water all up and down my veins, but it never got less. Sometimes it hardened and seemed to expand until I felt my guts were going to come spilling out or that I was going to choke or scream. This would always be at a moment when I was remembering some specific thing Sonny had once said or done.

When he was about as old as the boys in my classes his face had been bright and open, there was a lot of copper in it; and he'd had wonderfully direct brown eyes, and great gentleness and privacy. I wondered what he looked like now. He had been picked up, the evening before, in a raid on an apartment downtown, for peddling and using heroin.

I couldn't believe it: but what I mean by that is that I couldn't find any room for it anywhere inside me. I had kept it outside me for a long time. I hadn't wanted to know. I had had suspicions, but I didn't name them, I kept putting them away. I told myself that Sonny was wild, but he wasn't crazy. And he'd always been a good boy, he hadn't ever turned hard or evil or disrespectful, the way kids can, so quick, so quick, especially in Harlem. I didn't want to believe that I'd ever see my brother going down, coming to nothing, all that light in his face gone out, in the condition I'd already seen so many others. Yet it had happened and here I was, talking about algebra to a lot of boys who might, every one of them for all I knew, be popping off needles every time they went to the head. Maybe it did more for them than algebra could.

I was sure that the first time Sonny had ever had horse, he couldn't have been much older than these boys were now. These boys, now, were living as we'd been living then, they were growing up with a rush and their heads bumped abruptly against the low ceiling of their actual possibilities. They were filled with rage. All they really knew were two darknesses, the darkness of their lives, which was now closing in on them, and the darkness of the movies, which had blinded them to that other darkness, and in which they now, vindictively, dreamed, at once more together than they were at any other time, and more alone.

When the last bell rang, the last class ended, I let out my breath. It seemed I'd been holding it for all that time. My clothes were wet — I may have looked as though I'd been sitting in a steam bath, all dressed up, all afternoon. I sat alone in the classroom a long time. I listened to the boys outside, downstairs, shouting and cursing and laughing. Their laughter struck me for perhaps the first time. It was not the joyous laughter which — God knows why — one associates with children. It was mocking and insular, its intent to denigrate. It was disenchanted, and in this, also, lay the authority of their curses. Perhaps I was listening to them because I was thinking about my brother and in them I heard my brother. And myself.

One boy was whistling a tune, at once very complicated and very simple, it seemed to be pouring out of him as though he were a bird, and it sounded very cool and moving through all that harsh, bright air, only just holding its own through all those other sounds.

I stood up and walked over to the window and looked down into the court-yard. It was the beginning of the spring and the sap was rising in the boys. A teacher passed through them every now and again, quickly, as though he or she couldn't wait to get out of that courtyard, to get those boys out of their sight and off their minds. I started collecting my stuff. I thought I'd better get home and talk to Isabel.

The courtyard was almost deserted by the time I got downstairs. I saw this boy standing in the shadow of a doorway, looking just like Sonny. I almost called his name. Then I saw that it wasn't Sonny, but somebody we used to know, a boy from around our block. He'd been Sonny's friend. He'd never been mine, having been too young for me, and, anyway, I'd never liked him. And now, even though he was a grown-up man, he still hung around that block, still spent hours on the street corners, was always high and raggy. I used to run into him from time to time and he'd often work around to asking me for a quarter or fifty cents. He always had some real good excuse, too, and I always gave it to him, I don't know why.

But now, abruptly, I hated him. I couldn't stand the way he looked at me, partly like a dog, partly like a cunning child. I wanted to ask him what the hell he was doing in the school courtyard.

He sort of shuffled over to me, and he said, "I see you got the papers. So you already know about it."

"You mean about Sonny? Yes, I already know about it. How come they didn't get you?"

He grinned. It made him repulsive and it also brought to mind what he'd looked like as a kid. "I wasn't there. I stay away from them people."

"Good for you." I offered him a cigarette and I watched him through the smoke. "You come all the way down here just to tell me about Sonny?"

"That's right." He was sort of shaking his head and his eyes looked strange, as though they were about to cross. The bright sun deadened his damp dark brown skin and it made his eyes look yellow and showed up the dirt in his kinked hair. He smelled funky. I moved a little away from him and I said, "Well, thanks. But I already know about it and I got to get home."

"I'll walk you a little ways," he said. We started walking. There were a couple of kids still loitering in the courtyard and one of them said goodnight to me and looked strangely at the boy beside me.

"What're you going to do?" he asked me. "I mean, about Sonny?"

"Look. I haven't seen Sonny for over a year. I'm not sure I'm going to do anything. Anyway, what the hell *can* I do?"

"That's right," he said quickly, "ain't nothing you can do. Can't much help old Sonny no more, I guess."

It was what I was thinking and so it seemed to me he had no right to say it.

"I'm surprised at Sonny, though," he went on — he had a funny way of talking, he looked straight ahead as though he were talking to himself — "I thought Sonny was a smart boy, I thought he was too smart to get hung."

"I guess he thought so too," I said sharply, "and that's how he got hung. And how about you? You're pretty goddamn smart, I bet."

Then he looked directly at me, just for a minute. "I ain't smart," he said. "If I was smart, I'd have reached for a pistol a long time ago."

"Look. Don't tell *me* your sad story, if it was up to me, I'd give you one." Then I felt guilty — guilty, probably, for never having supposed that the poor bastard *had* a story of his own, much less a sad one, and I asked, quickly, "What's going to happen to him now?"

He didn't answer this. He was off by himself some place. "Funny thing," he said, and from his tone we might have been discussing the quickest way to get to Brooklyn, "when I saw the papers this morning, the first thing I asked myself was if I had anything to do with it. I felt sort of responsible."

I began to listen more carefully. The subway station was on the corner, just before us, and I stopped. He stopped, too. We were in front of a bar and he ducked slightly, peering in, but whoever he was looking for didn't seem to be there. The juke box was blasting away with something black and bouncy and I half watched the barmaid as she danced her way from the juke box to her place behind the bar. And I watched her face as she laughingly responded to something someone said to her, still keeping time to the music. When she smiled one saw the little girl, one sensed the doomed, still-struggling woman beneath the battered face of the semi-whore.

"I never *give* Sonny nothing," the boy said finally, "but a long time ago I come to school high and Sonny asked me how it felt." He paused, I couldn't bear to watch him, I watched the barmaid, and I listened to the music which seemed to be causing the pavement to shake. "I told him it felt great." The music stopped, the barmaid paused and watched the juke box until the music began again. "It did."

All this was carrying me some place I didn't want to go. I certainly didn't want to know how it felt. It filled everything, the people, the houses, the music, the dark, quicksilver barmaid, with menace; and this menace was their reality.

"What's going to happen to him now?" I asked again.

"They'll send him away some place and they'll try to cure him." He shook his head. "Maybe he'll even think he's kicked the habit. Then they'll let him loose" — he gestured, throwing his cigarette into the gutter. "That's all."

"What do you mean, that's *all*?"

But I knew what he meant.

"I *mean*, that's *all*." He turned his head and looked at me, pulling down the corners of his mouth. "Don't you know what I mean?" he asked, softly.

"How the hell *would* I know what you mean?" I almost whispered it, I don't know why.

"That's right," he said to the air, "how would *he* know what I mean?" He turned toward me again, patient and calm, and yet I somehow felt him shaking, shaking as though he were going to fall apart. I felt that ice in my guts again, the dread I'd felt all afternoon; and again I watched the barmaid, moving about the bar, washing glasses, and singing. "Listen. They'll let him out and then it'll just start all over again. That's what I mean."

"You mean — they'll let him out. And then he'll just start working his way back in again. You mean he'll never kick the habit. Is that what you mean?"

"That's right," he said, cheerfully. "*You* see what I mean."

"Tell me," I said at last, "why does he want to die? He must want to die, he's killing himself, why does he want to die?"

He looked at me in surprise. He licked his lips. "He don't want to die. He wants to live. Don't nobody want to die, ever."

Then I wanted to ask him — too many things. He could not have answered, or if he had, I could not have borne the answers. I started walking. "Well, I guess it's none of my business."

"It's going to be rough on old Sonny," he said. We reached the subway station. "This is your station?" he asked. I nodded. I took one step down. "Damn!" he said, suddenly. I looked up at him. He grinned again. "Damn it if I didn't leave all my money home. You ain't got a dollar on you, have you? Just for a couple of days, is all."

All at once something inside gave and threatened to come pouring out of me. I didn't hate him any more. I felt that in another moment I'd start crying like a child.

"Sure," I said. "Don't sweat." I looked in my wallet and didn't have a dollar, I only had a five. "Here," I said. "That hold you?"

He didn't look at it — he didn't want to look at it. A terrible closed look came over his face, as though he were keeping the number on the bill a secret from him and me. "Thanks," he said, and now he was dying to see me go. "Don't worry about Sonny. Maybe I'll write him or something."

"Sure," I said. "You do that. So long."

"Be seeing you," he said. I went on down the steps.

And I didn't write Sonny or send him anything for a long time. When I finally did, it was just after my little girl died, he wrote me back a letter which made me feel like a bastard.

Here's what he said:

Dear brother,

　　You don't know how much I needed to hear from you. I wanted to write you many a time but I dug how much I must have hurt you and so I didn't write. But now I feel like a man who's been trying to climb up out of some deep, real deep and funky hole and just saw the sun up there, outside. I got to get outside.

　　I can't tell you much about how I got here. I mean I don't know how to tell you. I guess I was afraid of something or I was trying to escape from something and you know I have never been very strong in the head (smile). I'm glad Mama and Daddy are dead and can't see what's happened to their son and I swear if I'd known what I was doing I would never have hurt you so, you and a lot of other fine people who were nice to me and who believed in me.

I don't want you to think it had anything to do with me being a musician. It's more than that. Or maybe less than that. I can't get anything straight in my head down here and I try not to think about what's going to happen to me when I get outside again. Sometime I think I'm going to flip and *never* get outside and sometime I think I'll come straight back. I tell you one thing, though, I'd rather blow my brains out than go through this again. But that's what they all say, so they tell me. If I tell you when I'm coming to New York and if you could meet me, I sure would appreciate it. Give my love to Isabel and the kids and I was sure sorry to hear about little Gracie. I wish I could be like Mama and say the Lord's will be done, but I don't know it seems to me that trouble is the one thing that never does get stopped and I don't know what good it does to blame it on the Lord. But maybe it does some good if you believe it.

Your brother,
Sonny

Then I kept in constant touch with him and I sent him whatever I could and I went to meet him when he came back to New York. When I saw him many things I thought I had forgotten came flooding back to me. This was because I had begun, finally, to wonder about Sonny, about the life that Sonny lived inside. This life, whatever it was, had made him older and thinner and it had deepened the distant stillness in which he had always moved. He looked very unlike my baby brother. Yet, when he smiled, when we shook hands, the baby brother I'd never known looked out from the depths of his private life, like an animal waiting to be coaxed into the light.

"How you been keeping?" he asked me.

"All right. And you?"

"Just fine." He was smiling all over his face. "It's good to see you again."

"It's good to see you."

The seven years' difference in our ages lay between us like a chasm: I wondered if these years would ever operate between us as a bridge. I was remembering, and it made it hard to catch my breath, that I had been there when he was born; and I had heard the first words he had ever spoken. When he started to walk, he walked from our mother straight to me. I caught him just before he fell when he took the first steps he ever took in this world.

"How's Isabel?"

"Just fine. She's dying to see you."

"And the boys?"

"They're fine, too. They're anxious to see their uncle."

"Oh, come on. You know they don't remember me."

"Are you kidding? Of course they remember you."

He grinned again. We got into a taxi. We had a lot to say to each other, far too much to know how to begin.

As the taxi began to move, I asked, "You still want to go to India?"

He laughed. "You still remember that. Hell, no. This place is Indian enough for me."

"It used to belong to them," I said.

And he laughed again. "They damn sure knew what they were doing when they got rid of it."

Years ago, when he was around fourteen, he'd been all hipped on the idea of going to India. He read books about people sitting on rocks, naked, in all kinds of weather, but mostly bad, naturally, and walking barefoot through hot coals and arriving at wisdom. I used to say that it sounded to me as though they were getting away from wisdom as fast as they could. I think he sort of looked down on me for that.

"Do you mind," he asked, "if we have the driver drive alongside the park? On the west side — I haven't seen the city in so long."

"Of course not," I said. I was afraid that I might sound as though I were humoring him, but I hoped he wouldn't take it that way.

So we drove along, between the green of the park and the stony, lifeless elegance of hotels and apartment buildings, toward the vivid, killing streets of our childhood. These streets hadn't changed, though housing projects jutted up out of them now like rocks in the middle of a boiling sea. Most of the houses in which we had grown up had vanished, as had the stores from which we had stolen, the basements in which we had first tried sex, the rooftops from which we had hurled tin cans and bricks. But houses exactly like the houses of our past yet dominated the landscape, boys exactly like the boys we once had been found themselves smothering in these houses, came down into the streets for light and air and found themselves encircled by disaster. Some escaped the trap, most didn't. Those who got out always left something of themselves behind, as some animals amputate a leg and leave it in the trap. It might be said, perhaps, that I had escaped, after all, I was a school teacher; or that Sonny had, he hadn't lived in Harlem for years. Yet, as the cab moved uptown through streets which seemed, with a rush, to darken with dark people, and as I covertly studied Sonny's face, it came to me that what we both were seeking through our separate cab windows was that part of ourselves which had been left behind. It's always at the hour of trouble and confrontation that the missing member aches.

We hit 110th Street and started rolling up Lenox Avenue. And I'd known this avenue all my life, but it seemed to me again, as it had seemed on the day I'd first heard about Sonny's trouble, filled with a hidden menace which was its very breath of life.

"We almost there," said Sonny.

"Almost." We were both too nervous to say anything more.

We live in a housing project. It hasn't been up long. A few days after it was up it seemed uninhabitably new, now, of course, it's already rundown. It looks like a parody of the good, clean, faceless life — God knows the people who live in it do their best to make it a parody. The beat-looking grass lying around isn't enough to make their lives green, the hedges will never hold out the streets, and they know it. The big windows fool no one, they aren't big enough to make space out of no space. They don't bother with the windows, they watch the TV screen instead. The playground is most popular with the children who don't play at jacks, or skip rope, or roller skate, or swing, and they can be found in it after dark. We moved in partly because it's not too far from where I teach, and partly for the kids; but it's really just like the houses in which Sonny and I grew up. The same things happen, they'll have the same things to remember. The moment Sonny and I started into the house I had the feeling that I was simply bringing him back into the danger he had almost died trying to escape.

Sonny has never been talkative. So I don't know why I was sure he'd be dying to talk to me when supper was over the first night. Everything went fine, the oldest boy remembered him, and the youngest boy liked him, and Sonny had remembered to bring something for each of them; and Isabel, who is really much nicer than I am, more open and giving, had gone to a lot of trouble about dinner and was genuinely glad to see him. And she's always been able to tease Sonny in a way that I haven't. It was nice to see her face so vivid again and to hear her laugh and watch her make Sonny laugh. She wasn't, or, anyway, she didn't seem to be, at all uneasy or embarrassed. She chatted as though there were no subject which had to be avoided and she got Sonny past his first, faint stiffness. And thank God she was there, for I was filled with that icy dread again. Everything I did seemed awkward to me, and everything I said sounded freighted with hidden meaning. I was trying to remember everything I'd heard about dope addiction and I couldn't help watching Sonny for signs. I wasn't doing it out of malice. I was trying to find out something about my brother. I was dying to hear him tell me he was safe.

"Safe!" my father grunted, whenever Mama suggested trying to move to a neighborhood which might be safer for children. "Safe, hell! Ain't no place safe for kids, nor nobody."

He always went on like this, but he wasn't, ever, really as bad as he sounded, not even on weekends, when he got drunk. As a matter of fact, he was always on the lookout for "something a little better," but he died before he found it. He died suddenly, during a drunken weekend in the middle of the war, when Sonny was fifteen. He and Sonny hadn't ever got on too well. And this was partly because Sonny was the apple of his father's eye. It was because he loved Sonny so much and was frightened for him, that he was always fighting with him. It doesn't do any good to fight with Sonny. Sonny just moves back, inside himself, where he can't be reached. But the principal reason that they never hit it off is that they were so much alike. Daddy was big and rough and loud-talking, just the opposite of Sonny, but they both had — that same privacy.

Mama tried to tell me something about this, just after Daddy died. I was home on leave from the army.

This was the last time I ever saw my mother alive. Just the same, this picture gets all mixed up in my mind with pictures I had of her when she was younger. The way I always see her is the way she used to be on a Sunday afternoon, say, when the old folks were talking after the big Sunday dinner. I always see her wearing pale blue. She'd be sitting on the sofa. And my father would be sitting in the easy chair, not far from her. And the living room would be full of church folks and relatives. There they sit, in chairs all around the living room, and the night is creeping up outside, but nobody knows it yet. You can see the darkness growing against the windowpanes and you hear the street noises every now and again, or maybe the jangling beat of a tambourine from one of the churches close by, but it's real quiet in the room. For a moment nobody's talking, but every face looks darkening, like the sky outside. And my mother rocks a little from the waist, and my father's eyes are closed. Everyone is looking at something a child can't see. For a minute they've forgotten the children. Maybe a kid is lying on the rug, half asleep. Maybe somebody's got a kid in his lap and is absent-mindedly stroking the kid's head. Maybe there's a kid, quiet and big-eyed, curled up in a big chair in the corner. The silence, the darkness coming, and the darkness in the faces frightens the child obscurely. He hopes that the hand which strokes his forehead will never stop — will never die. He hopes that there will never come a time when the old folks won't be sitting around the living room, talking about where they've come from, and what they've seen, and what's happened to them and their kinfolk.

But something deep and watchful in the child knows that this is bound to end, is already ending. In a moment someone will get up and turn on the light. Then the old folks will remember the children and they won't talk any more that day. And when light fills the room, the child is filled with darkness. He knows that every time this happens he's moved just a little closer to that darkness outside. The darkness outside is what the old folks have been talking about. It's what they've come from. It's what they endure. The child knows that they won't talk any more because if he knows too much about what's happened to *them*, he'll know too much too soon, about what's going to happen to *him*.

The last time I talked to my mother, I remember I was restless. I wanted to get out and see Isabel. We weren't married then and we had a lot to straighten out between us.

There Mama sat, in black, by the window. She was humming an old church song, *Lord, you brought me from a long ways off*. Sonny was out somewhere. Mama kept watching the streets.

"I don't know," she said, "if I'll ever see you again, after you go off from here. But I hope you'll remember the things I tried to teach you."

"Don't talk like that," I said, and smiled. "You'll be here a long time yet."

She smiled, too, but she said nothing. She was quiet for a long time. And I said, "Mama, don't you worry about nothing. I'll be writing all the time, and you be getting the checks. . . . "

"I want to talk to you about your brother," she said, suddenly. "If anything happens to me he ain't going to have nobody to look out for him."

"Mama," I said, "ain't nothing going to happen to you or Sonny. Sonny's all right. He's a good boy and he's got good sense."

"It ain't a question of his being a good boy," Mama said, "nor of his having good sense. It ain't only the bad ones, nor yet the dumb ones that gets sucked under." She stopped, looking at me. "Your Daddy once had a brother," she said, and she smiled in a way that made me feel she was in pain. "You didn't never know that, did you?"

"No," I said, "I never knew that," and I watched her face.

"Oh, yes," she said, "your Daddy had a brother." She looked out of the window again. "I know you never saw your Daddy cry. But *I* did — many a time, through all these years."

I asked her, "What happened to his brother? How come nobody's ever talked about him?"

This was the first time I ever saw my mother look old.

"His brother got killed," she said, "when he was just a little younger than you are now. I knew him. He was a fine boy. He was maybe a little full of the devil, but he didn't mean nobody no harm."

Then she stopped and the room was silent, exactly as it had sometimes been on those Sunday afternoons. Mama kept looking out into the streets.

"He used to have a job in the mill," she said, "and, like all young folks, he just liked to perform on Saturday nights. Saturday nights, him and your father would drift around to different places, go to dances and things like that, or just sit around with people they knew, and your father's brother would sing, he had a fine voice, and play along with himself on his guitar. Well, this particular Saturday night, him and your father was coming home from some place, and they were both a little drunk and there was a moon that night, it was bright like day. Your father's brother was feeling kind of good, and he was whistling to himself, and he had his guitar slung over his shoulder. They was coming down a hill and beneath them was a road that turned off from the highway. Well, your father's brother, being always kind of frisky, decided to run down this hill, and he did, with that guitar banging and clanging behind him, and he ran across the road, and he was making water behind a tree. And your father was sort of amused at him and he was still coming down the hill, kind of slow. Then he heard a car motor and that same minute his brother stepped from behind the tree, into the road, in the moonlight. And he started to cross the road. And your father started to run down the hill, he says he don't know why. This car was full of white men. They was all drunk, and when they seen your father's brother they let out a great whoop and holler and they aimed the car straight at him. They was having fun, they just wanted to scare him, the way they do sometimes, you know. But they was drunk. And I guess the boy, being drunk, too, and scared, kind of lost his head. By the time he jumped it was too late. Your father says he heard his brother scream when the car rolled over him, and he heard the wood of that guitar when it give, and he heard them strings go flying, and he heard them white men shouting, and the car kept on a-going and it ain't stopped till this day. And, time your father got down the hill, his brother weren't nothing but blood and pulp."

Tears were gleaming on my mother's face. There wasn't anything I could say.

"He never mentioned it," she said, "because I never let him mention it before you children. Your Daddy was like a crazy man that night and for many a night thereafter. He says he never in his life seen anything as dark as that road after the lights of that car had gone away. Weren't nothing, weren't nobody on that road, just your Daddy and his brother and that busted guitar. Oh, yes. Your Daddy never did really get right again. Till the day he died he weren't sure but that every white man he saw was the man that killed his brother."

She stopped and took out her handkerchief and dried her eyes and looked at me.

"I ain't telling you all this," she said, "to make you scared or bitter or to make you hate nobody. I'm telling you this because you got a brother. And the world ain't changed."

I guess I didn't want to believe this. I guess she saw this in my face. She turned away from me, toward the window again, searching those streets.

"But I praise my Redeemer," she said at last, "that He called your Daddy home before me. I ain't saying it to throw no flowers at myself, but, I declare, it keeps me from feeling too cast down to know I helped your father get safely through this world. Your father always acted like he was the roughest, strongest man on earth. And everybody took him to be like that. But if he hadn't had *me* there — to see his tears!"

She was crying again. Still, I couldn't move. I said, "Lord, Lord, Mama, I didn't know it was like that."

"Oh, honey," she said, "there's a lot that you don't know. But you are going to find it out." She stood up from the window and came over to me. "You got to hold on to your brother," she said, "and don't let him fall, no matter what it looks like is happening to him and no matter how evil you gets with him. You going to be evil with him many a time. But don't you forget what I told you, you hear?"

"I won't forget," I said. "Don't you worry, I won't forget. I won't let nothing happen to Sonny."

My mother smiled as though she were amused at something she saw in my face. Then, "You may not be able to stop nothing from happening. But you got to let him know you's *there*."

Two days later I was married, and then I was gone. And I had a lot of things on my mind and I pretty well forgot my promise to Mama until I got shipped home on a special furlough for her funeral.

And, after the funeral, with just Sonny and me alone in the empty kitchen, I tried to find out something about him.

"What do you want to do?" I asked him.

"I'm going to be a musician," he said.

For he had graduated, in the time I had been away, from dancing to the juke box to finding out who was playing what, and what they were doing with it, and he had bought himself a set of drums.

"You mean, you want to be a drummer?" I somehow had the feeling that being a drummer might be all right for other people but not for my brother Sonny.

"I don't think," he said, looking at me very gravely, "that I'll ever be a good drummer. But I think I can play a piano."

I frowned. I'd never played the role of the older brother quite so seriously before, had scarcely ever, in fact, *asked* Sonny a damn thing. I sensed myself in the presence of something I didn't really know how to handle, didn't understand. So I made my frown a little deeper as I asked: "What kind of musician do you want to be?"

He grinned. "How many kinds do you think there are?"

"Be *serious*," I said.

He laughed, throwing his head back, and then looked at me. "I *am* serious."

"Well, then, for Christ's sake, stop kidding around and answer a serious question. I mean, do you want to be a concert pianist, you want to play classical music and all that, or — or what?" Long before I finished he was laughing again. "For Christ's *sake*, Sonny!"

He sobered, but with difficulty. "I'm sorry. But you sound so — *scared!*" and he was off again.

"Well, you may think it's funny now, baby, but it's not going to be so funny when you have to make your living at it, let me tell you *that.*" I was furious because I knew he was laughing at me and I didn't know why.

"No," he said, very sober now, and afraid, perhaps, that he'd hurt me, "I don't want to be a classical pianist. That isn't what interests me. I mean" — he paused, looking hard at me, as though his eyes would help me to understand, and then gestured helplessly, as though perhaps his hand would help — "I mean, I'll have a lot of studying to do, and I'll have to study *everything*, but, I mean, I want to play *with* — jazz musicians." He stopped. "I want to play jazz," he said.

Well, the word had never before sounded as heavy, as real, as it sounded that afternoon in Sonny's mouth. I just looked at him and I was probably frowning a real frown by this time. I simply couldn't see why on earth he'd want to spend his time hanging around nightclubs, clowning around on bandstands, while people pushed each other around a dance floor. It seemed — beneath him, somehow. I had never thought about it before, had never been forced to, but I suppose I had always put jazz musicians in a class with what Daddy called "good-time people."

"Are you *serious*?"

"Hell, *yes*, I'm serious."

He looked more helpless than ever, and annoyed, and deeply hurt.

I suggested, helpfully: "You mean — like Louis Armstrong?"

His face closed as though I'd struck him. "No. I'm not talking about none of that old-time, down home crap."

"Well, look, Sonny, I'm sorry, don't get mad. I just don't altogether get it, that's all. Name somebody — you know, a jazz musician you admire."

"Bird."

"Who?"

"Bird! Charlie Parker! Don't they teach you nothing in the goddamn army?"

I lit a cigarette. I was surprised and then a little amused to discover that I was trembling. "I've been out of touch," I said. "You'll have to be patient with me. Now. Who's this Parker character?"

"He's just one of the greatest jazz musicians alive," said Sonny, sullenly, his hands in his pockets, his back to me. "Maybe *the* greatest," he added, bitterly, "that's probably why *you* never heard of him."

"All right," I said, "I'm ignorant. I'm sorry. I'll go out and buy all the cat's records right away, all right?"

"It don't," said Sonny, with dignity, "make any difference to me. I don't care what you listen to. Don't do me no favors."

I was beginning to realize that I'd never seen him so upset before. With another part of my mind I was thinking that this would probably turn out to be one of those things kids go through and that I shouldn't make it seem important by pushing it too hard. Still, I didn't think it would do any harm to ask: "Doesn't all this take a lot of time? Can you make a living at it?"

He turned back to me and half leaned, half sat, on the kitchen table. "Everything takes time," he said, "and—well, yes, sure, I can make a living at it. But what I don't seem to be able to make you understand is that it's the only thing I want to do."

"Well, Sonny," I said, gently, "you know people can't always do exactly what they *want* to do—"

"*No*, I don't know that," said Sonny, surprising me. "I think people *ought* to do what they want to do, what else are they alive for?"

"You getting to be a big boy," I said desperately, "it's time you started thinking about your future."

"I'm thinking about my future," said Sonny, grimly. "I think about it all the time."

I gave up. I decided, if he didn't change his mind, that we could always talk about it later. "In the meantime," I said, "you got to finish school." We had already decided that he'd have to move in with Isabel and her folks. I knew this wasn't the ideal arrangement because Isabel's folks are inclined to be dicty and they hadn't especially wanted Isabel to marry me. But I didn't know what else to do. "And we have to get you fixed up at Isabel's."

There was a long silence. He moved from the kitchen table to the window. "That's a terrible idea. You know it yourself."

"Do you have a *better* idea?"

He just walked up and down the kitchen for a minute. He was as tall as I was. He had started to shave. I suddenly had the feeling that I didn't know him at all.

He stopped at the kitchen table and picked up my cigarettes. Looking at me with a kind of mocking, amused defiance, he put one between his lips. "You mind?"

"You smoking already?"

He lit the cigarette and nodded, watching me through the smoke. "I just wanted to see if I'd have the courage to smoke in front of you." He grinned and blew a great cloud of smoke to the ceiling. "It was easy." He looked at my face. "Come on, now. I bet you was smoking at my age, tell the truth."

I didn't say anything but the truth was on my face, and he laughed. But now there was something very strained in his laugh. "Sure. And I bet that ain't all you was doing."

He was frightening me a little. "Cut the crap," I said. "We already decided that you was going to go and live at Isabel's. Now what's got into you all of a sudden?"

"*You* decided it," he pointed out. "*I* didn't decide nothing." He stopped in front of me, leaning against the stove, arms loosely folded. "Look, brother. I don't want to stay in Harlem no more, I really don't." He was very earnest. He looked at me, then over toward the kitchen window. There was something in his eyes I'd never seen before, some thoughtfulness, some worry all his own. He rubbed the muscle of one arm. "It's time I was getting out of here."

"Where do you want to *go*, Sonny?"

"I want to join the army. Or the navy, I don't care. If I say I'm old enough, they'll believe me."

Then I got mad. It was because I was so scared. "You must be crazy. You goddamn fool, what the hell do you want to go and join the *army* for?"

"I just told you. To get out of Harlem."

"Sonny, you haven't even finished *school*. And if you really want to be a musician, how do you expect to study if you're in the *army*?"

He looked at me, trapped, and in anguish. "There's ways. I might be able to work out some kind of deal. Anyway, I'll have the G.I. Bill when I come out."

"*If* you come out." We stared at each other. "Sonny, please. Be reasonable. I know the setup is far from perfect. But we got to do the best we can."

"I ain't learning nothing in school," he said. "Even when I go." He turned away from me and opened the window and threw his cigarette out into the narrow alley. I watched his back. "At least, I ain't learning nothing you'd want me to learn." He slammed the window so hard I thought the glass would fly out, and turned back to me. "And I'm sick of the stink of these garbage cans!"

"Sonny," I said, "I know how you feel. But if you don't finish school now, you're going to be sorry later that you didn't." I grabbed him by the shoulders. "And you only got another year. It ain't so bad. And I'll come back and I swear I'll help you do *whatever* you want to do. Just try to put up with it till I come back. Will you please do that? For me?"

He didn't answer and he wouldn't look at me.

"Sonny. You hear me?"

He pulled away. "I hear you. But you never hear anything I say."

I didn't know what to say to that. He looked out of the window and then back at me. "OK," he said, and sighed. "I'll try."

Then I said, trying to cheer him up a little, "They got a piano at Isabel's. You can practice on it."

And as a matter of fact, it did cheer him up for a minute. "That's right," he said to himself. "I forgot that." His face relaxed a little. But the worry, the thoughtfulness, played on it still, the way shadows play on a face which is staring into the fire.

———————

But I thought I'd never hear the end of that piano. At first, Isabel would write me, saying how nice it was that Sonny was so serious about his music and how, as soon as he came in from school, or wherever he had been when he was supposed to be at school, he went straight to that piano and stayed there until suppertime. And, after supper, he went back to that piano and stayed there until everybody went to bed. He was at the piano all day Saturday and all day Sunday. Then he bought a record player and started playing records. He'd play one record over and over again, all day long sometimes, and he'd improvise along with it on the piano. Or he'd play one section of the record, one chord, one change, one progression, then he'd do it on the piano. Then back to the record. Then back to the piano.

Well, I really don't know how they stood it. Isabel finally confessed that it wasn't like living with a person at all, it was like living with sound. And the sound didn't make any sense to her, didn't make any sense to any of them — naturally. They began, in a way, to be afflicted by this presence that was living in their home. It was as though Sonny were some sort of god, or monster. He moved in an atmosphere which wasn't like theirs at all. They fed him and he ate, he washed himself, he walked in and out of their door; he certainly wasn't nasty or unpleasant or rude, Sonny isn't any of those things; but it was as though he were all wrapped up in some cloud, some fire, some vision all his own; and there wasn't any way to reach him.

At the same time, he wasn't really a man yet, he was still a child, and they had to watch out for him in all kinds of ways. They certainly couldn't throw him out. Neither did they dare to make a great scene about that piano because even they dimly sensed, as I sensed, from so many thousands of miles away, that Sonny was at that piano playing for his life.

But he hadn't been going to school. One day a letter came from the school board and Isabel's mother got it — there had, apparently, been other letters but Sonny had torn them up. This day, when Sonny came in, Isabel's mother showed him the letter and asked where he'd been spending his time. And she finally got it out of him that he'd been down in Greenwich Village, with musicians and other characters, in a white girl's apartment. And this scared her and she started to scream at him and what came up, once she began — though she denies it to this day — was what sacrifices they were making to give Sonny a decent home and how little he appreciated it.

Sonny didn't play the piano that day. By evening, Isabel's mother had calmed down but then there was the old man to deal with, and Isabel herself. Isabel says she did her best to be calm but she broke down and started crying. She says she just watched Sonny's face. She could tell, by watching him, what was happening with him. And what was happening was that they penetrated his cloud, they had reached him. Even if their fingers had been a thousand times more gentle than human fingers ever are, he could hardly help feeling that they had stripped him naked and were spitting on that nakedness. For he also had to see that his presence, that music, which was life or death to him, had been torture for them and that they had endured it, not at all for his sake, but only for mine. And Sonny couldn't take that. He can take it a little better today than he could then but he's still not very good at it and, frankly, I don't know anybody who is.

The silence of the next few days must have been louder than the sound of all the music ever played since time began. One morning, before she went to work, Isabel was in his room for something and she suddenly realized that all of his records were gone. And she knew for certain that he was gone. And he was. He went as far as the navy would carry him. He finally sent me a postcard from some place in Greece and that was the first I knew that Sonny was still alive. I didn't see him any more until we were both back in New York and the war had long been over.

He was a man by then, of course, but I wasn't willing to see it. He came by the house from time to time, but we fought almost every time we met. I didn't like the way he carried himself, loose and dreamlike all the time, and I didn't like his friends, and his music seemed to be merely an excuse for the life he led. It sounded just that weird and disordered.

Then we had a fight, a pretty awful fight, and I didn't see him for months. By and by I looked him up, where he was living, in a furnished room in the Village, and I tried to make it up. But there were lots of people in the room and Sonny just lay on his bed, and he wouldn't come downstairs with me, and he treated these other people as though they were his family and I weren't. So I got mad and then he got mad, and then I told him that he might just as well be dead as live the way he was living. Then he stood up and he told me not to worry about him any more in life, that he *was* dead as far as I was concerned. Then he pushed me to the door and the other people looked on as though nothing were happening, and he slammed the door behind me. I stood in the hallway, staring at the door. I heard somebody laugh in the room and then the tears came to my eyes. I started down the steps, whistling to keep from crying, I kept whistling to myself, *You going to need me, baby, one of these cold, rainy days.*

I read about Sonny's trouble in the spring. Little Grace died in the fall. She was a beautiful little girl. But she only lived a little over two years. She died of polio and she suffered. She had a slight fever for a couple of days, but it didn't seem like anything and we just kept her in bed. And we would certainly have called the doctor, but the fever dropped, she seemed to be all right. So we thought it had just been a cold. Then, one day, she was up, playing, Isabel was in the kitchen fixing lunch for the two boys when they'd come in from school, and she heard Grace fall down in the living room. When you have a lot of children you don't always start running when one of them falls, unless they start screaming or something. And, this time, Grace was quiet. Yet, Isabel says that when she heard that *thump* and then that silence, something happened in her to make her afraid. And she ran to the living room and there was little Grace on the floor, all twisted up, and the reason she hadn't screamed was that she couldn't get her breath. And when she did scream, it was the worst sound, Isabel says, that she'd ever heard in all her life, and she still hears it sometimes in her dreams. Isabel will sometimes wake me up with a low, moaning, strangled sound and I have to be quick to awaken her and hold her to me and where Isabel is weeping against me seems a mortal wound.

I think I may have written Sonny the very day that little Grace was buried. I was sitting in the living room in the dark, by myself, and I suddenly thought of Sonny. My trouble made his real.

One Saturday afternoon, when Sonny had been living with us, or, anyway, been in our house, for nearly two weeks, I found myself wandering aimlessly about the living room, drinking from a can of beer, and trying to work up the courage to search Sonny's room. He was out, he was usually out whenever I was home, and Isabel had taken the children to see their grandparents. Suddenly I was standing still in front of the living room window, watching Seventh Avenue. The idea of searching Sonny's room made me still. I scarcely dared to admit to myself what I'd be searching for. I didn't know what I'd do if I found it. Or if I didn't.

On the sidewalk across from me, near the entrance to a barbecue joint, some people were holding an old-fashioned revival meeting. The barbecue cook, wearing a dirty white apron, his conked hair reddish and metallic in the pale sun, and a cigarette between his lips, stood in the doorway, watching them. Kids and older people paused in their errands and stood there, along with some older men and a couple of very tough-looking women who watched everything that happened on the avenue, as though they owned it, or were maybe owned by it. Well, they were watching this, too. The revival was being carried on by three sisters in black, and a brother. All they had were their voices and their Bibles and a tambourine. The brother was testifying and while he testified two of the sisters stood together, seeming to say, amen, and the third sister walked around with the tambourine outstretched and a couple of people dropped coins into it. Then the brother's testimony ended and the sister who had been taking up the collection dumped the coins into her palm and transferred them to the pocket of her long black robe. Then she raised both hands, striking the tambourine against the air, and then against one hand, and she started to sing. And the two other sisters and the brother joined in.

It was strange, suddenly, to watch, though I had been seeing these street meetings all my life. So, of course, had everybody else down there. Yet, they paused and watched and listened and I stood still at the window. "*Tis the old ship of Zion,*" they sang, and the sister with the tambourine kept a steady, jangling beat, "*it has rescued many a thousand!*" Not a soul under the sound of their voices was hearing this song for the first time, not one of them had been rescued. Nor had they seen much in the way of rescue work being done around them. Neither did they especially believe in the holiness of the three sisters and the brother, they knew too much about them, knew where they lived, and how. The woman with the tambourine, whose voice dominated the air, whose face was bright with joy, was divided by very little from the woman who stood watching her, a cigarette between her heavy, chapped lips, her hair a cuckoo's nest, her face scarred and swollen from many beatings, and her black eyes glittering like coal. Perhaps they both knew this, which was why, when, as rarely, they addressed each other, they addressed each other as Sister. As the singing filled the air the watching, listening faces underwent a change, the eyes focusing on something within; the music seemed to soothe a poison out of them; and time seemed, nearly, to fall away from the sullen, belligerent, battered faces, as though they were fleeing back to their first condition, while dreaming of their last. The barbecue cook half shook his head and smiled, and dropped his cigarette and disappeared into his joint. A man fumbled in his pockets for change and stood holding it in his hand impatiently, as though he had just remembered a pressing appointment further up the avenue. He looked furious. Then I saw Sonny, standing on the edge of the crowd. He was carrying a wide, flat notebook with a green cover, and it made him look, from where I was standing, almost like a schoolboy. The coppery sun brought out the copper in his skin, he was very faintly smiling, standing very still. Then the singing stopped, the tambourine turned into a collection plate again. The furious man dropped in his coins and vanished, so did a couple of the women, and Sonny dropped some change in the plate, looking directly at the woman with a little smile. He started across the avenue, toward the house. He has a slow, loping walk, something like the way Harlem hipsters walk, only he's imposed on this his own half-beat. I had never really noticed it before.

I stayed at the window, both relieved and apprehensive. As Sonny disappeared from my sight, they began singing again. And they were still singing when his key turned in the lock.

"Hey," he said.

"Hey, yourself. You want some beer?"

"No. Well, maybe." But he came up to the window and stood beside me, looking out. "What a warm voice," he said.

They were singing *If I could only hear my mother pray again!*

"Yes," I said, "and she can sure beat that tambourine."

"But what a terrible song," he said, and laughed. He dropped his notebook on the sofa and disappeared into the kitchen. "Where's Isabel and the kids?"

"I think they went to see their grandparents. You hungry?"

"No." He came back into the living room with his can of beer. "You want to come some place with me tonight?"

I sensed, I don't know how, that I couldn't possibly say no. "Sure. Where?"

He sat down on the sofa and picked up his notebook and started leafing through it. "I'm going to sit in with some fellows in a joint in the Village."

"You mean, you're going to play, tonight?"

"That's right." He took a swallow of his beer and moved back to the window. He gave me a sidelong look. "If you can stand it."

"I'll try," I said.

He smiled to himself and we both watched as the meeting across the way broke up. The three sisters and the brother, heads bowed, were singing *God be with you till we meet again*. The faces around them were very quiet. Then the song ended. The small crowd dispersed. We watched the three women and the lone man walk slowly up the avenue.

"When she was singing before," said Sonny, abruptly, "her voice reminded me for a minute of what heroin feels like sometimes — when it's in your veins. It makes you feel sort of warm and cool at the same time. And distant. And — and sure." He sipped his beer, very deliberately not looking at me. I watched his face. "It makes you feel — in control. Sometimes you've got to have that feeling."

"Do you?" I sat down slowly in the easy chair.

"Sometimes." He went to the sofa and picked up his notebook again. "Some people do."

"In order," I asked, "to play?" And my voice was very ugly, full of contempt and anger.

"Well" — he looked at me with great, troubled eyes, as though, in fact, he hoped his eyes would tell me things he could never otherwise say — "they *think* so. And *if* they think so —!"

"And what do *you* think?" I asked.

He sat on the sofa and put his can of beer on the floor. "I don't know," he said, and I couldn't be sure if he were answering my question or pursuing his thoughts. His face didn't tell me. "It's not so much to *play*. It's to *stand* it, to be able to make it at all. On any level." He frowned and smiled: "In order to keep from shaking to pieces."

"But these friends of yours," I said, "they seem to shake themselves to pieces pretty goddamn fast."

"Maybe." He played with the notebook. And something told me that I should curb my tongue, that Sonny was doing his best to talk, that I should listen. "But of course you only know the ones that've gone to pieces. Some don't — or at least they haven't *yet* and that's just about all *any* of us can say." He paused. "And then there are some who just live, really, in hell, and they know it and they see what's happening and they go right on. I don't know." He sighed, dropped the notebook, folded his arms. "Some guys, you can tell from the way they play, they on something *all* the time. And you can see that, well, it makes something real for them. But of course," he picked up his beer from the floor and sipped it and put the can down again, "they *want* to, too, you've got to see that. Even some of them that say they don't — *some*, not all."

"And what about you?" I asked — I couldn't help it. "What about you? Do *you* want to?"

He stood up and walked to the window and remained silent for a long time. Then he sighed. "Me," he said. Then: "While I was downstairs before, on my way here, listening to that woman sing, it struck me all of a sudden how much suffering she must have had to go through — to sing like that. It's *repulsive* to think you have to suffer that much."

I said: "But there's no way not to suffer — is there, Sonny?"

"I believe not," he said and smiled, "but that's never stopped anyone from trying." He looked at me. "Has it?" I realized, with this mocking look, that there stood between us, forever, beyond the power of time or forgiveness, the fact that I had held silence — so long! — when he had needed human speech to help him. He turned back to the window. "No, there's no way not to suffer. But you try all kinds of ways to keep from drowning in it, to keep on top of it, and to make it seem — well, like *you*. Like you did something, all right, and now you're suffering for it. You know?" I said nothing. "Well you know," he said, impatiently, "why *do* people suffer? Maybe it's better to do something to give it a reason, *any* reason."

"But we just agreed," I said, "that there's no way not to suffer. Isn't it better, then, just to — take it?"

"But nobody just takes it," Sonny cried, "that's what I'm telling you! *Everybody* tries not to. You're just hung up on the *way* some people try — it's not *your* way!"

The hair on my face began to itch, my face felt wet. "That's not true," I said, "that's not true. I don't give a damn what other people do, I don't even care how they suffer. I just care how *you* suffer." And he looked at me. "Please believe me," I said, "I don't want to see you — die — trying not to suffer."

"I won't," he said, flatly, "die trying not to suffer. At least, not any faster than anybody else."

"But there's no need," I said, trying to laugh, "is there? in killing yourself."

I wanted to say more, but I couldn't. I wanted to talk about will power and how life could be — well, beautiful. I wanted to say that it was all within; but was it? or, rather, wasn't that exactly the trouble? And I wanted to promise that I would never fail him again. But it would all have sounded — empty words and lies.

So I made the promise to myself and prayed that I would keep it.

"It's terrible sometimes, inside," he said, "that's what's the trouble. You walk these streets, black and funky and cold, and there's not really a living ass to talk to, and there's nothing shaking, and there's no way of getting it out — that storm inside. You can't talk it and you can't make love with it, and when you finally try to get with it and play it, you realize *nobody's* listening. So *you've* got to listen. You got to find a way to listen."

And then he walked away from the window and sat on the sofa again, as though all the wind had suddenly been knocked out of him. "Sometimes you'll do *anything* to play, even cut your mother's throat." He laughed and looked at me. "Or your brother's." Then he sobered. "Or your own." Then: "Don't worry. I'm all right now and I think I'll *be* all right. But I can't forget — where I've been. I don't mean just the physical place I've been, I mean where I've *been*. And *what* I've been."

"What have you been, Sonny?" I asked.

He smiled — but sat sideways on the sofa, his elbow resting on the back, his fingers playing with his mouth and chin, not looking at me. "I've been something I didn't recognize, didn't know I could be. Didn't know anybody could be." He stopped, looking inward, looking helplessly young, looking old. "I'm not talking about it now because I feel *guilty* or anything like that — maybe it would be better if I did, I don't know. Anyway, I can't really talk about it. Not to you, not to anybody," and now he turned and faced me. "Sometimes, you know, and it was actually when I was most *out* of the world, I felt that I was in it, that I was *with* it, really, and I could play or I didn't really have to *play*, it just came out of me, it was there. And I don't know how I played, thinking about it now, but I know I did awful things, those times, sometimes, to people. Or it wasn't that I *did* anything to them — it was that they weren't real." He picked up the beer can; it was empty; he rolled it between his palms: "And other times — well, I needed a fix, I needed to find a place to lean, I needed to clear a space to *listen* — and I couldn't find it, and I — went crazy, I did terrible things to *me*, I was terrible *for* me." He began pressing the beer can between his hands, I watched the metal begin to give. It glittered, as he played with it, like a knife, and I was afraid he would cut himself, but I said nothing. "Oh well. I can never tell you. I was all by myself at the bottom of something, stinking and sweating and crying and shaking, and I smelled it, you know? *my* stink, and I thought I'd die if I couldn't get away from it and yet, all the same, I knew that everything I was doing was just locking me in with it. And I didn't know," he paused, still flattening the beer can, "I didn't know, I still *don't* know, something kept telling me that maybe it was good to smell your own stink, but I didn't think that *that* was what I'd been trying to do — and — who can stand it?" and he abruptly dropped the ruined beer can, looking at me with a small, still smile, and then rose, walking to the window as though it were the lodestone rock. I watched his face, he watched the avenue. "I couldn't tell you when Mama died — but the reason I wanted to leave Harlem so bad was to get away from drugs. And then, when I ran away, that's what I was running from — really. When I came back, nothing had changed, *I* hadn't changed, I was just — older." And he stopped, drumming with his fingers on the windowpane. The sun had vanished, soon darkness would fall. I watched his face. "It can come again," he said, almost as though speaking to himself. Then he turned to me. "It can come again," he repeated. "I just want you to know that."

"All right," I said, at last. "So it can come again. All right."

He smiled, but the smile was sorrowful. "I had to try to tell you," he said.

"Yes," I said. "I understand that."

"You're my brother," he said, looking straight at me, and not smiling at all.

"Yes," I repeated, "yes. I understand that."

He turned back to the window, looking out. "All that hatred down there," he said, "all that hatred and misery and love. It's a wonder it doesn't blow the avenue apart."

We went to the only nightclub on a short, dark street, downtown. We squeezed through the narrow, chattering, jam-packed bar to the entrance of the big room, where the bandstand was. And we stood there for a moment, for the lights were very dim in this room and we couldn't see. Then, "Hello, boy," said a voice and an enormous black man, much older than Sonny or myself, erupted out of all that atmospheric lighting and put an arm around Sonny's shoulder. "I been sitting right here," he said, "waiting for you."

He had a big voice, too, and heads in the darkness turned toward us.

Sonny grinned and pulled a little away, and said, "Creole, this is my brother. I told you about him."

Creole shook my hand. "I'm glad to meet you, son," he said, and it was clear that he was glad to meet me *there*, for Sonny's sake. And he smiled, "You got a real musician in *your* family," and he took his arm from Sonny's shoulder and slapped him, lightly, affectionately, with the back of his hand.

"Well. Now I've heard it all," said a voice behind us. This was another musician, and a friend of Sonny's, a coal-black, cheerful-looking man, built close to the ground. He immediately began confiding to me, at the top of his lungs, the most terrible things about Sonny, his teeth gleaming like a lighthouse and his laugh coming up out of him like the beginning of an earthquake. And it turned out that everyone at the bar knew Sonny, or almost everyone; some were musicians, working there, or nearby, or not working, some were simply hangers-on, and some were there to hear Sonny play. I was introduced to all of them and they were all very polite to me. Yet, it was clear that, for them, I was only Sonny's brother. Here, I was in Sonny's world. Or, rather: his kingdom. Here, it was not even a question that his veins bore royal blood.

They were going to play soon and Creole installed me, by myself, at a table in a dark corner. Then I watched them, Creole, and the little black man, and Sonny, and the others, while they horsed around, standing just below the bandstand. The light from the bandstand spilled just a little short of them and, watching them laughing and gesturing and moving about, I had the feeling that they, nevertheless, were being most careful not to step into that circle of light too suddenly: that if they moved into the light too suddenly, without thinking, they would perish in flame. Then, while I watched, one of them, the small, black man, moved into the light and crossed the bandstand and started fooling around with his drums. Then — being funny and being, also, extremely ceremonious — Creole took Sonny by the arm and led him to the piano. A woman's voice called Sonny's name and a few hands started clapping. And Sonny, also being funny and being ceremonious, and so touched, I think, that he could have cried, but neither hiding it nor showing it, riding it like a man, grinned, and put both hands to his heart and bowed from the waist.

Creole then went to the bass fiddle and a lean, very bright-skinned brown man jumped up on the bandstand and picked up his horn. So there they were, and the atmosphere on the bandstand and in the room began to change and tighten. Someone stepped up to the microphone and announced them. Then there were all kinds of murmurs. Some people at the bar shushed others. The waitress ran around, frantically getting in the last orders, guys and chicks got closer to each other, and the lights on the bandstand, on the quartet, turned to a kind of indigo. Then they all looked different there. Creole looked about him for the last time, as though he were making certain that all his chickens were in the coop, and then he — jumped and struck the fiddle. And there they were.

All I know about music is that not many people ever really hear it. And even then, on the rare occasions when something opens within, and the music enters, what we mainly hear, or hear corroborated, are personal, private, vanishing evocations. But the man who creates the music is hearing something else, is dealing with the roar rising from the void and imposing order on it as it hits the air. What is evoked in him, then, is of another order, more terrible because it has no words, and triumphant, too, for that same reason. And his triumph, when he triumphs, is ours. I just watched Sonny's face. His face was troubled, he was working hard, but he wasn't with it. And I had the feeling that, in a way, everyone on the bandstand was waiting for him, both waiting for him and pushing him along. But as I began to watch Creole, I realized that it was Creole who held them all back. He had them on a short rein. Up there, keeping the beat with his whole body, wailing on the fiddle, with his eyes half closed, he was listening to everything, but he was listening to Sonny. He was having a dialogue with Sonny. He wanted Sonny to leave the shoreline and strike out for the deep water. He was Sonny's witness that deep water and drowning were not the same thing — he had been there, and he knew. And he wanted Sonny to know. He was waiting for Sonny to do the things on the keys which would let Creole know that Sonny was in the water.

And, while Creole listened, Sonny moved, deep within, exactly like someone in torment. I had never before thought of how awful the relationship must be between the musician and his instrument. He has to fill it, this instrument, with the breath of life, his own. He has to make it do what he wants it to do. And a piano is just a piano. It's made out of so much wood and wires and little hammers and big ones, and ivory. While there's only so much you can do with it, the only way to find this out is to try; to try and make it do everything.

And Sonny hadn't been near a piano for over a year. And he wasn't on much better terms with his life, not the life that stretched before him now. He and the piano stammered, started one way, got scared, stopped; started another way, panicked, marked time, started again; then seemed to have found a direction, panicked again, got stuck. And the face I saw on Sonny I'd never seen before. Everything had been burned out of it, and, at the same time, things usually hidden were being burned in, by the fire and fury of the battle which was occurring in him up there.

Yet, watching Creole's face as they neared the end of the first set, I had the feeling that something had happened, something I hadn't heard. Then they finished, there was scattered applause, and then, without an instant's warning, Creole started into something else, it was almost sardonic, it was *Am I Blue*. And, as though he commanded, Sonny began to play. Something began to happen. And Creole let out the reins. The dry, low, black man said something awful on the drums, Creole answered, and the drums talked back. Then the horn insisted, sweet and high, slightly detached perhaps, and Creole listened, commenting now and then, dry, and driving, beautiful and calm and old. Then they all came together again, and Sonny was part of the family again. I could tell this from his face. He seemed to have found, right there beneath his fingers, a damn brand-new piano. It seemed that he couldn't get over it. Then, for awhile, just being happy with Sonny, they seemed to be agreeing with him that brand-new pianos certainly were a gas.

Then Creole stepped forward to remind them that what they were playing was the blues. He hit something in all of them, he hit something in me, myself, and the music tightened and deepened, apprehension began to beat the air. Creole began to tell us what the blues were all about. They were not about anything very new. He and his boys up there were keeping it new, at the risk of ruin, destruction, madness, and death, in order to find new ways to make us listen. For, while the tale of how we suffer, and how we are delighted, and how we may triumph is never new, it always must be heard. There isn't any other tale to tell, it's the only light we've got in all this darkness.

And this tale, according to that face, that body, those strong hands on those strings, has another aspect in every country, and a new depth in every generation. Listen, Creole seemed to be saying, listen. Now these are Sonny's blues. He made the little black man on the drums know it, and the bright, brown man on the horn. Creole wasn't trying any longer to get Sonny in the water. He was wishing him Godspeed. Then he stepped back, very slowly, filling the air with the immense suggestion that Sonny speak for himself.

Then they all gathered around Sonny and Sonny played. Every now and again one of them seemed to say, amen. Sonny's fingers filled the air with life, his life. But that life contained so many others. And Sonny went all the way back, he really began with the spare, flat statement of the opening phrase of the song. Then he began to make it his. It was very beautiful because it wasn't hurried and it was no longer a lament. I seemed to hear with what burning he had made it his, with what burning we had yet to make it ours, how we could cease lamenting. Freedom lurked around us and I understood, at last, that he could help us to be free if we would listen, that he would never be free until we did. Yet, there was no battle in his face now. I heard what he had gone through, and would continue to go through until he came to rest in earth. He had made it his: that long line, of which we knew only Mama and Daddy. And he was giving it back, as everything must be given back, so that, passing through death, it can live forever. I saw my mother's face again, and felt, for the first time, how the stones of the road she had walked on must have bruised her feet. I saw the moonlit road where my father's brother died. And it brought something else back to me, and carried me past it. I saw my little girl again and felt Isabel's tears again, and I felt my own tears begin to rise. And I was yet aware that this was only a moment, that the world waited outside, as hungry as a tiger, and that trouble stretched above us, longer than the sky.

Then it was over. Creole and Sonny let out their breath, both soaking wet, and grinning. There was a lot of applause and some of it was real. In the dark, the girl came by and I asked her to take drinks to the bandstand. There was a long pause, while they talked up there in the indigo light and after awhile I saw the girl put a Scotch and milk on top of the piano for Sonny. He didn't seem to notice it, but just before they started playing again, he sipped from it and looked toward me, and nodded. Then he put it back on top of the piano. For me, then, as they began to play again, it glowed and shook above my brother's head like the very cup of trembling.

Toni Cade Bambara

Toni Cade Bambara (1939–1995) was born in New York City and grew up in Harlem and Bedford-Stuyvesant. As a child she began scribbling stories in the margins of her father's copies of the *New York Daily News* and on the squares of thin white cardboard her mother's stockings came wrapped around. She described herself militantly:

> I was raised by my family and community to be a combatant. Forays to the Apollo [Theater in Harlem] with my daddy and hanging tough on Speakers Corner with my mama taught me the power of the word, the importance of the resistance tradition, and the high standards our [black] community had regarding verbal performance. While my heart is a laughing gland and my favorite thing to be doing is laughing so hard I have to lower myself on the wall to keep from falling down, near that chamber is a blast furnace where a rifle pokes from the ribs.

In high school and at Queens College, Bambara remembered that she "hogged the lit journal." She took writing courses and wrote novels, stories, plays, film scripts, operas, "you-name-its." After her college graduation, she worked various jobs and studied for her M.A. at the City University of New York while she wrote fiction in "the predawn in-betweens." She began to publish her stories, and in 1972 she collected them in her first book, *Gorilla, My Love*. It wasn't until Bambara returned from a trip to Cuba in 1973 that she thought of herself as a writer: "There I learned what Langston Hughes and others, most especially my colleagues in the Neo-Black Arts Movement, had been teaching for years—that writing is a legitimate way, an important way, to participate in the empowerment of the community that names me." Her books of stories include *The Black Woman* (1970), *Tales and Stories for Black Folks* (1971), and *The Sea Birds Are Still Alive* (1977). She wrote two novels, *The Salt Eaters* (1980) and *If Blessing Comes* (1987). *Deep Sightings and Rescue Missions* was published in 1996.

Like Zora Neale Hurston, whom Bambara credited with giving her new ways to consider literary material (folkways as the basis of art) and new categories of perception (women's images), Bambara often used humor in her fiction. She said that "what I enjoy most in my work is the laughter and the outrage and the attention to language." Her stories, like "The Lesson," were often about children, but Bambara tried to avoid sentimentality. She attempted to keep her torrents of language and feeling in control by remembering the premises from which she proceeded as a black writer: "One, we are at war. Two, the natural response to oppression, ignorance, evil, and mystification is wide-awake resistance. Three, the natural response to stress and crisis is not breakdown and capitulation, but transformation and renewal."

RELATED STORY
ZZ Packer, "Brownies," page 1081.

The Lesson

1972

BACK IN THE DAYS when everyone was old and stupid or young and foolish and me and Sugar were the only ones just right, this lady moved on our block with nappy hair and proper speech and no makeup. And quite naturally we laughed at her, laughed the way we did at the junk man who went about his business like he was some big-time president and his sorry-ass horse his secretary. And we kinda hated her too, hated the way we did the winos who cluttered up our parks and pissed on our handball walls and stank up our hallways and stairs so you couldn't halfway play hide-and-seek without a goddamn gas mask. Miss Moore was her name. The only woman on the block with no first name. And she was black as hell, cept for her feet, which were fish-white and spooky. And she was always planning these boring-ass things for us to do, us being my cousin, mostly, who lived on the block cause we all moved North the same time and to the same apartment then spread out gradual to breathe. And our parents would yank our heads into some kinda shape and crisp up our clothes so we'd be presentable for travel with Miss Moore, who always looked like she was going to church, though she never did. Which is just one of the things the grownups talked about when they talked behind her back like a dog. But when she came calling with some sachet she'd sewed up or some gingerbread she'd made or some book, why then they'd all be too embarrassed to turn her down and we'd get handed over all spruced up. She'd been to college and said it was only right that she should take responsibility for the young ones' education, and she not even related by marriage or blood. So they'd go for it. Specially Aunt Gretchen. She was the main gofer in the family. You got some ole dumb shit foolishness you want somebody to go for, you send for Aunt Gretchen. She been screwed into the go-along for so long, it's a blood-deep natural thing with her. Which is how she got saddled with me and Sugar and Junior in the first place while our mothers were in a la-de-da apartment up the block having a good ole time.

So this one day, Miss Moore rounds us all up at the mailbox and it's pure-dee hot and she's knockin herself out about arithmetic. And school suppose to let up in summer I heard, but she don't never let up. And the starch in my pinafore scratching the shit outta me and I'm really hating this nappy-head bitch and her goddamn college degree. I'd much rather go to the pool or to the show where it's cool. So me and Sugar leaning on the mailbox being surly, which is a Miss Moore word. And Flyboy checking out what everybody brought for lunch. And Fat Butt already wasting his peanut-butter-and-jelly sandwich like the pig he is. And Junebug punchin on Q.T.'s arm for potato chips. And Rosie Giraffe shifting from one hip to the other waiting for somebody to step on her foot or ask her if she from Georgia so she can kick ass, preferably Mercedes'. And Miss Moore asking us do we know what money is, like we a bunch of retards. I mean real money, she say, like it's only poker chips or monopoly papers we lay on the grocer. So right away I'm tired of this and say so. And would much rather snatch Sugar and go to the Sunset and terrorize the West Indian kids and take their hair ribbons and their money too. And Miss Moore files that remark away for next week's lesson on brotherhood, I can tell. And finally I say we oughta get to the subway cause it's cooler and besides we might meet some cute boys. Sugar done swiped her mama's lipstick, so we ready.

So we heading down the street and she's boring us silly about what things cost and what our parents make and how much goes for rent and how money ain't divided up right in this country. And then she gets to the part about we all poor and live in the slums, which I don't feature. And I'm ready to speak on that, but she steps out in the street and hails two cabs just like that. Then she hustles half the crew in with her and hands me a five-dollar bill and tells me to calculate 10 percent tip for the driver. And we're off. Me and Sugar and Junebug and Flyboy hangin out the window and hollering to everybody, putting lipstick on each other cause Flyboy a faggot anyway, and making farts with our sweaty armpits. But I'm mostly trying to figure how to spend this money. But they all fascinated with the meter ticking and Junebug starts laying bets as to how much it'll read when Flyboy can't hold his breath no more. Then Sugar lays bets as to how much it'll be when we get there. So I'm stuck. Don't nobody want to go for my plan, which is to jump out at the next light and run off to the first bar-b-que we can find. Then the driver tells us to get the hell out cause we there already. And the meter reads eighty-five cents. And I'm stalling to figure out the tip and Sugar say give him a dime. And I decide he don't need it bad as I do, so later for him. But then he tries to take off with Junebug foot still in the door so we talk about his mama something ferocious. Then we check out that we on Fifth Avenue and everybody dressed up in stockings. One lady in a fur coat, hot as it is. White folks crazy.

"This is the place," Miss Moore say, presenting it to us in the voice she uses at the museum. "Let's look in the windows before we go in."

"Can we steal?" Sugar asks very serious like she's getting the ground rules squared away before she plays. "I beg your pardon," say Miss Moore, and we fall out. So she leads us around the windows of the toy store and me and Sugar screamin, "This is mine, that's mine, I gotta have that, that was made for me, I was born for that," till Big Butt drowns us out.

"Hey, I'm going to buy that there."

"That there? You don't even know what it is, stupid."

"I do so," he say punchin on Rosie Giraffe. "It's a microscope."

"Whatcha gonna do with a microscope, fool?"

"Look at things."

"Like what, Ronald?" ask Miss Moore. And Big Butt ain't got the first notion. So here go Miss Moore gabbing about the thousands of bacteria in a drop of water and the somethinorother in a speck of blood and the million and one living things in the air around us is invisible to the naked eye. And what she say that for? Junebug go to town on that "naked" and we rolling. Then Miss Moore ask what it cost. So we all jam into the window smudgin it up and the price tag say $300. So then she ask how long'd take for Big Butt and Junebug to save up their allowances. "Too long," I say. "Yeh," adds Sugar, "outgrown it by that time." And Miss Moore say no, you never outgrow learning instruments. "Why, even medical students and interns and," blah, blah, blah. And we ready to choke Big Butt for bringing it up in the first damn place.

"This here costs four hundred eighty dollars," say Rosie Giraffe. So we pile up all over her to see what she pointin out. My eyes tell me it's a chunk of glass cracked with something heavy, and different-color inks dripped into the splits, then the whole thing put into a oven or something. But for $480 it don't make sense.

"That's a paperweight made of semi-precious stones fused together under tremendous pressure," she explains slowly, with her hands doing the mining and all the factory work.

"So what's a paperweight?" ask Rosie Giraffe.

"To weigh paper with, dumbbell," say Flyboy, the wise man from the East.

"Not exactly," say Miss Moore, which is what she say when you warm or way off too. "It's to weigh paper down so it won't scatter and make your desk untidy." So right away me and Sugar curtsy to each other and then to Mercedes who is more the tidy type.

"We don't keep paper on top of the desk in my class," say Junebug, figuring Miss Moore crazy or lyin one.

"At home, then," she say. "Don't you have a calendar and a pencil case and a blotter and a letter-opener on your desk at home where you do your home-work?" And she know damn well what our homes look like cause she nosys around in them every chance she gets.

"I don't even have a desk," say Junebug. "Do we?"

"No. And I don't get no homework neither," say Big Butt.

"And I don't even have a home," say Flyboy like he do at school to keep the white folks off his back and sorry for him. Send this poor kid to camp posters, is his specialty.

"I do," says Mercedes. "I have a box of stationery on my desk and a picture of my cat. My godmother bought the stationery and the desk. There's a big rose on each sheet and the envelopes smell like roses."

"Who wants to know about your smelly-ass stationery," say Rosie Giraffe fore I can get my two cents in.

"It's important to have a work area all your own so that . . . "

"Will you look at this sailboat, please," say Flyboy, cutting her off and pointin to the thing like it was his. So once again we tumble all over each other to gaze at this magnificent thing in the toy store which is just big enough to maybe sail two kittens across the pond if you strap them to the posts tight. We all start reciting the price tag like we in assembly. "Handcrafted sailboat of fiberglass at one thousand one hundred ninety-five dollars."

"Unbelievable," I hear myself say and am really stunned. I read it again for myself just in case the group recitation put me in a trance. Same thing. For some reason this pisses me off. We look at Miss Moore and she lookin at us, waiting for I dunno what.

"Who'd pay all that when you can buy a sailboat set for a quarter at Pop's, a tube of glue for a dime, and a ball of string for eight cents? It must have a motor and a whole lot else besides," I say. "My sailboat cost me about fifty cents."

"But will it take water?" say Mercedes with her smart ass.

"Took mine to Alley Pond Park once," say Flyboy. "String broke. Lost it. Pity."

"Sailed mine in Central Park and it keeled over and sank. Had to ask my father for another dollar."

"And you got the strap," laugh Big Butt. "The jerk didn't even have a string on it. My old man wailed on his behind."

Little Q.T. was staring hard at the sailboat and you could see he wanted it bad. But he too little and somebody'd just take it from him. So what the hell. "This boat for kids, Miss Moore?"

"Parents silly to buy something like that just to get all broke up," say Rosie Giraffe.

"That much money it should last forever," I figure.

"My father'd buy it for me if I wanted it."

"Your father, my ass," say Rosie Giraffe getting a chance to finally push Mercedes.

"Must be rich people shop here," say Q.T.

"You are a very bright boy," say Flyboy. "What was your first clue?" And he rap him on the head with the back of his knuckles, since Q.T. the only one he could get away with. Though Q.T. liable to come up behind you years later and get his licks in when you half expect it.

"What I want to know is," I says to Miss Moore though I never talk to her, I wouldn't give the bitch that satisfaction, "is how much a real boat costs? I figure a thousand'd get you a yacht any day."

"Why don't you check that out," she says, "and report back to the group?" Which really pains my ass. If you gonna mess up a perfectly good swim day least you could do is have some answers. "Let's go in," she say like she got something up her sleeve. Only she don't lead the way. So me and Sugar turn the corner to where the entrance is, but when we get there I kinda hang back. Not that I'm scared, what's there to be afraid of, just a toy store. But I feel funny, shame. But what I got to be shamed about? Got as much right to go in as anybody. But somehow I can't seem to get hold of the door, so I step away from Sugar to lead. But she hangs back too. And I look at her and she looks at me and this is ridiculous. I mean, damn, I have never been shy about doing nothing or going nowhere. But then Mercedes steps up and then Rosie Giraffe and Big Butt crowd in behind and shove, and next thing we all stuffed into the doorway with only Mercedes squeezing past us, smoothing out her jumper and walking right down the aisle. Then the rest of us tumble in like a glued-together jigsaw done all wrong. And people lookin at us. And it's like the time me and Sugar crashed into the Catholic church on a dare. But once we got in there and everything so hushed and holy and the candles and the bowin and the handkerchiefs on all the drooping heads, I just couldn't go through with the plan. Which was for me to run up to the altar and do a tap dance while Sugar played the nose flute and messed around in the holy water. And Sugar kept givin me the elbow. Then later teased me so bad I tied her up in the shower and turned it on and locked her in. And she'd be there till this day if Aunt Gretchen hadn't finally figured I was lying about the boarder takin a shower.

Same thing in the store. We all walkin on tiptoe and hardly touchin the games and puzzles and things. And I watched Miss Moore who is steady watchin us like she waitin for a sign. Like Mama Drewery watches the sky and sniffs the air and takes note of just how much slant is in the bird formation. Then me and Sugar bump smack into each other, so busy gazing at the toys, 'specially the sailboat. But we don't laugh and go into our fat-lady bump-stomach routine. We just stare at that price tag. Then Sugar run a finger over the whole boat. And I'm jealous and want to hit her. Maybe not her, but I sure want to punch somebody in the mouth.

"Watcha bring us here for, Miss Moore?"

"You sound angry, Sylvia. Are you mad about something?" Givin me one of them grins like she tellin a grown-up joke that never turns out to be funny. And she's lookin very closely at me like maybe she plannin to do my portrait from memory. I'm mad, but I won't give her that satisfaction. So I slouch around the store being very bored and say, "Let's go."

Me and Sugar at the back of the train watchin the tracks whizzin by large then small then getting gobbled up in the dark. I'm thinkin about this tricky toy I saw in the store. A clown that somersaults on a bar then does chin-ups just cause you yank lightly at his leg. Cost $35. I could see me askin my mother for a $35 birthday clown. "You wanna who that costs what?" she'd say, cocking her head to the side to get a better view of the hole in my head. Thirty-five dollars could buy new bunk beds for Junior and Gretchen's boy. Thirty-five dollars and the whole household could go visit Grand-daddy Nelson in the country. Thirty-five dollars would pay for the rent and the piano bill too. Who are these people that spend that much for performing clowns and $1000 for toy sailboats? What kinda work they do and how they live and how come we ain't in on it? Where we are is who we are, Miss Moore always pointin out. But it don't necessarily have to be that way, she always adds then waits for somebody to say that poor people have to wake up and demand their share of the pie and don't none of us know what kind of pie she talking about in the first damn place. But she ain't so smart cause I still got her four dollars from the taxi and she sure ain't gettin it. Messin up my day with this shit. Sugar nudges me in my pocket and winks.

Miss Moore lines us up in front of the mailbox where we started from, seem like years ago, and I got a headache for thinkin so hard. And we lean all over each other so we can hold up under the draggy-ass lecture she always finishes us off with at the end before we thank her for borin us to tears. But she just looks at us like she readin tea leaves. Finally she say, "Well, what did you think of F.A.O. Schwarz?"

Rosie Giraffe mumbles, "White folks crazy."

"I'd like to go there again when I get my birthday money," says Mercedes, and we shove her out the pack so she has to lean on the mailbox by herself.

"I'd like a shower. Tiring day," say Flyboy.

Then Sugar surprises me by sayin, "You know, Miss Moore, I don't think all of us here put together eat in a year what that sailboat costs." And Miss Moore lights up like somebody goosed her. "And?" she say, urging Sugar on. Only I'm standin on her foot so she don't continue.

"Imagine for a minute what kind of society it is in which some people can spend on a toy what it would cost to feed a family of six or seven. What do you think?"

"I think," say Sugar pushing me off her feet like she never done before, cause I whip her ass in a minute, "that this is not much of a democracy if you ask me. Equal chance to pursue happiness means an equal crack at the dough, don't it?" Miss Moore is besides herself and I am disgusted with Sugar's treachery. So I stand on her foot one more time to see if she'll shove me. She shuts up, and Miss Moore looks at me, sorrowfully I'm thinkin. And somethin weird is goin on, I can feel it in my chest.

"Anybody else learn anything today?" lookin dead at me. I walk away and Sugar has to run to catch up and don't even seem to notice when I shrug her arm off my shoulder.

"Well, we got four dollars anyway," she says.

"Uh, hunh."

"We could go to Hascombs and get half a chocolate layer and then go to the Sunset and still have plenty money for potato chips and ice cream sodas."

"Uh, hunh."

"Race you to Hascombs," she say.

We start down the block and she gets ahead which is O.K. by me cause I'm going to the West End and then over to the Drive to think this day through. She can run if she want to and even run faster. But ain't nobody gonna beat me at nuthin.

Russell Banks

Russell Banks (b. 1940) was the son of an alcoholic father, the oldest of four children raised in a working-class New Hampshire family. He had what he calls "a turbulent, chaotic, and angry youth." At nineteen, he left his first wife and small child intending to go fight for Fidel Castro, but unable to speak Spanish, he never reached Cuba. Instead he stayed in southern Florida and took jobs as a window dresser and a furniture mover. Five years later, after his mother-in-law helped pay the tuition, Banks earned a B.A. at the University of North Carolina, graduating Phi Beta Kappa. With hindsight, Banks believes that "Writing in some way saved my life. It brought to my life a kind of order and discipline and connection to the world outside myself that I don't see how I could have obtained otherwise." Because he came from a deprived family background, he feels that he earned the right to become a writer "slowly over time, and I have depended heavily on the validation and encouragement of others."

Banks published six books of fiction, which sold modestly, while he supported himself and his family by teaching creative writing at Sarah Lawrence College, Columbia University, New York University, and Princeton University. In 1985, influenced by the work of several American writers of naturalist fiction, such as Sherwood Anderson and Richard Wright, Banks published *Continental Drift*, a novel about immigration. The book sold well and was a finalist for the Pulitzer Prize. Award-winning films were made of his later novels *Affliction* (1989) and *The Sweet Hereafter* (1991). In 1998 Banks retired from teaching to become a full-time writer. His next novel was *Cloudsplitter* (2000), about the nineteenth-century abolitionist and terrorist John Brown, who had been a hero to Banks in the 1960s when he was involved in the civil rights movement as a university student in North Carolina. *The Reserve* was published in 2008, the same year as his nonfiction collection *Dreaming Up America*. Another recent novel is *Lost Memory of Skin* (2011).

Throughout his career Banks has written stories in addition to novels, publishing four collections of short fiction and winning O. Henry and Best American Short Story awards. In 2000 he gathered what he considered his best stories in *The Angel on the Roof*, which includes "Black Man and White Woman in Dark Green Rowboat." Banks has said that his aim as a storyteller is to make his readers *see*, quoting Joseph Conrad: "Conrad meant literally visualize, not understand. That's the ambition for me as a writer too—so that my readers can see the world or themselves or other human beings in the world a little differently, a little more clearly. . . . with more compassion, with more understanding, more patience. I don't stereotype them so easily."

RELATED STORY
Ernest Hemingway, "Hills Like White Elephants," page 589.

Black Man and White Woman
in Dark Green Rowboat

1981

IT WAS THE THIRD DAY of an August heat wave. Within an hour of the sun's rising above the spruce and pine trees that grew along the eastern hills, a blue-gray haze had settled over the lake and trailerpark, so that from the short, sandy spit that served as a swimming place for the residents of the trailer park you couldn't see the far shore of the lake. Around seven, a man in plaid bathing trunks and white bathing cap, in his sixties but still straight and apparently in good physical condition, left one of the trailers and walked along the paved lane to the beach. He draped his white towel over the bow of a flaking, bottle green rowboat that had been dragged onto the sand and walked directly into the water and when the water was up to his waist he began to swim, smoothly, slowly, straight out in the still water for two hundred yards or so, where he turned, treaded water for a few moments, and then started swimming back toward shore. When he reached the shore, he dried himself and walked back to his trailer and went inside. By the time he closed his door the water was smooth again, a dark green plain beneath the thick, gray-blue sky. No birds moved or sang; even the insects were silent.

In the next few hours, people left their trailers to go to their jobs in town, those who had jobs — the nurse, the bank teller, the carpenter, the woman who worked in the office at the tannery, and her little girl, who would spend the day with a baby-sitter in town. They moved slowly, heavily, as if with regret, even the child.

Time passed, and the trailerpark was silent again, while the sun baked the metal roofs and sides of the trailers, heating them up inside, so that by mid-morning it was cooler outside than in, and the people came out and tried to find a shady place to sit. First to appear was a middle-aged woman in large sunglasses and white shorts and halter, her head hidden by a floppy, wide-brimmed, cloth hat. She carried a book and sat on the shaded side of her trailer in an aluminum and plastic-webbing lawn chair and began to read her book. Then from his trailer came the man in the plaid bathing trunks, bareheaded now and shirtless and tanned to a chestnut color, his skin the texture of old leather. He wore rubber sandals and proceeded to hook up a garden hose and water the small, meticulously weeded vegetable garden on the slope behind his trailer. Every now and then he aimed the hose down and sprayed his bony feet. From the first trailer in from the road, where a sign that said MANAGER had been attached over the door, a tall, thick-bodied woman in her forties with cropped, graying hair, wearing faded jeans cut off at midthigh and a floppy T-shirt that had turned pink in the wash, walked slowly out to the main road, a half mile, to get her mail. When she returned she sat on her steps and read the letters and advertisements and the newspaper. About that time a blond boy in his late teens with shoulder-length hair, skinny, tanned, shirtless, and barefoot in jeans, emerged from his trailer, sighed, and sat down on the stoop and smoked a joint. At the last trailer in the park, the one next to the beach, an old man smoking a cob pipe and wearing a sleeveless undershirt and beltless khaki trousers slowly scraped paint from the bottom of an overturned rowboat. He ceased working and watched carefully as, walking slowly past him toward a dark green rowboat on the sand, there came a young black man with a fishing rod in one hand and a tackle box in the other. The man was tall and, though slender, muscular. He wore jeans and a pale blue, unbuttoned, short-sleeved shirt.

The old man said it was too hot for fishing, they wouldn't feed in this weather, and the young man said he didn't care, it had to be cooler on the lake than here on shore. The old man agreed with that, but why bother carrying your fishing rod and tackle box with you when you don't expect to catch any fish?

"Right," the young man said, smiling. "Good question." Placing his box and the rod into the rowboat, he turned to wait for the young woman who was stepping away from the trailer where, earlier, the middle-aged woman in shorts, halter, and floppy hat had come out and sat in the lawn chair to read. The young woman was a girl, actually, twenty or maybe twenty-one. She wore a lime green terry-cloth bikini and carried a large yellow towel in one hand and a fashion magazine and small brown bottle of tanning lotion in the other. Her long, honey blond hair swung from side to side across her tanned shoulders as she walked down the lane to the beach, where both the young man and the old man watched her approach them. She made a brief remark about the heat to the old man, said good morning to the young man, placed her towel, magazine, and tanning lotion into the dark green rowboat, and helped the young man shove the boat off the hot sand into the water. Then she jumped into the boat and sat herself in the stern, and the man, barefoot, with the bottoms of his jeans rolled to his knees, waded out, got into the boat, and began to row.

For a while, as the man rowed and the girl rubbed tanning lotion slowly over her arms and legs and across her shoulders and belly, they said nothing. The man pulled smoothly on the oars and watched the girl, and she examined her light brown skin and stroked it and rubbed the oily, sweet-smelling fluid onto it. After a few moments, holding to the gunwales with her hands so that her entire body got exposed to the powerful sun, she leaned back, closed her eyes, and stretched her legs toward the man, placing her small, white feet over his large, dark feet. The man studied the wedge of her crotch, then her navel, where a puddle of sweat was collecting, then the rise of her small breasts, and finally her long throat glistening in the sunlight. The man was sweating from the effort of rowing and he said he should have brought a hat. He stopped rowing, let the blades of the oars float in the water, and removed his shirt and wrapped it around his head like a turban. The girl, realizing that he had ceased rowing, looked up and smiled at him. "You look like an Arab. A sheik."

"A galley slave, more likely."

"No, really. Honestly." She lay her head back again and closed her eyes, and the man took up the oars and resumed rowing. They were a long ways out now, perhaps a half-mile from the trailerpark. The trailers looked like pastel-colored shoe boxes from here, six of them lined up on one side of the lane, six on the other, with a cleared bit of low ground and marsh off to one side and the outlet of the lake, the Catamount River it was called, on the other. The water was deep there, and below the surface and buried in the mud were blocks of stone and wooden lattices, the remains of fishing weirs the Indians constructed here and used for centuries, until the arrival of the Europeans. In the fall when the lake was low you could see the tops of the huge boulders the Indians placed into the stream to make channels for their nets and traps. There were weirs like this all over northern New England, most of them considerably more elaborate than this, so no one here paid much attention to these, except perhaps to mention the fact of their existence to a visitor from Massachusetts or New York. It gave the place a history and a certain significance when outsiders were present that it did not otherwise seem to have.

The girl lifted her feet away from the man's feet, drawing them back so that her knees pointed straight at his. She turned slightly to one side and stroked her cheekbone and lower jaw with the fingertips and thumb of one hand, leaning her weight on the other forearm and hand. "I'm already putting on weight," she said.

"It doesn't work that way. You're just eating too much."

"I told Mother."

The man stopped rowing and looked at her.

"I told Mother," she repeated. Her eyes were closed and her face was directed toward the sun and she continued to stroke her cheekbone and lower jaw.

"When?"

"Last night."

"And?"

"And nothing. I told her that I love you very much."

"That's all?"

"No. I told her everything."

He started rowing again, faster this time and not as smoothly as before. They were nearing a small, tree-covered island. Large, rounded rocks lay around the island, half-submerged in the shallow water, like the backs of huge, coal-colored hippos. The man peered over his shoulder and observed the distance to the island, then drew in the oars and lifted a broken chunk of cinder block tied to a length of clothesline rope and slid it into the water. The rope went out swiftly and cleanly as the anchor sank and then suddenly stopped. The man opened his tackle box and started poking through it, searching for a deepwater spinner.

The girl was sitting up now, studying the island with her head canted to one side, as if planning a photograph. "Actually, Mother was a lot better than I'd expected her to be. If Daddy were alive, it would be different," she said. "Daddy . . . "

"Hated niggers."

"Jesus Christ!"

"And Mother loves 'em." He located the spinner and attached it to the line.

"My mother likes you. She's a decent woman, and she's tired and lonely. And she's not your enemy, any more than I am."

"You're sure of that." He made a long cast and dropped the spinner between two large rocks and started winding it back in. "No, I know your mamma's okay. I'm sorry. Tell me what she said."

"She thought it was great. She likes you. I'm happy, and that's what is really important to her, and she likes you. She worries about me a lot, you know. She's afraid for me, she thinks I'm *fragile*. Especially now, because I've had some close calls. At least that's how she sees them."

"Sees what?"

"Oh, you know. Depression."

"Yeah." He cast again, slightly to the left of where he'd put the spinner the first time.

"Listen, I don't know how to tell you this, but I might as well come right out and say it. I'm going to do it. This afternoon. Mother's coming with me. She called and set it up this morning."

He kept reeling in the spinner, slowly, steadily, as if he hadn't heard her, until the spinner clunked against the side of the boat and he lifted it dripping from the water, and he said, "I hate this whole thing. Hate! Just know that much, will you?"

She reached out and placed a hand on his arm. "I know you do. So do I. But it'll be all right again afterwards. I promise. It'll be just like it was."

"You can't promise that. No one can. It won't be all right afterwards. It'll be lousy."

"I suppose you'd rather I just did nothing."

"Yes. That's right."

"Well. We've been through all this before. A hundred times." She sat up straight and peered back at the trailerpark in the distance. "How long do you plan to fish?"

"An hour or so. Why? If you want to swim, I'll row you around to the other side of the island and drop you and come back and get you later."

"No. No. That's all right. There are too many rocks anyhow. I'll go in when we get back to the beach. I have to be ready to go by three-thirty."

"Yeah. I'll make sure you get there on time," he said, and he made a long cast off to his right in deeper water.

"I love to sweat," she said, lying back and showing herself once again to the full sun. "I love to just lie back and sweat."

The man fished, and the girl sunbathed. The water was as slick as oil, the air thick and still. After a while, the man reeled in his line and removed the silvery spinner and went back to poking through his tackle box. "Where the hell is the damn plug?" he mumbled.

The girl sat up and watched him, his long, dark back twisted toward her, the vanilla bottoms of his feet, the fluttering muscles of his shoulders and arms, when suddenly he yelped and yanked his hand free of the box and put the meat of his hand directly into his mouth. He looked up at the girl in rage.

"What? Are you all right?" She slid back in her seat and drew her legs up close to her and wrapped her arms around her knees.

In silence, still sucking on his hand, he reached with the other hand into the tackle box and came back with a pale green and scarlet plug with six double hooks attached to the sides and tail. He held it as if by the head delicately with thumb and forefinger and showed it to her.

The girl grimaced. "Ow! You poor thing."

He took his hand from his mouth and clipped the plug to his line and cast it toward the island, dropping it about twenty feet from the rocky shore, a short ways to the right of a pair of dog-sized boulders. The girl picked up her magazine and began to leaf through the pages, stopping every now and then to examine an advertisement or photograph. Again and again, the man cast the flashing plug into the water and drew it back to the boat, twitching its path from side to side to imitate the motions of an injured, fleeting, pale-colored animal.

Finally, lifting the plug from the water next to the boat, the man said, "Let's go. Old Merle was right, no sense fishing when the fish ain't feeding. The whole point is catching fish, right?" he said, and he removed the plug from the line and tossed it into his open tackle box.

"I suppose so. I don't like fishing anyhow." Then after a few seconds, as if she were pondering the subject, "But I guess it's relaxing. Even if you don't catch anything."

The man drew up the anchor, pulling in the wet rope hand over hand, and finally he pulled the cinder block free of the water and set it dripping behind him in the bow of the boat. They had drifted closer to the island now and were in the cooling shade of the thicket of oaks and birches that crowded together over the island. The water turned suddenly shallow here, only a few feet deep, and they could see the rocky bottom clearly.

"Be careful," the girl said. "We'll run aground in a minute." She watched the bottom nervously. "Take care."

The man looked over her head and beyond, all the way to the shore and the trailerpark. The shapes of the trailers were blurred together in the distance so that you could not tell where one trailer left off and another began. "I wish I could just leave you here," the man said, still not looking at her.

"What?"

The boat drifted silently in the smooth water between a pair of large rocks, barely disturbing the surface. The man's dark face was somber and ancient beneath the turban that covered his head and the back of his neck. He leaned forward on his seat, his forearms resting wearily on his thighs, his large hands hanging limply between his knees. "I said, I wish I could just leave you here," he said in a soft voice, and he looked down at his hands.

She looked nervously around her, as if for an ally or a witness. "We have to go back."

"You mean, you have to go back."

"That's right," she said.

He slipped the oars into the oarlocks and started rowing, turning the boat and shoving it quickly away from the island. Facing the trailerpark, he rowed along the side of the island, then around behind it, out of sight of the trailerpark and the people who lived there, emerging again in a few moments on the far side of the island, rowing steadily, smoothly, powerfully. Now his back was to the trailerpark, and the girl was facing it, looking grimly past the man toward the shore.

He rowed, and they said nothing more. In a while they had returned to shore and life among the people who lived there. A few of them were in the water and on the beach when the dark green rowboat touched land and the black man stepped out and drew the boat onto the sand. The old man in the white bathing cap was standing in waist-deep water, and the woman who was the manager of the trailerpark stood near the edge of the water, cooling her feet and ankles. The old man with the cob pipe was still chipping at the bottom of his rowboat, and next to him, watching and idly chatting, stood the kid with the long blond hair. They all watched silently as the black man turned away from the dark green rowboat and carried his fishing rod and tackle box away, and then they watched the girl, carrying her yellow towel, magazine, and bottle of tanning lotion, step carefully out of the boat and walk to where she lived with her mother.

Lynda Barry

Lynda Barry (b. 1956) was born in Richland Center, Wisconsin, and describes her ancestry as half Irish (each of her parents is half Irish), one-quarter German, and one-quarter Filipina. Her mother emigrated from the Philippines, and her father worked as a butcher. Until she was five years old, she lived with her parents and her two brothers in a trailer in Wisconsin with pictures taped to the walls. As a child she loved art, and at night in her bedroom she would wait for the pictures taped over her bed to come to life. She remembered that "Sometimes they fell. But this is not what I mean when I say they could move." After her family relocated in Seattle, her father deserted them, and they lived with Filipino relatives. By the time Barry graduated from high school at sixteen, she had disassociated herself from her family, supporting herself by working nights and weekends as a janitor at a hospital. There, she was exposed to many people's stories. She recalls, "I don't think it was good for me, necessarily, but I saw stuff, and I grew up really, really fast. . . . I lived at home, but that was it."

With the help of a scholarship, her savings, and work-study grants, Barry became a student at Evergreen State College in Olympia, Washington, where she took classes with art instructor Marilyn Frasca. Self-taught as an artist from childhood, Barry had always "kind of mixed up drawings and words." Frasca taught her an approach to creating art that essentially became Barry's method as a graphic artist, making pictures and stories happen "in a way that didn't involve thinking." In college Barry considered herself a hippie, and she struck up a friendship with a fellow student, Matt Groening, who later created the television series *The Simpsons*. Groening was the editor of the college newspaper, and Barry became a contributor, starting "to do cartoons, and it was mainly for Matt," who thought she had a terrific sense of humor. After graduation Barry settled in Seattle. When she was twenty-three, her comic strip "Ernie Pook's Comeek" was picked up by the *Chicago Reader*, one of the alternative weekly magazines then springing up around the country with a taste for what she called "oddball comics." Her strip about growing up featured Marlys, a spunky pigtailed kid as its protagonist. Barry's work appeared in over seventy papers, and she published several collections of her graphic art, including *The Good Times Are Killing Me* (1988), about her biracial childhood, and *Cruddy* (1999), a novel narrated by a sixteen-year-old. In 1991 *The Good Times Are Killing Me* was adapted as an off-Broadway musical, winning the Washington State Governor's Award.

Barry's early work, drawn with a pen, had a new-wave, 1980s look, but after she hurt her wrist, she gave up the pen for a brush, which gave her drawings their characteristically loose, childlike appearance. Then, as alternative weeklies fell victim to corporate acquisitions and mergers in the late 1990s, Barry's career faltered. After the publication of *One! Hundred! Demons!* in 2002, her publisher Sasquatch Books in Washington rejected her proposal for her next project, *What It Is*, and told her that they wouldn't publish any more of her work. "It was like an ax in the forehead," Barry said. Four years later, a small comics publisher in Montreal, Drawn & Quarterly, offered to print this book and reprint her old work, and her career was back on track. "San Francisco" is an excerpt from *One! Hundred! Demons!*, a graphic memoir that Barry calls "autobifictionalography."

When *What It Is* was finally published in 2008, she explained her method of creating a collage of ink brush, pen and pencil drawings, and watercolors, some on
ordinary yellow lined paper, in which she fashioned a loose narrative structure
out of the flow of her meditations, dreams, and memories to explore philosophical questions such as "What is an image?" (Barry believes that it is something "at
the center of everything we call the arts.")

   Currently, Barry lives with her husband, a prairie restoration expert, on a farm
in Wisconsin. They are a self-reliant couple, growing their own food and chopping wood for fuel. She also tours college campuses, offering two-day workshops
in "Writing the Unthinkable," teaching others the method of making art that
she learned long ago at Evergreen State. *Blabber Blabber Blabber: Volume I of
Everything* appeared in 2011.

RELATED CASEBOOK

See Casebook on Graphic Storytelling, pages 1647–1663, including Charles
Hatfield, "From *Alternative Comics:* Toward the Habit of Questioning," page 1649;
Michael Kupperman, "Are Comics Serious Literature?" page 1652.

Donald Barthelme

Donald Barthelme (1931–1989) was born in Philadelphia and raised in Texas, where his father was a prominent architect. While a high school student he won awards for his stories and poetry, and at the University of Houston he edited the campus newspaper and wrote film criticism for the *Houston Post*. At age thirty he became director of the Contemporary Arts Museum in Houston. In 1962 he moved to New York City, where he lived when he was not teaching at the University of Houston as Cullen Distinguished Professor of English.

During the twenty years that Barthelme contributed short fiction to *The New Yorker*, his minimalist style was often imitated. His stories amused some readers as magazine fiction, but they intrigued others who sensed the heavier substance beneath their light narrative surface, as in "At the Tolstoy Museum." Barthelme compared his style of writing short fiction with that of collage, saying that "the principle of collage is the central principle of all art in the twentieth century." Literary critics have noted that Barthelme, like the French poet Stéphane Mallarmé, whom he admired, played with the meanings of words, relying on poetic intuition to spark new connections of ideas buried in trite expressions and conventional responses.

Readers sometimes criticized Barthelme's stories—along with those of other authors in the group he called "the alleged postmodernists," such as John Barth and Italo Calvino—for being too obscure. Barthelme replied, "Art is not difficult because it wishes to be difficult, rather because it wishes to be art. However much the writer might long to be straight-forward, these virtues are no longer available to him. He discovers that in being simple, honest, straight-forward, nothing much happens." Barthelme published two novels, *Snow White* (1967) and *The Dead Father* (1975), and left a third novel, *The King*, ready for publication in 1992 after his death from cancer. Of his eight volumes of short stories, *Sixty Stories* (1981), which won the PEN/Faulkner Award for fiction, is the most representative. More recent publications are *The Teachings of Donald Barthelme* (1992) and *Not Knowing* (1997), a collection of essays and interviews.

RELATED STORY
Leo Tolstoy, "The Death of Ivan Ilych," page 1242.

At the Tolstoy Museum

1969

AT THE TOLSTOY MUSEUM we sat and wept. Paper streamers came out of our eyes. Our gaze drifted toward the pictures. They were placed too high on the wall. We suggested to the director that they be lowered six inches at least. He looked unhappy but said he would see to it. The holdings of the Tolstoy

Museum consist principally of some thirty thousand pictures of Count Leo Tolstoy.

After they had lowered the pictures we went back to the Tolstoy Museum. I don't think you can peer into one man's face too long — for too long a period. A great many human passions could be discerned, behind the skin.

Tolstoy means "fat" in Russian. His grandfather sent his linen to Holland to be washed. His mother *did not know* any bad words. As a youth he shaved off his eyebrows, hoping they would grow back bushier. He first contracted gonorrhea in 1847. He was once bitten on the face by a bear. He became a vegetarian in 1885. To make himself interesting, he occasionally bowed backward.

I was eating a sandwich at the Tolstoy Museum. The Tolstoy Museum is made of stone — many stones, cunningly wrought. Viewed from the street, it has the aspect of three stacked boxes: the first, second, and third levels. These are of increasing size. The first level is, say, the size of a shoebox, the second level the size of a case of whiskey, and the third level the size of a box that contained a new overcoat. The amazing cantilever of the third level has been much talked about. The glass floor there allows one to look straight down and provides a "floating" feeling. The entire building, viewed from the street, suggested that it is about to fall on you. This the architects relate to Tolstoy's moral authority.

Tolstoy's Coat.

In the basement of the Tolstoy Museum carpenters uncrated new pictures of Count Leo Tolstoy. The huge crates stenciled FRAGILE in red ink . . .

The guards at the Tolstoy Museum carry buckets in which there are stacks of clean white pocket handkerchiefs. More than any other museum, the Tolstoy Museum induces weeping. Even the bare title of a Tolstoy work, with its burden of love, can induce weeping — for example, the article titled "Who Should Teach Whom to Write, We the Peasant Children or the Peasant Children Us?" Many people stand before this article, weeping. Too, those who are caught by Tolstoy's eyes, in various portraits, room after room after room, are not unaffected by the experience. It is like, people say, committing a small crime and being discovered at it by your father, who stands in four doorways, looking at you.

I was reading a story of Tolstoy's at Tolstoy Museum. In this story a bishop is sailing on a ship. One of his fellow-passengers tells the Bishop about an island on which three hermits live. The hermits are said to be extremely devout. The Bishop is seized with a desire to see and talk with the hermits. He persuades the captain of the ship to anchor near the island. He goes ashore in a small boat. He speaks to the hermits. The hermits tell the Bishop how they worship God. They have a prayer that goes: "Three of You, three of us, have mercy on us." The Bishop feels that this is a prayer prayed in the wrong way. He undertakes to teach the hermits the Lord's Prayer. The hermits learn the Lord's Prayer but with the greatest difficulty. Night has fallen by the time they have got it correctly.

The Bishop returns to his ship, happy that he has been able to assist the hermits in their worship. The ship sails on. The Bishop sits alone on deck, thinking about the experience of the day. He sees a light in the sky, behind the ship. The light is cast by the three hermits floating over the water, hand in hand, without moving their feet. They catch up with the ship, saying: "We have forgotten, Servant of God, we have forgotten your teaching!" They ask him to teach them again. The Bishop crosses himself. Then he tells the hermits that their prayer, too, reaches God. "It is not for me to teach you. Pray for us sinners!" The Bishop bows to the deck. The hermits fly back over the sea, hand in hand, to their island.

Tolstoy as a Youth.

At Starogladkovskaya, about 1852.

Tiger Hunt, Siberia.

The story is written in a very simple style. It is said to originate in a folk tale. There is a version of it in St. Augustine. I was incredibly depressed by reading this story. Its beauty. Distance.

At the Tolstoy Museum, sadness grasped the 741 Sunday visitors. The Museum was offering a series of lectures on the text "Why Do Men Stupefy Themselves?" The visitors were made sad by these eloquent speakers, who were probably right.

The Ann-Vronsky Pavilion.

At the Disaster (Arrow Indicates Tolstoy).

People stared at tiny pictures of Turgenev, Nekrasov, and Fet. These and other small pictures hung alongside extremely large pictures of Count Leo Tolstoy.

In the plaza, a sinister musician played a wood trumpet while two children watched.

We considered the 640,086 pages (Jubilee Edition) of the author's published work. Some people wanted him to go away, but other people were glad we had him. "He has been a lifelong source of inspiration to me," one said.

I haven't made up my mind. Standing here in the "Summer in the Country" Room, several hazes passed over my eyes. Still, I think I will march on to "A Landlord's Morning." Perhaps something vivifying will happen to me there.

Museum Plaza with Monumental Head (Closed Mondays).

Ann Beattie

Ann Beattie (b. 1947) was born in Washington, D.C. She grew up in Chevy Chase, Maryland, the only child of parents who sent her to a suburban school that she called "a civilized concentration camp" because of its strict dress code and stern disciplinary system. She rebelled by bleaching her hair, wearing fishnet stockings, smoking cigarettes, and graduating in the bottom tenth of her class: "That took a little effort on my part." In 1969 she received a B.A. from American University, and the following year she went on to the University of Connecticut as a graduate student in English literature. Her short stories attracted the interest of Professor J. D. O'Hara there.

> He said that he heard that I wrote, and if I was so good at it, why didn't I let him see what I was doing? So I took one of the few stories I had and put it in his mailbox, and it came back with comments all over it—more comments than I'd ever seen, more words than there were in the story. I would put something in his mailbox every few days and he would return it. He taught me a lot . . . about the technical process of writing.

Beattie began to send her stories to magazines, and her first publication, "A Rose for Judy Garland's Casket," appeared in the *Western Humanities Review* in 1972. The next year another story won an *Atlantic Monthly* "first" award, and shortly thereafter she began publishing in *The New Yorker*. Beattie estimates that she sent thirteen stories to that magazine before one was accepted. "You see, I was living in Eastford, Connecticut, at the time and I was bored. You either wrote a story every night or watched television. I wrote a story every night."

Her first book of nineteen stories, *Distortions*, was published in 1976, the same year as her first novel, *Chilly Scenes of Winter*, which was later made into a film. In 1978 she published her second collection of stories, *Secrets and Surprises*, and a third collection, *The Burning House*, appeared in 1982. *Follies* was published the same year that Beattie won the 2005 Rea Award for the Short Story. *The New Yorker Stories* (2010) is a recent collection. Beattie's fiction has been compared to the work of John Cheever and John Updike for its exploration of American suburban life and its "weird domesticities." Beattie herself sees little resemblance: "I think they're fine writers, but I don't see any comparison in the world between us. . . . Updike's style, that learned elegance, that intrusion of self into the material, and that very careful way he orchestrates everything, and the same thing with Cheever—they're writing traditionally well-made stories." In stories such as "Janus" Beattie says she writes about anxiety and chaos, "and many of the simple flat statements that I bring together are usually non sequiturs or bordering on being non sequiturs—which reinforces the chaos. I write in these flat simple sentences because that's the way I think."

Janus

1985

THE BOWL WAS PERFECT. Perhaps it was not what you'd select if you faced a shelf of bowls, and not the sort of thing that would inevitably attract a lot of attention at a crafts fair, yet it had real presence. It was as predictably admired as a mutt who has no reason to suspect he might be funny. Just such a dog, in fact, was often brought out (and in) along with the bowl.

Andrea was a real estate agent, and when she thought that some prospective buyers might be dog lovers, she would drop off her dog at the same time she placed the bowl in the house that was up for sale. She would put a dish of water in the kitchen for Mondo, take his squeaking plastic frog out of her purse and drop it on the floor. He would pounce delightedly, just as he did every day at home, batting around his favorite toy. The bowl usually sat on a coffee table, though recently she had displayed it on top of a pine blanket chest and on a lacquered table. It was once placed on a cherry table beneath a Bonnard still life, where it held its own.

Everyone who has purchased a house or who has wanted to sell a house must be familiar with some of the tricks used to convince a buyer that the house is quite special: a fire in the fireplace in early evening; jonquils in a pitcher on the kitchen counter, where no one ordinarily has space to put flowers; perhaps the slight aroma of spring, made by a single drop of scent vaporizing from a lamp bulb.

The wonderful thing about the bowl, Andrea thought, was that it was both subtle and noticeable — a paradox of a bowl. Its glaze was the color of cream and seemed to glow no matter what light it was placed in. There were a few bits of color in it — tiny geometric flashes — and some of these were tinged with flecks of silver. They were as mysterious as cells seen under a microscope; it was difficult not to study them, because they shimmered, flashing for a split second, and then resumed their shape. Something about the colors and their random placement suggested motion. People who liked country furniture always commented on the bowl, but then it turned out that people who felt comfortable with Biedermeier loved it just as much. But the bowl was not at all ostentatious, or even so noticeable that anyone would suspect that it had been put in place deliberately. They might notice the height of the ceiling on first entering a room, and only when their eye moved down from that, or away from the refraction of sunlight on a pale wall, would they see the bowl. Then they would go immediately to it and comment. Yet they always faltered when they tried to say something. Perhaps it was because they were in the house for a serious reason, not to notice some object.

Once, Andrea got a call from a woman who had not put in an offer on a house she had shown her. That bowl, she said — would it be possible to find out where the owners had bought that beautiful bowl? Andrea pretended that she did not know what the woman was referring to. A bowl, somewhere in the house? Oh, on a table under the window. Yes, she would ask, of course. She let a couple of days pass, then called back to say that the bowl had been a present and the people did not know where it had been purchased.

When the bowl was not being taken from house to house, it sat on Andrea's coffee table at home. She didn't keep it carefully wrapped (although she transported it that way, in a box); she kept it on the table, because she liked to see it. It was large enough so that it didn't seem fragile, or particularly vulnerable if anyone sideswiped the table or Mondo blundered into it at play. She had asked her husband to please not drop his house key in it. It was meant to be empty.

When her husband first noticed the bowl, he had peered into it and smiled briefly. He always urged her to buy things she liked. In recent years, both of them had acquired many things to make up for all the lean years when they were graduate students, but now that they had been comfortable for quite a while, the pleasure of new possessions dwindled. Her husband had pronounced the bowl "pretty," and he had turned away without picking it up to examine it. He had no more interest in the bowl than she had in his new Leica.

She was sure that the bowl brought her luck. Bids were often put in on houses where she had displayed the bowl. Sometimes the owners, who were always asked to be away or to step outside when the house was being shown, didn't even know that the bowl had been in their house. Once — she could not imagine how — she left it behind, and then she was so afraid that something might have happened to it that she rushed back to the house and sighed with relief when the woman owner opened the door. The bowl, Andrea explained — she had purchased a bowl and set it on the chest for safekeeping while she toured the house with the prospective buyers, and she . . . She felt like rushing past the frowning woman and seizing her bowl. The owner stepped aside, and it was only when Andrea ran to the chest that the lady glanced at her a little strangely. In the few seconds before Andrea picked up the bowl, she realized that the owner must have just seen that it had been perfectly placed, that the sunlight struck the bluer part of it. Her pitcher had been moved to the far side of the chest, and the bowl predominated. All the way home, Andrea wondered how she could have left the bowl behind. It was like leaving a friend at an outing — just walking off. Sometimes there were stories in the paper about families forgetting a child somewhere and driving to the next city. Andrea had only gone a mile down the road before she remembered.

In time, she dreamed of the bowl. Twice, in a waking dream — early in the morning, between sleep and a last nap before rising — she had a clear vision of it. It came into sharp focus and startled her for a moment — the same bowl she looked at every day.

She had a very profitable year selling real estate. Word spread, and she had more clients than she felt comfortable with. She had the foolish thought that if only the bowl were an animate object she could thank it. There were times when she wanted to talk to her husband about the bowl. He was a stockbroker, and sometimes told people that he was fortunate to be married to a woman who had such a fine aesthetic sense and yet could also function in the real world. They were a lot alike, really — they had agreed on that. They were both quiet people — reflective, slow to make value judgments, but almost intractable once they had come to a conclusion. They both liked details, but while ironies attracted her, he was more impatient and dismissive when matters became many-sided or unclear. But they both knew this, it was the kind of thing they could talk about when they were alone in the car together, coming home from a party or after a weekend with friends. But she never talked to him about the bowl. When they were at dinner, exchanging their news of the day, or while they lay in bed at night listening to the stereo and murmuring sleepy disconnections, she was often tempted to come right out and say that she thought that the bowl in the living room, the cream-colored bowl, was responsible for her success. But she didn't say it. She couldn't begin to explain it. Sometimes in the morning, she would look at him and feel guilty that she had such a constant secret.

Could it be that she had some deeper connection with the bowl — a relationship of some kind? She corrected her thinking: how could she imagine such a thing, when she was a human being and it was a bowl? It was ridiculous. Just think of how people lived together and loved each other . . . But was that always so clear, always a relationship? She was confused by these thoughts, but they remained in her mind. There was something within her now, something real, that she never talked about.

The bowl was a mystery, even to her. It was frustrating, because her involvement with the bowl contained a steady sense of unrequited good fortune; it would have been easier to respond if some sort of demand were made in return. But that only happened in fairy tales. The bowl was just a bowl. She did not believe that for one second. What she believed was that it was something she loved.

In the past, she had sometimes talked to her husband about a new property she was about to buy or sell — confiding some clever strategy she had devised to persuade owners who seemed ready to sell. Now she stopped doing that, for all her strategies involved the bowl. She became more deliberate with the bowl, and more possessive. She put it in houses only when no one was there, and removed it when she left the house. Instead of just moving a pitcher or a dish, she would remove all the other objects from a table. She had to force herself to handle them carefully, because she didn't really care about them. She just wanted them out of sight.

She wondered how the situation would end. As with a lover, there was no exact scenario of how matters would come to a close. Anxiety became the operative force. It would be irrelevant if the lover rushed into someone else's arms, or wrote her a note and departed to another city. The horror was the possibility of the disappearance. That was what mattered.

She would get up at night and look at the bowl. It never occurred to her that she might break it. She washed and dried it without anxiety, and she moved it often, from coffee table to mahogany corner table or wherever, without fearing an accident. It was clear that she would not be the one who would do anything to the bowl. The bowl was only handled by her, set safely on one surface or another; it was not very likely that anyone would break it. A bowl was a poor conductor of electricity: it would not be hit by lightning. Yet the idea of damage persisted. She did not think beyond that — to what her life would be without the bowl. She only continued to fear that some accident would happen. Why not, in a world where people set plants where they did not belong, so that visitors touring a house would be fooled into thinking that dark corners got sunlight — a world full of tricks?

She had first seen the bowl several years earlier, at a crafts fair she had visited half in secret, with her lover. He had urged her to buy the bowl. She didn't *need* any more things, she told him. But she had been drawn to the bowl, and they had lingered near it. Then she went on to the next booth, and he came up behind her, tapping the rim against her shoulder as she ran her fingers over a wood carving. "You're still insisting that I buy that?" she said. "No," he said. "I bought it for you." He had bought her other things before this — things she liked more, at first — the child's ebony-and-turquoise ring that fitted her little finger; the wooden box, long and thin, beautifully dovetailed, that she used to hold paper clips; the soft gray sweater with a pouch pocket. It was his idea that when he could not be there to hold her hand she could hold her own — clasp her hands inside the lone pocket that stretched across the front. But in time she became more attached to the bowl than to any of his other presents. She tried to talk herself out of it. She owned other things that were more striking or valuable. It wasn't an object whose beauty jumped out at you; a lot of people must have passed it by before the two of them saw it that day.

Her lover had said that she was always too slow to know what she really loved. Why continue with her life the way it was? Why be two-faced, he asked her. He had made the first move toward her. When she would not decide in his favor, would not change her life and come to him, he asked her what made her think she could have it both ways. And then he made the last move and left. It was a decision meant to break her will, to shatter her intransigent ideas about honoring previous commitments.

Time passed. Alone in the living room at night, she often looked at the bowl sitting on the table, still and safe, unilluminated. In its way, it was perfect: the world cut in half, deep and smoothly empty. Near the rim, even in dim light, the eye moved toward one small flash of blue, a vanishing point on the horizon.

Alison Bechdel

Alison Bechdel (b. 1960) described her family background so meticulously in her best-selling graphic memoir *Fun Home* (2006) that her *New York Times* reviewer was moved to drive to Bechdel's hometown of Beech Creek, Pennsylvania, to check out her story: "two hundred miles west of Manhattan on I-80, then south on Route 150" past the spot where her father Bruce Bechdel was killed at the age of forty-four when he stepped in front of a truck. The reviewer also discovered that the Victorian mansion on Maple Avenue where Bechdel and her brother had grown up looked exactly as she had drawn it in her book. It was on the market for $279,900 with the realtor's sign in front reading, "Don't miss your chance to own a piece of history!"

Bechdel began keeping a journal when she was ten years old, but the scrupulously accurate drawings in *Fun Home* had their origin in an archive of family photographs, not her memory. Her graphic memoir consists of nearly a thousand panels drawn in black ink and shaded in green, drawings based on hundreds of reference photographs she took of herself using a digital camera with a timer. "It became really crazy and compulsive. I had to be my dad, I had to be my mom, I had to be my parents fighting with one another." She even posed as her father in his coffin—"I put on a jacket and tie and crossed my arms." Each chapter of *Fun Home*, such as the opening chapter, "Old Father, Old Artificer," begins with a drawing of an actual family photograph "to ground the story in real life. I wanted to keep reminding readers that the characters are real people, the events really happened." Finding out from her father's photographs that he led a secret homosexual life "right under our noses was like finding the key to a cryptogram," especially since Bechdel suspected while she was growing up that she was a lesbian. Her father, a high school English teacher, taught her to read literature closely. In college when she was studying James Joyce's *A Portrait of the Artist as a Young Man*, whose protagonist is named Stephen Dedalus and which includes the phrase "Old Father, Old Artificer," her father said, "Good. You damn well better identify with every page."

As a graphic artist Bechdel was first inspired by reading *Mad* magazine and the cartoons of Charles Addams. "I think I learned my biggest cartooning lesson from Addams—how to calibrate that crucial, tantalizing distance between the image and the word. Not too wide, not too narrow—just enough for the reader to complete the circle." From 1987 to 2008 Bechdel created comic strips about a lesbian household, what she calls "humorous real-life sitcoms," collected in *Dykes to Watch Out For* (2008). She feels that "Being a lesbian has been more of a boost to my career than a negative influence because I had a very cohesive, ready-made audience." *Fun Home* took her seven years to complete, first working on the text and then creating the drawings. "For some reason writing and drawing are very separate processes for me. I'll have an idea what a panel will look like while I'm writing, but I often don't touch a pencil until the text is completely finished. . . . It's almost like I'm two different people, first the writer, then the sketcher and inker." In *Are You My Mother? A Comic Drama* (2012), Bechdel explored her relationship with her mother in a second graphic memoir.

RELATED CASEBOOK

See Casebook on Graphic Storytelling, pages 1647–1663, including Alison Bechdel, "What the Little Old Ladies Feel," page 1647; Charles Hatfield, "From *Alternative Comics:* Toward the Habit of Questioning," page 1649; Michael Kupperman, "Are Comics Serious Literature?" page 1652.

2006

OLD FATHER, OLD ARTIFICER

LIKE MANY FATHERS, MINE COULD OCCASIONALLY BE PREVAILED ON FOR A SPOT OF "AIRPLANE."

AS HE LAUNCHED ME, MY FULL WEIGHT WOULD FALL ON THE PIVOT POINT BETWEEN HIS FEET AND MY STOMACH.

OOF!

IT WAS A DISCOMFORT WELL WORTH THE RARE PHYSICAL CONTACT, AND CERTAINLY WORTH THE MOMENT OF PERFECT BALANCE WHEN I SOARED ABOVE HIM.

IN THE CIRCUS, ACROBATICS WHERE ONE PERSON LIES ON THE FLOOR BALANCING ANOTHER ARE CALLED "ICARIAN GAMES."

CONSIDERING THE FATE OF ICARUS AFTER HE FLOUTED HIS FATHER'S ADVICE AND FLEW SO CLOSE TO THE SUN HIS WINGS MELTED, PERHAPS SOME DARK HUMOR IS INTENDED.

BUT BEFORE HE DID SO, HE MANAGED TO GET QUITE A LOT DONE.

HIS GREATEST ACHIEVEMENT, ARGUABLY, WAS HIS MONOMANIACAL RESTORATION OF OUR OLD HOUSE.

WHEN OTHER CHILDREN CALLED OUR HOUSE A MANSION, I WOULD DEMUR. I RESENTED THE IMPLICATION THAT MY FAMILY WAS RICH, OR UNUSUAL IN ANY WAY.

IN FACT, WE WERE UNUSUAL, THOUGH I WOULDN'T APPRECIATE EXACTLY HOW UNUSUAL UNTIL MUCH LATER. BUT WE WERE NOT RICH.

THE GILT CORNICES, THE MARBLE FIREPLACE, THE CRYSTAL CHANDELIERS, THE SHELVES OF CALF-BOUND BOOKS--THESE WERE NOT SO MUCH BOUGHT AS PRODUCED FROM THIN AIR BY MY FATHER'S REMARKABLE LEGERDEMAIN.

HISTORICAL RESTORATION WASN'T HIS JOB.

IT WAS HIS PASSION. AND I MEAN PASSION IN EVERY SENSE OF THE WORD.

OUR GOTHIC REVIVAL HOUSE HAD BEEN BUILT DURING THE SMALL PENNSYLVANIA TOWN'S ONE BRIEF MOMENT OF WEALTH, FROM THE LUMBER INDUSTRY, IN 1867.

BUT LOCAL FORTUNES HAD DECLINED STEADILY FROM THAT POINT, AND WHEN MY PARENTS BOUGHT THE PLACE IN 1962, IT WAS A SHELL OF ITS FORMER SELF.

THE SHUTTERS AND SCROLLWORK WERE GONE. THE CLAPBOARDS HAD BEEN SHEATHED WITH SCABROUS SHINGLES.

THE BARE LIGHTBULBS REVEALED DINGY WARTIME WALLPAPER AND WOODWORK PAINTED PASTEL GREEN.

ALL THAT WAS LEFT OF THE HOUSE'S LUMBER-ERA GLORY WERE THE EXUBERANT FRONT PORCH SUPPORTS.

BUT OVER THE NEXT EIGHTEEN YEARS, MY FATHER WOULD RESTORE THE HOUSE TO ITS ORIGINAL CONDITION, AND THEN SOME.

JESUS! THIS MUST BE THE PATTERN FOR THE ORIGINAL BARGEBOARD!

HE WOULD PERFORM, AS DAEDALUS DID, DAZZLING DISPLAYS OF ARTFULNESS.

HE WOULD CULTIVATE THE BARREN YARD... ...INTO A LUSH, FLOWERING LANDSCAPE.

HE WOULD MANIPULATE FLAGSTONES THAT WEIGHED HALF A TON... ...AND THE THINNEST, QUIVERING LAYERS OF GOLD LEAF.

IT COULD HAVE BEEN A ROMANTIC STORY, LIKE IN *IT'S A WONDERFUL LIFE*, WHEN JIMMY STEWART AND DONNA REED FIX UP THAT BIG OLD HOUSE AND RAISE THEIR FAMILY THERE.

HELLO, DARLING!

HELLO, DADDY!

Merry Christmas

BUT IN THE MOVIE WHEN JIMMY STEWART COMES HOME ONE NIGHT AND STARTS YELLING AT EVERYONE...

HOLD IT STRAIGHT.

TOMMY, STOP THAT! JANIE, HAVEN'T YOU LEARNED THAT SILLY TUNE YET?

ONE OF MY BROTHERS

...IT'S OUT OF THE ORDINARY.

THE NEEDLES ARE SHARP!

GODDAMN IT!

YOU PLAY IT OVER AND OVER--NOW STOP IT! **STOP IT!**

DAEDALUS, TOO, WAS INDIFFERENT TO THE HUMAN COST OF HIS PROJECTS.

DON'T HIT ME!

HE BLITHELY BETRAYED THE KING, FOR EXAMPLE, WHEN THE QUEEN ASKED HIM TO BUILD HER A COW DISGUISE SO SHE COULD SEDUCE THE WHITE BULL.

GEORGE, WHY MUST YOU TORTURE THE CHILDREN?

KUH-CLINK!

INDEED, THE RESULT OF THAT SCHEME--A HALF-BULL, HALF-MAN MONSTER--INSPIRED DAEDALUS'S GREATEST CREATION YET.

HE HID THE MINOTAUR IN THE LABYRINTH-- A MAZE OF PASSAGES AND ROOMS OPEN-ING ENDLESSLY INTO ONE ANOTHER...

...AND FROM WHICH, AS STRAY YOUTHS AND MAIDENS DISCOVERED TO THEIR PERIL...

...ESCAPE WAS IMPOSSIBLE.

THEN THERE ARE THOSE FAMOUS WINGS. WAS DAEDALUS REALLY STRICKEN WITH GRIEF WHEN ICARUS FELL INTO THE SEA?

OR JUST DISAPPOINTED BY THE DESIGN FAILURE?

SOMETIMES, WHEN THINGS WERE GOING WELL, I THINK MY FATHER ACTUALLY ENJOYED HAVING A FAMILY.

OR AT LEAST, THE AIR OF AUTHENTICITY WE LENT TO HIS EXHIBIT. A SORT OF STILL LIFE WITH CHILDREN.

AND OF COURSE, MY BROTHERS AND I WERE FREE LABOR. DAD CONSIDERED US EXTENSIONS OF HIS OWN BODY, LIKE PRECISION ROBOT ARMS.

PUT HOT, SOAPY WATER IN THE SINK AND GET SOME CLEAN RAGS.

IN THIS REGARD, IT WAS LIKE BEING RAISED NOT BY JIMMY BUT BY MARTHA STEWART.

IN THEORY, HIS ARRANGEMENT WITH MY MOTHER WAS MORE COOPERATIVE.

WHAT DO YOU THINK OF THIS GAS CHANDELIER?

BORDELLO.

AUCTION CATALOG

IN PRACTICE, IT WAS NOT.

I DEVELOPED A CONTEMPT FOR USE-LESS ORNAMENT. WHAT FUNCTION WAS SERVED BY THE SCROLLS, TASSELS, AND BRIC-A-BRAC THAT INFESTED OUR HOUSE?

IF ANYTHING, THEY OBSCURED FUNCTION. THEY WERE EMBELLISHMENTS IN THE WORST SENSE.

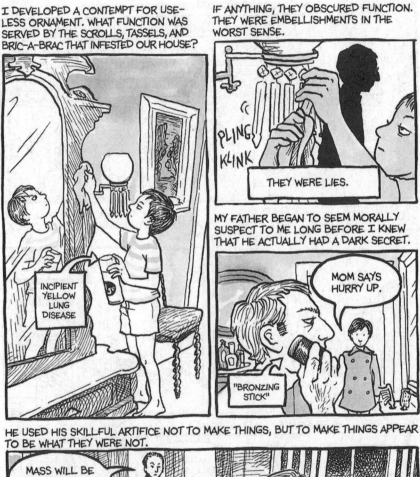

"PLING KLINK"

THEY WERE LIES.

INCIPIENT YELLOW LUNG DISEASE

MY FATHER BEGAN TO SEEM MORALLY SUSPECT TO ME LONG BEFORE I KNEW THAT HE ACTUALLY HAD A DARK SECRET.

MOM SAYS HURRY UP.

"BRONZING STICK"

HE USED HIS SKILLFUL ARTIFICE NOT TO MAKE THINGS, BUT TO MAKE THINGS APPEAR TO BE WHAT THEY WERE NOT.

MASS WILL BE OVER BEFORE WE GET THERE.

THAT IS TO SAY, IMPECCABLE.

THIS EMBARRASSMENT ON MY PART WAS A TINY SCALE MODEL OF MY FATHER'S MORE FULLY DEVELOPED SELF-LOATHING.

HIS SHAME INHABITED OUR HOUSE AS PERVASIVELY AND INVISIBLY AS THE AROMATIC MUSK OF AGING MAHOGANY.

IN FACT, THE METICULOUS, PERIOD INTERIORS WERE EXPRESSLY DESIGNED TO CONCEAL IT.

MIRRORS, DISTRACTING BRONZES, MULTIPLE DOORWAYS. VISITORS OFTEN GOT LOST UPSTAIRS.

GRACIOUS, I ALMOST WALKED RIGHT INTO THIS!

MY MOTHER, MY BROTHERS, AND I KNEW OUR WAY AROUND WELL ENOUGH, BUT IT WAS IMPOSSIBLE TO TELL IF THE MINOTAUR LAY BEYOND THE NEXT CORNER.

AND THE CONSTANT TENSION WAS HEIGHT- ENED BY THE FACT THAT SOME ENCOUN- TERS COULD BE QUITE PLEASANT.

HIS BURSTS OF KINDNESS WERE AS INCAN- DESCENT AS HIS TANTRUMS WERE DARK.

ALTHOUGH I'M GOOD AT ENUMERATING MY FATHER'S FLAWS, IT'S HARD FOR ME TO SUSTAIN MUCH ANGER AT HIM.

I EXPECT THIS IS PARTLY BECAUSE HE'S DEAD, AND PARTLY BECAUSE THE BAR IS LOWER FOR FATHERS THAN FOR MOTHERS.

STOP SPLASHING!

IN MY EYES!

HOLD STILL, DAMMIT!

MY MOTHER MUST HAVE BATHED ME HUNDREDS OF TIMES. BUT IT'S MY FATHER RINSING ME OFF WITH THE PURPLE METAL CUP THAT I REMEMBER MOST CLEARLY.

THE SUFFUSION OF WARMTH AS THE HOT WATER SLUICED OVER ME...

...THE SUDDEN, UNBEARABLE COLD OF ITS ABSENCE.

WAS HE A GOOD FATHER? I WANT TO SAY, "AT LEAST HE STUCK AROUND." BUT OF COURSE, HE DIDN'T.

AGAIN!

IT'S TRUE THAT HE DIDN'T KILL HIMSELF UNTIL I WAS NEARLY TWENTY.

BUT HIS ABSENCE RESONATED RETRO-ACTIVELY, ECHOING BACK THROUGH ALL THE TIME I KNEW HIM.

MAYBE IT WAS THE CONVERSE OF THE WAY AMPUTEES FEEL PAIN IN A MISSING LIMB.

HE REALLY WAS THERE ALL THOSE YEARS, A FLESH-AND-BLOOD PRESENCE STEAMING OFF THE WALLPAPER, DIGGING UP THE DOGWOODS, POLISHING THE FINIALS...

...SMELLING OF SAWDUST AND SWEAT AND DESIGNER COLOGNE.

BUT I ACHED AS IF HE WERE ALREADY GONE.

Ambrose Bierce

Ambrose Bierce (1842–1914?), the youngest of nine children, was born in a log cabin in Horse Cave Creek, Ohio. His father was a farmer, and Bierce had only one year of formal education at the Kentucky Military Institute when he was seventeen. During the Civil War he enlisted with the Ninth Indiana Infantry as a drummer boy. Wounded in 1864, he left the army and went to live with a brother in San Francisco. There he began his career as a newspaper writer, publishing his first story, "The Haunted Valley," in the *Overland Magazine* in 1871. When Bierce married the daughter of a wealthy Nevada miner, his father-in-law gave the young couple a wedding gift of $10,000, enabling them to live in London for five years. Homesick for California, Bierce returned with his wife and wrote for various newspapers, including William Randolph Hearst's *San Francisco Examiner*. In the 1880s he became very influential in his profession, although in literary circles outside California he was not widely known. Then his wife separated from him, his two sons died tragically, and he became embittered. In his seventies Bierce supervised publication of the twelve volumes of his *Collected Works*, revisited the Civil War battlefields of his youth, and then disappeared across the Mexican border. The Mexican writer Carlos Fuentes imagined Bierce's last months in the novel *The Old Gringo* (1985), which was made into a film.

Bierce is known as the author of the philosophical epigrams in *The Devil's Dictionary* (1906), but his two volumes of short stories are his finest achievement as a writer. He is considered a notable forerunner of American realists such as Stephen Crane. "An Occurrence at Owl Creek Bridge" was included in Bierce's first story collection, *In the Midst of Life*, published privately in San Francisco under the title *Tales of Soldiers and Civilians* (1891). His second collection, *Can Such Things Be?*, was published two years later.

Bierce preferred the short story to the novel, defining the novel as a "short story padded." He modeled his creation of suspense leading up to a dramatic crisis after the stories of Edgar Allan Poe, but Bierce described more realistic situations in his fiction. Dreams, flashbacks, and hallucinations, as in "An Occurrence at Owl Creek Bridge," provided vivid images but no escape from the violent death that was Bierce's obsession.

An Occurrence at Owl Creek Bridge

1891

I

A man stood upon a railroad bridge in Northern Alabama, looking down into the swift waters twenty feet below. The man's hands were behind his back, the wrists bound with a cord. A rope loosely encircled his neck. It was attached to a stout cross-timber above his head, and the slack fell to the level of his knees.

Some loose boards laid upon the sleepers supporting the metals of the railway supplied a footing for him and his executioners — two private soldiers of the Federal army, directed by a sergeant, who in civil life may have been a deputy sheriff. At a short remove upon the same temporary platform was an officer in the uniform of his rank, armed. He was a captain. A sentinel at each end of the bridge stood with his rifle in the position known as "support," that is to say, vertical in front of the left shoulder, the hammer resting on the forearm thrown straight across the chest — a formal and unnatural position, enforcing an erect carriage of the body. It did not appear to be the duty of these two men to know what was occurring at the centre of the bridge; they merely blockaded the two ends of the foot plank which traversed it.

Beyond one of the sentinels nobody was in sight; the railroad ran straight away into a forest for a hundred yards, then, curving, was lost to view. Doubt-less there was an outpost further along. The other bank of the stream was open ground — a gentle acclivity crowned with a stockade of vertical tree trunks, loop-holed for rifles, with a single embrasure through which protruded the muzzle of a brass cannon commanding the bridge. Midway of the slope between bridge and fort were the spectators — a single company of infantry in line, at "parade rest," the butts of the rifles on the ground, the barrels inclining slightly backward against the right shoulder, the hands crossed upon the stock. A lieutenant stood at the right of the line, the point of his sword upon the ground, his left hand resting upon his right. Excepting the group of four at the centre of the bridge not a man moved. The company faced the bridge, staring stonily, motionless. The sentinels, facing the banks of the stream, might have been statues to adorn the bridge. The captain stood with folded arms, silent, observing the work of his subordinates but making no sign. Death is a digni-tary who, when he comes announced, is to be received with formal manifesta-tions of respect, even by those most familiar with him. In the code of military etiquette silence and fixity are forms of deference.

The man who was engaged in being hanged was apparently about thirty-five years of age. He was a civilian, if one might judge from his dress, which was that of a planter. His features were good — a straight nose, firm mouth, broad forehead, from which his long, dark hair was combed straight back, fall-ing behind his ears to the collar of his well-fitted frock coat. He wore a mous-tache and pointed beard, but no whiskers; his eyes were large and dark grey and had a kindly expression which one would hardly have expected in one whose neck was in the hemp. Evidently this was no vulgar assassin. The liberal military code makes provision for hanging many kinds of people, and gentle-men are not excluded.

The preparations being complete, the two private soldiers stepped aside and each drew away the plank upon which he had been standing. The ser-geant turned to the captain, saluted and placed himself immediately behind that officer, who in turn moved apart one pace. These movements left the con-demned man and the sergeant standing on the two ends of the same plank, which spanned three of the cross-ties of the bridge. The end upon which the civilian stood almost, but not quite, reached a fourth. This plank had been held in place by the weight of the captain; it was now held by that of the sergeant. At a signal from the former, the latter would step aside, the plank would tilt and the condemned man go down between two ties. The arrangement commended itself to his judgment as simple and effective. His face had not been covered nor his eyes bandaged. He looked a moment at his "unsteadfast footing," then let his gaze wander to the swirling water of the stream racing madly beneath his feet. A piece of dancing driftwood caught his attention and his eyes followed it down the current. How slowly it appeared to move! What a sluggish stream!

He closed his eyes in order to fix his last thoughts upon his wife and children. The water, touched to gold by the early sun, the brooding mists under the banks at some distance down the stream, the fort, the soldiers, the piece of driftwood — all had distracted him. And now he became conscious of a new disturbance. Striking through the thought of his dear ones was a sound which he could neither ignore nor understand, a sharp, distinct, metallic percussion like the stroke of a blacksmith's hammer upon the anvil; it had the same ringing quality. He wondered what it was, and whether immeasurably distant or near by — it seemed both. Its recurrence was regular, but as slow as the tolling of a death knell. He awaited each stroke with impatience and — he knew not why — apprehension. The intervals of silence grew progressively longer; the delays became maddening. With their greater infrequency the sounds increased in strength and sharpness. They hurt his ear like the thrust of a knife; he feared he would shriek. What he heard was the ticking of his watch.

He unclosed his eyes and saw again the water below him. "If I could free my hands," he thought, "I might throw off the noose and spring into the stream. By diving I could evade the bullets, and, swimming vigorously, reach the bank, take to the woods, and get away home. My home, thank God, is as yet outside their lines; my wife and little ones are still beyond the invader's farthest advance."

As these thoughts, which have here to be set down in words, were flashed into the doomed man's brain rather than evolved from it, the captain nodded to the sergeant. The sergeant stepped aside.

II

Peyton Farquhar was a well-to-do planter, of an old and highly respected Alabama family. Being a slave owner, and, like other slave owners, a politician, he was naturally an original secessionist and ardently devoted to the Southern cause. Circumstances of an imperious nature which it is unnecessary to relate here, had prevented him from taking service with the gallant army which had fought the disastrous campaigns ending with the fall of Corinth, and he chafed under the inglorious restraint, longing for the release of his energies, the larger life of the soldier, the opportunity for distinction. That opportunity, he felt, would come, as it comes to all in war time. Meanwhile he did what he could. No service was too humble for him to perform in aid of the South, no adventure too perilous for him to undertake if consistent with the character of a civilian who was at heart a soldier, and who in good faith and without too much qualification assented to at least a part of the frankly villainous dictum that all is fair in love and war.

One evening while Farquhar and his wife were sitting on a rustic bench near the entrance to his grounds, a grey-clad soldier rode up to the gate and asked for a drink of water. Mrs. Farquhar was only too happy to serve him with her own white hands. While she was gone to fetch the water, her husband approached the dusty horseman and inquired eagerly for news from the front.

"The Yanks are repairing the railroads," said the man, "and are getting ready for another advance. They have reached the Owl Creek bridge, put it in order, and built a stockade on the other bank. The commandant has issued an order, which is posted everywhere, declaring that any civilian caught interfering with the railroad, its bridges, tunnels, or trains, will be summarily hanged. I saw the order."

"How far is it to the Owl Creek bridge?" Farquhar asked.

"About thirty miles."

"Is there no force on this side the creek?"

"Only a picket post half a mile out, on the railroad, and a single sentinel at this end of the bridge."

"Suppose a man — a civilian and student of hanging — should elude the picket post and perhaps get the better of the sentinel," said Farquhar, smiling, "what could he accomplish?"

The soldier reflected. "I was there a month ago," he replied. "I observed that the flood of last winter had lodged a great quantity of driftwood against the wooden pier at this end of the bridge. It is now dry and would burn like tow."

The lady had now brought the water, which the soldier drank. He thanked her ceremoniously, bowed to her husband, and rode away. An hour later, after nightfall, he repassed the plantation, going northward in the direction from which he had come. He was a Federal scout.

III

As Peyton Farquhar fell straight downward through the bridge, he lost consciousness and was as one already dead. From this state he was awakened — ages later, it seemed to him — by the pain of a sharp pressure upon his throat, followed by a sense of suffocation. Keen, poignant agonies seemed to shoot from his neck downward through every fibre of his body and limbs. These pains appeared to flash along well-defined lines of ramification, and to beat with an inconceivably rapid periodicity. They seemed like streams of pulsating fire heating him to an intolerable temperature. As to his head, he was conscious of nothing but a feeling of fullness — of congestion. These sensations were unaccompanied by thought. The intellectual part of his nature was already effaced; he had power only to feel, and feeling was torment. He was conscious of motion. Encompassed in a luminous cloud, of which he was now merely the fiery heart, without material substance, he swung through unthinkable arcs of oscillation, like a vast pendulum. Then all at once, with terrible suddenness, the light about him shot upward with the noise of a loud splash;

a frightful roaring was in his ears, and all was cold and dark. The power of thought was restored; he knew that the rope had broken and he had fallen into the stream. There was no additional strangulation; the noose about his neck was already suffocating him, and kept the water from his lungs. To die of hanging at the bottom of a river — the idea seemed to him ludicrous. He opened his eyes in the blackness and saw above him a gleam of light, but how distant, how inaccessible! He was still sinking, for the light became fainter and fainter until it was a mere glimmer. Then it began to grow and brighten, and he knew that he was rising toward the surface — knew it with reluctance, for he was now very comfortable. "To be hanged and drowned," he thought, "that is not so bad; but I do not wish to be shot. No; I will not be shot; that is not fair."

He was not conscious of an effort, but a sharp pain in his wrist apprised him that he was trying to free his hands. He gave the struggle his attention, as an idler might observe the feat of a juggler, without interest in the outcome. What splendid effort! — what magnificent, what superhuman strength! Ah, that was a fine endeavor! Bravo! The cord fell away; his arms parted and floated upward, the hands dimly seen on each side in the growing light. He watched them with a new interest as first one and then the other pounced upon the noose at his neck. They tore it away and thrust it fiercely aside, its undulations resembling those of a water-snake. "Put it back, put it back!" He thought he shouted these words to his hands, for the undoing of the noose had been succeeded by the direst pang which he had yet experienced. His neck ached horribly; his brain was on fire; his heart, which had been fluttering faintly, gave a great leap, trying to force itself out at his mouth. His whole body was racked and wrenched with an insupportable anguish! But his disobedient hands gave no heed to the command. They beat the water vigorously with quick, downward strokes, forcing him to the surface. He felt his head emerge; his eyes were blinded by the sunlight; his chest expanded convulsively, and with a supreme and crowning agony his lungs engulfed a great draught of air, which instantly he expelled in a shriek!

He was now in full possession of his physical senses. They were, indeed, preternaturally keen and alert. Something in the awful disturbance of his organic system had so exalted and refined them that they made record of things never before perceived. He felt the ripples upon his face and heard their separate sounds as they struck. He looked at the forest on the bank of the stream, saw the individual trees, the leaves and the veining of each leaf — saw the very insects upon them, the locusts, the brilliant-bodied flies, the grey spiders stretching their webs from twig to twig. He noted the prismatic colors in all the dewdrops upon a million blades of grass. The humming of the gnats that danced above the eddies of the stream, the beating of the dragon flies' wings, the strokes of the water spiders' legs, like oars which had lifted their boat — all these made audible music. A fish slid along beneath his eyes and he heard the rush of its body parting the water.

He had come to the surface facing down the stream; in a moment the visible world seemed to wheel slowly round, himself the pivotal point, and he saw the bridge, the fort, the soldiers upon the bridge, the captain, the sergeant, the two privates, his executioners. They were in silhouette against the blue sky.

They shouted and gesticulated, pointing at him; the captain had drawn his pistol, but did not fire; the others were unarmed. Their movements were grotesque and horrible, their forms gigantic.

Suddenly he heard a sharp report and something struck the water smartly within a few inches of his head, spattering his face with spray. He heard a second report, and saw one of the sentinels with his rifle at his shoulder, a light cloud of blue smoke rising from the muzzle. The man in the water saw the eye of the man on the bridge gazing into his own through the sights of the rifle. He observed that it was a grey eye, and remembered having read that grey eyes were keenest and that all famous marksmen had them. Nevertheless, this one had missed.

A counter swirl had caught Farquhar and turned him half round; he was again looking into the forest on the bank opposite the fort. The sound of a clear, high voice in a monotonous singsong now rang out behind him and came across the water with a distinctness that pierced and subdued all other sounds, even the beating of the ripples in his ears. Although no soldier, he had frequented camps enough to know the dread significance of that deliberate, drawling, aspirated chant; the lieutenant on shore was taking a part in the morning's work. How coldly and pitilessly — with what an even, calm intonation, presaging and enforcing tranquility in the men — with what accurately-measured intervals fell those cruel words:

"Attention, company.... Shoulder arms.... Ready.... Aim.... Fire."

Farquhar dived — dived as deeply as he could. The water roared in his ears like the voice of Niagara, yet he heard the dulled thunder of the volley, and rising again toward the surface, met shining bits of metal, singularly flattened, oscillating slowly downward. Some of them touched him on the face and hands, then fell away, continuing their descent. One lodged between his collar and neck; it was uncomfortably warm, and he snatched it out.

As he rose to the surface, gasping for breath, he saw that he had been a long time under water; he was perceptibly farther down stream — nearer to safety. The soldiers had almost finished reloading; the metal ramrods flashed all at once in the sunshine as they were drawn from the barrels, turned in the air, and thrust into their sockets. The two sentinels fired again, independently and ineffectually.

The hunted man saw all this over his shoulder; he was now swimming vigorously with the current. His brain was as energetic as his arms and legs; he thought with the rapidity of lightning.

"The officer," he reasoned, "will not make the martinet's error a second time. It is as easy to dodge a volley as a single shot. He has probably already given the command to fire at will. God help me, I cannot dodge them all!"

An appalling plash within two yards of him, followed by a loud rushing sound, *diminuendo*, which seemed to travel back through the air to the fort and died in an explosion which stirred the very river to its deeps! A rising sheet of water, which curved over him, fell down upon him, blinded him, strangled him! The cannon had taken a hand in the game. As he shook his head free from the commotion of the smitten water, he heard the deflected shot humming through the air ahead, and in an instant it was cracking and smashing the branches in the forest beyond.

"They will not do that again," he thought; "the next time they will use a charge of grape. I must keep my eye upon the gun; the smoke will apprise me — the report arrives too late; it lags behind the missile. It is a good gun."

Suddenly he felt himself whirled round and round — spinning like a top. The water, the banks, the forest, the now distant bridge, fort, and men — all were commingled and blurred. Objects were represented by their colors only; circular horizontal streaks of color — that was all he saw. He had been caught in a vortex and was being whirled on with a velocity of advance and gyration which made him giddy and sick. In a few moments he was flung upon the gravel at the foot of the left bank of the stream — the southern bank — and behind a projecting point which concealed him from his enemies. The sudden arrest of his motion, the abrasion of one of his hands on the gravel, restored him and he wept with delight. He dug his fingers into the sand, threw it over himself in handfuls and audibly blessed it. It looked like gold, like diamonds, rubies, emeralds; he could think of nothing beautiful which it did not resemble. The trees upon the bank were giant garden plants; he noted a definite order in their arrangement, inhaled the fragrance of their blooms. A strange, roseate light shone through the spaces among their trunks, and the wind made in their branches the music of æolian harps. He had no wish to perfect his escape, was content to remain in that enchanting spot until retaken.

A whizz and rattle of grapeshot among the branches high above his head roused him from his dream. The baffled cannoneer had fired him a random farewell. He sprang to his feet, rushed up the sloping bank, and plunged into the forest.

All that day he travelled, laying his course by the rounding sun. The forest seemed interminable; nowhere did he discover a break in it, not even a wood-man's road. He had not known that he lived in so wild a region. There was something uncanny in the revelation.

By nightfall he was fatigued, footsore, famishing. The thought of his wife and children urged him on. At last he found a road which led him in what he knew to be the right direction. It was as wide and straight as a city street, yet it seemed untravelled. No fields bordered it, no dwelling anywhere. Not so much as the barking of a dog suggested human habitation. The black bodies of the great trees formed a straight wall on both sides, terminating on the horizon in a point, like a diagram in a lesson in perspective. Overhead, as he looked up through this rift in the wood, shone great golden stars looking unfamiliar and grouped in strange constellations. He was sure they were arranged in some order which had a secret and malign significance. The wood on either side was full of singular noises, among which — once, twice, and again — he distinctly heard whispers in an unknown tongue.

His neck was in pain, and, lifting his hand to it, he found it horribly swollen. He knew that it had a circle of black where the rope had bruised it. His eyes felt congested; he could no longer close them. His tongue was swollen with thirst; he relieved its fever by thrusting it forward from between his teeth into the cool air. How softly the turf had carpeted the untravelled avenue! He could no longer feel the roadway beneath his feet!

Doubtless, despite his suffering, he fell asleep while walking, for now he sees another scene — perhaps he has merely recovered from a delirium. He stands at the gate of his own home. All is as he left it, and all bright and beautiful in the morning sunshine. He must have travelled the entire night. As he pushes open the gate and passes up the wide white walk, he sees a flutter of female garments; his wife, looking fresh and cool and sweet, steps down from the verandah to meet him. At the bottom of the steps she stands waiting, with a smile of ineffable joy, an attitude of matchless grace and dignity. Ah, how beautiful she is! He springs forward with extended arms. As he is about to clasp her, he feels a stunning blow upon the back of the neck; a blinding white light blazes all about him, with a sound like the shock of a cannon — then all is darkness and silence!

Peyton Farquhar was dead; his body, with a broken neck, swung gently from side to side beneath the timbers of the Owl Creek bridge.

Roberto Bolaño

Roberto Bolaño (1953–2003) was born in Chile, the son of a truck driver and boxer who moved his family to Mexico City in 1968. As a child Bolaño was dyslexic and did poorly in school. As a teenager in Mexico City he dropped out of school and worked briefly as a journalist. He became friends with Mario Santiago, who also loved literature and was trying to write poetry. In the 1970s they formed a group they called the Infrarealists, what Bolaño later described as "a kind of Dada à la Mexicana." Young poets and painters and hangers-on joined the group, and they lived a chaotic bohemian lifestyle modeled on what they imagined as the antics of the 1950s "beatnik" poets in the United States. When Bolaño was twenty, he left Mexico to return to Chile after the Chilean election of the Socialist President, Salvador Allende. After Augusto Pinochet's successful military coup against Allende on September 11, 1973, Bolaño allegedly was arrested as a suspected terrorist and spent eight days in prison, where he was supposedly rescued by two friends who worked as prison guards. Bolaño later described these experiences in his short stories "Dance Card" and "Detectives," later included in *Last Evenings on Earth* (2007). Recently Bolaño's claim to what is regarded in Latin America as the "badge of honor" of actively resisting the coup against President Allende in his generation's defining political experience has been questioned by people who actually participated in the events in Chile that he described. Manuel Llorente, the editor of the Spanish newspaper *El Mundo*, understood that "Bolaño was a writer who played with reality, who cultivated ambiguities and false identities, so I didn't care whether [his] narrative . . . was true or invented. To me, the only thing that mattered was its literary value."

In Mexico City, the birth of a son in 1990 caused Bolaño to give up his bohemian existence as a penniless poet and try to make a living from his writing. He moved to Spain, where he began to publish scores of short stories in magazines and newspapers. He had decided that "When I write, the only thing that interests me is the writing itself, that is, the form, the rhythm, the plot." His stories were later gathered in the collections published in English as *The Secret of Evil* (2012), *Last Evenings on Earth* (2010), and *The Insufferable Gaucho* (2010), whose title story is Bolaño's version of Borges' classic tale "The South." Bolaño's reputation as a major author is based on three of his most important novels – *By Night in Chile* (2003), *The Savage Detectives* (2007), and *2666* (2008), posthumously awarded the National Book Critics Circle Award. In 2003 Bolaño died from liver failure in Spain while awaiting a transplant.

The novelist Rodrigo Fresan understood that in a short story such as "Jim," Bolaño was writing "at a time when Latin America no longer believed in utopias, when paradise had become hell, and that sense of monstrousness and waking nightmares and constant flight from something horrid permeates . . . all his work. His books are political, but in a way that is more personal than militant or demagogic, that is closer to the mystique of the beatniks than the *Boom*." To the American writer Jonathan Lethem, "Reading Roberto Bolaño is like hearing the secret story, being shown the fabric of the particular, watching the tracks of art and life merge at the horizon and linger there like a dream from which we awake inspired to look more attentively at the world."

Jim

2003 / Translated by Chris Andrews

MANY YEARS AGO I had a friend named Jim, and he was the saddest North American I've ever come across. I've seen a lot of desperate men. But never one as sad as Jim. Once he went to Peru — supposedly for more than six months, but it wasn't long before I saw him again. The Mexican street kids used to ask him, what's poetry made of, Jim? Listening to them, Jim would stare at the clouds and then he'd start throwing up. Vocabulary, eloquence, the search for truth. Epiphany. Like when you have a vision of the Virgin. He was mugged several times in Central America, which is surprising, because he'd been a Marine and fought in Vietnam. No more fighting, Jim used to say. I'm a poet now, searching for the extraordinary, trying to express it in ordinary, every-day words. So you think there are ordinary, everyday words? I think there are, Jim used to say. His wife was a Chicana poet: every so often she'd threaten to leave him. He showed me a photo of her. She wasn't especially pretty. Her face betrayed suffering, and under that suffering, simmering rage. I imagined her in an apartment in San Francisco or a house in Los Angeles, with the windows shut and the curtains open, sitting at a table, eating sliced bread and a bowl of green soup. Jim liked dark women, apparently, history's secret women, he would say, without elaborating. As for me, I liked blondes. Once I saw him watching fire-eaters on a street in Mexico City. I saw him from behind, and I didn't say hello, but it was obviously Jim. The badly cut hair, the dirty white shirt and the stoop, as if he were still weighed down by his pack. Somehow his neck, his red neck, summoned up the image of a lynching in the country — a landscape in black and white, without billboards or gas station lights — the country as it is or ought to be: one expanse of idle land blurring into the next, brick-walled rooms or bunkers from which we have escaped, standing there, awaiting our return. Jim had his hands in his pockets. The fire-eater was wav-ing his torch and laughing fiercely. His blackened face was ageless: he could have been thirty-five or fifteen. He wasn't wearing a shirt and there was a ver-tical scar from his navel to his breastbone. Every so often he'd fill his mouth with flammable liquid and spit out a long snake of fire. The people in the street would watch him for a while, admire his skill, and continue on their way, except for Jim, who remained there on the edge of the sidewalk, stock-still, as if he expected something more from the fire-eater, a tenth signal (having deciphered the usual nine), or as if he'd seen in that discolored face the features of an old friend or of someone he'd killed. I watched him for a good long while. I was eighteen or nineteen at the time and believed I was immortal. If I'd real-ized that I wasn't, I would have turned around and walked away. After a while I got tired of looking at Jim's back and the fire-eater's grimaces. So I went over and called his name. Jim didn't seem to hear me. When he turned around I noticed that his face was covered with sweat. He seemed to be feverish, and it took him a while to work out who I was; he greeted me with a nod and then turned back to the fire-eater. Standing beside him, I noticed he was crying. He probably had a fever as well. I also discovered something that surprised me less at the time than it does now, writing this: the fire-eater was performing exclusively for Jim, as if all the other passersby on that corner in Mexico City simply didn't exist. Sometimes the flames came within a yard of where we were standing. What are you waiting for, I said, you want to get barbecued in the street? It was a stupid wisecrack, I said it without thinking, but then it hit me: that's exactly what Jim's waiting for. That year, I seem to remember, there was a song they kept playing in some of the funkier places with a refrain that went, *Chingado, hechizado (Fucked up, spellbound).* That was Jim: fucked up and spellbound. Mexico's spell had bound him and now he was looking his demons right in the face. Let's get out of here, I said. I also asked him if he was high, or feeling ill. He shook his head. The fire-eater was staring at us. Then, with his cheeks puffed out like Aeolus, the god of the winds, he began to approach us. In a fraction of a second I realized that it wasn't a gust of wind we'd be getting. Let's go, I said, and yanked Jim away from the fatal edge of that sidewalk. We took ourselves off down the street toward Reforma, and after a while we went our separate ways. Jim didn't say a word in all that time. I never saw him again.

Jorge Luis Borges

Jorge Luis Borges (1899–1986), an Argentinean writer of fiction, poetry, and criticism, was born in Buenos Aires. His father, a professor of psychology, amused him in childhood with various philosophical puzzles that continued to interest Borges when he grew up and became a writer. Educated in Europe, he began to write as a member of a Spanish avant-garde literary movement called *Ultraisme*, a development of expressionism in which image and metaphor were exaggerated to become more important than plot or character. Borges rejected this extreme view when he matured as a writer, but he remained an antirealist.

After his return to Buenos Aires in 1921, he worked in the National Library, becoming its director before the dictator Juan Perón hounded him out of the job for political reasons. Borges published his first book in 1923. In the 1930s he was most active as an essayist and editor; he also wrote detective stories under other names. Then he published *Fictions* (1944), a collection of short, often playful prose statements in which he examined various ideas to show that every human effort is a "fiction." Among his many books, *Labyrinths* (1962) and *The Aleph and Other Stories* (1970) are two important collections of sketches and stories. *Borges on Writing* (1973) contained his views on fiction, poetry, and translation. Until his death, Borges lived in Buenos Aires, where his progressive blindness circumscribed his life. He continued to write, and he occasionally lectured and taught in the United States.

Borges said that he wrote stories for the "sheer fun of it . . . I'm fond of short stories, but I'm far too lazy for novel writing. I'd get tired of the whole thing after writing ten or fifteen pages." He wrote his first short story, "Streetcorner Man," as a literary experiment after seeing a gangster film. He wanted to write a vivid, visual story, not a realistic one. "I knew quite well it was all unreal, but as I wasn't striving after reality I didn't mind." Borges' story "The South" was included in his collection *Artifices* (1944). In his foreword to that book he wrote, "Of 'The South,' which may be my best story, I shall tell the reader only that it is possible to read it both as a forthright narration of novelistic events and in quite another way as well." Borges' alternate reading was that his protagonist actually died on the operating table in the second paragraph of the story, only dreaming about his journey to the South.

Borges worked into every narrative the idea that he, as author, was not sure of all things, "because that's the way reality is." He was also speculative about his practices as a writer. From Ralph Waldo Emerson he got the idea that all literary works are one work and that all writers are one impersonal writer, one single all-knowing human being. Wondering if he had ever created a single original line in his writing, Borges said that if the reader looked long enough, a source might be found for everything he had written. Invention is just "mixing up memories. I don't think we're capable of creating in the way that God created the world."

RELATED CASEBOOK

See Casebook on Magical Realism, pages 1627–1646, including Jorge Luis Borges, "Borges and I," page 1631; Alejo Carpentier, "On the Marvelous Real in America," page 1633 and "The Baroque and the Marvelous Real," page 1635; Luis Leal, "Magical Realism in Spanish American Literature," page 1637; William Gass, "The First Seven Pages of the Boom," page 1639; Ursula K. Le Guin, "The Kind of Fiction Most Characteristic of Our Times," page 1641; Mario Vargas Llosa, "The Prose Style of Jorge Luis Borges and Gabriel García Márquez," 1645.

The South

1944 / Translated by Andrew Hurley

THE MAN THAT STEPPED off the boat in Buenos Aires in 1871 was a minister of the Evangelical Church; his name was Johannes Dahlmann. By 1939, one of his grandsons, Juan Dahlmann, was secretary of a municipal library on Calle Córdoba and considered himself profoundly Argentine. His maternal grandfather had been Francisco Flores, of the 2nd Infantry of the Line, who died on the border of Buenos Aires from a spear wielded by the Indians under Catriel. In the contrary pulls from his two lineages, Juan Dahlmann (perhaps impelled by his Germanic blood) chose that of his romantic ancestor, or that of a romantic death. That slightly willful but never ostentatious "Argentinization" drew sustenance from an old sword, a locket containing the daguerreotype of a bearded, inexpressive man, the joy and courage of certain melodies, the habit of certain verses in *Martín Fierro*, the passing years, a certain lack of spiritedness, and solitude. At the price of some self-denial, Dahlmann had managed to save the shell of a large country house in the South that had once belonged to the Flores family; one of the touchstones of his memory was the image of the eucalyptus trees and the long pink-colored house that had once been scarlet. His work, and perhaps his indolence, held him in the city. Summer after summer he contented himself with the abstract idea of possession and with the certainty that his house was waiting for him, at a precise place on the flatlands. In late February, 1939, something happened to him.

Though blind to guilt, fate can be merciless with the slightest distractions. That afternoon Dahlmann had come upon a copy (from which some pages were missing) of Weil's *Arabian Nights*; eager to examine his find, he did not wait for the elevator—he hurriedly took the stairs. Something in the dimness brushed his forehead—a bat? a bird? On the face of the woman who opened the door to him, he saw an expression of horror, and the hand he passed over his forehead came back red with blood. His brow had caught the edge of a recently painted casement window that somebody had forgotten to close. Dahlmann managed to sleep, but by the early hours of morning he was awake, and from that time on, the flavor of all things was monstrous to him. Fever wore him away, and illustrations from the *Arabian Nights* began to illuminate nightmares. Friends and members of his family would visit him and with exaggerated smiles tell him how well he looked. Dahlmann, in a kind of feeble stupor, would hear their words, and it would amaze him that they couldn't see he was in hell. Eight days passed, like eight hundred years. One afternoon, his usual physician appeared with a new man, and they drove Dahlmann to a sanatorium on Calle Ecuador; he needed to have an X ray. Sitting in the cab they had hired to drive them, Dahlmann reflected that he might, at last, in a room that was not his own, be able to sleep. He felt happy, he felt like talking, but the moment they arrived, his clothes were stripped from him, his head was shaved, he was strapped with metal bands to a table, he was blinded and dizzied with bright lights, his heart and lungs were listened to, and a man in a surgical mask stuck a needle in his arm. He awoke nauseated, bandaged, in a cell much like the bottom of a well, and in the days and nights that followed, he realized that until then he had been only somewhere on the outskirts of hell. Ice left but the slightest trace of coolness in his mouth. During these days, Dahlmann hated every inch of himself; he hated his identity, his bodily needs, his humiliation, the beard that prickled his face. He stoically suffered the treatments administered to him, which were quite painful, but when the surgeon told him he'd been on the verge of death from septicemia, Dahlmann, suddenly self-pitying, broke down and cried. The physical miseries, the unending anticipation of bad nights had not allowed him to think about anything as abstract as death. The next day, the surgeon told him he was coming right along, and that he'd soon be able to go out to the country house to convalesce. Incredibly, the promised day arrived.

Reality is partial to symmetries and slight anachronisms; Dahlmann had come to the sanatorium in a cab, and it was a cab that took him to the station at Plaza Constitución. The first cool breath of autumn, after the oppression of the summer, was like a natural symbol of his life brought back from fever and the brink of death. The city, at that seven o'clock in the morning, had not lost that look of a ramshackle old house that cities take on at night; the streets were like long porches and corridors, the plazas like interior courtyards. After his long stay in hospital, Dahlmann took it all in with delight and a touch of vertigo; a few seconds before his eyes registered them, he would recall the corners, the marquees, the modest variety of Buenos Aires. In the yellow light of the new day, it all came back to him.

Everyone knows that the South begins on the other side of Avenida Rivadavia. Dahlmann had often said that that was no mere saying, that by crossing Rivadavia one entered an older and more stable world. From the cab, he sought among the new buildings the window barred with wrought iron, the door knocker, the arch of a doorway; the long entryway, the almost-secret courtyard.

In the grand hall of the station he saw that he had thirty minutes before his train left. He suddenly remembered that there was a café on Calle Brasil (a few yards from Yrigoyen's house) where there was a huge cat that would let people pet it, like some disdainful deity. He went in. There was the cat, asleep. He ordered a cup of coffee, slowly spooned sugar into it, tasted it (a pleasure that had been forbidden him in the clinic), and thought, while he stroked the cat's black fur, that this contact was illusory, that he and the cat were separated as though by a pane of glass, because man lives in time, in successiveness, while the magical animal lives in the present, in the eternity of the instant.

The train, stretching along the next-to-last platform, was waiting. Dahlmann walked through the cars until he came to one that was almost empty. He lifted his bag onto the luggage rack; when the train pulled out, he opened his bag and after a slight hesitation took from it the first volume of *The Arabian Nights*. To travel with this book so closely linked to the history of his torment was an affirmation that the torment was past, and was a joyous, secret challenge to the frustrated forces of evil.

On both sides of the train, the city unraveled into suburbs; that sight, and later the sight of lawns and large country homes, led Dahlmann to put aside his reading. The truth is, Dahlmann read very little; the lodestone mountain and the genie sworn to kill the man who released him from the bottle were, as anyone will admit, wondrous things, but not much more wondrous than this morning and the fact of being. Happiness distracted him from Scheherazade and her superfluous miracles; Dahlmann closed the book and allowed himself simply to live.

Lunch (with bouillon served in bowls of shining metal, as in the now-distant summers of his childhood) was another quiet, savored pleasure.

Tomorrow I will wake up at my ranch, he thought, and it was as though he were two men at once; the man gliding along through the autumn day and the geography of his native land, and the other man, imprisoned in a sanatorium and subjected to methodical attentions. He saw unplastered brick houses, long and angular, infinitely watching the trains go by; he saw horsemen on the clod-strewn roads; he saw ditches and lakes and pastures; he saw long glowing clouds that seemed made of marble, and all these things were fortuitous, like some dream of the flat prairies. He also thought he recognized trees and crops that he couldn't have told one the name of — his direct knowledge of the country was considerably inferior to his nostalgic, literary knowledge.

From time to time he nodded off, and in his dreams there was the rushing momentum of the train. Now the unbearable white sun of midday was the yellow sun that comes before nightfall and that soon would turn to red. The car was different now, too; it was not the same car that had pulled out of the station in Buenos Aires — the plains and the hours had penetrated and transfigured it. Outside, the moving shadow of the train stretched out toward the horizon. The elemental earth was not disturbed by settlements or any other signs of humanity. All was vast, but at the same time intimate and somehow secret. In all the immense countryside, there would sometimes be nothing but a bull. The solitude was perfect, if perhaps hostile, and Dahlmann almost suspected that he was traveling not only into the South but into the past. From that fantastic conjecture he was distracted by the conductor, who seeing Dahlmann's ticket informed him that the train would not be leaving him at the usual station, but at a different one, a little before it, that Dahlmann barely knew. (The man added an explanation that Dahlmann didn't try to understand, didn't even listen to, because the mechanics of it didn't matter.)

The train came to its laborious halt in virtually the middle of the countryside. The station sat on the other side of the tracks, and was hardly more than a covered platform. They had no vehicle there, but the station-master figured Dahlmann might be able to find one at a store he directed him to — ten or twelve blocks away.

Dahlmann accepted the walk as a small adventure. The sun had sunk below the horizon now, but one final splendor brought a glory to the living yet silent plains before they were blotted out by night. Less to keep from tiring himself than to make those things last, Dahlmann walked slowly, inhaling with grave happiness the smell of clover.

The store had once been bright red, but the years had tempered its violent color (to its advantage). There was something in its sorry architecture that reminded Dahlmann of a steel engraving, perhaps from an old edition of *Paul et Virginie*. There were several horses tied to the rail in front. Inside, Dahlmann thought he recognized the owner; then he realized that he'd been fooled by the man's resemblance to one of the employees at the sanatorium. When the man heard Dahlmann's story, he said he'd have the calash harnessed up; to add yet another event to that day, and to pass the time, Dahlmann decided to eat there in the country store.

At one table some rough-looking young men were noisily eating and drinking; at first Dahlmann didn't pay much attention. On the floor, curled against the bar, lay an old man, as motionless as an object. The many years had worn him away and polished him, as a stone is worn smooth by running water or a saying is polished by generations of humankind. He was small, dark, and dried up, and he seemed to be outside time, in a sort of eternity. Dahlmann was warmed by the rightness of the man's hairband, the baize poncho he wore, his gaucho trousers, and the boots made out of the skin of a horse's leg, and he said to himself, recalling futile arguments with people from districts in the North, or from Entre Ríos, that only in the South did gauchos like that exist anymore.

Dahlmann made himself comfortable near the window. Little by little, darkness was enveloping the countryside, but the smells and sounds of the plains still floated in through the thick iron grate at the window. The storekeeper brought him sardines and then roast meat; Dahlmann washed them down with more than one glass of red wine. Idly, he savored the harsh bouquet of the wine and let his gaze wander over the store, which by now had turned a little sleepy. The kerosene lantern hung from one of the beams. There were three customers at the other table: two looked like laborers; the other, with coarse, Indian-like features, sat drinking with his wide-brimmed hat on. Dahlmann suddenly felt something lightly brush his face. Next to the tumbler of cloudy glass, on one of the stripes in the tablecloth, lay a little ball of wadded bread. That was all, but somebody had thrown it at him.

The drinkers at the other table seemed unaware of his presence. Dahlmann, puzzled, decided that nothing had happened, and he opened the volume of *The Arabian Nights*, as though to block out reality. Another wad of bread hit him a few minutes later, and this time the laborers laughed. Dahlmann told himself he wasn't scared, but that it would be madness for him, a sick man, to be dragged by strangers into some chaotic bar fight. He made up his mind to leave; he was already on his feet when the storekeeper came over and urged him, his voice alarmed: "Sr. Dahlmann, ignore those boys over there — they're just feeling their oats."

Dahlmann did not find it strange that the storekeeper should know his name by now but he sensed that the man's conciliatory words actually made the situation worse. Before, the men's provocation had been directed at an accidental face, almost at nobody; now it was aimed at him, at his name, and the men at the other table would know that name. Dahlmann brushed the storekeeper aside, faced the laborers, and asked them what their problem was.

The young thug with the Indian-looking face stood up, stumbling as he did so. At one pace from Dahlmann, he shouted insults at him, as though he were far away. He was playacting, exaggerating his drunkenness, and the exaggeration produced an impression both fierce and mocking. Amid curses and obscenities, the man threw a long knife into the air, followed it with his eyes, caught it, and challenged Dahlmann to fight. The storekeeper's voice shook as he objected that Dahlmann was unarmed. At that point, something unforeseeable happened.

From out of a corner, the motionless old gaucho in whom Dahlmann had seen a symbol of the South (the South that belonged to him) tossed him a naked dagger — it came to rest at Dahlmann's feet. It was as though the South itself had decided that Dahlmann should accept the challenge. Dahlmann bent to pick up the dagger, and as he did he sensed two things: first, that that virtually instinctive action committed him to fight, and second, that in his clumsy hand the weapon would serve less to defend him than to justify the other man's killing him. He had toyed with a knife now and then, as all men did, but his knowledge of knife fighting went no further than a vague recollection that thrusts should be aimed upward, and with the blade facing inward. *They'd never have allowed this sort of thing to happen in the sanatorium,* he thought.

"Enough stalling," the other man said. "Let's go outside."

They went outside, and while there was no hope in Dahlmann, there was no fear, either. As he crossed the threshold, he felt that on that first night in the sanatorium, when they'd stuck that needle in him, dying in a knife fight under the open sky, grappling with his adversary, would have been a liberation, a joy, and a fiesta. He sensed that had he been able to choose or dream his death that night, this is the death he would have dreamed or chosen.

Dahlmann firmly grips the knife, which he may have no idea how to manage, and steps out into the plains.

Tadeusz Borowski

Tadeusz Borowski (1922–1951), Polish short story writer and poet, created stories about his experiences in the concentration camp at Auschwitz during World War II that constitute one of the most harrowing literary statements of our time. Borowski was acquainted early with suffering and deprivation. His father was sent from the family's home in the Soviet Ukraine to an Arctic labor camp in 1926; his mother was transported to Siberia four years later, leaving Borowski to be raised by an aunt. In 1939 the family was reunited in Poland, but shortly afterward the Nazis occupied that country. Unable to attend school because the Nazis prohibited education for Poles, Borowski studied on his own and began to write poetry. He published his first mimeographed collection in 1942. Arrested soon after, he was transported to Auschwitz and tattooed with a camp serial number. As his friend Jan Kott said, Borowski was lucky: "Three weeks earlier 'Aryans' had stopped being sent to the gas chambers—except for special cases. From then on only Jews were gassed en masse."

Borowski remained in Auschwitz and Dachau for two years. At the end of the war, he was released and then repatriated to Poland in 1946. In 1948 he joined the Communist Party, working for them as a journalist in Warsaw until his suicide three years later. He is chiefly remembered for the hundred pages of short stories written a year after his release from the concentration camp; they are collected in the book *This Way for the Gas, Ladies and Gentlemen* (1967).

As Jan Kott realized, Borowski's writing is unique in the "literature of atrocity" produced by Holocaust survivors. "Among the tens of thousands of pages written about the Holocaust and the death camps, Borowski's slender book continues to occupy a place apart. The book is one of the cruelest of testimonies to what men did to men, and a pitiless verdict that anything can be done to a human being." In his stories Borowski identified with his first-person narrator, Vorarbeiter Tadeusz, to show that evil exists inside as well as outside us. Thus he assumed full moral responsibility for the terms of his survival at Auschwitz: following the orders of the Nazis. The detached, almost scientific descriptions in "This Way for the Gas, Ladies and Gentlemen" reflect all of existence turned into a concentration camp. In these stories Borowski grappled with his own question: "What will the world know of us if the Germans win?"

This Way for the Gas, Ladies and Gentlemen

1948 / Translated by Barbara Vedder

ALL OF US WALK AROUND naked. The delousing is finally over, and our striped suits are back from the tanks of Cyclone B solution, an efficient killer of lice in clothing and of men in gas chambers. Only the inmates in the blocks cut off from ours by the "Spanish goats"[1] still have nothing to wear. But all the same, all of us walk around naked: the heat is unbearable. The camp has been sealed off tight. Not a single prisoner, not one solitary louse, can sneak through the gate. The labour Kommandos have stopped working. All day, thousands of naked men shuffle up and down the roads, cluster around the squares, or lie against the walls and on top of the roofs. We have been sleeping on plain boards, since our mattresses and blankets are still being disinfected. From the rear blockhouses we have a view of the F.K.L. — *Frauen Konzentration Lager;*[2] there too the delousing is in full swing. Twenty-eight thousand women have been stripped naked and driven out of the barracks. Now they swarm around the large yard between the blockhouses.

The heat rises, the hours are endless. We are without even our usual diversion: the wide roads leading to the crematoria are empty. For several days now, no new transports have come in. Part of "Canada"[3] has been liquidated and detailed to a labour Kommando — one of the very toughest — at Harmenz. For there exists in the camp a special brand of justice based on envy: when the rich and mighty fall, their friends see to it that they fall to the very bottom. And Canada, our Canada, which smells not of maple forests but of French perfume, has amassed great fortunes in diamonds and currency from all over Europe.

Several of us sit on the top bunk, our legs dangling over the edge. We slice the neat loaves of crisp, crunchy bread. It is a bit coarse to the taste, the kind that stays fresh for days. Sent all the way from Warsaw — only a week ago my mother held this white loaf in her hands . . . dear Lord, dear Lord . . .

We unwrap the bacon, the onion, we open a can of evaporated milk. Henri, the fat Frenchman, dreams aloud of the French wine brought by the transports from Strasbourg, Paris, Marseille . . . Sweat streams down his body.

"Listen, *mon ami,*[4] next time we go up on the loading ramp, I'll bring you real champagne. You haven't tried it before, eh?"

"No. But you'll never be able to smuggle it through the gate, so stop teasing. Why not try and 'organize' some shoes for me instead — you know, the perforated kind, with a double sole, and what about that shirt you promised me long ago?"

"*Patience, patience.* When the new transports come, I'll bring all you want. We'll be going on the ramp again!"

"And what if there aren't any more 'cremo' transports?" I say spitefully. "Can't you see how much easier life is becoming around here: no limit on packages, no more beatings? You even write letters home . . . One hears all kind of talk, and, dammit, they'll run out of people!"

---

[1] Crossed wooden beams wrapped in barbed wire.

[2] Women's concentration camp. (Unless otherwise indicated, all foreign phrases are in German.)

[3] A designation of wealth and well-being in the camp. More specifically, the members of the labor gang, or Kommando, who helped to unload the incoming transports of people destined for the gas chambers.

[4] My friend (French).

"Stop talking nonsense." Henri's serious fat face moves rhythmically, his mouth is full of sardines. We have been friends for a long time, but I do not even know his last name. "Stop talking nonsense," he repeats, swallowing with effort. "They can't run out of people, or we'll starve to death in this blasted camp. All of us live on what they bring."

"All? We have our packages . . ."

"Sure, you and your friend, and ten other friends of yours. Some of you Poles get packages. But what about us, and the Jews, and the Russkis? And what if we had no food, no 'organization' from the transports, do you think you'd be eating those packages of yours in peace? We wouldn't let you!"

"You would, you'd starve to death like the Greeks. Around here, whoever has grub, has power."

"Anyway, you have enough, we have enough, so why argue?"

Right, why argue? They have enough, I have enough, we eat together and we sleep on the same bunks. Henri slices the bread, he makes a tomato salad. It tastes good with the commissary mustard.

Below us, naked sweat-drenched men crowd the narrow barracks aisles or lie packed in eights and tens in the lower bunks. Their nude, withered bodies stink of sweat and excrement; their cheeks are hollow. Directly beneath me, in the bottom bunk, lies a rabbi. He has covered his head with a piece of rag torn off a blanket and reads from a Hebrew prayer book (there is no shortage of this type of literature at the camp), wailing loudly, monotonously.

"Can't somebody shut him up? He's been raving as if he'd caught God himself by the feet."

"I don't feel like moving. Let him rave. They'll take him to the oven that much sooner."

"Religion is the opium of the people," Henri, who is a Communist and a *rentier*,[5] says sententiously. "If they didn't believe in God and eternal life, they'd have smashed the crematoria long ago."

"Why haven't you done it then?"

The question is rhetorical; the Frenchman ignores it.

"Idiot," he says simply, and stuffs a tomato in his mouth.

Just as we finish our snack, there is a sudden commotion at the door. The Muslims[6] scurry in fright to the safety of their bunks, a messenger runs into the Block Elder's shack. The Elder, his face solemn, steps out at once.

"Canada! *Antreten!*[7] But fast! There's a transport coming!"

"Great God!" yells Henri, jumping off the bunk. He swallows the rest of his tomato, snatches his coat, screams "*Raus*"[8] at the men below, and in a flash is at the door. We can hear a scramble in the other bunks. Canada is leaving for the ramp.

---

[5] Person of private or independent means (French).

[6] The camp name for a prisoner who had been destroyed physically and spiritually, and who had neither the strength nor the will to go on living — a man ripe for the gas chamber.

[7] "Get going."

[8] "Get out."

"Henri, the shoes!" I call after him.

"*Keine Angst!*"[9] he shouts back, already outside.

I proceed to put away the food. I tie a piece of rope around the suitcase where the onions and the tomatoes from my father's garden in Warsaw mingle with Portuguese sardines, bacon from Lublin (that's from my brother), and authentic sweetmeats from Salonica. I tie it all up, pull on my trousers, and slide off the bunk.

"*Platz!*"[10] I yell, pushing my way through the Greeks. They step aside. At the door I bump into Henri.

"*Was ist los?*"[11]

"Want to come with us on the ramp?"

"Sure, why not?"

"Come along then, grab your coat! We're short a few men. I've already told the Kapo," and he shoves me out of the barracks door.

We line up. Someone has marked down our numbers, someone up ahead yells, "March, march," and now we are running towards the gate, accompanied by the shouts of a multilingual throng that is already being pushed back to the barracks. Not everybody is lucky enough to be going on the ramp . . . We have almost reached the gate. *Links, zwei, drei, vier! Mützen ab!*[12] Erect, arms stretched stiffly along our hips, we march past the gate briskly, smartly, almost gracefully. A sleepy S.S. man with a large pad in his hand checks us off, waving us ahead in groups of five.

"*Hundert!*" he calls after we have all passed.

"*Stimmt!*"[13] comes a hoarse answer from out front.

We march fast, almost at a run. There are guards all around, young men with automatics. We pass camp II B, then some deserted barracks and a clump of unfamiliar green — apple and pear trees. We cross the circle of watchtowers and, running, burst on to the highway. We have arrived. Just a few more yards. There, surrounded by trees, is the ramp.

A cheerful little station, very much like any other provincial railway stop: a small square framed by tall chestnuts and paved with yellow gravel. Not far off, beside the road, squats a tiny wooden shed, uglier and more flimsy than the ugliest and flimsiest railway shack; farther along lie stacks of old rails, heaps of wooden beams, barracks' parts, bricks, paving stones. This is where they load freight for Birkenau: supplies for the construction of the camp, and people for the gas chambers. Trucks drive around, load up lumber, cement, people — a regular daily routine.

And now the guards are being posted along the rails, across the beams, in the green shade of the Silesian chestnuts, to form a tight circle around the ramp. They wipe the sweat from their faces and sip out of their canteens. It is unbearably hot; the sun stands motionless at its zenith.

---

[9] "Don't worry."

[10] "Place!" (In the sense of "Take your place!")

[11] "What's the matter?"

[12] "Left, two, three, four! Hats off!"

[13] "One hundred!" . . . "OK!"

"Fall out!"

We sit down in the narrow streaks of shade along the stacked rails. The hungry Greeks (several of them managed to come along, God only knows how) rummage underneath the rails. One of them finds some pieces of mildewed bread, another a few half-rotten sardines. They eat.

"*Schweinedreck*,"[14] spits a young, tall guard with corn-coloured hair and dreamy blue eyes. "For God's sake, any minute you'll have so much food to stuff down your guts, you'll bust!" He adjusts his gun, wipes his face with a handkerchief.

"Hey you, fatso!" His boot lightly touches Henri's shoulder. "*Pass mal auf*,[15] want a drink?"

"Sure, but I haven't got any marks," replies the Frenchman with a professional air.

"*Schade*, too bad."

"Come, come, Herr Posten, isn't my word good enough any more? Haven't we done business before? How much?"

"One hundred. *Gemacht?*"[16]

"*Gemacht*."

We drink the water, lukewarm and tasteless. It will be paid for by the people who have not yet arrived.

"Now you be careful," says Henri, turning to me. He tosses away the empty bottle. It strikes the rails and bursts into tiny fragments. "Don't take any money, they might be checking. Anyway, who the hell needs money? You've got enough to eat. Don't take suits, either, or they'll think you're planning to escape. Just get a shirt, silk only, with a collar. And a vest. And if you find something to drink, don't bother calling me. I know how to shift for myself, but you watch your step or they'll let you have it."

"Do they beat you up here?"

"Naturally. You've got to have eyes in your ass. *Arschaugen*."[17]

Around us sit the Greeks, their jaws working greedily, like huge human insects. They munch on stale lumps of bread. They are restless, wondering what will happen next. The sight of the large beams and the stacks of rails has them worried. They dislike carrying heavy loads.

"*Was wir arbeiten?*"[18] they ask.

"*Niks. Transport kommen, alles Krematorium, compris?*"[19]

"*Alles verstehen*,"[20] they answer in crematorium Esperanto. All is well — they will not have to move the heavy rails or carry the beams.

---

[14] "Filthy pigs."
[15] "Pay attention."
[16] "Done."
[17] "Ass eyes."
[18] "What will we be working on?"
[19] "Nothing. Transport coming, all Crematorium, understand?"
[20] "We understand."

In the meantime, the ramp has become increasingly alive with activity, increasingly noisy. The crews are being divided into those who will open and unload the arriving cattle cars and those who will be posted by the wooden steps. They receive instructions on how to proceed most efficiently. Motorcycles drive up, delivering S.S. officers, bemedalled, glittering with brass, beefy men with highly polished boots and shiny, brutal faces. Some have brought their briefcases, others hold thin, flexible whips. This gives them an air of military readiness and agility. They walk in and out of the commissary — for the miserable little shack by the road serves as their commissary, where in the summertime they drink mineral water, *Studentenquelle*, and where in winter they can warm up with a glass of hot wine. They greet each other in the state-approved way, raising an arm Roman fashion, then shake hands cordially, exchange warm smiles, discuss mail from home, their children, their families. Some stroll majestically on the ramp. The silver squares on their collars glitter, the gravel crunches under their boots, their bamboo whips snap impatiently.

We lie against the rails in the narrow streaks of shade, breathe unevenly, occasionally exchange a few words in our various tongues, and gaze listlessly at the majestic men in green uniforms, at the green trees, and at the church steeple of a distant village.

"The transport is coming," somebody says. We spring to our feet, all eyes turn in one direction. Around the bend, one after another, the cattle cars begin rolling in. The train backs into the station, a conductor leans out, waves his hand, blows a whistle. The locomotive whistles back with a shrieking noise, puffs, the train rolls slowly alongside the ramp. In the tiny barred windows appear pale, wilted, exhausted human faces, terror-stricken women with tangled hair, unshaven men. They gaze at the station in silence. And then, suddenly, there is a stir inside the cars and a pounding against the wooden boards.

"Water! Air!" — weary, desperate cries.

Heads push through the windows, mouths gasp frantically for air. They draw a few breaths, then disappear; others come in their place, then also disappear. The cries and moans grow louder.

A man in a green uniform covered with more glitter than any of the others jerks his head impatiently, his lips twist in annoyance. He inhales deeply, then with a rapid gesture throws his cigarette away and signals to the guard. The guard removes the automatic from his shoulder, aims, sends a series of shots along the train. All is quiet now. Meanwhile, the trucks have arrived, steps are being drawn up, and the Canada men stand ready at their posts by the train doors. The S.S. officer with the briefcase raises his hand.

"Whoever takes gold, or anything at all besides food, will be shot for stealing Reich property. Understand? *Verstanden?*"

"*Jawohl!*"[21] we answer eagerly.

"*Also los!* Begin!"

---

[21] "Yes, indeed!"

The bolts crack, the doors fall open. A wave of fresh air rushes inside the train. People . . . inhumanly crammed, buried under incredible heaps of luggage, suitcases, trunks, packages, crates, bundles of every description (everything that had been their past and was to start their future). Monstrously squeezed together, they have fainted from heat, suffocated, crushed one another. Now they push towards the opened doors, breathing like fish cast out on the sand.

"Attention! Out, and take your luggage with you! Take out everything. Pile all your stuff near the exits. Yes, your coats too. It is summer. March to the left. Understand?"

"Sir, what's going to happen to us?" They jump from the train on to the gravel, anxious, worn-out.

"Where are you people from?"

"Sosnowiec-Będzin. Sir, what's going to happen to us?" They repeat the question stubbornly, gazing into our tired eyes.

"I don't know. I don't understand Polish."

It is the camp law: people going to their death must be deceived to the very end. This is the only permissible form of charity. The heat is tremendous. The sun hangs directly over our heads, the white, hot sky quivers, the air vibrates, an occasional breeze feels like a sizzling blast from a furnace. Our lips are parched, the mouth fills with the salty taste of blood, the body is weak and heavy from lying in the sun. Water!

A huge, multicoloured wave of people loaded down with luggage pours from the train like a blind, mad river trying to find a new bed. But before they have a chance to recover, before they can draw a breath of fresh air and look at the sky, bundles are snatched from their hands, coats ripped off their backs, their purses and umbrellas taken away.

"But please, sir, it's for the sun, I cannot . . . "

"*Verboten!*[22] one of us barks through clenched teeth. There is an S.S. man standing behind your back, calm, efficient, watchful.

"*Meine Herrschaften,*[23] this way, ladies and gentlemen, try not to throw your things around, please. Show some goodwill," he says courteously, his restless hands playing with the slender whip.

"Of course, of course," they answer as they pass, and now they walk alongside the train somewhat more cheerfully. A woman reaches down quickly to pick up her handbag. The whip flies, the woman screams, stumbles, and falls under the feet of the surging crowd. Behind her, a child cries in a thin little voice "Mamele!" — a very small girl with tangled black curls.

The heaps grow. Suitcases, bundles, blankets, coats, handbags that open as they fall, spilling coins, gold, watches; mountains of bread pile up at the exits, heaps of marmalade, jams, masses of meat, sausages; sugar spills on the gravel. Trucks, loaded with people, start up with a deafening roar and drive off amidst the wailing and screaming of the women separated from their children, and

---

[22] "Forbidden!"
[23] "Distinguished ladies and gentlemen."

the stupefied silence of the men left behind. They are the ones who had been ordered to step to the right — the healthy and the young who will go to the camp. In the end, they too will not escape death, but first they must work.

Trucks leave and return, without interruption, as on a monstrous conveyor belt. A Red Cross van drives back and forth, back and forth, incessantly: it transports the gas that will kill these people. The enormous cross on the hood, red as blood, seems to dissolve in the sun.

The Canada men at the trucks cannot stop for a single moment, even to catch their breath. They shove the people up the steps, pack them in tightly, sixty per truck, more or less. Nearby stands a young, cleanshaven "gentleman," an S.S. officer with a notebook in his hand. For each departing truck he enters a mark; sixteen gone means one thousand people, more or less. The gentleman is calm, precise. No truck can leave without a signal from him, or a mark in his notebook: *Ordnung muss sein.*[24] The marks swell into thousands, the thousands into whole transports, which afterwards we shall simply call "from Salonica," "from Strasbourg," "from Rotterdam." This one will be called "Sosnowiec-Będzin." The new prisoners from Sosnowiec-Będzin will receive serial numbers 131–2 — thousand, of course, though afterwards we shall simply say 131–2, for short.

The transports swell into weeks, months, years. When the war is over, they will count up the marks in their notebooks — all four and a half million of them. The bloodiest battle of the war, the greatest victory of the strong, united Germany. *Ein Reich, ein Volk, ein Führer*[25] — and four crematoria.

The train has been emptied. A thin, pock-marked S.S. man peers inside, shakes his head in disgust, and motions to our group, pointing his finger at the door.

"*Rein.* Clean it up!"

We climb inside. In the corners amid human excrement and abandoned wrist-watches lie squashed, trampled infants, naked little monsters with enormous heads and bloated bellies. We carry them out like chickens, holding several in each hand.

"Don't take them to the trucks, pass them on to the women," says the S.S. man, lighting a cigarette. His cigarette lighter is not working properly; he examines it carefully.

"Take them, for God's sake!" I explode as the women run from me in horror, covering their eyes.

The name of God sounds strangely pointless, since the women and the infants will go on the trucks, every one of them, without exception. We all know what this means, and we look at each other with hate and horror.

"What, you don't want to take them?" asks the pock-marked S.S. man with a note of surprise and reproach in his voice, and reaches for his revolver.

"You mustn't shoot, I'll carry them." A tall, grey-haired woman takes the little corpses out of my hands and for an instant gazes straight into my eyes.

---

[24] There must be order.
[25] One Empire, one People, one Leader.

"My poor boy," she whispers and smiles at me. Then she walks away, staggering along the path. I lean against the side of the train. I am terribly tired. Someone pulls at my sleeve.

"*En avant*, to the rails, come on!"

I look up, but the face swims before my eyes, dissolves, huge and transparent, melts into the motionless trees and the sea of people . . . I blink rapidly: Henri.

"Listen, Henri, are we good people?"

"That's stupid. Why do you ask?"

"You see, my friend, you see, I don't know why, but I am furious, simply furious with these people — furious because I must be here because of them. I feel no pity. I am not sorry they're going to the gas chamber. Damn them all! I could throw myself at them, beat them with my fists. It must be pathological, I just can't understand . . ."

"Ah, on the contrary, it is natural, predictable, calculated. The ramp exhausts you, you rebel — and the easiest way to relieve your hate is to turn against someone weaker. Why, I'd even call it healthy. It's simple logic, *compris?*" He props himself up comfortably against the heap of rails. "Look at the Greeks, they know how to make the best of it! They stuff their bellies with anything they find. One of them has just devoured a full jar of marmalade."

"Pigs! Tomorrow half of them will die of the shits."

"Pigs? You've been hungry."

"Pigs!" I repeat furiously. I close my eyes. The air is filled with ghastly cries, the earth trembles beneath me, I can feel sticky moisture on my eyelids. My throat is completely dry.

The morbid procession streams on and on — trucks growl like mad dogs. I shut my eyes tight, but I can still see corpses dragged from the train, trampled infants, cripples piled on top of the dead, wave after wave . . . freight cars roll in, the heaps of clothing, suitcases, and bundles grow, people climb out, look at the sun, take a few breaths, beg for water, get into the trucks, drive away. And again freight cars roll in, again people . . . The scenes become confused in my mind — I am not sure if all of this is actually happening, or if I am dreaming. There is a humming inside my head; I feel that I must vomit.

Henri tugs at my arm.

"Don't sleep, we're off to load up the loot."

All the people are gone. In the distance, the last few trucks roll along the road in clouds of dust, the train has left, several S.S. officers promenade up and down the ramp. The silver glitters on their collars. Their boots shine, their red, beefy faces shine. Among them there is a woman — only now I realize she has been here all along — withered, flat-chested, bony, her thin, colourless hair pulled back and tied in a "Nordic" knot; her hands are in the pockets of her wide skirt. With a rat-like, resolute smile glued on her thin lips she sniffs around the corners of the ramp. She detests feminine beauty with the hatred of a woman who is herself repulsive, and knows it. Yes, I have seen her many times before and I know her well: she is the commandant of the F.K.L. She has come to look over the new crop of women, for some of them, instead of going on the trucks, will go on foot — to the concentration camp. There our boys, the barbers from Zauna, will shave their heads and will have a good laugh at their "outside world" modesty.

We proceed to load the loot. We lift huge trunks, heave them on to the trucks. There they are arranged in stacks, packed tightly. Occasionally somebody slashes one open with a knife, for pleasure or in search of vodka and perfume. One of the crates falls open; suits, shirts, books drop out on the ground . . . I pick up a small, heavy package. I unwrap it — gold, about two handfuls, bracelets, rings, brooches, diamonds . . .

"*Gib hier,*"[26] an S.S. man says calmly, holding up his briefcase already full of gold and colourful foreign currency. He locks the case, hands it to an officer, takes another, an empty one, and stands by the next truck, waiting. The gold will go to the Reich.

It is hot, terribly hot. Our throats are dry, each word hurts. Anything for a sip of water! Faster, faster, so that it is over, so that we may rest. At last we are done, all the trucks have gone. Now we swiftly clean up the remaining dirt: there must be "no trace left of the *Schweinerei.*"[27] But just as the last truck disappears behind the trees and we walk, finally, to rest in the shade, a shrill whistle sounds around the bend. Slowly, terribly slowly, a train rolls in, the engine whistles back with a deafening shriek. Again weary, pale faces at the windows, flat as though cut out of paper, with huge, feverishly burning eyes. Already trucks are pulling up, already the composed gentleman with the notebook is at his post, and the S.S. men emerge from the commissary carrying briefcases for the gold and money. We unseal the train doors.

It is impossible to control oneself any longer. Brutally we tear suitcases from their hands, impatiently pull off their coats. Go on, go on, vanish! They go, they vanish. Men, women, children. Some of them know.

Here is a woman — she walks quickly, but tries to appear calm. A small child with a pink cherub's face runs after her and, unable to keep up, stretches out his little arms and cries: "Mama! Mama!"

"Pick up your child, woman!"

"It's not mine, sir, not mine!" she shouts hysterically and runs on, covering her face with her hands. She wants to hide, she wants to reach those who will not ride the trucks, those who will go on foot, those who will stay alive. She is young, healthy, good-looking, she wants to live.

But the child runs after her, wailing loudly: "Mama, mama, don't leave me!"

"It's not mine, not mine, no!"

Andrei, a sailor from Sevastopol, grabs hold of her. His eyes are glassy from vodka and the heat. With one powerful blow he knocks her off her feet, then, as she falls, takes her by the hair and pulls her up again. His face twitches with rage.

---

[26] "Give it here."
[27] "Obscenity."

"Ah, you bloody Jewess! So you're running from your own child! I'll show you, you whore!" His huge hand chokes her, he lifts her in the air and heaves her on to the truck like a heavy sack of grain.

"Here! And take this with you, bitch!" and he throws the child at her feet.

"*Gut gemacht*, good work. That's the way to deal with degenerate mothers," says the S.S. man standing at the foot of the truck. "*Gut, gut, Russki.*"

"Shut your mouth," growls Andrei through clenched teeth, and walks away. From under a pile of rags he pulls out a canteen, unscrews the cork, takes a few deep swallows, passes it to me. The strong vodka burns the throat. My head swims, my legs are shaky, again I feel like throwing up.

And suddenly, above the teeming crowd pushing forward like a river driven by an unseen power, a girl appears. She descends lightly from the train, hops on to the gravel, looks around inquiringly, as if somewhat surprised. Her soft, blonde hair has fallen on her shoulders in a torrent, she throws it back impatiently. With a natural gesture she runs her hands down her blouse, casually straightens her skirt. She stands like this for an instant, gazing at the crowd, then turns and with a gliding look examines our faces, as though searching for someone. Unknowingly, I continue to stare at her, until our eyes meet.

"Listen, tell me, where are they taking us?"

I look at her without saying a word. Here, standing before me, is a girl, a girl with enchanting blonde hair, with beautiful breasts, wearing a little cotton blouse, a girl with a wise, mature look in her eyes. Here she stands, gazing straight into my face, waiting. And over there is the gas chamber: communal death, disgusting and ugly. And over in the other direction is the concentration camp: the shaved head, the heavy Soviet trousers in sweltering heat, the sickening, stale odour of dirty, damp female bodies, the animal hunger, the inhuman labour, and later the same gas chamber, only an even more hideous, more terrible death . . .

Why did she bring it? I think to myself, noticing a lovely gold watch on her delicate wrist. They'll take it away from her anyway.

"Listen, tell me," she repeats.

I remain silent. Her lips tighten.

"I know," she says with a shade of proud contempt in her voice, tossing her head. She walks off resolutely in the direction of the trucks. Someone tries to stop her; she boldly pushes him aside and runs up the steps. In the distance I can only catch a glimpse of her blonde hair flying in the breeze.

I go back inside the train; I carry out dead infants; I unload luggage. I touch corpses, but I cannot overcome the mounting, uncontrollable terror. I try to escape from the corpses, but they are everywhere: lined up on the gravel, on the cement edge of the ramp, inside the cattle cars. Babies, hideous naked women, men twisted by convulsions. I run off as far as I can go, but immediately a whip slashes across my back. Out of the corner of my eye I see an S.S. man, swearing profusely. I stagger forward and run, lose myself in the Canada group. Now, at last, I can once more rest against the stack of rails. The sun has leaned low over the horizon and illuminates the ramp with a reddish glow; the shadows of the trees have become elongated, ghostlike. In the silence that settles over nature at this time of day, the human cries seem to rise all the way to the sky.

Only from this distance does one have a full view of the inferno on the teeming ramp. I see a pair of human beings who have fallen to the ground locked in a last desperate embrace. The man has dug his fingers into the woman's flesh and has caught her clothing with his teeth. She screams hysterically, swears, cries, until at last a large boot comes down over her throat and she is silent. They are pulled apart and dragged like cattle to the truck. I see four Canada men lugging a corpse: a huge, swollen female corpse. Cursing, dripping wet from the strain, they kick out of their way some stray children who have been running all over the ramp, howling like dogs. The men pick them up by the collars, heads, arms, and toss them inside the trucks, on top of the heaps. The four men have trouble lifting the fat corpse on to the car, they call others for help, and all together they hoist up the mound of meat. Big, swollen, puffed-up corpses are being collected from all over the ramp; on top of them are piled the invalids, the smothered, the sick, the unconscious. The heap seethes, howls, groans. The driver starts the motor, the truck begins rolling.

"Halt! Halt!" an S.S. man yells after them. "Stop, damn you!"

They are dragging to the truck an old man wearing tails and a band around his arm. His head knocks against the gravel and pavement; he moans and wails in an uninterrupted monotone: "*Ich will mit dem Herrn Kommandanten sprechen* — I wish to speak with the commandant . . . " With senile stubbornness he keeps repeating these words all the way. Thrown on the truck, trampled by others, choked, he still wails: "*Ich will mit dem . . .*"

"Look here, old man!" a young S.S. man calls, laughing jovially. "In half an hour you'll be talking with the top commandant! Only don't forget to greet him with a Heil Hitler!"

Several other men are carrying a small girl with only one leg. They hold her by the arms and the one leg. Tears are running down her face and she whispers faintly: "Sir, it hurts, it hurts . . . " They throw her on the truck on top of the corpses. She will burn alive along with them.

The evening has come, cool and clear. The stars are out. We lie against the rails. It is incredibly quiet. Anaemic bulbs hang from the top of the high lamp-posts; beyond the circle of light stretches an impenetrable darkness. Just one step, and a man could vanish for ever. But the guards are watching, their automatics ready.

"Did you get the shoes?" asks Henri.

"No."

"Why?"

"My God, man, I am finished, absolutely finished!"

"So soon? After only two transports? Just look at me, I . . . since Christmas, at least a million people have passed through my hands. The worst of all are the transports from around Paris — one is always bumping into friends."

"And what do you say to them?"

"That first they will have a bath, and later we'll meet at the camp. What would you say?"

I do not answer. We drink coffee with vodka; somebody opens a tin of cocoa and mixes it with sugar. We scoop it up by the handful, the cocoa sticks to the lips. Again coffee, again vodka.

"Henri, what are we waiting for?"

"There'll be another transport."

"I'm not going to unload it! I can't take any more."

"So, it's got you down? Canada is nice, eh?" Henri grins indulgently and disappears into the darkness. In a moment he is back again.

"All right. Just sit here quietly and don't let an S.S. man see you. I'll try to find you your shoes."

"Just leave me alone. Never mind the shoes." I want to sleep. It is very late.

Another whistle, another transport. Freight cars emerge out of the darkness, pass under the lamp-posts, and again vanish in the night. The ramp is small, but the circle of lights is smaller. The unloading will have to be done gradually. Somewhere the trucks are growling. They back up against the steps, black, ghostlike, their searchlights flash across the trees. *Wasser! Luft!* The same all over again, like a late showing of the same film: a volley of shots, the train falls silent. Only this time a little girl pushes herself halfway through the small window and, losing her balance, falls out on to the gravel. Stunned, she lies still for a moment, then stands up and begins walking around in a circle, faster and faster, waving her rigid arms in the air, breathing loudly and spasmodically, whining in a faint voice. Her mind has given way in the inferno inside the train. The whining is hard on the nerves: an S.S. man approaches calmly, his heavy boot strikes between her shoulders. She falls. Holding her down with his foot, he draws his revolver, fires once, then again. She remains face down, kicking the gravel with her feet, until she stiffens. They proceed to unseal the train.

I am back on the ramp, standing by the doors. A warm, sickening smell gushes from inside. The mountain of people filling the car almost halfway up to the ceiling is motionless, horribly tangled, but still steaming.

"*Ausladen!*"[28] comes the command. An S.S. man steps out from the darkness. Across his chest hangs a portable searchlight. He throws a stream of light inside.

"Why are you standing about like sheep? Start unloading!" His whip flies and falls across our backs. I seize a corpse by the hand; the fingers close tightly around mine. I pull back with a shriek and stagger away. My heart pounds, jumps up to my throat. I can no longer control the nausea. Hunched under the train I begin to vomit. Then, like a drunk, I weave over to the stack of rails.

I lie against the cool, kind metal and dream about returning to the camp, about my bunk, on which there is no mattress, about sleep among comrades who are not going to the gas tonight. Suddenly I see the camp as a haven of peace. It is true, others may be dying, but one is somehow still alive, one has enough food, enough strength to work . . .

The lights on the ramp flicker with a spectral glow, the wave of people — feverish, agitated, stupefied people — flows on and on, endlessly. They think that now they will have to face a new life in the camp, and they prepare themselves emotionally for the hard struggle ahead. They do not know that in just

---

[28] "Unload."

a few moments they will die, that the gold, money, and diamonds which they have so prudently hidden in their clothing and on their bodies are now useless to them. Experienced professionals will probe into every recess of their flesh, will pull the gold from under the tongue and the diamonds from the uterus and the colon. They will rip out gold teeth. In tightly sealed crates they will ship them to Berlin.

The S.S. men's black figures move about, dignified, businesslike. The gentleman with the notebook puts down his final marks, rounds out the figures: fifteen thousand.

Many, very many, trucks have been driven to the crematoria today.

It is almost over. The dead are being cleared off the ramp and piled into the last truck. The Canada men, weighed down under a load of bread, marmalade, and sugar, and smelling of perfume and fresh linen, line up to go. For several days the entire camp will live off this transport. For several days the entire camp will talk about "Sosnowiec-Będzin." "Sosnowiec-Będzin" was a good, rich transport.

The stars are already beginning to pale as we walk back to the camp. The sky grows translucent and opens high above our heads — it is getting light.

Great columns of smoke rise from the crematoria and merge up above into a huge black river which very slowly floats across the sky over Birkenau and disappears beyond the forests in the direction of Trzebinia. The "Sosnowiec-Będzin" transport is already burning.

We pass a heavily armed S.S. detachment on its way to change guard. The men march briskly, in step, shoulder to shoulder, one mass, one will.

"*Und morgen die ganze Welt . . .*"[29] they sing at the top of their lungs.

"*Rechts ran!* To the right march!" snaps a command from up front. We move out of their way.

---

[29] "And tomorrow the whole world . . ."

T. Coraghessan Boyle

T. Coraghessan Boyle (b. 1948) was born in Peekskill, New York. Growing up he wasn't interested at all in literature—"I don't think I ever read a book until I was eighteen"—although he attended college and even taught high school for a short time. Until 1972, he says, he "was just hanging out." As "a way out of a dead end," he applied and was admitted to the Iowa Writers' Workshop program on the basis of a short story he had published in the *North American Review*. "The sole criterion for admittance to the workshop is the work itself; they didn't look at my grades, which were so bad I couldn't have gotten into graduate school."

At the University of Iowa, Boyle's talent flourished. He resumed writing and publishing short stories, passed his courses and preliminary examinations, and completed his doctorate with a story collection instead of a dissertation. Hired to teach at the University of Southern California, he earned tenure by publishing four books in seven years: *Descent of Man: Stories* (1979), *Water Music* (1981), *Budding Prospects* (1984), and *Greasy Lake and Other Stories* (1985). These were collected in *Stories* (1998). Boyle also received several literary awards and a National Endowment for the Arts Creative Writing Fellowship. What he called his "wild and woolly days" were well behind him.

Boyle continues to produce short stories as a relief from the concentration required by his novels. "Birnam Wood" appeared in *The New Yorker* in September 2012. *Descent of Man* made his reputation as an experimental writer, an inventor of literary parodies in the "playful" tradition of John Barth, Richard Brautigan, and Thomas Pynchon. Boyle believes that "humor resides in exaggeration, and humor is a quick cover for alarm and bewilderment." *Wild Child* (2010) and *T.C. Boyle Stories* (2013) are recent story collections.

Birnam Wood

2012

IT RAINED ALL THAT September, a grim, cold, bleached-out rain that found the holes in the roof and painted the corners with a black creeping mold that felt greasy to the touch. Heat would have dried it up, or at least curtailed it, but there was no heat — or insulation, either — because this was a summer rental, the price fixed for the season, Memorial Day to Labor Day, and the season was over. Long over. Back in May, when Nora was at school out West and I sent her a steady stream of wheedling letters begging her to come back to me, I'd described the place as a cottage. But it wasn't a cottage. It was a shack, a converted chicken coop from a time long gone, and the landlord collected his rent in summer, then drained the pipes and shut the place down over the winter, so that everything in it froze to the point where the mold died back and the mice, disillusioned, moved on to warmer precincts.

In the summer, we'd been outside most of the time, reading and lazing in the hammock till it got dark, after which we'd either listened to records or gone out to a club or somebody's house. We had a lot of friends — my friends, that is, people I'd grown up with — and we could just show up anytime, day or night, and get a party going. On weekends, I'd unfold the geological-survey maps of Fahnestock or Harriman Park and we'd pick out a lake in the middle of nowhere and hike in to see what it looked like in the shimmering world of color and movement. Almost always we'd have it to ourselves, and we'd swim, sunbathe, pass a joint and a bota bag of sweet red wine, and make love under the sun, while the trees swayed in the breeze and the only sound was the sound of the birds. Nora didn't have a tan line all summer. Neither did I.

But then it was September and it was raining and I had to go back to work. I was substitute-teaching at the time, a grinding, chaotic, thankless job, but I didn't really have a choice — we needed money to stay alive, same as anybody else. Nora could have worked — she had her degree now and she could have substituted, could have done anything — but the idea didn't appeal to her, and so, on the three or four days a week that I was summoned to one school or another, she was at home, listening to the rain drool from the eaves and trickle into the pots we'd set out under the worst of the leaks. I sprang for a cheap TV to keep her company, and then an electric heater the size of a six-pack of beer that nonetheless managed to make the meter spin like a 45. But we weren't paying utilities — the landlord was. I'd given him a lump sum at the end of May, and now we were getting our own back. One morning, when I was at work, he used his key to let himself in and found Nora in bed, the blankets pulled up to her neck and the TV rattling away, and he backed out the door, embarrassed, without saying a word. The next day, we got the eviction notice. The day after that, he cut off the electricity.

I was cooking by candlelight over the gas stove a few nights later (Chef Boyardee cheese ravioli, out of the can, with a side of iceberg lettuce cut in wedges), when Nora edged up beside me. We'd been drinking Burgundy out of the gallon jug we kept under the sink as a way of distracting ourselves from the obvious. The house crepitated around us. It wasn't raining, at least not right then, but there was a whole lot of dripping going on, dripping that had emerged as the defining soundtrack of our lives in the absence of music.

Her hair shone greasily in the candlelight. She'd twisted it into pigtails for convenience, because the water heater was defunct now, definitely defunct, and there was no way to take a shower unless we went over to a friend's house — and that involved the hassle of actually getting in the car and going someplace, when it was so much easier just to pile up the blankets on the bed, get stoned, and watch the shadows creep over the beams that did such an admirable job of holding up the slanted portion of the roof. Nora gazed into the pot on the stove. "I can't live like this," she said.

"No," I said, and I was in full agreement here. "Neither can I."

The first place we looked at was also a seasonal rental, though for a different season. It was another crumbling outbuilding, in the same summer colony, but it had been tricked up with heat and insulation because the landlady — eighty, ninety, maybe, with eyes like crushed glass and hair raked back so tightly you could make out the purple-splotched ruin of her scalp beneath — saw the advantage of renting through the winter and spring to whoever was left behind when the summer people went back to the city. I didn't begrudge her that. I didn't begrudge her anything. I didn't even know her. Nora had circled an ad in *The Pennysaver*, dialled the number, and now here she was, the old lady, waiting for us on the porch, out of the rain, and the minute we pulled into the driveway she began waving impatiently for us to jump out of the car, hurry up the steps, and get the business over with.

There were two problems with the house, the first apparent to all three of us, the second only to Nora and me. That problem, hovering over us before we even walked in the door, was that we were looking for a deal, because we didn't have the kind of money to put down for a deposit or first and last months' rent, just enough for now, for the current month — enough, we hoped, to get us out of the converted chicken coop and into someplace with heat and electricity till we could think what to do next. The old lady — Mrs. Fried — didn't look as if she would let things slide. Just the opposite. She gazed up at us out of her fractured eyes with the expectation of one thing only: money.

But then there was the first problem, which obviated the need to dwell on the second. The place was too small, smaller even than the shack we were living in, and we saw that the minute we stepped through the door. There were two rooms, bedroom and living room/kitchen, and to the right of the door, in a little recess, a bathroom the size of the sweatbox in "The Bridge on the River Kwai." We never got that far. We just stood there, the three of us, and gazed into the bedroom, which was off the narrow hall. The bedroom was too cramped for anything but the single bed that was squeezed into it. A second single, made up with an Army blanket and sheets gone gray with use, was pushed up against the wall in the hallway so that you had no more than a foot's leeway to get around it and into the front room. The old lady read our faces, read our minds — or thought she did — and gestured first at the bed in the hallway and then at the one in the bedroom. "Ven you vant," she said, shrugging, her delicate wheeze of a voice clinging to the hard consonants of her youth, "you come."

If Nora found it funny, laughing so hard that she couldn't seem to catch her breath as we ducked back into the car, I didn't. I was the one put in the awkward position here, I was the provider, and what was she? It was the sort of question you didn't ask, because it stirred resentment, and resentment was what had brought us down the first time around. I put the car in gear and drove along the dark tree-choked tunnel of the street, turned right, then right again, and swung into the muddy drive where the shack stood awaiting us. Inside, it smelled like a tomb. I could see my breath, even after I'd flicked on all four burners of the stove. Not sixty seconds went by before Nora said something that set me off, and I came right back at her — "We wouldn't be in this fucking mess if you'd get up off your ass and find a job" — and when we went to bed, early, to save on candles, it was for the warmth and nothing else.

There was no call the next morning, and I had mixed feelings about that. I dreaded the calls, but they meant money — and money was the beginning and end of everything there was, at least right then. When the phone did finally ring, it was half past twelve, and it went off like a flash bomb in the dream I was having, a dream that made me so much happier than the life I jolted awake to that I wanted it to go on forever. My eyes opened on the slanted ceiling, and my first thought was that even the chickens must have hated staring up at it, the sameness of it, day after day, until you lost your head and your feathers and somebody dropped you into a frying pan. Nora was propped up beside me, reading. Rain rapped insistently at the roof. "Well," she said. "Aren't you going to answer it?"

The cold pricked me everywhere, like acupuncture, and I clutched my jeans to my groin, fumbled with a sweatshirt, and hobbled across the room to snatch up the phone. It was my best friend, Artie, whom I'd known since elementary school. He didn't bother with a greeting. "You find a place yet?"

"Uh-uh, no."

"Well, I might've found something for you —"

I glanced at Nora. She'd put down her book and she was watching me now, her eyes squinted to slits in the fierceness of her concentration. "Who is it?" she mouthed, but I ignored her.

"I'm listening," I said.

"I didn't know if you'd be interested, because it's not a real rental — it's more like housesitting — and it's only temporary, like from next week through the end of April. It's a friend of my father's. An old guy and his wife. They go to Florida every winter and they want somebody in the house — or the apartment, there's an apartment in the basement, above ground, with windows and all — just so they don't get anybody breaking in. I was there once when I was a kid. It's nice. On a private lake. A place called Birnam Wood. You ever hear of it?"

"No," I said.

"Would you be interested at all?"

"You got a phone number?"

I told Nora not to get too excited, because chances were it wouldn't work out. Either we wouldn't want the place — there had to be something wrong with it, right? — or they, the old couple, wouldn't want us, once they got a look at us. Still, I phoned right away and the old man answered on the first ring. I introduced myself, talking fast, too fast maybe, because it wasn't till I dropped the name of Artie's father that the voice on the other end came to life. "Yes, we are expecting your call," the old man said, and he had some sort of accent, too, hesitating over the "w" in "we," as if afraid it would congeal on him, and in a sudden jolt of paranoia I wondered if he and Mrs. Fried were somehow in league — or, worse, if he was Mrs. Fried, throwing her voice to catch me unawares. But no, the place was miles away, buried in the woods in the hind end of Croton, well beyond the old lady's reach. He gave the address, then directions, but they were so elaborate I stopped listening midway through, thinking instead of what Artie had said: the place was on a lake. A private lake. I'd find it, no problem. How many private lakes could there be? I told the old man that we'd like to come have a look — at his earliest convenience, that is.

"When" — the hesitation again — "would you like to come?"

"I don't know — how about now? Now O.K.?"

There was a long pause, during which Nora flapped both hands at me as if to say, "Don't sound too eager," and then the old man, in his slow, deliberate way, said, "Yes, that will suit us."

We were late getting there, very late, actually, one snaking blacktop road looking much like the next, the rain hammering down, and Nora digging into me along the lines of "You're a real idiot, you know that?" and "Why in God's name didn't you write down the directions?" For a while, it looked like a lost cause, trees crowding the road, nobody and nothing around except for the odd mailbox and the watery flash of a picture window glimpsed through the veg-etation, but finally, after backing in and out of driveways and retracing our path half a dozen times, we came to a long low stone wall with a gated entrance flanked by two stone pillars. The gate — wrought iron coated in black enamel so slick it glowed — stood open. A brass plaque affixed to the pillar on the right read "Birnam Wood." I didn't want to bicker, but I couldn't help pointing out that we'd passed by the place at least three times already and Nora should have kept her eyes open, because I was the one driving and she was the one doing all the bitching, but she just ignored me, because the gravel of the private lane was crunching under our tires now and there were lawns and tennis courts opening up around us. Then the first house rose up out of the trees on our left, a huge towering thing of stone and glass with a glistening black slate roof and too many gables to count, even as the lake began to emerge from the mist on the other side of the road.

"Wow, you think that's it?" Nora's voice was pitched so low she might have been talking to herself. "Artie did say it was a mansion, right?" I could feel her eyes on me. "Well, didn't he?"

I didn't answer. A moment ago, I'd been worked up, hating her, hating the broken-down car with its bald tires and rusted-out panels that was the only thing we could afford, hating the trees and the rain, hating nature and rich people and the private lakes you couldn't find unless you were rich yourself, unless you had a helicopter, or a whole fleet of them, and now suddenly a dif-ferent mix of emotions was surging through me — surprise, yes, awe even, but a kind of desperation, too. Even as the next house came into view on the right — ivy-covered brick with three wings, half a dozen chimneys, and a whole fair-way of lawn sweeping down to the lake and the two red rowboats pulled up on a perfect little crescent of beach — I knew that I had to live here or die, and that I'd do anything it took, right down to licking the old man's shoes, to make that happen.

"What's the number?" I said. "You see a number on that house?"

She didn't. She'd lost her glasses — she was always losing her glasses — and in our rush to get out the door she hadn't bothered with her contacts, either. No matter. The road took us over a stone bridge and swept us directly into the driveway of the house we were looking for — No. 14. We got out of the car, the rain slackening now, and just stared up at the place, a big rearing brown-timbered Tudor that sat right on the lake itself. Around the corner I could make out a gazebo and a little dock with a rowboat tethered to it, this one painted green. And swans. Swans on the lake.

Everything seemed to brighten suddenly, as if the sun were about to break through. "All right," I said. "Here goes." And I took Nora by the hand and led her up the flagstone steps to the front door.

I introduced Nora as my wife, though that was a lie. Old people, that's what they wanted to hear. If you were married, you were mature, reliable, exactly like them, because in their day men and women didn't just live together — they made a commitment, they had children and went on cruises and built big houses on lakes and filled them with all the precious trinkets and manufactured artifacts they collected along the way. Mr. and Mrs. Kuenzli — Anton and Eva — were just like that. They met us at the door, two dwarfish old people who were almost identical, except that she was wearing a dress and had dyed her hair and he wasn't and hadn't. They gave us tea in a big room overlooking the lake and then escorted us around the house to show off their various collections — Mexican pottery, jade figurines, seascapes painted by a one-armed man they'd encountered in Manila. Every object had a story connected to it. They took turns filling in the details, no hurry at all. I knew what they were doing: checking us out, trying to get a read on us. I shrugged it off. If they were alarmed at the sight of us (this was in a time when people our age wore beads and serapes and cowboy boots and grew their hair long for the express purpose of sticking it to the bourgeoisie), they didn't show it. Still, it was a good hour before we went downstairs to the basement, which was where we were going to live, after all. That is, if things worked out.

They did. I made sure they did. The minute we walked down the stairs I was hooked — and I could see that Nora was, too. Here was a huge room — low-ceilinged, but the size of a basketball court — with a kitchen off to the left and next to it a bedroom with curtains, framed pictures on the walls, and twin beds separated by matching night tables fitted out with ashtrays and reading lamps, just like the room that every TV couple slept in, chastely and separately, so as not to confront the American family with the disturbing notion that people actually engaged in sexual relations. Nora gave me a furtive glance. "Ven you vant, you come," she said under her breath, and we both broke up.

Then it was back out into the main room and the real kicker, the deal-sealer, the sine qua non — a regulation-size slate-topped pool table. A pool table! All this — leather armchairs, Persian carpets, gleaming linoleum, heat, twin beds, the lake, the rowboat, swans — and a pool table, too? It was too much. Whatever the old man was asking for rent, because this wasn't strictly house-sitting and we were willing to make a token monthly payment, I was ready to double. Triple. Anything he wanted. I squeezed Nora's hand. She beamed up at me as the old couple looked on, smiling, moved now by the sight of us there in the depths of that house that had no doubt harbored children at one time, grandchildren even.

I felt a vast calm settle over me. "We'll take it," I said.

At the end of the first week, after checking on us six or seven times a day (or spying on us, as Nora insisted), Mrs. Kuenzli fretting over how we were

getting along — *Fine, thanks* — and even creaking down the stairs one night
with a pot of homemade chicken-spaetzle soup, the old couple climbed into
a limousine and went off to the airport, leaving us in possession. The main
house was sealed off, of course, but I didn't care about that. What I cared about
was getting out of the shack. What I cared about was Nora. Making her happy.
Making myself happy — and everybody else, too. Within days of the Kuenzlis'
departure, my friends began showing up unannounced for the purpose of
shooting eight ball and cranking up the volume on the Bang & Olufsen sound
system the Kuenzlis had at some point so fortuitously installed, then maybe
getting wrecked and taking the rowboat out on the glittering surface of the lake
while the trees flamed and the swans bobbed in our wake. Even the weather
cooperated. If September had been a loss, one of the coldest and rainiest on
record, October tiptoed in on a streak of pure sunshine and temperatures that
climbed into the seventies.

I was shooting pool one Saturday afternoon with Artie and another friend,
Richard, all three of us wired on black beauties and chain-drinking cheap beer,
when Nora came in the door, looking flushed. She had news. While we'd been
frittering our time away — that was how she put it, "frittering," but she was
smiling now, hardly able to contain herself — she'd gone out on her own to
interview for a job.

I loved her in that moment, loved the way the color came into her face
because she was addressing all three of us now, not just me, and that made her
self-conscious no matter the news, which was good, very good, I could see that
in an instant. "Well," I said, "you get it?"

The smile stalled, came back again. She nodded. "It's not much," she said,
already retreating. She looked from me to Artie and Richard. "Minimum
wage — but it's six nights a week."

I'd set down my pool cue and was coming across the room to her, that big
room with its buffed floors and the carpets thick enough for anything, when I
noticed she was all dressed up, and not in business clothes but in the fringed
boots and gauzy top she wore when we were going barhopping. "What is it," I
said, "that hostessing thing?"

She nodded.

"At Brennan's?"

Her smile was gone now. Her eyes — she was wearing her false lashes and
pale-blue eyeshadow — sank into mine. I was the one who'd told her about the
job, which Richard had heard about from the bartender there. "All you have
to do is smile," I'd told her. "All you have to do is say 'Party of four?' and let
them follow you to the table. You can do that, can't you?" I hadn't meant to be
demeaning. Or maybe I had. She was strong-willed, but I wanted to break her
down, make her dependent, make her mine, but at the same time I wanted her
to hold up her end, because we were a couple and that was what couples did.
They worked. Both of them.

I took her by the hand, tried to peck a kiss to her cheek, but she pulled
away.

"It means I'll be gone nights."

I shrugged. I could feel Artie and Richard watching me. There was a record on the stereo — I remember this clearly — something drum-based, with a churning polyrhythmic beat that seemed to fester under my words. "At least it's something," I said.

Artie lined up a shot. The balls clacked. Nothing dropped. "Hey, it's great news," he said, straightening up. "Congrats."

Nora gave him a look. "It's only temporary," she said.

We settled into a routine. The phone rang in the dark and I got up, answered it, and found out what school I was going to because somebody who just couldn't stand another day of it had called in sick — either that or hanged himself — and I was back home by three-thirty or four, at which point she'd be drinking coffee and making herself scrambled eggs and toast. Then I'd drive her to work and either sit there at the bar for a couple (depending on how I was feeling about our financial situation), or go back home and shoot pool by myself, pitting Player A against Player B and trying not to play favorites, until she got off, at ten, and I went to pick her up. Sometimes we'd linger at the bar, but most nights — weeknights, anyway — we'd go back home, because I needed the sleep. We climbed into our separate beds, snug enough, warm and dry and feeling pampered — or, if not pampered, at least secure — and when I switched off my lamp and turned to the wall the last image fading in my brain was of the steady bright nimbus of Nora's light and her face shining there above her book.

The weather held all that month, even as the leaves persisted and the lake rippled under the color of them. Whenever we could, we went out in the rowboat, and though we never acknowledged it, I suppose we were both thinking the same thing — that we'd better take advantage of it while we could, because each day of sun might be the last. I'd row and Nora would lie back against the seat in the stern, her eyes closed and her bare legs stretched out before her. What did I feel? Relaxed. As relaxed as I've ever felt in my life, before or since. There was something more to it, too. I felt powerful, the muscles of my arms flexing and releasing, while Nora dozed at my feet and the rest of the world went as still as held breath.

It was a feeling that couldn't last. And it didn't. Less than a week into November, there was frost on the windshield when I got up for school, and the sun seemed to have vanished, replaced by a low cloud cover and winds out of the north. Finally, reluctantly, I pulled the rowboat ashore and turned it over for the winter. Two days later, there was a rim of ice around the lake and the temperature went down into the teens overnight. But, as I said, the house was warm and well-insulated, with a furnace that could have heated six houses, and when we went to bed at night we couldn't resist joking about the shack, what we'd be suffering if we were still there. "My feet," Nora would say, "they'd freeze to the floor like when you touch the tip of your tongue to the ice-cube tray." "Yeah," I'd say, "yeah, but you wouldn't even notice because by then we'd be dried up and frozen like those mummies they found in the Andes." And she'd laugh, we'd both laugh, and listen to the whisper of the furnace as it clicked on and drove warm air through the bedroom and into the big room beyond, where the pool table stood draped in darkness.

And then came the night when I dropped her off at Brennan's and had my first drink and then another and didn't feel like going home. It was as if some gauge inside me had been turned up high, all the way, top of the dial. I felt like that a lot back then — and maybe it was just an overload of testosterone, maybe that was all it was — but on this night I sat at the bar and kept on drinking. I knew the regulars, an older crowd who came in for dinner and gradually gave way to people like Nora and me, the music shifting from a soft whisper of jazz to the rock and roll we wanted to hear, as the late diners gathered up their coats and gloves and doggie bags and headed out into the night. I'd been talking a lot of nothing to a guy in a sports coat who must have been in his thirties, a Martini drinker, and when he got up and left, a guy my own age slid onto the stool beside me. He asked me what was happening at the same time that I asked him, then he ordered a drink — tequila-and-tonic, very West Coast, or *hip*, that is — and we started talking. His name was Steve. He had rust-red hair, kinked out to his shoulders, and he wore a thin headband of braided leather.

What did we talk about? The usual — bands, drugs, what concerts we'd been to — but then we started in on books, and I was pleased and surprised, because most of the people I ran into in that time and place didn't extend themselves much beyond the Sunday comics. We were debating some fine point of "Slaughterhouse-Five," testing each other's bona fides — he could quote passages from memory, a talent I've never had — when Nora leaned in between us to brush a kiss to my lips, then straightened up and shook out her hair with a quick neat flip of her head. "My heels are killing me," she said. "And this top — Jesus, I'm freezing." She stole a look around, gave Steve a vacant smile, picked up my drink, and downed it in a single gulp. Then she was gone, back to her post at the station by the door.

Steve gave a low whistle. "Wow," he said. "That your old lady?"

I just shrugged, nonchalant, elevated in that instant above everybody in the place. I wouldn't have admitted it, but something stirred in me whenever I looked up and saw the way the men watched her as she tapped across the floor in her heels, trailing husbands and wives and sometimes even kids behind her, but it wasn't something good or admirable.

"Man, I'd love to — " he began, and then caught himself. "You are one lucky dude."

Another shrug. My feelings were complicated. I'd been drinking. And what I said next was inexcusable, I know that, and I didn't mean it, not in any literal sense, not in the real world of twin beds and Persian carpets and all the rest, but what I was trying to convey here was that I wasn't tied down — *old lady* — wasn't a husband, not yet, anyway, and that all my potentialities were intact. "I don't know," I said. "She can be a real pain in the ass." I took a sip of my drink, let out a long, withering sigh. "Sometimes I think she's more trouble than she's worth, know what I mean?"

That was all I said, or some variant of it, and then there was another drink and the conversation went deeper, and I guess somehow Steve must have got the impression that we weren't really all that committed, that living together was an experiment gone sour, that we were both — she and I — on the brink of something else. There was an exchange of phone numbers and addresses (*Birnam Wood? Cool. I used to swim in the lake there when I was a kid*), and then he was gone and the crowd at the bar began to thin. The minute he left I forgot him. Next thing I knew, Nora was there, dressed in her long coat and her knit hat and gloves, perched high on the platform of her heels.

"You've been drinking," she said.

"Yeah," I admitted.

She gave me a tired smile. "Have fun?"

"Yeah." I smiled back.

"Did you know it's snowing out?"

"Really?"

"Really." And then a beat. "You want me to drive?"

It was a long way home, twenty, twenty-five minutes in the best of conditions, but, with the snow and the worn tires and the fact that Nora didn't see too well at night, it must have taken us twice as long as that. We were the only ones on the road. The snow swept at the headlights and erased everything in front of us. I tried not to be critical, but every time we went around a curve the car sailed out of control and I suppose I got vocal about it, because at one point she pulled over, her lips drawn tight and her eyes furious in the sick yellow glare of the dashboard. "You want to drive?" she said. "Go ahead, be my guest."

When we got home (finally, miraculously), the phone was ringing. I could hear it from outside the door, making its demands. It took me a minute, pinning a glove under one arm and struggling to work the key in the lock as the snow sifted down and Nora stamped impatiently. "Hurry up, I have to pee," she said between clenched teeth. Then we were in, the phone ringing still — it must have been the sixth or seventh ring — and I flicked on the lights while Nora made a dash for the bathroom and I crossed the room to pick up the phone.

"Hello?" I gasped, out of breath and thinking it must be Artie, because who else would be calling at that hour?

"Hey, what's happening," the voice on the other end of the line said. "This Keith?"

"Yeah," I said. "Who's this?"

"Steve."

"Steve?"

"From the bar, you know. Like earlier? Brennan's?" I heard Nora flush the toilet. The cover was off the pool table because I'd left in the middle of a climactic match between Player A and Player B, all the angles still in play. I listened to the water rattle in the pipes. And then Steve's voice, low, confidential: "Hey, I was just wondering. Is Nora there?"

The bathroom door clicked open. There was a buzzing in my skull. Everything was wrong. "No," I said, shaking my head for emphasis, though there was no one there to see it. "She's not in."

"When'll she be back?"

I said nothing. I watched her swing open the bathroom door, saw her face there, the pristine towels on the rack, and the copper-and-gold wallpaper that Mrs. Kuenzli must have gone to some special store to pick out because she wanted the best, only the best. The voice on the other end of the line was saying something else, insinuating, whispering in my ear like a disease, and so I bent down to where the phone was plugged into the wall and pulled it out of the socket.

"Who was that?" Nora asked.

"Nobody," I said. "Wrong number."

She gave me a doubtful look. "You were on the line long enough."

I wanted to do something right for a change, wanted to take hold of her and press her to me, confess, tell her that I loved her, but I didn't. I just said, "You feel like a game of pool? I'll spot you two balls — "

"You play," she said. "I'm beat. I think I'll get ready for bed and read for a while." She paused at the bedroom door to give me a sweet, tired smile. "You've got to admit, Player B's a lot better than I am, anyway."

No argument there. I turned on the light over the table, cued up a record and took up the game where I'd left off. I was deep into my third game, on a real roll on behalf of Player A, the balls dropping as if I didn't even have to use the stick, as if I were willing them in, when suddenly there was a knock at the door. Two thumps. A pause. And then two thumps more.

I was just laying down the stick, any number of scenarios going through my head — it was a stranded motorist, the guy who drove the snowplow come to complain about the tail end of the car sticking out into the street, Artie braving the elements for a nightcap — when Nora came out of the bedroom, looking puzzled. She was in her pajamas, the kind kids wear, with a drawstring around the waist and a fold-down collar. Pink, with a flight of bluebirds running up and down her limbs and flapping across her chest. Her feet were bare. "Who's that?" she asked. "Artie?"

I didn't know what was coming, couldn't have guessed. I was in my own house, shooting pool and listening to music while the snow fell outside and the furnace hummed and my girlfriend stood there in her pajamas. "Must be," I said, even as the knock came again and a voice, muffled by the door, called out, "Keith? Nora? Knock-knock. Anybody home?"

I opened the door on Steve, his hair matted now and wet with snow. He was holding a bottle of tequila by the neck and he raised it in offering as he stamped in through the door. "Hey," he said, handing me the bottle, "cool place." He shrugged out of his jacket, dropping it right there on the floor. "Anybody down for a little action? Nora, how about you? A shot? Want to do a shot?"

She looked at him, bewildered — or maybe it was that she wasn't wearing her glasses and had to squint to take him in. I just stood there, the bottle like a brick in my hand — or no, a cement block, a weight, avoirdupois, dragging me down.

Steve never hesitated. He crossed the room to her, digging in his pocket for something, grinning and glassy-eyed. "Here," he said, producing an envelope. "After I saw you tonight? You're so beautiful. I don't even know if you know how beautiful — and sexy. You're really sexy." He handed her the envelope, but she wasn't looking at the envelope, she was looking at me. "I wrote you a poem," he said. "Go ahead. Read it."

"Steve," I was saying, "look, Steve, I think — " but I couldn't go on because of the way Nora was staring at me, her lips parted and her eyes come violently to life.

"Read it," he repeated. "I wrote it for you, just for you — "

"Look," I said, "it's late," and I moved toward him and actually took hold of his arm in an attempt to steer him away and out the door, back into the snow and out of our lives. "Nora's tired," I said.

He never turned, never even acknowledged me. "Let *her* say it. You're not tired, are you?"

For the first time, she shifted her eyes to him. "No," she said finally. "No, I'm not tired at all."

Before I knew what I was doing, I'd set the bottle down on the desk and I was pulling on my coat, furious suddenly, and then I was out the door and into the night, the snow swirling overhead and Steve's voice — "So you want a hit of tequila?" — trailing off behind me with a soft, hopeful, rising inflection.

Outside, the snow made a noise, a kind of hiss, as if the night had come alive. I walked twice around the house, cursing myself — but I wouldn't go back in, I wouldn't, not till whatever was going to happen had happened and he was gone — and then I found myself huddling under the gazebo. I turned my collar up, pulled on my gloves. There was a wind now and a taste of cold northern forest on the air. I walked out on the dock and stood there for I don't know how long, the lake locked up like a vault below me. That was when I noticed the light in the house directly across the lake from ours, the one with all the chimneys and the two red rowboats that were turned over now, twin humps like moguls in the snow. It was the only light visible anywhere, a single lamp burning in a window on the ground floor of the wing nearest the lake. What came over me I can't say — what the impulse was, I mean — but I lowered myself down off the edge of the dock and started across the lake. The wind was in my face. There were no stars. And the footing was bad, drifting powder over ice as clear as if it had come out of a machine. I went down twice, hard, but picked myself up and kept on.

When I got close, when I came up the crescent of beach past the rowboats and on up the slope of the whitening lawn, I saw that the curtains were open, which explained the resiliency of the light. The people there — and I didn't know them, not at all, not even by sight — must have left the curtains open purposely, I realized, because of the snow, the romance of it, the first snow of the season. It came to me that I was trespassing. Peeping. That, once the sun came up, anybody would be able to see my tracks. But, as soon as the thought entered my head, I dismissed it, because I didn't care about any of that — I'd gone out of myself, fixated on that light. Still, I kept to the shadows. I might even have crouched down in the bushes; I don't know.

What I saw was an ordinary room, a bedroom, lit like a stage. I saw a bed, an armoire, pictures on the wall. A shadow flickered across the room, then another, but for the longest time I didn't see anything. And then the man came into view, padding back and forth, undressing, getting ready for bed. How old was he? I couldn't tell, not really. Older than me, but not old. He settled into the bed — a double bed, queen-size, maybe — flicked on the lamp there and picked up a magazine and began reading. At some point, he set it down and seemed to be saying something to the other person in the room — the wife, I guessed — but of course it was just a murmur to me. And then, as if she'd heard her cue and stepped out of the wings, there she was, in a nightgown, fussing around her side of the bed before finally settling in and turning on her own light.

I felt guilty. I felt sick. And I didn't see anything revealing — or sexual, that is — no snuggling or stroking or even a kiss. They were night owls, those people. That light burned a long time. I know. Because I stayed there till it went out.

Ray Bradbury

Ray Bradbury (1920–2012) spent most of his childhood in the small community of Waukegan, Illinois. After his parents moved to California in 1934, he was educated at Los Angeles High School. While still in high school, Bradbury decided to become a professional writer, and at the age of fifteen he began submitting short stories to major national magazines. Two years later he joined the Los Angeles Science Fiction League, which published his first story, "Hollerbochen's Dilemma," in 1938. In his early twenties, he lived at home with his parents, selling newspapers for an income while he developed his literary style and began to place his stories in magazines. By the mid-1940s he was regularly publishing fantasy and horror stories; in 1949 he was voted the best science-fiction author of the year. Throughout his long career Bradbury wrote stories, poems, essays, plays, and film scripts. In 2003, *Bradbury Stories: 100 of His Most Celebrated Tales* was published. The following year he was the recipient of the National Medal of Arts.

Bradbury's best fiction, like his story "August 2026: There Will Come Soft Rains," dramatizes his heightened awareness of the major social problems of our time. The story is from his best-known work, *The Martian Chronicles* (1950), an accurate reflection of postwar America, with its fear of nuclear war, its problems with racism and book censorship, its confused values, and its longing for a simpler life. This book is a collection of previously published short stories linked with newly written passages to make a connected narrative. *Fahrenheit 451* (1953), Bradbury's first novel, was expanded from an earlier long story, "The Fireman." The firemen of the novel are determined to burn books because books confuse readers with their subtle, contradictory values and their ambivalent portrayals of human behavior.

Among Bradbury's most popular collections of short fiction are *The Illustrated Man* (1951), *Dandelion Wine* (1957), *I Sing the Body Electric* (1969), and *The Stories of Ray Bradbury* (1980). Bradbury credited several American short story writers—Sherwood Anderson, Katherine Anne Porter, and Eudora Welty—with helping him forge his poetic, yet spare, literary style. His style, as the critic Gilbert Highet has realized, is a "curious mixture of poetry and colloquialism." Bradbury has said that "I am not so much a science-fiction writer as I am a magician, an illusionist. From my beginnings as a boy conjurer I grew up frightening myself so as to frighten others so as to cure the midnight in our souls."

August 2026: There Will Come Soft Rains

1950

IN THE LIVING ROOM the voice-clock sang. *Tick-Tock, seven o'clock, time to get up, time to get up, seven o'clock!* as if it were afraid that nobody would. The morning house lay empty. The clock ticked on, repeating and repeating its sounds into the emptiness. *Seven-nine, breakfast time, seven-nine!*

In the kitchen the breakfast stove gave a hissing sigh and ejected from its warm interior eight pieces of perfectly browned toast, eight eggs sunnyside up, sixteen slices of bacon, two coffees, and two cool glasses of milk.

"Today is August 4, 2026," said a second voice from the kitchen ceiling, "in the city of Allendale, California." It repeated the date three times for memory's sake. "Today is Mr. Featherstone's birthday. Today is the anniversary of Tilita's marriage. Insurance is payable, as are the water, gas, and light bills."

Somewhere in the walls, relays clicked, memory tapes glided under electric eyes.

Eight-one, tick-tock, eight-one o'clock, off to school, off to work, run, run, eight-one! But no doors slammed, no carpets took the soft tread of rubber heels. It was raining outside. The weather box on the front door sang quietly: "Rain, rain, go away; rubbers, raincoats for today. . . ." And the rain tapped on the empty house, echoing.

Outside, the garage chimed and lifted its door to reveal the waiting car. After a long wait the door swung down again.

At eight-thirty the eggs were shriveled and the toast was like stone. An aluminum wedge scraped them into the sink, where hot water whirled them down a metal throat which digested and flushed them away to the distant sea. The dirty dishes were dropped into a hot washer and emerged twinkling dry.

Nine-fifteen, sang the clock, *time to clean.*

Out of warrens in the wall, tiny robot mice darted. The rooms were acrawl with the small cleaning animals, all rubber and metal. They thudded against chairs, whirling their mustached runners, kneading the rug nap, sucking gently at hidden dust. Then, like mysterious invaders, they popped into their burrows. Their pink electric eyes faded. The house was clean.

Ten o'clock. The sun came out from behind the rain. The house stood alone in a city of rubble and ashes. This was the one house left standing. At night the ruined city gave off a radioactive glow which could be seen for miles.

Ten-fifteen. The garden sprinklers whirled up in golden founts, filling the soft morning air with scatterings of brightness. The water pelted windowpanes, running down the charred west side where the house had been burned evenly free of its white paint. The entire west face of the house was black, save for five places. Here the silhouette in paint of a man mowing a lawn. Here, as in a photograph, a woman bent to pick flowers. Still farther over, their images burned on wood in one titanic instant, a small boy, hands flung into the air; higher up, the image of a thrown ball, and opposite him a girl, hands raised to catch a ball which never came down.

The five spots of paint — the man, the woman, the children, the ball — remained. The rest was a thin charcoaled layer.

The gentle sprinkler rain filled the garden with falling light.

Until this day, how well the house had kept its peace. How carefully it had inquired, "Who goes there? What's the password?" and, getting no answer from lonely foxes and whining cats, it had shut up its windows and drawn shades in an old-maidenly preoccupation with self-protection which bordered on a mechanical paranoia.

It quivered at each sound, the house did. If a sparrow brushed a window, the shade snapped up. The bird, startled, flew off! No, not even a bird must touch the house!

The house was an altar with ten thousand attendants, big, small, servicing, attending, in choirs. But the gods had gone away, and the ritual of the religion continued senselessly, uselessly.

Twelve noon.

A dog whined, shivering, on the front porch.

The front door recognized the dog voice and opened. The dog, once huge and fleshy, but now gone to bone and covered with sores, moved in and through the house, tracking mud. Behind it whirred angry mice, angry at having to pick up mud, angry at inconvenience.

For not a leaf fragment blew under the door but what the wall panels flipped open and the copper scrap rats flashed swiftly out. The offending dust, hair, or paper, seized in miniature steel jaws, was raced back to the burrows. There, down tubes which fed into the cellar, it was dropped into the sighing vent of an incinerator which sat like evil Baal in a dark corner.

The dog ran upstairs, hysterically yelping to each door, at last realizing, as the house realized, that only silence was here.

It sniffed the air and scratched the kitchen door. Behind the door, the stove was making pancakes which filled the house with a rich baked odor and the scent of maple syrup.

The dog frothed at the mouth, lying at the door, sniffing, its eyes turned to fire. It ran wildly in circles, biting at its tail, spun in a frenzy, and died. It lay in the parlor for an hour.

Two o'clock, sang a voice.

Delicately sensing decay at last, the regiments of mice hummed out as softly as blown gray leaves in an electrical wind.

Two-fifteen.

The dog was gone.

In the cellar, the incinerator glowed suddenly and a whirl of sparks leaped up the chimney.

Two thirty-five.

Bridge tables sprouted from patio walls. Playing cards fluttered onto pads in a shower of pips. Martinis manifested on an oaken bench with egg-salad sandwiches. Music played.

But the tables were silent and the cards untouched.

At four o'clock the tables folded like great butterflies back through the paneled walls.

Four-thirty.

The nursery walls glowed.

Animals took shape: yellow giraffes, blue lions, pink antelopes, lilac panthers cavorting in crystal substance. The walls were glass. They looked out upon color and fantasy. Hidden films clocked through well-oiled sprockets, and the walls lived. The nursery floor was woven to resemble a crisp, cereal meadow. Over this ran aluminum roaches and iron crickets, and in the hot still air butterflies of delicate red tissue wavered among the sharp aroma of animal spoors! There was the sound like a great matted yellow hive of bees within a dark bellows, the lazy bumble of a purring lion. And there was the patter of okapi feet and the murmur of a fresh jungle rain, like other hoofs, falling upon the summer-starched grass. Now the walls dissolved into distances of parched weed, mile on mile, and warm endless sky. The animals drew away into thorn brakes and water holes.

It was the children's hour.

Five o'clock. The bath filled with clear hot water.

Six, seven, eight o'clock. The dinner dishes manipulated like magic tricks, and in the study a *click.* In the metal stand opposite the hearth where a fire now blazed up warmly, a cigar popped out, half an inch of soft gray ash on it, smoking, waiting.

Nine o'clock. The beds warmed their hidden circuits, for nights were cool here.

Nine-five. A voice spoke from the study ceiling:

"Mrs. McClellan, which poem would you like this evening?"

The house was silent.

The voice said at last, "Since you express no preference, I shall select a poem at random." Quiet music rose to back the voice. "Sara Teasdale. As I recall, your favorite. . . .

There will come soft rains and the smell of the ground,
And swallows circling with their shimmering sound;

And frogs in the pools singing at night,
And wild plum trees in tremulous white;

Robins will wear their feathery fire,
Whistling their whims on a low fence-wire;

And not one will know of the war, not one
Will care at last when it is done.

Not one would mind, neither bird nor tree,
If mankind perished utterly;

And Spring herself, when she woke at dawn
Would scarcely know that we were gone."

The fire burned on the stone hearth and the cigar fell away into a mound of quiet ash on its tray. The empty chairs faced each other between the silent walls, and the music played.

At ten o'clock the house began to die.

The wind blew. A falling tree bough crashed through the kitchen window. Cleaning solvent, bottled, shattered over the stove. The room was ablaze in an instant!

"Fire!" screamed a voice. The house lights flashed, water pumps shot water from the ceilings. But the solvent spread on the linoleum, licking, eating, under the kitchen door, while the voices took it up in chorus: "Fire, fire, fire!"

The house tried to save itself. Doors sprang tightly shut, but the windows were broken by the heat and the wind blew and sucked upon the fire.

The house gave ground as the fire in ten billion angry sparks moved with flaming ease from room to room and then up the stairs. While scurrying water rats squeaked from the walls, pistoled their water, and ran for more. And the wall sprays let down showers of mechanical rain.

But too late. Somewhere, sighing, a pump shrugged to a stop. The quenching rain ceased. The reserve water supply which had filled baths and washed dishes for many quiet days was gone.

The fire crackled up the stairs. It fed upon Picassos and Matisses in the upper halls, like delicacies, baking off the oily flesh, tenderly crisping the canvases into black shavings.

Now the fire lay in beds, stood in windows, changed the colors of drapes!

And then, reinforcements.

From attic trapdoors, blind robot faces peered down with faucet mouths gushing green chemical.

The fire backed off, as even an elephant must at the sight of a dead snake. Now there were twenty snakes whipping over the floor, killing the fire with a clear cold venom of green froth.

But the fire was clever. It had sent flames outside the house, up through the attic to the pumps there. An explosion! The attic brain which directed the pumps was shattered into bronze shrapnel on the beams.

The fire rushed back into every closet and felt of the clothes hung there.

The house shuddered, oak bone on bone, its bared skeleton cringing from the heat, its wire, its nerves revealed as if a surgeon had torn the skin off to let the red veins and capillaries quiver in the scalded air. Help, help! Fire! Run, run! Heat snapped mirrors like the brittle winter ice. And the voices wailed Fire, fire, run, run, like a tragic nursery rhyme, a dozen voices, high, low, like children dying in a forest, alone, alone. And the voices fading as the wires popped their sheathings like hot chestnuts. One, two, three, four, five voices died.

In the nursery the jungle burned. Blue lions roared, purple giraffes bounded off. The panthers ran in circles changing color, and ten million animals, running before the fire, vanished off toward a distant steaming river. . . .

Ten more voices died. In the last instant under the fire avalanche, other choruses, oblivious, could be heard announcing the time, playing music, cutting the lawn by remote-control mower, or setting an umbrella frantically out and in the slamming and opening front door, a thousand things happening, like a clock shop when each clock strikes the hour insanely before or after the other, a scene of maniac confusion, yet unity; singing, screaming, a few last cleaning mice darting bravely out to carry the horrid ashes away! And one voice, with sublime disregard for the situation, read poetry aloud in the fiery study, until all the film spools burned, until all the wires withered and the circuits cracked.

The fire burst the house and let it slam flat down, puffing out skirts of spark and smoke.

In the kitchen, an instant before the rain of fire and timber, the stove could be seen making breakfasts at a psychopathic rate, ten dozen eggs, six loaves of toast, twenty dozen bacon strips, which, eaten by fire, started the stove working again, hysterically hissing!

The crash. The attic smashing into kitchen and parlor. The parlor into cellar, cellar into sub-cellar. Deep freeze, armchair, film tapes, circuits, beds, and all like skeletons thrown in a cluttered mound deep under.

Smoke and silence. A great quantity of smoke.

Dawn showed faintly in the east. Among the ruins, one wall stood alone. Within the wall, a last voice said, over and over again and again, even as the sun rose to shine upon the heaped rubble and steam:

"Today is August 5, 2026, today is August 5, 2026, today is . . ."

Albert Camus

Albert Camus (1913–1960), recipient of the Nobel Prize for literature in 1957, was born and educated in Algeria. Like the protagonist in his story "The Guest," Camus worked as a teacher in Algeria between 1940 and 1942 before serving as a member of the Resistance in France during the remainder of World War II. After the war he worked as a journalist, playwright, and novelist in Paris, having achieved recognition with the publication of his first novel, *The Stranger*, in 1942. A member of the Communist Party in his twenties, Camus became increasingly apolitical in his thirties, in contrast to his French colleague Jean-Paul Sartre, who gradually shifted in the 1950s from adherence to an existential philosophy to embrace a more hard-line Stalinist Marxism. Camus died in an automobile accident near Paris shortly after his forty-sixth birthday.

Exile and the Kingdom, published in 1957, was Camus's only collection of short fiction, the last major work completed before his death. It followed the production of several of his plays and the publication of his two novels *The Plague* (1947) and *The Fall* (1956) and his widely read book of essays, *The Rebel: An Essay on Man in Revolt* (1951). The critic A. H. T. Levi has recognized the thematic unity in "The Guest" and the other five stories constituting *Exile and the Kingdom*. They were written after the outbreak of the Franco-Algerian war in 1954, which became an eight-year-long bloody struggle between the colonists' military repression and the native terrorists' insurrection.

In his essays and short works of fiction, Camus tried to mediate the situation in Algeria by dramatizing the differences between the two countries in the belief, as he said, that "the aim of art, the aim of a life can only be to increase the sum of freedom and responsibility to be found in every man and in the world." In his "Appeal for a Civilian Truce" (1956), Camus stated his view of the situation in Algeria from his vantage point as an "Algerian Frenchman":

> On this soil there are a million Frenchmen who have been here for a century, millions of Muslims, either Arabs or Berbers, who have been here for centuries, and several vigorous religious communities. Those men must live together at the crossroads where history put them. They can do so if they will take a few steps toward each other in an open confrontation. Then our differences ought to help us instead of dividing us. As for me, here as in every domain, I believe only in differences and not in uniformity. First of all, because differences are the roots without which the tree of liberty, the sap of creation and of civilization, dries up.

The Guest

1957 / Translated by Justin O'Brien

THE SCHOOLMASTER WAS WATCHING the two men climb toward him. One was on horseback, the other on foot. They had not yet tackled the abrupt rise leading to the schoolhouse built on the hillside. They were toiling onward, making slow progress in the snow, among the stones, on the vast expanse of the high, deserted plateau. From time to time the horse stumbled. Without hearing anything yet, he could see the breath issuing from the horse's nostrils. One of the men, at least, knew the region. They were following the trail although it had disappeared days ago under a layer of dirty white snow. The schoolmaster calculated that it would take them half an hour to get onto the hill. It was cold; he went back into the school to get a sweater.

He crossed the empty, frigid classroom. On the blackboard the four rivers of France, drawn with four different colored chalks, had been flowing toward their estuaries for the past three days. Snow had suddenly fallen in mid-October after eight months of drought without the transition of rain, and the twenty pupils, more or less, who lived in the villages scattered over the plateau had stopped coming. With fair weather they would return. Daru now heated only the single room that was his lodging, adjoining the classroom and giving also onto the plateau to the east. Like the class windows, his window looked to the south. On that side the school was a few kilometers from the point where the plateau began to slope toward the south. In clear weather could be seen the purple mass of the mountain range where the gap opened onto the desert.

Somewhat warmed, Daru returned to the window from which he had first seen the two men. They were no longer visible. Hence they must have tackled the rise. The sky was not so dark, for the snow had stopped falling during the night. The morning had opened with a dirty light which had scarcely become brighter as the ceiling of clouds lifted. At two in the afternoon it seemed as if the day were merely beginning. But still this was better than those three days when the thick snow was falling amidst unbroken darkness with little gusts of wind that rattled the double door of the classroom. Then Daru had spent long hours in his room, leaving it only to go to the shed and feed the chickens or get some coal. Fortunately the delivery truck from Tadjid, the nearest village to the north, had brought his supplies two days before the blizzard. It would return in forty-eight hours.

Besides, he had enough to resist a siege, for the little room was cluttered with bags of wheat that the administration left as a stock to distribute to those of his pupils whose families had suffered from the drought. Actually they had all been victims because they were all poor. Every day Daru would distribute a ration to the children. They had missed it, he knew, during these bad days. Possibly one of the fathers or big brothers would come this afternoon and he could supply them with grain. It was just a matter of carrying them over to the next harvest. Now shiploads of wheat were arriving from France and the worst was over. But it would be hard to forget that poverty, that army of ragged ghosts wandering in the sunlight, the plateaus burned to a cinder month after month, the earth shriveled up little by little, literally scorched, every stone bursting into dust under one's foot. The sheep had died then by thousands and even a few men, here and there, sometimes without anyone's knowing.

In contrast with such poverty, he who lived almost like a monk in his remote schoolhouse, nonetheless satisfied with the little he had and with the rough life, had felt like a lord with his whitewashed walls, his narrow couch, his unpainted shelves, his well, and his weekly provision of water and food. And suddenly this snow, without warning, without the foretaste of rain. This is the way the region was, cruel to live in, even without men — who didn't help matters either. But Daru had been born here. Everywhere else, he felt exiled.

He stepped out onto the terrace in front of the schoolhouse. The two men were now halfway up the slope. He recognized the horseman as Balducci, the old gendarme he had known for a long time. Balducci was holding on the end of a rope an Arab who was walking behind him with hands bound and head lowered. The gendarme waved a greeting to which Daru did not reply, lost as he was in contemplation of the Arab dressed in a faded blue jellaba,[1] his feet in sandals but covered with socks of heavy raw wool, his head surmounted by a narrow, short chèche.[2] They were approaching. Balducci was holding back his horse in order not to hurt the Arab, and the group was advancing slowly.

Within earshot, Balducci shouted: "One hour to do the three kilometers from El Ameur!" Daru did not answer. Short and square in his thick sweater, he watched them climb. Not once had the Arab raised his head. "Hello," said Daru when they got up onto the terrace. "Come and warm up." Balducci painfully got down from his horse without letting go of the rope. From under his bristling mustache he smiled at the schoolmaster. His little dark eyes, deep-set under a tanned forehead, and his mouth surrounded with wrinkles made him look attentive and studious. Daru took the bridle, led the horse to the shed, and came back to the two men, who were now waiting for him in the school. He led them into his room. "I am going to heat up the classroom," he said. "We'll be more comfortable there." When he entered the room again Balducci was on the couch. He had undone the rope tying him to the Arab, who had squatted near the stove. His hands still bound, the chèche pushed back on his head, he was looking toward the window. At first Daru noticed only his huge lips, fat, smooth, almost Negroid; yet his nose was straight, his eyes were dark and full of fever. The chèche revealed an obstinate forehead and, under the weathered skin now rather discolored by the cold, the whole face had a restless and rebellious look that struck Daru when the Arab, turning his face toward him, looked him straight in the eyes. "Go into the other room," said the schoolmaster, "and I'll make you some mint tea." "Thanks," Balducci said. "What a chore! How I long for retirement." And addressing his prisoner in Arabic: "Come on, you." The Arab got up and, slowly, holding his bound wrists in front of him, went into the classroom.

With the tea, Daru brought a chair. But Balducci was already enthroned on the nearest pupil's desk and the Arab had squatted against the teacher's platform facing the stove, which stood between the desk and the window. When he held out the glass of tea to the prisoner, Daru hesitated at the sight of his bound hands. "He might perhaps be untied." "Sure," said Balducci. "That was for the trip." He started to get to his feet. But Daru, setting the glass on the

---

[1] A long, loose-fitting garment with full sleeves and a hood.
[2] A scarf or sash that serves as a turban.

floor, had knelt beside the Arab. Without saying anything, the Arab watched him with his feverish eyes. Once his hands were free, he rubbed his swollen wrists against each other, took the glass of tea, and sucked up the burning liquid in swift little sips.

"Good," said Daru. "And where are you headed?"

Balducci withdrew his mustache from the tea. "Here, son."

"Odd pupils! And you're spending the night?"

"No. I'm going back to El Ameur. And you will deliver this fellow to Tinguit. He is expected at police headquarters."

Balducci was looking at Daru with a friendly little smile.

"What's this story?" asked the schoolmaster. "Are you pulling my leg?"

"No, son. Those are the orders."

"The orders? I'm not . . ." Daru hesitated, not wanting to hurt the old Corsican. "I mean, that's not my job."

"What! What's the meaning of that? In wartime people do all kinds of jobs."

"Then I'll wait for the declaration of war!"

Balducci nodded.

"O.K. But the orders exist and they concern you too. Things are brewing, it appears. There is talk of a forthcoming revolt. We are mobilized, in a way."

Daru still had his obstinate look.

"Listen, son," Balducci said. "I like you and you must understand. There's only a dozen of us at El Ameur to patrol throughout the whole territory of a small department and I must get back in a hurry. I was told to hand this guy over to you and return without delay. He couldn't be kept there. His village was beginning to stir; they wanted to take him back. You must take him to Tinguit tomorrow before the day is over. Twenty kilometers shouldn't faze a husky fellow like you. After that, all will be over. You'll come back to your pupils and your comfortable life."

Behind the wall the horse could be heard snorting and pawing the earth. Daru was looking out the window. Decidedly, the weather was clearing and the light was increasing over the snowy plateau. When all the snow was melted, the sun would take over again and once more would burn the fields of stone. For days, still, the unchanging sky would shed its dry light on the solitary expanse where nothing had any connection with man.

"After all," he said, turning around toward Balducci, "what did he do?" And, before the gendarme had opened his mouth, he asked: "Does he speak French?"

"No, not a word. We had been looking for him for a month, but they were hiding him. He killed his cousin."

"Is he against us?"

"I don't think so. But you can never be sure."

"Why did he kill?"

"A family squabble, I think. One owed the other grain, it seems. It's not at all clear. In short, he killed his cousin with a billhook. You know, like a sheep, *kreezk!*"

Balducci made the gesture of drawing a blade across his throat and the Arab, his attention attracted, watched him with a sort of anxiety. Daru felt a sudden wrath against the man, against all men with their rotten spite, their tireless hates, their blood lust.

But the kettle was singing on the stove. He served Balducci more tea, hesitated, then served the Arab again, who, a second time, drank avidly. His raised arms made the jellaba fall open and the schoolmaster saw his thin, muscular chest.

"Thanks, kid," Balducci said. "And now, I'm off."

He got up and went toward the Arab, taking a small rope from his pocket.

"What are you doing?" Daru asked dryly.

Balducci, disconcerted, showed him the rope.

"Don't bother."

The old gendarme hesitated. "It's up to you. Of course, you are armed?"

"I have my shotgun."

"Where?"

"In the trunk."

"You ought to have it near your bed."

"Why? I have nothing to fear."

"You're crazy, son. If there's an uprising, no one is safe, we're all in the same boat."

"I'll defend myself. I'll have time to see them coming."

Balducci began to laugh, then suddenly the mustache covered the white teeth. "You'll have time? O.K. That's just what I was saying. You have always been a little cracked. That's why I like you, my son was like that."

At the same time he took out his revolver and put it on the desk.

"Keep it; I don't need two weapons from here to El Ameur."

The revolver shone against the black paint of the table. When the gendarme turned toward him, the schoolmaster caught the smell of leather and horse-flesh.

"Listen, Balducci," Daru said suddenly, "every bit of this disgusts me, and first of all your fellow here. But I won't hand him over. Fight, yes, if I have to. But not that."

The old gendarme stood in front of him and looked at him severely.

"You're being a fool," he said slowly. "I don't like it either. You don't get used to putting a rope on a man even after years of it, and you're even ashamed — yes, ashamed. But you can't let them have their way."

"I won't hand him over," Daru said again.

"It's an order, son, and I repeat it."

"That's right. Repeat to them what I've said to you: I won't hand him over."

Balducci made a visible effort to reflect. He looked at the Arab and at Daru. At last he decided.

"No, I won't tell them anything. If you want to drop us, go ahead; I'll not denounce you. I have an order to deliver the prisoner and I'm doing so. And now you'll just sign this paper for me."

"There's no need. I'll not deny that you left him with me."

"Don't be mean with me. I know you'll tell the truth. You're from here-abouts and you are a man. But you must sign, that's the rule."

Daru opened his drawer, took out a little square bottle of purple ink, the red wooden penholder with the "sergeant-major" pen he used for making models of penmanship, and signed. The gendarme carefully folded the paper and put it into his wallet. Then he moved toward the door.

"I'll see you off," Daru said.

"No," said Balducci. "There's no use being polite. You insulted me."

He looked at the Arab, motionless in the same spot, sniffed peevishly, and turned away toward the door. "Good-by, son," he said. The door shut behind him. Balducci appeared suddenly outside the window and then disappeared. His footsteps were muffled by the snow. The horse stirred on the other side of the wall and several chickens fluttered in fright. A moment later Balducci reappeared outside the window leading the horse by the bridle. He walked toward the little rise without turning around and disappeared from sight with the horse following him. A big stone could be heard bouncing down. Daru walked back toward the prisoner, who, without stirring, never took his eyes off him. "Wait," the schoolmaster said in Arabic and went toward the bedroom. As he was going through the door, he had a second thought, went to the desk, took the revolver, and stuck it in his pocket. Then, without looking back, he went into his room.

For some time he lay on his couch watching the sky gradually close over, listening to the silence. It was this silence that had seemed painful to him during the first days here, after the war. He had requested a post in the little town at the base of the foothills separating the upper plateaus from the desert. There, rocky walls, green and black to the north, pink and lavender to the south, marked the frontier of eternal summer. He had been named to a post farther north, on the plateau itself. In the beginning, the solitude and the silence had been hard for him on these wastelands peopled only by stones. Occasionally, furrows suggested cultivation, but they had been dug to uncover a certain kind of stone good for building. The only plowing here was to harvest rocks. Elsewhere a thin layer of soil accumulated in the hollows would be scraped out to enrich paltry village gardens. This is the way it was: bare rock covered three quarters of the region. Towns sprang up, flourished, then disappeared; men came by, loved one another or fought bitterly, then died. No one in this desert, neither he nor his guest, mattered. And yet, outside this desert neither of them, Daru knew, could have really lived.

When he got up, no noise came from the classroom. He was amazed at the unmixed joy he derived from the mere thought that the Arab might have fled and that he would be alone with no decision to make. But the prisoner was there. He had merely stretched out between the stove and the desk. With eyes open, he was staring at the ceiling. In that position, his thick lips were particularly noticeable, giving him a pouting look. "Come," said Daru. The Arab got up and followed him. In the bedroom, the schoolmaster pointed to a chair near the table under the window. The Arab sat down without taking his eyes off Daru.

"Are you hungry?"

"Yes," the prisoner said.

Daru set the table for two. He took flour and oil, shaped a cake in a frying-pan, and lighted the little stove that functioned on bottled gas. While the cake was cooking, he went out to the shed to get cheese, eggs, dates, and condensed milk. When the cake was done he set it on the window sill to cool, heated some condensed milk diluted with water, and beat up the eggs into an omelette. In one of his motions he knocked against the revolver stuck in his right pocket. He set the bowl down, went into the classroom, and put the revolver in his desk drawer. When he came back to the room, night was falling. He put on the light and served the Arab. "Eat," he said. The Arab took a piece of the cake, lifted it eagerly to his mouth, and stopped short.

"And you?" he asked.

"After you. I'll eat too."

The thick lips opened slightly. The Arab hesitated, then bit into the cake determinedly.

The meal over, the Arab looked at the schoolmaster. "Are you the judge?"

"No, I'm simply keeping you until tomorrow."

"Why do you eat with me?"

"I'm hungry."

The Arab fell silent. Daru got up and went out. He brought back a folding bed from the shed, set it up between the table and the stove, perpendicular to his own bed. From a large suitcase which, upright in a corner, served as a shelf for papers, he took two blankets and arranged them on the camp bed. Then he stopped, felt useless, and sat down on his bed. There was nothing more to do or to get ready. He had to look at this man. He looked at him, therefore, trying to imagine his face bursting with rage. He couldn't do so. He could see nothing but the dark yet shining eyes and the animal mouth.

"Why did you kill him?" he asked in a voice whose hostile tone surprised him.

The Arab looked away. "He ran away. I ran after him."

He raised his eyes to Daru and they were full of a sort of woeful interrogation. "Now what will they do to me?"

"Are you afraid?"

He stiffened, turning his eyes away.

"Are you sorry?"

The Arab stared at him openmouthed. Obviously he did not understand. Daru's annoyance was growing. At the same time he felt awkward and self-conscious with his big body wedged between the two beds.

"Lie down there," he said impatiently. "That's your bed."

The Arab didn't move. He called to Daru:

"Tell me!"

The schoolmaster looked at him.

"Is the gendarme coming back tomorrow?"

"I don't know."

"Are you coming with us?"

"I don't know. Why?"

The prisoner got up and stretched out on top of the blankets, his feet toward the window. The light from the electric bulb shone straight into his eyes and he closed them at once.

"Why?" Daru repeated, standing beside the bed.

The Arab opened his eyes under the blinding light and looked at him, trying not to blink.

"Come with us," he said.

In the middle of the night, Daru was still not asleep. He had gone to bed after undressing completely; he generally slept naked. But when he suddenly realized that he had nothing on, he hesitated. He felt vulnerable and the temptation came to him to put his clothes back on. Then he shrugged his shoulders; after all, he wasn't a child and, if need be, he could break his adversary in two. From his bed he could observe him, lying on his back, still motionless with his eyes closed under the harsh light. When Daru turned out the light, the darkness seemed to coagulate all of a sudden. Little by little, the night came back to life in the window where the starless sky was stirring gently. The schoolmaster soon made out the body lying at his feet. The Arab still did not move, but his eyes seemed open. A faint wind was prowling around the schoolhouse. Perhaps it would drive away the clouds and the sun would reappear.

During the night the wind increased. The hens fluttered a little and then were silent. The Arab turned over on his side with his back to Daru, who thought he heard him moan. Then he listened for his guest's breathing, become heavier and more regular. He listened to that breath so close to him and mused without being able to go to sleep. In this room where he had been sleeping alone for a year, this presence bothered him. But it bothered him also by imposing on him a sort of brotherhood he knew well but refused to accept in the present circumstances. Men who share the same rooms, soldiers or prisoners, develop a strange alliance as if, having cast off their armor with their clothing, they fraternized every evening, over and above their differences, in the ancient community of dream and fatigue. But Daru shook himself; he didn't like such musings, and it was essential to sleep.

A little later, however, when the Arab stirred slightly, the schoolmaster was still not asleep. When the prisoner made a second move, he stiffened, on the alert. The Arab was lifting himself slowly on his arms with almost the motion of a sleepwalker. Seated upright in bed, he waited motionless without turning his head toward Daru, as if he were listening attentively. Daru did not stir; it had just occurred to him that the revolver was still in the drawer of his desk. It was better to act at once. Yet he continued to observe the prisoner, who, with the same slithery motion, put his feet on the ground, waited again, then began to stand up slowly. Daru was about to call out to him when the Arab began to walk, in a quite natural but extraordinarily silent way. He was heading toward the door at the end of the room that opened into the shed. He lifted the latch with precaution and went out, pushing the door behind him but without shutting it. Daru had not stirred. "He is running away," he merely thought. "Good riddance!" Yet he listened attentively. The hens were not fluttering; the guest must be on the plateau. A faint sound of water reached him, and he didn't know what it was until the Arab again stood framed in the doorway, closed the door carefully, and came back to bed without a sound. Then Daru turned his back on him and fell asleep. Still later he seemed, from the depths of his sleep, to hear furtive steps around the schoolhouse. "I'm dreaming! I'm dreaming!" he repeated to himself. And he went on sleeping.

When he awoke, the sky was clear; the loose window let in a cold, pure air. The Arab was asleep, hunched up under the blankets now, his mouth open, utterly relaxed. But when Daru shook him, he started dreadfully, staring at Daru with wild eyes as if he had never seen him and such a frightened expression that the schoolmaster stepped back. "Don't be afraid. It's me. You must eat." The Arab nodded and said yes. Calm had returned to his face, but his expression was vacant and listless.

The coffee was ready. They drank it seated together on the folding bed as they munched their pieces of the cake. Then Daru led the Arab under the shed and showed him the faucet where he washed. He went back into the room, folded the blankets and the bed, made his own bed and put the room in order. Then he went through the classroom and out onto the terrace. The sun was already rising in the blue sky; a soft bright light was bathing the deserted plateau. On the ridge the snow was melting in spots. The stones were about to reappear. Crouched on the edge of the plateau, the schoolmaster looked at the deserted expanse. He thought of Balducci. He had hurt him, for he had sent him off in a way as if he didn't want to be associated with him. He could hear the gendarme's farewell and, without knowing why, he felt strangely empty and vulnerable. At that moment, from the other side of the schoolhouse, the prisoner coughed. Daru listened to him almost despite himself and then, furious, threw a pebble that whistled through the air before sinking into the snow. That man's stupid crime revolted him, but to hand him over was contrary to honor. Merely thinking of it made him smart with humiliation. And he cursed at one and the same time his own people who had sent him this Arab and the Arab too who had dared to kill and not managed to get away. Daru got up, walked in a circle on the terrace, waited motionless, and then went back into the schoolhouse.

The Arab, leaning over the cement floor of the shed, was washing his teeth with two fingers. Daru looked at him and said: "Come." He went back into the room ahead of the prisoner. He slipped a hunting-jacket on over his sweater and put on walking-shoes. Standing, he waited until the Arab had put on his chèche and sandals. They went into the classroom and the schoolmaster pointed to the exit, saying: "Go ahead." The fellow didn't budge. "I'm coming," said Daru. The Arab went out. Daru went back into the room and made a package of pieces of rusk, dates, and sugar. In the classroom, before going out, he hesitated a second in front of his desk, then crossed the threshold and locked the door. "That's the way," he said. He started toward the east, followed by the prisoner. But, a short distance from the schoolhouse, he thought he heard a slight sound behind them. He retraced his steps and examined the surroundings of the house; there was no one there. The Arab watched him without seeming to understand. "Come on," said Daru.

They walked for an hour and rested beside a sharp peak of limestone. The snow was melting faster and faster and the sun was drinking up the puddles at once, rapidly cleaning the plateau, which gradually dried and vibrated like the air itself. When they resumed walking, the ground rang under their feet. From time to time a bird rent the space in front of them with a joyful cry. Daru breathed in deeply the fresh morning light. He felt a sort of rapture before the vast familiar expanse, now almost entirely yellow under its dome of blue sky. They walked an hour or more, descending toward the south. They reached a level height made up of crumbly rocks. From there on, the plateau sloped down, eastward toward a low plain where there were a few spindly trees and, to the south, toward outcroppings of rock that gave the landscape a chaotic look.

Daru surveyed the two directions. There was nothing but the sky on the horizon. Not a man could be seen. He turned toward the Arab, who was looking at him blankly. Daru held out the package to him. "Take it," he said. "There are dates, bread, and sugar. You can hold out for two days. Here are a thousand francs too." The Arab took the package and the money but kept his full hands at chest level as if he didn't know what to do with what was being given him. "Now look," the schoolmaster said as he pointed in the direction of the east, "there's the way to Tinguit. You have a two-hour walk. At Tinguit you'll find the administration and the police. They are expecting you." The Arab looked toward the east, still holding the package and the money against his chest. Daru took his elbow and turned him rather roughly toward the south. At the foot of the height on which they stood could be seen a faint path. "That's the trail across the plateau. In a day's walk from here you'll find pasturelands and the first nomads. They'll take you in and shelter you according to their law." The Arab had now turned toward Daru and a sort of panic was visible in his expression. "Listen," he said. Daru shook his head: "No, be quiet. Now I'm leaving you." He turned his back on him, took two long steps in the direction of the school, looked hesitantly at the motionless Arab, and started off again. For a few minutes he heard nothing but his own step resounding on the cold ground and did not turn his head. A moment later, however, he turned around. The Arab was still there on the edge of the hill, his arms hanging now, and he was looking at the schoolmaster. Daru felt something rise in his throat. But he swore with impatience, waved vaguely, and started off again. He had already gone some distance when he again stopped and looked. There was no longer anyone on the hill.

Daru hesitated. The sun was now rather high in the sky and was beginning to beat down on his head. The schoolmaster retraced his steps, at first somewhat uncertainly, then with decision. When he reached the little hill, he was bathed in sweat. He climbed it as fast as he could and stopped, out of breath, at the top. The rock-fields to the south stood out sharply against the blue sky, but on the plain to the east a steamy heat was already rising. And in that slight haze, Daru, with heavy heart, made out the Arab walking slowly on the road to prison.

A little later, standing before the window of the classroom, the schoolmaster was watching the clear light bathing the whole surface of the plateau, but he hardly saw it. Behind him on the blackboard, among the winding French rivers, sprawled the clumsily chalked-up words he had just read: "You handed over our brother. You will pay for this." Daru looked at the sky, the plateau, and, beyond, the invisible lands stretching all the way to the sea. In the vast landscape he had loved so much, he was alone.

Alejo Carpentier

Alejo Carpentier (1904–1980) was born in Lausanne, Switzerland, to a French father and a Russian mother, though he later claimed that he was born in Cuba. His parents moved to Havana when he was a baby and his first language was French. Educated at private schools and the University of Havana, he continued to speak Spanish with a French accent. Carpentier began his career by working as a cultural journalist with a special interest in music and theater. In 1927 he helped start the journal *Revista de Avance*, a radical magazine encouraging nationalism and revolutionary cultural ideas. That year he was arrested for opposing Gerardo Machado's dictatorship and spent forty days in jail. There Carpentier began his first novel, completed in 1933. After his release from jail, he left Cuba to begin a voluntary exile in Paris that lasted a dozen years. He wrote in both French and Spanish, and he began to publish poetry and fiction, started a literary magazine, and became part of the surrealist movement. After the end of the Machado regime, Carpentier went back to Cuba briefly in 1936, but returned to Paris. Three years later, as he said, "without any other reason than the nostalgia of Cuba, I vacated my apartment and started the return to La Havana."

In 1943, on a trip to Haiti, Carpentier visited the fortress and palace built by the black King Henri Christophe. He was also reading Oswald Spengler's interpretation of history, *The Decline of the West*, and these experiences provided the inspiration for his second novel, a narrative about the Haitian revolution titled *The Kingdom of the World*, in 1949. He completed this book in Caracas, Venezuela, where he had moved at the outbreak of World War II. In a prologue to the novel, he expressed his belief in the special destiny of Latin America due to its unique cultural heritage, and later he referred to these ideas in an essay, "Marvelous Real in America." As he later wrote, "At every step, I found the marvelous reality realm, but at the same time I thought that the presence and permanence of the 'marvelous reality' was not the sole privilege of Haiti, but the heritage of the Americas as a whole. . . . But what is the history of the Americas about, but a chronicle of the marvelous reality?" He believed that to express this quality, a writer must make "use of metaphors, abundant images and colors, baroque, especially baroque to express the marvelous world of the Americas." His story "Journey to the Seed," published in 1958, employs this "baroque" literary style in its backward narrative return to the time before the birth of Don Marcial.

In 1959, after Fidel Castro's Communist revolution, Carpentier returned from Caracas to Havana. There he worked for the State Publishing House and completed *Explosion in a Cathedral* (1962), a meditation on the dangers of revolution as it gradually evolves into dictatorships. After Gabriel García-Márquez read this book, he is said to have destroyed an early draft of his novel *One Hundred Years of Solitude* and begun again. In 1962 Carpentier was appointed the Cuban ambassador to France. He settled in Paris for the remaining years of his life. There he wrote several more books and received many prizes and honors. He completed his last novel while suffering from terminal cancer and was buried in the Colon Cemetery in Havana alongside other prominent political and cultural figures in Cuban history.

RELATED CASEBOOK

See Casebook on Magical Realism, pages 1627–1646, including Jorge Luis Borges, "Borges and I," page 1631; Alejo Carpentier, "On the Marvelous Real in America," page 1633 and "The Baroque and the Marvelous Real," page 1635; Luis Leal, "Magical Realism in Spanish American Literature," page 1637; William Gass, "The First Seven Pages of the Boom," page 1639; Ursula K. Le Guin, "The Kind of Fiction Most Characteristic of Our Times," page 1641; Mario Vargas Llosa, "The Prose Style of Jorge Luis Borges and Gabriel García Márquez," page 1645.

Journey to the Seed

1954 / Translated by Jean Franco

I

"What do you want, old 'un?"

The question fell several times from the top of the scaffolding. But the old man did not reply. He went from one spot to another, poking about, a long monologue of incomprehensible phrases issuing from his throat. They had already brought down the roof-tiles which covered the faded pavings with their earthenware mosaic. Up above, the picks were loosening the masonry, sending the stones rolling down wooden channels in a great cloud of lime and chalk. And through each one of the embrasures which had been cut into the battlements appeared (their secret uncovered) smooth oval or square ceilings, cornices, garlands, denticles, mouldings and wallpaper which hung down from the friezes like old, cast-off snake skins. Watching the demolition, a Ceres with a broken nose, a discoloured robe and with a blackened crown of maize upon her head stood in her back court upon her fountain of faded masks. Visited by the sun in the dusky hours, the grey fish in her basin yawned in mossy, warm water, their round eyes watching those black workmen in the gap in the skyline who were gradually reducing the age-old height of the house. The old man had seated himself at the foot of the statue with his stick pointing at his chin. He watched the raising and lowering of buckets in which valuable remains were carried away. There was the sound of muffled street noises and, up above, the pulleys harmonized their disagreeable and grating bird-songs in a rhythm of iron upon stone.

Five o'clock struck. The cornices and entablatures emptied of people. There only remained the hand-ladders ready for the next day's assault. The breeze turned fresher, now that it was relieved of its load of sweat, curses, rope-creakings, axles shrieking for the oil-can, and the slapping of greasy bodies. Twilight arrived earlier for the denuded house. It was clothed in shadows at an hour when the now-fallen upper parapets had been wont to regale the façade with a sparkle of sunlight. Ceres tightened her lips. For the first time, the rooms slept without window-blinds, open on to a landscape of ruins.

Contrary to their wishes, several capitals lay in the grass. Their acanthus leaves revealed their vegetable condition. A climbing plant, attracted by the family resemblance, ventured to stretch its tendrils towards the Ionic scrolls. When night fell, the house was nearer the ground. A door-frame still stood on high with planks of shade hanging from its bewildered hinges.

II

Then the dark old man who had not moved from that place, gestured strangely and waved his stick over a cemetery of tiles.

The black and white marble squares flew back and covered the floors again. With sure leaps, stones closed the gaps in the battlements. The walnut panels, garnished with nails, fitted themselves into their frames whilst, with rapid rotations, the screws of the hinges buried themselves in their holes. Raised up by an effort from the flowers, the tiles on the faded pavings put together their broken fragments and in a noisy whirlwind of clay fell like rain upon the roof-tree. The house grew, returned again to its usual proportions, clothed and modest. Ceres was less grey. There were more fish in the fountain. And the murmur of water invoked forgotten begonias.

The old man put a key into the lock of the main door and began to open windows. His heels sounded hollow. When he lit the brass lamps, a yellow tremor ran along the oil of the family portraits and black-robed people murmured in all the galleries to the rhythm of spoons stirred in chocolate bowls.

Don Marcial, Marquis of Capellanías lay on his deathbed, his breast clad in medals, and with an escort of four candles with long beards of melted wax.

III

The candles grew slowly and lost their beads of sweat. When they regained their full height, a nun put them out and drew away her taper. The wicks became white and threw off their snuff. The house emptied of visitors and the carriages departed into the night. Don Marcial played on an invisible keyboard and opened his eyes.

The blurred and jumbled roof-beams fell gradually back into place. The flasks of medicine, the damask tassels, the scapulary over the head of the bed, the daguerrotypes and the palms of the balcony grille emerged from the mists. Whilst the doctor shook his head with professional condolence, the sick man felt better. He slept for a few hours and awoke with the black beetle-browed regard of Father Anastasio upon him. The confession changed from being frank, detailed, and full of sins to being reticent, halting, and full of concealments. And after all, what right had that Carmelite friar to interfere in his life? Suddenly Don Marcial felt himself drawn into the middle of the room. The weight on his forehead lifted and he got up with surprising speed. The naked woman who was lounging upon the brocade of the bed searched for her petticoats and bodices and took away with her, soon afterwards, the sound of crushed silk and perfume. Below, in the closed carriage, covering the seat studs, there was an envelope containing gold coins.

Don Marcial did not feel well. As he arranged his tie in front of the pierglass he found that he looked bloated. He went down to the office where legal men, solicitors and notaries were waiting for him to settle the auctioning of the house. It had all been useless. His belongings would go bit by bit to the highest bidder to the rhythm of hammer-blows upon the table. He greeted them and they left him alone. He thought of the mysteries of the written word, of those black threads which, ravelling and unravelling over wide, filigrained balance sheets, had ravelled and unravelled agreements, oaths, covenants, testimonies, declarations, surnames, titles, dates, lands, trees, and stones — a web of threads extracted from the inkwell, threads in which a man's legs became fouled and which formed barriers across the paths, access to which was denied by law; they formed a noose pressing at his throat and muffling his voice as he perceived the dreadful sound of words which floated free. His signature had betrayed him, getting involved in knots and tangles of parchments. Bound by it, the man of flesh became a man of paper.

It was dawn. The dining-room clock had just struck six in the afternoon.

IV

Months of mourning passed, overshadowed by a growing feeling of remorse. At first the idea of bringing another woman into that bedroom seemed almost reasonable to him. But, little by little, the need for a new body was replaced by increasing scruples which reached the point of flagellation. One night, Don Marcial drew blood from his flesh with a strap and immediately felt a more intense desire, though of short duration. It was then that the Marchioness returned, one afternoon, from her ride along the banks of the Almendares. The horses of the calash had no moisture on their manes other than that of their own sweat. But all the rest of the day, they kicked at the panels of the stable as if irritated by the stillness of the low clouds.

At twilight, a basin full of water fell in the Marchioness' bath and broke. Then the May rains made the tank overflow. And the dark old woman who had a touch of the tar-brush and who kept doves under her bed walked through the yard muttering: "Beware of rivers, child, beware of the running green." There wasn't a day on which water did not betray its presence. But this presence was finally nothing more than a bowlful spilled upon a Paris gown when they came back from the anniversary ball given by the Captain General of the colony.

Many relatives reappeared. Many friends returned. The chandeliers of the great drawing-room now sparkled very brightly. The cracks in the façades gradually closed. The piano again became a clavichord. The palm trees lost some rings. The climbing plants let go of the first cornice. The rings under Ceres' eyes grew whiter and the capitals seemed newly-carved. Marcial grew livelier and would spend whole afternoons embracing the Marchioness. Crowsfeet, frowns, and double chins were erased and the flesh regained its firmness. One day the smell of fresh paint filled the house.

V

The blushes were genuine. Every night the leaves of screens opened wider, skirts fell in the darker corners and there were new barriers of lace. Finally the Marchioness blew out the lamps. Only he spoke in the darkness.

They left for the sugar-mill in a great train of calashes — a shining of sorrel croups, of silver bits and of varnish in the sun. But in the shade of the poinsettias which made the inner portico of the house glow red, they realized that they hardly knew one another. Marcial gave permission for Negro tribal dances and drums in order to divert them a little on those days which were odorous with Cologne perfume, baths of benzoin, with loosened hair and sheets taken from the cupboards which, when opened, spilled out bunches of vetiver herb on to the tiles. A whiff of cane liquor whirled in the breeze with the prayer-bell. The low breezes wafted tidings of reluctant rains whose first, big, noisy drops were sucked in by roofs so dry that they gave out the sound of copper. After a dawn lengthened by an awkward embrace, their disagreements made up, the wound healed, they both went back to the city. The Marchioness changed her travelling dress for a bridal gown and as usual, the couple went to church to recover their liberty. They gave the presents back to relatives and friends and in a flurry of bronze bells, a parade of harnesses, each one took the road back to his own home. Marcial went on visiting María de las Mercedes for some time until the day when the rings were taken to the goldsmith's to be disengraved. There began a new life for Marcial. In the house with the high balconies, Ceres was replaced by an Italian Venus and the masks of the fountain almost imperceptibly pushed out their reliefs on seeing the flames of the oil-lamps still alight when dawn already dappled the sky.

VI

One night when he had been doing a lot of drinking and felt dizzied by the smell of stale tobacco left by his friends, Marcial had the strange sensation that all the clocks in the house were striking five, then half-past four, then half-past three. It was like a distant recognition of other possibilities. Just as one imagines oneself during the lassitude of a sleepless night able to walk on the smooth ceiling among furniture placed amidst the roof-beams and with the floor as a smooth ceiling above. It was a fleeting impression that left not the slightest trace in his mind which was now little inclined to meditation.

And there was a big party in the music-room on the day when he reached his minority. He was happy when he thought that his signature no longer had any legal value and that the moth-eaten registers and the notaries were erased from his world. He was reaching the stage where law courts were no longer to be feared by those whose persons were not held in any regard by the law codes. After getting tipsy on full-bodied wines, the young men took down from the wall a guitar encrusted with mother-of-pearl, a psaltery and a trombone. Someone wound up the clock which played the Tyrolean Cow Song and the Ballad of the Scottish Lakes. Another blew on the hunting horn that had lain coiled in its copper case upon the scarlet felt of a show-case alongside the transverse flute brought from Aránjuez. Marcial who was boldly courting the Campoflorido girl joined in the din and picked out the tune of Tripili-Trápala on the bass notes of the keyboard. Then they all went up into the attic, suddenly remembering that there, under the beams which were once again covered with plaster, were hoarded the dresses and liveries of the House of Capellanías. Along shelves frosted with camphor lay court-gowns, an Ambassador's sword, several braided military jackets, the cloak of a Prince of the Church, and long dress-coats with damask buttons and with damp marks in the folds. The shadows were tinted with amaranth ribbons, yellow crinolines, faded tunics, and velvet flowers. A thinker's costume with a tasselled hair-net made for a Carnival masquerade won applause. The Campoflorido rounded her shoulders underneath a shawl which was the colour of creole flesh and which had been used by a certain grandmother on a night of momentous family decision, in order to receive the waning fires of a rich treasurer of the Order of St Clare.

The young people returned to the music-room in fancy dress. Wearing an alderman's tricorne hat on his head, Marcial struck the floor three times with his stick, and started off the waltz which the mothers found terribly improper for young ladies with that clasping around the waist and the man's hand touching the whalebone supports of their corsets which they had all made from the latest pattern in the "Garden of Fashion." The doors were obscured by maidservants, stable-boys, servants who came from their far-off outbuildings and from stifling basements to marvel at such a riotous party. Later, they played blind man's buff and hide-and-seek. Marcial hid with the Campoflorido girl behind the Chinese screen and imprinted a kiss on her neck and in return received a perfumed handkerchief whose Brussels lace still held the soft warmth from her décolleté. And when, in the twilight, the girls went off to the watchtowers and fortresses which were silhouetted grey-black against the sea, the young men left for the Dance Hall where mulatto girls with huge bracelets swayed so gracefully without ever losing their little high-heeled shoes however agitated the dance. And from behind a neighbouring wall in a yard full of pomegranate trees the men of the Cabildo Arará Tres Ojos band beat out a drum roll just as if it were carnival time. Standing on tables and stools, Marcial and his friends applauded the grace of a Negress with greyish kinky hair who was beautiful, almost desirable again when she looked over her shoulder and danced with a proud gesture of defiance.

VII

The visits of Don Abundio, the family notary and executor, grew more frequent. He sat down gravely at the head of Marcial's bed, letting his stick of acana wood fall to the floor in order to wake him up before time. When he opened his eyes, they met an alpaca coat covered with dandruff, a coat whose shining sleeves gathered up titles and rents. There was finally only a small allowance left, one designed to put a check on any folly. It was then that Marcial resolved to enter the Royal Seminary of San Carlos.

After passing his examinations indifferently, he began to frequent the cloisters where he understood less and less of the teachers' explanations. The world of ideas was slowly becoming empty. What had first been a universal assembly of togas, doublets, ruffs and wigs, debaters and sophists took on the immobility of a waxworks museum. Marcial was now content with the scholastic exposition of system and accepted as true what was said in the text book. Over the copper engravings of Natural History were inscribed Lion, Ostrich, Whale, Jaguar. In the same way, Aristotle, Saint Thomas, Bacon, and Descartes headed the black pages on which boring catalogues of interpretations of the universe appeared in the margins of the lengthy chapters. Little by little, Marcial left off studying them and found that a great weight was lifted from him. His mind became light and happy when he accepted only an instinctive knowledge of things. Why think of the prism when the clear winter light gave added detail to the fortress of the door? An apple falling from the tree was only an incitement to the teeth. A foot in a bathtub was only a foot in a bathtub. The day on which he left the Seminary, he forgot his books. The gnomon recovered its fairy character; the spectrum became synonymous with the word spectre; the octander was an armour-plated insect with spines on its back.

Several times, he had walked quickly with an anxious heart to visit women who whispered behind blue doors at the foot of the battlements. The memory of one of them who wore embroidered shoes and basil leaves over her ear pursued him like a toothache on hot afternoons. But one day, the anger and threats of his confessor made him weep with fear. He fell for the last time between the sheets of hell and renounced forever his wanderings along quiet streets, and his last-minute cowardice which made him return home angrily after turning his back on a certain cracked pavement (the sign, when he was walking with his eyes lowered, of the half-turn he must make in order to enter the perfumed threshold).

Now he was living his religious crisis, full of amulets, paschal lambs and china doves, Virgins in sky-blue cloaks, angels with swan's wings, the Ass, the Ox, and a terrible Saint Dionysius who appeared to him in dreams with a big hollow between his shoulders and the hesitant walk of one who seeks for something he has lost. He stumbled against the bed and Marcial awoke in fear, grasping the rosary of muffled beads. The wicks in their oil vessels gave a sad light to the images which were recovering their pristine colours.

VIII

The furniture grew. It became more and more difficult to keep his arms on the edge of the dining-room table. The cupboards with carved cornices became wider at the front. Stretching their bodies, the Moors on the staircase brought their torches up to the balustrades of the landing. The arm-chairs were deeper and the rocking chairs tended to go over backwards. He no longer needed to bend his legs when he lay down at the bottom of the bathtub which had marble rings.

One morning, whilst reading a licentious book, Marcial suddenly felt like playing with the lead soldiers which lay in their wooden boxes. He hid the book again under the washbasin and opened a drawer covered with spiders' webs. The study table was too small to fit so many persons. For this reason, Marcial sat on the floor. He placed the grenadiers in lines of eight, then the officers on horseback, clustered round the standard-bearer and behind, the artillery with their cannons, gunwads, and matchstaffs. Bringing up the rear came fifes and kettledrums and an escort of drummers. The mortars were provided with a spring which enabled them to shoot glass marbles from a yard away.

Bang! Bang! Bang!

Horses fell, standard-bearers fell, drums fell. He had to be called three times by the Negro Eligio before he made up his mind to wash his hands and go down to the dining-room.

From then on, Marcial retained the habit of sitting on the tile floor. When he realized the advantages, he was surprised at not having thought of it before. Grown-ups with their addiction to velvet cushions sweat too much. Some smell of notary — like Don Abundio — because they know nothing of the coolness of marble (whatever the temperature) when one is lying full-length on the floor. It is only from the floor that all the angles and perspectives of a room can be appreciated. There are beauties of wood, mysterious insect paths, shadowy corners which are unknown from a man's height. When it rained, Marcial hid under the clavichord. Each roll of thunder made the box tremble and all the notes sang. From the sky fell thunderbolts which created a cavern full of improvisations — the sounds of an organ, of a pine grove in the wind, of a cricket's mandoline.

IX

That morning, they shut him in his room. He heard murmurs all over the house and the lunch they served him was too succulent for a weekday. There were six cakes from the confectioner's shop on the Alameda when only two could be eaten on Sundays after mass. He amused himself by looking at the travel engravings until the rising buzz which came from under the doors caused him to peep out between the Venetian blinds. Men dressed in black were arriving, carrying a box with bronze handles. He felt like crying but at that moment, Melchor the coachman appeared, displaying a toothy smile over his squeaky boots. They began to play chess. Melchor was knight. He was King. With the floor-tiles as the board, he could advance one at a time whilst Melchor had to jump one to the front and two sideways or vice versa. The game went on until nightfall when the Chamber of Commerce's Fire Brigade went past.

When he got up, he went to kiss the hand of his father who lay on his sick-bed. The Marquis was feeling better and spoke to his son with his normal looks and phrases. His "Yes, father" and "No, father" were fitted in between each bead in the rosary of questions like the responses of the acolyte in mass. Marcial respected the Marquis but for reasons which nobody would have guessed. He respected him because of his great height and because he appeared on ball nights with decorations sparkling across his breast; because he envied his sabre and his militia officer's epaulets, because at Christmas he had eaten a whole turkey stuffed with almonds and raisins to win a bet; because, on one occasion, perhaps because he wanted to beat her, he seized one of the mulatto girls who was sweeping in the rotunda and carried her in his arms to his room. Hidden behind a curtain, Marcial saw her emerge a short time later weeping and with her dress unbuttoned, and he was glad she had been punished because she was the one who always emptied the jam-pots that were returned to the larder.

His father was a terrible, magnanimous being whom he ought to love first after God. Marcial felt that he was more God than God because his gifts were daily and tangible. But he preferred the God of heaven because he interfered with him less.

X

When the furniture grew taller and Marcial knew better than anyone else what there was underneath beds, cupboards, and escritoires, he had a big secret; life held no charm away from Melchor, the coachman. Neither God nor his father, nor the gilded bishop in the Corpus processions were as important as Melchor.

Melchor came from far away. He was the grandson of conquered princes. In his kingdom, there were elephants, hippopotamus, tigers, and giraffes. There men did not work in dark rooms full of parchments like Don Abundio. They lived by being cleverer than the animals. One of them had caught a great crocodile in a blue lake by piercing it with a hook concealed in the tightly-packed bodies of twelve roast geese. Melchor knew songs that were easy to learn because the words had no meaning and were repeated a great deal. He stole sweets from the kitchen, got out at night through the stable door, and on one occasion had thrown stones at the police and then had disappeared into the shadows of Amargura street.

On rainy days, his boots were put to dry in front of the kitchen fire. Marcial would have liked to have had feet to fill such boots. The right-hand one was called Calambín. The left-hand one was called Calambán. The man who tamed unbroken horses just by putting his fingers on their lips, this lord of velvet and spurs who wore such tall top hats also knew how cool the marble floor was in summer and hid under the furniture a fruit or cake snatched from the trays which were destined for the big drawing-room. Marcial and Melchor had a secret store full of fruit and almonds which they held in common and called Urí, urí, urá, with understanding laughs. Both of them had explored the house from top to bottom and were the only ones who knew of the existence of a small basement full of Dutch flasks underneath the stables and of twelve dusty butterflies which had just lost their wings in a broken glass box in a disused attic over the maids' rooms.

XI

When Marcial acquired the habit of breaking things, he forgot about Melchor and drew closer to the dogs. There were several of them in the house. There was a big, striped one, a hound with dragging teats, a greyhound who was too old to play with, a woolly dog which the rest chased at certain periods and which the housemaids had to lock up.

Marcial liked Canelo best because he took shoes from out of the bedrooms and dug up the rose-bushes in the garden. He was always black from charcoal or covered with red earth and he used to devour the other dogs' meals, whine without reason, and hide stolen bones by the fountain. Occasionally he would finish off a newly-laid egg after sending the hen flying into the air with a swift levering movement of the muzzle. Everyone would kick Canelo. But Marcial fell ill when they took him away. And the dog returned in triumph, wagging its tail after having been abandoned at the other side of the Charity Hospital and recovered a position in the house which the other dogs with their skill at hunting or their alertness as watchdogs never occupied.

Canelo and Marcial used to pee together. Sometimes, they chose the Persian carpet in the drawing-room and upon the wool pile, they outlined the shapes of clouds which would grow slowly bigger. For this they were given the strap. But the beating did not hurt as much as the grown-ups thought. On the contrary, it was an excellent excuse for setting up a concert of howls and of arousing the sympathy of the neighbours. When the cross-eyed woman in the attic called his father a "savage," Marcial looked at Canelo and laughed with his eyes. They cried a bit more to get a biscuit and all was forgotten. Both of them used to eat earth, roll in the sun, drink from the fish-pond, and look for shade and perfume under the sweet basil. In hours of the greatest heat, the damp paving-stones were crowded. There was a grey goose with a bag hanging between its bow-legs; there was the old hen with a bare behind and the lizard that croaked and shot out a tongue like a pink tie issuing from its throat; there was the juba snake born in a city without females, and the mouse which walled up its hole with the seed of the carey bush. One day they showed Marcial a dog.

"Bow, wow," he said.

He spoke his own language. He had attained the supreme freedom. He already wanted to reach with his hands things which were out of reach of his hands.

XII

Hunger, thirst, heat, pain, cold. When Marcial had reduced his perception to these essential realities, he renounced light which was now incidental to him. He did not know his name. The baptism with its unpleasant salt was taken away from him and he did not now need smell, hearing, or sight. His hands brushed against pleasing forms. He was a totally sentient and tactile being. The universe entered him through all his pores. Then he closed his eyes which only perceived nebulous giants and penetrated into a warm, damp body full of shadows in which he died. The body, on feeling him wrapped in its own substance, slipped towards life.

But now time sped more rapidly and lessened its last hours. The minutes sounded like the slipping of cards under a gambler's thumb.

The birds returned to the egg in a rush of feathers. The fish coagulated into spawn leaving a snowstorm of scales at the bottom of the tank. The palms folded their fronds and disappeared into the earth like closed fans. Stalks sucked in the leaves and the ground drew in all that belonged to it. Thunder resounded in the corridors. Hair grew on the suède of gloves. Woollen shawls lost their dye and plumped out the fleece of distant sheep. Cupboards, escritoires, beds, crucifixes, tables, blinds flew into the night seeking their ancient roots in the jungles. Everything which had nails in it crumbled. A brig anchored (heaven knows where) hurriedly took the marble of the floor-tiles and the fountain back to Italy. The collection of arms, ironwork, the keys, copper-pans, horse-bits from the stables melted, swelling the river of metal which was channelled along roofless galleries into the earth. All was metamorphosed and went back to its primitive condition. The clay became clay again leaving a desert in place of a house.

XIII

When the workmen came at daybreak to continue the demolition, they found their work finished. Someone had taken away the statue of Ceres which had been sold the day before to an antique-dealer. After lodging a complaint with the Union, the men went and sat on the benches of the city park. Then one of them recalled the very vague story of a Marchioness of Capellanías who had been drowned one May afternoon among the lilies of the Almendares. But nobody paid any attention to the tale, because the sun was travelling from East to West and the hours which grow on the right-hand of clocks must become longer out of laziness since they are those which lead most surely to death.

Angela Carter

Angela Carter (1940–1992), the English writer, began her career as a journalist before studying literature at the University of Bristol. At the age of twenty-six she published her first novel, *Shadow Dance*, and decided "that life was too short to write journalism." She published books in many genres, including seven more novels, three short story collections, radio scripts, a screenplay, children's stories, a feminist study of the pornography of the Marquis de Sade, and a translation of Charles Perrault's classic French fairy tales.

"The Kiss" is from Carter's collection *Saints and Sinners* (1985). She has created a tale like Scheherezade, the most famous storyteller of all time, who lived in Persia before the 14th century reign of Tamburlaine. He was a devout Muslim who referred to himself as "the Sword of Islam." His multi-ethnic armies, who killed millions of people, were feared throughout Asia, Africa, and Europe. As the critic Charles Newman has said, Carter's narrative owes a great deal to the structure of fairy tales—"that authoritative voice out of the blue, avoiding dialogue whenever possible, embroidering seemingly opaque events with illuminating prologues and postludes. . . ."

Carter credited Jorge Luis Borges as a more important influence on her stories than the traditional fairy tales she enjoyed retelling in her own fashion. "I first read Borges in 1969, and it was like the Revelation—the extraordinary things he could do in his stories." Carter's fictions transcend the labels *magical realism* and *Gothic metafiction* often applied to them. They are fantasies spun by a remarkable imagination, evoking a terrifying atmosphere in which anything can happen and something violent often does. A complete collection of Carter's short fiction, *Burning Your Boats: The Collected Short Stories*, was published in 1996.

The Kiss

1985

THE WINTERS IN CENTRAL ASIA are piercing and bleak, while the sweating, foetid summers bring cholera, dysentery and mosquitoes, but, in April, the air caresses like the touch of the inner skin of the thigh and the scent of all the flowering trees douses this city's throat-catching whiff of cesspits.

Every city has its own internal logic. Imagine a city drawn in straightforward, geometric shapes with crayons from a child's colouring box, in ochre, in white, in pale terracotta. Low, blonde terraces of houses seem to rise out of the whitish, pinkish earth as if born from it, not built out of it. There is a faint, gritty dust over everything, like the dust those pastel crayons leave on your fingers.

Against these bleached pallors, the iridescent crusts of ceramic tiles that cover the ancient mausoleums ensorcellate the eye. The throbbing blue of Islam transforms itself to green while you look at it. Beneath a bulbous dome alternately lapis lazuli and veridian, the bones of Tamburlaine, the scourge of Asia, lie in a jade tomb. We are visiting an authentically fabulous city. We are in Samarkand.

The Revolution promised the Uzbek peasant women clothes of silk and on this promise, at least, did not welch. They wear tunics of flimsy satin, pink and yellow, red and white, black and white, red, green and white, in blotched stripes of brilliant colours that dazzle like an optical illusion, and they bedeck themselves with much jewellery made of red glass.

They always seem to be frowning because they paint a thick, black line straight across their foreheads that takes their eyebrows from one side of their faces to the other without a break. They rim their eyes with kohl. They look startling. They fasten their long hair in two or three dozen whirling plaits. Young girls wear little velvet caps embroidered with metallic thread and beadwork. Older women cover their heads with a couple of scarves of flower-printed wool, one bound tight over the forehead, the other hanging loosely on to the shoulders. Nobody has worn a veil for sixty years.

They walk as purposefully as if they did not live in an imaginary city. They do not know that they themselves and their turbanned, sheepskin jacketted, booted menfolk are creatures as extraordinary to the foreign eye as a unicorn. They exist, in all their glittering and innocent exoticism, in direct contradiction to history. They do not know what I know about them. They do not know that this city is not the entire world. All they know of the world is this city, beautiful as an illusion, where irises grow in the gutters. In the tea-house a green parrot nudges the bars of its wicker cage.

The market has a sharp, green smell. A girl with black-barred brows sprinkles water from a glass over radishes. In this early part of the year, you can buy only last summer's dried fruit — apricots, peaches, raisins — except for a few, precious, wrinkled pomegranates, stored in sawdust through the winter and now split open on the stall to show how a wet nest of garnets remains within. A local speciality of Samarkand is salted apricot kernels, more delicious, even, then pistachios.

An old woman sells arum lilies. This morning, she came from the mountains, where wild tulips have put out flowers like blown bubbles of blood, and the wheedling turtle-doves are nesting among the rocks. This old woman dips bread into a cup of buttermilk for her lunch and eats slowly. When she has sold her lilies, she will go back to the place where they are growing.

She scarcely seems to inhabit time. Or, it is as if she were waiting for Scheherezade to perceive a final dawn had come and, the last tale of all concluded, fall silent. Then, the lily-seller might vanish.

A goat is nibbling wild jasmine among the ruins of the mosque that was built by the beautiful wife of Tamburlaine.

Tamburlaine's wife started to build this mosque for him as a surprise, while he was away at the wars, but when she got word of his imminent return, one arch still remained unfinished. She went directly to the architect and begged him to hurry but the architect told her he would complete the work in time only if she gave him a kiss. One kiss, one single kiss.

Tamburlaine's wife was not only very beautiful and very virtuous but also very clever. She went to the market, bought a basket of eggs, boiled them hard and stained them a dozen different colours. She called the architect to the palace, showed him the basket and told him to choose any egg he liked and eat it. He took a red egg. What does it taste like? Like an egg. Eat another.

He took a green egg.

What does *that* taste like? Like the red egg. Try again.

He ate a purple egg.

One egg tastes just the same as any other egg, if they are fresh, he said. There you are! she said. Each of these eggs looks different to the rest but they all taste the same. So you may kiss any one of my serving women that you like but you must leave me alone.

Very well, said the architect. But soon he came back to her and this time he was carrying a tray with three bowls on it, and you would have thought the bowls were all full of water.

Drink from each of these bowls, he said.

She took a drink from the first bowl, then from the second; but how she coughed and spluttered when she took a mouthful from the third bowl, because it contained, not water, but vodka.

This vodka and that water both look alike but each tastes quite different, he said. And it is the same with love.

Then Tamburlaine's wife kissed the architect on the mouth. He went back to the mosque and finished the arch the same day that victorious Tamburlaine rode into Samarkand with his army and banners and his cases full of captive kings. But when Tamburlaine went to visit his wife, she turned away from him because no woman will return to the harem after she has tasted vodka. Tamburlaine beat her with a knout until she told him she had kissed the architect and then he sent his executioners hotfoot to the mosque.

The executioners saw the architect standing on top of the arch and ran up the stairs with their knives drawn but when he heard them coming he grew wings and flew away to Persia.

This is a story in simple, geometric shapes and the bold colours of a child's box of crayons. This Tamburlaine's wife of the story would have painted a black stripe laterally across her forehead and done up her hair in a dozen, dozen tiny plaits, like any other Uzbek woman. She would have bought red and white radishes from the market for her husband's dinner. After she ran away from him perhaps she made her living in the market. Perhaps she sold lilies there.

Raymond Carver

Raymond Carver (1938–1988) grew up in a logging town in Oregon, where his father worked in a sawmill and his mother held odd jobs. After graduating from high school, Carver married at the age of nineteen and had two children. Working hard to support his wife and family, he managed to enroll briefly in 1958 as a student at Chico State College in California, where he took a creative writing course from a then unknown young novelist named John Gardner. Carver remembered that he decided to try to become a writer because he liked to read pulp novels and magazines about hunting and fishing. He credited Gardner for giving him a strong sense of direction as a writer: "A writer's values and craft. This is what the man taught and what he stood for, and this is what I've kept by me in the years since that brief but all-important time."

In 1963 Carver received his B.A. degree from Humboldt State College in northern California. The following year he attended the Writers' Workshop at the University of Iowa. But the 1960s were difficult for him and his wife.

> I learned a long time ago when my kids were little and we had no money, and
> we were working our hearts out and weren't getting anywhere, even though
> we were giving it our best, my wife and I, that there were more important
> things than writing a poem or a story. That was a very hard realization for me
> to come to. But it came to me, and I had to accept it or die. Getting milk and
> food on the table, getting the rent paid, if a choice had to be made, then I
> had to forgo writing.

Carver's desire to be a writer was so strong that he kept on writing long after the "cold facts" of his life told him he ought to quit. His first collection of stories, *Will You Please Be Quiet, Please?*, was nominated for the National Book Award in 1976. Four more collections of stories followed, along with five books of poetry, before his death from lung cancer.

Critics have noted that the evolution of Carver's style causes his fiction to fall into three distinct periods. The tentative writing in his first book of stories — many of which were subsequently revised and republished — was followed by a paring down of his prose by his editor Gordon Lish. This resulted in the hard-edged, detached minimalist style of Carver's middle period, exemplified by the stories in his collection *What We Talk About When We Talk About Love* (1981). In his final period, Carver developed a more expansive style, as in the collection *Cathedral* (1983) and the new stories in his last collection, *Where I'm Calling From* (1988). Influenced by the cadence of Ernest Hemingway's sentences, Carver also believed in simplicity. He wrote:

> It's possible, in a poem or a short story, to write about commonplace things
> and objects using commonplace but precise language, and to endow those
> things — a chair, a window curtain, a fork, a stone, a woman's earring — with
> immense, even startling power. . . . If the words are heavy with the writer's
> own unbridled emotions, or if they are imprecise and inaccurate for some
> other reason — if the words are in any way blurred — the reader's eyes will slide
> right over them and nothing will be achieved. The reader's own artistic sense
> will simply not be engaged.

RELATED STORY
Nathan Englander, "What We Talk About When We Talk About Anne Frank," page 430.

RELATED CASEBOOK
See Casebook on Raymond Carver, pages 1556–1576, including Raymond Carver, "On Writing," page 1557; "Creative Writing 101," page 1560; "The Bath," page 1564; Tom Jenks, "The Origin of 'Cathedral,'" page 1569; Arthur M. Saltzman, "A Reading of 'What We Talk About When We Talk About Love,'" page 1570; and A. O. Scott, "Looking for Raymond Carver," page 1572.

Cathedral

1981

THIS BLIND MAN, an old friend of my wife's, he was on his way to spend the night. His wife had died. So he was visiting the dead wife's relatives in Connecticut. He called my wife from his in-laws'. Arrangements were made. He would come by train, a five-hour trip, and my wife would meet him at the station. She hadn't seen him since she worked for him one summer in Seattle ten years ago. But she and the blind man had kept in touch. They made tapes and mailed them back and forth. I wasn't enthusiastic about his visit. He was no one I knew. And his being blind bothered me. My idea of blindness came from the movies. In the movies, the blind moved slowly and never laughed. Sometimes they were led by seeing-eye dogs. A blind man in my house was not something I looked forward to.

That summer in Seattle she had needed a job. She didn't have any money. The man she was going to marry at the end of the summer was in officers' training school. He didn't have any money, either. But she was in love with the guy, and he was in love with her, etc. She'd seen something in the paper: HELP WANTED—*Reading to Blind Man*, and a telephone number. She phoned and went over, was hired on the spot. She'd worked with this blind man all summer. She read stuff to him, case studies, reports, that sort of thing. She helped him organize his little office in the county social-service department. They'd become good friends, my wife and the blind man. How do I know these things? She told me. And she told me something else. On her last day in the office, the blind man asked if he could touch her face. She agreed to this. She told me he touched his fingers to every part of her face, her nose—even her neck! She never forgot it. She even tried to write a poem about it. She was always trying to write a poem. She wrote a poem or two every year, usually after something really important had happened to her.

When we first started going out together, she showed me the poem. In the poem, she recalled his fingers and the way they had moved around over her face. In the poem, she talked about what she had felt at the time, about what went through her mind when the blind man touched her nose and lips. I can remember I didn't think much of the poem. Of course, I didn't tell her that. Maybe I just don't understand poetry. I admit it's not the first thing I reach for when I pick up something to read.

Anyway, this man who'd first enjoyed her favors, the officer-to-be, he'd been her childhood sweetheart. So okay. I'm saying that at the end of the summer she let the blind man run his hands over her face, said goodbye to him, married her childhood etc., who was now a commissioned officer, and she moved away from Seattle. But they'd kept in touch, she and the blind man. She made the first contact after a year or so. She called him up one night from an Air Force base in Alabama. She wanted to talk. They talked. He asked her to send him a tape and tell him about her life. She did this. She sent the tape. On the tape, she told the blind man about her husband and about their life together in the military. She told the blind man she loved her husband but she didn't like it where they lived and she didn't like it that he was a part of the military-industrial thing. She told the blind man she'd written a poem and he was in it. She told him that she was writing a poem about what it was like to be an Air Force officer's wife. The poem wasn't finished yet. She was still writing it. The blind man made a tape. He sent her the tape. She made a tape. This went on for years. My wife's officer was posted to one base and then another. She sent tapes from Moody AFB, McGuire, McConnell, and finally Travis, near Sacramento, where one night she got to feeling lonely and cut off from people she kept losing in that moving-around life. She got to feeling she couldn't go it another step. She went in and swallowed all the pills and capsules in the medicine chest and washed them down with a bottle of gin. Then she got into a hot bath and passed out.

But instead of dying, she got sick. She threw up. Her officer — why should he have a name? he was the childhood sweetheart, and what more does he want? — came home from somewhere, found her, and called the ambulance. In time, she put it all on a tape and sent the tape to the blind man. Over the years, she put all kinds of stuff on tapes and sent the tapes off lickety-split. Next to writing a poem every year, I think it was her chief means of recreation. On one tape, she told the blind man she'd decided to live away from her officer for a time. On another tape, she told him about her divorce. She and I began going out, and of course she told her blind man about it. She told him everything, or so it seemed to me. Once she asked me if I'd like to hear the latest tape from the blind man. This was a year ago. I was on the tape, she said. So I said okay, I'd listen to it. I got us drinks and we settled down in the living room. We made ready to listen. First she inserted the tape into the player and adjusted a couple of dials. Then she pushed a lever. The tape squeaked and someone began to talk in this loud voice. She lowered the volume. After a few minutes of harmless chitchat, I heard my own name in the mouth of this stranger, this blind man I didn't even know! And then this: "From all you've said about him, I can only conclude —" But we were interrupted, a knock at the door, something, and we didn't ever get back to the tape. Maybe it was just as well. I'd heard all I wanted to.

Now this same blind man was coming to sleep in my house.

"Maybe I could take him bowling," I said to my wife. She was at the draining board doing scalloped potatoes. She put down the knife she was using and turned around.

"If you love me," she said, "you can do this for me. If you don't love me, okay. But if you had a friend, any friend, and the friend came to visit, I'd make him feel comfortable." She wiped her hands with the dish towel.

"I don't have any blind friends," I said.

"You don't have *any* friends," she said. "Period. Besides," she said, "goddamn it, his wife's just died! Don't you understand that? The man's lost his wife!"

I didn't answer. She'd told me a little about the blind man's wife. Her name was Beulah. Beulah! That's a name for a colored woman.

"Was his wife Negro?" I asked.

"Are you crazy?" my wife said. "Have you just flipped or something?" She picked up a potato. I saw it hit the floor, then roll under the stove. "What's wrong with you?" she said. "Are you drunk?"

"I'm just asking," I said.

Right then my wife filled me in with more detail than I cared to know. I made a drink and sat at the kitchen table to listen. Pieces of the story began to fall into place.

Beulah had gone to work for the blind man the summer after my wife had stopped working for him. Pretty soon Beulah and the blind man had themselves a church wedding. It was a little wedding — who'd want to go to such a wedding in the first place? — just the two of them, plus the minister and the minister's wife. But it was a church wedding just the same. It was what Beulah had wanted, he'd said. But even then Beulah must have been carrying the cancer in her glands. After they had been inseparable for eight years — my wife's word, *inseparable* — Beulah's health went into a rapid decline. She died in a Seattle hospital room, the blind man sitting beside the bed and holding on to her hand. They'd married, lived and worked together, slept together — had sex, sure — and then the blind man had to bury her. All this without his having ever seen what the goddamned woman looked like. It was beyond my understanding. Hearing this, I felt sorry for the blind man for a little bit. And then I found myself thinking what a pitiful life this woman must have led. Imagine a woman who could never see herself as she was seen in the eyes of her loved one. A woman who could go on day after day and never receive the smallest compliment from her beloved. A woman whose husband could never read the expression on her face, be it misery or something better. Someone who could wear makeup or not — what difference to him? She could, if she wanted, wear green eye-shadow around one eye, a straight pin in her nostril, yellow slacks and purple shoes, no matter. And then to slip off into death, the blind man's hand on her hand, his blind eyes streaming tears — I'm imagining now — her last thought maybe this: that he never even knew what she looked like, and she on an express to the grave. Robert was left with a small insurance policy and half of a twenty-peso Mexican coin. The other half of the coin went into the box with her. Pathetic.

So when the time rolled around, my wife went to the depot to pick him up. With nothing to do but wait — sure, I blamed him for that — I was having a drink and watching the TV when I heard the car pull into the drive. I got up from the sofa with my drink and went to the window to have a look.

I saw my wife laughing as she parked the car. I saw her get out of the car and shut the door. She was still wearing a smile. Just amazing. She went around to the other side of the car to where the blind man was already starting to get out. This blind man, feature this, he was wearing a full beard! A beard on a blind man! Too much, I say. The blind man reached into the back seat and dragged out a suitcase. My wife took his arm, shut the car door, and, talking all the way, moved him down the drive and then up the steps to the front porch. I turned off the TV. I finished my drink, rinsed the glass, dried my hands. Then I went to the door.

My wife said, "I want you to meet Robert. Robert, this is my husband. I've told you all about him." She was beaming. She had this blind man by his coat sleeve.

The blind man let go of his suitcase and up came his hand.

I took it. He squeezed hard, held my hand, and then he let it go.

"I feel like we've already met," he boomed.

"Likewise," I said. I didn't know what else to say. Then I said, "Welcome. I've heard a lot about you." We began to move then, a little group, from the porch into the living room, my wife guiding him by the arm. The blind man was carrying his suitcase in his other hand. My wife said things like, "To your left here, Robert. That's right. Now watch it, there's a chair. That's it. Sit down right here. This is the sofa. We just bought this sofa two weeks ago."

I started to say something about the old sofa. I'd liked that old sofa. But I didn't say anything. Then I wanted to say something else, small-talk, about the scenic ride along the Hudson. How going *to* New York, you should sit on the right-hand side of the train, and coming *from* New York, the left-hand side.

"Did you have a good train ride?" I said. "Which side of the train did you sit on, by the way?"

"What a question, which side!" my wife said. "What's it matter which side?" she said.

"I just asked," I said.

"Right side," the blind man said. "I hadn't been on a train in nearly forty years. Not since I was a kid. With my folks. That's been a long time. I'd nearly forgotten the sensation. I have winter in my beard now," he said. "So I've been told, anyway. Do I look distinguished, my dear?" the blind man said to my wife.

"You look distinguished, Robert," she said. "Robert," she said. "Robert, it's just so good to see you."

My wife finally took her eyes off the blind man and looked at me. I had the feeling she didn't like what she saw. I shrugged.

I've never met, or personally known, anyone who was blind. This blind man was late forties, a heavy-set, balding man with stooped shoulders, as if he carried a great weight there. He wore brown slacks, brown shoes, a light-brown shirt, a tie, a sports coat. Spiffy. He also had this full beard. But he didn't use a cane and he didn't wear dark glasses. I'd always thought dark glasses were a must for the blind. Fact was, I wished he had a pair. At first glance, his eyes looked like anyone else's eyes. But if you look close, there was something different about them. Too much white in the iris, for one thing, and the pupils seemed to move around in the sockets without his knowing it or being able to stop it. Creepy. As I stared at his face, I saw the left pupil turn in toward his nose while the other made an effort to keep in one place. But it was only an effort, for that eye was on the roam without his knowing it or wanting it to be.

I said, "Let me get you a drink. What's your pleasure? We have a little of everything. It's one of our pastimes."

"Bub, I'm a Scotch man myself," he said fast enough in this big voice.

"Right," I said. Bub! "Sure you are, I knew it."

He let his fingers touch his suitcase, which was sitting alongside the sofa. He was taking his bearings. I didn't blame him for that.

"I'll move that up to your room," my wife said.

"No, that's fine," the blind man said loudly. "It can go up when I go up."

"A little water with the Scotch?" I said.

"Very little," he said.

"I knew it," I said.

He said, "Just a tad. The Irish actor, Barry Fitzgerald? I'm like that fellow. When I drink water, Fitzgerald said, I drink water. When I drink whiskey, I drink whiskey." My wife laughed. The blind man brought his hand up under his beard. He lifted his beard slowly and let it drop.

I did the drinks, three big glasses of Scotch with a splash of water in each. Then we made ourselves comfortable and talked about Robert's travels. First the long flight from the West Coast to Connecticut, we covered that. Then from Connecticut up here by train. We had another drink concerning that leg of the trip.

I remembered having read somewhere that the blind didn't smoke because, as speculation had it, they couldn't see the smoke they exhaled. I thought I knew that much and that much only about blind people. But this blind man smoked his cigarette down to the nubbin and then lit another one. This blind man filled his ashtray and my wife emptied it.

When we sat down at the table for dinner, we had another drink. My wife heaped Robert's plate with cube steak, scalloped potatoes, green beans. I buttered him up two slices of bread. I said, "Here's bread and butter for you." I swallowed some of my drink. "Now let us pray," I said, and the blind man lowered his head. My wife looked at me, her mouth agape. "Pray the phone won't ring and the food doesn't get cold," I said.

We dug in. We ate everything there was to eat on the table. We ate like there was no tomorrow. We didn't talk. We ate. We scarfed. We grazed that table. We were into serious eating. The blind man had right away located his foods, he knew just where everything was on his plate. I watched with admiration as he used his knife and fork on the meat. He'd cut two pieces of meat, fork the meat into his mouth, and then go all out for the scalloped potatoes, the beans next, and then he'd tear off a hunk of buttered bread and eat that. He'd follow this up with a big drink of milk. It didn't seem to bother him to use his fingers once in a while, either.

We finished everything, including half a strawberry pie. For a few moments, we sat as if stunned. Sweat beaded on our faces. Finally, we got up from the table and left the dirty plates. We didn't look back. We took ourselves into the living room and sank into our places again. Robert and my wife sat on the sofa. I took the big chair. We had us two or three more drinks while they talked about the major things that had come to pass for them in the past ten years. For the most part, I just listened. Now and then I joined in. I didn't want him to think I'd left the room, and I didn't want her to think I was feeling left out. They talked of things that had happened to them — to them! — these past ten years. I waited in vain to hear my name on my wife's sweet lips: "And then my dear husband came into my life" — something like that. But I heard nothing of the sort. More talk of Robert. Robert had done a little of everything, it seemed, a regular blind jack-of-all-trades. But most recently he and his wife had had an Amway distributorship, from which, I gathered, they'd earned their living, such as it was. The blind man was also a ham radio operator. He talked in his loud voice about conversations he'd had with fellow operators in Guam, in the Philippines, in Alaska, and even in Tahiti. He said he'd have a lot of friends there if he ever wanted to go visit those places. From time to time, he'd turn his blind face toward me, put his hand under his beard, ask me something. How long had I been in my present position? (Three years.) Did I like my work? (I didn't.) Was I going to stay with it? (What were the options?) Finally, when I thought he was beginning to run down, I got up and turned on the TV.

My wife looked at me with irritation. She was heading toward a boil. Then she looked at the blind man and said, "Robert, do you have a TV?"

The blind man said, "My dear, I have two TVs. I have a color set and a black-and-white thing, an old relic. It's funny, but if I turn the TV on, and I'm always turning it on, I turn on the color set. It's funny, don't you think?"

I didn't know what to say to that. I had absolutely nothing to say to that. No opinions. So I watched the news program and tried to listen to what the announcer was saying.

"This is a color TV," the blind man said. "Don't ask me how, but I can tell."

"We traded up a while ago," I said.

The blind man had another taste of his drink. He lifted his beard, sniffed it, and let it fall. He leaned forward on the sofa. He positioned his ashtray on the coffee table, then put the lighter to his cigarette. He leaned back on the sofa and crossed his legs at the ankles.

My wife covered her mouth, and then she yawned. She stretched. She said, "I think I'll go upstairs and put on my robe. I think I'll change into something else. Robert, you make yourself comfortable," she said.

"I'm comfortable," the blind man said.

"I want you to feel comfortable in this house," she said.

"I am comfortable," the blind man said.

After she'd left the room, he and I listened to the weather report and then to the sports roundup. By that time, she'd been gone so long I didn't know if she was going to come back. I thought she might have gone to bed. I wished she'd come back downstairs. I didn't want to be left alone with a blind man. I asked him if he wanted another drink, and he said sure. Then I asked if he wanted to smoke some dope with me. I said I'd just rolled a number. I hadn't, but I planned to do so in about two shakes.

"I'll try some with you," he said.

"Damn right," I said. "That's the stuff."

I got our drinks and sat down on the sofa with him. Then I rolled us two fat numbers. I lit one and passed it. I brought it to his fingers. He took it and inhaled.

"Hold it as long as you can," I said. I could tell he didn't know the first thing.

My wife came back downstairs wearing her pink robe and her pink slippers.

"What do I smell?" she said.

"We thought we'd have us some cannabis," I said.

My wife gave me a savage look. Then she looked at the blind man and said, "Robert, I didn't know you smoked."

He said, "I do now, my dear. There's a first time for everything. But I don't feel anything yet."

"This stuff is pretty mellow," I said. "This stuff is mild. It's dope you can reason with," I said. "It doesn't mess you up."

"Not much it doesn't, bub," he said, and laughed.

My wife sat on the sofa between the blind man and me. I passed her the number. She took it and toked and then passed it back to me. "Which way is this going?" she said. Then she said, "I shouldn't be smoking this. I can hardly keep my eyes open as it is. That dinner did me in. I shouldn't have eaten so much."

"It was the strawberry pie," the blind man said. "That's what did it," he said, and he laughed his big laugh. Then he shook his head.

"There's more strawberry pie," I said.

"Do you want some more, Robert?" my wife said.

"Maybe in a little while," he said.

We gave our attention to the TV. My wife yawned again. She said, "Your bed is made up when you feel like going to bed, Robert. I know you must have had a long day. When you're ready to go to bed, say so." She pulled his arm. "Robert?"

He came to and said, "I've had a real nice time. This beats tapes, doesn't it?"

I said, "Coming at you," and I put the number between his fingers. He inhaled, held the smoke, and then let it go. It was like he'd been doing it since he was nine years old.

"Thanks, bub," he said. "But I think this is all for me. I think I'm beginning to feel it," he said. He held the burning roach out for my wife.

"Same here," she said. "Ditto. Me, too." She took the roach and passed it to me. "I may just sit here for a while between you two guys with my eyes closed. But don't let me bother you, okay? Either one of you. If it bothers you, say so. Otherwise, I may just sit here with my eyes closed until you're ready to go to bed," she said. "Your bed's made up, Robert, when you're ready. It's right next to our room at the top of the stairs. We'll show you up when you're ready. You wake me up now, you guys, if I fall asleep." She said that and then she closed her eyes and went to sleep.

The news program ended. I got up and changed the channel. I sat back down on the sofa. I wished my wife hadn't pooped out. Her head lay across the back of the sofa, her mouth open. She'd turned so that her robe had slipped away from her legs, exposing a juicy thigh. I reached to draw her robe back over her, and it was then that I glanced at the blind man. What the hell! I flipped the robe open again.

"You say when you want some strawberry pie," I said.

"I will," he said.

I said, "Are you tired? Do you want me to take you up to your bed? Are you ready to hit the hay?"

"Not yet," he said. "No, I'll stay up with you, bub. If that's all right. I'll stay up until you're ready to turn in. We haven't had a chance to talk. Know what I mean? I feel like me and her monopolized the evening." He lifted his beard and he let it fall. He picked up his cigarettes and his lighter.

"That's all right," I said. Then I said, "I'm glad for the company."

And I guess I was. Every night I smoked dope and stayed up as long as I could before I fell asleep. My wife and I hardly ever went to bed at the same time. When I did go to sleep, I had these dreams. Sometimes I'd wake up from one of them, my heart going crazy.

Something about the church and the Middle Ages was on the TV. Not your run-of-the-mill TV fare. I wanted to watch something else. I turned to the other channels. But there was nothing on them, either. So I turned back to the first channel and apologized.

"Bub, it's all right," the blind man said. "It's fine with me. Whatever you want to watch is okay. I'm always learning something. Learning never ends. It won't hurt me to learn something tonight. I got ears," he said.

We didn't say anything for a time. He was leaning forward with his head turned at me, his right ear aimed in the direction of the set. Very disconcerting. Now and then his eyelids drooped and then they snapped open again. Now and then he put his fingers into his beard and tugged, like he was thinking about something he was hearing on the television.

On the screen, a group of men wearing cowls was being set upon and tormented by men dressed in skeleton costumes and men dressed as devils. The men dressed as devils wore devil masks, horns, and long tails. This pageant was part of a procession. The Englishman who was narrating the thing said it took place in Spain once a year. I tried to explain to the blind man what was happening.

"Skeletons," he said. "I know about skeletons," he said, and he nodded.

The TV showed this one cathedral. Then there was a long, slow look at another one. Finally, the picture switched to the famous one in Paris, with its flying buttresses and its spires reaching up to the clouds. The camera pulled away to show the whole of the cathedral rising above the skyline.

There were times when the Englishman who was telling the thing would shut up, would simply let the camera move around over the cathedrals. Or else the camera would tour the countryside, men in fields walking behind oxen. I waited as long as I could. Then I felt I had to say something. I said, "They're showing the outside of this cathedral now. Gargoyles. Little statues carved to look like monsters. Now I guess they're in Italy. Yeah, they're in Italy. There's paintings on the walls of this one church."

"Are those fresco paintings, bub?" he asked, and he sipped from his drink.

I reached for my glass. But it was empty. I tried to remember what I could remember. "You're asking me are those frescoes?" I said. "That's a good question. I don't know."

The camera moved to a cathedral outside Lisbon. The differences in the Portuguese cathedral compared with the French and Italian were not that great. But they were there. Mostly the interior stuff. Then something occurred to me, and I said, "Something has occurred to me. Do you have any idea what a cathedral is? What they look like, that is? Do you follow me? If somebody says cathedral to you, do you have any notion what they're talking about? Do you know the difference between that and a Baptist church, say?"

He let the smoke dribble from his mouth. "I know they took hundreds of workers fifty or a hundred years to build," he said. "I just heard the man say that, of course. I know generations of the same families worked on a cathedral. I heard him say that too. The men who began their life's work on them, they never lived to see the completion of their work. In that wise, bub, they're no different from the rest of us, right?" He laughed. Then his eyelids drooped again. His head nodded. He seemed to be snoozing. Maybe he was imagining himself in Portugal. The TV was showing another cathedral now. This one was in Germany. The Englishman's voice droned on. "Cathedrals," the blind man said. He sat up and rolled his head back and forth. "If you want the truth, bub, that's about all I know. What I just said. What I heard him say. But maybe you could describe one to me? I wish you'd do it. I'd like that. If you want to know, I really don't have a good idea."

I stared hard at the shot of the cathedral on the TV. How could I even begin to describe it? But say my life depended on it. Say my life was being threatened by an insane guy who said I had to do it or else.

I stared some more at the cathedral before the picture flipped off into the countryside. There was no use. I turned to the blind man and said, "To begin with, they're very tall." I was looking around the room for clues. "They reach way up. Up and up. Toward the sky. They're so big, some of them, they have to have these supports. To help hold them up, so to speak. These supports are called buttresses. They remind me of viaducts, for some reason. But maybe you don't know viaducts, either? Sometimes the cathedrals have devils and such carved into the front. Sometimes lords and ladies. Don't ask me why this is," I said.

He was nodding. The whole upper part of his body seemed to be moving back and forth.

"I'm not doing so good, am I?" I said.

He stopped nodding and leaned forward on the edge of the sofa. As he listened to me, he was running his fingers through his beard. I wasn't getting through to him, I could see that. But he waited for me to go on just the same. He nodded, like he was trying to encourage me. I tried to think what else to say. "They're really big," I said. "They're massive. They're built of stone. Marble, too, sometimes. In those olden days, when they built cathedrals, men wanted to be close to God. In those olden days, God was an important part of everyone's life. You could tell this from their cathedral-building. I'm sorry," I said, "but it looks like that's the best I can do for you. I'm just no good at it."

"That's all right, bub," the blind man said. "Hey, listen. I hope you don't mind my asking you. Can I ask you something? Let me ask you a simple question, yes or no. I'm just curious and there's no offense. You're my host. But let me ask if you are in any way religious? You don't mind my asking?"

I shook my head. He couldn't see that, though. A wink is the same as a nod to a blind man. "I guess I don't believe in it. In anything. Sometimes it's hard. You know what I'm saying?"

"Sure I do," he said.

"Right," I said.

The Englishman was still holding forth. My wife sighed in her sleep. She drew a long breath and went on with her sleeping.

"You'll have to forgive me," I said. "But I can't tell you what a cathedral looks like. It just isn't in me to do it. I can't do any more than I've done."

The blind man sat very still, his head down, as he listened to me.

I said, "The truth is, cathedrals don't mean anything special to me. Nothing. Cathedrals. They're something to look at on late-night TV. That's all they are."

It was then that the blind man cleared his throat. He brought something up. He took a handkerchief from his back pocket. Then he said, "I get it, bub. It's okay. It happens. Don't worry about it," he said. "Hey, listen to me. Will you do me a favor? I got an idea. Why don't you find us some heavy paper? And a pen. We'll do something. We'll draw one together. Get us a pen and some heavy paper. Go on, bub, get the stuff," he said.

So I went upstairs. My legs felt like they didn't have any strength in them. They felt like they did after I'd done some running. In my wife's room, I looked around. I found some ballpoints in a little basket on her table. And then I tried to think where to look for the kind of paper he was talking about.

Downstairs, in the kitchen, I found a shopping bag with onion skins in the bottom of the bag. I emptied the bag and shook it. I brought it into the living room and sat down with it near his legs. I moved some things, smoothed the wrinkles from the bag, spread it out on the coffee table.

The blind man got down from the sofa and sat next to me on the carpet.

He ran his fingers over the paper. He went up and down the sides of the paper. The edges, even the edges. He fingered the corners.

"All right," he said. "All right, let's do her."

He found my hand, the hand with the pen. He closed his hand over my hand. "Go ahead, bub, draw," he said. "Draw. You'll see. I'll follow along with you. It'll be okay. Just begin now like I'm telling you. You'll see. Draw," the blind man said.

So I began. First I drew a box that looked like a house. It could have been the house I lived in. Then I put a roof on it. At either end of the roof, I drew spires. Crazy.

"Swell," he said. "Terrific. You're doing fine," he said.

"Never thought anything like this could happen in your lifetime, did you, bub? Well, it's a strange life, we all know that. Go on now. Keep it up."

I put in windows with arches. I drew flying buttresses. I hung great doors. I couldn't stop. The TV station went off the air. I put down the pen and closed and opened my fingers. The blind man felt round over the paper. He moved the tips of his fingers over the paper, all over what I had drawn, and he nodded.

"Doing fine," the blind man said.

I took up the pen again, and he found my hand. I kept at it. I'm no artist. But I kept drawing just the same.

My wife opened up her eyes and gazed at us. She sat up on the sofa, her robe hanging open. She said, "What are you doing? Tell me, I want to know."

I didn't answer her.

The blind man said, "We're drawing a cathedral. Me and him are working on it. Press hard," he said to me. "That's right. That's good," he said. "Sure. You got it, bub. I can tell. You didn't think you could. But you can, can't you? You're cooking with gas now. You know what I'm saying? We're going to really have us something here in a minute. How's the old arm?" he said. "Put some people in there now. What's a cathedral without people?"

My wife said, "What's going on? Robert, what are you doing? What's going on?"

"It's all right," he said to her. "Close your eyes now," the blind man said to me.

I did it. I closed them just like he said.

"Are they closed?" he said. "Don't fudge."

"They're closed," I said.

"Keep them that way," he said. He said, "Don't stop now. Draw."

So we kept on with it. His fingers rode my fingers as my hand went over the paper. It was like nothing else in my life up to now.

Then he said, "I think that's it. I think you got it," he said. "Take a look. What do you think?"

But I had my eyes closed. I thought I'd keep them that way for a little longer. I thought it was something I ought to do.

"Well?" he said. "Are you looking?"

My eyes were still closed. I was in my house. I knew that. But I didn't feel like I was inside anything.

"It's really something," I said.

A Small, Good Thing

1983

SATURDAY AFTERNOON SHE DROVE to the bakery in the shopping center. After looking through a loose-leaf binder with photographs of cakes taped onto the pages, she ordered chocolate, the child's favorite. The cake she chose was decorated with a space ship and launching pad under a sprinkling of white stars, and a planet made of red frosting at the other end. His name, SCOTTY, would be in green letters beneath the planet. The baker, who was an older man with a thick neck, listened without saying anything when she told him the child would be eight years old next Monday. The baker wore a white apron that looked like a smock. Straps cut under his arms, went around in back and then to the front again, where they were secured under his heavy waist. He wiped his hands on his apron as he listened to her. He kept his eyes down on the photographs and let her talk. He let her take her time. He'd just come to work and he'd be there all night, baking, and he was in no real hurry.

She gave the baker her name, Ann Weiss, and her telephone number. The cake would be ready on Monday morning, just out of the oven, in plenty of time for the child's party that afternoon. The baker was not jolly. There were no pleasantries between them, just the minimum exchange of words, the necessary information. He made her feel uncomfortable, and she didn't like that. While he was bent over the counter with the pencil in his hand, she studied his coarse features and wondered if he'd ever done anything else with his life besides be a baker. She was a mother and thirty-three years old, and it seemed to her that everyone, especially someone the baker's age — a man old enough to be her father — must have children who'd gone through this special time of cakes and birthday parties. There must be that between them, she thought. But he was abrupt with her — not rude, just abrupt. She gave up trying to make friends with him. She looked into the back of the bakery and could see a long, heavy wooden table with aluminum pie pans stacked at one end; and beside the table a metal container filled with empty racks. There was an enormous oven. A radio was playing country-Western music.

The baker finished printing the information on the special order card and closed up the binder. He looked at her and said, "Monday morning." She thanked him and drove home.

On Monday morning, the birthday boy was walking to school with another boy. They were passing a bag of potato chips back and forth and the birthday boy was trying to find out what his friend intended to give him for his birthday that afternoon. Without looking, the birthday boy stepped off the curb at an intersection and was immediately knocked down by a car. He fell on his side with his head in the gutter and his legs out in the road. His eyes were closed, but his legs moved back and forth as if he were trying to climb over something. His friend dropped the potato chips and started to cry. The car had gone a hundred feet or so and stopped in the middle of the road. The man in the driver's seat looked back over his shoulder. He waited until the boy got unsteadily to his feet. The boy wobbled a little. He looked dazed, but okay. The driver put the car into gear and drove away.

The birthday boy didn't cry, but he didn't have anything to say about anything either. He wouldn't answer when his friend asked him what it felt like to be hit by a car. He walked home, and his friend went on to school. But after the birthday boy was inside his house and was telling his mother about it — she sitting beside him on the sofa, holding his hands in her lap, saying, "Scotty, honey, are you sure you feel all right, baby?" thinking she would call the doctor anyway — he suddenly lay back on the sofa, closed his eyes, and went limp.

When she couldn't wake him up, she hurried to the telephone and called her husband at work. Howard told her to remain calm, remain calm, and then he called an ambulance for the child and left for the hospital himself.

Of course, the birthday party was canceled. The child was in the hospital with a mild concussion and suffering from shock. There'd been vomiting, and his lungs had taken in fluid which needed pumping out that afternoon. Now he simply seemed to be in a very deep sleep — but no coma, Dr. Francis had emphasized, no coma, when he saw the alarm in the parents' eyes. At eleven o'clock that night, when the boy seemed to be resting comfortably enough after the many X-rays and the lab work, and it was just a matter of his waking up and coming around, Howard left the hospital. He and Ann had been at the hospital with the child since that afternoon, and he was going home for a short while to bathe and change clothes. "I'll be back in an hour," he said. She nodded. "It's fine," she said. "I'll be right here." He kissed her on the forehead, and they touched hands. She sat in the chair beside the bed and looked at the child. She was waiting for him to wake up and be all right. Then she could begin to relax.

Howard drove home from the hospital. He took the wet, dark streets very fast, then caught himself and slowed down. Until now, his life had gone smoothly and to his satisfaction — college, marriage, another year of college for the advanced degree in business, a junior partnership in an investment firm. Fatherhood. He was happy and, so far, lucky — he knew that. His parents were still living, his brothers and his sister were established, his friends from college had gone out to take their places in the world. So far, he had kept away from any real harm, from those forces he knew existed and that could cripple or bring down a man if the luck went bad, if things suddenly turned. He pulled into the driveway and parked. His left leg began to tremble. He sat in the car for a minute and tried to deal with the present situation in a rational manner. Scotty had been hit by a car and was in the hospital, but he was going to be all right. Howard closed his eyes and ran his hand over his face. He got out of the car and went up to the front door. The dog was barking inside the house. The telephone rang and rang while he unlocked the door and fumbled for the light switch. He shouldn't have left the hospital, he shouldn't have. "Goddamn it!" he said. He picked up the receiver and said, "I just walked in the door!"

"There's a cake here that wasn't picked up," the voice on the other end of the line said.

"What are you saying?" Howard asked.

"A cake," the voice said. "A sixteen-dollar cake."

Howard held the receiver against his ear, trying to understand. "I don't know anything about a cake," he said. "Jesus, what are you talking about?"

"Don't hand me that," the voice said.

Howard hung up the telephone. He went into the kitchen and poured himself some whiskey. He called the hospital. But the child's condition remained the same; he was still sleeping and nothing had changed there. While water poured into the tub, Howard lathered his face and shaved. He'd just stretched out in the tub and closed his eyes when the telephone rang again. He hauled himself out, grabbed a towel, and hurried through the house, saying, "Stupid,

stupid," for having left the hospital. But when he picked up the receiver and shouted, "Hello!" there was no sound at the other end of the line. Then the caller hung up.

He arrived back at the hospital a little after midnight. Ann still sat in the chair beside the bed. She looked up at Howard, and then she looked back at the child. The child's eyes stayed closed, the head was still wrapped in bandages. His breathing was quiet and regular. From an apparatus over the bed hung a bottle of glucose with a tube running from the bottle to the boy's arm.

"How is he?" Howard said. "What's all this?" waving at the glucose and the tube.

"Dr. Francis's orders," she said. "He needs nourishment. He needs to keep up his strength. Why doesn't he wake up, Howard? I don't understand, if he's all right."

Howard put his hand against the back of her head. He ran his fingers through her hair. "He's going to be all right. He'll wake up in a little while. Dr. Francis knows what's what."

After a time, he said, "Maybe you should go home and get some rest. I'll stay here. Just don't put up with this creep who keeps calling. Hang up right away."

"Who's calling?" she asked.

"I don't know who, just somebody with nothing better to do than call up people. You go on now."

She shook her head. "No," she said, "I'm fine."

"Really," he said. "Go home for a while, and then come back and spell me in the morning. It'll be all right. What did Dr. Francis say? He said Scotty's going to be all right. We don't have to worry. He's just sleeping now, that's all."

A nurse pushed the door open. She nodded at them as she went to the bed-side. She took the left arm out from under the covers and put her fingers on the wrist, found the pulse, then consulted her watch. In a little while, she put the arm back under the covers and moved to the foot of the bed, where she wrote something on a clipboard attached to the bed.

"How is he?" Ann said. Howard's hand was a weight on her shoulder. She was aware of the pressure from his fingers.

"He's stable," the nurse said. Then she said, "Doctor will be in again shortly. Doctor's back in the hospital. He's making rounds right now."

"I was saying maybe she'd want to go home and get a little rest," Howard said. "After the doctor comes," he said.

"She could do that," the nurse said. "I think you should both feel free to do that, if you wish." The nurse was a big Scandinavian woman with blond hair. There was the trace of an accent in her speech.

"We'll see what the doctor says," Ann said. "I want to talk to the doctor. I don't think he should keep sleeping like this. I don't think that's a good sign." She brought her hand up to her eyes and let her head come forward a little. Howard's grip tightened on her shoulder, and then his hand moved up to her neck, where his fingers began to knead the muscles there.

"Dr. Francis will be here in a few minutes," the nurse said. Then she left the room.

Howard gazed at his son for a time, the small chest quietly rising and falling under the covers. For the first time since the terrible minutes after Ann's telephone call to him at his office, he felt a genuine fear starting in his limbs. He began shaking his head. Scotty was fine, but instead of sleeping at home in his own bed, he was in a hospital bed with bandages around his head and a tube in his arm. But this help was what he needed right now.

Dr. Francis came in and shook hands with Howard, though they'd just seen each other a few hours before. Ann got up from the chair. "Doctor?"

"Ann," he said and nodded. "Let's just first see how he's doing," the doctor said. He moved to the side of the bed and took the boy's pulse. He peeled back one eyelid and then the other. Howard and Ann stood beside the doctor and watched. Then the doctor turned back the covers and listened to the boy's heart and lungs with his stethoscope. He pressed his fingers here and there on the abdomen. When he was finished, he went to the end of the bed and studied the chart. He noted the time, scribbled something on the chart, and then looked at Howard and Ann.

"Doctor, how is he?" Howard said. "What's the matter with him exactly?"

"Why doesn't he wake up?" Ann said.

The doctor was a handsome, big-shouldered man with a tanned face. He wore a three-piece blue suit, a striped tie, and ivory cufflinks. His gray hair was combed along the sides of his head, and he looked as if he had just come from a concert. "He's all right," the doctor said. "Nothing to shout about, he could be better, I think. But he's all right. Still, I wish he'd wake up. He should wake up pretty soon." The doctor looked at the boy again. "We'll know some more in a couple of hours, after the results of a few more tests are in. But he's all right, believe me, except for the hairline fracture of the skull. He does have that."

"Oh, no," Ann said.

"And a bit of a concussion, as I said before. Of course, you know he's in shock," the doctor said. "Sometimes you see this in shock cases. This sleeping."

"But he's out of any real danger?" Howard said. "You said before he's not in a coma. You wouldn't call this a coma, then — would you, doctor?" Howard waited. He looked at the doctor.

"No, I don't want to call it a coma," the doctor said and glanced over at the boy once more. "He's just in a very deep sleep. It's a restorative measure the body is taking on its own. He's out of any real danger, I'd say that for certain, yes. But we'll know more when he wakes up and the other tests are in," the doctor said.

"It's a coma," Ann said. "Of sorts."

"It's not a coma yet, not exactly," the doctor said. "I wouldn't want to call it coma. Not yet, anyway. He's suffered shock. In shock cases, this kind of reaction is common enough; it's a temporary reaction to bodily trauma. Coma. Well, coma is a deep, prolonged unconsciousness, something that could go on for days, or weeks even. Scotty's not in that area, not as far as we can tell. I'm certain his condition will show improvement by morning. I'm betting that it will. We'll know more when he wakes up, which shouldn't be long now. Of course, you may do as you like, stay here or go home for a time. But by all means feel free to leave the hospital for a while if you want. This is not easy, I know." The doctor gazed at the boy again, watching him, and then he turned to Ann and said, "You try not to worry, little mother. Believe me, we're doing all that can be done. It's just a question of a little more time now." He nodded at her, shook hands with Howard again, and then he left the room.

Ann put her hand over the child's forehead. "At least he doesn't have a fever," she said. Then she said, "My God, he feels so cold, though. Howard? Is he supposed to feel like this? Feel his head."

Howard touched the child's temples. His own breathing had slowed. "I think he's supposed to feel this way right now," he said. "He's in shock, remember? That's what the doctor said. The doctor was just in here. He would have said something if Scotty wasn't okay."

Ann stood there a while longer, working her lip with her teeth. Then she moved over to her chair and sat down.

Howard sat in the chair next to her chair. They looked at each other. He wanted to say something else and reassure her, but he was afraid, too. He took her hand and put it in his lap, and this made him feel better, her hand being there. He picked up her hand and squeezed it. Then he just held her hand. They sat like that for a while, watching the boy and not talking. From time to time, he squeezed her hand. Finally, she took her hand away.

"I've been praying," she said.

He nodded.

She said, "I almost thought I'd forgotten how, but it came back to me. All I had to do was close my eyes and say, 'Please God, help us — help Scotty,' and then the rest was easy. The words were right there. Maybe if you prayed, too," she said to him.

"I've already prayed," he said. "I prayed this afternoon — yesterday afternoon, I mean — after you called, while I was driving to the hospital. I've been praying," he said.

"That's good," she said. For the first time, she felt they were together in it, this trouble. She realized with a start that, until now, it had only been happening to her and to Scotty. She hadn't let Howard into it, though he was there and needed all along. She felt glad to be his wife.

The same nurse came in and took the boy's pulse again and checked the flow from the bottle hanging above the bed.

In an hour, another doctor came in. He said his name was Parsons, from Radiology. He had a bushy mustache. He was wearing loafers, a Western shirt, and a pair of jeans.

"We're going to take him downstairs for more pictures," he told them. "We need to do some more pictures, and we want to do a scan."

"What's that?" Ann said. "A scan?" She stood between this new doctor and the bed. "I thought you'd already taken all your X-rays."

"I'm afraid we need some more," he said. "Nothing to be alarmed about. We just need some more pictures, and we want to do a brain scan on him."

"My God," Ann said.

"It's perfectly normal procedure in cases like this," this new doctor said. "We just need to find out for sure why he isn't back awake yet. It's normal medical procedure, and nothing to be alarmed about. We'll be taking him down in a few minutes," this doctor said.

In a little while, two orderlies came into the room with a gurney. They were black-haired, dark-complexioned men in white uniforms, and they said a few words to each other in a foreign tongue as they unhooked the boy from the tube and moved him from his bed to the gurney. Then they wheeled him from the room. Howard and Ann got on the same elevator. Ann gazed at the child. She closed her eyes as the elevator began its descent. The orderlies stood at either end of the gurney without saying anything, though once one of the men made a comment to the other in their own language, and the other man nodded slowly in response.

Later that morning, just as the sun was beginning to lighten the windows in the waiting room outside the X-ray department, they brought the boy out and moved him back up to his room. Howard and Ann rode up on the elevator with him once more, and once more they took up their places beside the bed.

They waited all day, but still the boy did not wake up. Occasionally, one of them would leave the room to go downstairs to the cafeteria to drink coffee and then, as if suddenly remembering and feeling guilty, get up from the table and hurry back to the room. Dr. Francis came again that afternoon and examined the boy once more and then left after telling them he was coming along and could wake up at any minute now. Nurses, different nurses from the night before, came in from time to time. Then a young woman from the lab knocked and entered the room. She wore white slacks and a white blouse and carried a little tray of things which she put on the stand beside the bed. Without a word to them, she took blood from the boy's arm. Howard closed his eyes as the woman found the right place on the boy's arm and pushed the needle in.

"I don't understand this," Ann said to the woman.

"Doctor's orders," the young woman said. "I do what I'm told. They say draw that one, I draw. What's wrong with him, anyway?" she said. "He's a sweetie."

"He was hit by a car," Howard said. "A hit-and-run."

The young woman shook her head and looked again at the boy. Then she took her tray and left the room.

"Why won't he wake up?" Ann said. "Howard? I want some answers from these people."

Howard didn't say anything. He sat down again in the chair and crossed one leg over the other. He rubbed his face. He looked at his son and then he settled back in the chair, closed his eyes, and went to sleep.

Ann walked to the window and looked out at the parking lot. It was night, and cars were driving into and out of the parking lot with their lights on. She stood at the window with her hands gripping the sill, and knew in her heart that they were into something now, something hard. She was afraid, and her teeth began to chatter until she tightened her jaws. She saw a big car stop in front of the hospital and someone, a woman in a long coat, get into the car. She wished she were that woman and somebody, anybody, was driving her away from here to somewhere else, a place where she would find Scotty waiting for her when she stepped out of the car, ready to say *Mom* and let her gather him in her arms.

In a little while, Howard woke up. He looked at the boy again. Then he got up from the chair, stretched, and went over to stand beside her at the window. They both stared out at the parking lot. They didn't say anything. But they seemed to feel each other's insides now, as though the worry had made them transparent in a perfectly natural way.

The door opened and Dr. Francis came in. He was wearing a different suit and tie this time. His gray hair was combed along the sides of his head, and he looked as if he had just shaved. He went straight to the bed and examined the boy. "He ought to have come around by now. There's just no good reason for this," he said. "But I can tell you we're all convinced he's out of any danger. We'll just feel better when he wakes up. There's no reason, absolutely none, why he shouldn't come around. Very soon. Oh, he'll have himself a dilly of a headache when he does, you can count on that. But all of his signs are fine. They're as normal as can be."

"It is a coma, then?" Ann said.

The doctor rubbed his smooth cheek. "We'll call it that for the time being, until he wakes up. But you must be worn out. This is hard. I know this is hard. Feel free to go out for a bite," he said. "It would do you good. I'll put a nurse in here while you're gone if you'll feel better about going. Go and have yourselves something to eat."

"I couldn't eat anything," Ann said.

"Do what you need to do, of course," the doctor said. "Anyway, I wanted to tell you that all the signs are good, the tests are negative, nothing showed up at all, and just as soon as he wakes up he'll be over the hill."

"Thank you, doctor," Howard said. He shook hands with the doctor again. The doctor patted Howard's shoulder and went out.

"I suppose one of us should go home and check on things," Howard said. "Slug needs to be fed, for one thing."

"Call one of the neighbors," Ann said. "Call the Morgans. Anyone will feed a dog if you ask them to."

"All right," Howard said. After a while, he said, "Honey, why don't you do it? Why don't you go home and check on things, and then come back? It'll do you good. I'll be right here with him. Seriously," he said. "We need to keep up our strength on this. We'll want to be here for a while even after he wakes up."

"Why don't *you* go?" she said. "Feed Slug. Feed yourself."

"I already went," he said. "I was gone for exactly an hour and fifteen minutes. You go home for an hour and freshen up. Then come back."

She tried to think about it, but she was too tired. She closed her eyes and tried to think about it again. After a time, she said, "Maybe I will go home for a few minutes. Maybe if I'm not just sitting right here watching him every second, he'll wake up and be all right. You know? Maybe he'll wake up if I'm not here. I'll go home and take a bath and put on clean clothes. I'll feed Slug. Then I'll come back."

"I'll be right here," he said. "You go on home, honey. I'll keep an eye on things here." His eyes were bloodshot and small, as if he'd been drinking for a long time. His clothes were rumpled. His beard had come out again. She touched his face; and then she took her hand back. She understood he wanted to be by himself for a while, not have to talk or share his worry for a time. She picked her purse up from the nightstand, and he helped her into her coat.

"I won't be gone long," she said.

"Just sit and rest for a little while when you get home," he said. "Eat something. Take a bath. After you get out of the bath, just sit for a while and rest. It'll do you a world of good, you'll see. Then come back," he said. "Let's try not to worry. You heard what Dr. Francis said."

She stood in her coat for a minute trying to recall the doctor's exact words, looking for any nuances, any hint of something behind his words other than what he had said. She tried to remember if his expression had changed any when he bent over to examine the child. She remembered the way his features had composed themselves as he rolled back the child's eyelids and then listened to his breathing.

She went to the door, where she turned and looked back. She looked at the child, and then she looked at the father. Howard nodded. She stepped out of the room and pulled the door closed behind her.

She went past the nurses' station and down to the end of the corridor, looking for the elevator. At the end of the corridor, she turned to her right and entered a little waiting room where a Negro family sat in wicker chairs. There was a middle-aged man in a khaki shirt and pants, a baseball cap pushed back on his head. A large woman wearing a housedress and slippers was slumped in one of the chairs. A teenaged girl in jeans, hair done in dozens of little braids, lay stretched out in one of the chairs smoking a cigarette, her legs crossed at the ankles. The family swung their eyes to Ann as she entered the room. The little table was littered with hamburger wrappers and Styrofoam cups.

"Franklin," the large woman said as she roused herself. "Is it about Franklin?" Her eyes widened. "Tell me now, lady," the woman said. "Is it about Franklin?" She was trying to rise from her chair, but the man had closed his hand over her arm.

"Here, here," he said. "Evelyn."

"I'm sorry," Ann said. "I'm looking for the elevator. My son is in the hospital, and now I can't find the elevator."

"Elevator is down that way, turn left," the man said as he aimed a finger.

The girl drew on her cigarette and stared at Ann. Her eyes were narrowed to slits, and her broad lips parted slowly as she let the smoke escape. The Negro woman let her head fall on her shoulder and looked away from Ann, no longer interested.

"My son was hit by a car," Ann said to the man. She seemed to need to explain herself. "He has a concussion and a little skull fracture, but he's going to be all right. He's in shock now, but it might be some kind of coma, too. That's what really worries us, the coma part. I'm going out for a little while, but my husband is with him. Maybe he'll wake up while I'm gone."

"That's too bad," the man said and shifted in the chair. He shook his head. He looked down at the table, and then he looked back at Ann. She was still standing there. He said, "Our Franklin, he's on the operating table. Somebody cut him. Tried to kill him. There was a fight where he was at. At this party. They say he was just standing and watching. Not bothering nobody. But that don't mean nothing these days. Now he's on the operating table. We're just hoping and praying, that's all we can do now." He gazed at her steadily.

Ann looked at the girl again, who was still watching her, and at the older woman, who kept her head down, but whose eyes were now closed. Ann saw the lips moving silently, making words. She had an urge to ask what those words were. She wanted to talk more with these people who were in the same kind of waiting she was in. She was afraid, and they were afraid. They had that in common. She would have liked to have said something else about the accident, told them more about Scotty, that it had happened on the day of his birthday, Monday, and that he was still unconscious. Yet she didn't know how to begin. She stood looking at them without saying anything more.

She went down the corridor the man had indicated and found the elevator. She waited a minute in front of the closed doors, still wondering if she was doing the right thing. Then she put out her finger and touched the button.

She pulled into the driveway and cut the engine. She closed her eyes and leaned her head against the wheel for a minute. She listened to the ticking sounds the engine made as it began to cool. Then she got out of the car. She could hear the dog barking inside the house. She went to the front door, which was unlocked. She went inside and turned on lights and put on a kettle of water for tea. She opened some dogfood and fed Slug on the back porch. The dog ate in hungry little smacks. It kept running into the kitchen to see that she was going to stay. As she sat down on the sofa with her tea, the telephone rang.

"Yes!" she said as she answered. "Hello!"

"Mrs. Weiss," a man's voice said. It was five o'clock in the morning, and she thought she could hear machinery or equipment of some kind in the background.

"Yes, yes! What is it?" she said. "This is Mrs. Weiss. This is she. What is it, please?" She listened to whatever it was in the background. "Is it Scotty, for Christ's sake?"

"Scotty," the man's voice said. "It's about Scotty, yes. It has to do with Scotty, that problem. Have you forgotten about Scotty?" the man said. Then he hung up.

She dialed the hospital's number and asked for the third floor. She demanded information about her son from the nurse who answered the telephone. Then she asked to speak to her husband. It was, she said, an emergency.

She waited, turning the telephone cord in her fingers. She closed her eyes and felt sick at her stomach. She would have to make herself eat. Slug came in from the back porch and lay down near her feet. He wagged his tail. She pulled at his ear while he licked her fingers. Howard was on the line.

"Somebody just called here," she said. She twisted the telephone cord. "He said it was about Scotty," she cried.

"Scotty's fine," Howard told her. "I mean, he's still sleeping. There's been no change. The nurse has been in twice since you've been gone. A nurse or else a doctor. He's all right."

"This man called. He said it was about Scotty," she told him.

"Honey, you rest for a little while, you need the rest. It must be that same caller I had. Just forget it. Come back down here after you've rested. Then we'll have breakfast or something."

"Breakfast," she said. "I don't want any breakfast."

"You know what I mean," he said. "Juice, something. I don't know. I don't know anything, Ann. Jesus, I'm not hungry, either. Ann, it's hard to talk now. I'm standing here at the desk. Dr. Francis is coming again at eight o'clock this morning. He's going to have something to tell us then, something more definite. That's what one of the nurses said. She didn't know any more than that. Ann? Honey, maybe we'll know something more then. At eight o'clock. Come back here before eight. Meanwhile, I'm right here and Scotty's all right. He's still the same," he added.

"I was drinking a cup of tea," she said, "when the telephone rang. They said it was about Scotty. There was a noise in the background. Was there a noise in the background on that call you had, Howard?"

"I don't remember," he said. "Maybe the driver of the car, maybe he's a psychopath and found out about Scotty somehow. But I'm here with him. Just rest like you were going to do. Take a bath and come back by seven or so, and we'll talk to the doctor together when he gets here. It's going to be all right, honey. I'm here, and there are doctors and nurses around. They say his condition is stable."

"I'm scared to death," she said.

She ran water, undressed, and got into the tub. She washed and dried quickly, not taking the time to wash her hair. She put on clean underwear, wool slacks, and a sweater. She went into the living room, where the dog looked up at her and let its tail thump once against the floor. It was just starting to get light outside when she went out to the car.

She drove into the parking lot of the hospital and found a space close to the front door. She felt she was in some obscure way responsible for what had happened to the child. She let her thoughts move to the Negro family. She remembered the name Franklin and the table that was covered with hamburger papers, and the teenaged girl staring at her as she drew on her cigarette. "Don't have children," she told the girl's image as she entered the front door of the hospital. "For God's sake, don't."

She took the elevator up to the third floor with two nurses who were just going on duty. It was Wednesday morning, a few minutes before seven. There was a page for a Dr. Madison as the elevator doors slid open on the third floor.

She got off behind the nurses, who turned in the other direction and continued the conversation she had interrupted when she'd gotten into the elevator. She walked down the corridor to the little alcove where the Negro family had been waiting. They were gone now, but the chairs were scattered in such a way that it looked as if people had just jumped up from them the minute before. The tabletop was cluttered with the same cups and papers, the ashtray was filled with cigarette butts.

She stopped at the nurses' station. A nurse was standing behind the counter, brushing her hair and yawning.

"There was a Negro boy in surgery last night," Ann said. "Franklin was his name. His family was in the waiting room. I'd like to inquire about his condition."

A nurse who was sitting at a desk behind the counter looked up from a chart in front of her. The telephone buzzed and she picked up the receiver, but she kept her eyes on Ann.

"He passed away," said the nurse at the counter. The nurse held the hairbrush and kept looking at her. "Are you a friend of the family or what?"

"I met the family last night," Ann said. "My own son is in the hospital. I guess he's in shock. We don't know for sure what's wrong. I just wondered about Franklin, that's all. Thank you." She moved down the corridor. Elevator doors the same color as the walls slid open and a gaunt, bald man in white pants and white canvas shoes pulled a heavy cart off the elevator. She hadn't noticed these doors last night. The man wheeled the cart out into the corridor and stopped in front of the room nearest the elevator and consulted a clipboard. Then he reached down and slid a tray out of the cart. He rapped lightly on the door and entered the room. She could smell the unpleasant odors of warm food as she passed the cart. She hurried on without looking at any of the nurses and pushed open the door to the child's room.

Howard was standing at the window with his hands behind his back. He turned around as she came in.

"How is he?" she said. She went over to the bed. She dropped her purse on the floor beside the nightstand. It seemed to her she had been gone a long time. She touched the child's face. "Howard?"

"Dr. Francis was here a little while ago," Howard said. She looked at him closely and thought his shoulders were bunched a little.

"I thought he wasn't coming until eight o'clock this morning," she said quickly.

"There was another doctor with him. A neurologist."

"A neurologist," she said.

Howard nodded. His shoulders were bunching, she could see that. "What'd they say, Howard? For Christ's sake, what'd they say? What is it?"

"They said they're going to take him down and run more tests on him, Ann. They think they're going to operate, honey. Honey, they *are* going to operate. They can't figure out why he won't wake up. It's more than just shock or concussion, they know that much now. It's in his skull, the fracture, it has something, something to do with that, they think. So they're going to operate. I tried to call you, but I guess you'd already left the house."

"Oh, God," she said. "Oh, please, Howard, please," she said, taking his arms.

"Look!" Howard said. "Scotty! Look, Ann!" He turned her toward the bed.

The boy had opened his eyes, then closed them. He opened them again now. The eyes stared straight ahead for a minute, then moved slowly in his head until they rested on Howard and Ann, then traveled away again.

"Scotty," his mother said, moving to the bed.

"Hey, Scott," his father said. "Hey, son."

They leaned over the bed. Howard took the child's hand in his hands and began to pat and squeeze the hand. Ann bent over the boy and kissed his forehead again and again. She put her hands on either side of his face. "Scotty, honey, it's Mommy and Daddy," she said. "Scotty?"

The boy looked at them, but without any sign of recognition. Then his mouth opened, his eyes scrunched closed, and he howled until he had no more air in his lungs. His face seemed to relax and soften then. His lips parted as his last breath was puffed through his throat and exhaled gently through the clenched teeth.

The doctors called it a hidden occlusion and said it was a one-in-a-million circumstance. Maybe if it could have been detected somehow and surgery undertaken immediately, they could have saved him. But more than likely not. In any case, what would they have been looking for? Nothing had shown up in the tests or in the X-rays.

Dr. Francis was shaken. "I can't tell you how badly I feel. I'm so very sorry, I can't tell you," he said as he led them into the doctors' lounge. There was a doctor sitting in a chair with his legs hooked over the back of another chair, watching an early-morning TV show. He was wearing a green delivery-room outfit, loose green pants and green blouse, and a green cap that covered his hair. He looked at Howard and Ann and then looked at Dr. Francis. He got to his feet and turned off the set and went out of the room. Dr. Francis guided Ann to the sofa, sat down beside her, and began to talk in a low, consoling voice. At one point, he leaned over and embraced her. She could feel his chest rising and falling evenly against her shoulder. She kept her eyes open and let him hold her. Howard went into the bathroom, but he left the door open. After a violent fit of weeping, he ran water and washed his face. Then he came out and sat down at the little table that held a telephone. He looked at the telephone as though deciding what to do first. He made some calls. After a time, Dr. Francis used the telephone.

"Is there anything else I can do for the moment?" he asked them.

Howard shook his head. Ann stared at Dr. Francis as if unable to comprehend his words.

The doctor walked them to the hospital's front door. People were entering and leaving the hospital. It was eleven o'clock in the morning. Ann was aware of how slowly, almost reluctantly, she moved her feet. It seemed to her that Dr. Francis was making them leave when she felt they should stay, when it would be more the right thing to do to stay. She gazed out into the parking lot and then turned around and looked back at the front of the hospital. She began shaking her head. "No, no," she said. "I can't leave him here, no." She heard herself say that and thought how unfair it was that the only words that came out were the sort of words used on TV shows where people were stunned by violent or sudden deaths. She wanted her words to be her own. "No," she said, and for some reason the memory of the Negro woman's head lolling on the woman's shoulder came to her. "No," she said again.

"I'll be talking to you later in the day," the doctor was saying to Howard. "There are still some things that have to be done, things that have to be cleared up to our satisfaction. Some things that need explaining."

"An autopsy," Howard said.

Dr. Francis nodded.

"I understand," Howard said. Then he said, "Oh, Jesus. No, I don't understand, doctor. I can't, I can't. I just can't."

Dr. Francis put his arm around Howard's shoulders. "I'm sorry. God, how I'm sorry." He let go of Howard's shoulders and held out his hand. Howard looked at the hand, and then he took it. Dr. Francis put his arms around Ann once more. He seemed full of some goodness she didn't understand. She let her head rest on his shoulder, but her eyes stayed open. She kept looking at the hospital. As they drove out of the parking lot, she looked back at the hospital.

At home, she sat on the sofa with her hands in her coat pockets. Howard closed the door to the child's room. He got the coffee-maker going and then he found an empty box. He had thought to pick up some of the child's things that were scattered around the living room. But instead he sat down beside her on the sofa, pushed the box to one side, and leaned forward, arms between his knees. He began to weep. She pulled his head over into her lap and patted his shoulder. "He's gone," she said. She kept patting his shoulder. Over his sobs, she could hear the coffee-maker hissing in the kitchen. "There, there," she said tenderly. "Howard, he's gone. He's gone and now we'll have to get used to that. To being alone."

In a little while, Howard got up and began moving aimlessly around the room with the box, not putting anything into it, but collecting some things together on the floor at one end of the sofa. She continued to sit with her hands in her coat pockets. Howard put the box down and brought coffee into the living room. Later, Ann made calls to relatives. After each call had been placed and the party had answered, Ann would blurt out a few words and cry for a minute. Then she would quietly explain, in a measured voice, what had happened and tell them about arrangements. Howard took the box out to the garage, where he saw the child's bicycle. He dropped the box and sat down on the pavement beside the bicycle. He took hold of the bicycle awkwardly so that it leaned against his chest. He held it, the rubber pedal sticking into his chest. He gave the wheel a turn.

Ann hung up the telephone after talking to her sister. She was looking up another number when the telephone rang. She picked it up on the first ring.

"Hello," she said, and she heard something in the background, a humming noise. "Hello!" she said. "For God's sake," she said. "Who is this? What is it you want?"

"Your Scotty, I got him ready for you," the man's voice said. "Did you forget him?"

"You evil bastard!" she shouted into the receiver. "How can you do this, you evil son of a bitch?"

"Scotty," the man said. "Have you forgotten about Scotty?" Then the man hung up on her.

Howard heard the shouting and came in to find her with her head on her arms over the table, weeping. He picked up the receiver and listened to the dial tone.

Much later, just before midnight, after they had dealt with many things, the telephone rang again.

"You answer it," she said. "Howard, it's him, I know." They were sitting at the kitchen table with coffee in front of them. Howard had a small glass of whiskey beside his cup. He answered on the third ring.

"Hello," he said. "Who is this? Hello! Hello!" The line went dead. "He hung up," Howard said. "Whoever it was."

"It was him," she said. "That bastard. I'd like to kill him," she said. "I'd like to shoot him and watch him kick," she said.

"Ann, my God," he said.

"Could you hear anything?" she said. "In the background? A noise, machinery, something humming?"

"Nothing, really. Nothing like that," he said. "There wasn't much time. I think there was some radio music. Yes, there was a radio going, that's all I could tell. I don't know what in God's name is going on," he said.

She shook her head. "If I could, could get my hands on him." It came to her then. She knew who it was. Scotty, the cake, the telephone number. She pushed the chair away from the table and got up. "Drive me down to the shopping center," she said. "Howard."

"What are you saying?"

"The shopping center. I know who it is who's calling. I know who it is. It's the baker, the son-of-a-bitching baker, Howard. I had him bake a cake for Scotty's birthday. That's who's calling. That's who has the number and keeps calling us. To harass us about that cake. The baker, that bastard."

They drove down to the shopping center. The sky was clear and stars were out. It was cold, and they ran the heater in the car. They parked in front of the bakery. All of the shops and stores were closed, but there were cars at the far end of the lot in front of the movie theater. The bakery windows were dark, but when they looked through the glass they could see a light in the back room and, now and then, a big man in an apron moving in and out of the white, even light. Through the glass, she could see the display cases and some little tables with chairs. She tried the door. She rapped on the glass. But if the baker heard them, he gave no sign. He didn't look in their direction.

They drove around behind the bakery and parked. They got out of the car. There was a lighted window too high up for them to see inside. A sign near the back door said THE PANTRY BAKERY, SPECIAL ORDERS. She could hear faintly a radio playing inside and something creak—an oven door as it was pulled down? She knocked on the door and waited. Then she knocked again, louder. The radio was turned down and there was a scraping sound now, the distinct sound of something, a drawer, being pulled open and then closed.

Someone unlocked the door and opened it. The baker stood in the light and peered out at them. "I'm closed for business," he said. "What do you want at this hour? It's midnight. Are you drunk or something?"

She stepped into the light that fell through the open door. He blinked his heavy eyelids as he recognized her. "It's you," he said.

"It's me," she said. "Scotty's mother. This is Scotty's father. We'd like to come in."

The baker said. "I'm busy now. I have work to do."

She had stepped inside the doorway anyway. Howard came in behind her. The baker moved back. "It smells like a bakery in here. Doesn't it smell like a bakery in here, Howard?"

"What do you want?" the baker said. "Maybe you want your cake? That's it, you decided you want your cake. You ordered a cake, didn't you?"

"You're pretty smart for a baker," she said. "Howard, this is the man who's been calling us." She clenched her fists. She stared at him fiercely. There was a deep burning inside her, an anger that made her feel larger than herself, larger than either of these men.

"Just a minute here," the baker said. "You want to pick up your three-day-old cake? That it? I don't want to argue with you, lady. There it sits over there, getting stale. I'll give it to you for half of what I quoted you. No. You want it? You can have it. It's no good to me, no good to anyone now. It cost me time and money to make that cake. If you want it, okay, if you don't, that's okay, too. I have to get back to work." He looked at them and rolled his tongue behind his teeth.

"More cakes," she said. She knew she was in control of it, of what was increasing in her. She was calm.

"Lady, I work sixteen hours a day in this place to earn a living," the baker said. He wiped his hands on his apron. "I work night and day in here, trying to make ends meet." A look crossed Ann's face that made the baker move back and say, "No trouble, now." He reached to the counter and picked up a rolling pin with his right hand and began to tap it against the palm of his other hand. "You want the cake or not? I have to get back to work. Bakers work at night," he said again. His eyes were small, mean-looking, she thought, nearly lost in the bristly flesh around his cheeks. His neck was thick with fat.

"I know bakers work at night," Ann said. "They make phone calls at night, too. You bastard," she said.

The baker continued to tap the rolling pin against his hand. He glanced at Howard. "Careful, careful," he said to Howard.

"My son's dead," she said with a cold, even finality. "He was hit by a car Monday morning. We've been waiting with him until he died. But, of course, you couldn't be expected to know that, could you? Bakers can't know everything—can they, Mr. Baker? But he's dead. He's dead, you bastard!" Just as suddenly as it had welled in her, the anger dwindled, gave way to something else, a dizzy feeling of nausea. She leaned against the wooden table that was sprinkled with flour, put her hands over her face, and began to cry, her shoulders rocking back and forth. "It isn't fair," she said. "It isn't, isn't fair."

Howard put his hand at the small of her back and looked at the baker. "Shame on you," Howard said to him. "Shame."

The baker put the rolling pin back on the counter. He undid his apron and threw it on the counter. He looked at them, and then he shook his head slowly. He pulled a chair out from under the card table that held papers and receipts, an adding machine, and a telephone directory. "Please sit down," he said. "Let me get you a chair," he said to Howard. "Sit down now please." The baker went into the front of the shop and returned with two little wrought-iron chairs. "Please sit down, you people."

Ann wiped her eyes and looked at the baker. "I wanted to kill you," she said. "I wanted you dead."

The baker had cleared a space for them at the table. He shoved the adding machine to one side, along with the stacks of notepaper and receipts. He pushed the telephone directory onto the floor, where it landed with a thud. Howard and Ann sat down and pulled their chairs up to the table. The baker sat down, too.

"Let me say how sorry I am," the baker said, putting his elbows on the table. "God alone knows how sorry. Listen to me. I'm just a baker. I don't claim to be anything else. Maybe once, maybe years ago, I was a different kind of human being. I've forgotten, I don't know for sure. But I'm not any longer, if I ever was. Now I'm just a baker. That don't excuse my doing what I did, I know. But I'm deeply sorry. I'm sorry for your son, and sorry for my part in this," the baker said. He spread his hands out on the table and turned them over to reveal his palms. "I don't have any children myself, so I can only imagine what you must be feeling. All I can say to you now is that I'm sorry. Forgive me, if you can," the baker said. "I'm not an evil man, I don't think. Not evil, like you said on the phone. You got to understand what it comes down to is I don't know how to act anymore, it would seem. Please," the man said, "let me ask you if you can find it in your hearts to forgive me?"

It was warm inside the bakery. Howard stood up from the table and took off his coat. He helped Ann from her coat. The baker looked at them for a minute and then nodded and got up from the table. He went to the oven and turned off some switches. He found cups and poured coffee from an electric coffee-maker. He put a carton of cream on the table, and a bowl of sugar.

"You probably need to eat something," the baker said. "I hope you'll eat some of my hot rolls. You have to eat and keep going. Eating is a small, good thing in a time like this," he said.

He served them warm cinnamon rolls just out of the oven, the icing still runny. He put butter on the table and knives to spread the butter. Then the baker sat down at the table with them. He waited. He waited until they each took a roll from the platter and began to eat. "It's good to eat something," he said, watching them. "There's more. Eat up. Eat all you want. There's all the rolls in the world in here."

They ate rolls and drank coffee. Ann was suddenly hungry, and the rolls were warm and sweet. She ate three of them, which pleased the baker. Then he began to talk. They listened carefully. Although they were tired and in anguish, they listened to what the baker had to say. They nodded when the baker began to speak of loneliness, and of the sense of doubt and limitation that had come to him in his middle years. He told them what it was like to be childless all these years. To repeat the days with the ovens endlessly full and endlessly empty. The party food, the celebrations he'd worked over. Icing knuckle-deep. The tiny wedding couples stuck into cakes. Hundreds of them, no, thousands by now. Birthdays. Just imagine all those candles burning. He had a necessary trade. He was a baker. He was glad he wasn't a florist. It was better to be feeding people. This was a better smell anytime than flowers.

"Smell this," the baker said, breaking open a dark loaf. "It's a heavy bread, but rich." They smelled it, then he had them taste it. It had the taste of molasses and coarse grains. They listened to him. They ate what they could. They swallowed the dark bread. It was like daylight under the fluorescent trays of light. They talked on into the early morning, the high, pale cast of light in the windows, and they did not think of leaving.

What We Talk About
When We Talk About Love

1981

MY FRIEND MEL MCGINNIS was talking. Mel McGinnis is a cardiologist, and sometimes that gives him the right.

The four of us were sitting around his kitchen table drinking gin. Sunlight filled the kitchen from the big window behind the sink. There were Mel and me and his second wife, Teresa — Terri, we called her — and my wife, Laura. We lived in Albuquerque then. But we were all from somewhere else.

There was an ice bucket on the table. The gin and the tonic water kept going around, and we somehow got on the subject of love. Mel thought real love was nothing less than spiritual love. He said he'd spent five years in a seminary before quitting to go to medical school. He said he still looked back on those years in the seminary as the most important years in his life.

Terri said the man she lived with before she lived with Mel loved her so much he tried to kill her. Then Terri said, "He beat me up one night. He dragged me around the living room by my ankles. He kept saying, 'I love you, I love you, you bitch.' He went on dragging me around the living room. My head kept knocking on things." Terri looked around the table. "What do you do with love like that?"

She was a bone-thin woman with a pretty face, dark eyes, and brown hair that hung down her back. She liked necklaces made of turquoise, and long pendant earrings.

"My God, don't be silly. That's not love, and you know it," Mel said. "I don't know what you'd call it, but I sure know you wouldn't call it love."

"Say what you want to, but I know it was," Terri said. "It may sound crazy to you, but it's true just the same. People are different, Mel. Sure, sometimes he may have acted crazy. Okay. But he loved me. In his own way maybe, but he loved me. There was love there, Mel. Don't say there wasn't."

Mel let out his breath. He held his glass and turned to Laura and me. "The man threatened to kill me," Mel said. He finished his drink and reached for the gin bottle. "Terri's a romantic. Terri's of the kick-me-so-I'll-know-you-love-me school. Terri, hon, don't look that way." Mel reached across the table and touched Terri's cheek with his fingers. He grinned at her.

"Now he wants to make up," Terri said.

"Make up what?" Mel said. "What is there to make up? I know what I know. That's all."

"How'd we get started on this subject, anyway?" Terri said. She raised her glass and drank from it. "Mel always has love on his mind," she said. "Don't you, honey?" She smiled, and I thought that was the last of it.

"I just wouldn't call Ed's behavior love. That's all I'm saying, honey," Mel said. "What about you guys?" Mel said to Laura and me. "Does that sound like love to you?"

"I'm the wrong person to ask," I said. "I didn't even know the man. I've only heard his name mentioned in passing. I wouldn't know. You'd have to know the particulars. But I think what you're saying is that love is an absolute."

Mel said, "The kind of love I'm talking about is. The kind of love I'm talking about, you don't try to kill people."

Laura said, "I don't know anything about Ed, or anything about the situation. But who can judge anyone else's situation?"

I touched the back of Laura's hand. She gave me a quick smile. I picked up Laura's hand. It was warm, the nails polished, perfectly manicured. I encircled the broad wrist with my fingers, and I held her.

"When I left, he drank rat poison," Terri said. She clasped her arms with her hands. "They took him to the hospital in Sante Fe. That's where we lived then, about ten miles out. They saved his life. But his gums went crazy from it. I mean they pulled away from his teeth. After that, his teeth stood out like fangs. My God," Terri said. She waited a minute, then let go of her arms and picked up her glass.

"What people won't do!" Laura said.

"He's out of the action now," Mel said. "He's dead."

Mel handed me the saucer of limes. I took a section, squeezed it over my drink, and stirred the ice cubes with my finger.

"It gets worse," Terri said. "He shot himself in the mouth. But he bungled that too. Poor Ed," she said. Terri shook her head.

"Poor Ed nothing," Mel said. "He was dangerous."

Mel was forty-five years old. He was tall and rangy with curly soft hair. His face and arms were brown from the tennis he played. When he was sober, his gestures, all his movements, were precise, very careful.

"He did love me though, Mel. Grant me that," Terri said. "That's all I'm asking. He didn't love me the way you love me. I'm not saying that. But he loved me. You can grant me that, can't you?"

"What do you mean, he bungled it?" I said.

Laura leaned forward with her glass. She put her elbows on the table and held her glass in both hands. She glanced from Mel to Terri and waited with a look of bewilderment on her open face, as if amazed that such things happened to people you were friendly with.

"How'd he bungle it when he killed himself?" I said.

"I'll tell you what happened," Mel said. "He took this twenty-two pistol he'd bought to threaten Terri and me with. Oh, I'm serious, the man was always threatening. You should have seen the way we lived in those days. Like fugitives. I even bought a gun myself. Can you believe it? A guy like me? But I did. I bought one for self-defense and carried it in the glove compartment. Sometimes I'd have to leave the apartment in the middle of the night. To go to the hospital, you know? Terri and I weren't married then, and my first wife had the house and kids, the dog, everything, and Terri and I were living in this apartment here. Sometimes, as I say, I'd get a call in the middle of the night and have to go in to the hospital at two or three in the morning. It'd be dark out there in the parking lot, and I'd break into a sweat before I could even get to my car. I never knew if he was going to come up out of the shrubbery or from behind a car and start shooting. I mean, the man was crazy. He was capable of wiring a bomb, anything. He used to call my service at all hours and say he needed to talk to the doctor, and when I'd return the call, he'd say, 'Son of a bitch, your days are numbered.' Little things like that. It was scary, I'm telling you."

"I still feel sorry for him," Terri said.

"It sounds like a nightmare," Laura said. "But what exactly happened after he shot himself?"

Laura is a legal secretary. We'd met in a professional capacity. Before we knew it, it was a courtship. She's thirty-five, three years younger than I am. In addition to being in love, we like each other and enjoy one another's company. She's easy to be with.

"What happened?" Laura said.

Mel said, "He shot himself in the mouth in his room. Someone heard the shot and told the manager. They came in with a passkey, saw what had happened, and called an ambulance. I happened to be there when they brought him in, alive but past recall. The man lived for three days. His head swelled up to twice the size of a normal head. I'd never seen anything like it, and I hope I never do again. Terri wanted to go in and sit with him when she found out about it. We had a fight over it. I didn't think she should see him like that. I didn't think she should see him, and I still don't."

"Who won the fight?" Laura said.

"I was in the room with him when he died," Terri said. "He never came up out of it. But I sat with him. He didn't have anyone else."

"He was dangerous," Mel said. "If you call that love, you can have it."

"It was love," Terri said. "Sure, it's abnormal in most people's eyes. But he was willing to die for it. He did die for it."

"I sure as hell wouldn't call it love," Mel said. "I mean, no one knows what he did it for. I've seen a lot of suicides, and I couldn't say anyone ever knew what they did it for."

Mel put his hands behind his neck and tilted his chair back. "I'm not interested in that kind of love," he said. "If that's love, you can have it."

Terri said, "We were afraid. Mel even made a will out and wrote to his brother in California who used to be a Green Beret. Mel told him who to look for if something happened to him."

Terri drank from her glass. She said, "But Mel's right — we lived like fugitives. We were afraid. Mel was, weren't you, honey? I even called the police at one point, but they were no help. They said they couldn't do anything until Ed actually did something. Isn't that a laugh?" Terri said.

She poured the last of the gin into her glass and waggled the bottle. Mel got up from the table and went to the cupboard. He took down another bottle.

"Well, Nick and I know what love is," Laura said. "For us, I mean," Laura said. She bumped my knee with her knee. "You're supposed to say something now," Laura said, and turned her smile on me.

For an answer, I took Laura's hand and raised it to my lips. I made a big production out of kissing her hand. Everyone was amused.

"We're lucky," I said.

"You guys," Terri said. "Stop that now. You're making me sick. You're still on the honeymoon, for God's sake. You're still gaga, for crying out loud. Just wait. How long have you been together now? How long has it been? A year? Longer than a year?"

"Going on a year and a half," Laura said, flushed and smiling.

"Oh, now," Terri said. "Wait awhile."

She held her drink and gazed at Laura.

"I'm only kidding," Terri said.

Mel opened the gin and went around the table with the bottle.

"Here, you guys," he said. "Let's have a toast. I want to propose a toast. A toast to love. To true love," Mel said.

We touched glasses.

"To love," we said.

Outside in the backyard, one of the dogs began to bark. The leaves of the aspen that leaned past the window ticked against the glass. The afternoon sun was like a presence in this room, the spacious light of ease and generosity. We could have been anywhere, somewhere enchanted. We raised our glasses again and grinned at each other like children who had agreed on something forbidden.

"I'll tell you what real love is," Mel said. "I mean, I'll give you a good example. And then you can draw your own conclusions." He poured more gin into his glass. He added an ice cube and a sliver of lime. We waited and sipped our drinks. Laura and I touched knees again. I put a hand on her warm thigh and left it there.

"What do any of us really know about love?" Mel said. "It seems to me we're just beginners at love. We say we love each other and we do, I don't doubt it. I love Terri and Terri loves me, and you guys love each other too. You know the kind of love I'm talking about now. Physical love, that impulse that drives you to someone special, as well as love of the other person's being, his or her essence, as it were. Carnal love and, well, call it sentimental love, the day-to-day caring about the other person. But sometimes I have a hard time accounting for the fact that I must have loved my first wife too. But I did, I know I did. So I suppose I am like Terri in that regard. Terri and Ed." He thought about it and then he went on. "There was a time when I thought I loved my first wife more than life itself. But now I hate her guts. I do. How do you explain that? What happened to that love? What happened to it, is what I'd like to know. I wish someone could tell me. Then there's Ed. Okay, we're back to Ed. He loves Terri so much he tries to kill her and he winds up killing himself." Mel stopped talking and swallowed from his glass. "You guys have been together eighteen months and you love each other. It shows all over you. You glow with it. But you both loved other people before you met each other. You've both been married before, just like us. And you probably loved other people before that too, even. Terri and I have been together five years, been married for four. And the terrible thing, the terrible thing is, but the good thing too, the saving grace, you might say, is that if something happened to one of us — excuse me for saying this — but if something happened to one of us tomorrow I think the other one, the other person, would grieve for a while, you know, but then the surviving party would go out and love again, have someone else soon enough. All this, all of this love we're talking about, it would just be a memory. Maybe not even a memory. Am I wrong? Am I way off base? Because I want you to set me straight if you think I'm wrong. I want to know. I mean, I don't know anything, and I'm the first one to admit it."

"Mel, for God's sake," Terri said. She reached out and took hold of his wrist. "Are you getting drunk? Honey? Are you drunk?"

"Honey, I'm just talking," Mel said. "All right? I don't have to be drunk to say what I think. I mean, we're all just talking, right?" Mel said. He fixed his eyes on her.

"Sweetie, I'm not criticizing," Terri said.

She picked up her glass.

"I'm not on call today," Mel said. "Let me remind you of that. I am not on call," he said.

"Mel, we love you," Laura said.

Mel looked at Laura. He looked at her as if he could not place her, as if she was not the woman she was.

"Love you too, Laura," Mel said. "And you, Nick, love you too. You know something?" Mel said. "You guys are our pals," Mel said.

He picked up his glass.

Mel said, "I was going to tell you about something. I mean, I was going to prove a point. You see, this happened a few months ago, but it's still going on right now, and it ought to make us feel ashamed when we talk like we know what we're talking about when we talk about love."

"Come on now," Terri said. "Don't talk like you're drunk if you're not drunk."

"Just shut up for once in your life," Mel said very quietly. "Will you do me a favor and do that for a minute? So as I was saying, there's this old couple who had this car wreck out on the interstate. A kid hit them and they were all torn to shit and nobody was giving them much chance to pull through."

Terri looked at us and then back at Mel. She seemed anxious, or maybe that's too strong a word.

Mel was handing the bottle around the table.

"I was on call that night," Mel said. "It was May or maybe it was June. Terri and I had just sat down to dinner when the hospital called. There'd been this thing out on the interstate. Drunk kid, teenager, plowed his dad's pickup into this camper with this old couple in it. They were up in their mid-seventies, that couple. The kid—eighteen, nineteen, something—he was DOA. Taken the steering wheel through his sternum. The old couple, they were alive, you understand. I mean, just barely. But they had everything. Multiple fractures, internal injuries, hemorrhaging, contusions, lacerations, the works, and they each of them had themselves concussions. They were in a bad way, believe me. And, of course, their age was two strikes against them. I'd say she was worse off than he was. Ruptured spleen along with everything else. Both kneecaps broken. But they'd been wearing their seatbelts and, God knows, that's what saved them for the time being."

"Folks, this is an advertisement for the National Safety Council," Terri said. "This is your spokesman, Dr. Melvin R. McGinnis, talking." Terri laughed. "Mel," she said, "sometimes you're just too much. But I love you, hon," she said.

"Honey, I love you," Mel said.

He leaned across the table. Terri met him halfway. They kissed.

"Terri's right," Mel said as he settled himself again. "Get those seatbelts on. But seriously, they were in some shape, those oldsters. By the time I got down there, the kid was dead, as I said. He was off in a corner, laid out on a gurney. I took one look at the old couple and told the ER nurse to get me a neurologist and an orthopedic man and a couple of surgeons down there right away."

He drank from his glass. "I'll try to keep this short," he said. "So we took the two of them up to the OR and worked like fuck on them most of the night. They had these incredible reserves, those two. You see that once in a while. So we did everything that could be done, and toward morning we're giving them a fifty-fifty chance, maybe less than that for her. So here they are, still alive the next morning. So, okay, we move them into the ICU, which is where they both kept plugging away at it for two weeks, hitting it better and better on all the scopes. So we transfer them out to their own room."

Mel stopped talking. "Here," he said, "let's drink this cheapo gin the hell up. Then we're going to dinner, right? Terri and I know a new place. That's where we'll go, to this new place we know about. But we're not going until we finish up this cut-rate, lousy gin."

Terri said, "We haven't actually eaten there yet. But it looks good. From the outside, you know."

"I like food," Mel said. "If I had it to do all over again, I'd be a chef, you know? Right, Terri?" Mel said.

He laughed. He fingered the ice in his glass.

"Terri knows," he said. "Terri can tell you. But let me say this. If I could come back again in a different life, a different time and all, you know what? I'd like to come back as a knight. You were pretty safe wearing all that armor. It was all right being a knight until gunpowder and muskets and pistols came along."

"Mel would like to ride a horse and carry a lance," Terri said.

"Carry a woman's scarf with you everywhere," Laura said.

"Or just a woman," Mel said.

"Shame on you," Laura said.

Terri said, "Suppose you came back as a serf. The serfs didn't have it so good in those days," Terri said.

"The serfs never had it good," Mel said. "But I guess even the knights were vessels to someone. Isn't that the way it worked? But then everyone is always a vessel to someone. Isn't that right? Terri? But what I liked about knights, besides their ladies, was that they had that suit of armor, you know, and they couldn't get hurt very easy. No cars in those days, you know? No drunk teenagers to tear into your ass."

"Vassals," Terri said.

"What?" Mel said.

"Vassals," Terri said. "They were called vassals, not vessels."

"Vassals, vessels," Mel said, "what the fuck's the difference? You knew what I meant anyway. All right," Mel said. "So I'm not educated. I learned my stuff. I'm a heart surgeon, sure, but I'm just a mechanic. I go in and I fuck around and I fix things. Shit," Mel said.

"Modesty doesn't become you," Terri said.

"He's just a humble sawbones," I said. "But sometimes they suffocated in all that armor, Mel. They'd even have heart attacks if it got too hot and they were too tired and worn out. I read somewhere that they'd fall off their horses and not be able to get up because they were too tired to stand with all that armor on them. They got trampled by their own horses sometimes."

"That's terrible," Mel said. "That's a terrible thing, Nicky. I guess they'd just lay there and wait until somebody came along and made a shish kebab out of them."

"Some other vessel," Terri said.

"That's right," Mel said. "Some vassal would come along and spear the bastard in the name of love. Or whatever the fuck it was they fought over in those days."

"Same things we fight over these days," Terri said.

Laura said, "Nothing's changed."

The color was still high in Laura's cheeks. Her eyes were bright. She brought her glass to her lips.

Mel poured himself another drink. He looked at the label closely as if studying a long row of numbers. Then he slowly put the bottle down on the table and slowly reached for the tonic water.

"What about the old couple?" Laura said. "You didn't finish that story you started."

Laura was having a hard time lighting her cigarette. Her matches kept going out.

The sunshine inside the room was different now, changing, getting thinner. But the leaves outside the window were still shimmering, and I stared at the pattern they made on the panes and on the Formica counter. They weren't the same patterns, of course.

"What about the old couple?" I said.

"Older but wiser," Terri said.

Mel stared at her.

Terri said, "Go on with your story, hon. I was only kidding. Then what happened?"

"Terri, sometimes," Mel said.

"Please, Mel," Terri said. "Don't always be so serious, sweetie. Can't you take a joke?"

"Where's the joke?" Mel said.

He held his glass and gazed steadily at his wife.

"What happened?" Laura said.

Mel fastened his eyes on Laura. He said, "Laura, if I didn't have Terri and if I didn't love her so much, and if Nick wasn't my best friend, I'd fall in love with you, I'd carry you off, honey," he said.

"Tell your story," Terri said. "Then we'll go to that new place, okay?"

"Okay," Mel said. "Where was I?" he said. He stared at the table and then he began again.

"I dropped in to see each of them every day, sometimes twice a day if I was up doing other calls anyway. Casts and bandages, head to foot, the both of them. You know, you've seen it in the movies. That's just the way they looked, just like in the movies. Little eye-holes and nose-holes and mouth-holes. And she had to have her legs slung up on top of it. Well, the husband was very depressed for the longest while. Even after he found out that his wife was going to pull through, he was still very depressed. Not about the accident, though. I mean, the accident was one thing, but it wasn't everything. I'd get up to his mouth-hole, you know, and he'd say no, it wasn't the accident exactly but it was because he couldn't see her through his eye-holes. He said that was what was making him feel so bad. Can you imagine? I'm telling you, the man's heart was breaking because he couldn't turn his goddamn head and *see* his goddamn wife."

Mel looked around the table and shook his head at what he was going to say.

"I mean, it was killing the old fart just because he couldn't *look* at the fucking woman."

We all looked at Mel.

"Do you see what I'm saying?" he said.

Maybe we were a little drunk by then. I know it was hard keeping things in focus. The light was draining out of the room, going back through the window where it had come from. Yet nobody made a move to get up from the table to turn on the overhead light.

"Listen," Mel said. "Let's finish this fucking gin. There's about enough left here for one shooter all around. Then let's go eat. Let's go to the new place."

"He's depressed," Terri said. "Mel, why don't you take a pill?"

Mel shook his head. "I've taken everything there is."

"We all need a pill now and then," I said.

"Some people are born needing them," Terri said.

She was using her finger to rub at something on the table. Then she stopped rubbing.

"I think I want to call my kids," Mel said. "Is that all right with everybody? I'll call my kids," he said.

Terri said, "What if Marjorie answers the phone? You guys, you've heard us on the subject of Marjorie? Honey, you know you don't want to talk to Marjorie. It'll make you feel even worse."

"I don't want to talk to Marjorie," Mel said. "But I want to talk to my kids."

"There isn't a day goes by that Mel doesn't say he wishes she'd get married again. Or else die," Terri said. "For one thing," Terri said, "she's bankrupting us. Mel says it's just to spite him that she won't get married again. She has a boyfriend who lives with her and the kids, so Mel is supporting the boyfriend too."

"She's allergic to bees," Mel said. "If I'm not praying she'll get married again, I'm praying she'll get herself stung to death by a swarm of fucking bees."

"Shame on you," Laura said.

"Bzzzzzzz," Mel said, turning his fingers into bees and buzzing them at Terri's throat. Then he let his hands drop all the way to his sides.

"She's vicious," Mel said. "Sometimes I think I'll go up there dressed like a beekeeper. You know, that hat that's like a helmet with the plate that comes down over your face, the big gloves, and the padded coat? I'll knock on the door and let loose a hive of bees in the house. But first I'd make sure the kids were out, of course."

He crossed one leg over the other. It seemed to take him a lot of time to do it. Then he put both feet on the floor and leaned forward, elbows on the table, his chin cupped in his hands.

"Maybe I won't call the kids, after all. Maybe it isn't such a hot idea. Maybe we'll just go eat. How does that sound?"

"Sounds fine to me," I said. "Eat or not eat. Or keep drinking. I could head right on out into the sunset."

"What does that mean, honey?" Laura said.

"It just means what I said," I said. "It means I could just keep going. That's all it means."

"I could eat something myself," Laura said. "I don't think I've ever been so hungry in my life. Is there something to nibble on?"

"I'll put out some cheese and crackers," Terri said.

But Terri just sat there. She did not get up to get anything.

Mel turned his glass over. He spilled it out on the table.

"Gin's gone," Mel said.

Terri said, "Now what?"

I could hear my heart beating. I could hear everyone's heart. I could hear the human noise we sat there making, not one of us moving, not even when the room went dark.

Willa Cather

Willa Cather (1873–1947) once wrote that "a creative writer can do his best only with what lies within the range and character of his deepest sympathies." She was thirty-nine before she found her true subject. The oldest of seven children, Cather was raised in a loving home, but she hated the frontier prairie village of Red Cloud, Nebraska, where her family finally settled after leaving Virginia. She went to a preparatory school in Lincoln and continued at the University of Nebraska, studying classics. After her graduation in 1895, she moved to Pittsburgh, where she worked as a journalist for seven years before teaching English and Latin in high schools. At this time her stories and poems began to appear in popular magazines. Her first book was a volume of poetry, *April Twilights* (1903), followed in 1905 by *The Troll Gardens*, the first of four collections of short stories.

The most important influence on Cather's work was Sarah Orne Jewett, who taught her that beautiful writing is a consequence of steady concentration on a thoroughly understood subject. Cather met Jewett in Boston, and Jewett urged her to develop her talent, advising her to "find your own quiet center of life and write to the human heart, the great consciousness that all humanity goes to make up." It was not until 1912 that Cather found her subject, after a trip home to Red Cloud. When she no longer saw her adolescence on the prairie as deprived and stifling, she was able to feel that her own experience was significant enough to write about. *O Pioneers!* (1913), the first of her three novels about immigrant life on the western frontier, was followed in 1915 by *The Song of the Lark* and in 1918 by *My Ántonia*, a portrait of a pioneer woman that is generally regarded as her masterpiece.

Cather went on to publish a total of twelve novels and several collections of stories, many about artists, but she did not value her forty-four stories as highly as her novels, including only three of them in the definitive "Library Edition" that represents her final judgment of her work. She wrote "Paul's Case" (1905), a story about a sensitive boy who hungers for art and feels oppressed by everyday life, while she was still a high school teacher in Pittsburgh. Many critics have commented on the purity of Cather's prose style. Her early study of classical languages and her admiration of Flaubert helped form her attitudes toward rigorous control in her realistic fiction, but she later realized that as a young writer she had been inhibited by her awe of great writers: "Life began for me when I ceased to admire and began to remember." Cather was also a perceptive literary critic. She published a collection of essays, *On Writing* (1949), in which she analyzed the subtle magic of the storyteller's art: "Whatever is felt on the page without being specifically named there—that, one might say, is created."

Paul's Case

1905

IT WAS PAUL'S AFTERNOON to appear before the faculty of the Pittsburgh High School to account for his various misdemeanors. He had been suspended a week ago, and his father had called at the Principal's office and confessed his perplexity about his son. Paul entered the faculty room suave and smiling. His clothes were a trifle outgrown and the tan velvet on the collar of his open over-coat was frayed and worn; but for all that there was something of the dandy about him, and he wore an opal pin in his neatly knotted black four-in-hand, and a red carnation in his buttonhole. This latter adornment the faculty some-how felt was not properly significant of the contrite spirit befitting a boy under the ban of suspension.

Paul was tall for his age and very thin, with high, cramped shoulders and a narrow chest. His eyes were remarkable for a certain hysterical brilliancy and he continually used them in a conscious, theatrical sort of way, peculiarly offen-sive in a boy. The pupils were abnormally large, as though he were addicted to belladonna, but there was a glassy glitter about them which that drug does not produce.

When questioned by the Principal as to why he was there, Paul stated, politely enough, that he wanted to come back to school. This was a lie, but Paul was quite accustomed to lying; found it, indeed, indispensable for overcoming friction. His teachers were asked to state their respective charges against him, which they did with such a rancor and aggrievedness as evinced that this was not a usual case. Disorder and impertinence were among the offenses named, yet each of his instructors felt that it was scarcely possible to put into words the real cause of the trouble, which lay in a sort of hysterically defiant manner of the boy's; in the contempt which they all knew he felt for them, and which he seemingly made not the least effort to conceal. Once, when he had been making a synopsis of a paragraph at the blackboard, his English teacher had stepped to his side and attempted to guide his hand. Paul had started back with a shudder and thrust his hands violently behind him. The astonished woman could scarcely have been more hurt and embarrassed had he struck at her. The insult was so involuntary and definitely personal as to be unforgettable. In one way and another, he had made all his teachers, men and women alike, con-scious of the same feeling of physical aversion. In one class he habitually sat with his hand shading his eyes; in another he always looked out of the window during the recitation; in another he made a running commentary on the lec-ture, with humorous intention.

His teachers felt this afternoon that his whole attitude was symbolized by his shrug and his flippantly red carnation flower, and they fell upon him with-out mercy, his English teacher leading the pack. He stood through it smiling, his pale lips parted over his white teeth. (His lips were continually twitching, and he had a habit of raising his eyebrows that was contemptuous and irritat-ing to the last degree.) Older boys than Paul had broken down and shed tears under that baptism of fire, but his set smile did not once desert him, and his only sign of discomfort was the nervous trembling of the fingers that toyed with the buttons of his overcoat, and an occasional jerking of the other hand that held his hat. Paul was always smiling, always glancing about him, seeming to feel that people might be watching him and trying to detect something. This conscious expression, since it was as far as possible from boyish mirthfulness, was usually attributed to insolence or "smartness."

As the inquisition proceeded, one of his instructors repeated an impertinent remark of the boy's, and the Principal asked him whether he thought that a courteous speech to make to a woman. Paul shrugged his shoulders slightly and his eyebrows twitched.

"I don't know," he replied. "I didn't mean to be polite or impolite, either. I guess it's a sort of way I have of saying things regardless."

The Principal, who was a sympathetic man, asked him whether he didn't think that a way it would be well to get rid of. Paul grinned and said he guessed so. When he was told that he could go, he bowed gracefully and went out. His bow was but a repetition of the scandalous red carnation.

His teachers were in despair, and his drawing master voiced the feeling of them all when he declared there was something about the boy which none of them understood. He added: "I don't really believe that smile of his comes altogether from insolence; there's something sort of haunted about it. The boy is not strong, for one thing. I happen to know that he was born in Colorado, only a few months before his mother died out there of a long illness. There is something wrong about the fellow."

The drawing master had come to realize that, in looking at Paul, one saw only his white teeth and the forced animation of his eyes. One warm afternoon the boy had gone to sleep at his drawing-board, and his master had noted with amazement what a white, blue-veined face it was; drawn and wrinkled like an old man's about the eyes, the lips twitching even in his sleep, and stiff with a nervous tension that drew them back from his teeth.

His teachers left the building dissatisfied and unhappy; humiliated to have felt so vindictive toward a mere boy, to have uttered this feeling in cutting terms, and to have set each other on, as it were, in the gruesome game of intemperate reproach. Some of them remembered having seen a miserable street cat set at bay by a ring of tormentors.

As for Paul, he ran down the hill whistling the Soldiers' Chorus from *Faust,* looking wildly behind him now and then to see whether some of his teachers were not there to writhe under this light-heartedness. As it was now late in the afternoon and Paul was on duty that evening as usher at Carnegie Hall, he decided that he would not go home to supper. When he reached the concert hall the doors were not yet open and, as it was chilly outside, he decided to go up into the picture gallery — always deserted at this hour — where there were some of Raffelli's gay studies of Paris streets and an airy blue Venetian scene or two that always exhilarated him. He was delighted to find no one in the gallery but the old guard, who sat in one corner, a newspaper on his knee, a black patch over one eye and the other closed. Paul possessed himself of the place and walked confidently up and down, whistling under his breath. After a while he sat down before a blue Rico and lost himself. When he bethought him to look at his watch, it was after seven o'clock, and he rose with a start and ran downstairs, making a face at Augustus, peering out from the cast-room, and an evil gesture at the Venus of Milo as he passed her on the stairway.

When Paul reached the ushers' dressing-room half-a-dozen boys were there already, and he began excitedly to tumble into his uniform. It was one of the few that at all approached fitting, and Paul thought it very becoming — though he knew that the tight, straight coat accentuated his narrow chest, about which he was exceedingly sensitive. He was always considerably excited while he dressed, twanging all over to the tuning of the strings and the preliminary flourishes of the horns in the music-room; but tonight he seemed quite beside himself, and he teased and plagued the boys until, telling him that he was crazy, they put him down on the floor and sat on him.

Somewhat calmed by his suppression, Paul dashed out to the front of the house to seat the early comers. He was a model usher; gracious and smiling he ran up and down the aisles; nothing was too much trouble for him; he carried messages and brought programmes as though it were his greatest pleasure in life, and all the people in his section thought him a charming boy, feeling that he remembered and admired them. As the house filled, he grew more and more vivacious and animated, and the color came to his cheeks and lips. It was very much as though this were a great reception and Paul were the host. Just as the musicians came out to take their places, his English teacher arrived with checks for the seats which a prominent manufacturer had taken for the season. She betrayed some embarrassment when she handed Paul the tickets, and a *hauteur* which subsequently made her feel very foolish. Paul was startled for a moment, and had the feeling of wanting to put her out; what business had she here among all these fine people and gay colors? He looked her over and decided that she was not appropriately dressed and must be a fool to sit downstairs in such togs. The tickets had probably been sent her out of kindness, he reflected as he put down a seat for her, and she had about as much right to sit there as he had.

When the symphony began Paul sank into one of the rear seats with a long sigh of relief, and lost himself as he had done before the Rico. It was not that symphonies, as such, meant anything in particular to Paul, but the first sigh of the instruments seemed to free some hilarious and potent spirit within him; something that struggled there like the Genius in the bottle found by the Arab fisherman. He felt a sudden zest of life; the lights danced before his eyes and the concert hall blazed into unimaginable splendor. When the soprano soloist came on, Paul forgot even the nastiness of his teacher's being there and gave himself up to the peculiar stimulus such personages always had for him. The soloist chanced to be a German woman, by no means in her first youth, and the mother of many children; but she wore an elaborate gown and a tiara, and above all she had that indefinable air of achievement, that world-shine upon her, which, in Paul's eyes, made her a veritable queen of Romance.

After a concert was over Paul was always irritable and wretched until he got to sleep, and tonight he was even more than usually restless. He had the feeling of not being able to let down, of its being impossible to give up this delicious excitement which was the only thing that could be called living at all. During the last number he withdrew and, after hastily changing his clothes in the dressing-room, slipped out to the side door where the soprano's carriage stood. Here he began pacing rapidly up and down the walk, waiting to see her come out.

Over yonder the Schenley, in its vacant stretch, loomed big and square through the fine rain, the windows of its twelve stories glowing like those of a lighted cardboard house under a Christmas tree. All the actors and singers of the better class stayed there when they were in the city, and a number of the big manufacturers of the place lived there in the winter. Paul had often hung about the hotel, watching the people go in and out, longing to enter and leave school-masters and dull care behind him forever.

At last the singer came out, accompanied by the conductor, who helped her into her carriage and closed the door with a cordial *auf wiedersehen* which set Paul to wondering whether she were not an old sweetheart of his. Paul fol-lowed the carriage over to the hotel, walking so rapidly as not to be far from the entrance when the singer alighted and disappeared behind the swinging glass doors that were opened by a negro in a tall hat and a long coat. In the moment that the door was ajar it seemed to Paul that he, too, entered. He seemed to feel himself go after her up the steps, into the warm, lighted building, into an exotic, a tropical world of shiny, glistening surfaces and basking ease. He reflected upon the mysterious dishes that were brought into the dining-room, the green bottles in buckets of ice, as he had seen them in the supper party pictures of the *Sunday World* supplement. A quick gust of wind brought the rain down with sudden vehemence, and Paul was startled to find that he was still outside in the slush of the gravel driveway; that his boots were letting in the water and his scanty over-coat was clinging wet about him; that the lights in front of the concert hall were out, and that the rain was driving in sheets between him and the orange glow of the windows above him. There it was, what he wanted — tangibly before him, like the fairy world of a Christmas pantomime, but mocking spirits stood guard at the doors, and, as the rain beat in his face, Paul wondered whether he were destined always to shiver in the black night outside, looking up at it.

He turned and walked reluctantly toward the car tracks. The end had to come sometime; his father in his night-clothes at the top of the stairs, explana-tions that did not explain, hastily improvised fictions that were forever trip-ping him up, his upstairs room and its horrible yellow wall-paper, the creaking bureau with the greasy plush collar-box, and over his painted wooden bed the pictures of George Washington and John Calvin, and the framed motto, "Feed my Lambs," which had been worked in red worsted by his mother.

Half an hour later, Paul alighted from his car and went slowly down one of the side streets off the main thoroughfare. It was a highly respectable street, where all the houses were exactly alike, and where businessmen of mod-erate means begot and reared large families of children, all of whom went to Sabbath-school and learned the shorter catechism, and were interested in arithmetic; all of whom were as exactly alike as their homes, and of a piece of the monotony in which they lived. Paul never went up Cordelia Street without a shudder of loathing. His home was next to the house of the Cumberland minister. He approached it tonight with the nerveless sense of defeat, the hopeless feeling of sinking back forever into ugliness and commonness that he had always had when he came home. The moment he turned into Cordelia Street he felt the waters close above his head. After each of these orgies of living, he experienced all the physical depression which follows a debauch; the loathing of respectable beds, of common food, of a house penetrated by kitchen odors; a shuddering repulsion for the flavorless, colorless mass of every-day existence; a morbid desire for cool things and soft lights and fresh flowers.

The nearer he approached the house, the more absolutely unequal Paul felt to the sight of it all; his ugly sleeping chamber; the cold bathroom with the grimy zinc tub, the cracked mirror, the dripping spiggots; his father, at the top of the stairs, his hairy legs sticking out from his night-shirt, his feet thrust into carpet slippers. He was so much later than usual that there would certainly be inquiries and reproaches. Paul stopped short before the door. He felt that he could not be accosted by his father tonight; that he could not toss again on that miserable bed. He would not go in. He would tell his father that he had no car fare, and it was raining so hard he had gone home with one of the boys and stayed all night.

Meanwhile, he was wet and cold. He went around to the back of the house and tried one of the basement windows, found it open, raised it cautiously, and scrambled down the cellar wall to the floor. There he stood, holding his breath, terrified by the noise he had made, but the floor above him was silent, and there was no creak on the stairs. He found a soap-box, and carried it over to the soft ring of light that streamed from the furnace door, and sat down. He was horribly afraid of rats, so he did not try to sleep, but sat looking distrustfully at the dark, still terrified lest he might have awakened his father. In such reactions, after one of the experiences which made days and nights out of the dreary blanks of the calendar, when his senses were deadened, Paul's head was always singularly clear. Suppose his father had heard him getting in at the window and had come down and shot him for a burglar? Then, again, suppose his father had come down, pistol in hand, and he had cried out in time to save himself, and his father had been horrified to think how nearly he had killed him? Then, again, suppose a day should come when his father would remember that night, and wish there had been no warning cry to stay his hand? With this last supposition Paul entertained himself until daybreak.

The following Sunday was fine; the sodden November chill was broken by the last flash of autumnal summer. In the morning Paul had to go to church and Sabbath-school, as always. On seasonable Sunday afternoons the burghers of Cordelia Street always sat out on their front "stoops," and talked to their neighbors on the next stoop, or called to those across the street in neighborly fashion. The men usually sat on gay cushions placed upon the steps that led down to the sidewalk, while the women, in their Sunday "waists," sat in rockers on the cramped porches, pretending to be greatly at their ease. The children played in the streets; there were so many of them that the place resembled the recreation grounds of a kindergarten. The men on the steps — all in their shirt sleeves, their vests unbuttoned — sat with their legs well apart, their stomachs comfortably protruding, and talked of the prices of things, or told anecdotes of the sagacity of their various chiefs and overlords. They occasionally looked over the multitude of squabbling children, listened affectionately to their high-pitched, nasal voices, smiling to see their own proclivities reproduced in their offspring, and interspersed their legends of the iron kings with remarks about their sons' progress at school, their grades in arithmetic, and the amounts they had saved in their toy banks.

On this last Sunday of November, Paul sat all the afternoon on the lowest step of his "stoop," staring into the street, while his sisters, in their rockers, were talking to the minister's daughters next door about how many shirt-waists they had made in the last week, and how many waffles some one had eaten at the last church supper. When the weather was warm, and his father was in a particularly jovial frame of mind, the girls made lemonade, which was always brought out in a red-glass pitcher, ornamented with forget-me-nots in blue enamel. This the girls thought very fine, and the neighbors always joked about the suspicious color of the pitcher.

Today Paul's father sat on the top step, talking to a young man who shifted a restless baby from knee to knee. He happened to be the young man who was daily held up to Paul as a model, and after whom it was his father's dearest hope that he would pattern. This young man was of a ruddy complexion, with a compressed, red mouth, and faded, near-sighted eyes, over which he wore thick spectacles, with gold bows that curved about his ears. He was clerk to one of the magnates of a great steel corporation, and was looked upon in Cordelia Street as a young man with a future. There was a story that, some five years ago — he was now barely twenty-six — he had been a trifle dissipated but in order to curb his appetites and save the loss of time and strength that a sowing of wild oats might have entailed, he had taken his chief's advice, oft reiterated to his employees, and at twenty-one had married the first woman whom he could persuade to share his fortunes. She happened to be an angular school-mistress, much older than he, who also wore thick glasses, and who had now borne him four children, all near-sighted, like herself.

The young man was relating how his chief, now cruising in the Mediter-ranean, kept in touch with all the details of the business, arranging his office hours on his yacht just as though he were at home, and "knocking off work enough to keep two stenographers busy." His father told, in turn, the plan his corporation was considering, of putting in an electric railway plant at Cairo. Paul snapped his teeth; he had an awful apprehension that they might spoil it all before he got there. Yet he rather liked to hear these legends of the iron kings, that were told and retold on Sundays and holidays; these stories of pal-aces in Venice, yachts on the Mediterranean, and high play at Monte Carlo appealed to his fancy, and he was interested in the triumphs of these cash boys who had become famous, though he had no mind for the cash-boy stage.

After supper was over, and he had helped to dry the dishes, Paul nervously asked his father whether he could go to George's to get some help in his geom-etry, and still more nervously asked for car fare. This latter request he had to repeat, as his father, on principle, did not like to hear requests for money, whether much or little. He asked Paul whether he could not go to some boy who lived nearer, and told him that he ought not to leave his school work until Sunday; but he gave him the dime. He was not a poor man, but he had a worthy ambition to come up in the world. His only reason for allowing Paul to usher was, that he thought a boy ought to be earning a little.

Paul bounded upstairs, scrubbed the greasy odor of the dish-water from his hands with the ill-smelling soap he hated, and then shook over his fingers a few drops of violet water from the bottle he kept hidden in his drawer. He left the house with his geometry conspicuously under his arm, and the moment he got out of Cordelia Street and boarded a downtown car, he shook off the lethargy of two deadening days, and began to live again.

The leading juvenile of the permanent stock company which played at one of the downtown theatres was an acquaintance of Paul's, and the boy had been invited to drop in at the Sunday-night rehearsals whenever he could. For more than a year Paul had spent every available moment loitering about Charley Edwards's dressing-room. He had won a place among Edwards's following not only because the young actor, who could not afford to employ a dresser, often found him useful, but because he recognized in Paul something akin to what churchmen term "vocation."

It was at the theatre and at Carnegie Hall that Paul really lived; the rest was but a sleep and a forgetting. This was Paul's fairy tale, and it had for him all the allurement of a secret love. The moment he inhaled the gassy, painty, dusty odor behind the scenes, he breathed like a prisoner set free, and felt within him the possibility of doing or saying splendid, brilliant, poetic things. The moment the cracked orchestra beat out the overture from *Martha*, or jerked at the serenade from *Rigoletto*, all stupid and ugly things slid from him, and his senses were deliciously, yet delicately fired.

Perhaps it was because, in Paul's world, the natural nearly always wore the guise of ugliness, that a certain element of artificiality seemed to him necessary in beauty. Perhaps it was because his experience of life elsewhere was so full of Sabbath-school picnics, petty economies, wholesome advice as to how to succeed in life, and the unescapable odors of cooking, that he found this existence so alluring, these smartly-clad men and women so attractive, that he was so moved by these starry apple orchards that bloomed perennially under the lime-light.

It would be difficult to put it strongly enough how convincingly the stage entrance of that theatre was for Paul the actual portal of Romance. Certainly none of the company ever suspected it, least of all Charley Edwards. It was very like the old stories that used to float about London of fabulously rich Jews, who had subterranean halls there, with palms, and fountains, and soft lamps and richly apparelled women who never saw the disenchanting light of London day. So, in the midst of that smoke-palled city, enamored of figures and grimy toil, Paul had his secret temple, his wishing carpet, his bit of blue-and-white Mediterranean shore bathed in perpetual sunshine.

Several of Paul's teachers had a theory that his imagination had been perverted by garish fiction, but the truth was that he scarcely ever read at all.

The books at home were not such as would either tempt or corrupt a youthful mind, and as for reading the novels that some of his friends urged upon him — well, he got what he wanted much more quickly from music; any sort of music, from an orchestra to a barrel organ. He needed only the spark, the indescribable thrill that made his imagination master of his senses, and he could make plots and pictures enough of his own. It was equally true that he was not stage struck — not, at any rate, in the usual acceptation of that expression. He had no desire to become an actor, any more than he had to become a musician. He felt no necessity to do any of these things; what he wanted was to see, to be in the atmosphere, float on the wave of it, to be carried out, blue league after blue league, away from everything.

After a night behind the scenes, Paul found the school-room more than ever repulsive; the bare floors and naked walls; the prosy men who never wore frock coats, or violets in their buttonholes; the women with their dull gowns, shrill voices, and pitiful seriousness about prepositions that govern the dative. He could not bear to have the other pupils think, for a moment, that he took these people seriously; he must convey to them that he considered it all trivial, and was there only by way of a jest, anyway. He had autographed pictures of all the members of the stock company which he showed his classmates, telling them the most incredible stories of his familiarity with these people, of his acquaintance with the soloists who came to Carnegie Hall, his suppers with them and the flowers he sent them. When these stories lost their effect, and his audience grew listless, he became desperate and would bid all the boys good-bye, announcing that he was going to travel for a while; going to Naples, to Venice, to Egypt. Then, next Monday, he would slip back, conscious and nervously smiling; his sister was ill, and he should have to defer his voyage until spring.

Matters went steadily worse with Paul at school. In the itch to let his instructors know how heartily he despised them and their homilies, and how thoroughly he was appreciated elsewhere, he mentioned once or twice that he had no time to fool with theorems; adding — with a twitch of the eyebrows and a touch of that nervous bravado which so perplexed them — that he was helping the people down at the stock company; they were old friends of his.

The upshot of the matter was that the Principal went to Paul's father, and Paul was taken out of school and put to work. The manager at Carnegie Hall was told to get another usher in his stead; the door-keeper at the theatre was warned not to admit him to the house; and Charley Edwards remorsefully promised the boy's father not to see him again.

The members of the stock company were vastly amused when some of Paul's stories reached them — especially the women. They were hard-working women, most of them supporting indigent husbands or brothers, and they laughed rather bitterly at having stirred the boy to such fervid and florid inventions. They agreed with the faculty and with his father that Paul's was a bad case.

The east-bound train was ploughing through a January snow-storm; the dull dawn was beginning to show grey when the engine whistled a mile out of Newark. Paul started up from the seat where he had lain curled in uneasy slumber, rubbed the breath-misted window glass with his hand, and peered out. The snow was whirling in curling eddies above the white bottom lands, and the drifts lay already deep in the fields and along the fences, while here and there the long dead grass and dried weed stalks protruded black above it. Lights shone from the scattered houses, and a gang of laborers who stood beside the track waved their lanterns.

Paul had slept very little, and he felt grimy and uncomfortable. He had made the all-night journey in a day coach, partly because he was ashamed, dressed as he was, to go into a Pullman, and partly because he was afraid of being seen there by some Pittsburgh businessman, who might have noticed him in Denny & Carson's office. When the whistle awoke him, he clutched quickly at his breast pocket, glancing about him with an uncertain smile. But the little, clay-bespattered Italians were still sleeping, the slatternly women across the aisle were in open-mouthed oblivion, and even the crumby, crying babies were for the nonce stilled. Paul settled back to struggle with his impatience as best he could.

When he arrived at the Jersey City station, he hurried through his breakfast, manifestly ill at ease and keeping a sharp eye about him. After he reached the Twenty-third Street station, he consulted a cabman, and had himself driven to a men's furnishing establishment that was just opening for the day. He spent upward of two hours there, buying with endless reconsidering and great care. His new street suit he put on in the fitting-room; the frock coat and dress clothes he had bundled into the cab with his linen. Then he drove to a hatter's and a shoe house. His next errand was at Tiffany's, where he selected his silver and a new scarf-pin. He would not wait to have his silver marked, he said. Lastly, he stopped at a trunk shop on Broadway, and had his purchases packed into various travelling bags.

It was a little after one o'clock when he drove up to the Waldorf, and after settling with the cabman, went into the office. He registered from Washington; said his mother and father had been abroad, and that he had come down to await the arrival of their steamer. He told his story plausibly and had no trouble, since he volunteered to pay for them in advance, in engaging his rooms; a sleeping-room, sitting-room, and bath.

Not once, but a hundred times Paul had planned this entry into New York. He had gone over every detail of it with Charley Edwards, and in his scrap book at home there were pages of description about New York hotels, cut from the Sunday papers. When he was shown to his sitting-room on the eighth floor, he saw at a glance that everything was as it should be; there was but one detail in his mental picture that the place did not realize, so he rang for the bell boy and sent him down for flowers. He moved about nervously until the boy returned, putting away his new linen and fingering it delightedly as he did so. When the flowers came, he put them hastily into water, and then tumbled into a hot bath. Presently he came out of his white bath-room, resplendent in his new silk underwear, and playing with the tassels of his red robe. The snow was whirling so fiercely outside his windows that he could scarcely see across the street, but within the air was deliciously soft and fragrant. He put the violets and jonquils on the taboret beside the couch, and threw himself down, with a long sigh, covering himself with a Roman blanket. He was thoroughly tired; he had been in such haste, he had stood up to such a strain, covered so much ground in the last twenty-four hours, that he wanted to think how it had all come about. Lulled by the sound of the wind, the warm air, and the cool fragrance of the flowers, he sank into deep, drowsy retrospection.

It had been wonderfully simple; when they had shut him out of the theatre and concert hall, when they had taken away his bone, the whole thing was virtually determined. The rest was a mere matter of opportunity. The only thing that at all surprised him was his own courage — for he realized well enough that he had always been tormented by fear, a sort of apprehensive dread that, of late years, as the meshes of the lies he had told closed about him, had been pulling the muscles of his body tighter and tighter. Until now, he could not remember the time when he had not been dreading something. Even when he was a little boy, it was always there — behind him, or before, or on either side. There had always been the shadowed corner, the dark place into which he dared not look, but from which something seemed always to be watching him — and Paul had done things that were not pretty to watch, he knew.

But now he had a curious sense of relief, as though he had at last thrown down the gauntlet to the thing in the corner.

Yet it was but a day since he had been sulking in the traces; but yesterday afternoon that he had been sent to the bank with Denny & Carson's deposit, as usual — but this time he was instructed to leave the book to be balanced. There was above two thousand dollars in checks, and nearly a thousand in the bank notes which he had taken from the book and quietly transferred to his pocket. At the bank he had made out a new deposit slip. His nerves had been steady enough to permit of his returning to the office, where he had finished his work and asked for a full day's holiday tomorrow, Saturday, giving a perfectly reasonable pretext. The bank book, he knew, would not be returned before Monday or Tuesday, and his father would be out of town for the next week. From the time he slipped the bank notes into his pocket until he boarded the night train for New York, he had not known a moment's hesitation. It was not the first time Paul had steered through treacherous waters.

How astonishingly easy it had all been; here he was, the thing done; and this time there would be no awakening, no figure at the top of the stairs. He watched the snow flakes whirling by his window until he fell asleep.

When he awoke, it was three o'clock in the afternoon. He bounded up with a start; half of one of his precious days gone already! He spent more than an hour in dressing, watching every stage of his toilet carefully in the mirror. Everything was quite perfect; he was exactly the kind of boy he had always wanted to be.

When he went downstairs, Paul took a carriage and drove up Fifth Avenue toward the Park. The snow had somewhat abated; carriages and tradesmen's wagons were hurrying soundlessly to and fro in the winter twilight; boys in woollen mufflers were shovelling off the doorsteps; the avenue stages made fine spots of color against the white street. Here and there on the corners were stands, with whole flower gardens blooming under glass cases, against the sides of which the snow flakes stuck and melted; violets, roses, carnations, lilies of the valley—somewhat vastly more lovely and alluring that they blossomed thus unnaturally in the snow. The Park itself was a wonderful stage winterpiece.

When he returned, the pause of the twilight had ceased, and the tune of the streets had changed. The snow was falling faster, lights streamed from the hotels that reared their dozen stories fearlessly up into the storm, defying the raging Atlantic winds. A long, black stream of carriages poured down the avenue, intersected here and there by other streams, tending horizontally. There were a score of cabs about the entrance of his hotel, and his driver had to wait. Boys in livery were running in and out of the awning stretched across the sidewalk, up and down the red velvet carpet laid from the door to the street. Above, about, within it all was the rumble and roar, the hurry and toss of thousands of human beings as hot for pleasure as himself, and on every side of him towered the glaring affirmation of the omnipotence of wealth.

The boy set his teeth and drew his shoulders together in a spasm of realization: the plot of all dramas, the text of all romances, the nerve-stuff of all sensations was whirling about him like the snow flakes. He burnt like a faggot in a tempest.

When Paul went down to dinner, the music of the orchestra came floating up the elevator shaft to greet him. His head whirled as he stepped into the thronged corridor, and he sank back into one of the chairs against the wall to get his breath. The lights, the chatter, the perfumes, the bewildering medley of color—he had, for a moment, the feeling of not being able to stand it. But only for a moment; these were his own people, he told himself. He went slowly about the corridors, through the writing-rooms, smoking-rooms, reception-rooms, as though he were exploring the chambers of an enchanted palace, built and peopled for him alone.

When he reached the dining-room he sat down at a table near a window. The flowers, the white linen, the many-colored wine glasses, the gay toilettes of the women, the low popping of corks, the undulating repetitions of the *Blue Danube* from the orchestra, all flooded Paul's dream with bewildering radiance. When the roseate tinge of his champagne was added—that cold, precious, bubbling stuff that creamed and foamed in his glass—Paul wondered that there were honest men in the world at all. This was what all the world was fighting for, he reflected; this was what all the struggle was about. He doubted the reality of his past. Had he ever known a place called Cordelia Street, a place where fagged-looking businessmen got on the early car; mere rivets in a machine they seemed to Paul—sickening men, with combings of children's hair always hanging to their coats, and the smell of cooking in their clothes. Cordelia Street—Ah! that belonged to another time and country; had he not always been thus, had he not sat here night after night, from as far back as he could remember, looking pensively over just such shimmering textures, and slowly twirling the stem of a glass like this one between his thumb and middle finger? He rather thought he had.

He was not in the least abashed or lonely. He had no especial desire to meet or to know any of these people; all he demanded was the right to look on and conjecture, to watch the pageant. The mere stage properties were all he contended for. Nor was he lonely later in the evening, in his loge at the Metropolitan. He was now entirely rid of his nervous misgivings, of his forced aggressiveness, of the imperative desire to show himself different from his surroundings. He felt now that his surroundings explained him. Nobody questioned the purple; he had only to wear it passively. He had only to glance down at his attire to reassure himself that here it would be impossible for anyone to humiliate him.

He found it hard to leave his beautiful sitting-room to go to bed that night, and sat long watching the raging storm from his turret window. When he went to sleep it was with the lights turned on in his bedroom; partly because of his old timidity, and partly so that, if he should wake in the night, there would be no wretched moment of doubt, no horrible suspicion of yellow wall-paper, or of Washington or Calvin above his bed.

Sunday morning the city was practically snow-bound. Paul breakfasted late, and in the afternoon he fell in with a wild San Francisco boy, a freshman at Yale, who said he had run down for a "little flyer" over Sunday. The young man offered to show Paul the night side of the town, and the two boys went out together after dinner, not returning to the hotel until seven o'clock the next morning. They had started out in the confiding warmth of a champagne friendship, but their parting in the elevator was singularly cool. The freshman pulled himself together to make his train, and Paul went to bed. He awoke at two o'clock in the afternoon, very thirsty and dizzy, and rang for ice-water, coffee, and the Pittsburgh papers.

On the part of the hotel management, Paul excited no suspicion. There was this to be said for him, that he wore his spoils with dignity and in no way made himself conspicuous. Even under the glow of his wine he was never boisterous, though he found the stuff like a magician's wand for wonder-building. His chief greediness lay in his ears and eyes, and his excesses were not offensive ones. His dearest pleasures were the grey winter twilights in his sitting-room; his quiet enjoyment of his flowers, his clothes, his wide divan, his cigarette, and his sense of power. He could not remember a time when he had felt so at peace with himself. The mere release from the necessity of petty lying, lying every day and every day, restored his self-respect. He had never lied for pleasure, even at school; but to be noticed and admired, to assert his difference from other Cordelia Street boys; and he felt a good deal more manly, more honest, even, now that he had no need for boastful pretensions, now that he could, as his actor friends used to say, "dress the part." It was characteristic that remorse did not occur to him. His golden days went by without a shadow, and he made each as perfect as he could.

On the eighth day after his arrival in New York, he found the whole affair exploited in the Pittsburgh papers, exploited with a wealth of detail which indicated that local news of a sensational nature was at a low ebb. The firm of Denny & Carson announced that the boy's father had refunded the full amount of the theft, and that they had no intention of prosecuting. The Cumberland minister had been interviewed, and expressed his hope of yet reclaiming the motherless lad, and his Sabbath-school teacher declared that she would spare no effort to that end. The rumor had reached Pittsburgh that the boy had been seen in a New York hotel, and his father had gone East to find him and bring him home.

Paul had just come in to dress for dinner; he sank into a chair, weak to the knees, and clasped his head in his hands. It was to be worse than jail, even; the tepid waters of Cordelia Street were to close over him finally and forever. The grey monotony stretched before him in hopeless, unrelieved years; Sabbath-school, Young People's Meeting, the yellow-papered room, the damp dish-towels; it all rushed back upon him with a sickening vividness. He had the old feeling that the orchestra had suddenly stopped, the sinking sensation that the play was over. The sweat broke out on his face, and he sprang to his feet, looked about him with his white, conscious smile, and winked at himself in the mirror. With something of the old childish belief in miracles with which he had so often gone to class, all his lessons unlearned, Paul dressed and dashed whistling down the corridor to the elevator.

He had no sooner entered the dining-room and caught the measure of the music than his remembrance was lightened by his old elastic power of claiming the moment, mounting with it, and finding it all sufficient. The glare and glitter about him, the mere scenic accessories had again, and for the last time, their old potency. He would show himself that he was game, he would finish the thing splendidly. He doubted, more than ever, the existence of Cordelia Street, and for the first time he drank his wine recklessly. Was he not, after all, one of those fortunate beings born to the purple, was he not still himself and in his own place? He drummed a nervous accompaniment to the Pagliacci music and looked about him, telling himself over and over that it had paid.

He reflected drowsily, to the swell of the music and the chill sweetness of his wine, that he might have done it more wisely. He might have caught an outboard steamer and been well out of their clutches before now. But the other side of the world had seemed too far away and too uncertain then; he could not have waited for it; his need had been too sharp. If he had to choose over again, he would do the same thing tomorrow. He looked affectionately about the dining-room, now gilded with a soft mist. Ah, it had paid indeed!

Paul was awakened next morning by a painful throbbing in his head and feet. He had thrown himself across the bed without undressing, and had slept with his shoes on. His limbs and hands were lead heavy, and his tongue and throat were parched and burnt. There came upon him one of those fateful attacks of clear-headedness that never occurred except when he was physically exhausted and his nerves hung loose. He lay still and closed his eyes and let the tide of things wash over him.

His father was in New York; "stopping at some joint or other," he told himself. The memory of successive summers on the front stoop fell upon him like a weight of black water. He had not a hundred dollars left; and he knew now, more than ever, that money was everything, the wall that stood between all he loathed and all he wanted. The thing was winding itself up; he had thought of that on his first glorious day in New York, and had even provided a way to snap the thread. It lay on his dressing-table now; he had got it out last night when he came blindly up from dinner, but the shiny metal hurt his eyes, and he disliked the looks of it.

He rose and moved about with a painful effort, succumbing now and again to attacks of nausea. It was the old depression exaggerated; all the world had become Cordelia Street. Yet somehow he was not afraid of anything, was absolutely calm; perhaps because he had looked into the dark corner at last and knew. It was bad enough, what he saw there, but somehow not so bad as his long fear of it had been. He saw everything clearly now. He had a feeling that he had made the best of it, that he had lived the sort of life he was meant to live, and for half an hour he sat staring at the revolver. But he told himself that was not the way, so he went downstairs and took a cab to the ferry.

When Paul arrived at Newark, he got off the train and took another cab, directing the driver to follow the Pennsylvania tracks out of the town. The snow lay heavy on the roadways and had drifted deep in the open fields. Only here and there the dead grass or dried weed stalks projected, singularly black, above it. Once well into the country, Paul dismissed the carriage and walked, floundering along the tracks, his mind a medley of irrelevant things. He seemed to hold in his brain an actual picture of everything he had seen that morning. He remembered every feature of both his drivers, of the toothless old woman from whom he had bought the red flowers in his coat, the agent from whom he had got his ticket, and all of his fellow-passengers on the ferry. His mind, unable to cope with vital matters near at hand, worked feverishly and deftly at sorting and grouping these images. They made for him a part of the ugliness of the world, of the ache in his head, and the bitter burning on his tongue. He stopped and put a handful of snow into his mouth as he walked, but that, too, seemed hot. When he reached a little hillside, where the tracks ran through a cut some twenty feet below him, he stopped and sat down.

The carnations in his coat were drooping with the cold, he noticed; their red glory all over. It occurred to him that all the flowers he had seen in the glass cases that first night must have gone the same way, long before this. It was only one splendid breath they had, in spite of their brave mockery at the winter outside the glass; and it was a losing game in the end, it seemed, this revolt against the homilies by which the world is run. Paul took one of the blossoms carefully from his coat and scooped a little hole in the snow, where he covered it up. Then he dozed a while, from his weak condition, seemingly insensible to the cold.

The sound of an approaching train awoke him, and he started to his feet, remembering only his resolution, and afraid lest he should be too late. He stood watching the approaching locomotive, his teeth chattering, his lips drawn away from them in a frightened smile; once or twice he glanced nervously sidewise, as though he were being watched. When the right moment came, he jumped. As he fell, the folly of his haste occurred to him with merciless clearness, the vastness of what he had left undone. There flashed through his brain, clearer than ever before, the blue of Adriatic water, the yellow of Algerian sands.

He felt something strike his chest, and that his body was being thrown swiftly through the air, on and on, immeasurably far and fast, while his limbs were gently relaxed. Then, because the picture making mechanism was crushed, the disturbing visions flashed into black, and Paul dropped back into the immense design of things.

John Cheever

John Cheever (1912–1982), the leading exponent of the kind of carefully fashioned story of modern suburban manners that *The New Yorker* popularized, has been called by the reviewer John Leonard "the Chekhov of the suburbs." Cheever spent most of his life in New York City and in suburban towns similar to the ones he described in much of his fiction. Born in Quincy, Massachusetts, he was raised by parents who owned a prosperous business that failed after the 1929 stock market crash. His parents enjoyed reading literature to him, so at an early age he was acquainted with the fiction of Charles Dickens, Jack London, and Robert Louis Stevenson. He started his career at an unusually young age. Expelled from Thayer Academy for being, by his own account, a "quarrelsome, intractable . . . and lousy student," he moved to New York City, lived in a cell of a room on a bread-and-buttermilk diet, and wrote stories. When his first one, "Expelled," was accepted for publication by Malcolm Cowley, then editor of the *New Republic*, Cheever was launched as a teenager into a career as a writer of fiction. Earlier Cowley had told him that his stories were too long to get published by magazines that paid, so he made Cheever write a story of not more than a thousand words every day for four days to encourage discipline.

Cheever's first collection of stories, *The Way Some People Live*, appeared in 1942, while he was completing a four-year stint of army duty. In 1953 he strengthened his literary reputation with the book *The Enormous Radio and Other Stories*, a collection of fourteen of his *New Yorker* pieces. Six years later appeared another story collection, *The Housebreaker of Shady Hill*. In the 1960s and 1970s he published three more books of short stories and two widely acclaimed novels, *Bullet Park* (1969) and *Falconer* (1977). *The Stories of John Cheever*, published in 1978, won both the Pulitzer Prize and the National Book Critics Circle Award and became one of the few collections of short stories ever to make the *New York Times* best-seller list. In more than fifty years, Cheever published over 200 magazine stories; he figured that he earned "enough money to feed the family and buy a new suit every other year."

Usually a rapid writer, Cheever said he liked best the stories that he wrote in less than a week, although he spent months working on "The Swimmer" (1964). He originally wrote a draft of the plot as "a perfectly good" novel, but then he burned it. "I could very easily have sold the book," he said, "but the trick was to get the winter constellations in the midsummer sky without anyone knowing about it, and it didn't take 250 pages to do that."

RELATED COMMENTARY
John Cheever, "Why I Write Short Stories," page 1409.

The Swimmer

1964

IT WAS ONE OF THOSE midsummer Sundays when everyone sits around saying, "I *drank* too much last night." You might have heard it whispered by the parishioners leaving church, heard it from the lips of the priest himself, struggling with his cassock in the *vestiarium*, heard it from the golf links and the tennis courts, heard it from the wild-life preserve where the leader of the Audubon group was suffering from a terrible hangover. "I *drank* too much," said Donald Westerhazy. "We all *drank* too much," said Lucinda Merrill. "It must have been the wine," said Helen Westerhazy. "I *drank* too much of that claret."

This was the edge of the Westerhazys' pool. The pool, fed by an artesian well with a high iron content, was a pale shade of green. It was a fine day. In the west there was a massive stand of cumulus cloud so like a city seen from a distance — from the bow of an approaching ship — that it might have had a name. Lisbon. Hackensack. The sun was hot. Neddy Merrill sat by the green water, one hand in it, one around a glass of gin. He was a slender man — he seemed to have the especial slenderness of youth — and while he was far from young he had slid down his banister that morning and given the bronze backside of Aphrodite on the hall table a smack, as he jogged toward the smell of coffee in his dining room. He might have been compared to a summer's day, particularly the last hours of one, and while he lacked a tennis racket or a sail bag the impression was definitely one of youth, sport, and clement weather. He had been swimming and now he was breathing deeply, stertorously as if he could gulp into his lungs the components of that moment, the heat of the sun, the intenseness of his pleasure. It all seemed to flow into his chest. His own house stood in Bullet Park, eight miles to the south, where his four beautiful daughters would have had their lunch and might be playing tennis. Then it occurred to him that by taking a dogleg to the southwest he could reach his home by water.

His life was not confining and the delight he took in this observation could not be explained by its suggestion of escape. He seemed to see, with a cartographer's eye, that string of swimming pools, that quasi-subterranean stream that curved across the county. He had made a discovery, a contribution to modern geography; he would name the stream Lucinda after his wife. He was not a practical joker nor was he a fool but he was determinedly original and had a vague and modest idea of himself as a legendary figure. The day was beautiful and it seemed to him that a long swim might enlarge and celebrate its beauty.

He took off a sweater that was hung over his shoulders and dove in. He had an inexplicable contempt for men who did not hurl themselves into pools. He swam a choppy crawl, breathing either with every stroke or every fourth stroke and counting somewhere well in the back of his mind the one-two one-two of a flutter kick. It was not a serviceable stroke for long distances but the domestication of swimming had saddled the sport with some customs and in his part of the world a crawl was customary. To be embraced and sustained by the light green water was less a pleasure, it seemed, than the resumption of a natural condition, and he would have liked to swim without trunks, but this was not possible, considering his project. He hoisted himself up on the far curb — he never used the ladder — and started across the lawn. When Lucinda asked where he was going he said he was going to swim home.

The only maps and charts he had to go by were remembered or imaginary but these were clear enough. First there were the Grahams, the Hammers, the Lears, the Howlands, and the Crosscups. He would cross Ditmar Street to the Bunkers and come, after a short portage, to the Levys, the Welchers, and the public pool in Lancaster. Then there were the Hallorans, the Sachses, the Biswangers, Shirley Adams, the Gilmartins, and the Clydes. The day was lovely, and that he lived in a world so generously supplied with water seemed like a clemency, a beneficence. His heart was high and he ran across the grass. Making his way home by an uncommon route gave him the feeling that he was a pilgrim, an explorer, a man with a destiny, and he knew that he would find friends all along the way; friends would line the banks of the Lucinda River.

He went through a hedge that separated the Westerhazys' land from the Grahams', walked under some flowering apple trees, passed the shed that housed their pump and filter, and came out at the Grahams' pool. "Why, Neddy," Mrs. Graham said, "what a marvelous surprise. I've been trying to get you on the phone all morning. Here, let me get you a drink." He saw then, like any explorer, that the hospitable customs and traditions of the natives would have to be handled with diplomacy if he was ever going to reach his destination. He did not want to mystify or seem rude to the Grahams nor did he have the time to linger there. He swam the length of their pool and joined them in the sun and was rescued, a few minutes later, by the arrival of two carloads of friends from Connecticut. During the uproarious reunions he was able to slip away. He went down by the front of the Grahams' house, stepped over a thorny hedge, and crossed a vacant lot to the Hammers'. Mrs. Hammer, looking up from her roses, saw him swim by although she wasn't quite sure who it was. The Lears heard him splashing past the open windows of their living room. The Howlands and the Crosscups were away. After leaving the Howlands' he crossed Ditmar Street and started for the Bunkers', where he could hear, even at that distance, the noise of a party.

The water refracted the sound of voices and laughter and seemed to suspend it in midair. The Bunkers' pool was on a rise and he climbed some stairs to a terrace where twenty-five or thirty men and women were drinking. The only person in the water was Rusty Towers, who floated there on a rubber raft. Oh, how bonny and lush were the banks of the Lucinda River! Prosperous men and women gathered by the sapphire-colored waters while caterer's men in white coats passed them cold gin. Overhead a red de Haviland trainer was circling around and around and around in the sky with something like the glee of a child in a swing. Ned felt a passing affection for the scene, a tenderness for the gathering, as if it was something he might touch. In the distance he heard thunder. As soon as Enid Bunker saw him she began to scream: "Oh, look who's here! What a marvelous surprise! When Lucinda said you couldn't come I thought I'd *die*."

She made her way to him through the crowd, and when they had finished kissing she led him to the bar, a progress that was slowed by the fact that he stopped to kiss eight or ten other women and shake the hands of as many men. A smiling bartender he had seen at a hundred parties gave him a gin and tonic and he stood by the bar for a moment, anxious not to get stuck in any conversation that would delay his voyage. When he seemed about to be surrounded he dove in and swam close to the side to avoid colliding with Rusty's raft. At the far end of the pool he bypassed the Tomlinsons with a broad smile and jogged up the garden path. The gravel cut his feet but this was only unpleasantness. The party was confined to the pool, and as he went toward the house he heard the brilliant, watery sound of voices fade, heard the noise of a radio from the Bunkers' kitchen, where someone was listening to a ball game. Sunday afternoon. He made his way through the parked cars and down the grassy border of their driveway to Alewives Lane. He did not want to be seen on the road in his bathing trunks but there was no traffic and he made the short distance to the Levys' driveway, marked with a PRIVATE PROPERTY sign and a green tube for the *New York Times*. All the doors and windows of the big house were open but there were no signs of life; not even a dog barked. He went around the side of the house to the pool and saw that the Levys had only recently left. Glasses and bottles and dishes of nuts were on a table at the deep end, where there was a bathhouse or gazebo, hung with Japanese lanterns. After swimming the pool he got himself a glass and poured a drink. It was his fourth or fifth drink and he had swum nearly half the length of the Lucinda River. He felt tired, clean, and pleased at that moment to be alone; pleased with everything.

It would storm. The stand of cumulus cloud — that city — had risen and darkened, and while he sat there he heard the percussiveness of thunder again. The de Haviland trainer was still circling overhead and it seemed to Ned that he could almost hear the pilot laugh with pleasure in the afternoon; but when there was another peal of thunder he took off for home. A train whistle blew and he wondered what time it had gotten to be. Four? Five? He thought of the provincial station at that hour, where a waiter, his tuxedo concealed by a raincoat, a dwarf with some flowers wrapped in newspaper, and a woman who had been crying would be waiting for the local. It was suddenly growing dark; it was that moment when the pin-headed birds seemed to organize their song into some acute and knowledgeable recognition of the storm's approach. Then there was a fine noise of rushing water from the crown of an oak at his back, as if a spigot there had been turned. Then the noise of fountains came from the crowns of all the tall trees. Why did he love storms, what was the meaning of his excitement when the door sprang open and the rain wind fled rudely up the stairs, why had the simple task of shutting the windows of an old house seemed fitting and urgent, why did the first watery notes of a storm wind have for him the unmistakable sound of good news, cheer, glad tidings? Then there was an explosion, a smell of cordite, and rain lashed the Japanese lanterns that Mrs. Levy had bought in Kyoto the year before last, or was it the year before that?

He stayed in the Levys' gazebo until the storm had passed. The rain had cooled the air and he shivered. The force of the wind had stripped a maple of its red and yellow leaves and scattered them over the grass and the water. Since it was midsummer the tree must be blighted, and yet he felt a peculiar sadness at this sign of autumn. He braced his shoulders, emptied his glass, and started for the Welchers' pool. This meant crossing the Lindleys' riding ring and he was surprised to find it overgrown with grass and all the jumps dismantled. He wondered if the Lindleys had sold their horses or gone away for the summer and put them out to board. He seemed to remember having heard something about the Lindleys and their horses but the memory was unclear. On he went, barefoot through the wet grass, to the Welchers', where he found their pool was dry.

This breach in his chain of water disappointed him absurdly, and he felt like some explorer who seeks a torrential headwater and finds a dead stream. He was disappointed and mystified. It was common enough to go away for the summer but no one ever drained his pool. The Welchers had definitely gone away. The pool furniture was folded, stacked, and covered with a tarpaulin. The bathhouse was locked. All the windows of the house were shut, and when he went around to the driveway in front he saw a FOR SALE sign nailed to a tree. When had he last heard from the Welchers — when, that is, had he and Lucinda last regretted an invitation to dine with them? It seemed only a week or so ago. Was his memory failing or had he so disciplined it in the repression of unpleasant facts that he had damaged his sense of the truth? Then in the distance he heard the sound of a tennis game. This cheered him, cleared away all his apprehensions and let him regard the overcast sky and the cold air with indifference. This was the day that Neddy Merrill swam across the county. That was the day! He started off then for his most difficult portage.

Had you gone for a Sunday afternoon ride that day you might have seen him, close to naked, standing on the shoulders of Route 424, waiting for a chance to cross. You might have wondered if he was the victim of foul play, had his car broken down, or was he merely a fool. Standing barefoot in the deposits of the highway — beer cans, rags, and blowout patches — exposed to all kinds of ridicule, he seemed pitiful. He had known when he started that this was a part of his journey — it had been on his maps — but confronted with the lines of traffic, worming through the summery light, he found himself unprepared. He was laughed at, jeered at, a beer can was thrown at him, and he had no dignity or humor to bring to the situation. He could have gone back, back to the Westerhazys', where Lucinda would still be sitting in the sun. He had signed nothing, vowed nothing, pledged nothing, not even to himself. Why, believing as he did, that all human obduracy was susceptible to common sense, was he unable to turn back? Why was he determined to complete his journey even if it meant putting his life in danger? At what point had this prank, this joke, this piece of horseplay become serious? He could not go back, he could not even recall with any clearness the green water at the Westerhazys', the sense of inhaling the day's components, the friendly and relaxed voices saying that they had *drunk* too much. In the space of an hour, more or less, he had covered a distance that made his return impossible.

An old man, tooling down the highway at fifteen miles an hour, let him get to the middle of the road, where there was a grass divider. Here he was exposed to the ridicule of the northbound traffic, but after ten or fifteen minutes he was able to cross. From here he had only a short walk to the Recreation Center at the edge of the village of Lancaster, where there were some handball courts and a public pool.

The effect of the water on voices, the illusion of brilliance and suspense, was the same here as it had been at the Bunkers' but the sounds here were louder, harsher, and more shrill, and as soon as he entered the crowded enclosure he was confronted with regimentation. "ALL SWIMMERS MUST TAKE A SHOWER BEFORE USING THE POOL. ALL SWIMMERS MUST USE THE FOOTBATH. ALL SWIMMERS MUST WEAR THEIR IDENTIFICATION DISKS." He took a shower, washed his feet in a cloudy and bitter solution, and made his way to the edge of the water. It stank of chlorine and looked to him like a sink. A pair of lifeguards in a pair of towers blew police whistles at what seemed to be regular intervals and abused the swimmers through a public address system. Neddy remembered the sapphire water at the Bunkers' with longing and thought that he might contaminate himself — damage his own prosperousness and charm — by swimming in this murk, but he reminded himself that he was an explorer, a pilgrim, and that this was merely a stagnant bend in the Lucinda River. He dove, scowling with distaste, into the chlorine and had to swim with his head above water to avoid collisions, but even so he was bumped into, splashed, and jostled. When he got to the shallow end both lifeguards were shouting at him: "Hey, you, you without the identification disk, get outa the water." He did, but they had no way of pursuing him and he went through the reek of suntan oil and chlorine out through the hurricane fence and passed the handball courts. By crossing the road he entered the wooded part of the Halloran estate. The woods were not cleared and the footing was treacherous and difficult until he reached the lawn and the clipped beech hedge that encircled their pool.

The Hallorans were friends, an elderly couple of enormous wealth who seemed to bask in the suspicion that they might be Communists. They were zealous reformers but they were not Communists, and yet when they were accused, as they sometimes were, of subversion, it seemed to gratify and excite them. Their beech hedge was yellow and he guessed this had been blighted like the Levys' maple. He called hullo, hullo, to warn the Hallorans of his approach, to palliate his invasion of their privacy. The Hallorans, for reasons that had never been explained to him, did not wear bathing suits. No explanations were in order, really. Their nakedness was a detail in their uncompromising zeal for reform and he stepped politely out of his trunks before he went through the opening in the hedge.

Mrs. Halloran, a stout woman with white hair and a serene face, was reading the *Times*. Mr. Halloran was taking beech leaves out of the water with a scoop. They seemed not surprised or displeased to see him. Their pool was perhaps the oldest in the county, a fieldstone rectangle, fed by a brook. It had no filter or pump and its waters were the opaque gold of the stream.

"I'm swimming across the county," Ned said.

"Why, I didn't know one could," exclaimed Mrs. Halloran.

"Well, I've made it from the Westerhazys'," Ned said. "That must be about four miles."

He left his trunks at the deep end, walked to the shallow end, and swam this stretch. As he was pulling himself out of the water he heard Mrs. Halloran say, "We've been *terribly* sorry to hear about all your misfortunes, Neddy."

"My misfortunes?" Ned asked. "I don't know what you mean."

"Why we heard that you'd sold the house and that your poor children. . . ."

"I don't recall having sold the house," Ned said, "and the girls are at home."

"Yes," Mrs. Halloran sighed. "Yes. . . ." Her voice filled the air with an unseasonable melancholy and Ned spoke briskly. "Thank you for the swim."

"Well, have a nice trip," said Mrs. Halloran.

Beyond the hedge he pulled on his trunks and fastened them. They were loose and he wondered if, during the space of an afternoon, he could have lost some weight. He was cold and he was tired and the naked Hallorans and their dark water had depressed him. The swim was too much for his strength but how could he have guessed this, sliding down the banister that morning and sitting in the Westerhazys' sun? His arms were lame. His legs felt rubbery and ached at the joints. The worst of it was the cold in his bones and the feeling that he might never be warm again. Leaves were falling down around him and he smelled wood smoke on the wind. Who would be burning wood at this time of the year?

He needed a drink. Whiskey would warm him, pick him up, carry him through the last of his journey, refresh his feeling that it was original and valorous to swim across the county. Channel swimmers took brandy. He needed a stimulant. He crossed the lawn in front of the Hallorans' house and went down a little path to where they had built a house for their only daughter, Helen, and her husband, Eric Sachs. The Sachses' pool was small and he found Helen and her husband there.

"Oh, *Neddy*," Helen said. "Did you lunch at Mother's?"

"Not *really*," Ned said. "I *did* stop to see your parents." This seemed to be explanation enough. "I'm terribly sorry to break in on you like this but I've taken a chill and I wonder if you'd give me a drink."

"Why, I'd *love* to," Helen said, "but there hasn't been anything in this house to drink since Eric's operation. That was three years ago."

Was he losing his memory, had his gift for concealing painful facts let him forget that he had sold his house, that his children were in trouble, and that his friend had been ill? His eyes slipped from Eric's face to his abdomen, where he saw three pale, sutured scars, two of them at least a foot long. Gone was his navel, and what, Neddy thought, would the roving hand, bed-checking one's gifts at 3 A.M., make of a belly with no navel, no link to birth, this breach in the succession?

"I'm sure you can get a drink at the Biswangers'," Helen said. "They're having an enormous do. You can hear it from here. Listen!"

She raised her head and from across the road, the lawns, the gardens, the woods, the fields, he heard again the brilliant noise of voices over water. "Well, I'll get wet," he said, still feeling that he had no freedom of choice about his means of travel. He dove into the Sachses' cold water, and gasping, close to drowning, made his way from one end of the pool to the other. "Lucinda and I want *terribly* to see you," he said over his shoulder, his face set toward the Biswangers'. "We're sorry it's been so long and we'll call you *very* soon."

He crossed some fields to the Biswangers' and the sounds of revelry there. They would be honored to give him a drink, they would be happy to give him a drink. The Biswangers invited him and Lucinda for dinner four times a year, six weeks in advance. They were always rebuffed and yet they continued to send out their invitations, unwilling to comprehend the rigid and undemocratic realities of their society. They were the sort of people who discussed the price of things at cocktails, exchanged market tips during dinner, and after dinner told dirty stories to mixed company. They did not belong to Neddy's set — they were not even on Lucinda's Christmas card list. He went toward their pool with feelings of indifference, charity, and some unease, since it seemed to be getting dark and these were the longest days of the year. The party when he joined it was noisy and large. Grace Biswanger was the kind of hostess who asked the optometrist, the veterinarian, the real-estate dealer, and the dentist. No one was swimming and the twilight, reflected on the water of the pool, had a wintry gleam. There was a bar and he started for this. When Grace Biswanger saw him she came toward him, not affectionately as he had every right to expect, but bellicosely.

"Why, this party has everything," she said loudly, "including a gate crasher."

She could not deal him a social blow — there was no question about this and he did not flinch. "As a gate crasher," he asked politely, "do I rate a drink?"

"Suit yourself," she said. "You don't seem to pay much attention to invitations."

She turned her back on him and joined some guests, and he went to the bar and ordered a whiskey. The bartender served him but he served him rudely. His was a world in which the caterer's men kept the social score, and to be rebuffed by a part-time barkeep meant that he had suffered some loss of social esteem. Or perhaps the man was new and uninformed. Then he heard Grace at his back say: "They went for broke overnight — nothing but income — and he showed up drunk one Sunday and asked us to loan him five thousand dollars. . . ." She was always talking about money. It was worse than eating your peas off a knife. He dove into the pool, swam its length, and went away.

The next pool on his list, the last but two, belonged to his old mistress, Shirley Adams. If he had suffered any injuries at the Biswangers' they would be cured here. Love — sexual roughhouse in fact — was the supreme elixir, the pain killer, the brightly colored pill that would put the spring back into his step, the joy of life in his heart. They had had an affair last week, last month, last year. He couldn't remember. It was he who had broken it off, his was the upper hand, and he stepped through the gate of the wall that surrounded her pool with nothing so considered as self-confidence. It seemed in a way to be his pool, as the lover, particularly the illicit lover, enjoys the possessions of his mistress with an authority unknown to holy matrimony. She was there, her hair the color of brass, but her figure, at the edge of the lighted, cerulean water, excited in him no profound memories. It had been, he thought, a lighthearted affair, although she had wept when he broke it off. She seemed confused to see him and he wondered if she was still wounded. Would she, God forbid, weep again?

"What do you want?" she asked.

"I'm swimming across the county."

"Good Christ. Will you ever grow up?"

"What's the matter?"

"If you've come here for money," she said, "I won't give you another cent."

"You could give me a drink."

"I could but I won't. I'm not alone."

"Well, I'm on my way."

He dove in and swam the pool, but when he tried to haul himself up onto the curb he found that the strength in his arms and shoulders had gone, and he paddled to the ladder and climbed out. Looking over his shoulder he saw, in the lighted bathhouse, a young man. Going out onto the dark lawn he smelled chrysanthemums or marigolds — some stubborn autumnal fragrance — on the night air, strong as gas. Looking overhead he saw that the stars had come out, but why should he seem to see Andromeda, Cepheus, and Cassiopeia? What had become of the constellations of midsummer? He began to cry.

It was probably the first time in his adult life that he had ever cried, certainly the first time in his life that he had ever felt so miserable, cold, tired, and bewildered. He could not understand the rudeness of the caterer's barkeep or the rudeness of a mistress who had come to him on her knees and showered his trousers with tears. He had swum too long, he had been immersed too long, and his nose and his throat were sore from the water. What he needed then was a drink, some company, and some clean, dry clothes, and while he could have cut directly across the road to his home he went on to the Gilmartins' pool. Here, for the first time in his life, he did not dive but went down the steps into the icy water and swam a hobbled sidestroke that he might have learned as a youth. He staggered with fatigue on his way to the Clydes' and paddled the length of their pool, stopping again and again with his hand on the curb to rest. He climbed up the ladder and wondered if he had the strength to get home. He had done what he wanted, he had swum the county, but he was so stupefied with exhaustion that his triumph seemed vague. Stooped, holding on to the gateposts for support, he turned up the driveway of his own house.

The place was dark. Was it so late that they had all gone to bed? Had Lucinda stayed at the Westerhazys' for supper? Had the girls joined her there or gone someplace else? Hadn't they agreed, as they usually did on Sunday, to regret all their invitations and stay at home? He tried the garage doors to see what cars were in but the doors were locked and rust came off the handles onto his hands. Going toward the house, he saw the force of the thunderstorm had knocked one of the rain gutters loose. It hung down over the front door like an umbrella rib, but it could be fixed in the morning. The house was locked, and he thought that the stupid cook or the stupid maid must have locked the place up until he remembered that it had been some time since they had employed a maid or a cook. He shouted, pounded on the door, tried to force it with his shoulder, and then, looking in at the windows, saw that the place was empty.

Anton Chekhov

Anton Chekhov (1860–1904), the short story writer and playwright, wrote his first stories while he was a medical student at Moscow University, to help his family pay off debts. His grandfather had been a serf who had bought his freedom. His father was an unsuccessful grocer in Taganrog, in southwestern Russia. After completing medical school, Chekhov became an assistant to the district doctor in a small provincial town. His early sketches were mostly humorous stories that he first published in newspapers under different pen names, keeping his own name for his medical practice. But the popularity of these sketches made him decide to become a writer.

Chekhov's first two collections of short stories, published in 1886 and 1887, were acclaimed by readers, and from that time on he was able to give all his time to writing. He bought a small estate near Moscow, where he lived with his family and treated sick peasants at no charge. Chekhov's kindness and good works were not a matter of any political program or religious impulse but rather "the natural coloration of his talent," as Vladimir Nabokov put it. He was extremely modest about his extraordinary ability to empathize with the characters he created. Once he said to a visitor, "Do you know how I write my stories? Here's how!" And he glanced at his table, took up the first object that he saw—it was an ashtray—and said, "If you want it, you'll have a story tomorrow. It will be called 'The Ashtray.'" And it seemed to the visitor that Chekhov was conjuring up a story in front of his eyes: "Certain indefinite situations, adventures which had not yet found concrete form, were already beginning to crystallize about the ashtray."

In his stories Chekhov's technique appears disarmingly simple. Yet, as Virginia Woolf recognized, "as we read these little stories about nothing at all, the horizon widens; the soul gains an astonishing sense of freedom." Chekhov's remarkable absence of egotism can be seen in masterpieces such as "The Darling" and "The Lady with the Little Dog," both of which he wrote toward the end of his life. He once sent a sketch describing himself to the publisher who first encouraged him in which he gave a sense of the depth of his self-knowledge:

> Write a story, do, about a young man, the son of a serf, a former grocery boy, a choir singer, a high school pupil and university student, brought up to respect rank, to kiss the hands of priests, to truckle to the ideas of others—a young man who expressed thanks for every piece of bread, who was whipped many times, who went without galoshes to do his tutoring, who used his fists, tortured animals, was fond of dining with rich relatives, was a hypocrite in his dealings with God and men, needlessly, solely out of a realization of his own insignificance—write how this young man squeezes the slave out of himself, drop by drop, and how, on awaking one fine morning, he feels that the blood coursing through his veins is no longer that of a slave but that of a real human being.

Chekhov's more than 800 stories have influenced many writers of short fiction, including Sherwood Anderson, Katherine Mansfield, John Cheever, Raymond Carver, and Ann Beattie. Unconcerned with giving a social or ethical message in his work, he championed what he called "the holy of holies"—"love and absolute freedom—freedom from violence and lies, whatever their form." In 1902, Chekhov's stories began to be translated into English. The English versions published by Constance Garnett during the years 1916 to 1923 were the most widely reprinted. Here is the Garnett translation of "The Darling," along with a more recent translation of "The Lady with the Little Dog."

RELATED STORY
Joyce Carol Oates, "The Lady with the Pet Dog," page 964.

RELATED COMMENTARIES
Anton Chekhov, "Technique in Writing the Short Story," page 1411; Matthew C. Brennan, "Plotting against Chekhov: Joyce Carol Oates and 'The Lady with the Pet Dog,'" page 1400; Richard Ford, "Why We Like Chekhov," page 1426; Vladimir Nabokov, "A Reading of Chekhov's 'The Lady with the Little Dog,'" page 1486; Leo Tolstoy, "Chekhov's Intent in 'The Darling,'" page 1528. See also the student paper on reading Chekhov in Russian, page 1717.

The Darling

1899 / Translated by Constance Garnett

OLENKA, THE DAUGHTER of the retired collegiate assessor Plemyanniakov, was sitting on her back porch, lost in thought. It was hot, the flies were persistent and teasing, and it was pleasant to reflect that it would soon be evening. Dark rainclouds were gathering from the east, and bringing from time to time a breath of moisture in the air.

Kukin, who was the manager of an open-air theatre called the Tivoli, and who lived in the lodge, was standing in the middle of the garden looking at the sky.

"Again!" he observed despairingly. "It's going to rain again! Rain every day, as though to spite me. I might as well hang myself! It's ruin! Fearful losses every day."

He flung up his hands, and went on, addressing Olenka:

"There! that's the life we lead, Olga Semyonovna. It's enough to make one cry. One works and does one's utmost; one wears oneself out, getting no sleep at night, and racks one's brain what to do for the best. And then what happens? To begin with, one's public is ignorant, boorish. I give them the very best operetta, a dainty masque, first-rate music-hall artists. But do you suppose that's what they want? They don't understand anything of that sort. They want a clown; what they ask for is vulgarity. And then look at the weather! Almost every evening it rains. It started on the tenth of May, and it's kept it up all May and June. It's simply awful! The public doesn't come, but I've to pay the rent just the same, and pay the artists."

The next evening the clouds would gather again, and Kukin would say with an hysterical laugh:

"Well, rain away, then! Flood the garden, drown me! Damn my luck in this world and the next! Let the artists drag me into court! Send me to prison — to Siberia! — the scaffold! Ha, ha, ha!"

And the next day the same thing.

Olenka listened to Kukin with silent gravity, and sometimes tears came into her eyes. In the end his misfortunes touched her; she grew to love him. He was a small thin man, with a yellow face, and curls combed forward on his forehead. He spoke in a thin tenor; as he talked his mouth worked on one side, and there was always an expression of despair on his face; yet he aroused a deep and genuine affection in her. She was always fond of someone, and could not exist without loving. In earlier days she had loved her Papa, who now sat in a darkened room, breathing with difficulty; she had loved her aunt who used to come every other year from Bryansk; and before that, when she was at school, she had loved her French master. She was a gentle, soft-hearted, compassionate girl, with mild, tender eyes and very good health. At the sight of her full rosy cheeks, her soft white neck with a little dark mole on it, and the kind, naïve smile, which came into her face when she listened to anything pleasant, men thought, "Yes, not half bad," and smiled too, while lady visitors could not refrain from seizing her hand in the middle of a conversation, exclaiming in a gush of delight, "You darling!"

The house in which she had lived since her birth, and which was left her in her father's will, was at the extreme end of the town, not far from the Tivoli. In the evenings and at night she could hear the band playing, and the crackling and banging of fireworks, and it seemed to her that it was Kukin struggling with his destiny, storming the entrenchments of his chief foe, the indifferent public; there was a sweet thrill at her heart, she had no desire to sleep, and when he returned home at daybreak, she tapped softly at her bedroom window and, showing him only her face and one shoulder through the curtain; she gave him a friendly smile. . . .

He proposed to her, and they were married. And when he had a closer view of her neck and her plump, fine shoulders, he threw up his hands, and said:

"You darling!"

He was happy, but as it rained on the day and night of his wedding, his face still retained an expression of despair.

They got on very well together. She used to sit in his office, to look after things in the Tivoli, to put down the accounts and pay the wages. And her rosy cheeks, her sweet, naïve, radiant smile, were to be seen now at the office window, now in the refreshment bar or behind the scenes of the theatre. And already she used to say to her acquaintances that the theatre was the chief and most important thing in life, and that it was only through the drama that one could derive true enjoyment and become cultivated and humane.

"But do you suppose the public understands that?" she used to say. "What they want is a clown. Yesterday we gave *Faust Inside Out,* and almost all the boxes were empty; but if Vanichka and I had been producing some vulgar thing, I assure you the theatre would have been packed. Tomorrow Vanichka and I are doing *Orpheus in the Underworld.* Do come."

And what Kukin said about the theatre and the actors she repeated. Like him she despised the public for their ignorance and their indifference to art; she took part in the rehearsals, she corrected the actors, she kept an eye on the behavior of the musicians, and when there was an unfavorable notice in the local paper, she shed tears, and then went to the editor's office to set things right.

The actors were fond of her and used to call her "Vanichka and I," and "the darling"; she was sorry for them and used to lend them small sums of money, and if they deceived her, she used to shed a few tears in private, but did not complain to her husband.

They got on well in the winter too. They took the theatre in the town for the whole winter, and let it for short terms to a troupe from Little Russia, or to a conjurer, or to a local dramatic society. Olenka grew stouter, and was always beaming with satisfaction, while Kukin grew thinner and yellower, and continually complained of their terrible losses, although he had not done badly all the winter. He used to cough at night, and she used to give him hot raspberry tea or lime-flower water, to rub him with eau-de-Cologne and to wrap him in her warm shawls.

"You're such a sweet pet!" she used to say with perfect sincerity, stroking his hair. "You're such a pretty dear!"

Towards Lent he went to Moscow to collect a new troupe, and without him she could not sleep, but sat all night at her window, looking at the stars, and she compared herself with the hens, who are awake all night and uneasy when the cock is not in the henhouse. Kukin was detained in Moscow, and wrote that he would be back at Easter, adding some instructions about the Tivoli. But on the Sunday before Easter, late in the evening, came a sudden ominous knock at the gate; some one was hammering on the gate as though on a barrel — boom, boom, boom! The drowsy cook went flopping with her bare feet through the puddles, as she ran to open the gate.

"Please open," said some one outside in a thick bass. "There is a telegram for you."

Olenka had received telegrams from her husband before, but this time for some reason she felt numb with terror. With shaking hands she opened the telegram and read as follows:

Ivan Petrovich died suddenly to-day. Awaiting immate instructions fufuneral Tuesday.

That was how it was written in the telegram — "fufuneral," and the utterly incomprehensible word "immate." It was signed by the stage manager of the operatic company.

"My darling!" sobbed Olenka. "Vanichka, my precious, my darling! Why did I ever meet you! Why did I know you and love you! Your poor heartbroken Olenka is all alone without you!"

Kukin's funeral took place on Tuesday in Moscow, Olenka returned home on Wednesday, and as soon as she got indoors she threw herself on her bed and sobbed so loudly that it could be heard next door, and in the street.

"Poor darling!" the neighbors said, as they crossed themselves. "Olga Semyonovna, poor darling! How she does take on!"

Three months later Olenka was coming home from mass, melancholy and in deep mourning. It happened that one of her neighbors, Vassily Andreich

Pustovalov, returning home from church, walked back beside her. He was the manager at Babakayev's, the timber merchant's. He wore a straw hat, a white waistcoat, and a gold watch-chain, and looked more like a country gentleman than a man in trade.

"Everything happens as it is ordained, Olga Semyonovna," he said gravely, with a sympathetic note in his voice; "and if any of our dear ones die, it must be because it is the will of God, so we ought to have fortitude and bear it submissively."

After seeing Olenka to her gate, he said good-bye and went on. All day afterwards she heard his sedately dignified voice, and whenever she shut her eyes she saw his dark beard. She liked him very much. And apparently she had made an impression on him too, for not long afterwards an elderly lady, with whom she was only slightly acquainted, came to drink coffee with her, and as soon as she was seated at table began to talk about Pustovalov, saying that he was an excellent man whom one could thoroughly depend upon, and that any girl would be glad to marry him. Three days later Pustovalov himself came. He did not stay long, only about ten minutes, and he did not say much, but when he left, Olenka loved him — loved him so much that she lay awake all night in a perfect fever, and in the morning she sent for the elderly lady. The match was quickly arranged, and then came the wedding.

Pustovalov and Olenka got on very well together when they were married.

Usually he sat in the office till dinnertime, then he went out on business, while Olenka took his place, and sat in the office till evening, making up accounts and booking orders.

"Timber gets dearer every year; the price rises twenty per cent," she would say to her customers and friends. "Only fancy we used to sell local timber, and now Vassichka always has to go for wood to the Mogilev district. And the freight!" she would add, covering her cheeks with her hands in horror. "The freight!"

It seemed to her that she had been in the timber trade for ages and ages, and that the most important and necessary thing in life was timber; and there was something intimate and touching to her in the very sound of words such as "balk," "post," "beam," "pole," "scantling," "batten," "lath," "plank," etc.

At night when she was asleep she dreamed of perfect mountains of planks and boards, and long strings of wagons, carting timber somewhere far away. She dreamed that a whole regiment of six-inch beams forty feet high, standing on end, was marching upon the timberyard; that logs, beams, and boards knocked together with the resounding crash of dry wood, kept falling and getting up again, piling themselves on each other. Olenka cried out in her sleep, and Pustovalov said to her tenderly: "Olenka, what's the matter, darling? Cross yourself!"

Her husband's ideas were hers. If he thought the room was too hot, or that business was slack, she thought the same. Her husband did not care for entertainments, and on holidays he stayed at home. She did likewise.

"You are always at home or in the office," her friends said to her. "You should go to the theatre, darling, or to the circus."

"Vassichka and I have no time to go to theatres," she would answer sedately. "We have no time for nonsense. What's the use of these theatres?"

On Saturdays Pustovalov and she used to go to the evening service; on holidays to early mass, and they walked side by side with softened faces as they came home from church. There was a pleasant fragrance about them both, and her silk dress rustled agreeably. At home they drank tea, with fancy bread and jams of various kinds, and afterwards they ate pie. Every day at twelve o'clock there was a savory smell of beet-root soup and of mutton or duck in their yard, and on fast-days of fish, and no one could pass the gate without feeling hungry. In the office the samovar was always boiling, and customers were regaled with tea and biscuits. Once a week the couple went to the baths and returned side by side, both red in the face.

"Yes, we have nothing to complain of, thank God," Olenka used to say to her acquaintances. "I wish everyone were as well off as Vassichka and I."

When Pustovalov went away to buy wood in the Mogilev district, she missed him dreadfully, lay awake, and cried. A young veterinary surgeon in the army, called Smirnin, to whom they had let their lodge, used sometimes to come in in the evening. He used to talk to her and play cards with her, and this entertained her in her husband's absence. She was particularly interested in what he told her of his home life. He was married and had a little boy, but was separated from his wife because she had been unfaithful to him, and now he hated her and sent her forty rubles a month for the maintenance of their son. And hearing of all this, Olenka sighed and shook her head. She was sorry for him.

"Well, God keep you," she used to say to him at parting, as she lighted him down the stairs with a candle. "Thank you for coming to cheer me up, and may the Mother of God give you health."

And she always expressed herself with the same sedateness and dignity, the same reasonableness, in imitation of her husband. As the veterinary surgeon was disappearing behind the door below, she would say:

"You know, Vladimir Platonich, you'd better make it up with your wife. You should forgive her for the sake of your son. You may be sure the little fellow understands."

And when Pustovalov came back, she told him in a low voice about the veterinary surgeon and his unhappy home life, and both sighed and shook their heads and talked about the boy, who, no doubt, missed his father, and by some strange connection of ideas, they went up to the holy icons, bowed to the ground before them, and prayed that God would give them children.

And so the Pustovalovs lived for six years quietly and peaceably in love and complete harmony.

But behold! one winter day after drinking hot tea in the office, Vassily Andreich went out into the yard without his cap on to see about sending off some timber, caught cold, and was taken ill. He had the best doctors, but he grew worse and died after four months' illness. And Olenka was a widow once more.

"I've nobody, now you've left me, my darling," she sobbed, after her husband's funeral. "How can I live without you, in wretchedness and misery! Pity me, good people, all alone in the world!"

She went about dressed in black with "weepers,"[1] and gave up wearing hat and gloves for good. She hardly ever went out, except to church, or to her husband's grave, and led the life of a nun. It was not till six months later that she took off the weepers and opened the shutters of the windows. She was sometimes seen in the mornings, going with her cook to market for provisions, but what went on in her house and how she lived now could only be surmised. People guessed, from seeing her drinking tea in her garden with the veterinary surgeon, who read the newspaper aloud to her, and from the fact that, meeting a lady she knew at the post-office, she said to her:

"There is no proper veterinary inspection in our town, and that's the cause of all sorts of epidemics. One is always hearing of people's getting infection from the milk supply, or catching diseases from horses and cows. The health of domestic animals ought to be as well cared for as the health of human beings."

She repeated the veterinary surgeon's words, and was of the same opinion as he about everything. It was evident that she could not live a year without some attachment, and had found new happiness in the lodge. In anyone else this would have been censured, but no one could think ill of Olenka; everything she did was so natural. Neither she nor the veterinary surgeon said anything to other people of the change in their relations, and tried, indeed, to conceal it, but without success, for Olenka could not keep a secret. When he had visitors, men serving in his regiment, and she poured out tea or served the supper, she would begin talking of the cattle plague, of the foot and mouth disease, and of the municipal slaughterhouses. He was dreadfully embarrassed, and when the guests had gone, he would seize her by the hand and hiss angrily:

"I've asked you before not to talk about what you don't understand. When we veterinary surgeons are talking among ourselves, please don't put your word in. It's really annoying."

And she would look at him with astonishment and dismay, and ask him in alarm: "But Volodichka, what *am* I to talk about?"

And with tears in her eyes she would embrace him, begging him not to be angry, and they were both happy.

But this happiness did not last long. The veterinary surgeon departed, departed forever with his regiment, when it was transferred to a distant place—to Siberia, perhaps. And Olenka was left alone.

Now she was absolutely alone. Her father had long been dead, and his armchair lay in the attic, covered with dust and lame of one leg. She got thinner and plainer, and when people met her in the street they did not look at her as they used to, and did not smile to her; evidently her best years were over and left behind, and now a new sort of life had begun for her, which did not bear thinking about. In the evening Olenka sat in the porch, and heard the band playing and the fireworks popping in the Tivoli, but now the sound stirred no response. She looked into her yard without interest, thought of nothing, wished for nothing, and afterwards, when night came on she went to bed and dreamed of her empty yard. She ate and drank as it were unwillingly.

---

[1] White bands sewn on the sleeves of mourning dresses.

And what was worst of all, she had no opinions of any sort. She saw the objects about her and understood what she saw, but could not form any opinion about them, and did not know what to talk about. And how awful it is not to have any opinions! One sees a bottle, for instance, or the rain, or a peasant driving in his cart, but what the bottle is for, or the rain, or the peasant, and what is the meaning of it, one can't say, and could not even for a thousand rubles. When she had Kukin, or Pustovalov, or the veterinary surgeon, Olenka could explain everything, and give her opinion about anything you like, but now there was the same emptiness in her brain and in her heart as there was in her yard outside. And it was as harsh and as bitter as wormwood in the mouth.

Little by little the town grew in all directions. The road became a street, and where the Tivoli and the timberyard had been, there were new turnings and houses. How rapidly time passes! Olenka's house grew dingy, the roof got rusty, the shed sank on one side, and the whole yard was overgrown with docks and stinging-nettles. Olenka herself had grown plain and elderly; in summer she sat on the porch, and her soul, as before, was empty and dreary and full of bitterness. In winter she sat at her window and looked at the snow. When she caught the scent of spring, or heard the chime of the church bells, a sudden rush of memories from the past came over her, there was a tender ache in her heart, and her eyes brimmed over with tears; but this was only for a minute, and then came emptiness again and the sense of the futility of life. The black kitten, Briska, rubbed against her and purred softly, but Olenka was not touched by these feline caresses. That was not what she needed. She wanted a love that would absorb her whole being, her whole soul and reason — that would give her ideas and an object in life, and would warm her old blood. And she would shake the kitten off her skirt and say with vexation:

"Get along; I don't want you!"

And so it was, day after day and year after year, and no joy, and no opinions. Whatever Mavra, the cook, said she accepted.

One hot July day, towards evening, just as the cattle were being driven away, and the whole yard was full of dust, someone suddenly knocked at the gate. Olenka went to open it herself and was dumbfounded when she looked out: she saw Smirnin, the veterinary surgeon, gray-headed, and dressed as a civilian. She suddenly remembered everything. She could not help crying and letting her head fall on his breast without uttering a word, and in the violence of her feeling she did not notice how they both walked into the house and sat down to tea.

"My dear Vladimir Platonich! What fate has brought you?" she muttered, trembling with joy.

"I want to settle here for good, Olga Semyonovna," he told her. "I have resigned my post, and have come to settle down and try my luck on my own account. Besides, it's time for my boy to go to school. He's a big boy. I am reconciled with my wife, you know."

"Where is she?" asked Olenka.

"She's at the hotel with the boy, and I'm looking for lodgings."

"Good gracious, my dear soul! Lodgings? Why not have my house? Why shouldn't that suit you? Why, my goodness, I wouldn't take any rent!" cried

Olenka in a flutter, beginning to cry again. "You live here, and the lodge will do nicely for me. Oh dear! how glad I am!"

Next day the roof was painted and the walls were whitewashed, and Olenka, with her arms akimbo, walked about the yard giving directions. Her face was beaming with her old smile, and she was brisk and alert as though she had waked from a long sleep. The veterinary's wife arrived — a thin, plain lady, with short hair and a peevish expression. With her was her little Sasha, a boy of ten, small for his age, blue-eyed, chubby, with dimples in his cheeks. And scarcely had the boy walked into the yard when he ran after the cat, and at once there was the sound of his gay, joyous laugh.

"Is that your puss, Auntie?" he asked Olenka. "When she has little ones, do give us a kitten. Mamma is awfully afraid of mice."

Olenka talked to him, and gave him tea. Her heart warmed and there was a sweet ache in her bosom, as though the boy had been her own child. And when he sat at the table in the evening, going over his lessons, she looked at him with deep tenderness and pity as she murmured to herself:

"You pretty pet! . . . my precious! . . . Such a fair little thing, and so clever."

"'An island is a piece of land which is entirely surrounded by water,'" he read aloud.

"An island is a piece of land," she repeated, and this was the first opinion to which she gave utterance with positive conviction after so many years of silence and dearth of ideas.

Now she had opinions of her own, and at supper she talked to Sasha's parents, saying how difficult the lessons were at the high schools, but that yet the high school was better than a commercial one, since with a high-school education all careers were open to one, such as being a doctor or an engineer.

Sasha began going to the high school. His mother departed to Kharkov to her sister's and did not return; his father used to go off every day to inspect cattle, and would often be away from home for three days together, and it seemed to Olenka as though Sasha was entirely abandoned, that he was not wanted at home, that he was being starved, and she carried him off to her lodge and gave him a little room there.

And for six months Sasha had lived in the lodge with her. Every morning Olenka came into his bedroom and found him fast asleep, sleeping noiselessly with his hand under his cheek. She was sorry to wake him.

"Sashenka," she would say mournfully, "get up, darling. It's time for school."

He would get up, dress and say his prayers, and then sit down to breakfast, drink three glasses of tea, and eat two large biscuits and half a buttered roll. All this time he was hardly awake and a little ill-humored in consequence.

"You don't quite know your fable, Sashenka," Olenka would say, looking at him as though he were about to set off on a long journey. "What a lot of trouble I have with you! You must work and do your best, darling, and obey your teachers."

"Oh, do leave me alone!" Sasha would say.

Then he would go down the street to school, a little figure, wearing a big cap and carrying a satchel on his shoulder. Olenka would follow him noiselessly.

"Sashenka!" she would call after him, and she would pop into his hand a date or a caramel. When he reached the street where the school was, he would feel ashamed of being followed by a tall, stout woman; he would turn round and say:

"You'd better go home, Auntie. I can go the rest of the way alone."

She would stand still and look after him fixedly till he had disappeared at the school gate.

Ah, how she loved him! Of her former attachments not one had been so deep; never had her soul surrendered to any feeling so spontaneously, so disinterestedly, and so joyously as now that her maternal instincts were aroused. For this little boy with the dimple in his cheek and the big school cap, she would have given her whole life, she would have given it with joy and tears of tenderness. Why? Who can tell why?

When she had seen the last of Sasha, she returned home, contented and serene, brimming over with love; her face, which had grown younger during the last six months, smiled and beamed; people meeting her looked at her with pleasure.

"Good-morning, Olga Semyonovna, darling. How are you, darling?"

"The lessons at the high school are very difficult now," she would relate at the market. "It's too much; in the first class yesterday they gave him a fable to learn by heart, and a Latin translation and a problem. You know it's too much for a little chap."

And she would begin talking about the teachers, the lessons, and the schoolbooks, saying just what Sasha said.

At three o'clock they had dinner together: in the evening they learned their lessons together and cried. When she put him to bed, she would stay a long time making the Cross over him and murmuring a prayer; then she would go to bed and dream of that faraway misty future when Sasha would finish his studies and become a doctor or an engineer, would have a big house of his own with horses and a carriage, would get married and have children. . . . She would fall asleep still thinking of the same thing, and tears would run down her cheeks from her closed eyes, while the black cat lay purring beside her: "Mrr, mrr, mrr."

Suddenly there would come a loud knock at the gate.

Olenka would wake up breathless with alarm, her heart throbbing. Half a minute later would come another knock.

"It must be a telegram from Kharkov," she would think, beginning to tremble from head to foot. "Sasha's mother is sending for him from Kharkov. . . . Oh, mercy on us!"

She was in despair. Her head, her hands, and her feet would turn chill, and she would feel that she was the most unhappy woman in the world. But another minute would pass, voices would be heard: it would turn out to be the veterinary surgeon coming home from the club.

"Well, thank God!" she would think.

And gradually the load in her heart would pass off, and she would feel at ease. She would go back to bed thinking of Sasha, who lay sound asleep in the next room, sometimes crying out in his sleep:

"I'll give it to you! Get away! Shut up!"

The Lady with the Little Dog

1899 / Translated by Richard Pevear and Larissa Volokhonsky

I

The talk was that a new face had appeared on the embankment: a lady with a little dog. Dmitri Dmitrich Gurov, who had already spent two weeks in Yalta and was used to it, also began to take an interest in new faces. Sitting in a pavilion at Vernet's, he saw a young woman, not very tall, blond, in a beret, walking along the embankment; behind her ran a white spitz.

And after that he met her several times a day in the town garden or in the square. She went strolling alone, in the same beret, with the white spitz; nobody knew who she was, and they called her simply "the lady with the little dog."

"If she's here with no husband or friends," Gurov reflected, "it wouldn't be a bad idea to make her acquaintance."

He was not yet forty, but he had a twelve-year-old daughter and two sons in school. He had married young, while still a second-year student, and now his wife seemed half again his age. She was a tall woman with dark eyebrows, erect, imposing, dignified, and a thinking person, as she called herself. She read a great deal, used the new orthography, called her husband not Dmitri but Dimitri, but he secretly considered her none too bright, narrow-minded, graceless, was afraid of her, and disliked being at home. He had begun to be unfaithful to her long ago, was unfaithful often, and, probably for that reason, almost always spoke ill of women, and when they were discussed in his presence, he would say of them:

"An inferior race!"

It seemed to him that he had been taught enough by bitter experience to call them anything he liked, and yet he could not have lived without the "inferior race" even for two days. In the company of men he was bored, ill at ease, with them he was taciturn and cold, but when he was among women, he felt himself free and knew what to talk about with them and how to behave; and he was at ease even being silent with them. In his appearance, in his character, in his whole nature there was something attractive and elusive that disposed women towards him and enticed them; he knew that, and he himself was attracted to them by some force.

Repeated experience, and bitter experience indeed, had long since taught him that every intimacy, which in the beginning lends life such pleasant diversity and presents itself as a nice and light adventure, inevitably, with decent people — especially irresolute Muscovites, who are slow starters — grows into a major task, extremely complicated, and the situation finally becomes burdensome. But at every new meeting with an interesting woman, this experience somehow slipped from his memory, and he wanted to live, and everything seemed quite simple and amusing.

And so one time, towards evening, he was having dinner in the garden, and the lady in the beret came over unhurriedly to take the table next to his. Her expression, her walk, her dress, her hair told him that she belonged to decent society, was married, in Yalta for the first time, and alone, and that she was bored here . . . In the stories about the impurity of local morals there was much untruth, he despised them and knew that these stories were mostly invented by people who would eagerly have sinned themselves had they known how; but when the lady sat down at the next table, three steps away from him, he remembered those stories of easy conquests, of trips to the mountains, and the tempting thought of a quick, fleeting liaison, a romance with an unknown woman, of whose very name you are ignorant, suddenly took possession of him.

He gently called the spitz, and when the dog came over, he shook his finger at it. The spitz growled. Gurov shook his finger again.

The lady glanced at him and immediately lowered her eyes.

"He doesn't bite," she said and blushed.

"May I give him a bone?" and, when she nodded in the affirmative, he asked affably: "Have you been in Yalta long?"

"About five days."

"And I'm already dragging through my second week here."

They were silent for a while.

"The time passes quickly, and yet it's so boring here!" she said without looking at him.

"It's merely the accepted thing to say it's boring here. The ordinary man lives somewhere in his Belevo or Zhizdra and isn't bored, then he comes here: 'Ah, how boring! Ah, how dusty!' You'd think he came from Granada."

She laughed. Then they went on eating in silence, like strangers; but after dinner they walked off together — and a light, bantering conversation began, of free, contented people, who do not care where they go or what they talk about. They strolled and talked of how strange the light was on the sea; the water was of a lilac color, so soft and warm, and over it the moon cast a golden strip. They talked of how sultry it was after the hot day. Gurov told her he was a Muscovite, a philologist by education, but worked in a bank; had once been preparing to sing in an opera company, but had dropped it, owned two houses in Moscow . . . And from her he learned that she grew up in Petersburg, but was married in S., where she had now been living for two years, that she would be staying in Yalta for about a month, and that her husband might come to fetch her, because he also wanted to get some rest. She was quite unable to explain where her husband served — in the provincial administration or the zemstvo[1] council — and she herself found that funny. And Gurov also learned that her name was Anna Sergeevna.

Afterwards, in his hotel room, he thought about her, that tomorrow she would probably meet him again. It had to be so. Going to bed, he recalled that still quite recently she had been a schoolgirl, had studied just as his daughter was studying now, recalled how much timorousness and angularity there was in her laughter, her conversation with a stranger — it must have been the first

---

[1] County council.

time in her life that she was alone in such a situation, when she was followed, looked at, and spoken to with only one secret purpose, which she could not fail to guess. He recalled her slender, weak neck, her beautiful gray eyes.

"There's something pathetic in her all the same," he thought and began to fall asleep.

II

A week had passed since they became acquainted. It was Sunday. Inside it was stuffy, but outside the dust flew in whirls, hats blew off. They felt thirsty all day, and Gurov often stopped at the pavilion, offering Anna Sergeevna now a soft drink, now ice cream. There was no escape.

In the evening when it relented a little, they went to the jetty to watch the steamer come in. There were many strollers on the pier; they had come to meet people, they were holding bouquets. And here two particularities of the smartly dressed Yalta crowd distinctly struck one's eye: the elderly ladies were dressed like young ones, and there were many generals.

Owing to the roughness of the sea, the steamer arrived late, when the sun had already gone down, and it was a long time turning before it tied up. Anna Sergeevna looked at the ship and the passengers through her lorgnette, as if searching for acquaintances, and when she turned to Gurov, her eyes shone. She talked a lot, and her questions were abrupt, and she herself immediately forgot what she had asked; then she lost her lorgnette in the crowd.

The smartly dressed crowd was dispersing, the faces could no longer be seen, the wind had died down completely, and Gurov and Anna Sergeevna stood as if they were expecting someone else to get off the steamer. Anna Sergeevna was silent now and smelled the flowers, not looking at Gurov.

"The weather's improved towards evening," he said. "Where shall we go now? Shall we take a drive somewhere?"

She made no answer.

Then he looked at her intently and suddenly embraced her and kissed her on the lips, and he was showered with the fragrance and moisture of the flowers, and at once looked around timorously — had anyone seen them?

"Let's go to your place . . ." he said softly.

And they both walked quickly.

Her hotel room was stuffy and smelled of the perfumes she had bought in a Japanese shop. Gurov, looking at her now, thought: "What meetings there are in life!" From the past he had kept the memory of carefree, good-natured women, cheerful with love, grateful to him for their happiness, however brief; and of women — his wife, for example — who loved without sincerity, with superfluous talk, affectedly, with hysteria, with an expression as if it were not love, not passion, but something more significant; and of those two or three very beautiful, cold ones, in whose faces a predatory expression would suddenly flash, a stubborn wish to take, to snatch from life more than it could give, and these were women not in their first youth, capricious, unreasonable, domineering, unintelligent, and when Gurov cooled towards them, their beauty aroused hatred in him, and the lace of their underwear seemed to him like scales.

But here was all the timorousness and angularly of inexperienced youth, a feeling of awkwardness, and an impression of bewilderment, as if someone had suddenly knocked at the door. Anna Sergeevna, the "lady with the little dog," somehow took a special, very serious attitude towards what had happened, as if it were her fall—so it seemed, and that was strange and inopportune. Her features drooped and faded, and her long hair hung down sadly on both sides of her face, she sat pondering in a dejected pose, like the sinful woman in an old painting.

"It's not good," she said. "You'll be the first not to respect me now."

There was a watermelon on the table in the hotel room. Gurov cut himself a slice and unhurriedly began to eat it. At least half an hour passed in silence.

Anna Sergeevna was touching, she had about her a breath of the purity of a proper, naive, little-experienced woman; the solitary candle burning on the table barely lit up her face, but it was clear that her heart was uneasy.

"Why should I stop respecting you?" asked Gurov. "You don't know what you're saying yourself."

"God forgive me!" she said, and her eyes filled with tears. "This is terrible."

"It's like you're justifying yourself."

"How can I justify myself? I'm a bad, low woman, I despise myself and am not even thinking of any justification. It's not my husband I've deceived, but my own self! And not only now, I've been deceiving myself for a long time. My husband may be an honest and good man, but he's a lackey! I don't know what he does there, how he serves, I only know that he's a lackey. I married him when I was twenty, I was tormented by curiosity, I wanted something better. I told myself there must be a different life. I wanted to live! To live and live . . . I was burning with curiosity . . . you won't understand it, but I swear to God that I couldn't control myself any longer, something was happening to me, I couldn't restrain myself, I told my husband I was ill and came here . . . And here I go about as if in a daze, as if I'm out of my mind . . . and now I've become a trite, trashy woman, whom anyone can despise."

Gurov was bored listening, he was annoyed by the naive tone, by this repentance, so unexpected and out of place; had it not been for the tears in her eyes, one might have thought she was joking or playing a role.

"I don't understand," he said softly, "what is it you want?"

She hid her face on his chest and pressed herself to him.

"Believe me, believe me, I beg you . . ." she said. "I love an honest, pure life, sin is vile to me, I myself don't know what I'm doing. Simple people say, 'The unclean one beguiled me.' And now I can say of myself that the unclean one has beguiled me."

"Enough, enough . . ." he muttered.

He looked into her fixed, frightened eyes, kissed her, spoke softly and tenderly, and she gradually calmed down, and her gaiety returned. They both began to laugh.

Later, when they went out, there was not a soul on the embankment, the town with its cypresses looked completely dead, but the sea still beat noisily against the shore; one barge was rocking on the waves, and the lantern on it glimmered sleepily.

They found a cab and drove to Oreanda.

"I just learned your last name downstairs in the lobby: it was written on the board — von Dideritz," said Gurov. "Is your husband German?"

"No, his grandfather was German, I think, but he himself is Orthodox."

In Oreanda they sat on a bench not far from the church, looked down on the sea, and were silent. Yalta was barely visible through the morning mist, white clouds stood motionless on the mountaintops. The leaves of the trees did not stir, cicadas called, and the monotonous, dull noise of the sea, coming from below, spoke of the peace, of the eternal sleep that awaits us. So it had sounded below when neither Yalta nor Oreanda were there, so it sounded now and would go on sounding with the same dull indifference when we are no longer here. And in this constancy, in this utter indifference to the life and death of each of us, there perhaps lies hidden the pledge of our eternal salvation, the unceasing movement of life on earth, of unceasing perfection. Sitting beside the young woman, who looked so beautiful in the dawn, appeased and enchanted by the view of this magical décor — sea, mountains, clouds, the open sky — Gurov reflected that, essentially, if you thought of it, everything was beautiful in this world, everything except for what we ourselves think and do when we forget the higher goals of being and our human dignity.

Some man came up — it must have been a watchman — looked at them, and went away. And this detail seemed such a mysterious thing, and also beautiful. The steamer from Feodosia could be seen approaching in the glow of the early dawn, its lights out.

"There's dew on the grass," said Anna Sergeevna after a silence.

"Yes. It's time to go home."

They went back to town.

After that they met on the embankment every noon, had lunch together, dined, strolled, admired the sea. She complained that she slept poorly and that her heart beat anxiously, kept asking the same questions, troubled now by jealousy, now by fear that he did not respect her enough. And often on the square or in the garden, when there was no one near them, he would suddenly draw her to him and kiss her passionately. Their complete idleness, those kisses in broad daylight, with a furtive look around and the fear that someone might see them, the heat, the smell of the sea, and the constant flashing before their eyes of idle, smartly dressed, well-fed people, seemed to transform him; he repeatedly told Anna Sergeevna how beautiful she was, and how seductive, was impatiently passionate, never left her side, while she often brooded and kept asking him to admit that he did not respect her, did not love her at all, and saw in her only a trite woman. Late almost every evening they went somewhere out of town, to Oreanda or the cascade; these outings were successful, their impressions each time were beautiful, majestic.

They were expecting her husband to arrive. But a letter came from him in which he said that his eyes hurt and begged his wife to come home quickly. Anna Sergeevna began to hurry.

"It's good that I'm leaving," she said to Gurov. "It's fate itself."

She went by carriage, and he accompanied her. They drove for a whole day. When she had taken her seat in the express train and the second bell had rung, she said:

"Let me have one more look at you . . . One more look. There."

She did not cry, but was sad, as if ill, and her face trembled.

"I'll think of you . . . remember you," she said. "God be with you. Don't think ill of me. We're saying good-bye forever, it must be so, because we should never have met. Well, God be with you."

The train left quickly, its lights soon disappeared, and a moment later the noise could no longer be heard, as if everything were conspiring on purpose to put a speedy end to this sweet oblivion, this madness. And, left alone on the platform and gazing into the dark distance, Gurov listened to the chirring of the grasshoppers and the hum of the telegraph wires with a feeling as if he had just woken up. And he thought that now there was one more affair or adventure in his life, and it, too, was now over, and all that was left was the memory . . . He was touched, saddened, and felt some slight remorse; this young woman whom he was never to see again had not been happy with him; he had been affectionate with her, and sincere, but all the same, in his treatment of her, in his tone and caresses, there had been a slight shade of mockery, the somewhat coarse arrogance of a happy man, who was, moreover, almost twice her age. She had all the while called him kind, extraordinary, lofty; obviously, he had appeared to her not as he was in reality, and therefore he had involuntarily deceived her . . .

Here at the station there was already a breath of autumn, the wind was cool.

"It's time I headed north, too," thought Gurov, leaving the platform. "High time!"

III

At home in Moscow everything was already wintry, the stoves were heated, and in the morning, when the children were getting ready for school and drinking their tea, it was dark, and the nanny would light a lamp for a short time. The frosts had already set in. When the first snow falls, on the first day of riding in sleighs, it is pleasant to see the white ground, the white roofs; one's breath feels soft and pleasant, and in those moments one remembers one's youth. The old lindens and birches, white with hoarfrost, have a good-natured look, they are nearer one's heart than cypresses and palms, and near them one no longer wants to think of mountains and the sea.

Gurov was a Muscovite. He returned to Moscow on a fine, frosty day, and when he put on his fur coat and warm gloves and strolled down Petrovka, and when on Saturday evening he heard the bells ringing, his recent trip and the places he had visited lost all their charm for him. He gradually became immersed in Moscow life, now greedily read three newspapers a day and said that he never read the Moscow newspapers on principle. He was drawn to restaurants, clubs, to dinner parties, celebrations, and felt flattered that he had famous lawyers and actors among his clients, and that at the Doctors' Club he played cards with a professor. He could eat a whole portion of selyanka[2] from the pan . . .

A month would pass and Anna Sergeevna, as it seemed to him, would be covered by mist in his memory and would only appear to him in dreams with a touching smile, as other women did. But more than a month passed, deep winter came, and yet everything was as clear in his memory as if he had parted with Anna Sergeevna only the day before. And the memories burned brighter and brighter. Whether from the voices of his children doing their homework, which reached him in his study in the evening quiet, or from hearing a romance, or an organ in a restaurant, or the blizzard howling in the chimney, everything would suddenly rise up in his memory: what had happened on the jetty, and the early morning with mist on the mountains, and the steamer from Feodosia, and the kisses. He would pace the room for a long time, and remember, and smile, and then his memories would turn to reveries, and in his imagination the past would mingle with what was still to be. Anna Sergeevna was not a dream, she followed him everywhere like a shadow and watched him. Closing his eyes, he saw her as if alive, and she seemed younger, more beautiful, more tender than she was; and he also seemed better to himself than he had been then, in Yalta. In the evenings she gazed at him from the bookcase, the fireplace, the corner, he could hear her breathing, the gentle rustle of her skirts. In the street he followed women with his eyes, looking for one who resembled her . . .

And he was tormented now by a strong desire to tell someone his memories. But at home it was impossible to talk of his love, and away from home there was no one to talk with. Certainly not among his tenants nor at the bank. And what was there to say? Had he been in love then? Was there anything beautiful, poetic, or instructive, or merely interesting, in his relations with Anna Sergeevna? And he found himself speaking vaguely of love, of women, and no one could guess what it was about, and only his wife raised her dark eyebrows and said:

"You know, Dimitri, the role of fop doesn't suit you at all."

One night, as he was leaving the Doctors' Club together with his partner, an official, he could not help himself and said:

"If you only knew what a charming woman I met in Yalta!"

The official got into a sleigh and drove off, but suddenly turned around and called out:

"Dmitri Dmitrich!"

"What?"

"You were right earlier: the sturgeon was a bit off!"

Those words, so very ordinary, for some reason suddenly made Gurov indignant, struck him as humiliating, impure. Such savage manners, such faces! These senseless nights, and such uninteresting, unremarkable days! Frenzied card-playing, gluttony, drunkenness, constant talk about the same thing. Useless matters and conversations about the same thing took for their share the best part of

---

[2] Meat stewed with pickled cabbage and served in a pan.

one's time, the best of one's powers, and what was left in the end was some sort of curtailed, wingless life, some sort of nonsense, and it was impossible to get away or flee, as if you were sitting in a madhouse or a prison camp!

Gurov did not sleep all night and felt indignant, and as a result had a headache all the next day. And the following nights he slept poorly, sitting up in bed all the time and thinking, or pacing up and down. He was sick of the children, sick of the bank, did not want to go anywhere or talk about anything.

In December, during the holidays, he got ready to travel and told his wife he was leaving for Petersburg to solicit for a certain young man — and went to S. Why? He did not know very well himself. He wanted to see Anna Sergeevna and talk with her, to arrange a meeting, if he could.

He arrived at S. in the morning and took the best room in the hotel, where the whole floor was covered with gray army flannel and there was an inkstand on the table, gray with dust, with a horseback rider, who held his hat in his raised hand, but whose head was broken off. The hall porter gave him the necessary information: von Dideritz lives in his own house on Staro-Goncharnaya Street, not far from the hotel; he has a good life, is wealthy, keeps his own horses, everybody in town knows him. The porter pronounced it "Dridiritz."

Gurov walked unhurriedly to Staro-Goncharnaya Street, found the house. Just opposite the house stretched a fence, long, gray, with spikes.

"You could flee from such a fence," thought Gurov, looking now at the windows, now at the fence.

He reflected: today was not a workday, and the husband was probably at home. And anyhow it would be tactless to go in and cause embarrassment. If he sent a message, it might fall into the husband's hands, and that would ruin everything. It would be best to trust to chance. And he kept pacing up and down the street and near the fence and waited for his chance. He saw a beggar go in the gates and saw the dogs attack him, then, an hour later, he heard someone playing a piano, and the sounds reached him faintly, indistinctly. It must have been Anna Sergeevna playing. The front door suddenly opened and some old woman came out, the familiar white spitz running after her. Gurov wanted to call the dog, but his heart suddenly throbbed, and in his excitement he was unable to remember the spitz's name.

He paced up and down, and hated the gray fence more and more, and now he thought with vexation that Anna Sergeevna had forgotten him, and was perhaps amusing herself with another man, and that that was so natural in the situation of a young woman who had to look at this cursed fence from morning till evening. He went back to his hotel room and sat on the sofa for a long time, not knowing what to do, then had dinner, then took a long nap.

"How stupid and upsetting this all is," he thought, when he woke up and looked at the dark windows: it was already evening. "So I've had my sleep. Now what am I to do for the night?"

He sat on the bed, which was covered with a cheap, gray, hospital-like blanket, and taunted himself in vexation:

"Here's the lady with the little dog for you . . . Here's an adventure for you . . . Yes, here you sit."

That morning, at the train station, a poster with very big lettering had caught his eye: it was the opening night of *The Geisha*. He remembered it and went to the theater.

"It's very likely that she goes to opening nights," he thought.

The theater was full. And here, too, as in all provincial theaters generally, a haze hung over the chandeliers, the gallery stirred noisily; the local dandies stood in the front row before the performance started, their hands behind their backs; and here, too, in the governor's box, the governor's daughter sat in front, wearing a boa, while the governor himself modestly hid behind the portière, and only his hands could be seen; the curtain swayed, the orchestra spent a long time tuning up. All the while the public came in and took their seats, Gurov kept searching greedily with his eyes.

Anna Sergeevna came in. She sat in the third row, and when Gurov looked at her, his heart was wrung, and he realized clearly that there was now no person closer, dearer, or more important for him in the whole world; this small woman, lost in the provincial crowd, not remarkable for anything, with a vulgar lorgnette in her hand, now filled his whole life, was his grief, his joy, the only happiness he now wished for himself; and to the sounds of the bad orchestra, with its trashy local violins, he thought how beautiful she was. He thought and dreamed.

A man came in with Anna Sergeevna and sat down next to her, a young man with little side-whiskers, very tall, stooping; he nodded his head at every step, and it seemed he was perpetually bowing. This was probably her husband, whom she, in an outburst of bitter feeling that time in Yalta, had called a lackey. And indeed, in his long figure, his side-whiskers, his little bald spot, there was something of lackeyish modesty; he had a sweet smile, and the badge of some learned society gleamed in his buttonhole, like the badge of a lackey.

During the first intermission the husband went to smoke; she remained in her seat. Gurov, who was also sitting in the stalls, went up to her and said in a trembling voice and with a forced smile:

"How do you do?"

She looked at him and paled, then looked again in horror, not believing her eyes, and tightly clutched her fan and lorgnette in her hand, obviously struggling with herself to keep from fainting. Both were silent. She sat, he stood, alarmed at her confusion, not venturing to sit down next to her. The tuning-up violins and flutes sang out, it suddenly became frightening, it seemed that people were gazing at them from all the boxes. But then she got up and quickly walked to the exit, he followed her, and they both went confusedly through corridors and stairways, going up, then down, and the uniforms of the courts, the schools, and the imperial estates flashed before them, all with badges; ladies flashed by, fur coats on hangers, a drafty wind blew, drenching them with the smell of cigar stubs. And Gurov, whose heart was pounding, thought: "Oh, Lord! Why these people, this orchestra . . ."

And just then he suddenly recalled how, at the station in the evening after he had seen Anna Sergeevna off, he had said to himself that everything was over and they would never see each other again. But how far it still was from being over!

On a narrow, dark stairway with the sign "To the Amphitheater," she stopped.

"How you frightened me!" she said, breathing heavily, still pale, stunned. "Oh, how you frightened me! I'm barely alive. Why did you come? Why?"

"But understand, Anna, understand . . ." he said in a low voice, hurrying. "I beg you to understand . . ."

She looked at him with fear, with entreaty, with love, looked at him intently, the better to keep his features in her memory.

"I've been suffering so!" she went on, not listening to him. "I think only of you all the time, I've lived by my thoughts of you. And I've tried to forget, to forget, but why, why did you come?"

Further up, on the landing, two high-school boys were smoking and looking down, but Gurov did not care, he drew Anna Sergeevna to him and began kissing her face, her cheeks, her hands.

"What are you doing, what are you doing!" she repeated in horror, pushing him away from her. "We've both lost our minds. Leave today, leave at once . . . I adjure you by all that's holy, I implore you . . . Somebody's coming!"

Someone was climbing the stairs.

"You must leave . . ." Anna Sergeevna went on in a whisper. "Do you hear, Dmitri Dmitrich? I'll come to you in Moscow. I've never been happy, I'm unhappy now, and I'll never, never be happy, never! Don't make me suffer still more! I swear I'll come to Moscow. But we must part now! My dear one, my good one, my darling, we must part!"

She pressed his hand and quickly began going downstairs, turning back to look at him, and it was clear from her eyes that she was indeed not happy . . . Gurov stood for a little while, listened, then, when everything was quiet, found his coat and left the theater.

IV

And Anna Sergeevna began coming to see him in Moscow. Once every two or three months she left S., and told her husband she was going to consult a professor about her female disorder — and her husband did and did not believe her. Arriving in Moscow, she stayed at the Slavyansky Bazaar and at once sent a man in a red hat to Gurov. Gurov came to see her, and nobody in Moscow knew of it.

Once he was going to see her in that way on a winter morning (the messenger had come the previous evening but had not found him in). With him was his daughter, whom he wanted to see off to school, which was on the way. Big, wet snow was falling.

"It's now three degrees above freezing, and yet it's snowing," Gurov said to his daughter. "But it's warm only near the surface of the earth, while in the upper layers of the atmosphere the temperature is quite different."

"And why is there no thunder in winter, papa?"

He explained that, too. He spoke and thought that here he was going to a rendezvous, and not a single soul knew of it or probably would ever know. He had two lives: an apparent one, seen and known by all who needed it, filled with conventional truth and conventional deceit, which perfectly resembled the lives of his acquaintances and friends, and another that went on in secret. And by some strange coincidence, perhaps an accidental one, everything that he found important, interesting, necessary, in which he was sincere and did not deceive himself, which constituted the core of his life, occurred in secret from others, while everything that made up his lie, his shell, in which he hid in order to conceal the truth — for instance, his work at the bank, his arguments at the club, his "inferior race," his attending official celebrations with his wife — all this was in full view. And he judged others by himself, did not believe what he saw, and always supposed that every man led his own real and very interesting life under the cover of secrecy, as under the cover of night. Every personal existence was upheld by a secret, and it was perhaps partly for that reason that every cultivated man took such anxious care that his personal secret should be respected.

After taking his daughter to school, Gurov went to the Slavyansky Bazaar. He took his fur coat off downstairs, went up, and knocked softly at the door. Anna Sergeevna, wearing his favorite gray dress, tired from the trip and the expectation, had been waiting for him since the previous evening; she was pale, looked at him and did not smile, and he had barely come in when she was already leaning on his chest. Their kiss was long, lingering, as if they had not seen each other for two years.

"Well, how is your life there?" he asked. "What's new?"

"Wait, I'll tell you . . . I can't."

She could not speak because she was crying. She turned away from him and pressed a handkerchief to her eyes.

"Well, let her cry a little, and meanwhile I'll sit down," he thought, and sat down in an armchair.

Then he rang and ordered tea; and then, while he drank tea, she went on standing with her face turned to the window . . . She was crying from anxiety, from a sorrowful awareness that their life had turned out so sadly; they only saw each other in secret, they hid from people like thieves! Was their life not broken?

"Well, stop now," he said.

For him it was obvious that this love of theirs would not end soon, that there was no knowing when. Anna Sergeevna's attachment to him grew ever stronger, she adored him, and it would have been unthinkable to tell her that it all really had to end at some point; and she would not have believed it.

He went up to her and took her by the shoulders to caress her, to make a joke, and at that moment he saw himself in the mirror.

His hair was beginning to turn gray. And it seemed strange to him that he had aged so much in those last years, had lost so much of his good looks. The shoulders on which his hands lay were warm and trembled. He felt compassion for this life, still so warm and beautiful, but probably already near the point where it would begin to fade and wither, like his own life. Why did she love him so? Women had always taken him to be other than he was, and they had loved in him, not himself, but a man their imagination had created, whom they had greedily sought all their lives; and then, when they had noticed their mistake, they had still loved him. And not one of them had been happy with him. Time passed, he met women, became intimate, parted, but not once did he love; there was anything else, but not love.

And only now, when his head was gray, had he really fallen in love as one ought to — for the first time in his life.

He and Anna Sergeevna loved each other like very close, dear people, like husband and wife, like tender friends; it seemed to them that fate itself had destined them for each other, and they could not understand why he had a wife and she a husband; and it was as if they were two birds of passage, a male and a female, who had been caught and forced to live in separate cages. They had forgiven each other the things they were ashamed of in the past, they forgave everything in the present, and they felt that this love of theirs had changed them both.

Formerly, in sad moments, he had calmed himself with all sorts of arguments, whatever had come into his head, but now he did not care about any arguments, he felt deep compassion, he wanted to be sincere, tender . . .

"Stop, my good one," he said, "you've had your cry — and enough . . . Let's talk now, we'll think up something."

Then they had a long discussion, talked about how to rid themselves of the need for hiding, for deception, for living in different towns and not seeing each other for long periods. How could they free themselves from these unbearable bonds?

"How? How?" he asked, clutching his head. "How?"

And it seemed that, just a little more — and the solution would be found, and then a new, beautiful life would begin; and it was clear to both of them that the end was still far, far off, and that the most complicated and difficult part was just beginning.

Kate Chopin

Kate Chopin (1851–1904) was born in St. Louis. Her father died when she was four, and she was raised by her Creole mother's family. In 1870 she married Oscar Chopin, a cotton broker. They lived in Louisiana, first in New Orleans and then on a large plantation among the French-speaking Acadians. When her husband died in 1882, Chopin moved with her six children back to St. Louis. Friends encouraged her to write, and when she was nearly forty years old she published her first novel, *At Fault* (1890). Her stories began to appear in *Century* and *Harper's Magazine*, and two collections followed: *Bayou Folk* (1894) and *A Night in Arcadie* (1897). Working steadily from 1889 to 1901, she published two novels, thirteen essays, translations of Maupassant, poems, and over a hundred stories. Her last major work, the novel *The Awakening* (1899), is her masterpiece, but its sympathetic treatment of adultery shocked reviewers and readers throughout America. In St. Louis the novel was taken out of the libraries, and Chopin was denied membership in the St. Louis Fine Arts Club. When her third collection of stories was rejected by her publisher at the end of 1899, Chopin felt herself a literary outcast; she wrote very little in the last years of her life. She died at fifty-three of a brain hemorrhage.

What affronted the genteel readers of the 1890s was Chopin's attempt to write frankly about women's emotions in their relations with men, children, and their own sexuality. After her mother's death in 1885, she stopped being a practicing Catholic and accepted the Darwinian view of human evolution. Seeking God in nature rather than through the church, Chopin wrote freely on the subjects of sex and love, but she said she learned to her sorrow that for American authors, "the limitations imposed upon their art by their environment hamper a full and spontaneous expression." Magazine editors turned down her work if it challenged conventional social behavior, as it does in "The Story of an Hour," which feminist critics championed more than half a century after Chopin's death.

Chopin adopted Guy de Maupassant as a model after translating his stories from the French. She felt, "Here was life, not fiction; for where were the plots, the old fashioned mechanism and stage trappings that in a vague, unthinking way I had fancied were essential to the art of story making?" If her fiction is sometimes marred by stilted language or improbable coincidence, at her best, as in "Désirée's Baby," Chopin subtly emphasized character rather than plot in her dramatization of the tragic repercussions of racial prejudice.

RELATED COMMENTARY
Kate Chopin, "How I Stumbled upon Maupassant," page 1412.

Désirée's Baby

1892

AS THE DAY WAS PLEASANT, Madame Valmondé drove over to L'Abri to see Désirée and the baby.

It made her laugh to think of Désirée with a baby. Why, it seemed but yesterday that Désirée was little more than a baby herself; when Monsieur in riding through the gateway of Valmondé had found her lying asleep in the shadow of the big stone pillar.

The little one awoke in his arms and began to cry for "Dada." That was as much as she could do or say. Some people thought she might have strayed there of her own accord, for she was of the toddling age. The prevailing belief was that she had been purposely left by a party of Texans, whose canvas-covered wagon, late in the day, had crossed the ferry that Coton Maïs kept, just below the plantation. In time Madame Valmondé abandoned every speculation but the one that Désirée had been sent to her by a beneficent Providence to be the child of her affection, seeing that she was without child of the flesh. For the girl grew to be beautiful and gentle, affectionate and sincere, — the idol of Valmondé.

It was no wonder, when she stood one day against the stone pillar in whose shadow she had lain asleep, eighteen years before, that Armand Aubigny riding by and seeing her there, had fallen in love with her. That was the way all the Aubignys fell in love, as if struck by a pistol shot. The wonder was that he had not loved her before; for he had known her since his father brought him home from Paris, a boy of eight, after his mother died there. The passion that awoke in him that day, when he saw her at the gate, swept along like an avalanche, or like a prairie fire, or like anything that drives headlong over all obstacles.

Monsieur Valmondé grew practical and wanted things well considered: that is, the girl's obscure origin. Armand looked into her eyes and did not care. He was reminded that she was nameless. What did it matter about a name when he could give her one of the oldest and proudest in Louisiana? He ordered the *corbeille*[1] from Paris, and contained himself with what patience he could until it arrived; then they were married.

Madame Valmondé had not seen Désirée and the baby for four weeks. When she reached L'Abri she shuddered at the first sight of it, as she always did. It was a sad looking place, which for many years had not known the gentle presence of a mistress, old Monsieur Aubigny having married and buried his wife in France, and she having loved her own land too well ever to leave it. The roof came down steep and black like a cowl, reaching out beyond the wide galleries that encircled the yellow stuccoed house. Big, solemn oaks grew close to it, and their thick-leaved, far-reaching branches shadowed it like a pall. Young Aubigny's rule was a strict one, too, and under it his negroes had forgotten how to be gay, as they had been during the old master's easy-going and indulgent lifetime.

---

[1] Wedding presents (French).

The young mother was recovering slowly, and lay full length, in her soft white muslins and laces, upon a couch. The baby was beside her, upon her arm, where he had fallen sleep, at her breast. The yellow nurse woman sat beside a window fanning herself.

Madame Valmondé bent her portly figure over Désirée and kissed her, holding her an instant tenderly in her arms. Then she turned to the child.

"This is not the baby!" she exclaimed, in startled tones. French was the language spoken at Valmondé in those days.

"I knew you would be astonished," laughed Désirée, "at the way he has grown. The little *cochon de lait*![2] Look at his legs, mamma, and his hands and fingernails, — real fingernails. Zandrine had to cut them this morning. Isn't it true, Zandrine?"

The woman bowed her turbaned head majestically, "Mais si, Madame."

"And the way he cries," went on Désirée, "is deafening. Armand heard him the other day as far away as La Blanche's cabin."

Madame Valmondé had never removed her eyes from the child. She lifted it and walked with it over to the window that was lightest. She scanned the baby narrowly, then looked as searchingly at Zandrine, whose face was turned to gaze across the fields.

"Yes, the child has grown, has changed," said Madame Valmondé, slowly, as she replaced it beside its mother. "What does Armand say?"

Désirée's face became suffused with a glow that was happiness itself.

"Oh, Armand is the proudest father in the parish, I believe, chiefly because it is a boy, to bear his name; though he says not, — that he would have loved a girl as well. But I know it isn't true. I know he says that to please me. And mamma," she added, drawing Madame Valmondé's head down to her and speaking in a whisper, "he hasn't punished one of them — not one of them — since baby is born. Even Négrillon, who pretended to have burnt his leg that he might rest from work — he only laughed, and said Négrillon was a great scamp. Oh, mamma, I'm so happy; it frightens me."

What Désirée said was true. Marriage, and later the birth of his son had softened Armand Aubigny's imperious and exacting nature greatly. This was what made the gentle Désirée so happy, for she loved him desperately. When he frowned she trembled, but loved him. When he smiled, she asked no greater blessing of God. But Armand's dark, handsome face had not often been disfigured by frowns since the day he fell in love with her.

When the baby was about three months old, Désirée awoke one day to the conviction that there was something in the air menacing her peace. It was at first too subtle to grasp. It had only been a disquieting suggestion; an air of mystery among the blacks; unexpected visits from far-off neighbors who could hardly account for their coming. Then a strange, an awful change in her husband's manner, which she dared not ask him to explain. When he spoke to her, it was with averted eyes, from which the old love-light seemed to have gone

---

[2] An endearment (literally, "suckling pig" in French).

out. He absented himself from home; and when there, avoided her presence and that of her child, without excuse. And the very spirit of Satan seemed suddenly to take hold of him in his dealings with the slaves. Désirée was miserable enough to die.

She sat in her room, one hot afternoon, in her *peignoir*, listlessly drawing through her fingers the strands of her long, silky brown hair that hung about her shoulders. The baby, half naked, lay asleep upon her own great mahogany bed, that was like a sumptuous throne, with its satin-lined half-canopy. One of La Blanche's little quadroon boys — half naked too — stood fanning the child slowly with a fan of peacock feathers. Désirée's eyes had been fixed absently and sadly upon the baby, while she was striving to penetrate the threatening mist that she felt closing about her. She looked from her child to the boy who stood beside him, and back again; over and over. "Ah!" It was a cry that she could not help; which she was not conscious of having uttered. The blood turned like ice in her veins, and a clammy moisture gathered upon her face.

She tried to speak to the little quadroon boy; but no sound would come, at first. When he heard his name uttered, he looked up, and his mistress was pointing to the door. He laid aside the great, soft fan, and obediently stole away, over the polished floor, on his bare tiptoes.

She stayed motionless, with gaze riveted upon her child, and her face the picture of fright.

Presently her husband entered the room, and without noticing her, went to a table and began to search among some papers which covered it.

"Armand," she called to him, in a voice which must have stabbed him, if he was human. But he did not notice. "Armand," she said again. Then she rose and tottered towards him. "Armand," she panted once more, clutching his arm, "look at our child. What does it mean? Tell me."

He coldly but gently loosened her fingers from about his arm and thrust the hand away from him. "Tell me what it means!" she cried despairingly.

"It means," he answered lightly, "that the child is not white; it means that you are not white."

A quick conception of all that this accusation meant for her nerved her with unwonted courage to deny it. "It is a lie; it is not true, I am white! Look at my hair, it is brown; and my eyes are gray, Armand, you know they are gray. And my skin is fair," seizing his wrist. "Look at my hand; whiter than yours, Armand," she laughed hysterically.

"As white as La Blanche's," he returned cruelly; and went away leaving her alone with their child.

When she could hold a pen in her hand, she sent a despairing letter to Madame Valmondé.

"My mother, they tell me I am not white. Armand has told me I am not white. For God's sake tell them it is not true. You must know it is not true. I shall die. I must die. I cannot be so unhappy, and live."

The answer that came was as brief:

"My own Désirée: Come home to Valmondé; back to your mother who loves you. Come with your child."

When the letter reached Désirée she went with it to her husband's study, and laid it open upon the desk before which he sat. She was like a stone image: silent, white, motionless after she placed it there.

In silence he ran his cold eyes over the written words. He said nothing. "Shall I go, Armand?" she asked in tones sharp with agonized suspense.

"Yes, go."

"Do you want me to go?"

"Yes, I want you to go."

He thought Almighty God had dealt cruelly and unjustly with him; and felt, somehow, that he was paying Him back in kind when he stabbed thus into his wife's soul. Moreover he no longer loved her, because of the unconscious injury she had brought upon his home and his name.

She turned away like one stunned by a blow, and walked slowly towards the door, hoping he would call her back.

"Good-by, Armand," she moaned.

He did not answer her. That was his last blow at fate.

Désirée went in search of her child. Zandrine was pacing the sombre gallery with it. She took the little one from the nurse's arms with no word of explanation, and descending the steps, walked away, under the live-oak branches.

It was an October afternoon; the sun was just sinking. Out in the still fields the negroes were picking cotton.

Désirée had not changed the thin white garment nor the slippers which she wore. Her hair was uncovered and the sun's rays brought a golden gleam from its brown meshes. She did not take the broad, beaten road which led to the far-off plantation of Valmondé. She walked across a deserted field, where the stubble bruised her tender feet, so delicately shod, and tore her thin gown to shreds.

She disappeared among the reeds and willows that grew thick along the banks of the deep, sluggish bayou; and she did not come back again.

Some weeks later there was a curious scene enacted at L'Abri. In the centre of the smoothly swept back yard was a great bonfire. Armand Aubigny sat in the wide hallway that commanded a view of the spectacle; and it was he who dealt out to a half dozen negroes the material which kept this fire ablaze.

A graceful cradle of willow, with all its dainty furbishings, was laid upon the pyre, which had already been fed with the richness of a priceless *layette*. Then there were silk gowns, and velvet and satin ones added to these; laces, too, and embroideries; bonnets and gloves; for the *corbeille* had been of rare quality.

The last thing to go was a tiny bundle of letters; innocent little scribblings that Désirée had sent to him during the days of their espousal. There was the remnant of one back in the drawer from which he took them. But it was not Désirée's; it was part of an old letter from his mother to his father. He read it. She was thanking God for the blessing of her husband's love: —

"But, above all," she wrote, "night and day, I thank the good God for having so arranged our lives that our dear Armand will never know that his mother, who adores him, belongs to the race that is cursed with the brand of slavery."

The Story of an Hour

1894

KNOWING THAT MRS. MALLARD was afflicted with a heart trouble, great care was taken to break to her as gently as possible the news of her husband's death.

It was her sister Josephine who told her, in broken sentences; veiled hints that revealed in half concealing. Her husband's friend Richards was there, too, near her. It was he who had been in the newspaper office when intelligence of the railroad disaster was received, with Brently Mallard's name leading the list of "killed." He had only taken the time to assure himself of its truth by a second telegram, and had hastened to forestall any less careful, less tender friend in bearing the sad message.

She did not hear the story as many women have heard the same, with a paralyzed inability to accept its significance. She wept at once, with sudden, wild abandonment, in her sister's arms. When the storm of grief had spent itself she went away to her room alone. She would have no one follow her.

There stood, facing the open window, a comfortable, roomy armchair. Into this she sank, pressed down by a physical exhaustion that haunted her body and seemed to reach into her soul.

She could see in the open square before her house the tops of trees that were all aquiver with the new spring life. The delicious breath of rain was in the air. In the street below a peddler was crying his wares. The notes of a distant song which some one was singing reached her faintly, and countless sparrows were twittering in the eaves.

There were patches of blue sky showing here and there through the clouds that had met and piled one above the other in the west facing her window.

She sat with her head thrown back upon the cushion of the chair, quite motionless, except when a sob came up into her throat and shook her, as a child who had cried itself to sleep continues to sob in its dreams.

She was young, with a fair, calm face, whose lines bespoke repression and even a certain strength. But now there was a dull stare in her eyes, whose gaze was fixed away off yonder on one of those patches of blue sky. It was not a glance of reflection, but rather indicated a suspension of intelligent thought.

There was something coming to her and she was waiting for it, fearfully. What was it? She did not know; it was too subtle and elusive to name. But she felt it, creeping out of the sky, reaching toward her through the sounds, the scents, the color that filled the air.

Now her bosom rose and fell tumultuously. She was beginning to recognize this thing that was approaching to possess her, and she was striving to beat it back with her will — as powerless as her two white slender hands would have been.

When she abandoned herself a little whispered word escaped her slightly parted lips. She said it over and over under her breath: "free, free, free!" The vacant stare and the look of terror that had followed it went from her eyes.

They stayed keen and bright. Her pulses beat fast, and the coursing blood warmed and relaxed every inch of her body.

She did not stop to ask if it were or were not a monstrous joy that held her. A clear and exalted perception enabled her to dismiss the suggestion as trivial.

She knew that she would weep again when she saw the kind, tender hands folded in death; the face that had never looked save with love upon her, fixed and gray and dead. But she saw beyond that bitter moment a long procession of years to come that would belong to her absolutely. And she opened and spread her arms out to them in welcome.

There would be no one to live for her during those coming years: she would live for herself. There would be no powerful will bending hers in that blind persistence with which men and women believe they have a right to impose a private will upon a fellow-creature. A kind intention or a cruel intention made the act seem no less a crime as she looked upon it in that brief moment of illumination.

And yet she had loved him — sometimes. Often she had not. What did it matter! What could love, the unsolved mystery, count for in face of this posses-sion of self-assertion which she suddenly recognized as the strongest impulse of her being!

"Free! Body and soul free!" she kept whispering.

Josephine was kneeling before the closed door with her lips to the keyhole, imploring for admission. "Louise, open the door! I beg; open the door — you will make yourself ill. What are you doing, Louise? For heaven's sake open the door."

"Go away. I am not making myself ill." No; she was drinking in a very elixir of life through that open window.

Her fancy was running riot along those days ahead of her. Spring days, and summer days, and all sorts of days that would be her own. She breathed a quick prayer that life might be long. It was only yesterday she had thought with a shudder that life might be long.

She arose at length and opened the door to her sister's importunities. There was a feverish triumph in her eyes, and she carried herself unwittingly like a goddess of Victory. She clasped her sister's waist, and together they descended the stairs. Richards stood waiting for them at the bottom.

Some one was opening the front door with a latchkey. It was Brently Mallard who entered, a little travel-stained, composedly carrying his gripsack and umbrella. He had been far from the scene of the accident, and did not even know there had been one. He stood amazed at Josephine's piercing cry; at Richards' quick motion to screen him from the view of his wife.

But Richards was too late.

When the doctors came they said she had died of heart disease — of joy that kills.

Sandra Cisneros

Sandra Cisneros (b. 1954), the daughter of a Mexican father and a Chicana mother, grew up in ghetto neighborhoods in Chicago and began writing poetry when she was ten years old. Her six brothers so dominated the household that she remembers that she felt she had "seven fathers." Cisneros spoke Spanish at home with her father and on her frequent trips to Mexico to visit her grandmother, but she did not think of herself as a Chicana writer until she began a series of autobiographical sketches as a graduate student in the M.A. program at the University of Iowa's Writers' Workshop in 1977. Then she discovered her literary voice, realizing the uniqueness of her experience growing up as a poor Latina in Chicago:

> Everyone seemed to have some communal knowledge which I did not have. . . . This caused me to question myself, to become defensive. What did I, Sandra Cisneros, know? What could I know? My classmates were from the best schools in the country. They had been bred as fine hothouse flowers. I was a yellow weed among the city's cracks.

Cisneros says that she became a writer because she was "determined to fill a literary void . . . trying to write the stories that haven't been written." These early sketches developed into the book published as *The House on Mango Street* (1983), over forty short narratives that were highly praised by critics and won the 1985 Before Columbus American Book Award. Cisneros had found a way to write stories

> that were a cross between poetry and fiction. . . . [I] wanted to write a collection which could be read at any random point without having any knowledge of what came before or after. Or, that could be read in a series to tell one big story. I wanted stories like poems, compact and lyrical and ending with reverberation.

As Joyce Carol Oates has observed about stories such as "Barbie-Q," Cisneros's "emotionally rich subject is the Latino community, specifically the experience of growing up female in a male-dominated society; her work . . . might be as readily classified as prose poetry as prose fiction." To date Cisneros has published three books of poetry in addition to a second book of stories, *Woman Hollering Creek* (1991). *Caramelo* (2002) and *Have You Seen Marie* (2012) are recent novels.

RELATED STORY
Helena María Viramontes, "Miss Clairol," page 1301.

Barbie-Q

1991

For Licha

YOURS IS THE ONE with mean eyes and a ponytail. Striped swimsuit, stilettos, sunglasses, and gold hoop earrings. Mine is the one with bubble hair. Red swimsuit, stilettos, pearl earrings, and a wire stand. But that's all we can afford, besides one extra outfit apiece. Yours, "Red Flair," sophisticated A-line coatdress with a Jackie Kennedy pillbox hat, white gloves, handbag, and heels included. Mine, "Solo in the Spotlight," evening elegance in black glitter strapless gown with a puffy skirt at the bottom like a mermaid tail, formal-length gloves, pink chiffon scarf, and mike included. From so much dressing and undressing, the black glitter wears off where her titties stick out. This and a dress invented from an old sock when we cut holes here and here and here, the cuff rolled over for the glamorous, fancy-free, off-the-shoulder look.

Every time the same story. Your Barbie is roommates with my Barbie, and my Barbie's boyfriend comes over and your Barbie steals him, okay? Kiss kiss kiss. Then the two Barbies fight. You dumbbell! He's mine. Oh no he's not, you stinky! Only Ken's invisible, right? Because we don't have money for a stupid-looking boy doll when we'd both rather ask for a new Barbie outfit next Christmas. We have to make do with your mean-eyed Barbie and my bubblehead Barbie and our one outfit apiece not including the sock dress.

Until next Sunday when we are walking through the flea market on Maxwell Street and *there!* Lying on the street next to some tool bits, and platform shoes with the heels all squashed, and a fluorescent green wicker wastebasket, and aluminum foil, and hubcaps, and a pink shag rug, and windshield wiper blades, and dusty mason jars, and a coffee can full of rusty nails. *There!* Where? Two Mattel boxes. One with the "Career Gal" ensemble, snappy black-and-white business suit, three-quarter-length sleeve jacket with kick-pleat skirt, red sleeveless shell, gloves, pumps, and matching hat included. The other, "Sweet Dreams," dreamy pink-and-white plaid nightgown and matching robe, lace-trimmed slippers, hairbrush and hand mirror included. How much? Please, please, please, please, please, please, please, until they say okay.

On the outside you and me skipping and humming but inside we are doing loopity-loops and pirouetting. Until at the next vendor's stand, next to boxed pies, and bright orange toilet brushes, and rubber gloves, and wrench sets, and bouquets of feather flowers, and glass towel racks, and steel wool, and Alvin and the Chipmunks records, *there!* And *there!* And *there!* And *there!* and *there!* and *there!* and *there!* Bendable Legs Barbie with her new page-boy hairdo. Midge, Barbie's best friend. Ken, Barbie's boyfriend. Skipper, Barbie's little sister. Tutti and Todd, Barbie and Skipper's tiny twin sister and brother. Skipper's friends, Scooter and Ricky. Alan, Ken's buddy. And Francie, Barbie's MOD'ern cousin.

Everybody today selling toys, all of them damaged with water and smelling of smoke. Because a big toy warehouse on Halsted Street burned down yesterday — see there? — the smoke still rising and drifting across the Dan Ryan expressway. And now there is a big fire sale at Maxwell Street, today only.

So what if we didn't get our new Bendable Legs Barbie and Midge and Ken and Skipper and Tutti and Todd and Scooter and Ricky and Alan and Francie in nice clean boxes and had to buy them on Maxwell Street, all water-soaked and sooty. So what if our Barbies smell like smoke when you hold them up to your nose even after you wash and wash and wash them. And if the prettiest doll, Barbie's MOD'ern cousin Francie with real eyelashes, eyelash brush included, has a left foot that's melted a little — so? If you dress her in her new "Prom Pinks" outfit, satin splendor with matching coat, gold belt, clutch, and hair bow included, so long as you don't lift her dress, right? — who's to know.

Samuel Clemens (Mark Twain)

Mark Twain was the name under which Samuel Langhorne Clemens (1835–1910) published his writing. Clemens was born in the village of Florida, Missouri, the son of a lawyer from Virginia. When he was five, the family moved to Hannibal, Missouri, on the west bank of the Mississippi River — "a heavenly place for a boy," he later remembered. His formal schooling ended at age twelve, when his father died and he was apprenticed to his brother Orion, who edited a country newspaper. At this time he saw his first story printed — "The Dandy Frightening the Squatter," a typical piece of frontier humor. For years he worked as a journeyman printer in St. Louis, New York City, Philadelphia, and Cincinnati. Then he became an apprentice steamboat pilot on the Mississippi in 1857, and he remained on the river until the Civil War. In his book *Life on the Mississippi* (1883), Twain wrote that on the river he became "acquainted with all the different types of human nature that are to be found in fiction, biography or history." After considering enlisting in the Confederate army, he joined his brother Orion in the Nevada Territory, first prospecting for gold and then working for the Virginia City *Enterprise*. It was in his writing for this newspaper that he first used the pseudonym "Mark Twain," a call of the Mississippi pilots signifying a depth of two fathoms (twelve feet), just barely safe water for steamboats.

Twain's early work for newspapers was influenced by the topical humorists of his time. He first achieved recognition as a writer in 1865 with a tall tale, "Jim Smiley and His Jumping Frog," which was published in the *New York Saturday Press*. Twain later said he didn't think much of the story, but it was published in book form as "The Celebrated Jumping Frog of Calaveras County" with other sketches in 1867. Two years later his career was established with the travel book *The Innocents Abroad*. He achieved further fame (and fortune) with the popular success of his novels, *The Adventures of Tom Sawyer* (1876), *The Prince and the Pauper* (1882), *A Connecticut Yankee in King Arthur's Court* (1889), and many other books, including his masterpiece, *The Adventures of Huckleberry Finn* (1884).

Twain had a sensitive ear for the varied riches of American regional dialects, and he was our first author to write great works using a genuinely colloquial and native American speech. He published collections of short stories throughout his life, beginning with his first book, *The Celebrated Jumping Frog of Calaveras County and Other Sketches* (1867), and including such titles as *Mark Twain's Sketches* (1875), *Merry Tales* (1892), and *My Debut as a Literary Person, with Other Essays and Stories* (1903). *The Complete Stories of Mark Twain*, sixty in all, was published in 1957.

RELATED COMMENTARY
Samuel Clemens (Mark Twain), "Private History of the 'Jumping Frog' Story," page 1413.

The Celebrated Jumping Frog of Calaveras County

1865

IN COMPLIANCE WITH the request of a friend of mine, who wrote me from the East, I called on good-natured, garrulous old Simon Wheeler, and inquired after my friend's friend, *Leonidas W.* Smiley, as requested to do, and I hereunto append the result. I have a lurking suspicion that *Leonidas W.* Smiley is a myth; that my friend never knew such a personage; and that he only conjectured that, if I asked old Wheeler about him, it would remind him of his infamous *Jim* Smiley, and he would go to work and bore me nearly to death with some infernal reminiscence of him as long and tedious as it should be useless to me. If that was the design, it certainly succeeded.

I found Simon Wheeler dozing comfortably by the bar-room stove of the old, dilapidated tavern in the ancient mining camp of Angel's, and I noticed that he was fat and bald-headed, and had an expression of winning gentleness and simplicity upon his tranquil countenance. He roused up and gave me good-day. I told him a friend of mine had commissioned me to make some inquiries about a cherished companion of his boyhood named *Leonidas W.* Smiley — *Rev. Leonidas W.* Smiley — a young minister of the Gospel, who he had heard was at one time a resident of Angel's Camp. I added that, if Mr. Wheeler could tell me anything about this Rev. Leonidas W. Smiley, I would feel under many obligations to him.

Simon Wheeler backed me into a corner and blockaded me there with his chair, and then sat me down and reeled off the monotonous narrative which follows this paragraph. He never smiled, he never frowned, he never changed his voice from the gentle-flowing key to which he tuned the initial sentence, he never betrayed the slightest suspicion of enthusiasm; but all through the interminable narrative there ran a vein of impressive earnestness and sincerity, which showed me plainly that, so far from his imagining that there was anything ridiculous or funny about his story, he regarded it as a really important matter, and admired its two heroes as men of transcendent genius in finesse. To me, the spectacle of a man drifting serenely along through such a queer yarn without ever smiling, was exquisitely absurd. As I said before, I asked him to tell me what he knew of Rev. Leonidas W. Smiley, and he replied as follows. I let him go on in his own way, and never interrupted him once:

There was a feller here once by the name of *Jim* Smiley, in the winter of '49 — or maybe it was the spring of '50 — I don't recollect exactly, somehow, though what makes me think it was one or the other is because I remember the big flume wasn't finished when he first came to the camp; but anyway, he was the curiousest man about always betting on anything that turned up you ever see, if he could get anybody to bet on the other side; and if he couldn't, he'd change sides. Any way that suited the other man would suit him — any way just so's he got a bet, he was satisfied. But still he was lucky, uncommon lucky; he most always come out winner. He was always ready and laying for a chance; there couldn't be no solit'ry thing mentioned but that feller'd offer to bet on it, and take any side you please, as I was just telling you. If there was a horse race, you'd find him flush, or you'd find him busted at the end of it; if there was a dogfight, he'd bet on it; if there was a cat-fight, he'd bet on it; if there was a chicken-fight, he'd bet on it; why, if there was two birds setting on a fence, he would bet you which one would fly first; or if there was a camp meeting, he would be there reg'lar, to bet on Parson Walker, which he judged to be the best exhorter about here, and so he was, too, and a good man. If he even seen a straddlebug start to go anywheres, he would bet you how long it would take him to get wherever he was going to, and if you took him up, he would foller that straddlebug to Mexico but what he would find out where he was bound for and how long he was on the road. Lots of the boys here has seen that Smiley, and can tell you about him. Why, it never made no difference to *him* — he would bet on *anything* — the dangdest feller. Parson Walker's wife laid very sick once, for a good while, and it seemed as if they warn't going to save her; but one morning he come in, and Smiley asked how she was, and he said she was considerable better — thank the Lord for his inf'nit mercy — and coming on so smart that, with the blessing of Prov'dence, she'd get well yet; and Smiley, before he thought, says, "Well, I'll risk two-and-a-half that she don't, anyway."

Thish-yer Smiley had a mare — the boys called her the fifteen-minute nag, but that was only in fun, you know, because, of course, she was faster than that — and he used to win money on that horse, for all she was so slow and always had the asthma, or the distemper, or the consumption, or something of that kind. They used to give her two or three hundred yards start, and then pass her under way; but always at the fag end of the race she'd get excited and desperate-like, and come cavorting and straddling up, and scattering her legs around limber, sometimes in the air, and sometimes out to one side amongst the fences, and kicking up m-o-r-e dust, and raising m-o-r-e racket with her coughing and sneezing and blowing her nose — and always fetch up at the stand just about a neck ahead, as near as you could cipher it down.

And he had a little small bull pup, that to look at him you'd think he wan't worth a cent, but to set around and look ornery, and lay for a chance to steal something. But as soon as money was up on him, he was a different dog; his underjaw'd begin to stick out like the fo-castle of a steamboat, and his teeth would uncover, and shine savage like the furnaces. And a dog might tackle him, and bully-rag him, and bite him, and throw him over his shoulder two or three times, and Andrew Jackson — which was the name of the pup — Andrew Jackson would never let on but what *he* was satisfied, and hadn't expected nothing else — and the bets being doubled and doubled on the other side all the time, till the money was all up; and then all of a sudden he would grab that other dog jest by the j'int of his hind leg and freeze to it — not chaw, you understand, but only jest grip and hang on till they throwed up the sponge, if it was a year. Smiley always come out winner on that pup, till he harnessed a dog once that didn't have no hind legs, because they'd been sawed off by a circular saw, and when the thing had gone along far enough, and the money was all up, and he come to make a snatch for his pet holt, he saw in a minute how he'd been imposed on, and how the other dog had him in the door, so to speak, and he 'peared surprised, and then he looked sorter discouraged-like, and didn't try no more to win the fight, and so he got shucked out bad. He give Smiley a look, as much as to say his heart was broke, and it was *his* fault for putting up a dog that hadn't no hind legs for him to take holt of, which was his main dependence in a fight, and then he limped off a piece and laid down and died. It was a good pup, was that Andrew Jackson, and would have made a name for hisself if he'd lived, for the stuff was in him, and he had genius — I know it, because he hadn't had no opportunities to speak of, and it don't stand to reason that a dog could make such a fight as he could under them circumstances, if he hadn't no talent. It always makes me feel sorry when I think of that last fight of his'n, and the way it turned out.

Well, thish-yer Smiley had rat-tarriers, and chicken cocks, and tomcats, and all them kind of things, till you couldn't rest, and you couldn't fetch nothing for him to bet on but he'd match you. He ketched a frog one day, and took him home, and said he cal'klated to educate him; and so he never done nothing for three months but set in his back yard and learn that frog to jump. And you bet you he *did* learn him, too. He'd give him a little punch behind, and the next minute you'd see that frog whirling in the air like a doughnut — see him turn one summerset, or may be a couple, if he got a good start, and come down flatfooted and all right, like a cat. He got him up so in the matter of catching flies, and kept him in practice so constant, that he'd nail a fly every time as far as he could see him. Smiley said all a frog wanted was education, and he could do most anything — and I believe him. Why, I've seen him set Dan'l Webster down here on this floor — Dan'l Webster was the name of the frog — and sing out, "Flies, Dan'l, flies!" and quicker'n you could wink, he'd spring straight up, and snake a fly off'n the counter there, and flop down on the floor again as solid as a gob of mud, and fall to scratching the side of his head with his hind foot as indifferent as if he hadn't no idea he'd been doin' any more'n any frog might do. You never see a frog so modest and straightfor'ard as he was, for all he was so gifted. And when it come to fair and square jumping on a dead level, he could get over more ground at one straddle than any animal of his breed you ever see. Jumping on a dead level was his strong suit, you understand; and when it come to that, Smiley would ante up money on him as long as he had a red.[1] Smiley was monstrous proud of his frog, and well he might be, for fellers that had traveled and been everywheres, all said he laid over any frog that ever *they* see.

Well, Smiley kept the beast in a little lattice box, and he used to fetch him downtown sometimes and lay for a bet. One day a feller — a stranger in the camp, he was — come across him with his box, and says:

"What might it be that you've got in the box?"

And Smiley says, sorter indifferent like, "It might be a parrot, or it might be a canary, maybe, but it an't — it's only just a frog."

---

[1] A penny.

And the feller took it, and looked at it careful, and turned it round this way and that, and says, "H'm — so 'tis. Well, what's *he* good for?"

"Well," Smiley says, easy and careless, "he's good enough for *one* thing, I should judge — he can outjump any frog in Calaveras county."

The feller took the box again, and took another long, particular look, and give it back to Smiley, and says, very deliberate, "Well, I don't see no p'ints about that frog that's any better'n any other frog."

"Maybe you don't," Smiley says. "Maybe you understand frogs, and maybe you don't understand 'em; maybe you've had experience, and maybe you an't only a amature, as it were. Anyways, I've got *my* opinion, and I'll risk forty dollars that he can outjump any frog in Calaveras county."

And the feller studied a minute, and then says, kinder sad like, "Well, I'm only a stranger here, and I an't got no frog; but if I had a frog, I'd bet you."

And then Smiley says, "That's all right — that's all right — if you'll hold my box a minute, I'll go and get you a frog." And so the feller took the box, and put up his forty dollars along with Smiley's, and set down to wait.

So he set there a good while thinking and thinking to hisself, and then he got the frog out and prized his mouth open and took a teaspoon and filled him full of quail shot — filled him pretty near up to his chin — and set him on the floor. Smiley he went to the swamp and slopped around in the mud for a long time, and finally he ketched a frog, and fetched him in, and give him to this feller, and says:

"Now, if you're ready, set him alongside of Dan'l, with his fore-paws just even with Dan'l, and I'll give the word." Then he says, "One — two — three — jump!" and him and the feller touched up the frogs from behind, and the new frog hopped off, but Dan'l give a heave, and hysted up his shoulders — so — like a Frenchman, but it wan't no use — he couldn't budge; he was planted as solid as an anvil, and he couldn't no more stir than if he was anchored out. Smiley was a good deal surprised, and he was disgusted too, but he didn't have no idea what the matter was, of course.

The feller took the money and started away; and when he was going out at the door, he sorter jerked his thumb over his shoulders — this way — at Dan'l, and says again, very deliberate, "Well, *I* don't see no p'ints about that frog that's any better'n any other frog."

Smiley he stood scratching his head and looking down at Dan'l a long time, and at last he says, "I do wonder what in the nation that frog throw'd off for — I wonder if there an't something the matter with him — he 'pears to look mighty baggy, somehow." And he ketched Dan'l by the nap of the neck, and lifted him up and says, "Why, blame my cats, if he don't weigh five pound!" and turned him upside down, and he belched out a double handful of shot. And then he see how it was, and he was the maddest man — he set the frog down and took out after that feller, but he never ketched him. And —

[Here Simon Wheeler heard his name called from the front yard, and got up to see what was wanted.] And turning to me as he moved away, he said: "Just set where you are, stranger, and rest easy — I an't going to be gone a second."

But, by your leave, I did not think that a continuation of the history of the enterprising vagabond *Jim* Smiley would be likely to afford me much information concerning the Rev. *Leonidas W.* Smiley, and so I started away.

At the door I met the sociable Wheeler returning, and he buttonholed me and recommenced:

"Well, thish-yer Smiley had a yaller one-eyed cow that didn't have no tail, only jest a short stump like a bannanner, and —"

"Oh! hang Smiley and his afflicted cow," I muttered, good-naturedly, and bidding the old gentleman good-day, I departed.

Joseph Conrad

Joseph Conrad (1857–1924) was born Jozef Teodore Konrad Nalecz Korzeniowski near Kiev, in what was then Russian Poland. His parents died when he was young, and he was raised by his uncle. At the age of seventeen Conrad went to sea, and for many years he sailed in the French and British navies. He then took a job as steamboat captain on the Congo River, an experience that matured him: "Before I went to the Congo I was just a mere animal," he later wrote. After leaving Africa he settled in England to become a professional writer. Conrad did not learn English until after he was twenty (Polish was his first language, French his second), but he is considered one of the supreme English stylists despite having once complained that writing in English was like throwing mud at a wall. In 1895 he published his first novel, *Almayer's Folly*, followed by a stream of others: *An Outcast of the Islands* (1896), *The Nigger of the "Narcissus"* (1897), *Lord Jim* (1902), and *Nostromo* (1904). His later novels included *The Secret Agent* (1907), *Chance* (1913), and *Victory* (1915).

Conrad believed that his imagination was his most precious possession as a writer, and he did not consider himself bound by what he called the "fettering dogmas of some romantic, realistic, or naturalistic creed." He said that the avowed aim of his fiction was "to make you hear, to make you feel, above all to make you see." The epic sweep of his descriptions of nature often suggests a disquieting sense of the larger world's indifference to the fates of the mortal men and women whose stories he unfolds. In his use of rich symbolism and his subtle exploration of human psychology, he anticipated the direction modern fiction would take.

Conrad structured "Heart of Darkness" as a "frame story" to conform to a formula often used in *Blackwood's*, the English magazine for which he wrote it. But the depth of his psychological insight and the grandeur of his prose lifts "Heart of Darkness" far above a formula story. In Marlow's identification with Kurtz, Conrad explored another twist to the "double" theme, the idea that an honorable man might be attracted to his opposite. As the critic Tony Tanner has said, Conrad showed "that a hidden part of a man committed to order and the rules of society might suddenly embrace and identify itself with a being, a presence, an apparition which seems most antithetic to his own conscious self, a walking reminder of all that inner darkness and weakness which civilized man has suppressed in order to make group life possible."

Conrad felt that he might have made Kurtz "too symbolic" and that his story "pushed a little (but only very little)" beyond the actual facts of his four-month experience in the Congo. He justified his exaggeration, however, by his strong desire to give a political dimension to "Heart of Darkness." When the story was published, in 1899, it gave literary expression to an entire age's perception of the Congo as a place of horror and human degradation resulting from ruthless colonialism. In the story, the "Company" collecting "ivory" from the natives is a thinly disguised reference to the Anglo-Belgium India-Rubber Company. During the twenty years of King Leopold of Belgium's control of the company (he personally owned 50 percent of its stock), its agents killed an estimated 5 million people in the Congo, terrorizing and murdering the natives who failed to meet rubber quotas. Leopold himself cleared at least $20 million in profit before he lost his monopoly control of the trade as a result of the reform movement sparked by "Heart of Darkness" and other eyewitness reports.

RELATED COMMENTARIES
Chinua Achebe, "An Image of Africa: Racism in Conrad's 'Heart of Darkness,'" page 1385; Edward W. Said, "The Past and the Present: Joseph Conrad and the Fiction of Autobiography," page 1513; Leo Tolstoy, "The Works of Guy de Maupassant," page 1531.

Heart of Darkness

1899

I

The *Nellie*, a cruising yawl, swung to her anchor without a flutter of the sails, and was at rest. The flood had made, the wind was nearly calm, and being bound down the river, the only thing for it was to come to and wait for the turn of the tide.

The sea-reach of the Thames stretched before us like the beginning of an interminable waterway. In the offing the sea and the sky were welded together without a joint, and in the luminous space the tanned sails of the barges drifting up with the tide seemed to stand still in red clusters of canvas sharply peaked, with gleams of varnished sprits. A haze rested on the low shores that ran out to sea in vanishing flatness. The air was dark above Gravesend, and farther back still seemed condensed into a mournful gloom, brooding motionless over the biggest, and the greatest, town on earth.

The Director of Companies was our captain and our host. We four affectionately watched his back as he stood in the bows looking to seaward. On the whole river there was nothing that looked half so nautical. He resembled a pilot, which to a seaman is trustworthiness personified. It was difficult to realize his work was not out there in the luminous estuary, but behind him, within the brooding gloom.

Between us there was, as I have already said somewhere, the bond of the sea. Besides holding our hearts together through long periods of separation, it had the effect of making us tolerant of each other's yarns—and even convictions. The Lawyer—the best of old fellows—had, because of his many years and many virtues, the only cushion on deck, and was lying on the only rug. The accountant had brought out already a box of dominoes, and was toying architecturally with the bones. Marlow sat cross-legged right aft, leaning against the mizzen-mast. He had sunken cheeks, a yellow complexion, a straight back, and ascetic aspect, and, with his arms dropped, the palms of hands outwards, resembled an idol. The director, satisfied the anchor had good hold, made his way aft and sat down amongst us. We exchanged a few words lazily. Afterwards there was silence on board the yacht. For some reason or other we did not begin that game of dominoes. We felt meditative, and fit for nothing but placid staring. The day was ending in a serenity of still and exquisite brilliance. The water shone pacifically; the sky, without a speck, was a benign immensity of unstained light; the very mist on the Essex marshes was like a gauzy and radiant fabric, hung from the wooded rises inland, and draping the low shores in diaphanous folds. Only the gloom to the west, brooding over the upper reaches, became more somber every minute, as if angered by the approach of the sun.

And at last, in its curved and imperceptible fall, the sun sank low, and from glowing white changed to a dull red without rays and without heat, as if about to go out suddenly, stricken to death by the touch of that gloom brooding over a crowd of men.

Forthwith a change came over the water, and the serenity became less brilliant but more profound. The old river in its broad reach rested unruffled at the decline of day, after ages of good service done to the race that peopled its banks, spread out in the tranquil dignity of a waterway leading to the uttermost ends of the earth. We looked at the venerable stream not in the vivid flush of a short day that comes and departs forever, but in the august light of abiding memories. And indeed nothing is easier for a man who has, as the phrase goes, "followed the sea" with reverence and affection, than to evoke the great spirit of the past upon the lower reaches of the Thames. The tidal current runs to and fro in its unceasing service, crowded with memories of men and ships it had borne to the rest of home or to the battles of the sea. It had known and served all the men of whom the nation is proud, from Sir Francis Drake[1] to Sir John Franklin,[2] knights all, titled and untitled — the knights-errant of the sea. It had borne all the ships whose names are like jewels flashing in the night of time, from the *Golden Hind* returning with her round flanks full of treasure, to be visited by the Queen's Highness and thus pass out of the gigantic tale, to the *Erebus* and *Terror*, bound on other conquests — and that never returned. It had known the ships and the men. They had sailed from Deptford, from Greenwich, from Erith — the adventurers and the settlers; kings' ships and the ships of men on 'Change;[3] captains, admirals, the dark "interlopers" of the Eastern trade, and the commissioned "Generals" of East India fleets. Hunters for gold or pursuers of fame, they all had gone out on that stream, bearing the sword, and often the torch, messengers of the night within the land, bearers of a spark from the sacred fire. What greatness had not floated on the ebb of that river into the mystery of an unknown earth! . . . The dreams of men, the seed of commonwealths, the germs of empires.

---

[1] Sir Francis Drake (1540–1596), English navigator and pirate who sailed around the world (1577–1580) and led the fleet that defeated the Spanish Armada in 1588. The *Golden Hind* was his ship.

[2] Sir John Franklin (1786–1847), English explorer of the Arctic. His ships the *Erebus* and the *Terror* were lost in an expedition to find the Northwest Passage from the Atlantic to the Pacific.

[3] Investors at the London Stock Exchange.

The sun set; the dusk fell on the stream, and lights began to appear along the shore. The Chapman lighthouse, a three-legged thing erect on a mud-flat, shone strongly. Lights of ships moved in the fairway — a great stir of lights going up and going down. And farther west on the upper reaches the place of the monstrous town was still marked ominously on the sky, a brooding gloom in sunshine, a lurid glare under the stars.

"And this also," said Marlow suddenly, "has been one of the dark places on the earth."

He was the only man of us who still "followed the sea." The worst that could be said of him was that he did not represent his class. He was a seaman, but he was a wanderer, too, while most seamen lead, if one may so express it, a sedentary life. Their minds are of the stay-at-home order, and their home is always with them — the ship; and so is their country — the sea. One ship is very much like another, and the sea is always the same. In the immutability of their surroundings the foreign shores, the foreign faces, the changing immensity of life, glide past, veiled not by a sense of mystery but by a slightly disdainful ignorance; for there is nothing mysterious to a seaman unless it be the sea itself, which is the mistress of his existence and as inscrutable as Destiny. For the rest, after his hours of work, a casual stroll or a casual spree on shore suffices to unfold for him the secret of a whole continent, and generally he finds the secret not worth knowing. The yarns of seamen have a direct simplicity, the whole meaning of which lies within the shell of a cracked nut. But Marlow was not typical (if his propensity to spin yarns be excepted), and to him the meaning of an episode was not inside like a kernel but outside, enveloping the tale which brought it out only as a glow brings out a haze, in the likeness of one of these misty halos that sometimes are made visible by the special illumination of moonshine.

His remark did not seem at all surprising. It was just like Marlow. It was accepted in silence. No one took the trouble to grunt even; and presently he said, very slow —

"I was thinking of very old times, when the Romans first came here, nineteen hundred years ago — the other day. . . . Light came out of this river since — you say Knights? Yes; but it is like a running blaze on a plain, like a flash of lightning in the clouds. We live in the flicker — may it last as long as the old earth keeps rolling! But darkness was here yesterday. Imagine the feelings of a commander of a fine — what d'ye call 'em? — trireme in the Mediterranean, ordered suddenly to the north; run overland across the Gauls in a hurry; put in charge of one of these craft the legionaries — a wonderful lot of handy men they must have been, too — used to build, apparently by the hundred, in a month or two, if we may believe what we read. Imagine him here — the very end of the world, a sea the color of lead, a sky the color of smoke, a kind of ship about as rigid as a concertina — and going up this river with stores, or orders, or what you like. Sandbanks, marshes, forests, savages — precious little to eat fit for a civilized man, nothing but Thames water to drink. No Falernian wine[4] here, no going

---

[4] Legendary Roman wine.

ashore. Here and there a military camp lost in a wilderness, like a needle in a bundle of hay — cold, fog, tempests, disease, exile, and death — death skulking in the air, in the water, in the bush. They must have been dying like flies here. Oh, yes — he did it. Did it very well, too, no doubt, and without thinking much about it either, except afterwards to brag of what he had gone through in his time, perhaps. They were men enough to face the darkness. And perhaps he was cheered by keeping his eye on a chance of promotion to the fleet at Ravenna by and by, if he had good friends in Rome and survived the awful climate. Or think of a decent young citizen in a toga — perhaps too much dice, you know — coming out here in the train of some prefect, or taxgatherer, or trader even, to mend his fortunes. Land in a swamp, march through the woods, and in some inland post feel the savagery, the utter savagery, had closed round him — all that mysterious life of the wilderness that stirs in the forest, in the jungles, in the hearts of wild men. There's no initiation either into such mysteries. He has to live in the midst of the incomprehensible, which is also detestable. And it has a fascination, too, that goes to work upon him. The fascination of the abomination — you know, imagine the growing regrets, the longing to escape, the powerless disgust, the surrender, the hate."

He paused.

"Mind," he began again, lifting one arm from the elbow, the palm of the hand outwards, so that, with his legs folded before him, he had the pose of a Buddha preaching in European clothes and without a lotus-flower — "Mind, none of us would feel exactly like this. What saves us is efficiency — the devotion to efficiency. But these chaps were not much account, really. They were no colonists; their administration was merely a squeeze, and nothing more, I suspect. They were conquerors, and for that you want only brute force — nothing to boast of, when you have it, since your strength is just an accident arising from the weakness of others. They grabbed what they could get for the sake of what was to be got. It was just robbery with violence, aggravated murder on a great scale, and men going at it blind — as is very proper for those who tackle a darkness. The conquest of the earth, which mostly means the taking it away from those who have a different complexion or slightly flatter noses than ourselves, is not a pretty thing when you look into it too much. What redeems it is the idea only. An idea at the back of it; not a sentimental pretense but an idea; and an unselfish belief in the idea — something you can set up, and bow down before, and offer a sacrifice to . . ."

He broke off. Flames glided in the river, small green flames, red flames, white flames, pursuing, overtaking, joining, crossing each other — then separating slowly or hastily. The traffic of the great city went on in the deepening night upon the sleepless river. We looked on, waiting patiently — there was nothing else to do till the end of the flood; but it was more after a long silence, when he said, in a hesitating voice, "I suppose you fellows remember I did once turn fresh-water sailor for a bit," that we knew we were fated, before the ebb began to run, to hear one of Marlow's inconclusive experiences.

"I don't want to bother you much with what happened to me personally," he began, showing in this remark the weakness of many tellers of tales who seem so often unaware of what their audience would best like to hear; "yet to understand the effect of it on me you ought to know how I got out there, what I saw, how I went up that river to the place where I first met the poor chap. It was the farthest point of navigation and the culminating point of my experience. It seemed somehow to throw a kind of light on everything about me — and into my thoughts. It was somber enough, too — and pitiful — not extraordinary in any way — not very clear either. No, not very clear. And yet it seemed to throw a kind of light.

"I had then, as you remember, just returned to London after a lot of Indian Ocean, Pacific, China Seas — a regular dose of the East — six years or so, and I was loafing about, hindering you fellows in your work and invading your homes, just as though I had got a heavenly mission to civilize you. It was very fine for a time, but after a bit I did get tired of resting. Then I began to look for a ship — I should think the hardest work on earth. But the ships wouldn't even look at me. And I got tired of that game, too.

"Now when I was a little chap I had a passion for maps. I would look for hours at South America, or Africa, or Australia, and lose myself in all the glories of exploration. At that time there were many blank spaces on the earth, and when I saw one that looked particularly inviting on a map (but they all look that) I would put my finger on it and say, When I grow up I will go there. The North Pole was one of these places, I remember. Well, I haven't been there yet, and shall not try now. The glamour's off. Other places were scattered about the Equator, and in every sort of latitude all over the two hemispheres. I have been in some of them, and . . . well, we won't talk about that. But there was one yet — the biggest, the most blank, so to speak — that I had a hankering after.

"True, by this time it was not a blank space any more. It had got filled since my childhood with rivers and lakes and names. It had ceased to be a blank space of delightful mystery — a white patch for a boy to dream gloriously over. It had become a place of darkness. But there was in it one river especially, a mighty big river, that you could see on the map, resembling an immense snake uncoiled, with its head in the sea, its body at rest curving afar over a vast country, and its tail lost in the depths of the land. And as I looked at the map of it in a shop-window, it fascinated me as a snake would a bird — a silly little bird. Then I remembered there was a big concern, a Company for trade on that river. Dash it all! I thought to myself, they can't trade without using some kind of craft on that lot of fresh water — steamboats! Why shouldn't I try to get charge of one? I went on along Fleet Street, but could not shake off the idea. The snake had charmed me.

"You understand it was a Continental concern, that Trading society; but I have a lot of relations living on the Continent, because it's cheap and not so nasty as it looks, they say.

"I am sorry to own I began to worry them. This was already a fresh departure for me. I was not used to getting things that way, you know. I always went my own road and on my own legs where I had a mind to go. I wouldn't have believed it of myself; but, then — you see — I felt somehow I must get there by hook or by crook. So I worried them. The men said 'My dear fellow,' and did nothing. Then — would you believe it? — I tried the women. I, Charlie Marlow, set the women to work — to get a job. Heavens! Well, you see, the notion drove me. I had an aunt, a dear enthusiastic soul. She wrote: 'It will be delightful. I am ready to do anything, anything for you. It is a glorious idea. I know the wife of a very high personage in the Administration, and also a man who has lots of influence with,' etc., etc. She was determined to make no end of fuss to get me appointed skipper of a river steamboat, if such was my fancy.

"I got my appointment — of course; and I got it very quick. It appears the Company had received news that one of their captains had been killed in a scuffle with the natives. This was my chance, and it made me the more anxious to go. It was only months and months afterwards, when I made the attempt to recover what was left of the body, that I heard the original quarrel arose from a misunderstanding about some hens. Yes, two black hens. Fresleven — that was the fellow's name, a Dane — thought himself wronged somehow in the bargain, so he went ashore and started to hammer the chief of the village with a stick. Oh, it didn't surprise me in the least to hear this, and at the same time to be told that Fresleven was the gentlest, quietest creature that ever walked on two legs. No doubt he was; but he had been a couple of years already out there engaged in the noble cause, you know, and he probably felt the need at last of asserting his self-respect in some way. Therefore he whacked the old nigger mercilessly, while a big crowd of his people watched him, thunderstruck, till some man — I was told the chief's son — in desperation at hearing the old chap yell, made a tentative jab with a spear at the white man — and of course it went quite easy between the shoulder blades. Then the whole population cleared into the forest, expecting all kinds of calamities to happen, while, on the other hand, the steamer Fresleven commanded left also in a bad panic, in charge of the engineer, I believe. Afterwards nobody seemed to trouble much about Fresleven's remains, till I got out and stepped into his shoes. I couldn't let it rest, though; but when an opportunity offered at last to meet my predecessor, the grass growing through his ribs was tall enough to hide his bones. They were all there. The supernatural being had not been touched after he fell. And the village was deserted, the huts gaped black, rotting, all askew within the fallen enclosures. A calamity had come to it, sure enough. The people had vanished. Mad terror had scattered them, men, women, and children, through the bush, and they had never returned. What became of the hens I don't know either. I should think the cause of progress got them, anyhow. However, through this glorious affair I got my appointment, before I had fairly begun to hope for it.

"I flew around like mad to get ready, and before forty-eight hours I was crossing the Channel to show myself to my employers, and sign the contract. In a very few hours I arrived in a city that always makes me think of a whited sepulcher. Prejudice no doubt. I had no difficulty in finding the Company's offices. It was the biggest thing in the town, and everybody I met was full of it. They were going to run an over-sea empire, and make no end of coin by trade.

"A narrow and deserted street in deep shadow, high houses, innumerable windows with venetian blinds, a dead silence, grass sprouting between the stones, imposing carriage archways right and left, immense double doors standing ponderously ajar. I slipped through one of these cracks, went up a swept and ungarnished staircase, as arid as a desert, and opened the first door I came to. Two women, one fat and the other slim, sat on straw-bottomed chairs, knitting black wool. The slim one got up and walked straight at me — still knitting with downcast eyes — and only just as I began to think of getting out of her way, as you would for a somnambulist, stood still, and looked up. Her dress was as plain as an umbrella-cover, and she turned round without a word and preceded me into a waiting-room. I gave my name, and looked about. Deal table in the middle, plain chairs all around the walls, on one end a large shining map, marked with all the colors of a rainbow. There was a vast amount of red — good to see at any time, because one knows that some real work is done in there, a deuce of a lot of blue, a little green, smears of orange, and, on the East Coast, a purple patch, to show where the jolly pioneers of progress drink the jolly lagerbeer. However, I wasn't going into any of these. I was going into the yellow. Dead in the center. And the river was there — fascinating — deadly — like a snake. Ough! A door opened, a white-haired secretarial head, but wearing a compassionate expression, appeared, and a skinny forefinger beckoned me into the sanctuary. Its light was dim, and a heavy writing-desk squatted in the middle. From behind that structure came out an impression of pale plumpness in a frock-coat. The great man himself. He was five feet six, I should judge, and had his grip on the handle-end of ever so many millions. He shook hands, I fancy, murmured vaguely, was satisfied with my French. *Bon voyage.*

"In about forty-five seconds I found myself again in the waiting-room with the compassionate secretary, who, full of desolation and sympathy, made me sign some document. I believe I undertook amongst other things not to disclose any trade secrets. Well, I am not going to.

"I began to feel slightly uneasy. You know I am not used to such ceremonies, and there was something ominous in the atmosphere. It was just as though I had been let into some conspiracy — I don't know — something not quite right; and I was glad to get out. In the outer room the two women knitted black wool feverishly. People were arriving, and the younger one was walking back and forth introducing them. The old one sat on her chair. Her flat cloth slippers were propped up on a footwarmer, and a cat reposed on her lap. She wore a starched white affair on her head, had a wart on one cheek, and silver-rimmed spectacles hung on the tip of her nose. She glanced at me above the glasses. The swift and indifferent placidity of that look troubled me. Two youths with foolish and cheery countenances were being piloted over, and she threw at them the same quick glance of unconcerned wisdom. She seemed to know all about them and about me, too. An eerie feeling came over me. She seemed uncanny and fateful. Often far away there I thought of these two, guarding the door of Darkness, knitting black wool as for a warm pall, one introducing, introducing continuously to the unknown, the other scrutinizing the cheery and foolish faces with unconcerned old eyes. *Ave!* Old knitter of black wool. *Morituri te salutant.*[5] Not many of those she looked at ever saw her again — not half, by a long way.

---

[5] "Those who are about to die salute you" (Latin).

"There was yet a visit to the doctor. 'A simple formality,' assured me the secretary, with an air of taking an immense part in all my sorrows. Accordingly a young chap wearing his hat over the left eyebrow, some clerk I suppose — there must have been clerks in the business, though the house was as still as a house in a city of the dead — came from somewhere upstairs, and led me forth. He was shabby and careless, with inkstains on the sleeves of his jacket, and his cravat was large and billowy, under a chin shaped like the toe of an old boot. It was a little too early for the doctor, so I proposed a drink, and thereupon he developed a vein of joviality. As we sat over our vermouths he glorified the Company's business, and by and by I expressed casually my surprise at him not going out there. He became very cool and collected all at once. 'I am not such a fool as I look, quoth Plato to his disciples,' he said sententiously, emptied his glass with great resolution, and we rose.

"The old doctor felt my pulse, evidently thinking of something else the while. 'Good, good for there,' he mumbled, and then with a certain eagerness asked me whether I would let him measure my head. Rather surprised, I said Yes, when he produced a thing like calipers and got the dimensions back and front and every way, taking notes carefully. He was an unshaven little man in a threadbare coat like a gaberdine, with his feet in slippers, and I thought him a harmless fool. 'I always ask leave, in the interests of science, to measure the crania of those going out there,' he said. 'And when they come back, too?' I asked. 'Oh, I never see them,' he remarked; 'and, moreover, the changes take place inside, you know.' He smiled, as if at some quiet joke. 'So you are going out there. Famous. Interesting, too.' He gave me a searching glance, and made another note. 'Ever any madness in your family?' he asked, in a matter-of-fact tone. I felt very annoyed. 'Is that question in the interests of science, too?' 'It would be,' he said, without taking notice of my irritation, 'interesting for science to watch the mental changes of individuals, on the spot, but. . . .' 'Are you an alienist?' I interrupted. 'Every doctor should be — a little,' answered that original, imperturbably. 'I have a little theory which you Messieurs who go out there must help me to prove. This is my share in the advantages my country shall reap from the possession of such a magnificent dependency. The mere wealth I leave to others. Pardon my questions, but you are the first Englishman coming under my observation. . . .' I hastened to assure him I was not in the least typical. 'If I were,' said I, 'I wouldn't be talking like this with you.' 'What you say is rather profound, and probably erroneous,' he said, with a laugh. 'Avoid irritation more than exposure to the sun. Adieu. How do you English say, eh? Good-by. Ah! Good-by. Adieu. In the tropics one must before everything keep calm.' . . . He lifted a warning forefinger. . . . '*Du calme, du calme. Adieu.*'

"One thing more remained to do — say good-by to my excellent aunt. I found her triumphant. I had a cup of tea — the last decent cup of tea for many days — and in a room that most soothingly looked just as you would expect a lady's drawing-room to look, we had a long quiet chat by the fireside. In the course of these confidences it became quite plain to me I had been represented to the wife of the high dignitary, and goodness knows to how many more people besides, as an exceptional and gifted creature — a piece of good fortune for the Company — a man you don't get hold of every day. Good heavens! and I was going to take charge of a two-penny-half-penny river-steamboat with a penny whistle attached! It appeared, however, I was also one of the Workers, with a capital — you know. Something like an emissary of light, something like a lower sort of apostle. There had been a lot of such rot let loose in print and talk just about that time, and the excellent woman, living right in the rush of all that humbug, got carried off her feet. She talked about 'weaning those igno-rant millions from their horrid ways,' till, upon my word, she made me quite uncomfortable. I ventured to hint that the Company was run for profit.

"'You forget, dear Charlie, that the laborer is worthy of his hire,' she said, brightly. It's queer how out of touch with truth women are. They live in a world of their own, and there has never been anything like it, and never can be. It is too beautiful altogether, and if they were to set it up it would go to pieces before the first sunset. Some confounded fact we men have been living contentedly with ever since the day of creation would start up and knock the whole thing over.

"After this I got embraced, told to wear flannel, be sure to write often, and so on — and I left. In the street — I don't know why — a queer feeling came to me that I was an impostor. Odd thing that I, who used to clear out for any part of the world at twenty-four hours' notice, with less thought than most men give to the crossing of a street, had a moment — I won't say of hesitation, but of startled pause, before this commonplace affair. The best way I can explain it to you is by saying that, for a second or two, I felt as though, instead of going to the center of a continent, I were about to set off for the center of the earth.

"I left in a French steamer, and she called in every blamed port they have out there, for, as far as I could see, the sole purpose of landing soldiers and custom-house officers. I watched the coast. Watching a coast as it slips by the ship is like thinking about an enigma. There it is before you — smiling, frown-ing, inviting, grand, mean, insipid, or savage, and always mute with an air of whispering, Come and find out. This one was almost featureless, as if still in the making, with an aspect of monotonous grimness. The edge of a colossal jungle, so dark-green as to be almost black, fringed with white surf, ran straight, like a ruled line, far, far away along a blue sea whose glitter was blurred by a creeping mist. The sun was fierce, the land seemed to glisten and drip with steam. Here and there grayish-whitish specks showed up clustered inside the white surf, with a flag flying above them perhaps. Settlements some centuries old, and still no bigger than pinheads on the untouched expanse of their background. We pounded along, stopped, landed soldiers; went on, landed custom-house clerks to levy toll in what looked like a God-forsaken wilderness, with a tin shed and a flag-pole lost in it; landed more soldiers — to take care of the custom-house clerks, presumably. Some, I heard, got drowned in the surf; but whether they did or not, nobody seemed particularly to care. They were just flung out there, and on we went. Every day the coast looked the same, as though we had not moved; but we passed various places — trading places — with names like Gran' Bassam, Little Popo; names that seemed to belong to some sordid farce acted in front of a sinister backcloth. The idleness of a passenger, my isolation amongst all these men with whom I had no point of contact, the oily and languid sea, the uniform somberness of the coast, seemed to keep me away from the truth of things, within the toil of a mournful and senseless delusion. The voice of the surf heard now and then was a positive pleasure, like the speech of a brother. It was something natural, that had its reason, that had a meaning. Now and then a boat from the shore gave one a momentary contact with reality. It was paddled by black fellows. You could see from afar the white of their eyeballs glistening. They shouted, sang; their bodies streamed with perspiration; they had faces like grotesque masks — these chaps; but they had bone, muscle, a wild vitality, an intense energy of movement, that was as natural and true as the surf along their coast. They wanted no excuse for being there. They were a great comfort to look at. For a time I would feel I belonged still to a world of straightforward facts, but the feeling would not last long. Something would turn up to scare it away. Once, I remember, we came upon a man-of-war anchored off the coast. There wasn't even a shed there, and she was shelling the bush. It appears the French had one of their wars going on thereabouts. Her ensign dropped limp like a rag; the muzzles of the long six-inch guns stuck out all over the low hull; the greasy, slimy swell swung her up lazily and let her down, swaying her thin masts. In the empty immensity of earth, sky, and water, there she was, incomprehensible, firing into a continent. Pop, would go one of the six-inch guns; a small flame would dart and vanish, a little white smoke would disappear, a tiny projectile would give a feeble screech — and nothing happened. Nothing could happen. There was a touch of insanity in the proceeding, a sense of lugubrious drollery in the sight; and it was not dissipated by somebody on board assuring me earnestly there was a camp of natives — he called them enemies! — hidden out of sight somewhere.

"We gave her her letters (I heard the men in that lonely ship were dying of fever at the rate of three a day) and went on. We called at some more places with farcical names, where the merry dance of death and trade goes on in a still and earthy atmosphere as of an overheated catacomb; all along the formless coast bordered by dangerous surf, as if Nature herself had tried to ward off intruders; in and out of rivers, streams of death in life, whose banks were rotting into mud, whose waters, thickened into slime, invaded the contorted mangroves, that seemed to writhe at us in the extremity of an impotent despair. Nowhere did we stop long enough to get a particularized impression, but the general sense of vague and oppressive wonder grew upon me. It was like a weary pilgrimage amongst hints for nightmares.

"It was upward of thirty days before I saw the mouth of the big river. We anchored off the seat of the government. But my work would not begin till some two hundred miles farther on. So as soon as I could I made a start for a place thirty miles higher up.

"I had my passage on a little sea-going steamer. Her captain was a Swede, and knowing me for a seaman, invited me on the bridge. He was a young man, lean, fair, and morose, with lanky hair and a shuffling gait. As we left the miserable little wharf, he tossed his head contemptuously at the shore. 'Been living there?' he asked. I said, 'Yes.' 'Fine lot these government chaps — are they not?' he went on, speaking English with great precision and considerable bitterness. 'It is funny what some people will do for a few francs a month. I wonder what becomes of that kind when it goes upcountry?' I said to him I expected to see that soon. 'So-o-o!' he exclaimed. He shuffled athwart, keeping one eye ahead vigilantly. 'Don't be too sure,' he continued. 'The other day I took up a man who hanged himself on the road. He was a Swede, too.' 'Hanged himself! Why, in God's name?' I cried. I kept on looking out watchfully. 'Who knows? The sun was too much for him, or the country perhaps.'

"At last we opened a reach. A rocky cliff appeared, mounds of turned-up earth by the shore, houses on a hill, others with iron roofs, amongst a waste of excavations, or hanging to the declivity. A continuous noise of the rapids above hovered over this scene of inhabited devastation. A lot of people, mostly black and naked, moved about like ants. A jetty projected into the river. A blinding sunlight drowned all this at times in a sudden recrudescence of glare. 'There's your Company's station,' said the Swede, pointing to three wooden barrack-like structures on the rocky slope. 'I will send your things up. Four boxes did you say? So. Farewell.'

"I came upon a boiler wallowing in the grass, then found a path leading up the hill. It turned aside for the boulders, and also for an undersized railway-truck lying there on its back with its wheels in the air. One was off. The thing looked as dead as the carcass of some animal. I came upon more pieces of decaying machinery, a stack of rusty rails. To the left a clump of trees made a shady spot, where dark things seemed to stir feebly. I blinked, the path was steep. A horn tooted to the right, and I saw the black people run. A heavy and dull detonation shook the ground, a puff of smoke came out of the cliff, and that was all. No change appeared on the face of the rock. They were building a railway. The cliff was not in the way of anything; but the objectless blasting was all the work going on.

"A slight clinking behind me made me turn my head. Six black men advanced in a file, toiling up the path. They walked erect and slow, balancing small baskets full of earth on their heads, and the clink kept time with their footsteps. Black rags were wound round their loins, and the short ends behind waggled to and fro like tails. I could see every rib, the joints of their limbs were like knots in a rope; each had an iron collar on his neck, and all were connected together with a chain whose bights[6] swung between them, rhythmically clinking. Another report from the cliff made me think suddenly of that ship of war I had seen firing into a continent. It was the same kind of ominous voice; but these men could by no stretch of imagination be called enemies. They were called criminals, and the outraged law, like the bursting shells, had come to them, an insoluble mystery from the sea. All their meager breasts panted together, the violently dilated nostrils quivered, the eyes stared stonily uphill. They passed me within six inches, without a glance, with that complete,

---

[6] Loops.

deathlike indifference of unhappy savages. Behind this raw matter one of the reclaimed, the product of the new forces at work, strolled despondently, carrying a rifle by its middle. He had a uniform jacket with one button off, and seeing a white man on the path, hoisted his weapon to his shoulder with alacrity. This was simple prudence, white men being so much alike at a distance that he could not tell who I might be. He was speedily reassured, and with a large, white, rascally grin, and a glance at his charge, seemed to take me into partnership in his exalted trust. After that, I also was a part of the great cause of these high and just proceedings.

"Instead of going up, I turned and descended to the left. My idea was to let that chain-gang get out of sight before I climbed the hill. You know I am not particularly tender, I've had to strike and to fend off. I've had to resist and to attack sometimes — that's only one way of resisting — without counting the exact cost, according to the demands of such sort of life as I had blundered into. I've seen the devil of violence, and the devil of greed, and the devil of hot desire; but, by all the stars! these were strong, lusty, red-eyed devils, that swayed and drove men — men, I tell you. But as I stood on this hillside, I foresaw that in the blinding sunshine of that land I would become acquainted with a flabby, pretending, weak-eyed devil of a rapacious and pitiless folly. How insidious he could be, too, I was only to find out several months later and a thousand miles farther. For a moment I stood appalled, as though by a warning. Finally I descended the hill, obliquely, towards the trees I had seen.

"I avoided a vast artificial hole somebody had been digging on the slope, the purpose of which I found it impossible to divine. It wasn't a quarry or a sandpit, anyhow. It was just a hole. It might have been connected with the philanthropic desire of giving the criminals something to do. I don't know. Then I nearly fell into a very narrow ravine, almost no more than a scar in the hillside. I discovered that a lot of imported drainage-pipes for the settlement had been tumbled in there. There wasn't one that was not broken. It was a wanton smash-up. At last I got under the trees. My purpose was to stroll into the shade for a moment; but no sooner within than it seemed to me I had stepped into the gloomy circle of some Inferno. The rapids were near, and an uninterrupted, uniform, headlong, rushing noise filled the mournful stillness of the grove, where not a breath stirred, not a leaf moved, with a mysterious sound — as though the tearing pace of the launched earth had suddenly become audible.

"Black shapes crouched, lay, sat between the trees leaning against the trunks, clinging to the earth, half coming out, half effaced within the dim light, in all the attitudes of pain, abandonment, and despair. Another mine on the cliff went off, followed by a slight shudder of the soil under my feet. The work was going on. The work! and this was the place where some of the helpers had withdrawn to die.

"They were dying slowly — it was very clear. They were not enemies, they were not criminals, they were nothing earthly now — nothing but black shadows of disease and starvation, lying confusedly in the greenish gloom. Brought from all the recesses of the coast in all the legality of time contracts, lost in uncongenial surroundings, fed on unfamiliar food, they sickened, became inefficient, and were then allowed to crawl away and rest. These moribund shapes were free as air — and nearly as thin. I began to distinguish the gleam of the eyes under the trees. Then, glancing down, I saw a face near my hand. The black bones reclined at full length with one shoulder against the tree, and slowly the eyelids rose and the sunken eyes looked up at me, enormous and vacant, a kind of blind, white flicker in the depths of the orbs, which died out slowly. The man seemed young — almost a boy — but you know with them it's hard to tell. I found nothing else to do but to offer him one of my good Swede's ship's biscuits I had in my pocket. The fingers closed slowly on it and held — there was no other movement and no other glance. He had tied a bit of white worsted round his neck — Why? Where did he get it? Was it a badge — an ornament — a charm — a propitiatory act? Was there any idea at all connected with it? It looked startling round his black neck, this bit of white thread from beyond the seas.

"Near the same tree two more bundles of acute angles sat with their legs drawn up. One, with his chin propped on his knees, stared at nothing, in an intolerable and appalling manner: his brother phantom rested its forehead, as if overcome with a great weariness; and all about others were scattered in every pose of contorted collapse, as in some picture of a massacre or a pesti-lence. While I stood horror-struck, one of these creatures rose to his hands and knees, and went off on all-fours towards the river to drink. He lapped out of his hand, then sat up in the sunlight, crossing his shins in front of him, and after a time let his woolly head fall on his breastbone.

"I didn't want any more loitering in the shade, and I made haste towards the station. When near the buildings I met a white man, in such an unexpected elegance of get-up that in the first moment I took him for a sort of vision. I saw a high starched collar, white cuffs, a light alpaca jacket, snowy trousers, a clean necktie, and varnished boots. No hat. Hair parted, brushed, oiled, under a green-lined parasol held in a big white hand. He was amazing, and had a penholder behind his ear.

"I shook hands with this miracle, and I learned he was the Company's chief accountant, and that all the bookkeeping was done at this station. He had come out for a moment, he said, 'to get a breath of fresh air.' The expression sounded wonderfully odd, with its suggestion of sedentary desk life. I wouldn't have mentioned the fellow to you at all, only it was from his lips that I first heard the name of the man who is so indissolubly connected with the memories of that time. Moreover, I respected the fellow. Yes; I respected his collars, his vast cuffs, his brushed hair. His appearance was certainly that of a hairdresser's dummy; but in the great demoralization of the land he kept up his appearance. That's backbone. His starched collars and got-up shirt-fronts were achievements of character. He had been out nearly three years; and, later, I could not help ask-ing him how he managed to sport such linen. He had just the faintest blush, and said modestly, 'I've been teaching one of the native women about the sta-tion. It was difficult. She had a distaste for the work.' Thus this man had ver-ily accomplished something. And he was devoted to his books, which were in apple-pie order.

"Everything else in the station was in a muddle — heads, things, buildings. Strings of dusty niggers with splay feet arrived and departed; a stream of manufactured goods, rubbishy cottons, beads, and brass-wire sent into the depths of darkness, and in return came a precious trickle of ivory.

"I had to wait in the station for ten days — an eternity. I lived in a hut in the yard, but to be out of the chaos I would sometimes get into the accountant's office. It was built of horizontal planks, and so badly put together that, as he bent over his high desk, he was barred from neck to heels with narrow strips of sunlight. There was no need to open the big shutter to see. It was hot there, too; big flies buzzed fiendishly, and did not sting, but stabbed. I sat generally on the floor, while, of faultless appearance (and even slightly scented), perching on a high stool, he wrote. Sometimes he stood up for exercise. When a trucklebed with a sick man (some invalid agent from up-country) was put in there, he exhibited a gentle annoyance. 'The groans of this sick person,' he said, 'distract my attention. And without that it is extremely difficult to guard against clerical errors in this climate.'

"One day he remarked, without lifting his head, 'In the interior you will no doubt meet Mr. Kurtz.' On my asking who Mr. Kurtz was, he said he was a first-class agent; and seeing my disappointment at this information, he added slowly, laying down his pen, 'He is a very remarkable person.' Further questions elicited from him that Mr. Kurtz was at present in charge of a trading-post, a very important one, in the true ivory-country, at 'the very bottom of there. Sends in as much ivory as all the others put together. . . .' He began to write again. The sick man was too ill to groan. The flies buzzed in a great peace.

"Suddenly there was a growing murmur of voices and a great tramping of feet. A caravan had come in. A violent babble of uncouth sounds burst out on the other side of the planks. All the carriers were speaking together, and in the midst of the uproar the lamentable voice of the chief agent was heard 'giving it up' tearfully for the twentieth time that day. . . . He rose slowly. 'What a frightful row,' he said. He crossed the room gently to look at the sick man, and returning, said to me, 'He does not hear.' 'What! Dead?' I asked, startled. 'No, not yet,' he answered, with great composure. Then, alluding with a toss of the head to the tumult in the station-yard, 'When one has got to make correct entries, one comes to hate those savages — hate them to the death.' He remained thoughtful for a moment. 'When you see Mr. Kurtz,' he went on, 'tell him for me that everything here' — he glanced at the desk — 'is very satisfactory. I don't like to write to him — with those messengers of ours you never know who may get hold of your letter — at that Central Station.' He stared at me for a moment with his mild, bulging eyes. 'Oh, he will go far, very far,' he began again. 'He will be a somebody in the Administration before long. They, above — the Council in Europe, you know — mean him to be.'

"He turned to his work. The noise outside had ceased, and presently in going out I stopped at the door. In the steady buzz of flies the homeward-bound agent was lying flushed and insensible; the other, bent over his books, was making correct entries of perfectly correct transactions; and fifty feet below the doorstep I could see the still tree-tops of the grove of death.

"Next day I left the station at last, with a caravan of sixty men, for a two-hundred-mile tramp.

"No use telling you much about that. Paths, paths, everywhere; a stamped-in network of paths spreading over the empty land, through long grass, through burnt grass, through thickets, down and up chilly ravines, up and down stony hills ablaze with heat; and a solitude, a solitude, nobody, not a hut. The population had cleared out a long time ago. Well, if a lot of mysterious niggers armed with all kinds of fearful weapons suddenly took to traveling on the road between Deal and Gravesend, catching the yokels right and left to carry heavy loads for them, I fancy every farm and cottage thereabouts would get empty very soon. Only here the dwellings were gone, too. Still I passed through several abandoned villages. There's something pathetically childish in the ruins of grass walls. Day after day, with the stamp and shuffle of sixty pair of bare feet behind me, each pair under a sixty-pound load. Camp, cook, sleep, strike camp, march. Now and then a carrier dead in harness, at rest in the long grass near the path, with an empty water-gourd and his long staff lying by his side. A great silence around and above. Perhaps on some quiet night the tremor of far-off drums, sinking, swelling, a tremor vast, faint; a sound weird, appealing, suggestive, and wild — and perhaps with as profound a meaning as the sound of bells in a Christian country. Once a white man in an unbuttoned uniform, camping on the path with an armed escort of lank Zanzibaris, very hospitable and festive — not to say drunk. Was looking after the upkeep of the road, he declared. Can't say I saw any road or any upkeep, unless the body of a middle-aged Negro, with a bullet-hole in the forehead, upon which I absolutely stumbled three miles farther on, may be considered as a permanent improvement. I had a white companion, too, not a bad chap, but rather too fleshy and with the exasperating habit of fainting on the hot hillsides, miles away from the least bit of shade and water. Annoying, you know, to hold your own coat like a parasol over a man's head while he is coming to. I couldn't help asking him once what he meant by coming there at all. 'To make money, of course. What do you think?' he said, scornfully. Then he got fever, and had to be carried in a hammock slung under a pole. As he weighed sixteen stone[7] I had no end of rows with the carriers. They jibbed, ran away, sneaked off with their loads in the night — quite a mutiny. So, one evening, I made a speech in English with gestures, not one of which was lost to the sixty pairs of eyes before me, and the next morning I started the hammock off in front all right. An hour afterwards I came upon the whole concern wrecked in a bush — man, hammock, groans, blankets, horrors. The heavy pole had skinned his poor nose. He was very anxious for me to kill somebody, but there wasn't the shadow of a carrier near. I remember the old doctor — 'It would be interesting for science to watch the mental changes of individuals, on the spot.' I felt I was becoming scientifically interesting. However, all that is to no purpose. On the fifteenth day I came in sight of the big river again, and hobbled into the Central Station.

---

[7] 224 pounds (a *stone* is the equivalent of fourteen pounds).

It was a backwater surrounded by scrub and forest, with a pretty border of smelly mud on one side, and on the three others enclosed by a crazy fence of rushes. A neglected gap was all the gate it had, and the first glance at the place was enough to let you see the flabby devil was running that show. White men with long staves in their hands appeared languidly from amongst the buildings, strolling up to take a look at me, and then retired out of sight somewhere. One of them, a stout, excitable chap with black mustaches, informed me with great volubility and many digressions, as soon as I told him who I was, that my steamer was at the bottom of the river. I was thunderstruck. What, how, why? Oh, it was 'all right.' The 'manager himself' was there. All quite correct. 'Everybody had behaved splendidly! splendidly!' — 'you must,' he said in agitation, 'go and see the general manager at once. He is waiting!'

"I did not see the real significance of that wreck at once. I fancy I see it now, but I am not sure — not at all. Certainly the affair was too stupid — when I think of it — to be altogether natural. Still. . . . But at the moment it presented itself simply as a confounded nuisance. The steamer was sunk. They had started two days before in a sudden hurry up the river with the manager on board, in charge of some volunteer skipper, and before they had been out three hours they tore the bottom out of her on stones, and she sank near the south bank. I asked myself what I was to do there, now my boat was lost. As a matter of fact, I had plenty to do in fishing my command out of the river. I had to set about it the very next day. That, and the repairs when I brought the pieces to the station, took some months.

"My first interview with the manager was curious. He did not ask me to sit down after my twenty-mile walk that morning. He was commonplace in complexion, in feature, in manners, and in voice. He was of middle size and of ordinary build. His eyes, of the usual blue, were perhaps remarkably cold, and he certainly could make his glance fall on one as trenchant and heavy as an ax. But even at these times the rest of his person seemed to disclaim the intention. Otherwise there was only an indefinable, faint expression of his lips, something stealthy — a smile — not a smile — I remember it, but I can't explain. It was unconscious, this smile was, though just after he had said something it got intensified for an instant. It came at the end of his speeches like a seal applied on the words to make the meaning of the commonest phrase appear absolutely inscrutable. He was a common trader, from his youth up employed in these parts — nothing more. He was obeyed, yet he inspired neither love nor fear, nor even respect. He inspired uneasiness. That was it! Uneasiness. Not a definite mistrust — just uneasiness — nothing more. You have no idea how effective such a . . . a . . . faculty can be. He had no genius for organizing, for initiative, or for order even. That was evident in such things as the deplorable state of the station. He had no learning, and no intelligence. His position had come to him — why? Perhaps because he was never ill. . . . He had served three terms of three years out there. . . . Because triumphant health in the general rout of constitutions is a kind of power in itself. When he went home on leave he rioted on a large scale — pompously. Jack ashore — with a difference — in externals only. This one could gather from his casual talk.

He originated nothing, he could keep the routine going — that's all. But he was great. He was great by this little thing that it was impossible to tell what could control such a man. He never gave the secret away. Perhaps there was nothing within him. Such a suspicion made one pause — for out there there were no external checks. Once when various tropical diseases had laid low almost every 'agent' in the station, he was heard to say, 'Men who come out here should have no entrails.' He sealed the utterance with that smile of his, as though it had been a door opening into a darkness he had in his keeping. You fancied you had seen things — but the seal was on. When annoyed at meal-times by the constant quarrels of the white men about precedence, he ordered an immense round table to be made, for which a special house had to be built. This was the station's messroom. Where he sat was the first place — the rest were nowhere. One felt this to be his unalterable conviction. He was neither civil nor uncivil. He was quiet. He allowed his 'boy' — an overfed young Negro from the coast — to treat the white men, under his very eyes, with provoking insolence.

"He began to speak as soon as he saw me. I had been very long on the road. He could not wait. Had to start without me. The upriver stations had to be relieved. There had been so many delays already that he did not know who was dead and who was alive, and how they got on — and so on, and so on. He paid no attention to my explanations, and, playing with a stick of sealing-wax, repeated several times that the situation was 'very grave, very grave.' There were rumors that a very important station was in jeopardy, and its chief, Mr. Kurtz, was ill. Hoped it was not true. Mr. Kurtz was. . . . I felt weary and irri-table. Hang Kurtz, I thought. I interrupted him by saying I had heard of Mr. Kurtz on the coast. 'Ah! So they talk of him down there,' he murmured to him-self. Then he began again, assuring me Mr. Kurtz was the best agent he had, an exceptional man, of the greatest importance to the Company; therefore I could understand his anxiety. He was, he said, 'very, very uneasy.' Certainly he fidgeted on his chair a good deal, exclaimed, 'Ah, Mr. Kurtz!' broke the stick of sealing-wax and seemed dumfounded by the accident. Next thing he wanted to know 'how long it would take to. . . .' I interrupted him again. Being hungry, you know, and kept on my feet too, I was getting savage. 'How can I tell?' I said. 'I haven't even seen the wreck yet — some months, no doubt.' All this talk seemed to me so futile. 'Some months,' he said. 'Well, let us say three months before we can make a start. Yes. That ought to do the affair.' I flung out of his hut (he lived all alone in a clay hut with a sort of veranda) muttering to myself my opinion of him. He was a chattering idiot. Afterwards I took it back when it was borne in upon me startlingly with what extreme nicety he had estimated the time requisite for the 'affair.'

"I went to work the next day, turning, so to speak, my back on that station. In that way only it seemed to me I could keep my hold on the redeeming facts of life. Still, one must look about sometimes; and then I saw this station, these men strolling aimlessly about in the sunshine of the yard. I asked myself some-times what it all meant. They wandered here and there with their absurd long staves in their hands, like a lot of faithless pilgrims bewitched inside a rotten fence. The word 'ivory' rang in the air, was whispered, was sighed. You would think they were praying to it. A taint of imbecile rapacity blew through it all, like a whiff from some corpse. By Jove! I've never seen anything so unreal in my life. And outside, the silent wilderness surrounding this cleared speck on the earth struck me as something great and invincible, like evil or truth, waiting patiently for the passing away of this fantastic invasion.

"Oh, these months! Well, never mind. Various things happened. One evening a grass shed full of calico, cotton prints, beads, and I don't know what else, burst into a blaze so suddenly that you would have thought the earth had opened to let an avenging fire consume all the trash. I was smoking my pipe quietly by my dismantled steamer, and saw them all cutting capers in the light, with their arms lifted high, when the stout man with mustaches came tearing down to the river, a tin pail in his hand, assured me that everybody was 'behaving splendidly, splendidly,' dipped about a quart of water, and tore back again. I noticed there was a hole in the bottom of his pail.

"I strolled up. There was no hurry. You see the thing had gone off like a box of matches. It had been hopeless from the very first. The flame had leaped high, driven everybody back, lighted up everything — and collapsed. The shed was already a heap of embers glowing fiercely. A nigger was being beaten near by. They said he had caused the fire in some way; be that as it may, he was screeching most horribly. I saw him, later, for several days, sitting in a bit of shade looking very sick and trying to recover himself: afterwards he arose and went out — and the wilderness without a sound took him into its bosom again. As I approached the glow from the dark I found myself at the back of two men, talking. I heard the name of Kurtz pronounced, then the words, 'take advantage of this unfortunate accident.' One of the men was the manager. I wished him a good evening. 'Did you ever see anything like it — eh? it is incredible,' he said, and walked off. The other man remained. He was a first-class agent, young, gentlemanly, a bit reserved, with a forked little beard and a hooked nose. He was standoffish with the other agents, and they on their side said he was the manager's spy among them. As to me, I had hardly ever spoken to him before. We got into talk, and by and by we strolled away from the hissing ruins. Then he asked me to his room, which was in the main building of the station. He struck a match, and I perceived that this young aristocrat had not only a silver-mounted dressing-case but also a whole candle all to himself. Just at that time the manager was the only man supposed to have any right to candles. Native mats covered the clay walls; a collection of spears, assegais, shields, knives was hung up in trophies. The business intrusted to this fellow was the making of bricks — so I had been informed; but there wasn't a fragment of a brick anywhere in the station, and he had been there more than a year — waiting. It seems he could not make bricks without something, I don't know what — straw, maybe. Anyways, it could not be found there, and as it was not likely to be sent from Europe, it did not appear clear to me what he was waiting for. An act of special creation perhaps. However, they were all waiting — all the sixteen or twenty pilgrims of them — for something; and upon my word it did not seem an uncongenial occupation, from the way they took it, though the only thing that ever came to them was disease — as far as I could see. They beguiled the time by backbiting and intriguing against each other in a foolish kind of way. There was an air of plotting about that station, but nothing came of it, of course. It was as unreal as everything else — as the philanthropic pretense of the whole concern, as their talk, as their government, as their show of work. The only real feeling was a desire to get appointed to a trading-post where ivory was to be had, so that they could earn percentages. They intrigued and slandered and hated each other only on that account — but as to effectu- ally lifting a little finger — oh, no. By heavens! there is something after all in the world allowing one man to steal a horse while another must not look at the halter. Steal a horse straight out. Very well. He has done it. Perhaps he can ride. But there is a way of looking at a halter that would provoke the most charitable of saints into a kick.

"I had no idea why he wanted to be sociable, but as we chatted in there it suddenly occurred to me the fellow was trying to get at something — in fact, pumping me. He alluded constantly to Europe, to the people I was sup- posed to know there — putting leading questions as to my acquaintances in the sepulchral city, and so on. His little eyes glittered like mica discs — with curiosity — though he tried to keep up a bit of superciliousness. At first I was astonished, but very soon I became awfully curious to see what he would find out from me. I couldn't possibly imagine what I had in me to make it worth his while. It was very pretty to see how he baffled himself, for in truth my body was full only of chills, and my head had nothing in it but that wretched steam- boat business. It was evident he took me for a perfectly shameless prevarica- tor. At last he got angry, and, to conceal a movement of furious annoyance, he yawned. I rose. Then I noticed a small sketch in oils, on a panel, representing a woman, draped and blindfolded, carrying a lighted torch. The background was somber — almost black. The movement of the woman was stately, and the effect of the torchlight on the face was sinister.

"It arrested me, and he stood by civilly, holding an empty half-pint cham- pagne bottle (medical comforts) with the candle stuck in it. To my question he said Mr. Kurtz had painted this — in this very station more than a year ago — while waiting for means to go to his trading-post. 'Tell me, pray,' said I, 'who is this Mr. Kurtz?'

"'The chief of the Inner Station,' he answered in a short tone, looking away. 'Much obliged,' I said, laughing. 'And you are the brickmaker of the Central Station. Everyone knows that.' He was silent for a while. 'He is a prodigy,' he said at last. 'He is an emissary of pity, and science, and progress, and devil knows what else. We want,' he began to declaim suddenly, 'for the guidance of the cause intrusted to us by Europe, so to speak, higher intelligence, wide sympathies, a singleness of purpose.' 'Who says that?' I asked. 'Lots of them,' he replied. 'Some even write that; and so *he* comes here, a special being, as you ought to know.' 'Why ought I to know?' I interrupted, really surprised. He paid no attention. 'Yes. Today he is chief of the best station, next year he will be assistant-manager, two years more and . . . but I daresay you know what he will be in two years' time. You are of the new gang — the gang of virtue. The same people who sent him specially also recommended you. Oh, don't say no. I've my own eyes to trust.' Light dawned upon me. My dear aunt's influential acquaintances were producing an unexpected effect upon that young man. I nearly burst into a laugh. 'Do you read the Company's confidential correspondence?' I asked. He hadn't a word to say. It was great fun. 'When Mr. Kurtz,' I continued, severely, 'is General Manager, you won't have the opportunity.'

"He blew the candle out suddenly, and we went outside. The moon had risen. Black figures strolled about listlessly, pouring water on the glow, whence proceeded a sound of hissing; steam ascended in the moonlight, the beaten nigger groaned somewhere. 'What a row the brute makes!' said the indefatigable man with the mustaches, appearing near us. 'Serves him right. Transgression — punishment — bang! Pitiless, pitiless. That's the only way. This will prevent all conflagrations for the future. I was just telling the manager. . . .' He noticed my companion, and became crestfallen all at once. 'Not in bed yet,' he said, with a kind of servile heartiness; 'it's so natural. Ha! Danger — agitation.' He vanished. I went on to the riverside, and the other followed me. I heard a scathing murmur at my ear, 'Heap of muffs — go to.' The pilgrims could be seen in knots gesticulating, discussing. Several had still their staves in their hands. I verily believe they took these sticks to bed with them. Beyond the fence the forest stood up spectrally in the moonlight, and through the dim stir, through the faint sounds of that lamentable courtyard, the silence of the land went home to one's very heart — its mystery, its greatness, the amazing reality of its concealed life. The hurt nigger moaned feebly somewhere near by, and then fetched a deep sigh that made me mend my pace away from there. I felt a hand introducing itself under my arm. 'My dear sir,' said the fellow, 'I don't want to be misunderstood, and especially by you, you will see Mr. Kurtz long before I can have that pleasure. I wouldn't like him to get a false idea of my disposition. . . .'

"I let him run on, this papier-mâché Mephistopheles,[8] and it seemed to me that if I tried I could poke my forefinger through him, and would find nothing inside but a little loose dirt, maybe. He, don't you see, had been planning to be assistant-manager by and by under the present man, and I could see that the coming of that Kurtz had upset them both not a little. He talked precipitately, and I did not try to stop him. I had my shoulders against the wreck of my steamer, hauled up on the slope like a carcass of some big river animal. The smell of mud, of primeval mud, by Jove! was in my nostrils, the high stillness of primeval forest was before my eyes; there were shiny patches on the black creek. The moon had spread over everything a thin layer of silver — over the rank grass, over the mud, upon the wall of matted vegetation standing higher than the wall of a temple, over the great river I could see through a somber gap glittering, glittering, as it flowed broadly by without a murmur. All this was great, expectant, mute, while the man jabbered about himself. I wondered whether the stillness on the face of the immensity looking at us two were

---

[8] The Devil.

meant as an appeal or as a menace. What were we who had strayed in here? Could we handle that dumb thing, or would it handle us? I felt how big, how confoundedly big, was that thing that couldn't talk, and perhaps was deaf as well. What was in there? I could see a little ivory coming out from there, and I had heard Mr. Kurtz was in there. I had heard enough about it, too — God knows! Yet somehow it didn't bring any image with it — no more than if I had been told an angel or a fiend was in there. I believed it in the same way one of you might believe there are inhabitants in the planet Mars. I knew once a Scotch sailmaker who was certain, dead sure, there were people in Mars. If you asked him for some idea how they looked and behaved, he would get shy and mutter something about 'walking on all-fours.' If you as much as smiled, he would — though a man of sixty — offer to fight you. I would not have gone so far as to fight for Kurtz, but I went for him near enough to a lie. You know I hate, detest, and can't bear a lie, not because I am straighter than the rest of us, but simply because it appalls me. There is a taint of death, a flavor of mortality in lies — which is exactly what I hate and detest in the world — what I want to forget. It makes me miserable and sick, like biting something rotten would do. Temperament, I suppose. Well, I went near enough to it by letting the young fool there believe anything he liked to imagine as to my influence in Europe. I became in an instant as much of a pretense as the rest of the bewitched pilgrims. This simply because I had a notion it somehow would be of help to that Kurtz whom at the time I did not see — you understand. He was just a word for me. I did not see the man in the name any more than you do. Do you see him? Do you see the story? Do you see anything? It seems to me I am trying to tell you a dream — making a vain attempt, because no relation of a dream can convey the dream-sensation, that commingling of absurdity, surprise, and bewilderment in a tremor of struggling revolt, that notion of being captured by the incredible which is of the very essence of dreams . . ."

He was silent for a while.

". . . No, it is impossible; it is impossible to convey the life-sensation of any given epoch of one's existence — that which makes its truth, its meaning — its subtle and penetrating essence. It is impossible. We live, as we dream — alone . . ."

He paused again as if reflecting, then added —

"Of course in this you fellows see more than I could then. You see me, whom you know . . ."

It had become so pitch dark that we listeners could hardly see one another. For a long time already he, sitting apart, had been no more to us than a voice. There was not a word from anybody. The others might have been asleep, but I was awake. I listened, I listened on the watch for the sentence, for the word, that would give me the clue of the faint uneasiness inspired by this narrative that seemed to shape itself without human lips in the heavy night-air of the river.

". . . Yes — I let him run on," Marlow began again, "and think what he pleased about the powers that were behind me. I did! And there was nothing behind me! There was nothing but that wretched, old, mangled steamboat I was leaning against, while he talked fluently about 'the necessity for every man to get on.' 'And when one comes out here, you conceive, it is not to gaze at the moon.' Mr. Kurtz was a 'universal genius,' but even a genius would find it easier to work with 'adequate tools—intelligent men.' He did not make bricks—why, there was a physical impossibility in the way—as I was well aware; and if he did secretarial work for the manager, it was because 'no sensible man rejects wantonly the confidence of his superiors.' Did I see it? I saw it. What more did I want? What I really wanted was rivets, by heavens! Rivets. To get on with the work—to stop the hole. Rivets I wanted. There were cases of them down at the coast—cases—piled up—burst—split! You kicked a loose rivet at every second step in that station yard on the hillside. Rivets had rolled into the grove of death. You could fill your pockets with rivets for the trouble of stooping down—and there wasn't one rivet to be found where it was wanted. We had plates that would do, but nothing to fasten them with. And every week the messenger, a lone Negro, letter-bag on shoulder and staff in hand, left our station for the coast. And several times a week a coast caravan came in with trade goods—ghastly glazed calico that made you shudder only to look at it; glass beads, valued about a penny a quart, confounded spotted cotton handkerchiefs. And no rivets. Three carriers could have brought all that was wanted to set that steamboat afloat.

"He was becoming confidential now, but I fancy my unresponsive attitude must have exasperated him at last, for he judged it necessary to inform me he feared neither God nor devil, let alone any mere man. I said I could see that very well, but what I wanted was a certain quantity of rivets—and rivets were what really Mr. Kurtz wanted, if he had only known it. Now letters went to the coast every week. . . . 'My dear sir,' he cried, 'I write from dictation.' I demanded rivets. There was a way—for an intelligent man. He changed his manner; became very cold, and suddenly began to talk about a hippopotamus; wondered whether sleeping on board the steamer (I stuck to my salvage night and day) I wasn't disturbed. There was an old hippo that had the bad habit of getting out on the bank and roaming at night over the station grounds. The pilgrims used to turn out in a body and empty every rifle they could lay hands on at him. Some even had sat up o' nights for him. All this energy was wasted, though. 'That animal had a charmed life,' he said; 'but you can say this only of brutes in this country. No man—you apprehend me?—no man here bears a charmed life.' He stood there for a moment in the moonlight with his delicate hooked nose set a little askew, and his mica eyes glittering without a wink, then, with a curt good night, he strode off. I could see he was disturbed and considerably puzzled, which made me feel more hopeful than I had been for days. It was a great comfort to turn from that chap to my influential friend, the battered, twisted, ruined, tin-pot steamboat. I clambered on board. She rang under my feet like an empty Huntley & Palmer biscuit-tin kicked along a gutter; she was nothing so solid in make, and rather less pretty in shape, but I had expended enough hard work on her to make me love her. No influential friend would have served me better. She had given me a chance to come out a bit—to find out what I could do. No, I don't like work. I had rather laze about and think of all the fine things that can be done. I don't like work—no man does—but I like what is in the work—the chance to find yourself. Your own reality — for yourself, not for others — what no other man can ever know. They can only see the mere show, and never tell me what it really means.

"I was not surprised to see somebody sitting aft, on the deck, with his legs dangling over the mud. You see I rather chummed with the few mechanics there were in that station, whom the other pilgrims naturally despised — on account of their imperfect manners, I suppose. This was the foreman — a boiler-maker by trade — a good worker. He was a lank, bony, yellow-faced man, with big intense eyes. His aspect was worried, and his head was as bald as the palm of my hand; but his hair in falling seemed to have stuck to his chin; and had prospered in the new locality, for his beard hung down to his waist. He was a widower with six young children (he had left them in charge of a sister of his to come out there), and the passion of his life was pigeon-flying. He was an enthusiast and a connoisseur. He would rave about pigeons. After work hours he used sometimes to come over from his hut for a talk about his children and his pigeons; at work, when he had to crawl in the mud under the bottom of the steamboat, he would tie up that beard of his in a kind of white serviette he brought for the purpose. It had loops to go over his ears. In the evening he could be seen squatted on the bank rinsing that wrapper in the creek with great care, then spreading it solemnly on a bush to dry.

"I slapped him on the back and shouted, 'We shall have rivets!' He scrambled to his feet exclaiming, 'No! Rivets!' as though he couldn't believe his ears. Then in a low voice, 'You . . . eh?' I don't know why we behaved like lunatics. I put my finger to the side of my nose and nodded mysteriously. 'Good for you!' he cried, snapped his fingers above his head, lifting one foot. I tried a jig. We capered on the iron deck. A frightful clatter came out of that hulk, and the virgin forest on the other bank of the creek sent it back in a thundering roll upon the sleeping station. It must have made some of the pilgrims sit up in their hovels. A dark figure obscured the lighted doorway of the manager's hut, vanished, then, a second or so after, the doorway itself vanished, too. We stopped, and the silence driven away by the stamping of our feet flowed back again from the recesses of the land. The great wall of vegetation, an exuberant and entangled mass of trunks, branches, leaves, boughs, festoons, motionless in the moonlight, was like a rioting invasion of soundless life, a rolling wave of plants, piled up, crested, ready to topple over the creek, to sweep every little man of us out of his little existence. And it moved not. A deadened burst of mighty splashes and snorts reached us from afar as though an ichthyosaurus[9] had been taking a bath of glitter in the great river. 'After all,' said the boiler-maker in a reasonable tone, 'why shouldn't we get the rivets?' Why not, indeed! I did not know of any reason why we shouldn't. 'They'll come in three weeks,' I said confidently.

"But they didn't. Instead of rivets there came an invasion, an infliction, a visitation. It came in sections during the next three weeks, each section headed by a donkey carrying a white man in new clothes and tan shoes, bowing from that elevation right and left to the impressed pilgrims. A quarrelsome band of footsore sulky niggers trod on the heels of the donkeys; a lot of tents,

---

[9] Water-dwelling dinosaur.

campstools, tin boxes, white cases, brown bales would be shot down in the courtyard, and the air of mystery would deepen a little over the muddle of the station. Five such installments came, with their absurd air of disorderly flight with the loot of innumerable outfit shops and provision stores, that, one would think, they were lugging, after a raid, into the wilderness for equitable division. It was an extricable mess of things decent in themselves but that human folly made look like the spoils of thieving.

"This devoted band called itself the Eldorado Exploring Expedition, and I believe they were sworn to secrecy. Their talk, however, was the talk of sordid buccaneers: it was reckless without hardihood, greedy without audacity, and cruel without courage; there was not an atom of foresight or of serious intention in the whole batch of them, and they did not seem aware these things are wanted for the work of the world. To tear treasure out of the bowels of the land was their desire, with no more moral purpose at the back of it than there is in burglars breaking into a safe. Who paid the expenses of the noble enterprise I don't know; but the uncle of our manager was leader of that lot.

"In exterior he resembled a butcher in a poor neighborhood, and his eyes had a look of sleepy cunning. He carried his fat paunch with ostentation on his short legs, and during the time his gang infested the station spoke to no one but his nephew. You could see these two roaming about all day long with their heads close together in an everlasting confab.

"I had given up worrying myself about the rivets. One's capacity for that kind of folly is more limited than you would suppose. I said Hang! — and let things slide. I had plenty of time for meditation, and now and then I would give some thought to Kurtz. I wasn't very interested in him. No. Still, I was curious to see whether this man, who had come out equipped with moral ideas of some sort, would climb to the top after all and how he would set about his work when there."

II

"One evening as I was lying flat on the deck of my steamboat, I heard voices approaching — and there were the nephew and the uncle strolling along the bank. I laid my head on my arm again, and had nearly lost myself in a doze, when somebody said in my ear, as it were: 'I am as harmless as a little child, but I don't like to be dictated to. Am I the manager — or am I not? I was ordered to send him there. It's incredible.' . . . I became aware that the two were standing on the shore alongside the forepart of the steamboat, just below my head. I did not move; it did not occur to me to move: I was sleepy. 'It is unpleasant,' grunted the uncle. 'He has asked the Administration to be sent there,' said the other, 'with the idea of showing what he could do; and I was instructed accordingly. Look at the influence that man must have. Is it not frightful?' They both agreed it was frightful, then made several bizarre remarks: 'Make rain and fine weather — one man — the Council — by the nose' — bits of absurd sentences that got the better of my drowsiness, so that I had pretty near the whole of my wits about me when the uncle said, 'The climate may do away with this difficulty for you. Is he alone there?' 'Yes,' answered the manager; 'he sent his assistant down the river with a note to me in these terms: "Clear this poor devil out of the country, and don't bother sending more of that sort. I had rather be alone than have the kind of men you can dispose of with me." It was more than a year ago. Can you imagine such impudence!' 'Anything since then?' asked the other, hoarsely. 'Ivory,' jerked the nephew; 'lots of it — prime sort — lots — most annoying, from him.' 'And with that?' questioned the heavy rumble. 'Invoice,' was the reply fired out, so to speak. Then silence. They had been talking about Kurtz.

"I was broad awake by this time, but, lying perfectly at ease, remained still, having no inducement to change my position. 'How did that ivory come all this way?' growled the elder man, who seemed very vexed. The other explained that it had come with a fleet of canoes in charge of an English half-caste clerk Kurtz had with him; that Kurtz had apparently intended to return himself, the station being by that time bare of goods and stores, but after coming three hundred miles, he suddenly decided to go back, which he started to do alone in a small dugout with four paddlers, leaving the half-caste to continue down the river with the ivory. The two fellows there seemed astounded at anybody attempting such a thing. They were at a loss for an adequate motive. As to me, I seemed to see Kurtz for the first time. It was a distinct glimpse: the dugout, four paddling savages, and the lone white man turning his back suddenly on the headquarters, on relief, on thoughts of home — perhaps; setting his face towards the depths of the wilderness, towards his empty and desolate station. I did not know the motive. Perhaps he was just simply a fine fellow who stuck to his work for its own sake. His name, you understand, had not been pronounced once. He was 'that man.' The half-caste, who, as far as I could see, had conducted a difficult trip with great prudence and pluck, was invariably alluded to as 'that scoundrel.' The 'scoundrel' had reported that the 'man' had been very ill — had recovered imperfectly. . . . The two below me moved away then a few paces, and strolled back and forth at some little distance. I heard: 'Military post — doctor — two hundred miles — quite alone now — unavoidable delays — nine months — no news — strange rumors.' They approached again, just as the manager was saying, 'No one, as far as I know, unless a species of wandering trader — a pestilential fellow, snapping ivory from the natives.' Who was it they were talking about now? I gathered in snatches that this was some man supposed to be in Kurtz's district, and of whom the manager did not approve. 'We will not be free from unfair competition till one of these fellows is hanged for an example,' he said. 'Certainly,' grunted the other; 'get him hanged! Why not? Anything — anything can be done in this country. That's what I say; nobody here, you understand, *here*, can endanger your position. And why? You stand the climate — you outlast them all. The danger is in Europe; but there before I left I took care to —' They moved off and whispered, then their voices rose again. 'The extraordinary series of delays is not my fault. I did my best.' The fat man sighed. 'Very sad.' 'And the pestiferous absurdity of his talk,' continued the other; 'he bothered me enough when he was here. "Each station should be like a beacon on the road towards better things, a center for trade, of course, but also for humanizing, improving, instructing." Conceive you — that ass! And he wants to be manager! No it's —' Here he got choked by excessive indignation, and I lifted my head the least bit. I was surprised to see how near they were — right under me. I could have spat upon their hats. They were looking on the ground, absorbed in thought. The manager was switching his leg with a slender twig: his sagacious relative lifted his head. 'You have been well since you came out this time?' he asked. The other gave a start. 'Who? I? Oh! Like a charm — like a charm. But the rest — oh, my goodness! All sick. They die so quick, too, that I haven't the time to send them out of the country — it's incredible!' 'H'm. Just so,' grunted the uncle. 'Ah! my boy, trust to this — I say, trust to this.' I saw him extend his short flipper of an arm for a gesture that took in the forest, the creek, the mud, the river — seemed to beckon with a dishonoring flourish before the sunlit face of the land a treacherous appeal to the lurking death, to the hidden evil, to the profound darkness of its heart. It was so startling that I leaped to my feet and looked back at the edge of the forest, as though I had expected an answer of some sort to that black display of confidence. You know the foolish notions that come to one sometimes. The high stillness confronted these two figures with its ominous patience, waiting for the passing away of a fantastic invasion.

"They swore aloud together — out of sheer fright, I believe — then pretending not to know anything of my existence, turned back to the station. The sun was low; and leaning forward side by side, they seemed to be tugging painfully uphill their two ridiculous shadows of unequal length, that trailed behind them slowly over the tall grass without bending a single blade.

"In a few days the Eldorado Expedition went into the patient wilderness, that closed upon it as the sea closes over a diver. Long afterwards the news came that all the donkeys were dead. I know nothing as to the fate of the less valuable animals. They, no doubt, like the rest of us, found what they deserved. I did not inquire. I was then rather excited at the prospect of meeting Kurtz very soon. When I say very soon I mean it comparatively. It was just two months from the day we left the creek when we came to the bank below Kurtz's station.

"Going up that river was like traveling back to the earliest beginnings of the world, when vegetation rioted on the earth and the big trees were kings. An empty stream, a great silence, an impenetrable forest. The air was warm, thick, heavy, sluggish. There was no joy in the brilliance of sunshine. The long stretches of the waterway ran on, deserted, into the gloom of overshadowed distances. On silvery sandbanks hippos and alligators sunned themselves side by side. The broadening waters flowed through a mob of wooded islands; you lost your way on that river as you would in a desert, and butted all day long against shoals, trying to find the channel, till you thought yourself bewitched and cut off forever from everything you had known once — somewhere — far away — in another existence perhaps. There were moments when one's past came back to one, as it will sometimes when you have not a moment to spare to yourself; but it came in the shape of an unrestful and noisy dream, remembered with wonder amongst the overwhelming realities of this strange world of plants, and water, and silence. And this stillness of life did not in the least resemble a peace. It was the stillness of an implacable force brooding over an inscrutable intention. It looked at you with a vengeful aspect. I got used to it afterwards; I did not see it any more; I had no time. I had to keep guessing at the channel; I had to discern, mostly by inspiration, the signs of hidden banks; I watched for sunken stones; I was learning to clap my teeth smartly before my heart flew out, when I shaved by a fluke some infernal sly old snag that would have ripped the life out of the tin-pot steamboat and drowned all the pilgrims; I had to keep a lookout for the signs of dead wood we could cut up in the night for next day's steaming. When you have to attend to things of that sort, to the mere incidents of the surface, the reality — the reality, I tell you — fades. The inner truth is hidden — luckily, luckily. But I felt it all the same; I felt often its mysterious stillness watching me at my monkey tricks, just as it watches you fellows performing on your respective tightropes for — what is it? half-a-crown a tumble —"

"Try to be civil, Marlow," growled a voice, and I knew there was at least one listener awake besides myself.

"I beg your pardon. I forgot the heartache which makes up the rest of the price. And indeed what does the price matter, if the trick be well done? You do your tricks very well. And I didn't do badly either, since I managed not to sink that steamboat on my first trip. It's a wonder to me yet. Imagine a blindfolded man set to drive a van over a bad road. I sweated and shivered over the business considerably, I can tell you. After all, for a seaman, to scrape the bottom of the thing that's supposed to float all the time under his care is the unpardonable sin. No one may know of it, but you never forget the thump — eh? A blow on the very heart. You remember it, you dream of it, you wake up at night and think of it — years after — and go hot and cold all over. I don't pretend to say that steamboat floated all the time. More than once she had to wade for a bit, with twenty cannibals splashing around and pushing. We had enlisted some of these chaps on the way for a crew. Fine fellows — cannibals — in their place. They were men one could work with, and I am grateful to them. And, after all, they did not eat each other before my face: they had brought along a provision of hippo-meat which went rotten, and made the mystery of the wilderness stink in my nostrils. Phoo! I can sniff it now. I had the manager on board and three or four pilgrims with their staves — all complete. Sometimes we came upon a station close by the bank, clinging to the skirts of the unknown, and the white men rushing out of a tumble-down hovel, with great gestures of joy and surprise and welcome, seemed very strange — had the appearance of being held there captive by a spell. The word ivory would ring in the air for a while — and on we went again into the silence, along empty reaches, round the still bends, between the high walls of our winding way, reverberating in hollow claps the ponderous beat of the stern-wheel. Trees, trees, millions of trees, massive, immense, running up high; and at their foot, hugging the bank against the stream, crept the little begrimed steamboat, like a sluggish beetle crawling on the floor of a lofty portico. It made you feel very small, very lost, and yet it was not altogether depressing, that feeling. After all, if you were small, the grimy beetle crawled on — which was just what you wanted it to do. Where the pilgrims imagined it crawled to I don't know. To some place where they expected to get something, I bet! For me it crawled towards Kurtz — exclusively; but when the steam-pipes started leaking we crawled very slow. The reaches opened before us and closed behind, as if the forest had stepped leisurely across the water to bar the way for our return. We penetrated deeper and deeper into the heart of darkness. It was very quiet there. At night sometimes the roll of drums behind the curtain of trees would run up the river and remain sustained faintly, as if hovering in the air over our heads, till the first break of day. Whether it meant war, peace, or prayer we could not tell. The dawns were heralded by the descent of a chill stillness; the wood-cutters slept, their fires burned low; the snapping of a twig would make you start. We were wanderers on a prehistoric earth, on an earth that wore the aspect of an unknown planet. We could have fancied ourselves the first men taking posses- sion of an accursed inheritance, to be subdued at the cost of profound anguish and of excessive toil. But suddenly, as we struggled round a bend, there would be a glimpse of rush walls, of peaked grass-roofs, a burst of yells, a whirl of black limbs, a mass of hands clapping, of feet stamping, of bodies swaying, of eyes rolling, under the droop of heavy and motionless foliage. The steamer toiled along slowly on the edge of a black and incomprehensible frenzy. The prehistoric man was cursing us, praying to us, welcoming us — who could tell? We were cut off from the comprehension of our surroundings; we glided past like phantoms, wondering and secretly appalled, as sane men would be before an enthusiastic outbreak in a madhouse. We could not understand because we were too far and could not remember, because we were traveling in the night of first ages, of those ages that are gone, leaving hardly a sign — and no memories.

"The earth seemed unearthly. We are accustomed to look upon the shackled form of a conquered monster, but there — there you could look at a thing monstrous and free. It was unearthly, and the men were — No, they were not inhuman. Well, you know, that was the worst of it — this suspicion of their not being inhuman. It would come slowly to one. They howled and leaped, and spun, and made horrid faces; but what thrilled you was just the thought of their humanity — like yours — the thought of your remote kinship with this wild and passionate uproar. Ugly. Yes, it was ugly enough; but if you were man enough you would admit to yourself that there was in you just the faintest trace of a response to the terrible frankness of that noise, a dim suspi- cion of there being a meaning in it which you — you so remote from the night of first ages — could comprehend. And why not? The mind of man is capable of anything — because everything is in it, all the past as well as all the future. What was there after all? Joy, fear, sorrow, devotion, valor, rage — who can tell? — but truth — truth stripped of its cloak of time. Let the fool gape and shudder — the man knows, and can look on without a wink. But he must at least be as much of a man as these on the shore. He must meet the truth with his own true stuff — with his own inborn strength. Principles won't do. Acqui- sitions, clothes, pretty rags — rags that would fly off at the first good shake. No; you want a deliberate belief. An appeal to me in this fiendish row — is there? Very well; I hear; I admit, but I have a voice, too, and for good or evil mine is the speech that cannot be silenced. Of course, a fool, what with sheer fright and fine sentiments, is always safe. Who's that grunting? You wonder I didn't go ashore for a howl and a dance? Well, no — I didn't. Fine sentiments, you say? Fine sentiments, be hanged! I had no time. I had to mess about with white-lead and strips of woolen blanket helping to put bandages on those leaky steampipes — I tell you. I had to watch the steering, and circumvent those snags, and get the tin-pot along by hook or by crook. There was surface-truth enough in these things to save a wiser man. And between whiles I had to look after the savage who was fireman. He was an improved specimen; he could fire up a vertical boiler. He was there below me, and, upon my word, to look at him was as edifying as seeing a dog in a parody of breeches and a feather hat, walking on his hindlegs. A few months of training had done for that really fine chap. He squinted at the steam-gauge and at the water-gauge with an evident effort of intrepidity — and he had filed teeth, too, the poor devil, and the wool of his pate shaved into queer patterns, and three ornamental scars on each of his cheeks. He ought to have been clapping his hands and stamping his feet on the bank, instead of which he was hard at work, a thrall to strange witchcraft, full of improving knowledge. He was useful because he had been instructed; and what he knew was this — that should the water in that transparent thing disappear, the evil spirit inside the boiler would get angry through the greatness of his thirst, and take a terrible vengeance. So he sweated and fired up and watched the glass fearfully (with an impromptu charm, made of rags, tied to his arm, and a piece of polished bone, as big as a watch, stuck flatways through his lower lip), while the wooden banks slipped past us slowly, the short noise was left behind, the interminable miles of silence — and we crept on, towards Kurtz. But the snags were thick, the water was treacherous and shallow, the boiler seemed indeed to have a sulky devil in it, and thus neither that fireman nor I had any time to peer into our creepy thoughts.

"Some fifty miles below the Inner Station we came upon a hut of reeds, an inclined and melancholy pole, with the unrecognizable tatters of what had been a flag of some sort flying from it, and a neatly stacked woodpile. This was unexpected. We came to the bank, and on the stack of firewood found a flat piece of board with some faded pencil-writing on it. When deciphered it said: 'Wood for you. Hurry up. Approach cautiously.' There was a signature, but it was illegible — not Kurtz — a much longer word. 'Hurry up.' Where? Up the river? 'Approach cautiously.' We had not done so. But the warning could not have been meant for the place where it could be only found after approach. Something was wrong above. But what — and how much? That was the question. We commented adversely upon the imbecility of that telegraphic style. The bush around said nothing, and would not let us look very far, either. A torn curtain of red twill hung in the doorway of the hut, and flapped sadly in our faces. The dwelling was dismantled; but we could see a white man had lived there not very long ago. There remained a rude table — a plank on two posts; a heap of rubbish reposed in a dark corner, and by the door I picked up a book. It had lost its covers, and the pages had been thumbed into a state of extremely dirty softness; but the back had been lovingly stitched afresh with white cotton thread, which looked clean yet. It was an extraordinary find. Its title was, *An Inquiry into Some Points of Seamanship*, by a man Towser, Towson — some such name — Master in His Majesty's Navy. The matter looked dreary reading enough, with illustrative diagrams and repulsive tables of figures, and the copy was sixty years old. I handled this amazing antiquity with the greatest possible tenderness, lest it should dissolve in my hands. Within, Towson or Towser was inquiring earnestly into the breaking strain of ships' chains and tackle, and other such matters. Not a very enthralling book; but at the first glance you could see there a singleness of intention, an honest concern for the right way of going to work, which made these humble pages, thought out so many years ago, luminous with another than a professional light. The simple old sailor, with his talk of chains and purchases, made me forget the jungle and the pilgrims in a delicious sensation of having come upon something unmistakably real. Such a book being there was wonderful enough; but still more astounding were the notes penciled in the margin, and plainly referring to the text. I couldn't believe my eyes! They were in cipher! Yes, it looked like cipher. Fancy a man lugging with him a book of that description into this nowhere and studying it — and making notes — in cipher at that! It was an extravagant mystery.

"I had been dimly aware for some time of a worrying noise, and when I lifted my eyes I saw the woodpile was gone, and the manager, aided by all the pilgrims, was shouting at me from the riverside. I slipped the book into my pocket. I assure you to leave off reading was like tearing myself away from the shelter of an old and solid friendship.

"I started the lame engine ahead. 'It must be this miserable trader — this intruder,' exclaimed the manager, looking back malevolently at the place we had left. 'He must be English,' I said. 'It will not save him from getting into trouble if he is not careful,' muttered the manager darkly. I observed with assumed innocence that no man was safe from trouble in this world.

"The current was more rapid now, the steamer seemed at her last gasp, the stern-wheel flopped languidly, and I caught myself listening on tiptoe for the next beat of the float, for in sober truth I expected the wretched thing to give up every moment. It was like watching the last flickers of a life. But still we crawled. Sometimes I would pick out a tree a little way ahead to measure our progress towards Kurtz by, but I lost it invariably before we got abreast. To keep the eyes so long on one thing was too much for human patience. The manager displayed a beautiful resignation. I fretted and fumed and took to arguing with myself whether or not I would talk openly with Kurtz; but before I could come to any conclusion it occurred to me that my speech or my silence, indeed any action of mine, would be a mere futility. What did it matter what anyone knew or ignored? What did it matter who was manager? One gets sometimes such a flash of insight. The essentials of this affair lay deep under the surface, beyond my reach, and beyond my power of meddling.

"Towards the evening of the second day we judged ourselves about eight miles from Kurtz's station. I wanted to push on; but the manager looked grave, and told me the navigation up there was so dangerous that it would be advisable, the sun being very low already, to wait where we were till next morning.

Moreover, he pointed out that if the warning to approach cautiously were to be followed, we must approach in daylight — not at dusk, or in the dark. This was sensible enough. Eight miles meant nearly three hours' steaming for us, and I could also see suspicious ripples at the upper end of the reach. Nevertheless, I was annoyed beyond expression at the delay, and most unreasonably, too, since one night more could not matter much after so many months. As we had plenty of wood, and caution was the word, I brought up in the middle of the stream. The reach was narrow, straight, with high sides like a railway cutting. The dusk came gliding into it long before the sun had set. The current ran smooth and swift, but a dumb immobility sat on the banks. The living trees, lashed together by the creepers and every living bush of the undergrowth, might have been changed into stone, even to the slenderest twig, to the lightest leaf. It was not sleep — it seemed unnatural, like a state of trance. Not the faintest sound of any kind could be heard. You looked on amazed, and began to suspect yourself of being deaf — then the night came suddenly, and struck you blind as well. About three in the morning some large fish leaped, and the loud splash made me jump as though a gun had been fired. When the sun rose there was a white fog, very warm and clammy, and more blinding than the night. It did not shift or drive; it was just there, standing all around you like something solid. At eight or nine, perhaps, it lifted as a shutter lifts. We had a glimpse of the towering multitude of trees, of the immense matted jungle, with the blazing little ball of the sun hanging over it — all perfectly still — and then the white shutter came down again, smoothly, as if sliding in greased grooves. I ordered the chain, which we had begun to heave in, to be paid out again. Before it stopped running with a muffled rattle, a cry, a very loud cry, as of infinite desolation, soared slowly in the opaque air. It ceased. A complaining clamor, modulated in savage discords, filled our ears. The sheer unexpectedness of it made my hair stir under my cap. I don't know how it struck the others: to me it seemed as though the mist itself had screamed, so suddenly, and apparently from all sides at once, did this tumultuous and mournful uproar arise. It culminated in a hurried outbreak of almost intolerably excessive shrieking, which stopped short, leaving us stiffened in a variety of silly attitudes, and obstinately listening to the nearly as appalling and excessive silence. 'Good God! What is the meaning —' stammered at my elbow one of the pilgrims — a little fat man, with sandy hair and red whiskers, who wore side-spring boots, and pink pajamas tucked into his socks. Two others remained open-mouthed a whole minute, then dashed into the little cabin, to rush out incontinently and stand darting scared glances, with Winchesters at 'ready' in their hands. What we could see was just the steamer we were on, her outlines blurred as though she had been on the point of dissolving, and a misty strip of water, perhaps two feet broad, around her — and that was all. The rest of the world was nowhere, as far as our eyes and ears were concerned. Just nowhere. Gone, disappeared; swept off without leaving a whisper or a shadow behind.

"I went forward, and ordered the chain to be hauled in short, so as to be ready to trip the anchor and move the steamboat at once if necessary. 'Will they attack?' whispered an awed voice. 'We will be all butchered in this fog,' murmured another. The faces twitched with the strain, the hands trembling slightly, the eyes forgot to wink. It was very curious to see the contrast of expressions of the white men and of the black fellows of our crew, who were as much strangers to that part of the river as we, though their homes were only eight hundred miles away. The whites, of course, greatly discomposed, had besides a curious look of being painfully shocked by such an outrageous row. The others had an alert, naturally interested expression; but their faces were essentially quiet, even those of the one or two who grinned as they hauled at the chain. Several exchanged short, grunting phrases, which seemed to settle the matter to their satisfaction. Their headman, a young, broad-chested black, severely draped in dark-blue fringed cloths, with fierce nostrils and his hair all done up artfully in oily ringlets, stood near me. 'Aha!' I said, just for good fellowship's sake. 'Catch 'em,' he snapped, with a bloodshot widening of his eyes and a flash of sharp teeth — 'catch 'im. Give 'im to us.' 'To you, eh?' I asked; 'what would you do with them?' 'Eat 'em!' he said, curtly, and, leaning his elbow on the rail, looked out into the fog in a dignified and profoundly pensive attitude. I would no doubt have been properly horrified, had it not occurred to me that he and his chaps must be very hungry: that they must have been growing increasingly hungry for at least this month past. They had been engaged for six months (I don't think a single one of them had any clear idea of time, as we at the end of countless ages have. They still belonged to the beginnings of time — had no inherited experience to teach them as it were), and of course, as long as there was a piece of paper written over in accordance with some farcical law or other made down the river, it didn't enter anybody's head to trouble how they would live. Certainly they had brought with them some rotten hippo-meat, which couldn't have lasted very long, anyway, even if the pilgrims hadn't, in the midst of a shocking hullabaloo, thrown a considerable quantity of it overboard. It looked like a high-handed proceeding; but it was really a case of legitimate self-defense. You can't breathe dead hippo waking, sleeping, and eating, and at the same time keep your precarious grip on existence. Besides that, they had given them every week three pieces of brass wire, each about nine inches long; and the theory was they were to buy their provisions with that currency in riverside villages. You can see how *that* worked. There were either no villages, or the people were hostile, or the director, who like the rest of us fed out of tins, with an occasional old he-goat thrown in, didn't want to stop the steamer for some more or less recondite reason. So, unless they swallowed the wire itself, or made loops of it to snare the fishes with, I don't see what good their extravagant salary could be to them. I must say it was paid with a regularity worthy of a large and honorable trading company. For the rest, the only thing to eat — though it didn't look eatable in the least — I saw in their possession was a few lumps of some stuff like half-cooked dough, of a dirty lavender color, they kept wrapped in leaves, and now and then swallowed a piece of, but so small that it seemed done more for the looks of the thing than for any serious purpose of sustenance. Why in the name of all the gnawing devils of hunger they didn't go for us — they were thirty to five — and have a good tuck-in for once, amazes me now when I think of it. They were big powerful men, with not much capacity to weigh the consequences, with courage, with strength, even yet, though their skins were no longer glossy and their muscles no longer hard. And I saw that something restraining, one of those human secrets that baffle probability, had come into play there. I looked at them with a swift quickening of interest — not because it occurred to me I might be eaten by them before very long, though I own to you that just then I perceived — in a new light, as it were — how unwholesome the pilgrims looked, and I hoped, yes, I positively hoped, that my aspect was not so — what shall I say? — so — unappetizing: a touch of fantastic vanity which fitted well with the dream-sensation that pervaded all my days at that time. Perhaps I had a little fever, too. One can't live with one's finger everlastingly on one's pulse. I had often 'a little fever,' or a little touch of other things — the playful paw-strokes of the wilderness, the preliminary trifling before the more serious onslaught which came in due course. Yes; I looked at them as you would on any human being, with a curiosity of their impulses, motives, capacities, weaknesses, when brought to the test of an inexorable physical necessity. Restraint! What possible restraint! Was it superstition, disgust, patience, fear — or some kind of primitive honor? No fear can stand up to hunger, no patience can wear it out, disgust simply does not exist where hunger is; and as to superstition, beliefs, and what you may call principles, they are less than chaff in a breeze. Don't you know the devilry of lingering starvation, its exasperating torment, its black thoughts, its somber and brooding ferocity? Well, I do. It takes a man all his inborn strength to fight hunger properly. It's really easier to face bereavement, dishonor, and the perdition of one's soul — than this kind of prolonged hunger. Sad, but true. And these chaps, too, had no earthly reason for any kind of scruple. Restraint! I would just as soon have expected restraint from a hyena prowling amongst the corpses of a battlefield. But there was the fact facing me — the fact dazzling, to be seen, like the foam on the depths of the sea, like a ripple on an unfathomable enigma, a mystery greater — when I thought of it — than the curious, inexplicable note of desperate grief in this savage clamor that had swept by us on the riverbank, behind the blind whiteness of the fog.

"Two pilgrims were quarreling in hurried whispers as to which bank, 'Left.' 'No, no; how can you? Right, right, of course.' 'It is very serious,' said the manager's voice behind me; 'I would be desolated if anything should happen to Mr. Kurtz before we came up.' I looked at him, and had not the slightest doubt he was sincere. He was just the kind of man who would wish to preserve appearances. That was his restraint. But when he muttered something about going on at once, I did not even take the trouble to answer him. I knew, and he knew, that it was impossible. Were we to let go our hold of the bottom, we would be absolutely in the air — in space. We wouldn't be able to tell where we were going to — whether up or down stream, or across — till we fetched against one bank or the other — and then we wouldn't know at first which it was. Of course I made no move. I had no mind for a smash-up. You couldn't imagine a more deadly place for a shipwreck. Whether drowned at once or not, we were sure to perish speedily in one way or another. 'I authorize you to take all the risks,' he said, after a short silence. 'I refuse to take any,' I said, shortly;

which was just the answer he expected, though its tone might have surprised him. 'Well, I must defer to your judgment. You are captain,' he said, with marked civility. I turned my shoulder to him in sign of my appreciation, and looked into the fog. How long would it last? It was the most hopeless lookout. The approach to this Kurtz grubbing for ivory in the wretched bush was beset by as many dangers as though he had been an enchanted princess sleeping in a fabulous castle. 'Will they attack, do you think?' asked the manager, in a confidential tone.

"I did not think they would attack, for several obvious reasons. The thick fog was one. If they left the bank in their canoes they would get lost in it, as we would be if we attempted to move. Still, I had also judged the jungle of both banks quite impenetrable — and yet eyes were in it, eyes that had seen us. The riverside bushes were certainly very thick; but the undergrowth behind was evidently penetrable. However, during the short lift I had seen no canoes anywhere in the reach — certainly not abreast of the steamer. But what made the idea of attack inconceivable to me was the nature of the noise — of the cries we had heard. They had not the fierce character boding immediate hostile intention. Unexpected, wild, and violent as they had been, they had given me an irresistible impression of sorrow. The glimpse of the steamboat had for some reason filled those savages with unrestrained grief. The danger, if any, I expounded, was from our proximity to a great human passion let loose. Even extreme grief may ultimately vent itself in violence — but more generally takes the form of apathy. . . .

"You should have seen the pilgrims stare! They had no heart to grin, or even to revile me: but I believe they thought me gone mad — with fright, maybe. I delivered a regular lecture. My dear boys, it was no good bothering. Keep a lookout? Well, you may guess I watched the fog for the signs of lifting as a cat watches a mouse; but for anything else our eyes were of no more use to us than if we had been buried miles deep in a heap of cotton-wool. It felt like it, too — choking, warm, stifling. Besides, all I said, though it sounded extravagant, was absolutely true to fact. What we afterwards alluded to as an attack was really an attempt at repulse. The action was very far from being aggressive — it was not even defensive, in the usual sense: it was undertaken under the stress of desperation, and in its essence was purely protective.

"It developed itself, I should say, two hours after the fog lifted, and its commencement was at a spot, roughly speaking, about a mile and a half below Kurtz's station. We had just floundered and flopped round a bend, when I saw an islet, a mere grassy hummock of bright green, in the middle of the stream. It was the only thing of the kind; but as we opened the reach more, I perceived it was the head of a long sandbank, or rather of a chain of shallow patches stretching down the middle of the river. They were discolored, just awash, and the whole lot was seen just under the water, exactly as a man's backbone is seen running down the middle of his back under the skin. Now, as far as I did see, I could go to the right or to the left of this. I didn't know either channel, of course. The banks looked pretty well alike, the depth appeared the same; but as I had been informed the station was on the west side, I naturally headed for the western passage.

"No sooner had we fairly entered it than I became aware it was much narrower than I had supposed. To the left of us there was the long uninterrupted shoal, and to the right a high, steep bank heavily overgrown with bushes. Above the bush the trees stood in serried ranks. The twigs overhung the current thickly, and from distance to distance a large limb of some tree projected rigidly over the stream. It was then well on in the afternoon, the face of the forest was gloomy, and a broad strip of shadow had already fallen on the water. In this shadow we steamed up — very slowly, as you may imagine. I sheered her well inshore — the water being deepest near the bank, as the sounding-pole informed me.

"One of my hungry and forbearing friends was sounding in the bows just below me. This steamboat was exactly like a decked scow. On the deck, there were two little teak-wood houses, with doors and windows. The boiler was in the fore-end, and the machinery right astern. Over the whole there was a light roof, supported on stanchions. The funnel projected through that roof, and in front of the funnel a small cabin built of light planks served for a pilot-house. It contained a couch, two campstools, a loaded Martini-Henry[10] leaning in one corner, a tiny table, and the steering-wheel. It had a wide door in front and a broad shutter at each side. All these were always thrown open, of course. I spent my days perched up there on the extreme fore-end of that roof, before the door. At night I slept, or tried to, on the couch. An athletic black belonging to some coast tribe, and educated by my poor predecessor, was the helmsman. He sported a pair of brass earrings, wore a blue cloth wrapper from the waist to the ankles, and thought all the world of himself. He was the most unstable kind of fool I had ever seen. He steered with no end to a swagger while you were by; but if he lost sight of you, he became instantly the prey of an abject funk, and would let that cripple of a steamboat get the upper hand of him in a minute.

"I was looking down at the sounding-pole, and feeling much annoyed to see at each try a little more of it stick out that river, when I saw my poleman give up the business suddenly, and stretch himself flat on the deck, without even taking the trouble to haul his pole in. He kept hold on it though, and it trailed in the water. At the same time the fireman, whom I could also see below me, sat down abruptly before his furnace and ducked his head. I was amazed. Then I had to look at the river mighty quick, because there was a snag in the fairway. Sticks, little sticks, were flying about — thick: they were whizzing before my nose, dropping below me, striking behind me against my pilot-house. All this time the river, the shore, the woods, were very quiet — perfectly quiet. I could only hear the heavy splashing thump of the stern-wheel and the patter of these things. We cleared the snag clumsily. Arrows, by Jove! We were being shot at! I stepped in quickly to close the shutter on the land-side. That fool-helmsman, his hands on the spokes, was lifting his knees high, stamping his feet, champing his mouth, like a reined-in horse. Confound him! And we were staggering within ten feet of the bank. I had to lean right out to swing the heavy shutter, and I saw a face amongst the leaves on the level with my own, looking at me

---

[10] A heavy military rifle.

very fierce and steady; and then suddenly, as though a veil had been removed from my eyes, I made out, deep in the tangled gloom, naked breasts, arms, legs, glaring eyes — the bush was swarming with human limbs in movement, glistening, of bronze color. The twigs shook, swayed, and rustled, the arrows flew out of them, and then the shutter came to. 'Steer her straight,' I said to the helmsman. He held his head rigid, face forward; but his eyes rolled, he kept on lifting and setting down his feet gently, his mouth foamed a little. 'Keep quiet!' I said in a fury. I might just as well have ordered a tree not to sway in the wind. I darted out. Below me there was a great scuffle of feet on the iron deck; confused exclamations; a voice screamed, 'Can you turn back?' I caught sight of a V-shaped ripple on the water ahead. What? Another snag! A fusillade burst out under my feet. The pilgrims had opened with their Winchesters, and were simply squirting lead into that bush. A deuce of a lot of smoke came up and drove slowly forward. I swore at it. Now I couldn't see the ripple or the snag either. I stood in the doorway, peering, and the arrows came in swarms. They might have been poisoned, but they looked as though they wouldn't kill a cat. The bush began to howl. Our wood-cutters raised a war-like whoop; the report of a rifle just at my back deafened me. I glanced over my shoulder, and the pilot-house was yet full of noise and smoke when I made a dash at the wheel. The fool-nigger had dropped everything to throw the shutter open and let off that Martini-Henry. He stood before the wide opening, glaring, and I yelled at him to come back, while I straightened the sudden twist out of that steamboat. There was no room to turn even if I had wanted to, the snag was somewhere very near ahead in that confounded smoke, there was no time to lose, so I just crowded her into the bank — right into the bank, where I knew the water was deep.

"We tore slowly along the overhanging bushes in a whirl of broken twigs and flying leaves. The fusillade below stopped short, as I had foreseen it would when the squirts got empty. I threw my head back to a glinting whizz that traversed the pilot-house, in at one shutter-hole and out at the other. Looking past that mad helmsman, who was shaking the empty rifle and yelling at the shore, I saw vague forms of men running bent double, leaping, gliding, distinct, incomplete, evanescent. Something big appeared in the air before the shutter, the rifle went overboard, and the man stepped back swiftly, looked at me over his shoulder in an extraordinary, profound, familiar manner, and fell upon my feet. The side of his head hit the wheel twice, and the end of what appeared a long cane clattered round and knocked over a little campstool. It looked as though after wrenching that thing from somebody ashore he had lost his balance in the effort. The thin smoke had blown away, we were clear of the snag, and looking ahead I could see that in another hundred yards or so I would be free to sheer off, away from the bank; but my feet felt so very warm and wet that I had to look down. The man had rolled on his back and stared straight up at me; both his hands clutched that cane. It was the shaft of a spear that, either thrown or lunged through the opening, had caught him in the side just below the ribs; the blade had gone in out of sight, after making a frightful gash; my shoes were full; a pool of blood lay very still, gleaming dark-red under the wheel; his eyes shone with an amazing luster. The fusillade burst out again. He looked at me anxiously, gripping the spear like something precious, with an air of being afraid I would try to take it away from him. I had to make an effort to free my eyes from his gaze and attend to steering. With one hand I felt above my head for the line of the steam-whistle, and jerked out screech after screech hurriedly. The tumult of angry and warlike yells was checked instantly, and then from the depths of the woods went out such a tremulous and prolonged wail of mournful fear and utter despair as may be imagined to follow the flight of the last hope from the earth. There was a great commotion in the bush; the shower of arrows stopped, a few dropping shots rang out sharply—then silence, in which the languid beat of the stern-wheel came plainly to my ears. I put the helm hard a-starboard at the moment when the pilgrim in pink pajamas, very hot and agitated, appeared in the doorway. 'The manager sends me—' he began in an official tone, and stopped short. 'Good God!' he said, glaring at the wounded man.

"We two whites stood over him, and his lustrous and inquiring glance enveloped us both. I declare it looked as though he would presently put to us some question in an understandable language; but he died without uttering a sound, without moving a limb, without twitching a muscle. Only in the very last moment, as though in response to some sign we could not see, to some whisper we could not hear, he frowned heavily, and that frown gave to his black death-mask an inconceivably somber, brooding, and menacing expression. The luster of inquiring glance faded swiftly into vacant glassiness. 'Can you steer?' I asked the agent eagerly. He looked very dubious; but I made a grab at his arm, and he understood at once I meant him to steer whether or no. To tell you the truth, I was morbidly anxious to change my shoes and socks. 'He is dead,' murmured the fellow, immensely impressed. 'No doubt about it,' said I tugging like mad at the shoe-laces. 'And by the way, I suppose Mr. Kurtz is dead as well by this time.'

"For the moment that was the dominant thought. There was a sense of extreme disappointment, as though I had found out I had been striving after something altogether without a substance. I couldn't have been more disgusted if I had traveled all this way for the sole purpose of talking with Mr. Kurtz. Talking with.... I flung one shoe overboard, and became aware that that was exactly what I had been looking forward to—a talk with Kurtz. I made the strange discovery that I had never imagined him as doing, you know, but as discoursing. I didn't say to myself, 'Now I will never see him,' or 'Now I will never shake him by the hand,' but, 'Now I will never hear him.' The man presented himself as a voice. Not of course that I did not connect him with some sort of action. Hadn't I been told in all the tones of jealousy and admiration that he had collected, bartered, swindled, or stolen more ivory than all the other agents together? That was not the point. The point was in his being a gifted creature, and that of all his gifts the one that stood out preeminently, that carried with it a sense of real presence, was his ability to talk, his words—the gift of expression, the bewildering, the illuminating, the most exalted and the most contemptible, the pulsating stream of light, or the deceitful flow from the heart of an impenetrable darkness.

"The other shoe went flying unto the devil-god of that river. I thought, by Jove! it's all over. We are too late; he has vanished — the gift has vanished, by means of some spear, arrow, or club. I will never hear that chap speak after all — and my sorrow had a startling extravagance of emotion, even such as I had noticed in the howling sorrow of these savages in the bush. I couldn't have felt more lonely desolation somehow, had I been robbed of a belief or had missed my destiny in life. . . . Why do you sigh in this beastly way, somebody? Absurd? Well, absurd. Good Lord! mustn't a man ever — Here, give me some tobacco." . . .

There was a pause of profound stillness, then a match flared, and Marlow's lean face appeared, worn, hollow, with downward folds and drooped eyelids, with an aspect of concentrated attention; and as he took vigorous draws at his pipe, it seemed to retreat and advance out of the night in the regular flicker of the tiny flame. The match went out.

"Absurd!" he cried. "This is the worst of trying to tell. . . . Here you all are, each moored with two good addresses, like a hulk with two anchors, a butcher round one corner, a policeman round another, excellent appetites, and temperature normal — you hear — normal from year's end to year's end. And you say, Absurd! Absurd be — exploded! Absurd! My dear boys, what can you expect from a man who out of sheer nervousness had just flung overboard a pair of new shoes! Now I think of it, it is amazing I did not shed tears. I am, upon the whole, proud of my fortitude. I was cut to the quick at the idea of having lost the inestimable privilege of listening to the gifted Kurtz. Of course I was wrong. The privilege was waiting for me. Oh, yes, I heard more than enough. And I was right, too. A voice. He was very little more than a voice. And I heard — him — it — this voice — other voices — all of them were so little more than voices — and the memory of that time itself lingers around me, impalpable, like a dying vibration of one immense jabber, silly, atrocious, sordid, savage, or simply mean, without any kind of sense. Voices, voices — even the girl herself — now —"

He was silent for a long time.

"I laid the ghost of his gifts at last with a lie," he began, suddenly. "Girl! What? Did I mention a girl? Oh, she is out of it — completely. They — the women I mean — are out of it — should be out of it. We must help them to stay in that beautiful world of their own, lest ours gets worse. Oh, she had to be out of it. You should have heard the disinterred body of Mr. Kurtz saying, 'My Intended.' You would have perceived directly then how completely she was out of it. And the lofty frontal bone of Mr. Kurtz! They say the hair goes on growing sometimes, but this — ah — specimen, was impressively bald. The wilderness had patted him on the head, and, behold, it was like a ball — an ivory ball; it had caressed him, and — lo! — he had withered; it had taken him, loved him, embraced him, got into his veins, consumed his flesh, and sealed his soul to its own by the inconceivable ceremonies of some devilish initiation. He was its spoiled and pampered favorite. Ivory? I should think so. Heaps of it, stacks of it. The old mud shanty was bursting with it. You would think there was not a single tusk left either above or below the ground in the whole country. 'Mostly fossil,' the manager had remarked, disparagingly. It was no more fossil than I am; but they call it fossil when it is dug up. It appears these niggers do bury the tusks sometimes — but evidently they couldn't bury this parcel deep enough to save the gifted Mr. Kurtz from his fate. We filled the steamboat with it, and had to pile a lot on the deck. Thus he could see and enjoy as long as he could see, because the appreciation of this favor had remained with him to the last. You should have heard him say, 'My ivory.' Oh, yes, I heard him. 'My Intended, my ivory, my station, my river, my —' everything belonged to him. It made me hold my breath in expectation of hearing the wilderness burst into a prodigious peal of laughter that would shake the fixed stars in their places. Everything belonged to him — but that was a trifle. The thing was to know what he belonged to, how many powers of darkness claimed him for their own. That was the reflection that made you creepy all over. It was impossible — it was not good for one either — trying to imagine. He had taken a high seat amongst the devils of the land — I mean literally. You can't understand. How could you? — with solid pavement under your feet, surrounded by kind neighbors ready to cheer you or to fall on you, stepping delicately between the butcher and the policeman, in the holy terror of scandal and gallows and lunatic asylums — how can you imagine what particular region of the first ages a man's untrammeled feet may take him into by the way of solitude — utter solitude without a policeman — by the way of silence — utter silence, where no warning voice of a kind neighbor can be heard whispering of public opinion? These little things make all the great difference. When they are gone you must fall back upon your own innate strength, upon your own capacity for faithfulness. Of course you may be too much of a fool to go wrong — too dull even to know you are being assaulted by the powers of darkness. I take it, no fool ever made a bargain for his soul with the devil: the fool is too much of a fool, or the devil too much of a devil — I don't know which. Or you may be such a thunderingly exalted creature as to be altogether deaf and blind to anything but heavenly sights and sounds. Then the earth for you is only a standing place — and whether to be like this is your loss or your gain I won't pretend to say. But most of us are neither one nor the other. The earth for us is a place to live in, where we must put up with sights, with sounds, with smells, too, by Jove! — breathe dead hippo, so to speak and not be contaminated. And there, don't you see? your strength comes in, the faith in your ability for the digging of unostentatious holes to bury the stuff in — your power of devotion, not to yourself, but to an obscure, back-breaking business. And that's difficult enough. Mind, I am not trying to excuse or even explain — I am trying to account to myself for — for — Mr. Kurtz — for the shade of Mr. Kurtz. This initiated wraith from the back of Nowhere honored me with its amazing confidence before it vanished altogether. This was because it could speak English to me. The original Kurtz had been educated partly in England, and — as he was good enough to say himself — his sympathies were in the right place. His mother was half-English, his father was half-French. All Europe contributed to the making of Kurtz; and by and by I learned that, most appropriately, the International Society for the Suppression of Savage Customs had entrusted him with the making of a report, for its future guidance. And he had written it, too. I've seen it. I've read it. It was eloquent, vibrating with eloquence, but too high-strung, I think. Seventeen pages of close writing he had found time for! But this must have been before his — let us say — nerves, went wrong, and caused him to preside at certain midnight dances ending with unspeakable rites, which — as far as I reluctantly gathered from what I heard at various times — were offered up to him — do you understand? — to Mr. Kurtz himself. But it was a beautiful piece of writing. The opening paragraph, however, in the light of later information, strikes me now as ominous. He began with the argument that we whites, from the point of development he had arrived at, 'must necessarily appear to them [savages] in the nature of supernatural beings — we approach them with the might as of a deity,' and so on, and so on. 'By the simple exercise of our will we can exert a power for good practically unbounded,' etc., etc. From that point he soared and took me with him. The peroration was magnificent, though difficult to remember, you know. It gave me the notion of an exotic Immensity ruled by an august Benevolence. It made me tingle with enthusiasm. This was the unbounded power of eloquence — of words — of burning noble words. There were no practical hints to interrupt the magic current of phrases, unless a kind of note at the foot of the last page, scrawled evidently much later, in an unsteady hand, may be regarded as the exposition of a method. It was very simple, and at the end of that moving appeal to every altruistic sentiment it blazed at you, luminous and terrifying, like a flash of lightning in a serene sky: 'Exterminate all the brutes!' The curious part was that he had apparently forgotten all about that valuable postscriptum, because, later on, when he in a sense came to himself, he repeatedly entreated me to take good care of 'my pamphlet' (he called it), as it was sure to have in the future a good influence upon his career. I had full information about all these things, and, besides, as it turned out, I was to have the care of his memory. I've done enough for it to give me the indisputable right to lay it, if I choose, for an everlasting rest in the dust-bin of progress, amongst all the sweepings and, figuratively speaking, all the dead cats of civilization. But then, you see, I can't choose. He won't be forgotten. Whatever he was, he was not common. He had the power to charm or frighten rudimentary souls into an aggravated witch-dance in his honor; he could also fill the small souls of the pilgrims with bitter misgivings: he had one devoted friend at least, and he had conquered one soul in the world that was neither rudimentary nor tainted with self-seeking. No; I can't forget him, though I am not prepared to affirm the fellow was exactly worth the life we lost in getting to him. I missed my late helmsman awfully — I missed him even while his body was still lying in the pilot-house. Perhaps you will think it passing strange this regret for a savage who was no more account than a grain of sand in a black Sahara. Well, don't you see, he had done something, he had steered; for months I had him at my back — a help — an instrument. It was a kind of partnership. He steered for me — I had to look after him, I worried about his deficiencies, and thus a subtle bond had been created, of which I only became aware when it was suddenly broken. And the intimate profundity of that look he gave me when he received his hurt remains to this day in my memory — like a claim of distant kinship affirmed in a supreme moment.

"Poor fool! If he had only left that shutter alone. He had no restraint, no restraint—just like Kurtz—a tree swayed by the wind. As soon as I had put on a dry pair of slippers, I dragged him out, after first jerking the spear out of his side, which operation I confess I performed with my eyes shut tight. His heels leaped together over the little door-step; his shoulders were pressed to my breast; I hugged him from behind desperately. Oh! he was heavy, heavy; heavier than any man on earth, I should imagine. Then without more ado I tipped him overboard. The current snatched him as though he had been a wisp of grass, and I saw the body roll over twice before I lost sight of it forever. All the pilgrims and the manager were then congregated on the awning-deck about the pilot-house, chattering at each other like a flock of excited magpies, and there was a scandalized murmur at my heartless promptitude. What they wanted to keep that body hanging about for I can't guess. Embalm it, maybe. But I had also heard another, and a very ominous, murmur on the deck below. My friends the woodcutters were likewise scandalized, and with a better show of reason—though I admit that the reason itself was quite inadmissible. Oh, quite! I had made up my mind that if my late helmsman was to be eaten, the fishes alone should have him. He had been a very second-rate helmsman while alive, but now he was dead he might have become a first-class temptation, and possibly cause some startling trouble. Besides, I was anxious to take the wheel, the man in pink pajamas showing himself a hopeless duffer at the business.

"This I did directly the simple funeral was over. We were going half-speed, keeping right in the middle of the stream, and I listened to the talk about me. They had given up Kurtz, they had given up the station; Kurtz was dead, and the station had been burnt—and so on—and so on. The red-haired pilgrim was beside himself with the thought that at least this poor Kurtz had been properly avenged. 'Say! We must have made a glorious slaughter of them in the bush. Eh? What do you think? Say?' He positively danced, the blood-thirsty little gingery beggar. And he had nearly fainted when he saw the wounded man! I could not help saying, 'You made a glorious lot of smoke, anyhow.' I had seen, from the way the tops of the bushes rustled and flew, that almost all the shots had gone too high. You can't hit anything unless you take aim and fire from the shoulder; but these chaps fired from the hip with their eyes shut. The retreat, I maintained—and I was right—was caused by the screeching of the steam-whistle. Upon this they forgot Kurtz, and began to howl at me with indignant protests.

"The manager stood by the wheel murmuring confidentially about the necessity of getting well away down the river before dark at all events, when I saw in the distance a clearing on the riverside and the outlines of some sort of building. 'What's this?' I asked. He clapped his hands in wonder. 'The station!' he cried. I edged in at once, still going half-speed.

"Through my glasses I saw the slope of a hill interspersed with rare trees and perfectly free from undergrowth. A long decaying building on the summit was half buried in the high grass; the large holes in the peaked roof gaped black from afar; the jungle and the woods made a background. There was no enclosure or fence of any kind; but there had been one apparently, for near the house half-a-dozen slim posts remained in a row, roughly trimmed, and with their upper ends ornamented with round carved balls. The rails, or whatever there had been between, had disappeared. Of course the forest surrounded all that. The riverbank was clear, and on the waterside I saw a white man under a hat like a cart-wheel beckoning persistently with his whole arm. Examining the edge of the forest above and below, I was almost certain I could see movements — human forms gliding here and there. I steamed past prudently, then stopped the engines and let her drift down. The man on the shore began to shout, urging us to land. 'We have been attacked,' screamed the manager. 'I know — I know. It's all right,' yelled back the other, as cheerful as you please. 'Come along. It's all right, I am glad.'

"His aspect reminded me of something I had seen — something funny I had seen somewhere. As I maneuvered to get alongside, I was asking myself, 'What does this fellow look like?' Suddenly I got it. He looked like a harlequin. His clothes had been made of some stuff that was brown holland probably, but it was covered with patches all over, with bright patches, blue, red, and yellow — patches on the back, patches on the front, patches on elbows, on knees; colored binding around his jacket, scarlet edging at the bottom of his trousers; and the sunshine made him look extremely gay and wonderfully neat withal, because you could see how beautifully all this patching had been done. A beardless, boyish face, very fair, no features to speak of, nose peeling, little blue eyes, smiles and frowns chasing each other over that open countenance like sunshine and shadow on a windswept plain. 'Look out, captain!' he cried; 'there's a snag lodged in here last night.' What! Another snag? I confess I swore shamefully. I had nearly holed my cripple, to finish off that charming trip. The harlequin on the bank turned his little pug-nose up to me. 'You English?' he asked, all smiles. 'Are you?' I shouted from the wheel. The smiles vanished, and he shook his head as if sorry for my disappointment. Then he brightened up. 'Never mind!' he cried, encouragingly. 'Are we in time?' I asked. 'He is up there,' he replied with a toss of the head up the hill, and becoming gloomy all of a sudden. His face was like the autumn sky, overcast one moment and bright the next.

"When the manager, escorted by the pilgrims, all of them armed to the teeth, had gone to the house this chap came on board. 'I say, I don't like this. These natives are in the bush,' I said. He assured me earnestly it was all right. 'They are simple people,' he added; 'well, I am glad you came. It took me all my time to keep them off.' 'But you said it was all right,' I cried. 'Oh, they meant no harm,' he said; and as I stared he corrected himself, 'Not exactly.' Then vivaciously, 'My faith, your pilot-house wants a clean-up!' In the next breath he advised me to keep enough steam on the boiler to blow the whistle in case of any trouble. 'One good screech will do more for you than all your rifles. They are simple people,' he repeated. He rattled away at such a rate he quite overwhelmed me. He seemed to be trying to make up for lots of silence, and actually hinted, laughing, that such was the case. 'Don't you talk with Mr. Kurtz?' I said. 'You don't talk with that man — you listen to him,' he exclaimed with severe exaltation. 'But now —' He waved his arm, and in the twinkling of an eye was in the uttermost depths of despondency. In a moment he came up again with a jump, possessed himself of both my hands, and shook them continuously, while he gabbled: 'Brother sailor . . . honor . . . pleasure . . . delight . . . introduce myself . . . Russian . . . son of an arch-priest . . . Government of Tambov . . . What? Tobacco! English tobacco; the excellent English tobacco! Now, that's brotherly. Smoke? Where's a sailor that does not smoke?'

"The pipe soothed him, and gradually I made out he had run away from school, had gone to sea in a Russian ship; ran away again; served some time in English ships; was now reconciled with the arch-priest. He made a point of that. 'But when one is young one must see things, gather experience, ideas; enlarge the mind.' 'Here!' I interrupted. 'You can never tell! Here I met Mr. Kurtz,' he said, youthfully solemn and reproachful. I held my tongue after that. It appears he had persuaded a Dutch trading-house on the coast to fit him out with stores and goods, and had started for the interior with a light heart, and no more idea of what would happen to him than a baby. He had been wandering about that river for nearly two years alone, cut off from everybody and everything. 'I am not so young as I look. I am twenty-five,' he said. 'At first old Van Shuyten would tell me to go to the devil,' he narrated with keen enjoyment; 'but I stuck to him, and talked and talked, till at last he got afraid I would talk the hind-leg off his favorite dog, so he gave me some cheap things and a few guns, and told me he hoped he would never see my face again. Good old Dutchman, Van Shuyten. I've sent him one small lot of ivory a year ago, so that he can't call me a little thief when I get back. I hope he got it. And for the rest I don't care. I had some wood stacked for you. That was my old house. Did you see?'

"I gave him Towson's book. He made as though he would kiss me, but restrained himself. 'The only book I had left, and I thought I had lost it,' he said, looking at it ecstatically. 'So many accidents happen to a man going about alone, you know. Canoes get upset sometimes — and sometimes you've got to clear out so quick when the people get angry.' He thumbed the pages. 'You made notes in Russian?' I asked. He nodded. 'I thought they were written in cipher,' I said. He laughed, then became serious. 'I had lots of trouble to keep these people off,' he said. 'Did they want to kill you?' I asked. 'Oh, no!' he cried, and checked himself. 'Why did they attack us?' I pursued. He hesitated, then said shamefacedly, 'They don't want him to go.' 'Don't they?' I said, curiously. He nodded a nod full of mystery and wisdom. 'I tell you,' he cried, 'this man has enlarged my mind.' He opened his arms wide, staring at me with his little blue eyes that were perfectly round."

III

"I looked at him, lost in astonishment. There he was before me, in motley, as though he had absconded from a troupe of mimes, enthusiastic, fabulous. His very existence was improbable, inexplicable, and altogether bewildering. He was an insoluble problem. It was inconceivable how he had existed, how he had succeeded in getting so far, how he had managed to remain — why he did not instantly disappear. 'I went a little farther,' he said, 'then still a little farther — till

I had gone so far that I don't know how I'll ever get back. Never mind. Plenty time. I can manage. You take Kurtz away quick — quick — I tell you.' The glamour of youth enveloped his parti-colored rags, his destitution, his loneliness, the essential desolation of his futile wanderings. For months — for years — his life hadn't been worth a day's purchase; and there he was gallantly, thoughtlessly alive, to all appearance indestructible solely by the virtue of his few years and of his unreflecting audacity. I was seduced into something like admiration — like envy. Glamour urged him on, glamour kept him unscathed. He surely wanted nothing from the wilderness but space to breathe in and to push on through. His need was to exist, and to move onwards at the greatest possible risk, and with a maximum of privation. If the absolutely pure, uncalculating, unpractical spirit of adventure had ever ruled a human being, it ruled this be-patched youth. I almost envied him the possession of this modest and clear flame. It seemed to have consumed all thought of self so completely, that even while he was talking to you, you forgot that it was he — the man before your eyes — who had gone through these things. I did not envy him his devotion to Kurtz, though. He had not meditated over it. It came to him and he accepted it with a sort of eager fatalism. I must say that to me it appeared about the most dangerous thing in every way he had come upon so far.

"They had come together unavoidably, like two ships becalmed near each other, and lay rubbing sides at last. I suppose Kurtz wanted an audience, because on a certain occasion, when encamped in the forest, they had talked all night, or more probably Kurtz had talked. 'We talked of everything,' he said, quite transported at the recollection. 'I forgot there was such a thing as sleep. The night did not seem to last an hour. Everything! Everything! . . . Of love, too.' 'Ah, he talked to you of love!' I said, much amused. 'It isn't what you think,' he cried, almost passionately. 'It was in general. He made me see things — things.'

"He threw his arms up. We were on deck at the time, and the head-man of my wood-cutters, lounging near by, turned upon him his heavy and glittering eyes. I looked around, and I don't know why, but I assure you that never, never before, did this land, this river, this jungle, the very arch of this blazing sky, appear to me so hopeless and so dark, so impenetrable to human thought, so pitiless to human weakness. 'And, ever since, you have been with him, of course?' I said.

"On the contrary. It appears their intercourse had been very much broken by various causes. He had, as he informed me proudly, managed to nurse Kurtz through two illnesses (he alluded to it as you would to some risky feat), but as a rule Kurtz wandered alone far in the depths of the forest. 'Very often coming to this station, I had to wait days and days before he would turn up,' he said. 'Ah, it was worth waiting for! — sometimes.' 'What was he doing? exploring or what?' I asked. 'Oh, yes, of course'; he had discovered lots of villages, a lake, too — he did not know exactly in what direction; it was dangerous to inquire too much — but mostly his expeditions had been for ivory. 'But he had no goods to trade with by that time,' I objected. 'There's a good lot of cartridges left even yet,' he answered, looking away. 'To speak plainly, he raided the country,' I said. He nodded. 'Not alone, surely!' He muttered something about the

villages round that lake. 'Kurtz got the tribe to follow him, did he?' I suggested.
He fidgeted a little. 'They adored him,' he said. The tone of these words was
so extraordinary that I looked at him searchingly. It was curious to see his
mingled eagerness and reluctance to speak of Kurtz. The man filled his life,
occupied his thoughts, swayed his emotions. 'What can you expect?' he burst
out; 'he came to them with thunder and lightning, you know — and they had
never seen anything like it — and very terrible. He could be very terrible. You
can't judge Mr. Kurtz as you would an ordinary man. No, no, no! Now — just
to give you an idea — I don't mind telling you, he wanted to shoot me, too,
one day — but I don't judge him.' 'Shoot you!' I cried. 'What for?' 'Well, I had
a small lot of ivory the chief of that village near my house gave me. You see I
used to shoot game for them. Well, he wanted it, and wouldn't hear reason. He
declared he would shoot me unless I gave him the ivory and then cleared out
of the country, because he could do so, and had a fancy for it, and there was
nothing on earth to prevent him killing whom he jolly well pleased. And it was
true, too. I gave him the ivory. What did I care! But I didn't clear out. No, no. I
couldn't leave him. I had to be careful, of course, till we got friendly again for a
time. He had his second illness then. Afterwards I had to keep out of the way;
but I didn't mind. He was living for the most part in those villages on the lake.
When he came down to the river, sometimes he would take to me, and sometimes it was better for me to be careful. This man suffered too much. He hated
all this, and somehow he couldn't get away. When I had a chance I begged him
to try and leave while there was time; I offered to go back with him. And he
would say yes, and then he would remain; go off on another ivory hunt; disappear for weeks; forget himself amongst these people — forget himself — you
know.' 'Why! he's mad,' I said. He protested indignantly. Mr. Kurtz couldn't be
mad. If I had heard him talk, only two days ago, I wouldn't dare hint at such a
thing. . . . I had taken up my binoculars while we talked, and was looking at the
shore, sweeping the limit of the forest at each side and at the back of the house.
The consciousness of there being people in that bush, so silent, so quiet — as
silent and quiet as the ruined house on the hill — made me uneasy. There was
no sign on the face of nature of this amazing tale that was not so much told
as suggested to me in desolate exclamations, completed by shrugs, in interrupted phrases, in hints ending in deep sighs. The woods were unmoved, like
a mask — heavy, like the closed door of a prison — they looked with their air
of hidden knowledge, of patient expectation, of unapproachable silence. The
Russian was explaining to me that it was only lately that Mr. Kurtz had come
down to the river, bringing along with him all the fighting men of that lake
tribe. He had been absent for several months — getting himself adored, I suppose — and had come down unexpectedly, with the intention to all appearance
of making a raid either across the river or down stream. Evidently the appetite for more ivory had got the better of the — what shall I say? — less material
aspirations. However he had got much worse suddenly. 'I heard he was lying
helpless, and so I came up — took my chance,' said the Russian. 'Oh, he is bad,
very bad.' I directed my glass to the house. There were no signs of life, but there
was the ruined roof, the long mud wall peeping above the grass, with three

little square window-holes, no two of the same size; all this brought within reach of my hand, as it were. And then I made a brusque movement, and one of the remaining posts of that vanished fence leaped up in the field of my glass. You remember I told you I had been struck at the distance by certain attempts at ornamentation, rather remarkable in the ruinous aspect of the place. Now I had suddenly a nearer view, and its first result was to make me throw my head back as if before a blow. Then I went carefully from post to post with my glass, and I saw my mistake. These round knobs were not ornamental but symbolic; they were expressive and puzzling, striking and disturbing — food for thought and also for vultures if there had been any looking down from the sky; but at all events for such ants as were industrious enough to ascend the pole. They would have been even more impressive, those heads on the stakes, if their faces had not been turned to the house. Only one, the first I had made out, was facing my way. I was not so shocked as you may think. The start back I had given was really nothing but a movement of surprise. I had expected to see a knob of wood there, you know. I returned deliberately to the first I had seen — and there it was, black, dried, sunken, with closed eyelids — a head that seemed to sleep at the top of that pole, and with the shrunken dry lips showing a narrow white line of the teeth, was smiling, too, smiling continuously at some endless and jocose dream of that eternal slumber.

"I am not disclosing any trade secrets. In fact, the manager said afterwards that Mr. Kurtz's methods had ruined the district. I have no opinion on that point, but I want you clearly to understand that there was nothing exactly profitable in these heads being there. They only showed that Mr. Kurtz lacked restraint in the gratification of his various lusts, that there was something wanting in him — some small matter which, when the pressing need arose, could not be found under his magnificent eloquence. Whether he knew of this deficiency himself I can't say. I think the knowledge came to him at last — only at the very last. But the wilderness had found him out early, and had taken on him a terrible vengeance for the fantastic invasion. I think it had whispered to him things about himself which he did not know, things of which he had no conception till he took counsel with this great solitude — and the whisper had proved irresistibly fascinating. It echoed loudly within him because he was hollow at the core. . . . I put down the glass, and the head that had appeared near enough to be spoken to seemed at once to have leaped away from me into inaccessible distance.

"The admirer of Mr. Kurtz was a bit crestfallen. In a hurried indistinct voice he began to assure me he had not dared to take these — say, symbols — down. He was not afraid of the natives; they would not stir till Mr. Kurtz gave the word. His ascendancy was extraordinary. The camps of these people surrounded the place, and the chiefs came every day to see him. They would crawl. . . . 'I don't want to know anything of the ceremonies used when approaching Mr. Kurtz,' I shouted. Curious, this feeling that came over me that such details would be more intolerable than those heads drying on the stakes under Mr. Kurtz's windows. After all, that was only a savage sight, while I seemed at one bound to have been transported into some lightless region of subtle horrors, where pure, uncomplicated savagery was a positive relief, being something that had a right to exist — obviously — in the sunshine. The young man looked at me with surprise. I suppose it did not occur to him that Mr. Kurtz was no idol of mine. He forgot I hadn't heard any of these splendid monologues on, what was it? on love, justice, conduct of life — or what not. If it had come to crawling before Mr. Kurtz, he crawled as much as the veriest savage of them all. I had no idea of the conditions, he said: these heads were the heads of rebels. I shocked him excessively by laughing. Rebels! What would be the next definition I was to hear? There had been enemies, criminals, workers — and these were rebels. Those rebellious heads looked very subdued to me on their sticks. 'You don't know how such a life tries a man like Kurtz,' cried Kurtz's last disciple. 'Well, and you?' I said. 'I! I! I am a simple man. I have no great thoughts. I want nothing from anybody. How can you compare me to . . . ?' His feelings were too much for speech, and suddenly he broke down. 'I don't understand,' he groaned. 'I've been doing my best to keep him alive, and that's enough. I had no hand in all this. I have no abilities. There hasn't been a drop of medicine or a mouthful of invalid food for months here. He was shamefully abandoned. A man like this, with such ideas. Shamefully! Shamefully! I — I — haven't slept for the last ten nights. . . .'

"His voice lost itself in the calm of the evening. The long shadows of the forest had slipped downhill while we talked, had gone far beyond the ruined hovel, beyond the symbolic row of stakes. All this was in the gloom, while we down there were yet in the sunshine, and the stretch of the river abreast of the clearing glittered in a still and dazzling splendor, with a murky and over-shadowed bend above and below. Not a living soul was seen on the shore. The bushes did not rustle.

"Suddenly round the corner of the house a group of men appeared, as though they had come up from the ground. They waded waist-deep in the grass, in a compact body, bearing an improvised stretcher in their midst. Instantly, in the emptiness of the landscape, a cry arose while shrillness pierced the still air like a sharp arrow flying straight to the very heart of the land; and, as if by enchantment, streams of human beings — of naked human beings — with spears in their hands, with bows, with shields, with wild glances and savage movements, were poured into the clearing by the dark-faced and pensive for-est. The bushes shook, the grass swayed for a time, and then everything stood still in attentive immobility.

"'Now, if he does not say the right thing to them we are all done for,' said the Russian at my elbow. The knot of men with the stretcher had stopped, too, halfway to the steamer, as if petrified. I saw the man on the stretcher sit up, lank and with an uplifted arm, above the shoulders of the bearers. 'Let us hope that the man who can talk so well of love in general will find some particu-lar reason to spare us this time,' I said. I resented bitterly the absurd danger of our situation, as if to be at the mercy of that atrocious phantom had been a dishonoring necessity. I could not hear a sound, but through my glasses I saw the thin arm extended commandingly, the lower jaw moving, the eyes of that apparition shining darkly far in its bony head that nodded with grotesque jerks. Kurtz — Kurtz — that means short in German — don't it? Well, the name was as true as everything else in his life — and death. He looked at least seven feet long. His covering had fallen off, and his body emerged from it pitiful and appalling as from a winding-sheet. I could see the cage of his ribs all astir, the bones of his arm waving. It was as though an animated image of death carved out of old ivory had been shaking its hand with menaces at a motionless crowd of men made of dark and glittering bronze. I saw him open his mouth wide — it gave him a weirdly voracious aspect, as though he had wanted to swallow all the air, all the earth, all the men before him. A deep voice reached me faintly. He must have been shouting. He fell back suddenly. The stretcher shook as the bearers staggered forward again, and almost at the same time I noticed that the crowd of savages was vanishing without any perceptible movement of retreat, as if the forest that had ejected these beings so suddenly had drawn them in again as the breath is drawn in a long aspiration.

"Some of the pilgrims behind the stretcher carried his arms — two shot-guns, a heavy rifle, and a light revolver-carbine — the thunderbolts of that pitiful Jupiter. The manager bent over him murmuring as he walked beside his head. They laid him down in one of the little cabins — just a room for a bedplace and a campstool or two, you know. We had brought his belated correspondence, and a lot of torn envelopes and open letters littered his bed. His hand roamed feebly amongst these papers. I was struck by the fire in his eyes and the composed languor of his expression. It was not so much the exhaustion of disease. He did not seem in pain. This shadow looked satiated and calm, as though for the moment it had had its fill of all the emotions.

"He rustled one of the letters, and looking straight in my face said, 'I am glad.' Somebody had been writing to him about me. These special recommendations were turning up again. The volume of tone he emitted without effort, almost without the trouble of moving his lips, amazed me. A voice! a voice! It was grave, profound, vibrating, while the man did not seem capable of a whisper. However, he had enough strength in him — factitious no doubt — to very nearly make an end of us, as you shall hear directly.

"The manager appeared silently in the doorway; I stepped out at once and he drew the curtain after me. The Russian, eyed curiously by the pilgrims, was staring at the shore. I followed the direction of his glance.

"Dark human shapes could be made out in the distance, flitting indistinctly against the gloomy border of the forest, and near the river two bronze figures, leaning on tall spears, stood in the sunlight under fantastic headdresses of spotted skins, war-like and still in statuesque repose. And from right to left along the lighted shore moved a wild and gorgeous apparition of a woman.

"She walked with measured steps, draped in striped and fringed cloths, treading the earth proudly, with a slight jingle and flash of barbarous ornaments. She carried her head high; her hair was done in the shape of a helmet; she had brass leggings to the knee, brass wire gauntlets to the elbow, a crimson spot on her tawny cheek, innumerable necklaces of glass beads on her neck; bizarre things, charms, gifts of witchmen, that hung about her, glittered and trembled at every step. She must have had the value of several elephant tusks upon her. She was savage and superb, wild-eyed and magnificent; there was something ominous and stately in her deliberate progress. And in the hush that had fallen suddenly upon the whole sorrowful land, the immense wilderness, the colossal body of the fecund and mysterious life seemed to look at her, pensive, as though it had been looking at the image of its own tenebrous and passionate soul.

"She came abreast of the steamer, stood still, and faced us. Her long shadow fell to the water's edge. Her face had a tragic and fierce aspect of wild sorrow and of dumb pain mingled with the fear of some struggling, half-shaped resolve. She stood looking at us without a stir, and like the wilderness itself, with an air of brooding over an inscrutable purpose. A whole minute passed, and then she made a step forward. There was a low jingle, a glint of yellow metal, a sway of fringed draperies, and she stopped as if her heart had failed her. The young fellow by my side growled. The pilgrims murmured at my back. She looked at us all as if her life had depended upon the unswerving steadiness of her glance. Suddenly she opened her bared arms and threw them up rigid above her head, as though in an uncontrollable desire to touch the sky, and at the same time the swift shadows darted out on the earth, swept around on the river, gathering the steamer into a shadowy embrace. A formidable silence hung over the scene.

"She turned away slowly, walked on, followed the bank, and passed into the bushes to the left. Once only her eyes gleamed back at us in the dusk of the thickets before she disappeared.

" 'If she had offered to come aboard I really think I would have tried to shoot her,' said the man of patches, nervously. 'I have been risking my life every day for the last fortnight to keep her out of the house. She got in one day and kicked up a row about those miserable rags I picked up in the storeroom to mend my clothes with. I wasn't decent. At least it must have been that, for she talked like a fury to Kurtz for an hour, pointing at me now and then. I don't understand the dialect of this tribe. Luckily for me, I fancy Kurtz felt too ill that day to care, or there would have been mischief. I don't understand. . . . No — it's too much for me. Ah, well, it's all over now.'

"At this moment I heard Kurtz's deep voice behind the curtain: 'Save me! — save the ivory, you mean. Don't tell me. Save *me*! Why, I've had to save you. You are interrupting my plans now. Sick! Sick! Not so sick as you would like to believe. Never mind. I'll carry my ideas out yet — I will return. I'll show you what can be done. You with your little peddling notions — you are intefering with me. I will return. I . . .'

"The manager came out. He did me the honor to take me under the arm and lead me aside. 'He is very low, very low,' he said. He considered it necessary to sigh, but neglected to be consistently sorrowful. 'We have done all we could for him — haven't we? But there is no disguising the fact, Mr. Kurtz has done more harm than good to the Company. He did not see the time was not ripe for vigorous action. Cautiously, cautiously — that's my principle. We must be cautious yet. The district is closed to us for a time. Deplorable! Upon the whole, the trade will suffer. I don't deny there is a remarkable quantity of ivory — mostly fossil. We must save it, at all events — but look how precarious the position is — and why? Because the method is unsound.' 'Do you,' said I, looking at the shore, 'call it "unsound method"?' 'Without doubt,' he exclaimed, hotly. 'Don't you?' . . . 'No method at all,' I murmured after a while. 'Exactly,' he exulted. 'I anticipated this. Shows a complete want of judgment. It is my duty to point it out in the proper quarter.' 'Oh,' said I, 'that fellow — what's his name? — the brick-maker, will make a readable report for you.' He appeared confounded for a moment. It seemed to me I had never breathed an atmosphere so vile, and I turned mentally to Kurtz for relief — positively for relief. 'Nevertheless I think Mr. Kurtz is a remarkable man,' I said with emphasis. He started, dropped on me a cold heavy glance, said very quietly, 'he was,' and turned his back on me. My hour of favor was over; I found myself lumped along with Kurtz as a partisan of methods for which the time was not ripe: I was unsound! Ah! but it was something to have at least a choice of nightmares.

"I had turned to the wilderness really, not to Mr. Kurtz, who, I was ready to admit, was as good as buried. And for a moment it seemed to me as if I also were buried in a vast grave full of unspeakable secrets. I felt an intolerable weight oppressing my breast, the smell of the damp earth, the unseen presence of victorious corruption, the darkness of an impenetrable night. . . . The Russian tapped me on the shoulder. I heard him mumbling and stammering something about 'brother seaman — couldn't conceal — knowledge of matters that would affect Mr. Kurtz's reputation.' I waited. For him evidently Mr. Kurtz was not in his grave; I suspect that for him Mr. Kurtz was one of the immortals. 'Well,' said I at last, 'speak out. As it happens, I am Mr. Kurtz's friend — in a way.'

"He stated with a good deal of formality that had we not been 'of the same profession,' he would have kept the matter to himself without regard to consequences. 'He suspected there was an active ill will towards him on the part of these white men that —' 'You are right,' I said, remembering a certain conversation I had overheard. 'The manager thinks you ought to be hanged.' He showed a concern at this intelligence which amused me at first. 'I had better get out of the way quietly,' he said, earnestly. 'I can do no more for Kurtz now, and they would soon find some excuse. What's to stop them? There's a military post three hundred miles from here.' 'Well, upon my word,' said I, 'perhaps you had better go if you have any friends amongst the savages near by.' 'Plenty,' he said. 'They are simple people — and I want nothing, you know.' He stood biting his lip, then: 'I don't want any harm to happen to these whites here, but of course I was thinking of Mr. Kurtz's reputation — but you are a brother seaman and —' 'All right,' said I, after a time. 'Mr. Kurtz's reputation is safe with me.' I did not know how truly I spoke.

"He informed me, lowering his voice, that it was Kurtz who had ordered the attack to be made on the steamer. 'He hated sometimes the idea of being taken away — and then again. . . . But I don't understand these matters. I am a simple man. He thought it would scare you away — that you would give it up, thinking him dead. I could not stop him. Oh, I had an awful time of it this last month.' 'Very well,' I said. 'He is all right now.' 'Ye-e-es,' he muttered, not very convinced apparently. 'Thanks,' said I; 'I shall keep my eyes open.' 'But quiet — eh?' he urged, anxiously. 'It would be awful for his reputation if anybody here —' I promised a complete discretion with great gravity. 'I have a canoe and three black fellows waiting not very far. I am off. Could you give me a few Martini-Henry cartridges?' I could, and did, with proper secrecy. He helped himself, with a wink at me, to a handful of my tobacco. 'Between sailors — you know — good English tobacco.' At the door of the pilot-house he turned round — 'I say, haven't you a pair of shoes you could spare?' He raised one leg. 'Look.' The soles were tied with knotted strings sandal-wise under his bare feet. I rooted out an old pair, at which he looked with admiration before tucking them under his left arm. One of his pockets (bright red) was bulging with cartridges, from the other (dark blue) peeped 'Towson's Inquiry,' etc., etc. He seemed to think himself excellently well equipped for a renewed encounter with the wilderness. 'Ah! I'll never, never meet such a man again. You ought to have heard him recite poetry — his own, too, it was, he told me. Poetry!' He rolled his eyes at the recollection of these delights. 'Oh, he enlarged my mind!' 'Good-by,' said I. He shook hands and vanished in the night. Sometimes I ask myself whether I had ever really seen him — whether it was possible to meet such a phenomenon! . . .

"When I woke up shortly after midnight his warning came to my mind with its hint of danger that seemed, in the starred darkness, real enough to make me get up for the purpose of having a look around. On the hill a big fire burned, illuminating fitfully a crooked corner of the station-house. One of the agents with a picket of a few of our blacks, armed for the purpose, was keeping guard over the ivory; but deep within the forest, red gleams that wavered, that seemed to sink and rise from the ground amongst confused columnar shapes of intense blackness, showed the exact position of the camp where Mr. Kurtz's adorers were keeping their uneasy vigil. The monotonous beating of a big drum filled the air with muffled shocks and a lingering vibration. A steady droning sound of many men chanting each to himself some weird incantation came out from the black, flat wall of the wood as the humming of bees comes out of a hive, and had a strange narcotic effect upon my half-awake senses. I believe I dozed off leaning over the rail, till an abrupt burst of yells, an overwhelming outbreak of a pent-up and mysterious frenzy, woke me up in a bewildered wonder. It was cut short all at once, and the low droning went on with an effect of audible and soothing silence. I glanced casually into the little cabin. A light was burning within, but Mr. Kurtz was not there.

"I think I would have raised an outcry if I had believed my eyes. But I didn't believe them at first — the thing seemed so impossible. The fact is I was completely unnerved by a sheer blank fright, pure abstract terror, unconnected with any distinct shape of physical danger. What made this emotion so overpowering was — how shall I define it? — the moral shock I received, as if something altogether monstrous, intolerable to thought and odious to the soul, had been thrust upon me unexpectedly. This lasted of course the merest fraction of a second, and then the usual sense of commonplace, deadly danger, the possibility of a sudden onslaught and massacre, or something of the kind, which I saw impending, was positively welcome and composing. It pacified me, in fact, so much, that I did not raise an alarm.

"There was an agent buttoned up inside an ulster and sleeping on a chair on deck within three feet of me. The yells had not awakened him; he snored very slightly; I left him to his slumbers and leaped ashore. I did not betray Mr. Kurtz — it was ordered I should never betray him — it was written I should be loyal to the nightmare of my choice. I was anxious to deal with this shadow by myself alone — and to this day I don't know why I was so jealous of sharing with anyone the peculiar blackness of that experience.

"As soon as I got on the bank I saw a trail — a broad trail through the grass. I remember the exultation with which I said to myself, 'He can't walk — he is crawling on all-fours — I've got him.' The grass was wet with dew. I strode rapidly with clenched fists. I fancy I had some vague notion of falling upon him and giving him a drubbing. I don't know. I had some imbecile thoughts. The knitting old woman with the cat obtruded herself upon my memory as a most improper person to be sitting at the other end of such an affair. I saw a row of pilgrims squirting lead in the air out of Winchesters held to the hip. I thought I would never get back to the steamer, and imagined myself living alone and unarmed in the woods to an advanced age. Such silly things — you know. And I remember I confounded the beat of the drum with the beating of my heart, and was pleased at its calm regularity.

"I kept to the track though — then stopped to listen. The night was very clear; a dark blue space, sparkling with dew and starlight, in which black things stood very still. I thought I could see a kind of motion ahead of me. I was strangely cocksure of everything that night. I actually left the track and ran in a wide semicircle (I verily believe chuckling to myself) so as to get in front of that stir, of that motion I had seen — if indeed I had seen anything. I was circumventing Kurtz as though it had been a boyish game.

"I came upon him, and, if he had not heard me coming, I would have fallen over him, too, but he got up in time. He rose, unsteady, long, pale, indistinct, like a vapor exhaled by the earth, and swayed slightly, misty and silent before me; while at my back the fires loomed between the trees, and the murmur of many voices issued from the forest. I had cut him off cleverly; but when actually confronting him I seemed to come to my senses, I saw the danger in its right proportion. It was by no means over yet. Suppose he began to shout? Though he could hardly stand, there was still plenty of vigor in his voice. 'Go away — hide yourself,' he said, in that profound tone. It was very awful. I glanced back. We were within thirty yards from the nearest fire. A black figure stood up, strode on long black legs, waving long black arms, across the glow. It had horns — antelope horns, I think — on its head. Some sorcerer, some witchman, no doubt: it looked fiend-like enough. 'Do you know what you are doing?' I whispered. 'Perfectly,' he answered, raising his voice for that single word: it sounded to me far off and yet loud, like a hail through a speaking-trumpet. If he makes a row we are lost, I thought to myself. This clearly was not a case for fisticuffs, even apart from the very natural aversion I had to beat that Shadow — this wandering and tormented thing. 'You will be lost,' I said — 'utterly lost.' One gets sometimes such a flash of inspiration, you know. I did say the right thing, though indeed he could not have been more irretrievably lost than he was at this very moment, when the foundations of our intimacy were being laid — to endure — to endure — even to the end — even beyond.

"'I had immense plans,' he muttered irresolutely. 'Yes,' said I; 'but if you try to shout I'll smash your head with —' There was not a stick or a stone near. 'I will throttle you for good,' I corrected myself. 'I was on the threshold of great things,' he pleaded, in a voice of longing, with a wistfulness of tone that made my blood run cold. 'And now for this stupid scoundrel —' 'Your success in Europe is assured in any case,' I affirmed, steadily. I did not want to have the throttling of him, you understand — and indeed it would have been very little use for any practical purpose. I tried to break the spell — the heavy, mute spell of the wilderness — that seemed to draw him to its pitiless breast by the awakening of forgotten and brutal instincts, by the memory of gratified and monstrous passions. This alone, I was convinced, had driven him out to the edge of the forest, to the bush, towards the gleam of fires, the throb of drums, the drone of weird incantations; this alone had beguiled his unlawful soul beyond the bounds of permitted aspirations. And, don't you see, the terror of the position was not in being knocked on the head — though I had a very lively sense of that danger, too — but in this, that I had to deal with a being to whom I could not appeal in the name of anything high or low. I had, even like the niggers, to invoke him — himself — his own exalted and incredible degradation. There was nothing either above or below him, and I knew it. He had kicked himself loose of the earth. Confound the man! he had kicked the very earth to pieces. He was alone, and I before him did not know whether I stood on the ground or floated in the air. I've been telling you what we said — repeating the phrases we pronounced — but what's the good? They were common everyday words — the familiar, vague sounds exchanged on every waking day of life. But what of that? They had behind them, to my mind, the terrific suggestiveness of words heard in dreams, of phrases spoken in nightmares. Soul! If anybody had ever struggled with a soul, I am the man. And I wasn't arguing with a lunatic either. Believe me or not, his intelligence was perfectly clear — concentrated, it is true, upon himself with horrible intensity, yet clear; and therein was my only chance — barring, of course, the killing him there and then, which wasn't so good, on account of unavoidable noise. But his soul was mad. Being alone in the wilderness, it had looked within itself, and, by heavens! I tell you, it had gone mad. I had — for my sins, I suppose — to go through the ordeal of looking into it myself. No eloquence could have been so withering to one's belief in mankind as his final burst of sincerity. He struggled with himself, too. I saw it — I heard it. I saw the inconceivable mystery of a soul that knew no restraint, no faith, and no fear, yet struggling blindly with itself. I kept my head pretty well; but when I had him at last stretched on the couch, I wiped my forehead, while my legs shook under me as though I had carried half a ton on my back down that hill. And yet I had only supported him, his bony arm clasped round my neck — and he was not much heavier than a child.

"When next day we left at noon, the crowd, of whose presence behind the curtain of trees I had been acutely conscious all the time, flowed out of the woods again, filled the clearing, covered the slope with a mass of naked, breathing, quivering, bronze bodies. I steamed up a bit, then swung downstream, and two thousand eyes followed the evolutions of the splashing, thumping, fierce river-demon beating the water with its terrible tail and breathing black smoke into the air. In front of the first rank, along the river, three men, plastered with bright red earth from head to foot, strutted to and fro restlessly. When we came abreast again, they faced the river, stamped their feet, nodded their horned heads, swayed their scarlet bodies; they shook towards the fierce river-demon a bunch of black feathers, a mangy skin with a pendant tail — something that looked like a dried gourd; they shouted periodically together strings of amazing words that resembled no sounds of human language; and the deep murmurs of the crowd, interrupted suddenly, were like the responses of some satanic litany.

"We had carried Kurtz into the pilot-house: there was more air there. Lying on the couch, he stared through the open shutter. There was an eddy in the mass of human bodies, and the woman with helmeted head and tawny cheeks rushed out to the very brink of the stream. She put out her hands, shouted something, and all that wild mob took up the shout in a roaring chorus of articulated, rapid, breathless utterance.

"'Do you understand this?' I asked.

"He kept on looking out past me with fiery, longing eyes, with a mingled expression of wistfulness and hate. He made no answer, but I saw a smile, a smile of indefinable meaning, appear on his colorless lips that a moment after twitched convulsively. 'Do I not?' he said slowly, gasping, as if the words had been torn out of him by a supernatural power.

"I pulled the string of the whistle, and I did this because I saw the pilgrims on deck getting out their rifles with an air of anticipating a jolly lark. At the sudden screech there was a movement of abject terror through that wedged mass of bodies. 'Don't! don't you frighten them away,' cried someone on deck disconsolately. I pulled the string time after time. They broke and ran, they leaped, they crouched, they swerved, they dodged the flying terror of the sound. The three red chaps had fallen flat, face down on the shore, as though they had been shot dead. Only the barbarous and superb woman did not so much as flinch, and stretched tragically her bare arms after us over the somber and glittering river.

"And then that imbecile crowd down on the deck started their little fun, and I could see nothing more for smoke.

"The brown current ran swiftly out of the heart of darkness, bearing us down towards the sea with twice the speed of our upward progress; and Kurtz's life was running swiftly, too, ebbing out of his heart into the sea of inexorable time. The manager was very placid, he had no vital anxieties now, he took us both in with a comprehensive and satisfied glance: the 'affair' had come off as well as could be wished. I saw the time approaching when I would be left alone of the party of 'unsound method.' The pilgrims looked upon me with disfavor. I was, so to speak, numbered with the dead. It is strange how I accepted this unforeseen partnership, this choice of nightmares forced upon me in the tenebrous land invaded by these mean and greedy phantoms.

"Kurtz discoursed. A voice! a voice! It rang deep to the very last. It survived his strength to hide in the magnificent folds of eloquence the barren darkness of his heart. Oh, he struggled! he struggled! The wastes of his weary brain were haunted by shadowy images now — images of wealth and fame revolving obsequiously round his unextinguishable gift of noble and lofty expression. My Intended, my station, my career, my ideas — these were the objects for the occasional utterances of elevated sentiments. The shade of the original Kurtz frequented the bedside of the hollow sham, whose fate it was to be buried presently in the mold of primeval earth. But both the diabolic love and the unearthly hate of the mysteries it had penetrated fought for the possession of that soul satiated with primitive emotions, avid of lying fame, of sham distinction, of all the appearances of success and power.

"Sometimes he was contemptibly childish. He desired to have kings meet him at railway stations on his return from some ghastly Nowhere, where he intended to accomplish great things. 'You show them you have in you something that is really profitable, and then there will be no limits to the recognition of your ability,' he would say. 'Of course you must take care of the motives — right motives — always.' The long reaches that were like one and the same reach, monotonous bends that were exactly alike, slipped past the steamer with their multitude of secular trees looking patiently after this grimy fragment of another world, the forerunner of change, of conquest, of trade, of massacres, of blessings. I looked ahead — piloting. 'Close the shutter,' said Kurtz suddenly one day; 'I can't bear to look at this.' I did so. There was a silence. 'Oh, but I will wring your heart yet!' he cried at the invisible wilderness.

"We broke down — as I had expected — and had to lie up for repairs at the head of an island. This delay was the first thing that shook Kurtz's confidence. One morning he gave me a packet of papers and a photograph — the lot tied together with a shoestring. 'Keep this for me,' he said. 'This noxious fool' (meaning the manager) 'is capable of prying into my boxes when I am not looking.' In the afternoon I saw him. He was lying on his back with closed eyes, and I withdrew quietly, but I heard him mutter, 'Live rightly, die, die. . . .' I listened. There was nothing more. Was he rehearsing some speech in his sleep, or was it a fragment of a phrase from some newspaper article? He had been writing for the papers and meant to do so again, 'for the furthering of my ideas. It's a duty.'

"His was an impenetrable darkness. I looked at him as you peer down at a man who is lying at the bottom of a precipice where the sun never shines. But I had not much time to give him, because I was helping the engine-driver to take to pieces the leaky cylinders, to straighten a bent connecting-rod, and in other such matters. I lived in an infernal mess of rust, filings, nuts, bolts, spanners, hammers, ratchet-drills — things I abominate, because I don't get on with them. I tended the little forge we fortunately had aboard; I toiled wearily in a wretched scrap-heap — unless I had the shakes too bad to stand.

"One evening coming in with a candle I was startled to hear him say a little tremulously, 'I am lying here in the dark waiting for death.' The light was within a foot of his eyes. I forced myself to murmur, 'Oh, nonsense!' and stood over him as if transfixed.

"Anything approaching the change that came over his features I have never seen before, and hope never to see again. Oh, I wasn't touched. I was fascinated. It was as though a veil had been rent. I saw on that ivory face the expression of somber pride, of ruthless power, of craven terror — of an intense and hopeless despair. Did he live his life again in every detail of desire, temptation, and surrender during that supreme moment of complete knowledge? He cried in a whisper at some image, at some vision — he cried out twice, a cry that was no more than a breath —

"'The horror! The horror!'

"I blew the candle out and left the cabin. The pilgrims were dining in the messroom, and I took my place opposite the manager, who lifted his eyes to give me a questioning glance, which I successfully ignored. He leaned back, serene, with that peculiar smile of his sealing the unexpressed depths of his meanness. A continuous shower of small flies streamed upon the lamp, upon the cloth, upon our hands and faces. Suddenly the manager's boy put his insolent black head in the doorway, and said in a tone of scathing contempt —

"'Mistah Kurtz — he dead.'

"All the pilgrims rushed out to see. I remained, and went on with my dinner. I believe I was considered brutally callous. However, I did not eat much. There was a lamp in there — light, don't you know — and outside it was so beastly, beastly dark. I went no more near the remarkable man who had pronounced a judgment upon the adventures of his soul on this earth. The voice was gone. What else had been there? But I am of course aware that next day the pilgrims buried something in a muddy hole.

"And then they very nearly buried me.

"However, as you see, I did not go to join Kurtz there and then. I did not. I remained to dream the nightmare out to the end, and to show my loyalty to Kurtz once more. Destiny. My destiny! Droll thing life is — that mysterious arrangement of merciless logic for a futile purpose. The most you can hope from it is some knowledge of yourself — that comes too late — a crop of unextinguishable regrets. I have wrestled with death. It is the most unexciting contest you can imagine. It takes place in an impalpable grayness, with nothing underfoot, with nothing around, without spectators, without clamor, without glory, without the great desire of victory, without the great fear of defeat, in a sickly atmosphere of tepid skepticism, without much belief in your own right, and still less in that of your adversary. If such is the form of ultimate wisdom, then life is a greater riddle than some of us think it to be. I was within a hair's breadth of the last opportunity for pronouncement, and I found with humiliation that probably I would have nothing to say. This is the reason why I affirm that Kurtz was a remarkable man. He had something to say. He said it. Since I had peeped over the edge myself, I understand better the meaning of his stare, that could not see the flame of the candle, but was wide enough to embrace the whole universe, piercing enough to penetrate all the hearts that beat in the darkness. He had summed up — he had judged. 'The horror!' He was a remarkable man. After all, this was the expression of some sort of belief; it had candor, it had conviction, it had a vibrating note of revolt in its whisper, it had the appalling face of a glimpsed truth — the strange commingling of desire and hate. And it is not my own extremity I remember best — a vision of grayness without form filled with physical pain, and a careless contempt for the evanescence of all things — even of this pain itself. No! It is his extremity that I seem to have lived through. True, he had made that last stride, he had stepped over the edge, while I had been permitted to draw back my hesitating foot. And perhaps in this is the whole difference; perhaps all the wisdom, and all truth, and all sincerity, are just compressed into that inappreciable moment of time in which we step over the threshold of the invisible. Perhaps! I like to think my summing-up would not have been a word of careless contempt. Better his cry — much better. It was an affirmation, a moral victory paid for by innumerable defeats, by abominable terrors, by abominable satisfactions. But it was a victory! That is why I have remained loyal to Kurtz to the last, and even beyond, when a long time after I heard once more, not his own choice, but the echo of his magnificent eloquence thrown to me from a soul as translucently pure as a cliff of crystal.

"No, they did not bury me, though there is a period of time which I remember mistily, with a shuddering wonder, like a passage through some inconceivable world that had no hope in it and no desire. I found myself back in the sepulchral city resenting the sight of people hurrying through the streets to filch a little money from each other, to devour their infamous cookery, to gulp their unwholesome beer, to dream their insignificant and silly dreams. They trespassed upon my thoughts. They were intruders whose knowledge of life was to me an irritating pretense, because I felt so sure they could not possibly know the things I knew. Their bearing, which was simply the bearing of commonplace individuals going about their business in the assurance of perfect safety, was offensive to me like the outrageous flauntings of folly in the face of a danger it is unable to comprehend. I had no particular desire to enlighten them, but I had some difficulty in restraining myself from laughing in their faces, so full of stupid importance. I daresay I was not very well at that time. I tottered about the streets — there were various affairs to settle — grinning bitterly at perfectly respectable persons. I admit my behavior was inexcusable, but then my temperature was seldom normal in these days. My dear aunt's endeavors to 'nurse up my strength' seemed altogether beside the mark. It was not my strength that wanted nursing, it was my imagination that wanted soothing. I kept the bundle of papers given me by Kurtz, not knowing exactly what to do with it. His mother had died lately, watched over, as I was told, by his Intended. A clean-shaven man, with an official manner and wearing gold-rimmed spectacles, called on me one day and made inquiries, at first circuitous, afterwards suavely pressing, about what he was pleased to denominate certain 'documents.' I was not surprised, because I had had two rows with the manager on the subject out there. I had refused to give up the smallest scrap out of that package, and I took the same attitude with the spectacled man. He became darkly menacing at last, and with much heat argued that the Company had the right to every bit of information about its 'territories.' And he said, 'Mr. Kurtz's knowledge of unexplored regions must have been necessarily extensive and peculiar—owing to his great abilities and to the deplorable circumstances in which he had been placed: therefore —' I assured him Mr. Kurtz's knowledge, however extensive, did not bear upon the problems of commerce or administration. He invoked then the name of science. 'It would be an incalculable loss if,' etc., etc. I offered him the report on the 'Suppression of Savage Customs,' with the postscriptum torn off. He took it up eagerly, but ended by sniffing at it with an air of contempt. 'This is not what we had a right to expect,' he remarked. 'Expect nothing else,' I said. 'There are only private letters.' He withdrew upon some threat of legal proceedings, and I saw him no more; but another fellow, calling himself Kurtz's cousin, appeared two days later, and was anxious to hear all the details about his dear relative's last moments. Incidentally he gave me to understand that Kurtz had been essentially a great musician. 'There was the making of an immense success,' said the man, who was an organist, I believe, with lank gray hair flowing over a greasy coat-collar. I had no reason to doubt his statement; and to this day I am unable to say what was Kurtz's profession, whether he ever had any—which was the greatest of his talents. I had taken him for a painter who wrote for the papers, or else for a journalist who could paint—but even the cousin (who took snuff during the interview) could not tell me what he had been—exactly. He was a universal genius—on that point I agreed with the old chap, who thereupon blew his nose noisily into a large cotton handkerchief and withdrew in senile agitation, bearing off some family letters and memoranda without importance. Ultimately a journalist anxious to know something of the fate of his 'dear colleague' turned up. This visitor informed me Kurtz's proper sphere ought to have been politics 'on the popular side.' He had furry straight eyebrows, bristly hair cropped short, an eye-glass on a broad ribbon, and, becoming expansive, confessed his opinion that Kurtz really couldn't write a bit—'But heavens! how that man could talk. He electrified large meetings. He had faith—don't you see?—he had the faith. He could get himself to believe anything—anything. He would have been a splendid leader of an extreme party.' 'What party?' I asked. 'Any party,' answered the other. 'He was an—an—extremist.' Did I not think so? I assented. Did I know, he asked, with a sudden flash of curiosity, 'what it was that had induced him to go out there?' 'Yes,' said I, and forthwith handed him the famous Report for publication, if he thought fit. He glanced through it hurriedly, mumbling all the time, judged 'it would do,' and took himself off with this plunder.

"Thus I was left at last with a slim packet of letters and the girl's portrait. She struck me as beautiful—I mean she had a beautiful expression. I know that the sunlight can be made to lie, too, yet one felt that no manipulation of light and pose could have conveyed the delicate shade of truthfulness upon those features. She seemed ready to listen without mental reservation, without suspicion, without a thought for herself. I concluded I would go and give her back her portrait and those letters myself. Curiosity? Yes; and also some other feeling perhaps. All that had been Kurtz's had passed out of my hands: his soul, his body, his station, his plans, his ivory, his career. There remained only this memory and his Intended — and I wanted to give that up, too, to the past; in a way — to surrender personally all that remained of him with me to that oblivion which is the last word of our common fate. I don't defend myself. I had no clear perception of what it was I really wanted. Perhaps it was an impulse of unconscious loyalty, or the fulfillment of one of those ironic necessities, that lurk in the facts of human existence. I don't know. I can't tell. But I went.

"I thought his memory was like the other memories of the dead that accumulate in every man's life — a vague impress on the brain of shadows that had fallen on it in their swift and final passage; but before the high and ponderous door, between the tall houses of a street as still and decorous as a well-kept alley in a cemetery, I had a vision of him on the stretcher, opening his mouth voraciously, as if to devour all the earth with all its mankind. He lived then before me; he lived as much as he had ever lived — a shadow insatiable of splendid appearances, of frightful realities; a shadow darker than the shadow of the night, and draped nobly in the folds of a gorgeous eloquence. The vision seemed to enter the house with me — the stretcher, the phantom-bearers, the wild crowd of obedient worshipers, the gloom of the forests, the glitter of the reach between the murky bends, the beat of the drum, regular and muffled like the beating of a heart — the heart of a conquering darkness. It was a moment of triumph for the wilderness, an invading and vengeful rush which, it seemed to me, I would have to keep back alone for the salvation of another soul. And the memory of what I had heard him say afar there, with the honored shapes stirring at my back, in the glow of fires, within the patient woods, those broken phrases came back to me, were heard again in their ominous and terrifying simplicity. I remembered his abject pleading, his abject threats, the colossal scale of his vile desires, the meanness, the torment, the tempestuous anguish of his soul. And later on I seem to see his collected languid manner, when he said one day, 'This lot of ivory now is really mine. The Company did not pay for it. I collected it myself at a very great personal risk. I am afraid they will try to claim it as theirs though. H'm. It is a difficult case. What do you think I ought to do — resist? Eh? I want no more than justice.' . . . He wanted no more than justice — no more than justice. I rang the bell before a mahogany door on the first floor, and while I waited he seemed to stare at me out of the glassy panel — stare with that wide and immense stare embracing, condemning, loathing all the universe. I seemed to hear the whispered cry, 'The horror! The horror!'

"The dusk was falling. I had to wait in a lofty drawing-room with three long windows from floor to ceiling that were like three luminous and bedraped columns. The bent gilt legs and backs of the furniture shone in indistinct curves. The tall marble fireplace had a cold and monumental whiteness. A grand piano stood massively in a corner; with dark gleams on the flat surfaces like a somber and polished sarcophagus. A high door opened — closed. I rose.

"She came forward, all in black, with a pale head, floating towards me in the dusk. She was in mourning. It was more than a year since his death, more than a year since the news came; she seemed as though she would remember and mourn forever. She took both my hands in hers and murmured, 'I had heard you were coming.' I noticed she was not very young — I mean not girlish. She had a

mature capacity for fidelity, for belief, for suffering. The room seemed to have
grown darker, as if all the sad light of the cloudy evening had taken refuge on her
forehead. This fair hair, this pale visage, this pure brow, seemed surrounded by
an ashy halo from which the dark eyes looked out at me. Their glance was guileless, profound, confident, and trustful. She carried her sorrowful head as though
she were proud of that sorrow, as though she would say, I—I alone know how
to mourn him as he deserves. But while we were still shaking hands, such a look
of awful desolation came upon her face that I perceived she was one of those
creatures that are not the playthings of Time. For her he had died only yesterday. And, by Jove! the impression was so powerful that for me, too, he seemed
to have died only yesterday—nay, this very minute. I saw her and him in the
same instant of time—his death and her sorrow—I saw her sorrow in the very
moment of his death. Do you understand? I saw them together—I heard them
together. She had said, with a deep catch of the breath, 'I have survived' while
my strained ears seemed to hear distinctly, mingled with her tone of despairing regret, the summing up whisper of his eternal condemnation. I asked myself
what I was doing there, with a sensation of panic in my heart as though I had
blundered into a place of cruel and absurd mysteries not fit for a human being to
behold. She motioned me to a chair. We sat down. I laid the packet gently on the
little table, and she put her hand over it.... 'You knew him well,' she murmured,
after a moment of mourning silence.

"'Intimacy grows quickly out there,' I said. 'I knew him as well as it is possible for one man to know another.'

"'And you admired him,' she said. 'It was impossible to know him and not
to admire him. Was it?'

"'He was a remarkable man,' I said, unsteadily. Then before the appealing
fixity of her gaze, that seemed to watch for more words on my lips, I went on,
'It was impossible not to —'

"'Love him,' she finished eagerly, silencing me into an appalled dumbness.
'How true! how true! But when you think that no one knew him so well as I! I
had all his noble confidence. I knew him best.'

"'You knew him best,' I repeated. And perhaps she did. But with every
word spoken the room was growing darker, and only her forehead, smooth and
white, remained illumined by the unextinguishable light of belief and love.

"'You were his friend,' she went on. 'His friend,' she repeated, a little louder.
'You must have been, if he had given you this, and sent you to me. I feel I can
speak to you—and oh! I must speak. I want you—you have heard his last
words—to know I have been worthy of him.... It is not pride.... Yes! I am
proud to know I understood him better than anyone on earth—he told me so
himself. And since his mother died I have had no one—no one—to—to —'

"I listened. The darkness deepened. I was not even sure he had given me
the right bundle. I rather suspect he wanted me to take care of another batch
of his papers which, after his death, I saw the manager examining under the
lamp. And the girl talked, easing her pain in the certitude of my sympathy; she
talked as thirsty men drink. I had heard that her engagement with Kurtz had
been disapproved by her people. He wasn't rich enough or something. And

indeed I don't know whether he had not been a pauper all his life. He had given me some reason to infer that it was his impatience of comparative poverty that drove him out there.

"'. . . Who was not his friend who had heard him speak once?' she was saying. 'He drew men towards him by what was best in them.' She looked at me with intensity. 'It is the gift of the great,' she went on, and the sound of her low voice seemed to have the accompaniment of all the other sounds, full of mystery, desolation, and sorrow, I had ever heard — the ripple of the river, the soughing of the trees swayed by the wind, the murmurs of the crowds, the faint ring of incomprehensible words cried from afar, the whisper of a voice speaking from beyond the threshold of an external darkness. 'But you have heard him! You know!' she cried.

"'Yes, I know,' I said with something like despair in my heart, but bowing my head before the faith that was in her, before that great and saving illusion that shone with an unearthly glow in the darkness, in the triumphant darkness from which I could not have defended her — from which I could not even defend myself.

"'What a loss to me — to us!' — she corrected herself with beautiful generosity; then added in a murmur, 'To the world.' By the last gleams of twilight I could see the glitter of her eyes, full of tears — of tears that would not fall.

"'I have been very happy — very fortunate — very proud,' she went on. 'Too fortunate. Too happy for a little while. And now I am unhappy for — for life.'

"She stood up; her fair hair seemed to catch all the remaining light in a glimmer of gold. I rose, too.

"'And of all this,' she went on, mournfully, 'of all his promise, and of all his greatness, of his generous mind, of his noble heart, nothing remains — nothing but a memory. You and I —'

"'We shall always remember him,' I said, hastily.

"'No!' she cried. 'It is impossible that all this should be lost — that such a life should be sacrificed to leave nothing — but sorrow. You know what vast plans he had. I knew of them, too — I could not perhaps understand — but others knew of them. Something must remain. His words, at least, have not died.'

"'His words will remain,' I said.

"'And his example,' she whispered to herself. 'Men looked up to him — his goodness shone in every act. His example —'

"'True,' I said; 'his example, too. Yes, his example. I forgot that.'

"'But I do not. I cannot — I cannot believe — not yet. I cannot believe that I shall never see him again, that nobody will see him again, never, never, never.'

"She put out her arms as if after a retreating figure, stretching them back and with clasped pale hands across the fading and narrow sheen of the window. Never see him! I saw him clearly enough then. I shall see this eloquent phantom as long as I live, and I shall see her, too, a tragic and familiar Shade, resembling in this gesture another one, tragic also, and bedecked with powerless charms, stretching bare brown arms over the glitter of the infernal stream, the stream of darkness. She said suddenly very low, 'He died as he lived.'

"'His end,' said I, with dull anger stirring in me, 'was in every way worthy of his life.'

"'And I was not with him,' she murmured. My anger subsided before a feeling of infinite pity.

"'Everything that could be done —' I mumbled.

"'Ah, but I believed in him more than anyone on earth — more than his own mother, more than — himself. He needed me! Me! I would have treasured every sigh, every word, every sign, every glance.'

"I felt like a chill grip on my chest. 'Don't,' I said, in a muffled voice.

"'Forgive me. I — I have mourned so long in silence — in silence. . . . You were with him — to the last? I think of his loneliness. Nobody near to understand him as I would have understood. Perhaps no one to hear. . . .'

"'To the very end,' I said shakily. 'I heard his very last words. . . .' I stopped in a fright.

"'Repeat them,' she murmured in a heart-broken tone. 'I want — I want — something — something — to — live with.'

"I was on the point of crying at her, 'Don't you hear them?' The dusk was repeating them in a persistent whisper all around us, in a whisper that seemed to swell menacingly like the first whisper of a rising wind. 'The horror! The horror!'

"'His last word — to live with,' she insisted. 'Don't you understand I loved him — I loved him — I loved him!'

"I pulled myself together and spoke slowly.

"'The last word he pronounced was — your name.'

"I heard a light sigh and then my heart stood still, stopped dead short by an exulting and terrible cry, by the cry of inconceivable triumph and of unspeakable pain. 'I knew it — I was sure!' . . . She knew. She was sure. I heard her weeping, she had hidden her face in her hands. It seemed to me that the house would collapse before I could escape, that the heavens would fall upon my head. But nothing happened. The heavens do not fall for such a trifle. Would they have fallen, I wonder, if I had rendered Kurtz that justice which was his due? Hadn't he said he wanted only justice? But I couldn't. I could not tell her. It would have been too dark — too dark altogether. . . ."

Marlow ceased, and sat apart, indistinct and silent, in the pose of a meditating Buddha. Nobody moved for a time. "We have lost the first of the ebb," said the Director, suddenly. I raised my head. The offing was barred by a black bank of clouds, and the tranquil waterway leading to the uttermost ends of the earth flowed somber under an overcast sky — seemed to lead into the heart of an immense darkness.

Julio Cortázar

Julio Cortázar (1914–1984), an Argentinean short story writer, novelist, and translator, was born in Brussels but grew up in Buenos Aires. After a short time studying at the university, he taught school until he resigned after clashing with the Peronist government. In 1951 he moved to Paris, where he lived for the rest of his life, working as a translator for UNESCO.

Influenced as a young writer by the work of Jorge Luis Borges, Cortázar published his first collection of stories, *Bestiary*, the year he left Argentina. Seven more books of short fiction followed, including the collections *The End of the Game* (1965) and *We Love Glenda So Much* (1980). A prolific author, Cortázar also published poetry, essays, and novels, the most famous of which — *Hopscotch* (1963) — he called "the imperfect and desperate denunciation of the establishment of letters." His political engagement became more radical after he left Argentina, and in the last half of his life he worked for causes such as the Cuban Revolution and gave his royalties to support the Sandinistas in Nicaragua.

As the critic Jason Wilson has noted, Cortázar "learnt from the French Surrealists how to shake the lazy reader into an awareness that something threatens behind the conventions of everyday life without ever defining this elusive, often hostile otherness." The story "Axolotl" offered Cortázar the opportunity to create what he called "openings onto estrangement, instances of a dislocation in which the ordinary ceases to be tranquilizing because nothing is ordinary when submitted to a silent and sustained scrutiny."

Cortázar felt that he was possessed by the stories he had to tell:

> I refer to my own experience as a story writer, and I see a relatively happy and unremarkable man, caught up in the same trivialities and trips to the dentist as any inhabitant of a large city . . . who suddenly, instantaneously, in the subway, in a café, in a dream, in the office while revising a doubtful translation about Tanzanian illiteracy, stops being him-and-his-circumstances and, for no reason, without warning . . . without anything that gives him a chance to clench his teeth and take a deep breath, *he is a story*, a shapeless mass without words or faces or beginning or end, but still a story, something that can only be a story, and then, suddenly, Tanzania can go to hell, because he puts a paper in the typewriter and begins to write, even if his bosses and the whole United Nations scream in his ears.

RELATED STORY
Santiago Nazarian, "Fish Spine," page 961.

RELATED CASEBOOK
See Casebook on Magical Realism, pages 1627–1646, including Jorge Luis Borges, "Borges and I," page 1631; Alejo Carpentier, "On the Marvelous Real in America," page 1633 and "The Baroque and the Marvelous Real," page 1635; Luis Leal, "Magical Realism in Spanish American Literature," page 1637; William Gass, "The First Seven Pages of the Boom," page 1639; Ursula K. Le Guin, "The Kind of Fiction Most Characteristic of Our Times," page 1641; Mario Vargas Llosa, "The Prose Style of Jorge Luis Borges and Gabriel García Márquez," page 1645.

Axolotl

1967 / Translated by Paul Blackburn

THERE WAS A TIME when I thought a great deal about the axolotls. I went to see them in the aquarium at the Jardin des Plantes and stayed for hours watching them, observing their immobility, their faint movements. Now I am an axolotl.

I got to them by chance one spring morning when Paris was spreading its peacock tail after a wintry Lent. I was heading down the boulevard Port-Royal, then I took Saint-Marcel and L'Hôpital and saw green among all that grey and remembered the lions. I was friend of the lions and panthers, but had never gone into the dark, humid building that was the aquarium. I left my bike against the gratings and went to look at the tulips. The lions were sad and ugly and my panther was asleep. I decided on the aquarium, looked obliquely at banal fish until, unexpectedly, I hit it off with the axolotls. I stayed watching them for an hour and left, unable to think of anything else.

In the library at Sainte-Geneviève, I consulted a dictionary and learned that axolotls are the larval stage (provided with gills) of a species of salamander of the genus Ambystoma. That they were Mexican I knew already by looking at them and their little pink Aztec faces and the placard at the top of the tank. I read that specimens of them had been found in Africa capable of living on dry land during the periods of drought, and continuing their life under water when the rainy season came. I found their Spanish name, *ajolote*, and the mention that they were edible, and that their oil was used (no longer used, it said) like cod-liver oil.

I didn't care to look up any of the specialized works, but the next day I went back to the Jardin des Plantes. I began to go every morning, morning and afternoon some days. The aquarium guard smiled perplexedly taking my ticket. I would lean up against the iron bar in front of the tanks and set to watching them. There's nothing strange in this, because after the first minute I knew that we were linked, that something infinitely lost and distant kept pulling us together. It had been enough to detain me that first morning in front of the sheet of glass where some bubbles rose through the water. The axolotls huddled on the wretched narrow (only I can know how narrow and wretched) floor of moss and stone in the tank. There were nine specimens, and the majority pressed their heads against the glass, looking with their eyes of gold at whoever came near them. Disconcerted, almost ashamed, I felt it a lewdness to be peering at these silent and immobile figures heaped at the bottom of the tank. Mentally I isolated one, situated on the right and somewhat apart from the others, to study it better. I saw a rosy little body, translucent (I thought of those Chinese figurines of milky glass), looking like a small lizard about six inches long, ending in a fish's tail of extraordinary delicacy, the most sensitive part of our body. Along the back ran a transparent fin which joined with the tail, but what obsessed me was the feet, of the slenderest nicety, ending in tiny fingers with minutely human nails. And then I discovered its eyes, its face. Inexpressive features, with no other trait save the eyes, two orifices, like brooches, wholly of transparent gold, lacking any life but looking, letting themselves be penetrated by my look, which seemed to travel past the golden level and lose itself in a diaphanous interior mystery. A very slender black halo ringed the eye and etched it onto the pink flesh, onto the rosy stone of the head, vaguely triangular, but with curved and irregular sides which gave it a total likeness to a statuette corroded by time. The mouth was masked by the triangular plane of the face, its considerable size would be guessed only in profile; in front a delicate crevice barely slit the lifeless stone. On both sides of the head where the ears should have been, there grew three tiny sprigs red as coral, a vegetal outgrowth, the gills, I suppose. And they were the only thing quick about it; every ten or fifteen seconds the sprigs pricked up stiffly and again subsided. Once in a while a foot would barely move, I saw the diminutive toes poise mildly on the moss. It's that we don't enjoy moving a lot, and the tank is so cramped — we barely move in any direction and we're hitting one of the others with our tail or our head — difficulties arise, fights, tiredness. The time feels like it's less if we stay quietly.

It was their quietness that made me lean toward them fascinated the first time I saw the axolotls. Obscurely I seemed to understand their secret will, to abolish space and time with an indifferent immobility. I knew better later; the gill contraction, the tentative reckoning of the delicate feet on the stones, the abrupt swimming (some of them swim with a simple undulation of the body) proved to me that they were capable of escaping that mineral lethargy in which they spent whole hours. Above all else, their eyes obsessed me. In the standing tanks on either side of them, different fishes showed me the simple stupidity of their handsome eyes so similar to our own. The eyes of the axolotls spoke to me of the presence of a different life, of another way of seeing. Glueing my face to the glass (the guard would cough fussily once in a while), I tried to see better those diminutive golden points, that entrance to the infinitely slow and remote world of these rosy creatures. It was useless to tap with one finger on the glass directly in front of their faces; they never gave the least reaction. The golden eyes continued burning with their soft, terrible light; they continued looking at me from an unfathomable depth which made me dizzy.

And nevertheless they were close. I knew it before this, before being an axolotl. I learned it the day I came near them for the first time. The anthropomorphic features of a monkey reveal the reverse of what most people believe, the distance that is traveled from them to us. The absolute lack of similarity between axolotls and human beings proved to me that my recognition was valid, that I was not propping myself up with easy analogies. Only the little hands . . . But an eft, the common newt, has such hands also, and we are not at all alike. I think it was the axolotls' heads, that triangular pink shape with the tiny eyes of gold. That looked and knew. That laid the claim. They were not *animals.*

It would seem easy, almost obvious, to fall into mythology. I began seeing in the axolotls a metamorphosis which did not succeed in revoking a mysterious humanity. I imagined them aware, slaves of their bodies, condemned infinitely to the silence of the abyss, to a hopeless meditation. Their blind gaze, the diminutive gold disc without expression and nonetheless terribly shining, went through me like a message: "Save us, save us." I caught myself mumbling words of advice, conveying childish hopes. They continued to look at me, immobile; from time to time the rosy branches of the gills stiffened. In that instant I felt a muted pain; perhaps they were seeing me, attracting my strength to penetrate into the impenetrable thing of their lives. They were not human beings, but I had found in no animal such a profound relation with myself. The axolotls were like witnesses of something, and at times like horrible judges. I felt ignoble in front of them; there was such a terrifying purity in those transparent eyes. They were larvas, but larva means disguise and also phantom. Behind those Aztec faces, without expression but of an implacable cruelty, what semblance was awaiting its hour?

I was afraid of them. I think that had it not been for feeling the proximity of other visitors and the guard, I would not have been bold enough to remain alone with them. "You eat them alive with your eyes, hey," the guard said, laughing; he likely thought I was a little cracked. What he didn't notice was that it was they devouring me slowly with their eyes, in a cannibalism of gold. At any distance from the aquarium, I had only to think of them, it was as though I were being affected from a distance. It got to the point that I was going every day, and at night I thought of them immobile in the darkness slowly putting a hand out which immediately encountered another. Perhaps their eyes could see in the dead of night, and for them the day continued indefinitely. The eyes of axolotls have no lids.

I know now that there was nothing strange, that that had to occur. Leaning over in front of the tank each morning, the recognition was greater. They were suffering, every fiber of my body reached toward that stifled pain, that stiff torment at the bottom of the tank. They were lying in wait for something, a remote dominion destroyed, an age of liberty when the world had been that of the axolotls. Not possible that such a terrible expression which was attaining the overthrow of that forced blankness on their stone faces should carry any message other than one of pain, proof of that eternal sentence, of that liquid hell they were undergoing. Hopelessly, I wanted to prove to myself that my own sensibility was projecting a nonexistent consciousness upon the axolotls. They and I knew. So there was nothing strange in what happened. My face was pressed against the glass of the aquarium, my eyes were attempting once more to penetrate the mystery of those eyes of gold without iris, without pupil. I saw from very close up the face of an axolotl immobile next to the glass. No transition and no surprise, I saw my face against the glass, I saw it on the outside of the tank, I saw it on the other side of the glass. Then my face drew back and I understood.

Only one thing was strange: to go on thinking as usual, to know. To realize that was, for the first moment, like the horror of a man buried alive awaking to his fate. Outside, my face came close to the glass again, I saw my mouth, the lips compressed with the effort of understanding the axolotls. I was an axolotl and now I knew instantly that no understanding was possible. He was outside the aquarium, his thinking was a thinking outside the tank. Recognizing him, being him himself, I was an axolotl and in my world. The horror began — I learned in the same moment — of believing myself prisoner in the body of an axolotl, metamorphosed into him with my human mind intact, buried alive in an axolotl, condemned to move lucidly among unconscious creatures. But that stopped when a foot just grazed my face, when I moved just a little to one side and saw an axolotl next to me who was looking at me, and understood that he knew also, no communication possible, but very clearly. Or I was also in him, or all of us were thinking humanlike, incapable of expression, limited to the golden splendor of our eyes looking at the face of the man pressed against the aquarium.

He returned many times, but he comes less often now. Weeks pass without his showing up. I saw him yesterday, he looked at me for a long time and left briskly. It seemed to me that he was not so much interested in us any more, that he was coming out of habit. Since the only thing I do is think, I could think about him a lot. It occurs to me that at the beginning we continued to communicate, that he felt more than ever one with the mystery which was claiming him. But the bridges were broken between him and me, because what was his obsession is now an axolotl, alien to his human life. I think that at the beginning I was capable of returning to him in a certain way — ah, only in a certain way — and of keeping awake his desire to know us better. I am an axolotl for good now, and if I think like a man it's only because every axolotl thinks like a man inside his rosy stone semblance. I believe that all this succeeded in communicating something to him in those first days, when I was still he. And in this final solitude to which he no longer comes, I console myself by thinking that perhaps he is going to write a story about us, that, believing he's making up a story, he's going to write all this about axolotls.

Stephen Crane

Stephen Crane (1871–1900) wrote some of the most memorable fiction and poetry ever created by an American, publishing fourteen books in his short lifetime. The poet John Berryman, who wrote a biography of Crane, observed the essential truth about him: "Crane was a writer and nothing else: a man alone in a room with the English language, trying to get human feelings right." Crane's style in his short stories is as intensely personal as Edgar Allan Poe's or Nathaniel Hawthorne's, but he did not use the techniques of fantasy and allegory. "His eyes remained wide open on his world. He was almost illusionless, whether about his subjects or himself. Perhaps his sole illusion was the heroic one; and not even this, especially if he was concerned in it himself as a man, escaped his irony."

Crane was born in Newark, New Jersey, the youngest of fourteen children. His father, a Methodist minister, died when Crane was just a boy, and his mother supported the family by writing articles for Methodist papers and reporting for the *New York Tribune* and the *Philadelphia Press*. Crane briefly attended Lafayette College and Syracuse University before going to work in New York City as a freelance journalist. He became interested in life in the Bowery, one of the worst slums in New York, and he used this setting for his novel *Maggie: A Girl of the Streets*, a work so grimly naturalistic in its portrayal of slum life and so frank in its treatment of sex that Crane had to publish it at his own expense in 1893. Two years later he sold a long story about the Civil War to a syndicate for less than a hundred dollars. That work, *The Red Badge of Courage*, was such a vivid account of wartime experience—even though Crane had never been in a battle himself—that it established his literary reputation.

In the last five years of his life, before he died of tuberculosis in Germany, Crane traveled extensively as a reporter, first to the American West and then to Florida. He couldn't keep away from scenes of war or revolution, believing—as did Ernest Hemingway after him—that "the nearer a writer gets to life, the greater he becomes as an artist." Crane was en route to Florida on the steamship *Commodore* when the ship was wrecked on New Year's Day 1897. He based one of his finest short stories, "The Open Boat," on what happened to him in a lifeboat with the other survivors. He had first reported the disaster in an article for his newspaper shortly after the shipwreck. Joseph Conrad admired Crane's writing and said of "The Open Boat" that "by the deep and simple humanity of its presentation [the story] seems somehow to illustrate the essentials of life itself, like a symbolic tale."

RELATED COMMENTARY

Stephen Crane, "The Sinking of the *Commodore*," page 1417.

The Open Boat

A Tale Intended to Be after the Fact, Being the Experience of Four Men from the Sunk Steamer *Commodore*

1897

I

None of them knew the color of the sky. Their eyes glanced level, and were fastened upon the waves that swept toward them. These waves were of the hue of slate, save for the tops, which were of foaming white, and all of the men knew the colors of the sea. The horizon narrowed and widened, and dipped and rose, and at all times its edge was jagged with waves that seemed thrust up in points like rocks.

Many a man ought to have a bath-tub larger than the boat which here rode upon the sea. These waves were most wrongfully and barbarously abrupt and tall, and each froth-top was a problem in small boat navigation.

The cook squatted in the bottom and looked with both eyes at the six inches of gunwale which separated him from the ocean. His sleeves were rolled over his fat forearms, and the two flaps of his unbuttoned vest dangled as he bent to bail out the boat. Often he said: "Gawd! That was a narrow clip." As he remarked it he invariably gazed eastward over the broken sea.

The oiler, steering with one of the two oars in the boat, sometimes raised himself suddenly to keep clear of water that swirled in over the stern. It was a thin little oar and it seemed often ready to snap.

The correspondent, pulling at the other oar, watched the waves and wondered why he was there.

The injured captain, lying in the bow, was at this time buried in that profound dejection and indifference which comes, temporarily at least, to even the bravest and most enduring when, willy nilly, the firm fails, the army loses, the ship goes down. The mind of the master of a vessel is rooted deep in the timbers of her, though he command for a day or a decade, and this captain had on him the stern impression of a scene in the grays of dawn of seven turned faces, and later a stump of a top-mast with a white ball on it that slashed to and fro at the waves, went low and lower, and down. Thereafter there was something strange in his voice. Although steady, it was deep with mourning, and of a quality beyond oration or tears.

"Keep 'er a little more south, Billie," said he.

" 'A little more south,' sir," said the oiler in the stern.

A seat in this boat was not unlike a seat upon a bucking broncho, and, by the same token, a broncho is not much smaller. The craft pranced and reared, and plunged like an animal. As each wave came, and she rose for it, she seemed like a horse making at a fence outrageously high. The manner of her scramble over these walls of water is a mystic thing, and, moreover, at the top of them were ordinarily these problems in white water, the foam racing down from the summit of each wave, requiring a new leap, and a leap from the air. Then, after scornfully bumping a crest, she would slide, and race, and splash down a long incline and arrive bobbing and nodding in front of the next menace.

A singular disadvantage of the sea lies in the fact that after successfully surmounting one wave you discover that there is another behind it just as important and just as nervously anxious to do something effective in the way of swamping boats. In a ten-foot dingey one can get an idea of the resources of the sea in the line of waves that is not probable to the average experience, which is never at sea in a dingey. As each slaty wall of water approached, it shut all else from the view of the men in the boat, and it was not difficult to imagine that this particular wave was the final outburst of the ocean, the last effort of the grim water. There was a terrible grace in the move of the waves, and they came in silence, save for the snarling of the crests.

In the wan light, the faces of the men must have been gray. Their eyes must have glinted in strange ways as they gazed steadily astern. Viewed from a balcony, the whole thing would doubtlessly have been weirdly picturesque. But the men in the boat had no time to see it, and if they had had leisure there were other things to occupy their minds. The sun swung steadily up the sky, and they knew it was broad day because the color of the sea changed from slate to emerald-green, streaked with amber lights, and the foam was like tumbling snow. The process of the breaking day was unknown to them. They were aware only of this effect upon the color of the waves that rolled toward them.

In disjointed sentences the cook and the correspondent argued as to the difference between a life-saving station and a house of refuge. The cook had said: "There's a house of refuge just north of the Mosquito Inlet Light, and as soon as they see us, they'll come off in their boat and pick us up."

"As soon as who see us?" said the correspondent.

"The crew," said the cook.

"Houses of refuge don't have crews," said the correspondent. "As I understand them, they are only places where clothes and grub are stored for the benefit of shipwrecked people. They don't carry crews."

"Oh, yes, they do," said the cook.

"No, they don't," said the correspondent.

"Well, we're not there yet, anyhow," said the oiler, in the stern.

"Well," said the cook, "perhaps it's not a house of refuge that I'm thinking of as being near Mosquito Inlet Light. Perhaps it's a life-saving station."

"We're not there yet," said the oiler, in the stern.

II

As the boat bounced from the top of each wave, the wind tore through the hair of the hatless men, and as the craft plopped her stern down again the spray slashed past them. The crest of each of these waves was a hill, from the top of which the men surveyed, for a moment, a broad tumultuous expanse, shining and wind-riven. It was probably splendid. It was probably glorious, this play of the free sea, wild with lights of emerald and white and amber.

"Bully good thing it's an on-shore wind," said the cook. "If not where would we be? Wouldn't have a show."

"That's right," said the correspondent.

The busy oiler nodded his assent.

Then the captain, in the bow, chuckled in a way that expressed humor, contempt, tragedy, all in one. "Do you think we've got a show, now, boys?" said he.

Whereupon the three went silent, save for a trifle of hemming and hawing. To express any particular optimism at this time they felt to be childish and stupid, but they all doubtless possessed this sense of the situation in their mind. A young man thinks doggedly at such times. On the other hand, the ethics of their condition was decidedly against any open suggestion of hopelessness. So they were silent.

"Oh, well," said the captain, soothing his children, "we'll get ashore all right."

But there was that in his tone which made them think, so the oiler quoth: "Yes! If this wind holds!"

The cook was bailing. "Yes! If we don't catch hell in the surf."

Canton flannel gulls flew near and far. Sometimes they sat down on the sea, near patches of brown sea-weed that rolled over the waves with a movement like carpets on a line in a gale. The birds sat comfortably in groups, and they were envied by some in the dingey, for the wrath of the sea was no more to them than it was to a covey of prairie chickens a thousand miles inland. Often they came very close and stared at the men with black bead-like eyes. At these times they were uncanny and sinister in their unblinking scrutiny, and the men hooted angrily at them, telling them to be gone. One came, and evidently decided to alight on the top of the captain's head. The bird flew parallel to the boat and did not circle, but made short sidelong jumps in the air in chicken-fashion. His black eyes were wistfully fixed upon the captain's head. "Ugly brute," said the oiler to the bird. "You look as if you were made with a jack-knife." The cook and the correspondent swore darkly at the creature. The captain naturally wished to knock it away with the end of the heavy painter, but he did not dare do it, because anything resembling an emphatic gesture would have capsized this freighted boat, and so with his open hand, the captain gently and carefully waved the gull away. After it had been discouraged from the pursuit the captain breathed easier on account of his hair, and others breathed easier because the bird struck their minds at this time as being somehow gruesome and ominous.

In the meantime the oiler and the correspondent rowed. And also they rowed.

They sat together in the same seat, and each rowed an oar. Then the oiler took both oars; then the correspondent took both oars; then the oiler; then the correspondent. They rowed and they rowed. The very ticklish part of the business was when the time came for the reclining one in the stern to take his turn at the oars. By the very last star of truth, it is easier to steal eggs from under a hen than it was to change seats in the dingey. First the man in the stern slid his hand along the thwart and moved with care, as if he were of Sèvres.[1] Then the

---

[1] A delicate French porcelain.

man in the rowing seat slid his hand along the other thwart. It was all done with the most extraordinary care. As the two sidled past each other, the whole party kept watchful eyes on the coming wave, and the captain cried: "Look out now! Steady there!"

The brown mats of sea-weed that appeared from time to time were like islands, bits of earth. They were travelling, apparently, neither one way nor the other. They were, to all intents, stationary. They informed the men in the boat that it was making progress slowly toward the land.

The captain, rearing cautiously in the bow, after the dingey soared on a great swell, said that he had seen the light-house at Mosquito Inlet. Presently the cook remarked that he had seen it. The correspondent was at the oars, then, and for some reason he too wished to look at the light-house, but his back was toward the far shore and the waves were important, and for some time he could not seize an opportunity to turn his head. But at last there came a wave more gentle than the others, and when at the crest of it he swiftly scoured the western horizon.

"See it?" said the captain.

"No," said the correspondent, slowly, "I didn't see anything."

"Look again," said the captain. He pointed. "It's exactly in that direction."

At the top of another wave, the correspondent did as he was bid, and this time his eyes chanced on a small still thing on the edge of the swaying horizon. It was precisely like the point of a pin. It took an anxious eye to find a light-house so tiny.

"Think we'll make it, Captain?"

"If this wind holds and the boat don't swamp, we can't do much else," said the captain.

The little boat, lifted by each towering sea, and splashed viciously by the crests, made progress that in the absence of sea-weed was not apparent to those in her. She seemed just a wee thing wallowing, miraculously, top-up, at the mercy of five oceans. Occasionally, a great spread of water, like white flames, swarmed into her.

"Bail her, cook," said the captain, serenely.

"All right, Captain," said the cheerful cook.

III

It would be difficult to describe the subtle brotherhood of men that was here established on the seas. No one said that it was so. No one mentioned it. But it dwelt in the boat, and each man felt it warm him. They were a captain, an oiler, a cook, and a correspondent, and they were friends, friends in a more curiously iron-bound degree than may be common. The hurt captain, lying against the water-jar in the bow, spoke always in a low voice and calmly, but he could never command a more ready and swiftly obedient crew than the motley three of the dingey. It was more than a mere recognition of what was best for the common safety. There was surely in it a quality that was personal and heartfelt. And after this devotion to the commander of the boat there was this comrade-ship that the correspondent, for instance, who had been taught to be cynical of men, knew even at the time was the best experience of his life. But no one said that it was so. No one mentioned it.

"I wish we had a sail," remarked the captain. "We might try my overcoat on the end of an oar and give you two boys a chance to rest." So the cook and the correspondent held the mast and spread wide the overcoat. The oiler steered, and the little boat made good way with her new rig. Sometimes the oiler had to scull sharply to keep a sea from breaking into the boat, but otherwise sailing was a success.

Meanwhile the light-house had been growing slowly larger. It had now almost assumed color, and appeared like a little gray shadow on the sky. The man at the oars could not be prevented from turning his head rather often to try for a glimpse of this little gray shadow.

At last, from the top of each wave the men in the tossing boat could see land. Even as the light-house was an upright shadow on the sky, this land seemed but a long black shadow on the sea. It certainly was thinner than paper. "We must be about opposite New Smyrna," said the cook, who had coasted this shore often in schooners. "Captain, by the way, I believe they abandoned that life-saving station there about a year ago."

"Did they?" said the captain.

The wind slowly died away. The cook and the correspondent were not now obliged to slave in order to hold high the oar. But the waves continued their old impetuous swooping at the dingey, and the little craft, no longer under way, struggled woundily over them. The oiler or the correspondent took the oars again.

Shipwrecks are *apropos* of nothing. If men could only train for them and have them occur when the men had reached pink condition, there would be less drowning at sea. Of the four in the dingey none had slept any time worth mentioning for two days and two nights previous to embarking in the dingey, and in the excitement of clambering about the deck of a foundering ship they had also forgotten to eat heartily.

For these reasons, and for others, neither the oiler nor the correspondent was fond of rowing at this time. The correspondent wondered ingenuously how in the name of all that was sane could there be people who thought it amusing to row a boat. It was not an amusement; it was a diabolical punishment, and even a genius of mental aberrations could never conclude that it was anything but a horror to the muscles and a crime against the back. He mentioned to the boat in general how the amusement of rowing struck him, and the weary-faced oiler smiled in full sympathy. Previously to the foundering, by the way, the oiler had worked double-watch in the engine-room of the ship.

"Take her easy, now, boys," said the captain. "Don't spend yourselves. If we have to run a surf you'll need all your strength, because we'll sure have to swim for it. Take your time."

Slowly the land arose from the sea. From a black line it became a line of black and a line of white — trees and sand. Finally, the captain said that he could make out a house on the shore. "That's the house of refuge, sure," said the cook. "They'll see us before long, and come out after us."

The distant light-house reared high. "The keeper ought to be able to make us out now, if he's looking through a glass," said the captain. "He'll notify the life-saving people."

"None of those other boats could have got ashore to give word of the wreck," said the oiler, in a low voice. "Else the life-boat would be out hunting us."

Slowly and beautifully the land loomed out of the sea. The wind came again. It had veered from the northeast to the southeast. Finally, a new sound struck the ears of the men in the boat. It was the low thunder of the surf on the shore. "We'll never be able to make the light-house now," said the captain. "Swing her head a little more north, Billie."

"'A little more north,' sir," said the oiler.

Whereupon the little boat turned her nose once more down the wind, and all but the oarsman watched the shore grow. Under the influence of this expansion doubt and direful apprehension were leaving the minds of the men. The management of the boat was still most absorbing, but it could not prevent a quiet cheerfulness. In an hour, perhaps, they would be ashore.

Their back-bones had become thoroughly used to balancing in the boat and they now rode this wild colt of a dingey like circus men. The correspondent thought that he had been drenched to the skin, but happening to feel in the top pocket of his coat, he found therein eight cigars. Four of them were soaked with sea-water; four were perfectly scatheless. After a search, somebody produced three dry matches, and thereupon the four waifs rode impudently in their little boat, and with an assurance of an impending rescue shining in their eyes, puffed at the big cigars and judged well and ill of all men. Everybody took a drink of water.

IV

"Cook," remarked the captain, "there don't seem to be any signs of life about your house of refuge."

"No," replied the cook. "Funny they don't see us!"

A broad stretch of lowly coast lay before the eyes of the men. It was of dunes topped with dark vegetation. The roar of the surf was plain, and sometimes they could see the white lip of a wave as it spun up the beach. A tiny house was blocked out black upon the sky. Southward, the slim light-house lifted its little gray length.

Tide, wind, and waves were swinging the dingey northward. "Funny they don't see us," said the men.

The surf's roar was here dulled, but its tone was, nevertheless, thunderous and mighty. As the boat swam over the great rollers, the men sat listening to this roar. "We'll swamp sure," said everybody.

It is fair to say here that there was not a life-saving station within twenty miles in either direction, but the men did not know this fact and in consequence they made dark and opprobrious remarks concerning the eyesight of the nation's life-savers. Four scowling men sat in the dingey and surpassed records in the invention of epithets.

"Funny they don't see us."

The light-heartedness of a former time had completely faded. To their sharpened minds it was easy to conjure pictures of all kinds of incompetency and blindness and, indeed, cowardice. There was the shore of the populous land, and it was bitter and bitter to them that from it came no sign.

"Well," said the captain, ultimately, "I suppose we'll have to make a try for ourselves. If we stay out here too long, we'll none of us have strength left to swim after the boat swamps."

And so the oiler, who was at the oars, turned the boat straight for the shore. There was a sudden tightening of muscles. There was some thinking.

"If we don't all get ashore —" said the captain. "If we don't all get ashore, I suppose you fellows know where to send news of my finish?"

They then briefly exchanged some addresses and admonitions. As for the reflections of the men, there was a great deal of rage in them. Perchance they might be formulated thus: "If I am going to be drowned — if I am going to be drowned — if I am going to be drowned, why, in the name of the seven mad gods who rule the sea, was I allowed to come thus far and contemplate sand and trees? Was I brought here merely to have my nose dragged away as I was about to nibble the sacred cheese of life? It is preposterous. If this old ninny-woman, Fate, cannot do better than this, she should be deprived of the management of men's fortunes. She is an old hen who knows not her intention. If she has decided to drown me, why did she not do it in the beginning and save me all this trouble. The whole affair is absurd. . . . But, no, she cannot mean to drown me. She dare not drown me. She cannot drown me. Not after all this work." Afterward the man might have had an impulse to shake his fist at the clouds. "Just you drown me, now, and then hear what I call you!"

The billows that came at this time were more formidable. They seemed always just about to break and roll over the little boat in a turmoil of foam. There was a preparatory and long growl in the speech of them. No mind unused to the sea would have concluded that the dingey could ascend these sheer heights in time. The shore was still afar. The oiler was a wily surfman. "Boys," he said, swiftly, "she won't live three minutes more and we're too far out to swim. Shall I take her to sea again, Captain?"

"Yes! Go ahead!" said the captain.

This oiler, by a series of quick miracles, and fast and steady oarsmanship, turned the boat in the middle of the surf and took her safely to sea again.

There was a considerable silence as the boat bumped over the furrowed sea to deeper water. Then somebody in gloom spoke. "Well, anyhow, they must have seen us from the shore by now."

The gulls went in slanting flight up the wind toward the gray desolate east. A squall, marked by dingy clouds, and clouds brick-red, like smoke from a burning building, appeared from the southeast.

"What do you think of those life-saving people? Ain't they peaches?"

"Funny they haven't seen us."

"Maybe they think we're out here for sport! Maybe they think we're fishin'. Maybe they think we're damned fools."

It was a long afternoon. A changed tide tried to force them southward, but wind and wave said northward. Far ahead, where coast-line, sea, and sky formed their mighty angle, there were little dots which seemed to indicate a city on the shore.

"St. Augustine?"

The captain shook his head. "Too near Mosquito Inlet."

And the oiler rowed, and then the correspondent rowed. Then the oiler rowed. It was a weary business. The human back can become the seat of more aches and pains than are registered in books for the composite anatomy of a regiment. It is a limited area, but it can become the theatre of innumerable muscular conflicts, tangles, wrenches, knots, and other comforts.

"Did you ever like to row, Billie?" asked the correspondent.

"No," said the oiler, "Hang it."

When one exchanged the rowing-seat for a place in the bottom of the boat, he suffered a bodily depression that caused him to be careless of everything save an obligation to wiggle one finger. There was cold sea-water swashing to and fro in the boat, and he lay in it. His head, pillowed on a thwart, was within an inch of the swirl of a wave crest, and sometimes a particularly obstreperous sea came inboard and drenched him once more. But these matters did not annoy him. It is almost certain that if the boat had capsized he would have tumbled comfortably out upon the ocean as if he felt sure that it was a great soft mattress.

"Look! There's a man on the shore!"

"Where?"

"There! See 'im? See 'im?"

"Yes, sure! He's walking along."

"Now he's stopped. Look! He's facing us!"

"He's waving at us!"

"So he is! By thunder!"

"Ah, now, we're all right! There'll be a boat out here for us in half an hour."

"He's going on. He's running. He's going up to that house there."

The remote beach seemed lower than the sea, and it required a searching glance to discern the little black figure. The captain saw a floating stick and they rowed to it. A bath-towel was by some weird chance in the boat, and, tying this on the stick, the captain waved it. The oarsman did not dare turn his head, so he was obliged to ask questions.

"What's he doing now?"

"He's standing still again. He's looking, I think. . . . There he goes again. Toward the house. . . . Now he's stopped again."

"Is he waving at us?"

"No, not now! He was, though."

"Look! There comes another man!"

"He's running."

"Look at him go, would you."

"Why, he's on a bicycle. Now he's met the other man. They're both waving at us. Look!"

"There comes something up the beach."

"What the devil is that thing?"

"Why, it looks like a boat."

"Why, certainly it's a boat."

"No, it's on wheels."

"Yes, so it is. Well, that must be the life-boat. They drag them along shore on a wagon."

"That's the life-boat, sure."

"No, by, it's — it's an omnibus."

"I tell you it's a life-boat."

"It is not! It's an omnibus. I can see it plain. See? One of those big hotel omnibuses."

"By thunder, you're right. It's an omnibus, sure as fate. What do you suppose they are doing with an omnibus? Maybe they are going around collecting the life-crew, hey?"

"That's it, likely. Look! There's a fellow waving a little black flag. He's standing on the steps of the omnibus. There come those other two fellows. Now they're all talking together. Look at the fellow with the flag. Maybe he ain't waving it!"

"That ain't a flag, is it? That's his coat. Why, certainly, that's his coat."

"So it is. It's his coat. He's taken it off and is waving it around his head. But would you look at him swing it!"

"Oh, say, there isn't any life-saving station there. That's just a winter resort hotel omnibus that has brought over some of the boarders to see us drown."

"What's that idiot with the coat mean? What's he signaling, anyhow?"

"It looks as if he were trying to tell us to go north. There must be a life-saving station up there."

"No! He thinks we're fishing. Just giving us a merry hand. See? Ah, there, Willie."

"Well, I wish I could make something out of those signals. What do you suppose he means?"

"He don't mean anything. He's just playing."

"Well, if he'd just signal us to try the surf again, or to go to sea and wait, or go north, or go south, or go to hell — there would be some reason in it. But look at him. He just stands there and keeps his coat revolving like a wheel. The ass!"

"There come more people."

"Now there's quite a mob. Look! Isn't that a boat?"

"Where? Oh, I see where you mean. No, that's no boat."

"That fellow is still waving his coat."

"He must think we like to see him do that. Why don't he quit it. It don't mean anything."

"I don't know. I think he is trying to make us go north. It must be that there's a life-saving station there somewhere."

"Say, he ain't tired yet. Look at 'im wave."

"Wonder how long he can keep that up. He's been revolving his coat ever since he caught sight of us. He's an idiot. Why aren't they getting men to bring a boat out. A fishing boat — one of those big yawls — could come out here all right. Why don't he do something?"

"Oh, it's all right, now."

"They'll have a boat out here for us in less than no time, now that they've seen us."

A faint yellow tone came into the sky over the low land. The shadows on the sea slowly deepened. The wind bore coldness with it, and the men began to shiver.

"Holy smoke!" said one, allowing his voice to express his impious mood, "if we keep on monkeying out here! If we've got to flounder out here all night!"

"Oh, we'll never have to stay here all night! Don't you worry. They've seen us now, and it won't be long before they'll come chasing out after us."

The shore grew dusky. The man waving a coat blended gradually into this gloom, and it swallowed in the same manner the omnibus and the group of people. The spray, when it dashed uproariously over the side, made the voyagers shrink and swear like men who were being branded.

"I'd like to catch the chump who waved the coat. I feel like soaking him one, just for luck."

"Why? What did he do?"

"Oh, nothing, but then he seemed so damned cheerful."

In the meantime the oiler rowed, and then the correspondent rowed, and then the oiler rowed. Gray-faced and bowed forward, they mechanically, turn by turn, plied the leaden oars. The form of the light-house had vanished from the southern horizon, but finally a pale star appeared, just lifting from the sea. The streaked saffron in the west passed before the all-merging darkness, and the sea to the east was black. The land had vanished, and was expressed only by the low and drear thunder of the surf.

"If I am going to be drowned — if I am going to be drowned — if I am going to be drowned, why, in the name of the seven mad gods who rule the sea, was I allowed to come thus far and contemplate sand and trees? Was I brought here merely to have my nose dragged away as I was about to nibble the sacred cheese of life?"

The patient captain, drooped over the water-jar, was sometimes obliged to speak to the oarsman.

"Keep her head up! Keep her head up!"

" 'Keep her head up,' sir." The voices were weary and low.

This was surely a quiet evening. All save the oarsman lay heavily and listlessly in the boat's bottom. As for him, his eyes were just capable of noting the tall black waves that swept forward in a most sinister silence, save for an occasional subdued growl of a crest.

The cook's head was on a thwart, and he looked without interest at the water under his nose. He was deep in other scenes. Finally he spoke. "Billie," he murmured, dreamfully, "what kind of pie do you like best?"

V

"Pie," said the oiler and the correspondent, agitatedly. "Don't talk about those things, blast you!"

"Well," said the cook, "I was just thinking about ham sandwiches, and —"

A night on the sea in an open boat is a long night. As darkness settled finally, the shine of the light, lifting from the sea in the south, changed to full gold. On the northern horizon a new light appeared, a small bluish gleam on the edge of the waters. These two lights were the furniture of the world. Otherwise there was nothing but waves.

Two men huddled in the stern, and distances were so magnificent in the dingey that the rower was enabled to keep his feet partly warmed by thrusting them under his companions. Their legs indeed extended far under the rowing-seat until they touched the feet of the captain forward. Sometimes, despite the efforts of the tired oarsman, a wave came piling into the boat, an icy wave of the night, and the chilling water soaked them anew. They would twist their bodies for a moment and groan, and sleep the dead sleep once more, while the water in the boat gurgled about them as the craft rocked.

The plan of the oiler and the correspondent was for one to row until he lost the ability, and then arouse the other from his sea-water couch in the bottom of the boat.

The oiler plied the oars until his head drooped forward, and the overpowering sleep blinded him. And he rowed yet afterward. Then he touched a man in the bottom of the boat, and called his name. "Will you spell me for a little while?" he said, meekly.

"Sure, Billie," said the correspondent, awakening and dragging himself to a sitting position. They exchanged places carefully, and the oiler, cuddling down in the sea-water at the cook's side, seemed to go to sleep instantly.

The particular violence of the sea had ceased. The waves came without snarling. The obligation of the man at the oars was to keep the boat headed so that the tilt of the rollers would not capsize her, and to preserve her from filling when the crests rushed past. The black waves were silent and hard to be seen in the darkness. Often one was almost upon the boat before the oarsman was aware.

In a low voice the correspondent addressed the captain. He was not sure that the captain was awake, although this iron man seemed to be always awake. "Captain, shall I keep her making for that light north, sir?"

The same steady voice answered him. "Yes. Keep it about two points off the port bow."

The cook had tied a life-belt around himself in order to get even the warmth which this clumsy cork contrivance could donate, and he seemed almost stove-like when a rower, whose teeth invariably chattered wildly as soon as he ceased his labor, dropped down to sleep.

The correspondent, as he rowed, looked down at the two men sleeping under foot. The cook's arm was around the oiler's shoulders, and, with their fragmentary clothing and haggard faces, they were the babes of the sea, a grotesque rendering of the old babes in the wood.

Later he must have grown stupid at his work, for suddenly there was a growling of water, and a crest came with a roar and a swash into the boat, and it was a wonder that it did not set the cook afloat in his life-belt. The cook continued to sleep, but the oiler sat up, blinking his eyes and shaking with the new cold.

"Oh, I'm awful sorry, Billie," said the correspondent, contritely.

"That's all right, old boy," said the oiler, and lay down again and was asleep.

Presently it seemed that even the captain dozed, and the correspondent thought that he was the one man afloat on all the oceans. The wind had a voice as it came over the waves, and it was sadder than the end.

There was a long, loud swishing astern of the boat, and a gleaming trail of phosphorescence, like blue flame, was furrowed on the black waters. It might have been made by a monstrous knife.

Then there came a stillness, while the correspondent breathed with the open mouth and looked at the sea.

Suddenly there was another swish and another long flash of bluish light, and this time it was alongside the boat, and might almost have been reached with an oar. The correspondent saw an enormous fin speed like a shadow through the water, hurling the crystalline spray and leaving the long glowing trail.

The correspondent looked over his shoulder at the captain. His face was hidden, and he seemed to be asleep. He looked at the babes of the sea. They certainly were asleep. So, being bereft of sympathy, he leaned a little way to one side and swore softly into the sea.

But the thing did not then leave the vicinity of the boat. Ahead or astern, on one side or the other, at intervals long or short, fled the long sparkling streak, and there was to be heard the whirroo of the dark fin. The speed and power of the thing were greatly to be admired. It cut the water like a gigantic and keen projectile.

The presence of this biding thing did not affect the man with the same horror that it would if he had been a picnicker. He simply looked at the sea dully and swore in an undertone.

Nevertheless, it is true that he did not wish to be alone with the thing. He wished one of his companions to awaken by chance and keep him company with it. But the captain hung motionless over the water-jar and the oiler and the cook in the bottom of the boat were plunged in slumber.

VI

"If I am going to be drowned — if I am going to be drowned — if I am going to be drowned, why, in the name of the seven mad gods who rule the sea, was I allowed to come thus far and contemplate sand and trees?"

During this dismal night, it may be remarked that a man would conclude that it was really the intention of the seven mad gods to drown him, despite the abominable injustice of it. For it was certainly an abominable injustice to drown a man who had worked so hard, so hard. The man felt it would be a crime most unnatural. Other people had drowned at sea since galleys swarmed with painted sails, but still —

When it occurs to a man that nature does not regard him as important, and that she feels she would not maim the universe by disposing of him, he at first wishes to throw bricks at the temple, and he hates deeply the fact that there are no bricks and no temples. Any visible expression of nature would surely be pelleted with his jeers.

Then, if there be no tangible thing to hoot he feels, perhaps, the desire to confront a personification and indulge in pleas, bowed to one knee, and with hands supplicant, saying: "Yes, but I love myself."

A high cold star on a winter's night is the word he feels that she says to him. Thereafter he knows the pathos of his situation.

The men in the dingey had not discussed these matters, but each had, no doubt, reflected upon them in silence and according to his mind. There was seldom any expression upon their faces save the general one of complete weariness. Speech was devoted to the business of the boat.

To chime the notes of his emotion, a verse mysteriously entered the correspondent's head. He had even forgotten that he had forgotten this verse, but it suddenly was in his mind.

A soldier of the Legion lay dying in Algiers,
There was lack of woman's nursing, there was dearth of woman's tears;
But a comrade stood beside him, and he took that comrade's hand,
And he said: "I never more shall see my own, my native land."

In his childhood, the correspondent had been made acquainted with the fact that a soldier of the Legion lay dying in Algiers, but he had never regarded it as important. Myriads of his school-fellows had informed him of the soldier's plight, but the dinning had naturally ended by making him perfectly indifferent. He had never considered it his affair that a soldier of the Legion lay dying in Algiers, nor had it appeared to him as a matter for sorrow. It was less to him than the breaking of a pencil's point.

Now, however, it quaintly came to him as a human, living thing. It was no longer merely a picture of a few throes in the breast of a poet, meanwhile drinking tea and warming his feet at the grate; it was an actuality — stern, mournful, and fine.

The correspondent plainly saw the soldier. He lay on the sand with his feet out straight and still. While his pale left hand was upon his chest in an attempt to thwart the going of his life, the blood came between his fingers. In the far Algerian distance, a city of low square forms was set against a sky that was faint with the last sunset hues. The correspondent, plying the oars and dreaming of the slow and slower movements of the lips of the soldier, was moved by a profound and perfectly impersonal comprehension. He was sorry for the soldier of the Legion who lay dying in Algiers.

The thing which had followed the boat and waited had evidently grown bored at the delay. There was no longer to be heard the slash of the cut-water, and there was no longer the flame of the long trail. The light in the north still glimmered, but it was apparently no nearer to the boat. Sometimes the boom of the surf rang in the correspondent's ears, and he turned the craft seaward then and rowed harder. Southward, some one had evidently built a watch-fire on the beach. It was too low and too far to be seen, but it made a shimmering, roseate reflection upon the bluff back of it, and this could be discerned from the boat. The wind came stronger, and sometimes a wave suddenly raged out like a mountain-cat and there was to be seen the sheen and sparkle of a broken crest.

The captain, in the bow, moved on his water-jar and sat erect. "Pretty long night," he observed to the correspondent. He looked at the shore. "Those life-saving people take their time."

"Did you see that shark playing around?"

"Yes, I saw him. He was a big fellow, all right."

"Wish I had known you were awake."

Later the correspondent spoke into the bottom of the boat.

"Billie!" There was a slow and gradual disentanglement. "Billie, will you spell me?"

"Sure," said the oiler.

As soon as the correspondent touched the cold comfortable sea-water in the bottom of the boat, and had huddled close to the cook's life-belt he was deep in sleep, despite the fact that his teeth played all the popular airs. This sleep was so good to him that it was but a moment before he heard a voice call his name in a tone that demonstrated the last stages of exhaustion. "Will you spell me?"

"Sure, Billie."

The light in the north had mysteriously vanished, but the correspondent took his course from the wide-awake captain.

Later in the night they took the boat farther out to sea, and the captain directed the cook to take one oar at the stern and keep the boat facing the seas. He was to call out if he should hear the thunder of the surf. This plan enabled the oiler and the correspondent to get respite together. "We'll give those boys a chance to get into shape again," said the captain. They curled down and, after a few preliminary chatterings and trembles, slept once more the dead sleep. Neither knew they had bequeathed to the cook the company of another shark, or perhaps the same shark.

As the boat caroused on the waves, spray occasionally bumped over the side and gave them a fresh soaking, but this had no power to break their repose. The ominous slash of the wind and the water affected them as it would have affected mummies.

"Boys," said the cook, with the notes of every reluctance in his voice, "she's drifted in pretty close. I guess one of you had better take her to sea again." The correspondent, aroused, heard the crash of the toppled crests.

As he was rowing, the captain gave him some whiskey and water, and this steadied the chills out of him. "If I ever get ashore and anybody shows me even a photograph of an oar —"

At last there was a short conversation.

"Billie. . . . Billie, will you spell me?"

"Sure," said the oiler.

VII

When the correspondent again opened his eyes, the sea and the sky were each of the gray hue of the dawning. Later, carmine and gold was painted upon the waters. The morning appeared finally, in its splendor, with a sky of pure blue, and the sunlight flamed on the tips of the waves.

On the distant dunes were set many little black cottages, and a tall white wind-mill reared above them. No man, nor dog, nor bicycle appeared on the beach. The cottages might have formed a deserted village.

The voyagers scanned the shore. A conference was held in the boat. "Well," said the captain, "if no help is coming, we might better try a run through the surf right away. If we stay out here much longer we will be too weak to do anything for ourselves at all." The others silently acquiesced in this reasoning. The boat was headed for the beach. The correspondent wondered if none ever ascended the tall wind-tower, and if then they never looked seaward. This tower was a giant, standing with its back to the plight of the ants. It represented in a degree, to the correspondent, the serenity of nature amid the struggles of the individual — nature in the wind, and nature in the vision of men. She did not seem cruel to him then, nor beneficent, nor treacherous, nor wise. But she was indifferent, flatly indifferent. It is, perhaps, plausible that a man in this situation, impressed with the unconcern of the universe, should see the innumerable flaws of his life and have them taste wickedly in his mind and wish for another chance. A distinction between right and wrong seems absurdly clear to him, then, in this new ignorance of the grave-edge, and he understands that if he were given another opportunity he would mend his conduct and his words, and be better and brighter during an introduction, or at a tea.

"Now, boys," said the captain, "she is going to swamp sure. All we can do is to work her in as far as possible, and then when she swamps, pile out and scramble for the beach. Keep cool now, and don't jump until she swamps sure."

The oiler took the oars. Over his shoulders he scanned the surf. "Captain," he said, "I think I'd better bring her about, and keep her head-on to the seas and back her in."

"All right, Billie," said the captain. "Back her in." The oiler swung the boat then and, seated in the stern, the cook and the correspondent were obliged to look over their shoulders to contemplate the lonely and indifferent shore.

The monstrous inshore rollers heaved the boat high until the men were again enabled to see the white sheets of water scudding up the slanted beach. "We won't get in very close," said the captain. Each time a man could wrest his attention from the rollers, he turned his glance toward the shore, and in the expression of the eyes during this contemplation there was a singular quality. The correspondent, observing the others, knew that they were not afraid, but the full meaning of their glances was shrouded.

As for himself, he was too tired to grapple fundamentally with the fact. He tried to coerce his mind into thinking of it, but the mind was dominated at this time by the muscles, and the muscles said they did not care. It merely occurred to him that if he should drown it would be a shame.

There were no hurried words, no pallor, no plain agitation. The men simply looked at the shore. "Now, remember to get well clear of the boat when you jump," said the captain.

Seaward the crest of a roller suddenly fell with a thunderous crash, and the long white comber came roaring down upon the boat.

"Steady now," said the captain. The men were silent. They turned their eyes from the shore to the comber and waited. The boat slid up the incline, leaped at the furious top, bounced over it, and swung down the long back of the wave. Some water had been shipped and the cook bailed it out.

But the next crest crashed also. The tumbling boiling flood of white water caught the boat and whirled it almost perpendicular. Water swarmed in from all sides. The correspondent had his hands on the gunwale at this time, and when the water entered at that place he swiftly withdrew his fingers, as if he objected to wetting them.

The little boat, drunken with this weight of water, reeled and snuggled deeper into the sea.

"Bail her out, cook! Bail her out," said the captain.

"All right, Captain," said the cook.

"Now boys, the next one will do for us, sure," said the oiler. "Mind to jump clear of the boat."

The third wave moved forward, huge, furious, implacable. It fairly swallowed the dingey, and almost simultaneously the men tumbled into the sea. A piece of life-belt had lain in the bottom of the boat, and as the correspondent went overboard he held this to his chest with his left hand.

The January water was icy, and he reflected immediately that it was colder than he had expected to find it off the coast of Florida. This appeared to his dazed mind as a fact important enough to be noted at the time. The coldness of the water was sad; it was tragic. This fact was somehow so mixed and confused with his opinion of his own situation that it seemed almost a proper reason for tears. The water was cold.

When he came to the surface he was conscious of little but the noisy water. Afterward he saw his companions in the sea. The oiler was ahead in the race. He was swimming strongly and rapidly. Off to the correspondent's left, the cook's great white and corked back bulged out of the water, and in the rear the captain was hanging with his one good hand to the keel of the overturned dingey.

There is a certain immovable quality to a shore, and the correspondent wondered at it amid the confusion of the sea.

It seemed also very attractive, but the correspondent knew that it was a long journey, and he paddled leisurely. The piece of life-preserver lay under him, and sometimes he whirled down the incline of a wave as if he were on a hand-sled.

But finally he arrived at a place in the sea where travel was beset with difficulty. He did not pause swimming to inquire what manner of current had caught him, but there his progress ceased. The shore was set before him like a bit of scenery on a stage, and he looked at it and understood with his eyes each detail of it.

As the cook passed, much farther to the left, the captain was calling to him, "Turn over on your back, cook! Turn over on your back and use the oar."

"All right, sir." The cook turned on his back, and, paddling with an oar, went ahead as if he were a canoe.

Presently the boat also passed to the left of the correspondent with the captain clinging with one hand to the keel. He would have appeared like a man raising himself to look over a board fence, if it were not for the extraordinary gymnastics of the boat. The correspondent marvelled that the captain could still hold to it.

They passed on, nearer to shore — the oiler, the cook, the captain — and following them went the water-jar, bouncing gayly over the seas.

The correspondent remained in the grip of this strange new enemy — a current. The shore, with its white slope of sand and its green bluff, topped with little silent cottages, was spread like a picture before him. It was very near to him then, but he was impressed as one who in a gallery looks at a scene from Brittany or Holland.

He thought: "I am going to drown? Can it be possible? Can it be possible? Can it be possible?" Perhaps an individual must consider his own death to be the final phenomenon of nature.

But later a wave perhaps whirled him out of his small deadly current, for he found suddenly that he could again make progress toward the shore. Later still, he was aware that the captain, clinging with one hand to the keel of the dingey, had his face turned away from the shore and toward him, and was calling his name. "Come to the boat! Come to the boat!"

In his struggle to reach the captain and the boat, he reflected that when one gets properly wearied, drowning must really be a comfortable arrangement, a cessation of hostilities accompanied by a large degree of relief, and he was glad of it, for the main thing in his mind for some moments had been the horror of the temporary agony. He did not wish to be hurt.

Presently he saw a man running along the shore. He was undressing with most remarkable speed. Coat, trousers, shirt, everything flew magically off him.

"Come to the boat," called the captain.

"All right, Captain." As the correspondent paddled, he saw the captain let himself down to bottom and leave the boat. Then the correspondent performed his one little marvel of the voyage. A large wave caught him and flung him with ease and supreme speed completely over the boat and far beyond it. It struck him even then as an event in gymnastics, and a true miracle of the sea. An overturned boat in the surf is not a plaything to a swimming man.

The correspondent arrived in water that reached only to his waist, but his condition did not enable him to stand for more than a moment. Each wave knocked him into a heap, and the under-tow pulled at him.

Then he saw the man who had been running and undressing, and undressing and running, come bounding into the water. He dragged ashore the cook, and then waded toward the captain, but the captain waved him away, and sent him to the correspondent. He was naked, naked as a tree in winter, but a halo was about his head, and he shone like a saint. He gave a strong pull, and a long drag, and a bully heave at the correspondent's hand. The correspondent, schooled in the minor formulae, said: "Thanks, old man." But suddenly the man cried: "What's that?" He pointed a swift finger. The correspondent said: "Go."

In the shallows, face downward, lay the oiler. His forehead touched sand that was periodically, between each wave, clear of the sea.

The correspondent did not know all that transpired afterward. When he achieved safe ground he fell, striking the sand with each particular part of his body. It was as if he had dropped from a roof, but the thud was grateful to him.

It seems that instantly the beach was populated with men with blankets, clothes, and flasks, and women with coffee-pots and all the remedies sacred to their minds. The welcome of the land to the men from the sea was warm and generous, but a still and dripping shape was carried slowly up the beach, and the land's welcome for it could only be the different and sinister hospitality of the grave.

When it came night, the white waves paced to and fro in the moonlight, and the wind brought the sound of the great sea's voice to the men on shore, and they felt that they could then be interpreters.

Edwidge Danticat

Edwidge Danticat (b. 1969) was born in Port-au-Prince, Haiti. When she was two, her father immigrated to the United States to look for work. Two years later her mother followed him, leaving Edwidge and her younger brother in the care of their uncle, who was a minister. Danticat remembers her childhood fascination with the ritual of storytelling conducted by her aunt's grandmother in Haiti. When she told a story, her listeners said "Krik?" and she would answer "Krak!"

> She told stories when the people would gather — folk tales with her own spin on them, and stories about the family. It was call-and-response — if the audience seemed bored, the story would speed up, and if they were participating, a song would go in. The whole interaction was exciting to me. These cross-generational exchanges didn't happen often, because children were supposed to respect their elders. But when you were telling stories, it was more equal, and fun.

At the age of twelve, Danticat joined her parents in Brooklyn, where she began to learn English (the family still speaks Creole at home). Within a year she was writing articles for her high school newspaper, *New Youth Connections*. She majored in French literature at Barnard College, graduating in 1990, and went on to study in the M.F.A. program in creative writing at Brown University on a full scholarship. While still a graduate student she sold the manuscript of her first book, *Breath, Eyes, Memory*, to Soho, a small press she discovered in *Writer's Digest*. Published in 1994, the novel dramatized a young Haitian woman's coming of age in a troubled mother-daughter relationship and was chosen by Oprah Winfrey for the June 18, 1994, "meeting" of her television book club. With this endorsement, *Breath, Eyes, Memory* became a paperback best-seller.

The next year Danticat published *Krik? Krak!*, a collection of stories that included "Night Women." This book was nominated for a National Book Award, and she was chosen as one of the twenty "Best Young American Novelists" by *Granta* magazine. *The Farming of Bones*, her third book, published by Soho in 1998, describes the 1937 massacre on the Haitian-Dominican border, and *The Dew Breaker* (2005) focuses on the lives of dissidents tortured under the Duvalier regime. Danticat now works with the National Coalition for Haitian Rights on a grant from the Lila Acheson Wallace Foundation. As a spokesperson for her community, Danticat insists that she is free to write as she pleases in her fiction: "My characters are not representative of the community as a whole. As a writer, it's the person who is different from everybody else who might be interesting to you." Danticat's memoir, *Brother, I'm Dying* (2007), won the National Book Critics Circle Award. A collection of essays, *Create Dangerously: The Immigrant Artist at Work* (2010), and the novel *Claire of the Sea Light* (2013) are recent books.

Night Women

1991

I CRINGE FROM THE HEAT of the night on my face. I feel as bare as open flesh. Tonight I am much older than the twenty-five years that I have lived. The night is the time I dread most in my life. Yet if I am to live, I must depend on it.

Shadows shrink and spread over the lace curtain as my son slips into bed. I watch as he stretches from a little boy into the broom-size of a man, his height mounting the innocent fabric that splits our one-room house into two spaces, two mats, two worlds.

For a brief second, I almost mistake him for the ghost of his father, an old lover who disappeared with the night's shadows a long time ago. My son's bed stays nestled against the corner, far from the peeking jalousies. I watch as he digs furrows in the pillow with his head. He shifts his small body carefully so as not to crease his Sunday clothes. He wraps my long blood-red scarf around his neck, the one I wear myself during the day to tempt my suitors. I let him have it at night, so that he always has something of mine when my face is out of sight.

I watch his shadow resting still on the curtain. My eyes are drawn to him, like the stars peeking through the small holes in the roof that none of my suitors will fix for me, because they like to watch a scrap of the sky while lying on their naked backs on my mat.

A firefly buzzes around the room, finding him and not me. Perhaps it is a mosquito that has learned the gift of lighting itself. He always slaps the mosquitoes dead on his face without even waking. In the morning, he will have tiny blood spots on his forehead, as though he had spent the whole night kissing a woman with wide-open flesh wounds on her face.

In his sleep he squirms and groans as though he's already discovered that there is pleasure in touching himself. We have never talked about love. What would he need to know? Love is one of those lessons that you grow to learn the way one learns that one shoe is made to fit a certain foot, lest it cause discomfort.

There are two kinds of women: day women and night women. I am stuck between the day and night in a golden amber bronze. My eyes are the color of dirt, almost copper if I am standing in the sun. I want to wear my matted tresses in braids as soon as I learn to do my whole head without numbing my arms.

Most nights, I hear a slight whisper. My body freezes as I wonder how long it would take for him to cross the curtain and find me.

He says, "Mommy."

I say, "*Darling.*"

Somehow in the night, he always calls me in whispers. I hear the buzz of his transistor radio. It is shaped like a can of cola. One of my suitors gave it to him to plug into his ears so he can stay asleep while Mommy *works.*

There is a place in Ville Rose where ghost women ride the crests of waves while brushing the stars out of their hair. There they woo strollers and leave the stars on the path for them. There are nights that I believe that those ghost women are with me. As much as I know that there are women who sit up through the night and undo patches of cloth that they have spent the whole day weaving. These women, they destroy their toil so that they will always have more to do. And as long as there's work, they will not have to lie next to the lifeless soul of a man whose scent still lingers in another woman's bed.

The way my son reacts to my lips stroking his cheeks decides for me if he's asleep. He is like a butterfly fluttering on a rock that stands out naked in the middle of a stream. Sometimes I see in the folds of his eyes a longing for something that's bigger than myself. We are like faraway lovers, lying to one another, under different moons.

When my smallest finger caresses the narrow cleft beneath his nose, sometimes his tongue slips out of his mouth and he licks my fingernail. He moans and turns away, perhaps thinking that this too is a part of the dream.

I whisper my mountain stories in his ear, stories of the ghost women and the stars in their hair. I tell him of the deadly snakes lying at one end of a rainbow and the hat full of gold lying at the other end. I tell him that if I cross a stream of glass-clear hibiscus, I can make myself a goddess. I blow on his long eyelashes to see if he's truly asleep. My fingers coil themselves into visions of birds on his nose. I want him to forget that we live in a place where nothing lasts.

I know that sometimes he wonders why I take such painstaking care. Why do I draw half-moons on my sweaty forehead and spread crimson powders on the rise of my cheeks. We put on his ruffled Sunday suit and I tell him that we are expecting a sweet angel and where angels tread the hosts must be as beautiful as floating hibiscus.

In his sleep, his fingers tug his shirt ruffles loose. He licks his lips from the last piece of sugar candy stolen from my purse.

No more, no more, or your teeth will turn black. I have forgotten to make him brush the mint leaves against his teeth. He does not know that one day a woman like his mother may judge him by the whiteness of his teeth.

It doesn't take long before he is snoring softly. I listen for the shy laughter of his most pleasant dreams. Dreams of angels skipping over his head and occasionally resting their pink heels on his nose.

I hear him humming a song. One of the madrigals they still teach children on very hot afternoons in public schools. *Kompè Jako, domé vou?* Brother Jacques, are you asleep?

The hibiscus rustle in the night outside. I sing along to help him sink deeper into his sleep. I apply another layer of the Egyptian rouge to my cheeks. There are some sparkles in the powder, which make it easier for my visitor to find me in the dark.

Emmanuel will come tonight. He is a doctor who likes big buttocks on women, but my small ones will do. He comes on Tuesdays and Saturdays. He arrives bearing flowers as though he's come to court me. Tonight he brings me bougainvillea. It is always a surprise.

"How is your wife?" I ask.

"Not as beautiful as you."

On Mondays and Thursdays, it is an accordion player named Alexandre. He likes to make the sound of the accordion with his mouth in my ear. The rest of the night, he spends with his breadfruit head rocking on my belly button.

Should my son wake up, I have prepared my fabrication. One day, he will grow too old to be told that a wandering man is a mirage and that naked flesh is a dream. I will tell him that his father has come, that an angel brought him back from Heaven for a while.

The stars slowly slip away from the hole in the roof as the doctor sinks deeper and deeper beneath my body. He throbs and pants. I cover his mouth to keep him from screaming. I see his wife's face in the beads of sweat marching down his chin. He leaves with his body soaking from the dew of our flesh. He calls me an avalanche, a waterfall, when he is satisfied.

After he leaves at dawn, I sit outside and smoke a dry tobacco leaf. I watch the piece-worker women march one another to the open market half a day's walk from where they live. I thank the stars that at least I have the days to myself.

When I walk back into the house, I hear the rise and fall of my son's breath. Quickly, I lean my face against his lips to feel the calming heat from his mouth.

"Mommy, have I missed the angels again?" he whispers softly while reaching for my neck.

I slip into the bed next to him and rock him back to sleep.

"Darling, the angels have themselves a lifetime to come to us."

Lydia Davis

Lydia Davis (b. 1947) was born in Northampton, Massachusetts, the daughter of an English professor. After graduating from Barnard College, she lived abroad for three years in Ireland and France. While in Paris she began to translate from French to English, first working for the film industry and then translating works by Marcel Proust, Gustave Flaubert, and others. In 1992 she received an award for her translation of *Scratches* by the Surrealist author Leiris. In 2010 she published a translation of Flaubert's *Madame Bovary*.

Davis was living in the south of France while she wrote most of the short fiction in her first book, *The Thirteenth Woman and Other Stories* (1976). *Beat It Down* (1986) was her second collection, followed by her novel *The End of the Story* (1995) and *Almost No Memory* (1997), another book of stories. In her early work Davis explored, almost as a philosopher, the relationship between imagination and reality. She is particularly interested in the diversity of literary forms and the various possibilities for creating different realities through language, as in the stories from her collection *Varieties of Disturbance* (2007). This was her first book of stories after becoming the recipient of a MacArthur Fellowship in 2003.

Davis enjoys writing very short stories in addition to raising two children and teaching college, but she is less comfortable putting her experimental prose into the customary categories of flash fiction, sudden fiction, short shorts, or prose poems. "I think people may still be expecting a kind of miniature short story when they begin reading a piece of flash fiction, rather than the less usual offering that it might be—meditation, logic game, extended wordplay, diatribe—for which there is no good general name." She believes that a story "has to have a bit of narrative, if only 'she says,' and then enough of a creation of different time and place to transport the reader. But, of course, it is not a narrative poem. It is flatter, rhythmically different from a poem, and less elliptical." Her fondness for the form of very short stories goes back to the time in France after college when she found it difficult to write traditional narrative. After taking over two years to finish one story, she made herself write what she calls "two tiny stories" every day, each in the form of a single paragraph. "Blind Date" is from *The Collected Stories of Lydia Davis* (2009). Recently she translated Flaubert's *Madame Bovary* (2010) and Proust's *Swann's Way* (2010).

Blind Date

1999

"THERE ISN'T REALLY MUCH to tell," she said, but she would tell it if I liked. We were sitting in a midtown luncheonette. "I've only had one blind date in my life. And I didn't really have it. I can think of more interesting situations that are like a blind date — say when someone gives you a book as a present, when they fix you up with that book. I was once given a book of essays about reading, writing, book collecting. I felt it was a perfect match. I started reading it right away, in the back seat of the car. I stopped listening to the conversation in the front. I like to read about how other people read and collect books, even how they shelve their books. But by the time I was done with the book, I had taken a strong dislike to the author's personality. I won't have another date with *her*!" She laughed. Here we were interrupted by the waiter, and then a series of incidents followed that kept us from resuming our conversation that day.

The next time the subject came up, we were sitting in two Adirondack chairs looking out over a lake in, in fact, the Adirondacks. We were content to sit in silence at first. We were tired. We had been to the Adirondack Museum that day and seen many things of interest, including old guide boats and good examples of the original Adirondack chair. Now we watched the water and the edge of the woods, each thinking, I was sure, about James Fenimore Cooper. After some parties of canoers had gone by, older people in canvas boating hats, their quiet voices carrying far over the water to us, we went on talking. These were precious days of holiday together, and we were finishing many unfinished conversations.

"I was fifteen or sixteen, I guess," she said. "I was home from boarding school. Maybe it was summer. I don't know where my parents were. They were often away. They often left me alone there, sometimes for the evening, sometimes for weeks at a time. The phone rang. It was a boy I didn't know. He said he was a friend of a boy from school—I can't remember who. We talked a little and then he asked me if I wanted to have dinner with him. He sounded nice enough so I said I would, and we agreed on a day and a time and I told him where I lived.

"But after I got off the phone, I began thinking, worrying. What had this other boy said about me? What had the two of them said about me? Maybe I had some kind of a reputation. Even now I can't imagine that what they said was completely pure or innocent—for instance, that I was pretty and fun to be with. There had to be something nasty about it, two boys talking privately about a girl. The awful word that began to occur to me was *fast*. She's *fast*. I wasn't actually very fast. I was faster than some but not as fast as others. The more I imagined the two boys talking about me the worse I felt.

"I liked boys. I liked the boys I knew in a way that was much more innocent than they probably thought. I trusted them more than girls. Girls hurt my feelings, girls ganged up on me. I always had boys who were my friends, starting back when I was nine and ten and eleven. I didn't like this feeling that two boys were talking about me.

"Well, when the day came, I didn't want to go out to dinner with this boy. I just didn't want the difficulty of this date. It scared me—not because there was anything scary about the boy but because he was a stranger. I didn't know him. I didn't want to sit there face to face in some restaurant and start from the very beginning, knowing nothing. It didn't feel right. And there was the burden of that recommendation—'Give her a try.'

"Then again, maybe there were other reasons. Maybe I had been alone in that apartment so much by then that I had retreated into some kind of inner, unsociable space that was hard to come out of. Maybe I felt I had disappeared and I was comfortable that way and did not want to be forced back into existence. I don't know.

"At six o' clock, the buzzer rang. The boy was there, downstairs. I didn't answer it. It rang again. Still I did not answer it. I don't know how many times it rang or how long he leaned on it. I let it ring. At some point, I walked the length of the living room to the balcony. The apartment was four stories up. Across the street and down a flight of stone steps was a park. From the balcony on a clear day you could look out over the park and see all the way across town, maybe a mile, to the other river. At this point I think I ducked down or got down on my hands and knees and inched my way to the edge of the balcony. I think I looked over far enough to see him down there on the sidewalk below — looking up, as I remember it. Or he had gone across the street and was looking up. He didn't see me.

"I know that as I crouched there on the balcony or just back from it I had some impression of him being puzzled, disconcerted, disappointed, at a loss what to do now, not prepared for this — prepared for all sorts of other ways the date might go, other difficulties, but not for no date at all. Maybe he also felt angry or insulted, if it occurred to him then or later that maybe he hadn't made a mistake but that I had deliberately stood him up, and not the way I did it — alone up there in the apartment, uncomfortable and embarrassed, chickening out, hiding out — but, he would imagine, in collusion with someone else, a girlfriend or boyfriend, confiding in them, snickering over him.

"I don't know if he called me, or if I answered the phone if it rang. I could have given some excuse — I could have said I had gotten sick or had to go out suddenly. Or maybe I hung up when I heard his voice. In those days I did a lot of avoiding that I don't do now — avoiding confrontations, avoiding difficult encounters. And I did a fair amount of lying that I also don't do now.

"What was strange was how awful this felt. I was treating a person like a thing. And I was betraying not just him but something larger, some social contract. When you knew a decent person was waiting downstairs, someone you had made an appointment with, you did not just not answer the buzzer. What was even more surprising to me was what I felt about myself in that instant. I was behaving as though I had no responsibility to anyone or anything, and that made me feel as though I existed outside society, some kind of criminal, or didn't exist at all. I was annihilating myself even more than him. It was an awful violation."

She paused, thoughtful. We were sitting inside now, because it was raining. We had come inside to sit in a sort of lounge or recreation room provided for guests of that lakeside camp. The rain fell every afternoon there, sometimes for minutes, sometimes for hours. Across the water, the white pines and spruces were very still against the gray sky. The water was silver. We did not see any of the water birds we sometimes saw paddling around the edges of the lake — teals and loons. Inside, a fire burned in the fireplace. Over our heads hung a chandelier made of antlers. Between us stood a table constructed of a rough slab of wood resting on the legs of a deer, complete with hooves. On the table stood a lamp made from an old gun. She looked away from the lake and around the room. "In that book about the Adirondacks I was reading last night," she remarked, "he says this was what the Adirondacks was all about, I mean the Adirondacks style: things made from things."

A month or so later, when I was home again and she was back in the city, we were talking on the telephone and she said she had been hunting through one of the old diaries she had on her shelf there, that might say exactly what had happened — though of course, she said, she would just be filling in the details of something that did not actually happen. But she couldn't find this incident written down anywhere, which of course made her wonder if she had gotten the dates really wrong and she wasn't even in boarding school anymore by then. Maybe she was in college by then. But she decided to believe what she had told me. "But I'd forgotten how much I wrote about boys," she added. "Boys and books. What I wanted more than anything else at the age of sixteen was a great library."

Junot Díaz

Junot Díaz (b. 1968) was born in Santo Domingo, Dominican Republic. At the age of seven he immigrated with his mother, brother, and sister to the United States and grew up in a black and Hispanic neighborhood in New Jersey. After graduating from Rutgers University, he earned his M.F.A. studying fiction at Cornell University and began to write stories about immigrants from the Dominican Republic who were defining their American identity. In 1996 Díaz published his first book, *Drown*, a collection of ten stories, including "How to Date a Browngirl, Blackgirl, Whitegirl, or Halfie," to great critical acclaim. The reviewer Francine Prose admired his "spare, tense, powerful" depiction of the "rocky, dangerous road that leads his characters to adulthood—from the barrios and villages of the Dominican Republic to the crowded apartments and crack dens of New Jersey's inner cities." *Drown* became an alternate selection of the Book-of-the-Month Club and the Quality Paperback Book Club, and *Newsweek* named Díaz as one of the "New Faces of 1996."

In contrast to the media's fanfare, Díaz quietly expressed his thanks on the last page of *Drown* to the many people who had helped him to develop his voice as a writer. He began with a general acknowledgment of his debt to the Hispanic community in Barrio XXI and to his family, and he continued with a list of thirty-two people who had supported and mentored him over the years, including the Hispanic writer Helena María Viramontes and his agent Nicole Aragi: "You believed and people listened."

Díaz has said that, when he was seven, what he wanted most out of his family's move to the United States was McDonald's fast food and television. Looking back, he now sees that "the moment my family set foot in Kennedy Airport a world ended for me. You'd think that sort of cataclysm would make itself apparent quickly and with umbrage, but in actuality it took me years to notice. The end was not so much an apocalypse as it was a fading, a merging, and, ultimately, a metamorphosis." Díaz didn't return to the Dominican Republic until he was in college because

> that world which was almost but not entirely lost has always haunted me. When I write I try to remember it well. . . . A lot of my fiction concerns itself with the lives of Dominicans in the United States, but I don't think I would perceive the landscape of those experiences as well without another lens through which to view it.

In 2007 Díaz published *The Brief Wondrous Life of Oscar Wao*, which won many awards, including the 2008 Pulitzer Prize. *This is How You Lose Her*, his second book of stories, appeared in 2012.

How to Date a Browngirl, Blackgirl, Whitegirl, or Halfie

1996

WAIT FOR YOUR BROTHER and your mother to leave the apartment. You've already told them that you're feeling too sick to go to Union City to visit that tía[1] who likes to squeeze your nuts. (He's gotten big, she'll say.) And even though your moms knows you ain't sick you stuck to your story until finally she said, Go ahead and stay, malcriado.[2]

Clear the government cheese from the refrigerator. If the girl's from the Terrace stack the boxes behind the milk. If she's from the Park or Society Hill hide the cheese in the cabinet above the oven, way up where she'll never see. Leave yourself a reminder to get it out before morning or your moms will kick your ass. Take down any embarrassing photos of your family in the campo, especially the one with the half-naked kids dragging a goat on a rope leash. The kids are your cousins and by now they're old enough to understand why you're doing what you're doing. Hide the pictures of yourself with an Afro. Make sure the bathroom is presentable. Put the basket with all the crapped-on toilet paper under the sink. Spray the bucket with Lysol, then close the cabinet.

Shower, comb, dress. Sit on the couch and watch TV. If she's an outsider her father will be bringing her, maybe her mother. Neither of them want her seeing any boys from the Terrace — people get stabbed in the Terrace — but she's strong-headed and this time will get her way. If she's a whitegirl you know you'll at least get a hand job.

The directions were in your best handwriting, so her parents won't think you're an idiot. Get up from the couch and check the parking lot. Nothing. If the girl's local, don't sweat it. She'll flow over when she's good and ready. Sometimes she'll run into her other friends and a whole crowd will show up at your apartment and even though that means you ain't getting shit it will be fun anyway and you'll wish these people would come over more often. Sometimes the girl won't flow over at all and the next day in school she'll say sorry, smile and you'll be stupid enough to believe her and ask her out again.

Wait and after an hour go out to your corner. The neighborhood is full of traffic. Give one of your boys a shout and when he says, Are you still waiting on that bitch? say, Hell yeah.

Get back inside. Call her house and when her father picks up ask if she's there. He'll ask, Who is this? Hang up. He sounds like a principal or a police chief, the sort of dude with a big neck, who never has to watch his back. Sit and wait. By the time your stomach's ready to give out on you, a Honda or maybe a Jeep pulls in and out she comes.

---

[1] Aunt.

[2] A spoiled or ill-mannered child.

Hey, you'll say.

Look, she'll say. My mom wants to meet you. She's got herself all worried about nothing.

Don't panic. Say, Hey, no problem. Run a hand through your hair like the whiteboys do even though the only thing that runs easily through your hair is Africa. She will look good. The white ones are the ones you want the most, aren't they, but usually the out-of-towners are black, blackgirls who grew up with ballet and Girl Scouts, who have three cars in their driveways. If she's a halfie don't be surprised that her mother is white. Say, Hi. Her moms will say hi and you'll see that you don't scare her, not really. She will say that she needs easier directions to get out and even though she has the best directions in her lap give her new ones. Make her happy.

You have choices. If the girl's from around the way, take her to El Cibao for dinner. Order everything in your busted-up Spanish. Let her correct you if she's Latina and amaze her if she's black. If she's not from around the way, Wendy's will do. As you walk to the restaurant talk about school. A local girl won't need stories about the neighborhood but the other ones might. Supply the story about the loco who'd been storing canisters of tear gas in his basement for years, how one day the canisters cracked and the whole neighborhood got a dose of the military strength stuff. Don't tell her that your moms knew right away what it was, that she recognized its smell from the year the United States invaded your island.

Hope that you don't run into your nemesis, Howie, the Puerto Rican kid with the two killer mutts. He walks them all over the neighborhood and every now and then the mutts corner themselves a cat and tear it to shreds, Howie laughing as the cat flips up in the air, its neck twisted around like an owl, red meat showing through the soft fur. If his dogs haven't cornered a cat, he will walk behind you and ask, Hey, Yunior, is that your new fuckbuddy?

Let him talk. Howie weighs about two hundred pounds and could eat you if he wanted. At the field he will turn away. He has new sneakers, and doesn't want them muddy. If the girl's an outsider she will hiss now and say, What a fucking asshole. A homegirl would have been yelling back at him the whole time, unless she was shy. Either way don't feel bad that you didn't do anything. Never lose a fight on a first date or that will be the end of it.

Dinner will be tense. You are not good at talking to people you don't know. A halfie will tell you that her parents met in the Movement, will say, Back then people thought it a radical thing to do. It will sound like something her parents made her memorize. Your brother once heard that one and said, Man, that sounds like a whole lot of Uncle Tomming to me. Don't repeat this.

Put down your hamburger and say, It must have been hard.

She will appreciate your interest. She will tell you more. Black people, she will say, treat me real bad. That's why I don't like them. You'll wonder how she feels about Dominicans. Don't ask. Let her speak on it and when you're both finished eating walk back into the neighborhood. The skies will be magnificent. Pollutants have made Jersey sunsets one of the wonders of the world. Point it out. Touch her shoulder and say, That's nice, right?

Get serious. Watch TV but stay alert. Sip some of the Bermúdez your father left in the cabinet, which nobody touches. A local girl may have hips and a thick ass but she won't be quick about letting you touch. She has to live in the same neighborhood you do, has to deal with you being all up in her business. She might just chill with you and then go home. She might kiss you and then go, or she might, if she's reckless, give it up, but that's rare. Kissing will suffice. A whitegirl might just give it up right then. Don't stop her. She'll take her gum out of her mouth, stick it to the plastic sofa covers and then will move close to you. You have nice eyes, she might say.

Tell her that you love her hair, that you love her skin, her lips, because, in truth, you love them more than you love your own.

She'll say, I like Spanish guys, and even though you've never been to Spain, say, I like you. You'll sound smooth.

You'll be with her until about eight-thirty and then she will want to wash up. In the bathroom she will hum a song from the radio and her waist will keep the beat against the lip of the sink. Imagine her old lady coming to get her, what she would say if she knew her daughter had just lain under you and blown your name, pronounced with her eighth-grade Spanish, into your ear. While she's in the bathroom call one of your boys and say, Lo hice, loco.[3] Or just sit back on the couch and smile.

But usually it won't work this way. Be prepared. She will not want to kiss you. Just cool it, she'll say. The halfie might lean back, breaking away from you. She will cross her arms, say, I hate my tits. Stroke her hair but she will pull away. I don't like anybody touching my hair, she will say. She will act like somebody you don't know. In school she is known for her attention-grabbing laugh, as high and far-ranging as a gull, but here she will worry you. You will not know what to say.

You're the only kind of guy who asks me out, she will say. Your neighbors will start their hyena calls, now that the alcohol is in them. You and the blackboys.

Say nothing. Let her button her shirt, let her comb her hair, the sound of it stretching like a sheet of fire between you. When her father pulls in and beeps, let her go without too much of a good-bye. She won't want it. During the next hour the phone will ring. You will be tempted to pick it up. Don't. Watch the shows you want to watch, without a family around to debate you. Don't go downstairs. Don't fall asleep. It won't help. Put the government cheese back in its place before your moms kills you.

---

[3] (A boast about his sexual interactions with the girl, whether real or fabricated.)

Edith Eaton (Sui Sin Far)

Edith Eaton (Sui Sin Far) (1865–1914), was the first person of mixed Asian and European ancestry in the United States to publish fiction about her ethnic identity. Eaton was born in Macclesfield, England, as the oldest of sixteen children; she emigrated with her family first to the United States and then to Montreal, Canada, when she was nine years old. Her father was an Englishman who tried to support his large family by painting landscapes. Her mother was Chinese and was adopted by an English missionary couple who gave her an English education. Eaton took care of her younger siblings and later said that she "abhorred the work" of child care in the poverty-stricken household. Left in poor health after an attack of rheumatic fever, she taught herself shorthand and typing so she could work as a journalist for the *Montreal Star*, giving her wages to her parents to alleviate their financial distress. In 1888 she published the first of many articles in a Montreal magazine. Eight years later she began to use the pseudonym Sui Sin Far (a transliteration of the Cantonese symbol for water lily) for the stories she published in periodicals edited by her brother-in-law.

In 1898 Eaton's physician advised her to move to San Francisco for her health. After working there for two years as a typist for the Canadian Pacific Railroad, she relocated to Seattle, where she worked as an English teacher at a Baptist mission in Chinatown. There she wrote stories about the Chinese community that she placed in *Century, Ladies' Home Journal, Good Housekeeping*, and other magazines. In 1912 thirty of her linked stories were published as a novel, *Mrs. Spring Fragrance*. Eaton's earlier articles and sketches often exploited melodramatic situations and racial stereotypes, as in her story "The Gamblers" (1896), about a murder in an opium den. But as the writer matured, she dedicated herself to battling the racism oppressing the Chinese people in the United States, as in her two linked narratives "The Story of One White Woman Who Married a Chinese" and "Her Chinese Husband."

In 1909 Eaton said she had been advised that "if I wish to succeed in literature in America I should dress in Chinese costume, carry a fan in my hand, wear a pair of scarlet beaded slippers, live in New York City, and come of high birth." She was alluding to her sister Winnifred's success as a best-selling novelist who wrote under the pseudonym Onoto Watanna in the first years of the twentieth century. Winnifred exploited the vogue for things Japanese in the United States, wearing costly Japanese kimonos and claiming that her mother had been born a Japanese aristocrat. The short story writer Edith Eaton (Sui Sin Far) may have had a more modest career than her sister did, but she wrote honestly about what she knew. By embracing her Chinese heritage, she acquired the authenticity that makes her writing still relevant today.

The Story of One White Woman Who Married a Chinese

1910

I

Why did I marry Liu Kanghi, a Chinese? Well, in the first place because I loved him; in the second place, because I was weary of working, struggling, and fighting with the world; in the third place, because my child needed a home.

My first husband was an American fifteen years older than myself. For a few months I was very happy with him. I had been a working girl — a stenographer. A home of my own filled my heart with joy. It was a pleasure to me to wait upon James, cook him nice little dinners and suppers, read to him little pieces from the papers and magazines, and sing and play to him my little songs and melodies. And for a few months he seemed to be perfectly contented. I suppose I was a novelty to him, he having lived a bachelor existence until he was thirty-four. But it was not long before he left off smiling at my little jokes, grew restive and cross when I teased him, and when I tried to get him to listen to a story in which I was interested and longed to communicate, he would bid me not bother him. I was quick to see the change and realize that there was a gulf of differences between us. Nevertheless, I loved and was proud of him. He was considered a very bright and well-informed man, and although his parents had been uneducated working people he had himself been through the public schools. He was also an omnivorous reader of socialistic and new-thought literature. Woman suffrage was one of his particular hobbies. Whenever I had a magazine around he would pick it up and read aloud to me the columns of advice to women who were ambitious to become comrades to men and walk shoulder to shoulder with their brothers. Once I ventured to remark that much as I admired a column of men keeping step together, yet men and women thus ranked would, to my mind, make a very unbeautiful and disorderly spectacle. He frowned and answered that I did not understand him, and was too frivolous. He would often draw my attention to newspaper reports concerning women of marked business ability and enterprise. Once I told him that I did not admire clever business women, as I had usually found them, and so had other girls of my acquaintance, not nearly so kind-hearted, generous, and helpful as the humble drudges of the world — the ordinary working women. His answer to this was that I was jealous and childish.

But, in spite of his unkind remarks and evident contempt for me, I wished to please him. He was my husband and I loved him. Many an afternoon, when through with my domestic duties, did I spend in trying to acquire a knowledge of labor politics, socialism, woman suffrage, and baseball, the things in which he was most interested.

It was hard work, but I persevered until one day. It was about six months after our marriage. My husband came home a little earlier than usual, and found me engaged in trying to work out problems in subtraction and addition. He laughed sneeringly, "Give it up, Minnie," said he. "You weren't built for anything but taking care of kids. Gee! But there's a woman at our place who has a head for figures that makes her worth over a hundred dollars a month. *Her* husband would have a chance to develop himself."

This speech wounded me. I knew it was James's ambition to write a book on social reform.

The next day, unknown to my husband, I called upon the wife of the man who had employed me as a stenographer before I was married, and inquired of her whether she thought I could get back my old position.

"But, my dear," she exclaimed, "your husband is receiving a good salary! Why should you work?"

I told her that my husband had in mind the writing of a book on social reform, and I wished to help him in his ambition by earning some money towards its publication.

"Social reform!" she echoed. "What sort of social reformer is he who would allow his wife to work when he is well able to support her!"

She bade me go home and think no more of an office position. I was disappointed. I said: "Oh! I wish I could earn some money for James. If I were earning money, perhaps he would not think me so stupid."

"Stupid, my dear girl! You are one of the brightest little women I know," kindly comforted Mrs. Rogers.

But I knew differently and went on to tell her of my inability to figure with my husband how much he had made on certain sales, of my lack of interest in politics, labor questions, woman suffrage, and world reformation. "Oh!" I cried, "I am a narrow-minded woman. All I care for is for my husband to love me and be kind to me, for life to be pleasant and easy, and to be able to help a wee bit the poor and sick around me."

Mrs. Rogers looked very serious as she told me that there were differences of opinion as to what was meant by "narrow-mindedness," and that the majority of men had no wish to drag their wives into all their business perplexities, and found more comfort in a woman who was unlike rather than like themselves. Only that morning her husband had said to her: "I hate a woman who tries to get into every kink of a man's mind, and who must be forever at his elbow meddling with all his affairs."

I went home comforted. Perhaps after a while James would feel and see as did Mr. Rogers. Vain hope!

My child was six weeks old when I entered business life again as stenographer for Rutherford & Rutherford. My salary was fifty dollars a month — more than I had ever earned before — and James was well pleased, for he had feared that it would be difficult for me to obtain a paying place after having been out of practice for so long. This fifty dollars paid for all our living expenses, with the exception of rent, so that James would be able to put by his balance against the time when his book would be ready for publication.

He began writing his book, and Miss Moran, the young woman bookkeeper at his place, collaborated with him. They gave three evenings a week to the work, sometimes four. She came one evening when the baby was sick and James had gone for the doctor. She looked at the child with the curious eyes of one who neither loved nor understood children. "There is no necessity for its being sick," said she. "There must be an error somewhere." I made no answer, so she went on: "Sin, sorrow, and sickness all mean the same thing. We have no disease that we do not deserve, no trouble which we do not bring upon ourselves."

I did not argue with her, I knew that I could not; but as I looked at her standing there in the prime of her life and strength, broad-shouldered, masculine-featured, and, as it seemed to me, heartless, I disliked her more than I had ever disliked anyone before. My own father had died after suffering for many years from a terrible malady, contracted while doing his duty as a physician and surgeon. And my innocent child! What had sin to do with its measles?

When James came in she discussed with him the baseball game which had been played that afternoon, and also a woman suffrage meeting which she had attended the evening before.

After she had gone he seemed to be quite exhilarated, "That's a great woman!" he remarked.

"I do not think so!" I answered him. "One who would take from the sorrowful and suffering their hope of a happier existence hereafter, and add to their trials on earth by branding them as objects of aversion and contempt, is not only not a great woman but, to my mind, no woman at all."

He picked up a paper and walked into another room.

"What do you think now?" I cried after him.

"What would be the use of my explaining to you?" he returned. "You wouldn't understand."

How my heart yearned over my child those days! I would sit before the typewriter and in fancy hear her crying for her mother. Poor, sick little one, watched over by a strange woman, deprived of her proper nourishment. While I took dictation from my employer I thought only of her. The result, of course, was that I lost my place. My husband showed his displeasure at this in various ways and as the weeks went by and I was unsuccessful in obtaining another position, he became colder and more indifferent. He was neither a drinking nor an abusive man, but he could say such cruel and cutting things that I would a hundred times rather have been beaten and ill-used than compelled, as I was, to hear them. He even made me feel it a disgrace to be a woman and a mother. Once he said to me: "If you had had ambition of the right sort you would have perfected yourself in your stenography so that you could have taken cases in court. There's a little fortune in that business."

I was acquainted with a woman stenographer who reported divorce cases and who had described to me the work, so I answered: "I would rather die of hunger, my baby in my arms, than report divorce proceedings under the eyes of men in a court house."

"Other women, as good as you, have done and are doing it," he retorted.

"Other women, perhaps better than I, have done and are doing it," I replied, "but all women are not alike. I am not that kind."

"That's so," said he. "Well, they are the kind who are up to date. You are behind the times."

One evening I left James and Miss Moran engaged with their work and went across the street to see a sick friend. When I returned I let myself into the house very softly for fear of awakening the baby, whom I had left sleeping. As I stood in the hall I heard my husband's voice in the sitting room. This is what he was saying:

"I am a lonely man. There is no companionship between me and my wife."

"Nonsense!" answered Miss Moran, as I thought a little impatiently. "Look over this paragraph, please, and tell me if you do not think it would be well to have it follow after the one ending with the words 'ultimate concord,' in place of that beginning with 'These great principles.'"

"I cannot settle my mind upon the work tonight," said James in a sort of thick, tired voice. "I want to talk to you — to win your sympathy — your love."

I heard a chair pushed back. I knew Miss Moran had arisen.

"Good night!" I heard her say. "Much as I would like to see this work accomplished, I shall come no more!"

"But, my God! You cannot throw the thing up at this late date."

"I can and I will. Let me pass, sir."

"If there were no millstone around my neck, you would not say, 'Let me pass, sir,' in that tone of voice."

The next I heard was a heavy fall. Miss Moran had knocked my big husband down.

I pushed open the door. Miss Moran, cool and collected, was pulling on her gloves, James was struggling to his feet.

"Oh, Mrs. Carson!" exclaimed the former. "Your husband fell over the stool. Wasn't that stupid of him!"

James, of course, got his divorce six months after I deserted him. He did not ask for the child, and I was allowed to keep it.

II

I was on my way to the waterfront, the baby in my arms. I was walking quickly, for my state of mind was such that I could have borne twice my burden and not have felt it. Just as I turned down a hill which led to the docks, someone touched my arm and I heard a voice say:

"Pardon me, lady, but you have dropped your baby's shoe!"

"Oh, yes!" I answered, taking the shoe mechanically from an outstretched hand, and pushing on.

I could hear the waves lapping against the pier when the voice again fell upon my ear.

"If you go any further, lady, you will fall into the water!"

My answer was a step forward.

A strong hand was laid upon my arm and I was swung around against my will.

"Poor little baby," went on the voice, which was unusually soft for a man's. "Let me hold him!"

I surrendered my child to the voice.

"Better come over where it is light and you can see where to walk!"

I allowed myself to be led into the light.

Thus I met Liu Kanghi, the Chinese who afterwards became my husband. I followed him, obeyed him, trusted him from the very first. It never occurred to me to ask myself what manner of man was succoring me. I only knew that he was a man, and that I was being cared for as no one had ever cared for me since my father died. And my grim determination to leave a world which had been cruel to me, passed away — and in its place I experienced a strange calmness and content.

"I am going to take you to the house of a friend of mine," he said as he preceded me up the hill, the baby in his arms.

"You will not mind living with Chinese people?" he added.

An electric light under which we were passing flashed across his face.

I did not recoil — not even at first. It may have been because he was wearing American clothes, wore his hair cut, and, even to my American eyes, appeared a good-looking young man — and it may have been because of my troubles; but whatever it was I answered him, and I meant it: "I would much rather live with Chinese than Americans."

He did not ask me why, and I did not tell him until long afterwards the story of my unhappy marriage; my desertion of the man who had made it impossible for me to remain under his roof; the shame of the divorce, the averted faces of those who had been my friends; the cruelty of the world; the awful struggle for an existence for myself and child; sickness followed by despair.

The Chinese family with which he placed me were kind, simple folk. The father had been living in America for more than twenty years. The family consisted of his wife, a grown daughter, and several small sons and daughters, all of whom had been born in America. They made me very welcome and adored the baby. Liu Jusong, the father, was a working jeweler, but, because of an accident by which he had lost the use of one hand, he was partially incapacitated for work. Therefore, their family depended for maintenance chiefly upon their kinsman, Liu Kanghi, the Chinese who had brought me to them.

"We love much our cousin," said one of the little girls to me one day. "He teaches us so many games and brings us toys and sweets."

As soon as I recovered from the attack of nervous prostration which laid me low for over a month after being received into the Liu home, my mind began to form plans for my own and my child's maintenance. One morning I put on my hat and jacket and told Mrs. Liu I would go downtown and make an application for work as a stenographer at the different typewriting offices. She pleaded with me to wait a week longer — until, as she said, "your limbs are more fortified with strength"; but I assured her that I felt myself well able to begin to do for myself, and that I was anxious to repay some little part of the expense I had been to them.

"For all we have done for you," she answered, "our cousin has paid us doublefold."

"No money can recompense your kindness to myself and my child," I replied; "but if it is your cousin to whom I am indebted for board and lodging, all the greater is my anxiety to repay what I owe."

When I returned to the house that evening, tired out with my quest for work, I found Liu Kanghi tossing a ball with little Fong on the front porch.

Mrs. Liu bustled out to meet me and began scolding me in a motherly fashion.

"Oh, why you go downtown before you strong enough? See! You look all sick again!" said she.

She turned to Liu Kanghi and said something in Chinese. He threw the ball back to the boy and came towards me, his face grave and concerned.

"Please be so good as to take my cousin's advice," he urged.

"I am well enough to work now," I replied, "and I cannot sink deeper into your debt."

"You need not," said he. "I know a way by which you can quickly pay me off and earn a good living without wearing yourself out and leaving the baby all day. My cousin tells me that you can create most beautiful flowers on silk, velvet, and linen. Why not then you do some of that work for my store? I will buy all you can make."

"Oh!" I exclaimed. "I should be only too glad to do such work! But do you think I can earn a living in that way?"

"You certainly can," was his reply. "I am requiring an embroiderer, and if you will do the work for me I will try to pay you what it is worth."

So I gladly gave up my quest for office work. I lived in the Liu Jusong house and worked for Liu Kanghi. The days, weeks and months passed peacefully and happily. Artistic needlework had always been my favorite occupation, and when it became a source both of remuneration and pleasure, I began to feel that life was worth living, after all. I watched with complacency my child grow amongst the little Chinese children. My life's experience had taught me that the virtues do not all belong to the whites. I was interested in all that concerned the Liu household, became acquainted with all their friends, and lost altogether the prejudice against the foreigner in which I had been reared.

I had been living thus more than a year when, one afternoon as I was walking home from Liu Kanghi's store on Kearney Street, a parcel of silks and floss under my arm, and my little girl trudging by my side, I came face-to-face with James Carson.

"Well, now," said he, planting himself in front of me, "you are looking pretty well. How are you making out?"

I caught up my child and pushed past him without a word. When I reached the Liu house I was trembling in every limb, so great was my dislike and fear of the man who had been my husband.

About a week later a letter came to the house addressed to me. It read:

Dear Minnie, — If you are willing to forget the past and make up, I am, too. I was surprised to see you the other day, prettier than ever — and much more of a woman. Let me know your mind at an early date.

Your affectionate husband,
James

I ignored this letter, but a heavy fear oppressed me. Liu Kanghi, who called the evening of the day I received it, remarked as he arose to greet me that I was looking troubled, and hoped that it was not the embroidery flowers.

"It is the shadow from my big hat," I answered lightly. I was dressed for going downtown with Mrs. Liu, who was preparing her eldest daughter's trousseau.

"Someday," said Liu Kanghi earnestly, "I hope that you will tell to me all that is in your heart and mind."

I found comfort in his kind face.

"If you will wait until I return, I will tell you all tonight," I answered.

Strange as it may seem, although I had known Liu Kanghi now for more than a year, I had had little talk alone with him, and all he knew about me was what he had learned from Mrs. Liu; namely, that I was a divorced woman who, when saved from self-destruction, was homeless and starving.

That night, however, after hearing my story, he asked me to be his wife. He said: "I love you and would protect you from all trouble. Your child shall be as my own."

I replied: "I appreciate your love and kindness, but I cannot answer you just yet. Be my friend for a little while longer."

"Do you have for me the love feeling?" he asked.

"I do not know," I answered truthfully.

Another letter came. It was written in a different spirit from the first and contained a threat about the child.

There seemed but one course open to me. That was to leave my Chinese friends. I did. With much sorrow and regret I bade them good-bye, and took lodgings in a part of the city far removed from the outskirts of Chinatown, where my home had been with the Lius.

My little girl pined for her Chinese playmates, and I myself felt strange and lonely; but I knew that if I wished to keep my child I could no longer remain with my friends.

I still continued working for Liu Kanghi, and carried my embroidery to his store in the evening after the little one had been put to sleep. He usually escorted me back but never asked to be allowed, and I never invited him, to visit me, or even enter the house. I was a young woman, and alone, and, what I had suffered from scandal since I had left James Carson had made me wise.

It was a cold, wet evening in November when he accosted me once again. I had run over to a delicatessen store at the corner of the block where I lived. As I stepped out, his burly figure loomed up in the gloom before me. I started back with a little cry, but he grasped my arm and held it.

"Walk beside me quietly if you do not wish to attract attention," said he, "and by God, if you do, I will take the kid tonight!"

"You dare not!" I answered. "You have no right to her whatever. She is my child and I have supported her for the last two years alone."

"Alone! What will the judges say when I tell them about the Chinaman?"

"What will the judges say!" I echoed, "What can they say? Is there any disgrace in working for a Chinese merchant and receiving pay for my labor?"

"And walking in the evening with him, and living for over a year in a house for which he paid the rent. Ha! ha! ha! Ha! ha! ha!"

His laugh was low and sneering. He had evidently been making inquiries concerning the Liu family, and also watching me for some time. How a woman can loathe and hate the man she has once loved!

We were nearing my lodgings. Perhaps the child had awakened and was crying for me. I would not, however, have entered the house, had he not stopped at the door and pushed it open.

"Lead the way upstairs!" said he. "I want to see the kid."

"You shall not," I cried. In my desperation I wrenched myself from his grasp and faced him, blocking the stairs.

"If you use violence," I declared, "the lodgers will come to my assistance. They know me!"

He released my arm.

"Bah!" said he. "I've no use for the kid. It is you I'm after getting reconciled to. Don't you know, Minnie, that once your husband, always your husband? Since I saw you the other day on the street, I have been more in love with you than ever before. Suppose we forget all and begin over again!"

Though the tone of his voice had softened, my fear of him grew greater. I would have fled up the stairs had he not again laid his hand on my arm.

"Answer me, girl," said he.

And in spite of my fear, I shook off his hand and answered him: "No husband of mine are you, either legally or morally. And I have no feeling whatever for you other than contempt."

"Ah! So you have sunk!" — his expression was evil — "The oily little Chink has won you!"

I was no longer afraid of him.

"Won me!" I cried, unheeding who heard me. "Yes, honorably and like a man. And what are you that dare sneer at one like him. For all your six feet of grossness, your small soul cannot measure up to his great one. You were unwilling to protect and care for the woman who was your wife or the little child you caused to come into this world; but he succored and saved the stranger-woman, treated her as a woman, with reverence and respect; gave her child a home, and made them both independent, not only of others but of himself. Now, hearing you insult him behind his back, I know what I did not know before — that I love him, and all I have to say to you is, Go!"

And James Carson went. I heard of him again but once. That was when the papers reported his death of apoplexy while exercising at a public gymnasium.

Loving Liu Kanghi, I became his wife, and though it is true that there are many Americans who look down upon me for so becoming, I have never regretted it. No, not even when men cast upon me the glances they cast upon sporting women. I accept the lot of the American wife of a humble Chinaman in America. The happiness of the man who loves me is more to me than the approval or disapproval of those who in my dark days left me to die like a dog. My Chinese husband has his faults. He is hot-tempered and, at times, arbitrary; but he is always a man, and has never sought to take away from me the privilege of being but a woman. I can lean upon and trust in him. I feel him behind me, protecting and caring for me, and that, to an ordinary woman like myself, means more than anything else.

Only when the son of Liu Kanghi lays his little head upon my bosom do I question whether I have done wisely. For my boy, the son of a Chinese man, is possessed of a childish wisdom which brings the tears to my eyes; and as he stands between his father and myself, like yet unlike us both, so will he stand in after years between his father's and his mother's people. And if there is no kindliness nor understanding between them, what will my boy's fate be?

Her Chinese Husband

1910 / Sequel to The Story of One White Woman Who Married a Chinese

NOW THAT LIU KANGHI is no longer with me, I feel that it will ease my heart to record some memories of him — if I can. The task, though calling to me, is not an easy one, so strong to my mind the invincible proofs of his love for me, the things he has said and done. My memories of him are so vivid and pertinacious, my thoughts of him so tender.

To my Chinese husband I could go with all my little troubles and perplexities; to him I could talk as women love to do at times of the past and the future, the mysteries of religion, of life and death. He was not above discussing such things with me. With him I was never strange or embarrassed. My Chinese husband was simple in his tastes. He liked to hear a good story, and though unlearned in a sense, could discriminate between the good and bad in literature. This came of his Chinese education. He told me one day that he thought the stories in the Bible were more like Chinese than American stories, and added: "If you had not told me what you have about it, I should say that it was composed by the Chinese." Music had a soothing though not a deep influence over him. It could not sway his mind, but he enjoyed it just as he did a beautiful picture. Because I was interested in fancy work, so also was he. I can see his face, looking so grave and concerned, because one day by accident I spilt some ink on a piece of embroidery I was working. If he came home in the evenings and found me tired and out of sorts, he would cook the dinner himself, and go about it in such a way that I felt that he rather enjoyed showing off his skill as a cook. The next evening, if he found everything ready, he would humorously declare himself much disappointed that I was so exceedingly well.

At such times a gray memory of James Carson would arise. How his cold anger and contempt, as exhibited on like occasions, had shriveled me up in the long ago. And then — I would fall to musing on the difference between the two men as lovers and husbands.

James Carson had been much more of an ardent lover than ever had been Liu Kanghi. Indeed it was his passion, real or feigned, which had carried me off my feet. When wooing he had constantly reproached me with being cold, unfeeling, a marble statue, and so forth; and I, poor, ignorant little girl, would wonder how it was I appeared so when I felt so differently. For I had given James Carson my first love. Upon him my life had been concentrated as it has never been concentrated upon any other. Yet — !

There was nothing feigned about my Chinese husband. Simple and sincere as he was before marriage, so was he afterwards. As my union with James Carson had meant misery, bitterness, and narrowness, so my union with Liu Kanghi meant, on the whole, happiness, health, and development. Yet the former, according to American ideas, had been an educated broad-minded man; the other, just an ordinary Chinaman.

But the ordinary Chinaman that I would show to you was the sort of man that children, birds, animals, and some women love. Every morning he would go to the window and call to his pigeons, and they would flock around him, hearing and responding to his whispering and cooing. The rooms we lived in had been his rooms ever since he had come to America. They were above his store, and large and cool. The furniture had been brought from China, but there was nothing of tinsel about it. Dark wood, almost black, carved and antique, some of the pieces set with mother-of-pearl. On one side of the inner room stood a case of books and an ancestral tablet. I have seen Liu Kanghi touch the tablet with reverence, but the faith of his fathers was not strong enough to cause him to bow before it. The elegant simplicity of these rooms had surprised me much when I was first taken to them. I looked at him then, standing for a moment by the window, a solitary pigeon peeking in at him, perhaps wondering who had come to divert from her her friend's attention. So had he lived since he had come to this country — quietly and undisturbed — from twenty years of age to twenty-five. I felt myself an intruder. A feeling of pity for the boy — for such he seemed in his enthusiasm — arose in my breast. Why had I come to confuse his calm? Was it ordained, as he declared?

My little girl loved him better than she loved me. He took great pleasure in playing with her, curling her hair over his fingers, tying her sash, and all the simple tasks from which so many men turn aside.

Once the baby got hold of a set rat trap, and was holding it in such a way that the slightest move would have released the spring and plunged the cruel steel into her tender arms. Kanghi's eyes and mine beheld her thus at the same moment. I stood transfixed with horror. Kanghi quietly went up to the child and took from her the trap. Then he asked me to release his hand. I almost fainted when I saw it. "It was the only way," said he. We had to send for the doctor, and even as it was, came very near having a case of blood poisoning.

I have heard people say that he was a keen business man, this Liu Kanghi, and I imagine that he was. I did not, however, discuss his business with him. All I was interested in were the pretty things and the women who would come in and jest with him. He could jest too. Of course, the women did not know that I was his wife. Once a woman in rich clothes gave him her card and asked him to call upon her. After she had left he passed the card to me. I tore it up.

He took those things as a matter of course, and was not affected by them. "They are a part of Chinatown life," he explained.

He was a member of the Reform Club, a Chinese social club, and the Chinese Board of Trade. He liked to discuss business affairs and Chinese and American politics with his countrymen, and occasionally enjoyed an evening away from me. But I never needed to worry over him.

He had his littlenesses as well as his bignesses, had Liu Kanghi. For instance, he thought he knew better about what was good for my health and other things, purely personal, than I did myself, and if my ideas opposed or did not tally with his, he would very vigorously denounce what he called "the foolishness of women." If he admired a certain dress, he would have me wear it on every occasion possible, and did not seem to be able to understand that it was not always suitable.

"Wear the dress with the silver lines," he said to me one day somewhat authoritatively. I was attired for going out, but not as he wished to see me. I answered that the dress with the silver lines was unsuitable for a long and dusty ride on an open car.

"Never mind," said he, "whether it is unsuitable or not. I wish you to wear it."

"All right," I said, "I will wear it, but I will stay at home."

I stayed at home, and so did he.

At another time, he reproved me for certain opinions I had expressed in the presence of some of his countrymen. "You should not talk like that," said he. "They will think you are a bad woman."

My white blood rose at that, and I answered him in a way which grieves me to remember. For Kanghi had never meant to insult or hurt me. Imperious by nature, he often spoke before he thought — and he was so boyishly anxious for me to appear in the best light possible before his own people.

There were other things too: a sort of childish jealousy and suspicion which it was difficult to allay. But a woman can forgive much to a man, the sincerity and strength of whose love makes her own, though true, seem slight and mean.

Yes, life with Liu Kanghi was not without its trials and tribulations. There was the continual uncertainty about his own life here in America, the constant irritation caused by the assumption of the white men that a white woman does not love her Chinese husband, and their actions accordingly; also sneers and offensive remarks. There was also on Liu Kanghi's side an acute consciousness that, though belonging to him as his wife, yet in a sense I was not his, but of the dominant race, which claimed, even while it professed to despise me. This consciousness betrayed itself in words and ways which filled me with a passion of pain and humiliation. "Kanghi," I would sharply say, for I had to cloak my tenderness, "do not talk to me like that. You *are* my superior. . . . I would not love you if you were not."

But in spite of all I could do or say, it was there between us: that strange invisible — what? Was it the barrier of race — that consciousness?

Sometimes he would talk about returning to China. The thought filled me with horror. I had heard rumors of secondary wives. One afternoon the cousin of Liu Kanghi, with whom I had lived, came to see me, and showed me a letter which she had received from a little Chinese girl who had been born and brought up in America until the age of ten. The last paragraph in the letter read: "Emma and I are very sad and wish we were back in America." Kanghi's cousin explained that the father of the little girls, having no sons, had taken himself another wife, and the new wife lived with the little girls and their mother.

That was before my little boy was born. That evening I told Kanghi that he need never expect me to go to China with him.

"You see," I began, "I look upon you as belonging to me."

He would not let me say more. After a while he said: "It is true that in China a man may and occasionally does take a secondary wife, but that custom is custom, not only because sons are denied to the first wife, but because the first wife is selected by parents and guardians before a man is hardly a man. If a Chinese marries for love, his life is a filled-up cup, and he wants no secondary wife. No, not even for sake of a son. Take, for example, me, your great husband."

I sometimes commented upon his boyish ways and appearance, which was the reason why, when he was in high spirits, he would call himself my "great husband." He was not boyish always. I have seen him, when shouldering the troubles of kinfolk, the quarrels of his clan, and other responsibilities, acting and looking like a man of twice his years.

But for all the strange marriage customs of my husband's people, I considered them far more moral in their lives than the majority of Americans. I expressed myself thus to Liu Kanghi, and he replied: "The American people think higher. If only more of them lived up to what they thought, the Chinese would not be so confused in trying to follow their leadership."

If ever a man rejoiced over the birth of his child, it was Liu Kanghi. The boy was born with a veil over his face. "A prophet!" cried the old mulatto Jewess who nursed me. "A prophet has come into the world."

She told this to his father when he came to look upon him, and he replied: "He is my son, that is all I care about." But he was so glad, and there was feasting and rejoicing with his Chinese friends for over two weeks. He came in one evening and found me weeping over my poor little boy. I shall never forget the expression on his face.

"Oh, shame!" he murmured, drawing my head down to his shoulder. "What is there to weep about? The child is beautiful! The feeling heart, the understanding mind is his. And we will bring him up to be proud that he is of Chinese blood; he will fear none and, after him, the name of half-breed will no longer be one of contempt."

Kanghi as a youth had attended a school in Hong Kong, and while there had made the acquaintance of several half Chinese half English lads. "They were the brightest of all," he told me, "but they lowered themselves in the eyes of the Chinese by being ashamed of their Chinese blood and ignoring it."

His theory, therefore, was that if his own son was brought up to be proud instead of ashamed of his Chinese half, the boy would become a great man.

Perhaps he was right, but he could not see as could I, an American woman, the conflict before our boy.

After the little Kanghi had passed his first month, and we had found a reliable woman to look after him, his father began to take me around with him much more than formerly, and life became very enjoyable. We dined often at a Chinese restaurant kept by a friend of his, and afterwards attended theaters, concerts, and other places of entertainment. We frequently met Americans with whom he had become acquainted through business, and he would introduce them with great pride in me shining in his eyes. The little jealousies and suspicions of the first year seemed no longer to irritate him, and though I had still cause to shrink from the gaze of strangers, I know that my Chinese husband was for several years a very happy man.

Now, I have come to the end. He left home one morning followed to the gate by the little girl and boy (we had moved to a cottage in the suburbs).

"Bring me a red ball," pleaded the little girl.

"And me too," cried the boy.

"All right, chickens," he responded, waving his hand to them.

He was brought home at night shot through the head. There are some Chinese, just as there are some Americans, who are opposed to all progress, and who hate with a bitter hatred all who would enlighten or be enlightened.

But that I have not the heart to dwell upon. I can only remember that when they brought my Chinese husband home there were two red balls in his pocket. Such was Liu Kanghi—a man.

Larry Eigner

Larry Eigner (1927–1996), a writer almost completely paralyzed by cerebral palsy from a forceps injury at birth, spent the first fifty years of his life at home with his parents in Swampscott, Massachusetts, a town on the north shore of Massachusetts Bay. He was the oldest of three brothers. His mother, whom he remembered as the strongest member of his family, was his principal caretaker. Eigner described himself with stark objectivity in the third-person in *A Film on Larry Eigner, Poet* (1973). "He couldn't walk unless someone holds him or he holds onto a bar or railing, one hand is useless and his speech isn't good. He remembers he made up bad rhymes as a child and had his mother write them down. His brother was seven and he was thirteen years old when he began typing in earnest (with one finger) while he did a few strokes on a toy typewriter before." As the film's narrator understood, Larry got his life "together on pure willpower." To which his brother Richard added that Eigner also possessed the qualities of "a healthy irreverence, which enabled him to perceive the ironies of life; [and] an ear for hearing and an eye and mind for seeing the sounds, sights, and patterns of his world."

Initially home-schooled by his mother, Eigner went to stay at the Massachusetts Hospital School south of Boston for the sixth, seventh, and eighth grades. His eighth grade class operated a print shop where they published his first book, *Poems* (1941), when he was fourteen. After his graduation from high school in Swampscott, he took a few correspondence courses from the University of Chicago before deciding that he might as well read on his own. His real instructor as a poet was Cid Corman, who caught Eigner's attention by reading a poem by William Butler Yeats on a Boston radio station. With his brother Larry's help, Eigner began to exchange letters with Corman, who helped him discover the poetry of Ezra Pound, William Carlos Williams, Hart Crane, Robert Creeley, and Charles Olson. By the time Eigner read Olson's "Projective Verse" essay in the 1950 magazine *Poetry New York*, he was on his way to becoming what his mother called "the poetry expert," rejecting her favorite nineteenth-century rhymed poems in favor of Olson's idea of a poem as a field of energy based on the laws and possibilities of the breath.

Eigner's career as a writer began with the book *From the Sustaining Air*, edited by Creeley and published by his Divers Press in Mallorca in 1953. Over fifty volumes followed, all of them from small presses, including two books of short stories edited by Samuel Charters, *Clouding* (1968) and *Further North* (1969). In 1978 Eigner and his mother moved to California to live close to his brother Richard in Berkeley after his father's death. During the summer of 1993, the year his mother died, the University Art Museum of the University of California at Berkeley paid tribute to Eigner by exhibiting his poem "Again dawn" on the building's façade. His story "Act" was included in his 1978 volume of selected prose, *Country / Harbor / Quiet / Act / Around*, edited by Barrett Watten. It describes what Eigner observed one Sunday afternoon from his wheelchair in his glassed-in front porch in Swampscott as he watched a neighborhood drama unfold on a vacant lot close to his home.

Act

1978

ON SEPTEMBER 10TH, as I was sitting out front, they brought a cow to feed in the field opposite me. It was the first time a cow had ever been so close to home, though of course I had been as close to them or even closer on tours of farms and wasn't afraid in any case, and when they installed her they left her alone. I was taking the whole thing as a pleasant surprise because if you live long enough, and something happens for the first time in a long while, at any rate if it happens suddenly, then you are well satisfied and give yourself up to it, doing anything at all, even though you may have had quite enough of it as a child. Though I have very vivid memories of horses since for instance one used to power the milk-trucks on our route, if it had been a horse I suppose I would have been glad to see it again. I heard the cow moo while it was still out of sight, as I was sitting on the far side of the piazza, but thinking I might as well I moved over by the windows and looking through the sunroom I got glimpses of the animal between the upper parts of trees, and the lower ones, coming down the road, men leading the rather down-snouted head and then sometimes the tail, or, really, the hindquarters.

They must have been bringing it down from the big house opposite the head of the street, enterprise, really, establishment, with the big built-up rock garden in front and around the right-hand corner and in back to the left half-broken-down stables where they keep the town's remaining draft-animals by some arrangement, and plows, plough-horses for hire, I don't know whether one or two or more, along with some riding horse or other which I see being ridden maybe twice in a period of five years. For all I know, this was the first time they had a cow there, and there hasn't been one since then, but it must have been from there. All sorts of undertakings seem to go on from there, although actually, I suppose, there are just as many, even more, things going on at one of the many filling station garages, and though I've never really seen any signs of life there, at least in the parts of the stables behind the doorway, and have often wondered about this. But to this area, or parts of it, there is hardly a roof, and I don't know but that the building might extend all across the back of the house to the hedges on the other side. And there was for example a sleigh, the only one I have actually ever seen, which each day used to come out around six p.m. to give the children who used to coast there a ride, as I thought, anyway, just when it was time to go home and have supper in my family; and I can't tell just how many times I saw it, how many winters, before it didn't seem to be there any more — and I can't be sure it isn't there now. Why they should be keeping a cow there I don't know, but, after all, I can use my imagination to some extent, always, and Mr. Bursett, the knowing old head of the household, might deal in cattle on occasion, in addition to the other things.

It was Sunday. Even so (and the neighborhood had very recently filled up so that the three lots opposite me were now the only ones left to grow wild most of the time), there do not seem to have been many cars, and this is understandable, as even in the afternoon, when people are not only home but visiting, the cars aren't particularly noticeable by themselves — Sunday, any holiday, still seems rather a day of rest here, because it's a tradition, even the Fourth of July, Independence Day, feels that way, and always did in the days of private and sporadic firecracker bursts. There were two men in charge of the beast, which was quiet enough, and they came not too slowly down the quiet road, with only the slight but distinctly present sound of the lining trees, and their motions. She mooed again just a little while before they made the turn to enter the field, and I could see the definite wiseacre wrinkles that appeared around the mouth and nostrils to the eyes, momentarily and in few; in that skin which appears as an ancient heritage even in calves. They were far from entering spectacularly in front of my steps, about the midpoint, but went in calmly, while it did take two men, at the left corner, which was nearest to them and the shortest way possible. Just as they did with horses when they had plowed the land a few times in Spring and as they would do, with any animal.

And after untying her rope halter they left her alone to graze. If they had been plowing, of course, both of them would have stayed with the horse, one to dig in and hold the plow down into the furrow, and one to steer the horse, by its head, and to keep it going. There was more variety and interest then, as they rested a few times, while one would go for a bottle of pop to the corner store, for instance. And I knew them from way back, in the streets, and managed sometimes to shout a few words to them, and wondered somewhat what else to say, or whether they were perfectly all right without me. But this time the cow was left alone, to its own devices in its own natural element. There was no tether or fence, but she was waist-deep in her feed and that would have held her down, in any case. She had a lot of eating to do, and I suppose they knew about when to come back for her, without calculating much, either. You don't, of course, have to make an animal wildly hungry in order to eat at proper times. That is one possible paradox that man has been able to avoid.

This was a chance to have my longest "visit" with cows, and I did have quite enough of her. Although she was a good deal hidden in the growth. I could see a few of her distinctive movements as she went about her main business, mostly ruminating. She didn't raise her head any, as if to some distance or to look at the sky, hardly at all, but kept it at about its natural, apparently most enjoyable level, slightly nodding up and down; tail flicking a few times perhaps, while when she went to lean down and take a bite she moved her legs very slightly, especially the forelegs, taking very short steps, automatic, as if closing in on something quite directly, and with a little careless fling that lets a member go partly by its own weight. And I had read a paragraph or so about "mammals" with two stomachs, after many years of vaguely accepting the phrase "chewing the cud," and would have been glad to see any sign of where these bellies were, exactly, or what contours did they give, and so on — what went on. A camel with two humps is really something to watch, I'd say, while connecting-rods on the wheels of a locomotive pulling into a station are both more perplexing and varied. But in any event, anyway, I didn't want to look at a cow all day, and as I usually have in mind a number of things to do, after a while I went back to my reading.

The date may have been April or May rather than September, I don't know. Lately Spring and Fall have become associated with each other, not so much as they used to be, once, by reason of similar temperate weather or as being intermediate seasons, but because when Spring comes I think that fairly soon it will be Autumn and in great part it might well be, since they are greatly alike. I don't notice Spring any more until I am rather deeply into it, I don't sit around and wait for it to come or its later stages to develop, and I don't concern myself at all how I should make use of my summer or take advantage of it, make hay of it, as the saying goes. And so there is nevertheless some little sadness in Spring as in Fall, with all its other points, which is something, and when winter arrives I stay inside mostly and go on from there. While I don't mind the "distractions" of balmy weather, and am in fact glad of them, if the truth were known, there is still more to do inside, and more at hand.

After some pages, after a while when I looked up I found the cow facing right at me and however it was standing there motionless each time her jaws stopped working, for the few seconds before ducking in for another mouthful. I hadn't thought before about such things as what the eye-range of animals might be, whether an animal for instance can see the horizon, as a man does, whatever height he is at, or not. I don't suppose she was looking at me, though maybe cattle do when you are close enough, as dogs do, or as deer have done, the deer from a good distance off; she might have been looking at me at that, perhaps in some such way as I was regarding her, though again I have no way of knowing how close you have to get to this species for them to see you; but cows usually seem vacant, and this one was no exception. While in a general way perhaps it does depend on size, for all I know alertness may be even more important, a cat up in a tree might be able to see farther than a bovine in a tree or on a bluff, and I would say by looking at one that a horse, which is not too much bigger, can outsee a bull.

At the same time I did imagine this cow of mine under the circumstances had about as great a field of vision as I had myself; that is, she could see as much building, houses, mine and the man's next door, as well as the road and my driveway, as I could see the pasture. I thought that although she didn't have binocular vision, so that depth didn't appear to her very well, especially when there was no light-and-shade, her field was as wide as mine, and was just as cycloramic. And while if I waved at her with my handkerchief or anything nothing would happen, no interpretation would take place, that I could see, just the same, she must have her eyes for something. And, anyway, there was her hearing, by which she could perhaps hear things I could not, of higher or lower, slower pitch, say. If I mooed at her, or squeaked, or something, that might do something, though I wouldn't do that, I wasn't in the mood or whatever.

For some reason she was still headed this way for a good while afterwards, there were still plenty of weeds and wild plants flowering in all directions, and I looked up fairly often to see her still facing me. The head is more interesting than the tail anyway. But finally I got a little restless and I turned the wheelchair around to back up a bit and view the scenery as in the window-panes, and to have it on my right, and the storm-door which had either not had the glass panels removed yet or had had them put back in place of the screen sections just the day before. The screens were on the windows and sort of roughed everything over, slightly doubling images and thus giving them a distinct haziness. My own face, which is of course the nearest and biggest thing in a mirror, is not so much ugly as hesitant and uncertain, and it is for instance very strange, amusing or disconcerting sometimes, to see the distortions performed on heads, especially faces, by a flaw, of which there are a couple in one of our living-room windows, as people pass by it, perhaps even at the other end of the room. But my face has been becoming of late a very familiar thing and usually now I finish with it automatically, about the instant I see it; while at times, quite inconsistently, I have bucked myself up by facing it.

Other things in the window, at least when the screen is on it, are turned around, blended with a sort of honeycomb as if sound waves were to become visible, which move sort of reverberatingly as you move your head, softly but you think like buzzing flies— and a little romanticized, in places astonishingly vivid and good, because changed. The cow was there, in the field, her brown self, but more slenderly and keenly bulging, the fore-shoulders, as she stood there nevertheless squarely. It made me think of water-colors, animals airily planted with their feet firmly wide, almost but not quite cartoons, which I must have seen somewhere at some time. But that was not exactly this cow and she kept about her business and did not become too finely grained.

Then I must have become interested again in the matter I was reading about. Words followed words and while sometimes I find light or heavy reading dull, a good part of the time I read out of curiosity, simply to find out what can be said, and there are also times when I'm off, and really begin to construct, trying to take everything from the beginning into account, whether the author's thinking or something different I can't exactly say, half-imagining I am really getting a deep grasp for the moment. And whatever it was, if I stopped to try, quite likely it would take a little less time to reconstruct what I did then than was consumed in doing it in those particular surroundings. But I am never lost to the world and have never been able to get very oblivious. It seems that a hair can turn me and indeed it seems a mystery, and wonderful, too, that I am not turned more often. I don't know how long it was, but pretty soon four or five small boys came down the street, all in their Sunday clothes, of course, home from their various churches, and I think it may have been rather late for them to be on their way home, at that, and the sermons may have been unusually longish that day, it may have been one of the days when pulpits were exchanged this year. I don't remember as to that, because some things are done quite irregularly in this town, and anyhow, I suppose, I don't read the newspaper much, by our standards, just looking at the front page occasionally, very seldom going into the struggle with the inside sheets.

Small boys seem very well behaved nowadays, in this district, though it might be just because I don't see them all day and because I am grown up now. I sometimes wonder if playing hookey is still a legend current with children, as it was with me, or not. And on the other hand there do seem to be a couple of blooming toughs that I know of and so maybe more, even, lately moved into the side-street two lots down from me, which stretches way out back of me, recently built up with sunny and not-too-low-lying cottages. I heard the boys exclaiming a bit at the cow's being there in that field, right around the corner from them, and when I finally looked around they had just about gone past the cow-lots and were turning to their street. But then one of the boys halted completely for a while and the others were standing around. In another minute all of them went back, and produced a couple of balls from their pockets or somewhere. Some of them got into the field, where they were almost lost in the grass and weedstalks, and, shouting to think of it, began playing catch; and it so developed that almost immediately they began following the cow and tossing balls over her head. The cow did stay in one place, of course, practically, but once or twice she moved to a side and they kept tabs on her more and more closely. She would roll up her eyeballs and gaze at the thing very blankly as it sailed over, at not too great a height, then move the head a bit and face in the direction of one of the players.

In a few minutes she was beginning to quicken up in this process, but the boys suddenly varied their ideas and generally started moving around in a circle, with the cow in the vicinity of the center.

It was a miniature baseball or something of the sort they were using, which could be caught with the bare hands, though. They kept this up until finally, of course, the ball hit the cow on the flank, and dropped to the ground. They reasoned they could come back later and find it, however (for it would still be there if the cow hadn't grabbed it), and continued the game with the one remaining ball, going at it cautiously, though, and moving away from the cow, without any big ideas.

But after a while I saw one of them who was just standing at the moment doing nothing pick up a stone and throw it at the cow. It hit on the right hind leg just on the upper part where it begins to widen into the hip. The animal gave a jerk and turned around all in one heap, as it were, more quickly than I knew a cow could. But after taking a step and tilting her head in a clumsy sort of cock and staying that way, her foreleg lifted, she went to graze again. The boy had dropped out of sight in the grass. At the next opportunity he was up again and with a more purposeful but still pleasant face aimed for the buttocks and sprang forwards and sideways. And this time — the boy, with his back to me, watching with interest, I thought — the cow, mooing constantly, made for the nearest exit. At an unaccountable sort of gallop. It dashed behind the garage that is there fronting the road which is a block north from here, and went down the driveway, mooing, and up that street, of which I can't see much, but I got glimpses of it for a few seconds while it was still not too far up. Strangely enough the boys were not very fast in reacting. They sort of kept up with their game until the commotion at the end of the next street attracted them gradually, and impulsively they made up their minds to run around and see what was up.

I don't know what sort of damage there was, exactly, but whatever serious damage was caused it was freakish and not violently done. Very surprisingly they brought the cow down a couple of times more, this time, of course, standing guard over her. Though that may not be the sort of thing that happens more than once, I feel.

Ralph Ellison

Ralph Ellison (1914–1994) was born in Oklahoma City, Oklahoma. When he was three his father, a small-time vendor of ice and coal, died, and thereafter his mother worked as a domestic servant to support herself and her son. Ellison later credited his mother, who recruited black votes for the Socialist Party, for turning him into an activist. She also brought home discarded books and phonograph records from the white households where she worked, and as a boy Ellison developed an interest in literature and music. He played trumpet in his high school band, at the same time that he began to relate the works of fiction he was reading to real life. "I began to look at my own life through the lives of fictional characters. When I read Stendhal, I would search until I began to find patterns of a Stendhalian novel within the Negro communities in which I grew up. I began, in other words, quite early to connect the worlds projected in literature . . . with the life in which I found myself."

In 1933 Ellison entered Tuskegee Institute in Alabama, where he studied music for three years. Then he went to New York City and met the black writers Langston Hughes and Richard Wright, whose encouragement helped him to become a writer. Wright turned Ellison's attention to writing short stories and reading "those works in which writing was discussed as a craft . . . to Henry James's prefaces, to Conrad," and to other authors. In 1939 Ellison's short stories, essays, and reviews began to appear in periodicals. After World War II, he settled down to work on the novel *Invisible Man*. Published in 1952, it received the National Book Award for fiction, and in 1965 a *Book Week* poll listed it as the most distinguished American novel of the preceding twenty years. As the critic Richard D. Lyons recognized, the novel was "a chronicle of a young black man's awakening to racial discrimination and his battle against the refusal of Americans to see him apart from his ethnic background, which in turn leads to humiliation and disillusionment." "Battle Royal," an excerpt from *Invisible Man*, is often anthologized. It appears after the prologue describing the underground chamber in which the nameless protagonist has retreated from the chaos of life aboveground.

Insisting that "art by its nature is social," Ellison began *Invisible Man* with the words "I am an invisible man. No, I am not a spook like those who haunted Edgar Allan Poe; nor am I one of your Hollywood-movie ectoplasms. I am a man of substance, of flesh and bone, fiber and liquids — and I might even be said to possess a mind. I am invisible, understand, simply because people refuse to see me." At the time of his death from cancer, Ellison left an unfinished novel started in the late 1950s. His initial work on the manuscript was destroyed in a fire, and it was difficult for him to complete the book. After his death, Ellison's literary executor culled nearly 2,000 pages of manuscript to create *Juneteenth* (1999). In addition to *Invisible Man*, Ellison published two collections of essays, *Shadow and Act* (1964) and *Going to the Territory* (1986). He also held a chair as Albert Schweitzer Professor of Contemporary Literature and Culture at New York University. *Flying Home and Other Stories* was published in 1996.

RELATED COMMENTARY
Ralph Ellison, "The Influence of Folklore on 'Battle Royal,'" page 1420.

Battle Royal

1952

IT GOES A LONG WAY BACK, some twenty years. All my life I had been look-ing for something, and everywhere I turned someone tried to tell me what it was. I accepted their answers too, though they were often in contradiction and even self-contradictory. I was naïve. I was looking for myself and asking everyone except myself questions which I, and only I, could answer. It took me a long time and much painful boomeranging of my expectations to achieve a realization everyone else appears to have been born with: That I am nobody but myself. But first I had to discover that I am an invisible man!

And yet I am no freak of nature, nor of history. I was in the cards, other things having been equal (or unequal) eighty-five years ago. I am not ashamed of my grandparents for having been slaves. I am only ashamed of myself for having at one time been ashamed. About eighty-five years ago they were told that they were free, united with others of our country in everything pertain-ing to the common good, and, in everything social, separate like the fingers of the hand. And they believed it. They exulted in it. They stayed in their place, worked hard, and brought up my father to do the same. But my grandfather is the one. He was an odd old guy, my grandfather, and I am told I take after him. It was he who caused the trouble. On his deathbed he called my father to him and said, "Son, after I'm gone I want you to keep up the good fight. I never told you, but our life is a war and I have been a traitor all my born days, a spy in the enemy's country ever since I give up my gun back in the Reconstruction. Live with your head in the lion's mouth. I want you to overcome 'em with yeses, undermine 'em with grins, agree 'em to death and destruction, let 'em swoller you till they vomit or bust wide open." They thought the old man had gone out of his mind. He had been the meekest of men. The younger children were rushed from the room, the shades drawn, and the flame of the lamp turned so low that it sputtered on the wick like the old man's breathing. "Learn it to the younguns," he whispered fiercely; then he died.

But my folks were more alarmed over his last words than over his dying. It was as though he had not died at all, his words caused so much anxiety. I was warned emphatically to forget what he had said and, indeed, this is the first time it has been mentioned outside the family circle. It had a tremendous effect upon me, however. I could never be sure of what he meant. Grandfather had been a quiet old man who never made any trouble, yet on his deathbed he had called himself a traitor and a spy, and he had spoken of his meekness as a dangerous activity. It became a constant puzzle which lay unanswered in the back of my mind. And whenever things went well for me I remembered my grandfather and felt guilty and uncomfortable. It was as though I was car-rying out his advice in spite of myself. And to make it worse, everyone loved me for it. I was praised by the most lily-white men of the town. I was consid-ered an example of desirable conduct — just as my grandfather had been. And what puzzled me was that the old man had defined it as *treachery*. When I was praised for my conduct I felt a guilt that in some way I was doing something that was really against the wishes of the white folks, that if they had understood they would have desired me to act just the opposite, that I should have been sulky and mean, and that that really would have been what they wanted, even though they were fooled and thought they wanted me to act as I did. It made me afraid that some day they would look upon me as a traitor and I would be lost. Still I was more afraid to act any other way because they didn't like that at all. The old man's words were like a curse. On my graduation day I delivered an oration in which I showed that humility was the secret, indeed, the very essence of progress. (Not that I believed this — how could I, remembering my grandfather? — I only believed that it worked.) It was a great success. Everyone praised me and I was invited to give the speech at a gathering of the town's leading white citizens. It was a triumph for our whole community.

It was in the main ballroom of the leading hotel. When I got there I discovered that it was on the occasion of a smoker, and I was told that since I was to be there anyway I might as well take part in the battle royal to be fought by some of my schoolmates as part of the entertainment. The battle royal came first.

All of the town's big shots were there in their tuxedoes, wolfing down the buffet foods, drinking beer and whiskey and smoking black cigars. It was a large room with a high ceiling. Chairs were arranged in neat rows around three sides of a portable boxing ring. The fourth side was clear, revealing a gleaming space of polished floor. I had some misgivings over the battle royal, by the way. Not from a distaste for fighting, but because I didn't care too much for the other fellows who were to take part. They were tough guys who seemed to have no grandfather's curse worrying their minds. No one could mistake their toughness. And besides, I suspected that fighting a battle royal might detract from the dignity of my speech. In those pre-invisible days I visualized myself as a potential Booker T. Washington. But the other fellows didn't care too much for me either, and there were nine of them. I felt superior to them in my way, and I didn't like the manner in which we were all crowded together into the servants' elevator. Nor did they like my being there. In fact, as the warmly lighted floors flashed past the elevator we had words over the fact that I, by taking part in the fight, had knocked one of their friends out of a night's work.

We were led out of the elevator through a rococo hall into an anteroom and told to get into our fighting togs. Each of us was issued a pair of boxing gloves and ushered out into the big mirrored hall, which we entered looking cautiously about us and whispering, lest we might accidentally be heard above the noise of the room. It was foggy with cigar smoke. And already the whiskey was taking effect. I was shocked to see some of the most important men of the town quite tipsy. They were all there — bankers, lawyers, judges, doctors, fire chiefs, teachers, merchants. Even one of the more fashionable pastors. Something we could not see was going on up front. A clarinet was vibrating sensuously and the men were standing up and moving eagerly forward. We were a small tight group, clustered together, our bare upper bodies touching and shining with anticipatory sweat; while up front the big shots were becoming increasingly excited

over something we still could not see. Suddenly I heard the school superintendent, who had told me to come, yell, "Bring up the shines, gentlemen! Bring up
the little shines!"

We were rushed up to the front of the ballroom, where it smelled even more
strongly of tobacco and whiskey. Then we were pushed into place. I almost
wet my pants. A sea of faces, some hostile, some amused, ringed around us,
and in the center, facing us, stood a magnificent blonde — stark naked. There
was dead silence. I felt a blast of cold air chill me. I tried to back away, but
they were behind me and around me. Some of the boys stood with lowered
heads, trembling. I felt a wave of irrational guilt and fear. My teeth chattered,
my skin turned to goose flesh, my knees knocked. Yet I was strongly attracted
and looked in spite of myself. Had the price of looking been blindness, I would
have looked. The hair was yellow like that of a circus kewpie doll, the face heavily powdered and rouged, as though to form an abstract mask, the eyes hollow
and smeared a cool blue, the color of a baboon's butt. I felt a desire to spit upon
her as my eyes brushed slowly over her body. Her breasts were firm and round
as the domes of East Indian temples, and I stood so close as to see the fine skin
texture and beads of pearly perspiration glistening like dew around the pink
and erected buds of her nipples. I wanted at one and the same time to run
from the room, to sink through the floor, or go to her and cover her from my
eyes and the eyes of the others with my body; to feel the soft thighs, to caress
her and destroy her, to love her and murder her, to hide from her, and yet to
stroke where below the small American flag tattooed upon her belly her thighs
formed a capital V. I had a notion that of all in the room she saw only me with
her impersonal eyes.

And then she began to dance, a slow sensuous movement; the smoke of a
hundred cigars clinging to her like the thinnest of veils. She seemed like a fair
bird-girl girdled in veils calling to me from the angry surface of some gray and
threatening sea. I was transported. Then I became aware of the clarinet playing
and the big shots yelling at us. Some threatened us if we looked and others if
we did not. On my right I saw one boy faint. And now a man grabbed a silver
pitcher from a table and stepped close as he dashed ice water upon him and
stood him up and forced two of us to support him as his head hung and moans
issued from his thick bluish lips. Another boy began to plead to go home. He
was the largest of the group, wearing dark red fighting trunks much too small
to conceal the erection which projected from him as though in answer to the
insinuating low-registered moaning of the clarinet. He tried to hide himself
with his boxing gloves.

And all the while the blonde continued dancing, smiling faintly at the
big shots who watched her with fascination, and faintly smiling at our fear.
I noticed a certain merchant who followed her hungrily, his lips loose and
drooling. He was a large man who wore diamond studs in a shirtfront which
swelled with the ample paunch underneath, and each time the blonde swayed
her undulating hips he ran his hand through the thin hair of his bald head and,
with his arms upheld, his posture clumsy like that of an intoxicated panda,
wound his belly in a slow and obscene grind. This creature was completely

hypnotized. The music had quickened. As the dancer flung herself about with a detached expression on her face, the men began reaching out to touch her. I could see their beefy fingers sink into her soft flesh. Some of the others tried to stop them and she began to move around the floor in graceful circles, as they gave chase, slipping and sliding over the polished floor. It was mad. Chairs went crashing, drinks were spilt, as they ran laughing and howling after her. They caught her just as she reached a door, raised her from the floor, and tossed her as college boys are tossed at a hazing, and above her red fixed-smiling lips I saw the terror and disgust in her eyes, almost like my own terror and that which I saw in some of the other boys. As I watched, they tossed her twice and her soft breasts seemed to flatten against the air and her legs flung wildly as she spun. Some of the more sober ones helped her to escape. And I started off the floor, heading for the anteroom with the rest of the boys.

Some were still crying and in hysteria. But as we tried to leave we were stopped and ordered to get into the ring. There was nothing to do but what we were told. All ten of us climbed under the ropes and allowed ourselves to be blindfolded with broad bands of white cloth. One of the men seemed to feel a bit sympathetic and tried to cheer us up as we stood with our backs against the ropes. Some of us tried to grin. "See that boy over there?" one of the men said. "I want you to run across at the bell and give it to him right in the belly. If you don't get him, I'm going to get you. I don't like his looks." Each of us was told the same. The blindfolds were put on. Yet even then I had been going over my speech. In my mind each word was as bright as flame. I felt the cloth pressed into place, and frowned so that it would be loosened when I relaxed.

But now I felt a sudden fit of blind terror. I was unused to darkness. It was as though I had suddenly found myself in a dark room filled with poisonous cottonmouths. I could hear the bleary voices yelling insistently for the battle royal to begin.

"Get going in there!"

"Let me at that big nigger!"

I strained to pick up the school superintendent's voice, as though to squeeze some security out of that slightly more familiar sound.

"Let me at those black sonsabitches!" someone yelled.

"No, Jackson, no!" another voice yelled. "Here, somebody, help me hold Jack."

"I want to get at that ginger-colored nigger. Tear him limb from limb," the first voice yelled.

I stood against the ropes trembling. For in those days I was what they called ginger-colored, and he sounded as though he might crunch me between his teeth like a crisp ginger cookie.

Quite a struggle was going on. Chairs were being kicked about and I could hear voices grunting as with a terrific effort. I wanted to see, to see more desperately than ever before. But the blindfold was as tight as a thick skin-puckering scab and when I raised my gloved hands to push the layers of white aside a voice yelled, "Oh, no you don't, black bastard! Leave that alone!"

"Ring the bell before Jackson kills him a coon!" someone boomed in the sudden silence. And I heard the bell clang and the sound of the feet scuffling forward.

A glove smacked against my head. I pivoted, striking out stiffly as someone went past, and felt the jar ripple along the length of my arm to my shoulder. Then it seemed as though all nine of the boys had turned upon me at once. Blows pounded me from all sides while I struck out as best I could. So many blows landed upon me that I wondered if I were not the only blindfolded fighter in the ring, or if the man called Jackson hadn't succeeded in getting me after all.

Blindfolded, I could no longer control my motions. I had no dignity. I stumbled about like a baby or a drunken man. The smoke had become thicker and with each new blow it seemed to sear and further restrict my lungs. My saliva became like hot bitter glue. A glove connected with my head, filling my mouth with warm blood. It was everywhere. I could not tell if the moisture I felt upon my body was sweat or blood. A blow landed hard against the nape of my neck. I felt myself going over, my head hitting the floor. Streaks of blue light filled the black world behind the blindfold. I lay prone, pretending that I was knocked out, but felt myself seized by hands and yanked to my feet. "Get going, black boy! Mix it up!" My arms were like lead, my head smarting from blows. I managed to feel my way to the ropes and held on, trying to catch my breath. A glove landed in my mid-section and I went over again, feeling as though the smoke had become a knife jabbed into my guts. Pushed this way and that by the legs milling around me, I finally pulled erect and discovered that I could see the black, sweat-washed forms weaving in the smoky-blue atmosphere like drunken dancers weaving to the rapid drum-like thuds of blows.

Everyone fought hysterically. It was complete anarchy. Everybody fought everybody else. No group fought together for long. Two, three, four, fought one, then turned to fight each other, were themselves attacked. Blows landed below the belt and in the kidney, with the gloves open as well as closed, and with my eye partly opened now there was not so much terror. I moved carefully, avoiding blows, although not too many to attract attention, fighting from group to group. The boys groped about like blind, cautious crabs crouching to protect their mid-sections, their heads pulled in short against their shoulders, their arms stretched nervously before them, with their fists testing the smoke-filled air like the knobbed feelers of hypersensitive snails. In one corner I glimpsed a boy violently punching the air and heard him scream in pain as he smashed his hand against a ring post. For a second I saw him bent over holding his hand, then going down as a blow caught his unprotected head. I played one group against the other, slipping in and throwing a punch then stepping out of range while pushing the others into the melee to take the blows blindly aimed at me. The smoke was agonizing and there were no rounds, no bells at three minute intervals to relieve our exhaustion. The room spun round me, a swirl of lights, smoke, sweating bodies surrounded by tense white faces. I bled from both nose and mouth, the blood spattering upon my chest.

The men kept yelling, "Slug him, black boy! Knock his guts out!"

"Uppercut him! Kill him! Kill that big boy!"

Taking a fake fall, I saw a boy going down heavily beside me as though we were felled by a single blow, saw a sneaker-clad foot shoot into his groin as the two who had knocked him down stumbled upon him. I rolled out of range, feeling a twinge of nausea.

The harder we fought the more threatening the men became. And yet, I had begun to worry about my speech again. How would it go? Would they recognize my ability? What would they give me?

I was fighting automatically and suddenly I noticed that one after another of the boys was leaving the ring. I was surprised, filled with panic, as though I had been left alone with an unknown danger. Then I understood. The boys had arranged it among themselves. It was the custom for the two men left in the ring to slug it out for the winner's prize. I discovered this too late. When the bell sounded two men in tuxedoes leaped into the ring and removed the blindfold. I found myself facing Tatlock, the biggest of the gang. I felt sick at my stomach. Hardly had the bell stopped ringing in my ears than it clanged again and I saw him moving swiftly toward me. Thinking of nothing else to do I hit him smash on the nose. He kept coming, bringing the rank sharp violence of stale sweat. His face was a black blank of a face, only his eyes alive — with hate of me and aglow with a feverish terror from what had happened to us all. I became anxious. I wanted to deliver my speech and he came at me as though he meant to beat it out of me. I smashed him again and again, taking his blows as they came. Then on a sudden impulse I struck him lightly and as we clinched, I whispered, "Fake like I knocked you out, you can have the prize."

"I'll break your behind," he whispered hoarsely.

"For *them*?"

"For *me*, sonofabitch!"

They were yelling for us to break it up and Tatlock spun me half around with a blow, and as a joggled camera sweeps in a reeling scene, I saw the howling red faces crouching tense beneath the cloud of blue-gray smoke. For a moment the world wavered, unraveled, flowed, then my head cleared and Tatlock bounced before me. That fluttering shadow before my eyes was his jabbing left hand. Then falling forward, my head against his damp shoulder, I whispered,

"I'll make it five dollars more."

"Go to hell!"

But his muscles relaxed a trifle beneath my pressure and I breathed, "Seven!"

"Give it to your ma," he said, ripping me beneath the heart.

And while I still held him I butted him and moved away. I felt myself bombarded with punches. I fought back with hopeless desperation. I wanted to deliver my speech more than anything else in the world, because I felt that only these men could judge truly my ability, and now this stupid clown was ruining my chances. I began fighting carefully now, moving in to punch him and out again with my greater speed. A lucky blow to his chin and I had him going too — until I heard a loud voice yell, "I got my money on the big boy."

Hearing this, I almost dropped my guard. I was confused: Should I try to win against the voice out there? Would not this go against my speech, and was not this a moment for humility, for nonresistance? A blow to my head as I danced about sent my right eye popping like a jack-in-the-box and settled my dilemma. The room went red as I fell. It was a dream fall, my body languid and fastidious as to where to land, until the floor became impatient and smashed up to meet me. A moment later I came to. An hypnotic voice said FIVE emphatically. And I lay there, hazily watching a dark red spot of my own blood shaping itself into a butterfly, glistening and soaking into the soiled gray world of the canvas.

When the voice drawled TEN I was lifted up and dragged to a chair. I sat dazed. My eye pained and swelled with each throb of my pounding heart and I wondered if now I would be allowed to speak. I was wringing wet, my mouth still bleeding. We were grouped along the wall now. The other boys ignored me as they congratulated Tatlock and speculated as to how much they would be paid. One boy whimpered over his smashed hand. Looking up front, I saw attendants in white jackets rolling the portable ring away and placing a small square rug in the vacant space surrounded by chairs. Perhaps, I thought, I will stand on the rug to deliver my speech.

Then the M.C. called to us, "Come on up here boys and get your money."

We ran forward to where the men laughed and talked in their chairs, waiting. Everyone seemed friendly now.

"There it is on the rug," the man said. I saw the rug covered with coins of all dimensions and a few crumpled bills. But what excited me, scattered here and there, were the gold pieces.

"Boys, it's all yours," the man said. "You get all you grab."

"That's right, Sambo," a blond man said, winking at me confidentially.

I trembled with excitement, forgetting my pain. I would get the gold and the bills, I thought. I would use both hands. I would throw my body against the boys nearest me to block them from the gold.

"Get down around the rug now," the man commanded, "and don't anyone touch it until I give the signal."

"This ought to be good," I heard.

As told, we got around the square rug on our knees. Slowly the man raised his freckled hand as we followed it upward with our eyes.

I heard, "These niggers look like they're about to pray!"

Then, "Ready," the man said. "Go!"

I lunged for a yellow coin lying on the blue design of the carpet, touching it and sending a surprised shriek to join those rising around me. I tried frantically to remove my hand but could not let go. A hot, violent force tore through my body, shaking me like a wet rat. The rug was electrified. The hair bristled up on my head as I shook myself free. My muscles jumped, my nerves jangled, writhed. But I saw that this was not stopping the other boys. Laughing in fear and embarrassment, some were holding back and scooping up the coins knocked off by the painful contortions of the others. The men roared above us as we struggled.

"Pick it up, goddamnit, pick it up!" someone called like a bass-voiced parrot. "Go on, get it!"

I crawled rapidly around the floor, picking up the coins, trying to avoid the coppers and to get greenbacks and the gold. Ignoring the shock by laughing, as

I brushed the coins off quickly, I discovered that I could contain the electricity — a contradiction, but it works. Then the men began to push us onto the rug. Laughing embarrassedly, we struggled out of their hands and kept after the coins. We were all wet and slippery and hard to hold. Suddenly I saw a boy lifted into the air, glistening with sweat like a circus seal, and dropped, his wet back landing flush upon the charged rug, heard him yell and saw him literally dance upon his back, his elbows beating a frenzied tatoo upon the floor, his muscles twitching like the flesh of a horse stung by many flies. When he finally rolled off, his face was gray and no one stopped him when he ran from the floor amid booming laughter.

"Get the money," the M.C. called. "That's good hard American cash!"

And we snatched and grabbed, snatched and grabbed. I was careful not to come too close to the rug now, and when I felt the hot whiskey breath descend upon me like a cloud of foul air I reached out and grabbed the leg of a chair. It was occupied and I held on desperately.

"Leggo, nigger! Leggo!"

The huge face wavered down to mine as he tried to push me free. But my body was slippery and he was too drunk. It was Mr. Colcord, who owned a chain of movie houses and "entertainment palaces." Each time he grabbed me I slipped out of his hands. It became a real struggle. I feared the rug more than I did the drunk, so I held on, surprising myself for a moment by trying to topple *him* upon the rug. It was such an enormous idea that I found myself actually carrying it out. I tried not to be obvious, yet when I grabbed his leg, trying to tumble him out of the chair, he raised up roaring with laughter, and, looking at me with soberness dead in the eye, kicked me viciously in the chest. The chair leg flew out of my hand. I felt myself going and rolled. It was as though I had rolled through a bed of hot coals. It seemed a whole century would pass before I would roll free, a century in which I was seared through the deepest levels of my body to the fearful breath within me and the breath seared and heated to the point of explosion. It'll all be over in a flash, I thought as I rolled clear. It'll all be over in a flash.

But not yet, the men on the other side were waiting, red faces swollen as though from apoplexy as they bent forward in their chairs. Seeing their fingers coming toward me I rolled away as a fumbled football rolls off the receiver's fingertips, back into the coals. That time I luckily sent the rug sliding out of place and heard the coins ringing against the floor and the boys scuffling to pick them up and the M.C. calling, "All right, boys, that's all. Go get dressed and get your money."

I was limp as a dish rag. My back felt as though it had been beaten with wires.

When we had dressed the M.C. came in and gave us each five dollars, except Tatlock, who got ten for being last in the ring. Then he told us to leave. I was not to get a chance to deliver my speech, I thought. I was going out into the dim alley in despair when I was stopped and told to go back. I returned to the ballroom, where the men were pushing back their chairs and gathering in groups to talk.

The M.C. knocked on a table for quiet. "Gentlemen," he said, "we almost forgot an important part of the program. A most serious part, gentlemen. This boy was brought here to deliver a speech which he made at his graduation yesterday...."

"Bravo!"

"I'm told that he is the smartest boy we've got out there in Greenwood. I'm told that he knows more big words than a pocket-sized dictionary."

Much applause and laughter.

"So now, gentlemen, I want you to give him your attention."

There was still laughter as I faced them, my mouth dry, my eye throbbing. I began slowly, but evidently my throat was tense, because they began shouting, "Louder! Louder!"

"We of the younger generation extol the wisdom of that great leader and educator," I shouted, "who first spoke these flaming words of wisdom: 'A ship lost at sea for many days suddenly sighted a friendly vessel. From the mast of the unfortunate vessel was seen a signal: "Water, water; we die of thirst!" The answer from the friendly vessel came back: "Cast down your bucket where you are." The captain of the distressed vessel, at last heeding the injunction, cast down his bucket, and it came up full of fresh sparkling water from the mouth of the Amazon River.' And like him I say, and in his words, 'To those of my race who depend upon bettering their condition in a foreign land, or who underestimate the importance of cultivating friendly relations with the Southern white man, who is his next-door neighbor, I would say: "Cast down your bucket where you are" — cast it down in making friends in every manly way of the people of all races by whom we are surrounded...."

I spoke automatically and with such fervor that I did not realize that the men were still talking and laughing until my dry mouth, filling up with blood from the cut, almost strangled me. I coughed, wanting to stop and go to one of the tall brass, sand-filled spittoons to relieve myself, but a few of the men, especially the superintendent, were listening and I was afraid. So I gulped it down, blood, saliva, and all, and continued. (What powers of endurance I had during those days! What enthusiasm! What a belief in the rightness of things!) I spoke even louder in spite of the pain. But still they talked and still they laughed, as though deaf with cotton in dirty ears. So I spoke with greater emotional emphasis. I closed my ears and swallowed blood until I was nauseated. The speech seemed a hundred times as long as before, but I could not leave out a single word. All had to be said, each memorized nuance considered, rendered. Nor was that all. Whenever I uttered a word of three or more syllables a group of voices would yell for me to repeat it. I used the phrase "social responsibility" and they yelled:

"What's the word you say, boy?"

"Social responsibility," I said.

"What?"

"Social ..."

"Louder."

"... responsibility."

"More!"

"Respon —"

"Repeat!"

" — sibility."

The room filled with the uproar of laughter until, no doubt, distracted by having to gulp down my blood, I made a mistake and yelled a phrase I had often seen denounced in newspaper editorials, heard debated in private.

"Social . . ."

"What?" they yelled.

". . . equality —"

The laughter hung smokelike in the sudden stillness. I opened my eyes, puzzled. Sounds of displeasure filled the room. The M.C. rushed forward. They shouted hostile phrases at me. But I did not understand.

A small dry mustached man in the front row blared out, "Say that slowly, son!"

"What sir?"

"What you just said!"

"Social responsibility, sir," I said.

"You weren't being smart, were you, boy?" he said, not unkindly.

"No, sir!"

"You sure that about 'equality' was a mistake?"

"Oh, yes, sir," I said. "I was swallowing blood."

"Well, you had better speak more slowly so we can understand. We mean to do right by you, but you've got to know your place at all times. All right, now, go on with your speech."

I was afraid. I wanted to leave but I wanted also to speak and I was afraid they'd snatch me down.

"Thank you, sir," I said, beginning where I had left off, and having them ignore me as before.

Yet when I finished there was a thunderous applause. I was surprised to see the superintendent come forth with a package wrapped in white tissue paper, and, gesturing for quiet, address the men.

"Gentlemen, you see that I did not overpraise this boy. He makes a good speech and some day he'll lead his people in the proper paths. And I don't have to tell you that that is important in these days and times. This is a good, smart boy, and so to encourage him in the right direction, in the name of the Board of Education I wish to present him a prize in the form of this . . ."

He paused, removing the tissue paper and revealing a gleaming calfskin brief case.

". . . in the form of this first-class article from Shad Whitmore's shop."

"Boy," he said, addressing me, "take this prize and keep it well. Consider it a badge of office. Prize it. Keep developing as you are and some day it will be filled with important papers that will help shape the destiny of your people."

I was so moved that I could hardly express my thanks. A rope of bloody saliva forming a shape like an undiscovered continent drooled upon the leather and I wiped it quickly away. I felt an importance that I had never dreamed.

"Open it and see what's inside," I was told.

My fingers a-tremble, I complied, smelling the fresh leather and finding an official-looking document inside. It was a scholarship to the state college for Negroes. My eyes filled with tears and I ran awkwardly off the floor.

I was overjoyed; I did not even mind when I discovered that the gold pieces I had scrambled for were brass pocket tokens advertising a certain make of automobile.

When I reached home everyone was excited. Next day the neighbors came to congratulate me. I even felt safe from grandfather, whose deathbed curse usually spoiled my triumphs. I stood beneath his photograph with my brief case in hand and smiled triumphantly into his stolid black peasant's face. It was a face that fascinated me. The eyes seemed to follow everywhere I went.

That night I dreamed I was at a circus with him and that he refused to laugh at the clowns no matter what they did. Then later he told me to open my brief case and read what was inside and I did, finding an official envelope stamped with the state seal; and inside the envelope I found another and another, end-lessly, and I thought I would fall of weariness. "Them's years," he said. "Now open that one." And I did and in it I found an engraved document containing a short message in letters of gold. "Read it," my grandfather said. "Out loud."

"To Whom It May Concern," I intoned. "Keep This Nigger-Boy Running."

I awoke with the old man's laughter ringing in my ears.

(It was a dream I was to remember and dream again for many years after. But at the time I had no insight into its meaning. First I had to attend college.)

Nathan Englander

Nathan Englander (b. 1970) was born in West Hempstead, New York, and grew up as part of the Orthodox Jewish community in that Long Island town. He attended high school at the Hebrew Academy of Nassau County before he went to the State University of New York at Binghamton and the Iowa Writers' Workshop at the University of Iowa. In 1999 he published his first collection of short fiction, *For the Relief of Unbearable Urges*, to critical acclaim. In the following years Englander won the 2000 PEN/Malamud Award and a Guggenheim Fellowship, in addition to many other awards. In 2007 he published a historical novel, *The Ministry of Special Cases*, about Argentina's so-called "Dirty War" of 1976. His third book, the stories in *What We Talk About When We Talk About Anne Frank,* won the 2012 Frank O'Connor International Short Story Award. The title story first appeared in the December 12, 2011, issue of *The New Yorker.*

In the story "What We Talk About When We Talk About Anne Frank," the game played by the two married couples, a Hassidic couple and a secular Jewish couple, was something Englander actually played with what he called "dead seriousness" in his family. "We really were raised with the idea of a looming second Holocaust, and we would play this game wondering who would hide us. I remember my sister saying about a couple we knew, 'He would hide us, and she would turn us in.' And it struck me so deeply, and I just couldn't shake that thought for all these years, because it's true." Though his parents were third or fourth generation Americans, Englander told an interviewer that he spent his childhood in America feeling Jewish and not American. Then he lived in Israel for five years. "And it's only in Israel—it was those years there—where I got to be an American because everyone's a Jew." In Jerusalem, Englander met Jews who were secular atheists, and he broke off his Orthodox practice. He remembered thinking that God would punish him for riding a bus on the Sabbath, and when that didn't happen, he said "it felt like I wanted a cheeseburger." Yet he remains highly conscious of his Jewish heritage. "At the University of Iowa, one professor told me that I was writing all of my sentences in transliterated Yiddish. My mom's from Boston and my dad's from Brooklyn, but I hear everything [in a Yiddish] rhythm."

Recently Englander translated the *New American Haggadah* and cotranslated the Israeli writer Etgar Keret's *Suddenly a Knock at the Door.* Englander's stories have appeared in both *The O. Henry Prize Stories* and *The Best American Short Stories* annual volumes. He also teaches fiction at CUNY Hunter College's MFA Program in Creative Writing in New York City.

RELATED STORY
Raymond Carver, "What We Talk About When We Talk About Love," page 227.

What We Talk About When We Talk About Anne Frank

2011

THEY'RE IN OUR HOUSE maybe ten minutes and already Mark's lecturing us on the Israeli occupation. Mark and Lauren live in Jerusalem, and people from there think it gives them the right.

Mark is looking all stoic and nodding his head. "If we had what you have down here in South Florida," he says, and trails off. "Yup," he says, and he's nodding again. "We'd have no troubles at all."

"You do have what we have," I tell him. "All of it. Sun and palm trees. Old Jews and oranges and the worst drivers around. At this point, we've probably got more Israelis than you." Debbie, my wife, puts a hand on my arm—her signal that I'm either taking a tone, interrupting someone's story, sharing something private, or making an inappropriate joke. That's my cue, and I'm surprised, considering how often I get it, that she ever lets go of my arm.

"Yes, you've got everything now," Mark says. "Even terrorists."

I look at Lauren. She's the one my wife has the relationship with—the one who should take charge. But Lauren isn't going to give her husband any signal. She and Mark ran off to Israel twenty years ago and turned Hasidic, and neither of them will put a hand on the other in public. Not for this. Not to put out a fire.

"Wasn't Mohamed Atta living right here before 9/11?" Mark says, and now he pantomimes pointing out houses. "Goldberg, Goldberg, Goldberg — Atta, How'd you miss him in this place?"

"Other side of town," I say.

"That's what I'm talking about. That's what you have that we don't. Other sides of town. Wrong sides of the tracks. Space upon space." And now he's fingering the granite countertop in our kitchen, looking out into the living room and the dining room, staring through the kitchen windows at the pool. "All this house," he says, "and one son? Can you imagine?"

"No," Lauren says. And then she turns to us, backing him up. "You should see how we live with ten."

"Ten kids," I say. "We could get you a reality show with that here in the States. Help you get a bigger place."

The hand is back pulling at my sleeve. "Pictures," Debbie says, "I want to see the girls." We all follow Lauren into the den for her purse.

"Do you believe it?" Mark says. "Ten girls!" And the way it comes out of his mouth, it's the first time I like the guy. The first time I think about giving him a chance.

Facebook and Skype brought Deb and Lauren back together. They were glued at the hip growing up. Went all the way through school together. Yeshiva school. All girls. Out in Queens till high school and then riding the subway together to one called Central in Manhattan. They stayed best friends until I married Deb and turned her secular, and soon after that Lauren met Mark and they went off to the Holy Land and shifted from Orthodox to *ultra*-Orthodox, which to me sounds like a repackaged detergent — ORTHODOX ULTRA®, now with more deep-healing power. Because of that, we're supposed to call them Shoshana and Yerucham now. Deb's been doing it. I'm just not saying their names.

"You want some water?" I offer. "Coke in the can?"

" 'You'—which of us?" Mark says.

"You both," I say. "Or I've got whiskey. Whiskey's kosher, too, right?"

"If it's not, I'll kosher it up real fast," he says, pretending to be easygoing. And right then he takes off that big black hat and plops down on the couch in the den.

Lauren's holding the verticals aside and looking out at the yard. "Two girls from Forest Hills," she says. "Who ever thought we'd be the mothers of grownups?"

"Trevor's sixteen," Deb says. "You may think he's a grownup, and he may think he's a grownup — but we are not convinced."

Right then is when Trev comes padding into the den, all six feet of him, plaid pajama bottoms dragging on the floor and T-shirt full of holes. He's just woken up, and you can tell he's not sure if he's still dreaming. We told him we had guests. But there's Trev, staring at this man in the black suit, a beard resting on his belly. And Lauren, I met her once before, right when Deb and I got married, but ten girls and a thousand Shabbos dinners later — well, she's a big woman, in a bad dress and a giant blond Marilyn Monroe wig. Seeing them at the door, I can't say I wasn't shocked myself.

"Hey," he says.

And then Deb's on him, preening and fixing his hair and hugging him. "Trevy, this is my best friend from childhood," she says. "This is Shoshana, and this is —"

"Mark," I say.

"Yerucham," Mark says, and sticks out a hand. Trev shakes it. Then Trev sticks out his hand, polite, to Lauren. She looks at it, just hanging there in the air.

"I don't shake," she says. "But I'm so happy to see you. Like meeting my own son. I mean it." And here she starts to cry, and then she and Deb are hugging. And the boys, we just stand there until Mark looks at his watch and gets himself a good manly grip on Trev's shoulder.

"Sleeping until three on a Sunday? Man, those were the days," Mark says. "A regular little Rumpleforeskin." Trev looks at me, and I want to shrug, but Mark's also looking, so I don't move. Trev just gives us both his best teen-age glare and edges out of the room. As he does, he says, "Baseball practice," and takes my car keys off the hook by the door to the garage.

"There's gas," I say.

"They let them drive here at sixteen?" Mark says. "Insane."

"So what brings you here after all these years?" I say.

"My mother," Mark says. "She's failing, and my father's getting old — and they come to us for Sukkot every year. You know?"

"I know the holidays."

"They used to fly out to us. For Sukkot and Pesach, both. But they can't fly now, and I just wanted to get over while things are still good. We haven't been in America—"

"Oh, gosh," Lauren says. "I'm afraid to think how long it's been. More than ten years. Twelve," she says. "With the kids, it's just impossible until enough of them are big."

"How do you do it?" Deb says. "Ten kids? I really do want to hear."

That's when I remember, "I forgot your drink," I say to Mark.

"Yes, his drink. That's how," Lauren says. "That's how we cope."

And that's how the four of us end up back at the kitchen table with a bottle of vodka between us. I'm not one to get drunk on a Sunday afternoon, but, I tell you, when the plan is to spend the day with Mark I jump at the chance. Deb's drinking, too, but not for the same reason. I think she and Lauren are reliving a little bit of the wild times. The very small window when they were together, barely grown up, two young women living in New York on the edge of two worlds.

Deb says, "This is really racy for us. I mean, *really* racy. We try not to drink much at all these days. We think it sets a bad example for Trevor. It's not good to drink in front of them right at this age when they're all transgressive. He's suddenly so interested in that kind of thing."

"I'm just happy when he's interested in something," I say.

Deb slaps at the air, "I just don't think it's good to make drinking look like it's fun with a teen-ager around."

Lauren smiles and straightens her wig. "Does anything we do look fun to our kids?"

I laugh at that. Honestly, I'm liking her more and more.

"It's the age limit that does it," Mark says. "It's the whole American puritanical thing, the twenty-one-year-old drinking age and all that. We don't make a big deal about it in Israel, and so the kids, they don't even notice alcohol. Except for the foreign workers on Fridays, you hardly see anyone drunk at all."

"The workers and the Russians," Lauren says.

"The Russian immigrants," he says, "that's a whole separate matter. Most of them, you know, not even Jews."

"What does that mean?" I say.

"It means matrilineal descent, is what it means," Mark says. "With the Ethiopians there were conversions."

But Deb wants to keep us away from politics, and the way we're arranged, me in between them and Deb opposite (it's a round table, our kitchen table), she practically has to throw herself across to grab hold of my arm. "Fix me another," she says.

And here she switches the subject to Mark's parents. "How's the visit been going?" she says, her face all sombre. "How are your folks holding up?"

Deb is very interested in Mark's parents. They're Holocaust survivors. And Deb has what can only be called an unhealthy obsession with the idea of that generation being gone. Don't get me wrong. It's important to me, too. All I'm saying is there's healthy and unhealthy, and my wife, she gives the subject a *lot* of time.

"What can I say?" Mark says. "My mother's a very sick woman. And my father, he tries to keep his spirits up. He's a tough guy."

"I'm sure," I say. Then I look down at my drink, all serious, and give a shake of my head. "They really are amazing."

"Who?" Mark says. "Fathers?"

I look back up and they're all staring at me. "Survivors," I say, realizing I jumped the gun.

"There's good and bad," Mark says. "Like anyone else."

Lauren says, "The whole of Carmel Lake Village, it's like a D.P. camp with a billiards room."

"One tells the other, and they follow," Mark says, "From Europe to New York, and now, for the end of their lives, again the same place."

"Tell them that crazy story, Yuri," Lauren says.

"Tell us," Deb says.

"So you can picture my father," Mark says. "In the old country, he went to *heder*, had the *peyes* and all that. But in America a classic *galusmonger*. He looks more like you than me. It's not from him that I get this," he says, pointing at his beard. "Shoshana and I —"

"We know," I say.

"So my father. They've got a nice nine-hole course, a driving range, some greens for the practice putting. And my dad's at the clubhouse. I go with him. He wants to work out in the gym, he says. Tells me I should come. Get some exercise. And he tells me" — and here Mark points at his feet, sliding a leg out from under the table so we can see his big black clodhoppers — "'You can't wear those Shabbos shoes on the treadmill. You need the sneakers. You know, sports shoes?' And I tell him, 'I know what sneakers are, I didn't forget my English any more than your Yiddish is gone.' So he says, '*Ah shaynem dank dir in pupik*.' Just to show me who's who."

"Tell them the point," Lauren says.

"He's sitting in the locker room, trying to pull a sock on, which is, at that age, basically the whole workout in itself. It's no quick business. And I see, while I'm waiting, and I can't believe it — I nearly pass out. The guy next to him, the number on his arm, it's three before my father's number. You know, in sequence."

"What do you mean?" Deb says.

"I mean the number tattooed. It's the same as my father's camp number, digit for digit, but my father's ends in an eight. And this guy's, it ends in a five. That's the only difference. I mean, they're separated by two people. So I say, 'Excuse me, sir.' And the guy just says, 'You with the Chabad? I don't want anything but to be left alone. I already got candles at home.' I tell him, 'No. I'm not. I'm here visiting my father.' And to my father I say, 'Do you know this gentleman? Have you two met? I'd really like to introduce you, if you haven't.' And they look each other over for what, I promise you, is minutes. Actual minutes. It is — with *kavod* I say this, with respect for my father — but it is like watching a pair of big beige manatees sitting on a bench, each with one sock on. They're just looking each other up and down, everything slow. And then my father says, 'I seen him. Seen him around.' The other guy, he says, 'Yes, I've seen.' 'You're both survivors,' I tell them. 'Look. The numbers.' And they look. 'They're the same,' I say. And they both hold out their arms to look at the little ashen tattoos. To my father I say, 'Do you get it? The same, except his — it's right ahead of yours. Look! Compare.' So they look. They compare." Mark's eyes are popping out of his head. "Think about it," he says. "Around the world, surviving the un-survivable, these two old guys end up with enough money to retire to Carmel Lake and play golf every day. So I say to my dad, 'He's right ahead of you. Look, a five,' I say. 'And yours is an eight.' And my father says, 'All that means is he cut ahead of me in line. There same as here. This guy's a cutter. I just didn't want to say.' 'Blow it out your ear,' the other guy says. And that's it. Then they get back to putting on socks."

Deb looks crestfallen. She was expecting something empowering. Some story with which to educate Trevor, to reaffirm her belief in the humanity that, from inhumanity, forms.

But me, I love that kind of story. I'm starting to take a real shine to these two, and not just because I'm suddenly feeling sloshed.

"Good story, Yuri," I say, copying his wife. "Yerucham, that one's got zing."

Yerucham hoists himself up from the table, looking proud. He checks the label of our white bread on the counter, making sure it's kosher. He takes a slice, pulls off the crust, and rolls the white part against the countertop with the palm of his hand, making a little ball. He comes over and pours himself a shot and throws it back. Then he eats that crazy dough ball. Just tosses it in his mouth, as if it's the bottom of his own personal punctuation mark — you know, to underline his story.

"Is that good?" I say.

"Try it," he says. He goes to the counter and pitches me a slice of white bread, and says, "But first pour yourself a shot."

I reach for the bottle and find that Deb's got her hands around it, and her head's bowed down, like the bottle is anchoring her, keeping her from tipping back.

"Are you O.K., Deb?" Lauren says.

"It's because it was funny," I say.

"Honey!" Deb says.

"She won't tell you, but she's a little obsessed with the Holocaust. That story — no offense, Mark — it's not what she had in mind."

I should leave it be, I know. But it's not like someone from Deb's high school is around every day offering insights.

"It's like she's a survivor's kid, my wife. It's crazy, that education they give them. Her grandparents were all born in the Bronx, and here we are twenty minutes from downtown Miami but it's like it's 1937 and we live on the edge of Berlin."

"That's not it!" Deb says, openly defensive, her voice super high up in the register. "I'm not upset about that. It's the alcohol. All this alcohol. It's that and seeing Lauren. Seeing Shoshana, after all this time."

"Oh, she was always like this in high school," Shoshana says. "Sneak one drink, and she started to cry. You want to know what used to get her going, what would make her truly happy?" Shoshana says. "It was getting high. That's what always did it. Smoking up. It would make her laugh for hours and hours."

And, I tell you, I didn't see it coming. I'm as blindsided as Deb was by that numbers story.

"Oh, my God," Deb says, and she's pointing as me. "Look at my big bad secular husband. He really can't handle it. He can't handle his wife's having any history of naughtiness at all — Mr. Liberal Open-Minded." To me she says. "How much more chaste a wife can you dream of than a modern-day yeshiva girl who stayed a virgin until twenty-one? Honestly. What did you think Shoshana was going to say was so much fun?"

"Honestly-honestly?" I say. "I don't want to. It's embarrassing."

"Say it!" Deb says, positively glowing.

"Honestly, I thought you were going to say it was something like competing in the Passover Nut Roll, or making sponge cake. Something like that." I hang my head. And Shoshana and Deb are laughing so hard they can't breathe. They're grabbing at each other so that I can't tell if they're holding each other up or pulling each other down.

"I can't believe you told him about the nut roll," Shoshana says.

"And I can't believe," Deb says, "you just told my husband of twenty-two years how much we used to get high. I haven't touched a joint since before we were married," she says. "Have we, honey? Have we smoked since we got married?"

"No," I say. "It's been a very long time."

"So come on, Shosh. When was it? When was the last time you smoked?"

Now, I know I mentioned the beard on Mark. But I don't know if I mentioned how hairy a guy he is. That thing grows right up to his eyeballs. Like having eyebrows on top and bottom both. So when Deb asks the question, the two of them, Shosh and Yuri, are basically giggling like children, and I can tell, in the little part that shows, in the bit of skin I can see, that Mark's eyelids and earlobes are in full blush.

"When Shoshana said we drink to get through the days," Mark says, "she was kidding about the drinking."

"We don't drink much," Shoshana says.

"It's smoking that she means," he says.

"We still get high," Shoshana says. "I mean, all the time."

"Hasidim!" Deb screams. "You're not allowed."

"Everyone does in Israel. It's like the sixties there," Mark says. "It's the highest country in the world. Worse than Holland and India and Thailand put together. Worse than anywhere, even Argentina — though they may have us tied."

"Well, maybe that's why the kids aren't interested in alcohol," I say.

"Do you want to get high now?" Deb says. And we all three look at her. Me, with surprise. And those two with straight longing.

"We didn't bring," Shoshana says. "Though it's pretty rare anyone at customs peeks under the wig."

"Maybe you guys can find your way into the glaucoma underground over at Carmel Lake," I say. "I'm sure that place is rife with it."

"That's funny," Mark says.

"I'm funny," I say, now that we're all getting on.

"We've got pot," Deb says.

"We do?" I say. "I don't think we do."

Deb looks at me and bites at the cuticle on her pinkie.

"You're not secretly getting high all these years?" I say. I really don't feel well at all.

"Our son," Deb says. "He has pot."

"Our son?"

"Trevor," she says.

"Yes," I say. "I know which one."

It's a lot for one day, that kind of news. And it feels to me a lot like betrayal. Like my wife's old secret and my son's new secret are bound up together, and I've somehow been wronged. Also, I'm not one to recover quickly from any kind of slight from Deb — not when there are people around. I really need to talk stuff out. Some time alone, even five minutes, would fix it. But it's super apparent that Deb doesn't need any time alone with me. She doesn't seem troubled at all. What she seems is focussed. She's busy at the counter, using a paper tampon wrapper to roll a joint.

"It's an emergency-preparedness method we came up with in high school," Shoshana says. "The things teen-age girls will do when they're desperate."

"Do you remember that nice boy that we used to smoke in front of?" Deb says. "He'd just watch us. There'd be six or seven of us in a circle, girls and boys not touching — we were so religious. Isn't that crazy?" Deb is talking to me, as Shoshana and Mark don't think it's crazy at all. "The only place we touched was passing the joint, at the thumbs. And this boy, we had a nickname for him."

"Passover!" Shoshana yells.

"Yes," Deb says, "that's it. All we ever called him was Passover. Because every time the joint got to him he'd just pass it over to the next one of us. Passover Rand."

Shoshana takes the joint and lights it with a match, sucking deep. "It's a miracle when I remember anything these days," she says. "After my first was born, I forgot half of everything I knew. And then half again with each one after. Just last night, I woke up in a panic. I couldn't remember if there were fifty-two cards in a deck or fifty-two weeks in a year. The recall errors — I'm up all night worrying over them, just waiting for the Alzheimer's to kick in."

"It's not that bad," Mark tells her. "It's only everyone on one side of your family that has it."

"That's true," she says, passing her husband the joint. "The other side is blessed only with dementia. Anyway, which is it? Weeks or cards?"

"Same, same," Mark says, taking a hit.

When it's Deb's turn, she holds the joint and looks at me, like I'm supposed to nod or give her permission in some husbandly anxiety-absolving way. But instead of saying, "Go ahead," I pretty much bark at Deb. "When were you going to tell me about our son?"

At that, Deb takes a long hit, holding it deep, like an old pro.

"Really, Deb. How could you not tell me you knew?"

Deb walks over and hands me the joint. She blows the smoke in my face, not aggressive, just blowing.

"I've only known five days," she says. "I was going to tell you. I just wasn't sure how, or if I should talk to Trevy first, maybe give him a chance," she says.

"A chance to what?" I ask.

"To let him keep it as a secret between us. To let him know he could have my trust if he promised to stop."

"But he's the son," I say. "I'm the father. Even if it's a secret with him, it should be a double secret between me and you. I should always get to know — even if I pretend not to know — any secret with him."

"Do that double part again," Mark says. But I ignore him.

"That's how it's always been," I say to Deb. And, because I'm desperate and unsure, I follow it up with "Hasn't it?"

I mean, we really trust each other, Deb and I. And I can't remember feeling like so much has hung on one question in a long time. I'm trying to read her face, and something complex is going on, some formulation. And then she sits right there on the floor, at my feet.

"Oh, my God," she says. "I'm so fucking high. Like instantly. Like, like," and then she starts laughing. "Like, Mike," she says. "Like, kike," she says, turning completely serious. "Oh, my God, I'm really messed up."

"We should have warned you," Shoshana says.

As she says this, I'm holding my first hit in, and already trying to fight off the paranoia that comes rushing behind that statement.

"Warned us what?" I say, my voice high, and the smoke still sweet in my nose.

"This isn't your father's marijuana," Mark says. "The THC levels. One hit of this new hydroponic stuff, it's like if maybe you smoked a pound of the stuff we had when we were kids."

"I feel it," I say. And I do. I sit down with Deb on the floor and take her hands. I feel nice. Though I'm not sure if I thought that or said it, so I try it again, making sure it's out loud. "I feel nice," I say.

"I found the pot in the laundry hamper," Deb says. "Leave it to a teen-age boy to think that's the best place to hide something. His clean clothes show up folded in his room, and it never occurs to him that someone empties that hamper. To him, it's the loneliest, most forgotten space in the world. Point is I found an Altoids tin at the bottom, stuffed full." Deb gives my hands a squeeze. "Are we good now?"

"We're good," I say. And it feels like we're a team again, like it's us against them. Because Deb says, "Are you sure you guys are allowed to smoke pot that comes out of a tin that held non-kosher candy? I really don't know if that's O.K." And it's just exactly the kind of thing I'm thinking.

"First of all, we're not eating it. We're smoking it," Shoshana says. "And even so, it's cold contact, so it's probably all right either way."

" 'Cold contact'?" I say.

"It's a thing," Shoshana says. "Just forget about it and get up off the floor. Chop-chop." And they each offer us a hand and get us standing. "Come, sit back at the table," Shoshana says.

"I'll tell you," Mark says. "That's got to be the No. 1 most annoying thing about being Hasidic in the outside world. Worse than the rude stuff that gets said is the constant policing by civilians. Everywhere we go, people are checking on us. Ready to make some sort of liturgical citizen's arrest."

"Strangers!" Shoshana says. "Just the other day, on the way in from the airport. Yuri pulled into a McDonald's to pee, and some guy in a trucker hat came up to him as he went in and said, 'You allowed to go in there, brother?' Just like that."

"Not true!" Deb says.

"It's not that I don't see the fun in that," Mark says. "The allure. You know, we've got Mormons in Jerusalem. They've got a base there. A seminary. The rule is — the deal with the government — they can have their place, but they can't do outreach. No proselytizing. Anyway, I do some business with one of their guys."

"From Utah?" Deb says.

"From Idaho. His name is Jebediah, for real — do you believe it?"

"No, Yerucham and Shoshana," I say. "Jebediah is a very strange name." Mark rolls his eyes at that, handing me what's left of the joint. Without even asking, he gets up and gets the tin and reaches into his wife's purse for another tampon. And I'm a little less comfortable with this than with the white bread, with a guest coming into the house and smoking up all our son's pot. Deb must be thinking something similar, as she says, "After this story, I'm going to text Trev and make sure he's not coming back anytime soon."

"So when Jeb's at our house," Mark says, "when he comes by to eat and pours himself a Coke, I do that same religious-police thing. I can't resist. I say, 'Hey, Jeb, you allowed to have that?' People don't mind breaking their own rules, but they're real strict about someone else's."

"So are they allowed to have Coke?" Deb says.

"I don't know," Mark says. "All Jeb ever says back is 'You're thinking of coffee, and mind your own business, either way.'"

And then my Deb. She just can't help herself. "You heard about the scandal? The Mormons going through the Holocaust list."

"Like in 'Dead Souls,'" I say, explaining. "Like in the Gogol book, but real."

"Do you think we read that?" Mark says. "As Hasidim, or before?"

"They took the records of the dead," Deb says, "and they started running through them. They took these people who died as Jews and started converting them into Mormons. Converting the six million against their will."

"And this is what keeps an American Jew up at night?" Mark says.

"What does that mean?" Deb says.

"It means — " Mark says.

But Shoshana interrupts him. "Don't tell them what it means, Yuri. Just leave it unmeant."

"We can handle it," I say. "We are interested, even, in handling it."

"Your son, he seems like a nice boy."

"Do not talk about their son," Shoshana says.

"Do not talk about our son," Deb says. This time I reach across and lay a hand on her elbow.

"Talk," I say.

"He does not," Mark says, "seem Jewish to me."

"How can you say that?" Deb says. "What is wrong with you?" But Deb's upset draws less attention than my response. I'm laughing so hard that everyone turns toward me.

"What?" Mark says.

"Jewish to you?" I say. "The hat, the beard, the blocky shoes. A lot of pressure, I'd venture, to look Jewish to you. Like, say, maybe Ozzy Osbourne, or the guys from Kiss, like them telling Paul Simon, 'You do not look like a musician to me.'"

"It is not about the outfit," Mark says. "It's about building life in a vacuum. Do you know what I saw on the drive over here? Supermarket, supermarket, adult bookstore, supermarket, supermarket, firing range."

"Floridians do like their guns and porn," I say. "And their supermarkets."

"What I'm trying to say, whether you want to take it seriously or not, is that you can't build Judaism only on the foundation of one terrible crime," Mark says. "It's about this obsession with the Holocaust as a necessary sign of identity. As your only educational tool. Because for the children there is no connection otherwise. Nothing Jewish that binds."

"Wow, that's offensive," Deb says. "And close-minded. There is such a thing as Jewish culture. One can live a culturally rich life."

"Not if it's supposed to be a Jewish life. Judaism is a religion. And with religion comes ritual. Culture is nothing. Culture is some construction of the modern world. It is not fixed; it is ever changing, and a weak way to bind generations. It's like taking two pieces of metal, and instead of making a nice weld you hold them together with glue."

"What does that even mean?" Deb says. "Practically."

Mark raises a finger to make his point, to educate. "In Jerusalem we don't need to busy ourselves with symbolic efforts to keep our memories in place. Because we live exactly as our parents lived before the war. And this serves us in all things, in our relationships, too, in our marriages and parenting."

"Are you saying your marriage is better than ours?" Deb says. "Really? Just because of the rules you live by?"

"I'm saying your husband would not have the long face, worried his wife is keeping secrets. And your son, he would not get into the business of smoking without first coming to you. Because the relationships, they are defined. They are clear."

"Because they are welded together," I say, "and not glued."

"Yes," he says. "And I bet Shoshana agrees." But Shoshana is distracted. She is working carefully with an apple and a knife. She is making a little apple pipe, all the tampons gone.

"Did your daughters?" Deb says. "If they tell you everything, did they come to you first, before they smoked?"

"Our daughters do not have the taint of the world we grew up in. They have no interest in such things."

"So you think," I say.

"So I know," he says. "Our concerns are different, our worries."

"Let's hear 'em," Deb says.

"Let's not," Shoshana says. "Honestly, we're drunk, we're high, we are having a lovely reunion."

"Every time you tell him not to talk," I say, "it makes me want to hear what he's got to say even more."

"Our concern," Mark says, "is not the past Holocaust. It is the current one. The one that takes more than fifty per cent of the Jews of this generation. Our concern is intermarriage. It's the Holocaust that's happening now. You don't need to be worrying about some Mormons doing hocus-pocus on the murdered six million. You need to worry that your son marries a Jew."

"Oh, my God," Deb says. "Are you calling intermarriage a Holocaust?"

"You ask my feeling, that's my feeling. But this, no, it does not exactly apply to you, except in the example you set for the boy. Because you're Jewish, your son, he is as Jewish as me. No more, no less."

"I went to yeshiva, too, Born-Again Harry! You don't need to explain the rules to me."

"Did you just call me 'Born-Again Harry'?" Mark asks.

"I did," Deb says. And she and he, they start to laugh at that. They think 'Born-Again Harry' is the funniest thing they've heard in a while. And Shoshana laughs, and then I laugh, because laughter is infectious — and it is doubly so when you're high.

"You don't really think our family, my lovely, beautiful son, is headed for a Holocaust, do you?" Deb says. "Because that would really cast a pall on this beautiful day."

"No, I don't," Mark says. "It's a lovely house and a lovely family, a beautiful home that you've made for that strapping young man. You're a real *balabusta*," Mark says.

"That makes me happy," Deb says. And she tilts her head nearly ninety degrees to show her happy, sweet smile. "Can I hug you? I'd really like to give you a hug."

"No," Mark says, though he says it really politely. "But you can hug my wife. How about that?"

"That's a great idea," Deb says. Shoshana gets up and hands the loaded apple to me, and I smoke from the apple as the two women hug a tight, deep, dancing back-and-forth hug, tilting this way and that, so, once again, I'm afraid they might fall.

"It is a beautiful day," I say.

"It is," Mark says. And both of us look out the window, and both of us watch the perfect clouds in a perfect sky, so that we're both staring out as the sky suddenly darkens. It is a change so abrupt that the ladies undo their hug to watch.

"It's like that here," Deb says. And the clouds open up and torrential tropical rain drops straight down, battering. It is loud against the roof, and loud against the windows, and the fronds of the palm trees bend, and the floaties in the pool jump as the water boils.

Shoshana goes to the window. And Mark passes Deb the apple and goes to the window. "Really, it's always like this here?" Shoshana says.

"Sure," I say. "Every day. Stops as quick as it starts."

And both of them have their hands pressed up against the window. And they stay like that for some time, and when Mark turns around, harsh guy, tough guy, we see that he is weeping.

"You do not know," he says. "I forget what it's like to live in a place rich with water. This is a blessing above all others."

"If you had what we had," I say.

"Yes," he says, wiping his eyes.

"Can we go out?" Shoshana says. "In the rain?"

"Of course," Deb says. Then Shoshana tells me to close my eyes. Only me. And I swear I think she's going to be stark naked when she calls, "Open up."

She's taken off her wig is all, and she's wearing one of Trev's baseball caps in its place.

"I've only got the one wig this trip," she says. "If Trev won't mind."

"He won't mind," Deb says. And this is how the four of us find ourselves in the back yard, on a searingly hot day, getting pounded by all this cool, cool rain. It's just about the best feeling in the world. And, I have to say, Shoshana looks twenty years younger in that hat.

We do not talk in the rain. We are too busy frolicking and laughing and jumping around. And that's how it happens that I'm holding Mark's hand and sort of dancing, and Deb is holding Shoshana's hand, and they're doing their own kind of jig. And when I take Deb's hand, though neither Mark nor Shoshana is touching the other, somehow we've formed a broken circle. We've started dancing our own kind of hora in the rain.

It is the silliest and freest and most glorious I can remember feeling in years. Who would think that's what I'd be saying with these strict, suffocatingly austere people visiting our house? And then my Deb, my love, once again she is thinking what I'm thinking, and she says, face up into the rain, all of us spinning, "Are you sure this is O.K., Shoshana? That it's not mixed dancing? I don't want anyone feeling bad after."

"We'll be just fine," Shoshana says.

"We will live with the consequences." The question slows us, and stops us, though no one has yet let go.

"It's like the old joke," I say. Without waiting for anyone to ask which one, I say, "Why don't Hasidim have sex standing up?"

"Why?" Shoshana says.

"Because it might lead to mixed dancing."

Deb and Shoshana pretend to be horrified as we let go of hands, as we recognize that the moment is over, the rain disappearing as quickly as it came. Mark stands there staring into the sky, lips pressed tight. "That joke is very, very old," he says. "And mixed dancing makes me think of mixed nuts, and mixed grill, and *insalata mista*. The sound of 'mixed dancing' has made me wildly hungry. And I'm going to panic if the only kosher thing in the house is that loaf of bleached American bread."

"You have the munchies," I say.

"Diagnosis correct," he says.

Deb starts clapping at that, tiny claps, her hands held to her chest in prayer. She says to him, absolutely beaming, "You will not even believe what riches await."

The four of us stand in the pantry, soaking wet, hunting through the shelves and dripping on the floor. "Have you ever seen such a pantry?" Shoshana says, reaching her arms out. "It's gigantic." It is indeed large, and it is indeed stocked, an enormous amount of food, and an enormous selection of sweets, befitting a home that is often host to a swarm of teen-age boys.

"Are you expecting a nuclear winter?" Shoshana says.

"I'll tell you what she's expecting," I say. "You want to know how Holocaust-obsessed she really is? I mean, to what degree?"

"To no degree," Deb says. "We are done with the Holocaust."

"Tell us," Shoshana says.

"She's always plotting our secret hiding place," I say.

"No kidding," Shoshana says.

"Like, look at this. At the pantry, with a bathroom next to it, and the door to the garage. If you sealed it all up — like put drywall at the entrance to the den — you'd never suspect. If you covered that door inside the garage up good with, I don't know — if you hung your tools in front of it and hid hinges behind, maybe leaned the bikes and the mower against it, you'd have this closed area, with running water and a toilet and all this food. I mean, if someone sneaked into the garage to replenish things, you could rent out the house. Put in another family without their having any idea."

"Oh, my God," Shoshana says. "My short-term memory may be gone from having all those children — "

"And from the smoking," I say.

"And from that, too. But I remember from when we were kids," Shoshana says, turning to Deb. "You were always getting me to play games like that. To pick out spaces. And even worse, even darker — "

"Don't," Deb says.

"I know what you're going to say," I tell her, and I'm honestly excited. "The game, yes? She played that crazy game with you?"

"No," Deb says. "Enough. Let it go."

And Mark — who is utterly absorbed in studying kosher certifications, who is tearing through hundred-calorie snack packs and eating handfuls of roasted peanuts, and who has said nothing since we entered the pantry except "What's a Fig Newman?" — he stops and says, "I want to play this game."

"It's not a game," Deb says.

And I'm happy to hear her say that, as it's just what I've been trying to get her to admit for years. That it's not a game. That it's dead serious, and a kind of preparation, and an active pathology that I prefer not to indulge.

"It's the Anne Frank game," Shoshana says. "Right?"

Seeing how upset my wife is, I do my best to defend her. I say, "No, it's not a game. It's just what we talk about when we talk about Anne Frank."

"How do we play this non-game?" Mark says. "What do we do?"

"It's the Righteous Gentile game," Shoshana says.

"It's Who Will Hide Me?" I say.

"In the event of a second Holocaust," Deb says, giving in. "It's a serious exploration, a thought experiment that we engage in."

"That you play," Shoshana says.

"That, in the event of an American Holocaust, we sometimes talk about which of our Christian friends would hide us."

"I don't get it," Marks says.

"Of course you do," Shoshana says. "It's like this. If there was a Shoah, if it happened again — say we were in Jerusalem, and it's 1941 and the Grand Mufti got his way, what would Jebediah do?"

"What could he do?" Mark says.

"He could hide us. He could risk his life and his family's and everyone's around him. That's what the game is: would he — for real — would he do that for you?"

"He'd be good for that, a Mormon," Mark says. "Forget this pantry. They have to keep a year of food stored in case of the Rapture, or something like that. Water, too. A year of supplies. Or maybe it's that they have sex through a sheet. No, wait. I think that's supposed to be us."

"All right," Deb says. "Let's not play. Really, let's go back to the kitchen. I can order in from the glatt kosher place. We can eat outside, have a real dinner and not just junk."

"No, no," Mark says. "I'll play. I'll take it seriously."

"So would the guy hide you?" I say.

"The kids, too?" Mark says. "I'm supposed to pretend that in Jerusalem he's got a hidden motel or something where he can put the twelve of us?"

"Yes," Shoshana says. "In their seminary or something. Sure."

Mark thinks about this for a long, long time. He eats Fig Newmans and considers, and you can tell that he's taking it seriously — serious to the extreme.

"Yes," Mark says, looking choked up. "Jeb would do that for us. He would risk it all."

Shoshana nods. "Now you go," she says to us. "You take a turn."

"But we don't know any of the same people anymore," Deb says. "We usually just talk about the neighbors."

"Our across-the-street neighbors," I tell them. "They're the perfect example. Because the husband, Mitch, he would hide us. I know it. He'd lay down his life for what's right. But that wife of his."

"Yes," Deb says. "Mitch would hide us, but Gloria, she'd buckle. When he was at work one day, she'd turn us in."

"You could play against yourselves," Shoshana says. "What if one of you wasn't Jewish? Would you hide the other?"

"I'll do it," I say. "I'll be the Gentile, because I could pass best. A grown woman with an ankle-length denim skirt in her closet — they'd catch you in a flash."

"Fine," Deb says. And I stand up straight, put my shoulders back, like maybe I'm in a lineup. I stand there with my chin raised so my wife can study me. So she can decide if her husband really has what it takes. Would I have the strength, would I care enough — and it is not a light question, not a throwaway question — to risk my life to save her and our son?

Deb stares, and Deb smiles, and gives me a little push to my chest. "Of course he would," Deb says. She takes the half stride that's between us and gives me a tight hug that she doesn't release. "Now you," Deb says. "You and Yuri go."

"How does that even make sense?"Mark says. "Even for imagining."

"Sh-h-h," Shoshana says. "Just stand over there and be a good Gentile while I look."

"But if I weren't Jewish I wouldn't be me."

"That's for sure," I say.

"He agrees," Mark says. "We wouldn't even be married. We wouldn't have kids."

"Of course you can imagine it," Shoshana says. "Look," she says, and goes over and closes the pantry door. "Here we are, caught in South Florida for the second Holocaust. You're not Jewish, and you've got the three of us hiding in your pantry."

"But look at me!" he says.

"I've got a fix," I say. "You're a background singer for ZZ Top. You know that band?"

Deb lets go of me so she can give my arm a slap.

"Really," Shoshana says. "Look at the three of us like it's your house and we're your charges, locked up in this room."

"And what're you going to do while I do that?" Mark says.

"I'm going to look at you looking at us. I'm going to imagine."

"O.K.," he says, "*Nu*, get to it. I will stand, you imagine."

And that's what we do, the four of us. We stand there playing our roles, and we really get into it. I can see Deb seeing him, and him seeing us, and Shoshana just staring at her husband.

We stand there so long I can't tell how much time has passed, though the light changes ever so slightly — the sun outside again dimming — in the crack under the pantry door.

"So would I hide you?" he says. And for the first time that day he reaches out, as my Deb would, and puts his hand to his wife's hand. "Would I, Shoshi?"

And you can tell that Shoshana is thinking of her kids, though that's not part of the scenario. You can tell that she's changed part of the imagining. And she says, after a pause, yes, but she's not laughing. She says yes, but to him it sounds as it does to us, so that he is now asking and asking. But wouldn't I? Wouldn't I hide you? Even if it was life and death — if it would spare you, and they'd kill me alone for doing it? Wouldn't I?

Shoshana pulls back her hand.

She does not say it. And he does not say it. And of the four of us no one will say what cannot be said — that this wife believes her husband would not hide her. What to do? What will come of it? And so we stand like that, the four of us trapped in that pantry. Afraid to open the door and let out what we've locked inside.

Louise Erdrich

Louise Erdrich (b. 1954) is of German and Chippewa Indian descent. She grew up in Wahpeton, North Dakota, as a member of the Turtle Mountain Band of Chippewa. For many years her grandfather was tribal chair of the reservation. At Dartmouth College, Erdrich won several prizes for her fiction and poetry, including the American Academy of Poets Prize. After graduating in 1976, she returned to North Dakota, where she taught in the Poetry in the Schools Program. In 1979 she received her M.A. in creative writing from Johns Hopkins University. During her marriage to the late Michael Dorris, a professor of Native American studies at Dartmouth College, they collaborated on the novel *The Crown of Columbus* (1992).

Erdrich has been an editor of the Boston Indian Council newspaper, *The Circle*. Her stories have appeared in *Redbook*, the *New England Review*, the *Mississippi Valley Review*, and the anthologies *Earth Power Coming* and *That's What She Said*. In 1984 a collection of her poetry, *Jacklight*, was published and her first work of fiction, *Love Medicine*, won the National Book Critics Circle Award. Several of her later novels—including *The Beet Queen* (1986), *Tracks* (1988), *The Bingo Palace* (1994), and *Tales of Burning Love* (1996)—involve other generations of the families in *Love Medicine*. She is also the author of many recent novels as well as *The Red Convertible: Collected and New Stories, 1978–2008* (2009).

"The Red Convertible" is a chapter from *Love Medicine*. Each chapter is a self-enclosed narrative that also functions as a separate short story about the lives of two families, the Kashpaws and the Lamartines, on a North Dakota reservation between 1934 and 1984. "The Red Convertible" takes place in 1974 and is narrated by Lyman Lamartine.

Erdrich's work has won praise for its psychological depth and its literary excellence; it is a landmark achievement in its depiction of the lives of contemporary Native Americans. As the novelist Peter Matthiessen has recognized, *Love Medicine* is "quick with agile prose, taut speech, poetry, and power, conveying unflinchingly the funkiness, humor, and great unspoken sadness of the Indian reservations, and a people exiled to a no-man's-land between two worlds."

The Red Convertible

1984

Lyman Lamartine

I WAS THE FIRST ONE to drive a convertible on my reservation. And of course it was red, a red Olds. I owned that car along with my brother Henry Junior. We owned it together until his boots filled with water on a windy night and he bought out my share. Now Henry owns the whole car, and his younger brother Lyman (that's myself), Lyman walks everywhere he goes.

How did I earn enough money to buy my share in the first place? My own talent was I could always make money. I had a touch for it, unusual in a Chippewa. From the first I was different that way, and everyone recognized it. I was the only kid they let in the American Legion Hall to shine shoes, for example, and one Christmas I sold spiritual bouquets for the mission door to door. The nuns let me keep a percentage. Once I started, it seemed the more money I made the easier the money came. Everyone encouraged it. When I was fifteen I got a job washing dishes at the Joliet Café, and that was where my first big break happened.

It wasn't long before I was promoted to busing tables, and then the short-order cook quit and I was hired to take her place. No sooner than you know it I was managing the Joliet. The rest is history. I went on managing. I soon became part owner, and of course there was no stopping me then. It wasn't long before the whole thing was mine.

After I'd owned the Joliet for one year, it blew over in the worst tornado ever seen around here. The whole operation was smashed to bits. A total loss. The fryalator was up in a tree, the grill torn in half like it was paper. I was only sixteen. I had it all in my mother's name, and I lost it quick, but before I lost it I had every one of my relatives, and their relatives, to dinner, and I also bought that red Olds I mentioned, along with Henry.

The first time we saw it! I'll tell you when we first saw it. We had gotten a ride up to Winnipeg, and both of us had money. Don't ask me why, because we never mentioned a car or anything, we just had all our money. Mine was cash, a big bankroll from the Joliet's insurance. Henry had two checks — a week's extra pay for being laid off, and his regular check from the Jewel Bearing Plant.

We were walking down Portage anyway, seeing the sights, when we saw it. There it was, parked, large as life. Really as if it was alive. I thought of the word *repose*, because the car wasn't simply stopped, parked, or whatever. That car reposed, calm and gleaming, a for sale sign in its left front window. Then, before we had thought it over at all, the car belonged to us and our pockets were empty. We had just enough money for gas back home.

We went places in that car, me and Henry. We took off driving all one whole summer. We started off toward the Little Knife River and Mandaree in Fort Berthold and then we found ourselves down in Wakpala somehow, and then suddenly we were over in Montana on the Rocky Boy, and yet the summer was not even half over. Some people hang on to details when they travel, but we didn't let them bother us and just lived our everyday lives here to there.

I do remember this one place with willows. I remember I laid under those trees and it was comfortable. So comfortable. The branches bent down all around me like a tent or a stable. And quiet, it was quiet, even though there was a powwow close enough so I could see it going on. The air was not too still, not too windy either. When the dust rises up and hangs in the air around the dancers like that, I feel good. Henry was asleep with his arms thrown wide. Later on, he woke up and we started driving again. We were somewhere in Montana, or maybe on the Blood Reserve—it could have been anywhere. Anyway it was where we met the girl.

All her hair was in buns around her ears, that's the first thing I noticed about her. She was posed alongside the road with her arm out, so we stopped. That girl was short, so short her lumber shirt looked comical on her, like a nightgown. She had jeans on and fancy moccasins and she carried a little suitcase.

"Hop on in," says Henry. So she climbs in between us.

"We'll take you home," I says. "Where do you live?"

"Chicken," she says.

"Where the hell's that?" I ask her.

"Alaska."

"Okay," says Henry, and we drive.

We got up there and never wanted to leave. The sun doesn't truly set there in summer, and the night is more a soft dusk. You might doze off, sometimes, but before you know it you're up again, like an animal in nature. You never feel like you have to sleep hard or put away the world. And things would grow up there. One day just dirt or moss, the next day flowers and long grass. The girl's name was Susy. Her family really took to us. They fed us and put us up. We had our own tent to live in by their house, and the kids would be in and out of there all day and night. They couldn't get over me and Henry being brothers, we looked so different. We told them we knew we had the same mother, anyway.

One night Susy came in to visit us. We sat around in the tent talking of this and that. The season was changing. It was getting darker by that time, and the cold was even getting just a little mean. I told her it was time for us to go. She stood up on a chair.

"You never seen my hair," Susy said.

That was true. She was standing on a chair, but still, when she unclipped her buns the hair reached all the way to the ground. Our eyes opened. You couldn't tell how much hair she had when it was rolled up so neatly. Then my brother Henry did something funny. He went up to the chair and said, "Jump on my shoulders." So she did that, and her hair reached down past his waist, and he started twirling, this way and that, so her hair was flung out from side to side.

"I always wondered what it was like to have long pretty hair," Henry says. Well we laughed. It was a funny sight, the way he did it. The next morning we got up and took leave of those people.

On to greener pastures, as they say. It was down through Spokane and across Idaho then Montana and very soon we were racing the weather right along under the Canadian border through Columbus, Des Lacs, and then we were in Bottineau County and soon home. We'd made most of the trip, that summer, without putting up the car hood at all. We got home just in time, it turned out, for the army to remember Henry had signed up to join it.

I don't wonder that the army was so glad to get my brother that they turned him into a Marine. He was built like a brick outhouse anyway. We liked to tease him that they really wanted him for his Indian nose. He had a nose big and sharp as a hatchet, like the nose on Red Tomahawk, the Indian who killed Sitting Bull, whose profile is on signs all along the North Dakota highways. Henry went off to training camp, came home once during Christmas, then the next thing you know we got an overseas letter from him. It was 1970, and he said he was stationed up in the northern hill country. Whereabouts I did not know. He wasn't such a hot letter writer, and only got off two before the enemy caught him. I could never keep it straight, which direction those good Vietnam soldiers were from.

I wrote him back several times, even though I didn't know if those letters would get through. I kept him informed all about the car. Most of the time I had it up on blocks in the yard or half taken apart, because that long trip did a hard job on it under the hood.

I always had good luck with numbers, and never worried about the draft myself. I never even had to think about what my number was. But Henry was never lucky in the same way as me. It was at least three years before Henry came home. By then I guess the whole war was solved in the government's mind, but for him it would keep on going. In those years I'd put his car into almost perfect shape. I always thought of it as his car while he was gone, even though when he left he said, "Now it's yours," and threw me his key.

"Thanks for the extra key," I'd said. "I'll put it up in your drawer just in case I need it." He laughed.

When he came home, though, Henry was very different, and I'll say this: the change was no good. You could hardly expect him to change for the better, I know. But he was quiet, so quiet, and never comfortable sitting still anywhere but always up and moving around. I thought back to times we'd sat still for whole afternoons, never moving a muscle, just shifting our weight along the ground, talking to whoever sat with us, watching things. He'd always had a joke, then, too, and now you couldn't get him to laugh, or when he did it was more the sound of a man choking, a sound that stopped up the throats of other people around him. They got to leaving him alone most of the time, and I didn't blame them. It was a fact: Henry was jumpy and mean.

I'd bought a color TV set for my mom and the rest of us while Henry was away. Money still came very easy. I was sorry I'd ever bought it though, because of Henry. I was also sorry I'd bought color, because with black-and-white the pictures seem older and farther away. But what are you going to do? He sat in front of it, watching it, and that was the only time he was completely still. But it was the kind of stillness that you see in a rabbit when it freezes and before it will bolt. He was not easy. He sat in his chair gripping the armrests with all his might, as if the chair itself was moving at a high speed and if he let go at all he would rocket forward and maybe crash right through the set.

Once I was in the room watching TV with Henry and I heard his teeth click at something. I looked over, and he'd bitten through his lip. Blood was going down his chin. I tell you right then I wanted to smash that tube to pieces. I went over to it but Henry must have known what I was up to. He rushed from his chair and shoved me out of the way, against the wall. I told myself he didn't know what he was doing.

My mom came in, turned the set off real quiet, and told us she had made something for supper. So we went and sat down. There was still blood going down Henry's chin, but he didn't notice it and no one said anything, even though every time he took a bite of his bread his blood fell onto it until he was eating his own blood mixed in with the food.

While Henry was not around we talked about what was going to happen to him. There were no Indian doctors on the reservation, and my mom was afraid of trusting the old man, Moses Pillager, because he courted her long ago and was jealous of her husband. He might take revenge through her son. We were afraid that if we brought Henry to a regular hospital they would keep him.

"They don't fix them in those places," Mom said; "they just give them drugs."

"We wouldn't get him there in the first place," I agreed, "so let's just forget about it."

Then I thought about the car.

Henry had not even looked at the car since he'd gotten home, though like I said, it was in tip-top condition and ready to drive. I thought the car might bring the old Henry back somehow. So I bided my time and waited for my chance to interest him in the vehicle.

One night Henry was off somewhere. I took myself a hammer. I went out to that car and I did a number on its underside. Whacked it up. Bent the tail pipe double. Ripped the muffler loose. By the time I was done with the car it looked worse than any typical Indian car that has been driven all its life on reservation roads, which they always say are like government promises — full of holes. It just about hurt me, I'll tell you that! I threw dirt in the carburetor and I ripped all the electric tape off the seats. I made it look just as beat up as I could. Then I sat back and waited for Henry to find it.

Still, it took him over a month. That was all right, because it was just getting warm enough, not melting, but warm enough to work outside.

"Lyman," he says, walking in one day, "that red car looks like shit."

"Well it's old," I says. "You got to expect that."

"No way!" says Henry. "That car's a classic! But you went and ran the piss right out of it, Lyman, and you know it don't deserve that. I kept that car in A-one shape. You don't remember. You're too young. But when I left, that car was running like a watch. Now I don't even know if I can get it to start again, let alone get it anywhere near its old condition."

"Well you try," I said, like I was getting mad, "but I say it's a piece of junk."

Then I walked out before he could realize I knew he'd strung together more than six words at once.

After that I thought he'd freeze himself to death working on that car. He was out there all day, and at night he rigged up a little lamp, ran a cord out the window, and had himself some light to see by while he worked. He was better than he had been before, but that's still not saying much. It was easier for him to do the things the rest of us did. He ate more slowly and didn't jump up and down during the meal to get this or that or look out the window. I put my hand in the back of the TV set, I admit, and fiddled around with it good, so that it was almost impossible now to get a clear picture. He didn't look at it very often anyway. He was always out with that car or going off to get parts for it. By the time it was really melting outside, he had it fixed.

I had been feeling down in the dumps about Henry around this time. We had always been together before. Henry and Lyman. But he was such a loner now that I didn't know how to take it. So I jumped at the chance one day when Henry seemed friendly. It's not that he smiled or anything. He just said, "Let's take that old shitbox for a spin." Just the way he said it made me think he could be coming around.

We went out to the car. It was spring. The sun was shining very bright. My only sister, Bonita, who was just eleven years old, came out and made us stand together for a picture. Henry leaned his elbow on the red car's windshield, and he took his other arm and put it over my shoulder, very carefully, as though it was heavy for him to lift and he didn't want to bring the weight down all at once.

"Smile," Bonita said, and he did.

That picture, I never look at it anymore. A few months ago, I don't know why, I got his picture out and tacked it on the wall. I felt good about Henry at the time, close to him. I felt good having his picture on the wall, until one night when I was looking at television. I was a little drunk and stoned. I looked up at the wall and Henry was staring at me. I don't know what it was, but his smile had changed, or maybe it was gone. All I know is I couldn't stay in the same room with that picture. I was shaking. I got up, closed the door, and went into the kitchen. A little later my friend Ray came over and we both went back into that room. We put the picture in a brown bag, folded the bag over and over tightly, then put it way back in a closet.

I still see that picture now, as if it tugs at me, whenever I pass that closet door. The picture is very clear in my mind. It was so sunny that day Henry had to squint against the glare. Or maybe the camera Bonita held flashed like a mirror, blinding him, before she snapped the picture. My face is right out in the sun, big and round. But he might have drawn back, because the shadows on his face are deep as holes. There are two shadows curved like little hooks around the ends of his smile, as if to frame it and try to keep it there — that one, first smile that looked like it might have hurt his face. He has his field jacket on and the worn-in clothes he'd come back in and kept wearing ever since. After Bonita took the picture, she went into the house and we got into the car. There was a full cooler in the trunk. We started off, east, toward Pembina and the Red River because Henry said he wanted to see the high water.

The trip over there was beautiful. When everything starts changing, drying up, clearing off, you feel like your whole life is starting. Henry felt it, too. The top was down and the car hummed like a top. He'd really put it back in shape, even the tape on the seats was very carefully put down and glued back in layers. It's not that he smiled again or even joked, but his face looked to me as if it was clear, more peaceful. It looked as though he wasn't thinking of anything in particular except the bare fields and windbreaks and houses we were passing.

The river was high and full of winter trash when we got there. The sun was still out, but it was colder by the river. There were still little clumps of dirty snow here and there on the banks. The water hadn't gone over the banks yet, but it would, you could tell. It was just at its limit, hard swollen glossy like an old gray scar. We made ourselves a fire, and we sat down and watched the current go. As I watched it I felt something squeezing inside me and tightening and trying to let go all at the same time. I knew I was not just feeling it myself; I knew I was feeling what Henry was going through at that moment. Except that I couldn't stand it, the closing and opening. I jumped to my feet. I took Henry by the shoulders and I started shaking him. "Wake up," I says, "wake up, wake up, wake up!" I didn't know what had come over me. I sat down beside him again.

His face was totally white and hard. Then it broke, like stones break all of a sudden when water boils up inside them.

"I know it," he says. "I know it. I can't help it. It's no use."

We start talking. He said he knew what I'd done with the car. It was obvious it had been whacked out of shape and not just neglected. He said he wanted to give the car to me for good now, it was no use. He said he'd fixed it just to give it back and I should take it.

"No way," I says, "I don't want it."

"That's okay," he says, "you take it."

"I don't want it, though," I says back to him, and then to emphasize, just to emphasize, you understand, I touch his shoulder. He slaps my hand off.

"Take that car," he says.

"No," I say. "Make me," I say, and then he grabs my jacket and rips the arm loose. That jacket is a class act, suede with tags and zippers. I push Henry backwards, off the log. He jumps up and bowls me over. We go down in a clinch and come up swinging hard, for all we're worth, with our fists. He socks my jaw so hard I feel like it swings loose. Then I'm at his rib cage and land a good one under his chin so his head snaps back. He's dazzled. He looks at me and I look at him and then his eyes are full of tears and blood and at first I think he's crying. But no, he's laughing. "Ha! Ha!" he says. "Ha! Ha! Take good care of it."

"Okay," I says, "okay, no problem. Ha! Ha!"

I can't help it, and I start laughing, too. My face feels fat and strange, and after a while I get a beer from the cooler in the trunk, and when I hand it to Henry he takes his shirt and wipes my germs off. "Hoof-and-mouth disease," he says. For some reason this cracks me up, and so we're really laughing for a while, and then we drink all the rest of the beers one by one and throw them in the river and see how far, how fast, the current takes them before they fill up and sink.

"You want to go on back?" I ask after a while. "Maybe we could snag a couple nice Kashpaw girls."

He says nothing. But I can tell his mood is turning again.

"They're all crazy, the girls up here, every damn one of them."

"You're crazy too," I say, to jolly him up. "Crazy Lamartine boys!"

He looks as though he will take this wrong at first. His face twists, then clears, and he jumps up on his feet. "That's right!" he says. "Crazier 'n hell. Crazy Indians!"

I think it's the old Henry again. He throws off his jacket and starts swinging his legs out from the knees like a fancy dancer. He's down doing something between a grass dance and a bunny hop, no kind of dance I ever saw before, but neither has anyone else on all this green growing earth. He's wild. He wants to pitch whoopee! He's up and at me and all over. All this time I'm laughing so hard, so hard my belly is getting tied up in a knot.

"Got to cool me off!" he shouts all of a sudden. Then he runs over to the river and jumps in.

There's boards and other things in the current. It's so high. No sound comes from the river after the splash he makes, so I run right over. I look around. It's getting dark. I see he's halfway across the water already, and I know he didn't swim there but the current took him. It's far. I hear his voice, though, very clearly across it.

"My boots are filling," he says.

He says this in a normal voice, like he just noticed and he doesn't know what to think of it. Then he's gone. A branch comes by. Another branch. And I go in.

By the time I get out of the river, off the snag I pulled myself onto, the sun is down. I walk back to the car, turn on the high beams, and drive it up the bank. I put it in first gear and then I take my foot off the clutch. I get out, close the door, and watch it plow softly into the water. The headlights reach in as they go down, searching, still lighted even after the water swirls over the back end. I wait. The wires short out. It is all finally dark. And then there is only the water, the sound of it going and running and going and running and running.

William Faulkner

William Faulkner (1897–1962) was born in New Albany, Mississippi, into an old southern family. When he was a child, his parents moved to the isolated town of Oxford, Mississippi, and except for his service in World War I and some time in New Orleans and Hollywood, he spent the rest of his life there. "I discovered my own little postage stamp of native soil was worth writing about, and that I would never live long enough to exhaust it." His literary career began in New Orleans, where he lived for six months and wrote newspaper sketches and stories for the *Times-Picayune*. He met Sherwood Anderson in New Orleans, and Anderson helped him publish his first novel, *Soldier's Pay*, in 1926. Faulkner's major work was written in the late 1920s and the 1930s, when he created an imaginary county adjacent to Oxford, calling it Yoknapatawpha County and chronicling its history in a series of experimental novels, including *The Sound and the Fury* (1929), *As I Lay Dying* (1930), *Sanctuary* (1931), *Light in August* (1932), *Absalom, Absalom!* (1936), and *The Hamlet* (1940). In these works he showed himself to be a writer of genius, although "a willfully and perversely chaotic one," as Jorge Luis Borges noted, whose "labyrinthine world" required a no less labyrinthine prose technique to describe in epic manner the disintegration of the South through many generations. Faulkner was awarded the Nobel Prize for literature in 1952.

Faulkner experimented with using a child's point of view in "That Evening Sun," but he rarely included poetic imagery or stream-of-consciousness narration in his stories, which he wrote, he often said, to help him pay his rent. His biographer Frederick Karl noted that he used short fiction "as a means of working through, or toward, larger ideas." He wrote nearly a hundred stories, often revising them later to fit as sections into a novel. Four books of his stories were published in his lifetime, and Faulkner thought of each as a collection possessing a discernible internal organization. He wrote his editor Malcolm Cowley that "even to a collection of short stories, form, integration, is as important as to a novel—an entity of its own, single, set for one pitch, contrapuntal in integration, toward one end, one finale."

Although some readers found symbolism in "A Rose for Emily" that suggested he was implying a battle between the white characters in the South (Miss Emily herself) and in the North (Homer Barron), Faulkner denied a schematic interpretation. He said he had intended to write a ghost story, and "I think that the writer is too busy trying to create flesh-and-blood people that will stand up and cast a shadow to have time to be conscious of all the symbolism that he may put into what he does or what people may read into it."

RELATED COMMENTARY
William Faulkner, "The Meaning of 'A Rose for Emily,'" page 1424.

A Rose for Emily

1931

I

When Miss Emily Grierson died, our whole town went to her funeral: the men through a sort of respectful affection for a fallen monument, the women mostly out of curiosity to see the inside of her house, which no one save an old manservant — a combined gardener and cook — had seen in at least ten years.

It was a big, squarish frame house that had once been white, decorated with cupolas and spires and scrolled balconies in the heavily lightsome style of the seventies, set on what had once been our most select street. But garages and cotton gins had encroached and obliterated even the august names of that neighborhood; only Miss Emily's house was left, lifting its stubborn and coquettish decay above the cotton wagons and the gasoline pumps — an eyesore among eyesores. And now Miss Emily had gone to join the representatives of those august names where they lay in the cedar-bemused cemetery among the ranked and anonymous graves of Union and Confederate soldiers who fell at the battle of Jefferson.

Alive, Miss Emily had been a tradition, a duty, and a care; a sort of hereditary obligation upon the town, dating from that day in 1894 when Colonel Sartoris, the mayor — he who fathered the edict that no Negro woman should appear on the streets without an apron — remitted her taxes, the dispensation dating from the death of her father on into perpetuity. Not that Miss Emily would have accepted charity. Colonel Sartoris invented an involved tale to the effect that Miss Emily's father had loaned money to the town, which the town, as a matter of business, preferred this way of repaying. Only a man of Colonel Sartoris' generation and thought could have invented it, and only a woman could have believed it.

When the next generation, with its more modern ideas, became mayors and aldermen, this arrangement created some little dissatisfaction. On the first of the year they mailed her a tax notice. February came, and there was no reply. They wrote her a formal letter, asking her to call at the sheriff's office at her convenience. A week later the mayor wrote her himself, offering to call or to send his car for her, and received in reply a note on paper of an archaic shape, in a thin, flowing calligraphy in faded ink, to the effect that she no longer went out at all. The tax notice was also enclosed, without comment.

They called a special meeting of the Board of Aldermen. A deputation waited upon her, knocked at the door through which no visitor had passed since she ceased giving china-painting lessons eight or ten years earlier. They were admitted by the old Negro into a dim hall from which a stairway mounted into still more shadow. It smelled of dust and disuse — a close, dank smell. The Negro led them into the parlor. It was furnished in heavy, leather-covered furniture. When the Negro opened the blinds of one window, they could see that the leather was cracked; and when they sat down, a faint dust rose sluggishly about their thighs, spinning with slow motes in the single sun-ray. On a tarnished gilt easel before the fireplace stood a crayon portrait of Miss Emily's father.

They rose when she entered — a small, fat woman in black, with a thin gold chain descending to her waist and vanishing into her belt, leaning on an ebony cane with a tarnished gold head. Her skeleton was small and spare; perhaps that was why what would have been merely plumpness in another was obesity in her. She looked bloated, like a body long submerged in motionless water, and of that pallid hue. Her eyes, lost in the fatty ridges of her face, looked like two small pieces of coal pressed into a lump of dough as they moved from one face to another while the visitors stated their errand.

She did not ask them to sit. She just stood in the door and listened quietly until the spokesman came to a stumbling halt. Then they could hear the invisible watch ticking at the end of the gold chain.

Her voice was dry and cold. "I have no taxes in Jefferson. Colonel Sartoris explained it to me. Perhaps one of you can gain access to the city records and satisfy yourselves."

"But we have. We are the city authorities, Miss Emily. Didn't you get a notice from the sheriff, signed by him?"

"I received a paper, yes," Miss Emily said. "Perhaps he considers himself the sheriff. . . . I have no taxes in Jefferson."

"But there is nothing on the books to show that, you see. We must go by the —"

"See Colonel Sartoris. I have no taxes in Jefferson."

"But, Miss Emily —"

"See Colonel Sartoris." (Colonel Sartoris had been dead almost ten years.) "I have no taxes in Jefferson. Tobe!" The Negro appeared. "Show these gentlemen out."

II

So she vanquished them, horse and foot, just as she had vanquished their fathers thirty years before about the smell. That was two years after her father's death and a short time after her sweetheart — the one we believed would marry her — had deserted her. After her father's death she went out very little; after her sweetheart went away, people hardly saw her at all. A few of the ladies had the temerity to call, but were not received, and the only sign of life about the place was the Negro man — a young man then — going in and out with a market basket.

"Just as if a man — any man — could keep a kitchen properly," the ladies said; so they were not surprised when the smell developed. It was another link between the gross, teeming world and the high and mighty Griersons.

A neighbor, a woman, complained to the mayor, Judge Stevens, eighty years old.

"But what will you have me do about it, madam?" he said.

"Why, send her word to stop it," the woman said. "Isn't there a law?"

"I'm sure that won't be necessary," Judge Stevens said. "It's probably just a snake or a rat that nigger of hers killed in the yard. I'll speak to him about it."

The next day he received two more complaints, one from a man who came in diffident deprecation. "We really must do something about it, Judge. I'd be the last one in the world to bother Miss Emily, but we've got to do something." That night the Board of Aldermen met — three graybeards and one younger man, a member of the rising generation.

"It's simple enough," he said. "Send her word to have her place cleaned up. Give her a certain time to do it in, and if she don't. . . ."

"Dammit, sir," Judge Stevens said, "will you accuse a lady to her face of smelling bad?"

So the next night, after midnight, four men crossed Miss Emily's lawn and slunk about the house like burglars, sniffing along the base of the brickwork and at the cellar openings while one of them performed a regular sowing motion with his hand out of a sack slung from his shoulder. They broke open the cellar door and sprinkled lime there, and in all the outbuildings. As they recrossed the lawn, a window that had been dark was lighted and Miss Emily sat in it, the light behind her, and her upright torso motionless as that of an idol. They crept quietly across the lawn and into the shadow of the locusts that lined the street. After a week or two the smell went away.

That was when people had begun to feel really sorry for her. People in our town, remembering how old lady Wyatt, her great-aunt, had gone completely crazy at last, believed that the Griersons held themselves a little too high for what they really were. None of the young men were quite good enough for Miss Emily and such. We had long thought of them as a tableau, Miss Emily a slender figure in white in the background, her father a spraddled silhouette in the foreground, his back to her and clutching a horsewhip, the two of them framed by the back-flung front door. So when she got to be thirty and was still single, we were not pleased exactly, but vindicated; even with insanity in the family she wouldn't have turned down all of her chances if they had really materialized.

When her father died, it got about that the house was all that was left to her; and in a way, people were glad. At last they could pity Miss Emily. Being left alone, and a pauper, she had become humanized. Now she too would know the old thrill and the old despair of a penny more or less.

The day after his death all the ladies prepared to call at the house and offer condolence and aid, as is our custom. Miss Emily met them at the door, dressed as usual and with no trace of grief on her face. She told them that her father was not dead. She did that for three days, with the ministers calling on her, and the doctors, trying to persuade her to let them dispose of the body. Just as they were about to resort to law and force, she broke down, and they buried her father quickly.

We did not say she was crazy then. We believed she had to do that. We remembered all the young men her father had driven away, and we knew that with nothing left, she would have to cling to that which had robbed her, as people will.

III

She was sick for a long time. When we saw her again, her hair was cut short, making her look like a girl, with a vague resemblance to those angels in colored church windows — sort of tragic and serene.

The town had just let the contracts for paving the sidewalks, and in the summer after her father's death they began the work. The construction company came with niggers and mules and machinery, and a foreman named Homer Barron, a Yankee—a big, dark, ready man, with a big voice and eyes lighter than his face. The little boys would follow in groups to hear him cuss the niggers, and the niggers singing in time to the rise and fall of picks. Pretty soon he knew everybody in town. Whenever you heard a lot of laughing anywhere about the square, Homer Barron would be in the center of the group. Presently, we began to see him and Miss Emily on Sunday afternoons driving in the yellow-wheeled buggy and the matched team of bays from the livery stable.

At first we were glad that Miss Emily would have an interest, because the ladies all said, "Of course a Grierson would not think seriously of a Northerner, a day laborer." But there were still others, older people, who said that even grief could not cause a real lady to forget *noblesse oblige*—without calling it *noblesse oblige*. They just said, "Poor Emily. Her kinsfolk should come to her." She had some kin in Alabama; but years ago her father had fallen out with them over the estate of old lady Wyatt, the crazy woman, and there was no communication between the two families. They had not even been represented at the funeral.

And as soon as the old people said, "Poor Emily," the whispering began. "Do you suppose it's really so?" they said to one another. "Of course it is. What else could. . . ." This behind their hands; rustling of craned silk and satin behind jalousies closed upon the sun of Sunday afternoon as the thin, swift clop-clop-clop of the matched team passed: "Poor Emily."

She carried her head high enough—even when we believed that she was fallen. It was as if she demanded more than ever the recognition of her dignity as the last Grierson; as if it had wanted that touch of earthiness to reaffirm her imperviousness. Like when she bought the rat poison, the arsenic. That was over a year after they had begun to say "Poor Emily," and while the two female cousins were visiting her.

"I want some poison," she said to the druggist. She was over thirty then, still a slight woman, though thinner than usual, with cold, haughty black eyes in a face the flesh of which was strained across the temples and about the eye-sockets as you imagine a lighthouse-keeper's face ought to look. "I want some poison," she said.

"Yes, Miss Emily. What kind? For rats and such? I'd recom ——"

"I want the best you have. I don't care what kind."

The druggist named several. "They'll kill anything up to an elephant. But what you want is ——"

"Arsenic," Miss Emily said. "Is that a good one?"

"Is . . . arsenic? Yes, ma'am. But what you want ——"

"I want arsenic."

The druggist looked down at her. She looked back at him, erect, her face like a strained flag. "Why, of course," the druggist said. "If that's what you want. But the law requires you to tell what you are going to use it for."

Miss Emily just stared at him, her head tilted back in order to look him eye for eye, until he looked away and went and got the arsenic and wrapped it up. The Negro delivery boy brought her the package; the druggist didn't come back. When she opened the package at home there was written on the box, under the skull and bones: "For rats."

IV

So the next day we all said, "She will kill herself"; and we said it would be the best thing. When she had first begun to be seen with Homer Barron, we had said, "She will marry him." Then we said, "She will persuade him yet," because Homer himself had remarked — he liked men, and it was known that he drank with the younger men in the Elks' Club — that he was not a marrying man. Later we said, "Poor Emily" behind the jalousies as they passed on Sunday afternoon in the glittering buggy, Miss Emily with her head high and Homer Barron with his hat cocked and a cigar in his teeth, reins and whip in a yellow glove.

Then some of the ladies began to say that it was a disgrace to the town and a bad example to the young people. The men did not want to interfere, but at last the ladies forced the Baptist minister — Miss Emily's people were Episcopal — to call upon her. He would never divulge what happened during that interview, but he refused to go back again. The next Sunday they again drove about the streets, and the following day the minister's wife wrote to Miss Emily's relations in Alabama.

So she had blood-kin under her roof again and we sat back to watch developments. At first nothing happened. Then we were sure that they were to be married. We learned that Miss Emily had been to the jeweler's and ordered a man's toilet set in silver, with the letters H.B. on each piece. Two days later we learned that she had bought a complete outfit of men's clothing, including a nightshirt, and we said, "They are married." We were really glad. We were glad because the two female cousins were even more Grierson than Miss Emily had ever been.

So we were not surprised when Homer Barron — the streets had been finished some time since — was gone. We were a little disappointed that there was not a public blowing-off, but we believed that he had gone on to prepare for Miss Emily's coming, or to give her a chance to get rid of the cousins. (By that time it was a cabal, and we were all Miss Emily's allies to help circumvent the cousins.) Sure enough, after another week they departed. And, as we had expected all along, within three days Homer Barron was back in town. A neighbor saw the Negro man admit him at the kitchen door at dusk one evening.

And that was the last we saw of Homer Barron. And of Miss Emily for some time. The Negro man went in and out with the market basket, but the front door remained closed. Now and then we would see her at the window for a moment, as the men did that night when they sprinkled the lime, but for almost six months she did not appear on the streets. Then we knew that this was to be expected too; as if that quality of her father which had thwarted her woman's life so many times had been too virulent and too furious to die.

When we next saw Miss Emily, she had grown fat and her hair was turning gray. During the next few years it grew grayer and grayer until it attained an even pepper-and-salt iron-gray, when it ceased turning. Up to the day of her death at seventy-four it was still that vigorous iron-gray, like the hair of an active man.

From that time on her front door remained closed, save during a period of six or seven years, when she was about forty, during which she gave lessons in china-painting. She fitted up a studio in one of the downstairs rooms, where the daughters and granddaughters of Colonel Sartoris' contemporaries were sent to her with the same regularity and in the same spirit that they were sent to church on Sundays with a twenty-five-cent piece for the collection plate. Meanwhile her taxes had been remitted.

Then the newer generation became the backbone and the spirit of the town, and the painting pupils grew up and fell away and did not send their children to her with boxes of color and tedious brushes and pictures cut from the ladies' magazines. The front door closed upon the last one and remained closed for good. When the town got free postal delivery, Miss Emily alone refused to let them fasten the metal numbers above her door and attach a mailbox to it. She would not listen to them.

Daily, monthly, yearly we watched the Negro grow grayer and more stooped, going in and out with the market basket. Each December we sent her a tax notice, which would be returned by the post office a week later, unclaimed. Now and then we would see her in one of the downstairs windows — she had evidently shut up the top floor of the house — like the carven torso of an idol in a niche, looking or not looking at us, we could never tell which. Thus she passed from generation to generation — dear, inescapable, impervious, tranquil, and perverse.

And so she died. Fell ill in the house filled with dust and shadows, with only a doddering Negro man to wait on her. We did not even know she was sick; we had long since given up trying to get any information from the Negro. He talked to no one, probably not even to her, for his voice had grown harsh and rusty, as if from disuse.

She died in one of the downstairs rooms, in a heavy walnut bed with a curtain, her gray head propped on a pillow yellow and moldy with age and lack of sunlight.

V

The Negro met the first of the ladies at the front door and let them in, with their hushed, sibilant voices and their quick, curious glances, and then he disappeared. He walked right through the house and out the back and was not seen again.

The two female cousins came at once. They held the funeral on the second day, with the town coming to look at Miss Emily beneath a mass of bought flowers, with the crayon face of her father musing profoundly above the bier and the ladies sibilant and macabre; and the very old men — some in their brushed Confederate uniforms — on the porch and the lawn, talking of Miss

Emily as if she had been a contemporary of theirs, believing that they had danced with her and courted her perhaps, confusing time with its mathematical progression, as the old do, to whom all the past is not a diminishing road but, instead, a huge meadow which no winter ever quite touches, divided from them now by the narrow bottleneck of the most recent decade of years.

Already we knew that there was one room in that region above stairs which no one had seen in forty years, and which would have to be forced. They waited until Miss Emily was decently in the ground before they opened it.

The violence of breaking down the door seemed to fill this room with pervading dust. A thin, acrid pall as of the tomb seemed to lie everywhere upon this room decked and furnished as for a bridal: upon the valance curtains of faded rose color, upon the rose-shaded lights, upon the dressing table, upon the delicate array of crystal and the man's toilet things backed with tarnished silver, silver so tarnished that the monogram was obscured. Among them lay a collar and tie, as if they had just been removed, which, lifted, left upon the surface a pale crescent in the dust. Upon a chair hung the suit, carefully folded; beneath it the two mute shoes and the discarded socks.

The man himself lay in the bed.

For a long while we just stood there, looking down at the profound and fleshless grin. The body had apparently once lain in the attitude of an embrace, but now the long sleep that outlasts love, that conquers even the grimace of love, had cuckolded him. What was left of him, rotted beneath what was left of the nightshirt, had become inextricable from the bed in which he lay; and upon him and upon the pillow beside him lay that even coating of the patient and biding dust.

Then we noticed that in the second pillow was the indentation of a head. One of us lifted something from it, and leaning forward, that faint and invisible dust dry and acrid in the nostrils, we saw a long strand of iron-gray hair.

That Evening Sun

1931

I

Monday is no different from any other weekday in Jefferson now. The streets are paved now, and the telephone and electric companies are cutting down more and more of the shade trees — the water oaks, the maples and locusts and elms — to make room for iron poles bearing clusters of bloated and ghostly and bloodless grapes, and we have a city laundry which makes the rounds on Monday morning, gathering the bundles of clothes into bright-colored, specially-made motor cars: the soiled wearing of a whole week now flees apparitionlike behind alert and irritable electric horns, with a long diminishing noise of rubber and asphalt like tearing silk, and even the Negro women who still take in white people's washing after the old custom, fetch and deliver it in automobiles.

But fifteen years ago, on Monday morning the quiet, dusty, shady streets would be full of Negro women with, balanced on their steady, turbaned heads, bundles of clothes tied up in sheets, almost as large as cotton bales, carried so without touch of hand between the kitchen door of the white house and the blackened washpot beside a cabin door in Negro Hollow.

Nancy would set her bundle on the top of her head, then upon the bundle in turn she would set the black straw sailor hat which she wore winter and summer. She was tall, with a high, sad face sunken a little where her teeth were missing. Sometimes we would go a part of the way down the lane and across the pasture with her, to watch the balanced bundle and the hat that never bobbed nor wavered, even when she walked down into the ditch and up the other side and stooped through the fence. She would go down on her hands and knees and crawl through the gap, her head rigid, uptilted, the bundle steady as a rock or a balloon, and rise to her feet again and go on.

Sometimes the husbands of the washing women would fetch and deliver the clothes, but Jesus never did that for Nancy, even before father told him to stay away from our house, even when Dilsey was sick and Nancy would come to cook for us.

And then about half the time we'd have to go down the lane to Nancy's cabin and tell her to come on and cook breakfast. We would stop at the ditch, because father told us to not have anything to do with Jesus — he was a short black man, with a razor scar down his face — and we would throw rocks at Nancy's house until she came to the door, leaning her head around it without any clothes on.

"What yawl mean, chunking my house?" Nancy said. "What you little devils mean?"

"Father says for you to come on and get breakfast," Caddy said. "Father says it's over a half an hour now, and you've got to come this minute."

"I aint studying no breakfast," Nancy said. "I going to get my sleep out."

"I bet you're drunk," Jason said. "Father says you're drunk. Are you drunk, Nancy?"

"Who says I is?" Nancy said. "I got to get my sleep out. I ain't studying no breakfast."

So after a while we quit chunking the cabin and went back home. When she finally came, it was too late for me to go to school. So we thought it was whisky until that day they arrested her again and they were taking her to jail and they passed Mr Stovall. He was the cashier in the bank and a deacon in the Baptist church, and Nancy began to say:

"When you going to pay me, white man? When you going to pay me, white man? It's been three times now since you paid me a cent —" Mr Stovall knocked her down, but she kept on saying, "When you going to pay me, white man? It's been three times now since —" until Mr Stovall kicked her in the mouth with his heel and the marshal caught Mr Stovall back, and Nancy lying in the street, laughing. She turned her head and spat out some blood and teeth and said, "It's been three times now since he paid me a cent."

That was how she lost her teeth, and all that day they told about Nancy and Mr Stovall, and all that night the ones that passed the jail could hear Nancy singing and yelling. They could see her hands holding to the window bars, and a lot of them stopped along the fence, listening to her and to the jailer trying to make her stop. She didn't shut up until almost daylight, when the jailer began to hear a bumping and scraping upstairs and he went up there and found Nancy hanging from the window bar. He said that it was cocaine and not whisky, because no nigger would try to commit suicide unless he was full of cocaine, because a nigger full of cocaine wasn't a nigger any longer.

The jailer cut her down and revived her; then he beat her, whipped her. She had hung herself with her dress. She had fixed it all right, but when they arrested her she didn't have on anything except a dress and so she didn't have anything to tie her hands with and she couldn't make her hands let go of the window ledge. So the jailer heard the noise and ran up there and found Nancy hanging from the window, stark naked, her belly already swelling out a little, like a little balloon.

When Dilsey was sick in her cabin and Nancy was cooking for us, we could see her apron swelling out; that was before father told Jesus to stay away from the house. Jesus was in the kitchen, sitting behind the stove, with his razor scar on his black face like a piece of dirty string. He said it was a watermelon that Nancy had under her dress.

"It never come off of your vine, though," Nancy said.

"Off of what vine?" Caddy said.

"I can cut down the vine it did come off of," Jesus said.

"What makes you want to talk like that before these chillen?" Nancy said. "Whyn't you go on to work? You done et. You want Mr Jason to catch you hanging around his kitchen, talking that way before these chillen?"

"Talking what way?" Caddy said. "What vine?"

"I cant hang around white man's kitchen," Jesus said. "But white man can hang around mine. White man can come in my house, but I cant stop him. When white man want to come in my house, I aint got no house. I cant stop him, but he cant kick me outen it. He cant do that."

Dilsey was still sick in her cabin. Father told Jesus to stay off our place. Dilsey was still sick. It was a long time. We were in the library after supper.

"Isn't Nancy through in the kitchen yet?" mother said. "It seems to me that she has had plenty of time to have finished the dishes."

"Let Quentin go and see," father said. "Go and see if Nancy is through, Quentin. Tell her she can go on home."

I went to the kitchen. Nancy was through. The dishes were put away and the fire was out. Nancy was sitting in a chair, close to the cold stove. She looked at me.

"Mother wants to know if you are through," I said.

"Yes," Nancy said. She looked at me. "I done finished." She looked at me.

"What is it?" I said. "What is it?"

"I aint nothing but a nigger," Nancy said. "It aint none of my fault."

She looked at me, sitting in the chair before the cold stove, the sailor hat on her head. I went back to the library. It was the cold stove and all, when you think of a kitchen being warm and busy and cheerful. And with a cold stove and the dishes all put away, and nobody wanting to eat at that hour.

"Is she through?" mother said.

"Yessum," I said.

"What is she doing?" mother said.

"She's not doing anything. She's through."

"I'll go and see," father said.

"Maybe she's waiting for Jesus to come and take her home," Caddy said.

"Jesus is gone," I said. Nancy told us how one morning she woke up and Jesus was gone.

"He quit me," Nancy said. "Done gone to Memphis, I reckon. Dodging them city *po*-lice for a while, I reckon."

"And a good riddance," father said. "I hope he stays there."

"Nancy's scaired of the dark," Jason said.

"So are you," Caddy said.

"I'm not," Jason said.

"Scairy cat," Caddy said.

"I'm not," Jason said.

"You, Candace!" mother said. Father came back.

"I am going to walk down the lane with Nancy," he said. "She says that Jesus is back."

"Has she seen him?" mother said.

"No. Some Negro sent her word that he was back in town. I wont be long."

"You'll leave me alone, to take Nancy home?" mother said. "Is her safety more precious to you than mine?"

"I wont be long," father said.

"You'll leave these children unprotected, with that Negro about?"

"I'm going too," Caddy said. "Let me go, Father."

"What would he do with them, if he were unfortunate enough to have them?" father said.

"I want to go, too," Jason said.

"Jason!" mother said. She was speaking to father. You could tell that by the way she said the name. Like she believed that all day father had been trying to think of doing the thing she wouldn't like the most, and that she knew all the time that after a while he would think of it. I stayed quiet, because father and I both knew that mother would want him to make me stay with her if she just thought of it in time. So father didn't look at me. I was the oldest. I was nine and Caddy was seven and Jason was five.

"Nonsense," father said. "We wont be long."

Nancy had her hat on. We came to the lane. "Jesus always been good to me," Nancy said. "Whenever he had two dollars, one of them was mine." We walked in the lane. "If I can just get through the lane," Nancy said, "I be all right then."

The lane was always dark. "This is where Jason got scared on Hallowe'en," Caddy said.

"I didn't," Jason said.

"Cant Aunt Rachel do anything with him?" father said. Aunt Rachel was old. She lived in a cabin beyond Nancy's, by herself. She had white hair and she smoked a pipe in the door, all day long; she didn't work any more. They said she was Jesus' mother. Sometimes she said she was and sometimes she said she wasn't any kin to Jesus.

"Yes, you did," Caddy said. "You were scairder than Frony. You were scairder than T.P. even. Scairder than niggers."

"Cant nobody do nothing with him," Nancy said. "He say I done woke up the devil in him and aint but one thing going to lay it down again."

"Well, he's gone now," father said. "There's nothing for you to be afraid of now. And if you'd just let white men alone."

"Let what white men alone?" Caddy said. "How let them alone?"

"He aint gone nowhere," Nancy said. "I can feel him. I can feel him now, in this lane. He hearing us talk, every word, hid somewhere, waiting. I aint seen him, and I aint going to see him again but once more, with that razor in his mouth. That razor on that string down his back, inside his shirt. And then I aint going to be even surprised."

"I wasn't scaired," Jason said.

"If you'd behave yourself, you'd have kept out of this," father said. "But it's all right now. He's probably in St. Louis now. Probably got another wife by now and forgot all about you."

"If he has, I better not find out about it," Nancy said. "I'd stand there right over them, and every time he wropped her, I'd cut that arm off. I'd cut his head off and I'd slit her belly and I'd shove —"

"Hush," father said.

"Slit whose belly, Nancy?" Caddy said.

"I wasn't scaired," Jason said. "I'd walk right down this lane by myself."

"Yah," Caddy said. "You wouldn't dare to put your foot down in it if we were not here too."

II

Dilsey was still sick, so we took Nancy home every night until mother said, "How much longer is this going on? I to be left alone in this big house while you take home a frightened Negro?"

We fixed a pallet in the kitchen for Nancy. One night we waked up, hearing the sound. It was not singing and it was not crying, coming up the dark stairs. There was a light in mother's room and we heard father going down the hall, down the back stairs, and Caddy and I went into the hall. The floor was cold. Our toes curled away from it while we listened to the sound. It was like singing and it wasn't like singing, like the sounds that Negroes make.

Then it stopped and we heard father going down the back stairs, and we went to the head of the stairs. Then the sound began again, in the stairway, not loud, and we could see Nancy's eyes halfway up the stairs, against the wall. They looked like cat's eyes do, like a big cat against the wall, watching us. When we came down the steps to where she was, she quit making the sound again, and we stood there until father came back up from the kitchen, with his pistol in his hand. He went back down with Nancy and they came back with Nancy's pallet.

We spread the pallet in our room. After the light in mother's room went off, we could see Nancy's eyes again. "Nancy," Caddy whispered, "are you asleep, Nancy?"

Nancy whispered something. It was oh or no, I dont know which. Like nobody had made it, like it came from nowhere and went nowhere, until it was like Nancy was not there at all; that I had looked so hard at her eyes on the stairs that they had got printed on my eyeballs, like the sun does when you have closed your eyes and there is no sun. "Jesus," Nancy whispered. "Jesus."

"Was it Jesus?" Caddy said. "Did he try to come into the kitchen?"

"Jesus," Nancy said. Like this: Jeeeeeeeeeeeeeeeesus, until the sound went out, like a match or a candle does.

"It's the other Jesus she means," I said.

"Can you see us, Nancy?" Caddy whispered. "Can you see our eyes too?"

"I aint nothing but a nigger," Nancy said. "God knows. God knows."

"What did you see down there in the kitchen?" Caddy whispered. "What tried to get in?"

"God knows," Nancy said. We could see her eyes. "God knows."

Dilsey got well. She cooked dinner. "You'd better stay in bed a day or two longer," father said.

"What for?" Dilsey said. "If I had been a day later, this place would be to rack and ruin. Get on out of here now, and let me get my kitchen straight again."

Dilsey cooked supper too. And that night, just before dark, Nancy came into the kitchen.

"How do you know he's back?" Dilsey said. "You aint seen him."

"Jesus is a nigger," Jason said.

"I can feel him," Nancy said. "I can feel him laying yonder in the ditch."

"Tonight?" Dilsey said. "Is he there tonight?"

"Dilsey's a nigger too," Jason said.

"You try to eat something," Dilsey said.

"I dont want nothing," Nancy said.

"I aint a nigger," Jason said.

"Drink some coffee," Dilsey said. She poured a cup of coffee for Nancy. "Do you know he's out there tonight? How come you know it's tonight?"

"I know," Nancy said. "He's there, waiting. I know. I done lived with him too long. I know what he is fixing to do fore he know it himself."

"Drink some coffee," Dilsey said. Nancy held the cup to her mouth and blew into the cup. Her mouth pursed out like a spreading adder's, like a rubber mouth, like she had blown all the color out of her lips with blowing the coffee.

"I aint a nigger," Jason said. "Are you a nigger, Nancy?"

"I hellborn, child," Nancy said. "I wont be nothing soon. I going back where I come from soon."

III

She began to drink the coffee. While she was drinking, holding the cup in both hands, she began to make the sound again. She made the sound into the cup and the coffee sploshed out onto her hands and her dress. Her eyes looked at us and she sat there, her elbows on her knees, holding the cup in both hands, looking at us across the wet cup, making the sound. "Look at Nancy," Jason said. "Nancy cant cook for us now. Dilsey's got well now."

"You hush up," Dilsey said. Nancy held the cup in both hands, looking at us, making the sound, like there were two of them: one looking at us and the other making the sound. "Whyn't you let Mr Jason telefoam the marshal?" Dilsey said. Nancy stopped then, holding the cup in her long brown hands. She tried to drink some coffee again, but it sploshed out of the cup, onto her hands and her dress, and she put the cup down. Jason watched her.

"I cant swallow it," Nancy said. "I swallows but it wont go down me."

"You go down to the cabin," Dilsey said. "Frony will fix you a pallet and I'll be there soon."

"Wont no nigger stop him," Nancy said.

"I aint a nigger," Jason said. "Am I, Dilsey?"

"I reckon not," Dilsey said. She looked at Nancy. "I dont reckon so. What you going to do, then?"

Nancy looked at us. Her eyes went fast, like she was afraid there wasn't time to look, without hardly moving at all. She looked at us, at all three of us at one time. "You member that night I stayed in yawls' room?" she said. She told about how we waked up early the next morning, and played. We had to play quiet, on her pallet, until father woke up and it was time to get breakfast. "Go and ask your maw to let me stay here tonight," Nancy said. "I wont need no pallet. We can play some more."

Caddy asked mother. Jason went too. "I cant have Negroes sleeping in the bedrooms," mother said. Jason cried. He cried until mother said he couldn't have any dessert for three days if he didn't stop. Then Jason said he would stop if Dilsey would make a chocolate cake. Father was there.

"Why dont you do something about it?" mother said. "What do we have officers for?"

"Why is Nancy afraid of Jesus?" Caddy said. "Are you afraid of father, mother?"

"What could the officers do?" father said. "If Nancy hasn't seen him, how could the officers find him?"

"Then why is she afraid?" mother said.

"She says he is there. She says she knows he is there tonight."

"Yet we pay taxes," mother said. "I must wait here alone in this big house while you take a Negro woman home."

"You know that I am not lying outside with a razor," father said.

"I'll stop if Dilsey will make a chocolate cake," Jason said. Mother told us to go out and father said he didn't know if Jason would get a chocolate cake or not, but he knew what Jason was going to get in about a minute. We went back to the kitchen and told Nancy.

"Father said for you to go home and lock the door, and you'll be all right," Caddy said. "All right from what, Nancy? Is Jesus mad at you?" Nancy was holding the coffee cup in her hands again, her elbows on her knees and her hands holding the cup between her knees. She was looking into the cup. "What have you done that made Jesus mad?" Caddy said. Nancy let the cup go. It didn't break on the floor, but the coffee spilled out, and Nancy sat there with her hands still making the shape of the cup. She began to make the sound again, not loud. Not singing and not unsinging. We watched her.

"Here," Dilsey said. "You quit that, now. You get aholt of yourself. You wait here. I going to get Versh to walk home with you." Dilsey went out.

We looked at Nancy. Her shoulders kept shaking, but she quit making the sound. We watched her. "What's Jesus going to do to you?" Caddy said. "He went away."

Nancy looked at us. "We had fun that night I stayed in yawls' room, didn't we?"

"I didn't," Jason said. "I didn't have any fun."

"You were asleep in mother's room," Caddy said. "You were not there."

"Let's go down to my house and have some more fun," Nancy said.

"Mother wont let us," I said. "It's too late now."

"Dont bother her," Nancy said. "We can tell her in the morning. She wont mind."

"She wouldn't let us," I said.

"Dont ask her now," Nancy said. "Dont bother her now."

"She didn't say we couldn't go," Caddy said.

"We didn't ask," I said.

"If you go, I'll tell," Jason said.

"We'll have fun," Nancy said. "They won't mind, just to my house. I been working for yawl a long time. They won't mind."

"I'm not afraid to go," Caddy said. "Jason is the one that's afraid. He'll tell."

"I'm not," Jason said.

"Yes, you are," Caddy said. "You'll tell."

"I won't tell," Jason said. "I'm not afraid."

"Jason ain't afraid to go with me," Nancy said. "Is you, Jason?"

"Jason is going to tell," Caddy said. The lane was dark. We passed the pasture gate. "I bet if something was to jump out from behind that gate, Jason would holler."

"I wouldn't," Jason said. We walked down the lane. Nancy was talking loud.

"What are you talking so loud for, Nancy?" Caddy said.

"Who; me?" Nancy said. "Listen at Quentin and Caddy and Jason saying I'm talking loud."

"You talk like there was five of us here," Caddy said. "You talk like father was here too."

"Who; me talking loud, Mr Jason?" Nancy said.

"Nancy called Jason 'Mister,'" Caddy said.

"Listen how Caddy and Quentin and Jason talk," Nancy said.

"We're not talking loud," Caddy said. "You're the one that's talking like father —"

"Hush," Nancy said; "hush, Mr Jason."

"Nancy called Jason 'Mister' aguh —"

"Hush," Nancy said. She was talking loud when we crossed the ditch and stooped through the fence where she used to stoop through with the clothes on her head. Then we came to her house. We were going fast then. She opened the door. The smell of the house was like the lamp and the smell of Nancy was like the wick, like they were waiting for one another to begin to smell. She lit the lamp and closed the door and put the bar up. Then she quit talking loud, looking at us.

"What're we going to do?" Caddy said.

"What do yawl want to do?" Nancy said.

"You said we would have some fun," Caddy said.

There was something about Nancy's house; something you could smell besides Nancy and the house. Jason smelled it, even. "I don't want to stay here," he said. "I want to go home."

"Go home, then," Caddy said.

"I don't want to go by myself," Jason said.

"We're going to have some fun," Nancy said.

"How?" Caddy said.

Nancy stood by the door. She was looking at us, only it was like she had emptied her eyes, like she had quit using them. "What do you want to do?" she said.

"Tell us a story," Caddy said. "Can you tell a story?"

"Yes," Nancy said.

"Tell it," Caddy said. We looked at Nancy. "You don't know any stories."

"Yes," Nancy said. "Yes, I do."

She came and sat in a chair before the hearth. There was a little fire there. Nancy built it up, when it was already hot inside. She built a good blaze. She told a story. She talked like her eyes looked, like her eyes watching us and her voice talking to us did not belong to her. Like she was living somewhere else, waiting somewhere else. She was outside the cabin. Her voice was inside and the shape of her, the Nancy that could stoop under a barbed wire fence with a bundle of clothes balanced on her head as though without weight, like a balloon, was there. But that was all. "And so this here queen come walking up to the ditch, where that bad man was hiding. She was walking up to the ditch, and she say, 'If I can just get past this here ditch,' was what she say . . ."

"What ditch?" Caddy said. "A ditch like that one out there? Why did a queen want to go into a ditch?"

"To get to her house," Nancy said. She looked at us. "She had to cross the ditch to get into her house quick and bar the door."

"Why did she want to go home and bar the door?" Caddy said.

IV

Nancy looked at us. She quit talking. She looked at us. Jason's legs stuck straight out of his pants where he sat on Nancy's lap. "I don't think that's a good story," he said. "I want to go home."

"Maybe we had better," Caddy said. She got up from the floor. "I bet they are looking for us right now." She went toward the door.

"No," Nancy said. "Don't open it." She got up quick and passed Caddy. She didn't touch the door, the wooden bar.

"Why not?" Caddy said.

"Come back to the lamp," Nancy said. "We'll have fun. You don't have to go."

"We ought to go," Caddy said. "Unless we have a lot of fun." She and Nancy came back to the fire, the lamp.

"I want to go home," Jason said. "I'm going to tell."

"I know another story," Nancy said. She stood close to the lamp. She looked at Caddy, like when your eyes look up at a stick balanced on your nose. She had to look down to see Caddy, but her eyes looked like that, like when you are balancing a stick.

"I won't listen to it," Jason said. "I'll bang on the floor."

"It's a good one," Nancy said. "It's better than the other one."

"What's it about?" Caddy said. Nancy was standing by the lamp. Her hand was on the lamp, against the light, long and brown.

"Your hand is on that hot globe," Caddy said. "Don't it feel hot to your hand?"

Nancy looked at her hand on the lamp chimney. She took her hand away, slow. She stood there, looking at Caddy, wringing her long hand as though it were tied to her wrist with a string.

"Let's do something else," Caddy said.

"I want to go home," Jason said.

"I got some popcorn," Nancy said. She looked at Caddy and then at Jason and then at me and then at Caddy again. "I got some popcorn."

"I don't like popcorn," Jason said. "I'd rather have candy."

Nancy looked at Jason. "You can hold the popper." She was still wringing her hand; it was long and limp and brown.

"All right," Jason said. "I'll stay a while if I can do that. Caddy can't hold it. I'll want to go home again if Caddy holds the popper."

Nancy built up the fire. "Look at Nancy putting her hands in the fire," Caddy said. "What's the matter with you, Nancy?"

"I got popcorn," Nancy said. "I got some." She took the popper from under the bed. It was broken. Jason began to cry.

"Now we can't have any popcorn," he said.

"We ought to go home, anyway," Caddy said. "Come on, Quentin."

"Wait," Nancy said; "wait. I can fix it. Don't you want to help me fix it?"

"I don't think I want any," Caddy said. "It's too late now."

"You help me, Jason," Nancy said. "Don't you want to help me?"

"No," Jason said. "I want to go home."

"Hush," Nancy said; "hush. Watch. Watch me. I can fix it so Jason can hold it and pop the corn." She got a piece of wire and fixed the popper.

"It won't hold good," Caddy said.

"Yes, it will," Nancy said. "Yawl watch. Yawl help me shell some corn."

The popcorn was under the bed too. We shelled it into the popper and Nancy helped Jason hold the popper over the fire.

"It's not popping," Jason said. "I want to go home."

"You wait," Nancy said. "It'll begin to pop. We'll have fun then." She was sitting close to the fire. The lamp was turned up so high it was beginning to smoke.

"Why don't you turn it down some?" I said.

"It's all right," Nancy said. "I'll clean it. Yawl wait. The popcorn will start in a minute."

"I don't believe it's going to start," Caddy said. "We ought to start home, anyway. They'll be worried."

"No," Nancy said. "It's going to pop. Dilsey will tell um yawl with me. I been working for yawl long time. They won't mind if yawl at my house. You wait, now. It'll start popping any minute now."

Then Jason got some smoke in his eyes and he began to cry. He dropped the popper into the fire. Nancy got a wet rag and wiped Jason's face, but he didn't stop crying.

"Hush," she said. "Hush." But he didn't hush. Caddy took the popper out of the fire.

"It's burned up," she said. "You'll have to get some more popcorn, Nancy."

"Did you put all of it in?" Nancy said.

"Yes," Caddy said. Nancy looked at Caddy. Then she took the popper and opened it and poured the cinders into her apron and began to sort the grains, her hands long and brown, and we watching her.

"Haven't you got any more?" Caddy said.

"Yes," Nancy said; "yes. Look. This here ain't burnt. All we need to do is —"

"I want to go home," Jason said. "I'm going to tell."

"Hush," Caddy said. We all listened. Nancy's head was already turned toward the barred door, her eyes filled with red lamplight. "Somebody is coming," Caddy said.

Then Nancy began to make that sound again, not loud, sitting there above the fire, her long hands dangling between her knees; all of a sudden water began to come out on her face in big drops, running down her face, carrying in each one a little turning ball of firelight like a spark until it dropped off her chin. "She's not crying," I said.

"I ain't crying," Nancy said. Her eyes were closed. "I ain't crying. Who is it?"

"I don't know," Caddy said. She went to the door and looked out. "We've got to go now," she said. "Here comes father."

"I'm going to tell," Jason said. "Yawl made me come."

The water still ran down Nancy's face. She turned in her chair. "Listen. Tell him. Tell him we going to have fun. Tell him I take good care of yawl until in the morning. Tell him to let me come home with yawl and sleep on the floor. Tell him I won't need no pallet. We'll have fun. You member last time how we had so much fun?"

"I didn't have fun," Jason said. "You hurt me. You put smoke in my eyes. I'm going to tell."

V

Father came in. He looked at us. Nancy did not get up.

"Tell him," she said.

"Caddy made us come down here," Jason said. "I didn't want to."

Father came to the fire. Nancy looked up at him. "Can't you go to Aunt Rachel's and stay?" he said. Nancy looked up at father, her hands between her knees. "He's not here," father said. "I would have seen him. There's not a soul in sight."

"He in the ditch," Nancy said. "He waiting in the ditch yonder."

"Nonsense," father said. He looked at Nancy. "Do you know he's there?"

"I got the sign," Nancy said.

"What sign?"

"I got it. It was on the table when I come in. It was a hogbone, with blood meat still on it, laying by the lamp. He's out there. When yawl walk out that door, I gone."

"Gone where, Nancy?" Caddy said.

"I'm not a tattletale," Jason said.

"Nonsense," father said.

"He out there," Nancy said. "He looking through that window this minute, waiting for yawl to go. Then I gone."

"Nonsense," father said. "Lock up your house and we'll take you on to Aunt Rachel's."

"'Twont do no good," Nancy said. She didn't look at father now, but he looked down at her, at her long, limp, moving hands. "Putting it off wont do no good."

"Then what do you want to do?" father said.

"I don't know," Nancy said. "I can't do nothing. Just put it off. And that don't do no good. I reckon it belong to me. I reckon what I going to get ain't no more than mine."

"Get what?" Caddy said. "What's yours?"

"Nothing," father said. "You all must get to bed."

"Caddy made me come," Jason said.

"Go on to Aunt Rachel's," father said.

"It won't do no good," Nancy said. She sat before the fire, her elbows on her knees, her long hands between her knees. "When even your own kitchen wouldn't do no good. When even if I was sleeping on the floor in the room with your chillen, and the next morning there I am, and blood —"

"Hush," father said. "Lock the door and put out the lamp and go to bed."

"I scared of the dark," Nancy said. "I scared for it to happen in the dark."

"You mean you're going to sit right here with the lamp lighted?" father said. Then Nancy began to make the sound again, sitting before the fire, her long hands between her knees. "Ah, damnation," father said. "Come along, chillen. It's past bedtime."

"When yawl go home, I gone," Nancy said. She talked quieter now, and her face looked quiet, like her hands. "Anyway, I got my coffin money saved up with Mr. Lovelady." Mr. Lovelady was a short, dirty man who collected the Negro insurance, coming around to the cabins or the kitchens every Saturday morning, to collect fifteen cents. He and his wife lived at the hotel. One morning his wife committed suicide. They had a child, a little girl. He and the child went away. After a week or two he came back alone. We would see him going along the lanes and the back streets on Saturday mornings.

"Nonsense," father said. "You'll be the first thing I'll see in the kitchen tomorrow morning."

"You'll see what you'll see, I reckon," Nancy said. "But it will take the Lord to say what that will be."

VI

"Come and put the bar up," father said. But she didn't move. She didn't look at us again, sitting quietly there between the lamp and the fire. From some distance down the lane we could look back and see her through the open door.

"What, Father?" Caddy said. "What's going to happen?"

"Nothing," father said. Jason was on father's back, so Jason was the tallest of all of us. We went down into the ditch. I looked at it, quiet. I couldn't see much where the moonlight and the shadows tangled.

"If Jesus is hid here, he can see us, can't he?" Caddy said.

"He's not there," father said. "He went away a long time ago."

"You made me come," Jason said, high; against the sky it looked like father had two heads, a little one and a big one. "I didn't want to."

We went up out of the ditch. We could still see Nancy's house and the open door, but we couldn't see Nancy now, sitting before the fire with the door open, because she was tired. "I just done got tired," she said. "I just a nigger. It ain't no fault of mine."

But we could hear her, because she began just after we came up out of the ditch, the sound that was not singing and not unsinging. "Who will do our washing now, Father?" I said.

"I'm not a nigger," Jason said, high and close above father's head.

"You're worse," Caddy said, "you are a tattletale. If something was to jump out, you'd be scairder than a nigger."

"I wouldn't," Jason said.

"You'd cry," Caddy said.

"Caddy," father said.

"I wouldn't!" Jason said.

"Scairy cat," Caddy said.

"Candace!" father said.

F. Scott Fitzgerald

F. Scott Fitzgerald (1896–1940), regarded as the literary spokesman for the "Lost Generation" of the 1920s in America, was born in St. Paul, Minnesota. His family had some social standing but little money, and it was only with help from a maiden aunt that he was able to go to an eastern preparatory school and then on to Princeton, where he said his family hoped that he would attend to his studies and stop "wasting his time scribbling." He left college before graduating to accept a commission as a second lieutenant in the Regular Army during World War I, but he spent most of his time in the service writing his first novel, which he revised several times before it was published in 1920 as *This Side of Paradise*. The novel was such a success that magazines were eager to print Fitzgerald's stories, and his first story collection, *Flappers and Philosophers,* was rushed into print later the same year to take advantage of the novel's popularity. Another story collection, *Tales of the Jazz Age*, followed in 1922. Years later Fitzgerald would say, writing in the third person, that he was grateful to the Jazz Age because "it bore him up, flattered him, and gave him more money than he had dreamed of, simply for telling people that he felt as they did, that something had to be done with all the nervous energy stored up and unexpended in the War."

In 1925, with the publication of his novel *The Great Gatsby*, Fitzgerald reached the peak of his fame as a writer. His reputation declined rapidly in the harsher years of the 1930s. The Great Depression in the United States and around the world coincided with his own emotional and physical collapse, as his marriage and career fell apart because of his wife's mental illness and his alcoholism. Gertrude Stein had coined the term "Lost Generation" to describe the young men who had served in World War I and were forced to grow up "to find all Gods dead, all wars fought, all faiths in man shaken." But Fitzgerald's last years were truly lost, as he confronted the "waste and horror" of his dissipated talent, writing Hollywood screenplays and struggling unsuccessfully to finish his novel *The Last Tycoon*.

At the time of his death Fitzgerald had written about 160 stories. As one of his editors, Malcolm Cowley, said, the exact number is hard to set because some of his work was on the borderline between fiction and the essay or "magazine piece." Simple and clear in style, Fitzgerald's stories make up an informal history of his career, dating from before the publication of his first novel to after his final crack-up. "Winter Dreams," one of his early stories, is one of his best. As Cowley realized, it embodies "more dignity in the face of real sorrow."

Winter Dreams

1922

SOME OF THE CADDIES were poor as sin and lived in one-room houses with a neurasthenic cow in the front yard, but Dexter Green's father owned the second best grocery-store in Black Bear — the best one was "The Hub," patronized by the wealthy people from Sherry Island — and Dexter caddied only for pocket-money.

In the fall when the days became crisp and gray, and the long Minnesota winter shut down like the white lid of a box, Dexter's skis moved over the snow that hid the fairways of the golf course. At these times the country gave him a feeling of profound melancholy — it offended him that the links should lie in enforced fallowness, haunted by ragged sparrows for the long season. It was dreary, too, that on the tees where the gay colors fluttered in summer there were now only the desolate sand-boxes knee-deep in crusted ice. When he crossed the hills the wind blew cold as misery, and if the sun was out he tramped with his eyes squinted up against the hard dimensionless glare.

In April the winter ceased abruptly. The snow ran down into Black Bear Lake scarcely tarrying for the early golfers to brave the season with red and black balls. Without elation, without an interval of moist glory, the cold was gone.

Dexter knew that there was something dismal about this Northern spring, just as he knew there was something gorgeous about the fall. Fall made him clinch his hands and tremble and repeat idiotic sentences to himself, and make brisk abrupt gestures of command to imaginary audiences and armies. October filled him with hope which November raised to a sort of ecstatic triumph, and in this mood the fleeting brilliant impressions of the summer at Sherry Island were ready grist to his mill. He became a golf champion and defeated Mr. T. A. Hedrick in a marvellous match played a hundred times over the fairways of his imagination, a match each detail of which he changed about untiringly — sometimes he won with almost laughable ease, sometimes he came up magnificently from behind. Again, stepping from a Pierce-Arrow automobile, like Mr. Mortimer Jones, he strolled frigidly into the lounge of the Sherry Island Golf Club — or perhaps, surrounded by an admiring crowd, he gave an exhibition of fancy diving from the spring-board of the club raft. . . . Among those who watched him in open-mouthed wonder was Mr. Mortimer Jones.

And one day it came to pass that Mr. Jones — himself and not his ghost — came up to Dexter with tears in his eyes and said that Dexter was the —— best caddy in the club, and wouldn't he decide not to quit if Mr. Jones made it worth his while, because every other —— caddy in the club lost one ball a hole for him — regularly ——

"No, sir," said Dexter decisively, "I don't want to caddy any more." Then, after a pause: "I'm too old."

"You're not more than fourteen. Why the devil did you decide just this morning that you wanted to quit? You promised that next week you'd go over to the State tournament with me."

"I decided I was too old."

Dexter handed in his "A Class" badge, collected what money was due him from the caddy master, and walked home to Black Bear Village.

"The best —— caddy I ever saw," shouted Mr. Mortimer Jones over a drink that afternoon. "Never lost a ball! Willing! Intelligent! Quiet! Honest! Grateful!"

The little girl who had done this was eleven — beautifully ugly as little girls are apt to be who are destined after a few years to be inexpressibly lovely and bring no end of misery to a great number of men. The spark, however, was perceptible. There was a general ungodliness in the way her lips twisted down at the corners when she smiled, and in the — Heaven help us! — in the almost passionate quality of her eyes. Vitality is born early in such women. It was utterly in evidence now, shining through her thin frame in a sort of glow.

She had come eagerly out on to the course at nine o'clock with a white linen nurse and five small new golf-clubs in a white canvas bag which the nurse was carrying. When Dexter first saw her she was standing by the caddy house, rather ill at ease and trying to conceal the fact by engaging her nurse in an obviously unnatural conversation graced by startling and irrelevant grimaces from herself.

"Well, it's certainly a nice day, Hilda," Dexter heard her say. She drew down the corners of her mouth, smiled, and glanced furtively around her eyes in transit falling for an instant on Dexter.

Then to the nurse:

"Well, I guess there aren't very many people out here this morning, are there?"

The smile again — radiant, blatantly artificial — convincing.

"I don't know what we're supposed to do now," said the nurse looking nowhere in particular.

"Oh, that's all right. I'll fix it up."

Dexter stood perfectly still, his mouth slightly ajar. He knew that if he moved forward a step his stare would be in her line of vision — if he moved backward he would lose his full view of her face. For a moment he had not realized how young she was. Now he remembered having seen her several times the year before — in bloomers.

Suddenly, involuntarily, he laughed, a short abrupt laugh — then, startled by himself, he turned and began to walk quickly away.

"Boy!"

Dexter stopped.

"Boy —— "

Beyond question he was addressed. Not only that, but he was treated to that absurd smile, that preposterous smile — the memory of which at least a dozen men were to carry into middle age.

"Boy, do you know where the golf teacher is?"

"He's giving a lesson."

"Well, do you know where the caddy-master is?"

"He isn't here yet this morning."

"Oh." For a moment this baffled her. She stood alternately on her right and left foot.

"We'd like to get a caddy," said the nurse. "Mrs. Mortimer Jones sent us out to play golf, and we don't know how without we get a caddy."

Here she was stopped by an ominous glance from Miss Jones, followed immediately by the smile.

"There aren't any caddies here except me," said Dexter to the nurse, "and I got to stay here in charge until the caddy-master gets here."

"Oh."

Miss Jones and her retinue now withdrew, and at a proper distance from Dexter became involved in a heated conversation, which was concluded by Miss Jones taking one of the clubs and hitting it on the ground with violence. For further emphasis she raised it again and was about to bring it down smartly upon the nurse's bosom, when the nurse seized the club and twisted it from her hands.

"You damn little mean old *thing!*" cried Miss Jones wildly.

Another argument ensued. Realizing that the elements of comedy were implied in the scene, Dexter several times began to laugh, but each time restrained the laugh before it reached audibility. He could not resist the monstrous conviction that the little girl was justified in beating the nurse.

The situation was resolved by the fortuitous appearance of the caddy-master, who was appealed to immediately by the nurse.

"Miss Jones is to have a little caddy, and this one says he can't go."

"Mr. McKenna said I was to wait here till you came," said Dexter quickly.

"Well, he's here now." Miss Jones smiled cheerfully at the caddy-master. Then she dropped her bag and set off at a haughty mince toward the first tee.

"Well?" The caddy-master turned to Dexter. "What you standing there like a dummy for? Go pick up the young lady's clubs."

"I don't think I'll go out to-day," said Dexter.

"You don't——"

"I think I'll quit."

The enormity of his decision frightened him. He was a favorite caddy, and the thirty dollars a month he earned through the summer were not to be made elsewhere around the lake. But he had received a strong emotional shock, and his perturbation required a violent and immediate outlet.

It is not so simple as that, either. As so frequently would be the case in the future, Dexter was unconsciously dictated to by his winter dreams.

II

Now, of course, the quality and the seasonability of these winter dreams varied, but the stuff of them remained. They persuaded Dexter several years later to pass up a business course at the State university — his father, prospering now, would have paid his way — for the precarious advantage of attending an older and more famous university in the East, where he was bothered by his scanty funds. But do not get the impression, because his winter dreams happened to be concerned at first with musings on the rich, that there was anything merely snobbish in the boy. He wanted not association with glittering things and glittering people — he wanted the glittering things themselves. Often he reached out for the best without knowing why he wanted it — and sometimes he ran up against the mysterious denials and prohibitions in which life indulges. It is with one of those denials and not with his career as a whole that this story deals.

He made money. It was rather amazing. After college he went to the city from which Black Bear Lake draws its wealthy patrons. When he was only twenty-three and had been there not quite two years, there were already people who liked to say: "Now *there's* a boy — " All about him rich men's sons were peddling bonds precariously, or investing patrimonies precariously, or plodding through the two dozen volumes of the "George Washington Commercial Course," but Dexter borrowed a thousand dollars on his college degree and his confident mouth, and bought a partnership in a laundry.

It was a small laundry when he went into it, but Dexter made a specialty of learning how the English washed fine woollen golf-stockings without shrinking them, and within a year he was catering to the trade that wore knickerbockers. Men were insisting that their Shetland hose and sweaters go to his laundry, just as they had insisted on a caddy who could find golf-balls. A little later he was doing their wives' lingerie as well — and running five branches in different parts of the city. Before he was twenty-seven he owned the largest string of laundries in his section of the country. It was then that he sold out and went to New York. But the part of his story that concerns us goes back to the days when he was making his first big success.

When he was twenty-three Mr. Hart — one of the gray-haired men who liked to say "Now there's a boy" — gave him a guest card to the Sherry Island Golf Club for a week-end. So he signed his name one day on the register, and that afternoon played golf in a foursome with Mr. Hart and Mr. Sandwood and Mr. T. A. Hedrick. He did not consider it necessary to remark that he had once carried Mr. Hart's bag over this same links, and that he knew every trap and gully with his eyes shut — but he found himself glancing at the four caddies who trailed them, trying to catch a gleam or gesture that would remind him of himself, that would lessen the gap which lay between his present and his past.

It was a curious day, slashed abruptly with fleeting, familiar impressions. One minute he had the sense of being a trespasser — in the next he was impressed by the tremendous superiority he felt toward Mr. T. A. Hedrick, who was a bore and not even a good golfer any more. Then, because of a ball Mr. Hart lost near the fifteenth green, an enormous thing happened. While they were searching the stiff grasses of the rough there was a clear call of "Fore!" from behind a hill in their rear. And as they all turned abruptly from their search a bright new ball sliced abruptly over the hill and caught Mr. T. A. Hedrick in the abdomen.

"By Gad!" cried Mr. T. A. Hedrick, "they ought to put some of these crazy women off the course. It's getting to be outrageous."

A head and a voice came up together over the hill:

"Do you mind if we go through?"

"You hit me in the stomach!" declared Mr. Hedrick wildly.

"Did I?" The girl approached the group of men. "I'm sorry. I yelled 'Fore!' "

Her glance fell casually on each of the men — then scanned the fairway for her ball.

"Did I bounce into the rough?"

It was impossible to determine whether this question was ingenuous or malicious. In a moment, however, she left no doubt, for as her partner came up over the hill she called cheerfully:

"Here I am! I'd have gone on the green except that I hit something."

As she took her stance for a short mashie shot, Dexter looked at her closely. She wore a blue gingham dress, rimmed at throat and shoulders with a white edging that accentuated her tan. The quality of exaggeration, of thinness, which had made her passionate eyes and down-turning mouth absurd at eleven, was gone now. She was arrestingly beautiful. The color in her cheeks was centered like the color in a picture — it was not a "high" color, but a sort of fluctuating and feverish warmth, so shaded that it seemed at any moment it would recede and disappear. This color and the mobility of her mouth gave a continual impression of flux, of intense life, of passionate vitality — balanced only partially by the sad luxury of her eyes.

She swung her mashie impatiently and without interest, pitching the ball into a sand-pit on the other side of the green. With a quick, insincere smile and a careless "Thank you!" she went on after it.

"That Judy Jones!" remarked Mr. Hedrick on the next tee, as they waited — some moments — for her to play on ahead. "All she needs is to be turned up and spanked for six months and then to be married off to an old-fashioned cavalry captain."

"My God, she's good-looking!" said Mr. Sandwood, who was just over thirty.

"Good-looking!" cried Mr. Hedrick contemptuously, "she always looks as if she wanted to be kissed! Turning those big cow-eyes on every calf in town!"

It was doubtful if Mr. Hedrick intended a reference to the maternal instinct.

"She'd play pretty good golf if she'd try," said Mr. Sandwood.

"She has no form," said Mr. Hedrick solemnly.

"She has a nice figure," said Mr. Sandwood.

"Better thank the Lord she doesn't drive a swifter ball," said Mr. Hart, winking at Dexter.

Later in the afternoon the sun went down with a riotous swirl of gold and varying blues and scarlets, and left the dry, rustling night of Western summer. Dexter watched from the veranda of the Golf Club, watched the even overlap of the waters in the little wind, silver molasses under the harvest-moon. Then the moon held a finger to her lips and the lake became a clear pool, pale and quiet. Dexter put on his bathing-suit and swam out to the farthest raft, where he stretched dripping on the wet canvas of the springboard.

There was a fish jumping and a star shining and the lights around the lake were gleaming. Over on a dark peninsula a piano was playing the songs of last summer and of summers before that — songs from "Chin-Chin" and "The Count of Luxemburg" and "The Chocolate Soldier" — and because the sound of a piano over a stretch of water had always seemed beautiful to Dexter he lay perfectly quiet and listened.

The tune the piano was playing at that moment had been gay and new five years before when Dexter was a sophomore at college. They had played it at a prom once when he could not afford the luxury of proms, and he had stood outside the gymnasium and listened. The sound of the tune precipitated in him a sort of ecstasy and it was with that ecstasy he viewed what happened to him now. It was a mood of intense appreciation, a sense that, for once, he was magnificently attuned to life and that everything about him was radiating a brightness and a glamour he might never know again.

A low, pale oblong detached itself suddenly from the darkness of the Island, spitting forth the reverberated sound of a racing motor-boat. Two white streamers of cleft water rolled themselves out behind it and almost immediately the boat was beside him, drowning out the hot tinkle of the piano in the drone of its spray. Dexter raising himself on his arms was aware of a figure standing at the wheel, of two dark eyes regarding him over the lengthening space of water — then the boat had gone by and was sweeping in an immense and purposeless circle of spray round and round in the middle of the lake. With equal eccentricity one of the circles flattened out and headed back toward the raft.

"Who's that?" she called, shutting off her motor. She was so near now that Dexter could see her bathing suit, which consisted apparently of pink rompers.

The nose of the boat bumped the raft, and as the latter tilted rakishly he was precipitated toward her. With different degrees of interest they recognized each other.

"Aren't you one of those men we played through this afternoon?" she demanded.

He was.

"Well, do you know how to drive a motor-boat? Because if you do I wish you'd drive this one so I can ride on the surf-board behind. My name is Judy Jones" — she favored him with an absurd smirk — rather, what tried to be a smirk, for, twist her mouth as she might, it was not grotesque, it was merely beautiful — "and I live in a house over there on the Island, and in that house there is a man waiting for me. When he drove up at the door I drove out of the dock because he says I'm his ideal."

There was a fish jumping and a star shining and the lights around the lake were gleaming. Dexter sat beside Judy Jones and she explained how her boat was driven. Then she was in the water, swimming to the floating surf-board with a sinuous crawl. Watching her was without effort to the eye, watching a branch waving or a sea-gull flying. Her arms, burned to butternut, moved sinuously among the dull platinum ripples, elbow appearing first, casting the forearm back with a cadence of falling water, then reaching out and down, stabbing a path ahead.

They moved out into the lake; turning, Dexter saw that she was kneeling on the low rear of the now uptilted surf-board.

"Go faster," she called, "fast as it'll go."

Obediently he jammed the lever forward and the white spray mounted at the bow. When he looked around again the girl was standing up on the rushing board, her arms spread wide, her eyes lifted toward the moon.

"It's awful cold," she shouted. "What's your name?"

He told her.

"Well, why don't you come to dinner to-morrow night?"

His heart turned over like a fly-wheel of the boat, and, for the second time, her casual whim gave a new direction to his life.

III

Next evening while he waited for her to come down-stairs, Dexter peopled the soft deep summer room and the sun-porch that opened from it with the men who had already loved Judy Jones. He knew the sort of men they were — the men who when he first went to college had entered from the great prep schools with graceful clothes and the deep tan of healthy summers. He had seen that, in one sense, he was better than these men. He was newer and stronger. Yet in acknowledging to himself that he wished his children to be like them he was admitting that he was but the rough, strong stuff from which they eternally sprang.

When the time had come for him to wear good clothes, he had known who were the best tailors in America, and the best tailors in America had made him the suit he wore this evening. He had acquired that particular reserve peculiar to his university, that set it off from other universities. He recognized the value to him of such a mannerism and he had adopted it; he knew that to be careless in dress and manner required more confidence than to be careful. But carelessness was for his children. His mother's name had been Krimslich. She was a Bohemian of the peasant class and she had talked broken English to the end of her days. Her son must keep to the set patterns.

At a little after seven Judy Jones came down-stairs. She wore a blue silk afternoon dress, and he was disappointed at first that she had not put on something more elaborate. This feeling was accentuated when, after a brief greeting, she went to the door of a butler's pantry and pushing it open called: "You can serve dinner, Martha." He had rather expected that a butler would announce dinner, that there would be a cocktail. Then he put these thoughts behind him as they sat down side by side on a lounge and looked at each other.

"Father and mother won't be here," she said thoughtfully.

He remembered the last time he had seen her father, and he was glad the parents were not to be here to-night — they might wonder who he was. He had been born in Keeble, a Minnesota village fifty miles farther north, and he always gave Keeble as his home instead of Black Bear Village. Country towns were well enough to come from if they weren't inconveniently in sight and used as footstools by fashionable lakes.

They talked of his university, which she had visited frequently during the past two years, and of the near-by city which supplied Sherry Island with its patrons, and whither Dexter would return next day to his prospering laundries.

During dinner she slipped into a moody depression which gave Dexter a feeling of uneasiness. Whatever petulance she uttered in her throaty voice worried him. Whatever she smiled at — at him, at a chicken liver, at nothing — it disturbed him that her smile could have no root in mirth, or even in amusement.

When the scarlet corners of her lips curved down, it was less a smile than an invitation to a kiss.

Then, after dinner, she led him out on the dark sunporch and deliberately changed the atmosphere.

"Do you mind if I weep a little?" she said.

"I'm afraid I'm boring you," he responded quickly.

"You're not. I like you. But I've just had a terrible afternoon. There was a man I cared about, and this afternoon he told me out of a clear sky that he was poor as a church-mouse. He'd never even hinted it before. Does this sound horribly mundane?"

"Perhaps he was afraid to tell you."

"Suppose he was," she answered. "He didn't start right. You see, if I'd thought of him as poor — well, I've been mad about loads of poor men, and fully intended to marry them all. But in this case, I hadn't thought of him that way, and my interest in him wasn't strong enough to survive the shock. As if a girl calmly informed her fiancé that she was a widow. He might not object to widows, but——

"Let's start right," she interrupted herself suddenly. "Who are you, anyhow?"

For a moment Dexter hesitated. Then:

"I'm nobody," he announced. "My career is largely a matter of futures."

"Are you poor?"

"No," he said frankly, "I'm probably making more money than any man my age in the Northwest. I know that's an obnoxious remark, but you advised me to start right."

There was a pause. Then she smiled and the corners of her mouth drooped and an almost imperceptible sway brought her closer to him, looking up into his eyes. A lump rose in Dexter's throat, and he waited breathless for the experiment, facing the unpredictable compound that would form mysteriously from the elements of their lips. Then he saw — she communicated her excitement to him, lavishly, deeply, with kisses that were not a promise but a fulfillment. They aroused in him not hunger demanding renewal but surfeit that would demand more surfeit . . . kisses that were like charity, creating want by holding back nothing at all.

It did not take him many hours to decide that he had wanted Judy Jones ever since he was a proud, desirous little boy.

IV

It began like that — and continued, with varying shades of intensity, on such a note right up to the dénouement. Dexter surrendered a part of himself to the most direct and unprincipled personality with which he had ever come in contact. Whatever Judy wanted, she went after with the full pressure of her charm. There was no divergence of method, no jockeying for position or premeditation of effects — there was a very little mental side to any of her affairs. She simply made men conscious to the highest degree of her physical loveliness. Dexter had no desire to change her. Her deficiencies were knit up with a passionate energy that transcended and justified them.

When, as Judy's head lay against his shoulders that first night, she whispered, "I don't know what's the matter with me. Last night I thought I was in love with a man and to-night I think I'm in love with you —— " — it seemed to him a beautiful and romantic thing to say. It was the exquisite excitability that for the moment he controlled and owned. But a week later he was compelled to view this same quality in a different light. She took him in her roadster to a picnic supper, and after supper she disappeared, likewise in her roadster, with another man. Dexter became enormously upset and was scarcely able to be decently civil to the other people present. When she assured him that she had not kissed the other man, he knew she was lying — yet he was glad that she had taken the trouble to lie to him.

He was, as he found before the summer ended, one of a varying dozen who circulated about her. Each of them had at one time been favored above all others — about half of them still basked in the solace of occasional sentimental revivals. Whenever one showed signs of dropping out through long neglect, she granted him a brief honeyed hour, which encouraged him to tag along for a year or so longer. Judy made these forays upon the helpless and defeated without malice, indeed half unconscious that there was anything mischievous in what she did.

When a new man came to town every one dropped out — dates were automatically cancelled.

The helpless part of trying to do anything about it was that she did it all herself. She was not a girl who could be "won" in the kinetic sense — she was proof against cleverness, she was proof against charm; if any of these assailed her too strongly she would immediately resolve the affair to a physical basis, and under the magic of her physical splendor the strong as well as the brilliant played her game and not their own. She was entertained only by the gratification of her desires and by the direct exercise of her own charm. Perhaps from so much youthful love, so many youthful lovers, she had come, in self-defense, to nourish herself wholly from within.

Succeeding Dexter's first exhilaration came restlessness and dissatisfaction. The helpless ecstasy of losing himself in her was opiate rather than tonic. It was fortunate for his work during the winter that those moments of ecstasy came infrequently. Early in their acquaintance it had seemed for a while that there was a deep and spontaneous mutual attraction — that first August, for example — three days of long evenings on her dusky veranda, of strange wan kisses through the late afternoon, in shadowy alcoves or behind the protecting trellises of the garden arbors, of mornings when she was fresh as a dream and almost shy at meeting him in the clarity of the rising day. There was all the ecstasy of an engagement about it, sharpened by his realization that there was no engagement. It was during those three days that, for the first time, he had asked her to marry him. She said "Maybe some day," she said "kiss me," she said "I'd like to marry you," she said "I love you" — she said — nothing.

The three days were interrupted by the arrival of a New York man who visited at her house for half September. To Dexter's agony, rumor engaged them. The man was the son of the president of a great trust company. But at the end of a month it was reported that Judy was yawning. At a dance one night she sat all evening in a motor-boat with a local beau, while the New Yorker searched the club for her frantically. She told the local beau that she was bored with her visitor, and two days later he left. She was seen with him at the station, and it was reported that he looked very mournful indeed.

On this note the summer ended. Dexter was twenty-four, and he found himself increasingly in a position to do as he wished. He joined two clubs in the city and lived at one of them. Though he was by no means an integral part of the stag-lines at these clubs, he managed to be on hand at dances where Judy Jones was likely to appear. He could have gone out socially as much as he liked — he was an eligible young man, now, and popular with down-town fathers. His confessed devotion to Judy Jones had rather solidified his position. But he had no social aspirations and rather despised the dancing men who were always on tap for the Thursday or Saturday parties and who filled in at dinners with the younger married set. Already he was playing with the idea of going East to New York. He wanted to take Judy Jones with him. No disillusion as to the world in which she had grown up could cure his illusion as to her desirability.

Remember that — for only in the light of it can what he did for her be understood.

Eighteen months after he first met Judy Jones he became engaged to another girl. Her name was Irene Scheerer, and her father was one of the men who had always believed in Dexter. Irene was light-haired and sweet and honorable, and a little stout, and she had two suitors whom she pleasantly relinquished when Dexter formally asked her to marry him.

Summer, fall, winter, spring, another summer, another fall — so much he had given of his active life to the incorrigible lips of Judy Jones. She had treated him with interest, with encouragement, with malice, with indifference, with contempt. She had inflicted on him the innumerable little slights and indignities possible in such a case — as if in revenge for having ever cared for him at all. She had beckoned him and yawned at him and beckoned him again and he had responded often with bitterness and narrowed eyes. She had brought him ecstatic happiness and intolerable agony of spirit. She had caused him untold inconvenience and not a little trouble. She had insulted him, and she had ridden over him, and she had played his interest in her against his interest in his work — for fun. She had done everything to him except to criticise him — this she had not done — it seemed to him only because it might have sullied the utter indifference she manifested and sincerely felt toward him.

When autumn had come and gone again it occurred to him that he could not have Judy Jones. He had to beat this into his mind but he convinced himself at last. He lay awake at night for a while and argued it over. He told himself the trouble and the pain she had caused him, he enumerated her glaring deficiencies as a wife. Then he said to himself that he loved her, and after a while he fell asleep. For a week, lest he imagine her husky voice over the telephone or her eyes opposite him at lunch, he worked hard and late, and at night he went to his office and plotted out his years.

At the end of a week he went to a dance and cut in on her once. For almost the first time since they had met he did not ask her to sit out with him or tell her that she was lovely. It hurt him that she did not miss these things — that was all. He was not jealous when he saw that there was a new man to-night. He had been hardened against jealousy long before.

He stayed late at the dance. He sat for an hour with Irene Scheerer and talked about books and about music. He knew very little about either. But he was beginning to be master of his own time now, and he had a rather priggish notion that he — the young and already fabulously successful Dexter Green — should know more about such things.

That was in October, when he was twenty-five. In January, Dexter and Irene became engaged. It was to be announced in June, and they were to be married three months later.

The Minnesota winter prolonged itself interminably, and it was almost May when the winds came soft and the snow ran down into Black Bear Lake at last. For the first time in over a year Dexter was enjoying a certain tranquility of spirit. Judy Jones had been in Florida, and afterward in Hot Springs, and somewhere she had been engaged, and somewhere she had broken it off. At first, when Dexter had definitely given her up, it had made him sad that people still linked them together and asked for news of her, but when he began to be placed at dinner next to Irene Scheerer people didn't ask him about her any more — they told him about her. He ceased to be an authority on her.

May at last. Dexter walked the streets at night when the darkness was damp as rain, wondering that so soon, with so little done, so much of ecstasy had gone from him. May one year back had been marked by Judy's poignant, unforgivable, yet forgiven turbulence — it had been one of those rare times when he fancied she had grown to care for him. That old penny's worth of happiness he had spent for this bushel of content. He knew that Irene would be no more than a curtain spread behind him, a hand moving among gleaming teacups, a voice calling to children . . . fire and loveliness were gone, the magic of nights and the wonder of the varying hours and seasons . . . slender lips, down-turning, dropping to his lips and bearing him up into a heaven of eyes. . . . The thing was deep in him. He was too strong and alive for it to die lightly.

In the middle of May when the weather balanced for a few days on the thin bridge that led to deep summer he turned in one night at Irene's house. Their engagement was to be announced in a week now — no one would be surprised at it. And to-night they would sit together on the lounge at the University Club and look on for an hour at the dancers. It gave him a sense of solidity to go with her — she was so sturdily popular, so intensely "great."

He mounted the steps of the brownstone house and stepped inside.

"Irene," he called.

Mrs. Scheerer came out of the living-room to meet him.

"Dexter," she said, "Irene's gone up-stairs with a splitting headache. She wanted to go with you but I made her go to bed."

"Nothing serious, I —— "

"Oh, no. She's going to play golf with you in the morning. You can spare her for just one night, can't you, Dexter?"

Her smile was kind. She and Dexter liked each other. In the living-room he talked for a moment before he said good-night.

Returning to the University Club, where he had rooms, he stood in the doorway for a moment and watched the dancers. He leaned against the door-post, nodded at a man or two — yawned.

"Hello, darling."

The familiar voice at his elbow startled him. Judy Jones had left a man and crossed the room to him — Judy Jones, a slender enameled doll in cloth of gold: gold in a band at her head, gold in two slipper points at her dress's hem. The fragile glow of her face seemed to blossom as she smiled at him. A breeze of warmth and light blew through the room. His hands in the pockets of his dinner-jacket tightened spasmodically. He was filled with a sudden excitement.

"When did you get back?" he asked casually.

"Come here and I'll tell you about it."

She turned and he followed her. She had been away — he could have wept at the wonder of her return. She had passed through enchanted streets, doing things that were like provocative music. All mysterious happenings, all fresh and quickening hopes, had gone away with her, come back with her now.

She turned in the doorway.

"Have you a car here? If you haven't, I have."

"I have a coupé."

In then, with a rustle of golden cloth. He slammed the door. Into so many cars she had stepped — like this — like that — her back against the leather, so — her elbow resting on the door — waiting. She would have been soiled long since had there been anything to soil her — except herself — but this was her own self outpouring.

With an effort he forced himself to start the car and back into the street. This was nothing, he must remember. She had done this before, and he had put her behind him, as he would have crossed a bad account from his books.

He drove slowly down-town and, affecting abstraction, traversed the deserted streets of the business section, peopled here and there where a movie was giving out its crowd or where consumptive or pugilistic youth lounged in front of pool halls. The clink of glasses and the slap of hands on the bars issued from saloons, cloisters of glazed glass and dirty yellow light.

She was watching closely and the silence was embarrassing, yet in this crisis he could find no casual word with which to profane the hour. At a convenient turning he began to zigzag back toward the University Club.

"Have you missed me?" she asked suddenly.

"Everybody missed you."

He wondered if she knew of Irene Scheerer. She had been back only a day — her absence had been almost contemporaneous with his engagement.

"What a remark!" Judy laughed sadly — without sadness. She looked at him searchingly. He became absorbed in the dashboard.

"You're handsomer than you used to be," she said thoughtfully. "Dexter, you have the most rememberable eyes."

He could have laughed at this, but he did not laugh. It was the sort of thing that was said to sophomores. Yet it stabbed at him.

"I'm awfully tired of everything, darling." She called everyone darling, endowing the endearment with careless, individual comraderie. "I wish you'd marry me."

The directness of this confused him. He should have told her now that he was going to marry another girl, but he could not tell her. He could as easily have sworn that he had never loved her.

"I think we'd get along," she continued, on the same note, "unless probably you've forgotten me and fallen in love with another girl."

Her confidence was obviously enormous. She had said, in effect, that she found such a thing impossible to believe, that if it were true he had merely committed a childish indiscretion — and probably to show off. She would forgive him, because it was not a matter of any moment but rather something to be brushed aside lightly.

"Of course you could never love anybody but me," she continued, "I like the way you love me. Oh, Dexter, have you forgotten last year?"

"No, I haven't forgotten."

"Neither have I!"

Was she sincerely moved — or was she carried along by the wave of her own acting?

"I wish we could be like that again," she said, and he forced himself to answer: "I don't think we can."

"I suppose not. . . . I hear you're giving Irene Scheerer a violent rush."

There was not the faintest emphasis on the name, yet Dexter was suddenly ashamed.

"Oh, take me home," cried Judy suddenly; "I don't want to go back to that idiotic dance — with those children."

Then, as he turned up the street that led to the residence district, Judy began to cry quietly to herself. He had never seen her cry before.

The dark street lightened, the dwellings of the rich loomed up around them, he stopped his coupé in front of the great white bulk of the Mortimer Joneses house, somnolent, gorgeous, drenched with the splendor of the damp moonlight. Its solidity startled him. The strong walls, the steel of the girders, the breadth and beam and pomp of it were there only to bring out the contrast with the young beauty beside him. It was sturdy to accentuate her slightness — as if to show what a breeze could be generated by a butterfly's wing.

He sat perfectly quiet, his nerves in wild clamor, afraid that if he moved he would find her irresistibly in his arms. Two tears had rolled down her wet face and trembled on her upper lip.

"I'm more beautiful than anybody else," she said brokenly, "why can't I be happy?" Her moist eyes tore at his stability — her mouth turned slowly downward with an exquisite sadness: "I'd like to marry you if you'll have me, Dexter. I suppose you think I'm not worth having, but I'll be so beautiful for you, Dexter."

A million phrases of anger, pride, passion, hatred, tenderness fought on his lips. Then a perfect wave of emotion washed over him, carrying off with it a sediment of wisdom, of convention, of doubt, of honor. This was his girl who was speaking, his own, his beautiful, his pride.

"Won't you come in?" He heard her draw in her breath sharply.

Waiting.

"All right," his voice was trembling, "I'll come in."

V

It was strange that neither when it was over nor a long time afterward did he regret that night. Looking at it from the perspective of ten years, the fact that Judy's flare for him endured just one month seemed of little importance. Nor did it matter that by his yielding he subjected himself to a deeper agony in the end and gave serious hurt to Irene Scheerer and to Irene's parents, who had befriended him. There was nothing sufficiently pictorial about Irene's grief to stamp itself on his mind.

Dexter was at bottom hard-minded. The attitude of the city on his action was of no importance to him, not because he was going to leave the city, but because any outside attitude on the situation seemed superficial. He was completely indifferent to popular opinion. Nor, when he had seen that it was no use, that he did not possess in himself the power to move fundamentally or to hold Judy Jones, did he bear any malice toward her. He loved her, and he would love her until the day he was too old for loving — but he could not have her. So he tasted the deep pain that is reserved only for the strong, just as he had tasted for a little while the deep happiness.

Even the ultimate falsity of the grounds upon which Judy terminated the engagement — that she did not want to "take him away" from Irene — Judy, who had wanted nothing else — did not revolt him. He was beyond any revulsion or any amusement.

He went East in February with the intention of selling out his laundries and settling in New York — but the war came to America in March and changed his plans. He returned to the West, handed over the management of the business to his partner, and went into the first officers' training-camp in late April. He was one of those young thousands who greeted the war with a certain amount of relief, welcoming the liberation from webs of tangled emotion.

VI

This story is not his biography, remember, although things creep into it which have nothing to do with those dreams he had when he was young. We are almost done with them and with him now. There is only one more incident to be related here, and it happens seven years farther on.

It took place in New York, where he had done well — so well that there were no barriers too high for him. He was thirty-two years old, and, except for one flying trip immediately after the war, he had not been West in seven years. A man named Devlin from Detroit came into his office to see him in a business way, and then and there this incident occurred, and closed out, so to speak, this particular side of his life.

"So you're from the Middle West," said the man Devlin with careless curiosity. "That's funny — I thought men like you were probably born and raised on Wall Street. You know — wife of one of my best friends in Detroit came from your city. I was an usher at the wedding."

Dexter waited with no apprehension of what was coming.

"Judy Simms," said Devlin with no particular interest; "Judy Jones she was once."

"Yes, I knew her." A dull impatience spread over him. He had heard, of course, that she was married — perhaps deliberately he had heard no more.

"Awfully nice girl," brooded Devlin meaninglessly, "I'm sort of sorry for her."

"Why?" Something in Dexter was alert, receptive, at once.

"Oh, Lud Simms has gone to pieces in a way. I don't mean he ill-uses her, but he drinks and runs around —— "

"Doesn't she run around?"

"No. Stays at home with her kids."

"Oh."

"She's a little too old for him," said Devlin.

"Too old!" cried Dexter. "Why, man, she's only twenty-seven."

He was possessed with a wild notion of rushing out into the streets and taking a train to Detroit. He rose to his feet spasmodically.

"I guess you're busy," Devlin apologized quickly. "I didn't realize —— "

"No, I'm not busy," said Dexter, steadying his voice. "I'm not busy at all. Not busy at all. Did you say she was — twenty-seven? No, I said she was twenty-seven."

"Yes, you did," agreed Devlin dryly.

"Go on, then. Go on."

"What do you mean?"

"About Judy Jones."

Devlin looked at him helplessly.

"Well, that's — I told you all there is to it. He treats her like the devil. Oh, they're not going to get divorced or anything. When he's particularly outrageous she forgives him. In fact, I'm inclined to think she loves him. She was a pretty girl when she first came to Detroit."

A pretty girl! The phrase struck Dexter as ludicrous.

"Isn't she — a pretty girl, any more?"

"Oh, she's all right."

"Look here," said Dexter, sitting down suddenly. "I don't understand. You say she was a 'pretty girl' and now you say she's 'all right.' I don't understand what you mean — Judy Jones wasn't a pretty girl, at all. She was a great beauty. Why, I knew her, I knew her. She was —— "

Devlin laughed pleasantly.

"I'm not trying to start a row," he said. "I think Judy's a nice girl and I like her. I can't understand how a man like Lud Simms could fall madly in love with her, but he did." Then he added: "Most of the women like her."

Dexter looked closely at Devlin, thinking wildly that there must be a reason for this, some insensitivity in the man or some private malice.

"Lots of women fade just like that," Devlin snapped his fingers. "You must have seen it happen. Perhaps I've forgotten how pretty she was at her wedding. I've seen her so much since then, you see. She has nice eyes."

A sort of dullness settled down upon Dexter. For the first time in his life he felt like getting very drunk. He knew that he was laughing loudly at something Devlin had said, but he did not know what it was or why it was funny. When, in a few minutes, Devlin went he lay down on his lounge and looked out the window at the New York sky-line into which the sun was sinking in dull lovely shades of pink and gold.

He had thought that having nothing else to lose he was invulnerable at last — but he knew that he had just lost something more, as surely as if he had married Judy Jones and seen her fade away before his eyes.

The dream was gone. Something had been taken from him. In a sort of panic he pushed the palms of his hands into his eyes and tried to bring up a picture of the waters lapping on Sherry Island and the moonlit veranda, and gingham on the golf-links and the dry sun and the gold color of her neck's soft down. And her mouth damp to his kisses and her eyes plaintive with melancholy and her freshness like a new fine linen in the morning. Why, these things were no longer in the world! They had existed and they existed no longer.

For the first time in years the tears were streaming down his face. But they were for himself now. He did not care about mouth and eyes and moving hands. He wanted to care, and he could not care. For he had gone away and he could never go back any more. The gates were closed, the sun was gone down, and there was no beauty but the gray beauty of steel that withstands all time. Even the grief he could have borne was left behind in the country of illusion, of youth, of the richness of life, where his winter dreams had flourished.

"Long ago," he said, "long ago, there was something in me, but now that thing is gone. Now that thing is gone, that thing is gone. I cannot cry. I cannot care. That thing will come back no more."

Janet Frame

Janet Frame (1924–2004), who shares with Katherine Mansfield the distinction of being New Zealand's most acclaimed writer of short stories, was born the third of five children of working-class parents who emigrated to New Zealand from Scotland. Her father worked for the railways, and her mother served as a housemaid for some years to the wealthy family of Katherine Mansfield. Frame's childhood and adolescence were darkened after the deaths of two of her sisters in separate drowning accidents, and the onset of her beloved brother's severe epileptic seizures. In 1943 she began a course in teacher training though she aspired to be a poet. She managed to complete the first two years of the course, but during the third year of practical classroom experience, she attempted suicide by swallowing a bottle of aspirin tablets. After initiating therapy, she was sent to Seacliff Lunatic Asylum, an infamous local mental institution, where she stayed on and off for the next eight years. Diagnosed as suffering from schizophrenia, she was treated with over two hundred sessions of electroconvulsive therapy and insulin. In 1951, while still a patient at the hospital, her first book was published by New Zealand's Caxton Press. This was a collection titled *The Lagoon and Other Stories*. After it won the prestigious Hubert Church Memorial Award, Frame's doctors cancelled her scheduled lobotomy operation. Four years later, after her discharge from Seacliff, she rented a hut in the back garden of the writer Frank Sargeson at his home in an Auckland suburb. There with his encouragement she wrote her first novel, *Owls Do Cry* (1957).

In late 1956 Frame left New Zealand to live and write in Europe. During the next seven years she published several books despite her struggles with anxiety and depression. These included the novel *Faces in the Water* (1961), a fictionalized account of her experiences in the psychiatric wards of various hospitals. In this novel she polished her uniquely impressionistic literary style, avoiding the prevailing literary realism of her time and continuing in the tradition of Mansfield and Virginia Woolf's more experimental style. The success of this landmark novel gave Frame the confidence to live the solitary life she wanted, avoiding marriage and a family in order to devote herself to her writing. She returned to New Zealand, where she stayed the remainder of her life with frequent trips to the United States. In the 1980s she completed an autobiographical trilogy in an attempt to set the record straight. When it was adapted as a film for television by screenwriter Laura Jones and director Jane Campion, it was so successful that it introduced Frame to a new generation of readers.

In her lifetime Frame's literary works include eleven novels, four short story collections, and a book of poetry in addition to her three-volume autobiography. "The Two Sheep," an early fable, first appeared in *Snowman Snowman: Fables and Fantasies* in 1963. It was reprinted in *You Are Now Entering the Human Heart* (1983) and *The Daylight and the Dust: Selected Stories* (2010). Frame wrote her American publisher George Braziller a letter that suggests her individuality and her consummate commitment to her craft: "For me writing a book is a sealing process—there should be no seams showing, no hinges, no suggestion of the kitset novel, although, as nothing is forbidden, a writer may write a kitset novel if she wishes but transform it, transform it." She died at the age of seventy-nine from acute myeloid leukemia. Her posthumously published second volume of poetry was awarded New Zealand's top poetry prize in 2007.

RELATED STORY
Ursula K. Le Guin, "The Ones Who Walk Away from Omelas," page 814.

Two Sheep

1963

TWO SHEEP WERE TRAVELLING to the saleyards. The first sheep knew that after they had been sold their destination was the slaughterhouse at the freezing works. The second sheep did not know of their fate. They were being driven with the rest of the flock along a hot dusty valley road where the surrounding hills leaned in a sun-scorched wilderness of rock, tussock and old rabbit warrens. They moved slowly, for the drover in his trap was in no hurry, and had even taken one of the dogs to sit beside him while the other scrambled from side to side of the flock, guiding them.

"I think," said the first sheep who was aware of their approaching death, "that the sun has never shone so warm on my fleece, nor, from what I see with my small sheep's eye, has the sky seemed so flawless, without seams or tucks or cracks or blemishes."

"You are crazy," said the second sheep who did not know of their approaching death. "The sun is warm, yes, but how hot and dusty and heavy my wool feels! It is a burden to go trotting along this oven shelf. It seems our journey will never end,"

"How fresh and juicy the grass appears on the hill," the first sheep exclaimed. "And not a hawk in the sky!"

"I think," replied the second sheep, "that something has blinded you. Just look up in the sky and see those three hawks waiting to swoop and attack us!"

They trotted on further through the valley road. Now and again the second sheep stumbled.

"I feel so tired," he said. "I wonder how much longer we must walk on and on through this hot dusty valley?"

But the first sheep walked nimbly and his wool felt light upon him as if he had just been shorn. He could have gambolled like a lamb in August.

"I still think," he said, "that today is the most wonderful day I have known. I do not feel that the road is hot and dusty. I do not notice the stones and grit that you complain of. To me the hills have never seemed so green and enticing, the sun has never seemed so warm and comforting. I believe that I could walk through this valley forever, and never feel tired or hungry or thirsty."

"Whatever has come over you?" the second sheep asked crossly. "Here we are, trotting along hour after hour, and soon we shall stand in our pens in the saleyards while the sun leans over us with its branding irons and our overcoats are such a burden that they drag us to the floor of our pen where we are almost trampled to death by the so dainty feet of our fellow sheep. A fine life that is. It would not surprise me if after we are sold we are taken in trucks to the freezing works and killed in cold blood. But," he added, comforting himself, "that is not likely to happen. Oh no, that could never happen: I have it on authority that even when they are trampled by their fellows, sheep do not die. The tales we hear from time to time are but malicious rumours, and those vivid dreams which strike us in the night as we sleep in the sheltered hills, they are but illusions. Do you not agree?" he asks the first sheep.

They were turning now from the valley road, and the saleyards were in sight, while drawn up in the siding on the rusty railway lines, the red trucks stood waiting, spattered inside with sheep and cattle dirt and with white chalk marks, in cipher, on the outside. And still the first sheep did not reveal to his companion that they were being driven to certain death.

When they were jostled inside their pen the first sheep gave an exclamation of delight.

"What a pleasant little house they have let to us! I have never seen such smart red painted bars, and such four-square corners. And look at the elegant stairway which we will climb to enter those red caravans for our seaside holiday!"

"You make me tired," the second sheep said. "We are standing inside a dirty pen, nothing more, and I cannot move my feet in their nicely polished black shoes but I tread upon the dirt left by sheep which have been imprisoned here before us. In fact I have never been so badly treated in all my life!" And the second sheep began to cry. Just then a kind elderly sheep jostled through the flock and began to comfort him.

"You have been frightening your companion, I suppose," she said angrily to the first sheep. "You have been telling horrible tales of our fate. Some sheep never know when to keep things to themselves. There was no need to tell your companion the truth, that we are being led to certain death!"

But the first sheep did not answer. He was thinking that the sun had never blessed him with so much warmth, that no crowded pen had ever seemed so comfortable and luxurious. Then suddenly he was taken by surprise and hustled out a little gate and up the ramp into the waiting truck, and suddenly too the sun shone in its true colours, battering him about the head with gigantic burning bars, while the hawks congregated above, sizzling the sky with their wings, and a pall of dust clung to the barren used-up hills, and everywhere was commotion, pushing, struggling, bleating, trampling.

"This must be death," he thought, and he began to struggle and cry out.

The second sheep, having at last learned that he would meet his fate at the freezing works, stood unperturbed now in the truck with his nose against the wall and his eyes looking through the slits.

"You are right," he said to the first sheep. "The hill has never seemed so green, the sun has never been warmer, and this truck with its neat red walls is a mansion where I would happily spend the rest of my days."

But the first sheep did not answer. He had seen the approach of death. He could hide from it no longer. He had given up the struggle and was lying exhausted in a corner of the truck. And when the truck arrived at its destination, the freezing works, the man whose duty it was to unload the sheep noticed the first lying so still in the corner that he believed it was dead.

"We can't have dead sheep," he said, "How can you kill a dead sheep?"

So he heaved the first sheep out of the door of the truck onto the rusty railway line.

"I'll move it away later," he said to himself, "Meanwhile, here goes with this lot."

And while he was so busy moving the flock, the first sheep, recovering, sprang up and trotted away along the line, out the gate of the freezing works, up the road, along another road, until he saw a flock being driven before him.

"I will join the flock," he said. "No one will notice, and I shall be safe."

While the drover was not looking, the first sheep hurried in among the flock and was soon trotting along with them until they came to a hot dusty road through a valley where the hills leaned in a sun-scorched wilderness of rock, tussock, and old rabbit warrens.

By now he was feeling very tired. He spoke for the first time to his new companions.

"What a hot dusty road," he said. "How uncomfortable the heat is, and the sun seems to be striking me for its own burning purposes."

The sheep walking beside him looked surprised.

"It is a wonderful day," he exclaimed. "The sun is warmer than I have ever known it, the hills glow green with luscious grass, and there is not a hawk in the sky to threaten us!"

"You mean," the first sheep replied slyly, "that you are on your way to the saleyards, and then to the freezing works to be killed."

The other sheep gave a bleat of surprise.

"How did you guess?" he asked.

"Oh," said the first sheep wisely, "I know the code. And because I know the code I shall go around in circles all my life, not knowing whether to think that the hills are bare or whether they are green, whether the hawks are scarce or plentiful, whether the sun is friend or foe. For the rest of my life I shall not speak another word. I shall trot along the hot dusty valleys where the hills are both barren and lush with spring grass.

"What shall I do but keep silent?"

And so it happened, and over and over again the first sheep escaped death, and rejoined the flock of sheep who were travelling to the freezing works. He is still alive today. If you notice him in a flock, being driven along a hot dusty road, you will be able to distinguish him by his timidity, his uncertainty, the frenzied expression in his eyes when he tries, in his condemned silence, to discover whether the sky is at last free from hawks, or whether they circle in twos and threes above him, waiting to kill him.

Carlos Fuentes

Carlos Fuentes (1928–2012), the eminent Mexican novelist and short story writer, was born In Panama City. His father was a Mexican diplomat, so the family often lived abroad. After attending secondary schools in the United States, Chile, Argentina, and Mexico, Fuentes studied international law in Geneva from 1950 to 1952. In 1954 he published his first book, a collection of short stories titled *Masked Days*, and he began a career in the Mexican Ministry of Foreign Affairs. After the Cuban Revolution, he resigned from the diplomatic service to write full time, though in the 1970s Fuentes served as Mexican ambassador to France, among other assignments. He also lectured on Spanish and Latin American literature at several universities in the United States. His books include *The Death of Artemio Cruz* (1962), *Aura* (1962), and *Terra Nostra* (1975), an ambitious novel about Hispanic civilization. Other works include the story collection *Burnt Water* (1980) and *The Old Gringo* (1985), a novel that imagined the last days of the writer Ambrose Bierce in Mexico. It became the first bestseller in the United States written by a Mexican author.

Early in his writing, Fuentes concentrated on social issues in Latin America, but he also experimented with magical realism, contributing his share of narratives describing "the marvelous in the everyday" to the literary tradition developed by his friends Gabriel García Márquez and Julio Cortázar. "Pain" is an example of a third type of his fiction, a realistic psychological study revealing the obsessive, secret lives of ordinary people. It was included in *The Crystal Frontier: A Novel in Nine Stories* (1997).

Like the work of García Márquez, Fuentes's books have had a political impact by helping to create a Latin American identity and make Latin Americans more aware of their own culture. Fuentes has said, "One writes a lot for the future. I say to myself, 'O.K., there are a lot of illiterates in Mexico. Are they going to read *Terra Nostra*? Of course not. But what about tomorrow? What happens when they will be able to read? Will we be able to give them a cultural tradition?'"

RELATED COMMENTARY
Carlos Fuentes, "Mexico, the United States, and the Multicultural Future," p. 1430.

RELATED CASEBOOK
See Casebook on Magical Realism, pages 1627–1646, including Jorge Luis Borges, "Borges and I," page 1631; Alejo Carpentier, "On the Marvelous Real in America," page 1633 and "The Baroque and the Marvelous Real," page 1635; Luis Leal, "Magical Realism in Spanish American Literature," page 1637; William Gass, "The First Seven Pages of the Boom," page 1639; Ursula K. Le Guin, "The Kind of Fiction Most Characteristic of Our Times," page 1641; Mario Vargas Llosa, "The Prose Style of Jorge Luis Borges and Gabriel García Márquez," page 1645.

Pain

1997 / For Julio Ortega
Translated by Alfred MacAdam

I

Juan Zamora asked me to tell this story while he kept his back turned. What he means is that he wants to have his back to the reader the whole time. He says he's ashamed. Or, as he puts it himself, "I'm in pain." "Pain" as a synonym for "shame" is a peculiarity of Mexican speech, comparable to saying "senior citizens" for "old people" — so as not to offend — or saying "He's in a bad way" to soften the idea that someone's illness is terminal. Shame causes pain; sometimes pain causes shame.

So Juan Zamora will not offer you a view of his face over the course of this story. You'll be able to see only the nape of his neck, his back. I won't say "his ass," because that, too, is a loaded term in Mexico. Especially in the sense of "offering" your ass to someone, the lowest act of cowardice, a yielding or a type of abject courtesy. That's not the case with Juan Zamora. He wears a big university sweatshirt, size XXL, decorated in front with the emblem of the university in question, the kind of sweatshirt that hangs down to your thighs (though he wears it tucked into his jeans). No, Juan Zamora insists I tell you he won't be offering anything. He only wants to emphasize that his shame is equal to his pain. He doesn't blame anyone. It is true that he touched a world and that the world touched him.

But after all, everything that happened passed through him and happened inside him. This is what counts.

The story takes place during the time of the Mexican oil boom, at the end of the 1970s and beginning of the 1980s. Right from the start, that explains part of the pain-shame identification Juan Zamora is talking about. Shame because we celebrated the boom like a bunch of nouveaux riches. Pain because the wealth was badly used. Shame because the president said our problem now was to administer our wealth. Pain because the poor kept on getting poorer. Shame because we became frivolous spendthrifts, slaves of vulgar whims and our comic macho posturing. Pain because we were incapable of administering even our shame. Pain and shame because we were no good at being rich; the only things appropriate for us are poverty, dignity, effort. In Mexico, there have always been corrupt authoritarian figures with too much power. But they are forgiven everything if they are at least serious. (Is there one corruption that's serious and another that's frivolous?) Frivolity is intolerable, unforgivable, the mockery of all those who've been screwed. That's the source of the pain and the shame of those years when we were millionaires for a day, then woke up broke, out in the street, tears of laughter pouring down our faces before we began to laugh with pain.

Juan Zamora has his back to you. When he was twenty-three, he got to study at Cornell, thanks to a scholarship. He was a dedicated pre-med student at the National Preparatory School and then at the National University, and he

495

swears to you that that would have been enough for him if his mother hadn't got it into her head that during the Mexican boom period it was necessary to do some postgrad work at a Yankee university.

"Your father never knew how to take advantage of an opportunity. He was Don Leonardo Barroso's administrative lawyer for twenty years and died without a penny to his name. What could he have been thinking about? Well, not about you or me, Juanito, you can be sure of that."

"What did he say to you?"

"That honesty is its own reward. That he was an honorable professional. That he wasn't going to betray Mario de la Cueva and his other professors at the law school. That he'd been taught that law is an honorable profession. That you cannot defend the law if you're corrupt yourself. 'But it's not illegal, Gonzalo,' I'd say to your father, 'to accept a payment for doing favors. It's no crime drawing a matter to the attention of Minister Barroso. Everyone in government gets rich but you!'

" 'That's called a bribe, Lelia. It's a triple deception, besides being a lie. If the matter develops, it looks as if I was paid to move it along. If it fails, I look like a crook. In either case, I deceive the minister, the nation, and myself.'

" 'A little public-works contract, Gonzalo, that's all I'm asking you to request. You get your commission and bye-bye. No one will find out. With that money we could buy a house in Anzures. And get out of Colonia Santa María. We could send Juanito to a gringo university. What I mean is, the boy's a very good student and it would be a shame for him to go to waste with that riffraff at the National University.' "

Juan tells me to say that his mother recounted those things with a bitter smile on her face, a grimace that her son had only seen, from time to time, on cadavers he studied at school.

His father, Gonzalo Zamora, CPA, had to die for his widow to ask a single favor from Don Leonardo Barroso: would he see if he could get a scholarship for Juanito to study medicine in the United States? With great elegance, Don Leonardo said, Why, of course, he would be delighted to take care of it — why, that's the least the memory of good old Zamora deserved, such an honest lawyer, such a diligent functionary.

II

I'm following Juan Zamora, the Mexican student with his gray sweatshirt, through the sad streets of Ithaca, New York. I have no idea what he's looking for since there's so little to see here. The main street has barely any stores, two or three very bad restaurants, and immediately after that come mountains and gorges. Juanito feels — almost — as if he's in Mexico, in San Juan del Río or Tepeji, places he'd visited from time to time on holiday to breathe the air of forests and gorges, far from the pollution of the capital. The gorge in Ithaca is a deep and forbidding ravine, apparently a seductive abyss as well. Ithaca is famous for the number of suicides committed by desperate students who jump off the bridge spanning the gorge. One joke says that no professor will fail a bad student, for fear he'll dive into the chasm.

Since there isn't much to see around here on Sunday, Juan Zamora is going back to the house where he's living. It's a beautiful place of pale pink brick with a blue slate roof, surrounded by a well-kept lawn that becomes gravel around the house and extends into a tangled, thin, and somber woods behind it. Ivy climbs up the pink brick.

The seasons make up for Ithaca's lack of charm. Now it's late fall, and the forest is denuded, the trees on the mountainsides look like burned toothpicks, and the sky comes two or three steps down to communicate to all of us the silence and pain of God in the face of the fleeting death of the world. But winter in Ithaca gives a voice back to nature, which takes revenge on God by dressing in white, scattering frozen dust and snow stars, spreading large ivory mantles like sumptuous sheets on the earth — and an answer to heaven. Spring explodes, rapid and agonizing, in handfuls of splendid roses that perfume the air and leave a flash of forgotten things before summer takes over, heavy, sleepy, and slow, unlike the swift spring. Idle and lazy summer of stagnant waters, pesky mosquitoes, heavy, humid breathing, and intensely green mountains.

The gorge, too, reflects the seasons, but it also devours them, collapses them, and subjects them to the implacable death of gravity, a suffocating, final embrace of all things. The gorge is the vertigo in the order of this place.

Alongside the gorge, there is a munitions factory, a horrifying building of blackened brick with obscene chimneys, almost an evocation of the ugliness of the Nazis' "night and fog." The pistols produced by the Ithaca factory were the official side arm of the army of El Salvador, which is why officers and men there called them "itaquitas" — little Ithacas.

Juan Zamora asks me to tell all this while he turns his back on us because he was received as a guest in the residence of a prosperous businessman who in former years was connected with the munitions factory but now prefers to be an adviser to law firms negotiating defense contracts between the factory owners and the U.S. government. Tarleton Wingate and his family, in the days when Juan Zamora comes to live with them, are excited about the triumph of Ronald Reagan over Jimmy Carter. They watch television every night and applaud the decisions of the new president, his movie-star smile, his desire to put a halt to excessive government control, his optimism in declaring that a new day is dawning in America, his firmness in stopping the advances of Communism in Central America.

Wingate is a likable giant with fewer wrinkles on his fresh, juvenile face than an old saddle. His dull, sandy-colored hair contrasts with the platinum blond of his wife, Charlotte, and with the burnished, reddish-chestnut hair of the daughter of the house, Becky, who is thirteen. When the Wingates all sit down to watch television, they kindly invite Juan to join them. He doesn't understand if they are pained when terrible pictures of the war in El Salvador appear — nuns murdered along the roadside, rebels murdered by paramilitary death squads, an entire village machine-gunned by the army as the people flee across a river.

Juan Zamora turns his back to the screen and assures them that in Mexico they applaud President Reagan for saving us all from Communism, just as much as people do here. He also tells them that Mexico is interested in growing and prospering, as they can clearly see in the massive development of the oil industry by the government of López Portillo.

The gringos smile when they hear that, because they believe that prosperity is an inoculation against Communism. Juan Zamora wants to ask Mr. Wingate how his business with the Pentagon is going but decides he'd better keep quiet. What he insinuates first and then emphatically declares is that his family, the Zamoras, are adapting perfectly to Mexico's new wealth because they have always had lands, haciendas — the word has great prestige in the United States, where they pronounce the silent *h* — and oil wells. He realizes the Wingates don't know that oil is the property of the state in Mexico and are amazed at everything he tells them. Dogmatically but innocently, the Wingates believe that the expression *free world* is synonymous with *free enterprise*.

They have received Juan with pleasure, as part of a tradition. For a long time, foreign students have been hospitably taken into private homes near campuses in the United States. It surprises no one that rich young Latin Americans seek out such homes as extensions of their own and use them to accelerate their assimilation of English.

"There are kids," Tarleton Wingate assures him, "who have learned English spending hours in front of a TV set."

They all watch Peter Sellers's movie *Being There*, where the protagonist knows nothing except what he learns watching television, which is why he passes as a genius.

The Wingates ask Juan Zamora if Mexican television is good, and he has to answer truthfully that it isn't, that it's boring, vulgar, and censored, and that a very good writer, widely read by young people, Carlos Monsiváis, calls it "the idiot box." That seemed hilarious to Becky, who says she's going to tell it to her class — the idiot box. Don't put on intellectual airs, Charlotte tells her daughter; "egghead" she calls her, smiling as she tousles her hair. The redhead protests, don't tangle my hair, I'll have to fix it again before I baby-sit tonight. Juan Zamora is amazed at how gringo children work from the time they are young, baby-sitting, delivering papers, or selling lemonade during the summer. "It's to teach them the Protestant work ethic," Mr. Wingate says solemnly. And him? How did you ever grow up without television? Becky asks. Juan Zamora understands very well what Mr. Wingate is saying. Being rich and aristocratic in Mexico is a matter of land, haciendas, farm laborers, an elegant lifestyle, horses, dressing up as a *charro*, and having lots of servants — that's what being wealthy means in Mexico. Not watching television. And since his hosts have exactly the same idea in their heads, they understand it, praise it, envy it, and Becky goes out to earn five dollars as a babysitter. Charlotte puts on her apron to cook dinner, and Tarleton, with a profound sense of obligation, sits down to read the number-one book on the *New York Times* best-seller list, a spy novel that happens to confirm his paranoia about the red menace.

III

If the city of Ithaca is a kind of suburban Avernus, Cornell University is its Parnassus: a brilliant cream-colored temple with modern, sometimes almost Art

Deco lines and vast green and luminous spaces. Given the abrupt nature of the terrain, the campus is linked by beautiful terraces and grand stairways. Both lead to places that are centers of the life of the Mexican student Juan Zamora. One is the student union, which tries to make up for all of Ithaca's shortcomings with books, a stationery store, movies, theater, clothing, mailboxes, restaurants, and places to meet. Moving among those spaces, his back toward us, Juan Zamora tries to connect with the place. He takes special notice of the extreme sloppiness of the students. They wear baseball caps they don't even take off indoors or when they greet women. They rarely shave completely. They drink beer straight from the bottle. They wear sleeveless T-shirts, revealing at all hours their hairy underarms. Their jeans have torn knees, and at times they wear them cut off at the thigh and unraveling. They sit down to eat with their caps on and fill their mouths with hamburgers, french fries, and an entire menu pulled out of plastic bags. When they really want to be informal, they wear their baseball caps backward, with the visors cooling the napes of their necks.

One day, an athletic boy, blond, with pinched features, ordered a plate of spaghetti and began to eat it with his hands, by the fistful. Juan Zamora felt an uncontrollable revulsion that obliterated his appetite and forced him for the first and perhaps only time to criticize a fellow student. "That's disgusting! Didn't they teach you how to eat at home?" "Of course they did. My family's pretty rich, for your information." "So why do you eat like an animal?" "Because now I'm free," said the blond through a mouthful of pasta.

Juan Zamora arrived at Cornell not in a sports coat and tie but in blue jeans, a leather jacket, a sweater, and loafers. While alive, his father resigned himself to this scruffiness: "We used to wear suits and ties to class at law school . . ." Little by little, Juan assumed a more casual wardrobe — sweatshirt, Keds — but he always maintained (with his back turned) a minimal properness. He understood that the shabby disguise worn by the students was a way of equalizing social classes, so no one would ask about family background or economic status. All equal, equalized by sloppiness, the T-shirts, baseball caps, sneakers. Only in his refuge — the residence of the Wingate family — could Juan Zamora say, with impunity and with universal approval, even impressing them: "My family is very old. We've always been rich. We have haciendas, horses, servants. Now with the oil, we'll simply live as we always have, but with even more luxury. If only you could visit us in Mexico. My mother would be so happy to receive you and thank you for your kindness to me."

And Charlotte would sigh with admiration. She was the first platinum-dyed white woman Juan Zamora had ever seen wearing an apron. "How polite Spanish aristocrats are! Learn, Becky."

Charlotte never called Juan Zamora Mexican. She was afraid of offending him.

IV

The other space in the life of the Mexican student was the school of medicine, especially the amphitheater, built on Greek lines and as white as snow, but solid and crowning a hill as if intentionally, so that the smells of chloroform and formaldehyde would not contaminate the rest of the campus. Here the outlandish student outfits were replaced by the white uniform of medicine, although at times hairy legs and (almost always) blackened Keds would appear at the bottoms of the long clinic gowns.

Men and women, all in white, gave the place the air of a religious community. Young monks and nuns passed through its sparkling corridors. Juan thought chastity would be the rule in this order of young doctors. Besides, the white uniform (unless the hairy legs stuck out) accentuated the generational androgyny. Some girls wore their hair very short, while some boys wore it very long, so at times it was difficult to tell from behind what sex a person was.

Juan Zamora had had a couple of sexual relationships in Mexico. Sex was not his strong suit. He didn't like prostitutes. His female classmates at the National University were very demanding, very devouring and distracting, talking about having families or being independent, about living this way or that, about succeeding, and they talked with a decisiveness that made him feel out of place, guilty, ashamed of not being, ever, yet, all he could be. Juan Zamora's problem was that he confused each step of his life with something definitive, finished. Just as there are young people who let things flow and leave everything to chance, there are others who think the world ends every twenty-four hours. Juan was one of the latter. Without admitting it, he knew that his mother's anguish about their modest means, his father's upright pride, and his own uncertainties about his father's morality gave him a feeling of perpetual distress, of imminent doom that was mocked by the gray, implacable flow of daily life. If he had accepted that tranquil march of days, he might perhaps have entered a more or less stable relationship with a girl. But girls saw in Juan Zamora a boy who was too tense, frightened, insecure. A young man with his back turned, in pain.

"Why are you always looking behind you? Do you think someone's following us?"

"Don't be afraid to cross the street. There are no cars coming."

"Listen, stop ducking. No one's swinging at you."

Now, at Cornell, he put on his white robe and carefully washed his hands. He was going to perform his first autopsy, he and another student. Would it be a man or a woman? The question was important because it applied as well to the cadaver he would be studying.

The auditorium was dark.

Juan Zamora felt his way to the barely visible autopsy table. Then his back rubbed against someone else's. The two of them laughed nervously. In a flash, the blinding, implacable lights went on, like some vengeful Jehovah, and the janitor apologized for not getting there on time. He always tried to be more punctual than the students, he exclaimed, laughing, ashamed.

Which one would Juan Zamora look at first? The student or the cadaver? He looked down and saw the body covered by a sheet. He looked up and found that a very blond person with long hair and not very wide shoulders was looking away from him. He looked down again and uncovered the cadaver's face. It was impossible to know if the cadaver was a man or woman. Death had erased not only its time but its sexual personality. The only thing certain was that it was old. It was made of wax. You always had to think that the cadavers were made of wax. It made them easier to dissect. This one's eyes weren't closed tightly, and Juan was shocked to think they were still crying. But the thin nose stuffed with cotton balls, the rigid jaw, the sunken lips were no longer the cadaver's or ours. Death had stripped the individual of pronouns. It was no longer he or she, yours or mine. The other gloved hand held out a scalpel to him.

They worked in silence. They were masked. The blond person working with him, small but decisive, knew the guts of a dead person better than Juan did and guided him in the incisions he would have to make. He or she was an expert. Juan dared to look into the eyes opposite his own. They were gray, that hazel-tinted gray that sometimes appears in the most beautiful Anglo-Saxon eyes, where the unusual color is almost always accompanied by dreamy eyelids, depths of desire, fluidity, but also intensity.

Isolated by the latex, the masks, the robes, their gloved hands touched with the same feeling as when a man wears a condom. Only their eyes saw each other. Now Juan Zamora faces us, he turns to look at us, pulls off his mask, reveals his mestizo face, young, dark, with prominent, chiseled bones, his skin like some dessert — brown sugar, cinnamon candy, *café con leche* — his smooth, firm chin, his thick lower lip, his liquid black eyes that find the hazel-gray eyes. Juan Zamora no longer has his back turned. Instinctively, passionately, he turns his face toward us, he brings it close to the lips of the other, they join in a liberating, complete kiss that washes away all his insecurities, all his solitude, all his pain and shame. The two boys urgently, tremulously, ardently kiss in order to conquer death, if not for all time, then at least for this moment.

V

Jim was twenty-two, thin and refined, serious and studious, interested in politics and art: the other students called him Lord Jim. His blond head, his hazel-ringed eyes, and his small physique were accompanied by good muscles, good bones, a nervous agility, and, especially, extremely agile hands and long fingers. He would be a great doctor — Juan Zamora would say — though not because of his fingers and hands but because of his vocation. He was a little bit — Juan, despite the distance, orders us to say — like Juan's father, Gonzalo, a dedicated man, solid, though not worthy of compassion.

The two young men, a contrast of light and dark, looked good together. At first they attracted attention on campus, then they were accepted and even admired for the obvious affection they showed for each other and the spontaneousness of their relationship. In terms of love, Juan Zamora finally found himself satisfied, his feelings identified; at the same time, he was surprised. He really had had no idea about his homosexual tendencies, and to feel them revealed in this way, with this man, so completely and so passionately, with such satisfaction and understanding, filled him with a calm pride.

They continued studying and working together. Their conversation and their life had an immediacy, as if Juan Zamora's problem — the fear that each day would be the last, or at least the definitive, day — had become, thanks to Lord Jim, a blessing. For several weeks, there was no before and no after. Shared pleasure filled their days, kept other concerns and other times at bay.

One afternoon, as they were working together on an autopsy, Jim asked Juan for the first time about his studies in Mexico. Juan explained that he'd studied in the University City but that occasionally he'd passed through the old School of Medicine, located in the Plaza de Santo Domingo. It was a very beautiful colonial building that had housed the offices of the Inquisition. Lord Jim responded with a nervous laugh: it was the first time Juan had left him for a time that was not only remote but even forbidden and detested by the Anglo-Saxon soul. Juan persisted. There were no women doctors in Mexico until 1873, and the first one, Matilde Montoya, was allowed to do autopsies only in empty auditoriums, with the cadavers fully clothed.

Jim's nervous laugh was a small break in the tension or the distance (were they the same thing?) which that simple reference to the Holy Inquisition had introduced into the way they were together, the first irruption of a past into a relationship that the two boys lived only for the present. Juan Zamora had the ungraspable but desolating feeling that at that precise moment an even more dangerous perspective was also opening — the future. They slowly covered the cadaver of a beautiful girl who'd committed suicide and whose body no one had claimed.

Juan Zamora carefully timed his meetings with Lord Jim for the afternoons so he could return to the Wingates on time, have dinner with them, watch television, and make comments. Reagan was beginning his dirty secret war against Nicaragua, which was starting to annoy Juan Zamora, though he did not understand why. Tarleton, on the other hand, celebrated Reagan's decision to put a limit to Marxist expansion in the Americas. Perhaps that was the reason for the growing coolness of Charlotte and Tarleton Wingate and for the rather comic confusion of Becky, who was dispatched to her room as soon as Juan appeared, as if his mere appearance announced a plague. Did Juan Zamora look like a guerrilla and a Sandinista?

Of course, the Mexican student understood immediately that rumors of his homosexual association had filtered down from Parnassus to Suburbia — the community was small. But he decided not to give in and to go on normally, because his relationship was exactly that, normal, for the only people who had anything to say about it — he and Jim.

Jim was sensitive, he had good antennae, and he noticed a certain nervous malaise in his lover. He knew it had nothing to do with their relationship. In Jim's dormitory bed, wrapped in each other's arms, Juan tried to excuse himself because that afternoon he had not been able to perform. Jim, caressing Juan's head as it rested against his shoulder, told him it was normal, it happened to everyone. Both of them were doctors and were well acquainted with the stereotyped ideas surrounding sexual activity of all kinds, from masturbation, which supposedly drove adolescents insane, to the perfectly normal use of pornographic material by older people. But the myths of homosexuality were the worst. He understood. The Wingates would not tolerate a gay couple. It wasn't the racial or the social difference that bothered them. But Juan never played the role of rich boy with Jim. He said nothing. Jim wasn't interested in the past.

Juan tried to kiss Jim, but Jim stood up, naked, enraged, and said it was he who couldn't stand the repugnant Puritanism of these people, their disgusting disguise of goodness and their perpetual, inviolable sanctity in politics and sexuality. He turned to Juan in a fury.

"Do you know what your landlord, Mr. Tarleton Wingate, does for a living? He inflates the budgets of companies doing business with the Pentagon. Do you know how much Mr. Wingate charges the air force for lavatories for its planes? Two hundred thousand dollars each. Almost a quarter of a million dollars so someone can shit comfortably in midair! Who pays the expenses of the Defense Department and the earnings of Mr. Wingate? I do. The taxpayer."

"But he says he adores Reagan because he's eliminating government and lowering taxes."

"Just ask Mr. Wingate if he wants the government to stop defense spending, stop saving failed banks, or stop subsidizing inefficient farmers. Ask him and see what he says."

"He'd probably call me a Communist."

"They're a bunch of cynics. They want free enterprise in everything, except when it comes to weapons and rescuing thieving financiers."

It's hard for Juan Zamora to accept Jim's statements, accept something that breaks his rule about ingratiating himself with the Wingates, being accepted by them and, through them, by American society. But the criticism is coming from his lover, the being Juan loves most in the world, and his lover proclaims it in an implacable, angry tone, not caring how anyone, even Juan, reacts.

The Mexican student had feared something like this, something that would break their perfect, cloistered intimacy, the self-sufficiency of lovers. He hates the world, the busybody world, the cruel world, which gains nothing by poking its nose into the lives of lovers except that — the malicious pleasure of distancing them from each other. Could they ever enjoy the same sense of fullness they experienced before this little incident? Juan was confident they could, and he multiplied the proofs of his affection and loyalty to Lord Jim, his little pamperings, his attention. Perhaps the desire to reconstruct something so perfect it had to crack one day was all too obvious.

VI

Once again they are together, wearing their white masks, their gloves, dissecting another woman's body, this time an old one's. Lord Jim asks Juan to remember that place, the palace of the Inquisition in Mexico that became the medical school. He's amused by the idea of the same building's being used for torture one day and to bring relief to bodies the next. The Mexican student subtly changes the subject and tells him about the Plaza de Santo Domingo and the ancient tradition of the "evangelists," old men with old typewriters who sit in the doorways and type out the dictation of the illiterates who want to send letters to their parents, lovers, friends.

"How do they know these scribes are reliable?"

"They don't. They have to have faith."

"Confidence, Juan."

"Right."

Jim took off his mask and Juan gestured for him to be careful — they had to take precautions. Once before, the first time, they had kissed next to a cadaver, but the bacteria of the dead have killed more than one careless doctor. Jim gave him a strange look. He asked Juan to tell him the truth. About what? About his family, his house. Jim knew what people said around the university, that Juan was the scion of a rich family, hacienda owners, and so forth. Juan had never told Jim that, because they never talked about the past. Now Jim asked him to send a spoken letter, as if he, the gringo, were the "evangelist" in the plaza and Juan the illiterate.

"It's all lies," said Juan. His back was turned once again, but he spoke without hesitation. "Pure lies. We live in a very modest apartment. My father was a very honorable man who died penniless. My mother always threw it in his face. She'll die reproaching him. I feel pain and shame for the two of them. I feel pain for my father's useless morality, which no one remembers or values and which wasn't worth shit. On the other hand, people certainly would have celebrated him if he'd been rich. I'm ashamed that he didn't steal, that he was a poor devil. But I'd be just as ashamed if he were a thief. My dad. My poor, poor dad."

He felt relieved, clean. He'd been faithful to Lord Jim. From now on, there wouldn't be a single lie between them. He thought that and fleetingly he felt ill at ease. Lord Jim could be sincere with him as well.

"Explain to me 'pain and shame,' as you call them — which would be something like 'pity and shame' in English," said the American.

"My mother causes me pain, always complaining about what never was, heartsick about her life, which she should accept because it will never be different. I'm ashamed of her self-pity, you're right, that horrible sin of inflicting pain on yourself all day long. Yes, I think you're right. You've got to have compassion to cover the pain and shame you feel toward others."

He squeezed Lord Jim's hand and told him they shouldn't talk about the past because they understood each other so well in the present. The American shot him a strange look that he almost associated with the dead woman who would not resign herself to closing her eyes, the woman they never finished dissecting.

"I feel awful saying this to you, Juan, but we have to talk about the future."

The Mexican student made an involuntary but dramatic gesture, two swift and simultaneous, though repeated, movements, one hand raised to his mouth, as if he were begging silence and another extended forward, denying, stopping what was coming.

"I'm sorry, Juan. It really pains me to say this. It even shames me. You understand that no one controls his destiny absolutely."

VII

Juan turned his back — this time literally — on Cornell. He stopped studying and courteously said good-bye to the Wingates, who were surprised and upset, asking him why, did it have anything to do with them, with the way they'd treated him? But there was relief in their eyes and secret certainty: this had to end badly. He hoped to see them again someday. He would love to take them on a tour of the hacienda on horseback. Look me up if you come to Mexico.

The American family felt relieved but also guilty. Tarleton and Charlotte discussed the matter several times. The boy must have noticed the change in his hosts' attitude when he started to go out with Jim Rowlands. Had they broken the rules of hospitality? Had they allowed themselves to succumb to irrational prejudice? They certainly had. But prejudices could not be removed over night; they were very old, they had more reality—they did—than a political party or a bank account. Blacks, homosexuals, poor people, old people, women, foreigners: the list was interminable. And Becky—why expose her to a bad influence, a scandalous relationship? She was innocent. And innocence should be protected. Becky listened to them whisper while they imagined she was watching television, and she tried to keep a straight face. If they only knew. Thirteen years old and in a private school. How could they blame anything on her? What was money for? Day after day, all day, every day, the litany of the Me Generation was entitlement to every caprice, every pleasure; there was only one value: Me. Weren't her parents that way? Weren't they successful because they were that way? What did they want from her? For her to be a Puritan from the days of the Salem witch hunts? Then the girl immersed herself in what was happening on the screen so she wouldn't hear the voices of her parents, who didn't want to be heard, and she asked herself a question that confused her greatly: How can you enjoy everything and still seem a very moral, very puritanical person? Her blood tickled her, her body was changing, and Becky was anguished not to have answers. She hugged her stuffed rabbit and dared to ask him: What about you, Bunny, do you understand anything?

Up in the clouds, Juan, en route to Mexico City in his tourist-class seat on Eastern Airlines, tried to imagine a future without Lord Jim and accepted it with bitterness, desolation, as if his life had been canceled. The bad thing was to have admitted first the past, then the future. It was the painful act of leaving the moment when they loved each other without explanations, possessors of a single time, a single space, the Eden of a loving youth that excluded parents, friends, professors, bosses. But not other lovers.

Suspended in midair, Juan Zamora tried to remember everything, the good and the bad, once more and then to cancel it forever, never again think about what happened. Never again feel hatred, pain, shame, compassion for the past his poor parents lived. And never feel pity, shame for himself or for Lord Jim, for the future they were both going to live, separated forever: Juan Zamora's desolate future, Lord Jim's happy, comfortable, secure one, his marriage having been arranged since God knows when, since before he knew Juan. That was what the families of the rich professional class did in Seattle, on the other side of the continent, where it was expected that a young doctor with a future would marry and have children—things that would inspire respect and confidence. And anyway, in the Anglo-Saxon tradition a homosexual experience was an accepted part of a gentleman's education—there wasn't an Englishman at Oxford who hadn't had one, he'd say, if something about them should leak out. Cornell and Seattle were far apart, the country was immense, loves were fragile and small.

"And we rich people, I'll tell you by quoting a good writer, are not like other people," said Lord Jim, pounding in the final nail.

Juan remembered Jim's being angry only once, over Tarleton Wingate's hypocrisy. That's the Lord Jim he wanted to remember.

He pressed his burning head against the frozen window and turned his back on everything. Below, the Cornell gorge seemed insignificant to him, it didn't say anything to him, was not for him.

VIII

Four years later, the Wingates decided to take a vacation in Cancún. They stopped over in Mexico City so Becky could visit the marvelous Museum of Anthropology. Becky, now seventeen, was rather colorless even though she imitated her mother by dyeing her hair blond. Very curious, even liberated, she found herself a little Mexican boyfriend in the hotel lobby, and they went to spend a day in Cuernavaca. He was a very passionate boy, which seemed to annoy the driver, an angry, insecure man who tried to terrify tourists by taking curves at top speed.

It was Becky who encouraged her parents to pay a surprise visit on Juan Zamora, the Mexican student who'd lived with them in 1981. Did they remember him? How could they not remember Juan Zamora? And since Tarleton and Charlotte Wingate were still ashamed about the way in which Juan left their house, they accepted their daughter's idea. Besides, Juan Zamora himself had invited them to visit him.

Tarleton called Cornell and asked for Juan's address. The university computer instantly provided it, but it was not a country address. "But I want to see a hacienda," said Becky. "This must be his town house," said Charlotte. "Should we call him?" "No," Becky said excitedly, "let's surprise him." "You're a spoiled brat," answered her father, "but I agree. If we call him, he might figure out a way not to see us. I have the feeling he was angry when he left us."

The same driver who brought Becky to Cuernavaca now drove her along with her parents. The driver had a huge mocking smile on his face. If they'd only seen her the day before, kissing her face off with that low-life slob. Now, quite the young lady, the hypocrite, with that pair of distinguished gringos — sometimes even weirder things happen — searching for an impossible place.

"Colonia Santa María?" asked the driver, almost laughing. Leandro Reyes, Tarleton read on the chauffeur's license and noted mentally — just in case. "This is the first time anyone's ever asked me to take them there."

They crossed the densest urban spaces, spaces swirling around them noisy as a river made entirely of loose stones; they cut through the brown crust of polluted air; and they also crossed the time zones of Mexico City, disordered, anarchic, immortal — time overlapping its past and its future, like a child who will be father to his posterity, like a grandson who will be the only proof that his grandfather walked through these streets; they moved steadily north, along Mariano Escobedo to Ejército Nacional, to Puente de Alvarado, and Buenavista station, beyond San Rafael, which was increasingly underneath everything, uncertain if under construction or in collapse. What is new, what's old, what is being born in this city, what's dying — are they all the same thing?

The Wingates looked at one another, shocked, pained.

"Perhaps there's been a mistake."

"No," said the driver. "This is it. It's that apartment house right over there."

"Maybe it would be better if we just went back to the hotel," said Tarleton.

"No," Becky practically shouted. "We're here. I'm dying of curiosity."

"In that case, you can go in by yourself," said her mother.

They waited a while outside the lime-green building. Three stories high, it was in dire need of a good coat of paint. Clothes were hanging on the balconies to dry, and there was a TV antenna. At a soft-drink stand by the entrance, a red-cheeked girl wearing an apron but also sporting a permanent was busy putting bottles in the cooler. A wrinkled little old man in a straw hat poked his head out the door and stared at them curiously. On either side, a repair shop. A tamale vendor passed by shouting, Red, green, with chile, sweet, lard. The driver, Leandro Reyes, went on and on in English about debts, inflation, the cost of living, devaluations of the peso, pay cuts, useless pensions, everything messed up.

Becky reappeared and quickly got back in the car. "He wasn't there, but his mother was. She said it's been a long time since anyone's visited her, Juan's fine. He's working in a hospital. I made her swear she wouldn't tell him we were here."

IX

Every night, Juan Zamora has exactly the same dream. Occasionally he wishes he could dream something else. He goes to bed thinking about something else, but no matter how hard he tries, the dream always comes back punctually. Then he gives up and concedes the power of the dream, turning it into the inevitable comrade of his nights; a lover-dream, a dream that should adore the person it visits because it won't allow itself to be expelled from that second body of the former student and now young doctor in the social security system, Juan Zamora.

Night after night, it returns until it inhabits him, his twin, his double, the mythological shirt that can't be taken off without also pulling off the dreamer's skin. He dreams with a mixture of confusion, gratitude, rejection, and love. When he wishes to escape the dream, he does so by intensely desiring to be possessed again by it; when he wants to take control of the dream, his daily life appears with the bitter smile of all of Juan Zamora's dawns, sequestering him in the hospitals, ambulances, and morgues of his urban geography. Kidnapped by life, hostage of the dream, Juan Zamora returns each night to Cornell and walks hand in hand with Lord Jim toward the bridge over the gorge. It's fall, and the trees again look as bare as black needles. The sky has descended a bit, but the gorge is deeper than the firmament and summons the two young lovers with a false promise: heaven is down here, heaven is here, face up, breathing underbrush and brambles; its breath is green, its arms spiny. You have to earn heaven by giving yourself over to it: paradise, if it does exist, is in the very guts of the earth, its humid embrace awaiting us where flesh and clay mix, where the great maternal womb mixes with the mud of creation and life is born and reborn from its great reproductive depth, but never from its airy illusion, never from the airlines falsely connecting New York and Mexico, Atlantic and Pacific, in fact separating the lovers, breaking the marvelous unity of their perfect androgyny, their Siamese identity, their beautiful abnormality, their monstrous perfection, casting them to incompatible destinies, to opposite horizons. What time is it in Seattle when night falls in Mexico? Why does Jim's city face a panting sea while Juan's faces nervous dust? Why is the coastal air like crystal and the air of the plateau like excrement?

Juan and Jim sit on the bridge railing and look at each other deeply, to the depth of the Mexican's black eyes and the American's gray ones, not touching, possessed by their eyes, understanding everything, accepting everything, without rancor, without illusions, disposed nevertheless to have everything, the origin of love transformed into the destiny of love with no possible separation, no matter how daily life may split them apart.

They look at each other, they smile, they both stand at the edge of the bridge, they take each other by the hand, and they jump into the void. Their eyes are shut but they know that all the seasons have gathered to watch them die together — winter scattering frozen dust, autumn mourning the fleeting death of the world with a red and golden voice, slow, lazy, green summer, and finally another spring, no longer swift and imperceptible but eternal. A gorge replete with roses, a soft, fatal fall into the dew that bathes them as they still hold hands, their eyes closed, Lord Jim and Juan, brothers now.

X

Juan Zamora, that's right. He asked that I tell you all this. He feels pain, he feels shame, but he has compassion. He's turned his face toward us.

Mary Gaitskill

Mary Gaitskill (b. 1954) was born in Lexington, Kentucky, the daughter of a teacher and a social worker. She had what she describes as a difficult adolescence, running away from home at sixteen to become a stripper and spending time in mental institutions. She has said that

> this background is of limited relevance to my writing except for one thing: my experience of life as essentially unhappy and uncontrollable taught me to examine the way people, including myself, create survival systems and psychological "safe" places for themselves in unorthodox and sometimes apparently self-defeating ways. These inner worlds, although often unworkable and unattractive in social terms, can have a unique beauty and courage.

In 1981 Gaitskill graduated from the University of Michigan, where she won an award for her collection of short fiction, *The Woman Who Knew Judo and Other Stories*. Seven years later she published her first book of stories, *Bad Behavior*, with Poseidon Press. The critic Martin Waxman wrote in the Toronto *Globe and Mail* that her self-destructive characters are "outsiders whose behavior is 'bad' in that it is different ... unexpected."

In 1991 Gaitskill published her first novel, *Two Girls Fat and Thin*, in which she continued to develop what she called her characters' "confusion of violation with closeness." Her fiction often explores the theme of how people seek intimacy but don't know how to achieve it, as in her story "The Other Place." *Because They Wanted To* (1997) and *Don't Cry* (2009) are other collections of her stories. Gaitskill's novel *Veronica* (2005) was a National Book Award Finalist.

The Other Place

2011

MY SON, DOUGLAS, loves to play with toy guns. He is thirteen. He loves video games in which people get killed. He loves violence on TV, especially if it's funny. How did this happen? The way everything does, of course. One thing follows another, naturally.

Naturally, he looks like me: shorter than average, with a fine build, hazel eyes, and light-brown hair. Like me, he has a speech impediment and a condition called "essential tremor" that causes involuntary hand movements, which make him look more fragile than he is. He hates reading, but he is bright. He is interested in crows because he heard on a nature show that they are one of the only species that are more intelligent than they need to be to survive. He does beautiful, precise drawings of crows.

Mostly, though, he draws pictures of men holding guns. Or men hanging from nooses. Or men cutting up other men with chainsaws — in these pictures there are no faces, just figures holding chainsaws and figures being cut in two, with blood spraying out.

My wife, Marla, says that this is fine, as long as we balance it out with other things — family dinners, discussions of current events, sports, exposure to art and nature. But I don't know. Douglas and I were sitting together in the living room last week, half watching the TV and checking e-mail, when an advertisement for a movie flashed across the screen: it was called "Captivity" and the ad showed a terrified blond girl in a cage, a tear running down her face. Doug didn't speak or move. But I could feel his fascination, the suddenly deepening quality of it. And I don't doubt that he could feel mine. We sat there and felt it together.

And then she was there, the woman in the car. In the room with my son, her black hair, her hard laugh, the wrinkled skin under her hard eyes, the sudden blood filling the white of her blue eye. There was excited music on the TV and then the ad ended. My son's attention went elsewhere; she lingered.

When I was a kid, I liked walking through neighborhoods alone, looking at houses, seeing what people did to make them homes: the gardens, the statuary, the potted plants, the wind chimes. Late at night, if I couldn't sleep, I would sometimes slip out my bedroom window and just spend an hour or so walking around. I loved it, especially in late spring, when it was starting to be warm and there were night sounds — crickets, birds, the whirring of bats, the occasional whooshing car, some lonely person's TV. I loved the mysterious darkness of the trees, the way they moved against the sky if there was wind — big and heavy movements, but delicate, too, in all the subtle, reactive leaves. In that soft, blurry weather, people slept with their windows open; it was a small town and they weren't afraid. Some houses — I'm thinking of two in particular, where the Legges and the Myers lived — had yards that I would actually hang around in at night. Once, when I was sitting on the Legges' front porch, thinking about stealing a piece of their garden statuary, their cat came and sat with

me. I petted him and when I got up and went for the statuary he followed me
with his tail up. The Legges' statues were elves, not corny, cute elves but sinister, wicked-looking elves, and I thought that one would look good in my room.
But they were too heavy, so I just moved them around the yard.

I did things like that, dumb pranks that could only irritate those who
noticed them: rearranging statuary, leaving weird stuff in mailboxes, looking
into windows to see where people had dinner or left their personal things — or,
in the case of the Legges, where their daughter, Jenna, slept. She was on the
ground floor, her bed so close to the window that I could watch her chest rise
and fall the way I watched the grass on their lawn stirring in the wind. The
worst thing I did, probably, was put a giant marble in the Myers' gas tank,
which could've really caused a problem if it had rolled over the gas hole while
one of the Myers was driving on the highway, but I guess it never did.

Mostly, though, I wasn't interested in causing that kind of problem. I just
wanted to sit and watch, to touch other people's things, to drink in their lives.
I suspect that it's some version of these impulses that makes me the most successful real-estate agent in the Hudson Valley now: the ability to know what
physical objects and surroundings will most please a person's sense of identity
and make him feel at home.

I wish that Doug had this sensitivity to the physical world, and the ability
to drink from it. I've tried different things with him: I used to throw the ball
with him out in the yard, but he got tired of that; he hates hiking and likes biking only if he has to get someplace. What's working now a little bit is fishing,
fly-fishing hip deep in the Hudson. An ideal picture of normal childhood.

I believe I had a normal childhood. But you have to go pretty far afield
to find something people would call abnormal these days. My parents were
divorced, and then my mother had boyfriends — but this was true of about
half the kids I knew. She and my father fought, in the house, when they were
together, and they went on fighting, on the phone, after they separated — loud,
screaming fights sometimes. I didn't love it, but I understood it; people fight. I
was never afraid that my father was going to hurt her, or me. I had nightmares
occasionally, in which he turned into a murderer and came after me, chasing
me, getting closer, until I fell down, unable to make my legs move right. But
I've read that this is one of those primitive fears which everybody secretly has;
it bears little relation to what actually happens.

What actually happened: he forced me to play golf with him for hours
when I visited on Saturdays, even though it seemed only to make him miserable. He'd curse himself if he missed a shot and then that would make him miss
another one and he'd curse himself more. He'd whisper, "Oh, God," and wipe
his face if anything went wrong, or even if it didn't, as if just being there were
an ordeal, and then I had to feel sorry for him. He'd make these noises sometimes, painful grunts when he picked up the sack of clubs, and it put me on
edge and even disgusted me.

Now, of course, I see it differently. I remembered those Saturdays when I
was first teaching Doug how to cast, out in the back yard. I wasn't much good
myself yet, and I got tangled up in the bushes a couple of times. I could feel

the boy's flashing impatience; I felt my age, too. Then we went to work disentangling and he came closer to help me. We linked in concentration, and it occurred to me that the delicacy of the line and the fine movements needed to free it appealed to him the way drawing appealed to him, because of their beauty and precision.

Besides, he was a natural. When it was his turn to try, he kept his wrist stiff and gave the air a perfect little punch and *zip* — great cast. The next time, he got tangled up, but he was speedy about getting unstuck so that he could do it again. Even when the tremor acted up. Even when I lectured him on the laws of physics. It was a good day.

There is one not-normal thing you could point to in my childhood, which is that my mother, earlier in her life, before I was born, had occasionally worked as a prostitute. But I don't think that counts, because I didn't know about it as a child. I didn't learn about it until six years ago, when I was thirty-eight and my mother was sick with a strain of flu that had killed a lot of people, most of them around her age. She was in the hospital and she was feverish and thought she was dying. She held my hand as she told me, her eyes sad half-moons, her lips still full and provocative. She said that she wanted me to know because she thought it might help me to understand some of the terrible things I'd heard my father say to her — things I mostly hadn't even listened to. "It wasn't anything really bad," she said. "I just needed the money sometimes, between jobs. It's not like I was a drug addict — it was just hard to make it in Manhattan. I only worked for good escort places. I never had a pimp or went out on the street. I never did anything perverted — I didn't have to. I was beautiful. They'd pay just to be with me."

Later, when she didn't die, she was embarrassed that she'd told me. She laughed that raucous laugh of hers and said, "Way to go, Marcy! On your deathbed, tell your son you're a whore and then don't die!"

"It's O.K.," I said.

And it was. It frankly was not really even much of a surprise. It was her vanity that disgusted me, the way she undercut the confession with a preening, maudlin joke. I could not respect that even then.

I don't think that my mom's confession, or whatever it may have implied, had anything to do with what I think of as "it." When I was growing up, there was, after all, no evidence of her past, nothing that could have affected me. But suddenly, when I was about fourteen, I started getting excited by the thought of girls being hurt. Or killed. A horror movie would be on TV, a girl in shorts would be running and screaming with some guy chasing her, and to me it was like porn. Even a scene where a sexy girl was getting her legs torn off by a shark — bingo. It was like pushing a button. My mom would be in the kitchen making dinner and talking on the phone, stirring and striding around with the phone tucked between her shoulder and her chin. Outside, cars would go by, or a dog would run across the lawn. My homework would be slowly getting done in my lap while this sexy girl was screaming "God help me!" and having her legs torn off. And I would go invisibly into an invisible world that I called "the other place." Where I sometimes passively watched a killer and other times became one.

It's true that I started drinking and drugging right about then. All my friends did. My mom tried to lay down the law, but I found ways around her. We'd go into the woods, me and usually Chet Wotazak and Jim Bonham, and we'd smoke weed we'd got from Chet's brother, a local dealer named Dan, and drink cheap wine. We could sometimes get Chet's dad to lend us a gun — in my memory he had an AK-47, though I don't know how that's possible — and we'd go out to a local junk yard and take turns shooting up toilets, the long tubes of fluorescent lights, whatever was there. Then we'd go to Chet's house, up to his room, where we'd play loud music and tell dumb jokes and watch music videos in which disgusting things happened: snakes crawled over a little boy's sleeping face and he woke up being chased by a psychopath in a huge truck; a girl was turned into a pig and then a cake and then the lead singer bit off her head.

You might think that the videos and the guns were part of it, that they encouraged my violent thoughts. But Chet and Jim were watching and doing the same things and they were not like me. They said mean things about girls, and they were disrespectful sometimes, but they didn't want to hurt them, not really. They wanted to touch them and be touched by them; they wanted that more than anything. You could hear it in their voices and see it in their eyes, no matter what they said.

So I would sit with them and yet be completely apart from them, talking and laughing about normal things in a dark mash of music and snakes and children running from psychos and girls being eaten — images that took me someplace my friends couldn't see, although it was right there in the room with us.

It was the same at home. My mother made dinner, talked on the phone, fought with my dad, had guys over. Our cat licked itself and ate from its dish. Around us, people cared about one another. Jenna Legge slept peacefully. But in the other place sexy girls — and sometimes ugly girls or older women — ran and screamed for help as an unstoppable, all-powerful killer came closer and closer. There was no school or sports or mom or dad or caring, and it was great.

I've told my wife about most of this, the drinking, the drugs, the murder fantasies. She understands, because she has her past, too: extreme sex, vandalizing cars, talking vulnerable girls into getting more drunk than they should on behalf of some guy. There's a picture of her and another girl in bathing suits, the other girl chugging a beer that is being held by a guy so that it goes straight down her throat as her head is tipped way back.

Another guy is watching, and my smiling wife is holding the girl's hand. It's a picture that foreshadows some kind of cruelty or misery, or maybe just a funny story to tell about throwing up in the bathroom later. Privately, I see no similarity between it and my death obsession. For my wife, the connection is drugs and alcohol; she believes that we were that way because we were both addicts expressing our pain and anger through violent fantasies and blind actions. The first time I took Doug out to fish, it was me on the hot golf course all over again. As we walked to the lake in our heavy boots and clothes, I could feel his irritation at the bugs and the brightness, the squalor of nature in his fastidious eyes. I told him that fly-fishing was like driving a sports car, as opposed to the Subaru of rod and reel. I went on about how anything beautiful had to be conquered. He just turned down his mouth.

He got interested, though, in tying on the fly; the simple elegance of the knot (the "fish-killer") intrigued him. He laid it down the first time, too, placing the backcast perfectly in a space between trees. He gazed at the brown, light-wrinkled water with satisfaction. But when I put my hand on his shoulder I could feel him inwardly pull away.

As I got older, my night walks became rarer, with a different, sadder feeling to them. I would go out when I was not drunk or high but in a quiet mood, wanting to be somewhere that was neither the normal social world nor the other place. A world where I could sit and feel the power of nature come up through my feet, and be near other people without them being near me. Where I could believe in and for a moment possess the goodness of their lives. Jenna Legge still slept on the ground floor and sometimes I would look in her window and watch her breathe, and, if I was lucky, see one of her developing breasts swell out of her nightgown.

I never thought of killing Jenna. I didn't think about killing anyone I actually knew — not the girls I didn't like at school or the few I had sex with. The first times I had sex, I was so caught up in the feeling of it that I didn't even think about killing — I didn't think about anything at all. But I didn't have sex much. I was small, awkward, too quiet; I had that tremor. My expression must've been strange as I sat in class, feeling hidden in my other place, but outwardly visible to whoever looked — not that many did.

Then one day I was with Chet's brother, Dan, on a drug drop; he happened to be giving me a ride because his drop, at the local college, was on the way to wherever I was going. It was a guy buying, but, when we arrived, a girl opened the door. She was pretty and she knew it, but whatever confidence that knowledge gave her was superficial. We stayed for a while and smoked the product with her and her boyfriend. The girl sat very erect and talked too much, as if she were smart, but there was a question at the end of everything she said. When we left, Dan said, "That's the kind of lady I'd like to slap in the face." I asked, "Why?" But I knew. I don't remember what he said, because it didn't matter. I already knew. And later, instead of making up a girl, I thought of that one.

I forgot to mention: one night when I was outside Jenna's window, she opened her eyes and looked right at me. I was stunned, so stunned that I couldn't move. There was nothing between us but a screen with a hole in it. She looked at me and blinked. I said, "Hi." I held my breath; I had not spoken to her since third grade. But she just sighed, rolled over, and lay still. I stood there trembling for a long moment. And then, slowly and carefully, I walked through the yard and onto the sidewalk, back to my house.

I cut school the next day and the next, because I was scared that Jenna had told everybody and that I would be mocked. But eventually it became clear that nobody was saying anything, so I went back. In class, I looked at Jenna cautiously, then gratefully. But she did not return my look. At first, this moved me, made me consider her powerful. I tried insistently to catch her eye, to let her know what I felt. Finally our eyes met, and I realized that she didn't understand why I was looking at her. I realized that although her eyes had been open that night, she had still been asleep. She had looked right at me, but she had not seen me at all.

And so one night, or early morning, really, I got out of bed, into my mother's car, and drove to the campus to look for her — the college girl.

The campus was in a heavily wooded area bordering a nature preserve. The dorms were widely scattered, though some, resembling midsized family homes, were clustered together. The girl lived in one of those, but while I remembered the general location I couldn't be sure which one it was. I couldn't see into any of the windows, because even the open ones had blinds pulled down. While I was standing indecisively on a paved path between dorms, I saw two guys coming toward me. Quickly, I walked off into a section of trees and underbrush. I moved carefully through the thicket, coming to a wide field that led toward the nature preserve. The darkness deepened as I got farther from the dorms. I could feel things coming up from the ground — teeth and claws, eyes, crawling legs, and brainless eating mouths. A song played in my head, an enormously popular, romantic song about love and death that had supposedly made a bunch of teen-agers kill themselves.

Kids still listen to that song. I once heard it coming from the computer in our family room. When I went in and looked over Doug's hunched shoulder, I realized that the song was being used as the soundtrack for a graphic video about a little boy in a mask murdering people. It was spellbinding, the yearning, eerie harmony of the song juxtaposed with terrified screaming; I told Doug to turn it off. He looked pissed, but he did it and went slumping out the door. I found it and watched it by myself later.

I went back to the campus many times. I went to avoid my mother as much as anything. Her new boyfriend was an asshole, and she whined when he was around. When he wasn't around, she whined about him on the phone. Sometimes she called two people in a row to whine about exactly the same things that he'd said or done. Even when I played music loud so I couldn't hear her, I could *feel* her. When that happened, I'd leave my music on so that she'd think I was still in my room and I'd go to the campus. I'd follow lone female students as closely as I could, and I'd feel the other place running against the membrane of the world, almost touching it. Why does it make sense to put romantic music together with a story about a little boy murdering people? Because it does make sense — only I don't know how. It seems dimly to have to do with justice, with some wrong being avenged, but what? The hurts of childhood? The stupidity of life? The kid doesn't seem to be having fun. Random murder just seems like a job he has to do. But why? Soon enough I realized that the college campus was the wrong place to think about making it real. It wasn't an environment I could control; there were too many variables. I needed to get the girl someplace private. I needed to have certain things there. I needed to have a gun. I could find a place; there were deserted places. I could get a gun from Chet's house; I knew where his father kept his. But the girl?

Then, while I was in the car with my mom one day, we saw a guy hitch-hiking. He was middle-aged and fucked-up-looking, and my mom — we were stopped at a light — remarked that nobody in their right mind would pick him up. Two seconds later, somebody pulled over for him. My mom laughed.

I started hitchhiking. Most of the people who picked me up were men, but there were women, too. No one was scared of me. I was almost eighteen by then, but I was still small and quiet-looking. Women picked me up because they were concerned about me.

I didn't really plan to do it. I just wanted to feel the gun in my pocket and look at the woman and know that I *could* do it. There was this one — a thirty-ish blonde with breasts that I could see through her open coat. But then she said that she was pregnant and I started thinking about what if I was killing the baby?

Doug had a lot of nightmares when he was a baby, by which I mean between the ages of two and four. When he cried out in his sleep, it was usu-ally Marla who went to him. But one night she was sick and I told her to stay in bed while I went to comfort the boy. He was still crying "Mommy!" when I sat on the bed, and I felt his anxiety at seeing me instead of his mother, felt the moment of hesitation in his body before he came into my arms, vibrating rather than trembling, sweating and fragrant with emotion. He had dreamed that he was home alone and it was dark, and he was calling for his mother, but she wasn't there. "Daddy, Daddy," he wept, "there was a sick lady with red eyes and Mommy wouldn't come. Where is Mommy?"

That may've been the first time I truly remembered her, the woman in the car. It was so intense a moment that in a bizarre intersection of impossible feelings I got an erection with my crying child in my arms. But it lasted only a moment. I picked Doug up and carried him into our bedroom so that he could see his mother and nestle against her. I stayed awake nearly all night watching them.

The day it happened was a bright day, but windy and cold, and my mom would not shut up. I just wanted to watch a movie, but even with the TV turned up loud — I guess that's why she kept talking; she didn't think I could hear her — I couldn't blot out the sound of her yakking about how ashamed this asshole made her feel. I whispered, "If you're so ashamed, why do you talk about it?" She said, "It all goes back to being fucking molested." She lowered her voice; the only words I caught were "fucking corny." I went out into the hallway to listen. "The worst of it was that he wouldn't look at me," she said. I could almost hear her pacing around, the phone tucked against her shoulder. "That's why I fall for these passive-aggressive types who turn me on and then make me feel ashamed." Whoever she was talking to must have said something funny then, because she laughed. I left the TV on and walked out. I took the gun, but more for protection against perverts than the other thing.

I gave my boy that dream as surely as if I'd handed it to him. But I've given him a lot of other things, too. The first time he caught a fish he responded to my encouraging words with a bright glance that I will never forget. We let that one go, but only after he had held it in his hands, cold and quick, muscle with eyes and a heart, scales specked with yellow and red, and one tiny orange fin. Then the next one, bigger, leaping to break the rippling murk — I said, "Don't point the rod at the fish. Keep the tip up, keep it up" — and he listened to me and he brought it in. There is a picture of it on the corkboard in his room, the fish in the net, the lure bristling in its crude mouth. I have another picture, too, of him smiling triumphantly, holding it in his hands, its shining, still living body fully extended.

She was older than I'd wanted, forty or so, but still good-looking. She had a voice that was strong and lifeless at the same time. She had black hair and she wore tight black pants. She did not have a wedding ring, which meant that maybe no one would miss her. She picked me up on a lightly travelled forty-five-mile-an-hour road. She was listening to a talk show on the radio and she asked if I wanted to hear music instead. I said no, I liked talk shows.

"Yeah?" she said. "Why?"

"Because I'm interested in current events."

"I'm not," she said. "I just listen to this shit because the voices relax me. I don't really care what they're talking about."

They were talking about a war somewhere. Bombs were exploding in markets where people bought vegetables; somebody's legs had been blown off. We turned onto a road with a few cars, but none close to us.

"You don't care?"

"No, why should I? Oh, about this?" She paused. There was something about a little boy being rushed to an overcrowded hospital. "Yeah, that's bad. But it's not like we can do anything about it." On the radio, foreign people cried.

I took the gun out of my pocket.

I said, "Do you have kids?"

"No," she said. "Why?"

"Take me to Old Post Road. I'm going to the abandoned house there."

"I'm not going by there, but I can get you pretty close. So why do you care about current events? I didn't give a shit at your age."

"Take me there or I'll kill you."

She cocked her head and wrinkled her brow, as if she were trying to be sure she'd heard right. Then she looked down at the gun, and cut her eyes up at me; quickly, she looked back at the road. The car picked up speed.

"Take the next right or you'll die." My voice at that moment came not from me but from the other place. My whole body felt like an erection. She hit the right-turn signal. There was a long moment as we approached the crucial road. The voices on the radio roared ecstatically.

She pulled over to the shoulder.

"What are you doing?"

She put the car in park.

"Turn right or you die!"

She unbuckled her seat belt and turned to face me. "I'm ready," she said. She leaned back and gripped the steering wheel with one hand, as if to steady herself. With her free hand, she tapped herself between the eyes — bright, hot blue, rimmed with red. "Put it here," she said. "Go for it."

A car went by. Somebody in the passenger seat glanced at us blankly. "I don't want to do it here. There's witnesses. You need to take me to the place."

"What witnesses? That car's not stopping—nobody's going to stop unless the emergency lights are on and they're not, look."

"But if I shoot you in the head the blood will spray on the window and somebody could see." It was my own voice again: the power was gone. The people on the radio kept talking. Suddenly I felt my heart beating.

"O.K., then do it here." She opened her jacket to show me her chest. "Nobody'll hear. When you're done you can move me to the passenger seat and drive the car wherever."

"Get into the passenger seat now and I'll do it."

She laughed, hard. Her eyes were crazy. They were crazy the way an animal can be crazy in a tiny cage. "Hell, no. I'm not going to your place with you. You do it here, motherfucker."

I realized then that her hair was a wig, and a cheap one. For some reason, that made her seem even crazier. I held my gun hand against my body to hide the tremor.

"Come on, honey," she said. "Go for it."

Like a star, a red dot appeared in the white of her left eye. The normal place and the other place were turning into the same place, quick but slow, the way a car accident is quick but slow. I stared. The blood spread raggedly across her eye. She shifted her eyes from my face to a spot somewhere outside the car and fixed them there. I fought the urge to turn and see what she was looking at. She shifted her eyes again. She looked me deep in the face.

"Well?" she said. "Are you going to do it or not?"

Words appeared in my head, like a sign reading "I Don't Want To."

She leaned forward and turned on the emergency lights. "Get out of my car," she said quietly. "You're wasting my time."

As soon as I got out, she hit the gas and burned rubber. I walked into the field next to the road, without an idea of where I might go. I realized after she was gone that she might call the police, but I felt in my gut that she would not—in the other place there are no police, and she was from the other place.

Still, as I walked I took the bullets out of the gun and scattered them, kicking snow over them and stamping it down. I walked a long time, shivering horribly. I came across a drainage pipe and threw the empty gun into it. I thought, I should've gut-shot her—that's what I should've done. And then got her to the abandoned house. I should've gut-shot the bitch. But I knew why I hadn't. She'd been shot already, from the inside. If she had been somebody different I might actually have done it. But somehow the wig-haired woman had changed the channel and I don't even know if she'd meant to.

The fly bobbing on the brown, gentle water. The long grasses so green that they cast a fine, bright green on the brown water. The primitive fish mouth straining for water and finding it as my son releases it in the shallows. Its murky vanishing.

The blood bursting in her eye, poor woman, poor mother. My mother died of colon cancer just nine months ago. Shortly after that, it occurred to me that the woman had been wearing that awful wig because she was sick and undergoing chemo. Though of course I don't know.

The hurts of childhood that must be avenged: so small and so huge. Before I grew up and stopped thinking about her, I thought about that woman a lot. About what would've happened if I'd got her there, to the abandoned house. I don't remember anymore the details of these thoughts, only that they were distorted, swollen, blurred: broken face, broken voice, broken body left dying on the floor, watching me go with dimming, despairing eyes.

These pictures are faded now and far away. But they can still make me feel something.

The second time I put my hand on Doug's shoulder, he didn't move away inside; he was too busy tuning in to the line and the lure. Somewhere in him is the other place. It's quiet now, but I know it's there. I also know that he won't be alone with it. He won't know that I'm there with him, because we will never speak of it. But I will be there. He will not be alone with that.

Gabriel García Márquez

Gabriel García Márquez (b. 1928) was born in the remote small town of Aracataca in Magdalena province, near the Caribbean seacoast of Colombia. The oldest of twelve children of a poverty-stricken telegraph operator and his wife, he was raised by his maternal grandparents. When he was eight years old, he was sent to school near Bogotá, and after his graduation in 1946 he studied law. A writer from childhood, García Márquez published his first book, *Leaf Storm and Other Stories*, which includes "A Very Old Man with Enormous Wings," in 1955. He spent the next few years in Paris, where he wrote two short novels. After the Cuban Revolution, he returned to Central America and worked as a journalist and screenwriter. His great comic masterpiece, the novel *One Hundred Years of Solitude* (1967), was written while he lived in Mexico City. *The Autumn of the Patriarch* (1975), a novel about the life of a Latin American dictator, and the best-seller *Love in the Time of Cholera* (1988) are some other works. In 1982 he received the Nobel Prize for literature. His memoir *Living to Tell the Tale* was published in 2003. *Tales of My Melancholy Whores* (2005) is a recent novel.

García Márquez mingles realistic and fantastic details in all his fiction, including "A Very Old Man with Enormous Wings." He has said that the origin of his stories is always an image, "not an idea or a concept. The image grows in my head until the whole story takes shape as it might in real life." *Leaf Storm* was written after García Márquez returned from visiting the place where he grew up. As he later explained to an interviewer from the *Paris Review*:

> The atmosphere, the decadence, the heat in the village were roughly the same as what I had felt in Faulkner. It was a banana plantation region inhabited by a lot of Americans from the fruit companies which gave it the same sort of atmosphere I had found in the writers of the Deep South. Critics have spoken of the literary influence of Faulkner but I see it as a coincidence: I had simply found material that had to be dealt with in the same way that Faulkner had treated similar material. . . .
>
> What really happened to me in that trip to Aracataca was that I realized that everything that had occurred in my childhood had a literary value that I was only now appreciating. From the moment I wrote *Leaf Storm* I realized I wanted to be a writer and that nobody could stop me and that the only thing left for me to do was to be the best writer in the world.

Other collections of short fiction by García Márquez are *No One Writes to the Colonel and Other Stories* (1968), *Innocent Eréndira and Other Stories* (1978), *Collected Stories* (1984), and *Of Love and Other Demons* (1996).

In 1988 García Márquez coauthored (with Fernando Birri) a screenplay of "A Very Old Man with Enormous Wings" for Television Española. In a scene added to the film version of the story, the old man is revealed as a trickster or confidence man who takes off his wings when he is alone. The film also begins with a quotation from Hebrews 13:2: "Be not forgetful to entertain strangers: for thereby some have entertained angels unaware."

RELATED CASEBOOK
See Casebook on Magical Realism, pages 1627–1646, including Jorge Luis Borges, "Borges and I," page 1631; Alejo Carpentier, "On the Marvelous Real in America," page 1633 and "The Baroque and the Marvelous Real," page 1635; Luis Leal, "Magical Realism in Spanish American Literature," page 1637; William Gass, "The First Seven Pages of the Boom," page 1639; Ursula K. Le Guin, "The Kind of Fiction Most Characteristic of Our Times," page 1641; Mario Vargas Llosa, "The Prose Style of Jorge Luis Borges and Gabriel García Márquez," page 1645.

A Very Old Man with Enormous Wings

1955 / Translated by Gregory Rabassa

ON THE THIRD DAY of rain they had killed so many crabs inside the house that Pelayo had to cross his drenched courtyard and throw them into the sea, because the newborn child had a temperature all night and they thought it was due to the stench. The world had been sad since Tuesday. Sea and sky were a single ash-gray thing and the sands of the beach, which on March nights glimmered like powdered light, had become a stew of mud and rotten shellfish. The light was so weak at noon that when Pelayo was coming back to the house after throwing away the crabs, it was hard for him to see what it was that was moving and groaning in the rear of the courtyard. He had to go very close to see that it was an old man, a very old man, lying face down in the mud, who, in spite of his tremendous efforts, couldn't get up, impeded by his enormous wings.

Frightened by that nightmare, Pelayo ran to get Elisenda, his wife, who was putting compresses on the sick child, and he took her to the rear of the courtyard. They both looked at the fallen body with mute stupor. He was dressed like a ragpicker. There were only a few faded hairs left on his bald skull and very few teeth in his mouth, and his pitiful condition of a drenched great-grandfather had taken away any sense of grandeur he might have had. His huge buzzard wings, dirty and half-plucked, were forever entangled in the mud. They looked at him so long and so closely that Pelayo and Elisenda very soon overcame their surprise and in the end found him familiar. Then they dared speak to him, and he answered in an incomprehensible dialect with a strong sailor's voice. That was how they skipped over the inconvenience of the wings and quite intelligently concluded that he was a lonely castaway from some foreign ship wrecked by the storm. And yet, they called in a neighbor woman who knew everything about life and death to see him, and all she needed was one look to show them their mistake.

"He's an angel," she told them. "He must have been coming for the child, but the poor fellow is so old that the rain knocked him down."

On the following day everyone knew that a flesh-and-blood angel was held captive in Pelayo's house. Against the judgment of the wise neighbor woman, for whom angels in those times were the fugitive survivors of a celestial conspiracy, they did not have the heart to club him to death. Pelayo watched over him all afternoon from the kitchen, armed with his bailiff's club, and before going to bed he dragged him out of the mud and locked him up with the hens in the wire chicken coop. In the middle of the night, when the rain stopped, Pelayo and Elisenda were still killing crabs. A short time afterward the child woke up without a fever and with a desire to eat. Then they felt magnanimous and decided to put the angel on a raft with fresh water and provisions for three days and leave him to his fate on the high seas. But when they went out into the courtyard with the first light of dawn, they found the whole neighborhood in front of the chicken coop having fun with the angel, without the slightest reverence, tossing him things to eat through the openings in the wire as if he weren't a supernatural creature but a circus animal.

Father Gonzaga arrived before seven o'clock, alarmed at the strange news. By that time onlookers less frivolous than those at dawn had already arrived and they were making all kinds of conjectures concerning the captive's future. The simplest among them thought that he should be named mayor of the world. Others of sterner mind felt that he should be promoted to the rank of five-star general in order to win all wars. Some visionaries hoped that he could be put to stud in order to implant on earth a race of winged wise men who could take charge of the universe. But Father Gonzaga, before becoming a priest, had been a robust woodcutter. Standing by the wire, he reviewed his catechism in an instant and asked them to open the door so that he could take a close look at that pitiful man who looked more like a huge decrepit hen among the fascinated chickens. He was lying in a corner drying his open wings in the sunlight among the fruit peels and breakfast leftovers that the early risers had thrown him. Alien to the impertinences of the world, he only lifted his antiquarian eyes and murmured something in his dialect when Father Gonzaga went into the chicken coop and said good morning to him in Latin. The parish priest had his first suspicion of an impostor when he saw that he did not understand the language of God or know how to greet His ministers. Then he noticed that seen close up he was much too human: he had an unbearable smell of the outdoors, the back side of his wings was strewn with parasites and his main feathers had been mistreated by terrestrial winds, and nothing about him measured up to the proud dignity of angels. Then he came out of the chicken coop and in a brief sermon warned the curious against the risks of being ingenuous. He reminded them that the devil had the bad habit of making use of carnival tricks in order to confuse the unwary. He argued that if wings were not the essential element in determining the difference between a hawk and an airplane, they were even less so in the recognition of angels. Nevertheless, he promised to write a letter to his bishop so that the latter would write to his primate so that the latter would write to the Supreme Pontiff in order to get the final verdict from the highest courts.

His prudence fell on sterile hearts. The news of the captive angel spread with such rapidity that after a few hours the courtyard had the bustle of a marketplace and they had to call in troops with fixed bayonets to disperse the mob that was about to knock the house down. Elisenda, her spine all twisted from sweeping up so much marketplace trash, then got the idea of fencing in the yard and charging five cents admission to see the angel.

The curious came from far away. A traveling carnival arrived with a flying acrobat who buzzed over the crowd several times, but no one paid any attention to him because his wings were not those of an angel but, rather, those of a sidereal[1] bat. The most unfortunate invalids on earth came in search of health: a poor woman who since childhood had been counting her heartbeats and had run out of numbers; a Portuguese man who couldn't sleep because the noise of the stars disturbed him; a sleep-walker who got up at night to undo the things he had done while awake; and many others with less serious ailments. In the midst of that shipwreck disorder that made the earth tremble, Pelayo and Elisenda were happy with fatigue, for in less than a week they had crammed their rooms with money and the line of pilgrims waiting their turn to enter still reached beyond the horizon.

The angel was the only one who took no part in his own act. He spent his time trying to get comfortable in his borrowed nest, befuddled by the hellish heat of the oil lamps and sacramental candles that had been placed along the wire. At first they tried to make him eat some mothballs, which, according to the wisdom of the wise neighbor woman, were the food prescribed for angels. But he turned them down, just as he turned down the papal lunches that the penitents brought him, and they never found out whether it was because he was an angel or because he was an old man that in the end he ate nothing but eggplant mush. His only supernatural virtue seemed to be patience. Especially during the first days, when the hens pecked at him, searching for the stellar parasites that proliferated in his wings, and the cripples pulled out feathers to touch their defective parts with, and even the most merciful threw stones at him, trying to get him to rise so they could see him standing. The only time they succeeded in arousing him was when they burned his side with an iron for branding steers, for he had been motionless for so many hours that they thought he was dead. He awoke with a start, ranting in his hermetic language and with tears in his eyes, and he flapped his wings a couple of times, which brought on a whirlwind of chicken dung and lunar dust and a gale of panic that did not seem to be of this world. Although many thought that his reaction had been one not of rage but of pain, from then on they were careful not to annoy him, because the majority understood that his passivity was not that of a hero taking his ease but that of a cataclysm in repose.

Father Gonzaga held back the crowd's frivolity with formulas of maidservant inspiration while awaiting the arrival of a final judgment on the nature of the captive. But the mail from Rome showed no sense of urgency. They spent their time finding out if the prisoner had a navel, if his dialect had any connection with Aramaic, how many times he could fit on the head of a pin, or whether he wasn't just a Norwegian with wings. Those meager letters might have come and gone until the end of time if a providential event had not put an end to the priest's tribulations.

It so happened that during those days, among so many other carnival attractions, there arrived in town the traveling show of the woman who had been

---

[1] Coming from the stars.

changed into a spider for having disobeyed her parents. The admission to see her was not only less than the admission to see the angel, but people were permitted to ask her all manner of questions about her absurd state and to examine her up and down so that no one would ever doubt the truth of her horror. She was a frightful tarantula the size of a ram and with the head of a sad maiden. What was most heart-rending, however, was not her outlandish shape but the sincere affliction with which she recounted the details of her misfortune. While still practically a child she had sneaked out of her parents' house to go to a dance, and while she was coming back through the woods after having danced all night without permission, a fearful thunderclap rent the sky in two and through the crack came the lightning bolt of brimstone that changed her into a spider. Her only nourishment came from the meatballs that charitable souls chose to toss into her mouth. A spectacle like that, full of so much human truth and with such a fearful lesson, was bound to defeat without even trying that of a haughty angel who scarcely deigned to look at mortals. Besides, the few miracles attributed to the angel showed a certain mental disorder, like the blind man who didn't recover his sight but grew three new teeth, or the paralytic who didn't get to walk but almost won the lottery, and the leper whose sores sprouted sunflowers. Those consolation miracles, which were more like mocking fun, had already ruined the angel's reputation when the woman who had been changed into a spider finally crushed him completely. That was how Father Gonzaga was cured forever of his insomnia and Pelayo's courtyard went back to being as empty as during the time it had rained for three days and crabs walked through the bedrooms.

The owners of the house had no reason to lament. With the money they saved they built a two-story mansion with balconies and gardens and high netting so that crabs wouldn't get in during the winter, and with iron bars on the windows so that angels wouldn't get in. Pelayo also set up a rabbit warren close to town and gave up his job as bailiff for good, and Elisenda bought some satin pumps with high heels and many dresses of iridescent silk, the kind worn on Sunday by the most desirable women in those times. The chicken coop was the only thing that didn't receive any attention. If they washed it down with creolin and burned tears of myrrh inside it every so often, it was not in homage to the angel but to drive away the dungheap stench that still hung everywhere like a ghost and was turning the new house into an old one. At first, when the child learned to walk, they were careful that he not get too close to the chicken coop. But then they began to lose their fears and got used to the smell, and before the child got his second teeth he'd gone inside the chicken coop to play, where the wires were falling apart. The angel was no less standoffish with him than with other mortals, but he tolerated the most ingenious infamies with the patience of a dog who had no illusions. They both came down with chicken pox at the same time. The doctor who took care of the child couldn't resist the temptation to listen to the angel's heart, and he found so much whistling in the heart and so many sounds in his kidneys that it seemed impossible for him to be alive. What surprised him most, however, was the logic of his wings. They seemed so natural on that completely human organism that he couldn't understand why other men didn't have them too.

When the child began school it had been some time since the sun and rain had caused the collapse of the chicken coop. The angel went dragging himself about here and there like a stray dying man. They would drive him out of the bedroom with a broom and a moment later find him in the kitchen. He seemed to be in so many places at the same time that they grew to think that he'd been duplicated, that he was reproducing himself all through the house, and the exasperated and unhinged Elisenda shouted that it was awful living in that hell full of angels. He could scarcely eat and his antiquarian eyes had also become so foggy that he went about bumping into posts. All he had left were the bare cannulae[2] of his last feathers. Pelayo threw a blanket over him and extended him the charity of letting him sleep in the shed, and only then did they notice that he had a temperature at night, and was delirious with the tongue twisters of an old Norwegian. That was one of the few times they became alarmed, for they thought he was going to die and not even the wise neighbor woman had been able to tell them what to do with dead angels.

And yet he not only survived his worst winter, but seemed improved with the first sunny days. He remained motionless for several days in the farthest corner of the courtyard, where no one would see him, and at the beginning of December some large, stiff feathers began to grow on his wings, the feathers of a scarecrow, which looked more like another misfortune of decrepitude. But he must have known the reason for those changes, for he was quite careful that no one should notice them, that no one should hear the sea chanteys that he sometimes sang under the stars. One morning Elisenda was cutting some bunches of onions for lunch when a wind that seemed to come from the high seas blew into the kitchen. Then she went to the window and caught the angel in his first attempts at flight. They were so clumsy that his fingernails opened a furrow in the vegetable patch and he was on the point of knocking the shed down with the ungainly flapping that slipped on the light and couldn't get a grip on the air. But he did manage to gain altitude. Elisenda let out a sigh of relief, for herself and for him, when she saw him pass over the last houses, holding himself up in some way with the risky flapping of a senile vulture. She kept watching him even when she was through cutting the onions and she kept on watching until it was no longer possible for her to see him, because then he was no longer an annoyance in her life but an imaginary dot on the horizon of the sea.

---

[2] The tubular pieces by which feathers are attached to a body.

William Gass

William Gass (b. 1924) was born in Fargo, North Dakota. Soon after his birth his family moved to Warren, Ohio, where he attended local schools. After service as an ensign in the navy during World War II, he graduated from Kenyon College and went on to earn a doctorate in philosophy from Cornell University in 1954. His dissertation, "A Philosophical Investigation of Metaphor," was based on his training as a philosopher of language. In graduate school Gass read the work of Gertrude Stein, who influenced his writing experiments.

Earning a living for himself and his family from university teaching, Gass began to publish stories that were selected for inclusion in *The Best American Stories* of 1959, 1961, and 1962. In 1966 his first novel, *Omensetter's Luck*, about life in an Ohio small town in the 1890s, appeared. Critics praised his linguistic virtuosity, establishing Gass as an important writer of fiction. In 1968 he published *In the Heart of the Heart of the Country*, five stories dramatizing the theme of human isolation and the difficulty of love. The title story, originally published in *New American Review* in 1967, opens with a reference to Yeats's poem "Sailing to Byzantium," but Gass's verbal arrangement also suggests that he is punning on the words *to be*.

In 1971 Gass produced Willie Masters' *Lonesome Wife*, an experimental novella illustrated with photographs and typographical constructs intended to help readers free themselves from the linear conventions of narrative. As Gass explained in his essay "The Medium of Fiction," "It seems a country-headed thing to say: that literature is language, that stories and the places and the people in them are merely made of words as chairs are made of smoothed sticks and sometimes of cloth or metal tubes." *On Being Blue* (1976), his next book, is a long essay that the critic Larry McCaffrey read as an analysis of "blue" at "various levels as a word, color, state of mind, and Platonic ideal." Gass has published nine collections of essays, including *Finding a Form* (1996). He has retired from teaching as the David May Distinguished Professor in Humanities at Washington University in St. Louis. *Cartesian Sonata and Other Novellas* was published in 1998. "A Fugue" is a humorous section of his novel *The Tunnel* (1995), using words in formal repetitive patterns as if they were musical notes. The narrative structure is that of a fugue in three sections: an exposition, a development, and a recapitulation where the original subject returns to conclude the piece. Gass's most recent novel is *Middle C* (2013).

RELATED CASEBOOK
William Gass, "The First Seven Pages of the Boom," page 1639.

A Fugue

1995

MY DAD WOULDN'T LET ME have a dog. A dog? A dog we don't need. My mom made the neighbor's spitz her pal by poisoning it with the gin she sprinkled on the table scraps. Feed it somewhere else, my dad said. A dog we don't need. My dad wouldn't let me have a dog. Our neighbor's spitz — that mutt — he shits in the flower beds. Dog doo we don't need. At least feed it somewhere else, my dad said. My mom made the table scraps tasty for her pal, the neighbor's spitz — that mutt — by sprinkling them with gin. You're poisoning Pal, my dad said, but never mind, we don't need that mutt. My mom thought anything tasted better with a little gin to salt it up. That way my mom made the neighbor's spitz her pal, and maddened dad who wouldn't let me have a dog. He always said we didn't need one, they crapped on the carpet and put dirty paws on the pants leg of guests and yapped at cats or anyone who came to the door. A dog? A dog we don't need. We don't need chewed shoes and dog hairs on the sofa, fleas in the rug, dirty bowls in every corner of the kitchen, dog stink on our clothes. But my mom made the neighbor's spitz her pal anyway by poisoning it with the gin she sprinkled on the table scraps like she was baptising bones. At least feed it somewhere else, my dad said. My dad wouldn't let me have a pal. Who will have to walk that pal, he said. I will. And it's going to be snowing or it's going to be raining and who will be waiting by the vacant lot at the corner in the cold wet wind, waiting for the damn dog to do his business? Not you, Billy boy. Christ, you can't even be counted on to bring in the garbage cans or mow the lawn. So no dog. A mutt we don't need, we don't need dog doo in the flower beds, chewed shoes, fleas; what we need is the yard raked, like I said this morning. No damn dog. No mutt for your mother either even if she tries to get around me by feeding it when my back is turned, when I'm away at work earning her gin money so the sick thing can shit in a stream on the flower seeds; at least she should feed it somewhere else; it's always hanging around; is it a light string in the hall or a cloth on the table to be always hanging around? No. Chewed shoes, fleas, muddy paws and yappy daddle, bowser odor: a dog we don't need. Suppose it bites the postman: do you get sued? No. I am the one waiting at the corner vacant lot in the rain, the snow, the cold wet wind, waiting for the dog to do his damn business, and I get sued. You don't. Christ, you can't even be counted on to clip the hedge. You know: snicksnack. So no dog, my dad said. Though we had a dog nevertheless. That is, my mom made the neighbor's pal her mutt, and didn't let me have him for mine, either, because it just followed her around — yip nip — wanting to lap gin and nose its grease-sogged bread. So we did have a dog in the house, even though it just visited, and it would rest its white head in my mother's lap and whimper and my father would throw down his paper and say shit! and I would walk out of the house and neglect to mow or rake the yard, or snicksnack the hedge or bring the garbage cans around. My dad wouldn't let me have a dog. A dog? A dog we don't need, he said. So I was damned if I would fetch.

Dagoberto Gilb

Dagoberto Gilb (b. 1950) was born in Los Angeles. His mother was a Mexican who had crossed the border illegally and was terrified of being deported; his father was a man of German ancestry who spoke Spanish. They divorced before Gilb began kindergarten. After growing up in poverty, Gilb attended junior college in Los Angeles for three years before transferring to the University of California at Santa Barbara. In 1973 he earned a B.A. with a double major in philosophy and religious studies; in 1976 he completed an M.A. in religious studies. Yet as he told an interviewer on National Public Radio in 2001, he was unable to get a decent job with his two college degrees. "I'm a kind of big guy and particularly then. Now I look sweet and nice, but then I looked mean and ugly and scared people. And so I could never get these white-collar jobs. Men kind of backed away from me, and women kind of looked for their purse, kept it near."

For the next sixteen years Gilb worked as a skilled carpenter in Los Angeles and El Paso, a card-carrying journeyman in the United Brotherhood of Carpenters and Joiners. He also began writing short stories and keeping a journal of his experiences in a series of spiral notebooks. One day in El Paso he learned that Raymond Carver was teaching at the University of Texas across the street from a new building where Gilb was part of the construction crew. Gilb showed two of his stories to Carver, who also wrote about working-class people on the West Coast. Carver offered to help him get into the Iowa Writers' Workshop, but Gilb wasn't interested. It took him years to realize that Carver was trying to hasten the process of his recognition as a serious writer.

> What Carver was telling me . . . was the way the system works. You go to Iowa, you turn your story in to a professor who's a famous writer. And that famous professor-writer gets you to an editor. Whereas I was under the misconception that you put things in the mail, and some editor reads it and something happens, if it was good.

Having sent off his stories to magazines without the help of a "professor-writer" or a literary agent, Gilb estimates that his story, "Look on the Bright Side," was rejected 125 times before being accepted by *The Threepenny Review*. "Love in L.A." was included in his 1993 collection *The Magic of Blood*, which won the PEN/Hemingway Award for Fiction.

In 1994 Grove Press published Gilb's novel *The Last Known Residence of Mickey Acuna*, which was followed in 2001 by *Woodcuts of Women*, another story collection, and in 2003 by *Gritos*, a book of essays. Gilb is proud of his association with Grove Press because it "was always about the outsider, the not acceptable . . . for me it was writing that wasn't ordinary, by writers who didn't know how to live ordinary either"—earlier writers such as Jack Kerouac and William Burroughs, whom Gilb also admires. In 2006 he edited *Hecho en Tejas: An Anthology of Texas Mexican Literature*, a landmark collection. Annie Proulx, one of the judges who awarded the PEN/Hemingway Award to Gilb, recognized that in *The Magic of Blood*, "The stories are leavened with compassion and humor, and there is not a shred of sentimentality." *Before the End, After the Beginning* (2011) is a recent story collection.

Love in L.A.

1993

JAKE SLOUCHED IN A CLOT OF NEAR MOTIONLESS TRAFFIC, in the peculiar gray of concrete, smog, and early morning beneath the overpass of the Hollywood Freeway on Alvarado Street. He didn't really mind because he knew how much worse it could be trying to make a left onto the onramp. He certainly didn't do that every day of his life, and he'd assure anyone who'd ask that he never would either. A steady occupation had its advantages and he couldn't deny thinking about that too. He needed an FM radio in something better than this '58 Buick he drove. It would have crushed velvet interior with electric controls for the L.A. summer, a nice warm heater and defroster for the winter drives at the beach, a cruise control for those longer trips, mellow speakers front and rear of course, windows that hum closed, snuffing out that nasty exterior noise of freeways. The fact was that he'd probably have to change his whole style. Exotic colognes, plush, dark nightclubs, maitais and daquiris, necklaced ladies in satin gowns, misty and sexy like in a tequila ad. Jake could imagine lots of possibilities when he let himself, but none that ended up with him pressed onto a stalled freeway.

Jake was thinking about this freedom of his so much that when he glimpsed its green light he just went ahead and stared bye bye to the steadily employed. When he turned his head the same direction his windshield faced, it was maybe one second too late. He pounced the brake pedal and steered the front wheels away from the tiny brakelights but the smack was unavoidable. Just one second sooner and it would only have been close. One second more and he'd be crawling up the Toyota's trunk. As it was, it seemed like only a harmless smack, much less solid than the one against his back bumper.

Jake considered driving past the Toyota but was afraid the traffic ahead would make it difficult. As he pulled up against the curb a few carlengths ahead, it occurred to him that the traffic might have helped him get away too. He slammed the car door twice to make sure it was closed fully and to give himself another second more, then toured front and rear of his Buick for damage on or near the bumpers. Not an impressionable scratch even in the chrome. He perked up. Though the car's beauty was secondary to its ability to start and move, the body and paint were clean except for a few minor dings. This stood out as one of his few clearcut accomplishments over the years.

Before he spoke to the driver of the Toyota, whose looks he could see might present him with an added complication, he signaled to the driver of the car that hit him, still in his car and stopped behind the Toyota, and waved his hands and shook his head to let the man know there was no problem as far as he was concerned. The driver waved back and started his engine.

"It didn't even scratch my paint," Jake told her in that way of his. "So how you doin? Any damage to the car? I'm kinda hoping so, just so it takes a little more time and we can talk some. Or else you can give me your phone number now and I won't have to lay my regular b.s. on you to get it later."

He took her smile as a good sign and relaxed. He inhaled her scent like it was clean air and straightened out his less than new but not unhip clothes.

"You've got Florida plates. You look like you must be Cuban."

"My parents are from Venezuela."

"My name's Jake." He held out his hand.

"Mariana."

They shook hands like she'd never done it before in her life.

"I really am sorry about hitting you like that." He sounded genuine. He fondled the wide dimple near the cracked taillight. "It's amazing how easy it is to put a dent in these new cars. They're so soft they might replace waterbeds soon." Jake was confused about how to proceed with this. So much seemed so unlikely, but there was always possibility. "So maybe we should go out to breakfast somewhere and talk it over."

"I don't eat breakfast."

"Some coffee then."

"Thanks, but I really can't."

"You're not married, are you? Not that that would matter that much to me. I'm an openminded kinda guy."

She was smiling. "I have to get to work."

"That sounds boring."

"I better get your driver's license," she said.

Jake nodded, disappointed. "One little problem," he said. "I didn't bring it. I just forgot it this morning. I'm a musician," he exaggerated greatly, "and, well, I dunno, I left my wallet in the pants I was wearing last night. If you have some paper and a pen I'll give you my address and all that."

He followed her to the glove compartment side of her car.

"What if we don't report it to the insurance companies? I'll just get it fixed for you."

"I don't think my dad would let me do that."

"Your dad? It's not your car?"

"He bought it for me. And I live at home."

"Right." She was slipping away from him. He went back around to the back of her new Toyota and looked over the damage again. There was the trunk lid, the bumper, a rear panel, a taillight.

"You do have insurance?" she asked, suspicious, as she came around the back of the car.

"Oh yeah," he lied.

"I guess you better write the name of that down too."

He made up a last name and address and wrote down the name of an insurance company an old girlfriend once belonged to. He considered giving a real phone number but went against that idea and made one up.

"I act too," he lied to enhance the effect more. "Been in a couple of movies."

She smiled like a fan.

"So how about your phone number?" He was rebounding maturely.

She gave it to him.

"Mariana, you are beautiful," he said in his most sincere voice.

"Call me," she said timidly.

Jake beamed. "We'll see you, Mariana," he said holding out his hand. Her hand felt so warm and soft he felt like he'd been kissed.

Back in his car he took a moment or two to feel both proud and sad about his performance. Then he watched the rear view mirror as Mariana pulled up behind him. She was writing down the license plate numbers on his Buick, ones that he'd taken off a junk because the ones that belonged to his had expired so long ago. He turned the ignition key and revved the big engine and clicked into drive. His sense of freedom swelled as he drove into the now moving street traffic, though he couldn't stop the thought about that FM stereo radio and crushed velvet interior and the new car smell that would even make it better.

Charlotte Perkins Gilman

Charlotte Perkins Gilman (1860–1935) was born in Hartford, Connecticut. Her father deserted the family shortly after she was born and provided her mother with only meager support. As a teenager Gilman attended the Rhode Island School of Design for a brief period and worked as a commercial artist and teacher. Like her great-aunt Harriet Beecher Stowe, she was concerned at an early age with social injustice and wrote poetry about the hardship of women's lives.

In 1884 she married the artist Charles Walter Stetson. Suffering extreme depression after the birth of a daughter, she left her husband and moved to California in 1888. They were divorced, and she later married George Houghton Gilman, with whom she lived for thirty-four years. In the 1890s Gilman established her reputation as a lecturer and writer of feminist tracts. Her book *Women and Economics* (1898) is considered one of the most important works of the early years of the women's movement in the United States. Gilman's later books—*Concerning Children* (1900), *The Home* (1904), and *Human Work* (1904)—argue that women should be educated to become financially independent; then they could contribute more to the amelioration of systems of justice and the improvement of society. From 1909 to 1917 Gilman published her own journal, *The Forerunner*, for which she wrote voluminously. At the end of her life, suffering from cancer, she committed suicide with chloroform.

Today Gilman's best-known work is "The Yellow Wallpaper," written around 1890, shortly after her own nervous breakdown. A landmark story in its frank depiction of mental illness, it is part fantasy and part autobiography, an imaginative account of her suffering and treatment by the physician S. Weir Mitchell, who forbade her any activity, especially writing, the thing she most wanted to do. In setting the story Gilman used elements of the conventional gothic romances that were a staple in women's popular fiction—an isolated mansion, a distant but dominating male figure, and a mysterious household—all of which force the heroine into the role of passive victim of circumstances. But Gilman gave her own twist to the form. Using the brief paragraphs and simple sentences of popular fiction, she narrated her story in twelve artfully crafted sections with a clinical precision that avoided the trite language of typical romances.

RELATED STORY
Doris Lessing, "To Room 19," page 820.

RELATED CASEBOOK
See Casebook on Charlotte Perkins Gilman's "The Yellow Wallpaper," pages 1577–1588, including Charlotte Perkins Gilman, "Why I Wrote 'The Yellow Wallpaper,'" page 1578, and "Undergoing the Cure for Nervous Prostration," page 1579; Sandra M. Gilbert and Susan Gubar, "A Feminist Reading of Gilman's 'The Yellow Wallpaper,'" page 1581; and Elaine Showalter, "On 'The Yellow Wallpaper,'" page 1583.

The Yellow Wallpaper

1892

IT IS VERY SELDOM that mere ordinary people like John and myself secure ancestral halls for the summer.

A colonial mansion, a hereditary estate, I would say a haunted house, and reach the height of romantic felicity — but that would be asking too much of fate!

Still I will proudly declare that there is something queer about it.

Else, why should it be let so cheaply? And why have stood so long unten-anted?

John laughs at me, of course, but one expects that in marriage.

John is practical in the extreme. He has no patience with faith, an intense horror of superstition, and he scoffs openly at any talk of things not to be felt and seen and put down in figures.

John is a physician, and *perhaps* — (I would not say it to a living soul, of course, but this is dead paper and a great relief to my mind) — *perhaps* that is one reason I do not get well faster.

You see he does not believe I am sick!

And what can one do?

If a physician of high standing, and one's own husband, assures friends and relatives that there is really nothing the matter with one but temporary ner-vous depression — a slight hysterical tendency — what is one to do?

My brother is also a physician, and also of high standing, and he says the same thing.

So I take phosphates or phosphites — whichever it is, and tonics, and jour-neys, and air, and exercise, and am absolutely forbidden to "work" until I am well again.

Personally, I disagree with their ideas.

Personally, I believe that congenial work, with excitement and change, would do me good.

But what is one to do?

I did write for a while in spite of them; but it *does* exhaust me a good deal — having to be so sly about it, or else meet with heavy opposition.

I sometimes fancy that in my condition if I had less opposition and more society and stimulus — but John says the very worst thing I can do is to think about my condition, and I confess it always makes me feel bad.

So I will let it alone and talk about the house.

The most beautiful place! It is quite alone, standing well back from the road, quite three miles from the village. It makes me think of English places that you read about, for there are hedges and walls and gates that lock, and lots of separate little houses for the gardeners and people.

There is a *delicious* garden! I never saw such a garden — large and shady, full of box-bordered paths, and lined with long grape-covered arbors with seats under them.

There were greenhouses, too, but they are all broken now.

There was some legal trouble, I believe, something about the heirs and co-heirs; anyhow, the place has been empty for years.

That spoils my ghostliness, I am afraid, but I don't care — there is something strange about the house — I can feel it.

I even said so to John one moonlight evening, but he said what I felt was a *draught*, and shut the window.

I get unreasonably angry with John sometimes. I'm sure I never used to be so sensitive. I think it is due to this nervous condition.

But John says if I feel so, I shall neglect proper self-control; so I take pains to control myself — before him, at least, and that makes me very tired.

I don't like our room a bit. I wanted one downstairs that opened on the piazza and had roses all over the window, and such pretty old-fashioned chintz hangings! but John would not hear of it.

He said there was only one window and not room for two beds, and no near room for him if he took another.

He is very careful and loving, and hardly lets me stir without special direction.

I have a schedule prescription for each hour in the day; he takes all care from me, and so I feel basely ungrateful not to value it more.

He said we came here solely on my account, that I was to have perfect rest and all the air I could get. "Your exercise depends on your strength, my dear," said he, "and your food somewhat on your appetite; but air you can absorb all the time." So we took the nursery at the top of the house.

It is a big, airy room, the whole floor nearly, with windows that look all ways, and air and sunshine galore. It was nursery first and then playroom and gymnasium, I should judge; for the windows are barred for little children, and there are rings and things in the walls.

The paint and paper look as if a boys' school had used it. It is stripped off — the paper — in great patches all around the head of my bed, about as far as I can reach, and in a great place on the other side of the room low down. I never saw a worse paper in my life.

One of those sprawling flamboyant patterns committing every artistic sin.

It is dull enough to confuse the eye in following, pronounced enough to constantly irritate and provoke study, and when you follow the lame uncertain curves for a little distance they suddenly commit suicide — plunge off at outrageous angles, destroy themselves in unheard of contradictions.

The color is repellent, almost revolting; a smouldering unclean yellow, strangely faded by the slow-turning sunlight.

It is a dull yet lurid orange in some places, a sickly sulphur tint in others.

No wonder the children hated it! I should hate it myself if I had to live in this room long.

There comes John, and I must put this away, — he hates to have me write a word.

We have been here two weeks, and I haven't felt like writing before, since that first day.

I am sitting by the window now, up in this atrocious nursery, and there is nothing to hinder my writing as much as I please, save lack of strength.

John is away all day, and even some nights when his cases are serious.

I am glad my case is not serious!

But these nervous troubles are dreadfully depressing.

John does not know how much I really suffer. He knows there is no *reason* to suffer, and that satisfies him.

Of course it is only nervousness. It does weigh on me so not to do my duty in any way!

I meant to be such a help to John, such a real rest and comfort, and here I am a comparative burden already!

Nobody would believe what an effort it is to do what little I am able, — to dress and entertain, and order things.

It is fortunate Mary is so good with the baby. Such a dear baby!

And yet I *cannot* be with him, it makes me so nervous.

I suppose John never was nervous in his life. He laughs at me so about this wall-paper!

At first he meant to repaper the room, but afterwards he said that I was letting it get the better of me, and that nothing was worse for a nervous patient than to give way to such fancies.

He said that after the wall-paper was changed it would be the heavy bedstead, and then the barred windows, and then that gate at the head of the stairs, and so on.

"You know the place is doing you good," he said, "and really, dear, I don't care to renovate the house just for a three months' rental."

"Then do let us go downstairs," I said, "there are such pretty rooms there."

Then he took me in his arms and called me a blessed little goose, and said he would go down cellar, if I wished, and have it whitewashed into the bargain.

But he is right enough about the beds and windows and things.

It is an airy and comfortable room as any one need wish, and, of course, I would not be so silly as to make him uncomfortable just for a whim.

I'm really getting quite fond of the big room, all but that horrid paper.

Out of one window I can see the garden, those mysterious deep-shaded arbors, the riotous old-fashioned flowers, and bushes and gnarly trees.

Out of another I get a lovely view of the bay and a little private wharf belonging to the estate. There is a beautiful shaded lane that runs down there from the house. I always fancy I see people walking in these numerous paths and arbors, but John has cautioned me not to give way to fancy in the least. He says that with my imaginative power and habit of story-making, a nervous weakness like mine is sure to lead to all manner of excited fancies, and that I ought to use my will and good sense to check the tendency. So I try.

I think sometimes that if I were only well enough to write a little it would relieve the press of ideas and rest me.

But I find I get pretty tired when I try.

It is so discouraging not to have any advice and companionship about my work. When I get really well, John says we will ask Cousin Henry and Julia down for a long visit; but he says he would as soon put fireworks in my pillow-case as to let me have those stimulating people about now.

I wish I could get well faster.

But I must not think about that. This paper looks to me as if it *knew* what a vicious influence it had!

There is a recurrent spot where the pattern lolls like a broken neck and two bulbous eyes stare at you upside down.

I get positively angry with the impertinence of it and the everlastingness. Up and down and sideways they crawl, and those absurd, unblinking eyes are everywhere. There is one place where two breadths didn't match, and the eyes go all up and down the line, one a little higher than the other.

I never saw so much expression in an inanimate thing before, and we all know how much expression they have! I used to lie awake as a child and get more entertainment and terror out of blank walls and plain furniture than most children could find in a toy-store.

I remember what a kindly wink the knobs of our big, old bureau used to have, and there was one chair that always seemed like a strong friend.

I used to feel that if any of the other things looked too fierce I could always hop into that chair and be safe.

The furniture in this room is no worse than inharmonious, however, for we had to bring it all from downstairs. I suppose when this was used as a play-room they had to take the nursery things out, and no wonder! I never saw such ravages as the children have made here.

The wall-paper, as I said before, is torn off in spots, and it sticketh closer than a brother — they must have had perseverance as well as hatred.

Then the floor is scratched and gouged and splintered, the plaster itself is dug out here and there, and this great heavy bed which is all we found in the room, looks as if it had been through the wars.

But I don't mind it a bit — only the paper.

There comes John's sister. Such a dear girl as she is, and so careful of me! I must not let her find me writing.

She is a perfect and enthusiastic housekeeper, and hopes for no better profession. I verily believe she thinks it is the writing which made me sick!

But I can write when she is out, and see her a long way off from these windows.

There is one that commands the road, a lovely shaded winding road, and one that just looks off over the country. A lovely country, too, full of great elms and velvet meadows.

This wall-paper has a kind of sub-pattern in a different shade, a particularly irritating one, for you can only see it in certain lights, and not clearly then.

But in the places where it isn't faded and where the sun is just so — I can see a strange, provoking, formless sort of figure, that seems to skulk about behind that silly and conspicuous front design.

There's sister on the stairs!

———

Well, the Fourth of July is over! The people are all gone and I am tired out. John thought it might do me good to see a little company, so we just had mother and Nellie and the children down for a week.

Of course I didn't do a thing. Jennie sees to everything now.

But it tired me all the same.

John says if I don't pick up faster he shall send me to Weir Mitchell[1] in the fall.

But I don't want to go there at all. I had a friend who was in his hands once, and she says he is just like John and my brother, only more so!

Besides, it is such an undertaking to go so far.

I don't feel as if it was worth while to turn my hand over for anything, and I'm getting dreadfully fretful and querulous.

I cry at nothing, and cry most of the time.

Of course I don't when John is here, or anybody else, but when I am alone.

And I am alone a good deal just now. John is kept in town very often by serious cases, and Jennie is good and lets me alone when I want her to.

So I walk a little in the garden or down that lovely lane, sit on the porch under the roses, and lie down up here a good deal.

I'm getting really fond of the room in spite of the wall-paper. Perhaps *because* of the wall-paper.

It dwells in my mind so!

I lie here on this great immovable bed — it is nailed down, I believe — and follow that pattern about by the hour. It is as good as gymnastics, I assure you. I start, we'll say, at the bottom, down in the corner over there where it has not been touched, and I determine for the thousandth time that I *will* follow that pointless pattern to some sort of a conclusion.

I know a little of the principle of design, and I know this thing was not arranged on any laws of radiation, or alternation, or repetition, or symmetry, or anything else that I ever heard of.

It is repeated, of course, by the breadths, but not otherwise.

Looked at in one way each breadth stands alone, the bloated curves and flourishes — a kind of "debased Romanesque" with *delirium tremens* — go waddling up and down in isolated columns of fatuity.

But, on the other hand, they connect diagonally, and the sprawling outlines run off in great slanting waves of optic horror, like a lot of wallowing seaweeds in full chase.

The whole thing goes horizontally, too, at least it seems so, and I exhaust myself in trying to distinguish the order of its going in that direction.

They have used a horizontal breadth for a frieze, and that adds wonderfully to the confusion.

There is one end of the room where it is almost intact, and there, when the crosslights fade and the low sun shines directly upon it, I can almost fancy

---

[1] Dr. S. Weir Mitchell (1829–1914) was an eminent Philadelphia neurologist who advocated "rest cures" for nervous disorders. He was the author of *Diseases of the Nervous System, Especially of Women* (1881).

radiation after all, — the interminable grotesques seem to form around a common centre and rush off in headlong plunges of equal distraction.

It makes me tired to follow it. I will take a nap I guess.

———————

I don't know why I should write this.

I don't want to.

I don't feel able.

And I know John would think it absurd. But I *must* say what I feel and think in some way — it is such a relief!

But the effort is getting to be greater than the relief.

Half the time now I am awfully lazy, and lie down ever so much.

John says I mustn't lose my strength, and has me take cod liver oil and lots of tonics and things, to say nothing of ale and wine and rare meat.

Dear John! He loves me very dearly, and hates to have me sick. I tried to have a real earnest reasonable talk with him the other day, and tell him how I wish he would let me go and make a visit to Cousin Henry and Julia.

But he said I wasn't able to go, nor able to stand it after I got there; and I did not make out a very good case for myself, for I was crying before I had finished.

It is getting to be a great effort for me to think straight. Just this nervous weakness I suppose.

And dear John gathered me up in his arms, and just carried me upstairs and laid me on the bed, and sat by me and read to me till it tired my head.

He said I was his darling and his comfort and all he had, and that I must take care of myself for his sake, and keep well.

He says no one but myself can help me out of it, that I must use my will and self-control and not let any silly fancies run away with me.

There's one comfort, the baby is well and happy, and does not have to occupy this nursery with the horrid wallpaper.

If we had not used it, that blessed child would have! What a fortunate escape! Why, I wouldn't have a child of mine, an impressionable little thing, live in such a room for worlds.

I never thought of it before, but it is lucky that John kept me here after all, I can stand it so much easier than a baby, you see.

Of course I never mention it to them any more — I am too wise, — but I keep watch of it all the same.

There are things in that paper that nobody knows but me, or ever will.

Behind that outside pattern the dim shapes get clearer every day.

It is always the same shape, only very numerous.

And it is like a woman stooping down and creeping about behind that pattern. I don't like it a bit. I wonder — I begin to think — I wish John would take me away from here!

———————

It is so hard to talk to John about my case, because he is so wise, and because he loves me so.

But I tried it last night.

It was moonlight. The moon shines in all around just as the sun does.

I hate to see it sometimes, it creeps so slowly, and always comes in by one window or another.

John was asleep and I hated to waken him, so I kept still and watched the moonlight on that undulating wallpaper till I felt creepy.

The faint figure behind seemed to shake the pattern, just as if she wanted to get out.

I got up softly and went to feel and see if the paper *did* move, and when I came back John was awake.

"What is it, little girl?" he said. "Don't go walking about like that — you'll get cold."

I thought it was a good time to talk, so I told him that I really was not gaining here, and that I wished he would take me away.

"Why, darling!" said he, "our lease will be up in three weeks, and I can't see how to leave before.

"The repairs are not done at home, and I cannot possibly leave town just now. Of course if you were in any danger, I could and would, but you really are better, dear, whether you can see it or not. I am a doctor, dear, and I know. You are gaining flesh and color, your appetite is better, I feel really much easier about you."

"I don't weigh a bit more," said I, "nor as much; and my appetite may be better in the evening when you are here, but it is worse in the morning when you are away!"

"Bless her little heart!" said he with a big hug, "she shall be as sick as she pleases! But now let's improve the shining hours by going to sleep, and talk about it in the morning!"

"And you won't go away?" I asked gloomily.

"Why, how can I, dear? It is only three weeks more and then we will take a nice little trip of a few days while Jennie is getting the house ready. Really dear you are better!"

"Better in body perhaps —" I began, and stopped short, for he sat up straight and looked at me with such a stern, reproachful look that I could not say another word.

"My darling," said he, "I beg of you, for my sake and for our child's sake, as well as for your own, that you will never for one instant let that idea enter your mind! There is nothing so dangerous, so fascinating, to a temperament like yours. It is a false and foolish fancy. Can you not trust me as a physician when I tell you so?"

So of course I said no more on that score, and we went to sleep before long. He thought I was asleep first, but I wasn't, and lay there for hours trying to decide whether that front pattern and the back pattern really did move together or separately.

On a pattern like this, by daylight, there is a lack of sequence, a defiance of law, that is a constant irritant to a normal mind.

The color is hideous enough, and unreliable enough, and infuriating enough, but the pattern is torturing.

You think you have mastered it, but just as you get well underway in following, it turns a back-somersault and there you are. It slaps you in the face, knocks you down, and tramples upon you. It is like a bad dream.

The outside pattern is a florid arabesque, reminding one of a fungus. If you can imagine a toadstool in joints, an interminable string of toadstools, budding and sprouting in endless convolutions — why, that is something like it.

That is, sometimes!

There is one marked peculiarity about this paper, a thing nobody seems to notice but myself, and that is that it changes as the light changes.

When the sun shoots in through the east window — I always watch for that first long, straight ray — it changes so quickly that I never can quite believe it.

That is why I watch it always.

By moonlight — the moon shines in all night when there is a moon — I wouldn't know it was the same paper.

At night in any kind of light, in twilight, candlelight, lamplight, and worst of all by moonlight, it becomes bars! The outside pattern I mean, and the woman behind it is as plain as can be.

I didn't realize for a long time what the thing was that showed behind, that dim sub-pattern, but now I am quite sure it is a woman.

By daylight she is subdued, quiet. I fancy it is the pattern that keeps her so still. It is so puzzling. It keeps me quiet by the hour.

I lie down ever so much now. John says it is good for me, and to sleep all I can.

Indeed he started the habit by making me lie down for an hour after each meal.

It is a very bad habit I am convinced, for you see I don't sleep.

And that cultivates deceit, for I don't tell them I'm awake — O no!

The fact is I am getting a little afraid of John.

He seems very queer sometimes, and even Jennie has an inexplicable look.

It strikes me occasionally, just as a scientific hypothesis, — that perhaps it is the paper!

I have watched John when he did not know I was looking, and come into the room suddenly on the most innocent excuses, and I've caught him several times *looking at the paper!* And Jennie too. I caught Jennie with her hand on it once.

She didn't know I was in the room, and when I asked her in a quiet, a very quiet voice, with the most restrained manner possible, what she was doing with the paper — she turned around as if she had been caught stealing, and looked quite angry — asked me why I should frighten her so!

Then she said that the paper stained everything it touched, that she had found yellow smooches on all my clothes and John's, and she wished we would be more careful!

Did not that sound innocent? But I know she was studying that pattern, and I am determined that nobody shall find it out but myself!

Life is very much more exciting now than it used to be. You see I have something more to expect, to look forward to, to watch. I really do eat better, and am more quiet than I was.

John is so pleased to see me improve! He laughed a little the other day, and said I seemed to be flourishing in spite of my wall-paper.

I turned it off with a laugh. I had no intention of telling him it was *because* of the wall-paper — he would make fun of me. He might even want to take me away.

I don't want to leave now until I have found it out. There is a week more, and I think that will be enough.

I'm feeling ever so much better! I don't sleep much at night, for it is so interesting to watch developments; but I sleep a good deal in the daytime.

In the daytime it is tiresome and perplexing.

There are always new shoots on the fungus, and new shades of yellow all over it. I cannot keep count of them, though I have tried conscientiously.

It is the strangest yellow, that wall-paper! It makes me think of all the yellow things I ever saw — not beautiful ones like buttercups, but old foul, bad yellow things.

But there is something else about that paper — the smell! I noticed it the moment we came into the room, but with so much air and sun it was not bad. Now we have had a week of fog and rain, and whether the windows are open or not, the smell is here.

It creeps all over the house.

I find it hovering in the dining-room, skulking in the parlor, hiding in the hall, lying in wait for me on the stairs.

It gets into my hair.

Even when I go to ride, if I turn my head suddenly and surprise it — there is that smell!

Such a peculiar odor, too! I have spent hours in trying to analyze it, to find what it smelled like.

It is not bad — at first, and very gentle, but quite the subtlest, most enduring odor I ever met.

In this damp weather it is awful, I wake up in the night and find it hanging over me.

It used to disturb me at first. I thought seriously of burning the house — to reach the smell.

But now I am used to it. The only thing I can think of that it is like is the *color* of the paper! A yellow smell.

There is a very funny mark on this wall, low down, near the mopboard. A streak that runs around the room. It goes behind every piece of furniture, except the bed, a long, straight, even *smooch*, as if it had been rubbed over and over.

I wonder how it was done and who did it, and what they did it for. Round and round and round — round and round and round — it makes me dizzy!

I really have discovered something at last.

Through watching so much at night, when it changes so, I have finally found out.

The front pattern *does* move — and no wonder! The woman behind shakes it!

Sometimes I think there are a great many women behind, and sometimes only one, and she crawls around fast, and her crawling shakes it all over.

Then in the very bright spots she keeps still, and in the very shady spots she just takes hold of the bars and shakes them hard.

And she is all the time trying to climb through. But nobody could climb through that pattern — it strangles so; I think that is why it has so many heads.

They get through, and then the pattern strangles them off and turns them upside down, and makes their eyes white!

If those heads were covered or taken off it would not be half so bad.

I think that woman gets out in the daytime!

And I'll tell you why — privately — I've seen her!

I can see her out of every one of my windows!

It is the same woman, I know, for she is always creeping, and most women do not creep by daylight.

I see her in that long shaded lane, creeping up and down. I see her in those dark grape arbors, creeping all around the garden.

I see her on that long road under the trees, creeping along, and when a carriage comes she hides under the blackberry vines.

I don't blame her a bit. It must be very humiliating to be caught creeping by daylight!

I always lock the door when I creep by daylight. I can't do it at night, for I know John would suspect something at once.

And John is so queer now, that I don't want to irritate him. I wish he would take another room! Besides, I don't want anybody to get that woman out at night but myself.

I often wonder if I could see her out of all the windows at once.

But, turn as fast as I can, I can only see out of one at one time.

And though I always see her, she *may* be able to creep faster than I can turn!

I have watched her sometimes away off in the open country, creeping as fast as a cloud shadow in a high wind.

If only that top pattern could be gotten off from the under one! I mean to try it, little by little.

I have found out another funny thing, but I shan't tell it this time! It does not do to trust people too much.

There are only two more days to get this paper off, and I believe John is beginning to notice. I don't like the look in his eyes.

And I heard him ask Jennie a lot of professional questions about me. She had a very good report to give.

She said I slept a good deal in the daytime.

John knows I don't sleep very well at night, for all I'm so quiet!

He asked me all sorts of questions, too, and pretended to be very loving and kind.

As if I couldn't see through him!

Still, I don't wonder he acts so, sleeping under this paper for three months.

It only interests me, but I feel sure John and Jennie are secretly affected by it.

Hurrah! This is the last day, but it is enough. John is to stay in town over night, and won't be out until this evening.

Jennie wanted to sleep with me — the sly thing! But I told her I should undoubtedly rest better for a night all alone.

That was clever, for really I wasn't alone a bit! As soon as it was moonlight and that poor thing began to crawl and shake the pattern, I got up and ran to help her.

I pulled and she shook, I shook and she pulled, and before morning we had peeled off yards of that paper.

A strip about as high as my head and half around the room.

And then when the sun came and that awful pattern began to laugh at me, I declared I would finish it to-day!

We go away to-morrow, and they are moving all my furniture down again to leave things as they were before.

Jennie looked at the wall in amazement, but I told her merrily that I did it out of pure spite at the vicious thing.

She laughed and said she wouldn't mind doing it herself, but I must not get tired.

How she betrayed herself that time!

But I am here, and no person touches this paper but me, — not *alive!*

She tried to get me out of the room — it was too patent! But I said it was so quiet and empty and clean now that I believed I would lie down again and sleep all I could; and not to wake me even for dinner — I would call when I woke.

So now she is gone, and the servants are gone, and the things are gone, and there is nothing left but that great bedstead nailed down, with the canvas mattress we found on it.

We shall sleep downstairs to-night, and take the boat home to-morrow.

I quite enjoy the room, now it is bare again.

How those children did tear about here!

This bedstead is fairly gnawed!

But I must get to work.

I have locked the door and thrown the key down into the front path.

I don't want to go out, and I don't want to have anybody come in, till John comes.

I want to astonish him.

I've got a rope up here that even Jennie did not find. If that woman does get out, and tries to get away, I can tie her!

But I forgot I could not reach far without anything to stand on!

This bed will *not* move!

I tried to lift and push it until I was lame, and then I got so angry I bit off a little piece at one corner — but it hurt my teeth.

Then I peeled off all the paper I could reach standing on the floor. It sticks horribly and the pattern just enjoys it! All those strangled heads and bulbous eyes and waddling fungus growths just shriek with derision!

I am getting angry enough to do something desperate. To jump out of the window would be admirable exercise, but the bars are too strong even to try.

Besides I wouldn't do it. Of course not. I know well enough that a step like that is improper and might be misconstrued.

I don't like to *look* out of the windows even — there are so many of those creeping women, and they creep so fast.

I wonder if they all come out of that wall-paper as I did?

But I am securely fastened now by my well-hidden rope — you don't get *me* out in the road there!

I suppose I shall have to get back behind the pattern when it comes night, and that is hard!

It is so pleasant to be out in this great room and creep around as I please!

I don't want to go outside. I won't, even if Jennie asks me to.

For outside you have to creep on the ground, and everything is green instead of yellow.

But here I can creep smoothly on the floor, and my shoulder just fits in that long smooch around the wall, so I cannot lose my way.

Why there's John at the door!

It is no use, young man, you can't open it!

How he does call and pound!

Now he's crying for an axe.

It would be a shame to break down that beautiful door!

"John dear!" said I in the gentlest voice, "the key is down by the front steps, under a plantain leaf!"

That silenced him for a few moments.

Then he said — very quietly indeed, "Open the door, my darling!"

"I can't," said I. "The key is down by the front door under a plantain leaf!"

And then I said it again, several times, very gently and slowly, and said it so often that he had to go and see, and he got it of course, and came in. He stopped short by the door.

"What is the matter?" he cried. "For God's sake, what are you doing!"

I kept on creeping just the same, but I looked at him over my shoulder.

"I've got out at last," said I, "in spite of you and Jane. And I've pulled off most of the paper, so you can't put me back!"

Now why should that man have fainted? But he did, and right across my path by the wall, so that I had to creep over him every time!

Nikolai Gogol

Nikolai Gogol (1809–1852) broke through the eighteenth-century literary conventions that prevailed in his time. He is considered the father of Russian realism—"We all came out from under Gogol's 'Overcoat'" is a remark attributed to the novelists Ivan Turgenev, Leo Tolstoy, and Fyodor Dostoevsky, each of whom is supposed to have said it as a tribute to the story's importance. As today's readers can agree, Gogol used romanticism and fantasy in his fiction as well.

Born in Sorochintsky in the Russian Ukraine, Gogol was sent away to a boarding school as a boy; he was so physically unattractive that the other students gave him the name "the mysterious dwarf." In 1828, after he left school, Gogol moved to St. Petersburg (then the capital of Russia), passed the civil service examinations, and held various government jobs; he also became a friend of Alexander Pushkin, the great Russian poet. In 1831 and 1832 Gogol published *Evenings on a Farm near Dikanka*; in 1835 he followed it with *Arabesques*, stories like "The Overcoat" and "The Diary of a Madman" that imagined a nightmare world of fear and frustration. In 1836 his play *The Inspector General*, a satire ridiculing Russian officials, was considered so scandalous that Gogol was forced into exile in Rome, where he wrote the novel *Dead Souls*, which he considered his most important book. In his last years his health declined; sinking into a severe depression, he slowly starved himself to death at the age of forty-three.

In *The Lonely Voice* (1963), his study of the short story, Frank O'Connor maintained that the expression "We all came out from under Gogol's 'Overcoat'" has a validity beyond its relevance for Russian writers. O'Connor identified this story as "the first appearance in fiction of the Little Man." He went on to define the special impact of the short story as a literary form that offers an intense awareness of human isolation. To O'Connor, the short story (unlike the novel) never features a true hero. Instead, it portrays "a submerged population group," which changes character from writer to writer and generation to generation: "It may be Gogol's officials . . . Maupassant's prostitutes, Chekhov's doctors and teachers, Sherwood Anderson's provincials, always dreaming of escape." Everything about Akaky Akakievich in "The Overcoat"—his absurd name, his absurd family, his absurd job—is on the same level of mediocrity, yet something about the little clerk moves us to pity and sympathy. When others torment him, we seem to hear him say, "Leave me alone! Why do you insult me? I am your brother."

RELATED COMMENTARY
Vladimir Nabokov, "Gogol's Genius in 'The Overcoat,'" page 1483.

The Overcoat

1840 / Translated by Constance Garnett

IN THE DEPARTMENT OF . . . but I had better not mention which department. There is nothing in the world more touchy than a department, a regiment, a government office, and, in fact, any sort of official body. Nowadays every private individual considers all society insulted in his person. I have been told that very lately a complaint was lodged by a police inspector of which town I don't remember, and that in this complaint he set forth clearly that the institutions of the State were in danger and that his sacred name was being taken in vain; and, in proof thereof, he appended to his complaint an enormously long volume of some romantic work in which a police inspector appeared on every tenth page, occasionally, indeed, in an intoxicated condition. And so, to avoid any unpleasantness, we had better call the department of which we are speaking "a certain department."

And so, in a *certain department* there was a *certain clerk*; a clerk of whom it cannot be said that he was very remarkable; he was short, somewhat pockmarked, with rather reddish hair and rather dim, bleary eyes, with a small bald patch on the top of his head, with wrinkles on both sides of his cheeks and the sort of complexion which is usually described as hemorrhoidal . . . nothing can be done about that, it is the Petersburg climate. As for his grade in the civil service (for among us a man's rank is what must be established first) he was what is called a perpetual titular councilor, a class at which, as we all know, various writers who indulge in the praiseworthy habit of attacking those who cannot defend themselves jeer and jibe to their hearts' content. This clerk's surname was Bashmachkin. From the very name it is clear that it must have been derived from a shoe (*bashmak*); but when and under what circumstances it was derived from a shoe, it is impossible to say. Both his father and his grandfather and even his brother-in-law, and all the Bashmachkins without exception wore boots, which they simply resoled two or three times a year. His name was Akaky Akakievich. Perhaps it may strike the reader as a rather strange and contrived name, but I can assure him that it was not contrived at all, that the circumstances were such that it was quite out of the question to give him any other name. Akaky Akakievich was born toward nightfall, if my memory does not deceive me, on the twenty-third of March. His mother, the wife of a government clerk, a very good woman, made arrangements in due course to christen the child. She was still lying in bed, facing the door, while on her right hand stood the godfather, an excellent man called Ivan Ivanovich Yeroshkin, one of the head clerks in the Senate, and the godmother, the wife of a police official and a woman of rare qualities, Arina Semeonovna Belobriushkova. Three names were offered to the happy mother for selection — Mokky, Sossy, or the name of the martyr Khozdazat. "No," thought the poor lady, "they are all such names!" To satisfy her, they opened the calendar at another page, and the names which turned up were: Trifily, Dula, Varakhasy. "What an infliction!" said the mother. "What names they all are! I really never heard such names.

Varadat or Varukh would be bad enough, but Trifily and Varakhasy!" They turned over another page and the names were: Pavsikakhy and Vakhisy. "Well, I see," said the mother, "it is clear that it is his fate. Since that is how it is, he had better be named after his father; his father is Akaky; let the son be Akaky, too." This was how he came to be Akaky Akakievich. The baby was christened and cried and made sour faces during the ceremony, as though he foresaw that he would be a titular councilor. So that was how it all came to pass. We have reported it here so that the reader may see for himself that it happened quite inevitably and that to give him any other name was out of the question.

No one has been able to remember when and how long ago he entered the department, nor who gave him the job. Regardless of how many directors and higher officials of all sorts came and went, he was always seen in the same place, in the same position, at the very same duty, precisely the same copying clerk, so that they used to declare that he must have been born a copying clerk, uniform, bald patch, and all. No respect at all was shown him in the department. The porters, far from getting up from their seats when he came in, took no more notice of him than if a simple fly had flown across the reception room. His superiors treated him with a sort of despotic aloofness. The head clerk's assistant used to throw papers under his nose without even saying "Copy this" or "Here is an interesting, nice little case" or some agreeable remark of the sort, as is usually done in well-bred offices. And he would take it, gazing only at the paper without looking to see who had put it there and whether he had the right to do so; he would take it and at once begin copying it. The young clerks jeered and made jokes at him to the best of their clerkly wit, and told before his face all sorts of stories of their own invention about him; they would say of his landlady, an old woman of seventy, that she beat him, would ask when the wedding was to take place, and would scatter bits of paper on his head, calling them snow. Akaky Akakievich never answered a word, however, but behaved as though there were no one there. It had no influence on his work; in the midst of all this teasing, he never made a single mistake in his copying. It was only when the jokes became too unbearable, when they jolted his arm, and prevented him from going on with his work, that he would say: "Leave me alone! Why do you insult me?" and there was something touching in the words and in the voice in which they were uttered. There was a note in it of something that aroused compassion, so that one young man, new to the office, who, following the example of the rest, had allowed himself to tease him, suddenly stopped as though cut to the heart, and from that time on, everything was, as it were, changed and appeared in a different light to him. Some unseen force seemed to repel him from the companions with whom he had become acquainted because he thought they were well-bred and decent men. And long afterward, during moments of the greatest gaiety, the figure of the humble little clerk with a bald patch on his head appeared before him with his heart-rending words: "Leave me alone! Why do you insult me?" and within those moving words he heard others: "I am your brother." And the poor young man hid his face in his hands, and many times afterward in his life he shuddered, seeing how much inhumanity there is in man, how much savage brutality lies hidden under refined, cultured politeness, and, my God! even in a man whom the world accepts as a gentleman and a man of honor. . . .

It would be hard to find a man who lived for his work as did Akaky Akakievich. To say that he was zealous in his work is not enough; no, he loved his work. In it, in that copying, he found an interesting and pleasant world of his own. There was a look of enjoyment on his face; certain letters were favorites with him, and when he came to them he was delighted; he chuckled to himself and winked and moved his lips, so that it seemed as though every letter his pen was forming could be read in his face. If rewards had been given according to the measure of zeal in the service, he might to his amazement have even found himself a civil councilor; but all he gained in the service, as the wits, his fellow clerks, expressed it, was a button in his buttonhole[1] and hemorrhoids where he sat. It cannot be said, however, that no notice had ever been taken of him. One director, being a good-natured man and anxious to reward him for his long service, sent him something a little more important than his ordinary copying; he was instructed to make some sort of report from a finished document for another office; the work consisted only of altering the headings and in places changing the first person into the third. This cost him so much effort that he was covered with perspiration: he mopped his brow and said at last, "No, I'd rather copy something."

From that time on they left him to his copying forever. It seemed as though nothing in the world existed for him except his copying. He gave no thought at all to his clothes; his uniform was — well, not green but some sort of rusty, muddy color. His collar was very low and narrow, so that, although his neck was not particularly long, yet, standing out of the collar, it looked as immensely long as those of the dozens of plaster kittens with nodding heads which foreigners carry about on their heads and peddle in Russia. And there were always things sticking to his uniform, either bits of hay or threads; moreover, he had a special knack of passing under a window at the very moment when various garbage was being flung out into the street, and so was continually carrying off bits of melon rind and similar litter on his hat. He had never once in his life noticed what was being done and what was going on in the street, all those things at which, as we all know, his colleagues, the young clerks, always stare, utilizing their keen sight so well that they notice anyone on the other side of the street with a strap hanging loose — an observation which always calls forth a sly grin. Whatever Akaky Akakievich looked at, he saw nothing but his clear, evenly written lines, and it was only perhaps when a horse suddenly appeared from nowhere and placed its head on his shoulder, and with its nostrils blew a real gale upon his cheek, that he would notice that he was not in the middle of his writing, but rather in the middle of the street.

On reaching home, he would sit down at once at the table, hurriedly eat his soup and a piece of beef with an onion; he did not notice the taste at all but ate

---

[1] Whereas most clerks of long service wore a medal of achievement. (Leonard J. Kent, ed., *The Complete Tales of Nikolai Gogol*, vol. 2 [Chicago: University of Chicago Press, 1985].)

it all with the flies and anything else that Providence happened to send him. When he felt that his stomach was beginning to be full, he would get up from the table, take out a bottle of ink, and begin copying the papers he had brought home with him. When he had none to do, he would make a copy especially for his own pleasure, particularly if the document were remarkable not for the beauty of its style but because it was addressed to some new or distinguished person.

Even at those hours when the gray Petersburg sky is completely overcast and the whole population of clerks have dined and eaten their fill, each as best he can, according to the salary he receives and his personal tastes; when they are all resting after the scratching of pens and bustle of the office, their own necessary work and other people's, and all the tasks that an overzealous man voluntarily sets himself even beyond what is necessary; when the clerks are hastening to devote what is left of their time to pleasure; some more enterprising are flying to the theater, others to the street to spend their leisure staring at women's hats, some to spend the evening paying compliments to some attractive girl, the star of a little official circle, while some—and this is the most frequent of all—go simply to a fellow clerk's apartment on the third or fourth story, two little rooms with a hall or a kitchen, with some pretensions to style, with a lamp or some such article that has cost many sacrifices of dinners and excursions—at the time when all the clerks are scattered about the apartments of their friends, playing a stormy game of whist, sipping tea out of glasses, eating cheap biscuits, sucking in smoke from long pipes, telling, as the cards are dealt, some scandal that has floated down from higher circles, a pleasure which the Russian can never by any possibility deny himself, or, when there is nothing better to talk about, repeating the everlasting anecdote of the commanding officer who was told that the tail had been cut off the horse on the Falconet monument[2]—in short, even when everyone was eagerly seeking entertainment, Akaky Akakievich did not indulge in any amusement. No one could say that they had ever seen him at an evening party. After working to his heart's content, he would go to bed, smiling at the thought of the next day and wondering what God would send him to copy. So flowed on the peaceful life of a man who knew how to be content with his fate on a salary of four hundred rubles, and so perhaps it would have flowed on to extreme old age, had it not been for the various disasters strewn along the road of life, not only of titular, but even of privy, actual court, and all other councilors, even those who neither give counsel to others nor accept it themselves.

There is in Petersburg a mighty foe of all who receive a salary of about four hundred rubles. That foe is none other than our northern frost, although it is said to be very good for the health. Between eight and nine in the morning, precisely at the hour when the streets are filled with clerks going to their departments, the frost begins indiscriminately giving such sharp and stinging nips at all their noses that the poor fellows don't know what to do with them.

---

[2] Famous statue of Peter the First. (Kent, ed.)

At that time, when even those in the higher grade have a pain in their brows and tears in their eyes from the frost, the poor titular councilors are sometimes almost defenseless. Their only protection lies in running as fast as they can through five or six streets in a wretched, thin little overcoat and then warming their feet thoroughly in the porter's room, till all their faculties and talents for their various duties thaw out again after having been frozen on the way. Akaky Akakievich had for some time been feeling that his back and shoulders were particularly nipped by the cold, although he did try to run the regular distance as fast as he could. He wondered at last whether there were any defects in his overcoat. After examining it thoroughly in the privacy of his home, he discovered that in two or three places, on the back and the shoulders, it had become a regular sieve; the cloth was so worn that you could see through it and the lining was coming out. I must note that Akaky Akakievich's overcoat had also served as a butt for the jokes of the clerks. It had even been deprived of the honorable name of overcoat and had been referred to as the "dressing gown."[3] It was indeed of rather a peculiar make. Its collar had been growing smaller year by year as it served to patch the other parts. The patches were not good specimens of the tailor's art, and they certainly looked clumsy and ugly. On seeing what was wrong, Akaky Akakievich decided that he would have to take the overcoat to Petrovich, a tailor who lived on the fourth floor up a back staircase, and, in spite of having only one eye and being pockmarked all over his face, was rather successful in repairing the trousers and coats of clerks and others — that is, when he was sober, be it understood, and had no other enterprise on his mind. Of this tailor I ought not, of course, say much, but since it is now the rule that the character of every person in a novel must be completely described, well, there's nothing I can do but describe Petrovich too. At first he was called simply Grigory, and was a serf belonging to some gentleman or other. He began to be called Petrovich[4] from the time that he got his freedom and began to drink rather heavily on every holiday, at first only on the main holidays, but afterward, on all church holidays indiscriminately, wherever there was a cross in the calendar. In this he was true to the customs of his forefathers, and when he quarreled with his wife he used to call her a worldly woman and a German. Since we have now mentioned the wife, it will be necessary to say a few words about her, too, but unfortunately not much is known about her, except indeed that Petrovich had a wife and that she wore a cap and not a kerchief, but apparently she could not boast of beauty; anyway, none but soldiers of the guard peered under her cap when they met her, and they twitched their mustaches and gave vent to a rather peculiar sound.

As he climbed the stairs leading to Petrovich's — which, to do them justice, were all soaked with water and slops and saturated through and through with that smell of ammonia which makes the eyes smart, and is, as we all know, inseparable from the backstairs of Petersburg houses — Akaky Akakievich was

---

[3] *Kapot*, usually a woman's garment. (Kent, ed.)

[4] Customarily, serfs were addressed by first name only, while free men were addressed either by first name and patronymic or just the patronymic. (Kent, ed.)

already wondering how much Petrovich would ask for the job, and inwardly resolving not to give more than two rubles. The door was open, because Petrovich's wife was frying some fish and had so filled the kitchen with smoke that you could not even see the cockroaches. Akaky Akakievich crossed the kitchen unnoticed by the good woman, and walked at last into a room where he saw Petrovich sitting on a big, wooden, unpainted table with his legs tucked under him like a Turkish pasha. The feet, as is usual with tailors when they sit at work, were bare; and the first object that caught Akaky Akakievich's eye was the big toe, with which he was already familiar, with a misshapen nail as thick and strong as the shell of a tortoise. Around Petrovich's neck hung a skein of silk and another of thread and on his knees was a rag of some sort. He had for the last three minutes been trying to thread his needle, but could not get the thread into the eye and so was very angry with the darkness and indeed with the thread itself, muttering in an undertone: "She won't go in, the savage! You wear me out, you bitch." Akaky Akakievich was unhappy that he had come just at the minute when Petrovich was in a bad humor; he liked to give him an order when he was a little "elevated," or, as his wife expressed it, "had fortified himself with vodka, the one-eyed devil." In such circumstances Petrovich was as a rule very ready to give way and agree, and invariably bowed and thanked him. Afterward, it is true, his wife would come wailing that her husband had been drunk and so had asked too little, but adding a single ten-kopek piece would settle that. But on this occasion Petrovich was apparently sober and consequently curt, unwilling to bargain, and the devil knows what price he would be ready to demand. Akaky Akakievich realized this, and was, as the saying is, beating a retreat, but things had gone too far, for Petrovich was screwing up his solitary eye very attentively at him and Akaky Akakievich involuntarily said: "Good day, Petrovich!"

"I wish you a good day, sir," said Petrovich, and squinted at Akaky Akakievich's hands, trying to discover what sort of goods he had brought.

"Here I have come to you, Petrovich, do you see . . . !"

It must be noticed that Akaky Akakievich for the most part explained himself by apologies, vague phrases, and meaningless parts of speech which have absolutely no significance whatever. If the subject were a very difficult one, it was his habit indeed to leave his sentences quite unfinished, so that very often after a sentence had begun with the words, "It really is, don't you know . . ." nothing at all would follow and he himself would be quite oblivious to the fact that he had not finished his thought, supposing he had said all that was necessary.

"What is it?" said Petrovich, and at the same time with his solitary eye he scrutinized his whole uniform from the collar to the sleeves, the back, the skirts, the buttonholes — with all of which he was very familiar since they were all his own work. Such scrutiny is habitual with tailors; it is the first thing they do on meeting one.

"It's like this, Petrovich . . . the overcoat, the cloth . . . you see everywhere else it is quite strong; it's a little dusty and looks as though it were old, but it is new and it is only in one place just a little . . . on the back, and just a little worn on one shoulder and on this shoulder, too, a little . . . do you see? that's all, and it's not much work . . ."

Petrovich took the "dressing gown," first spread it out over the table, examined it for a long time, shook his head, and put his hand out to the window sill for a round snuffbox with a portrait on the lid of some general — which general I can't exactly say, for a finger had been thrust through the spot where a face should have been, and the hole had been pasted over with a square piece of paper. After taking a pinch of snuff, Petrovich held the "dressing gown" up in his hands and looked at it against the light, and again he shook his head; then he turned it with the lining upward and once more shook his head; again he took off the lid with the general pasted up with paper and snuffed a pinch into his nose, shut the box, put it away, and at last said: "No, it can't be repaired; a wretched garment!" Akaky Akakievich's heart sank at those words.

"Why can't it, Petrovich?" he said, almost in the imploring voice of a child. "Why, the only thing is, it is a bit worn on the shoulders; why, you have got some little pieces . . ."

"Yes, the pieces will be found all right," said Petrovich, "but it can't be patched, the stuff is rotten; if you put a needle in it, it would give way."

"Let it give way, but you just put a patch on it."

"There is nothing to put a patch on. There is nothing for it to hold on to; there is a great strain on it; it is not worth calling cloth; it would fly away at a breath of wind."

"Well, then, strengthen it with something — I'm sure, really, this is . . ."

"No," said Petrovich resolutely, "there is nothing that can be done, the thing is no good at all. You had far better, when the cold winter weather comes, make yourself leg wrappings out of it, for there is no warmth in stockings; the Germans invented them just to make money." (Petrovich enjoyed a dig at the Germans occasionally.) "And as for the overcoat, it is obvious that you will have to have a new one."

At the word "new" there was a mist before Akaky Akakievich's eyes, and everything in the room seemed blurred. He could see nothing clearly but the general with the piece of paper over his face on the lid of Petrovich's snuffbox.

"A new one?" he said, still feeling as though he were in a dream; "why, I haven't the money for it."

"Yes, a new one," Petrovich repeated with barbarous composure.

"Well, and if I did have a new one, how much would it . . . ?"

"You mean what will it cost?"

"Yes."

"Well, at least one hundred and fifty rubles," said Petrovich, and he compressed his lips meaningfully. He was very fond of making an effect; he was fond of suddenly disconcerting a man completely and then squinting sideways to see what sort of a face he made.

"A hundred and fifty rubles for an overcoat!" screamed poor Akaky Akakievich — it was perhaps the first time he had screamed in his life, for he was always distinguished by the softness of his voice.

"Yes," said Petrovich, "and even then it depends on the coat. If I were to put marten on the collar, and add a hood with silk linings, it would come to two hundred."

"Petrovich, please," said Akaky Akakievich in an imploring voice, not hearing and not trying to hear what Petrovich said, and missing all his effects, "repair it somehow, so that it will serve a little longer."

"No, that would be wasting work and spending money for nothing," said Petrovich, and after that Akaky Akakievich went away completely crushed, and when he had gone Petrovich remained standing for a long time with his lips pursed up meaningfully before he began his work again, feeling pleased that he had not demeaned himself or lowered the dignity of the tailor's art.

When he got into the street, Akaky Akakievich felt as though he was in a dream. "So that is how it is," he said to himself. "I really did not think it would be this way . . ." and then after a pause he added, "So that's it! So that's how it is at last! and I really could never have supposed it would be this way. And there . . ." There followed another long silence, after which he said: "So that's it! well, it really is so utterly unexpected . . . who would have thought . . . what a circumstance . . ." Saying this, instead of going home he walked off in quite the opposite direction without suspecting what he was doing. On the way a clumsy chimney sweep brushed the whole of his sooty side against him and blackened his entire shoulder; a whole hatful of plaster scattered upon him from the top of a house that was being built. He noticed nothing of this, and only after he had jostled against a policeman who had set his halberd down beside him and was shaking some snuff out of his horn into his rough fist, he came to himself a little and then only because the policeman said: "Why are you poking yourself right in one's face, haven't you enough room on the street?" This made him look around and turn homeward; only there he began to collect his thoughts, to see his position in a clear and true light, and began talking to himself no longer incoherently but reasonably and openly as with a sensible friend with whom one can discuss the most intimate and vital matters. "No," said Akaky Akakievich, "it is no use talking to Petrovich now; just now he really is . . . his wife must have been giving it to him. I had better go to him on Sunday morning; after Saturday night he will have a crossed eye and be sleepy, so he'll want a little drink and his wife won't give him a kopek. I'll slip ten kopeks into his hand and then he will be more accommodating and maybe take the overcoat . . ."

So reasoning with himself, Akaky Akakievich cheered up and waited until the next Sunday; then, seeing from a distance Petrovich's wife leaving the house, he went straight in. Petrovich certainly had a crossed eye after Saturday. He could hardly hold his head up and was very drowsy; but, despite all that, as soon as he heard what Akaky Akakievich was speaking about, it seemed as though the devil had nudged him. "I can't," he said, "you must order a new one." Akaky Akakievich at once slipped a ten-kopek piece into his hand. "I thank you, sir, I will have just a drop to your health, but don't trouble yourself about the overcoat; it is no good for anything. I'll make you a fine new coat; you can have faith in me for that."

Akaky Akakievich would have said more about repairs, but Petrovich, without listening, said: "A new one I'll make you without fail; you can rely on that; I'll do my best. It could even be like the fashion that is popular, with the collar to fasten with silver-plated hooks under a flap."

Then Akaky Akakievich saw that there was no escape from a new overcoat and he was utterly depressed. How indeed, for what, with what money could he get it? Of course he could to some extent rely on the bonus for the coming holiday, but that money had long been appropriated and its use determined beforehand. It was needed for new trousers and to pay the cobbler an old debt for putting some new tops on some old boots, and he had to order three shirts from a seamstress as well as two items of undergarments which it is indecent to mention in print; in short, all that money absolutely must be spent, and even if the director were to be so gracious as to give him a holiday bonus of forty-five or even fifty, instead of forty rubles, there would be still left a mere trifle, which would be but a drop in the ocean compared to the fortune needed for an overcoat. Though, of course, he knew that Petrovich had a strange craze for suddenly demanding the devil knows what enormous price, so that at times his own wife could not help crying out: "Why, you are out of your wits, you idiot! Another time he'll undertake a job for nothing, and here the devil has bewitched him to ask more than he is worth himself." Though, of course, he knew that Petrovich would undertake to make it for eighty rubles, still where would he get those eighty rubles? He might manage half of that sum; half of it could be found, perhaps even a little more; but where could he get the other half? . . . But, first of all, the reader ought to know where that first half was to be found. Akaky Akakievich had the habit every time he spent a ruble of putting aside two kopeks in a little box which he kept locked, with a slit in the lid for dropping in the money. At the end of every six months he would inspect the pile of coppers there and change them for small silver. He had done this for a long time, and in the course of many years the sum had mounted up to forty rubles and so he had half the money in his hands, but where was he to get the other half; where was he to get another forty rubles? Akaky Akakievich thought and thought and decided at last that he would have to diminish his ordinary expenses, at least for a year; give up burning candles in the evening, and if he had to do any work he must go into the landlady's room and work by her candle; that as he walked along the streets he must walk as lightly and carefully as possible, almost on tiptoe, on the cobbles and flagstones, so that his soles might last a little longer than usual; that he must send his linen to the wash less frequently, and that, to preserve it from being worn, he must take it off every day when he came home and sit in a thin cotton dressing gown, a very ancient garment which Time itself had spared. To tell the truth, he found it at first rather difficult to get used to these privations, but after a while it became a habit and went smoothly enough — he even became quite accustomed to being hungry in the evening; on the other hand, he had spiritual nourishment, for he carried ever in his thoughts the idea of his future overcoat. His whole existence had in a sense become fuller, as though he had married, as though some other person were present with him, as though he were no longer alone but an agreeable companion had consented to walk the path of life hand in hand with him, and that companion was none other than the new overcoat with its thick padding and its strong, durable lining. He became, as it were, more alive, even more strong-willed, like a man who has set before himself a definite goal.

Uncertainty, indecision, in fact all the hesitating and vague characteristics, vanished from his face and his manners. At times there was a gleam in his eyes; indeed, the most bold and audacious ideas flashed through his mind. Why not really have marten on the collar? Meditation on the subject always made him absent-minded. On one occasion when he was copying a document, he very nearly made a mistake, so that he almost cried out "ough" aloud and crossed himself. At least once every month he went to Petrovich to talk about the overcoat: where it would be best to buy the cloth, and what color it should be, and what price; and, though he returned home a little anxious, he was always pleased at the thought that at last the time was at hand when everything would be bought and the overcoat would be made. Things moved even faster than he had anticipated. Contrary to all expectations, the director bestowed on Akaky Akakievich a bonus of no less than sixty rubles. Whether it was that he had an inkling that Akaky Akakievich needed a coat, or whether it happened by luck, owing to this he found he had twenty rubles extra. This circumstance hastened the course of affairs. Another two or three months of partial starvation and Akaky Akakievich had actually saved up nearly eighty rubles. His heart, as a rule very tranquil, began to throb.

The very first day he set out with Petrovich for the shops. They bought some very good cloth, and no wonder, since they had been thinking of it for more than six months, and scarcely a month had passed without their going out to the shop to compare prices; now Petrovich himself declared that there was no better cloth to be had. For the lining they chose calico, but of such good quality, that in Petrovich's words it was even better than silk, and actually as strong and handsome to look at. Marten they did not buy, because it was too expensive, but instead they chose cat fur, the best to be found in the shop — cat which in the distance might almost be taken for marten. Petrovich was busy making the coat for two weeks, because there was a great deal of quilting; otherwise it would have been ready sooner. Petrovich charged twelve rubles for the work; less than that it hardly could have been; everything was sewn with silk, with fine double seams, and Petrovich went over every seam afterwards with his own teeth, imprinting various patterns with them. It was . . . it is hard to say precisely on what day, but probably on the most triumphant day in the life of Akaky Akakievich, that Petrovich at last brought the overcoat. He brought it in the morning, just before it was time to set off for the department. The overcoat could not have arrived at a more opportune time, because severe frosts were just beginning and seemed threatening to become even harsher. Petrovich brought the coat himself as a good tailor should. There was an expression of importance on his face, such as Akaky Akakievich had never seen there before. He seemed fully conscious of having completed a work of no little importance and of having shown by his own example the gulf that separates tailors who only put in linings and do repairs from those who make new coats. He took the coat out of the huge handkerchief in which he had brought it (the handkerchief had just come home from the wash); he then folded it up and put it in his pocket for future use. After taking out the overcoat, he looked at it with much pride and holding it in both hands, threw it very deftly over Akaky

Akakievich's shoulders, then pulled it down and smoothed it out behind with his hands; then draped it about Akaky Akakievich somewhat jauntily. Akaky Akakievich, a practical man, wanted to try it with his arms in the sleeves. Petrovich helped him to put it on, and it looked splendid with his arms in the sleeves, too. In fact, it turned out that the overcoat was completely and entirely successful. Petrovich did not let slip the occasion for observing that it was only because he lived in a small street and had no signboard, and because he had known Akaky Akakievich so long, that he had done it so cheaply, and that on Nevsky Prospekt they would have asked him seventy-five rubles for the tailoring alone. Akaky Akakievich had no inclination to discuss this with Petrovich; besides he was frightened of the big sums that Petrovich was fond of flinging airily about in conversation. He paid him, thanked him, and went off, with his new overcoat on, to the department. Petrovich followed him out and stopped in the street, staring for a long time at the coat from a distance and then purposely turned off and, taking a short cut through a side street, came back into the street, and got another view of the coat from the other side, that is, from the front.

Meanwhile Akaky Akakievich walked along in a gay holiday mood. Every second he was conscious that he had a new overcoat on his shoulders, and several times he actually laughed from inward satisfaction. Indeed, it had two advantages: one that it was warm and the other that it was good. He did not notice how far he had walked at all and he suddenly found himself in the department; in the porter's room he took off the overcoat, looked it over, and entrusted it to the porter's special care. I cannot tell how it happened, but all at once everyone in the department learned that Akaky Akakievich had a new overcoat and that the "dressing gown" no longer existed. They all ran out at once into the cloakroom to look at Akaky Akakievich's new overcoat; they began welcoming him and congratulating him so that at first he could do nothing but smile and then felt positively embarrassed. When, coming up to him, they all began saying that he must "sprinkle" the new overcoat and that he ought at least to buy them all a supper, Akaky Akakievich lost his head completely and did not know what to do, how to get out of it, nor what to answer. A few minutes later, flushing crimson, he even began assuring them with great simplicity that it was not a new overcoat at all, that it wasn't much, that it was an old overcoat. At last one of the clerks, indeed the assistant of the head clerk of the room, probably in order to show that he wasn't too proud to mingle with those beneath him, said: "So be it, I'll give a party instead of Akaky Akakievich and invite you all to tea with me this evening; as luck would have it, it is my birthday." The clerks naturally congratulated the assistant head clerk and eagerly accepted the invitation. Akaky Akakievich was beginning to make excuses, but they all declared that it was uncivil of him, that it would be simply a shame and a disgrace and that he could not possibly refuse. So, he finally relented, and later felt pleased about it when he remembered that through this he would have the opportunity of going out in the evening, too, in his new overcoat. That whole day was for Akaky Akakievich the most triumphant and festive day in his life. He returned home in the happiest frame of mind, took off the overcoat, and hung it carefully on the wall, admiring the cloth and lining once more, and then pulled out his old "dressing gown," now completely falling apart, and put it next to his new overcoat to compare the two. He glanced at it and laughed: the difference was enormous! And long afterwards he went on laughing at dinner, as the position in which the "dressing gown" was placed recurred to his mind. He dined in excellent spirits and after dinner wrote nothing, no papers at all, but just relaxed for a little while on his bed, till it got dark; then, without putting things off, he dressed, put on his overcoat, and went out into the street. Where precisely the clerk who had invited him lived we regret to say we cannot tell; our memory is beginning to fail sadly, and everything there in Petersburg, all the streets and houses, are so blurred and muddled in our head that it is a very difficult business to put anything in orderly fashion. Regardless of that, there is no doubt that the clerk lived in the better part of the town and consequently a very long distance from Akaky Akakievich. At first Akaky Akakievich had to walk through deserted streets, scantily lighted, but as he approached his destination the streets became more lively, more full of people, and more brightly lighted; passers-by began to be more frequent, ladies began to appear, here and there beautifully dressed, and beaver collars were to be seen on the men. Cabmen with wooden, railed sledges, studded with brass-topped nails, were less frequently seen; on the other hand, jaunty drivers in raspberry-colored velvet caps, with lacquered sledges and bearskin rugs, appeared and carriages with decorated boxes dashed along the streets, their wheels crunching through the snow.

Akaky Akakievich looked at all this as a novelty; for several years he had not gone out into the streets in the evening. He stopped with curiosity before a lighted shop window to look at a picture in which a beautiful woman was represented in the act of taking off her shoe and displaying as she did so the whole of a very shapely leg, while behind her back a gentleman with whiskers and a handsome imperial on his chin was sticking his head in at the door. Akaky Akakievich shook his head and smiled and then went on his way. Why did he smile? Was it because he had come across something quite unfamiliar to him, though every man retains some instinctive feeling on the subject, or was it that he reflected, like many other clerks, as follows: "Well, those Frenchmen! It's beyond anything! If they go in for anything of the sort, it really is . . . !" Though possibly he did not even think that; there is no creeping into a man's soul and finding out all that he thinks. At last he reached the house in which the assistant head clerk lived in fine style; there was a lamp burning on the stairs, and the apartment was on the second floor. As he went into the hall Akaky Akakievich saw rows of galoshes. Among them in the middle of the room stood a hissing samovar puffing clouds of steam. On the walls hung coats and cloaks among which some actually had beaver collars or velvet lapels. From the other side of the wall there came noise and talk, which suddenly became clear and loud when the door opened and the footman came out with a tray full of empty glasses, a jug of cream, and a basket of biscuits. It was evident that the clerks had arrived long before and had already drunk their first glass of tea. Akaky Akakievich, after hanging up his coat with his own hands, went into the room, and at the same moment there flashed before his eyes a vision of candles, clerks, pipes, and card tables, together with the confused sounds of conversation rising up on all sides and the noise of moving chairs. He stopped very awkwardly in the middle of the room, looking about and trying to think of what to do, but he was noticed and received with a shout and they all went at once into the hall and again took a look at his overcoat. Though Akaky Akakievich was somewhat embarrassed, yet, being a simple-hearted man, he could not help being pleased at seeing how they all admired his coat. Then of course they all abandoned him and his coat, and turned their attention as usual to the tables set for whist. All this — the noise, the talk, and the crowd of people — was strange and wonderful to Akaky Akakievich. He simply did not know how to behave, what to do with his arms and legs and his whole body; at last he sat down beside the players, looked at the cards, stared first at one and then at another of the faces, and in a little while, feeling bored, began to yawn — especially since it was long past the time at which he usually went to bed. He tried to say goodbye to his hosts, but they would not let him go, saying that he absolutely must have a glass of champagne in honor of the new coat. An hour later supper was served, consisting of salad, cold veal, pastry and pies from the bakery, and champagne. They made Akaky Akakievich drink two glasses, after which he felt that things were much more cheerful, though he could not forget that it was twelve o'clock, and that he ought to have been home long ago. That his host might not take it into his head to detain him, he slipped out of the room, hunted in the hall for his coat, which he found, not without regret, lying on the floor, shook it, removed some fluff from it, put it on, and went down the stairs into the street. It was still light in the streets. Some little grocery shops, those perpetual clubs for servants and all sorts of people, were open; others which were closed showed, however, a long streak of light at every crack of the door, proving that they were not yet deserted, and probably maids and menservants were still finishing their conversation and discussion, driving their masters to utter perplexity as to their whereabouts. Akaky Akakievich walked along in a cheerful state of mind; he was even on the point of running, goodness knows why, after a lady of some sort who passed by like lightning with every part of her frame in violent motion. He checked himself at once, however, and again walked along very gently, feeling positively surprised at the inexplicable impulse that had seized him. Soon the deserted streets, which are not particularly cheerful by day and even less so in the evening, stretched before him. Now they were still more dead and deserted; the light of street lamps was scantier, the oil evidently running low; then came wooden houses and fences; not a soul anywhere; only the snow gleamed on the streets and the low-pitched slumbering hovels looked black and gloomy with their closed shutters. He approached the spot where the street was intersected by an endless square, which looked like a fearful desert with its houses scarcely visible on the far side.

In the distance, goodness knows where, there was a gleam of light from some sentry box which seemed to be at the end of the world. Akaky Akakievich's lightheartedness faded. He stepped into the square, not without uneasiness, as though his heart had a premonition of evil. He looked behind him and to both sides — it was as though the sea were all around him. "No, better not look," he thought, and walked on, shutting his eyes, and when he opened them to see whether the end of the square was near, he suddenly saw standing before him, almost under his very nose, some men with mustaches; just what they were like he could not even distinguish. There was a mist before his eyes, and a throbbing in his chest. "Why, that overcoat is mine!" said one of them in a voice like a clap of thunder, seizing him by the collar. Akaky Akakievich was on the point of shouting "Help" when another put a fist the size of a clerk's head against his lips, saying: "You just shout now." Akaky Akakievich felt only that they took the overcoat off, and gave him a kick with their knees, and he fell on his face in the snow and was conscious of nothing more. A few minutes later he recovered consciousness and got up on his feet, but there was no one there. He felt that it was cold on the ground and that he had no overcoat, and began screaming, but it seemed as though his voice would not carry to the end of the square. Overwhelmed with despair and continuing to scream, he ran across the square straight to the sentry box beside which stood a policeman leaning on his halberd and, so it seemed, looking with curiosity to see who the devil the man was who was screaming and running toward him from the distance. As Akaky Akakievich reached him, he began breathlessly shouting that he was asleep and not looking after his duty not to see that a man was being robbed. The policeman answered that he had seen nothing, that he had only seen him stopped in the middle of the square by two men, and supposed that they were his friends, and that, instead of abusing him for nothing, he had better go the next day to the police inspector, who would certainly find out who had taken the overcoat. Akaky Akakievich ran home in a terrible state: his hair, which was still comparatively abundant on his temples and the back of his head, was completely disheveled; his sides and chest and his trousers were all covered with snow. When his old landlady heard a fearful knock at the door, she jumped hurriedly out of bed and, with only one slipper on, ran to open it, modestly holding her chemise over her bosom; but when she opened it she stepped back, seeing in what a state Akaky Akakievich was. When he told her what had happened, she clasped her hands in horror and said that he must go straight to the district commissioner, because the local police inspector would deceive him, make promises, and lead him a dance; that it would be best of all to go to the district commissioner, and that she knew him, because Anna, the Finnish girl who was once her cook, was now in service as a nurse at the commissioner's; and that she often saw him himself when he passed by their house, and that he used to be every Sunday at church too, saying his prayers and at the same time looking good-humoredly at everyone, and that therefore by every token he must be a kindhearted man. After listening to this advice, Akaky Akakievich made his way very gloomily to his room, and how he spent that night I leave to the imagination of those who are in the least able to picture the position of others.

Early in the morning he set off to the police commissioner's but was told that he was asleep. He came at ten o'clock, he was told again that he was asleep;

he came at eleven and was told that the commissioner was not at home; he came at dinnertime, but the clerks in the anteroom would not let him in, and insisted on knowing what was the matter and what business had brought him and exactly what had happened; so that at last Akaky Akakievich for the first time in his life tried to show the strength of his character and said curtly that he must see the commissioner himself, and they dare not refuse to admit him, that he had come from the department on government business, and that if he made complaint of them they would see. The clerks dared say nothing to this, and one of them went to summon the commissioner. The latter received his story of being robbed of his overcoat in an extremely peculiar manner. Instead of attending to the main point, he began asking Akaky Akakievich questions: why had he been coming home so late? wasn't he going, or hadn't he been, to some bawdy house? so that Akaky Akakievich was overwhelmed with confusion, and went away without knowing whether or not the proper measures would be taken regarding his overcoat. He was absent from the office all that day (the only time that it had happened in his life). Next day he appeared with a pale face, wearing his old "dressing gown," which had become a still more pitiful sight. The news of the theft of the overcoat — though there were clerks who did not let even this chance slip of jeering at Akaky Akakievich — touched many of them. They decided on the spot to get up a collection for him, but collected only a very trifling sum, because the clerks had already spent a good deal contributing to the director's portrait and on the purchase of a book, at the suggestion of the head of their department, who was a friend of the author, and so the total realized was very insignificant. One of the clerks, moved by compassion, ventured at any rate to assist Akaky Akakievich with good advice, telling him not to go to the local police inspector, because, though it might happen that the latter might succeed in finding his overcoat because he wanted to impress his superiors, it would remain in the possession of the police unless he presented legal proofs that it belonged to him; he urged that by far the best thing would be to appeal to a Person of Consequence; that the Person of Consequence, by writing and getting into communication with the proper authorities, could push the matter through more successfully. There was nothing else to do. Akaky Akakievich made up his mind to go to the Person of Consequence. What precisely was the nature of the functions of the Person of Consequence has remained a matter of uncertainty. It must be noted that this Person of Consequence had only lately become a person of consequence, and until recently had been a person of no consequence. Though, indeed, his position even now was not reckoned of consequence in comparison with others of still greater consequence. But there is always to be found a circle of persons to whom a person of little consequence in the eyes of others is a person of consequence. It is true that he did his utmost to increase the consequence of his position in various ways, for instance by insisting that his subordinates should come out onto the stairs to meet him when he arrived at his office; that no one should venture to approach him directly but all proceedings should follow the strictest chain of command; that a collegiate registrar should report the matter to the governmental secretary; and the governmental secretary to the titular councilors or whomsoever it might be, and that business should only reach him through this channel. Everyone in Holy Russia has a craze for imitation; everyone apes and mimics his superiors. I have actually been told that a titular councilor who was put in charge of a small separate office, immediately partitioned off a special room for himself, calling it the head office, and posted lackeys at the door with red collars and gold braid, who took hold of the handle of the door and opened it for everyone who went in, though the "head office" was so tiny that it was with difficulty that an ordinary writing desk could be put into it. The manners and habits of the Person of Consequence were dignified and majestic, but hardly subtle. The chief foundation of his system was strictness; "strictness, strictness, and — strictness!" he used to say, and at the last word he would look very significantly at the person he was addressing, though, indeed, he had no reason to do so, for the dozen clerks who made up the whole administrative mechanism of his office stood in appropriate awe of him; any clerk who saw him in the distance would leave his work and remain standing at attention till his superior had left the room. His conversation with his subordinates was usually marked by severity and almost confined to three phrases: "How dare you? Do you know to whom you are speaking? Do you understand who I am?" He was, however, at heart a good-natured man, pleasant and obliging with his colleagues; but his advancement to a high rank had completely turned his head. When he received it, he was perplexed, thrown off his balance, and quite at a loss as to how to behave. If he chanced to be with his equals, he was still quite a decent man, a very gentlemanly man, in fact, and in many ways even an intelligent man; but as soon as he was in company with men who were even one grade below him, there was simply no doing anything with him: he sat silent and his position excited compassion, the more so as he himself felt that he might have been spending his time to so much more advantage. At times there could be seen in his eyes an intense desire to join in some interesting conversation, but he was restrained by the doubt whether it would not be too much on his part, whether it would not be too great a familiarity and lowering of his dignity, and in consequence of these reflections he remained everlastingly in the same mute condition, only uttering from time to time monosyllabic sounds, and in this way he gained the reputation of being a terrible bore.

So this was the Person of Consequence to whom our friend Akaky Akakievich appealed, and he appealed to him at a most unpropitious moment, very unfortunate for himself, though fortunate, indeed, for the Person of Consequence. The latter happened to be in his study, talking in the very best of spirits with an old friend of his childhood who had only just arrived and whom he had not seen for several years. It was at this moment that he was informed that a man called Bashmachkin was asking to see him. He asked abruptly, "What sort of man is he?" and received the answer, "A government clerk." "Ah! he can wait. I haven't time now," said the Person of Consequence. Here I must observe that this was a complete lie on the part of the Person of Consequence; he had time; his friend and he had long ago said all they had to say to each other and their conversation had begun to be broken by very long pauses during which they

merely slapped each other on the knee, saying, "So that's how things are, Ivan
Abramovich!" — "So that's it, Stepan Varlamovich!" but, despite that, he told
the clerk to wait in order to show his friend, who had left the civil service some
years before and was living at home in the country, how long clerks had to wait
for him. At last, after they had talked or rather been silent, to their heart's content and had smoked a cigar in very comfortable armchairs with sloping backs,
he seemed suddenly to recollect, and said to the secretary, who was standing at
the door with papers for his signature: "Oh, by the way, there is a clerk waiting,
isn't there? Tell him he can come in." When he saw Akaky Akakievich's meek
appearance and old uniform, he turned to him at once and said: "What do you
want?" in a firm and abrupt voice, which he had purposely rehearsed in his
own room in solitude before the mirror for a week before receiving his present post and the grade of a general. Akaky Akakievich, who was overwhelmed
with appropriate awe beforehand, was somewhat confused and, as far as his
tongue would allow him, explained to the best of his powers, with even more
frequent "ers" than usual, that he had had a perfectly new overcoat and now he
had been robbed of it in the most inhuman way, and that now he had come to
beg him by his intervention either to correspond with his honor, the head police
commissioner, or anybody else, and find the overcoat. This mode of proceeding
struck the general for some reason as too familiar. "What next, sir?" he went
on abruptly. "Don't you know the way to proceed? To whom are you addressing
yourself? Don't you know how things are done? You ought first to have handed
in a petition to the office; it would have gone to the head clerk of the room, and
to the head clerk of the section; then it would have been handed to the secretary
and the secretary would have brought it to me . . ."

"But, your Excellency," said Akaky Akakievich, trying to gather the drop
of courage he possessed and feeling at the same time that he was perspiring all
over, "I ventured, your Excellency, to trouble you because secretaries . . . er . . .
are people you can't depend on . . ."

"What? what? what?" said the Person of Consequence, "where did you get
hold of that attitude? where did you pick up such ideas? What insubordina-
tion is spreading among young men against their superiors and their chiefs!"
The Person of Consequence did not apparently observe that Akaky Akakievich
was well over fifty, and therefore if he could have been called a young man it
would only have been in comparison to a man of seventy. "Do you know to
whom you are speaking? Do you understand who I am? Do you understand
that, I ask you?" At this point he stamped, and raised his voice to such a powerful note that Akaky Akakievich was not the only one to be terrified. Akaky
Akakievich was positively petrified; he staggered, trembling all over, and could
not stand; if the porters had not run up to support him, he would have flopped
on the floor; he was led out almost unconscious. The Person of Consequence,
pleased that the effect had surpassed his expectations and enchanted at the
idea that his words could even deprive a man of consciousness, stole a sideway
glance at his friend to see how he was taking it, and perceived not without satisfaction that his friend was feeling very uncertain and even beginning to be a
little terrified himself.

How he got downstairs, how he went out into the street — of all that Akaky Akakievich remembered nothing; he had no feeling in his arms or his legs. In all his life he had never been so severely reprimanded by a general, and this was by one of another department, too. He went out into the snowstorm that was whistling through the streets, with his mouth open, and as he went he stumbled off the pavement; the wind, as its way is in Petersburg, blew upon him from all points of the compass and from every side street. In an instant it had blown a quinsy into his throat, and when he got home he was not able to utter a word; he went to bed with a swollen face and throat. That's how violent the effects of an appropriate reprimand can be!

Next day he was in a high fever. Thanks to the gracious assistance of the Petersburg climate, the disease made more rapid progress than could have been expected, and when the doctor came, after feeling his pulse he could find nothing to do but prescribe a poultice, and that simply so that the patient might not be left without the benefit of medical assistance; however, two days later he informed him that his end was at hand, after which he turned to Akaky Akakievich's landlady and said: "And you had better lose no time, my good woman, but order him now a pine coffin, for an oak one will be too expensive for him." Whether Akaky Akakievich heard these fateful words or not, whether they produced a shattering effect upon him, and whether he regretted his pitiful life, no one can tell, for he was constantly in delirium and fever. Apparitions, each stranger than the one before, were continually haunting him: first he saw Petrovich and was ordering him to make an overcoat trimmed with some sort of traps for robbers, who were, he believed, continually under the bed, and he was calling his landlady every minute to pull out a thief who had even got under the quilt; then he kept asking why his old "dressing gown" was hanging before him when he had a new overcoat; then he thought he was standing before the general listening to the appropriate reprimand and saying, "I am sorry, your Excellency"; then finally he became abusive, uttering the most awful language, so that his old landlady positively crossed herself, having never heard anything of the kind from him before, and the more horrified because these dreadful words followed immediately upon the phrase "your Excellency." Later on, his talk was merely a medley of nonsense, so that it was quite unintelligible; all that was evident was that his incoherent words and thoughts were concerned with nothing but the overcoat. At last poor Akaky Akakievich gave up the ghost. No seal was put upon his room nor upon his things, because, in the first place, he had no heirs and, in the second, the property left was very small, to wit, a bundle of quills, a quire of white government paper, three pairs of socks, two or three buttons that had come off his trousers, and the "dressing gown" with which the reader is already familiar. Who came into all his wealth God only knows; even I who tell the tale must admit that I have not bothered to inquire. And Petersburg carried on without Akaky Akakievich, as though, indeed, he had never been in the city. A creature had vanished and departed whose cause no one had championed, who was dear to no one, of interest to no one, who never attracted the attention of a naturalist, though the latter does not disdain to fix a common fly upon a pin and look at him under the microscope — a creature who bore patiently the jeers of the office and for no particular reason went to his grave, though even he at the very end of his life was visited by an exalted guest in the form of an overcoat that for one instant brought color into his poor, drab life—a creature on whom disease fell as it falls upon the heads of the mighty ones of this world . . . !

Several days after his death, a messenger from the department was sent to his lodgings with instructions that he should go at once to the office, for his chief was asking for him; but the messenger was obliged to return without him, explaining that he could not come, and to the inquiry "Why?" he added, "Well, you see, the fact is he is dead; he was buried three days ago." This was how they learned at the office of the death of Akaky Akakievich, and the next day there was sitting in his seat a new clerk who was very much taller and who wrote not in the same straight handwriting but made his letters more slanting and crooked.

But who could have imagined that this was not all there was to tell about Akaky Akakievich, that he was destined for a few days to make his presence felt in the world after his death, as though to make up for his life having been unnoticed by anyone? But so it happened, and our little story unexpectedly finishes with a fantastic ending.

Rumors were suddenly floating about Petersburg that in the neighborhood of the Kalinkin Bridge and for a little distance beyond, a corpse[5] had begun appearing at night in the form of a clerk looking for a stolen overcoat, and stripping from the shoulders of all passers-by, regardless of grade and calling, overcoats of all descriptions—trimmed with cat fur or beaver or padded, lined with raccoon, fox, and bear—made, in fact of all sorts of skin which men have adapted for the covering of their own. One of the clerks of the department saw the corpse with his own eyes and at once recognized it as Akaky Akakievich; but it excited in him such terror that he ran away as fast as his legs could carry him and so could not get a very clear view of him, and only saw him hold up his finger threateningly in the distance.

From all sides complaints were continually coming that backs and shoulders, not of mere titular councilors, but even of upper court councilors, had been exposed to catching cold, as a result of being stripped of their overcoats. Orders were given to the police to catch the corpse regardless of trouble or expense, dead or alive, and to punish him severely, as an example to others, and, indeed, they very nearly succeeded in doing so. The policeman of one district in Kiryushkin Alley snatched a corpse by the collar on the spot of the crime in the very act of attempting to snatch a frieze overcoat from a retired musician, who used, in his day, to play the flute. Having caught him by the collar, he shouted until he had brought two other policemen whom he ordered to hold the corpse while he felt just a minute in his boot to get out a snuffbox in order to revive his nose which had six times in his life been frostbitten, but

---

[5] Mrs. Garnett excepted, this is often translated "ghost," but there is no doubt of Gogol's intention. He uses the word *mertverts* ("corpse") and not *pridivenye* ("ghost"). To confuse the two is damaging to Gogol's delight in the fantastic, and seriously alters the tone of the story. (Kent, ed.)

the snuff was probably so strong that not even a dead man could stand it. The policeman had hardly had time to put his finger over his right nostril and draw up some snuff in the left when the corpse sneezed violently right into the eyes of all three. While they were putting their fists up to wipe their eyes, the corpse completely vanished, so that they were not even sure whether he had actually been in their hands. From that time forward, the policemen had such a horror of the dead that they were even afraid to seize the living and confined themselves to shouting from the distance: "Hey, you! Move on!" and the clerk's body began to appear even on the other side of the Kalinkin Bridge, terrorizing all timid people.

We have, however, quite neglected the Person of Consequence, who may in reality almost be said to be the cause of the fantastic ending of this perfectly true story. To begin with, my duty requires me to do justice to the Person of Consequence by recording that soon after poor Akaky Akakievich had gone away crushed to powder, he felt something not unlike regret. Sympathy was a feeling not unknown to him; his heart was open to many kindly impulses, although his exalted grade very often prevented them from being shown. As soon as his friend had gone out of his study, he even began brooding over poor Akaky Akakievich, and from that time forward, he was almost every day haunted by the image of the poor clerk who had been unable to survive the official reprimand. The thought of the man so worried him that a week later he actually decided to send a clerk to find out how he was and whether he really could help him in any way. And when they brought him word that Akaky Akakievich had died suddenly in a delirium and fever, it made a great impression on him; his conscience reproached him and he was depressed all day. Anxious to distract his mind and to forget the unpleasant incident, he went to spend the evening with one of his friends, where he found respectable company, and what was best of all, almost everyone was of the same grade so that he was able to be quite uninhibited. This had a wonderful effect on his spirits. He let himself go, became affable and genial — in short, spent a very agreeable evening. At supper he drank a couple of glasses of champagne — a proceeding which we all know is not a bad recipe for cheerfulness. The champagne made him inclined to do something unusual, and he decided not to go home yet but to visit a lady of his acquaintance, a certain Karolina Ivanovna — a lady apparently of German extraction, for whom he entertained extremely friendly feelings. It must be noted that the Person of Consequence was a man no longer young. He was an excellent husband, and the respectable father of a family. He had two sons, one already serving in an office, and a nice-looking daughter of sixteen with a rather turned-up, pretty little nose, who used to come every morning to kiss his hand, saying: "*Bon jour, Papa.*" His wife, who was still blooming and decidedly good-looking, indeed, used first to give him her hand to kiss and then turning his hand over would kiss it. But though the Person of Consequence was perfectly satisfied with the pleasant amenities of his domestic life, he thought it proper to have a lady friend in another quarter of the town. This lady friend was not a bit better looking nor younger than his wife, but these puzzling things exist in the world and it is not our business to criticize them. And so the Person of Consequence went downstairs, got into his sledge, and said to his coachman, "To Karolina Ivanovna." While luxuriously wrapped in his warm fur coat he remained in that agreeable frame of mind sweeter to a Russian than anything that could be invented, that is, when one thinks of nothing while thoughts come into the mind by themselves, one pleasanter than the other, without your having to bother following them or looking for them. Full of satisfaction, he recalled all the amusing moments of the evening he had spent, all the phrases that had started the intimate circle of friends laughing; many of them he repeated in an undertone and found them as amusing as before, and so, very naturally, laughed very heartily at them again. From time to time, however, he was disturbed by a gust of wind which, blowing suddenly, God knows why or where from, cut him in the face, pelting him with flakes of snow, puffing out his coat collar like a sail, or suddenly flinging it with unnatural force over his head and giving him end-less trouble to extricate himself from it. All at once, the Person of Consequence felt that someone had clutched him very tightly by the collar. Turning around he saw a short man in a shabby old uniform, and not without horror recognized him as Akaky Akakievich. The clerk's face was white as snow and looked like that of a corpse, but the horror of the Person of Consequence was beyond all bounds when he saw the mouth of the corpse distorted into speech, and breath-ing upon him the chill of the grave, it uttered the following words: "Ah, so here you are at last! At last I've . . . er . . . caught you by the collar. It's your overcoat I want; you refused to help me and abused me in the bargain! So now give me yours!" The poor Person of Consequence very nearly dropped dead. Resolute and determined as he was in his office and before subordinates in general, and though anyone looking at his manly air and figure would have said: "Oh, what a man of character!" yet in this situation he felt, like very many persons of heroic appearance, such terror that not without reason he began to be afraid he would have some sort of fit. He actually flung his overcoat off his shoulders as far as he could and shouted to his coachman in an unnatural voice: "Drive home! Let's get out of here!" The coachman, hearing the tone which he had only heard in critical moments and then accompanied by something even more tangible, hunched his shoulders up to his ears in case of worse following, swung his whip, and flew on like an arrow. In a little over six minutes, the Person of Conse-quence was at the entrance of his own house. Pale, panic-stricken, and without his overcoat, he arrived home instead of at Karolina Ivanovna's, dragged himself to his own room, and spent the night in great distress, so that next morning his daughter said to him at breakfast, "You look very pale today, Papa"; but her papa remained mute and said not a word to anyone of what had happened to him, where he had been, and where he had been going. The incident made a great impression upon him. Indeed, it happened far more rarely that he said to his subordinates, "How dare you? Do you understand who I am?" and he never uttered those words at all until he had first heard all the facts of the case.

What was even more remarkable is that from that time on the apparition of the dead clerk ceased entirely; apparently the general's overcoat had fitted him perfectly; anyway nothing more was heard of overcoats being snatched from anyone. Many restless and anxious people refused, however, to be pacified, and still maintained that in remote parts of the town the dead clerk went on appearing. One policeman, in Kolomna, for instance, saw with his own eyes an apparition appear from behind a house; but, being by natural constitution somewhat frail — so much so that on one occasion an ordinary grown-up suckling pig, making a sudden dash out of some private building, knocked him off his feet to the great amusement of the cabmen standing around, whom he fined two kopeks each for snuff for such disrespect — he did not dare to stop it, and so followed it in the dark until the apparition suddenly looked around and, stopping, asked him: "What do you want?" displaying a huge fist such as you never see among the living. The policeman said: "Nothing," and turned back on the spot. This apparition, however, was considerably taller and adorned with immense mustaches, and, directing its steps apparently toward Obukhov Bridge, vanished into the darkness of the night.

Nathaniel Hawthorne

Nathaniel Hawthorne (1804–1864), writer of short stories and novels, was born in Salem, Massachusetts, into an eminent family who traced their lineage back to the Puritans. After his graduation from Bowdoin College in 1825, Hawthorne lived at home while he wrote works of short fiction he called "tales" or "articles" that he tried to sell to periodicals. American magazines of the time were mostly interested in publishing ghost stories, Indian legends, and "village tales" based on historical anecdotes. Hawthorne (like his contemporary Edgar Allan Poe) created stories that transcended the limitations of these conventions; his imagination was stirred by what he called "an inveterate love of allegory."

Hawthorne published his first collection of stories, *Twice-Told Tales*, in 1837; a second book of stories, *Mosses from an Old Manse*, appeared in 1846. That year he stopped writing to earn a better living for his family as surveyor of customs for the port of Salem. This was a political appointment, and after the Whigs won the presidency three years later, Hawthorne—a Democrat—was out of a job. He returned to writing fiction, sketching his "official life" at the Custom House in the introduction to his novel *The Scarlet Letter* in 1850. During the last decade of his career as a writer he published three other novels, several books for children, and another collection of tales. In "The Custom House," Hawthorne humorously suggested that his profession would not have impressed his Puritan ancestors:

> "What is he?" murmurs one grey shadow of my forefathers to the other. "A writer of story-books! What kind of business in life, what manner of glorifying God, or being serviceable to mankind in his day and generation, may that be? Why, the degenerate fellow might as well have been a fiddler!" Such are the compliments bandied between my great-grandsires and myself across the gulf of time! And yet, let them scorn me as they will, strong traits of their nature have intertwined themselves with mine.

Despite Hawthorne's portrait of himself as an unappreciated artist, he was recognized by contemporaries such as Herman Melville and Edgar Allan Poe as a "genius of a very lofty order." Hawthorne wrote about 120 short tales and sketches in addition to his novels. His notebooks are filled with ideas for stories, more often jottings of abstract ideas than detailed observations of "real" individuals. "The Minister's Black Veil" and "Young Goodman Brown" are two of his most famous moral tales.

RELATED COMMENTARIES
Herman Melville, "Blackness in Hawthorne's 'Young Goodman Brown,'" page 1473; Edgar Allan Poe, "The Importance of the Single Effect in a Prose Tale," page 1509.

The Minister's Black Veil

1836 / A Parable

THE SEXTON stood in the porch of Milford meeting-house, pulling busily at the bell-rope. The old people of the village came stooping along the street. Children, with bright faces, tripped merrily beside their parents, or mimicked a graver gait, in the conscious dignity of their Sunday clothes. Spruce bachelors looked sidelong at the pretty maidens, and fancied that the Sabbath sunshine made them prettier than on week days. When the throng had mostly streamed into the porch, the sexton began to toll the bell, keeping his eye on the Reverend Mr. Hooper's door. The first glimpse of the clergyman's figure was the signal for the bell to cease its summons.

"But what has good Parson Hooper got upon his face?" cried the sexton in astonishment.

All within hearing immediately turned about, and beheld the semblance of Mr. Hooper, pacing slowly his meditative way towards the meeting-house. With one accord they started, expressing more wonder than if some strange minister were coming to dust the cushions of Mr. Hooper's pulpit.

"Are you sure it is our parson?" inquired Goodman Gray of the sexton.

"Of a certainty it is good Mr. Hooper," replied the sexton. "He was to have exchanged pulpits with Parson Shute, of Westbury; but Parson Shute sent to excuse himself yesterday, being to preach a funeral sermon."

The cause of so much amazement may appear sufficiently slight. Mr. Hooper, a gentlemanly person, of about thirty, though still a bachelor, was dressed with due clerical neatness, as if a careful wife had starched his band, and brushed the weekly dust from his Sunday's garb. There was but one thing remarkable in his appearance. Swathed about his forehead, and hanging down over his face, so low as to be shaken by his breath, Mr. Hooper had on a black veil. On a nearer view it seemed to consist of two folds of crape, which entirely concealed his features, except the mouth and chin, but probably did not intercept his sight, further than to give a darkened aspect to all living and inanimate things. With this gloomy shade before him, good Mr. Hooper walked onward, at a slow and quiet pace, stooping somewhat, and looking on the ground, as is customary with abstracted men, yet nodding kindly to those of his parishioners who still waited on the meeting-house steps. But so wonder-struck were they that his greeting hardly met with a return.

"I can't really feel as if good Mr. Hooper's face was behind that piece of crape," said the sexton.

"I don't like it," muttered an old woman, as she hobbled into the meeting-house. "He has changed himself into something awful, only by hiding his face."

"Our parson has gone mad!" cried Goodman Gray, following him across the threshold.

A rumor of some unaccountable phenomenon had preceded Mr. Hooper into the meeting-house, and set all the congregation astir. Few could refrain from twisting their heads towards the door; many stood upright, and turned directly about; while several little boys clambered upon the seats, and came down again with a terrible racket. There was a general bustle, a rustling of the women's gowns and shuffling of the men's feet, greatly at variance with that hushed repose which should attend the entrance of the minister. But Mr. Hooper appeared not to notice the perturbation of his people. He entered with an almost noiseless step, bent his head mildly to the pews on each side, and bowed as he passed his oldest parishioner, a white-haired great-grandsire, who occupied an arm-chair in the centre of the aisle. It was strange to observe how slowly this venerable man became conscious of something singular in the appearance of his pastor. He seemed not fully to partake of the prevailing wonder, till Mr. Hooper had ascended the stairs, and showed himself in the pulpit, face to face with his congregation, except for the black veil. That mysterious emblem was never once withdrawn. It shook with his measured breath, as he gave out the psalm; it threw its obscurity between him and the holy page, as he read the Scriptures; and while he prayed, the veil lay heavily on his uplifted countenance. Did he seek to hide it from the dread Being whom he was addressing?

Such was the effect of this simple piece of crape, that more than one woman of delicate nerves was forced to leave the meeting-house. Yet perhaps the pale-faced congregation was almost as fearful a sight to the minister, as his black veil to them.

Mr. Hooper had the reputation of a good preacher, but not an energetic one: he strove to win his people heavenward by mild, persuasive influences, rather than to drive them thither by the thunders of the Word. The sermon which he now delivered was marked by the same characteristics of style and manner as the general series of his pulpit oratory. But there was something, either in the sentiment of the discourse itself, or in the imagination of the auditors, which made it greatly the most powerful effort that they had ever heard from their pastor's lips. It was tinged, rather more darkly than usual, with the gentle gloom of Mr. Hooper's temperament. The subject had reference to secret sin, and those sad mysteries which we hide from our nearest and dearest, and would fain conceal from our own consciousness, even forgetting that the Omniscient can detect them. A subtle power was breathed into his words. Each member of the congregation, the most innocent girl, and the man of hardened breast, felt as if the preacher had crept upon them, behind his awful veil, and discovered their hoarded iniquity of deed or thought. Many spread their clasped hands on their bosoms. There was nothing terrible in what Mr. Hooper said, at least, no violence; and yet, with every tremor of his melancholy voice, the hearers quaked. An unsought pathos came hand in hand with awe. So sensible were the audience of some unwonted attribute in their minister, that they longed for a breath of wind to blow aside the veil, almost believing that a stranger's visage would be discovered, though the form, gesture, and voice were those of Mr. Hooper.

At the close of the services, the people hurried out with indecorous confusion, eager to communicate their pent-up amazement, and conscious of lighter spirits the moment they lost sight of the black veil. Some gathered in little circles, huddled closely together, with their mouths all whispering in the centre; some went homeward alone, wrapt in silent meditation; some talked loudly, and profaned the Sabbath day with ostentatious laughter. A few shook their sagacious heads, intimating that they could penetrate the mystery; while one or two affirmed that there was no mystery at all, but only that Mr. Hooper's eyes were so weakened by the midnight lamp, as to require a shade. After a brief interval, forth came good Mr. Hooper also, in the rear of his flock. Turning his veiled face from one group to another, he paid due reverence to the hoary heads, saluted the middle aged with kind dignity as their friend and spiritual guide, greeted the young with mingled authority and love, and laid his hands on the little children's heads to bless them. Such was always his custom on the Sabbath day. Strange and bewildered looks repaid him for his courtesy. None, as on former occasions, aspired to the honor of walking by their pastor's side. Old Squire Saunders, doubtless by an accidental lapse of memory, neglected to invite Mr. Hooper to his table, where the good clergyman had been wont to bless the food, almost every Sunday since his settlement. He returned, therefore, to the parsonage, and, at the moment of closing the door, was observed to look back upon the people, all of whom had their eyes fixed upon the minister. A sad smile gleamed faintly from beneath the black veil, and flickered about his mouth, glimmering as he disappeared.

"How strange," said a lady, "that a simple black veil, such as any woman might wear on her bonnet, should become such a terrible thing on Mr. Hooper's face!"

"Something must surely be amiss with Mr. Hooper's intellects," observed her husband, the physician of the village. "But the strangest part of the affair is the effect of this vagary, even on a sober-minded man like myself. The black veil, though it covers only our pastor's face, throws its influence over his whole person, and makes him ghostlike from head to foot. Do you not feel it so?"

"Truly do I," replied the lady; "and I would not be alone with him for the world. I wonder he is not afraid to be alone with himself!"

"Men sometimes are so," said her husband.

The afternoon service was attended with similar circumstances. At its conclusion, the bell tolled for the funeral of a young lady. The relatives and friends were assembled in the house, and the more distant acquaintances stood about the door, speaking of the good qualities of the deceased, when their talk was interrupted by the appearance of Mr. Hooper, still covered with his black veil. It was now an appropriate emblem. The clergyman stepped into the room where the corpse was laid, and bent over the coffin, to take a last farewell of his deceased parishioner. As he stooped, the veil hung straight down from his forehead, so that, if her eyelids had not been closed forever, the dead maiden might have seen his face. Could Mr. Hooper be fearful of her glance, that he so hastily caught back the black veil? A person who watched the interview between the dead and living, scrupled not to affirm, that, at the instant when the clergyman's features were disclosed, the corpse had slightly shuddered, rustling the shroud and muslin cap, though the countenance retained the composure of death. A superstitious old woman was the only witness of this prodigy. From the coffin Mr. Hooper passed into the chamber of the mourners, and thence to the head of the staircase, to make the funeral prayer. It was a tender and heart-dissolving prayer, full of sorrow, yet so imbued with celestial hopes, that the music of a heavenly harp, swept by the fingers of the dead, seemed faintly to be heard among the saddest accents of the minister. The people trembled, though they but darkly understood him when he prayed that they, and himself, and all of mortal race, might be ready, as he trusted this young maiden had been, for the dreadful hour that should snatch the veil from their faces. The bearers went heavily forth, and the mourners followed, saddening all the street, with the dead before them, and Mr. Hooper in his black veil behind.

"Why do you look back?" said one in the procession to his partner.

"I had a fancy," replied she, "that the minister and the maiden's spirit were walking hand in hand."

"And so had I, at the same moment," said the other.

That night, the handsomest couple in Milford village were to be joined in wedlock. Though reckoned a melancholy man, Mr. Hooper had a placid cheerfulness for such occasions, which often excited a sympathetic smile where livelier merriment would have been thrown away. There was no quality of his disposition which made him more beloved than this. The company at the wedding awaited his arrival with impatience, trusting that the strange awe, which had gathered over him throughout the day, would now be dispelled. But such was not the result. When Mr. Hooper came, the first thing that their eyes rested on was the same horrible black veil, which had added deeper gloom to the funeral, and could portend nothing but evil to the wedding. Such was its immediate effect on the guests that a cloud seemed to have rolled duskily from beneath the black crape, and dimmed the light of the candles. The bridal pair stood up before the minister. But the bride's cold fingers quivered in the tremulous hand of the bridegroom, and her deathlike paleness caused a whisper that the maiden who had been buried a few hours before was come from her grave to be married. If ever another wedding were so dismal, it was that famous one where they tolled the wedding knell. After performing the ceremony, Mr. Hooper raised a glass of wine to his lips, wishing happiness to the new-married couple in a strain of mild pleasantry that ought to have brightened the features of the guests, like a cheerful gleam from the hearth. At that instant, catching a glimpse of his figure in the looking-glass, the black veil involved his own spirit in the horror with which it overwhelmed all others. His frame shuddered, his lips grew white, he spilt the untasted wine upon the carpet, and rushed forth into the darkness. For the Earth, too, had on her Black Veil.

The next day, the whole village of Milford talked of little else than Parson Hooper's black veil. That, and the mystery concealed behind it, supplied a topic for discussion between acquaintances meeting in the street, and good women gossiping at their open windows. It was the first item of news that the tavern-keeper told to his guests. The children babbled of it on their way to school. One imitative little imp covered his face with an old black handkerchief, thereby so affrighting his playmates that the panic seized himself, and he well-nigh lost his wits by his own waggery.

It was remarkable that of all the busybodies and impertinent people in the parish, not one ventured to put the plain question to Mr. Hooper, wherefore he did this thing. Hitherto, whenever there appeared the slightest call for such interference, he had never lacked advisers, nor shown himself adverse to be guided by their judgment. If he erred at all, it was by so painful a degree of self-distrust, that even the mildest censure would lead him to consider an indifferent action as a crime. Yet, though so well acquainted with this amiable weakness, no individual among his parishioners chose to make the black veil a subject of friendly remonstrance. There was a feeling of dread, neither plainly confessed nor carefully concealed, which caused each to shift the responsibility upon another, till at length it was found expedient to send a deputation of the church, in order to deal with Mr. Hooper about the mystery, before it should grow into a scandal. Never did an embassy so ill discharge its duties. The minister received them with friendly courtesy, but became silent, after they were seated, leaving to his visitors the whole burden of introducing their important business. The topic, it might be supposed, was obvious enough. There was the black veil swathed round Mr. Hooper's forehead, and concealing every feature above his placid mouth, on which, at times, they could perceive the glimmering of a melancholy smile. But that piece of crape, to their imagination, seemed to hang down before his heart, the symbol of a fearful secret between him and them. Were the veil but cast aside, they might speak freely of it, but not till then. Thus they sat a considerable time, speechless, confused, and shrinking uneasily from Mr. Hooper's eye, which they felt to be fixed upon them with an invisible glance. Finally, the deputies returned abashed to their constituents, pronouncing the matter too weighty to be handled, except by a council of the churches, if, indeed, it might not require a general synod.

But there was one person in the village unappalled by the awe with which the black veil had impressed all beside herself. When the deputies returned without an explanation, or even venturing to demand one, she, with the calm energy of her character, determined to chase away the strange cloud that appeared to be settling round Mr. Hooper, every moment more darkly than before. As his plighted wife, it should be her privilege to know what the black veil concealed. At the minister's first visit, therefore, she entered upon the subject with a direct simplicity, which made the task easier both for him and her. After he had seated himself, she fixed her eyes steadfastly upon the veil, but could discern nothing of the dreadful gloom that had so overawed the multitude: it was but a double fold of crape, hanging down from his forehead to his mouth, and slightly stirring with his breath.

"No," said she aloud, and smiling, "there is nothing terrible in this piece of crape, except that it hides a face which I am always glad to look upon. Come, good sir, let the sun shine from behind the cloud. First lay aside your black veil: then tell me why you put it on."

Mr. Hooper's smile glimmered faintly.

"There is an hour to come," said he, "when all of us shall cast aside our veils. Take it not amiss, beloved friend, if I wear this piece of crape till then."

"Your words are a mystery, too," returned the young lady. "Take away the veil from them, at least."

"Elizabeth, I will," said he, "so far as my vow may suffer me. Know, then, this veil is a type and a symbol, and I am bound to wear it ever, both in light and darkness, in solitude and before the gaze of multitudes, and as with strangers, so with my familiar friends. No mortal eye will see it withdrawn. This dismal shade must separate me from the world: even you, Elizabeth, can never come behind it!"

"What grievous affliction hath befallen you," she earnestly inquired, "that you should thus darken your eyes forever?"

"If it be a sign of mourning," replied Mr. Hooper, "I, perhaps, like most other mortals, have sorrows dark enough to be typified by a black veil."

"But what if the world will not believe that it is the type of an innocent sorrow?" urged Elizabeth. "Beloved and respected as you are, there may be whispers that you hide your face under the consciousness of secret sin. For the sake of your holy office, do away this scandal!"

The color rose into her cheeks as she intimated the nature of the rumors that were already abroad in the village. But Mr. Hooper's mildness did not forsake him. He even smiled again — that same sad smile, which always appeared like a faint glimmering of light, proceeding from the obscurity beneath the veil.

"If I hide my face for sorrow, there is cause enough," he merely replied; "and if I cover it for secret sin, what mortal might not do the same?"

And with this gentle, but unconquerable obstinacy did he resist all her entreaties. At length Elizabeth sat silent. For a few moments she appeared lost in thought, considering, probably, what new methods might be tried to withdraw her lover from so dark a fantasy, which, if it had no other meaning, was perhaps a symptom of mental disease. Though of a firmer character than his own, the tears rolled down her cheeks. But, in an instant, as it were, a new feeling took the place of sorrow: her eyes were fixed insensibly on the black veil, when, like a sudden twilight in the air, its terrors fell around her. She arose, and stood trembling before him.

"And do you feel it then, at last?" said he mournfully.

She made no reply, but covered her eyes with her hand, and turned to leave the room. He rushed forward and caught her arm.

"Have patience with me, Elizabeth!" cried he, passionately. "Do not desert me, though this veil must be between us here on earth. Be mine, and hereafter there shall be no veil over my face, no darkness between our souls! It is but a mortal veil — it is not for eternity! O! you know not how lonely I am, and how frightened, to be alone behind my black veil. Do not leave me in this miserable obscurity forever!"

"Lift the veil but once, and look me in the face," said she.

"Never! It cannot be!" replied Mr. Hooper.

"Then farewell!" said Elizabeth.

She withdrew her arm from his grasp, and slowly departed, pausing at the door, to give one long shuddering gaze, that seemed almost to penetrate the mystery of the black veil. But, even amid his grief, Mr. Hooper smiled to think that only a material emblem had separated him from happiness, though the horrors, which it shadowed forth, must be drawn darkly between the fondest of lovers.

From that time no attempts were made to remove Mr. Hooper's black veil, or, by a direct appeal, to discover the secret which it was supposed to hide. By persons who claimed a superiority to popular prejudice, it was reckoned merely an eccentric whim, such as often mingles with the sober actions of men otherwise rational, and tinges them all with its own semblance of insanity. But with the multitude, good Mr. Hooper was irreparably a bugbear. He could not walk the street with any peace of mind, so conscious was he that the gentle and timid would turn aside to avoid him, and that others would make it a point of hardihood to throw themselves in his way. The impertinence of the latter class compelled him to give up his customary walk at sunset to the burial ground; for when he leaned pensively over the gate, there would always be faces behind the gravestones, peeping at his black veil. A fable went the rounds that the stare of the dead people drove him thence. It grieved him, to the very depth of his kind heart, to observe how the children fled from his approach, breaking up their merriest sports, while his melancholy figure was yet afar off. Their instinctive dread caused him to feel more strongly than aught else, that a preternatural horror was interwoven with the threads of the black crape. In truth, his own antipathy to the veil was known to be so great, that he never willingly passed before a mirror, nor stooped to drink at a still fountain, lest, in its peaceful bosom, he should be affrighted by himself. This was what gave plausibility to the whispers, that Mr. Hooper's conscience tortured him for some great crime too horrible to be entirely concealed, or otherwise than so obscurely intimated. Thus, from beneath the black veil, there rolled a cloud into the sunshine, an ambiguity of sin or sorrow, which enveloped the poor minister, so that love or sympathy could never reach him. It was said that ghost and fiend consorted with him there. With self-shudderings and outward terrors, he walked continually in its shadow, groping darkly within his own soul, or gazing through a medium that saddened the whole world. Even the lawless wind, it was believed, respected his dreadful secret, and never blew aside the veil. But still good Mr. Hooper sadly smiled at the pale visages of the worldly throng as he passed by.

Among all its bad influences, the black veil had the one desirable effect, of making its wearer a very efficient clergyman. By the aid of his mysterious emblem — for there was no other apparent cause — he became a man of awful power over souls that were in agony for sin. His converts always regarded him with a dread peculiar to themselves, affirming, though but figuratively, that, before he brought them to celestial light, they had been with him behind the black veil. Its gloom, indeed, enabled him to sympathize with all dark affections. Dying sinners cried aloud for Mr. Hooper, and would not yield their breath till he appeared; though ever, as he stooped to whisper consolation, they shuddered at the veiled face so near their own. Such were the terrors of the black veil, even when Death had bared his visage! Strangers came long distances to attend service at his church, with the mere idle purpose of gazing at his figure, because it was forbidden them to behold his face. But many were made to quake ere they departed! Once, during Governor Belcher's administration, Mr. Hooper was appointed to preach the election sermon. Covered with his black veil, he stood before the chief magistrate, the council, and the representatives, and wrought so deep an impression that the legislative measures of that year were characterized by all the gloom and piety of our earliest ancestral sway.

In this manner Mr. Hooper spent a long life, irreproachable in outward act, yet shrouded in dismal suspicions; kind and loving, though unloved, and dimly feared; a man apart from men, shunned in their health and joy, but ever summoned to their aid in mortal anguish. As years wore on, shedding their snows above his sable veil, he acquired a name throughout the New England churches, and they called him Father Hooper. Nearly all his parishioners, who were of mature age when he was settled, had been borne away by many a funeral: he had one congregation in the church, and a more crowded one in the churchyard; and having wrought so late into the evening, and done his work so well, it was now good Father Hooper's turn to rest.

Several persons were visible by the shaded candle-light, in the death chamber of the old clergyman. Natural connections he had none. But there was the decorously grave, though unmoved physician, seeking only to mitigate the last pangs of the patient whom he could not save. There were the deacons, and other eminently pious members of his church. There, also, was the Reverend Mr. Clark, of Westbury, a young and zealous divine, who had ridden in haste to pray by the bedside of the expiring minister. There was the nurse, no hired handmaiden of death, but one whose calm affection had endured thus long in secrecy, in solitude, amid the chill of age, and would not perish, even at the dying hour. Who, but Elizabeth! And there lay the hoary head of good Father Hooper upon the death pillow, with the black veil still swathed about his brow, and reaching down over his face, so that each more difficult gasp of his faint breath caused it to stir. All through life that piece of crape had hung between him and the world: it had separated him from cheerful brotherhood and woman's love, and kept him in that saddest of all prisons, his own heart; and still it lay upon his face, as if to deepen the gloom of his darksome chamber, and shade him from the sunshine of eternity.

For some time previous, his mind had been confused, wavering doubtfully between the past and the present, and hovering forward, as it were, at intervals, into the indistinctness of the world to come. There had been feverish turns, which tossed him from side to side, and wore away what little strength he had. But in his most convulsive struggles, and in the wildest vagaries of his intellect, when no other thought retained its sober influence, he still showed an awful solicitude lest the black veil should slip aside. Even if his bewildered soul could have forgotten, there was a faithful woman at his pillow, who, with averted eyes, would have covered that aged face, which she had last beheld in the comeliness of manhood. At length the death-stricken old man lay quietly in the torpor of mental and bodily exhaustion, with an imperceptible pulse, and breath that grew fainter and fainter, except when a long, deep, and irregular inspiration seemed to prelude the flight of his spirit.

The minister of Westbury approached the bedside.

"Venerable Father Hooper," said he, "the moment of your release is at hand. Are you ready for the lifting of the veil that shuts in time from eternity?"

Father Hooper at first replied merely by a feeble motion of his head; then, apprehensive, perhaps, that his meaning might be doubtful, he exerted himself to speak.

"Yea," said he, in faint accents, "my soul hath a patient weariness until that veil be lifted."

"And is it fitting," resumed the Reverend Mr. Clark, "that a man so given to prayer, of such a blameless example, holy in deed and thought, so far as mortal judgment may pronounce; is it fitting that a father in the church should leave a shadow on his memory, that may seem to blacken a life so pure? I pray you, my venerable brother, let not this thing be! Suffer us to be gladdened by your triumphant aspect as you go to your reward. Before the veil of eternity be lifted, let me cast aside this black veil from your face!"

And thus speaking, the Reverend Mr. Clark bent forward to reveal the mystery of so many years. But, exerting a sudden energy, that made all the beholders stand aghast, Father Hooper snatched both his hands from beneath the bedclothes, and pressed them strongly on the black veil, resolute to struggle, if the minister of Westbury would contend with a dying man.

"Never!" cried the veiled clergyman. "On earth, never!"

"Dark old man!" exclaimed the affrighted minister, "with what horrible crime upon your soul are you now passing to the judgment?"

Father Hooper's breath heaved; it rattled in his throat; but, with a mighty effort, grasping forward with his hands, he caught hold of life, and held it back till he should speak. He even raised himself in bed; and there he sat, shivering with the arms of death around him, while the black veil hung down, awful at that last moment, in the gathered terrors of a lifetime. And yet the faint, sad smile, so often there, now seemed to glimmer from its obscurity, and linger on Father Hooper's lips.

"Why do you tremble at me alone?" cried he, turning his veiled face round the circle of pale spectators. "Tremble also at each other! Have men avoided me, and women shown no pity, and children screamed and fled, only for my black veil? What, but the mystery which it obscurely typifies, has made this piece of crape so awful? When the friend shows his inmost heart to his friend; the lover to his best beloved; when man does not vainly shrink from the eye of his Creator, loathsomely treasuring up the secret of his sin; then deem me a monster, for the symbol beneath which I have lived, and die! I look around me, and, lo! on every visage a Black Veil!"

While his auditors shrank from one another, in mutual affright, Father Hooper fell back upon his pillow, a veiled corpse, with a faint smile lingering on the lips. Still veiled, they laid him in his coffin, and a veiled corpse they bore him to the grave. The grass of many years has sprung up and withered on that grave, the burial stone is moss-grown, and good Mr. Hooper's face is dust; but awful is still the thought that it mouldered beneath the Black Veil!

NOTE. Another clergyman in New England, Mr. Joseph Moody, of York, Maine, who died about eighty years since, made himself remarkable by the same eccentricity that is here related of the Reverend Mr. Hooper. In his case, however, the symbol had a different import. In early life he had accidentally killed a beloved friend; and from that day till the hour of his own death, he hid his face from men.

Young Goodman Brown

1835

YOUNG GOODMAN BROWN came forth at sunset into the street at Salem village; but put his head back, after crossing the threshold, to exchange a parting kiss with his young wife. And Faith, as the wife was aptly named, thrust her own pretty head into the street, letting the wind play with the pink ribbons of her cap while she called to Goodman Brown.

"Dearest heart," whispered she, softly and rather sadly, when her lips were close to his ear, "prithee put off your journey until sunrise and sleep in your own bed to-night. A lone woman is troubled with such dreams and such thoughts that she's afeared of herself sometimes. Pray tarry with me this night, dear husband, of all nights in the year."

"My love and my Faith," replied young Goodman Brown, "of all nights in the year, this one night must I tarry away from thee. My journey, as thou callest it, forth and back again, must needs be done 'twixt now and sunrise. What, my sweet, pretty wife, dost thou doubt me already, and we but three months married?"

"Then God bless you!" said Faith, with the pink ribbons; "and may you find all well when you come back."

"Amen!" cried Goodman Brown. "Say thy prayers, dear Faith, and go to bed at dusk, and no harm will come to thee."

So they parted; and the young man pursued his way until, being about to turn the corner by the meeting-house, he looked back and saw the head of Faith still peeping after him with a melancholy air, in spite of her pink ribbons.

"Poor little Faith!" thought he, for his heart smote him. "What a wretch am I to leave her on such an errand! She talks of dreams, too. Methought as she spoke there was trouble in her face, as if a dream had warned her what work is to be done to-night. But no, no; 't would kill her to think it. Well, she's a blessed angel on earth, and after this one night I'll cling to her skirts and follow her to heaven."

With this excellent resolve for the future, Goodman Brown felt himself justified in making more haste on his present evil purpose. He had taken a dreary road, darkened by all the gloomiest trees of the forest, which barely stood aside to let the narrow path creep through, and closed immediately behind. It was all as lonely as could be; and there is this peculiarity in such a solitude, that the traveller knows not who may be concealed by the innumerable trunks and the thick boughs overhead; so that with lonely footsteps he may yet be passing through an unseen multitude.

"There may be a devilish Indian behind every tree," said Goodman Brown to himself; and he glanced fearfully behind him as he added, "What if the devil himself should be at my very elbow!"

His head being turned back, he passed a crook of the road, and, looking forward again, beheld the figure of a man, in grave and decent attire, seated at the foot of an old tree. He arose at Goodman Brown's approach and walked onward side by side with him.

"You are late, Goodman Brown," said he. "The clock of the Old South was striking as I came through Boston, and that is full fifteen minutes agone."

"Faith kept me back a while," replied the young man, with a tremor in his voice, caused by the sudden appearance of his companion, though not wholly unexpected.

It was now deep dusk in the forest, and deepest in that part of it where these two were journeying. As nearly as could be discerned, the second traveller was about fifty years old, apparently in the same rank of life as Goodman Brown, and bearing a considerable resemblance to him, though perhaps more in expression than features. Still they might have been taken for father and son. And yet, though the elder person was as simply clad as the younger, and as simple in manner too, he had an indescribable air of one who knew the world, and who would not have felt abashed at the governor's dinner table or in King William's court, were it possible that his affairs should call him thither. But the only thing about him that could be fixed upon as remarkable was his staff, which bore the likeness of a great black snake, so curiously wrought that it might almost be seen to twist and wriggle itself like a living serpent. This, of course, must have been an ocular deception, assisted by the uncertain light.

"Come, Goodman Brown," cried his fellow-traveller, "this is a dull pace for the beginning of a journey. Take my staff, if you are so soon weary."

"Friend," said the other, exchanging his slow pace for a full stop, "having kept covenant by meeting thee here, it is my purpose now to return whence I came. I have scruples touching the matter thou wot'st of."

"Sayest thou so?" replied he of the serpent, smiling apart. "Let us walk on, nevertheless, reasoning as we go; and if I convince thee not thou shalt turn back. We are but a little way in the forest yet."

"Too far! too far!" exclaimed the goodman, unconsciously resuming his walk. "My father never went into the woods on such an errand, nor his father before him. We have been a race of honest men and good Christians since the days of the martyrs; and shall I be the first of the name of Brown that ever took this path and kept —"

"Such company, thou wouldst say," observed the elder person, interpreting his pause. "Well said, Goodman Brown! I have been as well acquainted with your family as with ever a one among the Puritans; and that's no trifle to say. I helped your grandfather, the constable, when he lashed the Quaker woman so smartly through the streets of Salem; and it was I that brought your father a pitch-pine knot, kindled at my own hearth, to set fire to an Indian village, in King Philip's war.[1] They were my good friends, both; and many a pleasant walk have we had along this path, and returned merrily after midnight. I would fain be friends with you for their sake."

"If it be as thou sayest," replied Goodman Brown, "I marvel they never spoke of these matters; or, verily, I marvel not, seeing that the least rumor of the sort would have driven them from New England. We are a people of prayer, and good works to boot, and abide no such wickedness."

"Wickedness or not," said the traveller with the twisted staff, "I have a very general acquaintance here in New England. The deacons of many a church have drunk the communion wine with me; the selectmen of divers towns make me their chairman; and a majority of the Great and General Court are firm supporters of my interest. The governor and I, too — But these are state secrets."

"Can this be so?" cried Goodman Brown, with a stare of amazement at his undisturbed companion. "Howbeit, I have nothing to do with the governor and council; they have their own ways, and are no rule for a simple husbandman like me. But, were I to go on with thee, how should I meet the eye of that good old man, our minister, at Salem village? Oh, his voice would make me tremble both Sabbath day and lecture day."

Thus far the elder traveller had listened with due gravity; but now burst into a fit of irrepressible mirth, shaking himself so violently that his snake-like staff actually seemed to wriggle in sympathy.

"Ha! ha! ha!" shouted he again and again; then composing himself, "Well, go on, Goodman Brown, go on; but, prithee, don't kill me with laughing."

"Well, then, to end the matter at once," said Goodman Brown, considerably nettled, "there is my wife, Faith. It would break her dear little heart; and I'd rather break my own."

"Nay, if that be the case," answered the other, "e'en go thy ways, Goodman Brown. I would not for twenty old women like the one hobbling before us that Faith should come to any harm."

As he spoke he pointed his staff at a female figure on the path, in whom Goodman Brown recognized a very pious and exemplary dame, who had taught him his catechism in youth, and was still his moral and spiritual adviser, jointly with the minister and Deacon Gookin.

"A marvel, truly that Goody Cloyse should be so far in the wilderness at nightfall," said he. "But with your leave, friend, I shall take a cut through the woods until we have left this Christian woman behind. Being a stranger to you, she might ask whom I was consorting with and whither I was going."

"Be it so," said his fellow-traveller. "Betake you to the woods, and let me keep the path."

Accordingly the young man turned aside, but took care to watch his companion, who advanced softly along the road until he had come within a staff's length of the old dame. She, meanwhile, was making the best of her way, with

---

[1] King Philip, a Wampanoag chief, spearheaded the most destructive Indian war ever waged against the New England colonists (1675–1676).

singular speed for so aged a woman, and mumbling some indistinct words — a prayer, doubtless — as she went. The traveller put forth his staff and touched her withered neck with what seemed the serpent's tail.

"The devil!" screamed the pious old lady.

"Then Goody Cloyse knows her old friend?" observed the traveller, confronting her and leaning on his writhing stick.

"Ah, forsooth, and is it your worship indeed?" cried the good dame. "Yea, truly is it, and in the very image of my old gossip, Goodman Brown, the grandfather of the silly fellow that now is. But — would your worship believe it? — my broomstick hath strangely disappeared, stolen, as I suspect, by that unhanged witch, Goody Cory, and that, too, when I was all anointed with the juice of smallage, and cinquefoil, and wolf's bane —"

"Mingled with fine wheat and the fat of a new-born babe," said the shape of old Goodman Brown.

"Ah, your worship knows the recipe," cried the old lady, cackling aloud. "So, as I was saying, being all ready for the meeting, and no horse to ride on, I made up my mind to foot it; for they tell me there is a nice young man to be taken into communion to-night. But now your good worship will lend me your arm, and we shall be there in a twinkling."

"That can hardly be," answered her friend. "I may not spare you my arm, Goody Cloyse; but here is my staff, if you will."

So saying, he threw it down at her feet, where, perhaps, it assumed life, being one of the rods which its owner had formerly lent to the Egyptian magi. Of this fact, however, Goodman Brown could not take cognizance. He had cast up his eyes in astonishment, and, looking down again, beheld neither Goody Cloyse nor the serpentine staff, but his fellow-traveller alone, who waited for him as calmly as if nothing had happened.

"That old woman taught me my catechism," said the young man; and there was a world of meaning in this simple comment.

They continued to walk onward, while the elder traveller exhorted his companion to make good speed and persevere in the path, discoursing so aptly that his arguments seemed rather to spring up in the bosom of his auditor than to be suggested by himself. As they went, he plucked a branch of maple to serve for a walking stick, and began to strip it of the twigs and little boughs, which were wet with evening dew. The moment his fingers touched them they became strangely withered and dried up as with a week's sunshine. Thus the pair proceeded, at a good free pace, until suddenly, in a gloomy hollow of the road, Goodman Brown sat himself down on the stump of a tree and refused to go any farther.

"Friend," he said, stubbornly, "my mind is made up. Not another step will I budge on this errand. What if a wretched old woman do choose to go to the devil when I thought she was going to heaven: is that any reason why I should quit my dear Faith and go after her?"

"You will think better of this by and by," said his acquaintance, composedly. "Sit here and rest yourself a while; and when you feel like moving again, there is my staff to help you along."

Without more words, he threw his companion the maple stick, and was as speedily out of sight as if he had vanished into the deepening gloom. The young man sat a few moments by the roadside, applauding himself greatly, and thinking with how clear a conscience he should meet the minister in his morning walk, nor shrink from the eye of good old Deacon Gookin. And what calm sleep would be his that very night, which was to have been spent so wickedly, but so purely and sweetly now, in the arms of Faith! Amidst these pleasant and praiseworthy meditations, Goodman Brown heard the tramp of horses along the road, and deemed it advisable to conceal himself within the verge of the forest, conscious of the guilty purpose that had brought him thither, though now so happily turned from it.

On came the hoof tramps and the voices of the riders, two grave old voices, conversing soberly as they drew near. These mingled sounds appeared to pass along the road, within a few yards of the young man's hiding-place; but, owing doubtless to the depth of the gloom at that particular spot, neither the travellers nor their steeds were visible. Though their figures brushed the small boughs by the wayside, it could not be seen that they intercepted, even for a moment, the faint gleam from the strip of bright sky athwart which they must have passed. Goodman Brown alternately crouched and stood on tiptoe, pulling aside the branches and thrusting forth his head as far as he durst without discerning so much as a shadow. It vexed him the more, because he could have sworn, were such a thing possible, that he recognized the voices of the minister and Deacon Gookin, jogging along quietly, as they were wont to do, when bound to some ordination or ecclesiastical council. While yet within hearing, one of the riders stopped to pluck a switch.

"Of the two, reverend sir," said the voice like the deacon's, "I had rather miss an ordination dinner than to-night's meeting. They tell me that some of our community are to be here from Falmouth and beyond, and others from Connecticut and Rhode Island, besides several of the Indian powwows, who, after their fashion, know almost as much deviltry as the best of us. Moreover, there is a goodly young woman to be taken into communion."

"Mighty well, Deacon Gookin!" replied the solemn old tones of the minister. "Spur up, or we shall be late. Nothing can be done, you know, until I get on the ground."

The hoofs clattered again; and the voices, talking so strangely in the empty air, passed on through the forest, where no church had ever been gathered or solitary Christian prayed. Whither, then, could these holy men be journeying so deep into the heathen wilderness? Young Goodman Brown caught hold of a tree for support, being ready to sink down on the ground, faint and overburdened with the heavy sickness of his heart. He looked up to the sky, doubting whether there really was a heaven above him. Yet there was the blue arch, and the stars brightening in it.

"With heaven above and Faith below, I will yet stand firm against the devil!" cried Goodman Brown.

While he still gazed upward into the deep arch of the firmament and had lifted his hands to pray, a cloud, though no wind was stirring, hurried across the zenith and hid the brightening stars. The blue sky was still visible, except directly overhead, where this black mass of cloud was sweeping swiftly northward. Aloft in the air, as if from the depths of the cloud, came a confused and doubtful sound of voices. Once the listener fancied that he could distinguish the accents of towns-people of his own, men and women, both pious and ungodly, many of whom he had met at the communion table, and had seen others rioting at the tavern. The next moment, so indistinct were the sounds, he doubted whether he had heard aught but the murmur of the old forest, whispering without a wind. Then came a stronger swell of those familiar tones, heard daily in the sunshine at Salem village, but never until now from a cloud of night. There was one voice, of a young woman, uttering lamentations, yet with an uncertain sorrow, and entreating for some favor, which, perhaps, it would grieve her to obtain; and all the unseen multitude, both saints and sinners, seemed to encourage her onward.

"Faith!" shouted Goodman Brown, in a voice of agony and desperation; and the echoes of the forest mocked him, crying, "Faith! Faith!" as if bewildered wretches were seeking her all through the wilderness.

The cry of grief, rage, and terror was yet piercing the night, when the unhappy husband held his breath for a response. There was a scream, drowned immediately in a louder murmur of voices, fading into far-off laughter, as the dark cloud swept away, leaving the clear and silent sky above Goodman Brown. But something fluttered lightly down through the air and caught on the branch of a tree. The young man seized it, and beheld a pink ribbon.

"My Faith is gone!" cried he after one stupefied moment. "There is no good on earth; and sin is but a name. Come, devil; for to thee is this world given."

And, maddened with despair, so that he laughed loud and long, did Goodman Brown grasp his staff and set forth again, at such a rate that he seemed to fly along the forest path rather than to walk or run. The road grew wilder and drearier and more faintly traced, and vanished at length, leaving him in the heart of the dark wilderness, still rushing onward with the instinct that guides mortal man to evil. The whole forest was peopled with frightful sounds — the creaking of the trees, the howling of wild beasts, and the yell of Indians; while sometimes the wind tolled like a distant church bell, and sometimes gave a broad roar around the traveller, as if all Nature were laughing him to scorn. But he was himself the chief horror of the scene, and shrank not from its other horrors.

"Ha! ha! ha!" roared Goodman Brown when the wind laughed at him. "Let us hear which will laugh loudest. Think not to frighten me with your deviltry. Come witch, come wizard, come Indian powwow, come devil himself, and here comes Goodman Brown. You may as well fear him as he fear you."

In truth, all through the haunted forest there could be nothing more frightful than the figure of Goodman Brown. On he flew among the black pines, brandishing his staff with frenzied gestures, now giving vent to an inspiration of horrid blasphemy, and now shouting forth such laughter as set all the echoes of the forest laughing like demons around him. The fiend in his own shape is less hideous than when he rages in the breast of man. Thus sped the demoniac on his course, until, quivering among the trees, he saw a red light before him, as when the felled trunks and branches of a clearing have been set on fire, and throw up their lurid blaze against the sky, at the hour of midnight. He paused, in a lull of the tempest that had driven him onward, and heard the swell of what seemed a hymn, rolling solemnly from a distance with the weight of many voices. He knew the tune; it was a familiar one in the choir of the village meeting-house. The verse died heavily away, and was lengthened by a chorus, not of human voices, but of all the sounds of the benighted wilderness pealing in awful harmony together. Goodman Brown cried out, and his cry was lost to his own ear by its unison with the cry of the desert.

In the interval of silence he stole forward until the light glared full upon his eyes. At one extremity of an open space, hemmed in by the dark wall of the forest, arose a rock, bearing some rude, natural resemblance either to an altar or a pulpit, and surrounded by four blazing pines, their tops aflame, their stems untouched, like candles at an evening meeting. The mass of foliage that had overgrown the summit of the rock was all on fire, blazing high into the night and fitfully illuminating the whole field. Each pendent twig and leafy festoon was in a blaze. As the red light arose and fell, a numerous congregation alternately shone forth, then disappeared in shadow, and again grew, as it were, out of the darkness, peopling the heart of the solitary woods at once.

"A grave and dark-clad company," quoth Goodman Brown.

In truth they were such. Among them, quivering to and fro between gloom and splendor, appeared faces that would be seen next day at the council board of the province, and others which, Sabbath after Sabbath, looked devoutly heavenward, and benignantly over the crowded pews, from the holiest pulpits in the land. Some affirm that the lady of the governor was there. At least there were high dames well known to her, and wives of honored husbands, and widows, a great multitude, and ancient maidens, all of excellent repute, and fair young girls, who trembled lest their mothers should espy them. Either the sudden gleams of light flashing over the obscure field bedazzled Goodman Brown, or he recognized a score of the church members of Salem village famous for their especial sanctity. Good old Deacon Gookin had arrived, and waited at the skirts of that venerable saint, his revered pastor. But, irreverently consorting with these grave, reputable, and pious people, these elders of the church, these chaste dames and dewy virgins, there were men of dissolute lives and women of spotted fame, wretches given over to all mean and filthy vice, and suspected even of horrid crimes. It was strange to see that the good shrank not from the wicked, nor were the sinners abashed by the saints. Scattered also among their pale-faced enemies were the Indian priests, or powwows, who had often scared their native forest with more hideous incantations than any known to English witchcraft.

"But where is Faith?" thought Goodman Brown; and, as hope came into his heart, he trembled.

Another verse of the hymn arose, a slow and mournful strain, such as the pious love, but joined to words which expressed all that our nature can conceive of sin, and darkly hinted at far more. Unfathomable to mere mortals is the lore of fiends. Verse after verse was sung; and still the chorus of the desert swelled between like the deepest tone of a mighty organ; and with the final peal of that dreadful anthem there came a sound, as if the roaring wind, the rushing streams, the howling beasts, and every other voice of the unconcerted wilderness were mingling and according with the voice of guilty man in homage to the prince of all. The four blazing pines threw up a loftier flame, and obscurely discovered shapes and visages of horror on the smoke wreaths above the impious assembly. At the same moment the fire on the rock shot redly forth and formed a flowing arch above its base, where now appeared a figure. With reverence be it spoken, the figure bore no slight similitude, both in garb and manner, to some grave divine of the New England churches.

"Bring forth the converts!" cried a voice that echoed through the field and rolled into the forest.

At the word, Goodman Brown stepped forth from the shadow of the trees and approached the congregation, with whom he felt a loathful brotherhood by the sympathy of all that was wicked in his heart. He could have well-nigh sworn that the shape of his own dead father beckoned him to advance, looking downward from a smoke wreath, while a woman, with dim features of despair, threw out her hand to warn him back. Was it his mother? But he had no power to retreat one step, nor to resist, even in thought, when the minister and good old Deacon Gookin seized his arms and led him to the blazing rock. Thither came also the slender form of a veiled female, led between Goody Cloyse, that pious teacher of the catechism, and Martha Carrier, who had received the devil's promise to be queen of hell. A rampant hag was she. And there stood the proselytes beneath the canopy of fire.

"Welcome, my children," said the dark figure, "to the communion of your race. Ye have found thus young your nature and your destiny. My children, look behind you!"

They turned; and flashing forth, as it were, in a sheet of flame, the fiend worshippers were seen; the smile of welcome gleamed darkly on every visage.

"There," resumed the sable form, "are all whom ye have reverenced from youth. Ye deemed them holier than yourselves and shrank from your own sin, contrasting it with their lives of righteousness and prayerful aspirations heavenward. Yet here are they all in my worshipping assembly. This night it shall be granted you to know their secret deeds: how hoary-bearded elders of the church have whispered wanton words to the young maids of their households; how many a woman, eager for widows' weeds, has given her husband a drink at bedtime and let him sleep his last sleep in her bosom; how beardless youths have made haste to inherit their fathers' wealth; and how fair damsels — blush not, sweet ones — have dug little graves in the garden, and bidden me, the sole guest, to an infant's funeral. By the sympathy of your human hearts for sin ye shall scent out all the places — whether in church, bedchamber, street, field, or forest — where crime has been committed, and shall exult to behold the whole earth one stain of guilt, one mighty blood spot. Far more than this. It shall be yours to penetrate, in every bosom, the deep mystery of sin, the fountain of all wicked arts, and which inexhaustibly supplies more evil impulses than human power — than my power at its utmost — can make manifest in deeds. And now, my children, look upon each other."

They did so; and, by the blaze of the hell-kindled torches, the wretched man beheld his Faith, and the wife her husband, trembling before that unhallowed altar.

"Lo, there ye stand, my children," said the figure, in a deep and solemn tone, almost sad with its despairing awfulness, as if his once angelic nature could yet mourn for our miserable race. "Depending upon one another's hearts, ye had still hoped that virtue were not all a dream. Now are ye undeceived. Evil is the nature of mankind. Evil must be your only happiness. Welcome again, my children, to the communion of your race."

"Welcome," repeated the fiend worshippers, in one cry of despair and triumph.

And there they stood, the only pair, as it seemed, who were yet hesitating on the verge of wickedness in this dark world. A basin was hallowed, naturally, in the rock. Did it contain water, reddened by the lurid light? or was it blood? or, perchance, a liquid flame? Herein did the shape of evil dip his hand and prepare to lay the mark of baptism upon their foreheads, that they might be partakers of the mystery of sin, more conscious of the secret guilt of others, both in deed and thought, than they could now be of their own. The husband cast one look at his pale wife, and Faith at him. What polluted wretches would the next glance show them to each other, shuddering alike at what they disclosed and what they saw!

"Faith! Faith!" cried the husband, "look up to heaven, and resist the wicked one."

Whether Faith obeyed he knew not. Hardly had he spoken when he found himself amid calm night and solitude, listening to a roar of the wind which died heavily away through the forest. He staggered against the rock, and felt it chill and damp; while a hanging twig, that had been all on fire, besprinkled his cheek with the coldest dew.

The next morning young Goodman Brown came slowly into the street of Salem village, staring around him like a bewildered man. The good old minister was taking a walk along the graveyard to get an appetite for breakfast and meditate his sermon, and bestowed a blessing, as he passed, on Goodman Brown. He shrank from the venerable saint as if to avoid an anathema. Old Deacon Gookin was at domestic worship, and the holy words of his prayer were heard through the open window. "What God doth the wizard pray to?" quoth Goodman Brown. Goody Cloyse, that excellent old Christian, stood in the early sunshine at her own lattice, catechizing a little girl who had brought her a pint of morning's milk. Goodman Brown snatched away the child as from the grasp of the fiend himself. Turning the corner by the meeting-house, he spied the head of Faith, with the pink ribbons, gazing anxiously forth, and bursting into such joy at sight of him that she skipped along the street and almost kissed her husband before the whole village. But Goodman Brown looked sternly and sadly into her face, and passed on without a greeting.

Had Goodman Brown fallen asleep in the forest and only dreamed a wild dream of a witch-meeting?

Be it so if you will; but, alas! it was a dream of evil omen for young Goodman Brown. A stern, a sad, a darkly meditative, a distrustful, if not a desperate man did he become from the night of that fearful dream. On the Sabbath day, when the congregation were singing a holy psalm, he could not listen because an anthem of sin rushed loudly upon his ear and drowned all the blessed strain. When the minister spoke from the pulpit with power and fervid eloquence, and, with his hand on the open Bible, of the sacred truths of our religion, and of saint-like lives and triumphant deaths, and of future bliss or misery unutterable, then did Goodman Brown turn pale, dreading lest the roof should thunder down upon the gray blasphemer and his hearers. Often, awaking suddenly at midnight, he shrank from the bosom of Faith; and at morning or eventide, when the family knelt down at prayer, he scowled and muttered to himself, and gazed sternly at his wife, and turned away. And when he had lived long, and was borne to his grave a hoary corpse, followed by Faith, an aged woman, and children and grandchildren, a goodly procession, besides neighbors not a few, they carved no hopeful verse upon his tombstone, for his dying hour was gloom.

Ernest Hemingway

Ernest Hemingway (1899–1961) was born in Oak Park, Illinois, but he spent most of his boyhood in Michigan, where his father, a doctor, encouraged his enthusiasm for camping and hunting. Active as a reporter for his high school newspaper, Hemingway decided not to go on to college. Instead he worked as a reporter on the *Kansas City Star* for a few months before volunteering to serve in an American ambulance unit in France during World War I. Then he went to Italy, served at the front, and was severely wounded in action just before his nineteenth birthday. After the war he was too restless to settle down in the United States, so he lived in Paris and supported himself and his wife as a newspaper correspondent. He worked hard at learning how to write fiction; as he later said, "I found the greatest difficulty, aside from knowing what you really felt, rather than what you were supposed to feel, or had been taught to feel, was to put down what really happened in action: what the actual things were which produced the emotion that you experienced."

In America Hemingway had admired the work of Sherwood Anderson, especially the colloquial, "unliterary" tone of his stories, and in Paris he came under the influence of Gertrude Stein, telling Anderson in a letter of 1922 that "Gertrude Stein and me are just like brothers." As many critics have recognized, Hemingway was receptive to several diverse influences as a young writer forging his literary style. He was also aware of the work of the experimental poet Ezra Pound, whose advice in essays written in 1913 on the composition of imagist poetry is suggested in the style developed in Hemingway's early fiction:

1. Direct treatment of the "thing," without evasion or cliché.
2. The use of absolutely no word that does not contribute to the general design.
3. Fidelity to the rhythms of natural speech.
4. The natural object is always the adequate symbol.

Hemingway's first book, *In Our Time* (1925), is a collection of stories and sketches. His early novels, *The Sun Also Rises* (1926) and *A Farewell to Arms* (1929), established him as a master stylist, probably the most influential writer of American prose in the first half of the twentieth century. In 1938 he collected what he considered his best short fiction, forty-nine stories. After publication of *The Old Man and the Sea*, he was awarded the Nobel Prize for literature in 1954. Seven years later, in poor health and haunted by the memory of the suicide of his father, who had shot himself with a Civil War pistol in 1929, Hemingway killed himself with a shotgun in his Idaho hunting lodge.

Hemingway's concise way of developing a plot through dialogue, as in "Hills Like White Elephants," attracted many imitators. He once explained how he achieved an intense compression by comparing his method to the principle of the iceberg: "There is seven-eighths of it under water for every part that shows. Anything you know you can eliminate and it only strengthens your iceberg. It is the part that doesn't show. If a writer omits something because he does not know it then there is a hole in the story." The most authoritative collection of Hemingway's stories, *The Complete Short Stories of Ernest Hemingway: The Finca-Vigia Edition*, was published in 1991.

RELATED STORY
Russell Banks, "Black Man and White Woman in Dark Green Rowboat," page 71.

Hills Like White Elephants

1927

THE HILLS ACROSS THE VALLEY of the Ebro were long and white. On this side there was no shade and no trees and the station was between two lines of rails in the sun. Close against the side of the station there was the warm shadow of the building and a curtain, made of strings of bamboo beads, hung across the open door into the bar, to keep out flies. The American and the girl with him sat at a table in the shade, outside the building. It was very hot and the express from Barcelona would come in forty minutes. It stopped at this junction for two minutes and went on to Madrid.

"What should we drink?" the girl asked. She had taken off her hat and put it on the table.

"It's pretty hot," the man said.

"Let's drink beer."

"*Dos cervezas*," the man said into the curtain.

"Big ones?" a woman asked from the doorway.

"Yes. Two big ones."

The woman brought two glasses of beer and two felt pads. She put the felt pads and the beer glasses on the table and looked at the man and the girl. The girl was looking off at the line of hills. They were white in the sun and the country was brown and dry.

"They look like white elephants," she said.

"I've never seen one," the man drank his beer.

"No, you wouldn't have."

"I might have," the man said. "Just because you say I wouldn't have doesn't prove anything."

The girl looked at the bead curtain. "They've painted something on it," she said. "What does it say?"

"Anis del Toro. It's a drink."

"Could we try it?"

The man called "Listen" through the curtain. The woman came out from the bar.

"Four reales."

"We want two Anis del Toro."

"With water?"

"Do you want it with water?"

"I don't know," the girl said. "Is it good with water?"

"It's all right."

"You want them with water?" asked the woman.

"Yes, with water."

"It tastes like licorice," the girl said and put the glass down.

"That's the way with everything."

"Yes," said the girl. "Everything tastes of licorice. Especially all the things you've waited so long for, like absinthe."

"Oh, cut it out."

"You started it," the girl said. "I was being amused. I was having a fine time."

"Well, let's try and have a fine time."

"All right. I was trying. I said the mountains looked like white elephants. Wasn't that bright?"

"That was bright."

"I wanted to try this new drink: That's all we do, isn't it — look at things and try new drinks?"

"I guess so."

The girl looked across at the hills.

"They're lovely hills," she said. "They don't really look like white elephants. I just meant the coloring of their skin through the trees."

"Should we have another drink?"

"All right."

The warm wind blew the bead curtain against the table.

"The beer's nice and cool," the man said.

"It's lovely," the girl said.

"It's really an awfully simple operation, Jig," the man said. "It's not really an operation at all."

The girl looked at the ground the table legs rested on.

"I know you wouldn't mind it, Jig. It's really not anything. It's just to let the air in."

The girl did not say anything.

"I'll go with you and I'll stay with you all the time. They just let the air in and then it's all perfectly natural."

"Then what will we do afterward?"

"We'll be fine afterward. Just like we were before."

"What makes you think so?"

"That's the only thing that bothers us. It's the only thing that's made us unhappy."

The girl looked at the bead curtain, put her hand out, and took hold of two of the strings of beads.

"And you think then we'll be all right and be happy."

"I know we will. You don't have to be afraid. I've known lots of people that have done it."

"So have I," said the girl. "And afterward they were all so happy."

"Well," the man said, "if you don't want to you don't have to. I wouldn't have you do it if you didn't want to. But I know it's perfectly simple."

"And you really want to?"

"I think it's the best thing to do. But I don't want you to do it if you don't really want to."

"And if I do it you'll be happy and things will be like they were and you'll love me?"

"I love you now. You know I love you."

"I know. But if I do it, then it will be nice again if I say things are like white elephants, and you'll like it?"

"I'll love it. I love it now but I just can't think about it. You know how I get when I worry."

"If I do it you won't ever worry?"

"I won't worry about that because it's perfectly simple."

"Then I'll do it. Because I don't care about me."

"What do you mean?"

"I don't care about me."

"Well, I care about you."

"Oh, yes. But I don't care about me. And I'll do it and then everything will be fine."

"I don't want you to do it if you feel that way."

The girl stood up and walked to the end of the station. Across, on the other side, were fields of grain and trees along the banks of the Ebro. Far away, beyond the river, were mountains. The shadow of a cloud moved across the field of grain and she saw the river through the trees.

"And we could have all this," she said. "And we could have everything and every day we make it more impossible."

"What did you say?"

"I said we could have everything."

"We can have everything."

"No, we can't."

"We can have the whole world."

"No, we can't."

"We can go everywhere."

"No, we can't. It isn't ours any more."

"It's ours."

"No, it isn't. And once they take it away, you never get it back."

"But they haven't taken it away."

"We'll wait and see."

"Come on back in the shade," he said. "You mustn't feel that way."

"I don't feel any way," the girl said. "I just know things."

"I don't want you to do anything that you don't want to do —"

"Nor that isn't good for me," she said. "I know. Could we have another beer?"

"All right. But you've got to realize —"

"I realize," the girl said. "Can't we maybe stop talking?"

They sat down at the table and the girl looked across at the hills on the dry side of the valley and the man looked at her and at the table.

"You've got to realize," he said, "that I don't want you to do it if you don't want to. I'm perfectly willing to go through with it if it means anything to you."

"Doesn't it mean anything to you? We could get along."

"Of course it does. But I don't want anybody but you. I don't want any one else. And I know it's perfectly simple."

"Yes, you know it's perfectly simple."

"It's all right for you to say that, but I do know it."

"Would you do something for me now?"

"I'd do anything for you."

"Would you please please please please please please please stop talking?"

He did not say anything but looked at the bags against the wall of the station. There were labels on them from all the hotels where they had spent nights.

"But I don't want you to," he said, "I don't care anything about it."

"I'll scream," the girl said.

The woman came out through the curtains with two glasses of beer and put them down on the damp felt pads. "The train comes in five minutes," she said.

"What did she say?" asked the girl.

"That the train is coming in five minutes."

The girl smiled brightly at the woman, to thank her.

"I'd better take the bags over to the other side of the station," the man said. She smiled at him.

"All right. Then come back and we'll finish the beer."

He picked up the two heavy bags and carried them around the station to the other tracks. He looked up the tracks but could not see the train. Coming back, he walked through the barroom, where people waiting for the train were drinking. He drank an Anis at the bar and looked at the people. They were all waiting reasonably for the train. He went out through the bead curtain. She was sitting at the table and smiled at him.

"Do you feel better?" he asked.

"I feel fine," she said. "There's nothing wrong with me. I feel fine."

Zora Neale Hurston

Zora Neale Hurston (1891–1960) was born to a family of sharecroppers in Notasulga, Alabama. When she was very young she moved to Eatonville, Florida, a town founded by African Americans. After her mother died in 1904, her father, a Baptist preacher, couldn't raise their eight children, so Hurston was forced to move from one relative's home to another. She never finished grade school, but when she was old enough to support herself, she attended Howard University in Washington, D.C. In 1921 she published her first story, "John Redding Goes to Sea," in the student literary magazine.

In 1925 Hurston went to New York City and became active in the cultural renaissance in Harlem, collaborating with Langston Hughes on a folk comedy, *Mule Bone*. Like Hughes, she was deeply interested in the abiding folk spirit inherent in southern life. With several other writers of that time, she tried to express her cultural heritage by writing short stories. *The Eatonville Anthology* (1927), which included "Sweat," was the collection that first brought Hurston's work to the attention of a national audience. After Hurston studied with the famous anthropologist Franz Boas at Barnard College, she returned to Florida to record the oral traditions of her native community. As critics have noted, from this time to the end of her life she tried to achieve a balance in her literary work between the folk culture of her racial background and her individuality as a developing artist. Realizing that average white people used stereotypes to keep African Americans, Asian Americans, Hispanic Americans, and Native Americans in their "place," Hurston insisted that it was

> urgent to realize that minorities do think, and think about something other than the race problem. That they are very human and internally, according to natural endowment, are just like everybody else. So long as this is not conceived, there must remain that feeling of unsurmountable difference, and difference to the average man means something bad. If people were made right, they would be just like him.

During the Great Depression of the 1930s, Hurston turned all her energies to writing. "The Gilded Six-Bits" appeared in *Story* in 1933. She published *Mules and Men* (1935), based on material from her field trips to Florida, and *Their Eyes Were Watching God* (1937), a novel about a woman's search for love and personal identity, in addition to several other books, including an autobiography. Although she published more than any other African American woman writer of her time, in the last two decades of her life she earned very little from her writing. Fifteen years after Hurston's death, her work was rediscovered by black authors such as Alice Walker, and she is now honored as an important American writer.

RELATED COMMENTARIES

Zora Neale Hurston, "How It Feels to Be Colored Me," page 1434; Zora Neale Hurston, "What White Publishers Won't Print," page 1438; Alice Walker, "Zora Neale Hurston: A Cautionary Tale and a Partisan View," page 1535.

The Gilded Six-Bits

1933

IT WAS A NEGRO YARD around a Negro house in a Negro settlement that looked to the payroll of the G and G Fertilizer works for its support.

But there was something happy about the place. The front yard was parted in the middle by a sidewalk from gate to doorstep, a sidewalk edged on either side by quart bottles driven neck down to the ground on a slant. A mess of homey flowers planted without a plan but blooming cheerily from their helter-skelter places. The fence and house were whitewashed. The porch and steps scrubbed white.

The front door stood open to the sunshine so that the floor of the front room could finish drying after its weekly scouring. It was Saturday. Everything clean from the front gate to the privy house. Yard raked so that the strokes of the rake would make a pattern. Fresh newspaper cut in fancy-edge on the kitchen shelves.

Missie May was bathing herself in the galvanized washtub in the bedroom. Her dark-brown skin glistened under the soapsuds that skittered down from her wash rag. Her stiff young breasts thrust forward aggressively like broad-based cones with the tips lacquered in black.

She heard men's voices in the distance and glanced at the dollar clock on the dresser.

"Humph! Ah'm way behind time t'day! Joe gointer be heah 'fore Ah git mah clothes on if Ah don't make haste."

She grabbed the clean meal sack at hand and dried herself hurriedly and began to dress. But before she could tie her slippers, there came the ring of singing metal on wood. Nine times.

Missie May grinned with delight. She had not seen the big tall man come stealing in the gate and creep up the walk grinning happily at the joyful mischief he was about to commit. But she knew that it was her husband throwing silver dollars in the door for her to pick up and pile beside her plate at dinner. It was this way every Saturday afternoon. The nine dollars hurled into the open door, he scurried to a hiding place behind the cape jasmine bush and waited.

Missie May promptly appeared at the door in mock alarm.

"Who dat chunkin' money in mah do'way?" she demanded. No answer from the yard. She leaped off the porch and began to search the shrubbery. She peeped under the porch and hung over the gate to look up and down the road. While she did this, the man behind the jasmine darted to the chinaberry tree. She spied him and gave chase.

"Nobody ain't gointer be chunkin' money at me and Ah not do'em nothin'," she shouted in mock anger. He ran around the house with Missie May at his heels. She overtook him at the kitchen door. He ran inside but could not close it after him before she crowded in and locked with him in a rough and tumble. For several minutes the two were a furious mass of male and female energy. Shouting, laughing, twisting, turning, and Joe trying, but not too hard, to get away.

"Missie May, take yo' hand out mah pocket!" Joe shouted out between laughs.

"Ah ain't, Joe, not lessen you gwine gimme whateve' it is good you got in yo' pocket. Turn it go Jo, do Ah'll tear yo' clothes."

"Go on tear 'em. You de one dat pushes de needles round heah. Move yo' hand Missie May."

"Lemme git dat paper sack out yo' pocket. Ah bet its candy kisses."

"Tain't. Move yo' hand. Woman ain't got no business in a man's clothes nowhow. Go 'way."

Missie May gouged way down and gave an upward jerk and triumphed.

"Unhhunh! Ah got it. It 'tis so candy kisses. Ah knowed you had somethin' for me in yo' clothes. Now Ah got to see whut's in every pocket you got."

Joe smiled indulgently and let his wife go through all of his pockets and take out the things that he had hidden there for her to find. She bore off the chewing gum, the cake of sweet soap, the pocket handkerchief as if she had wrested them from him, as if they had not been bought for the sake of this friendly battle.

"Whew! dat play-fight done got me all warmed up," Joe exclaimed. "Got me some water in de kittle?"

"Yo' water is on de fire and yo' clean things is cross de bed. Hurry up and wash yo'self and git changed so we kin eat. Ah'm hongry." As Missie said this, she bore the steaming kettle into the bedroom.

"You ain't hongry, sugar," Joe contradicted her. "Youse jes's little empty. Ah'm de one whut's hongry. Ah could eat up camp meetin', back off 'sociation, and drink Jurdan dry. Have it on de table when Ah git out de tub."

"Don't you mess wid mah business, man. You git in yo' clothes. Ah'm a real wife, not no dress and breath. Ah might not look lak one, but if you burn me, you won't git a thing but wife ashes."

Joe splashed in the bedroom and Missie May fanned around in the kitchen. A fresh red and white checked cloth on the table. Big pitcher of buttermilk beaded with pale drops of butter from the churn. Hot fried mullet, crackling bread, ham hocks atop a mound of string beans and new potatoes, and perched on the window-sill a pone of spicy potato pudding.

Very little talk during the meal but that little consisted of banter that pretended to deny affection but in reality flaunted it. Like when Missie May reached for a second helping of the tater pone. Joe snatched it out of her reach. After Missie May had made two or three unsuccessful grabs at the pan, she begged, "Aw, Joe gimme some mo' dat tater pone."

"Nope, sweetenin' is for us men-folks. Y'all pritty li'l frail eels don't need nothin' lak dis. You too sweet already."

"Please, Joe."

"Naw, naw. Ah don't want you to get no sweeter than whut you is already. We goin' down de road al li'l piece t'night so you go put on yo' Sunday-go-to-meetin' things."

Missie May looked at her husband to see if he was playing some prank. "Sho' nuff, Joe?"

"Yeah. We goin' to de ice cream parlor."

"Where de ice cream parlor at, Joe?"

"A new man done come heah from Chicago and he done got a place and took and opened it up for a ice cream parlor, and bein' as it's real swell, Ah wants you to be one de first ladies to walk in dere and have some set down."

"Do Jesus, Ah ain't knowed nothin' 'bout it. Who de man done it?"

"Mister Otis D. Slemmons, of spots and places — Memphis, Chicago, Jacksonville, Philadelphia, and so on."

"Dat heavy-set man wid his mouth full of gold teethes?"

"Yeah. Where did you see 'im at?"

"Ah went down to de sto' tuh git a box of lye and Ah seen 'im standin' on de corner talkin' to some of de mens, and Ah come on back and went to scrubbin' de floor, and he passed and tipped his hat whilst Ah was scourin' de steps. Ah thought never Ah seen *him* befo'."

Joe smiled pleasantly. "Yeah, he's up to date. He got de finest clothes Ah ever seen on a colored man's back."

"Aw, he don't look no better in his clothes than you do in yourn. He got a puzzlegut on 'im and he so chuckle-headed, he got a pone behind his neck."

Joe looked down at his own abdomen and said wistfully, "Wisht Ah had a build on me lak he got. He ain't puzzle-gutted, honey. He jes' got a corperation. Dat make 'm look lak a rich white man. All rich mens is got some belly on 'em."

"Ah seen de pitchers of Henry Ford and he's a spare-built man and Rockefeller look lak he ain't got but one gut. But Ford and Rockefeller and dis Slemmons and all de rest kin be as many-gutted as dey please, ah'm satisfied wid you jes' lak you is, baby. God took pattern after a pine tree and built you noble. Youse a pritty still man, and if Ah knowed any way to make you mo' pritty still Ah'd take and do it."

Joe reached over gently and toyed with Missie May's ear. "You jes' say dat cause you love me, but Ah know Ah can't hold no light to Otis D. Slemmons. Ah ain't never been nowhere and Ah ain't got nothin' but you."

"How you know dat, Joe."

"He tole us so hisself."

"Dat don't make it so. His mouf is cut cross-ways, ain't it? Well, he kin lie jes' lak anybody els."

"Good Lawd, Missie! You womens sho' is hard to sense into things. He's got a five-dollar gold piece for a stick-pin and he got a ten-dollar gold piece on his watch chain and his mouf is jes' crammed full of gold teethes. Sho' wisht it wuz mine. And whut make it so cool, he got money 'cumulated. And womens give it all to 'im."

"Ah don't see whut de womens see on 'im. Ah wouldn't give 'im a wind if de sherff wuz after 'im."

"Well, he tole us how de white womens in Chicago give 'im all dat gold money. So he don't 'low nobody to touch it at all. Not even put dey finger on it. Dey tole 'im not to. You kin make 'miration at it, but don't tetch it."

"Whyn't he stay up dere where dey so crazy 'bout 'im?"

"Ah reckon dey done made 'im vast-rich and he wants to travel some. He say dey wouldn't leave 'im hit a lick of work. He got mo' lady people crazy 'bout him than he kin shake a stick at."

"Joe, Ah hates to see you so dumb. Dat stray nigger jes' tell y'all anything and y'all b'lieve it."

"Go 'head on now, honey and put on yo' clothes. He talkin' 'bout his pritty womens — Ah want 'im to see *mine.*"

Missie May went off to dress and Joe spent the time trying to make his stomach punch out like Slemmons' middle. He tried the rolling swagger of the stranger, but found that his tall bone-and-muscle stride fitted ill with it. He just had time to drop back into his seat before Missie May came in dressed to go.

On the way home that night Joe was exultant. "Didn't Ah say ole Otis was swell? Can't he talk Chicago talk? Wuzn't dat funny whut he said when great big fat ole Ida Armstrong come in? He asted me, 'Who is dat broad wid de forty shake?' Dat's a new word. Us always thought forty was a set of figgers but he showed us where it means a whole heap of things. Sometimes he don't say forty, he jes' say thirty-eight and two and dat mean de same thing. Know whut he tole me when Ah was payin' for our ice cream? He say, 'Ah have to hand it to you, Joe. Dat wife of yours is jes' thirty-eight and two. Yessuh, she's forty!' Ain't he killin'?"

"He'll do in case of a rush. But he sho' is got uh heap uh gold on 'im. Dat's de first time Ah ever seed gold money. It lookted good on him sho' nuff, but it'd look a whole heap better on you."

"Who, me? Missie May was youse crazy! Where would a po' man lak me git gold money from?"

Missie May was silent for a minute, then she said, "Us might find some goin' long de road some time. Us could."

"Who would be losin' gold money 'round heah? We ain't even seen none dese white folks wearin' no gold money on dey watch chain. You must be figgeren' Mister Packard or Mister Cadillac goin' pass through heah . . ."

"You don't know whut been lost 'round heah. Maybe somebody way back in memorial times lost they gold money and went on off and it ain't never been found. And then if we wuz to find it, you could wear some 'thout havin' no gang of womens lak dat Slemmons say he got."

Joe laughed and hugged her. "Don't be so wishful 'bout me. Ah'm satisfied de way Ah is. So long as Ah be yo' husband, Ah don't keer 'bout nothin' else. Ah'd ruther all de other womens in de world to be dead than for you to have de toothache. Less we go to bed and git our night rest."

It was Saturday night once more before Joe could parade his wife in Slemmons' ice cream parlor again. He worked the night shift and Saturday was his only night off. Every other evening around six o'clock he left home, and dying dawn saw him hustling home around the lake where the challenging sun flung a flaming sword from east to west across the trembling water.

That was the best part of life — going home to Missie May. Their whitewashed house, the mock battle on Saturday, the dinner and ice cream parlor afterwards, church on Sunday nights when Missie outdressed any woman in town — all, everything was right.

One night around eleven the acid ran out at the G and G. The foreman knocked off the crew and let the steam die down. As Joe rounded the lake on his way home, a lean moon rode the lake in a silver boat. If anybody had asked Joe about the moon on the lake, he would have said he hadn't paid it any attention. But he saw it with his feelings. It made him yearn painfully for Missie. Creation obsessed him. He thought about children. They had been married for more than a year now. They had money put away. They ought to be making little feet for shoes. A little boy child would be about right.

He saw a dim light in the bedroom and decided to come in through the kitchen door. He could wash the fertilizer dust off himself before presenting himself to Missie May. It would be nice for her not to know that he was there until he slipped into his place in bed and hugged her back. She always liked that.

He eased the kitchen door open slowly and silently, but when he went to set his dinner bucket on the table he bumped it into a pile of dishes, and something crashed to the floor. He heard his wife gasp in fright and hurried to reassure her.

"Iss me, honey. Don't get skeered."

There was a quick, large movement in the bedroom. A rustle, a thud, and a stealthy silence. The light went out.

What? Robbers? Murderers? Some varmint attacking his helpless wife, perhaps. He struck a match, threw himself on guard, and stepped over the doorsill into the bedroom.

The great belt on the wheel of Time slipped and eternity stood still. By the match light he could see the man's legs fighting with his breeches in his frantic desire to get them on. He had both chance and time to kill the intruder in his helpless condition — half-in and half-out of his pants — but he was too weak to take action. The shapeless enemies of humanity that live in the hours of Time had waylaid Joe. He was assaulted in his weakness. Like Samson awakening after his haircut. So he just opened his mouth and laughed.

The match went out and he struck another and lit the lamp. A howling wind raced across his heart, but underneath its fury he heard his wife sobbing and Slemmons pleading for his life. Offering to buy it with all that he had. "Please, suh, don't kill me. Sixty-two dollars at de sto' gold money."

Joe just stood. Slemmons looked at the window, but it was screened. Joe stood out like a rough-backed mountain between him and the door. Barring him from escape, from sunrise, from life.

He considered a surprise attack upon the big clown that stood there laughing like a chessy cat. But before his fist could travel an inch, Joe's own rushed out to crush him like a battering ram. Then Joe stood over him.

"Git into yo' damn rags, Slemmons, and dat quick."

Slemmons scrambled to his feet and into his vest and coat. As he grabbed his hat, Joe's fury overrode his intentions and he grabbed at Slemmons with his left hand and struck at him with his right. The right landed. The left grazed the front of his vest. Slemmons was knocked a somersault into the kitchen and fled through the open door. Joe found himself alone with Missie May, with the golden watch charm clutched in his left fist. A short bit of broken chain dangled between his fingers.

Missie May was sobbing. Wails of weeping without words. Joe stood, and after awhile he found out that he had something in his hand. And then he stood and felt without thinking and without seeing with his natural eyes. Missie May kept on crying and Joe kept on feeling so much and not knowing what to do with all his feelings, he put Slemmons' watch charm in his pants pocket and took a good laugh and went to bed.

"Missie May, whut you crying for?"

"Cause Ah love you so hard and Ah know you don't love *me* no mo'."

Joe sank his face into the pillow for a spell then he said huskily, "You don't know de feelings of dat yet, Missie May."

"Oh Joe, honey, he said he wuz gointer gimme dat gold money and he jes' kept on after me —"

Joe was very still and silent for a long time. Then he said, "Well, don't cry no mo', Missie May. Ah got yo' gold piece for you."

The hours went past on their rusty ankles. Joe still and quiet on one bed-rail and Missie May wrung dry of sobs on the other. Finally the sun's tide crept upon the shore of night and drowned all its hours. Missie May with her face stiff and streaked towards the window saw the dawn come into her yard. It was day. Nothing more. Joe wouldn't be coming home as usual. No need to fling open the front door and sweep off the porch, making it nice for Joe. Never no more breakfast to cook; no more washing and starching of Joe's jumper-jackets and pants. No more nothing. So why get up?

With this strange man in her bed, she felt embarrassed to get up and dress. She decided to wait till he had dressed and gone. Then she would get up, dress quickly, and be gone forever beyond reach of Joe's looks and laughs. But he never moved. Red light turned to yellow, then white.

From beyond the no-man's land between them came a voice. A strange voice that yesterday had been Joe's.

"Missie May, ain't you gonna fix me no breakfus'?"

She sprang out of bed. "Yeah, Joe. Ah didn't reckon you wuz hongry."

No need to die today. Joe needed her for a few more minutes anyhow.

Soon there was a roaring fire in the cook stove. Water bucket full and two chickens killed. Joe loved fried chicken and rice. She didn't deserve a thing and good Joe was letting her cook him some breakfast. She rushed hot biscuits to the table as Joe took his seat.

He ate with his eyes on his plate. No laughter, no banter.

"Missie May, you ain't eatin' yo' breakfus'."

"Ah don't choose none, Ah thank yuh."

His coffee cup was empty. She sprang to refill it. When she turned from the stove and bent to set the cup beside Joe's plate, she saw the yellow coin on the table between them.

She slumped into her seat and wept into her arms.

Presently Joe said calmly, "Missie May, you cry too much. Don't look back lak Lot's wife and turn to salt."

The sun, the hero of every day, the impersonal old man that beams as brightly on death as on birth, came up every morning and raced across the blue dome and dipped into the sea of fire every evening. Water ran down hill and birds nested.

Missie knew why she didn't leave Joe. She couldn't. She loved him too much. But she couldn't understand why Joe didn't leave her. He was polite, even kind at times, but aloof.

There were no more Saturday romps. No ringing silver dollars to stack beside her plate. No pockets to rifle. In fact the yellow coin in his trousers was like a monster hiding in the cave of his pockets to destroy her.

She often wondered if he still had it, but nothing could have induced her to ask nor yet to explore his pockets to see for herself. Its shadow was in the house whether or no.

One night Joe came home around midnight and complained of pains in the back. He asked Missie to rub him down with liniment. It had been three months since Missie had touched his body and it all seemed strange. But she rubbed him. Grateful for the chance. Before morning, youth triumphed and Missie exulted. But the next day, as she joyfully made up their bed, beneath her pillow she found the piece of money with the bit of chain attached.

Alone to herself, she looked at the thing with loathing, but look she must. She took it into her hands with trembling and saw first thing that it was no gold piece. It was a gilded half-dollar. Then she knew why Slemmons had forbidden anyone to touch his gold. He trusted village eyes at a distance not to recognize his stick-pin as a gilded quarter, and his watch charm as a four-bit piece.

She was glad at first that Joe had left it there. Perhaps he was through with her punishment. They were man and wife again. Then another thought came clawing at her. He had come home to buy from her as if she were any woman in the long house. Fifty cents for her love. As if to say that he could pay as well as Slemmons. She slid the coin into his Sunday pants pocket and dressed herself and left his house.

Halfway between her house and the quarters she met her husband's mother, and after a short talk she turned and went back home. If she had not the substance of marriage, she had the outside show. Joe must leave *her*. She let him see she didn't want his old gold four-bits too.

She saw no more of the coin for some time though she knew that Joe could not help finding it in his pocket. But his health kept poor, and he came home at least every ten days to be rubbed.

The sun swept around the horizon, trailing its robes of weeks and days. One morning as Joe came in from work, he found Missie May chopping wood. Without a word he took the ax and chopped a huge pile before he stopped.

"You ain't got no business choppin' wood, and you know it."

"How come? Ah been choppin' it for de last longest."

"Ah ain't blind. You makin' feet for shoes."

"Won't you be glad to have a li'l baby chile, Joe?"

"You know dat 'thout astin' me."

"Iss gointer be a boy chile and de very spit of you."

"You reckon, Missie May?"

"Who else could it look lak?"

Joe said nothing, but he thrust his hand deep into his pocket and fingered something there.

It was almost six months later Missie May took to bed and Joe went and got his mother to come wait on the house.

Missie May delivered a fine boy. Her travail was over when Joe came in from work one morning. His mother and the old women were drinking great bowls of coffee around the fire in the kitchen.

The minute Joe came into the room his mother called him aside.

"How did Missie May make out?" he asked quickly.

"Who, dat gal? She strong as a ox. She gointer have plenty mo'. We done fixed her wid de sugar and lard to sweeten her for de nex' one."

Joe stood silent awhile.

"You ain't ast 'bout de baby, Joe. You oughter be mighty proud cause he sho' is de spittin' image of yuh, son. Dat's yourn all right, if you never git another one, dat un is yourn. And you know Ah'm mighty proud too, son, cause Ah never thought well of you marryin' Missie May cause her ma used tuh fan her foot 'round right smart and Ah been mighty skeered dat Missie May wuz gointer git misput on her road."

Joe said nothing. He fooled around the house till late in the day then just before he went to work, he went and stood at the foot of the bed and asked his wife how she felt. He did this every day during the week.

On Saturday he went to Orlando to make his market. It had been a long time since he had done that.

Meat and lard, meal and flour, soap and starch. Cans of corn and tomatoes. All the staples. He fooled around town for awhile and bought bananas and apples. Way after while he went around to the candy store.

"Hellow, Joe," the clerk greeted him. "Ain't seen you in a long time."

"Nope, Ah ain't been heah. Been 'round spots and places."

"Want some of them molasses kisses you always buy?"

"Yessuh." He threw the gilded half-dollar on the counter. "Will dat spend?"

"Whut is it, Joe? Well, I'll be doggone! A gold-plated four-bit piece. Where'd you git it, Joe?"

"Offen a stray nigger dat come through Eatonville. He had it on his watch chain for a charm — goin' 'round making out iss gold money. Ha ha! He had a quarter on his tie pin and it wuz all golded up too. Tryin' to fool people. Makin' out he so rich and everything. Ha! Ha! Tryin' to tole off folkses wives from home."

"How did you git it, Joe? Did he fool you, too?"

"Who, me? Naw suh! He ain't fooled me none. Know whut Ah done? He come 'round me wid his smart talk. Ah hauled off and knocked 'im down and took his old four-bits 'way from 'im. Gointer buy my wife some good ole 'lasses kisses wid it. Gimme fifty cents worth of dem candy kisses."

"Fifty cents buys a mightly lot of candy kisses, Joe. Why don't you split it up and take some chocolate bars, too. They eat good, too."

"Yessuh, de do, but Ah wants all dat in kisses. Ah got a li'l boy chile home now. Tain't a week old yet, but he kin suck a sugar tit and maybe eat one them kisses hisself."

Joe got his candy and left the store. The clerk turned to the next customer. "Wisht I could be like these darkies. Laughin' all the time. Nothin' worries 'em."

Back in Eatonville, Joe reached his own front door. There was the ring of singing metal on wood. Fifteen times. Missie May couldn't run to the door, but she crept there as quickly as she could.

"Joe Banks, Ah hear you chunkin' money in mah do'way. You wait till Ah got mah strength back and Ah'm gointer fix you for dat."

Sweat

1926

I

It was eleven o'clock of a Spring night in Florida. It was Sunday. Any other night, Delia Jones would have been in bed for two hours by this time. But she was a washwoman, and Monday morning meant a great deal to her. So she collected the soiled clothes on Saturday when she returned the clean things. Sunday night after church, she sorted and put the white things to soak. It saved her almost a half-day's start. A great hamper in the bedroom held the clothes that she brought home. It was so much neater than a number of bundles lying around.

She squatted on the kitchen floor beside the great pile of clothes, sorting them into small heaps according to color, and humming a song in a mournful key, but wondering through it all where Sykes, her husband, had gone with her horse and buckboard.

Just then something long, round, limp, and black fell upon her shoulders and slithered to the floor beside her. A great terror took hold of her. It softened her knees and dried her mouth so that it was a full minute before she could cry out or move. Then she saw that it was the big bull whip her husband liked to carry when he drove.

She lifted her eyes to the door and saw him standing there bent over with laughter at her fright. She screamed at him.

"Sykes, what you throw dat whip on me like dat? You know it would skeer me — looks just like a snake, an' you knows how skeered Ah is of snakes."

"Course Ah knowed it! That's how come Ah done it." He slapped his leg with his hand and almost rolled on the ground in his mirth. "If you such a big fool dat you got to have a fit over a earth worm or a string, Ah don't keer how bad Ah skeer you."

"You ain't got no business doing it. Gawd knows it's a sin. Some day Ah'm gointuh drop dead from some of yo' foolishness. 'Nother thing, where you been wid mah rig? Ah feeds dat pony. He ain't fuh you to be drivin' wid no bull whip."

"You sho' is one aggravatin' nigger woman!" he declared and stepped into the room. She resumed her work and did not answer him at once. "Ah done tole you time and again to keep them white folks' clothes outa dis house."

He picked up the whip and glared at her. Delia went on with her work. She went out into the yard and returned with a galvanized tub and set it on the washbench. She saw that Sykes had kicked all of the clothes together again, and now stood in her way truculently, his whole manner hoping, *praying*, for an argument. But she walked calmly around him and commenced to re-sort the things.

"Next time, Ah'm gointer kick 'em outdoors," he threatened as he struck a match along the leg of his corduroy breeches.

Delia never looked up from her work, and her thin, stooped shoulders sagged further.

"Ah ain't for no fuss t'night, Sykes. Ah just come from taking sacrament at the church house."

He snorted scornfully. "Yeah, you just come from de church house on a Sunday night, but heah you is gone to work on them clothes. You ain't nothing but a hypocrite. One of them amen-corner Christians — sing, whoop, and shout, then come home and wash white folks' clothes on the Sabbath."

He stepped roughly upon the whitest pile of things, kicking them helter-skelter as he crossed the room. His wife gave a little scream of dismay, and quickly gathered them together again.

"Sykes, you quit grindin' dirt into these clothes! How can Ah git through by Sat'day if Ah don't start on Sunday?"

"Ah don't keer if you never git through. Anyhow, Ah done promised Gawd and a couple of other men, Ah ain't gointer have it in mah house. Don't gimme no lip neither, else Ah'll throw 'em out and put mah fist up side yo' head to boot."

Delia's habitual meekness seemed to slip from her shoulders like a blown scarf. She was on her feet; her poor little body, her bare knuckly hands bravely defying the strapping hulk before her.

"Looka heah, Sykes, you done gone too fur. Ah been married to you fur fifteen years, and Ah been takin' in washin' fur fifteen years. Sweat, sweat, sweat! Work and sweat, cry and sweat, pray and sweat!"

"What's that got to do with me?" he asked brutally.

"What's it got to do with you, Sykes? Mah tub of suds is filled yo' belly with vittles more times than yo' hands is filled it. Mah sweat is done paid for this house and Ah reckon Ah kin keep on sweatin' in it."

She seized the iron skillet from the stove and struck a defensive pose, which act surprised him greatly, coming from her. It cowed him and he did not strike her as he usually did.

"Naw you won't," she panted, "that ole snaggle-toothed black woman you runnin' with ain't comin' heah to pile up on *mah* sweat and blood. You ain't paid for nothin' on this place, and Ah'm gointer stay right heah till Ah'm toted out foot foremost."

"Well, you better quit gittin' me riled up, else they'll be totin' you out sooner than you expect. Ah'm so tired of you Ah don't know whut to do. Gawd! How Ah hates skinny wimmen!"

A little awed by this new Delia, he sidled out of the door and slammed the back gate after him. He did not say where he had gone, but she knew too well. She knew very well that he would not return until nearly daybreak also. Her work over, she went on to bed but not to sleep at once. Things had come to a pretty pass!

She lay awake, gazing upon the debris that cluttered their matrimonial trail. Not an image left standing along the way. Anything like flowers had long ago been drowned in the salty stream that had been pressed from her heart. Her tears, her sweat, her blood. She had brought love to the union and he had brought a longing after the flesh. Two months after the wedding, he had given her the first brutal beating. She had the memory of his numerous trips to Orlando with all of his wages when he had returned to her penniless, even before the first year had passed. She was young and soft then, but now she thought of her knotty, muscled limbs, her harsh knuckly hands, and drew herself up into an unhappy little ball in the middle of the big feather bed. Too late now to hope for love, even if it were not Bertha it would be someone else. This case differed from the others only in that she was bolder than the others. Too late for everything except her little home. She had built it for her old days, and planted one by one the trees and flowers there. It was lovely to her, lovely.

Somehow, before sleep came, she found herself saying aloud: "Oh well, whatever goes over the Devil's back, is got to come under his belly. Sometime or ruther, Sykes, like everybody else, is gointer reap his sowing." After that she was able to build a spiritual earthworks against her husband. His shells could no longer reach her. AMEN. She went to sleep and slept until he announced his presence in bed by kicking her feet and rudely snatching the covers away.

"Gimme some kivah heah, an' git yo' damn foots over on yo' own side! Ah oughter mash you in yo' mouf fuh drawing dat skillet on me."

Delia went clear to the rail without answering him. A triumphant indifference to all that he was or did.

II

The week was full of work for Delia as all other weeks, and Saturday found her behind her little pony, collecting and delivering clothes.

It was a hot, hot day near the end of July. The village men on Joe Clarke's porch even chewed cane listlessly. They did not hurl the cane-knots as usual. They let them dribble over the edge of the porch. Even conversation had collapsed under the heat.

"Heah come Delia Jones," Jim Merchant said, as the shaggy pony came 'round the bend of the road toward them. The rusty buckboard was heaped with baskets of crisp, clean laundry.

"Yep," Joe Lindsay agreed. "Hot or col', rain or shine, jes'ez reg'lar ez de weeks roll roun' Delia carries 'em an' fetches 'em on Sat'day."

"She better if she wanter eat," said Moss. "Syke Jones ain't wuth de shot an' powder hit would tek tuh kill 'em. Not to *huh* he ain't."

"He sho' ain't," Walter Thomas chimed in. "It's too bad, too, cause she wuz a right pretty li'l trick when he got huh. Ah'd uh mah'ied huh mahself if he hadnter beat me to it."

Delia nodded briefly at the men as she drove past.

"Too much knockin' will ruin *any* 'oman. He done beat huh 'nough tuh kill three women, let 'lone change they looks," said Elijah Moseley. "How Syke kin stommuck dat big black greasy Mogul he's layin' roun' wid, gits me.

Ah swear dat eight-rock couldn't kiss a sardine can Ah done thowed out de back do' 'way las' yeah."

"Aw, she's fat, thass how come. He's allus been crazy 'bout fat women," put in Merchant. "He'd a' been tied up wid one long time ago if he could a' found one tuh have him. Did Ah tell yuh 'bout him come sidlin' roun' *mah* wife — bringin' her a basket uh peecans outa his yard fuh a present? Yessir, mah wife! She tol' him tuh take 'em right straight back home, 'cause Delia works so hard ovah dat washtub she reckon everything on de place taste lak sweat an' soapsuds. Ah jus' wisht Ah'd a' caught 'im 'roun' dere! Ah'd a' made his hips ketch on fiah down dat shell road."

"Ah know he done it, too. Ah sees 'im grinnin' at every 'oman dat passes," Walter Thomas said. "But even so, he useter eat some mighty big hunks uh humble pie tuh git dat li'l 'oman he got. She wuz ez pritty ez a speckled pup! Dat wuz fifteen years ago. He useter be so skeered uh losin' huh, she could make him do some parts of a husband's duty. Dey never wuz de same in de mind."

"There oughter be a law about him," said Lindsay. "He ain't fit tuh carry guts tuh a bear."

Clarke spoke for the first time. "'Tain't no law on earth dat kin make a man be decent if it ain't in 'im. There's plenty men dat takes a wife lak dey do a joint uh sugar-cane. It's round, juicy, an' sweet when dey gits it. But dey squeeze an' grind, squeeze an' grind an' wring tell dey wring every drop uh pleasure dat's in 'em out. When dey's satisfied dat dey is wrung dry, dey treats 'em jes' lak dey do a cane-chew. Dey thows 'em away. Dey knows whut dey is doin' while dey is at it, an' hates theirselves fuh it but they keeps on hangin' after huh tell she's empty. Den dey hates huh fuh bein' a cane-chew an' in de way."

"We oughter take Syke an' dat stray 'oman uh his'n down in Lake Howell swamp an' lay on de rawhide till they cain't say Lawd a' mussy. He allus wuz uh ovahbearin niggah, but since dat white 'oman from up north done teached 'im how to run a automobile, he done got too beggety to live — an' we oughter kill 'im," Old Man Anderson advised.

A grunt of approval went around the porch. But the heat was melting their civic virtue and Elijah Moseley began to bait Joe Clarke.

"Come on, Joe, git a melon outa dere an' slice it up for yo' customers. We'se all sufferin' wid de heat. De bear's done got *me*!"

"Thass right, Joe, a watermelon is jes' whut Ah needs tuh cure de eppizudicks," Walter Thomas joined forces with Moseley. "Come on dere, Joe. We all is steady customers an' you ain't set us up in a long time. Ah chooses dat long, bowlegged Floridy favorite."

"A god, an' be dough. You all gimme twenty cents and slice away," Clarke retorted. "Ah needs a col' slice m'self. Heah, everybody chip in. Ah'll lend y'all mah meat knife."

The money was all quickly subscribed and the huge melon brought forth. At that moment, Sykes and Bertha arrived. A determined silence fell on the porch and the melon was put away again.

Merchant snapped down the blade of his jacknife and moved toward the store door.

"Come on in, Joe, an' gimme a slab uh sow belly an' uh pound uh coffee — almost fuhgot 'twas Sat'day. Got to git on home." Most of the men left also.

Just then Delia drove past on her way home, as Sykes was ordering magnificently for Bertha. It pleased him for Delia to see.

"Git whutsoever yo' heart desires, Honey. Wait a minute, Joe. Give huh two bottles uh strawberry soda-water, uh quart parched ground-peas, an' a block uh chewin' gum."

With all this they left the store, with Sykes reminding Bertha that this was his town and she could have it if she wanted it.

The men returned soon after they left, and held their watermelon feast.

"Where did Syke Jones git da 'oman from nohow?" Lindsay asked.

"Ovah Apopka. Guess dey musta been cleanin' out de town when she lef.' She don't look lak a thing but a hunk uh liver wid hair on it."

"Well, she sho' kin squall," Dave Carter contributed. "When she gits ready tuh laff, she jes' opens huh mouf an' latches it back tuh de las' notch. No ole granpa alligator down in Lake Bell ain't got nothin' on huh."

III

Bertha had been in town three months now. Sykes was still paying her room-rent at Della Lewis' — the only house in town that would have taken her in. Sykes took her frequently to Winter Park to "stomps." He still assured her that he was the swellest man in the state.

"Sho' you kin have dat li'l ole house soon's Ah git dat 'oman outa dere. Everything b'longs tuh me an' you sho' kin have it. Ah sho' 'bominates uh skinny 'oman. Lawdy, you sho' is got one portly shape on you! You kin git *anything* you wants. Dis is *mah* town an' you sho' kin have it."

Delia's work-worn knees crawled over the earth in Gethsemane[1] and up the rocks of Calvary many, many times during these months. She avoided the villagers and meeting places in her efforts to be blind and deaf. But Bertha nullified this to a degree, by coming to Delia's house to call Sykes out to her at the gate.

Delia and Sykes fought all the time now with no peaceful interludes. They slept and ate in silence. Two or three times Delia had attempted a timid friendliness, but she was repulsed each time. It was plain that the breaches must remain agape.

The sun had burned July to August. The heat streamed down like a million hot arrows, smiting all things living upon the earth. Grass withered, leaves browned, snakes went blind in shedding, and men and dogs went mad. Dog days!

Delia came home one day and found Sykes there before her. She wondered, but started to go on into the house without speaking, even though he was standing in the kitchen door and she must either stoop under his arm or ask him to move. He made no room for her. She noticed a soap box beside the steps, but paid no particular attention to it, knowing that he must have brought

---

[1]A reference to the garden where Jesus was betrayed (in the Gospels) before being tried and crucified on Calvary or Golgotha, the "hill of skulls."

it there. As she was stooping to pass under his outstretched arm, he suddenly pushed her backward, laughingly.

"Look in de box dere Delia, Ah done brung yuh somethin'!"

She nearly fell upon the box in her stumbling, and when she saw what it held, she all but fainted outright.

"Syke! Syke, mah Gawd! You take dat rattlesnake 'way from heah! You *got-tuh*. Oh, Jesus, have mussy!"

"Ah ain't got tuh do nuthin' uh de kin'—fact is Ah ain't got tuh do nothin' but die. Tain't no use uh you puttin' on airs makin' out lak you skeered uh dat snake—he's gointer stay right heah tell he die. He wouldn't bite me cause Ah knows how tuh handle 'im. Nohow he wouldn't risk breakin' out his fangs 'gin yo skinny laigs."

"Naw, now Syke, don't keep dat thing 'round tryin' tuh skeer me tuh death. You knows Ah'm even feared uh earth worms. Thass de biggest snake Ah evah did se. Kill 'im Syke, please."

"Doan ast me tuh do nothin' fuh yuh. Goin' 'round tryin' tuh be so damn asterperious. Naw, Ah ain't gonna kill it. Ah think uh damn sight mo' uh him dan you! Dat's a nice snake an' anybody doan lak 'im kin jes' hit de grit."

The village soon heard that Sykes had the snake, and came to see and ask questions.

"How de hen-fire did you ketch dat six-foot rattler, Syke?" Thomas asked.

"He's full uh frogs so he cain't hardly move, thass how Ah eased up on 'm. But Ah'm a snake charmer an' knows how tuh handle 'em. Shux, dat ain't nothin'. Ah could ketch one eve'y day if Ah so wanted tuh."

"Whut he needs is a heavy hick'ry club leaned real heavy on his head. Dat's de bes' way tuh charm a rattlesnake."

"Naw, Walt, y'all jes' don't understand dese diamon' backs lak Ah do," said Sykes in a superior tone of voice.

The village agreed with Walter, but the snake stayed on. His box remained by the kitchen door with its screen wire covering. Two or three days later it had digested its meal of frogs and literally came to life. It rattled at every movement in the kitchen or the yard. One day as Delia came down the kitchen steps she saw his chalky-white fangs curved like scimitars hung in the wire meshes. This time she did not run away with averted eyes as usual. She stood for a long time in the doorway in a red fury that grew bloodier for every second that she regarded the creature that was her torment.

That night she broached the subject as soon as Sykes sat down to the table.

"Syke, Ah wants you tuh take dat snake 'way fum heah. You done starved me an' Ah put up widcher, you done beat me an Ah took dat, but you don kilt all mah insides bringin' dat varmint heah."

Sykes poured out a saucer full of coffee and drank it deliberately before he answered her.

"A whole lot Ah keer 'bout how you feels inside uh out. Dat snake ain't goin' no damn wheah till Ah gits ready fuh 'im tuh go. So fur as beatin' is concerned, yuh ain't took near all dat you gointer take ef yuh stay 'round *me*."

Delia pushed back her plate and got up from the table. "Ah hates you, Sykes," she said calmly. "Ah hates you tuh de same degree dat Ah useter love yuh. Ah done took an' took till mah belly is full up tuh mah neck. Dat's de reason Ah got mah letter fum de church an' moved mah membership tuh Woodbridge — so Ah don't haftuh take no sacrament wid yuh. Ah don't wantuh see yuh 'round me atall. Lay 'round wid dat 'oman all yuh wants tuh, but gwan 'way from me an' mah house. Ah hates yuh lak uh suck-egg dog."

Sykes almost let the huge wad of corn bread and collard greens he was chewing fall out of his mouth in amazement. He had a hard time whipping himself up to the proper fury to try to answer Delia.

"Well, Ah'm glad you does hate me. Ah'm sho' tiahed uh you hangin' ontuh me. Ah don't want yuh. Look at yuh stringey ole neck! Yo' rawbony laigs an' arms is enough tuh cut uh man tuh death. You looks jes' lak de devvul's doll-baby tuh *me*. You cain't hate me no worse dan Ah hates you. Ah been hatin' *you* fuh years."

"Yo' ole black hide don't look lak nothin' tuh me, but uh passle uh wrinkled up rubber, wid yo' big ole yeahs flappin' on each side lak uh paih uh buzzard wings. Don't think Ah'm gointuh be run 'way fum mah house neither. Ah'm goin' tuh de white folks 'bout *you*, mah young man, de very nex' time you lay yo' han's on me. Mah cup is done run ovah." Delia said this with no signs of fear and Sykes departed from the house, threatening her, but made not the slightest move to carry out any of them.

That night he did not return at all, and the next day being Sunday, Delia was glad she did not have to quarrel before she hitched up her pony and drove the four miles to Woodbridge.

She stayed to the night service — "love feast" — which was very warm and full of spirit. In the emotional winds her domestic trials were borne far and wide so that she sang as she drove homeward,

> Jurden water, black an' col
> Chills de body, not de soul
> An' Ah wantah cross Jurden in uh calm time.

She came from the barn to the kitchen door and stopped.

"Whut's de mattah, ol' Satan, you ain't kicken' up yo' racket?" She addressed the snake's box. Complete silence. She went on into the house with a new hope in its birth struggles. Perhaps her threat to go to the white folks had frightened Sykes! Perhaps he was sorry! Fifteen years of misery and suppression had brought Delia to the place where she would hope *anything* that looked towards a way over or through her wall of inhibitions.

She felt in the match-safe behind the stove at once for a match. There was only one there.

"Dat niggah wouldn't fetch nothin' heah tuh save his rotten neck, but he kin run thew whut Ah brings quick enough. Now he done toted off nigh on tuh haff uh box uh matches. He done had dat 'oman heah in mah house, too."

Nobody but a woman could tell how she knew this even before she struck the match. But she did and it put her into a new fury.

Presently she brought in the tubs to put the white things to soak. This time she decided she need not bring the hamper out of the bedroom; she would go in there and do the sorting. She picked up the pot-bellied lamp and went in. The room was small and the hamper stood hard by the foot of the white iron bed. She could sit and reach through the bedposts — resting as she worked.

"Ah wantah cross Jurden in uh calm time." She was singing again. The mood of the "love feast" had returned. She threw back the lid of the basket almost gaily. Then, moved by both horror and terror, she sprang back toward the door. *There lay the snake in the basket!* He moved sluggishly at first, but even as she turned round and round, jumped up and down in an insanity of fear, he began to stir vigorously. She saw him pouring his awful beauty from the basket upon the bed, then she seized the lamp and ran as fast as she could to the kitchen. The wind from the open door blew out the light and the darkness added to her terror. She sped to the darkness of the yard, slamming the door after her before she thought to set down the lamp. She did not feel safe even on the ground, so she climbed up in the hay barn.

There for an hour or more she lay sprawled upon the hay a gibbering wreck.

Finally she grew quiet, and after that came coherent thought. With this stalked through her a cold, bloody rage. Hours of this. A period of introspection, a space of retrospection, then a mixture of both. Out of this an awful calm.

"Well, Ah done de bes' Ah could. If things ain't right, Gawd knows tain't mah fault."

She went to sleep — a twitch sleep — and woke up to a faint gray sky. There was a loud hollow sound below. She peered out. Sykes was at the wood-pile, demolishing a wire-covered box.

He hurried to the kitchen door, but hung outside there some minutes before he entered, and stood some minutes more inside before he closed it after him.

The gray in the sky was spreading. Delia descended without fear now, and crouched beneath the low bedroom window. The drawn shade shut out the dawn, shut in the night. But the thin walls held back no sound.

"Dat ol' scratch is woke up now!" She mused at the tremendous whirr inside, which every woodsman knows, is one of the sound illusions. The rattler is a ventriloquist. His whirr sounds to the right, to the left, straight ahead, behind, close under foot — everywhere but where it is. Woe to him who guesses wrong unless he is prepared to hold up his end of the argument! Sometimes he strikes without rattling at all.

Inside, Sykes heard nothing until he knocked a pot lid off the stove while trying to reach the match-safe in the dark. He had emptied his pockets at Bertha's.

The snake seemed to wake up under the stove and Sykes made a quick leap into the bedroom. In spite of the gin he had had, his head was clearing now.

"Mah Gawd!" he chattered, "ef Ah could on'y strack uh light!"

The rattling ceased for a moment as he stood paralyzed. He waited. It seemed that the snake waited also.

"Oh, fuh de light! Ah thought he'd be too sick" — Sykes was muttering to himself when the whirr began again, closer, right underfoot this time. Long before this, Sykes' ability to think had been flattened down to primitive instinct and he leaped — onto the bed.

Outside Delia heard a cry that might have come from a maddened chimpanzee, a stricken gorilla. All the terror, all the horror, all the rage that man possibly could express, without a recognizable human sound.

A tremendous stir inside there, another series of animal screams, the intermittent whirr of the reptile. The shade torn violently down from the window, letting in the red dawn, a huge brown hand seizing the window stick, great dull blows upon the wooden floor punctuating the gibberish of sound long after the rattle of the snake had abruptly subsided. All this Delia could see and hear from her place beneath the window, and it made her ill. She crept over to the four o'clocks and stretched herself on the cool earth to recover.

She lay there. "Delia, Delia!" She could hear Sykes calling in a most despairing tone as one who expected no answer. The sun crept on up, and he called. Delia could not move — her legs had gone flabby. She never moved, he called, and the sun kept rising.

"Mah Gawd!" She heard him moan, "Mah Gawd fum Heben!" She heard him stumbling about and got up from her flower-bed. The sun was growing warm. As she approached the door she heard him call out hopefully, "Delia, is dat you Ah heah?"

She saw him on his hands and knees as soon as she reached the door. He crept an inch or two toward her — all that he was able, and she saw his horribly swollen neck and his one open eye shining with hope. A surge of pity too strong to support bore her away from that eye that must, could not, fail to see the tubs. He would see the lamp. Orlando with its doctors was too far. She could scarcely reach the chinaberry tree, where she waited in the growing heat while inside she knew the cold river was creeping up and up to extinguish that eye which must know by now that she knew.

Washington Irving

Washington Irving (1783–1859), named after George Washington, was the youngest of eleven children born in New York City to a mother of English descent and a Scottish father who was a prosperous merchant. After studying law with Judge Josiah Hoffman, Irving went on a grand tour of Europe for two years. Returning to New York City, he published the *Salmagundi Papers* (1807–1808) and a comic *History of New York* (1809), in which he invented the figure of a talkative elderly narrator named Diedrich Knickerbocker who told anecdotes about the early history of the Dutch colony. Irving's writing was so successful that his comical gentleman "Knickerbocker" came to personify New York City, and the name survives today in the professional basketball team the New York Knicks.

Anguished by the death of his fiancée, Judge Hoffman's daughter, Irving left New York in 1815 to join his brother Peter in the European branch of the family's business in Liverpool. When the venture failed, Irving moved to London and began to meet British authors, including Sir Walter Scott, one of the most successful playwrights and novelists of his time. They shared an enthusiasm for German literature, which Irving read in translation. He began an intensive study of German, making his own translation of the folktale "Peter Klaus the Goatherd" and other stories. Then Irving started "scribbling" original short prose tales based on his translations. In one especially inspired day he produced "Rip Van Winkle," which most scholars describe as the first successful American short story. It was published in London in 1819–1820 as part of Irving's two-volume collection *The Sketch Book*, which included another masterpiece, "The Legend of Sleepy Hollow," also based on German folklore.

In "Rip Van Winkle" Irving went to ingenious lengths to disguise his borrowing. First he invented the tongue-in-cheek character "Geoffrey Crayon" as the author of *The Sketch Book*, attempting to hide that he was an American writer trying to interest English readers in his work. Then Irving created a frame for "Rip Van Winkle," with Crayon telling the reader that he found the tale "among the papers of the late Diedrich Knickerbocker." Irving's use of pseudonyms and mock documentation in the opening and closing paragraphs of "Rip Van Winkle" underscores the humorous tone of his tale, which gave the story an enduring new life as an American legend. *The Sketch Book* was so popular that Scott followed Irving's lead and published the first short story in British literature, "The Two Drovers," in 1827. After years abroad Irving returned to New York in 1832 and settled in Tarrytown on the Hudson. He involved himself in politics and continued to publish books, most notably the travel sketches *A Tour on the Prairies* (1835) and the multivolume *Life of Washington* (1859).

RELATED COMMENTARY
J. C. C. Nachtigal, "Peter Klaus the Goatherd," page 1491.

Rip Van Winkle

1819–1820

A Posthumous Writing of Diedrich Knickerbocker

By Woden, God of Saxons,
From whence comes Wensday, that is Wodensday,
Truth is a thing that ever I will keep
Unto thylke day in which I creep into
My sepulchre —

— Cartwright[1]

[THE FOLLOWING TALE WAS FOUND among the papers of the late Diedrich Knickerbocker, an old gentleman of New York, who was very curious in the Dutch history of the province, and the manners of the descendants from its primitive settlers. His historical researches, however, did not lie so much among books as among men; for the former are lamentably scanty on his favorite topics; whereas he found the old burghers, and still more their wives, rich in that legendary lore so invaluable to true history. Whenever, therefore, he happened upon a genuine Dutch family, snugly shut up in its low-roofed farmhouse, under a spreading sycamore, he looked upon it as a little clasped volume of black-letter, and studied it with the zeal of a book-worm.

The result of all these researches was a history of the province during the reign of the Dutch governors, which he published some years since. There have been various opinions as to the literary character of his work, and, to tell the truth, it is not a whit better than it should be. Its chief merit is its scrupulous accuracy, which indeed was a little questioned on its first appearance, but has since been completely established; and it is now admitted into all historical collections as a book of unquestionable authority.

The old gentleman died shortly after the publication of his work; and now that he is dead and gone, it cannot do much harm to his memory to say that his time might have been much better employed in weightier labors. He, however, was apt to ride his hobby his own way; and though it did now and then kick up the dust a little in the eyes of his neighbors, and grieve the spirit of some friends, for whom he felt the truest deference and affection, yet his errors and follies are remembered "more in sorrow than in anger," and it begins to be suspected that he never intended to offend. But however his memory may be appreciated by critics, it is still held dear by many folk whose good opinion is well worth having; particularly by certain biscuit-makers, who have gone so far as to imprint his likeness on their New-Year cakes; and have thus given him a chance for immortality, almost equal to being stamped on a Waterloo Medal, or a Queen Anne's Farthing.]

---

[1]William Cartwright (1611–1643) was an English playwright. The lines are from his play *The Ordinary* (III. i. 1050–54).

Whoever has made a voyage up the Hudson must remember the Kaatskill mountains. They are a dismembered branch of the great Appalachian family, and are seen away to the west of the river, swelling up to a noble height, and lording it over the surrounding country. Every change of season, every change of weather, indeed, every hour of the day, produces some change in the magical hues and shapes of these mountains, and they are regarded by all the good wives, far and near, as perfect barometers. When the weather is fair and settled, they are clothed in blue and purple, and print their bold outlines on the clear evening sky; but sometimes, when the rest of the landscape is cloudless, they will gather a hood of gray vapors about their summits, which, in the last rays of the setting sun, will glow and light up like a crown of glory.

At the foot of these fairy mountains, the voyager may have descried the light smoke curling up from a village, whose shingle-roofs gleam among the trees, just where the blue tints of the upland melt away into the fresh green of the nearer landscape. It is a little village, of great antiquity, having been founded by some of the Dutch colonists in the early times of the province, just about the beginning of the government of the good Peter Stuyvesant, (may he rest in peace!) and there were some of the houses of the original settlers standing within a few years, built of small yellow bricks brought from Holland, having latticed windows and gable fronts, surmounted with weathercocks.

In that same village, and in one of these very houses (which, to tell the precise truth, was sadly time-worn and weather-beaten), there lived, many years since, while the country was yet a province of Great Britain, a simple, good-natured fellow, of the name of Rip Van Winkle. He was a descendant of the Van Winkles who figured so gallantly in the chivalrous days of Peter Stuyvesant, and accompanied him to the siege of Fort Christina. He inherited, however, but little of the martial character of his ancestors. I have observed that he was a simple, good-natured man; he was, moreover, a kind neighbor, and an obedient, hen-pecked husband. Indeed, to the latter circumstance might be owing that meekness of spirit which gained him such universal popularity; for those men are most apt to be obsequious and conciliating abroad, who are under the discipline of shrews at home. Their tempers, doubtless, are rendered pliant and malleable in the fiery furnace of domestic tribulation; and a curtain-lecture is worth all the sermons in the world for teaching the virtues of patience and long-suffering. A termagant wife may, therefore, in some respects, be considered a tolerable blessing; and if so, Rip Van Winkle was thrice blessed.

Certain it is, that he was a great favorite among all the good wives of the village, who, as usual with the amiable sex, took his part in all family squabbles; and never failed, whenever they talked those matters over in their evening gossipings, to lay all the blame on Dame Van Winkle. The children of the village, too, would shout with joy whenever he approached. He assisted at their sports, made their playthings, taught them to fly kites and shoot marbles, and told them long stories of ghosts, witches, and Indians. Whenever he went dodging about the village, he was surrounded by a troop of them, hanging on his skirts, clambering on his back, and playing a thousand tricks on him with impunity; and not a dog would bark at him throughout the neighborhood.

The great error in Rip's composition was an insuperable aversion to all kinds of profitable labor. It could not be from the want of assiduity or perseverance; for he would sit on a wet rock, with a rod as long and heavy as a Tartar's lance, and fish all day without a murmur, even though he should not be encouraged by a single nibble. He would carry a fowling-piece on his shoulder for hours together, trudging through woods and swamps, and up hill and down dale, to shoot a few squirrels or wild pigeons. He would never refuse to assist a neighbor even in the roughest toil, and was a foremost man at all country frolics for husking Indian corn, or building stone fences; the women of the village, too, used to employ him to run their errands, and to do such little odd jobs as their less obliging husbands would not do for them. In a word, Rip was ready to attend to anybody's business but his own; but as to doing family duty, and keeping his farm in order, he found it impossible.

In fact, he declared it was of no use to work on his farm; it was the most pestilent little piece of ground in the whole country; everything about it went wrong, and would go wrong, in spite of him. His fences were continually falling to pieces; his cow would either go astray, or get among the cabbages; weeds were sure to grow quicker in his fields than anywhere else; the rain always made a point of setting in just as he had some out-door work to do; so that though his patrimonial estate had dwindled away under his management, acre by acre, until there was little more left than a mere patch of Indian corn and potatoes, yet it was the worst conditioned farm in the neighborhood.

His children, too, were as ragged and wild as if they belonged to nobody. His son Rip, an urchin begotten in his own likeness, promised to inherit the habits, with the old clothes, of his father. He was generally seen trooping like a colt at his mother's heels, equipped in a pair of his father's cast-off galligaskins,[2] which he had much ado to hold up with one hand, as a fine lady does her train in bad weather.

Rip Van Winkle, however, was one of those happy mortals, of foolish, well-oiled dispositions, who take the world easy, eat white bread or brown, whichever can be got with least thought or trouble, and would rather starve on a penny than work for a pound. If left to himself, he would have whistled life away in perfect contentment; but his wife kept continually dinning in his ears about his idleness, his carelessness, and the ruin he was bringing on his family. Morning, noon, and night, her tongue was incessantly going, and everything he said or did was sure to produce a torrent of household eloquence. Rip had but one way of replying to all lectures of the kind, and that, by frequent use, had grown into a habit. He shrugged his shoulders, shook his head, cast up his eyes, but said nothing. This, however, always provoked a fresh volley from his wife; so that he was fain to draw off his forces, and take to the outside of the house — the only side which, in truth, belongs to a hen-pecked husband.

Rip's sole domestic adherent was his dog Wolf, who was as much hen-pecked as his master; for Dame Van Winkle regarded them as companions in idleness, and even looked upon Wolf with an evil eye, as the cause of his master's going

---

[2]Large, loose breeches.

so often astray. True it is, in all points of spirit befitting an honorable dog, he was as courageous an animal as ever scoured the woods; but what courage can withstand the ever-enduring and all-besetting terrors of a woman's tongue? The moment Wolf entered the house his crest fell, his tail drooped to the ground, or curled between his legs, he sneaked about with a gallows air, casting many a sidelong glance at Dame Van Winkle, and at the least flourish of a broomstick or ladle he would fly to the door with yelping precipitation.

Times grew worse and worse with Rip Van Winkle as years of matrimony rolled on; a tart temper never mellows with age, and a sharp tongue is the only edged tool that grows keener with constant use. For a long while he used to console himself, when driven from home, by frequenting a kind of perpetual club of the sages, philosophers, and other idle personages of the village, which held its sessions on a bench before a small inn, designated by a rubicund portrait of His Majesty George the Third. Here they used to sit in the shade through a long, lazy summer's day, talking listlessly over village gossip, or telling endless sleepy stories about nothing. But it would have been worth any statesman's money to have heard the profound discussions that sometimes took place, when by chance an old newspaper fell into their hands from some passing traveller. How solemnly they would listen to the contents, as drawled out by Derrick Van Bummel, the schoolmaster, a dapper learned little man, who was not to be daunted by the most gigantic word in the dictionary; and how sagely they would deliberate upon public events some months after they had taken place.

The opinions of this junto[3] were completely controlled by Nicholas Vedder, patriarch of the village, and landlord of the inn, at the door of which he took his seat from morning till night, just moving sufficiently to avoid the sun and keep in the shade of a large tree; so that the neighbors could tell the hour by his movements as accurately as by a sun-dial. It is true he was rarely heard to speak, but smoked his pipe incessantly. His adherents, however (for every great man has his adherents), perfectly understood him, and knew how to gather his opinions. When anything that was read or related displeased him, he was observed to smoke his pipe vehemently, and to send forth short, frequent, and angry puffs; but when pleased, he would inhale the smoke slowly and tranquilly, and emit it in light and placid clouds; and sometimes, taking the pipe from his mouth, and letting the fragrant vapor curl about his nose, would gravely nod his head in token of perfect approbation.

From even this stronghold the unlucky Rip was at length routed by his termagant wife, who would suddenly break in upon the tranquillity of the assemblage and call the members all to naught; nor was that august personage, Nicholas Vedder himself, sacred from the daring tongue of this terrible virago, who charged him outright with encouraging her husband in habits of idleness.

Poor Rip was at last reduced almost to despair; and his only alternative, to escape from the labor of the farm and clamor of his wife, was to take gun in hand and stroll away into the woods. Here he would sometimes seat himself at the foot of a tree, and share the contents of his wallet with Wolf, with whom

---

[3]A group brought together by a common purpose.

he sympathized as a fellow-sufferer in persecution. "Poor Wolf," he would say, "thy mistress leads thee a dog's life of it, but never mind, my lad, whilst I live thou shalt never want a friend to stand by thee!" Wolf would wag his tail, look wistfully in his master's face, and if dogs can feel pity, I verily believe he reciprocated the sentiment with all his heart.

In a long ramble of the kind on a fine autumnal day, Rip had unconsciously scrambled to one of the highest parts of the Kaatskill mountains. He was after his favorite sport of squirrel-shooting, and the still solitudes had echoed and reechoed with the reports of his gun. Panting and fatigued, he threw himself, late in the afternoon, on a green knoll, covered with mountain herbage, that crowned the brow of a precipice. From an opening between the trees he could overlook all the lower country for many a mile of rich woodland. He saw at a distance the lordly Hudson, far, far below him, moving on its silent but majestic course, with the reflection of a purple cloud, or the sail of a lagging bark, here and there sleeping on its glassy bosom, and at last losing itself in the blue highlands.

On the other side he looked down into a deep mountain glen, wild, lonely, and shagged, the bottom filled with fragments from the impending cliffs, and scarcely lighted by the reflected rays of the setting sun. For some time Rip lay musing on this scene; evening was gradually advancing; the mountains began to throw their long blue shadows over the valleys; he saw that it would be dark long before he could reach the village, and he heaved a heavy sigh when he thought of encountering the terrors of Dame Van Winkle.

As he was about to descend, he heard a voice from a distance, hallooing, "Rip Van Winkle, Rip Van Winkle!" He looked around, but could see nothing but a crow winging its solitary flight across the mountain. He thought his fancy must have deceived him, and turned again to descend, when he heard the same cry ring through the still evening air: "Rip Van Winkle! Rip Van Winkle!"—at the same time Wolf bristled up his back, and giving a low growl, skulked to his master's side, looking fearfully down into the glen. Rip now felt a vague apprehension stealing over him; he looked anxiously in the same direction, and perceived a strange figure slowly toiling up the rocks, and bending under the weight of something he carried on his back. He was surprised to see any human being in this lonely and unfrequented place; but supposing it to be some one of the neighborhood in need of his assistance, he hastened down to yield it.

On nearer approach he was still more surprised at the singularity of the stranger's appearance. He was a short, square-built old fellow, with thick bushy hair, and a grizzled beard. His dress was of the antique Dutch fashion—a cloth jerkin strapped around the waist—several pair of breeches, the outer one of ample volume, decorated with rows of buttons down the sides, and bunches at the knees. He bore on his shoulders a stout keg, that seemed full of liquor, and made signs for Rip to approach and assist him with the load. Though rather shy and distrustful of this new acquaintance, Rip complied with his usual alacrity; and mutually relieving one another, they clambered up a narrow gully, apparently the dry bed of a mountain torrent. As they ascended, Rip every now and then heard long, rolling peals, like distant thunder, that seemed to issue out of a deep ravine, or rather cleft, between lofty rocks, toward which their rugged path conducted. He paused for an instant, but supposing it to be the muttering of one of those transient thunder-showers which often take place in mountain heights, he proceeded. Passing through the ravine, they came to a hollow, like a small amphitheatre, surrounded by perpendicular precipices, over the brinks of which impending trees shot their branches, so that you only caught glimpses of the azure sky and the bright evening cloud. During the whole time Rip and his companion had labored on in silence; for though the former marvelled greatly what could be the object of carrying a keg of liquor up this wild mountain, yet there was something strange and incomprehensible about the unknown, that inspired awe and checked familiarity.

On entering the amphitheatre, new objects of wonder presented themselves. On a level spot in the centre was a company of odd-looking personages playing at ninepins. They were dressed in a quaint, outlandish fashion; some wore short doublets, others jerkins, with long knives in their belts, and most of them had enormous breeches, of similar style with that of the guide's. Their visages, too, were peculiar: one had a large beard, broad face, and small piggish eyes; the face of another seemed to consist entirely of nose, and was surmounted by a white sugar-loaf hat, set off with a little red cock's tail. They all had beards, of various shapes and colors. There was one who seemed to be the commander. He was a stout old gentleman, with a weather-beaten countenance; he wore a laced doublet, broad belt and hanger, high crowned hat and feather, red stockings, and high-heeled shoes, with roses in them. The whole group reminded Rip of the figures in an old Flemish painting, in the parlor of Dominie Van Shaick, the village parson, and which had been brought over from Holland at the time of the settlement.

What seemed particularly odd to Rip was, that, though these folks were evidently amusing themselves, yet they maintained the gravest faces, the most mysterious silence, and were, withal, the most melancholy party of pleasure he had ever witnessed. Nothing interrupted the stillness of the scene but the noise of the balls, which, whenever they rolled, echoed along the mountains like rumbling peals of thunder.

As Rip and his companion approached them, they suddenly desisted from their play, and stared at him with such fixed, statue-like gaze, and such strange, uncouth, lack-lustre countenances, that his heart turned within him, and his knees smote together. His companion now emptied the contents of the keg into large flagons, and made signs to him to wait upon the company. He obeyed with fear and trembling; they quaffed the liquor in profound silence, and then returned to their game.

By degrees Rip's awe and apprehension subsided. He even ventured, when no eye was fixed upon him, to taste the beverage, which he found had much of the flavor of excellent Hollands. He was naturally a thirsty soul, and was soon tempted to repeat the draught. One taste provoked another; and he reiterated his visits to the flagon so often that at length his senses were overpowered, his eyes swam in his head, his head gradually declined, and he fell into a deep sleep.

On waking, he found himself on the green knoll whence he had first seen the old man of the glen. He rubbed his eyes — it was a bright sunny morning.

The birds were hopping and twittering among the bushes, and the eagle was wheeling aloft, and breasting the pure mountain breeze. "Surely," thought Rip, "I have not slept here all night." He recalled the occurrences before he fell asleep. The strange man with a keg of liquor—the mountain ravine—the wild retreat among the rocks—the woe-begone party at ninepins—the flagon—"Oh! that flagon! that wicked flagon!" thought Rip, "what excuse shall I make to Dame Van Winkle?"

He looked round for his gun, but in place of the clean, well-oiled fowling-piece, he found an old firelock lying by him, the barrel encrusted with rust, the lock falling off, and the stock worm-eaten. He now suspected that the grave roisters of the mountains had put a trick upon him, and, having dosed him with liquor, had robbed him of his gun. Wolf, too, had disappeared, but he might have strayed away after a squirrel or partridge. He whistled after him, and shouted his name, but all in vain; the echoes repeated his whistle and shout, but no dog was to be seen.

He determined to revisit the scene of the last evening's gambol, and if he met with any of the party, to demand his dog and gun. As he rose to walk, he found himself stiff in the joints, and wanting in his usual activity. "These mountain beds do not agree with me," thought Rip, "and if this frolic should lay me up with a fit of the rheumatism, I shall have a blessed time with Dame Van Winkle." With some difficulty he got down into the glen: he found the gully up which he and his companion had ascended the preceding evening; but to his astonishment a mountain stream was now foaming down it, leaping from rock to rock, and filling the glen with babbling murmurs. He, however, made shift to scramble up its sides, working his toilsome way through thickets of birch, sassafras, and witch-hazel, and sometimes tripped up or entangled by the wild grape-vines that twisted their coils or tendrils from tree to tree, and spread a kind of network in his path.

At length he reached to where the ravine had opened through the cliffs to the amphitheatre; but no traces of such opening remained. The rocks presented a high, impenetrable wall, over which the torrent came tumbling in a sheet of feathery foam, and fell into a broad deep basin, black from the shadows of the surrounding forest. Here, then, poor Rip was brought to a stand. He again called and whistled after his dog; he was only answered by the cawing of a flock of idle crows, sporting high in air about a dry tree that overhung a sunny precipice; and who, secure in their elevation, seemed to look down and scoff at the poor man's perplexities. What was to be done? the morning was passing away, and Rip felt famished for want of his breakfast. He grieved to give up his dog and gun; he dreaded to meet his wife; but it would not do to starve among the mountains. He shook his head, shouldered the rusty firelock, and, with a heart full of trouble and anxiety, turned his footsteps homeward.

As he approached the village he met a number of people, but none whom he knew, which somewhat surprised him, for he had thought himself acquainted with every one in the country round. Their dress, too, was of a different fashion from that to which he was accustomed. They all stared at him with equal marks of surprise, and whenever they cast their eyes upon him, invariably stroked their chins. The constant recurrence of this gesture induced Rip, involuntarily, to do the same, when, to his astonishment, he found his beard had grown a foot long!

He had now entered the skirts of the village. A troop of strange children ran at his heels, hooting after him, and pointing at his gray beard. The dogs, too, not one of which he recognized for an old acquaintance, barked at him as he passed. The very village was altered; it was larger and more populous. There were rows of houses which he had never seen before, and those which had been his familiar haunts had disappeared. Strange names were over the doors — strange faces at the windows — everything was strange. His mind now misgave him; he began to doubt whether both he and the world around him were not bewitched. Surely this was his native village, which he had left but the day before. There stood the Kaatskill mountains — there ran the silver Hudson at a distance — there was every hill and dale precisely as it had always been. Rip was sorely perplexed. "That flagon last night," thought he, "has addled my poor head sadly!"

It was with some difficulty that he found the way to his own house, which he approached with silent awe, expecting every moment to hear the shrill voice of Dame Van Winkle. He found the house gone to decay — the roof fallen in, the windows shattered, and the doors off the hinges. A half-starved dog that looked like Wolf was skulking about it. Rip called him by name, but the cur snarled, showed his teeth, and passed on. This was an unkind cut indeed. "My very dog," sighed poor Rip, "has forgotten me!"

He entered the house, which to tell the truth, Dame Van Winkle had always kept in neat order. It was empty, forlorn, and apparently abandoned. This desolateness overcame all his connubial fears — he called loudly for his wife and children — the lonely chambers rang for a moment with his voice, and then all again was silence.

He now hurried forth, and hastened to his old resort, the village inn, but it too was gone. A large rickety wooden building stood in its place, with great gaping windows, some of them broken and mended with old hats and petticoats, and over the door was painted, "The Union Hotel, by Jonathan Doolittle." Instead of the great tree that used to shelter the quiet little Dutch inn of yore, there now was reared a tall naked pole, with something on top that looked like a red night-cap, and from it was fluttering a flag, on which was a singular assemblage of stars and stripes — all this was strange and incomprehensible. He recognized on the sign, however, the ruby face of King George, under which he had smoked so many a peaceful pipe; but even this was singularly metamorphosed. The red coat was changed for one of blue and buff, a sword was held in the hand instead of a sceptre, the head was decorated with a cocked hat, and underneath was painted in large characters, GENERAL WASHINGTON.

There was, as usual, a crowd of folk about the door, but none that Rip recollected. The very character of the people seemed changed. There was a busy, bustling, disputatious tone about it, instead of the accustomed phlegm and drowsy tranquillity. He looked in vain for the sage Nicholas Vedder, with his broad face, double chin, and fair long pipe, uttering clouds of tobacco-smoke instead of idle speeches; or Van Bummel, the schoolmaster, doling forth the contents of an ancient newspaper. In place of these, a lean, bilious-looking fellow, with his pockets full of handbills, was haranguing vehemently about rights of citizens — elections — members of congress — liberty — Bunker's Hill — heroes of seventy-six — and other words, which were a perfect Babylonish jargon to the bewildered Van Winkle.

The appearance of Rip, with his long, grizzled beard, his rusty fowling-piece, his uncouth dress, and an army of women and children at his heels, soon attracted the attention of the tavern-politicians. They crowded round him, eyeing him from head to foot with great curiosity. The orator bustled up to him, and, drawing him partly aside, inquired "On which side he voted?" Rip stared in vacant stupidity. Another short but busy little fellow pulled him by the arm, and, rising on tiptoe, inquired in his ear, "Whether he was Federal or Democrat?" Rip was equally at a loss to comprehend the question; when a knowing, self-important old gentleman, in a sharp cocked hat, made his way through the crowd, putting them to the right and left with his elbows as he passed, and planting himself before Van Winkle, with one arm akimbo, the other resting on his cane, his keen eyes and sharp hat penetrating, as it were, into his very soul, demanded in an austere tone, "What brought him to the election with a gun on his shoulder, and a mob at his heels; and whether he meant to breed a riot in the village?" — "Alas! gentlemen," cried Rip, somewhat dismayed, "I am a poor quiet man, a native of the place, and a loyal subject of the King, God bless him!"

Here a general shout burst from the by-standers — "A tory! a tory! a spy! a refugee! hustle him! away with him!" It was with great difficulty that the self-important man in the cocked hat restored order; and, having assumed a ten-fold austerity of brow, demanded again of the unknown culprit, what he came there for, and whom he was seeking? The poor man humbly assured him that he meant no harm, but merely came there in search of some of his neighbors, who used to keep about the tavern.

"Well — who are they? — name them."

Rip bethought himself a moment, and inquired, "Where's Nicholas Vedder?"

There was a silence for a little while, when an old man replied, in a thin piping voice, "Nicholas Vedder! why, he is dead and gone these eighteen years! There was a wooden tombstone in that churchyard that used to tell all about him, but that's rotten and gone too."

"Where's Brom Dutcher?"

"Oh, he went off to the army in the beginning of the war; some say he was killed at the storming of Stony Point — others say he was drowned in a squall at the foot of Antony's Nose. I don't know — he never came back again."

"Where's Van Bummel, the schoolmaster?"

"He went off to the wars too, was a great militia general, and is now in congress."

Rip's heart died away at hearing of these sad changes in his home and friends, and finding himself thus alone in the world. Every answer puzzled him too, by treating of such enormous lapses of time, and of matters which he could not understand: war — congress — Stony Point — he had no courage to ask after any more friends, but cried out in despair, "Does nobody here know Rip Van Winkle?"

"Oh, Rip Van Winkle!" exclaimed two or three. "Oh, to be sure! that's Rip Van Winkle yonder, leaning against the tree."

Rip looked, and he beheld a precise counterpart of himself, as he went up the mountain; apparently as lazy, and certainly as ragged. The poor fellow was now completely confounded. He doubted his own identity, and whether he was himself or another man. In the midst of his bewilderment, the man in the cocked hat demanded who he was, and what was his name.

"God knows," exclaimed he, at his wit's end; "I'm not myself — I'm somebody else — that's me yonder — no — that's somebody else got into my shoes — I was myself last night, but I fell asleep on the mountain, and they've changed my gun, and everything's changed, and I'm changed, and I can't tell what's my name, or who I am!"

The by-standers began now to look at each other, nod, wink significantly, and tap their fingers against their foreheads. There was a whisper, also, about securing the gun, and keeping the old fellow from doing mischief, at the very suggestion of which the self-important man in the cocked hat retired with some precipitation. At this critical moment a fresh, comely woman pressed through the throng to get a peep at the gray-bearded man. She had a chubby child in her arms, which, frightened at his looks, began to cry. "Hush, Rip," cried she, "hush, you little fool; the old man won't hurt you." The name of the child, the air of the mother, the tone of her voice, all awakened a train of recollections in his mind. "What is your name, my good woman?" asked he.

"Judith Gardenier."

"And your father's name?"

"Ah, poor man, Rip Van Winkle was his name, but it's twenty years since he went away from home with his gun, and never has been heard of since — his dog came home without him; but whether he shot himself, or was carried away by the Indians, nobody can tell. I was then but a little girl."

Rip had but one question more to ask; but he put it with a faltering voice:

"Where's your mother?"

"Oh, she too died but a short time since; she broke a blood vessel in a fit of passion at a New England peddler."

There was a drop of comfort, at least, in this intelligence. The honest man could contain himself no longer. He caught his daughter and her child in his arms. "I am your father!" cried he — "Young Rip Van Winkle once — old Rip Van Winkle now! — Does nobody know poor Rip Van Winkle?"

All stood amazed, until an old woman, tottering out from among the crowd, put her hand to her brow, and peering under it in his face for a moment, exclaimed, "Sure enough! it is Rip Van Winkle — it is himself! Welcome home again, old neighbor. Why, where have you been these twenty long years?"

Rip's story was soon told, for the whole twenty years had been to him but as one night. The neighbors stared when they heard it; some were seen to wink at each other, and put their tongues in their cheeks: and the self-important man in the cocked hat, who, when the alarm was over, had returned to the field, screwed down the corners of his mouth, and shook his head — upon which there was a general shaking of the head throughout the assemblage.

It was determined, however, to take the opinion of old Peter Vanderdonk, who was seen slowly advancing up the road. He was a descendant of the historian of that name, who wrote one of the earliest accounts of the province. Peter was the most ancient inhabitant of the village, and well versed in all the wonderful events and traditions of the neighborhood. He recollected Rip at once, and corroborated his story in the most satisfactory manner. He assured the company that it was a fact, handed down from his ancestor the historian, that the Kaatskill mountains had always been haunted by strange beings. That it was affirmed that the great Hendrick Hudson, the first discoverer of the river and country, kept a kind of vigil there every twenty years, with his crew of the *Half-moon*; being permitted in this way to revisit the scenes of his enterprise, and keep a guardian eye upon the river and the great city called by his name. That his father had once seen them in their old Dutch dresses playing at nine-pins in a hollow of the mountain; and that he himself had heard, one summer afternoon, the sound of their balls, like distant peals of thunder.

To make a long story short, the company broke up and returned to the more important concerns of the election. Rip's daughter took him home to live with her; she had a snug, well-furnished house, and a stout, cheery farmer for a husband, whom Rip recollected for one of the urchins that used to climb upon his back. As to Rip's son and heir, who was the ditto of himself, seen leaning against the tree, he was employed to work on the farm; but evinced an hereditary disposition to attend to anything else but his business.

Rip now resumed his old walks and habits; he soon found many of his former cronies, though all rather the worse for the wear and tear of time; and preferred making friends among the rising generation, with whom he soon grew into great favor.

Having nothing to do at home, and being arrived at that happy age when a man can be idle with impunity, he took his place once more on the bench at the inn-door, and was reverenced as one of the patriarchs of the village, and a chronicle of the old times "before the war." It was some time before he could get into the regular track of gossip, or could be made to comprehend the strange events that had taken place during his torpor. How that there had been a revolutionary war — that the country had thrown off the yoke of old England — and that, instead of being a subject of his Majesty George the Third, he was now a free citizen of the United States. Rip, in fact, was no politician; the changes of states and empires made but little impression to him; but there was one species of despotism under which he long groaned, and that was — petticoat government. Happily that was at an end; he had got his neck out of the yoke of matrimony, and could go in and out whenever he pleased, without dreading the tyranny of Dame Van Winkle. Whenever her name was mentioned, however, he shook his head, shrugged his shoulders, and cast up his eyes; which might pass either for an expression of resignation to his fate, or joy at his deliverance.

He used to tell his story to every stranger that arrived at Mr. Doolittle's hotel. He was observed, at first, to vary on some points every time he told it, which was, doubtless, owing to his having so recently awaked. It at last settled down precisely to the tale I have related, and not a man, woman, or child in the neighborhood but knew it by heart. Some always pretended to doubt the reality of it, and insisted that Rip had been out of his head, and that this was one point on which he always remained flighty. The old Dutch inhabitants, however, almost universally gave it full credit. Even to this day they never hear a thunderstorm of a summer afternoon about the Kaatskill, but they say Hendrick Hudson and his crew are at their game of ninepins; and it is a common wish of all hen-pecked husbands in the neighborhood, when life hangs heavy on their hands, that they might have a quieting draught out of Rip Van Winkle's flagon.

Note
The foregoing Tale, one would suspect, had been suggested to Mr. Knickerbocker by a little German superstition about the Emperor Frederick *der Rothbart*, and the Kypphäuser mountain: the subjoined note, however, which he had appended to the tale, shows that it is an absolute fact, narrated with his usual fidelity.

"The story of Rip Van Winkle may seem incredible to many, but nevertheless I give it my full belief, for I know the vicinity of our old Dutch settlements to have been very subject to marvellous events and appearances. Indeed, I have heard many stranger stories than this, in the villages along the Hudson; all of which were too well authenticated to admit of a doubt. I have even talked with Rip Van Winkle myself, who, when last I saw him, was a very venerable old man, and so perfectly rational and consistent on every other point, that I think no conscientious person could refuse to take this into the bargain; nay, I have seen a certificate on the subject taken before a country justice and signed with a cross, in the justice's own handwriting. The story, therefore, is beyond the possibility of doubt." — "D.K."

Shirley Jackson

Shirley Jackson (1919–1965) was born in San Francisco, California, her mother a housewife and her father an employee of a lithographing company. Most of her early life was spent in Burlingame, California, which she later used as the setting for her first novel, *The Road Through the Wall* (1948). As a child she was interested in writing; she won a poetry prize at age twelve, and in high school she began keeping a diary to record her writing progress. After high school she briefly attended the University of Rochester but left because of an attack of the mental depression that was to recur periodically in her later years. She recovered her health by living quietly at home and writing, conscientiously turning out 1,000 words of prose a day. In 1937 she entered Syracuse University, where she published stories in the student literary magazine. There she met Stanley Edgar Hyman, who was to become a noted literary critic. They were married in 1940, the year she received her degree. They had four children while both continued active literary careers, settling to raise their family in a large Victorian house in Vermont, where Hyman taught literature at Bennington College.

Jackson's first national publication was a humorous story written after a job at a department store during the Christmas rush: "My Life with R. H. Macy" appeared in *The New Republic* in 1941. Her first child was born the next year, but she wrote every day on a disciplined schedule, selling her stories to magazines and publishing three novels. She refused to take herself too seriously as a writer: "I can't persuade myself that writing is honest work. It is a very personal reaction, but 50 percent of my life is spent washing and dressing the children, cooking, washing dishes and clothes, and mending. After I get it all to bed, I turn around to my typewriter and try to—well, to create concrete things again. It's great fun, and I love it. But it doesn't tie any shoes."

Jackson's best-known work, "The Lottery," is often anthologized, dramatized, and televised. She regarded it as a tale in the sense that Nathaniel Hawthorne used the term—a moral allegory revealing the hidden evil in the human soul. She wrote later that "explaining just what I had hoped the story to say is very difficult. I supposed, I hoped, by setting a particularly brutal ancient rite in the present and in my own village, to shock the story's readers with a graphic dramatization of the pointless violence and general inhumanity in their own lives." *Just an Ordinary Day: The Uncollected Stories of Shirley Jackson* was published in 1997.

RELATED COMMENTARY

Shirley Jackson, "The Morning of June 28, 1948, and 'The Lottery,'" page 1443.

The Lottery

1948

THE MORNING OF JUNE 27TH was clear and sunny, with the fresh warmth of a full-summer day; the flowers were blossoming profusely and the grass was richly green. The people of the village began to gather in the square, between the post office and the bank, around ten o'clock; in some towns there were so many people that the lottery took two days and had to be started on June 26th, but in this village, where there were only about three hundred people, the whole lottery took less than two hours, so it could begin at ten o'clock in the morning and still be through in time to allow the villagers to get home for noon dinner.

The children assembled first, of course. School was recently over for the summer, and the feeling of liberty sat uneasily on most of them; they tended to gather together quietly for a while before they broke into boisterous play, and their talk was still of the classroom and teacher, of books and reprimands. Bobby Martin had already stuffed his pockets full of stones, and the other boys soon followed his example, selecting the smoothest and roundest stones; Bobby and Harry Jones and Dickie Delacroix—the villagers pronounced this name "Dellacroy"—eventually made a great pile of stones in one corner of the square and guarded it against the raids of the other boys. The girls stood aside, talking among themselves, looking over their shoulders at the boys, and the very small children rolled in the dust or clung to the hands of their older brothers or sisters.

Soon the men began to gather, surveying their own children, speaking of planting and rain, tractors and taxes. They stood together, away from the pile of stones in the corner, and their jokes were quiet and they smiled rather than laughed. The women, wearing faded house dresses and sweaters, came shortly after their menfolk. They greeted one another and exchanged bits of gossip as they went to join their husbands. Soon the women, standing by their husbands, began to call to their children, and the children came reluctantly, having to be called four or five times. Bobby Martin ducked under his mother's grasping hand and ran, laughing, back to the pile of stones. His father spoke up sharply, and Bobby came quickly and took his place between his father and his oldest brother.

The lottery was conducted—as were the square dances, the teen-age club, the Halloween program—by Mr. Summers, who had time and energy to devote to civic activities. He was a round-faced, jovial man and he ran the coal business, and people were sorry for him, because he had no children and his wife was a scold. When he arrived in the square, carrying the black wooden box, there was a murmur of conversation among the villagers, and he waved and called, "Little late today, folks." The postmaster, Mr. Graves, followed him, carrying a three-legged stool, and the stool was put in the center of the square and Mr. Summers set the black box down on it. The villagers kept their distance, leaving a space between themselves and the stool, and when Mr. Summers said, "Some of you fellows want to give me a hand?" there was a hesitation before two men, Mr. Martin and his oldest son, Baxter, came forward to hold the box steady on the stool while Mr. Summers stirred up the papers inside it.

The original paraphernalia for the lottery had been lost long ago, and the black box now resting on the stool had been put into use even before Old Man Warner, the oldest man in town, was born. Mr. Summers spoke frequently to the villagers about making a new box, but no one liked to upset even as much tradition as was represented by the black box. There was a story that the present box had been made with some pieces of the box that had preceded it, the one that had been constructed when the first people settled down to make a village here. Every year, after the lottery, Mr. Summers began talking again about a new box, but every year the subject was allowed to fade off without anything's being done. The black box grew shabbier each year; by now it was no longer completely black but splintered badly along one side to show the original wood color, and in some places faded or stained.

Mr. Martin and his oldest son, Baxter, held the black box securely on the stool until Mr. Summers had stirred the papers thoroughly with his hand. Because so much of the ritual had been forgotten or discarded, Mr. Summers had been successful in having slips of paper substituted for the chips of wood that had been used for generations. Chips of wood, Mr. Summers had argued, had been all very well when the village was tiny, but now that the population was more than three hundred and likely to keep on growing, it was necessary to use something that would fit more easily into the black box. The night before the lottery, Mr. Summers and Mr. Graves made up the slips of paper and put them in the box, and it was then taken to the safe of Mr. Summers's coal company and locked up until Mr. Summers was ready to take it to the square next morning. The rest of the year, the box was put away, sometimes one place, sometimes another; it had spent one year in Mr. Graves's barn and another year underfoot in the post office, and sometimes it was set on a shelf in the Martin grocery and left there.

There was a great deal of fussing to be done before Mr. Summers declared the lottery open. There were the lists to make up — of heads of families, heads of households in each family, members of each household in each family. There was the proper swearing-in of Mr. Summers by the postmaster, as the official of the lottery; at one time, some people remembered, there had been a recital of some sort, performed by the official of the lottery, a perfunctory, tuneless chant that had been rattled off duly each year; some people believed that the official of the lottery used to stand just so when he said or sang it, others believed that he was supposed to walk among the people, but years and years ago this part of the ritual had been allowed to lapse. There had been, also, a ritual salute, which the official of the lottery had had to use in addressing each person who came up to draw from the box, but this also had changed with time, until now it was felt necessary only for the official to speak to each person approaching. Mr. Summers was very good at all this; in his clean white shirt and blue jeans, with one hand resting carelessly on the black box, he seemed very proper and important as he talked interminably to Mr. Graves and the Martins.

Just as Mr. Summers finally left off talking and turned to the assembled villagers, Mrs. Hutchinson came hurriedly along the path to the square, her sweater thrown over her shoulders, and slid into place in the back of the crowd. "Clean forgot what day it was," she said to Mrs. Delacroix, who stood next to her, and they both laughed softly. "Thought my old man was out back stacking wood," Mrs. Hutchinson went on, "and then I looked out the window and the kids was gone, and then I remembered it was the twenty-seventh and came a-running." She dried her hands on her apron, and Mrs. Delacroix said, "You're in time, though. They're still talking away up there."

Mrs. Hutchinson craned her neck to see through the crowd and found her husband and children standing near the front. She tapped Mrs. Delacroix on the arm as a farewell and began to make her way through the crowd. The people separated good-humoredly to let her through; two or three people said, in voices just loud enough to be heard across the crowd, "Here comes your Missus, Hutchinson," and "Bill, she made it after all." Mrs. Hutchinson reached her husband, and Mr. Summers, who had been waiting, said cheerfully, "Thought we were going to have to get on without you, Tessie." Mrs. Hutchinson said, grinning, "Wouldn't have me leave m'dishes in the sink, now, would you, Joe?" and soft laughter ran through the crowd as the people stirred back into position after Mrs. Hutchinson's arrival.

"Well, now," Mr. Summers said soberly, "guess we better get started, get this over with, so's we can go back to work. Anybody ain't here?"

"Dunbar," several people said. "Dunbar, Dunbar."

Mr. Summers consulted his list. "Clyde Dunbar," he said. "That's right. He's broke his leg, hasn't he? Who's drawing for him?"

"Me, I guess," a woman said, and Mr. Summers turned to look at her. "Wife draws for her husband," Mr. Summers said. "Don't you have a grown boy to do it for you, Janey?" Although Mr. Summers and everyone else in the village knew the answer perfectly well, it was the business of the official of the lottery to ask such questions formally. Mr. Summers waited with an expression of polite interest while Mrs. Dunbar answered.

"Horace's not but sixteen yet," Mrs. Dunbar said regretfully. "Guess I gotta fill in for the old man this year."

"Right," Mr. Summers said. He made a note on the list he was holding. Then he asked, "Watson boy drawing this year?"

A tall boy in the crowd raised his hand. "Here," he said. "I'm drawing for m'mother and me." He blinked his eyes nervously and ducked his head as several voices in the crowd said things like "Good fellow, Jack," and "Glad to see your mother's got a man to do it."

"Well," Mr. Summers said, "guess that's everyone. Old Man Warner make it?"

"Here," a voice said, and Mr. Summers nodded.

A sudden hush fell on the crowd as Mr. Summers cleared his throat and looked at the list. "All ready?" he called. "Now, I'll read the names — heads of families first — and the men come up and take a paper out of the box. Keep the paper folded in your hand without looking at it until everyone has had a turn. Everything clear?"

The people had done it so many times that they only half listened to the directions; most of them were quiet, wetting their lips, not looking around. Then Mr. Summers raised one hand high and said, "Adams." A man disengaged himself from the crowd and came forward. "Hi, Steve," Mr. Summers said, and Mr. Adams said, "Hi, Joe." They grinned at one another humorlessly and nervously. Then Mr. Adams reached into the black box and took out a folded paper. He held it firmly by one corner as he turned and went hastily back to his place in the crowd, where he stood a little apart from his family, not looking down at his hand.

"Allen," Mr. Summers said, "Anderson.... Bentham."

"Seems like there's no time at all between lotteries any more," Mrs. Delacroix said to Mrs. Graves in the back row. "Seems like we got through with the last one only last week."

"Time sure goes fast," Mrs. Graves said.

"Clark.... Delacroix."

"There goes my old man," Mrs. Delacroix said. She held her breath while her husband went forward.

"Dunbar," Mr. Summers said, and Mrs. Dunbar went steadily to the box while one of the women said, "Go on, Janey," and another said, "There she goes."

"We're next," Mrs. Graves said. She watched while Mr. Graves came around from the side of the box, greeted Mr. Summers gravely, and selected a slip of paper from the box. By now, all through the crowd there were men holding the small folded papers in their large hands, turning them over and over nervously. Mrs. Dunbar and her two sons stood together, Mrs. Dunbar holding the slip of paper.

"Harburt.... Hutchinson."

"Get up there, Bill," Mrs. Hutchinson said, and the people near her laughed.

"Jones."

"They do say," Mr. Adams said to Old Man Warner, who stood next to him, "that over in the north village they're talking of giving up the lottery."

Old Man Warner snorted. "Pack of crazy fools," he said. "Listening to the young folks, nothing's good enough for *them*. Next thing you know, they'll be wanting to go back to living in caves, nobody work any more, live *that* way for a while. Used to be a saying about 'Lottery in June, corn be heavy soon.' First thing you know, we'd all be eating stewed chickweed and acorns. There's *always* been a lottery," he added petulantly. "Bad enough to see young Joe Summers up there joking with everybody."

"Some places have already quit lotteries," Mrs. Adams said.

"Nothing but trouble in *that*," Old Man Warner said stoutly. "Pack of young fools."

"Martin." And Bobby Martin watched his father go forward. "Overdyke.... Percy."

"I wish they'd hurry," Mrs. Dunbar said to her older son. "I wish they'd hurry."

"They're almost through," her son said.

"You get ready to run tell Dad," Mrs. Dunbar said.

Mr. Summers called his own name and then stepped forward precisely and selected a slip from the box. Then he called, "Warner."

"Seventy-seventh year I been in the lottery," Old Man Warner said as he went through the crowd. "Seventy-seventh time."

"Watson." The tall boy came awkwardly through the crowd. Someone said, "Don't be nervous, Jack," and Mr. Summers said, "Take your time, son."

"Zanini."

After that, there was a long pause, a breathless pause, until Mr. Summers, holding his slip of paper in the air, said, "All right, fellows." For a minute, no one moved, and then all the slips of paper were opened. Suddenly, all the women began to speak at once, saying, "Who is it?" "Who's got it?" "Is it the Dunbars?" "Is it the Watsons?" Then the voices began to say, "It's Hutchinson. It's Bill," "Bill Hutchinson's got it."

"Go tell your father," Mrs. Dunbar said to her older son.

People began to look around to see the Hutchinsons. Bill Hutchinson was standing quiet, staring down at the paper in his hand. Suddenly, Tessie Hutchinson shouted to Mr. Summers, "You didn't give him time enough to take any paper he wanted. I saw you. It wasn't fair!"

"Be a good sport, Tessie," Mrs. Delacroix called, and Mrs. Graves said, "All of us took the same chance."

"Shut up, Tessie," Bill Hutchinson said.

"Well, everyone," Mr. Summers said, "that was done pretty fast, and now we've got to be hurrying a little more to get done in time." He consulted his next list. "Bill," he said, "you draw for the Hutchinson family. You got any other households in the Hutchinsons?"

"There's Don and Eva," Mrs. Hutchinson yelled. "Make *them* take their chance!"

"Daughters drew with their husbands' families, Tessie," Mr. Summers said gently. "You know that as well as anyone else."

"It wasn't *fair*," Tessie said.

"I guess not, Joe," Bill Hutchinson said regretfully. "My daughter draws with her husband's family, that's only fair. And I've got no other family except the kids."

"Then, as far as drawing for families is concerned, it's you," Mr. Summers said in explanation, "and as far as drawing for households is concerned, that's you, too. Right?"

"Right," Bill Hutchinson said.

"How many kids, Bill?" Mr. Summers asked formally.

"Three," Bill Hutchinson said. "There's Bill, Jr., and Nancy, and little Dave. And Tessie and me."

"All right, then," Mr. Summers said. "Harry, you got their tickets back?"

Mr. Graves nodded and held up the slips of paper. "Put them in the box, then," Mr. Summers directed. "Take Bill's and put it in."

"I think we ought to start over," Mrs. Hutchinson said, as quietly as she could. "I tell you it wasn't *fair*. You didn't give him time enough to choose. *Every*body saw that."

Mr. Graves had selected the five slips and put them in the box, and he dropped all the papers but those onto the ground, where the breeze caught them and lifted them off.

"Listen, everybody," Mrs. Hutchinson was saying to the people around her.

"Ready, Bill?" Mr. Summers asked, and Bill Hutchinson, with one quick glance around at his wife and children, nodded.

"Remember," Mr. Summers said, "take the slips and keep them folded until each person has taken one. Harry, you help little Dave." Mr. Graves took the hand of the little boy, who came willingly with him up to the box. "Take a paper out of the box, Davy," Mr. Summers said. Davy put his hand into the box and laughed. "Take just *one* paper," Mr. Summers said. "Harry, you hold it for him." Mr. Graves took the child's hand and removed the folded paper from the tight fist and held it while little Dave stood next to him and looked up at him wonderingly.

"Nancy next," Mr. Summers said. Nancy was twelve, and her school friends breathed heavily as she went forward, switching her skirt, and took a slip daintily from the box. "Bill, Jr.," Mr. Summers said, and Billy, his face red and his feet overlarge, nearly knocked the box over as he got a paper out. "Tessie," Mr. Summers said. She hesitated for a minute, looking around defiantly, and then set her lips and went up to the box. She snatched a paper out and held it behind her.

"Bill," Mr. Summers said, and Bill Hutchinson reached into the box and felt around, bringing his hand out at last with the slip of paper in it.

The crowd was quiet. A girl whispered, "I hope it's not Nancy," and the sound of the whisper reached the edges of the crowd.

"It's not the way it used to be," Old Man Warner said clearly. "People ain't the way they used to be."

"All right," Mr. Summers said. "Open the papers. Harry, you open little Dave's."

Mr. Graves opened the slip of paper and there was a general sigh through the crowd as he held it up and everyone could see that it was blank. Nancy and Bill, Jr., opened theirs at the same time, and both beamed and laughed, turning around to the crowd and holding their slips of paper above their heads.

"Tessie," Mr. Summers said. There was a pause, and then Mr. Summers looked at Bill Hutchinson, and Bill unfolded his paper and showed it. It was blank.

"It's Tessie," Mr. Summers said, and his voice was hushed. "Show us her paper, Bill."

Bill Hutchinson went over to his wife and forced the slip of paper out of her hand. It had a black spot on it, the black spot Mr. Summers had made the night before with the heavy pencil in the coal-company office. Bill Hutchinson held it up and there was a stir in the crowd.

"All right, folks," Mr. Summers said. "Let's finish quickly."

Although the villagers had forgotten the ritual and lost the original black box, they still remembered to use stones. The pile of stones the boys had made earlier was ready; there were stones on the ground with the blowing scraps of paper that had come out of the box. Mrs. Delacroix selected a stone so large she had to pick it up with both hands and turned to Mrs. Dunbar. "Come on," she said. "Hurry up."

Mrs. Dunbar had small stones in both hands, and she said, gasping for breath, "I can't run at all. You'll have to go ahead and I'll catch up with you."

The children had stones already, and someone gave little Davy Hutchinson a few pebbles.

Tessie Hutchinson was in the center of a cleared space by now, and she held her hands out desperately as the villagers moved in on her. "It isn't fair," she said. A stone hit her on the side of the head.

Old Man Warner was saying, "Come on, come on, everyone." Steve Adams was in the front of the crowd of villagers, with Mrs. Graves beside him.

"It isn't fair, it isn't right," Mrs. Hutchinson screamed and then they were upon her.

Henry James

Henry James (1843–1916) was born in New York City. His father was a religious philosopher, and his brother William James was a noted physician, philosopher, and psychologist. Educated mostly by tutors in the United States and Europe, James published his first story at the age of twenty-one. In 1875 he chose to live permanently in England. He formed friendships with several European writers, including Gustave Flaubert and Guy de Maupassant. During the first phase of James's long career, he explored personal relationships, most notably in the novel *The Portrait of a Lady* (1881). Then he turned to themes of social reform, as in *The Bostonians* (1886). He constantly experimented with ways to refine his writing and commented on his "art of fiction" in many essays, prefaces, letters, and notebooks. The dense, symbolic style of his later work whose fundamental theme is the innocence and exuberance of the New World clashing with the experience and corruption of the Old, can be seen in his three last novels, *The Wings of the Dove* (1902), *The Ambassadors* (1903), and *The Golden Bowl* (1904).

In his lifetime James wrote more than seventy stories. He began as a modest imitator of Nathaniel Hawthorne and ended as a great creative writer of fiction and literary criticism; the progression was the result of his professionalism, his constant self-examination, his self-knowledge, and his self-control. He felt that experience assumes meaning only when the proper form for its expression is found. One of his favorite words was "awareness," and he tried to make his own awareness encompass everything he could observe, relate, weigh, and judge. Thus, his was a world of connections continually subjected to a controlled and harmonious ordering. In the essay "The Art of Fiction," he said that the source of fiction is not mere raw experience but "the power to guess the unseen from the seen, to trace the implication of things, to judge the whole piece by the pattern, the condition of feeling life in general so completely that you are well on your way to knowing any particular corner of it."

James's stories lack the characteristic compression and dramatic action typical of this literary form. Instead, through the device he called a "central intelligence," he revealed the world through the silent thought of one of his characters, proceeding at a stately, leisurely pace. Yet in 1891, when James wrote in his notebook the idea that was the genesis of the story "The Real Thing," he apparently had in mind something else, a compressed short story in the manner of Guy de Maupassant, which he hoped would be easier to sell to a magazine than a longer work. He regarded this story as a great challenge: "To look at a thing hard and straight and seriously—to fix it."

RELATED COMMENTARY
Henry James, "The Genesis of 'The Real Thing,'" page 1446.

The Real Thing

1891

I

When the porter's wife, who used to answer the house-bell, announced "A gentleman and a lady, sir," I had, as I often had in those days — the wish being father to the thought — an immediate vision of sitters. Sitters my visitors in this case proved to be; but not in the sense I should have preferred. There was nothing at first however to indicate that they mightn't have come for a portrait. The gentleman, a man of fifty, very high and very straight, with a moustache slightly grizzled and a dark grey walking-coat admirably fitted, both of which I noted professionally — I don't mean as a barber or yet as a tailor — would have struck me as a celebrity if celebrities often were striking. It was a truth of which I had for some time been conscious that a figure with a good deal of frontage was, as one might say, almost never a public institution. A glance at the lady helped to remind me of this paradoxical law: she also looked too distinguished to be a "personality." Moreover one would scarcely come across two variations together.

Neither of the pair immediately spoke — they only prolonged the preliminary gaze suggesting that each wished to give the other a chance. They were visibly shy; they stood there letting me take them in — which, as I afterwards perceived, was the most practical thing they could have done. In this way their embarrassment served their cause. I had seen people painfully reluctant to mention that they desired anything so gross as to be represented on canvas; but the scruples of my new friends appeared almost insurmountable. Yet the gentleman might have said "I should like a portrait of my wife," and the lady might have said "I should like a portrait of my husband." Perhaps they weren't husband and wife — this naturally would make the matter more delicate. Perhaps they wished to be done together — in which case they ought to have brought a third person to break the news.

"We come from Mr. Rivet," the lady finally said with a dim smile that had the effect of a moist sponge passed over a "sunk" piece of painting, as well as of a vague allusion to vanished beauty. She was as tall and straight, in her degree, as her companion, and with ten years less to carry. She looked as sad as a woman could look whose face was not charged with expression; that is her tinted oval mask showed waste as an exposed surface shows friction. The hand of time had played over her freely, but to an effect of elimination. She was slim and stiff, and so well-dressed, in dark blue cloth, with lappets and pockets and buttons, that it was clear she employed the same tailor as her husband. The couple had an indefinable air of prosperous thrift — they evidently got a good deal of luxury for their money. If I was to be one of their luxuries it would behoove me to consider my terms.

"Ah Claude Rivet recommended me?" I echoed; and I added that it was very kind of him, though I could reflect that, as he only painted landscape, this wasn't a sacrifice.

The lady looked very hard at the gentleman, and the gentleman looked round the room. Then staring at the floor a moment and stroking his moustache, he rested his pleasant eyes on me with the remark: "He said you were the right one."

"I try to be, when people want to sit."

"Yes, we should like to," said the lady anxiously.

"Do you mean together?"

My visitors exchanged a glance. "If you could do anything with *me* I suppose it would be double," the gentleman stammered.

"Oh yes, there's naturally a higher charge for two figures than for one."

"We should like to make it pay," the husband confessed.

"That's very good of you," I returned, appreciating so unwonted a sympathy — for I supposed he meant pay the artist.

A sense of strangeness seemed to dawn on the lady. "We mean for the illustrations — Mr. Rivet said you might put one in."

"Put in — an illustration?" I was equally confused.

"Sketch her off, you know," said the gentleman, coloring.

It was only then that I understood the service Claude Rivet had rendered me; he had told them how I worked in black-and-white, for magazines, for storybooks, for sketches of contemporary life, and consequently had copious employment for models. These things were true, but it was not less true — I may confess it now; whether because the aspiration was to lead to everything or to nothing I leave the reader to guess — that I couldn't get the honors, to say nothing of the emoluments, of a great painter of portraits out of my head. My "illustrations" were my pot-boilers; I looked to a different branch of art — far and away the most interesting it had always seemed to me — to perpetuate my fame. There was no shame in looking to it also to make my fortune; but that fortune was by so much further from being made from the moment my visitors wished to be "done" for nothing. I was disappointed; for in the pictorial sense I had immediately *seen* them. I had seized their type — I had already settled what I would do with it. Something that wouldn't absolutely have pleased them, I afterwards reflected.

"Ah you're — you're — a?" I began as soon as I had mastered my surprise. I couldn't bring out the dingy word "models": it seemed so little to fit the case.

"We haven't had much practice," said the lady.

"We've got to *do* something, and we've thought that an artist in your line might perhaps make something of us," her husband threw off. He further mentioned that they didn't know many artists and that they had gone first, on the off-chance — he painted views of course, but sometimes put in figures; perhaps I remembered — to Mr. Rivet, whom they had met a few years before at a place in Norfolk where he was sketching.

"We used to sketch a little ourselves," the lady hinted.

"It's very awkward, but we absolutely *must* do something," her husband went on.

"Of course we're not so *very* young," she admitted with a wan smile.

With the remark that I might as well know something more about them the husband had handed me a card extracted from a neat new pocket-book — their appurtenances were all of the freshest — and inscribed with the words "Major

Monarch." Impressive as these words were they didn't carry my knowledge much further; but my visitor presently added: "I've left the army and we've had the misfortune to lose our money. In fact our means are dreadfully small."

"It's awfully trying — a regular strain," said Mrs. Monarch.

They evidently wished to be discreet — to take care not to swagger because they were gentlefolk. I felt them willing to recognize this as something of a drawback, at the same time that I guessed at an underlying sense — their consolation in adversity — that they *had* their points. They certainly had; but these advantages struck me as preponderantly social; such for instance as would help to make a drawing-room look well. However, a drawing-room was always, or ought to be, a picture.

In consequence of his wife's allusion to their age Major Monarch observed: "Naturally, it's more for the figure that we thought of going in. We can still hold ourselves up." On the instant I saw that the figure was indeed their strong point. His "naturally" didn't sound vain, but it lighted up the question. "*She* has got the best," he continued, nodding at his wife, with a pleasant after-dinner absence of circumlocution. I could only reply, as if we were in fact sitting over our wine, that this didn't prevent his own from being very good; which led him in turn to rejoin: "We thought that if you ever have to do people like us, we might be something like it. *She*, particularly — for a lady in a book, you know."

I was so amused by them that, to get more of it, I did my best to take their point of view; and though it was an embarrassment to find myself appraising physically, as if they were animals on hire or useful blacks, a pair whom I should have expected to meet only in one of the relations in which criticism is tacit, I looked at Mrs. Monarch judicially enough to be able to exclaim, after a moment, with conviction: "Oh yes, a lady in a book!" She was singularly like a bad illustration.

"We'll stand up, if you like," said the Major; and he raised himself before me with a really grand air.

I could take his measure at a glance — he was six feet two and a perfect gentleman. It would have paid any club in process of formation and in want of a stamp to engage him at a salary to stand in the principal window. What struck me immediately was that in coming to me they had rather missed their vocation; they could surely have been turned to better account for advertising purposes. I couldn't of course see the thing in detail, but I could see them make someone's fortune — I don't mean their own. There was something in them for a waistcoat-maker, an hotel-keeper, or a soap-vendor. I could imagine "We always use it" pinned on their bosoms with the greatest effect; I had a vision of the promptitude with which they would launch a table d'hôte.

Mrs. Monarch sat still, not from pride but from shyness, and presently her husband said to her: "Get up my dear and show how smart you are." She obeyed, but she had no need to get up to show it. She walked to the end of the studio, and then she came back blushing, with her fluttered eyes on her husband. I was reminded of an incident I had accidentally had a glimpse of in Paris — being with a friend there, a dramatist about to produce a play — when an actress came to him to ask to be intrusted with a part. She went through her paces before him, walked up and down as Mrs. Monarch was doing. Mrs. Monarch did it quite as well, but I abstained from applauding. It was very odd to see such people apply for such poor pay. She looked as if she had ten thousand a year. Her husband had used the word that described her: she was in the London current jargon essentially and typically "smart." Her figure was, in the same order of ideas, conspicuously and irreproachably "good." For a woman of her age her waist was surprisingly small; her elbow moreover had the orthodox crook. She held her head at the conventional angle, but why did she come to *me*? She ought to have tried on jackets at a big shop. I feared my visitors were not only destitute but "artistic" — which would be a great complication. When she sat down again I thanked her, observing that what a draughtsman most valued in his model was the faculty of keeping quiet.

"Oh *she* can keep quiet," said Major Monarch. Then he added jocosely: "I've always kept her quiet."

"I'm not a nasty fidget, am I?" It was going to wring tears from me, I felt, the way she hid her head, ostrich-like, in the other broad bosom.

The owner of this expanse addressed his answer to me. "Perhaps it isn't out of place to mention — because we ought to be quite businesslike, oughtn't we? — that when I married her she was known as the Beautiful Statue."

"Oh dear!" said Mrs. Monarch ruefully.

"Of course I should want a certain amount of expression," I rejoined.

"Of *course*!" — and I had never heard such unanimity.

"And then I suppose you know that you'll get awfully tired."

"Oh, we *never* get tired!" they eagerly cried.

"Have you had any kind of practice?"

They hesitated — they looked at each other. "We've been photographed — *immensely*," said Mrs. Monarch.

"She means the fellows have asked us themselves," added the Major.

"I see — because you're so good-looking."

"I don't know what they thought, but they were always after us."

"We always got our photographs for nothing," smiled Mrs. Monarch.

"We might have brought some, my dear," her husband remarked.

"I'm not sure we have any left. We've given quantities away," she explained to me.

"With our autographs and that sort of thing," said the Major.

"Are they to be got in the shops?" I enquired as a harmless pleasantry.

"Oh yes, *hers* — they used to be."

"Not now," said Mrs. Monarch, with her eyes on the floor.

II

I could fancy the "sort of thing" they put on the presentation copies of their photographs, and I was sure they wrote a beautiful hand. It was odd how quickly I was sure of everything that concerned them. If they were now so poor as to have to earn shillings and pence they could never have had much of a margin. Their good looks had been their capital, and they had good-humoredly made the most of the career that this resource marked out for them. It was in their faces, the blankness, the deep intellectual repose of the twenty years of country-house visiting that had given them pleasant intonations. I could see the sunny drawing-rooms, sprinkled with periodicals she didn't read, in which Mrs. Monarch had continually sat; I could see the wet shrubberies in which she had walked, equipped to admiration for either exercise. I could see the rich covers the Major had helped to shoot and the wonderful garments in which, late at night, he repaired to the smoking-room to talk about them. I could imagine their leggings and waterproofs, their knowing tweeds and rugs, their rolls of sticks and cases of tackle and neat umbrellas; and I could evoke the exact appearance of their servants and the compact variety of their luggage on the platforms of country stations.

They gave small tips, but they were liked; they didn't do anything themselves, but they were welcome. They looked so well everywhere; they gratified the general relish for stature, complexion, and "form." They knew it without fatuity or vulgarity, and they respected themselves in consequence. They weren't superficial; they were thorough and kept themselves up — it had been their line. People with such a taste for activity had to have some line. I could feel how even in a dull house they could have been counted on for the joy of life. At present something had happened — it didn't matter what, their little income had grown less, it had grown least — and they had to do something for pocket-money. Their friends could like them, I made out, without liking to support them. There was something about them that represented credit — their clothes, their manners, their type; but if credit is a large empty pocket in which an occasional chink reverberates, the chink at least must be audible. What they wanted of me was to help to make it so. Fortunately they had no children — I soon divined that. They would also perhaps wish our relations to be kept secret: this was why it was "for the figure"— the reproduction of the face would betray them.

I liked them — I felt, quite as their friends must have done — they were so simple; and I had no objection to them if they would suit. But somehow with all their perfections I didn't easily believe in them. After all they were amateurs, and the ruling passion of my life was the detestation of the amateur. Combined with this was another perversity — an innate preference for the represented subject over the real one: the defect of the real one was so apt to be a lack of representation. I like things that appeared; then one was sure. Whether they *were* or not was a subordinate and almost always a profitless question. There were other considerations, the first of which was that I already had two or three recruits in use, notably a young person with big feet, in alpaca, from Kilburn, who for a couple of years had come to me regularly for my illustrations and with whom I was still — perhaps ignobly — satisfied. I frankly explained to my visitors how the case stood, but they had taken more precautions than I supposed. They had reasoned out their opportunity, for Claude Rivet had told them of the projected *édition de luxe* of one of the writers of our day — the rarest of the novelists — who, long neglected by the multitudinous vulgar and dearly prized by the attentive (need I mention Philip Vincent?), had had the happy fortune of seeing, late in life, the dawn and then the full light of a higher criticism; an estimate in which on the part of the public there was something really of expiation. The edition preparing, planned by a publisher of taste, was practically an act of high reparation; the wood-cuts with which it was to be enriched were the homage of English art to one of the most independent representatives of English letters. Major and Mrs. Monarch confessed to me they had hoped I might be able to work *them* into my branch of the enterprise. They knew I was to do the first of the books, "Rutland Ramsay," but I had to make clear to them that my participation in the rest of the affair — this first book was to be a test — must depend on the satisfaction I should give. If this should be limited my employers would drop me with scarce common forms. It was therefore a crisis for me, and naturally I was making special preparations, looking about for new people, should they be necessary, and securing the best types. I admitted however that I should like to settle down to two or three good models who would do for everything.

"Should we have often to — a — put on special clothes?" Mrs. Monarch timidly demanded.

"Dear yes — that's half the business."

"And should we be expected to supply our own costumes?"

"Oh no; I've got a lot of things. A painter's models put on — or put off — anything he likes."

"And you mean — a — the same?"

"The same?"

Mrs. Monarch looked at her husband again.

"Oh she was just wondering," he explained, "if the costumes are in *general* use." I had to confess that they were, and I mentioned further that some of them — I had a lot of genuine greasy last-century things — had served their time, a hundred years ago, on living world-stained men and women; on figures not perhaps so far removed, in that vanished world, from *their* type, the Monarchs', *quoi!* of a breeched and bewigged age. "We'll put on anything that *fits*," said the Major.

"Oh I arrange that — they fit in the pictures."

"I'm afraid I should do better for the modern books. I'd come as you like," said Mrs. Monarch.

"She has got a lot of clothes at home: they might do for contemporary life," her husband continued.

"Oh I can fancy scenes in which you'd be quite natural." And indeed I could see the slipshod rearrangements of stale properties — the stories I tried to produce pictures for without the exasperation of reading them — whose sandy tracts the good lady might help to people. But I had to return to the fact that for this sort of work — the daily mechanical grind — I was already equipped: the people I was working with were fully adequate.

"We only thought we might be more like *some* characters," said Mrs. Monarch mildly, getting up.

Her husband also rose; he stood looking at me with a dim wistfulness that was touching in so fine a man. "Wouldn't it be rather a pull sometimes to have — a — to have — ?" He hung fire; he wanted me to help him by phrasing what he meant. But I couldn't — I didn't know. So he brought it out awkwardly: "The *real* thing; a gentleman, you know, or a lady." I was quite ready to give a general assent — I admitted that there was a great deal in that. This encouraged Major Monarch to say, following up his appeal with an unacted gulp: "It's awfully hard — we've tried everything." The gulp was communicative; it proved too much for his wife. Before I knew it Mrs. Monarch had dropped again upon a divan and burst into tears. Her husband sat down beside her, holding one of her hands; whereupon she quickly dried her eyes with the other, while I felt embarrassed as she looked up at me. "There isn't a confounded job I haven't applied for — waited for — prayed for. You can fancy we'd be pretty bad first. Secretaryships and that sort of thing? You might as well ask for a peerage. I'd be *anything* — I'm strong; a messenger or a coalheaver. I'd put on a gold-laced cap and open carriage doors in front of the haberdasher's; I'd hang about a station to carry portmanteaux; I'd be a postman. But they won't *look* at you; there are thousands as good as yourself already on the ground. *Gentlemen*, poor beggars, who've drunk their wine, who've kept their hunters!"

I was as reassuring as I knew how to be, and my visitors were presently on their feet again while, for the experiment, we agreed on an hour. We were discussing it when the door opened and Miss Churm came in with a wet umbrella. Miss Churm had to take the omnibus to Maida Vale and then walk half a mile. She looked a trifle blowsy and slightly splashed. I scarcely ever saw her come in without thinking afresh how odd it was that, being so little in herself, she should yet be so much in others. She was a meagre little Miss Churm, but was such an ample heroine of romance. She was only a freckled cockney, but she could represent everything, from a fine lady to a shepherdess; she had the faculty as she might have had a fine voice or long hair. She couldn't spell and she loved beer, but she had two or three "points," and practice, and a knack, and mother-wit, and a whimsical sensibility, and a love of the theatre, and seven sisters, and not an ounce of respect, especially for the *h*. The first thing my visitors saw was that her umbrella was wet, and in their spotless perfection they visibly winced at it. The rain had come on since their arrival.

"I'm all in a soak; there *was* a mess of people in the 'bus. I wish you lived near a stytion," said Miss Churm. I requested her to get ready as quickly as possible, and she passed into the room in which she always changed her dress. But before going out she asked me what she was to get into this time.

"It's the Russian princess, don't you know?" I answered; "the one with the 'golden eyes,' in black velvet, for the long thing in the *Cheapside*."

"Golden eyes? I *say*!" cried Miss Churm, while my companions watched her with intensity as she withdrew. She always arranged herself, when she was late, before I could turn round; and I kept my visitors a little on purpose, so that they might get an idea, from seeing her, what would be expected of themselves. I mentioned that she was quite my notion of an excellent model — she was really very clever.

"Do you think she looks like a Russian princess?" Major Monarch asked with lurking alarm.

"When I make her, yes."

"Oh if you have to *make* her — !" he reasoned, not without point.

"That's the most you can ask. There are so many who are not makeable."

"Well now, *here's* a lady" — and with a persuasive smile he passed his arm into his wife's — "who's already made!"

"Oh I'm not a Russian princess," Mrs. Monarch protested a little coldly. I could see she had known some and didn't like them. There at once was a complication of a kind I never had to fear with Miss Churm.

This young lady came back in black velvet — the gown was rather rusty and very low on her lean shoulders — and with a Japanese fan in her red hands. I reminded her that in the scene I was doing she had to look over some one's head. "I forget whose it is; but it doesn't matter. Just look over a head."

"I'd rather look over a stove," said Miss Churm; and she took her station near the fire. She fell into position, settled herself into a tall attitude, gave a certain backward inclination to her head and a certain forward droop to her fan, and looked, at least to my prejudiced sense, distinguished and charming, foreign and dangerous. We left her looking so while I went downstairs with Major and Mrs. Monarch.

"I believe I could come about as near it as that," said Mrs. Monarch.

"Oh you think she's shabby, but you must allow for the alchemy of art."

However, they went off with an evident increase of comfort founded on their demonstrable advantage in being the real thing. I could fancy them shuddering over Miss Churm. She was very droll about them when I went back, for I told her what they wanted.

"Well, if *she* can sit I'll tyke to book-keeping," said my model.

"She's very ladylike," I replied as an innocent form of aggravation.

"So much the worse for *you*. That means she can't turn round."

"She'll do for the fashionable novels."

"Oh yes, she'll *do* for them!" my model humorously declared. "Ain't they bad enough without her?" I had often sociably denounced them to Miss Churm.

III

It was for the elucidation of a mystery in one of these works that I first tried Mrs. Monarch. Her husband came with her, to be useful if necessary — it was sufficiently clear that as a general thing he would prefer to come with her. At first I wondered if this were for "propriety's" sake — if he were going to be jealous and meddling. The idea was too tiresome, and if it had been confirmed it would speedily have brought our acquaintance to a close. But I soon saw there was nothing in it and that if he accompanied Mrs. Monarch it was — in addition to the chance of being wanted — simply because he had nothing else to do. When they were separate his occupation was gone and they never *had* been separate. I judged rightly that in their awkward situation their close union was their main comfort and that this union had no weak spot. It was a real marriage, an encouragement to the hesitating, a nut for pessimists to crack. Their address was humble — I remember afterwards thinking it had been the only thing about them that was really professional — and I could fancy the lamentable lodgings in which the Major would have been left alone. He could sit there more or less grimly with his wife — he couldn't sit there anyhow without her.

He had too much tact to try and make himself agreeable when he couldn't be useful; so when I was too absorbed in my work to talk he simply sat and waited. But I liked to hear him talk — it made my work, when not interrupting it, less mechanical, less special. To listen to him was to combine the excitement of going out with the economy of staying at home. There was only one hindrance — that I seemed not to know any of the people this brilliant couple had known. I think he wondered extremely, during the term of our intercourse, whom the deuce I *did* know. He hadn't a stray sixpence of an idea to fumble for, so we didn't spin it very fine; we confined ourselves to questions of leather and even of liquor — saddlers and breeches-makers and how to get excellent claret cheap — and matters like "good trains" and the habits of small game. His lore on these last subjects was astonishing — he managed to interweave the station-master with the ornithologist. When he couldn't talk about greater things he could talk cheerfully about smaller, and since I couldn't accompany him into reminiscences of the fashionable world he could lower the conversation without a visible effort to my level.

So earnest a desire to please was touching in a man who could so easily have knocked one down. He looked after the fire and had an opinion on the draught of the stove without my asking him, and I could see that he thought many of my arrangements not half knowing. I remember telling him that if I were only rich I'd offer him a salary to come and teach me how to live. Sometimes he gave a random sigh of which the essence might have been: "Give me even such a bare old barrack as *this*, and I'd do something with it!" When I wanted to use him he came alone; which was an illustration of the superior courage of women. His wife could bear her solitary second floor, and she was in general more discreet; showing by various small reserves that she was alive to the propriety of keeping our relations markedly professional — not letting them slide into sociability. She wished it to remain clear that she and the Major were employed, not cultivated, and if she approved of me as a superior, who could be kept in his place, she never thought me quite good enough for an equal.

She sat with great intensity, giving the whole of her mind to it, and was capable of remaining for an hour almost as motionless as before a photographer's lens. I could see she had been photographed often, but somehow the very habit that made her good for that purpose unfitted her for mine. At first I was extremely pleased with her ladylike air, and it was a satisfaction, on coming to follow her lines, to see how good they were and how far they could lead the pencil. But after a little skirmishing I began to find her too insurmountably stiff; do what I would with it my drawing looked like a photograph or a copy of a photograph. Her figure had no variety of expression — she herself had no sense of variety. You may say that this was my business and was only a question of placing her. Yet I placed her in every conceivable position and she managed to obliterate their differences. She was always a lady certainly, and into the bargain was always the same lady. She was the real thing, but always the same thing. There were moments when I rather writhed under the serenity of her confidence that she *was* the real thing.

All her dealings with me and all her husband's were an implication that this was lucky for *me*. Meanwhile I found myself trying to invent types that approached her own, instead of making her own transform itself—in the clever way that was not impossible for instance to poor Miss Churm. Arrange as I would and take the precautions I would, she always came out, in my pictures, too tall—landing me in the dilemma of having represented a fascinating woman as seven feet high, which (out of respect perhaps to my own very much scantier inches) was far from my idea of such a personage.

The case was worse with the Major—nothing I could do would keep *him* down, so that he became useful only for the representation of brawny giants. I adored variety and range, I cherished human accidents, the illustrative note; I wanted to characterize closely, and the thing in the world I most hated was the danger of being ridden by a type. I had quarreled with some of my friends about it; I had parted company with them for maintaining that one *had* to be, and that if the type was beautiful—witness Raphael and Leonardo—the servitude was only a gain. I was neither Leonardo nor Raphael—I might only be a presumptuous young modern searcher; but I held that everything was to be sacrificed sooner than character. When they claimed that the obsessional form could easily *be* character I retorted, perhaps superficially, "Whose?" It couldn't be everybody's—it might end in being nobody's.

After I had drawn Mrs. Monarch a dozen times I felt surer even than before that the value of such a model as Miss Churm resided precisely in the fact that she had no positive stamp, combined of course with the other fact that what she did have was a curious and inexplicable talent for imitation. Her usual appearance was like a curtain which she could draw up at request for a capital performance. This performance was simply suggestive; but it was a word to the wise—it was vivid and pretty. Sometimes even I thought it, though she was plain herself, too insipidly pretty; I made it a reproach to her that the figures drawn from her were monotonously (*bêtement*, as we used to say) graceful. Nothing made her more angry; it was so much her pride to feel she could sit for characters that had nothing in common with each other. She would accuse me at such moments of taking away her "reputytion."

It suffered a certain shrinkage, this queer quantity, from the repeated visits of my new friends. Miss Churm was greatly in demand, never in want of employment, so I had no scruple in putting her off occasionally, to try them more at my ease. It was certainly amusing at first to do the real thing—it was amusing to do Major Monarch's trousers. They *were* the real thing, even if he did come out colossal. It was amusing to do his wife's back hair—it was so mathematically neat—and the particular "smart" tension of her tight stays. She lent herself especially to positions in which the face was somewhat averted or blurred; she abounded in ladylike back views and *profils perdus*.[1] When she stood erect she took naturally one of the attitudes in which court-painters represent queens and princesses; so that I found myself wondering whether, to draw

---

[1] Profiles in which the face is averted and its features remain unseen.

out this accomplishment, I couldn't get the editor of the *Cheapside* to publish a really royal romance, "A Tale of Buckingham Palace." Sometimes however the real thing and the make-believe came into contact; by which I mean that Miss Churm, keeping an appointment or coming to make one on days when I had much work in hand, encountered her invidious rivals. The encounter was not on their part, for they noticed her no more than if she had been the housemaid; not from intentional loftiness, but simply because as yet, professionally, they didn't know how to fraternize, as I could imagine they would have liked — or at least that the Major would. They couldn't talk about the omnibus — they always walked; and they didn't know what else to try — she wasn't interested in good trains or cheap claret. Besides, they must have felt — in the air — that she was amused at them, secretly derisive of their ever knowing how. She wasn't a person to conceal the limits of her faith if she had had a chance to show them. On the other hand Mrs. Monarch didn't think her tidy; for why else did she take pains to say to me — it was going out of the way, for Mrs. Monarch — that she didn't like dirty women?

One day when my young lady happened to be present with my other sitters — she even dropped in, when it was convenient, for a chat — I asked her to be so good as to lend a hand in getting tea, a service with which she was familiar and which was one of a class that, living as I did in a small way, with slender domestic resources, I often appealed to my models to render. They liked to lay hands on my property, to break the sitting, and sometimes the china — it made them feel Bohemian. The next time I saw Miss Churm after this incident she surprised me greatly by making a scene about it — she accused me of having wished to humiliate her. She hadn't resented the outrage at the time, but had seemed obliging and amused, enjoying the comedy of asking Mrs. Monarch, who sat vague and silent, whether she would have cream and sugar, and putting an exaggerated simper into the question. She had tried intonations — as if she too wished to pass for the real thing — till I was afraid my other visitors would take offense.

Oh they were determined not to do this, and their touching patience was the measure of their great need. They would sit by the hour, uncomplaining, till I was ready to use them; they would come back on the chance of being wanted and would walk away cheerfully if it failed. I used to go to the door with them to see in what magnificent order they retreated. I tried to find other employment for them — I introduced them to several artists. But they didn't "take," for reasons I could appreciate, and I became rather anxiously aware that after such disappointments they fell back upon me with a heavier weight. They did me the honor to think me most *their* form. They weren't romantic enough for the painters, and in those days there were few serious workers in black-and-white. Besides, they had an eye to the great job I had mentioned to them — they had secretly set their hearts on supplying the right essence for my pictorial vindication of our fine novelist. They knew that for this undertaking I should want no costume-effects, none of the frippery of past ages — that it was a case in which everything would be contemporary and satirical and presumably genteel. If I could work them into it their future would be assured, for the labor would of course be long and the occupation steady.

One day Mrs. Monarch came without her husband — she explained his absence by his having had to go to the City. While she sat there in her usual relaxed majesty there came at the door a knock which I immediately recognized as the subdued appeal of a model out of work. It was followed by the entrance of a young man whom I at once saw to be a foreigner and who proved in fact an Italian acquainted with no English word but my name, which he uttered in a way that made it seem to include all others. I hadn't then visited his country, nor was I proficient in his tongue; but as he was not so meanly constituted — what Italian is? — as to depend only on that member for expression he conveyed to me, in familiar but graceful mimicry, that he was in search of exactly the employment in which the lady before me was engaged. I was not struck with him at first, and while I continued to draw I dropped few signs of interest or encouragement. He stood his ground however — not importunately, but with a dumb dog-like fidelity in his eyes that amounted to innocent impudence, the manner of a devoted servant — he might have been in the house for years — unjustly suspected. Suddenly it struck me that this very attitude and expression made a picture; whereupon I told him to sit down and wait till I should be free. There was another picture in the way he obeyed me, and I observed as I worked that there were others still in the way he looked wonderingly, with his head thrown back, about the high studio. He might have been crossing himself in Saint Peter's. Before I finished I said to myself "The fellow's a bankrupt orange-monger, but a treasure."

When Mrs. Monarch withdrew he passed across the room like a flash to open the door for her, standing there with the rapt pure gaze of the young Dante spellbound by the young Beatrice. As I never insisted, in such situations, on the blankness of the British domestic, I reflected that he had the making of a servant — and I needed one, but couldn't pay him to be only that — as well as of a model; in short I resolved to adopt my bright adventurer if he would agree to officiate in the double capacity. He jumped at my offer, and in the event my rashness — for I had really known nothing about him — wasn't brought home to me. He proved a sympathetic though a desultory ministrant, and had in a wonderful degree the *sentiment de la pose*. It was uncultivated, instinctive, a part of the happy instinct that had guided him to my door and helped him to spell out my name on the card nailed to it. He had had no other introduction to me than a guess, from the shape of my high north window, seen outside, that my place was a studio and that as a studio it would contain an artist. He had wandered to England in search of fortune, like other itinerants, and had embarked, with a partner and a small green hand-cart, on the sale of penny ices. The ices had melted away and the partner had dissolved in their train. My young man wore tight yellow trousers with reddish stripes and his name was Oronte. He was sallow but fair, and when I put him into some old clothes of my own he looked like an Englishman. He was as good as Miss Churm, who could look, when requested, like an Italian.

IV

I thought Mrs. Monarch's face slightly convulsed when, on her coming back with her husband, she found Oronte installed. It was strange to have to recognize in

a scrap of a lazzarone[2] a competitor to her magnificent Major. It was she who
scented danger first, for the Major was anecdotically unconscious. But Oronte
gave us tea, with a hundred eager confusions — he had never been concerned
in so queer a process — and I think she thought better of me for having at last
an "establishment." They saw a couple of drawings that I had made of the establishment, and Mrs. Monarch hinted that it never would have struck her he had
sat for them. "Now the drawings you make from *us*, they look exactly like us,"
she reminded me, smiling in triumph; and I recognized that this was indeed
just their defect. When I drew the Monarchs I couldn't anyhow get away from
them — get into the character I wanted to represent; and I hadn't the least desire
my model should be discoverable in my picture. Miss Churm never was, and
Mrs. Monarch thought I hid her, very properly, because she was vulgar; whereas
if she was lost it was only as the dead who go to heaven are lost — in the gain of
an angel the more.

By this time I had got a certain start with "Rutland Ramsay," the first novel
in the great projected series; that is I had produced a dozen drawings, several
with the help of the Major and his wife, and I had sent them in for approval.
My understanding with the publishers, as I have already hinted, had been
that I was to be left to do my work, in this particular case, as I liked, with the
whole book committed to me; but my connection with the rest of the series
was only contingent. There were moments when, frankly, it *was* a comfort to
have the real thing under one's hand; for there were characters in "Rutland
Ramsay" that were very much like it. There were people presumably as erect
as the Major and women of as good a fashion as Mrs. Monarch. There was a
great deal of country-house life — treated, it is true, in a fine fanciful ironical
generalized way — and there was a considerable implication of knickerbockers
and kilts. There were certain things I had to settle at the outset; such things for
instance as the exact appearance of the hero and the particular bloom and figure of the heroine. The author of course gave me a lead, but there was a margin
for interpretation. I took the Monarchs into my confidence, I told them frankly
what I was about, I mentioned my embarrassments and alternatives. "Oh take
him!" Mrs. Monarch murmured sweetly, looking at her husband; and "What
could you want better than my wife?" the Major enquired with the comfortable candor that now prevailed between us.

I wasn't obliged to answer these remarks — I was only obliged to place my
sitters. I wasn't easy in mind, and I postponed a little timidly perhaps the solving of my question. The book was a large canvas, the other figures were numerous, and I worked off at first some of the episodes in which the hero and the
heroine were not concerned. When once I had set *them* up I should have to
stick to them — I couldn't make my young man seven feet high in one place
and five feet nine in another. I inclined on the whole to the latter measurement,
though the Major more than once reminded me that *he* looked about as young
as any one. It was indeed quite possible to arrange him, for the figure, so that it

---

[2] The name given to homeless beggars in Naples.

would have been difficult to detect his age. After the spontaneous Oronte had been with me a month, and after I had given him to understand several times over that his native exuberance would presently constitute an insurmountable barrier to our further intercourse, I waked to a sense of his heroic capacity. He was only five feet seven, but the remaining inches were latent. I tried him almost secretly at first, for I was really rather afraid of the judgment my other models would pass on such a choice. If they regarded Miss Churm as little better than a snare what would they think of the representation by a person so little the real thing as an Italian street-vendor of a protagonist formed by a public school?

If I went a little in fear of them it wasn't because they bullied me, because they had got an oppressive foothold, but because in their really pathetic decorum and mysteriously permanent newness they counted on me so intensely. I was therefore very glad when Jack Hawley came home: he was always of such good counsel. He painted badly himself, but there was no one like him for putting his finger on the place. He had been absent from England for a year; he had been somewhere — I don't remember where — to get a fresh eye. I was in a good deal of dread of any such organ, but we were old friends; he had been away for months and a sense of emptiness was creeping into my life. I hadn't dodged a missile for a year.

He came back with a fresh eye, but with the same old black velvet blouse, and the first evening he spent in my studio we smoked cigarettes till the small hours. He had done no work himself, he had only got the eye; so the field was clear for the production of my little things. He wanted to see what I had produced for the *Cheapside*, but he was disappointed in the exhibition. That at least seemed the meaning of two or three comprehensive groans which, as he lounged on my big divan, his leg folded under him, looking at my latest drawings, issued from his lips with the smoke of the cigarette.

"What's the matter with you?" I asked.

"What's the matter with *you*?"

"Nothing save that I'm mystified."

"You are indeed. You're quite off the hinge. What's the meaning of this new fad?" And he tossed me, with visible irreverence, a drawing in which I happened to have depicted both my elegant models. I asked if he didn't think it good, and he replied that it struck him as execrable, given the sort of thing I had always represented myself to him as wishing to arrive at; but I let that pass — I was so anxious to see exactly what he meant. The two figures in the picture looked colossal, but I supposed this was *not* what he meant, inasmuch as, for aught he knew to the contrary, I might have been trying for some such effect. I maintained that I was working exactly in the same way as when he last had done me the honor to tell me I might do something some day. "Well, there's a screw loose somewhere," he answered; "wait a bit and I'll discover it." I depended upon him to do so: where else was the fresh eye? But he produced at last nothing more luminous than "I don't know — I don't like your types." This was lame for a critic who had never consented to discuss with me anything but the question of execution, the direction of strokes, and the mystery of values.

"In the drawings you've been looking at I think my types are very hand-some."

"Oh they won't do!"

"I've been working with new models."

"I see you have. *They* won't do."

"Are you very sure of that?"

"Absolutely — they're stupid."

"You mean *I* am — for I ought to get round that."

"You *can't* — with such people. Who are they?"

I told him, so far as was necessary, and he concluded heartlessly: *"Ce sont des gens qu'il faut mettre à la porte."*[3]

"You've never seen them; they're awfully good" — I flew to their defense.

"Not seen them? Why all this recent work of yours drops to pieces with them. It's all I want to see of them."

"No one else has said anything against it — the *Cheapside* people are pleased."

"Every one else is an ass, and the *Cheapside* people the biggest asses of all. Come, don't pretend at this time of day to have pretty illusions about the public, especially about publishers and editors. It's not for *such* animals you work — it's for those you know, *coloro che sanno;*[4] so keep straight for *me* if you can't keep straight for yourself. There was a certain sort of thing you used to try for — and a very good thing it was. But this twaddle isn't *in* it." When I talked with Hawley later about "Rutland Ramsay" and its possible successors he declared that I must get back into my boat again or I should go to the bottom. His voice in short was the voice of warning.

I noted the warning, but I didn't turn my friends out of doors. They bored me a good deal; but the very fact that they bored me admonished me not to sacrifice them — if there was anything to be done with them — simply to irritation. As I look back at this phase they seem to me to have pervaded my life not a little. I have a vision of them as most of the time in my studio, seated against the wall on an old velvet bench to be out of the way, and resembling the while a pair of patient courtiers in a royal ante-chamber. I'm convinced that during the coldest weeks of the winter they held their ground because it saved them fire. Their new-ness was losing its gloss, and it was impossible not to feel them objects of charity. Whenever Miss Churm arrived they went away, and after I was fairly launched in "Rutland Ramsay" Miss Churm arrived pretty often. They managed to express to me tacitly that they supposed I wanted her for the low life of the book, and I let them suppose it, since they had attempted to study the work — it was lying about the studio — without discovering that it dealt only with the highest circles. They had dipped into the most brilliant of our novelists without deciphering many passages. I still took an hour from them, now and again, in spite of Jack Hawley's warning: it would be time enough to dismiss them, if dismissal should

---

[3] "You'll have to throw them out" (French).

[4] "The ones who understand" (Italian).

be necessary, when the rigor of the season was over. Hawley had made their acquaintance — he had met them at my fireside — and thought them a ridiculous pair. Learning that he was a painter they tried to approach him, to show him too that they were the real thing; but he looked at them, across the big room, as if they were miles away: they were a compendium of everything he most objected to in the social system of his country. Such people as that, all convention and patent-leather, with ejaculations that stopped conversation, had no business in a studio. A studio was a place to learn to see, and how could you see through a pair of featherbeds?

The main inconvenience I suffered at their hands was that at first I was shy of letting it break upon them that my artful little servant had begun to sit to me for "Rutland Ramsay." They knew I had been odd enough — they were prepared by this time to allow oddity to artists — to pick a foreign vagabond out of the streets when I might have had a person with whiskers and credentials; but it was some time before they learned how high I rated his accomplishments. They found him in an attitude more than once, but they never doubted I was doing him as an organ-grinder. There were several things they never guessed, and one of them was that for a striking scene in the novel, in which a footman briefly figured, it occurred to me to make use of Major Monarch as the menial. I kept putting this off, I didn't like to ask him to don the livery — besides the difficulty of finding a livery to fit him. At last, one day late in the winter, when I was at work on the despised Oronte, who caught one's idea on the wing, and was in the glow of feeling myself go very straight, they came in, the Major and his wife, with their society laugh about nothing (there was less and less to laugh at); came in like country-callers — they always reminded me of that — who have walked across the park after church and are presently persuaded to stay to luncheon. Luncheon was over, but they could stay to tea — I knew they wanted it. The fit was on me, however, and I couldn't let my ardor cool and my work wait, with the fading daylight, while my model prepared it. So I asked Mrs. Monarch if she would mind laying it out — a request which for an instant brought all the blood to her face. Her eyes were on her husband's for a second, and some mute telegraphy passed between them. Their folly was over the next instant; his cheerful shrewdness put an end to it. So far from pitying their wounded pride, I must add, I was moved to give it as complete a lesson as I could. They bustled about together and got out the cups and saucers and made the kettle boil. I know they felt as if they were waiting on my servant, and when the tea was prepared I said: "He'll have a cup, please — he's tired." Mrs. Monarch brought him one where he stood, and he took it from her as if he had been a gentleman at a party squeezing a crush-hat with an elbow.

Then it came over me that she had made a great effort for me — made it with a kind of nobleness — and that I owed her a compensation. Each time I saw her after this I wondered what the compensation could be. I couldn't go on doing the wrong thing to oblige them. Oh it *was* the wrong thing, the stamp of the work for which they sat — Hawley was not the only person to say it now. I sent in a large number of the drawings I had made for "Rutland Ramsay," and I received a warning that was more to the point than Hawley's. The artistic adviser of the house for which I was working was of opinion that many of my illustrations were not what had been looked for. Most of these illustrations were the subjects in which the Monarchs had figured. Without going into the question of what *had* been looked for, I had to face the fact that at this rate I shouldn't get the other books to do. I hurled myself in despair on Miss Churm — I put her through all her paces. I not only adopted Oronte publicly as my hero, but one morning when the Major looked in to see if I didn't require him to finish a *Cheapside* figure for which he had begun to sit the week before, I told him I had changed my mind — I'd do the drawing from my man. At this my visitor turned pale and stood looking at me. "Is *he* your idea of an English gentleman?" he asked.

I was disappointed, I was nervous, I wanted to get on with my work; so I replied with irritation: "Oh my dear Major — I can't be ruined for *you!*"

It was a horrid speech, but he stood another moment — after which, without a word, he quitted the studio. I drew a long breath, for I said to myself that I shouldn't see him again. I hadn't told him definitely that I was in danger of having my work rejected, but I was vexed at his not having felt the catastrophe in the air, read with me the moral of our fruitless collaboration, the lesson that in the deceptive atmosphere of art even the highest respectability may fail of being plastic.

I didn't owe my friends money, but I did see them again. They reappeared together three days later; and, given all the other facts, there was something tragic in that one. It was a clear proof they could find nothing else in life to do. They had threshed the matter out in a dismal conference — they had digested the bad news that they were not in for the series. If they weren't useful to me for the *Cheapside* their function seemed difficult to determine, and I could only judge at first that they had come, forgivingly, decorously, to take a last leave. This made me rejoice in secret that I had little leisure for a scene; for I had placed both my other models in position together and I was pegging away at a drawing from which I hoped to derive glory. It had been suggested by the passage in which Rutland Ramsay, drawing up a chair to Artemisia's piano-stool, says extraordinary things to her while she ostensibly fingers out a difficult piece of music. I had done Miss Churm at the piano before — it was an attitude in which she knew how to take on an absolutely poetic grace. I wished the two figures to "compose" together with intensity, and my little Italian had entered perfectly into my conception. The pair were vividly before me, the piano had been pulled out; it was a charming show of blended youth and murmured love, which I had only to catch and keep. My visitors stood and looked at it, and I was friendly to them over my shoulder.

They made no response, but I was used to silent company and went on with my work, only a little disconcerted — even though exhilarated by the sense that *this* was at least the ideal thing — at not having got rid of them after all. Presently I heard Mrs. Monarch's sweet voice beside or rather above me: "I wish her hair were a little better done." I looked up and she was staring with a strange fixedness at Miss Churm, whose back was turned to her. "Do you mind my just touching it?" she went on — a question which made me spring up for an instant as with the instinctive fear that she might do the young lady a harm. But she quieted me with a glance I shall never forget — I confess I should like to have been able to paint *that* — and went for a moment to my model. She spoke to her softly, laying a hand on her shoulder and bending over her; and as the girl, understanding, gratefully assented, she disposed her rough curls, with a few quick passes, in such a way as to make Miss Churm's head twice as charming. It was one of the most heroic personal services I've ever seen rendered. Then Mrs. Monarch turned away with a low sigh and, looking about her as if for something to do, stooped to the floor with a noble humility and picked up a dirty rag that had dropped out of my paint-box.

The Major meanwhile had also been looking for something to do, and, wandering to the other end of the studio, saw before him my breakfast-things neglected, unremoved. "I say, can't I be useful *here*?" he called out to me with an irrepressible quaver. I assented with a laugh that I fear was awkward, and for the next ten minutes, while I worked, I heard the light clatter of china and the tinkle of spoons and glass. Mrs. Monarch assisted her husband — they washed up my crockery, they put it away. They wandered off into my little scullery, and I afterwards found that they had cleaned my knives and that my slender stock of plate had an unprecedented surface. When it came over me, the latent eloquence of what they were doing, I confess that my drawing was blurred for a moment — the picture swam. They had accepted their failure, but they couldn't accept their fate. They had bowed their heads in bewilderment to the perverse and cruel law in virtue of which the real thing could be so much less precious than the unreal; but they didn't want to starve. If my servants were my models, then my models might be my servants. They would reverse the parts — the others would sit for the ladies and gentlemen and *they* would do the work. They would still be in the studio — it was an intense dumb appeal to me not to turn them out. "Take us on," they wanted to say "we'll do *anything*."

My pencil dropped from my hand; my sitting was spoiled and I got rid of my sitters, who were also evidently rather mystified and awestruck. Then, alone with the Major and his wife I had a most uncomfortable moment. He put their prayer into a single sentence: "I say, you know — just let *us* do for you, can't you?" I couldn't — it was dreadful to see them emptying my slops; but I pretended I could, to oblige them, for about a week. Then I gave them a sum of money to go away, and I never saw them again. I obtained the remaining books, but my friend Hawley repeats that Major and Mrs. Monarch did me a permanent harm, got me into false ways. If it be true I'm content to have paid the price — for the memory.

Sarah Orne Jewett

Sarah Orne Jewett (1849–1909) was born in South Berwick, Maine. Her father was a country doctor, and she often accompanied him on his horse-and-buggy rounds among sick people on the local farms. She later said that she got her real education from these trips, rather than from her classes at Miss Rayne's School and the Berwick Academy. She had a fine ear for local speech and the native idiom, which she used to good effect in her stories. Impressed as a girl by the sympathetic depiction of *local color* (the people and life of a particular geographical setting) in the fiction of Harriet Beecher Stowe, Jewett began to write stories herself, publishing her earliest one, "Jenny Garrow's Lovers," in a Boston weekly when she was eighteen years old. Shortly after her twentieth birthday, her work was accepted by the prestigious *Atlantic Monthly*, and her career was launched. Jewett published her first collection of linked sketches, *Deephaven*, in 1877. She read the work of Gustave Flaubert, Émile Zola, Leo Tolstoy, and Henry James, and her style gradually matured, as is evident in the stories that make up the 1886 volume *A White Heron and Other Stories*.

Jewett took her favorite motto from Flaubert: "One should write of ordinary life as if one were writing history." Her masterpiece, *The Country of the Pointed Firs* (1896), is a book of scrupulously observed short sketches linked by the narrator's account of her stay in a Maine seacoast village and her growing involvement in the quiet lives of its people. Many stories were written about New England in Jewett's time, but hers have a unique quality stemming from her deep sympathy for the native characters and her ear for local speech. Once she laughingly told the younger writer Willa Cather that her head was full of dear old houses and dear old women, and when an old house and an old woman came together in her brain with a click, she knew a story was under way.

Although it is true that Jewett's realism heightens the attractive aspects of the rural New England character at the same time that it diminishes the harsher qualities, her literary technique is so candid and true to the larger aspects of human nature that the darker undercurrents of deprivation, both physical and psychological, are evident beneath the surface of her descriptions. Henry James recognized that Jewett was "surpassed only by Hawthorne as producer of the most finished and penetrating of the numerous 'short stories' that have the domestic life of New England for their general and their doubtless somewhat lean subject." In her time she was lauded for possessing an exquisitely simple, natural, and graceful style; now she is regarded as one of our most distinguished American regionalist writers, as evidenced by "A White Heron."

RELATED COMMENTARY
Sarah Orne Jewett, "Looking Back on Girlhood," page 1450.

A White Heron

1886

I

The woods were already filled with shadows one June evening, just before eight o'clock, though a bright sunset still glimmered faintly among the trunks of the trees. A little girl was driving home her cow, a plodding, dilatory, provoking creature in her behavior, but a valued companion for all that. They were going away from the western light, and striking deep into the dark woods, but their feet were familiar with the path, and it was no matter whether their eyes could see it or not.

There was hardly a night the summer through when the old cow could be found waiting at the pasture bars; on the contrary, it was her greatest pleasure to hide herself away among the high huckleberry bushes, and though she wore a loud bell she had made the discovery that if one stood perfectly still it would not ring. So Sylvia had to hunt for her until she found her and call Co'! Co'! with never an answering Moo, until her childish patience was quite spent. If the creature had not given good milk and plenty of it, the case would have seemed very different to her owners. Besides, Sylvia had all the time there was, and very little use to make of it. Sometimes in pleasant weather it was a consolation to look upon the cow's pranks as an intelligent attempt to play hide and seek, and as the child had no playmates she lent herself to this amusement with a good deal of zest. Though this chase had been so long that the wary animal herself had given an unusual signal of her whereabouts, Sylvia had only laughed when she came upon Mistress Moolly at the swamp-side, and urged her affectionately homeward with a twig of birch leaves. The old cow was not inclined to wander farther, she even turned in the right direction for once as they left the pasture, and stepped along the road at a good pace. She was quite ready to be milked now, and seldom stopped to browse. Sylvia wondered what her grandmother would say because they were so late. It was a great while since she had left home at half past five o'clock, but everybody knew the difficulty of making this errand a short one. Mrs. Tilley had chased the horned torment too many summer evenings herself to blame any one else for lingering, and was only thankful as she waited that she had Sylvia, nowadays, to give such valuable assistance. The good woman suspected that Sylvia loitered occasionally on her own account; there never was such a child for straying about out-of-doors since the world was made! Everybody said that it was a good change for a little maid who had tried to grow for eight years in a crowded manufacturing town, but, as for Sylvia herself, it seemed as if she never had been alive at all before she came to live at the farm. She thought often with wistful compassion of a wretched dry geranium that belonged to a town neighbor.

"'Afraid of folks,'" old Mrs. Tilley said to herself, with a smile, after she had made the unlikely choice of Sylvia from her daughter's houseful of children, and was returning to the farm. "'Afraid of folks,' they said! I guess she won't be troubled no great with 'em up to the old place!" When they reached the door of the lonely house and stopped to unlock it, and the cat came to purr loudly, and rub against them, a deserted pussy, indeed, but fat with young robins, Sylvia whispered that this was a beautiful place to live in, and she never should wish to go home.

The companions followed the shady wood-road, the cow taking slow steps, and the child very fast ones. The cow stopped long at the brook to drink, as if the pasture were not half a swamp, and Sylvia stood still and waited, letting her bare feet cool themselves in the shoal water, while the great twilight moths struck softly against her. She waded on through the brook as the cow moved away, and listened to the thrushes with a heart that beat fast with pleasure. There was a stirring in the great boughs overhead. They were full of little birds and beasts that seemed to be wide-awake, and going about their world, or else saying good-night to each other in sleepy twitters. Sylvia herself felt sleepy as she walked along. However, it was not much farther to the house, and the air was soft and sweet. She was not often in the woods so late as this, and it made her feel as if she were a part of the gray shadows and the moving leaves. She was just thinking how long it seemed since she first came to the farm a year ago, and wondering if everything went on in the noisy town just the same as when she was there; the thought of the great red-faced boy who used to chase and frighten her made her hurry along the path to escape from the shadow of the trees.

Suddenly this little woods-girl is horror-stricken to hear a clear whistle not very far away. Not a bird's whistle, which would have a sort of friendliness, but a boy's whistle, determined, and somewhat aggressive. Sylvia left the cow to whatever sad fate might await her, and stepped discreetly aside into the bushes, but she was just too late. The enemy had discovered her, and called out in a very cheerful and persuasive tone, "Halloa, little girl, how far is it to the road?" and trembling Sylvia answered almost inaudibly, "A good ways."

She did not dare to look boldly at the tall young man, who carried a gun over his shoulder, but she came out of her bush and again followed the cow, while he walked alongside.

"I have been hunting for some birds," the stranger said kindly, "and I have lost my way, and need a friend very much. Don't be afraid," he added gallantly. "Speak up and tell me what your name is, and whether you think I can spend the night at your house, and go out gunning early in the morning."

Sylvia was more alarmed than before. Would not her grandmother consider her much to blame? But who could have foreseen such an accident as this? It did not appear to be her fault, and she hung her head as if the stem of it were broken, but managed to answer, "Sylvy," with much effort when her companion again asked her name.

Mrs. Tilley was standing in the doorway when the trio came into view. The cow gave a loud moo by way of explanation.

"Yes, you'd better speak up for yourself, you old trial! Where'd she tucked herself away this time, Sylvy?" Sylvia kept an awed silence; she knew by instinct that her grandmother did not comprehend the gravity of the situation. She must be mistaking the stranger for one of the farmer-lads of the region.

The young man stood his gun beside the door, and dropped a heavy game-bag beside it; then he bade Mrs. Tilley good-evening, and repeated his way-farer's story, and asked if he could have a night's lodging.

"Put me anywhere you like," he said. "I must be off early in the morning, before day; but I am very hungry, indeed. You can give me some milk at any rate, that's plain."

"Dear sakes, yes," responded the hostess, whose long slumbering hospitality seemed to be easily awakened. "You might fare better if you went out on the main road a mile or so, but you're welcome to what we've got. I'll milk right off, and you make yourself at home. You can sleep on husks or feathers," she proffered graciously. "I raised them all myself. There's good pasturing for geese just below here towards the ma'sh. Now step round and set a plate for the gentleman, Sylvy!" And Sylvia promptly stepped. She was glad to have something to do, and she was hungry herself.

It was a surprise to find so clean and comfortable a little dwelling in this New England wilderness. The young man had known the horrors of its most primitive housekeeping, and the dreary squalor of that level of society which does not rebel at the companionship of hens. This was the best thrift of an old-fashioned farmstead, though on such a small scale that it seemed like a hermitage. He listened eagerly to the old woman's quaint talk, he watched Sylvia's pale face and shining gray eyes with ever growing enthusiasm, and insisted that this was the best supper he had eaten for a month; then, afterward, the new-made friends sat down in the doorway together while the moon came up.

Soon it would be berry-time, and Sylvia was a great help at picking. The cow was a good milker, though a plaguy thing to keep track of, the hostess gossiped frankly, adding presently that she had buried four children, so that Sylvia's mother, and a son (who might be dead) in California were all the children she had left. "Dan, my boy, was a great hand to go gunning," she explained sadly. "I never wanted for pa'tridges or gray squer'ls while he was to home. He's been a great wand'rer, I expect, and he's no hand to write letters. There, I don't blame him, I'd ha' seen the world myself if it had been so I could.

"Sylvia takes after him," the grandmother continued affectionately, after a minute's pause. "There ain't a foot o' ground she don't know her way over, and the wild creatur's counts her one o' themselves. Squer'ls she'll tame to come an' feed right out o' her hands, and all sorts o' birds. Last winter she got the jay-birds to bangeing here, and I believe she'd 'a' scanted herself of her own meals to have plenty to throw out amongst 'em, if I hadn't kep' watch. Anything but crows, I tell her, I'm willin' to help support, — though Dan he went an' tamed one o' them that did seem to have reason same as folks. It was round here a good spell after he went away. Dan an' his father they didn't hitch, — but he never held up his head ag'in after Dan had dared him an' gone off."

The guest did not notice this hint of family sorrows in his eager interest in something else.

"So Sylvy knows all about birds, does she?" he exclaimed, as he looked round at the little girl who sat, very demure but increasingly sleepy, in the moonlight. "I am making a collection of birds myself. I have been at it ever since I was a boy." (Mrs. Tilley smiled.) "There are two or three very rare ones I have been hunting for these five years. I mean to get them on my own ground if they can be found."

"Do you cage 'em up?" asked Mrs. Tilley doubtfully, in response to this enthusiastic announcement.

"Oh, no, they're stuffed and preserved, dozens and dozens of them," said the ornithologist, "and I have shot or snared every one myself. I caught a glimpse of a white heron three miles from here on Saturday, and I have followed it in this direction. They have never been found in this district at all. The little white heron, it is," and he turned again to look at Sylvia with the hope of discovering that the rare bird was one of her acquaintances.

But Sylvia was watching a hop-toad in the narrow footpath.

"You would know the heron if you saw it," the stranger continued eagerly. "A queer tall white bird with soft feathers and long thin legs. And it would have a nest perhaps in the top of a high tree, made of sticks, something like a hawk's nest."

Sylvia's heart gave a wild beat; she knew that strange white bird, and had once stolen softly near where it stood in some bright green swamp grass, away over at the other side of the woods. There was an open place where the sunshine always seemed strangely yellow and hot, where tall, nodding rushes grew, and her grandmother had warned her that she might sink in the soft black mud underneath and never be heard of more. Not far beyond were the salt marshes and beyond those was the sea, the sea which Sylvia wondered and dreamed about, but never had looked upon, though its great voice could often be heard above the noise of the woods on stormy nights.

"I can't think of anything I should like so much as to find that heron's nest," the handsome stranger was saying. "I would give ten dollars to anybody who could show it to me," he added desperately, "and I mean to spend my whole vacation hunting for it if need be. Perhaps it was only migrating, or had been chased out of its own region by some bird of prey."

Mrs. Tilley gave amazed attention to all this, but Sylvia still watched the toad, not divining, as she might have done at some calmer time, that the creature wished to get to its hole under the doorstep, and was much hindered by the unusual spectators at that hour of the evening. No amount of thought, that night, could decide how many wished-for treasures the ten dollars, so lightly spoken of, would buy.

The next day the young sportsman hovered about the woods, and Sylvia kept him company, having lost her first fear of the friendly lad, who proved to be most kind and sympathetic. He told her many things about the birds and what they knew and where they lived and what they did with themselves. And he gave her a jack-knife, which she thought as great a treasure as if she were a desert-islander. All day long he did not once make her troubled or afraid except when he brought down some unsuspecting singing creature from its bough. Sylvia would have liked him vastly better without his gun; she could not understand why he killed the very birds he seemed to like so much. But as the day waned, Sylvia still watched the young man with loving admiration. She had never seen anybody so charming and delightful; the woman's heart, asleep in the child, was vaguely thrilled by a dream of love. Some premonition of that great power stirred and swayed these young foresters who traversed the solemn woodlands with soft-footed silent care. They stopped to listen to a bird's song; they pressed forward again eagerly, parting the branches — speaking to each other rarely and in whispers; the young man going first and Sylvia following, fascinated, a few steps behind, with her gray eyes dark with excitement.

She grieved because the longed-for white heron was elusive, but she did not lead the guest, she only followed, and there was no such thing as speaking first. The sound of her own unquestioned voice would have terrified her — it was hard enough to answer yes or no when there was need of that. At last evening began to fall, and they drove the cow home together, and Sylvia smiled with pleasure when they came to the place where she heard the whistle and was afraid only the night before.

II

Half a mile from home, at the farther edge of the woods, where the land was highest, a great pine-tree stood, the last of its generation. Whether it was left for a boundary mark, or for what reason, no one could say; the woodchoppers who had felled its mates were dead and gone long ago, and a whole forest of sturdy trees, pines and oaks and maples, had grown again. But the stately head of this old pine towered above them all and made a landmark for sea and shore miles and miles away. Sylvia knew it well. She had always believed that whoever climbed to the top of it could see the ocean; and the little girl had often laid her hand on the great rough trunk and looked up wistfully at those dark boughs that the wind always stirred, no matter how hot and still the air might be below. Now she thought of the tree with a new excitement, for why, if one climbed it at break of day, could not one see all the world, and easily discover whence the white heron flew, and mark the place, and find the hidden nest?

What a spirit of adventure, what wild ambition! What fancied triumph and delight and glory for the later morning when she could make known the secret! It was almost too real and too great for the childish heart to bear.

All night the door of the little house stood open, and the whippoorwills came and sang upon the very step. The young sportsman and his old hostess were sound asleep, but Sylvia's great design kept her broad awake and watching. She forgot to think of sleep. The short summer night seemed as long as the winter darkness, and at last when the whippoorwills ceased, and she was afraid the morning would after all come too soon, she stole out of the house and followed the pasture path through the woods, hastening toward the open ground beyond, listening with a sense of comfort and companionship to the drowsy twitter of a half-awakened bird, whose perch she had jarred in passing. Alas, if the great wave of human interest which flooded for the first time this dull little life should sweep away the satisfactions of an existence heart to heart with nature and the dumb life of the forest!

There was the huge tree asleep yet in the paling moonlight, and small and hopeful Sylvia began with utmost bravery to mount to the top of it, with tingling, eager blood coursing the channels of her whole frame, with her bare feet and fingers, that pinched and held like bird's claws to the monstrous ladder reaching up, up, almost to the sky itself. First she must mount the white oak tree that grew alongside, where she was almost lost among the dark branches and the green leaves heavy and wet with dew; a bird fluttered off its nest, and a red squirrel ran to and fro and scolded pettishly at the harmless housebreaker. Sylvia felt her way easily. She had often climbed there, and knew that higher still one of the oak's upper branches chafed against the pine trunk, just where its lower boughs were set close together. There, when she made the dangerous pass from one tree to the other, the great enterprise would really begin.

She crept out along the swaying oak limb at last, and took the daring step across into the old pine-tree. The way was harder than she thought; she must reach far and hold fast, the sharp dry twigs caught and held her and scratched her like angry talons, the pitch made her thin little fingers clumsy and stiff as she went round and round the tree's great stem, higher and higher upward. The sparrows and robins in the woods below were beginning to wake and twitter to the dawn, yet it seemed much lighter there aloft in the pine-tree, and the child knew that she must hurry if her project were to be of any use.

The tree seemed to lengthen itself out as she went up, and to reach farther and farther upward. It was like a great main-mast to the voyaging earth; it must truly have been amazed that morning through all its ponderous frame as it felt this determined spark of human spirit creeping and climbing from higher branch to branch. Who knows how steadily the least twigs held themselves to advantage this light, weak creature on her way! The old pine must have loved his new dependent. More than all the hawks, and bats, and moths, and even the sweet-voiced thrushes, was the brave, beating heart of the solitary gray-eyed child. And the tree stood still and held away the winds that June morning while the dawn grew bright in the east.

Sylvia's face was like a pale star, if one had seen it from the ground, when the last thorny bough was past, and she stood trembling and tired but wholly triumphant, high in the tree-top. Yes, there was the sea with the dawning sun making a golden dazzle over it, and toward that glorious east flew two hawks with slow-moving pinions. How low they looked in the air from that height when before one had only seen them far up, and dark against the blue sky. Their gray feathers were as soft as moths; they seemed only a little way from the tree, and Sylvia felt as if she too could go flying away among the clouds. Westward, the woodlands and farms reached miles and miles into the distance; here and there were church steeples, and white villages; truly it was a vast and awesome world.

The birds sang louder and louder. At last the sun came up bewilderingly bright. Sylvia could see the white sails of ships out at sea, and the clouds that were purple and rose-colored and yellow at first began to fade away. Where was the white heron's nest in the sea of green branches, and was this wonderful sight and pageant of the world the only reward for having climbed to such a giddy height? Now look down again, Sylvia, where the green marsh is set among the shining birches and dark hemlocks; there where you saw the white heron once you will see him again; look, look! a white spot of him like a single floating feather comes up from the dead hemlock and grows larger, and rises, and comes close at last, and goes by the landmark pine with steady sweep of wing and outstretched slender neck and crested head. And wait! wait! do not move a foot or a finger, little girl, do not send an arrow of light and consciousness from your two eager eyes, for the heron has perched on a pine bough not far beyond yours, and cries back to his mate on the nest, and plumes his feathers for the new day!

The child gives a long sigh a minute later when a company of shouting catbirds comes also to the tree, and vexed by their fluttering and lawlessness the solemn heron goes away. She knows his secret now, the wild, light, slender bird that floats and wavers, and goes back like an arrow presently to his home in the green world beneath. Then Sylvia, well satisfied, makes her perilous way down again, not daring to look far below the branch she stands on, ready to cry sometimes because her fingers ache and her lamed feet slip. Wondering over and over again what the stranger would say to her, and what he would think when she told him how to find his way straight to the heron's nest.

"Sylvy, Sylvy!" called the busy old grandmother again and again, but nobody answered, and the small husk bed was empty, and Sylvia had disappeared.

The guest waked from a dream, and remembering his day's pleasure hurried to dress himself that it might sooner begin. He was sure from the way the shy little girl looked once or twice yesterday that she had at least seen the white heron, and now she must really be persuaded to tell. Here she comes now, paler than ever, and her worn old frock is torn and tattered, and smeared with pine pitch. The grandmother and the sportsman stand in the door together and question her, and the splendid moment had come to speak of the dead hemlock-tree by the green marsh.

But Sylvia does not speak after all, though the old grandmother fretfully rebukes her, and the young man's kind appealing eyes are looking straight in her own. He can make them rich with money; he has promised it, and they are poor now. He is so well worth making happy, and he waits to hear the story she can tell.

No, she must keep silence! What is it that suddenly forbids her and makes her dumb? Has she been nine years growing, and now, when the great world for the first time puts out a hand to her, must she thrust it aside for a bird's sake? The murmur of the pine's green branches is in her ears, she remembers how the white heron came flying through the golden air and how they watched the sea and the morning together, and Sylvia cannot speak; she cannot tell the heron's secret and give its life away.

Dear loyalty, that suffered a sharp pang as the guest went away disappointed later in the day, that could have served and followed him and loved him as a dog loves! Many a night Sylvia heard the echo of his whistle haunting the pasture path as she came home with the loitering cow. She forgot even her sorrow at the sharp report of his gun and the piteous sight of thrushes and sparrows dropping silent to the ground, their songs hushed and their pretty feathers stained and wet with blood. Were the birds better friends than their hunter might have been, — who can tell? Whatever treasures were lost to her, woodlands and summer-time, remember! Bring your gifts and graces and tell your secrets to this lonely country child!

Ha Jin

Ha Jin (b. 1956) was born Xuefei Jin in mainland China shortly before the start of the Cultural Revolution, which closed schools and colleges throughout the country. The son of an army officer, he volunteered at age fourteen for the army and served for nearly five years on the Russian border. He recalls that "In the beginning, I was basically illiterate. I couldn't read. Then in the second year, the border calmed down. We knew there would be no war, we would live in peace, and I began to think of education." Working as a telegrapher at a railroad company, he taught himself English from a radio course of study. In 1977, when colleges reopened in China, he left the army and enrolled as an English major at a university in Harbin. Jin earned a B.A. in English in 1981 and an M.A. in 1984. The next year he left China to become a doctoral student at Brandeis University, intending to return to China as an English teacher and translator. The atrocity of the June 4, 1989, massacre at Tiananmen Square, where Chinese soldiers killed dissident students and civilians demonstrating against the repressive government, convinced him that he should stay in the United States with his Chinese wife and son. Jin said he became an American citizen because he felt he could never write honestly in China.

Accepting permanent exile, Jin began writing poetry and fiction in English at Brandeis, where he completed his doctorate in 1993. Under the pen name Ha Jin, he published his first book of poetry, *Between Silences*, in 1990. Working as a busboy, waiter, and night watchman because he couldn't find a job teaching Chinese literature, Jin supported his family while writing short stories. *Ocean of Words* (1996), his first story collection, won the PEN/Hemingway Award, while *Under the Red Flag* (1997) received the Flannery O'Connor Award for Short Fiction. Jin's novella *In the Pond* (1998) was selected as the best fiction book of that year by the *Chicago Tribune*. His short stories were included in *The Best American Short Stories* (1997 and 1999) and three Pushcart Prize anthologies. His novel *Waiting* won both the 1999 National Book Award for Fiction and the 2000 PEN/Faulkner Award. His novel *War Trash* was published in 2004. In 2008 he published an essay collection, *The Writer as Migrant*.

Jin has told the interviewer Rich Rennicks that he feels "more at home" writing short fiction than poetry or novels.

> Poetry largely depends on luck. You never know when you can write the next poem. As for a novel, you need time and leisure—which I don't often have. You have to let yourself live in the novel for a long time, possessed by the characters. When I am teaching, this is difficult. But short fiction is possible. You can work on a story intensely for two or three hours a day, then go to teach your class.

In stories such as "Saboteur," Jin has stated that he is not attempting to explain Chinese culture to his Western readers. He believes that "at heart we are all the same. Literature operates on the principle of similarity and identity, not on difference." This story is from Jin's collection *The Bridegroom* and was included in the 2000 edition of *The Best American Short Stories*. *A Good Fall* (2010) is a recent story collection.

Saboteur

2000

MR. CHIU AND HIS BRIDE were having lunch in the square before Muji Train Station. On the table between them were two bottles of soda spewing out brown foam and two paper boxes of rice and sautéed cucumber and pork. "Let's eat," he said to her, and broke the connected ends of the chopsticks. He picked up a slice of streaky pork and put it into his mouth. As he was chewing, a few crinkles appeared on his thin jaw.

To his right, at another table, two railroad policemen were drinking tea and laughing; it seemed that the stout, middle-aged man was telling a joke to his young comrade, who was tall and of athletic build. Now and again they would steal a glance at Mr. Chiu's table.

The air smelled of rotten melon. A few flies kept buzzing above the couple's lunch. Hundreds of people were rushing around to get on the platform or to catch buses to downtown. Food and fruit vendors were crying for customers in lazy voices. About a dozen young women, representing the local hotels, held up placards which displayed the daily prices and words as large as a palm, like FREE MEALS, AIR-CONDITIONING, and ON THE RIVER. In the center of the square stood a concrete statue of Chairman Mao, at whose feet were peasants were napping, their backs on the warm granite and their faces toward the sunny sky. A flock of pigeons perched on the Chairman's raised hand and forearm.

The rice and cucumber tasted good, and Mr. Chiu was eating unhurriedly. His sallow face showed exhaustion. He was glad that the honeymoon was finally over and that he and his bride were heading back for Harbin. During the two weeks' vacation, he had been worried about his liver, because three months ago he had suffered from acute hepatitis; he was afraid he might have a relapse. But he had had no severe symptoms, despite his liver being still big and tender. On the whole he was pleased with his health, which could endure even the strain of a honeymoon; indeed, he was on the course of recovery. He looked at his bride, who took off her wire glasses, kneading the root of her nose with her fingertips. Beads of sweat coated her pale cheeks.

"Are you all right, sweetheart?" he asked.

"I have a headache. I didn't sleep well last night."

"Take an aspirin, will you?"

"It's not that serious. Tomorrow is Sunday and I can sleep in. Don't worry."

As they were talking, the stout policeman at the next table stood up and threw a bowl of tea in their direction. Both Mr. Chiu's and his bride's sandals were wet instantly.

"Hooligan!" she said in a low voice.

Mr. Chiu got to his feet and said out loud, "Comrade Policeman, why did you do this?" He stretched out his right foot to show the wet sandal.

"Do what?" the stout man asked huskily, glaring at Mr. Chiu while the young fellow was whistling.

"See, you dumped tea on our feet."

"You're lying. You wet your shoes yourself."

"Comrade Policemen, your duty is to keep order, but you purposely tortured us common citizens. Why violate the law you are supposed to enforce?" As Mr. Chiu was speaking, dozens of people began gathering around.

With a wave of his hand, the man said to the young fellow, "Let's get hold of him!"

They grabbed Mr. Chiu and clamped handcuffs around his wrists. He cried, "You can't do this to me. This is utterly unreasonable."

"Shut up!" The man pulled out his pistol. "You can use your tongue at our headquarters."

The young fellow added, "You're a saboteur, you know that? You're disrupting public order."

The bride was too petrified to say anything coherent. She was a recent college graduate, had majored in fine arts, and had never seen the police make an arrest. All she could say was, "Oh, please, please!"

The policemen were pulling Mr. Chiu, but he refused to go with them, holding the corner of the table and shouting, "We have a train to catch. We already bought the tickets."

The stout man punched him in the chest. "Shut up. Let your ticket expire." With the pistol butt he chopped Mr. Chiu's hands, which at once released the table. Together the two men were dragging him away to the police station.

Realizing he had to go with them, Mr. Chiu turned his head and shouted to his bride, "Don't wait for me here. Take the train. If I'm not back by tomorrow morning, send someone over to get me out."

She nodded, covering her sobbing mouth with her palm.

After removing his belt, they locked Mr. Chiu into a cell in the back of the Railroad Police Station. The single window in the room was blocked by six steel bars; it faced a spacious yard, in which stood a few pines. Beyond the trees, two swings hung from an iron frame, swaying gently in the breeze. Somewhere in the building a cleaver was chopping rhythmically. There must be a kitchen upstairs, Mr. Chiu thought.

He was too exhausted to worry about what they would do to him, so he lay down on the narrow bed and shut his eyes. He wasn't afraid. The Cultural Revolution was over already, and recently the Party had been propagating the idea that all citizens were equal before the law. The police ought to be a law-abiding model for common people. As long as he remained coolheaded and reasoned with them, they probably wouldn't harm him.

Late in the afternoon he was taken to the Interrogation Bureau on the second floor. On his way there, in the stairwell, he ran into the middle-aged policeman who had manhandled him. The man grinned, rolling his bulgy eyes and pointing his fingers at him as if firing a pistol. Egg of a tortoise! Mr. Chiu cursed mentally.

The moment he sat down in the office, he burped, his palm shielding his mouth. In front of him, across a long desk, sat the chief of the bureau and a donkey-faced man. On the glass desktop was a folder containing information on his case. He felt it bizarre that in just a matter of hours they had accumulated a small pile of writing about him. On second thought he began to wonder whether they had kept a file on him all the time. How could this have happened? He lived and worked in Harbin, more than three hundred miles away, and this was his first time in Muji City.

The chief of the bureau was a thin, bald man who looked serene and intelligent. His slim hands handled the written pages in the folder in the manner of a lecturing scholar. To Mr. Chiu's left sat a young scribe, with a clipboard on his knee and a black fountain pen in his hand.

"Your name?" the chief asked, apparently reading out the question from a form.

"Chiu Maguang."

"Age?"

"Thirty-four."

"Profession?"

"Lecturer."

"Work unit?"

"Harbin University."

"Political status?"

"Communist Party member."

The chief put down the paper and began to speak. "Your crime is sabotage, although it hasn't induced serious consequences yet. Because you are a Party member, you should be punished more. You have failed to be a model for the masses and you —"

"Excuse me, sir," Mr. Chiu cut him off.

"What?"

"I didn't do anything. Your men are the saboteurs of our social order. They threw hot tea on my feet and on my wife's feet. Logically speaking, you should criticize them, if not punish them."

"That statement is groundless. You have no witness. Why should I believe you?" the chief said matter-of-factly.

"This is my evidence." He raised his right hand. "Your man hit my fingers with a pistol."

"That doesn't prove how your feet got wet. Besides, you could have hurt your fingers yourself."

"But I am telling the truth!" Anger flared up in Mr. Chiu. "Your police station owes me an apology. My train ticket has expired, my new leather sandals are ruined, and I am late for a conference in the provincial capital. You must compensate me for the damage and losses. Don't mistake me for a common citizen who would tremble when you sneeze. I'm a scholar, a philosopher, and an expert in dialectical materialism. If necessary, we will argue about this in *The Northeastern Daily*, or we will go to the highest People's Court in Beijing. Tell me, what's your name?" He got carried away with his harangue, which was by no means trivial and had worked to his advantage on numerous occasions.

"Stop bluffing us," the donkey-faced man broke in. "We have seen a lot of your kind. We can easily prove you are guilty. Here are some of the statements given by eyewitnesses." He pushed a few sheets of paper toward Mr. Chiu.

Mr. Chiu was dazed to see the different handwritings, which all stated that he had shouted in the square to attract attention and refused to obey the police. One of the witnesses had identified herself as a purchasing agent from a shipyard in Shanghai. Something stirred in Mr. Chiu's stomach, a pain rising to his rib. He gave out a faint moan.

"Now you have to admit you are guilty," the chief said. "Although it's a serious crime, we won't punish you severely, provided you write out a self-criticism and promise that you won't disrupt the public order again. In other words, your release will depend on your attitude toward this crime."

"You're daydreaming!" Mr. Chiu cried. "I won't write a word, because I'm innocent. I demand that you provide me with a letter of apology so I can explain to my university why I'm late."

Both the interrogators smiled contemptuously. "Well, we've never done that," said the chief, taking a puff of his cigarette.

"Then make this a precedent."

"That's unnecessary. We are pretty certain that you will comply with our wishes." The chief blew a column of smoke toward Mr. Chiu's face.

At the tilt of the chief's head, two guards stepped forward and grabbed the criminal by the arms. Mr. Chiu meanwhile went on saying, "I shall report you to the Provincial Administration. You'll have to pay for this! You are worse than the Japanese military police."

They dragged him out of the room.

After dinner, which consisted of a bowl of millet porridge, a corn bun, and a piece of pickled turnip, Mr. Chiu began to have a fever, shaking with a chill and sweating profusely. He knew that the fire of anger had gotten into his liver and that he was probably having a relapse. No medicine was available, because his briefcase had been left with his bride. At home it would have been time for him to sit in front of their color TV, drinking jasmine tea and watching the evening news. It was so lonesome in here. The orange bulb above the single bed was the only source of light, which enabled the guards to keep him under surveillance at night. A moment ago he had asked them for a newspaper or a magazine to read, but they turned him down.

Through the small opening on the door noises came in. It seemed that the police on duty were playing cards or chess in a nearby office; shouts and laughter could be heard now and then. Meanwhile, an accordion kept coughing from a remote corner in the building. Looking at the ballpoint and the letter paper left for him by the guards when they took him back from the Interrogation Bureau, Mr. Chiu remembered the old saying, "When a scholar runs into soldiers, the more he argues, the muddier his point becomes." How ridiculous this whole thing was. He ruffled his thick hair with his fingers.

He felt miserable, massaging his stomach continually. To tell the truth, he was more upset than frightened, because he would have to catch up with his work once he was back home — a paper that was due at the printers next week, and two dozen books he ought to read for the courses he was going to teach in the fall.

A human shadow flitted across the opening. Mr. Chiu rushed to the door and shouted through the hole, "Comrade Guard, Comrade Guard!"

"What do you want?" a voice rasped.

"I want you to inform your leaders that I'm very sick. I have heart disease and hepatitis. I may die here if you keep me like this without medication."

"No leader is on duty on the weekend. You have to wait till Monday."

"What? You mean I'll stay in here tomorrow?"

"Yes."

"Your station will be held responsible if anything happens to me."

"We know that. Take it easy, you won't die."

It seemed illogical that Mr. Chiu slept quite well that night, though the light above his head had been on all the time and the straw mattress was hard and infested with fleas. He was afraid of ticks, mosquitoes, cockroaches — any kind of insect but fleas and bedbugs. Once, in the countryside, where his school's faculty and staff had helped the peasants harvest crops for a week, his colleagues had joked about his flesh, which they said must have tasted nonhuman to fleas. Except for him, they were all afflicted with hundreds of bites.

More amazing now, he didn't miss his bride a lot. He even enjoyed sleeping alone, perhaps because the honeymoon had tired him out and he needed more rest.

The backyard was quiet on Sunday morning. Pale sunlight streamed through the pine branches. A few sparrows were jumping on the ground, catching caterpillars and ladybugs. Holding the steel bars, Mr. Chiu inhaled the morning air, which smelled meaty. There must have been an eatery or a cooked-meat stand nearby. He reminded himself that he should take this detention with ease. A sentence that Chairman Mao had written to a hospitalized friend rose in his mind: "Since you are already in here, you may as well stay and make the best of it."

His desire for peace of mind originated in his fear that his hepatitis might get worse. He tried to remain unperturbed. However, he was sure that his liver was swelling up, since the fever still persisted. For a whole day he lay in bed, thinking about his paper on the nature of contradictions. Time and again he was overwhelmed by anger, cursing aloud, "A bunch of thugs!" He swore that once he was out, he would write an article about this experience. He had better find out some of the policemen's names.

It turned out to be a restful day for the most part; he was certain that his university would send somebody to his rescue. All he should do now was remain calm and wait patiently. Sooner or later the police would have to release him, although they had no idea that he might refuse to leave unless they wrote him an apology. Damn those hoodlums, they had ordered more than they could eat!

When he woke up on Monday morning, it was already light. Somewhere a man was moaning; the sound came from the backyard. After a long yawn, and kicking off the tattered blanket, Mr. Chiu climbed out of bed and went to the window. In the middle of the yard, a young man was fastened to a pine, his wrists handcuffed around the trunk from behind. He was wriggling and swearing loudly, but there was no sight of anyone else in the yard. He looked familiar to Mr. Chiu.

Mr. Chiu squinted his eyes to see who it was. To his astonishment, he recognized the man, who was Fenjin, a recent graduate from the Law Department at Harbin University. Two years ago Mr. Chiu had taught a course in Marxist materialism, in which Fenjin had enrolled. Now, how on earth had this young devil landed here?

Then it dawned on him that Fenjin must have been sent over by his bride. What a stupid woman! A bookworm, who only knew how to read foreign novels! He had expected that she would contact the school's Security Section, which would for sure send a cadre here. Fenjin held no official position; he merely worked in a private law firm that had just two lawyers; in fact, they had little business except for some detective work for men and women who suspected their spouses of having extramarital affairs. Mr. Chiu was overcome with a wave of nausea.

Should he call out to let his student know he was nearby? He decided not to because he didn't know what had happened. Fenjin must have quarreled with the police to incur such a punishment. Yet this could never have occurred if Fenjin hadn't come to his rescue. So no matter what, Mr. Chiu had to do something. But what could he do?

It was going to be a scorcher. He could see purple steam shimmering and rising from the ground among the pines. Poor devil, he thought, as he raised a bowl of corn glue to his mouth, sipped, and took a bite of a piece of salted celery.

When a guard came to collect the bowl and the chopsticks, Mr. Chiu asked him what had happened to the man in the backyard. "He called our boss 'bandit,'" the guard said. "He claimed he was a lawyer or something. An arrogant son of a rabbit."

Now it was obvious to Mr. Chiu that he had to do something to help his rescuer. Before he could figure out a way, a scream broke out in the backyard. He rushed to the window and saw a tall policeman standing before Fenjin, an iron bucket on the ground. It was the same young fellow who had arrested Mr. Chiu in the square two days before. The man pinched Fenjin's nose, then raised his hand, which stayed in the air for a few seconds, then slapped the lawyer across the face. As Fenjin was groaning, the man lifted up the bucket and poured water on his head.

"This will keep you from getting sunstroke, boy. I'll give you some more every hour," the man said loudly.

Fenjin kept his eyes shut, yet his wry face showed that he was struggling to hold back from cursing the policeman, or, more likely, that he was sobbing in silence. He sneezed, then raised his face and shouted, "Let me go take a piss."

"Oh, yeah?" the man bawled. "Pee in your pants."

Still Mr. Chiu didn't make any noise, gripping the steel bars with both hands, his fingers white. The policeman turned and glanced at the cell's window; his pistol, partly holstered, glittered in the sun. With a snort he spat his cigarette butt to the ground and stamped it into the dust.

Then the door opened and the guards motioned Mr. Chiu to come out. Again they took him upstairs to the Interrogation Bureau.

The same men were in the office, though this time the scribe was sitting there empty-handed. At the sight of Mr. Chiu the chief said, "Ah, here you are. Please be seated."

After Mr. Chiu sat down, the chief waved a white silk fan and said to him, "You may have seen your lawyer. He's a young man without manners, so our director had him taught a crash course in the backyard."

"It's illegal to do that. Aren't you afraid to appear in a newspaper?"

"No, we are not, not even on TV. What else can you do? We are not afraid of any story you make up. We call it fiction. What we do care about is that you cooperate with us. That is to say, you must admit your crime."

"What if I refuse to cooperate?"

"Then your lawyer will continue his education in the sunshine."

A swoon swayed Mr. Chiu, and he held the arms of the chair to steady himself. A numb pain stung him in the upper stomach and nauseated him, and his head was throbbing. He was sure that the hepatitis was finally attacking him. Anger was flaming up in his chest; his throat was tight and clogged.

The chief resumed, "As a matter of fact, you don't even have to write out your self-criticism. We have your crime described clearly here. All we need is your signature."

Holding back his rage, Mr. Chiu said, "Let me look at that."

With a smirk the donkey-faced man handed him a sheet which carried these words:

> I hereby admit that on July 13 I disrupted public order at Muji Train Station, and that I refused to listen to reason when the railroad police issued their warning. Thus I myself am responsible for my arrest. After two days' detention, I have realized the reactionary nature of my crime. From now on, I shall continue to educate myself with all my effort and shall never commit this kind of crime again.

A voice started screaming in Mr. Chiu's ears, "Lie, lie!" But he shook his head and forced the voice away. He asked the chief, "If I sign this, will you release both my lawyer and me?"

"Of course, we'll do that." The chief was drumming his fingers on the blue folder — their file on him.

Mr. Chiu signed his name and put his thumbprint under his signature.

"Now you are free to go," the chief said with a smile, and handed him a piece of paper to wipe his thumb with.

Mr. Chiu was so sick that he couldn't stand up from the chair at first try. Then he doubled his effort and rose to his feet. He staggered out of the building to meet his lawyer in the backyard, having forgotten to ask for his belt back. In his chest he felt as though there were a bomb. If he were able to, he would have razed the entire police station and eliminated all their families. Though he knew he could do nothing like that, he made up his mind to do something.

"I'm sorry about this torture, Fenjin," Mr. Chiu said when they met.

"It doesn't matter. They are savages." The lawyer brushed a patch of dirt off his jacket with trembling fingers. Water was still dribbling from the bottoms of his trouser legs.

"Let's go now," the teacher said.

The moment they came out of the police station, Mr. Chiu caught sight of a tea stand. He grabbed Fenjin's arm and walked over to the old woman at the table. "Two bowls of black tea," he said and handed her a one-yuan note.

After the first bowl, they each had another one. Then they set out for the train station. But before they walked fifty yards, Mr. Chiu insisted on eating a bowl of tree-ear soup at a food stand. Fenjin agreed. He told his teacher, "You mustn't treat me like a guest."

"No, I want to eat something myself."

As if dying of hunger, Mr. Chiu dragged his lawyer from restaurant to restaurant near the police station, but at each place he ordered no more than two bowls of food. Fenjin wondered why his teacher wouldn't stay at one place and eat his fill.

Mr. Chiu bought noodles, wonton, eight-grain porridge, and chicken soup, respectively, at four restaurants. While eating, he kept saying through his teeth, "If only I could kill all the bastards!" At the last place he merely took a few sips of the soup without tasting the chicken cubes and mushrooms.

Fenjin was baffled by his teacher, who looked ferocious and muttered to himself mysteriously, and whose jaundiced face was covered with dark puckers. For the first time Fenjin thought of Mr. Chiu as an ugly man.

Within a month over eight hundred people contracted acute hepatitis in Muji. Six died of the disease, including two children. Nobody knew how the epidemic had started.

Denis Johnson

Denis Johnson (b. 1949) was born in Munich, Germany, and raised in Tokyo, Manila, and Washington. For a few months in 1973, while his parents lived in Arizona, he traveled up and down the West Coast. Describing the experience later in *The New Yorker*, Johnson recalled that in February when he landed in Berkeley he believed himself to be "a young man convinced that everything that happened to him was something he'd someday write about." He discovered that he and the other druggies he met on the streets believed "that we'd broken the bonds of mindless materialism and hypocritical conformity and were now just natually floundering around until the new shape of human freedom manifested itself." Two months later he left "the maniac road" to return to his parents and a job before he "headed back to college, where I stayed for as long as they'd have me."

Johnson published his first book, *The Incognito Lounge and Other Poems*, in 1982 and followed it with four novels before publishing the volume of short fiction, *Jesus' Son* (1992), that was heralded as a landmark in drug literature by an American author. "Work" is a story from that collection. Johnson told interviewer Andrea Clark for an article in the *San Francisco Reader* the he was "straight" when he wrote *Jesus' Son*: "I didn't write it under the influence. I don't know how you can. I mean, your hands get real big. How could you type?" Johnson recalled that

> What's funny about *Jesus' Son* is that I never even wrote that book, I just wrote it down. I would tell these stories apropos of nothing about when I was drinking and using and people would say, "You should write these things down." I was probably 35 when I wrote the first story. The voice is kind of a mix in that it has a young voice, but it's also someone who's looking back. I like that kind of double vision. So I worked on them once in a while, then I started using stories I heard other people tell, and then I started making some up. Pretty soon it was fiction. Then I just forgot about it. I thought, I'm not going to parade my defects, my history of being a spiritual cripple, out in front of other people. But once in a while I'd write a little more—I would just hear the voices.

Johnson's writing has appeared in *The Paris Review*, *The New Yorker*, and *McSweeney's*. In addition to poetry and fiction, he has also written plays for Campo Santo, a San Francisco theater company. He told Clark, "If you write fiction, you're by yourself. There are certain advantages to that in that you don't have to explain anything to anybody. But when you get in with others who share the loneliness of the whole enterprise, you're not alone anymore." Johnson's recent novels are *Tree of Smoke* (2007), winner of a National Book Award, and *Nobody Move* (2009). In 2012 he published *Soul of a Whore and Purvis: Two Plays in Verse*.

Work

1992

I'D BEEN STAYING AT THE Holiday Inn with my girlfriend, honestly the most beautiful woman I'd ever known, for three days under a phony name, shooting heroin. We made love in the bed, ate steaks at the restaurant, shot up in the john, puked, cried, accused one another, begged of one another, forgave, promised, and carried one another to heaven.

But there was a fight. I stood outside the motel hitchhiking, dressed up in a hurry, shirtless under my jacket, with the wind crying through my earring. A bus came. I climbed aboard and sat on the plastic seat while the things of our city turned in the windows like the images in a slot machine.

Once, as we stood arguing at a streetcorner, I punched her in the stomach. She doubled over and broke down crying. A car full of young college men stopped beside us.

"She's feeling sick," I told them.

"Bullshit," one of them said. "You elbowed her right in the *gut*."

"He did, he did, he did," she said, weeping.

I don't remember what I said to them. I remember loneliness crushing first my lungs, then my heart, then my balls. They put her in the car with them and drove away.

But she came back.

This morning, after the fight, after sitting on the bus for several blocks with a thoughtless, red mind, I jumped down and walked into the Vine.

The Vine was still and cold. Wayne was the only customer. His hands were shaking. He couldn't lift his glass.

I put my left hand on Wayne's shoulder, and with my right, opiated and steady, I brought his shot of bourbon to his lips.

"How would you feel about making some money?" he asked me.

"I was just going to go over here in the corner and nod out," I informed him.

"I decided," he said, "in my mind, to make some money."

"So what?" I said.

"Come with me," he begged.

"You mean you need a ride."

"I have the tools," he said. "All we need is that sorry-ass car of yours to get around in."

We found my sixty-dollar Chevrolet, the finest and best thing I ever bought, considering the price, in the streets near my apartment. I liked that car. It was the kind of thing you could bang into a phone pole with and nothing would happen at all.

Wayne cradled his burlap sack of tools in his lap as we drove out of town to where the fields bunched up into hills and then dipped down toward a cool river mothered by benevolent clouds.

All the houses on the riverbank—a dozen or so—were abandoned. The same company, you could tell, had built them all, and then painted them four different colors. The windows in the lower stories were empty of glass. We passed alongside them and I saw that the ground floors of these buildings were covered with silt. Sometime back a flood had run over the banks, cancelling everything. But now the river was flat and slow. Willows stroked the waters with their hair.

"Are we doing a burglary?" I asked Wayne.

"You can't burgulate a forgotten, empty house," he said, horrified at my stupidity.

I didn't say anything.

"This is a salvage job," he said. "Pull up to that one, right about there."

The house we parked in front of just had a terrible feeling about it. I knocked.

"Don't do that," Wayne said. "It's stupid."

Inside, our feet kicked up the silt the river had left here. The watermark wandered the walls of the downstairs about three feet above the floor. Straight, stiff grass lay all over the place in bunches, as if someone had stretched them there to dry.

Wayne used a pry bar, and I had a shiny hammer with a blue rubber grip. We put the pry points in the seams of the wall and started tearing away the Sheetrock. It came loose with a noise like old men coughing. Whenever we exposed some of the wiring in its white plastic jacket, we ripped it free of its connections, pulled it out, and bunched it up. That's what we were after. We intended to sell the copper wire for scrap.

By the time we were on the second floor, I could see we were going to make some money. But I was getting tired. I dropped the hammer, went to the bathroom. I was sweaty and thirsty. But of course the water didn't work.

I went back to Wayne, standing in one of two small empty bedrooms, and started dancing around and pounding the walls, breaking through the Sheetrock and making a giant racket, until the hammer got stuck. Wayne ignored this misbehavior.

I was catching my breath.

I asked him, "Who owned these houses, do you think?"

He stopped doing anything, "This is my house."

"It is?"

"It was."

He gave the wire a long, smooth yank, a gesture full of the serenity of hatred, popping its staples and freeing it into the room.

We balled up big gobs of wire in the center of each room, working for over an hour. I boosted Wayne through the trapdoor into the attic, and he pulled me up after him, both of us sweating and our pores leaking the poisons of drink, which smelled like old citrus peelings, and we made a mound of white-jacketed wire in the top of his former home, pulling it up out of the floor.

I felt weak. I had to vomit in the corner—just a thimbleful of grey bile. "All this work," I complained, "is fucking with my high. Can't you figure out some easier way of making a dollar?"

Wayne went to the window. He rapped it several times with his pry bar, each time harder, until it was loudly destroyed. We threw the stuff out there onto the mud-flattened meadow that came right up below us from the river.

It was quiet in this strange neighborhood along the bank except for the steady breeze in the young leaves. But now we heard a boat coming upstream. The sound curlicued through the riverside saplings like a bee, and in a minute a flat-nosed sports boat cut up the middle of the river going thirty or forty, at least.

This boat was pulling behind itself a tremendous triangular kite on a rope. From the kite, up in the air a hundred feet or so, a woman was suspended, belted in somehow, I would have guessed. She had long red hair. She was delicate and white, and naked except for her beautiful hair. I don't know what she was thinking as she floated past these ruins.

"What's she doing?" was all I could say, though we could see that she was flying.

"Now, that is a beautiful sight," Wayne said.

On the way to town, Wayne asked me to make a long detour onto the Old Highway. He had me pull up to a lopsided farmhouse set on a hill of grass.

"I'm not going in but for two seconds," he said. "You want to come in?"

"Who's here?" I said.

"Come and see," he told me.

It didn't seem anyone was home when we climbed the porch and he knocked. But he didn't knock again, and after a full three minutes a woman opened the door, a slender redhead in a dress printed with small blossoms. She didn't smile. "Hi," was all she said to us.

"Can we come in?" Wayne asked.

"Let me come onto the porch," she said, and walked past us to stand looking out over the fields.

I waited at the other end of the porch, leaning against the rail, and didn't listen. I don't know what they said to one another. She walked down the steps, and Wayne followed. He stood hugging himself and talking down at the earth. The wind lifted and dropped her long red hair. She was about forty, with a bloodless, waterlogged beauty. I guessed Wayne was the storm that had stranded her here.

In a minute he said to me, "Come on." He got in the driver's seat and started the car — you didn't need a key to start it.

I came down the steps and got in beside him. He looked at her through the windshield. She hadn't gone back inside yet, or done anything at all.

"That's my wife," he told me, as if it wasn't obvious.

I turned around in the seat and studied Wayne's wife as we drove off.

What word can be uttered about those fields? She stood in the middle of them as on a high mountain, with her red hair pulled out sideways by the wind, around her the green and grey plains pressed down flat, and all the grasses of Iowa whistling one note.

I knew who she was.

"That was her, wasn't it?" I said.

Wayne was speechless.

There was no doubt in my mind. She was the woman we'd seen flying over the river. As nearly as I could tell, I'd wandered into some sort of dream that Wayne was having about his wife, and his house. But I didn't say anything more about it.

Because, after all, in small ways, it was turning out to be one of the best days of my life, whether it was somebody else's dream or not. We turned in the scrap wire for twenty-eight dollars — each — at a salvage yard near the gleaming tracks at the edge of town, and went back to the Vine.

Who should be pouring drinks there but a young woman whose name I can't remember. But I remember the way she poured. It was like doubling your money. She wasn't going to make her employers rich. Needless to say, she was revered among us.

"I'm buying," I said.

"No way in hell," Wayne said.

"Come on."

"It is," Wayne said, "my sacrifice."

Sacrifice? Where had he gotten a word like sacrifice? Certainly I had never heard of it.

I'd seen Wayne look across the poker table in a bar and accuse — I do not exaggerate — the biggest, blackest man in Iowa of cheating, accuse him for no other reason than that he, Wayne, was a bit irked by the run of the cards. That was my idea of sacrifice, tossing yourself away, discarding your body. The black man stood up and circled the neck of a beer bottle with his fingers. He was taller than anyone who had ever entered that barroom.

"Step outside," Wayne said.

And the man said, "This ain't school."

"What the goddamn fucking piss-hell," Wayne said, "is that suppose to mean?"

"I ain't stepping outside like you do at school. Make your try right here and now."

"This ain't a place for our kind of business," Wayne said, "not inside here with women and children and dogs and cripples."

"Shit," the man said. "You're just drunk."

"I don't care," Wayne said. "To me you don't make no more noise than a fart in a paper bag."

The huge, murderous man said nothing.

"I'm going to sit down now," Wayne said, "and I'm going to play my game, and fuck you."

The man shook his head. He sat down too. This was an amazing thing. By reaching out one hand and taking hold of it for two or three seconds, he could have popped Wayne's head like an egg.

And then came one of those moments. I remember living through one when I was eighteen and spending the afternoon in bed with my first wife, before we were married. Our naked bodies started glowing, and the air turned such a strange color I thought my life must be leaving me, and with every young fiber and cell I wanted to hold on to it for another breath. A clattering sound was tearing up my head as I staggered upright and opened the door on a vision I will never see again: Where are my women now, with their sweet wet words and ways, and the miraculous balls of hail popping in a green translucence in the yards?

We put on our clothes, she and I, and walked out into a town flooded ankle-deep with white, buoyant stones. Birth should have been like that.

That moment in the bar, after the fight was narrowly averted, was like the green silence after the hailstorm. Somebody was buying a round of drinks. The cards were scattered on the table, face up, face down, and they seemed to foretell that whatever we did to one another would be washed away by liquor or explained away by sad songs.

Wayne was a part of all that.

The Vine was like a railroad club car that had somehow run itself off the tracks into a swamp of time where it awaited the blows of the wrecking ball. And the blows really were coming. Because of Urban Renewal, they were tearing up and throwing away the whole downtown.

And here we were, this afternoon, with nearly thirty dollars each, and our favorite, our very favorite, person tending bar. I wish I could remember her name, but I remember only her grace and her generosity.

All the really good times happened when Wayne was around. But this afternoon, somehow, was the best of all those times. We had money. We were grimy and tired. Usually we felt guilty and frightened, because there was something wrong with us, and we didn't know what it was; but today we had the feeling of men who had worked.

The Vine had no jukebox, but a real stereo continually playing tunes of alcoholic self-pity and sentimental divorce. "Nurse," I sobbed. She poured doubles like an angel, right up to the lip of a cocktail glass, no measuring. "You have a lovely pitching arm." You had to go down to them like a humming-bird over a blossom. I saw her much later, not too many years ago, and when I smiled she seemed to believe I was making advances. But it was only that I remembered. I'll never forget you. Your husband will beat you with an extension cord and the bus will pull away leaving you standing there in tears, but you were my mother.

James Joyce

James Joyce (1882–1941) was born James Augustine Aloysius Joyce in Rathgar, a suburb of Dublin, during a turbulent era of political change in Ireland. His parents sent him at the age of six to the best Jesuit school, Clongowes Wood College, where he spent three years; but in 1891 his father was no longer able to afford the tuition, and he was withdrawn. During the period of his parents' financial decline, Joyce — a brilliant student — was educated at home and then given free tuition at Belvedere College, where he won prizes for his essays. Shortly after taking his bachelor's degree in 1902 from University College, Dublin, he left Ireland for Paris, where he attended one class at the Collège de Médecine but dropped out because he could not afford the fees. Nearly starving, he remained in Paris and wrote what he called "Epiphanies." These were notebook jottings of overheard conversations or passing observations that he later incorporated into his fiction, thinking that they illuminated in a flash the meaning of a group of apparently unrelated phenomena. In April 1903 Joyce returned to Dublin because his mother was dying. He remained in Ireland for a short time as a teacher, but the following year he went to live abroad again, disillusioned by his home country's political corruption and religious hypocrisy.

Dubliners (1914), a group of fifteen short stories begun in 1904, was Joyce's attempt to "write a chapter of the moral history" of Ireland. He chose Dublin for the setting because that city seemed to him "the center of paralysis," but he also thought of following the book with another titled "Provincials." As if to prove his perception of the extent of stifling moral repression in his country, he had great difficulties getting the book published — a struggle lasting nine years. This so angered and frustrated Joyce that he never again lived in Ireland; he settled in Trieste, Zurich, and Paris and wrote the novels that established him as one of the greatest authors of modern times: *A Portrait of the Artist as a Young Man* (1916), *Ulysses* (1922), and *Finnegans Wake* (1939).

Joyce's stories about the lives of young people, servants, politicians, and the complacent middle class were intended to represent a broad spectrum of Dublin life, not "a collection of tourist impressions" but a penetrating account of the spiritual waste of his time. Today's reader finds it difficult to believe that some stories in *Dubliners* could have appeared so scandalous to Joyce's publishers that at one point the plates were destroyed at the printers. "Araby" and "The Dead" suggest the periods of youth, adolescence, and maturity that Joyce included in his book. His technique blends a detached sympathy for his subject with a "scrupulous meanness" of observed detail. Instead of dramatic plots, he structured his stories around "epiphanies" — evanescent moments that reveal "a sudden spiritual manifestation, whether in the vulgarity of speech or of gesture or in a memorable expression of the mind itself."

RELATED STORY
John Updike, "A & P," page 1290.

RELATED COMMENTARIES
Richard Ellmann, "A Biographical Perspective on Joyce's 'The Dead,'" page 1422; Frank O'Connor, "Style and Form in Joyce's 'The Dead,'" page 1497.

Araby

1914

NORTH RICHMOND STREET, being blind, was a quiet street except at the hour when the Christian Brothers' School set the boys free. An uninhabited house of two storeys stood at the blind end, detached from its neighbours in a square ground. The other houses of the street, conscious of decent lives within them, gazed at one another with brown imperturbable faces.

The former tenant of our house, a priest, had died in the back drawing-room. Air, musty from having been long enclosed, hung in all the rooms, and the waste room behind the kitchen was littered with old useless papers. Among these I found a few paper-covered books, the pages of which were curled and damp: *The Abbot*, by Walter Scott, *The Devout Communicant*, and *The Memoirs of Vidocq*. I liked the last best because its leaves were yellow. The wild garden behind the house contained a central apple-tree and a few straggling bushes under one of which I found the late tenant's rusty bicycle-pump. He had been a very charitable priest; in his will he had left all his money to institutions and the furniture of his house to his sister.

When the short days of winter came dusk fell before we had well eaten our dinners. When we met in the street the houses had grown sombre. The space of sky above us was the colour of ever-changing violet and towards it the lamps of the street lifted their feeble lanterns. The cold air stung us and we played till our bodies glowed. Our shouts echoed in the silent street. The career of our play brought us through the dark muddy lanes behind the houses where we ran the gauntlet of the rough tribes from the cottages, to the back doors of the dark dripping gardens where odours arose from the ashpits, to the dark odorous stables where a coachman smoothed and combed the horse or shook music from the buckled harness. When we returned to the street light from the kitchen windows had filled the areas. If my uncle was seen turning the corner we hid in the shadow until we had seen him safely housed. Or if Mangan's sister came out on the doorstep to call her brother in to his tea we watched her from our shadow peer up and down the street. We waited to see whether she would remain or go in and, if she remained, we left our shadow and walked up to Mangan's steps resignedly. She was waiting for us, her figure defined by the light from the half-opened door. Her brother always teased her before he obeyed and I stood by the railings looking at her. Her dress swung as she moved her body and the soft rope of her hair tossed from side to side.

Every morning I lay on the floor in the front parlour watching her door. The blind was pulled down to within an inch of the sash so that I could not be seen. When she came out on the doorstep my heart leaped. I ran to the hall, seized my books, and followed her. I kept her brown figure always in my eye and, when we came near the point at which our ways diverged, I quickened my pace and passed her. This happened morning after morning. I had never spoken to her, except for a few casual words, and yet her name was like a sum-mons to all my foolish blood.

Her image accompanied me even in places the most hostile to romance. On Saturday evenings when my aunt went marketing I had to go to carry some of the parcels. We walked through the flaring streets, jostled by drunken men and bargaining women, amid the curses of labourers, the shrill litanies of shop-boys who stood on guard by the barrel of pigs' cheeks, the nasal chanting of street-singers, who sang a *come-all-you* about O'Donovan Rossa,[1] or a ballad about the troubles in our native land. These noises converged in a single sensa-tion of life for me: I imagined that I bore my chalice safely through a throng of foes. Her name sprang to my lips at moments in strange prayers and praises which I myself did not understand. My eyes were often full of tears (I could not tell why) and at times a flood from my heart seemed to pour itself out into my bosom. I thought little of the future. I did not know whether I would ever speak to her or not or, if I spoke to her, how I could tell her of my confused adoration. But my body was like a harp and her words and gestures were like fingers running upon the wires.

One evening I went into the back drawing-room in which the priest had died. It was a dark rainy evening and there was no sound in the house. Through one of the broken panes I heard the rain impinge upon the earth, the fine incessant needles of water playing in the sodden beds. Some distant lamp or lighted window gleamed below me. I was thankful that I could see so little. All my senses seemed to desire to veil themselves and, feeling that I was about to slip from them, I pressed the palms of my hands together until they trembled, murmuring: "*O love! O love!*" many times.

At last she spoke to me. When she addressed the first words to me I was so confused that I did not know what to answer. She asked me was I going to *Araby*. I forgot whether I answered yes or no. It would be a splendid bazaar, she said she would love to go.

"And why can't you?" I asked.

While she spoke she turned a silver bracelet round and round her wrist. She could not go, she said, because there would be a retreat that week in her convent. Her brother and two other boys were fighting for their caps and I was alone at the railings. She held one of the spikes, bowing her head towards me. The light from the lamp opposite our door caught the white curve of her neck, lit up her hair that rested there and, falling, lit up the hand upon the railing. It fell over one side of her dress and caught the white border of a petticoat, just visible as she stood at ease.

"It's well for you," she said.

"If I go," I said, "I will bring you something."

What innumerable follies laid waste my waking and sleeping thoughts after that evening! I wished to annihilate the tedious intervening days. I chafed against the work of school. At night in my bedroom and by day in the classroom her image came between me and the page I strove to read. The

---

[1] Jeremiah O'Donovan (1831–1915), born in Ross Carberry of County Cork, was nicknamed "Dynamite Rossa" for championing violent means to achieve Irish independence.

syllables of the word *Araby* were called to me through the silence in which my soul luxuriated and cast an Eastern enchantment over me. I asked for leave to go to the bazaar on Saturday night. My aunt was surprised and hoped it was not some Freemason affair. I answered few questions in class. I watched my master's face pass from amiability to sternness; he hoped I was not beginning to idle. I could not call my wandering thoughts together. I had hardly any patience with the serious work of life which, now that it stood between me and my desire, seemed to me child's play, ugly monotonous child's play.

On Saturday morning I reminded my uncle that I wished to go to the bazaar in the evening. He was fussing at the hallstand, looking for the hat-brush, and answered me curtly:

"Yes, boy, I know."

As he was in the hall I could not go into the front parlour and lie at the window. I left the house in bad humour and walked slowly towards the school. The air was pitilessly raw and already my heart misgave me.

When I came home to dinner my uncle had not yet been home. Still it was early. I sat staring at the clock for some time and, when its ticking began to irritate me, I left the room. I mounted the staircase and gained the upper part of the house. The high cold empty gloomy rooms liberated me and I went from room to room singing. From the front window I saw my companions playing below in the street. Their cries reached me weakened and indistinct and, leaning my forehead against the cool glass, I looked over at the dark house where she lived. I may have stood there for an hour, seeing nothing but the brown-clad figure cast by my imagination, touched discreetly by the lamplight at the curved neck, at the hand upon the railings and at the border below the dress.

When I came downstairs again I found Mrs. Mercer sitting at the fire. She was an old garrulous woman, a pawnbroker's widow, who collected used stamps for some pious purpose. I had to endure the gossip of the tea-table. The meal was prolonged beyond an hour and still my uncle did not come. Mrs. Mercer stood up to go: she was sorry she couldn't wait any longer, but it was after eight o'clock and she did not like to be out late, as the night air was bad for her. When she had gone I began to walk up and down the room, clenching my fists. My aunt said:

"I'm afraid you may put off your bazaar for this night of Our Lord."

At nine o'clock I heard my uncle's latchkey in the halldoor. I heard him talking to himself and heard the hallstand rocking when it had received the weight of his overcoat. I could interpret these signs. When he was midway through his dinner I asked him to give me the money to go to the bazaar. He had forgotten.

"The people are in bed and after their first sleep now," he said.

I did not smile. My aunt said to him energetically:

"Can't you give him the money and let him go? You've kept him late enough as it is."

My uncle said he was very sorry he had forgotten. He said he believed in the old saying: "All work and no play makes Jack a dull boy." He asked me where I was going and, when I had told him a second time, he asked me did I know *The Arab's Farewell to his Steed*. When I left the kitchen he was about to recite the opening lines of the piece to my aunt.

I held a florin[2] tightly in my hand as I strode down Buckingham Street towards the station. The sight of the streets thronged with buyers and glaring with gas recalled to me the purpose of my journey. I took my seat in a third-class carriage of a deserted train. After an intolerable delay the train moved out of the station slowly. It crept onward among ruinous houses and over the twinkling river. At Westland Row Station a crowd of people pressed to the carriage doors; but the porters moved them back, saying that it was a special train for the bazaar. I remained alone in the bare carriage. In a few minutes the train drew up beside an improvised wooden platform. I passed out on to the road and saw by the lighted dial of a clock that it was ten minutes to ten. In front of me was a large building which displayed the magical name.

I could not find any sixpenny entrance and, fearing that the bazaar would be closed, I passed in quickly through a turnstile, handing a shilling to a weary-looking man. I found myself in a big hall girdled at half its height by a gallery. Nearly all the stalls were closed and the greater part of the hall was in darkness. I recognised a silence like that which pervades a church after a service. I walked into the centre of the bazaar timidly. A few people were gathered about the stalls which were still open. Before a curtain, over which the words *Café Chantant* were written in coloured lamps, two men were counting money on a salver. I listened to the fall of the coins.

Remembering with difficulty why I had come I went over to one of the stalls and examined porcelain vases and flowered tea-sets. At the door of the stall a young lady was talking and laughing with two young gentlemen. I remarked their English accents and listened vaguely to their conversation.

"O, I never said such a thing!"

"O, but you did!"

"O, but I didn't!"

"Didn't she say that?"

"Yes. I heard her."

"O, there's a . . . fib!"

Observing me the young lady came over and asked me did I wish to buy anything. The tone of her voice was not encouraging; she seemed to have spoken to me out of a sense of duty. I looked humbly at the great jars that stood like eastern guards at either side of the dark entrance to the stall and murmured:

"No, thank you."

The young lady changed the position of one of the vases and went back to the two young men. They began to talk of the same subject. Once or twice the young lady glanced at me over her shoulder.

I lingered before her stall, though I knew my stay was useless, to make my interest in her wares seem the more real. Then I turned away slowly and

---

[2] A silver coin worth two shillings.

walked down the middle of the bazaar. I allowed the two pennies to fall against the sixpence in my pocket. I heard a voice call from one end of the gallery that the light was out. The upper part of the hall was now completely dark.

Gazing up into the darkness I saw myself as a creature driven and derided by vanity; and my eyes burned with anguish and anger.

The Dead

1914

LILY, THE CARETAKER'S DAUGHTER, was literally run off her feet. Hardly had she brought one gentleman into the little pantry behind the office on the ground floor and helped him off with his overcoat than the wheezy hall-door bell clanged again and she had to scamper along the bare hallway to let in another guest. It was well for her she had not to attend to the ladies also. But Miss Kate and Miss Julia had thought of that and had converted the bathroom upstairs into a ladies' dressing-room. Miss Kate and Miss Julia were there, gossiping and laughing and fussing, walking after each other to the head of the stairs, peering down over the banisters and calling down to Lily to ask her who had come.

It was always a great affair, the Misses Morkan's annual dance. Everybody who knew them came to it, members of the family, old friends of the family, the members of Julia's choir, any of Kate's pupils that were grown up enough and even some of Mary Jane's pupils too. Never once had it fallen flat. For years and years it had gone off in splendid style as long as anyone could remember; ever since Kate and Julia, after the death of their brother Pat, had left the house in Stoney Batter and taken Mary Jane, their only niece, to live with them in the dark gaunt house on Usher's Island, the upper part of which they had rented from Mr Fulham, the corn-factor on the ground floor. That was a good thirty years ago if it was a day. Mary Jane, who was then a little girl in short clothes, was now the main prop of the household for she had the organ in Haddington Road. She had been through the Academy and gave a pupils' concert every year in the upper room of the Antient Concert Rooms. Many of her pupils belonged to better-class families on the Kingstown and Dalkey line. Old as they were, her aunts also did their share. Julia, though she was quite grey, was still the leading soprano in Adam and Eve's, and Kate, being too feeble to go about much, gave music lessons to beginners on the old square piano in the back room. Lily, the caretaker's daughter, did housemaid's work for them. Though their life was modest they believed in eating well; the best of everything: diamond-bone sirloins, three-shilling tea and the best bottled stout. But Lily seldom made a mistake in the orders so that she got on well with her three mistresses. They were fussy, that was all. But the only thing they would not stand was back answers.

Of course they had good reason to be fussy on such a night. And then it was long after ten o'clock and yet there was no sign of Gabriel and his wife. Besides they were dreadfully afraid that Freddy Malins might turn up screwed. They would not wish for worlds that any of Mary Jane's pupils should see him under the influence; and when he was like that it was sometimes very hard to manage him. Freddy Malins always came late but they wondered what could be keeping Gabriel: and that was what brought them every two minutes to the banisters to ask Lily had Gabriel or Freddy come.

— O, Mr Conroy, said Lily to Gabriel when she opened the door for him, Miss Kate and Miss Julia thought you were never coming. Good-night, Mrs Conroy.

— I'll engage they did, said Gabriel, but they forget that my wife here takes three mortal hours to dress herself.

He stood on the mat, scraping the snow from his goloshes, while Lily led his wife to the foot of the stairs and called out:

— Miss Kate, here's Mrs Conroy.

Kate and Julia came toddling down the dark stairs at once. Both of them kissed Gabriel's wife, said she must be perished alive and asked was Gabriel with her.

— Here I am as right as the mail, Aunt Kate! Go on up. I'll follow, called out Gabriel from the dark.

He continued scraping his feet vigorously while the three women went upstairs, laughing, to the ladies' dressing-room. A light fringe of snow lay like a cape on the shoulders of his overcoat and like toecaps on the toes of his goloshes; and, as the buttons of his overcoat slipped with a squeaking noise through the snow-stiffened frieze, a cold fragrant air from out-of-doors escaped from crevices and folds.

— Is it snowing again, Mr Conroy? asked Lily.

She had preceded him into the pantry to help him off with his overcoat. Gabriel smiled at the three syllables she had given his surname and glanced at her. She was a slim, growing girl, pale in complexion and with hay-coloured hair. The gas in the pantry made her look still paler. Gabriel had known her when she was a child and used to sit on the lowest step nursing a rag doll.

— Yes, Lily, he answered, and I think we're in for a night of it.

He looked up at the pantry ceiling, which was shaking with the stamping and shuffling of feet on the floor above, listened for a moment to the piano and then glanced at the girl, who was folding his overcoat carefully at the end of a shelf.

— Tell me, Lily, he said in a friendly tone, do you still go to school?

— O no, sir, she answered. I'm done schooling this year and more.

— O, then, said Gabriel gaily, I suppose we'll be going to your wedding one of these fine days with your young man, eh?

The girl glanced back at him over her shoulder and said with great bitterness:

—The men that is now is only all palaver and what they can get out of you.

Gabriel coloured as if he felt he had made a mistake and, without looking at her, kicked off his goloshes and flicked actively with his muffler at his patent-leather shoes.

He was a stout tallish young man. The high colour of his cheeks pushed upwards even to his forehead where it scattered itself in a few formless patches of pale red; and on his hairless face there scintillated restlessly the polished lenses and the bright gilt rims of the glasses which screened his delicate and restless eyes. His glossy black hair was parted in the middle and brushed in a long curve behind his ears where it curled slightly beneath the groove left by his hat.

When he had flicked lustre into his shoes he stood up and pulled his waistcoat down more tightly on his plump body. Then he took a coin rapidly from his pocket.

—O Lily, he said, thrusting it into her hands, it's Christmas-time, isn't it? Just . . . here's a little. . . .

He walked rapidly towards the door.

—O no, sir! cried the girl, following him. Really, sir, I wouldn't take it.

—Christmas-time! Christmas-time! said Gabriel, almost trotting to the stairs and waving his hand to her in deprecation.

The girl, seeing that he had gained the stairs, called out after him:

—Well, thank you, sir.

He waited outside the drawing-room door until the waltz should finish, listening to the skirts that swept against it and to the shuffling of feet. He was still discomposed by the girl's bitter and sudden retort. It had cast a gloom over him which he tried to dispel by arranging his cuffs and the bows of his tie. Then he took from his waistcoat pocket a little paper and glanced at the headings he had made for his speech. He was undecided about the lines from Robert Browning for he feared they would be above the heads of his hearers. Some quotation that they could recognise from Shakespeare or from the Melodies[1] would be better. The indelicate clacking of the men's heels and the shuffling of their soles reminded him that their grade of culture differed from his. He would only make himself ridiculous by quoting poetry to them which they could not understand. They would think that he was airing his superior education. He would fail with them just as he had failed with the girl in the pantry. He had taken up a wrong tone. His whole speech was a mistake from first to last, an utter failure.

Just then his aunts and his wife came out of the ladies' dressing-room. His aunts were two small plainly dressed old women. Aunt Julia was an inch or so the taller. Her hair, drawn low over the tops of her ears, was grey; and grey also, with darker shadows, was her large flaccid face. Though she was stout in build and stood erect her slow eyes and parted lips gave her the appearance

---

[1] *Irish Melodies* is a collection of poems by Thomas Moore (1779–1852) that generated goodwill and support for Irish nationalists.

of a woman who did not know where she was or where she was going. Aunt Kate was more vivacious. Her face, healthier than her sister's, was all puckers and creases, like a shrivelled red apple, and her hair, braided in the same old-fashioned way, had not lost its ripe nut colour.

They both kissed Gabriel frankly. He was their favourite nephew, the son of their dead elder sister, Ellen, who had married T. J. Conroy of the Port and Docks.

— Gretta tells me you're not going to take a cab back to Monkstown tonight, Gabriel, said Aunt Kate.

— No, said Gabriel, turning to his wife, we had quite enough of that last year, hadn't we? Don't you remember, Aunt Kate, what a cold Gretta got out of it? Cab windows rattling all the way, and the east wind blowing in after we passed Merrion. Very jolly it was. Gretta caught a dreadful cold.

Aunt Kate frowned severely and nodded her head at every word.

— Quite right, Gabriel, quite right, she said. You can't be too careful.

— But as for Gretta there, said Gabriel, she'd walk home in the snow if she were let.

Mrs Conroy laughed.

— Don't mind him, Aunt Kate, she said. He's really an awful bother, what with green shades for Tom's eyes at night and making him do the dumb-bells, and forcing Eva to eat the stirabout. The poor child! And she simply hates the sight of it! . . . O, but you'll never guess what he makes me wear now!

She broke out into a peal of laughter and glanced at her husband, whose admiring and happy eyes had been wandering from her dress to her face and hair. The two aunts laughed heartily too, for Gabriel's solicitude was a standing joke with them.

— Goloshes! said Mrs Conroy. That's the latest. Whenever it's wet under-foot I must put on my goloshes. To-night even he wanted me to put them on, but I wouldn't. The next thing he'll buy me will be a diving suit.

Gabriel laughed nervously and patted his tie reassuringly while Aunt Kate nearly doubled herself, so heartily did she enjoy the joke. The smile soon faded from Aunt Julia's face and her mirthless eyes were directed towards her nephew's face. After a pause she asked:

— And what are goloshes, Gabriel?

— Goloshes, Julia! exclaimed her sister. Goodness me, don't you know what goloshes are? You wear them over your . . . over your boots, Gretta, isn't it?

— Yes, said Mrs Conroy. Guttapercha things. We both have a pair now. Gabriel says everyone wears them on the continent.

— O, on the continent, murmured Aunt Julia, nodding her head slowly.

Gabriel knitted his brows and said, as if he were slightly angered:

— It's nothing very wonderful but Gretta thinks it very funny because she says the word reminds her of Christy Minstrels.

— But tell me, Gabriel, said Aunt Kate, with brisk tact. Of course, you've seen about the room. Gretta was saying . . .

— O, the room is all right, replied Gabriel. I've taken one in the Gresham.

— To be sure, said Aunt Kate, by far the best thing to do. And the children, Gretta, you're not anxious about them?

— O, for one night, said Mrs Conroy. Besides, Bessie will look after them.

— To be sure, said Aunt Kate again. What a comfort it is to have a girl like that, one you can depend on! There's that Lily, I'm sure I don't know what has come over her lately. She's not the girl she was at all.

Gabriel was about to ask his aunt some questions on this point but she broke off suddenly to gaze after her sister who had wandered down the stairs and was craning her neck over the banisters.

— Now, I ask you, she said, almost testily, where is Julia going? Julia! Julia! Where are you going?

Julia, who had gone halfway down one flight, came back and announced blandly:

— Here's Freddy.

At the same moment a clapping of hands and a final flourish of the pianist told that the waltz had ended. The drawing-room door was opened from within and some couples came out. Aunt Kate drew Gabriel aside hurriedly and whispered into his ear:

— Slip down, Gabriel, like a good fellow and see if he's all right, and don't let him up if he's screwed. I'm sure he's screwed. I'm sure he is.

Gabriel went to the stairs and listened over the banisters. He could hear two persons talking in the pantry. Then he recognised Freddy Malins' laugh. He went down the stairs noisily.

— It's such a relief, said Aunt Kate to Mrs Conroy, that Gabriel is here. I always feel easier in my mind when he's here. . . . Julia, there's Miss Daly and Miss Power will take some refreshment. Thanks for your beautiful waltz, Miss Daly. It made lovely time.

A tall wizen-faced man, with a stiff grizzled moustache and swarthy skin, who was passing out with his partner said:

— And may we have some refreshment, too, Miss Morkan?

— Julia, said Aunt Kate summarily, and here's Mr Browne and Miss Furlong. Take them in, Julia, with Miss Daly and Miss Power.

— I'm the man for the ladies, said Mr Browne, pursing his lips until his moustache bristled and smiling in all his wrinkles. You know, Miss Morkan, the reason they are so fond of me is —

He did not finish his sentence, but, seeing that Aunt Kate was out of ear-shot, at once led the three young ladies into the back room. The middle of the room was occupied by two square tables placed end to end, and on these Aunt Julia and the caretaker were straightening and smoothing a large cloth. On the sideboard were arrayed dishes and plates, and glasses and bundles of knives and forks and spoons. The top of the closed square piano served also as a side-board for viands and sweets. At a smaller sideboard in one corner two young men were standing, drinking hop-bitters.

Mr Browne led his charges thither and invited them all, in jest, to some ladies' punch, hot, strong and sweet. As they said they never took anything strong he opened three bottles of lemonade for them. Then he asked one of the young men to move aside, and, taking hold of the decanter, filled out for himself a goodly measure of whisky. The young men eyed him respectfully while he took a trial sip.

— God help me, he said, smiling, it's the doctor's orders.

His wizened face broke into a broader smile, and the three young ladies laughed in musical echo to his pleasantry, swaying their bodies to and fro, with nervous jerks of their shoulders. The boldest said:

— O, now, Mr Browne, I'm sure the doctor never ordered anything of the kind.

Mr Browne took another sip of his whisky and said, with sidling mimicry:

— Well, you see, I'm like the famous Mrs Cassidy, who is reported to have said: *Now, Mary Grimes, if I don't take it, make me take it, for I feel I want it.*

His hot face had leaned forward a little too confidentially and he had assumed a very low Dublin accent so that the young ladies, with one instinct, received his speech in silence. Miss Furlong, who was one of Mary Jane's pupils, asked Miss Daly what was the name of the pretty waltz she had played; and Mr Browne, seeing that he was ignored, turned promptly to the two young men who were more appreciative.

A red-faced young woman, dressed in pansy, came into the room, excitedly clapping her hands and crying:

— Quadrilles! Quadrilles!

Close on her heels came Aunt Kate, crying:

— Two gentlemen and three ladies, Mary Jane!

— O, here's Mr Bergin and Mr Kerrigan, said Mary Jane. Mr Kerrigan, will you take Miss Power? Miss Furlong, may I get you a partner, Mr Bergin. O, that'll just do now.

— Three ladies, Mary Jane, said Aunt Kate.

The two young gentlemen asked the ladies if they might have the pleasure, and Mary Jane turned to Miss Daly.

— O, Miss Daly, you're really awfully good, after playing for the last two dances, but really we're so short of ladies to-night.

— I don't mind in the least, Miss Morkan.

— But I've a nice partner for you, Mr Bartell D'Arcy, the tenor. I'll get him to sing later on. All Dublin is raving about him.

— Lovely voice, lovely voice! said Aunt Kate.

As the piano had twice begun the prelude to the first figure Mary Jane led her recruits quickly from the room. They had hardly gone when Aunt Julia wandered slowly into the room, looking behind her at something.

— What is the matter, Julia? asked Aunt Kate anxiously. Who is it?

Julia, who was carrying in a column of table-napkins, turned to her sister and said, simply, as if the question had surprised her:

— It's only Freddy, Kate, and Gabriel with him.

In fact right behind her Gabriel could be seen piloting Freddy Malins across the landing. The latter, a young man of about forty, was of Gabriel's size and build, with very round shoulders. His face was fleshy and pallid, touched with colour only at the thick hanging lobes of his ears and at the wide wings of his nose. He had coarse features, a blunt nose, a convex and receding brow, tumid and protruded lips. His heavy-lidded eyes and the disorder of his scanty hair made him look sleepy. He was laughing heartily in a high key at a story which he had been telling Gabriel on the stairs and at the same time rubbing the knuckles of his left fist backwards and forwards into his left eye.

— Good-evening, Freddy, said Aunt Julia.

Freddy Malins bade the Misses Morkan good-evening in what seemed an offhand fashion by reason of the habitual catch in his voice and then, seeing that Mr Browne was grinning at him from the sideboard, crossed the room on rather shaky legs and began to repeat in an undertone the story he had just told to Gabriel.

— He's not so bad, is he? said Aunt Kate to Gabriel.

Gabriel's brows were dark but he raised them quickly and answered:

— O no, hardly noticeable.

— Now, isn't he a terrible fellow! she said. And his poor mother made him take the pledge on New Year's Eve. But come on, Gabriel, into the drawing-room.

Before leaving the room with Gabriel she signalled to Mr Browne by frowning and shaking her forefinger in warning to and fro. Mr Browne nodded in answer and, when she had gone, said to Freddy Malins:

— Now, then, Teddy, I'm going to fill you out a good glass of lemonade just to buck you up.

Freddy Malins, who was nearing the climax of his story, waved the offer aside impatiently but Mr Browne, having first called Freddy Malins' attention to a disarray in his dress, filled out and handed him a full glass of lemonade. Freddy Malins' left hand accepted the glass mechanically, his right hand being engaged in the mechanical readjustment of his dress. Mr Browne, whose face was once more wrinkling with mirth, poured out for himself a glass of whisky while Freddy Malins exploded, before he had well reached the climax of his story, in a kink of high-pitched bronchitic laughter and, setting down his untasted and overflowing glass, began to rub the knuckles of his left fist backwards and forwards into his left eye, repeating words of his last phrase as well as his fit of laughter would allow him.

————————

Gabriel could not listen while Mary Jane was playing her Academy piece, full of runs and difficult passages, to the hushed drawing-room. He liked music but the piece she was playing had no melody for him and he doubted whether it had any melody for the other listeners, though they had begged Mary Jane to play something. Four young men, who had come from the refreshment-room to stand in the doorway at the sound of the piano, had gone away quietly in couples after a few minutes. The only persons who seemed to follow the music were Mary Jane herself, her hands racing along the key-board or lifted from it at the pauses like those of a priestess in momentary imprecation, and Aunt Kate standing at her elbow to turn the page.

Gabriel's eyes, irritated by the floor, which glittered with beeswax under the heavy chandelier, wandered to the wall above the piano. A picture of the balcony scene in *Romeo and Juliet* hung there and beside it was a picture of the two murdered princes in the Tower which Aunt Julia had worked in red, blue and brown wools when she was a girl. Probably in the school they had gone to as girls that kind of work had been taught, for one year his mother had worked for him as a birthday present a waistcoat of purple tabinet, with little foxes' heads upon it, lined with brown satin and having round mulberry buttons. It was strange that his mother had had no musical talent though Aunt Kate used to call her the brains carrier of the Morkan family. Both she and Julia had always seemed a little proud of their serious and matronly sister. Her photograph stood before the pierglass. She held an open book on her knees and was pointing out something in it to Constantine who, dressed in a man-o'-war suit, lay at her feet. It was she who had chosen the names for her sons for she was very sensible of the dignity of family life. Thanks to her, Constantine was now senior curate in Balbriggan and, thanks to her, Gabriel himself had taken his degree in the Royal University. A shadow passed over his face as he remembered her sullen opposition to his marriage. Some slighting phrases she had used still rankled in his memory; she had once spoken of Gretta as being country cute and that was not true of Gretta at all. It was Gretta who had nursed her during all her last long illness in their house at Monkstown.

He knew that Mary Jane must be near the end of her piece for she was playing again the opening melody with runs of scales after every bar and while he waited for the end the resentment died down in his heart. The piece ended with a trill of octaves in the treble and a final deep octave in the bass. Great applause greeted Mary Jane as, blushing and rolling up her music nervously, she escaped from the room. The most vigorous clapping came from the four young men in the doorway who had gone away to the refreshment-room at the beginning of the piece but had come back when the piano had stopped.

Lancers were arranged. Gabriel found himself partnered with Miss Ivors. She was a frank-mannered talkative young lady, with a freckled face and prominent brown eyes. She did not wear a low-cut bodice and the large brooch which was fixed in the front of her collar bore on it an Irish device.

When they had taken their places she said abruptly:

—I have a crow to pluck with you.

—With me? said Gabriel.

She nodded her head gravely.

—What is it? asked Gabriel, smiling at her solemn manner.

—Who is G.C.? answered Miss Ivors, turning her eyes upon him.

Gabriel coloured and was about to knit his brows, as if he did not understand, when she said bluntly:

—O, innocent Amy! I have found out that you write for *The Daily Express.* Now, aren't you ashamed of yourself?

—Why should I be ashamed of myself? asked Gabriel, blinking his eyes and trying to smile.

—Well, I'm ashamed of you, said Miss Ivors frankly. To say you'd write for a rag like that. I didn't think you were a West Briton.

A look of perplexity appeared on Gabriel's face. It was true that he wrote a literary column every Wednesday in *The Daily Express*, for which he was paid fifteen shillings. But that did not make him a West Briton surely. The books he received for review were almost more welcome than the paltry cheque. He loved to feel the covers and turn over the pages of newly printed books. Nearly every day when his teaching in the college was ended he used to wander down the quays to the second-hand booksellers, to Hickey's on Bachelor's Walk, to Webb's or Massey's on Aston's Quay, or to O'Clohissey's in the by-street. He did not know how to meet her charge. He wanted to say that literature was above politics. But they were friends of many years' standing and their careers had been parallel, first at the University and then as teachers: he could not risk a grandiose phrase with her. He continued blinking his eyes and trying to smile and murmured lamely that he saw nothing political in writing reviews of books.

When their turn to cross had come he was still perplexed and inattentive. Miss Ivors promptly took his hand in a warm grasp and said in a soft friendly tone:

— Of course, I was only joking. Come, we cross now.

When they were together again she spoke of the University question and Gabriel felt more at ease. A friend of hers had shown her his review of Browning's poems. That was how she had found out the secret: but she liked the review immensely. Then she said suddenly:

— O, Mr Conroy, will you come for an excursion to the Aran Isles this summer? We're going to stay there a whole month. It will be splendid out in the Atlantic. You ought to come. Mr Clancy is coming, and Mr Kilkelly and Kathleen Kearney. It would be splendid for Gretta too if she'd come. She's from Connacht, isn't she?

— Her people are, said Gabriel shortly.

— But you will come, won't you? said Miss Ivors, laying her warm hand eagerly on his arm.

— The fact is, said Gabriel, I have already arranged to go —

— Go where? asked Miss Ivors.

— Well, you know, every year I go for a cycling tour with some fellows and so —

— But where? asked Miss Ivors.

— Well, we usually go to France or Belgium or perhaps Germany, said Gabriel awkwardly.

— And why do you go to France and Belgium, said Miss Ivors, instead of visiting your own land?

— Well, said Gabriel, it's partly to keep in touch with the languages and partly for a change.

— And haven't you your own language to keep in touch with — Irish? asked Miss Ivors.

— Well, said Gabriel, if it comes to that, you know, Irish is not my language.

Their neighbours had turned to listen to the cross-examination. Gabriel glanced right and left nervously and tried to keep his good humour under the ordeal which was making a blush invade his forehead.

— And haven't you your own land to visit, continued Miss Ivors, that you know nothing of, your own people, and your own country?

— O, to tell you the truth, retorted Gabriel suddenly, I'm sick of my own country, sick of it!

— Why? asked Miss Ivors.

Gabriel did not answer for his retort had heated him.

— Why? repeated Miss Ivors.

They had to go visiting together and, as he had not answered her, Miss Ivors said warmly:

— Of course, you've no answer.

Gabriel tried to cover his agitation by taking part in the dance with great energy. He avoided her eyes for he had seen a sour expression on her face. But when they met in the long chain he was surprised to feel his hand firmly pressed. She looked at him from under her brows for a moment quizzically until he smiled. Then, just as the chain was about to start again, she stood on tiptoe and whispered into his ear:

— West Briton!

When the lancers were over Gabriel went away to a remote corner of the room where Freddy Malins' mother was sitting. She was a stout feeble old woman with white hair. Her voice had a catch in it like her son's and she stuttered slightly. She had been told that Freddy had come and that he was nearly all right. Gabriel asked her whether she had had a good crossing. She lived with her married daughter in Glasgow and came to Dublin on a visit once a year. She answered placidly that she had had a beautiful crossing and that the captain had been most attentive to her. She spoke also of the beautiful house her daughter kept in Glasgow, and of all the nice friends they had there. While her tongue rambled on Gabriel tried to banish from his mind all memory of the unpleasant incident with Miss Ivors. Of course the girl or woman, or whatever she was, was an enthusiast but there was a time for all things. Perhaps he ought not to have answered her like that. But she had no right to call him a West Briton before people, even in joke. She had tried to make him ridiculous before people, heckling him and staring at him with her rabbit's eyes.

He saw his wife making her way towards him through the waltzing couples. When she reached him she said into his ear:

— Gabriel, Aunt Kate wants to know won't you carve the goose as usual. Miss Daly will carve the ham and I'll do the pudding.

— All right, said Gabriel.

— She's sending in the younger ones first as soon as this waltz is over so that we'll have the tables to ourselves.

— Were you dancing? asked Gabriel.

— Of course I was. Didn't you see me? What words had you with Molly Ivors?

— No words. Why? Did she say so?

— Something like that. I'm trying to get that Mr D'Arcy to sing. He's full of conceit, I think.

— There were no words, said Gabriel moodily, only she wanted me to go for a trip to the west of Ireland and I said I wouldn't.

His wife clasped her hands excitedly and gave a little jump.

— O, do go, Gabriel, she cried. I'd love to see Galway again.

— You can go if you like, said Gabriel coldly.

She looked at him for a moment, then turned to Mrs Malins and said:

— There's a nice husband for you, Mrs Malins.

While she was threading her way back across the room Mrs Malins, without adverting to the interruption, went on to tell Gabriel what beautiful places there were in Scotland and beautiful scenery. Her son-in-law brought them every year to the lakes and they used to go fishing. Her son-in-law was a splendid fisher. One day he caught a fish, a beautiful big big fish, and the man in the hotel boiled it for their dinner.

Gabriel hardly heard what she said. Now that supper was coming near he began to think again about his speech and about the quotation. When he saw Freddy Malins coming across the room to visit his mother Gabriel left the chair free for him and retired into the embrasure of the window. The room had already cleared and from the back room came the clatter of plates and knives. Those who still remained in the drawing-room seemed tired of dancing and were conversing quietly in little groups. Gabriel's warm trembling fingers tapped the cold pane of the window. How cool it must be outside! How pleasant it would be to walk out alone, first along by the river and then through the park! The snow would be lying on the branches of the trees and forming a bright cap on the top of the Wellington Monument. How much more pleasant it would be there than at the supper-table!

He ran over the headings of his speech: Irish hospitality, sad memories, the Three Graces, Paris, the quotation from Browning. He repeated to himself a phrase he had written in his review: *One feels that one is listening to a thought-tormented music.* Miss Ivors had praised the review. Was she sincere? Had she really any life of her own behind all her propagandism? There had never been any ill-feeling between them until that night. It unnerved him to think that she would be at the supper-table, looking up at him while he spoke with her critical quizzing eyes. Perhaps she would not be sorry to see him fail in his speech. An idea came into his mind and gave him courage. He would say, alluding to Aunt Kate and Aunt Julia: *Ladies and Gentlemen, the generation which is now on the wane among us may have had its faults but for my part I think it had certain qualities of hospitality, of humour, of humanity, which the new and very serious and hypereducated generation that is growing up around us seems to me to lack.* Very good: that was one for Miss Ivors. What did he care that his aunts were only two ignorant old women?

A murmur in the room attracted his attention. Mr Browne was advancing from the door, gallantly escorting Aunt Julia, who leaned upon his arm, smiling and hanging her head. An irregular musketry of applause escorted her also as far as the piano and then, as Mary Jane seated herself on the stool, and Aunt Julia, no longer smiling, half turned so as to pitch her voice fairly into the room, gradually ceased. Gabriel recognised the prelude. It was that of an old song of Aunt Julia's — *Arrayed for the Bridal.* Her voice, strong and clear in tone, attacked with great spirit the runs which embellish the air and though she sang very rapidly she did not miss even the smallest of the grace notes. To follow the voice, without looking at the singer's face, was to feel and share the excitement of swift and secure flight. Gabriel applauded loudly with all the others at the close of the song and loud applause was borne in from the invisible supper-table. It sounded so genuine that a little colour struggled into Aunt Julia's face as she bent to replace in the music-stand the old leather-bound song-book that had her initials on the cover. Freddy Malins, who had listened with his head perched sideways to hear her better, was still applauding when everyone else had ceased and talking animatedly to his mother who nodded her head gravely and slowly in acquiescence. At last, when he could clap no more, he stood up suddenly and hurried across the room to Aunt Julia whose hand he seized and held in both his hands, shaking it when words failed him or the catch in his voice proved too much for him.

— I was just telling my mother, he said, I never heard you sing so well, never. No, I never heard your voice so good as it is to-night. Now! Would you believe that now? That's the truth. Upon my word and honour that's the truth. I never heard your voice sound so fresh and so . . . so clear and fresh, never.

Aunt Julia smiled broadly and murmured something about compliments as she released her hand from his grasp. Mr Browne extended his open hand towards her and said to those who were near him in the manner of a showman introducing a prodigy to an audience:

— Miss Julia Morkan, my latest discovery!

He was laughing very heartily at this himself when Freddy Malins turned to him and said:

— Well, Browne, if you're serious you might make a worse discovery. All I can say is I never heard her sing half so well as long as I am coming here. And that's the honest truth.

— Neither did I, said Mr Browne. I think her voice has greatly improved.

Aunt Julia shrugged her shoulders and said with meek pride:

— Thirty years ago I hadn't a bad voice as voices go.

— I often told Julia, said Aunt Kate emphatically, that she was simply thrown away in that choir. But she never would be said by me.

She turned as if to appeal to the good sense of the others against a refractory child while Aunt Julia gazed in front of her, a vague smile of reminiscence playing on her face.

— No, continued Aunt Kate, she wouldn't be said or led by anyone, slaving there in that choir night and day, night and day. Six o'clock on Christmas morning! And all for what?

— Well, isn't it for the honour of God, Aunt Kate? asked Mary Jane, twisting round on the piano-stool and smiling.

Aunt Kate turned fiercely on her niece and said:

— I know all about the honour of God, Mary Jane, but I think it's not at all honourable for the pope to turn out the women out of the choirs that have slaved there all their lives and put little whipper-snappers of boys over their heads. I suppose it is for the good of the Church if the pope does it. But it's not just, Mary Jane, and it's not right.

She had worked herself into a passion and would have continued in defence of her sister for it was a sore subject with her but Mary Jane, seeing that all the dancers had come back, intervened pacifically:

— Now, Aunt Kate, you're giving scandal to Mr Browne who is of the other persuasion.

Aunt Kate turned to Mr Browne, who was grinning at this allusion to his religion, and said hastily:

— O, I don't question the pope's being right. I'm only a stupid old woman and I wouldn't presume to do such a thing. But there's such a thing as common everyday politeness and gratitude. And if I were in Julia's place I'd tell that Father Healy straight up to his face. . . .

— And besides, Aunt Kate, said Mary Jane, we really are all hungry and when we are hungry we are all very quarrelsome.

— And when we are thirsty we are also quarrelsome, added Mr Browne.

— So that we had better go to supper, said Mary Jane, and finish the discussion afterwards.

On the landing outside the drawing-room Gabriel found his wife and Mary Jane trying to persuade Miss Ivors to stay for supper. But Miss Ivors, who had put on her hat and was buttoning her cloak, would not stay. She did not feel in the least hungry and she had already overstayed her time.

— But only for ten minutes, Molly, said Mrs Conroy. That won't delay you.

— To take a pick itself, said Mary Jane, after all your dancing.

— I really couldn't, said Miss Ivors.

— I am afraid you didn't enjoy yourself at all, said Mary Jane hopelessly.

— Ever so much, I assure you, said Miss Ivors, but you really must let me run off now.

— But how can you get home? asked Mrs Conroy.

— O, it's only two steps up the quay.

Gabriel hesitated a moment and said:

— If you will allow me, Miss Ivors, I'll see you home if you really are obliged to go.

But Miss Ivors broke away from them.

— I won't hear of it, she cried. For goodness sake go in to your suppers and don't mind me. I'm quite well able to take care of myself.

— Well, you're the comical girl, Molly, said Mrs Conroy frankly.

— *Beannacht libh,*[2] cried Miss Ivors, with a laugh, as she ran down the staircase.

Mary Jane gazed after her, a moody puzzled expression on her face, while Mrs Conroy leaned over the banisters to listen for the hall-door. Gabriel asked himself was he the cause of her abrupt departure. But she did not seem to be in ill humour: she had gone away laughing. He stared blankly down the staircase.

---

[2] "A blessing on you" (Irish — traditional way of saying "farewell").

At that moment Aunt Kate came toddling out of the supper-room, almost wringing her hands in despair.

— Where is Gabriel? she cried. Where on earth is Gabriel? There's everyone waiting in there, stage to let, and nobody to carve the goose!

— Here I am, Aunt Kate! cried Gabriel, with sudden animation, ready to carve a flock of geese, if necessary.

A fat brown goose lay at one end of the table and at the other end, on a bed of creased paper strewn with sprigs of parsley, lay a great ham, stripped of its outer skin and peppered over with crust crumbs, a neat paper frill round its shin and beside this was a round of spiced beef. Between these rival ends ran parallel lines of side-dishes: two little minsters of jelly, red and yellow; a shallow dish full of blocks of blancmange and red jam, a large green leaf-shaped dish with a stalk-shaped handle, on which lay bunches of purple raisins and peeled almonds, a companion dish on which lay a solid rectangle of Smyrna figs, a dish of custard topped with grated nutmeg, a small bowl full of chocolates and sweets wrapped in gold and silver papers and a glass vase in which stood some tall celery stalks. In the centre of the table there stood, as sentries to a fruit-stand which upheld a pyramid of oranges and American apples, two squat old-fashioned decanters of cut glass, one containing port and the other dark sherry. On the closed square piano a pudding in a huge yellow dish lay in waiting and behind it were three squads of bottles of stout and ale and minerals, drawn up according to the colours of their uniforms, the first two black, with brown and red labels, the third and smallest squad white, with transverse green sashes.

Gabriel took his seat boldly at the head of the table and, having looked to the edge of the carver, plunged his fork firmly into the goose. He felt quite at ease now for he was an expert carver and liked nothing better than to find himself at the head of a well-laden table.

— Miss Furlong, what shall I send you? he asked. A wing or a slice of the breast?

— Just a small slice of the breast.

— Miss Higgins, what for you?

— O, anything at all, Mr Conroy.

While Gabriel and Miss Daly exchanged plates of goose and plates of ham and spiced beef Lily went from guest to guest with a dish of hot floury potatoes wrapped in a white napkin. This was Mary Jane's idea and she had also suggested apple sauce for the goose but Aunt Kate had said that plain roast goose without apple sauce had always been good enough for her and she hoped she might never eat worse. Mary Jane waited on her pupils and saw that they got the best slices and Aunt Kate and Aunt Julia opened and carried across from the piano bottles of stout and ale for the gentlemen and bottles of minerals for the ladies. There was a great deal of confusion and laughter and noise, the noise of orders and counter-orders, of knives and forks, of corks and glass-stoppers. Gabriel began to carve second helpings as soon as he had finished the first round without serving himself. Everyone protested loudly so that he compromised by taking a long draught of stout for he had found the carving hot work. Mary Jane settled down quietly to her supper but Aunt Kate and Aunt Julia were still toddling round the table, walking on each other's heels, getting in each other's way and giving each other unheeded orders. Mr Browne begged of them to sit down and eat their suppers and so did Gabriel but they said there was time enough so that, at last, Freddy Malins stood up and, capturing Aunt Kate, plumped her down on her chair amid general laughter.

When everyone had been well served Gabriel said, smiling:

— Now, if anyone wants a little more of what vulgar people call stuffing let him or her speak.

A chorus of voices invited him to begin his own supper and Lily came forward with three potatoes which she had reserved for him.

— Very well, said Gabriel amiably, as he took another preparatory draught, kindly forget my existence, ladies and gentlemen, for a few minutes.

He set to his supper and took no part in the conversation with which the table covered Lily's removal of the plates. The subject of talk was the opera company which was then at the Theatre Royal. Mr Bartell D'Arcy, the tenor, a dark-complexioned young man with a smart moustache, praised very highly the leading contralto of the company but Miss Furlong thought she had a rather vulgar style of production. Freddy Malins said there was a negro chieftain singing in the second part of the Gaiety pantomime who had one of the finest tenor voices he had ever heard.

— Have you heard him? he asked Mr Bartell D'Arcy across the table.

— No, answered Mr Bartell D'Arcy carelessly.

— Because, Freddy Malins explained, now I'd be curious to hear your opinion of him. I think he has a grand voice.

— It takes Teddy to find out the really good things, said Mr Browne familiarly to the table.

— And why couldn't he have a voice too? asked Freddy Malins sharply. Is it because he's only a black?

Nobody answered this question and Mary Jane led the table back to the legitimate opera. One of her pupils had given her a pass for *Mignon.* Of course it was very fine, she said, but it made her think of poor Georgina Burns. Mr Browne could go back farther still, to the old Italian companies that used to come to Dublin — Tietjens, Ilma de Murzka, Campanini, the great Trebelli, Giuglini, Ravelli, Aramburo. Those were the days, he said, when there was something like singing to be heard in Dublin. He told too of how the top gallery of the old Royal used to be packed night after night, of how one night an Italian tenor had sung five encores to *Let Me Like a Soldier Fall,* introducing a high C every time, and of how the gallery boys would sometimes in their enthusiasm unyoke the horses from the carriage of some great *prima donna* and pull her themselves through the streets to her hotel. Why did they never play the grand old operas now, he asked, *Dinorah, Lucrezia Borgia?* Because they could not get the voices to sing them: that was why.

— O, well, said Mr Bartell D'Arcy, I presume there are as good singers today as there were then.

— Where are they? asked Mr Browne defiantly.

— In London, Paris, Milan, said Mr Bartell D'Arcy warmly. I suppose Caruso, for example, is quite as good, if not better than any of the men you have mentioned.

— Maybe so, said Mr Browne. But I may tell you I doubt it strongly.

— O, I'd give anything to hear Caruso sing, said Mary Jane.

— For me, said Aunt Kate, who had been picking a bone, there was only one tenor. To please me, I mean. But I suppose none of you ever heard of him.

— Who was he, Miss Morkan? asked Mr Bartell D'Arcy politely.

— His name, said Aunt Kate, was Parkinson. I heard him when he was in his prime and I think he had then the purest tenor voice that was ever put into a man's throat.

— Strange, said Mr Bartell D'Arcy. I never even heard of him.

— Yes, yes, Miss Morkan is right, said Mr Browne. I remember hearing of old Parkinson but he's too far back for me.

— A beautiful pure sweet mellow English tenor, said Aunt Kate with enthusiasm.

Gabriel having finished, the huge pudding was transferred to the table. The clatter of forks and spoons began again. Gabriel's wife served out spoonfuls of the pudding and passed the plates down the table. Midway down they were held up by Mary Jane, who replenished them with raspberry or orange jelly or with blanc-mange and jam. The pudding was of Aunt Julia's making and she received praises for it from all quarters. She herself said that it was not quite brown enough.

— Well, I hope, Miss Morkan, said Mr Browne, that I'm brown enough for you because, you know, I'm all brown.

All the gentlemen, except Gabriel, ate some of the pudding out of compliment to Aunt Julia. As Gabriel never ate sweets the celery had been left for him. Freddy Malins also took a stalk of celery and ate it with his pudding. He had been told that celery was a capital thing for the blood and he was just then under the doctor's care. Mrs Malins, who had been silent all through the supper, said that her son was going down to Mount Melleray in a week or so. The table then spoke of Mount Melleray, how bracing the air was down there, how hospitable the monks were and how they never asked for a penny-piece from their guests.

— And do you mean to say, asked Mr Browne incredulously, that a chap can go down there and put up there as if it were a hotel and live on the fat of the land and then come away without paying a farthing?

— O, most people give some donation to the monastery when they leave, said Mary Jane.

— I wish we had an institution like that in our Church, said Mr Browne candidly.

He was astonished to hear that the monks never spoke, got up at two in the morning and slept in their coffins. He asked what they did it for.

— That's the rule of the order, said Aunt Kate firmly.

— Yes, but why? asked Mr Browne.

Aunt Kate repeated that it was the rule, that was all. Mr Browne still seemed not to understand. Freddy Malins explained to him, as best he could, that the monks were trying to make up for the sins committed by all the sinners in the outside world. The explanation was not very clear for Mr Browne grinned and said:

— I like that idea very much but wouldn't a comfortable spring bed do them as well as a coffin?

— The coffin, said Mary Jane, is to remind them of their last end.

As the subject had grown lugubrious it was buried in a silence of the table during which Mrs Malins could be heard saying to her neighbour in an indistinct undertone:

— They are very good men, the monks, very pious men.

The raisins and almonds and figs and apples and oranges and chocolates and sweets were now passed about the table and Aunt Julia invited all the guests to have either port or sherry. At first Mr Bartell D'Arcy refused to take either but one of his neighbours nudged him and whispered something to him upon which he allowed his glass to be filled. Gradually as the last glasses were being filled the conversation ceased. A pause followed, broken only by the noise of the wine and by unsettlings of chairs. The Misses Morkan, all three, looked down at the tablecloth. Someone coughed once or twice and then a few gentlemen patted the table gently as a signal for silence. The silence came and Gabriel pushed back his chair and stood up.

The patting at once grew louder in encouragement and then ceased altogether. Gabriel leaned his ten trembling fingers on the tablecloth and smiled nervously at the company. Meeting a row of upturned faces he raised his eyes to the chandelier. The piano was playing a waltz tune and he could hear the skirts sweeping against the drawing-room door. People, perhaps, were standing in the snow on the quay outside, gazing up at the lighted windows and listening to the waltz music. The air was pure there. In the distance lay the park where the trees were weighted with snow. The Wellington Monument wore a gleaming cap of snow that flashed westward over the white field of Fifteen Acres.

He began:

— Ladies and Gentlemen.

— It has fallen to my lot this evening, as in years past, to perform a very pleasing task but a task for which I am afraid my poor powers as a speaker are all too inadequate.

— No, no! said Mr Browne.

— But, however that may be, I can only ask you to-night to take the will for the deed and to lend me your attention for a few moments while I endeavour to express to you in words what my feelings are on this occasion.

— Ladies and Gentlemen. It is not the first time that we have gathered together under this hospitable roof, around this hospitable board. It is not the first time that we have been the recipients — or perhaps, I had better say, the victims — of the hospitality of certain good ladies.

He made a circle in the air with his arm and paused. Everyone laughed or smiled at Aunt Kate and Aunt Julia and Mary Jane who all turned crimson with pleasure. Gabriel went on more boldly:

— I feel more strongly with every recurring year that our country has no tradition which does it so much honour and which it should guard so jealously as that of its hospitality. It is a tradition that is unique as far as my experience goes (and I have visited not a few places abroad) among the modern nations. Some would say, perhaps, that with us it is rather a failing than anything to be boasted of. But granted even that, it is, to my mind, a princely failing, and one that I trust will long be cultivated among us. Of one thing, at least, I am sure. As long as this one roof shelters the good ladies aforesaid — and I wish from my heart it may do so for many and many a long year to come — the tradition of genuine warm-hearted courteous Irish hospitality, which our forefathers have handed down to us and which we in turn must hand down to our descendants, is still alive among us.

A hearty murmur of assent ran round the table. It shot through Gabriel's mind that Miss Ivors was not there and that she had gone away discourteously: and he said with confidence in himself:

— Ladies and Gentlemen.

— A new generation is growing up in our midst, a generation actuated by new ideas and new principles. It is serious and enthusiastic for these new ideas and its enthusiasm, even when it is misdirected, is, I believe, in the main sincere. But we are living in a sceptical and, if I may use the phrase, a thought-tormented age: and sometimes I fear that this new generation, educated or hypereducated as it is, will lack those qualities of humanity, of hospitality, of kindly humour which belonged to an older day. Listening tonight to the names of all those great singers of the past it seemed to me, I must confess, that we were living in a less spacious age. Those days might, without exaggeration, be called spacious days: and if they are gone beyond recall let us hope, at least, that in gatherings such as this we shall still speak of them with pride and affection, still cherish in our hearts the memory of those dead and gone great ones whose fame the world will not willingly let die.

— Hear, hear! said Mr Browne loudly.

— But yet, continued Gabriel, his voice falling into a softer inflection, there are always in gatherings such as this sadder thoughts that will recur to our minds: thoughts of the past, of youth, of changes, of absent faces that we miss here to-night. Our path through life is strewn with many such sad memories: and were we to brood upon them always we could not find the heart to go on bravely with our work among the living. We have all of us living duties and living affections which claim, and rightly claim, our strenuous endeavours.

— Therefore, I will not linger on the past. I will not let any gloomy moralising intrude upon us here to-night. Here we are gathered together for a brief moment from the bustle and rush of our everyday routine. We are met here as friends, in the spirit of good-fellowship, as colleagues, also to a certain extent, in the true spirit of *camaraderie*, and as the guests of — what shall I call them? — the Three Graces of the Dublin musical world.

The table burst into applause and laughter at this sally. Aunt Julia vainly asked each of her neighbours in turn to tell her what Gabriel had said.

— He says we are the Three Graces, Aunt Julia, said Mary Jane.

Aunt Julia did not understand but she looked up, smiling, at Gabriel, who continued in the same vein:

—Ladies and Gentlemen.

—I will not attempt to play to-night the part that Paris played on another occasion. I will not attempt to choose between them. The task would be an invidious one and one beyond my poor powers. For when I view them in turn, whether it be our chief hostess herself, whose good heart, whose too good heart, has become a byword with all who knew her, or her sister, who seems to be gifted with perennial youth and whose singing must have been a surprise and a revelation to us all to-night, or, last but not least, when I consider our youngest hostess, talented, cheerful, hard-working and the best of nieces, I confess, Ladies and Gentlemen, that I do not know to which of them I should award the prize.

Gabriel glanced down at his aunts and, seeing the large smile on Aunt Julia's face and the tears which had risen to Aunt Kate's eyes, hastened to close. He raised his glass of port gallantly, while every member of the company fingered a glass expectantly, and said loudly:

—Let us toast them all three together. Let us drink to their health, wealth, long life, happiness and prosperity and may they long continue to hold the proud and self-won position which they hold in their profession and the position of honour and affection which they hold in our hearts.

All the guests stood up, glass in hand, and, turning towards the three seated ladies, sang in unison, with Mr Browne as leader:

> For they are jolly gay fellows,
> For they are jolly gay fellows,
> For they are jolly gay fellows,
> Which nobody can deny.

Aunt Kate was making frank use of her handkerchief and even Aunt Julia seemed moved. Freddy Malins beat time with his pudding-fork and the singers turned towards one another, as if in melodious conference, while they sang, with emphasis:

> Unless he tells a lie,
> Unless he tells a lie.

Then, turning once more towards their hostesses, they sang:

> For they are jolly gay fellows,
> For they are jolly gay fellows,
> For they are jolly gay fellows,
> Which nobody can deny.

The acclamation which followed was taken up beyond the door of the supper-room by many of the other guests and renewed time after time, Freddy Malins acting as officer with his fork on high.

The piercing morning air came into the hall where they were standing so that Aunt Kate said:

— Close the door, somebody. Mrs Malins will get her death of cold.

— Browne is out there, Aunt Kate, said Mary Jane.

— Browne is everywhere, said Aunt Kate, lowering her voice.

Mary Jane laughed at her tone.

— Really, she said archly, he is very attentive.

— He has been laid on here like the gas, said Aunt Kate in the same tone, all during the Christmas.

She laughed herself this time good-humouredly and then added quickly:

— But tell him to come in, Mary Jane, and close the door. I hope to goodness he didn't hear me.

At that moment the hall-door was opened and Mr Browne came in from the doorstep, laughing as if his heart would break. He was dressed in a long green overcoat with mock astrakhan cuffs and collar and wore on his head an oval fur cap. He pointed down the snow-covered quay from where the sound of shrill prolonged whistling was borne in.

— Teddy will have all the cabs in Dublin out, he said.

Gabriel advanced from the little pantry behind the office, struggling into his overcoat and, looking round the hall, said:

— Gretta not down yet?

— She's getting on her things, Gabriel, said Aunt Kate.

— Who's playing up there? asked Gabriel.

— Nobody. They're all gone.

— O no, Aunt Kate, said Mary Jane. Bartell D'Arcy and Miss O'Callaghan aren't gone yet.

— Someone is strumming at the piano, anyhow, said Gabriel.

Mary Jane glanced at Gabriel and Mr Browne and said with a shiver:

— It makes me feel cold to look at you two gentlemen muffled up like that. I wouldn't like to face your journey home at this hour.

— I'd like nothing better this minute, said Mr Browne stoutly, than a rattling fine walk in the country or a fast drive with a good spanking goer between the shafts.

— We used to have a very good horse and trap at home, said Aunt Julia sadly.

— The never-to-be-forgotten Johnny, said Mary Jane, laughing.

Aunt Kate and Gabriel laughed too.

— Why, what was wonderful about Johnny? asked Mr Browne.

— The late lamented Patrick Morkan, our grandfather, that is, explained Gabriel, commonly known in his later years as the old gentleman, was a glue-boiler.

— O, now, Gabriel, said Aunt Kate, laughing, he had a starch mill.

— Well, glue or starch, said Gabriel, the old gentleman had a horse by the name of Johnny. And Johnny used to work in the old gentleman's mill, walking round and round in order to drive the mill. That was all very well; but now comes the tragic part about Johnny. One fine day the old gentleman thought he'd like to drive out with the quality to a military review in the park.

— The Lord have mercy on his soul, said Aunt Kate compassionately.

— Amen, said Gabriel. So the old gentleman, as I said, harnessed Johnny and put on his very best tall hat and his very best stock collar and drove out in grand style from his ancestral mansion somewhere near Back Lane, I think.

Everyone laughed, even Mrs Malins, at Gabriel's manner and Aunt Kate said:

— O now, Gabriel, he didn't live in Back Lane, really. Only the mill was there.

— Out from the mansion of his forefathers, continued Gabriel, he drove with Johnny. And everything went on beautifully until Johnny came in sight of King Billy's statue: and whether he fell in love with the horse King Billy sits on or whether he thought he was back again in the mill, anyhow he began to walk round the statue.

Gabriel paced in a circle round the hall in his goloshes amid the laughter of the others.

— Round and round he went, said Gabriel, and the old gentleman, who was a very pompous old gentleman, was highly indignant. *Go on, sir! What do you mean, sir? Johnny! Johnny! Most extraordinary conduct! Can't understand the horse!*

The peals of laughter which followed Gabriel's imitation of the incident were interrupted by a resounding knock at the hall-door. Mary Jane ran to open it and let in Freddy Malins. Freddy Malins, with his hat well back on his head and his shoulders humped with cold, was puffing and steaming after his exertions.

— I could only get one cab, he said.

— O, we'll find another along the quay, said Gabriel.

— Yes, said Aunt Kate. Better not keep Mrs Malins standing in the draught.

Mrs Malins was helped down the front steps by her son and Mr Browne and, after many manœuvres, hoisted into the cab. Freddy Malins clambered in after her and spent a long time settling her on the seat, Mr Browne helping him with advice. At last she was settled comfortably and Freddy Malins invited Mr Browne into the cab. There was a good deal of confused talk, and then Mr Browne got into the cab. The cabman settled his rug over his knees, and bent down for the address. The confusion grew greater and the cabman was directed differently by Freddy Malins and Mr Browne, each of whom had his head out through a window of the cab. The difficulty was to know where to drop Mr Browne along the route and Aunt Kate, Aunt Julia and Mary Jane helped the discussion from the doorstep with cross-directions and contradictions and abundance of laughter. As for Freddy Malins he was speechless with laughter. He popped his head in and out of the window every moment, to the great danger of his hat, and told his mother how the discussion was progressing till at last Mr Browne shouted to the bewildered cabman above the din of everybody's laughter:

— Do you know Trinity College?

— Yes, sir, said the cabman.

— Well, drive bang up against Trinity College gates, said Mr Browne, and then we'll tell you where to go. You understand now?

— Yes, sir, said the cabman.

— Make like a bird for Trinity College.

— Right, sir, cried the cabman.

The horse was whipped up and the cab rattled off along the quay amid a chorus of laughter and adieus.

Gabriel had not gone to the door with the others. He was in a dark part of the hall gazing up the staircase. A woman was standing near the top of the first flight, in the shadow also. He could not see her face but he could see the terra-cotta and salmonpink panels of her skirt which the shadow made appear black and white. It was his wife. She was leaning on the banisters, listening to something. Gabriel was surprised at her stillness and strained his ear to listen also. But he could hear little save the noise of laughter and dispute on the front steps, a few chords struck on the piano and a few notes of a man's voice singing.

He stood still in the gloom of the hall, trying to catch the air that the voice was singing and gazing up at his wife. There was grace and mystery in her attitude as if she were a symbol of something. He asked himself what is a woman standing on the stairs in the shadow, listening to distant music, a symbol of. If he were a painter he would paint her in that attitude. Her blue felt hat would show off the bronze of her hair against the darkness and the dark panels of her skirt would show off the light ones. *Distant Music* he would call the picture if he were a painter.

The hall-door closed; and Aunt Kate, Aunt Julia and Mary Jane came down the hall, still laughing.

— Well, isn't Freddy terrible? said Mary Jane. He's really terrible.

Gabriel said nothing but pointed up the stairs towards where his wife was standing. Now that the hall-door was closed the voice and the piano could be heard more clearly. Gabriel held up his hand for them to be silent. The song seemed to be in the old Irish tonality and the singer seemed uncertain both of his words and of his voice. The voice, made plaintive by distance and by the singer's hoarseness, faintly illuminated the cadence of the air with words expressing grief:

O, the rain falls on my heavy locks
And the dew wets my skin,
My babe lies cold . . .

— O, exclaimed Mary Jane. It's Bartell D'Arcy singing and he wouldn't sing all the night. O, I'll get him to sing a song before he goes.

— O do, Mary Jane, said Aunt Kate.

Mary Jane brushed past the others and ran to the staircase but before she reached it the singing stopped and the piano was closed abruptly.

— O, what a pity! she cried. Is he coming down, Gretta?

Gabriel heard his wife answer yes and saw her come down towards them. A few steps behind her were Mr Bartell D'Arcy and Miss O'Callaghan.

— O, Mr D'Arcy, cried Mary Jane, it's downright mean of you to break off like that when we were all in raptures listening to you.

— I have been at him all the evening, said Miss O'Callaghan, and Mrs Conroy too and he told us he had a dreadful cold and couldn't sing.

— O, Mr D'Arcy, said Aunt Kate, now that was a great fib to tell.

— Can't you see that I'm as hoarse as a crow? said Mr D'Arcy roughly.

He went into the pantry hastily and put on his overcoat. The others, taken aback by his rude speech, could find nothing to say. Aunt Kate wrinkled her brows and made signs to the others to drop the subject. Mr D'Arcy stood swathing his neck carefully and frowning.

— It's the weather, said Aunt Julia, after a pause.

— Yes, everybody has colds, said Aunt Kate readily, everybody.

— They say, said Mary Jane, we haven't had snow like it for thirty years; and I read this morning in the newspapers that the snow is general all over Ireland.

— I love the look of snow, said Aunt Julia sadly.

— So do I, said Miss O'Callaghan. I think Christmas is never really Christmas unless we have the snow on the ground.

— But poor Mr D'Arcy doesn't like the snow, said Aunt Kate, smiling.

Mr D'Arcy came from the pantry, fully swathed and buttoned, and in a repentant tone told them the history of the cold. Everyone gave him advice and said it was a great pity and urged him to be very careful of his throat in the night air. Gabriel watched his wife who did not join in the conversation. She was standing right under the dusty fanlight and the flame of the gas lit up the rich bronze of her hair which he had seen her drying at the fire a few days before. She was in the same attitude and seemed unaware of the talk about her. At last she turned towards them and Gabriel saw that there was colour on her cheeks and that her eyes were shining. A sudden tide of joy went leaping out of his heart.

— Mr D'Arcy, she said, what is the name of that song you were singing?

— It's called *The Lass of Aughrim*, said Mr D'Arcy, but I couldn't remember it properly. Why? Do you know it?

— *The Lass of Aughrim*, she repeated. I couldn't think of the name.

— It's a very nice air, said Mary Jane. I'm sorry you were not in voice tonight.

— Now, Mary Jane, said Aunt Kate, don't annoy Mr D'Arcy. I won't have him annoyed.

Seeing that all were ready to start she shepherded them to the door where good-night was said:

— Well, good-night, Aunt Kate, and thanks for the pleasant evening.

— Good-night, Gabriel. Good-night, Gretta!

— Good-night, Aunt Kate, and thanks ever so much. Good-night, Aunt Julia.

— O, good-night, Gretta, I didn't see you.

— Good-night, Mr D'Arcy. Good-night, Miss O'Callaghan.

— Good-night, Miss Morkan.

— Good-night, again.

— Good-night, all. Safe home.

— Good-night. Good-night.

The morning was still dark. A dull yellow light brooded over the houses and the river; and the sky seemed to be descending. It was slushy underfoot;

and only streaks and patches of snow lay on the roofs, on the parapets of the quay and on the area railings. The lamps were still burning redly in the murky air and, across the river, the palace of the Four Courts stood out menacingly against the heavy sky.

She was walking on before him with Mr Bartell D'Arcy, her shoes in a brown parcel tucked under one arm and her hands holding her skirt up from the slush. She had no longer any grace of attitude but Gabriel's eyes were still bright with happiness. The blood went bounding along his veins; and the thoughts were rioting through his brain, proud, joyful, tender, valorous.

She was walking on before him so lightly and so erect that he longed to run after her noiselessly, catch her by the shoulders and say something foolish and affectionate into her ear. She seemed to him so frail that he longed to defend her against something and then to be alone with her. Moments of their secret life together burst like stars upon his memory. A heliotrope envelope was lying beside his breakfast-cup and he was caressing it with his hand. Birds were twittering in the ivy and the sunny web of the curtain was shimmering along the floor: he could not eat for happiness. They were standing on the crowded platform and he was placing a ticket inside the warm palm of her glove. He was standing with her in the cold, looking in through a grated window at a man making bottles in a roaring furnace. It was very cold. Her face, fragrant in the cold air, was quite close to his; and suddenly she called out to the man at the furnace.

— Is the fire hot, sir?

But the man could not hear her with the noise of the furnace. It was just as well. He might have answered rudely.

A wave of yet more tender joy escaped from his heart and went coursing in warm flood along his arteries. Like the tender fires of stars moments of their life together, that no one knew of or would ever know of, broke upon and illumined his memory. He longed to recall to her those moments, to make her forget the years of their dull existence together and remember only their moments of ecstasy. For the years, he felt, had not quenched his soul or hers. Their children, his writing, her household cares had not quenched all their souls' tender fire. In one letter that he had written to her then he had said: *Why is it that words like these seem to me so dull and cold? Is it because there is no word tender enough to be your name?*

Like distant music these words that he had written years before were borne towards him from the past. He longed to be alone with her. When the others had gone away, when he and she were in their room in the hotel, then they would be alone together. He would call her softly:

— Gretta!

Perhaps she would not hear at once: she would be undressing. Then something in his voice would strike her. She would turn and look at him. . . .

At the corner of Winetavern Street they met a cab. He was glad of its rattling noise as it saved him from conversation. She was looking out of the window and seemed tired. The others spoke only a few words, pointing out some building or street. The horse galloped along wearily under the murky morning sky, dragging his old rattling box after his heels, and Gabriel was again in a cab with her, galloping to catch the boat, galloping to their honeymoon.

As the cab drove across O'Connell Bridge[3] Miss O'Callaghan said:

— They say you never cross O'Connell Bridge without seeing a white horse.

— I see a white man this time, said Gabriel.

— Where? asked Mr Bartell D'Arcy.

Gabriel pointed to the statue, on which lay patches of snow. Then he nodded familiarly to it and waved his hand.

— Good-night, Dan, he said gaily.

When the cab drew up before the hotel Gabriel jumped out and, in spite of Mr Bartell D'Arcy's protest, paid the driver. He gave the man a shilling over his fare. The man saluted and said:

— A prosperous New Year to you, sir.

— The same to you, said Gabriel cordially.

She leaned for a moment on his arm in getting out of the cab and while standing at the curbstone, bidding the others good-night. She leaned lightly on his arm, as lightly as when she had danced with him a few hours before. He had felt proud and happy then, happy that she was his, proud of her grace and wifely carriage. But now, after the kindling again of so many memories, the first touch of her body, musical and strange and perfumed, sent through him a keen pang of lust. Under cover of her silence he pressed her arm closely to his side; and, as they stood at the hotel door, he felt that they had escaped from their lives and duties, escaped from home and friends and run away together with wild and radiant hearts to a new adventure.

An old man was dozing in a great hooded chair in the hall. He lit a candle in the office and went before them to the stairs. They followed him in silence, their feet falling in soft thuds on the thickly carpeted stairs. She mounted the stairs behind the porter, her head bowed in the ascent, her frail shoulders curved as with a burden, her skirt girt tightly about her. He could have flung his arms about her hips and held her still for his arms were trembling with desire to seize her and only the stress of his nails against the palms of his hands held the wild impulse of his body in check. The porter halted on the stairs to settle his guttering candle. They halted too on the steps below him. In the silence Gabriel could hear the falling of the molten wax into the tray and the thumping of his own heart against his ribs.

The porter led them along a corridor and opened a door. Then he set his unstable candle down on a toilet-table and asked at what hour they were to be called in the morning.

— Eight, said Gabriel.

The porter pointed to the tap of the electric-light and began a muttered apology but Gabriel cut him short.

---

[3] The central bridge in Dublin, named after the patriot Daniel O'Connell (1775–1847) whose statue stands nearby.

— We don't want any light. We have enough light from the street. And I say, he added, pointing to the candle, you might remove that handsome article, like a good man.

The porter took up his candle again, but slowly for he was surprised by such a novel idea. Then he mumbled good-night and went out. Gabriel shot the lock to.

A ghostly light from the street lamp lay in a long shaft from one window to the door. Gabriel threw his overcoat and hat on a couch and crossed the room towards the window. He looked down into the street in order that his emotion might calm a little. Then he turned and leaned against a chest of drawers with his back to the light. She had taken off her hat and cloak and was standing before a large swinging mirror, unhooking her waist. Gabriel paused for a few moments, watching her, and then said:

— Gretta!

She turned away from the mirror slowly and walked along the shaft of light towards him. Her face looked so serious and weary that the words would not pass Gabriel's lips. No, it was not the moment yet.

— You look tired, he said.

— I am a little, she answered.

— You don't feel ill or weak?

— No, tired: that's all.

She went on to the window and stood there, looking out. Gabriel waited again and then, fearing that diffidence was about to conquer him, he said abruptly:

— By the way, Gretta!

— What is it?

— You know that poor fellow Malins? he said quickly.

— Yes. What about him?

— Well, poor fellow, he's a decent sort of chap after all, continued Gabriel in a false voice. He gave me back that sovereign I lent him and I didn't expect it really. It's a pity he wouldn't keep away from that Browne, because he's not a bad fellow at heart.

He was trembling now with annoyance. Why did she seem so abstracted? He did not know how he could begin. Was she annoyed, too, about something? If she would only turn to him or come to him of her own accord! To take her as she was would be brutal. No, he must see some ardour in her eyes first. He longed to be master of her strange mood.

— When did you lend him the pound? she asked, after a pause.

Gabriel strove to restrain himself from breaking out into brutal language about the sottish Malins and his pound. He longed to cry to her from his soul, to crush her body against his, to overmaster her. But he said:

— O, at Christmas, when he opened that little Christmas-card shop in Henry Street.

He was in such a fever of rage and desire that he did not hear her come from the window. She stood before him for an instant, looking at him strangely. Then, suddenly raising herself on tiptoe and resting her hands lightly on his shoulders, she kissed him.

— You are a very generous person, Gabriel, she said.

Gabriel, trembling with delight at her sudden kiss and at the quaintness of her phrase, put his hands on her hair and began smoothing it back, scarcely touching it with his fingers. The washing had made it fine and brilliant. His heart was brimming over with happiness. Just when he was wishing for it she had come to him of her own accord. Perhaps her thoughts had been running with his. Perhaps she had felt the impetuous desire that was in him and then the yielding mood had come upon her. Now that she had fallen to him so easily he wondered why he had been so diffident.

He stood, holding her head between his hands. Then, slipping one arm swiftly about her body and drawing her towards him, he said softly:

— Gretta dear, what are you thinking about?

She did not answer nor yield wholly to his arm. He said again, softly:

— Tell me what it is, Gretta. I think I know what is the matter. Do I know?

She did not answer at once. Then she said in an outburst of tears:

— O, I am thinking about that song, *The Lass of Aughrim.*

She broke loose from him and ran to the bed and, throwing her arms across the bed-rail, hid her face. Gabriel stood stock-still for a moment in astonishment and then followed her. As he passed in the way of the cheval-glass he caught sight of himself in full length, his broad, well-filled shirtfront, the face whose expression always puzzled him when he saw it in a mirror and his glimmering gilt-rimmed eyeglasses. He halted a few paces from her and said:

— What about the song? Why does that make you cry?

She raised her head from her arms and dried her eyes with the back of her hand like a child. A kinder note than he had intended went into his voice.

— Why, Gretta? he asked.

— I am thinking about a person long ago who used to sing that song.

— And who was the person long ago? asked Gabriel, smiling.

— It was a person I used to know in Galway when I was living with my grandmother, she said.

The smile passed away from Gabriel's face. A dull anger began to gather again at the back of his mind and the dull fires of his lust began to glow angrily in his veins.

— Someone you were in love with? he asked ironically.

— It was a young boy I used to know, she answered, named Michael Furey. He used to sing that song, *The Lass of Aughrim.* He was very delicate.

Gabriel was silent. He did not wish her to think that he was interested in this delicate boy.

— I can see him so plainly, she said after a moment. Such eyes as he had: big dark eyes! And such an expression in them — an expression!

— O, then, you were in love with him? said Gabriel.

— I used to go out walking with him, she said, when I was in Galway.

A thought flew across Gabriel's mind.

— Perhaps that was why you wanted to go to Galway with that Ivors girl? he said coldly.

She looked at him and asked in surprise:

— What for?

Her eyes made Gabriel feel awkward. He shrugged his shoulders and said:

— How do I know? To see him perhaps.

She looked away from him along the shaft of light towards the window in silence.

— He is dead, she said at length. He died when he was only seventeen. Isn't that a terrible thing to die so young as that?

— What was he? asked Gabriel, still ironically.

— He was in the gasworks, she said.

Gabriel felt humiliated by the failure of his irony and by the evocation of this figure from the dead, a boy in the gasworks. While he had been full of memories of their secret life together, full of tenderness and joy and desire, she had been comparing him in her mind with another. A shameful consciousness of his own person assailed him. He saw himself as a ludicrous figure, acting as a pennyboy for his aunts, a nervous well-meaning sentimentalist, orating to vulgarians and idealising his own clownish lusts, the pitiable fatuous fellow he had caught a glimpse of in the mirror. Instinctively he turned his back more to the light lest she might see the shame that burned upon his forehead.

He tried to keep up his tone of cold interrogation but his voice when he spoke was humble and indifferent.

— I suppose you were in love with this Michael Furey, Gretta, he said.

— I was great with him at that time, she said.

Her voice was veiled and sad. Gabriel, feeling now how vain it would be to try to lead her whither he had purposed, caressed one of her hands and said, also sadly:

— And what did he die of so young, Gretta? Consumption, was it?

— I think he died for me, she answered.

A vague terror seized Gabriel at this answer as if, at that hour when he had hoped to triumph, some impalpable and vindictive being was coming against him, gathering forces against him in its vague world. But he shook himself free of it with an effort of reason and continued to caress her hand. He did not question her again for he felt that she would tell him of herself. Her hand was warm and moist: it did not respond to his touch but he continued to caress it just as he had caressed her first letter to him that spring morning.

— It was in the winter, she said, about the beginning of the winter when I was going to leave my grandmother's and come up here to the convent. And he was ill at the time in his lodgings in Galway and wouldn't be let out and his people in Oughterard were written to. He was in decline, they said, or something like that. I never knew rightly.

She paused for a moment and sighed.

— Poor fellow, she said. He was very fond of me and he was such a gentle boy. We used to go out together, walking, you know, Gabriel, like the way they do in the country. He was going to study singing only for his health. He had a very good voice, poor Michael Furey.

— Well; and then? asked Gabriel.

— And then when it came to the time for me to leave Galway and come up to the convent he was much worse and I wouldn't be let see him so I wrote a letter saying I was going up to Dublin and would be back in the summer and hoping he would be better then.

She paused for a moment to get her voice under control and then went on:

— Then the night before I left I was in my grandmother's house in Nuns' Island, packing up, and I heard gravel thrown up against the window. The window was so wet I couldn't see so I ran downstairs as I was and slipped out the back into the garden and there was the poor fellow at the end of the garden, shivering.

— And did you not tell him to go back? asked Gabriel.

— I implored of him to go home at once and told him he would get his death in the rain. But he said he did not want to live. I can see his eyes as well as well! He was standing at the end of the wall where there was a tree.

— And did he go home? asked Gabriel.

— Yes, he went home. And when I was only a week in the convent he died and he was buried in Oughterard where his people came from. O, the day I heard that, that he was dead!

She stopped, choking with sobs, and, overcome by emotion, flung herself face downward on the bed, sobbing in the quilt. Gabriel held her hand for a moment longer, irresolutely, and then, shy of intruding on her grief, let it fall gently and walked quietly to the window.

She was fast asleep.

Gabriel, leaning on his elbow, looked for a few moments unresentfully on her tangled hair and half-open mouth, listening to her deep-drawn breath. So she had had that romance in her life: a man had died for her sake. It hardly pained him now to think how poor a part he, her husband, had played in her life. He watched her while she slept as though he and she had never lived together as man and wife. His curious eyes rested long upon her face and on her hair: and, as he thought of what she must have been then, in that time of her first girlish beauty, a strange friendly pity for her entered his soul. He did not like to say even to himself that her face was no longer beautiful but he knew that it was no longer the face for which Michael Furey had braved death.

Perhaps she had not told him all the story. His eyes moved to the chair over which she had thrown some of her clothes. A petticoat string dangled to the floor. One boot stood upright, its limp upper fallen down: the fellow of it lay upon its side. He wondered at his riot of emotions of an hour before. From what had it proceeded? From his aunt's supper, from his own foolish speech, from the wine and dancing, the merry-making when saying good-night in the hall, the pleasure of the walk along the river in the snow. Poor Aunt Julia! She, too, would soon be a shade with the shade of Patrick Morkan and his horse. He had caught that haggard look upon her face for a moment when she was singing *Arrayed for the Bridal*. Soon, perhaps, he would be sitting in that same drawing-room, dressed in black, his silk hat on his knees. The blinds would be drawn down and Aunt Kate would be sitting beside him, crying and blowing her nose and telling him how Julia had died. He would cast about his mind for some words that might console her, and would find only lame and useless ones. Yes, yes: that would happen very soon.

The air of the room chilled his shoulders. He stretched himself cautiously along under the sheets and lay down beside his wife. One by one they were all becoming shades. Better pass boldly into that other world, in the full glory of some passion, than fade and wither dismally with age. He thought of how she who lay beside him had locked in her heart for so many years that image of her lover's eyes when he had told her that he did not wish to live.

Generous tears filled Gabriel's eyes. He had never felt like that himself towards any woman but he knew that such a feeling must be love. The tears gathered more thickly in his eyes and in the partial darkness he imagined he saw the form of a young man standing under a dripping tree. Other forms were near. His soul had approached that region where dwell the vast hosts of the dead. He was conscious of, but could not apprehend, their wayward and flickering existence. His own identity was fading out into a grey impalpable world: the solid world itself which these dead had one time reared and lived in was dissolving and dwindling.

A few light taps upon the pane made him turn to the window. It had begun to snow again. He watched sleepily the flakes, silver and dark, falling obliquely against the lamplight. The time had come for him to set out on his journey westward. Yes, the newspapers were right: snow was general all over Ireland. It was falling on every part of the dark central plain, on the treeless hills, falling softly upon the Bog of Allen and, farther westward, softly falling into the dark mutinous Shannon waves. It was falling, too, upon every part of the lonely churchyard on the hill where Michael Furey lay buried. It lay thickly drifted on the crooked crosses and headstones, on the spears of the little gate, on the barren thorns. His soul swooned slowly as he heard the snow falling faintly through the universe and faintly falling, like the descent of their last end, upon all the living and the dead.

Franz Kafka

Franz Kafka (1883–1924), who said that a book should serve as "an axe to break up the frozen sea within us," led a life whose events are simple and sad. He was born into a Jewish family in Prague, and from youth onward he feared his authoritarian father so much that he stuttered in his presence, although he spoke easily with others. In 1906 he received a doctorate in jurisprudence, and for many years he worked a tedious job as a civil service lawyer investigating claims at the state Workers' Accident Insurance Institute. He never married and lived for the most part with his parents, writing fiction at night (he was an insomniac) and publishing only a few slim volumes of stories during his lifetime. *Meditation*, a collection of sketches, appeared in 1912; "The Stoker: A Fragment" in 1913; "The Metamorphosis" in 1915; "The Judgment" in 1916; "In the Penal Colony" in 1919; and "A Country Doctor" in 1920. Only a few of his friends knew that Kafka was also at work on the great novels that were published after his death from tuberculosis: *Amerika*, *The Trial*, and *The Castle*. (He asked his literary executor, Max Brod, to burn these works in manuscript, but Brod refused.) Kafka's despair with his writing, his job, his father, and his life was complete. Like Gustave Flaubert—whom he admired—he used his fiction as a "rock" to which he clung in order not to be drowned in the waves of the world around him. With typical irony, however, he saw the effort as futile: "By scribbling I run ahead of myself in order to catch myself up at the finishing post. I cannot run away from myself."

In his diaries Kafka recorded his obsession with literature. "What will be my fate as a writer is very simple. My talent for portraying my dreamlike inner life has thrust all other matters into the background." The translator Joachim Neugroschel noted that in Kafka's earliest stories, he tested "certain expressionist and even surrealist innovations, shredding syntax, short-circuiting imagery, condensing emotions and tableaux into brief, sometimes even tiny shards and prose poems to evoke a moody and sometimes wistful lyricism." The late story "A Hunger Artist" is one of Kafka's most striking "parables of alienation," as his biographer Ernst Pawel noted, but the "dreamlike" quality of his imagination is apparent in all of Kafka's work.

Kafka is perhaps best known as the author of the waking nightmare "The Metamorphosis," whose remarkable first sentence is one of the most famous in short story literature. The hero of "The Metamorphosis," Gregor Samsa (pronounced *Zamza*), is the son of philistine, middle-class parents in Prague, as was Kafka, and literary critics have tended to interpret the story as an autobiographical fiction, in which Kafka projected his sense of inadequacy before his demanding father. Though Kafka probably took Fyodor Dostoevsky's novella "The Double" (1846) as the inspiration for the plot, the mood, and the pace of his story, Vladimir Nabokov suggested that the greatest literary influence on Kafka was Flaubert, who also used language with ironic precision. The visionary, nightmarish quality of Kafka's fiction is in striking contrast to its precise and formal style, the clarity of which intensifies the dark richness of the fantasy.

RELATED COMMENTARIES
Ann Charters, "Translating Kafka," page 1405; Gustav Janouch, "Kafka's View of 'The Metamorphosis,'" page 1448.

A Hunger Artist

1924 / Translated by Ann Charters

IN RECENT DECADES the public's interest in the art of fasting has suffered a marked decline. While formerly it used to pay very well to stage large exhibitions of this kind under private management, today this is quite impossible. Those were different times. Back then the whole town was engaged with the hunger artist; during his fast, the audience's involvement grew from day to day; everyone wanted to see the hunger artist at least once a day; during the later stages subscribers used to sit in specially reserved seats in front of the small barred cage all day long; there were even exhibitions at night by torchlight to heighten the effect; on fine days his cage was carried out into the open, and that was particularly the time when the hunger artist was shown to children; while for the adults he was often just an entertainment in which they took part because it happened to be in fashion, for the children, who stood open-mouthed, holding each other's hands for safety's sake, watching him as he sat there on the straw spread out for him, even spurning a chair, he was a pale figure in a black leotard with enormously protruding ribs, sometimes nodding politely, answering questions with a forced smile, occasionally even stretching his arm through the bars to let them feel how skinny he was, but then again withdrawing completely into himself, paying attention to no one, not even noticing the striking of the clock, so important for him, the only piece of furniture in his cage, but merely staring into space with his eyes almost shut, taking a sip now and then from a tiny glass of water to moisten his lips.

Besides the changing spectators there were also permanent guards selected by the public — strangely enough, usually butchers — who had the job of watching the hunger artist day and night always three at a time to make sure that he didn't consume any nourishment in some secret manner. But this was no more than a formality introduced to reassure the public, because insiders knew well enough that during his fast, the hunger artist would never, under any circumstances, not even under duress, swallow the smallest crumb; his code of honor as an artist forbade it. Not every watchman, of course, was capable of understanding this; often there were groups of night guards who were very lax in carrying out their duties and deliberately congregated in a far corner and absorbed themselves in a game of cards, obviously intending to give the hunger artist the chance to take a little refreshment, which they assumed he could produce from some secret stash. Nothing was more tormenting to the hunger artist than such watchmen; they made him miserable; they made his fasting seem terribly difficult; sometimes he would overcome his physical weakness and sing for as long as he could keep it up during their watch, to show how unfair their suspicions were. But that was of little use; they only marveled at his skill in being able to eat even while singing. He much preferred the guards who sat right up against the bars and who weren't satisfied with the dim night lighting in the hall and so trained on him the beams of the flashlights supplied to them by his manager. The harsh light didn't disturb him at all, since he wasn't able to sleep deeply anyway, whereas he could always doze off a little whatever the light or the hour, even in the overcrowded, noisy hall. He was quite prepared to spend the whole night entirely without sleep with such watchmen; he was prepared to swap jokes with them, to tell them stories about his nomadic life and listen to their stories in turn, anything just to keep them awake, to be able to show them again and again that he had nothing to eat in his cage and that he was fasting like no one of them could fast. But he was happiest when morning came and a lavish breakfast was served to them at his expense, on which they threw themselves with the appetites of healthy men after a weary night's vigil. Of course there were even people who would see this breakfast as an attempt to bribe the guards, but that was really going too far, and when these people were asked if they would be willing to take over the night watch without breakfast, just for the sake of the cause, they slunk away, though they stuck to their suspicions all the same.

But suspicions of this nature were really inseparable from fasting. No one, after all, was capable of spending all his days and nights continuously watching the hunger artist, so no one could be absolutely certain from firsthand knowledge that his fasting had truly been an unbroken and faultless performance; only the hunger artist himself could know that, and only he, therefore, could be at the same time both the performer and the satisfied spectator of his own fasting. Yet there was another reason why he was never satisfied; perhaps it wasn't only his fasting that made him so emaciated that many people, much to their regret, couldn't attend his performances because they couldn't bear the sight of him; perhaps he had become so emaciated from dissatisfaction with himself. For he alone knew something that not even other insiders knew: how easy it was to fast. It was the easiest thing in the world. He made no secret of this, either, though no one believed him; at best some thought him modest, but mostly they regarded him as a publicity seeker or even took him for a fraud, a person for whom fasting was easy because he knew how to make it easy and then also even had the audacity more or less to admit it. He was forced to endure all of this, he'd even grown accustomed to it all in the course of time, but inwardly his own dissatisfaction gnawed at him, yet never after a single fasting period — you had to grant him this much — had he voluntarily left his cage. The manager had set forty days as the maximum period of the fasting; he would never allow a fast to run beyond this limit, not even in the major cities, and for good reason. Experience had shown that the public's interest in any town could be stimulated for about forty days by increasing the advertisements, but then the public lost interest, and a substantial drop in attendance was noted; naturally there were small variations in this matter between the different towns and regions, but as a rule forty days was the limit. So then on the fortieth day the gate of the flower-decorated cage was opened, an enthusiastic crowd of spectators filled the hall, a military band played, two doctors entered the cage to take the hunger artist's vital measurements, the results were announced to the audience through a megaphone, and finally two young ladies came forward, pleased that they had won the lottery for the honor of leading the hunger artist out of the cage and down a few steps toward a small table where a carefully prepared invalid's meal was served. And at this point, the hunger artist always resisted. True, he willingly surrendered his bony arms to the outstretched hands of these solicitous ladies as they bent down to him, but he refused to stand up. Why stop now, after just forty days? He could have kept going for much longer, infinitely longer; why stop now when he was at his best — indeed, when he had not yet even reached his best fasting form? Why did they want to rob him of the glory of fasting longer, not only of being the greatest hunger artist of all time, which he probably already was — but also of surpassing himself to achieve the unimaginable, because he felt that his capacity to fast was limitless. Why had this audience, which pretended to admire him so much, had so little patience with him; if he could endure fasting longer, why couldn't they endure it? Besides, he was tired, he was comfortable sitting in straw, and now he was supposed to stand upright and go to a meal; the thought alone nauseated him to such a point that he was prevented from expressing it with great difficulty, only out of regard for the ladies. And he gazed up into the eyes of the ladies, who appeared so friendly but were actually so cruel, and shook his head, which weighed heavily on his feeble neck. But then what happened was always what happened. The manager came forward, silently raised his arms over the hunger artist — the band music made speech impossible — as if he were calling upon heaven to look down on its handiwork there in the straw; on this pathetic martyr, which the hunger artist certainly was, only in an entirely different sense; he grasped the hunger artist around his emaciated waist with exaggerated care as if to suggest what a feeble object he had to deal with here; and giving him a secret shake or two, so that the hunger artist's legs and upper body wobbled to and fro, he handed him over to the care of the ladies, who had turned deathly pale in the meantime. Now the hunger artist submitted to everything; his head lay on his chest, as if it had rolled there by chance and stopped itself inexplicably; his body was hollowed out; his legs were squeezed tightly together at the knees in some instinct of self-preservation, but his feet were scraping at the ground, as if it weren't the real ground — they were still seeking the real ground; and the entire weight of his body, admittedly very modest, lay on one of the ladies, who — looking around for help, with panting breath — this wasn't how she had pictured her position of honor — first craned her neck back as far as possible, at least to keep her face from touching the hunger artist, then finding this impossible, when her more fortunate companion didn't come to her aid, instead contenting herself with carrying before her the small bundle of bones that was the hunger artist's hand, the first lady burst into tears amid the audience's delighted laughter and had to be replaced by an attendant who had been standing by in readiness. Then came the meal, a little of which the manager spooned into the nearly unconscious, comatose hunger artist to the accompaniment of cheerful patter designed to divert attention away from the hunger artist's condition; then came the toast drunk to the audience, which the hunger artist allegedly whispered to the manager; the band concluded everything with a great fanfare; the crowd melted away, and nobody had any cause to feel dissatisfied with the show, no one, only the hunger artist, always just him alone.

So he lived for many years with regular short periods of rest, in apparent glory honored by the world, yet in spite of that mostly in a dark mood that became even darker because no one took it seriously. And indeed, how could anyone have comforted him? What more could he wish for? And if once in awhile some good natured soul came along and felt sorry for him and tried to explain to him that his depression was probably caused by his fasting, it sometimes happened, especially if his fast were well advanced, that the hunger artist responded with a burst of rage and to everyone's alarm began to shake the bars of his cage like a wild beast. But the manager had a method of punishment that he was fond of using in such cases. He would apologize publicly to the assembled audience for the hunger artist, admitting that his behavior could only be excused as an irritable condition brought on by his fasting, something that well-fed people by no means could easily understand; in this connection, he would go on to speak of the hunger artist's claim that he was able to fast for a much longer time than he did fast; the manager praised the high aspirations, the good will, the great measure of self-denial undoubtedly implicit in this claim; but then he would seek to refute this claim simply enough by producing photographs, which were at the same time offered for sale to the public; for these pictures showed the hunger artist on his fortieth day of fasting, in bed, almost dead from exhaustion. This perversion of the truth, which assuredly was familiar to the hunger artist, always unnerved him anew and was too much for him. Here the result of the premature ending of his fast was presented as its cause! To fight against this lack of understanding, against this world of ignorance, was impossible. Up to that point he always stood clinging to the bars of his cage, listening eagerly to the manager in good faith, but as soon as the photographs appeared he would let go and sink back with a groan onto his straw, and the reassured public could come close again and inspect him.

When the witnesses to such scenes recalled them a few years later, they often failed to understand them at all. For in the meantime, the previously mentioned decline of the public's interest in fasting had occurred; it seemed to happen almost overnight; there may have been deeper reasons for it, but who cared about digging them up; in any case, the day came when the hunger artist found himself deserted by the pleasure-seeking crowds, who went streaming past him toward other exhibitions. For one last time his manager dragged him across half Europe to see if the old interest might be revived here and there; all in vain, it was as if a repulsion for exhibition fasting had set in everywhere by secret pact. In reality it couldn't have come about so suddenly, of course, and people now belatedly recalled a number of warning signs that had neither been adequately noted nor adequately dealt with in the flush of success, but now it was too late for countermeasures. Of course fasting would surely make a comeback some day, but that was no comfort to the living. What should the hunger artist do now? He who had been applauded by thousands couldn't appear as a sideshow in village fairs, and as for starting a new profession, the hunger artist was not merely too old, but he was also, above all, too fanatically devoted to his fasting. So he took leave of his manager, his companion throughout an unparalleled career, and found an engagement for himself with a large circus; in order to spare his own feelings, he avoided reading the terms of his contract.

A large circus, with its immense number of personnel and animals and apparatus, all constantly replacing and supplementing one another, can always find a use for anyone at any time, even a hunger artist, provided, of course, that his demands are sufficiently modest, and furthermore in this particular case it wasn't just the hunger artist himself who was being booked, but also his long-famous name; indeed, considering the peculiar nature of his art, which doesn't decrease with advancing age, one couldn't even say that he was a superannuated artist, past his prime, and seeking refuge in a quiet circus job; on the contrary, the hunger artist pledged that he could fast just as well as ever, which was clearly believable; in fact, he even claimed that if they let him have his way, as they readily promised him, he would truly astound the world by setting a new record, a claim that only provoked a smile from the experts, considering the public's current mood, which the hunger artist, in his enthusiasm, was apt to forget.

Basically, however, the hunger artist hadn't lost his sense of the real situation, and he accepted it as self-evident that he and his cage would not be placed as a star attraction in the center ring, but rather would be offered as a sideshow in a readily accessible site near the animal cages. Large, brightly colored posters made a frame for his cage and proclaimed what was to be seen there. When the audience came pouring out during the intermission to look at the animals, they almost inevitably had to pass the hunger artist's cage and stop there for a moment; they would perhaps have stayed longer, if those pressing them from behind in the narrow passageway, who couldn't understand the delay on the path to the animals they were so eager to see, hadn't made a longer, more leisurely contemplation impossible. This was also the reason why the hunger artist, who naturally looked forward to these visiting periods as his purpose in life, trembled at their prospect as well. At first he could hardly wait for the intermissions; he had been delighted watching the crowds come surging toward him, until it was made clear to him only too soon — not even the most obstinate, almost deliberate self-deception could obscure the fact — that most of these people, to judge from their actions, were again and again without exception on their way to the wild animals. And that first sight of them from a distance always remained the best. For as soon as they had reached him, he was immediately deafened by the shouting and cursing from the two contending factions which kept continuously forming — those who wanted to stop and stare at him (and the hunger artist soon found them the more distasteful) out of no real interest but only just as a whim or out of defiance, and those others who only wanted to go straight to the animal cages. Once the first rush was over, then came the stragglers, and these, who had nothing to prevent them from stopping as long as they liked, hurried by with long strides, without hardly even a side glance at him, as they rushed to see the animals in the remaining time. And it was an all too rare stroke of luck when the father of a family came along with his children, pointed to the hunger artist, explained in detail what was happening, told stories about earlier years when he himself had witnessed similar but incomparably more splendid performances, but then the children, since they hadn't been sufficiently prepared by either school or life, remained rather uncomprehending — what was fasting to them? — yet the gleam of their inquisitive eyes suggested something new to come, better and more merciful times. Perhaps, the hunger artist sometimes said to himself, things could become a little better if his cage were located not so close to the animal cages. That made the choice of destination too easy for people, to say nothing of how the stench of the stables, the restlessness of the animals at night, the serving of raw meat to the beasts of prey, and the roars at feeding time constantly offended and depressed him. But he did not dare to complain to the management; after all, he had the animals to thank for the throng of visitors, among them here and there even someone who was there just to see him; and who could tell where they might hide him if he called attention to his existence and thereby to the fact that, strictly speaking, he was no more than an obstacle in the path to the animals.

A small obstacle, to be sure, an obstacle growing smaller all the time. It has become customary nowadays to want to find it strange to call attention to a hunger artist, and in accordance with this custom his fate was sealed. He might fast as much as he could, and indeed he did, but nothing could save him now, people passed him by. Just try to explain the art of fasting to someone! Someone who doesn't feel it cannot be made to understand it. The colorful posters became dirty and illegible, they were torn down and no one thought to replace them; the little signboard tallying the number of days fasted, which at first had been carefully changed every day, had long remained the same, for after the first few weeks the staff had grown tired of even this small task; and so the hunger artist just went on fasting as he had once dreamed of doing, and it was indeed no trouble for him to do so, as he had always predicted, but no one counted the days; no one, not even the hunger artist himself, knew how great his achievement was, and his heart grew heavy. And once in a while, when some casual passer-by stopped, ridiculed the outdated number on the board, and talked about a hoax, that was in its way the stupidest lie ever invented by indifference and inherent malice, since the hunger artist didn't cheat, he was working honestly, but the world was cheating him of his reward.

So again many more days passed and there came an end to that as well. One day a supervisor happened to notice the cage, and he asked the attendants why this perfectly useful cage with the rotten straw in it was left unoccupied; no one knew, until somebody with the help of the signboard remembered the hunger artist. They poked into the straw with sticks and found the hunger artist underneath. "Are you still fasting?" asked the supervisor. "When on earth do you mean to stop?" "Forgive me, everybody," whispered the hunger artist; only the supervisor, who pressed his ear against the bars, understood him. "Certainly," said the supervisor, tapping his finger at the side of his forehead to suggest the hunger artist's condition to the staff, "we forgive you." "I always wanted you to admire my fasting," said the hunger artist. "We do admire it," said the supervisor obligingly. "But you shouldn't admire it," said the hunger artist. "All right, then, we don't admire it," said the supervisor, "but why shouldn't we admire it?" "Because I have to fast, I can't help it," said the hunger artist. "How about that," said the supervisor. "Why can't you help it?" "Because," said the hunger artist, lifting his shriveled head a little, and puckering his lips as if for a kiss, he spoke right into the supervisor's ear, so that nothing would be missed, "because I couldn't find the food I liked. If I had found it, believe me, I shouldn't have made any fuss and stuffed myself just like you and everyone else." These were his last words, but in his dying eyes there remained the firm, if no longer proud, conviction that he was still continuing to fast.

"Now clear this out!" said the supervisor, and they buried the hunger artist, straw and all. Then they put a young panther into the cage. Even the most insensitive felt it was refreshing to see this wild creature leaping about in a cage that had been neglected for so long. He lacked for nothing. The food that he liked was brought to him by his keepers without hesitation; he didn't even appear to miss his freedom; that noble body, full to almost bursting with all he needed, seemed to carry freedom itself around with it; it appeared to be placed somewhere in his jaws; and the joy of life streamed with such ardent passion from his throat, that it wasn't easy for the onlookers to withstand it. But they braced themselves, surrounded the cage, and never wanted to move on.

The Metamorphosis

1915 / Translated by Ann Charters

I

As Gregor Samsa awoke one morning from troubled dreams, he found himself transformed in his bed into a monstrous insect. He was lying on his hard, armor-plated back, and when he lifted his head a little he could see his dome-like brown belly divided into bow-shaped ridges, on top of which the precariously perched bed quilt was about to slide off completely. His numerous legs, pitiably thin compared to the rest of him, fluttered helplessly before his eyes.

"What has happened to me?" he thought. It was no dream. His room — a normal, though rather small, human bedroom — lay quiet within its four familiar walls. Above the table, where a collection of cloth samples was unpacked and laid out — Samsa was a traveling salesman — hung the picture that he had recently cut from an illustrated magazine and put in a pretty gilt frame. It showed a lady wearing a small fur hat and a fur stole, sitting upright, holding out to the viewer a heavy fur muff into which her entire forearm had vanished.

Then Gregor looked toward the window, and the dreary weather — he heard the rain falling on the metal ledge of the window — made him feel quite melancholy. "What if I went back to sleep again for awhile and forgot about all this nonsense?" he thought, but it was absolutely impossible, since he was used to sleeping on his right side, and he was unable to get into that position in his present state. No matter how hard he tried to heave himself over onto his right side, he always rocked onto his back again. He tried a hundred times, closing his eyes so he wouldn't have to look at his wriggly legs, and he didn't give up until he began to feel a faint, dull ache in his side that he had never felt before.

"Oh God," he thought, "what a hard job I picked for myself! Traveling day in and day out. Much more stressful than working in the home office; on top of that, the strain of traveling, the worry about making connections, the bad meals at all hours, meeting new people, no real human contact, no one who ever becomes a friend. The devil take it all!" He felt a slight itch on top of his belly; slowly he pushed himself on his back closer to the bedpost, so he could lift his head better; he found the itchy place, which was covered with little white spots he couldn't identify; he tried to touch the place with one of his legs, but he immediately drew it back, for the contact sent icy shudders through his entire body.

He slid back to his former position. "Getting up so early like this," he thought, "makes you quite stupid. A man has to have his sleep. Other traveling salesmen live like women in a harem. For instance, when I return to the hotel during the morning to write up my orders, I find these gentlemen just sitting down to breakfast. I should try that with my boss; I would be fired on the spot. Anyway, who knows if that wouldn't be a good thing for me after all. If it weren't for my parents, I would have quit long ago, I would have gone to the boss and told him off. That would knock him off his desk! It's a strange thing, too, the way he sits on top of his desk and talks down to his employees from this height, especially since he's hard of hearing and we have to come so close to him. Now, I haven't totally given up hope; as soon as I've saved the money to pay back what my parents owe him — that should take another five or six years — I'll certainly do it. Then I'll take the big step. Right now, though, I have to get up, because my train leaves at five."

He looked over at the alarm clock, which was ticking on the chest of drawers. "Heavenly Father," he thought. It was half past six, and the hands of the clock were quietly moving forward; in fact, it was after half past, it was nearly quarter to seven. Was it possible the alarm hadn't rung? He saw from the bed that it was correctly set at four o'clock; surely it had rung. Yes, but was it possible to sleep peacefully right through that furniture-rattling noise? Well, he hadn't exactly slept peacefully, but probably all the more soundly. What should he do now? The next train left at seven o'clock; to catch it, he would have to rush like mad, and his samples weren't even packed yet, and he definitely didn't feel particularly fresh and rested. And even if he did catch the train, he wouldn't escape a scene with his boss, since the firm's office boy would have been waiting at the five o'clock train and would have reported back to the office long ago that he hadn't turned up. The office boy was the boss's own creature, without backbone or brains. Now, what if he called in sick? But that would be embarrassing, and it would look suspicious, because in the five years he'd been with the company, he'd never been sick before. His boss would be sure to show up with the doctor from the Health Insurance; he'd reproach his parents for their son's laziness, and he'd cut short any excuses by repeating the doctor's argument that people don't get sick, they're just lazy. And in this case, would he be so wrong? The fact was that except for being drowsy, which was certainly unnecessary after his long sleep, Gregor felt quite well, and he was even hungrier than usual.

As he was hurriedly turning all these thoughts over in his mind, still not able to decide to get out of bed—the alarm clock was just striking a quarter to seven—he heard a cautious tap on the door, close by the head of his bed. "Gregor"—someone called—it was his mother—"it's a quarter to seven. Didn't you want to leave?" That gentle voice! Gregor was shocked when he heard his own voice reply; it was unmistakably his old familiar voice, but mixed with it could be heard an irrepressible undertone of painful squeaking, which left the words clear for only a moment, immediately distorting their sound so that you didn't know if you had really heard them right. Gregor would have liked to answer fully and explain everything, but under the circumstances, he contented himself by saying, "Yes, yes, thank you, mother. I'm just getting up." No doubt the wooden door between them must have kept her from noticing the change in Gregor's voice, for his mother was reassured with his announcement and shuffled off. But because of this brief conversation, the other family members had become aware that Gregor unexpectedly was still at home, and soon his father began knocking on a side door softly, but with his fist. "Gregor, Gregor," he called, "what's the matter with you?" And after a little while, in a deeper, warning tone, "Gregor! Gregor!" At the other side door, his sister was asking plaintively, "Gregor, aren't you feeling well? Do you need anything?" To both sides of the room, Gregor answered, "I'm getting ready," and he forced himself to pronounce each syllable carefully and to separate his words by inserting long pauses, so his voice sounded normal. His father went back to his breakfast, but his sister whispered, "Gregor, open the door, please do." But Gregor had no intention of opening the door, and he congratulated himself on having developed the prudent habit during his travels of always locking all doors during the night, even at home.

As a start, he would get up quietly and undisturbed, get dressed, and—what was most important—eat breakfast, and then he would consider what to do next, since he realized that he would never come to a sensible conclusion about the situation if he stayed in bed. He remembered how many times before, perhaps when he was lying in bed in an unusual position, he had felt slight pains that turned out to be imaginary when he got up, and he was looking forward to finding out how this morning's fantasy would fade away. As for the change in his voice, he didn't doubt at all that it was nothing more than the first warning of a serious cold, a traveling salesman's occupational hazard.

It was easy to push off the quilt; all he had to do was to take a deep breath and it fell off by itself. But things got difficult with the next step, especially since he was now much broader. He could have used hands and arms to prop himself up, but all he had were his numerous little legs that never stopped moving in all directions and that he couldn't control at all. Whenever he tried to bend one of his legs, that was the first one to straighten itself out; and when it was finally doing what he wanted it to do, then all the other legs waved uncontrollably, in very painful agitation. "There's simply no use staying idle in bed," said Gregor to himself.

The first thing he meant to do was get the lower part of his body out of bed, but this lower part, which he still hadn't seen, and couldn't imagine either, proved to be too difficult to move, it shifted so slowly; and when finally, growing almost frantic, he gathered his strength and lurched forward, he miscalculated the direction, and banged himself violently into the bottom bedpost, and from the burning pain he felt, he realized that for the moment, it was the lower part of his body that was the most sensitive.

Next he tried to get the upper part of his body out first, and cautiously brought his head to the edge of the bed. This he managed easily, and eventually the rest of his body, despite its width and weight, slowly followed the direction of his head. But when he finally had moved his head off the bed into open space, he became afraid of continuing any further, because if he were to fall in this position, it would be a miracle if he didn't injure his head. And no matter what happened, he must not lose consciousness just now; he would be better off staying in bed.

But when he repeated his efforts and, sighing, found himself stretched out just as before, and again he saw his little legs struggling if possible even more wildly than ever, despairing of finding a way to bring discipline and order to this random movement, he once again realized that it was impossible to stay in bed, and that the wisest course was to make every sacrifice, if there was even the slightest hope of freeing himself from the bed. But at the same time, he continued to remind himself that it was always better to think calmly and coolly than make desperate decisions. In such stressful moments he usually turned his eyes toward the window, but unfortunately the view of the morning fog didn't inspire confidence or comfort; it was so thick that it obscured the other side of the narrow street. "Already seven o'clock," he said as the alarm clock rang again, "already seven o'clock and still such a heavy fog." And for a little while longer he lay quietly, breathing very gently as if expecting perhaps that the silence would restore real and normal circumstances.

But then he told himself, "Before it reaches quarter past seven, I must absolutely be out of bed without fail. Besides, by then someone from the office will be sent here to ask about me, since it opens at seven." And he began to rock the entire length of his body in a steady rhythm to swing it out of bed. If he maneuvered out of bed in this way, then his head, which he intended to lift up as he fell, would presumably escape injury. His back seemed to be hard; it wouldn't be harmed if he fell on the carpet. His biggest worry was the loud crash he was bound to make, which would certainly cause anxiety, perhaps even alarm, behind all the doors. Still, he had to take the risk.

When Gregor was already jutting halfway out of bed — his new approach was more a game than an exertion, for all he needed was to seesaw himself on his back — it occurred to him how easy his task would become if only he had help. Two strong people — he thought of his father and the maid — would have been enough; all they had to do was to slide their arms under his round back, lift him out of bed, bend down with their burden, and then wait patiently while he swung himself onto the ground, where he hoped that his little legs would find some purpose. Well, quite aside from the fact that the doors were locked, should he really have called for help? Despite his misery, he couldn't help smiling at the very thought of it.

By now he had pushed himself so far off the bed with his steady rocking that he could feel himself losing his balance, and he would finally have to decide what he was going to do, because in five minutes it would be quarter after seven — when the front doorbell rang. "That's somebody from the office," he said to himself, and his body became rigid, while his little legs danced in the air even faster. For a moment everything was quiet. "They won't open the door," Gregor told himself, with a surge of irrational hope. But then, as usual, the maid walked to the door with her firm step and opened it. Gregor needed only to hear the first words of greeting from the visitor to know who it was — the office manager himself. Why on earth was Gregor condemned to work for a company where the slightest sign of negligence was seized upon with the gravest suspicion? Were the employees, without exception, all scoundrels? Was no one among them a loyal and dedicated man, who, if he did happen to miss a few hours of work one morning, might drive himself so crazy with remorse that he couldn't get out of bed? Wouldn't it have been enough to send an apprentice to inquire — if inquiries were really necessary — did the manager himself have to come, and make it clear to the whole innocent family that any investigation into this suspicious matter could only be entrusted to a manager? And responding to these irritating thoughts more than to any conscious decision, Gregor swung himself out of bed with all his strength. There was a loud thud, but not really a crash. The carpet softened his fall, and his back was more resilient than Gregor had thought, so the resulting thud wasn't so noticeable. Only he hadn't held his head carefully enough and had banged it; he twisted it and rubbed it against the carpet in pain and annoyance.

"Something fell in there," said the manager in the adjoining room on the left. Gregor tried to imagine whether something similar to what had happened to him today might happen one day to the office manager; one really had to admit this possibility. But, as if in brusque reply, the manager took a few decisive steps in the next room, which made his patent leather boots creak. And in the adjoining room to the right, Gregor's sister whispered, as if warning him, "Gregor, the office manager is here." "I know," said Gregor to himself; but he didn't dare to raise his voice high enough so that his sister could hear.

"Gregor," said his father from the room to his left, "the office manager has come and wants to know why you didn't catch the early train. We don't know what to tell him. Besides, he wants to talk to you in person. So, please, open the door. Surely he will be kind enough to excuse the disorder in your room." "Good morning, Mr. Samsa," the manager was calling in a friendly tone. "He's not well," said his mother to the manager, while his father continued talking through the door. "He's not well, believe me, sir. Why else would Gregor miss a train! That boy doesn't have anything in his head but business. I'm almost upset, as it is, that he never goes out at night; he's been in town for the past week, but he's stayed home every evening. He just sits here with us at the table, quietly reading the newspaper or studying the railroad timetables. His only recreation is when he occupies himself with his fretsaw. For instance, during the past two or three evenings, he's made a small picture frame; you'd be surprised how pretty it is; it's hanging in his room; you'll see it as soon as Gregor opens up. I'm really glad you've come, sir, we haven't been able to persuade Gregor to open the door; he's so obstinate; and he must definitely be feeling unwell, although he denied it earlier this morning." "I'll be right there," said Gregor slowly and deliberately, but he didn't move, so as not to miss a word of the conversation. "Dear madam, I can think of no other explanation, either," said the office manager. "Let us only hope it's nothing serious. Though, on the other hand, I must say, that we business people — fortunately or unfortunately — often very simply must overlook a slight indisposition in order to get on with business." "Well, can the office manager come in now?" asked his father impatiently and knocked again on the door. "No," said Gregor. In the room to the left, there was an embarrassed silence; in the room to the right, his sister began sobbing.

Why hadn't she joined the others? Probably she had just gotten out of bed and hadn't yet begun dressing. And why was she crying? Because he hadn't gotten up and let the office manager in, because he was in danger of losing his job, and because his boss would pester his parents again about their old debts? But surely for the moment these were unnecessary worries. Gregor was still here and would never consider abandoning the family. True, at this very moment he was lying on the carpet, and no one who could have seen his condition, could seriously expect him to open his door for the office manager. But Gregor could hardly be fired for this small discourtesy, for which he could easily find a plausible excuse later on. And it seemed to Gregor, that it would be much more sensible, just to leave him in peace for now, instead of pestering him with tears and speeches. But it was just this uncertainty about him that upset the others and excused their behavior.

"Mr. Samsa," the office manager now called out, raising his voice, "what is the matter with you? You are barricading yourself in your room, answering with only Yes and No, causing your parents serious and needless worries, and — I mention this only in passing — now suddenly you neglect your duties to the firm in an absolutely shocking manner. I'm speaking here in the name of your parents and your employer, and I must ask you to give an immediate and satisfactory explanation. I'm amazed, amazed! I took you for a quiet, sensible person, and now suddenly you seem intent on behaving in an absolutely strange manner. Early this morning, the head of the firm did suggest to me a possible explanation for your absence — it concerned the cash payment for sales that you received recently — but I practically gave him my word of honor that this couldn't be true. But now that I'm witness to your unbelievable obstinacy here, I haven't the slightest desire to defend you in any way whatsoever. And your job is by no means secure. I'd originally intended to confide this to you privately, but since you force me to waste my time here needlessly, I see no reason why your parents shouldn't hear it as well. For some time your sales have been quite unsatisfactory; to be sure, it's not the best season for business, we recognize that, but a season for doing no business at all just doesn't exist, Mr. Samsa, it *must* not exist."

"But, sir," Gregor called out, beside himself and forgetting everything in his agitation, "I'll open the door immediately, this very minute. A slight indisposition, a dizzy spell, kept me from getting up. I'm still lying in bed. But I feel completely well again. I'm just climbing out of bed. Please be patient for a moment. It's not going quite so well as I thought. But I'm really all right. How suddenly a thing like this can happen to a person! Just last night I felt fine, my parents know that, or rather last night I already had a slight foreboding. It must have been noticeable. Why didn't I let them know at the office! But you always think that you can recover from an illness without having to stay at home. Please, sir, please spare my parents! Because there are no grounds for all the accusations you just made; no one has ever said a word to me about them. Perhaps you haven't seen the last orders that I sent in. Anyway, I can still catch the eight o'clock train; the last couple hours of rest have made me feel much stronger. Don't delay here any longer, sir; I'll soon be back at work, and please be kind enough to report that to the office, and put in a good word for me with the head of the firm."

And while Gregor was hastily blurting all this out, hardly aware of what he was saying, he had easily reached the chest of drawers, perhaps as a result of his practice in bed, and he was trying to raise himself up against it. He actually wanted to open his door, he actually looked forward to showing himself and speaking with the manager; he was eager to find out what the others, who so wanted to see him, would say when they caught sight of him. If they were frightened, then Gregor was no longer responsible and he could rest in peace. But if they took everything calmly, then he, too, had no grounds for alarm, and could still get to the station in time for the eight o'clock train — if he hurried. At first he kept sliding a few times down the side of the polished chest, but finally, giving one last heave, he stood upright; he no longer paid attention to the pain in his lower abdomen, though it hurt a lot. Then he let himself fall against the back of a nearby chair, clinging to its edges with his little legs. By doing this, he gained control over himself, and he stayed very quiet so he could listen to the office manager.

"Did you understand even a single word?" the manager asked the parents. "Surely he can't be trying to make fools of us?" "For Heaven's sake," cried his mother, already in tears, "perhaps he's seriously ill, and we're torturing him. Grete! Grete!" she then called. "Mother?" answered his sister from the other side—they were communicating across Gregor's room. "You must get the doctor immediately. Gregor is sick. Hurry, run for the doctor. Didn't you hear Gregor talking just now?" "That was an animal voice," said the office manager, in a tone much lower than the mother's shouting. "Anna! Anna!" yelled the father through the hallway into the kitchen, clapping his hands. "Get the locksmith at once!" And already the two young girls were running through the hallway with a rustling of skirts—how had his sister gotten dressed so quickly?—and tearing open the front door to the apartment. There was no sound of the door closing; they must have just left it open, as you sometimes do in homes where a great misfortune had occurred.

But Gregor had grown calmer. Apparently no one understood his words any longer, though they were sufficiently clear to himself, even clearer than before; perhaps his ears were getting adjusted to the sound. But at least people knew now that something was wrong with him and were ready to help him. His parents' first orders had been given with such confidence and dispatch that he already felt comforted. Once more he'd been drawn back into the circle of humanity, and he expected miraculous results from both the doctor and the locksmith, without distinguishing precisely between them. In order to make his voice as clear as possible for the conversations he anticipated in the future, he coughed a little, but as quietly as he could, because it might not sound like a human cough, and he could no longer trust his judgment. Meanwhile, it had become completely quiet in the next room. Perhaps his parents sat at the table whispering with the office manager; perhaps they were all leaning against his door and listening.

Gregor pushed himself along slowly to the door holding onto the chair, then he let go of it and fell against the door, holding himself upright—the balls of his little feet secreted a sticky substance—and rested there a moment from his efforts. Then he attempted to use his mouth to turn the key in the lock. It seemed, unfortunately, that he had no real teeth—then how was he to hold onto the key?—but to compensate for that, his jaws were certainly very powerful; with their help, he succeeded in getting the key to turn, ignoring the fact that he was undoubtedly somehow injuring himself, since a brown fluid was streaming out of his mouth, oozing over the lock and dripping onto the floor. "Listen to that," said the office manager in the next room, "he's turning the key." Gregor felt greatly encouraged; but he felt that all of them, mother and father too, should have been cheering him on. "Keep it up, Gregor," they should have shouted, "Keep going, keep working on that lock!" And imagining that everyone was eagerly following his efforts, he bit down on the key with all the strength he had in his jaws. As the key began to turn, he danced around the lock; hanging on with only his mouth, he used the full weight of his body to either push up on the key or press down on it. The clear click of the lock as it finally snapped open, broke Gregor's concentration. With a sigh of relief, he said to himself, "I didn't need the locksmith after all," and he laid his head down on the handle so the door could open wide.

Since he had to open the door in this manner, it could open out fairly widely while he himself wasn't yet visible. Next he had to turn his body slowly around one half of the double door, moving very carefully so he wouldn't fall flat on his back while crossing over the threshold. He was concentrating on this difficult maneuver, not thinking of anything else, when he heard the manager exclaim a loud "Oh" — it sounded like the wind howling — and then he could see him too, standing closest to the door, pressing his hand against his open mouth and slowly staggering back, as if driven by some invisible and intensely powerful force. His mother — despite the presence of the manager, she was standing in the room with untidy hair sticking out in all directions from the night before — first looked toward his father with her hands clasped; then she took two steps toward Gregor and collapsed on the floor, her skirts billowing out around her and her face hidden on her breast. His father clenched his fist with a menacing air, as if he wanted to knock Gregor back into his room; then he looked uncertainly around the living room, covered his eyes with his hands, and sobbed so hard that his powerful chest heaved.

Now Gregor decided not to enter the room after all; instead he leaned against his side of the firmly bolted wing of the double door, so that only half of his body was visible, his head tilting above it while he peered at the others. Meanwhile, it had become much brighter; across the street a section of an endlessly long, dark gray building was clearly visible — it was a hospital — with its facade starkly broken by regularly placed windows; it was still raining, but now large individual drops were falling, striking the ground one at a time. On the table, the breakfast dishes were set out in a lavish display, since his father considered breakfast the most important meal of the day; he lingered over it for hours, reading various newspapers. Directly on the opposite wall hung a photograph of Gregor, taken during his military service, wearing a lieutenant's uniform, his hand on his sword, with a carefree smile, demanding respect for his bearing and his rank. The door to the entrance hall was open, and since the apartment door also stood open, you could see out to the landing and the top of the descending stairs.

"Well, now," said Gregor, and he was quite aware that he was the only one who had remained calm. "I'll get dressed at once, pack my samples, and be on my way. Will you, will you all let me go catch my train? Now you see, sir, I'm not obstinate, and I'm glad to work; traveling is a hard job, but I couldn't live without it. Where are you going, sir? Back to the office? Yes? Will you give a true account of everything? A man may temporarily seem incapable of working, but that is precisely the moment to remember his past accomplishments and to consider that later on, after overcoming his obstacles, he's sure to work all the harder and more diligently. As you know very well, I'm deeply obligated to the head of the firm. And then I have to take care of my parents and my sister. I'm in a tight spot, but I'll work myself out of it again. Please don't make it harder for me than it already is. I beg you to put in a good word for me at the office. Traveling salesmen aren't regarded highly there, I know. They think we make lots of money and lead easy lives. They have no particular reason to think differently. But you, sir, you have a better idea of what's really going on than the rest of the office, why — speaking just between ourselves — you have an even better idea than the head of the firm himself, who, in his role as our employer, lets his judgment be swayed against his employees. You know very well that a traveling salesman, who's out of the office most of the year, can easily become a victim of gossip, coincidences, and unfounded complaints, against which he can't possibly defend himself, since he almost never hears about them, except perhaps after he returns exhausted from a trip, and then he himself personally suffers the grim consequences without understanding the reasons for them. Sir, please don't leave without having told me that you think I'm at least partly right!"

But at Gregor's very first words the office manager had already turned away, and now with open mouth, he simply stared back at him over a twitching shoulder. And during Gregor's speech, he never stood still for a moment, but — without taking his eyes off Gregor — he kept moving very gradually toward the door, as if there were a secret ban on leaving the room. He was already in the front hall, and from the abrupt way that he pulled his leg out of the living room, you might have thought that he had just scorched the sole of his foot. In the hall, however, he stretched out his right hand as far as he could toward the stairs, as if some supernatural deliverance were awaiting him there.

Gregor realized that he must not let the office manager leave in this frame of mind, or his position in the firm would be seriously compromised. His parents didn't quite understand the situation; over the years they'd convinced themselves that Gregor was set up for life in this firm, and besides, they were now so preoccupied by their immediate worries that they'd lost any sense of the future. But Gregor had more foresight. The office manager must be stopped, calmed down, persuaded, and finally won over; Gregor's future and that of his family depended on it! If only his sister had been here! She had understood, she had even started to cry when Gregor was still lying quietly on his back. And the office manager, a ladies' man, would certainly have listened to her; she would have shut the front door and talked him out of his fright in the hall. But she wasn't there; Gregor would have to handle the situation by himself. And forgetting that he was still completely unfamiliar with his present powers of movement, and also that very possibly, indeed probably once again his words hadn't been understood, he let go of the wing of the door, shoved himself through the opening, and tried to move toward the office manager, who was already on the landing, foolishly clutching the banister with both hands; but instead, groping for support, Gregor fell down with a small cry upon his many little legs. The instant that happened he felt a sense of physical well-being for the first time that morning; his little legs had solid ground under them; he was delighted to discover that they obeyed him perfectly; they even seemed eager to carry him off in whatever direction he chose; and now he felt sure that the end to all his suffering was at hand. But at that same moment, as he lay on the floor rocking with suppressed motion, not far away from his mother, directly opposite her, she — who had seemed so completely self-absorbed — suddenly jumped up, stretched out her arms, spread her fingers out wide, crying "Help, for Heaven's sake, help!" She craned her head forward, as if she wanted to get a better look at Gregor, but then inconsistently, she backed away instead; forgetting that the table laden with breakfast dishes was right behind her, she sat down on it hastily, as if distracted, and then failed to notice that next to her, the coffee was pouring out of the big, overturned pot in a steady stream onto the carpet.

"Mother, mother," Gregor said softly and looked up at her. For a moment, the office manager had completely slipped from his mind; on the other hand, at the sight of the flowing coffee, he couldn't help snapping his jaws a few times. That made his mother scream again; she fled from the table and collapsed into his father's arms as he was rushing towards her. But Gregor had no time now for his parents; the office manager was already on the stairs; his chin on the banister, he was taking a final look back. Gregor leaped forward, moving as fast as he could to catch him; the office manager must have anticipated this, for he jumped down several steps and vanished; but he was still yelling "Aaah!" and the sound echoed through the entire staircase. Unfortunately, the manager's flight seemed to confuse Gregor's father, who had remained relatively calm until now; for instead of running after the office manager himself, or at least not preventing Gregor from going after him, his father seized with his right hand the manager's cane — it had been left behind on a chair along with his hat and overcoat — and with his left hand, he picked up a large newspaper from the table, and stamping his feet, he began to brandish the cane and the newspaper to drive Gregor back to his room. No plea of Gregor's helped; indeed, no plea was understood; no matter how humbly he bent his head, his father only stamped his feet harder. Across the room, his mother had flung open a window despite the cold weather, and she was leaning far out of it with her face buried in her hands. A strong draft was created between the street and the staircase, so that the window curtains billowed up, the newspapers rustled on the table, and a few pages flew across the floor. Relentlessly, his father charged, making hissing noises like a savage. Since Gregor had as yet no practice in moving backwards, it was really slow going. If Gregor had only been able to turn around, he would have returned to his room right away, but he was afraid of making his father impatient by his slow rotation, while at any moment now the cane in his father's hand threatened a deadly blow to his back or his head. Finally, however, Gregor had no other choice when he realized with dismay that while moving backwards he had no control over his direction; and so with constant, fearful glances at his father, he began to turn himself around as quickly as he could, which was in reality very slowly. Perhaps his father sensed Gregor's good intentions, since he didn't interfere — occasionally he even steered the movement from a distance with the tip of the cane. If only his father would stop that unbearable hissing! It made Gregor lose his head completely. He had almost turned totally around, when distracted by the hissing, he made a mistake and briefly shifted the wrong way back again. But when at last he successfully brought his head around to the doorway, he discovered that his body was too wide to squeeze through. Naturally, in his father's present mood it didn't occur to him to open the other wing of the double door and create a passage wide enough for Gregor. He was simply obsessed with the idea that Gregor must return to his room as fast as possible. And he would never have allowed the intricate maneuvers that Gregor needed, in order to pull himself upright and try to fit through the door this way. Instead, as if there were no obstacles, he drove Gregor forward, making a lot of noise; the noise behind Gregor didn't sound any longer like the voice of a single father; now this was really getting serious, and Gregor — regardless of what would happen — jammed into the doorway. One side of his body lifted up, he lay lopsided in the opening, one of his sides was scraped raw, ugly blotches appeared on the white door, soon he was wedged in tightly and unable to move any further by himself; on one side his little legs were trembling in midair, while on the other side they were painfully crushed against the floor — when his father gave him a strong shove from behind that was truly his deliverance, so that he flew far into his room, bleeding profusely. The door was slammed shut with the cane, and at last there was silence.

II

Not until dusk did Gregor awaken from his heavy, torpid sleep. He would certainly have awakened by himself before long, even without being disturbed, for he felt that he had rested and slept long enough, but it seemed to him that a furtive step and a cautious closing of the hall door had aroused him. The light of the electric street lamps were reflected in pale patches here and there on the ceiling and on the upper parts of the furniture, but down below where Gregor lay, it was dark. Slowly, still groping awkwardly with his antennae, which he was just beginning to appreciate, he dragged himself toward the door to see what had been going on there. His left side felt like a single long, unpleasantly tightening scab, and he actually had to limp on his two rows of legs. One little leg, moreover, had been badly hurt during the morning's events — it seemed almost a miracle that only one had been injured — and it dragged along lifelessly.

Only when he reached the door did he discover what had really attracted him: it was the smell of something edible. For there stood a bowl filled with fresh milk in which floated small slices of white bread. He practically laughed with joy, since he was even hungrier now than in the morning, and he immediately plunged his head into the milk almost over his eyes. But he soon pulled it out again in disappointment; not only did he find eating difficult on account of his tender left side — and he could only eat if his whole heaving body joined in — but he also didn't care at all for the milk, which used to be his favorite drink, and that was surely why his sister had placed it there for him; in fact, he turned away from the bowl almost with disgust and crawled back into the middle of the room.

Through the crack in the double door, Gregor could look into the living room where the gas was lit, but while during this time his father was usually in the habit of reading the afternoon newspaper in a loud voice to his mother and sometimes to his sister as well, there wasn't a sound at present. Well, perhaps this practice of reading aloud that his sister was always telling him about and often mentioned in her letters, had recently been dropped altogether. But it was silent in all the other rooms too, though the apartment was certainly not empty. "What a quiet life the family's been leading," Gregor said to himself, and while he sat there staring into the darkness, he felt a great sense of pride that he had been able to provide such a life in so beautiful an apartment for his parents and sister. But what if all the peace, all the comfort, all the contentment were now to come to a terrible end? Rather than lose himself in such thoughts, Gregor decided to start moving and crawled up and down the room.

Once during the long evening, first one of the side doors and then the other was opened a tiny crack and quickly closed again; probably someone had felt the need to come in and then decided against it. Gregor now settled himself directly in front of the living room door, determined to persuade the hesitating visitor to come in or else at least to discover who it might be; but the door wasn't opened again, and Gregor waited in vain. That morning, when the doors had been locked, they all had wanted to come in to see him; now after he had opened one of the doors himself and the others had obviously been unlocked during the day, no one came in, and the keys were even put into the locks on the other side of the doors.

It wasn't until late at night that the light in the living room was turned off, and Gregor could easily tell that his parents and sister had stayed awake until then, because as he could clearly hear, all three of them were tiptoeing away. Certainly now no one would come into Gregor's room until morning; so he had ample time to reflect in peace and quiet about how he should restructure his life. But the high-ceilinged, spacious room in which he had to lie flat on the floor filled him with an anxiety he couldn't explain, since it was his own room and he had lived in it for the past five years; and with a half-unconscious movement — and not without a slight feeling of shame — he scurried under the sofa, where even though his back was slightly squeezed and he couldn't raise his head, he immediately felt quite comfortable, regretting only that his body was too wide to fit completely under the sofa.

There he stayed the entire night, which he spent either dozing and waking up from hunger with a start, or else fretting with vague hopes, but it all led him to the same conclusion, that for now he would have to stay calm and, by exercising patience and trying to be as considerate as possible, help the family to endure the inconveniences he was bound to cause them in his present condition.

Very early in the morning — it was still almost night — Gregor had the opportunity to test the strength of his new resolutions, because his sister, nearly fully dressed, opened the door from the hall and peered in uncertainly. She couldn't locate him immediately, but when she caught sight of him under the sofa — God, he had to be somewhere, he couldn't have flown away, could he? — she was so startled that, unable to control herself, she slammed the door shut again from the outside. But, apparently regretting her behavior, she immediately opened the door again and came in on tiptoe as if she were visiting someone seriously ill or even a complete stranger. Gregor had pushed his head forward just to the edge of the sofa and was watching her. Would she notice that he had left the milk standing, certainly not because he wasn't hungry, and would she bring in some other kind of food he liked better? If she didn't do it on her own, he would rather starve than bring it to her attention, though he felt a tremendous urge to dart out from under the sofa, throw himself at her feet and beg for something good to eat. But, to Gregor's surprise, his sister noticed at once that his bowl was still full, except for a little milk that had spilled around the edges; she immediately picked it up, to be sure not with her bare hands but with an old rag, and carried it out. Gregor was wildly curious to know what she would bring in its place, and he made various guesses about it. But he could never have guessed what his sister, in the goodness of her heart, actually did. To find out what he liked, she brought him a wide selection that she spread out on an old newspaper. There were old, half-rotten vegetables, bones left over from the evening meal covered with a congealed white sauce, a few raisins and almonds, some cheese that Gregor had considered inedible two days ago, a slice of dry bread, a slice of bread and butter, and a slice of bread and butter with some salt. In addition, she set down the bowl, now presumably reserved for Gregor's exclusive use, into which she had poured some water. And from a sense of delicacy, since she understood that Gregor was unlikely to eat in her presence, she quickly left the room and even turned the key in the lock outside so that Gregor would understand that he could indulge himself as freely as he liked. Gregor's little legs whirled as he hurried toward the food. His injuries must have fully healed already; he no longer felt any handicap, which amazed him, and made him think that over a month ago he had nicked his finger with a knife, and that this injury had still been hurting him the day before yesterday. "Could I have become less sensitive?" he wondered, sucking greedily at the cheese, which he was drawn to immediately, more than the other foods. Quickly, one after another, with tears of contentment streaming from his eyes, he devoured the cheese, the vegetables, and the white sauce; on the other hand, the fresh food didn't appeal to him; he couldn't stand the smell, and he even dragged the things he wanted to eat a little distance away. He had finished with everything long ago and was just resting lazily in the same spot, when his sister slowly turned the key in the lock as a signal that he should withdraw. That startled him at once, even though he was almost dozing off, and he scuttled back under the sofa again. But it took a lot of self-control to stay there, even for the brief time that his sister was in the room, because his body was bloated after his heavy meal, and he could hardly breathe in that cramped space. In between brief bouts of near suffocation, he watched with somewhat bulging eyes as his unsuspecting sister swept up with a broom not only the scraps he hadn't eaten, but also the foods that he hadn't touched, as if they were also no longer fit to eat, and then she hastily dumped everything into a bucket which she covered with a wooden lid, and carried it out. She had scarcely turned her back when Gregor came out from under the sofa to stretch himself and let his belly expand.

In this way Gregor was fed each day, once in the morning while his parents and the maid were still sleeping, and the second time in the afternoon after the family's meal, while his parents took a short nap and his sister sent the maid on some errand or other. Certainly they didn't want Gregor to starve either, but perhaps they couldn't stand to know about his feeding arrangements except by hearsay; or perhaps his sister also wished to spare them anything even mildly distressing, since they were already suffering enough as it was.

Gregor couldn't discover what excuses had been made that first morning to get rid of the doctor and the locksmith, for since the others couldn't understand him, no one thought that he could understand them — including his sister — and so whenever she was in his room, he had to content himself with hearing her occasional sighs and appeals to the saints. Not until later on, when she had become a little more used to it all — of course her complete adjustment was out of the question — Gregor sometimes caught a remark that was meant to be friendly or could be interpreted that way. "Today he really liked it," she said, when Gregor had gobbled up his food, or when he hadn't eaten much, as was gradually happening more and more frequently, she would say almost sadly, "Now he hasn't touched anything again."

But while Gregor couldn't get any news directly, he overheard many things from the adjoining rooms, and as soon as he heard the sound of voices, he would immediately run to the corresponding door and press his entire body against it. Especially in the early days, there was no conversation that didn't refer to him somehow, if only indirectly. For two whole days, there were family discussions at every meal about what they should do now; but they also talked about the same subject between meals, because now there were always at least two family members at home, since probably no one wanted to stay alone in the apartment. And yet, on no account could they leave it empty. Besides, on the very first day, the cook — it wasn't entirely clear what or how much she knew of the situation — had begged his mother on bended knees to let her leave at once, and when she departed fifteen minutes later, she thanked them tearfully for her dismissal as if it were the greatest favor they had ever bestowed on her in this house, and without being asked, she swore a solemn oath, promising not to say a word about what had happened to anyone.

So now his sister, together with his mother, had to do the cooking as well; this wasn't much trouble, of course, since they ate almost nothing. Again and again Gregor would hear how one encouraged another to eat, always getting the answer, "Thanks, I've had enough" or something similar. They didn't seem to drink anything either. Often his sister asked his father if he wanted some beer, and she kindly offered to get it herself; and then when his father didn't answer, she suggested that if he didn't want her to bother, she could send the janitor's wife for it, but in the end his father answered with a firm "No," and there wasn't any further discussion.

In the course of the very first day his father explained the family's financial situation and prospects to both the mother and sister. Every now and then he stood up from the table to get some receipt or account book from the small safe that he'd managed to salvage from the collapse of his business five years earlier. He could be heard opening the complicated lock, taking out what he was looking for, and closing it again. The father's explanations, to some extent, were the first encouraging news that Gregor had heard since his captivity. He had always supposed that his father had nothing at all left from his old business, at least his father had never told him anything to the contrary, though Gregor had never actually asked him about it. In those days Gregor's only concern had been to do all that he could to help the family forget as quickly as possible the business catastrophe that had plunged them all into complete despair. And so he had begun to work with exceptional zeal and was promoted almost overnight from a junior clerk to a traveling salesman, who naturally had a much greater earning potential, and his successes were immediately converted by way of commissions into cash that he could bring home and lay on the table for the astonished and delighted family. Those had been happy times, and they had never been repeated, at least not with such splendor, even though Gregor was eventually earning so much money that he was capable of meeting the expenses of the entire family, and in fact did so. They had simply grown used to it, the family as well as Gregor; they accepted the money gratefully and he gave it gladly, but it didn't arouse any especially warm feelings any longer. Only Gregor's sister had stayed close to him, and it was his secret plan that she, who — unlike Gregor — loved music and could play the violin very movingly, should be sent to the conservatory next year despite the considerable expense involved, and which he would certainly have to meet somehow. During Gregor's brief visits home, the conservatory was often mentioned in his conversations with his sister, but it was always only as a beautiful dream that could never come true, and his parents even disliked hearing those innocent allusions; but Gregor had definitely set his mind on it and had intended to announce his plan solemnly on Christmas Eve.

Such were the thoughts, quite futile in his present condition, that passed through his mind as he stood upright, glued to the door, eavesdropping. Sometimes he grew so weary that he could no longer listen and let his head bump carelessly against the door, but then he held it up again immediately, because even the slightest noise that he inadvertently made was enough to be heard next door and to reduce everyone to silence. "Just what's he up to now?" his father would say after a pause, obviously turning toward the door, and only then would the interrupted conversation gradually resume.

Gregor now had ample opportunity to discover — since his father would often repeat his explanations, partly because he hadn't concerned himself with these matters for a long time, and also partly because his mother couldn't always grasp everything the first time — that despite all their misfortune, a sum of money, to be sure a very small one, still remained from the old days and had even increased slightly in the meantime since the interest had never been touched. And besides that, the money Gregor had been bringing home every month — he'd only kept a little for himself — had not been entirely spent and had accumulated into a modest capital. Behind his door, Gregor nodded his head eagerly, delighted at this unexpected foresight and thrift. In fact, he could have used this surplus money to pay off more of his father's debt to the head of the firm, so the day when he could have quit his job would have been a lot closer, but now things were doubtless better the way his father had arranged them.

However, this money was by no means sufficient to allow the family to live off the interest; it might be enough to support them for a year, or for two at the most, but no more than that. It was really just a sum that shouldn't be touched, but instead saved for an emergency; money to live on would have to be earned. Now his father was still certainly healthy, but he was an old man who hadn't done any work for the past five years and couldn't be expected to take on very much; in those five years, which was his first vacation in his hardworking if unsuccessful life, he had put on weight and as a result, had become very sluggish. And as for his old mother, should she really start trying to earn money, when she suffered from asthma and found it a strain just to walk through the apartment, and spent every second day gasping for breath on the couch by the open window? And should his sister go out to work, she who was still a child at seventeen and whose life it would be a pity to disturb, since it consisted of wearing nice clothes, sleeping late, helping out with the housework, enjoying a few modest amusements, and most of all, playing the violin? At first, whenever the conversation turned to the necessity of earning money, Gregor would always let go of the door immediately and then throw himself down on the cool leather sofa beside it, because he felt so flushed with shame and grief.

Often he lay there throughout the long nights, not sleeping a wink and just scrabbling on the leather for hours. Or else, undaunted by the great effort of shoving an armchair to the window, he would crawl to the sill and, propping himself up on the chair, lean against the panes, evidently inspired by some memory of the sense of freedom that he used to experience looking out the window. Because, in fact, from day to day he saw objects only a short distance away becoming more indistinct; the hospital across the street, which he used to curse because he saw it all too often, he now couldn't see at all, and if he weren't certain that he lived on the quiet but decidedly urban Charlotte Street, he might have believed that he was gazing out of his window into a barren wasteland where the gray sky and the gray earth merged indistinguishably. Only twice had his attentive sister needed to see the armchair standing by the window; from then on whenever she cleaned the room, she carefully pushed the chair back to the window, and now she even left the inside windowpane open.

If Gregor had only been able to speak to his sister and thank her for all she had to do for him, he could have endured her services more easily, but as it was, they oppressed him. To be sure, she tried to ease the embarrassment of the situation as much as possible, and the longer time went on, the better she became at it, but in time Gregor too became more keenly aware of everything. Even the way she came in was terrible for him. Hardly had she entered the room when — not even taking time to close the door, though she was usually so careful to spare everyone the sight of Gregor's room — she'd run straight to the window and tear it open with impatient fingers, almost as if she were suffocating, and then she stayed there for a while, taking deep breaths no matter how cold it was. With this hustle and bustle, she scared Gregor twice a day; he lay quaking under the sofa the entire time, and yet he knew perfectly well that she would surely have spared him if she had only found it possible to stand being in a room with him with the windows closed.

One time — it must have been a month since Gregor's transformation, so there was no particular reason for his sister to be surprised by his appearance any more — she came a little earlier than usual and caught Gregor as he was looking out the window, motionless and terrifyingly upright. It wouldn't have surprised Gregor if she hadn't come in, since his position prevented her from opening the window immediately, but not only did she not enter, she also actually jumped back and shut the door; a stranger might easily have thought that Gregor had been lying in wait for her and meant to bite her. Gregor naturally hid at once under the sofa, but he had to wait until noon before she came back, and she seemed much more uneasy than usual. From this he concluded that the sight of him was still unbearable to her and was bound to remain unbearable in the future, and that she probably was exercising great self-control not to run away at the sight of even the small portion of his body that protruded from under the sofa. To spare her even this sight, he draped the sheet on his back and dragged it over to the sofa one day — he needed four hours for this task — and placed it in such a way so as to conceal himself completely, so that she couldn't see him even if she stooped down. If she considered this sheet unnecessary, then of course she could remove it, because it was clear enough that Gregor was hardly shutting himself off so completely for his own sake; but she left the sheet the way it was, and Gregor believed he caught a grateful look when he once cautiously raised the sheet a little with his head to see how she was reacting to the new arrangement.

During the first two weeks his parents couldn't bring themselves to come in to him, and often he heard them say how much they appreciated his sister's work, whereas previously they'd been annoyed with her because she'd appeared to be a little useless. But often now, both his father and mother waited outside of Gregor's room while his sister was cleaning up inside, and as soon as she emerged, she had to give a detailed report about how the room looked, what Gregor had eaten, how he had behaved this time, and whether perhaps some slight improvement was noticeable. Gregor's mother, incidentally, wanted to visit him relatively soon, but at first his father and sister put her off with sensible arguments, which Gregor listened to most attentively and fully endorsed. But later his mother had to be held back by force, and when she cried out, "Let me go to Gregor; after all, he's my unfortunate son! Don't you understand that I must go to him?" then Gregor thought that perhaps it would be a good idea after all if she did come in; not every day, of course, but perhaps once a week; she surely understood everything much better than his sister, who for all her courage, was still only a child, and had perhaps, in the final analysis, merely taken on this demanding task out of childish recklessness.

Gregor's wish to see his mother was soon fulfilled. During the daytime Gregor didn't want to show himself at the window, if only out of consideration for his parents, but he couldn't crawl very far on his few square yards of floor space, either, nor could he bear to lie still during the night; eating had soon ceased to give him the slightest pleasure, and so as a distraction he got into the habit of crawling crisscross over the walls and ceiling. He especially enjoyed hanging from the ceiling; it was quite different from lying on the floor;

he could breathe more freely, and a mild tingle ran through his body; and in the almost blissful oblivion in which Gregor found himself up there, it could happen that, to his surprise, he let himself go and crashed onto the floor. But now of course he had much greater control over his body than before, and he never hurt himself by even this great fall. Gregor's sister immediately noticed the new pastime that he had found for himself—after all, he left some traces of the sticky tracks of his crawling here and there—and she then took it into her head to enable Gregor to crawl around to the greatest possible extent, so she decided to remove the furniture that stood in his way, first of all, the chest of drawers and the desk. But she couldn't do this alone; she didn't dare ask her father for help; and the maid would most certainly not help her, because this girl (about sixteen years old) was bravely staying on since the previous cook had quit, but she'd asked permission to keep the kitchen locked at all times and to open it only when expressly called; so his sister had no other choice than to get her mother one day when her father was out. And indeed, with cries of eager delight, Gregor's mother approached his room, but she fell silent at the door. Of course his sister first looked in to check that everything in the room was in order; only then did she let her mother enter. Gregor had hastily pulled the sheet even lower down in tighter folds; the whole thing really looked like a sheet casually tossed over the sofa. This time Gregor also refrained from peering out from under the sheet; he denied himself the sight of his mother, and was only pleased to know that she had finally come. "Come on in, you can't see him," said his sister, and evidently she was leading her mother by the hand. Now Gregor heard the two weak women shifting the really heavy old chest of drawers from its place, and how his sister obstinately took on the hardest part of the work for herself, ignoring the warnings of her mother, who was afraid she'd strain herself. It took a very long time. After about a quarter of an hour's work, Gregor's mother said that it would be better to leave the chest where it was, because for one thing, it was just too heavy, they would not be finished before the father arrived, and with the chest in the middle of the room, Gregor's path would be blocked; and for the second, it wasn't at all certain that they were doing Gregor a favor to move the furniture. It seemed to her that the opposite was true; the sight of the bare walls made her heart ache; and why shouldn't Gregor also feel the same way, since after all he'd been accustomed to the furniture for so long and might feel abandoned in an empty room. "And doesn't it really look," concluded his mother very softly, in fact she'd been almost whispering the whole time, as if she were anxious that Gregor, whose exact whereabouts she didn't know, couldn't hear even the sound of her voice, for of course she was convinced that he couldn't understand her words, "and doesn't it look as if by moving the furniture we were showing that we'd given up all hope for improvement and were callously abandoning him to his own resources? I think it would be best if we tried to keep the room just as it was, so that when Gregor comes back to us again, everything will be unchanged and it can be easier to forget what happened in the meantime."

Hearing his mother's words, Gregor realized that the lack of all direct human exchange, together with his monotonous life in the midst of the family, must have confused his mind during these past two months, because otherwise he couldn't explain to himself how he could seriously have wanted his room cleared out. Had he really wanted his warm room, with its comfortable old family furniture, to be transformed into a cave in which he could crawl freely around in all directions, no doubt, but only at the cost of swiftly and totally losing his human past? Indeed, he was already on the verge of forgetting it, and only his mother's voice, which he hadn't heard for so long, had brought him to his senses. Nothing should be removed; everything must stay; he couldn't do without the beneficial effects of the furniture on his state of mind; and if the furniture interfered with his mindless crawling about, then it was not a loss but a great gain.

But unfortunately his sister thought differently; she had grown accustomed, to be sure not entirely without reason, to being the great expert on Gregor in any discussion with her parents, and so now her mother's proposal was cause enough for the sister to insist on removing not only the chest of drawers and the desk, as she had originally planned, but also the rest of the furniture in the room except for the indispensable sofa. It was, of course, not only her childish defiance and the self-confidence she had recently and so unexpectedly gained at such cost that led to this determination; but she had also in fact observed that Gregor needed more space to crawl around in, while on the other hand, as far as she could see, he never used the furniture. But, perhaps, what also played some part was the romantic spirit of girls of her age, which seeks satisfaction at every opportunity and tempted Grete to make Gregor's predicament even more frightening so that she might then be able to do even more for him than before. For most likely no one but Grete would ever dare to enter into a room where Gregor ruled the bare walls all by himself.

And so she refused to be dissuaded from her resolve by her mother, who in any case seemed unsure of herself in that room and who soon fell silent out of sheer nervousness, and helped the sister as best she could to move the chest of drawers out of the room. Well, Gregor could do without the chest, if necessary, but the desk had to stay. And no sooner had the two women, groaning and shoving the chest, left the room, when Gregor poked his head out from under the sofa to see how he could intervene as cautiously and tactfully as possible. Unfortunately, it was his mother who returned first, while Grete kept her arms around the chest in the next room, rocking it back and forth, and naturally unable to move it by herself from its spot. Gregor's mother, however, was not used to the sight of him; it might make her sick, and so Gregor scurried backwards in alarm to the other end of the sofa, though not in time to prevent the front of the sheet from stirring a little. That was enough to catch his mother's attention. She stopped short, stood still a moment, and then went back to Grete.

Although Gregor kept telling himself that nothing out of the ordinary was happening, that just a couple of pieces of furniture were being moved around, all the same he soon had to admit to himself that this walking back and forth by the women, their little cries to each other, the scraping of the furniture along the floor, were affecting him on all sides like a tremendous uproar, and no matter how tightly he tucked in his head and legs and pressed his body against the floor, he was forced to admit that he couldn't endure the fuss much longer. They were emptying out his room, stripping him of everything he loved; they had already removed the chest, which contained his fretsaw and other tools; and now they were prying loose the desk, which was almost embedded in the floor, and at which he'd done his homework when he was in business school, high school, and even as far back as elementary school — at this point he really had no more time to consider the good intentions of the two women, whose existence he had indeed almost forgotten, because by now they were working away in silence from sheer exhaustion, and he heard only the heavy shuffling of their feet.

And so he broke out — just at the moment the women were in the next room, leaning against the desk to catch their breath — and he changed direction four times, not really knowing what he should rescue first, and then he spotted the picture of the lady dressed in nothing but furs, hanging conspicuously on what was otherwise a bare wall opposite him; he crawled rapidly up to it and pressed himself against the glass, which held him fast and soothed his hot belly. At least this picture, which Gregor now completely covered, was definitely not going to be removed by anyone. He twisted his head around toward the door of the living room to observe the women on their return.

They had not given themselves much of a rest and were already coming back; Grete had put her arm around her mother and was almost carrying her. "Well, what should we take now?" said Grete and looked around. Then her eyes met Gregor's on the wall. No doubt it was only due to the presence of her mother that she kept her composure, lowered her head to keep her mother from looking about, and said, although rather shakily and without thinking, "Come on, why don't we go back to the living room for a moment?" Grete's intention was clear to Gregor; she wanted to get her mother to safety and then chase him down from the wall. Well, just let her try! He clung to his picture and wouldn't give it up. He would rather fly in Grete's face.

But Grete's words had made her mother even more anxious; she stepped to one side, caught sight of the huge brown splotch on the flowered wallpaper, and before realizing that what she saw was Gregor, she cried out in a hoarse, shrieking voice, "Oh God, oh God," and collapsed across the sofa with outstretched arms, as if giving up completely, and didn't move. "You, Gregor," cried the sister, raising her fist and glaring at him. These were the first words that she had addressed directly to him since his transformation. She ran into the next room to get some sort of medicine to revive her mother from her fainting fit; Gregor also wanted to help — there was time enough to save his picture later on — but he was stuck fast to the glass and had to wrench himself free; then he also ran into the next room, as if he could give some advice to his sister as in the old days; but once there he had to stand uselessly behind her while she was rummaging among various little bottles; she got frightened when she turned around; one of the bottles fell to the floor and shattered; a splinter of glass sliced Gregor's face, and some kind of burning medicine splashed around him; then without further delay, Grete grabbed as many bottles as she could hold and ran back to her mother with them; she slammed the door closed with her foot. Gregor was now cut off from his mother, who was perhaps nearly dying because of him; he dared not open the door for fear of frightening away his sister, who had to stay with his mother; now he had nothing to do but wait; and so, in an agony of self-reproach and anxiety, he began to crawl, to crawl over everything, walls, furniture, and ceiling; until finally when the entire room was spinning, he dropped in despair onto the middle of the big table.

A little while passed. Gregor lay worn out, all was quiet, perhaps that was a good sign. Then the doorbell rang. The maid, of course, was locked in the kitchen, and Grete had to open the door. Father was back. "What's happened?" were his first words; Grete's face must have told him everything. Grete replied in a muffled voice, evidently with her face pressing against her father's chest. "Mother fainted. But she's better now. Gregor's broken loose." "Just what I expected," said his father. "Just what I've always told you, but you women wouldn't listen." It was clear to Gregor that his father had misinterpreted Grete's all too brief statement and assumed that Gregor was guilty of some act of violence. That meant that he must now try to pacify his father, for he had neither the time nor the means to explain things to him. And so Gregor fled to the door of his room and pressed himself against it, so that as soon as his father came in from the hall, he should see that Gregor had the best intention of returning to his room immediately, and that it was unnecessary to drive him back; but that someone only had to open the door, and he would immediately disappear.

But his father was in no mood to observe such subtlety; "Ah ha!" he cried as soon as he entered, in a tone both furious and elated. Gregor drew his head back from the door and raised it toward his father. He hadn't really pictured his father at all, standing that way; admittedly he had been too preoccupied by the new sensation of crawling around to concern himself with what was going on in the rest of the household as before, and he really ought to have been prepared for some changes. And yet, and yet, was this really his father? The same man who used to lie wearily in bed when Gregor left early on one of his business trips; who always greeted him on his return in the evening wearing a robe and sitting in an armchair; who was actually hardly capable of standing up, but had merely raised his arms to show his pleasure; and who, during the rare family walks on a few Sundays a year and on the high holidays, would always shuffle laboriously along between Gregor and his mother, who walked slowly anyway, walking even a little slower than they walked, bundled in his old overcoat, planting his cane before him for each step he took, and when he wanted to say something, nearly always standing still and gathering his escorts around him? Now, however, he held himself erect, dressed in a tight blue uniform with gold buttons, like that worn by bank messengers; his heavy double chin bulged over the high stiff collar of his jacket; from under his bushy eyebrows, his black eyes flashed alert and observant glances; his previously tousled white hair was combed flat, meticulously parted and gleaming. He tossed his cap, on which was a gold monogram, probably that of some bank, right across the room in a wide arc onto the couch, and started toward Gregor with a grimly set face, the ends of his long uniform jacket thrown back, and his hands in his pockets. Probably he didn't know himself what he intended; nevertheless, he lifted his feet unusually high, and Gregor was astonished at the gigantic size of his boot soles. But Gregor didn't dwell on his reflections; he had known from the very first day of his new life that his father considered only the strictest measures appropriate for dealing with him. And so he fled from his father, pausing only when his father stood still, and immediately hurrying on again when he made any kind of a move. In that way they circled the room several times, without anything decisive happening; in fact, they proceeded in such a slow tempo that it didn't have the appearance of a chase. For this reason, Gregor stayed on the floor for the time being, especially since he feared his father might regard any escape onto the walls or ceiling as a particularly wicked act. At the same time, Gregor had to admit that he couldn't keep up with this kind of running for long; for while his father took a single step, he had to carry out a countless number of movements. Shortness of breath was beginning to appear, and even in his earlier days his lungs had never been entirely reliable. As he went staggering along, saving all his energy for running, hardly keeping his eyes open, in his stupor not even thinking of any other refuge than running, and having almost forgotten that the walls were available, though admittedly here these walls were blocked by elaborately carved furniture full of sharp points and corners — suddenly something came sailing past him, lightly tossed; it landed next to him and rolled away in front of him. It was an apple; immediately a second one came flying after it; Gregor stopped dead in fright; any further running was useless, because his father was determined to bombard him. He had filled his pockets from the fruit bowl on the sideboard and now, without taking careful aim, he was throwing one apple after another. These small red apples rolled around on the floor as if electrified, colliding with one another. One weakly thrown apple grazed Gregor's back and glanced off harmlessly. But another one thrown directly afterwards actually penetrated into Gregor's back; Gregor wanted to drag himself further, as if the surprising and unbelievable pain might pass if he changed his position; but he felt as if nailed to the spot and stretched himself flat out, all his senses in complete confusion. Now with his last conscious sight he saw how the door of his room was flung open, and his mother rushed out in her chemise, ahead of his screaming sister, for his sister had undressed her when she had fainted to make it easier for her to breathe; he saw his mother running to his father, shedding her loosened petticoats one by one on the floor behind her, and stumbling over her petticoats to fling herself upon his father, and embracing him, in complete union with him — but now Gregor's vision failed him — begging him, with her hands clasped around his father's neck, to spare Gregor's life.

III

Gregor suffered from his serious injury for over a month — the apple remained embedded in his flesh as a visible reminder since no one dared to remove it — and it even seemed to bring home to his father that despite Gregor's present deplorable and repulsive shape, he was still a member of the family who ought not to be treated as an enemy, but that on the contrary, family duty required them to swallow their disgust and put up with him, simply put up with him.

And now, although Gregor had probably suffered some permanent loss of mobility as a result of his injury and for the present needed long, long minutes to cross his room like an old invalid — crawling up the walls was out of the question — yet he thought he was granted entirely satisfactory compensation for this deterioration of his condition, since every day toward evening the living room door, which he used to watch intently for an hour or two beforehand, would be opened, so that lying in the darkness of his room and not visible from the living room, he could see the entire family at the lamp-lit table and could listen to the conversation as if by general consent, not at all as he had been obliged earlier to eavesdrop.

Of course, there were no longer the lively discussions of earlier days that Gregor used to recall wistfully in small hotel rooms whenever he had to sink down wearily into the damp bedding. Now it was mostly very quiet. The father fell asleep in his armchair shortly after supper; the mother and sister would caution each other to keep quiet; the mother, hunched forward under the light, stitched away at fine lingerie for a fashion boutique; the sister, who had taken a job as a salesgirl, studied shorthand and French every evening, in the hope of getting a better job some day. Occasionally the father woke up, and as if he didn't know he'd been sleeping, he said to the mother, "How long you've been sewing again today!" and instantly he'd doze off again, while the mother and sister smiled wearily at each other.

With a kind of perverse obstinacy, the father refused to take off his messenger's uniform even in the house, and while his robe hung uselessly on the clothes hook, he slept fully dressed in his chair, as if he were ever ready for duty and waiting for his superior's call even here. As a result, his uniform — not new to begin with — started to look less clean despite all the efforts of the mother and sister, and Gregor would often spend whole evenings staring at the soiled and spotted uniform, with its gleaming, constantly polished gold buttons, in which the old man slept in great discomfort and yet very peacefully.

As soon as the clock struck ten, the mother tried to wake up the father with a few gentle words, trying to persuade him to go to bed, because here he couldn't get any proper rest, which the father sorely needed, since he had to go on duty at six. But with the obstinacy that had possessed him since he'd become a bank messenger, he always insisted on staying at the table a little longer, though he regularly fell asleep, and it was then only with the greatest effort that he could be coaxed into exchanging his armchair for his bed. No matter how much the mother and sister cajoled and admonished him, he would go on shaking his head slowly for a quarter of an hour, keeping his eyes shut and refusing to get up. The mother plucked at his sleeve, whispering sweet words into his ear; the sister would leave her homework to help her mother, but none of this had any effect on the father. He merely sank deeper into his chair. He would open his eyes only when the two women took hold of him under his arms, look back and forth at the mother and sister, and usually say, "What a life. Such is the peace of my old age." And supported by both women, he rose to his feet laboriously, as if he himself were his greatest burden, and allowed the women to lead him to the door, where he waved them away and went on by himself, while the mother hastily dropped her sewing and the sister her pen, to run after the father and provide further assistance.

Who in this overworked and exhausted family had time to worry about Gregor any more than was absolutely necessary? The household was neglected even more; the maid was dismissed after all; a gigantic, bony cleaning woman with white hair fluttering around her head now came every morning and evening to do the heaviest chores; everything else was taken care of by the mother, along with all her sewing. It even came to pass that various pieces of family jewelry, which the mother and sister used to wear with great pleasure at parties and on great occasions, had to be sold, as Gregor learned in the evenings from the family's discussion of the prices they had fetched. But always their greatest complaint was that they couldn't leave this apartment, which was much too large for their present circumstances, since no one could imagine how to move Gregor. But Gregor fully understood that it was not only concern for him that prevented a move, for he could easily have been shipped in a suitable crate with a few air holes; what mostly stopped them was the complete hopelessness of their situation and their sense that they had been struck by a misfortune unlike anyone else in their entire circle of friends and relations. They were suffering to the limit what the world requires of poor people: the father brought in breakfast for junior bank clerks; the mother sacrificed herself sewing underwear for strangers; the sister ran to and fro behind a counter at the bidding of customers, but the family had no more strength beyond that. And the wound in Gregor's back began to hurt again whenever the mother and sister returned after putting the father to bed, dropped their work, drew close together, and sat cheek to cheek; then the mother, pointing to Gregor's room, said "Close the door, Grete," so that Gregor was again left in darkness while in the next room, the women mingled their tears or stared dry eyed at the table.

Gregor spent his nights and days almost entirely without sleep. Sometimes he fancied that the next time the door opened, he would once again take charge of the family affairs just as he had done in the past; in his thoughts there reappeared, as after a long absence, the director and the office manager, the clerks and the trainees, the slow-witted office boy, two or three friends from other firms, a maid in a country hotel (a charming, fleeting memory), a cashier in a hat shop whom he'd courted earnestly but too slowly — they all appeared mixed up with strangers or people he'd forgotten, but instead of helping him and his family, they were all inaccessible, and he was glad when they disappeared. But at other times he was in no mood to worry about his family; he was filled with rage over how badly he was looked after; and even though he couldn't imagine having an appetite for anything, he still invented plans for getting into the pantry so he could help himself to the food that was coming to him, even if he wasn't hungry. No longer considering what might give Gregor some special pleasure, the sister now quickly pushed any old food into Gregor's room with her foot before she rushed off to work both in the morning and at noon; then in the evening, not caring whether the food had only been nibbled at or — most frequently — left completely untouched, she swept it out with a swing of her broom. The cleaning of his room, which she now always took care of in the evening, couldn't have been more perfunctory. Grimy dirt streaked the walls, and balls of dust and filth lay here and there. At first Gregor would stand in particularly offensive corners when the sister came in, as if intending to reproach her. But he could have waited there for weeks without the sister making any improvement; she could see the dirt just as well as he could, of course, but she had simply made up her mind to leave it there. At the same time, with a touchiness that was new to her, and that indeed was felt in the entire family, she made certain that the cleaning of Gregor's room remained her exclusive responsibility. Once Gregor's mother subjected his room to a thorough cleaning, which she managed only by using several buckets of water — the resulting dampness made Gregor sick, of course, and he lay stretched out on the sofa, embittered and immobile — but the mother didn't escape her punishment. Because that evening, the moment Gregor's sister noticed the change in his room, she ran into the living room, deeply insulted, and although the mother raised her hands imploringly, the sister broke out in a fit of weeping, while the parents — the father had of course been frightened out of his armchair — gaped in helpless astonishment, until they too started in; the father reproached the mother on his right for not leaving the cleaning of Gregor's room to the sister, and he shouted at the sister on his left, warning her that she would never again be allowed to clean Gregor's room; meanwhile the mother tried to drag the father, who was beside himself with rage, into the bedroom; the sister, shaking with sobs, beat the table with her small fists; and Gregor hissed loudly in his fury because no one thought of closing the door and sparing him this spectacle and commotion.

But even if Gregor's sister, exhausted by her work at the shop, was fed up with taking care of him as before, it was by no means necessary for the mother to take her place to make sure that Gregor wouldn't be neglected. For now the cleaning woman was there. This old widow, who in her long life must have weathered the worst thanks to her sturdy constitution, wasn't really repelled by Gregor. Without being in the least nosy, she happened one day to open the door to Gregor's room, and at the sight of Gregor, who was completely taken by surprise and began scrambling back and forth though no one was chasing him, she had merely stood still in amazement, her hands folded on her stomach. Since then, she never failed to open his door a crack every morning and night to peep in at Gregor. Initially she would even call him over with words she probably considered friendly, such as "Come on over here, you old dung beetle," or "Just look at that old dung beetle!" Gregor never responded to such calls, but remained motionless where he stood, as if the door had never been opened. If only they had ordered this woman to clean out his room every day, instead of letting her disturb him whenever she pleased! Once, early in the morning — a heavy rain, perhaps a sign of the coming spring, was pelting the windowpanes — Gregor was so annoyed when the cleaning woman again launched into her phrases that he charged toward her as if to attack, but slowly and feebly. Instead of being frightened, the cleaning woman simply raised a chair placed near the door and stood there with her mouth wide open, obviously not intending to close it again until the chair in her hand came crashing down on Gregor's back. "So you're not coming any closer?" she asked, when Gregor turned around again, and she calmly put the chair back in the corner.

By this time Gregor was eating next to nothing. Only when he happened by chance to pass by the food spread out for him, would he take a bite in his mouth just for pleasure, hold it there for hours, and then mostly spit it back out again. At first he thought it was distress at the condition of his room that kept him from eating, but he soon became adjusted to these very changes. The family had gotten into the habit of putting things that had no other place into his room, and now there were plenty of such things, because they had rented a bedroom in the apartment to three boarders. These serious gentlemen — all three had full beards, as Gregor once observed through a crack in the door — were obsessed with order, not only in their room, but also, since they were paying rent there, throughout the apartment, particularly the kitchen. They couldn't stand any kind of useless odds and ends, let alone dirty ones. Furthermore, they had for the most part brought along their own furnishings. For this reason, many things had become superfluous that couldn't be sold but also couldn't be thrown away. All these things ended up in Gregor's room. As did the ash bucket and the garbage pail from the kitchen. Whatever was not being used at the moment was simply flung into Gregor's room by the cleaning woman, who was always in a hurry; Gregor was usually fortunate enough to see only the object in question and the hand that held it. Perhaps the cleaning woman intended to retrieve these objects when she had time and opportunity to do so, or else to throw out everything at once, but in fact they lay wherever they happened to land, unless Gregor waded through the junk pile and set it in motion, at first out of necessity because there was no free space to crawl; but later on with growing pleasure, though after such excursions he would lie still for hours, dead tired and miserable.

Since the boarders also sometimes took their evening meal at home in the common living room, Gregor's door stayed shut on many evenings, but he found it very easy to give up the open door, for when it was left open on many earlier evenings he had already not taken advantage of it, but without the family's notice, he had lain in the darkest corner of his room. Once, however, the cleaning woman had left the door to the living room open a small crack; and it stayed open, even when the boarders entered in the evening and the lamp was lit. They sat at the head of the table where the father, mother, and Gregor had sat in the old days, unfolded their napkins and picked up their knives and forks. Immediately the mother appeared in the doorway with a platter of meat, and right behind her was the sister with a platter piled high with potatoes. The food gave off thick clouds of steam. The boarders bent over the platters placed in front of them as if to examine them before eating, and in fact the man sitting in the middle (whom the other two seemed to regard as an authority) cut up a piece of meat on the platter, obviously in order to determine whether it was tender enough or should perhaps need to be sent back to the kitchen. He was satisfied, and so the mother and sister, who had been watching anxiously, breathed freely again and began to smile.

The family itself ate in the kitchen. Nevertheless, before the father headed for the kitchen, he came into the living room, bowed once, his cap in hand, and walked around the table. The boarders all rose simultaneously and muttered something into their beards. When they were alone again, they ate in almost complete silence. It seemed strange to Gregor that out of the various noises of eating, he could always distinguish the sound of their chomping teeth, as if to demonstrate to Gregor that teeth were necessary for eating, and that even the most wonderful toothless jaws could accomplish nothing. "I do have an appetite," said Gregor mournfully to himself, "but not for these things. How those boarders gorge themselves, and I'm starving to death."

On that very evening — Gregor couldn't remember having once heard the violin during all this time — it was heard from the kitchen. The boarders had already finished their supper, the middle one had taken out a newspaper, handing over a sheet apiece to the two others, and they were now leaning back, reading and smoking. When the violin began to play, they noticed it, stood up, and tiptoed to the hall, where they paused, huddled together. They must have been heard from the kitchen, because the father called, "Are the gentlemen disturbed by the music, perhaps? It can be stopped at once." "On the contrary," said the middle boarder, "wouldn't the young lady like to come in here with us and play in the living room, which is more spacious and comfortable?" "Oh, with pleasure," cried the father, as if he were the violinist. The boarders went back into the living room and waited. Soon the father came with the music stand, the mother with the sheet music, and the sister with the violin. The sister calmly got everything ready to play; the parents, who'd never rented rooms before and therefore were excessively polite to the boarders, didn't dare to sit on their own chairs; the father leaned against the door, his right hand thrust between two buttons of his closed uniform jacket; the mother, however, was offered a chair by one of the boarders and sat down on it just where he happened to put it, off to the side in a corner.

The sister began to play; the father and mother on either side of her followed the movements of her hands attentively. Gregor, attracted by her playing, had ventured out a little further, and his head was already in the living room. He was hardly surprised that he had recently begun to show so little concern for others; previously such thoughtfulness had been his pride. And yet right now he would have had even more reason than ever to stay hidden, because he was completely covered with dust as a result of the particles that lay everywhere in his room and flew about with his slightest movement; bits of fluff, hair, and food remnants also stuck to his back and trailed from his sides; his indifference to everything was much too great for him to lie on his back and rub himself against the carpet, as he had once done several times a day. And in spite of his condition, he felt no shame in edging forward a little onto the immaculate floor of the living room.

To be sure, no one paid any attention to him. The family was completely absorbed by the violin playing; on the other hand, the boarders, with their hands in their pockets, stood at first much too closely behind the sister's music stand so that they all would have been able to read the music, which surely must have distracted the sister, but they soon retreated to the window and stayed there with lowered heads, softly talking with each other, while the father watched them anxiously. Indeed it now appeared all too clearly that they seemed disappointed in their hopes of hearing beautiful or entertaining violin playing, as if they had had enough of the recital and were merely suffering this disturbance of their peace out of politeness. In particular, the way in which they all blew their cigar smoke through their nose and mouth into the air suggested their high degree of irritability. And yet the sister was playing so beautifully. Her face was inclined to one side, her eyes followed the notes of the music with a searching and sorrowful look. Gregor crawled a little bit further forward and kept his head close to the floor so that it might be possible for their eyes to meet. Was he an animal, that music could move him so? It seemed as if he were being shown the way to the unknown nourishment he longed for. He was determined to push his way up to his sister and tug at her skirt, and thus suggest that she should come into his room with her violin, for nobody here was worthy of her playing as he would be worthy of it. He would never let her out of his room again, at least not so long as he lived; his terrible shape would be useful to him for the first time; he would stand guard at all the doors of his room simultaneously, hissing at the intruders; his sister, however, wouldn't be forced to stay with him but should remain of her own free will; she should sit next to him on the sofa, bending her ear down to him, and then he would confide to her that he had made a firm resolve to send her to the Conservatory, and that if misfortune hadn't intervened, he would have announced this to everyone at Christmas — had Christmas passed already? — without listening to any objections. After this declaration his sister would burst into tears of emotion, and Gregor would raise himself up to her shoulder and kiss her on the neck, which — now that she went out to work — she kept free of ribbon or collar.

"Mr. Samsa!" cried the middle boarder to the father, and without wasting another word, he pointed with his forefinger at Gregor, who was slowly crawling forward. The violin fell silent, the middle boarder first smiled at his friends with a shake of his head and then looked at Gregor again. The father seemed to think that it was more urgent to pacify the boarders than to drive Gregor out, though they weren't at all upset, and Gregor seemed to entertain them more than the violin playing. With outstretched arms, the father rushed to them and tried to herd them back to their room, while simultaneously blocking their view of Gregor with his body. Now they really became a bit angry; it wasn't clear whether the father's behavior was to blame or whether the realization was dawning on them that they had unknowingly had a next door neighbor like Gregor. They demanded explanations from the father, waving their arms at him, nervously plucking their beards, and then they backed toward their room very reluctantly. In the meantime, the sister had recovered from the bewildered state she had fallen into with the sudden interruption of her music; after having dangled her violin and bow listlessly for awhile in her slack hands, continuing to gaze at the music as if she were still playing, she had suddenly pulled herself together, placed her instrument in her mother's lap (her mother was still sitting in her chair, gasping for breath with heaving lungs) and run into the next room, which the boarders were approaching more rapidly now under pressure from the father. One could see the blankets and pillows on the beds obeying the sister's skillful hands and arranging themselves neatly. Before the boarders had even reached their room, she finished making the beds and slipped out. Once again the father seemed so overcome by his obstinacy that he was forgetting any respect he still owed his boarders. He kept crowding them and crowding them until, just at the doorway to their room, the middle boarder thunderously stamped his foot and brought the father to a halt. "I hereby declare," he said, raising his hand and looking around for the mother and sister too, "that in view of the disgusting conditions prevailing in this household and family" — here he promptly spit on the floor — "I give immediate notice. I will of course not pay a cent for the days that I have been living here, either; on the contrary, I will think seriously about taking some sort of legal action against you, with claims — believe me — that would be very easy to substantiate." He was silent and looked straight ahead of him, as if he were expecting something. And in fact his two friends immediately chimed in with the words, "We're also leaving tomorrow." Thereupon he seized the door handle and banged the door shut.

Gregor's father staggered with groping hands to his armchair and let himself fall into it; he looked as if he were stretching out for his usual evening nap, but the rapid nodding of his head, as if it were out of control, showed that he was anything but asleep. All this time Gregor had been lying still in the same place where the boarders had caught sight of him. His disappointment over the failure of his plan, and perhaps also the weakness caused by his great hunger, made it impossible for him to move. With a fair degree of certainty, he feared that in the very next moment everything would collapse over him, and he was waiting. He was not even startled when the violin slipped through the mother's trembling fingers, fell off her lap, and gave off a reverberating clang.

"My dear parents," the sister said, striking the table with her hand by way of introduction, "things can't go on like this. Perhaps you don't realize that, but I do. I refuse to utter my brother's name in the presence of this monster, and so I say: we have to try to get rid of it. We've done everything humanly possible to take care of it and put up with it; I think no one could reproach us in the slightest."

"She's right a thousand times over," the father said to himself. Still struggling to catch her breath, a wild look in her eyes, the mother began to cough hollowly into her hand.

The sister rushed to the mother and held her forehead. The father's thoughts seemed to have become clearer as a result of the sister's words; he had sat up straight and was playing with his uniform cap among the dishes that still lay on the table from the boarder's supper, and from time to time he glanced over at Gregor, who remained motionless.

"We must try to get rid of it," said the sister, now only addressing the father, since the mother couldn't hear anything over her coughing. "It'll kill both of you, I can see that coming. When we all have to work as hard as we do, how

can we stand this constant torment at home? At least I can't stand it anymore."
And she burst out into such violent weeping that her tears flowed down onto
her mother's face, where she mechanically wiped them away.

"My child," said the father compassionately and with remarkable comprehension, "but what are we supposed to do?"

The sister just shrugged her shoulders to show the helplessness that
had now come over her during her crying fit, in contrast to her former self-
confidence.

"If he understood us," said the father, half-questioningly; the sister, still
sobbing, waved her hand vehemently to show how unthinkable it was.

"If he understood us," repeated the father, closing his eyes to absorb the
sister's conviction that this was impossible, "then perhaps we might be able to
come to some sort of agreement with him. But as it is —"

"He's got to go," cried the sister, "that's the only answer, father. You must
just try to stop thinking that this is Gregor. The fact that we've believed it for
so long is actually our true misfortune. But how can it be Gregor? If it were
Gregor, he would long since have understood that it's impossible for people
to live together with such a creature, and he would have gone away of his own
free will. Then we wouldn't have a brother, but we could go on living and honor
his memory. But instead this creature persecutes us, drives away the boarders,
obviously wants to take over the entire apartment and let us sleep out in the
street. Just look, father," she suddenly shrieked, "he's at it again!" And — in a
state of panic that was totally incomprehensible to Gregor — the sister even
abandoned her mother, literally bolting away from her chair as if she would
rather sacrifice her mother than stay near Gregor, and she rushed behind her
father, who got to his feet as well, alarmed at her behavior, and half raised his
arms as if to protect her.

But Gregor hadn't the slightest intention of frightening anyone, least of all
his sister. He had merely begun to turn himself around so as to return to his
room, and that admittedly did attract attention, since in his feeble condition he
had to use his head to achieve these difficult turns, raising it and bumping it
against the floor several times. He paused and looked around. His good intentions seemed to have been recognized; it had only been a momentary alarm.
Now they all watched him, silent and sad. His mother lay back in her chair, her
legs stretched out and pressed together, her eyes almost shut from exhaustion;
his father and sister were sitting side by side, his sister had placed her hand
around her father's neck.

"Perhaps I'm allowed to turn around now," Gregor thought, and he resumed
his work. He couldn't suppress his panting from the exertion and also had to
stop and rest every once in awhile. Otherwise no one hurried him, it was all
left entirely to him. When he had completed the turn, he started to crawl back
in a straight line. He was astonished at the great distance separating him from
his room and couldn't comprehend how in his weak condition he could have
covered the same ground a short time ago almost without noticing it. So intent
was he on crawling rapidly, he scarcely noticed that no word or outcry from the
family was disturbing his progress. Only when he was already in the doorway

did he turn his head, not completely, for he felt his neck stiffening, but enough to see that nothing had changed behind him, except that his sister had stood up. His final gaze fell on his mother, who was now sound asleep.

No sooner was he inside his room than the door was hurriedly slammed shut, firmly bolted, and locked. The sudden noise behind him frightened Gregor so much that his little legs buckled. It was his sister who had been in such a hurry. She had been standing there ready and waiting, then she had swiftly leaped forward, Gregor hadn't even heard her coming, and she had cried "At last!" to her parents as she turned the key in the lock.

"And now?" Gregor asked himself, and peered around in the darkness. He soon made the discovery that he couldn't move at all. It didn't surprise him; rather it seemed unnatural to him that until now he had actually been able to get around on those thin little legs. Otherwise he felt relatively comfortable. He had pains throughout his body, of course, but it seemed to him that they were gradually getting weaker and weaker and would eventually disappear completely. The rotten apple in his back and the inflamed area around it, completely covered over by soft dust, scarcely bothered him. His thoughts went back to his family with tenderness and love. His conviction that he must disappear was, if possible, even stronger than his sister's. He remained in this state of empty, peaceful meditation until the tower clock struck three in the morning. He was just conscious of the beginning of the dawn outside his window. Then his head sank down completely, involuntarily, and his last breath issued faintly from his nostrils.

Early in the morning when the cleaning woman arrived — from sheer energy and impatience she would slam all the doors so loudly, no matter how many times she'd been asked not to do so, that it was impossible to sleep peacefully anywhere in the apartment — she found nothing unusual at first during her customary brief visit to Gregor. She thought that he was deliberately lying motionless like that, acting insulted; she credited him with unlimited intelligence. Since she happened to be holding the long broom in her hand, she tried to tickle Gregor with it from the doorway. When this produced no response, she became annoyed and jabbed Gregor a little, and it was only when she had moved him from his place without his resistance that she began to take notice. When she quickly grasped the fact of the matter, she opened her eyes wide and gave a low whistle, but she didn't stay there long; instead she tore open the bedroom door and shouted at the top of her voice into the darkness, "Come and take a look; it's croaked; it's lying there, completely and totally croaked!"

The Samsa parents sat up in their marriage bed and had to overcome the shock that the cleaning woman had given them before they could finally grasp her message. Then Mr. and Mrs. Samsa quickly climbed out of bed, one from each side; Mr. Samsa wrapped the blanket around his shoulders, Mrs. Samsa came out only in her nightgown; in this way they entered Gregor's room. Meanwhile the living room door had also opened; Grete had been sleeping there since the boarders had moved in; she was fully dressed, as if she'd not slept at all, and her pale face seemed to confirm this. "Dead?" asked Mrs. Samsa, and looked up inquiringly at the cleaning woman, though she could have examined everything herself, and the situation was plain enough without her doing so. "I'll say!" replied the cleaning woman, and to prove it she pushed Gregor's corpse with her broom off to one side. Mrs. Samsa made a movement as if she wanted to hold back the broom, but she didn't do it. "Well," said Mr. Samsa, "now we can thank God." He crossed himself, and the three women followed his example. Grete, who never took her eyes off the corpse, said, "Just look how thin he was. After all, he hadn't been eating anything for so long. The food came out of his room again just the way it went in." As a matter of fact, Gregor's body was completely flat and dry; this was really evident now for the first time when he was no longer lifted up by his little legs and also when nothing else diverted their gaze.

"Come in with us, Grete, for a little while," said Mrs. Samsa with a melancholy smile, and Grete followed her parents into their bedroom, not without looking back at the corpse. The cleaning woman shut Gregor's door and opened his window wide. Although it was early in the morning, the fresh air held a touch of mildness. By now it was nearly the end of March.

The three boarders emerged from their room and looked around in astonishment for their breakfast; they had been forgotten. "Where is breakfast?" the middle one gruffly asked the cleaning woman. But she put her finger to her lips and hastily and silently beckoned them to come into Gregor's room. In they went and stood with their hands in the pockets of their somewhat shabby jackets in a circle around Gregor's corpse in the room that by now was filled with light.

Just then the bedroom door opened, and Mr. Samsa appeared in his uniform with his wife on one arm and his daughter on the other. They all looked as if they had been crying; from time to time Grete pressed her face against her father's sleeve.

"Leave my apartment at once!" said Mr. Samsa and pointed to the door without letting go of the women. "What do you mean?" asked the middle boarder, somewhat dismayed and with a sugary smile. The two others held their hands behind their backs and rubbed them together incessantly, as if in gleeful anticipation of a major quarrel that could only turn out in their favor. "I mean exactly what I say," answered Mr. Samsa, and he marched in a line with his two women companions toward the boarder. At first the boarder quietly stood still and looked at the floor, as if he were rearranging matters in his head. "Well, then, we'll go," he said, and suddenly overcome with humility he looked up at Mr. Samsa as if he were seeking new approval for this decision. Mr. Samsa merely nodded several times, staring at him hard. At that the boarder immediately took long strides into the hall; his two friends, who had been listening for awhile, their hands entirely still, now practically went hopping right after him, as if afraid that Mr. Samsa would reach the hall ahead of them and cut them off from their leader. In the hall, all three took their hats from the coat rack, drew their canes out of the umbrella stand, bowed silently and left the apartment. Impelled by a mistrust that proved to be entirely unfounded, Mr. Samsa and the two women stepped out onto the landing and, leaning over the banister, they watched the three boarders slowly but surely descend the long staircase, disappearing on each floor at a certain turn and then reappearing a few moments later; the lower they got, the more the Samsa family's interest in them dwindled, and when a butcher's boy proudly carrying a tray on his head swung past them on up the stairs, Mr. Samsa and the women left the banister and, as if relieved, all went back to the apartment.

They decided to spend this day resting and going for a walk; they not only deserved a break from their work, they also desperately needed it. And so they sat down at the table to write their letters of excuse, Mr. Samsa to the bank manager, Mrs. Samsa to her employer, and Grete to the store owner. While they were writing, the cleaning woman came in to announce that she was going because her morning work was finished. The three letter writers merely nodded at first without looking up, but as the cleaning woman still kept lingering, they all looked up irritably. "Well?" asked Mr. Samsa. The cleaning woman stood smiling in the doorway as if she had some great news for the family but would only tell it if they questioned her properly. The little ostrich feather sticking up almost straight on her hat, which had annoyed Mr. Samsa during all the time she had been working for them, was fluttering in all directions. "Well, what is it you really want?" asked Mrs. Samsa, for whom the cleaning woman still had the most respect. "Well," answered the cleaning woman, and she couldn't go on immediately for her own good natured chuckling, "well, you don't have to worry about getting rid of the thing next door. It's already been taken care of." Mrs. Samsa and Grete bent their heads down over their letters, as if they intended to resume writing; Mr. Samsa, who realized that the cleaning woman was now eager to start describing everything in detail, cut her short with an outstretched hand. But since she couldn't tell her story, she remembered that she was in a great hurry and cried out, obviously offended, "Goodbye, everyone," then whirled around wildly and left the apartment with a thunderous slamming of the door.

"She'll be fired tonight," said Mr. Samsa, but he received no reply from either his wife or his daughter, because the cleaning woman seemed to have disturbed the peace of mind they had just recently acquired. They got up, went over to the window, and stayed there, their arms around each other. Mr. Samsa turned toward them in his chair and watched them quietly for awhile. Then he called, "Oh, come on over here. Stop brooding over the past. And have a little consideration for me, too." The women obeyed him at once, rushed over to him, caressed him, and hurriedly finished their letters.

Then they all three left the apartment together, which they hadn't done in months, and took the trolley out to the open country on the outskirts of the city. The car, in which they were the only passengers, was flooded with warm sunshine. Leaning back comfortably in their seats, they discussed their prospects for the future and it turned out that, on closer inspection, these weren't bad at all, because all three had positions which—though they hadn't ever really asked one another about them in any detail—were thoroughly advantageous and especially promising for the future. The greatest immediate improvement in their situation would easily result, of course, from a change in apartments; now they would move to a smaller and cheaper apartment, but one better located and in general more practical than their present one, which Gregor had chosen. While they were talking in this way, it occurred almost simultaneously to both Mr. and Mrs. Samsa, as they watched their daughter's increasing liveliness, that despite all the recent cares that had made her cheeks pale, she had blossomed into a good looking and well-developed girl. Growing quieter and almost unconsciously communicating through glances, they thought it would soon be time, too, to find a good husband for her. And it was like a confirmation of their new dreams and good intentions when at the end of their ride, their daughter stood up first and stretched her young body.

Etgar Keret

Etgar Keret (b. 1967) was born in the Israeli industrial center of Ramat Gan during the year of the Six-Day War between Israel and Egypt. His name *Keret* means "city," and *Etgar* means "challenge," since he was delivered by cesarean section after a six-month pregnancy his mother had been advised to terminate. His parents were Holocaust survivors. His mother's family had perished in the Warsaw ghetto; his father had stayed alive by spending two years hidden in a hole in the Soviet Union. While Keret was growing up, they never talked about their war experiences, and he believes that being raised by parents who insisted that they could request anything of their children as long as they provided a good enough reason inadequately prepared him for the complexities of real life. Their rationality forced him to repress the heavy emotions that now fuel his fiction. "The reason I write is that I'm not in dialogue with my emotions; writing puts me in touch with myself." He considers his siblings to be a microcosm of the contradictions in contemporary Israeli society. His older brother, a computer genius, is also an extreme left-wing anarchist heading a movement to legalize marijuana, while his sister is an ultra-Orthodox mother of eleven children who lived until recently in a kibbutz settlement and whose conservative religious beliefs prohibit her from reading Keret's fiction.

Keret decided to become a writer when he was nineteen, after he began his military service with the Israeli army. Two weeks after his best friend committed suicide in the service, Keret wrote his first story, "Pipes," in an attempt to answer his friend's act. He told an interviewer he was "trying to say that you have to find a way out. For me the way out was stories. . . . Since then I haven't stopped writing." Later he joked that "saying whatever comes to mind, in the army, is not necessarily the best way to obtain a weekend leave. Writing is much safer: most of your commanders, even if they find a page of your writing, won't feel like reading it. Especially if it's a short and weird story." After his discharge, Keret began university studies in Israel. One of his professors left for a job in a publishing house and offered to bring out a book of Keret's short fiction. In 1992 he published *Pipelines*, his first story collection. Two years later appeared his second book of stories, *Missing Kissinger*, coauthored by Palestinian writer Samir El-Youssef (titled *Gaza Blues* in English translation). This volume was followed by several other books in Hebrew, including children's books and graphic novels coauthored with Rutu Modan. Keret is one of Israel's most controversial younger writers, and his books have been published in more than twenty languages throughout the world; these books include *The Nimrod Flip-Out*, another story collection published in English. His 2004 story collection *The Bus Driver Who Wanted to Be God*, translated into Arabic from English, is the only book by an Israeli author to be published in the Palestinian Authority since the beginning of the latest intifada. Keret's early story "Not Human Beings" was included in *The Girl on the Fridge* (2008). *Suddenly, a Knock on the Door* (2012) is a recent story collection.

As the American critic Stephen Marche observed in the Jewish newspaper *Forward*, "Kafka said that literature should be an ax to break the frozen sea within us. Keret is a writer wailing at the ice with a Wiffle Ball bat." Keret says he writes about the violence that he grew up with in contemporary Israel, where compulsory military service is an accepted way of life.

> In a country where, for three years out of their lives, everybody who is eighteen lives in a reality where he may kill people or see people get killed next to him, he may do things Americans would never do. I didn't serve in the occupied territories, but people who do know that if you knock on a door and it doesn't open, you kick it open. You can play the guitar, read Nietzsche, become a very good dentist, but you'll still do it. And once you cross that line, it's very difficult to uncross it. When your girlfriend won't talk to you and locks the door, you will still know how to kick it open.

RELATED STORY
Isaac Babel, "My First Goose," page 36.

Not Human Beings

1994 / Translated by Miriam Shlesinger and Sondra Silverston

DAVIDOFF, THE REGIMENT COMMANDER'S driver, was the first to see him. "Here comes trouble," he said, getting up from the empty ammo box he was sitting on.

"He's just a Border Police officer," said Stein, completely focused on the backgammon board.

"You know what that means," said Davidoff, still standing there and staring at the officer in the strange olive green uniform.

"No, I don't know," Stein muttered impatiently, "so how about sitting down already. It's your turn."

"It means they're going to move one of our guys over to them, 'personnel reinforcement' they call it. This isn't the first time."

"So they'll move someone over to them, big deal. Shoot the dice already, Davidoff."

"Maybe for you it's no big deal, but for the poor — "

"I swear, Davidoff, if you don't shoot the fucking dice, I'll go to the personnel officer right now and ask him to send *me*. Maybe with those guys. I'll at least be able to finish a game."

"You know, Stein," Davidoff said, ungluing his eyes from the Border Police officer, "sometimes you can be such an asshole. One day with them" — he pointed at the officer — "one day with them, and you'll sing a different tune. You never met guys like that, they'll eat you alive. Especially an Ashkenazi[1] putz like you." Davidoff gave a dry laugh. "They'll have to scrape you off the bumper of their jeep."

"Fuck it, we're never going to get through this game today," Stein said, pissed off. He'd just stood up when Shaharabani, all sweaty, came over and said the personnel officer wanted to talk to him.

---

[1] Jews of European descent.

"Those Border Police pricks, they're a different army, they don't think like us at all. They're wild animals," the personnel officer said, digging around in his ear with his pen. "And that's exactly why I have to send them a good soldier who won't react to their provocations, not a hot-tempered one like Ackerman or Shaharabani who, best-case scenario, ends up in jail, worst-case in the hospital."

Stein packed his things and got into the jeep with the officer. He could've done without that compliment. "It's not so bad. Only a week," he thought, trying to cheer himself up. He could see Hamama's you-have-my-condolences face in the distance as they drove off.

"Okay, who's the prick that stole my commando knife?" asked the squat, hairy guy who was walking around the tent buck naked.

"Cool it, Zanzuri, I just took it for a second to cut the duct tape." A sweaty black soldier handed him a huge knife with a compass on the handle. Zanzuri snatched the knife and, in the same gesture, pressed it against the black guy's throat. "Shafik, you Bedouin asshole. You put your sweaty hands on my things one more time and I'll stick this knife up your black ass. You hear me?"

The officer who came into the tent ignored the incident. "Your bunk's over there," he said, pointing to the far end. "What did you say your name was?"

"Stein, Shmulik Stein," Stein mumbled.

"Your bunk's over there, Stein." He pointed to the same bed again. "Patrol in two hours, be ready."

Whenever he went out on patrol in one of those armored, rock-resistant jeeps, there were always riots. They couldn't drive down a single street without a brick flying at them. But now, from the open Border Police jeep, Gaza looked like a ghost town. There were four of them. Zanzuri drove, and apart from Stein, there was the sweaty black guy and a redhead. The redhead took a piece of Bazooka out of his vest pocket, put it in his mouth, and threw out the wrapper.

"Hey, Russki, toss a piece over here," Zanzuri demanded when he saw him in the rearview mirror.

"All gone," the redhead said and smiled, showing rotten teeth.

"Fuck," Zanzuri said and spat a wad of phlegm over the side of the jeep. "The first Arab I catch today is going to be one sorry son of a bitch!" The second jeep passed them. The driver was a skinny, scar-faced soldier, and the officer was in the passenger seat. A hundred meters in front of them, an old Arab man was trudging down the road. Stein saw Scar Face spin the wheel sharply to the left, lunge onto the sidewalk, and hit the old Arab, who landed on his face a few meters away and lay there motionless. "The mute's all hopped up today," Zanzuri said with a snicker. "Did you see how he sent the towel-head flying?" Stein, not understanding what exactly had happened, turned and saw the body on the sidewalk, saw Zanzuri laughing and the Russian chewing gum. He tried to put all the images together into a single, coherent reality, but he couldn't. The other jeep stopped at the corner of an alley, and Zanzuri pulled up right behind it.

Stein jumped out, ran over to the mute, and grabbed him by the shirt. "You ran him over on purpose, you psycho, you ran over a human being on purpose. He didn't do anything to you." The Russian grabbed Stein from behind with an iron grip and pulled him away from the mute.

"He didn't run over a human being," Zanzuri corrected. "He ran over an Arab, so what the fuck is your problem?" Stein felt the Russian's repulsive, hot breath on his neck and knew that if he opened his mouth to say something, he'd burst out crying.

"That roof there," the officer said, pointing, ignoring everything that had happened, "there's someone on it. I want Zanzuri and the Russki to bring him down here."

The Russian let go of Stein. He and Zanzuri disappeared into the alley the officer had pointed to. They were back two minutes later, dragging someone with his hands tied behind him and a wide strip of duct tape over his mouth.

"I shut him up," Zanzuri said. "I hate it when they start begging."

The mute sighed in agreement and nodded. He went over to the trussed-up Arab and pretended to bend down but straightened abruptly and butted him in the face.

"Did you find anything on him?" the officer asked in a bored tone.

"This!" Zanzuri said, proudly holding up a bottle of root beer with a soaked rag tied around its neck. "And he had a brick, too." The mute kept punching the Arab, who was now lying on the ground, moaning faintly.

"Enough!" Stein shouted, stepping toward them. The mute stood up, pulled his truncheon out of his vest, and glared at him.

"You're starting to get on my nerves, Stein," the officer muttered, an unlit cigarette in the corner of his mouth. He put the crushed pack of unfiltered Ascots into his pouch and rummaged around for something in his pocket. When he didn't find it, he went on: "What are you, Stein, the Red Cross? Those scum have only one thing on their minds — killing you. It's their only reason for living. Get that into your head. They might look like us on the outside, but they're not."

The Arab's bound body writhed on the ground, and Stein tried to go over and help him. The mute blocked his way.

"You just don't get it, do you?" the officer said. "Okay, like they say: a picture is worth a thousand words. Russki, pick him up," he ordered. The Russian stood the Arab up from the back and held on to him so he wouldn't fall. The Arab's face was caked with blood and dirt. "Zanzuri, the knife," the officer said, holding out his hand, the unlit cigarette still between his lips. Zanzuri took the knife out of his vest and slapped it into the officer's outstretched palm. The officer looked at the knife for a minute and tapped the handle with his finger. "The compass on the handle isn't working," he said.

"Yes, I know," Zanzuri said with a nod. "That asshole Bedouin broke it." He pointed at the black soldier, whose sweat-soaked uniform looked darker than the others.

"Fuck it," the officer said and ripped open the Arab's shirt. The buttons scattered on the ground, and Stein saw a hairy chest rising and falling rapidly.

"No!" Stein yelled, managing to take a step toward the officer. The mute smashed the back of his neck with the heavy wooden truncheon, and Stein fell to the ground.

"Hold him with his head up," Stein heard the officer command.

"Not the Arab, you moron," said the Russian, "the bleeding heart." He snickered.

Stein was on his knees now, the mute supporting him under an armpit with one hand, pulling his hair back with the other. Three meters away from him, the officer was moving the knife to the Arab's trembling stomach, and there was nothing he could do. With a quick slice, the officer cut the stomach in two, and rolled-up flags, flyers, candy, and phone tokens came spilling out of it.

"Don't touch the candy," the officer warned them. "It's poisoned." He handed the knife back to Zanzuri. The Russian unrolled one of the flags. It was a PLO flag. Zanzuri and the black soldier filled their pockets with phone tokens. The Russian stripped the Arab, who was lying on the ground flat as a sheet after being emptied out. He folded him in eight and laid him on the jeep's spare tire.

"Hey, Russki, what are you going to do with him?" Zanzuri asked.

"A cover for my motor scooter, a cape, who knows," said the Russian, and he shrugged. "It must be good for something."

"Man, those Russians are stingy," Zanzuri whispered to the black soldier, the tokens jingling in his pockets. Even though more than five minutes had gone by since the mute had hit him with his truncheon, Stein decided that the time had come to faint.

———————

Stein woke up on his bed in the tent, wearing his clothes and shoes, the pain so agonizing that he could barely move his neck. Everyone was sleeping now. The needle of the broken compass on Zanzuri's knife handle glowed brightly in the dark. Stein got up quietly, pulled the knife out of its sheath, and started walking where the phosphorescent needle led him.

Jamaica Kincaid

Jamaica Kincaid (b. 1949) was born and educated in St. Johns, Antigua, in the West Indies. Her father was a carpenter, and her family doted upon her when she was growing up. Kincaid remembers the early influence of her family:

> My mother did keep everything I ever wore, and basically until I was quite grown up my past was sort of a museum to me. Clearly, the way I became a writer was that my mother wrote my life for me and told it to me. I can't help but think that it made me interested in the idea of myself as an object. I can't account for the reason I became a writer any other way, because I certainly didn't know writers. And not only that. I thought writing was something that people just didn't do anymore, that went out of fashion, like the bustle. I really didn't read a book that was written in the twentieth century until I was about seventeen and away from home.

Kincaid left Antigua to study in the United States, but she found college "a dismal failure," so she educated herself. She began writing and published her stories in *Rolling Stone*, the *Paris Review*, and *The New Yorker*, where she became a staff writer in 1978. Six years later she published her first book, *At the Bottom of the River*, a collection of stories, which won the Morton Dauwen Zabel Award of the American Academy and Institute of Arts and Letters. In 1985 her book of interrelated stories *Annie John*, about a girl's coming of age in the West Indies, was also much praised. In her autobiographical writing, Kincaid often explores the idea that her deep affection for her family and her native country developed into a conflicting need for separation and independence as she grew up.

Typically Kincaid writes in a deliberately precise rhythmic style about intense emotions, as in her story "Girl," which first appeared in a 1978 issue of *The New Yorker* and was later collected in *At the Bottom of the River* (1984). Her fiction is free from conventional plots, characters, and dialogue. The critic Suzanne Freeman has recognized that "what Kincaid has to tell me, she tells, with her sing-song style, in a series of images that are as sweet and mysterious as the secrets that children whisper in your ear." Although Kincaid is married to an American and lives in Vermont, she feels that the British West Indies will continue to be the source for her fiction. "What I really feel about America is that it's given me a place to be myself—but myself as I was formed somewhere else." *A Small Place* (1988), another book about the West Indies, was described by the novelist Salman Rushdie as "a jeremiad of great clarity and a force that one might have called torrential were the language not so finely controlled." Some other books are *Lucy* (1990), *Autobiography of My Mother* (1996), *My Brother* (1997), and *Among the Flowers: A Walk in the Himalayas* (2005). *See Now Then* (2013) is a recent novel.

RELATED COMMENTARY
Jamaica Kincaid, "On 'Girl,'" page 1454.

Girl

1978

WASH THE WHITE CLOTHES on Monday and put them on the stone heap; wash the color clothes on Tuesday and put them on the clothesline to dry; don't walk barehead in the hot sun; cook pumpkin fritters in very hot sweet oil; soak your little cloths right after you take them off; when buying cotton to make yourself a nice blouse, be sure that it doesn't have gum on it, because that way it won't hold up well after a wash; soak salt fish overnight before you cook it; is it true that you sing benna[1] in Sunday school?; always eat your food in such a way that it won't turn someone else's stomach; on Sundays try to walk like a lady and not like the slut you are so bent on becoming; don't sing benna in Sunday school; you mustn't speak to wharf-rat boys, not even to give directions; don't eat fruits on the street — flies will follow you; *but I don't sing benna on Sundays at all and never in Sunday school*; this is how to sew on a button; this is how to make a button-hole for the button you have just sewed on; this is how to hem a dress when you see the hem coming down and so to prevent yourself from looking like the slut I know you are so bent on becoming; this is how you iron your father's khaki shirt so that it doesn't have a crease; this is how you iron your father's khaki pants so that they don't have a crease; this is how you grow okra — far from the house, because okra tree harbors red ants; when you are growing dasheen, make sure it gets plenty of water or else it makes your throat itch when you are eating it; this is how you sweep a corner; this is how you sweep a whole house; this is how you sweep a yard; this is how you smile to someone you don't like too much; this is how you smile to someone you don't like at all; this is how you smile to someone you like completely; this is how you set a table for tea; this is how you set a table for dinner; this is how you set a table for dinner with an important guest; this is how you set a table for lunch; this is how you set a table for breakfast; this is how to behave in the presence of men who don't know you very well, and this way they won't recognize immediately the slut I have warned you against becoming; be sure to wash every day, even if it is with your own spit; don't squat down to play marbles — you are not a boy, you know; don't pick people's flowers — you might catch something; don't throw stones at blackbirds, because it might not be a blackbird at all; this is how to make a bread pudding; this is how to make doukona;[2] this is how to make pepper pot; this is how to make a good medicine for a cold; this is how to make a good medicine to throw away a child before it even becomes a child; this is how to catch a fish; this is how to throw back a fish you don't like, and that way something bad won't fall on you; this is how to bully a man; this is how a man bullies you; this is how to love a man, and if this doesn't work there are other ways, and

---

[1] Calypso music.
[2] A spicy plantain pudding.

if they don't work don't feel too bad about giving up; this is how to spit up in the air if you feel like it, and this is how to move quick so that it doesn't fall on you; this is how to make ends meet; always squeeze bread to make sure it's fresh; *but what if the baker won't let me feel the bread?*; you mean to say that after all you are really going to be the kind of woman who the baker won't let near the bread?

Nora Krug

Nora Krug (b. 1977), artist and writer, was born in Karlsruhe, Germany. At nineteen she left to study stage and graphic design at Paul McCartney's Institute for Performing Arts in Liverpool before she completed her degree in illustration and documentary film in Berlin. In 2004 she earned her M.F.A. in illustration at The School of Visual Arts in New York City. She then worked as a freelance illustrator for publications such as the *New York Times* and *The Guardian* as well as on Comedy Central and MTV. Krug is a recipient of Guggenheim and Fulbright fellowships. In 2005 she was awarded a DAAD grant from the German Academic Exchange Service, which enabled her to return to Germany as a professor of illustration and drawing at the Muthesius Academy of Fine Arts and Design in Kiel. She accepted the grant as a first step along the path to what she considered to be "an internationally oriented way of life." Currently she is an associate professor in the illustration program at Parsons The New School for Design in New York City.

Krug's publications include two books, *Red Riding Hood Redux*, a wordless reinterpretation of the classic fairy tale drawn from the different perspectives of Red Riding Hood, the wolf, the hunter, the mother, and the grandmother; and the award-winning *Shadow Atlas*, an illustrated encyclopedia of ghosts and spirits. It was screen printed in four colors and hand-bound in a limited edition of 400 copies in Italy. Krug's animated guide to Japanese business etiquette, *How to Bow*, was shown at the Sundance Film Festival. Her story "Kamikaze" was included in both *The Best American Comics of 2012* and *The Best American Non-Required Reading*.

Krug has described the role of drawing in her work:

> Drawing is a kind of research for me, and with every new story I create, I try to find out something about an issue I am interested in. It's not only the historic, textual research that inspires me. I see the act of drawing itself as a research tool. Visualizing stories and situations that I didn't witness myself helps me imagine what experiencing a certain situation must have been like, and it helps me develop empathy for the characters whom my stories are about. I used to make documentary films, and I see my visual biographies as a continuation of my documentaries.
>
> "Kamikaze" is one in a series of biographies about people whose lives have been impacted by war. . . . I wanted to find out what being a kamikaze pilot really meant in Japan during WWII. In the west, we perceive kamikaze pilots as patriotic fanatics. In reality, a lot of these young men, however, didn't want to die, and reading their biographies and farewell letters to their fiancées or parents is heartbreaking. I think our idea of war is often too simplistic, and we are very influenced by how the idea of it is represented in the press and entertainment culture, but for the most part know very little about the complexities of war. Through my visual narratives, I hope to create a more complex understanding of how war was and is experienced in different cultures.

RELATED CASEBOOK
See Casebook on Graphic Storytelling, pages 1647–1663, including Charles Hatfield, "From *Alternative Comics*: Toward the Habit of Questioning," page 1649; Michael Kupperman, "Are Comics Serious Literature?" page 1652.

He saw a man who was alive, but whose intestines hung down from his belly.

He saw someone whose face was swollen to a degree that it was impossible to make out the person's eyes, nose and mouth.

Ena felt as though his soul was cleansed.

Why did you return alive?

He swore to never again be involved in any form of war.

On August 15th, the emperor broadcast his capitulation. Ena was no longer a soldier, but, as a surviving Kamikaze pilot, despised by some.

Club soda makes you feel less hungry

Ena went back to university in Tokyo. Only half of his former college friends had survived.

Ena and Shibata met frequently in Tokyo.

Oh absolutely delighted.

A few years after the war, Ena returned to Kuroshima. Shibata asked him to find Shina, the girl who had looked after him, and to ask her if she would marry Shibata.

In 2004, Ena erected a Buddhist statue on Kuroshima, and he decided that he would commemorate his friends who had died as Kamikaze pilots every year on the island.

Ena Takehiko is in his late 80s and lives as a retired soy-bean exporter in Japan. Sources: Wings of Defeat (Dir. Risa Morimoto), Kamikaze in Color (Dir. Ron Marans), Kamikaze Diaries (Auth. Emiko Ohnuki-Tierney), Tokkou no Machi: Chiran (Auth. Sanae Sato). Thank you to: Ena Takehiko, Ai Tarebayashi, William Gordon (Wesley University).

Jhumpa Lahiri

Jhumpa Lahiri (b. 1967) was born in London, the daughter of Bengali parents. As a child she often made trips to Calcutta, and she feels that her sense of culture has been influenced by both India and the United States. To Lahiri, India "is the place where my parents are from, a place I visited frequently for extended time and formed relationships with people and with my relatives and felt a tie over time even though it was a sort of parenthesis in my life to be there." Lahiri grew up in Rhode Island and started writing fiction in her grade school notebooks. After graduating with a B.A. from Barnard College, she applied to creative writing programs in several graduate schools, but her applications were rejected by all of them. She began working on her first book of short fiction while in an office job as a research assistant in Cambridge, Massachusetts, at a nonprofit organization. She remembers,

> For the first time I had a computer of my own at my desk, and I started writing fiction again, more seriously. I used to stay late and come in to work on stories. Eventually I had enough material to apply to the creative writing program at Boston University. But once that ended, unsure of what to do next, I went on to graduate school and got my Ph.D. [in Renaissance Studies]. In the process, it became clear to me that I was not meant to be a scholar. It was something I did out of a sense of duty and practicality, but it was never something I loved. I still wrote stories on the side, publishing things here and there. The year I finished my dissertation [1997], I was also accepted to the Fine Arts Work Center in Provincetown, and that changed everything. It was something of a miracle. In seven months I got an agent, sold a book, and had a story published in *The New Yorker*. I've been extremely lucky. It's been the happiest possible ending.

As a new writer, Lahiri has explained that "the characters I'm drawn to all face some barrier of communication. I like to write about people who think in a way they can't fully express." At first she began to place her stories in *Agni*, *Epoch*, *The Louisville Review*, *Harvard Review*, and *Story Quarterly*. In 1993 she was awarded a Transatlantic Review fellowship from the Henfield Foundation, and in 1997 she won a fiction prize from *The Louisville Review*. In 1999 Lahiri published her first collection of short fiction, *Interpreter of Maladies*, a total of nine stories. Her book won the Pulitzer Prize for Fiction in 2000, winning over the short story collections that year of two other finalists, Ha Jin (*Waiting*) and Annie Proulx (*Close Range*). In 2003 she published her first novel, *The Namesake*. A second collection of stories, *Unaccustomed Earth*, appeared in 2008, and her second novel, *The Lowland*, in 2013.

RELATED COMMENTARY
Simon Lewis, "Lahiri's 'Interpreter of Maladies,'" page 1463.

Interpreter of Maladies

1999

AT THE TEA STALL Mr. and Mrs. Das bickered about who should take Tina to the toilet. Eventually Mrs. Das relented when Mr. Das pointed out that he had given the girl her bath the night before. In the rearview mirror Mr. Kapasi watched as Mrs. Das emerged slowly from his bulky white Ambassador, dragging her shaved, largely bare legs across the back seat. She did not hold the little girl's hand as they walked to the rest room.

They were on their way to see the Sun Temple at Konarak. It was a dry, bright Saturday, the mid-July heat tempered by a steady ocean breeze, ideal weather for sightseeing. Ordinarily Mr. Kapasi would not have stopped so soon along the way, but less than five minutes after he'd picked up the family that morning in front of Hotel Sandy Villa, the little girl had complained. The first thing Mr. Kapasi had noticed when he saw Mr. and Mrs. Das, standing with their children under the portico of the hotel, was that they were very young, perhaps not even thirty. In addition to Tina they had two boys, Ronny and Bobby, who appeared very close in age and had teeth covered in a network of flashing silver wires. The family looked Indian but dressed as foreigners did, the children in stiff, brightly colored clothing and caps with translucent visors. Mr. Kapasi was accustomed to foreign tourists; he was assigned to them regularly because he could speak English. Yesterday he had driven an elderly couple from Scotland, both with spotted faces and fluffy white hair so thin it exposed their sunburnt scalps. In comparison, the tanned, youthful faces of Mr. and Mrs. Das were all the more striking. When he'd introduced himself, Mr. Kapasi had pressed his palms together in greeting, but Mr. Das squeezed hands like an American so that Mr. Kapasi felt it in his elbow. Mrs. Das, for her part, had flexed one side of her mouth, smiling dutifully at Mr. Kapasi, without displaying any interest in him.

As they waited at the tea stall, Ronny, who looked like the older of the two boys, clambered suddenly out of the back seat, intrigued by a goat tied to a stake in the ground.

"Don't touch it," Mr. Das said. He glanced up from his paperback tour book, which said "INDIA" in yellow letters and looked as if it had been published abroad. His voice, somehow tentative and a little shrill, sounded as though it had not yet settled into maturity.

"I want to give it a piece of gum," the boy called back as he trotted ahead.

Mr. Das stepped out of the car and stretched his legs by squatting briefly to the ground. A clean-shaven man, he looked exactly like a magnified version of Ronny. He had a sapphire blue visor, and was dressed in shorts, sneakers, and a T-shirt. The camera slung around his neck, with an impressive telephoto lens and numerous buttons and markings, was the only complicated thing he wore. He frowned, watching as Ronny rushed toward the goat, but appeared to have no intention of intervening. "Bobby, make sure that your brother doesn't do anything stupid."

"I don't feel like it," Bobby said, not moving. He was sitting in the front seat beside Mr. Kapasi, studying a picture of the elephant god taped to the glove compartment.

"No need to worry," Mr. Kapasi said. "They are quite tame." Mr. Kapasi was forty-six years old, with receding hair that had gone completely silver, but his butterscotch complexion and his unlined brow, which he treated in spare moments to dabs of lotus-oil balm, made it easy to imagine what he must have looked like at an earlier age. He wore gray trousers and a matching jacket-style shirt, tapered at the waist, with short sleeves and a large pointed collar, made of a thin but durable synthetic material. He had specified both the cut and the fabric to his tailor — it was his preferred uniform for giving tours because it did not get crushed during his long hours behind the wheel. Through the windshield he watched as Ronny circled around the goat, touched it quickly on its side, then trotted back to the car.

"You left India as a child?" Mr. Kapasi asked when Mr. Das had settled once again into the passenger seat.

"Oh, Mina and I were both born in America," Mr. Das announced with an air of sudden confidence. "Born and raised. Our parents live here now, in Assansol. They retired. We visit them every couple years." He turned to watch as the little girl ran toward the car, the wide purple bows of her sundress flopping on her narrow brown shoulders. She was holding to her chest a doll with yellow hair that looked as if it had been chopped, as a punitive measure, with a pair of dull scissors. "This is Tina's first trip to India, isn't it, Tina?"

"I don't have to go to the bathroom anymore," Tina announced.

"Where's Mina?" Mr. Das asked.

Mr. Kapasi found it strange that Mr. Das should refer to his wife by her first name when speaking to the little girl. Tina pointed to where Mrs. Das was purchasing something from one of the shirtless men who worked at the tea stall. Mr. Kapasi heard one of the shirtless men sing a phrase from a popular Hindi love song as Mrs. Das walked back to the car, but she did not appear to understand the words of the song, for she did not express irritation, or embarrassment, or react in any other way to the man's declarations.

He observed her. She wore a red-and-white-checkered skirt that stopped above her knees, slip-on shoes with a square wooden heel, and a close-fitting blouse styled like a man's undershirt. The blouse was decorated at chest-level with a calico appliqué in the shape of a strawberry. She was a short woman, with small hands like paws, her frosty pink fingernails painted to match her lips, and was slightly plump in her figure. Her hair, shorn only a little longer than her husband's, was parted far to one side. She was wearing large dark brown sunglasses with a pinkish tint to them, and carried a big straw bag, almost as big as her torso, shaped like a bowl, with a water bottle poking out of it. She walked slowly, carrying some puffed rice tossed with peanuts and chili peppers in a large packet made from newspapers. Mr. Kapasi turned to Mr. Das.

"Where in America do you live?"

"New Brunswick, New Jersey."

"Next to New York."

"Exactly. I teach middle school there."

"What subject?"

"Science. In fact, every year I take my students on a trip to the Museum of Natural History in New York City. In a way we have a lot in common, you could say, you and I. How long have you been a tour guide, Mr. Kapasi?"

"Five years."

Mrs. Das reached the car. "How long's the trip?" she asked, shutting the door.

"About two and a half hours," Mr. Kapasi replied.

At this Mrs. Das gave an impatient sigh, as if she had been traveling her whole life without pause. She fanned herself with a folded Bombay film magazine written in English.

"I thought that the Sun Temple is only eighteen miles north of Puri," Mr. Das said, tapping on the tour book.

"The roads to Konarak are poor. Actually it is a distance of fifty-two miles," Mr. Kapasi explained.

Mr. Das nodded, readjusting the camera strap where it had begun to chafe the back of his neck.

Before starting the ignition, Mr. Kapasi reached back to make sure the cranklike locks on the inside of each of the back doors were secured. As soon as the car began to move the little girl began to play with the lock on her side, clicking it with some effort forward and backward, but Mrs. Das said nothing to stop her. She sat a bit slouched at one end of the back seat, not offering her puffed rice to anyone. Ronny and Tina sat on either side of her, both snapping bright green gum.

"Look," Bobby said as the car began to gather speed. He pointed with his finger to the tall trees that lined the road. "Look."

"Monkeys!" Ronny shrieked. "Wow!"

They were seated in groups along the branches, with shining black faces, silver bodies, horizontal eyebrows, and crested heads. Their long gray tails dangled like a series of ropes among the leaves. A few scratched themselves with black leathery hands, or swung their feet, staring as the car passed.

"We call them the hanuman," Mr. Kapasi said. "They are quite common in the area."

As soon as he spoke, one of the monkeys leaped into the middle of the road, causing Mr. Kapasi to brake suddenly. Another bounced onto the hood of the car, then sprang away. Mr. Kapasi beeped his horn. The children began to get excited, sucking in their breath and covering their faces partly with their hands. They had never seen monkeys outside of a zoo, Mr. Das explained. He asked Mr. Kapasi to stop the car so that he could take a picture.

While Mr. Das adjusted his telephoto lens, Mrs. Das reached into her straw bag and pulled out a bottle of colorless nail polish, which she proceeded to stroke on the tip of her index finger.

The little girl stuck out a hand. "Mine too. Mommy, do mine too."

"Leave me alone," Mrs. Das said, blowing on her nail and turning her body slightly. "You're making me mess up."

The little girl occupied herself by buttoning and unbuttoning a pinafore on the doll's plastic body.

"All set," Mr. Das said, replacing the lens cap.

The car rattled considerably as it raced along the dusty road, causing them all to pop up from their seats every now and then, but Mrs. Das continued to polish her nails. Mr. Kapasi eased up on the accelerator, hoping to produce a smoother ride. When he reached for the gearshift the boy in front accommodated him by swinging his hairless knees out of the way. Mr. Kapasi noted that this boy was slightly paler than the other children. "Daddy, why is the driver sitting on the wrong side in this car, too?" the boy asked.

"They all do that here, dummy," Ronny said.

"Don't call your brother a dummy," Mr. Das said. He turned to Mr. Kapasi. "In America, you know . . . it confuses them."

"Oh yes, I am well aware," Mr. Kapasi said. As delicately as he could, he shifted gears again, accelerating as they approached a hill in the road. "I see it on *Dallas*, the steering wheels are on the left-hand side."

"What's *Dallas*?" Tina asked, banging her now naked doll on the seat behind Mr. Kapasi.

"It went off the air," Mr. Das explained. "It's a television show."

They were all like siblings, Mr. Kapasi thought as they passed a row of date trees. Mr. and Mrs. Das behaved like an older brother and sister, not parents. It seemed that they were in charge of the children only for the day; it was hard to believe they were regularly responsible for anything other than themselves. Mr. Das tapped on his lens cap, and his tour book, dragging his thumbnail occasionally across the pages so that they made a scraping sound. Mrs. Das continued to polish her nails. She had still not removed her sunglasses. Every now and then Tina renewed her plea that she wanted her nails done, too, and so at one point Mrs. Das flicked a drop of polish on the little girl's finger before depositing the bottle back inside her straw bag.

"Isn't this an air-conditioned car?" she asked, still blowing on her hand. The window on Tina's side was broken and could not be rolled down.

"Quit complaining," Mr. Das said. "It isn't so hot."

"I told you to get a car with air-conditioning," Mrs. Das continued. "Why do you do this, Raj, just to save a few stupid rupees. What are you saving us, fifty cents?"

Their accents sounded just like the ones Mr. Kapasi heard on American television programs, though not like the ones on *Dallas*.

"Doesn't it get tiresome, Mr. Kapasi, showing people the same thing every day?" Mr. Das asked, rolling down his own window all the way. "Hey, do you mind stopping the car. I just want to get a shot of this guy."

Mr. Kapasi pulled over to the side of the road as Mr. Das took a picture of a barefoot man, his head wrapped in a dirty turban, seated on top of a cart of grain sacks pulled by a pair of bullocks. Both the man and the bullocks were emaciated. In the back seat Mrs. Das gazed out another window, at the sky, where nearly transparent clouds passed quickly in front of one another.

"I look forward to it, actually," Mr. Kapasi said as they continued on their way. "The Sun Temple is one of my favorite places. In that way it is a reward for me. I give tours on Fridays and Saturdays only. I have another job during the week."

"Oh? Where?" Mr. Das asked.

"I work in a doctor's office."

"You're a doctor?"

"I am not a doctor. I work with one. As an interpreter."

"What does a doctor need an interpreter for?"

"He has a number of Gujarati patients. My father was Gujarati, but many people do not speak Gujarati in this area, including the doctor. And so the doctor asked me to work in his office, interpreting what the patients say."

"Interesting. I've never heard of anything like that," Mr. Das said.

Mr. Kapasi shrugged. "It is a job like any other."

"But so romantic," Mrs. Das said dreamily, breaking her extended silence. She lifted her pinkish brown sunglasses and arranged them on top of her head like a tiara. For the first time, her eyes met Mr. Kapasi's in the rearview mirror: pale, a bit small, their gaze fixed but drowsy.

Mr. Das craned to look at her. "What's so romantic about it?"

"I don't know. Something." She shrugged, knitting her brows together for an instant. "Would you like a piece of gum, Mr. Kapasi?" she asked brightly. She reached into her straw bag and handed him a small square wrapped in green-and-white-striped paper. As soon as Mr. Kapasi put the gum in his mouth a thick sweet liquid burst onto his tongue.

"Tell us more about your job, Mr. Kapasi," Mrs. Das said.

"What would you like to know, madame?"

"I don't know," she shrugged, munching on some puffed rice and licking the mustard oil from the corners of her mouth. "Tell us a typical situation." She settled back in her seat, her head tilted in a patch of sun, and closed her eyes. "I want to picture what happens."

"Very well. The other day a man came in with a pain in his throat."

"Did he smoke cigarettes?"

"No. It was very curious. He complained that he felt as if there were long pieces of straw stuck in his throat. When I told the doctor he was able to prescribe the proper medication."

"That's so neat."

"Yes," Mr. Kapasi agreed after some hesitation.

"So these patients are totally dependent on you," Mrs. Das said. She spoke slowly, as if she were thinking aloud. "In a way, more dependent on you than the doctor."

"How do you mean? How could it be?"

"Well, for example, you could tell the doctor that the pain felt like a burning, not straw. The patient would never know what you had told the doctor, and the doctor wouldn't know that you had told the wrong thing. It's a big responsibility."

"Yes, a big responsibility you have there, Mr. Kapasi," Mr. Das agreed.

Mr. Kapasi had never thought of his job in such complimentary terms. To him it was a thankless occupation. He found nothing noble in interpreting people's maladies, assiduously translating the symptoms of so many swollen bones, countless cramps of bellies and bowels, spots on people's palms that changed color, shape, or size. The doctor, nearly half his age, had an affinity for bell-bottom trousers and made humorless jokes about the Congress party. Together they worked in a stale little infirmary where Mr. Kapasi's smartly tailored clothes clung to him in the heat, in spite of the blackened blades of a ceiling fan churning over their heads.

The job was a sign of his failings. In his youth he'd been a devoted scholar of foreign languages, the owner of an impressive collection of dictionaries. He had dreamed of being an interpreter for diplomats and dignitaries, resolving conflicts between people and nations, settling disputes of which he alone could understand both sides. He was a self-educated man. In a series of notebooks, in the evenings before his parents settled his marriage, he had listed the common etymologies of words, and at one point in his life he was confident that he could converse, if given the opportunity, in English, French, Russian, Portuguese, and Italian, not to mention Hindi, Bengali, Orissi, and Gujarati. Now only a handful of European phrases remained in his memory, scattered words for things like saucers and chairs. English was the only non-Indian language he spoke fluently anymore. Mr. Kapasi knew it was not a remarkable talent. Sometimes he feared that his children knew better English than he did, just from watching television. Still, it came in handy for the tours.

He had taken the job as an interpreter after his first son, at the age of seven, contracted typhoid — that was how he had first made the acquaintance of the doctor. At the time Mr. Kapasi had been teaching English in a grammar school, and he bartered his skills as an interpreter to pay the increasingly exorbitant medical bills. In the end the boy had died one evening in his mother's arms, his limbs burning with fever, but then there was the funeral to pay for, and the other children who were born soon enough, and the newer, bigger house, and the good schools and tutors, and the fine shoes and the television, and the countless other ways he tried to console his wife and to keep her from crying in her sleep, and so when the doctor offered to pay him twice as much as he earned at the grammar school, he accepted. Mr. Kapasi knew that his wife had little regard for his career as an interpreter. He knew it reminded her of the son she'd lost, and that she resented the other lives he helped, in his own small way, to save. If ever she referred to his position, she used the phrase "doctor's assistant," as if the process of interpretation were equal to taking someone's temperature, or changing a bedpan. She never asked him about the patients who came to the doctor's office, or said that his job was a big responsibility.

For this reason it flattered Mr. Kapasi that Mrs. Das was so intrigued by his job. Unlike his wife, she had reminded him of its intellectual challenges. She had also used the word "romantic." She did not behave in a romantic way toward her husband, and yet she had used the word to describe him. He wondered if Mr. and Mrs. Das were a bad match, just as he and his wife were.

Perhaps they, too, had little in common apart from three children and a decade of their lives. The signs he recognized from his own marriage were there — the bickering, the indifference, the protracted silences. Her sudden interest in him, an interest she did not express in either her husband or her children, was mildly intoxicating. When Mr. Kapasi thought once again about how she had said "romantic," the feeling of intoxication grew.

He began to check his reflection in the rearview mirror as he drove, feeling grateful that he had chosen the gray suit that morning and not the brown one, which tended to sag a little in the knees. From time to time he glanced through the mirror at Mrs. Das. In addition to glancing at her face he glanced at the strawberry between her breasts, and the golden brown hollow in her throat. He decided to tell Mrs. Das about another patient, and another: the young woman who had complained of a sensation of raindrops in her spine, the gentleman whose birthmark had begun to sprout hairs. Mrs. Das listened attentively, stroking her hair with a small plastic brush that resembled an oval bed of nails, asking more questions, for yet another example. The children were quiet, intent on spotting more monkeys in the trees, and Mr. Das was absorbed by his tour book, so it seemed like a private conversation between Mr. Kapasi and Mrs. Das. In this manner the next half hour passed, and when they stopped for lunch at a roadside restaurant that sold fritters and omelette sandwiches, usually something Mr. Kapasi looked forward to on his tours so that he could sit in peace and enjoy some hot tea, he was disappointed. As the Das family settled together under a magenta umbrella fringed with white and orange tassels, and placed their orders with one of the waiters who marched about in tricornered caps, Mr. Kapasi reluctantly headed toward a neighboring table.

"Mr. Kapasi, wait. There's room here," Mrs. Das called out. She gathered Tina onto her lap, insisting that he accompany them. And so, together, they had bottled mango juice and sandwiches and plates of onions and potatoes deep-fried in graham-flour batter. After finishing two omelette sandwiches Mr. Das took more pictures of the group as they ate.

"How much longer?" he asked Mr. Kapasi as he paused to load a new roll of film in the camera.

"About half an hour more."

By now the children had gotten up from the table to look at more monkeys perched in a nearby tree, so there was a considerable space between Mrs. Das and Mr. Kapasi. Mr. Das placed the camera to his face and squeezed one eye shut, his tongue exposed at one corner of his mouth. "This looks funny. Mina, you need to lean in closer to Mr. Kapasi."

She did. He could smell a scent on her skin, like a mixture of whiskey and rosewater. He worried suddenly that she could smell his perspiration, which he knew had collected beneath the synthetic material of his shirt. He polished off his mango juice in one gulp and smoothed his silver hair with his hands. A bit of the juice dripped onto his chin. He wondered if Mrs. Das had noticed.

She had not. "What's your address, Mr. Kapasi?" she inquired, fishing for something inside her straw bag.

"You would like my address?"

"So we can send you copies," she said. "Of the pictures." She handed him a scrap of paper which she had hastily ripped from a page of her film magazine. The blank portion was limited, for the narrow strip was crowded by lines of text and a tiny picture of a hero and heroine embracing under a eucalyptus tree.

The paper curled as Mr. Kapasi wrote his address in clear, careful letters. She would write to him, asking about his days interpreting at the doctor's office, and he would respond eloquently, choosing only the most entertaining anecdotes, ones that would make her laugh out loud as she read them in her house in New Jersey. In time she would reveal the disappointment of her marriage, and he his. In this way their friendship would grow, and flourish. He would possess a picture of the two of them, eating fried onions under a magenta umbrella, which he would keep, he decided, safely tucked between the pages of his Russian grammar. As his mind raced, Mr. Kapasi experienced a mild and pleasant shock. It was similar to a feeling he used to experience long ago when, after months of translating with the aid of a dictionary, he would finally read a passage from a French novel, or an Italian sonnet, and understand the words, one after another, unencumbered by his own efforts. In those moments Mr. Kapasi used to believe that all was right with the world, that all struggles were rewarded, that all of life's mistakes made sense in the end. The promise that he would hear from Mrs. Das now filled him with the same belief.

When he finished writing his address Mr. Kapasi handed her the paper, but as soon as he did so he worried that he had either misspelled his name, or accidentally reversed the numbers of his postal code. He dreaded the possibility of a lost letter, the photograph never reaching him, hovering somewhere in Orissa, close but ultimately unattainable. He thought of asking for the slip of paper again, just to make sure he had written his address accurately, but Mrs. Das had already dropped it into the jumble of her bag.

They reached Konarak at two-thirty. The temple, made of sandstone, was a massive pyramid-like structure in the shape of a chariot. It was dedicated to the great master of life, the sun, which struck three sides of the edifice as it made its journey each day across the sky. Twenty-four giant wheels were carved on the north and south sides of the plinth. The whole thing was drawn by a team of seven horses, speeding as if through the heavens. As they approached, Mr. Kapasi explained that the temple had been built between A.D. 1243 and 1255, with the efforts of twelve hundred artisans, by the great ruler of the Ganga dynasty, King Narasimhadeva the First, to commemorate his victory against the Muslim army.

"It says the temple occupies about a hundred and seventy acres of land," Mr. Das said, reading from his book.

"It's like a desert," Ronny said, his eyes wandering across the sand that stretched on all sides beyond the temple.

"The Chandrabhaga River once flowed one mile north of here. It is dry now," Mr. Kapasi said, turning off the engine.

They got out and walked toward the temple, posing first for pictures by the pair of lions that flanked the steps. Mr. Kapasi led them next to one of the wheels of the chariot, higher than any human being, nine feet in diameter.

"'The wheels are supposed to symbolize the wheel of life,'" Mr. Das read. "'They depict the cycle of creation, preservation, and achievement of realization.' Cool." He turned the page of his book. "'Each wheel is divided into eight thick and thin spokes, dividing the day into eight equal parts. The rims are carved with designs of birds and animals, whereas the medallions in the spokes are carved with women in luxurious poses, largely erotic in nature.'"

What he referred to were the countless friezes of entwined naked bodies, making love in various positions, women clinging to the necks of men, their knees wrapped eternally around their lovers' thighs. In addition to these were assorted scenes from daily life, of hunting and trading, of deer being killed with bows and arrows and marching warriors holding swords in their hands.

It was no longer possible to enter the temple, for it had filled with rubble years ago, but they admired the exterior, as did all the tourists Mr. Kapasi brought there, slowly strolling along each of its sides. Mr. Das trailed behind, taking pictures. The children ran ahead, pointing to figures of naked people, intrigued in particular by the Nagamithunas, the half-human, half-serpentine couples who were said, Mr. Kapasi told them, to live in the deepest waters of the sea. Mr. Kapasi was pleased that they liked the temple, pleased especially that it appealed to Mrs. Das. She stopped every three or four paces, staring silently at the carved lovers, and the processions of elephants, and the topless female musicians beating on two-sided drums.

Though Mr. Kapasi had been to the temple countless times, it occurred to him, as he, too, gazed at the topless women, that he had never seen his own wife fully naked. Even when they had made love she kept the panels of her blouse hooked together, the string of her petticoat knotted around her waist. He had never admired the backs of his wife's legs the way he now admired those of Mrs. Das, walking as if for his benefit alone. He had, of course, seen plenty of bare limbs before, belonging to the American and European ladies who took his tours. But Mrs. Das was different. Unlike the other women, who had an interest only in the temple, and kept their noses buried in a guidebook, or their eyes behind the lens of a camera, Mrs. Das had taken an interest in him.

Mr. Kapasi was anxious to be alone with her, to continue their private conversation, yet he felt nervous to walk at her side. She was lost behind her sunglasses, ignoring her husband's requests that she pose for another picture, walking past her children as if they were strangers. Worried that he might disturb her, Mr. Kapasi walked ahead, to admire, as he always did, the three life-sized bronze avatars of Surya, the sun god, each emerging from its own niche on the temple facade to greet the sun at dawn, noon, and evening. They wore elaborate headdresses, their languid, elongated eyes closed, their bare chests draped with carved chains and amulets. Hibiscus petals, offerings from previous visitors, were strewn at their gray-green feet. The last statue, on the northern wall of the temple, was Mr. Kapasi's favorite. This Surya had a tired expression, weary after a hard day of work, sitting astride a horse with folded legs. Even his horse's eyes were drowsy. Around his body were smaller sculptures of women in pairs, their hips thrust to one side.

"Who's that?" Mrs. Das asked. He was startled to see that she was standing beside him.

"He is the Astachala-Surya," Mr. Kapasi said. "The setting sun."

"So in a couple of hours the sun will set right here?" She slipped a foot out of one of her square-heeled shoes, rubbed her toes on the back of her other leg.

"That is correct."

She raised her sunglasses for a moment, then put them back on again. "Neat."

Mr. Kapasi was not certain exactly what the word suggested, but he had a feeling it was a favorable response. He hoped that Mrs. Das had understood Surya's beauty, his power. Perhaps they would discuss it further in their letters. He would explain things to her, things about India, and she would explain things to him about America. In its own way this correspondence would fulfill his dream, of serving as an interpreter between nations. He looked at her straw bag, delighted that his address lay nestled among its contents. When he pictured her so many thousands of miles away he plummeted, so much so that he had an overwhelming urge to wrap his arms around her, to freeze with her, even for an instant, in an embrace witnessed by his favorite Surya. But Mrs. Das had already started walking.

"When do you return to America?" he asked, trying to sound placid.

"In ten days."

He calculated: A week to settle in, a week to develop the pictures, a few days to compose her letter, two weeks to get to India by air. According to his schedule, allowing room for delays, he would hear from Mrs. Das in approximately six weeks' time.

The family was silent as Mr. Kapasi drove them back, a little past four-thirty, to Hotel Sandy Villa. The children had bought miniature granite versions of the chariot's wheels at a souvenir stand, and they turned them round in their hands. Mr. Das continued to read his book. Mrs. Das untangled Tina's hair with her brush and divided it into two little ponytails.

Mr. Kapasi was beginning to dread the thought of dropping them off. He was not prepared to begin his six-week wait to hear from Mrs. Das. As he stole glances at her in the rearview mirror, wrapping elastic bands around Tina's hair, he wondered how he might make the tour last a little longer. Ordinarily he sped back to Puri using a shortcut, eager to return home, scrub his feet and hands with sandalwood soap, and enjoy the evening newspaper and a cup of tea that his wife would serve him in silence. The thought of that silence, something to which he'd long been resigned, now oppressed him. It was then that he suggested visiting the hills at Udayagiri and Khandagiri, where a number of monastic dwellings were hewn out of the ground, facing one another across a defile. It was some miles away, but well worth seeing, Mr. Kapasi told them.

"Oh yeah, there's something mentioned about it in this book," Mr. Das said. "Built by a Jain king or something."

"Shall we go then?" Mr. Kapasi asked. He paused at a turn in the road. "It's to the left."

Mr. Das turned to look at Mrs. Das. Both of them shrugged.

"Left, left," the children chanted.

Mr. Kapasi turned the wheel, almost delirious with relief. He did not know what he would do or say to Mrs. Das once they arrived at the hills. Perhaps he would tell her what a pleasing smile she had. Perhaps he would compliment her strawberry shirt, which he found irresistibly becoming. Perhaps, when Mr. Das was busy taking a picture, he would take her hand.

He did not have to worry. When they got to the hills, divided by a steep path thick with trees, Mrs. Das refused to get out of the car. All along the path, dozens of monkeys were seated on stones, as well as on the branches of the trees. Their hind legs were stretched out in front and raised to shoulder level, their arms resting on their knees.

"My legs are tired," she said, sinking low in her seat. "I'll stay here."

"Why did you have to wear those stupid shoes?" Mr. Das said. "You won't be in the pictures."

"Pretend I'm there."

"But we could use one of these pictures for our Christmas card this year. We didn't get one of all five of us at the Sun Temple. Mr. Kapasi could take it."

"I'm not coming. Anyway, those monkeys give me the creeps."

"But they're harmless," Mr. Das said. He turned to Mr. Kapasi. "Aren't they?"

"They are more hungry than dangerous," Mr. Kapasi said. "Do not provoke them with food, and they will not bother you."

Mr. Das headed up the defile with the children, the boys at his side, the little girl on his shoulders. Mr. Kapasi watched as they crossed paths with a Japanese man and woman, the only other tourists there, who paused for a final photograph, then stepped into a nearby car and drove away. As the car disappeared out of view some of the monkeys called out, emitting soft whooping sounds, and then walked on their flat black hands and feet up the path. At one point a group of them formed a little ring around Mr. Das and the children. Tina screamed in delight. Ronny ran in circles around his father. Bobby bent down and picked up a fat stick on the ground. When he extended it, one of the monkeys approached him and snatched it, then briefly beat the ground.

"I'll join them," Mr. Kapasi said, unlocking the door on his side. "There is much to explain about the caves."

"No. Stay a minute," Mrs. Das said. She got out of the back seat and slipped in beside Mr. Kapasi. "Raj has his dumb book anyway." Together, through the windshield, Mrs. Das and Mr. Kapasi watched as Bobby and the monkey passed the stick back and forth between them.

"A brave little boy," Mr. Kapasi commented.

"It's not so surprising," Mrs. Das said.

"No?"

"He's not his."

"I beg your pardon?"

"Raj's. He's not Raj's son."

Mr. Kapasi felt a prickle on his skin. He reached into his shirt pocket for the small tin of lotus-oil balm he carried with him at all times, and applied it to three spots on his forehead. He knew that Mrs. Das was watching him, but he did not turn to face her. Instead he watched as the figures of Mr. Das and the children grew smaller, climbing up the steep path, pausing every now and then for a picture, surrounded by a growing number of monkeys.

"Are you surprised?" The way she put it made him choose his words with care.

"It's not the type of thing one assumes," Mr. Kapasi replied slowly. He put the tin of lotus-oil balm back in his pocket.

"No, of course not. And no one knows, of course. No one at all. I've kept it a secret for eight whole years." She looked at Mr. Kapasi, tilting her chin as if to gain a fresh perspective. "But now I've told you."

Mr. Kapasi nodded. He felt suddenly parched, and his forehead was warm and slightly numb from the balm. He considered asking Mrs. Das for a sip of water, then decided against it.

"We met when we were very young," she said. She reached into her straw bag in search of something, then pulled out a packet of puffed rice. "Want some?"

"No, thank you."

She put a fistful in her mouth, sank into the seat a little, and looked away from Mr. Kapasi, out the window on her side of the car. "We married when we were still in college. We were in high school when he proposed. We went to the same college, of course. Back then we couldn't stand the thought of being separated, not for a day, not for a minute. Our parents were best friends who lived in the same town. My entire life I saw him every weekend, either at our house or theirs. We were sent upstairs to play together while our parents joked about our marriage. Imagine! They never caught us at anything, though in a way I think it was all more or less a setup. The things we did those Friday and Saturday nights, while our parents sat downstairs drinking tea . . . I could tell you stories, Mr. Kapasi."

As a result of spending all her time in college with Raj, she continued, she did not make many close friends. There was no one to confide in about him at the end of a difficult day, or to share a passing thought or a worry. Her parents now lived on the other side of the world, but she had never been very close to them, anyway. After marrying so young she was overwhelmed by it all, having a child so quickly, and nursing, and warming up bottles of milk and testing their temperature against her wrist while Raj was at work, dressed in sweaters and corduroy pants, teaching his students about rocks and dinosaurs. Raj never looked cross or harried, or plump as she had become after the first baby.

Always tired, she declined invitations from her one or two college girl-friends, to have lunch or shop in Manhattan. Eventually the friends stopped calling her, so that she was left at home all day with the baby, surrounded by toys that made her trip when she walked or wince when she sat, always cross and tired. Only occasionally did they go out after Ronny was born, and even more rarely did they entertain. Raj didn't mind; he looked forward to coming home from teaching and watching television and bouncing Ronny on his knee. She had been outraged when Raj told her that a Punjabi friend, someone whom she had once met but did not remember, would be staying with them for a week for some job interviews in the New Brunswick area.

Bobby was conceived in the afternoon, on a sofa littered with rubber teething toys, after the friend learned that a London pharmaceutical company had hired him, while Ronny cried to be freed from his playpen. She made no protest when the friend touched the small of her back as she was about to make a pot of coffee, then pulled her against his crisp navy suit. He made love to her swiftly, in silence, with an expertise she had never known, without the meaningful expressions and smiles Raj always insisted on afterward. The next day Raj drove the friend to JFK. He was married now, to a Punjabi girl, and they lived in London still, and every year they exchanged Christmas cards with Raj and Mina, each couple tucking photos of their families into the envelopes. He did not know that he was Bobby's father. He never would.

"I beg your pardon, Mrs. Das, but why have you told me this information?" Mr. Kapasi asked when she had finally finished speaking, and had turned to face him once again.

"For God's sake, stop calling me Mrs. Das. I'm twenty-eight. You probably have children my age."

"Not quite." It disturbed Mr. Kapasi to learn that she thought of him as a parent. The feeling he had had toward her, that had made him check his reflection in the rearview mirror as they drove, evaporated a little.

"I told you because of your talents." She put the packet of puffed rice back into her bag without folding over the top.

"I don't understand," Mr. Kapasi said.

"Don't you see? For eight years I haven't been able to express this to anybody, not to friends, certainly not to Raj. He doesn't even suspect it. He thinks I'm still in love with him. Well, don't you have anything to say?"

"About what?"

"About what I've just told you. About my secret, and about how terrible it makes me feel. I feel terrible looking at my children, and at Raj, always terrible. I have terrible urges, Mr. Kapasi, to throw things away. One day I had the urge to throw everything I own out the window, the television, the children, everything. Don't you think it's unhealthy?"

He was silent.

"Mr. Kapasi, don't you have anything to say? I thought that was your job."

"My job is to give tours, Mrs. Das."

"Not that. Your other job. As an interpreter."

"But we do not face a language barrier. What need is there for an interpreter?"

"That's not what I mean. I would never have told you otherwise. Don't you realize what it means for me to tell you?"

"What does it mean?"

"It means that I'm tired of feeling so terrible all the time. Eight years, Mr. Kapasi, I've been in pain eight years. I was hoping you could help me feel better, say the right thing. Suggest some kind of remedy."

He looked at her, in her red plaid skirt and strawberry T-shirt, a woman not yet thirty, who loved neither her husband nor her children, who had already fallen out of love with life. Her confession depressed him, depressed him all the more when he thought of Mr. Das at the top of the path, Tina clinging to his shoulders, taking pictures of ancient monastic cells cut into the hills to show his students in America, unsuspecting and unaware that one of his sons was not his own. Mr. Kapasi felt insulted that Mrs. Das should ask him to interpret her common, trivial little secret. She did not resemble the patients in the doctor's office, those who came glassy-eyed and desperate, unable to sleep or breathe or urinate with ease, unable, above all, to give words to their pains. Still, Mr. Kapasi believed it was his duty to assist Mrs. Das. Perhaps he ought to tell her to confess the truth to Mr. Das. He would explain that honesty was the best policy. Honesty, surely, would help her feel better, as she'd put it. Perhaps he would offer to preside over the discussion, as a mediator. He decided to begin with the most obvious question, to get to the heart of the matter, and so he asked, "Is it really pain you feel, Mrs. Das, or is it guilt?"

She turned to him and glared, mustard oil thick on her frosty pink lips. She opened her mouth to say something, but as she glared at Mr. Kapasi some certain knowledge seemed to pass before her eyes, and she stopped. It crushed him; he knew at that moment that he was not even important enough to be properly insulted. She opened the car door and began walking up the path, wobbling a little on her square wooden heels, reaching into her straw bag to eat handfuls of puffed rice. It fell through her fingers, leaving a zigzagging trail, causing a monkey to leap down from a tree and devour the little white grains. In search of more, the monkey began to follow Mrs. Das. Others joined him, so that she was soon being followed by about half a dozen of them, their velvety tails dragging behind.

Mr. Kapasi stepped out of the car. He wanted to holler, to alert her in some way, but he worried that if she knew they were behind her, she would grow nervous. Perhaps she would lose her balance. Perhaps they would pull at her bag or her hair. He began to jog up the path, taking a fallen branch in his hand to scare away the monkeys. Mrs. Das continued walking, oblivious, trailing grains of puffed rice. Near the top of the incline, before a group of cells fronted by a row of squat stone pillars, Mr. Das was kneeling on the ground, focusing the lens of his camera. The children stood under the arcade, now hiding, now emerging from view.

"Wait for me," Mrs. Das called out. "I'm coming."

Tina jumped up and down. "Here comes Mommy!"

"Great," Mr. Das said without looking up. "Just in time. We'll get Mr. Kapasi to take a picture of the five of us."

Mr. Kapasi quickened his pace, waving his branch so that the monkeys scampered away, distracted, in another direction.

"Where's Bobby?" Mrs. Das asked when she stopped.

Mr. Das looked up from the camera. "I don't know. Ronny, where's Bobby?"

Ronny shrugged. "I thought he was right here."

"Where is he?" Mrs. Das repeated sharply. "What's wrong with all of you?"

They began calling his name, wandering up and down the path a bit. Because they were calling, they did not initially hear the boy's screams. When they found him, a little farther down the path under a tree, he was surrounded by a group of monkeys, over a dozen of them, pulling at his T-shirt with their long black fingers. The puffed rice Mrs. Das had spilled was scattered at his feet, raked over by the monkeys' hands. The boy was silent, his body frozen, swift tears running down his startled face. His bare legs were dusty and red with welts from where one of the monkeys struck him repeatedly with the stick he had given to it earlier.

"Daddy, the monkey's hurting Bobby," Tina said.

Mr. Das wiped his palms on the front of his shorts. In his nervousness he accidentally pressed the shutter on his camera; the whirring noise of the advancing film excited the monkeys, and the one with the stick began to beat Bobby more intently. "What are we supposed to do? What if they start attacking?"

"Mr. Kapasi," Mrs. Das shrieked, noticing him standing to one side. "Do something, for God's sake, do something!"

Mr. Kapasi took his branch and shooed them away, hissing at the ones that remained, stomping his feet to scare them. The animals retreated slowly, with a measured gait, obedient but unintimidated. Mr. Kapasi gathered Bobby in his arms and brought him back to where his parents and siblings were standing. As he carried him he was tempted to whisper a secret into the boy's ear. But Bobby was stunned, and shivering with fright, his legs bleeding slightly where the stick had broken the skin. When Mr. Kapasi delivered him to his parents, Mr. Das brushed some dirt off the boy's T-shirt and put the visor on him the right way. Mrs. Das reached into her straw bag to find a bandage which she taped over the cut on his knee. Ronny offered his brother a fresh piece of gum. "He's fine. Just a little scared, right, Bobby?" Mr. Das said, patting the top of his head.

"God, let's get out of here," Mrs. Das said. She folded her arms across the strawberry on her chest. "This place gives me the creeps."

"Yeah. Back to the hotel, definitely," Mr. Das agreed.

"Poor Bobby," Mrs. Das said. "Come here a second. Let Mommy fix your hair." Again she reached into her straw bag, this time for her hairbrush, and began to run it around the edges of the translucent visor. When she whipped out the hairbrush, the slip of paper with Mr. Kapasi's address on it fluttered away in the wind. No one but Mr. Kapasi noticed. He watched as it rose, carried higher and higher by the breeze, into the trees where the monkeys now sat, solemnly observing the scene below. Mr. Kapasi observed it too, knowing that this was the picture of the Das family he would preserve forever in his mind.

D. H. Lawrence

David Herbert Lawrence (1885–1930) was born the son of a coal miner in the industrial town of Eastwood, in Nottinghamshire, England. His mother had been a schoolteacher, and she was frustrated by the hard existence of a coal miner's wife. Through her financial sacrifices, Lawrence was able to complete high school; then he studied to become a teacher. In 1909, shortly after he began teaching in South London, he published his first novel, *The White Peacock*, but he was not established as a major literary figure until the publication of *Sons and Lovers* (1913). Much of his fiction, like this novel and the story "Odour of Chrysanthemums," is about characters caught between their unsatisfactory relationships with others and their struggle to break free. Lawrence sought an ideal balance or, as he wrote in the novel *Women in Love* (1920), a "star equilibrium," in which two beings are attracted to each other but never lose their individuality. He felt that "no emotion is supreme, or exclusively worth living for. All emotions go to the achieving of a living relationship between a human being and the other human being or creature or thing he becomes purely related to."

A prolific writer, Lawrence suffered from tuberculosis and spent years wandering in Italy, Australia, Mexico, New Mexico, and southern France, seeking a warm, sunny climate. He also fled to primitive societies to escape the industrialization and commercialism of Western life. A virulent social critic, he was frequently harassed by censorship because his short stories, novels, and poetry were often explicitly sexual and he always challenged conventional moral attitudes. Literature, for Lawrence, had two great functions: providing an emotional experience, and then, if the reader had the courage of his or her own feelings and could live imaginatively, becoming "a mine of practical truth."

Lawrence wrote stories all his life, publishing a first collection, *The Prussian Officer*, in 1914; it was followed by four other collections. In 1961 his stories were compiled in a three-volume paperback edition that has gone through numerous reprintings. The style of the early stories is harshly realistic, but Lawrence's depiction of his characters' emotional situations changed in his later work, where he created fantasies like his chilling story "The Rocking-Horse Winner."

RELATED STORY
John Steinbeck, "The Chrysanthemums," page 1223.

RELATED COMMENTARIES
D. H. Lawrence, "On 'The Fall of the House of Usher' and 'The Cask of Amontillado,'" page 1458; Janice H. Harris, "Levels of Meaning in Lawrence's 'The Rocking-Horse Winner,'" page 1432; Jay Parini, "Lawrence's and Steinbeck's 'Chrysanthemums,'" page 1507.

Odour of Chrysanthemums

1909

I

The small locomotive engine, Number 4, came clanking, stumbling down from Selston with seven full waggons. It appeared round the corner with loud threats of speed, but the colt that it startled from among the gorse, which still flickered indistinctly in the raw afternoon, outdistanced it at a canter. A woman, walking up the railway line to Underwood, drew back into the hedge, held her basket aside, and watched the footplate of the engine advancing. The trucks thumped heavily past, one by one, with slow inevitable movement, as she stood insignificantly trapped between the jolting black waggons and the hedge; then they curved away towards the coppice where the withered oak leaves dropped noiselessly, while the birds, pulling at the scarlet hips beside the track, made off into the dusk that had already crept into the spinney.[1] In the open, the smoke from the engine sank and cleaved to the rough grass. The fields were dreary and forsaken, and in the marshy strip that led to the whimsey, a reedy pit-pond, the fowls had already abandoned their run among the alders, to roost in the tarred fowl-house. The pit-bank loomed up beyond the pond, flames like red sores licking its ashy sides, in the afternoon's stagnant light. Just beyond rose the tapering chimneys and the clumsy black headstocks of Brinsley Colliery. The two wheels were spinning fast up against the sky, and the winding-engine rapped out its little spasms. The miners were being turned up.

The engine whistled as it came into the wide bay of railway lines beside the colliery, where rows of trucks stood in harbour.

Miners, single, trailing and in groups, passed like shadows diverging home. At the edge of the ribbed level of sidings squat a low cottage, three steps down from the cinder track. A large bony vine clutched at the house, as if to claw down the tiled roof. Round the bricked yard grew a few wintry primroses. Beyond, the long garden sloped down to a bush-covered brook course. There were some twiggy apple trees, winter-crack trees, and ragged cabbages. Beside the path hung dishevelled pink chrysanthemums, like pink cloths hung on bushes. A woman came stooping out of the felt-covered fowl-house, half-way down the garden. She closed and padlocked the door, then drew herself erect, having brushed some bits from her white apron.

She was a tall woman of imperious mien, handsome, with definite black eyebrows. Her smooth black hair was parted exactly. For a few moments she stood steadily watching the miners as they passed along the railway: then she turned towards the brook course. Her face was calm and set, her mouth was closed with disillusionment. After a moment she called:

"John!" There was no answer. She waited, and then said distinctly:

"Where are you?"

---

[1] A small wood with undergrowth.

"Here!" replied a child's sulky voice from among the bushes. The woman looked piercingly through the dusk.

"Are you at that brook?" she asked sternly.

For answer the child showed himself before the raspberry-canes that rose like whips. He was a small, sturdy boy of five. He stood quite still, defiantly.

"Oh!" said the mother, conciliated. "I thought you were down at that wet brook — and you remember what I told you — "

The boy did not move or answer.

"Come, come on in," she said more gently, "it's getting dark. There's your grandfather's engine coming down the line!"

The lad advanced slowly, with resentful, taciturn movement. He was dressed in trousers and waistcoat of cloth that was too thick and hard for the size of the garments. They were evidently cut down from a man's clothes.

As they went slowly towards the house he tore at the ragged wisps of chrysanthemums and dropped the petals in handfuls along the path.

"Don't do that — it does look nasty," said his mother. He refrained, and she, suddenly pitiful, broke off a twig with three or four wan flowers and held them against her face. When mother and son reached the yard her hand hesitated, and instead of laying the flower aside, she pushed it in her apron-band. The mother and son stood at the foot of the three steps looking across the bay of lines at the passing home of the miners. The trundle of the small train was imminent. Suddenly the engine loomed past the house and came to a stop opposite the gate.

The engine-driver, a short man with round grey beard, leaned out of the cab high above the woman.

"Have you got a cup of tea?" he said in a cheery, hearty fashion.

It was her father. She went in, saying she would mash. Directly, she returned.

"I didn't come to see you on Sunday," began the little grey-bearded man.

"I didn't expect you," said his daughter.

The engine-driver winced; then, reassuming his cheery, airy manner, he said:

"Oh, have you heard then? Well, and what do you think ——?"

"I think it is soon enough," she replied.

At her brief censure the little man made an impatient gesture, and said coaxingly, yet with dangerous coldness:

"Well, what's a man to do? It's no sort of life for a man of my years, to sit at my own hearth like a stranger. And if I'm going to marry again it may as well be soon as late — what does it matter to anybody?"

The woman did not reply, but turned and went into the house. The man in the engine-cab stood assertive, till she returned with a cup of tea and a piece of bread and butter on a plate. She went up the steps and stood near the footplate of the hissing engine.

"You needn't 'a' brought me bread an' butter," said her father. "But a cup of tea" — he sipped appreciatively — "it's very nice." He sipped for a moment or two, then: "I hear as Walter's got another bout on," he said.

"When hasn't he?" said the woman bitterly.

"I heered tell of him in the 'Lord Nelson' braggin' as he was going to spend that b—— afore he went: half a sovereign that was."

"When?" asked the woman.

"A' Sat'day night — I know that's true."

"Very likely," she laughed bitterly. "He gives me twenty-three shillings."

"Aye, it's a nice thing, when a man can do nothing with his money but make a beast of himself!" said the grey-whiskered man. The woman turned her head away. Her father swallowed the last of his tea and handed her the cup.

"Aye," he sighed, wiping his mouth. "It's a settler, it is —— "

He put his hand on the lever. The little engine strained and groaned, and the train rumbled towards the crossing. The woman again looked across the metals. Darkness was settling over the spaces of the railway and trucks: the miners, in grey sombre groups, were still passing home. The winding-engine pulsed hurriedly, with brief pauses. Elizabeth Bates looked at the dreary flow of men, then she went indoors. Her husband did not come.

The kitchen was small and full of firelight; red coals piled glowing up the chimney mouth. All the life of the room seemed in the white, warm hearth and the steel fender reflecting the red fire. The cloth was laid for tea; cups glinted in the shadows. At the back, where the lowest stairs protruded, into the room, the boy sat struggling with a knife and a piece of whitewood. He was almost hidden in the shadow. It was half-past four. They had but to await the father's coming to begin tea. As the mother watched her son's sullen little struggle with the wood, she saw herself in his silence and pertinacity; she saw the father in her child's indifference to all but himself. She seemed to be occupied by her husband. He had probably gone past his home, slunk past his own door, to drink before he came in, while his dinner spoiled and wasted in waiting. She glanced at the clock, then took the potatoes to strain them in the yard. The garden and fields beyond the brook were closed in uncertain darkness. When she rose with the saucepan, leaving the drain steaming into the night behind her, she saw the yellow lamps were lit along the high road that went up the hill away beyond the space of the railway lines and the field.

Then again she watched the men trooping home, fewer now and fewer.

Indoors the fire was sinking and the room was dark red. The woman put her saucepan on the hob, and set a batter pudding near the mouth of the oven. Then she stood unmoving. Directly, gratefully, came quick young steps to the door. Someone hung on the latch a moment, then a little girl entered and began pulling off her outdoor things, dragging a mass of curls, just ripening from gold to brown, over her eyes with her hat.

Her mother chid her for coming late from school, and said she would have to keep her at home the dark winter days.

"Why, mother, it's hardly a bit dark yet. The lamp's not lighted, and my father's not home."

"No, he isn't. But it's a quarter to five! Did you see anything of him?"

The child became serious. She looked at her mother with large, wistful blue eyes.

"No, mother, I've never seen him. Why? Has he come up an' gone past, to Old Brinsley? He hasn't, mother, 'cos I never saw him."

"He'd watch that," said the mother bitterly, "he'd take care as you didn't see him. But you may depend upon it, he's seated in the 'Prince o' Wales.' He wouldn't be this late."

The girl looked at her mother piteously.

"Let's have our teas, mother, should we?" said she.

The mother called John to table. She opened the door once more and looked out across the darkness of the lines. All was deserted: she could not hear the winding-engines.

"Perhaps," she said to herself, "he's stopped to get some ripping done."

They sat down to tea. John, at the end of the table near the door, was almost lost in the darkness. Their faces were hidden from each other. The girl crouched against the fender slowly moving a thick piece of bread before the fire. The lad, his face a dusky mark on the shadow, sat watching her who was transfigured in the red glow.

"I do think it's beautiful to look in the fire," said the child.

"Do you?" said her mother. "Why?"

"It's so red, and full of little caves — and it feels so nice, and you can fair smell it."

"It'll want mending directly," replied her mother, "and then if your father comes he'll carry on and say there never is a fire when a man comes home sweating from the pit. — A public-house is always warm enough."

There was silence till the boy said complainingly: "Make haste, our Annie."

"Well, I am doing! I can't make the fire do it no faster, can I?"

"She keeps wafflin' it about so's to make 'er slow," grumbled the boy.

"Don't have such an evil imagination, child," replied the mother.

Soon the room was busy in the darkness with the crisp sound of crunching. The mother ate very little. She drank her tea determinedly, and sat thinking. When she rose her anger was evident in the stern unbending of her head. She looked at the pudding in the fender, and broke out:

"It is a scandalous thing as a man can't even come home to his dinner! If it's crozzled up to a cinder I don't see why I should care. Past his very door he goes to get to a public-house, and here I sit with his dinner waiting for him —— "

She went out. As she dropped piece after piece of coal on the red fire, the shadows fell on the walls, till the room was almost in total darkness.

"I canna see," grumbled the invisible John. In spite of herself, the mother laughed.

"You know the way to your mouth," she said. She set the dustpan outside the door. When she came again like a shadow on the hearth, the lad repeated, complaining sulkily:

"I canna see."

"Good gracious!" cried the mother irritably, "you're as bad as your father if it's a bit dusk!"

Nevertheless she took a paper spill from a sheaf on the mantelpiece and proceeded to light the lamp that hung from the ceiling in the middle of the room. As she reached up, her figure displayed itself just rounding with maternity.

"Oh, mother —— !" exclaimed the girl.

"What?" said the woman, suspended in the act of putting the lamp-glass over the flame. The copper reflector shone handsomely on her, as she stood with uplifted arm, turning to face her daughter.

"You've got a flower in your apron!" said the child, in a little rapture at this unusual event.

"Goodness me!" exclaimed the woman, relieved. "One would think the house was afire." She replaced the glass and waited a moment before turning up the wick. A pale shadow was seen floating vaguely on the floor.

"Let me smell!" said the child, still rapturously, coming forward and putting her face to her mother's waist.

"Go along, silly!" said the mother, turning up the lamp. The light revealed their suspense so that the woman felt it almost unbearable. Annie was still bending at her waist. Irritably, the mother took the flowers out from her apron-band.

"Oh, mother — don't take them out!" Annie cried, catching her hand and trying to replace the sprig.

"Such nonsense!" said the mother, turning away. The child put the pale chrysanthemums to her lips, murmuring:

"Don't they smell beautiful!"

Her mother gave a short laugh.

"No," she said, "not to me. It was chrysanthemums when I married him, and chrysanthemums when you were born, and the first time they ever brought him home drunk, he'd got brown chrysanthemums in his button-hole."

She looked at the children. Their eyes and their parted lips were wondering. The mother sat rocking in silence for some time. Then she looked at the clock.

"Twenty minutes to six!" In a tone of fine bitter carelessness she continued: "Eh, he'll not come now till they bring him. There he'll stick! But he needn't come rolling in here in his pit-dirt, for *I* won't wash him. He can lie on the floor —— Eh, what a fool I've been, what a fool! And this is what I came here for, to this dirty hole, rats and all, for him to slink past his very door. Twice last week — he's begun now —— "

She silenced herself, and rose to clear the table.

While for an hour or more the children played, subduedly intent, fertile of imagination, united in fear of the mother's wrath, and in dread of their father's home-coming, Mrs. Bates sat in her rocking-chair making a "singlet" of thick cream-coloured flannel, which gave a dull wounded sound as she tore off the grey edge. She worked at her sewing with energy, listening to the children, and her anger wearied itself, lay down to rest, opening its eyes from time to time and steadily watching, its ears raised to listen. Sometimes even her anger quailed and shrank, and the mother suspended her sewing, tracing the footsteps that thudded along the sleepers outside; she would lift her head sharply to bid the children "hush," but she recovered herself in time, and the footsteps went past the gate, and the children were not flung out of their play-world.

But at last Annie sighed, and gave in. She glanced at her waggon of slippers, and loathed the game. She turned plaintively to her mother.

"Mother!" — but she was inarticulate.

John crept out like a frog from under the sofa. His mother glanced up.

"Yes," she said, "just look at those shirtsleeves!"

The boy held them out to survey them, saying nothing. Then somebody called in a hoarse voice away down the line, and suspense bristled in the room, till two people had gone by outside, talking.

"It is time for bed," said the mother.

"My father hasn't come," wailed Annie plaintively. But her mother was primed with courage.

"Never mind. They'll bring him when he does come — like a log." She meant there would be no scene. "And he may sleep on the floor till he wakes himself. I know he'll not go to work tomorrow after this!"

The children had their hands and faces wiped with a flannel. They were very quiet. When they had put on their nightdresses, they said their prayers, the boy mumbling. The mother looked down at them, at the brown silken bush of intertwining curls in the nape of the girl's neck, at the little black head of the lad, and her heart burst with anger at their father who caused all three such distress. The children hid their faces in her skirts for comfort.

When Mrs. Bates came down, the room was strangely empty, with a tension of expectancy. She took up her sewing and stitched for some time without raising her head. Meantime her anger was tinged with fear.

II

The clock struck eight and she rose suddenly, dropping her sewing on her chair. She went to the stairfoot door, opened it, listening. Then she went out, locking the door behind her.

Something scuffled in the yard, and she started, though she knew it was only the rats with which the place was overrun. The night was very dark. In the great bay of railway lines, bulked with trucks, there was no trace of light, only away back she could see a few yellow lamps at the pit-top, and the red smear of the burning pit-bank on the night. She hurried along the edge of the track, then, crossing the converging lines, came to the stile by the white gates, whence she emerged on the road. Then the fear which had led her shrank. People were walking up to New Brinsley; she saw the lights in the houses; twenty yards further on were the broad windows of the "Prince of Wales," very warm and bright, and the loud voices of men could be heard distinctly. What a fool she had been to imagine that anything had happened to him! He was merely drinking over there at the "Prince of Wales." She faltered. She had never yet been to fetch him, and she never would go. So she continued her walk towards the long straggling line of houses, standing blank on the highway. She entered a passage between the dwellings.

"Mr. Rigley? — Yes! Did you want him? No, he's not in at this minute."

The raw-boned woman leaned forward from her dark scullery and peered at the other, upon whom fell a dim light through the blind of the kitchen window.

"Is it Mrs. Bates?" she asked in a tone tinged with respect.

"Yes. I wondered if your Master was at home. Mine hasn't come yet."

" 'Asn't 'e! Oh, Jack's been 'ome an' 'ad 'is dinner an' gone out. 'E's just gone for 'alf an hour afore bedtime. Did you call at the 'Prince of Wales'?"

"No——"

"No, you didn't like——! It's not very nice." The other woman was indulgent. There was an awkward pause. "Jack never said nothink about—about your Mester," she said.

"No!—I expect he's stuck in there!"

Elizabeth Bates said this bitterly, and with recklessness. She knew that the woman across the yard was standing at her door listening, but she did not care. As she turned:

"Stop a minute! I'll just go an' ask Jack if 'e knows anythink," said Mrs. Rigley.

"Oh, no—I wouldn't like to put——!"

"Yes, I will, if you'll just step inside an' see as th' childer doesn't come downstairs and set theirselves afire."

Elizabeth Bates, murmuring a remonstrance, stepped inside. The other woman apologized for the state of the room.

The kitchen needed apology. There were little frocks and trousers and childish undergarments on the squab and on the floor, and a litter of playthings everywhere. On the black American cloth of the table were pieces of bread and cake, crusts, slops, and a teapot with cold tea.

"Eh, ours is just as bad," said Elizabeth Bates, looking at the woman, not at the house. Mrs. Rigley put a shawl over her head and hurried out, saying:

"I shanna be a minute."

The other sat, noting with faint disapproval the general untidiness of the room. Then she fell to counting the shoes of various sizes scattered over the floor. There were twelve. She sighed and said to herself, "No wonder!"—glancing at the litter. There came the scratching of two pairs of feet on the yard, and the Rigleys entered. Elizabeth Bates rose. Rigley was a big man, with very large bones. His head looked particularly bony. Across his temple was a blue scar, caused by a wound got in the pit, a wound in which the coal-dust remained blue like tattooing.

" 'Asna 'e come whoam yit?" asked the man, without any form of greeting, but with deference and sympathy. "I couldna say wheer he is—'e's non ower theer!"—he jerked his head to signify the "Prince of Wales."

" 'E's 'appen gone up to th' 'Yew,' " said Mrs. Rigley.

There was another pause. Rigley had evidently something to get off his mind:

"Ah left 'im finishin' a stint," he began. "Loose-all 'ad bin gone about ten minutes when we com'n away, an' I shouted, 'Are ter comin', Walt?' an' 'e said, 'Go on, Ah shanna be but a'ef a minnit,' so we com'n ter th' bottom, me an' Bowers, thinkin' as 'e wor just behint, an' 'ud come up i' th' next bantle——"

He stood perplexed, as if answering a charge of deserting his mate. Elizabeth Bates, now again certain of disaster, hastened to reassure him:

"I expect 'e's gone up to th' 'Yew Tree,' as you say. It's not the first time. I've fretted myself into a fever before now. He'll come home when they carry him."

"Ay, isn't it too bad!" deplored the other woman.

"I'll just step up to Dick's an' see if 'e *is* theer," offered the man, afraid of appearing alarmed, afraid of taking liberties.

"Oh, I wouldn't think of bothering you that far," said Elizabeth Bates, with emphasis, but he knew she was glad of his offer.

As they stumbled up the entry, Elizabeth Bates heard Rigley's wife run across the yard and open her neighbour's door. At this, suddenly all the blood in her body seemed to switch away from her heart.

"Mind!" warned Rigley. "Ah've said many a time as Ah'd fill up them ruts in this entry, sumb'dy 'll be breakin' their legs yit."

She recovered herself and walked quickly along with the miner.

"I don't like leaving the children in bed, and nobody in the house," she said.

"No, you dunna!" he replied courteously. They were soon at the gate of the cottage.

"Well, I shanna be many minnits. Dunna you be frettin' now, 'e'll be all right," said the butty.[2]

"Thank you very much, Mr. Rigley," she replied.

"You're welcome!" he stammered, moving away. "I shanna be many minnits."

The house was quiet. Elizabeth Bates took off her hat and shawl, and rolled back the rug. When she had finished, she sat down. It was a few minutes past nine. She was startled by the rapid chuff of the winding-engine at the pit, and the sharp whirr of the brakes on the rope as it descended. Again she felt the painful sweep of her blood, and she put her hand to her side, saying aloud, "Good gracious! — it's only the nine o'clock deputy going down," rebuking herself.

She sat still, listening. Half an hour of this, and she was wearied out.

"What am I working myself up like this for?" she said pitiably to herself, "I s'll only be doing myself some damage."

She took out her sewing again.

At a quarter to ten there were footsteps. One person! She watched for the door to open. It was an elderly woman, in a black bonnet and a black woollen shawl — his mother. She was about sixty years old, pale, with blue eyes, and her face all wrinkled and lamentable. She shut the door and turned to her daughter-in-law peevishly.

"Eh, Lizzie, whatever shall we do, whatever shall we do!" she cried.

Elizabeth drew back a little, sharply.

"What is it, mother?" she said.

The elder woman seated herself on the sofa.

"I don't know, child, I can't tell you!" — she shook her head slowly. Elizabeth sat watching her, anxious and vexed.

_____

[2]A fellow workman in a colliery.

"I don't know," replied the grandmother, sighing very deeply. "There's no end to my troubles, there isn't. The things I've gone through, I'm sure it's enough —— !" She wept without wiping her eyes, the tears running.

"But, mother," interrupted Elizabeth, "what do you mean? What is it?"

The grandmother slowly wiped her eyes. The fountains of her tears were stopped by Elizabeth's directness. She wiped her eyes slowly.

"Poor child! Eh, you poor thing!" she moaned. "I don't know what we're going to do, I don't — and you as you are — it's a thing, it is indeed!"

Elizabeth waited.

"Is he dead?" she asked, and at the words her heart swung violently, though she felt a slight flush of shame at the ultimate extravagance of the question. Her words sufficiently frightened the old lady, almost brought her to herself.

"Don't say so, Elizabeth! We'll hope it's not as bad as that; no, may the Lord spare us that, Elizabeth. Jack Rigley came just as I was sittin' down to a glass afore going to bed, an' 'e said, ' 'Appen you'll go down th' line, Mrs. Bates. Walt's had an accident. 'Appen you'll go an' sit wi' 'er till we can get him home.' I hadn't time to ask him a word afore he was gone. An' I put my bonnet on an' come straight down, Lizzie. I thought to myself, 'Eh, that poor blessed child, if anybody should come an' tell her of a sudden, there's no knowin' what'll 'appen to 'er.' You mustn't let it upset you, Lizzie — or you know what to expect. How long is it, six months — or is it five, Lizzie? Ay!" — the old woman shook her head — "time slips on, it slips on! Ay!"

Elizabeth's thoughts were busy elsewhere. If he was killed — would she be able to manage on the little pension and what she could earn? — she counted up rapidly. If he was hurt — they wouldn't take him to the hospital — how tiresome he would be to nurse! — but perhaps she'd be able to get him away from the drink and his hateful ways. She would — while he was ill. The tears offered to come to her eyes at the picture. But what sentimental luxury was this she was beginning? — She turned to consider the children. At any rate she was absolutely necessary for them. They were her business.

"Ay!" repeated the old woman, "it seems but a week or two since he brought me his first wages. Ay — he was a good lad, Elizabeth, he was, in his way. I don't know why he got to be such a trouble, I don't. He was a happy lad at home, only full of spirits. But there's no mistake he's been a handful of trouble, he has! I hope the Lord'll spare him to mend his ways. I hope so, I hope so. You've had a sight o' trouble with him, Elizabeth, you have indeed. But he was a jolly enough lad wi' me, he was, I can assure you. I don't know how it is. . . ."

The old woman continued to muse aloud, a monotonous irritating sound, while Elizabeth thought concentratedly, startled once, when she heard the winding-engine chuff quickly, and the brakes skirr with a shriek. Then she heard the engine more slowly, and the brakes made no sound. The old woman did not notice. Elizabeth waited in suspense. The mother-in-law talked, with lapses into silence.

"But he wasn't your son, Lizzie, an' it makes a difference. Whatever he was, I remember him when he was little, an' I learned to understand him and to make allowances. You've got to make allowances for them —"

It was half-past ten, and the old woman was saying: "But it's trouble from beginning to end; you're never too old for trouble, never too old for that —— " when the gate banged back, and there were heavy feet on the steps.

"I'll go, Lizzie, let me go," cried the old woman, rising. But Elizabeth was at the door. It was a man in pit-clothes.

"They're bringin' 'im, Missis," he said. Elizabeth's heart halted a moment. Then it surged on again, almost suffocating her.

"Is he — is it bad?" she asked.

The man turned away, looking at the darkness:

"The doctor says 'e'd been dead hours. 'E saw 'im i' th' lamp-cabin."

The old woman, who stood just behind Elizabeth, dropped into a chair, and folded her hands, crying: "Oh, my boy, my boy!"

"Hush!" said Elizabeth, with a sharp twitch of a frown. "Be still, mother, don't waken th' children: I wouldn't have them down for anything!"

The old woman moaned softly, rocking herself. The man was drawing away. Elizabeth took a step forward.

"How was it?" she asked.

"Well, I couldn't say for sure," the man replied, very ill at ease. "'E wor finishin' a stint an' th' butties 'ad gone, an' a lot o' stuff come down atop 'n 'im."

"And crushed him?" cried the widow, with a shudder.

"No," said the man, "it fell at th' back of 'im. 'E wor under th' face, an' it niver touched 'im. It shut 'im in. It seems 'e wor smothered."

Elizabeth shrank back. She heard the old woman behind her cry:

"What? — what did 'e say it was?"

The man replied, more loudly: "'E wor smothered!"

Then the old woman wailed aloud, and this relieved Elizabeth.

"Oh, mother," she said, putting her hand on the old woman, "don't waken th' children, don't waken th' children."

She wept a little, unknowing, while the old mother rocked herself and moaned. Elizabeth remembered that they were bringing him home, and she must be ready. "They'll lay him in the parlour," she said to herself, standing a moment pale and perplexed.

Then she lighted a candle and went into the tiny room. The air was cold and damp, but she could not make a fire, there was no fireplace. She set down the candle and looked round. The candlelight glittered on the lustre-glasses, on the two vases that held some of the pink chrysanthemums, and on the dark mahogany. There was a cold, deathly smell of chrysanthemums in the room. Elizabeth stood looking at the flowers. She turned away, and calculated whether there would be room to lay him on the floor, between the couch and the chiffonier. She pushed the chairs aside. There would be room to lay him down and to step round him. Then she fetched the old red tablecloth, and another old cloth, spreading them down to save her bit of carpet. She shivered on leaving the parlour; so, from the dresser-drawer she took a clean shirt and put it at the fire to air. All the time her mother-in-law was rocking herself in the chair and moaning.

"You'll have to move from there, mother," said Elizabeth. "They'll be bringing him in. Come in the rocker."

The old mother rose mechanically, and seated herself by the fire, continuing to lament. Elizabeth went into the pantry for another candle, and there, in the little penthouse under the naked tiles, she heard them coming. She stood still in the pantry doorway, listening. She heard them pass the end of the house, and come awkwardly down the three steps, a jumble of shuffling footsteps and muttering voices. The old woman was silent. The men were in the yard.

Then Elizabeth heard Matthews, the manager of the pit, say: "You go in first, Jim. Mind!"

The door came open, and the two women saw a collier backing into the room, holding one end of a stretcher, on which they could see the nailed pit-boots of the dead man. The two carriers halted, the man at the head stooping to the lintel of the door.

"Wheer will you have him?" asked the manager, a short, white-bearded man.

Elizabeth roused herself and came from the pantry carrying the unlighted candle.

"In the parlour," she said.

"In there, Jim!" pointed the manager, and the carriers backed round into the tiny room. The coat with which they had covered the body fell off as they awkwardly turned through the two doorways, and the women saw their man, naked to the waist, lying stripped for work. The old woman began to moan in a low voice of horror.

"Lay th' stretcher at th' side," snapped the manager, "an' put 'im on th' cloths. Mind now, mind! Look you now ——!"

One of the men had knocked off a vase of chrysanthemums. He stared awkwardly, then they set down the stretcher. Elizabeth did not look at her husband. As soon as she could get in the room, she went and picked up the broken vase and the flowers.

"Wait a minute!" she said.

The three men waited in silence while she mopped up the water with a duster.

"Eh, what a job, what a job, to be sure!" the manager was saying, rubbing his brow with trouble and perplexity. "Never knew such a thing in my life, never! He'd no business to ha' been left. I never knew such a thing in my life! Fell over him clean as a whistle, an' shut him in. Not four foot of space, there wasn't — yet it scarce bruised him."

He looked down at the dead man, lying prone, half naked, all grimed with coal-dust.

" 'Sphyxiated,' the doctor said. It *is* the most terrible job I've ever known. Seems as if it was done o' purpose. Clean over him, an' shut 'im in, like a mouse-trap" — he made a sharp, descending gesture with his hand.

The colliers standing by jerked aside their heads in hopeless comment.

The horror of the thing bristled upon them all.

Then they heard the girl's voice upstairs calling shrilly: "Mother, mother — who is it? Mother, who is it?"

Elizabeth hurried to the foot of the stairs and opened the door:

"Go to sleep!" she commanded sharply. "What are you shouting about? Go to sleep at once — there's nothing —— "

Then she began to mount the stairs. They could hear her on the boards, and on the plaster floor of the little bedroom. They could hear her distinctly:

"What's the matter now? — what's the matter with you, silly thing?" — her voice was much agitated, with an unreal gentleness.

"I thought it was some men come," said the plaintive voice of the child. "Has he come?"

"Yes, they've brought him. There's nothing to make a fuss about. Go to sleep now, like a good child."

They could hear her voice in the bedroom, they waited whilst she covered the children under the bedclothes.

"Is he drunk?" asked the girl, timidly, faintly.

"No! No — he's not! He — he's asleep."

"Is he asleep downstairs?"

"Yes — and don't make a noise."

There was silence for a moment, then the men heard the frightened child again:

"What's that noise?"

"It's nothing, I tell you, what are you bothering for?"

The noise was the grandmother moaning. She was oblivious of everything, sitting on her chair rocking and moaning. The manager put his hand on her arm and bade her "Sh — sh!!"

The old woman opened her eyes and looked at him. She was shocked by this interruption, and seemed to wonder.

"What time is it?" — the plaintive thin voice of the child, sinking back unhappily into sleep, asked this last question.

"Ten o'clock," answered the mother more softly. Then she must have bent down and kissed the children.

Matthews beckoned to the men to come away. They put on their caps and took up the stretcher. Stepping over the body, they tiptoed out of the house. None of them spoke till they were far from the wakeful children.

When Elizabeth came down she found her mother alone on the parlour floor, leaning over the dead man, the tears dropping on him.

"We must lay him out," the wife said. She put on the kettle, then returning knelt at the feet, and began to unfasten the knotted leather laces. The room was clammy and dim with only one candle, so that she had to bend her face almost to the floor. At last she got off the heavy boots and put them away.

"You must help me now," she whispered to the old woman. Together they stripped the man.

When they arose, saw him lying in the naive dignity of death, the women stood arrested in fear and respect. For a few moments they remained still, looking down, the old mother whimpering. Elizabeth felt countermanded. She saw him, how utterly inviolable he lay in himself. She had nothing to do with him. She could not accept it. Stooping, she laid her hand on him, in claim. He was still warm, for the mine was hot where he had died. His mother had his face between her hands, and was murmuring incoherently. The old tears fell in succession as drops from wet leaves; the mother was not weeping, merely her tears flowed. Elizabeth embraced the body of her husband, with cheek and lips. She seemed to be listening, inquiring, trying to get some connection. But she could not. She was driven away. He was impregnable.

She rose, went into the kitchen, where she poured warm water into a bowl, brought soap and flannel and a soft towel.

"I must wash him," she said.

Then the old mother rose stiffly, and watched Elizabeth as she carefully washed his face, carefully brushing the big blonde moustache from his mouth with the flannel. She was afraid with a bottomless fear, so she ministered to him. The old woman, jealous, said:

"Let me wipe him!" — and she knelt on the other side drying slowly as Elizabeth washed, her big black bonnet sometimes brushing the dark head of her daughter. They worked thus in silence for a long time. They never forgot it was death, and the touch of the man's dead body gave them strange emotions, different in each of the women; a great dread possessed them both, the mother felt the lie was given to her womb, she was denied; the wife felt the utter isolation of the human soul, the child within her was a weight apart from her.

At last it was finished. He was a man of handsome body, and his face showed no traces of drink. He was blonde, full-fleshed, with fine limbs. But he was dead.

"Bless him," whispered his mother, looking always at his face, and speaking out of sheer terror. "Dear lad — bless him!" She spoke in a faint, sibilant ecstasy of fear and mother love.

Elizabeth sank down again to the floor, and put her face against his neck, and trembled and shuddered. But she had to draw away again. He was dead, and her living flesh had no place against his. A great dread and weariness held her: she was so unavailing. Her life was gone like this.

"White as milk he is, clear as a twelve-month baby, bless him, the darling!" the old mother murmured to herself. "Not a mark on him, clear and clean and white, beautiful as ever a child was made," she murmured with pride. Elizabeth kept her face hidden.

"He went peaceful, Lizzie — peaceful as sleep. Isn't he beautiful, the lamb? Ay — he must ha' made his peace, Lizzie. 'Appen he made it all right, Lizzie, shut in there. He'd have time. He wouldn't look like this if he hadn't made his peace. The lamb, the dear lamb. Eh, but he had a hearty laugh. I loved to hear it. He had the heartiest laugh, Lizzie, as a lad —— "

Elizabeth looked up. The man's mouth was fallen back, slightly open under the cover of the moustache. The eyes, half shut, did not show glazed in the obscurity. Life with its smoky burning gone from him, had left him apart and utterly alien to her. And she knew what a stranger he was to her. In her womb was ice of fear, because of this separate stranger with whom she had been living as one flesh. Was this what it all meant — utter, intact separateness, obscured by heat of living? In dread she turned her face away. The fact was too deadly. There had been nothing between them, and yet they had come together, exchanging their nakedness repeatedly. Each time he had taken her, they had been two isolated beings, far apart as now. He was no more responsible than she. The child was like ice in her womb. For as she looked at the dead man, her mind, cold and detached, said clearly: "Who am I? What have I been doing? I have been fighting a husband who did not exist. *He* existed all the time. What wrong have I done? What was that I have been living with? There lies the reality, this man." — And her soul died in her for fear: she knew she had never seen him, he had never seen her, they had met in the dark and had fought in the dark, not knowing whom they met nor whom they fought. And now she saw, and turned silent in seeing. For she had been wrong. She had said he was something he was not; she had felt familiar with him. Whereas he was apart all the while, living as she never lived, feeling as she never felt.

In fear and shame she looked at his naked body, that she had known falsely. And he was the father of her children. Her soul was torn from her body and stood apart. She looked at his naked body and was ashamed, as if she had denied it. After all, it was itself. It seemed awful to her. She looked at his face, and she turned her own face to the wall. For his look was other than hers, his way was not her way. She had denied him what he was — she saw it now. She had refused him as himself. — And this had been her life, and his life. — She was grateful to death, which restored the truth. And she knew she was not dead.

And all the while her heart was bursting with grief and pity for him. What had he suffered? What stretch of horror for this helpless man! She was rigid with agony. She had not been able to help him. He had been cruelly injured, this naked man, this other being, and she could make no reparation. There were the children — but the children belonged to life. This dead man had nothing to do with them. He and she were only channels through which life had flowed to issue in the children. She was a mother — but how awful she knew it now to have been a wife. And he, dead now, how awful he must have felt it to be a husband. She felt that in the next world he would be a stranger to her. If they met there, in the beyond, they would only be ashamed of what had been before. The children had come, for some mysterious reason, out of both of them. But the children did not unite them. Now he was dead, she knew how eternally he was apart from her, how eternally he had nothing more to do with her. She saw this episode of her life closed. They had denied each other in life. Now he had withdrawn. An anguish came over her. It was finished then: it had become hopeless between them long before he died. Yet he had been her husband. But how little!

"Have you got his shirt, 'Lizabeth?"

Elizabeth turned without answering, though she strove to weep and behave as her mother-in-law expected. But she could not, she was silenced. She went into the kitchen and returned with the garment.

"It is aired," she said, grasping the cotton shirt here and there to try. She was almost ashamed to handle him; what right had she or anyone to lay hands on him; but her touch was humble on his body. It was hard work to clothe him. He was so heavy and inert. A terrible dread gripped her all the while: that he could be so heavy and utterly inert, unresponsive, apart. The horror of the distance between them was almost too much for her — it was so infinite a gap she must look across.

At last it was finished. They covered him with a sheet and left him lying, with his face bound. And she fastened the door of the little parlour, lest the children should see what was lying there. Then, with peace sunk heavy on her heart, she went about making tidy the kitchen. She knew she submitted to life, which was her immediate master. But from death, her ultimate master, she winced with fear and shame.

The Rocking-Horse Winner

1926

THERE WAS A WOMAN who was beautiful, who started with all the advantages, yet she had no luck. She married for love, and the love turned to dust. She had bonny children, yet she felt they had been thrust upon her, and she could not love them. They looked at her coldly, as if they were finding fault with her. And hurriedly she felt she must cover up some fault in herself. Yet what it was that she must cover up she never knew. Nevertheless, when her children were present, she always felt the center of her heart go hard. This troubled her, and in her manner she was all the more gentle and anxious for her children, as if she loved them very much. Only she herself knew that at the center of her heart was a hard little place that could not feel love, no, not for anybody. Everybody else said of her: "She is such a good mother. She adores her children." Only she herself, and her children themselves, knew it was not so. They read it in each other's eyes.

There were a boy and two little girls. They lived in a pleasant house, with a garden, and they had discreet servants, and felt themselves superior to anyone in the neighborhood.

Although they lived in style, they felt always an anxiety in the house. There was never enough money. The mother had a small income, and the father had a small income, but not nearly enough for the social position which they had to keep up. The father went into town to some office. But though he had good prospects, these prospects never materialized. There was always the grinding sense of the shortage of money, though the style was always kept up.

At last the mother said: "I will see if *I* can't make something." But she did not know where to begin. She racked her brains, and tried this thing and the other, but could not find anything successful. The failure made deep lines come into her face. Her children were growing up, they would have to go to school. There must be more money, there must be more money. The father, who was always very handsome and expensive in his tastes, seemed as if he never *would* be able to do anything worth doing. And the mother, who had a great belief in herself, did not succeed any better, and her tastes were just as expensive.

And so the house came to be haunted by the unspoken phrase: *There must be more money! There must be more money!* The children could hear it all the time though nobody said it aloud. They heard it at Christmas, when the expensive and splendid toys filled the nursery. Behind the shining modern rocking horse, behind the smart doll's house, a voice would start whispering: "There *must* be more money! There *must* be more money!" And the children would stop playing, to listen for a moment. They would look into each other's eyes, to see if they had all heard. And each one saw in the eyes of the other two that they too had heard. "There *must* be more money! There *must* be more money!"

It came whispering from the springs of the still-swaying rocking horse, and even the horse, bending his wooden, champing head, heard it. The big doll, sitting so pink and smirking in her new pram, could hear it quite plainly, and seemed to be smirking all the more self-consciously because of it. The foolish puppy, too, that took the place of the teddy bear, he was looking so extraordinarily foolish for no other reason but that he heard the secret whisper all over the house: "There *must* be more money!"

Yet nobody ever said it aloud. The whisper was everywhere, and therefore no one spoke it. Just as no one ever says: "We are breathing!" in spite of the fact that breath is coming and going all the time.

"Mother," said the boy Paul one day, "why don't we keep a car of our own? Why do we always use Uncle's, or else a taxi?"

"Because we're the poor members of the family," said the mother.

"But why *are* we, Mother?"

"Well — I suppose," she said slowly and bitterly, "it's because your father has no luck."

The boy was silent for some time.

"Is luck money, Mother?" he asked rather timidly.

"No, Paul. Not quite. It's what causes you to have money."

"Oh!" said Paul vaguely. "I thought when Uncle Oscar said *filthy lucker*, it meant money."

"*Filthy lucre* does mean money," said the mother. "But it's lucre, not luck."

"Oh!" said the boy. "Then what *is* luck, Mother?"

"It's what causes you to have money. If you're lucky you have money. That's why it's better to be born lucky than rich. If you're rich, you may lose your money. But if you're lucky, you will always get more money."

"Oh! Will you? And is Father not lucky?"

"Very unlucky, I should say," she said bitterly.

The boy watched her with unsure eyes.

"Why?" he asked.

"I don't know. Nobody ever knows why one person is lucky and another unlucky."

"Don't they? Nobody at all? Does *nobody* know?"

"Perhaps God. But He never tells."

"He ought to, then. And aren't you lucky either, Mother?"

"I can't be, if I married an unlucky husband."

"But by yourself, aren't you?"

"I used to think I was, before I married. Now I think I am very unlucky indeed."

"Why?"

"Well — never mind! Perhaps I'm not really," she said.

The child looked at her, to see if she meant it. But he saw, by the lines of her mouth, that she was only trying to hide something from him.

"Well, anyhow," he said stoutly, "I'm a lucky person."

"Why?" said his mother, with a sudden laugh.

He stared at her. He didn't even know why he had said it.

"God told me," he asserted, brazening it out.

"I hope He did, dear!" she said, again with a laugh, but rather bitter.

"He did, Mother!"

"Excellent!" said the mother.

The boy saw she did not believe him; or, rather, that she paid no attention to his assertion. This angered him somewhat, and made him want to compel her attention.

He went off by himself, vaguely, in a childish way, seeking for the clue to "luck." Absorbed, taking no heed of other people, he went about with a sort of stealth, seeking inwardly for luck. He wanted luck, he wanted it, he wanted it. When the two girls were playing dolls in the nursery, he would sit on his big rocking horse, charging madly into space, with a frenzy that made the little girls peer at him uneasily. Wildly the horse careered, the waving dark hair of the boy tossed, his eyes had a strange glare in them. The little girls dared not speak to him.

When he had ridden to the end of his mad little journey, he climbed down and stood in front of his rocking horse, staring fixedly into its lowered face. Its red mouth was slightly open, its big eye was wide and glassy-bright.

Now! he could silently command the snorting steed. Now, take me to where there is luck! Now take me!

And he would slash the horse on the neck with the little whip he had asked Uncle Oscar for. He *knew* the horse could take him to where there was luck, if only he forced it. So he would mount again, and start on his furious ride, hoping at last to get there. He knew he could get there.

"You'll break your horse, Paul!" said the nurse.

"He's always riding like that! I wish he'd leave off!" said his elder sister Joan.

But he only glared down on them in silence. Nurse gave him up. She could make nothing of him. Anyhow he was growing beyond her.

One day his mother and his uncle Oscar came in when he was on one of his furious rides. He did not speak to them.

"Hallo, you young jockey! Riding a winner?" said his uncle.

"Aren't you growing too big for a rocking horse? You're not a very little boy any longer, you know," said his mother.

But Paul only gave a blue glare from his big, rather close-set eyes. He would speak to nobody when he was in full tilt. His mother watched him with an anxious expression on her face.

At last he suddenly stopped forcing his horse into the mechanical gallop, and slid down.

"Well, I got there!" he announced fiercely, his blue eyes still flaring, and his sturdy long legs straddling apart.

"Where did you get to?" asked his mother.

"Where I wanted to go," he flared back at her.

"That's right, son!" said Uncle Oscar. "Don't you stop till you get there. What's the horse's name?"

"He doesn't have a name," said the boy.

"Gets on without all right?" asked the uncle.

"Well, he has different names. He was called Sansovino last week."

"Sansovino, eh? Won the Ascot. How did you know his name?"

"He always talks about horse races with Bassett," said Joan.

The uncle was delighted to find that his small nephew was posted with all the racing news. Bassett, the young gardener, who had been wounded in the left foot in the war and had got his present job through Oscar Cresswell, whose batman he had been, was a perfect blade of the "turf." He lived in the racing events, and the small boy lived with him.

Oscar Cresswell got it all from Bassett.

"Master Paul comes and asks me, so I can't do more than tell him, sir," said Bassett, his face terribly serious, as if he were speaking of religious matters.

"And does he ever put anything on a horse he fancies?"

"Well—I don't want to give him away—he's a young sport, a fine sport, sir. Would you mind asking him himself? He sort of takes a pleasure in it, and perhaps he'd feel I was giving him away, sir, if you don't mind."

Bassett was serious as a church.

The uncle went back to his nephew and took him off for a ride in the car.

"Say, Paul, old man, do you ever put anything on a horse?" the uncle asked.

The boy watched the handsome man closely.

"Why, do you think I oughtn't to?" he parried.

"Not a bit of it! I thought perhaps you might give me a tip for the Lincoln."

The car sped on into the country, going down to Uncle Oscar's place in Hampshire.

"Honor bright?" said the nephew.

"Honor bright, son!" said the uncle.

"Well, then, Daffodil."

"Daffodil! I doubt it, sonny. What about Mirza?"

"I only know the winner," said the boy. "That's Daffodil."

"Daffodil, eh?"

There was a pause. Daffodil was an obscure horse comparatively.

"Uncle!"

"Yes, son?"

"You won't let it go any further, will you? I promised Bassett."

"Bassett be damned, old man! What's he got to do with it?"

"We're partners. We've been partners from the first. Uncle, he lent me my first five shillings, which I lost. I promised him, honor bright, it was only between me and him; only you gave me that ten-shilling note I started winning with, so I thought you were lucky. You won't let it go any further, will you?"

The boy gazed at his uncle from those big, hot, blue eyes, set rather close together. The uncle stirred and laughed uneasily.

"Right you are, son! I'll keep your tip private. Daffodil, eh? How much are you putting on him?"

"All except twenty pounds," said the boy. "I keep that in reserve."

The uncle thought it a good joke.

"You keep twenty pounds in reserve, do you, you young romancer? What are you betting, then?"

"I'm betting three hundred," said the boy gravely. "But it's between you and me, Uncle Oscar! Honor bright?"

The uncle burst into a roar of laughter.

"It's between you and me all right, you young Nat Gould,"[1] he said, laughing. "But where's your three hundred?"

"Bassett keeps it for me. We're partners."

"You are, are you! And what is Bassett putting on Daffodil?"

"He won't go quite as high as I do, I expect. Perhaps he'll go a hundred and fifty."

"What, pennies?" laughed the uncle.

"Pounds," said the child, with a surprised look at his uncle. "Bassett keeps a bigger reserve than I do."

Between wonder and amusement Uncle Oscar was silent. He pursued the matter no further, but he determined to take his nephew with him to the Lincoln races.

"Now, son," he said, "I'm putting twenty on Mirza, and I'll put five for you on any horse you fancy. What's your pick?"

"Daffodil, Uncle."

"No, not the fiver on Daffodil!"

"I should if it was my own fiver," said the child.

"Good! Good! Right you are! A fiver for me and a fiver for you on Daffodil."

The child had never been to a race meeting before, and his eyes were blue fire. He pursed his mouth tight, and watched. A Frenchman just in front had put his money on Lancelot. Wild with excitement, he flailed his arms up and down, yelling *"Lancelot! Lancelot!"* in his French accent.

Daffodil came in first, Lancelot second, Mirza third. The child, flushed and with eyes blazing, was curiously serene. His uncle brought him four five-pound notes, four to one.

"What am I to do with these?" he cried, waving them before the boy's eyes.

---

[1] Nathaniel Gould (1857–1919), British novelist and sports columnist known best for a series of novels about horse racing.

"I suppose we'll talk to Bassett," said the boy. "I expect I have fifteen hundred now; and twenty in reserve; and this twenty."

His uncle studied him for some moments.

"Look here, son!" he said. "You're not serious about Bassett and that fifteen hundred, are you?"

"Yes, I am. But it's between you and me, Uncle. Honor bright!"

"Honor bright all right, son! But I must talk to Bassett."

"If you'd like to be a partner, Uncle, with Bassett and me, we could all be partners. Only, you'd have to promise, honor bright, Uncle, not to let it go beyond us three. Bassett and I are lucky, and you must be lucky, because it was your ten shillings I started winning with. . . ."

Uncle Oscar took both Bassett and Paul into Richmond Park for an afternoon, and there they talked.

"It's like this, you see, sir," Bassett said. "Master Paul would get me talking about racing events, spinning yarns, you know, sir. And he was always keen on knowing if I'd made or if I'd lost. It's about a year since, now, that I put five shillings on Blush of Dawn for him — and we lost. Then the luck turned, with that ten shillings he had from you, that we put on Singhalese. And since then, it's been pretty steady, all things considering. What do you say, Master Paul?"

"We're all right when we're sure," said Paul. "It's when we're not quite sure that we go down."

"Oh, but we're careful then," said Bassett.

"But when are you *sure*?" Uncle Oscar smiled.

"It's Master Paul, sir," said Bassett, in a secret, religious voice. "It's as if he had it from heaven. Like Daffodil, now, for the Lincoln. That was as sure as eggs."

"Did you put anything on Daffodil?" asked Oscar Cresswell.

"Yes, sir. I made my bit."

"And my nephew?"

Bassett was obstinately silent, looking at Paul.

"I made twelve hundred, didn't I, Bassett? I told Uncle I was putting three hundred on Daffodil."

"That's right," said Bassett, nodding.

"But where's the money?" asked the uncle.

"I keep it safe locked up, sir. Master Paul he can have it any minute he likes to ask for it."

"What, fifteen hundred pounds?"

"And twenty! And *forty*, that is, with the twenty he made on the course."

"It's amazing!" said the uncle.

"If Master Paul offers you to be partners, sir, I would, if I were you; if you'll excuse me," said Bassett.

Oscar Cresswell thought about it.

"I'll see the money," he said.

They drove home again, and sure enough, Bassett came round to the garden house with fifteen hundred pounds in notes. The twenty pounds reserve was left with Joe Glee, in the Turf Commission deposit.

"You see, it's all right, Uncle, when I'm *sure*! Then we go strong, for all we're worth. Don't we, Bassett?"

"We do that, Master Paul."

"And when are you sure?" said the uncle, laughing.

"Oh, well, sometimes I'm *absolutely* sure, like about Daffodil," said the boy; "and sometimes I have an idea; and sometimes I haven't even an idea, have I, Bassett? Then we're careful, because we mostly go down."

"You do, do you! And when you're sure, like about Daffodil, what makes you sure, sonny?"

"Oh, well, I don't know," said the boy uneasily. "I'm sure, you know, Uncle; that's all."

"It's as if he had it from heaven, sir," Bassett reiterated.

"I should say so!" said the uncle.

But he became a partner. And when the Leger was coming on, Paul was "sure" about Lively Spark, which was a quite inconsiderable horse. The boy insisted on putting a thousand on the horse, Bassett went for five hundred, and Oscar Cresswell two hundred. Lively Spark came in first, and the betting had been ten to one against him. Paul had made ten thousand.

"You see," he said, "I was absolutely sure of him."

Even Oscar Cresswell had cleared two thousand.

"Look here, son," he said, "this sort of thing makes me nervous."

"It needn't, Uncle! Perhaps I shan't be sure again for a long time."

"But what are you going to do with your money?" asked the uncle.

"Of course," said the boy. "I started it for Mother. She said she had no luck, because Father is unlucky, so I thought if *I* was lucky, it might stop whispering."

"What might stop whispering?"

"Our house. I *hate* our house for whispering."

"What does it whisper?"

"Why — why" — the boy fidgeted — "why, I don't know. But it's always short of money, you know, Uncle."

"I know it, son, I know it."

"You know people send Mother writs, don't you, Uncle?"

"I'm afraid I do," said the uncle.

"And then the house whispers, like people laughing at you behind your back. It's awful, that is! I thought if I was lucky. . . ."

"You might stop it," added the uncle.

The boy watched him with big blue eyes, that had an uncanny cold fire in them, and he said never a word.

"Well, then!" said the uncle. "What are we doing?"

"I shouldn't like Mother to know I was lucky," said the boy.

"Why not, son?"

"She'd stop me."

"I don't think she would."

"Oh!" — and the boy writhed in an odd way — "I *don't* want her to know, Uncle."

"All right, son! We'll manage it without her knowing."

They managed it very easily. Paul, at the other's suggestion, handed over five thousand pounds to his uncle, who deposited it with the family lawyer, who was then to inform Paul's mother that a relative had put five thousand pounds into his hands, which sum was to be paid out a thousand pounds at a time, on the mother's birthday, for the next five years.

"So she'll have a birthday present of a thousand pounds for five successive years," said Uncle Oscar. "I hope it won't make it all the harder for her later."

Paul's mother had her birthday in November. The house had been "whispering" worse than ever lately, and, even in spite of his luck, Paul could not bear up against it. He was very anxious to see the effect of the birthday letter, telling his mother about the thousand pounds.

When there were no visitors, Paul now took his meals with his parents, as he was beyond the nursery control. His mother went into town nearly every day. She had discovered that she had an odd knack of sketching furs and dress materials, so she worked secretly in the studio of a friend who was the chief artist for the leading drapers. She drew the figures of ladies in furs and ladies in silk and sequins for the newspaper advertisements. This young woman artist earned several thousand pounds a year, but Paul's mother only made several hundreds, and she was again dissatisfied. She so wanted to be first in something, and she did not succeed, even in making sketches for drapery advertisements.

She was down to breakfast on the morning of her birthday. Paul watched her face as she read her letters. He knew the lawyer's letter. As his mother read it, her face hardened and became more expressionless. Then a cold, determined look came on her mouth. She hid the letter under the pile of others, and said not a word about it.

"Didn't you have anything nice in the post for your birthday, Mother?" said Paul.

"Quite moderately nice," she said, her voice cold and absent.

She went away to town without saying more.

But in the afternoon Uncle Oscar appeared. He said Paul's mother had had a long interview with the lawyer, asking if the whole five thousand could not be advanced at once, as she was in debt.

"What do you think, Uncle?" said the boy.

"I leave it to you, son."

"Oh, let her have it, then! We can get some more with the other," said the boy.

"A bird in the hand is worth two in the bush, laddie!" said Uncle Oscar.

"But I'm sure to *know* for the Grand National; or the Lincolnshire; or else the Derby. I'm sure to know for *one* of them," said Paul.

So Uncle Oscar signed the agreement, and Paul's mother touched the whole five thousand. Then something very curious happened. The voices in the house suddenly went mad, like a chorus of frogs on a spring evening. There were certain new furnishings, and Paul had a tutor. He was *really* going to Eton, his father's school, in the following autumn. There were flowers in the winter, and a blossoming of the luxury Paul's mother had been used to. And yet the voices in the house, behind the sprays of mimosa and almond blossom, and from under the piles of iridescent cushions, simply trilled and screamed in a sort of ecstasy: "There *must* be more money! Oh-h-h; there *must* be more money. Oh, now, now-w! Now-w-w — there *must* be more money! — more than ever! More than ever!"

It frightened Paul terribly. He studied away at his Latin and Greek. But his intense hours were spent with Bassett. The Grand National had gone by; he had not "known," and had lost a hundred pounds. Summer was at hand. He was in agony for the Lincoln. But even for the Lincoln he didn't "know," and he lost fifty pounds. He became wild-eyed and strange, as if something were going to explode in him.

"Let it alone, son! Don't you bother about it!" urged Uncle Oscar. But it was as if the boy couldn't really hear what his uncle was saying.

"I've got to know for the Derby! I've got to know for the Derby!" the child reiterated, his big blue eyes blazing with a sort of madness.

His mother noticed how overwrought he was.

"You'd better go to the seaside. Wouldn't you like to go now to the seaside, instead of waiting? I think you'd better," she said, looking down at him anxiously, her heart curiously heavy because of him.

But the child lifted his uncanny blue eyes. "I couldn't possibly go before the Derby, Mother!" he said. "I couldn't possibly!"

"Why not?" she said, her voice becoming heavy when she was opposed. "Why not? You can still go from the seaside to see the Derby with your uncle Oscar, if that's what you wish. No need for you to wait here. Besides, I think you care too much about these races. It's a bad sign. My family has been a gambling family, and you won't know till you grow up how much damage it has done. But it has done damage. I shall have to send Bassett away, and ask Uncle Oscar not to talk racing to you, unless you promise to be reasonable about it; go away to the seaside and forget it. You're all nerves!"

"I'll do what you like, Mother, so long as you don't send me away till after the Derby," the boy said.

"Send you away from where? Just from this house?"

"Yes," he said, gazing at her.

"Why, you curious child, what makes you care about this house so much, suddenly? I never knew you loved it."

He gazed at her without speaking. He had a secret within a secret, something he had not divulged, even to Bassett or to his uncle Oscar.

But his mother, after standing undecided and a little bit sullen for some moments, said:

"Very well, then! Don't go to the seaside till after the Derby, if you don't wish it. But promise me you won't let your nerves go to pieces. Promise you won't think so much about horse racing and *events,* as you call them!"

"Oh, no," said the boy casually. "I won't think much about them, Mother. You needn't worry. I wouldn't worry, Mother, if I were you."

"If you were me and I were you," said his mother, "I wonder what we *should* do!"

"But you know you needn't worry, Mother, don't you?" the boy repeated.

"I should be awfully glad to know it," she said wearily.

"Oh, well you *can*, you know. I mean, you *ought* to know you needn't worry," he insisted.

"Ought I? Then I'll see about it," she said.

Paul's secret of secrets was his wooden horse, that which had no name. Since he was emancipated from a nurse and a nursery governess, he had had his rocking horse removed to his own bedroom at the top of the house.

"Surely, you're too big for a rocking horse!" his mother had remonstrated.

"Well, you see, Mother, till I can have a *real* horse, I like to have *some* sort of animal about," had been his quaint answer.

"Do you feel he keeps you company?" She laughed.

"Oh, yes! He's very good, he always keeps me company, when I'm there," said Paul.

So the horse, rather shabby, stood in an arrested prance in the boy's bedroom.

The Derby was drawing near, and the boy grew more and more tense. He hardly heard what was spoken to him, he was very frail, and his eyes were really uncanny. His mother had sudden strange seizures of uneasiness about him. Sometimes, for half an hour, she would feel a sudden anxiety about him that was almost anguish. She wanted to rush to him at once, and know he was safe.

Two nights before the Derby, she was at a big party in town, when one of her rushes of anxiety about her boy, her firstborn, gripped her heart till she could hardly speak. She fought with the feeling, might and main, for she believed in common sense. But it was too strong. She had to leave the dance and go downstairs to telephone to the country. The children's nursery governess was terribly surprised and startled at being rung up in the night.

"Are the children all right, Miss Wilmot?"

"Oh, yes, they are quite all right."

"Master Paul? Is he all right?"

"He went to bed as right as a trivet. Shall I run up and look at him?"

"No," said Paul's mother reluctantly. "No! Don't trouble. It's all right. Don't sit up. We shall be home fairly soon." She did not want her son's privacy intruded upon.

"Very good," said the governess.

It was about one o'clock when Paul's mother and father drove up to their house. All was still. Paul's mother went to her room and slipped off her white fur cloak. She had told her maid not to wait up for her. She heard her husband downstairs, mixing a whisky and soda.

And then, because of the strange anxiety at her heart, she stole upstairs to her son's room. Noiselessly she went along the upper corridor. Was there a faint noise? What was it?

She stood, with arrested muscles, outside his door, listening. There was a strange, heavy, and yet not loud noise. Her heart stood still. It was a soundless noise, yet rushing and powerful. Something huge, in violent, hushed motion.

What was it? What in God's name was it? She ought to know. She felt that she knew the noise. She knew what it was.

Yet she could not place it. She couldn't say what it was. And on and on it went, like a madness.

Softly, frozen with anxiety and fear, she turned the door handle.

The room was dark. Yet in the space near the window, she heard and saw something plunging to and fro. She gazed in fear and amazement.

Then suddenly she switched on the light, and saw her son, in his green pajamas, madly surging on the rocking horse. The blaze of light suddenly lit him up, as he urged the wooden horse, and lit her up, as she stood, blonde, in her dress of pale green and crystal, in the doorway.

"Paul!" she cried. "Whatever are you doing?"

"It's Malabar!" he screamed, in a powerful, strange voice. "It's Malabar!"

His eyes blazed at her for one strange and senseless second, as he ceased urging his wooden horse. Then he fell with a crash to the ground, and she, all her tormented motherhood flooding upon her, rushed to gather him up.

But he was unconscious, and unconscious he remained, with some brain fever. He talked and tossed, and his mother sat stonily by his side.

"Malabar! It's Malabar! Bassett, Bassett, I *know*! It's Malabar!"

So the child cried, trying to get up and urge the rocking horse that gave him his inspiration.

"What does he mean by Malabar?" asked the heart-frozen mother.

"I don't know," said the father stonily.

"What does he mean by Malabar?" she asked her brother Oscar.

"It's one of the horses running for the Derby," was the answer.

And, in spite of himself, Oscar Cresswell spoke to Bassett, and himself put a thousand on Malabar: at fourteen to one.

The third day of the illness was critical: they were waiting for a change. The boy, with his rather long, curly hair, was tossing ceaselessly on the pillow. He never slept nor regained consciousness, and his eyes were like blue stones. His mother sat, feeling her heart had gone, turned actually into a stone.

In the evening, Oscar Cresswell did not come, but Bassett sent a message, saying could he come up for one moment, just one moment? Paul's mother was very angry at the intrusion, but on second thought she agreed. The boy was the same. Perhaps Bassett might bring him to consciousness.

The gardener, a shortish fellow with a little brown mustache, and sharp little brown eyes, tiptoed into the room, touched his imaginary cap to Paul's mother, and stole to the bedside, staring with glittering, smallish eyes at the tossing, dying child.

"Master Paul!" he whispered. "Master Paul! Malabar came in first all right, a clean win. I did as you told me. You've made over seventy thousand pounds, you have; you've got over eighty thousand. Malabar came in all right, Master Paul."

"Malabar! Malabar! Did I say Malabar, Mother? Did I say Malabar? Do you think I'm lucky, Mother? I knew Malabar, didn't I? Over eighty thousand pounds! I call that lucky, don't you, Mother? Over eighty thousand pounds! I knew, didn't I know I knew? Malabar came in all right. If I ride my horse till

I'm sure, then I tell you, Bassett, you can go as high as you like. Did you go for all you were worth, Bassett?"

"I went a thousand on it, Master Paul."

"I never told you, Mother, that if I can ride my horse, and *get there*, then I'm absolutely sure — oh, absolutely! Mother, did I ever tell you? I *am* lucky!"

"No, you never did," said the mother.

But the boy died in the night.

And even as he lay dead, his mother heard her brother's voice saying to her: "My God, Hester, you're eighty-odd thousand to the good, and a poor devil of a son to the bad. But, poor devil, poor devil, he's best gone out of a life where he rides his rocking horse to find a winner."

Ursula K. Le Guin

Ursula K. Le Guin (b. 1929) is the daughter of Theodora Kroeber, a writer, and Alfred Louis Kroeber, a pioneering anthropologist at the University of California at Berkeley. From her family background Le Guin acquired a double orientation, humanistic and scientific, that shows in all her writing. She was educated at Radcliffe College and Columbia University, where she completed a master's thesis in medieval romance literature. In 1953 she married the historian Charles Le Guin, with whom she had three children. Although she wrote her first science-fiction story at the age of twelve, she didn't begin publishing until twenty years later. One of her stories, "Semley's Necklace," grew into her first published novel, *Rocannon's World* (1966). Another story, "Winter's King," introduced the setting she developed for her first major success, the novel *The Left Hand of Darkness* (1969). These stories and novels, along with *Planet of Exile* (1966), *City of Illusions* (1967), *The Dispossessed* (1974), the novella *The Word for World Is Forest* (1976), and stories in *The Wind's Twelve Quarters* (1976), form the Hainish cycle, a series of independent works sharing an imaginary historic background. To date Le Guin has published over twenty novels, eleven volumes of short stories, four essay collections, and six books of poetry.

Although Le Guin's earliest work primarily attracted a devoted audience of science-fiction readers, her later work—starting with *The Left Hand of Darkness*—has wider appeal. In that novel she explored the theme of androgyny on the planet Winter (Gethen), where inhabitants may adopt alternately male and female roles. Le Guin insists on Aristotle's definition of *Homo sapiens* as social animals, and she shows how difficult it is to think of our fellow humans as people, rather than as men and women.

Le Guin brings to fantasy fiction a wealth of literary scholarship, crediting Leo Tolstoy, Anton Chekhov, and Virginia Woolf (among others) as her primary influences. Most of her stories, like "The Ones Who Walk Away from Omelas," are about reciprocal relationships, illustrating "the sort of golden rule that whatever you touch, touches you." This maxim has scientific backings in ecology and philosophical echoes in Taoism and Zen. Le Guin has said that she works best with what she calls "fortune cookie ideas" suggested by someone else. Through her stories she shows how simple concepts hide a mass of complexity and contradiction that can create anarchy when human beings try to act on them. In 1990 Le Guin published *Dancing at the Edge of the World: Thoughts on Words, Women, Places*; in 1998 she wrote *Steering the Craft: Exercises and Discussions on Story Writing for the Lone Navigator or the Mutinous Crew*. *Cheek by Jowl* (2009) is a recent essay collection.

RELATED STORY
Janet Frame, "Two Sheep," page 491.

RELATED COMMENTARY
Ursula K. Le Guin, "The Scapegoat in Omelas," page 1462.

RELATED CASEBOOK
Ursula K. Le Guin, "The Kind of Fiction Most Characteristic of Our Time," page 1641.

The Ones Who Walk Away from Omelas

1976

WITH A CLAMOR of bells that set the swallows soaring, the Festival of Summer came to the city. Omelas, bright-towered by the sea. The rigging of the boats in harbor sparkled with flags. In the streets between houses with red roofs and painted walls, between old moss-grown gardens and under avenues of trees, past great parks and public buildings, processions moved. Some were decorous: old people in long stiff robes of mauve and grey, grave master workmen, quiet, merry women carrying their babies and chatting as they walked. In other streets the music beat faster, a shimmering of gong and tambourine, and the people went dancing, the procession was a dance. Children dodged in and out, their high calls rising like the swallows' crossing flights over the music and the singing. All the processions wound towards the north side of the city, where on the great water-meadow called the Green Fields boys and girls, naked in the bright air, with mud-stained feet and ankles and long, lithe arms, exercised their restive horses before the race. The horses wore no gear at all but a halter without bit. Their manes were braided with streamers of silver, gold, and green. They flared their nostrils and pranced and boasted to one another; they were vastly excited, the horse being the only animal who has adopted our ceremonies as his own. Far off to the north and west the mountains stood up half encircling Omelas on her bay. The air of morning was so clear that the snow still crowning the Eighteen Peaks burned with white-gold fire across the miles of sunlit air, under the dark blue of the sky. There was just enough wind to make the banners that marked the racecourse snap and flutter now and then. In the silence of the broad green meadows one could hear the music winding through the city streets, farther and nearer and ever approaching, a cheerful faint sweetness of the air that from time to time trembled and gathered together and broke out into the great joyous clanging of the bells.

Joyous! How is one to tell about joy? How describe the citizens of Omelas?

They were not simple folk, you see, though they were happy. But we do not say the words of cheer much any more. All smiles have become archaic. Given a description such as this one tends to make certain assumptions. Given a description such as this one tends to look next for the King, mounted on a splendid stallion and surrounded by his noble knights, or perhaps in a golden litter borne by great-muscled slaves. But there was no king. They did not use swords, or keep slaves. They were not barbarians. I do not know the rules and laws of their society, but I suspect that they were singularly few. As they did without monarchy and slavery, so they also got on without the stock exchange, the advertisement, the secret police, and the bomb. Yet I repeat that these were not simple folk, not dulcet shepherds, noble savages, bland utopians. They were not less complex than us. The trouble is that we have a bad habit, encouraged by pedants and sophisticates, of considering happiness as something rather stupid. Only pain is intellectual, only evil interesting. This is the treason of the artist: a refusal to admit the banality of evil and the terrible boredom of pain. If you can't lick 'em, join 'em. If it hurts, repeat it. But to praise despair is to condemn delight, to embrace violence is to lose hold of everything else. We have almost lost hold; we can no longer describe a happy man, nor make any celebration of joy. How can I tell you about the people of Omelas? They were not naïve and happy children — though their children were, in fact, happy. They were mature, intelligent, passionate adults whose lives were not wretched. O miracle! but I wish I could describe it better. I wish I could convince you. Omelas sounds in my words like a city in a fairy tale, long ago and far away, once upon a time. Perhaps it would be best if you imagined it as your own fancy bids, assuming it will rise to the occasion, for certainly I cannot suit you all. For instance, how about technology? I think that there would be no cars or helicopters in and above the streets; this follows from the fact that the people of Omelas are happy people. Happiness is based on a just discrimination of what is necessary, what is neither necessary nor destructive, and what is destructive. In the middle category, however — that of the unnecessary but undestructive, that of comfort, luxury, exuberance, etc. — they could perfectly well have central heating, subway trains, washing machines, and all kinds of marvelous devices not yet invented here, floating light-sources, fuelless power, a cure for the common cold. Or they could have none of that: it doesn't matter. As you like it. I incline to think that people from towns up and down the coast have been coming in to Omelas during the last days before the Festival on very fast little trains and double-decked trams and that the train station of Omelas is actually the handsomest building in town, though plainer than the magnificent Farmers' Market. But even granted trains, I fear that Omelas so far strikes some of you as goody-goody. Smiles, bells, parades, horses, bleh. If so, please add an orgy. If an orgy would help, don't hesitate. Let us not, however, have temples from which issue beautiful nude priests and priestesses already half in ecstasy and ready to copulate with any man or woman, lover or stranger, who desires union with the deep godhead of the blood, although that was my first idea. But really it would be better not to have any temples in Omelas — at least, not manned temples. Religion yes, clergy no. Surely the beautiful nudes can just wander about, offering themselves like divine soufflés to the hunger of the needy and the rapture of the flesh. Let them join the processions. Let tambourines be struck above the copulations, and the glory of desire be proclaimed upon the gongs, and (a not unimportant point) let the offspring of these delightful rituals be beloved and looked after by all. One thing I know there is none of in Omelas is guilt. But what else should there be? I thought at first there were no drugs, but that is puritanical. For those who like it, the faint insistent sweetness of *drooz* may perfume the ways of the city, *drooz* which first brings a great lightness and brilliance to the mind and limbs, and then after some hours a dreamy languor, and wonderful visions at last of the very arcana and inmost secrets of the Universe, as well as exciting the pleasure of sex beyond all belief; and it is not habit-forming. For more modest tastes I think there ought to be beer. What else, what else belongs in the joyous city? The sense of victory, surely, the celebration of courage. But as we did without clergy, let us do without soldiers. The joy built upon successful slaughter is not the right kind of joy; it will not do; it is fearful and it is trivial. A boundless and generous contentment, a magnanimous triumph felt not against some outer enemy but in communion with the finest and fairest in the souls of all men everywhere and the splendor of the world's summer: this is what swells the hearts of the people of Omelas, and the victory they celebrate is that of life. I really don't think many of them need to take *drooz*.

Most of the processions have reached the Green Fields by now. A marvelous smell of cooking goes forth from the red and blue tents of the provisioners. The faces of small children are amiably sticky; in the benign grey beard of a man a couple of crumbs of rich pastry are entangled. The youths and girls have mounted their horses and are beginning to group around the starting line of the course. An old woman, small, fat, and laughing, is passing out flowers from a basket, and tall young men wear her flowers in their shining hair. A child of nine or ten sits at the edge of the crowd, alone, playing on a wooden flute. People pause to listen, and they smile, but they do not speak to him, for he never ceases playing and never sees them, his dark eyes wholly rapt in the sweet, thin magic of the tune.

He finishes, and slowly lowers his hands holding the wooden flute.

As if that little private silence were the signal, all at once a trumpet sounds from the pavillion near the starting line: imperious, melancholy, piercing. The horses rear on their slender legs, and some of them neigh in answer. Sober-faced, the young riders stroke the horses' necks and soothe them, whispering, "Quiet, quiet, there my beauty, my hope. . . ." They begin to form in rank along the starting line. The crowds along the racecourse are like a field of grass and flowers in the wind. The Festival of Summer has begun.

Do you believe? Do you accept the festival, the city, the joy? No? Then let me describe one more thing.

In a basement under one of the beautiful public buildings of Omelas, or perhaps in the cellar of one of its spacious private homes, there is a room. It has one locked door, and no window. A little light seeps in dustily between cracks in the boards, secondhand from a cobwebbed window somewhere across the cellar. In one corner of the little room a couple of mops, with stiff, clotted, foul-smelling heads, stand near a rusty bucket. The floor is dirt, a little damp to the touch, as cellar dirt usually is. The room is about three paces long and two wide: a mere broom closet or disused tool room. In the room a child is sitting. It could be a boy or a girl. It looks about six, but actually is nearly ten. It is feeble-minded. Perhaps it was born defective, or perhaps it has become imbecile through fear, malnutrition, and neglect. It picks its nose and occasionally fumbles vaguely with its toes or genitals, as it sits hunched in the corner farthest from the bucket and the two mops. It is afraid of the mops. It finds them horrible. It shuts its eyes, but it knows the mops are still standing there; and the door is locked; and nobody will come. The door is always locked; and nobody ever comes, except that sometimes — the child has no understanding of time or interval — sometimes the door rattles terribly and opens, and a person, or several people, are there. One of them may come in and kick the child to make it stand up. The others never come close, but peer in at it with frightened, disgusted eyes. The food bowl and the water jug are hastily filled, the door is locked, the eyes disappear. The people at the door never say anything, but the child, who has not always lived in the tool room, and can remember sunlight and its mother's voice, sometimes speaks. "I will be good," it says. "Please let me out. I will be good!" They never answer. The child used to scream for help at night, and cry a good deal, but now it only makes a kind of whining, "eh-haa, eh-haa," and it speaks less and less often. It is so thin there are no calves to its legs; its belly protrudes; it lives on a half-bowl of corn meal and grease a day. It is naked. Its buttocks and thighs are a mass of festered sores, as it sits in its own excrement continually.

They all know it is there, all the people of Omelas. Some of them have come to see it, others are content merely to know it is there. They all know that it has to be there. Some of them understand why, and some do not, but they all understand that their happiness, the beauty of their city, the tenderness of their friendships, the health of their children, the wisdom of their scholars, the skill of their makers, even the abundance of their harvest and the kindly weathers of their skies, depend wholly on this child's abominable misery.

This is usually explained to children when they are between eight and twelve, whenever they seem capable of understanding; and most of those who come to see the child are young people, though often enough an adult comes, or comes back, to see the child. No matter how well the matter has been explained to them, these young spectators are always shocked and sickened at the sight. They feel disgust, which they had thought themselves superior to. They feel anger, outrage, impotence, despite all the explanations. They would like to do something for the child. But there is nothing they can do. If the child were brought up into the sunlight out of that vile place, if it were cleaned and fed and comforted, that would be a good thing, indeed; but if it were done, in that day and hour all the prosperity and beauty and delight of Omelas would wither and be destroyed. Those are the terms. To exchange all the goodness and grace of every life in Omelas for that single, small improvement: to throw away the happiness of thousands for the chance of the happiness of one: that would be to let guilt within the walls indeed.

The terms are strict and absolute; there may not even be a kind word spoken to the child.

Often the young people go home in tears, or in a tearless rage, when they have seen the child and faced this terrible paradox. They may brood over it for weeks or years. But as time goes on they begin to realize that even if the child could be released, it would not get much good of its freedom: a little vague pleasure of warmth and food, no doubt, but little more. It is too degraded and imbecile to know any real joy. It has been afraid too long ever to be free of fear. Its habits are too uncouth for it to respond to humane treatment. Indeed, after so long it would probably be wretched without walls about it to protect it, and darkness for its eyes, and its own excrement to sit in. Their tears at the bitter injustice dry when they begin to perceive the terrible justice of reality and to accept it. Yet it is their tears and anger, the trying of their generosity and the acceptance of their helplessness, which are perhaps the true source of the splendor of their lives. Theirs is no vapid, irresponsible happiness. They know that they, like the child, are not free. They know compassion. It is the existence of the child, and their knowledge of its existence, that makes possible the nobility of their architecture, the poignancy of their music, the profundity of their science. It is because of the child that they are so gentle with children. They know that if the wretched one were not there snivelling in the dark, the other one, the flute-player, could make no joyful music as the young riders line up in their beauty for the race in the sunlight of the first morning of summer.

Now do you believe in them? Are they not more credible? But there is one more thing to tell, and this is quite incredible.

At times one of the adolescent girls or boys who go to see the child does not go home to weep or rage, does not, in fact, go home at all. Sometimes also a man or woman much older falls silent for a day or two, and then leaves home. These people go out into the street, and walk down the street alone. They keep walking, and walk straight out of the city of Omelas, through the beautiful gates. They keep walking across the farmlands of Omelas. Each one goes alone, youth or girl, man or woman. Night falls; the traveler must pass down village streets, between the houses with yellow-lit windows, and on out into the darkness of the fields. Each alone, they go west or north, towards the mountains. They go on. They leave Omelas, they walk ahead into the darkness, and they do not come back. The place they go towards is a place even less imaginable to most of us than the city of happiness. I cannot describe it at all. It is possible that it does not exist. But they seem to know where they are going, the ones who walk away from Omelas.

Doris Lessing

Doris Lessing (1919–2013) was born in Persia (now Iran), where her father managed a bank. When she was five, her family moved to a farm in Rhodesia (now Zimbabwe), in an isolated part of Africa that had not been settled before by white people. Lessing left school at the age of fourteen in rebellion against her mother. After a first marriage failed, she married again and had one son. She was a Communist for some years in her twenties, when she "learned a great deal, chiefly about the nature of political power, how groups of people operate." Then in 1949 she left her husband in Rhodesia and came with her son to London, where she spent the rest of her life as a professional writer. In 2007 she was awarded the Nobel Prize in Literature.

Africa remained in Lessing's consciousness as "an inexplicable majestic silence lying just over the border of memory or of thought. Africa gives you the knowledge that man is a small creature, among other creatures, in a large landscape." Lessing's first two books, the novel *The Grass Is Singing* (1950) and a volume of short stories *This Was the Old Chief's Country* (1951), are based on her experiences in Rhodesia. These early stories develop the theme of the exploitation of blacks by white people—although Lessing also considers racial prejudice "only one aspect of the atrophy of the imagination that prevents us from seeing ourselves in every creature that breathes under the sun." She published many novels, but perhaps the most influential was *The Golden Notebook* (1962), an experimental book exploring the destructive relationships between men and women that mirror the lack of coherence and order in our fragmented, materialistic society.

Lessing's short stories have often been compared to those of D. H. Lawrence. Like him, she was highly receptive to emotions that surface during the writing of fiction:

> This question of I, who am I, what different levels there are inside of us, is
> very relevant to writing, to the process of creative writing about which we
> know nothing whatsoever. Every writer feels he, she, hits a different level. A
> certain kind of writing or emotion comes from it. But you don't know who it is
> who lives there.

Like Lawrence, Lessing was not always confident of rational solutions to the problems of modern life. In her fiction she went beyond Lawrence, however, to explore the possibilities for change. Two of her collections are *The Doris Lessing Reader* (1989) and *The Real Thing*, stories and sketches published in 1992. Her recent novels include *The Cleft* (2007) and *Alfred and Emily* (2008). "To Room 19" is a powerful early story included in *A Man and Two Women* (1963).

RELATED STORY
Charlotte Perkins Gilman, "The Yellow Wallpaper," page 533.

To Room 19

1963

THIS IS A STORY, I suppose, about a failure in intelligence: the Rawlings' marriage was grounded in intelligence.

They were older when they married than most of their married friends: in their well-seasoned late twenties. Both had had a number of affairs, sweet rather than bitter; and when they fell in love — for they did fall in love — had known each other for some time. They joked that they had saved each other "for the real thing." That they had waited so long (but not too long) for this real thing was to them a proof of their sensible discrimination. A good many of their friends had married young, and now (they felt) probably regretted lost opportunities; while others, still unmarried, seemed to them arid, self-doubting, and likely to make desperate or romantic marriages.

Not only they, but others, felt they were well-matched: their friends' delight was an additional proof of their happiness. They had played the same roles, male and female, in this group or set, if such a wide, loosely connected, constantly changing constellation of people could be called a set. They had both become, by virtue of their moderation, their humour, and their abstinence from painful experience, people to whom others came for advice. They could be, and were, relied on. It was one of those cases of a man and a woman linking themselves whom no one else had ever thought of linking, probably because of their similarities. But then everyone exclaimed: Of course! How right! How was it we never thought of it before!

And so they married amid general rejoicing, and because of their foresight and their sense for what was probable, nothing was a surprise to them.

Both had well-paid jobs. Matthew was a subeditor on a large London newspaper, and Susan worked in an advertising firm. He was not the stuff of which editors or publicised journalists are made, but he was much more than "a subeditor," being one of the essential background people who in fact steady, inspire, and make possible the people in the limelight. He was content with this position. Susan had a talent for commercial drawing. She was humorous about the advertisements she was responsible for, but she did not feel strongly about them one way or the other.

Both, before they married, had had pleasant flats, but they felt it unwise to base a marriage on either flat, because it might seem like a submission of personality on the part of the one whose flat it was not. They moved into a new flat in South Kensington on the clear understanding that when their marriage had settled down (a process they knew would not take long, and was in fact more a humorous concession to popular wisdom than what was due to themselves) they would buy a house and start a family.

And this is what happened. They lived in their charming flat for two years, giving parties and going to them, being a popular young married couple, and then Susan became pregnant, she gave up her job, and they bought a house in Richmond. It was typical of this couple that they had a son first, then a daughter, then twins, son and daughter. Everything right, appropriate, and what everyone would wish for, if they could choose. But people did feel these two had chosen; this balanced and sensible family was no more than what was due to them because of their infallible sense for *choosing* right.

And so they lived with their four children in their gardened house in Richmond and were happy. They had everything they had wanted and had planned for.

And yet....

Well, even this was expected, that there must be a certain flatness....

Yes, yes, of course, it was natural they sometimes felt like this. Like what?

Their life seemed to be like a snake biting its tail. Matthew's job for the sake of Susan, children, house, and garden—which caravanserai needed a well-paid job to maintain it. And Susan's practical intelligence for the sake of Matthew, the children, the house, and the garden—which unit would have collapsed in a week without her.

But there was no point about which either could say: "For the sake of *this* is all at rest." Children? But children can't be a centre of life and a reason for being. They can be a thousand things that are delightful, interesting, satisfying, but they can't be a wellspring to live from. Or they shouldn't be. Susan and Matthew knew that well enough.

Matthew's job? Ridiculous. It was an interesting job, but scarcely a reason for living. Matthew took pride in doing it well, but he could hardly be expected to be proud of the newspaper; the newspaper he read, *his* newspaper, was not the one he worked for.

Their love for each other? Well, that was nearest it. If this wasn't a centre, what was? Yes, it was around this point, their love, that the whole extraordinary structure revolved. For extraordinary it certainly was. Both Susan and Matthew had moments of thinking so, of looking in secret disbelief at this thing they had created: marriage, four children, big house, garden, charwomen, friends, cars ... and this *thing*, this entity, all of it had come into existence, been blown into being out of nowhere, because Susan loved Matthew and Matthew loved Susan. Extraordinary. So that was the central point, the wellspring.

And if one felt that it simply was not strong enough, important enough, to support it all, well whose fault was that? Certainly neither Susan's nor Matthew's. It was in the nature of things. And they sensibly blamed neither themselves nor each other.

On the contrary, they used their intelligence to preserve what they had created from a painful and explosive world: they looked around them, and took lessons. All around them, marriages collapsing, or breaking, or rubbing along (even worse, they felt). They must not make the same mistakes, they must not.

They had avoided the pitfall so many of their friends had fallen into—of buying a house in the country *for the sake of the children,* so that the husband became a weekend husband, a weekend father, and the wife always careful not to ask what went on in the town flat which they called (in joke) a bachelor flat. No, Matthew was a full-time husband, a full-time father, and at night, in the big married bed in the big married bedroom (which had an attractive view of the river), they lay beside each other talking and he told her about his day, and what he had done, and whom he had met; and she told him about her day (not as interesting, but that was not her fault), for both knew of the hidden resentments and deprivations of the woman who has lived her own life — and above all, has earned her own living — and is now dependent on a husband for outside interests and money.

Nor did Susan make the mistake of taking a job for the sake of her independence, which she might very well have done, since her old firm, missing her qualities of humour, balance, and sense, invited her often to go back. Children needed their mother to a certain age, that both parents knew and agreed on; and when these four healthy wisely brought up children were of the right age, Susan would work again, because she knew, and so did he, what happened to women of fifty at the height of their energy and ability, with grownup children who no longer needed their full devotion.

So here was this couple, testing their marriage, looking after it, treating it like a small boat full of helpless people in a very stormy sea. Well, of course, so it was. . . . The storms of the world were bad, but not too close — which is not to say they were selfishly felt: Susan and Matthew were both well-informed and responsible people. And the inner storms and quicksands were understood and charted. So everything was all right. Everything was in order. Yes, things were under control.

So what did it matter if they felt dry, flat? People like themselves, fed on a hundred books (psychological, anthropological, sociological), could scarcely be unprepared for the dry, controlled wistfulness which is the distinguishing mark of the intelligent marriage. Two people, endowed with education, with discrimination, with judgement, linked together voluntarily from their will to be happy together and to be of use to others — one sees them everywhere, one knows them, one even is that thing oneself: sadness because so much is after all so little. These two, unsurprised, turned towards each other with even more courtesy and gentle love: this was life, that two people, no matter how carefully chosen, could not be everything to each other. In fact, even to say so, to think in such a way, was banal; they were ashamed to do it.

It was banal, too, when one night Matthew came home late and confessed he had been to a party, taken a girl home, and slept with her. Susan forgave him, of course. Except that forgiveness is hardly the word. Understanding, yes. But if you understand something, you don't forgive it, you are the thing itself: forgiveness is for what you *don't* understand. Nor had he *confessed* — what sort of word is that?

The whole thing was not important. After all, years ago they had joked: Of course I'm not going to be faithful to you, no one can be faithful to one other person for a whole lifetime. (And there was the word "faithful" — stupid, all these words, stupid, belonging to a savage old world.) But the incident left both of them irritable. Strange, but they were both bad-tempered, annoyed. There was something unassimilable about it.

Making love splendidly after he had come home that night, both had felt that the idea that Myra Jenkins, a pretty girl met at a party, could be even relevant was ridiculous. They had loved each other for over a decade, would love each other for years more. Who, then, was Myra Jenkins?

Except, thought Susan, unaccountably bad-tempered, she was (is?) the first. In ten years. So either the ten years' fidelity was not important, or she isn't. (No, no, there is something wrong with this way of thinking, there must be.) But if she isn't important, presumably it wasn't important either when Matthew and I first went to bed with each other that afternoon whose delight even now (like a very long shadow at sundown) lays a long, wandlike finger over us. (Why did I say sundown?) Well, if what we felt that afternoon was not important, nothing is important, because if it hadn't been for what we felt, we wouldn't be Mr. and Mrs. Rawlings with four children, et cetera, et cetera. The whole thing is *absurd* — for him to have come home and told me was absurd. For him not to have told me was absurd. For me to care or, for that matter, not to care, is absurd ... and who is Myra Jenkins? Why, no one at all.

There was only one thing to do, and of course these sensible people did it, they put the thing behind them, and consciously, knowing what they were doing, moved forward into a different phase of their marriage, giving thanks for the past good fortune as they did so.

For it was inevitable that the handsome, blond, attractive, manly man, Matthew Rawlings, should be at times tempted (oh, what a word!) by the attractive girls at parties she could not attend because of the four children; and that sometimes he would succumb (a word even more repulsive, if possible) and that she, a goodlooking woman in the big well-tended garden at Richmond, would sometimes be pierced as by an arrow from the sky with bitterness. Except that bitterness was not in order, it was out of court. Did the casual girls touch the marriage? They did not. Rather it was they who knew defeat because of the handsome Matthew Rawlings' marriage body and soul to Susan Rawlings.

In that case why did Susan feel (though luckily not for longer than a few seconds at a time) as if life had become a desert, and that nothing mattered, and that her children were not her own?

Meanwhile her intelligence continued to assert that all was well. What if her Matthew did have an occasional sweet afternoon, the odd affair? For she knew quite well, except in her moments of aridity, that they were very happy, that the affairs were not important.

Perhaps that was the trouble? It was in the nature of things that the adventures and delights could no longer be hers, because of the four children and the big house that needed so much attention. But perhaps she was secretly wishing, and even knowing that she did, that the wildness and the beauty could be his. But he was married to her. She was married to him. They were married inextricably. And therefore the gods could not strike him with the real magic, not really. Well, was it Susan's fault that after he came home from an adventure he looked harassed rather than fulfilled? (In fact, that was how she knew he had been *unfaithful*, because of his sullen air, and his glances at her, similar to hers at him: What is it that I share with this person that shields all delight from me?) But none of it by anybody's fault. (But what did they feel ought to be somebody's fault?) Nobody's fault, nothing to be at fault, no one to blame, no one to offer or to take it ... and nothing wrong, either, except that

Matthew never was really struck, as he wanted to be, by joy; and that Susan was more and more often threatened by emptiness. (It was usually in the garden that she was invaded by this feeling: she was coming to avoid the garden, unless the children or Matthew were with her.) There was no need to use the dramatic words "unfaithful," "forgive," and the rest: intelligence forbade them. Intelligence barred, too, quarrelling, sulking, anger, silences of withdrawal, accusations, and tears. Above all, intelligence forbids tears.

A high price has to be paid for the happy marriage with the four healthy children in the large white gardened house.

And they were paying it, willingly, knowing what they were doing. When they lay side by side or breast to breast in the big civilised bedroom overlooking the wild sullied river, they laughed, often, for no particular reason; but they knew it was really because of these two small people, Susan and Matthew, supporting such an edifice on their intelligent love. The laugh comforted them; it saved them both, though from what, they did not know.

They were now both fortyish. The older children, boy and girl, were ten and eight, at school. The twins, six, were still at home. Susan did not have nurses or girls to help her: childhood is short; and she did not regret the hard work. Often enough she was bored, since small children can be boring; she was often very tired; but she regretted nothing. In another decade, she would turn herself back into being a woman with a life of her own.

Soon the twins would go to school, and they would be away from home from nine until four. These hours, so Susan saw it, would be the preparation for her own slow emancipation away from the role of hub-of-the-family into woman-with-her-own-life. She was already planning for the hours of freedom when all the children would be "off her hands." That was the phrase used by Matthew and by Susan and by their friends, for the moment when the youngest child went off to school. "They'll be off your hands, darling Susan, and you'll have time to yourself." So said Matthew, the intelligent husband, who had often enough commended and consoled Susan, standing by her in spirit during the years when her soul was not her own, as she said, but her children's.

What it amounted to was that Susan saw herself as she had been at twenty-eight, unmarried; and then again somewhere about fifty, blossoming from the root of what she had been twenty years before. As if the essential Susan were in abeyance, as if she were in cold storage. Matthew said something like this to Susan one night: and she agreed that it was true — she did feel something like that. What, then, was this essential Susan? She did not know. Put like that it sounded ridiculous, and she did not really feel it. Anyway, they had a long discussion about the whole thing before going off to sleep in each other's arms.

So the twins went off to their school, two bright affectionate children who had no problems about it, since their older brother and sister had trodden this path so successfully before them. And now Susan was going to be alone in the big house, every day of the school term, except for the daily woman who came in to clean.

It was now, for the first time in this marriage, that something happened which neither of them had foreseen.

This is what happened. She returned, at nine-thirty, from taking the twins to the school by car, looking forward to seven blissful hours of freedom. On the first morning she was simply restless, worrying about the twins "naturally enough" since this was their first day away at school. She was hardly able to contain herself until they came back. Which they did happily, excited by the world of school, looking forward to the next day. And the next day Susan took them, dropped them, came back, and found herself reluctant to enter her big and beautiful home because it was as if something was waiting for her there that she did not wish to confront. Sensibly, however, she parked the car in the garage, entered the house, spoke to Mrs. Parkes, the daily woman, about her duties, and went up to her bedroom. She was possessed by a fever which drove her out again, downstairs, into the kitchen, where Mrs. Parkes was making cake and did not need her, and into the garden. There she sat on a bench and tried to calm herself looking at trees, at a brown glimpse of the river. But she was filled with tension, like a panic: as if an enemy was in the garden with her. She spoke to herself severely, thus: All this is quite natural. First, I spent twelve years of my adult life working, *living my own life*. Then I married, and from the moment I became pregnant for the first time I signed myself over, so to speak, to other people. To the children. Not for one moment in twelve years have I been alone, had time to myself. So now I have to learn to be myself again. That's all.

And she went indoors to help Mrs. Parkes cook and clean, and found some sewing to do for the children. She kept herself occupied every day. At the end of the first term she understood she felt two contrary emotions. First: secret astonishment and dismay that during those weeks when the house was empty of children she had in fact been more occupied (had been careful to keep herself occupied) than ever she had been when the children were around her needing her continual attention. Second: that now she knew the house would be full of them, and for five weeks, she resented the fact she would never be alone. She was already looking back at those hours of sewing, cooking (but by herself) as at a lost freedom which would not be hers for five long weeks. And the two months of term which would succeed the five weeks stretched alluringly open to her — freedom. But what freedom — when in fact she had been so careful *not* to be free of small duties during the last weeks? She looked at herself, Susan Rawlings, sitting in a big chair by the window in the bedroom, sewing shirts or dresses, which she might just as well have bought. She saw herself making cakes for hours at a time in the big family kitchen: yet usually she bought cakes. What she saw was a woman alone, that was true, but she had not felt alone. For instance, Mrs. Parkes was always somewhere in the house. And she did not like being in the garden at all, because of the closeness there of the enemy — irritation, restlessness, emptiness, whatever it was — which keeping her hands occupied made less dangerous for some reason.

Susan did not tell Matthew of these thoughts. They were not sensible. She did not recognise herself in them. What should she say to her dear friend and husband, Matthew? "When I go into the garden, that is, if the children are not there, I feel as if there is an enemy there waiting to invade me." "What enemy, Susan darling?" "Well I don't know, really. . . ." "Perhaps you should see a doctor?"

No, clearly this conversation should not take place. The holidays began and Susan welcomed them. Four children, lively, energetic, intelligent, demanding: she was never, not for a moment of her day, alone. If she was in a room, they would be in the next room, or waiting for her to do something for them; or it would soon be time for lunch or tea, or to take one of them to the dentist. Something to do: five weeks of it, thank goodness.

On the fourth day of these so welcome holidays, she found she was storming with anger at the twins; two shrinking beautiful children who (and this is what checked her) stood hand in hand looking at her with sheer dismayed disbelief. This was their calm mother, shouting at them. And for what? They had come to her with some game, some bit of nonsense. They looked at each other, moved closer for support, and went off hand in hand, leaving Susan holding on to the windowsill of the living room, breathing deep, feeling sick. She went to lie down, telling the older children she had a headache. She heard the boy Harry telling the little ones: "It's all right, Mother's got a headache." She heard that *It's all right* with pain.

That night she said to her husband: "Today I shouted at the twins, quite unfairly." She sounded miserable, and he said gently: "Well, what of it?"

"It's more of an adjustment than I thought, their going to school."

"But Susie, Susie darling. . . ." For she was crouched weeping on the bed. He comforted her: "Susan, what is all this about? You shouted at them? What of it? If you shouted at them fifty times a day it wouldn't be more than the little devils deserve." But she wouldn't laugh. She wept. Soon he comforted her with his body. She became calm. Calm, she wondered what was wrong with her, and why she should mind so much that she might, just once, have behaved unjustly with the children. What did it matter? They had forgotten it all long ago: Mother had a headache and everything was all right.

It was a long time later that Susan understood that that night, when she had wept and Matthew had driven the misery out of her with his big solid body, was the last time, ever in their married life, that they had been — to use their mutual language — with each other. And even that was a lie, because she had not told him of her real fears at all.

The five weeks passed, and Susan was in control of herself, and good and kind, and she looked forward to the holidays with a mixture of fear and longing. She did not know what to expect. She took the twins off to school (the elder children took themselves to school) and she returned to the house determined to face the enemy wherever he was, in the house, or the garden or — where?

She was again restless, she was possessed by restlessness. She cooked and sewed and worked as before, day after day, while Mrs. Parkes remonstrated: "Mrs. Rawlings, what's the need for it? I can do that, it's what you pay me for."

And it was so irrational that she checked herself. She would put the car in the garage, go up to her bedroom, and sit, hands in her lap, forcing herself to be quiet. She listened to Mrs. Parkes moving around the house. She looked out into the garden and saw the branches shake the trees. She sat defeating the enemy, restlessness. Emptiness. She ought to be thinking about her life, about herself. But she did not. Or perhaps she could not. As soon as she forced her mind to think about Susan (for what else did she want to be alone for?), it skipped off to thoughts of butter or school clothes. Or it thought of Mrs. Parkes. She realised that she sat listening for the movements of the cleaning woman, following her every turn, bend, thought. She followed her in her mind from kitchen to bathroom, from table to oven, and it was as if the duster, the cleaning cloth, the saucepan, were in her own hand. She would hear herself saying: No, not like that, don't put that there. . . . Yet she did not give a damn what Mrs. Parkes did, or if she did it at all. Yet she could not prevent herself from being conscious of her, every minute. Yes, this was what was wrong with her: she needed, when she was alone, to be really alone, with no one near. She could not endure the knowledge that in ten minutes or in half an hour Mrs. Parkes would call up the stairs: "Mrs. Rawlings, there's no silver polish. Madam, we're out of flour."

So she left the house and went to sit in the garden where she was screened from the house by trees. She waited for the demon to appear and claim her, but he did not.

She was keeping him off, because she had not, after all, come to an end of arranging herself.

She was planning how to be somewhere where Mrs. Parkes would not come after her with a cup of tea, or a demand to be allowed to telephone (always irritating, since Susan did not care who she telephoned or how often), or just a nice talk about something. Yes, she needed a place, or a state of affairs, where it would not be necessary to keep reminding herself: In ten minutes I must telephone Matthew about . . . and at half past three I must leave early for the children because the car needs cleaning. And at ten o'clock tomorrow I must remember. . . . She was possessed with resentment that the seven hours of freedom in every day (during weekdays in the school term) were not free, that never, not for one second, ever, was she free from the pressure of time, from having to remember this or that. She could never forget herself; never really let herself go into forgetfulness.

Resentment. It was poisoning her. (She looked at this emotion and thought it was absurd. Yet she felt it.) She was a prisoner. (She looked at this thought too, and it was no good telling herself it was a ridiculous one.) She must tell Matthew—but what? She was filled with emotions that were utterly ridiculous, that she despised, yet that nevertheless she was feeling so strongly she could not shake them off.

The school holidays came round, and this time they were for nearly two months, and she behaved with a conscious controlled decency that nearly drove her crazy. She would lock herself in the bathroom, and sit on the edge of the bath, breathing deep, trying to let go into some kind of calm. Or she went up into the spare room, usually empty, where no one would expect her to be. She heard the children calling "Mother, Mother," and kept silent, feeling guilty. Or she went to the very end of the garden, by herself, and looked at the slow-moving brown river; she looked at the river and closed her eyes and breathed slow and deep, taking it into her being, into her veins.

Then she returned to the family, wife and mother, smiling and responsible, feeling as if the pressure of these people — four lively children and her husband — were a painful pressure on the surface of her skin, a hand pressing on her brain. She did not once break down into irritation during these holidays, but it was like living out a prison sentence, and when the children went back to school, she sat on a white stone near the flowing river, and she thought: It is not even a year since the twins went to school, since *they were off my hands* (What on earth did I think I meant when I used the stupid phrase?), and yet I'm a different person. I'm simply not myself. I don't understand it.

Yet she had to understand it. For she knew that this structure — big white house, on which the mortgage still cost four hundred a year, a husband, so good and kind and insightful; four children, all doing so nicely; and the garden where she sat; and Mrs. Parkes, the cleaning woman — all this depended on her, and yet she could not understand why, or even what it was she contributed to it.

She said to Matthew in their bedroom: "I think there must be something wrong with me."

And he said: "Surely not, Susan? You look marvellous — you're as lovely as ever."

She looked at the handsome blond man, with his clear, intelligent, blue-eyed face, and thought: Why is it I can't tell him? Why not? And she said: "I need to be alone more than I am."

At which he swung his slow blue gaze at her, and she saw what she had been dreading: Incredulity. Disbelief. And fear. An incredulous blue stare from a stranger who was her husband, as close to her as her own breath.

He said: "But the children are at school and off your hands."

She said to herself: I've got to force myself to say: Yes, but do you realize that I never feel free? There's never a moment I can say to myself: There's nothing I have to remind myself about, nothing I have to do in half an hour, or an hour, or two hours....

But she said: "I don't feel well."

He said: "Perhaps you need a holiday."

She said, appalled: "But not without you, surely?" For she could not imagine herself going off without him. Yet that was what he meant. Seeing her face, he laughed, and opened his arms, and she went into them, thinking: Yes, yes, but why can't I say it? And what is it I have to say?

She tried to tell him, about never being free. And he listened and said: "But Susan, what sort of freedom can you possibly want — short of being dead! Am I ever free? I go to the office, and I have to be there at ten — all right, half past ten, sometimes. And I have to do this or that, don't I? Then I've got to come home at a certain time — I don't mean it, you know I don't — but if I'm not going to be back home at six I telephone you. When can I ever say to myself: I have nothing to be responsible for in the next six hours?"

Susan, hearing this, was remorseful. Because it was true. The good marriage, the house, the children, depended just as much on his voluntary bondage as it did on hers. But why did he not feel bound? Why didn't he chafe and become restless? No, there was something really wrong with her and this proved it.

And that word "bondage" — why had she used it? She had never felt marriage, or the children, as bondage. Neither had he, or surely they wouldn't be together lying in each other's arms content after twelve years of marriage.

No, her state (whatever it was) was irrelevant, nothing to do with her real good life with her family. She had to accept the fact that, after all, she was an irrational person and to live with it. Some people had to live with crippled arms, or stammers, or being deaf. She would have to live knowing she was subject to a state of mind she could not own.

Nevertheless, as a result of this conversation with her husband, there was a new regime next holidays.

The spare room at the top of the house now had a cardboard sign saying: PRIVATE! DO NOT DISTURB! on it. (This sign had been drawn in coloured chalks by the children, after a discussion between the parents in which it was decided this was psychologically the right thing.) The family and Mrs. Parkes knew this was "Mother's Room" and that she was entitled to her privacy. Many serious conversations took place between Matthew and the children about not taking Mother for granted. Susan overheard the first, between father and Harry, the older boy, and was surprised at her irritation over it. Surely she could have a room somewhere in that big house and retire into it without such a fuss being made? Without it being so solemnly discussed? Why couldn't she simply have announced: "I'm going to fit out the little top room for myself, and when I'm in it I'm not to be disturbed for anything short of fire"? Just that, and finished; instead of long earnest discussions. When she heard Harry and Matthew explaining it to the twins with Mrs. Parkes coming in — "Yes, well, a family sometimes gets on top of a woman" — she had to go right away to the bottom of her garden until the devils of exasperation had finished their dance in her blood.

But now there was a room, and she could go there when she liked, she used it seldom: she felt even more caged there than in her bedroom! One day she had gone up there after a lunch for ten children she had cooked and served because Mrs. Parkes was not there, and had sat alone for a while looking into the garden. She saw the children stream out from the kitchen and stand looking up at the window where she sat behind the curtains. They were all — her children and their friends — discussing Mother's Room. A few minutes later, the chase of children in some game came pounding up the stairs, but ended as abruptly as if they had fallen over a ravine, so sudden was the silence. They had remembered she was there, and had gone silent in a great gale of "Hush! Shhhhhh! Quiet, you'll disturb her. . . ." And they went tiptoeing downstairs like criminal conspirators.

When she came down to make tea for them, they all apologised. The twins put their arms around her, from front and back, making a human cage of loving limbs, and promised it would never occur again. "We forgot, Mummy, we forgot all about it!"

What it amounted to was that Mother's Room, and her need for privacy, had become a valuable lesson in respect for other people's rights. Quite soon Susan was going up to the room only because it was a lesson it was a pity to drop. Then she took sewing up there, and the children and Mrs. Parkes came in and out: it had become another family room.

She sighed, and smiled, and resigned herself—she made jokes at her own expense with Matthew over the room. That is, she did from the self she liked, she respected. But at the same time, something inside her howled with impatience, with rage. . . . And she was frightened. One day she found herself kneeling by her bed and praying: "Dear God, keep it away from me, keep him away from me." She meant the devil, for she now thought of it, not caring if she was irrational, as some sort of demon. She imagined him, or it, as a youngish man, or perhaps a middle-aged man pretending to be young. Or a man young-looking from immaturity? At any rate, she saw the young-looking face which, when she drew closer, had dry lines about mouth and eyes. He was thinnish, meagre in build. And he had a reddish complexion, and ginger hair. That was he—a gingery, energetic man, and he wore a reddish hairy jacket, unpleasant to the touch.

Well, one day she saw him. She was standing at the bottom of the garden, watching the river ebb past, when she raised her eyes and saw this person, or being, sitting on the white stone bench. He was looking at her, and grinning. In his hand was a long crooked stick, which he had picked off the ground, or broken off the tree above him. He was absent-mindedly, out of an absent-minded or freakish impulse of spite, using the stick to stir around in the coils of a blindworm or a grass snake (or some kind of snake-like creature: it was whitish and unhealthy to look at, unpleasant). The snake was twisting about, flinging its coils from side to side in a kind of dance of protest against the teasing prodding stick.

Susan looked at him, thinking: Who is the stranger? What is he doing in our garden? Then she recognised the man around whom her terrors had crystallised. As she did so, he vanished. She made herself walk over to the bench. A shadow from a branch lay across thin emerald grass, moving jerkily over its roughness, and she could see why she had taken it for a snake, lashing and twisting. She went back to the house thinking: Right, then, so I've seen him with my own eyes, so I'm not crazy after all—there is a danger because I've seen him. He is lurking in the garden and some-times even in the house, and he wants to *get into me and to take me over.*

She dreamed of having a room or a place, anywhere, where she could go and sit, by herself, no one knowing where she was.

Once, near Victoria, she found herself outside a news agent that had Rooms to Let advertised. She decided to rent a room, telling no one. Sometimes she could take the train into Richmond and sit alone in it for an hour or two. Yet how could she? A room would cost three or four pounds a week, and she earned no money, and how could she explain to Matthew that she needed such a sum? What for? It did not occur to her that she was taking it for granted she wasn't going to tell him about the room.

Well, it was out of the question, having a room; yet she knew she must.

One day, when a school term was well established, and none of the children had measles or other ailments, and everything seemed in order, she did the shopping early, explained to Mrs. Parkes she was meeting an old school friend, took the train to Victoria, searched until she found a small quiet hotel, and asked for a room for the day. They did not let rooms by the day, the manageress said, looking doubtful, since Susan so obviously was not the kind of woman who needed a room for unrespectable reasons. Susan made a long explanation about not being well, being unable to shop without frequent rests for lying down. At last she was allowed to rent the room provided she paid a full night's price for it. She was taken up by the manageress and a maid, both concerned over the state of her health . . . which must be pretty bad if, living at Richmond (she had signed her name and address in the register), she needed a shelter at Victoria.

The room was ordinary and anonymous, and was just what Susan needed. She put a shilling in the gas fire, and sat, eyes shut, in a dingy arm-chair with her back to a dingy window. She was alone. She was alone. She was alone. She could feel pressures lifting off her. First the sounds of traffic came very loud; then they seemed to vanish; she might even have slept a little. A knock on the door: it was Miss Townsend, the manageress, bringing her a cup of tea with her own hands, so concerned was she over Susan's long silence and possible illness.

Miss Townsend was a lonely woman of fifty, running this hotel with all the rectitude expected of her, and she sensed in Susan the possibility of understanding companionship. She stayed to talk. Susan found herself in the middle of a fantastic story about her illness, which got more and more impossible as she tried to make it tally with the large house at Richmond, well-off husband, and four children. Suppose she said instead: Miss Townsend, I'm here in your hotel because I need to be alone for a few hours, above all *alone and with no one knowing where I am*. She said it mentally, and saw, mentally, the look that would inevitably come on Miss Townsend's elderly maiden's face. "Miss Townsend, my four children and my husband are driving me insane, do you understand that? Yes, I can see from the gleam of hysteria in your eyes that comes from loneliness controlled but only just contained that I've got everything in the world you've ever longed for. Well, Miss Townsend, I don't want any of it. You can have it, Miss Townsend. I wish I was absolutely alone in the world, like you. Miss Townsend, I'm besieged by seven devils, Miss Townsend, Miss Townsend, let me stay here in your hotel where the devils can't get me. . . ." Instead of saying all this, she described her anaemia, agreed to try Miss Townsend's remedy for it, which was raw liver, minced, between whole-meal bread, and said yes, perhaps it would be better if she stayed at home and let a friend do shopping for her. She paid her bill and left the hotel, defeated.

At home Mrs. Parkes said she didn't really like it, no, not really, when Mrs. Rawlings was away from nine in the morning until five. The teacher had telephoned from school to say Joan's teeth were paining her, and she hadn't known what to say; and what was she to make for the children's tea, Mrs. Rawlings hadn't said.

All this was nonsense, of course. Mrs. Parkes's complaint was that Susan had withdrawn herself spiritually, leaving the burden of the big house on her.

Susan looked back at her day of "freedom" which had resulted in her becoming a friend of the lonely Miss Townsend, and in Mrs. Parkes's remonstrances. Yet she remembered the short blissful hour of being alone, really alone. She was determined to arrange her life, no matter what it cost, so that she could have that solitude more often. An absolute solitude, where no one knew her or cared about her.

But how? She thought of saying to her old employer: I want you to back me up in a story with Matthew that I am doing part-time work for you. The truth is that. . . . But she would have to tell him a lie too, and which lie? She could not say: I want to sit by myself three or four times a week in a rented room. And besides, he knew Matthew, and she could not really ask him to tell lies on her behalf, apart from being bound to think it meant a lover.

Suppose she really took a part-time job, which she could get through fast and efficiently, leaving time for herself. What job? Addressing envelopes? Canvassing?

And there was Mrs. Parkes, working widow, who knew exactly what she was prepared to give to the house, who knew by instinct when her mistress withdrew in spirit from her responsibilities. Mrs. Parkes was one of the servers of this world, but she needed someone to serve. She had to have Mrs. Rawlings, her madam, at the top of the house or in the garden, so that she could come and get support from her: "Yes, the bread's not what it was when I was a girl. . . . Yes, Harry's got a wonderful appetite, I wonder where he puts it all. . . . Yes, it's lucky the twins are so much of a size, they can wear each other's shoes, that's a saving in these hard times. . . . Yes, the cherry jam from Switzerland is not a patch on the jam from Poland, and three times the price. . . ." And so on. That sort of talk Mrs. Parkes must have, every day, or she would leave, not knowing herself why she left.

Susan Rawlings, thinking these thoughts, found that she was prowling through the great thicketed garden like a wild cat: she was walking up the stairs, down the stairs, through the rooms into the garden, along the brown running river, back, up through the house, down again. . . . It was a wonder Mrs. Parkes did not think it strange. But, on the contrary, Mrs. Rawlings could do what she liked, she could stand on her head if she wanted, provided she was *there*. Susan Rawlings prowled and muttered through her house, hating Mrs. Parkes, hating poor Miss Townsend, dreaming of her hour of solitude in the dingy respectability of Miss Townsend's hotel bedroom, and she knew quite well she was mad. Yes, she was mad.

She said to Matthew that she must have a holiday. Matthew agreed with her. This was not as things had been once — how they had talked in each other's arms in the marriage bed. He had, she knew, diagnosed her finally as *unreasonable*. She had become someone outside himself that he had to manage. They were living side by side in this house like two tolerably friendly strangers.

Having told Mrs. Parkes — or rather, asked for her permission — she went off on a walking holiday in Wales. She chose the remotest place she knew of. Every morning the children telephoned her before they went off to school, to encourage and support her, just as they had over Mother's Room. Every evening she telephoned them, spoke to each child in turn, and then to Matthew. Mrs. Parkes, given permission to telephone for instructions or advice, did so every day at lunchtime. When, as happened three times, Mrs. Rawlings was out on the mountainside, Mrs. Parkes asked that she should ring back at such-and-such a time, for she would not be happy in what she was doing without Mrs. Rawlings's blessing.

Susan prowled over wild country with the telephone wire holding her to her duty like a leash. The next time she must telephone, or wait to be telephoned, nailed her to her cross. The mountains themselves seemed trammelled by her unfreedom. Everywhere on the mountains, where she met no one at all, from breakfast time to dusk, excepting sheep, or a shepherd, she came face to face with her own craziness, which might attack her in the broadest valleys, so that they seemed too small, or on a mountain top from which she could see a hundred other mountains and valleys, so that they seemed too low, too small, with the sky pressing down too close. She would stand gazing at a hillside brilliant with ferns and bracken, jewelled with running water, and see nothing but her devil, who lifted inhuman eyes at her from where he leaned negligently on a rock, switching at his ugly yellow boots with a leafy twig.

She returned to her home and family, with the Welsh emptiness at the back of her mind like a promise of freedom.

She told her husband she wanted to have an *au pair* girl.

They were in their bedroom, it was late at night, the children slept. He sat, shirted and slippered, in a chair by the window, looking out. She sat brushing her hair and watching him in the mirror. A time-hallowed scene in the connubial bedroom. He said nothing, while she heard the arguments coming into his mind, only to be rejected because every one was *reasonable*.

"It seems strange to get one now; after all, the children are in school most of the day. Surely the time for you to have help was when you were stuck with them day and night. Why don't you ask Mrs. Parkes to cook for you? She's even offered to — I can understand if you are tired of cooking for six people. But you know that an *au pair* girl means all kinds of problems; it's not like having an ordinary char in during the day. . . ."

Finally he said carefully: "Are you thinking of going back to work?"

"No," she said, "no, not really." She made herself sound vague, rather stupid. She went on brushing her black hair and peering at herself so as to be oblivious of the short uneasy glances her Matthew kept giving her. "Do you think we can't afford it?" she went on vaguely, not at all the old efficient Susan who knew exactly what they could afford.

"It's not that," he said, looking out of the window at dark trees, so as not to look at her. Meanwhile she examined a round, candid, pleasant face with clear dark brows and clear grey eyes. A sensible face. She brushed thick healthy black hair and thought: Yet that's the reflection of a mad-woman. How very strange! Much more to the point if what looked back at me was the gingery green-eyed demon with his dry meagre smile. . . . Why wasn't Matthew agreeing? After all, what else could he do? She was breaking her part of the bargain and there was no way of forcing her to keep it: that her spirit, her soul, should live in this house, so that the people in it could grow like plants in water, and Mrs. Parkes remain content in their service. In return for this, he would be a good loving husband, and responsible towards the children. Well, nothing like this had been true of either of them for a long time. He did his duty, perfunctorily; she did not even pretend to do hers. And he had become like other husbands, with his real life in his work and the people he met there, and very likely a serious affair. All this was her fault.

At last he drew heavy curtains, blotting out the trees, and turned to force her attention: "Susan, are you really sure we need a girl?" But she would not meet his appeal at all. She was running the brush over her hair again and again, lifting fine black clouds in a small hiss of electricity. She was peering in and smiling as if she were amused at the clinging hissing hair that followed the brush.

"Yes, I think it would be a good idea, on the whole," she said, with the cunning of a madwoman evading the real point.

In the mirror she could see her Matthew lying on his back, his hands behind his head, staring upwards, his face sad and hard. She felt her heart (the old heart of Susan Rawlings) soften and call out to him. But she set it to be indifferent.

He said: "Susan, the children?" It was an appeal that *almost* reached her. He opened his arms, lifting them palms up, empty. She had only to run across and fling herself into them, onto his hard, warm chest, and melt into herself, into Susan. But she could not. She would not see his lifted arms. She said vaguely: "Well, surely it'll be even better for them? We'll get a French or a German girl and they'll learn the language."

In the dark she lay beside him, feeling frozen, a stranger. She felt as if Susan had been spirited away. She disliked very much this woman who lay here, cold and indifferent beside a suffering man, but she could not change her.

Next morning she set about getting a girl, and very soon came Sophie Traub from Hamburg, a girl of twenty, laughing, healthy, blue-eyed, intending to learn English. Indeed, she already spoke a good deal. In return for a room — "Mother's Room" — and her food, she undertook to do some light cooking, and to be with the children when Mrs. Rawlings asked. She was an intelligent girl and understood perfectly what was needed. Susan said: "I go off sometimes, for the morning or for the day — well, sometimes the children run home from school, or they ring up, or a teacher rings up. I should be here, really. And there's the daily woman. . . ." And Sophie laughed her deep fruity *Fräulein's* laugh, showed her fine white teeth and her dimples, and said: "You want some person to play mistress of the house sometimes, not so?"

"Yes, that is just so," said Susan, a bit dry, despite herself, thinking in secret fear how easy it was, how much nearer to the end she was than she thought. Healthy Fräulein Traub's instant understanding of their position proved this to be true.

The *au pair* girl, because of her own commonsense, or (as Susan said to herself, with her new inward shudder) because she had been *chosen* so well by

Susan, was a success with everyone, the children liking her, Mrs. Parkes forgetting almost at once that she was German, and Matthew finding her "nice to have around the house." For he was now taking things as they came, from the surface of life, withdrawn both as a husband and a father from the household.

One day Susan saw how Sophie and Mrs. Parkes were talking and laughing in the kitchen, and she announced that she would be away until tea time. She knew exactly where to go and what she must look for. She took the District Line to South Kensington, changed to the Circle, got off at Paddington, and walked around looking at the smaller hotels until she was satisfied with one which had FRED'S HOTEL painted on windowpanes that needed cleaning. The facade was a faded shiny yellow, like unhealthy skin. A door at the end of a passage said she must knock; she did, and Fred appeared. He was not at all attractive, not in any way, being fattish, and run-down, and wearing a tasteless striped suit. He had small sharp eyes in a white creased face, and was quite prepared to let Mrs. Jones (she chose the farcical name deliberately, staring him out) have a room three days a week from ten until six. Provided of course that she paid in advance each time she came? Susan produced fifteen shillings (no price had been set by him) and held it out, still fixing him with a bold unblinking challenge she had not known until then she could use at will. Looking at her still, he took up a ten-shilling note from her palm between thumb and forefinger, fingered it; then shuffled up two half-crowns, held out his own palm with these bits of money displayed thereon, and let his gaze lower broodingly at them. They were standing in the passage, a red-shaded light above, bare boards beneath, and a strong smell of floor polish rising about them. He shot his gaze up at her over the still-extended palm, and smiled as if to say: What do you take me for? "I shan't," said Susan, "be using this room for the purposes of making money." He still waited. She added another five shillings, at which he nodded and said: "You pay, and I ask no questions." "Good," said Susan. He now went past her to the stairs, and there waited a moment: the light from the street door being in her eyes, she lost sight of him momentarily. Then she saw a sober-suited, white-faced, white-balding little man trotting up the stairs like a waiter, and she went after him. They proceeded in utter silence up the stairs of this house where no questions were asked — Fred's Hotel, which could afford the freedom for its visitors that poor Miss Townsend's hotel could not. The room was hideous. It had a single window, with thin green brocade curtains, a three-quarter bed that had a cheap green satin bedspread on it, a fireplace with a gas fire and a shilling meter by it, a chest of drawers, and a green wicker armchair.

"Thank you," said Susan, knowing that Fred (if this was Fred, and not George, or Herbert, or Charlie) was looking at her, not so much with curiosity, an emotion he would not own to, for professional reasons, but with a philosophical sense of what was appropriate. Having taken her money and shown her up and agreed to everything, he was clearly disapproving of her for coming here. She did not belong here at all, so his look said. (But she knew, already, how very much she did belong: the room had been waiting for her to join it.) "Would you have me called at five o'clock, please?" and he nodded and went downstairs.

It was twelve in the morning. She was free. She sat in the armchair, she simply sat, she closed her eyes and sat and let herself be alone. She was alone and no one knew where she was. When a knock came on the door she was annoyed, and prepared to show it: but it was Fred himself; it was five o'clock and he was calling her as ordered. He flicked his sharp little eyes over the room—bed, first. It was undisturbed. She might never have been in the room at all. She thanked him, said she would be returning the day after tomorrow, and left. She was back home in time to cook supper, to put the children to bed, to cook a second supper for her husband and herself later. And to welcome Sophie back from the pictures where she had gone with a friend. All these things she did cheerfully, willingly. But she was thinking all the time of the hotel room; she was longing for it with her whole being.

Three times a week. She arrived promptly at ten, looked Fred in the eyes, gave him twenty shillings, followed him up the stairs, went into the room, and shut the door on him with gentle firmness. For Fred, disapproving of her being here at all, was quite ready to let friendship, or at least acquaintanceship, follow his disapproval, if only she would let him. But he was content to go off on her dismissing nod, with the twenty shillings in his hand.

She sat in the armchair and shut her eyes.

What did she *do* in the room? Why, nothing at all. From the chair, when it had rested her, she went to the window, stretching her arms, smiling, treasuring her anonymity, to look out. She was no longer Susan Rawlings, mother of four, wife of Matthew, employer of Mrs. Parkes and of Sophie Traub, with these and those relations with friends, school-teachers, tradesmen. She no longer was mistress of the big white house and garden, owning clothes suitable for this and that activity or occasion. She was Mrs. Jones, and she was alone, and she had no past and no future. Here I am, she thought, after all these years of being married and having children and playing those roles of responsibility—and I'm just the same. Yet there have been times I thought that nothing existed of me except the roles that went with being Mrs. Matthew Rawlings. Yes, here I am, and if I never saw any of my family again, here I would still be . . . how very strange that is! And she leaned on the sill, and looked into the street, loving the men and women who passed, because she did not know them. She looked at the down-trodden buildings over the street, and at the sky, wet and dingy, or sometimes blue, and she felt she had never seen buildings or sky before. And then she went back to the chair, empty, her mind a blank. Sometimes she talked aloud, saying nothing—an exclamation, meaningless, followed by a comment about the floral pattern on the thin rug, or a stain on the green satin coverlet. For the most part, she wool-gathered—what word is there for it?—brooded, wandered, simply went dark, feeling emptiness run deliciously through her veins like the movement of her blood.

This room had become more her own than the house she lived in. One morning she found Fred taking her a flight higher than usual. She stopped, refusing to go up, and demanded her usual room, Number 19. "Well, you'll have to wait half an hour, then," he said. Willingly she descended to the dark disinfectant-smelling hall, and sat waiting until the two, man and woman, came down the stairs, giving her swift indifferent glances before they hurried out into the street, separating at the door. She went up to the room, *her* room, which they had just vacated. It was no less hers, though the windows were set wide open, and a maid was straightening the bed as she came in.

After these days of solitude, it was both easy to play her part as mother and wife, and difficult — because it was so easy: she felt an imposter. She felt as if her shell moved here, with her family, answering to Mummy, Mother, Susan, Mrs. Rawlings. She was surprised no one saw through her, that she wasn't turned out of doors, as a fake. On the contrary, it seemed the children loved her more; Matthew and she "got on" pleasantly, and Mrs. Parkes was happy in her work under (for the most part, it must be confessed) Sophie Traub. At night she lay beside her husband, and they made love again, apparently just as they used to, when they were really married. But she, Susan, or the being who answered so readily and improbably to the name of Susan, was not there: she was in Fred's Hotel, in Paddington, waiting for the easing hours of solitude to begin.

Soon she made a new arrangement with Fred and with Sophie. It was for five days a week. As for the money, five pounds, she simply asked Matthew for it. She saw that she was not even frightened he might ask what for: he would give it to her, she knew that, and yet it was terrifying it could be so, for this close couple, these partners, had once known the destination of every shilling they must spend. He agreed to give her five pounds a week. She asked for just so much, not a penny more. He sounded indifferent about it. It was as if he were paying her, she thought: *paying her off* — yes, that was it. Terror came back for a moment when she understood this, but she stilled it: things had gone too far for that. Now, every week, on Sunday nights, he gave her five pounds, turning away from her before their eyes could meet on the transaction. As for Sophie Traub, she was to be somewhere in or near the house until six at night, after which she was free. She was not to cook, or to clean; she was simply to be there. So she gardened or sewed, and asked friends in, being a person who was bound to have a lot of friends. If the children were sick, she nursed them. If teachers telephoned, she answered them sensibly. For the five daytimes in the school week, she was altogether the mistress of the house.

One night in the bedroom, Matthew asked: "Susan, I don't want to interfere — don't think that, please — but are you sure you are well?"

She was brushing her hair at the mirror. She made two more strokes on either side of her head, before she replied: "Yes, dear, I am sure I am well."

He was again lying on his back, his blond head on his hands, his elbows angled up and part-concealing his face. He said: "Then Susan, I have to ask you this question, though you must understand, I'm not putting any sort of pressure on you." (Susan heard the word "pressure" with dismay, because this was inevitable; of course she could not go on like this.) "Are things going to go on like this?"

"Well," she said, going vague and bright and idiotic again, so as to escape: "Well, I don't see why not."

He was jerking his elbows up and down, in annoyance or in pain, and, looking at him, she saw he had got thin, even gaunt; and restless angry movements were not what she remembered of him. He said: "Do you want a divorce, is that it?"

At this, Susan only with the greatest difficulty stopped herself from laughing: she could hear the bright bubbling laughter she *would* have emitted, had she let herself. He could only mean one thing: she had a lover, and that was why she spent her days in London, as lost to him as if she had vanished to another continent.

Then the small panic set in again: she understood that he hoped she did have a lover, he was begging her to say so, because otherwise it would be too terrifying.

She thought this out as she brushed her hair, watching the fine black stuff fly up to make its little clouds of electricity, hiss, hiss, hiss. Behind her head, across the room, was a blue wall. She realised she was absorbed in watching the black hair making shapes against the blue. She should be answering him. "Do *you* want a divorce, Matthew?"

He said: "That surely isn't the point, is it?"

"You brought it up, I didn't," she said, brightly, suppressing meaningless tinkling laughter.

Next day she asked Fred: "Have enquiries been made for me?"

He hesitated, and she said: "I've been coming here a year now. I've made no trouble, and you've been paid every day. I have a right to be told."

"As a matter of fact, Mrs. Jones, a man did come asking."

"A man from a detective agency?"

"Well, he could have been, couldn't he?"

"I was asking you. . . . Well, what did you tell him?"

"I told him a Mrs. Jones came every weekday from ten until five or six and stayed in Number 19 by herself."

"Describing me?"

"Well, Mrs. Jones, I had no alternative. Put yourself in my place."

"By rights I should deduct what that man gave you for the information."

He raised shocked eyes: she was not the sort of person to make jokes like this! Then he chose to laugh: a pinkish wet slit appeared across his white crinkled face; his eyes positively begged her to laugh, otherwise he might lose some money. She remained grave, looking at him.

He stopped laughing and said: "You want to go up now?" — returning to the familiarity, the comradeship, of the country where no questions are asked, on which (and he knew it) she depended completely.

She went up to sit in her wicker chair. But it was not the same. Her husband had searched her out. (The world had searched her out.) The pressures were on her. She was here with his connivance. He might walk in at any moment, here, into Room 19. She imagined the report from the detective agency: "A woman calling herself Mrs. Jones, fitting the description of your wife (et cetera, et cetera, et cetera), stays alone all day in Room No. 19. She insists on this room, waits for it if it is engaged. As far as the proprietor knows, she receives no visitors there, male or female." A report something on these lines Matthew must have received.

Well, of course he was right: things couldn't go on like this. He had put an end to it all simply by sending a detective after her.

She tried to shrink herself back into the shelter of the room, a snail pecked out of its shell and trying to squirm back. But the peace of the room had gone. She was trying consciously to revive it, trying to let go into the dark creative trance (or whatever it was) that she had found there. It was no use, yet she craved for it, she was as ill as a suddenly deprived addict.

Several times she returned to the room, to look for herself there, but instead she found the unnamed spirit of restlessness, a pricking fevered hunger for movement, an irritable self-consciousness that made her brain feel as if it had coloured lights going on and off inside it. Instead of the soft dark that had been the room's air, were now waiting for her demons that made her dash blindly about, muttering words of hate; she was impelling herself from point to point like a moth dashing itself against a windowpane, sliding to the bottom, fluttering off on broken wings, then crashing into the invisible barrier again. And again and again. Soon she was exhausted, and she told Fred that for a while she would not be needing the room, she was going on a holiday. Home she went, to the big white house by the river. The middle of a weekday, and she felt guilty at returning to her own home when not expected. She stood unseen, looking in at the kitchen window. Mrs. Parkes, wearing a discarded floral overall of Susan's, was stooping to slide something into the oven. Sophie, arms folded, was leaning her back against a cupboard and laughing at some joke made by a girl not seen before by Susan — a dark foreign girl, Sophie's visitor. In an armchair Molly, one of the twins, lay curled, sucking her thumb and watching the grownups. She must have some sickness, to be kept from school. The child's listless face, the dark circles under her eyes, hurt Susan: Molly was looking at the three grownups working and talking in exactly the same way Susan looked at the four through the kitchen window: she was remote, shut off from them.

But then, just as Susan imagined herself going in, picking up the little girl, and sitting in an armchair with her, stroking her probably heated forehead, Sophie did just that: she had been standing on one leg, the other knee flexed, its foot set against the wall. Now she let her foot in its ribbon-tied red shoe slide down the wall, stood solid on two feet, clapping her hands before and behind her, and sang a couple of lines in German, so that the child lifted her heavy eyes at her and began to smile. Then she walked, or rather skipped, over to the child, swung her up, and let her fall into her lap at the same moment she sat herself. She said "Hopla! Hopla! Molly . . ." and began stroking the dark untidy young head that Molly laid on her shoulder for comfort.

Well. . . . Susan blinked the tears of farewell out of her eyes, and went quietly up through the house to her bedroom. There she sat looking at the river through the trees. She felt at peace, but in a way that was new to her. She had no desire to move, to talk, to do anything at all. The devils that had haunted the house, the garden, were not there; but she knew it was because her soul was in Room 19 in Fred's Hotel; she was not really here at all. It was a sensation that should have been frightening: to sit at her own bedroom window, listening to

Sophie's rich young voice sing German nursery songs to her child, listening to Mrs. Parkes clatter and move below, and to know that all this had nothing to do with her: she was already out of it.

Later, she made herself go down and say she was home: it was unfair to be here unannounced. She took lunch with Mrs. Parkes, Sophie, Sophie's Italian friend Maria, and her daughter Molly, and felt like a visitor.

A few days later, at bedtime, Matthew said: "Here's your five pounds," and pushed them over at her. Yet he must have known she had not been leaving the house at all.

She shook her head, gave it back to him, and said, in explanation, not in accusation: "As soon as you knew where I was, there was no point."

He nodded, not looking at her. He was turned away from her: thinking, she knew, how best to handle this wife who terrified him.

He said: "I wasn't trying to. . . . It's just that I was worried."

"Yes, I know."

"I must confess that I was beginning to wonder. . . ."

"You thought I had a lover?"

"Yes, I am afraid I did."

She knew that he wished she had. She sat wondering how to say: "For a year now I've been spending all my days in a very sordid hotel room. It's the place where I'm happy. In fact, without it I don't exist." She heard herself saying this, and understood how terrified he was that she might. So instead she said: "Well, perhaps you're not far wrong."

Probably Matthew would think the hotel proprietor lied: he would want to think so.

"Well," he said, and she could hear his voice spring up, so to speak with relief, "in that case I must confess I've got a bit of an affair on myself."

She said, detached and interested: "Really? Who is she?" and saw Matthew's startled look because of this reaction.

"It's Phil. Phil Hunt."

She had known Phil Hunt well in the old unmarried days. She was thinking: No, she won't do, she's too neurotic and difficult. She's never been happy yet. Sophie's much better. Well, Matthew will see that himself as sensible as he is.

This line of thought went on in silence, while she said aloud: "It's no point telling you about mine, because you don't know him."

Quick, quick, invent, she thought. Remember how you invented all that nonsense for Miss Townsend.

She began slowly, careful not to contradict herself: "His name is Michael" (*Michael What?*) — "Michael Plant." (What a silly name!) "He's rather like you — in looks, I mean." And indeed, she could imagine herself being touched by no one but Matthew himself. "He's a publisher." (Really? Why?) "He's got a wife already and two children."

She brought out this fantasy, proud of herself.

Matthew said: "Are you two thinking of marrying?"

She said, before she could stop herself: "Good God, *no!*"

She realised, if Matthew wanted to marry Phil Hunt, that this was too emphatic, but apparently it was all right, for his voice sounded relieved as he said: "It is a bit impossible to imagine oneself married to anyone else, isn't it?" With which he pulled her to him, so that her head lay on his shoulder. She turned her face into the dark of his flesh, and listened to the blood pounding through her ears saying: I am alone, I am alone, I am alone.

In the morning Susan lay in bed while he dressed.

He had been thinking things out in the night, because now he said: "Susan, why don't we make a foursome?"

Of course, she said to herself, of course he would be bound to say that. If one is sensible, if one is reasonable, if one never allows oneself a base thought or an envious emotion, naturally one says: Let's make a foursome!

"Why not?" she said.

"We could all meet for lunch. I mean, it's ridiculous, you sneaking off to filthy hotels, and me staying late at the office, and all the lies everyone has to tell."

What on earth did I say his name was? — she panicked, then said: "I think it's a good idea, but Michael is away at the moment. When he comes back, though — and I'm sure you two would like each other."

"He's away, is he? So that's why you've been. . . ." Her husband put his hand to the knot of his tie in a gesture of male coquetry she would not before have associated with him; and he bent to kiss her cheek with the expression that goes with the words: Oh you naughty little puss! And she felt its answering look, naughty and coy, come onto her face.

Inside she was dissolving in horror at them both, at how far they had both sunk from honesty of emotion.

So now she was saddled with a lover, and he had a mistress! How ordinary, how reassuring, how jolly! And now they would make a foursome of it, and go about to theatres and restaurants. After all, the Rawlings could well afford that sort of thing, and presumably the publisher Michael Plant could afford to do himself and his mistress quite well. No, there was nothing to stop the four of them developing the most intricate relationship of civilised tolerance, all enveloped in a charming afterglow of autumnal passion. Perhaps they would all go off on holidays together? She had known people who did. Or perhaps Matthew would draw the line there? Why should he, though, if he was capable of talking about "foursomes" at all?

She lay in the empty bedroom, listening to the car drive off with Matthew in it, off to work. Then she heard the children clattering off to school to the accompaniment of Sophie's cheerfully ringing voice. She slid down into the hollow of the bed, for shelter against her own irrelevance. And she stretched out her hand to the hollow where her husband's body had lain, but found no comfort there: he was not her husband. She curled herself up in a small tight ball under the clothes: she could stay here all day, all week, indeed, all her life.

But in a few days she must produce Michael Plant, and — but how? She must presumably find some agreeable man prepared to impersonate a publisher called Michael Plant. And in return for which she would — what?

Well, for one thing they would make love. The idea made her want to cry with sheer exhaustion. Oh no, she had finished with all that — the proof of it was that the words "make love," or even imagining it, trying hard to revive no more than the pleasures of sensuality, let alone affection, or love, made her want to run away and hide from the sheer effort of the thing. . . . Good Lord, why make love at all? Why make love with anyone? Or if you are going to make love, what does it matter who with? Why shouldn't she simply walk into the street, pick up a man, and have a roaring sexual affair with him? Why not? Or even with Fred? What difference did it make?

But she had let herself in for it — an interminable stretch of time with a lover, called Michael, as part of a gallant civilised foursome. Well, she could not, and she would not.

She got up, dressed, went down to find Mrs. Parkes, and asked her for the loan of a pound, since Matthew, she said, had forgotten to leave her money. She exchanged with Mrs. Parkes variations on the theme that husbands are all the same, they don't think, and without saying a word to Sophie, whose voice could be heard upstairs from the telephone, walked to the underground, travelled to South Kensington, changed to the Inner Circle, got out at Paddington, and walked to Fred's Hotel. There she told Fred that she wasn't going on holiday after all, she needed the room. She would have to wait an hour, Fred said. She went to a busy tearoom-cum-restaurant around the corner, and sat watching the people flow in and out the door that kept swinging open and shut, watched them mingle and merge, and separate, felt her being flow into them, into their movement. When the hour was up, she left a half-crown for her pot of tea, and left the place without looking back at it, just as she had left her house, the big, beautiful white house, without another look, but silently dedicating it to Sophie. She returned to Fred, received the key of Number 19, now free, and ascended the grimy stairs slowly, letting floor after floor fall away below her, keeping her eyes lifted, so that floor after floor descended jerkily to her level of vision, and fell away out of sight.

Number 19 was the same. She saw everything with an acute, narrow, checking glance: the cheap shine of the satin spread, which had been replaced carelessly after the two bodies had finished their convulsions under it; a trace of powder on the glass that topped the chest of drawers; an intense green shade in a fold of the curtain. She stood at the window, looking down, watching people pass and pass and pass until her mind went dark from the constant movement. Then she sat in the wicker chair, letting herself go slack. But she had to be careful, because she did not want, today, to be surprised by Fred's knock at five o'clock.

The demons were not here. They had gone forever, because she was buying her freedom from them. She was slipping already into the dark fructifying dream that seemed to caress her inwardly, like the movement of her blood . . . but she had to think about Matthew first. Should she write a letter for the coroner? But what should she say? She would like to leave him with the look on his face she had seen this morning — banal, admittedly, but at least confidently healthy. Well, that was impossible, one did not look like that with a wife dead from suicide. But how to leave him believing she was dying because of a man — because of the fascinating publisher Michael Plant? Oh, how ridiculous! How absurd! How humiliating! But she decided not to trouble about it, simply not to think about the living. If he wanted to believe she had a lover, he would believe it. And he *did* want to believe it. Even when he had found out that there was no publisher in London called Michael Plant, he would think: Oh poor Susan, she was afraid to give me his real name.

And what did it matter whether he married Phil Hunt or Sophie? Though it ought to be Sophie, who was already the mother of those children . . . and what hypocrisy to sit here worrying about the children, when she was going to leave them because she had not got the energy to stay.

She had about four hours. She spent them delightfully, darkly, sweetly, letting herself slide gently, gently, to the edge of the river. Then, with hardly a break in her consciousness, she got up, pushed the thin rug against the door, made sure the windows were tight shut, put two shillings in the meter, and turned on the gas. For the first time since she had been in the room she lay on the hard bed that smelled stale, that smelled of sweat and sex.

She lay on her back on the green satin cover, but her legs were chilly. She got up, found a blanket folded in the bottom of the chest of drawers, and carefully covered her legs with it. She was quite content lying there, listening to the faint soft hiss of the gas that poured into the room, into her lungs, into her brain, as she drifted off into the dark river.

Clarice Lispector

Clarice Lispector (1925–1977) was born of Russian parents in the Ukraine, but two months after her birth, her family moved to Brazil. As a teenager growing up in Rio de Janeiro, she began to write stories and plays while embarking on an ambitious study of contemporary Brazilian and European literature, particularly the fiction of Katherine Mansfield and Virginia Woolf, with whom she felt a special affinity, and the existentialist philosophy of Albert Camus and Jean-Paul Sartre. In 1944 she graduated from the National Faculty of Law and worked as one of Brazil's first female journalists. Shortly afterward Lispector married a diplomat and published her first novel, *Close to the Savage Heart* (1944).

Living in Europe and the United States with her husband from 1945 to 1960, Lispector wrote many stories and novels in which she explored her preoccupation with existential themes. Literary critics singled out the stories in *Family Ties* (1960), from which "The Smallest Woman in the World" is taken, for particular praise. In this story Lispector created a world both exotic and familiar, dramatizing the instinct for survival that directs the thoughts and actions of every living creature. As the critic Giovanni Pontiero has observed, Lispector's stories suggest a surreal quality in their portrayal of the everyday lives of her characters. "Free from psychological conflicts, they show a greater participation in what is real—the greater space that includes all spaces."

Lispector believed that the essence of all art and literature is experimental, and she was fascinated by the creative process. "My inspiration does not come from the supernatural, but from unconscious elaboration, which comes to the surface as a kind of revelation." Her nine prize-winning novels and nine collections of stories established her as a leading Brazilian author. *An Apprenticeship, or the Book of Pleasures* (1969) was one of the books that introduced her work in translation to an American audience. Her last novel, *The Hour of the Star*, was published the same year as her death from cancer. Lispector's most recently translated collection of short fiction is *The Foreign-Legion: Stories and Chronicles* (1986).

The Smallest Woman in the World

1960 / Translated by Elizabeth Bishop

IN THE DEPTHS OF Equatorial Africa the French explorer, Marcel Pretre, hunter and man of the world, came across a tribe of surprisingly small pygmies. Therefore he was even more surprised when he was informed that a still smaller people existed, beyond forests and distances. So he plunged farther on.

In the Eastern Congo, near Lake Kivu, he really did discover the smallest pygmies in the world. And — like a box within a box within a box — obedient, perhaps, to the necessity nature sometimes feels of outdoing herself — among the smallest pygmies in the world there was the smallest of the smallest pygmies in the world.

Among mosquitoes and lukewarm trees, among leaves of the most rich and lazy green, Marcel Pretre found himself facing a woman seventeen and three-quarter inches high, full-grown, black, silent — "Black as a monkey," he informed the press — who lived in a treetop with her little spouse. In the tepid miasma of the jungle, that swells the fruits so early and gives them an almost intolerable sweetness, she was pregnant.

So there she stood, the smallest woman in the world. For an instant, in the buzzing heat, it seemed as if the Frenchman had unexpectedly reached his final destination. Probably only because he was not insane, his soul neither wavered nor broke its bounds. Feeling an immediate necessity for order and for giving names to what exists, he called her Little Flower. And in order to be able to classify her among the recognizable realities, he immediately began to collect facts about her.

Her race will soon be exterminated. Few examples are left of this species, which, if it were not for the sly dangers of Africa, might have multiplied. Besides disease, the deadly effluvium of the water, insufficient food, and ranging beasts, the great threat to the Likoualas are the savage Bahundes, a threat that surrounds them in the silent air, like the dawn of battle. The Bahundes hunt them with nets, like monkeys. And eat them. Like that: they catch them in nets and *eat* them. The tiny race, retreating, always retreating, has finished hiding away in the heart of Africa, where the lucky explorer discovered it. For strategic defense, they live in the highest trees. The women descend to grind and cook corn and to gather greens; the men, to hunt. When a child is born, it is left free almost immediately. It is true that, what with the beasts, the child frequently cannot enjoy this freedom for very long. But then it is true that it cannot be lamented that for such a short life there had been any long, hard work. And even the language that the child learns is short and simple, merely the essentials, The Likoualas use few names; they name things by gestures and animal noises. As for things of the spirit, they have a drum. While they dance to the sound of the drum, a little male stands guard against the Bahundes, who come from no one knows where.

That was the way, then, that the explorer discovered, standing at his very feet, the smallest existing human thing. His heart beat, because no emerald in the world is so rare. The teachings of the wise men of India are not so rare. The richest man in the world has never set eyes on such strange grace. Right there was a woman that the greed of the most exquisite dream could never have imagined. It was then that the explorer said timidly, and with a delicacy of feeling of which his wife would never have thought him capable: "You are Little Flower."

At that moment, Little Flower scratched herself where no one scratches. The explorer — as if he were receiving the highest prize for chastity to which an idealistic man dares aspire — the explorer, experienced as he was, looked the other way.

A photograph of Little Flower was published in the colored supplement of the Sunday Papers, life-size. She was wrapped in a cloth, her belly already very big. The flat nose, the black face, the splay feet. She looked like a dog.

On that Sunday, in an apartment, a woman seeing the picture of Little Flower in the paper didn't want to look a second time because "It gives me the creeps."

In another apartment, a lady felt such perverse tenderness for the smallest of the African women that — an ounce of prevention being worth a pound of cure — Little Flower could never be left alone to the tenderness of that lady. Who knows to what murkiness of love tenderness can lead? The woman was upset all day, almost as if she were missing something. Besides, it was spring and there was a dangerous leniency in the air.

In another house, a little girl of five, seeing the picture and hearing the comments, was extremely surprised. In a houseful of adults, this little girl had been the smallest human being up until now. And, if this was the source of all caresses, it was also the source of the first fear of the tyranny of love. The existence of Little Flower made the little girl feel — with a deep uneasiness that only years and years later, and for very different reasons, would turn into thought — made her feel, in her first wisdom, that "sorrow is endless."

In another house, in the consecration of spring, a girl about to be married felt an ecstasy of pity: "Mama, look at her little picture, poor little thing! Just look how sad she is!"

"But," said the mother, hard and defeated and proud, "it's the sadness of an animal. It isn't human sadness."

"Oh, Mama!" said the girl, discouraged.

In another house, a clever little boy had a clever idea; "Mummy, if I could put this little woman from Africa in little Paul's bed when he's asleep? When he woke up wouldn't he be frightened? Wouldn't he howl? When he saw her sitting on his bed? And then we'd play with her! She would be our toy!"

His mother was setting her hair in front of the bathroom mirror at the moment, and she remembered what a cook had told her about life in an orphanage. The orphans had no dolls, and, with terrible maternity already throbbing in their hearts, the little girls had hidden the death of one of the children from the nun. They kept the body in a cupboard and when the nun went out they played with the dead child, giving her baths and things to eat, punishing her only to be able to kiss and console her. In the bathroom, the mother remembered this, and let fall her thoughtful hands, full of curlers. She considered the cruel necessity of loving. And she considered the malignity of our desire for happiness. She considered how ferociously we need to play. How many times we will kill for love. Then she looked at her clever child as if she were looking at a dangerous stranger. And she had a horror of her own soul that, more than her body, had engendered that being, adept at life and happiness. She looked at him attentively and with uncomfortable pride, that child who had already lost two front teeth, evolution evolving itself, teeth falling out to give place to those that could bite better. "I'm going to buy him a new suit," she decided, looking at him, absorbed. Obstinately, she adorned her gap-toothed son with fine clothes; obstinately, she wanted him very clean, as if his cleanliness could emphasize a soothing superficiality, obstinately perfecting the polite side of beauty. Obstinately drawing away from, and drawing him away from, something that ought to be "black as a monkey." Then, looking in the bathroom mirror, the mother gave a deliberately refined and social smile, placing a distance of insuperable millenniums between the abstract lines of her features and the crude face of Little Flower. But with years of practice, she knew that this was going to be a Sunday on which she would have to hide from herself anxiety, dreams, and lost millenniums.

In another house, they gave themselves up to the enthralling task of measuring the seventeen and three-quarter inches of Little Flower against the wall. And, really, it was a delightful surprise: she was even smaller than the sharpest imagination could have pictured. In the heart of each member of the family was born, nostalgic, the desire to have that tiny and indomitable thing for itself, that thing spared having been eaten, that permanent source of charity. The avid family soul wanted to devote itself. To tell the truth, who hasn't wanted to own a human being just for himself? Which, it is true, wouldn't always be convenient; there are times when one doesn't want to have feelings.

"I bet if she lived here it would end in a fight," said the father, sitting in the armchair and definitely turning the page of the newspaper. "In this house everything ends in a fight."

"Oh, you, José — always a pessimist," said the mother.

"But, Mama, have you thought of the size her baby's going to be?" said the oldest little girl, aged thirteen, eagerly.

The father stirred uneasily behind his paper.

"It should be the smallest black baby in the world," the mother answered, melting with pleasure. "Imagine her serving our table, with her big little belly!"

"That's enough!" growled father.

"But you have to admit" said the mother, unexpectedly offended, "that it is something very rare. You're the insensitive one."

And the rare thing itself?

In the meanwhile, in Africa, the rare thing herself, in her heart — and who knows if the heart wasn't black, too, since once nature has erred she can no longer be trusted — the rare thing herself had something even rarer in her heart, like the secret of her own secret: a minimal child. Methodically, the explorer studied that little belly of the smallest mature human being. It was at this moment that the explorer, for the first time since he had known her, instead of feeling curiosity, or exhalation, or victory, or the scientific spirit, felt sick.

The smallest woman in the world was laughing.

She was laughing, warm, warm — Little Flower was enjoying life. The rare thing herself was experiencing the ineffable sensation of not having been eaten yet. Not having been eaten yet was something that at any other time would have given her the agile impulse to jump from branch to branch. But in this moment of tranquility, amid the thick leaves of the Eastern Congo, she was not putting this impulse into action — it was entirely concentrated in the smallness of the rare thing itself. So she was laughing. It was a laugh such as only one who does not speak laughs. It was a laugh that the explorer, constrained, couldn't classify. And she kept on enjoying her own soft laugh, she who wasn't being devoured. Not to be devoured is the most perfect feeling. Not to be devoured is the secret goal of a whole life. While she was not being eaten, her bestial laughter was as delicate as joy is delicate. The explorer was baffled.

In the second place, if the rare thing herself was laughing, it was because, within her smallness, a great darkness had begun to move.

The rare thing herself felt in her breast a warmth that might be called love. She loved that sallow explorer. If she could have talked and had told him that she loved him, he would have been puffed up with vanity. Vanity that would have collapsed when she added that she also loved the explorer's ring very much, and the explorer's boots. And when that collapse had taken place Little Flower would not have understood why. Because her love for the explorer — one might even say "profound love," since, having no other resources, she was reduced to profundity — her profound love for the explorer would not have been at all diminished by the fact that she also loved his boots. There is an old misunderstanding about the word love, and, if many children are born from this misunderstanding, many others have lost the unique chance of being born, only because of the susceptibility that demands that it be me! me! that is loved, and not my money. But in the humidity of the forest these cruel refinements do not exist, and love is not to be eaten, love is to find a boot pretty, love is to like the strange color of a man who isn't black, is to laugh for love of a shiny ring. Little Flower blinked with love, and laughed warmly, small, gravid, warm.

The explorer tried to smile back, without knowing exactly to what abyss his smile responded, and then he was embarrassed as only a very big man can be embarrassed. He pretended to adjust his explorer's hat better; he colored, prudishly. He turned a lovely color, a greenish-pink, like a lime at sunrise. He was undoubtedly sour.

Perhaps adjusting the symbolic helmet helped the explorer to get control of himself, severely recapture the discipline of his work, and go on with his note-taking. He had learned how to understand some of the tribe's few articulate words, and to interpret their signs. By now, he could ask questions.

Little Flower answered "Yes." That it was very nice to have a tree of her own to live in. Because — she didn't say this but her eyes became so dark that they said it — because it is good to own, good to own, good to own. The explorer winked several times.

Marcel Pretre had some difficult moments with himself. But at least he kept busy taking notes. Those who didn't take notes had to manage as best they could:

"Well," suddenly declared one old lady, folding up the newspaper decisively, "well, as I always say: God knows what He's doing."

Jack London

Jack London (1876–1916), unlike Bret Harte, Mark Twain, and most of the early American writers who wrote stories about the American West, was born in that region—in San Francisco. He had a hard childhood, forced to earn his own living by manual labor in a canning factory starting at age fifteen. Later he worked in a laundry, and still later he was a sailor. Descriptive writing came naturally to him, and two years before he graduated from Oakland High School he won first prize in a local newspaper's article contest for "Story of a Typhoon off the Coast of Japan." He attended the University of California at Berkeley for one semester, but he regarded himself as self-taught, reading Karl Marx and Friedrich Engels, Herbert Spencer, and Friedrich Nietzsche as a young man. He joined the Socialist Labor Party after he had become convinced that it was impossible for workers to secure better conditions without organizing to take over the means of production. In 1897 he joined the Klondike gold rush and spent the winter in the Yukon. Two years later, after his return from Alaska on a 2,000-mile boat trip down the Yukon River, he published his first professional story, "To the Man on the Trail," in the *Overland Monthly*, and began to write for his living. London's first collection of fiction, *Son of the Wolf*, appeared in 1900. His novel *The Call of the Wild* (1903) was his biggest success, selling 1.5 million copies, and he became the highest-paid author of his time. He regarded his adventure stories as inferior to his political writing, however; they were merely a means of making money to meet his expanding interests in social reform as a Socialist speaker and political candidate. He covered the Russo-Japanese War as a correspondent and wrote articles on the San Francisco earthquake of 1906 and the Mexican Revolution of 1914. Shortly before his death at the age of forty, he resigned from the Socialist Party "because of its lack of fire and fight, and its loss of emphasis on the class struggle." London's death, possibly by his own hand, strangely echoed the events of his semi-autobiographical novel *Martin Eden* (1909), in which a writer achieves success, but after rejecting Socialist aims finds his life meaningless and commits suicide.

London produced almost fifty volumes of prose, including several collections of short stories such as *Son of the Wolf*, *South Sea Tales* (1911) and *The House of Pride and Other Tales of Hawaii* (1912). He learned to tell stories, he claimed, when he was bumming across the United States and had to decide exactly the right line to pitch between the moment the housewife opened the door and the moment she asked him what he wanted. He felt that poverty had made him hustle, but that only his good luck had prevented it from destroying him. Claiming "no mentor but myself" as a writer, he placed the highest value on original experience; the stamp of self on a writer's work was "a trademark of far greater value than copyright."

London's reputation as a storyteller has declined in the United States in recent times, but he remains one of our most translated authors. His literary style is simple, often journalistic, and his stories are known to countless readers around the world for championing social protest and dramatizing this country's rugged pioneer experience. As Jorge Luis Borges has observed, the vitality which permeated London's life is apparent in his best work. "To Build a Fire" tells the story of a man's struggle against nature, trying to survive against impossible odds in a universe indifferent to an individual's fate.

RELATED COMMENTARY
Jack London, "Letter to the Editor on 'To Build a Fire,'" page 1467.

To Build a Fire

1908

DAY HAD BROKEN cold and grey, exceedingly cold and grey, when the man turned aside from the main Yukon trail and climbed the high earth-bank, where a dim and little-travelled trail led eastward through the fat spruce timberland. It was a steep bank, and he paused for breath at the top, excusing the act to himself by looking at his watch. It was nine o'clock. There was no sun nor hint of sun, though there was not a cloud in the sky. It was a clear day, and yet there seemed an intangible pall over the face of things, a subtle gloom that made the day dark, and that was due to the absence of sun. This fact did not worry the man. He was used to the lack of sun. It had been days since he had seen the sun, and he knew that a few more days must pass before that cheerful orb, due south, would just peep above the skyline and dip immediately from view.

The man flung a look back along the way he had come. The Yukon lay a mile wide and hidden under three feet of ice. On top of this ice were as many feet of snow. It was all pure white, rolling in gentle undulations where the ice jams of the freeze-up had formed. North and south, as far as his eye could see, it was unbroken white, save for a dark hairline that curved and twisted from around the spruce-covered island to the south, and that curved and twisted away into the north, where it disappeared behind another spruce-covered island. This dark hairline was the trail — the main trail — that led south five hundred miles to the Chilcoot Pass, Dyea, and salt water; and that led north seventy miles to Dawson, and still on to the north a thousand miles to Nulato, and finally to St. Michael, on Bering Sea, a thousand miles and half a thousand more.

But all this — the mysterious, far-reaching hairline trail, the absence of sun from the sky, the tremendous cold, and the strangeness and weirdness of it all — made no impression on the man. It was not because he was long used to it. He was a newcomer in the land, a *chechaquo*, and this was his first winter. The trouble with him was that he was without imagination. He was quick and alert in the things of life, but only in the things, and not in the significances. Fifty degrees below zero meant eighty-odd degrees of frost. Such fact impressed him as being cold and uncomfortable, and that was all. It did not lead him to meditate upon his frailty as a creature of temperature, and upon man's frailty in general, able only to live within certain narrow limits of heat and cold; and from there on it did not lead him to the conjectural field of immortality and man's place in the universe. Fifty degrees below zero stood for a bite of frost that hurt and that must be guarded against by the use of mittens, ear flaps, warm moccasins, and thick socks. Fifty degrees below zero. That there should be anything more to it than that was a thought that never entered his head.

As he turned to go on, he spat speculatively. There was a sharp explosive crackle that startled him. He spat again. And again, in the air, before it could fall to the snow, the spittle crackled. He knew that at fifty below spittle crackled on the snow, but this spittle had crackled in the air. Undoubtedly it was colder than fifty below—how much colder he did not know. But the temperature did not matter. He was bound for the old claim on the left fork of Henderson Creek, where the boys were already. They had come over across the divide from the Indian Creek country, while he had come the roundabout way to take a look at the possibilities of getting out logs in the spring from the islands in the Yukon. He would be in to camp by six o'clock; a bit after dark, it was true, but the boys would be there, a fire would be going, and a hot supper would be ready. As for lunch, he pressed his hand against the protruding bundle under his jacket. It was also under his shirt, wrapped up in a handkerchief and lying against the naked skin. It was the only way to keep the biscuits from freezing. He smiled agreeably to himself as he thought of those biscuits, each cut open and sopped in bacon grease, and each enclosing a generous slice of fried bacon.

He plunged in among the big spruce trees. The trail was faint. A foot of snow had fallen since the last sled had passed over, and he was glad he was without a sled, travelling light. In fact, he carried nothing but the lunch wrapped in the handkerchief. He was surprised, however, at the cold. It certainly was cold, he concluded, as he rubbed his numb nose and cheekbones with his mittened hand. He was a warm-whiskered man, but the hair on his face did not protect the high cheekbones and the eager nose that thrust itself aggressively into the frosty air.

At the man's heels trotted a dog, a big native husky, the proper wolf-dog, grey-coated and without any visible or temperamental difference from its brother, the wild wolf. The animal was depressed by the tremendous cold. It knew that it was no time for travelling. Its instinct told it a truer tale than was told to the man by the man's judgment. In reality, it was not merely colder than fifty below zero; it was colder than sixty below, than seventy below. It was seventy-five below zero. Since the freezing point is thirty-two above zero, it meant that one hundred and seven degrees of frost obtained. The dog did not know anything about thermometers. Possibly in its brain there was no sharp consciousness of a condition of very cold such as was in the man's brain. But the brute had its instinct. It experienced a vague but menacing apprehension that subdued it and made it slink along at the man's heels, and that made it question eagerly every unwonted movement of the man as if expecting him to go into camp or to seek shelter somewhere and build a fire. The dog had learned fire, and it wanted fire, or else to burrow under the snow and cuddle its warmth away from the air.

The frozen moisture of its breathing had settled on its fur in a fine powder of frost, and especially were its jowls, muzzle, and eyelashes whitened by its crystal breath. The man's red beard and moustache were likewise frosted, but more solidly, the deposit taking the form of ice and increasing with every warm, moist breath he exhaled. Also, the man was chewing tobacco, and the muzzle of ice held his lips so rigidly that he was unable to clear his chin when he expelled the juice. The result was a crystal beard of the color and solidity of amber that was increasing its length on his chin. If he fell down it would shatter itself, like glass, into brittle fragments. But he did not mind the appendage. It was the penalty all tobacco chewers paid in that country, and he had been out before in two cold snaps. They had not been so cold as this, he knew, but by the spirit thermometer at Sixty Mile he knew they had been registered at fifty below and at fifty-five.

He held on through the level stretch of woods for several miles, crossed a wide flat of nigger heads,[1] and dropped down a bank to the frozen bed of a small stream. This was Henderson Creek, and he knew he was ten miles from the forks. He looked at his watch. It was ten o'clock. He was making four miles an hour, and he calculated that he would arrive at the forks at half-past twelve. He decided to celebrate that event by eating his lunch there.

The dog dropped in again at his heels, with a tail drooping discouragement, as the man swung along the creek bed. The furrow of the old sled trail was plainly visible, but a dozen inches of snow covered up the marks of the last runners. In a month no man had come up or down that silent creek. The man held steadily on. He was not much given to thinking, and just then particularly he had nothing to think about save that he would eat lunch at the forks and that at six o'clock he would be in camp with the boys. There was nobody to talk to; and, had there been, speech would have been impossible because of the ice muzzle on his mouth. So he continued monotonously to chew tobacco and to increase the length of his amber beard.

Once in a while the thought reiterated itself that it was very cold and that he had never experienced such cold. As he walked along he rubbed his cheekbones and nose with the back of his mittened hand. He did this automatically, now and again changing hands. But, rub as he would, the instant he stopped his cheekbones went numb, and the following instant the end of his nose went numb. He was sure to frost his cheeks; he knew that, and experienced a pang of regret that he had not devised a nose strap of the sort Bud wore in cold snaps. Such a strap passed across the cheeks, as well, and saved them. But it didn't matter much, after all. What were frosted cheeks? A bit painful, that was all; they were never serious.

Empty as the man's mind was of thoughts, he was keenly observant, and he noticed the changes in the creeks, the curves and bends and timber jams, and always he sharply noted where he placed his feet. Once, coming round a bend, he shied abruptly, like a startled horse, curved away from the place where he had been walking, and retreated several paces back along the trail. The creek he knew was frozen clear to the bottom — no creek could contain water in that arctic winter — but he knew also that there were springs that

---

[1] Hard tussocks in the tundra.

bubbled out from the hillsides and ran along under the snow and on top of the ice of the creek. He knew that the coldest snaps never froze these springs, and he knew likewise their danger. They were traps. They hid pools of water under the snow that might be three inches deep, or three feet. Sometimes a skin of ice half an inch thick covered them, and in turn was covered by the snow. Sometimes there were alternate layers of water and ice skin, so that when one broke through he kept on breaking through for a while, sometimes wetting himself to the waist.

That was why he had shied in such a panic. He had felt the give under his feet and heard the crackle of a snow-hidden ice skin. And to get his feet wet in such a temperature meant trouble and danger. At the very least it meant delay, for he would be forced to stop and build a fire, and under its protection to bare his feet while he dried his socks and moccasins. He stood and studied the creek bed and its banks, and decided that the flow of water came from the right. He reflected awhile, rubbing his nose and cheeks, then skirted to the left, stepping gingerly and testing the footing for each step. Once clear of the danger, he took a fresh chew of tobacco and swung along at his four-mile gait.

In the course of the next two hours he came upon several similar traps. Usually the snow above the hidden pools had a sunken, candied appearance that advertised the danger. Once again, however, he had a close call; and once, suspecting danger, he compelled the dog to go on in front. The dog did not want to go. It hung back until the man shoved it forward, and then it went quickly across the white, unbroken surface. Suddenly it broke through, floundered to one side, and got away to firmer footing. It had wet its forefeet and legs, and almost immediately the water that clung to it turned to ice. It made quick efforts to lick the ice off its legs, then dropped down in the snow and began to bite out the ice that had formed between the toes. This was a matter of instinct. To permit the ice to remain would mean sore feet. It did not know this. It merely obeyed the mysterious prompting that arose from the deep crypts of its being. But the man knew, having achieved a judgment on the subject, and he removed the mitten from his right hand and helped to tear out the ice particles. He did not expose his fingers more than a minute, and was astonished at the swift numbness that smote them. It certainly was cold. He pulled on the mitten hastily, and beat the hand savagely across his chest.

At twelve o'clock the day was at its brightest. Yet the sun was too far south on its winter journey to clear the horizon. The bulge of the earth intervened between it and Henderson Creek, where the man walked under a clear sky at noon and cast no shadow. At half-past twelve, to the minute, he arrived at the forks of the creek. He was pleased at the speed he had made. If he kept it up, he would certainly be with the boys by six. He unbuttoned his jacket and shirt and drew forth his lunch. The action consumed no more than a quarter of a minute, yet in that brief moment the numbness laid hold of the exposed fingers. He did not put the mitten on, but, instead, struck the fingers a dozen sharp smashes against his leg. Then he sat down on a snow-covered log to eat. The sting that followed upon the striking of his fingers against his leg ceased so quickly that he was startled. He had had no chance to take a bite of biscuit.

He struck the fingers repeatedly and returned them to the mitten, baring the other hand for the purpose of eating. He tried to take a mouthful, but the ice muzzle prevented. He had forgotten to build a fire and thaw out. He chuckled at his foolishness, and as he chuckled he noted the numbness creeping into the exposed fingers. Also, he noted that the stinging which had first come to his toes when he sat down was already passing away. He wondered whether the toes were warm or numb. He moved them inside the moccasins and decided that they were numb.

He pulled the mitten on hurriedly and stood up. He was a bit frightened. He stamped up and down until the stinging returned into the feet. It certainly was cold, was his thought. That man from Sulphur Creek had spoken the truth when telling how cold it sometimes got in the country. And he had laughed at him at the time! That showed one must not be too sure of things. There was no mistake about it, it *was* cold. He strode up and down, stamping his feet and threshing his arms, until reassured by the returning warmth. Then he got out matches and proceeded to make a fire. From the undergrowth, where high water of the previous spring had lodged a supply of seasoned twigs, he got his firewood. Working carefully from a small beginning, he soon had a roaring fire, over which he thawed the ice from his face and in the protection of which he ate his biscuits. For the moment the cold of space was outwitted. The dog took satisfaction in the fire, stretching out close enough for warmth and far enough away to escape being singed.

When the man had finished, he filled his pipe and took his comfortable time over a smoke. Then he pulled on his mittens, settled the ear flaps of his cap firmly about his ears, and took the creek trail up the left fork. The dog was disappointed and yearned back towards the fire. This man did not know cold. Possibly all the generations of his ancestry had been ignorant of cold, of real cold, of cold one hundred and seven degrees below freezing point. But the dog knew; all its ancestry knew, and it had inherited the knowledge. And it knew that it was not good to walk abroad in such fearful cold. It was the time to lie snug in a hole in the snow and wait for a curtain of cloud to be drawn across the face of outer space whence this cold came. On the other hand, there was no keen intimacy between the dog and the man. The one was the toil slave of the other, and the only caresses it had ever received were the caresses of the whip lash and of harsh and menacing throat sounds that threatened the whip lash. So the dog made no effort to communicate its apprehension to the man. It was not concerned in the welfare of the man; it was for its own sake that it yearned back towards the fire. But the man whistled, and spoke to it with the sound of whip lashes, and the dog swung in at the man's heels and followed after.

The man took a chew of tobacco and proceeded to start a new amber beard. Also, his moist breath quickly powdered with white his moustache, eyebrows, and lashes. There did not seem to be so many springs on the left fork of the Henderson, and for half an hour the man saw no signs of any. And then it happened. At a place where there were no signs, where the soft, unbroken snow seemed to advertise solidity beneath, the man broke through. It was not deep. He wet himself half-way to the knees before he floundered out of the firm crust.

He was angry, and cursed his luck aloud. He had hoped to get into camp with the boys at six o'clock, and this would delay him an hour, for he would have to build a fire and dry out his footgear. This was imperative at that low temperature — he knew that much; and he turned aside to the bank, which he climbed. On top, tangled in the underbrush about the trunks of several small spruce trees, was a high-water deposit of dry firewood — sticks and twigs, principally, but also larger portions of seasoned branches and fine, dry, last year's grasses. He threw down several large pieces on top of the snow. This served for a foundation and prevented the young flame from drowning itself in the snow it otherwise would melt. The flame he got by touching a match to a small shred of birch bark that he took from his pocket. This burned even more readily than paper. Placing it on the foundation, he fed the young flame with wisps of dry grass and with the tiniest dry twigs.

He worked slowly and carefully, keenly aware of his danger. Gradually, as the flame grew stronger, he increased the size of the twigs with which he fed it. He squatted in the snow pulling the twigs out from their entanglement in the brush and feeding directly to the flame. He knew there must be no failure. When it is seventy-five below zero, a man must not fail in his first attempt to build a fire — that is, if his feet are wet. If his feet are dry, and he fails, he can run along the trail for half a mile and restore his circulation. But the circulation of wet and freezing feet cannot be restored by running when it is seventy-five below. No matter how fast he runs, the wet feet will freeze the harder.

All this the man knew. The old-timer on Sulphur Creek had told him about it the previous fall, and now he was appreciating the advice. Already all sensation had gone out of his feet. To build the fire he had been forced to remove his mittens, and the fingers had quickly gone numb. His pace of four miles an hour had kept his heart pumping blood to the surface of his body and to all the extremities. But the instant he stopped, the action of the pump eased down. The cold of space smote the unprotected tip of the planet, and he, being on that unprotected tip, received the full force of the blow. The blood of his body recoiled before it. The blood was alive, like the dog, and like the dog it wanted to hide away and cover itself up from the fearful cold. So long as he walked four miles an hour, he pumped that blood, willy-nilly, to the surfaces; but now it ebbed away and sank down into the recesses of his body. The extremities were the first to feel its absence. His wet feet froze the faster, and his exposed fingers numbed the faster, though they had not yet begun to freeze. Nose and cheeks were already freezing, while the skin of all his body chilled as it lost its blood.

But he was safe. Toes and nose and cheeks would be only touched by the frost, for the fire was beginning to burn with strength. He was feeding it with twigs the size of his finger. In another minute he would be able to feed it with branches the size of his wrist, and then he could remove his wet footgear, and, while it dried, he could keep his naked feet warm by the fire, rubbing them at first, of course, with snow. The fire was a success. He was safe. He remembered the advice of the old-timer on Sulphur Creek, and smiled. The old-timer had been very serious in laying down the law that no man must travel alone in the Klondike after fifty below. Well, here he was; he had had the accident; he was alone; and he had saved himself. Those old-timers were rather womanish, some of them, he thought. All a man had to do was to keep his head, and he was all right. Any man who was a man could travel alone. But it was surprising, the rapidity with which his cheeks and nose were freezing. And he had not thought his fingers could go lifeless in so short a time. Lifeless they were, for he could scarcely make them move together to grip a twig, and they seemed remote from his body and from him. When he touched a twig, he had to look and see whether or not he had hold of it. The wires were pretty well down between him and his finger ends.

All of which counted for little. There was the fire, snapping and crackling and promising life with every dancing flame. He started to untie his moccasins. They were coated with ice; the thick German socks were like sheaths of iron halfway to the knees; and the moccasin strings were like rods of steel all twisted and knotted as by some conflagration. For a moment he tugged with his numb fingers, then, realizing the folly of it, he drew his sheath knife.

But before he could cut the strings, it happened. It was his own fault or, rather, his mistake. He should not have built the fire under the spruce tree. He should have built it in the open. But it had been easier to pull the twigs from the brush and drop them directly on the fire. Now the tree under which he had done this carried a weight of snow on its boughs. No wind had blown for weeks, and each bough was fully freighted. Each time he had pulled a twig he had communicated a slight agitation to the tree — an imperceptible agitation, so far as he was concerned, but an agitation sufficient to bring about the disaster. High up in the tree one bough capsized its load of snow. This fell on the boughs beneath, capsizing them. This process continued, spreading out and involving the whole tree. It grew like an avalanche, and it descended without warning upon the man and the fire, and the fire was blotted out! Where it had burned was a mantle of fresh and disordered snow.

The man was shocked. It was as though he had just heard his own sentence of death. For a moment he sat and stared at the spot where the fire had been. Then he grew very calm. Perhaps the old-timer on Sulphur Creek was right. If he had only had a trail mate he would have been in no danger now. The trail mate could have built the fire. Well, it was up to him to build the fire over again, and this second time there must be no failure. Even if he succeeded, he would most likely lose some toes. His feet must be badly frozen by now, and there would be some time before the second fire was ready.

Such were his thoughts, but he did not sit and think them. He was busy all the time they were passing through his mind. He made a new foundation for a fire, this time in the open, where no treacherous tree could blot it out. Next he gathered dry grasses and tiny twigs from the high-water flotsam. He could not bring his fingers together to pull them out, but he was able to gather them by the handful. In this way he got many rotten twigs and bits of green moss that were undesirable, but it was the best he could do. He worked methodically, even collecting an armful of the larger branches to be used later when the fire gathered strength. And all the while the dog sat and watched him, a certain yearning wistfulness in its eyes, for it looked upon him as the fire provider, and the fire was slow in coming.

When all was ready, the man reached in his pocket for a second piece of birch bark. He knew the bark was there, and, though he could not feel it with his fingers, he could hear its crisp rustling as he fumbled for it. Try as he would, he could not clutch hold of it. And all the time, in his consciousness, was the knowledge that each instant his feet were freezing. This thought tended to put him in a panic, but he fought against it and kept calm. He pulled on his mittens with his teeth, and threshed his arms back and forth, beating his hands with all his might against his sides. He did this sitting down, and he stood up to do it; and all the while the dog sat in the snow, its wolf brush of a tail curled around warmly over its forefront, its sharp wolf ears pricked forward intently as it watched the man. And the man, as he beat and threshed with his arms and hands, felt a great surge of envy as he regarded the creature that was warm and secure in its natural covering.

After a time he was aware of the first faraway signals of sensation in his beaten fingers. The faint tingling grew stronger till it evolved into a stinging ache that was excruciating, but which the man hailed with satisfaction. He stripped the mitten from his right hand and fetched forth the birch bark. The exposed fingers were quickly going numb again. Next he brought out his bunch of sulphur matches. But the tremendous cold had already driven the life out of his fingers. In his effort to separate one match from the others, the whole bunch fell in the snow. He tried to pick it out of the snow, but failed. The dead fingers could neither touch nor clutch. He was very careful. He drove the thought of his freezing feet, and nose, and cheeks, out of his mind, devoting his whole soul to the matches. He watched, using the sense of vision in place of that to touch, and when he saw his fingers on each side the bunch, he closed them — that is, he willed to close them, for the wires were down, and the fingers did not obey. He pulled the mitten on the right hand, and beat it fiercely against his knee. Then with both mittened hands, he scooped the bunch of matches, along with much snow, into his lap. Yet he was no better off.

After some manipulation he managed to get the bunch between the heels of his mittened hands. In this fashion he carried it to his mouth. The ice crackled and snapped when by a violent effort he opened his mouth. He drew the lower jaw in, curled the upper lip out of the way, and scraped the bunch with his upper teeth in order to separate a match. He succeeded in getting one, which he dropped on his lap. He was no better off. He could not pick it up. Then he devised a way. He picked it up in his teeth and scratched it on his leg. Twenty times he scratched before he succeeded in lighting it. As it flamed he held it with his teeth to the birch bark. But the burning brimstone went up his nostrils and into his lungs, causing him to cough spasmodically. The match fell into the snow and went out.

The old-timer on Sulphur Creek was right, he thought in the moment of controlled despair that ensued: after fifty below, a man should travel with a partner. He beat his hands, but failed in exciting any sensation. Suddenly he bared both hands, removing the mittens with his teeth. He caught the whole bunch between the heels of his hands. His arm muscles not being frozen enabled him to press the hand heels tightly against the matches. Then he scratched the bunch along his leg. It flared into flame, seventy sulphur matches at once! There was no wind to blow them out. He kept his head to one side to escape the strangling fumes, and held the blazing bunch to the birch bark. As he so held it, he became aware of sensation in his hand. His flesh was burning. He could smell it. Deep down below the surface he could feel it. The sensation developed into pain that grew acute. And still he endured it, holding the flame of the matches clumsily to the bark that would not light readily because his own burning hands were in the way, absorbing most of the flame.

At last, when he could endure no more, he jerked his hands apart. The blazing matches fell sizzling into the snow, but the birch bark was alight. He began laying dry grasses and the tiniest twigs on the flame. He could not pick and choose, for he had to lift the fuel between the heels of his hands. Small pieces of rotten wood and green moss clung to the twigs, and he bit them off as well as he could with his teeth. He cherished the flame carefully and awkwardly. It meant life, and it must not perish. The withdrawal of blood from the surface of his body now made him begin to shiver, and he grew more awkward. A large piece of green moss fell squarely on the little fire. He tried to poke it out with his fingers, but his shivering frame made him poke too far, and he disrupted the nucleus of the little fire, the burning grasses and tiny twigs separating and scattering. He tried to poke them together again, but in spite of the tenseness of the effort, his shivering got away with him, and the twigs were hopelessly scattered. Each twig gushed a puff of smoke and went out. The fire provider had failed. As he looked apathetically about him, his eyes chanced on the dog, sitting across the ruins of the fire from him, in the snow, making restless, hunching movements, slightly lifting one forefoot and then the other, shifting its weight back and forth on them with wistful eagerness.

The sight of the dog put a wild idea into his head. He remembered the tale of the man, caught in a blizzard, who killed a steer and crawled inside the carcass, and so was saved. He would kill the dog and bury his hands in the warm body until the numbness went out of them. Then he could build another fire. He spoke to the dog, calling it to him; but in his voice was a strange note of fear that frightened the animal, who had never known the man to speak in such a way before. Something was the matter, and its suspicious nature sensed danger — it knew not what danger, but somewhere, somehow, in its brain arose an apprehension of the man. It flattened its ears down at the sound of the man's voice, and its restless, hunching movements and the liftings and shiftings of its forefeet became more pronounced; but it would not come to the man. He got on his hands and knees and crawled towards the dog. This unusual posture again excited suspicion, and the animal sidled mincingly away.

The man sat up in the snow for a moment and struggled for calmness. Then he pulled on his mittens, by means of his teeth, and got upon his feet. He glanced down at first in order to assure himself that he was really standing up, for the absence of sensation in his feet left him unrelated to the earth. His erect position in itself started to drive the webs of suspicion from the dog's mind; and when he spoke peremptorily, with the sound of whip lashes in his voice, the dog rendered its customary allegiance and came to him. As it came within reaching distance, the man lost his control. His arms flashed out to the dog, and he experienced genuine surprise when he discovered that his hands could not clutch, that there was neither bend nor feeling in the fingers. He had forgotten for the moment that they were frozen and that they were freezing more and more. All this happened quickly, and before the animal could get away, he encircled its body with his arms. He sat down in the snow, and in this fashion held the dog, while it snarled and whined and struggled.

But it was all he could do, hold its body encircled in his arms and sit there. He realized he could not kill the dog. There was no way to do it. With his helpless hands he could neither draw nor hold his sheath knife nor throttle the animal. He released it, and it plunged wildly away, with tail between its legs, and still snarling. It halted forty feet away and surveyed him curiously, with ears sharply pricked forward.

The man looked down at his hands in order to locate them, and found them hanging on the ends of his arms. It struck him as curious that one should have to use his eyes in order to find out where his hands were. He began threshing his arms back and forth, beating the mittened hands against his sides. He did this for five minutes, violently, and his heart pumped enough blood up to the surface to put a stop to his shivering. But no sensation was aroused in the hands. He had an impression that they hung like weights on the ends of his arms, but when he tried to run the impression down, he could not find it.

A certain fear of death, dull and oppressive, came to him. This fear quickly became poignant as he realized that it was no longer a mere matter of freezing his fingers and toes, or of losing his hands and feet, but that it was a matter of life and death with the chances against him. This threw him into a panic, and he turned and ran up the creek bed along the old, dim trail. The dog joined in behind him and kept up with him. He ran blindly, without intention, in fear such as he had never known in his life. Slowly, as he ploughed and floundered through the snow, he began to see things again — the banks of the creek, the old timber jams, the leafless aspens, and the sky. The running made him feel better. He did not shiver. Maybe, if he ran on, his feet would thaw out; and, anyway, if he ran far enough, he would reach camp and the boys. Without doubt he would lose some fingers and toes and some of his face; but the boys would take care of him, and save the rest of him when he got there. And at the same time there was another thought in his mind that said he would never get to the camp and the boys; that it was too many miles away, that the freezing had too great a start on him, and that he would soon be stiff and dead. This thought he kept in the background and refused to consider. Sometimes it pushed itself forward and demanded to be heard, but he thrust it back and strove to think of other things.

It struck him as curious that he could run at all on feet so frozen that he could not feel them when they struck the earth and took the weight of his body. He seemed to himself to skim along above the surface, and to have no connection with the earth. Somewhere he had once seen a winged Mercury, and he wondered if Mercury felt as he felt when skimming over the earth.

His theory of running until he reached camp and the boys had one flaw in it: he lacked the endurance. Several times he stumbled, and finally he tottered, crumpled up, and fell. When he tried to rise, he failed. He must sit and rest, he decided, and next time he would merely walk and keep on going. As he sat and regained his breath, he noted that he was feeling quite warm and comfortable. He was not shivering, and it even seemed that a warm glow had come to his chest and trunk. And yet, when he touched his nose or cheeks, there was no sensation. Running would not thaw them out. Nor would it thaw out his hands and feet. Then the thought came to him that the frozen portions of his body must be extending. He tried to keep this thought down, to forget it, to think of something else; he was aware of the panicky feeling that it caused, and he was afraid of the panic. But the thought asserted itself, and persisted, until it produced a vision of his body totally frozen. This was too much, and he made another wild run along the trail. Once he slowed down to a walk, but the thought of the freezing extending itself made him run again.

And all the time the dog ran with him, at his heels. When he fell down a second time, it curled its tail over its forefeet and sat in front of him, facing him, curiously eager and intent. The warmth and security of the animal angered him, and he cursed it till it flattened down its ears appeasingly. This time the shivering came more quickly upon the man. He was losing in his battle with the frost. It was creeping into his body from all sides. The thought of it drove him on, but he ran no more than a hundred feet, when he staggered and pitched headlong. It was his last panic. When he had recovered his breath and control, he sat up and entertained in his mind the conception of meeting death with dignity. However, the conception did not come to him in such terms. His idea of it was that he had been making a fool of himself, running around like a chicken with its head cut off—such was the simile that occurred to him. Well, he was bound to freeze anyway, and he might as well take it decently. With this new-found peace of mind came the first glimmerings of drowsiness. A good idea, he thought, to sleep off to death. It was like taking an anaesthetic. Freezing was not so bad as people thought. There were lots worse ways to die.

He pictured the boys finding his body next day. Suddenly he found himself with them, coming along the trail looking for himself. And, still with them, he came around a turn in the trail and found himself lying in the snow. He did not belong with himself any more, for even then he was out of himself, standing with the boys and looking at himself in the snow. It certainly was cold, was his thought. When he got back to the States he could tell the folks what real cold was. He drifted on from this to a vision of the old-timer on Sulphur Creek. He could see him quite clearly, warm and comfortable, and smoking a pipe.

"You were right, old hoss; you were right," the man mumbled to the old-timer of Sulphur Creek.

Then the man drowsed off into what seemed to him the most comfortable and satisfying sleep he had ever known. The dog sat facing him and waiting. The brief day drew to a close in a long, slow twilight. There were no signs of a fire to be made, and, besides, never in the dog's experience had it known a man to sit like that in the snow and make no fire. As the twilight drew on, its eager yearning for the fire mastered it, and with a great lifting and shifting of forefeet, it whined softly, then flattened its ears down in anticipation of being chidden by the man. But the man remained silent. Later the dog whined loudly. And still later it crept close to the man and caught the scent of death. This made the animal bristle and back away. A little longer it delayed, howling under the stars that leaped and danced and shone brightly in the cold sky. Then it turned and trotted up the trail in the direction of the camp it knew, where were the other food providers and fire providers.

Katherine Mansfield

Katherine Mansfield (1888–1923) was born Kathleen Mansfield Beauchamp in Wellington, New Zealand. In 1903 she persuaded her father, a banker and industrialist, to send her to London to study the cello. After a brief return to New Zealand, she went back to London with a small allowance from her family, deciding to become a writer instead of a musician after meeting D. H. Lawrence and Virginia Woolf. Mansfield's first book of short stories, *In a German Pension*, was published in 1911. In the same year she met the literary critic John Middleton Murry, who became her husband in 1918. *Bliss and Other Stories* (1920) established her reputation and was followed by *The Garden-Party* (1922).

Mansfield took Anton Chekhov as her model, but after she was stricken with tuberculosis in 1918, she found it difficult to work. In her posthumously published *Journal* (1927), she often upbraided herself when she felt too ill to write: "Look at the stories that wait and wait just at the threshold. Why don't I let them in? And their place would be taken by others who are lurking beyond just there — waiting for the chance." Finally she sought a cure for her illness at the Gurdjieff Institute in France, run by the noted Armenian mystic Georges Ivanovitch Gurdjieff, whose methods combined spiritual and physical healing. She died at the institute a few months after her thirty-fourth birthday.

Eighty-eight of Mansfield's stories have been published (including fifteen left unfinished), and they have had a great influence on the development of the literary form. As did Chekhov and James Joyce, Mansfield simplified plot to intensify its emotional impact, dramatizing small moments to reveal the larger significance in people's lives, or, as Willa Cather observed, approaching "the major forces of life through comparatively trivial incidents." Mansfield developed her own technique of narration in which she transformed a chance incident into a terse psychological drama. As would a symbolist poet, she used concrete images — such as the fur piece in "Miss Brill" — to convey her characters' feelings, or what she called "the state of the soul." Her stories have affected later writers as powerfully as Chekhov's affected her.

RELATED COMMENTARY
Katherine Mansfield, "Review of Woolf's 'Kew Gardens,'" page 1468.

Miss Brill

1920

ALTHOUGH IT WAS SO brilliantly fine — the blue sky powdered with gold and great spots of light like white wine splashed over the Jardins Publiques — Miss Brill was glad that she had decided on her fur. The air was motionless, but when you opened your mouth there was just a faint chill, like a chill from a glass of iced water before you sip, and now and again a leaf came drifting — from nowhere, from the sky. Miss Brill put up her hand and touched her fur. Dear little thing!

It was nice to feel it again. She had taken it out of its box that afternoon, shaken out the moth-powder, given it a good brush, and rubbed the life back into the dim little eyes. "What has been happening to me?" said the sad little eyes. Oh, how sweet it was to see them snap at her again from the red eiderdown! . . . But the nose, which was of some black composition, wasn't at all firm. It must have had a knock, somehow. Never mind — a little dab of black sealing-wax when the time came — when it was absolutely necessary. . . . Little rogue! Yes, she really felt like that about it. Little rogue biting its tail just by her left ear. She could have taken it off and laid it on her lap and stroked it. She felt a tingling in her hands and arms, but that came from walking, she supposed. And when she breathed, something light and sad — no, not sad, exactly — something gentle seemed to move in her bosom.

There were a number of people out this afternoon, far more than last Sunday. And the band sounded louder and gayer. That was because the Season had begun. For although the band played all the year round on Sundays, out of season it was never the same. It was like some one playing with only the family to listen; it didn't care how it played if there weren't any strangers present. Wasn't the conductor wearing a new coat, too? She was sure it was new. He scraped with his foot and flapped his arms like a rooster about to crow, and the bandsmen sitting in the green rotunda blew out their cheeks and glared at the music. Now there came a little "flutey" bit — very pretty! — a little chain of bright drops. She was sure it would be repeated. It was; she lifted her head and smiled.

Only two people shared her "special" seat: a fine old man in a velvet coat, his hands clasped over a huge carved walking-stick, and a big old woman, sitting upright, with a roll of knitting on her embroidered apron. They did not speak. This was disappointing, for Miss Brill always looked forward to the conversation. She had become really quite expert, she thought, at listening as though she didn't listen, at sitting in other people's lives just for a minute while they talked round her.

She glanced, sideways, at the old couple. Perhaps they would go soon. Last Sunday, too, hadn't been as interesting as usual. An Englishman and his wife, he wearing a dreadful Panama hat and she button boots. And she'd gone on the whole time about how she ought to wear spectacles; she knew she needed them; but that it was no good getting any; they'd be sure to break and they'd never keep on. And he'd been so patient. He'd suggested everything — gold rims, the kind that curved round your ears, little pads inside the bridge. No, nothing would please her. "They'll always be sliding down my nose!" Miss Brill had wanted to shake her.

The old people sat on the bench, still as statues. Never mind, there was always the crowd to watch. To and fro, in front of the flower-beds and the band rotunda, the couples and groups paraded, stopped to talk, to greet, to buy a handful of flowers from the old beggar who had his tray fixed to the railings. Little children ran among them, swooping and laughing; little boys with big white silk bows under their chins, little girls, little French dolls, dressed up in velvet and lace. And sometimes a tiny staggerer came suddenly rocking into the open from under the trees, stopped, stared, as suddenly sat down "flop," until its small high-stepping mother, like a young hen, rushed scolding to its rescue.

Other people sat on the benches and green chairs, but they were nearly always the same, Sunday after Sunday, and — Miss Brill had often noticed — there was something funny about nearly all of them. They were odd, silent, nearly all old, and from the way they stared they looked as though they'd just come from dark little rooms or even — even cupboards!

Behind the rotunda the slender trees with yellow leaves down drooping, and through them just a line of sea, and beyond the blue sky with gold-veined clouds.

Tum-tum-tum tiddle-um! tiddle-um! tum tiddley-um turn ta! blew the band.

Two young girls in red came by and two young soldiers in blue met them, and they laughed and paired and went off arm-in-arm. Two peasant women with funny straw hats passed, gravely, leading beautiful smoke-coloured donkeys. A cold, pale nun hurried by. A beautiful woman came along and dropped her bunch of violets, and a little boy ran after to hand them to her, and she took them and threw them away as if they'd been poisoned. Dear me! Miss Brill didn't know whether to admire that or not! And now an ermine toque and a gentleman in grey met just in front of her. He was tall, stiff, dignified, and she was wearing the ermine toque she'd bought when her hair was yellow. Now everything, her hair, her face, even her eyes, was the same colour as the shabby ermine, and her hand, in its cleaned glove, lifted to dab her lips, was a tiny yellowish paw. Oh, she was so pleased to see him — delighted! She rather thought they were going to meet that afternoon. She described where she'd been — everywhere, here, there, along by the sea. The day was so charming — didn't he agree? And wouldn't he, perhaps? . . . But he shook his head, lighted a cigarette, slowly breathed a great deep puff into her face, and, even while she was still talking and laughing, flicked the match away and walked on. The ermine toque was alone; she smiled more brightly than ever. But even the band seemed to know what she was feeling and played more softly, played tenderly, and the drum beat, "The Brute! The Brute!" over and over. What would she do? What was going to happen now? But as Miss Brill wondered, the ermine toque turned, raised her hand as though she'd seen some one else, much nicer, just over there, and pattered away. And the band changed again and played more quickly, more gaily than ever, and the old couple on Miss Brill's seat got up and marched away, and such a funny old man with long whiskers hobbled along in time to the music and was nearly knocked over by four girls walking abreast.

Oh, how fascinating it was! How she enjoyed it! How she loved sitting here, watching it all! It was like a play. It was exactly like a play. Who could believe the sky at the back wasn't painted? But it wasn't till a little brown dog trotted on solemn and then slowly trotted off, like a little "theatre" dog, a little dog that had been drugged, that Miss Brill discovered what it was that made it so exciting. They were all on the stage. They weren't only the audience, not only looking on; they were acting. Even she had a part and came every Sunday. No doubt somebody would have noticed if she hadn't been there; she was part of the performance after all. How strange she'd never thought of it like that before! And yet it explained why she made such a point of starting from home at just the same time each week — so as not to be late for the performance — and it also explained why she had quite a queer, shy feeling at telling her English pupils how she spent her Sunday afternoons. No wonder! Miss Brill nearly laughed out loud. She was on the stage. She thought of the old invalid gentleman to whom she read the newspaper four afternoons a week while he slept in the garden. She had got quite used to the frail head on the cotton pillow, the hollowed eyes, the open mouth and the high pinched nose. If he'd been dead she mightn't have noticed for weeks; she wouldn't have minded. But suddenly he knew he was having the paper read to him by an actress! "An actress!" The old head lifted; two points of light quivered in the old eyes. "An actress — are ye?" And Miss Brill smoothed the newspaper as though it were the manuscript of her part and said gently: "Yes, I have been an actress for a long time."

The band had been having a rest. Now they started again. And what they played was warm, sunny, yet there was just a faint chill — something, what was it? — not sadness — no, not sadness — a something that made you want to sing. The tune lifted, lifted, the light shone; and it seemed to Miss Brill that in another moment all of them, all the whole company, would begin singing. The young ones, the laughing ones who were moving together, they would begin, and the men's voices, very resolute and brave, would join them. And then she too, she too, and the others on the benches — they would come in with a kind of accompaniment — something low, that scarcely rose or fell, something so beautiful — moving. . . . And Miss Brill's eyes filled with tears and she looked smiling at all the other members of the company. Yes, we understand, we understand, she thought — though what they understood she didn't know.

Just at that moment a boy and a girl came and sat down where the old couple had been. They were beautifully dressed; they were in love. The hero and heroine, of course, just arrived from his father's yacht. And still soundlessly singing, still with that trembling smile, Miss Brill prepared to listen.

"No, not now," said the girl. "Not here, I can't."

"But why? Because of that stupid old thing at the end there?" asked the boy. "Why does she come here at all — who wants her? Why doesn't she keep her silly old mug at home?"

"It's her fu-fur which is so funny," giggled the girl. "It's exactly like a fried whiting."

"Ah, be off with you!" said the boy in an angry whisper. Then: "Tell me, ma petite chérie — "

"No, not here," said the girl. "Not *yet*."

On her way home she usually bought a slice of honey-cake at the baker's. It was her Sunday treat. Sometimes there was an almond in her slice, sometimes not. It made a great difference. If there was an almond it was like carrying home a tiny present — a surprise — something that might very well not have been there. She hurried on the almond Sundays and struck the match for the kettle in quite a dashing way.

But to-day she passed the baker's by, climbed the stairs, went into the little dark room — her room like a cupboard — and sat down on the red eiderdown. She sat there for a long time. The box that the fur came out of was on the bed. She unclasped the necklet quickly; quickly, without looking, laid it inside. But when she put the lid on she thought she heard something crying.

Bobbie Ann Mason

Bobbie Ann Mason (b. 1942) grew up on a farm outside Mayfield, Kentucky. As a child she loved to read, and her parents always made sure she had books, mostly popular fiction about the Bobbsey Twins and the Nancy Drew mysteries. After majoring in journalism at the University of Kentucky, she took several jobs in New York City with movie magazines, writing articles about Annette Funicello, Troy Donahue, Fabian, and other teen stars. Next she went to graduate school at the University of Connecticut, where she received her Ph.D. in literature with a dissertation on Vladimir Nabokov's *Ada*. This study was later published in paperback as *Nabokov's Garden* (1974).

After graduate school, Mason wrote *The Girl Sleuth: A Feminist Guide to the Bobbsey Twins, Nancy Drew, and Their Sisters* (1975) about her favorite childhood reading; then, in her late thirties, she started writing short stories. In 1980 *The New Yorker* published her first story. "It took me a long time to discover my material," she says. "It wasn't a matter of developing writing skills, it was a matter of knowing how to see things. And it took me a very long time to grow up. I'd been writing for a long time, but was never able to see what there was to write about. And I always aspired to things away from home, so it took me a long time to look back at home and realize that that's where the center of my thoughts was." Mason writes about the working-class people of western Kentucky, and her stories have contributed to a renaissance of regional fiction in America, helping to create a literary style that critics have labeled "shopping mall realism."

Mason's first collection, *Shiloh and Other Stories*, won the 1982 Hemingway Foundation Award. In 1985 reviewers of her novel *In Country* compared her to Ann Beattie and other "writers of her generation who chronicle aimless lives in prose that tends to be as laconic and stripped down as her characters' emotional range." Mason doesn't regard herself as a feminist writer, despite her depiction of the unfulfilled wife in her story "Shiloh." Her most recent collections of stories are *Zigzagging Down a Wild Trail* (2002) and *Nancy Culpepper* (2006). In her introduction to *Midnight Magic: Selected Stories* (1998), Mason explained her thinking process in "Shiloh":

> As I began writing "Shiloh," I did not know the characters were going to the Civil War battleground. They didn't know either. The notion came up spontaneously, with them and with me. At the point where Mabel says to her daughter, "Y'all ought to take a little run to Shiloh," Shiloh dreamily sailed back into my head from my high school days when history classes took field trips to the battleground. I never went on one of those trips, but I heard of them so often that going to Shiloh had a mystique about it, and it broke free from my memory at the appropriate moment. . . . Shiloh is actually that darkest place of Southern history, where 24,000 soldiers were wounded, and 3,500 of them died in battle.

Shiloh

1982

LEROY MOFFITT'S WIFE, Norma Jean, is working on her pectorals. She lifts three-pound dumbbells to warm up, then progresses to a twenty-pound barbell. Standing with her legs apart, she reminds Leroy of Wonder Woman.

"I'd give anything if I could just get these muscles to where they're real hard," says Norma Jean. "Feel this arm. It's not as hard as the other one."

"That's 'cause you're right-handed," says Leroy, dodging as she swings the barbell in an arc.

"Do you think so?"

"Sure."

Leroy is a truckdriver. He injured his leg in a highway accident four months ago, and his physical therapy, which involves weights and a pulley, prompted Norma Jean to try building herself up. Now she is attending a body-building class. Leroy has been collecting temporary disability since his tractor-trailer jackknifed in Missouri, badly twisting his left leg in its socket. He has a steel pin in his hip. He will probably not be able to drive his rig again. It sits in the backyard, like a gigantic bird that has flown home to roost. Leroy has been home in Kentucky for three months, and his leg is almost healed, but the accident frightened him and he does not want to drive any more long hauls. He is not sure what to do next. In the meantime, he makes things from craft kits. He started by building a miniature log cabin from notched Popsicle sticks. He varnished it and placed it on the TV set, where it remains. It reminds him of a rustic Nativity scene. Then he tried string art (sailing ships on black velvet), a macramé owl kit, a snap-together B-17 Flying Fortress, and a lamp made out of a model truck, with a light fixture screwed on the top of the cab. At first the kits were diversions, something to kill time, but now he is thinking about building a full-scale log house from a kit. It would be considerably cheaper than building a regular house, and besides, Leroy has grown to appreciate how things are put together. He has begun to realize that in all the years he was on the road he never took time to examine anything. He was always flying past scenery.

"They won't let you build a log cabin in any of the new subdivisions," Norma Jean tells him.

"They will if I tell them it's for you," he says, teasing her. Ever since they were married, he has promised Norma Jean he would build her a new home one day. They have always rented, and the house they live in is small and nondescript. It does not even feel like a home, Leroy realizes now.

Norma Jean works at the Rexall drugstore, and she has acquired an amazing amount of information about cosmetics. When she explains to Leroy the three stages of complexion care, involving creams, toners, and moisturizers, he thinks happily of other petroleum products — axle grease, diesel fuel. This is a connection between him and Norma Jean. Since he has been home, he has felt unusually tender about his wife and guilty over his long absences. But he can't tell what she feels about him. Norma Jean has never complained about his traveling; she has never made hurt remarks, like calling his truck a "widow-maker." He is reasonably certain she has been faithful to him, but he wishes she would celebrate his permanent homecoming more happily. Norma Jean is often startled to find Leroy at home, and he thinks she seems a little disappointed about it. Perhaps he reminds her too much of the early days of their marriage, before he went on the road. They had a child who died as an infant, years ago. They never speak about their memories of Randy, which have almost faded, but now that Leroy is home all the time, they sometimes feel awkward around each other, and Leroy wonders if one of them should mention the child. He has the feeling that they are waking up out of a dream together — that they must create a new marriage, start afresh. They are lucky they are still married. Leroy has read that for most people losing a child destroys the marriage — or else he heard this on *Donahue*. He can't always remember where he learns things anymore.

At Christmas, Leroy bought an electric organ for Norma Jean. She used to play the piano when she was in high school. "It don't leave you," she told him once. "It's like riding a bicycle."

The new instrument had so many keys and buttons that she was bewildered by it at first. She touched the keys tentatively, pushed some buttons, then pecked out "Chopsticks." It came out in an amplified fox-trot rhythm, with marimba sounds.

"It's an orchestra!" she cried.

The organ had a pecan-look finish and eighteen preset chords, with optional flute, violin, trumpet, clarinet, and banjo accompaniments. Norma Jean mastered the organ almost immediately. At first she played Christmas songs. Then she bought *The Sixties Songbook* and learned every tune in it, adding variations to each with the rows of brightly colored buttons.

"I didn't like these old songs back then," she said. "But I have this crazy feeling I missed something."

"You didn't miss a thing," said Leroy.

Leroy likes to lie on the couch and smoke a joint and listen to Norma Jean play "Can't Take My Eyes Off You" and "I'll Be Back." He is back again. After fifteen years on the road, he is finally settling down with the woman he loves. She is still pretty. Her skin is flawless. Her frosted curls resemble pencil trimmings.

Now that Leroy has come home to stay, he notices how much the town has changed. Subdivisions are spreading across western Kentucky like an oil slick. The sign at the edge of town says "Pop: 11,500" — only seven hundred more than it said twenty years before. Leroy can't figure out who is living in all the new houses. The farmers who used to gather around the courthouse square on Saturday afternoons to play checkers and spit tobacco juice have gone. It has been years since Leroy has thought about the farmers, and they have disappeared without his noticing.

Leroy meets a kid named Stevie Hamilton in the parking lot at the new shopping center. While they pretend to be strangers meeting over a stalled car, Stevie tosses an ounce of marijuana under the front seat of Leroy's car. Stevie is wearing orange jogging shoes and a T-shirt that says CHATTAHOOCHEE SUPER-RAT. His father is a prominent doctor who lives in one of the expensive subdivisions in a new white-columned brick house that looks like a funeral parlor. In the phone book under his name there is a separate number, with the listing "Teenagers."

"Where do you get this stuff?" asks Leroy. "From your pappy?"

"That's for me to know and you to find out," Stevie says. He is slit-eyed and skinny.

"What else you got?"

"What you interested in?"

"Nothing special. Just wondered."

Leroy used to take speed on the road. Now he has to go slowly. He needs to be mellow. He leans back against the car and says, "I'm aiming to build me a log house, soon as I get time. My wife, though, I don't think she likes the idea."

"Well, let me know when you want me again," Stevie says. He has a cigarette in his cupped palm, as though sheltering it from the wind. He takes a long drag, then stomps it on the asphalt and slouches away.

Stevie's father was two years ahead of Leroy in high school. Leroy is thirty-four. He married Norma Jean when they were both eighteen, and their child Randy was born a few months later, but he died at the age of four months and three days. He would be about Stevie's age now. Norma Jean and Leroy were at the drive-in, watching a double feature (*Dr. Strangelove* and *Lover Come Back*), and the baby was sleeping in the back seat. When the first movie ended, the baby was dead. It was the sudden infant death syndrome. Leroy remembers handing Randy to a nurse at the emergency room, as though he were offering her a large doll as a present. A dead baby feels like a sack of flour. "It just happens sometimes," said the doctor, in what Leroy always recalls as a nonchalant tone. Leroy can hardly remember the child anymore, but he still sees vividly a scene from *Dr. Strangelove* in which the President of the United States was talking in a folksy voice on the hot line to the Soviet premier about the bomber accidentally headed toward Russia. He was in the War Room, and the world map was lit up. Leroy remembers Norma Jean standing catatonically beside him in the hospital and himself thinking: Who is this strange girl? He had forgotten who she was. Now scientists are saying that crib death is caused by a virus. Nobody knows anything, Leroy thinks. The answers are always changing.

When Leroy gets home from the shopping center, Norma Jean's mother, Mabel Beasley, is there. Until this year, Leroy has not realized how much time she spends with Norma Jean. When she visits, she inspects the closets and then the plants, informing Norma Jean when a plant is droopy or yellow. Mabel calls the plants "flowers," although there are never any blooms. She always notices if Norma Jean's laundry is piling up. Mabel is a short, overweight woman whose tight, brown-dyed curls look more like a wig than the actual wig she sometimes wears. Today she has brought Norma Jean an off-white dust ruffle she made for the bed; Mabel works in a custom-upholstery shop.

"This is the tenth one I made this year," Mabel says. "I got started and couldn't stop."

"It's real pretty," says Norma Jean.

"Now we can hide things under the bed," says Leroy, who gets along with his mother-in-law primarily by joking with her. Mabel has never really forgiven him for disgracing her by getting Norma Jean pregnant. When the baby died, she said that fate was mocking her.

"What's that thing?" Mabel says to Leroy in a loud voice, pointing to a tangle of yarn on a piece of canvas.

Leroy holds it up for Mabel to see. "It's my needlepoint," he explains. "This is a *Star Trek* pillow cover."

"That's what a woman would do," says Mabel. "Great day in the morning!"

"All the big football players on TV do it," he says.

"Why, Leroy, you're always trying to fool me. I don't believe you for one minute. You don't know what to do with yourself — that's the whole trouble. Sewing!"

"I'm aiming to build us a log house," says Leroy. "Soon as my plans come."

"Like *heck* you are," says Norma Jean. She takes Leroy's needlepoint and shoves it into a drawer. "You have to find a job first. Nobody can afford to build now anyway."

Mabel straightens her girdle and says, "I still think before you get tied down y'all ought to take a little run to Shiloh."

"One of these days, Mama," Norma Jean says impatiently.

Mabel is talking about Shiloh, Tennessee. For the past few years, she has been urging Leroy and Norma Jean to visit the Civil War battleground there. Mabel went there on her honeymoon — the only real trip she ever took. Her husband died of a perforated ulcer when Norma Jean was ten, but Mabel, who was accepted into the United Daughters of the Confederacy in 1975, is still preoccupied with going back to Shiloh.

"I've been to kingdom come and back in that truck out yonder," Leroy says to Mabel, "but we never yet set foot in that battleground. Ain't that something? How did I miss it?"

"It's not even that far," Mabel says.

After Mabel leaves, Norma Jean reads to Leroy from a list she has made. "Things you could do," she announces. "You could get a job as a guard at Union Carbide, where they'd let you set on a stool. You could get on at the lumberyard. You could do a little carpenter work, if you want to build so bad. You could —"

"I can't do something where I'd have to stand up all day."

"You ought to try standing up all day behind a cosmetics counter. It's amazing that I have strong feet, coming from two parents that never had strong feet at all." At the moment Norma Jean is holding on to the kitchen counter, raising her knees one at a time as she talks. She is wearing two-pound ankle weights.

"Don't worry," says Leroy. "I'll do something."

"You could truck calves to slaughter for somebody. You wouldn't have to drive any big old truck for that."

"I'm going to build you this house," says Leroy. "I want to make you a real home."

"I don't want to live in any log cabin."

"It's not a cabin. It's a house."

"I don't care. It looks like a cabin."

"You and me together could lift those logs. It's just like lifting weights."

Norma Jean doesn't answer. Under her breath, she is counting. Now she is marching through the kitchen. She is doing goose steps.

Before his accident, when Leroy came home he used to stay in the house with Norma Jean, watching TV in bed and playing cards. She would cook fried chicken, picnic ham, chocolate pie — all his favorites. Now he is home alone much of the time. In the mornings, Norma Jean disappears, leaving a cooling place in the bed. She eats a cereal called Body Buddies, and she leaves the bowl on the table, with the soggy tan balls floating in a milk puddle. He sees things about Norma Jean that he never realized before. When she chops onions, she stares off into a corner, as if she can't bear to look. She puts on her house slippers almost precisely at nine o'clock every evening and nudges her jogging shoes under the couch. She saves bread heels for the birds. Leroy watches the birds at the feeder. He notices the peculiar way goldfinches fly past the window. They close their wings, then fall, then spread their wings to catch and lift themselves. He wonders if they close their eyes when they fall. Norma Jean closes her eyes when they are in bed. She wants the lights turned out. Even then, he is sure she closes her eyes.

He goes for long drives around town. He tends to drive a car rather carelessly. Power steering and an automatic shift make a car feel so small and inconsequential that his body is hardly involved in the driving process. His injured leg stretches out comfortably. Once or twice he has almost hit something, but even the prospect of an accident seems minor in a car. He cruises the new subdivisions, feeling like a criminal rehearsing for a robbery. Norma Jean is probably right about a log house being inappropriate here in the new subdivisions. All the houses look grand and complicated. They depress him.

One day when Leroy comes home from a drive he finds Norma Jean in tears. She is in the kitchen making a potato and mushroom-soup casserole, with grated-cheese topping. She is crying because her mother caught her smoking.

"I didn't hear her coming. I was standing here puffing away pretty as you please," Norma Jean says, wiping her eyes.

"I knew it would happen sooner or later," says Leroy, putting his arm around her.

"She don't know the meaning of the word 'knock,'" says Norma Jean. "It's a wonder she hadn't caught me years ago."

"Think of it this way," Leroy says. "What if she caught me with a joint?"

"You better not let her!" Norma Jean shrieks. "I'm warning you, Leroy Moffitt!"

"I'm just kidding. Here, play me a tune. That'll help you relax."

Norma Jean puts the casserole in the oven and sets the timer. Then she plays a ragtime tune, with horns and banjo, as Leroy lights up a joint and lies on the couch, laughing to himself about Mabel's catching him at it. He thinks of Stevie Hamilton—a doctor's son pushing grass. Everything is funny. The whole town seems crazy and small. He is reminded of Virgil Mathis, a boastful policeman Leroy used to shoot pool with. Virgil recently led a drug bust in a back room at a bowling alley, where he seized ten thousand dollars' worth of marijuana. The newspaper had a picture of him holding up the bags of grass and grinning widely. Right now, Leroy can imagine Virgil breaking down the door and arresting him with a lungful of smoke. Virgil would probably have been alerted to the scene because of all the racket Norma Jean is making. Now she sounds like a hard-rock band. Norma Jean is terrific. When she switches to a Latin-rhythm version of "Sunshine Superman," Leroy hums along. Norma Jean's foot goes up and down, up and down.

"Well, what do you think?" Leroy says, when Norma Jean pauses to search through her music.

"What do I think about what?"

His mind had gone blank. Then he says, "I'll sell my rig and build us a house." That wasn't what he wanted to say. He wanted to know what she thought — what she *really* thought — about them.

"Don't start in on that again," says Norma Jean. She begins playing "Who'll Be the Next in Line?"

Leroy used to tell hitchhikers his whole life story—about his travels, his hometown, the baby. He would end with a question: "Well, what do you think?" It was just a rhetorical question. In time, he had the feeling that he'd been telling the same story over and over to the same hitchhikers. He quit talking to hitchhikers when he realized how his voice sounded—whining and self-pitying, like some teenage-tragedy song. Now Leroy has the sudden impulse to tell Norma Jean about himself, as if he had just met her. They have known each other so long they have forgotten a lot about each other. They could become reacquainted. But when the oven timer goes off and she runs to the kitchen, he forgets why he wants to do this.

The next day, Mabel drops by. It is Saturday and Norma Jean is cleaning. Leroy is studying the plans for his log house, which have finally come in the mail. He has them spread out on the table—big sheets of stiff blue paper, with diagrams and numbers printed in white. While Norma Jean runs the vacuum, Mabel drinks coffee. She sets her coffee cup on a blueprint.

"I'm just waiting for time to pass," she says to Leroy, drumming her fingers on the table.

As soon as Norma Jean switches off the vacuum, Mabel says in a loud voice, "Did you hear about the datsun dog that killed the baby?"

Norma Jean says, "The word is 'dachshund.'"

"They put the dog on trial. It chewed the baby's legs off. The mother was in the next room all the time." She raises her voice. "They thought it was neglect."

Norma Jean is holding her ears. Leroy manages to open the refrigerator and get some Diet Pepsi to offer Mabel. Mabel still has some coffee and she waves away the Pepsi.

"Datsuns are like that," Mabel says. "They're jealous dogs. They'll tear a place to pieces if you don't keep an eye on them."

"You better watch out what you're saying, Mabel," says Leroy.

"Well, facts is facts."

Leroy looks out the window at his rig. It is like a huge piece of furniture gathering dust in the backyard. Pretty soon it will be an antique. He hears the vacuum cleaner. Norma Jean seems to be cleaning the living room rug again.

Later, she says to Leroy, "She just said that about the baby because she caught me smoking. She's trying to pay me back."

"What are you talking about?" Leroy says, nervously shuffling blueprints.

"You know good and well," Norma Jean says. She is sitting in a kitchen chair with her feet up and her arms wrapped around her knees. She looks small and helpless. She says, "The very idea, her bringing up a subject like that! Saying it was neglect."

"She didn't mean that," Leroy says.

"She might not have *thought* she meant it. She always says things like that. You don't know how she goes on."

"But she didn't really mean it. She was just talking."

Leroy opens a king-sized bottle of beer and pours it into two glasses, dividing it carefully. He hands a glass to Norma Jean and she takes it from him mechanically. For a long time, they sit by the kitchen window watching the birds at the feeder.

Something is happening. Norma Jean is going to night school. She has graduated from her six-week body-building course and now she is taking an adult-education course in composition at Paducah Community College. She spends her evenings outlining paragraphs.

"First you have a topic sentence," she explains to Leroy. "Then you divide it up. Your secondary topic has to be connected to your primary topic."

To Leroy, this sounds intimidating. "I never was any good in English," he says.

"It makes a lot of sense."

"What are you doing this for, anyhow?"

She shrugs. "It's something to do." She stands up and lifts her dumbbells a few times.

"Driving a rig, nobody cared about my English."

"I'm not criticizing your English."

Norma Jean used to say, "If I lose ten minutes' sleep, I just drag all day." Now she stays up late, writing compositions. She got a B on her first paper — a how-to theme on soup-based casseroles. Recently Norma Jean has been cooking unusual foods — tacos, lasagna, Bombay chicken. She doesn't play the organ anymore, though her second paper was called "Why Music Is Important to Me." She sits at the kitchen table, concentrating on her outlines, while Leroy plays with his log house plans, practicing with a set of Lincoln Logs. The thought of getting a truckload of notched, numbered logs scares him, and he wants to be prepared. As he and Norma Jean work together at the kitchen table, Leroy has the hopeful thought that they are sharing something, but he knows he is a fool to think this. Norma Jean is miles away. He knows he is going to lose her. Like Mabel, he is just waiting for time to pass.

One day, Mabel is there before Norma Jean gets home from work, and Leroy finds himself confiding in her. Mabel, he realizes, must know Norma Jean better than he does.

"I don't know what's got into that girl," Mabel says. "She used to go to bed with the chickens. Now you say she's up all hours. Plus her a-smoking. I like to died."

"I want to make her this beautiful home," Leroy says, indicating the Lincoln Logs. "I think she even wants it. Maybe she was happier with me gone."

"She don't know what to make of you, coming home like this."

"Is that it?"

Mabel takes the roof off his Lincoln Log cabin. "You couldn't get *me* in a log cabin," she says. "I was raised in one. It's no picnic, let me tell you."

"They're different now," says Leroy.

"I tell you what," Mabel says, smiling oddly at Leroy.

"What?"

"Take her down to Shiloh. Y'all need to get out together, stir a little. Her brain's all balled up over them books."

Leroy can see traces of Norma Jean's features in her mother's face. Mabel's worn face has the texture of crinkled cotton, but suddenly she looks pretty. It occurs to Leroy that Mabel has been hinting all along that she wants them to take her with them to Shiloh.

"Let's all go to Shiloh," he says. "You and me and her. Come Sunday."

Mabel throws up her hand in protest. "Oh, no, not me. Young folks want to be by themselves."

When Norma Jean comes in with groceries, Leroy says excitedly, "Your mama here's been dying to go to Shiloh for thirty-five years. It's about time we went, don't you think?"

"I'm not going to butt in on anybody's second honeymoon," Mabel says.

"Who's going on a honeymoon, for Christ's sake?" Norma Jean says loudly.

"I never raised no daughter of mine to talk that-a-way," Mabel says.

"You ain't seen nothing yet," says Norma Jean. She starts putting away boxes and cans, slamming cabinet doors.

"There's a log cabin at Shiloh," Mabel says. "It was there during the battle. There's bullet holes in it."

"When are you going to *shut up* about Shiloh, Mama?" asks Norma Jean.

"I always thought Shiloh was the prettiest place, so full of history," Mabel goes on. "I just hoped y'all could see it once before I die, so you could tell me about it." Later, she whispers to Leroy, "You do what I said. A little change is what she needs."

"Your name means 'the king,'" Norma Jean says to Leroy that evening. He is trying to get her to go to Shiloh, and she is reading a book about another century.

"Well, I reckon I ought to be right proud."

"I guess so."

"Am I still king around here?"

Norma Jean flexes her biceps and feels them for hardness. "I'm not fooling around with anybody, if that's what you mean," she says.

"Would you tell me if you were?"

"I don't know."

"What does *your* name mean?"

"It was Marilyn Monroe's real name."

"No kidding!"

"Norma comes from the Normans. They were invaders," she says. She closes her book and looks hard at Leroy. "I'll go to Shiloh with you if you'll stop staring at me."

On Sunday, Norma Jean packs a picnic and they go to Shiloh. To Leroy's relief, Mabel says she does not want to come with them. Norma Jean drives, and Leroy, sitting beside her, feels like some boring hitchhiker she has picked up. He tries some conversation, but she answers him in monosyllables. At Shiloh, she drives aimlessly through the park, past bluffs and trails and steep ravines. Shiloh is an immense place, and Leroy cannot see it as a battleground. It is not what he expected. He thought it would look like a golf course. Monuments are everywhere, showing through the thick clusters of trees. Norma Jean passes the log cabin Mabel mentioned. It is surrounded by tourists looking for bullet holes.

"That's not the kind of log house I've got in mind," says Leroy apologetically.

"I know *that*."

"This is a pretty place. Your mama was right."

"It's O.K.," says Norma Jean. "Well, we've seen it. I hope she's satisfied."

They burst out laughing together.

At the park museum, a movie on Shiloh is shown every half hour, but they decide that they don't want to see it. They buy a souvenir Confederate flag for Mabel, and then they find a picnic spot near the cemetery. Norma Jean has brought a picnic cooler, with pimiento sandwiches, soft drinks, and Yodels. Leroy eats a sandwich and then smokes a joint, hiding it behind the picnic cooler. Norma Jean has quit smoking altogether. She is picking cake crumbs from the cellophane wrapper, like a fussy bird.

Leroy says, "So the boys in gray ended up in Corinth. The Union soldiers zapped 'em finally. April 7, 1862."

They both know that he doesn't know any history. He is just talking about some of the historical plaques they have read. He feels awkward, like a boy on a date with an older girl. They are still just making conversation.

"Corinth is where Mama eloped to," says Norma Jean.

They sit in silence and stare at the cemetery for the Union dead and, beyond, at a tall cluster of trees. Campers are parked nearby, bumper to bumper, and small children in bright clothing are cavorting and squealing. Norma Jean wads up the cake wrapper and squeezes it tightly in her hand. Without looking at Leroy, she says, "I want to leave you."

Leroy takes a bottle of Coke out of the cooler and flips off the cap. He holds the bottle poised near his mouth but cannot remember to take a drink. Finally he says, "No, you don't."

"Yes, I do."

"I won't let you."

"You can't stop me."

"Don't do me that way."

Leroy knows Norma Jean will have her own way. "Didn't I promise to be home from now on?" he says.

"In some ways, a woman prefers a man who wanders," says Norma Jean. "That sounds crazy, I know."

"You're not crazy."

Leroy remembers to drink from his Coke. Then he says, "Yes, you *are* crazy. You and me could start all over again. Right back at the beginning."

"We *have* started all over again," says Norma Jean. "And this is how it turned out."

"What did I do wrong?"

"Nothing."

"Is this one of those women's lib things?" Leroy asks.

"Don't be funny."

The cemetery, a green slope dotted with white markers, looks like a subdivision site. Leroy is trying to comprehend that his marriage is breaking up, but for some reason he is wondering about white slabs in a graveyard.

"Everything was fine till Mama caught me smoking," says Norma Jean, standing up. "That set something off."

"What are you talking about?"

"She won't leave me alone — *you* won't leave me alone." Norma Jean seems to be crying, but she is looking away from him. "I feel eighteen again. I can't face that all over again." She starts walking away. "No, it *wasn't* fine. I don't know what I'm saying. Forget it."

Leroy takes a lungful of smoke and closes his eyes as Norma Jean's words sink in. He tries to focus on the fact that thirty-five hundred soldiers died on the grounds around him. He can only think of that war as a board game with plastic soldiers. Leroy almost smiles, as he compares the Confederates' daring attack on the Union camps and Virgil Mathis's raid on the bowling alley. General Grant, drunk and furious, shoved the southerners back to Corinth, where Mabel and Jet Beasley were married years later, when Mabel was still thin and good-looking. The next day, Mabel and Jet visited the battleground, and then Norma Jean was born, and then she married Leroy and they had a baby, which they lost, and now Leroy and Norma Jean are here at the same battleground. Leroy knows he is leaving out a lot. He is leaving out the insides of history. History was always just names and dates to him. It occurs to him that building a house out of logs is similarly empty — too simple. And the real inner workings of a marriage, like most of history, have escaped him. Now he sees that building a log house is the dumbest idea he could have had. It was clumsy of him to think Norma Jean would want a log house. It was a crazy idea. He'll have to think of something else, quickly. He will wad the blueprints into tight balls and fling them into the lake. Then he'll get moving again. He opens his eyes. Norma Jean has moved away and is walking through the cemetery, following a serpentine brick path.

Leroy gets up to follow his wife, but his good leg is asleep and his bad leg still hurts him. Norma Jean is far away, walking rapidly toward the bluff by the river, and he tries to hobble toward her. Some children run past him, screaming noisily. Norma Jean has reached the bluff, and she is looking out over the Tennessee River. Now she turns toward Leroy and waves her arms. Is she beckoning to him? She seems to be doing an exercise for her chest muscles. The sky is unusually pale — the color of the dust ruffle Mabel made for their bed.

Guy de Maupassant

Guy de Maupassant (1850–1893) was born in Normandy, the son of a wealthy stockbroker. Unable to accept discipline in school, he joined the army during the Franco-Prussian War of 1870–1871. Then for seven years he apprenticed himself to Gustave Flaubert, a distant relative, who attempted to teach him to write. Maupassant remembered, "I wrote verses, short stories, longer stories, even a wretched play. Nothing survived. The master read everything. Then, the following Sunday at lunch, he developed his criticisms." Flaubert taught Maupassant that talent "is nothing other than a long patience. Work."

The essence of Flaubert's now famous teaching is that the writer must look at everything to find some aspect of it that no one has yet seen or expressed. "Everything contains some element of the unexplored because we are accustomed to use our eyes only with the memory of what other people before us have thought about the object we are looking at. The least thing has a bit of the unknown about it. Let us find this." In 1880 Maupassant caused a sensation with the publication of his story "Boule de Suif" ("Ball of Fat"), a dramatic account of prostitution and bourgeois hypocrisy in France. During the next decade he published nearly 300 stories before his gradual incapacitation and death from syphilis, which afflicted him along with many of his contemporaries.

Characterized by compact and dramatic narrative lines, Maupassant's stories eliminated the moral judgments and the long digressions favored by earlier writers. Along with the Russian writer Anton Chekhov, Maupassant is credited with technical advances that moved the short story toward an austerity that has marked it ever since. These two writers influenced nearly everyone who has written short fiction after them. As Joseph Conrad recognized, "Facts, and again facts, are his [Maupassant's] unique concern. That is why he is not always properly understood." Maupassant's lack of sentimentality toward his characters, as in his depiction of the "little" clerk's wife in "The Necklace," laid him open to charges of cynicism and hardness. Even if Maupassant's stories display a greater distance from his characters and a less sympathetic irony than Chekhov's, both writers were the most accomplished of narrators in their powers of exact observation and independent judgment and in their supple, practiced knowledge of their craft.

RELATED COMMENTARIES
Guy de Maupassant, "The Writer's Goal," page 1471; Kate Chopin, "How I Stumbled upon Maupassant," page 1412.

The Necklace

1884 / Translated by Marjorie Laurie

SHE WAS ONE of those pretty and charming girls who are sometimes, as if by a mistake of destiny, born in a family of clerks. She had no dowry, no expectations, no means of being known, understood, loved, wedded by any rich and distinguished man; and she let herself be married to a little clerk at the Ministry of Public Instructions.

She dressed plainly because she could not dress well, but she was as unhappy as though she had really fallen from her proper station, since with women there is neither caste nor rank: and beauty, grace, and charm act instead of family and birth. Natural fineness, instinct for what is elegant, suppleness of wit, are the sole hierarchy, and make from women of the people the equals of the very greatest ladies.

She suffered ceaselessly, feeling herself born for all the delicacies and all the luxuries. She suffered from the poverty of her dwelling, from the wretched look of the walls, from the worn-out chairs, from the ugliness of the curtains. All those things, of which another woman of her rank would never even have been conscious, tortured her and made her angry. The sight of the little Breton peasant who did her humble housework aroused in her regrets which were despairing, and distracted dreams. She thought of the silent antechambers hung with Oriental tapestry, lit by tall bronze candelabra, and of the two great footmen in knee breeches who sleep in the big armchairs, made drowsy by the heavy warmth of the hot-air stove. She thought of the long *salons* fitted up with ancient silk, of the delicate furniture carrying priceless curiosities, and of the coquettish perfumed boudoirs made for talks at five o'clock with intimate friends, with men famous and sought after, whom all women envy and whose attention they all desire.

When she sat down to dinner, before the round table covered with a tablecloth three days old, opposite her husband, who uncovered the soup tureen and declared with an enchanted air, "Ah, the good *pot-au-feu*! I don't know anything better than that," she thought of dainty dinners, of shining silverware, of tapestry which peopled the walls with ancient personages and with strange birds flying in the midst of a fairy forest; and she thought of delicious dishes served on marvelous plates, and of the whispered gallantries which you listen to with a sphinxlike smile, while you are eating the pink flesh of a trout or the wings of a quail.

She had no dresses, no jewels, nothing. And she loved nothing but that; she felt made for that. She would so have liked to please, to be envied, to be charming, to be sought after.

She had a friend, a former schoolmate at the convent, who was rich, and whom she did not like to go and see any more, because she suffered so much when she came back.

But one evening, her husband returned home with a triumphant air, and holding a large envelope in his hand.

"There," said he. "Here is something for you."

She tore the paper sharply, and drew out a printed card which bore these words:

"The Minister of Public Instruction and Mme. Georges Ramponneau request the honor of M. and Mme. Loisel's company at the palace of the Ministry on Monday evening, January eighteenth."

Instead of being delighted, as her husband hoped, she threw the invitation on the table with disdain, murmuring:

"What do you want me to do with that?"

"But, my dear, I thought you would be glad. You never go out, and this is such a fine opportunity. I had awful trouble to get it. Everyone wants to go; it is very select, and they are not giving many invitations to clerks. The whole official world will be there."

She looked at him with an irritated glance, and said, impatiently:

"And what do you want me to put on my back?"

He had not thought of that; he stammered:

"Why, the dress you go to the theater in. It looks very well, to me."

He stopped, distracted, seeing his wife was crying. Two great tears descended slowly from the corners of her eyes toward the corners of her mouth. He stuttered:

"What's the matter? What's the matter?"

But, by violent effort, she had conquered her grief, and she replied, with a calm voice, while she wiped her wet cheeks:

"Nothing. Only I have no dress and therefore I can't go to this ball. Give your card to some colleague whose wife is better equipped than I."

He was in despair. He resumed:

"Come, let us see, Mathilde. How much would it cost, a suitable dress, which you could use on other occasions. Something very simple?"

She reflected several seconds, making her calculations and wondering also what sum she could ask without drawing on herself an immediate refusal and a frightened exclamation from the economical clerk.

Finally, she replied, hesitatingly:

"I don't know exactly, but I think I could manage it with four hundred francs."

He had grown a little pale, because he was laying aside just that amount to buy a gun and treat himself to a little shooting next summer on the plain of Nanterre, with several friends who went to shoot larks down there, of a Sunday.

But he said:

"All right. I will give you four hundred francs. And try to have a pretty dress."

The day of the ball drew near, and Mme. Loisel seemed sad, uneasy, anxious. Her dress was ready, however. Her husband said to her one evening:

"What is the matter? Come, you've been so queer these last three days."

And she answered:

"It annoys me not to have a single jewel, not a single stone, nothing to put on. I shall look like distress. I should almost rather not go at all."

He resumed:

"You might wear natural flowers. It's very stylish at this time of the year. For ten francs you can get two or three magnificent roses."

She was not convinced.

"No; there's nothing more humiliating than to look poor among other women who are rich."

But her husband cried:

"How stupid you are! Go look up your friend Mme. Forestier, and ask her to lend you some jewels. You're quite thick enough with her to do that."

She uttered a cry of joy:

"It's true. I never thought of it."

The next day she went to her friend and told of her distress.

Mme. Forestier went to a wardrobe with a glass door, took out a large jewelbox, brought it back, opened it, and said to Mme. Loisel:

"Choose, choose, my dear."

She saw first of all some bracelets, then a pearl necklace, then a Venetian cross, gold and precious stones of admirable workmanship. She tried on the ornaments before the glass, hesitated, could not make up her mind to part with them, to give them back. She kept asking:

"Haven't you any more?"

"Why, yes. Look. I don't know what you like."

All of a sudden she discovered, in a black satin box, a superb necklace of diamonds, and her heart began to beat with an immoderate desire. Her hands trembled as she took it. She fastened it around her throat, outside her high necked dress, and remained lost in ecstasy at the sight of herself.

Then she asked, hesitating, filled with anguish:

"Can you lend me that, only that?"

"Why, yes, certainly."

She sprang upon the neck of her friend, kissed her passionately, then fled with her treasure.

The day of the ball arrived. Mme. Loisel made a great success. She was prettier than them all, elegant, gracious, smiling, and crazy with joy. All the men looked at her, asked her name, endeavored to be introduced. All the attachés of the Cabinet wanted to waltz with her. She was remarked by the minister himself.

She danced with intoxication, with passion, made drunk by pleasure, forgetting all, in the triumph of her beauty, in the glory of her success, in a sort of cloud of happiness composed of all this homage, of all this admiration, of all these awakened desires, and of that sense of complete victory which is so sweet to a woman's heart.

She went away about four o'clock in the morning. Her husband had been sleeping since midnight, in a little deserted anteroom, with three other gentlemen whose wives were having a good time. He threw over her shoulders the wraps which he had brought, modest wraps of common life, whose poverty contrasted with the elegance of the ball dress. She felt this, and wanted to escape so as not to be remarked by the other women, who were enveloping themselves in costly furs.

Loisel held her back.

"Wait a bit. You will catch cold outside. I will go and call a cab."

But she did not listen to him, and rapidly descended the stairs. When they were in the street they did not find a carriage; and they began to look for one, shouting after the cabmen whom they saw passing by at a distance.

They went down toward the Seine, in despair, shivering with cold. At last they found on the quay one of those ancient noctambulant coupés[1] which, exactly as if they were ashamed to show their misery during the day, are never seen round Paris until after nightfall.

It took them to their door in the Rue des Martyrs, and once more, sadly, they climbed up homeward. All was ended, for her. And as to him, he reflected that he must be at the Ministry at ten o'clock.

She removed the wraps which covered her shoulders before the glass, so as once more to see herself in all her glory. But suddenly she uttered a cry. She no longer had the necklace around her neck!

Her husband, already half undressed, demanded:

"What is the matter with you?"

She turned madly toward him:

"I have — I have — I've lost Mme. Forestier's necklace."

He stood up, distracted.

"What! — how? — impossible!"

And they looked in the folds of her dress, in the folds of her cloak, in her pockets, everywhere. They did not find it.

He asked:

"You're sure you had it on when you left the ball?"

"Yes, I felt it in the vestibule of the palace."

"But if you had lost it in the street we should have heard it fall. It must be in the cab."

"Yes. Probably. Did you take his number?"

"No. And you, didn't you notice it?"

"No."

They looked, thunderstruck, at one another. At last Loisel put on his clothes.

"I shall go back on foot," said he, "over the whole route which we have taken to see if I can find it."

And he went out. She sat waiting on a chair in her ball dress, without strength to go to bed, overwhelmed, without fire, without a thought.

Her husband came back about seven o'clock. He had found nothing.

He went to Police Headquarters, to the newspaper offices, to offer a reward; he went to the cab companies — everywhere, in fact, whither he was urged by the least suspicion of hope.

She waited all day, in the same condition of mad fear before this terrible calamity.

Loisel returned at night with a hollow, pale face; he had discovered nothing.

"You must write to your friend," said he, "that you have broken the clasp of her necklace and that you are having it mended. That will give us time to turn round."

---

[1] An enclosed four-wheeled carriage.

She wrote at his dictation.

At the end of a week they had lost all hope.

And Loisel, who had aged five years, declared:

"We must consider how to replace that ornament."

The next day they took the box which had contained it, and they went to the jeweler whose name was found within. He consulted his books.

"It was not I, madame, who sold that necklace; I must simply have furnished the case."

Then they went from jeweler to jeweler, searching for a necklace like the other, consulting their memories, sick both of them with chagrin and anguish.

They found, in a shop at the Palais Royal, a string of diamonds which seemed to them exactly like the one they looked for. It was worth forty thousand francs. They could have it for thirty-six.

So they begged the jeweler not to sell it for three days yet. And they made a bargain that he should buy it back for thirty-four thousand francs, in case they found the other one before the end of February.

Loisel possessed eighteen thousand francs which his father had left him. He would borrow the rest.

He did borrow, asking a thousand francs of one, five hundred of another, five louis here, three louis there. He gave notes, took up ruinous obligations, dealt with usurers and all the race of lenders. He compromised all the rest of his life, risked his signature without even knowing if he could meet it; and, frightened by the pains yet to come, by the black misery which was about to fall upon him, by the prospect of all physical privation and of all the moral tortures which he was to suffer, he went to get the new necklace, putting down upon the merchant's counter thirty-six thousand francs.

When Mme. Loisel took back the necklace, Mme. Forestier said to her, with a chilly manner:

"You should have returned it sooner; I might have needed it."

She did not open the case, as her friend had so much feared. If she had detected the substitution, what would she have thought, what would she have said? Would she not have taken Mme. Loisel for a thief?

Mme. Loisel now knew the horrible existence of the needy. She took her part, moreover, all of a sudden, with heroism. That dreadful debt must be paid. She would pay it. They dismissed their servant; they changed their lodgings; they rented a garret under the roof.

She came to know what heavy housework meant and the odious cares of the kitchen. She washed the dishes, using her rosy nails on the greasy pots and pans. She washed the dirty linen, the shirts, and the dishcloths, which she dried upon a line; she carried the slops down to the street every morning, and carried up the water, stopping for breath at every landing. And, dressed like a woman of the people, she went to the fruiterer, the grocer, the butcher, her basket on her arm, bargaining, insulted, defending her miserable money sou by sou.

Each month they had to meet some notes, renew others, obtain more time.

Her husband worked in the evening making a fair copy of some tradesman's accounts, and late at night he often copied manuscript for five sous a page.

And this life lasted for ten years.

At the end of ten years, they had paid everything, everything, with the rates of usury, and the accumulations of the compound interest.

Mme. Loisel looked old now. She had become the woman of impoverished households — strong and hard and rough. With frowsy hair, skirts askew, and red hands, she talked loud while washing the floor with great swishes of water. But sometimes, when her husband was at the office, she sat down near the window, and she thought of that gay evening of long ago, of that ball where she had been so beautiful and so fêted.

What would have happened if she had not lost that necklace? Who knows? Who knows? How life is strange and changeful! How little a thing is needed for us to be lost or to be saved!

But, one Sunday, having gone to take a walk in the Champs Elysées to refresh herself from the labor of the week, she suddenly perceived a woman who was leading a child. It was Mme. Forestier, still young, still beautiful, still charming.

Mme. Loisel felt moved. Was she going to speak to her? Yes, certainly. And now that she had paid, she was going to tell her all about it. Why not?

She went up.

"Good-day, Jeanne."

The other, astonished to be familiarly addressed by this plain goodwife, did not recognize her at all, and stammered.

"But — madam! — I do not know — you must be mistaken."

"No. I am Mathilde Loisel."

Her friend uttered a cry.

"Oh, my poor Mathilde! How you are changed!"

"Yes, I have had days hard enough, since I have seen you, days wretched enough — and that because of you!"

"Of me! How so?"

"Do you remember that diamond necklace which you lent me to wear at the ministerial ball?"

"Yes. Well?"

"Well, I lost it."

"What do you mean? You brought it back."

"I brought you back another just like it. And for this we have been ten years paying. You can understand that it was not easy for us, who had nothing. At last it is ended, and I am very glad."

Mme. Forestier had stopped.

"You say that you bought a necklace of diamonds to replace mine?"

"Yes. You never noticed it, then! They were very like."

And she smiled with a joy which was proud and naïve at once.

Mme. Forestier, strongly moved, took her two hands.

"Oh, my poor Mathilde! Why, my necklace was paste. It was worth at most five hundred francs!"

Herman Melville

Herman Melville (1819–1891) published his first short story in 1853 as "Bartleby, the Scrivener: A Story of Wall Street." Behind him were seven years of writing novels beginning with the burst of creative energy that produced his early books of sea adventure: *Typee* (1846), *Omoo* (1847), *Mardi* (1849), *Redburn* (1849), and *White-Jacket* (1850). All of these were based on his experiences on board ship. Melville had been left in poverty at the age of fifteen when his father went bankrupt, and in 1839 he went to sea as a cabin boy. Two years later he sailed on a whaler bound for the Pacific, but he deserted in the Marquesas Islands and lived for a time with cannibals. Having little formal education, Melville later boasted that "a whale ship was my Yale College and my Harvard." His most ambitious book was *Moby-Dick* (1851), a work of great allegorical complexity heavily indebted to the influence of Nathaniel Hawthorne, Melville's neighbor in the Berkshires at the time he wrote it. *Moby-Dick* was not a commercial success, however, and the novel that followed it, *Pierre* (1852), was dismissed by critics as incomprehensible trash.

It was at this point that Melville turned to the short story. Between 1853 and 1856 he published fifteen sketches and stories and a serialized historical novel, promising the popular magazines that his stories would "contain nothing of any sort to shock the fastidious." But when this work and another novel (*The Confidence Man*, 1857) failed to restore his reputation, he ceased trying to support his family by his pen. He moved from his farm in the Berkshires to a house in New York City bought for him by his father-in-law, and worked for more than twenty years as an inspector of customs. He published a few books of poems and wrote a short novel, *Billy Budd*, which critics acclaimed as one of his greatest works when it was published—thirty years after his death.

Melville stood at the crossroads in the early history of American short fiction. When he began to publish in magazines, Hawthorne and Edgar Allan Poe had already done their best work in the romantic vein of tales and sketches, and the realistic local-color school of short stories had not yet been established. Melville created something new in "Bartleby, the Scrivener," a fully developed, if discursive, short story set in a contemporary social context. It baffled readers of *Putnam's Monthly Magazine* in 1853, when it was published in two installments. One reviewer called it "a Poeish tale with an infusion of more natural sentiment." For the rest of his stories, Melville used the conventional form of old-fashioned tales mostly set in remote times or places.

RELATED STORY
Daniel Orozco, "Orientation," page 1061.

RELATED COMMENTARIES
Herman Melville, "Blackness in Hawthorne's 'Young Goodman Brown,'" page 1473; J. Hillis Miller, "A Deconstructive Reading of Melville's 'Bartleby, the Scrivener,'" page 1477.

Bartleby, the Scrivener

1853

A Story of Wall Street

I AM A RATHER ELDERLY man. The nature of my avocations, for the last thirty years, has brought me into more than ordinary contact with what would seem an interesting and somewhat singular set of men, of whom, as yet, nothing, that I know of, has ever been written — I mean, the law-copyists, or scriveners. I have known very many of them, professionally and privately, and, if I pleased, could relate divers histories, at which good-natured gentlemen might smile, and sentimental souls might weep. But I waive the biographies of all other scriveners, for a few passages in the life of Bartleby, who was a scrivener, the strangest I ever saw, or heard of. While, of other law-copyists, I might write the complete life, of Bartleby nothing of that sort can be done. I believe that no materials exist, for a full and satisfactory biography of this man. It is an irreparable loss to literature. Bartleby was one of those beings of whom nothing is ascertainable, except from the original sources, and, in his case, those are very small. What my own astonished eyes saw of Bartleby, *that* is all I know of him, except, indeed, one vague report, which will appear in the sequel.

Ere introducing the scrivener, as he first appeared to me, it is fit I make some mention of myself, my *employés*, my business, my chambers, and general surroundings, because some such description is indispensable to an adequate understanding of the chief character about to be presented. Imprimis:[1] I am a man who, from his youth upwards, has been filled with a profound conviction that the easiest way of life is the best. Hence, though I belong to a profession proverbially energetic and nervous, even to turbulence, at times, yet nothing of that sort have I ever suffered to invade my peace. I am one of those unambitious lawyers who never address a jury, or in any way draw down public applause; but, in the cool tranquillity of a snug retreat, do a snug business among rich men's bonds, and mortgages, and title-deeds. All who know me, consider me an eminently *safe* man. The late John Jacob Astor, a personage little given to poetic enthusiasm, had no hesitation in pronouncing my first grand point to be prudence; my next, method. I do not speak it in vanity, but simply record the fact, that I was not unemployed in my profession by the late John Jacob Astor; a name which, I admit, I love to repeat; for it hath a rounded and orbicular sound to it, and rings like unto bullion. I will freely add, that I was not insensible to the late John Jacob Astor's good opinion.

Some time prior to the period at which this little history begins, my avocations had been largely increased. The good old office, now extinct in the State of New York, of a Master in Chancery, had been conferred upon me. It was not a very arduous office, but very pleasantly remunerative. I seldom lose my temper; much more seldom indulge in dangerous indignation at wrongs and

---

[1]In the first place (Latin).

outrages; but I must be permitted to be rash here and declare, that I consider the sudden and violent abrogation of the office of Master in Chancery, by the new Constitution, as a —— premature act; inasmuch as I had counted upon a life-lease of the profits, whereas I only received those of a few short years. But this is by the way.

My chambers were up stairs, at No. — Wall Street. At one end, they looked upon the white wall of the interior of a spacious skylight shaft, penetrating the building from top to bottom.

This view might have been considered rather tame than otherwise, deficient in what landscape painters call "life." But, if so, the view from the other end of my chambers offered, at least, a contrast, if nothing more. In that direction, my windows commanded an unobstructed view of a lofty brick wall, black by age and everlasting shade; which wall required no spy-glass to bring out its lurking beauties, but, for the benefit of all near-sighted spectators, was pushed up to within ten feet of my window-panes. Owing to the great height of the surrounding buildings, and my chambers being on the second floor, the interval between this wall and mine not a little resembled a huge square cistern.

At the period just preceding the advent of Bartleby, I had two persons as copyists in my employment, and a promising lad as an office-boy. First, Turkey; second, Nippers; third, Ginger Nut. These may seem names, the like of which are not usually found in the Directory. In truth, they were nicknames, mutually conferred upon each other by my three clerks, and were deemed expressive of their respective persons or characters. Turkey was a short, pursy Englishman, of about my own age — that is, somewhere not far from sixty. In the morning, one might say, his face was of a fine florid hue, but after twelve o'clock, meridian — his dinner hour — it blazed like a grate full of Christmas coals; and continued blazing — but, as it were, with a gradual wane — till six o'clock, P.M., or thereabouts; after which, I saw no more of the proprietor of the face, which, gaining its meridian with the sun, seemed to set with it, to rise, culminate, and decline the following day, with the like regularity and undiminished glory. There are many singular coincidences I have known in the course of my life, not the least among which was the fact, that, exactly when Turkey displayed his fullest beams from his red and radiant countenance, just then, too, at that critical moment, began the daily period when I considered his business capacities as seriously disturbed for the remainder of the twenty-four hours. Not that he was absolutely idle, or averse to business then; far from it. The difficulty was, he was apt to be altogether too energetic. There was a strange, inflamed, flurried, flighty recklessness of activity about him. He would be incautious in dipping his pen into his inkstand. All his blots upon my documents were dropped there after twelve o'clock, meridian. Indeed, not only would he be reckless, and sadly given to making blots in the afternoon, but, some days, he went further, and was rather noisy. At such times, too, his face flamed with augmented blazonry, as if cannel coal had been heaped on anthracite. He made an unpleasant racket with his chair; spilled his sand-box; in mending his pens, impatiently split them all to pieces, and threw them on the floor in a sudden passion; stood up, and leaned over his table, boxing his papers about in a most indecorous manner, very sad to behold in an elderly man like him. Nevertheless, as he was in many ways a most valuable person to me, and all the time before twelve o'clock, meridian, was the quickest, steadiest creature, too, accomplishing a great deal of work in a style not easily to be matched — for these reasons, I was willing to overlook his eccentricities, though, indeed, occasionally, I remonstrated with him. I did this very gently, however, because, though the civilest, nay, the blandest and most reverential of men in the morning, yet, in the afternoon, he was disposed, upon provocation, to be slightly rash with his tongue — in fact, insolent. Now, valuing his morning services as I did, and resolved not to lose them — yet, at the same time, made uncomfortable by his inflamed ways after twelve o'clock — and being a man of peace, unwilling by my admonitions to call forth unseemly retorts from him, I took upon me, one Saturday noon (he was always worse on Saturdays) to hint to him, very kindly, that, perhaps, now that he was growing old, it might be well to abridge his labors; in short, he need not come to my chambers after twelve o'clock, but, dinner over, had best go home to his lodgings, and rest himself till tea-time. But no; he insisted upon his afternoon devotions. His countenance became intolerably fervid, as he oratorically assured me — gesticulating with a long ruler at the other end of the room — that if his services in the morning were useful, how indispensable, then, in the afternoon?

"With submission, sir," said Turkey, on this occasion, "I consider myself your right-hand man. In the morning I but marshal and deploy my columns; but in the afternoon I put myself at their head, and gallantly charge the foe, thus" — and he made a violent thrust with the ruler.

"But the blots, Turkey," intimated I.

"True; but, with submission, sir, behold these hairs! I am getting old. Surely, sir, a blot or two of a warm afternoon is not to be severely urged against gray hairs. Old age — even if it blot the page — is honorable. With submission, sir, we *both* are getting old."

This appeal to my fellow-feeling was hardly to be resisted. At all events, I saw that go he would not. So, I made up my mind to let him stay, resolving, nevertheless, to see to it that, during the afternoon, he had to do with my less important papers.

Nippers, the second on my list, was a whiskered, sallow, and, upon the whole, rather piratical-looking young man, of about five-and-twenty. I always deemed him the victim of two evil powers — ambition and indigestion. The ambition was evinced by a certain impatience of the duties of a mere copyist, an unwarrantable usurpation of strictly professional affairs such as the original drawing up of legal documents. The indigestion seemed betokened in an occasional nervous testiness and grinning irritability, causing the teeth to audibly grind together over mistakes committed in copying; unnecessary maledictions, hissed, rather than spoken, in the heat of business; and especially by a continual discontent with the height of the table where he worked. Though of a very ingenious mechanical turn, Nippers could never get this table to suit him. He put chips under it, blocks of various sorts, bits of pasteboard, and at last went so far as to attempt an exquisite adjustment, by final pieces of folded blotting paper. But no invention would answer. If, for the sake of easing his back, he brought the table-lid at a sharp angle well up towards his chin, and wrote there like a man using the steep roof of a Dutch house for his desk, then he declared that it stopped the circulation in his arms. If now he lowered the table to his waistbands, and stooped over it in writing, then there was a sore aching in his back. In short, the truth of the matter was, Nippers knew not what he wanted. Or, if he wanted anything, it was to be rid of a scrivener's table altogether. Among the manifestations of his diseased ambition was a fondness he had for receiving visits from certain ambiguous-looking fellows in seedy coats, whom he called his clients. Indeed, I was aware that not only was he, at times, considerable of a ward-politician, but he occasionally did a little business at the justices' courts, and was not unknown on the steps of the Tombs.[2] I have good reason to believe, however, that one individual who called upon him at my chambers, and who, with a grand air, he insisted was his client, was no other than a dun, and the alleged title-deed, a bill. But, with all his failings, and the annoyances he caused me, Nippers, like his compatriot Turkey, was a very useful man to me; wrote a neat, swift hand; and, when he chose, was not deficient in a gentlemanly sort of deportment. Added to this, he always dressed in a gentlemanly sort of way; and so, incidentally, reflected credit upon my chambers. Whereas, with respect to Turkey, I had much ado to keep him from being a reproach to me. His clothes were apt to look oily, and smell of eating-houses. He wore his pantaloons very loose and baggy in summer. His coats were execrable, his hat not to be handled. But while the hat was a thing of indifference to me, inasmuch as his natural civility and deference, as a dependent Englishman, always led him to doff it the moment he entered the room, yet his coat was another matter. Concerning his coats, I reasoned with him; but with no effect. The truth was, I suppose, that a man with so small an income could not afford to sport such a lustrous face and a lustrous coat at one and the same time. As Nippers once observed, Turkey's money went chiefly for red ink. One winter day, I presented Turkey with a highly respectable-looking coat of my own — a padded gray coat, of a most comfortable warmth, and which buttoned straight up from the knee to the neck. I thought Turkey would appreciate the favor, and abate his rashness and obstreperousness of afternoons. But no; I verily believe that buttoning himself up in so downy and blanket-like a coat had a pernicious effect upon him upon the same principle that too much oats are bad for horses. In fact, precisely as a rash, restive horse is said to feel his oats, so Turkey felt his coat. It made him insolent. He was a man whom prosperity harmed.

Though, concerning the self-indulgent habits of Turkey, I had my own private surmises, yet, touching Nippers, I was well persuaded that, whatever might be his faults in other respects, he was, at least, a temperate young man. But, indeed, nature herself seemed to have been his vintner, and, at his birth, charged him so thoroughly with an irritable, brandy-like disposition, that all subsequent potations were needless. When I consider how, amid the stillness

---

[2]A prison in New York City.

of my chambers, Nippers would sometimes impatiently rise from his seat, and stooping over his table, spread his arms wide apart, seize the whole desk, and move it, and jerk it, with a grim, grinding motion on the floor, as if the table were a perverse voluntary agent, intent on thwarting and vexing him, I plainly perceive that, for Nippers, brandy-and-water were altogether superfluous.

It was fortunate for me that, owing to its peculiar cause — indigestion — the irritability and consequent nervousness of Nippers were mainly observable in the morning, while in the afternoon he was comparatively mild. So that, Turkey's paroxysms only coming on about twelve o'clock, I never had to do with their eccentricities at one time. Their fits relieved each other, like guards. When Nippers' was on, Turkey's was off; and *vice versa*. This was a good natural arrangement, under the circumstances.

Ginger Nut, the third on my list, was a lad, some twelve years old. His father was a carman, ambitious of seeing his son on the bench instead of a cart, before he died. So he sent him to my office, as student at law, errand-boy, cleaner, and sweeper, at the rate of one dollar a week. He had a little desk to himself, but he did not use it much. Upon inspection, the drawer exhibited a great array of the shells of various sorts of nuts. Indeed, to this quick-witted youth, the whole noble science of the law was contained in a nutshell. Not the least among the employments of Ginger Nut, as well as one which he discharged with the most alacrity, was his duty as cake and apple purveyor for Turkey and Nippers. Copying lawpapers being proverbially a dry, husky sort of business, my two scriveners were fain to moisten their mouths very often with Spitzenbergs, to be had at the numerous stalls nigh the Custom House and Post Office. Also, they sent Ginger Nut very frequently for that peculiar cake — small, flat, round, and very spicy — after which he had been named by them. Of a cold morning, when business was but dull, Turkey would gobble up scores of these cakes, as if they were mere wafers — indeed, they sell them at the rate of six or eight for a penny — the scrape of his pen blending with the crunching of the crisp particles in his mouth. Of all the fiery afternoon blunders and flurried rashness of Turkey, was his once moistening a ginger-cake between his lips, and clapping it on to a mortgage, for a seal. I came within an ace of dismissing him then. But he mollified me by making an oriental bow, and saying —

"With submission, sir, it was generous of me to find you in stationery on my own account."

Now my original business — that of a conveyancer and title hunter, and drawer-up of recondite documents of all sorts — was considerably increased by receiving the Master's office. There was now great work for scriveners. Not only must I push the clerks already with me, but I must have additional help.

In answer to my advertisement, a motionless young man one morning stood upon my office threshold, the door being open, for it was summer. I can see that figure now — pallidly neat, pitiably respectable, incurably forlorn! It was Bartleby.

After a few words touching his qualifications, I engaged him, glad to have among my corps of copyists a man of so singularly sedate an aspect, which I thought might operate beneficially upon the flighty temper of Turkey, and the fiery one of Nippers.

I should have stated before that ground-glass folding-doors divided my premises into two parts, one of which was occupied by my scriveners, the other by myself. According to my humor, I threw open these doors, or closed them. I resolved to assign Bartleby a corner by the folding-doors, but on my side of them, so as to have this quiet man within easy call, in case any trifling thing was to be done. I placed his desk close up to a small side-window in that part of the room, a window which originally had afforded a lateral view of certain grimy brickyards and bricks, but which, owing to subsequent erections, commanded at present no view at all, though it gave some light. Within three feet of the panes was a wall, and the light came down from far above, between two lofty buildings, as from a very small opening in a dome. Still further to a satisfactory arrangement, I procured a high green folding screen, which might entirely isolate Bartleby from my sight, though not remove him from my voice. And thus, in a manner, privacy and society were conjoined.

At first, Bartleby did an extraordinary quantity of writing. As if long famishing for something to copy, he seemed to gorge himself on my documents. There was no pause for digestion. He ran a day and night line, copying by sunlight and by candle-light. I should have been quite delighted with his application, had he been cheerfully industrious. But he wrote on silently, palely, mechanically.

It is, of course, an indispensable part of a scrivener's business to verify the accuracy of his copy, word by word. Where there are two or more scriveners in an office, they assist each other in this examination, one reading from the copy, the other holding the original. It is a very dull, wearisome, and lethargic affair. I can readily imagine that, to some sanguine temperaments, it would be altogether intolerable. For example, I cannot credit that the mettlesome poet, Byron, would have contentedly sat down with Bartleby to examine a law document of, say five hundred pages, closely written in a crimpy hand.

Now and then, in the haste of business, it had been my habit to assist in comparing some brief document myself, calling Turkey or Nippers for this purpose. One object I had, in placing Bartleby so handy to me behind the screen, was, to avail myself of his services on such trivial occasions. It was on the third day, I think, of his being with me, and before any necessity had arisen for having his own writing examined, that, being much hurried to complete a small affair I had in hand, I abruptly called to Bartleby. In my haste and natural expectancy of instant compliance, I sat with my head bent over the original on my desk, and my right hand sideways, and somewhat nervously extended with the copy, so that, immediately upon emerging from his retreat, Bartleby might snatch it and proceed to business without the least delay.

In this very attitude did I sit when I called to him, rapidly stating what it was I wanted him to do — namely, to examine a small paper with me. Imagine my surprise, nay, my consternation, when, without moving from his privacy, Bartleby, in a singularly mild, firm voice, replied, "I would prefer not to."

I sat awhile in perfect silence, rallying my stunned faculties. Immediately it occurred to me that my ears had deceived me, or Bartleby had entirely misunderstood my meaning. I repeated my request in the clearest tone I could assume; but in quite as clear a one came the previous reply, "I would prefer not to."

"Prefer not to," echoed I, rising in high excitement, and crossing the room with a stride. "What do you mean? Are you moonstruck? I want you to help me compare this sheet here — take it," and I thrust it towards him.

"I would prefer not to," said he.

I looked at him steadfastly. His face was leanly composed; his gray eye dimly calm. Not a wrinkle of agitation rippled him. Had there been the least uneasiness, anger, impatience, or impertinence in his manner; in other words, had there been anything ordinarily human about him, doubtless I should have violently dismissed him from the premises. But as it was, I should have as soon thought of turning my pale plaster-of-paris bust of Cicero out of doors. I stood gazing at him awhile, as he went on with his own writing, and then reseated myself at my desk. This is very strange, thought I. What had one best do? But my business hurried me. I concluded to forget the matter for the present, reserving it for my future leisure. So, calling Nippers from the other room, the paper was speedily examined.

A few days after this, Bartleby concluded four lengthy documents, being quadruplicates of a week's testimony taken before me in my High Court of Chancery. It became necessary to examine them. It was an important suit, and great accuracy was imperative. Having all things arranged, I called Turkey, Nippers, and Ginger Nut, from the next room, meaning to place the four copies in the hands of my four clerks, while I should read from the original. Accordingly, Turkey, Nippers, and Ginger Nut had taken their seats in a row, each with his document in his hand, when I called to Bartleby to join this interesting group.

"Bartleby! quick, I am waiting."

I heard a slow scrape of his chair legs on the uncarpeted floor, and soon he appeared standing at the entrance of his hermitage.

"What is wanted?" said he, mildly.

"The copies, the copies," said I, hurriedly. "We are going to examine them. There" — and I held towards him the fourth quadruplicate.

"I would prefer not to," he said, and gently disappeared behind the screen.

For a few moments I was turned into a pillar of salt, standing at the head of my seated column of clerks. Recovering myself, I advanced towards the screen, and demanded the reason for such extraordinary conduct.

"*Why* do you refuse?"

"I would prefer not to."

With any other man I should have flown outright into a dreadful passion, scorned all further words, and thrust him ignominiously from my presence. But there was something about Bartleby that not only strangely disarmed me, but, in a wonderful manner, touched and disconcerted me. I began to reason with him.

"These are your own copies we are about to examine. It is labor saving to you, because one examination will answer for your four papers. It is common usage. Every copyist is bound to help examine his copy. Is it not so? Will you not speak? Answer!"

"I prefer not to," he replied in a flute-like tone. It seemed to me that, while I had been addressing him, he carefully revolved every statement that I made;

fully comprehended the meaning; could not gainsay the irresistible conclusion; but, at the same time, some paramount consideration prevailed with him to reply as he did.

"You are decided, then, not to comply with my request — a request made according to common usage and common sense?"

He briefly gave me to understand, that on that point my judgment was sound. Yes: his decision was irreversible.

It is not seldom the case that, when a man is browbeaten in some unprecedented and violently unreasonable way, he begins to stagger in his own plainest faith. He begins, as it were, vaguely to surmise that, wonderful as it may be, all the justice and all the reason is on the other side. Accordingly, if any disinterested persons are present, he turns to them for some reinforcement for his own faltering mind.

"Turkey," said I, "what do you think of this? Am I not right?"

"With submission, sir," said Turkey, in his blandest tone, "I think that you are."

"Nippers," said I, "what do *you* think of it?"

"I think I should kick him out of the office."

(The reader of nice perceptions will have perceived that, it being morning, Turkey's answer is couched in polite and tranquil terms, but Nippers replies in ill-tempered ones. Or, to repeat a previous sentence, Nippers' ugly mood was on duty, and Turkey's off.)

"Ginger Nut," said I, willing to enlist the smallest suffrage in my behalf, "what do *you* think of it?"

"I think, sir, he's a little *luny*," replied Ginger Nut, with a grin.

"You hear what they say," said I, turning towards the screen, "come forth and do your duty."

But he vouchsafed no reply. I pondered a moment in sore perplexity. But once more business hurried me. I determined again to postpone the consideration of this dilemma to my future leisure. With a little trouble we made out to examine the papers without Bartleby, though at every page or two Turkey deferentially dropped his opinion, that this proceeding was quite out of the common; while Nippers, twitching in his chair with a dyspeptic nervousness, ground out, between his set teeth, occasional hissing maledictions against the stubborn oaf behind the screen. And for his (Nippers') part, this was the first and the last time he would do another man's business without pay.

Meanwhile Bartleby sat in his hermitage, oblivious to everything but his own peculiar business there.

Some days passed, the scrivener being employed upon another lengthy work. His late remarkable conduct led me to regard his ways narrowly. I observed that he never went to dinner; indeed, that he never went anywhere. As yet I had never, of my personal knowledge, known him to be outside of my office. He was a perpetual sentry in the corner. At about eleven o'clock though, in the morning, I noticed that Ginger Nut would advance towards the opening in Bartleby's screen, as if silently beckoned thither by a gesture invisible to me where I sat. The boy would then leave the office, jingling a few pence, and reappear with a handful of ginger-nuts, which he delivered in the hermitage, receiving two of the cakes for his trouble.

He lives, then, on ginger-nuts, thought I; never eats a dinner, properly speaking; he must be a vegetarian, then, but no; he never eats even vegetables, he eats nothing but ginger-nuts. My mind then ran on in reveries concerning the probable effects upon the human constitution of living entirely on ginger-nuts. Ginger-nuts are so called, because they contain ginger as one of their peculiar constituents, and the final flavoring one. Now, what was ginger? A hot, spicy thing. Was Bartleby hot and spicy? Not at all. Ginger, then, had no effect upon Bartleby. Probably he preferred it should have none.

Nothing so aggravates an earnest person as a passive resistance. If the individual so resisted be of a not inhumane temper, and the resisting one perfectly harmless in his passivity, then, in the better moods of the former, he will endeavor charitably to construe to his imagination what proves impossible to be solved by his judgment. Even so, for the most part, I regarded Bartleby and his ways. Poor fellow! thought I, he means no mischief; it is plain he intends no insolence; his aspect sufficiently evinces that his eccentricities are involuntary. He is useful to me. I can get along with him. If I turn him away, the chances are he will fall in with some less indulgent employer, and then he will be rudely treated, and perhaps driven forth miserably to starve. Yes. Here I can cheaply purchase a delicious self-approval. To befriend Bartleby; to humor him in his strange wilfulness, will cost me little or nothing, while I lay up in my soul what will eventually prove a sweet morsel for my conscience. But this mood was not invariable with me. The passiveness of Bartleby sometimes irritated me. I felt strangely goaded on to encounter him in new opposition — to elicit some angry spark from him answerable to my own. But, indeed, I might as well have essayed to strike fire with my knuckles against a bit of Windsor soap. But one afternoon the evil impulse in me mastered me, and the following little scene ensued:

"Bartleby," said I, "when those papers are all copied, I will compare them with you."

"I would prefer not to."

"How? Surely you do not mean to persist in that mulish vagary?"

No answer.

I threw open the folding-doors nearby, and turning upon Turkey and Nippers, exclaimed:

"Bartleby a second time says, he won't examine his papers. What do you think of it, Turkey?"

It was afternoon, be it remembered. Turkey sat glowing like a brass boiler; his bald head steaming; his hands reeling among his blotted papers.

"Think of it?" roared Turkey. "I think I'll just step behind his screen, and black his eyes for him!"

So saying, Turkey rose to his feet and threw his arms into a pugilistic position. He was hurrying away to make good his promise, when I detained him, alarmed at the effect of incautiously rousing Turkey's combativeness after dinner.

"Sit down, Turkey," said I, "and hear what Nippers has to say. What do you think of it, Nippers? Would I not be justified in immediately dismissing Bartleby?"

"Excuse me, that is for you to decide, sir. I think his conduct quite unusual, and, indeed, unjust, as regards Turkey and myself. But it may only be a passing whim."

"Ah," exclaimed I, "you have strangely changed your mind, then — you speak very gently of him now."

"All beer," cried Turkey; "gentleness is effects of beer — Nippers and I dined together to-day. You see how gentle *I* am, sir. Shall I go and black his eyes?"

"You refer to Bartleby, I suppose. No, not to-day, Turkey," I replied; "pray, put up your fists."

I closed the doors, and again advanced towards Bartleby. I felt additional incentives tempting me to my fate. I burned to be rebelled against again. I remembered that Bartleby never left the office.

"Bartleby," said I, "Ginger Nut is away; just step around to the Post Office, won't you?" (it was but a three minutes' walk) "and see if there is anything for me."

"I would prefer not to."

"You *will* not?"

"I *prefer* not."

I staggered to my desk, and sat there in a deep study. My blind inveteracy returned. Was there any other thing in which I could procure myself to be ignominiously repulsed by this lean, penniless wight? my hired clerk? What added thing is there, perfectly reasonable, that he will be sure to refuse to do?

"Bartleby!"

No answer.

"Bartleby," in a louder tone.

No answer.

"Bartleby," I roared.

Like a very ghost, agreeably to the laws of magical invocation, at the third summons, he appeared at the entrance of his hermitage.

"Go to the next room, and tell Nippers to come to me."

"I would prefer not to," he respectfully and slowly said, and mildly disappeared.

"Very good, Bartleby," said I, in a quiet sort of serenely-severe self-possessed tone, intimating the unalterable purpose of some terrible retribution very close at hand. At the moment I half intended something of the kind. But upon the whole, as it was drawing towards my dinner-hour, I thought it best to put on my hat and walk home for the day, suffering much from perplexity and distress of mind.

Shall I acknowledge it? The conclusion of this whole business was, that it soon became a fixed fact of my chambers, that a pale young scrivener, by the name of Bartleby, had a desk there; that he copied for me at the usual rate of four cents a folio (one hundred words); but he was permanently exempt from examining the work done by him, that duty being transferred to Turkey and Nippers, out of compliment, doubtless, to their superior acuteness; moreover, said Bartleby was never, on any account, to be dispatched on the most trivial errand of any sort; and that even if entreated to take upon him such a matter, it was generally understood that he would "prefer not to" — in other words, that he would refuse point blank.

As days passed on, I became considerably reconciled to Bartleby. His steadiness, his freedom from all dissipation, his incessant industry (except when he chose to throw himself into a standing revery behind his screen), his great stillness, his unalterableness of demeanor under all circumstances, made him a valuable acquisition. One prime thing was this — *he was always there* — first in the morning, continually through the day, and the last at night. I had a singular confidence in his honesty. I felt my most precious papers perfectly safe in his hands. Sometimes, to be sure, I could not, for the very soul of me, avoid falling into sudden spasmodic passions with him. For it was exceeding difficult to bear in mind all the time those strange peculiarities, privileges, and unheard-of exemptions, forming the tacit stipulations on Bartleby's part under which he remained in my office. Now and then, in the eagerness of dispatching pressing business, I would inadvertently summon Bartleby, in a short, rapid tone, to put his finger, say, on the incipient tie of a bit of red tape with which I was about compressing some papers. Of course, from behind the screen the usual answer, "I prefer not to," was sure to come; and then, how could a human creature, with the common infirmities of our nature, refrain from bitterly exclaiming upon such perverseness — such unreasonableness? However, every added repulse of this sort which I received only tended to lessen the probability of my repeating the inadvertence.

Here it must be said, that, according to the custom of most legal gentlemen occupying chambers in densely populated law buildings, there were several keys to my door. One was kept by a woman residing in the attic, which person weekly scrubbed and daily swept and dusted my apartments. Another was kept by Turkey for convenience sake. The third I sometimes carried in my own pocket. The fourth I knew not who had.

Now, one Sunday morning I happened to go to Trinity Church, to hear a celebrated preacher, and finding myself rather early on the ground I thought I would walk round to my chambers for a while. Luckily I had my key with me; but upon applying it to the lock, I found it resisted by something inserted from the inside. Quite surprised, I called out; when to my consternation a key was turned from within; and thrusting his lean visage at me, and holding the door ajar, the apparition of Bartleby appeared, in his shirt-sleeves, and otherwise in a strangely tattered *deshabille*, saying quietly that he was sorry, but he was deeply engaged just then, and preferred not admitting me at present. In a brief word or two, he moreover added, that perhaps I had better walk round the block two or three times, and by that time he would probably have concluded his affairs.

Now, the utterly unsurmised appearance of Bartleby, tenanting my lawchambers of a Sunday morning, with his cadaverously gentlemanly *nonchalance*, yet withal firm and self-possessed, had such a strange effect upon me, that incontinently I slunk away from my own door, and did as desired. But not without sundry twinges of impotent rebellion against the mild effrontery of this unaccountable scrivener. Indeed, it was his wonderful mildness chiefly, which not only disarmed me, but unmanned me, as it were. For I consider that one, for the time, is sort of unmanned when he tranquilly permits his hired clerk to dictate to him, and order him away from his own premises. Furthermore, I was full of uneasiness as to what Bartleby could possibly be doing in my office in his shirt-sleeves, and in an otherwise dismantled condition on a Sunday morning. Was anything amiss going on? Nay, that was out of the question. It was not to be thought of for a moment that Bartleby was an immoral person. But what could he be doing there? — copying? Nay again, whatever might be his eccentricities, Bartleby was an eminently decorous person. He would be the last man to sit down to his desk in any state approaching to nudity. Besides, it was Sunday; and there was something about Bartleby that forbade the supposition that he would by any secular occupation violate the proprieties of the day.

Nevertheless, my mind was not pacified; and full of a restless curiosity, at last I returned to the door. Without hindrance I inserted my key, opened it, and entered. Bartleby was not to be seen. I looked round anxiously, peeped behind his screen; but it was very plain that he was gone. Upon more closely examining the place, I surmised that for an indefinite period Bartleby must have ate, dressed, and slept in my office, and that too without plate, mirror, or bed. The cushioned seat of a rickety old sofa in one corner bore the faint impress of a lean, reclining form. Rolled away under his desk, I found a blanket; under the empty grate, a blacking box and brush; on a chair, a tin basin, with soap and a ragged towel; in a newspaper a few crumbs of ginger-nuts and a morsel of cheese. Yes, thought I, it is evident enough that Bartleby has been making his home here, keeping bachelor's hall all by himself. Immediately then the thought came sweeping across me, what miserable friendlessness and loneliness are here revealed! His poverty is great; but his solitude, how horrible! Think of it. Of a Sunday, Wall Street is deserted as Petra;[3] and every night of every day it is an emptiness. This building, too, which of week-days hums with industry and life, at nightfall echoes with sheer vacancy, and all through Sunday is forlorn. And here Bartleby makes his home; sole spectator of a solitude which he has seen all populous — a sort of innocent and transformed Marius[4] brooding among the ruins of Carthage!

For the first time in my life a feeling of overpowering stinging melancholy seized me. Before, I had never experienced aught but a not unpleasing sadness. The bond of a common humanity now drew me irresistibly to gloom. A fraternal melancholy! For both I and Bartleby were sons of Adam. I remembered the bright silks and sparkling faces I had seen that day, in gala trim,

---

[3]A city in what is now Jordan, once the center of an Arab kingdom. It was deserted for more than ten centuries, until its rediscovery by explorers in 1812.

[4]Gaius Marius (157?–86 B.C.), a Roman general, several times elected consul. Marius's greatest military successes came in the Jugurthine War, in Africa. Later, when his opponents gained power and he was banished, he fled to Africa. Carthage was a city in North Africa.

swan-like sailing down the Mississippi of Broadway; and I contrasted them with the pallid copyist, and thought to myself, Ah, happiness courts the light, so we deem the world is gay; but misery hides aloof, so we deem that misery there is none. These sad fancyings — chimeras, doubtless, of a sick and silly brain — led on to other and more special thoughts, concerning the eccentricities of Bartleby. Presentiments of strange discoveries hovered round me. The scrivener's pale form appeared to me laid out, among uncaring strangers, in its shivering winding-sheet.

Suddenly I was attracted by Bartleby's closed desk, the key in open sight left in the lock.

I mean no mischief, seek the gratification of no heartless curiosity, thought I; besides, the desk is mine, and its contents, too, so I will make bold to look within. Everything was methodically arranged, the papers smoothly placed. The pigeon-holes were deep, and removing the files of documents, I groped into their recesses. Presently I felt something there, and dragged it out. It was an old bandanna handkerchief, heavy and knotted. I opened it, and saw it was a savings' bank.

I now recalled all the quiet mysteries which I had noted in the man. I remembered that he never spoke but to answer; that, though at intervals he had considerable time to himself, yet I had never seen him reading — no, not even a newspaper; that for long periods he would stand looking out, at his pale window behind the screen, upon the dead brick wall; I was quite sure he never visited any refectory or eating-house; while his pale face clearly indicated that he never drank beer like Turkey; or tea and coffee even, like other men; that he never went anywhere in particular that I could learn; never went out for a walk, unless, indeed, that was the case at present; that he had declined telling who he was, or whence he came, or whether he had any relatives in the world; that though so thin and pale, he never complained of ill-health. And more than all, I remembered a certain unconscious air of pallid — how shall I call it? — of pallid haughtiness, say, or rather an austere reserve about him, which has positively awed me into my tame compliance with his eccentricities, when I had feared to ask him to do the slightest incidental thing for me, even though I might know, from his long-continued motionlessness, that behind his screen he must be standing in one of those dead-wall reveries of his.

Revolving all these things, and coupling them with the recently discovered fact, that he made my office his constant abiding place and home, and not forgetful of his morbid moodiness; revolving all these things, a prudential feeling began to steal over me. My first emotions had been those of pure melancholy and sincerest pity; but just in proportion as the forlornness of Bartleby grew and grew to my imagination, did that same melancholy merge into fear, that pity into repulsion. So true it is, and so terrible, too, that up to a certain point the thought or sight of misery enlists our best affections; but, in certain special cases, beyond that point it does not. They err who would assert that invariably this is owing to the inherent selfishness of the human heart. It rather proceeds from a certain hopelessness of remedying excessive and organic ill. To a sensitive being, pity is not seldom pain. And when at last it is perceived that such pity cannot lead to effectual succor, common sense bids the soul be rid of it. What I saw that morning persuaded me that the scrivener was the victim of innate and incurable disorder. I might give alms to his body; but his body did not pain him; it was his soul that suffered, and his soul I could not reach.

I did not accomplish the purpose of going to Trinity Church that morning. Somehow, the things I had seen disqualified me for the time from church-going. I walked homeward, thinking what I would do with Bartleby. Finally, I resolved upon this — I would put certain calm questions to him the next morning, touching his history, etc., and if he declined to answer them openly and unreservedly (and I supposed he would prefer not), then to give him a twenty dollar bill over and above whatever I might owe him, and tell him his services were no longer required; but that if in any other way I could assist him, I would be happy to do so, especially if he desired to return to his native place, wherever that might be, I would willingly help to defray the expenses. Moreover, if, after reaching home, he found himself at any time in want of aid, a letter from him would be sure of a reply.

The next morning came.

"Bartleby," said I, gently calling to him behind his screen.

No reply.

"Bartleby," said I, in a still gentler tone, "come here; I am not going to ask you to do anything you would prefer not to do — I simply wish to speak to you."

Upon this he noiselessly slid into view.

"Will you tell me, Bartleby, where you were born?"

"I would prefer not to."

"Will you tell me *anything* about yourself?"

"I would prefer not to."

"But what reasonable objection can you have to speak to me? I feel friendly towards you."

He did not look at me while I spoke, but kept his glance fixed upon my bust of Cicero, which, as I then sat, was directly behind me, some six inches above my head.

"What is your answer, Bartleby?" said I, after waiting a considerable time for a reply, during which his countenance remained immovable, only there was the faintest conceivable tremor of the white attenuated mouth.

"At present I prefer to give no answer," he said, and retired into his hermitage.

It was rather weak in me I confess, but his manner, on this occasion, nettled me. Not only did there seem to lurk in it a certain calm disdain, but his perverseness seemed ungrateful, considering the undeniable good usage and indulgence he had received from me.

Again I sat ruminating what I should do. Mortified as I was at his behavior, and resolved as I had been to dismiss him when I entered my office, nevertheless I strangely felt something superstitious knocking at my heart, and forbidding me to carry out my purpose, and denouncing me for a villain if I dared to breathe one bitter word against this forlornest of mankind. At last, familiarly drawing my chair behind his screen, I sat down and said: "Bartleby, never mind, then, about revealing your history; but let me entreat you, as a friend, to comply as far as may be with the usages of this office. Say now, you will help to examine papers tomorrow or next day: in short, say now, that in a day or two you will begin to be a little reasonable: — say so, Bartleby."

"At present I would prefer not to be a little reasonable," was his mildly cadaverous reply.

Just then the folding-doors opened, and Nippers approached. He seemed suffering from an unusually bad night's rest, induced by severer indigestion than common. He overheard those final words of Bartleby.

"*Prefer not*, eh?" gritted Nippers — "I'd *prefer* him, if I were you, sir," addressing me — "I'd *prefer* him; I'd give him preferences, the stubborn mule! What is it, sir, pray, that he *prefers* not to do now?"

Bartleby moved not a limb.

"Mr. Nippers," said I, "I'd prefer that you would withdraw for the present."

Somehow, of late, I had got into the way of involuntarily using this word "prefer" upon all sorts of not exactly suitable occasions. And I trembled to think that my contact with the scrivener had already and seriously affected me in a mental way. And what further and deeper aberration might it not yet produce? This apprehension had not been without efficacy in determining me to summary measures.

As Nippers, looking very sour and sulky, was departing, Turkey blandly and deferentially approached.

"With submission, sir," said he, "yesterday I was thinking about Bartleby here, and I think that if he would but prefer to take a quart of good ale every day, it would do much towards mending him, and enabling him to assist in examining his papers."

"So you have got the word, too," said I, slightly excited.

"With submission, what word, sir?" asked Turkey, respectfully crowding himself into the contracted space behind the screen, and by so doing, making me jostle the scrivener. "What word, sir?"

"I would prefer to be left alone here," said Bartleby, as if offended at being mobbed in his privacy.

"*That's* the word, Turkey," said I — "*that's* it."

"Oh, *prefer*? oh yes — queer word. I never use it myself. But, sir, as I was saying, if he would but prefer —"

"Turkey," interrupted I, "you will please withdraw."

"Oh certainly, sir, if you prefer that I should."

As he opened the folding-door to retire, Nippers at his desk caught a glimpse of me, and asked whether I would prefer to have a certain paper copied on blue paper or white. He did not in the least roguishly accent the word "prefer." It was plain that it involuntarily rolled from his tongue. I thought to myself, surely I must get rid of a demented man, who already has in some degree turned the tongues, if not the heads of myself and clerks. But I thought it prudent not to break the dismission at once.

The next day I noticed that Bartleby did nothing but stand at his window in his dead-wall revery. Upon asking him why he did not write, he said that he had decided upon doing no more writing.

"Why, how now? what next?" exclaimed I, "do no more writing?"

"No more."

"And what is the reason?"

"Do you not see the reason for yourself?" he indifferently replied.

I looked steadfastly at him, and perceived that his eyes looked dull and glazed. Instantly it occurred to me, that his unexampled diligence in copying by his dim window for the first few weeks of his stay with me might have temporarily impaired his vision.

I was touched. I said something in condolence with him. I hinted that of course he did wisely in abstaining from writing for a while; and urged him to embrace that opportunity of taking wholesome exercise in the open air. This, however, he did not do. A few days after this, my other clerks being absent, and being in a great hurry to dispatch certain letters by the mail, I thought that, having nothing else earthly to do, Bartleby would surely be less inflexible than usual, and carry these letters to the Post Office. But he blankly declined. So, much to my inconvenience, I went myself.

Still added days went by. Whether Bartleby's eyes improved or not, I could not say. To all appearance, I thought they did. But when I asked him if they did he vouchsafed no answer. At all events, he would do no copying. At last, in replying to my urgings, he informed me that he had permanently given up copying.

"What!" exclaimed I; "suppose your eyes should get entirely well—better than ever before—would you not copy then?"

"I have given up copying," he answered, and slid aside.

He remained as ever, a fixture in my chamber. Nay—if that were possible—he became still more of a fixture than before. What was to be done? He would do nothing in the office; why should he stay there? In plain fact, he had now become a millstone to me, not only useless as a necklace, but afflictive to bear. Yet I was sorry for him. I speak less than truth when I say that, on his own account, he occasioned me uneasiness. If he would but have named a single relative or friend, I would instantly have written, and urged their taking the poor fellow away to some convenient retreat. But he seemed alone, absolutely alone in the universe. A bit of wreck in the mid-Atlantic. At length, necessities connected with my business tyrannized over all other considerations. Decently as I could, I told Bartleby that in six days' time he must unconditionally leave the office. I warned him to take measures, in the interval, for procuring some other abode. I offered to assist him in this endeavor, if he himself would but take the first step towards a removal. "And when you finally quit me, Bartleby," added I, "I shall see that you go not away entirely unprovided. Six days from this hour, remember."

At the expiration of that period, I peeped behind the screen, and lo! Bartleby was there.

I buttoned up my coat, balanced myself; advanced slowly towards him, touched his shoulder, and said, "The time has come; you must quit this place; I am sorry for you; here is money; but you must go."

"I would prefer not," he replied, with his back still towards me.

"You *must.*"

He remained silent.

Now I had an unbounded confidence in this man's common honesty. He had frequently restored to me sixpences and shillings carelessly dropped upon the floor, for I am apt to be very reckless in such shirt-button affairs. The proceeding, then, which followed will not be deemed extraordinary.

"Bartleby," said I, "I owe you twelve dollars on account; here are thirty-two; the odd twenty are yours — Will you take it?" and I handed the bills towards him.

But he made no motion.

"I will leave them here, then," putting them under a weight on the table. Then taking my hat and cane and going to the door, I tranquilly turned and added — "After you have removed your things from these offices, Bartleby, you will of course lock the door — since every one is now gone for the day but you — and if you please, slip your key underneath the mat, so that I may have it in the morning. I shall not see you again; so good-bye to you. If, hereafter, in your new place of abode, I can be of any service to you, do not fail to advise me by letter. Good-bye, Bartleby, and fare you well."

But he answered not a word; like the last column of some ruined temple, he remained standing mute and solitary in the middle of the otherwise deserted room.

As I walked home in a pensive mood, my vanity got the better of my pity. I could not but highly plume myself on my masterly management in getting rid of Bartleby. Masterly I call it, and such it must appear to any dispassionate thinker. The beauty of my procedure seemed to consist in its perfect quietness. There was no vulgar bullying, no bravado of any sort, no choleric hectoring, and striding to and fro across the apartment, jerking out vehement commands for Bartleby to bundle himself off with his beggarly traps. Nothing of the kind. Without loudly bidding Bartleby depart — as an inferior genius might have done — I *assumed* the ground that depart he must; and upon that assumption built all I had to say. The more I thought over my procedure, the more I was charmed with it. Nevertheless, next morning, upon awakening, I had my doubts — I had somehow slept off the fumes of vanity. One of the coolest and wisest hours a man has, is just after he awakes in the morning. My procedure seemed as sagacious as ever — but only in theory. How it would prove in practice — there was the rub. It was truly a beautiful thought to have assumed Bartleby's departure; but, after all, that assumption was simply my own, and none of Bartleby's. The great point was, not whether I had assumed that he would quit me, but whether he would prefer to do so. He was more a man of preferences than assumptions.

After breakfast, I walked down town, arguing the probabilities *pro* and *con*. One moment I thought it would prove a miserable failure, and Bartleby would be found all alive at my office as usual; the next moment it seemed certain that I should find his chair empty. And so I kept veering about. At the corner of Broadway and Canal Street, I saw quite an excited group of people standing in earnest conversation.

"I'll take odds he doesn't," said a voice as I passed.

"Doesn't go? — done!" said I, "put up your money."

I was instinctively putting my hand in my pocket to produce my own, when I remembered that this was an election day. The words I had overheard bore no reference to Bartleby, but to the success or non-success of some candidate for the mayoralty. In my intent frame of mind, I had, as it were, imagined that all Broadway shared in my excitement, and were debating the same question with me. I passed on, very thankful that the uproar of the street screened my momentary absent-mindedness.

As I had intended, I was earlier than usual at my office door. I stood listening for a moment. All was still. He must be gone. I tried the knob. The door was locked. Yes, my procedure had worked to a charm; he indeed must be vanished. Yet a certain melancholy mixed with this: I was almost sorry for my brilliant success. I was fumbling under the door mat for the key, which Bartleby was to have left there for me, when accidentally my knee knocked against a panel, producing a summoning sound, and in response a voice came to me from within — "Not yet; I am occupied."

It was Bartleby.

I was thunderstruck. For an instant I stood like the man who, pipe in mouth, was killed one cloudless afternoon long ago in Virginia, by summer lightning; at his own warm open window he was killed, and remained leaning out there upon the dreamy afternoon, till someone touched him, when he fell.

"Not gone!" I murmured at last. But again obeying that wondrous ascendancy which the inscrutable scrivener had over me, and from which ascendancy, for all my chafing, I could not completely escape, I slowly went down stairs and out into the street, and while walking round the block, considered what I should next do in this unheard-of perplexity. Turn the man out by an actual thrusting I could not; to drive him away by calling him hard names would not do; calling in the police was an unpleasant idea; and yet, permit him to enjoy his cadaverous triumph over me — this, too, I could not think of. What was to be done? or, if nothing could be done, was there anything further that I could *assume* in the matter? Yes, as before I had prospectively assumed that Bartleby would depart, so now I might retrospectively assume that departed he was. In the legitimate carrying out of this assumption, I might enter my office in a great hurry, and pretending not to see Bartleby at all, walk straight against him as if he were air. Such a proceeding would in a singular degree have the appearance of a home-thrust. It was hardly possible that Bartleby could withstand such an application of the doctrine of assumption. But upon second thoughts the success of the plan seemed rather dubious. I resolved to argue the matter over with him again.

"Bartleby," said I, entering the office, with a quietly severe expression, "I am seriously displeased. I am pained, Bartleby. I had thought better of you. I had imagined you of such a gentlemanly organization, that in any delicate dilemma a slight hint would suffice — in short, an assumption. But it appears I am deceived. Why," I added, unaffectedly starting, "you have not even touched that money yet," pointing to it, just where I had left it the evening previous.

He answered nothing.

"Will you, or will you not, quit me?" I now demanded in a sudden passion, advancing close to him.

"I would prefer *not* to quit you," he replied, gently emphasizing the *not*.

"What earthly right have you to stay here? Do you pay any rent? Do you pay my taxes? Or is this property yours?"

He answered nothing.

"Are you ready to go on and write now? Are your eyes recovered? Could you copy a small paper for me this morning? or help examine a few lines? or step round to the Post Office? In a word, will you do anything at all, to give a coloring to your refusal to depart the premises?"

He silently retired into his hermitage.

I was now in such a state of nervous resentment that I thought it but prudent to check myself at present from further demonstrations. Bartleby and I were alone. I remembered the tragedy of the unfortunate Adams and the still more unfortunate Colt in the solitary office of the latter; and how poor Colt, being dreadfully incensed by Adams, and imprudently permitting himself to get wildly excited, was at unawares hurried into his fatal act — an act which certainly no man could possibly deplore more than the actor himself.[5] Often it had occurred to me in my ponderings upon the subject that had that altercation taken place in the public street, or at a private residence, it would not have terminated as it did. It was the circumstance of being alone in a solitary office, upstairs, of a building entirely unhallowed by humanizing domestic associations — an uncarpeted office, doubtless, of a dusty, haggard sort of appearance — this it must have been, which greatly helped to enhance the irritable desperation of the hapless Colt.

But when this old Adam of resentment rose in me and tempted me concerning Bartleby, I grappled him and threw him. How? Why, simply by recalling the divine injunction: "A new commandment give I unto you, that ye love one another." Yes, this it was that saved me. Aside from higher considerations, charity often operates as a vastly wise and prudent principle — a great safeguard to its possessor. Men have committed murder for jealousy's sake, and anger's sake, and hatred's sake, and selfishness' sake, and spiritual pride's sake; but no man, that ever I heard of, ever committed a diabolical murder for sweet charity's sake. Mere self-interest, then, if no better motive can be enlisted, should, especially with high-tempered men, prompt all beings to charity and philanthropy. At any rate, upon the occasion in question, I strove to drown my exasperated feelings towards the scrivener by benevolently construing his conduct. Poor fellow, poor fellow! thought I, he don't mean anything; and besides, he has seen hard times, and ought to be indulged.

I endeavored, also, immediately to occupy myself, and at the same time to comfort my despondency. I tried to fancy, that in the course of the morning, at such time as might prove agreeable to him, Bartleby, of his own free accord,

---

[5] John C. Colt murdered Samuel Adams in January 1842. Later that year, after his conviction, Colt committed suicide a half-hour before he was to be hanged. The case received wide and sensationalistic press coverage at the time.

would emerge from his hermitage and take up some decided line of march in the direction of the door. But no. Half-past twelve o'clock came; Turkey began to glow in the face, overturn his inkstand, and become generally obstreperous; Nippers abated down into quietude and courtesy; Ginger Nut munched his noon apple; and Bartleby remained standing at his window in one of his profoundest dead-wall reveries. Will it be credited? Ought I to acknowledge it? That afternoon I left the office without saying one further word to him.

Some days now passed, during which, at leisure intervals I looked a little into "Edwards[6] on the Will," and "Priestley[7] on Necessity." Under the circumstances, those books induced a salutary feeling. Gradually I slid into the persuasion that these troubles of mine, touching the scrivener, had been all predestined from eternity, and Bartleby was billeted upon me for some mysterious purpose of an all-wise Providence, which it was not for a mere mortal like me to fathom. Yes, Bartleby, stay there behind your screen, thought I; I shall persecute you no more; you are harmless and noiseless as any of these old chairs; in short, I never feel so private as when I know you are here. At last I see it, I feel it; I penetrate to the predestined purpose of my life. I am content. Others may have loftier parts to enact; but my mission in this world, Bartleby, is to furnish you with office-room for such period as you may see fit to remain.

I believe that this wise and blessed frame of mind would have continued with me, had it not been for the unsolicited and uncharitable remarks obtruded upon me by my professional friends who visited the rooms. But thus it often is, that the constant friction of illiberal minds wears out at last the best resolves of the more generous. Though to be sure, when I reflected upon it, it was not strange that people entering my office should be struck by the peculiar aspect of the unaccountable Bartleby, and so be tempted to throw out some sinister observations concerning him. Sometimes an attorney, having business with me, and calling at my office, and finding no one but the scrivener there, would undertake to obtain some sort of precise information from him touching my whereabouts; but without heeding his idle talk, Bartleby would remain standing immovable in the middle of the room. So after contemplating him in that position for a time, the attorney would depart, no wiser than he came.

Also, when a reference was going on, and the room full of lawyers and witnesses, and business driving fast, some deeply-occupied legal gentleman present, seeing Bartleby wholly unemployed, would request him to run round to his (the legal gentleman's) office and fetch some papers for him. Thereupon, Bartleby would tranquilly decline, and yet remain idle as before. Then the

---

[6]Jonathan Edwards, *Freedom of the Will* (1754). Edwards was an important American theologian, a rigidly orthodox Calvinist who believed in the doctrine of predestination and a leader of the Great Awakening, the religious revival that swept the North American colonies in the 1740s.

[7]Joseph Priestley (1733–1803), English scientist and clergyman. Priestley began as a Unitarian but developed his own radical ideas on "natural determinism." As a scientist, he did early experiments with electricity and was one of the first to discover the existence of oxygen. As a political philosopher, he championed the French Revolution — a cause so unpopular in England that he had to flee that country and spend the last decade of his life in the United States.

lawyer would give a great stare, and turn to me. And what could I say? At last I was made aware that all through the circle of my professional acquaintance, a whisper of wonder was running round, having reference to the strange creature I kept at my office. This worried me very much. And as the idea came upon me of his possibly turning out a long-lived man, and keeping occupying my chambers, and denying my authority; and perplexing my visitors; and scandalizing my professional reputation; and casting a general gloom over the premises; keeping soul and body together to the last upon his savings (for doubtless he spent but half a dime a day), and in the end perhaps outlive me, and claim possession of my office by right of his perpetual occupancy: as all these dark anticipations crowded upon me more and more, and my friends continually intruded their relentless remarks upon the apparition in my room; a great change was wrought in me. I resolved to gather all my faculties together, and forever rid me of this intolerable incubus.

Ere revolving any complicated project, however, adapted to this end, I first simply suggested to Bartleby the propriety of his permanent departure. In a calm and serious tone, I commended the idea to his careful and mature consideration. But, having taken three days to meditate upon it, he apprised me, that his original determination remained the same; in short, that he still preferred to abide with me.

What shall I do? I now said to myself, buttoning up my coat to the last button. What shall I do? what ought I to do? what does conscience say I *should* do with this man, or, rather, ghost. Rid myself of him, I must; go, he shall. But how? You will not thrust him, the poor, pale, passive mortal you will not thrust such a helpless creature out of your door? you will not dishonor yourself by such cruelty? No, I will not, I cannot do that. Rather would I let him live and die here, and then mason up his remains in the wall. What, then, will you do? For all your coaxing, he will not budge. Bribes he leaves under your own paper-weight on your table; in short, it is quite plain that he prefers to cling to you.

Then something severe, something unusual must be done. What! surely you will not have him collared by a constable, and commit his innocent pallor to the common jail? And upon what ground could you procure such a thing to be done? — a vagrant, is he? What! he a vagrant, a wanderer, who refuses to budge? It is because he will not be a vagrant, then, that you seek to count him *as* a vagrant. That is too absurd. No visible means of support: there I have him. Wrong again: for indubitably he *does* support himself, and that is the only unanswerable proof that any man can show of his possessing the means so to do. No more, then. Since he will not quit me, I must quit him. I will change my offices; I will move elsewhere, and give him fair notice, that if I find him on my new premises I will then proceed against him as a common trespasser.

Acting accordingly, next day I thus addressed him: "I find these chambers too far from the City Hall; the air is unwholesome. In a word, I propose to remove my offices next week, and shall no longer require your services. I tell you this now, in order that you may seek another place."

He made no reply, and nothing more was said.

On the appointed day I engaged carts and men, proceeded to my chambers, and, having but little furniture, everything was removed in a few hours. Throughout, the scrivener remained standing behind the screen, which I directed to be removed the last thing. It was withdrawn; and, being folded up like a huge folio, left him the motionless occupant of a naked room. I stood in the entry watching him a moment, while something from within me upbraided me.

I re-entered, with my hand in my pocket — and — and my heart in my mouth.

"Good-bye, Bartleby; I am going — good-bye, and God some way bless you; and take that," slipping something in his hand. But it dropped upon the floor, and then — strange to say — I tore myself from him whom I had so longed to be rid of.

Established in my new quarters, for a day or two I kept the door locked, started at every footfall in the passages. When I returned to my rooms, after any little absence, I would pause at the threshold for an instant, and attentively listen, ere applying my key. But these fears were needless. Bartleby never came nigh me.

I thought all was going well, when a perturbed-looking stranger visited me, inquiring whether I was the person who had recently occupied rooms at No. — Wall Street.

Full of forebodings, I replied that I was.

"Then, sir," said the stranger, who proved a lawyer, "you are responsible for the man you left there. He refuses to do any copying; he refuses to do anything; he says he prefers not to; and he refuses to quit the premises."

"I am very sorry, sir," said I, with assumed tranquillity, but an inward tremor, "but, really, the man you allude to is nothing to me — he is no relation or apprentice of mine, that you should hold me responsible for him."

"In mercy's name, who is he?"

"I certainly cannot inform you. I know nothing about him. Formerly I employed him as a copyist; but he has done nothing for me now for some time past."

"I shall settle him, then — good morning, sir."

Several days passed, and I heard nothing more; and, though I often felt a charitable prompting to call at the place and see poor Bartleby, yet a certain squeamishness, of I know not what, withheld me.

All is over with him, by this time, thought I, at last, when, through another week, no further intelligence reached me. But, coming to my room the day after, I found several persons waiting at my door in a high state of nervous excitement.

"That's the man here — he comes," cried the foremost one, whom I recognized as the lawyer who had previously called upon me alone.

"You must take him away, sir, at once," cried a portly person among them, advancing upon me, and whom I knew to be the landlord of No. — Wall Street. "These gentlemen, my tenants, cannot stand it any longer; Mr. B——" pointing to the lawyer, "has turned him out of his room, and he now persists in haunting the building generally, sitting upon the banisters of the stairs by day, and sleeping in the entry by night. Everybody is concerned; clients are leaving the offices; some fears are entertained of a mob; something you must do, and that without delay."

Aghast at this torrent, I fell back before it, and would fain have locked myself in my new quarters. In vain I persisted that Bartleby was nothing to me — no more than to any one else. In vain — I was the last person known to have anything to do with him, and they held me to the terrible account. Fearful, then, of being exposed in the papers (as one person present obscurely threatened), I considered the matter, and, at length, said, that if the lawyer would give me a confidential interview with the scrivener, in his (the lawyer's) own room, I would, that afternoon, strive my best to rid them of the nuisance they complained of.

Going upstairs to my old haunt, there was Bartleby silently sitting upon the banister at the landing.

"What are you doing here, Bartleby?" said I.

"Sitting upon the banister," he mildly replied.

I motioned him into the lawyer's room, who then left us.

"Bartleby," said I, "are you aware that you are the cause of great tribulation to me, by persisting in occupying the entry after being dismissed from the office?"

No answer.

"Now one of two things must take place. Either you must do something, or something must be done to you. Now what sort of business would you like to engage in? Would you like to re-engage in copying for some one?"

"No; I would prefer not to make any change."

"Would you like a clerkship in a dry-goods store?"

"There is too much confinement about that. No, I would not like a clerkship; but I am not particular."

"Too much confinement," I cried, "why, you keep yourself confined all the time!"

"I would prefer not to take a clerkship," he rejoined, as if to settle that little item at once.

"How would a bar-tender's business suit you? There is no trying of the eyesight in that."

"I would not like it at all; though, as I said before, I am not particular."

His unwonted wordiness inspired me. I returned to the charge.

"Well, then, would you like to travel through the country collecting bills for the merchants? That would improve your health."

"No, I would prefer to be doing something else."

"How, then, would going as a companion to Europe, to entertain some young gentleman with your conversation — how would that suit you?"

"Not at all. It does not strike me that there is anything definite about that. I like to be stationary. But I am not particular."

"Stationary you shall be, then," I cried, now losing all patience, and, for the first time in all my exasperating connections with him, fairly flying into a passion. "If you do not go away from these premises before night, I shall feel bound — indeed, I *am* bound — to — to — to quit the premises myself!" I rather absurdly concluded, knowing not with what possible threat to try to frighten his immobility into compliance. Despairing of all further efforts, I was precipitately leaving him, when a final thought occurred to me — one which had not been wholly unindulged before.

"Bartleby," said I, in the kindest tone I could assume under such exciting circumstances, "will you go home with me now not to my office, but my dwelling — and remain there till we can conclude upon some convenient arrangement for you at our leisure? Come, let us start now, right away."

"No: at present I would prefer not to make any change at all."

I answered nothing; but, effectually dodging every one by the suddenness and rapidity of my flight, rushed from the building, ran up Wall Street towards Broadway, and, jumping into the first omnibus, was soon removed from pursuit. As soon as tranquillity returned, I distinctly perceived that I had now done all that I possibly could, both in respect to the demands of the landlord and his tenants, and with regard to my own desire and sense of duty, to benefit Bartleby, and shield him from rude persecution. I now strove to be entirely care-free and quiescent; and my conscience justified me in the attempt; though, indeed, it was not so successful as I could have wished. So fearful was I of being again hunted out by the incensed landlord and his exasperated tenants, that, surrendering my business to Nippers, for a few days, I drove about the upper part of the town and through the suburbs, in my rockaway; crossed over to Jersey City and Hoboken, and paid fugitive visits to Manhattanville and Astoria. In fact, I almost lived in my rockaway for the time.

When again I entered my office, lo, a note from the landlord lay upon the desk. I opened it with trembling hands. It informed me that the writer had sent to the police, and had Bartleby removed to the Tombs as a vagrant. Moreover, since I knew more about him than any one else, he wished me to appear at that place, and make a suitable statement of the facts. These tidings had a conflicting effect upon me. At first I was indignant; but, at last, almost approved. The landlord's energetic, summary disposition, had led him to adopt a procedure which I do not think I would have decided upon myself; and yet, as a last resort, under such peculiar circumstances, it seemed the only plan.

As I afterwards learned, the poor scrivener, when told that he must be conducted to the Tombs, offered not the slightest obstacle, but, in his pale, unmoving way, silently acquiesced.

Some of the compassionate and curious by-standers joined the party; and headed by one of the constables arm-in-arm with Bartleby, the silent procession filed its way through all the noise, and heat, and joy of the roaring thoroughfares at noon.

The same day I received the note, I went to the Tombs, or, to speak more properly, the Halls of Justice. Seeking the right officer, I stated the purpose of my call, and was informed that the individual I described was, indeed, within. I then assured the functionary that Bartleby was a perfectly honest man, and greatly to be compassionated, however unaccountably eccentric. I narrated all I knew, and closed by suggesting the idea of letting him remain in as indulgent confinement as possible, till something less harsh might be done — though, indeed, I hardly knew what. At all events, if nothing else could be decided upon, the alms-house must receive him. I then begged to have an interview.

Being under no disgraceful charge, and quite serene and harmless in all his ways, they had permitted him freely to wander about the prison, and, especially, in the inclosed grass-platted yards thereof. And so I found him there, standing all alone in the quietest of the yards, his face towards a high wall, while all around, from the narrow slits of the jail windows, I thought I saw peering out upon him the eyes of murderers and thieves.

"Bartleby!"

"I know you," he said, without looking round — "and I want nothing to say to you."

"It was not I that brought you here, Bartleby," said I, keenly pained at his implied suspicion. "And to you, this should not be so vile a place. Nothing reproachful attaches to you by being here. And see, it is not so sad a place as one might think. Look, there is the sky, and here is the grass."

"I know where I am," he replied, but would say nothing more, and so I left him.

As I entered the corridor again, a broad meat-like man, in an apron, accosted me, and, jerking his thumb over my shoulder, said "Is that your friend?"

"Yes."

"Does he want to starve? If he does, let him live on the prison fare, that's all."

"Who are you?" asked I, not knowing what to make of such an unofficially speaking person in such a place.

"I am the grub-man. Such gentlemen as have friends here, hire me to provide them with something good to eat."

"Is this so?" said I, turning to the turnkey.

He said it was.

"Well, then," said I, slipping some silver into the grub-man's hands (for so they called him), "I want you to give particular attention to my friend there; let him have the best dinner you can get. And you must be as polite to him as possible."

"Introduce me, will you?" said the grub-man, looking at me with an expression which seemed to say he was all impatience for an opportunity to give a specimen of his breeding.

Thinking it would prove of benefit to the scrivener, I acquiesced; and, asking the grub-man his name, went up with him to Bartleby.

"Bartleby, this is a friend; you will find him very useful to you."

"Your sarvant, sir, your sarvant," said the grub-man, making a low salutation behind his apron. "Hope you find it pleasant here, sir; nice grounds — cool apartments — hope you'll stay with us some time — try to make it agreeable. What will you have for dinner to-day?"

"I prefer not to dine to-day," said Bartleby, turning away. "It would disagree with me; I am unused to dinners." So saying, he slowly moved to the other side of the inclosure, and took up a position fronting the dead-wall.

"How's this?" said the grub-man, addressing me with a stare of astonishment. "He's odd, ain't he?"

"I think he is a little deranged," said I, sadly.

"Deranged? deranged is it? Well, now, upon my word, I thought that friend of yourn was a gentleman forger; they are always pale and genteel-like, them forgers. I can't help pity 'em — can't help it, sir. Did you know Monroe Edwards?" he added, touchingly, and paused. Then, laying his hand piteously on my shoulder, sighed, "he died of consumption at Sing-Sing. So you weren't acquainted with Monroe?"

"No, I was never socially acquainted with any forgers. But I cannot stop longer. Look to my friend yonder. You will not lose by it. I will see you again."

Some few days after this, I again obtained admission to the Tombs, and went through the corridors in quest of Bartleby; but without finding him.

"I saw him coming from his cell not long ago," said a turnkey, "may be he's gone to loiter in the yards."

So I went in that direction.

"Are you looking for the silent man?" said another turnkey, passing me. "Yonder he lies — sleeping in the yard there. 'Tis not twenty minutes since I saw him lie down."

The yard was entirely quiet. It was not accessible to the common prisoners. The surrounding walls, of amazing thickness, kept off all sounds behind them. The Egyptian character of the masonry weighed upon me with its gloom. But a soft imprisoned turf grew under foot. The heart of the eternal pyramids, it seemed, wherein, by some strange magic, through the clefts, grass-seed, dropped by birds, had sprung.

Strangely huddled at the base of the wall, his knees drawn up, and lying on his side, his head touching the cold stones, I saw the wasted Bartleby. But nothing stirred. I paused; then went close up to him; stooped over, and saw that his dim eyes were open; otherwise he seemed profoundly sleeping. Something prompted me to touch him. I felt his hand, when a tingling shiver ran up my arm and down my spine to my feet.

The round face of the grub-man peered upon me now. "His dinner is ready. Won't he dine to-day, either? Or does he live without dining?"

"Lives without dining," said I, and closed the eyes.

"Eh! — He's asleep, ain't he?"

"With kings and counselors,"[8] murmured I.

There would seem little need for proceeding further in this history. Imagination will readily supply the meagre recital of poor Bartleby's interment. But, ere parting with the reader, let me say, that if this little narrative has sufficiently interested him, to awaken curiosity as to who Bartleby was, and what

------

[8]A reference to Job 3:14. Job, who has lost his family and all his property and been stricken by a terrible disease, wishes he had never been born: "then had I been at rest with kings and counselors of the earth, which built desolate places for themselves."

manner of life he led prior to the present narrator's making his acquaintance, I can only reply, that in such curiosity I fully share, but am wholly unable to gratify it. Yet here I hardly know whether I should divulge one little item of rumor, which came to my ear a few months after the scrivener's decease. Upon what basis it rested, I could never ascertain; and hence, how true it is I cannot now tell. But, inasmuch as this vague report has not been without a certain suggestive interest to me, however sad, it may prove the same with some others; and so I will briefly mention it. The report was this: that Bartleby had been a subordinate clerk in the Dead Letter Office at Washington, from which he had been suddenly removed by a change in the administration. When I think over this rumor, hardly can I express the emotions which seize me. Dead letters! does it not sound like dead men? Conceive a man by nature and misfortune prone to a pallid hopelessness, can any business seem more fitted to heighten it than that of continually handling these dead letters, and assorting them for the flames? For by the cart-load they are annually burned. Sometimes from out the folded paper the pale clerk takes a ring: — the finger it was meant for, perhaps, moulders in the grave; a bank-note sent in swiftest charity: — he whom it would relieve, nor eats nor hungers any more; pardon for those who died despairing; hope for those who died unhoping; good tidings for those who died stifled by unrelieved calamities. On errands of life, these letters speed to death.

Ah, Bartleby! Ah, humanity!

Steven Millhauser

Steven Millhauser (b. 1943) was born in Brooklyn, New York, and moved to Stratford, Connecticut, when he was four years old. His parents were both teachers, and Millhauser recalls that their combined salaries were enough only to permit them to live in a working-class neighborhood. "My friends and classmates all had names like Zielski, Stoccatore, Saksa, Mancini, Pavluvcik, Ciccarelli, Leitkowski, Cerino, DiCicio, Politano, Recupido. Names like these, as sheer sounds, have the power to move me like chords struck on an old piano."

Millhauser incorporated his early memories of Stratford as a magically illuminated place of childhood innocence in his first novel, *Edwin Mullhouse* (1972), particularly "what an American small-town street feels like and smells like, what kitchens and cellars and attics are like, what roadside weeds and telephone poles are like." He followed this book with another novel and three books of short fiction — *In the Penny Arcade* (1986), *The Barnum Museum* (1990), and *Little Kingdoms: Three Novellas* (1993) — before publishing his novel *Martin Dressler: The Tale of an American Dreamer*, which won the Pulitzer Prize in 1997. "Flying Carpets" is from *The Knife Thrower and Other Stories* (1998). Other recent collections of short fiction are *The King in the Tree: Three Novellas* (2003), *Dangerous Laughter* (2008), and *We Others: New and Selected Stories* (2011).

In an interview with Jim Shepard, Millhauser reminisced about his childhood and his ideas about the craft of fiction, especially his interest in shorter forms of fiction and the intensity of feeling he experiences when he's writing well:

> The novella isn't really a form at all. . . . In this it's no different from the short story or the novel, which are frequently called "forms" but are in fact nothing but rough lengths. A true literary form exists only in the fixed poetic forms: the sonnet, the villanelle, the sestina, and so on. . . . The challenge and the glory of the short story lie exactly there, in its shortness. But shortness encourages certain effects and not others. It encourages, for instance, the close-up view, the revelatory detail, the single significant moment. . . . [When things are going well, I feel] that the entire universe is streaming in on me. It's a feeling of strength, of terrifying health, of much-more-aliveness. It's the kind of feeling that probably should never be talked about, as if one were confessing to a shameful deed.

RELATED COMMENTARY
Daniel Orozco, "On Steven Millhauser's 'Flying Carpets,'" page 1499.

Flying Carpets

1998

IN THE LONG SUMMERS of my childhood, games flared up suddenly, burned to a brightness, and vanished forever. The summers were so long that they gradually grew longer than the whole year, they stretched out slowly beyond the edges of our lives, but at every moment of their vastness they were drawing to an end, for that's what summers mostly did: they taunted us with endings, marched always into the long shadow thrown backward by the end of vacation. And because our summers were always ending, and because they lasted forever, we grew impatient with our games, we sought new and more intense ones; and as the crickets of August grew louder, and a single red leaf appeared on branches green with summer, we threw ourselves as if desperately into new adventures, while the long days never changing, grew heavy with boredom and longing.

I first saw the carpets in the back yards of other neighborhoods. Glimpses of them came to me from behind garages, flickers of color at the corners of two-family houses where clotheslines on pulleys stretched from upper porches to high gray poles, and old Italian men in straw hats stood hoeing between rows of tomatoes and waist-high corn. I saw one once at the far end of a narrow strip of grass between two stucco houses, skimming lightly over the ground at the level of the garbage cans. Although I took note of them, they were of no more interest to me than games of jump rope I idly watched on the school playground, or dangerous games with jackknives I saw the older boys playing at the back of the candy store. One morning I noticed one in a back yard in my neighborhood; four boys stood tensely watching. I was not surprised a few days later when my father came home from work with a long package under his arm, wrapped in heavy brown paper, tied with a straw-colored twine from which little prickly hairs stuck up.

The colors were duller than I had expected, less magical — only maroon and green: dark green curlings and loopings against a maroon that was nearly brown. At each end the fringes were thickish rough strings. I had imagined crimson, emerald, the orange of exotic birds. The underside of the carpet was covered with a coarse, scratchy material like burlap; in one corner I noticed a small black mark, circled in red, shaped like a capital *H* with a slanting middle line. In the back yard I practiced cautiously, close to the ground, following the blurred blue directions printed on a piece of paper so thin I could see my fingertips touching the other side. It was all a matter of artfully shifted weight: seated cross-legged just behind the center of the carpet, you leaned forward slightly to send the carpet forward, left to make it turn left; right, right. The carpet rose when you lifted both sides with fingers cupped beneath, lowered when you pushed lightly down. It slowed to a stop when the bottom felt the pressure of a surface.

At night I kept it rolled up in the narrow space at the foot of my bed, alongside old puzzle boxes at the bottom of my bookcase.

For days I was content to practice gliding back and forth about the yard, passing under the branches of the crab-apple trees, squeezing between the swing and ladder of the yellow swing set, flying into the bottoms of sheets on the clothesline, drifting above the row of zinnias at the edge of the garden to skim along the carrots and radishes and four rows of corn, passing back and forth over the wooden floor of the old chicken coop that was nothing but a roof and posts at the back of the garage, while my mother watched anxiously from the kitchen window. I was no more tempted to rise into the sky than I was tempted to plunge downhill on my bike with my arms crossed over my chest. Sometimes I liked to watch the shadow of my carpet moving on the ground, a little below me and to one side; and now and then, in a nearby yard, I would see an older boy rise on his carpet above the kitchen window, or pass over the sunlit shingles of a garage roof.

Sometimes my friend Joey came skimming over his low picket fence into my yard. Then I followed him around and around the crab-apple trees and through the open chicken coop. He went faster than I did, leaning far forward, tipping sharply left or right. He even swooped over my head, so that for a moment a shadow passed over me. One day he landed on the flat tar-papered roof of the chicken coop, where I soon joined him. Standing with my hands on my hips, the sun burning down on my face, I could see over the tall back-yard hedge into the weed-grown lot where in past summers I had hunted for frogs and garden snakes. Beyond the lot I saw houses and telephone wires rising on the hill beside the curving sun-sparkling road; and here and there, in back yards hung with clotheslines, against the white-shingled backs of houses, over porch rails and sloping cellar doors and the water arcs of lawn sprinklers shot through with faint rainbows, I could see the children on their red and green and blue carpets, riding through the sunny air.

One afternoon when my father was at work and my mother lay in her darkened bedroom, breathing damply with asthma, I pulled out the carpet at the foot of the bed, unrolled it, and sat down on it to wait. I wasn't supposed to ride my carpet unless my mother was watching from the kitchen window. Joey was in another town, visiting his cousin Marilyn, who lived near a department store with an escalator. The thought of riding up one escalator and down the next, up one and down the next, while the stairs flattened out or lifted up, filled me with irritation and boredom. Through the window screen I could hear the sharp, clear blows of a hammer, like the ticking of a gigantic clock. I could hear the clish-clish of the hedge clippers, which made me think of movie sword fights; the uneven hum of a rising and falling bee. I lifted the edges of the carpet and began to float about the room. After a while I passed through the door and down the stairs into the small living room and big yellow kitchen, but I kept bumping into pots and chair tops; and soon I came skimming up the stairs and landed on my bed and looked out the window into the back yard. The shadow of the swing frame showed sharp and black against the grass. I felt a tingling or tugging in my legs and arms. Dreamily I pushed the window higher and raised the screen.

For a while I glided about the room, then bent low as I approached the open window and began to squeeze the carpet through. The wooden bottom of the raised window scraped along my back, the sides of the frame pressed against me. It was like the dream where I tried to push myself through the small door-way, tried and tried, though my bones hurt, and my skin burned, till suddenly I pulled free. For a moment I seemed to sit suspended in the air beyond my window; below I saw the green hose looped on its hook, the handles and the handle shadows on the tops of the metal garbage cans, the mountain laurel bush pressed against the cellar window; then I was floating out over the top of the swing and the crab-apple trees; below me I saw the shadow of the carpet rippling over grass; and drifting high over the hedge and out over the vacant lot, I looked down on the sunny tall grass, the milkweed pods and pink thistles, a green Coke bottle gleaming in the sun; beyond the lot the houses rose behind each other on the hill, the red chimneys clear against the blue sky; and all was sunny, all was peaceful and still; the hum of insects; the far sound of a hand mower, like distant scissors; soft shouts of children in the warm, drowsy air; heavily my eyelids began to close, but far below I saw a boy in brown shorts looking up at me, shading his eyes, and seeing him there, I felt suddenly where I was, way up in the dangerous air; and leaning fearfully to one side I steered the carpet back to my yard, dropped past the swing, and landed on the grass near the back steps. As I sat safe in my yard I glanced up at the high, open window, and far above the window the red shingles of the roof glittered in the sun.

I dragged the heavy carpet up to my room, but the next day I rose high above Joey as he passed over the top of the swing. In a distant yard I saw some-one skim over the top of a garage roof and sink out of sight. At night I lay awake planning voyages, pressing both hands against my heart to slow its vio-lent beating.

One night I woke to a racket of crickets. Through the window screen I could see the shadow of the swing frame in the moonlit back yard. I could see the streetlamp across from the bakery down by the field and the three streetlamps rising with the road as it curved out of sight at the top of the hill. The night sky was the color of a dark blue marble I liked to hold up to a bulb in the table lamp. I dressed quickly, pulled out my carpet, and slowly, so as not to make scraping noises, pushed up the window and the screen. From the foot of the bed I lifted the rolled rug. It suddenly spilled open, like a dark liquid rush-ing from a bottle. The wood of the window pressed against my back as I bent my way through.

In the blue night I sailed over the back yard, passing high over the hedge and into the lot, where I saw the shadow of the carpet rippling over the moon-lit high grass. I turned back to the yard, swooped over the garage roof and circled the house at the level of the upper windows, watching myself pass in the glittery black glass; and rising a little higher, into the dark and dream-blue air, I looked down to see that I was passing over Joey's yard toward Ciccarelli's lot, where older boys had rock fights in the choked paths twisting among high weeds and thornbushes; and as when, standing up to my waist in water, I sud-denly bent my legs and felt the cold wetness covering my shoulders, so now I plunged into the dark blue night, crossing Ciccarelli's lot, passing over a street, sailing over garage roofs, till rising higher I looked down on the telephone wires glistening as if wet with moonlight, on moon-greened treetops stuffed with blackness, on the slanting rafters and open spaces of a half-built house crisscrossed with shadows; in the distance I could see a glassy stream going under a road; spots of light showed the shapes of far streets; and passing over a roof close by a chimney, I saw each brick so sharp and clear in the moonlight that I could make out small bumps and holes in the red and ocher surfaces; and sweeping upward with the wind in my hair I flew over moon-flooded rooftops striped with chimney shadows, until I saw below me the steeple of a white church, the top of the firehouse, the big red letters of the five-and-dime, the movie marquee sticking out like a drawer, the shop windows dark-shining in the light of the streetlamps, the street with its sheen of red from the traffic light; then out over rows of rooftops on the far side of town, a black factory with lit-up windows and white smoke that glowed like light; a field stretching away; gleaming water; till I felt I'd strayed to the farthest edge of things; and turning back I flew high above the moonlit town, when suddenly I saw the hill with three streetlamps, the bakery, the swing frame, the chicken coop—and landing for a moment on the roof of the garage, sitting with my legs astride the peak, exultant, unafraid, I saw, high in the blue night sky, passing slowly across the white moon, another carpet with its rider.

With a feeling of exhilaration and weariness—a weariness like sadness—I rose slowly toward my window, and bending my way through, I plunged into sleep.

The next morning I woke sluggish and heavy-headed. Outside, Joey was waiting for me on his carpet. He wanted to race around the house. But I had no heart for carpets that day, stubbornly I swung on the old swing, threw a tennis ball onto the garage roof and caught it as it came rushing over the edge, squeezed through the hedge into the vacant lot where I'd once caught a frog in a jar. At night I lay remembering my journey in sharp detail—the moon-glistening telephone wires above their shadow stripes, the clear bricks in the chimney—while through the window screen I heard the chik-chik-chik of crickets. I sat up in bed and shut the window and turned the metal lock on top.

I had heard tales of other voyages, out beyond the ends of the town, high up into the clouds. Joey knew a boy who'd gone up so high you couldn't see him anymore, like a balloon that grows smaller and smaller and vanishes—as if suddenly—into blue regions beyond the reach of sight. There were towns up there, so they said; I didn't know; white cloud towns, with towers. Up there, in the blue beyond the blue, there were rivers you could go under the way you could walk under a bridge; birds with rainbow-colored tails; ice mountains and cities of snow; flattened shining masses of light like whirling discs; blue gardens; slow-moving creatures with leathery wings; towns inhabited by the dead. My father had taught me not to believe stories about Martians and spaceships, and these tales were like those stories: even as you refused to believe them, you saw them, as if the sheer effort of not believing them made them glow in your mind. Beside such stories, my forbidden night journey over the rooftops seemed tame as a stroll. I could feel dark desires ripening within me; stubbornly I returned to my old games, as carpets moved in back yards, forming bars of red and green across white shingles.

Came a day when my mother let me stay home while she went shopping at the market at the top of the hill. I wanted to call out after her: Stop! Make me go with you! I saw her walking across the lawn toward the open garage. My father had taken the bus to work. In my room I raised the blinds and looked out at the brilliant blue sky. For a long time I looked at that sky before unlocking the window, pushing up the glass and screen.

I set forth high over the back yard and rose smoothly into the blue. I kept my eyes ahead and up, though now and then I let my gaze fall over the carpet's edge. Down below I saw little red and black roofs, the shadows of houses thrown all on one side, a sunny strip of road fringed with sharp-bent tree shadows, as if they had been blown sideways by a wind — and here and there, on neat squares of lawn, little carpets flying above their moving shadows. The sky was blue, pure blue. When I next glanced down I saw white puff-balls hanging motionless over factory smokestacks, oil tanks like white coins by a glittering brown river. Up above, in all that blue, I saw only a small white cloud, with a little rip at the bottom, as if someone had started to tear it in half. The empty sky was so blue, so richly and thickly blue, that it seemed a thing I ought to be able to feel, like lake water or snow. I had read a story once about a boy who walked into a lake and came to a town on the bottom, and now it seemed to me that I was plunging deep into a lake, even though I was climbing. Below me I saw a misty patch of cloud, rectangles of dark green and butterscotch and brown. The blue stretched above like fields of snow, like fire. I imagined myself standing in my yard, looking up at my carpet growing smaller and smaller until it vanished into the blue. I felt myself vanishing into blue. He was vanishing into blue. Below my carpet I saw only blue. In this blue beyond blue, all nothing everywhere, was I still I? I had passed out of sight, the string holding me to earth had snapped, and in these realms of blue I saw no rivers and white towns, no fabulous birds, but only shimmering distances of sky-blue heaven-blue blue. In that blaze of blue I tried to remember whether the boy in the lake had ever come back; and looking down at that ungraspable blue, which plunged away on both sides, I longed for the hardness under green grass, tree bark scraping my back, sidewalks, dark stones. Maybe it was the fear of never coming back, maybe it was the blue passing into me and soaking me through and through, but a dizziness came over me, I closed my eyes — and it seemed to me that I was falling through the sky, that my carpet had blown away, that the rush of my falling had knocked the wind out of me, that I had died, was about to die, as in a dream when I felt myself falling toward the sharp rocks, that I was running, tumbling, crawling, pursued by blue; and opening my eyes I saw that I had come down within sight of housetops, my hands clutching the edges of my carpet like claws. I swooped lower and soon recognized the rooftops of my neighborhood. There was Joey's yard, there was my garden, there was my chicken coop, my swing; and landing in the yard I felt the weight of the earth streaming up through me like a burst of joy.

At dinner I could scarcely keep my eyes open; by bedtime I had a temperature. There were no fits of coughing, no itchy eyes, or raw red lines under runny nostrils — only a steady burning, a heavy weariness, lasting three days. In my bed, under the covers, behind closed blinds, I lay reading a book that kept falling on my chest. On the fourth day I woke feeling alert and cool skinned. My mother, who for three days had been lowering her hand gently to my forehead and staring at me with grave, searching eyes, now walked briskly about the room, opening blinds with a sharp thin sound, drawing them up with a clatter. In the morning I was allowed to play quietly in the yard. In the afternoon I stood behind my mother on an escalator leading up to boys' pants. School was less than two weeks away; I had outgrown everything; Grandma was coming up for a visit; Joey's uncle had brought real horseshoes with him; there was no time, no time for anything at all; and as I walked to school along hot sidewalks shaded by maples, along the sandy roadside past Ciccarelli's lot, up Franklin Street and along Collins Street, I saw, in the warm and summery September air, like a gigantic birthmark, a brilliant patch of red leaves among the green.

One rainy day when I was in my room looking for a slipper, I found my rolled-up carpet under the bed. Fluffs of dust stuck to it like bees. Irritably I lugged it down into the cellar and laid it on top of an old trunk under the stairs. On a snowy afternoon in January I chased a Ping-Pong ball into the light-striped darkness under the cellar stairs. Long spiderwebs like delicate rigging had grown in the dark space, stretching from the rims of barrels to the undersides of the steps. My old carpet lay on the crumbly floor between the trunk and a wooden barrel. "I've got it!" I cried, seizing the white ball with its sticky little clump of spiderweb, rubbing it clean with my thumb, bending low as I ducked back into the yellow light of the cellar. The sheen on the dark green table made it look silky. Through a high window I could see the snow slanting down, falling steadily, piling up against the glass.

Lorrie Moore

Lorrie Moore (b. 1957) was born in Glens Falls, New York, daughter of an insurance executive and a housewife. After completing her studies at St. Lawrence University and Cornell University, where she earned an M.F.A. in 1982, Moore began teaching at the University of Wisconsin. As an undergraduate she won a *Seventeen* magazine short story contest in 1976, and she has been publishing her fiction in magazines such as *Cosmopolitan*, *Ms.*, and *The New Yorker* ever since.

Self-Help, Moore's first collection of short stories, appeared in 1985. As the title of the book suggests, several of the humorous stories were narrated in what Moore calls "second person, mock-imperative" voices as she parodied the self-improvement manuals popular with American readers. In the book Moore included sketches to cover various situations—"The Kid's Guide to Divorce," "How to Talk to Your Mother," "How to Be an Other Woman," and "How to Become a Writer."

Reviewers noted that typically the fictional characters narrating Moore's stories were intelligent people whose self-knowledge only contributed to their sense of distress, so they reacted by attempting to distance themselves from their dilemmas through humor. A character in Moore's second collection, *Like Life* (1990), is told, "Everything's a joke with you." She replies, "Nothing's a joke with me. It just all comes out like one." Acknowledging that her recent story "Referential" is a tribute to Vladimir Nabokov's story "Signs and Symbols," Moore told interviewer Deborah Treisman that the two stories share several common elements, such as the phone ringing at the end. Moore felt that having the two adults not married in her story "was a more contemporary situation with its own dilemmas and twists." Moore's books include *Anagrams* (1987), *Who Will Run the Frog Hospital?* (1994), and *Birds of America* (1998). Her most recent novel is *A Gate at the Stairs* (2009).

RELATED STORY
Vladimir Nabokov, "Signs and Symbols," page 956.

Referential

2012

FOR THE THIRD TIME in three years, they talked about what would be a suitable birthday present for her deranged son. There was so little they were actually allowed to bring; almost everything could be transformed into a weapon, and so most items had to be left at the front desk and then, if requested, brought in later by a big blond aide, who would look the objects over beforehand for their wounding possibilities. Pete had brought a basket of jams, but they were in glass jars and so not permitted. "I forgot about that," he said. The jars were arranged by color, from the brightest marmalade to cloudberry to fig, as if they contained the urine tests of an increasingly ill person. Just as well they'll be confiscated, she thought. They would find something else to bring.

By the time her son was twelve, and had begun his dazed and quiet muttering, had given up brushing his teeth, Pete had been in their lives for six years, and now four more years had passed. The love they had for Pete was long and winding, with hidden turns but no real halts. Her son thought of him as a kind of stepfather. She and Pete had got old together, though it showed more on her, with her black shirtdresses worn for slimming and her now graying hair undyed and often pinned up with strands hanging down like Spanish moss. Once her son had been stripped and gowned and placed in the facility, she, too, had removed her necklaces, earrings, scarves — all her prosthetic devices, she said to Pete, trying to amuse — and put them in a latched accordion file under her bed. She was not allowed to wear them when visiting, so she would no longer wear them at all, a kind of solidarity with her child, a new widowhood on top of the widowhood she already possessed. Unlike other women her age (who tended to try too hard, with lurid lingerie and flashing jewelry), she now felt that that sort of effort was ludicrous, and she went out into the world like an Amish woman, or perhaps, even worse, when the unforgiving light of spring hit her face, an Amish man. If she was going to be old, let her be a full-fledged citizen of the old country! "To me, you always look so beautiful," Pete no longer said.

Pete had lost his job in the recent economic downturn. At one point, he had been poised to live with her, but her child's deepening troubles had caused him to pull back. He said that he loved her but could not find the space he needed for himself in her life or in her house. (He did not blame her son — or did he?) He eyed with somewhat visible covetousness and sour remarks the front room, which her son, when home, lived in with large blankets and empty ice-cream pints, an Xbox, and DVDs.

She no longer knew where Pete went, sometimes for weeks at a time. She thought it an act of vigilance and attachment that she did not ask, tried not to care. She once grew so hungry for touch that she went to the Stressed Tress salon around the corner just to have her hair washed. The few times she had flown to Buffalo to see her brother and his family, at airport security she had chosen the pat-downs and the wandings rather than the scanning machine.

"Where is Pete?" her son cried out during visits she made alone, his face scarlet with acne, swollen and wide with the effects of medications that had been changed, then changed again, and she said that Pete was busy today, but soon, soon, maybe next week, he would come. A maternal vertigo beset her, the room circled, and the thin scars on her son's arms sometimes seemed to spell out Pete's name, the loss of fathers etched primitively in an algebra of skin. In the carrousel spin of the room, those white webbed lines resembled coarse, campground graffiti, as when young people used to stiffly carve the words "PEACE" and "FUCK" into picnic tables and trees, the "C" three-quarters of a square. Mutilation was a language. And vice versa. The cutting endeared her boy to the girls, many of whom were cutters themselves and seldom saw a boy who was one, and so in the group sessions he became popular, which he neither minded nor perhaps really noticed. When no one was looking, he sometimes cut the bottoms of his feet — with crisp paper from crafts hour. In group, he pretended to read the girls' soles like palms, announcing the arrival of strangers and the progress toward romance — "toe-mances," he called them — and sometimes seeing his own fate in what they had cut there.

Now she and Pete went to see her son without the jams but with a soft deckle-edged book about Daniel Boone, pulled from her own bookcase, which was allowed, even though her son would believe that it contained messages for him, believe that, although it was a story about a long-ago person, it was also the story of his own sorrow and heroism in the face of every manner of wilderness, defeat, and abduction, that his own life could be draped over the book, which was simply a noble armature for the revelation of tales of *him*. There would be clues in the words on pages with numbers that added up to his age: 97, 88, 466. There would be other veiled references to his existence. There always were.

They sat at the visitors' table together, and her son set the book aside and did try to smile at both of them. There was still sweetness in his eyes, the sweetness he'd been born with, even if fury could dart in a scattershot fashion across them. Someone had cut his tawny hair — or, at least, had tried. Perhaps the staff person hadn't wanted the scissors to stay near him for a prolonged period and had snipped quickly, then leaped away, approached again, grabbed and snipped, then jumped back. That's what it looked like. Her son had wavy hair that had to be cut carefully. Now it no longer cascaded down but was close to his head, springing out at angles that would likely matter to no one but a mother.

"So where have you been?" her son asked Pete.

"Good question," Pete said, as if praising the thing would make it go away. How could people be mentally well in such a world?

"Do you miss us?" the boy asked.

Pete did not answer.

"Do you think of me when you look at the black capillaries of the trees at night?"

"I suppose I do." Pete stared back at him, so as not to shift in his seat. "I am always hoping that you are O.K. and that they treat you well here."

"Do you think of my mom when you stare up at the clouds and all they hold?"

Pete fell silent again.

"That's enough," she said to her son, who turned to her with a change of expression.

"There's supposed to be cake this afternoon for someone's birthday," he said.

"That will be nice!" she said, smiling back.

"No candles, of course. Or forks. We'll just have to grab the frosting and mash it into our eyes for blinding. Do you ever think about how, at that moment of the candles, time stands still, even as the moments carry away the smoke? It's like the fire of burning love. Do you ever wonder why so many people have things they don't deserve but how absurd all those things are to begin with? Do you really think a wish can come true if you never ever ever ever ever ever tell it to anyone?"

On the ride home, she and Pete did not exchange a word, and every time she looked at his aging hands, arthritically clasping the steering wheel, the familiar thumbs slung low in their slightly simian way, she understood anew the desperate place they both were in, though their desperations were separate, not shared, and her eyes then felt the stabbing pressure of tears.

The last time her son had tried to do it, his method had been, in the doctor's words, morbidly ingenious. He might have succeeded, but a fellow-patient, a girl from group, had stopped him at the last minute. There had been blood to be mopped. For a time, her son had wanted only a distracting pain, but eventually he had wanted to tear a hole in himself and flee through it. Life, for him, was full of spies and preoccupying espionage. Yet sometimes the spies would flee as well, and someone might have to go after them, over the rolling fields of dream, into the early-morning mountains of dawning signification, in order, paradoxically, to escape them altogether.

There was a storm looming, and lightning did its quick, purposeful zigzag among the clouds. She did not need such stark illustration that horizons could be shattered, filled with messages and broken codes, yet there it was. A spring snow began to fall with the lightning still cracking, and Pete put the windshield wipers on so that they could peer through the cleared semicircles at the darkening road before them. She knew that the world had not been created to speak just to her, and yet, as for her son, sometimes things did. The fruit trees had bloomed early, for instance—the orchards they passed were pink—but the premature warmth precluded bees, and there would be little fruit. Most of the dangling blossoms would fall in this very storm.

When they arrived at her house and went in, Pete glanced at himself in the hallway mirror. Perhaps he needed assurance that he was still alive and not the ghost he seemed.

"Would you like a drink?" she asked, hoping he would stay. "I have some good vodka. I could make you a nice white Russian!"

"Just vodka," he said reluctantly. "Straight."

She opened the freezer to find the vodka, and when she closed it again she stood there for a moment, looking at the photo magnets she'd stuck to the refrigerator door. As a baby, her son had seemed happier than most babies. As a six-year-old, he was still smiling and hamming it up, his arms and legs shooting out like starbursts, his perfectly gapped teeth flashing, his hair in honeyed coils. At ten, he had a vaguely brooding and fearful expression, though there was light in his eyes, and his lovely cousins beside him. There he was, a plumpish teen-ager, his arm around Pete. And there, in the corner, he was an infant again, held by his dignified, handsome father, whom he did not recall, because he had died so long ago. All this had to be accepted. Living did not mean one joy piled upon another. It was merely the hope for less pain, hope played like a playing card upon another hope, a wish for kindnesses and mercies to emerge like kings and queens in an unexpected twist in the game. One could hold the cards oneself or not: they would land the same way, regardless. Tenderness did not enter into it, except in a damaged way.

"You don't want ice?"

"No," Pete said. "No, thank you."

She placed two glasses of vodka on the kitchen table. She sank into the chair across from him.

"Perhaps this will help you sleep," she said.

"Don't know if anything can do that," he said, taking a swig. Insomnia plagued him.

"I am going to bring him home this week," she said. "He needs his home back, his house, his room. He is no danger to anyone."

Pete drank some more, sipping noisily. She could see that he wanted no part of this, but she felt that she had no choice but to proceed. "Perhaps you could help. He looks up to you."

"Help how?" Pete asked with a flash of anger. There was the clink of his glass on the table.

"We could each spend part of the night near him," she said carefully.

The telephone rang. The Radio Shack wall phone brought almost nothing but bad news, and so the sound of it ringing, especially in the evening, always startled her. She repressed a shudder but still her shoulders hunched, as if she were anticipating a blow. She stood.

"Hello?" she said, answering it on the third ring, her heart pounding. But the person on the other end hung up. She sat back down. "I guess it was a wrong number," she said, adding, "Perhaps you would like more vodka."

"Only a little. Then I should go."

She poured him some more. She'd said what she needed to say and did not want to have to persuade him. She would wait for him to step forward with the right words. Unlike some of her meaner friends, who kept warning her, she believed that there was a deep good side of Pete and she was always patient for it. What else could she be?

The phone rang again.

"Probably telemarketers," he said.

"I hate them," she said. "Hello?" she said more loudly into the receiver.

This time when the caller hung up she glanced at the lit panel on the phone, which was supposed to reveal the number of the person who was calling.

She sat back down and pooled herself more vodka. "Someone is phoning here from your apartment," she said.

He threw back the rest of his drink. "I should go," he said, and got up. She followed him. At the door, she watched him grasp the knob and twist it firmly. He opened it wide, blocking the mirror.

"Good night," he said. His expression had already forwarded itself to some-place far away.

She threw her arms around him to kiss him, but he turned his head abruptly so that her mouth landed on his ear. She remembered that he had made this evasive move ten years ago, when they had first met, and he was in a condition of romantic overlap.

"Thank you for coming with me," she said.

"You're welcome," he replied, then hurried down the steps to his car, which was parked at the curb out front. She did not attempt to walk him to it. She closed the front door and locked it as the telephone began to ring again.

She went into the kitchen. She had not actually been able to read the caller I.D. without her glasses, and had invented the part about its being Pete's number, but he had made it the truth anyway, which was the black magic of lies and good guesses, nimble bluffs. Now she braced herself. She planted her feet.

"Hello?" she said, answering on the fifth ring. The plastic panel where the number should appear was clouded as if by a scrim, a page of onionskin over the onion — or, rather, a picture of an onion. One depiction on top of another.

"Good evening," she said loudly. What would burst forth? A monkey's paw. A lady. A tiger.

But there was nothing at all.

Alice Munro

Alice Munro (b. 1931) grew up on a farm in a rural community near Lake Huron in Ontario, Canada, where her father raised silver foxes. After attending the University of Western Ontario for two years, she married and moved to British Columbia. Munro remembers that she began writing things down when she was about twelve, and at age fifteen she decided she would soon write a great novel: "But I thought perhaps I wasn't ready so I would write a short story in the meantime." She began publishing her stories when she was a university student, but her writing progressed very slowly during the next several years after she remarried and raised a family. "I never intended to be a short story writer," she has explained. "I started writing them because I didn't have time to write anything else—I had three children. And then I got used to writing stories, so I saw my material that way, and now I don't think I'll ever write a novel."

In 1968 Munro published her first collection of stories, *Dance of the Happy Shades*, which won the Governor General's Award in Canada. Three years later she published her second book, *Lives of Girls and Women*. Another collection of stories, *Something I've Been Meaning to Tell You*, appeared in 1974, and a series of connected stories titled *Who Do You Think You Are?* was published in 1978, giving Munro her second Governor General's Award. She won her third with *The Progress of Love* in 1987. *The Love of a Good Woman* (1998), *Hateship, Friendship, Courtship, Loveship, Marriage* (2001), *Runaway* (2004), and *The View from Castle Rock* (2006) are recent collections. "Age of Faith" was a chapter in *Lives of Girls and Women*.

Literary critics have observed that Munro's stories about small town Canadian life are reminiscent of the fiction of the American writer Eudora Welty. Most of Munro's stories are set in southern Ontario, where she grew up. She sees herself as an anachronism, "because I write about places where your roots are and most people don't live that kind of life any more at all. Most writers, probably, the writers who are most in tune with our time, write about places that have no texture because this is where most of us live." Her story collection *Dear Life* was published in 2012. The following year Munro was awarded the Nobel Prize in Literature.

RELATED STORY
Philip Roth, "The Conversion of the Jews" page 1167.

RELATED COMMENTARY
Alice Munro, "How I Write Short Stories," page 1481.

Age of Faith

1971

WHEN WE LIVED IN that house at the end of the Flats Road, and before my mother knew how to drive a car, she and I used to walk to town; town being Jubilee, a mile away. While she locked the door I had to run to the gate and look up and down the road and make sure there was nobody coming. Who could there ever be, on that road, besides the mailman and Uncle Benny? When I shook my head no she would hide the key under the second post of the veranda, where the wood had rotted and made a little hole. She believed in burglars.

Turning our backs on the Grenoch Swamp, the Wawanash River, and some faraway hills, both bare and wooded, which though not ignorant of the facts of geography I did sometimes believe to be the end of the world, we followed the Flats Road which was not much more, at this end, than two wheel tracks, with a vigorous growth of plantain and chickweed down the middle. My mind would be on burglars. I saw them black and white, with melancholy dedicated faces, professional clothes. I imagined them waiting somewhere not too far away, say in those ferny boggy fields along the edge of the swamp, waiting and holding in their minds the most exact knowledge of our house and everything in it. They knew about the cups with butterfly handles, painted gold; my coral necklace which I thought ugly and scratchy but had been taught to consider valuable, since it had been sent from Australia by my father's Aunt Helen on her trip around the world; a silver bracelet bought by my father for my mother before they were married; a black bowl with Japanese figures painted on it, very peaceful to look at, a wedding present; and my mother's greenish white Laocoön inkwell awarded for highest marks and general proficiency when she graduated from high school—the serpent so cunningly draped around the three male figures that I could never discover whether there were or were not marble genitals underneath. Burglars coveted these things, I understood, but would not move unless we gave them cause, by our carelessness. Their knowledge, their covetousness, made each thing seem confirmed in its value and uniqueness. Our world was steadfastly reflected in burglar minds.

Later on of course I began to doubt the existence of burglars or at least to doubt that they could operate in this manner. Much more likely, I saw, that their methods were haphazard and their knowledge hazy, their covetousness unfocused, their relationship to us next thing to accidental. I could go more easily up the river to the swamp when my belief in them had faded, but I missed them, I missed the thought of them, for quite a while.

I had never had a picture of God so clear and uncomplicated as my picture of the burglars. My mother was not so ready to refer to him. We belonged—at least my father and my father's family belonged—to the United Church in Jubilee, and my brother Owen and I had both been baptized there when we were babies, which showed a surprising weakness or generosity on my mother's part; perhaps childbirth mellowed and confused her.

The United Church was the most modern, the largest, the most prosperous church in Jubilee. It had taken in all the former Methodists and Congregationalists and a good chunk of Presbyterians (that was what my father's family had been) at the time of Church Union. There were four other churches in town but they were all small, all relatively poor, and all, by United Church standards, went to extremes. The Catholic church was the most extreme. White and wooden, with a plain mission cross, it stood on a hill at the north end of town and dispensed peculiar services to Catholics, who seemed bizarre and secretive as Hindus, with their idols and confessions and black spots on Ash Wednesday. At school the Catholics were a small but unintimidated tribe, mostly Irish, who did not stay in the classroom for Religious Education but were allowed to go down to the basement, where they banged on the pipes. It was hard to connect their simple rowdiness with their exotic dangerous faith. My father's aunts, my great-aunts, lived across from the Catholic church and used to make jokes about "nipping in for a bit of a confession" but they knew, they could tell you, all there was beyond jokes, babies' skeletons, and strangled nuns under the convent floors, yes, fat priests and fancy women and the black old popes. It was all true, they had books about it. All true. Like the Irish at school, the church building seemed inadequate; too bare and plain and straightforward-looking to be connected with such voluptuousness and scandal.

The Baptists were extreme as well, but in a completely unsinister, slightly comic way. No person of any importance or social standing went to the Baptist Church, and so somebody like Pork Childs, who delivered coal and collected garbage for the town, could get to be a leading figure, an elder, in it. Baptists could not dance or go to movies; Baptist ladies could not wear lipstick. But their hymns were loud, rollicking, and optimistic, and in spite of the austerity of their lives their religion had more vulgar cheerfulness about it than anybody else's. Their church was not far from the house we later rented on River Street; it was modest, but modern and hideous, being built of gray cement blocks, with pebbled glass windows.

As for the Presbyterians, they were leftovers, people who had refused to become United. They were mostly elderly, and campaigned against hockey practice on Sundays, and sang psalms.

The fourth church was the Anglican, and nobody knew or spoke much about it. It did not have, in Jubilee, any of the prestige or money which attached to it in towns where there was a remnant of the old Family Compact, or some sort of military or social establishment to keep it going. The people who settled Wawanash County and built up Jubilee were Scotch Presbyterians, Congregationalists, Methodists from the north of England. To be Anglican was therefore not fashionable as it was in some places, and it was not so interesting as being Catholic or Baptist, not even proof of stubborn conviction like being Presbyterian. However the church had a bell, the only church bell in town, and that seemed to me a lovely thing for a church to have.

In the United Church the pews, of glossy golden oak, were placed in a democratic fan-shaped sort of arrangement, with the pulpit and choir at the heart of the fan. There was no altar, only a powerful display of organ pipes. The stained-glass windows showed Christ performing useful miracles (though not the water into wine) or else they illustrated parables. On Communion Sunday the wine went round on trays, in little, thick, glass cups; it was like everybody having refreshments. And it was not even wine, but grape juice. This was the church the Legion attended, uniformed, on a certain Sunday; also the Lions Club, carrying their purple-tassled hats. Doctors, lawyers, merchants passed the plate.

My parents went to church seldom. My father in his unaccustomed suit seemed deferential but self-contained. During the prayer he would put his elbow on his knee, rest his forehead on his hand, close his eyes, with an air of courtesy and forebearance. My mother, on the other hand, never closed her eyes a minute and barely inclined her head. She would sit looking all around, cautious but unabashed, like an anthropologist taking note of the behavior of a primitive tribe. She listened to the sermon bolt upright, bright-eyed, skeptically chewing at her lipstick; I was afraid that at any moment she might jump up and challenge something. The hymns she ostentatiously did not sing.

After we rented the house in town we had a boarder, Fern Dogherty, who sang in the United Church choir. I would go to church with her and sit by myself, the only member of our family present. My father's aunts lived at the other end of town and did not take this long walk often; the service was broadcast, anyway, over the Jubilee radio station.

Why did I do this? At first, it was probably to bother my mother, though she made no outright objection to it, and to make myself interesting. I could imagine people looking at me, saying afterwards, "Do you see that little Jordan girl there, all by herself, Sunday after Sunday?" I hoped that people would be intrigued and touched by my devoutness and persistence, knowing my mother's beliefs or nonbeliefs, as they did. Sometimes I thought of the population of Jubilee as nothing but a large audience, for me; and so in a way it was; for every person who lived there, the rest of the town was an audience.

But the second winter we lived in town — the winter I was twelve years old — my reasons had changed, or solidified. I wanted to settle the question of God. I had been reading books about the Middle Ages; I was attracted more and more to the idea of faith. God had always been a possibility for me; now I was prey to a positive longing for Him. He was a necessity. But I wanted reassurance, proof that He actually was there. That was what I came to church for, but could not mention to anybody.

On wet windy Sundays, snowy Sundays, sore-throat Sundays, I came and sat in the United Church full of this unspeakable hope; that God would display Himself, to me at least, like a dome of light, a bubble radiant and indisputable above the modern pews; that He would flower suddenly as a bank of day lilies below the organ pipes. I felt I must rigidly contain this hope; to reveal it, in fervor of tone or word or gesture, would have been inappropriate as farting. What was chiefly noticeable in people's faces during the earlier, more God-directed parts of the service (the sermon tended to take off into topical areas) was a kind of cohesive tact, the very thing my mother offended against, with that cross inquiring look, as if she was going to pull up shortly and demand that everything make sense.

The question of whether God existed or not never came up in Church. It was only a matter of what He approved of, or usually of what He did not approve of. After the benediction there would be a stir, a comfortable release in the church as if everybody had yawned, though of course no one had, and people rose and greeted each other in a pleased, relieved, congratulatory way. I felt at such times itchy, hot, heavy, despondent.

I did not think of taking my problem to any believer, even to Mr. McLaughlin the minister. It would have been unthinkably embarrassing. Also, I was afraid. I was afraid the believer might falter in defending his beliefs, or defining them, and this would be a setback for me. If Mr. McLaughlin, for instance, turned out to have no firmer a grasp on God than I did, it would be a huge though not absolute discouragement. I preferred to believe his grasp was good, and not try it out.

However I did think of taking it to another church, to the Anglican church. It was because of the bell, and because I was curious to see what another church was like inside and how they went about things, and the Anglican was the only one it was possible to try. I did not tell anybody what I was doing, naturally, but walked with Fern Dogherty to the steps of the United Church, where we parted, she to go round to the vestry to get into her choir gown. When she was out of sight I turned and doubled back across town, and came to the Anglican church, in answer to the invitation of that bell. I hoped nobody saw me. I went in.

There was a storm porch set up outside the main door, to keep the wind out. Then a little cold entry with a strip of brown matting, hymn books piled on the window-ledge. I entered the church itself.

They had no furnace, evidently, just a space heater by the door, making its steady domestic noise. A strip of the same brown matting went across the back and up the aisle; otherwise there was just the wooden floor, not varnished or painted, rather wide boards occasionally springy underfoot. Seven or eight pews on either side, no more. A couple of choir benches at right angles to the pews, a pump organ at one side and the pulpit — I didn't know at first that was what it was — stuck up like a hen roost at the other side. Beyond that a railing, a step up, a tiny chancel. The floor of the chancel had an old parlor carpet. Then there was a table, with a pair of silver candlesticks, a baize-lined collection plate, and a cross which looked as if it might be cardboard covered with silver paper, like a stage crown. Above the table was a reproduction of the Holman Hunt painting of Christ knocking at the door. I had not seen this picture before. The Christ in it differed in some small but important way from the Christ performing miracles in the United Church window. He looked more regal and more tragic, and the background against which he appeared was gloomier and richer, more pagan somehow, or at least Mediterranean. I was used to seeing him limp and shepherdly in Sunday-school pastels.

Altogether there were about a dozen people in the church. There was Dutch Monk, the butcher, and his wife and his daughter Gloria, who was in Grade Five at school. She and I were the only people under the age of forty. There were some old women.

I was barely in time. The bell had stopped ringing and the organ began to play a hymn, and the minister entered from the side door which must have led to the vestry, at the head of the choir, which was three ladies and two men. He was a round-headed, cheerful-looking young man I had never seen before. I knew that the Anglican Church could not afford a minister all its own and shared one with Porterfield and Blue River; he must have lived in one of those places. He had snowboots on under his robes.

He had an English accent, *Dearly beloved brethren, the scripture moveth us in sundry places to acknowledge and confess our manifold sins and wickedness. . . .*

There was a board in front of each bench, to kneel on. Everybody slid forward, rustling open prayer books, and when the minister finished his part, everybody else began saying something back. I looked through the prayer book I had found on the shelf in front of me but I could not find the place, so I gave up and listened to what they were saying. Across the aisle from us, and one pew ahead, was a tall, bony old lady in a black-velvet turban. She had not opened her prayer book, she did not need it. Kneeling erectly, lifting her chalky wolfish profile skyward — it reminded me of the profile of a Crusader's effigy, in the encyclopedia at home — she led all the other voices in the congregation, indeed dominated them so that they were no more than a fuzzy edge of hers, which was loud, damp, melodic, mournfully exultant.

> . . . left undone those things which we ought to have done, And we have done those things which we ought not to have done; And there is no health in us. But thou, O Lord, have mercy upon us, miserable offenders. Spare thou them, O God, which confess their faults. Restore thou them that are penitent; According to thy promises declared unto mankind in Christ Jesu our Lord. . . .

And further along this line, and the minister took it up in his fine, harmonizing, though perhaps more restrained, English voice, and this dialogue continued, steadily paced, rising and falling, always with confidence, with lively emotion safely contained in the most elegant channels of language, and coming together, finally, in perfect quiet and reconciliation.

> *Lord, have mercy upon us.*
> Christ, have mercy upon us.
> *Lord, have mercy upon us.*

So here was what I had not known, but must always have suspected, existed, what all those Methodists and Congregationalists and Presbyterians had fearfully abolished — the theatrical in religion. From the very first I was strongly delighted. Many things pleased me — the kneeling down on the hard board, getting up and kneeling down again and bobbing the head at the altar at the mention of Jesus' name, the recitation of the Creed which I loved for its litany of strange splendid things in which to believe. I liked the idea of calling Jesus *Jesu* sometimes; it made Him sound more kingly and magical, like a wizard or an Indian god; I liked the IHS on the pulpit banner, rich, ancient, threadbare design. The poverty, smallness, shabbiness, and bareness of the church pleased me, that smell of mold or mice, frail singing of the choir, isolation of the worshippers. *If they are here*, I felt, *then it is probably all true.* Ritual which in other circumstances might have seemed wholly artificial, lifeless, had here a kind of last-ditch dignity. The richness of the words against the poverty of the place. If I could not quite get a scent of God then at least I could get the scent of His old times of power, real power, not what He enjoyed in the United Church today; I could remember His dim fabled hierarchy, His lovely moldered calendar of feasts and saints. There they were in the prayer book, I opened on them by accident — saints' days. Did anybody keep them? Saints' days made me think of something so different from Jubilee — open mows and half-timbered farmhouses and the Angelus and candles, a procession of nuns in the snow, cloister walks, all quiet, a world of tapestry, secure in faith. Safety. If God could be discovered, or recalled, everything would be safe. Then you would see things that I saw — just the dull grain of wood in the floor boards, the windows of plain glass filled with thin branches and snowy sky — and the strange, anxious pain that just seeing things could create would be gone. It seemed plain to me that this was the only way the world could be borne, *the only way it could be borne* — if all those atoms, galaxies of atoms, were safe all the time, whirling away in God's mind. How could people rest, how could they even go on breathing and existing, until they were sure of this? They did go on, so they must be sure.

How about my mother? Being my mother, she did not quite count. But even she, when cornered, would say yes, oh yes, there must be something — some *design.* But it was no use wasting time thinking about it, she warned, because we could never understand it anyway; there was quite enough to think about if we started trying to improve life in the here and now for a change; when we were dead we would find out about the rest of it, if there was any rest of it.

Not even she was prepared to say *Nothing*, and see herself and every stick and stone and feather in the world floating loose on that howling hopeless dark. No.

The idea of God did not connect for me with any idea of being good, which is perhaps odd, considering all about sins and wickedness that I did listen to. I believed in being saved by faith alone, by some great grab of the soul. But did I really, *did I really want it to happen to me*? Yes and no. I wanted it to happen, but I saw it would have to be a secret. How could I go on living with my mother and father and Fern Dogherty and my friend Naomi and everybody else in Jubilee otherwise?

The minister spoke to me at the door in a breezy way.

"Nice to see the good-looking young ladies out this nippy morning."

I shook his hand with difficulty. I had a stolen prayer book under my coat, held in place by my crooked arm.

"Couldn't see where you were in church," Fern said. The Anglican service was shorter than ours, economizing on sermon, so I had had time to get back to the United Church steps to meet her when she came out.

"I was behind a post."

My mother wanted to know what the sermon had been about.

"Peace," said Fern. "And the United Nations. Et cetera, et cetera."

"Peace," said my mother enjoyably. "Well, is he for it or against it?"

"He's all in favor of the United Nations."

"I guess God is too then. What a relief. Only a short time ago He and Mr. McLaughlin were all for the war. They are a changeable pair."

Next week when I was with my mother in the Walker store the tall old lady in the black turban walked by, and spoke to her, and I was afraid she would say she had seen me in the Anglican Church, but she did not.

My mother said to Fern Dogherty, "I saw old Mrs. Sherriff in the Walker store today. She still has the same hat. It makes me think of an English bobby's."

"She comes in the post office all the time and creates a scene if her paper isn't there by three o'clock," Fern said. "She's a tartar."

Then from a conversation between Fern and my mother during which my mother tried unsuccessfully to send me out of the room — she would do this as a kind of formality, I think, for once she had told me to go she did not bother much about whether I went — I learned that Mrs. Sherriff had had bizarre troubles in her family which either resulted from, or had resulted in, a certain amount of eccentricity and craziness in herself. Her oldest son had died of drink, her second son was in and out of the asylum (this was what the mental hospital was always called, in Jubilee), and her daughter had committed suicide, drowning herself in fact, in the Wawanash River. Her husband? He owned a dry-goods store and was a pillar of the community, said my mother dryly. Maybe he had syphilis, suggested Fern, and passed it on, it attacks the brains in the second generation, they were all hypocrites, those old boys with the stiff collars. My mother said that Mrs. Sherriff for many years wore her dead daughter's clothes, around the house and to do the gardening in, until she got them worn out.

Another story: once the Red Front Grocery had forgotten to put a pound of butter in her order, and she had come after the grocery boy with a hatchet.

Christ, have mercy upon us.

Also that week I did a vulgar thing. I asked God to prove himself by answering a prayer. The prayer had to do with something called "Household Science," which we had at school once a week, on Thursday afternoons. In Household Science we learned to knit and crochet and embroider and run a sewing machine, and everything we did was more impossible than the last thing; my hands would be slimy with sweat and the Household Science room itself with its three ancient sewing machines and its cutting tables and battered dummies looked to me like an arena of torture. And so it was. Mrs. Forbes the teacher was a fat little woman with the painted face of a celluloid doll and with most girls she was jolly. But my stupidity, my stubby blundering hands crumpling up the grimy handkerchief I was supposed to be hemming, or the miserable crocheting, put her into a dancing rage.

"Look at the filthy work, filthy work! I've heard about you, you think you're so clever with your memory work (I was famous for memorizing poems fast) and here you take stitches any six-year-old would be ashamed of!"

Now she had me trying to learn to thread the sewing machine. And I could not learn. We were making aprons, with appliquéd tulips. Some girls were already finishing the tulips or doing the hem and I had not even sewn the waistband on yet, because I could not get the sewing machine threaded, and

Mrs. Forbes said she was not going to show me again. It did not do any good when she showed me anyhow; her quick hands in front of me astonished and blinded and paralyzed me, with their close flashes of contempt.

So I prayed: please let me not have to thread the sewing machine on Thursday afternoon. I said this over several times in my head, quickly, seriously, unemotionally, as if trying out a spell. I did not use any special pleading or bargaining. I did not ask for anything extraordinary, like a fire in the Household Science room or Mrs. Forbes slipping on the street and breaking a leg; nothing but a little unspecific intervention.

Nothing happened. She had not forgotten about me. At the beginning of the class I was sent to the machine. I sat there trying to figure out where to put the thread—I did not have any hope of putting it in the right place but had to put it some place, to show her I was trying—and she came and stood behind me, breathing disgustedly; as usual my legs began to shake, and shook so badly I moved the pedal and the machine began to run, weakly, with no thread in it.

"All right, Del," said Mrs. Forbes. I was surprised at her voice, which was not kind, certainly, but not angry, only worn out.

"I said all right. You can get up."

She picked up the pieces of the apron that I had desperately basted together, crumpled them up, and threw them in the wastebasket.

"You cannot learn to sew," she said, "any more than a person who is tone deaf can learn to sing. I have tried and I am beaten. Come with me."

She handed me a broom. "If you know how to sweep I want you to sweep this room and throw the scraps in the wastebasket, and be responsible for keeping the floor clean, and when you are not doing that you can sit at the table back here and—memorize poetry, for all I care."

I was weak with relief and joy, in spite of public shame, which I was used to. I swept the floor conscientiously and then got my library book about Mary Queen of Scots and read, disgraced, but unburdened, alone at the back of the room. I thought at first that what had happened was plainly miraculous, an answer to my prayer. But presently I began to wonder; suppose I hadn't prayed, suppose it was going to happen anyway? I had no way of knowing; there was no control for my experiment. Minute by minute I turned more niggardly, ungrateful. How could I be sure? And surely too it was rather petty, rather obvious of God to concern Himself so quickly with such a trivial request? It was almost as if He were showing off. I wanted Him to move in a more mysterious way.

I wanted to tell somebody but I could not tell Naomi. I had asked her if she believed in God and she had said promptly and scornfully, "Well of course I do, I'm not like your old lady. Do you think I want to go to Hell?" I never discussed it with her again.

I picked on my brother Owen to tell. He was three years younger than I was. At one time he had been impressionable and trusting. Once out on the farm we had a shelter of old boards that we played house in, and he sat on the end of a board and I served him mountain-ash berries, telling him they were his cornflakes. He ate them all. While he was still eating it occurred to me they might be poisonous, but I did not tell him, for reasons of my own prestige and the importance of the game, and afterwards I prudently decided not to tell anyone else. Now he had learned to skate, and went to hockey practice, and leaned over the bannisters and spat on my head, an ordinary boy.

But there were angles, still, from which he looked frail and young, pursuits of his that seemed to me lost and hopeless. He entered contests. This was my mother's nature showing in him, her boundless readiness to take up the challenges and promises of the outside world. He believed in prizes; telescopes he could see the craters of the moon through, magicians' kits with which he could make things disappear, chemistry sets that would enable him to manufacture explosives. He would have been an alchemist, if he had known about it. However, he was not religious.

He sat on the floor of his room cutting out tiny cardboard figures of hockey players, which he would then arrange in teams and play games with; such godlike games he played with trembling absorption, and then seemed to me to inhabit a world so far from my own (the real one), a world so irrelevant, heartbreakingly flimsy in its deceptions.

I sat on the bed behind him.

"Owen."

He didn't answer; when he was playing his games he never wanted anyone around.

"What do you think happens to someone when they die?"

"*I* don't know," said Owen mutinously.

"Do you believe God keeps your soul alive? Do you know what your soul is? Do you believe in God?"

Owen turned his head and gave me a trapped look. He had nothing to hide, nothing to show but his pure-hearted indifference.

"You better believe in God," I said. "Listen." I told him about my prayer, and Household Science. He listened unhappily. The need I felt was not in him. It made me angry to discover this; he seemed dazed, defenseless but resilient, a hard rubber ball. He would listen, if I insisted, agree with me, if I insisted on that, but in his heart, I thought, he was not paying any attention. Stupidity.

I would often hector him like this from now on, when I could get him alone. *Don't tell Mother*, I said. He was all I had to try my faith out on; I had to have somebody. His deep lack of interest, the satisfaction he seemed to take in a world without God were what I really could not bear, and kept hammering at; also I felt that because he was younger, and had been in my power so long, he had an obligation to follow me; for him not to acknowledge it was a sign of insurrection.

In my room, with the door shut, I read from the Book of Common Prayer.

Sometimes walking along the street I would shut my eyes (the way Owen and I used to do, playing blind) and say to myself— frowning, praying— "God. God. *God*." Then I would imagine for a few precarious seconds a dense bright cloud descending on Jubilee, wrapping itself around my skull. But my eyes flew open in alarm; I was not able to let that in, or me out. Also I was afraid of bumping into something, being seen, making a fool of myself.

Good Friday came. I was going out. My mother came into the hall and said, "What have you got your beret on for?"

It was time to take a stand. "I'm going to church."

"There is no church."

"I'm going to the Anglican Church. They have church on Good Friday."

My mother had to sit down on the steps. She gave me as searching, pale, exasperated a look as she had examined me with a year before when she found a drawing Naomi and I had done in my scribbler, of a fat naked lady with balloon breasts and a huge, inky, sprouting nest of pubic hair.

"Do you know what Good Friday is in memory of?"

"Crucifixion," I said tersely.

"That's the day Christ died for our sins. That's what they tell us. Now. Do you believe that?"

"Yes."

"Christ died for our sins," said my mother, jumping up. In the hall mirror she peered aggressively at her own dim face. "Well, well, *well*. Redeemed by the blood. That is a lovely notion. You might as well take the Aztecs cutting out live hearts because they thought the sun wouldn't rise and set if they didn't. Christianity is no better. What do you think of a God that asks for blood? Blood, blood, blood. Listen to their hymns, that's all they're ever about. What about a God who isn't satisfied until he has got somebody hanging on a cross for six hours, nine hours, whatever it was? If I was God I wouldn't be so bloodthirsty. Ordinary people wouldn't be so bloodthirsty. I don't count Hitler. At one time maybe they would be but not now. Do you know what I'm saying, do you know what I'm leading up to?"

"No," I said honestly.

"God was made by man! Not the other way around! God was made by *man*. Man at a lower and bloodthirstier stage of his development than he is at now, we hope. Man made God in his own image. I've argued that with ministers. I'll argue it with anybody. I've never met anybody who could argue against it and make sense."

"Can I go?"

"I'm not stopping you," said my mother, though she had actually moved in front of the door. "Go and get your fill of it. You'll see I'm right. Maybe you take after my mother." She looked hard in my face for traces of the religious fanatic. "If you do, I suppose it's out of my hands."

I was not discouraged by my mother's arguments, not so much as I would have been if they had come from someone else. Nevertheless, crossing town, I looked for proof of the opposite point of view. I took simple comfort from the fact that the stores were locked, the blinds down in all their windows. That proved something, didn't it? If I knocked on the doors of all the houses along my route and asked a question — *Did Christ die for our sins?* — the answer, no doubt startled and embarrassed, would be yes.

I realized that I did not care a great deal, myself, about Christ dying for our sins. I only wanted God. But if Christ dying for our sins was the avenue to God, I would work on it.

Good Friday was, unsuitably, a mild sunny sort of day, with icicles dripping and crashing, roofs steaming, little streams running down the streets. Sunlight poured through the ordinary glass windows of the church. I was late, because of my mother. The minister was already up in front. I slid into the back pew and the lady in the velvet turban, Mrs. Sherriff, gave me a white angry look; perhaps not angry; just magnificently startled; it was as if I had sat down beside an eagle on its perch.

I was heartened to see her, though. I was glad to see them all — the six or eight or ten people, real people, who had put on their hats and left their houses and walked through the streets crossing rivulets of melted snow and presented themselves here; they would not do that without a reason.

I wanted to find a believer, a true believer, on whom I could rest my doubts. I wanted to watch and take heart from such a person, not talk to them. At first I had thought it might be Mrs. Sherriff, but she would not do; her craziness disqualified her. My believer must be luminously sane.

> O Lord, arise, help us, and deliver us for thy
>   Name's sake.
> O Lord, arise, help us, and deliver us for
>   thine honor.
> Behold the Lamb of God which taketh away
>   the sin of the world.

I set myself to think of Christ's sufferings. I held my hands together in such a way that I could press a single fingernail with all possible force into each palm. I dug and twisted but could not even get blood; I felt abashed, knowing this did not make me a participant in suffering. God, if He had any taste, would despise such foolishness (but had He? Look at the things that saints had done, and got approval for). He would know what I was really thinking, and trying to beat down in my mind. It was: *Were Christ's sufferings really that bad?*

Were they that bad, when you knew, and He knew, and everybody knew, that He would rise up whole and bright and everlasting and sitteth on the right hand of God the Father Almighty from whence He shall come to judge the quick and the dead? Many people — not all, perhaps, or even most people, but quite a few — would submit their flesh to similar pains if they could be sure of getting what He got, afterwards. Many had, in fact; saints and martyrs.

All right, but there was a difference. He was God; it was more of a comedown, more of a submission, for Him. Was He God, or God's earthly son only, at that time? I could not get it straight. Did He understand how the whole thing was being done on purpose, and it would all be all right in the end, or was His God-ness temporarily blacked out, so that He saw only this collapse? *My God, my God, why hast thou forsaken me?*

After the long psalm with the prophecies in it about the raiment, and casting lots, the minister went up into the pulpit and said he would preach a short sermon on the last words of Christ on the cross. The very thing I had been thinking of. But it turned out there were more last words than the ones I knew about. He started off with *I thirst*, which showed, he said, that Christ suffered in body just as much as we would in the same situation, not a bit less, and He was not ashamed to admit it, and ask for help, and give the poor soldiers a chance of obtaining grace, with the sponge soaked in vinegar. *Woman, behold thy son . . . son, behold thy mother*, showed that his last or almost his last thoughts were for others, arranging for them to be a comfort to each other when He was gone (though never really gone). Even in the hour of His agony and passion He did not forget human relationships, how beautiful and important they were. *Today thou shalt be with me in Paradise* showed of course his continuing concern for the sinner, the wrongdoer cast out by society and hanging there on the companion cross. *O Lord who hatest nothing that thou hast made and . . . desirest not the death of a sinner but rather that he may turn from his wickedness and live—*

But why — I could not stop this thinking though I knew it could bring me no happiness — why should God hate anything that He had made? If He was going to hate it, why make it? And if He had made everything the way He wanted it then nothing was to blame for being the way it was, and this more or less threw out, didn't it, the whole idea of sin? So why should Christ have to die for our sins? The sermon was having a bad effect on me; it made me bewildered and argumentative. It even made me feel, though I could not admit it, a distaste for Christ Himself, because of the way His perfections were being continually pointed out. *My God, my God, why hast thou forsaken me?* Briefly, the minister said, oh very briefly, Jesus had lost touch with God. Yes, it had happened, even to Him. He had lost the connection, and then in the darkness He had cried out in despair. But this too was part of the plan, it was necessary. It was so we should know in our own blackest moments that our doubts, our misery had been shared by Christ Himself, and then, knowing this, our doubts would all the more quickly pass.

But why? Why should they all the more quickly pass? Suppose that was the last true cry of Christ, the last true thing ever heard of Him? We had to at least suppose that, didn't we? We had to consider it. Suppose He cried that, and died, and never did rise again, never did discover it was all God's difficult drama? There was suffering. Yes; think of Him suddenly realizing: *it was not true. None of it was true.* Pain of torn hands and feet was nothing to that. To look through the slats of the world, having come all that way, and say what He had said, and then see — nothing. *Talk about that!* I cried inwardly to the minister. Oh, talk about that, drag it into the open, and then — defeat it!

But we do what we can, the minister could not do any more.

I met Mrs. Sheriff on the street a few days later. I was by myself this time.

"I know you. What are you doing all the time at the Anglican Church? I thought you were United."

When most of the snow had melted and the river had gone down, Owen and I went out the Flats Road, separately, on Saturdays, to the farm. The house, where Uncle Benny had been living all winter and my father had been living most of the time, except for those weekends when he came in to stay with us, was so dirty that it no longer had to be a house at all; it was like some sheltered extension of the out-of-doors. The pattern of the kitchen linoleum was lost; dirt itself made a pattern. Uncle Benny said to me, "Now here's the cleaning lady, just the thing we need," but I did not think so. The whole place smelled of fox. There would be no fire in the stove till evening and the door stood open. Outside were crows cawing over the muddy fields, the river high and silver, the pattern of the horizon exactly, magically the same as remembered and forgotten and remembered. The foxes were nervous, yelping, because it was the time of year the females had their pups. Owen and I were not allowed to go near the pens.

Owen was swinging on the rope under the ash tree, where our swing had been last summer.

"Major killed a sheep!"

Major was our dog, now thought of as Owen's dog, though he did not pay any particular attention to Owen; Owen paid it to him. He was a big golden-brown mongrel collie, who had grown too lazy last summer even to chase cars, but napped in the shade; awake or asleep, he had a slow senatorial sort of dignity. And now he was chasing sheep; he had taken up criminality in his old age, just as a proud and hitherto careful old senator might publicly take up vice. Owen and I went to have a look at him, Owen telling on the way that the sheep belonged to the Potters, whose land adjoined ours, and that the Potter boys had seen Major, from their truck, and had stopped and jumped over fences and yelled, but Major had separated his sheep from the others and kept right on after it and killed it.

Killed it. I imagined it all bloody, torn apart; Major had never hunted or killed a thing in his life. "Did he want it to *eat?*" I asked in bewilderment and repugnance, and Owen was obliged to explain that the killing had been, in a way, incidental. It seemed that sheep could be run to death, frightened to death, they were so weak and fat and panicky; though Major had taken, as a trophy, a mouthful of warm wool from the neck, had pounced on that and worried it a bit, for form's sake. Then he had to streak for home (if he could streak, Major!) because the Potter boys were coming.

He was tied up inside the barn, the door open to give him some light and air. Owen jumped astride his back to wake him up — Major always woke so quickly and gravely, without fuss, that it was hard to know whether he was really asleep, or shamming — and then rolled over on the floor with him, trying to make him play. "Old sheep killer, old sheep killer," said Owen, punching him proudly. Major put up with this, but was no more playful than usual; he did not seem to have regained his youth in any but the one astounding way. He licked the top of Owen's head in a patronizing manner, and settled down to sleep again when Owen let go.

"He has to be tied up so he won't go after sheep again, old sheep killer. Potters said they'd shoot him if they ever caught him again."

This was true. Major was indeed in the limelight. My father and Uncle Benny came to look at him, in his sham dignity and innocence on the barn floor. Uncle Benny saw him as doomed. In his opinion no dog who took up chasing sheep had any hope of getting over it. "Once he's got the taste," Uncle Benny said, fondling Major's head, "he's got the taste. You can't let him live, a sheep killer."

"You mean shoot him?" I cried not exactly out of love for Major but because it seemed such a brutal ending to what everybody was considering a rather comic story. It was like leading the white-haired senator out to public execution for his embarrassing pranks.

"Can't keep a sheep killer. He'd have you poor, paying for all the sheep he killed. Anyways somebody else'd put an end to him, if you didn't."

My father, appealed to, said that perhaps Major would not chase any more sheep. He was tied up, anyway. He could stay tied up the rest of his life, if necessary, or at least until he got over his second childhood and became too feeble for chasing anything; that should not be too long now.

But my father was wrong. Uncle Benny with his grinning pessimism, his mournful satisfied predictions, was right. Major broke out of captivity, during the early morning hours. The barn door was shut but he tore some wire netting from a window that had no glass in it, and jumped out, and raced to Potter's to take up again his lately discovered pleasures. He was home by breakfast, but the broken rope and window and the dead sheep in Potter's pasture were there to tell the story.

We were at breakfast. My father had spent the night in town. Uncle Benny phoned him and told him, and my father when he came back to the table said, "Owen. We have to get rid of Major."

Owen began to quiver but he did not say a word. My father in a few words told about the breakout and the dead sheep.

"Well he's an old dog," said my mother with false heartiness. "He's an old dog and he's had a good life and who knows what's going to happen to him now anyway, all the diseases and miseries of old age."

"He could come and live here," said Owen weakly. "Then he wouldn't know where a sheep was."

"A dog like that can't live in town. And no guarantee he wouldn't get back at it anyway."

"Think of him tied up in town, Owen," said my mother reproachfully.

Owen got up and left the table without saying anything else. My mother did not call him back to say *excuse me*.

I was used to things being killed. Uncle Benny went hunting, and trapping muskrats, and every fall my father killed foxes and sold the pelts for our livelihood. Throughout the year he killed old and crippled or simply useless horses for the foxes' food. I had had two bad dreams about this, both some time ago, that I still remembered. Once I dreamed that I went down to my father's meat house, a screened shed beyond the barn where in summer he kept parts of skinned and butchered horses hanging on hooks. The shed was in the shade of a crab-apple tree; the screens would be black with flies. I dreamed that I looked inside and found, not unexpectedly, that what he really had hanging there were skinned and dismembered human bodies. The other dream owed something to English history, which I had been reading about in the encyclopedia. I dreamed my father had set up an ordinary, humble block of wood on the grass outside the kitchen door, and was lining us up — Owen and my mother and me — to cut off our heads. *It won't hurt*, he told us, as if that was all we had to be afraid of, *it'll all be over in a minute*. He was kind and calm, reasonable, tiredly persuasive, explaining that it was all somehow for our own good. Thoughts of escape struggled in my mind like birds caught in oil, their wings out, helpless. I was paralyzed by this reasonableness, the arrangements so simple and familiar and taken for granted, the reassuring face of insanity.

In the daytime I was not so frightened as these dreams would suggest. It never bothered me to go past the meat house, or to hear the gun go off. But when I thought of Major being shot, when I pictured my father loading the gun unhurriedly, ritualistically as he always did, and calling Major who would not suspect anything, being used to men with guns, and the two of them walking past the barn, my father looking for a good spot — I did see again the outline of that reasonable, blasphemous face. It was the deliberateness I dwelt on, deliberate choice to send the bullet into the brain to stop the systems working — in this choice and act, no matter how necessary and reasonable, was the assent to anything. Death was made possible. And not because it could not be prevented but because it was what was wanted — *wanted*, by all those adults, and managers, and executioners, with their kind implacable faces.

And by me? I did not want it to happen, I did not want Major to be shot, but I was full of a tense excitement as well as regret. That scene of execution which I imagined, and which gave me such a flash of darkness — was that altogether unwelcome? No. I dwelt on Major's trustfulness, his affection for my father — whom he did like, in his self-possessed way, as much as he could like anybody — his half-blind cheerful eyes. I went upstairs to see how Owen was taking it.

He was sitting on the bedroom floor fooling with some jacks. He was not crying. I had vague hopes that he might be persuaded to make trouble, not because I thought it would do any good, but because I felt the occasion demanded it.

"If you prayed for Major not to get shot would he not get shot?" said Owen in a demanding voice.

The thought of praying had never crossed my mind.

"You prayed you wouldn't have to thread the sewing machine anymore and you didn't."

I saw with dismay the unavoidable collision coming, of religion and life.

He got up and stood in front of me and said tensely, "*Pray*. How do you do it? Start now!"

"You can't pray," I said, "about a thing like that."

"Why not?"

Why not? Because, I could have said to him, we do not pray for things to happen or not happen, but for the strength and grace to bear what does. A fine way out, that smells abominably of defeat. But I did not think of it. I simply thought, and knew, that praying was not going to stop my father going out and getting his gun and calling, "Major! Here, Major — " Praying would not alter that.

God would not alter it. If God was on the side of goodness and mercy and compassion, then why had he made these things so difficult to get at? Never mind saying, *so they will be worth the trouble*; never mind all that. Praying for an act of execution not to take place was useless simply because God was not interested in such objections; they were not His.

Could there be God not contained in the churches' net at all, not made manageable by any spells and crosses, God real, and really in the world, and alien and unacceptable as death? Could there be God amazing, indifferent, beyond faith?

"How do you do it?" said Owen stubbornly. "Do you have to get down on your knees?"

"It doesn't matter."

But he had already knelt down, and clenched his hands at his sides. Then not bowing his head he screwed up his face with strong effort.

"Get up, Owen!" I said roughly. "It's not going to do any good. It won't work, it doesn't work, Owen get up, be a good boy, darling."

He swiped at me with his clenched fists, not taking time out to open his eyes. With the making of his prayer his face went through several desperate, private grimaces, each of which seemed to me a reproach and an exposure, hard to look at as skinned flesh. Seeing somebody have faith, close up, is no easier than seeing someone chop a finger off.

Do missionaries ever have these times, of astonishment and shame?

Haruki Murakami

Haruki Murakami (b. 1949) was born in Kobe, Japan, to parents who were teachers of literature. After completing an undergraduate degree in classics at Waseda University, he began his career by translating the works of modern American writers. The critic Naomi Matsuoka has observed that he is one of a new generation of Japanese writers who took American literature, rather than their own native literature, as the foundation of their writing. "Murakami had found particular affinity to the literature of the American 1920s, especially to F. Scott Fitzgerald. However, his extensive reading list includes Raymond Chandler, Kurt Vonnegut, Truman Capote, John Updike, John Cheever, John Barth, Thomas Pynchon, John Irving, and Tim O'Brien."

In 1982 Murakami debuted as a novelist in Japan with *A Wild Sheep Chase*, based on Raymond Chandler's detective novel *The Long Goodbye*. Four other novels have also been translated into English, including *The Wind-Up Bird Chronicle* (1997) and *Sputnik Sweetheart* (2001). In Murakami's early short fiction, he often modeled his work on the stories of Raymond Carver, whom Murakami translated into Japanese and interviewed in 1984. When Carver asked what Japanese readers liked about his fiction, Murakami replied, "There is something in common between your stories and traditional Japanese short stories. There is some subtle change in a domestic situation, and the situation is altered although there is no change in the essential level and the stories cut off at that point." Later, in *Ultramarine* (1986), Carver dedicated his poem "The Projectile" to Murakami.

Murakami's story "UFO in Kushiro," published in *After the Quake* (2002), was his response to the 7.33-magnitude earthquake in Kobe, Japan, in 1995. He says that he now writes spontaneously, rather than following the tracks of his earlier literary heroes. In 2006 he won the Franz Kafka Prize. As a marathon runner, he published a best-selling memoir *What I Talk About When I Talk About Running* in 2008. *IQ84* (2013) is a recent novel.

UFO in Kushiro

2001 / Translated by Jay Rubin

FIVE STRAIGHT DAYS she spent in front of the television, staring at crumbled banks and hospitals, whole blocks of stores in flames, severed rail lines and expressways. She never said a word. Sunk deep in the cushions of the sofa, her mouth clamped shut, she wouldn't answer when Komura spoke to her. She wouldn't shake her head or nod. Komura could not be sure the sound of his voice was even getting through to her.

Komura's wife came from way up north in Yamagata and, as far as he knew, she had no friends or relatives who could have been hurt in Kobe. Yet she stayed rooted in front of the television from morning to night. In his presence, at least, she ate nothing and drank nothing and never went to the toilet. Aside from an occasional flick of the remote control to change the channel, she hardly moved a muscle.

Komura would make his own toast and coffee, and head off to work. When he came home in the evening, he'd fix himself a snack with whatever he found in the refrigerator and eat alone. She'd still be glaring at the late news when he dropped off to sleep. A stone wall of silence surrounded her. Komura gave up trying to break through.

When he came home from work that Sunday, the sixth day, his wife had disappeared.

Komura was a salesman at one of the oldest hi-fi-equipment specialty stores in Tokyo's Akihabara "Electronics Town." He handled top-of-the-line stuff and earned a sizeable commission whenever he made a sale. Most of his clients were doctors, wealthy independent businessmen, and rich provincials. He had been doing this for eight years and had a decent income right from the start. The economy was healthy, real-estate prices were rising, and Japan was overflowing with money. People's wallets were bursting with ten-thousand-yen bills, and everyone was dying to spend them. The most expensive items were the first to sell out.

Komura was tall and slim and a stylish dresser. He was good with people. In his bachelor days he had dated a lot of women. But after getting married, at twenty-six, he found that his desire for sexual adventures simply — and mysteriously — vanished. He hadn't slept with any woman but his wife during the five years of their marriage. Not that the opportunity had never presented itself — but he had lost all interest in fleeting affairs and one-night stands. He much preferred to come home early, have a relaxed meal with his wife, talk with her for a while on the sofa, then go to bed and make love. This was everything he wanted.

Komura's friends and colleagues were puzzled by his marriage. Alongside him with his clean, classic good looks, his wife could not have seemed more ordinary. She was short with thick arms, and she had a dull, even stolid appearance. And it wasn't just physical: there was nothing attractive about her personality either. She rarely spoke and always wore a sullen expression.

Still, though he did not quite understand why, Komura always felt his tension dissipate when he and his wife were together under one roof; it was the only time he could truly relax. He slept well with her, undisturbed by the strange dreams that had troubled him in the past. His erections were hard; his sex life was warm. He no longer had to worry about death or venereal disease or the vastness of the universe.

His wife, on the other hand, disliked Tokyo's crowds and longed for Yamagata. She missed her parents and her two elder sisters, and she would go home to see them whenever she felt the need. Her parents operated a successful inn, which kept them financially comfortable. Her father was crazy about his youngest daughter and happily paid her round-trip fares. Several times, Komura had come home from work to find his wife gone and a note on the kitchen table telling him that she was visiting her parents for a while. He never objected. He just waited for her to come back, and she always did, after a week or ten days, in a good mood.

But the letter his wife left for him when she vanished five days after the earthquake was different: *I am never coming back*, she had written, then went on to explain, simply but clearly, why she no longer wanted to live with him.

The problem is that you never give me anything, she wrote. *Or, to put it more precisely, you have nothing inside you that you can give me. You are good and kind and handsome, but living with you is like living with a chunk of air. It's not entirely your fault, though. There are lots of women who will fall in love with you. But please don't call me. Just get rid of all the stuff I'm leaving behind.*

In fact, she hadn't left much of anything behind. Her clothes, her shoes, her umbrella, her coffee mug, her hair dryer: all were gone. She must have packed them in boxes and shipped them out after he left for work that morning. The only things still in the house that could be called "her stuff" were the bike she used for shopping and a few books. The Beatles and Bill Evans CDs that Komura had been collecting since his bachelor days had also vanished.

The next day, he tried calling his wife's parents in Yamagata. His mother-in-law answered the phone and told him that his wife didn't want to talk to him. She sounded somewhat apologetic. She also told him that they would be sending him the necessary forms soon and that he should put his seal on them and send them back right away.

Komura answered that he might not be able to send them "right away." This was an important matter, and he wanted time to think it over.

"You can think it over all you want, but I know it won't change anything," his mother-in-law said.

She was probably right. Komura told himself. No matter how much he thought or waited, things would never be the same. He was sure of that.

Shortly after he had sent the papers back with his seal stamped on them, Komura asked for a week's paid leave. His boss had a general idea of what had been happening, and February was a slow time of the year, so he let Komura go without a fuss. He seemed on the verge of saying something to Komura, but finally said nothing.

Sasaki, a colleague of Komura's, came over to him at lunch and said, "I hear you're taking time off. Are you planning to do something?"

"I don't know," Komura said. "What *should* I do?"

Sasaki was a bachelor, three years younger than Komura. He had a delicate build and short hair, and he wore round, gold-rimmed glasses. A lot of people thought he talked too much and had a rather arrogant air, but he got along well enough with the easygoing Komura.

"What the hell — as long as you're taking the time off, why not make a nice trip out of it?"

"Not a bad idea." Komura said.

Wiping his glasses with his handkerchief, Sasaki peered at Komura as if looking for some kind of clue.

"Have you ever been to Hokkaido?" he asked.

"Never."

"Would you like to go?"

"Why do you ask?"

Sasaki narrowed his eyes and cleared his throat. "To tell you the truth, I've got a small package I'd like to send to Kushiro, and I'm hoping you'll take it there for me. You'd be doing me a big favor, and I'd be glad to pay for a round-trip ticket. I could cover your hotel in Kushiro, too."

"A small package?"

"Like this." Sasaki said, shaping a four-inch cube with his hands. "Nothing heavy."

"Something to do with work?"

Sasaki shook his head. "Not at all," he said. "Strictly personal, I just don't want it to get knocked around, which is why I can't mail it. I'd like you to deliver it by hand, if possible. I really ought to do it myself, but I haven't got time to fly all the way to Hokkaido."

"Is it something important?"

His closed lips curling slightly, Sasaki nodded. "It's nothing fragile, and there are no 'hazardous materials.' There's no need to worry about it. They're not going to stop you when they X-ray it at the airport. I promise I'm not going to get you in trouble. And it weighs practically nothing. All I'm asking is that you take it along the way you'd take anything else. The only reason I'm not mailing it is I just don't *feel* like mailing it."

Hokkaido in February would be freezing cold. Komura knew, but cold or hot it was all the same to him.

"So who do I give the package to?"

"My sister. My younger sister. She lives up there."

Komura decided to accept Sasaki's offer. He hadn't thought about how to spend his week off, and making plans now would have been too much trouble. Besides, he had no reason for not wanting to go to Hokkaido. Sasaki called the airline then and there, reserving a ticket to Kushiro. The flight would leave two days later, in the afternoon.

At work the next day, Sasaki handed Komura a box like the ones used for human ashes, only smaller, wrapped in manila paper. Judging from the feel, it was made of wood. As Sasaki had said, it weighed practically nothing. Broad strips of transparent tape went all around the package over the paper. Komura held it in his hands and studied it a few seconds. He gave it a little shake but he couldn't feel or hear anything moving inside.

"My sister will pick you up at the airport. And she'll be arranging a room for you," Sasaki said. "All you have to do is stand outside the gate with the package in your hands where she can see it. Don't worry, the airport's not very big."

Komura left home with the box in his suitcase, wrapped in a thick undershirt. The plane was far more crowded than he had expected. Why were all these people going from Tokyo to Kushiro in the middle of winter? he wondered.

The morning paper was full of earthquake reports. He read it from beginning to end on the plane. The number of dead was rising. Many areas were still without water or electricity, and countless people had lost their homes. Each article reported some new tragedy, but to Komura the details seemed oddly lacking in depth. All sounds reached him as far-off, monotonous echos. The only thing he could give any serious thought to was his wife as she retreated ever farther into the distance.

Mechanically he ran his eyes over the earthquake reports, stopped now and then to think about his wife, then went back to the paper. When he grew tired of this, he closed his eyes and napped. And when he woke, he thought about his wife again. Why had she followed the TV earthquake reports with such intensity, from morning to night, without eating or sleeping? What could she have seen in them?

Two young women wearing overcoats of similar design and color approached Komura at the airport. One was fair-skinned and maybe five feet six, with short hair. The area from her nose to her full upper lip was oddly extended in a way that made Komura think of shorthaired ungulates. Her companion was more like five feet one and would have been quite pretty if her nose hadn't been so small. Her long hair fell straight to her shoulders. Her ears were exposed, and there were two moles on her right earlobe which were emphasized by the earrings she wore. Both women looked to be in their midtwenties. They took Komura to a café in the airport.

"I'm Keiko Sasaki," the taller woman said. "My brother told me how helpful you've been to him. This is my friend Shimao."

"Nice to meet you," Komura said.

"Hi." Shimao said.

"My brother tells me your wife recently passed away," Keiko Sasaki said with a respectful expression.

Komura waited a moment before answering. "No, she didn't die."

"I just talked to my brother the day before yesterday. I'm sure he said quite clearly that you'd lost your wife."

"I did. She divorced me. But as far as I know she's alive and well."

"That's odd. I couldn't possibly have misheard something so important." She gave him an injured look. Komura put a small amount of sugar in his coffee and gave it a gentle stir before taking a sip. The liquid was thin, with no taste to speak of, more sign than substance. What the hell am I doing here? he wondered.

"Well, I guess I did mishear it. I can't imagine how else to explain the mistake." Keiko Sasaki said, apparently satisfied now. She drew in a deep breath and chewed her lower lip. "Please forgive me. I was very rude."

"Don't worry about it. Either way, she's gone."

Shimao said nothing while Komura and Keiko spoke, but she smiled and kept her eyes on Komura. She seemed to like him. He could tell from her expression and her subtle body language. A brief silence fell over the three of them.

"Anyway, let me give you the important package I brought," Komura said. He unzipped his suitcase and pulled the box out of the folds of the thick ski undershirt he had wrapped it in. The thought struck him then: I was supposed to be holding this when I got off the plane. That's how they were going to recognize me. How did they know who I was?

Keiko Sasaki stretched her hands across the table, her expressionless eyes fixed on the package. After testing its weight, she did as Komura had done and gave it a few shakes by her ear. She flashed him a smile as if to signal that everything was fine, and slipped the box into her oversize shoulder bag.

"I have to make a call," she said. "Do you mind if I excuse myself for a moment?"

"Not at all," Komura said. "Feel free."

Keiko slung the bag over her shoulder and walked off toward a distant phone booth. Komura studied the way she walked. The upper half of her body was still, while everything from the hips down made large, smooth, mechanical movements. He had the strange impression that he was witnessing some moment from the past, shoved with random suddenness into the present.

"Have you been to Hokkaido before?" Shimao asked.

Komura shook his head.

"Yeah, I know. It's a long way to come."

Komura nodded, then turned to survey his surroundings. "Funny," he said, "sitting here like this, it doesn't feel as if I've come all that far."

"Because you flew. Those planes are too damn fast. Your mind can't keep up with your body."

"You may be right."

"Did you want to make such a long trip?"

"I guess so." Komura said.

"Because your wife left?"

He nodded.

"No matter how far you travel, you can never get away from yourself," Shimao said.

Komura was staring at the sugar bowl on the table as she spoke, but then he raised his eyes to hers.

"It's true," he said. "No matter how far you travel, you can never get away from yourself. It's like your shadow. It follows you everywhere."

Shimao looked hard at Komura. "I'll bet you loved her, didn't you?"

Komura dodged the question. "You're a friend of Keiko Sasaki's?"

"Right. We do stuff together."

"What kind of stuff?"

Instead of answering him, Shimao asked, "Are you hungry?"

"I wonder," Komura said. "I feel kind of hungry and kind of not."

"Let's go and eat something warm, the three of us. It'll help you relax."

Shimao drove a small four-wheel-drive Subaru. It had to have way over a hundred thousand miles on it, judging from how battered it was. The rear bumper had a huge dent in it. Keiko Sasaki sat next to Shimao, and Komura had the cramped rear seat to himself. There was nothing particularly wrong with Shimao's driving, but the noise in back was terrible, and the suspension was nearly shot. The automatic transmission slammed into gear whenever it downshifted, and the heater blew hot and cold. Shutting his eyes, Komura felt as if he had been imprisoned in a washing machine.

No snow had been allowed to gather on the streets in Kushiro, but dirty, icy mounds stood at random intervals on both sides of the road. Dense clouds hung low and, although it was not yet sunset, everything was dark and desolate. The wind tore through the city in sharp squeals. There were no pedestrians. Even the traffic lights looked frozen.

"This is one part of Hokkaido that doesn't get much snow," Keiko Sasaki explained in a loud voice, glancing back at Komura. "We're on the coast and the wind is strong, so whatever piles up gets blown away. It's cold, though, *freezing* cold. Sometimes it feels like it's taking your ears off."

"You hear about drunks who freeze to death sleeping on the street," Shimao said.

"Do you get bears around here?" Komura asked.

Keiko giggled and turned to Shimao. "Bears, he says."

Shimao gave the same kind of giggle.

"I don't know much about Hokkaido," Komura said by way of explanation.

"I know a good story about bears," Keiko said. "Right, Shimao?"

"A *great* story!" Shimao said.

But their talk broke off at that point, and neither of them told the bear story. Komura didn't ask to hear it. Soon they reached their destination, a big noodle shop on the highway. They parked in the lot and went inside. Komura had a beer and a hot bowl of ramen noodles. The place was dirty and empty, and the chairs and tables were rickety, but the ramen was excellent, and when he had finished eating, Komura did, in fact, feel a little more relaxed.

"Tell me, Mr. Komura," Keiko Sasaki said, "do you have something you want to do in Hokkaido? My brother tells me you're going to spend a week here."

Komura thought about it for a moment, but couldn't come up with anything he wanted to do.

"How about a hot spring? Would you like a nice, long soak in a tub? I know a little country place not far from here."

"Not a bad idea," Komura said.

"I'm sure you'd like it. It's really nice. No bears or anything."

The two women looked at each other and laughed again.

"Do you mind if I ask you about your wife?" Keiko said.

"I don't mind."

"When did she leave?"

"Hmm . . . five days after the earthquake, so that's more than two weeks ago now."

"Did it have something to do with the earthquake?"

Komura shook his head. "Probably not. I don't think so."

"Still, I wonder if things like that aren't connected somehow," Shimao said with a tilt of the head.

"Yeah," Keiko said. "It's just that you can't see how."

"Right," Shimao said, "Stuff like that happens all the time."

"Stuff like what?" Komura asked.

"Like, say, what happened with somebody I know," Keiko said.

"You mean Mr. Saeki?" Shimao asked.

"Exactly," Keiko said. "There's this guy — Saeki. He lives in Kushiro. He's about forty. A hairstylist. His wife saw a UFO last year, in the autumn. She was driving on the edge of town all by herself in the middle of the night and she saw a huge UFO land in a field. *Whoosh!* Like in *Close Encounters.* A week later, she left home. They weren't having any domestic problems or anything. She just disappeared and never came back."

"Into thin air," Shimao said.

"And it was because of the UFO?" Komura asked.

"I don't know why," Keiko said. "She just walked out. No note or anything. She had two kids in elementary school, too. The whole week before she left, all she'd do was tell people about the UFO. You couldn't get her to stop. She'd go on and on about how big and beautiful it was."

She paused to let the story sink in.

"My wife left a note," Komura said. "And we don't have any kids."

"So your situation's a little better than Saeki's," Keiko said.

"Yeah. Kids make a big difference," Shimao said, nodding.

"Shimao's father left home when she was seven," Keiko explained with a frown. "Ran off with his wife's younger sister."

"All of a sudden. One day," Shimao said, smiling.

A silence settled over the group.

"Maybe Mr. Saeki's wife didn't run away but was captured by aliens from the UFO," Komura said to smooth things over.

"It's possible," Shimao said with a somber expression. "You hear stories like that all the time."

"You mean like you're-walking-along-the-street-and-a-bear-eats-you kind of thing?" Keiko asked. The two women laughed again.

The three of them left the noodle shop and went to a nearby love hotel. It was on the edge of town, on a street where love hotels alternated with gravestone dealers. The hotel Shimao had chosen was an odd building, constructed to look like a European castle. A triangular red flag flew on its highest tower.

Keiko got the key at the front desk, and the three of them took the elevator to the room. The windows were tiny, compared with the absurdly big bed. Komura hung his down jacket on a hanger and went into the toilet. During the few minutes he was in there, the two women managed to run a bath, dim the lights, check the heat, turn on the television, examine the delivery menus from local restaurants, test the light switches at the head of the bed, and check the contents of the minibar.

"The owners are friends of mine," Keiko said. "I had them get their biggest room ready. It is a love hotel, but don't let that bother you. You're not bothered, are you?"

"Not at all," Komura said.

"I thought this would make a lot more sense than sticking you in a cramped little room in some cheap business hotel by the station."

"You may be right," Komura said.

"Why don't you take a bath? I filled the tub."

Komura did as he was told. The tub was huge. He felt uneasy soaking in it alone. The couples who came to this hotel probably took baths together.

When he emerged from the bathroom, Komura was surprised to find that Keiko Sasaki had left. Shimao was still there, drinking beer and watching TV.

"Keiko went home," Shimao said. "She wanted me to apologize and tell you that she'll be back tomorrow morning. Do you mind if I stay here a little while and have a beer?"

"Fine," Komura said.

"You're sure it's no problem? Like, you want to be alone or you can't relax if somebody else is around or something?"

Komura insisted it was no problem. Drinking a beer and drying his hair with a towel, he watched TV with Shimao. It was a news special on the Kobe earthquake. The usual images appeared again and again: tilted buildings, buckled streets, old women weeping, confusion and aimless anger. When a commercial came on, Shimao used the remote to switch off the TV.

"Let's talk," she said, "as long as we're here."

"Fine," Komura said.

"Hmm, what should we talk about?"

"In the car, you and Keiko said something about a bear, remember? You said it was a great story."

"Oh yeah," she said, nodding. "The bear story."

"You want to tell it to me?"

"Sure, why not?"

Shimao got a fresh beer from the minibar and filled both their glasses.

"It's a little raunchy," she said. "You don't mind?"

Komura shook his head.

"I mean, some men don't like hearing a woman tell certain kinds of stories."

"I'm not like that."

"It's something that actually happened to me, so it's a little embarrassing."

"I'd like to hear it if you're OK with it."

"I'm OK, if you're OK."

"I'm OK," Komura said.

"Three years ago — back around the time I entered junior college — I was dating this guy. He was a year older than me, a college student. He was the first guy I had sex with. One day the two of us were out hiking — in the mountains way up north."

She took a sip of beer.

"It was fall, and the hills were full of bears. That's the time of year when the bears are getting ready to hibernate, so they're out looking for food and they're really dangerous. Sometimes they attack people. They did an awful job on one hiker just three days before we went out. So somebody gave us a bell to carry — about the same size as a wind-bell. You're supposed to shake it when you walk so the bears know there are people around and won't come out. Bears don't attack people on purpose. I mean, they're pretty much vegetarians. They don't *have* to attack people. What happens is they suddenly bump into people in their territory and they get surprised or angry and they attack out of reflex. So if you walk along ringing your bell, they'll avoid you. Get it?"

"I get it."

"So that's what we were doing, walking along and ringing the bell. We got to this place where there was nobody else around, and all of a sudden he said he wanted to . . . do it. I kind of liked the idea, too, so I said OK and we went into this bushy place off the trail where nobody could see us, and we spread out a piece of plastic. But I was afraid of the bears. I mean, think how awful it would be to have some bear attack you from behind and kill you when you're having sex! I would never want to die that way. Would you?"

Komura agreed that he would not want to die that way.

"So there we were, shaking the bell with one hand and having sex. Kept it up from start to finish. *Ding-a-ling! Ding-a-ling!*"

"Which one of you shook the bell?"

"We took turns. We'd trade off when our hands got tired. It was so weird, shaking this bell the whole time we were doing it! I think about it sometimes even now, when I'm having sex, and I start laughing."

Komura gave a little laugh, too.

Shimao clapped her hands. "Oh, that's wonderful," she said. "You *can* laugh after all!"

"Of course I can laugh," Komura said, but come to think of it, this was the first time he had laughed in quite a while. When was the last time?

"Do you mind if I take a bath, too?" Shimao asked.

"Fine," he said.

While she was bathing, Komura watched a variety show emceed by some comedian with a loud voice. He didn't find it the least bit funny, but he couldn't tell whether that was the show's fault or his own. He drank a beer and opened a pack of nuts from the minibar. Shimao stayed in the bath for a very long time. Finally, she came out wearing nothing but a towel and sat on the edge of the bed. Dropping the towel, she slid in between the sheets like a cat and lay there looking straight at Komura.

"When was the last time you did it with your wife?" she asked.

"At the end of December, I think."

"And nothing since?"

"Nothing."

"Not with anybody?"

Komura closed his eyes and shook his head.

"You know what *I* think," Shimao said. "You need to lighten up and learn to enjoy life a little more. I mean, think about it: tomorrow there could be an earthquake; you could be kidnapped by aliens; you could be eaten by a bear. Nobody knows what's going to happen."

"Nobody knows what's going to happen," Komura echoed.

"Ding-a-ling," Shimao said.

After several failed attempts to have sex with Shimao, Komura gave up. This had never happened to him before.

"You must have been thinking about your wife," Shimao said.

"Yup," Komura said, but in fact what he had been thinking about was the earthquake. Images of it had come to him one after another, as if in a slide show, flashing on the screen and fading away. Highways, flames, smoke, piles of rubble, cracks in streets. He couldn't break the chain of silent images.

Shimao pressed her ear against his naked chest.

"These things happen," she said.

"Uh-huh."

"You shouldn't let it bother you."

"I'll try not to," Komura said.

"Men always let it bother them, though."

Komura said nothing.

Shimao played with his nipple.

"You said your wife left a note, didn't you?"

"I did."

"What did it say?"

"That living with me was like living with a chunk of air."

"A chunk of air?" Shimao tilted her head back to look up at Komura. "What does *that* mean?"

"That there's nothing inside me, I guess."

"Is it true?"

"Could be," Komura said. "I'm not sure, though. I may have nothing inside me, but what would *something* be?"

"Yeah, really, come to think of it. What *would* something be? My mother was crazy about salmon skin. She always used to wish there were a kind of salmon made of nothing but skin. So there may be some cases when it's *better* to have nothing inside. Don't you think?"

Komura tried to imagine what a salmon made of nothing but skin would be like. But even supposing there were such a thing, wouldn't the skin itself be the *something* inside? Komura took a deep breath, raising and then lowering Shimao's head on his chest.

"I'll tell you this, though," Shimao said, "I don't know whether you've got nothing or something inside you, but I think you're terrific. I'll bet the world is full of women who would understand you and fall in love with you."

"It said that, too."

"What? Your wife's note?"

"Uh-huh."

"No kidding," Shimao said, lowering her head to Komura's chest again. He felt her earring against his skin like a secret object.

"Come to think of it," Komura said, "what's the *something* inside that box I brought up here?"

"Is it bothering you?"

"It wasn't bothering me before. But now, I don't know, it's starting to."

"Since when?"

"Just now."

"All of a sudden?"

"Yeah, once I started thinking about it, all of a sudden."

"I wonder why it's started to bother you now, all of a sudden?"

Komura glared at the ceiling for a minute to think. "I wonder."

They listened to the moaning of the wind. The wind: it came from someplace unknown to Komura, and it blew past to someplace unknown to him.

"I'll tell you why," Shimao said in a low voice. "It's because that box contains the *something* that was inside you. You didn't know that when you carried it here and gave it to Keiko with your own hands. Now, you'll never get it back."

Komura lifted himself from the mattress and looked down at the woman. Tiny nose, moles on the earlobe. In the room's deep silence, his heart beat with a loud, dry sound. His bones cracked as he leaned forward. For one split second, Komura realized that he was on the verge of committing an act of overwhelming violence.

"Just kidding," Shimao said when she saw the look on his face. "I said the first thing that popped into my head. It was a lousy joke. I'm sorry. Try not to let it bother you. I didn't mean to hurt you."

Komura forced himself to calm down and, after a glance around the room, sank his head into his pillow again. He closed his eyes and took a deep breath. The huge bed stretched out around him like a nocturnal sea. He heard the freezing wind. The fierce pounding of his heart shook his bones.

"Are you starting to feel a *little* as if you've come a long way?" Shimao asked.

"Hmm. Now I feel as if I've come a *very* long way," Komura answered honestly.

Shimao traced a complicated design on Komura's chest with her fingertip, as if casting a magic spell.

"But really," she said, "you're just at the beginning."

Vladimir Nabokov

Vladimir Nabokov (1899–1977), claiming that "the nationality of a worthwhile writer is of secondary importance," resists classification as a Russian, American, or even Swiss writer. Born into an aristocratic and wealthy family in St. Petersburg (now Leningrad), he was educated at the Prince Tenishev School there. As a boy he was an avid reader and loved literature: "Between the ages of ten and fifteen in St. Petersburg, I must have read more fiction and poetry—English, Russian, and French—than in any other five-year period in my life." He published a collection of his own poems at the age of sixteen. When the Bolsheviks seized power after the Russian Revolution of 1917, Nabokov fled to Europe with his family. He took a degree in French and Russian literature at Cambridge University in 1922, the same year his father, who had been a liberal politician in Russia, was assassinated in Berlin by right-wing Russians. Nabokov lived as an émigré in Germany and France until the outbreak of World War II forced him, his wife Vera, and their young son Dmitri to move to the United States. He had published many novels in Europe and had begun to write in English, but he made his living in the United States as a lecturer on Russian language and literature at Stanford, Wellesley, Harvard, and Cornell, ascending "from lean lecturer to full professor." In his time away from teaching, he wrote fiction, selling occasional stories to *The Atlantic Monthly* and *The New Yorker* before the financial success of his novel *Lolita* (1955), a best-seller when it finally found an American publisher in 1958, enabled him to give up teaching and return to Europe. In 1961 he settled at the Palace Hotel in Montreux, Switzerland, where he remained with his wife and continued to write until his death. The more than thirty volumes of his complete works include such novels as *The Real Life of Sebastian Knight* (1941), *Pnin* (1957), *Pale Fire* (1962), and *Ada, or Ardor: A Family Chronicle* (1969). His lectures at Cornell on European and Russian literature, published in 1980 and 1981, show him teaching his students to be good readers of great literature by insisting that style and structure are the essence of a book; "caress the details," he would intone, rolling the *r*—"the divine details!"

Nabokov once told an interviewer that "the writer's art is his real passport. His identity should be immediately recognized by a special pattern or unique coloration." His "special pattern" as a writer was a passionate interest in language and experience that led him to create works where memories of the past mingled with an ironic sense of the precariousness of the present. A meticulous craftsman, he revised his manuscripts to polish his wit and style to razor sharpness: "I think like a genius, I write like a distinguished author, and I speak like a child. . . . At parties, if I attempt to entertain people with a good story, I have to go back to every other sentence for oral erasures and inserts. Even the dream I describe to my wife across the breakfast table is only a first draft."

A half-dozen books of Nabokov's short stories were published in his lifetime, many of them translated from Russian into English by his son. The early collections show him learning his craft in Berlin; perhaps the best collection is *Nabokov's Dozen* (1958), thirteen stories written in Berlin in the 1930s, Boston in the 1940s, and Ithaca in the 1950s. "Signs and Symbols" is from this book.

RELATED STORY
Lorrie Moore, "Referential," page 920.

RELATED COMMENTARIES
Vladimir Nabokov, "Gogol's Genius in 'The Overcoat,'" page 1483; Vladimir Nabokov, "A Reading of Chekhov's 'The Lady with the Little Dog,'" page 1486.

Signs and Symbols

1958

I

For the fourth time in as many years they were confronted with the problem of what birthday present to bring a young man who was incurably deranged in his mind. He had no desires. Man-made objects were to him either hives of evil, vibrant with a malignant activity that he alone could perceive, or gross comforts for which no use could be found in his abstract world. After eliminating a number of articles that might offend him or frighten him (anything in the gadget line for instance was taboo), his parents chose a dainty and innocent trifle: a basket with ten different fruit jellies in ten little jars.

At the time of his birth they had been married already for a long time; a score of years had elapsed, and now they were quite old. Her drab gray hair was done anyhow. She wore cheap black dresses. Unlike other women of her age (such as Mrs. Sol, their next-door neighbor, whose face was all pink and mauve with paint and whose hat was a cluster of brookside flowers), she presented a naked white countenance to the fault-finding light of spring days. Her husband, who in the old country had been a fairly successful businessman, was now wholly dependent on his brother Isaac, a real American of almost forty years standing. They seldom saw him and had nicknamed him "the Prince."

That Friday everything went wrong. The underground train lost its life current between two stations, and for a quarter of an hour one could hear nothing but the dutiful beating of one's heart and the rustling of newspapers. The bus they had to take next kept them waiting for ages; and when it did come, it was crammed with garrulous high-school children. It was raining hard as they walked up the brown path leading to the sanitarium. There they waited again; and instead of their boy shuffling into the room as he usually did (his poor face blotched with acne, ill-shaven, sullen, and confused), a nurse they knew, and did not care for, appeared at last and brightly explained that he had again attempted to take his life. He was all right, she said, but a visit might disturb him. The place was so miserably understaffed, and things got mislaid or mixed up so easily, that they decided not to leave their present in the office but to bring it to him next time they came.

She waited for her husband to open his umbrella and then took his arm. He kept clearing his throat in a special resonant way he had when he was upset. They reached the bus-stop shelter on the other side of the street and he closed his umbrella. A few feet away, under a swaying and dripping tree, a tiny half-dead unfledged bird was helplessly twitching in a puddle.

During the long ride to the subway station, she and her husband did not exchange a word; and every time she glanced at his old hands (swollen veins, brown-spotted skin), clasped and twitching upon the handle of his umbrella, she felt the mounting pressure of tears. As she looked around trying to hook her mind onto something, it gave her a kind of soft shock, a mixture of compassion and wonder, to notice that one of the passengers, a girl with dark hair and grubby red toenails, was weeping on the shoulder of an older woman. Whom did that woman resemble? She resembled Rebecca Borisovna, whose daughter had married one of the Soloveichiks — in Minsk,[1] years ago.

The last time he had tried to do it, his method had been, in the doctor's words, a masterpiece of inventiveness; he would have succeeded, had not an envious fellow patient thought he was learning to fly — and stopped him. What he really wanted to do was to tear a hole in his world and escape.

The system of his delusions had been the subject of an elaborate paper in a scientific monthly, but long before that she and her husband had puzzled it out for themselves. "Referential mania," Herman Brink had called it. In these very rare cases the patient imagines that everything happening around him is a veiled reference to his personality and existence. He excludes real people from the conspiracy — because he considers himself to be so much more intelligent than other men. Phenomenal nature shadows him wherever he goes. Clouds in the staring sky transmit to one another, by means of slow signs, incredibly detailed information regarding him. His inmost thoughts are discussed at nightfall, in manual alphabet,[2] by darkly gesticulating trees. Pebbles or stains or sun flecks form patterns representing in some awful way messages which he must intercept. Everything is a cipher and of everything he is the theme. Some of the spies are detached observers, such as glass surfaces and still pools; others, such as coats in store windows, are prejudiced witnesses, lynchers at heart; others again (running water, storms) are hysterical to the point of insanity, have a distorted opinion of him and grotesquely misinterpret his actions. He must be always on his guard and devote every minute and module of life to the decoding of the undulation of things. The very air he exhales is indexed and filed away. If only the interest he provokes were limited to his immediate surroundings — but alas it is not! With distance the torrents of wild scandal increase in volume and volubility. The silhouettes of his blood corpuscles, magnified a million times, flit over vast plains; and still farther, great mountains of unbearable solidity and height sum up in terms of granite and groaning firs the ultimate truth of his being.

II

When they emerged from the thunder and foul air of the subway, the last dregs of the day were mixed with the street lights. She wanted to buy some fish for supper, so she handed him the basket of jelly jars, telling him to go home. He walked up to the third landing and then remembered he had given her his keys earlier in the day.

In silence he sat down on the steps and in silence rose when some ten minutes later she came, heavily trudging upstairs, wanly smiling, shaking her head in deprecation of her silliness. They entered their two-room flat and he at once went to the mirror. Straining the corners of his mouth apart by means of his thumbs, with a horrible masklike grimace, he removed his new hopelessly uncomfortable dental plate and severed the long tusks of saliva connecting him to it. He read his

---

[1] A city in western Russia.
[2] Sign language used by the deaf.

Russian-language newspaper while she laid the table. Still reading, he ate the pale victuals that needed no teeth. She knew his moods and was also silent.

When he had gone to bed, she remained in the living room with her pack of soiled cards and her old albums. Across the narrow yard where the rain tinkled in the dark against some battered ash cans, windows were blandly alight and in one of them a black-trousered man with his bare elbows raised could be seen lying supine on an untidy bed. She pulled the blind down and examined the photographs. As a baby he looked more surprised than most babies. From a fold in the album, a German maid they had had in Leipzig and her fat-faced fiancé fell out. Minsk, the Revolution, Leipzig,[3] Berlin, Leipzig, a slanting house front badly out of focus. Four years old, in a park: moodily, shyly, with puckered forehead, looking away from an eager squirrel as he would from any other stranger. Aunt Rose, a fussy, angular, wild-eyed old lady, who had lived in a tremulous world of bad news, bankruptcies, train accidents, cancerous growths — until the Germans put her to death, together with all the people she had worried about. Age six — that was when he drew wonderful birds with human hands and feet, and suffered from insomnia like a grown-up man. His cousin, now a famous chess player. He again, aged about eight, already difficult to understand, afraid of the wallpaper in the passage, afraid of a certain picture in a book which merely showed an idyllic landscape with rocks on a hillside and an old cart wheel hanging from the branch of a leafless tree. Aged ten: the year they left Europe. The shame, the pity, the humiliating difficulties, the ugly, vicious, backward children he was with in that special school. And then came a time in his life, coinciding with a long convalescence after pneumonia, when those little phobias of his which his parents had stubbornly regarded as the eccentricities of a prodigiously gifted child hardened as it were into a dense tangle of logically interacting illusions, making him totally inaccessible to normal minds.

This, and much more, she accepted — for after all living did mean accepting the loss of one joy after another, not even joys in her case — mere possibilities of improvement. She thought of the endless waves of pain that for some reason or other she and her husband had to endure; of the invisible giants hurting her boy in some unimaginable fashion; of the incalculable amount of tenderness contained in the world; of the fate of this tenderness, which is either crushed, or wasted, or transformed into madness; of neglected children humming to themselves in unswept corners; of beautiful weeds that cannot hide from the farmer and helplessly have to watch the shadow of his simian stoop leave mangled flowers in its wake, as the monstrous darkness approaches.

III

It was past midnight when from the living room she heard her husband moan; and presently he staggered in, wearing over his nightgown the old overcoat with astrakhan[4] collar which he much preferred to the nice blue bathrobe he had.

---

[3] Leipzig is a city in Germany. The Revolution is the Russian Revolution of 1917–20.
[4] Lustrous, tight-curled wool (from Astrakhan, a city in southeast Russia).

"I can't sleep," he cried.

"Why," she asked, "why can't you sleep? You were so tired."

"I can't sleep because I am dying," he said and lay down on the couch.

"Is it your stomach? Do you want me to call Dr. Solov?"

"No doctors, no doctors," he moaned. "To the devil with doctors! We must get him out of there quick. Otherwise we'll be responsible. Responsible!" he repeated and hurled himself into a sitting position, both feet on the floor, thumping his forehead with his clenched fist.

"All right," she said quietly, "we shall bring him home tomorrow morning."

"I would like some tea," said her husband and retired to the bathroom.

Bending with difficulty, she retrieved some playing cards and a photograph or two that had slipped from the couch to the floor: knave of hearts, nine of spades, ace of spades, Elsa and her bestial beau.

He returned in high spirits, saying in a loud voice:

"I have it all figured out. We will give him the bedroom. Each of us will spend part of the night near him and the other part on this couch. By turns. We will have the doctor see him at least twice a week. It does not matter what the Prince says. He won't have to say much anyway because it will come out cheaper."

The telephone rang. It was an unusual hour for their telephone to ring. His left slipper had come off and he groped for it with his heel and toe as he stood in the middle of the room, and childishly, toothlessly, gaped at his wife. Having more English than he did, it was she who attended to calls.

"Can I speak to Charlie," said a girl's dull little voice.

"What number you want? No. That is not the right number."

The receiver was gently cradled. Her hand went to her old tired heart.

"It frightened me," she said.

He smiled a quick smile and immediately resumed his excited monologue. They would fetch him as soon as it was day. Knives would have to be kept in a locked drawer. Even at his worst he presented no danger to other people.

The telephone rang a second time. The same toneless anxious young voice asked for Charlie.

"You have the incorrect number. I will tell you what you are doing: you are turning the letter O instead of zero."

They sat down to their unexpected festive midnight tea. The birthday present stood on the table. He sipped noisily; his face was flushed; every now and then he imparted a circular motion to his raised glass so as to make the sugar dissolve more thoroughly. The vein on the side of his bald head where there was a large birthmark stood out conspicuously and, although he had shaved that morning, a silvery bristle showed on his chin. While she poured him another glass of tea, he put on his spectacles and re-examined with pleasure the luminous yellow, green, red little jars. His clumsy moist lips spelled out their eloquent labels: apricot, grape, beech plum, quince. He had got to crab apple, when the telephone rang again.

Santiago Nazarian

Santiago Nazarian (b. 1977), fiction writer, translator, and screenwriter, was born in Sao Paulo, Brazil. He is the son of a mother who loved books and a father who loved art. He remembers his home as "a battleground between literature and the visual arts. Every year my mom took one of my dad's canvases down from the wall to make room for another bookcase." After graduating from the university with a degree in advertising, Nazarian worked as a copywriter for a few years. In 2003 his first novel, *Olivio*, won the Conrado Wessel Literature Prize. He followed this book with four more novels before publishing a collection of short fiction, *Pornoghost*, in 2011. His story "Fish Spine" was included in the anthology *The Future Is Not for Us* (2012), published by Open Letter, the nonprofit translation press at the University of Rochester, New York. This anthology was created, as the prologue states, "to fight the internal editorial isolation in which the region [of Latin America] is submerged. It's very difficult, for instance, for an Ecuadorian or a Uruguayan to read a book published by a Paraguayan or a Guatemalan. This collection seeks to recover the active exchange with the reader who gives literature its only pertinent fire."

Nazarian's short fiction has appeared in many journals in Brazil and Latin America, as well as in Europe and the United States. He makes use of new technical media, understanding that his "literary generation has emerged with a new scenario, using blogs to say what you want, without the guarantee of a publisher." In 2007 he was chosen by the Hay Festival as one of the most talented Latin American writers under the age of thirty-nine.

As editor Diego Trelles Paz understood, in his fiction Nazarian writes a poetic prose that communicates a sense of being a "highly polished exercise in style, minimalistic and highly symbolic." The almost obsessive progression of short sentences that drive the narration in "Fish Spine" vividly suggest the poor working class protagonist's insecurity as he tries desperately to impress the girl he loves. In an interview, Nazarian stated that writing was his passion, his attempt "to materialize an inner universe." He feels that the short sentences he uses in his fiction "are more intuitive than conscious. . . . I can see the rhythm of the sentences, the words, the way I speak. . . . So if he 'left on the horse alone,' maybe I see it: 'He left. On the horse. Alone.'"

RELATED STORY
Julio Cortázar, "Axolotl," page 362.

Fish Spine

2012 / Translated by Janet Hendrickson

HAU TURNED THE FAUCET on with careful fingers. He would have to turn it off after washing his hands. They smelled like fish, fresh fish, like something rotting. Always. Scales on his fingers. He didn't want to contaminate the faucet. He would have to turn it off again, with clean hands. He washed them.

He bent over the sink and felt his back ache. He bent over the sink and felt his spine. He placed his hands on his back; he straightened up before the mirror. He looked into his eyes. He saw himself. No scales. No spine. No reflection of fish in his slanted eyes, in his adolescent face. Hau remained the same, despite his hands.

He took a hand off his back and turned off the faucet. He brought his fingers to his nose. He smelled. Still there. His spine hurt. The fish screamed. His slanted eyes squeezed even tighter before the mirror.

The whole day. Every morning. He helped his parents at their market stall. Knife on spine, fish on ice, lowered eyes, like his voice, though he spoke Portuguese better than they. He wrapped. Newspaper. Black ink. Stained fingers, sinking in the water. Frozen fingers, wrapping the fish, packing the scraps, the end of his adolescence.

Hau spent the whole morning waiting for his reflection in the mirror. His fingers under his nose. Soap, vanilla, to remove a daily life that wasn't his. Only a job. Only family. It wouldn't contaminate his poetry. In his fingers, it wouldn't contaminate his paper. He wrapped. He packed. He folded origami in his free time.

For her. When she passed. She lowered her eyes. She lowered her head. He hoped she didn't see, even if she felt. Even if she felt the smell of the stall miles away. She always passed by in a hurry. She never looked at him. Or maybe it was he who lowered his eyes. And she couldn't perceive him.

They met each other later. In the evening. When she asked him what he did. Or what was he going to do? Philosophy. Together in class, waiting for the entrance exam. Together at the bus stop, waiting for the bus to arrive. And goodnight. Tomorrow I wake up early to help my father.

They didn't go much further. They didn't give each other kisses or caresses, but they said hello. They shook hands and their fingers touched. He hoped his fingers didn't denounce him. The smell of fish. Everything in its place at the end of the day. Until dawn again, when the fish awaited him.

Brushing his teeth, he heard the first birdsongs; he looked at his own reflection in the mirror, foaming at the mouth. He spit. He brought his fingers to his mouth. He no longer felt his spine. At least the pain and smell didn't build up day after day; they disappeared after work without leaving long-term effects. One day his past would erase itself forever. And not even he would remember what fish smelled like.

Perfume. On a Friday night, to see his friends, to see her, until the morning. At a bar, over beers, they would celebrate a birthday. It wasn't his. It wasn't hers. But they would be together, and that was what mattered. He would be on the left, with the boys. Laughing, drinking, distilled, fermented. She would be there in front, with the women, beckoning, perfuming the atmosphere with colorful cocktails. Sitting on the edge of the street, in the gutter, where the market stalls would go up later.

The alcohol opened up his appetite, and the menu opened up his spine, with fish, dried cod, cod cakes, one piece per couple. A piece of provolone. Pies. Ketchup. Mayonnaise. Napkins to clean your fingers.

She pulled off a feat. She only used one. One napkin and she wiped her lipstick. Only one napkin and she handled. The mayonnaise. Ketchup. Provolone, pies, and fish spines, cod cakes. He accompanied the boys; he gathered a mountain of paper. Their napkins with ketchup, mayonnaise. He looked at her and swallowed. He looked at her and everything sweetened. He cleaned his hands on a stack of napkins.

Such women are needed, to make boys behave. Women are needed, so that boys use napkins. To drink a little more, to smile and hide, to hide the fish spines in their teeth. To hide the scales between their fingers. He looked at her and hid behind the paper. A piece, folded, origami.

She was there through it all on the right side of the table. Beside her friends, smiling with composure. The boys mocking. He, working. His fingers for her. His fingers shaking. His fingers working. His sweetened fingers, on paper, transforming into poetry all that he felt.

What did he feel? The gutter calling him. His friends calling for a drink. Beer, fermented, going down the wolves' mouths, fish spines. Hours later he would be there, his fingers frozen. With his fingers in the fish, on that same street, wrapping the women's dinners in paper, the dinners of the mothers, the mothers of their girls.

And poetry would just be black ink. The news would be mayonnaise, stained, on newsprint, on fish spines. He would just be another one. Squinting at the market. Eyes lowered like his voice, quiet.

He would work for the fish, fresh, dead, the true interest of all the women who approached him. They wouldn't sense the perfume on his neck. They wouldn't sense the pain in his spine.

With his fingers working quickly he concluded, though drunk, a job well done. Fish spine. Bar napkin. Origami. Perfect. Figures and poems for her, on a stainless piece of paper. A paper fish. "To dive with you."

She took the fish in her hands, with a smile on her lips. It was lovely. Origami. Her smile. It made the whole market sink beneath the sea and the marine life prevail. She brought it to her mouth, to her lipstick, and kissed it. "Oh, how funny, it even smells like fish."

Joyce Carol Oates

Joyce Carol Oates (b. 1938) was born in Lockport, New York, one of three children in a Roman Catholic family. She began to put picture stories down on paper even before she could write, and she remembers that her parents "dutifully" supplied her with lined tablets and gave her a typewriter when she was fourteen. In 1956, after Oates graduated from high school, she went on a scholarship to major in English at Syracuse University, but she did not devote most of her time to writing until after she received her M.A. from the University of Wisconsin in 1961. Discovering by chance that one of her stories had been cited in the honor roll of Martha Foley's annual *The Best American Short Stories*, Oates assembled the fourteen stories in her first book, *By the North Gate* (1963). Her career was launched, and as John Updike speculated, she "was perhaps born a hundred years too late; she needs a lustier audience, a race of Victorian word-eaters to be worthy of her astounding productivity, her tireless gift of self-enthrallment."

One of our most prolific authors, Oates has published many books, including over a hundred stories. She also writes poetry and literary criticism, including the volume *New Heaven, New Earth* (1974), analyzing the "visionary experience in literature" as exemplified in the work of Henry James, Virginia Woolf, Franz Kafka, D. H. Lawrence, Flannery O'Connor, and others. As a writer, critic, and professor at Princeton University, Oates dedicates her life to "promoting and exploring literature. . . . I am not conscious of being in any particular literary tradition, though I share with my contemporaries an intense interest in the formal aspects of writing; each of my books is an experiment of a kind, an investigation of the relationship between a certain consciousness and its formal aesthetic expression."

The story "Where Are You Going, Where Have You Been?" was first published in *Epoch* in 1966; it was included in *The Best American Short Stories* of 1967 and *Prize Stories: The O. Henry Awards 1968* and was made into a film. Oates has said that this story, based on a 1966 article by Dan Moser in *Life* magazine about a Tucson, Arizona, murderer, has been "constantly misunderstood by one generation, and intuitively understood by another." She sees the story as dealing with a human being "struggling heroically to define personal identity in the face of incredible opposition, even in the face of death itself." She also had in mind Bob Dylan songs such as "Like a Rolling Stone" and "It's All Over Now, Baby Blue." Some recent Oates' collections are *Heat and Other Stories* (1992), *Haunted: Tales of the Grotesque* (1994), *Will You Always Love Me and Other Stories* (1996), *I Am No One You Know* (2004), *Wild Nights* (2008), and *The Corn Maiden and Other Nightmares* (2011).

RELATED STORY
Anton Chekhov, "The Lady with the Little Dog," page 271.

RELATED COMMENTARIES
Matthew C. Brennan, "Plotting against Chekhov: Joyce Carol Oates and 'The Lady with the Dog,'" page 1400.

RELATED CASEBOOK
Joyce Carol Oates, "The Parables of Flannery O'Connor," page 1600; See Casebook on Joyce Carol Oates's "Where Are You Going, Where Have You Been?," pages 1616–1617, including Joyce Carol Oates, "Stories That Define Me: The Making of a Writer," page 1617; Joyce Carol Oates, "*Smooth Talk*: Short Story into Film," page 1619; Don Moser, "The Pied Piper of Tucson: He Cruised in a Golden Car, Looking for the Action," page 1622.

The Lady with the Pet Dog

1972

I

Strangers parted as if to make way for him.

There he stood. He was there in the aisle, a few yards away, watching her.

She leaned forward at once in her seat, her hand jerked up to her face as if to ward off a blow — but then the crowd in the aisle hid him, he was gone. She pressed both hands against her cheeks. He was not there, she had imagined him.

"My God," she whispered.

She was alone. Her husband had gone out to the foyer to make a telephone call; it was intermission at the concert, a Thursday evening.

Now she saw him again, clearly. He was standing there. He was staring at her. Her blood rocked in her body, draining out of her head . . . she was going to faint. . . . They stared at each other. They gave no sign of recognition. Only when he took a step forward did she shake her head *no — no — keep away*. It was not possible.

When her husband returned, she was staring at the place in the aisle where her lover had been standing. Her husband leaned forward to interrupt that stare.

"What's wrong?" he said. "Are you sick?"

Panic rose in her in long shuddering waves. She tried to get to her feet, panicked at the thought of fainting here, and her husband took hold of her. She stood like an aged woman, clutching the seat before her.

At home he helped her up the stairs and she lay down. Her head was like a large piece of crockery that had to be held still, it was so heavy. She was still panicked. She felt it in the shallows of her face, behind her knees, in the pit of her stomach. It sickened her, it made her think of mucus, of something thick and gray congested inside her, stuck to her, that was herself and yet not herself — a poison.

She lay with her knees drawn up toward her chest, her eyes hotly open, while her husband spoke to her. She imagined that other man saying, *Why did you run away from me?* Her husband was saying other words. She tried to listen to them. He was going to call the doctor, he said, and she tried to sit up. "No, I'm all right now," she said quickly. The panic was like lead inside her, so thickly congested. How slow love was to drain out of her, how fluid and sticky it was inside her head!

Her husband believed her. No doctor. No threat. Grateful, she drew her husband down to her. They embraced, not comfortably. For years now they had not been comfortable together, in their intimacy and at a distance, and now they struggled gently as if the paces of this dance were too rigorous for them. It was something they might have known once, but had now outgrown. The panic in her thickened at this double betrayal: she drew her husband to her, she caressed him wildly, she shut her eyes to think about that other man.

A crowd of men and women parting, unexpectedly, and there he stood — there he stood — she kept seeing him, and yet her vision blotched at the memory. It had been finished between them, six months before, but he had come out here . . . and she had escaped him, now she was lying in her husband's arms, in his embrace, her face pressed against his. It was a kind of sleep, this love-making. She felt herself falling asleep, her body falling from her. Her eyes shut.

"I love you," her husband said fiercely, angrily.

She shut her eyes and thought of that other man, as if betraying him would give her life a center.

"Did I hurt you? Are you — ?" her husband whispered.

Always this hot flashing of shame between them, the shame of her husband's near failure, the clumsiness of his love —

"You didn't hurt me," she said.

II

They had said good-by six months before. He drove her from Nantucket, where they had met, to Albany, New York, where she visited her sister. The hours of intimacy in the car had sealed something between them, a vow of silence and impersonality: she recalled the movement of the highways, the passing of other cars, the natural rhythms of the day hypnotizing her toward sleep while he drove. She trusted him, she could sleep in his presence. Yet she could not really fall asleep in spite of her exhaustion, and she kept jerking awake, frightened, to discover that nothing had changed — still the stranger who was driving her to Albany, still the highway, the sky, the antiseptic odor of the rented car, the sense of a rhythm behind the rhythm of the air that might unleash itself at any second. Everywhere on this highway, at this moment, there were men and women driving together, bonded together — what did that mean, to be together? What did it mean to enter into a bond with another person?

No, she did not really trust him; she did not really trust men. He would glance at her with his small cautious smile and she felt a declaration of shame between them.

Shame.

In her head she rehearsed conversations. She said bitterly, "You'll be relieved when we get to Albany. Relieved to get rid of me." They had spent so many days talking, confessing too much, driven to a pitch of childish excitement, laughing together on the beach, breaking into that pose of laughter that seems to eradicate the soul, so many days of this that the silence of the trip was like the silence of a hospital — all these surface noises, these rattles and hums, but an interior silence, a befuddlement. She said to him in her imagination, "One of us should die." Then she leaned over to touch him. She caressed the back of his neck. She said, aloud, "Would you like me to drive for a while?"

They stopped at a picnic area where other cars were stopped — couples, families — and walked together, smiling at their good luck. He put his arm around her shoulders and she sensed how they were in a posture together, a man and a woman forming a posture, a figure, that someone might sketch and show to them. She said slowly, "I don't want to go back. . . ."

Silence. She looked up at him. His face was heavy with her words, as if she had pulled at his skin with her fingers. Children ran nearby and distracted him — yes, he was a father too, his children ran like that, they tugged at his skin with their light, busy fingers.

"Are you so unhappy?" he said.

"I'm not unhappy, back there. I'm nothing. There's nothing to me," she said.

They stared at each other. The sensation between them was intense, exhausting. She thought that this man was her savior, that he had come to her at a time in her life when her life demanded completion, an end, a permanent fixing of all that was troubled and shifting and deadly. And yet it was absurd to think this. No person could save another. So she drew back from him and released him.

A few hours later they stopped at a gas station in a small city. She went to the women's rest room, having to ask the attendant for a key, and when she came back her eye jumped nervously onto the rented car — why? did she think he might have driven off without her? — onto the man, her friend, standing in conversation with the young attendant. Her friend was as old as her husband, over forty, with lanky, sloping shoulders, a full body, his hair thick, a dark, burnished brown, a festive color that made her eye twitch a little — and his hands were always moving, always those rapid conversational circles, going nowhere, gestures that were at once a little aggressive and apologetic.

She put her hand on his arm, a claim. He turned to her and smiled and she felt that she loved him, that everything in her life had forced her to this moment and that she had no choice about it.

They sat in the car for two hours, in Albany, in the parking lot of a Howard Johnson's restaurant, talking, trying to figure out their past. There was no future. They concentrated on the past, the several days behind them, lit up with a hot, dazzling August sun, like explosions that already belonged to other people, to strangers. Her face was faintly reflected in the green-tinted curve of the windshield, but she could not have recognized that face. She began to cry; she told herself: *I am not here, this will pass, this is nothing.* Still, she could not stop crying. The muscles of her face were springy, like a child's, unpredictable muscles. He stroked her arms, her shoulders, trying to comfort her. "This is so hard . . . this is impossible . . ." he said. She felt panic for the world outside this car, all that was not herself and this man, and at the same time she understood that she was free of him, as people are free of other people, she would leave him soon, safely, and within a few days he would have fallen into the past, the impersonal past. . . .

"I'm so ashamed of myself!" she said finally.

She returned to her husband and saw that another woman, a shadow-woman, had taken her place — noiseless and convincing, like a dancer performing certain difficult steps. Her husband folded her in his arms and talked to her of his own loneliness, his worries about his business, his health, his mother, kept tranquilized and mute in a nursing home, and her spirit detached itself from her and drifted about the rooms of the large house she lived in with her husband, a shadow-woman delicate and imprecise. There was no boundary to her, no edge. Alone, she took hot baths and sat exhausted in the steaming water, wondering at her perpetual exhaustion. All that winter she noticed the limp, languid weight of her arms, her veins bulging slightly with the pressure of her extreme weariness. *This is fate*, she thought, to be here and not there, to be one person and not another, a certain man's wife and not the wife of another man. The long, slow pain of this certainty rose in her, but it never became clear, it was baffling and imprecise. She could not be serious about it; she kept congratulating herself on her own good luck, to have escaped so easily, to have freed herself. So much love had gone into the first several years of her marriage that there wasn't much left, now, for another man. . . . She was certain of that. But the bath water made her dizzy, all that perpetual heat, and one day in January she drew a razor blade lightly across the inside of her arm, near the elbow, to see what would happen.

Afterward she wrapped a small towel around it, to stop the bleeding. The towel soaked through. She wrapped a bath towel around that and walked through the empty rooms of her home, lightheaded, hardly aware of the stubborn seeping of blood. There was no boundary to her in this house, no precise limit. She could flow out like her own blood and come to no end.

She sat for a while on a blue love seat, her mind empty. Her husband telephoned her when he would be staying late at the plant. He talked to her always about his plans, his problems, his business friends, his future. It was obvious that he had a future. As he spoke she nodded to encourage him, and her heartbeat quickened with the memory of her own, personal shame, the shame of this man's particular, private wife. One evening at dinner he leaned forward and put his head in his arms and fell asleep, like a child. She sat at the table with him for a while, watching him. His hair had gone gray, almost white, at the temples — no one would guess that he was so quick, so careful a man, still fairly young about the eyes. She put her hand on his head, lightly, as if to prove to herself that he was real. He slept, exhausted.

One evening they went to a concert and she looked up to see her lover there, in the crowded aisle, in this city, watching her. He was standing there, with his overcoat on, watching her. She went cold. That morning the telephone had rung while her husband was still home, and she had heard him answer it, heard him hang up — it must have been a wrong number — and when the telephone rang again, at 9:30, she had been afraid to answer it. She had left home to be out of the range of that ringing, but now, in this public place, in this busy auditorium, she found herself staring at that man, unable to make any sign to him, any gesture of recognition. . . .

He would have come to her but she shook her head. *No. Stay away.*

Her husband helped her out of the row of seats, saying, "Excuse us, please. Excuse us," so that strangers got to their feet, quickly, alarmed, to let them pass. Was that woman about to faint? What was wrong?

At home she felt the blood drain slowly back into her head. Her husband embraced her hips, pressing his face against her, in that silence that belonged to the earliest days of their marriage. She thought, *He will drive it out of me.* He made love to her and she was back in the auditorium again, sitting alone, now that the concert was over. The stage was empty; the heavy velvet curtains had not been drawn; the musicians' chairs were empty, everything was silent and expectant; in the aisle her lover stood and smiled at her — her husband was impatient. He was apart from her, working on her, operating on her; and then, stricken, he whispered, "Did I hurt you?"

The telephone rang the next morning. Dully, sluggishly, she answered it. She recognized his voice at once — that "Anna?" with its lifting of the second syllable, questioning and apologetic and making its claim — "Yes, what do you want?" she said.

"Just to see you. Please —"

"I can't."

"Anna, I'm sorry, I didn't mean to upset you —"

"I can't see you."

"Just for a few minutes — I have to talk to you —"

"But why, why now? Why now?" she said.

She heard her voice rising, but she could not stop it. He began to talk again, drowning her out. She remembered his rapid conversation. She remembered his gestures, the witty energetic circling of his hands.

"Please don't hang up!" he cried.

"I can't — I don't want to go through it again —"

"I'm not going to hurt you. Just tell me how you are."

"Everything is the same."

"Everything is the same with me."

She looked up at the ceiling, shyly. "Your wife? Your children?"

"The same."

"Your son?"

"He's fine —"

"I'm glad to hear that. I —"

"Is it still the same with you, your marriage? Tell me what you feel. What are you thinking?"

"I don't know. . . ."

She remembered his intense, eager words, the movement of his hands, that impatient precise fixing of the air by his hands, the jabbing of his fingers.

"Do you love me?" he said.

She could not answer.

"I'll come over to see you," he said.

"No," she said.

What will come next, what will happen?

Flesh hardening on his body, aging. Shrinking. He will grow old, but not soft like her husband. They are two different types: he is nervous, lean, energetic, wise. She will grow thinner, as the tension radiates out from her backbone, wearing down her flesh. Her collarbones will jut out of her skin. Her husband, caressing her in their bed, will discover that she is another woman — she is not there with him — instead she is rising in an elevator in a downtown hotel, carrying a book as a prop, or walking quickly away from that hotel, her head bent and filled with secrets. Love, what to do with it? . . . Useless as moths' wings, as moths' fluttering. . . . She feels the flutterings of silky, crazy wings in her chest.

He flew out to visit her every several weeks, staying at a different hotel each time. He telephoned her, and she drove down to park in an underground garage at the very center of the city.

She lay in his arms while her husband talked to her, miles away, one body fading into another. He will grow old, his body will change, she thought, pressing her cheek against the back of one of these men. If it was her lover, they were in a hotel room: always the propped-up little booklet describing the hotel's many services, with color photographs of its cocktail lounge and dining room and coffee shop. Grow old, leave me, die, go back to your neurotic wife and your sad, ordinary children, she thought, but still her eyes closed gratefully against his skin and she felt how complete their silence was, how they had come to rest in each other.

"Tell me about your life here. The people who love you," he said, as he always did.

One afternoon they lay together for four hours. It was her birthday and she was intoxicated with her good fortune, this prize of the afternoon, this man in her arms! She was a little giddy, she talked too much. She told him about her parents, about her husband. . . . "They were all people I believed in, but it turned out wrong. Now, I believe in you. . . ." He laughed as if shocked by her words. She did not understand. Then she understood. "But I believe truly in you. I can't think of myself without you," she said. . . . He spoke of his wife, her ambitions, her intelligence, her use of the children against him, her use of his younger son's blindness, all of his words gentle and hypnotic and convincing in the late afternoon peace of this hotel room . . . and she felt the terror of laughter, threatening laughter. Their words, like their bodies, were aging.

She dressed quickly in the bathroom, drawing her long hair up around the back of her head, fixing it as always, anxious that everything be the same. Her face was slightly raw, from his face. The rubbing of his skin. Her eyes were too bright, wearily bright. Her hair was blond but not so blond as it had been that summer in the white Nantucket air.

She ran water and splashed it on her face. She blinked at the water. Blind. Drowning. She thought with satisfaction that soon, soon, he would be back home, in that house on Long Island she had never seen, with that woman she had never seen, sitting on the edge of another bed, putting on his shoes. She wanted nothing except to be free of him. Why not be free? *Oh,* she thought suddenly, *I will follow you back and kill you. You and her and the little boy. What is there to stop me?*

She left him. Everyone on the street pitied her, that look of absolute zero.

III

A man and a child, approaching her. The sharp acrid smell of fish. The crashing of waves. Anna pretended not to notice the father with his son — there was something strange about them. That frank, silent intimacy, too gentle, the man's bare feet in the water and the boy a few feet away, leaning away from his father. He was about nine years old and still his father held his hand.

A small yipping dog, a golden dog, bounded near them.

Anna turned shyly back to her reading; she did not want to have to speak to these neighbors. She saw the man's shadow falling over her legs, then over the pages of her book, and she had the idea that he wanted to see what she was reading. The dog nuzzled her; the man called him away.

She watched them walk down the beach. She was relieved that the man had not spoken to her.

She saw them in town later that day, the two of them brown-haired and patient, now wearing sandals, walking with that same look of care. The man's white shorts were soiled and a little baggy. His pullover shirt was a faded green. His face was broad, the cheekbones wide, spaced widely apart, the eyes stark in their sockets, as if they fastened onto objects for no reason, ponderous and edgy. The little boy's face was pale and sharp; his lips were perpetually parted.

Anna realized that the child was blind.

The next morning, early, she caught sight of them again. For some reason she went to the back door of her cottage. She faced the sea breeze eagerly. Her heart hammered. . . . She had been here, in her family's old house, for three days, alone, bitterly satisfied at being alone, and now it was a puzzle to her how her soul strained to fly outward, to meet with another person. She watched the man with his son, his cautious, rather stooped shoulders above the child's small shoulders.

The man was carrying something, it looked like a notebook. He sat on the sand, not far from Anna's spot of the day before, and the dog rushed up to them. The child approached the edge of the ocean, timidly. He moved in short jerky steps, his legs stiff. The dog ran around him. Anna heard the child crying out a word that sounded like "Ty" — it must have been the dog's name — and then the man joined in, his voice heavy and firm.

"Ty —"

Anna tied her hair back with a yellow scarf and went down to the beach.

The man glanced around at her. He smiled. She stared past him at the waves. To talk to him or not to talk — she had the freedom of that choice. For a moment she felt that she had made a mistake, that the child and the dog would not protect her, that behind this man's ordinary, friendly face there was a certain arrogant maleness — then she relented, she smiled shyly.

"A nice house you've got there," the man said.

She nodded her thanks.

The man pushed his sunglasses up on his forehead. Yes, she recognized the eyes of the day before — intelligent and nervous, the sockets pale, untanned.

"Is that your telephone ringing?" he said.

She did not bother to listen. "It's a wrong number," she said.

Her husband calling: she had left home for a few days, to be alone.

But the man, settling himself on the sand, seemed to misinterpret this. He smiled in surprise, one corner of his mouth higher than the other. He said nothing. Anna wondered: *What is he thinking?* The dog was leaping about her, panting against her legs, and she laughed in embarrassment. She bent to pet it, grateful for its busyness. "Don't let him jump up on you," the man said. "He's a nuisance."

The dog was a small golden retriever, a young dog. The blind child, standing now in the water, turned to call the dog to him. His voice was shrill and impatient.

"Our house is the third one down — the white one," the man said.

She turned, startled. "Oh, did you buy it from Dr. Patrick? Did he die?"

"Yes, finally. . . ."

Her eyes wandered nervously over the child and the dog. She felt the nervous beat of her heart out to the very tips of her fingers, the fleshy tips of her fingers: little hearts were there, pulsing. *What is he thinking?* The man had opened his notebook. He had a piece of charcoal and he began to sketch something.

Anna looked down at him. She saw the top of his head, his thick brown hair, the freckles on his shoulders, the quick, deft movement of his hand. Upside down, Anna herself being drawn. She smiled in surprise.

"Let me draw you. Sit down," he said.

She knelt awkwardly a few yards away. He turned the page of the sketch pad. The dog ran to her and she sat, straightening out her skirt beneath her, flinching from the dog's tongue. "Ty!" cried the child. Anna sat, and slowly the pleasure of the moment began to glow in her; her skin flushed with gratitude.

She sat there for nearly an hour. The man did not talk much. Back and forth the dog bounded, shaking itself. The child came to sit near them, in silence. Anna felt that she was drifting into a kind of trance while the man sketched her, half a dozen rapid sketches, the surface of her face given up to him. "Where are you from?" the man asked.

"Ohio. My husband lives in Ohio."

She wore no wedding band.

"Your wife —" Anna began.

"Yes?"

"Is she here?"

"Not right now."

She was silent, ashamed. She had asked an improper question. But the man did not seem to notice. He continued drawing her, bent over the sketch pad. When Anna said she had to go, he showed her the drawings — one after another of her, Anna, recognizably Anna, a woman in her early thirties, her hair smooth and flat across the top of her head, tied behind by a scarf. "Take the one you like best," he said, and she picked one of her with the dog in her lap, sitting very straight, her brows and eyes clearly defined, her lips girlishly pursed, the dog and her dress suggested by a few quick irregular lines.

"Lady with pet dog," the man said.

She spent the rest of that day reading, nearer her cottage. It was not really a cottage—it was a two-story house, large and ungainly and weathered. It was mixed up in her mind with her family, her own childhood, and she glanced up from her book, perplexed, as if waiting for one of her parents or her sister to come up to her. Then she thought of that man, the man with the blind child, the man with the dog, and she could not concentrate on her reading. Someone—probably her father—had marked a passage that must be important, but she kept reading and rereading it: *We try to discover in things, endeared to us on that account, the spiritual glamour which we ourselves have cast upon them; we are disillusioned, and learn that they are in themselves barren and devoid of the charm that they owed, in our minds, to the association of certain ideas. . . .*

She thought again of the man on the beach. She lay the book aside and thought of him: his eyes, his aloneness, his drawings of her.

They began seeing each other after that. He came to her front door in the evening, without the child; he drove her into town for dinner. She was shy and extremely pleased. The darkness of the expensive restaurant released her; she heard herself chatter; she leaned forward and seemed to be offering her face up to him, listening to him. He talked about his work on a Long Island newspaper and she seemed to be listening to him, as she stared at his face, arranging her own face into the expression she had seen in that charcoal drawing. Did he see her like that, then?—girlish and withdrawn and patrician? She felt the weight of his interest in her, a force that fell upon her like a blow. A repeated blow. Of course he was married, he had children—of course she was married, permanently married. This flight from her husband was not important. She had left him before, to be alone, it was not important. Everything in her was slender and delicate and not important.

They walked for hours after dinner, looking at the other strollers, the weekend visitors, the tourists, the couples like themselves. Surely they were mistaken for a couple, a married couple. *This is the hour in which everything is decided*, Anna thought. They had both had several drinks and they talked a great deal. Anna found herself saying too much, stopping and starting giddily. She put her hand to her forehead, feeling faint.

"It's from the sun—you've had too much sun—" he said.

At the door to her cottage, on the front porch, she heard herself asking him if he would like to come in. She allowed him to lead her inside, to close the door. *This is not important*, she thought clearly, *he doesn't mean it, he doesn't love me, nothing will come of it*. She was frightened, yet it seemed to her necessary to give in; she had to leave Nantucket with that act completed, an act of adultery, an accomplishment she would take back to Ohio and to her marriage.

Later, incredibly, she heard herself asking: "Do you . . . do you love me?"

"You're so beautiful!" he said, amazed.

She felt this beauty, shy and glowing and centered in her eyes. He stared at her. In this large, drafty house, alone together, they were like accomplices, conspirators. She could not think: how old was she? which year was this? They had done something unforgivable together, and the knowledge of it was tugging at their faces. A cloud seemed to pass over her. She felt herself smiling shrilly.

Afterward, a peculiar raspiness, a dryness of breath. He was silent. She felt a strange, idle fear, a sense of the danger outside this room and this old, comfortable bed — a danger that would not recognize her as the lady in that drawing, the lady with the pet dog. There was nothing to say to this man, this stranger. She felt the beauty draining out of her face, her eyes fading.

"I've got to be alone," she told him.

He left, and she understood that she would not see him again. She stood by the window of the room, watching the ocean. A sense of shame overpowered her: it was smeared everywhere on her body, the smell of it, the richness of it. She tried to recall him, and his face was confused in her memory: she would have to shout to him across a jumbled space, she would have to wave her arms wildly. *You love me! You must love me!* But she knew he did not love her, and she did not love him; he was a man who drew everything up into himself, like all men, walking away, free to walk away, free to have his own thoughts, free to envision her body, all the secrets of her body. . . . And she lay down again in the bed, feeling how heavy this body had become, her insides heavy with shame, the very backs of her eyelids coated with shame.

"This is the end of one part of my life," she thought.

But in the morning the telephone rang. She answered it. It was her lover: they talked brightly and happily. She could hear the eagerness in his voice, the love in his voice, that same still, sad amazement — she understood how simple life was, there were no problems.

They spent most of their time on the beach, with the child and the dog. He joked and was serious at the same time. He said, once, "You have defined my soul for me," and she laughed to hide her alarm. In a few days it was time for her to leave. He got a sitter for the boy and took the ferry with her to the mainland, then rented a car to drive her up to Albany. She kept thinking: *Now something will happen. It will come to an end.* But most of the drive was silent and hypnotic. She wanted him to joke with her, to say again that she had defined his soul for him, but he drove fast, he was serious, she distrusted the hawkish look of his profile — she did not know him at all. At a gas station she splashed her face with cold water. Alone in the grubby little rest room, shaky and very much alone. In such places are women totally alone with their bodies. The body grows heavier, more evil, in such silence. . . . On the beach everything had been noisy with sunlight and gulls and waves; here, as if run to earth, everything was cramped and silent and dead.

She went outside, squinting. There he was, talking with the station attendant. She could not think as she returned to him whether she wanted to live or not.

She stayed in Albany for a few days, then flew home to her husband. He met her at the airport, near the luggage counter, where her three pieces of pale-brown luggage were brought to him on a conveyer belt, to be claimed by him. He kissed her on the cheek. They shook hands, a little embarrassed. She had come home again.

"How will I live out the rest of my life?" she wondered.

In January her lover spied on her: she glanced up and saw him, in a public place, in the DeRoy Symphony Hall. She was paralyzed with fear. She nearly fainted. In this faint she felt her husband's body, loving her, working its love upon her, and she shut her eyes harder to keep out the certainty of his love — sometimes he failed at loving her, sometimes he succeeded, it had nothing to do with her or her pity or her ten years of love for him, it had nothing to do with a woman at all. It was a private act accomplished by a man, a husband or a lover, in communion with his own soul, his manhood.

Her husband was forty-two years old now, growing slowly into middle age, getting heavier, softer. Her lover was about the same age, narrower in the shoulders, with a full, solid chest, yet lean, nervous. She thought, in her paralysis, of men and how they love freely and eagerly so long as their bodies are capable of love, love for a woman; and then, as love fades in their bodies, it fades from their souls and they become immune and immortal and ready to die.

Her husband was a little rough with her, as if impatient with himself. "I love you," he said fiercely, angrily. And then, ashamed, he said, "Did I hurt you? . . ."

"You didn't hurt me," she said.

Her voice was too shrill for their embrace.

While he was in the bathroom she went to her closet and took out that drawing of the summer before. There she was, on the beach at Nantucket, a lady with a pet dog, her eyes large and defined, the dog in her lap hardly more than a few snarls, a few coarse soft lines of charcoal . . . her dress smeared, her arms oddly limp . . . her hands not well drawn at all. . . . She tried to think: did she love the man who had drawn this? did he love her? The fever in her husband's body had touched her and driven her temperature up, and now she stared at the drawing with a kind of lust, fearful of seeing an ugly soul in that woman's face, fearful of seeing the face suddenly through her lover's eyes. She breathed quickly and harshly, staring at the drawing.

And so, the next day, she went to him at his hotel. She wept, pressing against him, demanding of him, "What do you want? Why are you here? Why don't you let me alone?" He told her that he wanted nothing. He expected nothing. He would not cause trouble.

"I want to talk about last August," he said.

"Don't —" she said.

She was hypnotized by his gesturing hands, his nervousness, his obvious agitation. He kept saying, "I understand. I'm making no claims upon you."

They became lovers again.

He called room service for something to drink and they sat side by side on his bed, looking through a copy of *The New Yorker*, laughing at the cartoons. It was so peaceful in this room, so complete. They were on a holiday. It was a secret holiday. Four-thirty in the afternoon, on a Friday, an ordinary Friday: a secret holiday.

"I won't bother you again," he said.

He flew back to see her again in March, and in late April. He telephoned her from his hotel — a different hotel each time — and she came down to him at once. She rose to him in various elevators, she knocked on the doors of various rooms, she stepped into his embrace, breathless and guilty and already angry with him, pleading with him. One morning in May, when he telephoned, she pressed her forehead against the doorframe and could not speak. He kept saying, "What's wrong? Can't you talk? Aren't you alone?" She felt that she was going insane. Her head would burst. Why, why did he love her, why did he pursue her? Why did he want her to die?

She went to him in the hotel room. A familiar room: had they been here before? "Everything is repeating itself. Everything is stuck," she said. He framed her face in his hands and said that she looked thinner — was she sick? — what was wrong? She shook herself free. He, her lover, looked about the same. There was a small, angry pimple on his neck. He stared at her, eagerly and suspiciously. Did she bring bad news?

"So you love me? You love me?" she asked.

"Why are you so angry?"

"I want to be free of you. The two of us free of each other."

"That isn't true — you don't want that —"

He embraced her. She was wild with that old, familiar passion for him, her body clinging to his, her arms not strong enough to hold him. Ah, what despair! — what bitter hatred she felt! — she needed this man for her salvation, he was all she had to live for, and yet she could not believe in him. He embraced her thighs, her hips, kissing her, pressing his warm face against her, and yet she could not believe in him, not really. She needed him in order to live, but he was not worth her love, he was not worth her dying. . . . She promised herself this: when she got back home, when she was alone, she would draw the razor more deeply across her arm.

The telephone rang and he answered it: a wrong number.

"Jesus," he said.

They lay together, still. She imagined their posture like this, the two of them one figure, one substance; and outside this room and this bed there was a universe of disjointed, separate things, blank things, that had nothing to do with them. She would not be Anna out there, the lady in the drawing. He would not be her lover.

"I love you so much . . ." she whispered.

"Please don't cry! We have only a few hours, please. . . ."

It was absurd, their clinging together like this. She saw them as a single figure in a drawing, their arms and legs entwined, their heads pressing mutely together. Helpless substance, so heavy and warm and doomed. It was absurd that any human being should be so important to another human being. She wanted to laugh: a laugh might free them both.

She could not laugh.

Sometime later he said, as if they had been arguing, "Look. It's you. You're the one who doesn't want to get married. You lie to me —"

"Lie to you?"

"You love me but you won't marry me, because you want something left over — something not finished — all your life you can attribute your misery to me, to our not being married — you are using me —"

"Stop it! You'll make me hate you!" she cried.

"You can say to yourself that you're miserable because of *me*. We will never be married, you will never be happy, neither one of us will ever be happy —"

"I don't want to hear this!" she said.

She pressed her hands flatly against her face.

She went to the bathroom to get dressed. She washed her face and part of her body, quickly. The fever was in her, in the pit of her belly. She would rush home and strike a razor across the inside of her arm and free that pressure, that fever.

The impatient bulging of the veins: an ordeal over.

The demand of the telephone's ringing: that ordeal over.

The nuisance of getting the car and driving home in all that five o'clock traffic: an ordeal too much for a woman.

The movement of this stranger's body in hers: over, finished.

Now, dressed, a little calmer, they held hands and talked. They had to talk swiftly, to get all their news in: he did not trust the people who worked for him, he had faith in no one, his wife had moved to a textbook publishing company and was doing well, she had inherited a Ben Shahn painting from her father and wanted to "touch it up a little" — she was crazy! — his blind son was at another school, doing fairly well, in fact his children were all doing fairly well in spite of the stupid mistake of their parents' marriage — and what about her? what about her life? She told him in a rush the one thing he wanted to hear: that she lived with her husband lovelessly, the two of them polite strangers, sharing a bed, lying side by side in the night in that bed, bodies out of which souls had fled. There was no longer even any shame between them.

"And what about me? Do you feel shame with me still?" he asked.

She did not answer. She moved away from him and prepared to leave.

Then, a minute later, she happened to catch sight of his reflection in the bureau mirror — he was glancing down at himself, checking himself mechanically, impersonally, preparing also to leave. He too would leave this room: he too was headed somewhere else.

She stared at him. It seemed to her that in this instant he was breaking from her, the image of her lover fell free of her, breaking from her . . . and she realized that he existed in a dimension quite apart from her, a mysterious being. And suddenly, joyfully, she felt a miraculous calm. This man was her husband, truly — they were truly married, here in this room — they had been married haphazardly and accidentally for a long time. In another part of the city she had another husband, a "husband," but she had not betrayed that man, not really. This man, whom she loved above any other person in the world, above even her own self-pitying sorrow and her own life, was her truest lover, her destiny. And she did not hate him, she did not hate herself any longer; she did not wish to die; she was flooded with a strange certainty, a sense of gratitude, of pure selfless energy. It was obvious to her that she had, all along, been behaving correctly; out of instinct.

What triumph, to love like this in any room, anywhere, risking even the craziest of accidents!

"Why are you so happy? What's wrong?" he asked, startled. He stared at her. She felt the abrupt concentration in him, the focusing of his vision on her, almost a bitterness in his face, as if he feared her. What, was it beginning all over again? Their love beginning again, in spite of them? "How can you look so happy?" he asked. "We don't have any right to it. Is it because . . . ?"

"Yes," she said.

Where Are You Going, Where Have You Been?

1966

For Bob Dylan

HER NAME WAS Connie. She was fifteen and she had a quick nervous giggling habit of craning her neck to glance into mirrors, or checking other people's faces to make sure her own was all right. Her mother, who noticed everything and knew everything and who hadn't much reason any longer to look at her own face, always scolded Connie about it. "Stop gawking at yourself, who are you? You think you're so pretty?" she would say. Connie would raise her eyebrows at these familiar complaints and look right through her mother, into a shadowy vision of herself as she was right at that moment: she knew she was pretty and that was everything. Her mother had been pretty once too, if you could believe those old snapshots in the album, but now her looks were gone and that was why she was always after Connie.

"Why don't you keep your room clean like your sister? How've you got your hair fixed — what the hell stinks? Hair spray? You don't see your sister using that junk."

Her sister June was twenty-four and still lived at home. She was a secretary in the high school Connie attended, and if that wasn't bad enough — with her in the same building — she was so plain and chunky and steady that Connie had to hear her praised all the time by her mother and her mother's sisters. June did this, June did that, she saved money and helped clean the house and cooked and Connie couldn't do a thing, her mind was all filled with trashy daydreams. Their father was away at work most of the time and when he came home he wanted supper and he read the newspaper at supper and after supper he went to bed. He didn't bother talking much to them, but around his bent head Connie's mother kept picking at her until Connie wished her mother was dead and she herself was dead and it was all over. "She makes me want to throw up sometimes," she complained to her friends. She had a high, breathless, amused voice which made everything she said a little forced, whether it was sincere or not.

There was one good thing: June went places with girl friends of hers, girls who were just as plain and steady as she, and so when Connie wanted to do that her mother had no objections. The father of Connie's best girl friend drove the girls the three miles to town and left them off at a shopping plaza, so that they could walk through the stores or go to a movie, and when he came to pick them up again at eleven he never bothered to ask what they had done.

They must have been familiar sights, walking around that shopping plaza in their shorts and flat ballerina slippers that always scuffed the sidewalk, with charm bracelets jingling on their thin wrists; they would lean together to whisper and laugh secretly if someone passed by who amused or interested them. Connie had long dark blond hair that drew anyone's eye to it, and she wore part of it pulled up on her head and puffed out and the rest of it she let fall down her back. She wore a pullover jersey blouse that looked one way when she was at home and another way when she was away from home. Everything about her had two sides to it, one for home and one for anywhere that was not home: her walk that could be childlike and bobbing, or languid enough to make anyone think she was hearing music in her head, her mouth which was pale and smirking most of the time, but bright and pink on these evenings out, her laugh which was cynical and drawling at home — "Ha, ha, very funny" — but high-pitched and nervous anywhere else, like the jingling of the charms on her bracelet.

Sometimes they did go shopping or to a movie, but sometimes they went across the highway, ducking fast across the busy road, to a drive-in restaurant where older kids hung out. The restaurant was shaped like a big bottle, though squatter than a real bottle, and on its cap was a revolving figure of a grinning boy who held a hamburger aloft. One night in midsummer they ran across, breathless with daring, and right away someone leaned out a car window and invited them over, but it was just a boy from high school they didn't like. It made them feel good to be able to ignore him. They went up through the maze of parked and cruising cars to the bright-lit, fly-infested restaurant, their faces pleased and expectant as if they were entering a sacred building that loomed out of the night to give them what haven and what blessing they yearned for. They sat at the counter and crossed their legs at the ankles, their thin shoulders rigid with excitement and listened to the music that made everything so good: the music was always in the background like music at a church service, it was something to depend upon.

A boy named Eddie came in to talk with them. He sat backwards on his stool, turning himself jerkily around in semi-circles and then stopping and turning again, and after a while he asked Connie if she would like something to eat. She said she did and so she tapped her friend's arm on her way out — her friend pulled her face up into a brave droll look — and Connie said she would meet her at eleven, across the way. "I just hate to leave her like that," Connie said earnestly, but the boy said that she wouldn't be alone for long. So they went out to his car and on the way Connie couldn't help but let her eyes wander over the windshields and faces all around her, her face gleaming with the joy that had nothing to do with Eddie or even this place; it might have been the music. She drew her shoulders up and sucked in her breath with the pure pleasure of being alive, and just at that moment she happened to glance at a face just a few feet from hers. It was a boy with shaggy black hair, in a convertible jalopy painted gold. He stared at her and then his lips widened into a grin. Connie slit her eyes at him and turned away, but she couldn't help glancing back and there he was still watching her. He wagged a finger and laughed and said, "Gonna get you, baby," and Connie turned away again without Eddie noticing anything.

She spent three hours with him, at the restaurant where they ate hamburgers and drank Cokes in wax cups that were always sweating, and then down an alley a mile or so away, and when he left her off at five to eleven only the movie house was still open at the plaza. Her girl friend was there, talking with a boy. When Connie came up the two girls smiled at each other and Connie said, "How was the movie?" and the girl said, "*You* should know." They rode off with the girl's father, sleepy and pleased, and Connie couldn't help but look at the darkened shopping plaza with its big empty parking lot and its signs that were faded and ghostly now, and over at the drive-in restaurant where cars were still circling tirelessly. She couldn't hear the music at this distance.

Next morning June asked her how the movie was and Connie said, "So-so."

She and that girl and occasionally another girl went out several times a week that way, and the rest of the time Connie spent around the house — it was summer vacation — getting in her mother's way and thinking, dreaming, about the boys she met. But all the boys fell back and dissolved into a single face that was not even a face, but an idea, a feeling, mixed up with the urgent insistent pounding of the music and the humid night air of July. Connie's mother kept dragging her back to the daylight by finding things for her to do or saying suddenly, "What's this about the Pettinger girl?"

And Connie would say nervously, "Oh, her. That dope." She always drew thick clear lines between herself and such girls, and her mother was simple and kindly enough to believe her. Her mother was so simple, Connie thought, that it was maybe cruel to fool her so much. Her mother went scuffling around the house in old bedroom slippers and complained over the telephone to one sister about the other, then the other called up and the two of them complained about the third one. If June's name was mentioned her mother's tone was approving, and if Connie's name was mentioned it was disapproving. This did not really mean she disliked Connie and actually Connie thought that her mother preferred her to June because she was prettier, but the two of them kept up a pretense of exasperation, a sense that they were tugging and struggling over something of little value to either of them. Sometimes, over coffee, they were almost friends, but something would come up — some vexation that was like a fly buzzing suddenly around their heads — and their faces went hard with contempt.

One Sunday Connie got up at eleven — none of them bothered with church — and washed her hair so that it could dry all day long, in the sun. Her parents and sister were going to a barbecue at an aunt's house and Connie said no, she wasn't interested, rolling her eyes, to let mother know just what she thought of it. "Stay home alone then," her mother said sharply. Connie sat out back in a lawn chair and watched them drive away, her father quiet and bald, hunched around so that he could back the car out, her mother with a look that was still angry and not at all softened through the windshield, and in the back seat poor old June all dressed up as if she didn't know what a barbecue was, with all the running yelling kids and the flies. Connie sat with her eyes closed in the sun, dreaming and dazed with the warmth about her as if this were a kind of love, the caresses of love, and her mind slipped over onto thoughts of the boy she had been with the night before and how nice he had been, how sweet it always was, not the way someone like June would suppose but sweet, gentle, the way it was in movies and promised in songs; and when she opened her eyes she hardly knew where she was, the back yard ran off into weeds and a fenceline of trees and behind it the sky was perfectly blue and still. The asbestos "ranch house" that was now three years old startled her — it looked small. She shook her head as if to get awake.

It was too hot. She went inside the house and turned on the radio to drown out the quiet. She sat on the edge of her bed, barefoot, and listened for an hour and a half to a program called XYZ Sunday Jamboree, record after record of hard, fast, shrieking songs she sang along with, interspersed by exclamations from "Bobby King": "An' look here you girls at Napoleon's — Son and Charley want you to pay real close attention to this song coming up!"

And Connie paid close attention herself, bathed in a glow of slow-pulsed joy that seemed to rise mysteriously out of the music itself and lay languidly about the airless little room, breathed in and breathed out with each gentle rise and fall of her chest.

After a while she heard a car coming up the drive. She sat up at once, startled, because it couldn't be her father so soon. The gravel kept crunching all the way in from the road — the driveway was long — and Connie ran to the window. It was a car she didn't know. It was an open jalopy, painted a bright gold that caught the sun opaquely. Her heart began to pound and her fingers snatched at her hair, checking it, and she whispered "Christ. Christ," wondering how bad she looked. The car came to a stop at the side door and the horn sounded four short taps as if this were a signal Connie knew.

She went into the kitchen and approached the door slowly, then hung out the screen door, her bare toes curling down off the step. There were two boys in the car and now she recognized the driver: he had shaggy, shabby black hair that looked crazy as a wig and he was grinning at her.

"I ain't late, am I?" he said.

"Who the hell do you think you are?" Connie said.

"Toldja I'd be out, didn't I?"

"I don't even know who you are."

She spoke sullenly, careful to show no interest or pleasure, and he spoke in a fast bright monotone. Connie looked past him to the other boy, taking her time. He had fair brown hair, with a lock that fell onto his forehead. His sideburns gave him a fierce, embarrassed look, but so far he hadn't even bothered to glance at her. Both boys wore sunglasses. The driver's glasses were metallic and mirrored everything in miniature.

"You wanta come for a ride?" he said.

Connie smirked and let her hair fall loose over one shoulder.

"Don'tcha like my car? New paint job," he said. "Hey."

"What?"

"You're cute."

She pretended to fidget, chasing flies away from the door.

"Don'tcha believe me, or what?" he said.

"Look, I don't even know who you are," Connie said in disgust.

"Hey, Ellie's got a radio, see. Mine's broke down." He lifted his friend's arm and showed her the little transistor the boy was holding, and now Connie began to hear the music. It was the same program that was playing inside the house.

"Bobby King?" she said.

"I listen to him all the time. I think he's great."

"He's kind of great," Connie said reluctantly.

"Listen, that guy's great. He knows where the action is."

Connie blushed a little, because the glasses made it impossible for her to see just what this boy was looking at. She couldn't decide if she liked him or if he was just a jerk, and so she dawdled in the doorway and wouldn't come down or go back inside. She said, "What's all that stuff painted on your car?"

"Can'tcha read it?" He opened the door very carefully, as if he was afraid it might fall off. He slid out just as carefully, planting his feet firmly on the ground, the tiny metallic world in his glasses slowing down like gelatine hardening and in the midst of it Connie's bright green blouse. "This here is my name, to begin with," he said. ARNOLD FRIEND was written in tar-like black letters on the side, with a drawing of a round grinning face that reminded Connie of a pumpkin, except it wore sunglasses. "I wanta introduce myself, I'm Arnold Friend and that's my real name and I'm gonna be your friend, honey, and inside the car's Ellie Oscar, he's kinda shy." Ellie brought his transistor up to his shoulder and balanced it there. "Now these numbers are a secret code, honey," Arnold Friend explained. He read off the numbers 33, 19, 17 and raised his eyebrows at her to see what she thought of that, but she didn't think much of it. The left rear fender had been smashed and around it was written, on the gleaming gold background: DONE BY CRAZY WOMAN DRIVER. Connie had to laugh at that. Arnold Friend was pleased at her laughter and looked up at her. "Around the other side's a lot more — you wanta come and see them?"

"No."

"Why not?"

"Why should I?"

"Don'tcha wanta see what's on the car? Don'tcha wanta go for a ride?"

"I don't know."

"Why not?"

"I got things to do."

"Like what?"

"Things."

He laughed as if she had said something funny. He slapped his thighs. He was standing in a strange way, leaning back against the car as if he were balancing himself. He wasn't tall, only an inch or so taller than she would be if she came down to him. Connie liked the way he was dressed, which was the way all of them dressed: tight faded jeans stuffed into black, scuffed boots, a belt that pulled his waist in and showed how lean he was, and a white pullover shirt that was a little soiled and showed the hard small muscles of his arms and shoulders. He looked as if he probably did hard work, lifting and carrying things. Even his neck looked muscular. And his face was a familiar face, somehow: the jaw and chin and cheeks slightly darkened, because he hadn't shaved for a day or two, and the nose long and hawk-like, sniffing as if she were a treat he was going to gobble up and it was all a joke.

"Connie, you ain't telling the truth. This is your day set aside for a ride with me and you know it," he said, still laughing. The way he straightened and recovered from his fit of laughing showed that it had been all fake.

"How do you know what my name is?" she said suspiciously.

"It's Connie."

"Maybe and maybe not."

"I know my Connie," he said, wagging his finger. Now she remembered him even better, back at the restaurant, and her cheeks warmed at the thought of how she sucked in her breath just at the moment she passed him — how she must have looked to him. And he had remembered her. "Ellie and I come out here especially for you," he said. "Ellie can sit in back. How about it?"

"Where?"

"Where what?"

"Where're we going?"

He looked at her. He took off the sunglasses and she saw how pale the skin around his eyes was, like holes that were not in shadow but instead in light. His eyes were like chips of broken glass that catch the light in an amiable way. He smiled. It was as if the idea of going for a ride somewhere, to some place, was a new idea to him.

"Just for a ride, Connie sweetheart."

"I never said my name was Connie," she said.

"But I know what it is. I know your name and all about you, lots of things," Arnold Friend said. He had not moved yet but stood still leaning back against the side of his jalopy. "I took a special interest in you, such a pretty girl, and found out all about you like I know your parents and sister are gone somewheres and I know where and how long they're going to be gone, and I know who you were with last night, and your best friend's name is Betty. Right?"

He spoke in a simple lilting voice, exactly as if he were reciting the words to a song. His smile assured her that everything was fine. In the car Ellie turned up the volume on his radio and did not bother to look around at them.

"Ellie can sit in the back seat," Arnold Friend said. He indicated his friend with a casual jerk of his chin, as if Ellie did not count and she could not bother with him.

"How'd you find out all that stuff?" Connie said.

"Listen: Betty Schultz and Tony Fitch and Jimmy Pettinger and Nancy Pettinger," he said, in a chant. "Raymond Stanley and Bob Hutter —"

"Do you know all those kids?"

"I know everybody."

"Look, you're kidding. You're not from around here."

"Sure."

"But — how come we never saw you before?"

"Sure you saw me before," he said. He looked down at his boots, as if he were a little offended. "You just don't remember."

"I guess I'd remember you," Connie said.

"Yeah?" He looked up at this, beaming. He was pleased. He began to mark time with the music from Ellie's radio, tapping his fists lightly together. Connie looked away from his smile to the car, which was painted so bright it almost hurt her eyes to look at it. She looked at that name, ARNOLD FRIEND. And up at the front fender was an expression that was familiar — MAN THE FLYING SAUCERS. It was an expression kids had used the year before, but didn't use this year. She looked at it for a while as if the words meant something to her that she did not yet know.

"What're you thinking about? Huh?" Arnold Friend demanded. "Not worried about your hair blowing around in the car, are you?"

"No."

"Think I maybe can't drive good?"

"How do I know?"

"You're a hard girl to handle. How come?" he said. "Don't you know I'm your friend? Didn't you see me put my sign in the air when you walked by?"

"What sign?"

"My sign." And he drew an X in the air, leaning out toward her. They were maybe ten feet apart. After his hand fell back to his side the X was still in the air, almost visible. Connie let the screen door close and stood perfectly still inside it, listening to the music from her radio and the boy's blend together. She stared at Arnold Friend. He stood there so stiffly relaxed, pretending to be relaxed, with one hand idly on the door handle as if he were keeping himself up that way and had no intention of ever moving again. She recognized most things about him, the tight jeans that showed his thighs and buttocks and the greasy leather boots and the tight shirt, and even that slippery friendly smile of his, that sleepy dreamy smile that all the boys used to get across ideas they didn't want to put into words. She recognized all this and also the singsong way he talked, slightly mocking, kidding, but serious and a little melancholy, and she recognized the way he tapped one fist against the other in homage to the perpetual music behind him. But all these things did not come together.

She said suddenly, "Hey, how old are you?"

His smile faded. She could see then that he wasn't a kid, he was much older — thirty, maybe more. At this knowledge her heart began to pound faster.

"That's a crazy thing to ask. Can'tcha see I'm your own age?"

"Like hell you are."

"Or maybe a coupla years older, I'm eighteen."

"Eighteen?" she said doubtfully.

He grinned to reassure her and lines appeared at the corners of his mouth. His teeth were big and white. He grinned so broadly his eyes became slits and she saw how thick the lashes were, thick and black as if painted with a black tarlike material. Then he seemed to become embarrassed, abruptly, and looked over his shoulder at Ellie. "*Him*, he's crazy," he said. "Ain't he a riot, he's a nut, a real character." Ellie was still listening to the music. His sunglasses told nothing about what he was thinking. He wore a bright orange shirt unbuttoned halfway to show his chest, which was a pale, bluish chest and not muscular like Arnold Friend's. His shirt collar was turned up all around and the very tips of the collar pointed out past his chin as if they were protecting him. He was pressing the transistor radio up against his ear and sat there in a kind of daze, right in the sun.

"He's kinda strange," Connie said.

"Hey, she says you're kinda strange! Kinda strange!" Arnold Friend cried. He pounded on the car to get Ellie's attention. Ellie turned for the first time and Connie saw with shock that he wasn't a kid either — he had a fair, hairless face, cheeks reddened slightly as if the veins grew too close to the surface of his skin, the face of a forty-year-old baby. Connie felt a wave of dizziness rise in her at this sight and she stared at him as if waiting for something to change the shock of the moment, make it all right again. Ellie's lips kept shaping words, mumbling along with the words blasting his ear.

"Maybe you two better go away," Connie said faintly.

"What? How come?" Arnold Friend cried. "We come out here to take you for a ride. It's Sunday." He had the voice of the man on the radio now. It was the same voice, Connie thought. "Don'tcha know it's Sunday all day and honey, no matter who you were with last night today you're with Arnold Friend and don't you forget it! — Maybe you better step out here," he said, and this last was in a different voice. It was a little flatter, as if the heat was finally getting to him.

"No. I got things to do."

"Hey."

"You two better leave."

"We ain't leaving until you come with us."

"Like hell I am —"

"Connie, don't fool around with me. I mean — I mean, don't fool *around*," he said, shaking his head. He laughed incredulously. He placed his sunglasses on top of his head, carefully, as if he were indeed wearing a wig, and brought the stems down behind his ears. Connie stared at him, another wave of dizziness and fear rising in her so that for a moment he wasn't even in focus but was just a blur, standing there against his gold car, and she had the idea that he had driven up the driveway all right but had come from nowhere before that and belonged nowhere and that everything about him and even the music that was so familiar to her was only half real.

"If my father comes and sees you —"

"He ain't coming. He's at a barbecue."

"How do you know that?"

"Aunt Tillie's. Right now they're — uh — they're drinking. Sitting around," he said vaguely, squinting as if he were staring all the way to town and over to Aunt Tillie's back yard. Then the vision seemed to clear and he nodded energetically. "Yeah. Sitting around. There's your sister in a blue dress, huh? And high heels, the poor sad bitch — nothing like you, sweetheart! And your mother's helping some fat woman with the corn, they're cleaning the corn — husking the corn —"

"What fat woman?" Connie cried.

"How do I know what fat woman. I don't know every goddamn fat woman in the world!" Arnold Friend laughed.

"Oh, that's Mrs. Hornby. . . . Who invited her?" Connie said. She felt a little light-headed. Her breath was coming quickly.

"She's too fat. I don't like them fat. I like them the way you are, honey," he said, smiling sleepily at her. They stared at each other for a while, through the screen door. He said softly, "Now what you're going to do is this: you're going to come out that door. You're going to sit up front with me and Ellie's going to sit in the back, the hell with Ellie, right? This isn't Ellie's date. You're my date. I'm your lover, honey."

"What? You're crazy —"

"Yes, I'm your lover. You don't know what that is but you will," he said. "I know that too. I know all about you. But look: it's real nice and you couldn't ask for nobody better than me, or more polite. I always keep my word. I'll tell you how it is, I'm always nice at first, the first time. I'll hold you so tight you won't think you have to try to get away or pretend anything because you'll know you can't. And I'll come inside you where it's all secret and you'll give in to me and you'll love me —"

"Shut up! You're crazy!" Connie said. She backed away from the door. She put her hands against her ears as if she'd heard something terrible, something not meant for her. "People don't talk like that, you're crazy," she muttered. Her heart was almost too big now for her chest and its pumping made sweat break out all over her. She looked out to see Arnold Friend pause and then take a step toward the porch lurching. He almost fell. But, like a clever drunken man, he managed to catch his balance. He wobbled in his high boots and grabbed hold of one of the porch posts.

"Honey?" he said. "You still listening?"

"Get the hell out of here!"

"Be nice, honey. Listen."

"I'm going to call the police —"

He wobbled again and out of the side of his mouth came a fast spat curse, an aside not meant for her to hear. But even this "Christ!" sounded forced. Then he began to smile again. She watched this smile come, awkward as if he were smiling from inside a mask. His whole face was a mask, she thought wildly, tanned down onto his throat but then running out as if he had plastered make-up on his face but had forgotten about his throat.

"Honey — ? Listen, here's how it is. I always tell the truth and I promise you this: I ain't coming in that house after you."

"You better not! I'm going to call the police if you — if you don't —"

"Honey," he said, talking right through her voice, "honey, I'm not coming in there but you are coming out here. You know why?"

She was panting. The kitchen looked like a place she had never seen before, some room she had run inside but which wasn't good enough, wasn't going to help her. The kitchen window had never had a curtain, after three years, and there were dishes in the sink for her to do — probably — and if you ran your hand across the table you'd probably feel something sticky there.

"You listening, honey? Hey?"

" — going to call the police —"

"Soon as you touch the phone I don't need to keep my promise and can come inside. You won't want that."

She rushed forward and tried to lock the door. Her fingers were shaking. "But why lock it," Arnold Friend said gently, talking right into her face. "It's just a screen door. It's just nothing." One of his boots was at a strange angle, as if his foot wasn't in it. It pointed out to the left, bent at the ankle. "I mean, anybody can break through a screen door and glass and wood and iron or anything else if he needs to, anybody at all and specially Arnold Friend. If the place got lit up with a fire, honey, you'd come runnin' out into my arms, right into my arms an' safe at home — like you knew I was your lover and'd stopped fooling around, I don't mind a nice shy girl but I don't like no fooling around." Part of those words were spoken with a slight rhythmic lilt, and Connie somehow recognized them — the echo of a song from last year, about a girl rushing into her boyfriend's arms and coming home again —

Connie stood barefoot on the linoleum floor, staring at him. "What do you want?" she whispered.

"I want you," he said.

"What?"

"Seen you that night and thought, that's the one, yes sir. I never needed to look any more."

"But my father's coming back. He's coming to get me. I had to wash my hair first —" She spoke in a dry, rapid voice, hardly raising it for him to hear.

"No, your daddy is not coming and yes, you had to wash your hair and you washed it for me. It's nice and shining and all for me. I thank you, sweetheart," he said, with a mock bow, but again he almost lost his balance. He had to bend and adjust his boots. Evidently his feet did not go all the way down; the boots must have been stuffed with something so that he would seem taller. Connie stared out at him and behind him at Ellie in the car, who seemed to be looking off toward Connie's right, into nothing. Then Ellie said, pulling the words out of the air one after another as if he were just discovering them, "You want me to pull out the phone?"

"Shut your mouth and keep it shut," Arnold Friend said, his face red from bending over or maybe from embarrassment because Connie had seen his boots. "This ain't none of your business."

"What — what are you doing? What do you want?" Connie said. "If I call the police they'll get you, they'll arrest you —"

"Promise was not to come in unless you touch that phone, and I'll keep that promise," he said. He resumed his erect position and tried to force his shoulders back. He sounded like a hero in a movie, declaring something important. He spoke too loudly and it was as if he were speaking to someone behind Connie. "I ain't made plans for coming in that house where I don't belong but just for you to come out to me, the way you should. Don't you know who I am?"

"You're crazy," she whispered. She backed away from the door but did not want to go into another part of the house, as if this would give him permission to come through the door. "What do you . . . You're crazy, you. . . ."

"Huh? What're you saying, honey?"

Her eyes darted everywhere in the kitchen. She could not remember what it was, this room.

"This is how it is, honey: you come out and we'll drive away, have a nice ride. But if you don't come out we're gonna wait till your people come home and then they're all going to get it."

"You want that telephone pulled out?" Ellie said. He held the radio away from his ear and grimaced, as if without the radio the air was too much for him.

"I toldja shut up, Ellie," Arnold Friend said, "you're deaf, get a hearing aid, right? Fix yourself up. This little girl's no trouble and's gonna be nice to me, so Ellie keep to yourself, this ain't your date — right? Don't hem in on me, don't hog, don't crush, don't bird dog, don't trail me," he said in a rapid, meaningless voice, as if he were running through all the expressions he'd learned but was no longer sure which one of them was in style, then rushing on to new ones, making them up with his eyes closed. "Don't crawl under my fence, don't squeeze in my chipmunk hole, don't sniff my glue, suck my popsicle, keep your own greasy fingers on yourself!" He shaded his eyes and peered in at Connie, who was backed against the kitchen table. "Don't mind him, honey, he's just a creep. He's a dope. Right? I'm the boy for you and like I said, you come out here nice like a lady and give me your hand, and nobody else gets hurt, I mean, your nice old bald-headed daddy and your mummy and your sister in her high heels. Because listen: why bring them in this?"

"Leave me alone," Connie whispered.

"Hey, you know that old woman down the road, the one with the chickens and stuff — you know her?"

"She's dead!"

"Dead? What? You know her?" Arnold Friend said.

"She's dead —"

"Don't you like her?"

"She's dead — she's — she isn't here any more —"

"But don't you like her, I mean, you got something against her? Some grudge or something?" Then his voice dipped as if he were conscious of rudeness. He touched the sunglasses on top of his head as if to make sure they were still there. "Now you be a good girl."

"What are you going to do?"

"Just two things, or maybe three," Arnold Friend said. "But I promise it won't last long and you'll like me that way you get to like people you're close to. You will. It's all over for you here, so come on out. You don't want your people in any trouble, do you?"

She turned and bumped against a chair or something, hurting her leg, but she ran into the back room and picked up the telephone. Something roared in her ear, a tiny roaring, and she was so sick with fear that she could do nothing but listen to it—the telephone was clammy and very heavy and her fingers groped down to the dial but were too weak to touch it. She began to scream into the phone, into the roaring. She cried out, she cried for her mother, she felt her breath start jerking back and forth in her lungs as if it were something Arnold Friend was stabbing her with again and again with no tenderness. A noisy sorrowful wailing rose all about her and she was locked inside it the way she was locked inside this house.

After a while she could hear again. She was sitting on the floor, with her wet back against the wall.

Arnold Friend was saying from the door, "That's a good girl. Put the phone back."

She kicked the phone away from her.

"No, honey. Pick it up. Put it back right."

She picked it up and put it back. The dial tone stopped.

"That's a good girl. Now you come outside."

She was hollow with what had been fear but what was now just an empti-ness. All that screaming had blasted it out of her. She sat, one leg cramped under her, and deep inside her brain was something like a pinpoint of light that kept going and would not let her relax. She thought, I'm not going to see my mother again. She thought, I'm not going to sleep in my bed again. Her bright green blouse was all wet.

Arnold Friend said, in a gentle-loud voice that was like a stage voice, "The place where you came from ain't there any more, and where you had in mind to go is cancelled out. This place you are now—inside your daddy's house—is nothing but a cardboard box I can knock down any time. You know that and always did know it. You hear me?"

She thought, I have got to think. I have got to know what to do.

"We'll go out to a nice field, out in the country here where it smells so nice and it's sunny," Arnold Friend said. "I'll have my arms tight around you so you won't need to try to get away and I'll show you what love is like, what it does. The hell with this house! It looks solid all right," he said. He ran a fingernail down the screen and the noise did not make Connie shiver, as it would have the day before. "Now put your hand on your heart, honey. Feel that? That feels solid too but we know better. Be nice to me, be sweet like you can because what else is there for a girl like you but to be sweet and pretty and give in?—and get away before her people get back?"

She felt her pounding heart. Her hand seemed to enclose it. She thought for the first time in her life that it was nothing that was hers, that belonged to her, but just a pounding, living thing inside this body that wasn't really hers either.

"You don't want them to get hurt," Arnold Friend went on. "Now get up, honey. Get up all by yourself."

She stood.

"Now turn this way. That's right. Come over to me—Ellie, put that away, didn't I tell you? You dope. You miserable creepy dope," Arnold Friend said. His words were not angry but only part of an incantation. The incantation was kindly. "Now come out through the kitchen to me honey and let's see a smile, try it, you're a brave sweet little girl and now they're eating corn and hotdogs cooked to bursting over an outdoor fire, and they don't know one thing about you and never did and honey you're better than them because not a one of them would have done this for you."

Connie felt the linoleum under her feet; it was cool. She brushed her hair back out of her eyes. Arnold Friend let go of the post tentatively and opened his arms for her, his elbows pointing in toward each other and his wrists limp, to show that this was an embarrassed embrace and a little mocking, he didn't want to make her self-conscious.

She put out her hand against the screen. She watched herself push the door slowly open as if she were back safe somewhere in the other doorway, watching this body and this head of long hair moving out into the sunlight where Arnold Friend waited.

"My sweet little blue-eyed girl," he said in a half-sung sigh that had nothing to do with her brown eyes but was taken up just the same by the vast sunlit reaches of the land behind him and on all sides of him — so much land that Connie had never seen before and did not recognize except to know that she was going to it.

Tim O'Brien

Tim O'Brien (b. 1946) was born in Austin, Minnesota, and educated at Macalester College and Harvard University. Drafted into the army during the Vietnam War, he attained the rank of sergeant and received the Purple Heart.

O'Brien's first book, *If I Die in a Combat Zone, Box Me Up and Ship Me Home* (1973), is an account of his combat experience presented as "autofiction," a mixture of autobiography and fiction. His next book, *Northern Lights* (1974), depicts a conflict between two brothers. But O'Brien produced his finest work to date in the novel *Going after Cacciato* (1978), which won the National Book Award and was judged by many critics to be the best book by an American about the Vietnam War. This was followed by the novels *The Nuclear Age* (1985), about the ominous future of the human race, *In the Lake of the Woods* (1994), and *Tom Cat in Love* (1999). *July, July* (2003) is a recent novel.

"Soldiers are dreamers," a line by the English poet Siegfried Sassoon, who survived a sniper's bullet during World War I, is the epigraph for *Going after Cacciato*. Dreams play an important role in all O'Brien's fiction, yet the note they sound in a story such as "The Things They Carried" is not surrealistic. The dream is always rooted so firmly in reality that it survives, paradoxically, as the most vital element in an O'Brien story. "The Things They Carried" first appeared in *Esquire* magazine and was included in *The Best American Short Stories* when Ann Beattie edited the volume in 1987. It is also included in O'Brien's collection *The Things They Carried* (1990).

RELATED STORY
Saïd Sayrafiezadeh, A Brief Encounter with the Enemy, page 1198.

RELATED COMMENTARIES
Tim O'Brien, "Alpha Company," page 1494; Matt Steinglass, "Reading Tim O'Brien in Hanoi," page 1522.

The Things They Carried

1986

FIRST LIEUTENANT JIMMY CROSS carried letters from a girl named Martha, a junior at Mount Sebastian College in New Jersey. They were not love letters, but Lieutenant Cross was hoping, so he kept them folded in plastic at the bottom of his rucksack. In the late afternoon, after a day's march, he would dig his foxhole, wash his hands under a canteen, unwrap the letters, hold them with the tips of his fingers, and spend the last hour of light pretending. He would imagine romantic camping trips into the White Mountains in New Hampshire. He would sometimes taste the envelope flaps, knowing her tongue had been there. More than anything, he wanted Martha to love him as he loved her, but the letters were mostly chatty, elusive on the matter of love. She was a virgin, he was almost sure. She was an English major at Mount Sebastian, and she wrote beautifully about her professors and roommates and midterm exams, about her respect for Chaucer and her great affection for Virginia Woolf. She often quoted lines of poetry; she never mentioned the war, except to say, Jimmy, take care of yourself. The letters weighed ten ounces. They were signed "Love, Martha," but Lieutenant Cross understood that "Love" was only a way of signing and did not mean what he sometimes pretended it meant. At dusk, he would carefully return the letters to his rucksack. Slowly, a bit distracted, he would get up and move among his men, checking the perimeter, then at full dark he would return to his hole and watch the night and wonder if Martha was a virgin.

The things they carried were largely determined by necessity. Among the necessities or near necessities were P-38 can openers, pocket knives, heat tabs, wrist watches, dog tags, mosquito repellant, chewing gum, candy, cigarettes, salt tablets, packets of Kool-Aid, lighters, matches, sewing kits, Military Payment Certificates, C rations, and two or three canteens of water. Together, these items weighed between fifteen and twenty pounds, depending upon a man's habits or rate of metabolism. Henry Dobbins, who was a big man, carried extra rations; he was especially fond of canned peaches in heavy syrup over pound cake. Dave Jensen, who practiced field hygiene, carried a toothbrush, dental floss, and several hotel-size bars of soap he'd stolen on R&R in Sydney, Australia. Ted Lavender, who was scared, carried tranquilizers until he was shot in the head outside the village of Than Khe in mid-April. By necessity, and because it was SOP,[1] they all carried steel helmets that weighed five pounds including the liner and camouflage cover. They carried the standard fatigue jackets and trousers. Very few carried underwear. On their feet they carried jungle boots — 2.1 pounds — and Dave Jensen carried three pairs of socks and a can of Dr. Scholl's foot powder as a precaution against trench foot. Until he was shot, Ted Lavender carried six or seven ounces of premium dope, which for him was a necessity. Mitchell Sanders, the RTO,[2] carried condoms. Norman Bowker carried a diary. Rat Kiley carried comic books. Kiowa, a devout Baptist, carried an illustrated New Testament that had been presented to him by his father, who taught Sunday school in Oklahoma City, Oklahoma. As a hedge against bad times, however, Kiowa also carried his grandmother's distrust of the white man, his grandfather's old hunting hatchet. Necessity dictated. Because the land was mined and booby-trapped, it was SOP for each man to carry a steel-centered, nylon-covered flak jacket, which weighed 6.7 pounds, but which on hot days seemed much heavier. Because you could die so quickly, each man carried at least one large compress bandage, usually in the helmet band for easy access. Because the nights were cold, and because the monsoons were wet, each carried a green plastic poncho that could be used as

---

[1] Standard operating procedure.
[2] Radiotelephone operator.

a raincoat or ground sheet or makeshift tent. With its quilted liner, the poncho weighed almost two pounds, but it was worth every ounce. In April, for instance, when Ted Lavender was shot, they used his poncho to wrap him up, then to carry him across the paddy, then to lift him into the chopper that took him away.

––––––––

They were called legs or grunts.

To carry something was to "hump" it, as when Lieutenant Jimmy Cross humped his love for Martha up the hills and through the swamps. In its intransitive form, "to hump" meant "to walk," or "to march," but it implied burdens far beyond the intransitive.

Almost everyone humped photographs. In his wallet, Lieutenant Cross carried two photographs of Martha. The first was a Kodachrome snapshot signed "Love," though he knew better. She stood against a brick wall. Her eyes were gray and neutral, her lips slightly open as she stared straight-on at the camera. At night, sometimes, Lieutenant Cross wondered who had taken the picture, because he knew she had boyfriends, because he loved her so much, and because he could see the shadow of the picture taker spreading out against the brick wall. The second photograph had been clipped from the 1968 Mount Sebastian yearbook. It was an action shot — women's volleyball — and Martha was bent horizontal to the floor, reaching, the palms of her hands in sharp focus, the tongue taut, the expression frank and competitive. There was no visible sweat. She wore white gym shorts. Her legs, he thought, were almost certainly the legs of a virgin, dry and without hair, the left knee cocked and carrying her entire weight, which was just over one hundred pounds. Lieutenant Cross remembered touching that left knee. A dark theater, he remembered, and the movie was *Bonnie and Clyde*, and Martha wore a tweed skirt, and during the final scene, when he touched her knee, she turned and looked at him in a sad, sober way that made him pull his hand back, but he would always remember the feel of the tweed skirt and the knee beneath it and the sound of the gunfire that killed Bonnie and Clyde, how embarrassing it was, how slow and oppressive. He remembered kissing her good night at the dorm door. Right then, he thought, he should've done something brave. He should've carried her up the stairs to her room and tied her to the bed and touched that left knee all night long. He should've risked it. Whenever he looked at the photographs, he thought of new things he should've done.

––––––––

What they carried was partly a function of rank, partly of field specialty.

As a first lieutenant and platoon leader, Jimmy Cross carried a compass, maps, code books, binoculars, and a .45-caliber pistol that weighed 2.9 pounds fully loaded. He carried a strobe light and the responsibility for the lives of his men.

As an RTO, Mitchell Sanders carried the PRC-25 radio, a killer, twenty-six pounds with its battery.

As a medic, Rat Kiley carried a canvas satchel filled with morphine and plasma and malaria tablets and surgical tape and comic books and all the things a medic must carry, including M&M's for especially bad wounds, for a total weight of nearly twenty pounds.

As a big man, therefore a machine gunner, Henry Dobbins carried the M-60, which weighed twenty-three pounds unloaded, but which was almost always loaded. In addition, Dobbins carried between ten and fifteen pounds of ammunition draped in belts across his chest and shoulders.

As PFCs or Spec 4s, most of them were common grunts and carried the standard M-16 gas-operated assault rifle. The weapon weighed 7.5 pounds unloaded, 8.2 pounds with its full twenty-round magazine. Depending on numerous factors, such as topography and psychology, the riflemen carried anywhere from twelve to twenty magazines, usually in cloth bandoliers, adding on another 8.4 pounds at minimum, fourteen pounds at maximum. When it was available, they also carried M-16 maintenance gear—rods and steel brushes and swabs and tubes of LSA oil—all of which weighed about a pound. Among the grunts, some carried the M-79 grenade launcher, 5.9 pounds unloaded, a reasonably light weapon except for the ammunition, which was heavy. A single round weighed ten ounces. The typical load was twenty-five rounds. But Ted Lavender, who was scared, carried thirty-four rounds when he was shot and killed outside Than Khe, and he went down under an exceptional burden, more than twenty pounds of ammunition, plus the flak jacket and helmet and rations and water and toilet paper and tranquilizers and all the rest, plus the unweighed fear. He was dead weight. There was no twitching or flopping. Kiowa, who saw it happen, said it was like watching a rock fall, or a big sandbag or something—just boom, then down—not like the movies where the dead guy rolls around and does fancy spins and goes ass over teakettle—not like that, Kiowa said, the poor bastard just flat-fuck fell. Boom. Down. Nothing else. It was a bright morning in mid-April. Lieutenant Cross felt the pain. He blamed himself. They stripped off Lavender's canteens and ammo, all the heavy things, and Rat Kiley said the obvious, the guy's dead, and Mitchell Sanders used his radio to report one U.S. KIA[3] and to request a chopper. Then they wrapped Lavender in his poncho. They carried him out to a dry paddy, established security, and sat smoking the dead man's dope until the chopper came. Lieutenant Cross kept to himself. He pictured Martha's smooth young face, thinking he loved her more than anything, more than his men, and now Ted Lavender was dead because he loved her so much and could not stop thinking about her. When the dust-off arrived, they carried Lavender aboard. Afterward they burned Than Khe. They marched until dusk, then dug their holes, and that night Kiowa kept explaining how you had to be there, how fast it was, how the poor guy just dropped like so much concrete. Boom-down, he said. Like cement.

In addition to the three standard weapons—the M-60, M-16, and M-79—they carried whatever presented itself, or whatever seemed appropriate as a means of killing or staying alive. They carried catch-as-catch-can. At various times, in various situations, they carried M-14s and CAR-15s and Swedish Ks and grease

---

[3] Killed in action.

guns and captured AK-47s and Chi-Coms and RPGs and Simonov carbines and black-market Uzis and .38-caliber Smith & Wesson handguns and 66 mm LAWs and shotguns and silencers and blackjacks and bayonets and C-4 plastic explosives. Lee Strunk carried a slingshot; a weapon of last resort, he called it. Mitchell Sanders carried brass knuckles. Kiowa carried his grandfather's feathered hatchet. Every third or fourth man carried a Claymore antipersonnel mine — 3.5 pounds with its firing device. They all carried fragmentation grenades — fourteen ounces each. They all carried at least one M-18 colored smoke grenade — twenty-four ounces. Some carried CS or tear-gas grenades. Some carried white-phosphorus grenades. They carried all they could bear, and then some, including a silent awe for the terrible power of the things they carried.

In the first week of April, before Lavender died, Lieutenant Jimmy Cross received a good-luck charm from Martha. It was a simple pebble, an ounce at most. Smooth to the touch, it was a milky-white color with flecks of orange and violet, oval-shaped, like a miniature egg. In the accompanying letter, Martha wrote that she had found the pebble on the Jersey shoreline, precisely where the land touched water at high tide, where things came together but also separated. It was this separate-but-together quality, she wrote, that had inspired her to pick up the pebble and to carry it in her breast pocket for several days, where it seemed weightless, and then to send it through the mail, by air, as a token of her truest feelings for him. Lieutenant Cross found this romantic. But he wondered what her truest feelings were, exactly, and what she meant by separate-but-together. He wondered how the tides and waves had come into play on that afternoon along the Jersey shoreline when Martha saw the pebble and bent down to rescue it from geology. He imagined bare feet. Martha was a poet, with the poet's sensibilities, and her feet would be brown and bare, the toenails unpainted, the eyes chilly and somber like the ocean in March, and though it was painful, he wondered who had been with her that afternoon. He imagined a pair of shadows moving along the strip of sand where things came together but also separated. It was phantom jealousy, he knew, but he couldn't help himself. He loved her so much. On the march, through the hot days of early April, he carried the pebble in his mouth, turning it with his tongue, tasting sea salts and moisture. His mind wandered. He had difficulty keeping his attention on the war. On occasion he would yell at his men to spread out the column, to keep their eyes open, but then he would slip away into daydreams, just pretending, walking barefoot along the Jersey shore, with Martha, carrying nothing. He would feel himself rising. Sun and waves and gentle winds, all love and lightness.

What they carried varied by mission.

When a mission took them to the mountains, they carried mosquito netting, machetes, canvas tarps, and extra bug juice.

If a mission seemed especially hazardous, or if it involved a place they knew to be bad, they carried everything they could. In certain heavily mined AOs,[4]

---

[4] Areas of operations.

where the land was dense with Toe Poppers and Bouncing Betties, they took turns humping a twenty-eight-pound mine detector. With its headphones and big sensing plate, the equipment was a stress on the lower back and shoulders, awkward to handle, often useless because of the shrapnel in the earth, but they carried it anyway, partly for safety, partly for the illusion of safety.

On ambush, or other night missions, they carried peculiar little odds and ends. Kiowa always took along his New Testament and a pair of moccasins for silence. Dave Jensen carried night-sight vitamins high in carotin. Lee Strunk carried his slingshot; ammo, he claimed, would never be a problem. Rat Kiley carried brandy and M&M's. Until he was shot, Ted Lavender carried the starlight scope, which weighed 6.3 pounds with its aluminum carrying case. Henry Dobbins carried his girlfriend's pantyhose wrapped around his neck as a comforter. They all carried ghosts. When dark came, they would move out single file across the meadows and paddies to their ambush coordinates, where they would quietly set up the Claymores and lie down and spend the night waiting.

Other missions were more complicated and required special equipment. In mid-April, it was their mission to search out and destroy the elaborate tunnel complexes in the Than Khe area south of Chu Lai. To blow the tunnels, they carried one-pound blocks of pentrite high explosives, four blocks to a man, sixty-eight pounds in all. They carried wiring, detonators, and battery-powered clackers. Dave Jensen carried earplugs. Most often, before blowing the tunnels, they were ordered by higher command to search them, which was considered bad news, but by and large they just shrugged and carried out orders. Because he was a big man, Henry Dobbins was excused from tunnel duty. The others would draw numbers. Before Lavender died there were seventeen men in the platoon, and whoever drew the number seventeen would strip off his gear and crawl in head first with a flashlight and Lieutenant Cross's .45-caliber pistol. The rest of them would fan out as security. They would sit down or kneel, not facing the hole, listening to the ground beneath them, imagining cobwebs and ghosts, whatever was down there — the tunnel walls squeezing in — how the flashlight seemed impossibly heavy in the hand and how it was tunnel vision in the very strictest sense, compression in all ways, even time, and how you had to wiggle in — ass and elbows — a swallowed-up feeling — and how you found yourself worrying about odd things — will your flashlight go dead? Do rats carry rabies? If you screamed, how far would the sound carry? Would your buddies hear it? Would they have the courage to drag you out? In some respects, though not many, the waiting was worse than the tunnel itself. Imagination was a killer.

On April 16, when Lee Strunk drew the number seventeen, he laughed and muttered something and went down quickly. The morning was hot and very still. Not good, Kiowa said. He looked at the tunnel opening, then out across a dry paddy toward the village of Than Khe. Nothing moved. No clouds or birds or people. As they waited, the men smoked and drank Kool-Aid, not talking much, feeling sympathy for Lee Strunk but also feeling the luck of the draw. You win some, you lose some, said Mitchell Sanders, and sometimes you settle for a rain check. It was a tired line and no one laughed.

Henry Dobbins ate a tropical chocolate bar. Ted Lavender popped a tranquilizer and went off to pee.

After five minutes, Lieutenant Jimmy Cross moved to the tunnel, leaned down, and examined the darkness. Trouble, he thought — a cave-in maybe. And then suddenly, without willing it, he was thinking about Martha. The stresses and fractures, the quick collapse, the two of them buried alive under all that weight. Dense, crushing love. Kneeling, watching the hole, he tried to concentrate on Lee Strunk and the war, all the dangers, but his love was too much for him, he felt paralyzed, he wanted to sleep inside her lungs and breathe her blood and be smothered. He wanted her to be a virgin and not a virgin, all at once. He wanted to know her. Intimate secrets — why poetry? Why so sad? Why the grayness in her eyes? Why so alone? Not lonely, just alone — riding her bike across campus or sitting off by herself in the cafeteria. Even dancing, she danced alone — and it was the aloneness that filled him with love. He remembered telling her that one evening. How she nodded and looked away. And how, later, when he kissed her, she received the kiss without returning it, her eyes wide open, not afraid, not a virgin's eyes, just flat and uninvolved.

Lieutenant Cross gazed at the tunnel. But he was not there. He was buried with Martha under the white sand at the Jersey shore. They were pressed together, and the pebble in his mouth was her tongue. He was smiling. Vaguely, he was aware of how quiet the day was, the sullen paddies, yet he could not bring himself to worry about matters of security. He was beyond that. He was just a kid at war, in love. He was twenty-two years old. He couldn't help it.

A few moments later Lee Strunk crawled out of the tunnel. He came up grinning, filthy but alive. Lieutenant Cross nodded and closed his eyes while the others clapped Strunk on the back and made jokes about rising from the dead.

Worms, Rat Kiley said. Right out of the grave. Fuckin' zombie.

The men laughed. They all felt great relief.

Spook City, said Mitchell Sanders.

Lee Strunk made a funny ghost sound, a kind of moaning, yet very happy, and right then, when Strunk made that high happy moaning sound, when he went *Ahhooooo*, right then Ted Lavender was shot in the head on his way back from peeing. He lay with his mouth open. The teeth were broken. There was a swollen black bruise under his left eye. The cheekbone was gone. Oh shit, Rat Kiley said, the guy's dead. The guy's dead, he kept saying, which seemed profound — the guy's dead. I mean really.

The things they carried were determined to some extent by superstition. Lieutenant Cross carried his good-luck pebble. Dave Jensen carried a rabbit's foot. Norman Bowker, otherwise a very gentle person, carried a thumb that had been presented to him as a gift by Mitchell Sanders. The thumb was dark brown, rubbery to the touch, and weighed four ounces at most. It had been cut from a VC corpse, a boy of fifteen or sixteen. They'd found him at the bottom of an irrigation ditch, badly burned, flies in his mouth and eyes. The boy wore black shorts and sandals. At the time of his death he had been carrying a pouch of rice, a rifle, and three magazines of ammunition.

You want my opinion, Mitchell Sanders said, there's a definite moral here.

He put his hand on the dead boy's wrist. He was quiet for a time, as if counting a pulse, then he patted the stomach, almost affectionately, and used Kiowa's hunting hatchet to remove the thumb.

Henry Dobbins asked what the moral was.

Moral?

You know. *Moral.*

Sanders wrapped the thumb in toilet paper and handed it across to Norman Bowker. There was no blood. Smiling, he kicked the boy's head, watched the flies scatter, and said, It's like with that old TV show — Paladin. Have gun, will travel.

Henry Dobbins thought about it.

Yeah, well, he finally said. I don't see no moral.

There it *is*, man.

Fuck off.

―――――――――

They carried USO stationery and pencils and pens. They carried Sterno, safety pins, trip flares, signal flares, spools of wire, razor blades, chewing tobacco, liberated joss sticks and statuettes of the smiling Buddha, candles, grease pencils, *The Stars and Stripes*, fingernail clippers, Psy Ops[5] leaflets, bush hats, bolos, and much more. Twice a week, when the resupply choppers came in, they carried hot chow in green Mermite cans and large canvas bags filled with iced beer and soda pop. They carried plastic water containers, each with a two-gallon capacity. Mitchell Sanders carried a set of starched tiger fatigues for special occasions. Henry Dobbins carried Black Flag insecticide. Dave Jensen carried empty sandbags that could be filled at night for added protection. Lee Strunk carried tanning lotion. Some things they carried in common. Taking turns, they carried the big PRC-77 scrambler radio, which weighed thirty pounds with its battery. They shared the weight of memory. They took up what others could no longer bear. Often, they carried each other, the wounded or weak. They carried infections. They carried chess sets, basketballs, Vietnamese-English dictionaries, insignia of rank, Bronze Stars and Purple Hearts, plastic cards imprinted with the Code of Conduct. They carried diseases, among them malaria and dysentery. They carried lice and ringworm and leeches and paddy algae and various rots and molds. They carried the land itself — Vietnam, the place, the soil — a powdery orange-red dust that covered their boots and fatigues and faces. They carried the sky. The whole atmosphere, they carried it, the humidity, the monsoons, the stink of fungus and decay, all of it, they carried gravity. They moved like mules. By daylight they took sniper fire, at night they were mortared, but it was not

――――――――――――――――――――――――

[5] Psychological operations.

battle, it was just the endless march, village to village, without purpose, nothing won or lost. They marched for the sake of the march. They plodded along slowly, dumbly, leaning forward against the heat, unthinking, all blood and bone, simple grunts, soldiering with their legs, toiling up the hills and down into the paddies and across the rivers and up again and down, just humping, one step and then the next and then another, but no volition, no will, because it was automatic, it was anatomy, and the war was entirely a matter of posture and carriage, the hump was everything, a kind of inertia, a kind of emptiness, a dullness of desire and intellect and conscience and hope and human sensibility. Their principles were in their feet. Their calculations were biological. They had no sense of strategy or mission. They searched the villages without knowing what to look for, not caring, kicking over jars of rice, frisking children and old men, blowing tunnels, sometimes setting fires and sometimes not, then forming up and moving on to the next village, then other villages, where it would always be the same. They carried their own lives. The pressures were enormous. In the heat of early afternoon, they would remove their helmets and flak jackets, walking bare, which was dangerous but which helped ease the strain. They would often discard things along the route of march. Purely for comfort, they would throw away rations, blow their Claymores and grenades, no matter, because by nightfall the resupply choppers would arrive with more of the same, then a day or two later still more, fresh watermelons and crates of ammunition and sunglasses and woolen sweaters — the resources were stunning — sparklers for the Fourth of July, colored eggs for Easter. It was the great American war chest — the fruits of science, the smokestacks, the canneries, the arsenals at Hartford, the Minnesota forests, the machine shops, the vast fields of corn and wheat — they carried like freight trains; they carried it on their backs and shoulders — and for all the ambiguities of Vietnam, all the mysteries and unknowns, there was at least the single abiding certainty that they would never be at a loss for things to carry.

After the chopper took Lavender away, Lieutenant Jimmy Cross led his men into the village of Than Khe. They burned everything. They shot chickens and dogs, they trashed the village well, they called in artillery and watched the wreckage, then they marched for several hours through the hot afternoon, and then at dusk, while Kiowa explained how Lavender died, Lieutenant Cross found himself trembling.

He tried not to cry. With his entrenching tool, which weighed five pounds, he began digging a hole in the earth.

He felt shame. He hated himself. He had loved Martha more than his men, and as a consequence Lavender was now dead, and this was something he would have to carry like a stone in his stomach for the rest of the war.

All he could do was dig. He used his entrenching tool like an ax, slashing, feeling both love and hate, and then later, when it was full dark, he sat at the bottom of his foxhole and wept. It went on for a long while. In part, he was grieving for Ted Lavender, but mostly it was for Martha, and for himself, because she belonged to another world, which was not quite real, and because she was a junior at Mount Sebastian College in New Jersey, a poet and a virgin and uninvolved, and because he realized she did not love him and never would.

Like cement, Kiowa whispered in the dark. I swear to God — boom-down. Not a word.

I've heard this, said Norman Bowker.

A pisser, you know? Still zipping himself up. Zapped while zipping.

All right, fine. That's enough.

Yeah, but you had to see it, the guy just —

I *heard*, man. Cement. So why not shut the fuck *up*?

Kiowa shook his head sadly and glanced over at the hole where Lieutenant Jimmy Cross sat watching the night. The air was thick and wet. A warm, dense fog had settled over the paddies and there was the stillness that precedes rain.

After a time Kiowa sighed.

One thing for sure, he said. The Lieutenant's in some deep hurt. I mean that crying jag — the way he was carrying on — it wasn't fake or anything, it was real heavy-duty hurt. The man cares.

Sure, Norman Bowker said.

Say what you want, the man does care.

We all got problems.

Not Lavender.

No, I guess not, Bowker said. Do me a favor, though.

Shut up?

That's a smart Indian. Shut up.

Shrugging, Kiowa pulled off his boots. He wanted to say more, just to lighten up his sleep, but instead he opened his New Testament and arranged it beneath his head as a pillow. The fog made things seem hollow and unattached. He tried not to think about Ted Lavender, but then he was thinking how fast it was, no drama, down and dead, and how it was hard to feel anything except surprise. It seemed un-Christian. He wished he could find some great sadness, or even anger, but the emotion wasn't there and he couldn't make it happen. Mostly he felt pleased to be alive. He liked the smell of the New Testament under his cheek, the leather and ink and paper and glue, whatever the chemicals were. He liked hearing the sounds of night. Even his fatigue, it felt fine, the stiff muscles and the prickly awareness of his own body, a floating feeling. He enjoyed not being dead. Lying there, Kiowa admired Lieutenant Jimmy Cross's capacity for grief. He wanted to share the man's pain, he wanted to care as Jimmy Cross cared. And yet when he closed his eyes, all he could think was Boom-down, and all he could feel was the pleasure of having his boots off and the fog curling in around him and the damp soil and the Bible smells and the plush comfort of night.

After a moment Norman Bowker sat up in the dark.

What the hell, he said. You want to *talk*, talk. Tell it to me.

Forget it.

No, man, go on. One thing I hate, it's a silent Indian.

For the most part they carried themselves with poise, a kind of dignity. Now and then, however, there were times of panic, when they squealed or wanted to squeal but couldn't, when they twitched and made moaning sounds and covered their heads and said Dear Jesus and flopped around on the earth and fired their weapons blindly and cringed and sobbed and begged for the noise to stop and went wild and made stupid promises to themselves and to God and to their mothers and fathers, hoping not to die. In different ways, it happened to all of them. Afterward, when the firing ended, they would blink and peek up. They would touch their bodies, feeling shame, then quickly hiding it. They would force themselves to stand. As if in slow motion, frame by frame, the world would take on the old logic — absolute silence, then the wind, then sunlight, then voices. It was the burden of being alive. Awkwardly, the men would reassemble themselves, first in private, then in groups, becoming soldiers again. They would repair the leaks in their eyes. They would check for casualties, call in dust-offs, light cigarettes, try to smile, clear their throats and spit and begin cleaning their weapons. After a time someone would shake his head and say, No lie, I almost shit my pants, and someone else would laugh, which meant it was bad, yes, but the guy had obviously not shit his pants, it wasn't that bad, and in any case nobody would ever do such a thing and then go ahead and talk about it. They would squint into the dense, oppressive sunlight. For a few moments, perhaps, they would fall silent, lighting a joint and tracking its passage from man to man, inhaling, holding in the humiliation. Scary stuff, one of them might say. But then someone else would grin or flick his eyebrows and say, Roger-dodger, almost cut me a new asshole, *almost.*

There were numerous such poses. Some carried themselves with a sort of wistful resignation, others with pride or stiff soldierly discipline or good humor or macho zeal. They were afraid of dying but they were even more afraid to show it.

They found jokes to tell.

They used a hard vocabulary to contain the terrible softness. *Greased,* they'd say. *Offed, lit up, zapped while zipping.* It wasn't cruelty, just stage presence. They were actors and the war came at them in 3-D. When someone died, it wasn't quite dying, because in a curious way it seemed scripted, and because they had their lines mostly memorized, irony mixed with tragedy, and because they called it by other names, as if to encyst and destroy the reality of death itself. They kicked corpses. They cut off thumbs. They talked grunt lingo. They told stories about Ted Lavender's supply of tranquilizers, how the poor guy didn't feel a thing, how incredibly tranquil he was.

There's a moral here, said Mitchell Sanders.

They were waiting for Lavender's chopper, smoking the dead man's dope.

The moral's pretty obvious, Sanders said, and winked. Stay away from drugs. No joke, they'll ruin your day every time.

Cute, said Henry Dobbins.

Mind-blower, get it? Talk about wiggy — nothing left, just blood and brains.

They made themselves laugh.

There it is, they'd say, over and over, as if the repetition itself were an act of poise, a balance between crazy and almost crazy, knowing without going. There it is, which meant be cool, let it ride, because oh yeah, man, you can't change what can't be changed, there it is, there it absolutely and positively and fucking well *is*.

They were tough.

They carried all the emotional baggage of men who might die. Grief, terror, love, longing — these were intangibles, but the intangibles had their own mass and specific gravity, they had tangible weight. They carried shameful memories. They carried the common secret of cowardice barely restrained, the instinct to run or freeze or hide, and in many respects this was the heaviest burden of all, for it could never be put down, it required perfect balance and perfect posture. They carried their reputations. They carried the soldier's greatest fear, which was the fear of blushing. Men killed, and died, because they were embarrassed not to. It was what had brought them to the war in the first place, nothing positive, no dreams of glory or honor, just to avoid the blush of dishonor. They died so as not to die of embarrassment. They crawled into tunnels and walked point and advanced under fire. Each morning, despite the unknowns, they made their legs move. They endured. They kept humping. They did not submit to the obvious alternative, which was simply to close the eyes and fall. So easy, really. Go limp and tumble to the ground and let the muscles unwind and not speak and not budge until your buddies picked you up and lifted you into the chopper that would roar and dip its nose and carry you off to the world. A mere matter of falling, yet no one ever fell. It was not courage, exactly; the object was not valor. Rather, they were too frightened to be cowards.

By and large they carried these things inside, maintaining the masks of composure. They sneered at sick call. They spoke bitterly about guys who had found release by shooting off their own toes or fingers. Pussies, they'd say. Candyasses. It was fierce, mocking talk, with only a trace of envy or awe, but even so, the image played itself out behind their eyes.

They imagined the muzzle against flesh. They imagined the quick, sweet pain, then the evacuation to Japan, then a hospital with warm beds and cute geisha nurses.

They dreamed of freedom birds.

At night, on guard, staring into the dark, they were carried away by jumbo jets. They felt the rush of takeoff. *Gone!* they yelled. And then velocity, wings and engines, a smiling stewardess — but it was more than a plane, it was a real bird, a big sleek silver bird with feathers and talons and high screeching. They were flying. The weights fell off, there was nothing to bear. They laughed and held on tight, feeling the cold slap of wind and altitude, soaring, thinking *It's over, I'm gone!* — they were naked, they were light and free — it was all lightness, bright and fast and buoyant, light as light, a helium buzz in the brain, a giddy bubbling in the lungs as they were taken up over the clouds and the war, beyond duty, beyond gravity and mortification and global entanglements — *Sin loi!*[6] they yelled, *I'm sorry, motherfuckers, but I'm out of it, I'm goofed, I'm on a space cruise, I'm gone!* — and it was a restful, disencumbered sensation, just riding the light waves, sailing that big silver freedom bird over the mountains and oceans, over America, over the farms and great sleeping cities and cemeteries and highways and the golden arches of McDonald's. It was flight, a kind of fleeing, a kind of falling, falling higher and higher, spinning off the edge of the earth and beyond the sun and through the vast, silent vacuum where there were no burdens and where everything weighed exactly nothing. *Gone!* they screamed, *I'm sorry but I'm gone!* And so at night, not quite dreaming, they gave themselves over to lightness, they were carried, they were purely borne.

On the morning after Ted Lavender died, First Lieutenant Jimmy Cross crouched at the bottom of his foxhole and burned Martha's letters. Then he burned the two photographs. There was a steady rain falling, which made it difficult, but he used heat tabs and Sterno to build a small fire, screening it with his body, holding the photographs over the tight blue flame with the tips of his fingers.

He realized it was only a gesture. Stupid, he thought. Sentimental, too, but mostly just stupid.

Lavender was dead. You couldn't burn the blame.

Besides, the letters were in his head. And even now, without photographs, Lieutenant Cross could see Martha playing volleyball in her white gym shorts and yellow T-shirt. He could see her moving in the rain.

When the fire died out, Lieutenant Cross pulled his poncho over his shoulders and ate breakfast from a can.

There was no great mystery, he decided.

In those burned letters Martha had never mentioned the war, except to say, Jimmy, take care of yourself. She wasn't involved. She signed the letters "Love," but it wasn't love, and all the fine lines and technicalities did not matter.

The morning came up wet and blurry. Everything seemed part of everything else, the fog and Martha and the deepening rain.

It was a war, after all.

Half smiling, Lieutenant Jimmy Cross took out his maps. He shook his head hard, as if to clear it, then bent forward and began planning the day's march. In ten minutes, or maybe twenty, he would rouse the men and they would pack up and head west, where the maps showed the country to be green and inviting. They would do what they had always done. The rain might add some weight, but otherwise it would be one more day layered upon all the other days.

---

[6] "Sorry about that!" (Vietnamese).

He was realistic about it. There was that new hardness in his stomach.

No more fantasies, he told himself.

Henceforth, when he thought about Martha, it would be only to think that she belonged elsewhere. He would shut down the daydreams. This was not Mount Sebastian, it was another world, where there were no pretty poems or midterm exams, a place where men died because of carelessness and gross stupidity. Kiowa was right. Boom-down, and you were dead, never partly dead.

Briefly, in the rain, Lieutenant Cross saw Martha's gray eyes gazing back at him.

He understood.

It was very sad, he thought. The things men carried inside. The things men did or felt they had to do.

He almost nodded at her, but didn't.

Instead he went back to his maps. He was now determined to perform his duties firmly and without negligence. It wouldn't help Lavender, he knew that, but from this point on he would comport himself as a soldier. He would dispose of his good-luck pebble. Swallow it, maybe, or use Lee Strunk's slingshot, or just drop it along the trail. On the march he would impose strict field discipline. He would be careful to send out flank security, to prevent straggling or bunching up, to keep his troops moving at the proper pace and at the proper interval. He would insist on clean weapons. He would confiscate the remainder of Lavender's dope. Later in the day, perhaps, he would call the men together and speak to them plainly. He would accept the blame for what had happened to Ted Lavender. He would be a man about it. He would look them in the eyes, keeping his chin level, and he would issue the new SOPs in a calm, impersonal tone of voice, an officer's voice, leaving no room for argument or discussion. Commencing immediately, he'd tell them, they would no longer abandon equipment along the route of march. They would police up their acts. They would get their shit together, and keep it together, and maintain it neatly and in good working order.

He would not tolerate laxity. He would show strength, distancing himself.

Among the men there would be grumbling, of course, and maybe worse, because their days would seem longer and their loads heavier, but Lieutenant Cross reminded himself that his obligation was not to be loved but to lead. He would dispense with love; it was not now a factor. And if anyone quarreled or complained, he would simply tighten his lips and arrange his shoulders in the correct command posture. He might give a curt little nod. Or he might not. He might just shrug and say Carry on, then they would saddle up and form into a column and move out toward the villages of Than Khe.

Flannery O'Connor

Mary Flannery O'Connor (1925–1964) was born in Savannah, Georgia, the only child of Roman Catholic parents. When she was thirteen her father was found to have disseminated lupus, an incurable disease in which antibodies in the immune system attack the body's own substances. After her father's death in 1941, O'Connor attended Georgia State College for Women in Milledgeville, where she published stories and edited the literary magazine. On the strength of these stories, she was awarded a fellowship at the Writers' Workshop at the University of Iowa and earned her M.F.A. degree there. Late in 1950 she became ill with what was diagnosed as lupus, and she returned to Milledgeville to start a series of treatments that temporarily arrested the disease. Living with her mother on the family's 500-acre dairy farm, O'Connor began to work again, writing from nine to twelve in the morning and spending the rest of the day resting, reading, writing letters, and raising peacocks.

O'Connor's first book, *Wise Blood*, a complex comic novel attacking the contemporary secularization of religion, was published in 1952. It was followed in 1955 by a collection of stories, *A Good Man Is Hard to Find*. O'Connor was able to see a second novel, *The Violent Bear It Away*, through to publication in 1960, but she died of lupus in 1964, having completed enough stories for a second collection, *Everything That Rises Must Converge* (1965). Her total output of just thirty-one stories, collected in her *Complete Stories*, won the National Book Award for fiction in 1972.

Despite her illness, O'Connor was never a recluse; she accepted as many lecture invitations as her health would permit. A volume of her lectures and occasional pieces was published in 1969 as *Mystery and Manners*. It is a valuable companion to her stories and novels, because she often reflected on her writing and interpreted her fiction. As a devout Roman Catholic, O'Connor was uncompromising in her religious views: "For I am no disbeliever in spiritual purpose and no vague believer. This means that for me the meaning of life is centered in our Redemption by Christ and what I see in the world I see in relation to that." As Joyce Carol Oates recognized in her essay "The Visionary Art of Flannery O'Connor," O'Connor is one of the great religious writers of modern times, unique "in her celebration of the necessity of succumbing to the divine through violence that is immediate and irreparable. There is no mysticism in her work that is only spiritual; it is physical as well." O'Connor's stories, like the three included here, frequently involve family relationships, but they are not meant to be read as realistic fiction, despite her remarkable ear for dialogue. O'Connor said she wrote them as parables, as the epigraph to "A Good Man Is Hard to Find" attests.

RELATED CASEBOOK
See Casebook on Flannery O'Connor, pages 1589–1615, including Flannery O'Connor, "From Letters, 1954–55," page 1590; "Writing Short Stories," page 1592; "A Reasonable Use of the Unreasonable," page 1597; Joyce Carol Oates, "The Parables of Flannery O'Connor," page 1600; Wayne C. Booth, "A Rhetorical

Reading of O'Connor's 'Everything That Rises Must Converge,'" page 1608; Dorothy Tuck McFarland, "On 'Good Country People,'" page 1611.

Everything That Rises Must Converge

1965

HER DOCTOR HAD TOLD Julian's mother that she must lose twenty pounds on account of her blood pressure, so on Wednesday nights Julian had to take her downtown on the bus for a reducing class at the Y. The reducing class was designed for working girls over fifty, who weighed from 165 to 200 pounds. His mother was one of the slimmer ones, but she said ladies did not tell their age or weight. She would not ride the buses by herself at night since they had been integrated, and because the reducing class was one of her few pleasures, necessary for her health, and *free*, she said Julian could at least put himself out to take her, considering all she did for him. Julian did not like to consider all she did for him, but every Wednesday night he braced himself and took her.

She was almost ready to go, standing before the hall mirror, putting on her hat, while he, his hands behind him, appeared pinned to the door frame, waiting like Saint Sebastian for the arrows to begin piercing him. The hat was new and had cost her seven dollars and a half. She kept saying, "Maybe I shouldn't have paid that for it. No, I shouldn't have. I'll take it off and return it tomorrow. I shouldn't have bought it."

Julian raised his eyes to heaven. "Yes, you should have bought it," he said. "Put it on and let's go." It was a hideous hat. A purple velvet flap came down on one side of it and stood up on the other; the rest of it was green and looked like a cushion with the stuffing out. He decided it was less comical than jaunty and pathetic. Everything that gave her pleasure was small and depressed him.

She lifted the hat one more time and set it down slowly on top of her head. Two wings of gray hair protruded on either side of her florid face, but her eyes, sky-blue, were as innocent and untouched by experience as they must have been when she was ten. Were it not that she was a widow who had struggled fiercely to feed and clothe and put him through school and who was supporting him still, "until he got on his feet," she might have been a little girl that he had to take to town.

"It's all right, it's all right," he said. "Let's go." He opened the door himself and started down the walk to get her going. The sky was a dying violet and the houses stood out darkly against it, bulbous liver-colored monstrosities of a uniform ugliness though no two were alike. Since this had been a fashionable neighborhood forty years ago, his mother persisted in thinking they did well to have an apartment in it. Each house had a narrow collar of dirt around it in which sat, usually, a grubby child. Julian walked with his hands in his pockets, his head down and thrust forward, and his eyes glazed with the determination to make himself completely numb during the time he would be sacrificed to her pleasure.

The door closed and he turned to find the dumpy figure, surmounted by the atrocious hat, coming toward him. "Well," she said, "you only live once and paying a little more for it, I at least won't meet myself coming and going."

"Some day I'll start making money," Julian said gloomily — he knew he never would — "and you can have one of those jokes whenever you take the fit." But first they would move. He visualized a place where the nearest neighbor would be three miles away on either side.

"I think you're doing fine," she said, drawing on her gloves. "You've only been out of school a year. Rome wasn't built in a day."

She was one of the few members of the Y reducing class who arrived in hat and gloves and who had a son who had been to college. "It takes time," she said, "and the world is in such a mess. This hat looked better on me than any of the others, though when she brought it out I said, 'Take that thing back. I wouldn't have it on my head,' and she said, 'Now wait till you see it on,' and when she put it on me, I said, 'We-ull,' and she said, 'If you ask me, that hat does something for you and you do something for the hat, and besides,' she said, 'with that hat, you won't meet yourself coming and going.'"

Julian thought he could have stood his lot better if she had been selfish, if she had been an old hag who drank and screamed at him. He walked along, saturated in depression, as if in the midst of his martyrdom he had lost his faith. Catching sight of his long, hopeless, irritated face, she stopped suddenly with a grief-stricken look, and pulled back on his arm. "Wait on me," she said. "I'm going back to the house and take this thing off and tomorrow I'm going to return it. I was out of my head. I can pay the gas bill with the seven-fifty."

He caught her arm in a vicious grip. "You are not going to take it back," he said. "I like it."

"Well," she said, "I don't think I ought . . ."

"Shut up and enjoy it," he muttered, more depressed than ever.

"With the world in the mess it's in," she said, "it's a wonder we can enjoy anything. I tell you, the bottom rail is on the top."

Julian sighed.

"Of course," she said, "if you know who you are, you can go anywhere." She said this every time he took her to the reducing class. "Most of them in it are not our kind of people," she said, "but I can be gracious to anybody. I know who I am."

"They don't give a damn for your graciousness," Julian said savagely. "Knowing who you are is good for one generation only. You haven't the foggiest idea where you stand now or who you are."

She stopped and allowed her eyes to flash at him. "I most certainly do know who I am," she said, "and if you don't know who you are, I'm ashamed of you."

"Oh hell," Julian said.

"Your great-grandfather was a former governor of this state," she said. "Your grandfather was a prosperous landowner. Your grandmother was a Godhigh."

"Will you look around you," he said tensely, "and see where you are now?" and he swept his arm jerkily out to indicate the neighborhood, which the growing darkness at least made less dingy.

"You remain what you are," she said. "Your great-grandfather had a planta- tion and two hundred slaves."

"There are no more slaves," he said irritably.

"They were better off when they were," she said. He groaned to see that she was off on that topic. She rolled onto it every few days like a train on an open track. He knew every stop, every junction, every swamp along the way, and knew the exact point at which her conclusion would roll majestically into the station: "It's ridiculous. It's simply not realistic. They should rise, yes, but on their own side of the fence."

"Let's skip it," Julian said.

"The ones I feel sorry for," she said, "are the ones that are half white. They're tragic."

"Will you skip it?"

"Suppose we were half white. We would certainly have mixed feelings."

"I have mixed feelings now," he groaned.

"Well let's talk about something pleasant," she said. "I remember going to Grandpa's when I was a little girl. Then the house had double stairways that went up to what was really the second floor — all the cooking was done on the first. I used to like to stay down in the kitchen on account of the way the walls smelled. I would sit with my nose pressed against the plaster and take deep breaths. Actually the place belonged to the Godhighs but your grandfather Chestny paid the mortgage and saved it for them. They were in reduced circumstances," she said, "but reduced or not, they never forgot who they were."

"Doubtless that decayed mansion reminded them," Julian muttered. He never spoke of it without contempt or thought of it without longing. He had seen it once when he was a child before it had been sold. The double stairways had rotted and had been torn down. Negroes were living in it. But it remained in his mind as his mother had known it. It appeared in his dreams regularly. He would stand on the wide porch, listening to the rustle of oak leaves, then wander through the high-ceilinged hall into the parlor that opened onto it and gaze at the worn rugs and faded draperies. It occurred to him that it was he, not she, who could have appreciated it. He preferred its threadbare elegance to anything he could name and it was because of it that all the neighborhoods they had lived in had been a torment to him — whereas she had hardly known the difference. She called her insensitivity "being adjustable."

"And I remember the old darky who was my nurse, Caroline. There was no better person in the world. I've always had a great respect for my colored friends," she said. "I'd do anything in the world for them and they'd . . ."

"Will you for God's sake get off that subject?" Julian said. When he got on a bus by himself, he made it a point to sit down beside a Negro, in reparation as it were for his mother's sins.

"You're mighty touchy tonight," she said. "Do you feel all right?"

"Yes I feel all right," he said. "Now lay off."

She pursed her lips. "Well, you certainly are in a vile humor," she observed. "I just won't speak to you at all."

They had reached the bus stop. There was no bus in sight and Julian, his hands still jammed in his pockets and his head thrust forward, scowled down the empty street. The frustration of having to wait on the bus as well as ride on it began to creep up his neck like a hot hand. The presence of his mother was borne in upon him as she gave a pained sigh. He looked at her bleakly. She was holding herself very erect under the preposterous hat, wearing it like a banner of her imaginary dignity. There was in him an evil urge to break her spirit. He suddenly unloosened his tie and pulled it off and put it in his pocket.

She stiffened. "Why must you look like *that* when you take me to town?" she said. "Why must you deliberately embarrass me?"

"If you'll never learn where you are," he said, "you can at least learn where I am."

"You look like a — thug," she said.

"Then I must be one," he murmured.

"I'll just go home," she said. "I will not bother you. If you can't do a little thing like that for me . . ."

Rolling his eyes upward, he put his tie back on. "Restored to my class," he muttered. He thrust his face toward her and hissed, "True culture is in the mind, the *mind*," he said, and tapped his head, "the mind."

"It's in the heart," she said, "and in how you do things and how you do things is because of who you *are*."

"Nobody in the damn bus cares who you are."

"I care who I am," she said icily.

The lighted bus appeared on top of the next hill and as it approached, they moved out into the street to meet it. He put his hand under her elbow and hoisted her up on the creaking step. She entered with a little smile, as if she were going into a drawing room where everyone had been waiting for her. While he put in the tokens, she sat down on one of the broad front seats for three which faced the aisle. A thin woman with protruding teeth and long yellow hair was sitting on the end of it. His mother moved up beside her and left room for Julian beside herself. He sat down and looked at the floor across the aisle where a pair of thin feet in red and white canvas sandals were planted.

His mother immediately began a general conversation meant to attract anyone who felt like talking. "Can it get any hotter?" she said and removed from her purse a folding fan, black with a Japanese scene on it, which she began to flutter before her.

"I reckon it might could," the woman with the protruding teeth said, "but I know for a fact my apartment couldn't get no hotter."

"It must get the afternoon sun," his mother said. She sat forward and looked up and down the bus. It was half filled. Everybody was white. "I see we have the bus to ourselves," she said. Julian cringed.

"For a change," said the woman across the aisle, the owner of the red and white canvas sandals. "I come on one the other day and they were thick as fleas — up front and all through."

"The world is in a mess everywhere," his mother said. "I don't know how we've let it get in this fix."

"What gets my goat is all those boys from good families stealing automobile tires," the woman with the protruding teeth said. "I told my boy, I said you may not be rich but you been raised right and if I ever catch you in any such mess, they can send you on to the reformatory. Be exactly where you belong."

"Training tells," his mother said. "Is your boy in high school?"

"Ninth grade," the woman said.

"My son just finished college last year. He wants to write but he's selling typewriters until he gets started," his mother said.

The woman leaned forward and peered at Julian. He threw her such a malevolent look that she subsided against the seat. On the floor across the aisle there was an abandoned newspaper. He got up and got it and opened it out in front of him. His mother discreetly continued the conversation in a lower tone but the woman across the aisle said in a loud voice, "Well that's nice. Selling typewriters is close to writing. He can go right from one to the other."

"I tell him," his mother said, "that Rome wasn't built in a day."

Behind the newspaper Julian was withdrawing into the inner compartment of his mind where he spent most of his time. This was a kind of mental bubble in which he established himself when he could not bear to be part of what was going on around him. From it he could see out and judge but in it he was safe from any kind of penetration from without. It was the only place where he felt free of the general idiocy of his fellows. His mother had never entered it but from it he could see her with absolute clarity.

The old lady was clever enough and he thought that if she had started from any of the right premises, more might have been expected of her. She lived according to the laws of her own fantasy world, outside of which he had never seen her set foot. The law of it was to sacrifice herself for him after she had first created the necessity to do so by making a mess of things. If he had permitted her sacrifices, it was only because her lack of foresight had made them necessary. All of her life had been a struggle to act like a Chestny without the Chestny goods, and to give him everything she thought a Chestny ought to have; but since, said she, it was fun to struggle, why complain? And when you had won, as she had won, what fun to look back on the hard times! He could not forgive her that she had enjoyed the struggle and that she thought *she* had won.

What she meant when she said she had won was that she had brought him up successfully and had sent him to college and that he had turned out so well — good looking (her teeth had gone unfilled, so that his could be straightened), intelligent (he realized he was too intelligent to be a success), and with a future ahead of him (there was of course no future ahead of him). She excused his gloominess on the grounds that he was still growing up and his radical ideas on his lack of practical experience. She said he didn't yet know a thing about "life," that he hadn't even entered the real world — when already he was as disenchanted with it as a man of fifty.

The further irony of all this was that in spite of her, he had turned out so well. In spite of going to only a third-rate college, he had, on his own initiative, come out with a first-rate education; in spite of growing up dominated by a small mind, he had ended up with a large one; in spite of all her foolish views, he was free of prejudice and unafraid to face facts. Most miraculous of all, instead of being blinded by love for her as she was for him, he had cut himself emotionally free of her and could see her with complete objectivity. He was not dominated by his mother.

The bus stopped with a sudden jerk and shook him from his meditation. A woman from the back lurched forward with little steps and barely escaped falling in his newspaper as she righted herself. She got off and a large Negro got on. Julian kept his paper lowered to watch. It gave him a certain satisfaction to see injustice in daily operation. It confirmed his view that with a few exceptions there was no one worth knowing within a radius of three hundred miles. The Negro was well dressed and carried a briefcase. He looked round and then sat down on the other end of the seat where the woman with the red and white canvas sandals was sitting. He immediately unfolded a newspaper and obscured himself behind it. Julian's mother's elbow at once prodded insistently into his ribs. "Now you see why I won't ride on these buses by myself," she whispered.

The woman with the red and white canvas sandals had risen at the same time the Negro sat down and had gone further back in the bus and taken the seat of the woman who had got off. His mother leaned forward and cast her an approving look.

Julian rose, crossed the aisle, and sat down in the place of the woman with the canvas sandals. From this position, he looked serenely across at his mother. Her face had turned an angry red. He stared at her, making his eyes the eyes of a stranger. He felt his tension suddenly lift as if he had openly declared war on her.

He would have liked to get in conversation with the Negro and to talk with him about art or politics or any subject that would be above the comprehension of those around them, but the man remained entrenched behind his paper. He was either ignoring the change of seating or had never noticed it. There was no way for Julian to convey his sympathy.

His mother kept her eyes fixed reproachfully on his face. The woman with the protruding teeth was looking at him avidly as if he were a type of monster new to her.

"Do you have a light?" he asked the Negro.

Without looking away from his paper, the man reached in his pocket and handed him a packet of matches.

"Thanks," Julian said. For a moment he held the matches foolishly. A NO SMOKING sign looked down upon him from over the door. This alone would not have deterred him; he had no cigarettes. He had quit smoking some months before because he could not afford it. "Sorry," he muttered and handed back the matches. The Negro lowered the paper and gave him an annoyed look. He took the matches and raised the paper again.

His mother continued to gaze at him but she did not take the advantage of his momentary discomfort. Her eyes retained their battered look. Her face seemed to be unnaturally red, as if her blood pressure had risen. Julian allowed no glimmer of sympathy to show on his face. Having got the advantage, he wanted desperately to keep it and carry it through. He would have liked to teach her a lesson that would last her a while, but there seemed no way to continue the point. The Negro refused to come out from behind his paper.

Julian folded his arms and looked stolidly before him, facing her but as if he did not see her, as if he had ceased to recognize her existence. He visualized a scene in which, the bus having reached their stop, he would remain in his seat and when she said, "Aren't you going to get off?" he would look at her as a stranger who had rashly addressed him. The corner they got off on was usually deserted, but it was well lighted and it would not hurt her to walk by herself the four blocks to the Y. He decided to wait until the time came and then decide whether or not he would let her get off by herself. He would have to be at the Y at ten to bring her back, but he could leave her wondering if he was going to show up. There was no reason for her to think she could always depend on him.

He retired again into the high-ceilinged room sparsely settled with large pieces of antique furniture. His soul expanded momentarily but then he became aware of his mother across from him and the vision shriveled. He studied her coldly. Her feet in little pumps dangled like a child's and did not quite reach the floor. She was training on him an exaggerated look of reproach. He felt completely detached from her. At that moment he could with pleasure have slapped her as he would have slapped a particularly obnoxious child in his charge.

He began to imagine various unlikely ways by which he could teach her a lesson. He might make friends with some distinguished Negro professor or lawyer and bring him home to spend the evening. He would be entirely justified but her blood pressure would rise to 300. He could not push her to the extent of making her have a stroke, and moreover, he had never been successful at making any Negro friends. He had tried to strike up an acquaintance on the bus with some of the better types, with ones that looked like professors or ministers or lawyers. One morning he had sat down next to a distinguished-looking dark brown man who had answered his questions with a sonorous solemnity but who had turned out to be an undertaker. Another day he had sat down beside a cigar-smoking Negro with a diamond ring on his finger, but after a few stilted pleasantries, the Negro had rung the buzzer and risen, slipping two lottery tickets into Julian's hand as he climbed over him to leave.

He imagined his mother lying desperately ill and his being able to secure only a Negro doctor for her. He toyed with that idea for a few minutes and then dropped it for a momentary vision of himself participating as a sympathizer in a sit-in demonstration. This was possible but he did not linger with it. Instead, he approached the ultimate horror. He brought home a beautiful suspiciously

Negroid woman. Prepare yourself, he said. There is nothing you can do about it. This is the woman I've chosen. She's intelligent, dignified, even good, and she's suffered and she hasn't thought it *fun*. Now persecute us, go ahead and persecute us. Drive her out of here, but remember, you're driving me too. His eyes were narrowed and through the indignation he had generated, he saw his mother across the aisle, purplefaced, shrunken to the dwarf-like proportions of her moral nature, sitting like a mummy beneath the ridiculous banner of her hat.

He was tilted out of his fantasy again as the bus stopped. The door opened with a sucking hiss and out of the dark a large, gaily dressed, sullen-looking colored woman got on with a little boy. The child, who might have been four, had on a short plaid suit and a Tyrolean hat with a blue feather in it. Julian hoped that he would sit down beside him and that the woman would push in beside his mother. He could think of no better arrangement.

As she waited for her tokens, the woman was surveying the seating possibilities — he hoped with the idea of sitting where she was least wanted. There was something familiar-looking about her but Julian could not place what it was. She was a giant of a woman. Her face was set not only to meet opposition but to seek it out. The downward tilt of her large lower lip was like a warning sign: DON'T TAMPER WITH ME. Her bulging figure was encased in a green crepe dress and her feet overflowed in red shoes. She had on a hideous hat. A purple velvet flap came down on one side of it and stood up on the other; the rest of it was green and looked like a cushion with the stuffing out. She carried a mammoth red pocketbook that bulged throughout as if it were stuffed with rocks.

To Julian's disappointment, the little boy climbed up on the empty seat beside his mother. His mother lumped all children, black and white, into the common category, "cute," and she thought little Negroes were on the whole cuter than little white children. She smiled at the little boy as he climbed on the seat.

Meanwhile the woman was bearing down upon the empty seat beside Julian. To his annoyance, she squeezed herself into it. He saw his mother's face change as the woman settled herself next to him and he realized with satisfaction that this was more objectionable to her than it was to him. Her face seemed almost gray and there was a look of dull recognition in her eyes, as if suddenly she had sickened at some awful confrontation. Julian saw that it was because she and the woman had, in a sense, swapped sons. Though his mother would not realize the symbolic significance of this, she would feel it. His amusement showed plainly on his face.

The woman next to him muttered something unintelligible to herself. He was conscious of a kind of bristling next to him, muted growling like that of an angry cat. He could not see anything but the red pocketbook upright on the bulging green thighs. He visualized the woman as she had stood waiting for her tokens — the ponderous figure, rising from the red shoes upward over the solid hips, the mammoth bosom, the haughty face, to the green and purple hat.

His eyes widened.

The vision of the two hats, identical, broke upon him with the radiance of a brilliant sunrise. His face was suddenly lit with joy. He could not believe that Fate had thrust upon his mother such a lesson. He gave a loud chuckle so that she would look at him and see that he saw. She turned her eyes on him slowly. The blue in them seemed to have turned a bruised purple. For a moment he had an uncomfortable sense of her innocence, but it lasted only a second before principle rescued him. Justice entitled him to laugh. His grin hardened until it said to her as plainly as if he were saying aloud: Your punishment exactly fits your pettiness. This should teach you a permanent lesson.

Her eyes shifted to the woman. She seemed unable to bear looking at him and to find the woman preferable. He became conscious again of the bristling presence at his side. The woman was rumbling like a volcano about to become active. His mother's mouth began to twitch slightly at one corner. With a sinking heart, he saw incipient signs of recovery on her face and realized that this was going to strike her suddenly as funny and was going to be no lesson at all. She kept her eyes on the woman and an amused smile came over her face as if the woman were a monkey that had stolen her hat. The little Negro was looking up at her with large fascinated eyes. He had been trying to attract her attention for some time.

"Carver," the woman said suddenly. "Come heah!"

When he saw that the spotlight was on him at last, Carver drew his feet up and turned himself toward Julian's mother and giggled.

"Carver!" the woman said. "You heah me? Come Heah!"

Carver slid down from the seat but remained squatting with his back against the base of it, his head turned slowly around toward Julian's mother, who was smiling at him. The woman reached a hand across the aisle and snatched him to her. He righted himself and hung backwards on her knees, grinning at Julian's mother. "Isn't he cute?" Julian's mother said to the woman with the protruding teeth.

"I reckon he is," the woman said without conviction.

The Negress yanked him upright but he eased out of her grip and shot across the aisle and scrambled, giggling wildly, onto the seat beside his love.

"I think he likes me," Julian's mother said, and smiled at the woman. It was the smile she used when she was being particularly gracious to an inferior. Julian saw everything lost. The lesson had rolled off her like rain on a roof.

The woman stood up and yanked the little boy off the seat as if she were snatching him from contagion. Julian could feel the rage in her at having no weapon like his mother's smile. She gave the child a sharp slap across his leg. He howled once and then thrust his head into her stomach and kicked his feet against her shins. "Behave," she said vehemently.

The bus stopped and the Negro who had been reading the newspaper got off. The woman moved over and set the little boy down with a thump between herself and Julian. She held him firmly by the knee. In a moment he put his hands in front of his face and peeped at Julian's mother through his fingers.

"I see yoooooooo!" she said and put her hand in front of her face and peeped at him.

The woman slapped his hand down. "Quit yo' foolishness," she said, "before I knock the living Jesus out of you!"

Julian was thankful that the next stop was theirs. He reached up and pulled the cord. The woman reached up and pulled it at the same time. Oh my God, he thought. He had the terrible intuition that when they got off the bus together, his mother would open her purse and give the little boy a nickel. The gesture would be as natural to her as breathing. The bus stopped and the woman got up and lunged to the front, dragging the child, who wished to stay on, after her. Julian and his mother got up and followed. As they neared the door, Julian tried to relieve her of her pocketbook.

"No," she murmured, "I want to give the little boy a nickel."

"No!" Julian hissed. "No!"

She smiled down at the child and opened her bag. The bus door opened and the woman picked him up by the arm and descended with him, hanging at her hip. Once in the street she set him down and shook him.

Julian's mother had to close her purse while she got down the bus step but as soon as her feet were on the ground, she opened it again and began to rummage inside. "I can't find but a penny," she whispered, "but it looks like a new one."

"Don't do it!" Julian said fiercely between his teeth. There was a streetlight on the corner and she hurried to get under it so that she could better see into her pocketbook. The woman was heading off rapidly down the street with the child still hanging backward on her hand.

"Oh little boy!" Julian's mother called and took a few quick steps and caught up with them just beyond the lamppost. "Here's a bright new penny for you," and she held out the coin, which shone bronze in the dim light.

The huge woman turned and for a moment stood, her shoulders lifted and her face frozen with frustrated rage, and stared at Julian's mother. Then all at once she seemed to explode like a piece of machinery that had been given one ounce of pressure too much. Julian saw the black fist swing out with the red pocketbook. He shut his eyes and cringed as he heard the woman shout, "He don't take nobody's pennies!" When he opened his eyes, the woman was disappearing down the street with the little boy staring wide-eyed over her shoulder. Julian's mother was sitting on the sidewalk.

"I told you not to do that," Julian said angrily. "I told you not to do that!"

He stood over her for a minute, gritting his teeth. Her legs were stretched out in front of her and her hat was on her lap. He squatted down and looked her in the face. It was totally expressionless. "You got exactly what you deserved," he said. "Now get up."

He picked up her pocketbook and put what had fallen out back in it. He picked the hat up off her lap. The penny caught his eye on the sidewalk and he picked that up and let it drop before her eyes into the purse. Then he stood up and leaned over and held his hands out to pull her up. She remained immobile. He sighed. Rising above them on either side were black apartment buildings, marked with irregular rectangles of light. At the end of the block a man came out of a door and walked off in the opposite direction. "All right," he said, "suppose somebody happens by and wants to know why you're sitting on the sidewalk?"

She took the hand and, breathing hard, pulled heavily up on it and then stood for a moment, swaying slightly as if the spots of light in the darkness were circling around her. Her eyes, shadowed and confused, finally settled on his face. He did not try to conceal his irritation. "I hope this teaches you a lesson," he said. She leaned forward and her eyes raked his face. She seemed trying to determine his identity. Then, as if she found nothing familiar about him, she started off with a headlong movement in the wrong direction.

"Aren't you going to the Y?" he asked.

"Home," she muttered.

"Well, are we walking?"

For answer she kept going. Julian followed along, his hands behind him. He saw no reason to let the lesson she had had go without backing it up with an explanation of its meaning. She might as well be made to understand what had happened to her. "Don't think that was just an uppity Negro woman," he said. "That was the whole colored race which will no longer take your condescending pennies. That was your black double. She can wear the same hat as you, and to be sure," he added gratuitously (because he thought it was funny), "it looked better on her than it did on you. What all this means," he said, "is that the old world is gone. The old manners are obsolete and your graciousness is not worth a damn." He thought bitterly of the house that had been lost for him. "You aren't who you think you are," he said.

She continued to plow ahead, paying no attention to him. Her hair had come undone on one side. She dropped her pocketbook and took no notice. He stopped and picked it up and handed it to her but she did not take it.

"You needn't act as if the world had come to an end," he said, "because it hasn't. From now on you've got to live in a new world and face a few realities for a change. Buck up," he said, "it won't kill you."

She was breathing fast.

"Let's wait on the bus," he said.

"Home," she said thickly.

"I hate to see you behave like this," he said. "Just like a child. I should be able to expect more of you." He decided to stop where he was and make her stop and wait for a bus. "I'm not going any farther," he said, stopping. "We're going on the bus."

She continued to go on as if she had not heard him. He took a few steps and caught her arm and stopped her. He looked into her face and caught his breath. He was looking into a face he had never seen before. "Tell Grandpa to come get me," she said.

He stared, stricken.

"Tell Caroline to come get me," she said.

Stunned, he let her go and she lurched forward again, walking as if one leg were shorter than the other. A tide of darkness seemed to be sweeping her from him. "Mother!" he cried. "Darling, sweetheart, wait!" Crumpling, she fell to the pavement. He dashed forward and fell at her side, crying, "Mamma,

Mamma!" He turned her over. Her face was fiercely distorted. One eye, large and staring, moved slightly to the left as if it had become unmoored. The other remained fixed on him, raked his face again, found nothing, and closed.

"Wait here, wait here!" he cried and jumped up and began to run for help toward a cluster of lights he saw in the distance ahead of him. "Help, help!" he shouted, but his voice was thin, scarcely a thread of sound. The lights drifted farther away the faster he ran and his feet moved numbly as if they carried him nowhere. The tide of darkness seemed to sweep him back to her, postponing from moment to moment his entry into the world of guilt and sorrow.

Good Country People

1955

BESIDES THE NEUTRAL EXPRESSION that she wore when she was alone, Mrs. Freeman had two others, forward and reverse, that she used for all her human dealings. Her forward expression was steady and driving like the advance of a heavy truck. Her eyes never swerved to left or right but turned as the story turned as if they followed a yellow line down the center of it. She seldom used the other expression because it was not often necessary for her to retract a statement, but when she did, her face came to a complete stop, there was an almost imperceptible movement of her black eyes, during which they seemed to be receding, and then the observer would see that Mrs. Freeman, though she might stand there as real as several grain sacks thrown on top of each other, was no longer there in spirit. As for getting anything across to her when this was the case, Mrs. Hopewell had given it up. She might talk her head off. Mrs. Freeman could never be brought to admit herself wrong on any point. She would stand there and if she could be brought to say anything, it was something like, "Well, I wouldn't of said it was and I wouldn't of said it wasn't," or letting her gaze range over the top kitchen shelf where there was an assortment of dusty bottles, she might remark, "I see you ain't ate many of them figs you put up last summer."

They carried on their most important business in the kitchen at breakfast. Every morning Mrs. Hopewell got up at seven o'clock and lit her gas heater and Joy's. Joy was her daughter, a large blonde girl who had an artificial leg. Mrs. Hopewell thought of her as a child though she was thirty-two years old and highly educated. Joy would get up while her mother was eating and lumber into the bathroom and slam the door, and before long, Mrs. Freeman would arrive at the back door. Joy would hear her mother call, "Come on in," and then they would talk a while in low voices that were indistinguishable in the bathroom. By the time Joy came in, they had usually finished the weather report and were on one or the other of Mrs. Freeman's daughters, Glynese or Carramae, Joy called them Glycerin and Caramel. Glynese, a redhead, was eighteen and had many admirers; Carramae, a blonde, was only fifteen but already married and pregnant. She could not keep anything on her stomach. Every morning Mrs. Freeman told Mrs. Hopewell how many times she had vomited since the last report.

Mrs. Hopewell liked to tell people that Glynese and Carramae were two of the finest girls she knew and that Mrs. Freeman was a *lady* and that she was never ashamed to take her anywhere or introduce her to anybody they might meet. Then she would tell how she had happened to hire the Freemans in the first place and how they were a godsend to her and how she had had them four years. The reason for her keeping them so long was that they were not trash. They were good country people. She had telephoned the man whose name they had given as a reference and he had told her that Mr. Freeman was a good farmer but that his wife was the nosiest woman ever to walk the earth. "She's got to be into everything," the man said. "If she don't get there before the dust settles, you can bet she's dead, that's all. She'll want to know all your business. I can stand him real good," he had said, "but me nor my wife neither could have stood that woman one more minute on this place." That had put Mrs. Hopewell off for a few days.

She had hired them in the end because there were no other applicants but she had made up her mind beforehand exactly how she would handle the woman. Since she was the type who had to be into everything, then, Mrs. Hopewell had decided, she would not only let her be into everything, she would *see to it* that she was into everything—she would give her the responsibility of everything, she would put her in charge. Mrs. Hopewell had no bad qualities of her own but she was able to use other people's in such a constructive way that she never felt the lack. She had hired the Freemans and she had kept them four years.

Nothing is perfect. This was one of Mrs. Hopewell's favorite sayings. Another was: that is life! And still another, the most important, was: well, other people have their opinions too. She would make these statements, usually at the table, in a tone of gentle insistence as if no one held them but her, and the large hulking Joy, whose constant outrage had obliterated every expression from her face, would stare just a little to the side of her, her eyes icy blue, with the look of someone who has achieved blindness by an act of will and means to keep it.

When Mrs. Hopewell said to Mrs. Freeman that life was like that, Mrs. Freeman would say, "I always said so myself." Nothing had been arrived at by anyone that had not first been arrived at by her. She was quicker than Mr. Freeman. When Mrs. Hopewell said to her after they had been on the place a while, "You know, you're the wheel behind the wheel," and winked, Mrs. Freeman had said, "I know it. I've always been quick. It's some that are quicker than others."

"Everybody is different," Mrs. Hopewell said.

"Yes, most people is," Mrs. Freeman said.

"It takes all kinds to make the world."

"I always said it did myself."

The girl was used to this kind of dialogue for breakfast and more of it for dinner; sometimes they had it for supper too. When they had no guest they ate in the kitchen because that was easier. Mrs. Freeman always managed to arrive at some point during the meal and to watch them finish it. She would stand in the doorway if it were summer but in the winter she would stand with one elbow on top of the refrigerator and look down on them, or she would stand by the gas heater, lifting the back of her skirt slightly. Occasionally she would stand against the wall and roll her head from side to side. At no time was she in any hurry to leave. All this was very trying on Mrs. Hopewell but she was a woman of great patience. She realized that nothing is perfect and that in the Freemans she had good country people and that if, in this day and age, you get good country people, you had better hang onto them.

She had had plenty of experience with trash. Before the Freemans she had averaged one tenant family a year. The wives of these farmers were not the kind you would want to be around you for very long. Mrs. Hopewell, who had divorced her husband long ago, needed someone to walk over the fields with her; and when Joy had to be impressed for these services, her remarks were usually so ugly and her face so glum that Mrs. Hopewell would say, "If you can't come pleasantly, I don't want you at all," to which the girl, standing square and rigid-shouldered with her neck thrust slightly forward, would reply, "If you want me, here I am — LIKE I AM."

Mrs. Hopewell excused this attitude because of the leg (which had been shot off in a hunting accident when Joy was ten). It was hard for Mrs. Hopewell to realize that her child was thirty-two now and that for more than twenty years she had had only one leg. She thought of her still as a child because it tore her heart to think instead of the poor stout girl in her thirties who had never danced a step or had any *normal* good times. Her name was really Joy but as soon as she was twenty-one and away from home, she had had it legally changed. Mrs. Hopewell was certain that she had thought and thought until she had hit upon the ugliest name in any language. Then she had gone and had the beautiful name, Joy, changed without telling her mother until after she had done it. Her legal name was Hulga.

When Mrs. Hopewell thought the name Hulga, she thought of the broad blank hull of a battleship. She would not use it. She continued to call her Joy to which the girl responded but in a purely mechanical way.

Hulga had learned to tolerate Mrs. Freeman who saved her from taking walks with her mother. Even Glynese and Carramae were useful when they occupied attention that might otherwise have been directed at her. At first she had thought she could not stand Mrs. Freeman for she had found that it was not possible to be rude to her. Mrs. Freeman would take on strange resentments and for days together she would be sullen but the source of her displeasure was always obscure; a direct attack, a positive leer, blatant ugliness to her face — these never touched her. And without warning one day, she began calling her Hulga.

She did not call her that in front of Mrs. Hopewell who would have been incensed but when she and the girl happened to be out of the house together, she would say something and add the name Hulga to the end of it, and the big spectacled Joy-Hulga would scowl and redden as if her privacy had been intruded upon. She considered the name her personal affair. She had arrived at it first purely on the basis of its ugly sound and then the full genius of its fitness had struck her. She had a vision of the name working like the ugly sweating Vulcan who stayed in the furnace and to whom, presumably, the goddess had to come when called. She saw it as the name of her highest creative act. One of her major triumphs was that her mother had not been able to turn her dust into Joy, but the greater one was that she had been able to turn it herself into Hulga. However, Mrs. Freeman's relish for using the name only irritated her. It was as if Mrs. Freeman's beady steel-pointed eyes had penetrated far enough behind her face to reach some secret fact. Something about her seemed to fascinate Mrs. Freeman and then one day Hulga realized that it was the artificial leg. Mrs. Freeman had a special fondness for the details of secret infections, hidden deformities, assaults upon children. Of diseases, she preferred the lingering or incurable. Hulga had heard Mrs. Hopewell give her the details of the hunting accident, how the leg had been literally blasted off, how she had never lost consciousness. Mrs. Freeman could listen to it any time as if it had happened an hour ago.

When Hulga stumped into the kitchen in the morning (she could walk without making the awful noise but she made it—Mrs. Hopewell was certain—because it was ugly-sounding), she glanced at them and did not speak. Mrs. Hopewell would be in her red kimono with her hair tied around her head in rags. She would be sitting at the table, finishing her breakfast and Mrs. Freeman would be hanging by her elbow outward from the refrigerator, looking down at the table. Hulga always put her eggs on the stove to boil and then stood over them with her arms folded, and Mrs. Hopewell would look at her—a kind of indirect gaze divided between her and Mrs. Freeman—and would think that if she would only keep herself up a little, she wouldn't be so bad looking. There was nothing wrong with her face that a pleasant expression wouldn't help. Mrs. Hopewell said that people who looked on the bright side of things would be beautiful even if they were not.

Whenever she looked at Joy this way, she could not help but feel that it would have been better if the child had not taken the Ph.D. It had certainly not brought her out any and now that she had it, there was no more excuse for her to go to school again. Mrs. Hopewell thought it was nice for girls to go to school to have a good time but Joy had "gone through." Anyhow, she would not have been strong enough to go again. The doctors had told Mrs. Hopewell that with the best of care, Joy might see forty-five. She had a weak heart. Joy had made it plain that if it had not been for this condition, she would be far from these red hills and good country people. She would be in a university lecturing to people who knew what she was talking about. And Mrs. Hopewell could very well picture her there, looking like a scarecrow and lecturing to more of the same. Here she went about all day in a six-year-old skirt and a yellow sweat shirt with a faded cowboy on a horse embossed on it. She thought this was funny; Mrs. Hopewell thought it was idiotic and showed simply that she was still a child. She was brilliant but she didn't have a grain of sense. It seemed to Mrs. Hopewell that every year she grew less like other people and more like herself—bloated, rude, and squint-eyed. And she said such strange things! To her own mother she had said—without warning, without excuse, standing up in the middle of a meal with her face purple and her mouth half full—"Woman! do you ever look inside? Do you ever look inside and see what you are *not*? God!" she had cried sinking down again and staring at her plate, "Malebranche was right: we are not our own light. We are not our own light!" Mrs. Hopewell had no idea to this day what brought that on. She had only made the remark, hoping Joy would take it in, that a smile never hurt anyone.

The girl had taken the Ph.D. in philosophy and this left Mrs. Hopewell at a complete loss. You could say, "My daughter is a nurse," or "My daughter is a schoolteacher," or even, "My daughter is a chemical engineer." You could not say, "My daughter is a philosopher." That was something that had ended with the Greeks and Romans. All day Joy sat on her neck in a deep chair, reading. Sometimes she went for walks but she didn't like dogs or cats or birds or flowers or nature or nice young men. She looked at nice young men as if she could smell their stupidity.

One day Mrs. Hopewell had picked up one of the books the girl had just put down and opening it at random, she read, "Science, on the other hand, has to assert its soberness and seriousness afresh and declare that it is concerned solely with what-is. Nothing—how can it be for science anything but a horror and a phantasm? If science is right, then one thing stands firm: science wishes to know nothing of nothing. Such is after all the strictly scientific approach to Nothing. We know it by wishing to know nothing of Nothing." These words had been underlined with a blue pencil and they worked on Mrs. Hopewell like some evil incantation in gibberish. She shut the book quickly and went out of the room as if she were having a chill.

This morning when the girl came in, Mrs. Freeman was on Carramae. "She thrown up four times after supper," she said, "and was up twict in the night after three o'clock. Yesterday she didn't do nothing but ramble in the bureau drawer. All she did. Stand up there and see what she could run up on."

"She's got to eat," Mrs. Hopewell muttered, sipping her coffee, while she watched Joy's back at the stove. She was wondering what the child had said to the Bible salesman. She could not imagine what kind of a conversation she could possibly have had with him.

He was a tall gaunt hatless youth who had called yesterday to sell them a Bible. He had appeared at the door, carrying a large black suitcase that weighted him so heavily on one side that he had to brace himself against the door facing. He seemed on the point of collapse but he said in a cheerful voice, "Good morning, Mrs. Cedars!" and set the suitcase down on the mat. He was not a bad-looking young man though he had on a bright blue suit and yellow socks that were not pulled up far enough. He had prominent face bones and a streak of sticky-looking brown hair falling across his forehead.

"I'm Mrs. Hopewell," she said.

"Oh!" he said, pretending to look puzzled but with his eyes sparkling, "I saw it said 'The Cedars' on the mailbox so I thought you was Mrs. Cedars!" and he burst out in a pleasant laugh. He picked up the satchel and under cover of a pant, he fell forward into her hall. It was rather as if the suitcase had moved first, jerking him after it. "Mrs. Hopewell!" he said and grabbed her hand. "I hope you are well!" and he laughed again and then all at once his face sobered completely. He paused and gave her a straight earnest look and said, "Lady, I've come to speak of serious things."

"Well, come in," she muttered, none too pleased because her dinner was almost ready. He came into the parlor and sat down on the edge of a straight chair and put the suitcase between his feet and glanced around the room as if he were sizing her up by it. Her silver gleamed on the two sideboards; she decided he had never been in a room as elegant as this.

"Mrs. Hopewell," he began, using her name in a way that sounded almost intimate, "I know you believe in Chrustian service."

"Well yes," she murmured.

"I know," he said and paused, looking very wise with his head cocked on one side, "that you're a good woman. Friends have told me."

Mrs. Hopewell never liked to be taken for a fool. "What are you selling?" she asked.

"Bibles," the young man said and his eye raced around the room before he added, "I see you have no family Bible in your parlor, I see that is the one lack you got!"

Mrs. Hopewell could not say, "My daughter is an atheist and won't let me keep the Bible in the parlor." She said, stiffening slightly, "I keep my Bible by my bedside." This was not the truth. It was in the attic somewhere.

"Lady," he said, "the word of God ought to be in the parlor."

"Well, I think that's a matter of taste," she began. "I think . . ."

"Lady," he said, "for a Chrustian, the word of God ought to be in every room in the house besides in his heart. I know you're a Chrustian because I can see it in every line of your face."

She stood up and said, "Well, young man, I don't want to buy a Bible and I smell my dinner burning."

He didn't get up. He began to twist his hands and looking down at them he said softly, "Well lady, I'll tell you the truth — not many people want to buy one nowadays and besides, I know I'm real simple. I don't know how to say a thing but to say it. I'm just a country boy." He glanced up into her unfriendly face. "People like you don't like to fool with country people like me!"

"Why!" she cried, "good country people are the salt of the earth! Besides, we all have different ways of doing, it takes all kinds to make the world go 'round. That's life!"

"You said a mouthful," he said.

"Why, I think there aren't enough good country people in the world!" she said, stirred. "I think that's what's wrong with it!"

His face had brightened. "I didn't inraduce myself," he said. "I'm Manley Pointer from out in the country around Willohobie, not even from a place, just from near a place."

"You wait a minute," she said. "I have to see about my dinner." She went out to the kitchen and found Joy standing near the door where she had been listening.

"Get rid of the salt of the earth," she said, "and let's eat."

Mrs. Hopewell gave her a pained look and turned the heat down under the vegetables. "*I* can't be rude to anybody," she murmured and went back into the parlor.

He had opened the suitcase and was sitting with a Bible on each knee.

"You might as well put those up," she told him. "I don't want one."

"I appreciate your honesty," he said. "You don't see any more real honest people unless you go way out in the country."

"I know," she said, "real genuine folks!" Through the crack in the door she heard a groan.

"I guess a lot of boys come telling you they're working their way through college," he said, "but I'm not going to tell you that. Somehow," he said, "I don't want to go to college. I want to devote my life to Chrustian service. See," he said, lowering his voice, "I got this heart condition. I may not live long. When you know it's something wrong with you and you may not live long, well then, lady . . ." He paused, with his mouth open, and stared at her.

He and Joy had the same condition! She knew that her eyes were filling with tears but she collected herself quickly and murmured, "Won't you stay for dinner? We'd love to have you!" and was sorry the instant she heard herself say it.

"Yes mam," he said in an abashed voice, "I would sher love to do that!"

Joy had given him one look on being introduced to him and then throughout the meal had not glanced at him again. He had addressed several remarks to her, which she had pretended not to hear. Mrs. Hopewell could not understand deliberate rudeness, although she lived with it, and she felt she had always to overflow with hospitality to make up for Joy's lack of courtesy. She urged him to talk about himself and he did. He said he was the seventh child of twelve and that his father had been crushed under a tree when he himself was eight years old. He had been crushed very badly, in fact, almost cut in two and was practically not recognizable. His mother had got along the best she could by hard working and she had always seen that her children went to Sunday School and that they read the Bible every evening. He was now nineteen years old and he had been selling Bibles for four months. In that time he had sold seventy-seven Bibles and had the promise of two more sales. He wanted to become a missionary because he thought that was the way you could do most for people. "He who losest his life shall find it," he said simply and he was so sincere, so genuine and earnest that Mrs. Hopewell would not for the world have smiled. He prevented his peas from sliding onto the table by blocking them with a piece of bread which he later cleaned his plate with. She could see Joy observing sidewise how he handled his knife and fork and she saw too that every few minutes, the boy would dart a keen appraising glance at the girl as if he were trying to attract her attention.

After dinner Joy cleared the dishes off the table and disappeared and Mrs. Hopewell was left to talk with him. He told her again about his childhood and his father's accident and about various things that had happened to him. Every five minutes or so she would stifle a yawn. He sat for two hours until finally she told him she must go because she had an appointment in town. He packed his Bibles and thanked her and prepared to leave, but in the doorway he stopped and wrung her hand and said that not on any of his trips had he met a lady as nice as her and he asked if he could come again. She had said she would always be happy to see him.

Joy had been standing in the road, apparently looking at something in the distance, when he came down the steps toward her, bent to the side with his heavy valise. He stopped where she was standing and confronted her directly. Mrs. Hopewell could not hear what he said but she trembled to think what Joy would say to him. She could see that after a minute Joy said something and that then the boy began to speak again, making an excited gesture with his free hand. After a minute Joy said something else at which the boy began to speak once more. Then to her amazement, Mrs. Hopewell saw the two of them walk off together, toward the gate. Joy had walked all the way to the gate with him and Mrs. Hopewell could not imagine what they had said to each other, and she had not yet dared to ask.

Mrs. Freeman was insisting upon her attention. She had moved from the refrigerator to the heater so that Mrs. Hopewell had to turn and face her in order to seem to be listening. "Glynese gone out with Harvey Hill again last night," she said. "She had this sty."

"Hill," Mrs. Hopewell said absently, "is that the one who works in the garage?"

"Nome, he's the one that goes to chiropractor school," Mrs. Freeman said. "She had this sty. Been had it two days. So she says when he brought her in the other night he says, 'Lemme get rid of that sty for you,' and she says, 'How?' and he says, 'You just lay yourself down acrost the seat of that car and I'll show you.' So she done it and he popped her neck. Kept on a-popping it several times until she made him quit. This morning," Mrs. Freeman said, "she ain't got no sty. She ain't got no traces of a sty."

"I never heard of that before," Mrs. Hopewell said.

"He ast her to marry him before the Ordinary," Mrs. Freeman went on, "and she told him she wasn't going to be married in no *office*."

"Well, Glynese is a fine girl," Mrs. Hopewell said. "Glynese and Carramae are both fine girls."

"Carramae said when her and Lyman was married Lyman said it sure felt sacred to him. She said he said he wouldn't take five hundred dollars for being married by a preacher."

"How much would he take?" the girl asked from the stove.

"He said he wouldn't take five hundred dollars," Mrs. Freeman repeated.

"Well we all have work to do," Mrs. Hopewell said.

"Lyman said it just felt more sacred to him," Mrs. Freeman said. "The doctor wants Carramae to eat prunes. Says instead of medicine. Says them cramps is coming from pressure. You know where I think it is?"

"She'll be better in a few weeks," Mrs. Hopewell said.

"In the tube," Mrs. Freeman said. "Else she wouldn't be as sick as she is."

Hulga had cracked her two eggs into a saucer and was bringing them to the table along with a cup of coffee that she had filled too full. She sat down carefully and began to eat, meaning to keep Mrs. Freeman there by questions if for any reason she showed an inclination to leave. She could perceive her mother's eye on her. The first round-about question would be about the Bible salesman and she did not wish to bring it on. "How did he pop her neck?" she asked.

Mrs. Freeman went into a description of how he had popped her neck. She said he owned a '55 Mercury but that Glynese said she would rather marry a man with only a '36 Plymouth who would be married by a preacher. The girl asked what if he had a '32 Plymouth and Mrs. Freeman said what Glynese had said was a '36 Plymouth.

Mrs. Hopewell said there were not many girls with Glynese's common sense. She said what she admired in those girls was their common sense. She said that reminded her that they had had a nice visitor yesterday, a young man selling Bibles. "Lord," she said, "he bored me to death but he was so sincere and genuine I couldn't be rude to him. He was just good country people, you know," she said, "— just the salt of the earth."

"I seen him walk up," Mrs. Freeman said, "and then later — I seen him walk off," and Hulga could feel the slight shift in her voice, the slight insinuation, that he had not walked off alone, had he? Her face remained expressionless but the color rose into her neck and she seemed to swallow it down with the next spoonful of egg. Mrs. Freeman was looking at her as if they had a secret together.

"Well, it takes all kinds of people to make the world go 'round," Mrs. Hopewell said. "It's very good we aren't all alike."

"Some people are more alike than others," Mrs. Freeman said.

Hulga got up and stumped, with about twice the noise that was necessary, into her room and locked the door. She was to meet the Bible salesman at ten o'clock at the gate. She had thought about it half the night. She had started thinking of it as a great joke and then she had begun to see profound implications in it. She had lain in bed imagining dialogues for them that were insane on the surface but that reached below to depths that no Bible salesman would be aware of. Their conversation yesterday had been of this kind.

He had stopped in front of her and had simply stood there. His face was bony and sweaty and bright, with a little pointed nose in the center of it, and his look was different from what it had been at the dinner table. He was gazing at her with open curiosity, with fascination, like a child watching a new fantastic animal at the zoo, and he was breathing as if he had run a great distance to reach her. His gaze seemed somehow familiar but she could not think where she had been regarded with it before. For almost a minute he didn't say anything. Then on what seemed an insuck of breath, he whispered, "You ever ate a chicken that was two days old?"

The girl looked at him stonily. He might have just put this question up for consideration at the meeting of a philosophical association. "Yes," she presently replied as if she had considered it from all angles.

"It must have been mighty small!" he said triumphantly and shook all over with little nervous giggles, getting very red in the face, and subsiding finally into his gaze of complete admiration, while the girl's expression remained exactly the same.

"How old are you?" he asked softly.

She waited some time before she answered. Then in a flat voice she said, "Seventeen."

His smiles came in succession like waves breaking on the surface of a little lake. "I see you got a wooden leg," he said. "I think you're brave. I think you're real sweet."

The girl stood blank and solid and silent.

"Walk to the gate with me," he said. "You're a brave sweet little thing and I liked you the minute I seen you walk in the door."

Hulga began to move forward.

"What's your name?" he asked, smiling down on the top of her head.

"Hulga," she said.

"Hulga," he murmured, "Hulga. Hulga. I never heard of anybody name Hulga before. You're shy, aren't you, Hulga?" he asked.

She nodded, watching his large red hand on the handle of the giant valise.

"I like girls that wear glasses," he said. "I think a lot. I'm not like these people that a serious thought don't ever enter their heads. It's because I may die."

"I may die too," she said suddenly and looked up at him. His eyes were very small and brown, glittering feverishly.

"Listen," he said, "don't you think some people was meant to meet on account of what all they got in common and all? Like they both think serious thoughts and all?" He shifted the valise to his other hand so that the hand nearest her was free. He caught hold of her elbow and shook it a little. "I don't work on Saturday," he said. "I like to walk in the woods and see what Mother Nature is wearing. O'er the hills and far away. Pic-nics and things. Couldn't we go on a pic-nic tomorrow? Say yes, Hulga," he said and gave her a dying look as if he felt his insides about to drop out of him. He had even seemed to sway slightly toward her.

During the night she had imagined that she seduced him. She imagined that the two of them walked on the place until they came to the storage barn beyond the two back fields and there, she imagined, that things came to such a pass that she very easily seduced him and that then, of course, she had to reckon with his remorse. True genius can get an idea across even to an inferior mind. She imagined that she took his remorse in hand and changed it into a deeper understanding of life. She took all his shame away and turned it into something useful.

She set off for the gate at exactly ten o'clock, escaping without drawing Mrs. Hopewell's attention. She didn't take anything to eat, forgetting that food is usually taken on a pic-nic. She wore a pair of slacks and a dirty white shirt, and as an afterthought, she had put some Vapex on the collar of it since she did not own any perfume. When she reached the gate no one was there.

She looked up and down the empty highway and had the furious feeling that she had been tricked, that he had only meant to make her walk to the gate after the idea of him. Then suddenly he stood up, very tall, from behind a bush on the opposite embankment. Smiling, he lifted his hat which was new and wide-brimmed. He had not worn it yesterday and she wondered if he had bought it for the occasion. It was toast-colored with a red and white band around it and was slightly too large for him. He stepped from behind the bush still carrying the black valise. He had on the same suit and the same yellow socks sucked down in his shoes from walking. He crossed the highway and said, "I knew you'd come!"

The girl wondered acidly how he had known this. She pointed to the valise and asked, "Why did you bring your Bibles?"

He took her elbow, smiling down on her as if he could not stop. "You can never tell when you'll need the word of God, Hulga," he said. She had a moment in which she doubted that this was actually happening and then they began to climb the embankment. They went down into the pasture toward the woods. The boy walked lightly by her side, bouncing on his toes. The valise did not seem to be heavy today; he even swung it. They crossed half the pasture without saying anything and then, putting his hand easily on the small of her back, he asked softly, "Where does your wooden leg join on?"

She turned an ugly red and glared at him and for an instant the boy looked abashed. "I didn't mean you no harm," he said. "I only meant you're so brave and all. I guess God takes care of you."

"No," she said, looking forward and walking fast, "I don't even believe in God."

At this he stopped and whistled. "No!" he exclaimed as if he were too astonished to say anything else.

She walked on and in a second he was bouncing at her side, fanning with his hat. "That's very unusual for a girl," he remarked, watching her out of the corner of his eye. When they reached the edge of the wood, he put his hand on her back again and drew her against him without a word and kissed her heavily.

The kiss, which had more pressure than feeling behind it, produced that extra surge of adrenalin in the girl that enables one to carry a packed trunk out of a burning house, but in her, the power went at once to the brain. Even before he released her, her mind, clear and detached and ironic anyway, was regarding him from a great distance, with amusement but with pity. She had never been kissed before and she was pleased to discover that it was an unexceptional experience and all a matter of the mind's control. Some people might enjoy drain water if they were told it was vodka. When the boy, looking expectant but uncertain, pushed her gently away, she turned and walked on, saying nothing as if such business, for her, were common enough.

He came along panting at her side, trying to help her when he saw a root that she might trip over. He caught and held back the long swaying blades of thorn vine until she had passed beyond them. She led the way and he came breathing heavily behind her. Then they came out on a sunlit hillside, sloping softly into another one a little smaller. Beyond, they could see the rusted top of the old barn where the extra hay was stored.

The hill was sprinkled with small pink weeds. "Then you ain't saved?" he asked suddenly, stopping.

The girl smiled. It was the first time she had smiled at him at all. "In my economy," she said, "I'm saved and you are damned but I told you I didn't believe in God."

Nothing seemed to destroy the boy's look of admiration. He gazed at her now as if the fantastic animal at the zoo had put its paw through the bars and given him a loving poke. She thought he looked as if he wanted to kiss her again and she walked on before he had the chance.

"Ain't there somewheres we can sit down sometime?" he murmured, his voice softening toward the end of the sentence.

"In that barn," she said.

They made for it rapidly as if it might slide away like a train. It was a large two-story barn, cool and dark inside. The boy pointed up the ladder that led into the loft and said, "It's too bad we can't go up there."

"Why can't we?" she asked.

"Yer leg," he said reverently.

The girl gave him a contemptuous look and putting both hands on the ladder, she climbed it while he stood below, apparently awestruck. She pulled herself expertly through the opening and then looked down at him and said, "Well, come on if you're coming," and he began to climb the ladder, awkwardly bringing the suitcase with him.

"We won't need the Bible," she observed.

"You never can tell," he said, panting. After he had got into the loft, he was a few seconds catching his breath. She had sat down in a pile of straw. A wide sheath of sunlight, filled with dust particles, slanted over her. She lay back against a bale, her face turned away, looking out the front opening of the barn where hay was thrown from a wagon into the loft. The two pink-speckled hillsides lay back against a dark ridge of woods. The sky was cloudless and cold blue. The boy dropped down by her side and put one arm under her and the other over her and began methodically kissing her face, making little noises like a fish. He did not remove his hat but it was pushed far enough back not to interfere. When her glasses got in his way, he took them off of her and slipped them into his pocket.

The girl at first did not return any of the kisses but presently she began to and after she had put several on his cheek, she reached his lips and remained there, kissing him again and again as if she were trying to draw all the breath out of him. His breath was clear and sweet like a child's and the kisses were sticky like a child's. He mumbled about loving her and about knowing when he first seen her that he loved her, but the mumbling was like the sleepy fretting of a child being put to sleep by his mother. Her mind, throughout this, never stopped or lost itself for a second to her feelings. "You ain't said you loved me none," he whispered finally, pulling back from her. "You got to say that."

She looked away from him off into the hollow sky and then down at a black ridge and then down farther into what appeared to be two green swelling lakes. She didn't realize he had taken her glasses but this landscape could not seem exceptional to her for she seldom paid any close attention to her surroundings.

"You got to say it," he repeated. "You got to say you love me."

She was always careful how she committed herself. "In a sense," she began, "if you use the word loosely, you might say that. But it's not a word I use. I don't have illusions. I'm one of those people who see *through* to nothing."

The boy was frowning. "You got to say it. I said it and you got to say it," he said.

The girl looked at him almost tenderly. "You poor baby," she murmured. "It's just as well you don't understand," and she pulled him by the neck, face-down, against her. "We are all damned," she said, "but some of us have taken off our blindfolds and see that there's nothing to see. It's a kind of salvation."

The boy's astonished eyes looked blankly through the ends of her hair. "Okay," he almost whined, "but do you love me or don'tcher?"

"Yes," she said and added, "in a sense. But I must tell you something. There mustn't be anything dishonest between us." She lifted his head and looked him in the eye. "I am thirty years old," she said. "I have a number of degrees."

The boy's look was irritated but dogged. "I don't care," he said. "I don't care a thing about what all you done. I just want to know if you love me or don'tcher?" and he caught her to him and wildly planted her face with kisses until she said, "Yes, yes."

"Okay then," he said, letting her go. "Prove it."

She smiled, looking dreamily out on the shifty landscape. She had seduced him without even making up her mind to try. "How?" she asked, feeling that he should be delayed a little.

He leaned over and put his lips to her ear. "Show me where your wooden leg joins on," he whispered.

The girl uttered a sharp little cry and her face instantly drained of color. The obscenity of the suggestion was not what shocked her. As a child she had sometimes been subject to feelings of shame but education had removed the last traces of that as a good surgeon scrapes for cancer; she would no more have felt it over what he was asking than she would have believed in his Bible. But she was as sensitive about the artificial leg as a peacock about his tail. No one ever touched it but her. She took care of it as someone else would his soul, in private and almost with her own eyes turned away. "No," she said.

"I known it," he muttered, sitting up. "You're just playing me for a sucker."

"Oh no no!" she cried. "It joins on at the knee. Only at the knee. Why do you want to see it?"

The boy gave her a long penetrating look. "Because," he said, "it's what makes you different. You ain't like anybody else."

She sat staring at him. There was nothing about her face or her round freezing-blue eyes to indicate that this had moved her; but she felt as if her heart had stopped and left her mind to pump her blood. She decided that for the first time in her life she was face to face with real innocence. This boy, with an instinct that came from beyond wisdom, had touched the truth about her. When after a minute, she said in a hoarse high voice, "All right," it was like surrendering to him completely. It was like losing her own life and finding it again, miraculously, in his.

Very gently he began to roll the slack leg up. The artificial limb, in a white sock and brown flat shoe, was bound in a heavy material like canvas and ended in an ugly jointure where it was attached to the stump. The boy's face and his voice were entirely reverent as he uncovered it and said, "Now show me how to take it off and on."

She took it off for him and put it back on again and then he took it off himself, handling it as tenderly as if it were a real one. "See!" he said with a delighted child's face. "Now I can do it myself!"

"Put it back on," she said. She was thinking that she would run away with him and that every night he would take the leg off and every morning put it back on again. "Put it back on," she said.

"Not yet," he murmured, setting it on its foot out of her reach. "Leave it off for a while. You got me instead."

She gave a little cry of alarm but he pushed her down and began to kiss her again. Without the leg she felt entirely dependent on him. Her brain seemed to have stopped thinking altogether and to be about some other function that it was not very good at. Different expressions raced back and forth over her face. Every now and then the boy, his eyes like two steel spikes, would glance behind him where the leg stood. Finally she pushed him off and said, "Put it back on me now."

"Wait," he said. He leaned the other way and pulled the valise toward him and opened it. It had a pale blue spotted lining and there were only two Bibles in it. He took one of these out and opened the cover of it. It was hollow and contained a pocket flask of whiskey, a pack of cards, and a small blue box with printing on it. He laid these out in front of her one at a time in an evenly-spaced row, like one presenting offerings at the shrine of a goddess. He put the blue box in her hand. THIS PRODUCT TO BE USED ONLY FOR THE PREVENTION OF DISEASE, she read, and dropped it. The boy was unscrewing the top of the flask. He stopped and pointed, with a smile, to the deck of cards. It was not an ordinary deck but one with an obscene picture on the back of each card. "Take a swig," he said, offering her the bottle first. He held it in front of her, but like one mesmerized, she did not move.

Her voice when she spoke had an almost pleading sound. "Aren't you," she murmured, "aren't you just good country people?"

The boy cocked his head. He looked as if he were just beginning to understand that she might be trying to insult him. "Yeah," he said, curling his lip slightly, "but it ain't held me back none. I'm as good as you any day in the week."

"Give me my leg," she said.

He pushed it farther away with his foot. "Come on now, let's begin to have us a good time," he said coaxingly. "We ain't got to know one another good yet."

"Give me my leg!" she screamed and tried to lunge for it but he pushed her down easily.

"What's the matter with you all of a sudden?" he asked, frowning as he screwed the top on the flask and put it quickly back inside the Bible. "You just a while ago said you didn't believe in nothing. I thought you was some girl!"

Her face was almost purple. "You're a Christian!" she hissed. "You're a fine Christian! You're just like them all — say one thing and do another. You're a perfect Christian, you're . . ."

The boy's mouth was set angrily. "I hope you don't think," he said in a lofty indignant tone, "that I believe in that crap! I may sell Bibles but I know which end is up and I wasn't born yesterday and I know where I'm going!"

"Give me my leg!" she screeched. He jumped up so quickly that she barely saw him sweep the cards and the blue box into the Bible and throw the Bible into the valise. She saw him grab the leg and then she saw it for an instant slanted forlornly across the inside of the suitcase with a Bible at either side of its opposite ends. He slammed the lid shut and snatched up the valise and swung it down the hole and then stepped through himself.

When all of him had passed but his head, he turned and regarded her with a look that no longer had any admiration in it. "I've gotten a lot of interesting things," he said. "One time I got a woman's glass eye this way. And you needn't to think you'll catch me because Pointer ain't really my name. I use a different name at every house I call at and don't stay nowhere long. And I'll tell you another thing, Hulga," he said, using the name as if he didn't think much of it, "you ain't so smart. I been believing in nothing ever since I was born!" and then the toast-colored hat disappeared down the hole and the girl was left, sitting on the straw in the dusty sunlight. When she turned her churning face toward the opening, she saw his blue figure struggling successfully over the green speckled lake.

Mrs. Hopewell and Mrs. Freeman, who were in the back pasture, digging up onions, saw him emerge a little later from the woods and head across the meadow toward the highway. "Why, that looks like that nice dull young man that tried to sell me a Bible yesterday," Mrs. Hopewell said, squinting. "He must have been selling them to the Negroes back in there. He was so simple," she said, "but I guess the world would be better off if we were all that simple."

Mrs. Freeman's gaze drove forward and just touched him before he disappeared under the hill. Then she returned her attention to the evil-smelling onion shoot she was lifting from the ground. "Some can't be that simple," she said. "I know I never could."

A Good Man Is Hard to Find

1955

> The dragon is by the side of the road, watching those who pass. Beware lest
> he devour you. We go to the Father of Souls, but it is necessary to pass by the
> dragon.
>
> — St. Cyril of Jerusalem

THE GRANDMOTHER DIDN'T WANT to go to Florida. She wanted to visit
some of her connections in east Tennessee and she was seizing at every
chance to change Bailey's mind. Bailey was the son she lived with, her only
boy. He was sitting on the edge of his chair at the table, bent over the orange
sports section of the *Journal*. "Now look here, Bailey," she said, "see here, read
this," and she stood with one hand on her thin hip and the other rattling the
newspaper at his bald head. "Here this fellow that calls himself The Misfit is
aloose from the Federal Pen and headed toward Florida and you read here
what it says he did to these people. Just you read it. I wouldn't take my children
in any direction with a criminal like that aloose in it. I couldn't answer to my
conscience if I did."

Bailey didn't look up from his reading so she wheeled around then and
faced the children's mother, a young woman in slacks, whose face was as broad
and innocent as a cabbage and was tied around with a green headkerchief
that had two points on the top like rabbit's ears. She was sitting on the sofa,
feeding the baby his apricots out of a jar. "The children have been to Florida
before," the old lady said. "You all ought to take them somewhere else for a
change so they would see different parts of the world and be broad. They never
have been to east Tennessee."

The children's mother didn't seem to hear her but the eight-year-old boy,
John Wesley, a stocky child with glasses, said, "If you don't want to go to Florida,
why dontcha stay at home?" He and the little girl, June Star, were reading the
funny papers on the floor.

"She wouldn't stay at home to be queen for a day," June Star said without
raising her yellow head.

"Yes and what would you do if this fellow, The Misfit, caught you?" the
grandmother asked.

"I'd smack his face," John Wesley said.

"She wouldn't stay at home for a million bucks," June Star said. "Afraid she'd
miss something. She has to go everywhere we go."

"All right, Miss," the grandmother said. "Just remember that the next time
you want me to curl your hair."

June Star said her hair was naturally curly.

The next morning the grandmother was the first one in the car, ready to go.
She had her big black valise that looked like the head of a hippopotamus in one
corner, and underneath it she was hiding a basket with Pitty Sing, the cat, in it.
She didn't intend for the cat to be left alone in the house for three days because

he would miss her too much and she was afraid he might brush against one of the gas burners and accidentally asphyxiate himself. Her son, Bailey, didn't like to arrive at a motel with a cat.

She sat in the middle of the back seat with John Wesley and June Star on either side of her. Bailey and the children's mother and the baby sat in front and they left Atlanta at eight forty-five with the mileage on the car at 55890. The grandmother wrote this down because she thought it would be interesting to say how many miles they had been when they got back. It took them twenty minutes to reach the outskirts of the city.

The old lady settled herself comfortably, removing her white cotton gloves and putting them up with her purse on the shelf in front of the back window. The children's mother still had on slacks and still had her head tied up in a green kerchief, but the grandmother had on a navy blue straw sailor hat with a bunch of white violets on the brim and a navy blue dress with a small white dot in the print. Her collars and cuffs were white organdy trimmed with lace and at her neckline she had pinned a purple spray of cloth violets containing a sachet. In case of an accident, anyone seeing her dead on the highway would know at once that she was a lady.

She said she thought it was going to be a good day for driving, neither too hot nor too cold, and she cautioned Bailey that the speed limit was fifty-five miles an hour and that the patrolmen hid themselves behind billboards and small clumps of trees and sped out after you before you had a chance to slow down. She pointed out interesting details of the scenery: Stone Mountain; the blue granite that in some places came up to both sides of the highway; the brilliant red clay banks slightly streaked with purple; and the various crops that made rows of green lace-work on the ground. The trees were full of silver-white sunlight and the meanest of them sparkled. The children were reading comic magazines and their mother had gone back to sleep.

"Let's go through Georgia fast so we won't have to look at it much," John Wesley said.

"If I were a little boy," said the grandmother, "I wouldn't talk about my native state that way. Tennessee has the mountains and Georgia has the hills."

"Tennessee is just a hillbilly dumping ground," John Wesley said, "and Georgia is a lousy state too."

"You said it," June Star said.

"In my time," said the grandmother, folding her thin veined fingers, "children were more respectful of their native states and their parents and everything else. People did right then. Oh look at the cute little pickaninny!" she said and pointed to a Negro child standing in the door of a shack. "Wouldn't that make a picture, now?" she asked and they all turned and looked at the little Negro out of the back window. He waved.

"He didn't have any britches on," June Star said.

"He probably didn't have any," the grandmother explained. "Little niggers in the country don't have things like we do. If I could paint, I'd paint that picture," she said.

The children exchanged comic books.

The grandmother offered to hold the baby and the children's mother passed him over the front seat to her. She set him on her knee and bounced him and told him about the things they were passing. She rolled her eyes and screwed up her mouth and stuck her leathery thin face into his smooth bland one. Occasionally he gave her a faraway smile. They passed a large cotton field with five or six graves fenced in the middle of it, like a small island. "Look at the graveyard!" the grandmother said, pointing it out. "That was the old family burying ground. That belonged to the plantation."

"Where's the plantation?" John Wesley asked.

"Gone with the Wind," said the grandmother. "Ha. Ha."

When the children finished all the comic books they had brought, they opened the lunch and ate it. The grandmother ate a peanut butter sandwich and an olive and would not let the children throw the box and the paper napkins out the window. When there was nothing else to do they played a game by choosing a cloud and making the other two guess what shape it suggested. John Wesley took one the shape of a cow and June Star guessed a cow and John Wesley said, no, an automobile, and June Star said he didn't play fair, and they began to slap each other over the grandmother.

The grandmother said she would tell them a story if they would keep quiet. When she told a story, she rolled her eyes and waved her head and was very dramatic. She said once when she was a maiden lady she had been courted by a Mr. Edgar Atkins Teagarden from Jasper, Georgia. She said he was a very good-looking man and a gentleman and that he brought her a watermelon every Saturday afternoon with his initials cut in it, E. A. T. Well, one Saturday, she said, Mr. Teagarden brought the watermelon and there was nobody at home and he left it on the front porch and returned in his buggy to Jasper, but she never got the watermelon, she said, because a nigger boy ate it when he saw the initials, E. A. T.! This story tickled John Wesley's funny bone and he giggled and giggled but June Star didn't think it was any good. She said she wouldn't marry a man that just brought her a watermelon on Saturday. The grandmother said she would have done well to marry Mr. Teagarden because he was a gentleman and had bought Coca-Cola stock when it first came out and that he had died only a few years ago, a very wealthy man.

They stopped at The Tower for barbecued sandwiches. The Tower was a part stucco and part wood filling station and dance hall set in a clearing outside of Timothy. A fat man named Red Sammy Butts ran it and there were signs stuck here and there on the building and for miles up and down the highway saying, TRY RED SAMMY'S FAMOUS BARBECUE. NONE LIKE FAMOUS RED SAMMY'S! RED SAM! THE FAT BOY WITH THE HAPPY LAUGH. A VETERAN! RED SAMMY'S YOUR MAN!

Red Sammy was lying on the bare ground outside The Tower with his head under a truck while a gray monkey about a foot high, chained to a small chinaberry tree, chattered nearby. The monkey sprang back into the tree and got on the highest limb as soon as he saw the children jump out of the car and run toward him.

Inside, The Tower was a long dark room with a counter at one end and tables at the other and dancing space in the middle. They all sat down at a board table next to the nickelodeon and Red Sam's wife, a tall burnt-brown woman with hair and eyes lighter than her skin, came and took their order. The children's mother put a dime in the machine and played "The Tennessee Waltz," and the grandmother said that tune always made her want to dance. She asked Bailey if he would like to dance but he only glared at her. He didn't have a naturally sunny disposition like she did and trips made him nervous. The grandmother's brown eyes were very bright. She swayed her head from side to side and pretended she was dancing in her chair. June Star said play something she could tap to so the children's mother put in another dime and played a fast number and June Star stepped out onto the dance floor and did her tap routine.

"Ain't she cute?" Red Sam's wife said, leaning over the counter. "Would you like to come be my little girl?"

"No I certainly wouldn't," June Star said. "I wouldn't live in a broken-down place like this for a million bucks!" and she ran back to the table.

"Ain't she cute?" the woman repeated, stretching her mouth politely.

"Aren't you ashamed?" hissed the grandmother.

Red Sam came in and told his wife to quit lounging on the counter and hurry up with these people's order. His khaki trousers reached just to his hip bones and his stomach hung over them like a sack of meal swaying under his shirt. He came over and sat down at a table nearby and let out a combination sigh and yodel. "You can't win," he said. "You can't win," and he wiped his sweating red face off with a gray handkerchief. "These days you don't know who to trust," he said. "Ain't that the truth?"

"People are certainly not nice like they used to be," said the grandmother.

"Two fellers come in here last week," Red Sammy said, "driving a Chrysler. It was a old beat-up car but it was a good one and these boys looked all right to me. Said they worked at the mill and you know I let them fellers charge the gas they bought? Now why did I do that?"

"Because you're a good man!" the grandmother said at once.

"Yes'm, I suppose so," Red Sam said as if he were struck with this answer.

His wife brought the orders, carrying the five plates all at once without a tray, two in each hand and one balanced on her arm. "It isn't a soul in this green world of God's that you can trust," she said. "And I don't count nobody out of that, not nobody," she repeated, looking at Red Sammy.

"Did you read about that criminal, The Misfit, that's escaped?" asked the grandmother.

"I wouldn't be a bit surprised if he didn't attact this place right here," said the woman. "If he hears about it being here, I wouldn't be none surprised to see him. If he hears it's two cent in the cash register, I wouldn't be a tall surprised if he . . ."

"That'll do," Red Sam said. "Go bring these people their Co'-Colas," and the woman went off to get the rest of the order.

"A good man is hard to find," Red Sammy said. "Everything is getting terrible. I remember the day you could go off and leave your screen door unlatched. Not no more."

He and the grandmother discussed better times. The old lady said that in her opinion Europe was entirely to blame for the way things were now. She said the way Europe acted you would think we were made of money and Red Sam said it was no use talking about it, she was exactly right. The children ran outside into the white sunlight and looked at the monkey in the lacy chinaberry tree. He was busy catching fleas on himself and biting each one carefully between his teeth as if it were a delicacy.

They drove off again into the hot afternoon. The grandmother took cat naps and woke up every few minutes with her own snoring. Outside of Toombsboro she woke up and recalled an old plantation that she had visited in this neighborhood once when she was a young lady. She said the house had six white columns across the front and that there was an avenue of oaks leading up to it and two little wooden trellis arbors on either side in front where you sat down with your suitor after a stroll in the garden. She recalled exactly which road to turn off to get to it. She knew that Bailey would not be willing to lose any time looking at an old house, but the more she talked about it, the more she wanted to see it once again and find out if the little twin arbors were still standing. "There was a secret panel in this house," she said craftily, not telling the truth but wishing that she were, "and the story went that all the family silver was hidden in it when Sherman came through but it was never found . . ."

"Hey!" John Wesley said. "Let's go see it! We'll find it! We'll poke all the woodwork and find it! Who lives there? Where do you turn off at? Hey Pop, can't we turn off there?"

"We never have seen a house with a secret panel!" June Star shrieked. "Let's go to the house with the secret panel! Hey Pop, can't we go see the house with the secret panel!"

"It's not far from here, I know," the grandmother said. "It wouldn't take over twenty minutes."

Bailey was looking straight ahead. His jaw was as rigid as a horseshoe. "No," he said.

The children began to yell and scream that they wanted to see the house with the secret panel. John Wesley kicked the back of the front seat and June Star hung over her mother's shoulder and whined desperately into her ear that they never had any fun even on their vacation, that they could never do what THEY wanted to do. The baby began to scream and John Wesley kicked the back of the seat so hard that his father could feel the blows in his kidney.

"All right!" he shouted and drew the car to a stop at the side of the road. "Will you all shut up? Will you all just shut up for one second? If you don't shut up, we won't go anywhere."

"It would be very educational for them," the grandmother murmured.

"All right," Bailey said, "but get this: this is the only time we're going to stop for anything like this. This is the one and only time."

"The dirt road that you have to turn down is about a mile back," the grandmother directed. "I marked it when we passed."

"A dirt road," Bailey groaned.

After they had turned around and were headed toward the dirt road, the grandmother recalled other points about the house, the beautiful glass over the front doorway and the candle-lamp in the hall. John Wesley said that the secret panel was probably in the fireplace.

"You can't go inside this house," Bailey said. "You don't know who lives there."

"While you all talk to the people in front, I'll run around behind and get in a window," John Wesley suggested.

"We'll all stay in the car," his mother said.

They turned onto the dirt road and the car raced roughly along in a swirl of pink dust. The grandmother recalled the times when there were no paved roads and thirty miles was a day's journey. The dirt road was hilly and there were sudden washes in it and sharp curves on dangerous embankments. All at once they would be on a hill, looking down over the blue tops of trees for miles around, then the next minute, they would be in a red depression with the dust-coated trees looking down on them.

"This place had better turn up in a minute," Bailey said, "or I'm going to turn around."

The road looked as if no one had traveled on it in months.

"It's not much farther," the grandmother said and just as she said it, a horrible thought came to her. The thought was so embarrassing that she turned red in the face and her eyes dilated and her feet jumped up, upsetting her valise in the corner. The instant the valise moved, the newspaper top she had over the basket under it rose with a snarl and Pitty Sing, the cat, sprang onto Bailey's shoulder.

The children were thrown to the floor and their mother, clutching the baby, was thrown out the door onto the ground; the old lady was thrown into the front seat. The car turned over once and landed right-side-up in a gulch off the side of the road. Bailey remained in the driver's seat with the cat — gray-striped with a broad white face and an orange nose — clinging to his neck like a caterpillar.

As soon as the children saw they could move their arms and legs, they scrambled out of the car, shouting, "We've had an ACCIDENT!" The grandmother was curled up under the dashboard, hoping she was injured so that Bailey's wrath would not come down on her all at once. The horrible thought she had had before the accident was that the house she had remembered so vividly was not in Georgia but in Tennessee.

Bailey removed the cat from his neck with both hands and flung it out the window against the side of a pine tree. Then he got out of the car and started looking for the children's mother. She was sitting against the side of the red gutted ditch, holding the screaming baby, but she only had a cut down her face and a broken shoulder. "We've had an ACCIDENT!" the children screamed in a frenzy of delight.

"But nobody's killed," June Star said with disappointment as the grandmother limped out of the car, her hat still pinned to her head but the broken front brim standing up at a jaunty angle and the violet spray hanging off the side. They all sat down in the ditch, except the children, to recover from the shock. They were all shaking.

"Maybe a car will come along," said the children's mother hoarsely.

"I believe I have injured an organ," said the grandmother, pressing her side, but no one answered her. Bailey's teeth were clattering. He had on a yellow sport shirt with bright blue parrots designed in it and his face was as yellow as the shirt. The grandmother decided that she would not mention that the house was in Tennessee.

The road was about ten feet above and they could only see the tops of the trees on the other side of it. Behind the ditch they were sitting in there were more woods, tall and dark and deep. In a few minutes they saw a car some distance away on top of a hill, coming slowly as if the occupants were watching them. The grandmother stood up and waved both arms dramatically to attract their attention. The car continued to come on slowly, disappeared around a bend and appeared again, moving even slower, on top of the hill they had gone over. It was a big black battered hearse-like automobile. There were three men in it.

It came to a stop just over them and for some minutes, the driver looked down with a steady expressionless gaze to where they were sitting, and didn't speak. Then he turned his head and muttered something to the other two and they got out. One was a fat boy in black trousers and a red sweat shirt with a silver stallion embossed on the front of it. He moved around on the right side of them and stood staring, his mouth partly open in a kind of loose grin. The other had on khaki pants and a blue striped coat and a gray hat pulled very low, hiding most of his face. He came around slowly on the left side. Neither spoke.

The driver got out of the car and stood by the side of it, looking down at them. He was an older man than the other two. His hair was just beginning to gray and he wore silver-rimmed spectacles that gave him a scholarly look. He had a long creased face and didn't have on any shirt or undershirt. He had on blue jeans that were too tight for him and was holding a black hat and a gun. The two boys also had guns.

"We've had an ACCIDENT!" the children screamed.

The grandmother had the peculiar feeling that the bespectacled man was someone she knew. His face was as familiar to her as if she had known him all her life but she could not recall who he was. He moved away from the car and began to come down the embankment, placing his feet carefully so that he wouldn't slip. He had on tan and white shoes and no socks, and his ankles were red and thin. "Good afternoon," he said. "I see you all had you a little spill."

"We turned over twice!" said the grandmother.

"Oncet," he corrected. "We seen it happen. Try their car and see will it run, Hiram," he said quietly to the boy with the gray hat.

"What you got that gun for?" John Wesley asked. "Whatcha gonna do with that gun?"

"Lady," the man said to the children's mother, "would you mind calling them children to sit down by you? Children make me nervous. I want all you all to sit down right together there where you're at."

"What are you telling US what to do for?" June Star asked.

Behind them the line of woods gaped like a dark open mouth. "Come here," said the mother.

"Look here now," Bailey began suddenly, "we're in a predicament! We're in . . ."

The grandmother shrieked. She scrambled to her feet and stood staring. "You're The Misfit!" she said. "I recognized you at once!"

"Yes'm," the man said, smiling slightly as if he were pleased in spite of himself to be known, "but it would have been better for all of you, lady, if you hadn't of reckernized me."

Bailey turned his head sharply and said something to his mother that shocked even the children. The old lady began to cry and The Misfit reddened.

"Lady," he said, "don't you get upset. Sometimes a man says things he don't mean. I don't reckon he meant to talk to you thataway."

"You wouldn't shoot a lady, would you?" the grandmother said and removed a clean handkerchief from her cuff and began to slap at her eyes with it.

The Misfit pointed the toe of his shoe into the ground and made a little hole and then covered it up again. "I would hate to have to," he said.

"Listen," the grandmother almost screamed, "I know you're a good man. You don't look a bit like you have common blood. I know you must come from nice people!"

"Yes mam," he said, "finest people in the world." When he smiled he showed a row of strong white teeth. "God never made a finer woman than my mother and my daddy's heart was pure gold," he said. The boy with the red sweat shirt had come around behind them and was standing with his gun at his hip. The Misfit squatted down on the ground. "Watch them children, Bobby Lee," he said. "You know they make me nervous." He looked at the six of them huddled together in front of him and he seemed to be embarrassed as if he couldn't think of anything to say. "Ain't a cloud in the sky," he remarked, looking up at it. "Don't see no sun but don't see no cloud neither."

"Yes, it's a beautiful day," said the grandmother. "Listen," she said, "you shouldn't call yourself The Misfit because I know you're a good man at heart. I can just look at you and tell."

"Hush!" Bailey yelled. "Hush! Everybody shut up and let me handle this!" He was squatting in the position of a runner about to sprint forward but he didn't move.

"I pre-chate that, lady," The Misfit said and drew a little circle in the ground with the butt of his gun.

"It'll take a half a hour to fix this here car," Hiram called, looking over the raised hood of it.

"Well, first you and Bobby Lee get him and that little boy to step over yonder with you," The Misfit said, pointing to Bailey and John Wesley. "The boys want to ast you something," he said to Bailey. "Would you mind stepping back in them woods there with them?"

"Listen," Bailey began, "we're in a terrible predicament! Nobody realizes what this is," and his voice cracked. His eyes were as blue and intense as the parrots in his shirt and he remained perfectly still.

The grandmother reached up to adjust her hat brim as if she were going to the woods with him but it came off in her hand. She stood staring at it and after a second she let it fall on the ground. Hiram pulled Bailey up by the arm as if he were assisting an old man. John Wesley caught hold of his father's hand and

Bobby Lee followed. They went off toward the woods and just as they reached the dark edge, Bailey turned and supporting himself against a gray naked pine trunk, he shouted, "I'll be back in a minute, Mamma, wait on me!"

"Come back this instant!" his mother shrilled but they all disappeared into the woods.

"Bailey Boy!" the grandmother called in a tragic voice but she found she was looking at The Misfit squatting on the ground in front of her. "I just know you're a good man," she said desperately. "You're not a bit common!"

"Nome, I ain't a good man," The Misfit said after a second as if he had considered her statement carefully, "but I ain't the worst in the world neither. My daddy said I was a different breed of dog from my brothers and sisters. 'You know,' Daddy said, 'it's some that can live their whole life out without asking about it and it's others has to know why it is, and this boy is one of the latters. He's going to be into everything!' " He put on his black hat and looked up suddenly and then away deep into the woods as if he were embarrassed again. "I'm sorry I don't have on a shirt before you ladies," he said, hunching his shoulders slightly. "We buried our clothes that we had on when we escaped and we're just making do until we can get better. We borrowed these from some folks we met," he explained.

"That's perfectly all right," the grandmother said. "Maybe Bailey has an extra shirt in his suitcase."

"I'll look and see terrectly," The Misfit said.

"Where are they taking him?" the children's mother screamed.

"Daddy was a card himself," The Misfit said. "You couldn't put anything over on him. He never got in trouble with the Authorities though. Just had the knack of handling them."

"You could be honest too if you'd only try," said the grandmother. "Think how wonderful it would be to settle down and live a comfortable life and not have to think about somebody chasing you all the time."

The Misfit kept scratching in the ground with the butt of his gun as if he were thinking about it. "Yes'm, somebody is always after you," he murmured.

The grandmother noticed how thin his shoulder blades were just behind his hat because she was standing up looking down at him. "Do you ever pray?" she asked.

He shook his head. All she saw was the black hat wiggle between his shoulder blades. "Nome," he said.

There was a pistol shot from the woods, followed closely by another. Then silence. The old lady's head jerked around. She could hear the wind move through the tree tops like a long satisfied insuck of breath. "Bailey Boy!" she called.

"I was a gospel singer for a while," The Misfit said. "I been most everything. Been in the arm service, both land and sea, at home and abroad, been twict married, been an undertaker, been with the railroads, plowed Mother Earth, been in a tornado, seen a man burnt alive oncet," and he looked up at the children's mother and the little girl who were sitting close together, their faces white and their eyes glassy; "I even seen a woman flogged," he said.

"Pray, pray," the grandmother began, "pray, pray . . ."

"I never was a bad boy that I remember of," The Misfit said in an almost dreamy voice, "but somewheres along the line I done something wrong and got sent to the penitentiary. I was buried alive," and he looked up and held her attention to him by a steady stare.

"That's when you should have started to pray," she said. "What did you do to get sent to the penitentiary, that first time?"

"Turn to the right, it was a wall," The Misfit said, looking up again at the cloudless sky. "Turn to the left, it was a wall. Look up it was a ceiling, look down it was a floor. I forgot what I done, lady. I set there and set there, trying to remember what it was I done and I ain't recalled it to this day. Oncet in a while, I would think it was coming to me, but it never come."

"Maybe they put you in by mistake," the old lady said vaguely.

"Nome," he said. "It wasn't no mistake. They had the papers on me."

"You must have stolen something," she said.

The Misfit sneered slightly. "Nobody had nothing I wanted," he said. "It was a head-doctor at the penitentiary said what I had done was kill my daddy but I known that for a lie. My daddy died in nineteen ought nineteen of the epidemic flu and I never had a thing to do with it. He was buried in the Mount Hopewell Baptist churchyard and you can go there and see for yourself."

"If you would pray," the old lady said, "Jesus would help you."

"That's right," The Misfit said.

"Well then, why don't you pray?" she asked trembling with delight suddenly.

"I don't want no hep," he said. "I'm doing all right by myself."

Bobby Lee and Hiram came ambling back from the woods. Bobby Lee was dragging a yellow shirt with bright blue parrots in it.

"Thow me that shirt, Bobby Lee," The Misfit said. The shirt came flying at him and landed on his shoulder and he put it on. The grandmother couldn't name what the shirt reminded her of. "No, lady," The Misfit said while he was buttoning it up, "I found out the crime don't matter. You can do one thing or you can do another, kill a man or take a tire off his car, because sooner or later you're going to forget what it was you done and just be punished for it."

The children's mother had begun to make heaving noises as if she couldn't get her breath. "Lady," he asked, "would you and that little girl like to step off yonder with Bobby Lee and Hiram and join your husband?"

"Yes, thank you," the mother said faintly. Her left arm dangled helplessly and she was holding the baby, who had gone to sleep, in the other. "Hep that lady up, Hiram," The Misfit said as she struggled to climb out of the ditch, "and Bobby Lee, you hold onto that little girl's hand."

"I don't want to hold hands with him," June Star said. "He reminds me of a pig."

The fat boy blushed and laughed and caught her by the arm and pulled her off into the woods after Hiram and her mother.

Alone with The Misfit, the grandmother found that she had lost her voice. There was not a cloud in the sky nor any sun. There was nothing around her but woods. She wanted to tell him that he must pray. She opened and closed her mouth several times before anything came out. Finally she found herself saying, "Jesus. Jesus," meaning, Jesus will help you, but the way she was saying it, it sounded as if she might be cursing.

"Yes'm," The Misfit said as if he agreed. "Jesus thown everything off balance. It was the same case with Him as with me except He hadn't committed any crime and they could prove I had committed one because they had the papers on me. Of course," he said, "they never shown me my papers. That's why I sign myself now. I said long ago, you get you a signature and sign everything you do and keep a copy of it. Then you'll know what you done and you can hold up the crime to the punishment and see do they match and in the end you'll have something to prove you ain't been treated right. I call myself The Misfit," he said, "because I can't make what all I done wrong fit what all I gone through in punishment."

There was a piercing scream from the woods, followed closely by a pistol report. "Does it seem right to you, lady, that one is punished a heap and another ain't punished at all?"

"Jesus!" the old lady cried. "You've got good blood! I know you wouldn't shoot a lady! I know you come from nice people! Pray! Jesus, you ought not to shoot a lady. I'll give you all the money I've got!"

"Lady," The Misfit said, looking beyond her far into the woods, "there never was a body that give the undertaker a tip."

There were two more pistol reports and the grandmother raised her head like a parched old turkey hen crying for water and called, "Bailey Boy, Bailey Boy!" as if her heart would break.

"Jesus was the only One that ever raised the dead," The Misfit continued, "and He shouldn't have done it. He thown everything off balance. If He did what He said, then it's nothing for you to do but thow away everything and follow Him, and if He didn't, then it's nothing for you to do but enjoy the few minutes you got left the best you can — by killing somebody or burning down his house or doing some other meanness to him. No pleasure but meanness," he said and his voice had become almost a snarl.

"Maybe He didn't raise the dead," the old lady mumbled, not knowing what she was saying and feeling so dizzy that she sank down in the ditch with her legs twisted under her.

"I wasn't there so I can't say He didn't," The Misfit said. "I wisht I had of been there," he said, hitting the ground with his fist. "It ain't right I wasn't there because if I had of been there I would of known. Listen lady," he said in a high voice, "if I had of been there I would of known and I wouldn't be like I am now." His voice seemed about to crack and the grandmother's head cleared for an instant. She saw the man's face twisted close to her own as if he were going to cry and she murmured, "Why you're one of my babies. You're one of my own children!" She reached out and touched him on the shoulder. The Misfit sprang back as if a snake had bitten him and shot her three times through the chest. Then he put his gun down on the ground and took off his glasses and began to clean them.

Hiram and Bobby Lee returned from the woods and stood over the ditch, looking down at the grandmother who half sat and half lay in a puddle of blood with her legs crossed under her like a child's and her face smiling up at the cloudless sky.

Without his glasses, The Misfit's eyes were red-rimmed and pale and defenseless-looking. "Take her off and thow her where you thown the others," he said, picking up the cat that was rubbing itself against his leg.

"She was a talker, wasn't she?" Bobby Lee said, sliding down the ditch with a yodel.

"She would of been a good woman," The Misfit said, "if it had been somebody there to shoot her every minute of her life."

"Some fun!" Bobby Lee said.

"Shut up, Bobby Lee," The Misfit said. "It's no real pleasure in life."

Frank O'Connor

Frank O'Connor was the pseudonym for Michael Francis O'Donovan (1903–1966), who was born in Cork, Ireland. His parents were so poor that he attended school only through the fourth grade, at the Christian Brothers School in Cork. During the Irish struggle for independence from England (1918–1921), he was briefly a member of the Irish Republican Army. For several years thereafter he worked as a librarian in Cork and Dublin; it was at this time that he began using his pseudonym so that he would not jeopardize his job as a public official. He had started to write stories as a boy, and for a while he could not decide whether to be a painter or a writer: "I discovered by the time I was sixteen or seventeen that paints cost too much money, so I became a writer because you could be a writer with a pencil and a penny notebook."

When O'Connor was twenty-eight years old, the *Atlantic Monthly* published his story "Guests of the Nation," which he later said was an imitation of Isaac Babel's stories in *Red Cavalry*. His first collection of stories appeared that same year (1931), and from then on he made his living as a writer. During the 1950s he lived in the United States, teaching at Harvard and Northwestern universities and publishing two excellent critical works, *The Mirror in the Roadway* (1956), a study of the modern novel, and *The Lonely Voice* (1963), a history of the short story. O'Connor was a prolific writer, editor, critic, and translator, with almost fifty books to his credit, including fourteen volumes of short stories. He often rewrote his stories several times, even after they were published, so many of them appear in different versions in his various volumes.

O'Connor's greatest achievement was in the short story. Primarily indebted to Anton Chekhov, he declared himself to be an old-fashioned storyteller, believing that a story should have the sound of a person speaking. This conviction gives his fiction an engaging tone, confirming—as do Chekhov's stories—the author's basic sympathy toward his characters. In praising O'Connor's stories, the noted Irish poet William Butler Yeats said that he was "doing for Ireland what Chekhov did for Russia."

RELATED STORIES
Issac Babel, "My First Goose," page 36; Etgar Keret, "Not Human Beings," page 752.

RELATED COMMENTARIES
Frank O'Connor, "The Nearest Thing to Lyric Poetry Is the Short Story," page 1495; Frank O'Connor, "Style and Form in Joyce's 'The Dead,'" page 1497.

Guests of the Nation

1954

I

At dusk the big Englishman, Belcher, would shift his long legs out of the ashes and say "Well, chums, what about it?" and Noble or me would say "All right, chum" (for we had picked up some of their curious expressions), and the little Englishman, Hawkins, would light the lamp and bring out the cards. Sometimes Jeremiah Donovan would come up and supervise the game and get excited over Hawkins's cards, which he always played badly, and shout at him as if he was one of our own "Ah, you divil, you, why didn't you play the tray?"

But ordinarily Jeremiah was a sober and contented poor devil like the big Englishman, Belcher, and was looked up to only because he was a fair hand at documents, though he was slow enough even with them. He wore a small cloth hat and big gaiters over his long pants, and you seldom saw him with his hands out of his pockets. He reddened when you talked to him, tilting from toe to heel and back, and looking down all the time at his big farmer's feet. Noble and me used to make fun of his broad accent, because we were from the town.

I couldn't at the time see the point of me and Noble guarding Belcher and Hawkins at all, for it was my belief that you could have planted that pair down anywhere from this to Claregalway and they'd have taken root there like a native weed. I never in my short experience seen two men to take to the country as they did.

They were handed on to us by the Second Battalion when the search for them became too hot, and Noble and myself, being young, took over with a natural feeling of responsibility, but Hawkins made us look like fools when he showed that he knew the country better than we did.

"You're the bloke they calls Bonaparte," he says to me. "Mary Brigid O'Connell told me to ask you what you done with the pair of her brother's socks you borrowed."

For it seemed, as they explained it, that the Second used to have little evenings, and some of the girls of the neighborhood turned in, and, seeing they were such decent chaps, our fellows couldn't leave the two Englishmen out of them. Hawkins learned to dance "The Walls of Limerick," "The Siege of Ennis," and "The Waves of Tory" as well as any of them, though, naturally, he couldn't return the compliment, because our lads at that time did not dance foreign dances on principle.

So whatever privileges Belcher and Hawkins had with the Second they just naturally took with us, and after the first day or two we gave up all pretense of keeping a close eye on them. Not that they could have got far, for they had accents you could cut with a knife and wore khaki tunics and overcoats with civilian pants and boots. But it's my belief that they never had any idea of escaping and were quite content to be where they were.

It was a treat to see how Belcher got off with the old woman of the house where we were staying. She was a great warrant to scold, and cranky even with us, but before ever she had a chance of giving our guests, as I may call them, a lick of her tongue, Belcher had made her his friend for life. She was breaking sticks, and Belcher, who hadn't been more than ten minutes in the house, jumped up from his seat and went over to her.

"Allow me, madam," he says, smiling his queer little smile, "please allow me"; and he takes the bloody hatchet. She was struck too paralytic to speak, and after that, Belcher would be at her heels, carrying a bucket, a basket, or a load of turf, as the case might be. As Noble said, he got into looking before she leapt, and hot water, or any little thing she wanted, Belcher would have it ready for her. For such a huge man (and though I am five foot ten myself I had to look up at him) he had an uncommon shortness or should I say lack? of speech. It took us some time to get used to him, walking in and out, like a ghost, without a word. Especially because Hawkins talked enough for a platoon, it was strange to hear big Belcher with his toes in the ashes come out with a solitary "Excuse me, chum" or "That's right, chum." His one and only passion was cards, and I will say for him that he was a good card-player. He could have fleeced myself and Noble, but whatever we lost to him Hawkins lost to us, and Hawkins played with the money Belcher gave him.

Hawkins lost to us because he had too much old gab, and we probably lost to Belcher for the same reason. Hawkins and Noble would spit at one another about religion into the early hours of the morning, and Hawkins worried the soul out of Noble, whose brother was a priest, with a string of questions that would puzzle a cardinal. To make it worse even in treating of holy subjects, Hawkins had a deplorable tongue. I never in all my career met a man who could mix such a variety of cursing and bad language into an argument. He was a terrible man, and a fright to argue. He never did a stroke of work, and when he had no one else to talk to, he got stuck in the old woman.

He met his match in her, for one day when he tried to get her to complain profanely of the drought, she gave him a great come-down by blaming it entirely on Jupiter Pluvius (a deity neither Hawkins nor I have ever heard of, though Noble said that among the pagans it was believed that he had something to do with the rain). Another day he was swearing at the capitalists for starting the German war when the old lady laid down her iron, puckered up her little crab's mouth, and said: "Mr. Hawkins, you can say what you like about the war, and think you'll deceive me because I'm only a simple poor country-woman, but I know what started the war. It was the Italian Count that stole the heathen divinity out of the temple in Japan. Believe me, Mr. Hawkins, nothing but sorrow and want can follow the people that disturb the hidden powers."

A queer old girl, all right.

II

We had our tea one evening, and Hawkins lit the lamp and we all sat into cards. Jeremiah Donovan came in too, and sat down and watched us for a while, and it suddenly struck me that he had no great love for the two Englishmen. It came as a great surprise to me, because I hadn't noticed anything about him before.

Late in the evening a really terrible argument blew up between Hawkins and Noble, about capitalists and priests and love of your country.

"The capitalists," says Hawkins with an angry gulp, "pays the priests to tell you about the next world so as you won't notice what the bastards are up to in this."

"Nonsense, man!" says Noble, losing his temper. "Before ever a capitalist was thought of, people believed in the next world."

Hawkins stood up as though he was preaching a sermon.

"Oh, they did, did they?" he says with a sneer. "They believed all the things you believe, isn't that what you mean? And you believe that God created Adam, and Adam created Shem, and Shem created Jehoshophat. You believe all that silly old fairytale about Eve and Eden and the apple. Well, listen to me, chum. If you're entitled to hold a silly belief — like that, I'm entitled to hold my silly belief which is that the first thing your God created was a bleeding capitalist, with morality and Rolls-Royce complete. Am I right, chum?" he says to Belcher.

"You're right, chum," says Belcher with his amused smile, and got up from the table to stretch his long legs into the fire and stroke his moustache. So, seeing that Jeremiah Donovan was going, and that there was no knowing when the argument about religion would be over, I went out with him. We strolled down to the village together, and then he stopped and started blushing and mumbling and saying I ought to be behind, keeping guard on the prisoners. I didn't like the tone he took with me, and anyway I was bored with life in the cottage, so I replied by asking him what the hell we wanted guarding them at all for. I told him I'd talked it over with Noble, and that we'd both rather be out with a fighting column.

"What use are those fellows to us?" says I.

He looked at me in surprise and said: "I thought you knew we were keeping them as hostages."

"Hostages?" I said.

"The enemy have prisoners belonging to us," he says, "and now they're talking of shooting them. If they shoot our prisoners, we'll shoot theirs."

"Shoot them?" I said.

"What else did you think we were keeping them for?" he says.

"Wasn't it very unforeseen of you not to warn Noble and myself of that in the beginning?" I said.

"How was it?" says he. "You might have known it."

"We couldn't know it, Jeremiah Donovan," says I. "How could we when they were on our hands so long?"

"The enemy have our prisoners as long and longer," says he.

"That's not the same thing at all," says I.

"What difference is there?" says he.

I couldn't tell him, because I knew he wouldn't understand. If it was only an old dog that was going to the vet's, you'd try and not get too fond of him, but Jeremiah Donovan wasn't a man that would ever be in danger of that.

"And when is this thing going to be decided?" says I.

"We might hear tonight," he says. "Or tomorrow or the next day at latest. So if it's only hanging round here that's a trouble to you, you'll be free soon enough."

It wasn't the hanging round that was a trouble to me at all by this time. I had worse things to worry about. When I got back to the cottage the argument was still on. Hawkins was holding forth in his best style, maintaining that there was no next world, and Noble was maintaining that there was; but I could see that Hawkins had had the best of it.

"Do you know what, chum?" he was saying with a saucy smile. "I think you're just as big a bleeding unbeliever as I am. You say you believe in the next world, and you know just as much about the next world as I do, which is sweet damn-all. What's heaven? You don't know. Where's heaven? You don't know. You know sweet damn-all! I ask you again, do they wear wings?"

"Very well, then," says Noble, "they do. Is that enough for you? They do wear wings."

"Where do they get them, then? Who makes them? Have they a factory for wings? Have they a sort of store where you hands in your chit and takes your bleeding wings?"

"You're an impossible man to argue with," says Noble. "Now, listen to me—" And they were off again.

It was long after midnight when we locked up and went to bed. As I blew out the candle I told Noble what Jeremiah Donovan was after telling me. Noble took it very quietly. When we'd been in bed about an hour he asked me did I think we ought to tell the Englishmen. I didn't think we should, because it was more than likely that the English wouldn't shoot our men, and even if they did, the brigade officers, who were always up and down with the Second Battalion and knew the Englishmen well, wouldn't be likely to want them plugged. "I think so too," says Noble. "It would be great cruelty to put the wind up them now."

"It was very unforeseen of Jeremiah Donovan anyhow," says I.

It was next morning that we found it so hard to face Belcher and Hawkins. We went about the house all day scarcely saying a word. Belcher didn't seem to notice; he was stretched into the ashes as usual, with his usual look of waiting in quietness for something unforeseen to happen, but Hawkins noticed and put it down to Noble's being beaten in the argument of the night before.

"Why can't you take a discussion in the proper spirit?" he says severely. "You and your Adam and Eve! I'm a Communist, that's what I am. Communist or anarchist, it all comes to much the same thing." And for hours he went round the house, muttering when the fit took him. "Adam and Eve! Adam and Eve! Nothing better to do with their time than picking bleeding apples!"

III

I don't know how we got through that day, but I was very glad when it was over, the tea things were cleared away, and Belcher said in his peaceable way: "Well, chums, what about it?" We sat round the table and Hawkins took out the cards, and just then I heard Jeremiah Donovan's footstep on the path and a dark presentiment crossed my mind. I rose from the table and caught him before he reached the door.

"What do you want?" I asked.

"I want those two soldier friends of yours," he says, getting red.

"Is that the way, Jeremiah Donovan?" I asked.

"That's the way. There were four of our lads shot this morning, one of them a boy of sixteen."

"That's bad," I said.

At that moment Noble followed me out, and the three of us walked down the path together, talking in whispers. Feeney, the local intelligence officer, was standing by the gate.

"What are you going to do about it?" I asked Jeremiah Donovan.

"I want you and Noble to get them out; tell them they're being shifted again; that'll be the quietest way."

"Leave me out of that," says Noble under his breath.

Jeremiah Donovan looks at him hard.

"All right," he says. "You and Feeney get a few tools from the shed and dig a hole by the far end of the bog. Bonaparte and myself will be after you. Don't let anyone see you with the tools. I wouldn't like it to go beyond ourselves."

We saw Feeney and Noble go round to the shed and went in ourselves. I left Jeremiah Donovan to do the explanations. He told them that he had orders to send them back to the Second Battalion. Hawkins let out a mouthful of curses, and you could see that though Belcher didn't say anything, he was a bit upset too. The old woman was for having them stay in spite of us, and she didn't stop advising them until Jeremiah Donovan lost his temper and turned on her. He had a nasty temper, I noticed. It was pitch-dark in the cottage by this time, but no one thought of lighting the lamp, and in the darkness the two Englishmen fetched their topcoats and said good-bye to the old woman.

"Just as a man makes a home of a bleeding place, some bastard at headquarters thinks you're too cushy and shunts you off," says Hawkins, shaking her hand.

"A thousand thanks, madam," says Belcher. "A thousand thanks for everything" — as though he'd made it up.

We went round to the back of the house and down towards the bog. It was only then that Jeremiah Donovan told them. He was shaking with excitement.

"There were four of our fellows shot in Cork this morning and now you're to be shot as a reprisal."

"What are you talking about?" snaps Hawkins. "It's bad enough being mucked about as we are without having to put up with your funny jokes."

"It isn't a joke," says Donovan. "I'm sorry, Hawkins, but it's true," and begins on the usual rigmarole about duty and how unpleasant it is.

I never noticed that people who talk a lot about duty find it much of a trouble to them.

"Oh, cut it out!" says Hawkins.

"Ask Bonaparte," says Donovan, seeing that Hawkins isn't taking him seriously. "Isn't it true, Bonaparte?"

"It is," I say, and Hawkins stops.

"Ah, for Christ's sake, chum!"

"I mean it, chum," I say.

"You don't sound as if you mean it."

"If he doesn't mean it, I do," says Donovan, working himself up.

"What have you against me, Jeremiah Donovan?"

"I never said I had anything against you. But why did your people take out four of our prisoners and shoot them in cold blood?"

He took Hawkins by the arm and dragged him on, but it was impossible to make him understand that we were in earnest. I had the Smith and Wesson in my pocket and I kept fingering it and wondering what I'd do if they put up a fight for it or ran, and wishing to God they'd do one or the other. I knew if they did run for it, that I'd never fire on them. Hawkins wanted to know was Noble in it, and when we said yes, he asked us why Noble wanted to plug him. Why did any of us want to plug him? What had he done to us? Weren't we all chums? Didn't we understand him and didn't he understand us? Did we imagine for an instant that he'd shoot us for all the so-and-so officers in the so-and-so British Army?

By this time we'd reached the bog, and I was so sick I couldn't even answer him. We walked along the edge of it in the darkness, and every now and then Hawkins would call a halt and begin all over again, as if he was wound up, about our being chums, and I knew that nothing but the sight of the grave would convince him that we had to do it. And all the time I was hoping that something would happen; that they'd run for it or that Noble would take over the responsibility from me. I had the feeling that it was worse on Noble than on me.

IV

At last we saw the lantern in the distance and made towards it. Noble was carrying it, and Feeney was standing somewhere in the darkness behind him, and the picture of them so still and silent in the bogland brought it home to me that we were in earnest, and banished the last bit of hope I had.

Belcher, on recognizing Noble, said: "Hallo, chum," in his quiet way, but Hawkins flew at him at once, and the argument began all over again, only this time Noble had nothing to say for himself and stood with his head down, holding the lantern between his legs.

It was Jeremiah Donovan who did the answering. For the twentieth time, as though it was haunting his mind, Hawkins asked if anybody thought he'd shoot Noble.

"Yes, you would," says Jeremiah Donovan.

"No, I wouldn't, damn you!"

"You would, because you'd know you'd be shot for not doing it."

"I wouldn't, not if I was to be shot twenty times over. I wouldn't shoot a pal. And Belcher wouldn't — isn't that right, Belcher?"

"That's right, chum," Belcher said, but more by way of answering the question than of joining in the argument. Belcher sounded as though whatever unforeseen thing he'd always been waiting for had come at last.

"Anyway, who says Noble would be shot if I wasn't? What do you think I'd do if I was in his place, out in the middle of a blasted bog?"

"What would you do?" asks Donovan.

"I'd go with him wherever he was going, of course. Share my last bob with him and stick by him through thick and thin. No one can ever say of me that I let down a pal."

"We had enough of this," says Jeremiah Donovan, cocking his revolver. "Is there any message you want to send?"

"No, there isn't."

"Do you want to say your prayers?"

Hawkins came out with a cold-blooded remark that even shocked me and turned on Noble again.

"Listen to me, Noble," he says. "You and me are chums. You can't come over to my side, so I'll come over to your side. That show you I mean what I say? Give me a rifle and I'll go along with you and the other lads."

Nobody answered him. We knew that was no way out.

"Hear what I'm saying?" he says. "I'm through with it. I'm a deserter or anything else you like. I don't believe in your stuff, but it's no worse than mine. That satisfy you?"

Noble raised his head, but Donovan began to speak and he lowered it again without replying.

"For the last time, have you any messages to send?" says Donovan in a cool, excited sort of voice.

"Shut up, Donovan! You don't understand me, but these lads do. They're not the sort to make a pal and kill a pal. They're not the tools of any capitalist."

I alone of the crowd saw Donovan raise his Webley to the back of Hawkins's neck, and as he did so I shut my eyes and tried to pray. Hawkins had begun to say something else when Donovan fired, and as I opened my eyes at the bang, I saw Hawkins stagger at the knees and lie out flat at Noble's feet, slowly and as quiet as a kid falling asleep, with the lantern-light on his lean legs and bright farmer's boots. We all stood very still, watching him settle out in the last agony.

Then Belcher took out a handkerchief and began to tie it about his own eyes (in our excitement we'd forgotten to do the same for Hawkins), and, seeing it wasn't big enough, turned and asked for the loan of mine. I gave it to him and he knotted the two together and pointed with his foot at Hawkins.

"He's not quite dead," he says. "Better give him another."

Sure enough, Hawkins's left knee is beginning to rise. I bend down and put my gun to his head; then, recollecting myself, I get up again. Belcher understands what's in my mind.

"Give him his first," he says. "I don't mind. Poor bastard, we don't know what's happening to him now."

I knelt and fired. By this time I didn't seem to know what I was doing. Belcher, who was fumbling a bit awkwardly with the handkerchiefs, came out with a laugh as he heard the shot. It was the first time I heard him laugh and it sent a shudder down my back; it sounded so unnatural.

"Poor bugger!" he said quietly. "And last night he was so curious about it all. It's very queer, chums, I always think. Now he knows as much about it as they'll ever let him know, and last night he was all in the dark."

Donovan helped him to tie the handkerchiefs about his eyes. "Thanks, chum," he said. Donovan asked if there were any messages he wanted sent.

"No, chum," he says, "not for me. If any of you would like to write to Hawkins's mother, you'll find a letter from her in his pocket. He and his mother were great chums. But my missus left me eight years ago. Went away with another fellow and took the kid with her. I like the feeling of a home, as you may have noticed, but I couldn't start again after that."

It was an extraordinary thing, but in those few minutes Belcher said more than in all the weeks before. It was just as if the sound of the shot had started a flood of talk in him and he could go on the whole night like that, quite happily, talking about himself. We stood round like fools now that he couldn't see us any longer. Donovan looked at Noble, and Noble shook his head. Then Donovan raised his Webley, and at that moment Belcher gives his queer laugh again. He may have thought we were talking about him, or perhaps he noticed the same thing I'd noticed and couldn't understand it.

"Excuse me, chums," he says. "I feel I'm talking the hell of a lot, and so silly, about my being so handy about a house and things like that. But this thing came on me suddenly. You'll forgive me, I'm sure."

"You don't want to say a prayer?" asks Donovan.

"No, chum," he says. "I don't think it would help. I'm ready, and you boys want to get it over."

"You understand that we're only doing our duty?" says Donovan.

Belcher's head was raised like a blind man's, so that you could only see his chin and the tip of his nose in the lantern-light.

"I never could make out what duty was myself," he said. "I think you're all good lads, if that's what you mean. I'm not complaining."

Noble, just as if he couldn't bear any more of it, raised his fist at Donovan, and in a flash Donovan raised his gun and fired. The big man went over like a sack of meal, and this time there was no need of a second shot.

I don't remember much about the burying, but that it was worse than all the rest because we had to carry them to the grave. It was all mad lonely with nothing but a patch of lantern-light between ourselves and the dark, and birds hooting and screeching all round, disturbed by the guns. Noble went through Hawkins's belongings to find the letter from his mother, and then joined his hands together. He did the same with Belcher. Then, when we'd filled the grave, we separated from Jeremiah Donovan and Feeney and took our tools back to the shed. All the way we didn't speak a word. The kitchen was dark and cold as we'd left it, and the old woman was sitting over the hearth, saying her beads. We walked past her into the room, and Noble struck a match to light the lamp. She rose quietly and came to the doorway with all her cantankerousness gone.

"What did ye do with them?" she asked in a whisper, and Noble started so that the match went out in his hand.

"What's that?" he asked without turning around.

"I heard ye," she said.

"What did you hear?" asked Noble.

"I heard ye. Do ye think I didn't hear ye, putting the spade back in the houseen?"

Noble struck another match and this time the lamp lit for him.

"Was that what ye did to them?" she asked.

Then, by God, in the very doorway, she fell on her knees and began praying, and after looking at her for a minute or two Noble did the same by the fireplace. I pushed my way out past her and left them at it. I stood at the door, watching the stars and listening to the shrieking of the birds dying out over the bogs. It is so strange what you feel at times like that that you can't describe it. Noble says he saw everything ten times the size, as though there were nothing in the whole world but that little patch of bog with the two Englishmen stiffening into it, but with me it was as if the patch of bog where the Englishmen were was a million miles away, and even Noble and the old woman, mumbling behind me, and the birds and the bloody stars were all far away, and I was somehow very small and very lost and lonely like a child astray in the snow. And anything that happened to me afterwards, I never felt the same about again.

Tillie Olsen

Tillie Olsen (1913–2007) was born in Omaha, Nebraska, the daughter of political refugees fleeing the Russian Czarist pogroms after the failed revolution of 1905. Her father was a farmer, packing-house worker, house painter, and jack-of-all-trades; her mother was a factory worker. At the age of sixteen Olsen dropped out of high school to help support her family during the Depression. She was a member of the Young Communist League, involved in the Warehouse Union's labor disputes in Kansas City. At age nineteen she began her first novel, *Yonnondio*. Four chapters of this book about a poverty-stricken working-class family were completed in the next four years, during which time she married, gave birth to her first child, and was left with the baby by her husband because, as she later wrote in her autobiographical story "I Stand Here Ironing," he "could no longer endure sharing want" with them. In 1934 a section of the first chapter of her novel was published in *Partisan Review*, but she abandoned the unfinished book in 1937. The year before she had married Jack Olsen, with whom she had three more children; raising the children and working for political causes took up all her time. In the 1940s she was a factory worker; in the 1950s, a secretary; and not until 1953, when her youngest daughter started school, could she begin writing again.

That year Olsen enrolled in a class in fiction writing at San Francisco State College. She was awarded a Stanford University creative writing fellowship for 1955 and 1956. During the 1950s she wrote the four stories collected in *Tell Me a Riddle*, which established her reputation when the book was published as a paperback in 1961. Identified as a champion of the reemerging feminist movement, Olsen wrote a biographical introduction to Rebecca Harding Davis's nineteenth-century proletarian story, "Life in the Iron-Mills," republished by the Feminist Press in 1972. Two years later, after several grants and creative writing fellowships, she published the still-unfinished *Yonnondio*. *Silences*, a collection of essays exploring the different circumstances that obstruct or silence literary creation, appeared in 1978.

The Canadian author Margaret Atwood understood Olsen's value as a writer:

> Few writers have gained such wide respect on such a small body of published work. . . . Among women writers in the United States, "respect" is too pale a word: "reverence" is more like it. This is presumably because women writers, even more than their male counterparts, recognize what a heroic feat it is to have held down a job, raised four children, and still somehow managed to become and to remain a writer.

A radical feminist, Olsen has said that she felt no personal guilt as a single working parent over her daughter's predicament, as described in her narrative "I Stand Here Ironing," since "guilt is a word used far too sloppily, to cover up harmful situations in society that must be changed." Her four stories have appeared in more than fifty anthologies and have been translated into many languages. In 1994 she was awarded the Rea Award for the Short Story, a literary prize that honors a living American author who has made "a significant contribution to the short story as an art form."

I Stand Here Ironing

1961

I STAND HERE IRONING, and what you asked me moves tormented back and forth with the iron.

"I wish you would manage the time to come in and talk with me about your daughter. I'm sure you can help me understand her. She's a youngster who needs help and whom I'm deeply interested in helping."

"Who needs help." . . . Even if I came, what good would it do? You think because I am her mother I have a key, or that in some way you could use me as a key? She has lived for nineteen years. There is all that life that has happened outside of me, beyond me.

And when is there time to remember, to sift, to weigh, to estimate, to total? I will start and there will be an interruption and I will have to gather it all together again. Or I will become engulfed with all I did or did not do, with what should have been and what cannot be helped.

She was a beautiful baby. The first and only one of our five that was beautiful at birth. You do not guess how new and uneasy her tenancy in her now-loveliness. You did not know her all those years she was thought homely, or see her poring over her baby pictures, making me tell her over and over how beautiful she had been — and would be, I would tell her — and was now, to the seeing eye. But the seeing eyes were few or nonexistent. Including mine.

I nursed her. They feel that's important nowadays, I nursed all the children, but with her, with all the fierce rigidity of first motherhood, I did like the books then said. Though her cries battered me to trembling and my breasts ached with swollenness, I waited till the clock decreed.

Why do I put that first? I do not even know if it matters, or if it explains anything.

She was a beautiful baby. She blew shining bubbles of sound. She loved motion, loved light, loved color and music and textures. She would lie on the floor in her blue overalls patting the surface so hard in ecstasy her hands and feet would blur. She was a miracle to me, but when she was eight months old I had to leave her daytimes with the woman downstairs to whom she was no miracle at all, for I worked or looked for work and for Emily's father, who "could no longer endure" (he wrote in his good-bye note) "sharing want with us."

I was nineteen. It was the pre-relief, pre-WPA world of the depression. I would start running as soon as I got off the streetcar, running up the stairs, the place smelling sour, and awake or asleep to startle awake, when she saw me she would break into a clogged weeping that could not be comforted, a weeping I can hear yet.

After a while I found a job hashing at night so I could be with her days, and it was better. But it came to where I had to bring her to his family and leave her.

It took a long time to raise the money for her fare back. Then she got chicken pox and I had to wait longer. When she finally came, I hardly knew her, walking quick and nervous like her father, looking like her father, thin, and dressed in a shoddy red that yellowed her skin and glared at the pockmarks. All the baby loveliness gone.

She was two. Old enough for nursery school they said, and I did not know then what I know now — the fatigue of the long day, and the lacerations of group life in the kinds of nurseries that are only parking places for children.

Except that it would have made no difference if I had known. It was the only place there was. It was the only way we could be together, the only way I could hold a job.

And even without knowing, I knew. I knew the teacher that was evil because all these years it has curdled into my memory, the little boy hunched in the corner, her rasp, "why aren't you outside, because Alvin hits you? that's no reason, go out, scaredy." I knew Emily hated it even if she did not clutch and implore "don't go Mommy" like the other children, mornings.

She always had a reason why we should stay home. Momma, you look sick. Momma, I feel sick. Momma, the teachers aren't there today, they're sick. Momma, we can't go, there was a fire there last night. Momma, it's a holiday today, no school, they told me.

But never a direct protest, never rebellion. I think of our others in their three-, four-year-oldness — the explosions, the tempers, the denunciations, the demands — and I feel suddenly ill. I put the iron down. What in me demanded that goodness in her? And what was the cost, the cost to her of such goodness?

The old man living in the back once said in his gentle way: "You should smile at Emily more when you look at her." What *was* in my face when I looked at her? I loved her. There were all the acts of love.

It was only with the others I remembered what he said, and it was the face of joy, and not of care or tightness or worry I turned to them — too late for Emily. She does not smile easily, let alone almost always as her brothers and sisters do. Her face is closed and sombre, but when she wants, how fluid. You must have seen it in her pantomimes, you spoke of her rare gift for comedy on the stage that rouses laughter out of the audience so dear they applaud and applaud and do not want to let her go.

Where does it come from, that comedy? There was none of it in her when she came back to me that second time, after I had to send her away again. She had a new daddy now to learn to love, and I think perhaps it was a better time.

Except when we left her alone nights, telling ourselves she was old enough.

"Can't you go some other time, Mommy, like tomorrow?" she would ask. "Will it be just a little while you'll be gone? Do you promise?"

The time we came back, the front door open, the clock on the floor in the hall. She rigid awake. "It wasn't just a little while. I didn't cry. Three times I called you, just three times, and then I ran downstairs to open the door so you could come faster. The clock talked loud. I threw it away, it scared me what it talked."

She said the clock talked loud again that night I went to the hospital to have Susan. She was delirious with the fever that comes before red measles, but she was fully conscious all the week I was gone and the week after we were home when she could not come near the new baby or me.

She did not get well. She stayed skeleton thin, not wanting to eat, and night after night she had nightmares. She would call for me, and I would rouse from exhaustion to sleepily call back: "You're all right, darling, go to sleep, it's just a dream," and if she still called, in a sterner voice, "now go to sleep, Emily, there's nothing to hurt you." Twice, only twice, when I had to get up for Susan anyhow, I went in to sit with her.

Now when it is too late (as if she would let me hold her and comfort her like I do the others) I get up and go to her at once at her moan or restless stirring. "Are you awake, Emily? Can I get you something?" And the answer is always the same: "No, I'm all right, go back to sleep, Mother."

They persuaded me at the clinic to send her away to a convalescent home in the country where "she can have the kind of food and care you can't manage for her, and you'll be free to concentrate on the new baby." They still send children to that place. I see pictures on the society page of sleek young women planning affairs to raise money for it, or dancing at the affairs, or decorating Easter eggs or filling Christmas stockings for the children.

They never have a picture of the children so I do not know if the girls still wear those gigantic red bows and the ravaged looks on the every other Sunday when parents can come to visit "unless otherwise notified" — as we were notified the first six weeks.

Oh it is a handsome place, green lawns and tall trees and fluted flower beds. High up on the balconies of each cottage the children stand, the girls in their red bows and white dresses, the boys in white suits and giant red ties. The parents stand below shrieking up to be heard and the children shriek down to be heard, and between them the invisible wall "Not To Be Contaminated by Parental Germs or Physical Affection."

There was a tiny girl who always stood hand in hand with Emily. Her parents never came. One visit she was gone. "They moved her to Rose Cottage," Emily shouted in explanation. "They don't like you to love anybody here."

She wrote once a week, the labored writing of a seven-year-old. "I am fine. How is the baby. If I write my leter nicly I will have a star. Love." There never was a star. We wrote every other day, letters she could never hold or keep but only hear read — once. "We simply do not have room for children to keep any personal possessions," they patiently explained when we pieced one Sunday's shrieking together to plead how much it would mean to Emily, who loved so to keep things, to be allowed to keep her letters and cards.

Each visit she looked frailer. "She isn't eating," they told us.

(They had runny eggs for breakfast or mush with lumps, Emily said later, I'd hold it in my mouth and not swallow. Nothing ever tasted good, just when they had chicken.)

It took us eight months to get her released home, and only the fact that she gained back so little of her seven lost pounds convinced the social worker.

I used to try to hold and love her after she came back, but her body would stay stiff, and after a while she'd push away. She ate little. Food sickened her, and I think much of life too. Oh she had physical lightness and brightness, twinkling by on skates, bouncing like a ball up and down up and down over the jump rope, skimming over the hill; but these were momentary.

She fretted about her appearance, thin and dark and foreign-looking at a time when every little girl was supposed to look or thought she should look a chubby blonde replica of Shirley Temple. The doorbell sometimes rang for her, but no one seemed to come and play in the house or to be a best friend. Maybe because we moved so much.

There was a boy she loved painfully through two school semesters. Months later she told me how she had taken pennies from my purse to buy him candy. "Licorice was his favorite and I brought him some every day, but he still liked Jennifer better'n me. Why, Mommy?" The kind of question for which there is no answer.

School was a worry for her. She was not glib or quick in a world where glibness and quickness were easily confused with ability to learn. To her over-worked and exasperated teachers she was an overconscientious "slow learner" who kept trying to catch up and was absent entirely too often.

I let her be absent, though sometimes the illness was imaginary. How different from my now-strictness about attendance with the others. I wasn't work-ing. We had a new baby. I was home anyhow. Sometimes, after Susan grew old enough, I would keep her home from school, too, to have them all together.

Mostly Emily had asthma, and her breathing, harsh and labored, would fill the house with a curiously tranquil sound. I would bring the two old dresser mirrors and her boxes of collections to her bed. She would select beads and single earrings, bottle tops and shells, dried flowers and pebbles, old postcards and scraps, all sorts of oddments; then she and Susan would play Kingdom, setting up landscapes and furniture, peopling them with action.

Those were the only times of peaceful companionship between her and Susan. I have edged away from it, that poisonous feeling between them, that terrible balancing of hurts and needs I had to do between the two, and did so badly, those earlier years.

Oh there were conflicts between the others too, each one human, needing, demanding, hurting, taking — but only between Emily and Susan, no, Emily toward Susan that corroding resentment. It seems so obvious on the surface, yet it is not obvious; Susan, the second child, Susan, golden- and curly-haired and chubby, quick and articulate and assured, everything in appearance and manner Emily was not; Susan, not able to resist Emily's precious things, losing or sometimes clumsily breaking them; Susan telling jokes and riddles to com-pany for applause while Emily sat silent (to say to me later: that was *my* riddle, Mother, I told it to Susan); Susan, who for all the five years' difference in age was just a year behind Emily in developing physically.

I am glad for that slow physical development that widened the difference between her and her contemporaries, though she suffered over it. She was too vulnerable for that terrible world of youthful competition, of preening and parading, of constant measuring of yourself against every other, of envy, "If I had that copper hair," "If I had that skin. . . ." She tormented herself enough about not looking like the others, there was enough of unsureness, the having to be conscious of words before you speak, the constant caring — what are they thinking of me? without having it all magnified by the merciless physical drives.

Ronnie is calling. He is wet and I change him. It is rare there is such a cry now. That time of motherhood is almost behind me when the ear is not one's own but must always be racked and listening for the child cry, the child call. We sit for a while and I hold him, looking out over the city spread in charcoal with its soft aisles of light. "*Shoogily*," he breathes and curls closer. I carry him back to bed, asleep. *Shoogily*. A funny word, a family word, inherited from Emily, invented by her to say: *comfort*.

In this and other ways she leaves her seal, I say aloud. And startle at my saying it. What do I mean? What did I start to gather together, to try and make coherent? I was at the terrible, growing years. War years. I do not remember them well. I was working, there were four smaller ones now, there was not time for her. She had to help be a mother, and housekeeper, and shopper. She had to get her seal. Mornings of crisis and near hysteria trying to get lunches packed, hair combed, coats and shoes found, everyone to school or Child Care on time, the baby ready for transportation. And always the paper scribbled on by a smaller one, the book looked at by Susan then mislaid, the homework not done. Running out to that huge school where she was one, she was lost, she was a drop; suffering over the unpreparedness, stammering and unsure in her classes.

There was so little time left at night after the kids were bedded down. She would struggle over books, always eating (it was in those years she developed her enormous appetite that is legendary in our family) and I would be ironing, or preparing food for the next day, or writing V-mail to Bill, or tending the baby. Sometimes, to make me laugh, or out of her despair, she would imitate happenings or types at school.

I think I said once: "Why don't you do something like this in the school amateur show?" One morning she phoned me at work, hardly understandable through the weeping: "Mother, I did it. I won, I won; they gave me first prize; they clapped and clapped and wouldn't let me go."

Now suddenly she was Somebody, and as imprisoned in her difference as she had been in anonymity.

She began to be asked to perform at other high schools, even in colleges, then at city and statewide affairs. The first one we went to, I only recognized her that first moment when thin, shy, she almost drowned herself into the curtains. Then: Was this Emily? The control, the command, the convulsing and deadly clowning, the spell, then the roaring, stamping audience, unwilling to let this rare and precious laughter out of their lives.

Afterwards: You ought to do something about her with a gift like that — but without money or knowing how, what does one do? We have left it all to her, and the gift has so often eddied inside, clogged and clotted, as been used and growing.

She is coming. She runs up the stairs two at a time with her light graceful step, and I know she is happy tonight. Whatever it was that occasioned your call did not happen today.

"Aren't you ever going to finish the ironing, Mother? Whistler painted his mother in a rocker. I'd have to paint mine standing over an ironing board." This is one of her communicative nights and she tells me everything and nothing as she fixes herself a plate of food out of the icebox.

She is so lovely. Why did you want me to come in at all? Why were you concerned? She will find her way.

She starts up the stairs to bed. "Don't get me up with the rest in the morning." "But I thought you were having midterms." "Oh, those," she comes back in, kisses me, and says quite lightly, "in a couple of years when we'll all be atom-dead they won't matter a bit."

She has said it before. She *believes* it. But because I have been dredging the past, and all that compounds a human being is so heavy and meaningful in me, I cannot endure it tonight.

I will never total it all. I will never come in to say: She was a child seldom smiled at. Her father left me before she was a year old. I had to work her first six years when there was work, or I sent her home and to his relatives. There were years she had care she hated. She was dark and thin and foreign-looking in a world where the prestige went to blondeness and curly hair and dimples, she was slow where glibness was prized. She was a child of anxious, not proud, love. We were poor and could not afford for her the soil of easy growth. I was a young mother, I was a distracted mother. There were other children pushing up, demanding. Her younger sister seemed all that she was not. There were years she did not want me to touch her. She kept too much in herself, her life was such she had to keep too much in herself. My wisdom came too late. She has much to her and probably little will come of it. She is a child of her age, of depression, of war, of fear.

Let her be. So all that is in her will not bloom — but in how many does it? There is still enough left to live by. Only help her to know — help make it so there is cause for her to know — that she is more than this dress on the ironing board, helpless before the iron.

Daniel Orozco

Daniel Orozco (b. 1958) grew up in San Francisco and earned his B.A. at Stanford University in 1979 and his M.F.A. at the University of Washington in 1994. "Orientation," his best-known story, originally appeared in *The Seattle Review* and was chosen for inclusion in the *Best American Short Stories* 1995. Since that time Orozco has been the recipient of many prizes and fellowships, including the Pushcart Prize in 1997, a National Endowment for the Arts fellowship in 2006, and the William Saroyan International Prize for Writing after the publication of *Orientation and Other Stories* in 2011. His stories have appeared in magazines such as *Harper's, Zoetrope, McSweeney's, and Story Quarterly.* Currently he teaches creative writing at the University of Idaho and is working on his first novel.

In his answer to an interviewer's question about what drew him to the subject matter of the office work environment in "Orientation," Orozco replied that "On the job is where we all have to be, whether we like it or not. My mother packed licorice in a factory for over twenty years, and came home tired but still human, and I am in awe of how she managed that. . . . In the arena of the workplace, the drama of identity is a drama of extremity, sharp and distilled. The workplace is where we reveal our true selves. It's Hemingway's 'grace under pressure.'"

Orozco is known for his painstaking approach to writing his fiction and admits that he is daunted by the challenge of creating a novel. "As slow as I may be writing a story, a story's compass is brief, its drama tight, its structure precisely defined. . . . Short story or novel, I think that structure is the primary narrative problem." As an instructor of creative writing, he believes that "Ultimately teaching writing is the flip-side of teaching reading, by which I mean creating readers who are able to critically and thoughtfully respond to texts. . . . I don't care if you like it or not—*how does it work*? This is about learning craft. . . . Once you understand what went into crafting that story, then you understand where your response comes from, and that makes you a smart reader."

RELATED STORY
Herman Melville, "Bartleby, the Scrivener," page 886.

RELATED COMMENTARY
Daniel Orozco, "On Steven Millhauser's 'Flying Carpets,'" page 1499.

Orientation

1994

THOSE ARE THE OFFICES and these are the cubicles. That's my cubicle there, and this is your cubicle. This is your phone. Never answer your phone. Let the Voicemail System answer it. This is your Voicemail System Manual. There are no personal phone calls allowed. We do, however, allow for emergencies. If you must make an emergency phone call, ask your supervisor first. If you can't find your supervisor, ask Phillip Spiers, who sits over there. He'll check with Clarissa Nicks, who sits over there. If you make an emergency phone call without asking, you may be let go.

These are your IN and OUT boxes. All the forms in your IN box must be logged in by the date shown in the upper left-hand corner, initialed by you in the upper right-hand corner, and distributed to the Processing Analyst whose name is numerically coded in the lower left-hand corner. The lower right-hand corner is left blank. Here's your Processing Analyst Numerical Code Index. And here's your Forms Processing Procedures Manual.

You must pace your work. What do I mean? I'm glad you asked that. We pace our work according to the eight-hour workday. If you have twelve hours of work in your IN box, for example, you must compress that work into the eight-hour day. If you have one hour of work in your IN box, you must expand that work to fill the eight-hour day. That was a good question. Feel free to ask questions. Ask too many questions, however, and you may be let go.

That is our receptionist. She is a temp. We go through receptionists here. They quit with alarming frequency. Be polite and civil to the temps. Learn their names, and invite them to lunch occasionally. But don't get close to them, as it only makes it more difficult when they leave. And they always leave. You can be sure of that.

The men's room is over there. The women's room is over there. John LaFountaine, who sits over there, uses the women's room occasionally. He says it is accidental. We know better, but we let it pass. John LaFountaine is harmless, his forays into the forbidden territory of the women's room simply a benign thrill, a faint blip on the dull flat line of his life.

Russell Nash, who sits in the cubicle to your left, is in love with Amanda Pierce, who sits in the cubicle to your right. They ride the same bus together after work. For Amanda Pierce, it is just a tedious bus ride made less tedious by the idle nattering of Russell Nash. But for Russell Nash, it is the highlight of his day. It is the highlight of his life. Russell Nash has put on forty pounds, and grows fatter with each passing month, nibbling on chips and cookies while peeking glumly over the partitions at Amanda Pierce, and gorging himself at home on cold pizza and ice cream while watching adult videos on TV.

Amanda Pierce, in the cubicle to your right, has a six-year old son named Jamie, who is autistic. Her cubicle is plastered from top to bottom with the boy's crayon artwork — sheet after sheet of precisely drawn concentric circles and ellipses, in black and yellow. She rotates them every other Friday. Be sure to comment on them. Amanda Pierce also has a husband, who is a lawyer. He subjects her to an escalating array of painful and humiliating sex games, to which Amanda Pierce reluctantly submits. She comes to work exhausted and freshly wounded every morning, wincing from the abrasions on her breasts, or the bruises on her abdomen, or the second-degree burns on the backs of her thighs.

But we're not supposed to know any of this. Do not let on. If you let on, you may be let go.

Amanda Pierce, who tolerates Russell Nash, is in love with Albert Bosch, whose office is over there. Albert Bosch, who only dimly registers Amanda Pierce's existence, has eyes only for Ellie Tapper, who sits over there. Ellie Tapper, who hates Albert Bosch, would walk through fire for Curtis Lance. But Curtis Lance hates Ellie Tapper. Isn't the world a funny place? Not in the ha-ha sense, of course.

Anika Bloom sits in that cubicle. Last year, while reviewing quarterly reports in a meeting with Barry Hacker, Anika Bloom's left palm began to bleed. She fell into a trance, stared into her hand, and told Barry Hacker when and how his wife would die. We laughed it off. She was, after all, a new employee. But Barry Hacker's wife is dead. So unless you want to know exactly when and how you'll die, never talk to Anika Bloom.

Colin Heavey sits in that cubicle over there. He was new once, just like you. We warned him about Anika Bloom. But at last year's Christmas Potluck, he felt sorry for her when he saw that no one was talking to her. Colin Heavey brought her a drink. He hasn't been himself since. Colin Heavey is doomed. There's nothing he can do about it, and we are powerless to help him. Stay away from Colin Heavey. Never give any of your work to him. If he asks to do something, tell him you have to check with me. If he asks again, tell him I haven't gotten back to you.

This is the Fire Exit. There are several on this floor, and they are marked accordingly. We have a Floor Evacuation Review every three months, and an Escape Route Quiz once a month. We have our Biannual Fire Drill twice a year, and our Annual Earthquake Drill once a year. These are precautions only. These things never happen.

For your information, we have a comprehensive health plan. Any catastrophic illness, any unforeseen tragedy is completely covered. All dependents are completely covered. Larry Bagdikian, who sits over there, has six daughters. If anything were to happen to any of his girls, or to all of them, if all six were to simultaneously fall victim to illness or injury — stricken with a hideous degenerative muscle disease or some rare toxic blood disorder, sprayed with semiautomatic gunfire while on a class field trip, or attacked in their bunk beds by some prowling nocturnal lunatic — if any of this were to pass, Larry's girls would all be taken care of. Larry Bagdikian would not have to pay one dime. He would have nothing to worry about.

We also have a generous vacation and sick leave policy. We have an excellent disability insurance plan. We have a stable and profitable pension fund. We get group discounts for the symphony, and block seating at the ballpark.

We get commuter ticket books for the bridge. We have Direct Deposit. We are all members of Costco.

This is our kitchenette. And this, this is our Mr. Coffee. We have a coffee pool, into which we each pay two dollars a week for coffee, filters, sugar, and CoffeeMate. If you prefer Cremora, or half-and-half to CoffeeMate, there is a special pool for three dollars a week. If you prefer Sweet 'n Low to sugar, there is a special pool for two-fifty a week. We do not do decaf. You are allowed to join the coffee pool of your choice, but you are not allowed to touch the Mr. Coffee.

This is the microwave oven. You are allowed to *heat* food in the microwave oven. You are not, however, allowed to *cook* food in the microwave oven.

We get one hour for lunch. We also get one fifteen-minute break in the morning, and one fifteen-minute break in the afternoon. Always take your breaks. If you skip a break, it is gone forever. For your information, your break is a privilege, not a right. If you abuse the break policy, we are authorized to rescind your breaks. Lunch, however, is a right, not a privilege. If you abuse the lunch policy, our hands will be tied, and we will be forced to look the other way. We will not enjoy that.

This is the refrigerator. You may put your lunch in it. Barry Hacker, who sits over there, steals food from this refrigerator. His petty theft is an outlet for his grief. Last New Year's Eve, while kissing his wife, a blood vessel burst in her brain. Barry Hacker's wife was two months pregnant at the time, and lingered in a coma for a half a year before dying. It was a tragic loss for Barry Hacker. He hasn't been himself since. Barry Hacker's wife was a beautiful woman. She was also completely covered. Barry Hacker did not have to pay one dime. But his dead wife haunts him. She haunts all of us. We have seen her, reflected in the monitors of our computers, moving past our cubicles. We have seen the dim shadow of her face in our photocopies. She pencils herself in the receptionist's appointment book, with the notation: To see Barry Hacker. She has left messages in the receptionist's Voicemail box, messages garbled by the electronic chirrups and buzzes in the phone line, her voice echoing from an immense distance within the ambient hum. But the voice is hers. And beneath her voice, beneath the tidal *whoosh* of static and hiss, the gurgling and crying of a baby can be heard.

In any case, if you bring a lunch, put a little something extra in the bag for Barry Hacker. We have four Barrys in this office. Isn't that a coincidence?

This is Matthew Payne's office. He is our Unit Manager, and his door is always closed. We have never seen him, and you will never see him. But he is here. You can be sure of that. He is all around us.

This is the Custodian's Closet. You have no business in the Custodian's Closet.

And this, this is our Supplies Cabinet. If you need supplies, see Curtis Lance. He will log you in on the Supplies Cabinet Authorization Log, then give you a Supplies Authorization Slip. Present your pink copy of the Supplies Authorization Slip to Ellie Tapper. She will log you in on the Supplies Cabinet Key Log, then give you the key. Because the Supplies Cabinet is located outside the Unit Manager's office, you must be very quiet. Gather your supplies quietly. The Supplies Cabinet is divided into four sections. Section One contains letterhead stationery, blank paper and envelopes, memo and note pads, and so on. Section Two contains pens and pencils and typewriter and printer ribbons, and the like. In Section Three we have erasers, correction fluids, transparent tapes, glue sticks, et cetera. And in Section Four we have paper clips and push pins and scissors and razor blades. And here are the spare blades for the shredder. Do not touch the shredder, which is located over there. The shredder is of no concern to you.

Gwendolyn Stich sits in that office there. She is crazy about penguins, and collects penguin knickknacks: penguin posters and coffee mugs and stationery, penguin stuffed animals, penguin jewelry, penguin sweaters and T-shirts and socks. She has a pair of penguin fuzzy slippers she wears when working late at the office. She has a tape cassette of penguin sounds which she listens to for relaxation. Her favorite colors are black and white. She has personalized license plates that read PEN GWEN. Every morning, she passes through all the cubicles to wish each of us a *good* morning. She brings Danish on Wednesdays for Hump Day morning break, and doughnuts on Fridays for TGIF afternoon break. She organizes the Annual Christmas Potluck, and is in charge of the Birthday List. Gwendolyn Stich's door is always open to all of us. She will always lend an ear, and put in a good word for you; she will always give you a hand, or the shirt off her back, or a shoulder to cry on. Because her door is always open, she hides and cries in a stall in the women's room. And John LaFountaine — who, enthralled when a woman enters, site quietly in his stall with his knees to his chest — John LaFountaine has heard her vomiting in there. We have come upon Gwendolyn Stich huddled in the stairwell, shivering in the updraft, sipping a Diet Mr. Pibb and hugging her knees. She does not let any of this interfere with her work. If it interfered with her work, she might have to be let go.

Kevin Howard sits in that cubicle over there. He is a serial killer, the one they call the Carpet Cutter, responsible for the mutilations across town. We're not supposed to know that, so do not let on. Don't worry. His compulsion inflicts itself on strangers only, and the routine established is elaborate and unwavering. The victim must be a white male, a young adult no older than thirty, heavyset, with dark hair and eyes, and the like. The victim must be chosen at random, before sunset, from a public place; the victim is followed home, and must put up a struggle; et cetera. The carnage inflicted is precise: the angle and direction of the incisions; the layering of skin and muscle tissue; the rearrangement of the visceral organs; and so on. Kevin Howard does not let any of this interfere with his work. He is, in fact, our fastest typist. He types as if he were on fire. He has a secret crush on Gwendolyn Stich, and leaves a red-foil-wrapped Hershey's Kiss on her desk every afternoon. But he hates Anika Bloom, and keeps well away from her. In his presence, she has uncontrollable fits of shaking and trembling. Her left palm does not stop bleeding.

In any case, when Kevin Howard gets caught, act surprised. Say that he seemed like a nice person, a bit of a loner, perhaps, but always quiet and polite.

This is the photocopier room. And this, this is our view. It faces southwest. West is down there, toward the water. North is back there. Because we are on the seventeenth floor, we are afforded a magnificent view. Isn't it beautiful? It overlooks the park, where the tops of those trees are. You can see a segment of the bay between those two buildings there. You can see the sun set in the gap between those two buildings over there. You can see this building reflected in the glass panels of that building across the way. There. See? That's you, waving. And look there. There's Anika Bloom in the kitchenette, waving back.

Enjoy this view while photocopying. If you have problems with the photocopier, see Russell Nash. If you have any questions, ask your supervisor. If you can't find your supervisor, ask Phillip Spiers. He sits over there. He'll check with Clarissa Nicks. She sits over there. If you can't find them, feel free to ask me. That's my cubicle. I sit in there.

Julie Otsuka

Julie Otsuka (b. 1962) was born in Palo Alto, California, where her father worked as an engineer and her mother as a lab technician. Her grandparents had immigrated to the United States from Japan. After Otsuka studied art at Yale University, she began her career as a painter before enrolling in graduate school at Columbia University, where she earned her M.F.A. in creative writing. Her first novel, *When the Emperor Was Divine* (2002), about the internment of a Japanese-American family during World War II, was based on Otsuka's own family story. Her grandfather was arrested as a suspected spy the day after the bombing of Pearl Harbor, and her mother, uncle, and grandmother were confined to a camp in Topaz, Utah, for the duration of the war. In 2004 Otsuka was the recipient of a Guggenheim Fellowship. This support helped her create her second novel, *The Buddha in the Attic* (2011), a bestseller about a group of young Japanese "picture brides" who were brought to the United States a century ago to wed Japanese men who knew them only by their photographs. It was a National Book Award finalist and won the Langum Prize for American Historical Fiction. "The Children" is an extract from this novel.

In an interview published in the magazine *Granta*, which excerpted Otsuka's second novel in two issues, she explained that in *The Buddha in the Attic*, the central character is everyone in the group of brides, what Otsuka called "the collective 'we.' No one 'I' is more important than any other. Using the 'we' voice allowed me to tell a much larger story than I would have been able to tell otherwise. . . . It's a very capacious and infinitely expandable voice. Each sentence gives you a brief window into somebody's life—it's like catching a glimpse of someone's house from a train—and then we move on. Also, since Japan is a very group-oriented culture. . . it made sense to speak of the picture brides as a collective unity."

Otsuka also stated that her writing was very intuitive and she often read her sentences aloud as part of her creative process. "I was obsessed with the rhythm of the language while writing this novel. I was constantly reading my sentences out loud. . . . I could hear where the accents fell. I could often hear the rhythmic pattern of the next sentence I wanted to write before I knew the exact words to drop into that pattern. And at times I found myself doing things like searching for the right three-syllable town in California where they had Japanese migrant laborers working in the peach orchards. . . . A two-syllable town with orange groves just would not do."

The Children

WE LAID THEM DOWN GENTLY, in ditches and furrows and wicker baskets beneath the trees. We left them lying naked, atop blankets, on woven straw mats at the edges of the fields. We placed them in wooden apple boxes and nursed them every time we finished hoeing a row of beans. When they were older, and more rambunctious, we sometimes tied them to chairs. We strapped them on to our backs in the dead of winter in Redding and went out to prune the grapevines, but some mornings it was so cold that their ears froze and bled. In early summer, in Stockton, we left them in nearby gullies while we dug up onions and began picking the first plums. We gave them sticks to play with in our absence and called out to them from time to time to let them know we were still there. *Don't bother the dogs. Don't touch the bees. Don't wander away or Papa will get mad.* When they tired and began to cry out for us we kept on working because if we didn't we knew we would never pay off the debt on our lease. *Mama can't come.* After a while their voices grew fainter and their crying came to a stop. And at the end of the day when there was no more light in the sky, we woke them up from wherever it was they lay sleeping and brushed the dirt from their hair. *It's time to go home.*

Some of them were stubborn and wilful and would not listen to a word we said. Others were more serene than the Buddha. *He came into the world smiling.* One loved her father more than anyone else. One hated bright colours. One would not go anywhere without his tin pail. One weaned herself at the age of thirteen months by pointing to a glass of milk on the counter and telling us, 'I want.' Several were wise beyond their years. *The fortune-teller told us he was born with the soul of an old man.* They ate at the table like grown-ups. They never cried. They never complained. They never left their chopsticks standing upright in their rice. They played by themselves all day long in the fields while we worked, without making a sound. They drew pictures in the dirt for hours. And whenever we tried to pick them up and carry them home they shook their heads and said, 'I'm too heavy,' or 'Mama, rest.' They worried about us when we were tired. They worried about us when we were sad. They knew, without our telling them, when our knees were bothering us or it was our time of the month. They slept with us, at night, like puppies, on wooden boards covered with hay, and for the first time since coming to America we did not mind having someone else beside us in the bed.

Always, we had favourites. Perhaps it was our firstborn, Ichiro, who made us feel so much less lonely than we had been before. *My husband has not spoken to me in more than two years.* Or our second son, Yoichi, who taught himself how to read English by the time he was four. *He's a genius.* Or Sunoko, who always tugged at our sleeve with such fierce urgency and then forgot what it was she wanted to say. 'It will come to you later,' we would tell her, even though it never did. Some of us preferred our daughters, who were gentle and good, and some of us, like our mothers before us, preferred our sons. *They're the better gain on the farm.* We fed them more than we did their sisters. We sided with them in arguments. We dressed them in nicer clothes. We scraped up our last pennies to take them to the doctor whenever they came down with fever, while our daughters we cared for at home. *I applied a mustard plaster to her chest and said a prayer to the god of wind and bad colds.* Because we knew that our daughters would leave us the moment they married, but our sons would provide for us in our old age.

Usually, our husbands had nothing to do with them. They never changed a single diaper. They never washed a dirty dish. They never touched a broom. In the evening, no matter how tired we were when we came in from the fields, they sat down and read the paper while we cooked dinner for the children and stayed up until late washing and mending piles of clothes. They never let us go to sleep before them. They never let us rise after the sun. *You'll set a bad example for the children.* They were silent, weathered men who tramped in and out of the house in their muddy overalls muttering to themselves about sucker growth, the price of green beans, how many crates of celery they thought we could pull from the fields. They rarely spoke to their children, or even seemed to remember their names. *Tell number three boy not to slouch when he walks.* And if things grew too noisy at the table, they clapped their hands and shouted out, 'That's enough!' Their children, in turn, preferred not to speak to their fathers at all. Whenever one of them had something to say it always went through us. *Tell Papa I need a nickel. Tell Papa there's something wrong with one of the horses. Tell Papa he missed a spot shaving. Ask Papa how come he's so old.*

As soon as we could we put them to work in the fields. They picked strawberries with us in San Martin. They picked peas with us in Los Osos. They crawled behind us through the vineyards of Hughson and Del Rey as we cut down the raisin grapes and laid them out to dry on wooden trays in the sun. They hauled water. They cleared brush. They shovelled weeds. They chopped wood. They hoed in the blazing summer heat of the Imperial Valley before their bones were fully formed. Some of them were slow-moving and dreamy and planted entire rows of cauliflower sprouts upside down by mistake. Others could sort tomatoes faster than the fastest of the hired help. Many complained. They had stomach aches. Headaches. Their eyes were itching like crazy from the dust. Some of them pulled on their boots every morning without having to be told. One of them had a favourite pair of clippers, which he sharpened every evening in the barn after supper and would not let anyone else touch. One could not stop thinking about bugs. *They're everywhere.* One sat down one day in the middle of an onion patch and said she wished she'd never been born. And we wondered if we had done the right thing, bringing them into this world.

And yet they played for hours like calves in the fields. They made swords out of broken grape-stakes and duelled beneath the trees. They made kites out of newspaper and balsa wood and tied knives to the strings and had dogfights on windy days in the sky. They made twist-up dolls out of wire and straw and did evil things to them with sharpened chopsticks in the woods. They played shadow catch shadow on moonlit nights in the orchards, just as we had back home in Japan. They played kick the can and mumblety-peg and *jan ken po.* They had contests to see who could nail together the most packing crates the night before we went to market and who could hang the longest from the walnut tree without letting go. They folded squares of paper into airplanes and birds and watched them fly away. They collected crows' nests and snakeskins, beetle shells, acorns, rusty iron stakes from down by the tracks. They learned the names of the planets. They read each other's palms. *Your lifeline is unusually short.* They told each other's fortunes. *One day you will take a long journey on a train.* They went out into the barn after supper with their kerosene lanterns and played mama and papa in the loft. *Now slap your belly and make a sound like you're dying.* And on hot summer nights, when it was ninety-eight degrees, they spread their blankets out beneath the peach trees and dreamed of picnics down by the river, a new eraser, a book, a ball, a china doll with blinking violet eyes, leaving home, one day, for the great world beyond.

Beyond the farm, they'd heard, there were strange pale children who grew up entirely indoors and knew nothing of the fields and streams. Some of these children, they'd heard, had never even seen a tree. *Their mothers won't let them go outside and play in the sun.* Beyond the farm, they'd heard, there were fancy white houses with gold-framed mirrors and crystal doorknobs and porcelain toilets that flushed with the yank of a chain. *And they don't even make a smell.* Beyond the farm, they'd heard, there were mattresses stuffed with hard metal springs that were somehow as soft as a cloud. (Goro's sister had gone away to work as a maid in the city, and when she came back she said that the beds there were so soft she had to sleep on the floor.) Beyond the farm, they'd heard, there were mothers who ate their breakfast every morning in bed and fathers who sat on cushioned chairs all day long in their offices shouting orders into a phone — and for this, they got paid. Beyond the farm, they'd heard, wherever you went you were always a stranger and if you got on the wrong bus by mistake you might never find your way home.

They caught tadpoles and dragonflies down by the creek and put them into glass jars. They watched us kill the chickens. They found the places in the hills where the deer had last slept and lay down in their round nests in the tall, flattened grass. They pulled the tails off lizards to see how long it would take them to grow back. *Nothing's happening.* They brought home baby sparrows that had fallen from the trees and fed them sweetened rice gruel with a toothpick but in the morning, when they woke, the sparrows were dead. "Nature doesn't care," we told them. They sat on the fence and watched the farmer in the next field over leading his cow up to meet with the bull. They saw a mother cat eating her own kittens. "It happens," we explained. They heard us being taken late at night by our husbands, who would not leave us alone even though we had long ago lost our looks. "It doesn't matter what you look like in the dark," we were told. They bathed with us every evening, out of doors, in giant wooden tubs heated over a fire, and sank down to their chins in the hot steaming water. They leaned back their heads. They closed their eyes. They reached out for our hands. They asked us questions. *How do you know when you're dead? What if there were no birds? What if you have red spots all over your body but nothing hurts? Is it true that the Chinese really eat pigs' feet?*

They had things to keep them safe. A red bottle cap. A glass marble. A postcard of two Russian beauties strolling along the Songhua River sent to them by an uncle who was stationed in Manchuria. They had lucky white feathers that they carried with them at all times in their pockets, and stones wrapped in soft cloth that they pulled out of drawers and held — just for a moment, until the bad feeling went away — in their hands. They had secret words that they whispered to themselves whenever they felt afraid. They had favourite trees that they climbed up into whenever they warned to be alone. *Everyone please go away.* They had favourite sisters in whose arms they could instantly fall asleep. They had hated older brothers with whom they refused to be left alone in a room. *He'll kill me.* They had dogs from whom they were inseparable and to whom they could tell all the things they could not tell anyone else. *I broke Papa's pipe and buried it under a tree.* They had their own rules. *Never sleep with your pillow facing toward the north* (Hoshiko had gone to sleep with her pillow facing north and in the middle of the night she stopped breathing and died). They had their own rituals. *You must always throw salt where a hobo has been.* They had their own beliefs. *If you see a spider in the morning you will have good luck. If you lie down after eating you will turn into a cow. If you wear a basket on your head you will stop growing. A single flower means death.*

We told them stories about tongue-cut sparrows and grateful cranes and baby doves that always remembered to let their parents perch on the higher branch. We tried to teach them manners. *Never point with your chopsticks. Never suck on your chopsticks. Never take the last piece of food from a plate.* We praised them when they were kind to others but told them not to expect to be rewarded for their good deeds. We scolded them whenever they tried to talk back. We taught them never to accept a handout. We taught them never to brag. We taught them everything we knew. *A fortune begins with a penny. It is better to suffer ill than to do ill. You must give back whatever you receive. Don't be loud like the Americans. Stay away from the Chinese. They don't like us.* Watch out for the Koreans. *They hate us.* Be careful around the Filipinos. *They're worse than the Koreans.* Never marry an Okinawan. *They're not real Japanese.*

In the countryside, especially, we often lost them early. To diphtheria and the measles. Tonsillitis. Whooping cough. Mysterious infections that turned gangrenous overnight. One of them was bitten by a poisonous black spider in the outhouse and came down with fever. One was kicked in the stomach by our favourite grey mule. One disappeared while we were sorting the peaches in the packing shed and even though we looked under every rock and tree for her we never did find her and after that we were never the same. *I lost the will to live.* One tumbled out of the truck while we were driving the rhubarb to market and fell into a coma from which he never awoke. One was kidnapped by a pear-picker from a nearby orchard whose advances we had repeatedly rebuffed. *I should have just told him yes.* Another was badly burned when the moonshine still exploded out back behind the barn and lived for only a day. *The last thing she said to me was, 'Mama, don't forget to look up at the sky.'* Several drowned. One in the Calaveras River. One in the Nacimiento. One in an irrigation ditch. One in a laundry tub we knew we should not have left out overnight. And every year, in August, on the Feast of the Dead, we lit white paper lanterns on their gravestones and welcomed their spirits back to Earth for a day. And at the end of that day, when it was time for them to leave, we set the paper lanterns afloat on the river to guide them safely home. For they were Buddhas now, who resided in the Land of Bliss.

A few of us were unable to have them, and this was the worst fate of all. For without an heir to carry on the family name the spirits of our ancestors would cease to exist. *I feel like I came all the way to America for nothing.* Sometimes we tried going to the faith healer, who told us that our uterus was the wrong shape and there was nothing that could be done. 'Your destiny is in the hands of the gods,' she said to us, and then she showed us to the door. Or we consulted the acupuncturist, Dr Ishida, who took one look at us and said, 'Too much yang,' and gave us herbs to nourish our yin and blood. And three months later we found ourselves miscarrying yet again. Sometimes we were sent by our husband back home to Japan, where the rumours would follow us for the rest of our lives. 'Divorced,' the neighbours would whisper. And, 'I hear she's dry as a gourd.' Sometimes we tried cutting off all our hair and offering it to the goddess of fertility if only she would make us conceive, but still, every month, we continued to bleed. And even though our husband had told us it made no difference to him whether he became a father or not — the only thing that mattered, he had said to us, was that we grew old side by side — we could not stop thinking of the children we'd never had. *Every night I can hear them playing in the fields outside my window.*

In J-Town they lived with us eight and nine to a room behind our barbershops and bathhouses and in tiny unpainted apartments that were so dark we had to leave the lights on all day long. They chopped carrots for us in our restaurants. They stacked apples for us at our fruit stands. They climbed up on to their bicycles and delivered bags of groceries to our customers' back doors. They separated the colours from the whites in our basement laundries and quickly learned to tell the difference between a red-wine stain and blood. They swept the floors of our boarding houses. They changed towels. They stripped sheets. They made up the beds. They opened doors on things that should never be seen. *I thought he was praying but he was dead.* They brought supper every evening to the elderly widow in 4A from Nagasaki, Mrs Kawamura, who worked as a chambermaid at the Hotel Drexel and had no children of her own. *My husband was a gambler who left me with only forty-five cents.* They played *go* in the lobby with the bachelor, Mr Morita, who started out as a presser at the Empress Hand Laundry thirty years ago and still worked there to this day. *It all went by so fast.* They trailed their fathers from one yard to the next as they made their gardening rounds and learned how to trim the hedges and mow the grass. They waited for us on wooden slatted benches in the park while we finished cleaning the houses across the street. *Don't talk to strangers,* we told them. *Study hard. Be patient. Whatever you do, don't end up like me.*

At school they sat in the back of the classroom in their homemade clothes with the Mexicans and spoke in timid, faltering voices. They never raised their hands. They never smiled. At recess they huddled together in a corner of the schoolyard and whispered among themselves in their secret, shameful language. In the cafeteria they were always last in line for lunch. Some of them — our first-borns — hardly knew any English and whenever they were called upon to speak their knees began to shake. One of them, when asked her name by the teacher, replied, 'Six,' and the laughter rang in her ears for days. Another said his name was Pencil, and for the rest of his life that was what he was called. Many of them begged us not to be sent back, but within weeks, it seemed, they could name all the animals in English and read aloud every sign that they saw whenever we went shopping downtown — the street of the tall timber poles, they told us, was called State Street, and the street of the unfriendly barbers was Grove, and the bridge from which Mr Itami had jumped after the stock market collapsed was the Last Chance Bridge — and wherever they went they were able to make their desires known. *One chocolate malt, please.*

One by one all the old words we had taught them began to disappear from their heads. They forgot the names of the flowers in Japanese. They forgot the names of the colours. They forgot the names of the fox god and the thunder god and the god of poverty, whom we could never escape. *No matter how long we live in this country they'll never let us buy land.* They forgot the name of the water goddess, Mizu Gami, who protected our rivers and streams and insisted that we keep our wells clean. They forgot the words for snow-light and bell cricket and fleeing in the night. They forgot what to say at the altar to our dead ancestors, who watched over us night and day. They forgot how to count. They forgot how to pray. They spent their days now living in the new language, whose twenty-six letters still eluded us even though we had been in America for years. *All I learned was the letter X so I could sign my name at the bank.* They pronounced their Ls and Rs with ease. And even when we sent them to the Buddhist temple on Saturdays to study Japanese they did not learn a thing. *The only reason my children go is to get out of working in the store.* But whenever we heard them talking out loud in their sleep the words that came out of their mouths came out — we were sure of it — in Japanese.

They gave themselves new names we had not chosen for them and could barely pronounce. One called herself Doris. One called herself Peggy. Many called themselves George. Saburo was called Chinky by all the others because he looked just like a Chinaman. Toshitachi was called Harlem because his skin was so dark. Etsuko was given the name Esther by her teacher, Mr Slater, on her first day of school. "It's his mother's name," she explained. To which we replied, "So is yours." Sumire called herself Violet. Shizuko was Sugar. Makoto was just Mac. Shigeharu Takagi joined the Methodist Church at the age of nine and changed his name to Paul. Edison Kobayashi was born lazy but had a photographic memory and could tell you the name of every person he'd ever met. Grace Sugita didn't like ice cream. *Too cold.* Kitty Matsutaro expected nothing and got nothing in return. Six-foot-four Tiny Honda was the biggest Japanese we'd ever seen. Mop Yamasaki had long hair and liked to dress like a girl. Lefty Hayashi was the star pitcher at Emerson Junior High. Sam Nishimura had been sent to Tokyo to receive a proper Japanese education and had just returned to America after six and a half years. *They made him start all over again in the first grade.* Daisy Takada had perfect posture and liked to do things in sets of four. Mabel Ota's father had gone bankrupt three times. Lester Nakano's family bought all their clothes at the Goodwill. Tommy Takayama's mother was — everyone knew it — a whore. *She has six different children by five different men. And two of them are twins.*

Soon we could barely recognize them. They were taller than we were, and heavier. They were loud beyond belief. *I feel like a duck that's hatched goose's eggs.* They preferred their own company to ours and pretended not to understand a word that we said. Our daughters took big long steps, in the American manner, and moved with undignified haste. They wore their garments too loose. They swayed their hips like mares. They chartered away like coolies the moment they came home from school and said whatever popped into their minds. *Mr Dempsey has a folded ear.* Our sons grew enormous. They insisted on eating bacon and eggs every morning for breakfast instead of bean-paste soup. They refused to use chopsticks. They drank gallons of milk. They poured ketchup all over their rice. They spoke perfect English just like on the radio and whenever they caught us bowing before the kitchen god in the kitchen and clapping our hands they rolled their eyes and said, 'Mama, *please.*'

Mostly, they were ashamed of us. Our floppy straw hats and threadbare clothes. Our heavy accents. *Every sing oh righ?* Our cracked, calloused palms. Our deeply lined faces black from years of picking peaches and staking grape plants in the sun. They longed for real fathers with briefcases who went to work in a suit and tie and only mowed the grass on Sundays. They wanted different and better mothers who did not look so worn out. *Can't you put on a little lipstick?* They dreaded rainy days in the country when we came to pick them up after school in our old battered pickups. They never invited friends over to our crowded homes in J-Town. *We live like beggars.* They would not be seen with us at the temple on the Emperor's birthday. They would not celebrate the annual Freeing of the Insects with us at the end of summer in the park. They refused to join hands and dance with us in the streets on the Festival of the Autumnal Equinox. They laughed at us whenever we insisted that they bow to us first thing in the morning and with each passing day they seemed to slip further and further from our grasp.

Some of them developed unusually good vocabularies and became the best students in the class. They won prizes for best essay on California wild flowers. They received highest honours in science. They had more gold stars than anyone else on the teacher's chart. Others fell behind every year during harvest season and had to repeat the same grade twice. One got pregnant at fourteen and was sent away to live with her grandparents on a silkworm farm in remote western Japan. *Every week she writes to me asking when she can come home.* One took his own life. Several quit school. A few ran wild. They formed their own gangs. They made up their own rules. *No knives, No girls. No Chinese allowed.* They went around late at night looting for other people to fight. *Let's go beat up some Filipinos.* And when they were too lazy to leave the neighbourhood they stayed at home and fought among themselves. *You goddamn Jap!* Others kept their heads down and tried not to be seen. They went to no parties (they were invited to no parties). They played no instruments. They never got valentines (they never sent valentines). They didn't like to dance (they didn't have the right shoes). They floated ghostlike through the halls, with their eyes turned away and their books clutched to their chests, as though lost in a dream. If someone called them a name behind their back they did not hear it. If someone called them a name to their face they just nodded and walked on. If they were given the oldest textbooks to use in math class they shrugged and took it in stride. *I never really liked algebra anyway.* If their pictures appeared at the end of the yearbook they pretended not to mind. "That's just the way it is," they said to themselves. And, "So what?" And, "Who cares?" Because they knew that no matter what they did they would never really fit in.

They learned which mothers would let them come over (Mrs Henke, Mrs Woodruff, Mrs Alfred Chandler III) and which would not (all the other mothers). They learned which barbers would cut their hair (the Negro barbers) and which barbers to avoid (the grumpy barbers on the south side of Grove). They learned that there were certain things that would never be theirs: higher noses, fairer complexions, longer legs that might be noticed from afar. *Every morning I do my stretching exercises but it doesn't seem to help.* They learned when they could go swimming at the YMCA — *Coloured days are on Mondays* — and when they could go to the picture show at the Pantages Theater downtown (never). They learned that they should always call the restaurant first. *Do you serve Japanese?* They learned not to go out alone during the daytime and what to do if they found themselves cornered in an alley after dark. *Just tell them you know judo.* And if that didn't work, they learned to fight back with their fists. *They respect you when you're strong.* They learned to find protectors. They learned to hide their anger. *No, of course. I don't mind. That's fine. Go ahead.* They learned never to show their fear. They learned that some people are born luckier than others and that things in this world do not always go as you plan.

Still, they dreamed. One swore she would one day marry a preacher so she wouldn't have to pick berries on Sundays. One wanted to save up enough money to buy his own farm. One wanted to become a tomato-grower like his father. One wanted to become anything but. One wanted to plant a vineyard. One wanted to start his own label. *I'd call it Fukuda Orchards.* One could not wait until the day she got off the ranch. One wanted to go to college even though no one she knew had ever left the town. *I know it's crazy, but . . .* One loved living out in the country and never wanted to leave. *It's better here. Nobody knows who we are.* One wanted something more but could not say exactly what it was. *This just isn't enough.* One wanted a Swing King drum set with hi-hat cymbals. One wanted a spotted pony. One wanted his own paper route. One wanted her own room, with a lock on the door. *Anyone who came in would have to knock first.* One wanted to become an artist and live in a garret in Paris. One wanted to go to refrigeration school. *You can do it through the mail.* One wanted to build bridges. One wanted to play the piano. One wanted to operate his own fruit stand alongside the highway instead of working for somebody else. One wanted to learn shorthand at the Merritt Secretarial Academy and get an inside job in an office. *Then I'd have it made.* One wanted to become the next Great Togo on the professional wrestling circuit. One wanted to become a state senator. One wanted to cut hair and open her own salon. One had polio and just wanted to breathe without her iron lung. One wanted to become a master seamstress. One wanted to become a teacher. One wanted to become a doctor. One wanted to become his sister. One wanted to become a gangster. One wanted to become a star. And even though we saw the darkness coming we said nothing and let them dream on.

Cynthia Ozick

Cynthia Ozick (b. 1928) sees a clear distinction between art and life: "As for life, I don't like it. I notice no 'interplay of life and art.' Life is that which—pressingly, persistently, unfailingly, imperially—interrupts." In Ozick's life there has been a long time between what Grace Paley called "knowing and telling." Ozick was born in New York City, the daughter of a pharmacist. She received a B.A. from New York University in 1949 and an M.A. from Ohio State University in 1950 with a thesis titled "Parable in Henry James." She didn't publish her first work, the novel *Trust*, until 1966. Three collections of short fiction followed: *The Pagan Rabbi and Other Stories* (1971), *Bloodshed and Three Novellas* (1976), and *Levitation* (1981). In 1989 she published *Metaphor and Memory: Essays* and *The Shawl*, a novella developing the short story included here.

In her essay "The Lesson of the Master" in *Art and Ardor* (1983), Ozick described how as a young writer she was betrayed by Henry James. After college she worshiped literature, seeing herself "a priest at that altar, and that altar was all of my life." She felt that James was trying to teach her a lesson through his fiction, that an aspiring writer ought "to live immaculately, unspoiled by what we mean when we say 'life'—relationship, family mess, distraction, exhaustion, anxiety, above all disappointment." Ozick remembers herself as a nearsighted twenty-two-year-old "infected with the commonplace intention of writing a novel" and trying to live "like the elderly bald-headed Henry James." Years later she realized her mistake. To be a writer,

> one must keep one's psychological distance from the supreme artists. . . .
> The true Lesson of the Master, then, is, simply, never to venerate what is complete, burnished, whole . . . never to worship ripe Art or the ripened artist; but instead to seek to be young while young, primitive while primitive, ungainly when ungainly — to look for crudeness and rudeness, to husband one's own stupidity or ungenius.

Yet Ozick also understands that life "interrupts," and the journey to art is beset with difficulties. In her best short fiction, such as the Holocaust story "The Shawl," she accepts the challenge of her craft, writing in a swiftly imagistic style. She admits that "in beginning a story I know nothing at all: surely not where I am going, and hardly at all how to get there." Some other books are *What Henry James Knew* (1993), *The Cynthia Ozick Reader* (1996), *The Puttermesser Papers* (1997), *Heir to the Glimmering World* (2004), and *Foreign Bodies* (2010).

RELATED COMMENTARY
Cynthia Ozick, "Isaac Babel: 'Let Me Finish,'" page 1500.

The Shawl

1980

STELLA, COLD, COLD, the coldness of hell. How they walked on the roads together, Rosa with Magda curled up between sore breasts, Magda wound up in the shawl. Sometimes Stella carried Magda. But she was jealous of Magda. A thin girl of fourteen, too small, with thin breasts of her own, Stella wanted to be wrapped in a shawl, hidden away, asleep, rocked by the march, a baby, a round infant in arms. Magda took Rosa's nipple, and Rosa never stopped walking, a walking cradle. There was not enough milk; sometimes Magda sucked air; then she screamed. Stella was ravenous. Her knees were tumors on sticks, her elbows chicken bones.

Rosa did not feel hunger; she felt light, not like someone walking but like someone in a faint, in trance, arrested in a fit, someone who is already a floating angel, alert and seeing everything, but in the air, not there, not touching the road. As if teetering on the tips of her fingernails. She looked into Magda's face through a gap in the shawl: a squirrel in a nest, safe, no one could reach her inside the little house of the shawl's windings. The face, very round, a pocket mirror of a face: but it was not Rosa's bleak complexion, dark like cholera, it was another kind of face altogether, eyes blue as air, smooth feathers of hair nearly as yellow as the Star sewn into Rosa's coat. You could think she was one of *their* babies.

Rosa, floating, dreamed of giving Magda away in one of the villages. She could leave the line for a minute and push Magda into the hands of any woman on the side of the road. But if she moved out of line they might shoot. And even if she fled the line for half a second and pushed the shawl-bundle at a stranger, would the woman take it? She might be surprised, or afraid; she might drop the shawl, and Magda would fall out and strike her head and die. The little round head. Such a good child, she gave up screaming, and sucked now only for the taste of the drying nipple itself. The neat grip of the tiny gums. One mite of a tooth tip sticking up in the bottom gum, how shining, an elfin tombstone of white marble, gleaming there. Without complaining, Magda relinquished Rosa's teats, first the left, then the right; both were cracked, not a sniff of milk. The duct crevice extinct, a dead volcano, blind eye, chill hole, so Magda took the corner of the shawl and milked it instead. She sucked and sucked, flooding the threads with wetness. The shawl's good flavor, milk of linen.

It was a magic shawl, it could nourish an infant for three days and three nights. Magda did not die, she stayed alive, although very quiet. A peculiar smell, of cinnamon and almonds, lifted out of her mouth. She held her eyes open every moment, forgetting how to blink or nap, and Rosa and sometimes Stella studied their blueness. On the road they raised one burden of a leg after another and studied Magda's face. "Aryan," Stella said, in a voice grown as thin as a string; and Rosa thought how Stella gazed at Magda like a young cannibal. And the time that Stella said "Aryan," it sounded to Rosa as if Stella had really said, "Let us devour her."

But Magda lived to walk. She lived that long, but she did not walk very well, partly because she was only fifteen months old, and partly because the spindles of her legs could not hold up her fat belly. It was fat with air, full and round. Rosa gave almost all her food to Magda, Stella gave nothing; Stella was ravenous, a growing child herself, but not growing much. Stella did not menstruate. Rosa did not menstruate. Rosa was ravenous, but also not; she learned from Magda how to drink the taste of a finger in one's mouth. They were in a place without pity, all pity was annihilated in Rosa, she looked at Stella's bones without pity. She was sure that Stella was waiting for Magda to die so she could put her teeth into the little thighs.

Rosa knew Magda was going to die very soon; she should have been dead already, but she had been buried away deep inside the magic shawl, mistaken there for the shivering mound of Rosa's breasts; Rosa clung to the shawl as if it covered only herself. No one took it away from her. Magda was mute. She never cried. Rosa hid her in the barracks, under the shawl, but she knew that one day someone would inform; or one day someone, not even Stella, would steal Magda to eat her. When Magda began to walk Rosa knew that Magda was going to die very soon, something would happen. She was afraid to fall asleep; she slept with the weight of her thigh on Magda's body; she was afraid she would smother Magda under her thigh. The weight of Rosa was becoming less and less, Rosa and Stella were slowly turning into air.

Magda was quiet, but her eyes were horribly alive, like blue tigers. She watched. Sometimes she laughed — it seemed a laugh, but how could it be? Magda had never seen anyone laugh. Still, Magda laughed at her shawl when the wind blew its corners, the bad wind with pieces of black in it, that made Stella's and Rosa's eyes tear. Magda's eyes were always clear and tearless. She watched like a tiger. She guarded her shawl. No one could touch it; only Rosa could touch it. Stella was not allowed. The shawl was Magda's own baby, her pet, her little sister. She tangled herself up in it and sucked on one of the corners when she wanted to be very still.

Then Stella took the shawl away and made Magda die.

Afterward Stella said: "I was cold."

And afterward she was always cold, always. The cold went into her heart: Rosa saw that Stella's heart was cold. Magda flopped onward with her little pencil legs scribbling this way and that, in search of the shawl; the pencils faltered at the barracks opening, where the light began. Rosa saw and pursued. But already Magda was in the square outside the barracks, in the jolly light. It was the roll-call arena. Every morning Rosa had to conceal Magda under the shawl against a wall of the barracks and go out and stand in the arena with Stella and hundreds of others, sometimes for hours, and Magda, deserted, was quiet under the shawl, sucking on her corner. Every day Magda was silent, and so she did not die. Rosa saw that today Magda was going to die, and at the same time a fearful joy ran in Rosa's two palms, her fingers were on fire, she was astonished, febrile: Magda, in the sunlight, swaying on her pencil legs, was howling. Ever since the drying up of Rosa's nipples, ever since Magda's last scream on the road, Magda had been devoid of any syllable; Magda was a mute. Rosa believed that something had gone wrong with her vocal cords, with her windpipe, with the cave of her larynx; Magda was defective, without a voice; perhaps she was deaf; there might be something amiss with her intelligence; Magda was dumb. Even the laugh that came when the ash-stippled wind made a clown out of Magda's shawl was only the air-blown showing of her teeth. Even when the lice, head lice and body lice, crazed her so that she became as wild as one of the big rats that plundered the barracks at daybreak looking for carrion, she rubbed and scratched and kicked and bit and rolled without a whimper. But now Magda's mouth was spilling a long viscous rope of clamor.

"Maaaa —"

It was the first noise Magda had ever sent out from her throat since the drying up of Rosa's nipples.

"Maaaa . . . aaa!"

Again! Magda was wavering in the perilous sunlight of the arena, scribbling on such pitiful little bent shins. Rosa saw. She saw that Magda was grieving the loss of her shawl, she saw that Magda was going to die. A tide of commands hammered in Rosa's nipples: Fetch, get, bring! But she did not know which to go after first, Magda or the shawl. If she jumped out into the arena to snatch Magda up, the howling would not stop, because Magda would still not have the shawl; but if she ran back into the barracks to find the shawl, and if she found it, and if she came after Magda holding it and shaking it, then she would get Magda back, Magda would put the shawl in her mouth and turn dumb again.

Rosa entered the dark. It was easy to discover the shawl. Stella was heaped under it, asleep in her thin bones. Rosa tore the shawl free and flew — she could fly, she was only air — into the arena. The sunheat murmured of another life, of butterflies in summer. The light was placid, mellow. On the other side of the steel fence, far away, there were green meadows speckled with dandelions and deep-colored violets; beyond them, even farther, innocent tiger lilies, tall, lifting their orange bonnets. In the barracks they spoke of "flowers," of "rain": excrement, thick turd-braids, and the slow stinking maroon waterfall that slunk down from the upper bunks, the stink mixed with a bitter fatty floating smoke that greased Rosa's skin. She stood for an instant at the margin of the arena. Sometimes the electricity inside the fence would seem to hum; even Stella said it was only an imagining, but Rosa heard real sounds in the wire: grainy sad voices. The farther she was from the fence, the more clearly the voices crowded at her. The lamenting voices strummed so convincingly, so passionately, it was impossible to suspect them of being phantoms. The voices told her to hold up the shawl, high; the voices told her to shake it, to whip with it, to unfurl it like a flag. Rosa lifted, shook, whipped, unfurled. Far off, very far, Magda leaned across her air-fed belly, reaching out with the rods of her arms. She was high up, elevated, riding someone's shoulder. But the shoulder that carried Magda was not coming toward Rosa and the shawl, it was drifting away, the speck of Magda was moving more and more into the smoky distance. Above the shoulder a helmet glinted. A light tapped the helmet and sparkled it into a goblet. Below the helmet a black body like a domino and a pair of black boots hurled themselves in the direction of the electrified fence. The electric voices began to chatter wildly. "Maamaa, maaamaaa," they all hummed together. How far Magda was from Rosa now, across the whole square, past a dozen barracks, all the way on the other side! She was no bigger than a moth.

All at once Magda was swimming through the air. The whole of Magda traveled through loftiness. She looked like a butterfly touching a silver vine. And the moment Magda's feathered round head and her pencil legs and balloonish belly and zigzag arms splashed against the fence, the steel voices went mad in their growling, urging Rosa to run and run to the spot where Magda had fallen from her flight against the electrified fence; but of course Rosa did not obey them. She only stood, because if she ran they would shoot, and if she tried to pick up the sticks of Magda's body they would shoot, and if she let the wolf's screech ascending now through the ladder of her skeleton break out, they would shoot; so she took Magda's shawl and filled her own mouth with it, stuffed it in and stuffed it in, until she was swallowing up the wolf's screech and tasting the cinnamon and almond depth of Magda's saliva; and Rosa drank Magda's shawl until it dried.

ZZ Packer

ZZ Packer (b. 1973) was named Zuwena, a Swahili name that means "good," before she became ZZ, a nickname given to her in childhood. Born in Chicago, she grew up in Atlanta and Louisville. She recalled in an interview with Robert Birnbaum that, while in high school, she was able to formulate a clear plan for college:

> I was in this math and science program in the summers, and one of the things they did, which was amazing, was show us all these different colleges. There is no way in Louisville, Kentucky, that I would have been able to see these colleges. So we went on these trips and they were trying to get us to these Ivy League colleges.

When Packer began to attend Yale University, she was undecided about whether she wanted to major in the humanities or in the sciences, but after her graduation from Yale, she went on to a writing program at Johns Hopkins University. There, in a workshop with Francine Prose, she decided to become a writer.

To support herself, Packer taught public high school for two years. She stopped because the job didn't leave her sufficient time to continue writing. "Teaching, the students really need you. You can't just say, 'No, I am going to do this really selfish thing, scribble.'" A fellowship to the writers' program at the University of Iowa enabled Packer to continue working on her short fiction. She then moved on to the writing program at Stanford University on Wallace Stegner and Truman Capote fellowships, where she began to publish her stories in magazines such as *The New Yorker*, *Seventeen*, *Harper's*, and *Ploughshares*.

Packer's stories often contain what she calls "autobiographical elements, details and settings and that sort of thing." She chose the eight stories for her first collection, *Drinking Coffee Elsewhere* (2003), including "Brownies," from the fifty or so works of short fiction in her computer.

> I keep them on the hard drive and I keep long hand drafts and file them away. Every once in awhile, when I'm procrastinating while I'm supposed to be writing, I'll look through this very long list of the abandoned ones. I just keep them there to see. . . . I will sometimes cannibalize an old story. Nothing in here was good except this one line I could actually use.

In addition to teaching workshops at both Iowa and Stanford, Packer has been hailed by *Oprah Magazine* as a "thrilling new voice" and become the subject of photo spreads in *Vogue* and *Entertainment Weekly*. Despite the fanfare, she is currently teaching and working on a first novel.

RELATED STORY
Toni Cade Bambara, "The Lesson," page 64.

Brownies

1999

BY OUR SECOND DAY at Camp Crescendo, the girls in my Brownie troop had decided to kick the asses of each and every girl in Brownie Troop 909. Troop 909 was doomed from the first day of camp; they were white girls, their complexions a blend of ice cream: strawberry, vanilla. They turtled out from their bus in pairs, their rolled-up sleeping bags chromatized with Disney characters: Sleeping Beauty, Snow White, Mickey Mouse; or the generic ones cheap parents bought: washed-out rainbows, unicorns, curly-eyelashed frogs. Some clutched Igloo coolers and still others held on to stuffed toys like pacifiers, looking all around them like tourists determined to be dazzled.

Our troop was wending its way past their bus, past the ranger station, past the colorful trail guide drawn like a treasure map, locked behind glass.

"Man, did you smell them?" Arnetta said, giving the girls a slow once-over, "They smell like Chihuahuas. *Wet* Chihuahuas." Their troop was still at the entrance, and though we had passed them by yards, Arnetta raised her nose in the air and grimaced.

Arnetta said this from the very rear of the line, far away from Mrs. Margolin, who always strung our troop behind her like a brood of obedient ducklings. Mrs. Margolin even looked like a mother duck — she had hair cropped close to a small ball of a head, almost no neck, and huge, miraculous breasts. She wore enormous belts that looked like the kind that weightlifters wear, except hers would be cheap metallic gold or rabbit fur or covered with gigantic fake sunflowers, and often these belts would become nature lessons in and of themselves. "See," Mrs. Margolin once said to us, pointing to her belt, "this one's made entirely from the feathers of baby pigeons."

The belt layered with feathers was uncanny enough, but I was more disturbed by the realization that I had never actually *seen* a baby pigeon. I searched weeks for one, in vain — scampering after pigeons whenever I was downtown with my father.

But nature lessons were not Mrs. Margolin's top priority. She saw the position of troop leader as an evangelical post. Back at the A.M.E. church where our Brownie meetings were held, Mrs. Margolin was especially fond of imparting religious aphorisms by means of acrostics — "Satan" was the "Serpent Always Tempting and Noisome"; she'd refer to the "Bible" as "Basic Instructions Before Leaving Earth." Whenever she quizzed us on these, expecting to hear the acrostics parroted back to her, only Arnetta's correct replies soared over our vague mumblings. "Jesus?" Mrs. Margolin might ask expectantly, and Arnetta alone would dutifully answer, "Jehovah's Example, Saving Us Sinners."

Arnetta always made a point of listening to Mrs. Margolin's religious talk and giving her what she wanted to hear. Because of this, Arnetta could have blared through a megaphone that the white girls of Troop 909 were "wet Chihuahuas" without so much as a blink from Mrs. Margolin. Once, Arnetta killed the troop goldfish by feeding it a french fry covered in ketchup, and when Mrs. Margolin demanded that she explain what had happened, claimed the goldfish had been eyeing her meal for *hours*, then the fish — giving in to temptation — had leapt up and snatched a whole golden fry from her fingertips.

"*Serious* Chihuahua," Octavia added, and though neither Arnetta nor Octavia could *spell* "Chihuahua," had ever *seen* a Chihuahua, trisyllabic words had gained a sort of exoticism within our fourth-grade set at Woodrow Wilson Elementary. Arnetta and Octavia would flip through the dictionary, determined to work the vulgar-sounding ones like "Djibouti" and "asinine" into conversation.

"*Caucasian* Chihuahuas," Arnetta said.

That did it. The girls in my troop turned elastic: Drema and Elise doubled up on one another like inextricably entwined kites; Octavia slapped her belly; Janice jumped straight up in the air, then did it again, as if to slam-dunk her own head. They could not stop laughing. No one had laughed so hard since a boy named Martez had stuck a pencil in the electric socket and spent the whole day with a strange grin on his face.

"Girls, girls," said our parent helper, Mrs. Hedy. Mrs. Hedy was Octavia's mother, and she wagged her index finger perfunctorily, like a windshield wiper. "Stop it, now. Be good." She said this loud enough to be heard, but lazily, bereft of any feeling of indication that she meant to be obeyed, as though she could say these words again at the exact same pitch if a button somewhere on her were pressed.

But the rest of the girls didn't stop; they only laughed louder. It was the word "Caucasian" that got them all going. One day at school, about a month before the Brownie camping trip, Arnetta turned to a boy wearing impossibly high-ankled floodwater jeans and said, "What are you? *Caucasian?*" The word took off from there, and soon everything was Caucasian. If you ate too fast you ate like a Caucasian, if you ate too slow you ate like a Caucasian. The biggest feat anyone at Woodrow Wilson could do was to jump off the swing in midair, at the highest point in its arc, and if you fell (as I had, more than once) instead of landing on your feet, knees bent Olympic gymnast — style, Arnetta and Octavia were prepared to comment. They'd look at each other with the silence of passengers who'd narrowly escaped an accident, then nod their heads, whispering with solemn horror, "*Caucasian.*"

Even the only white kid in our school, Dennis, got in on the Caucasian act. That time when Martez stuck a pencil in the socket, Dennis had pointed and yelled, "That was *so* Caucasian!"

When you lived in the south suburbs of Atlanta, it was easy to forget about whites. Whites were like those baby pigeons: real and existing, but rarely seen or thought about. Everyone had been to Rich's to go clothes shopping, everyone had seen white girls and their mothers coo-cooing over dresses; everyone had gone to the downtown library and seen white businessmen swish by importantly, wrists flexed in front of them to check the time as though they would change from Clark Kent into Superman at any second. But those images were as fleeting as cards shuffled in a deck, whereas the ten white girls behind us — *invaders*, Arnetta would later call them — were instantly real and memorable, with their long, shampoo-commercial hair, straight as spaghetti from the box. This alone was reason for envy and hatred. The only black girl most of us had ever seen with hair that long was Octavia, whose hair hung past her butt like a Hawaiian hula dancer's. The sight of Octavia's mane prompted other girls to listen to her reverentially, as though whatever she had to say would somehow activate their own follicles. For example, when, on the first day of camp, Octavia made as if to speak, and everyone fell silent. "Nobody," Octavia said, "calls us niggers."

At the end of that first day, when half of our troop made their way back to the cabin after tag-team restroom visits, Arnetta said she'd heard one of the Troop 909 girls call Daphne a nigger. The other half of the girls and I were helping Mrs. Margolin clean up the pots and pans from the campfire ravioli dinner. When we made our way to the restrooms to wash up and brush our teeth, we met up with Arnetta midway.

"Man, I completely heard the girl," Arnetta reported. "Right, Daphne?"

Daphne hardly ever spoke, but when she did, her voice was petite and tinkly, the voice one might expect from a shiny new earring. She'd written a poem once, for Langston Hughes Day, a poem brimming with all the teacher-winning ingredients — trees and oceans, sunsets and moons — but what cinched the poem for the grown-ups, snatching the win from Octavia's musical ode to Grandmaster Flash and the Furious Five, were Daphne's last lines:

> You are my father, the veteran
> When you cry in the dark
> It rains and rains and rains in my heart

She'd always worn clean, though faded, jumpers and dresses when Chic jeans were the fashion, but when she went up to the dais to receive her prize journal, pages trimmed in gold, she wore a new dress with a velveteen bodice and a taffeta skirt as wide as an umbrella. All the kids clapped, though none of them understood the poem. I'd read encyclopedias the way others read comics, and I didn't get it. But those last lines pricked me, they were so eerie, and as my father and I ate cereal, I'd whisper over my Froot Loops, like a mantra, "*You are my father, the veteran. You are my father, the veteran, the veteran, the veteran*," until my father, who acted in plays as Caliban and Othello and was not a veteran, marched me up to my teacher one morning and said, "Can you tell me what's wrong with this kid?"

I thought Daphne and I might become friends, but I think she grew spooked by me whispering those lines to her, begging her to tell me what they meant, and I soon understood that two quiet people like us were better off quiet alone.

"Daphne? Didn't you hear them call you a nigger?" Arnetta asked, giving Daphne a nudge.

The sun was setting behind the trees, and their leafy tops formed a canopy of black lace for the flame of the sun to pass through. Daphne shrugged her shoulders at first, then slowly nodded her head when Arnetta gave her a hard look.

Twenty minutes later, when my restroom group returned to the cabin, Arnetta was still talking about Troop 909. My restroom group had passed by some of the 909 girls. For the most part, they deferred to us, waving us into the restrooms, letting us go even though they'd gotten there first.

We'd seen them, but from afar, never within their orbit enough to see whether their faces were the way all white girls appeared on TV — ponytailed and full of energy, bubbling over with love and money. All I could see was that some of them rapidly fanned their faces with their hands, though the heat of the day had long passed. A few seemed to be lolling their heads in slow circles, half purposefully, as if exercising the muscles of their necks, half ecstatically, like Stevie Wonder.

"We can't let them get away with that," Arnetta said, dropping her voice to a laryngitic whisper. "We can't let them get away with calling us niggers. I say we teach them a lesson." She sat down cross-legged on a sleeping bag, an embittered Buddha, eyes glimmering acrylic-black. "We can't go telling Mrs. Margolin, either. Mrs. Margolin'll say something about doing unto others and the path of righteousness and all. Forget that shit." She let her eyes flutter irreverently till they half closed, as though ignoring an insult not worth returning. We could all hear Mrs. Margolin outside, gathering the last of the metal campware.

Nobody said anything for a while. Usually people were quiet after Arnetta spoke. Her tone had an upholstered confidence that was somehow both regal and vulgar at once. It demanded a few moments of silence in its wake, like the ringing of a church bell or the playing of taps. Sometimes Octavia would ditto or dissent to whatever Arnetta had said, and this was the signal that others could speak. But this time Octavia just swirled a long cord of hair into pretzel shapes.

"*Well?*" Arnetta said. She looked as if she had discerned the hidden severity of the situation and was waiting for the rest of us to catch up. Everyone looked from Arnetta to Daphne. It was, after all, Daphne who had supposedly been called the name, but Daphne sat on the bare cabin floor, flipping through the pages of the Girl Scout handbook, eyebrows arched in mock wonder, as if the handbook were a catalogue full of bright and startling foreign costumes. Janice broke the silence. She clapped her hands to broach her idea of a plan.

"They gone be sleeping," she whispered conspiratorially, "then we gone sneak into they cabin, then we'll put daddy longlegs in they sleeping bags. Then they'll wake up. Then we gone beat 'em up till they're as flat as frying pans!" She jammed her fist into the palm of her hand, then made a sizzling sound.

Janice's country accent was laughable, her looks homely, her jumpy acrobatics embarrassing to behold. Arnetta and Octavia volleyed amused, arrogant smiles whenever Janice opened her mouth, but Janice never caught the hint, spoke whenever she wanted, fluttered around Arnetta and Octavia futilely offering her opinions to their departing backs. Whenever Arnetta and Octavia shooed her away, Janice loitered until the two would finally sigh and ask, "What *is* it, Miss Caucasoid? What do you *want*?"

"Shut up, Janice," Octavia said, letting a fingered loop of hair fall to her waist as though just the sound of Janice's voice had ruined the fun of her hair twisting.

Janice obeyed, her mouth hung open in a loose grin, unflappable, unhurt.

"All right," Arnetta said, standing up. "We're going to have a secret meeting and talk about what we're going to do."

Everyone gravely nodded her head. The word "secret" had a built-in importance, the modifier form of the word carried more clout than the noun. A secret meant nothing; it was like gossip: just a bit of unpleasant knowledge about someone who happened to be someone other than yourself. A secret *meeting*, or a secret *club* was entirely different.

That was when Arnetta turned to me as though she knew that doing so was both a compliment and a charity.

"Snot, you're not going to be a bitch and tell Mrs. Margolin, are you?"

I had been called "Snot" ever since first grade, when I'd sneezed in class and two long ropes of mucus had splattered a nearby girl.

"Hey," I said. "Maybe you didn't hear them right — I mean —"

"Are you gonna tell on us or not?" was all Arnetta wanted to know, and by the time the question was asked, the rest of our Brownie troop looked at me as though they'd already decided their course of action, me being the only impediment.

Camp Crescendo used to double as a high-school-band and field hockey camp until an arcing field hockey ball landed on the clasp of a girl's metal barrette, knifing a skull nerve and paralyzing the right side of her body. The camp closed down for a few years and the girl's teammates built a memorial, filling the spot on which the girl fell with hockey balls, on which they had painted — all in nail polish — get-well tidings, flowers, and hearts. The balls were still stacked there, like a shrine of ostrich eggs embedded in the ground.

On the second day of camp, Troop 909 was dancing around the mound of hockey balls, their limbs jangling awkwardly, their cries like the constant summer squeal of an amusement park. There was a stream that bordered the field hockey lawn, and the girls from my troop settled next to it, scarfing down the last of lunch: sandwiches made from salami and slices of tomato that had gotten waterlogged from the melting ice in the cooler. From the stream bank, Arnetta eyed the Troop 909 girls, scrutinizing their movements to glean inspiration for battle.

"Man," Arnetta said, "we could bumrush them right now if that damn lady would *leave*."

The 909 troop leader was a white woman with the severe pageboy hairdo of an ancient Egyptian. She lay on a picnic blanket, sphinx-like, eating a banana, sometimes holding it out in front of her like a microphone. Beside her sat a girl slowly flapping one hand like a bird with a broken wing. Occasionally, the leader would call out the names of girls who'd attempted leapfrogs and flips, or of girls who yelled too loudly or strayed far from the circle.

"I'm just glad Big Fat Mama's not following us here," Octavia said. "At least we don't have to worry about her." Mrs. Margolin, Octavia assured us, was having her Afternoon Devotional, shrouded in mosquito netting, in a clearing she'd found. Mrs. Hedy was cleaning mud from her espadrilles in the cabin.

"I handled them." Arnetta sucked on her teeth and proudly grinned. "I told her we was going to gather leaves."

"Gather leaves," Octavia said, nodding respectfully. "That's a good one. Especially since they're so mad-crazy about this camping thing." She looked from ground to sky, sky to ground. Her hair hung down her back in two braids like a squaw's. "I mean, I really don't know why it's even called *camping*—all we ever do with Nature is find some twigs and say something like, 'Wow, this fell from a tree.'" She then studied her sandwich. With two disdainful fingers, she picked out a slice of dripping tomato, the sections congealed with red slime. She pitched it into the stream embrowned with dead leaves and the murky effigies of other dead things, but in the opaque water, a group of small silver-brown fish appeared. They surrounded the tomato and nibbled.

"Look!" Janice cried. "Fishes! Fishes?" As she scrambled to the edge of the stream to watch, a covey of insects threw up tantrums from the wheatgrass and nettle, a throng of tiny electric machines, all going at once. Octavia sneaked up behind Janice as if to push her in. Daphne and I exchanged terrified looks. It seemed as though only we knew that Octavia was close enough—and bold enough—to actually push Janice into the stream. Janice turned around quickly, but Octavia was already staring serenely into the still water as though she was gathering some sort of courage from it. "What's so funny?" Janice said, eyeing them all suspiciously.

Elise began humming the tune to "Karma Chameleon," all the girls joining in, their hums light and facile. Janice also began to hum, against everyone else, the high-octane opening chords of "Beat It."

"I love me some Michael Jackson," Janice said when she'd finished humming, smacking her lips as though Michael Jackson were a favorite meal. "I *will* marry Michael Jackson."

Before anyone had a chance to impress upon Janice the impossibility of this, Arnetta suddenly rose, made a sun visor of her hand, and watched Troop 909 leave the field hockey lawn.

"Dammit!" she said, "We've got to get them *alone*."

"They won't ever be alone." I said. All the rest of the girls looked at me, for I usually kept quiet. If I spoke even a word, I could count on someone calling me Snot. Everyone seemed to think that we could beat up these girls; no one entertained the thought that they might fight *back*. "The only time they'll be unsupervised is in the bathroom."

"Oh shut up, Snot," Octavia said.

But Arnetta slowly nodded her head. "The bathroom," she said. "The bathroom," she said, again and again. "The bathroom! The bathroom!"

According to Octavia's watch, it took us five minutes to hike to the restrooms, which were midway between our cabin and Troop 909's. Inside, the mirrors above the sinks returned only the vaguest of reflections, as though someone had taken a scouring pad to their surfaces to obscure the shine. Pine needles, leaves, and dirty, flattened wads of chewing gum covered the floor like a mosaic. Webs of hair matted the drain in the middle of the floor. Above the sinks and below the mirrors, stacks of folded white paper towels lay on a long metal counter. Shaggy white balls of paper towels sat on the sinktops in a line like corsages on display. A thread of floss snaked from a wad of tissues dotted with the faint red-pink of blood. One of those white girls, I thought, had just lost a tooth.

Though the restroom looked almost the same as it had the night before, it somehow seemed stranger now. We hadn't noticed the wooden rafters coming together in great V's. We were, it seemed, inside a whale, viewing the ribs of the roof of its mouth.

"Wow. It's a mess," Elise said.

"You can say that again."

Arnetta leaned against the doorjamb of a restroom stall. "This is where they'll be again," she said. Just seeing the place, just having a plan seemed to satisfy her. "We'll go in and talk to them. You know, 'How you doing? How long'll you be here?' That sort of thing. Then Octavia and I are gonna tell them what happens when they call any one of us a nigger."

"I'm going to say something, too," Janice said.

Arnetta considered this. "Sure," she said. "Of course. Whatever you want."

Janice pointed her finger like a gun at Octavia and rehearsed the line she'd thought up, "'We're gonna teach you a *lesson!*' That's what I'm going to say." She narrowed her eyes like a TV mobster. "'We're gonna teach you little girls a lesson!'"

With the back of her hand, Octavia brushed Janice's finger away. "You couldn't teach me to shit in a toilet."

"But," I said, "what if they say, 'We didn't say that? We didn't call anyone an N-I-G-G-E-R.'"

"Snot," Arnetta said, and then sighed. "Don't think. Just fight. If you even know how."

Everyone laughed except Daphne. Arnetta gently laid her hand on Daphne's shoulder. "Daphne. You don't have to fight. We're doing this for you."

Daphne walked to the counter, took a clean paper towel, and carefully unfolded it like a map. With it, she began to pick up the trash all around. Everyone watched.

"C'mon," Arnetta said to everyone. "Let's beat it." We all ambled toward the doorway, where the sunshine made one large white rectangle of light. We were immediately blinded, and we shielded our eyes with our hands and our forearms.

"Daphne?" Arnetta asked. "Are you coming?"

We all looked back at the bending girl, the thin of her back hunched like the back of a custodian sweeping a stage, caught in limelight. Stray strands of her hair were lit near-transparent, thin fiber-optic threads. She did not nod yes to the question, nor did she shake her head no. She abided, bent. Then she began again, picking up leaves, wads of paper, the cotton fluff innards from a torn stuffed toy. She did it so methodically, so exquisitely, so humbly, she must have been trained. I thought of those dresses she wore, faded and old, yet so pressed and clean. I then saw the poverty in them; I then could imagine her mother, cleaning the houses of others, returning home, weary.

"I guess she's not coming."

We left her and headed back to our cabin, over pine needles and leaves, taking the path full of shade.

"What about our secret meeting?" Elise asked.

Arnetta enunciated her words in a way that defied contradiction: "We just had it."

It was nearing our bedtime, but the sun had not yet set.

"Hey, your mama's coming," Arnetta said to Octavia when she saw Mrs. Hedy walk toward the cabin, sniffling. When Octavia's mother wasn't giving bored, parochial orders, she sniffled continuously, mourning an imminent divorce from her husband. She might begin a sentence, "I don't know what Robert will do when Octavia and I are gone. Who'll buy him cigarettes?" and Octavia would hotly whisper, "*Mama*," in a way that meant: Please don't talk about our problems in front of everyone. Please shut up.

But when Mrs. Hedy began talking about her husband, thinking about her husband, seeing clouds shaped like the head of her husband, she couldn't be quiet, and no one could dislodge her from the comfort of her own woe. Only one thing could perk her up — Brownie songs. If the girls were quiet, and Mrs. Hedy was in her dopey, sorrowful mood, she would say, "Y'all know I like those songs, girls. Why don't you sing one?" Everyone would groan, except me and Daphne. I, for one, liked some of the songs.

"C'mon, everybody," Octavia said drearily, "She likes the Brownie song best."

We sang, loud enough to reach Mrs. Hedy:

"I've got something in my pocket;
It belongs across my face.
And I keep it very close at hand
    in a most convenient place.
I'm sure you couldn't guess it
If you guessed a long, long while.
So I'll take it out and put it on —
It's a great big Brownie smile!"

The Brownie song was supposed to be sung cheerfully, as though we were elves in a workshop, singing as we merrily cobbled shoes, but everyone except me hated the song so much that they sang it like a maudlin record, played on the most sluggish of rpms.

"That was good," Mrs. Hedy said, closing the cabin door behind her. "Wasn't that nice, Linda?"

"Praise God," Mrs. Margolin answered without raising her head from the chore of counting out Popsicle sticks for the next day's craft session.

"Sing another one," Mrs. Hedy said. She said it with a sort of joyful aggression, like a drunk I'd once seen who'd refused to leave a Korean grocery.

"God, Mama, get over it," Octavia whispered in a voice meant only for Arnetta, but Mrs. Hedy heard it and started to leave the cabin.

"Don't go," Arnetta said. She ran after Mrs. Hedy and held her by the arm. "We haven't finished singing." She nudged us with a single look. "Let's sing the 'Friends Song.' For Mrs. Hedy."

Although I liked some of the songs, I hated this one:

Make new friends
But keep the o-old,
One is silver
And the other gold.

If most of the girls in the troop could be any type of metal, they'd be bunched-up wads of tinfoil, maybe, or rusty iron nails you had to get tetanus shots for.

"No, no, no," Mrs. Margolin said before anyone could start in on the "Friends Song." "An uplifting song. Something to lift her up and take her mind off all these earthly burdens."

Arnetta and Octavia rolled their eyes. Everyone knew what song Mrs. Margolin was talking about, and no one, no one, wanted to sing it.

"Please, no," a voice called out. "Not 'The Doughnut Song.'"

"Please not 'The Doughnut Song,'" Octavia pleaded.

"I'll brush my teeth two times if I don't have to sing 'The Doughnut—'"

"Sing!" Mrs. Margolin demanded.

We sang:

"Life without Jesus is like a do-ough-nut!
Like a do-ooough-nut!
Like a do-ooough-nut!
Life without Jesus is like a do-ough-nut!
There's a hole in the middle of my soul!"

There were other verses, involving other pastries, but we stopped after the first one and cast glances toward Mrs. Margolin to see if we could gain a reprieve. Mrs. Margolin's eyes fluttered blissfully. She was half asleep.

"Awww," Mrs. Hedy said, as though giant Mrs. Margolin were a cute baby, "Mrs. Margolin's had a long day."

"Yes indeed," Mrs. Margolin answered. "If you don't mind, I might just go to the lodge where the beds are. I haven't been the same since the operation."

I had not heard of this operation, or when it had occurred, since Mrs. Margolin had never missed the once-a-week Brownie meetings, but I could see from Daphne's face that she was concerned, and I could see that the other girls had decided that Mrs. Margolin's operation must have happened long ago in some remote time unconnected to our own. Nevertheless, they put on sad faces. We had all been taught that adulthood was full of sorrow and pain, taxes and bills, dreaded work and dealings with whites, sickness and death. I tried to do what the others did. I tried to look silent.

"Go right ahead, Linda," Mrs. Hedy said, "I'll watch the girls." Mrs. Hedy seemed to forget about divorce for a moment; she looked at us with dewy eyes, as if we were mysterious, furry creatures. Meanwhile, Mrs. Margolin walked through the maze of sleeping bags until she found her own. She gathered a neat stack of clothes and pajamas slowly, as though doing so was almost painful. She took her toothbrush, her toothpaste, her pillow. "All right!" Mrs. Margolin said, addressing us all from the threshold of the cabin. "Be in bed by nine." She said it with a twinkle in her voice, letting us know she was allowing us to be naughty and stay up till nine-fifteen.

"C'mon everybody," Arnetta said after Mrs. Margolin left. "Time for us to wash up."

Everyone watched Mrs. Hedy closely, wondering whether she would insist on coming with us since it was night, making a fight with Troop 909 nearly impossible. Troop 909 would soon be in the bathroom, washing their faces, brushing their teeth — completely unsuspecting of our ambush.

"We won't be long," Arnetta said. "We're old enough to go to the restrooms by ourselves."

Ms. Hedy pursed her lips at this dilemma. "Well, I guess you Brownies are almost Girl Scouts, right?"

"Right!"

"Just one more badge," Drema said.

"And about," Octavia droned, "a million more cookies to sell." Octavia looked at all of us, *Now's our chance*, her face seemed to say, but our chance to do *what*, I didn't exactly know.

Finally, Mrs. Hedy walked to the doorway where Octavia stood dutifully waiting to say goodbye but looking bored doing it. Mrs. Hedy held Octavia's chin. "You'll be good?"

"Yes, Mama."

"And remember to pray for me and your father? If I'm asleep when you get back?"

"Yes, Mama."

When the other girls had finished getting their toothbrushes and washcloths and flashlights for the group restroom trip, I was drawing pictures of tiny birds with too many feathers. Daphne was sitting on her sleeping bag, reading.

"You're not going to come?" Octavia asked.

Daphne shook her head.

"I'm gonna stay, too," I said. "I'll go to the restroom when Daphne and Mrs. Hedy go."

Arnetta leaned down toward me and whispered so that Mrs. Hedy, who'd taken over Mrs. Margolin's task of counting Popsicle sticks, couldn't hear. "No, Snot. If we get in trouble, you're going to get in trouble with the rest of us."

We made our way through the darkness by flashlight. The tree branches that had shaded us just hours earlier, along the same path, now looked like arms sprouting menacing hands. The stars sprinkled the sky like spilled salt. They seemed fastened to the darkness, high up and holy, their places fixed and definite as we stirred beneath them.

Some, like me, were quiet because we were afraid of the dark; others were talking like crazy for the same reason.

"Wow!" Drema said, looking up. "Why are all the stars out here? I never see stars back on Oneida Street."

"It's a camping trip, that's why," Octavia said. "You're supposed to see stars on camping trips."

Janice said, "This place smells like my mother's air freshener."

"These woods are *pine*," Elise said. "Your mother probably uses *pine* air freshener."

Janice mouthed an exaggerated "Oh," nodding her head as though she just then understood one of the world's great secrets.

No one talked about fighting. Everyone was afraid enough just walking through the infinite deep of the woods. Even though I didn't fight to fight, was afraid of fighting, I felt I was part of the rest of the troop; like I was defending something. We trudged against the slight incline of the path, Arnetta leading the way.

"You know," I said, "their leader will be there. Or they won't even be there. It's dark already. Last night the sun was still in the sky. I'm sure they're already finished."

Arnetta acted as if she hadn't heard me. I followed her gaze with my flashlight, and that's when I saw the squares of light in the darkness. The bathroom was just ahead.

But the girls were there. We could hear them before we could see them.

"Octavia and I will go in first so they'll think there's just two of us, then wait till I say, 'We're gonna teach you a lesson,'" Arnetta said. "Then, bust in. That'll surprise them."

"That's what I was supposed to say," Janice said.

Arnetta went inside, Octavia next to her. Janice followed, and the rest of us waited outside.

They were in there for what seemed like whole minutes, but something was wrong. Arnetta hadn't given the signal yet. I was with the girls outside when I heard one of the Troop 909 girls say, "NO. That did NOT happen!"

That was to be expected, that they'd deny the whole thing. What I hadn't expected was *the voice* in which the denial was said. The girl sounded as though her tongue were caught in her mouth. "That's a BAD word!" the girl continued. "We don't say BAD words!"

"Let's go in," Elise said.

"No," Drema said, "I don't want to. What if we get beat up?"

"Snot?" Elise turned to me, her flashlight blinding. It was the first time anyone had asked my opinion, though I knew they were just asking because they were afraid.

"I say we go inside, just to see what's going on."

"But Arnetta didn't give us the signal," Drema said. "She's supposed to say, 'We're gonna teach you a lesson,' and I didn't hear her say it."

"C'mon," I said. "Let's just go in."

We went inside. There we found the white girls — about five girls huddled up next to one big girl. I instantly knew she was the owner of the voice we'd heard. Arnetta and Octavia inched toward us as soon as we entered.

"Where's Janice?" Elise asked, then we heard a flush. "Oh."

"I think," Octavia said, whispering to Elise, "they're retarded."

"We ARE NOT retarded!" the big girl said, though it was obvious that she was. That they all were. The girls around her began to whimper.

"They're just pretending," Arnetta said, trying to convince herself. "I know they are."

Octavia turned to Arnetta. "Arnetta. Let's just leave."

Janice came out of a stall, happy and relieved, then she suddenly remembered her line, pointed to the big girl, and said, "We're gonna teach you a lesson."

"Shut up, Janice," Octavia said, but her heart was not in it. Arnetta's face was set in a lost, deep scowl. Octavia turned to the big girl and said loudly, slowly, as if they were all deaf, "We're going to leave. It was nice meeting you, O.K.? You don't have to tell anyone that we were here. O.K.?"

"Why not?" said the big girl, like a taunt. When she spoke, her lips did not meet, her mouth did not close. Her tongue grazed the roof of her mouth, like a little pink fish. "You'll get in trouble. I know. *I* know."

Arnetta got back her old cunning. "If you said anything, then you'd be a tattletale."

The girl looked sad for a moment, then perked up quickly. A flash of genius crossed her face. "I *like* tattletale."

"It's all right, girls. It's gonna be all right!" the 909 troop leader said. All of Troop 909 burst into tears. It was as though someone had instructed them all to cry at once. The troop leader had girls under her arm, and all the rest of the girls crowded about her. It reminded me of a hog I'd seen on a field trip, where all the little hogs gathered about the mother at feeding time, latching onto her teats. The 909 troop leader had come into the bathroom, shortly after the big girl had threatened to tell. Then the ranger came, then, once the ranger had radioed the station, Mrs. Margolin arrived with Daphne in tow.

The ranger had left the restroom area, but everyone else was huddled just outside, swatting mosquitoes.

"Oh. They *will* apologize," Mrs. Margolin said to the 909 troop leader, but she said this so angrily, I knew she was speaking more to us than to the other troop leader. "When their parents find out, every one a them will be on punishment."

"It's all right, it's all right," the 909 troop leader reassured Mrs. Margolin. Her voice lilted in the same way it had when addressing the girls. She smiled the whole time she talked. She was like one of those TV-cooking-show women who talk and dice onions and smile all at the same time.

"See. It could have happened. I'm not calling your girls fibbers or anything." She shook her head ferociously from side to side, her Egyptian-style pageboy flapping against her cheeks like heavy drapes. "It *could* have happened. See. Our girls are *not* retarded. They are *delayed* learners." She said this in a syrupy instructional voice, as though our troop might be delayed learners as well, "We're from the Decatur Children's Academy. Many of them just have special needs."

"Now we won't be able to walk to the bathroom by ourselves!" the big girl said.

"Yes you will," the troop leader said, "but maybe we'll wait till we get back to Decatur —"

"I don't want to wait!" the girl said. "I want my Independence badge!"

The girls in my troop were entirely speechless. Arnetta looked stoic, as though she were soon to be tortured but was determined not to appear weak. Mrs. Margolin pursed her lips solemnly and said, "Bless them, Lord. Bless them."

In contrast, the Troop 909 leader was full of words and energy. "Some of our girls are echolalic —" She smiled and happily presented one of the girls hanging onto her, but the girl widened her eyes in horror, and violently withdrew herself from the center of attention, sensing she was being sacrificed for the village sins. "Echolalic," the troop leader continued. "That means they will say whatever they hear, like an echo — that's where the word comes from. It comes from 'echo.'" She ducked her head apologetically, "I mean, not all of them have the most *progressive* of parents, so if they heard a bad word, they might have repeated it. But I guarantee it would not have been *intentional*."

Arnetta spoke. "I saw her say the word. I heard her." She pointed to a small girl, smaller than any of us, wearing an oversized T-shirt that read: "Eat Bertha's Mussels."

The troop leader shook her head and smiled, "That's impossible. She doesn't speak. She can, but she doesn't."

Arnetta furrowed her brow. "No. It wasn't her. That's right. It was *her*."

The girl Arnetta pointed to grinned as though she'd been paid a compliment. She was the only one from either troop actually wearing a full uniform: the mocha-colored A-line shift, the orange ascot, the sash covered with badges, though all the same one — the Try-It patch. She took a few steps toward Arnetta and made a grand sweeping gesture toward the sash. "See," she said, full of self-importance, "I'm a Brownie." I had a hard time imagining this girl calling anyone a "nigger"; the girl looked perpetually delighted, as though she would have cuddled up with a grizzly if someone had let her.

On the fourth morning, we boarded the bus to go home.

The previous day had been spent building miniature churches from Popsicle sticks. We hardly left the cabin. Mrs. Margolin and Mrs. Hedy guarded us so closely, almost no one talked for the entire day.

Even on the day of departure from Camp Crescendo, all was serious and silent. The bus ride began quietly enough. Arnetta had to sit beside Mrs. Margolin; Octavia had to sit beside her mother. I sat beside Daphne, who gave me her prize journal without a word of explanation.

"You don't want it?"

She shook her head no. It was empty.

Then Mrs. Hedy began to weep. "Octavia," Mrs. Hedy said to her daughter without looking at her, "I'm going to sit with Mrs. Margolin. All right?"

Arnetta exchanged seats with Mrs. Hedy. With the two women up front, Elise felt it safe to speak. "Hey," she said, then she set her face into a placid, vacant stare, trying to imitate that of a Troop 909 girl. Emboldened, Arnetta made a gesture of mock pride toward an imaginary sash, the way the girl in full uniform had done. Then they all made a game of it, trying to do the most exaggerated imitations of the Troop 909 girls, all without speaking, all without laughing loud enough to catch the women's attention.

Daphne looked down at her shoes, white with sneaker polish. I opened the journal she'd given me. I looked out the window, trying to decide what to write, searching for lines, but nothing could compare with what Daphne had written, "*My father, the veteran*," my favorite line of all time. It replayed itself in my head, and I gave up trying to write.

By then, it seemed that the rest of the troop had given up making fun of the girls in Troop 909. They were now quietly gossiping about who had passed notes to whom in school. For a moment the gossiping fell off, and all I heard was the hum of the bus as we sped down the road and the muffled sounds of Mrs. Hedy and Mrs. Margolin talking about serious things.

"You know," Octavia whispered, "why did *we* have to be stuck at a camp with retarded girls? You know?"

"*You* know why," Arnetta answered. She narrowed her eyes like a cat. "My mama and I were in the mall in Buckhead, and this white lady just kept looking at us. I mean, like we were foreign or something. Like we were from China."

"What did the woman say?" Elise asked.

"Nothing," Arnetta said. "She didn't say nothing."

A few girls quietly nodded their heads.

"There was this time," I said, "when my father and I were in the mall and —"

"Oh shut up, Snot," Octavia said.

I stared at Octavia, then rolled my eyes from her to the window. As I watched the trees blur, I wanted nothing more than to be through with it all: the bus ride, the troop, school — all of it. But we were going home. I'd see the same girls in school the next day. We were on a bus, and there was nowhere else to go.

"Go on, Laurel," Daphne said to me. It seemed like the first time she'd spoken the whole trip, and she'd said my name. I turned to her and smiled weakly so as not to cry, hoping she'd remember when I'd tried to be her friend, thinking maybe that her gift of the journal was an invitation of friendship. But she didn't smile back. All she said was, "What happened?"

I studied the girls, waiting for Octavia to tell me to shut up again before I even had a chance to utter another word, but everyone was amazed that Daphne had spoken. The bus was silent. I gathered my voice. "Well," I said. "My father and I were in this mall, but *I* was the one doing the staring." I stopped and glanced from face to face. I continued. "There were these white people dressed like Puritans or something, but they weren't Puritans. They were Mennonites.

They're these people who, if you ask them to do a favor, like paint your porch or something, they have to do it. It's in their rules."

"That sucks," someone said.

"C'mon," Arnetta said. "You're lying."

"I am not."

"How do you know that's not just some story someone made up?" Elise asked, her head cocked full of daring. "I mean, who's gonna do whatever you ask?"

"It's not made up. I know because when I was looking at them, my father said, 'See those people? If you ask them to do something, they'll do it. Anything you want.'"

No one would call anyone's father a liar — then they'd have to fight the person. But Drema parsed her words carefully. "How does your *father* know that's not just some story? Huh?"

"Because," I said, "he went up to the man and asked him would he paint our porch, and the man said yes. It's their religion."

"Man, I'm glad I'm a Baptist," Elise said, shaking her head in sympathy for the Mennonites.

"So did the guy do it?" Drema asked, scooting closer to hear if the story got juicy.

"Yeah," I said. "His whole family was with him. My dad drove them to our house. They all painted our porch. The woman and girl were in bonnets and long, long skirts with buttons up to their necks. The guy wore this weird hat and these huge suspenders."

"Why," Arnetta asked archly, as though she didn't believe a word, "would someone pick a *porch*? If they'll do anything, why not make them paint the whole *house*? Why not ask for a hundred bucks?"

I thought about it, and then remembered the words my father had said about them painting our porch, though I had never seemed to think about his words after he'd said them.

"He said," I began, only then understanding the words as they uncoiled from my mouth, "it was the only time he'd have a white man on his knees doing something for a black man for free."

I now understood what he meant, and why he did it, though I didn't like it. When you've been made to feel bad for so long, you jump at the chance to do it to others. I remembered the Mennonites bending the way Daphne had bent when she was cleaning the restroom. I remembered the dark blue of their bonnets, the black of their shoes. They painted the porch as though scrubbing a floor. I was already trembling before Daphne asked quietly, "Did he thank them?"

I looked out the window. I could not tell which were the thoughts and which were the trees. "No," I said, and suddenly knew there was something mean in the world that I could not stop.

Arnetta laughed. "If I asked them to take off their long skirts and bonnets and put on some jeans, would they do it?"

And Daphne's voice, quiet, steady: "Maybe they would. Just to be nice."

Grace Paley

Grace Paley (1922–2007) was born in New York City. She studied at Hunter College and New York University, and in 1942 she married for the first time. She had two children from that marriage. In the 1950s she turned from writing poetry to short fiction. Her first book of stories, *The Little Disturbances of Man* (1959), established her reputation as a writer with a remarkably supple gift for language. As Susan Sontag later said, "She is that rare kind of writer, a natural with a voice like no one else's—funny, sad, lean, modest, energetic, acute." When this book went out of print in 1965, its reputation survived, strengthened by the infrequent appearances of her new stories in magazines such as the *Atlantic Monthly*, *Esquire*, the *Noble Savage*, *Genesis West*, the *New American Review*, *Ararat*, and *Fiction*.

During the 1960s and 1970s Paley was prominent as a nonviolent activist protesting the Vietnam War. She was secretary of the Greenwich Village Peace Center, spent time in jail for her antiwar activities, and visited Hanoi and Moscow as a member of peace delegations, defining herself as a "somewhat combative pacifist and cooperative anarchist." During the World Peace Congress in Moscow in 1973, she condemned the Soviet Union for silencing political dissidents; the congress disassociated itself from her statement. Paley was a feminist and active in the antinuclear movement. In 1974 her second volume of stories, *Enormous Changes at the Last Minute*, was published. It is a quieter, more openly personal collection of seventeen stories, many of them, such as "A Conversation with My Father," autobiographical. Her third book of stories, *Later the Same Day*, which includes "Mother," appeared in 1985. In 1988 Paley was designated the first official New York State Author by an act of the state legislature.

Paley refused to blame her teaching jobs or her involvements as an activist for her relatively low productivity as a writer. As she put it, "There is a long time in me between knowing and telling." She said that she wrote "from distress." What she tried to get at in her stories was "a history of everyday life," and her subject matter and prose style are unmistakable. Dividing her time between a Vermont farm and a Manhattan apartment close to the Greenwich Village School (P.S. 41), Little Tony's Unisex Haircutters, the Famous Ray's Pizza, the H & H Fruit and Vegetable Market, and the Jefferson Market Branch of the New York Public Library, Paley observed her neighbors, friends, and family with compassion, humor, and hope. Her spare dissection of her characters was never performed at the expense of sympathy for the human condition. *The Collected Stories of Grace Paley* was published in 1994.

RELATED STORY
Grace Paley, "Samuel," page 1667.

RELATED COMMENTARIES
Grace Paley, "A Conversation with Ann Charters," page 1503.

A Conversation with My Father

1974

MY FATHER IS EIGHTY-SIX years old and in bed. His heart, that bloody motor, is equally old and will not do certain jobs any more. It still floods his head with brainy light. But it won't let his legs carry the weight of his body around the house. Despite my metaphors, this muscle failure is not due to his old heart, he says, but to a potassium shortage. Sitting on one pillow, leaning on three, he offers last-minute advice and makes a request.

"I would like you to write a simple story just once more," he says, "the kind de Maupassant wrote, or Chekhov, the kind you used to write. Just recognizable people and then write down what happened to them next."

I say, "Yes, why not? That's possible." I want to please him, though I don't remember writing that way. I *would* like to try to tell such a story, if he means the kind that begins: "There was a woman . . ." followed by plot, the absolute line between two points which I've always despised. Not for literary reasons, but because it takes all hope away. Everyone, real or invented, deserves the open destiny of life.

Finally I thought of a story that had been happening for a couple of years right across the street. I wrote it down, then read it aloud. "Pa," I said, "how about this? Do you mean something like this?"

> Once in my time there was a woman and she had a son. They lived nicely, in a small apartment in Manhattan. This boy at about fifteen became a junkie, which is not unusual in our neighborhood. In order to maintain her close friendship with him, she became a junkie too. She said it was part of the youth culture, with which she felt very much at home. After a while, for a number of reasons, the boy gave it all up and left the city and his mother in disgust. Hopeless and alone, she grieved. We all visit her.

"O.K., Pa, that's it," I said, "an unadorned and miserable tale."

"But that's not what I mean," my father said. "You misunderstood me on purpose. You know there's a lot more to it. You know that. You left everything out. Turgenev wouldn't do that. Chekhov wouldn't do that. There are in fact Russian writers you never heard of, you don't have an inkling of, as good as anyone, who can write a plain ordinary story, who would not leave out what you have left out. I object not to facts but to people sitting in trees talking senselessly, voices from who knows where. . . ."

"Forget that one, Pa, what have I left out now? In this one?"

"Her looks, for instance."

"Oh. Quite handsome, I think. Yes."

"Her hair?"

"Dark, with heavy braids, as though she were a girl or a foreigner."

"What were her parents like, her stock? That she became such a person. It's interesting, you know."

"From out of town. Professional people. The first to be divorced in their county. How's that? Enough?" I asked.

"With you, it's all a joke," he said. "What about the boy's father? Why didn't you mention him? Who was he? Or was the boy born out of wedlock?"

"Yes," I said. "He was born out of wedlock."

"For Godsakes, doesn't anyone in your stories get married? Doesn't anyone have the time to run down to City Hall before they jump into bed?"

"No," I said. "In real life, yes. But in my stories, no."

"Why do you answer me like that?"

"Oh, Pa, this is a simple story about a smart woman who came to N.Y.C. full of interest love trust excitement very up to date, and about her son, what a hard time she had in this world. Married or not, it's of small consequence."

"It is of great consequence," he said.

"O.K.," I said.

"O.K. O.K. yourself," he said, "but listen. I believe you that she's good-looking, but I don't think she was so smart."

"That's true," I said. "Actually that's the trouble with stories. People start out fantastic. You think they're extraordinary, but it turns out as the work goes along, they're just average with a good education. Sometimes the other way around, the person's a kind of dumb innocent, but he outwits you and you can't even think of an ending good enough."

"What do you do then?" he asked. He had been a doctor for a couple of decades and then an artist for a couple of decades and he's still interested in details, craft, technique.

"Well, you just have to let the story lie around till some agreement can be reached between you and the stubborn hero."

"Aren't you talking silly now?" he asked. "Start again," he said. "It so happens I'm not going out this evening. Tell the story again. See what you can do this time."

"O.K.," I said. "But it's not a five-minute job." Second attempt:

Once, across the street from us, there was a fine handsome woman, our neighbor. She had a son whom she loved because she'd known him since birth (in helpless chubby infancy, and in the wrestling, hugging ages, seven to ten, as well as earlier and later). This boy, when he fell into the fist of adolescence, became a junkie. He was not a hopeless one. He was in fact hopeful, an ideologue and successful converter. With his busy brilliance, he wrote persuasive articles for his high-school newspaper. Seeking a wider audience, using important connections, he drummed into Lower Manhattan newsstand distribution a periodical called *Oh! Golden Horse!*

In order to keep him from feeling guilty (because guilt is the stony heart of nine tenths of all clinically diagnosed cancers in America today, she said), and because she had always believed in giving bad habits room at home where one could keep an eye on them, she too became a junkie. Her kitchen was famous for a while — a center for intellectual addicts who knew what they were doing. A few felt artistic like Coleridge[1] and others

---

[1]Samuel Taylor Coleridge (1772–1834), English Romantic poet, was an opium addict.

were scientific and revolutionary like Leary.[2] Although she was often high herself, certain good mothering reflexes remained, and she saw to it that there was lots of orange juice around and honey and milk and vitamin pills. However, she never cooked anything but chili, and that no more than once a week. She explained, when we talked to her, seriously, with neighborly concern, that it was her part in the youth culture and she would rather be with the young, it was an honor, than with her own generation.

One week, while nodding through an Antonioni film, this boy was severely jabbed by the elbow of a stern and proselytizing girl, sitting beside him. She offered immediate apricots and nuts for his sugar level, spoke to him sharply, and took him home.

She had heard of him and his work and she herself published, edited, and wrote a competitive journal called *Man Does Live by Bread Alone*. In the organic heat of her continuous presence he could not help but become interested once more in his muscles, his arteries, and nerve connections. In fact he began to love them, treasure them, praise them with funny little songs in *Man Does Live*. . . .

> the fingers of my flesh transcend
> my transcendental soul
> the tightness in my shoulders end
> my teeth have made me whole

To the mouth of his head (that glory of will and determination) he brought hard apples, nuts, wheat germ, and soybean oil. He said to his old friends, From now on, I guess I'll keep my wits about me. I'm going on the natch. He said he was about to begin a spiritual deep-breathing journey. How about you too, Mom? he asked kindly.

His conversion was so radiant, splendid, that neighborhood kids his age began to say that he had never been a real addict at all, only a journalist along for the smell of the story. The mother tried several times to give up what had become without her son and his friends a lonely habit. This effort only brought it to supportable levels. The boy and his girl took their electronic mimeograph and moved to the bushy edge of another borough. They were very strict. They said they would not see her again until she had been off drugs for sixty days.

At home alone in the evening, weeping, the mother read and reread the seven issues of *Oh! Golden Horse!* They seemed to her as truthful as ever. We often crossed the street to visit and console. But if we mentioned any of our children who were at college or in the hospital or dropouts at home, she would cry out, My baby! My baby! and burst into terrible, face-scarring, time-consuming tears. The End.

First my father was silent, then he said, "Number One: You have a nice sense of humor. Number Two: I see you can't tell a plain story. So don't waste

---

[2]Timothy Leary (1920–1996), sometime Harvard professor of psychology and early advocate of the use of LSD.

time." Then he said sadly, "Number Three: I suppose that means she was alone, she was left like that, his mother. Alone. Probably sick?"

I said, "Yes."

"Poor woman. Poor girl, to be born in a time of fools, to live among fools. The end. The end. You were right to put that down. The end."

I didn't want to argue, but I had to say, "Well, it is not necessarily the end, Pa."

"Yes," he said, "what a tragedy. The end of a person."

"No, Pa," I begged him. "It doesn't have to be. She's only about forty. She could be a hundred different things in this world as time goes on. A teacher or a social worker. An ex-junkie! Sometimes it's better than having a master's in education."

"Jokes," he said. "As a writer that's your main trouble. You don't want to recognize it. Tragedy! Plain tragedy! Historical tragedy! No hope. The end."

"Oh, Pa," I said. "She could change."

"In your own life, too, you have to look it in the face." He took a couple of nitroglycerin. "Turn to five," he said, pointing to the dial on the oxygen tank. He inserted the tubes into his nostrils and breathed deep. He closed his eyes and said, "No."

I had promised the family to always let him have the last word when arguing, but in this case I had a different responsibility. That woman lives across the street. She's my knowledge and my invention. I'm sorry for her. I'm not going to leave her there in that house crying. (Actually neither would Life, which unlike me has no pity.)

Therefore: She did change. Of course her son never came home again. But right now, she's the receptionist in a storefront community clinic in the East Village. Most of the customers are young people, some old friends. The head doctor has said to her, "If we only had three people in this clinic with your experiences. . . ."

"The doctor said that?" My father took the oxygen tubes out of his nostrils and said, "Jokes. Jokes again."

"No, Pa, it could really happen that way, it's a funny world nowadays."

"No," he said. "Truth first. She will slide back. A person must have character. She does not."

"No, Pa," I said. "That's it. She's got a job. Forget it. She's in that storefront working."

"How long will it be?" he asked. "Tragedy! You too. When will you look it in the face?"

Mother

1985

ONE DAY I WAS listening to the AM radio. I heard a song: "Oh, I Long to See My Mother in the Doorway." By God! I said, I understand that song. I have often longed to see my mother in the doorway. As a matter of fact, she did stand frequently in various doorways looking at me. She stood one day, just so, at the front door, the darkness of the hallway behind her. It was New Year's Day. She said sadly, If you come home at 4 A.M. when you're seventeen, what time will you come home when you're twenty? She asked this question without humor or meanness. She had begun her worried preparations for death. She would not be present, she thought, when I was twenty. So she wondered.

Another time she stood in the doorway of my room. I had just issued a political manifesto attacking the family's position on the Soviet Union. She said, Go to sleep for godsakes, you damn fool, you and your Communist ideas. We saw them already, Papa and me, in 1905. We guessed it all.

At the door of the kitchen she said, You never finish your lunch. You run around senselessly. What will become of you?

Then she died.

Naturally for the rest of my life I longed to see her, not only in doorways, in a great number of places — in the dining room with my aunts, at the window looking up and down the block, in the country garden among zinnias and marigolds, in the living room with my father.

They sat in comfortable leather chairs. They were listening to Mozart. They looked at one another amazed. It seemed to them that they'd just come over on the boat. They'd just learned the first English words. It seemed to them that he had just proudly handed in a 100 percent correct exam to the American anatomy professor. It seemed as though she'd just quit the shop for the kitchen.

I wish I could see her in the doorway of the living room.

She stood there a minute. Then she sat beside him. They owned an expensive record player. They were listening to Bach. She said to him, Talk to me a little. We don't talk so much anymore.

I'm tired, he said. Can't you see? I saw maybe thirty people today. All sick, all talk talk talk talk. Listen to the music, he said. I believe you once had perfect pitch. I'm tired, he said.

Then she died.

Octavio Paz

Octavio Paz (1914–1998), the 1990 Nobel Prize–winning Mexican poet and essayist, was born in Mexico City. He said that he "came from a typical Mexican family," European on his mother's side and Mexican Indian on his father's side, but his father was a distinguished lawyer who took part in the Mexican Revolution and defended Emiliano Zapata, the peasant revolutionary leader advocating agrarian reform. Paz recalled that his "family had been impoverished by the revolution and the civil war. Our house, full of antique furniture, books, and other objects, was gradually crumbling to bits." While still a teenager, Paz began to publish poetry in literary journals. His first book of seven poems, *Rustic Moon,* was published in 1933.

In 1937 Paz went abroad to attend a congress of antifascist writers in Spain. He also spent a short time in Paris, where he met many surrealist writers. "My experiences in Spain confirmed my revolutionary ardor," he noted, "but at the same time made me mistrust revolutionary theories. This brought me closer to the political attitude of the surrealists" rather than the official social realism doctrines of the Communist bureaucracy in the Soviet Union. Back in Mexico City, Paz worked as a journalist supporting the cause of the Spanish Republicans until the German-Soviet pact at the outbreak of World War II made him withdraw from politics. In 1944 Paz received a Guggenheim fellowship that enabled him to live in San Francisco for a year, where he studied the work of a number of American poets, among them e. e. cummings, Wallace Stevens, and William Carlos Williams, who translated Paz's poetry into English. As a poet, Paz felt that "my career wasn't brilliant and my advancement was slow."

The need for financial security led Paz to enter the diplomatic service after publishing a book of essays about Mexican culture, *The Labyrinth of Solitude,* in 1956. In the 1960s he was the Mexican ambassador to India, until he resigned in 1968 in protest of his government's use of violence against a student uprising in Mexico City. After 1968 Paz lived for the most part in Mexico when not lecturing at American universities. He published numerous books of poetry and essays and a few short stories, including the surrealist story "My Life with the Wave," which was included in *Eagle or Sun?* (1970). In the story Paz uses what the critic Jason Wilson has recognized as images that "refer to wholesome, natural archetypes dormant and unconscious [in human beings]. . . . Paz links water symbolism with woman and prenatal paradise; water is fertility and self-knowledge, and is both creative and destructive."

Although Paz was primarily a poet and wrote little short fiction, he regarded the prose fragment to be the form "that best reflects the ever-changing reality that we live and are." In an essay in *Alternating Current* (1973) commenting on the fragmentary nature of contemporary life, Paz defined literature as "metaphors of the world" within a writer: "I've always thought of literature as a language, but by language I mean the plurality of visions in the world."

My Life with the Wave

1949 / Translated by Eliot Weinberger

WHEN I LEFT THAT SEA, a wave moved ahead of the others. She was tall and light. In spite of the shouts of the others who grabbed her by her floating clothes, she clutched my arm and went off with me leaping. I didn't want to say anything to her, because it hurt me to shame her in front of her friends. Besides, the furious stares of the elders paralyzed me. When we got to town, I explained to her that it was impossible, that life in the city was not what she had been able to imagine with the ingenuity of a wave that had never left the sea. She watched me gravely: "No, your decision is made. You can't go back." I tried sweetness, hardness, irony. She cried, screamed, hugged, threatened. I had to apologize.

The next day my troubles began. How could we get on the train without being seen by the conductor, the passengers, the police? Certainly the rules say nothing in respect to the transport of waves on the railroad, but this same reserve was an indication of the severity with which our act would be judged. After much thought I arrived at the station an hour before departure, took my seat, and, when no one was looking, emptied the water tank for the passengers; then, carefully, poured in my friend.

The first incident came about when the children of a nearby couple declared their noisy thirst. I stopped them and promised them refreshments and lemonade. They were at the point of accepting when another thirsty passenger approached. I was about to invite her also, but the stare of her companion stopped me. The lady took a paper cup, approached the tank, and turned the faucet. Her cup was barely half full when I leaped between the woman and my friend. She looked at me astonished. While I apologized, one of the children turned the faucet again. I closed it violently. The lady brought the cup to her lips:

"Agh, this water is salty."

The boy echoed her. Various passengers rose. The husband called the conductor:

"This man put salt in the water."

The conductor called the Inspector:

"So you put substances in the water?"

The Inspector in turn called the police:

"So you poisoned the water?"

The police in turn called the Captain:

"So you're the poisoner?"

The captain called three agents. The agents took me to an empty car amid the stares and whispers of the passengers. At the next station they took me off and pushed and dragged me to the jail. For days no one spoke to me, except during the long interrogations. When I explained my story no one believed me, not even the jailer, who shook his head, saying: "The case is grave, truly grave. You didn't want to poison the children?" One day they brought me before the Magistrate.

"Your case is difficult," he repeated. "I will assign you to the Penal Judge."

A year passed. Finally they judged me. As there were no victims, my sentence was light. After a short time, my day of liberty arrived.

The Chief of the Prison called me in:

"Well, now you're free. You were lucky. Lucky there were no victims. But don't do it again, because the next time won't be so short . . ."

And he stared at me with the same grave stare with which everyone watched me.

The same afternoon I took the train and after hours of uncomfortable traveling arrived in Mexico City. I took a cab home. At the door of my apartment I heard laughter and singing. I felt a pain in my chest, like the smack of a wave of surprise when surprise smacks us across the chest: my friend was there, singing and laughing as always.

"How did you get back?"

"Simple: in the train. Someone, after making sure that I was only salt water, poured me in the engine. It was a rough trip: soon I was a white plume of vapor, soon I fell in a fine rain on the machine. I thinned out a lot. I lost many drops."

Her presence changed my life. The house of dark corridors and dusty furniture was filled with air, with sun, with sounds and green and blue reflections, a numerous and happy populace of reverberations and echoes. How many waves is one wave, and how it can make a beach or a rock or jetty out of a wall, a chest, a forehead that it crowns with foam! Even the abandoned corners, the abject corners of dust and debris were touched by her light hands. Everything began to laugh and everywhere shined with teeth. The sun entered the old rooms with pleasure and stayed in my house for hours, abandoning the other houses, the district, the city, the country. And some nights, very late, the scandalized stars watched it sneak from my house.

Love was a game, a perpetual creation. All was beach, sand, a bed of sheets that were always fresh. If I embraced her, she swelled with pride, incredibly tall, like the liquid stalk of a poplar; and soon that thinness flowered into a fountain of white feathers, into a plume of smiles that fell over my head and back and covered me with whiteness. Or she stretched out in front of me, infinite as the horizon, until I too became horizon and silence. Full and sinuous, it enveloped me like music or some giant lips. Her present was a going and coming of caresses, of murmurs, of kisses. Entered in her waters I was drenched to the socks and in a wink of an eye I found myself up above, at the height of vertigo, mysteriously suspended, to fall like a stone and feel myself gently deposited on the dryness, like a feather. Nothing is comparable to sleeping in those waters, to wake pounded by a thousand happy light lashes, by a thousand assaults that withdrew laughing.

But never did I reach the center of her being. Never did I touch the nakedness of pain and of death. Perhaps it does not exist in waves, that secret site that renders a woman vulnerable and mortal, that electric button where all interlocks, twitches, and straightens out to then swoon. Her sensibility, like that of women, spread in ripples, only they weren't concentric ripples, but rather eccentric, spreading each time farther, until they touched other galaxies. To love her was to extend to remote contacts, to vibrate with far-off stars we never suspected. But her center . . . no, she had no center, just an emptiness as in a whirlwind, that sucked me in and smothered me.

Stretched out side by side, we exchanged confidences, whispers, smiles. Curled up, she fell on my chest and there unfolded like a vegetation of murmurs. She sang in my ear, a little snail. She became humble and transparent, clutching my feet like a small animal, calm water. She was so clear I could read all of her thoughts. Certain nights her skin was covered with phosphorescence and to embrace her was to embrace a piece of night tattooed with fire. But she also became black and bitter. At unexpected hours she roared, moaned, twisted. Her groans woke the neighbors. Upon hearing her, the sea wind would scratch at the door of the house or rave in a loud voice on the roof. Cloudy days irritated her; she broke furniture, said bad words, covered me with insults and green and gray foam. She spit, cried, swore, prophesied. Subject to the moon, to the stars, to the influence of the light of other worlds, she changed her moods and appearance in a way that I thought fantastic, but it was as fatal as the tide.

She began to miss solitude. The house was full of snails and conches, of small sailboats that in her fury she had shipwrecked (together with the others, laden with images, that each night left my forehead and sank in her ferocious or pleasant whirlwinds). How many little treasures were lost in that time! But my boats and the silent song of the snails was not enough. I had to install in the house a colony of fish. I confess that it was not without jealousy that I watched them swimming in my friend, caressing her breasts, sleeping between her legs, adorning her hair with light flashes of color.

Among all those fish there were a few particularly repulsive and ferocious ones, little tigers from the aquarium, with large fixed eyes and jagged and bloodthirsty mouths. I don't know by what aberration my friend delighted in playing with them, shamelessly showing them a preference whose significance I preferred to ignore. She passed long hours confined with those horrible creatures. One day I couldn't stand it any more; I threw open the door and launched after them. Agile and ghostly they escaped my hands while she laughed and pounded me until I fell. I thought I was drowning. And when I was at the point of death, and purple, she deposited me on the bank and began to kiss me, saying I don't know what things. I felt very weak, fatigued, and humiliated. And at the same time her voluptuousness made me close my eyes, because her voice was sweet and she spoke to me of the delicious death of the drowned. When I recovered, I began to fear and hate her.

I had neglected my affairs. Now I began to visit friends and renew old and dear relations. I met an old girlfriend. Making her swear to keep my secret, I told her of my life with the wave. Nothing moves women so much as the possibility of saving a man. My redeemer employed all of her arts, but what could a woman, master of a limited number of souls and bodies, do in front of my friend who was always changing — and always identical to herself in her incessant metamorphoses.

Winter came. The sky turned gray. Fog fell on the city. Frozen drizzle rained. My friend cried every night. During the day she isolated herself, quiet and sinister, stuttering a single syllable, like an old woman who grumbles in a corner. She became cold; to sleep with her was to shiver all night and to feel freeze, little by little, the blood, the bones, the thoughts. She turned deep, impenetrable, restless. I left frequently and my absences were each time more prolonged. She, in her corner, howled loudly. With teeth like steel and a corrosive tongue she gnawed the walls, crumbled them. She passed the nights in mourning, reproaching me. She had nightmares, deliriums of the sun, of warm beaches. She dreamt of the pole and of changing into a great block of ice, sailing beneath black skies in nights long as months. She insulted me. She cursed and laughed; filled the house with guffaws and phantoms. She called up the monsters of the depths, blind ones, quick ones, blunt. Charged with electricity, she carbonized all she touched; full of acid, she dissolved whatever she brushed against. Her sweet embraces became knotty cords that strangled me. And her body, greenish and elastic, was an implacable whip that lashed, lashed, lashed. I fled. The horrible fish laughed with ferocious smiles.

There in the mountains, among the tall pines and precipices, I breathed the cold thin air like a thought of liberty. At the end of a month I returned. I had decided. It had been so cold that over the marble of the chimney, next to the extinct fire, I found a statue of ice. I was unmoved by her weary beauty. I put her in a big canvas sack and went out to the streets with the sleeper on my shoulders. In a restaurant in the outskirts I sold her to a waiter friend who immediately began to chop her into little pieces, which he carefully deposited in the buckets where bottles are chilled.

Edgar Allan Poe

Edgar Allan Poe (1809–1849), the son of poor traveling actors, was adopted by the merchant John Allan of Richmond, Virginia, after the death of Poe's mother when Poe was three years old. He was educated in England and Virginia, enlisted and served two years in the army, then entered the military academy at West Point, from which he was expelled for absenteeism after a year. When John Allan disinherited him, Poe became a writer to earn his living.

In 1833 Poe's story "A MS. Found in a Bottle" won a fifty-dollar prize for the best story in a popular Baltimore periodical, and soon afterward he assumed editorship of the *Southern Literary Messenger.* In 1836 he married his cousin Virginia Clemm, shortly before her fourteenth birthday. Poe's brilliant reviews, poems, and stories attracted wide attention, but in 1837 he quarreled with the owner of the *Messenger* over his salary and the degree of his independence as an editor, and he resigned from the magazine.

In 1841 Poe became an editor of *Graham's Magazine,* and during his yearlong tenure he quadrupled subscriptions by publishing his own stories and articles. He left *Graham's* to start his own magazine, which failed. His remaining years as a freelance writer were a struggle with poverty, depression, poor health aggravated by addiction to drugs and alcohol, and—after 1847—grief over the death of his wife. The writer Jorge Luis Borges observed that Poe's life "was short and unhappy, if unhappiness can be short."

Poe's first collection of twenty-five short stories appeared in two volumes in 1840, *Tales of the Grotesque and Arabesque.* His second collection of twelve stories, *Tales,* published in 1845, was so successful that it was followed by *The Raven and Other Poems* the same year. Poe was industrious, and his books of short fiction and poetry sold well, but his total income from them in his lifetime was less than three hundred dollars.

Most of Poe's best stories can be divided into two categories: melodramatic tales of gothic terror, symbolic psychological fiction that became the source of the modern horror story, such as "The Cask of Amontillado," "The Fall of the House of Usher," and "The Tell-Tale Heart"; and stories of intellect or reason, analytic tales that were precursors of the modern detective story. After critics accused Poe of imitating the extravagant "mysticism" of German romantic writers in his monologues of inspired madness, Poe asserted his originality in the preface to his first story collection: "If in many of my productions terror has been the thesis, I maintain that terror is not of Germany, but of the soul."

Known as a literary critic as well as a poet and writer of short fiction, Poe published more than seventy tales. He is important as one of the earliest writers to attempt to formulate an aesthetic theory about the short story form, or "prose tale" as it was called in his time. Some of his most extensive comments on this subject are found in his reviews of Hawthorne's *Twice-Told Tales* for *Graham's Magazine* in 1842 and *Godey's Lady's Book* in 1847. In these essays he also described his own philosophy of composition. Poe believed that unity of a "single effect" was the most essential quality of all successful short fiction. He praised Hawthorne for his "invention, creation, imagination, originality"— qualities Poe himself possessed in abundance. In June 1846, Hawthorne returned the compliment by sending Poe a graceful letter with a copy of his second collection, *Mosses from an Old Manse,* saying that he would never fail to recognize Poe's "force and originality" as a writer of tales even if he sometimes disagreed with Poe's opinions as a critic.

Poe's stories were widely translated, and he became the first American writer of short fiction to be internationally celebrated. Interpretations of his creative work by writers living abroad usually focused on aspects of his genius that supported their views of America. The Russian novelist Fyodor Dostoevsky admired Poe's "strangely material" imagination and recognized that Poe, unlike the German romantic writers, did not give a large role to supernatural agents in his gothic tales. Instead, Dostoevsky felt that the "power of details" in Poe's descriptions was presented "with such stupendous plasticity that you cannot but believe in the reality or possibility of a fact which actually never has occurred."

The French poet Charles Baudelaire, who translated Poe's tales and championed his genius, regarded Poe from a completely different perspective when he identified him as an alienated artist—"le poète maudit"— a writer outside his society who reflected the derangement of a hypocritical country that professed individual freedom yet permitted slavery in the southern states and bigamy among the Mormons in Utah.

Other readers were more critical—for instance, the transcendentalist writer Margaret Fuller, who took Poe to task for what she considered his careless use of language. Perhaps the most sweeping dismissal of Poe's writing originated with Henry James, who—despite his interest in the psychological presentation of fictional characters—declared that "an enthusiasm for Poe is the mark of a decidedly primitive stage of reflection." Later critics are more appreciative and continue to engage in a lively conversation about Poe's work.

RELATED COMMENTARIES
Edgar Allan Poe, "The Importance of the Single Effect in a Prose Tale," page 1509; D. H. Lawrence, "On 'The Fall of the House of Usher' and 'The Cask of Amontillado,'" page 1458; Cleanth Brooks and Robert Penn Warren, "A New Critical Reading of 'The Fall of the House of Usher,'" page 1402.

The Cask of Amontillado

1846

THE THOUSAND INJURIES of Fortunato I had borne as I best could; but when he ventured upon insult, I vowed revenge. You, who so well know the nature of my soul, will not suppose, however, that I gave utterance to a threat. *At length* I would be avenged; this was a point definitely settled — but the very definitiveness with which it was resolved precluded the idea of risk. I must not only punish, but punish with impunity. A wrong is unredressed when retribution overtakes its redresser. It is equally unredressed when the avenger fails to make himself felt as such to him who has done the wrong.

It must be understood, that neither by word nor deed had I given Fortunato cause to doubt my good-will. I continued, as was my wont, to smile in his face, and he did not perceive that my smile *now* was at the thought of his immolation.

He had a weak point — this Fortunato — although in other regards he was a man to be respected and even feared. He prided himself on his connoisseurship in wine. Few Italians have the true virtuoso spirit. For the most part their enthusiasm is adopted to suit the time and opportunity — to practise imposture upon the British and Austrian *millionaires*. In painting and gemmary Fortunato, like his countrymen, was a quack — but in the matter of old wines he was sincere. In this respect I did not differ from him materially: I was skilful in the Italian vintages myself, and bought largely whenever I could.

It was about dusk, one evening during the supreme madness of the carnival season, that I encountered my friend. He accosted me with excessive warmth, for he had been drinking much. The man wore motley. He had on a tight-fitting parti-striped dress, and his head was surmounted by the conical cap and bells. I was so pleased to see him, that I thought I should never have done wringing his hand.

I said to him: "My dear Fortunato, you are luckily met. How remarkably well you are looking to-day! But I have received a pipe[1] of what passes for Amontillado, and I have my doubts."

"How?" said he. "Amontillado? A pipe? Impossible! And in the middle of the carnival!"

"I have my doubts," I replied; "and I was silly enough to pay the full Amontillado price without consulting you in the matter. You were not to be found, and I was fearful of losing a bargain."

"Amontillado!"

"I have my doubts."

"Amontillado!"

"And I must satisfy them."

"Amontillado!"

"As you are engaged, I am on my way to Luchesi. If any one has a critical turn, it is he. He will tell me ——"

"Luchesi cannot tell Amontillado from Sherry."

"And yet some fools will have it that his taste is a match for your own."

"Come, let us go."

"Whither?"

"To your vaults."

"My friend, no; I will not impose upon your good nature. I perceive you have an engagement. Luchesi ——"

"I have no engagement; — come."

"My friend, no. It is not the engagement, but the severe cold with which I perceive you are afflicted. The vaults are insufferably damp. They are encrusted with nitre."

---

[1] A large cask or keg.

"Let us go, nevertheless. The cold is merely nothing. Amontillado! You have been imposed upon. And as for Luchesi, he cannot distinguish Sherry from Amontillado."

Thus speaking, Fortunato possessed himself of my arm. Putting on a mask of black silk, and drawing a *roquelaire*[2] closely about my person, I suffered him to hurry me to my palazzo.

There were no attendants at home; they had absconded to make merry in honor of the time. I had told them that I should not return until the morning, and had given them explicit orders not to stir from the house. These orders were sufficient, I well knew, to insure their immediate disappearance, one and all, as soon as my back was turned.

I took from their sconces two flambeaux, and giving one to Fortunato, bowed him through several suites of rooms to the archway that led into the vaults. I passed down a long and winding staircase, requesting him to be cautious as he followed. We came at length to the foot of the descent, and stood together on the damp ground of the catacombs of the Montresors.

The gait of my friend was unsteady, and the bells upon his cap jingled as he strode.

"The pipe?" said he.

"It is farther on," said I; "but observe the white web-work which gleams from these cavern walls."

He turned toward me, and looked into my eyes with two filmy orbs that distilled the rheum of intoxication.

"Nitre?" he asked, at length.

"Nitre," I replied. "How long have you had that cough?"

"Ugh! ugh! ugh!—ugh! ugh! ugh!—ugh! ugh! ugh!—ugh! ugh! ugh!—ugh! ugh! ugh!"

My poor friend found it impossible to reply for many minutes.

"It is nothing," he said, at last.

"Come," I said, with decision, "we will go back; your health is precious. You are rich, respected, admired, beloved; you are happy, as once I was. You are a man to be missed. For me it is no matter. We will go back; you will be ill, and I cannot be responsible. Besides, there is Luchesi——"

"Enough," he said; "the cough is a mere nothing; it will not kill me. I shall not die of a cough."

"True—true," I replied; "and, indeed, I had no intention of alarming you unnecessarily; but you should use all proper caution. A draught of this Medoc will defend us from the damps."

Here I knocked off the neck of a bottle which I drew from a long row of its fellows that lay upon the mould.

"Drink," I said, presenting him the wine.

He raised it to his lips with a leer. He paused and nodded to me familiarly, while his bells jingled.

---

[2]A short cloak.

"I drink," he said, "to the buried that repose around us."

"And I to your long life."

He again took my arm, and we proceeded.

"These vaults," he said, "are extensive."

"The Montresors," I replied, "were a great and numerous family."

"I forget your arms."

"A huge human foot d'or,[3] in a field azure; the foot crushes a serpent rampant whose fangs are imbedded in the heel."

"And the motto?"

"*Nemo me impune lacessit.*"[4]

"Good!" he said.

The wine sparkled in his eyes and the bells jingled. My own fancy grew warm with the Medoc. We had passed through walls of piled bones, with casks and puncheons intermingling into the inmost recesses of the catacombs. I paused again, and this time I made bold to seize Fortunato by an arm above the elbow.

"The nitre!" I said; "see, it increases. It hangs like moss upon the vaults. We are below the river's bed. The drops of moisture trickle among the bones. Come, we will go back ere it is too late. Your cough ——"

"It is nothing," he said; "let us go on. But first, another draught of the Medoc."

I broke and reached him a flagon of De Grâve. He emptied it at a breath. His eyes flashed with a fierce light. He laughed and threw the bottle upward with a gesticulation I did not understand.

I looked at him in surprise. He repeated the movement — a grotesque one.

"You do not comprehend?" he said.

"Not I," I replied.

"Then you are not of the brotherhood."

"How?"

"You are not of the masons."

"Yes, yes," I said; "yes, yes."

"You? Impossible! A mason?"

"A mason," I replied.

"A sign," he said.

"It is this," I answered, producing a trowel from beneath the folds of my *roquelaire.*

"You jest," he exclaimed, recoiling a few paces. "But let us proceed to the Amontillado."

"Be it so," I said, replacing the tool beneath the cloak, and again offering him my arm. He leaned upon it heavily. We continued our route in search of the Amontillado. We passed through a range of low arches, descended, passed on, and descending again, arrived at a deep crypt, in which the foulness of the air caused our flambeaux rather to glow than flame.

At the most remote end of the crypt there appeared another less spacious. Its walls had been lined with human remains, piled to the vault overhead, in the

---

[3] Of gold.

[4] "No one wounds me with impunity"; the motto of the royal arms of Scotland.

fashion of the great catacombs of Paris. Three sides of this interior crypt were still ornamented in this manner. From the fourth the bones had been thrown down, and lay promiscuously upon the earth, forming at one point a mound of some size. Within the wall thus exposed by the displacing of the bones, we perceived a still interior recess, in depth about four feet, in width three, in height six or seven. It seemed to have been constructed for no especial use within itself, but formed merely the interval between two of the colossal supports of the roof of the cata-combs, and was backed by one of their circumscribing walls of solid granite.

It was in vain that Fortunato, uplifting his dull torch, endeavored to pry into the depth of the recess. Its termination the feeble light did not enable us to see.

"Proceed," I said; "herein is the Amontillado. As for Luchesi ——"

"He is an ignoramus," interrupted my friend, as he stepped unsteadily for-ward, while I followed immediately at his heels. In an instant he had reached the extremity of the niche, and finding his progress arrested by the rock, stood stupidly bewildered. A moment more and I had fettered him to the granite. In its surface were two iron staples, distant from each other about two feet, horizontally. From one of these depended a short chain, from the other a padlock. Throwing the links about his waist, it was but the work of a few seconds to secure it. He was too much astounded to resist. Withdrawing the key I stepped back from the recess.

"Pass your hand," I said, "over the wall; you cannot help feeling the nitre. Indeed it is *very* damp. Once more let me *implore* you to return. No? Then I must positively leave you. But I must first render you all the little attentions in my power."

"The Amontillado!" ejaculated my friend, not yet recovered from his astonishment.

"True," I replied; "the Amontillado."

As I said these words I busied myself among the pile of bones of which I have before spoken. Throwing them aside, I soon uncovered a quantity of building stone and mortar. With these materials and with the aid of my trowel, I began vigorously to wall up the entrance of the niche.

I had scarcely laid the first tier of the masonry when I discovered that the intoxication of Fortunato had in a great measure worn off. The earliest indica-tion I had of this was a low moaning cry from the depth of the recess. It was *not* the cry of a drunken man. There was then a long and obstinate silence. I laid the second tier, and the third, and the fourth; and then I heard the furious vibrations of the chain. The noise lasted for several minutes, during which, that I might hearken to it with the more satisfaction, I ceased my labors and sat down upon the bones. When at last the clanking subsided, I resumed the trowel, and finished without interruption the fifth, the sixth, and the seventh tier. The wall was now nearly upon a level with my breast. I again paused, and holding the flambeaux over the masonwork, threw a few feeble rays upon the figure within.

A succession of loud and shrill screams, bursting suddenly from the throat of the chained form, seemed to thrust me violently back. For a brief moment I hesitated — I trembled. Unsheathing my rapier, I began to grope with it about the recess; but the thought of an instant reassured me. I placed my hand upon the solid fabric of the catacombs, and felt satisfied. I reapproached the wall.

I replied to the yells of him who clamored. I reechoed—I aided—I surpassed them in volume and in strength. I did this, and the clamorer grew still.

It was now midnight, and my task was drawing to a close. I had completed the eighth, the ninth, and the tenth tier. I had finished a portion of the last and the eleventh; there remained but a single stone to be fitted and plastered in. I struggled with its weight; I placed it partially in its destined position. But now there came from out the niche a low laugh that erected the hairs upon my head. It was succeeded by a sad voice, which I had difficulty in recognizing as that of the noble Fortunato. The voice said—

"Ha! ha! ha!—he! he!—a very good joke indeed—an excellent jest. We will have many a rich laugh about it at the palazzo—he! he! he!—over our wine—he! he! he!"

"The Amontillado!" I said.

"He! he! he!—he! he! he!—yes, the Amontillado. But is it not getting late? Will not they be awaiting us at the palazzo, the Lady Fortunato and the rest? Let us be gone."

"Yes," I said, "let us be gone."

"For the love of God, Montresor!"

"Yes," I said, "for the love of God!"

But to these words I hearkened in vain for a reply. I grew impatient. I called aloud:

"Fortunato!"

No answer. I called again:

"Fortunato!"

No answer still, I thrust a torch through the remaining aperture and let it fall within. There came forth in return only a jingling of the bells. My heart grew sick—on account of the dampness of the catacombs. I hastened to make an end of my labor. I forced the last stone into its position; I plastered it up. Against the new masonry I re-erected the old rampart of bones. For the half of a century no mortal has disturbed them. *In pace requiescat!*[5]

---

[5]In peace may he rest (Latin).

The Fall of the House of Usher

1839

Son cœur est un luth suspendu;
Sitôt qu'on le touche il résonne.[1]

—De Béranger

DURING THE WHOLE of a dull, dark, and soundless day in the autumn of the year, when the clouds hung oppressively low in the heavens, I had been passing alone, on horseback, through a singularly dreary tract of country, and at length found myself, as the shades of the evening drew on, within view of the melancholy House of Usher. I know not how it was — but, with the first glimpse of the building, a sense of insufferable gloom pervaded my spirit. I say insufferable; for the feeling was unrelieved by any of that half-pleasurable, because poetic, sentiment, with which the mind usually receives even the sternest natural images of the desolate or terrible. I looked upon the scene before me — upon the mere house, and the simple landscape features of the domain — upon the bleak walls — upon the vacant eye-like windows — upon a few rank sedges — and upon a few white trunks of decayed trees — with an utter depression of soul which I can compare to no earthly sensation more properly than to the after-dream of the reveller upon opium — the bitter lapse into every-day life — the hideous dropping off of the veil. There was an iciness, a sinking, a sickening of the heart — an unredeemed dreariness of thought which no goading of the imagination could torture into aught of the sublime. What was it — I paused to think — what was it that so unnerved me in the contemplation of the House of Usher? It was a mystery all insoluble; nor could I grapple with the shadowy fancies that crowded upon me as I pondered. I was forced to fall back upon the unsatisfactory conclusion, that while, beyond doubt, there *are* combinations of very simple natural objects which have the power of thus affecting us, still the analysis of this power lies among considerations beyond our depth. It was possible, I reflected, that a mere different arrangement of the particulars of the scene, of the details of the picture, would be sufficient to modify, or perhaps to annihilate its capacity for sorrowful impression; and, acting upon this idea, I reined my horse to the precipitous brink of a black and lurid tarn that lay in unruffled lustre by the dwelling, and gazed down — but with a shudder even more thrilling than before — upon the remodelled and inverted images of the gray sedge, and the ghastly tree-stems, and the vacant and eye-like windows.

Nevertheless, in this mansion of gloom I now proposed to myself a sojourn of some weeks. Its proprietor, Roderick Usher, had been one of my boon companions in boyhood; but many years had elapsed since our last meeting. A letter, however, had lately reached me in a distant part of the country — a letter from him — which, in its wildly importunate nature, had admitted of no

---

[1] His heart is a suspended lute; / Which resonates as soon as touched.

other than a personal reply. The MS. gave evidence of nervous agitation. The writer spoke of acute bodily illness — of a mental disorder which oppressed him — and of an earnest desire to see me, as his best, and indeed his only personal friend, with a view of attempting, by the cheerfulness of my society, some alleviation of his malady. It was the manner in which all this, and much more, was said — it was the apparent *heart* that went with his request — which allowed me no room for hesitation; and I accordingly obeyed forthwith what I still considered a very singular summons.

Although, as boys, we had been even intimate associates, yet I really knew little of my friend. His reserve had been always excessive and habitual. I was aware, however, that his very ancient family had been noted, time out of mind, for a peculiar sensibility of temperament, displaying itself, through long ages, in many works of exalted art, and manifested, of late, in repeated deeds of munificent yet unobtrusive charity, as well as in a passionate devotion to the intricacies, perhaps even more than to the orthodox and easily recognizable beauties, of musical science. I had learned, too, the very remarkable fact, that the stem of the Usher race, all time-honoured as it was, had put forth, at no period, any enduring branch; in other words, that the entire family lay in the direct line of descent, and had always, with very trifling and very temporary variation, so lain. It was this deficiency, I considered, while running over in thought the perfect keeping of the character of the premises with the accredited character of the people, and while speculating upon the possible influence which the one, in the long lapse of centuries, might have exercised upon the other — it was this deficiency, perhaps of collateral issue, and the consequent undeviating transmission, from sire to son, of the patrimony with the name, which had, at length, so identified the two as to merge the original title of the estate in the quaint and equivocal appellation of the "House of Usher" — an appellation which seemed to include, in the minds of the peasantry who used it, both the family and the family mansion.

I have said that the sole effect of my somewhat childish experiment — that of looking down within the tarn — had been to deepen the first singular impression. There can be no doubt that the consciousness of the rapid increase of my superstition — for why should I not so term it? — served mainly to accelerate the increase itself. Such, I have long known, is the paradoxical law of all sentiments having terror as a basis. And it might have been for this reason only, that, when I again uplifted my eyes to the house itself, from its image in the pool, there grew in my mind a strange fancy — a fancy so ridiculous, indeed, that I but mention it to show the vivid force of the sensations which oppressed me. I had so worked upon my imagination as really to believe that about the whole mansion and domain there hung an atmosphere peculiar to themselves and their immediate vicinity — an atmosphere which had no affinity with the air of heaven, but which had reeked up from the decayed trees, and the gray wall, and the silent tarn — a pestilent and mystic vapour, dull, sluggish, faintly discernible, and leaden-hued.

Shaking off from my spirit what *must* have been a dream, I scanned more narrowly the real aspect of the building. Its principal feature seemed to be that of an excessive antiquity. The discoloration of ages had been great. Minute fungi overspread the whole exterior, hanging in a fine tangled web-work from the eaves. Yet all this was apart from an extraordinary dilapidation. No portion of the masonry had fallen; and there appeared to be a wild inconsistency between its still perfect adaptation of parts, and the crumbling condition of the individual stones. In this there was much that reminded me of the specious totality of the old woodwork which has rotted for long years in some neglected vault, with no disturbance from the breath of the external air. Beyond this indication of extensive decay, however, the fabric gave little token of instability. Perhaps the eye of a scrutinizing observer might have discovered a barely perceptible fissure, which, extending from the roof of the building in front, made its way down the wall in a zigzag direction, until it became lost in the sullen waters of the tarn.

Noticing these things, I rode over a short causeway to the house. A servant in waiting took my horse, and I entered the Gothic archway of the hall. A valet, of stealthy step, thence conducted me, in silence, through many dark and intricate passages in my progress to the *studio* of his master. Much that I encountered on the way contributed, I know not how, to heighten the vague sentiments of which I have already spoken. While the objects around me — while the carvings of the ceilings, the sombre tapestries of the walls, the ebon blackness of the floors, and the phantasmagoric armorial trophies which rattled as I strode, were but matters to which, or to such as which, I had been accustomed from my infancy — while I hesitated not to acknowledge how familiar was all this — I still wondered to find how unfamiliar were the fancies which ordinary images were stirring up. On one of the staircases, I met the physician of the family. His countenance, I thought, wore a mingled expression of low cunning and perplexity. He accosted me with trepidation and passed on. The valet now threw open a door and ushered me into the presence of his master.

The room in which I found myself was very large and lofty. The windows were long, narrow, and pointed, and at so vast a distance from the black oaken floor as to be altogether inaccessible from within. Feeble gleams of encrimsoned light made their way through the trellised panes, and served to render sufficiently distinct the more prominent objects around; the eye, however, struggled in vain to reach the remoter angles of the chamber, or the recesses of the vaulted and fretted ceiling. Dark draperies hung upon the walls. The general furniture was profuse, comfortless, antique, and tattered. Many books and musical instruments lay scattered about, but failed to give any vitality to the scene. I felt that I breathed an atmosphere of sorrow. An air of stern, deep, and irredeemable gloom hung over and pervaded all.

Upon my entrance, Usher arose from a sofa on which he had been lying at full length, and greeted me with a vivacious warmth which had much in it, I at first thought, of an overdone cordiality — of the constrained effort of the *ennuyé* man of the world. A glance, however, at his countenance convinced me of his perfect sincerity. We sat down; and for some moments, while he spoke not, I gazed upon him with a feeling half of pity, half of awe. Surely, man had never before so terribly altered, in so brief a period, as had Roderick Usher! It was with difficulty that I could bring myself to admit the identity of the wan being before me with the companion of my early boyhood. Yet the character of his face had been at all times remarkable. A cadaverousness of complexion; an eye large, liquid, and luminous beyond comparison; lips somewhat thin and very pallid, but of a surpassingly beautiful curve; a nose of a delicate Hebrew model, but with a breadth of nostril unusual in similar formations; a finely moulded chin, speaking, in its want of prominence, of a want of moral energy; hair of a more than web-like softness and tenuity; these features, with an inordinate expansion above the regions of the temple, made up altogether a countenance not easily to be forgotten. And now in the mere exaggeration of the prevailing character of these features, and of the expression they were wont to convey, lay so much of change that I doubted to whom I spoke. The now ghastly pallor of the skin, and the now miraculous lustre of the eye, above all things startled and even awed me. The silken hair, too, had been suffered to grow all unheeded, and as, in its wild gossamer texture, it floated rather than fell about the face, I could not, even with effort, connect its Arabesque expression with any idea of simple humanity.

In the manner of my friend I was at once struck with an incoherence — an inconsistency; and I soon found this to arise from a series of feeble and futile struggles to overcome an habitual trepidancy — an excessive nervous agitation. For something of this nature I had indeed been prepared, no less by his letter, than by reminiscences of certain boyish traits, and by conclusions deduced from his peculiar physical conformation and temperament. His action was alternately vivacious and sullen. His voice varied rapidly from a tremulous indecision (when the animal spirits seemed utterly in abeyance) to that species of energetic concision — that abrupt, weighty, unhurried, and hollow-sounding enunciation — that leaden, self-balanced, and perfectly modulated guttural utterance, which may be observed in the lost drunkard, or the irreclaimable eater of opium, during the periods of his most intense excitement.

It was thus that he spoke of the object of my visit, of his earnest desire to see me, and of the solace he expected me to afford him. He entered, at some length, into what he conceived to be the nature of his malady. It was, he said, a constitutional and a family evil, and one for which he despaired to find a remedy — a mere nervous affection, he immediately added, which would undoubtedly soon pass off. It displayed itself in a host of unnatural sensations. Some of these, as he detailed them, interested and bewildered me; although, perhaps, the terms and the general manner of their narration had their weight. He suffered much from a morbid acuteness of the senses; the most insipid food was alone endurable; he could wear only garments of certain texture; the odours of all flowers were oppressive; his eyes were tortured by even a faint light; and there were but peculiar sounds, and these from stringed instruments, which did not inspire him with horror.

To an anomalous species of terror I found him a bounden slave. "I shall perish," said he, "I *must* perish in this deplorable folly. Thus, thus, and not otherwise, shall I be lost. I dread the events of the future, not in themselves, but in their results. I shudder at the thought of any, even the most trivial, incident, which may operate upon this intolerable agitation of soul. I have, indeed, no abhorrence of danger, except in its absolute effect — in terror. In this unnerved — in this pitiable condition — I feel that the period will sooner or later arrive when I must abandon life and reason together, in some struggle with the grim phantasm, FEAR."

I learned, moreover, at intervals, and through broken and equivocal hints, another singular feature of his mental condition. He was enchained by certain superstitious impressions in regard to the dwelling which he tenanted, and whence, for many years, he had never ventured forth—in regard to an influence whose supposititious force was conveyed in terms too shadowy here to be re-stated—an influence which some peculiarities in the mere form and substance of his family mansion had, by dint of long sufferance, he said, obtained over his spirit—an effect which the *physique* of the gray wall and turrets, and of the dim tarn into which they all looked down, had, at length, brought about upon the *morale* of his existence.

He admitted, however, although with hesitation, that much of the peculiar gloom which thus afflicted him could be traced to a more natural and far more palpable origin—to the severe and long-continued illness—indeed to the evidently approaching dissolution—of a tenderly beloved sister, his sole companion for long years, his last and only relative on earth. "Her decease," he said, with a bitterness which I can never forget, "would leave him (him the hopeless and the frail) the last of the ancient race of the Ushers." While he spoke, the lady Madeline (for so was she called) passed slowly through a remote portion of the apartment, and, without having noticed my presence, disappeared. I regarded her with an utter astonishment not unmingled with dread—and yet I found it impossible to account for such feelings. A sensation of stupor oppressed me, as my eyes followed her retreating steps. When a door, at length, closed upon her, my glance sought instinctively and eagerly the countenance of the brother—but he had buried his face in his hands, and I could only perceive that a far more than ordinary wanness had overspread the emaciated fingers through which trickled many passionate tears.

The disease of the lady Madeline had long baffled the skill of her physicians. A settled apathy, a gradual wasting away of the person, and frequent although transient affections of a partially cataleptical character were the unusual diagnosis. Hitherto she had steadily borne up against the pressure of her malady, and had not betaken herself finally to bed; but on the closing in of the evening of my arrival at the house, she succumbed (as her brother told me at night with inexpressible agitation) to the prostrating power of the destroyer; and I learned that the glimpse I had obtained of her person would thus probably be the last I should obtain—that the lady, at least while living, would be seen by me no more.

For several days ensuing, her name was unmentioned by either Usher or myself: and during this period I was busied in earnest endeavours to alleviate the melancholy of my friend. We painted and read together, or I listened, as if in a dream, to the wild improvisations of his speaking guitar. And thus, as a closer and still closer intimacy admitted me more unreservedly into the recesses of his spirit, the more bitterly did I perceive the futility of all attempt at cheering a mind from which darkness, as if an inherent positive quality, poured forth upon all objects of the moral and physical universe in one unceasing radiation of gloom.

I shall ever bear about me a memory of the many solemn hours I thus spent alone with the master of the House of Usher. Yet I should fail in any attempt to convey an idea of the exact character of the studies, or of the occupations, in which he involved me, or led me the way. An excited and highly distempered ideality threw a sulphureous lustre over all. His long improvised dirges will ring forever in my ears. Among other things, I hold painfully in mind a certain singular perversion and amplification of the wild air of the last waltz of Von Weber. From the paintings over which his elaborate fancy brooded, and which grew, touch by touch, into vagueness at which I shuddered the more thrillingly, because I shuddered knowing not why; — from these paintings (vivid as their images now are before me) I would in vain endeavour to educe more than a small portion which should lie within the compass of merely written words. By the utter simplicity, by the nakedness of his designs, he arrested and overawed attention. If ever mortal painted an idea, that mortal was Roderick Usher. For me at least — in the circumstances then surrounding me — there arose out of the pure abstractions which the hypochondriac contrived to throw upon his canvas, an intensity of intolerable awe, no shadow of which I felt ever yet in the contemplation of the certainly glowing yet too concrete reveries of Fuseli.

One of the phantasmagoric conceptions of my friend, partaking not so rigidly of the spirit of abstraction, may be shadowed forth, although feebly, in words. A small picture presented the interior of an immensely long and rectangular vault or tunnel, with low walls, smooth, white, and without interruption or device. Certain accessory points of the design served well to convey the idea that this excavation lay at an exceeding depth below the surface of the earth. No outlet was observed in any portion of its vast extent, and no torch or other artificial source of light was discernible; yet a flood of intense rays rolled throughout, and bathed the whole in a ghastly and inappropriate splendour.

I have just spoken of that morbid condition of the auditory nerve which rendered all music intolerable to the sufferer, with the exception of certain effects of stringed instruments. It was, perhaps, the narrow limits to which he thus confined himself upon the guitar, which gave birth, in great measure, to the fantastic character of his performances. But the fervid *facility* of his *impromptus* could not be so accounted for. They must have been, and were, in the notes, as well as in the words of his wild fantasias (for he not unfrequently accompanied himself with rhymed verbal improvisations), the result of that intense mental collectedness and concentration to which I have previously alluded as observable only in particular moments of the highest artificial excitement. The words of one of these rhapsodies I have easily remembered. I was, perhaps, the more forcibly impressed with it, as he gave it, because, in the under or mystic current of its meaning, I fancied that I perceived, and for the first time, a full consciousness on the part of Usher, of the tottering of his lofty reason upon her throne. The verses, which were entitled "The Haunted Palace," ran very nearly, if not accurately, thus:

I

In the greenest of our valleys,
    By good angels tenanted,
Once a fair and stately palace —
    Radiant palace — reared its head.

In the monarch Thought's dominion —
 It stood there!
Never seraph spread a pinion
 Over fabric half so fair.

II

Banners yellow, glorious, golden,
 On its roof did float and flow;
(This — all this — was in the olden
 Time long ago)
And every gentle air that dallied,
 In that sweet day,
Along the ramparts plumed and pallid,
 A winged odour went away.

III

Wanderers in that happy valley
 Through two luminous windows saw
Spirits moving musically
 To a lute's well-tunèd law,
Round about a throne, where sitting
 (Porphyrogene!)
In state his glory well befitting,
 The ruler of the realm was seen.

IV

And all with pearl and ruby glowing
 Was the fair palace door,
Through which came flowing, flowing, flowing
 And sparkling evermore,
A troop of Echoes whose sweet duty
 Was but to sing,
In voices of surpassing beauty,
 The wit and wisdom of their king.

V

But evil things, in robes of sorrow,
 Assailed the monarch's high estate;
(Ah, let us mourn, for never morrow
 Shall dawn upon him, desolate!)
And, round about his home, the glory
 That blushed and bloomed
Is but a dim-remembered story
 Of the old time entombed.

VI

And travellers now within that valley,
 Through the red-litten windows see

Vast forms that move fantastically
  To a discordant melody;
While, like a rapid ghastly river,
  Through the pale door,
A hideous throng rush out forever,
  And laugh — but smile no more.

I well remember that suggestions arising from this ballad led us into a train of thought wherein there became manifest an opinion of Usher's which I mention not so much on account of its novelty (for other men[2] have thought thus), as on account of the pertinacity with which he maintained it. This opinion, in its general form, was that of the sentience of all vegetable things. But, in his disordered fancy, the idea had assumed a more daring character, and trespassed, under certain conditions, upon the kingdom of inorganization. I lack words to express the full extent, or the earnest *abandon* of his persuasion. The belief, however, was connected (as I have previously hinted) with the gray stones of the home of his forefathers. The conditions of the sentience had been here, he imagined, fulfilled in the method of collocation of these stones — in the order of their arrangement, as well as in that of the many *fungi* which overspread them, and of the decayed trees which stood around — above all, in the long undisturbed endurance of this arrangement, and in its reduplication in the still waters of the tarn. Its evidence — the evidence of the sentience — was to be seen, he said (and I here started as he spoke), in the gradual yet certain condensation of an atmosphere of their own about the waters and the walls. The result was discoverable, he added, in that silent yet importunate and terrible influence which for centuries had moulded the destinies of his family, and which made *him* what I now saw him — what he was. Such opinions need no comment, and I will make none.

Our books — the books which, for years, had formed no small portion of the mental existence of the invalid — were, as might be supposed, in strict keeping with his character of phantasm. We pored together over such works as the Ververt et Chartreuse of Gresset; the Belphegor of Machiavelli; the Heaven and Hell of Swedenborg; the Subterranean Voyage of Nicholas Klimm of Holberg; the Chiromancy of Robert Flud, of Jean D'Indaginé, and of De la Chambre; the Journey into the Blue Distance of Tieck; and the City of the Sun of Campanella. One favourite volume was a small octavo edition of the *Directorium Inquisitorum,* by the Dominican Eymeric de Gironne; and there were passages in Pomponius Mela, about the old African Satyrs and Ægipans, over which Usher would sit dreaming for hours. His chief delight, however, was found in the perusal of an exceedingly rare and curious book in quarto Gothic — the manual of a forgotten church — the *Vigiliæ Mortuorum secundum Chorum Ecclesiæ Maguntinæ.*

I could not help thinking of the wild ritual of this work, and of its probable influence upon the hypochondriac, when, one evening, having informed me

---

[2] Watson, Dr. Percival, Spallanzani, and especially the Bishop of Landaff. — See *Chemical Essays,* vol. v. [Poe's note.]

abruptly that the lady Madeline was no more, he stated his intention of preserving her corpse for a fortnight, (previously to its final interment), in one of the numerous vaults within the main walls of the building. The worldly reason, however, assigned for this singular proceeding, was one which I did not feel at liberty to dispute. The brother had been led to his resolution (so he told me) by consideration of the unusual character of the malady of the deceased, of certain obtrusive and eager inquiries on the part of her medical men, and of the remote and exposed situation of the burial-ground of the family. I will not deny that when I called to mind the sinister countenance of the person whom I met upon the staircase, on the day of my arrival at the house, I had no desire to oppose what I regarded as at best but a harmless, and by no means an unnatural, precaution.

At the request of Usher, I personally aided him in the arrangements for the temporary entombment. The body having been encoffined, we two alone bore it to its rest. The vault in which we placed it (and which had been so long unopened that our torches, half smothered in its oppressive atmosphere, gave us little opportunity for investigation) was small, damp, and entirely without means of admission for light; lying, at great depth, immediately beneath that portion of the building in which was my own sleeping apartment. It had been used, apparently, in remote feudal times, for the worst purposes of a donjon-keep, and, in later days, as a place of deposit for powder, or some other highly combustible substance, as a portion of its floor, and the whole interior of a long archway through which we reached it, were carefully sheathed with copper. The door, of massive iron, had been, also, similarly protected. Its immense weight caused an unusually sharp grating sound, as it moved upon its hinges.

Having deposited our mournful burden upon tressels within this region of horror, we partially turned aside the yet unscrewed lid of the coffin, and looked upon the face of the tenant. A striking similitude between the brother and sister now first arrested my attention; and Usher, divining, perhaps, my thoughts, murmured out some few words from which I learned that the deceased and himself had been twins, and that sympathies of a scarcely intelligible nature had always existed between them. Our glances, however, rested not long upon the dead — for we could not regard her unawed. The disease which had thus entombed the lady in the maturity of youth, had left, as usual in all maladies of a strictly cataleptical character, the mockery of a faint blush upon the bosom and the face, and that suspiciously lingering smile upon the lip which is so terrible in death. We replaced and screwed down the lid, and, having secured the door of iron, made our way, with toil, into the scarcely less gloomy apartments of the upper portion of the house.

And now, some days of bitter grief having elapsed, an observable change came over the features of the mental disorder of my friend. His ordinary manner had vanished. His ordinary occupations were neglected or forgotten. He roamed from chamber to chamber with hurried, unequal, and objectless step. The pallor of his countenance had assumed, if possible, a more ghastly hue — but the luminousness of his eye had utterly gone out. The once occasional huskiness of his tone was heard no more; and a tremulous quaver, as if of extreme terror, habitually characterized his utterance. There were times, indeed, when I thought his unceasingly agitated mind was labouring with some oppressive secret, to divulge which he struggled for the necessary courage. At times, again, I was obliged to resolve all into the mere inexplicable vagaries of madness, for I beheld him gazing upon vacancy for long hours, in an attitude of the profoundest attention, as if listening to some imaginary sound. It was no wonder that his condition terrified — that it infected me. I felt creeping upon me, by slow yet certain degrees, the wild influences of his own fantastic yet impressive superstitions.

It was, especially, upon retiring to bed late in the night of the seventh or eighth day after the placing of the lady Madeline within the donjon, that I experienced the full power of such feelings. Sleep came not near my couch — while the hours waned and waned away. I struggled to reason off the nervousness which had dominion over me. I endeavoured to believe that much, if not all of what I felt, was due to the bewildering influence of the gloomy furniture of the room — of the dark and tattered draperies, which, tortured into motion by the breath of a rising tempest, swayed fitfully to and fro upon the walls, and rustled uneasily about the decorations of the bed. But my efforts were fruitless. An irrepressible tremour gradually pervaded my frame; and, at length, there sat upon my very heart an incubus of utterly causeless alarm. Shaking this off with a gasp and a struggle, I uplifted myself upon the pillows, and, peering earnestly within the intense darkness of the chamber, hearkened — I know not why, except that an instinctive spirit prompted me — to certain low and indefinite sounds which came, through the pauses of the storm, at long intervals, I knew not whence. Overpowered by an intense sentiment of horror, unaccountable yet unendurable, I threw on my clothes with haste (for I felt that I should sleep no more during the night), and endeavoured to arouse myself from the pitiable condition into which I had fallen, by pacing rapidly to and fro through the apartment.

I had taken but few turns in this manner, when a light step on an adjoining staircase arrested my attention. I presently recognised it as that of Usher. In an instant afterward he rapped, with a gentle touch, at my door, and entered, bearing a lamp. His countenance was, as usual, cadaverously wan — but, moreover, there was a species of mad hilarity in his eyes — an evidently restrained *hysteria* in his whole demeanour. His air appalled me — but anything was preferable to the solitude which I had so long endured, and I even welcomed his presence as a relief.

"And you have not seen it?" he said abruptly, after having stared about him for some moments in silence — "you have not then seen it? — but, stay! you shall." Thus speaking, and having carefully shaded his lamp, he hurried to one of the casements, and threw it freely open to the storm.

The impetuous fury of the entering gust nearly lifted us from our feet. It was, indeed, a tempestuous yet sternly beautiful night, and one wildly singular in its terror and its beauty. A whirlwind had apparently collected its force in our vicinity; for there were frequent and violent alterations in the direction of the wind; and the exceeding density of the clouds (which hung so low as to press upon the turrets of the house) did not prevent our perceiving the life-like velocity with which they flew careering from all points against each other, without passing away into the distance. I say that even their exceeding density did not prevent our perceiving this — yet we had no glimpse of the moon or stars — nor was there any flashing forth of the lightning. But the under surfaces of the huge masses of agitated vapour, as well as all terrestrial objects immediately around us, were glowing in the unnatural light of a faintly luminous and distinctly visible gaseous exhalation which hung about and enshrouded the mansion.

"You must not — you shall not behold this!" said I, shudderingly, to Usher, as I led him, with a gentle violence, from the window to a seat. "These appearances, which bewilder you, are merely electrical phenomena not uncommon — or it may be that they have their ghastly origin in the rank miasma of the tarn. Let us close this casement; — the air is chilling and dangerous to your frame. Here is one of your favourite romances. I will read, and you shall listen; — and so we will pass away this terrible night together."

The antique volume which I had taken up was the "Mad Trist" of Sir Launcelot Canning; but I had called it a favourite of Usher's more in sad jest than in earnest; for, in truth, there is little in its uncouth and unimaginative prolixity which could have had interest for the lofty and spiritual ideality of my friend. It was, however, the only book immediately at hand; and I indulged a vague hope that the excitement which now agitated the hypochondriac might find relief (for the history of mental disorder is full of similar anomalies) even in the extremeness of the folly which I could read. Could I have judged, indeed, by the wild overstrained air of vivacity with which he hearkened, or apparently hearkened, to the words of the tale, I might well have congratulated myself upon the success of my design.

I had arrived at that well-known portion of the story where Ethelred, the hero of the Trist, having sought in vain for peaceable admission into the dwelling of the hermit, proceeds to make good an entrance by force. Here, it will be remembered, the words of the narrative run thus:

"And Ethelred, who was by nature of a doughty heart, and who was now mighty withal, on account of the powerfulness of the wine which he had drunken, waited no longer to hold parley with the hermit, who, in sooth, was of an obstinate and maliceful turn, but, feeling the rain upon his shoulders, and fearing the rising of the tempest, uplifted his mace outright, and, with blows, made quickly room in the plankings of the door for his gauntleted hand; and now pulling therewith sturdily, he so cracked, and ripped, and tore all asunder, that the noise of the dry and hollow-sounding wood alarmed and reverberated throughout the forest."

At the termination of this sentence I started and, for a moment, paused; for it appeared to me (although I at once concluded that my excited fancy had deceived me) — it appeared to me that, from some very remote portion of the mansion, there came, indistinctly, to my ears, what might have been, in its exact similarity of character, the echo (but a stifled and dull one certainly) of the very cracking and ripping sound which Sir Launcelot had so particularly described. It was, beyond doubt, the coincidence alone which had arrested my attention; for, amid the rattling of the sashes of the casements, and the ordinary commingled noises of the still increasing storm, the sound, in itself, had nothing, surely, which should have interested or disturbed me. I continued the story:

"But the good champion Ethelred, now entering within the door, was sore enraged and amazed to perceive no signal of the maliceful hermit; but, in the stead thereof, a dragon of a scaly and prodigious demeanour, and of a fiery tongue, which sate in guard before a palace of gold, with a floor of silver; and upon the wall there hung a shield of shining brass with this legend enwritten —

> Who entereth herein, a conqueror hath bin;
> Who slayeth the dragon, the shield he shall win.

And Ethelred uplifted his mace, and struck upon the head of the dragon, which fell before him, and gave up his pesty breath, with a shriek so horrid and harsh, and withal so piercing, that Ethelred had fain to close his ears with his hands against the dreadful noise of it, the like whereof was never before heard."

Here again I paused abruptly, and now with a feeling of wild amazement — for there could be no doubt whatever that, in this instance, I did actually hear (although from what direction it proceeded I found it impossible to say) a low and apparently distant, but harsh, protracted, and most unusual screaming or grating sound — the exact counterpart of what my fancy had already conjured up for the dragon's unnatural shriek as described by the romancer.

Oppressed, as I certainly was, upon the occurrence of the second and most extraordinary coincidence, by a thousand conflicting sensations, in which wonder and extreme terror were predominant, I still retained sufficient presence of mind to avoid exciting, by any observation, the sensitive nervousness of my companion. I was by no means certain that he had noticed the sounds in question; although, assuredly, a strange alteration had, during the last few minutes, taken place in his demeanour. From a position fronting my own, he had gradually brought round his chair, so as to sit with his face to the door of the chamber; and thus I could but partially perceive his features, although I saw that his lips trembled as if he were murmuring inaudibly. His head had dropped upon his breast — yet I knew that he was not asleep, from the wide and rigid opening of the eye as I caught a glance of it in profile. The motion of his body, too, was at variance with this idea — for he rocked from side to side with a gentle yet constant and uniform sway. Having rapidly taken notice of all this, I resumed the narrative of Sir Launcelot, which thus proceeded:

"And now, the champion, having escaped from the terrible fury of the dragon, bethinking himself of the brazen shield, and of the breaking up of the enchantment which was upon it, removed the carcass from out of the way before him, and approached valorously over the silver pavement of the castle to where the shield was upon the wall; which in sooth tarried not for his full coming, but fell down at his feet upon the silver floor, with a mighty great and terrible ringing sound."

No sooner had these syllables passed my lips, than — as if a shield of brass had indeed, at the moment, fallen heavily upon a floor of silver — I became aware of a distinct, hollow, metallic, and clangorous, yet apparently muffled reverberation. Completely unnerved, I leaped to my feet; but the measured rocking movement of Usher was undisturbed. I rushed to the chair in which he sat. His eyes were bent fixedly before him, and throughout his whole countenance there reigned a stony rigidity. But, as I placed my hand upon his shoulder, there came a strong shudder over his whole person; a sickly smile quivered about his lips; and I saw that he spoke in a low, hurried, and gibbering murmur, as if unconscious of my presence. Bending closely over him, I at length drank in the hideous import of his words.

"Not hear it? — yes, I hear it, and *have* heard it. Long — long — long — many minutes, many hours, many days, have I heard it — yet I dared not — oh, pity me, miserable wretch that I am! — I dared not — I *dared* not speak! *We have put her living in the tomb!* Said I not that my senses were acute? I *now* tell you that I heard her first feeble movements in the hollow coffin. I heard them — many, many days ago — yet I dared not — I *dared not speak*! And now — to-night — Ethelred — ha! ha! — the breaking of the hermit's door, and the death-cry of the dragon, and the clangour of the shield! — say, rather, the rending of her coffin, and the grating of the iron hinges of her prison, and her struggles within the coppered archway of the vault! Oh whither shall I fly? Will she not be here anon? Is she not hurrying to upbraid me for my haste? Have I not heard her footsteps on the stair? Do I not distinguish that heavy and horrible beating of her heart? MADMAN!"— here he sprang furiously to his feet, and shrieked out his syllables, as if in the effort he were giving up his soul — "MADMAN! I TELL YOU THAT SHE NOW STANDS WITHOUT THE DOOR!"

As if in the superhuman energy of his utterance there had been found the potency of a spell — the huge antique panels to which the speaker pointed threw slowly back, upon the instant, their ponderous and ebony jaws. It was the work of the rushing gust — but then without those doors there *did* stand the lofty and enshrouded figure of the lady Madeline of Usher. There was blood upon her white robes, and the evidence of some bitter struggle upon every portion of her emaciated frame. For a moment she remained trembling and reeling to and fro upon the threshold, then, with a low moaning cry, fell heavily inward upon the person of her brother, and in her violent and now final death-agonies, bore him to the floor a corpse, and a victim to the terrors he had anticipated.

From that chamber, and from that mansion, I fled aghast. The storm was still abroad in all its wrath as I found myself crossing the old causeway. Suddenly there shot along the path a wild light, and I turned to see whence a gleam so unusual could have issued; for the vast house and its shadows were alone behind me. The radiance was that of the full, setting, and blood-red moon, which now shone vividly through that once barely discernible fissure, of which I have before spoken as extending from the roof of the building, in a zigzag direction, to the base. While I gazed, this fissure rapidly widened — there came a fierce breath of the whirlwind — the entire orb of the satellite burst at once upon my sight — my brain reeled as I saw the mighty walls rushing asunder — there was a long tumultuous shouting sound like the voice of a thousand waters — and the deep and dank tarn at my feet closed sullenly and silently over the fragments of the "HOUSE OF USHER."

The Tell-Tale Heart

1843

TRUE! — NERVOUS — VERY, VERY DREADFULLY nervous I had been and am; but why *will* you say that I am mad? The disease had sharpened my senses — not destroyed — not dulled them. Above all was the sense of hearing acute. I heard all things in the heaven and in the earth. I heard many things in hell. How, then, am I mad? Hearken! and observe how healthily — how calmly I can tell you the whole story.

It is impossible to say how first the idea entered my brain; but once conceived, it haunted me day and night. Object there was none. Passion there was none. I loved the old man. He had never wronged me. He had never given me insult. For his gold I had no desire. I think it was his eye! yes, it was this! One of his eyes resembled that of a vulture — a pale blue eye, with a film over it. Whenever it fell upon me, my blood ran cold; and so by degrees — very gradually — I made up my mind to take the life of the old man, and thus rid myself of the eye for ever.

Now this is the point. You fancy me mad. Madmen know nothing. But you should have seen *me*. You should have seen how wisely I proceeded — with what caution — with what foresight — with what dissimulation I went to work! I was never kinder to the old man than during the whole week before I killed him. And every night, about midnight, I turned the latch of his door and opened it — oh, so gently! And then, when I had made an opening sufficient for my head, I put in a dark lantern, all closed, closed, so that no light shone out, and then I thrust in my head. Oh, you would have laughed to see how cunningly I thrust it in! I moved it slowly — very, very slowly, so that I might not disturb the old man's sleep. It took me an hour to place my whole head within the opening so far that I could see him as he lay upon his bed. Ha — would a madman have been so wise as this? And then, when my head was well in the room, I undid the lantern cautiously — oh, so cautiously — cautiously (for the hinges creaked) — I undid it just so much that a single thin ray fell upon the vulture eye. And this I did for seven long nights — every night just after midnight — but I found the eye always closed; and so it was impossible to do the work; for it was not the old man who vexed me, but his Evil Eye. And every morning, when the day broke, I went boldly into the chamber, and spoke courageously to him, calling him by name in a hearty tone, and inquiring how he had passed the night. So you see he would have been a very profound old man, indeed, to suspect that every night, just at twelve, I looked in upon him while he slept.

Upon the eighth night I was more than usually cautious in opening the door. A watch's minute hand moves more quickly than did mine. Never before that night had I *felt* the extent of my own powers — of my sagacity. I could scarcely contain my feelings of triumph. To think that there I was, opening the door, little by little, and he not even to dream of my secret deeds or thoughts. I fairly chuckled at the idea; and perhaps he heard me; for he moved on the bed suddenly, as if startled. Now you may think that I drew back — but no. His room was as black as pitch with the thick darkness (for the shutters were close fastened, through fear of robbers), and so I knew that he could not see the opening of the door, and I kept pushing it on steadily, steadily.

I had my head in, and was about to open the lantern, when my thumb slipped upon the tin fastening, and the old man sprang up in the bed, crying out — "Who's there?"

I kept quite still and said nothing. For a whole hour I did not move a muscle, and in the meantime I did not hear him lie down. He was still sitting up in the bed listening; — just as I have done, night after night, hearkening to the death watches in the wall.

Presently I heard a slight groan, and I knew it was the groan of mortal terror. It was not a groan of pain or of grief — oh, no! — it was the low stifled sound that arises from the bottom of the soul when overcharged with awe. I knew the sound well. Many a night, just at midnight, when all the world slept, it has welled up from my own bosom, deepening with its dreadful echo, the terrors that distracted me. I say I knew it well. I knew what the old man felt, and pitied him, although I chuckled at heart. I knew that he had been lying awake ever since the first slight noise, when he had turned in the bed. His fears had been ever since growing upon him. He had been trying to fancy them causeless, but could not. He had been saying to himself — "It is nothing but the wind in the chimney — it is only a mouse crossing the floor," or "it is merely a cricket which has made a single chirp." Yes, he has been trying to comfort himself with these suppositions; but he had found all in vain. *All in vain*; because Death, in approaching him, had stalked with his black shadow before him, and enveloped the victim. And it was the mournful influence of the unperceived shadow that caused him to feel — although he neither saw nor heard — to *feel* the presence of my head within the room.

When I had waited a long time, very patiently, without hearing him lie down, I resolved to open a little — a very, very little crevice in the lantern. So I opened it — you cannot imagine how stealthily, stealthily — until, at length, a single dim ray, like the thread of the spider, shot from out the crevice and full upon the vulture eye.

It was open — wide, wide open — and I grew furious as I gazed upon it. I saw it with perfect distinctness — all a dull blue, with a hideous veil over it that chilled the very marrow in my bones, but I could see nothing else of the old man's face or person: for I had directed the ray as if by instinct, precisely upon the damned spot.

And now have I not told you that what you mistake for madness is but over-acuteness of the senses? — now, I say, there came to my ears a low, dull, quick sound, such as a watch makes when enveloped in cotton. I knew *that* sound well too. It was the beating of the old man's heart. It increased my fury, as the beating of a drum stimulates the soldier into courage.

But even yet I refrained and kept still. I scarcely breathed. I held the lantern motionless. I tried how steadily I could maintain the ray upon the eye. Meantime the hellish tattoo of the heart increased. It grew quicker and quicker, and louder and louder every instant. The old man's terror *must* have been extreme! It grew louder, I say, louder every moment! — do you mark me well? I have told you that I am nervous: so I am. And now at the dead hour of the night, amid the dreadful silence of that old house, so strange a noise as this excited me to uncontrollable terror. Yet, for some minutes longer I refrained and stood still. But the beating grew louder, louder! I thought the heart must burst. And now a new anxiety seized me — the sound would be heard by a neighbor! The old man's hour had come! With a loud yell, I threw open the lantern and leaped into the room. He shrieked once — once only. In an instant I dragged him to the floor, and pulled the heavy bed over him. I then smiled gaily, to find the deed so far done. But, for many minutes, the heart beat on with a muffled sound. This, however, did not vex me; it would not be heard through the wall. At length it ceased. The old man was dead. I removed the bed and examined the corpse. Yes, he was stone, stone dead. I placed my hand upon the heart and held it there many minutes. There was no pulsation. He was stone dead. His eye would trouble me no more.

If still you think me mad, you will think so no longer when I describe the wise precautions I took for the concealment of the body. The night waned, and I worked hastily, but in silence. First of all I dismembered the corpse. I cut off the head and the arms and the legs.

I then took up three planks from the flooring of the chamber, and deposited all between the scantlings. I then replaced the boards so cleverly, so cunningly, that no human eye — not even *his* — could have detected anything wrong. There was nothing to wash out — no stain of any kind — no blood-spot whatever. I had been too wary for that. A tub had caught all — ha! ha!

When I had made an end of these labors, it was four o'clock — still dark as midnight. As the bell sounded the hour, there came a knocking at the street door. I went down to open it with a light heart — for what had I *now* to fear? There entered three men, who introduced themselves, with perfect suavity, as officers of the police. A shriek had been heard by a neighbor during the night; suspicion of foul play had been aroused; information had been lodged at the police office, and they (the officers) had been deputed to search the premises.

I smiled — for *what* had I to fear? I bade the gentlemen welcome. The shriek, I said, was my own in a dream. The old man, I mentioned, was absent in the country. I took my visitors all over the house. I bade them search — search *well*. I led them, at length, to *his* chamber. I showed them his treasures, secure, undisturbed. In the enthusiasm of my confidence, I brought chairs into the room, and desired them *here* to rest from their fatigues, while I myself, in the wild audacity of my perfect triumph, placed my own seat upon the very spot beneath which reposed the corpse of the victim.

The officers were satisfied. My *manner* had convinced them. I was singularly at ease. They sat, and while I answered cheerily, they chatted familiar things. But, ere long, I felt myself getting pale and wished them gone. My head ached, and I fancied a ringing in my ears: but still they sat and still they chatted. The ringing became more distinct: — it continued and became more distinct: I talked more freely to get rid of the feeling: but it continued and gained definitiveness — until, at length, I found that the noise was *not* within my ears.

No doubt I now grew *very* pale; — but I talked more fluently, and with a heightened voice. Yet the sound increased — and what could I do? It was *a low, dull, quick sound — much such a sound as a watch makes when enveloped in cotton.* I gasped for breath — and yet the officers heard it not. I talked more quickly — more vehemently; but the noise steadily increased. I arose and argued about trifles, in a high key and with violent gesticulations, but the noise steadily increased. Why *would* they not be gone? I paced the floor to and fro with heavy strides, as if excited to fury by the observation of the men — but the noise steadily increased. Oh God! what *could* I do? I foamed — I raved — I swore! I swung the chair upon which I had been sitting, and grated it upon the boards, but the noise arose over all and continually increased. It grew louder — louder — *louder*! And still the men chatted pleasantly, and smiled. Was it possible they heard not? Almighty God! — no, no! They heard! — they suspected! — they *knew*! — they were making a mockery of my horror! — this I thought, and this I think. But any thing was better than this agony! Any thing was more tolerable than this derision! I could bear those hypocritical smiles no longer! I felt that I must scream or die! — and now — again! — hark! louder! louder! louder! *louder!* —

"Villains!" I shrieked, "dissemble no more! I admit the deed! — tear up the planks! — here, here! — it is the beating of his hideous heart!"

Katherine Anne Porter

Katherine Anne Porter (1890–1980) was born Callie Russell Porter in Indian Creek, Texas. When she was only two years old her mother died. Educated at boarding schools and an Ursuline convent, Porter worked briefly as a reporter in Chicago and Denver. As a child she had wanted to be a writer, but it took fifteen years of serious writing before she trusted herself enough as a stylist to approach a publisher. Most of her life during this time was a financial struggle; she spent only 10 percent of her energies on writing, and "the other 90 percent went to keeping my head above water." She nearly lost her life in the influenza epidemic that swept the United States at the end of World War I, and when she recovered, she went to Mexico to study Aztec and Mayan art.

There she found herself "smack into the Obregón revolution" of 1921, the setting of her story "Flowering Judas." She published her first story, "Maria Concepción," in *Century* magazine one year later, and achieved acclaim as a writer with her first collection of short stories, *Flowering Judas and Other Stories*, in 1930. Her most productive decade as a writer was the 1930s, when she published *Noon Wine* (1937) and *Pale Horse, Pale Rider: Three Short Novels* (1939). She supported herself with lecture tours and teaching jobs at various universities while she worked on her novel *Ship of Fools* (1962), which took over two decades to complete. In 1965 her *Collected Stories* won both the Pulitzer Prize and the National Book Award.

Porter's style is not so recognizably "southern" as William Faulkner's or Flannery O'Connor's. She was a southerner by tradition and inheritance, but she had thought of herself since childhood as "always restless, always a roving spirit." She was very conscious of her own art as a storyteller, and of the art of fiction in general; she wrote personal essays on Willa Cather, Katherine Mansfield, Flannery O'Connor, Eudora Welty, and Virginia Woolf. Particularly indebted in her best stories to Mansfield, Porter attempted to dramatize a character's state of mind rather than develop a complicated plot. Her analysis of Mansfield's literary practice in the essay "The Art of Katherine Mansfield" can also be applied to a story such as "Maria Concepción":

> With fine objectivity, she bares a moment of experience, real experience,
> in the life of some one human being; she states no belief, gives no motives,
> airs no theories, but simply presents to the reader a situation, a place, and a
> character, and there it is; and the emotional content is present as implicitly
> as the germ is in the grain of wheat.

Maria Concepción

1922

MARIA CONCEPCIÓN WALKED CAREFULLY, keeping to the middle of the white, dusty road, where the maguey thorns and the treacherous curved spines of organa cactus had not gathered so profusely. She would have enjoyed resting for a moment in the dark shade by the roadside, but she had no time to waste drawing cactus needles from her feet. Juan and his *jefe* would be waiting for their food in the damp trenches of the buried city.

She carried about a dozen living fowls slung over her right shoulder, their feet fastened together. Half of them fell upon the flat of her back, the balance dangled uneasily over her breast. They wriggled their benumbed and swollen legs against her neck, they twisted their stupefied, half-blind eyes upward, seeming to peer into her face inquiringly. She did not see them or think of them. Her left arm was a trifle tired with the weight of the food basket, and she was hungry after her long morning's work.

Under her clean bright-blue cotton rebozo her straight back outlined itself strongly. Instinctive serenity softened her black eyes, shaped like almonds set far apart, and tilted a bit endwise. She walked with the free, natural, yet guarded, ease of the primitive woman carrying an unborn child. The shape of her body, was easy, the swelling life was not a distortion, but the right, inevitable proportions of a woman. She was entirely contented, calmly filled with a sense of the goodness of life.

Her small house was half-way up a shallow hill, under a clump of peru-trees, a wall of organa cactus inclosing it on the side nearest the road. Now she came down into the valley, divided by the narrow spring, and crossed a bridge of loose stones near the hut where Maria Rosa the bee-keeper lived with her old godmother, Lupe, the medicine-woman. Maria Concepción had no faith in the charred owl bones, the singed rabbit fur, the messes and ointments sold by Lupe to the ailing of the village. She was a good Christian, and bought her remedies, bottled, with printed directions that she could not read, at the drug-store near the city market, where she went almost daily with her fowls. But she often purchased a jar of honey from young Maria Rosa, a pretty, shy child only fifteen years old.

Maria Concepción and her husband, Juan Villegas, were each a little past their eighteenth year. She had a good reputation with the neighbors as an energetic, religious woman. It was commonly known that if she wished to buy a new rebozo for herself or a shirt for Juan, she could bring out a sack of hard silver pesos for the purpose.

She had paid for the license, nearly a year ago, the potent bit of stamped paper which permits people to be married in the church. She had given money to the priest before she and Juan walked together up to the altar the Monday after Holy Week. It had been the adventure of the villagers to go, three Sundays one after another, to hear the banns called by the priest for Juan de Dios Villegas and Maria Concepción Gutierrez. After the wedding she had called herself Maria Concepción Gutierrez de Villegas, as though she owned a whole hacienda.

She paused on the bridge and dabbled her feet in the water, her eyes resting themselves from the sun-rays in a fixed, dreaming gaze to the far-off mountains, deeply blue under their hanging drift of clouds. It came to her that she would like a fresh crust of honey. The delicious aroma of bees, their slow, thrilling hum poured upon her, awakening a pleasant desire for a crisp flake of sweetness in her mouth.

"If I do not eat it now, I shall mark my child," she thought, peering through the crevices in the thick hedge of cactus that sheered up nakedly, like prodigious bared knife-blades cast protectingly around the small clearing. The place was so silent that she doubted if Maria Rosa and Lupe were at home.

The leaning *jacal* of dried rush-withes and corn-sheaves, bound to tall saplings thrust into the earth, roofed with yellowed maguey-leaves flattened and overlapping like shingles, sat drowsy and fragrant in the warmth of noonday. The hives, similarly constructed, were scattered toward the back of the clearing, like small mounds of clean vegetable refuse. Over each mound there hung a dusty golden shimmer of bees.

A light, gay scream of laughter rose from behind the hut; a man's short laugh joined in. "Ah, Maria Rosa has a *novio!*" Maria Concepción stopped short, smiling, shifted her burden slightly, bending forward to see more clearly through the hedge spaces, shading her eyes.

Maria Rosa ran, dodging between beehives, parting two stunted jasmine-bushes as she came, lifting her knees in swift leaps, looking over her shoulder and laughing in a quivering, excited way. A heavy jar, swung by the handle to her wrist, knocked against her thighs as she ran. Her toes pushed up sudden spurts of dust, her half-unbraided hair showered around her shoulders in long crinkled wisps.

Juan Villegas ran after her, also laughing strangely, his teeth set, both rows gleaming behind the small, soft black beard growing sparsely on his lips, his chin, leaving his brown cheeks girl-smooth. When he seized her, he clenched so hard that her chemise gave way and slipped off her shoulder. Frightened, she stopped laughing, pushed him away, and stood silent, trying to pull up the ripped sleeve with one hand. Her pointed chin and dark-red mouth moved in an uncertain way, as if she wished to laugh again; her long black lashes flickered with the tiny quick-moving lights in her half-hidden eyes.

Maria Concepción realized that she had not stirred or breathed for some seconds. Her forehead was cold, and yet boiling water seemed to be pouring slowly along her spine. An unaccountable pain was in her knees, as though pieces of ice had got into them. She was afraid Juan and Maria Rosa would feel her eyes fixed upon them, and find her there, unable to move. But they did not pass beyond the inclosure, or even glance toward the gap in the wall opening upon the road.

Juan lifted one of Maria Rosa's half-bound braids and slapped her neck with it, playfully. She smiled with soft, expectant shyness. Together they moved back through the hives of honey-comb. Juan flourished his wide hat back and forth, walking very proudly. Maria Rosa balanced her jar on one hip, and swung her long, full petticoats with every step.

Maria Concepción came out of the heavy darkness which seemed to enwrap her head and bind her at the throat, and found herself walking onward, keeping the road by instinct, feeling her way delicately, her ears strumming as if all Maria Rosa's bees had hived in them. Her careful sense of duty kept her moving toward the buried city where Juan's chief, the American archæologist, was taking his midday rest, waiting for his dinner.

Juan and Maria Rosa! She burned all over now, as if a layer of those tiny fig-cactus bristles, as insidious and petty-cruel as spun glass, had crawled under her skin. She wished to sit down quietly and wait for her death without finishing what she had set out to do, remembering no more those two strange people, Juan and Maria Rosa, laughing and kissing in the sweet-smelling sunshine. Once, years before, when she was a young girl, she had returned from market to find her *jacal* burned to a pile of ash and her few pesos gone. An incredibly lost and empty feeling had possessed her; she had kept moving about the place, unbelieving, somehow expecting it all to take shape again before her eyes, restored unchanged. But it was all gone. And now here was a worse thing. This was something that could not happen. But it was true. Maria Rosa, that sinful girl, shameless!

She heard herself saying a harsh, true word about Maria Rosa, saying it aloud as if she expected some one to answer, "Yes, you are right." At this moment the gray, untidy head of Givens appeared over the edges of the newest trench he had caused to be dug in his field of excavations. The long, deep crevasses, in which a man might stand without being seen, lay crisscrossed like orderly gashes of a giant scalpel. Nearly all the men of the small community were employed by Givens in this work of uncovering the lost city of their ancestors. They worked all the year through and prospered, digging all day for those small clay heads and bits of pottery for which there was no use on earth, they being all broken and covered with earth. They themselves could make better ones, perfectly stout and new. But the unearthly delight of the *jefe* in finding these things was an endless puzzle. He would fairly roar for joy at times, waving a shattered pot or a human rib-bone above his head, shouting for his photographer to come and make a picture of this!

Now he emerged, and his young enthusiast's eyes welcomed Maria Concepción from his old-man face, covered with hard wrinkles, burned to the color of red earth under the countless suns of his explorer's life.

"I hope you've brought me a nice fat one." He selected a fowl from the bunch dangling nearest him as Maria Concepción, wordless, leaned over the trench. "Dress it for me, there's a good girl. I'll broil it."

Maria Concepción took the fowl by the head, and silently, swiftly drew the knife across the throat, twisting off the head with the casual firmness one might use with the top of a beet.

"*Dios*, woman, but you have valor!" said Givens, watching her. "I can't do that. It makes me creep."

"My home country is Guadalajara," answered Maria Concepción, without bravado. "There we have valor for everything."

She stood and regarded Givens condescendingly, that diverting white man who had no woman to cook for him, and, moreover, appeared not to feel any loss of dignity in preparing his own food. He knelt now, eyes squinted tightly, nose wrinkled, trying to avoid the smoke, turning the roasting fowl busily on a stick. Juan's *jefe*, therefore to be humored, to be placated.

"The tortillas are fresh and hot, Señor," she murmured. "By permission, I will now go to market."

"Yes, yes, run along; bring me another to-morrow." Givens turned his head to look at her again. Her grand manner reminded him of royalty in exile. He noticed her unnatural paleness. "The sun is too hot, eh?" he asked.

"*Si*, Señor. Pardon me, but Juan will be here soon?"

"He should be, the scamp. Leave his food. The others will eat it."

She moved away; the blue of her rebozo became a dancing spot in the heat vibrations that appeared to rise from the gray-red soil. Givens considered her exceptionally intelligent. He liked to tell stories of Juan's escapades also, of how often he had saved him, within the last five years, from going to jail, or even from being shot, for his varied and highly imaginative misdemeanors.

"I am never a minute too soon," he would say indulgently. "Well, why not? He is a good worker. He never intentionally did harm in his life."

After Juan was married, he used to twit him, with exactly the right shade of condescension, on his many infidelities to Maria Concepción. He was fond of saying, "She'll discover you yet, young demon!" which would please Juan immensely.

Maria Concepción did not think of telling Juan she had found him out, but she kept saying to herself, "If I had been a young girl like Maria Rosa, and a man had caught hold of me so, I would have broken my jar over his head." Her anger was all against Maria Rosa because she had not done this.

Less than a week after this the two culprits went away to war, Juan as a common soldier, Maria Rosa as his *soldadera*. She bowed her neck under a heavy and onerous yoke of duties: she carried the blankets and the cooking-pots, she slept on stones or dry branches, she marched ahead of the troops, with the battalion of experienced women of war, in search of provisions. She ate with them what was left after the men had eaten. After battles she went out on the field with the others to salvage clothing and guns and ammunition from the slain before they should begin to spoil in the heat.

This was the life the little bee-keeper found at the end of her runaway journey. There was no particular scandal in the village. People shrugged. It was far better for every one that they were gone. There was a popular belief among her neighbors that Maria Concepción was not so mild as she seemed.

When she learned about her man and that shameless girl she did not weep. Later, when the baby was born, and died within four days, she did not weep. "She is mere stone," said old Lupe, who had offered all her charms for the preservation of the little life, and had been rebuffed with a ferocity that appalled her.

If Maria Concepción had not gone so regularly to church, lighting candles before the saints and receiving holy communion at the altar every month, there might have been talk of her being devil-possessed, her face was so changed and blind-looking. But this was impossible when, after all, she had been married by the priest. It must be, they reasoned, that she was being punished for her pride. They decided this was the true reason: she was altogether too proud.

During the two years that Juan and Maria Rosa were gone Maria Concepción sold her fowls and looked after her house, and her sack of hard pesos grew. Lupe had no talent for bees, and the hives did not prosper. She used to see Maria Concepción in the market or at church, and afterward she always said that no one could tell by looking that she was a woman who had such a heavy grief.

"I pray God everything goes well with Maria Concepción from this out," she would say, "for she has had her share of trouble."

When some idle person repeated this to the deserted woman, she went down to Lupe's house and stood within the clearing, and called to the medicine-woman, who sat in her doorway stirring a jar of fresh snake's grease and rabbit blood, a cure for sores:

"Keep your prayers to yourself, Lupe, or offer them for others who need them. I will ask God for what I want in this world."

"And will you get it, you think, Maria Concepción?" asked Lupe, tittering cruelly, and smelling the mixture clinging to the wooden spoon. "Did you pray for what you have now?"

Afterward every one noticed that Maria Concepción went more often to church, and less to the village to talk with the other women as they sat along the curb, eating fruit and nursing their infants, at the end of the market-day.

"After all, she is wrong to take us for her enemies," said grave old Sole-dad, who always thought such things out. "All women have these troubles. Well, we should suffer together."

But Maria Concepción lived alone. She was thin, as if something was gnawing her away inside, her eyes were sunken, and she spoke no more than was necessary. She worked harder than ever, and her butchering knife was scarcely ever out of her hand.

Juan and Maria Rosa, tired of military life, came home one day without asking permission of any authority whatever. The field of war had unrolled itself, a long scroll of vexations, until the end had frayed out within twenty miles of Juan's village. So he and his *soldadera*, now as lean as a wolf, and burdened with a child daily expected, set out with no ostentation and walked home.

They arrived one morning about daybreak. Juan was picked up on sight by a group of military police from the small *cuartel* on the edge of town, who told him with impersonal cheerfulness that he would add one to a group of ten waiting to be shot next morning as deserters.

Maria Rosa, screaming, and falling on her face in the road, was taken under the armpits by two guards and helped briskly to her own *jacal*, now sadly run down. She was received with professional calm by Lupe, who hastily set about the business obviously in hand.

Limping with foot weariness, a layer of dust concealing his fine new clothes, got mysteriously from somewhere, Juan appeared before the captain of the *cuartel.* The captain recognized him as the chief digger for his good friend Givens. He despatched a note in haste to that kindly and eccentric person.

Shortly afterward, Givens showed up at the *cuartel*, and Juan was delivered to him, with the urgent request that nothing be made public about so humane and sensible an operation on the part of military authority.

Juan walked out of the rather stifling atmosphere of the drumhead court, a definite air of swagger about him. His hat, incredibly huge and embroidered with silver thread, hung over one eyebrow, secured at the back by a cord of silver dripping with cobalt-blue tassels. His shirt was of a checkerboard pattern in green and black, his white cotton trousers were bound by a belt of yellow leather tooled in red. His feet were bare, the beautifully arched and muscled feet of the Indian, with long, flexible toes.

He removed his cigarette from the corner of his full-lipped, wide mouth. He removed the splendid hat. His black hair, pressed damply to his forehead, sprang up suddenly in a cloudy thatch on his crown.

"You young devil," said Givens, a trifle shaken, "some day I shall be five minutes too late!"

Juan bowed to the officer, who appeared to be gazing at a vacuum. He swung his arm wide in a free circle up-soaring toward the prison window, where forlorn heads poked over the window-sill, hot eyes following the lucky departing one. Two or three of them flipped a hand in response, with a gallant effort to imitate his own casual and heady manner.

He kept up this insufferable pantomime until they rounded the first sheltering clump of fig-cactus. Then he seized Givens's hand, and his eyes blazed adoration and gratitude.

"With all my life, all my life, I thank thee!" he said. "It is nothing to be shot, *mi jefe*, — certainly you know I was not afraid, — but to be shot in a drove of deserters, against a cold wall, by order of that — "

Glittering epithets tumbled over one another like explosions of a rocket. All the scandalous analogies from the animal and vegetable worlds were applied in a vivid, unique, and personal way to the life, loves, and family history of the harmless young officer who had just set him free. But Juan cared nothing for this; his gratitude to his *jefe* excluded all other possible obligations.

"What will Maria Concepción say to all this?" asked Givens. "You are very informal, Juan, for a man who was married in the church."

Juan put on his hat.

"Oh, Maria Concepción! That's nothing! Look you, *mi jefe*, to be married in the church is a great misfortune to a man. After that he is not himself any more. How can that woman complain when I do not drink, not even on days of fiesta, more than a glass of pulque? I do not beat her; never, never. We were always at peace. I say to her, 'Come here,' and she comes straight. I say, 'Go there,' and she goes quickly. Yet sometimes I looked at her and thought, 'Now I am married to that woman in the church,' and I felt a sinking inside, as if something were lying heavy on my stomach. With Maria Rosa it is all different. She is not silent; she talks. When she talks too much, I slap her and say, 'Silence, thou simpleton!' and she weeps. She is just a girl with whom I do as

I please. You know how she used to keep those clean little bees in their hives? She always smelt of their honey. I swear it. I would not harm Maria Concepción because I am married to her in the church; but also, *mi jefe,* I will not leave Maria Rosa, because she pleases me more than any other woman."

"Let me tell you, Juan, Maria Concepción will some day take your head off with that sharp knife she uses on the fowls. Then you will remember what I have said."

Juan's expression was the proper blend of sentimental triumph and melancholy. It was pleasant to think of himself in the role of romantic hero to two such desirable women. His present situation was ineffably perfect. He had just escaped from the threat of a disagreeable end. His clothes were new and handsome. He was on his way to work and civilian life with his patient *jefe.* He was little more than twenty years old. Life tasted good, for a certainty. He fairly smacked his lips on its savor.

The early sunshine, the light, clear air, full of the good smell of ripening cactus-figs, peaches, and melons, of pungent pepper-berries dangling in bright red clusters on the peru-trees, the very smell of his cigarette, shook him with a merry ecstasy of good-will for all life, whatever it was.

"Señor,"—he addressed his friend handsomely, as one man to another, — "women are good things, but not at this moment. By your permission, I will now go to the village and eat. To-morrow morning very early I will come to the buried city and work. Let us forget Maria Concepción and Maria Rosa. Each one in her place. I will manage them when the time comes."

News of Juan's adventure soon got abroad, and Juan found many friends about him during the morning. They frankly commended his leaving the army. *Por Dios!* a man could do no better thing than that! The new hero ate a great deal and drank a little, the occasion being better than a feast-day. It was almost noon before he returned to visit Maria Rosa.

He found her sitting on a straw mat, rubbing oil on her three-hour-old son. Before this felicitous vision Juan's emotions so twisted him that he returned to the village and invited every man in the "Death and Resurrection" *pulqueria* to drink with him.

Having thus taken leave of his balance, he found himself unaccountably back in his own house after his long absence, attempting to beat Maria Concepción by way of reestablishing himself in his legal household.

Maria Concepción, knowing what had happened in the withe hut of her enemy, knowing all the events of that unhappy day, refused to be beaten by Juan drunk when Juan sober had never thought of such a thing. She did not scream; she stood her ground and resisted; she even struck at him.

Juan, amazed, only half comprehending his own actions, stepped back and gazed at her questioningly through a leisurely whirling film which seemed to have lodged behind his eyes. Certainly here was a strange thing. He had not intended to touch her. Oh, well, no harm done. He gave up, turned away. Sleep was better. He lay down amiably in a shadowed corner and floated away dreamlessly.

Maria Concepción, seeing that Juan was quiet, began automatically to bind the legs of her fowls. It was market-day, and she would be late.

Her movements were quick and rigid, like a doll jerked about on strings. She fumbled and tangled the bits of cord in her haste, and set off across the plowed, heavy fields instead of taking the accustomed road. She ran grotesquely, in uneven, jolting leaps between furrows, a crazy panic in her head, in her stumbling legs. She seemed not to know her directions. Now and then she would stop and look about, trying to place herself, then proceed a few steps.

At once, with an inner quivering, she came to her senses completely, recognized the thing that troubled her so terribly, was certain of what she wanted. She sat down quietly under a sheltering thorny bush and gave herself over to her long and devouring sorrow; flinched and shuddered away for the first time from that pain in the heart that pressed and pressed intolerably, until she wished to tear out the heart with her hands to be eased of it. The thing which had for so long squeezed her whole body into a tight, dumb knot of suffering suddenly broke with painful and shocking violence. She jerked with the involuntary recoil of one who receives a blow, and the tears poured from her eyes as if the wounds of her whole life were shedding their salt ichor. Drawing her rebozo over her head, she bowed her forehead on her arms, folded upon her updrawn knees, and wept.

After a great while she sat up, throwing the rebozo off her face, and leaned against the clustered saplings of the bush, arms relaxed at her sides, her face still, her eyes swollen, the lids closed and heavy. She sat there in deadly silence and immobility, the tears still forming steadily under the lashes, as if poured from an inexhaustible, secret, slow-moving river. She seemed to be crying in her sleep. From time to time she would lift the corner of her rebozo to wipe her face dry; and silently the tears would run again, streaking her face, drenching the front of her chemise. She had that complete and horrifying realization of calamity which is not a thing of the mind, but a physical experience as sharp and certain as the bite of thorns. All her being was a dark, confused memory of an endless loss, of grief burning in the heart by night, of deadly baffled anger eating at her by day, until her feet were as heavy as if she were mired in the muddy roads during the time of rains.

Juan awakened slowly, with long yawns and grumblings, alternated with short relapses into sleep full of visions and clamorous noises. A blur of orange light seared his eyeballs when he tried to unseal his lids. There came from somewhere a rapid confusion of words, a low voice weeping without tears, speaking awful meaningless phrases over and over. He began to listen. He strained and tugged at the leash of his stupor, he sweated to grasp those words which should have fearful meanings, yet somehow he could not comprehend them. Then he came awake with frightening suddenness, sitting up, eyes straining at the long, lashing streak of gilded light piercing the corn-husk walls from the level, disappearing sun.

Maria Concepción stood in the doorway, looming colossally tall to his shocked eyes. She was talking quickly, calling to him. Then he saw her clearly.

"*Por Dios!*" thought Juan, frozen with amazement, "here I am facing my death!" for the long knife she wore habitually at her belt was in her hand. But instead, she threw it away, clear from her, and got down on her knees, crawling toward him as he had seen her crawl toward the shrine at Guadalupe many times. Never had she knelt before him! He watched her approach with superstitious horror. Falling forward upon her face, she kissed his feet. She huddled upon his knees, lips moving urgently in a thrilling whisper. Her words became clear, and Juan understood them all.

For a second he could not speak. He sat immovable. Then he took her head between both his hands, and supported her somewhat in this way, saying swiftly, anxiously reassuring, almost in a babble:

"Oh, thou poor creature! Oh, thou dear woman! Oh, my Maria Concepción, unfortunate! Listen! do not fear! Hear me! I will hide thee away, I, thy own man, will protect thee! Quiet! Not a sound!"

Trying to collect himself, he held and soothed her as they sat together in the new darkness. Maria Concepción bent over, face almost upon his knees, her feet folded under her, seeking security of him. For the first time in his careless, utterly unafraid existence Juan was aware of danger. This was danger. Maria Concepción would be dragged away between two gendarmes, with him helpless and unarmed, to spend her days in Belem Prison, maybe. Danger! The night was peopled with tangible menaces. He stood up, dragging the woman to her feet with him. She was silent now, perfectly rigid, holding to him with resistless strength, her hands frozen on his arms.

"Get me the knife," he told her in a whisper. She obeyed, her feet slipping along the hard earth floor, her shoulders straight, her arms stiffened downward. He lighted a candle. Maria Concepción held the knife out to him. It was stained and dark even to the end of the handle, a thick stain with a viscous gleam.

He frowned at her harshly, noting the same stains on her chemise and hands.

"Take off thy clothes and wash thy hands," he ordered. He washed the knife carefully, and threw the water wide of the doorway. She watched him, and did likewise with the bowl where she had bathed.

"Light thy brasero and cook food for me," he told her in the same peremptory tone. He took her garments and went out. When he returned, she was wearing an old soiled dress, and was fanning the foe in the charcoal-burner. Seating himself cross-legged near her, he stared at her as at a creature unknown to him, who bewildered him utterly, for whom there was no possible explanation. She did not turn her head, but kept an oblivious silence and stillness, save for the movement of her strong hands fanning the blaze which cast sparks and small jets of white smoke, flaring and dying rhythmically with the motion of the fan, lighting her face and leaving it in darkness by turns.

"*Tu mujer*," —Juan's voice barely disturbed the silence, — "listen now to me carefully, and answer my questions as I ask them, and later, when the gendarmes come here for us, thou shalt have nothing to fear. But there will be something to settle between us afterward."

She turned her head slowly at this. The light from the fire cast small red sparks into the corners of her eyes; a yellow phosphorescence glimmered behind the dark iris.

"For me it is all settled, *Juanito mio*," she answered, without fear, in a tone so tender, so grave, so heavy with sorrow, that Juan felt his vitals contract. He wished to weep openly not as a man, but as a very small child. He could not fathom this woman, or the mysterious fortunes of life grown so instantly tangled where all had seemed so gay and simple. He felt, too, that she had become unique and invaluable, a woman without an equal in a million women, and he could not tell why. He drew an enormous sigh that rattled in his chest.

"*Si, si*, it is all settled. I shall not go away again. We shall stay here together, you and I, forever."

In whispers he questioned her, and she answered whispering, and he instructed her over and over until she had her lesson by heart. The profound blackness of the night encroached upon them, flowing over the narrow threshold, invading their hearts. It brought with it sighs and murmurs, the pad of ghostly feet in the near-by road, the sharp staccato whimper of wind through the cactus-leaves. All these familiar cadences were now invested with sinister terrors; a dread, formless and uncontrollable, possessed them both.

"Light another candle," said Juan, aloud, suddenly, in too resolute, in too hard a tone. "Let us eat now."

They sat facing each other and ate from the same dish, after their old habit. Neither tasted what they ate. With food half-way to his mouth, Juan listened. The sound of voices grew, spread, widened at the turn of the road, along the organa wall. A spray of lantern-light filtered through the hedge, a single voice slashed the blackness, literally ripped the fragile layer of stillness which hovered above the hut.

"Juan Villegas!"

"Pass, friends!" Juan cried cheerfully.

They stood in the doorway, simple, cautious gendarmes from the village, partly Indian themselves, personally known to all the inhabitants. They flashed their lanterns almost apologetically upon the pleasant, harmless scene of a man eating supper with his wife.

"Pardon, Brother," said the leader. "Some one has killed the woman Maria Rosa, and we must ask questions of all her neighbors and friends." He paused, and added with an attempt at severity, "Naturally!"

"Naturally," agreed Juan. "I was a good friend of Maria Rosa. I regret her bad fortune."

They all went away together, the men walking in a group, Maria Concepción following a trifle to one side, a few steps in the rear, but near Juan, This was the custom. There was no thought of changing it even for such an important occasion.

The two points of candle-light at Maria Rosa's head fluttered uneasily; the shadows shifted and dodged on the stained, darkened walls. To Maria Concepción everything in the smothering, inclosing room shared an evil restlessness. The watchful faces of those called as witnesses, those familiar faces of old friends, were made alien by that look of speculation in the eyes. The ridges of the rose-colored silk rebozo thrown over the body varied continually, as though the thing it covered was not perfectly in repose. Her eyes swerved over the body from the candle-tips at the head to the feet, jutting up thinly, the small, scarred soles protruding, freshly washed, a mass of crooked, half-healed wounds, thorn-pricks and cuts of sharp stones. Her gaze went back to the candle-flare, to Juan's eyes warning her, to the gendarmes talking among themselves. Her eyes would not be controlled.

With a leap that shook her her gaze settled upon the face of Maria Rosa. Instantly, her blood ran smoothly again: there was nothing to fear. Even the restless light could not give a look of life to that fixed countenance. She was dead. Maria Concepción felt her muscles give way softly; her heart began beating without effort. She knew no more rancor against that pitiable thing, lying indifferently on its new mat under the fine silk rebozo. The mouth drooped sharply at the corners in a grimace of weeping arrested half-way. The brows were strangely distressed; the dead could not cast off some dark, final obsession of terror. It was all finished. Maria Rosa had eaten too much honey and had had too much love. Now she must sit in hell, crying over her sins and her hard death forever and ever.

Old Lupe's cackling voice arose. She had spent the morning helping Maria Rosa. The child had spat blood the moment it was born, a bad sign. She thought then that bad luck would come to the house. Well, about sunset she was in the yard at the back of the house grinding tomatoes and pepper. She had left mother and babe asleep. She heard a strange noise in the house, a choking and smothered calling, like some one in the nightmare. Well, such a thing is only natural. But there followed a light, quick, thudding sound —

"Like the blows of a fist?" interrupted the officer.

"No, not at all like such a thing."

"How do you know?"

"I am acquainted with that sound, Señor," retorted Lupe. "This noise was something else."

But she was at a loss to describe it exactly. Immediately, there was a slight rattle of pebbles rolling and slipping under feet; then she knew some one had been there and was running away.

"Why did you wait so long before going to see?"

"I am old and hard in the joints," said Lupe; "I cannot run after people. I walked as fast as I could to the organa hedge, for it is only by this way that any one can enter. There was no one in the road, Señor, no one. Three cows, with a dog driving them; nothing else. When I got to Maria Rosa, she was lying all tangled up, and from her neck to her middle she was full of knife-holes. It was a sight to move the Blessed Image Himself! Her mouth and eyes were — "

"Never mind. Who came oftenest to her house? Who were her enemies?"

The old face congealed, closed. Her spongy skin drew into a network of secretive wrinkles. She turned withdrawn and expressionless eyes upon the gendarmes.

"I am an old woman; I do not see well; I cannot hurry on my feet. I did not see any one leave the clearing."

"You did not hear splashing in the spring near the bridge?"

"No, Señor."

"Why, then, do our dogs follow a scent there and lose it?"

"*Solo Dios sabe*, Señor. I am an old wo —"

"How did the footfalls sound?" broke in the officer, hastily.

"Like the tread of an evil spirit!" intoned Lupe in a swelling oracular tone startling to the listeners. The Indians stirred among themselves, watchfully. To them the medicine-woman was an incalculable force. They half expected her to pronounce a charm that would produce the evil spirit among them at once.

The gendarme's politeness began to wear thin.

"No, poor fool; I mean, were they heavy or light? The footsteps of a man or of a woman? Was the person shod or barefoot?"

A glance at the listening circle assured Lupe of their thrilled attention. She enjoyed the prominence, the menacing importance, of her situation. What she had not seen she could not describe, thank God! No one could harm her because her knees were stiff and she could not run even to seize a murderer. As for knowing the difference between footfalls, shod or bare, man or woman, nay, even as between devil and human, who ever heard of such madness?

"My ears are not eyes, Señor," she ended grandly; "but upon my heart I swear those footsteps fell as the tread of the spirit of evil!"

"*Loca!*" yapped the gendarme in a shrill voice. "Take her away somebody! Juan Villegas, tell me —"

Juan told him everything he knew, patiently, several times over. He had returned to his wife that day. She had gone to market as usual. He had helped her prepare her fowls. She had returned about mid-afternoon, they had talked, she had cooked, they had eaten. Nothing was amiss. Then the gendarmes came. That was all. Yes, Maria Rosa had gone away with him, but there had been no bad blood on this account between him and his wife or Maria Rosa. Everybody knew that his wife was a quiet woman.

Maria Concepción heard her own voice answering without a break. It was true at first she was troubled when her husband went away, but after that she had not cared. It was the way of men, she believed. Well, he had come home, thank God! She had gone to market, but had returned early, because now she had her man to cook for. That was all.

Other voices followed. A toothless old man said, "But she is a woman of good repute among us, and Maria Rosa was not." A smiling young mother, Anita, baby at breast, said: "But if no one thinks so, how can you accuse her? Should not a woman's own husband know best where she was at all times?" Another: "Maria Rosa had a strange life, apart from us. How do we know who may have wished her evil?"

Maria Concepción suddenly felt herself guarded, surrounded, upborne by her faithful friends. They were all about her, speaking for her, defending her, refusing to admit ill of her. The forces of life were ranged invincibly with her against the vanquished dead. Maria Rosa had forfeited her share in their loyalty. What did they really believe? How much had old Lupe seen? She looked from one to the other of the circling faces. Their eyes gave back reassurance, understanding, a secret and mighty sympathy.

The gendarmes were at a loss. They, too, felt that sheltering wall cast impenetrably around the woman they had meant to accuse of murder. They watched her closely. They questioned several people over again. There was no prying open the locked doors of their defenses.

A small bundle lying against the wall at the head of the body squirmed like an eel. A wail, a mere sliver of sound, issued. Maria Concepción took the almost forgotten son of Maria Rosa in her arms.

"He is mine," she said clearly; "I will take him with me."

No one assented in words, but she felt an approving nod, a bare breath of friendly agreement, run around the tight, hot room.

The gendarmes gave up. Nobody could be accused; there was not a shred of true evidence. Well, then, good night to everybody. Many pardons for having intruded. Good health!

Maria Concepción, carrying the child, followed Juan from the clearing. The hut was left with its lighted candles and a group of old women who would sit up all night, drinking coffee and smoking and relating pious tales of horror.

Juan's exaltation had burned down. There was not an ember of excitement left in him. He was tired; the high sense of adventure was faded. Maria Rosa was vanished, to come no more forever. Their days of marching, of eating, of fighting, of making love, were all over. To-morrow he would go back to dull and endless labor, he would descend into the trenches of the buried city as Maria Rosa would go into her grave. He felt his veins fill up with bitterness, with black and unendurable melancholy. *O Dios!* what strange fortunes overtake a man!

Well, there was no way out of it. For the moment he craved to forget in sleep. He found himself so drowsy he could hardly guide his feet. The occasional light touch of the woman at his elbow was unreal, as ghostly as the brushing of a leaf against his face. Having secured her safety, compelled by an instinct he could not in the least comprehend, he forgot her. There survived in him only a vast blind hurt like a covered wound.

He entered the *jacal,* and, without waiting to light a candle, threw off his clothing, sitting just within the door. He moved with lagging, half-awake hands, seeking to strip his outwearied body of its heavy finery. With a long groaning sigh of relief he fell straight back on the floor, almost instantly asleep, his arms flung up and out in the simple attitude of exhaustion.

Maria Concepción, a small clay jar in her hand, approached the gentle little mother goat tethered to a sapling, which gave and yielded as she pulled at the rope's-end after the farthest reaches of grass about her. The kid, tied up a few yards away, rose bleating, its feathery fleece shivering in the fresh wind. Sitting on her heels, holding his tether, she allowed him to suckle a few moments. Afterward — all her movements very deliberate and even — she drew a supply of milk for the child.

She sat against the wall of her house, near the doorway. The child, fed and asleep, was cradled in the hollow of her crossed legs. The silence overfilled the world, the skies flowed down evenly to the rim of the valley, the stealthy moon crept slantwise to the shelter of the mountains. She felt soft and warm all over; she dreamed that the newly born child was her own, and she was resting deliciously.

Maria Concepción could hear Juan's breathing. The sound vapored from the low doorway, calmly; the house seemed to be resting after a burdensome day. She breathed, too, very slowly and quietly, each inspiration saturating her with repose. The child's light, faint breath was a mere shadowy moth of sound flitting in the silver air. The night, the earth under her, seemed to swell and recede together with a vast, unhurried, benign breathing. She drooped and closed her eyes, feeling the slow rise and fall within her own body. She did not know what it was, but it eased her all through. Even as she was falling asleep, head bowed over the child, she was still aware of a strange, wakeful happiness.

William Sydney Porter (O. Henry)

William Sydney Porter (1862–1910), who wrote under the name O. Henry, was born in Greensboro, North Carolina. After rudimentary schooling he worked in a drugstore; then at the age of fourteen he moved to Texas, where he took a series of jobs over the next twenty years as a rancher, a bank teller, and the editor of a humorous weekly magazine called the *Rolling Stone.* In 1896 he fled to Honduras after being indicted for alleged embezzlement of funds from the bank that had employed him. He protested his innocence, but he was arrested and convicted of the crime when he returned to the United States to be with his dying wife. While serving three years in the federal penitentiary in Columbus, Ohio, Porter began to write short stories under the pseudonym of O. Henry. It is thought that he got the idea for the name from a reference book he used at his job in the prison pharmacy.

After his release from prison, Porter settled in New York City and began to contribute stories to the *New York World* on a regular basis, turning out a story a week for thirty months. He took as his first subject adventure and revolution in Latin America when he debuted with a book of tales, *Cabbages and Kings,* in 1904. This collection became a best-seller, and before Porter's death from alcoholism only six years later he followed it with twelve more volumes of short stories set in the United States, including *The Four Million* (1906), *Heart of the West* (1907), *The Trimmed Lamp* (1907), *The Gentle Grafter* (1908), *The Voice of the City* (1908), *Options* (1909), *Roads of Destiny* (1909), *Whirligigs* (1910), and *Strictly Business* (1910).

A prolific writer of short stories, Porter was called "a Yankee Maupassant" after the French writer, whose tales in English translation were gaining popularity with American readers about the time Porter started his career. Like several of Maupassant's works of short fiction, the typical O. Henry story concludes with a surprise twist to the plot, or what he called a "snapper" ending, as in his story "The Gift of the Magi." Contemporary critics often fault the predictability of his stock story formulas and the facetiousness of his garrulous, breezy narrative style, but the literary historian Arthur Voss has pointed out that in O. Henry's stories the author is trying to "make the point that the humble, insignificant little people of New York are just as admirable and their lives as worthy of attention and interest" as the wealthiest members of society. In recognition of Porter's popularization of the short story in America, the publisher Frank Doubleday established the O. Henry Awards in 1918, an annual anthology consisting of twenty "winners" representing the year's best short stories, currently selected from more than three thousand stories in American and Canadian magazines.

The Gift of the Magi

1906

ONE DOLLAR AND EIGHTY-SEVEN cents. That was all. And sixty cents of it was in pennies. Pennies saved one and two at a time by bulldozing the grocer and the vegetable man and the butcher until one's cheek burned with the silent imputation of parsimony that such close dealing implied. Three times Della counted it. One dollar and eighty-seven cents. And the next day would be Christmas.

There was clearly nothing left to do but flop down on the shabby little couch and howl. So Della did it. Which instigates the moral reflection that life is made up of sobs, sniffles, and smiles, with sniffles predominating.

While the mistress of the home is gradually subsiding from the first stage to the second, take a look at the home. A furnished flat at $8 per week. It did not exactly beggar description, but it certainly had that word on the lookout for the mendicancy squad.

In the vestibule below was a letter-box into which no letter would go, and an electric button from which no mortal finger could coax a ring. Also appertaining thereunto was a card bearing the name "Mr. James Dillingham Young."

The "Dillingham" had been flung to the breeze during a former period of prosperity when its possessor was being paid $30 per week. Now, when the income was shrunk to $20, the letters of "Dillingham" looked blurred, as though they were thinking seriously of contracting to a modest and unassuming D. But whenever Mr. James Dillingham Young came home and reached his flat above he was called "Jim" and greatly hugged by Mrs. James Dillingham Young, already introduced to you as Della. Which is all very good.

Della finished her cry and attended to her cheeks with the powder rag. She stood by the window and looked out dully at a grey cat walking a grey fence in a grey backyard. To-morrow would be Christmas Day, and she had only $1.87 with which to buy Jim a present. She had been saving every penny she could for months, with this result. Twenty dollars a week doesn't go far. Expenses had been greater than she had calculated. They always are. Only $1.87 to buy a present for Jim. Her Jim. Many a happy hour she had spent planning for something nice for him. Something fine and rare and sterling—something just a little bit near to being worthy of the honour of being owned by Jim.

There was a pier-glass between the windows of the room. Perhaps you have seen a pier-glass in an $8 flat. A very thin and very agile person may, by observing his reflection in a rapid sequence of longitudinal strips, obtain a fairly accurate conception of his looks. Della, being slender, had mastered the art.

Suddenly she whirled from the window and stood before the glass. Her eyes were shining brilliantly, but her face had lost its colour within twenty seconds. Rapidly she pulled down her hair and let it fall to its full length.

Now, there were two possessions of the James Dillingham Youngs in which they both took a mighty pride. One was Jim's gold watch that had been his father's and his grandfather's. The other was Della's hair. Had the Queen of

Sheba lived in the flat across the airshaft, Della would have let her hair hang out the window some day to dry just to depreciate Her Majesty's jewels and gifts. Had King Solomon been the janitor, with all his treasures piled up in the basement, Jim would have pulled out his watch every time he passed, just to see him pluck at his beard from envy.

So now Della's beautiful hair fell about her, rippling and shining like a cascade of brown waters. It reached below her knee and made itself almost a garment for her. And then she did it up again nervously and quickly. Once she faltered for a minute and stood still while a tear or two splashed on the worn red carpet.

On went her old brown jacket; on went her old brown hat. With a whirl of skirts and with the brilliant sparkle still in her eyes, she fluttered out of the door and down the stairs to the street.

Where she stopped the sign read: "Mme. Sofronie. Hair Goods of All Kinds." One flight up Della ran, and collected herself, panting. Madame, large, too white, chilly, hardly looked the "Sofronie."

"Will you buy my hair?" asked Della.

"I buy hair," said Madame. "Take yer hat off and let's have a sight at the looks of it."

Down rippled the brown cascade.

"Twenty dollars," said Madame, lifting the mass with a practised hand.

"Give it to me quick," said Della.

Oh, and the next two hours tripped by on rosy wings. Forget the hashed metaphor. She was ransacking the stores for Jim's present.

She found it at last. It surely had been made for Jim and no one else. There was no other like it in any of the stores, and she had turned all of them inside out. It was a platinum fob chain simple and chaste in design, properly proclaiming its value by substance alone and not by meretricious ornamentation — as all good things should do. It was even worthy of The Watch. As soon as she saw it she knew that it must be Jim's. It was like him. Quietness and value — the description applied to both. Twenty-one dollars they took from her for it, and she hurried home with the 87 cents. With that chain on his watch Jim might be properly anxious about the time in any company. Grand as the watch was, he sometimes looked at it on the sly on account of the old leather strap that he used in place of a chain.

When Della reached home her intoxication gave way a little to prudence and reason. She got out her curling irons and lighted the gas and went to work repairing the ravages made by generosity added to love. Which is always a tremendous task, dear friends — a mammoth task.

Within forty minutes her head was covered with tiny, close-lying curls that made her look wonderfully like a truant schoolboy. She looked at her reflection in the mirror long, carefully, and critically.

"If Jim doesn't kill me," she said to herself, "before he takes a second look at me, he'll say I look like a Coney Island chorus girl. But what could I do — oh! what could I do with a dollar and eighty-seven cents?"

At seven o'clock the coffee was made and the frying-pan was on the back of the stove, hot and ready to cook the chops.

Jim was never late. Della doubled the fob chain in her hand and sat on the corner of the table near the door that he always entered. Then she heard his step on the stair away down on the first flight, and she turned white for just a moment. She had a habit of saying little silent prayers about the simplest everyday things, and now she whispered: "Please God, make him think I am still pretty."

The door opened and Jim stepped in and closed it. He looked thin and very serious. Poor fellow, he was only twenty-two — and to be burdened with a family! He needed a new overcoat and he was without gloves.

Jim stepped inside the door, as immovable as a setter at the scent of quail. His eyes were fixed upon Della, and there was an expression in them that she could not read, and it terrified her. It was not anger, nor surprise, nor disapproval, nor horror, nor any of the sentiments that she had been prepared for. He simply stared at her fixedly with that peculiar expression on his face.

Della wriggled off the table and went for him.

"Jim, darling," she cried, "don't look at me that way. I had my hair cut off and sold it because I couldn't have lived through Christmas without giving you a present. It'll grow out again — you won't mind, will you? I just had to do it. My hair grows awfully fast. Say 'Merry Christmas!' Jim, and let's be happy. You don't know what a nice — what a beautiful, nice gift I've got for you."

"You've cut off your hair?" asked Jim, laboriously, as if he had not arrived at that patent fact yet even after the hardest mental labour.

"Cut it off and sold it," said Della. "Don't you like me just as well, anyhow? I'm me without my hair, ain't I?"

Jim looked about the room curiously.

"You say your hair is gone?" he said with an air almost of idiocy.

"You needn't look for it," said Della. "It's sold, I tell you — sold and gone, too. It's Christmas Eve, boy. Be good to me, for it went for you. Maybe the hairs of my head were numbered," she went on with a sudden serious sweetness, "but nobody could ever count my love for you. Shall I put the chops on, Jim?"

Out of his trance Jim seemed quickly to wake. He enfolded his Della. For ten seconds let us regard with discreet scrutiny some inconsequential object in the other direction. Eight dollars a week or a million a year — what is the difference? A mathematician or a wit would give you the wrong answer. The magi brought valuable gifts, but that was not among them. This dark assertion will be illuminated later on.

Jim drew a package from his overcoat pocket and threw it upon the table.

"Don't make any mistake, Dell," he said, "about me. I don't think there's anything in the way of a haircut or a shave or a shampoo that could make me like my girl any less. But if you'll unwrap that package you may see why you had me going awhile at first."

White fingers and nimble tore at the string and paper. And then an ecstatic scream of joy; and then, alas! a quick feminine change to hysterical tears and wails, necessitating the immediate employment of all the comforting powers of the lord of the flat.

For there lay The Combs — the set of combs, side and back, that Della had worshipped for long in a Broadway window. Beautiful combs, pure tortoiseshell, with jewelled rims — just the shade to wear in the beautiful vanished hair. They were expensive combs, she knew, and her heart had simply craved and yearned over them without the least hope of possession. And now they were hers, but the tresses that should have adorned the coveted adornments were gone.

But she hugged them to her bosom, and at length she was able to look up with dim eyes and a smile and say: "My hair grows so fast, Jim!"

And then Della leaped up like a little singed cat and cried, "Oh, oh!"

Jim had not yet seen his beautiful present. She held it out to him eagerly upon her open palm. The dull precious metal seemed to flash with a reflection of her bright and ardent spirit.

"Isn't it a dandy, Jim? I hunted all over town to find it. You'll have to look at the time a hundred times a day now. Give me your watch. I want to see how it looks on it."

Instead of obeying, Jim tumbled down on the couch and put his hands under the back of his head and smiled.

"Dell," said he, "let's put our Christmas presents away and keep 'em awhile. They're too nice to use just at present. I sold the watch to get the money to buy your combs. And now suppose you put the chops on."

The magi, as you know, were wise men — wonderfully wise men — who brought gifts to the Babe in the manger. They invented the art of giving Christmas presents. Being wise, their gifts were no doubt wise ones, possibly bearing the privilege of exchange in case of duplication. And here I have lamely related to you the uneventful chronicle of two foolish children in a flat who most unwisely sacrificed for each other the greatest treasures of their house. But in a last word to the wise of these days, let it be said that of all who give gifts these two were the wisest. Of all who give and receive gifts, such as they are wisest. Everywhere they are wisest. They are the magi.

Annie Proulx

Annie Proulx (b. 1935) was born in Norwich, Connecticut, the oldest of five sisters. Her mother was a painter and an amateur naturalist whose family had lived in Connecticut since 1635 as farmers, millworkers, inventors, and artists. Her father was the vice president of a textile company, and Proulx remembers that "we moved frequently when I was a child, North Carolina, Vermont, Maine, Rhode Island, town after town." She credits her mother for encouraging her to observe the environment closely. "From the time I was extremely small, I was told, 'Look at that.' . . . everything—from the wale of corduroy to the broken button to the loose thread to the disheveled mustache to the clouded eye." Proulx attended Colby College, the University of Vermont, and Concordia University, earning a B.A. and an M.A., as well as passing her doctoral oral examinations in history. In 1975, with few teaching jobs available, she abandoned work on her Ph.D. and began a perilous career in freelance journalism. In the 1980s she published six "how-to" books on a variety of subjects, including *Plan and Make Your Own Fences and Gates, Walkways, Walls and Drives* (1983). During this time she also raised her sons from her third marriage while living in an isolated cabin in a rural town in Vermont. Later she said that this life made her "very alert and aware of everything, from tree branches and wild mushrooms to animal tracks. It's an excellent training for the eye. Most of us stagger around deaf and dumb."

Supporting herself and her sons on her meager income as a journalist, Proulx began to write stories for fun, creating one or two a year. "It was my pleasure, my indulgence, when I wanted to do something that wasn't fishing or canoeing." Most of these early stories were written for a men's magazine about hunting and fishing, where her first editor told her that she had to publish under a masculine name, "something like Joe or Zack, retrievers' names," she complained. They compromised on using her initials, E. A. Proulx, the E standing for her first name, Edna. In 1983 and 1987, two of her stories were listed among the "Distinguished Short Stories" in *Best American Short Stories*. In 1988, Proulx published her first book of fiction, the nine stories set in northern Vermont constituting *Heart Songs and Other Stories*.

Proulx's contract with her publisher Charles Scribner's Sons for *Heart Songs* also required her to produce a novel. She felt she "had not a clue about writing a novel, or even the faintest desire. I thought of myself as a short story writer. Period, period, period." Proulx found the inspiration for her first work of long fiction in a group of old postcards, and after her novel *Postcards* appeared in 1992, she told interviewer Esther Fein, "It was astonishing how easy writing a novel was compared to writing a short story. I was so used to cramping thoughts and sections and cutting, and suddenly I had room to expand." In 1993 Proulx was the recipient of the PEN/Faulkner Award for *Postcards*. The following year her second novel, *The Shipping News*, won the National Book Award and the Pulitzer Prize. This was followed by the novel *Accordion Crimes* in 1996. "Job History," was included in *Close Range: Wyoming Stories* (2000). She also published a second set of Wyoming stories, *Bad*

Dirt, in 2004. In 2005 her story "Brokeback Mountain," originally published in *The New Yorker* and made into a film, won the Best Picture Award at the Venice International Film Festival.

Job History

1999

LEELAND LEE is born at home in Cora, Wyoming, November 17, 1947, the youngest of six. In the 1950s his parents move to Unique when his mother inherits a small dog-bone ranch. The ranch lies a few miles outside town. They raise sheep, a few chickens and some hogs. The father is irascible and, as soon as they can, the older children disperse. Leeland can sing "That Doggie in the Window" all the way through. His father strikes him with a flyswatter and tells him to shut up. There is no news on the radio. A blizzard has knocked out the power.

Leeland's face shows heavy bone from his mother's side. His neck is thick and his red-gold hair plastered down in bangs. Even as a child his eyes are as pouchy as those of a middle-aged alcoholic, the brows rod-straight above wandering, out-of-line eyes. His nose lies broad and close to his face, his mouth seems to have been cut with a single chisel blow into easy flesh. In the fifth grade, horsing around with friends, he falls off the school's fire escape and breaks his pelvis. He is in a body cast for three months. On the news an announcer says that the average American eats 8.6 pounds of margarine a year but only 8.3 pounds of butter. He never forgets this statistic.

When Leeland is seventeen he marries Lori Bovee. They quit school. Lori is pregnant and Leeland is proud of this. His pelvis gives him no trouble. She is a year younger than he, with an undistinguished, oval face, hair of medium length. She is a little stout but looks a confection in pastel sweater sets. Leeland and his mother fight over this marriage and Leeland leaves the ranch. He takes a job pumping gas at Egge's Service Station. Ed Egge says, "You may fire when ready, Gridley," and laughs. The station stands at the junction of highway 16 and a county road. Highway 16 is the main tourist road to Yellowstone. Leeland buys Lori's father's old truck for fifty dollars and Ed rebuilds the engine. Vietnam and Selma, Alabama, are on the news.

The federal highway program puts through the new four-lane interstate forty miles south of highway 16 and parallel with it. Overnight the tourist business in Unique falls flat. One day a hundred cars stop for gas and oil, hamburgers, cold soda. The next day only two cars pull in, both driven by locals asking how business is. In a few months there is a FOR SALE sign on the inside window of the service station. Ed Egge gets drunk and, driving at speed, hits two steers on the county road.

Leeland joins the army, puts in for the motor pool. He is stationed in Germany for six years and never learns a word of the language. He comes back to

Wyoming heavier, moodier. He works with a snow-fence crew during spring and summer, then moves Lori and the children — the boy and a new baby girl — to Casper where he drives oil trucks. They live in a house trailer on Poison Spider Road, jammed between two rioting neighbors. On the news they hear that an enormous diamond has been discovered somewhere. The second girl is born. Leeland can't seem to get along with the oil company dispatcher. After a year they move back to Unique. Leeland and his mother make up their differences.

Lori is good at saving money and she has put aside a small nest egg. They set up in business for themselves. Leeland believes people will be glad to trade at a local ranch supply store that saves a long drive into town. He rents the service station from Mrs. Egge who has not been able to sell it after Ed's death. They spruce it up, Leeland doing all the carpenter work, Lori painting the interior and exterior. On the side Leeland raises hogs with his father. His father was born and raised in Iowa and knows hogs.

It becomes clear that people relish the long drive to a bigger town where they can see something different, buy fancy groceries, clothing, bakery goods as well as ranch supplies. One intensely cold winter when everything freezes from God to gizzard, Leeland and his father lose 112 hogs. They sell out. Eighteen months later the ranch supply business goes under. The new color television set goes back to the store.

After the bankruptcy proceedings Leeland finds work on a road construction crew. He is always out of town, it seems, but back often enough for what he calls "a good ride" and so makes Lori pregnant again. Before the baby is born he quits the road crew. He can't seem to get along with the foreman. No one can, and turnover is high. On his truck radio he hears that hundreds of religious cult members have swallowed Kool-Aid and cyanide.

Leeland takes a job at Tongue River Meat Locker and Processing. Old Man Brose owns the business. Leeland is the only employee. He has an aptitude for sizing up and cutting large animals. He likes wrapping the tidy packages, the smell of damp bone and chill. He can throw his cleaver unerringly and when mice run along the wall they do not run far if Leeland is there. After months of discussion with Old Man Brose, Leeland and Lori sign a ten-year lease on the meat locker operation. Their oldest boy graduates from high school, the first in the family to do so, and joins the army. He signs up for six years. There is something on the news about school lunches and ketchup is classed as a vegetable. Old Man Brose moves to Albuquerque.

The economy takes a dive. The news is full of talk about recession and unemployment. Thrifty owners of small ranches go back to doing their own butchering, cutting and freezing. The meat locker lease payments are high and electricity jumps up. Leeland and Lori have to give up the business. Old Man Brose returns from Albuquerque. There are bad feelings. It didn't work out, Leeland says, and that's the truth of it.

It seems like a good time to try another place. The family moves to Thermopolis where Leeland finds a temporary job at a local meat locker during hunting season. A hunter from Des Moines, not far from where Leeland's father was born, tips him $100 when he loads packages of frozen elk and the elk's head onto the man's single-engine plane. The man has been drinking. The plane goes down in the Medicine Bow range to the southeast.

During this long winter Leeland is out of work and stays home with the baby. Lori works in the school cafeteria. The baby is a real crier and Leeland quiets him down with spoonsful of beer.

In the spring they move back to Unique and Leeland tries truck driving again, this time in long-distance rigs on coast-to-coast journeys that take him away two and three months at a time. He travels all over the continent, to Texas, Alaska, Montreal and Corpus Christi. He says every place is the same. Lori works now in the kitchen of the Hi-Lo Café in Unique. The ownership of the café changes three times in two years. West Klinker, an elderly rancher, eats three meals a day at the Hi-Lo. He is sweet on Lori. He reads her an article from the newspaper — a strange hole has appeared in the ozone layer. He confuses ozone with oxygen.

One night while Leeland is somewhere on the east coast the baby goes into convulsions following a week's illness of fever and cough. Lori makes a frightening drive over icy roads to the distant hospital. The baby survives but he is slow. Lori starts a medical emergency response group in Unique. Three women and two men sign up to take the first aid course. They drive a hundred miles to the first aid classes. Only two of them pass the test on the first try. Lori is one of the two. The other is Stuttering Bob, an old bachelor. One of the failed students says Stuttering Bob has nothing to do but study the first aid manual as he enjoys the leisured life that goes with a monthly social security check.

Leeland quits driving trucks and again tries raising hogs with his father on the old ranch. He becomes a volunteer fireman and is at the bad February fire that kills two children. It takes the fire truck three hours to get in to the ranch through the wind-drifted snow. The family is related to Lori. When something inside explodes, Leeland tells, an object flies out of the house and strikes the fire engine hood. It is a Nintendo player and not even charred.

Stuttering Bob has cousins in Muncie, Indiana. One of the cousins works at the Muncie Medical Center. The cousin arranges for the Medical Center to donate an old ambulance to the Unique Rescue Squad although they had intended to give it to a group in Mississippi. Bob's cousin, who has been to Unique, persuades them. Bob is afraid to drive through congested cities so Leeland and Lori take a series of buses to Muncie to pick up the vehicle. It is their first vacation. They take the youngest boy with them. On the return trip Lori leaves her purse on a chair in a restaurant. The gas money for the return trip is in the purse. They go back to the restaurant, wild with anxiety. The purse has been turned in and nothing is missing. Lori and Leeland talk about the goodness of people, even strangers. In their absence Stuttering Bob is elected president of the rescue squad.

A husband and wife from California move to Unique and open a taxidermy business. They say they are artists and arrange the animals in unusual poses. Lori gets work cleaning their workshop. The locals make jokes about the coyote in their window, posed lifting a leg against sagebrush where a trap is set. The taxidermists hold out for almost two years, then move to Oregon. Leeland's and Lori's oldest son telephones from overseas. He is making a career of the service.

Leeland's father dies and they discover the hog business is deeply in debt, the ranch twice-mortgaged. The ranch is sold to pay off debts. Leeland's mother moves in with them. Leeland continues long-distance truck driving. His mother watches television all day. Sometimes she sits in Lori's kitchen, saying almost nothing, picking small stones from dried beans.

The youngest daughter baby-sits. One night, on the way home, her employer feels her small breasts and asks her to squeeze his penis, because, he says, she ate the piece of chocolate cake he was saving. She does it but runs crying into the house and tells Lori who advises her to keep quiet and stay home from now on. The man is Leeland's friend; they hunt elk and antelope together.

Leeland quits truck driving. Lori has saved a little money. Once more they decide to go into business for themselves. They lease the old gas station where Leeland had his first job and where they tried the ranch supply store. Now it is a gas station again, but also a convenience store. They try surefire gimmicks: plastic come-on banners that pop and tear in the wind, free ice cream cones with every fill-up, prize drawings. Leeland has been thinking of the glory days when a hundred cars stopped. Now highway 16 seems the emptiest road in the country. They hold on for a year; then Leeland admits that it hasn't worked out and he is right. He is depressed for days when San Francisco beats Denver in the Super Bowl.

Their oldest boy is discharged from the service and will not say why but Leeland knows it is chemical substances, drugs. Leeland is driving long-distance trucks again despite his back pain. The oldest son is home, working as a ranch hand in Pie. Leeland studies him, looking for signs of addiction. The son's eyes are always red and streaming.

The worst year comes. Leeland's mother dies, Leeland hurts his back, and, in the same week, Lori learns that she has breast cancer and is pregnant again. She is forty-six. Lori's doctor advises an abortion. Lori refuses.

The oldest son is discovered to have an allergy to horses and quits the ranch job. He tells Leeland he wants to try raising hogs. Pork prices are high. For a few days Leeland is excited. He can see it clearly: Leeland Lee & Son, Livestock. But the son changes his mind when a friend he knew in the service comes by on a motorcycle. The next morning both of them leave for Phoenix.

Lori spontaneously aborts in the fifth month of the pregnancy and then the cancer burns her up. Leeland is at the hospital with her every day. Lori dies. The daughters, both married now, curse Leeland. No one knows how to reach the oldest son and he misses the funeral. The youngest boy cries inconsolably. They decide he will live in Billings, Montana, with the oldest sister who is expecting her first child.

Two springs after Lori's death a middle-aged woman from Ohio buys the café, paints it orange, renames it Unique Eats and hires Leeland to cook. He is good with meat, knows how to choose the best cuts and grill or do them chicken-fried style to perfection. He has never cooked anything at home and everyone is surprised at this long-hidden skill. The oldest son comes back and next year they plan to lease the old gas station and convert it to a motorcycle repair shop and steak house. Nobody has time to listen to the news.

Jamie Quatro

Jamie Quatro (b. 1970) was born in San Diego, California, and raised in Tucson, Arizona. Her father was a physician and her mother a classical pianist. Quatro earned her B.A. in English from Pepperdine University and her M.A. in English from the College of William and Mary. In 2000, continuing her graduate studies in British Romantic Poetry on a Presidential Fellowship at Princeton University, she left the doctoral program in her first year when she became pregnant with the first of her and her husband's four children.

In 2009 Quatro completed her M.F.A. in Fiction from Bennington College, after she and her husband and children had moved to the Georgia side of Lookout Mountain near Chattanooga. That year she began to publish her short stories and essays in many literary journals, including *The Antioch Review, Tin House, Ploughshares, The Kenyon Reivew, McSweeney's,* and *Oxford American.* She was also the recipient of fellowships from Yaddo and the MacDowell Colony, which offered her additional time for her writing. Quatro understands the process: "Writers write. It is isolated and terrifying and every day, when you sit down in the chair, a thousand forces will do their best to pluck what little vision you have from you."

In 2013, Quatro published her first story collection, *I Want to Show You More,* to glowing reviews. She has said that the story writer she most admires is Alice Munro, but Quatro is also highly conscious of the writing of Eudora Welty. "Eudora Welty's parents weren't from the South, and it seemed to give her a certain detachment from her own Southern landscape that served her work. I think that when you move to a particular region from elsewhere, you have a kind of clear-eyed vision about what makes that region distinctive." Quatro would also be in sympathy with Welty's statement, "I am a writer who came from a sheltered life. A sheltered life can be a daring life as well. For all serious daring starts from within."

RELATED STORY
Eudora Welty, "A Worn Path," page 1323.

I.7 to Tennessee

2013

EVA BOCK MADE her way along the shoulder of Lula Lake Road. She was eighty-nine — tall, bent forward from the waist. Her white pants hung from her hips so the hemlines of the legs pooled onto the tops of her tennis shoes. Her narrow lips were painted orange-red, and her steel-gray hair, tied up in a bun, smelled faintly of lemon. Loose strands hung about her cheeks and trailed down her spine. She wore a pair of headphones that created a furrow across the center pile of her hair. The cord fed into a chunky cassette deck/FM radio hooked onto the waistband of her pants. She was listening to NPR.

In her pocket was a letter, addressed: *Pres. George W. Bush, Penn. Ave., Wash. D.C.* Seven envelopes she had thrown away before she felt her handwriting passed for that of an adult. The letter itself she dictated to Quentin Jenkins, one of the McCallie boys who went down the mountain for her groceries. Quentin wrote in cursive on a college-ruled sheet of paper. She preferred he type it, and considered offering to pay him an extra dollar to do so, but when she finished her dictation and Quentin read the letter back to her, she grew excited and snatched the paper from him, folding and stuffing it into an envelope. Then she realized she hadn't signed the letter, so she had to open the envelope and borrow the boy's pen. Quentin offered to mail it for her but she had made up her mind to deliver it to the post office herself. She took great pride in the fact that she, an eighty-nine-year-old woman, still had things to say to the President of the United States. It was a formal letter, protesting the war. She felt it her duty to place it, personally, into the hands of the government.

A yellow Penske truck approached, honking. Eva set her feet a little ways apart and froze, looking straight ahead. She swayed from side to side, as if holding her balance on a log. In her freckled hand she carried a furled green umbrella, the tip of which she planted into the pavement to steady herself against the truck's tailwind.

When it passed she continued on, watching her feet take turns appearing and vanishing beneath her. One of her shoe-laces was untied. The Lookout Mountain residents never honked. She had been walking this route, mornings, for as long as she could remember. Most locals slowed and made half-circles around her so she wouldn't feel obliged to step off the pavement. The tourists would run her off the road if she did not stand her ground to remind them this was a residential suburb, where folks lived and worked and took morning walks.

Eva felt short of breath, a bit light-headed. She'd been unable to finish her toast that morning, so eager she'd been to set off upon her errand. Three houses before the elementary school she stopped to tie her shoe. Sitting on the stone retaining wall beside the Sutherlands' driveway, she crossed her left foot over her right knee. The angle was awkward; the laces draped against her inside arch. She rested, looking up Lula Lake Road, visualizing her route. Just past the school's pillared entrance were a small pond and wooden gazebo; beyond the gazebo she could see the spire of the Methodist church, and beyond that were the bakery, City Hall, gas station, and convenience mart. Next came the Mountain Market and Bed and Breakfast. A brief stretch of houses. And then — with difficulty, Eva pictured herself reaching it — the four-way stop where Lookout Mountain, Georgia, became Lookout Mountain, Tennessee.

It was here, at the border, that Eva usually turned around, so that by the time she came home to the Adirondack rocker on her front patio, she had covered just over a mile of ground. Today would be different. The post office was on the Tennessee side, 1.7 miles from her front door. She'd had Quentin look it up on his laptop computer. Round trip: 3.4. She had not walked this far in twenty years.

She stood and, clutching the handle of her umbrella, again began her slow, measured steps. With her free hand she brushed off the backs of her pant legs and adjusted her top. She was wearing a threadbare sweater with an orange "P" knitted into the black fabric. It had been a gift from her son Thomas, who, after one semester at Princeton, joined the Army and was killed in a village in the Batangan Penninsula when he went into the jungle to relieve himself and stepped onto a booby-trapped 105 round. One arm was found hanging by its sleeve from a branch twenty feet above the ground. At least this was the story she heard coming out of her mouth when people asked about the sweater. Sometimes she forgot and said she didn't know where the sweater came from, and when she said this, it was as true as when she told the story about the dead son. She wasn't always sure if the thing had actually happened or if it was just something she read in a book. When she told the story, she felt she had not even known the boy in the jungle; she told it without emotion, as if describing a scene from a stage play, the boy who stepped onto the booby trap just an actor who was now carrying on another life somewhere.

When she finished telling the story she would berate herself. "His own mother," she would think. *What kind of mother stops feeling grief for her son? What kind of mother must I have been?* She could not remember. And there was no one left whom she could ask.

But no one talked to her about the sweater anymore. If anyone spoke to her at all, it was, "Miss Eva, why must you take your walk along this busy road? You know when the fog sets in we can't see you coming or going. Miss Eva, you're going to get yourself run over." But most people in town could not imagine what it would be like to drive along Lula Lake without watching for Miss Eva. Single-handedly, between 7:30 and 8:45 A.M., Eva Bock kept the speed limit in check.

The truth was she could no longer remember why she walked this road. "It's the way I know," she said when people asked. When she'd formed the habit, Lula Lake was not paved. Where the gas station and pharmacy stood had once been a grove of peach trees. But these were details that, most of the time, she could not recall. This morning, for example, she could think back only as far as yesterday's walk, when Phyllis Driver came out of the convenience mart and offered her a cup of Barnies coffee. She turned it down. The cup was brown with a picture of a man wearing glasses drawn in yellow lines. Phyllis was wearing a watch for people with vision trouble, large black numbers on an oversized white face. It read 8:10. Eva could remember these things — the time, watch, cup, "Barnies." She could not remember her own son.

Sometimes she did remember things, usually when the season was in a time of change, but they were memories from her childhood. When one of these memories broke over her she would laugh and clap her hands against her thighs. One October morning, she stepped into the Mountain Market, flushed and shaking. Lorna Ellis, the cashier, put out her cigarette. "Gambling!" Eva shouted, "At the college!" Except for smears of red in the corners, her lips were colorless and wet with saliva. The skin on her face was like a delicate system of roots. Miss Eva beckoned and Lorna followed her out onto the stoop. With her umbrella, Eva pointed to the ridge above the Methodist church, where the trees around the Westminster campus shone red and yellow. "That's where Granddaddy showed me how to play blackjack. Held me on his knee and taught me to add up cards."

When she did remember her son, Eva Bock prayed. It was the only time she prayed, and since she rarely remembered, she prayed infrequently. She began with the Lord's Prayer but usually wound up arguing about the funeral with Hugh, her husband, dead thirty-two years now. "Thy will be done, on earth as it is in Heaven," she would recite, imagining Thomas's soul continuing to fly upward while the rest of him fell back to earth. "And get rid of the flag," she told Hugh. "It's sullying his coffin." When they sent Thomas home in a bag with a zipper, Hugh oversaw the entire affair: the guns, flag-folding, honors from a country that served Thomas up in the name of — what? It was a question she'd asked so many times it was boiled down, the feeling refined out of it. Just a quiet string of words she wished God would tell her the answer to. Sometimes during these prayers, when she got to the part where she meant to argue about the funeral, a young Hugh Bock would appear before her, expressionless and shining in a white linen suit. He was handsome and when she saw him like this she would forget what it was she wanted to say. She would feel girlish and shy and want to adorn him in some way, perhaps slide a daisy into the buttonhole on his lapel.

Today she did not remember Hugh or her son. She thought only of hand-delivering the letter in her pocket. It was cold out, close to freezing, in fact, and her knuckles ached around the handle of the umbrella. *Should have put on my coat. But there's no sense in turning around.* She was passing the pond and gazebo beside the school. Children — looking impossibly tiny to her, dwarfed by oversized backpacks — were emerging from side streets and parked cars. They wore brightly colored rubber shoes and hats with tassels. Mothers and fathers looked at her but did not wave or say hello, which was the way Eva wanted it. It was the reason she'd started wearing the headphones. The muscles of her face no longer betrayed any expression, so that it was difficult for anyone to tell if she was feeling friendly, which she usually was not. More than anything else, while she walked, Eva Bock wanted to be left alone.

Two boys wearing hooded sweatshirts flicked thin branches over the pond like fly rods. Sunlight and shadow spotted the muddy water, the surface of which buoyed a thousand brightly colored leaves. A yellow dog sat on the bank beside the boys.

"Careful," Eva said. She had not intended to say the word aloud.

They turned to look at her. One boy laughed, then, leaned over and said something to the other.

"What are you listening to?" the second boy called out.

Eva kept up her wide, even steps. "Floods in Mexico," she said. "A mountain fell into the sea and the wave washed away a village in Chiapas."

The bell rang. The boys ran across the school's front lawn, the dog following, their shoes kicking up little moist tufts of grass.

Something in the way the boys ran off . . . Eva felt as if a stack of papers were shifting inside her head. *Remember.* But as soon as she tried there was only the road ahead of her, a line up of latecoming cars, children's faces like pale moons in backseat windows. Eva planted her feet and stood, waiting for the cars to pass. She listened to the British announcer reporting the collapse of a bridge in Dubai. She thought of her letter and reached into her pocket, afraid she might forget her errand and turn around at the four-way stop. She rubbed her fingers along the edge of the envelope, feeling the stamps. She'd had to lick four of them to make enough postage. Almost a half-dollar to mail a letter to the President.

She continued on, past City Hall with its wooden sign hanging by only one hook so the words *Lookout Mountain, Ga.* had to be read sideways. She passed the Fairy Bakery with its morning smells of cinnamon rolls and coffee. The bakery had opened in September and some mornings the line came out the door.

At the McFarland intersection, in front of the gas station, she had to stop to rest. There was a bench in the tiny center island, placed there by the Fairyland Garden Club. Violas had been planted around the bench and Eva accidentally crushed two of them beneath her shoe. She sat down, folding her hands around her knees. *Only a quarter-mile, Miss Eva. How are you going to make it all the way into Tennessee?* Little black spots dotted the outside edges of her vision. She swiped at them with her hand.

Coming toward her, crossing Lula Lake from Oberon Road, was the new family — the professor's wife and her two children. Eva had seen them before. They were late for school but the mother did not seem in a hurry. The boy had hair like a mushroom cap and carried a long stick. The girl's brown hair was pulled into pigtails and she wore a skirt with stockings. The mother watched the boy, who, when they reached the island, pointed the stick at Eva and pretended to fire. The mother said something and Eva pushed back an earphone.

"Sorry to interrupt. We've seen you out walking." She put her hands on the tops of the children's heads. "This is Myra and Grady. I'm Jocelyn Corley." She held out a hand. She seemed eager to be touched.

Eva took her hand and looked up. The woman had a scarf tied around her neck. *Sarkozy,* Eva heard in one ear, *like President Bush, is a teetotaler. He enjoys mountain biking. He and Bush are discussing a Franco-American holiday in honor of Lafayette.*

"We've been so charmed, seeing you out here every day," the mother said. "We even made up a limerick about it. We thought, with your permission, we could send it to the *Mountain Mirror.*"

"Let's hear it then," Eva said. She was annoyed by this distraction from her errand and by the fact that these new folks had already formed opinions about her. Again she reached to feel for the letter in her pocket. In one ear Sarkozy was speaking. *France was there for the United States at the beginning. United States was there for France during the wars in Europe. We must remind our people of this.*

The little girl stepped behind her mother, shy; but Jocelyn and the boy recited:

> "There once was a woman named Bock,
>   who every day went for a walk.
>   Rain or snow,
>   still she would go,
>   each step like the tick of a clock."

"Carrying a dirty sock," said the boy. "Looking for a cool rock."

"He comes up with alternate endings," the mother said.

"What's on your iPod?" the girl asked. When Eva didn't answer the girl pointed to her hip.

"Oh. It's a radio." She lifted the corner of her sweater so the girl could see the cassette player. "I've got my news program on. The war."

The boy sat down on the bench and unzipped his backpack. "Are you for blue or gray?"

Eva wiped her eyes with the back of her hand. The spots were elongating, drifting toward the center of her vision.

"Watch this," said the boy, pulling something from his bag. It was a large magnolia seedpod. He turned it over in his hand. "Incoming!" he said. He plunked the seedpod down onto the bed of violas and made a crackling noise inside his mouth.

Eva removed her headphones. "Where did you learn that?"

"Since we moved here he's become obsessed with weapons," the mother said. "All this Civil War history everywhere."

For a moment Eva thought she might reach out and shake the boy by the shoulders. *In the name of what?* But then she could not remember what her question meant.

Now the mother was smiling; she was taking the children away. As they crossed McFarland the boy looked back and waved.

Eva lifted her chin and put her headphones back on.

On she went, past the Mountain Market with its green awning and smells of pipe tobacco and lard from the deep fryer, past the Garden Walk Inn with its trellised porch and dollhouse mailbox. And now began the stretch of large homes set back from the road. Two more blocks and she would reach the four-way stop. This was still familiar ground. But Eva was beginning to worry.

In the first place, she realized, now that she was near the border, she could not remember if the post office in Tennessee was actually on Lula Lake Road. She thought there might be a turn somewhere. In the second place — whether from excitement or just the anticipation of the extra length of her walk — her heart was clattering beneath her sweater like teeth in the cold. She turned off the radio, though she left the headphones on to discourage talkers. She put her hand into her pocket and rubbed the letter between her thumb and forefinger. The black spots floated up, and up, in front of her.

Past Elfin, past Robin Hood Trail. She had to stop three times to steady herself for passing cars, all of which slowed and crossed the double yellow line into the opposite lane. She saw Megan Compson wave from inside her silver van. Eva walked on, trying not to bend her knees too much. Beside the road were smears of color, red and yellow, purple and orange; twiggy bushes and small trees with dead brown leaves under them; low stone walls and white fences with latched gates. Vines with chalky periwinkle berries dragged at her sleeve and pant legs. The sun laid orange slats of fight across rooftops. Dogs strolled out from porches and sniffed at her legs; the ones that barked she held off with her umbrella.

She rounded the last curve and saw the single pulsing red light above the intersection of Lula Lake and Lee Avenue. She could not remember why she was supposed to cross rather than turn around. Something about solemn duty and the government.

She reached the intersection and stood, breathing. Her lips felt dry. Beside her was a wrought-iron sign with arrows and words: LOOKOUT MOUNTAIN BIRD SANCTUARY. POINT PARK, CRAVENS HOUSE, RUBY FALLS. Another sign, shaped like a choo-choo train, read TAKE SCENIC HIGHWAY DOWN TO HISTORIC CHATTANOOGA!

Something about the government. Something about a funeral. The post office. She was going to tell President Johnson how she felt about things in North . . . She reached into her pocket and her heart rattled beneath her ribs. Surely the post office would not be in the direction of all those damned tourist traps. She turned onto Lee.

After walking thirty yards Eva realized she had made a mistake. The road curved and began to climb a hill. She had not planned on climbing any hills. She turned to go back to the intersection and the asphalt rushed up toward her. She would have fallen were it not for the umbrella, which she threw out in front of her and held on to with both hands — she had to lean back and squat to avoid falling. There was nothing for it but to continue uphill, and to do so she was forced to lean forward and bend her knees, using her umbrella like a cane. She was considerably irked by the black spots, which moved around and around in the trees on either side of her. Pinestraw blanketed the pavement beneath her; it was slippery and she moved toward the center of the road. Why wasn't she on Lula Lake Road? Why wasn't she on her way home? The sun was already above the tops of the tallest pines.

The hill became steeper; now if she stopped at all she would not be able to hold her balance. Eva made up her mind to signal the next car that drove past and request a ride back home. No, that wasn't right. She was supposed to mail a letter. She would request a ride to the post office, and then home. She removed her headphones and left them hanging in an arc about her neck.

Ahead of her was a sharp blind curve. If she didn't cross the street she might be struck by an oncoming vehicle. Eva listened for cars; hearing nothing, with slow steps she crossed to the right side of the road.

Where the pavement ended, there was a steep drop-off. Below, fifty yards down the rocky hillside, Eva could see a track. A woman was running laps.

Next to the track was a baseball diamond, the grass still green. Silver bleachers gleamed on either side of the "baselines; beyond the field was a play-ground with swings and picnic tables. The Commons, on the Tennessee/Georgia bor-der *grass stains on his pants. The smell of leather oil and sweat. Watch this hit, I'll fly it to the moon. Crepe myrtle blossoms in a jar on the kitchen table* . . . and now a black dog was bounding up the hillside. Eva saw him for only a second before he reached her. She did not have time to steady herself. She hit at him with her umbrella, then lost her balance and fell. Her thin body hurtled down the side of the hill toward the baseball field until she struck the trunk of a maple tree with her left hip bone.

She lay on her side among rocks and fallen leaves. For a space of time — seconds? hours? — she thought she had finished with her walk and was now resting in her own bed, and for this she felt an overwhelming gratitude. Interrupting her sleep was a dog's bark, abrupt like the scrape of a chair being pushed back from a table. A leaf blower droned, a bird sang. The sifting of leaves, then a quick panting, very close to her ear.

She opened her eyes. The black dog was in front of her; she saw his paws, toes spread on the uneven rocky hillside, cluster of silver rags hanging from a purple collar. He barked and Eva threw an arm over the ear that was facing upward.

The sleeve of her sweater was torn and pocked with hitchhiker burrs. She noticed her earphones were gone. The dog stopped barking and began to sniff around her face. Warm tongue on her cheek. The dog whimpered and backed away, then disappeared down the hillside.

The trunk before her was twisted about with a vine of bright pink leaves. In her confusion, Eva thought they were hands clamoring to reach the top branches, each leaf five fingers pressing into the bark, staking its claim. She rolled her head and saw that the vine ended halfway up the trunk; at the top of the tree the branches were thin and white, with only a few yellow leaves still attached. Through the branches the sky was an exhilarating blue.

She remembered: She was going to the post office in Tennessee. She was going to deliver a letter to President Bush.

What foolishness! She should never have attempted such a thing. Twenty years she had stood up to speeding tourists, and all anyone would remember was that she had fallen off the side of the road because of a dog. And what did she know about the war? Listening to NPR had only given her ideas, had made her forget who she was. She was an eighty-nine-year-old pacifist who could not find her way to the post office. Who could not remember her own son.

What do you know about the decisions of our government? It was Hugh's voice. He was standing in the driveway next to her; in her hand was the garden hose.

I know our son is dead. Cheated out of his birthright by his own country. I know the President is a liar.

Hugh slapped her across the face. She stumbled backward into the hydran-gea bush. *Your son died in the name of this country. And here you are, setting your goddamn table with goddamn linen napkins.* She lay in the bush, looking up at the sky.

But something, was not right with the sky. The black spots had returned and now swirled in front of the blue and branches and the yellow dangling leaves. Eva let her head roll back so she was again looking at the vine on the tree trunk and the black spots came with her, they went out to join the leaves, or the leaves peeled off and joined the spots, she couldn't tell. They were coming together, the colors merging into a subdued gray, approaching her, arranging themselves in a dark processional.

In her mind, Eva righted herself to meet them.

The spots drifting toward her were soldiers in uniform. They were all identical — all her son. She cried out and tried to touch one of them but the sons did not look at her as they came on. As they neared, Eva saw Thomas's face over and over again — his high cheekbones; the slight depression across the bridge of his nose, left there when he broke it against the handlebars of his two-wheel bicycle; the scar below the downy blond arch of his right eyebrow; the cowlick at the center of his part above his forehead. She used to wet down the cowlick Sunday mornings before church. His hair was soft and during the sermons she twirled it through her fingertips.

The faces came on. She could see the green and gold of Thomas's eyes. None of them saw her. The sons drifted past and out of her vision in a regular, stolid rhythm.

"Look at me," she said. "I want to ask you a question."

One of them stopped and turned his head. His face remained expressionless and the others waited patiently behind. She understood that he was waiting for her to ask the question and it was terrible, this passionless waiting man who was her son, terrible that he did not recognize her. She felt certain that, were she able to kiss his cheek, she would remember how to feel sadness and grief, love and longing.

In his gray uniform the son continued to wait. Eva could bear it no longer. "In the name of *what*?" she cried out to the son in front of her. "*Of what*?" she asked the waiting ones behind him. The son smiled and for a moment Eva thought he would comfort her. She saw his lips move but no sound came out. The others smiled in exactly the same way as the first.

And then they were pulling back, all of them, one by one. With horror she realized they were leaving her and she felt at the very least she should say something to put Thomas at rest. But the sons were not at rest — they were only apart, winnowed from victories and failures. While she watched they withdrew into the sky, grown dark now. They began to circle above her with a hard, impartial energy, like the stars.

Now the dark sky and circling soldiers started to descend and she understood that the darkness would cover her like a hood. Eva saw the last gray soldier turn. This time it was Hugh Bock's face before her and when he spoke it was only a whisper.

"Unanswerable," he said. And the host of orbiting sons repeated the word until it became a kind of song, the sound of air moving in summer trees: *Unanswerable, unanswerable*.

Beneath them, Eva listened.

The dog was, in fact, a female retriever named Pearl. Her barking alerted her owner, Sharon Miller, who was running laps on the track at the Commons. Pearl led her up the hillside to Eva Bock's body, her leg wrapped around the trunk of a tree. One of her shoes was missing and her thin foot in its dirty white stocking looked like a child's. Her hair was spread out across the rocks and colored leaves in a way that would have been almost sensual had she been merely asleep. Her eyes were open, wide and antique, and there was a vertical gash shaped like a parallelogram from her temple to her jaw. The frail skin looked as if it had been freshly shucked. Sharon Miller could see the grayish skullbone. She vomited, then called 911 and the Lookout Mountain, Georgia City Hall. She also called her husband, who called Liza at the *Mountain Mirror*. Assuming Miss Eva had been, as long predicted, run off the road by a tourist, Liza posted the information on the *Mountain Mirror's* website, so that, for a time after her death, the Lookout Mountain residents felt a sense of indignation at the license plates from anywhere but Georgia or Tennessee.

Because she had fallen on the Tennessee side, the ambulance came not from the Walker County, Georgia, response unit six miles away, but from St. Elmo at the base of the mountain. It took seventeen minutes, during which time residents gathered and peered down the side of the hill. Dr. Bailey was called — he was young and took the steep hillside with ease — and was able to determine that Miss Eva was, indeed, dead. Just the same, he administered CPR until the EMTs came. Everyone felt it was a heroic gesture.

Before the night-shift CNA at Memorial Hospital threw out the white pants — bloody at the knees, both pant legs cut off the victim from the hemline up through the waistband — he found the envelope in the pocket. He was an immigrant from Haiti, nineteen years old, and had never seen 15-cent stamps. He felt this must be an important letter; he was surprised the EMTs had not removed it from the pocket for the next-of-kin. He could not read the words on the front but he opened the letter to see if there was any money inside. Then, feeling guilty and superstitious, he went into the supply closet and resealed the envelope with Scotch tape.

When he clocked out the next morning, the CNA gave the letter to the woman who volunteered at the front desk, who placed it in a stack of outgoing mail.

Seven months after Eva Bock's funeral (during which the local police closed 58 South to tourists, to ensure that the funeral procession could head down to the cemetery in St. Elmo unimpeded; the residents, who had already simplified Miss Eva the way the living do, felt it was her final triumph), a letter in an eight-by-ten white linen stock envelope, addressed to Mrs. Eva Bock, arrived at the Lookout Mountain Post Office. Steven Ruske, Receiving, had never seen a letter from the White House. He was supposed to shred it (there was no next-of-kin listed on the Bock account) but who would know?

On his lunch break, despite the fact that it was a felony — didn't he, of all people, know it! — Steven Ruske took the letter out to his car, which was parked on Lula Lake Road across from the post office. He opened the envelope beneath his steering wheel. It was only a form letter with a stamped signature. He read it anyhow.

> *Dear Mrs. Eva Bock,*
>
>   *Thank you for writing to express your concerns regarding our efforts to improve the lives of the Iraqi people. I want to assure you, personally, that I and my administration are doing everything within our power to minimize casualties, both military and civilian. Please continue to keep our troops in your thoughts and prayers as we look forward to a future in which the freedoms we enjoy as Americans — including the freedom of speech, which allows citizens like yourself to speak out against oppression and injustice — are made available to our fellow citizens at the far reaches of the globe.*
>
>   *Sincerely,*
>   *President George W. Bush*

Steven Ruske slid the letter back into the envelope. He finished eating his sandwich, placing the letter in his lap to catch the crumbs. He stuffed the leftover crusts, foil wrapper, and envelope into his brown lunch sack. Then he crossed the street and, before returning to work, tossed the sack into the dumpster next to the Lookout Mountain Café.

Philip Roth

Philip Roth (b. 1933) was born in Newark, New Jersey, and grew up in a Jewish neighborhood there. His father was an insurance salesman whose parents had emigrated from Austria-Hungary. Roth worked on the high school newspaper and studied literature at Rutgers and at Bucknell University before earning his M.A. in literature from the University of Chicago, where he later taught English. He launched his career as a writer with a short novel, *Goodbye, Columbus* (1959), published together with five short stories, including "The Conversion of the Jews," which appeared earlier the same year in the *Paris Review*. The book was so successful — it won a National Book Award — that Roth decided to give up teaching. Three years later he followed it with his first full-length novel, *Letting Go.* In 1975 a second collection of stories appeared, *Reading Myself and Others.*

Over the years Roth's work has ranged from realistic, serious depictions of characters and events to surreal, comic attacks on such favorite American institutions as baseball and the cult of success to bittersweet, introspective examinations of the personal and moral dilemmas of a writer living among the people he writes about. The autobiographical character Nathan Zuckerman is featured in *The Ghost Writer* (1979), *Zuckerman Unbound* (1981), *The Counterlife* (1986), and several other novels, including *Exit Ghost* (2007). Roth has published the prize-winning trilogy of novels, *American Pastoral* (1997), *I Married a Communist* (1998), and *The Human Stain* (2000). *Nemesis* (2010) is a recent novel.

In May 2006 *The New York Times Book Review* contacted "a couple of hundred prominent writers, critics, editors, and other literary sages, asking them to please identify 'the single best work of American fiction published in the last twenty-five years.'" Of the twenty-two books cited, six of Roth's novels were selected: *American Pastoral, The Counterlife, Operation Shylock, Sabbath's Theater, The Human Stain,* and *The Plot against America.* The accompanying essay, "In Search of the Best," by A. O. Scott, stated, "If we had asked for the single best writer of fiction of the past twenty-five years, [Roth] would have won."

RELATED STORY
Alice Munro, "Age of Faith," page 927.

The Conversion of the Jews

1959

"YOU'RE A REAL ONE for opening your mouth in the first place," Itzie said. "What do you open your mouth all the time for?"

"I didn't bring it up, Itz, I didn't," Ozzie said.

"What do you care about Jesus Christ for anyway?"

"I didn't bring up Jesus Christ. He did. I didn't even know what he was talking about. Jesus is historical, he kept saying. Jesus is historical." Ozzie mimicked the monumental voice of Rabbi Binder.

"Jesus was a person that lived like you and me," Ozzie continued. "That's what Binder said —"

"Yeah? . . . So what! What do I give two cents whether he lived or not. And what do you gotta open your mouth!" Itzie Lieberman favored closed-mouthedness, especially when it came to Ozzie Freedman's questions. Mrs. Freedman had to see Rabbi Binder twice before about Ozzie's questions and this Wednesday at four-thirty would be the third time. Itzie preferred to keep *his* mother in the kitchen; he settled for behind-the-back subtleties such as gestures, faces, snarls, and other less delicate barnyard noises.

"He was a real person, Jesus, but he wasn't like God, and we don't believe he is God." Slowly, Ozzie was explaining Rabbi Binder's position to Itzie, who had been absent from Hebrew School the previous afternoon.

"The Catholics," Itzie said helpfully, "they believe in Jesus Christ, that he's God." Itzie Lieberman used "the Catholics" in its broadest sense — to include the Protestants.

Ozzie received Itzie's remark with a tiny head bob, as though it were a footnote, and went on. "His mother was Mary, and his father probably was Joseph," Ozzie said. "But the New Testament says his real father was God."

"His *real* father?"

"Yeah," Ozzie said, "that's the big thing, his father's supposed to be God."

"Bull."

"That's what Rabbi Binder says, that it's impossible —"

"Sure it's impossible. That stuff's all bull. To have a baby you gotta get laid," Itzie theologized. "Mary hadda get laid."

"That's what Binder says: 'The only way a woman can have a baby is to have intercourse with a man.'"

"He said *that*, Ozz?" For a moment it appeared that Itzie had put the theological question aside. "He said that, intercourse?" A little curled smile shaped itself in the lower half of Itzie's face like a pink mustache. "What you guys do, Ozz, you laugh or something?"

"I raised my hand."

"Yeah? Whatja say?"

"That's when I asked the question."

Itzie's face lit up. "Whatja ask about — intercourse?"

"No, I asked the question about God, how if He could create the heaven and earth in six days, and make all the animals and the fish and the light in six days — the light especially, that's what always gets me, that He could make the light. Making fish and animals, that's pretty good —"

"That's damn good." Itzie's appreciation was honest but unimaginative: it was as though God had just pitched a one-hitter.

"But making light . . . I mean when you think about it, it's really something," Ozzie said. "Anyway, I asked Binder if He could make all that in six days, and He could *pick* the six days he wanted right out of nowhere, why couldn't He let a woman have a baby without having intercourse."

"You said intercourse, Ozz, to Binder?"

"Yeah."

"Right in class?"

"Yeah."

Itzie smacked the side of his head.

"I mean, no kidding around," Ozzie said, "that'd really be nothing. After all that other stuff, that'd practically be nothing."

Itzie considered a moment. "What'd Binder say?"

"He started all over again explaining how Jesus was historical and how he lived like you and me but he wasn't God. So I said I under*stood* that. What I wanted to know was different."

What Ozzie wanted to know was always different. The first time he had wanted to know how Rabbi Binder could call the Jews "The Chosen People" if the Declaration of Independence claimed all men to be created equal. Rabbi Binder tried to distinguish for him between political equality and spiritual legitimacy, but what Ozzie wanted to know, he insisted vehemently, was different. That was the first time his mother had to come.

Then there was the plane crash. Fifty-eight people had been killed in a plane crash at La Guardia. In studying a casualty list in the newspaper his mother had discovered among the list of those dead eight Jewish names (his grandmother had nine but she counted Miller as a Jewish name); because of the eight she said the plane crash was "a tragedy." During free-discussion time on Wednesday Ozzie had brought to Rabbi Binder's attention this matter of "some of his relations" always picking out the Jewish names. Rabbi Binder had begun to explain cultural unity and some other things when Ozzie stood up at his seat and said that what he wanted to know was different. Rabbi Binder insisted that he sit down and it was then that Ozzie shouted that he wished all fifty-eight were Jews. That was the second time his mother came.

"And he kept explaining about Jesus being historical, and so I kept asking him. No kidding, Itz, he was trying to make me look stupid."

"So what he finally do?"

"Finally he starts screaming that I was deliberately simple-minded and a wise guy, and that my mother had to come, and this was the last time. And that I'd never get bar-mitzvahed if he could help it. Then, Itz, then he starts talking in that voice like a statue, real slow and deep, and he says that I better think over what I said about the Lord. He told me to go to his office and think it over." Ozzie leaned his body towards Itzie. "Itz, I thought it over for a solid hour, and now I'm convinced God could do it."

Ozzie had planned to confess his latest transgression to his mother as soon as she came home from work. But it was a Friday night in November and already dark, and when Mrs. Freedman came through the door she tossed off her coat, kissed Ozzie quickly on the face, and went to the kitchen table to light the three yellow candles, two for the Sabbath and one for Ozzie's father.

When his mother lit the candles she would move her two arms slowly towards her, dragging them through the air, as though persuading people whose minds were half made up. And her eyes would get glassy with tears.

Even when his father was alive Ozzie remembered that her eyes had gotten glassy, so it didn't have anything to do with his dying. It had something to do with lighting the candles.

As she touched the flaming match to the unlit wick of a Sabbath candle, the phone rang, and Ozzie, standing only a foot from it, plucked it off the receiver and held it muffled to his chest. When his mother lit candles Ozzie felt there should be no noise; even breathing, if you could manage it, should be softened. Ozzie pressed the phone to his breast and watched his mother dragging whatever she was dragging, and he felt his own eyes get glassy. His mother was a round, tired, gray-haired penguin of a woman whose gray skin had begun to feel the tug of gravity and the weight of her own history. Even when she was dressed up she didn't look like a chosen person. But when she lit candles she looked like something better; like a woman who knew momentarily that God could do anything.

After a few mysterious minutes she was finished. Ozzie hung up the phone and walked to the kitchen table where she was beginning to lay the two places for the four-course Sabbath meal. He told her that she would have to see Rabbi Binder next Wednesday at four-thirty, and then he told her why. For the first time in their life together she hit Ozzie across the face with her hand.

All through the chopped liver and chicken soup part of the dinner Ozzie cried; he didn't have any appetite for the rest.

On Wednesday, in the largest of the three basement classrooms of the synagogue, Rabbi Marvin Binder, a tall, handsome, broad-shouldered man of thirty with thick strong-fibered black hair, removed his watch from his pocket and saw that it was four o'clock. At the rear of the room Yakov Blotnik, the seventy-one-year-old custodian, slowly polished the large window, mumbling to himself, unaware that it was four o'clock or six o'clock, Monday or Wednesday. To most of the students Yakov Blotnik's mumbling, along with his brown curly beard, scythe nose, and two heel-trailing black cats, made of him an object of wonder, a foreigner, a relic, towards whom they were alternately fearful and disrespectful. To Ozzie the mumbling had always seemed a monotonous, curious prayer; what made it curious was that old Blotnik had been mumbling so steadily for so many years, Ozzie suspected he had memorized the prayers and forgotten all about God.

"It is now free-discussion time," Rabbi Binder said. "Feel free to talk about any Jewish matter at all — religion, family, politics, sports —"

There was silence. It was a gusty, clouded November afternoon and it did not seem as though there ever was or could be a thing called baseball. So nobody this week said a word about that hero from the past, Hank Greenberg — which limited free discussion considerably.

And the soul-battering Ozzie Freedman had just received from Rabbi Binder had imposed its limitation. When it was Ozzie's turn to read aloud from the Hebrew book the rabbi had asked him petulantly why he didn't read more rapidly. He was showing no progress. Ozzie said he could read faster but that if he did he was sure not to understand what he was reading. Nevertheless, at the rabbi's repeated suggestion Ozzie tried, and showed a great talent, but in the midst of a long passage he stopped short and said he didn't understand a word he was reading, and started in again at a drag-footed pace. Then came the soul-battering.

Consequently, when free-discussion time rolled around none of the students felt too free. The rabbi's invitation was answered only by the mumbling of feeble old Blotnik.

"Isn't there anything at all you would like to discuss?" Rabbi Binder asked again, looking at his watch. "No questions or comments?"

There was a small grumble from the third row. The rabbi requested that Ozzie rise and give the rest of the class the advantage of his thought.

Ozzie rose. "I forget it now," he said, and sat down in his place.

Rabbi Binder advanced a seat towards Ozzie and poised himself on the edge of the desk. It was Itzie's desk and the rabbi's frame only a dagger's-length away from his face snapped him to sitting attention.

"Stand up again, Oscar," Rabbi Binder said calmly, "and try to assemble your thoughts."

Ozzie stood up. All his classmates turned in their seats and watched as he gave an unconvincing scratch to his forehead.

"I can't assemble any," he announced, and plunked himself down.

"Stand up!" Rabbi Binder advanced from Itzie's desk to the one directly in front of Ozzie; when the rabbinical back was turned Itzie gave it five-fingers off the tip of his nose, causing a small titter in the room. Rabbi Binder was too absorbed in squelching Ozzie's nonsense once and for all to bother with titters. "Stand up, Oscar. What's your question about?"

Ozzie pulled a word out of the air. It was the handiest word. "Religion."

"Oh, now you remember?"

"Yes."

"What is it?"

Trapped, Ozzie blurted the first thing that came to him. "Why can't He make anything He wants to make!"

As Rabbi Binder prepared an answer, a final answer, Itzie, ten feet behind him, raised one finger on his left hand, gestured it meaningfully towards the rabbi's back, and brought the house down.

Binder twisted quickly to see what had happened and in the midst of the commotion Ozzie shouted into the rabbi's back what he couldn't have shouted to his face. It was a loud, toneless sound that had the timbre of something stored inside for about six days.

"You don't know! You don't know anything about God!"

The rabbi spun back towards Ozzie. "What?"

"You don't know — you don't —"

"Apologize, Oscar, apologize!" It was a threat.

"You don't —"

Rabbi Binder's hand flicked out at Ozzie's cheek. Perhaps it had only been meant to clamp the boy's mouth shut, but Ozzie ducked and the palm caught him squarely on the nose.

The blood came in a short, red spurt on to Ozzie's shirt front.

The next moment was all confusion. Ozzie screamed, "You bastard, you bastard!" and broke for the classroom door. Rabbi Binder lurched a step backwards, as though his own blood had started flowing violently in the opposite direction, then gave a clumsy lurch forward and bolted out the door after Ozzie. The class followed after the rabbi's huge blue-suited back, and before old Blotnik could turn from his window, the room was empty and everyone was headed full speed up the three flights leading to the roof.

If one should compare the light of day to the life of man: sunrise to birth; sunset — the dropping down over the edge — to death; then as Ozzie Freedman wiggled through the trapdoor of the synagogue roof, his feet kicking backwards bronco-style at Rabbi Binder's outstretched arms — at that moment the day was fifty years old. As a rule, fifty or fifty-five reflects accurately the age of late afternoons in November, for it is in that month, during those hours, that one's awareness of light seems no longer a matter of seeing, but of hearing: light begins clicking away. In fact, as Ozzie locked shut the trapdoor in the rabbi's face, the sharp click of the bolt into the lock might momentarily have been mistaken for the sound of the heavier gray that had just throbbed through the sky.

With all his weight Ozzie kneeled on the locked door; any instant he was certain that Rabbi Binder's shoulder would fling it open, splintering the wood into shrapnel and catapulting his body into the sky. But the door did not move and below him he heard only the rumble of feet, first loud then dim, like thunder rolling away.

A question shot through his brain. "Can this be *me*?" For a thirteen-year-old who had just labeled his religious leader a bastard, twice, it was not an improper question. Louder and louder the question came to him — "Is it me? It is me?"— until he discovered himself no longer kneeling, but racing crazily towards the edge of the roof, his eyes crying, his throat screaming, and his arms flying everywhichway as though not his own.

"Is it me? Is it me Me ME ME ME! It has to be me — but is it!"

It is the question a thief must ask himself the night he jimmies open his first window, and it is said to be the question with which bridegrooms quiz themselves before the altar.

In the few wild seconds it took Ozzie's body to propel him to the edge of the roof, his self-examination began to grow fuzzy. Gazing down at the street, he became confused as to the problem beneath the question: was it, is-it-me-who-called-Binder-a-bastard? or, is-it-me-prancing-around-on-the-roof? However, the scene below settled all, for there is an instant in any action when whether it is you or somebody else is academic. The thief crams the money in his pockets and scoots out the window. The bridegroom signs the hotel register for two. And the boy on the roof finds a streetful of people gaping at him, necks stretched backwards, faces up, as though he were the ceiling of the Hayden Planetarium. Suddenly you know it's you.

"Oscar! Oscar Freedman!" A voice rose from the center of the crowd, a voice that, could it have been seen, would have looked like the writing on a scroll. "Oscar Freedman, get down from there. Immediately!" Rabbi Binder was pointing one arm stiffly up at him; and at the end of that arm, one finger aimed menacingly. It was the attitude of a dictator, but one — the eyes confessed all — whose personal valet had spit neatly in his face.

Ozzie didn't answer. Only for a blink's length did he look towards Rabbi Binder. Instead his eyes began to fit together the world beneath him, to sort out people from places, friends from enemies, participants from spectators. In little jagged starlike clusters his friends stood around Rabbi Binder, who was still pointing. The topmost point on a star compounded not of angels but of five adolescent boys was Itzie. What a world it was, with those stars below, Rabbi Binder below . . . Ozzie, who a moment earlier hadn't been able to control his own body, started to feel the meaning of the word control: he felt Peace and he felt Power.

"Oscar Freedman, I'll give you three to come down."

Few dictators give their subjects three to do anything; but, as always, Rabbi Binder only looked dictatorial.

"Are you ready, Oscar?"

Ozzie nodded his head yes, although he had no intention in the world — the lower one or the celestial one he'd just entered — of coming down even if Rabbi Binder should give him a million.

"All right then," said Rabbi Binder. He ran a hand through his black Samson hair as though it were the gesture prescribed for uttering the first digit. Then, with his other hand cutting a circle out of the small piece of sky around him, he spoke. "One!"

There was no thunder. On the contrary, at that moment, as though "one" was the cue for which he had been waiting, the world's least thunderous person appeared on the synagogue steps. He did not so much come out the synagogue door as lean out, onto the darkening air. He clutched at the doorknob with one hand and looked up at the roof.

"Oy!"

Yakov Blotnik's old mind hobbled slowly, as if on crutches, and though he couldn't decide precisely what the boy was doing on the roof, he knew it wasn't good — that is, it wasn't-good-for-the-Jews. For Yakov Blotnik life had fractionated itself simply: things were either good-for-the-Jews or no-good-for-the-Jews.

He smacked his free hand to his in-sucked cheek, gently. "Oy, Gut!" And then quickly as he was able, he jacked down his head and surveyed the street. There was Rabbi Binder (like a man at an auction with only three dollars in his pocket, he had just delivered a shaky "Two!"); there were the students, and that was all. So far it-wasn't-so-bad-for-the-Jews. But the boy had to come down immediately, before anybody saw. The problem: how to get the boy off the roof?

Anybody who has ever had a cat on the roof knows how to get him down. You call the fire department. Or first you call the operator and you ask her for the fire department. And the next thing there is great jamming of brakes and clanging of bells and shouting of instructions. And then the cat is off the roof. You do the same thing to get a boy off the roof.

That is, you do the same thing if you are Yakov Blotnik and you once had a cat on the roof.

When the engines, all four of them, arrived, Rabbi Binder had four times given Ozzie the count of three. The big hook-and-ladder swung around the corner and one of the firemen leaped from it, plunging headlong towards the yellow fire hydrant in front of the synagogue. With a huge wrench he began to unscrew the top nozzle. Rabbi Binder raced over to him and pulled at his shoulder.

"There's no fire . . ."

The fireman mumbled back over his shoulder and, heatedly, continued working at the nozzle.

"But there's no fire, there's no fire . . ." Binder shouted. When the fireman mumbled again, the rabbi grasped his face with both his hands and pointed it up at the roof.

To Ozzie it looked as though Rabbi Binder was trying to tug the fireman's head out of his body, like a cork from a bottle. He had to giggle at the picture they made: it was a family portrait—rabbi in black skullcap, fireman in red fire hat, and the little yellow hydrant squatting beside like a kid brother, bareheaded. From the edge of the roof Ozzie waved at the portrait, a one-handed, flapping, mocking wave; in doing it his right foot slipped from under him. Rabbi Binder covered his eyes with his hands.

Firemen work fast. Before Ozzie had even regained his balance, a big, round, yellowed net was being held on the synagogue lawn. The firemen who held it looked up at Ozzie with stern, feelingless faces.

One of the firemen turned his head towards Rabbi Binder. "What, is the kid nuts or something?"

Rabbi Binder unpeeled his hands from his eyes, slowly, painfully, as if they were tape. Then he checked: nothing on the sidewalk, no dents in the net.

"Is he gonna jump, or what?" the fireman shouted.

In a voice not at all like a statue, Rabbi Binder finally answered. "Yes, Yes, I think so . . . He's been threatening to . . ."

Threatening to? Why, the reason he was on the roof, Ozzie remembered, was to get away; he hadn't even thought about jumping. He had just run to get away, and the truth was that he hadn't really headed for the roof as much as he'd been chased there.

"What's his name, the kid?"

"Freedman," Rabbi Binder answered. "Oscar Freedman."

The fireman looked up at Ozzie. "What is it with you, Oscar? You gonna jump, or what?"

Ozzie did not answer. Frankly, the question had just arisen.

"Look, Oscar, if you're gonna jump, jump—and if you're not gonna jump, don't jump. But don't waste our time, willya?"

Ozzie looked at the fireman and then at Rabbi Binder. He wanted to see Rabbi Binder cover his eyes one more time.

"I'm going to jump."

And then he scampered around the edge of the roof to the corner, where there was no net below, and he flapped his arms at his sides, swishing the air and smacking his palms to his trousers on the downbeat. He began screaming like some kind of engine, "Wheeeee . . . wheeeeee," and leaning way out over the edge with the upper half of his body. The firemen whipped around to cover the ground with the net. Rabbi Binder mumbled a few words to Somebody and covered his eyes. Everything happened quickly, jerkily, as in a silent movie. The crowd, which had arrived with the fire engines, gave out a long, Fourth-of-July fireworks oooh-aahhh. In the excitement no one had paid the crowd much heed, except, of course, Yakov Blotnik, who swung from the doorknob counting heads. "Fier und tsvantsik . . . finf und tsvantsik . . . Oy, Gut!" It wasn't like this with the cat.

Rabbi Binder peeked through his fingers, checked the sidewalk and net. Empty. But there was Ozzie racing to the other corner. The firemen raced with him but were unable to keep up. Whenever Ozzie wanted to he might jump and splatter himself upon the sidewalk, and by the time the firemen scooted to the spot all they could do with their net would be to cover the mess.

"Wheeeee . . . wheeeee . . ."

"Hey, Oscar," the winded fireman yelled, "What the hell is this, a game or something?"

"Wheeeee . . . wheeeee . . ."

"Hey, Oscar —"

But he was off now to the other corner, flapping his wings fiercely. Rabbi Binder couldn't take it any longer — the fire engines from nowhere, the screaming suicidal boy, the net. He fell to his knees, exhausted, and with his hands curled together in front of his chest like a little dome, he pleaded, "Oscar, stop it, Oscar. Don't jump, Oscar. Please come down . . . Please don't jump."

And further back in the crowd a single voice, a single young voice, shouted a lone word to the boy on the roof.

"Jump!"

It was Itzie. Ozzie momentarily stopped flapping.

"Go ahead, Ozz — jump!" Itzie broke off his point of the star and courageously, with the inspiration not of a wise-guy but of a disciple, stood alone. "Jump, Ozz, jump!"

Still on his knees, his hands still curled, Rabbi Binder twisted his body back. He looked at Itzie, then, agonizingly, back to Ozzie.

"Oscar, Don't Jump! Please, Don't Jump . . . please, please . . ."

"Jump!" This time it wasn't Itzie but another point of the star. By the time Mrs. Freedman arrived to keep her four-thirty appointment with Rabbi Binder, the whole little upside down heaven was shouting and pleading for Ozzie to jump, and Rabbi Binder no longer was pleading with him not to jump, but was crying into the dome of his hands.

Understandably Mrs. Freedman couldn't figure out what her son was doing on the roof. So she asked.

"Ozzie, my Ozzie, what are you doing? My Ozzie, what is it?"

Ozzie stopped wheeeeeing and slowed his arms down to a cruising flap, the kind birds use in soft winds, but he did not answer. He stood against the low, clouded, darkening sky — light clicked down swiftly now, as on a small gear — flapping softly and gazing down at the small bundle of a woman who was his mother.

"What are you doing, Ozzie?" She turned towards the kneeling Rabbi Binder and rushed so close that only a paper-thickness of dusk lay between her stomach and his shoulders.

"What is my baby doing?"

Rabbi Binder gaped up at her but he too was mute. All that moved was the dome of his hands; it shook back and forth like a weak pulse.

"Rabbi, get him down! He'll kill himself. Get him down, my only baby . . ."

"I can't," Rabbi Binder said, "I can't . . ." and he turned his handsome head towards the crowd of boys behind him. "It's them. Listen to them."

And for the first time Mrs. Freedman saw the crowd of boys, and she heard what they were yelling.

"He's doing it for them. He won't listen to me. It's them." Rabbi Binder spoke like one in a trance.

"For them?"

"Yes."

"Why for them?"

"They want him to . . ."

Mrs. Freedman raised her two arms upward as though she were conducting the sky. "For them he's doing it!" And then in a gesture older than pyramids, older than prophets and floods, her arms came slapping down to her sides. "A martyr I have. Look!" She tilted her head to the roof. Ozzie was still flapping softly. "My martyr."

"Oscar, come down, *please*," Rabbi Binder groaned.

In a startlingly even voice Mrs. Freedman called to the boy on the roof. "Ozzie, come down, Ozzie. Don't be a martyr, my baby."

As though it were a litany, Rabbi Binder repeated her words. "Don't be a martyr, my baby. Don't be a martyr."

"Gawhead, Ozz — *be* a Martin!" It was Itzie. "Be a Martin, be a Martin," and all the voices joined in singing for Martindom, whatever it was. "Be a Martin, be a Martin . . ."

———

Somehow when you're on a roof the darker it gets the less you can hear. All Ozzie knew was that two groups wanted two new things: his friends were spirited and musical about what they wanted; his mother and the rabbi were even-toned, chanting, about what they didn't want. The rabbi's voice was without tears now and so was his mother's.

The big net stared up at Ozzie like a sightless eye. The big, clouded sky pushed down. From beneath it looked like a gray corrugated board. Suddenly, looking up into that unsympathetic sky, Ozzie realized all the strangeness of what these people, his friends, were asking: they wanted him to jump, to kill himself; they were singing about it now — it made them that happy. And there was an even greater strangeness: Rabbi Binder was on his knees, trembling. If there was a question to be asked now it was not "Is it me?" but rather "Is it us? . . . Is it us?"

Being on the roof, it turned out, was a serious thing. If he jumped would the singing become dancing? Would it? What would jumping stop? Yearningly, Ozzie wished he could rip open the sky, plunge his hands through, and pull out the sun; and on the sun, like a coin, would be stamped JUMP or DON'T JUMP.

Ozzie's knees rocked and sagged a little under him as though they were setting him for a dive. His arms tightened, stiffened, froze, from shoulders to fingernails. He felt as if each part of his body were going to vote as to whether he should kill himself or not — and each part as though it were independent of *him*.

The light took an unexpected click down and the new darkness, like a gag, hushed the friends singing for this and the mother and rabbi chanting for that.

Ozzie stopped counting votes, and in a curiously high voice, like one who wasn't prepared for speech, he spoke.

"Mamma?"

"Yes, Oscar."

"Mamma, get down on your knees, like Rabbi Binder."

"Oscar —"

"Get down on your knees," he said, "or I'll jump."

Ozzie heard a whimper, then a quick rustling, and when he looked down where his mother had stood he saw the top of a head and beneath that a circle of dress. She was kneeling beside Rabbi Binder.

He spoke again. "Everybody kneel." There was the sound of everybody kneeling.

Ozzie looked around. With one hand he pointed towards the synagogue entrance. "Make *him* kneel."

There was a noise, not of kneeling, but of body-and-cloth stretching. Ozzie could hear Rabbi Binder saying in a gruff whisper, ". . . or he'll *kill* himself," and when next he looked there was Yakov Blotnik off the doorknob and for the first time in his life upon his knees in the Gentile posture of prayer.

As for the firemen — it is not as difficult as one might imagine to hold a net taut while you are kneeling.

Ozzie looked around again; and then he called to Rabbi Binder.

"Rabbi?"

"Yes, Oscar."

"Rabbi Binder, do you believe in God?"

"Yes."

"Do you believe God can do Anything?" Ozzie leaned his head out into the darkness. "Anything?"

"Oscar, I think —"

"Tell me you believe God can do Anything."

There was a second's hesitation. Then: "God can do Anything."

"Tell me you believe God can make a child without intercourse."

"He can."

"Tell me!"

"God," Rabbi Binder admitted, "can make a child without intercourse."

"Mamma, you tell me."

"God can make a child without intercourse," his mother said.

"Make *him* tell me." There was no doubt who *him* was.

In a few moments Ozzie heard an old comical voice say something to the increasing darkness about God.

Next, Ozzie made everybody say it. And then he made them all say they believed in Jesus Christ — first one at a time, then all together.

When the catechizing was through it was the beginning of evening. From the street it sounded as if the boy on the roof might have sighed.

"Ozzie?" A woman's voice dared to speak. "You'll come down now?"

There was no answer, but the woman waited, and when a voice finally did speak it was thin and crying, and exhausted as that of an old man who has just finished pulling the bells.

"Mamma, don't you see — you shouldn't hit me. He shouldn't hit me. You shouldn't hit me about God, Mamma. You should never hit anybody about God —"

"Ozzie, please come down now."

"Promise me, promise me you'll never hit anybody about God."

He had asked only his mother, but for some reason everyone kneeling in the street promised he would never hit anybody about God.

Once again there was silence.

"I can come down now, Mamma," the boy on the roof finally said. He turned his head both ways as though checking the traffic lights. "Now I can come down . . ."

And he did, right into the center of the yellow net that glowed in the evening's edge like an overgrown halo.

Joe Sacco

Joe Sacco (b. 1960) was born on the Mediterranean island of Malta, the son of an engineer (father) and a teacher (mother). As a boy he lived in Australia before moving to the West Coast of the United States when he was twelve. Growing up in Los Angeles and Portland, he read *Mad* magazine and war comics; after high school he studied journalism at the University of Oregon in Eugene, from which he graduated in 1981. In the 1980s he traveled in Europe and Malta, working as a cartoonist and editor for various comics publishers. He also produced six issues of his own comic book *Yahoo* for Fantagraphics Books in Seattle. While living in Berlin in the early 1990s, he decided to travel in the Middle East with the idea that the ordinary news channels weren't telling the whole story about the conflicts there. In 1992 he visited Israel and the occupied territories, which gave him the material for his groundbreaking book *Palestine*, created after Sacco returned to the United States. This book combined the techniques of eyewitness reportage with the medium of graphic storytelling. It was first published as a two-part comic book in 1995 and won the American Book Award.

Later Sacco explained that in his book he wasn't trying to reconcile the differences between Israelis and Palestinians. Instead he wanted, in a small way, to give the Palestinians a voice and provide a clear "lens through which people could see their lives." Sacco had also traveled in Sarajevo, and in 1998 Art Spiegelman, comix editor of *Details* magazine, commissioned him to cover the Bosnian war crimes trials in The Hague, Netherlands. Two years later Sacco's experiences resulted in *Safe Area Gorazde: The War in Eastern Bosnia 1992–1995*, a graphic narrative that exposed the political impotence of the U.N. operations during the Bosnian War. In 2001 he received a Guggenheim Fellowship. *But I Like It*, a collection of his cartoon strips about the blues and rock and roll, was published in 2006.

As reviewer Chris Hedges commented, in Sacco's stories of what he encountered in the Middle East, he "survives by making friends and living in the same conditions as those he covers. This gives his work a kind of street-level grit and insight, and it also makes it hard to romanticize the people he writes about. . . . His drawings are stark, realistic visions of the gray, depressing world of a land mangled by artillery shells and deformed by poverty." Sacco never studied art formally and doesn't consider himself a particularly good artist, saying "I kind of bludgeon my way through the page." Moving quickly through war-torn countries, he sometimes uses a camera instead of relying on sketches to capture the background scenes. What makes his work so powerful is his lack of self-righteousness and his attention to odd, humanizing details as he chronicles his encounters with devastated landscapes. At first Sacco wasn't sure that anyone would even print his kind of storytelling—"I thought it was almost commercial suicide." Now he feels that creating graphic fiction gives him a valuable freedom.

> The main benefit [to comics] is that you can make your subject very accessible. You open the book and suddenly you're in the place. Maybe there's also a guilty pleasure as people think back to their childhood days reading comics and they think, "This might be fun, it might be an easy way to learn something about this." It's a very subversive medium, it's appealing but what's in the comic itself could be very hard, even difficult material.

RELATED CASEBOOK

See Casebook on Graphic Storytelling, pages 1647–1663, including Charles Hatfield, "From *Alternative Comics*: Toward the Habit of Questioning," page 1649; Michael Kupperman, "Are Comics Serious Literature?," page 1652; Joe Sacco, "Some Reflections on *Palestine*," page 1655; Edward W. Said, "Homage to Joe Sacco," page 1658.

Marjane Satrapi

Marjane Satrapi (b. 1969) was born in Rasht, Iran, and raised in Tehran. She is the only child of a father who was a successful architect and a mother who was a dress designer, and she is the granddaughter of the last Qadjar emperor of Persia. In 1984, five years after the Iranian Revolution, at the beginning of the war between Iran and Iraq that left a million dead, her parents sent her to live in Vienna, fearing that she would be arrested as an outspoken rebellious teenager in fundamentalist Tehran. Feeling exiled as an art student in Austria, Satrapi failed to fit in. She spent months on the street, became suicidal, and was hospitalized. In 1989, when she returned home to the domestic repression of the totalitarian regime in Iran, she found that "everything was settled down. The revolution was far behind, ten years before. . . . We were so fed up with the eight years of war [with Iraq]; it was so good that the war was finished. People just wanted to live. . . . We didn't talk about politics because we were so scared. This new generation is different. They haven't lived what we have gone through. They don't have the same fears."

After a brief marriage Satrapi left Tehran for Paris in 1994, where she attended a comic book workshop called "The Association," which included Pierre-François Beauchard, whose black-and-white graphic novels, published under the name David B., dramatize family trauma. As a child Satrapi never dreamed that she would become a graphic artist, since she did not like to read comic books. While she was growing up, her cousins tried to interest her in the popular Tintin adventure series created by the Belgian artist Hergé, who incorporated actual news stories from 1929 to 1983 into his graphic narratives. Satrapi claims that Tintin—a peripatetic young journalist who traveled the world with his dog Snowy—didn't stop anywhere long enough to interact with young women characters, so she couldn't identify with him. It was encountering Art Spiegelman's Holocaust story *Maus* that captivated her. "When I read him I thought . . . it's possible to tell a story and make a point this way. It was amazing." She realized that she could express her ideas and feelings through pictures in a way that words alone could not communicate.

> Image is an international language. The first writing of the human being was drawing, not writing. That appeared much before the alphabet. And when you draw a situation—someone is scared or angry or happy—it means the same thing in all cultures. You cannot draw someone crying, and in one culture they think that he is happy. He would have the same expression. There's something direct about the image. Also, it is more accessible. People don't take it so seriously. And when you want to use a little bit of humor, it's much easier to use pictures.

"The Veil," a story told from the perspective of a ten-year-old girl, is from *Persepolis 1* (2003), subtitled "The Story of a Childhood," which describes Satrapi's life in Iran during the Revolution and the first years of the war with Iraq. *Persepolis 2* (2004), called "The Story of a Return," begins with her arrival in Austria and ends with her return to her ravaged homeland. She wrote them after she moved to Paris, which has become her home. *Persepolis* is dedicated to her parents, but she didn't show them her first book based on their life together until just before it was published. She feels that

> maturity is knowing to say what to whom and when. Sometimes saying stuff
> is not a very good idea. You want to make yourself feel a little bit lighter,
> so you take your shit and you put it on somebody else's back. Well, that's
> extremely egoistic. One should know also how to hold things back and
> assume his or her own responsibility.

Describing her method, Satrapi, who writes in French, says she first decides how many frames she wants to put on each page and what she wants to say in each frame. Then she sketches a stick figure or the outline of a scene in each frame. "After that, I take a pencil and draw them. Once that is finished, I put my paper over the light box and ink it. It's a long process." Satrapi's other books include *Embroideries* (2005) and *Chicken with Plums* (2006). *Persepolis* is available as a film distributed by Sony Classics.

RELATED CASEBOOK
See Casebook on Graphic Storytelling, pages 1647–1663, including Charles Hatfield, "From *Alternative Comics*: Toward the Habit of Questioning," page 1649; Michael Kupperman, "Are Comics Serious Literature?," page 1652; Sydney Plum, "Reading 'The Veil,' by Marjane Satrapi," page 1653.

From *Persepolis:* The Veil

2003

George Saunders

George Saunders (b. 1958) was born and raised on the south side of Chicago. He attended the Colorado School of Mines and earned a B.S. in geophysical engineering in 1981. Then, as he described in a "Personal History" (2003) column for The *New Yorker*, followed some years of confusion, as apparently he tried to emulate the inimitable lives of the authors he admired as a young aspiring writer: Ernest Hemingway, Thomas Wolfe, and Jack Kerouac. "At twenty-six, at the embarrassing end of a series of attempts at channeling Kerouac, I was beyond broke, back in my home town, living in my aunt and uncle's basement." After a short, brutal winter job on a roofing crew in Chicago, Saunders read in *People* magazine about the Creative Writing graduate program at Syracuse University. He was accepted into the program and received his M.A. in 1988.

From 1989 to 1996, Saunders worked as a technical writer and geophysical engineer while writing the stories collected in his first book, *CivilWarLand in Bad Decline: Stories and a Novella* (1996). Since 1997, he has taught creative writing at Syracuse University and conducted writing workshops throughout the United States. *Pastoralia*, his second collection, appeared in 2000. His short fiction has won the National Magazine Award for Fiction and the O. Henry Prize. *The Brief and Frightening Reign of Phil* was published in 2005.

As Joyce Carol Oates recognized, Saunders's "hyperkinetic dark-fantasist-satiric prose" is an acquired taste, but it's also "a taste quickly acquired." His vision of America as a land peopled with "entrepreneurial zealots whom he satirizes" sometimes "spills over into sheer comic-book silliness," but often "engages us unexpectedly." Abandoning his earlier literary models, Saunders has forged his own style in the "stream-of-consciousness black humor" tradition of contemporary American novelists Thomas Pynchon, Robert Coover, and Don DeLillo. Saunders cares for his cartoon characters, as in "Sticks." His people are life's losers, but they continue to persevere against all the odds, hoping things will get better. Saunders practices Nyingma Buddhism, a Tibetan Buddhist tradition that has led him to the path of the spiritual warrior whose weapons are "gentleness, clarity of mind, and an open heart." Some other Saunders's books are *In Persuasion Nation* (2006), a story collection, and *The Braindead Megaphone* (2007), his collected essays. *Tenth of December Stories* appeared in 2013.

Sticks

1994

EVERY YEAR THANKSGIVING NIGHT we flocked out behind Dad as he dragged the Santa suit to the road and draped it over a kind of crucifix he'd built out of metal pole in the yard. Super Bowl week the pole was dressed in a jersey and Rod's helmet and Rod had to clear it with Dad if he wanted to take the helmet off. On Fourth of July the pole was Uncle Sam, on Veterans Day a soldier, on Halloween a ghost. The pole was Dad's one concession to glee. We were allowed a single Crayola from the box at a time. One Christmas Eve he shrieked at Kimmie for wasting an apple slice. He hovered over us as we poured ketchup, saying, Good enough good enough good enough. Birthday parties consisted of cupcakes, no ice cream. The first time I brought a date over she said, What's with your dad and that pole? and I sat there blinking.

We left home, married, had children of our own, found the seeds of meanness blooming also within us. Dad began dressing the pole with more complexity and less discernible logic. He draped some kind of fur over it on Groundhog Day and lugged out a floodlight to ensure a shadow. When an earthquake struck Chile he laid the pole on its side and spray-painted a rift in the earth. Mom died and he dressed the pole as Death and hung from the crossbar photos of Mom as a baby. We'd stop by and find odd talismans from his youth arranged around the base: army medals, theater tickets, old sweatshirts, tubes of Mom's makeup. One autumn he painted the pole bright yellow. He covered it with cotton swabs that winter for warmth and provided offspring by hammering in six crossed sticks around the yard. He ran lengths of string between the pole and the sticks, and taped to the string letters of apology, admissions of error, pleas for understanding, all written in a frantic hand on index cards. He painted a sign saying LOVE and hung it from the pole and another that said FORGIVE? and then he died in the hall with the radio on and we sold the house to a young couple who yanked out the pole and left it by the road on garbage day.

Saïd Sayrafiezadeh

Saïd Sayrafiezadeh (b. 1968) was born in Brooklyn, New York, to a Jewish mother and an Iranian Muslim father. His mother was a committed member of the Socialist Workers Party who moved to Pittsburgh with Sayrafiezadeh and raised him there as a single parent. He remembered that she was often depressed because "much of her energy and passion was put into realizing the working-class revolution. . . . The cataclysmic event that we were anticipating was going to take place sometime in the future, the distant future, perhaps not even in our lifetime. And until then there could be no real excitement; there could be only meetings and petitionings and militant newspaper sales on Saturday morning." Otherwise "we lived in a simple apartment and ate simple meals and did simple things. Things stayed the same." In his early twenties he left Pittsburgh for New York City and became an actor and a writer. He believes that his stories are a way for him "to imagine how things would have played out had I never left. There's catharsis in this: I'm reliving trauma."

Sayrafiezadeh began his career by writing plays. When he turned to writing fiction, he felt that his playwrighting experience had given him "an absolute awareness" of the reader. "It's been invaluable as a writer. I consider the reader when I create my scenes. What would they want to see happen next? How would they want to see it? Sometimes I give it to them, and sometimes I don't, but I'm always thinking about them. It's about the reader as much as it's about me."

In 2009, after publishing his memoir *When Skateboards Will Be Free: A Memoir of a Political Childhood* about his experiences being raised by a Socialist mother, Sayrafiezadeh continued writing nonfiction and fiction for magazines such as *Granta* and *The Paris Review*. His story "A Brief Encounter with the Enemy" came out of his imagination, as he never served in the armed forces. Instead of being faithful to actual events or personal experience, he is inspired by what he calls "the drama" of the Marxist idea "that war is inevitable under capitalism." While writing the story, Sayrafiezadeh says that he knew what was going to happen at the end of it, because "That's why I wrote it. The event on the hill is the story I wanted to tell. The ending takes up probably about five hundred words, but it's the first five thousand words that are really the key — that's where the hard work went. . . . All I could do was draw him [his protagonist] and his surroundings as vividly as possible and hope for the best."

RELATED STORY:
Tim O'Brien, "The Things They Carried," page 990.

A Brief Encounter with the Enemy

2012

TO GET TO THE HILL you have to first take the path. The path is narrow and steep and lined with trees that are so dark they could be purple, and so dense it feels as though you're walking alongside a brick wall. You can't see in and you hope that no one can see out.

The first time I went up the path it was terrifying. I could barely take a full breath, let alone put one foot in front of the other. If I'd had to run, I wouldn't have remembered how. Besides, I was loaded down with fifty pounds of equipment that clanged and banged with every step. I might as well have been carrying a refrigerator on my back. But after the first month the fear dissipated and the path started to become fascinating, even charming. I was able to appreciate the "beauty of the surroundings" — as the brochure had said — even the trees that I was constantly bumping against. "What kind of trees are these?" I asked out loud. I wanted to learn everything I could. I wanted to get everything there was to get out of this experience.

"Christmas trees," someone answered back. He was being funny, of course, and everyone laughed, even though we were missing Christmas.

The sergeant wanted to know what was funny. We told him nothing was funny, sir. He said that that was true — nothing was funny, that if you could get shot in the face at any moment then nothing could be funny.

So we were quiet again, the fifty of us, we were fearful again, but it didn't last too long, because fear can't persist unless you have at least a little evidence to sustain it. Fascination can't persist, either. What can persist, however, is boredom. I had come all this way hoping for something groundbreaking to happen, and nothing had happened. Now twelve months had passed, and tomorrow I was flying back home.

That's what I was thinking about when I walked up the path for the last time.

I was also thinking about Becky.

"Ooh," she had said when I told her the news. "You're going on an adventure, Luke!" She'd clapped her hands like a little girl.

"I sure am," I said.

We'd run into each other in the lobby. She was coming down with a cigarette and I was going up with a sandwich. I hadn't seen her since the afternoon I'd tried to casually ask her out and she'd said no, point-blank. "Do you want to get some ice cream?" I had said. I'd known her since high school, and the Mister Softee truck was parked right outside.

"No, thanks," she'd told me. "I'm on a diet." I couldn't tell if that was an excuse. Her body looked fine to me.

Six months later, though, she was all smiles, standing close to me in the lobby and batting her eyelashes as the other office workers came and went around us in a big wave of suits.

I was deploying in two weeks, but I tried to make it sound as if it was no big deal. In fact it *was* no big deal. Everyone thought that the war was coming to an end. Everyone thought that it was only a matter of time. We'd taken the peninsula and we'd secured the border and we'd advanced to within twenty-five miles of the capital. Any day now, everyone said. My main concern had been that I wouldn't make it over in time to see any action.

She said, "You going to keep in touch, Luke?" And she made a pouting face, as if I'd been the one to turn down her invitation for ice cream.

"You know I will," I said.

She had big lips and long lashes. She had a little gray in her hair, but I didn't care about that. She'd been married and was now divorced. I didn't care about that, either. I'd just hit twenty-seven and was getting soft around the middle. I was hoping to get back in shape. "Push yourself to your physical limits," the brochure had said.

She wrote her e-mail address in purple ink on the bottom of my sandwich bag. When she walked off, I took a long look at her ass. She didn't need a diet.

In the first couple of months, I made a point of e-mailing her. We were each allotted fifteen minutes a day at the Internet café, and I sent her updates when I could.

"What's going on down there, Luke?" she wanted to know. "Tell me everything." She ended her e-mails with "xoxo***."

"What's that mean?" I had to ask one of the guys.

"Hugs and kisses," he said.

"But what do the asterisks mean?"

He didn't know.

There wasn't much to report about what was going on. The enemy had yet to make his appearance. So I told her that we had an Internet café, and a bowling alley, and a Burger King. "They have everything down here," I wrote.

It wasn't entirely true. They didn't have things like boots. It was the rainy season and it rained every day. To be fair, there were ponchos, but ponchos don't keep you from slipping and sliding when you're going along the path on patrol in Skechers. If you got caught in a particularly bad downpour you might as well be ice-skating, and you'd come back to base at least an hour late. The sergeant would mark this down in his blue book. He'd make sure you saw him marking it down. What happened after that was anyone's guess. "You get ten of those, you get court-martialled," the most paranoid among us speculated.

Boots did finally arrive. This was about three months into our tour. They came from Timberland, no less, donated free of charge so that not everything would have to fall on the taxpayers. Half the guys sold their boots right off, they sold them to the other half of the guys who could afford to buy them and have two pairs. Then they used the proceeds to purchase things like cigarettes and instant soup. There was a guy named Chaz who wanted to give me twenty-five dollars for my boots. He acted like he was doing me a favor. "I'll tell you what I'll do," he said. He sat down on my cot and took out his money. "Whaddya say?" He was trying to be chummy about it. He was trying to be down-home. He'd gone to a good college and his parents sent him money every two weeks and we had nothing in common except that we both wanted boots. He was one of those guys who had joined for all the wrong reasons. He had joined not because he believed in anything but because he wanted to put it down on his résumé and jump-start his career.

I told him, "You're here for the wrong reasons, Chaz."

He said, "What reasons are those?" As if he didn't know.

Twenty years from now, I'd probably see him on television asking for my vote. He used phrases like "in the long term," regarding my boots.

I e-mailed Becky to tell her that we'd got new boots from Timberland.

She e-mailed back:

But what else is going on?
xoxo***

It wasn't the rainy season now. It was the hot and dry season. No one needed boots anymore. I made it to the end of the path in fifteen minutes. I could have done it in flip-flops. I could have done it barefoot.

It was getting close to evening, and things were cooling down a bit, but the flies were buzzing and I was sweating badly because I was dressed as if I were heading into battle. I felt less like a soldier and more like I was going trick-or-treating dressed as a soldier — all I needed was a bag for my candy. Everything about me was superfluous and ridiculous — the boots but also the helmet, the jacket, and the backpack, which rattled on my back like a gumball machine. The gun was unnecessary, too, but it was the lightest thing on me. That was the contradiction. It was three feet long and it looked like it was made of iron, but it felt like plastic. It could have been a squirt gun, except for the fact that it had all sorts of gadgets and meters on it that told you things like the time and the temperature. Plus it could kill a man from a mile away. You hardly even had to pull the trigger. If you put your finger in the proximity of the trigger, it sensed what you wanted to do and it pulled itself. *Poof* went the bullet, and the gun would vibrate gently, as if you were getting a call on your cell phone.

The first time I'd ever shot a gun was when my dad had taken me and my sister down to the woods to go hunting. This was about ten years ago, when the war had just started. There were supposed to be things like deer and elk lurking around in those woods. At least, that was how it had been when my dad was a kid and his dad had taken him hunting. But times had changed, and the factories were up and running for the war effort, and the woods had been dug through to make way for a new train line. Plus there was smoke. It was spring or fall, and the smoke smelled like barbecue and ammonia. Not only were there no deer or elk, there weren't even any chipmunks. So instead of teaching us how to hunt, my dad drew a bull's-eye on the side of a tree using a piece of chalk. Inside the bull's-eye he drew the face of the enemy. It was a surprisingly good representation, although he exaggerated the nose and eyes and ears for comic effect.

"This is how you hold it, Luke," he told me. "This is how you cock it. This is how you aim it."

I remember that the gun was heavy like a brick, and when I pulled the trigger it felt as if my right hand and ear had caught on fire. "Look what you did, Luke!" my father screamed. Sure enough, I had hit the bull's-eye right in the center. "Try again, Luke," he said, but I didn't want anything more to do with it.

My sister, on the other hand, had a great time. She blasted away at the target, *blam, blam, blam,* pretending it was really the enemy. Most of the time she missed everything, including the tree, but she thought the experience was fun and funny. "He's dead!" she kept saying. "The enemy's dead!" She looked like a pro, even though she was only twelve. I threw stones in the river, waiting for the shooting to be over so I could go back home and play video games. By the time evening came and the bullets ran out, she'd blasted a hole through the tree.

"They're all dead," she said.

Ten years later, it was the sergeant asking us if we wanted to end up dead. No sir, we said. He had us at target practice two hours a day. Lying on our bellies, crawling through the mud. We were training like mad, because we thought we were going to be doing some real fighting. One week after we arrived, the war had taken a turn for the worse, just like that, and there was no longer a chance that it was going to be ending anytime soon. We had lost the peninsula and we had mishandled the border and we had been forced back from the capital. Each day, the reports would come through listing the number of casualties. It seemed always to fall somewhere between two and two hundred, and by the time word spread around the base no one could be sure if the numbers were being exaggerated up or down. It was anyone's guess how many we were losing. I say "we," but we had nothing to do with it. We had landed on the other side of the country, far from the fighting, and we hadn't lost anything — it was the poor bastards a thousand miles away trying to push back toward the capital who had something to worry about.

I wrote to Becky a few times. "Can you tell me what is happening, please?" When her e-mail came back it would be almost entirely redacted:

Dear Luke,

███

xoxo***

According to my state-of-the-art gun, it was now six-oh-two and eighty-five degrees. Back home, it was twelve hours earlier and sixty degrees colder. Tomorrow morning we were flying home, and we didn't care that we were going back to cold weather. We were flying home on American Airlines, which had donated the plane free of charge. "Travelling in style," the guys said. They said that it was the least American Airlines could do. The fact was that twelve months had passed and we hadn't done much of anything. In fact, our main accomplishment might have been the bridge that I was now walking across. My boots echoed in the valley. It was sturdy, the bridge, and it was steel, and it would no doubt still be here, sitting at the end of the path, in ten thousand years, when the war was finally over. We had built the bridge in order to get across the valley. We had to get across the valley so we could get up the hill. The hill was the goal. The hill was where the enemy was waiting for us.

"Eight hundred and eighty hiding," our sergeant had told us. How he'd come up with that number, we didn't know. It was so specific we thought it must be true.

Ten hours a day we worked on that bridge. We'd wake up in the morning when it was still dark, and we'd eat our powdered eggs in darkness, and by the time we walked up the path and reached the valley the sun would just be rising, and the light would seem to be actually emanating upward from the valley, golden and warm, with traces of pinks and reds. One of the guys, who worked at a used-car dealership, said that if he was going to make a car commercial he'd use the valley as a backdrop to portray things like power and eternity, and everyone said that was right, that they'd buy that car for sure.

But the truth was that no one really wanted to get the bridge built, because no one wanted to get over the hill. We didn't say this out loud, of course; instead, we just worked as slowly as possible, and as incompetently. We accidentally dropped tools into the valley. I once dropped my blowtorch. It slipped from my hands like a bar of soap and bounced down the cliff until it took flight into the abyss.

"Do you know how much that blowtorch cost?" my sergeant screamed. He screamed like the money was coming out of his own pocket. He screamed like I had dropped his daughter in the valley. He stared at me for so long, one inch from my face, breathing like he'd run a race, his breath smelling like powdered eggs, that I thought he was actually asking me if I knew how much it cost.

"A hundred and thirty-five dollars?" I guessed.

This caught him by surprise. "It cost forty dollars," he said.

That didn't seem like all that much.

"I should drop you in the valley," he said. He made me do pushups, right then and there, thirty pushups. I got down on the ground, but I couldn't do them. He told me to take my backpack off and try again, but I still couldn't do them. This pissed him off even more. He put me to work cleaning the bathrooms, which was fine by me. I could have scrubbed toilets for the rest of my tour and been perfectly content. I could have scrubbed toilets for the rest of may life. Anything not to get over that hill and find eight hundred and eighty enemy waiting. But the next day I was back working on the bridge, bright and early. He needed all the help he could get. His superiors were probably screaming at him an inch from his face. Their superiors were screaming at them, and so on and so forth, until you got all the way up to the President screaming and panting as if he'd just run a race. Meanwhile, on the other side of the country, the casualties were mounting.

Day after day, we hammered and welded. Fifty guys pounding at the same time. The sounds echoed through the valley from morning to night, so that, if the enemy didn't know we were coming, they knew now.

One night, one of the guys said that we should go on strike. He was a farm boy from Iowa or Idaho, big and pink. Half the guys were farm boys. The other half were black boys. There was a smattering of others, like me and the future politician, but those were the basic demographics.

"Put down the tools of your trade, men," the farm boy said. He'd heard that somewhere.

"I'm not putting a damn thing down," one of the black boys said. "I'm trying to learn a skill." Then he whispered to everyone, "I pay attention. I ask questions. I watch everything." He made it sound as if he were planning to rob a bank. Which, I suppose, is how you feel when you've joined the Army not because you have beliefs but because you want to get a job.

So we spent the better part of four months working on that bridge, but even when you work slowly and incompetently you still make progress. And, when we finally arrived at the other side of the valley, we couldn't help but have a twisted feeling of pride. Yet the moment we stepped off the bridge and faced the hill we knew we had entered no man's land. We had colluded in our own demise.

The hill wasn't like the path. It was rocky and gray with no growth and no place to hide. It looked like a giant bowl of uncooked oatmeal. It looked like a place you could easily bury fifty bodies and no one would know.

"No time like the present," the sergeant said. And we put our backpacks on and our visors down and we raised our guns and started up.

The truth was that none of us had joined for the right reasons. I might have thought I had in the very beginning, when I'd gone to the Career Center to sign the papers and take the physical and get the brochure that promised a "life-altering experience" and which showed half a dozen young men in uniform standing on a beach and looking like they were having the time of their lives. It was easy to delude myself because everyone was congratulating me for living up to my ideals. Who would want to argue with that? There were three hundred people at my going-away party at work, chanting, "Luke! Luke! Luke! U.S.A.! U.S.A.!" There were people there who had never said a word to me, who had never even looked at me in the hallway, including the managing director. Now they were acting like they'd known my name all along, like I was a movie star making a guest appearance at their company. All the guys were shaking my hand, and all the girls were kissing my cheek. The managing director gave an impromptu speech about "men like Luke," and about how my job would still be there when I got back in a year, because that was company policy. It was the most boring job in the world, and I didn't want it to still be there when I got back. I was sure that something miraculous was going to happen to change my situation and make me into someone new. All I did was sit in a cubicle eight hours a day, five days a week, staring at a computer as I filled in the little empty blocks on a spreadsheet. *Click, drag, drop. Click, drag, drop.* Half the time there wasn't even anything to do, and I would just sit there staring at the blank screen, pretending that I was working and wishing I could go online and look at porn. *Click, drag, drop.* This is what happens when you have an associate's degree.

But at my going-away party I soaked up the applause. I thanked the managing director for all his support. I thanked everyone for coming. They stood around smiling and waiting for me to say something special, something profound. Three hundred people staring at me with my face covered in lipstick. Then someone in the back yelled, "Shoot some of those motherfuckers for me, Luke!" And this broke the ice and made everyone laugh, and we sliced up the big red-white-and-blue cake that they had all chipped in for.

It wasn't until the moment we started up that hill that I understood that I'd come here for all the wrong reasons. Vanity and pride topped the list. Girls, too — if I was being completely honest. In other words, ideals were very low. Staring at a hilltop that was getting closer and closer, I would have traded all of it never to have to see what was on the other side.

When we got to the top, the sergeant at our rear, we peered over like scared little boys, our heads low and our eyes half closed, and that's when we realized there was no one there. Not a soul. All that existed was a wide open space, a prairie almost, bordered on one side by a lake and on the other by more prairie. It surprised everyone, this desolation, including the sergeant, who now wanted to move up front and commanded us to follow him into the great unknown where there was no sign of life.

That first day we explored and came up empty. The next day, twenty-five guys went back to discover nothing. After that, fifteen guys went, then ten, then it was decided that it was a waste of time and energy, that the reconnaissance had been wrong and the enemy was nowhere around, and that all we needed was one guy to go along the path and over the bridge and up the hill once a day just to make sure there was nothing out of the ordinary.

Which is what I was doing right now when I reached the top of the hill. It was six-forty-three. It was still eighty-five degrees.

After we'd discovered nothing is when the boredom set in. Excruciating boredom. We'd eat, we'd shower, we'd clean, we'd train. In that order. Then we stopped training, because there was no point. That was about the fifth month.

During the sixth month, I went to the movie theatre almost every day. Something had got mixed up in the supplies, though, and the theatre had only two movies, both Indiana Jones, one of which was dubbed in Spanish. I watched them over and over, even the Spanish one, and then I never went back. A couple of the guys asked the sergeant if we'd be getting any more movies, and his response was "You're worried about movies when our boys are being killed a thousand miles away?" He had a point.

The days dragged on. Instead of getting in shape, I started to get fatter. If I ever let myself reflect on matters of spirit or psyche, I reflected that at the end of my tour all I would have to show for my effort was that I was one year older. In short, I was going to get out of the Army and be exactly the same person I was before I joined. I was going to go back to that same cubicle with those same spreadsheets. At night, I would dream of fantastic adventures, full of action, shot in vivid color, not unlike the Indiana Jones movies. I dreamed of being possessed by exceptional courage and heroism. I dreamed of confronting the enemy. In the morning, I'd wake with disappointment, eat, shower, clean the dorm, and then go bowling. My bowling improved.

Becky would send e-mails saying that she was worried about me, wanting to know what was going on, wanting to know if I was O.K. Eighty per cent of her messages would be redacted. For a while, I fanned her concern by responding with ambiguous statements like "We'll just have to wait and see." But soon her concern started to make me feel foolish, and I stopped going to the Internet café as often. When I did go, I would use my fifteen minutes to look at porn.

About the only thing we could do for the war effort was cheer for the planes that flew overhead on their way to drop their payload on the other side of the country. They sounded like thunder when they appeared, always around noon, two dozen or so, their bellies silver and red. We'd jump up and down, fifty of us guys, screaming at them, waving our hands as if we were on a desert island, hoping that the pilots would give a signal that they'd seen us. In the evening, they'd pass back going the other way, flying faster because they were lighter.

One day our sergeant said, "What are you waving at them for? There's no one in those planes. Those are drones."

I came to the top of the hill. It was seven-twelve, according to my gun. It was starting to get dusky and gray. I stood and surveyed the great expanse of nothingness. North to south, as I had been trained. Then east to west. The water, the prairie. Nothing.

It was silent up there on the hill, except for the occasional buzzing of the flies. It was always silent, of course, but today it seemed even more so. I had a surge of nostalgia: this was the last time I was going to be standing here. It was similar to that phenomenon that prisoners experience, becoming nostalgic for their cells the moment they are released.

I unzipped my backpack and took out my meal, which came in a little plastic container with an American flag. It was dinnertime, but I hadn't eaten my lunch yet. Today, it was ham and cheese with an apple and a cookie. Yesterday, it had been turkey and cheese with an apple and a cookie. Tomorrow, I would be making my own lunch. Two days after that, I'd be back at the office in a cubicle looking at spreadsheets. I sat down on a rock and ate my sandwich. The flies buzzed. I felt nostalgic for the Army lunches.

And it was then that I saw him. At first, I had no idea what I was seeing. In fact, at first I thought it might be an animal. All I could detect was some faint movement way out in the prairie, maybe a mile away, a rustling of the grass. It's just the breeze, I thought. But as I continued to watch I suddenly saw the unmistakable shape of a human head appear above the tall grass. I put my sandwich down and picked up my backpack. My hands were shaking as I took out my binoculars, and I had to clamp my elbows together to steady my gaze. Sure enough, there he was. A tall, bald, fat man, maybe fifty, maybe younger: the enemy.

He was walking with something, a sheep or a goat, I guessed, although I could scarcely see it in the grass. I imagined that he was moving stealthily, the man, that he was trying to keep himself concealed, but when the grass parted it was clear that he wasn't trying to hide from anyone. It was as if he had just gone out for an afternoon stroll. His nonchalance irritated me. It flew in the face of my boredom. Everything I had done for the past twelve months had been in relation to this man's existence — or nonexistence — and now here he was, seemingly unperturbed by what lay beyond the hill on which I was now sitting. He didn't even know we had built a bridge.

He was moving toward the water, perhaps bringing the goat or sheep to drink. I watched the man carefully through my binoculars. It felt slightly invasive to be watching him so closely, slightly pathetic. Years ago, I had made the discovery that a window in the hallway of my apartment building faced the bedroom window in a neighboring apartment. I was probably about ten years old, and had just become tall enough to be able to peer over the high window ledge. The bedroom belonged to a woman, and I remember that she was rather disappointingly plain, and that she had long plain blown hair, dishwater hair, and she dressed always in baggy pajamas, sacklike, that revealed nothing. All she did was lie in her bed and read. For hours she read. For hours I would stand there in the hallway watching her, hoping that she would do something exciting, like take off her clothes and masturbate. But she read, and I watched. And then around ten o'clock she would put her book down on her nightstand and turn her light off and I would go back to our apartment, where my father would ask me what I'd been doing for the last two or three hours in the hallway.

"Nothing, Dad," I'd say. Which was true — I'd done nothing.

Standing there now on the crest of the hill, I did something: I picked up my gun and released the safety. I hadn't handled the gun in a while and it felt strangely heavy, unwieldy even, as if I were trying to hoist a manhole cover with my bare hands. It pressed down painfully on my shoulder as I peered through the sights. The man was standing at the edge of the lake, and he was peeing. He had his hand on his hip and he was leaning backward in a posture of bliss, and his face was not all that different from the face my father had once drawn on that tree years ago.

I observed the man in the crosshairs. He was 1.1 miles away. He was five feet ten inches tall. He jiggled himself dry, buttoned up, and started to walk leisurely along the edge of the lake back toward the prairie. Soon he was 1.2 miles away. Then he turned in toward the plains, toward the high grass, and just when he was about to disappear for good I put my finger in the proximity of the trigger. *Poof.* The gun vibrated gently with its message.

He stumbled and fell face first onto the ground. It happened so quickly that I thought he must have tripped over something. Surely it couldn't have been because of me. But, no, a small pool of blood began to form under him as he lay there.

The sheep or goat that had been by his side was not a sheep or a goat, after all, but a little boy. He darted around in a panicked circle. I watched him through the crosshairs. His mania increased until it looked as if he might actually begin to dig a hole in the ground with his feet. He disappeared into the high grass, only to return a moment later to lift the man's arm and try to drag him off. He couldn't, of course, and for a moment I had the thought that I would run down the hill and help the boy. I would help the boy and then I would send an e-mail to Becky telling her what I had done. "Dear Becky, Today I helped one of the local boys."

Poof.

The boy fell right where he stood, he fell straight down as if he were melting into the ground in a puddle of blood. Once he'd fallen, he didn't stir. Only the man was moving now, struggling to push himself up, but it was obvious that he had no strength. Eventually, he stopped altogether and just lay on the ground as if he were napping. The pool of blood spread out and ran into the high grass.

I stood there for a while. It was beginning to get dark. It was seven-fifty-three. Back home, it was seven-fifty-three. A few minutes later, the prairie was immersed in a dark-gray light and I could hardly see anything. The only sound was the buzzing of the flies.

I turned and went back down the hill, the last time I'd be going down the hill, and then I went across the bridge and along the path. My gun and backpack banged against the solid wall of trees. It was almost completely dark now, and in the dark I could hear my father saying, over and over, "What have you been doing, Luke? What have you been doing for the last two or three hours?"

Nothing. I've done nothing.

The next day we flew back home in style, just like we'd been promised.

Leslie Marmon Silko

Leslie Marmon Silko (b. 1948), a Laguna Pueblo Native American, was born and grew up in New Mexico. She was educated at Bureau of Indian Affairs schools in Laguna, a Catholic school in Albuquerque, and the University of New Mexico, where she received her B.A. in English in 1969. After teaching at various colleges, she became a professor of English at the University of Arizona at Tucson. Silko's first novel, *Ceremony* (1977), is regarded as one of the most important books in modern Native American literature. In it she forged a connection between the shared past of the tribe and the individual life of a Native American returning home after World War II. Silko has received a National Endowment for the Arts fellowship, a Pushcart Prize, and a three-year grant from the MacArthur Foundation, which enabled her to take time off from teaching and become "a little less beholden to the everyday world."

Storyteller (1981), a collection of tribal folktales, family anecdotes, photographs by her grandfather, and her own poems and stories, is Silko's personal anthology of the Laguna Pueblo culture. "Yellow Woman" is from that collection. It illustrates Silko's skill in retelling a traditional Native American legend in a realistic contemporary context that confirms its emotional truth and makes it accessible to a larger audience.

Tales about a "ka'tsina" mountain spirit who seduces the Yellow Woman away from her husband and family were first told to the fictional heroine by her grandfather. The Yellow Woman in the traditional captivity narratives can be interpreted in several ways—as a girl who runs off with a man outside the tribe, as a raped and kidnapped married woman, as a spirit, as a fertility archetype. In creating fiction, Silko works with all the implied meanings of the old legends; she has said that she writes "because I like seeing how I can translate [a] sort of feeling or flavor or sense of a story that's told and heard onto the page." Other books by Silko include *The Almanac of the Dead* (1991), *Sacred Water* (1993), *Yellow Woman and a Beauty of the Spirit: Essays on Native American Life* (1996), and *Gardens in the Dunes* (1999). *The Turquoise Ledge: A Memoir* was published in 2010.

RELATED COMMENTARIES

Leslie Marmon Silko, "Language and Literature from a Pueblo Indian Perspective," page 1516; Paula Gunn Allen, "Whirlwind Man Steals Yellow Woman," page 1393.

Yellow Woman

1974

I

My thigh clung to his with dampness, and I watched the sun rising up through the tamaracks and willows. The small brown water birds came to the river and hopped across the mud, leaving brown scratches in the alkali-white crust. They bathed in the river silently. I could hear the water, almost at our feet where the narrow fast channel bubbled and washed green ragged moss and fern leaves. I looked at him beside me, rolled in the red blanket on the white river sand. I cleaned the sand out of the cracks between my toes, squinting because the sun was above the willow trees. I looked at him for the last time, sleeping on the white river sand.

I felt hungry and followed the river south the way we had come the afternoon before, following our footprints that were already blurred by the lizard tracks and bug trails. The horses were still lying down, and the black one whinnied when he saw me but he did not get up — maybe it was because the corral was made out of thick cedar branches and the horses had not yet felt the sun like I had. I tried to look beyond the pale red mesas to the pueblo. I knew it was there, even if I could not see it, on the sand rock hill above the river, the same river that moved past me now and had reflected the moon last night.

The horse felt warm underneath me. He shook his head and pawed the sand. The bay whinnied and leaned against the gate trying to follow, and I remembered him asleep in the red blanket beside the river. I slid off the horse and tied him close to the other horse. I walked north with the river again, and the white sand broke loose in footprints over footprints.

"Wake up."

He moved in the blanket and turned his face to me with his eyes still closed. I knelt down to touch him.

"I'm leaving."

He smiled now, eyes still closed. "You are coming with me, remember?" He sat up now with his bare dark chest and belly in the sun.

"Where?"

"To my place."

"And will I come back?"

He pulled his pants on. I walked away from him, feeling him behind me and smelling the willows.

"Yellow Woman," he said.

I turned to face him. "Who are you?" I asked.

He laughed and knelt on the low, sandy bank, washing his face in the river. "Last night you guessed my name, and you knew why I had come."

I stared past him at the shallow moving water and tried to remember the night, but I could only see the moon in the water and remember his warmth around me.

"But I only said that you were him and that I was Yellow Woman — I'm not really her — I have my own name and I come from the pueblo on the other side of the mesa. Your name is Silva and you are a stranger I met by the river yesterday afternoon."

He laughed softly. "What happened yesterday has nothing to do with what you will do today, Yellow Woman."

"I know — that's what I'm saying — the old stories about the ka'tsina spirit[1] and Yellow Woman can't mean us."

My old grandpa liked to tell those stories best. There is one about Badger and Coyote who went hunting and were gone all day, and when the sun was going down they found a house. There was a girl living there alone, and she had light hair and eyes and she told them that they could sleep with her. Coyote wanted to be with her all night so he sent Badger into a prairie-dog hole, telling him he thought he saw something in it. As soon as Badger crawled in, Coyote blocked up the entrance with rocks and hurried back to Yellow Woman.

"Come here," he said gently.

He touched my neck and I moved close to him to feel his breathing and to hear his heart. I was wondering if Yellow Woman had known who she was — if she knew that she would become part of the stories. Maybe she'd had another name that her husband and relatives called her so that only the ka'tsina from the north and the storytellers would know her as Yellow Woman. But I didn't go on; I felt him all around me, pushing me down into the white river sand.

Yellow Woman went away with the spirit from the north and lived with him and his relatives. She was gone for a long time, but then one day she came back and she brought twin boys.

"Do you know the story?"

"What story?" He smiled and pulled me close to him as he said this. I was afraid lying there on the red blanket. All I could know was the way he felt, warm, damp, his body beside me. This is the way it happens in the stories, I was thinking, with no thought beyond the moment she meets the ka'tsina spirit and they go.

"I don't have to go. What they tell in stories was real only then, back in time immemorial, like they say."

He stood up and pointed at my clothes tangled in the blanket. "Let's go," he said.

I walked beside him, breathing hard because he walked fast, his hand around my wrist. I had stopped trying to pull away from him, because his hand felt cool and the sun was high, drying the river bed into alkali. I will see someone, eventually I will see someone, and then I will be certain that he is only a man — some man from nearby — and I will be sure that I am not Yellow Woman. Because she is from out of time past and I live now and I've been to school and there are highways and pickup trucks that Yellow Woman never saw.

It was an easy ride north on horseback. I watched the change from the cottonwood trees along the river to the junipers that brushed past us in the foothills, and finally there were only piñons, and when I looked up at the rim of

---

[1] A mountain spirit of the Pueblo Indians.

the mountain plateau I could see pine trees growing on the edge. Once I stopped to look down, but the pale sandstone had disappeared and the river was gone and the dark lava hills were all around. He touched my hand, not speaking, but always singing softly a mountain song and looking into my eyes.

I felt hungry and wondered what they were doing at home now — my mother, my grandmother, my husband, and the baby. Cooking breakfast, saying, "Where did she go? — maybe kidnapped," and Al going to the tribal police with the details: "She went walking along the river."

The house was made with black lava rock and red mud. It was high above the spreading miles of arroyos and long mesas. I smelled a mountain smell of pitch and buck brush. I stood there beside the black horse, looking down on the small, dim country we had passed, and I shivered.

"Yellow Woman, come inside where it's warm."

II

He lit a fire in the stove. It was an old stove with a round belly and an enamel coffeepot on top. There was only the stove, some faded Navajo blankets, and a bedroll and cardboard box. The floor was made of smooth adobe plaster, and there was one small window facing east. He pointed at the box.

"There's some potatoes and the frying pan." He sat on the floor with his arms around his knees pulling them close to his chest and he watched me fry the potatoes. I didn't mind him watching me because he was always watching me — he had been watching me since I came upon him sitting on the river bank trimming leaves from a willow twig with his knife. We ate from the pan and he wiped the grease from his fingers on his Levis.

"Have you brought women here before?" He smiled and kept chewing, so I said, "Do you always use the same tricks?"

"What tricks?" He looked at me like he didn't understand.

"The story about being a ka'tsina from the mountains. The story about Yellow Woman."

Silva was silent; his face was calm.

"I don't believe it. Those stories couldn't happen now," I said.

He shook his head and said softly, "But someday they will talk about us, and they will say, 'Those two lived long ago when things like that happened.'"

He stood up and went out. I ate the rest of the potatoes and thought about things — about the noise the stove was making and the sound of the mountain wind outside. I remembered yesterday and the day before, and then I went outside.

I walked past the corral to the edge where the narrow trail cut through the black rim rock. I was standing in the sky with nothing around me but the wind that came down from the blue mountain peak behind me. I could see faint mountain images in the distance miles across the vast spread of mesas and valleys and plains. I wondered who was over there to feel the mountain wind on those sheer blue edges — who walks on the pine needles in those blue mountains.

"Can you see the pueblo?" Silva was standing behind me.

I shook my head. "We're too far away."

"From here I can see the world." He stepped out on the edge. "The Navajo reservation begins over there." He pointed to the east. "The Pueblo boundaries are over here." He looked below us to the south, where the narrow trail seemed to come from. "The Texans have their ranches over there, starting with that valley, the Concho Valley. The Mexicans run some cattle over there too."

"Do you ever work for them?"

"I steal from them," Silva answered. The sun was dropping behind us and shadows were filling the land below. I turned away from the edge that dropped forever into the valleys below.

"I'm cold," I said; "I'm going inside." I started wondering about this man who could speak the Pueblo language so well but who lived on a mountain and rustled cattle. I decided that this man Silva must be Navajo, because Pueblo men didn't do things like that.

"You must be a Navajo."

Silva shook his head gently. "Little Yellow Woman," he said, "you never give up, do you? I have told you who I am. The Navajo people know me, too." He knelt down and unrolled the bedroll and spread the extra blankets out on a piece of canvas. The sun was down, and the only light in the house came from outside — the dim orange light from sundown.

I stood there and waited for him to crawl under the blankets.

"What are you waiting for?" he said, and I lay down beside him. He undressed me slowly like the night before beside the river — kissing my face gently and running his hands up and down my belly and legs. He took off my pants and then he laughed.

"Why are you laughing?"

"You are breathing so hard."

I pulled away from him and turned my back to him.

He pulled me around and pinned me down with his arms and chest. "You don't understand, do you, little Yellow Woman? You will do what I want."

And again he was all around me with his skin slippery against mine, and I was afraid because I understood that his strength could hurt me. I lay underneath him and I knew that he could destroy me. But later, while he slept beside me, I touched his face and I had a feeling — the kind of feeling for him that overcame me that morning along the river. I kissed him on the forehead and he reached out for me.

When I woke up in the morning he was gone. It gave me a strange feeling because for a long time I sat there on the blankets and looked around the little house for some object of his — some proof that he had been there or maybe that he was coming back. Only the blankets and the cardboard box remained. The .30–30[2] that had been leaning in the corner was gone, and so was the knife I had used the night before. He was gone, and I had my chance to go now. But first I had to eat, because I knew it would be a long walk home.

I found some dried apricots in the cardboard box, and I sat down on a rock at the edge of the plateau rim. There was no wind and the sun warmed me. I was surrounded by silence. I drowsed with apricots in my mouth, and I didn't believe that there were highways or railroads or cattle to steal.

---

[2] A rifle.

When I woke up, I stared down at my feet in the black mountain dirt. Little black ants were swarming over the pine needles around my foot. They must have smelled the apricots. I thought about my family far below me. They would be wondering about me, because this had never happened to me before. The tribal police would file a report. But if old Grandpa weren't dead he would tell them what happened — he would laugh and say, "Stolen by a ka'tsina, a mountain spirit. She'll come home — they usually do." There are enough of them to handle things. My mother and grandmother will raise the baby like they raised me. Al will find someone else, and they will go on like before, except that there will be a story about the day I disappeared while I was walking along the river. Silva had come for me; he said he had. I did not decide to go. I just went. Moonflowers blossom in the sand hills before dawn, just as I followed him. That's what I was thinking as I wandered along the trail through the pine trees.

It was noon when I got back. When I saw the stone house I remembered that I had meant to go home. But that didn't seem important any more, maybe because there were little blue flowers growing in the meadow behind the stone house and the gray squirrels were playing in the pines next to the house. The horses were standing in the corral, and there was a beef carcass hanging on the shady side of a big pine in front of the house. Flies buzzed around the clotted blood that hung from the carcass. Silva was washing his hands in a bucket full of water. He must have heard me coming because he spoke to me without turning to face me.

"I've been waiting for you."

"I went walking in the big pine trees."

I looked into the bucket full of bloody water with brown-and-white animal hairs floating in it. Silva stood there letting his hand drip, examining me intently.

"Are you coming with me?"

"Where?" I asked him.

"To sell the meat in Marquez."

"If you're sure it's O.K."

"I wouldn't ask you if it wasn't," he answered.

He sloshed the water around in the bucket before he dumped it out and set the bucket upside down near the door. I followed him to the corral and watched him saddle the horses. Even beside the horses he looked tall, and I asked him again if he wasn't Navajo. He didn't say anything; he just shook his head and kept cinching up the saddle.

"But Navajos are tall."

"Get on the horse," he said, "and let's go."

The last thing he did before we started down the steep trail was to grab the .30–30 from the corner. He slid the rifle into the scabbard that hung from his saddle.

"Do they ever try to catch you?" I asked.

"They don't know who I am."

"Then why did you bring the rifle?"

"Because we are going to Marquez where the Mexicans live."

III

The trail leveled out on a narrow ridge that was steep on both sides like an animal spine. On one side I could see where the trail went around the rocky gray hills and disappeared into the southeast where the pale sandrock mesas stood in the distance near my home. On the other side was a trail that went west, and as I looked far into the distance I thought I saw the little town. But Silva said no, that I was looking in the wrong place, that I just thought I saw houses. After that I quit looking off into the distance; it was hot and the wildflowers were closing up their deep-yellow petals. Only the waxy cactus flowers bloomed in the bright sun, and I saw every color that a cactus blossom can be; the white ones and the red ones were still buds, but the purple and the yellow were blossoms, open full and the most beautiful of all.

Silva saw him before I did. The white man was riding a big gray horse, coming up the trail toward us. He was traveling fast and the gray horse's feet sent rocks rolling off the trail into the dry tumbleweeds. Silva motioned for me to stop and we watched the white man. He didn't see us right away, but finally his horse whinnied at our horses and he stopped. He looked at us briefly before he loped the gray horse across the three hundred yards that separated us. He stopped his horse in front of Silva, and his young fat face was shadowed by the brim of his hat. He didn't look mad, but his small, pale eyes moved from the blood-soaked gunny sacks hanging from my saddle to Silva's face and then back to my face.

"Where did you get the fresh meat?" the white man asked.

"I've been hunting," Silva said, and when he shifted his weight in the saddle the leather creaked.

"The hell you have, Indian. You've been rustling cattle. We've been looking for the thief for a long time."

The rancher was fat, and sweat began to soak through his white cowboy shirt and the wet cloth stuck to the thick rolls of belly fat. He almost seemed to be panting from the exertion of talking, and he smelled rancid, maybe because Silva scared him.

Silva turned to me and smiled. "Go back up the mountain, Yellow Woman."

The white man got angry when he heard Silva speak in a language he couldn't understand. "Don't try anything, Indian. Just keep riding to Marquez. We'll call the state police from there."

The rancher must have been unarmed because he was very frightened and if he had a gun he would have pulled it out then. I turned my horse around and the rancher yelled, "Stop!" I looked at Silva for an instant and there was something ancient and dark — something I could feel in my stomach — in his eyes, and when I glanced at his hand I saw his finger on the trigger of the .30–30 that was still in the saddle scabbard. I slapped my horse across the flank and the sacks of raw meat swung against my knees as the horse leaped up the trail. It was hard to keep my balance, and once I thought I felt the saddle slipping backward; it was because of this that I could not look back.

I didn't stop until I reached the ridge where the trail forked. The horse was breathing deep gasps and there was a dark film of sweat on its neck. I looked down in the direction I had come from, but I couldn't see the place. I waited. The wind came up and pushed warm air past me. I looked up at the sky, pale blue and full of thin clouds and fading vapor trails left by jets.

I think four shots were fired — I remember hearing four hollow explosions that reminded me of deer hunting. There could have been more shots after that, but I couldn't have heard them because my horse was running again and the loose rocks were making too much noise as they scattered around his feet.

Horses have a hard time running downhill, but I went that way instead of uphill to the mountain because I thought it was safer. I felt better with the horse running southeast past the round gray hills that were covered with cedar trees and black lava rock. When I got to the plain in the distance I could see the dark green patches of tamaracks that grew along the river; and beyond the river I could see the beginning of the pale sandrock mesas. I stopped the horse and looked back to see if anyone was coming; then I got off the horse and turned the horse around, wondering if it would go back to its corral under the pines on the mountain. It looked back at me for a moment and then plucked a mouthful of green tumbleweeds before it trotted back up the trail with its ears pointed forward, carrying its head daintily to one side to avoid stepping on the dragging reins. When the horse disappeared over the last hill, the gunny sacks full of meat were still swinging and bouncing.

IV

I walked toward the river on a wood-hauler's road that I knew would eventually lead to the paved road. I was thinking about waiting beside the road for someone to drive by, but by the time I got to the pavement I had decided it wasn't very far to walk if I followed the river back the way Silva and I had come.

The river water tasted good, and I sat in the shade under a cluster of silvery willows. I thought about Silva, and I felt sad at leaving him; still, there was something strange about him, and I tried to figure it out all the way back home.

I came back to the place on the river bank where he had been sitting the first time I saw him. The green willow leaves that he had trimmed from the branch were still lying there, wilted in the sand. I saw the leaves and I wanted to go back to him — to kiss him and to touch him — but the mountains were too far away now. And I told myself, because I believe it, he will come back sometime and be waiting again by the river.

I followed the path up from the river into the village. The sun was getting low, and I could smell supper cooking when I got to the screen door of my house. I could hear their voices inside — my mother was telling my grandmother how to fix the Jell-O and my husband, Al, was playing with the baby. I decided to tell them that some Navajo had kidnapped me, but I was sorry that old Grandpa wasn't alive to hear my story because it was the Yellow Woman stories he liked to tell best.

Art Spiegelman

Art Spiegelman (b. 1948), the only child of two Polish Holocaust survivors, was born in Sweden and taken to the United States when he was three to live in Rego Park in Queens, where he grew up. From childhood he knew he wanted to become a cartoonist. As a student at New York's High School of Art and Design, he drew baseball cards and Bazooka comics for Topps, a chewing gum company. He studied art and philosophy at the State University of New York at Binghamton before being hospitalized for a mental breakdown. "Prisoner on the Hell Planet," a story created for *Short Order Comics* in 1972, depicts his state of shock after his mother's suicide. Spiegelman dropped out of college and went to live in San Francisco from 1970 to 1975. There he connected with the world of "comix," comics with X-rated content sold in headshops along with psychedelic posters and drug paraphernalia. His friendship with cartoonist Bill Griffith gave him what he called "needed stability in the land of lotus-eaters." On the West Coast Spiegelman drew and wrote for a number of underground publications, including *Bizarre Sex*, *Choice Meat*, *Real Pulp*, and *Young Lust*, and he edited *Arcade* and *Douglas Comix*.

In 1972, while teaching at the San Francisco Academy of Art, Spiegelman began experimenting with the concept of mice being tormented by cats as a metaphor for the Nazi persecution of the Jews during the Holocaust. His Pulitzer Prize–winning *Maus: A Survivor's Tale* (1991) began as a three-page strip in a comics anthology and grew to become a two-volume narrative about Spiegelman's complex relationship with his father, an Auschwitz concentration camp survivor. As he created his story, Spiegelman's graphic drawings evolved in stages, reflecting the influence of German expressionist paintings and Walt Disney cartoons before he found his own style. As critic Scott McCloud understood, the book's "great innovation—unmatched and possibly unmatchable—was in the combination of style and subject. Somehow the old cartoon vocabulary—the familiar imagery of cats and mice—made the Holocaust bearable and approachable, strange and yet familiar."

Maus first appeared through installments in *Raw*, Spiegelman's large-format publication begun in 1980 with Françoise Mouly, his French-born wife. All the nearly 300 pages of the book, along with the artist's preparatory drawings, photographs, and tape-recorded interviews with his father, were exhibited at the Museum of Modern Art shortly before Spiegelman received a Pulitzer Prize in 1992. "Prisoner on the Hell Planet," reprinted in *Maus*, is drawn in a style reminiscent of Lynd Ward's woodblock artistry and the imagery of German expressionism. Spiegelman's later style can be seen in books such as *In the Shadow of No Towers* (2004), his personal experience of the 9/11 World Trade Center disaster, and his magazine cover drawings for *The New Yorker*, including the issue of February 14, 2000, when Spiegelman paid homage to "Peanuts" cartoonist Charles Schulz by portraying him as a chain-smoking mouse. *Breakdowns* (2008) contains a long essay about what Spiegelman called his "stumbling apprenticeship," an account of how he developed into the artist who created *Maus* after his interests "began to diverge from an underground comix scene still dominated by sex, dope, and transgressive genre stories. I became consumed with finding out how narrative comics had to be comics at all, infatuated with the cross-pollination of High and Low." Spiegelman understood that he had "smashed into the wall that separated cartoonists from Artists." Yet earlier, "in the claustrophobic confines of my immigrant parents' home, comics were my picture window onto American culture." *METAMAUS* was published in 2011.

RELATED CASEBOOK

See Casebook on Graphic Storytelling, pages 1647–1663, including Charles Hatfield, "From *Alternative Comics*: Toward the Habit of Questioning," page 1649; and Michael Kupperman, "Are Comics Serious Literature?," page 1652.

1972

John Steinbeck

John Steinbeck (1902–1968) was born in Salinas and raised near Monterey in the fertile farm country of the Salinas Valley in California, the locale for his story "The Chrysanthemums." His mother was a former schoolteacher; his father was the county treasurer. In high school Steinbeck wrote for the school newspaper and was president of his class. He enjoyed literature from an early age and read novels by Gustave Flaubert, Fyodor Dostoevsky, and Thomas Hardy in the family library. Enrolled at Stanford University as an English major, Steinbeck dropped out before graduating and worked at odd jobs—fruit picker, caretaker, laboratory assistant—while he made his first efforts at writing fiction. Several times he took short-term jobs with the Spreckels Sugar Company and gained a perspective on labor problems, which he would later describe in his novels.

In 1929 Steinbeck began his literary career by publishing *Cup of Gold*, a fictionalized biography of Henry Morgan, the seventeenth-century Welsh pirate. His next book, *The Pastures of Heaven* (1932), is a collection of short stories about the people in a farm community in California. The critic Brian Barbour has stated that Steinbeck realized early in his career that the short story form was not congenial to his talents. He felt that he needed the more expansive form of the novel to give his characters a chance for what he considered real growth. In 1936 Steinbeck wrote *In Dubious Battle*, his first major political novel. He then published four more novels and another book of short fiction before his greatest work, *The Grapes of Wrath* (1939). This book, about a family from the Dust Bowl who emigrate to California and struggle to make a living despite agricultural exploitation, won Steinbeck the Pulitzer Prize. Among his many other successful novels are *East of Eden* (1952) and *The Winter of Our Discontent* (1961). He received the Nobel Prize for literature in 1962.

One of the most accomplished popular novelists in the United States, Steinbeck excelled—as did Ernest Hemingway—in the creation of exciting conflicts, convincing dialogue, and recognizable characters to dramatize his philosophy of life. Although his production of short stories was relatively slight, his work is often anthologized because of his clear, realistic treatment of social themes as his characters struggle to forge meaningful lives. "The Chrysanthemums" echoes the D. H. Lawrence story "Odour of Chrysanthemums" in its concerns with sexual roles and the difficulty of striking a balance between self-interest and the needs of others. Steinbeck's biographer, Jackson J. Benson, also commented that the excellence of "The Chrysanthemums" lies in "its delicate, indirect handling of a woman's emotions . . . [especially] the difficulty of the woman in finding a creative significant role in a male-dominated society."

RELATED STORY
D. H. Lawrence, "Odour of Chrysanthemums," page 787.

RELATED COMMENTARY
Jay Parini, "Lawrence's and Steinbeck's 'Chrysanthemums,'" page 1507.

The Chrysanthemums

1938

THE HIGH GREY-FLANNEL fog of winter closed off the Salinas Valley from the sky and from all the rest of the world. On every side it sat like a lid on the mountains and made of the great valley a closed pot. On the broad, level land floor the gang plows bit deep and left the black earth shining like metal where the shares had cut. On the foothill ranches across the Salinas River, the yellow stubble fields seemed to be bathed in pale cold sunshine, but there was no sunshine in the valley now in December. The thick willow scrub along the river flamed with sharp and positive yellow leaves.

It was a time of quiet and of waiting. The air was cold and tender. A light wind blew up from the southwest so that the farmers were mildly hopeful of a good rain before long; but fog and rain do not go together.

Across the river, on Henry Allen's foothill ranch there was little work to be done, for the hay was cut and stored and the orchards were plowed up to receive the rain deeply when it should come. The cattle on the higher slopes were becoming shaggy and rough-coated.

Elisa Allen, working in her flower garden, looked down across the yard and saw Henry, her husband, talking to two men in business suits. The three of them stood by the tractor shed, each man with one foot on the side of the little Fordson. They smoked cigarettes and studied the machine as they talked.

Elisa watched them for a moment and then went back to her work. She was thirty-five. Her face was lean and strong and her eyes were as clear as water. Her figure looked blocked and heavy in her gardening costume, a man's black hat pulled low down over her eyes, clod-hopper shoes, a figured print dress almost completely covered by a big corduroy apron with four big pockets to hold the snips, the trowel and scratcher, the seeds, and the knife she worked with. She wore heavy leather gloves to protect her hands while she worked.

She was cutting down the old year's chrysanthemum stalks with a pair of short and powerful scissors. She looked down toward the men by the tractor shed now and then. Her face was eager and mature and handsome; even her work with the scissors was overeager, overpowerful. The chrysanthemum stems seemed too small and easy for her energy.

She brushed a cloud of hair out of her eyes with the back of her glove, and left a smudge of earth on her cheek in doing it. Behind her stood the neat white farm house with red geraniums close-banked around it as high as the windows. It was a hard-swept looking little house with hard-polished windows, and a clean mud-mat on the front steps.

Elisa cast another glance toward the tractor shed. The strangers were getting into their Ford coupe. She took off a glove and put her strong fingers down into the forest of new green chrysanthemum sprouts that were growing around the old roots. She spread the leaves and looked down among the close-growing stems. No aphids were there, no sowbugs or snails or cutworms. Her terrier fingers destroyed such pests before they could get started.

Elisa started at the sound of her husband's voice. He had come near quietly, and he leaned over the wire fence that protected her flower garden from cattle and dogs and chickens.

"At it again," he said. "You've got a strong new crop coming."

Elisa straightened her back and pulled on the gardening glove again. "Yes. They'll be strong this coming year." In her tone and on her face there was a little smugness.

"You've got a gift with things," Henry observed. "Some of those yellow chrysanthemums you had this year were ten inches across. I wish you'd work out in the orchard and raise some apples that big."

Her eyes sharpened. "Maybe I could do it, too. I've a gift with things, all right. My mother had it. She could stick anything in the ground and make it grow. She said it was having planters' hands that knew how to do it."

"Well, it sure works with flowers," he said.

"Henry, who were those men you were talking to?"

"Why, sure, that's what I came to tell you. They were from the Western Meat Company. I sold thirty head of three-year-old steers. Got nearly my own price, too."

"Good," she said. "Good for you."

"And I thought," he continued, "I thought how it's Saturday afternoon, and we might go into Salinas for dinner at a restaurant, and then to a picture show — to celebrate, you see."

"Good," she repeated. "Oh, yes. That will be good."

Henry put on his joking tone. "There's fights tonight. How'd you like to go to the fights?"

"Oh, no," she said breathlessly. "No, I wouldn't like fights."

"Just fooling, Elisa. We'll go to a movie. Let's see. It's two now. I'm going to take Scotty and bring down those steers from the hill. It'll take us maybe two hours. We'll go in town about five and have dinner at the Cominos Hotel. Like that?"

"Of course I'll like it. It's good to eat away from home."

"All right, then. I'll go get up a couple of horses."

She said, "I'll have plenty of time to transplant some of these sets, I guess."

She heard her husband calling Scotty down by the barn. And a little later she saw the two men ride up the pale yellow hillside in search of the steers.

There was a little square sandy bed kept for rooting the chrysanthemums. With her trowel she turned the soil over and over, and smoothed it and patted it firm. Then she dug ten parallel trenches to receive the sets. Back at the chrysanthemum bed she pulled out the little crisp shoots, trimmed off the leaves at each one with her scissors, and laid it on a small orderly pile.

A squeak of wheels and plod of hoofs came from the road. Elisa looked up. The country road ran along the dense bank of willows and cottonwoods that bordered the river, and up this road came a curious vehicle, curiously drawn. It was an old spring-wagon, with a round canvas top on it like the corner of a prairie schooner. It was drawn by an old bay horse and a little grey-and-white burro. A big stubble-bearded man sat between the cover flaps and drove the crawling team. Underneath the wagon, between the hind wheels, a lean and rangy mongrel dog walked sedately. Words were painted on the canvas, in clumsy, crooked letters. "Pots, pans, knives, sisors, lawn mores, Fixed." Two rows of articles, and the triumphantly definitive "Fixed" below. The black paint had run down in little sharp points beneath each letter.

Elisa, squatting on the ground, watched to see the crazy, loose-jointed wagon pass by. But it didn't pass. It turned into the farm road in front of her house, crooked old wheels skirling and squeaking. The rangy dog darted from between the wheels and ran ahead. Instantly the two ranch shepherds flew out at him. Then all three stopped, and with stiff and quivering tails, with taut straight legs, with ambassadorial dignity, they slowly circled, sniffing daintily. The caravan pulled up to Elisa's wire fence and stopped. Now the newcomer dog, feeling outnumbered, lowered his tail and retired under the wagon with raised hackles and bared teeth.

The man on the seat called out, "That's a bad dog in a fight when he gets started."

Elisa laughed. "I see he is. How soon does he generally get started?"

The man caught up her laughter and echoed it heartily. "Sometimes not for weeks and weeks," he said. He climbed stiffly down, over the wheel. The horse and the donkey drooped like unwatered flowers.

Elisa saw that he was a very big man. Although his hair and beard were greying, he did not look old. His worn black suit was wrinkled and spotted with grease. The laughter had disappeared from his face and eyes the moment his laughing voice ceased. His eyes were dark, and they were full of the brooding that gets in the eyes of teamsters and of sailors. The calloused hands he rested on the wire fence were cracked, and every crack was a black line. He took off his battered hat.

"I'm off my general road, ma'am," he said. "Does this dirt road cut over across the river to the Los Angeles highway?"

Elisa stood up and shoved the thick scissors in her apron pocket. "Well, yes, it does, but it winds around and then fords the river. I don't think your team could pull through the sand."

He replied with some asperity, "It might surprise you what them beasts can pull through."

"When they get started?" she asked.

He smiled for a second. "Yes. When they get started."

"Well," said Elisa, "I think you'll save time if you go back to the Salinas road and pick up the highway there."

He drew a big finger down the chicken wire and made it sing. "I ain't in any hurry, ma'am. I go from Seattle to San Diego and back every year. Takes all my time. About six months each way. I aim to follow nice weather."

Elisa took off her gloves and stuffed them in the apron pocket with the scissors. She touched the under edge of her man's hat, searching for fugitive hairs. "That sounds like a nice kind of a way to live," she said.

He leaned confidentially over the fence. "Maybe you noticed the writing on my wagon. I mend pots and sharpen knives and scissors. You got any of them things to do?"

"Oh, no," she said, quickly. "Nothing like that." Her eyes hardened with resistance.

"Scissors is the worst thing," he explained. "Most people just ruin scissors trying to sharpen 'em, but I know how. I got a special tool. It's a little bobbit kind of thing, and patented. But it sure does the trick."

"No. My scissors are all sharp."

"All right, then. Take a pot," he continued earnestly, "a bent pot, or a pot with a hole. I can make it like new so you don't have to buy no new ones. That's a savings for you."

"No," she said shortly. "I tell you I have nothing like that for you to do."

His face fell to an exaggerated sadness. His voice took on a whining undertone. "I ain't had a thing to do today. Maybe I won't have no supper tonight. You see I'm off my regular road. I know folks on the highway clear from Seattle to San Diego. They save their things for me to sharpen up because they know I do it so good and save them money."

"I'm sorry," Elisa said irritably. "I haven't anything for you to do."

His eyes left her face and fell to searching the ground. They roamed about until they came to the chrysanthemum bed where she had been working. "What's them plants, ma'am?"

The irritation and resistance melted from Elisa's face. "Oh, those are chrysanthemums, giant whites and yellows. I raise them every year, bigger than anybody around here."

"Kind of a long-stemmed flower? Looks like a quick puff of colored smoke?" he asked.

"That's it. What a nice way to describe them."

"They smell kind of nasty till you get used to them," he said.

"It's a good bitter smell," she retorted, "not nasty at all."

He changed his tone quickly, "I like the smell myself."

"I had ten-inch blooms this year," she said.

The man leaned farther over the fence. "Look. I know a lady down the road a piece, has got the nicest garden you ever seen. Got nearly every kind of flower but no chrysanthemums. Last time I was mending a copper-bottom washtub for her (that's a hard job but I do it good), she said to me, 'If you ever run acrost some nice chrysanthemums I wish you'd try to get me a few seeds.' That's what she told me."

Elisa's eyes grew alert and eager. "She couldn't have known much about chrysanthemums. You *can* raise them from seed, but it's much easier to root the little sprouts you see there."

"Oh," he said. "I s'pose I can't take none to her, then."

"Why yes you can," Elisa cried. "I can put some in damp sand, and you can carry them right along with you. They'll take root in the pot if you keep them damp. And then she can transplant them."

"She'd sure like to have some, ma'am. You say they're nice ones?"

"Beautiful," she said. "Oh, beautiful." Her eyes shone. She tore off the battered hat and shook out her dark pretty hair. "I'll put them in a flower pot, and you can take them right with you. Come into the yard."

While the man came through the picket gate Elisa ran excitedly along the geranium-bordered path to the back of the house. And she returned carrying a big red flower pot. The gloves were forgotten now. She kneeled on the ground by the starting bed and dug up the sandy soil with her fingers and scooped it into the bright new flower pot. Then she picked up the little pile of shoots she had prepared. With her strong fingers she pressed them into the sand and tamped around them with her knuckles. The man stood over her. "I'll tell you what to do," she said. "You remember so you can tell the lady."

"Yes, I'll try to remember."

"Well, look. These will take root in about a month. Then she must set them out, about a foot apart in good rich earth like this, see?" She lifted a handful of dark soil for him to look at. "They'll grow fast and tall. Now remember this: In July tell her to cut them down, about eight inches from the ground."

"Before they bloom?" he asked.

"Yes, before they bloom." Her face was tight with eagerness. "They'll grow right up again. About the last of September the buds will start."

She stopped and seemed perplexed. "It's the budding that takes the most care," she said hesitantly. "I don't know how to tell you." She looked deep into his eyes, searchingly. Her mouth opened a little, and she seemed to be listening. "I'll try to tell you," she said. "Did you ever hear of planting hands?"

"Can't say I have, ma'am."

"Well, I can only tell you what it feels like. It's when you're picking off the buds you don't want. Everything goes right down into your fingertips. You watch your fingers work. They do it themselves. You can feel how it is. They pick and pick the buds. They never make a mistake. They're with the plant. Do you see? Your fingers and the plant. You can feel that, right up your arm. They know. They never make a mistake. You can feel it. When you're like that you can't do anything wrong. Do you see that? Can you understand that?"

She was kneeling on the ground looking up at him. Her breast swelled passionately.

The man's eyes narrowed. He looked away self-consciously. "Maybe I know," he said. "Sometimes in the night in the wagon there—"

Elisa's voice grew husky. She broke in on him, "I've never lived as you do, but I know what you mean. When the night is dark—why, the stars are sharp-pointed, and there's quiet. Why, you rise up and up! Every pointed star gets driven into your body. It's like that. Hot and sharp and—lovely."

Kneeling there, her hand went out toward his legs in the greasy black trousers. Her hesitant fingers almost touched the cloth. Then her hand dropped to the ground. She crouched low like a fawning dog.

He said, "It's nice, just like you say. Only when you don't have no dinner, it ain't."

She stood up then, very straight, and her face was ashamed. She held the flower pot out to him and placed it gently in his arms. "Here. Put it in your wagon, on the seat, where you can watch it. Maybe I can find something for you to do."

At the back of the house she dug in the can pile and found two old and battered aluminum saucepans. She carried them back and gave them to him. "Here, maybe you can fix these."

His manner changed. He became professional. "Good as new I can fix them." At the back of his wagon he set a little anvil, and out of an oily tool box dug a small machine hammer. Elisa came through the gate to watch him while he pounded out the dents in the kettles. His mouth grew sure and knowing. At a difficult part of the work he sucked his underlip.

"You sleep right in the wagon?" Elisa asked.

"Right in the wagon, ma'am. Rain or shine I'm dry as a cow in there."

"It must be nice," she said. "It must be very nice. I wish women could do such things."

"It ain't the right kind of a life for a woman."

Her upper lip raised a little, showing her teeth. "How do you know? How can you tell?" she said.

"I don't know, ma'am," he protested. "Of course I don't know. Now here's your kettles, done. You don't have to buy no new ones."

"How much?"

"Oh, fifty cents'll do. I keep my prices down and my work good. That's why I have all them satisfied customers up and down the highway."

Elisa brought him a fifty-cent piece from the house and dropped it in his hand. "You might be surprised to have a rival some time. I can sharpen scissors, too. And I can beat the dents out of little pots. I could show you what a woman might do."

He put his hammer back in the oily box and shoved the little anvil out of sight. "It would be a lonely life for a woman, ma'am, and a scary life, too, with animals creeping under the wagon all night." He climbed over the singletree, steadying himself with a hand on the burro's white rump. He settled himself in the seat, picked up the lines. "Thank you kindly, ma'am," he said. "I'll do like you told me; I'll go back and catch the Salinas road."

"Mind," she called, "if you're long in getting there, keep the sand damp."

"Sand, ma'am? . . . Sand? Oh, sure. You mean around the chrysanthemums. Sure I will." He clucked his tongue. The beasts leaned luxuriously into their collars. The mongrel dog took his place between the back wheels. The wagon turned and crawled out the entrance road and back the way it had come, along the river.

Elisa stood in front of her wire fence watching the slow progress of the caravan. Her shoulders were straight, her head thrown back, her eyes half-closed, so that the scene came vaguely into them. Her lips moved silently, forming the words "Good-bye — good-bye." Then she whispered, "That's a bright direction. There's a glowing there." The sound of her whisper startled her. She shook herself free and looked about to see whether anyone had been listening. Only the dogs had heard. They lifted their heads toward her from their sleeping in the dust, and then stretched out their chins and settled asleep again. Elisa turned and ran hurriedly into the house.

In the kitchen she reached behind the stove and felt the water tank. It was full of hot water from the noonday cooking. In the bathroom she tore off her soiled clothes and flung them into the corner. And then she scrubbed herself with a little block of pumice, legs and thighs, loins and chest and arms, until her skin was scratched and red. When she had dried herself she stood in front of a mirror in her bedroom and looked at her body. She tightened her stomach and threw out her chest. She turned and looked over her shoulder at her back.

After a while she began to dress, slowly. She put on her newest underclothing and her nicest stockings and the dress which was the symbol of her prettiness. She worked carefully on her hair, penciled her eyebrows and rouged her lips.

Before she was finished she heard the little thunder of hoofs and the shouts of Henry and his helper as they drove the red steers into the corral. She heard the gate bang shut and set herself for Henry's arrival.

His step sounded on the porch. He entered the house calling, "Elisa, where are you?"

"In my room, dressing. I'm not ready. There's hot water for your bath. Hurry up. It's getting late."

When she heard him splashing in the tub, Elisa laid his dark suit on the bed, and shirt and socks and tie beside it. She stood his polished shoes on the floor beside the bed. Then she went to the porch and sat primly and stiffly down. She looked toward the river road where the willow-line was still yellow with frosted leaves so that under the high grey fog they seemed a thin band of sunshine. This was the only color in the grey afternoon. She sat unmoving for a long time. Her eyes blinked rarely.

Henry came banging out of the door, shoving his tie inside his vest as he came. Elisa stiffened and her face grew tight. Henry stopped short and looked at her. "Why — why, Elisa. You look so nice!"

"Nice? You think I look nice? What do you mean by 'nice'?"

Henry blundered on. "I don't know. I mean you look different, strong and happy."

"I am strong? Yes, strong. What do you mean 'strong'?"

He looked bewildered. "You're playing some kind of a game," he said helplessly. "It's a kind of a play. You look strong enough to break a calf over your knee, happy enough to eat it like a watermelon."

For a second she lost her rigidity. "Henry! Don't talk like that. You didn't know what you said." She grew complete again. "I'm strong," she boasted, "I never knew before how strong."

Henry looked down toward the tractor shed, and when he brought his eyes back to her, they were his own again. "I'll get out the car. You can put on your coat while I'm starting."

Elisa went into the house. She heard him drive to the gate and idle down his motor, and then she took a long time to put on her hat. She pulled it here and pressed it there. When Henry turned the motor off she slipped into her coat and went out.

The little roadster bounced along on the dirt road by the river, raising the birds and driving the rabbits into the brush. Two cranes flapped heavily over the willow-line and dropped into the river-bed.

Far ahead on the road Elisa saw a dark speck. She knew.

She tried not to look as they passed it, but her eyes would not obey. She whispered to herself sadly, "He might have thrown them off the road. That wouldn't have been much trouble, not very much. But he kept the pot," she explained. "He had to keep the pot. That's why he couldn't get them off the road."

The roadster turned a bend and she saw the caravan ahead. She swung full around toward her husband so she could not see the little covered wagon and the mismatched team as the car passed them.

In a moment it was over. The thing was done. She did not look back.

She said loudly, to be heard above the motor. "It will be good, tonight, a good dinner."

"Now you're changed again," Henry complained. He took one hand from the wheel and patted her knee. "I ought to take you in to dinner oftener. It would be good for both of us. We get so heavy out on the ranch."

"Henry," she asked, "could we have wine at dinner?"

"Sure we could. Say! That will be fine."

She was silent for a while; then she said, "Henry, at those prize fights, do the men hurt each other very much?"

"Sometimes a little, not often. Why?"

"Well, I've read how they break noses, and blood runs down their chests. I've read how the fighting gloves get heavy and soggy with blood."

He looked around at her. "What's the matter, Elisa? I didn't know you read things like that." He brought the car to a stop, then turned to the right over the Salinas River bridge.

"Do any women ever go to the fights?" she asked.

"Oh, sure, some. What's the matter Elisa? Do you want to go? I don't think you'd like it, but I'll take you if you really want to go."

She relaxed limply in the seat. "Oh, no. No. I don't want to go. I'm sure I don't." Her face was turned away from him. "It will be enough if we can have wine. It will be plenty." She turned up her coat collar so he could not see that she was crying weakly — like an old woman.

Amy Tan

Amy Tan (b. 1952) was born in Oakland, California. Her father was educated as an engineer in Beijing; her mother left China in 1949, just before the communist revolution. Tan remembers that as a child she felt like an American girl trapped in a Chinese body: "There was shame and self-hate. There is this myth that America is a melting pot, but what happens in assimilation is that we end up deliberately choosing the American things—hot dogs and apple pie—and ignoring the Chinese offerings."

After her father's death, Tan and her mother lived in Switzerland, where she attended high school. "I was a novelty," she recalls. "There were so few Asians in Europe that everywhere I went people stared. Europeans asked me out. I had never been asked out in America." After attending a small college in Oregon, she worked for IBM as a writer of computer manuals. In 1984 Tan and her mother visited China and met her relatives; there she made the important discovery, as she has said, that "I belonged to my family and my family belonged to China." A year later, back in San Francisco, Tan read Louise Erdrich's *Love Medicine* and was so impressed by the power of its interlocking stories about another cultural minority, Native Americans, that she began to write short stories herself. One of them was published in a little magazine read by a literary agent in San Diego, who urged Tan to outline a book about the conflicts between different generations of Chinese mothers and daughters in the United States. After her agent negotiated a $50,000 advance from Putnam, Tan worked full-time on the first draft of her book *The Joy Luck Club* (1989) and finished it in four months.

"Two Kinds" is a story from that book. At first Tan thought her book contract was "all a token minority thing. I thought they had to fill a quota since there weren't many Chinese Americans writing." But her book was a best-seller and was nominated for a National Book Award. As the novelist Valerie Miner has recognized, Tan's special gifts are her storytelling ability and her "remarkable ear for dialogue and dialect, representing the choppy English of the mother and the sloppy California vernacular of the daughter with a sensitive authenticity." At the heart of Tan's book is the resilient bond between mother and daughter. "I'm my own person," the daughter says. "How can she be her own person," the mother answers. "When did I give her up?" Tan's other books include *The Kitchen God's Wife* (1991); a children's book, *The Moon Lady* (1992); *The Hundred Secret Senses* (1995); *The Bonesetter's Daughter* (2001); *The Opposite of Fate* (2003); *Saving Fish from Drowning* (2005); and *Valley of Amazement* (2013).

RELATED COMMENTARY
Amy Tan, "In the Canon, for All the Wrong Reasons," page 1524.

Two Kinds

1989

MY MOTHER BELIEVED you could be anything you wanted to be in America. You could open a restaurant. You could work for the government and get good retirement. You could buy a house with almost no money down. You could become rich. You could become instantly famous.

"Of course you can be prodigy, too," my mother told me when I was nine. "You can be best anything. What does Auntie Lindo know? Her daughter, she is only best tricky."

America was where all my mother's hopes lay. She had come here in 1949 after losing everything in China: her mother and father, her family home, her first husband, and two daughters, twin baby girls. But she never looked back with regret. There were so many ways for things to get better.

We didn't immediately pick the right kind of prodigy. At first my mother thought I could be a Chinese Shirley Temple. We'd watch Shirley's old movies on TV as though they were training films. My mother would poke my arm and say, "*Ni kan*" — You watch. And I would see Shirley tapping her feet, or singing a sailor song, or pursing her lips into a very round O while saying, "Oh my goodness."

"*Ni kan*," said my mother as Shirley's eyes flooded with tears. "You already know how. Don't need talent for crying!"

Soon after my mother got this idea about Shirley Temple, she took me to a beauty training school in the Mission district and put me in the hands of a student who could barely hold the scissors without shaking. Instead of getting big fat curls, I emerged with an uneven mass of crinkly black fuzz. My mother dragged me off to the bathroom and tried to wet down my hair.

"You look like Negro Chinese," she lamented, as if I had done this on purpose.

The instructor of the beauty training school had to lop off these soggy clumps to make my hair even again. "Peter Pan is very popular these days," the instructor assured my mother. I now had hair the length of a boy's, with straight-across bangs that hung at a slant two inches above my eyebrows. I liked the haircut and it made me actually look forward to my future fame.

In fact, in the beginning, I was just as excited as my mother, maybe even more so. I pictured this prodigy part of me as many different images, trying each one on for size. I was a dainty ballerina girl standing by the curtains, waiting to hear the right music that would send me floating on my tiptoes. I was like the Christ child lifted out of the straw manger, crying with holy indignity. I was Cinderella stepping from her pumpkin carriage with sparkly cartoon music filling the air.

In all of my imaginings, I was filled with a sense that I would soon become *perfect*. My mother and father would adore me. I would be beyond reproach. I would never feel the need to sulk for anything.

But sometimes the prodigy in me became impatient. "If you don't hurry up and get me out of here, I'm disappearing for good," it warned. "And then you'll always be nothing."

———————

Every night after dinner, my mother and I would sit at the Formica kitchen table. She would present new tests, taking her examples from stories of amazing children she had read in *Ripley's Believe It or Not,* or *Good Housekeeping, Reader's Digest,* and a dozen other magazines she kept in a pile in our bathroom. My mother got these magazines from people whose houses she cleaned. And since she cleaned many houses each week, we had a great assortment. She would look through them all, searching for stories about remarkable children.

The first night she brought out a story about a three-year-old boy who knew the capitals of all the states and even most of the European countries. A teacher was quoted as saying the little boy could also pronounce the names of the foreign cities correctly.

"What's the capital of Finland?" my mother asked me, looking at the magazine story.

All I knew was the capital of California, because Sacramento was the name of the street we lived on in Chinatown. "Nairobi!" I guessed, saying the most foreign word I could think of. She checked to see if that was possibly one way to pronounce "Helsinki" before showing me the answer.

The tests got harder — multiplying numbers in my head, finding the queen of hearts in a deck of cards, trying to stand on my head without using my hands, predicting the daily temperatures in Los Angeles, New York, and London.

One night I had to look at a page from the Bible for three minutes and then report everything I could remember. "Now Jehoshaphat had riches and honor in abundance and . . . that's all I remember, Ma," I said.

And after seeing my mother's disappointed face once again, something inside of me began to die. I hated the tests, the raised hopes and failed expectations. Before going to bed that night, I looked in the mirror above the bathroom sink and when I saw only my face staring back — and that it would always be this ordinary face — I began to cry. Such a sad, ugly girl! I made high-pitched noises like a crazed animal, trying to scratch out the face in the mirror.

And then I saw what seemed to be the prodigy side of me — because I had never seen that face before. I looked at my reflection, blinking so I could see more clearly. The girl staring back at me was angry, powerful. This girl and I were the same. I had new thoughts, willful thoughts, or rather thoughts filled with lots of won'ts. I won't let her change me, I promised myself. I won't be what I'm not.

So now on nights when my mother presented her tests, I performed listlessly, my head propped on one arm. I pretended to be bored. And I was. I got so bored I started counting the bellows of the foghorns out on the bay while my mother drilled me in other areas. The sound was comforting and reminded me of the cow jumping over the moon. And the next day, I played a game with myself, seeing if my mother would give up on me before eight bellows. After a while I usually counted only one, maybe two bellows at most. At last she was beginning to give up hope.

Two or three months had gone by without any mention of my being a prodigy again. And then one day my mother was watching *The Ed Sullivan Show* on TV. The TV was old and the sound kept shorting out. Every time my mother got halfway up from the sofa to adjust the set, the sound would go back on and Ed would be talking. As soon as she sat down, Ed would go silent again. She got up, the TV broke into loud piano music. She sat down. Silence. Up and down, back and forth, quiet and loud. It was like a stiff embraceless dance between her and the TV set. Finally she stood by the set with her hand on the sound dial.

She seemed entranced by the music, a little frenzied piano piece with this mesmerizing quality, sort of quick passages and then teasing lilting ones before it returned to the quick playful parts.

"*Ni kan*," my mother said, calling me over with hurried hand gestures. "Look here."

I could see why my mother was fascinated by the music. It was being pounded out by a little Chinese girl, about nine years old, with a Peter Pan haircut. The girl had the sauciness of a Shirley Temple. She was proudly modest like a proper Chinese child. And she also did this fancy sweep of a curtsy, so that the fluffy skirt of her white dress cascaded slowly to the floor like the petals of a large carnation.

In spite of these warning signs, I wasn't worried. Our family had no piano and we couldn't afford to buy one, let alone reams of sheet music and piano lessons. So I could be generous in my comments when my mother bad-mouthed the little girl on TV.

"Play note right, but doesn't sound good! No singing sound," complained my mother.

"What are you picking on her for?" I said carelessly. "She's pretty good. Maybe she's not the best, but she's trying hard." I knew almost immediately I would be sorry I said that.

"Just like you," she said. "Not the best. Because you not trying." She gave a little huff as she let go of the sound dial and sat down on the sofa.

The little Chinese girl sat down also to play an encore of "Anitra's Dance" by Grieg. I remember the song, because later on I had to learn how to play it.

Three days after watching *The Ed Sullivan Show,* my mother told me what my schedule would be for piano lessons and piano practice. She had talked to Mr. Chong, who lived on the first floor of our apartment building. Mr. Chong was a retired piano teacher and my mother had traded housecleaning services for weekly lessons and a piano for me to practice on every day, two hours a day, from four until six.

When my mother told me this, I felt as though I had been sent to hell. I whined and then kicked my foot a little when I couldn't stand it anymore.

"Why don't you like me the way I am? I'm *not* a genius! I can't play the piano. And even if I could, I wouldn't go on TV if you paid me a million dollars!" I cried.

My mother slapped me. "Who ask you be genius?" she shouted. "Only ask you be your best. For you sake. You think I want you be genius? Hnnh! What for! Who ask you!"

"So ungrateful," I heard her mutter in Chinese. "If she had as much talent as she has temper, she would be famous now."

Mr. Chong, whom I secretly nicknamed Old Chong, was very strange, always tapping his fingers to the silent music of an invisible orchestra. He looked ancient in my eyes. He had lost most of the hair on top of his head and he wore thick glasses and had eyes that always looked tired and sleepy. But he must have been younger than I thought, since he lived with his mother and was not yet married.

I met Old Lady Chong once and that was enough. She had this peculiar smell like a baby that had done something in its pants. And her fingers felt like a dead person's, like an old peach I once found in the back of the refrigerator; the skin just slid off the meat when I picked it up.

I soon found out why Old Chong had retired from teaching piano. He was deaf. "Like Beethoven!" he shouted to me. "We're both listening only in our head!" And he would start to conduct his frantic silent sonatas.

Our lessons went like this. He would open the book and point to different things, explaining their purpose: "Key! Treble! Bass! No sharps or flats! So this is C major! Listen now and play after me!"

And then he would play the C scale a few times, a simple chord, and then, as if inspired by an old, unreachable itch, he gradually added more notes and running trills and a pounding bass until the music was really something quite grand.

I would play after him, the simple scale, the simple chord, and then I just played some nonsense that sounded like a cat running up and down on top of garbage cans. Old Chong smiled and applauded and then said, "Very good! But now you must learn to keep time!"

So that's how I discovered that Old Chong's eyes were too slow to keep up with the wrong notes I was playing. He went through the motions in half-time. To help me keep rhythm, he stood behind me, pushing down on my right shoulder for every beat. He balanced pennies on top of my wrists so I would keep them still as I slowly played scales and arpeggios. He had me curve my hand around an apple and keep that shape when playing chords. He marched stiffly to show me how to make each finger dance up and down, staccato like an obedient little soldier.

He taught me all these things, and that was how I also learned I could be lazy and get away with mistakes, lots of mistakes. If I hit the wrong notes because I hadn't practiced enough, I never corrected myself. I just kept playing in rhythm. And Old Chong kept conducting his own private reverie.

So maybe I never really gave myself a fair chance. I did pick up the basics pretty quickly, and I might have become a good pianist at that young age. But I was so determined not to try, not to be anybody different that I learned to play only the most ear-splitting preludes, the most discordant hymns.

Over the next year, I practiced like this, dutifully in my own way. And then one day I heard my mother and her friend Lindo Jong both talking in a loud bragging tone of voice so others could hear. It was after church, and I was leaning against the brick wall wearing a dress with stiff white petticoats. Auntie Lindo's daughter, Waverly, who was about my age, was standing farther down the wall about five feet away. We had grown up together and shared all the closeness of two sisters squabbling over crayons and dolls. In other words, for the most part, we hated each other. I thought she was snotty. Waverly Jong had gained a certain amount of fame as "Chinatown's Littlest Chinese Chess Champion."

"She bring home too many trophy," lamented Auntie Lindo that Sunday. "All day she play chess. All day I have no time do nothing but dust off her winnings." She threw a scolding look at Waverly, who pretended not to see her.

"You lucky you don't have this problem," said Auntie Lindo with a sigh to my mother.

And my mother squared her shoulders and bragged: "Our problem worser than yours. If we ask Jing-mei wash dish, she hear nothing but music. It's like you can't stop this natural talent."

And right then, I was determined to put a stop to her foolish pride.

A few weeks later, Old Chong and my mother conspired to have me play in a talent show which would be held in the church hall. By then, my parents had saved up enough to buy me a secondhand piano, a black Wurlitzer spinet with a scarred bench. It was the showpiece of our living room.

For the talent show, I was to play a piece called "Pleading Child" from Schumann's *Scenes from Childhood*. It was a simple, moody piece that sounded more difficult than it was. I was supposed to memorize the whole thing, playing the repeat parts twice to make the piece sound longer. But I dawdled over it, playing a few bars and then cheating, looking up to see what notes followed. I never really listened to what I was playing. I daydreamed about being somewhere else, about being someone else.

The part I liked to practice best was the fancy curtsy: right foot out, touch the rose on the carpet with a pointed foot, sweep to the side, left leg bends, look up and smile.

My parents invited all the couples from the Joy Luck Club to witness my debut. Auntie Lindo and Uncle Tin were there. Waverly and her two older brothers had also come. The first two rows were filled with children both younger and older than I was. The littlest ones got to go first. They recited simple nursery rhymes, squawked out tunes on miniature violins, twirled Hula Hoops, pranced in pink ballet tutus, and when they bowed or curtsied, the audience would sigh in unison, "Awww," and then clap enthusiastically.

When my turn came, I was very confident. I remember my childish excitement. It was as if I knew, without a doubt, that the prodigy side of me really did exist. I had no fear whatsoever, no nervousness. I remember thinking to myself, This is it! This is it! I looked out over the audience, at my mother's blank face, my father's yawn, Auntie Lindo's stiff-lipped smile, Waverly's sulky expression. I had on a white dress layered with sheets of lace, and a pink bow in my Peter Pan haircut. As I sat down I envisioned people jumping to their feet and Ed Sullivan rushing up to introduce me to everyone on TV.

And I started to play. It was so beautiful. I was so caught up in how lovely I looked that at first I didn't worry how I would sound. So it was a surprise to me when I hit the first wrong note and I realized something didn't sound quite right. And then I hit another and another followed that. A chill started at the top of my head and began to trickle down. Yet I couldn't stop playing, as though my hands were bewitched. I kept thinking my fingers would adjust themselves back, like a train switching to the right track. I played this strange jumble through two repeats, the sour notes staying with me all the way to the end.

When I stood up, I discovered my legs were shaking. Maybe I had just been nervous and the audience, like Old Chong, had seen me go through the right motions and had not heard anything wrong at all. I swept my right foot out, went down on my knee, looked up and smiled. The room was quiet, except for Old Chong, who was beaming and shouting, "Bravo! Bravo! Well done!" But then I saw my mother's face, her stricken face. The audience clapped weakly, and as I walked back to my chair, with my whole face quivering as I tried not to cry, I heard a little boy whisper loudly to his mother, "That was awful," and the mother whispered back, "Well, she certainly tried."

And now I realized how many people were in the audience, the whole world it seemed. I was aware of eyes burning into my back. I felt the shame of my mother and father as they sat stiffly throughout the rest of the show.

We could have escaped during intermission. Pride and some strange sense of honor must have anchored my parents to their chairs. And so we watched it all: the eighteen-year-old boy with a fake mustache who did a magic show and juggled flaming hoops while riding a unicycle. The breasted girl with white makeup who sang from *Madama Butterfly* and got honorable mention. And the eleven-year-old boy who won first prize playing a tricky violin song that sounded like a busy bee.

After the show, the Hsus, the Jongs, and the St. Clairs from the Joy Luck Club came up to my mother and father.

"Lots of talented kids," Auntie Lindo said vaguely, smiling broadly.

"That was somethin' else," said my father, and I wondered if he was referring to me in a humorous way, or whether he even remembered what I had done.

Waverly looked at me and shrugged her shoulders. "You aren't a genius like me," she said matter-of-factly. And if I hadn't felt so bad, I would have pulled her braids and punched her stomach.

But my mother's expression was what devastated me: a quiet, blank look that said she had lost everything. I felt the same way, and it seemed as if everybody were now coming up, like gawkers at the scene of an accident, to see what parts were actually missing. When we got on the bus to go home, my father was humming the busy-bee tune and my mother was silent. I kept thinking she wanted to wait until we got home before shouting at me. But when my father unlocked the door to our apartment, my mother walked in and then went to the back, into the bedroom. No accusations. No blame. And in a way, I felt disappointed. I had been waiting for her to start shouting, so I could shout back and cry and blame her for all my misery.

I assumed my talent-show fiasco meant I never had to play the piano again. But two days later, after school, my mother came out of the kitchen and saw me watching TV.

"Four clock," she reminded me as if it were any other day. I was stunned, as though she were asking me to go through the talent-show torture again. I wedged myself more tightly in front of the TV.

"Turn off TV," she called from the kitchen five minutes later.

I didn't budge. And then I decided. I didn't have to do what my mother said anymore. I wasn't her slave. This wasn't China. I had listened to her before and look what happened. She was the stupid one.

She came out from the kitchen and stood in the arched entryway of the living room. "Four clock," she said once again, louder.

"I'm not going to play anymore," I said nonchalantly. "Why should I? I'm not a genius."

She walked over and stood in front of the TV. I saw her chest was heaving up and down in an angry way.

"No!" I said, and I now felt stronger, as if my true self had finally emerged. So this was what had been inside me all along.

"No! I won't!" I screamed.

She yanked me by the arm, pulled me off the floor, snapped off the TV. She was frighteningly strong, half pulling, half carrying me toward the piano as I kicked the throw rugs under my feet. She lifted me up and onto the hard bench. I was sobbing by now, looking at her bitterly. Her chest was heaving even more and her mouth was open, smiling crazily as if she were pleased I was crying.

"You want me to be someone that I'm not!" I sobbed. "I'll never be the kind of daughter you want me to be!"

"Only two kinds of daughters," she shouted in Chinese. "Those who are obedient and those who follow their own mind! Only one kind of daughter can live in this house. Obedient daughter!"

"Then I wish I wasn't your daughter. I wish you weren't my mother," I shouted. As I said these things I got scared. I felt like worms and toads and slimy things were crawling out of my chest, but it also felt good, as if this awful side of me had surfaced, at last.

"Too late change this," said my mother shrilly.

And I could sense her anger rising to its breaking point. I wanted to see it spill over. And that's when I remembered the babies she had lost in China, the ones we never talked about. "Then I wish I'd never been born!" I shouted. "I wish I were dead! Like them."

It was as if I had said the magic words, Alakazam! — and her face went blank, her mouth closed, her arms went slack, and she backed out of the room, stunned, as if she were blowing away like a small brown leaf, thin, brittle, lifeless.

———————

It was not the only disappointment my mother felt in me. In the years that followed, I failed her so many times, each time asserting my own will, my right to fall short of expectations. I didn't get straight As. I didn't become class president. I didn't get into Stanford. I dropped out of college.

For unlike my mother, I did not believe I could be anything I wanted to be. I could only be me.

And for all those years, we never talked about the disaster at the recital or my terrible accusations afterward at the piano bench. All that remained unchecked, like a betrayal that was now unspeakable. So I never found a way to ask her why she had hoped for something so large that failure was inevitable.

And even worse, I never asked her what frightened me the most: Why had she given up hope?

For after our struggle at the piano, she never mentioned my playing again. The lessons stopped, the lid to the piano was closed, shutting out the dust, my misery, and her dreams.

So she surprised me. A few years ago, she offered to give me the piano, for my thirtieth birthday. I had not played in all those years. I saw the offer as a sign of forgiveness, a tremendous burden removed.

"Are you sure?" I asked shyly. "I mean, won't you and Dad miss it?"

"No, this your piano," she said firmly. "Always your piano. You only one can play."

"Well, I probably can't play anymore," I said. "It's been years."

"You pick up fast," said my mother, as if she knew this was certain. "You have natural talent. You could been genius if you want to."

"No I couldn't."

"You just not trying," said my mother. And she was neither angry nor sad. She said it as if to announce a fact that could never be disproved. "Take it," she said.

But I didn't at first. It was enough that she had offered it to me. And after that, every time I saw it in my parents' living room, standing in front of the bay windows, it made me feel proud, as if it were a shiny trophy I had won back.

———————

Last week I sent a tuner over to my parents' apartment and had the piano reconditioned, for purely sentimental reasons. My mother had died a few months before and I had been getting things in order for my father, a little bit at a time. I put the jewelry in special silk pouches. The sweaters she had knitted in yellow, pink, bright orange — all the colors I hated — I put those in moth-proof boxes. I found some old Chinese silk dresses, the kind with little slits up the sides. I rubbed the old silk against my skin, then wrapped them in tissue and decided to take them home with me.

After I had the piano tuned, I opened the lid and touched the keys. It sounded even richer than I remembered. Really, it was a very good piano. Inside the bench were the same exercise notes with handwritten scales, the same secondhand music books with their covers held together with yellow tape.

I opened up the Schumann book to the dark little piece I had played at the recital. It was on the left-hand side of the page, "Pleading Child." It looked more difficult than I remembered. I played a few bars, surprised at how easily the notes came back to me.

And for the first time, or so it seemed, I noticed the piece on the right-hand side. It was called "Perfectly Contented." I tried to play this one as well. It had a lighter melody but the same flowing rhythm and turned out to be quite easy. "Pleading Child" was shorter but slower; "Perfectly Contented" was longer but faster. And after I played them both a few times, I realized they were two halves of the same song.

Leo Tolstoy

Leo Tolstoy (1828–1910) is generally considered the greatest Russian writer of prose fiction. Born on his parents' estate in the province of Tula, he spent his years at the university drinking and gambling like many other noblemen, but in his twenties he joined the Russian army and began writing sketches of military life. After he left the army and traveled in Europe, he settled down to writing. He produced his two great novels, *War and Peace* and *Anna Karenina*, in 1869 and 1877, respectively. As Tolstoy grew older, he began to be dissatisfied with literature, reaching the conclusion that art is ungodly because it is founded on imagination. Vladimir Nabokov described Tolstoy's obsession thus: "Somehow, the process of seeking the Truth seemed more important to him than the easy, vivid, brilliant discovery of the illusion of truth through the medium of his artistic genius." In his eighties Tolstoy decided that by living comfortably on his country estate he was betraying his ideal of simple, saintly existence, so he wandered away from his home, heading for a monastery. He died in the waiting room of a little railway station, refusing to let his wife come near him. They had quarreled over his belief that he should give away all his copyrights "to the people" instead of leaving them to the couple's many children.

In "The Works of Guy de Maupassant" (1894), an essay about the French author, Tolstoy expressed his view of the moral duty of a writer. He felt that

> the cement which binds every artistic production into one whole and so produces the illusion of a reflection of life is not the unity of persons and situations, but the unity of the original, moral relation of the author to his subject. . . . And so an author who has no definite, clear, new view of the world, and still more so the one who does not consider this to be necessary, cannot give an artistic production. He can write beautifully, and a great deal but there will be no artistic production.

The chief theme of Tolstoy's writing, as in his great story "The Death of Ivan Ilych" (1886), is that the only certain happiness is to live for others. This helps to explain the tragedy of Ivan Ilych, who just before his death realizes that he has not lived as he should have. The story took Tolstoy two years to finish. In its first version, it was told in the first person by a colleague, who was given the diary Ivan Ilych kept during his fatal illness. The narrator begins, "It is impossible, absolutely impossible, to live as I have lived, and as we all live. I realized that as a result of the death of an acquaintance of mine, Ivan Ilych, and of the diary he left behind." Finally Tolstoy told the story in the third person, without using the diary.

RELATED STORY
Donald Barthelme, "At the Tolstoy Museum," page 84.

RELATED COMMENTARY
Leo Tolstoy, "Chekhov's Intent in 'The Darling,'" page 1528; Leo Tolstoy, "The Works of Guy de Maupassant," page 1531.

The Death of Ivan Ilych

1886 / Translated by Louise Maude and Aylmer Maude

I

During an interval in the Melvinski trial in the large building of the Law Courts, the members and public prosecutor met in Ivan Egorovich Shebek's private room, where the conversation turned on the celebrated Krasovski case. Fëdor Vasilievich warmly maintained that it was not subject to their jurisdiction, Ivan Egorovich maintained the contrary, while Peter Ivanovich, not having entered into the discussion at the start, took no part in it but looked through the *Gazette* which had just been handed in.

"Gentlemen," he said, "Ivan Ilych has died!"

"You don't say so!"

"Here, read it yourself," replied Peter Ivanovich, handing Fëdor Vasilievich the paper still damp from the press. Surrounded by a black border were the words: "Praskovya Fëdorovna Golovina, with profound sorrow, informs relatives and friends of the demise of her beloved husband Ivan Ilych Golovin, Member of the Court of Justice, which occurred on February the 4th of this year 1882. The funeral will take place on Friday at one o'clock in the afternoon."

Ivan Ilych had been a colleague of the gentlemen present and was liked by them all. He had been ill for some weeks with an illness said to be incurable. His post had been kept open for him, but there had been conjectures that in case of his death Alexeev might receive his appointment, and that either Vinnikov or Shtabel would succeed Alexeev. So on receiving the news of Ivan Ilych's death the first thought of each of the gentlemen in that private room was of the changes and promotions it might occasion among themselves or their acquaintances.

"I shall be sure to get Shtabel's place or Vinnikov's," thought Fëdor Vasilievich. "I was promised that long ago, and the promotion means an extra eight hundred rubles a year for me besides the allowance."

"Now I must apply for my brother-in-law's transfer from Kaluga," thought Peter Ivanovich. "My wife will be very glad, and then she won't be able to say that I never do anything for her relations."

"I thought he would never leave his bed again," said Peter Ivanovich aloud. "It's very sad."

"But what really was the matter with him?"

"The doctors couldn't say—at least they could, but each of them said something different. When last I saw him I thought he was getting better."

"And I haven't been to see him since the holidays. I always meant to go."

"Had he any property?"

"I think his wife had a little — but something quite trifling."

"We shall have to go to see her, but they live so terribly far away."

"Far away from you, you mean. Everything's far away from your place."

"You see, he never can forgive my living on the other side of the river," said Peter Ivanovich, smiling at Shebek. Then, still talking of the distances between different parts of the city, they returned to the Court.

Besides considerations as to the possible transfers and promotions likely to result from Ivan Ilych's death, the mere fact of the death of a near acquaintance aroused, as usual, in all who heard of it the complacent feeling that, "it is he who is dead and not I."

Each one thought or felt, "Well, he's dead but I'm alive!" But the more intimate of Ivan Ilych's acquaintances, his so-called friends, could not help thinking also that they would now have to fulfill the very tiresome demands of propriety by attending the funeral service and paying a visit of condolence to the widow.

Fëdor Vasilievich and Peter Ivanovich had been his nearest acquaintances. Peter Ivanovich had studied law with Ivan Ilych and had considered himself to be under obligations to him.

Having told his wife at dinner-time of Ivan Ilych's death and of his conjecture that it might be possible to get her brother transferred to their circuit, Peter Ivanovich sacrificed his usual nap, put on his evening clothes, and drove to Ivan Ilych's house.

At the entrance stood a carriage and two cabs. Leaning against the wall in the hall downstairs near the cloak-stand was a coffin-lid covered with cloth of gold, ornamented with gold cord and tassels, that had been polished up with metal powder. Two ladies in black were taking off their fur cloaks. Peter Ivanovich recognized one of them as Ivan Ilych's sister, but the other was a stranger to him. His colleague Schwartz was just coming downstairs, but on seeing Peter Ivanovich enter he stopped and winked at him, as if to say: "Ivan Ilych has made a mess of things — not like you and me."

Schwartz's face, with his Piccadilly whiskers and his slim figure in evening dress, had as usual an air of elegant solemnity which contrasted with the playfulness of his character and had a special piquancy here, or so it seemed to Peter Ivanovich.

Peter Ivanovich allowed the ladies to precede him and slowly followed them upstairs. Schwartz did not come down but remained where he was, and Peter Ivanovich understood that he wanted to arrange where they should play bridge that evening. The ladies went upstairs to the widow's room, and Schwartz, with seriously compressed lips but a playful look in his eyes, indicated by a twist of his eyebrows the room to the right where the body lay.

Peter Ivanovich, like everyone else on such occasions, entered feeling uncertain what he would have to do. All he knew was that at such times it is always safe to cross oneself. But he was not quite sure whether one should make obeisances while doing so. He therefore adopted a middle course. On entering the room he began crossing himself and made a slight movement resembling a bow. At the same time, as far as the motion of his head and arm allowed, he surveyed the room. Two young men — apparently nephews, one of whom was a high-school pupil — were leaving the room, crossing themselves as they did so. An old woman was standing motionless, and a lady with

strangely arched eyebrows was saying something to her in a whisper. A vigorous, resolute Church Reader, in a frock-coat, was reading something in a
loud voice with an expression that precluded any contradiction. The butler's
assistant, Gerasim, stepping lightly in front of Peter Ivanovich, was strewing
something on the floor. Noticing this, Peter Ivanovich was immediately aware
of a faint odor of a decomposing body.

The last time he had called on Ivan Ilych, Peter Ivanovich had seen Gerasim in the study. Ivan Ilych had been particularly fond of him and he was performing the duty of a sick nurse.

Peter Ivanovich continued to make the sign of the cross, slightly inclining
his head in an intermediate direction between the coffin, the Reader, and the
icons on the table in a corner of the room. Afterwards, when it seemed to him
that this movement of his arm in crossing himself had gone on too long, he
stopped and began to look at the corpse.

The dead man lay, as dead men always lie, in a specially heavy way, his rigid
limbs sunk in the soft cushions of the coffin, with the head forever bowed on
the pillow. His yellow waxen brow with bald patches over his sunken temples
was thrust up in the way peculiar to the dead, the protruding nose seeming
to press on the upper lip. He was much changed and had grown even thinner since Peter Ivanovich had last seen him, but, as is always the case with the
dead, his face was handsomer and above all more dignified than when he was
alive. The expression on the face said that what was necessary had been accomplished, and accomplished rightly. Besides this there was in that expression a
reproach and a warning to the living. This warning seemed to Peter Ivanovich
out of place, or at least not applicable to him. He felt a certain discomfort
and so he hurriedly crossed himself once more and turned and went out the
door — too hurriedly and too regardless of propriety, as he himself was aware.

Schwartz was waiting for him in the adjoining room with legs spread wide
apart and both hands toying with his top-hat behind his back. The mere sight
of that playful, well-groomed, and elegant figure refreshed Peter Ivanovich. He
felt that Schwartz was above all these happenings and would not surrender to
any depressing influences. His very look said that this incident of a church service for Ivan Ilych could not be a sufficient reason for infringing the order of the
session — in other words, that it would certainly not prevent his unwrapping
a new pack of cards and shuffling them that evening while a footman placed
four fresh candles on the table: in fact, that there was no reason for supposing
that this incident would hinder their spending the evening agreeably. Indeed
he said this in a whisper as Peter Ivanovich passed him, proposing that they
should meet for a game at Fëdor Vasilievich's. But apparently Peter Ivanovich
was not destined to play bridge that evening. Praskovya Fëdorovna (a short,
fat woman who despite all efforts to the contrary had continued to broaden
steadily from her shoulders downwards and who had the same extraordinarily
arched eyebrows as the lady who had been standing by the coffin), dressed all
in black, her head covered with lace, came out of her own room with some
other ladies, conducted them to the room where the dead body lay, and said:
"The service will begin immediately. Please go in."

Schwartz, making an indefinite bow, stood still, evidently neither accepting nor declining this invitation. Praskovya Fëdorovna, recognizing Peter Ivanovich, sighed, went close up to him, took his hand, and said: "I know you were a true friend to Ivan Ilych . . ." and looked at him awaiting some suitable response. And Peter Ivanovich knew that, just as it had been the right thing to cross himself in that room, so what he had to do here was to press her hand, sigh, and say, "Believe me. . . ." So he did all this and as he did it felt that the desired result had been achieved: that both he and she were touched.

"Come with me. I want to speak to you before it begins," said the widow. "Give me your arm."

Peter Ivanovich gave her his arm and they went to the inner rooms, passing Schwartz, who winked at Peter Ivanovich compassionately.

"That does for our bridge! Don't object if we find another player. Perhaps you can cut in when you do escape," said his playful look.

Peter Ivanovich sighed still more deeply and despondently, and Praskovya Fëdorovna pressed his arm gratefully. When they reached the drawing-room, upholstered in pink cretonne and lighted by a dim lamp, they sat down at the table — she on a sofa and Peter Ivanovich on a low pouffe, the springs of which yielded spasmodically under his weight. Praskovya Fëdorovna had been on the point of warning him to take another seat, but felt that such a warning was out of keeping with her present condition and so changed her mind. As he sat down on the pouffe Peter Ivanovich recalled how Ivan Ilych had arranged this room and had consulted him regarding this pink cretonne with green leaves. The whole room was full of furniture and knick-knacks, and on her way to the sofa the lace of the widow's black shawl caught on the carved edge of the table. Peter Ivanovich rose to detach it, and the springs of the pouffe, relieved of his weight, rose also and gave him a push. The widow began detaching her shawl herself, and Peter Ivanovich again sat down, suppressing the rebellious springs of the pouffe under him. But the widow had not quite freed herself and Peter Ivanovich got up again, and again the pouffe rebelled and even creaked. When this was all over she took out a clean cambric handkerchief and began to weep. The episode with the shawl and the struggle with the pouffe had cooled Peter Ivanovich's emotions and he sat there with a sullen look on his face. This awkward situation was interrupted by Sokolov, Ivan Ilych's butler, who came to report that the plot in the cemetery that Praskovya Fëdorovna had chosen would cost two hundred rubles. She stopped weeping and, looking at Peter Ivanovich with the air of a victim, remarked in French that it was very hard for her. Peter Ivanovich made a silent gesture signifying his full conviction that it must indeed be so.

"Please smoke," she said in a magnanimous yet crushed voice, and turned to discuss with Sokolov the price of the plot for the grave.

Peter Ivanovich while lighting his cigarette heard her inquiring very circumstantially into the price of different plots in the cemetery and finally decided which she would take. When that was done she gave instructions about engaging the choir. Sokolov then left the room.

"I look after everything myself," she told Peter Ivanovich, shifting the albums that lay on the table; and noticing that the table was endangered by his cigarette-ash, she immediately passed him an ashtray, saying as she did so: "I consider it an affectation to say that my grief prevents my attending to practical affairs. On the contrary, if anything can — I won't say console me, but — distract me, it is seeing to everything concerning him." She again took out her handkerchief as if preparing to cry, but suddenly, as if mastering her feeling, she shook herself and began to speak calmly. "But there is something I want to talk to you about."

Peter Ivanovich bowed, keeping control of the springs of the pouffe, which immediately began quivering under him.

"He suffered terribly the last few days."

"Did he?" said Peter Ivanovich.

"Oh, terribly! He screamed unceasingly, not for minutes but for hours. For the last three days he screamed incessantly. It was unendurable. I cannot understand how I bore it; you could hear him three rooms off. Oh, what I have suffered!"

"Is it possible that he was conscious all that time?" asked Peter Ivanovich.

"Yes," she whispered. "To the last moment. He took leave of us a quarter of an hour before he died, and asked us to take Vasya away."

The thought of the sufferings of this man he had known so intimately, first as a merry little boy, then as a school-mate, and later as a grown-up colleague, suddenly struck Peter Ivanovich with horror, despite an unpleasant consciousness of his own and this woman's dissimulation. He again saw that brow, and that nose pressing down on the lip, and felt afraid for himself.

"Three days of frightful suffering and then death! Why, that might suddenly, at any time, happen to me," he thought, and for a moment felt terrified. But — he did not himself know how — the customary reflection at once occurred to him that this had happened to Ivan Ilych and not to him, and that it should not and could not happen to him, and that to think that it could would be yielding to depression which he ought not to do, as Schwartz's expression plainly showed. After which reflection Peter Ivanovich felt reassured, and began to ask with interest about the details of Ivan Ilych's death, as though death was an accident natural to Ivan Ilych but certainly not to himself.

After many details of the really dreadful physical sufferings Ivan Ilych had endured (which details he learnt only from the effect those sufferings had produced on Praskoyva Fëdorovna's nerves) the widow apparently found it necessary to get to business.

"Oh, Peter Ivanovich, how hard is it! How terribly, terribly hard!" and she again began to weep.

Peter Ivanovich sighed and waited for her to finish blowing her nose. When she had done so he said, "Believe me . . ." and she again began talking and brought out what was evidently her chief concern with him — namely, to question him as to how she could obtain a grant of money from the government on the occasion of her husband's death. She made it appear that she was asking Peter Ivanovich's advice about her pension, but he soon saw that she already knew about that to the minutest detail, more even than he did himself. She knew how much could be got out of the government in consequence of her husband's death, but wanted to find out whether she could not possibly extract something more. Peter Ivanovich tried to think of some means of doing so, but after reflecting for a while and, out of propriety, condemning the government for its niggardliness, he said he thought that nothing more could be got. Then she sighed and evidently began to devise means of getting rid of her visitor. Noticing this, he put out his cigarette, rose, pressed her hand, and went out into the anteroom.

In the dining-room where the clock stood that Ivan Ilych had liked so much and had bought at an antique shop, Peter Ivanovich met a priest and a few acquaintances who had come to attend the service, and he recognized Ivan Ilych's daughter, a handsome young woman. She was in black and her slim figure appeared slimmer than ever. She had a gloomy, determined, almost angry expression, and bowed to Peter Ivanovich as though he were in some way to blame. Behind her, with the same offended look, stood a wealthy young man, an examining magistrate, whom Peter Ivanovich also knew and who was her fiancé, as he had heard. He bowed mournfully to them and was about to pass into the death-chamber, when from under the stairs appeared the figure of Ivan Ilych's schoolboy son, who was extremely like his father. He seemed a little Ivan Ilych, such as Peter Ivanovich remembered when they studied law together. His tear-stained eyes had in them the look that is seen in the eyes of boys of thirteen or fourteen who are not pure-minded. When he saw Peter Ivanovich he scowled morosely and shamefacedly. Peter Ivanovich nodded to him and entered the death-chamber. The service began: candles, groans, incense, tears, and sobs. Peter Ivanovich stood looking gloomily down at his feet. He did not look once at the dead man, did not yield to any depressing influence, and was one of the first to leave the room. There was no one in the anteroom, but Gerasim darted out of the dead man's room, rummaged with his strong hands among the fur coats to find Peter Ivanovich's, and helped him on with it.

"Well, friend Gerasim," said Peter Ivanovich, so as to say something. "It's a sad affair, isn't it?"

"It's God's will. We shall all come to it some day," said Gerasim, displaying his teeth — the even, white teeth of a healthy peasant — and, like a man in the thick of urgent work, he briskly opened the front door, called the coachman, helped Peter Ivanovich into the sledge, and sprang back to the porch as if in readiness for what he had to do next.

Peter Ivanovich found the fresh air particularly pleasant after the smell of incense, the dead body, and carbolic acid.

"Where to, sir?" asked the coachman.

"It's not too late even now. . . . I'll call round on Fëdor Vasilievich."

He accordingly drove there and found them just finishing the first rubber, so that it was quite convenient for him to cut in.

II

Ivan Ilych's life had been most simple and most ordinary and therefore most terrible.

He had been a member of the Court of Justice, and died at the age of forty-five. His father had been an official who after serving in various ministries and departments in Petersburg had made the sort of career which brings men to positions from which by reason of their long service they cannot be dismissed, though they were obviously unfit to hold any responsible position, and for whom therefore posts are specially created, which though fictitious carry salaries of from six to ten thousand rubles that are not fictitious, and in receipt of which they live on to a great age.

Such was the Privy Councillor and superfluous member of various superfluous institutions, Ilya Epimovich Golovin.

He had three sons, of whom Ivan Ilych was the second. The eldest son was following in his father's footsteps only in another department, and was already approaching that stage in the service at which a similar sinecure would be reached. The third son was a failure. He had ruined his prospects in a number of positions and was now serving in the railway department. His father and brothers, and still more their wives, not merely disliked meeting him, but avoided remembering his existence unless compelled to do so. His sister had married Baron Greff, a Petersburg official of her father's type. Ivan Ilych was *le phénix de la famille*[1] as people said. He was neither as cold and formal as his elder brother nor as wild as the younger, but was a happy mean between them — an intelligent, polished, lively, and agreeable man. He had studied with his younger brother at the School of Law, but the latter had failed to complete the course and was expelled when he was in the fifth class. Ivan Ilych finished the course well. Even when he was at the School of Law he was just what he remained for the rest of his life: a capable, cheerful, good-natured, and sociable man, though strict in the fulfillment of what he considered to be his duty: and he considered his duty to be what was so considered by those in authority. Neither as a boy nor as a man was he a toady, but from early youth was by nature attracted to people of high station as a fly is drawn to the light, assimilating their ways and views of life and establishing friendly relations with them. All the enthusiasms of childhood and youth passed without leaving much trace on him; he succumbed to sensuality, to vanity, and latterly among the highest classes to liberalism, but always within limits which his instinct unfailingly indicated to him as correct.

At school he had done things which had formerly seemed to him very horrid and made him feel disgusted with himself when he did them; but when later on he saw that such actions were done by people of good position and that they did not regard them as wrong, he was able not exactly to regard them as right, but to forget about them entirely or not be at all troubled at remembering them.

Having graduated from the School of Law and qualified for the tenth rank of the civil service, and having received money from his father for his equipment, Ivan Ilych ordered himself clothes at Scharmer's, the fashionable tailor, hung a medallion inscribed *respice finem*[2] on his watch-chain, took leave of his professor and the prince who was patron of the school, had a farewell dinner

---

[1] The pride of the family. (Unless otherwise indicated, all foreign phrases are in French — often the everyday language of middle-class and upper-class Russians of Tolstoy's time.)

[2] "Consider your end" — that is, your death (Latin).

with his comrades at Donon's first-class restaurant, and with his new and fashionable portmanteau, linen, clothes, shaving and other toilet appliances, and a traveling rug, all purchased at the best shops, he set off for one of the provinces where, through his father's influence, he had been attached to the Governor as an official for special service.

In the province Ivan Ilych soon arranged as easy and agreeable a position for himself as he had had at the School of Law. He performed his official tasks, made his career, and at the same time amused himself pleasantly and decorously. Occasionally he paid official visits to country districts, where he behaved with dignity both to his superiors and inferiors, and performed the duties entrusted to him, which related chiefly to the sectarians,[3] with an exactness and incorruptible honesty of which he could not but feel proud.

In official matters, despite his youth and taste for frivolous gaiety, he was exceedingly reserved, punctilious, and even severe; but in society he was often amusing and witty, and always good-natured, correct in his manner, and *bon enfant*,[4] as the governor and his wife — with whom he was like one of the family — used to say of him.

In the province he had an affair with a lady who made advances to the elegant young lawyer, and there was also a milliner; and there were carousals with aides-de-camp who visited the district, and after-supper visits to a certain outlying street of doubtful reputation; and there was too some obsequiousness to his chief and even to his chief's wife, but all this was done with such a tone of good breeding that no hard names could be applied to it. It all came under the heading of the French saying: "*Il faut que jeunesse se passe.*"[5] It was all done with clean hands, in clean linen, with French phrases, and above all among people of the best society and consequently with the approval of people of rank.

So Ivan Ilych served for five years and then came a change in his official life. The new and reformed judicial institutions were introduced, and new men were needed. Ivan Ilych became such a new man. He was offered the post of examining magistrate, and he accepted it though the post was in another province and obliged him to give up the connections he had formed and to make new ones. His friends met to give him a send-off; they had a group-photograph taken and presented him with a silver cigarette-case, and he set off to his new post.

As examining magistrate Ivan Ilych was just as *comme il faut*[6] and decorous a man, inspiring general respect and capable of separating his official duties from his private life, as he had been when acting as an official on special service. His duties now as examining magistrate were far more interesting and attractive than before. In his former position it had been pleasant to wear an undress uniform made by Scharmer, and to pass through the crowd of petitioners and officials who were timorously awaiting an audience with the governor, and who envied him as with free and easy gait he went straight into his chief's private room to have a cup of tea and a cigarette with him. But not many people had then been directly

---

[3] "Old Believers," dissenters from the Orthodox Church.
[4] One of the boys (literally, "a good child").
[5] "Youth will have its day."
[6] Proper (literally, "as it should be").

dependent on him—only police officials and the sectarians when he went on special missions—and he liked to treat them politely, almost as comrades, as if he were letting them feel that he who had the power to crush them was treating them in this simple, friendly way. There were then but few such people. But now, as an examining magistrate, Ivan Ilych felt that everyone without exception, even the most important and self-satisfied, was in his power, and that he need only write a few words on a sheet of paper with a certain heading, and this or that important, self-satisfied person would be brought before him in the role of an accused person or a witness, and if he did not choose to allow him to sit down, would have to stand before him and answer his questions. Ivan Ilych never abused his power; he tried on the contrary to soften its expression, but the consciousness of it and of the possibility of softening its effect, supplied the chief interest and attraction of his office. In his work itself, especially in his examinations, he very soon acquired a method of eliminating all considerations irrelevant to the legal aspect of the case, and reducing even the most complicated case to a form in which it would be presented on paper only in its externals, completely excluding his personal opinion of the matter, while above all observing every prescribed formality. The work was new and Ivan Ilych was one of the first men to apply the new Code of 1864.[7]

On taking up the post of examining magistrate in a new town, he made new acquaintances and connections, placed himself on a new footing, and assumed a somewhat different tone. He took up an attitude of rather dignified aloofness towards the provincial authorities, but picked out the best circle of legal gentlemen and wealthy gentry living in the town and assumed a tone of slight dissatisfaction with the government, of moderate liberalism, and of enlightened citizenship. At the same time, without at all altering the elegance of his toilet, he ceased shaving his chin and allowed his beard to grow as it pleased.

Ivan Ilych settled down very pleasantly in this new town. The society there, which inclined towards opposition to the Governor, was friendly, his salary was larger, and he began to play vint,[8] which he found added not a little to the pleasure of life, for he had a capacity for cards, played good-humoredly, and calculated rapidly and astutely, so that he usually won.

After living there for two years he met his future wife, Praskovya Fëdorovna Mikhel, who was the most attractive, clever, and brilliant girl of the set in which he moved, and among other amusements and relaxations from his labors as examining magistrate, Ivan Ilych established light and playful relations with her.

While he had been an official on special service he had been accustomed to dance, but now as an examining magistrate it was exceptional for him to do so. If he danced now, he did it as if to show that though he served under the reformed order of things, and had reached the fifth official rank, yet when it came to dancing he could do it better than most people. So at the end of an evening he sometimes danced with Praskovya Fëdorovna, and it was chiefly

---

[7] The emancipation of the serfs in 1861 was followed by a thorough, all-round reform of judicial proceedings. [Translators' note]

[8] A form of bridge. [Translators' note]

during these dances that he captivated her. She fell in love with him. Ivan Ilych had at first no definite intention of marrying, but when the girl fell in love with him he said to himself: "Really, why shouldn't I marry?"

Praskovya Fëdorovna came of a good family, was not bad looking, and had some little property. Ivan Ilych might have aspired to a more brilliant match, but even this was good. He had his salary, and she, he hoped, would have an equal income. She was well connected, and was a sweet, pretty, and thoroughly correct young woman. To say that Ivan Ilych married because he fell in love with Praskovya Fëdorovna and found that she sympathized with his views of life would be as incorrect as to say that he married because his social circle approved of the match. He was swayed by both these considerations: the marriage gave him personal satisfaction, and at the same time it was considered the right thing by the most highly placed of his associates.

So Ivan Ilych got married.

The preparations for marriage and the beginning of married life, with its conjugal caresses, the new furniture, new crockery, and new linen, were very pleasant until his wife became pregnant — so that Ivan Ilych had begun to think that marriage would not impair the easy, agreeable, gay, and always decorous character of his life, approved of by society and regarded by himself as natural, but would even improve it. But from the first months of his wife's pregnancy, something new, unpleasant, depressing, and unseemly, and from which there was no way of escape, unexpectedly showed itself.

His wife, without any reason — *de gaieté de coeur*[9] as Ivan Ilych expressed it to himself — began to disturb the pleasure and propriety of their life. She began to be jealous without any cause, expected him to devote his whole attention to her, found fault with everything, and made coarse and ill-mannered scenes.

At first Ivan Ilych hoped to escape from the unpleasantness of this state of affairs by the same easy and decorous relation to life that had served him heretofore: he tried to ignore his wife's disagreeable moods, continued to live in his usual easy and pleasant way, invited friends to his house for a game of cards, and also tried going out to his club or spending his evenings with friends. But one day his wife began upbraiding him so vigorously, using such coarse words, and continued to abuse him every time he did not fulfil her demands, so resolutely and with such evident determination not to give way till he submitted — that is, till he stayed at home and was bored just as she was — that he became alarmed. He now realized that matrimony — at any rate with Praskovya Fëdorovna — was not always conducive to the pleasures and amenities of life, but on the contrary often infringed both comfort and propriety, and that he must therefore entrench himself against such infringement. And Ivan Ilych began to seek for means of doing so. His official duties were the one thing that imposed upon Praskovya Fëdorovna, and by means of his official work and the duties attached to it he began struggling with his wife to secure his own independence.

With the birth of their child, the attempts to feed it and the various failures in doing so, and with the real and imaginary illnesses of mother and child, in

---

[9] From sheer exuberance (literally, "from happiness of heart").

which Ivan Ilych's sympathy was demanded but about which he understood nothing, the need of securing for himself an existence outside his family life became still more imperative.

As his wife grew more irritable and exacting and Ivan Ilych transferred the center of gravity of his life more and more to his official work so did he grow to like his work better and became more ambitious than before.

Very soon, within a year of his wedding, Ivan Ilych had realized that marriage, though it may add some comforts to life, is in fact a very intricate and difficult affair towards which in order to perform one's duty, that is, to lead a decorous life approved of by society, one must adopt a definite attitude just as towards one's official duties.

And Ivan Ilych evolved such an attitude towards married life. He only required of it those conveniences — dinner at home, housewife, and bed — which it could give him, and above all that propriety of external forms required by public opinion. For the rest he looked for light-hearted pleasure and propriety, and was very thankful when he found them, but if he met with antagonism and querulousness he at once retired into his separate fenced-off world of official duties, where he found satisfaction.

Ivan Ilych was esteemed a good official, and after three years was made Assistant Public Prosecutor. His new duties, their importance, the possibility of indicting and imprisoning anyone he chose, the publicity his speeches received, and the success he had in all these things made his work still more attractive.

More children came. His wife became more and more querulous and ill-tempered, but the attitude Ivan Ilych had adopted towards his home life rendered him almost impervious to her grumbling.

After seven years' service in that town he was transferred to another province as Public Prosecutor. They moved, but were short of money and his wife did not like the place they moved to. Though the salary was higher the cost of living was greater, besides which two of their children died and family life became still more unpleasant for him.

Praskovya Fëdorovna blamed her husband for every inconvenience they encountered in their new home. Most of the conversations between husband and wife, especially as to the children's education, led to topics which recalled former disputes, and those disputes were apt to flare up again at any moment. There remained only those rare periods of amorousness which still came to them at times but did not last long. These were islets at which they anchored for a while and then again set out upon that ocean of veiled hostility which showed itself in their aloofness from one another. This aloofness might have grieved Ivan Ilych had he considered that it ought not to exist, but he now regarded the position as normal, and even made it the goal at which he aimed in family life. His aim was to free himself more and more from those unpleasantnesses and to give them a semblance of harmlessness and propriety. He attained this by spending less and less time with his family, and when obliged to be at home he tried to safeguard his position by the presence of outsiders. The chief thing however was that he had his official duties. The whole interest of his life now centered in the official world and that interest absorbed him. The consciousness of his power, being able to ruin anybody he wished to ruin, the importance, even the external dignity of his entry into court, or meetings with his subordinates, his success with superiors and inferiors, and above all his masterly handling of cases, of which he was conscious — all this gave him pleasure and filled his life, together with chats with his colleagues, dinners, and bridge. So that on the whole Ivan Ilych's life continued to flow as he considered it should do — pleasantly and properly.

So things continued for another seven years. His eldest daughter was already sixteen, another child had died, and only one son was left, a schoolboy and a subject of dissension. Ivan Ilych wanted to put him in the School of Law, but to spite him Praskovya Fëdorovna entered him at the High School. The daughter had been educated at home and had turned out well: the boy did not learn badly either.

III

So Ivan Ilych lived for seventeen years after his marriage. He was already a Public Prosecutor of long standing, and had declined several proposed transfers while awaiting a more desirable post, when an unanticipated and unpleasant occurrence quite upset the peaceful course of his life. He was expecting to be offered the post of presiding judge in a University town, but Happe somehow came to the front and obtained the appointment instead. Ivan Ilych became irritable, reproached Happe, and quarreled both with him and with his immediate superiors — who became colder to him and again passed him over when other appointments were made.

This was in 1880, the hardest year of Ivan Ilych's life. It was then that it became evident on the one hand that his salary was insufficient for them to live on, and on the other that he had been forgotten, and not only this, but that what was for him the greatest and most cruel injustice appeared to others a quite ordinary occurrence. Even his father did not consider it his duty to help him. Ivan Ilych felt himself abandoned by everyone, and that they regarded his position with a salary of 3,500 rubles as quite normal and even fortunate. He alone knew that with the consciousness of the injustices done him, with his wife's incessant nagging, and with the debts he had contracted by living beyond his means, his position was far from normal.

In order to save money that summer he obtained leave of absence and went with his wife to live in the country at her brother's place.

In the country, without his work, he experienced *ennui* for the first time in his life, and not only *ennui* but intolerable depression, and he decided that it was impossible to go on living like that, and that it was necessary to take energetic measures.

Having passed a sleepless night pacing up and down the veranda, he decided to go to Petersburg and bestir himself, in order to punish those who had failed to appreciate him and to get transferred to another ministry.

Next day, despite many protests from his wife and her brother, he started for Petersburg with the sole object of obtaining a post with a salary of five thousand rubles a year. He was no longer bent on any particular department, or tendency, or kind of activity. All he now wanted was an appointment to another post with a salary of five thousand rubles, either in the administration, in the banks, with the railways, in one of the Empress Marya's Institutions,[10] or even in the customs — but it had to carry with it a salary of five thousand rubles and be in a ministry other than that in which they had failed to appreciate him.

And this quest of Ivan Ilych's was crowned with remarkable and unexpected success. At Kursk an acquaintance of his, F. I. Ilyin, got into the first-class carriage, sat down beside Ivan Ilych, and told him of a telegram just received by the Governor of Kursk announcing that a change was about to take place in the ministry: Peter Ivanovich was to be superseded by Ivan Semënovich.

The proposed change, apart from its significance for Russia, had a special significance for Ivan Ilych, because by bringing forward a new man, Peter Petrovich, and consequently his friend Zachar Ivanovich, it was highly favorable for Ivan Ilych, since Zachar Ivanovich was a friend and colleague of his.

In Moscow this news was confirmed, and on reaching Petersburg Ivan Ilych found Zachar Ivanovich and received a definite promise of an appointment in his former department of Justice.

A week later he telegraphed to his wife: "Zachar in Miller's place. I shall receive appointment on presentation of report."

Thanks to this change of personnel, Ivan Ilych had unexpectedly obtained an appointment in his former ministry which placed him two stages above his former colleagues besides giving him five thousand rubles salary and three thousand five hundred rubles for expenses connected with his removal. All his ill humor towards his former enemies and the whole department vanished, and Ivan Ilych was completely happy.

He returned to the country more cheerful and contented than he had been for a long time. Praskovya Fëdorovna also cheered up and a truce was arranged between them. Ivan Ilych told of how he had been fêted by everybody in Petersburg, how all those who had been his enemies were put to shame and now fawned on him, how envious they were of his appointment, and how much everybody in Petersburg had liked him.

Praskovya Fëdorovna listened to all this and appeared to believe it. She did not contradict anything, but only made plans for their life in the town to which they were going. Ivan Ilych saw with delight that these plans were his plans, that he and his wife agreed, and that, after a stumble, his life was regaining its due and natural character of pleasant lightheartedness and decorum.

Ivan Ilych had come back for a short time only, for he had to take up his new duties on the 10th of September. Moreover, he needed time to settle into the new place, to move all his belongings from the province, and to buy and order many additional things: in a word, to make such arrangements as he had resolved on, which were almost exactly what Praskovya Fëdorovna too had decided on.

Now that everything had happened so fortunately, and that he and his wife were at one in their aims and moreover saw so little of one another, they got on

---

[10] Orphanages founded by the wife of Czar Paul I, who ruled from 1796 to 1801.

together better than they had done since the first years of marriage. Ivan Ilych had thought of taking his family away with him at once, but the insistence of his wife's brother and her sister-in-law, who had suddenly become particularly amiable and friendly to him and his family, induced him to depart alone.

So he departed, and the cheerful state of mind induced by his success and by the harmony between his wife and himself, the one intensifying the other, did not leave him. He found a delightful house, just the thing both he and his wife had dreamt of. Spacious, lofty reception rooms in the old style, a convenient and dignified study, rooms for his wife and daughter, a study for his son — it might have been specially built for them. Ivan Ilych himself superintended the arrangements, chose the wallpapers, supplemented the furniture (preferably with antiques which he considered particularly *comme il faut*), and supervised the upholstering. Everything progressed and progressed and approached the ideal he had set himself: even when things were only half completed they exceeded his expectations. He saw what a refined and elegant character, free from vulgarity, it would all have when it was ready. On falling asleep he pictured to himself how the reception-room would look. Looking at the yet unfinished drawing-room he could see the fireplace, the screen, the what-not, the little chairs dotted here and there, the dishes and plates on the walls, and the bronzes, as they would be when everything was in place. He was pleased by the thought of how his wife and daughter, who shared his taste in this matter, would be impressed by it. They were certainly not expecting as much. He had been particularly successful in finding, and buying cheaply, antiques which gave a particularly aristocratic character to the whole place. But in his letters he intentionally understated everything in order to be able to surprise them. All this so absorbed him that his new duties — though he liked his official work — interested him less than he had expected. Sometimes he even had moments of absent-mindedness during the Court Sessions, and would consider whether he should have straight or curved cornices for his curtains. He was so interested in it all that he often did things himself, rearranging the furniture, or rehanging the curtains. Once when mounting a step-ladder to show the upholsterer, who did not understand, how he wanted the hangings draped, he made a false step and slipped, but being a strong and agile man he clung on and only knocked his side against the knob of the window frame. The bruised place was painful but the pain soon passed, and he felt particularly bright and well just then. He wrote: "I feel fifteen years younger." He thought he would have everything ready by September, but it dragged on till mid-October. But the result was charming not only in his eyes but to everyone who saw it.

In reality it was just what is usually seen in the houses of people of moderate means who want to appear rich, and therefore succeed only in resembling others like themselves: there were damasks, dark wood, plants, rugs, and dull and polished bronzes — all the things people of a certain class have in order to resemble other people of that class. His house was so like the others that it would never have been noticed, but to him it all seemed to be quite exceptional. He was very happy when he met his family at the station and brought them to the newly furnished house all lit up, where a footman in a white tie opened the

door into the hall decorated with plants, and when they went on into the drawing room and the study uttering exclamations of delight. He conducted them
everywhere, drank in their praises eagerly, and beamed with pleasure. At tea
that evening, when Praskovya Fëdorovna among other things asked him about
his fall, he laughed and showed them how he had gone flying and had frightened the upholsterer.

"It's a good thing I'm a bit of an athlete. Another man might have been
killed, but I merely knocked myself, just here; it hurts when it's touched, but it's
passing off already — it's only a bruise."

So they began living in their new home — in which, as always happens,
when they got thoroughly settled in they found they were just one room
short — and with the increased income, which as always was just a little (some
five hundred rubles) too little, but it was all very nice.

Things went particularly well at first, before everything was finally arranged
and while something had still to be done: this thing bought, that thing ordered,
another thing moved, and something else adjusted. Though there were some disputes between husband and wife, they were both so well satisfied and had so much
to do that it all passed off without any serious quarrels. When nothing was left to
arrange it became rather dull and something seemed to be lacking, but they were
then making acquaintances, forming habits, and life was growing fuller.

Ivan Ilych spent his mornings at the law court and came home to dinner,
and at first he was generally in a good humor, though he occasionally became
irritable just on account of his house. (Every spot on the tablecloth or the uphol-
stery, and every broken windowblind string, irritated him. He had devoted so
much trouble to arranging it all that every disturbance of it distressed him.)
But on the whole his life ran its course as he believed life should do: easily,
pleasantly, and decorously.

He got up at nine, drank his coffee, read the paper, and then put on his undress
uniform and went to the law courts. There the harness in which he worked had
already been stretched to fit him and he donned it without a hitch: petitioners,
inquiries at the chancery, the chancery itself, and the sittings public and administrative. In all this the thing was to exclude everything fresh and vital, which
always disturbs the regular course of official business, and to admit only official
relations with people, and then only on official grounds. A man would come,
for instance, wanting some information. Ivan Ilych, as one in whose sphere the
matter did not lie, would have nothing to do with him: but if the man had some
business with him in his official capacity, something that could be expressed
on officially stamped paper, he would do everything, positively everything he
could within the limits of such relations, and in doing so would maintain the
semblance of friendly human relations, that is, would observe the courtesies of
life. As soon as the official relations ended, so did everything else. Ivan Ilych possessed this capacity to separate his real life from the official side of affairs and
not mix the two, in the highest degree, and by long practice and natural aptitude
had brought it to such a pitch that sometimes, in the manner of a virtuoso, he
would even allow himself to let the human and official relations mingle. He let
himself do this just because he felt that he could at any time he chose resume

the strictly official attitude again and drop the human relation. And he did it all easily, pleasantly, correctly, and even artistically. In the intervals between the sessions he smoked, drank tea, chatted a little about politics, a little about general topics, a little about cards, but most of all about official appointments. Tired, but with the feelings of a virtuoso — one of the first violins who has played his part in an orchestra with precision — he would return home to find that his wife and daughter had been out paying calls, or had a visitor, and that his son had been to school, had done his homework with his tutor, and was duly learning what is taught at High Schools. Everything was as it should be. After dinner, if they had no visitors, Ivan Ilych sometimes read a book that was being much discussed at the time, and in the evening settled down to work, that is, read official papers, compared the depositions of witnesses, and noted paragraphs of the Code applying to them. This was neither dull nor amusing. It was dull when he might have been playing bridge, but if no bridge was available it was at any rate better than doing nothing or sitting with his wife. Ivan Ilych's chief pleasure was giving little dinners to which he invited men and women of good social position, and just as his drawing-room resembled all other drawing-rooms so did his enjoyable little parties resemble all other such parties.

Once they even gave a dance. Ivan Ilych enjoyed it and everything went off well, except that it led to a violent quarrel with his wife about the cakes and sweets. Praskovya Fëdorovna had made her own plans, but Ivan Ilych insisted on getting everything from an expensive confectioner and ordered too many cakes, and the quarrel occurred because some of those cakes were left over and the confectioner's bill came to forty-five rubles. It was a great and disagreeable quarrel. Praskovya Fëdorovna called him "a fool and an imbecile," and he clutched at his head and made angry allusions to divorce.

But the dance itself had been enjoyable. The best people were there, and Ivan Ilych had danced with Princess Trufonova, a sister of the distinguished founder of the Society "Bear My Burden."

The pleasures connected with his work were pleasures of ambition; his social pleasures were those of vanity; but Ivan Ilych's greatest pleasure was playing bridge. He acknowledged that whatever disagreeable incident happened in his life, the pleasure that beamed like a ray of light about everything else was to sit down to bridge with good players, not noisy partners, and of course to four-handed bridge (with five players it was annoying to have to stand out, though one pretended not to mind), to play a clever and serious game (when the cards allowed it), and then to have supper and drink a glass of wine. After a game of bridge, especially if he had won a little (to win a large sum was unpleasant), Ivan Ilych went to bed in specially good humor.

So they lived. They formed a circle of acquaintances among the best people and were visited by people of importance and by young folk. In their views as to their acquaintances, husband, wife, and daughter were entirely agreed, and tacitly and unanimously kept at arm's length and shook off the various shabby friends and relations who, with much show of affection, gushed into the drawing-room with its Japanese plates on the walls. Soon these shabby friends ceased to obtrude themselves and only the best people remained in the Golovins' set.

Young men made up to Lisa, and Petrishchev, an examining magistrate and Dmitri Ivanovich Petrishchev's son and sole heir, began to be so attentive to her that Ivan Ilych had already spoken to Praskovya Fëdorovna about it, and considered whether they should not arrange a party for them, or get up some private theatricals.

So they lived, and all went well, without change, and life flowed pleasantly.

IV

They were all in good health. It could not be called ill health if Ivan Ilych sometimes said that he had a queer taste in his mouth and felt some discomfort in his left side.

But this discomfort increased and, though not exactly painful, grew into a sense of pressure in his side accompanied by ill humor. And his irritability became worse and worse and began to mar the agreeable, easy, and correct life that had established itself in the Golovin family. Quarrels between husband and wife became more and more frequent, and soon the ease and amenity disappeared and even the decorum was barely maintained. Scenes again became frequent, and very few of those islets remained on which husband and wife could meet without explosion. Praskovya Fëdorovna now had good reason to say that her husband's temper was trying. With characteristic exaggeration she said he had always had a dreadful temper, and that it had needed all her good nature to put up with it for twenty years. It was true that now the quarrels were started by him. His bursts of temper always came just before dinner, often just as he began to eat his soup. Sometimes he noticed that a plate or dish was chipped, or the food was not right, or his son put his elbow on the table, or his daughter's hair was not done as he liked it, and for all this he blamed Praskovya Fëdorovna. At first she retorted and said disagreeable things to him, but once or twice he fell into such a rage at the beginning of dinner that she realized it was due to some physical derangement brought on by taking food, and so she restrained herself and did not answer, but only hurried to get the dinner over. She regarded this self-restraint as highly praiseworthy. Having come to the conclusion that her husband had a dreadful temper and made her life miserable, she began to feel sorry for herself, and the more she pitied herself the more she hated her husband. She began to wish he would die; yet she did not want him to die because then his salary would cease. And this irritated her against him still more. She considered herself dreadfully unhappy just because not even his death could save her, and though she concealed her exasperation, that hidden exasperation of hers increased his irritation also.

After one scene in which Ivan Ilych had been particularly unfair and after which he had said in explanation that he certainly was irritable but that it was due to his not being well, she said that if he was ill it should be attended to, and insisted on his going to see a celebrated doctor.

He went. Everything took place as he had expected and as it always does. There was the usual waiting and the important air assumed by the doctor, with which he was so familiar (resembling that which he himself assumed in court), and the sounding and listening, and the questions which called for answers that were foregone conclusions and were evidently unnecessary, and the look of importance which implied that "if only you put yourself in our hands we will arrange everything — we know indubitably how it has to be done, always in the same way for everybody alike." It was all just as it was in the law courts. The doctor put on just the same air towards him as he himself put on towards an accused person.

The doctor said that so-and-so indicated that there was so-and-so inside the patient, but if the investigation of so-and-so did not confirm this, then he must assume that and that. If he assumed that and that, then . . . and so on. To Ivan Ilych only one question was important: was his case serious or not? But the doctor ignored that inappropriate question. From his point of view it was not the one under consideration, the real question was to decide between a floating kidney, chronic catarrh, or appendicitis. It was not a question of Ivan Ilych's life or death, but one between a floating kidney and appendicitis. And that question the doctor solved brilliantly, as it seemed to Ivan Ilych, in favor of the appendix, with the reservation that should an examination of the urine give fresh indications the matter would be reconsidered. All this was just what Ivan Ilych had himself brilliantly accomplished a thousand times in dealing with men on trial. The doctor summed up just as brilliantly, looking over his spectacles triumphantly and even gaily at the accused. From the doctor's summing up Ivan Ilych concluded that things were bad, but that for the doctor, and perhaps for everybody else, it was a matter of indifference, though for him it was bad. And this conclusion struck him painfully, arousing in him a great feeling of pity for himself and of bitterness towards the doctor's indifference to a matter of such importance.

He said nothing of this, but rose, placed the doctor's fee on the table, and remarked with a sigh: "We sick people probably often put inappropriate questions. But tell me, in general, is this complaint dangerous, or not? . . ."

The doctor looked at him sternly over his spectacles with one eye, as if to say: "Prisoner, if you will not keep to the questions put to you, I shall be obliged to have you removed from the court."

"I have already told you what I consider necessary and proper. The analysis may show something more." And the doctor bowed.

Ivan Ilych went out slowly, seated himself disconsolately in his sledge, and drove home. All the way home he was going over what the doctor had said, trying to translate those complicated, obscure, scientific phrases into plain language and find in them an answer to the question: "Is my condition bad? Is it very bad? Or is there as yet nothing much wrong?" And it seemed to him that the meaning of what the doctor had said was that it was very bad. Everything in the streets seemed depressing. The cabmen, the houses, the passers-by, and the shops, were dismal. His ache, this dull gnawing ache that never ceased for a moment, seemed to have acquired a new and more serious significance from the doctor's dubious remarks. Ivan Ilych now watched it with a new and oppressive feeling.

He reached home and began to tell his wife about it. She listened, but in the middle of his account his daughter came in with her hat on, ready to go out with her mother. She sat down reluctantly to listen to this tedious story, but could not stand it long, and her mother too did not hear him to the end.

"Well, I am very glad," she said. "Mind now to take your medicine regularly. Give me the prescription and I'll send Gerasim to the chemist's." And she went to get ready to go out.

While she was in the room Ivan Ilych had hardly taken time to breathe, but he sighed deeply when she left it.

"Well," he thought, "perhaps it isn't so bad after all."

He began taking his medicine and following the doctor's directions, which had been altered after the examination of the urine. But then it happened that there was a contradiction between the indications drawn from the examination of the urine and the symptoms that showed themselves. It turned out that what was happening differed from what the doctor had told him, and that he had either forgotten, or blundered, or hidden something from him. He could not, however, be blamed for that, and Ivan Ilych still obeyed his orders implicitly and at first derived some comfort from doing so.

From the time of his visit to the doctor, Ivan Ilych's chief occupation was the exact fulfilment of the doctor's instructions regarding hygiene and the taking of medicine, and the observation of his pain and his excretions. His chief interests came to be people's ailments and people's health. When sickness, deaths, or recoveries were mentioned in his presence, especially when the illness resembled his own, he listened with agitation which he tried to hide, asked questions, and applied what he heard to his own case.

The pain did not grow less, but Ivan Ilych made efforts to force himself to think that he was better. And he could do this so long as nothing agitated him. But as soon as he had any unpleasantness with his wife, any lack of success in his official work, or held bad cards at bridge, he was at once acutely sensible of his disease. He had formerly borne such mischances, hoping soon to adjust what was wrong, to master it and attain success, or make a grand slam. But now every mischance upset him and plunged him into despair. He would say to himself: "There now, just as I was beginning to get better and the medicine had begun to take effect, comes this accursed misfortune, or unpleasantness. . . ." And he was furious with the mishap, or with the people who were causing the unpleasantness and killing him, for he felt that this fury was killing him but could not restrain it. One would have thought that it should have been clear to him that this exasperation with circumstances and people aggravated his illness, and that he ought therefore to ignore unpleasant occurrences. But he drew the very opposite conclusion: he said that he needed peace, and he watched for everything that might disturb it and became irritable at the slightest infringement of it. His condition was rendered worse by the fact that he read medical books and consulted doctors. The progress of his disease was so gradual that he could deceive himself when comparing one day with another — the difference was so slight. But when he consulted the doctors it seemed to him that he was getting worse, and even very rapidly. Yet despite this he was continually consulting them.

That month he went to see another celebrity, who told him almost the same as the first had done but put his questions rather differently, and the interview with this celebrity only increased Ivan Ilych's doubts and fears. A friend of a friend of his, a very good doctor, diagnosed his illness again quite differently from the others, and though he predicted recovery, his questions and suppositions bewildered Ivan Ilych still more and increased his doubts. A homeopathist diagnosed the disease in yet another way, and prescribed medicine which Ivan Ilych took secretly for a week. But after a week, not feeling any improvement and having lost confidence both in the former doctor's treatment and in this one's, he became still more despondent. One day a lady acquaintance mentioned a cure effected by a wonder-working icon. Ivan Ilych caught himself listening attentively and beginning to believe that it had occurred. This incident alarmed him. "Has my mind really weakened to such an extent?" he asked himself. "Nonsense! It's all rubbish. I mustn't give way to nervous fears but having chosen a doctor must keep strictly to his treatment. That is what I will do. Now it's all settled. I won't think about it, but will follow the treatment seriously till summer, and then we shall see. From now there must be no more of this wavering!" This was easy to say but impossible to carry out. The pain in his side oppressed him and seemed to grow worse and more incessant, while the taste in his mouth grew stranger and stranger. It seemed to him that his breath had a disgusting smell, and he was conscious of a loss of appetite and strength. There was no deceiving himself: something terrible, new, and more important than anything before in his life, was taking place within him of which he alone was aware. Those about him did not understand or would not understand it, but thought everything in the world was going on as usual. That tormented Ivan Ilych more than anything. He saw that his household, especially his wife and daughter who were in a perfect whirl of visiting, did not understand anything of it and were annoyed that he was so depressed and so exacting, as if he were to blame for it. Though they tried to disguise it he saw that he was an obstacle in their path, and that his wife had adopted a definite line in regard to his illness and kept to it regardless of anything he said or did. Her attitude was this: "You know," she would say to her friends, "Ivan Ilych can't do as other people do, and keep to the treatment prescribed for him. One day he'll take his drops and keep strictly to his diet and go to bed in good time, but the next day unless I watch him he'll suddenly forget his medicine, eat sturgeon — which is forbidden — and sit up playing cards till one o'clock in the morning."

"Oh, come, when was that?" Ivan Ilych would ask in vexation. "Only once at Peter Ivanovich's."

"And yesterday with Shebek."

"Well, even if I hadn't stayed up, this pain would have kept me awake."

"Be that as it may you'll never get well like that, but will always make us wretched."

Praskovya Fëdorovna's attitude to Ivan Ilych's illness, as she expressed it both to others and to him, was that it was his own fault and was another of the annoyances he caused her. Ivan Ilych felt that this opinion escaped her involuntarily — but that did not make it easier for him.

At the law courts too, Ivan Ilych noticed, or thought he noticed, a strange attitude towards himself. It sometimes seemed to him that people were watching him inquisitively as a man whose place might soon be vacant. Then again, his friends would suddenly begin to chaff him in a friendly way about his low spirits, as if the awful, horrible, and unheard-of thing that was going on within him, incessantly gnawing at him and irresistibly drawing him away, was a very agreeable subject for jests. Schwartz in particular irritated him by his jocularity, vivacity, and *savoir-faire*, which reminded him of what he himself had been ten years ago.

Friends came to make up a set and they sat down to cards. They dealt, bending the new cards to soften them, and he sorted the diamonds in his hand and found he had seven. His partner said "No trumps" and supported him with two diamonds. What more could be wished for? It ought to be jolly and lively. They would make a grand slam. But suddenly Ivan Ilych was conscious of that gnawing pain, that taste in his mouth, and it seemed ridiculous that in such circumstances he should be pleased to make a grand slam.

He looked at his partner Mikhail Mikhaylovich, who rapped the table with his strong hand and instead of snatching up the tricks pushed the cards courteously and indulgently towards Ivan Ilych that he might have the pleasure of gathering them up without the trouble of stretching out his hand for them. "Does he think I am too weak to stretch out my arm?" thought Ivan Ilych, and forgetting what he was doing he over-trumped his partner, missing the grand slam by three tricks. And what was most awful of all was that he saw how upset Mikhail Mikhaylovich was about it but did not himself care. And it was dreadful to realize why he did not care.

They all saw that he was suffering and said: "We can stop if you are tired. Take a rest." Lie down? No, he was not at all tired, and he finished the rubber. All were gloomy and silent. Ivan Ilych felt that he had diffused this gloom over them and could not dispel it. They had supper and went away, and Ivan Ilych was left alone with the consciousness that his life was poisoned and was poisoning the lives of others, and that this poison did not weaken but penetrated more and more deeply into his whole being.

With this consciousness, and with physical pain besides the terror, he must go to bed, often to lie awake the greater part of the night. Next morning he had to get up again, dress, go to the law courts, speak, and write; or if he did not go out, spend at home those twenty-four hours a day each of which was a torture. And he had to live thus all alone on the brink of an abyss, with no one who understood or pitied him.

V

So one month passed and then another. Just before the New Year his brother-in-law came to town and stayed at their house. Ivan Ilych was at the law courts and Praskovya Fëdorovna had gone shopping. When Ivan Ilych came home and entered his study he found his brother-in-law there—a healthy, florid man—unpacking his portmanteau himself. He raised his head on hearing Ivan Ilych's footsteps and looked up at him for a moment without a word. That stare told Ivan Ilych everything. His brother-in-law opened his mouth to utter an exclamation of surprise but checked himself, and that action confirmed it all.

"I have changed, eh?"

"Yes, there is a change."

And after that, try as he would to get his brother-in-law to return to the subject of his looks, the latter would say nothing about it. Praskovya Fëdorovna came home and her brother went out to her. Ivan Ilych locked the door and began to examine himself in the glass, first full face, then in profile. He took up a portrait of himself taken with his wife, and compared it with what he saw in the glass. The change in him was immense. Then he bared his arms to the elbow, looked at them, drew the sleeves down again, sat down on an ottoman, and grew blacker than night.

"No, no, this won't do!" he said to himself, and jumped up, went to the table, took up some law papers and began to read them, but could not continue. He unlocked the door and went into the reception-room. The door leading to the drawing room was shut. He approached it on tiptoe and listened.

"No, you are exaggerating!" Praskovya Fëdorovna was saying.

"Exaggerating! Don't you see it? Why, he's a dead man! Look at his eyes — there's no light in them. But what is it that is wrong with him?"

"No one knows. Nikolaevich said something, but I don't know what. And Leshchetitsky[11] said quite the contrary. . . ."

Ivan Ilych walked away, went to his own room, lay down, and began musing: "The kidney, a floating kidney." He recalled all the doctors had told him of how it detached itself and swayed about. And by an effort of imagination he tried to catch that kidney and arrest it and support it. So little was needed for this, it seemed to him. "No, I'll go to see Peter Ivanovich again." He rang, ordered the carriage, and got ready to go.

"Where are you going, Jean?" asked his wife, with a specially sad and exceptionally kind look.

This exceptionally kind look irritated him. He looked morosely at her.

"I must go to see Peter Ivanovich."[12]

He went to see Peter Ivanovich, and together they went to see his friend, the doctor. He was in, and Ivan Ilych had a long talk with him.

Reviewing the anatomical and physiological details of what in the doctor's opinion was going on inside him, he understood it all.

There was something, a small thing, in the vermiform appendix. It might all come right. Only stimulate the energy of one organ and check the activity of another, then absorption would take place and everything would come right. He got home rather late for dinner, ate his dinner, and conversed cheerfully, but could not for a long time bring himself to go back to work in his room. At last, however, he went to his study and did what was necessary, but the consciousness that he had put something aside — an important, intimate matter which he would revert to when his work was done — never left him. When he had finished his work he remembered that this intimate matter was the thought of his vermiform appendix. But he did not give himself up to it, and went to

---

[11] Two doctors, the latter a celebrated specialist. [Translators' note]

[12] That was the friend whose friend was a doctor. [Translators' note]

the drawing-room for tea. There were callers there, including the examining magistrate who was a desirable match for his daughter, and they were conversing, playing the piano, and singing. Ivan Ilych, as Praskovya Fëdorovna remarked, spent that evening more cheerfully than usual, but he never for a moment forgot that he had postponed the important matter of the appendix. At eleven o'clock he said good-night and went to his bedroom. Since his illness he had slept alone in a small room next to his study. He undressed and took up a novel by Zola,[13] but instead of reading it he fell into thought, and in his imagination that desired improvement in the vermiform appendix occurred. There were the absorption and evacuation and the re-establishment of normal activity. "Yes, that's it!" he said to himself. "One need only assist nature, that's all." He remembered his medicine, rose, took it, and lay down on his back watching for the beneficent action of the medicine and for it to lessen the pain. "I need only take it regularly and avoid all injurious influences. I am already feeling better, much better." He began touching his side: it was not painful to the touch. "There, I really don't feel it. It's much better already." He put out the light and turned on his side. . . . "The appendix is getting better, absorption is occurring." Suddenly he felt the old, familiar, dull, gnawing pain, stubborn and serious. There was the same familiar loathsome taste in his mouth. His heart sank and he felt dazed. "My God! My God!" he muttered. "Again, again! and it will never cease." And suddenly the matter presented itself in a quite different aspect. "Vermiform appendix! Kidney!" he said to himself. "It's not a question of appendix or kidney, but of life and . . . death. Yes, life was there and now it is going, going and I cannot stop it. Yes. Why deceive myself? Isn't it obvious to everyone but me that I'm dying, and that it's only a question of weeks, days . . . it may happen this moment. There was light and now there is darkness. I was here and now I'm going there! Where?" A chill came over him, his breathing ceased, and he felt only the throbbing of his heart.

"When I am not, what will there be? There will be nothing. Then where shall I be when I am no more? Can this be dying? No, I don't want to!" He jumped up and tried to light the candle, felt for it with trembling hands, dropped candle and candlestick on the floor, and fell back on his pillow.

"What's the use? It makes no difference," he said to himself, staring with wide-open eyes into the darkness. "Death. Yes, death. And none of them know or wish to know it, and they have no pity for me. Now they are playing." (He heard through the door the distant sound of a song and its accompaniment.) "It's all the same to them, but they will die too! Fools! I first, and they later, but it will be the same for them. And now they are merry . . . the beasts!"

Anger choked him and he was agonizingly, unbearably miserable. "It is impossible that all men have been doomed to suffer this awful horror!" He raised himself.

"Something must be wrong. I must calm myself—must think it all over from the beginning." And he again began thinking. "Yes, the beginning of my illness: I knocked my side, but I was still quite well that day and the next. It hurt a little, then

---

[13] Émile Zola (1840–1902) was a French novelist.

rather more. I saw the doctors, then followed despondency and anguish, more doctors, and I drew nearer to the abyss. My strength grew less and I kept coming nearer and nearer, and now I have wasted away and there is no light in my eyes. I think of the appendix — but this is death! I think of mending the appendix, and all the while here is death! Can it really be death?" Again terror seized him and he gasped for breath. He leant down and began feeling for the matches, pressing with his elbow on the stand beside the bed. It was in his way and hurt him, he grew furious with it, pressed on it still harder, and upset it. Breathless and in despair he fell on his back, expecting death to come immediately.

Meanwhile the visitors were leaving. Praskovya Fëdorovna was seeing them off. She heard something fall and came in.

"What has happened?"

"Nothing. I knocked it over accidentally."

She went out and returned with a candle. He lay there panting heavily, like a man who has run a thousand yards, and stared upwards at her with a fixed look.

"What is it, Jean?"

"No . . . no . . . thing. I upset it." ("Why speak of it? She won't understand," he thought.)

And in truth she did not understand. She picked up the stand, lit his candle, and hurried away to see another visitor off. When she came back he still lay on his back, looking upwards.

"What is it? Do you feel worse?"

"Yes."

She shook her head and sat down.

"Do you know, Jean, I think we must ask Leshchetitsky to come and see you here."

This meant calling in the famous specialist, regardless of expense. He smiled malignantly and said "No." She remained a little longer and then went up to him and kissed his forehead.

While she was kissing him he hated her from the bottom of his soul and with difficulty refrained from pushing her away.

"Good-night. Please God you'll sleep."

"Yes."

VI

Ivan Ilych saw that he was dying, and he was in continual despair.

In the depth of his heart he knew he was dying, but not only was he not accustomed to the thought, he simply did not and could not grasp it.

The syllogism he had learnt from Kiezewetter's Logic:[14] "Caius is a man, men are mortal, therefore Caius is mortal," had always seemed to him correct as applied to Caius, but certainly not as applied to himself. That Caius — man in the

---

[14]Klaus Kiezewetter (1766–1819) wrote *The Outline of Logic According to Kantian Principles,* a popular text in Russia, based on the teachings of German philosopher Immanuel Kant (1722–1804).

abstract—was mortal, was perfectly correct, but he was not Caius, not an abstract man, but a creature quite, quite separate from all others. He had been little Vanya, with a mama and a papa, with Mitya and Volodya, with the toys, a coachman and a nurse, afterwards with Katenka and with all the joys, griefs, and delights of childhood, boyhood, and youth. What did Caius know of the smell of that striped leather ball Vanya had been so fond of? Had Caius kissed his mother's hand like that, and did the silk of her dress rustle so for Caius? Had he rioted like that at school when the pastry was bad? Had Caius been in love like that? Could Caius preside at a session as he did? "Caius really was mortal, and it was right for him to die; but for me, little Vanya, Ivan Ilych, with all my thoughts and emotions, it's altogether a different matter. It cannot be that I ought to die. That would be too terrible."

Such was his feeling.

"If I had to die like Caius I should have known it was so. An inner voice would have told me so, but there was nothing of the sort in me and I and all my friends felt that our case was quite different from that of Caius. And now here it is!" he said to himself. "It can't be. It's impossible! But here it is. How is this? How is one to understand it?"

He could not understand it, and tried to drive this false, incorrect, morbid thought away and to replace it by other proper and healthy thoughts. But that thought, and not the thought only but the reality itself, seemed to come and confront him.

And to replace that thought he called up a succession of others, hoping to find in them some support. He tried to get back into the former current of thoughts that had once screened the thought of death from him. But strange to say, all that had formerly shut off, hidden, and destroyed his consciousness of death, no longer had that effect. Ivan Ilych now spent most of his time in attempting to re-establish that old current. He would say to himself: "I will take up my duties again—after all I used to live by them." And banishing all doubts he would go to the law courts, enter into conversation with his colleagues, and sit carelessly as was his wont, scanning the crowd with a thoughtful look and leaning both his emaciated arms on the arms of his oak chair; bending over as usual to a colleague and drawing his papers nearer he would interchange whispers with him, and then suddenly raising his eyes and sitting erect would pronounce certain words and open the proceedings. But suddenly in the midst of those proceedings the pain in his side, regardless of the stage the proceedings had reached, would begin its own gnawing work. Ivan Ilych would turn his attention to it and try to drive the thought of it away, but without success. *It* would come and stand before him and look at him, and he would be petrified and the light would die out of his eyes, and he would again begin asking himself whether *It* alone was true. And his colleagues and subordinates would see with surprise and distress that he, the brilliant and subtle judge, was becoming confused and making mistakes. He would shake himself, try to pull himself together, manage somehow to bring the sitting to a close, and return home with the sorrowful consciousness that his judicial labors could not as formerly hide from him what he wanted them to hide, and could not deliver him from *It*. And what was worst of all was that *It* drew his attention to itself not in order to make him take some action but only that he should look at *It*, look it straight in the face: look at it and without doing anything, suffer inexpressibly.

And to save himself from this condition Ivan Ilych looked for consolations — new screens — and new screens were found and for a while seemed to save him, but then they immediately fell to pieces or rather became transparent, as if *It* penetrated them and nothing could veil *It*.

In these latter days he would go into the drawing-room he had arranged — that drawing-room where he had fallen and for the sake of which (how bitterly ridiculous it seemed) he had sacrificed his life — for he knew that his illness originated with that knock. He would enter and see that something had scratched the polished table. He would look for the cause of this and find that it was the bronze ornamentation of an album, that had got bent. He would take up the expensive album which he had lovingly arranged, and feel vexed with his daughter and her friends for their untidiness — for the album was torn here and there and some of the photographs turned upside down. He would put it carefully in order and bend the ornamentation back into position. Then it would occur to him to place all those things in another corner of the room, near the plants. He could call the footman, but his daughter or wife would come to help him. They would not agree, and his wife would contradict him, and he would dispute and grow angry. But that was all right, for then he did not think about *It*. *It* was invisible.

But then, when he was moving something himself, his wife would say: "Let the servants do it. You will hurt yourself again." And suddenly *It* would flash through the screen and he would see it. It was just a flash, and he hoped it would disappear, but he would involuntarily pay attention to his side. "It sits there as before, gnawing just the same!" And he could no longer forget *It*, but could distinctly see it looking at him from behind the flowers. "What is it all for?"

"It really is so! I lost my life over that curtain as I might have done when storming a fort. Is that possible? How terrible and how stupid. It can't be true! It can't, but it is."

He would go to his study, lie down, and again be alone with *It*: face to face with *It*. And nothing could be done with *It* except to look at it and shudder.

VII

How it happened it is impossible to say because it came about step by step, unnoticed, but in the third month of Ivan Ilych's illness, his wife, his daughter, his son, his acquaintances, the doctors, the servants, and above all he himself, were aware that the whole interest he had for other people was whether he would soon vacate his place, and at last release the living from the discomfort caused by his presence and be himself released from his sufferings.

He slept less and less. He was given opium and hypodermic injections of morphine, but this did not relieve him. The dull depression he experienced in a somnolent condition at first gave him a little relief, but only as something new, afterwards it became as distressing as the pain itself or even more so.

Special foods were prepared for him by the doctors' orders, but all those foods became increasingly distasteful and disgusting to him.

For his excretions also special arrangements had to be made, and this was a torment to him every time — a torment from the uncleanliness, the unseemliness, and the smell, and from knowing that another person had to take part in it.

But just through this most unpleasant matter, Ivan Ilych obtained comfort. Gerasim, the butler's young assistant, always came in to carry the things out. Gerasim was a clean, fresh peasant lad, grown stout on town food and always cheerful and bright. At first the sight of him, in his clean Russian peasant costume, engaged on that disgusting task embarrassed Ivan Ilych.

Once when he got up from the commode too weak to draw up his trousers, he dropped into a soft armchair and looked with horror at his bare, enfeebled thighs with the muscles so sharply marked on them.

Gerasim with a firm light tread, his heavy boots emitting a pleasant smell of tar and fresh winter air, came in wearing a clean Hessian apron, the sleeves of his print shirt tucked up over his strong bare young arms; and refraining from looking at his sick master out of consideration for his feelings, and restraining the joy of life that beamed from his face, he went up to the commode.

"Gerasim!" said Ivan Ilych in a weak voice.

Gerasim started, evidently afraid he might have committed some blunder, and with a rapid movement turned his fresh, kind, simple young face which just showed the first downy signs of a beard.

"Yes, sir?"

"That must be very unpleasant for you. You must forgive me. I am helpless."

"Oh, why, sir," and Gerasim's eyes beamed and he showed his glistening white teeth, "what's a little trouble? It's a case of illness with you, sir."

And his deft strong hands did their accustomed task, and he went out of the room stepping lightly. Five minutes later he as lightly returned.

Ivan Ilych was still sitting in the same position in the armchair.

"Gerasim," he said when the latter had replaced the freshly-washed utensil. "Please come here and help me." Gerasim went up to him. "Lift me up. It is hard for me to get up, and I have sent Dmitri away."

Gerasim went up to him, grasped his master with his strong arms deftly but gently, in the same way that he stepped — lifted him, supported him with one hand, and with the other drew up his trousers and would have set him down again, but Ivan Ilych asked to be led to the sofa. Gerasim, without an effort and without apparent pressure, led him, almost lifting him, to the sofa and placed him on it.

"Thank you. How easily and well you do it all!"

Gerasim smiled again and turned to leave the room. But Ivan Ilych felt his presence such a comfort that he did not want to let him go.

"One thing more, please move up that chair. No, the other one — under my feet. It is easier for me when my feet are raised."

Gerasim brought the chair, set it down gently in place, and raised Ivan Ilych's legs on to it. It seemed to Ivan Ilych that he felt better while Gerasim was holding up his legs.

"It's better when my legs are higher," he said. "Place that cushion under them."

Gerasim did so. He again lifted the legs and placed them, and again Ivan Ilych felt better while Gerasim held his legs. When he set them down Ivan Ilych fancied he felt worse.

"Gerasim," he said. "Are you busy now?"

"Not at all, sir," said Gerasim, who had learnt from the townsfolk how to speak to gentlefolk.

"What have you still to do?"

"What have I to do? I've done everything except chopping the logs for tomorrow."

"Then hold my legs up a bit higher, can you?"

"Of course I can. Why not?" And Gerasim raised his master's legs higher and Ivan Ilych thought that in that position he did not feel any pain at all.

"And how about the logs?"

"Don't trouble about that, sir. There's plenty of time."

Ivan Ilych told Gerasim to sit down and hold his legs, and began to talk to him. And strange to say it seemed to him that he felt better while Gerasim held his legs up.

After that Ivan Ilych would sometimes call Gerasim and get him to hold his legs on his shoulders, and he liked talking to him. Gerasim did it all easily, willingly, simply, and with a good nature that touched Ivan Ilych. Health, strength, and vitality in other people were offensive to him, but Gerasim's strength and vitality did not mortify but soothed him.

What tormented Ivan Ilych most was the deception, the lie, which for some reason they all accepted, that he was not dying but was simply ill, and that he only need keep quiet and undergo a treatment and then something very good would result. He however knew that do what they would nothing would come of it, only still more agonizing suffering and death. This deception tortured him — their not wishing to admit what they all knew and what he knew, but wanting to lie to him concerning his terrible condition, and wishing and forcing him to participate in that lie. Those lies — lies enacted over him on the eve of his death and destined to degrade this awful, solemn act to the level of their visitings, their curtains, their sturgeon for dinner — were a terrible agony for Ivan Ilych. And strangely enough, many times when they were going through their antics over him he had been within a hair-breadth of calling out to them: "Stop lying! You know and I know that I am dying. Then at least stop lying about it!" But he had never had the spirit to do it. The awful, terrible act of his dying was, he could see, reduced by those about him to the level of a casual, unpleasant, and almost indecorous incident (as if someone entered a drawing-room diffusing an unpleasant odor) and this was done by that very decorum which he had served all his life long. He saw that no one felt for him, because no one even wished to grasp his position. Only Gerasim recognized it and pitied him. And so Ivan Ilych felt at ease only with him. He felt comforted when Gerasim supported his legs (sometimes all night long) and refused to go to bed, saying, "Don't you worry, Ivan Ilych. I'll get sleep enough later on," or when he suddenly became familiar and exclaimed: "If you weren't sick it would be another matter, but as it is, why should I grudge a little trouble?" Gerasim alone did not lie; everything showed that he alone understood the facts of the case and did not consider it necessary to disguise them, but simply felt sorry for his emaciated and enfeebled master. Once when Ivan Ilych was sending him away he even said straight out: "We shall all of us die, so why should I grudge a little trouble?" — expressing the fact that he did not think his work burdensome, because he was doing it for a dying man and hoped someone would do the same for him when his time came.

Apart from this lying, or because of it, what most tormented Ivan Ilych was that no one pitied him as he wished to be pitied. At certain moments after prolonged suffering he wished most of all (though he would have been ashamed to confess it) for someone to pity him as a sick child is pitied. He longed to be petted and comforted. He knew he was an important functionary, that he had a beard turning grey, and that therefore what he longed for was impossible, but still he longed for it. And in Gerasim's attitude towards him there was something akin to what he wished for, and so that attitude comforted him. Ivan Ilych wanted to weep, wanted to be petted and cried over, and then his colleague Shebek would come, and instead of weeping and being petted, Ivan Ilych would assume a serious, severe, and profound air, and by force of habit would express his opinion on a decision of the Court of Cassation and would stubbornly insist on that view. This falsity around him and within him did more than anything else to poison his last days.

VIII

It was morning. He knew it was morning because Gerasim had gone, and Peter the footman had come and put out the candles, drawn back one of the curtains, and begun quietly to tidy up. Whether it was morning or evening, Friday or Sunday, made no difference, it was all just the same: the gnawing, unmitigated, agonizing pain, never ceasing for an instant, the consciousness of life inexorably waning but not yet extinguished, the approach of that ever dreaded and hateful Death which was the only reality, and always the same falsity. What were days, weeks, hours, in such a case?

"Will you have some tea, sir?"

"He wants things to be regular, and wishes the gentlefolk to drink tea in the morning," thought Ivan Ilych, and only said: "No."

"Wouldn't you like to move onto the sofa, sir?"

"He wants to tidy up the room, and I'm in the way. I am uncleanliness and disorder," he thought, and said only:

"No, leave me alone."

The man went on bustling about. Ivan Ilych stretched out his hand. Peter came up, ready to help.

"What is it, sir?"

"My watch."

Peter took the watch which was close at hand and gave it to his master.

"Half-past eight. Are they up?"

"No, sir, except Vasily Ivanich" (the son) "who has gone to school. Praskovya Fëdorovna ordered me to wake her if you asked for her. Shall I do so?"

"No, there's no need to." "Perhaps I'd better have some tea," he thought, and added aloud: "Yes, bring me some tea."

Peter went to the door, but Ivan Ilych dreaded being left alone. "How can I keep him here? Oh yes, my medicine." "Peter, give me my medicine." "Why not? Perhaps it may still do me some good." He took a spoonful and swallowed it. "No, it won't help. It's all tomfoolery, all deception," he decided as soon as he became aware of the familiar, sickly, hopeless taste. "No, I can't believe in it any longer. But the pain, why this pain? If it would only cease just for a moment!" And he moaned. Peter turned towards him. "It's all right. Go and fetch me some tea."

Peter went out. Left alone Ivan Ilych groaned not so much with pain, terrible though that was, as from mental anguish. Always and for ever the same, always these endless days and nights. If only it would come quicker! If only *what* would come quicker? Death, darkness? . . . No, no! Anything rather than death!

When Peter returned with the tea on a tray, Ivan Ilych stared at him for a time in perplexity, not realizing who and what he was. Peter was disconcerted by that look and his embarrassment brought Ivan Ilych to himself.

"Oh, tea! All right, put it down. Only help me to wash and put on a clean shirt."

And Ivan Ilych began to wash. With pauses for rest, he washed his hands and then his face, cleaned his teeth, brushed his hair, and looked in the glass. He was terrified by what he saw, especially by the limp way in which his hair clung to his pallid forehead.

While his shirt was being changed he knew that he would be still more frightened at the sight of his body, so he avoided looking at it. Finally he was ready. He drew on a dressing gown, wrapped himself in a plaid, and sat down in the armchair to take his tea. For a moment he felt refreshed, but as soon as he began to drink the tea he was again aware of the same taste, and the pain also returned. He finished it with an effort, and then lay down stretching out his legs, and dismissed Peter.

Always the same. Now a spark of hope flashes up, then a sea of despair rages, and always pain; always pain, always despair, and always the same. When alone he had a dreadful and distressing desire to call someone, but he knew beforehand that with others present it would be still worse. "Another dose of morphine—to lose consciousness. I will tell him, the doctor, that he must think of something else. It's impossible, impossible, to go on like this."

An hour and another pass like that. But now there is a ring at the door bell. Perhaps it's the doctor? It is. He comes in fresh, hearty, plump, and cheerful, with that look on his face that seems to say: "There now, you're in a panic about something, but we'll arrange it all for you directly!" The doctor knows this expression is out of place here, but he has put it on once for all and can't take it off—like a man who has put on a frock-coat in the morning to pay a round of calls.

The doctor rubs his hands vigorously and reassuringly.

"Brr! How cold it is! There's such a sharp frost; just let me warm myself!" he says, as if it were only a matter of waiting till he was warm, and then he would put everything right.

"Well now, how are you?"

Ivan Ilych feels that the doctor would like to say: "Well, how are our affairs?" but that even he feels that this would not do, and says instead: "What sort of a night have you had?"

Ivan Ilych looks at him as much as to say: "Are you really never ashamed of lying?" But the doctor does not wish to understand this question, and Ivan Ilych says: "Just as terrible as ever. The pain never leaves me and never subsides. If only something. . . ."

"Yes, you sick people are always like that. . . . There, now I think I am warm enough. Even Praskovya Fëdorovna, who is so particular, could find no fault with my temperature. Well, now I can say good-morning," and the doctor presses his patient's hand.

Then, dropping his former playfulness, he begins with a most serious face to examine the patient, feeling his pulse and taking his temperature, and then begins the sounding and auscultation.

Ivan Ilych knows quite well and definitely that all this is nonsense and pure deception, but when the doctor, getting down on his knee, leans over him, putting his ear first higher then lower, and performs various gymnastic movements over him with a significant expression on his face, Ivan Ilych submits to it all as he used to submit to the speeches of the lawyers, though he knew very well that they were all lying and why they were lying.

The doctor, kneeling on the sofa, is still sounding him when Praskovya Fëdorovna's silk dress rustles at the door and she is heard scolding Peter for not having let her know of the doctor's arrival.

She comes in, kisses her husband, and at once proceeds to prove that she has been up a long time already, and only owing to a misunderstanding failed to be there when the doctor arrived.

Ivan Ilych looks at her, scans her all over, sets against her the whiteness and plumpness and cleanness of her hands and neck, the gloss of her hair, and the sparkle of her vivacious eyes. He hates her with his whole soul. And the thrill of hatred he feels for her makes him suffer from her touch.

Her attitude towards him and his disease is still the same. Just as the doctor had adopted a certain relation to his patient which he could not abandon, so had she formed one towards him—that he was not doing something he ought to do and was himself to blame, and that she reproached him lovingly for this—and she could not now change that attitude.

"You see he doesn't listen to me and doesn't take his medicine at the proper time. And above all he lies in a position that is no doubt bad for him—with his legs up."

She described how he made Gerasim hold his legs up.

The doctor smiled with a contemptuous affability that said: "What's to be done? These sick people do have foolish fancies of that kind, but we must forgive them."

When the examination was over the doctor looked at his watch, and then Praskovya Fëdorovna announced to Ivan Ilych that it was of course as he pleased, but she had sent today for a celebrated specialist who would examine him and have a consultation with Michael Danilovich (their regular doctor).

"Please don't raise any objections. I am doing this for my own sake," she said ironically, letting it be felt that she was doing it all for his sake and only said this to leave him no right to refuse. He remained silent, knitting his brows. He felt that he was so surrounded and involved in a mesh of falsity that it was hard to unravel anything.

Everything she did for him was entirely for her own sake, and she told him she was doing for herself what she actually was doing for herself, as if that was so incredible that he must understand the opposite.

At half-past eleven the celebrated specialist arrived. Again the sounding began and the significant conversations in his presence and in another room, about the kidneys and the appendix, and the questions and answers, with such an air of importance that again, instead of the real question of life and death which now alone confronted him, the question arose of the kidney and appendix which were not behaving as they ought to and would now be attacked by Michael Danilovich and the specialist and forced to amend their ways.

The celebrated specialist took leave of him with a serious though not hopeless look, and in reply to the timid question Ivan Ilych, with eyes glistening with fear and hope, put to him as to whether there was a chance of recovery, said that he could not vouch for it but there was a possibility. The look of hope with which Ivan Ilych watched the doctor out was so pathetic that Praskovya Fëdorovna, seeing it, even wept as she left the room to hand the doctor his fee.

The gleam of hope kindled by the doctor's encouragement did not last long. The same room, the same pictures, curtains, wallpaper, medicine bottles, were all there, and the same aching suffering body, and Ivan Ilych began to moan. They gave him a subcutaneous injection and he sank into oblivion.

It was twilight when he came to. They brought him his dinner and he swallowed some beef tea with difficulty, and then everything was the same again and night was coming on.

After dinner, at seven o'clock, Praskovya Fëdorovna came into the room in evening dress, her full bosom pushed up by her corset, and with traces of powder on her face. She had reminded him in the morning that they were going to the theater. Sarah Bernhardt was visiting the town and they had a box, which he had insisted on their taking. Now he had forgotten about it and her toilet offended him, but he concealed his vexation when he remembered that he had himself insisted on their securing a box and going because it would be an instructive and aesthetic pleasure for the children.

Praskovya Fëdorovna came in, self-satisfied but yet with a rather guilty air. She sat down and asked how he was, but, as he saw, only for the sake of asking and not in order to learn about it, knowing that there was nothing to learn — and then went on to what she really wanted to say: that she would not on any account have gone but that the box had been taken and Helen and their daughter were going, as well as Petrishchev (the examining magistrate, their daughter's fiancé) and that it was out of the question to let them go alone; but that she would have much preferred to sit with him for a while; and he must be sure to follow the doctor's orders while she was away.

"Oh, and Fëdor Petrovich" (the fiancé) "would like to come in. May he? And Lisa?"

"All right."

Their daughter came in in full evening dress, her fresh young flesh exposed (making a show of that very flesh which in his own case caused so much suffering), strong, healthy, evidently in love, and impatient with illness, suffering, and death, because they interfered with her happiness.

Fëdor Petrovich came in too, in evening dress, his hair curled *à la Capoul*,[15] a tight stiff collar round his long sinewy neck, an enormous white shirt-front and narrow black trousers tightly stretched over his strong thighs. He had one white glove tightly drawn on, and was holding his opera hat in his hand.

Following him the schoolboy crept in unnoticed, in a new uniform, poor little fellow, and wearing gloves. Terribly dark shadows showed under his eyes, the meaning of which Ivan Ilych knew well.

His son had always seemed pathetic to him, and now it was dreadful to see the boy's frightened look of pity. It seemed to Ivan Ilych that Vasya was the only one besides Gerasim who understood and pitied him.

They all sat down and again asked how he was. A silence followed. Lisa asked her mother about the opera-glasses, and there was an altercation between mother and daughter as to who had taken them and where they had been put. This occasioned some unpleasantness.

Fëdor Petrovich inquired of Ivan Ilych whether he had ever seen Sarah Bernhardt. Ivan Ilych did not at first catch the question, but then replied: "No, have you seen her before?"

"Yes, in *Adrienne Lecouvreur*."[16]

Praskovya Fëdorovna mentioned some rôles in which Sarah Bernhardt was particularly good. Her daughter disagreed. Conversation sprang up as to the elegance and realism of her acting — the sort of conversation that is always repeated and is always the same.

In the midst of the conversation Fëdor Petrovich glanced at Ivan Ilych and became silent. The others also looked at him and grew silent. Ivan Ilych was staring with glittering eyes straight before him, evidently indignant with them. This had to be rectified, but it was impossible to do so. The silence had to be broken, but for a time no one dared to break it and they all became afraid that the conventional deception would suddenly become obvious and the truth become plain to all. Lisa was the first to pluck up courage and break that silence, but by trying to hide what everybody was feeling, she betrayed it.

"Well, if we are going it's time to start," she said, looking at her watch, a present from her father, and with a faint and significant smile at Fëdor Petrovich relating to something known only to them. She got up with a rustle of her dress.

They all rose, said good-night, and went away.

When they had gone it seemed to Ivan Ilych that he felt better; the falsity had gone with them. But the pain remained — that same pain and that same

---

[15] An elaborate hair styling for men. Capoul was a famous French singer.
[16] Comedy by French playwrights Eugène Scribe and Ernest Legouvé.

fear that made everything monotonously alike, nothing harder and nothing easier. Everything was worse.

Again minute followed minute and hour followed hour. Everything remained the same and there was no cessation. And the inevitable end of it all became more and more terrible.

"Yes, send Gerasim here," he replied to a question Peter asked.

IX

His wife returned late at night. She came in on tiptoe, but he heard her, opened his eyes, and made haste to close them again. She wished to send Gerasim away and to sit with him herself, but he opened his eyes and said: "No, go away."

"Are you in great pain?"

"Always the same."

"Take some opium."

He agreed and took some. She went away.

Till about three in the morning he was in a state of stupefied misery. It seemed to him that he and his pain were being thrust into a narrow, deep black sack, but though they were pushed further and further in they could not be pushed to the bottom. And this, terrible enough in itself, was accompanied by suffering. He was frightened yet wanted to fall through the sack, he struggled but yet cooperated. And suddenly he broke through, fell, and regained consciousness. Gerasim was sitting at the foot of the bed dozing quietly and patiently, while he himself lay with his emaciated stockinged legs resting on Gerasim's shoulders; the same shaded candle was there and the same unceasing pain.

"Go away, Gerasim," he whispered.

"It's all right, sir. I'll stay a while."

"No. Go away."

He removed his legs from Gerasim's shoulders, turned sideways onto his arm, and felt sorry for himself. He only waited till Gerasim had gone into the next room and then restrained himself no longer but wept like a child. He wept on account of his helplessness, his terrible loneliness, the cruelty of man, the cruelty of God, and the absence of God.

"Why hast Thou done all this? Why hast Thou brought me here? Why, why dost Thou torment me so terribly?"

He did not expect an answer and yet wept because there was no answer and could be none. The pain again grew more acute, but he did not stir and did not call. He said to himself: "Go on! Strike me! But what is it for? What have I done to Thee? What is it for?"

Then he grew quiet and not only ceased weeping but even held his breath and became all attention. It was as though he were listening not to an audible voice but to the voice of his soul, to the current of thoughts arising within him.

"What is it you want?" was the first clear conception capable of expression in words, that he heard.

"What do you want? What do you want?" he repeated to himself.

"What do I want? To live and not to suffer," he answered.

And again he listened with such concentrated attention that even his pain did not distract him.

"To live? How?" asked his inner voice.

"Why, to live as I used to — well and pleasantly."

"As you lived before, well and pleasantly?" the voice repeated.

And in imagination he began to recall the best moments of his pleasant life. But strange to say none of those best moments of his pleasant life now seemed at all what they had then seemed — none of them except the first recollections of childhood. There, in childhood, there had been something really pleasant with which it would be possible to live if it could return. But the child who had experienced that happiness existed no longer, it was like a reminiscence of somebody else.

As soon as the period began which had produced the present Ivan Ilych, all that had then seemed joys now melted before his sight and turned into something trivial and often nasty.

And the further he departed from childhood and the nearer he came to the present the more worthless and doubtful were the joys. This began with the School of Law. A little that was really good was still found there — there was lightheartedness, friendship, and hope. But in the upper classes there had already been fewer of such good moments. Then during the first years of his official career, when he was in the service of the Governor, some pleasant moments again occurred: they were the memories of love for a woman. Then all became confused and there was still less of what was good; later on again there was still less that was good, and the further he went the less there was. His marriage, a mere accident, then the disenchantment that followed it, his wife's bad breath and the sensuality and hypocrisy: then the deadly official life and those preoccupations about money, a year of it, and two, and ten, and twenty, and always the same thing. And the longer it lasted the more deadly it became. "It is as if I had been going downhill while I imagined I was going up. And that is really what it was. I was going up in public opinion, but to the same extent life was ebbing away from me. And now it is all done and there is only death."

"Then what does it mean? Why? It can't be that life is so senseless and horrible. But if it really has been so horrible and senseless, why must I die and die in agony? There is something wrong!"

"Maybe I did not live as I ought to have done," it suddenly occurred to him. "But how could that be, when I did everything properly?" he replied, and immediately dismissed from his mind this, the sole solution of all the riddles of life and death, as something quite impossible.

"Then what do you want now? To live? Live how? Live as you lived in the law courts when the usher proclaimed 'The judge is coming!' The judge is coming, the judge!" he repeated to himself. "Here he is, the judge. But I am not guilty!" he exclaimed angrily. "What is it for?" And he ceased crying, but turning his face to the wall continued to ponder on the same question: Why, and for what purpose, is there all this horror? But however much he pondered he found no answer. And whenever the thought occurred to him, as it often did, that it all resulted from his not having lived as he ought to have done, he at once recalled the correctness of his whole life and dismissed so strange an idea.

X

Another fortnight passed. Ivan Ilych now no longer left his sofa. He would not lie in bed but lay on the sofa, facing the wall nearly all the time. He suffered ever the same unceasing agonies and in his loneliness pondered always on the same insoluble question: "What is this? Can it be that it is Death?" And the inner voice answered: "Yes, it is Death."

"Why these sufferings?" And the voice answered, "For no reason — they just are so." Beyond and besides this there was nothing.

From the very beginning of his illness, ever since he had first been to see the doctor, Ivan Ilych's life had been divided between two contrary and alternating moods: now it was despair and the expectation of this uncomprehended and terrible death, and now hope and an intently interested observation of the functioning of his organs. Now before his eyes there was only a kidney or an intestine that temporarily evaded its duty, and now only that incomprehensible and dreadful death from which it was impossible to escape.

These two states of mind had alternated from the very beginning of his illness, but the further it progressed the more doubtful and fantastic became the conception of the kidney, and the more real the sense of impending death.

He had but to call to mind what he had been three months before and what he was now, to call to mind with what regularity he had been going downhill, for every possibility of hope to be shattered.

Latterly during that loneliness in which he found himself as he lay facing the back of the sofa, a loneliness in the midst of a populous town and surrounded by numerous acquaintances and relations but that yet could not have been more complete anywhere — either at the bottom of the sea or under the earth — during that terrible loneliness Ivan Ilych had lived only in memories of the past. Pictures of his past rose before him one after another. They always began with what was nearest in time and then went back to what was most remote — to his childhood — and rested there. If he thought of the stewed prunes that had been offered him that day, his mind went back to the raw shrivelled French plums of his childhood, their peculiar flavor and the flow of saliva when he sucked their stones, and along with the memory of that taste came a whole series of memories of those days: his nurse, his brother, and their toys. "No, I mustn't think of that. . . . It is too painful," Ivan Ilych said to himself, and brought himself back to the present — to the button on the back of the sofa and the creases in its morocco. "Morocco is expensive, but it does not wear well: there had been a quarrel about it. It was a different kind of quarrel and a different kind of morocco that time when we tore father's portfolio and were punished, and mama brought us some tarts. . . ." And again his thoughts dwelt on his childhood, and again it was painful and he tried to banish them and fix his mind on something else.

Then again together with that chain of memories another series passed through his mind — of how his illness had progressed and grown worse. There also the further back he looked the more life there had been. There had been more of what was good in life and more of life itself. The two merged together.

"Just as the pain went on getting worse and worse, so my life grew worse and worse," he thought. "There is one bright spot there at the back, at the beginning of life, and afterwards all becomes blacker and blacker and proceeds more and more rapidly — in inverse ratio to the square of the distance from death," thought Ivan Ilych. And the example of a stone falling downwards with increasing velocity entered his mind. Life, a series of increasing sufferings, flies further and further towards its end — the most terrible suffering. "I am flying. . . ." He shuddered, shifted himself, and tried to resist, but was already aware that resistance was impossible, and again with eyes weary of gazing but unable to cease seeing what was before them, he stared at the back of the sofa and waited — awaiting that dreadful fall and shock and destruction.

"Resistance is impossible!" he said to himself. "If I could only understand what it is all for! But that too is impossible. An explanation would be possible if it could be said that I have not lived as I ought to. But it is impossible to say that," and he remembered all the legality, correctitude, and propriety of his life. "That at any rate can certainly not be admitted," he thought, and his lips smiled ironically as if someone could see that smile and be taken in by it. "There is no explanation! Agony, death. . . . What for?"

XI

Another two weeks went by in this way and during that fortnight an event occurred that Ivan Ilych and his wife had desired. Petrishchev formally proposed. It happened in the evening. The next day Praskovya Fëdorovna came into her husband's room considering how best to inform him of it, but that very night there had been a fresh change for the worse in his condition. She found him still lying on the sofa but in a different position. He lay on his back, groaning and staring fixedly straight in front of him.

She began to remind him of his medicines, but he turned his eyes towards her with such a look that she did not finish what she was saying; so great an animosity, to her in particular, did that look express.

"For Christ's sake let me die in peace!" he said.

She would have gone away, but just then their daughter came in and went up to say good morning. He looked at her as he had done at his wife, and in reply to her inquiry about his health said dryly that he would soon free them all of himself. They were both silent and after sitting with him for a while went away.

"Is it our fault?" Lisa said to her mother. "It's as if we were to blame! I am sorry for papa, but why should we be tortured?"

The doctor came at his usual time. Ivan Ilych answered "Yes" and "No," never taking his angry eyes from him, and at last said: "You know you can do nothing for me, so leave me alone."

"We can ease your sufferings."

"You can't even do that. Let me be."

The doctor went into the drawing-room and told Praskovya Fëdorovna that the case was very serious and that the only resource left was opium to allay her husband's sufferings, which must be terrible.

It was true, as the doctor said, that Ivan Ilych's physical sufferings were terrible, but worse than the physical sufferings were his mental sufferings, which were his chief torture.

His mental sufferings were due to the fact that that night, as he looked at Gerasim's sleepy, good-natured face with its prominent cheek-bones, the question suddenly occurred to him: "What if my whole life has really been wrong?"

It occurred to him that what had appeared perfectly impossible before, namely that he had not spent his life as he should have done, might after all be true. It occurred to him that his scarcely perceptible attempts to struggle against what was considered good by the most highly placed people, those scarcely noticeable impulses which he had immediately suppressed, might have been the real thing, and all the rest false. And his professional duties and the whole arrangement of his life and of his family, and all his social and official interests, might all have been false. He tried to defend all those things to himself and suddenly felt the weakness of what he was defending. There was nothing to defend.

"But if that is so," he said to himself, "and I am leaving this life with the consciousness that I have lost all that was given me and it is impossible to rectify it — what then?"

He lay on his back and began to pass his life in review in quite a new way. In the morning when he saw first his footman, then his wife, then his daughter, and then the doctor, their every word and movement confirmed to him the awful truth that had been revealed to him during the night. In them he saw himself — all that for which he had lived — and saw clearly that it was not real at all, but a terrible and huge deception which had hidden both life and death. This consciousness intensified his physical suffering tenfold. He groaned and tossed about, and pulled at his clothing which choked and stifled him. And he hated them on that account.

He was given a large dose of opium and became unconscious, but at noon his sufferings began again. He drove everybody away and tossed from side to side.

His wife came to him and said:

"Jean, my dear, do this for me. It can't do any harm and often helps. Healthy people often do it."

He opened his eyes wide.

"What? Take communion? Why? It's unnecessary! However. . . ."

She began to cry.

"Yes, do, my dear. I'll send for our priest. He is such a nice man."

"All right. Very well," he muttered.

When the priest came and heard his confession, Ivan Ilych was softened and seemed to feel a relief from his doubts and consequently from his sufferings, and for a moment there came a ray of hope. He again began to think of the vermiform appendix and the possibility of correcting it. He received the sacrament with tears in his eyes.

When they laid him down again afterwards he felt a moment's ease, and the hope that he might live awoke in him again. He began to think of the operation that had been suggested to him. "To live! I want to live!" he said to himself.

His wife came in to congratulate him after his communion, and when uttering the usual conventional words she added:

"You feel better, don't you?"

Without looking at her he said "Yes."

Her dress, her figure, the expression of her face, the tone of her voice, all revealed the same thing. "This is wrong, it is not as it should be. All you have lived for and still live for is falsehood and deception, hiding life and death from you." And as soon as he admitted that thought, his hatred and his agonizing physical suffering again sprang up, and with that suffering a consciousness of the unavoidable, approaching end. And to this was added a new sensation of grinding shooting pain and a feeling of suffocation.

The expression of his face when he uttered that "yes" was dreadful. Having uttered it, he looked her straight in the eyes, turned on his face with a rapidity extraordinary in his weak state and shouted:

"Go away! Go away and leave me alone!"

XII

From that moment the screaming began that continued for three days, and was so terrible that one could not hear it through two closed doors without horror. At the moment he answered his wife he realized that he was lost, that there was no return, that the end had come, the very end, and his doubts were still unsolved and remained doubts.

"Oh! Oh! Oh!" he cried in various intonations. He had begun by screaming "I won't!" and continued screaming on the letter O.

For three whole days, during which time did not exist for him, he struggled in that black sack into which he was being thrust by an invisible, resistless force. He struggled as a man condemned to death struggles in the hands of the executioner, knowing that he cannot save himself. And every moment he felt that despite all his efforts he was drawing nearer and nearer to what terrified him. He felt that his agony was due to his being thrust into that black hole and still more to his not being able to get right into it. He was hindered from getting into it by his conviction that his life had been a good one. That very justification of his life held him fast and prevented his moving forward, and it caused him most torment of all.

Suddenly some force struck him in the chest and side, making it still harder to breathe, and he fell through the hole and there at the bottom was a light. What had happened to him was like the sensation one sometimes experiences in a railway carriage when one thinks one is going backwards while one is really going forwards and suddenly becomes aware of the real direction.

"Yes, it was all not the right thing," he said to himself, "but that's no matter. It can be done. But what *is* the right thing?" he asked himself, and suddenly grew quiet.

This occurred at the end of the third day, two hours before his death. Just then his schoolboy son had crept softly in and gone up to the bedside. The dying man was still screaming desperately and waving his arms. His hand fell on the boy's head, and the boy caught it, pressed it to his lips, and began to cry.

At that very moment Ivan Ilych fell through and caught sight of the light, and it was revealed to him that though his life had not been what it should have been, this could still be rectified. He asked himself, "What *is* the right thing?" and grew still, listening. Then he felt that someone was kissing his hand. He opened his eyes, looked at his son, and felt sorry for him. His wife came up to him and he glanced at her. She was gazing at him open-mouthed, with undried tears on her nose and cheek and a despairing look on her face. He felt sorry for her too.

"Yes, I am making them wretched," he thought. "They are sorry, but it will be better for them when I die." He wished to say this but had not the strength to utter it. "Besides, why speak? I must act," he thought. With a look at his wife he indicated his son and said: "Take him away . . . sorry for him . . . sorry for you too. . . ." He tried to add, "forgive me," but said "forgo" and waved his hand, knowing that He whose understanding mattered would understand.

And suddenly it grew clear to him that what had been oppressing him and would not leave him was all dropping away at once from two sides, from ten sides, and from all sides. He was sorry for them, he must act so as not to hurt them: release them and free himself from these sufferings. "How good and how simple!" he thought. "And the pain?" he asked himself. "What had become of it? Where are you, pain?"

He turned his attention to it.

"Yes, here it is. Well, what of it? Let the pain be."

"And death . . . where is it?"

He sought his former accustomed fear of death and did not find it. "Where is it? What death?" There was no fear because there was no death.

In place of death there was light.

"So that's what it is!" he suddenly exclaimed aloud. "What joy!"

To him all this happened in a single instant, and the meaning of that instant did not change. For those present his agony continued for another two hours. Something rattled in his throat, his emaciated body twitched, then the gasping and rattle became less and less frequent.

"It is finished!" said someone near him.

He heard these words and repeated them in his soul.

"Death is finished," he said to himself. "It is no more!"

He drew in a breath, stopped in the midst of a sigh, stretched out, and died.

Jean Toomer

Jean Toomer (1894–1967), author of *Cane,* generally considered the literary master-piece of the Harlem or "New Negro" Renaissance of the 1920s, was born in Washing-ton, D.C. When his father deserted his mother soon after his birth, Toomer was raised in the household of his maternal grandfather, Pinckney B. S. Pinchbeck, described in the *Dictionary of American Biography* as "the typical Negro politician of the Recon-struction." A crusader for African American rights, Pinchbeck had served as acting governor of Louisiana before Toomer's birth. In 1890 Pinchbeck had moved his family from New Orleans to Washington, D.C., but he was twice denied a seat in the U.S. Senate because of the claim that he had been fraudulently elected. Toomer formed a close attachment to his grandfather. After brief enrollments at several colleges, Toomer took a job in New York City in 1918 and began to write poetry, fiction, essays, and reviews. Two years later he returned to Washington, D.C., to help nurse his ailing grandfather. There he immersed himself in a study of the conditions of life for blacks in America, believing that the United States could serve as a melting pot transform-ing all races into one race. As Toomer later wrote in the *Liberator* magazine, "From my own point of view I am naturally and inevitably an American. I have strived for a spiritual fusion analogous to the fact of racial inter-mingling."

Exhausted by the strain of nursing his grandfather, who was finally hospi-talized, Toomer accepted an offer in 1922 to work as the head of a school for African Americans in Sparta, Georgia. There he found what he later said was "the starting point" of his book *Cane.* In a later autobiographical sketch, Toomer wrote that his three months in Georgia were a revelation to him:

> The setting was crude in a way, but strangely rich and beautiful. . . . There was
> a valley, the valley of *Cane,* with smoke-wreaths during the day and mist at
> night. A family of back-country Negroes had only recently moved into a shack
> not too far away [from where he was living]. They sang. And this was the first
> time I'd ever heard the folk-songs and spirituals. They were very rich and sad
> and joyous and beautiful. But I learned that the Negroes of the town objected
> to them. They called them "shouting." They had victrolas and player-pianos.
> So, I realized with deep regret, that the spirituals, meeting ridicule, would be
> certain to die out. . . . And this was the feeling I put into *Cane. Cane* was a
> swan-song. It was a song of the end.

Toomer began writing the impressionistic sketches—such as "Blood-Burning Moon"—that made up *Cane* while riding the train back to Washington, D.C., to stay with his grandfather, who died a few weeks later. Magazines and journals such as the *Liberator, Broom,* and *Prairie,* which first published "Blood-Burning Moon" (1923), began to accept his work, and his book was published in 1923 to great critical praise. He published one other work, *Essentials* (1931), a privately printed book of aphorisms. Toomer spent the rest of his life in a search for self-realization through Eastern religions and psychoanalysis. He stated that "why people have expected me to write a second and a third and a fourth book like *Cane* is one of the queer misunderstandings of my life." The expressive style of works like "Blood-Burning Moon" influenced younger writers such as Zora Neale Hurston and Langston Hughes, who participated in the Harlem Renaissance.

Blood-Burning Moon

1923

1

Up from the skeleton stone walls, up from the rotting floor boards and the solid hand-hewn beams of oak of the pre-war cotton factory, dusk came up. Up from the dusk the full moon came. Glowing like a fired pine-knot, it illumined the great door and soft showered the Negro shanties aligned along the single street of factory town. The full moon in the great door was an omen. Negro women improvised songs against its spell.

Louisa sang as she came over the crest of the hill from the white folks' kitchen. Her skin was the color of oak leaves on young trees in fall. Her breasts, firm and up-pointed like ripe acorns. And her singing had the low murmur of winds in fig trees. Bob Stone, younger son of the people she worked for, loved her. By the way the world reckons things, he had won her. By measure of that warm glow which came into her mind at thought of him, he had won her. Tom Burwell, whom the whole town called Big Boy, also loved her. But working in the fields all day, and far away from her, gave him no chance to show it. Though often enough of evenings he had tried to. Somehow, he never got along. Strong as he was with hands upon the ax or plow, he found it difficult to hold her. Or so he thought. But the fact was that he held her to factory town more firmly than he thought for. His black balanced, and pulled against, the white of Stone, when she thought of them. And her mind was vaguely upon them as she came over the crest of the hill, coming from the white folks' kitchen. As she sang softly at the evil face of the full moon.

A strange stir was in her. Indolently, she tried to fix upon Bob or Tom as the cause of it. To meet Bob in the canebrake, as she was going to do an hour or so later, was nothing new. And Tom's proposal which she felt on its way to her could be indefinitely put off. Separately, there was no unusual significance to either one. But for some reason, they jumbled when her eyes gazed vacantly at the rising moon. And from the jumble came the stir that was strangely within her. Her lips trembled. The slow rhythm of her song grew agitant and restless. Rusty black and tan spotted hounds, lying in the dark corners of porches or prowling around back yards, put their noses in the air and caught its tremor. They began plaintively to yelp and howl. Chickens woke up and cackled. Intermittently, all over the countryside dogs barked and roosters crowed as if heralding a weird dawn or some ungodly awakening. The women sang lustily. Their songs were cotton-wads to stop their ears. Louisa came down into factory town and sank wearily upon the step before her home. The moon was rising towards a thick cloud-bank which soon would hide it.

Red nigger moon. Sinner!
Blood-burning moon. Sinner!
Come out that fact'ry door.

2

Up from the deep dusk of a cleared spot on the edge of the forest a mellow glow arose and spread fan-wise into the low-hanging heavens. And all around the air was heavy with scent of boiling cane. A large pile of cane-stalks lay like ribboned shadows upon the ground. A mule, harnessed to a pole, trudged lazily round and round the pivot of the grinder. Beneath a swaying oil lamp, a Negro alternately whipped out at the mule, and fed cane-stalks to the grinder. A fat boy waddled pails of fresh ground juice between the grinder and the boiling stove. Steam came from the copper boiling pan. The scent of cane came from the copper pan and drenched the forest and the hill that sloped to factory town, beneath its fragrance. It drenched the men in circle seated around the stove. Some of them chewed at the white pulp of stalks, but there was no need for them to, if all they wanted was to taste the cane. One tasted it in factory town. And from factory town one could see the soft haze thrown by the glowing stove upon the low-hanging heavens.

   Old David Georgia stirred the thickening syrup with a long ladle, and ever so often drew it off. Old David Georgia tended his stove and told tales about the white folks, about moon-shining and cotton picking, and about sweet nigger gals, to the men who sat there about his stove to listen to him. Tom Burwell chewed cane-stalk and laughed with the others till someone mentioned Louisa. Till some one said something about Louisa and Bob Stone, about the silk stockings she must have gotten from him. Blood ran up Tom's neck hotter than the glow that flooded from the stove. He sprang up. Glared at the men and said, "She's my gal." Will Manning laughed. Tom strode over to him. Yanked him up and knocked him to the ground. Several of Manning's friends got up to fight for him. Tom whipped out a long knife and would have cut them to shreds if they hadnt ducked into the woods. Tom had had enough. He nodded to Old David Georgia and swung down the path to factory town. Just then, the dogs started barking and the roosters began to crow. Tom felt funny. Away from the fight, away from the stove, chill got to him. He shivered. He shuddered when he saw the full moon rising towards the cloud-bank. He who didnt give a godam for the fears of old women. He forced his mind to fasten on Louisa. Bob Stone. Better not be. He turned into the street and saw Louisa sitting before her home. He went towards her, ambling, touched the brim of a marvelously shaped, spotted, felt hat, said he wanted to say something to her, and then found that he didnt know what he had to say, or if he did, that he couldnt say it. He shoved his big fists in his overalls, grinned, and started to move off.

   "Youall want me, Tom?"

   "Thats what us wants, sho, Louisa."

   "Well, here I am —"

   "An here I is, but that aint ahelpin none, all th same."

   "You wanted to say something? . . ."

   "I did that, sho. But words is like the spots on dice: no matter how y fumbles em, there's times when they jes wont come. I dunno why. Seems like th love I feels fo yo done stole'm tongue. I got it now. Whee! Louisa, honey, I oughtnt tell y, I feel I oughtnt cause yo is young an goes t church an I has had other gals, but Louisa I sho do love y. Lil gal, Ise watched y from them first days when youall sat right here befo yo door befo th well an sang sometimes in a way that like t broke m heart. Ise carried y with me into th fields, day after day, an after that, an I sho can plow when yo is there, an I can pick cotton. Yassur! Come near beatin Barlo yesterday. I sho did. Yassur! And next year if ole Stone'll trust me, I'll have a farm. My own. My bales will buy yo what y gets from white folks now. Silk stockings an purple dresses — course I dont believe what some folks been whisperin as t how y gets them things now. White folks always did do for niggers what they likes. An they jes cant help alikin yo, Louisa. Bob Stone likes y. Course he does. But not th way folks is awhisperin. Does he, hon?"

"I dont know what you mean, Tom."

"Course y dont. Ise already cut two niggers. Had t hon, t tell em so. Niggers always tryin t make somethin out a nothin. An then besides, white folks aint up t them tricks so much nowadays. Godam better not be. Leastawise not with yo. Cause I wouldnt stand f it. Nassur."

"What would you do, Tom?"

"Cut him just like I cut a nigger."

"No, Tom —"

"I said I would and there aint no mo to it. But that aint th talk f now. Sing, honey Louisa, an while I'm listenin t y I'll be makin love."

Tom took her hand in his. Against the tough thickness of his own, hers felt soft and small. His huge body slipped down to the step beside her. The full moon sank upward into the deep purple of the cloud-bank. An old woman brought a lighted lamp and hung it on the common well whose bulk shadow squatted in the middle of the road, opposite Tom and Louisa. The old woman lifted the well-lid, took hold the chain, and began drawing up the heavy bucket. As she did so, she sang. Figures shifted, restless-like, between lamp and window in the front rooms of the shanties. Shadows of the figures fought each other on the gray dust of the road. Figures raised the windows and joined the old woman in song. Louisa and Tom, the whole street, singing:

> Red nigger moon. Sinner!
> Blood-burning moon. Sinner!
> Come out that fact'ry door.

3

Bob Stone sauntered from his veranda out into the gloom of fir trees and magnolias. The clear white of his skin paled, and the flush of his cheeks turned purple. As if to balance this outer change, his mind became consciously a white man's. He passed the house with its huge open hearth which, in the days of slavery, was the plantation cookery. He saw Louisa bent over the hearth. He went in as a master should and took her. Direct, honest, bold. None of this sneaking that he had to go through now. The contrast was repulsive to him. His family had lost ground. Hell no, his family still owned the niggers, practically. Damned if they did, or he wouldnt have to duck around so. What would they think if they knew? His mother? His sister? He shouldnt mention them, shouldnt think of them in this connection. There in the dusk he blushed at doing so. Fellows about town were all right, but how about his friends up North? He could see them incredible, repulsed. They didnt know. The thought first made him laugh. Then, with their eyes still upon him, he began to feel embarrassed. He felt the need of explaining things to them. Explain hell. They wouldnt understand, and moreover, who ever heard of a Southerner getting on his knees to any Yankee, or anyone. No sir. He was going to see Louisa to-night, and love her. She was lovely — in her way. Nigger way. What way was that? Damned if he knew. Must know. He'd known her long enough to know. Was there something about niggers that you couldnt know? Listening to them at church didnt tell you anything. Looking at them didnt tell you anything. Talking to them didnt tell you anything — unless it was gossip, unless they wanted to talk. Of course, about farming, and licker, and craps — but those werent nigger. Nigger was something more. How much more? Something to be afraid of, more? Hell no. Who ever heard of being afraid of a nigger? Tom Burwell. Cartwell had told him that Tom went with Louisa after she reached home. No sir. No nigger had ever been with his girl. He'd like to see one try. Some position for him to be in. Him, Bob Stone, of the old Stone family, in a scrap with a nigger over a nigger girl. In the good old days . . . Ha! Those were the days. His family had lost ground. Not so much, though. Enough for him to have to cut through old Lemon's canefield by way of the woods, that he might meet her. She was worth it. Beautiful nigger gal. Why nigger? Why not, just gal? No, it was because she was nigger that he went to her. Sweet . . . The scent of boiling cane came to him. Then he saw the rich glow of the stove. He heard the voices of the men circled around it. He was about to skirt the clearing when he heard his own name mentioned. He stopped. Quivering. Leaning against a tree, he listened.

"Bad nigger. Yassur, he sho is one bad nigger when he gets started."

"Tom Burwell's been on th gang three times fo cuttin men."

"What y think he's agwine t do t Bob Stone?"

"Dunno yet. He aint found out. When he does — Baby!"

"Aint no tellin."

"Young Stone aint no quitter and I ken tell y that. Blood of th old uns in his veins."

"Thats right. He'll scrap, sho."

"Be gettin too hot f niggers round this away."

"Shut up, nigger. Y dont know what y talkin bout."

Bob Stone's ears burned as though he had been holding them over the stove. Sizzling heat welled up within him. His feet felt as if they rested on red-hot coals. They stung him to quick movement. He circled the fringe of the glowing. Not a twig cracked beneath his feet. He reached the path that led to factory town. Plunged furiously down it. Halfway along, a blindness within him veered him aside. He crashed into the bordering canebrake. Cane leaves cut his face and lips. He tasted blood. He threw himself down and dug his fingers in the ground. The earth was cool. Cane-roots took the fever from his hands.

After a long while, or so it seemed to him, the thought came to him that it must be time to see Louisa. He got to his feet and walked calmly to their meeting place. No Louisa. Tom Burwell had her. Veins in his forehead bulged and distended. Saliva moistened the dried blood on his lips. He bit down on his lips. He tasted blood. Not his own blood; Tom Burwell's blood. Bob drove through the cane and out again upon the road. A hound swung down the path before him towards factory town. Bob couldnt see it. The dog loped aside to let him pass. Bob's blind rushing made him stumble over it. He fell with a thud that dazed him. The hound yelped. Answering yelps came from all over the countryside. Chickens cackled. Roosters crowed, heralding the blood-shot eyes of southern awakening. Singers in the town were silenced. They shut their windows down. Palpitant between the rooster crows, a chill hush settled upon the huddled forms of Tom and Louisa. A figure rushed from the shadow and stood before them. Tom popped to his feet.

"Whats y want?"

"I'm Bob Stone."

"Yassur — an I'm Tom Burwell. Whats y want?"

Bob lunged at him. Tom side-stepped, caught him by the shoulder, and flung him to the ground. Straddled him.

"Let me up."

"Yassur — but watch yo doins, Bob Stone."

A few dark figures, drawn by the sound of scuffle, stood about them. Bob sprang to his feet.

"Fight like a man, Tom Burwell, and I'll lick y."

Again he lunged. Tom side-stepped and flung him to the ground. Straddled him.

"Get off me, you godam nigger you."

"Yo sho has started somethin now. Get up."

Tom yanked him up and began hammering at him. Each blow sounded as if it smashed into a precious, irreplaceable soft something. Beneath them, Bob staggered back. He reached in his pocket and whipped out a knife.

"That my game, sho."

Blue flash, a steel blade slashed across Bob Stone's throat. He had a sweetish sick feeling. Blood began to flow. Then he felt a sharp twitch of pain. He let his knife drop. He slapped one hand against his neck. He pressed the other on top of his head as if to hold it down. He groaned. He turned, and staggered towards the crest of the hill in the direction of white town. Negroes who had seen the fight slunk into their homes and blew the lamps out. Louisa, dazed, hysterical, refused to go indoors. She slipped, crumbled, her body loosely propped against the woodwork of the well. Tom Burwell leaned against it. He seemed rooted there.

Bob reached Broad Street. White men rushed up to him. He collapsed in their arms.

"Tom Burwell. . . ."

White men like ants upon a forage rushed about. Except for the taut hum of their moving, all was silent. Shotguns, revolvers, rope, kerosene, torches. Two

high-powered cars with glaring search-lights. They came together. The taut hum
rose to a low roar. Then nothing could be heard but the flop of their feet in the
thick dust of the roar. The moving body of their silence preceded them over the
crest of the hill into factory town. It flattened the Negroes beneath it. It rolled to
the wall of the factory, where it stopped. Tom knew that they were coming. He
couldnt move. And then he saw the search-lights of the two cars glaring down
on him. A quick shock went through him. He stiffened. He started to run. A yell
went up from the mob. Tom wheeled about and faced them. They poured down
on him. They swarmed. A large man with dead-white face and flabby cheeks
came to him and almost jabbed a gun-barrel through his guts.

"Hands behind y, nigger."

Tom's wrists were bound. The big man shoved him to the well. Burn him
over it, and when the woodwork caved in, his body would drop to the bottom.
Two deaths for a godam nigger. Louisa was driven back. The mob pushed in.
Its pressure, its momentum was too great. Drag him to the factory. Wood and
stakes already there. Tom moved in the direction indicated. But they had to drag
him. They reached the great door. Too many to get in there. The mob divided
and flowed around the walls to either side. The big man shoved him through
the door. The mob pressed in from the sides. Taut humming. No words. A stake
was sunk into the ground. Rotting floor boards piled around it. Kerosene poured
on the rotting floor boards. Tom bound to the stake. His breast was bare. Nails
scratches let little lines of blood trickle down and mat into the hair. His face, his
eyes were set and stony. Except for irregular breathing, one would have thought
him already dead. Torches were flung onto the pile. A great flare muffled in black
smoke shot upward. The mob yelled. The mob was silent. Now Tom could be
seen within the flames. Only his head, erect, lean, like a blackened stone. Stench
of burning flesh soaked the air. Tom's eyes popped. His head settled downward.
The mob yelled. Its yell echoed against the skeleton stone walls and sounded like
a hundred yells. Like a hundred mobs yelling. Its yell thudded against the thick
front wall and fell back. Ghost of a yell slipped through the flames and out the
great door of the factory. It fluttered like a dying thing down the single street of
factory town. Louisa, upon the step before her home, did not hear it, but her eyes
opened slowly. They saw the full moon glowing in the great door. The full moon,
an evil thing, an omen, soft showering the homes of folks she knew. Where were
they, these people? She'd sing, and perhaps they'd come out and join her. Perhaps
Tom Burwell would come. At any rate, the full moon in the great door was an
omen which she must sing to:

Red nigger moon. Sinner!
Blood-burning moon. Sinner!
Come out that fact'ry door.

John Updike

John Updike (1932–2009) was born in Shillington, Pennsylvania, an only child. His father taught algebra in a local high school, and his mother wrote short stories and novels. His mother's consciousness of a special destiny, combined with his family's meager income—they lived with his mother's parents for the first thirteen years of Updike's life—made him "both arrogant and shy" as a teenager. He wrote stories, drew cartoons, and clowned for the approval of his peers. After getting straight A's in high school, he went to Harvard University on a full scholarship, studying English and graduating summa cum laude in 1954. He spent a year at Oxford on a fellowship, then joined the staff of *The New Yorker*. In 1959 Updike published both his first book of short fiction, *The Same Door*, and his first novel, *The Poorhouse Fair*. That year he also moved from New York City to a coastal town in Massachusetts, where he lived for nearly fifty years.

In the 1960s, 1970s, and early 1980s, Updike continued to alternate novels and collections of stories, adding occasional volumes of verse, collections of essays, and one play. His novels include *Rabbit, Run* (1960), *Couples* (1968), *Rabbit Redux* (1971), and *Marry Me* (1976). *Rabbit Is Rich* (1981), continuing the story of Harry "Rabbit" Angstrom, a suburban Pennsylvanian whom Updike traced through adolescence, marriage, fatherhood, and middle age, won virtually every major American literary award for the year it appeared; Updike concluded the series with *Rabbit at Rest* (1991). Updike's collections of stories include *Pigeon Feathers* (1962), *Museums and Women* (1972), and *Problems and Other Stories* (1981). In 1983 Updike won the National Book Critics Circle Award for his collection of essays and criticism *Hugging the Shore*. In 1989 he published his memoirs, *Self-Consciousness*. Other books are *The Afterlife and Other Stories* (1994) and *The Complete Henry Bech* (*Twenty Stories*) in 2001. Updike's collected *Early Stories* (2003) contains his short fiction from 1953 to 1975; his *Collected Later Stories* appeared in 2013.

Updike said he was indebted to Ernest Hemingway and J. D. Salinger's stories for the literary form he adopted to describe the painful experience of adolescence: "I learned a lot from Salinger's short stories; he did remove the short narrative from the wise-guy, slice-of-life stories of the thirties and forties. Like most innovative artists, he made new room for shapelessness, for life as it is lived." Updike wrote realistic narrative, believing that "fiction is a tissue of lies that refreshes and informs our sense of actuality. Reality is—chemically, atomically, biologically—a fabric of microscopic accuracies." His fiction, such as the story "A & P," concentrated on these "microscopic accuracies," tiny details of characterization and setting brilliantly described. The critic Louis Menand understood that Hemingway "would probably not have given" the boy in "A & P" his thought in the last sentence of the story, "or would not have permitted him to express it. But it is the sentence—in a story that somehow squeezes the whole pathos of Cold War life into a tiny, perfect anecdote—that produces the click," the effect of the story.

RELATED STORY
James Joyce, "Araby," page 675.

A & P

1961

IN WALKS THESE THREE GIRLS in nothing but bathing suits. I'm in the third checkout slot, with my back to the door, so I don't see them until they're over by the bread. The one that caught my eye first was the one in the plaid green two-piece. She was a chunky kid, with a good tan and a sweet broad soft-looking can with those two crescents of white just under it, where the sun never seems to hit, at the top of the backs of her legs. I stood there with my hand on a box of HiHo crackers trying to remember if I rang it up or not. I ring it up again and the customer starts giving me hell. She's one of these cash-register-watchers, a witch about fifty with rouge on her cheekbones and no eyebrows, and I know it made her day to trip me up. She'd been watching cash registers for fifty years and probably never seen a mistake before.

By the time I got her feathers smoothed and her goodies into a bag — she gives me a little snort in passing, if she'd been born at the right time they would have burned her over in Salem — by the time I get her on her way the girls had circled around the bread and were coming back, without a pushcart, back my way along the counters, in the aisle between the checkouts and the Special bins. They didn't even have shoes on. There was this chunky one, with the two-piece — it was bright green and the seams on the bra were still sharp and her belly was still pretty pale so I guessed she just got it (the suit) — there was this one, with one of those chubby berry-faces, the lips all bunched together under her nose, this one, and a tall one, with black hair that hadn't quite frizzed right, and one of these sunburns right across under the eyes, and a chin that was too long — you know, the kind of girl other girls think is very "striking" and "attractive" but never quite makes it, as they very well know, which is why they like her so much — and then the third one, that wasn't quite so tall. She was the queen. She kind of led them, the other two peeking around and making their shoulders round. She didn't look around, not this queen, she just walked straight on slowly, on these long white prima-donna legs. She came down a little hard on her heels, as if she didn't walk in her bare feet that much, putting down her heels and then letting the weight move along to her toes as if she was testing the floor with every step, putting a little deliberate extra action into it. You never know for sure how girls' minds work (do you really think it's a mind in there or just a little buzz like a bee in a glass jar?) but you got the idea she had talked the other two into coming in here with her, and now she was showing them how to do it, walk slow and hold yourself straight.

She had on a kind of dirty-pink — beige maybe, I don't know — bathing suit with a little nubble all over it, and what got me, the straps were down. They were off her shoulders looped loose around the cool tops of her arms, and I guess as a result the suit had slipped a little on her, so all around the top of the cloth there was this shining rim. If it hadn't been there you wouldn't have known there could have been anything whiter than those shoulders. With the straps pushed off, there was nothing between the top of the suit and the top of her head except just *her*, this clean bare plane of the top of her chest down from the shoulder bones like a dented sheet of metal tilted in the light. I mean, it was more than pretty.

She had sort of oaky hair that the sun and salt had bleached, done up in a bun that was unravelling, and a kind of prim face. Walking into the A & P with your straps down, I suppose it's the only kind of face you *can* have. She held her head so high her neck, coming up out of those white shoulders, looked kind of stretched, but I didn't mind. The longer her neck was, the more of her there was.

She must have felt in the corner of her eye me and over my shoulder Stokesie in the second slot watching, but she didn't tip. Not this queen. She kept her eyes moving across the racks, and stopped, and turned so slow it made my stomach rub the inside of my apron, and buzzed to the other two, who kind of huddled against her for relief, and then they all three of them went up the cat-and-dog-food-breakfast-cereal-macaroni-rice-raisins-seasonings-spreads-spaghetti-soft-drinks-crackers-and-cookies aisle. From the third slot I look straight up this aisle to the meat counter, and I watched them all the way. The fat one with the tan sort of fumbled with the cookies, but on second thought she put the package back. The sheep pushing their carts down the aisle — the girls were walking against the usual traffic (not that we have one-way signs or anything) — were pretty hilarious. You could see them, when Queenie's white shoulders dawned on them, kind of jerk, or hop, or hiccup, but their eyes snapped back to their own baskets and on they pushed. I bet you could set off dynamite in an A & P and the people would by and large keep reaching and checking oatmeal off their lists and muttering "Let me see, there was a third thing, began with A, asparagus, no, ah, yes, applesauce!" or whatever it is they do mutter. But there was no doubt, this jiggled them. A few houseslaves in pin curlers even looked around after pushing their carts past to make sure what they had seen was correct.

You know, it's one thing to have a girl in a bathing suit down on the beach, where what with the glare nobody can look at each other much anyway, and another thing in the cool of the A & P, under the fluorescent lights, against all those stacked packages, with her feet paddling along naked over our check-board green-and-cream rubber-tile floor.

"Oh Daddy," Stokesie said beside me. "I feel so faint."

"Darling," I said. "Hold me tight." Stokesie's married, with two babies chalked up on his fuselage already, but as far as I can tell that's the only difference. He's twenty-two, and I was nineteen this April.

"Is it done?" he asks, the responsible married man finding his voice. I forgot to say he thinks he's going to be manager some sunny day, maybe in 1990 when it's called the Great Alexandrov and Petrooshki Tea Company or something.

What he meant was, our town is five miles from a beach, with a big summer colony out on the Point, but we're right in the middle of town, and the women generally put on a shirt or shorts or something before they get out of the car into the street. And anyway these are usually women with six children and varicose veins mapping their legs and nobody, including them, could care less. As I say, we're right in the middle of town, and if you stand at our front doors you can see two banks and the Congregational church and the newspaper store and three real-estate offices and about twenty-seven old freeloaders tearing up Central Street because the sewer broke again. It's not as if we're on the Cape; we're north of Boston and there's people in this town haven't seen the ocean for twenty years.

The girls had reached the meat counter and were asking McMahon something. He pointed, they pointed, and they shuffled out of sight behind a pyramid of Diet Delight peaches. All that was left for us to see was old McMahon patting his mouth and looking after them sizing up their joints. Poor kids, I began to feel sorry for them, they couldn't help it.

Now here comes the sad part of the story, at least my family says it's sad, but I don't think it's so sad myself. The store's pretty empty, it being Thursday afternoon, so there was nothing much to do except lean on the register and wait for the girls to show up again. The whole store was like a pinball machine and I didn't know which tunnel they'd come out of. After a while they come around out of the far aisle, around the light bulbs, records at discount of the Caribbean Six or Tony Martin Sings or some such gunk you wonder they waste the wax on, sixpacks of candy bars, and plastic toys done up in cellophane that fall apart when a kid looks at them anyway. Around they come, Queenie still leading the way, and holding a little gray jar in her hand. Slots Three through Seven are unmanned and I could see her wondering between Stokes and me, but Stokesie with his usual luck draws an old party in baggy gray pants who stumbles up with four giant cans of pineapple juice (what do these bums *do* with all that pineapple juice? I've often asked myself) so the girls come to me. Queenie puts down the jar and I take it into my fingers icy cold. Kingfish Fancy Herring Snacks in Pure Sour Cream: 49¢. Now her hands are empty, not a ring or a bracelet, bare as God made them, and I wonder where the money's coming from. Still with that prim look she lifts a folded dollar bill out of the hollow at the center of her nubbled pink top. The jar went heavy in my hand. Really, I thought that was so cute.

Then everybody's luck begins to run out. Lengel comes in from haggling with a truck full of cabbages on the lot and is about to scuttle into that door marked MANAGER behind which he hides all day when the girls touch his eye. Lengel's pretty dreary, teaches Sunday school and the rest, but he doesn't miss that much. He comes over and says, "Girls, this isn't the beach."

Queenie blushes, though maybe it's just a brush of sunburn I was noticing for the first time, now that she was so close. "My mother asked me to pick up a jar of herring snacks." Her voice kind of startled me, the way voices do when you see the people first, coming out so flat and dumb yet kind of tony, too, the way it ticked over "pick up" and "snacks." All of a sudden I slid right down her voice into her living room. Her father and the other men were standing around in ice-cream coats and bow ties and the women were in sandals picking up herring snacks on toothpicks off a big glass plate and they were all holding drinks the color of water with olives and sprigs of mint in them. When my parents have somebody over they get lemonade and if it's a real racy affair Schlitz in tall glasses with "They'll Do It Every Time" cartoons stencilled on.

"That's all right," Lengel said. "But this isn't the beach." His repeating this struck me as funny, as if it had just occurred to him, and he had been thinking all these years the A & P was a great big sand dune and he was the head lifeguard. He didn't like my smiling — as I say he doesn't miss much — but he concentrates on giving the girls that sad Sunday-school–superintendent stare.

Queenie's blush is no sunburn now, and the plump one in plaid, that I liked better from the back — a really sweet can — pipes up, "We weren't doing any shopping. We just came in for the one thing."

"That makes no difference," Lengel tells her, and I could see from the way his eyes went that he hadn't noticed she was wearing a two-piece before. "We want you decently dressed when you come in here."

"We *are* decent," Queenie says suddenly, her lower lip pushing, getting sore now that she remembers her place, a place from which the crowd that runs the A & P must look pretty crummy. Fancy Herring Snacks flashed in her very blue eyes.

"Girls, I don't want to argue with you. After this come in here with your shoulders covered. It's our policy." He turns his back. That's policy for you. Policy is what the kingpins want. What the others want is juvenile delinquency.

All this while, the customers had been showing up with their carts but, you know, sheep, seeing a scene, they had all bunched up on Stokesie, who shook open a paper bag as gently as peeling a peach, not wanting to miss a word. I could feel in the silence everybody getting nervous, most of all Lengel, who asks me, "Sammy, have you rung up their purchase?"

I thought and said "No" but it wasn't about that I was thinking. I go through the punches, 4, 9, GROC, TOT — it's more complicated than you think, and after you do it often enough, it begins to make a little song, that you hear words to, in my case "Hello (*bing*) there, you (*gung*) hap-py *pee-pul* (*splat*)!" — the *splat* being the drawer flying out. I uncrease the bill, tenderly as you may imagine, it just having come from between the two smoothest scoops of vanilla I had ever known were there, and pass a half and a penny into her narrow pink palm, and nestle the herrings in a bag and twist its neck and hand it over, all the time thinking.

The girls, and who'd blame them, are in a hurry to get out, so I say "I quit" to Lengel enough for them to hear, hoping they'll stop and watch me, their unsuspected hero. They keep right on going, into the electric eye; the door flies open and they flicker across the lot to their car, Queenie and Plaid and Big Tall Goony-Goony (not that as raw material she was so bad), leaving me with Lengel and a kink in his eyebrow.

"Did you say something, Sammy?"

"I said I quit."

"I thought you did."

"You didn't have to embarrass them."

"It was they who were embarrassing us."

I started to say something that came out "Fiddle-de-doo." It's a saying of my grandmother's, and I know she would have been pleased.

"I don't think you know what you're saying," Lengel said.

"I know you don't," I said. "But I do." I pull the bow at the back of my apron and start shrugging it off my shoulders. A couple customers that had been heading for my slot begin to knock against each other, like scared pigs in a chute.

Lengel sighs and begins to look very patient and old and gray. He's been a friend of my parents for years. "Sammy, you don't want to do this to your Mom and Dad," he tells me. It's true, I don't. But it seems to me that once you begin a gesture it's fatal not to go through with it. I fold the apron, "Sammy" stitched in red on the pocket, and put it on the counter, and drop the bow tie on top of it. The bow tie is theirs, if you've ever wondered. "You'll feel this for the rest of your life," Lengel says, and I know that's true, too, but remembering how he made that pretty girl blush makes me so scrunchy inside I punch the No Sale tab and the machine whirs "pee-pul" and the drawer splats out. One advantage to this scene taking place in summer, I can follow this up with a clean exit, there's no fumbling around getting your coat and galoshes, I just saunter into the electric eye in my white shirt that my mother ironed the night before, and the door heaves itself open, and outside the sunshine is skating around on the asphalt.

I look around for my girls, but they're gone, of course. There wasn't anybody but some young married screaming with her children about some candy they didn't get by the door of a powder-blue Falcon station wagon. Looking back in the big windows, over the bags of peat moss and aluminum lawn furniture stacked on the pavement, I could see Lengel in my place in the slot, checking the sheep through. His face was dark gray and his back stiff, as if he'd just had an injection of iron, and my stomach kind of fell as I felt how hard the world was going to be to me hereafter.

Luis Alberto Urrea

Luis Alberto Urrea (b. 1955) was born in Tijuana, Mexico, to an American mother from New York City and a Mexican father. He lived in his grandmother's house with his aunt and cousins, speaking Spanish, and his mother would go off to work in San Diego every day. Later he realized "how lonely it must have been for this woman from Manhattan to be stuck in Tijuana with people who didn't like her culture, didn't like *her*—and with a language she didn't understand and a child who didn't understand her." When he was five years old, his parents moved to a Mexican barrio in San Diego, where Urrea learned "that on my dad's side I was considered to be Mexican and on my mom's side I was considered to be American. My dad always called me Luis and my mom always called me Louis." Finally, as he recalled, "My mom got the upper hand. She spent the most time with me because he [his dad] was very macho and had girlfriends and other families." His mother read to Urrea every night and introduced him to novels by Charles Dickens and Mark Twain. In some way, he says, "that pushed me to be a writer also."

At the University of California at San Diego, Urrea earned a B.A. in creative writing. In 1977, during his senior year in college, his father died in a car accident and Urrea was responsible for his funeral. Urrea's story about this traumatic event, "Father Returns from the Mountain," which he rewrote several times, was accepted for publication in an anthology titled *Edges*, edited by Ursula K. Le Guin in 1980. It was the first story he wrote what he would see in print, and it gave him the confidence to become a professional writer. Honored by many literary prizes and awards, Urrea is the author of a collection of short stories, *Six Kinds of Sky* (2002), as well as several novels, a memoir, poetry, and works of nonfiction.

As an instructor of creative writing at the University of Illinois at Chicago, Urea tells his students "that before Picasso painted cubism, he learned how to draw and how to paint. . . . a lot of writers in graduate school are stone cold experimentalists—mostly, I think, because they don't know how to tell a clear story. They do whatever trick they can do to avert your attention. . . . I always want to make sure that people can actually communicate something first."

RELATED COMMENTARY
Luis Alberto Urrea, "On Writing 'Father Returns from the Mountain,'" page 1532.

Father Returns from the Mountain

1980

THE CAR IS RED. It has a sun-baked and peeling black top. Little flakes of fake leather blow away in the wind. The roof is crushed. Windows are shattered. The front end is crumpled. The axles are split and the tires slant crookedly. Dry blood on the hood. The steering wheel is twisted. Details of violence. An American Motors Rambler 440, 1966 model. Slivers of glass are stuck in the carpets. Dust settles on the stains. A photograph of my father and me is caught under the seat, fluttering like a flag, like a bird trapped in the wind. There is a dime in the broken driver's seat. Blood where the radio should be. / This is the truth. The truth is a diamond, or at least a broken mirror. There are many reflective surfaces, and we observe the ones we choose. We see what we can. / The car is red. It stands in a dusty compound among other crushed machines. A note to my father in a flowery woman's hand blows out of the glove compartment. It whispers "Querido Alberto" a hundred times as it spins away. There is a chain-link fence that rattles in a breeze that smells of dogs and perfume. A yellow sticker is pasted to the hood because there is no glass to hold it. Children scare each other by touching the crusty patches of my father's blood. "He'll come back to eat you!" The dead man, the dead man. / A Mexican cop slides down the slope. He squints in the early morning sun. He can hardly see my father in the wreckage. He runs back up and calls for help. The blue light atop his car flashes, flashes, casting marching shadows over the rocks. Pink urine spreads across my father's clothing. The pain is a sound that hums inside his gut, that pierces his skull. Darkness. Sleep. / The telephone feels warm. I look out the window at a Monday sky. "Hello," he says. It is a family friend. "Do you remember me?" The morning sunlight reaches through the trees. "Of course I remember you. What's up?" His silence buzzes for a moment. When he speaks, he speaks carefully. "Your father . . . has had an accident." "Is he hurt?" "Yes." "Badly?" "Yes." I lean forward. I think of my father being hurt. I think of him in pain. The tiny agony of tears pinches the corners of my eyes. / We are on a balcony in Puerto Vallarta. I am in love with the most inconceivable girl in Rosario, Sinaloa. Ebony crabs have come in from the jungle, mad with the rain that hasn't stopped for two days. They climb the stairs of the hotel, wait before our doors, attack us when we come out. His hand is on my shoulder. I cannot contain the feelings as we watch lightning bombard the hilltops. Rain undermines the streets and floods the river that eats great rifts in the jungle. We spend the entire night in each other's confidence. And when the tears come, he lets me cry. / My father is severely damaged. His eyes are open, but will not function. They scrape up and down, but they cannot break the thick shell of darkness that covers them. His body will not move — he tells it to — to get the hell up, get back in the car, light a cigarette, go bowling, something. Anything. But he is frozen. His mouth is a traitor that will not function. It fills slowly with liquid. When it reaches his lips, there is a gradual, endless snail of red slipping down his cheek and hiding in his ear. I am sitting in my room listening to music. / "How bad?" I ask, a little afraid, a little unwilling, a little uncertain. "Very bad. He flew off a mountain. He fell in the desert." The sun is bright. / The car is red. The police compound is quiet. A scrawny cat licks the speedometer. / The police lift him into the ambulance. He tries to talk, he tries to see he is a slab of meat and it makes him angry. The pain makes him angry. The cuts on his face sting. And through the morning, dawn scorching the paper-sheet horizon, ravens smelling the blood and exploding off the road before them, the ambulance crew flies. To a hospital — well, a clinic. Scorpions drowsing in its shade. And there, the nurses find him almost dead, and strip him bare, and shoot a load of morphine in his fallen veins, and tie him down in case he kicks, and leave him naked — God, he's mad. But the poppies blooming in his arms send out their odors, their perfume already bubbles up his throat, and down, down, beyond his belly, to where the memories dwell. The blood has made his throat black. / I sit alone in the funeral home. There is little sound from without: even downtown Tijuana has to sleep. 3:00 A.M. No sleep for me. Me and the body, we're wired. / I open the coffin lid and look at him. He is broken. His chin is a black openness. He was always shaved pink and now little gray whiskers are pushing their heads up through the wounds. His shirt is stained. I put my face to the side of the box and stare and stare. I watch for a flicker, a twitch. I wait for a microscopic flare of the nostrils. The sealed eyelids seem ready to pop, to rise and lower. I want, in terror, to see him lick his lips so that I can break the Mexican sealing glass, pull him up, save him, embrace him. There is no movement. There is no sound. / I found a photograph just yesterday. In it, my father stands with the president, with generals, senators. His captain's uniform looks as crisp as a salad. At times, I shuffle through his official papers and look at his federal police badge. His smiles look like mine. We are connected by the lips. The grin is our chain. / I lie on the floor beneath the coffin. He's up on a table laid out like God's buffet. I close my eyes to sleep, my last night beside him. I am a poet at the instant. A shadow passes over my face. I jump up, thinking that someone is approaching. There is nothing. Again the shadow. Again nothing. Again and again. I imagine him waving farewell. As I slip into sleep, I have a vision of a stiff hand reaching for me over the edge. / The dreams have come in a series. They are diamonds. They are broken mirrors. In the first, I am run over by a truck. My half-brother stands on the curb and smiles down at me. I pull at people's legs from the black street. / Death is here now. I am finally aware of it. Perhaps childhood is not knowing that it is grinning at you from the corner. It has pressed its face against the windows, it has stalked in with the fog and awaits its turn. / At 8:00 P.M. he tried to open his eyes. His straining led to nothing. My father was born in Rosario, little gem at the southern end of Sinaloa. He died in San Luis Rio Colorado, a dry husk in the north of Sonora. I can imagine his gray hair against the pillow. His lips, white, rolling back almost in a smile. His abdomen searing red hot, then tingling pink as he passed through to the new side. Possibly music, a fragment of a tune wafting through the haze. I hope he heard music. / The family friend calls again. "Tell me," I say. "His condition deteriorated for several hours." "And?" "And your señor . . . rested." "Dead?" "Dead." "Just now?" "Yes." "Thank you." "Are you all right?" "Thank you." / No one comes to the funeral home to spell me. It's a wake, and I'm awake. I have watched the corpse for seven hours. I have closed the lid. I have not eaten since the day before. "I hate waiting," I say out loud. His voice: "I know, Son. I always hated it too. It's boring." I spin around, but the lid remains closed. There's nobody else in the room. "Do you hear me?" I ask. "Yes," he replies. "I love you." I say. "I know," he says. / Mexicans love the dead. They are a lovely treat with which to terrify each other. Dawn's light, and people passing in the street push open the door to peek at the coffin. "What are you looking at, you vampires?" I yell at them. "El muerto," they whisper. "El muerto." / We carry the coffin to the graveside. I have to go to the bathroom. Dogs are running on the graves. Whores and cops and ice cream men are working downtown. People are eating and laughing and sweating and making love all over the world and my father is dead. The world has not even hesitated. Nobody has noticed. / The hard part is watching the box go down. Watching it being pushed into the black mouth, knowing that his flesh is being hid from you, and if you should search for a touch of it again you will find dusty corruption. The body goes. I walk away from the weeping. White clouds on the border. I keep my back to the mourners. Tijuana looks pretty from a distance. I was born there. / I sit in my house alone, working on the third draft of a book no-one will ever read. I hear a car in the driveway. When I open the door, the car is red. My dead father is leaning on the steering wheel. His hair is in disorder, his eyes are uncertain. I go to him, take his cold hand, lead him inside. He sits on the couch, settling like a white feather. "What happened?" he asks. I look into his face. He doesn't know. He doesn't know he's dead. Maybe I can fool him. Keep him alive. But I know as I hope it is impossible. I kneel at his feet. "Papá, you were killed." "Killed! But I'm right here!" "You were killed in an accident." "But the car's in the driveway. Brand new." "No." "It can't be," he says. I am afraid of hurting him, but I must. "Papá," I say, "go away. You're dead." "I can't be dead," he insists, pain and frustration mixing on his face. / As a child, I would ride standing beside him as he drove, holding tight to his shoulder. / I take his pant-legs in my hands. "Papá, go away. You can't stay here. You're dead!" He shakes his head sadly. I weep like his little boy wept, with my head on his knees. "You're dead, you're dead, you're dead." / A stonemason gets in the grave and spreads concrete over the box. We don't have enough money for a headstone. Maybe a tree will grow here, or a stand of mustard, goldenrod. Other mourners file in to feed the hole beside my father's. / The car is red. The cold desert wind moans in it at night. There is a scar on the mountain where he crashed. His glasses bend the moonlight between the crumbled rocks. / I hear his engine again. He looks much better. "Get in," he says. I get in. He takes me through miles and miles of dreamlands. Things that do and do not exist pass by, one after one. We are free to go anywhere we choose. He wants to go home to Rosario. / "Did it hurt to die?" I finally ask. "Well," he says, "it hurt before I died." "Were you afraid?" "Of course. I listened for you, but you never came." My stomach tightens. "I wanted to be there. I couldn't get to you. Don't you think it hurt me to let you die?" He smiles. "I know," he says. We pass the ruins of a railyard. "Your grandfather is proud of you," he says. I look at him. The tears come. I try to stop them, but they force their way out anyway. "I don't want to be without you," I blurt. He looks at me for a long while, then taps me on the knee. "You've got to stop crying. You sound like a little girl." Then: "You aren't without me. Remember that." His eyes are clear. "Where are your glasses?" I ask. "Back on the side of the road," he says. "But that's all right. I won't be needing them now." "Were you cognizant at the hospital?" I ask. "Yes," he says with disgust. "I was trapped inside that damned dead body. I hated that." "I'm sorry, Papá," I tell him. He looks at me. "Don't be sorry. You waste so much time that you need for yourself." I nod. "I closed the coffin," I say. "Thank you. I didn't want to be on display." I touch his arm. "Papá, did you . . . did you see God?" He smiles at me and turns on the radio. / When I was fourteen, my father and I spent hours laughing in the night about nothing, nothing at all. / The car is red. The driver's seat is torn. A beehive swells inside it. Bees fly where his eyes used to be. They fly through the air that used to touch his lips. They walk on the bent wheel that cracked his ribs. They sit where he used to sit. A slow, warm cascade of honey spreads over the traces of demolition. It is gold. It catches the sunlight and reflects the clouds that move in its depths, minute and sparkling white. Droplets reflect the blue of the sky. They hint at the smile in my father's eyes.

> Rosario, my earth
> little town in which I learned to love
> I dream of you, I miss you
> thinking someday I'll return
>
> Life took me from you,
> but I never, never forgot you
> my grandest illusion now
> is to return to you once more
> in the years of my nightfall

> — ALBERTO URREA
> June 2, 1915–January 10, 1977

Helena María Viramontes

Helena María Viramontes (b. 1954) was born in East Los Angeles, the daughter of a construction worker and a Chicana housewife who raised six daughters and three sons in a community that offered refuge for relatives and friends crossing the border from Mexico into California. As a child Viramontes witnessed "late night kitchen meetings where everyone talked and laughed in low voices" about having reached the United States, *el otro lado* ("the other side"). After graduation from Garfield High School, Viramontes worked twenty hours a week while earning her B.A. from Immaculate Heart College, one of five Chicanas in her class. She then entered the graduate program at the University of California at Irvine as a creative writing student, but she left in 1981 and completed the requirements for the M.E.A. degree after the publication of her stories.

As the critic Maria Herrera-Sobek has observed, "the 1980s decade witnessed an explosion in the literary output of Chicana authors," when Chicano-oriented publishers began to "risk investing in Mexican American women writers." Viramontes began to place her stories in small magazines such as *Maize* and *XhismArte Magazine* as well as the anthology *Cuentos: Stories by Latinas* (1983). Her first book, *The Moths and Other Stories*, was published in 1985 by Arte Publico Press in Houston, Texas. The same year the University of California at Irvine sponsored the first national conference on Mexican American women writers, resulting in the volume *Beyond Stereotypes: A Critical Analysis of Chicana Literature* (1985). Three years later Viramontes helped organize a second Chicana writers conference at Irvine and coedited the anthology *Chicana Creativity and Criticism* (1988), in which "Miss Clairol" was first published. In 1989 Viramontes received a National Endowment for the Arts Fellowship grant; she was also selected by Gabriel García Márquez to participate in a ten-day storytelling workshop sponsored by the Sundance Institute in Utah. After this experience she began adapting one of her short stories into a film script. In 1993 she published her second book of short stories, *Paris Rats in E.L.A.* Her first novel, *Under the Feet of Jesus*, followed in 1995.

As a woman of color, Viramontes believes that language is her most powerful tool for survival. She explains in "Why I Write" (1993) that "through writing, I have learned to protect the soles of my feet from the broken glass. . . . Writing is the only way I know how to pray." In 2007 she published *Their Dogs Came with Them*.

RELATED STORY
Sandra Cisneros, "Barbie-Q," page 290.

RELATED COMMENTARY
Carlos Fuentes, "Mexico, the United States, and the Multicultural Future," page 1430.

Miss Clairol

1988

ARLENE AND CHAMP WALK TO K-MART. The store is full of bins mounted with bargain buys from T-shirts to rubber sandals. They go to aisle 23, Cosmetics. Arlene, wearing bell bottom jeans two sizes too small, can't bend down to the Miss Clairol boxes, asks Champ.

— Which one mamá — says Champ, chewing her thumb nail.

— Shit, mija, I dunno. — Arlene smacks her gum, contemplating the decision—Maybe I need a change, tú sabes. What do you think? — She holds up a few blond strands with black roots. Arlene has burned the softness of her hair with peroxide; her hair is stiff, breaks at the ends and the needs plenty of Aqua Net hairspray to tease and tame her ratted hair, then folds it back into a high lump behind her head. For the last few months she has been a platinum "Light Ash" blond, before that a Miss Clairol "Flame" redhead, before that Champ couldn't even identify the color — somewhere between orange and brown, a "Sun Bronze." The only way Champ knows her mother's true hair color is by her roots which, like death, inevitably rise to the truth.

— I hate it, tú sabes, when I can't decide. — Arlene is wearing a pink, strapless tube top. Her stomach spills over the hip hugger jeans. Spits the gum onto the floor. — Fuck it. — And Champ follows her to the rows of nailpolish, next to the Maybelline rack of make-up, across the false eyelashes that look like insects on display in clear, plastic boxes. Arlene pulls out a particular color of nailpolish, looks at the bottom of the bottle for the price, puts it back, gets another. She has a tattoo of purple XXX's on her finger like a ring. She finally settles for a purple-blackish color, Ripe Plum, that Champ thinks looks like the color of Frankenstein's nails. She looks at her own stubby nails, chewed and gnawed.

Walking over to the eyeshadows, Arlene slowly slinks out another stick of gum from her back pocket, unwraps and crumbles the wrapper into a little ball, lets it fall to her feet. Smacks the gum.

— Grandpa Ham used to make chains with these gum wrappers — she says, toeing the wrapper on the floor with her rubber sandals, her toes dotted with old nailpolish. — He started one, tú sabes, that went from room to room. That was before he went nuts — she says, looking at the price of magenta eyeshadow. — Sabes que? What do you think? — lifting the eyeshadow to Champ.

— I dunno — responds Champ, shrugging her shoulders the way she always does when she is listening to something else, her own heartbeat, what Gregorio said on the phone yesterday, shrugs her shoulders when Miss Smith says OFELIA, answer my question. She is too busy thinking of things people otherwise dismiss like parentheses, but sticks to her like gum, like a hole on a shirt, like a tattoo, and sometimes she wishes she weren't born with such adhesiveness. The chain went from room to room, round and round like a web, she remembers. That was before he went nuts.

—Champ. You listening? Or in lala land again? —Arlene has her arms akimbo on a fold of flesh, pissed.

—I said, I dunno. —Champ whines back, still looking at the wrapper on the floor.

—Well you better learn, tú sabes, and fast too. Now think, will this color go good with Pancha's blue dress? —Pancha is Arlene's comadre. Since Arlene has a special date tonight, she lent Arlene her royal blue dress that she keeps in a plastic bag at the end of her closet. The dress is made of chiffon, with satin-like material underlining, so that when Arlene first tried it on and strutted about, it crinkled sounds of elegance. The dress fits too tight. Her plump arms squeeze through, her hips breathe in and hold their breath, the seams do all they can to keep the body contained. But Arlene doesn't care as long as it sounds right.

—I think it will —Champ says, and Arlene is very pleased.

—Think so? So do I mija. —

They walk out the double doors and Champ never remembers her mother paying.

It is four in the afternoon, but already Arlene is preparing for the date. She scrubs the tub, Art Labo on the radio, drops crystals of Jean Nate into the running water, lemon scent rises with the steam. the bathroom door ajar, she removes her top and her breasts flop and sag, pushes her jeans down with some difficulty, kicks them off, and steps in the tub.

—Mija. MIJA —she yells. —Mija, give me a few bobby pins. —She is worried about her hair frizzing and so wants to pin it up.

Her mother's voice is faint because Champ is in the closet. There are piles of clothes on the floor, hangers thrown askew and tangled, shoes all piled up or thrown on the top shelf. Champ is looking for her mother's special dress. Pancha says every girl has one at the end of her closet.

—Goddamn it Champ. —

Amidst the dirty laundry, the black hole of the closet, she finds nothing.

—NOW —

—Alright, ALRIGHT. Cheeze amá, stop yelling —says Champ, and goes in the steamy bathroom, checks the drawers. Hairbrushes jump out, rollers, strands of hair. Rummages through bars of soap, combs, eyeshadows, finds nothing; pulls open another drawer, powder, empty bottles of oil, manicure scissors, kotex, dye instructions crinkled and botched, finally, a few bobby pins.

After Arlene pins up her hair, she asks Champ, —Sabes que? Should I wear my hair up? Do I look good with it up? —Champ is sitting on the toilet.

—Yea, amá, you look real pretty. —

—Thanks mija —says Arlene. —Sabes que? When you get older I'll show you how you can look just as pretty —and she puts her head back, relaxes, like the Calgon commercials.

Champ lays on her stomach, T.V. on to some variety show with pogo stick dancers dressed in outfits of stretchy material and glitter. She is wearing one of Gregorio's white T-shirts, the ones he washes and bleaches himself so that the whiteness is impeccable. It drapes over her deflated ten year old body like a dress.

She is busy cutting out Miss Breck models from the stacks of old magazines Pancha found in the back of her mother's garage. Champ collects the array of honey colored haired women, put them in a shoe box with all her other special things.

Arlene is in the bathroom, wrapped in a towel. She has painted her eyebrows so that the two are arched and even, penciled thin and high. The magenta shades her eyelids. The towel slips, reveals one nipple blind from a cigarette burn, a date to forget. She rewraps the towel, likes her reflection, turns to her profile for additional inspection. She feels good, turns up the radio to . . . your love. For you loveeeee, I will do anything, I will do anything, forrr your love. For your kiss . . .

Champ looks on. From the open bathroom door, she can see Arlene, anticipation burning like a cigarette from her lips, sliding her shoulders to the ahhhh ahhhhh, and pouting her lips until the song ends. And Champ likes her mother that away.

Arlene carefully stretches black eyeliner, like a fallen question mark, outlines each eye. The work is delicate, her hand trembles cautiously, stops the process to review the face with each line. Arlene the mirror is not Arlene the face who has worn too many relationships, gotten too little sleep. The last touch is the chalky, beige lipstick.

By the time she is finished, her ashtray is full of cigarette butts, Champ's variety show is over, and Jackie Gleason's dancing girls come on to make kaleidoscope patterns with their long legs and arms. Gregorio is still not home, and Champ goes over to the window, checks the houses, the streets, corners, roams the sky with her eyes.

Arlene sits on the toilet, stretches up her nylons, clips them to her girdle. She feels good thinking about the way he will unsnap her nylons, and she will unroll them slowly, point her toes when she does.

Champ opens a can of Campbell soup, finds a perfect pot in the middle of a stack of dishes, pulls it out to the threatening rumble of the tower. She washes it out, pours the contents of the red can, turns the knob. After it boils, she puts the pot on the sink for it to cool down. She searches for a spoon.

Arlene is romantic. When Champ begins her period, she will tell her things that only women can know. She will tell her about the first time she made love with a boy, her awkwardness and shyness forcing them to go under the house, where the cool, refined soil made a soft mattress. How she closed her eyes and wondered what to expect, or how the penis was the softest skin she had ever felt against her, how it tickled her, searched for a place to connect. She was eleven and his name was Harry.

She will not tell Champ that her first fuck was a guy named Puppet who ejaculated prematurely, at the sight of her apricot vagina, so plump and fuzzy. — Pendejo — she said — you got it all over me. — She rubbed the gooey substance off her legs, her belly in disgust. Ran home to tell Rat and Pancha, her mouth open with laughter.

Arlene powder puffs under her arms, between her breasts, tilts a bottle of *Love Cries* perfume and dabs behind her ears, neck and breasts for those tight caressing songs which permit them to grind their bodies together until she can feel a bulge in his pants and she knows she's in for the night.

Jackie Gleason is a bartender in a saloon. He wears a black bow tie, a white apron, and is polishing a glass. Champ is watching him, sitting in the radius of the gray light, eating her soup from the pot.

Arlene is a romantic. She will dance until Pancha's dress turns a different color, dance until her hair becomes undone, her hips jiggering and quaking beneath a new pair of hosiery, her mascara shadowing under her eyes from the perspiration of the ritual, dance spinning herself into Miss Clairol, and stopping only when it is time to return to the sewing factory, time to wait out the next date, time to change hair color. Time to remember or to forget.

Champ sees Arlene from the window. She can almost hear Arlene's nylons rubbing against one another, hear the crinkling sound of satin when she gets in the blue and while shark-finned Dodge. Champ yells goodbye. It all sounds so right to Arlene who is too busy cranking up the window to hear her daughter.

Kurt Vonnegut Jr.

Kurt Vonnegut Jr. (1922–2007) was born on November 11 in Indianapolis, Indiana. The son of an architect and a homemaker, he attended Cornell University and Carnegie-Mellon University before the outbreak of World War II, when he interrupted his studies to serve in the U.S. Army. As a prisoner of war in Dresden, Germany, he survived a devastating air raid on February 13, 1945, by staying in a meat locker under a slaughterhouse during the bombing. After World War II, Vonnegut worked in public relations at the General Electric Company in Schenectady, New York, before becoming a freelance writer. *Player Piano*, his first novel, appeared in 1952, followed by a second fantasy novel, *The Sirens of Titan*, in 1959. Two years later he published *Mother Night*, a first-person fictional narrative about World War II. In 1969 Vonnegut published another novel that has become a classic based on his own experience of the Allies' fire-bombing of Dresden. Vonnegut titled it *Slaughterhouse-Five; or, The Children's Crusade: A Duty-Dance with Death, by Kurt Vonnegut, Jr., a Fourth-Generation German-American Now Living in Easy Circumstances on Cape Cod (and Smoking Too Much) Who, as an American Infantry Scout Hors de Combat, as a Prisoner of War, Witnessed the Fire-Bombing of Dresden, Germany, the Florence of the Elbe, Long Time Ago, and Survived to Tell the Tale; This Is a Novel Somewhat in the Telegraphic Schizophrenic Manner of Tales of the Planet Tralfamadore, Where the Flying Saucers Come From.*

After *Slaughterhouse-Five* was made into a film in 1972, Vonnegut's books achieved cult status. The critic Jerome Klinkowitz has observed that there was a "shift in taste" in the late 1960s and early 1970s that brought more serious appreciation to Vonnegut's fiction after a new generation of writers—Donald Barthelme, John Barth, Richard Brautigan, Jerzy Kosinski, Don DeLillo, Thomas Pynchon, and others—began publishing. "Ten years and several books their elder, Vonnegut by his long exile underground was well prepared to be the senior member of the new disruptive group."

Before Vonnegut's breakthrough as a novelist, he published short stories, like the fantasy tale "Harrison Bergeron," in *Canary in a Cathouse* (1961) and *Welcome to the Monkey House* (1968). John Updike understood that Vonnegut "began as a published writer with the so-called slick magazines"—*The Saturday Evening Post*, *Collier's*, and *The Ladies' Home Journal*. In the 1950s, slickness "was a verbal mechanism that raised the spectre of pain and then too easily delivered us from it. Yet the pain in Vonnegut was always real. Through the transpositions of science fiction, he found a way . . . to vaporize it, to scatter it on the plane of the cosmic and the comic." *Armageddon in Retrospect*, a collection of unpublished short stories, was published in 2008, posthumously.

Harrison Bergeron

1961

THE YEAR WAS 2081, and everybody was finally equal. They weren't only equal before God and the law. They were equal every which way. Nobody was smarter than anybody else. Nobody was better looking than anybody else. Nobody was stronger or quicker than anybody else. All this equality was due to the 211th, 212th, and 213th Amendments to the Constitution, and to the unceasing vigilance of agents of the United States Handicapper General.

Some things about living still weren't quite right, though. April, for instance, still drove people crazy by not being springtime. And it was in that clammy month that the H-G men took George and Hazel Bergeron's fourteen-year-old son, Harrison, away.

It was tragic, all right, but George and Hazel couldn't think about it very hard. Hazel had a perfectly average intelligence, which meant she couldn't think about anything except in short bursts. And George, while his intelligence was way above normal, had a little mental handicap radio in his ear. He was required by law to wear it at all times. It was tuned to a government transmitter. Every twenty seconds or so, the transmitter would send out some sharp noise to keep people like George from taking unfair advantage of their brains.

George and Hazel were watching television. There were tears on Hazel's cheeks, but she'd forgotten for the moment what they were about.

On the television screen were ballerinas.

A buzzer sounded in George's head. His thoughts fled in panic, like bandits from a burglar alarm.

"That was a real pretty dance, that dance they just did," said Hazel.

"Huh?" said George.

"That dance — it was nice," said Hazel.

"Yup," said George. He tried to think a little about the ballerinas. They weren't really very good — no better than anybody else would have been, anyway. They were burdened with sashweights and bags of birdshot, and their faces were masked, so that no one, seeing a free and graceful gesture or a pretty face, would feel like something the cat drug in. George was toying with the vague notion that maybe dancers shouldn't be handicapped. But he didn't get very far with it before another noise in his ear radio scattered his thoughts.

George winced. So did two out of the eight ballerinas.

Hazel saw him wince. Having no mental handicap herself, she had to ask George what the latest sound had been.

"Sounded like somebody hitting a milk bottle with a ball peen hammer," said George.

"I'd think it would be real interesting, hearing all the different sounds," said Hazel, a little envious. "All the things they think up."

"Um," said George.

"Only, if I was Handicapper General, you know what I would do?" said Hazel. Hazel, as a matter of fact, bore a strong resemblance to the Handicapper

General, a woman named Diana Moon Glampers. "If I was Diana Moon Glampers," said Hazel, "I'd have chimes on Sunday — just chimes. Kind of in honor of religion."

"I could think, if it was just chimes," said George.

"Well — maybe make 'em real loud," said Hazel. "I think I'd make a good Handicapper General."

"Good as anybody else," said George.

"Who knows better'n I do what normal is?" said Hazel.

"Right," said George. He began to think glimmeringly about his abnormal son who was now in jail, about Harrison, but a twenty-one-gun salute in his head stopped that.

"Boy!" said Hazel, "that was a doozy, wasn't it?"

It was such a doozy that George was white and trembling, and tears stood on the rims of his red eyes. Two of the eight ballerinas had collapsed to the studio floor, were holding their temples.

"All of a sudden you look so tired," said Hazel. "Why don't you stretch out on the sofa, so's you can rest your handicap bag on the pillows, honeybunch." She was referring to the forty-seven pounds of birdshot in a canvas bag, which was padlocked around George's neck. "Go on and rest the bag for a little while," she said. "I don't care if you're not equal to me for a while."

George weighed the bag with his hands. "I don't mind it" he said. "I don't notice it any more. It's just a part of me."

"You been so tired lately — kind of wore out," said Hazel. "If there was just some way we could make a little hole in the bottom of the bag, and just take out a few of them lead balls. Just a few."

"Two years in prison and two thousand dollars fine for every ball I took out," said George. "I don't call that a bargain."

"If you could just take a few out when you came home from work," said Hazel. "I mean — you don't compete with anybody around here. You just set around."

"If I tried to get away with it," said George, "then other people'd get away with it — and pretty soon we'd be right back to the dark ages again, with everybody competing against everybody else. You wouldn't like that, would you?"

"I'd hate it," said Hazel.

"There you are," said George. "The minute people start cheating on laws, what do you think happens to society?"

If Hazel hadn't been able to come up with an answer to this question, George couldn't have supplied one. A siren was going off in his head.

"Reckon it'd fall all apart," said Hazel.

"What would?" said George blankly.

"Society," said Hazel uncertainly. "Wasn't that what you just said?"

"Who knows?" said George.

The television program was suddenly interrupted for a news bulletin. It wasn't clear at first as to what the bulletin was about, since the announcer, like all announcers, had a serious speech impediment. For about half a minute, and in a state of high excitement, the announcer tried to say, "Ladies and gentlemen — "

He finally gave up, handed the bulletin to a ballerina to read.

"That's all right —" Hazel said of the announcer, "he tried. That's the big thing. He tried to do the best he could with what God gave him. He should get a nice raise for trying so hard."

"Ladies and gentlemen —" said the ballerina, reading the bulletin. She must have been extraordinarily beautiful, because the mask she wore was hideous. And it was easy to see that she was the strongest and most graceful of all the dancers, for her handicap bags were as big as those worn by two-hundred-pound men.

And she had to apologize at once for her voice, which was a very unfair voice for a woman to use. Her voice was a warm, luminous, timeless melody. "Excuse me —" she said, and she began again, making her voice absolutely uncompetitive.

"Harrison Bergeron, age fourteen," she said in a grackle squawk, "has just escaped from jail, where he was held on suspicion of plotting to overthrow the government. He is a genius and an athlete, is under-handicapped, and should be regarded as extremely dangerous."

A police photograph of Harrison Bergeron was flashed on the screen — upside down, then sideways, upside down again, then right side up. The picture showed the full length of Harrison against a background calibrated in feet and inches. He was exactly seven feet tall.

The rest of Harrison's appearance was Halloween and hardware. Nobody had ever born heavier handicaps. He had outgrown hindrances faster than the H-G men could think them up. Instead of a little ear radio for a mental handicap, he wore a tremendous pair of earphones, and spectacles with thick wavy lenses. The spectacles were intended to make him not only half blind, but to give him whanging headaches besides.

Scrap metal was hung all over him. Ordinarily, there was a certain symmetry, a military neatness to the handicaps issued to strong people, but Harrison looked like a walking junkyard. In the race of life, Harrison carried three hundred pounds.

And to offset his good looks, the H-G men required that he wear at all times a red rubber ball for a nose, keep his eyebrows shaved off, and cover his even white teeth with black caps at snaggle-tooth random.

"If you see this boy," said the ballerina, "do not — I repeat, do not — try to reason with him."

There was the shriek of a door being torn from its hinges.

Screams and barking cries of consternation came from the television set. The photograph of Harrison Bergeron on the screen jumped again and again, as though dancing to the tune of an earthquake.

George Bergeron correctly identified the earthquake, and well he might have — for many was the time his own home had danced to the same crashing tune. "My God —" said George, "that must be Harrison!"

The realization was blasted from his mind instantly by the sound of an automobile collision in his head.

When George could open his eyes again, the photograph of Harrison was gone. A living, breathing Harrison filled the screen.

Clanking, clownish, and huge, Harrison stood in the center of the studio. The knob of the uprooted studio door was still in his hand. Ballerinas, technicians, musicians, and announcers cowered on their knees before him, expecting to die.

"I am the Emperor!" cried Harrison. "Do you hear? I am the Emperor! Everybody must do what I say at once!" He stamped his foot and the studio shook.

"Even as I stand here — " he bellowed, "crippled, hobbled, sickened — I am a greater ruler than any man who ever lived! Now watch me become what I *can* become!"

Harrison tore the straps of his handicap harness like wet tissue paper, tore straps guaranteed to support five thousand pounds.

Harrison's scrap-iron handicaps crashed to the floor.

Harrison thrust his thumbs under the bars of the padlock that secured his head harness. The bar snapped like celery. Harrison smashed his headphones and spectacles against the wall.

He flung away his rubber-ball nose, revealed a man that would have awed Thor, the god of thunder.

"I shall now select my Empress!" he said, looking down on the cowering people. "Let the first woman who dares rise to her feet claim her mate and her throne!"

A moment passed, and then a ballerina arose, swaying like a willow.

Harrison plucked the mental handicap from her ear, snapped off her physical handicaps with marvelous delicacy. Last of all, he removed her mask.

She was blindingly beautiful.

"Now — " said Harrison, taking her hand, "shall we show the people the meaning of the word dance? Music!" he commanded.

The musicians scrambled back into their chairs, and Harrison stripped them of their handicaps, too. "Play your best," he told them, "and I'll make you barons and dukes and earls."

The music began. It was normal at first — cheap, silly, false. But Harrison snatched two musicians from their chairs, waved them like batons as he sang the music as he wanted it played. He slammed them back into their chairs.

The music began again and was much improved.

Harrison and his Empress merely listened to the music for a while — listened gravely, as though synchronizing their heartbeats with it.

They shifted their weights to their toes.

Harrison placed his big hands on the girl's tiny waist, letting her sense the weightlessness that would soon be hers.

And then, in an explosion of joy and grace, into the air they sprang!

Not only were the laws of the land abandoned, but the law of gravity and the laws of motion as well.

They reeled, whirled, swiveled, flounced, capered, gamboled, and spun.

They leaped like deer on the moon.

The studio ceiling was thirty feet high, but each leap brought the dancers nearer to it.

It became their obvious intention to kiss the ceiling.

They kissed it.

And then, neutralizing gravity with love and pure will, they remained suspended in air inches below the ceiling, and they kissed each other for a long, long time.

It was then that Diana Moon Glampers, the Handicapper General, came into the studio with a double-barreled ten-gauge shotgun. She fired twice, and the Emperor and the Empress were dead before they hit the floor.

Diana Moon Glampers loaded the gun again. She aimed at the musicians and told them they had ten seconds to get their handicaps back on.

It was then that the Bergerons' television tube burned out.

Hazel turned to comment about the blackout to George. But George had gone out into the kitchen for a can of beer.

George came back in with the beer, paused while a handicap signal shook him up. And then he sat down again. "You been crying?" he said to Hazel.

"Yup," she said.

"What about?" he said.

"I forgot," she said. "Something real sad on television."

"What was it?" he said.

"It's all kind of mixed up in my mind," said Hazel.

"Forget sad things," said George.

"I always do," said Hazel.

"That's my girl," said George. He winced. There was the sound of a rivetting gun in his head.

"Gee — I could tell that one was a doozy," said Hazel.

"You can say that again," said George.

"Gee — " said Hazel, "I could tell that one was a doozy."

Alice Walker

Alice Walker (b. 1944) was the eighth and youngest child of Willie Lee and Minnie Lou Grant Walker, sharecroppers in Eatonton, Georgia. Walker did well in school, encouraged by her teachers and her mother, whose stories she loved as "a walking history of our community." For two years, Walker attended Spelman College in Atlanta, the oldest college for black women in the United States. Then she studied at Sarah Lawrence College in New York, where she began her writing career by publishing a book of poetry, *Once* (1968). Since that time Walker has published several collections of poetry, novels, volumes of short stories, and *Living by the Word* (1988), a book of essays. Her best-known novel, *The Color Purple* (1982), made her the first black woman to win the Pulitzer Prize. Some later books are *The Temple of My Familiar* (1989), *Possessing the Secret of Joy* (1992), *Anything We Love Can Be Saved: A Writer's Activism* (1997), *We Are the Ones We Have Been Waiting For* (2006), and *The World Will Follow Joy* (2012).

Walker's works express her commitment to the idea of radical social change. She was active in the civil rights movement in Mississippi, where she met and married a civil rights lawyer from whom she separated after the birth of their daughter. In confronting the painful struggle of black history, Walker asserts that the creativity of black women, the extent to which they are permitted to express themselves, is a measure of the health of the entire American society. She calls herself a "womanist," her term for a feminist of color. In her definition, "womanism" is preferable to "feminism" because, as she has said,

> part of our tradition as black women is that we are universalists. Black children, yellow children, red children, brown children, that is the black woman's normal, day-to-day relationship. In my family alone, we are about four different colors. When a black woman looks at the world, it is so different . . . when I look at the people in Iran they look like kinfolk. When I look at the people in Cuba, they look like my uncles and nieces.

Walker credits many writers for influencing her prose style in her short fiction. Virginia Woolf, Zora Neale Hurston, and Gabriel García Márquez seem to Walker to be "like musicians; at one with their cultures and their historical subconscious." Her two books of stories show a clear progression of theme. The women of *In Love and Trouble* (1973) struggle against injustice almost in spite of themselves, as does the protagonist in "Everyday Use" from that collection; the heroines of *You Can't Keep a Good Woman Down* (1981) consciously challenge conventions. Walker has said, "Writing really helps you heal yourself. I think if you write long enough, you will be a healthy person. That is, if you write what you need to write, as opposed to what will make money, or what will make fame." "Everyday Use" was first published in *Harper's* in 1973.

RELATED COMMENTARY
Alice Walker, "Zora Neale Hurston: A Cautionary Tale and a Partisan View," page 1535.

Everyday Use

1973

I WILL WAIT FOR HER in the yard that Maggie and I made so clean and wavy yesterday afternoon. A yard like this is more comfortable than most people know. It is not just a yard. It is like an extended living room. When the hard clay is swept clean as a floor and the fine sand around the edges lined with tiny, irregular grooves, anyone can come and sit and look up into the elm tree and wait for the breezes that never come inside the house.

Maggie will be nervous until after her sister goes: she will stand hopelessly in corners, homely and ashamed of the burn scars down her arms and legs, eyeing her sister with a mixture of envy and awe. She thinks her sister has held life always in the palm of one hand, that "no" is a word the world never learned to say to her.

You've no doubt seen those TV shows where the child who has "made it" is confronted, as a surprise, by her own mother and father, tottering in weakly from backstage. (A pleasant surprise, of course: What would they do if parent and child came on the show only to curse out and insult each other?) On TV mother and child embrace and smile into each other's faces. Sometimes the mother and father weep, the child wraps them in her arms and leans across the table to tell how she would not have made it without their help. I have seen these programs.

Sometimes I dream a dream in which Dee and I are suddenly brought together on a TV program of this sort. Out of a dark and soft-seated limousine I am ushered into a bright room filled with many people. There I meet a smiling, gray, sporty man like Johnny Carson who shakes my hand and tells me what a fine girl I have. Then we are on the stage and Dee is embracing me with tears in her eyes. She pins on my dress a large orchid, even though she has told me once that she thinks orchids are tacky flowers.

In real life I am a large, big-boned woman with rough, man-working hands. In the winter I wear flannel nightgowns to bed and overalls during the day. I can kill and clean a hog as mercilessly as a man. My fat keeps me hot in zero weather. I can work outside all day, breaking ice to get water for washing; I can eat pork liver cooked over the open fire minutes after it comes steaming from the hog. One winter I knocked a bull calf straight in the brain between the eyes with a sledge hammer and had the meat hung up to chill before nightfall. But of course all this does not show on television. I am the way my daughter would want me to be: a hundred pounds lighter, my skin like an uncooked barley pancake. My hair glistens in the hot bright lights. Johnny Carson has much to do to keep up with my quick and witty tongue.

But that is a mistake. I know even before I wake up. Who ever knew a Johnson with a quick tongue? Who can even imagine me looking a strange white man in the eye? It seems to me I have talked to them always with one foot raised in flight, with my head turned in whichever way is farthest from them. Dee, though. She would always look anyone in the eye. Hesitation was no part of her nature.

"How do I look, Mama?" Maggie says, showing just enough of her thin body enveloped in pink skirt and red blouse for me to know she's there, almost hidden by the door.

"Come out into the yard," I say.

Have you ever seen a lame animal, perhaps a dog run over by some careless person rich enough to own a car, sidle up to someone who is ignorant enough to be kind to him? That is the way my Maggie walks. She has been like this, chin on chest, eyes on ground, feet in shuffle, ever since the fire that burned the other house to the ground.

Dee is lighter than Maggie, with nicer hair and a fuller figure. She's a woman now, though sometimes I forget. How long ago was it that the other house burned? Ten, twelve years? Sometimes I can still hear the flames and feel Maggie's arms sticking to me, her hair smoking and her dress falling off her in little black papery flakes. Her eyes seemed stretched open, blazed open by the flames reflected in them. And Dee. I see her standing off under the sweet gum tree she used to dig gum out of; a look of concentration on her face as she watched the last dingy gray board of the house fall in toward the red-hot brick chimney. Why don't you do a dance around the ashes? I'd wanted to ask her. She had hated the house that much.

I used to think she hated Maggie, too. But that was before we raised the money, the church and me, to send her to Augusta to school. She used to read to us without pity; forcing words, lies, other folks' habits, whole lives upon us two, sitting trapped and ignorant underneath her voice. She washed us in a river of make-believe, burned us with a lot of knowledge we didn't necessarily need to know. Pressed us to her with the serious way she read, to shove us away at just the moment, like dimwits, we seemed about to understand.

Dee wanted nice things. A yellow organdy dress to wear to her graduation from high school; black pumps to match a green suit she'd made from an old suit somebody gave me. She was determined to stare down any disaster in her efforts. Her eyelids would not flicker for minutes at a time. Often I fought off the temptation to shake her. At sixteen she had a style of her own: and knew what style was.

I never had an education myself. After second grade the school was closed down. Don't ask me why: in 1927 colored asked fewer questions than they do now. Sometimes Maggie reads to me. She stumbles along good-naturedly but can't see well. She knows she is not bright. Like good looks and money, quickness passed her by. She will marry John Thomas (who has mossy teeth in an earnest face) and then I'll be free to sit here and I guess just sing church songs to myself. Although I never was a good singer. Never could carry a tune. I was always better at a man's job. I used to love to milk till I was hooked in the side in '49. Cows are soothing and slow and don't bother you, unless you try to milk them the wrong way.

I have deliberately turned my back on the house. It is three rooms, just like the one that burned, except the roof is tin; they don't make shingle roofs any more. There are no real windows, just some holes cut in the sides, like the portholes in a ship, but not round and not square, with rawhide holding the shutters up on the outside. This house is in a pasture, too, like the other one. No doubt when Dee sees it she will want to tear it down. She wrote me once that no matter where we "choose" to live, she will manage to come see us. But she will never bring her friends. Maggie and I thought about this and Maggie asked me, "Mama, when did Dee ever *have* any friends?"

She had a few. Furtive boys in pink shirts hanging about on washday after school. Nervous girls who never laughed. Impressed with her they worshiped the well-turned phrase, the cute shape, the scalding humor that erupted like bubbles in lye. She read to them.

When she was courting Jimmy T she didn't have much time to pay to us, but turned all her faultfinding power on him. He *flew* to marry a cheap city gal from a family of ignorant flashy people. She hardly had time to recompose herself.

When she comes I will meet — but there they are!

Maggie attempts to make a dash for the house, in her shuffling way, but I stay her with my hand. "Come back here," I say. And she stops and tries to dig a well in the sand with her toe.

It is hard to see them clearly through the strong sun. But even the first glimpse of leg out of the car tells me it is Dee. Her feet were always neat-looking, as if God himself had shaped them with a certain style. From the other side of the car comes a short, stocky man. Hair is all over his head a foot long and hanging from his chin like a kinky mule tail. I hear Maggie suck in her breath. "Uhnnnh," is what it sounds like. Like when you see the wriggling end of a snake just in front of your foot on the road. "Uhnnnh."

Dee next. A dress down to the ground, in this hot weather. A dress so loud it hurts my eyes. There are yellows and oranges enough to throw back the light of the sun. I feel my whole face warming from the heat waves it throws out. Earrings gold, too, and hanging down to her shoulders. Bracelets dangling and making noises when she moves her arm up to shake the folds of the dress out of her armpits. The dress is loose and flows, and as she walks closer, I like it. I hear Maggie go "Uhnnnh" again. It is her sister's hair. It stands straight up like the wool on a sheep. It is black as night and around the edges are two long pigtails that rope about like small lizards disappearing behind her ears.

"Wa-su-zo-Tean-o!" she says, coming on in that gliding way the dress makes her move. The short stocky fellow with the hair to his navel is all grinning and he follows up with "Asalamalakim, my mother and sister!" He moves to hug Maggie but she falls back, right up against the back of my chair. I feel her trembling there and when I look up I see the perspiration falling off her chin.

"Don't get up," says Dee. Since I am stout it takes something of a push. You can see me trying to move a second or two before I make it. She turns, showing white heels through her sandals, and goes back to the car. Out she peeks next with a Polaroid. She stoops down quickly and lines up picture after picture of me sitting there in front of the house with Maggie cowering behind me. She never takes a shot without making sure the house is included. When a cow comes nibbling around the edge of the yard she snaps it and me *and* the house. Then she puts the Polaroid in the back seat of the car, and comes up and kisses me on the forehead.

Meanwhile Asalamalakim is going through the motions with Maggie's hand. Maggie's hand is as limp as a fish, and probably as cold, despite the sweat, and she keeps trying to pull it back. It looks like Asalamalakim wants to shake hands but wants to do it fancy. Or maybe he don't know how people shake hands. Anyhow, he soon gives up on Maggie.

"Well," I say. "Dee."

"No, Mama," she says. "Not 'Dee,' Wangero Leewanika Kemanjo!"

"What happened to 'Dee'?" I wanted to know.

"She's dead," Wangero said. "I couldn't bear it any longer being named after the people who oppress me."

"You know as well as me you was named after your aunt Dicie," I said. Dicie is my sister. She named Dee. We called her "Big Dee" after Dee was born.

"But who was *she* named after?" asked Wangero.

"I guess after Grandma Dee," I said.

"And who was she named after?" asked Wangero.

"Her mother," I said, and saw Wangero was getting tired. "That's about as far back as I can trace it," I said. Though, in fact, I probably could have carried it back beyond the Civil War through the branches.

"Well," said Asalamalakim, "there you are."

"Uhnnnh," I heard Maggie say.

"There I was not," I said, "before 'Dicie' cropped up in our family, so why should I try to trace it that far back?"

He just stood there grinning, looking down on me like somebody inspecting a Model A car. Every once in a while he and Wangero sent eye signals over my head.

"How do you pronounce this name?" I asked.

"You don't have to call me by it if you don't want to," said Wangero.

"Why shouldn't I?" I asked. "If that's what you want us to call you, we'll call you."

"I know it might sound awkward at first," said Wangero.

"I'll get used to it," I said. "Ream it out again."

Well, soon we got the name out of the way. Asalamalakim had a name twice as long and three times as hard. After I tripped over it two or three times he told me to just call him Hakim-a-barber. I wanted to ask him was he a barber, but I didn't really think he was, so I didn't ask.

"You must belong to those beef-cattle peoples down the road," I said. They said "Asalamalakim" when they met you, too, but they didn't shake hands. Always too busy: feeding the cattle, fixing the fences, putting up salt-lick shelters, throwing down hay. When the white folks poisoned some of the herd the men stayed up all night with rifles in their hands. I walked a mile and a half just to see the sight.

Hakim-a-barber said, "I accept some of their doctrines, but farming and raising cattle is not my style." (They didn't tell me, and I didn't ask, whether Wangero [Dee] had really gone and married him.)

We sat down to eat and right away he said he didn't eat collards and pork was unclean. Wangero, though, went on through the chitlins and corn bread, the greens and everything else. She talked a blue streak over the sweet potatoes. Everything delighted her. Even the fact that we still used the benches her daddy made for the table when we couldn't afford to buy chairs.

"Oh, Mama!" she cried. Then turned to Hakim-a-barber. "I never knew how lovely these benches are. You can feel the rump prints," she said, running her hands underneath her and along the bench. Then she gave a sigh and her hand closed over Grandma Dee's butter dish. "That's it!" she said. "I knew there was something I wanted to ask you if I could have." She jumped up from the table and went over in the corner where the churn stood, the milk in it clabber by now. She looked at the churn and looked at it.

"This churn top is what I need," she said. "Didn't Uncle Buddy whittle it out of a tree you all used to have?"

"Yes," I said.

"Uh-huh," she said happily. "And I want the dasher, too."

"Uncle Buddy whittle that, too?" asked the barber.

Dee (Wangero) looked up at me.

"Aunt Dee's first husband whittled the dash," said Maggie so low you almost couldn't hear her. "His name was Henry, but they called him Stash."

"Maggie's brain is like an elephant's," Wangero said, laughing. "I can use the churn top as a centerpiece for the alcove table," she said, sliding a plate over the churn, "and I'll think of something artistic to do with the dasher."

When she finished wrapping the dasher the handle stuck out. I took it for a moment in my hands. You didn't even have to look close to see where hands pushing the dasher up and down to make butter had left a kind of sink in the wood. In fact, there were a lot of small sinks; you could see where thumbs and fingers had sunk into the wood. It was beautiful light yellow wood, from a tree that grew in the yard where Big Dee and Stash had lived.

After dinner Dee (Wangero) went to the trunk at the foot of my bed and started rifling through it. Maggie hung back in the kitchen over the dishpan. Out came Wangero with two quilts. They had been pieced by Grandma Dee and then Big Dee and me had hung them on the quilt frames on the front porch and quilted them. One was in the Lone Star pattern. The other was Walk Around the Mountain. In both of them were scraps of dresses Grandma Dee had worn fifty and more years ago. Bits and pieces of Grandpa Jarrell's Paisley shirts. And one teeny faded blue piece, about the size of a penny matchbox, that was from Great Grandpa Ezra's uniform that he wore in the Civil War.

"Mama," Wangero said sweet as a bird. "Can I have these old quilts?"

I heard something fall in the kitchen, and a minute later the kitchen door slammed.

"Why don't you take one or two of the others?" I asked. "These old things was just done by me and Big Dee from some tops your grandma pieced before she died."

"No," said Wangero. "I don't want those. They are stitched around the borders by machine."

"That'll make them last better," I said.

"That's not the point," said Wangero. "These are all pieces of dresses Grandma used to wear. She did all this stitching by hand. Imagine!" She held the quilts securely in her arms, stroking them.

"Some of the pieces, like those lavender ones, come from old clothes her mother handed down to her," I said, moving up to touch the quilts. Dee (Wangero) moved back just enough so that I couldn't reach the quilts. They already belonged to her.

"Imagine!" she breathed again, clutching them closely to her bosom.

"The truth is," I said, "I promised to give them quilts to Maggie, for when she marries John Thomas."

She gasped like a bee had stung her.

"Maggie can't appreciate these quilts!" she said. "She'd probably be backward enough to put them to everyday use."

"I reckon she would," I said. "God knows I been saving 'em for long enough with nobody using 'em. I hope she will!" I didn't want to bring up how I had offered Dee (Wangero) a quilt when she went away to college. Then she had told me they were old-fashioned, out of style.

"But they're *priceless*!" she was saying now, furiously; for she has a temper. "Maggie would put them on the bed and in five years they'd be in rags. Less than that!"

"She can always make some more," I said. "Maggie knows how to quilt."

Dee (Wangero) looked at me with hatred. "You just will not understand. The point is these quilts, *these* quilts!"

"Well," I said, stumped. "What would *you* do with them?"

"Hang them," she said. As if that was the only thing you *could* do with quilts.

Maggie by now was standing in the door. I could almost hear the sound her feet made as they scraped over each other.

"She can have them, Mama," she said, like somebody used to never winning anything, or having anything reserved for her. "I can 'member Grandma Dee without the quilts."

I looked at her hard. She had filled her bottom lip with checkerberry snuff and it gave her face a kind of dopey, hangdog look. It was Grandma Dee and Big Dee who taught her how to quilt herself. She stood there with her scarred hands hidden in the folds of her skirt. She looked at her sister with something like fear but she wasn't mad at her. This was Maggie's portion. This was the way she knew God to work.

When I looked at her like that something hit me in the top of my head and ran down to the soles of my feet. Just like when I'm in church and the spirit of God touches me and I get happy and shout. I did something I never had done before: hugged Maggie to me, then dragged her on into the room, snatched the quilts out of Miss Wangero's hands and dumped them into Maggie's lap. Maggie just sat there on my bed with her mouth open.

"Take one or two of the others," I said to Dee.

But she turned without a word and went out to Hakim-a-barber.

"You just don't understand," she said, as Maggie and I came out to the car.

"What don't I understand?" I wanted to know.

"Your heritage," she said. And then she turned to Maggie, kissed her, and said, "You ought to try to make something of yourself, too, Maggie. It's really a new day for us. But from the way you and Mama still live you'd never know it."

She put on some sunglasses that hid everything above the tip of her nose and her chin.

Maggie smiled; maybe at the sunglasses. But a real smile, not scared. After we watched the car dust settle I asked Maggie to bring me a dip of snuff. And then the two of us sat there just enjoying, until it was time to go in the house and go to bed.

David Foster Wallace

David Foster Wallace (1962–2008) was born and raised in Urbana, the son of a philosophy professor at the University of Illinois. Wallace graduated from Amherst College in 1986. Soon afterwards he published his first two books of fiction, the novel *The Broom of the System* (1987) and the short story collection *Girl with Curious Hair* (1990), which included "Everything is Green." In the late 1980s and early 1990s, after a brief enrollment in Harvard University's doctoral program in philosophy, he said that he "went through a real bad three years" of depression when he lived in Boston and Syracuse. During this time he coauthored the non-fiction book *Signifying Rappers: Rap and Race in the Urban Present* (1990) with Mark Costello.

In 1993 Wallace began teaching creative writing and English literature at Illinois State University, where he completed his grandly conceived second novel, *Infinite Jest* (1996). In this book he tried to avoid what he considered the excesses of avant-garde fiction, which he described as "hellaciously unfun to read," and the vapid superficiality of most commercial fiction. Dense and dark, at 981 pages it became his breakthrough novel, an ingenious satire on contemporary American life. After its publication, Wallace became the recipient of a MacArthur Foundation "genius grant" and taught creative writing at Pomona College.

Wallace's extravagant treatment of everyday events has been called "hysterical realism," a term coined by critic James Wood in an essay on Zadie Smith's novel *White Teeth*, reprinted in Wood's book *The Irresponsible Self: On Laughter and the Novel* (2004). This sort of inflated, manic prose is also found in Wallace's next two collections of short fiction, *Brief Interviews with Hideous Men* (1999) and *Oblivion* (2004). This unfinished novel *The Pale King* (2011) was published posthumously after his suicide.

Everything Is Green

1989

SHE SAYS I DO NOT CARE if you believe me or not, it is the truth, go on and believe what you want to. So it is for sure that she is lying. When it is the truth she will go crazy trying to get you to believe her. So I feel like I know.

She lights up and looks off away from me, looking sly with her cigarette in light through a wet window, and I can not feel what to say.

I say Mayfly I can not feel what to do or say or believe you any more. But there is things I know. I know I am older and you are not. And I give to you all I got to give you, with my hands and my heart both. Every thing that is inside me I have gave you. I have been keeping it together and working steady every day. I have made you the reason I got for what I always do. I have tried to make a home to give to you, for you to be in, and for it to be nice.

I light up myself and I throw the match in the sink with other matches and dishes and a sponge and such things.

I say Mayfly my heart has been down the road and back for you but I am forty-eight years old. It is time I have got to not let things just carry me by any more. I got to use some time that is still mine to try to make everything feel right. I got to try to feel how I need to. In me there is needs which you can not even see any more, because there is too many needs in you that are in the way.

She does not say any thing and I look at her window and I can feel that she knows I know about it, and she shifts her self on my sofa lounger. She brings her legs up underneath her in some shorts.

I say it really does not matter what I seen or what I think I seen. That is not it any more. I know I am older and you are not. But now I am feeling like there is all of me going in to you and nothing of you is coming back any more.

Her hair is up with a barret and pins and her chin is in her hand, it's early, she looks like she is dreaming out at the clean light through the wet window over my sofa lounger.

Everything is green she says. Look how green it all is Mitch. How can you say the things you say you feel like when everything outside is green like it is.

The window over the sink of my kitchenet is cleaned off from the hard rain last night and it is a morning with a sun, it is still early, and there is a mess of green out. The trees are green and some grass out past the speed bumps is green and slicked down. But every thing is not green. The other trailers are not green and my card table out with puddles in lines and beer cans and butts floating in the ash trays is not green, or my truck, or the gravel of the lot, or the big wheel toy that is on its side under a clothes line without clothes on it by the next trailer, where the guy has got him some kids.

Everything is green she is saying. She is whispering it and the whisper is not to me no more I know.

I chuck my smoke and turn hard from the morning with the taste of something true in my mouth. I turn hard toward her in the light on the sofa lounger.

She is looking outside, from where she is sitting, and I look at her, and there is something in me that can not close up, in that looking. Mayfly has a body. And she is my morning. Say her name.

Eudora Welty

Eudora Welty (1909–2001) was born in Jackson, Mississippi, where she spent nearly her whole life. She had a predominately tranquil view of the South, so her stories and novels provide a strong contrast to the turbulent fiction of William Faulkner and Richard Wright, who also wrote about Mississippi. Welty grew up as one of three children in a close-knit family living two blocks from the state capitol. Her father was the president of an insurance company, and her mother was a thrifty housewife who kept a Jersey cow in a little pasture behind the backyard. An insatiable reader as a child, Welty began writing spontaneously and continued, without any particular encouragement or any plan to be a writer, during her years in college. In her mid-twenties she started to publish stories in the *Southern Review,* but she credited the persistence of her New York literary agent with helping her get a story published in the *Atlantic Monthly* in 1941. This event led directly to the publication of her first book of stories, *A Curtain of Green,* the same year.

During World War II Welty was a staff member of the *New York Times Book Review* while she lived at home with her mother and continued to write short fiction. Another collection was published in 1943 as *The Wide Net and Other Stories.* After leaving her newspaper work, she turned a short story into her first novel, *Delta Wedding* (1946), on the advice of her agent. She produced several other story collections over the years. Her novel *The Optimist's Daughter* won the Pulitzer Prize in 1972. In 1980 *The Collected Stories of Eudora Welty* appeared, forty-one stories in all. Welty was also a fine critic of the short story. Her essays and reviews of the work of writers such as Anton Chekhov, Willa Cather, Katherine Anne Porter, Virginia Woolf, and Isak Dinesen, as well as some comments on her own work, were collected in *The Eye of the Story* (1977). Eight years later the book *Conversations with Eudora Welty* was a best-seller.

In the preface to her collected stories, Welty stated,

> I have been told, both in approval and in accusation, that I seem to love all my characters. What I do in writing of any character is to try to enter into the mind, heart, and skin of a human being who is not myself. Whether this happens to be a man or a woman, old or young, with skin black or white, the primary challenge lies in making the jump itself. It is the act of a writer's imagination that I set most high.

Welty's usual manner was a calm celebration of her characters' minor victories, as in "A Worn Path." The e-mail software used by millions of people was named after her and her story "Why I Live at the P.O." According to inventor Steve Dorner, he felt as if he "lived at the post office" while developing e-mail, so he transposed the short story title into his slogan, "Bringing the P.O. to Where You Live." Later Dorner publicly apologized for being "presumptuous" enough to name his e-mail program Eudora, after a living person, but Welty's literary agent said the writer had been "pleased and amused" to hear of the tribute.

RELATED STORY
Jamie Quatro, "I.7 to Tennessee," page 1157.

RELATED COMMENTARY
Eudora Welty, "Is Phoenix Jackson's Grandson Really Dead?" page 1536.

A Worn Path

1941

IT WAS DECEMBER — a bright frozen day in the early morning. Far out in the country there was an old Negro woman with her head tied in a red rag, coming along a path through the pinewoods. Her name was Phoenix Jackson. She was very old and small and she walked slowly in the dark pine shadows, moving a little from side to side in her steps, with the balanced heaviness and light- ness of a pendulum in a grandfather clock. She carried a thin, small cane made from an umbrella, and with this she kept tapping the frozen earth in front of her. This made a grave and persistent noise in the still air, that seemed medita- tive like the chirping of a solitary little bird.

She wore a dark striped dress reaching down to her shoe tops, and an equally long apron of bleached sugar sacks, with a full pocket: all neat and tidy, but every time she took a step she might have fallen over her shoelaces, which dragged from her unlaced shoes. She looked straight ahead. Her eyes were blue with age. Her skin had a pattern all its own of numberless branch- ing wrinkles and as though a whole little tree stood in the middle of her fore- head, but a golden color ran underneath, and the two knobs of her cheeks were illumined by a yellow burning under the dark. Under the red rag her hair came down on her neck in the frailest of ringlets, still black, and with an odor like copper.

Now and then there was a quivering in the thicket. Old Phoenix said, "Out of my way, all you foxes, owls, beetles, jack rabbits, coons and wild ani- mals!... Keep out from under these feet, little bobwhites.... Keep the big wild hogs out of my path. Don't let none of those come running my direction. I got a long way." Under her small black-freckled hand her cane, limber as a buggy whip, would switch at the brush as if to rouse up any hiding things.

On she went. The woods were deep and still. The sun made the pine needles almost too bright to look at, up where the wind rocked. The cones dropped as light as feathers. Down in the hollow was the mourning dove — it was not too late for him.

The path ran up a hill. "Seem like there is chains about my feet, time I get this far," she said, in the voice of argument old people keep to use with themselves. "Something always take a hold of me on this hill — pleads I should stay."

After she got to the top she turned and gave a full, severe look behind her where she had come. "Up through pines," she said at length. "Now down through oaks."

Her eyes opened their widest, and she started down gently. But before she got to the bottom of the hill a bush caught her dress.

Her fingers were busy and intent, but her skirts were full and long, so that before she could pull them free in one place they were caught in another. It was not possible to allow the dress to tear. "I in the thorny bush," she said. "Thorns, you doing your appointed work. Never want to let folks pass, no sir. Old eyes thought you was a pretty little *green* bush."

Finally, trembling all over, she stood free, and after a moment dared to stoop for her cane.

"Sun so high!" she cried, leaning back and looking, while the thick tears went over her eyes. "The time getting all gone here."

At the foot of this hill was a place where a log was laid across the creek.

"Now comes the trial," said Phoenix.

Putting her right foot out, she mounted the log and shut her eyes. Lifting her skirt, leveling her cane fiercely before her, like a festival figure in some parade, she began to march across. Then she opened her eyes and she was safe on the other side.

"I wasn't as old as I thought," she said.

But she sat down to rest. She spread her skirts on the bank around her and folded her hands over her knees. Up above her was a tree in a pearly cloud of mistletoe. She did not dare to close her eyes, and when a little boy brought her a plate with a slice of marble-cake on it she spoke to him. "That would be acceptable," she said. But when she went to take it there was just her own hand in the air.

So she left that tree, and had to go through a barbed-wire fence. There she had to creep and crawl, spreading her knees and stretching her fingers like a baby trying to climb the steps. But she talked loudly to herself: she could not let her dress be torn now, so late in the day, and she could not pay for having her arm or her leg sawed off if she got caught fast where she was.

At last she was safe through the fence and risen up out in the clearing. Big dead trees, like black men with one arm, were standing in the purple stalks of the withered cotton field. There sat a buzzard.

"Who you watching?"

In the furrow she made her way along.

"Glad this not the season for bulls," she said, looking sideways, "and the good Lord made his snakes to curl up and sleep in the winter. A pleasure I don't see no two-headed snake coming around that tree, where it come once. It took a while to get by him, back in the summer."

She passed through the old cotton and went into a field of dead corn. It whispered and shook and was taller than her head. "Through the maze now," she said, for there was no path.

Then there was something tall, black, and skinny there, moving before her.

At first she took it for a man. It could have been a man dancing in the field. But she stood still and listened, and it did not make a sound. It was as silent as a ghost.

"Ghost," she said sharply, "who be you the ghost of? For I have heard of nary death close by."

But there was no answer — only the ragged dancing in the wind.

She shut her eyes, reached out her hand, and touched a sleeve. She found a coat and inside that an emptiness, cold as ice.

"You scarecrow," she said. Her face lighted. "I ought to be shut up for good," she said with laughter. "My senses is gone. I too old. I the oldest people I ever know. Dance, old scarecrow," she said, "while I dancing with you."

She kicked her foot over the furrow, and with mouth drawn down, shook her head once or twice in a little strutting way. Some husks blew down and whirled in streamers about her skirts.

Then she went on, parting her way from side to side with the cane, through the whispering field. At last she came to the end, to a wagon track where the silver grass blew between the red ruts. The quail were walking around like pullets, seeming all dainty and unseen.

"Walk pretty," she said. "This the easy place. This the easy going."

She followed the track, swaying through the quiet bare fields, through the little strings of trees silver in their dead leaves, past cabins silver from weather, with the doors and windows boarded shut, all like old women under a spell sitting there. "I walking in their sleep," she said, nodding her head vigorously.

In a ravine she went where a spring was silently flowing through a hollow log. Old Phoenix bent and drank. "Sweet-gum makes the water sweet," she said, and drank more. "Nobody know who made this well, for it was here when I was born."

The track crossed a swampy part where the moss hung as white as lace from every limb. "Sleep on, alligators, and blow your bubbles." Then the track went into the road.

Deep, deep the road went down between the high green-colored banks. Overhead the live-oaks met, and it was as dark as a cave.

A black dog with a lolling tongue came up out of the weeds by the ditch. She was meditating, and not ready, and when he came at her she only hit him a little with her cane. Over she went in the ditch, like a little puff of milkweed.

Down there, her senses drifted away. A dream visited her, and she reached her hand up, but nothing reached down and gave her a pull. So she lay there and presently went to talking. "Old woman," she said to herself, "that black dog come up out of the weeds to stall you off, and now there he sitting on his fine tail, smiling at you."

A white man finally came along and found her — a hunter, a young man, with his dog on a chain.

"Well, Granny!" he laughed. "What are you doing there?"

"Lying on my back like a June-bug waiting to be turned over, mister," she said, reaching up her hand.

He lifted her up, gave her a swing in the air, and set her down. "Anything broken, Granny?"

"No sir, them old dead weeds is springy enough," said Phoenix, when she had got her breath. "I thank you for your trouble."

"Where do you live, Granny?" he asked, while the two dogs were growling at each other.

"Away back yonder, sir, behind the ridge. You can't even see it from here."

"On your way home?"

"No sir, I going to town."

"Why, that's too far! That's as far as I walk when I come out myself, and I get something for my trouble." He patted the stuffed bag he carried, and there hung down a little closed claw. It was one of the bobwhites, with its beak hooked bitterly to show it was dead. "Now you go on home, Granny!"

"I bound to go to town, mister," said Phoenix. "The time come around."

He gave another laugh, filling the whole landscape. "I know you old colored people! Wouldn't miss going to town to see Santa Claus!"

But something held old Phoenix very still. The deep lines in her face went into a fierce and different radiation. Without warning, she had seen with her own eyes a flashing nickel fall out of the man's pocket onto the ground.

"How old are you, Granny?" he was saying.

"There is no telling, mister," she said, "no telling."

Then she gave a little cry and clapped her hands and said, "Git on away from here, dog! Look! Look at that dog!" She laughed as if in admiration. "He ain't scared of nobody. He a big black dog." She whispered, "Sic him!"

"Watch me get rid of that cur," said the man. "Sic him, Pete! Sic him!"

Phoenix heard the dogs fighting, and heard the man running and throwing sticks. She even heard a gunshot. But she was slowly bending forward by that time, further and further forward, the lid stretched down over her eyes, as if she were doing this in her sleep. Her chin was lowered almost to her knees. The yellow palm of her hand came out from the fold of her apron. Her fingers slid down and along the ground under the piece of money with the grace and care they would have in lifting an egg from under a setting hen. Then she slowly straightened up, she stood erect, and the nickel was in her apron pocket. A bird flew by. Her lips moved. "God watching me the whole time. I come to stealing."

The man came back, and his own dog panted about them. "Well, I scared him off that time," he said, and then he laughed and lifted his gun and pointed it at Phoenix.

She stood straight and faced him.

"Doesn't the gun scare you?" he said, still pointing it.

"No, sir, I seen plenty go off closer by, in my day, and for less than what I done," she said, holding utterly still.

He smiled, and shouldered the gun. "Well, Granny," he said, "you must be a hundred years old, and scared of nothing. I'd give you a dime if I had any money with me. But you take my advice and stay home, and nothing will happen to you."

"I bound to go on my way, mister," said Phoenix. She inclined her head in the red rag. Then they went in different directions, but she could hear the gun shooting again and again over the hill.

She walked on. The shadows hung from the oak trees to the road like curtains. Then she smelled wood-smoke, and smelled the river, and she saw a steeple and the cabins on their steep steps. Dozens of little black children whirled around her. There ahead was Natchez shining. Bells were ringing. She walked on.

In the paved city it was Christmas time. There were red and green electric lights strung and crisscrossed everywhere, and all turned on in the daytime. Old Phoenix would have been lost if she had not distrusted her eyesight and depended on her feet to know where to take her.

She paused quietly on the sidewalk where people were passing by. A lady came along in the crowd, carrying an armful of red-, green-, and silver-wrapped presents; she gave off perfume like the red roses in hot summer, and Phoenix stopped her.

"Please, missy, will you lace up my shoe?" She held up her foot.

"What do you want, Grandma?"

"See my shoe," said Phoenix. "Do all right for out in the country, but wouldn't look right to go in a big building."

"Stand still then, Grandma," said the lady. She put her packages down on the sidewalk beside her and laced and tied both shoes tightly.

"Can't lace 'em with a cane," said Phoenix. "Thank you, missy. I doesn't mind asking a nice lady to tie up my shoe, when I gets out on the street."

Moving slowly and from side to side, she went into the big building, and into a tower of steps, where she walked up and around and around until her feet knew to stop.

She entered a door, and there she saw nailed up on the wall the document that had been stamped with the gold seal and framed in the gold frame, which matched the dream that was hung up in her head.

"Here I be," she said. There was a fixed and ceremonial stiffness over her body.

"A charity case, I suppose," said an attendant who sat at the desk before her.

But Phoenix only looked above her head. There was sweat on her face, the wrinkles in her skin shone like a bright net.

"Speak up, Grandma," the woman said. "What's your name? We must have your history, you know. Have you been here before? What seems to be the trouble with you?"

Old Phoenix only gave a twitch to her face as if a fly were bothering her.

"Are you deaf?" cried the attendant.

But then the nurse came in.

"Oh, that's just old Aunt Phoenix," she said. "She doesn't come for herself — she has a little grandson. She makes these trips just as regular as clockwork. She lives away back off the Old Natchez Trace." She bent down. "Well, Aunt Phoenix, why don't you just take a seat? We won't keep you standing after your long trip." She pointed.

The old woman sat down, bolt upright in the chair.

"Now, how is the boy?" asked the nurse.

Old Phoenix did not speak.

"I said, how is the boy?"

But Phoenix only waited and stared straight ahead, her face very solemn and withdrawn into rigidity.

"Is his throat any better?" asked the nurse. "Aunt Phoenix, don't you hear me? Is your grandson's throat any better since the last time you came for the medicine?"

With her hands on her knees, the old woman waited, silent, erect and motionless, just as if she were in armor.

"You mustn't take up our time this way, Aunt Phoenix," the nurse said. "Tell us quickly about your grandson, and get it over. He isn't dead, is he?"

At last there came a flicker and then a flame of comprehension across her face, and she spoke.

"My grandson. It was my memory had left me. There I sat and forgot why I made my long trip."

"Forgot?" The nurse frowned. "After you came so far?"

Then Phoenix was like an old woman begging a dignified forgiveness for waking up frightened in the night. "I never did go to school, I was too old at the Surrender," she said in a soft voice. "I'm an old woman without an education. It was my memory fail me. My little grandson, he is just the same, and I forgot it in the coming."

"Throat never heals, does it?" said the nurse, speaking in a loud, sure voice to old Phoenix. By now she had a card with something written on it, a little list. "Yes. Swallowed lye. When was it? — January — two, three years ago — "

Phoenix spoke unasked now. "No, missy, he not dead, he just the same. Every little while his throat began to close up again, and he not able to swallow. He not get his breath. He not able to help himself. So the time come around, and I go on another trip for the soothing medicine."

"All right. The doctor said as long as you came to get it, you could have it," said the nurse. "But it's an obstinate case."

"My little grandson, he sit up there in the house all wrapped up, waiting by himself," Phoenix went on. "We is the only two left in the world. He suffer and it don't seem to put him back at all. He got a sweet look. He going to last. He wear a little patch quilt and peep out holding his mouth open like a little bird. I remembers so plain now. I not going to forget him again, no, the whole enduring time. I could tell him from all the others in creation."

"All right." The nurse was trying to hush her now. She brought her a bottle of medicine. "Charity," she said, making a check mark in a book.

Old Phoenix held the bottle close to her eyes, and then carefully put it into her pocket.

"I thank you," she said.

"It's Christmas time, Grandma," said the attendant. "Could I give you a few pennies out of my purse?"

"Five pennies is a nickel," said Phoenix stiffly.

"Here's a nickel," said the attendant.

Phoenix rose carefully and held out her hand. She received the nickel and then fished the other nickel out of her pocket and laid it beside the new one. She stared at her palm closely, with her head on one side.

Then she gave a tap with her cane on the floor.

"This is what come to me to do," she said. "I going to the store and buy my child a little windmill they sells, made out of paper. He going to find it hard to believe there such a thing in the world. I'll march myself back where he waiting, holding it straight up in this hand."

She lifted her free hand, gave a little nod, turned around, and walked out of the doctor's office. Then her slow step began on the stairs, going down.

Edith Wharton

Edith Wharton (1862–1937) was born into a wealthy family in New York City. She later wrote, "My little-girl life, safe, guarded, monotonous, was cradled in the only world about which, according to Goethe [the German poet], it is impossible to write poetry. The small society into which I was born was 'good' in the most prosaic sense of the term, and its only interest, for the generality of readers, lies in the fact of its sudden and total extinction." She was raised by governesses and tutors in the family homes in Paris, New York City, and Newport, Rhode Island. At an early age she decided to become a writer, and when she was only thirteen she disregarded Goethe and published, at her own expense, a collection of verse.

After her marriage in 1885, Wharton began to write stories for popular magazines. Her first collection of stories, *The Greater Inclination* (1899), was followed by books of fiction almost every year for more than a quarter of a century, a total of eleven collections of stories and sixteen novels. She lived most of her life in Paris, but her periodic visits to her country estate in the Berkshires, near Lenox, Massachusetts, helped her write with authority about life in America. Her best works include the early novel *The House of Mirth* (1905); *Ethan Frome* (1911), a laconically powerful New England tragedy; and *The Age of Innocence* (1920), a novel about old New York society. As a rule, Wharton's conventional novels of manners develop characterizations; her short stories, more satiric, emphasize plots. In both forms her point of view is always poised, her prose style elegant and tightly controlled.

One of Wharton's good friends was another expatriate and keen observer of the society they knew so well, Henry James. James, who also visited her in the Berkshires, had a profound influence on her writing, encouraging her to set a high standard. Like James, Wharton enjoyed defining her artistic methods as a storyteller. In 1925 she published *The Writing of Fiction*, where in analyzing the French and Russian contributions to the short story form, she recognized that "instead of a loose web spread over the surface of life they have made it, at its best, a shaft driven straight into the heart of human experience." "The Other Two" is an early story that first appeared in *Collier's Weekly* in 1904 and was collected in *The Descent of Man* the same year.

The Other Two

1904

I

Waythorn, on the drawing-room hearth, waited for his wife to come down to dinner.

It was their first night under his own roof, and he was surprised at his thrill of boyish agitation. He was not so old, to be sure—his glass gave him little more than the five-and-thirty years to which his wife confessed—but he had fancied himself already in the temperate zone; yet here he was listening for her step with a tender sense of all it symbolized, with some old trail of verse about

the garlanded nuptial doorposts floating through his enjoyment of the pleasant room and the good dinner just beyond it.

They had been hastily recalled from their honeymoon by the illness of Lily
Haskett, the child of Mrs. Waythorn's first marriage. The little girl, at Waythorn's
desire, had been transferred to his house on the day of her mother's wedding,
and the doctor, on their arrival, broke the news that she was ill with typhoid,
but declared that all the symptoms were favorable. Lily could show twelve
years of unblemished health, and the case promised to be a light one. The
nurse spoke as reassuringly, and after a moment of alarm Mrs. Waythorn had
adjusted herself to the situation. She was very fond of Lily — her affection for
the child had perhaps been her decisive charm in Waythorn's eyes — but she
had the perfectly balanced nerves which her little girl had inherited, and no
woman ever wasted less tissue in unproductive worry. Waythorn was therefore
quite prepared to see her come in presently, a little late because of a last look at
Lily, but as serene and well-appointed as if her good-night kiss had been laid
on the brow of health. Her composure was restful to him; it acted as ballast
to his somewhat unstable sensibilities. As he pictured her bending over the
child's bed he thought how soothing her presence must be in illness: her very
step would prognosticate recovery.

His own life had been a gray one, from temperament rather than circumstance, and he had been drawn to her by the unperturbed gaiety which kept
her fresh and elastic at an age when most women's activities are growing either
slack or febrile. He knew what was said about her; for, popular as she was, there
had always been a faint undercurrent of detraction. When she had appeared in
New York, nine or ten years earlier, as the pretty Mrs. Haskett whom Gus
Varick had unearthed somewhere — was it in Pittsburg or Utica? — society,
while promptly accepting her, had reserved the right to cast a doubt on its own
indiscrimination. Inquiry, however, established her undoubted connection
with a socially reigning family, and explained her recent divorce as the natural
result of a runaway match at seventeen; and as nothing was known of Mr. Haskett
it was easy to believe the worst of him.

Alice Haskett's remarriage with Gus Varick was a passport to the set
whose recognition she coveted, and for a few years the Varicks were the
most popular couple in town. Unfortunately the alliance was brief and
stormy, and this time the husband had his champions. Still, even Varick's
stanchest supporters admitted that he was not meant for matrimony, and
Mrs. Varick's grievances were of a nature to bear the inspection of the New
York courts. A New York divorce is in itself a diploma of virtue, and in the
semiwidowhood of this second separation Mrs. Varick took on an air of
sanctity, and was allowed to confide her wrongs to some of the most scrupulous ears in town. But when it was known that she was to marry Waythorn
there was a momentary reaction. Her best friends would have preferred to
see her remain in the role of the injured wife, which was as becoming to her
as crepe to a rosy complexion. True, a decent time had elapsed, and it was
not even suggested that Waythorn had supplanted his predecessor. People
shook their heads over him, however, and one grudging friend, to whom

he affirmed that he took the step with his eyes open, replied oracularly: "Yes — and with your ears shut."

Waythorn could afford to smile at these innuendos. In the Wall Street phrase, he had "discounted" them. He knew that society has not yet adapted itself to the consequences of divorce, and that till the adaptation takes place every woman who uses the freedom the law accords her must be her own social justification. Waythorn had an amused confidence in his wife's ability to justify herself. His expectations were fulfilled, and before the wedding took place Alice Varick's group had rallied openly to her support. She took it all imperturbably; she had a way of surmounting obstacles without seeming to be aware of them, and Waythorn looked back with wonder at the trivialities over which he had worn his nerves thin. He had the sense of having found refuge in a richer, warmer nature than his own, and his satisfaction, at the moment, was humorously summed up in the thought that his wife, when she had done all she could for Lily, would not be ashamed to come down and enjoy a good dinner.

The anticipation of such enjoyment was not, however, the sentiment expressed by Mrs. Waythorn's charming face when she presently joined him. Though she had put on her most engaging tea gown she had neglected to assume the smile that went with it, and Waythorn thought he had never seen her look so nearly worried.

"What is it?" he asked. "Is anything wrong with Lily?"

"No; I've just been in and she's still sleeping." Mrs. Waythorn hesitated. "But something tiresome has happened."

He had taken her two hands, and now perceived that he was crushing a paper between them.

"This letter?"

"Yes — Mr. Haskett has written — I mean his lawyer has written."

Waythorn felt himself flush uncomfortably. He dropped his wife's hands.

"What about?"

"About seeing Lily. You know the courts —"

"Yes, yes," he interrupted nervously.

Nothing was known about Haskett in New York. He was vaguely supposed to have remained in the outer darkness from which his wife had been rescued, and Waythorn was one of the few who were aware that he had given up his business in Utica and followed her to New York in order to be near his little girl. In the days of his wooing, Waythorn had often met Lily on the doorstep, rosy and smiling, on her way "to see papa."

"I am so sorry," Mrs. Waythorn murmured.

He roused himself. "What does he want?"

"He wants to see her. You know she goes to him once a week."

"Well — he doesn't expect her to go to him now, does he?"

"No — he has heard of her illness; but he expects to come here."

"*Here?*"

Mrs. Waythorn reddened under his gaze. They looked away from each other.

"I'm afraid he has the right. . . . You'll see. . . ." She made a proffer of the letter.

Waythorn moved away with a gesture of refusal. He stood staring about the softly-lighted room, which a moment before had seemed so full of bridal intimacy.

"I'm so sorry," she repeated. "If Lily could have been moved —"

"That's out of the question," he returned impatiently.

"I suppose so."

Her lip was beginning to tremble, and he felt himself a brute.

"He must come, of course," he said. "When is — his day?"

"I'm afraid — tomorrow."

"Very well. Send a note in the morning."

The butler entered to announce dinner.

Waythorn turned to his wife. "Come — you must be tired. It's beastly, but try to forget about it," he said, drawing her hand through his arm.

"You're so good, dear. I'll try," she whispered back.

Her face cleared at once, and as she looked at him across the flowers, between the rosy candleshades, he saw her lips waver back into a smile.

"How pretty everything is!" she sighed luxuriously.

He turned to the butter. "The champagne at once, please. Mrs. Waythorn is tired."

In a moment or two their eyes met above the sparkling glasses. Her own were quite clear and untroubled: he saw that she had obeyed his injunction and forgotten.

II

Waythorn, the next morning, went downtown earlier than usual. Haskett was not likely to come till the afternoon, but the instinct of flight drove him forth. He meant to stay away all day — he had thoughts of dining at his club. As his door closed behind him he reflected that before he opened it again it would have admitted another man who had as much right to enter it as himself, and the thought filled him with a physical repugnance.

He caught the elevated at the employees' hour, and found himself crushed between two layers of pendulous humanity. At Eighth Street the man facing him wriggled out, and another took his place. Waythorn glanced up and saw that it was Gus Varick. The men were so close together that it was impossible to ignore the smile of recognition on Varick's handsome overblown face. And after all — why not? They had always been on good terms, and Varick had been divorced before Waythorn's intentions to his wife began. The two exchanged a word on the perennial grievance of the congested trains, and when a seat at their side was miraculously left empty the instinct of self-preservation made Waythorn slip into it after Varick.

The latter drew the stout man's breath of relief. "Lord — I was beginning to feel like a pressed flower." He leaned back, looking unconcernedly at Waythorn. "Sorry to hear that Sellers is knocked out again."

"Sellers?" echoed Waythorn, starting at his partner's name.

Varick looked surprised. "You didn't know he was laid up with the gout?"

"No. I've been away — I only got back last night." Waythorn felt himself reddening in anticipation of the other's smile.

"Ah — yes; to be sure. And Sellers' attack came on two days ago. I'm afraid he's pretty bad. Very awkward for me, as it happens, because he was just putting through a rather important thing for me."

"Ah?" Waythorn wondered vaguely since when Varick had been dealing in "important things." Hitherto he had dabbled only in the shallow pools of speculation, with which Waythorn's office did not usually concern itself.

It occurred to him that Varick might be talking at random, to relieve the strain of their propinquity. That strain was becoming momentarily more apparent to Waythorn, and when, at Cortlandt Street, he caught sight of an acquaintance and had a sudden vision of the picture he and Varick must present to an initiated eye, he jumped up with a muttered excuse.

"I hope you'll find Sellers better," said Varick civilly, and he stammered back: "If I can be of any use to you — " and let the departing crowd sweep him to the platform.

At his office he heard that Sellers was in fact ill with the gout, and would probably not be able to leave the house for some weeks.

"I'm sorry it should have happened so, Mr. Waythorn," the senior clerk said with affable significance. "Mr. Sellers was very much upset at the idea of giving you such a lot of extra work just now."

"Oh, that's no matter," said Waythorn hastily. He secretly welcomed the pressure of additional business, and was glad to think, when the day's work was over, he would have to call at his partner's on the way home.

He was late for luncheon, and turned in at the nearest restaurant instead of going back to his club. The place was full, and the waiter hurried him to the back of the room to capture the only vacant table. In the cloud of cigar smoke Waythorn did not at once distinguish his neighbors: but presently, looking about him, he saw Varick seated a few feet off. This time, luckily, they were too far apart for conversation, and Varick, who faced another way, had probably not even seen him; but there was an irony in their renewed nearness.

Varick was said to be fond of good living, and as Waythorn sat dispatching his hurried luncheon he looked across half enviously at the other's leisurely degustation of his meal. When Waythorn first saw him he had been helping himself with critical deliberation to a bit of Camembert at the ideal point of liquefaction, and now, the cheese removed, he was just pouring his *cafe double* from its little two-storied earthen pot. He poured slowly, his ruddy profile bent over the task, and one beringed white hand steadying the lid of the coffeepot; then he stretched his other hand to the decanter of cognac at his elbow, filled a liqueur glass, took a tentative sip, and poured the brandy into his coffee cup.

Waythorn watched him in a kind of fascination. What was he thinking of — only of the flavor of the coffee and the liqueur? Had the morning's meeting left no more trace in his thoughts than on his face? Had his wife so completely passed out of his life that even this odd encounter with her present husband, within a week after her remarriage, was no more than an incident in his day? And as Waythorn mused, another idea struck him: had Haskett ever met Varick as Varick and he had just met? The recollection of Haskett perturbed him, and he rose and left the restaurant, taking a circuitous way out to escape the placid irony of Varick's nod.

It was after seven when Waythorn reached home. He thought the footman who opened the door looked at him oddly.

"How is Miss Lily?" he asked in haste.

"Doing very well, sir. A gentleman — "

"Tell Barlow to put off dinner for half an hour," Waythorn cut him off, hurrying upstairs.

He went straight to his room and dressed without seeing his wife. When he reached the drawing room she was there, fresh and radiant. Lily's day had been good; the doctor was not coming back that evening.

At dinner Waythorn told her of Sellers' illness and of the resulting complications. She listened sympathetically, adjuring him not to let himself be overworked, and asking vague feminine questions about the routine of the office. Then she gave him the chronicle of Lily's day; quoted the nurse and doctor, and told him who had called to inquire. He had never seen her more serene and unruffled. It struck him, with a curious pang, that she was very happy in being with him, so happy that she found a childish pleasure in rehearsing the trivial incidents of her day.

After dinner they went to the library, and the servant put the coffee and liqueurs on a low table before her and left the room. She looked singularly soft and girlish in her rosy-pale dress, against the dark leather of one of his bachelor armchairs. A day earlier the contrast would have charmed him.

He turned away now, choosing a cigar with affected deliberation.

"Did Haskett come?" he asked, with his back to her.

"Oh, yes — he came."

"You didn't see him, of course?"

She hesitated a moment. "I let the nurse see him."

That was all. There was nothing more to ask. He swung round toward her, applying a match to his cigar. Well, the thing was over for a week, at any rate. He would try not to think of it. She looked up at him, a trifle rosier than usual, with a smile in her eyes.

"Ready for your coffee, dear?"

He leaned against the mantelpiece, watching her as she lifted the coffeepot. The lamplight struck a gleam from her bracelets and tipped her soft hair with brightness. How light and slender she was, and how each gesture flowed into the next! She seemed a creature all compact of harmonies. As the thought of Haskett receded, Waythorn felt himself yielding again to the joy of possessorship. They were his, those white hands with flitting motions, his the light haze of hair, the lips and eyes. . . .

She set down the coffeepot, and reaching for the decanter of cognac, measured off a liqueur glass and poured it into his cup.

Waythorn uttered a sudden exclamation.

"What is the matter?" she said, startled.

"Nothing; only — I don't take cognac in my coffee."

"Oh, how stupid of me," she cried.

Their eyes met, and she blushed a sudden agonized red.

III

Ten days later, Mr. Sellers, still housebound, asked Waythorn to call on his way downtown.

The senior partner, with his swaddled foot propped up by the fire, greeted his associate with an air of embarrassment.

"I'm sorry, my dear fellow; I've got to ask you to do an awkward thing for me."

Waythorn waited, and the other went on, after a pause apparently given to the arrangement of his phrases: "The fact is, when I was knocked out I had just gone into a rather complicated piece of business for — Gus Varick."

"Well?" said Waythorn, with an attempt to put him at his ease.

"Well — it's this way: Varick came to me the day before my attack. He had evidently had an inside tip from somebody, and had made about a hundred thousand. He came to me for advice, and I suggested his going in with Vanderlyn."

"Oh, the deuce!" Waythorn exclaimed. He saw in a flash what had happened. The investment was an alluring one, but required negotiation. He listened quietly while Sellers put the case before him, and, the statement ended, he said: "You think I ought to see Varick?"

"I'm afraid I can't as yet. The doctor is obdurate. And this thing can't wait. I hate to ask you, but no one else in the office knows the ins and outs of it."

Waythorn stood silent. He did not care a farthing for the success of Varick's venture, but the honor of the office was to be considered, and he could hardly refuse to oblige his partner.

"Very well," he said, "I'll do it."

That afternoon, apprised by telephone, Varick called at the office. Waythorn, waiting in his private room, wondered what the others thought of it. The newspapers, at the time of Mrs. Waythorn's marriage, had acquainted their readers with every detail of her previous matrimonial ventures, and Waythorn could fancy the clerks smiling behind Varick's back as he was ushered in.

Varick bore himself admirably. He was easy without being undignified, and Waythorn was conscious of cutting a much less impressive figure. Varick had no experience of business, and the talk prolonged itself for nearly an hour while Waythorn set forth with scrupulous precision the details of the proposed transaction.

"I'm awfully obliged to you," Varick said as he rose. "The fact is I'm not used to having much money to look after, and I don't want to make an ass of myself — " He smiled, and Waythorn could not help noticing that there was something pleasant about his smile. "It feels uncommonly queer to have enough cash to pay one's bills. I'd have sold my soul for it a few years ago!"

Waythorn winced at the allusion. He had heard it rumoured that a lack of funds had been one of the determining causes of the Varick separation, but it did not occur to him that Varick's words were intentional. It seemed more likely that the desire to keep clear of embarrassing topics had fatally drawn him into one. Waythorn did not wish to be outdone in civility.

"We'll do the best we can for you," he said. "I think this is a good thing you're in."

"Oh, I'm sure it's immense. It's awfully good of you —" Varick broke off, embarrassed. "I suppose the thing's settled now — but if —"

"If anything happens before Sellers is about, I'll see you again," said Waythorn quietly. He was glad, in the end, to appear the more self-possessed of the two.

The course of Lily's illness ran smooth, and as the days passed Waythorn grew used to the idea of Haskett's weekly visit. The first time the day came round, he stayed out late, and questioned his wife as to the visit on his return. She replied at once that Haskett had merely seen the nurse downstairs, as the doctor did not wish anyone in the child's sickroom till after the crisis.

The following week Waythorn was again conscious of the recurrence of the day, but had forgotten it by the time he came home to dinner. The crisis of the disease came a few days later, with a rapid decline of fever, and the little girl was pronounced out of danger. In the rejoicing which ensued the thought of Haskett passed out of Waythorn's mind, and one afternoon, letting himself into the house with a latchkey, he went straight to his library without noticing a shabby hat and umbrella in the hall.

In the library he found a small effaced-looking man with a thinnish gray beard sitting on the edge of a chair. The stranger might have been a piano tuner, or one of those mysteriously efficient persons who are summoned in emergencies to adjust some detail of the domestic machinery. He blinked at Waythorn through a pair of gold-rimmed spectacles and said mildly: "Mr. Waythorn, I presume? I am Lily's father."

Waythorn flushed. "Oh —" he stammered uncomfortably. He broke off, disliking to appear rude. Inwardly he was trying to adjust the actual Haskett to the image of him projected by his wife's reminiscences. Waythorn had been allowed to infer that Alice's first husband was a brute.

"I am sorry to intrude," said Haskett, with his over-the-counter politeness.

"Don't mention it," returned Waythorn, collecting himself. "I suppose the nurse has been told?"

"I presume so. I can wait," said Haskett. He had a resigned way of speaking, as though life had worn down his natural powers of resistance.

Waythorn stood on the threshold, nervously pulling off his gloves.

"I'm sorry you've been detained. I will send for the nurse," he said, and as he opened the door he added with an effort: "I'm glad we can give you a good report of Lily." He winced as the *we* slipped out, but Haskett seemed not to notice it.

"Thank you, Mr. Waythorn. It's been an anxious time for me."

"Ah, well, that's past. Soon she'll be able to go to you." Waythorn nodded and passed out.

In his own room he flung himself down with a groan. He hated the woman-ish sensibility which made him suffer so acutely from the grotesque chances of life. He had known when he married that his wife's former husbands were both living, and that amid the multiplied contacts of modern existence there were a thousand chances to one that he would run against one or the other, yet he found himself as much disturbed by his brief encounter with Haskett as though the law had not obligingly removed all difficulties in the way of their meeting.

Waythorn sprang up and began to pace the room nervously. He had not suffered half as much from his two meetings with Varick. It was Haskett's presence in his own house that made the situation so intolerable. He stood still, hearing steps in the passage.

"This way, please," he heard the nurse say. Haskett was being taken upstairs, then: not a corner of the house but was open to him. Waythorn dropped into another chair, staring vaguely ahead of him. On his dressing table stood a photograph of Alice, taken when he had first known her. She was Alice Varick then — how fine and exquisite he had thought her! Those were Varick's pearls about her neck. At Waythorn's insistence they had been returned before her marriage. Had Haskett ever given her any trinkets — and what had become of them, Waythorn wondered? He realized suddenly that he knew very little of Haskett's past or present situation; but from the man's appearance and manner of speech he could reconstruct with curious precision the surroundings of Alice's first marriage. And it startled him to think that she had, in the background of her life, a phase of existence so different from anything with which he had connected her. Varick, whatever his faults, was a gentleman, in the conventional, traditional sense of the term: the sense which at that moment seemed, oddly enough, to have most meaning to Waythorn. He and Varick had the same social habits, spoke the same language, understood the same allusions. But this other man . . . it was grotesquely uppermost in Waythorn's mind that Haskett had worn a made-up tie attached with an elastic. Why should that ridiculous detail symbolize the whole man? Waythorn was exasperated by his own paltriness, but the fact of the tie expanded, forced itself on him, became as it were the key to Alice's past. He could see her, as Mrs. Haskett, sitting in a "front parlor" furnished in plush, with a pianola, and a copy of *Ben Hur* on the center table. He could see her going to the theater with Haskett — or perhaps even to a "Church Sociable" — she in the "picture hat" and Haskett in a black frock coat, a little creased, with the made-up tie on an elastic. On the way home they would stop and look at the illuminated shop windows, lingering over the photographs of New York actresses. On Sunday afternoons Haskett would take her for a walk, pushing Lily ahead of them in a white enameled perambulator, and Waythorn had a vision of the people they would stop and talk to. He could fancy how pretty Alice must have looked, in a dress adroitly constructed from the hints of a New York fashion paper, and how she must have looked down on the other women, chafing at her life, and secretly feeling that she belonged in a bigger place.

For the moment his foremost thought was one of wonder at the way in which she had shed the phase of existence which her marriage with Haskett implied. It was as if her whole aspect, every gesture, every inflection, every allusion, were a studied negation of that period of her life. If she had denied being married to Haskett she could hardly have stood more convicted of duplicity than in this obliteration of the self which had been his wife.

Waythorn started up, checking himself in the analysis of her motives. What right had he to create a fantastic effigy of her and then pass judgment on it? She had spoken vaguely of her first marriage as unhappy, had hinted, with becoming reticence, that Haskett had wrought havoc among her young illusions. . . . It was a pity for Waythorn's peace of mind that Haskett's very inoffensiveness shed a new light on the nature of those illusions. A man would rather think that his wife has been brutalized by her first husband than that the process has been reversed.

IV

"Mr. Waythorn, I don't like that French governess of Lily's."

Haskett, subdued and apologetic, stood before Waythorn in the library, revolving his shabby hat in his hand.

Waythorn, surprised in his armchair over the evening paper, stared back perplexedly at his visitor.

"You'll excuse my asking to see your," Haskett continued. "But this is my last visit, and I thought if I could have a word with you it would be a better way than writing to Mrs. Waythorn's lawyer."

Waythorn rose uneasily. He did not like the French governess either; but that was irrelevant.

"I am not so sure of that," he returned stiffly; "but since you wish it I will give your message to — my wife." He always hesitated over the possessive pronoun in addressing Haskett.

The latter sighed. "I don't know as that will help much. She didn't like it when I spoke to her."

Waythorn turned red. "When did you see her?" he asked.

"Not since the first day I came to see Lily — right after she was taken sick. I remarked to her then that I didn't like the governess."

Waythorn made no answer. He remembered distinctly that, after that first visit, he had asked his wife if she had seen Haskett. She had lied to him then, but she had respected his wishes since; and the incident cast a curious light on her character. He was sure she would not have seen Haskett that first day if she had divined that Waythorn would object, and the fact that she did not divine it was almost as disagreeable to the latter as the discovery that she had lied to him.

"I don't like the woman," Haskett was repeating with mild persistency. "She ain't straight, Mr. Waythorn — she'll teach the child to be underhand. I've noticed a change in Lily — she's too anxious to please — and she don't always tell the truth. She used to be the straightest child, Mr. Waythorn —" He broke off, his voice a little thick. "Not but what I want her to have a stylish education," he ended.

Waythorn was touched. "I'm sorry, Mr. Haskett; but frankly, I don't quite see what I can do."

Haskett hesitated. Then he laid his hat on the table, and advanced to the hearthrug, on which Waythorn was standing. There was nothing aggressive in his manner, but he had the solemnity of a timid man resolved on a decisive measure.

"There's just one thing you can do, Mr. Waythorn," he said. "You can remind Mrs. Waythorn that, by the decree of the courts, I am entitled to have a voice in Lily's bringing-up." He paused, and went on more deprecatingly: "I'm not the kind to talk about enforcing my rights, Mr. Waythorn. I don't know as I think a man is entitled to rights he hasn't known how to hold on to; but this business of the child is different. I've never let go there—and I never mean to."

The scene left Waythorn deeply shaken. Shamefacedly, in indirect ways, he had been finding out about Haskett; and all that he had learned was favorable. The little man, in order to be near his daughter, had sold out his share in a profitable business in Utica, and accepted a modest clerkship in a New York manufacturing house. He boarded in a shabby street and had few acquaintances. His passion for Lily filled his life. Waythorn felt that this exploration of Haskett was like groping about with a dark lantern in his wife's past; but he saw now that there were recesses his lantern had not explored. He had never inquired into the exact circumstances of his wife's first matrimonial rupture. On the surface all had been fair. It was she who had obtained the divorce, and the court had given her the child. But Waythorn knew how many ambiguities such a verdict might cover. The mere fact that Haskett retained a right over his daughter implied an unsuspected compromise. Waythorn was an idealist. He always refused to recognize unpleasant contingencies till he found himself confronted with them, and then he saw them followed by a spectral train of consequences. His next days were thus haunted, and he determined to try to lay the ghosts by conjuring them up in his wife's presence.

When he repeated Haskett's request a flame of anger passed over her face; but she subdued it instantly and spoke with a slight quiver of outraged motherhood.

"It is very ungentlemanly of him," she said.

The word grated on Waythorn. "That is neither here nor there. It's a bare question of rights."

She murmured: "It's not as if he could ever be a help to Lily—"

Waythorn flushed. This was even less to his taste. "The question is," he repeated, "what authority has he over her?"

She looked downward, twisting herself a little in her seat. "I am willing to see him—I thought you objected," she faltered.

In a flash he understood that she knew the extent of Haskett's claims. Perhaps it was not the first time she had resisted them.

"My objecting has nothing to do with it," he said coldly; "if Haskett has a right to be consulted you must consult him."

She burst into tears, and he saw that she expected him to regard her as a victim.

Haskett did not abuse his rights. Waythorn had felt miserably sure that he would not. But the governess was dismissed, and from time to time the little man demanded an interview with Alice. After the first outburst she accepted the situation with her usual adaptability. Haskett had once reminded Waythorn of the piano tuner, and Mrs. Waythorn, after a month or two, appeared to class him with that domestic familiar. Waythorn could not but respect the father's tenacity. At first he had tried to cultivate the suspicion that Haskett might be "up to" something, that he had an object in securing a foothold in the house. But in his heart Waythorn was sure of Haskett's single-mindedness; he even guessed in the latter a mild contempt for such advantages as his relation with the Waythorns might offer. Haskett's sincerity of purpose made him invulnerable, and his successor had to accept him as a lien on the property.

Mr. Sellers was sent to Europe to recover from his gout, and Varick's affairs hung on Waythorn's hands. The negotiations were prolonged and complicated; they necessitated frequent conferences between the two men, and the interests of the firm forbade Waythorn's suggesting that his client should transfer his business to another officer.

Varick appeared well in the transaction. In moments of relaxation his coarse streak appeared, and Waythorn dreaded his geniality; but in the office he was concise and clear-headed, with a flattering deference to Waythorn's judgment. Their business relations being so affably established, it would have been absurd for the two men to ignore each other in society. The first time they met in a drawing-room, Varick took up their intercourse in the same easy key, and his hostess' grateful glance obliged Waythorn to respond to it. After that they ran across each other frequently, and one evening at a ball Waythorn, wandering through the remoter rooms, came upon Varick seated beside his wife. She colored a little, and faltered in what she was saying; but Varick nodded to Waythorn without rising, and the latter strolled on.

In the carriage, on the way home, he broke out nervously: "I didn't know you spoke to Varick."

Her voice trembled a little. "It's the first time — he happened to be standing near me; I didn't know what to do. It's so awkward, meeting everywhere — and he said you had been very kind about some business."

"That's different," said Waythorn.

She paused a moment. "I'll do just as you wish," she returned pliantly. "I thought it would be less awkward to speak to him when we meet."

Her pliancy was beginning to sicken him. Had she really no will of her own — no theory about her relation to these men? She had accepted Haskett — did she mean to accept Varick? It was "less awkward," as she had said, and her instinct was to evade difficulties or to circumvent them. With sudden vividness Waythorn saw how the instinct had developed. She was "as easy as an old shoe" — a shoe that too many feet had worn. Her elasticity was the result of tension in too many different directions. Alice Haskett — Alice Varick — Alice Waythorn — she had been each in turn, and had left hanging to each name a little of her privacy, a little of her personality, a little of the inmost self where the unknown god abides.

"Yes — it's better to speak to Varick," said Waythorn wearily.

V

The winter wore on, and society took advantage of the Waythorns' acceptance of Varick. Harassed hostesses were grateful to them for bridging over a social difficulty, and Mrs. Waythorn was held up as a miracle of good taste. Some experimental spirits could not resist the diversion of throwing Varick and his former wife together, and there were those who thought he found a zest in the propinquity. But Mrs. Waythorn's conduct remained irreproachable. She neither avoided Varick nor sought him out. Even Waythorn could not but admit that she had discovered the solution of the newest social problem.

He had married her without giving much thought to that problem. He had fancied that a woman can shed her past like a man. But now he saw that Alice was bound to hers both by the circumstances which forced her into continued relation with it, and by the traces it had left on her nature. With grim irony Waythorn compared himself to a member of a syndicate. He held so many shares in his wife's personality and his predecessors were his partners in the business. If there had been any element of passion in the transaction he would have felt less deteriorated by it. The fact that Alice took her change of husbands like a change of weather reduced the situation to mediocrity. He could have forgiven her for blunders, for excesses; for resisting Haskett, for yielding to Varick; for anything but her acquiescence and her tact. She reminded him of a juggler tossing knives; but the knives were blunt and she knew they would never cut her.

And then, gradually, habit formed a protecting surface for his sensibilities. If he paid for each day's comfort with the small change of his illusions, he grew daily to value the comfort more and set less store upon the coin. He had drifted into a dulling propinquity with Haskett and Varick and he took refuge in the cheap revenge of satirizing the situation. He even began to reckon up the advantages which accrued from it, to ask himself if it were not better to own a third of a wife who knew how to make a man happy than a whole one who had lacked opportunity to acquire the art. For it was an art, and made up, like all others, of concessions, eliminations, and embellishments; of lights judiciously thrown and shadows skillfully softened. His wife knew exactly how to manage the lights, and he knew exactly to what training she owed her skill. He even tried to trace the source of his obligations, to discriminate between the influences which had combined to produce his domestic happiness: he perceived that Haskett's commonness had made Alice worship good breeding, while Varick's liberal construction of the marriage bond had taught her to value the conjugal virtues; so that he was directly indebted to his predecessors for the devotion which made his life easy if not inspiring.

From this phase he passed into that of complete acceptance. He ceased to satirize himself because time dulled the irony of the situation and the joke lost its humor with its sting. Even the sight of Haskett's hat on the hall table had ceased to touch the springs of epigram. The hat was often seen there now, for it had been decided that it was better for Lily's father to visit her than for the little girl to go to his boardinghouse. Waythorn, having acquiesced in this arrangement, had been surprised to find how little difference it made. Haskett was never obtrusive, and the few visitors who met him on the stairs were unaware of his identity. Waythorn did not know how often he saw Alice, but with himself Haskett was seldom in contact.

One afternoon, however, he learned on entering that Lily's father was waiting to see him. In the library he found Haskett occupying a chair in his usual provisional way. Waythorn always felt grateful to him for not leaning back.

"I hope you'll excuse me, Mr. Waythorn," he said rising. "I wanted to see Mrs. Waythorn about Lily, and your man asked me to wait here till she came in."

"Of course," said Waythorn, remembering that a sudden leak had that morning given over the drawing room to the plumbers.

He opened his cigar case and held it out to his visitor, and Haskett's acceptance seemed to mark a fresh stage in their intercourse. The spring evening was chilly, and Waythorn invited his guest to draw up his chair to the fire. He meant to find an excuse to leave Haskett in a moment; but he was tired and cold, and after all the little man no longer jarred on him.

The two were enclosed in the intimacy of their blended cigar smoke when the door opened and Varick walked into the room. Waythorn rose abruptly. It was the first time that Varick had come to the house, and the surprise of seeing him, combined with the singular inopportuneness of his arrival, gave a new edge to Waythorn's blunted sensibilities. He stared at his visitor without speaking.

Varick seemed too preoccupied to notice his host's embarrassment.

"My dear fellow," he exclaimed in his most expansive tone, "I must apologize for tumbling in on you in this way, but I was too late to catch you downtown, and so I thought — "

He stopped short, catching sight of Haskett, and his sanguine color deepened to a flush which spread vividly under his scant blond hair. But in a moment he recovered himself and nodded slightly. Haskett returned the bow in silence, and Waythorn was still groping for speech when the footman came in carrying a tea table.

The intrusion offered a welcome vent to Waythorn's nerves. "What the deuce are you bringing this here for?" he said sharply.

"I beg your pardon, sir, but the plumbers are still in the drawing room, and Mrs. Waythorn said she would have tea in the library." The footman's perfectly respectful tone implied a reflection on Waythorn's reasonableness.

"Oh, very well," said the latter resignedly, and the footman proceeded to open the folding tea table and set out its complicated appointments. While this interminable process continued the three men stood motionless, watching it with a fascinated stare, till Waythorn, to break the silence, said to Varick, "Won't you have a cigar?"

He held out the case he had just tendered to Haskett, and Varick helped himself with a smile. Waythorn looked about for a match, and finding none, proffered a light from his own cigar. Haskett, in the background, held his ground mildly, examining his cigar tip now and then, and stepping forward at the right moment to knock its ash into the fire.

The footman at last withdrew, and Varick immediately began: "If I could just say half a word to you about this business — "

"Certainly," stammered Waythorn; "in the dining room — "

But as he placed his hand on the door it opened from without, and his wife appeared on the threshold.

She came in fresh and smiling, in her street dress and hat, shedding a fragrance from the boa which she loosened in advancing.

"Shall we have tea in here, dear?" she began; and then she caught sight of Varick. Her smiled deepened, veiling a slight tremor of surprise. "Why, how do you do?" she said with a distinct note of pleasure.

As she shook hands with Varick she saw Haskett standing behind him. Her smile faded for a moment, but she recalled it quickly, with a scarcely perceptible side glance at Waythorn.

"How do you do, Mr. Haskett?" she said, and shook hands with him a shade less cordially.

The three men stood awkwardly before her, till Varick, always the most self-possessed, dashed into an explanatory phrase.

"We — I had to see Waythorn a moment on business," he stammered, brick-red from chin to nape.

Haskett stepped forward with his air of mild obstinacy. "I am sorry to intrude; but you appointed five o'clock — " he directed his resigned glance to the timepiece on the mantel.

She swept aside their embarrassment with a charming gesture of hospitality.

"I'm so sorry — I'm always late; but the afternoon was so lovely." She stood drawing off her gloves, propitiatory and graceful, diffusing about her a sense of ease and familiarity in which the situation lost its grotesqueness. "But before talking business," she added brightly, "I'm sure everyone wants a cup of tea."

She dropped into her low chair by the tea table, and the two visitors, as if drawn by her smile, advanced to receive the cups she held out.

She glanced about for Waythorn, and he took the third cup with a laugh.

John Edgar Wideman

John Edgar Wideman (b. 1941) was born in Washington, D.C., and grew up in the Homewood section of Pittsburgh, Pennsylvania, an inner-city ghetto he has written about frequently in his fiction. At the University of Pennsylvania, Wideman was both a star athlete and a brilliant scholar: He earned All-Ivy honors in basketball as well as a place in the Philadelphia Big Five Basketball Hall of Fame, and he was one of two African Americans to receive a Rhodes scholarship in 1963, the year he graduated. Wideman spent the next three years at Oxford University studying English literature and followed this experience with a year at the University of Iowa Writers' Workshop as a Kent fellow. He is now retired from his position as Distinguished Professor of English at the University of Massachusetts, Amherst.

Wideman published three novels in the 1960s and 1970s before his first book of stories, *Damballah*, appeared in 1981. This was a volume in what he called the Homewood Trilogy, three books describing the Pittsburgh community of Homewood, founded by a runaway slave. The other two books in the trilogy are the novels *Hiding Place* (1981) and *Sent for You Yesterday* (1983), which won a PEN/Faulkner Award. Wideman received this award a second time for his novel *Philadelphia Fire* (1990). *All Stories Are True: The Stories of John Edgar Wideman*—comprising a total of thirty-five stories, including those in *Fever* (1989), his second book of short fiction—appeared in 1992. *Fatheralong: A Meditation on Fathers and Sons, Race and Society* (1994) and *Hoop Roots* (2001) are two other nonfiction books. *Briefs, Stories for the Palm of the Mind,* appeared in 2010.

"newborn thrown in trash and dies," which first appeared in *All Stories Are True*, is reminiscent of an earlier story in third-person narration about "dead children in garbage cans" titled "Daddy Garbage" in *Damballah*. Later Wideman read a newspaper account of a newborn infant murdered in New York City, and he said that he felt compelled "out of a sense of sadness, frustration, and pain to create the voice of a child who is witness to its own death and never got a chance to speak." Wideman felt that "the challenge of the story was to give dignity to the short life, and to slow down time when the course of its life was so short." As a teacher of aspiring writers, Wideman told his students to "find the material that you have a stake in, that you care about immensely, that pins you down." In 1998 he was the recipient of the prestigious Rea Award for the Short Story.

newborn thrown in trash and dies

1992

THEY SAY YOU SEE your whole life pass in review the instant before you die. How would *they* know. If you die after the instant replay, you aren't around to tell anybody anything. So much for they and what they say. So much for the wish to be a movie star for once in your life because I think that's what people are hoping, what people are pretending when they say you see your life that way at the end. Death doesn't turn your life into a five-star production. The end is the end. And what you know at the end goes down the tube with you. I can speak to you now only because I haven't reached bottom yet. I'm on my way, faster than I want to be traveling and my journey won't take long, but I'm just beginning the countdown to zero. Zero's where I started also so I know a little bit about zero. Know what they say isn't necessarily so. In fact the opposite's true. You begin and right in the eye of that instant storm your life plays itself out for you in advance. That's the theater of your fate, there's where you're granted a preview, the coming attractions of everything that must happen to you. Your life rolled into a ball so dense, so superheavy it would drag the universe down to hell if this tiny, tiny lump of whatever didn't dissipate as quickly as it formed. Quicker. The weight of it is what you recall some infinitesimal fraction of when you stumble and crawl through your worst days on earth.

Knowledge of what's coming gone as quickly as it flashes forth. Quicker. Faster. Gone before it gets here, so to speak. Any other way and nobody would stick around to play out the cards they're dealt. No future in it. You begin forgetting before the zero's entirely wiped off the clock face, before the next digit materializes. What they say is assbackwards, a saying by the way, assbackwards itself. Whether or not you're treated to a summary at the end, you get the whole thing handed to you, neatly packaged as you begin. Then you forget it. Or try to forget. Live your life as if it hasn't happened before, as if the tape has not been prepunched full of holes, the die cast.

I remember because I won't receive much of a life. A measure of justice in the world, after all. I receive a compensatory bonus. Since the time between my wake-up call and curfew is so cruelly brief, the speeded-up preview of what will come to pass, my life, my portion, my destiny, my career, slowed down just enough to let me peek. Not slow enough for me to steal much, but I know some of what it contains, its finality, the groaning, fatal weight of it around my neck.

Call it a trade-off. A standoff. Intensity for duration. I won't get much and this devastating flash isn't much either, but I get it. Zingo.

But the future remains mysterious. Even if we all put our heads together and became one gigantic brain, a brain lots smarter than the sum of each of our smarts, an intelligence as great as the one that guides ants, whales or birds, because they're smarter, they figure things out not one by one, each individual locked in the cell of its head, its mortality, but collectively, doing what the group needs to do to survive, relate to the planet. If we were smarter even than birds and bees, we'd still have only a clue about what's inside the first flash of being. I know it happened and that I receive help from it. Scattered help. Sometimes I catch on. Sometimes I don't. But stuff from it's being pumped out always. I know things I have no business knowing. Things I haven't been around long enough to learn myself. For instance, many languages. A vast palette of feelings. The names of unseen things. Nostalgia for a darkness I've never experienced, a darkness another sense I can't account for assures me I will enter again. Large matters. Small ones. Naked as I am I'm dressed so to speak for my trip. Down these ten swift flights to oblivion.

Floor Ten. Nothing under the sun, they say, is new. This time they're right. They never stop talking so percentages guarantee they'll be correct sometimes. Especially since they speak out of both sides of their mouths at once: *Birds of a feather flock together. Opposites attract.* Like the billion billion monkeys at typewriters who sooner or later will bang out this story I think is uniquely mine. Somebody else, a Russian, I believe, with a long, strange-sounding name, has already written about his life speeding past as he topples slow-motion from a window high up in a tall apartment building. But it was in another country. And alas, the Russian's dead.

Floor Nine. In this building they shoot craps. One of many forms of gambling proliferating here. Very little new wealth enters this cluster of buildings that are like high-rise covered wagons circled against the urban night, so what's here is cycled and recycled by games of chance, by murder and other violent forms of exchange. Kids do it. Adults. Birds and bees. The law here is the same one ruling the jungle, they say. They say this is a jungle of the urban asphalt concrete variety. Since I've never been to Africa or the Amazon I can't agree or disagree. But you know what I think about what they say.

Seven come eleven. Snake eyes. Boxcars. Fever in the funkhouse searching for a five. Talk to me, baby. Talk. Talk. Please. Please. Please.

They cry and sing and curse and pray all night long over these games. On one knee they chant magic formulas to summon luck. They forget luck is rigged. Some of the men carry a game called Three Card Monte downtown. They cheat tourists who are stupid enough to trust in luck. Showmen with quick hands shuffling cards to a blur, fast feet carrying them away from busy intersections when cops come to break up their scam or hit on them for a cut. Flimflam artists, con men who daily use luck as bait and hook, down on their knees in a circle of other men who also should know better, trying to sweet-talk luck into their beds. Luck is the card you wish for, the card somebody else holds. You learn luck by its absence. Luck is what separates you from what you want. Luck is always turning its back and you lose.

Like other potions and powders they sell and consume here luck creates dependency. In their rooms people sit and wait for a hit. A yearning unto death for more, more, more till the little life they've been allotted dies in a basket on the doorstep where they abandoned it.

The Floor of Facts. Seventeen stories in this building. The address is 2950 West 23rd Street. My mother is nineteen years old. The trash chute down which I was dropped is forty-five feet from the door of the apartment my mother was visiting. I was born and will die Monday, August 12, 1991. The small door in the yellow cinder block wall is maroon. I won't know till the last second why my mother pushes it open. In 1990 nine discarded babies were discovered in New York City's garbage. As of August this year seven have been found. 911 is the number to call if you find a baby in the trash. Ernesto Mendez, forty-four, a Housing Authority caretaker, will notice my head, shoulders, and curly hair in a black plastic bag he slashes open near the square entrance of the trash compactor on the ground floor of this brown-brick public housing project called the Gerald J. Carey Gardens. Gardens are green places where seeds are planted, tended, nurtured. The headline above my story reads "Newborn Is Thrown in Trash and Dies." The headline will remind some readers of a similar story with a happy ending that appeared in March. A baby rescued and surviving after she was dropped down a trash chute by her twelve-year-old mother. The reporter, a Mr. George James who recorded many of the above facts, introduced my unhappy story in the Metro Section of the *New York Times* on Wednesday, August 14, with this paragraph: "A young Brooklyn woman gave birth on Monday afternoon in a stairwell in a Coney Island housing project and then dropped the infant down a trash chute into a compactor ten stories below, the police said yesterday." And that's about it. What's fit to print. My tale in a nutshell followed by a relation of facts obtained by interview and reading official documents. Trouble is I could not be reached for comment. No one's fault. Certainly no negligence on the reporter's part. He gave me sufficient notoriety. Many readers must have shaken their heads in dismay or sighed or blurted Jesus Christ, did you see this, handing the Metro Section across the breakfast table or passing it to somebody at work. As grateful as I am to have my story made public you should be able to understand why I feel cheated, why the newspaper account is not enough, why I want my voice to be part of the record. The awful silence is not truly broken until we speak for ourselves. One chance to speak was snatched away. Then I didn't cry out as I plunged through the darkness. I didn't know any better. Too busy thinking to myself, *This is how it is, this is how it is, how it is . . .* accustoming myself to what it seemed life brings, what life is. Spinning, tumbling, a breathless rush, terror, exhilaration, and wonder, wondering is this it, am I doing it right. I didn't know any better. The floors, the other lives packed into this building were going on their merry way as I flew past them in the darkness of my tunnel. No one waved. No one warned me. Said hello or good-bye. And of course I was too busy flailing, trying to catch my breath, trying to stop shivering in the sudden, icy air, welcoming almost the thick, pungent draft rushing up at me as if another pair of thighs were opening below to replace the ones from which I'd been ripped.

In the quiet dark of my passage I did not cry out. Now I will not be still.

A Floor of Questions. Why.

A Floor of Opinions. I believe the floor of fact should have been the ground floor, the foundation, the solid start, the place where all else is firmly rooted. I believe there should be room on the floor of fact for what I believe, for this opinion and others I could not venture before arriving here. I believe some facts are unnecessary and that unnecessary borders on untrue. I believe facts sometimes speak for themselves but never speak for us. They are never anyone's voice and voices are what we must learn to listen to if we wish ever to be heard. I believe my mother did not hate me. I believe somewhere I have a father, who if he is reading this and listening carefully will recognize me as his daughter and be ashamed, heartbroken. I must believe these things. What else do I have. Who has made my acquaintance or noticed or cared or forgotten me. How could anyone be aware of what hurtles by faster than light, blackly, in a dark space beyond the walls of the rooms they live in, beyond the doors they lock, shades they draw when they have rooms and the rooms have windows and the windows have shades and the people believe they possess something worth concealing.

In my opinion my death will serve no purpose. The streetlamps will pop on. Someone will be run over by an expensive car in a narrow street and the driver will hear a bump but consider it of no consequence. Junkies will leak out the side doors of this gigantic mound, nodding, buzzing, greeting their kind with hippy-dip vocalizations full of despair and irony and stylized to embrace the very best that's being sung, played, and said around them. A young woman will open a dresser drawer and wonder whose baby that is sleeping peaceful on a bed of dishtowels, T-shirts, a man's ribbed sweat socks. She will feel something slither through the mud of her belly and splash into the sluggish river that meanders through her. She hasn't eaten for days, so that isn't it. Was it a deadly disease. Or worse, some new life she must account for. She opens and shuts the baby's drawer, pushes and pulls, opens and shuts.

I believe all floors are not equally interesting. Less reason to notice some than others. Equality would become boring, predictable. Though we may slight some and rattle on about others, that does not change the fact that each floor exists and the life on it is real, whether we pause to notice or not. As I gather speed and weight during my plunge, each floor adds its share. When I hit bottom I will bear witness to the truth of each one.

Floor of Wishes. I will miss Christmas. They say no one likes being born on Christmas. You lose your birthday, they say. A celebration already on December 25 and nice things happen to everyone on that day anyway, you give and receive presents, people greet you smiling and wish you peace and goodwill. The world is decorated. Colored bulbs draped twinkling in windows and trees, doorways hung with wild berries beneath which you may kiss a handsome stranger. Music everywhere. Even wars truced for twenty-four hours and troops served home-cooked meals, almost. Instead of at least two special days a year, if your birthday falls on Christmas, you lose one. Since my portion's less than a day, less than those insects called ephemera receive, born one morning dead the next, and I can't squeeze a complete life cycle as they do into the time allotted, I wish today were Christmas. Once would be enough. If it's as special as they say. And in some matters we yearn to trust them. Need to trust something, someone, so we listen, wish what they say is true. The holiday of Christmas seems to be the best time to be on earth, to be a child and awaken with your eyes full of dreams and expectations and believe for a while at least that all good things are possible — peace, goodwill, love, merriment, the raven-maned rocking horse you want to ride forever. No conflict of interest for me. I wouldn't lose a birthday to Christmas. Rather than this smoggy heat I wish I could see snow. The city, this building snug under a blanket of fresh snow. No footprints of men running, men on their knees, men bleeding. No women forced out into halls and streets, away from their children. I wish this city, this tower were stranded in a gentle snowstorm and Christmas happens day after day and the bright fires in every hearth never go out, and the carols ring true chorus after chorus, and the gifts given and received precipitate endless joys. The world trapped in Christmas for a day dancing on forever.

I wish I could transform the ten flights of my falling into those twelve days in the Christmas song. *On the first day of Christmas my true love said to me . . .* angels, a partridge in a pear tree, ten maids a milking, five gold rings, two turtledoves. I wish those would be the sights greeting me instead of darkness, the icy winter heart of this August afternoon I have been pitched without a kiss through a maroon door.

Floor of Power. El Presidente inhabits this floor. Some say he owns the whole building. He believes he owns it, collects rent, treats the building and its occupants with contempt. He is a bold-faced man. Cheeks slotted nose to chin like a puppet's. Chicken lips. This floor is entirely white. A floury, cracked white some say used to gleam. El Presidente is white also. Except for the pink dome of his forehead. Once, long ago, his flesh was pink head to toe. Then he painted himself white to match the white floor of power. Paint ran out just after the brush stroke that permanently sealed his eyes. Since El Presidente is cheap and mean he refused to order more paint. Since El Presidente is vain and arrogant he pretended to look at his unfinished self in the mirror and proclaimed he liked what he saw, the coat of cakey white, the raw, pink dome pulsing like a bruise.

El Presidente often performs on TV. We can watch him jog, golf, fish, travel, lie, preen, mutilate the language. But these activities are not his job; his job is keeping things in the building as they are, squatting on the floor of power like a broken generator or broken furnace or broken heart, occupying the space where one that works should be.

Floor of Regrets. One thing bothers me a lot. I regret not knowing what is on the floors above the one where I began my fall. I hope it's better up there. Real gardens perhaps or even a kind of heaven for the occupants lucky enough to live above the floors I've seen. Would one of you please mount the stairs, climb slowly up from floor ten, examine carefully, one soft, warm night, the topmost floors and sing me a lullaby of what I missed.

Floor of Love. I'm supposed to be sleeping. I could be sleeping. Early morning and my eyes don't want to open and legs don't want to push me out of bed yet. Two rooms away I can hear Mom in the kitchen. She's fixing breakfast. Daddy first, then I will slump into the kitchen Mom has made bright and smelling good already this morning. Her perkiness, the sizzling bacon, water boiling, wheat bread popping up like jack-in-the-box from the shiny toaster, the Rice Krispies crackling, fried eggs hissing, the FM's sophisticated patter and mincing string trios would wake the dead. And it does. Me and Daddy slide into our places. Hi, Mom. Good morning, Dearheart. The day begins. Smells wonderful. I awaken now to his hand under the covers with me, rubbing the baby fat of my tummy where he's shoved my nightgown up past my panties. He says I shouldn't wear them. Says it ain't healthy to sleep in your drawers. Says no wonder you get those rashes. He rubs and pinches. Little nips. Then the flat of his big hand under the elastic waistband wedges my underwear down. I raise my hips a little bit to help. No reason not to. The whole thing be over with sooner. Don't do no good to try and stop him or slow him down. He said my Mama knows. He said go on fool and tell her she'll smack you for talking nasty. He was right. She beat me in the kitchen. Then took me in to their room and he stripped me butt-naked and beat me again while she watched. So I kinda hump up, wiggle, and my underwear's down below my knees, his hand's on its way back up to where I don't even understand how to grow hairs yet.

The Floor That Stands for All the Other Floors Missed or Still to Come. My stepbrother Tommy was playing in the schoolyard and they shot him dead. Bang. Bang. Gang banging and poor Tommy caught a cap in his chest. People been in and out the apartment all day. Sorry. Sorry. Everybody's so sorry. Some brought cakes, pies, macaroni casseroles, lunch meat, liquor. Two Ebony Cobras laid a joint on Tommy's older brother who hadn't risen from the kitchen chair he's straddling, head down, nodding, till his boys bop through the door. They know who hit Tommy. They know tomorrow what they must do. Today one of those everybody-in-the-family-and-friends-in-dark-clothes-funeral days, the mothers, sisters, aunts, grandmothers weepy, the men motherfucking everybody from god on down. You can't see me among the mourners. My time is different from this time. You can't understand my time. Or name it. Or share it. Tommy is beginning to remember me. To join me where I am falling unseen through your veins and arteries down down to where the heart stops, the square opening through which trash passes to the compactor.

William Carlos Williams

William Carlos Williams (1883–1963), the poet, novelist, playwright, and short story writer, was born in Rutherford, New Jersey. After graduating from the University of Pennsylvania Medical School, he returned to Rutherford, where he practiced medicine as a pediatrician for the rest of his life. While still an undergraduate, he began to write poetry, influenced by his friends, the poets Ezra Pound and Hilda Doolittle. Williams published his first book, *Poems*, in 1909. Initially he devoted himself to poetry, but his experimental writing in the 1920s led him to the novel and the short story. The story became for him a way to emphasize his social and humanitarian concerns, which influenced the gritty, down-to-earth realism of his literary style.

Williams wrote most of his stories during the Depression, when his patients in Rutherford were the poor people characterized by President Franklin Delano Roosevelt in 1933 as "ill-fed, ill-housed, and ill-clothed." Williams's patients were often down and out, but he saw them as splendidly vital people. When asked how he managed the two careers of medicine and writing, Williams answered, "It's no strain. In fact, the one [medicine] nourishes the other [writing], even if at times I've groaned to the contrary."

Like the doctor-writer Anton Chekhov before him, Williams understood the moral responsibility of his calling, and he was vigilant against his feelings of arrogance and self-importance. "There's nothing like a difficult patient to show us ourselves," he once told a medical student. "I would learn so much on my rounds, or making home visits. At times I felt like a thief because I heard words, lines, saw people and places—and used it all in my writing. I guess I've told people that, and no one's so surprised! There was something deeper going on, though—the force of all those encounters. I was put off guard again and again, and the result was—well, a descent into myself."

Williams collected his stories in four volumes: *The Knife of the Times* (1932), *Life along the Passaic River* (1938), *Make Light of It* (1950), and *The Farmers' Daughters* (1961). In 1984 Robert Coles compiled *The Doctor Stories*. As Coles understood, in "The Use of Force," Williams "extends to us, really, moments of a doctor's self-recognition—rendered in such a way that the particular becomes the universal." Williams used vernacular American speech and direct observation in all his writing. His work includes twenty books of poetry, four novels, several books of nonfiction, a collection of plays, and an autobiography.

The Use of Force

1938

THEY WERE NEW PATIENTS to me, all I had was the name, Olson. Please come down as soon as you can, my daughter is very sick. When I arrived I was met by the mother, a big startled looking woman, very clean and apologetic who merely said, Is this the doctor? and let me in. In the back, she added. You must excuse us, doctor, we have her in the kitchen where it is warm. It is very damp here sometimes.

The child was fully dressed and sitting on her father's lap near the kitchen table. He tried to get up, but I motioned for him not to bother, took off my overcoat and started to look things over. I could see that they were all very nervous, eyeing me up and down distrustfully. As often, in such cases, they weren't telling me more than they had to, it was up to me to tell them; that's why they were spending three dollars on me.

The child was fairly eating me up with her cold, steady eyes, and no expression to her face whatever. She did not move and seemed, inwardly, quiet; an unusually attractive little thing, and as strong as a heifer in appearance. But her face was flushed, she was breathing rapidly, and I realized that she had a high fever. She had magnificent blonde hair, in profusion. One of those picture children often reproduced in advertising leaflets and the photogravure sections of the Sunday papers.

She's had a fever for three days, began the father and we don't know what it comes from. My wife has given her things, you know, like people do, but it don't do no good. And there's been a lot of sickness around. So we tho't you'd better look her over and tell us what is the matter.

As doctors often do I took a trial shot at it as a point of departure. Has she had a sore throat?

Both parents answered me together, No . . . No, she says her throat don't hurt her.

Does your throat hurt you? added the mother to the child. But the little girl's expression didn't change nor did she move her eyes from my face.

Have you looked?

I tried to, said the mother, but I couldn't see.

As it happens we had been having a number of cases of diphtheria in the school to which this child went during that month and we were all, quite apparently, thinking of that, though no one had as yet spoken of the thing.

Well, I said, suppose we take a look at the throat first. I smiled in my best professional manner and asking for the child's first name I said, come on, Mathilda, open your mouth and let's take a look at your throat.

Nothing doing.

Aw, come on, I coaxed, just open your mouth wide and let me take a look. Look, I said opening both hands wide, I haven't anything in my hands. Just open up and let me see.

Such a nice man, put in the mother. Look how kind he is to you. Come on, do what he tells you to. He won't hurt you.

At that I ground my teeth in disgust. If only they wouldn't use the word "hurt" I might be able to get somewhere. But I did not allow myself to be hurried or disturbed but speaking quietly and slowly I approached the child again.

As I moved my chair a little nearer suddenly with one catlike movement both her hands clawed instinctively for my eyes and she almost reached them too. In fact she knocked my glasses flying and they fell, though unbroken, several feet away from me on the kitchen floor.

Both the mother and father almost turned themselves inside out in embarrassment and apology. You bad girl, said the mother, taking her and shaking her by one arm. Look what you've done. The nice man . . .

For heaven's sake, I broke in. Don't call me a nice man to her. I'm here to look at her throat on the chance that she might have diphtheria and possibly die of it. But that's nothing to her. Look here, I said to the child, we're going to look at your throat. You're old enough to understand what I'm saying. Will you open it now by yourself or shall we have to open it for you?

Not a move. Even her expression hadn't changed. Her breaths however were coming faster and faster. Then the battle began. I had to do it. I had to have a throat culture for her own protection. But first I told the parents that it was entirely up to them. I explained the danger but said that I would not insist on a throat examination so long as they would take the responsibility.

If you don't do what the doctor says you'll have to go to the hospital, the mother admonished her severely.

Oh yeah? I had to smile to myself. After all, I had already fallen in love with the savage brat, the parents were contemptible to me. In the ensuing struggle they grew more and more abject, crushed, exhausted while she surely rose to magnificent heights of insane fury of effort bred of her terror of me.

The father tried his best, and he was a big man but the fact that she was his daughter, his shame at her behavior and his dread of hurting her made him release her just at the critical times when I had almost achieved success, till I wanted to kill him. But his dread also that she might have diphtheria made him tell me to go on, go on though he himself was almost fainting, while the mother moved back and forth behind us raising and lowering her hands in an agony of apprehension.

Put her in front of you on your lap, I ordered, and hold both her wrists.

But as soon as he did the child let out a scream. Don't, you're hurting me. Let go of my hands. Let them go I tell you. Then she shrieked terrifyingly, hysterically. Stop it! Stop it! You're killing me!

Do you think she can stand it, doctor! said the mother.

You get out, said the husband to his wife. Do you want her to die of diphtheria?

Come on now, hold her, I said.

Then I grasped the child's head with my left hand and tried to get the wooden tongue depressor between her teeth. She fought, with clenched teeth, desperately! But now I also had grown furious — at a child. I tried to hold myself down but I couldn't. I know how to expose a throat for inspection. And I did my best. When finally I got the wooden spatula behind the last teeth and just the point of it into the mouth cavity, she opened up for an instant but before I could see anything she came down again and gripped the wooden blade between her molars. She reduced it to splinters before I could get it out again.

Aren't you ashamed, the mother yelled at her. Aren't you ashamed to act like that in front of the doctor?

Get me a smooth-handled spoon of some sort, I told the mother. We're going through with this. The child's mouth was already bleeding. Her tongue was cut and she was screaming in wild hysterical shrieks. Perhaps I should have desisted and come back in an hour or more. No doubt it would have been better. But I have seen at least two children lying dead in bed of neglect in such cases, and feeling that I must get a diagnosis now or never I went at it again. But the worst of it was that I too had got beyond reason. I could have torn the child apart in my own fury and enjoyed it. It was a pleasure to attack her. My face was burning with it.

The damned little brat must be protected against her own idiocy, one says to one's self at such times. Others must be protected against her. It is a social necessity. And all these things are true. But a blind fury, a feeling of adult shame, bred of a longing for muscular release are the operatives. One goes on to the end.

In the final unreasoning assault I overpowered the child's neck and jaws. I forced the heavy silver spoon back of her teeth and down her throat till she gagged. And there it was — both tonsils covered with membrane. She had fought valiantly to keep me from knowing her secret. She had been hiding that sore throat for three days at least and lying to her parents in order to escape just such an outcome as this.

Now truly she was furious. She had been on the defensive before but now she attacked. Tried to get off her father's lap and fly at me while tears of defeat blinded her eyes.

Tobias Wolff

Tobias Wolff (b. 1945) began *This Boy's Life*, his best-selling memoir, by writing, "My first stepfather used to say that what I didn't know would fill a book. Well, here it is." A compassionate sense of paradox and irony permeates his writing, as in "Bullet in the Brain" and "Say Yes," adding an emotional color to the transparently clear prose of his narratives.

Born in Birmingham, Alabama, Wolff followed his mother to the Pacific Northwest when his parents divorced. It is this period in his life that is the subject of *This Boy's Life* (1989), which was later made into a movie. After being expelled from prep school, he served in the U.S. Army in Vietnam between 1964 and 1968. Then he studied at Oxford University and Stanford University, where in 1975–1976 he received a Wallace Stegner fellowship in creative writing. Two National Endowment for the Arts fellowships followed, along with a Mary Roberts Rinehart grant, an Arizona Council on the Arts fellowship, a Guggenheim fellowship, three O. Henry short story prizes, and the PEN/Faulkner Award for fiction for *The Barracks Thief* (1984), a novella about his army experience. Wolff's first book was a collection of short stories, *In the Garden of the North American Martyrs* (1981). *The Night in Question* (1997) is another story collection, and a recent novel is *Old School* (2004). *Our Story Begins*, his latest story collection, was published in 2008.

Wolff credits several writers as influences on his fiction: Ernest Hemingway, Anton Chekhov, Paul Bowles, Sherwood Anderson, John Cheever, Flannery O'Connor, and Raymond Carver—"the list has no end so I'd better stop here." He prefers writing short stories to novels because "when I write a short story, I feel like I'm somehow cooperating with the story; when I try to work in longer forms, I feel like I'm beating them into existence. I feel a kind of clumsiness that I don't feel when I'm writing short stories." Wolff regards writing as an "essentially optimistic art," because

> the very act of writing assumes, to begin with, that someone cares to
> hear what you have to say. It assumes that people share, that people
> can be reached, that people can be touched and even in some cases
> changed. . . . So many of the things in our world tend to lead us to despair. It
> seems to me that the final symptom of despair is silence, and that storytell-
> ing is one of the sustaining arts; it's one of the affirming arts. . . . A writer may
> have a certain pessimism in his outlook, but the very act of being a writer
> seems to me to be an optimistic act.

Bullet in the Brain

1995

ANDERS COULDN'T GET TO THE BANK until just before it closed, so of course the line was endless and he got stuck behind two women whose loud, stupid conversation put him in a murderous temper. He was never in the best of tempers anyway, Anders—a book critic known for the weary, elegant savagery with which he dispatched almost everything he reviewed.

With the line still doubled around the rope, one of the tellers stuck a "POSITION CLOSED" sign in her window and walked to the back of the bank, where she leaned against a desk and began to pass the time with a man shuffling papers. The women in front of Anders broke off their conversation and watched the teller with hatred. "Oh, that's nice," one of them said. She turned to Anders and added, confident of his accord, "One of those little human touches that keep us coming back for more."

Anders had conceived his own towering hatred of the teller, but he immediately turned it on the presumptuous crybaby in front of him. "Damned unfair," he said. "Tragic, really. If they're not chopping off the wrong leg, or bombing your ancestral village, they're closing their positions."

She stood her ground. "I didn't say it was tragic," she said. "I just think it's a pretty lousy way to treat your customers."

"Unforgivable," Anders said. "Heaven will take note."

She sucked in her cheeks but stared past him and said nothing. Anders saw that the other woman, her friend, was looking in the same direction. And then the tellers stopped what they were doing, and the customers slowly turned, and silence came over the bank. Two men wearing black ski masks and blue business suits were standing to the side of the door. One of them had a pistol pressed against the guard's neck. The guard's eyes were closed, and his lips were moving. The other man had a sawed-off shotgun. "Keep your big mouth shut!" the man with the pistol said, though no one had spoken a word. "One of you tellers hits the alarm, you're all dead meat. Got it?"

The tellers nodded.

"Oh, bravo, " Anders said. "Dead meat." He turned to the woman in front of him. "Great script, eh? The stern, brass-knuckled poetry of the dangerous classes."

She looked at him with drowning eyes.

The man with the shotgun pushed the guard to his knees. He handed up the shotgun to his partner and yanked the guard's wrists up behind his back and locked them together with a pair of handcuffs. He toppled him onto the floor with a kick between the shoulder blades. Then he took his shotgun back and went over to the security gate at the end of the counter. He was short and heavy and moved with peculiar slowness, even torpor. "Buzz him in," his partner said. The man with the shotgun opened the gate and sauntered along the line of tellers, handing each of them a Hefty bag. When he came to the empty position he looked over at the man with the pistol, who said, "Whose slot is that?"

Anders watched the teller. She put her hand to her throat and turned to the man she'd been talking to. He nodded. "Mine," she said.

"Then get your ugly ass in gear and fill that bag."

"There you go," Anders said to the woman in front of him. "Justice is done."

"Hey! Bright boy! Did I tell you talk?"

"No," Anders said.

"Then shut your trap."

"Did you hear that?" Anders said. "Bright boy. Right out of 'The Killers.'"

"Please be quiet," the woman said.

"Hey, you deaf or what?" The man with the pistol walked over to Anders. He poked the weapon into Anders' gut. "You think I'm playing games?"

"No," Anders said, but the barrel tickled like a stiff finger and he had to fight back the titters. He did this by making himself stare into the man's eyes, which were clearly visible behind the holes in the mask: pale blue, and rawly red-rimmed. The man's left eyelid kept twitching. He breathed out a piercing, ammoniac smell that shocked Anders more than anything that had happened, and he was beginning to develop a sense of unease when the man prodded him again with the pistol.

"You like me, bright boy?" he said. "You want to suck my dick?"

"No," Anders said.

"Then stop looking at me."

Anders fixed his gaze on the man's shiny wing-top shoes.

"Not down there. Up there." He stuck the pistol under Anders' chin and pushed it upward until Anders was looking at the ceiling.

Anders had never paid much attention to that part of the bank, a pompous old building with marble floors and counters and pillars, and gilt scrollwork over the tellers' cages. The domed ceiling had been decorated with mythological figures whose fleshy, toga-draped ugliness Anders had taken in at a glance many years earlier and afterward declined to notice. Now he had no choice but to scrutinize the painter's work. It was even worse than he remembered, and all of it executed with the utmost gravity. The artist had a few tricks up his sleeve and used them again and again — a certain rosy blush on the underside of the clouds, a coy backward glance on the faces of the cupids and fauns. The ceiling was crowded with various dramas, but the one that caught Anders' eye was Zeus and Europa — portrayed, in this rendition, as a bull ogling a cow from behind a haystack. To make the cow sexy, the painter had canted her hips suggestively and given her long, droopy eyelashes through which she gazed back at the bull with sultry welcome. The bull wore a smirk and his eyebrows were arched. If there'd been a bubble coming out of his mouth, it would have said, "Hubba hubba."

"What's so funny, bright boy?"

"Nothing."

"You think I'm comical? You think I'm some kind of clown?"

"No."

"You think you can fuck with me?"

"No."

"Fuck with me again, you're history. *Capiche?*"

Anders burst our laughing. He covered his mouth with both hands and said, "I'm sorry, I'm sorry," then snorted helplessly through his fingers and said, "*Capiche* — oh, God, *capiche*," and at that the man with the pistol raised the pistol and shot Anders right in the head.

The bullet smashed Anders' skull and ploughed through his brain and exited behind his right ear, scattering shards of bone into the cerebral cortex, the corpus callosum, back toward the basal ganglia, and down into the thalamus. But before all this occurred, the first appearance of the bullet in the cerebrum set off a crackling chain of ion transports and neurotransmissions. Because of their peculiar origin these traced a peculiar patter, flukishly calling to life a summer afternoon some forty years past, and long since lost to memory. After striking the cranium the bullet was moving at 900 feet per second, a pathetically sluggish, glacial pace compared to the synaptic lighting that flashed around it. Once in the brain, that is, the bullet came under the mediation of brain time, which gave Anders plenty of leisure to contemplate the scene that, in a phrase he would have abhorred, "passed before his eyes."

It is worth noting what Anders did not remember, given what he did remember. He did not remember his first lover, Sherry, or what he had most madly loved about her, before it came to irritate him — her unembarrassed carnality, and especially the cordial way she had with his unit, which she called Mr. Mole, as in, "Uh-oh, looks like Mr. Mole wants to play," and "Let's hide Mr. Mole!" Anders did not remember his wife, whom he had also loved before she exhausted him with her predictability, or his daughter, now a sullen professor of economics at Dartmouth. He did not remember standing just outside his daughter's door as she lectured her bear about his naughtiness and described the truly appalling punishments Paws would receive unless he changed his ways. He did not remember a single line of the hundreds of poems he had committed to memory in his youth so that he could give himself the shivers at will — not "Silent, upon a peak in Darien," or "My God, I heard this day," or "All my pretty ones? Did you say all? O hell-kite! All?" None of these did he remember; not one. Anders did not remember his dying mother saying of his father, "I should have stabbed him in his sleep."

He did not remember Professor Josephs telling his class how Athenian prisoners in Sicily had been released if they could recite Aeschylus, and then reciting Aeschylus himself, right there, in the Greek. Anders did not remember how his eyes had burned at those sounds. He did not remember the surprise of seeing a college classmate's name on the jacket of a novel not long after they graduated, or the respect he had felt after reading the book. He did not remember the pleasure of giving respect.

Nor did Anders remember seeing a woman leap to her death from the building opposite his own just days after his daughter was born. He did not remember shouting, "Lord have mercy!" He did not remember deliberately crashing his father's car in to a tree, of having his ribs kicked in by three policemen at an anti-war rally, or waking himself up with laughter. He did not remember when he began to regard the heap of books on his desk with boredom and dread, or when he grew angry at writers for writing them. He did not remember when everything began to remind him of something else.

This is what he remembered. Heat. A baseball field. Yellow grass, the whirr of insects, himself leaning against a tree as the boys of the neighborhood gather for a pickup game. He looks on as the others argue the relative genius of Mantle and Mays. They have been worrying this subject all summer, and it has become tedious to Anders: an oppression, like the heat.

Then the last two boys arrive, Coyle and a cousin of his from Mississippi. Anders has never met Coyle's cousin before and will never see him again. He says hi with the rest but takes no further notice of him until they've chosen sides and someone asks the cousin what position he wants to play. "Shortstop," the boy says. "Short's the best position they is." Anders turns and looks at him. He wants to hear Coyle's cousin repeat what he's just said, but he knows better than to ask. The others will think he's being a jerk, ragging the kid for his grammar. But that isn't it, not at all — it's that Anders is strangely roused, elated, by those final two words, their pure unexpectedness and their music. He takes the field in a trance, repeating them to himself.

The bullet is already in the brain; it won't be outrun forever, or charmed to a halt. In the end it will do its work and leave the troubled skull behind, dragging its comet's tail of memory and hope and talent and love into the marble hall of commerce. That can't be helped. But for now Anders can still make time. Time for the shadows to lengthen on the grass, time for the tethered dog to bark at the flying ball, time for the boy in right field to smack his sweat-blackened mitt and softly chant, *They is, they is, they is.*

Say Yes

1985

THEY WERE DOING the dishes, his wife washing while he dried. He'd washed the night before. Unlike most men he knew, he really pitched in on the housework. A few months earlier he'd overheard a friend of his wife's congratulate her on having such a considerate husband, and he thought, *I try.* Helping out with the dishes was a way of showing how considerate he was.

They talked about different things and somehow got on the subject of whether white people should marry black people. He said that all things considered, he thought it was a bad idea.

"Why?" she asked.

Sometimes his wife got this look where she pinched her brows together and bit her lower lip and stared down at something. When he saw her like this he knew he should keep his mouth shut, but he never did. Actually it made him talk more. She had that look now.

"Why?" she asked again, and stood there with her hand inside a bowl, not washing it but just holding it above the water.

"Listen," he said, "I went to school with blacks, and I've worked with blacks and lived on the same street with blacks, and we've always gotten along just fine. I don't need you coming along now and implying that I'm a racist."

"I didn't imply anything," she said, and began washing the bowl again, turning it around in her hand as though she were shaping it. "I just don't see what's wrong with a white person marrying a black person, that's all."

"They don't come from the same culture as we do. Listen to them sometime — they even have their own language. That's okay with me, I *like* hearing them talk" — he did; for some reason it always made him feel happy — "but it's different. A person from their culture and a person from our culture could never really *know* each other."

"Like you know me?" his wife asked.

"Yes. Like I know you."

"But if they love each other," she said. She was washing faster now, not looking at him.

Oh boy, he thought. He said, "Don't take my word for it. Look at the statistics. Most of those marriages break up."

"Statistics." She was piling dishes on the drainboard at a terrific rate, just swiping at them with the cloth. Many of them were greasy, and there were flecks of food between the tines of the forks. "All right," she said, "what about foreigners? I suppose you think the same thing about two foreigners getting married."

"Yes," he said, "as a matter of fact I do. How can you understand someone who comes from a completely different background?"

"Different," said his wife. "Not the same, like us."

"Yes, different," he snapped, angry with her for resorting to this trick of repeating his words so that they sounded crass, or hypocritical. "These are dirty," he said, and dumped all the silverware back into the sink.

The water had gone flat and gray. She stared down at it, her lips pressed tight together, then plunged her hands under the surface. "Oh!" she cried, and jumped back. She took her right hand by the wrist and held it up. Her thumb was bleeding.

"Ann, don't move," he said. "Stay right there." He ran upstairs to the bathroom and rummaged in the medicine chest for alcohol, cotton, and a Band-Aid. When he came back down she was leaning against the refrigerator with her eyes closed, still holding her hand. He took the hand and dabbed at her thumb with the cotton. The bleeding had stopped. He squeezed it to see how deep the wound was and a single drop of blood welled up, trembling and bright, and fell to the floor. Over the thumb she stared at him accusingly. "It's shallow," he said. "Tomorrow you won't even know it's there." He hoped that she appreciated how quickly he had come to her aid. He'd acted out of concern for her, with no thought of getting anything in return, but now the thought occurred to him that it would be a nice gesture on her part not to start up that conversation again, as he was tired of it. "I'll finish up here," he said. "You go and relax."

"That's okay," she said. "I'll dry."

He began to wash the silverware again, giving a lot of attention to the forks.

"So," she said, "you wouldn't have married me if I'd been black."

"For Christ's sake, Ann!"

"Well, that's what you said, didn't you?"

"No, I did not. The whole question is ridiculous. If you had been black we probably wouldn't even have met. You would have had your friends and I would have had mine. The only black girl I ever really knew was my partner in the debating club, and I was already going out with you by then."

"But if we had met, and I'd been black?"

"Then you probably would have been going out with a black guy." He picked up the rinsing nozzle and sprayed the silverware. The water was so hot that the metal darkened to pale blue, then turned silver again.

"Let's say I wasn't," she said. "Let's say I am black and unattached and we meet and fall in love."

He glanced over at her. She was watching him and her eyes were bright. "Look," he said, taking a reasonable tone, "this is stupid. If you were black you wouldn't be you." As he said this he realized it was absolutely true. There was no possible way of arguing with the fact that she would not be herself if she were black. So he said it again: "If you were black you wouldn't be you."

"I know," she said, "but let's just say."

He took a deep breath. He had won the argument but he still felt cornered. "Say what?" he asked.

"That I'm black, but still me, and we fall in love. Will you marry me?"

He thought about it.

"Well?" she said, and stepped close to him. Her eyes were even brighter. "Will you marry me?"

"I'm thinking," he said.

"You won't, I can tell. You're going to say no."

"Let's not move too fast on this," he said. "There are lots of things to consider. We don't want to do something we would regret for the rest of our lives."

"No more considering. Yes or no."

"Since you put it that way —"

"Yes or no."

"Jesus, Ann. All right. No."

She said, "Thank you," and walked from the kitchen into the living room. A moment later he heard her turning the pages of a magazine. He knew that she was too angry to be actually reading it, but she didn't snap through the pages the way he would have done. She turned them slowly, as if she were studying every word. She was demonstrating her indifference to him, and it had the effect he knew she wanted it to have. It hurt him.

He had no choice but to demonstrate his indifference to her. Quietly, thoroughly, he washed the rest of the dishes. Then he dried them and put them away. He wiped the counters and the stove and scoured the linoleum where the drop of blood had fallen. While he was at it, he decided, he might as well mop the whole floor. When he was done the kitchen looked new, the way it looked when they were first shown the house, before they had ever lived here.

He picked up the garbage pail and went outside. The night was clear and he could see a few stars to the west, where the lights of the town didn't blur them out.

On El Camino the traffic was steady and light, peaceful as a river. He felt ashamed that he had let his wife get him into a fight. In another thirty years or so they would both be dead. What would all that stuff matter then? He thought of the years they had spent together, and how close they were, and how well they knew each other, and his throat tightened so that he could hardly breathe. His face and neck began to tingle. Warmth flooded his chest. He stood there for a while, enjoying these sensations, then picked up the pail and went out the back gate.

The two mutts from down the street had pulled over the garbage can again. One of them was rolling around on his back and the other had something in her mouth. Growling, she tossed it into the air, leaped up and caught it, growled again and whipped her head from side to side. When they saw him coming they trotted away with short, mincing steps. Normally he would heave rocks at them, but this time he let them go.

The house was dark when he came back inside. She was in the bathroom. He stood outside the door and called her name. He heard bottles clinking, but she didn't answer him. "Ann, I'm really sorry," he said. "I'll make it up to you, I promise."

"How?" she asked.

He wasn't expecting this. But from a sound in her voice, a level and definite note that was strange to him, he knew that he had to come up with the right answer. He leaned against the door. "I'll marry you," he whispered.

"We'll see," she said. "Go on to bed. I'll be out in a minute."

He undressed and got under the covers. Finally he heard the bathroom door open and close.

"Turn off the light," she said from the hallway.

"What?"

"Turn off the light."

He reached over and pulled the chain on the bedside lamp. The room went dark. "All right," he said. He lay there, but nothing happened. "All right," he said again. Then he heard a movement across the room. He sat up, but he couldn't see a thing. The room was silent. His heart pounded the way it had on their first night together the way it still did when he woke at a noise in the darkness and waited to hear it again — the sound of someone moving through the house, a stranger.

Virginia Woolf

Virginia Woolf (1882–1941) is best known as a novelist, critic, and essayist; she published only one book of short stories, early in her career. The daughter of Sir Leslie Stephen, a scholar and editor of the monumental *Dictionary of National Biography*, she was educated at home in her father's library, keenly aware that if she had been born a boy, she would have gone on to Cambridge or Oxford. Later, guided by this sense of injustice, she wrote two feminist works, *A Room of One's Own* (1929) and *Three Guineas* (1938). In frail health all her life, she married the journalist Leonard Woolf in 1912, and they lived in Bloomsbury, the fashionably bohemian section of London. Her first novel, *The Voyage Out*, was published in 1915. Two years later the Woolfs set two stories by "L. and V. Woolf" on an old handpress and published them under the imprint of the Hogarth Press. The little pamphlet was so successful that their press became a thriving enterprise, publishing the work of authors such as Katherine Mansfield and T. S. Eliot. In 1921 the Hogarth Press published *Monday or Tuesday*, Woolf's collection of short stories, and the following year—sustained by the freedom of having her own printing press—she began to publish the unconventional novels that made her reputation: *Jacob's Room* (1922), *Mrs. Dalloway* (1925), *To the Lighthouse* (1927), and *The Waves* (1931).

Dissatisfied with realistic fiction, Woolf explored the psychological nature of consciousness. She believed that beneath the appearance of change and disorder that marks daily life is a timeless reality that becomes apparent only during pure "moments of being," when the self is transcended and the individual consciousness becomes an undifferentiated part of a greater whole. For Woolf, the description of the immediate flow of her characters' thoughts and feelings, as in "Kew Gardens," was more important than the realistic depiction of their physical behavior. Her good friend E.M. Forster admired "the style and sensitiveness" of Woolf's early stories "Kew Gardens" and "The Mark on the Wall." He later remembered that "none of us guessed that out of the pollen of those flowers would come the trees of the future," her experimental novels.

Throughout her life, Woolf wrote short stories to relax between the arduous bouts of work on her novels, usually sketching a story out in rough form, then putting the draft away in a drawer. She felt that in her fiction she revealed "some order" about the world, "a token of some real thing behind appearances; and I make it real by putting it into words." If an editor asked her for a short story, she would take out a sketch and rewrite it several times. She discussed with her husband the possibility of republishing *Monday or Tuesday* with her later stories, and after her suicide, Leonard Woolf saw this book through to publication as *A Haunted House and Other Stories* (1953).

RELATED COMMENTARY
Katherine Mansfield, "Review of Woolf's 'Kew Gardens,'" page 1468.

Kew Gardens

1919

FROM THE OVAL-SHAPED flower bed there rose perhaps a hundred stalks spreading into heart-shaped or tongue-shaped leaves half way up and unfurling at the tip red or blue or yellow petals marked with spots of colour raised upon the surface; and from the red, blue, or yellow gloom of the throat emerged a straight bar, rough with gold dust and slightly clubbed at the end. The petals were voluminous enough to be stirred by the summer breeze, and when they moved, the red, blue, and yellow lights passed one over the other, staining an inch of the brown earth beneath with a spot of the most intricate colour. The light fell either upon the smooth grey back of a pebble, or, falling into a raindrop or, the shell of a snail with its brown, circular veins, or falling into a raindrop, it expanded with such intensity of red, blue, and yellow the thin walls of water that one expected them to burst and disappear. Instead, the drop was left in a second silver grey once more, and the light now settled upon the flesh of a leaf, revealing the branching thread of fibre beneath the surface, and again it moved on and spread its illumination in the vast green spaces beneath the dome of the heart-shaped and tongue-shaped leaves. Then the breeze stirred rather more briskly overhead and the colour was flashed into the air above, into the eyes of the men and women who walk in Kew Gardens in July.

The figures of these men and women straggled past the flower bed with a curiously irregular movement not unlike that of the white and blue butterflies who crossed the turf in zig-zag flights from bed to bed. The man was about six inches in front of the woman, strolling carelessly, while she bore on with greater purpose, only turning her head now and then to see that the children were not too far behind. The man kept this distance in front of the woman purposely, though perhaps unconsciously, for he wished to go on with his thoughts.

"Fifteen years ago I came here with Lily," he thought. "We sat somewhere over there by a lake, and I begged her to marry me all through the hot afternoon. How the dragonfly kept circling round us: how clearly I see the dragonfly and her shoe with the square silver buckle at the toe. All the time I spoke I saw her shoe and when it moved impatiently I knew without looking up what she was going to say: the whole of her seemed to be in her shoe. And my love, my desire, were in the dragonfly; for some reason I thought that if it settled there, on that leaf, the broad one with the red flower in the middle of it, if the dragon fly settled on the leaf she would say 'Yes' at once. But the dragonfly went round and round: it never settled anywhere — of course not, happily not, or I shouldn't be walking here with Eleanor and the children — Tell me, Eleanor, d'you ever think of the past?"

"Why do you ask, Simon?"

"Because I've been thinking of the past. I've been thinking of Lily, the woman I might have married . . . Well, why are you silent? Do you mind my thinking of the past?"

"Why should I mind, Simon? Doesn't one always think of the past, in a garden with men and women lying under the trees? Aren't they one's past, all that remains of it, those men and women, those ghosts lying under the trees, . . . one's happiness, one's reality?"

"For me, a square silver shoe-buckle and a dragonfly — "

"For me, a kiss. Imagine six little girls sitting before their easels twenty years ago, down by the side of a lake, painting the water-lilies, the first red water-lilies I'd ever seen. And suddenly a kiss, there on the back of my neck. And my hand shook all the afternoon so that I couldn't paint. I took out my watch and marked the hour when I would allow myself to think of the kiss for five minutes only — it was so precious — the kiss of an old grey-haired woman with a wart on her nose, the mother of all my kisses all my life. Come, Caroline, come, Hubert."

They walked on past the flowerbed, now walking four abreast, and soon diminished in size among the trees and looked half transparent as the sunlight and shade swam over their backs in large trembling irregular patches.

In the oval flower bed the snail, whose shell had been stained red, blue, and yellow for the space of two minutes or so, now appeared to be moving very slightly in its shell, and next began to labour over the crumbs of loose earth which broke away and rolled down as it passed over them. It appeared to have a definite goal in front of it, differing in this respect from the singular high-stepping angular green insect who attempted to cross in front of it, and waited for a second with its antennae trembling as if in deliberation, and then stepped off as rapidly and strangely in the opposite direction. Brown cliffs with deep green lakes in the hollows, flat, blade-like trees that waved from root to tip, round boulders of grey stone, vast crumpled surfaces of a thin crackling texture — all these objects lay across the snail's progress between one stalk and another to his goal. Before he had decided whether to circumvent the arched tent of a dead leaf or to breast it there came past the bed the feet of other human beings.

This time they were both men. The younger of the two wore an expression of perhaps unnatural calm; he raised his eyes and fixed them very steadily in front of him while his companion spoke, and directly his companion had done speaking he looked on the ground again and sometimes opened his lips only after a long pause and sometimes did not open them at all. The elder man had a curiously uneven and shaky method of walking, jerking his hand forward and throwing up his head abruptly, rather in the manner of an impatient carriage horse tired of waiting outside a house; but in the man these gestures were irresolute and pointless. He talked almost incessantly; he smiled to himself and again began to talk, as if the smile had been an answer. He was talking about spirits — the spirits of the dead, who, according to him, were even now telling him all sorts of odd things about their experiences in Heaven.

"Heaven was known to the ancients as Thessaly, William, and now, with this war, the spirit matter is rolling between the hills like thunder." He paused, seemed to listen, smiled, jerked his head, and continued: —

"You have a small electric battery and a piece of rubber to insulate the wire — isolate? — insulate? — well, we'll skip the details, no good going into details that wouldn't be understood — and in short the little machine stands in any convenient position by the head of the bed, we will say, on a neat mahogany stand. All arrangements being properly fixed by workmen under my direction, the widow applies her ear and summons the spirit by sign as agreed. Women! Widows! Women in black — "

Here he seemed to have caught sight of a woman's dress in the distance, which in the shade looked a purple black. He took off his hat, placed his hand upon his heart, and hurried towards her muttering and gesticulating feverishly. But William caught him by the sleeve and touched a flower with the tip of his walking-stick in order to divert the old man's attention. After looking at it for a moment in some confusion the old man bent his ear to it and seemed to answer a voice speaking from it, for he began talking about the forests of Uruguay which he had visited hundreds of years ago in company with the most beautiful young woman in Europe. He could be heard murmuring about forests of Uruguay blanketed with the wax petals of tropical roses, nightingales, sea beaches, mermaids, and women drowned at sea, as he suffered himself to be moved on by William, upon whose face the look of stoical patience grew slowly deeper and deeper.

Following his steps so closely as to be slightly puzzled by his gestures came two elderly women of the lower middle class, one stout and ponderous, the other rosy-cheeked and nimble. Like most people of their station they were frankly fascinated by any signs of eccentricity betokening a disordered brain, especially in the well-to-do; but they were too far off to be certain whether the gestures were merely eccentric or genuinely mad. After they had scrutinised the old man's back in silence for a moment and given each other a queer, sly look, they went on energetically piecing together their very complicated dialogue:

"Nell, Bert, Lot, Cess, Phil, Pa, he says, I says, she says, I says, I says, I says — "
"My Bert, Sis, Bill, Grandad, the old man, sugar,

Sugar, flour, kippers, greens,
Sugar, sugar, sugar."

The ponderous woman looked through the pattern of falling words at the flowers standing cool, firm, and upright in the earth, with a curious expression. She saw them as a sleeper waking from a heavy sleep sees a brass candlestick reflecting the light in an unfamiliar way, and closes his eyes and opens them, and seeing the brass candlestick again, finally starts broad awake and stares at the candlestick with all his powers. So the heavy woman came to a standstill opposite the oval-shaped flower bed, and ceased even to pretend to listen to what the other woman was saying. She stood there letting the words fall over her, swaying the top part of her body slowly backwards and forwards, looking at the flowers. Then she suggested that they should find a seat and have their tea.

The snail had now considered every possible method of reaching his goal without going round the dead leaf or climbing over it. Let alone the effort needed for climbing a leaf, he was doubtful whether the thin texture which vibrated with such an alarming crackle when touched even by the tip of his horns would bear his weight; and this determined him finally to creep beneath it, for there was a point where the leaf curved high enough from the ground to admit him. He had just inserted his head in the opening and was taking stock of the high brown roof and was getting used to the cool brown light when two other people came past outside on the turf. This time they were both young, a young man and a young woman. They were both in the prime of youth, or even in that season which precedes the prime of youth, the season before the smooth pink folds of the flower have burst their gummy case, when the wings of the butterfly, though fully grown, are motionless in the sun.

"Lucky it isn't Friday," he observed.

"Why? D'you believe in luck?"

"They make you pay sixpence on Friday."

"What's sixpence anyway? Isn't it worth sixpence?"

"What's 'it' — what do you mean by 'it'?"

"O anything — I mean — you know what I mean."

Long pauses came between each of these remarks, they were uttered in toneless and monotonous voices. The couple stood still on the edge of the flowerbed, and together pressed the end of her parasol deep down into the soft earth. The action and the fact that his hand rested on the top of hers expressed their feelings in a strange way, as these short insignificant words also expressed something, words with short wings for their heavy body of meaning, inadequate to carry them far and thus alighting awkwardly upon the very common objects that surrounded them and were to their inexperienced touch so massive, but who knows (so they thought as they pressed the parasol into the earth) what precipices aren't concealed in them, or what slopes of ice don't shine in the sun on the other side? Who knows? Who has ever seen this before? Even when she wondered what sort of tea they gave you at Kew, he felt that something loomed up behind her words, and stood vast and solid behind them; and the mist very slowly rose and uncovered — O Heavens, what were those shapes? — little white tables, and waitresses who looked first at her and then at him; and there was a bill that he would pay with a real two shilling piece, and it was real, all real, he assured himself, fingering the coin in his pocket, real to everyone except to him and to her; even to him it began to seem real; and then — but it was too exciting to stand and think any longer, and he pulled the parasol out of the earth with a jerk and was impatient to find the place where one had tea with other people, like other people.

"Come along Trissie; it's time we had our tea."

"Wherever *does* one have one's tea?" she asked with the oddest thrill of excitement in her voice, looking vaguely round and letting herself be drawn on down the grass path, trailing her parasol, turning her head this way and that way, forgetting her tea, wishing to go down there and then down there, remembering orchids and cranes among wild flowers, a Chinese pagoda and a crimson-crested bird; but he bore her on.

Thus one couple after another with much the same irregular and aimless movement passed the flower bed and were enveloped in layer after layer of greenblue vapour, in which at first their bodies had substance and a dash of colour, but later both substance and colour dissolved in the green blue atmosphere. How hot it was! So hot that even the thrush chose to hop, like a mechanical bird, in the shadow of the flowers, with long pauses between one movement and the next; instead of rambling vaguely the white butterflies danced one above another, making with their white shifting flakes the outline of a shattered marble column above the tallest flowers; the glass roofs of the palm house shone as if a whole market full of shiny green umbrellas had opened in the sun; and in the drone of the aeroplane the voice of the summer sky murmured its fierce soul. Yellow and black, pink and snow white, shapes of all these colours, men, women, and children were spotted for a second upon the horizon, and then, seeing the breadth of yellow that lay upon the grass, they wavered and sought shade beneath the trees, dissolving like drops of water in the yellow and green atmosphere, staining it faintly with red and blue. It seemed as if all gross and heavy bodies had sunk down in the heat motionless and lay huddled upon the ground, but their voices went wavering from them as if they were flames lolling from the thick waxen bodies of candles. Voices, yes, voices, wordless voices, breaking the silence suddenly with such depth of contentment, such passion of desire, or, in the voices of children, such freshness of surprise; breaking the silence? But there was no silence; all the time the motor omnibuses were turning their wheels and changing their gear; like a vast nest of Chinese boxes all of wrought steel turning ceaselessly one within another the city murmured; on the top of which the voices cried aloud and the petals of myriads of flowers flashed their colours into the air.

Richard Wright

Richard Wright (1908–1960) was born on a plantation near Natchez, Mississippi, the son of a farmhand and a country schoolteacher. His home life was disrupted when his father deserted the family, and Wright later said it was only through reading that he managed to keep himself alive. As soon as he could, he moved north, to Memphis, Chicago, and then to New York City, where he became involved in radical politics. He was a member of the Communist Party from 1932 to 1944. In the 1930s he worked as a reporter for *New Masses*, a correspondent for the Harlem bureau of the *Daily Worker*, and an editor for *New Challenge*, a left-wing magazine that published his "Blueprint for Negro Writing," an effort to bridge the gap between Marxism and black nationalism, in 1938. He was also then writing the stories that appeared in *Uncle Tom's Children* (1938), which won first prize in a contest for writers in the Federal Writers' Project during the Depression. Wright's early fiction was strongly influenced by Ernest Hemingway's way of writing stories, but Wright also set himself the problem of how to use a modernist style to write about social issues as a radicalized African American:

> Practically all of us, young writers, were influenced by Ernest Hemingway. We liked the simple, direct way in which he wrote, but a great many of us wanted to write about social problems. The question came up: How could we write about social problems and use a simple style? Hemingway's style is so concentrated on naturalistic detail that there is no room for social comment. One boy said that one way was to dig deeper into the character and try to get something that will live. I decided to try it.

The result was the five stories published in *Uncle Tom's Children*. Next Wright turned to his first novel, *Native Son* (1940), an American classic dramatizing a brutal story of racial conflict. This was followed by *Black Boy* (1945), a brilliant autobiography written when he was not yet forty. The next year he left the United States to spend the last fourteen years of his life in Paris, feeling himself alienated from American values. In 1960, the year Wright died, he gathered for publication his second book of short stories, *Eight Men*, made up of fiction that had appeared over the years in magazines and anthologies, including "The Man Who Was Almost a Man," written in the 1930s.

Telling stories from a realistic view of his own experience, Wright experimented with literary techniques in all his fiction. His short stories dramatize the same themes as his novels and are equally experimental. "The Man Who Was Almost a Man" weaves the black farm boy's speech so skillfully with standard English narration that most readers are unaware of the effect of the deliberate juxtaposition, but this technique brings us closer to the boy's world while making an implicit social comment about his exclusion from the exploitative white society engulfing him.

The Man Who Was Almost a Man

1961

DAVE STRUCK OUT across the fields, looking homeward through paling light. Whut's the use talkin wid em niggers in the field? Anyhow, his mother was putting supper on the table. Them niggers can't understan nothing. One of these days he was going to get a gun and practice shooting, then they couldn't talk to him as though he were a little boy. He slowed, looking at the ground. Shucks, Ah ain scareda them even ef they are biggern me! Aw, Ah know whut Ahma do. Ahm going by ol Joe's sto n git that Sears Roebuck catlog n look at them guns. Mebbe Ma will lemme buy one when she gits mah pay from ol man Hawkins. Ahma beg her t gimme some money. Ahm ol ernough to hava gun. Ahm seventeen. Almost a man. He strode, feeling his long loose-jointed limbs. Shucks, a man oughta hava little gun aftah he done worked hard all day.

He came in sight of Joe's store. A yellow lantern glowed on the front porch. He mounted steps and went through the screen door, hearing it bang behind him. There was a strong smell of coal oil and mackerel fish. He felt very confident until he saw fat Joe walk in through the rear door, then his courage began to ooze.

"Howdy, Dave! Whutcha want?"

"How yuh, Mistah Joe? Aw, Ah don wanna buy nothing. Ah jus wanted t see ef yuhd lemme look at tha catlog erwhile."

"Sure! You wanna see it here?"

"Nawsuh. Ah wants t take it home wid me. Ah'll bring it back termorrow when Ah come in from the fiels."

"You plannin on buying something?"

"Yessuh."

"Your ma lettin you have your own money now?"

"Shucks. Mistah Joe, Ahm gittin t be a man like anybody else!"

Joe laughed and wiped his greasy white face with a red bandanna.

"Whut you plannin on buyin?"

Dave looked at the floor, scratched his head, scratched his thigh, and smiled. Then he looked up shyly.

"Ah'll tell yuh, Mistah Joe, ef yuh promise yuh won't tell."

"I promise."

"Waal, Ahma buy a gun."

"A gun? What you want with a gun?"

"Ah wanna keep it."

"You ain't nothing but a boy. You don't need a gun."

"Aw, lemme have the catlog, Mistah Joe. Ah'll bring it back."

Joe walked through the rear door. Dave was elated. He looked around at barrels of sugar and flour. He heard Joe coming back. He craned his neck to see if he were bringing the book. Yeah, he's got it. Gawddog, he's got it!

"Here, but be sure you bring it back. It's the only one I got."

"Sho, Mistah Joe."

"Say, if you wanna buy a gun, why don't you buy one from me? I gotta gun to sell."

"Will it shoot?"

"Sure it'll shoot."

"Whut kind is it?"

"Oh, it's kinda old . . . a left-hand Wheeler. A pistol. A big one."

"Is it got bullets in it?"

"It's loaded."

"Kin Ah see it?"

"Where's your money?"

"What yuh wan fer it?"

"I'll let you have it for two dollars."

"Just two dollahs? Shucks, Ah could buy tha when Ah git mah pay."

"I'll have it here when you want it."

"Awright, suh. Ah be in fer it."

He went through the door, hearing it slam again behind him. Ahma git some money from Ma n buy me a gun! Only two dollahs! He tucked the thick catalogue under his arm and hurried.

"Where yuh been, boy?" His mother held a steaming dish of black-eyed peas.

"Aw, Ma, Ah jus stopped down the road t talk wid the boys."

"Yuh know bettah t keep suppah waitin."

He sat down, resting the catalogue on the edge of the table.

"Yuh git up from there and git to the well n wash yosef! Ah ain feedin no hogs in mah house!"

She grabbed his shoulder and pushed him. He stumbled out of the room, then came back to get the catalogue.

"Whut this?"

"Aw, Ma, it's jusa catlog."

"Who yuh git it from?"

"From Joe, down at the sto."

"Waal, thas good. We kin use it in the outhouse."

"Naw, Ma." He grabbed for it. "Gimme ma catlog, Ma."

She held onto it and glared at him.

"Quit hollerin at me! Whut's wrong wid yuh? Yuh crazy?"

"But Ma, please. It ain mine! It's Joe's! He tol me t bring it back t im termorrow."

She gave up the book. He stumbled down the back steps, hugging the thick book under his arm. When he had splashed water on his face and hands, he groped back to the kitchen and fumbled in a corner for the towel. He bumped into a chair; it clattered to the floor. The catalogue sprawled at his feet. When he had dried his eyes he snatched up the book and held it again under his arm. His mother stood watching him.

"Now, ef yuh gonna act a fool over that ol book, Ah'll take it n burn it up."

"Naw, Ma, please."

"Waal, set down n be still!"

He sat down and drew the oil lamp close. He thumbed page after page, unaware of the food his mother set on the table. His father came in. Then his small brother.

"Whutcha got there, Dave?" his father asked.

"Jusa catlog," he answered, not looking up.

"Yeah, here they is!" His eyes glowed at blue-and-black revolvers. He glanced up, feeling sudden guilt. His father was watching him. He eased the book under the table and rested it on his knees. After the blessing was asked, he ate. He scooped up peas and swallowed fat meat without chewing. Buttermilk helped to wash it down. He did not want to mention money before his father. He would do much better by cornering his mother when she was alone. He looked at his father uneasily out of the edge of his eye.

"Boy, how come yuh don quit foolin wid tha book n eat yo suppah?"

"Yessuh."

"How you n ol man Hawkins gitten erlong?"

"Suh?"

"Can't yuh hear? Why don yuh lissen? Ah ast yu how wuz yuh n ol man Hawkins gittin erlong?"

"Oh, swell, Pa. Ah plows mo lan than anybody over there."

"Waal, yuh oughta keep you mind on whut yuh doin."

"Yessuh."

He poured his plate full of molasses and sopped it up slowly with a chunk of cornbread. When his father and brother had left the kitchen, he still sat and looked again at the guns in the catalogue, longing to muster courage enough to present his case to his mother. Lawd, ef Ah only had tha pretty one! He could almost feel the slickness of the weapon with his fingers. If he had a gun like that he would polish it and keep it shining so it would never rust. N Ah'd keep it loaded, by Gawd!

"Ma?" His voice was hesitant.

"Hunh?"

"Ol man Hawkins give yuh mah money yit?"

"Yeah, but ain no usa yuh thinking bout throwin nona it erway. Ahm keeping tha money sos yuh kin have cloes t go to school this winter."

He rose and went to her side with the open catalogue in his palms. She was washing dishes, her head bent low over a pan. Shyly he raised the book. When he spoke, his voice was husky, faint.

"Ma, Gawd knows Ah wans one of these."

"One of whut?" she asked, not raising her eyes.

"One of these," he said again, not daring even to point. She glanced up at the page, then at him with wide eyes.

"Nigger, is yuh gone plumb crazy?"

"Aw, Ma —"

"Git outta here! Don yuh talk t me bout no gun! Yuh a fool!"

"Ma, Ah kin buy one fer two dollahs."

"Not ef Ah knows it, yuh ain!"

"But yuh promised me one —"

"Ah don care what Ah promised! Yuh ain nothing but a boy yit!"

"Ma, ef yuh lemme buy one Ah'll *never* ast yuh fer nothing no mo."

"Ah tol yuh t git outta here! Yuh ain gonna toucha penny of tha money fer no gun! Thas how come Ah has Mistah Hawkins t pay yo wages t me, cause Ah knows yuh ain got no sense."

"But, Ma, we needa gun. Pa ain got no gun. We needa gun in the house. Yuh kin never tell whut might happen."

"Now don yuh try to maka fool outta me, boy! Ef we did hava gun, yuh wouldn't have it!"

He laid the catalogue down and slipped his arm around her waist.

"Aw, Ma, Ah done worked hard alla summer n ain ast yuh fer nothing, is Ah, now?"

"Thas whut yuh spose t do!"

"But Ma, Ah wans a gun. Yuh kin lemme have two dollahs outta mah money. Please, Ma. I kin give it to Pa. . . . Please, Ma! Ah loves yuh, Ma."

When she spoke her voice came soft and low.

"What yu wan wida gun, Dave? Yuh don need no gun. Yuh'll git in trouble. N ef yo pa jus thought Ah let yuh have money t buy a gun he'd hava fit."

"Ah'll hide it, Ma. It ain but two dollahs."

"Lawd, chil, whut's wrong wid yuh?"

"Ain nothin wrong, Ma. Ahm almos a man now. Ah wans a gun."

"Who gonna sell yuh a gun?"

"Ol Joe at the sto."

"N it don cos but two dollahs?"

"Thas all, Ma. Jus two dollahs. Please, Ma."

She was stacking the plates away; her hands moved slowly, reflectively. Dave kept an anxious silence. Finally, she turned to him.

"Ah'll let yuh git tha gun ef yuh promise me one thing."

"What's tha, Ma?"

"Yuh bring it straight back t me, yuh hear? It be fer Pa."

"Yessum! Lemme go now, Ma."

She stooped, turned slightly to one side, raised the hem of her dress, rolled down the top of her stocking, and came up with a slender wad of bills.

"Here," she said. "Lawd knows yuh don need no gun. But yer pa does. Yuh bring it right back t me, yuh hear? Ahma put it up. Now ef yuh don, Ahma have yuh pa lick yuh so hard yuh won fergit it."

"Yessum."

He took the money, ran down the steps, and across the yard.

"Dave! Yuuuuuh Daaaaave!"

He heard, but he was not going to stop now. "Now, Lawd!"

The first movement he made the following morning was to reach under his pillow for the gun. In the gray light of dawn he held it loosely, feeling a sense of power. Could kill a man with a gun like this. Kill anybody, black or white. And if he were holding his gun in his hand, nobody could run over him; they would have to respect him. It was a big gun, with a long barrel and a heavy handle. He raised and lowered it in his hand, marveling at its weight.

He had not come straight home with it as his mother had asked; instead he had stayed out in the fields, holding the weapon in his hand, aiming it now and then at some imaginary foe. But he had not fired it; he had been afraid that his father might hear. Also he was not sure he knew how to fire it.

To avoid surrendering the pistol he had not come into the house until he knew that they were all asleep. When his mother had tiptoed to his bedside late that night and demanded the gun, he had first played possum; then he had told her that the gun was hidden outdoors, that he would bring it to her in the morning. Now he lay turning it slowly in his hands. He broke it, took out the cartridges, felt them, and then put them back.

He slid out of bed, got a long strip of old flannel from a trunk, wrapped the gun in it, and tied it to his naked thigh while it was still loaded. He did not go in to breakfast. Even though it was not yet daylight, he started for Jim Hawkins' plantation. Just as the sun was rising he reached the barns where the mules and plows were kept.

"Hey! That you, Dave?"

He turned. Jim Hawkins stood eying him suspiciously.

"What're yuh doing here so early?"

"Ah didn't know Ah wuz gittin up so early, Mistah Hawkins. Ah was fixin t hitch up ol Jenny n take her t the fiels."

"Good. Since you're so early, how about plowing that stretch down by the woods?"

"Suits me, Mistah Hawkins."

"O.K. Go to it!"

He hitched Jenny to a plow and started across the fields. Hot dog! This was just what he wanted. If he could get down by the woods, he could shoot his gun and nobody would hear. He walked behind the plow, hearing the traces creaking, feeling the gun tied tight to his thigh.

When he reached the woods, he plowed two whole rows before he decided to take out the gun. Finally, he stopped, looked in all directions, then untied the gun and held it in his hand. He turned to the mule and smiled.

"Know whut this is, Jenny? Naw, yuh wouldn know! Yuhs jusa ol mule! Anyhow, this is a gun, n it kin shoot, by Gawd!"

He held the gun at arm's length. Whut t hell, Ahma shoot this thing! He looked at Jenny again.

"Lissen here, Jenny! When Ah pull this ol trigger, Ah don wan yuh t run n acka fool now!"

Jenny stood with head down, her short ears pricked straight. Dave walked off about twenty feet, held the gun far out from him at arm's length, and turned his head. Hell, he told himself, Ah ain afraid. The gun felt loose in his fingers; he waved it wildly for a moment. Then he shut his eyes and tightened his forefinger. Bloom! A report half deafened him and he thought his right hand was torn from his arm. He heard Jenny whinnying and galloping over the field, and he found himself on his knees, squeezing his fingers hard between his legs. His hand was numb; he jammed it into his mouth, trying to warm it, trying to stop the pain. The gun lay at his feet. He did not quite know what had happened. He stood up and stared at the gun as though it were a living thing. He gritted his teeth and kicked the gun. Yuh almos broke mah arm! He turned to look for Jenny; she was far over the fields, tossing her head and kicking wildly.

"Hol on there, ol mule!"

When he caught up with her she stood trembling, walling her big white eyes at him. The plow was far away; the traces had broken. Then Dave stopped short, looking, not believing. Jenny was bleeding. Her left side was red and wet with blood. He went closer. Lawd, have mercy! Wondah did Ah shoot this mule? He grabbed for Jenny's mane. She flinched, snorted, whirled, tossing her head.

"Hol on now! Hol on."

Then he saw the hole in Jenny's side, right between the ribs. It was round, wet, red. A crimson stream streaked down the front leg, flowing fast. Good Gawd! Ah wuzn't shootin at tha mule. He felt panic. He knew he had to stop that blood, or Jenny would bleed to death. He had never seen so much blood in all his life. He chased the mule for half a mile, trying to catch her. Finally she stopped, breathing hard, stumpy tail half arched. He caught her mane and led her back to where the plow and gun lay. Then he stopped and grabbed handfuls of damp black earth and tried to plug the bullet hole. Jenny shuddered, whinnied, and broke from him.

"Hol on! Hol on now!"

He tried to plug it again, but blood came anyhow. His fingers were hot and sticky. He rubbed dirt into his palms, trying to dry them. Then again he attempted to plug the bullet hole, but Jenny shied away, kicking her heels high. He stood helpless. He had to do something. He ran at Jenny; she dodged him. He watched a red stream of blood flow down Jenny's leg and form a bright pool at her feet.

"Jenny . . . Jenny," he called weakly.

His lips trembled. She's bleeding t death! He looked in the direction of home, wanting to go back, wanting to get help. But he saw the pistol lying in the damp black clay. He had a queer feeling that if he only did something, this would not be; Jenny would not be there bleeding to death.

When he went to her this time, she did not move. She stood with sleepy, dreamy eyes; and when he touched her she gave a low-pitched whinny and knelt to the ground, her front knees slopping in blood.

"Jenny . . . Jenny . . ." he whispered.

For a long time she held her neck erect; then her head sank, slowly. Her ribs swelled with a mighty heave and she went over.

Dave's stomach felt empty, very empty. He picked up the gun and held it gingerly between his thumb and forefinger. He buried it at the foot of a tree. He took a stick to cover the pool of blood with dirt — but what was the use? There was Jenny lying with her mouth open and her eyes walled and glassy. He could not tell Jim Hawkins he had shot his mule. But he had to tell something. Yeah, Ah'll tell em Jenny started gittin wil n fell on the joint of the plow. . . . But that would hardly happen to a mule. He walked across the field slowly, head down.

It was sunset. Two of Jim Hawkins' men were over near the edge of the woods digging a hole in which to bury Jenny. Dave was surrounded by a knot of people, all of whom were looking down at the dead mule.

"I don't see how in the world it happened," said Jim Hawkins for the tenth time.

The crowd parted and Dave's mother, father, and small brother pushed into the center.

"Where Dave?" his mother called.

"There he is," said Jim Hawkins.

His mother grabbed him.

"Whut happened, Dave? Whut yuh done?"

"Nothin."

"C mon, boy, talk," his father said.

Dave took a deep breath and told the story he knew nobody believed.

"Waal," he drawled. "Ah brung ol Jenny down here sos Ah could do mah plowin. Ah plowed bout two rows, just like yuh see." He stopped and pointed at the long rows of upturned earth. "Then somethin musta been wrong wid ol Jenny. She wouldn ack right a-tall. She started snortin n kickin her heels. Ah tried t hol her, but she pulled erway, rearin n goin in. Then when the point of the plow was stickin up in the air, she swung erroun n twisted herself back on it. . . . She stuck herself n started t bleed. N fo Ah could do anything, she wuz dead."

"Did you ever hear of anything like that in all your life?" asked Jim Hawkins.

There were white and black standing in the crowd. They murmured. Dave's mother came close to him and looked hard into his face. "Tell the truth, Dave," she said.

"Looks like a bullet hole to me," said one man.

"Dave, whut yuh do wid the gun?" his mother asked.

The crowd surged in, looking at him. He jammed his hands into his pockets, shook his head slowly from left to right, and backed away. His eyes were wide and painful.

"Did he hava gun?" asked Jim Hawkins.

"By Gawd, Ah tol yuh tha wuz a gun wound," said a man, slapping his thigh.

His father caught his shoulders and shook him till his teeth rattled.

"Tell whut happened, yuh rascal! Tell whut. . . ."

Dave looked at Jenny's stiff legs and began to cry.

"Whut yuh do wid tha gun?" his mother asked.

"What wuz he doin wida gun?" his father asked.

"Come on and tell the truth," said Hawkins. "Ain't nobody going to hurt you. . . ."

His mother crowded close to him.

"Did yuh shoot tha mule, Dave?"

Dave cried, seeing blurred white and black faces.

"Ahh ddinn gggo tt sshooot hher.... Ah ssswear ffo Gawd Ahh ddin.... Ah wuz a-tryin t sssee ef the old gggun would sshoot — "

"Where yuh git the gun from?" his father asked.

"Ah got it from Joe, at the sto."

"Where yuh git the money?"

"Ma give it t me."

"He kept worryin me, Bob. Ah had t. Ah tol im t bring the gun right back t me.... It was fer yuh, the gun."

"But how yuh happen to shoot that mule?" asked Jim Hawkins.

"Ah wuzn shootin at the mule, Mistah Hawkins. The gun jumped when Ah pulled the trigger.... N fo Ah knowed anythin Jenny was there a-bleedin."

Somebody in the crowd laughed. Jim Hawkins walked close to Dave and looked into his face.

"Well, looks like you have bought you a mule, Dave."

"Ah swear fo Gawd, Ah didn go t kill the mule, Mistah Hawkins!"

"But you killed her!"

All the crowd was laughing now. They stood on tiptoe and poked heads over one another's shoulders.

"Well, boy, looks like yuh done bought a dead mule! Hahaha!"

"Ain tha ershame."

"Hohohohoho."

Dave stood, head down, twisting his feet in the dirt.

"Well, you needn't worry about it, Bob," said Jim Hawkins to Dave's father. "Just let the boy keep on working and pay me two dollars a month."

"Whut yuh wan fer yo mule, Mistah Hawkins?"

Jim Hawkins screwed up his eyes.

"Fifty dollars."

"Whut yuh do wid tha gun?" Dave's father demanded.

Dave said nothing.

"Yuh wan me t take a tree n beat yuh till yuh talk!"

"Nawsuh!"

"Whut yuh do wid it?"

"Ah throwed it erway."

"Where?"

"Ah ... Ah throwed it in the creek."

"Waal, c mon home. N firs thing in the mawnin git to tha creek n fin tha gun."

"Yessuh."

"Whut yuh pay fer it?"

"Two dollahs."

"Take tha gun n git yo money back n carry it to Mistah Hawkins, yuh hear? N don fergit Ahma lam you black bottom good fer this! Now march yosef on home, suh!"

Dave turned and walked slowly. He heard people laughing. Dave glared, his eyes welling with tears. Hot anger bubbled in him. Then he swallowed and stumbled on.

———————

That night Dave did not sleep. He was glad that he had gotten out of killing the mule so easily, but he was hurt. Something hot seemed to turn over inside him each time he remembered how they had laughed. He tossed on his bed, feeling his hard pillow. N Pa says he's gonna beat me. . . . He remembered other beatings, and his back quivered. Naw, naw, Ah sho don wan im t beat me tha way no mo. Dam em all! Nobody ever gave him anything. All he did was work. They treat me like a mule, n then they beat me. He gritted his teeth. N Ma had t tell on me.

Well, if he had to, he would take old man Hawkins that two dollars. But that meant selling the gun. And he wanted to keep that gun. Fifty dollars for a dead mule.

He turned over, thinking how he had fired the gun. He had an itch to fire it again. Ef other men kin shoota gun, by Gawd, Ah kin! He was still, listening. Mebbe they all sleepin now. The house was still. He heard the soft breathing of his brother. Yes, now! He would go down and get that gun and see if he could fire it! He eased out of bed and slipped into overalls.

The moon was bright. He ran almost all the way to the edge of the woods. He stumbled over the ground, looking for the spot where he had buried the gun. Yeah, here it is. Like a hungry dog scratching for a bone, he pawed it up. He puffed his black cheeks and blew dirt from the trigger and barrel. He broke it and found four cartridges unshot. He looked around; the fields were filled with silence and moonlight. He clutched the gun stiff and hard in his fingers. But, as soon as he wanted to pull the trigger, he shut his eyes and turned his head. Naw, Ah can't shoot wid mah eyes closed n mah head turned. With effort he held his eyes open; then he squeezed. *Blooooom!* He was stiff, not breathing. The gun was still in his hands. Dammit, he'd done it! He fired again. *Blooooom!* He smiled. *Bloooom! Blooooom! Click, click.* There! It was empty. If anybody could shoot a gun, he could. He put the gun into his hip pocket and started across the fields.

When he reached the top of a ridge he stood straight and proud in the moonlight, looking at Jim Hawkins' big white house, feeling the gun sagging in his pocket. Lawd, ef Ah had just one mo bullet Ah'd taka shot at tha house. Ah'd like t scare ol man Hawkins jusa little. . . . Jusa enough t let im know Dave Saunders is a man.

To his left the road curved, running to the tracks of the Illinois Central. He jerked his head, listening. From far off came a faint *hoooof-hoooof; hoooof-hoooof.* . . . He stood rigid. Two dollahs a mont. Les see now. . . . Tha means it'll take bout two years. Shucks! Ah'll be dam!

He started down the road, toward the tracks. Yeah, here she comes! He stood beside the track and held himself stiffly. Here she comes, erroun the ben. . . . C mon, yuh slow poke! C mon! He had his hand on his gun; something quivered in his stomach. Then the train thundered past, the gray and brown box cars rumbling and clinking. He gripped the gun tightly; then he jerked his hand out of his pocket. Ah betcha Bill wouldn't do it! Ah betcha. . . . The cars slid past, steel grinding upon steel. Ahm ridin yuh ternight, so hep me Gawd! He was hot all over. He hesitated just a moment; then he grabbed, pulled atop of a car, and lay flat. He felt his pocket; the gun was still there. Ahead the long rails were glinting in the moonlight, stretching away, away to somewhere, somewhere where he could be a man. . . .

PART TWO

COMMENTARIES

The next part of this book consists of comments by writers and critics on the short story form, on the writing process, and on various individual stories. In the preface to his story collection *Twice-Told Tales*, Nathaniel Hawthorne wrote that a writer "would have reason to be ashamed if he could not criticize his own work as fairly as another man's, and — though it is little his business, and perhaps still less his interest — he can hardly resist a temptation to achieve something of the sort. If writers were allowed to do so, and would perform the task with perfect sincerity and unreserve, their opinions of their own productions would often be more valuable and instructive than the works themselves." Although Hawthorne was not entirely serious in this last statement, there is some truth in what he said. Writers' comments about creating short fiction can often clarify their work, place their stories in a larger context of literary history, and shed light on the creative process.

Reading literary criticism can also help stimulate your response to the stories. "Criticism is not literature, and the pleasure of criticism is not the pleasure of literature," observed the noted teacher and critic Lionel Trilling. "But experience suggests that the two pleasures go together, and the pleasure of criticism makes literature and its pleasure the more readily accessible."

The commentaries in this section are arranged alphabetically by author. The headnotes to the stories in Part One of the anthology refer you to the related commentaries in this and the next part of the book.

Chinua Achebe

Chinua Achebe delivered "An Image of Africa: Racism in Conrad's 'Heart of Darkness'" as a public lecture at the University of Massachusetts, Amherst, in 1974. It was later included in his book *Hopes and Impediments: Selected Essays* (1988). In his preface to that book, Achebe notes that the great African American W. E. B. Du Bois wrote in *The Souls of Black Folk* that "the problem of the Twentieth Century is the problem of the colour line." Achebe points out that Du Bois wrote that sentence in 1903, only one year after Conrad wrote "Heart of Darkness." Achebe continues, "This chronology is of the utmost importance. Therefore the defence sometimes proffered: that Conrad should not be judged by the standards of later times; that racism had not become an issue in the world when he wrote his famous African novel, will have to clarify whose world it is talking about."

An Image of Africa: Racism in Conrad's "Heart of Darkness"

1974

Heart of Darkness projects the image of Africa as "the other world," the antithesis of Europe and therefore of civilization, a place where man's vaunted intelligence and refinement are finally mocked by triumphant bestiality. The book opens on the River Thames, tranquil, resting peacefully "at the decline of day after ages of good service done to the race that peopled its banks." But the actual story will take place on the River Congo, the very antithesis of the Thames. The River Congo is quite decidedly not a River Emeritus. It has rendered no service and enjoys no old-age pension. We are told that "going up that river was like travelling back to the earliest beginning of the world."

Is Conrad saying then that these two rivers are very different, one good, the other bad? Yes, but that is not the real point. It is not the differentness that worries Conrad but the lurking hint of kinship, of common ancestry. For the Thames too "has been one of the dark places of the earth." It conquered its darkness, of course, and is now in daylight and at peace. But if it were to visit its primordial relative, the Congo, it would run the terrible risk of hearing grotesque echoes of its own forgotten darkness, and falling victim to an avenging recrudescence of the mindless frenzy of the first beginnings.

These suggestive echoes comprise Conrad's famed evocation of the African atmosphere in *Heart of Darkness*. In the final consideration, his method amounts to no more than a steady, ponderous, fake-ritualistic repetition of two antithetical sentences, one about silence and the other about frenzy. We can inspect samples of this: (a) "It was the stillness of an implacable force brooding over an inscrutable intention" and (b) "The steamer toiled along slowly on the edge of a black and incomprehensible frenzy." Of course, there is a judicious change of adjective from time to time, so that instead of "inscrutable," for example, you might have "unspeakable," even plain "mysterious," etc., etc.

The eagle-eyed English critic F. R. Leavis drew attention long ago to Conrad's "adjectival insistence upon inexpressible and incomprehensible mystery." That insistence must not be dismissed lightly, as many Conrad critics have tended to do, as a mere stylistic flaw; for it raises serious questions of artistic good faith. When a writer while pretending to record scenes, incidents, and their impact is in reality engaged in inducing hypnotic stupor in his readers through a bombardment of emotive words and other forms of trickery, much more has to be at stake than stylistic felicity. Generally, normal readers are well armed to detect and resist such underhand activity. But Conrad chose his subject well — one which was guaranteed not to put him in conflict with the psychological predisposition of his readers or raise the need for him to contend with their resistance. He chose the role of purveyor of comforting myths.

The most interesting and revealing passages in *Heart of Darkness* are, however, about people. I must crave the indulgence of my reader to quote almost a whole page from about the middle of the story when representatives of Europe in a steamer going down the Congo encounter the denizens of Africa:

> We were wanderers on a prehistoric earth, on an earth that wore the aspect of an unknown planet. We could have fancied ourselves the first of men taking possession of an accursed inheritance, to be subdued at the cost of profound anguish and of excessive toil. But suddenly, as we struggled round a bend, there would be a glimpse of rush walls, of peaked grass-roofs, a burst of yells, a whirl of black limbs, a mass of hands clapping, of feet stamping, of bodies swaying, of eyes rolling, under the droop of heavy and motionless foliage. The steamer toiled along slowly on the edge of the black and incomprehensible frenzy. The prehistoric man was cursing us, praying to us, welcoming us — who could tell? We were cut off from the comprehension of our surroundings; we glided past like phantoms, wondering and secretly appalled, as sane men would be before an enthusiastic outbreak in a madhouse. We could not understand because we were too far and could not remember because we were travelling in the night of first ages, of those ages that are gone, leaving hardly a sign — and no memories.
>
> The earth seemed unearthly. We are accustomed to look upon the shackled form of a conquered monster, but there — there you could look at a thing monstrous and free. It was unearthly, and the men were — No, they were not inhuman. Well, you know, that was the worst of it — this suspicion of their not being inhuman. It would come slowly to one. They howled and leaped, and spun, and made horrid faces; but what thrilled you was just

the thought of their humanity — like yours — the thought of your remote kinship with this wild and passionate uproar. Ugly. Yes, it was ugly enough; but if you were man enough you would admit to yourself that there was in you just the faintest trace of a response to the terrible frankness of that noise, a dim suspicion of there being a meaning in it which you — you so remote from the night of first ages — could comprehend.

Herein lies the meaning of *Heart of Darkness* and the fascination it holds over the Western mind: "What thrilled you was just the thought of their humanity — like yours. . . . Ugly."

Having shown us Africa in the mass, Conrad then zeros in, half a page later, on a specific example, giving us one of his rare descriptions of an African who is not just limbs or rolling eyes:

> And between whiles I had to look after the savage who was fireman. He was an improved specimen; he could fire up a vertical boiler. He was there below me, and, upon my word, to look at him was as edifying as seeing a dog in a parody of breeches and a feather hat, walking on his hind legs. A few months of training had done for that really fine chap. He squinted at the steam gauge and at the water gauge with an evident effort of intrepidity — and he had filed his teeth, too, the poor devil, and the wool of his pate shaved into queer patterns, and three ornamental scars on each of his cheeks. He ought to have been clapping his hands and stamping his feet on the bank, instead of which he was hard at work, a thrall to strange witchcraft, full of improving knowledge.

As everybody knows, Conrad is a romantic on the side. He might not exactly admire savages clapping their hands and stamping their feet but they have at least the merit of being in their place, unlike this dog in a parody of breeches. For Conrad, things being in their place is of the utmost importance.

"Fine fellows — cannibals — in their place," he tells us pointedly. Tragedy begins when things leave their accustomed place, like Europe leaving its safe stronghold between the policeman and the baker to take a peep into the heart of darkness.

Before the story takes us into the Congo basin proper we are given this nice little vignette as an example of things in their place:

> Now and then a boat from the shore gave one a momentary contact with reality. It was paddled by black fellows. You could see from afar the white of their eyeballs glistening. They shouted, sang; their bodies streamed with perspiration; they had faces like grotesque masks — these chaps; but they had bone, muscle, a wild vitality, an intense energy of movement, that was as natural and true as the surf along their coast. They wanted no excuse for being there. They were a great comfort to look at.

Towards the end of the story Conrad lavishes a whole page quite unexpectedly on an African woman who has obviously been some kind of mistress to Mr. Kurtz and now presides (if I may be permitted a little liberty) like a formidable mystery over the inexorable imminence of his departure: "She was savage and superb, wild-eyed and magnificent. . . . She stood looking at us without a stir and like the wilderness itself, with an air of brooding over an inscrutable purpose."

This Amazon is drawn in considerable detail, albeit of a predictable nature, for two reasons. First, she is in her place and so can win Conrad's special brand of approval; and second, she fulfils a structural requirement of the story; a savage counterpart to the refined, European woman who will step forth to end the story: "She came forward, all in black with a pale head, floating toward me in the dusk. She was in mourning. . . . She took both my hands in hers and murmured, 'I had heard you were coming.' . . . She had a mature capacity for fidelity, for belief, for suffering."

The difference in the attitude of the novelist to these two women is conveyed in too many direct and subtle ways to need elaboration. But perhaps the most significant difference is the one implied in the author's bestowal of human expression to the one and the withholding of it from the other. It is clearly not part of Conrad's purpose to confer language on the "rudimentary souls" of Africa. In place of speech they made "a violent babble of uncouth sounds." They "exchanged short grunting phrases" even among themselves. But most of the time they were too busy with their frenzy. There are two occasions in the book, however, when Conrad departs somewhat from his practice and confers speech, even English speech, on the savages. The first occurs when cannibalism gets the better of them: "'Catch 'im,' he snapped, with a bloodshot widening of his eyes and a flash of sharp white teeth—'catch 'im. Give 'im to us.' 'To you, eh?' I asked; 'what would you do with them?' 'Eat 'im!' he said curtly."

The other occasion was the famous announcement: "Mistah Kurtz—he dead."

At first sight these instances might be mistaken for unexpected acts of generosity from Conrad. In reality they constitute some of his best assaults. In the case of the cannibals the incomprehensible grunts that had thus far served them for speech suddenly proved inadequate for Conrad's purpose of letting the European glimpse the unspeakable craving in their hearts. Weighing the necessity for consistency in the portrayal of the dumb brutes against the sensational advantages of securing their conviction by clear, unambiguous evidence issuing out of their own mouths, Conrad chose the latter. As for the announcement of Mr. Kurtz's death by the "insolent black head in the doorway," what better or more appropriate *finis* could be written to the horror story of that wayward child of civilization who willfully had given his soul to the powers of darkness and "taken a high seat amongst the devils of the land" than the proclamation of his physical death by the forces he had joined?

It might be contended, of course, that the attitude to the African in *Heart of Darkness* is not Conrad's but that of his fictional narrator, Marlow, and that far from endorsing it Conrad might indeed be holding it up to irony and criticism. Certainly, Conrad appears to go to considerable pains to set up layers of insulation between himself and the moral universe of his story. He has, for example, a narrator behind a narrator. The primary narrator is Marlow, but his account is given to us through the filter of a second, shadowy person. But if Conrad's intention is to draw a *cordon sanitaire* between himself and the moral and psychological *malaise* of his narrator, his care seems to me totally wasted because he neglects to hint, clearly and adequately, at an alternative frame of reference by which we may judge the actions and opinions of his characters. It would not have been beyond Conrad's power to make that provision if he had thought it necessary. Conrad seems to me to approve of Marlow, with only minor reservations — a fact reinforced by the similarities between their two careers.

Marlow comes through to us not only as a witness of truth, but one holding those advanced and humane views appropriate to the English liberal tradition which required all Englishmen of decency to be deeply shocked by atrocities in Bulgaria or the Congo of King Leopold of the Belgians or wherever.

Thus, Marlow is able to toss out such bleeding-heart sentiments as these:

> They were all dying slowly — it was very clear. They were not enemies, they were not criminals, they were nothing earthly now — nothing but black shadows of disease and starvation, lying confusedly in the greenish gloom. Brought from all the recesses of the coast in all the legality of time contracts, lost in uncongenial surroundings, fed on unfamiliar food, they sickened, became inefficient, and were then allowed to crawl away and rest.

The kind of liberalism espoused here by Marlow/Conrad touched all the best minds of the age in England, Europe, and America. It took different forms in the minds of different people but almost always managed to sidestep the ultimate question of equality between white people and black people. That extraordinary missionary Albert Schweitzer, who sacrificed brilliant careers in music and theology in Europe for a life of service to Africans in much the same area as Conrad writes about, epitomizes the ambivalence. In a comment which has often been quoted Schweitzer says: "The African is indeed my brother but my junior brother." And so he proceeded to build a hospital appropriate to the needs of junior brothers with standards of hygiene reminiscent of medical practice in the days before the germ theory of disease came into being. Naturally he became a sensation in Europe and America. Pilgrims flocked, and I believe still flock even after he has passed on, to witness the prodigious miracle in Lambaréné, on the edge of the primeval forest.

Conrad's liberalism would not take him quite as far as Schweitzer's, though. He would not use the word "brother" however qualified; the farthest he would go was "kinship." When Marlow's African helmsman falls down with a spear in his heart he gives his white master one final disquieting look: "And the intimate profundity of that look he gave me when he received his hurt remains to this day in my memory — like a claim of distant kinship affirmed in a supreme moment."

It is important to note that Conrad, careful as ever with his words, is concerned not so much about "distant kinship" as about someone *laying a claim* on it. The black man lays a claim on the white man which is well-nigh intolerable. It is the laying of this claim which frightens and at the same time fascinates Conrad, "the thought of their humanity — like yours. . . . Ugly."

The point of my observations should be quite clear by now, namely that Joseph Conrad was a thoroughgoing racist. That this simple truth is glossed over in criticisms of his work is due to the fact that white racism against Africa is such a normal way of thinking that its manifestations go completely unremarked. Students of *Heart of Darkness* will often tell you that Conrad is concerned not so much with Africa as with the deterioration of one European mind caused by solitude and sickness. They will point out to you that Conrad is, if anything, less charitable to the Europeans in the story than he is to the natives, that the point of the story is to ridicule Europe's civilizing mission in Africa. A Conrad student informed me in Scotland that Africa is merely a setting for the disintegration of the mind of Mr. Kurtz.

Which is partly the point. Africa as setting and backdrop which eliminates the African as human factor. Africa as a metaphysical battlefield devoid of all recognizable humanity, into which the wandering European enters at his peril. Can nobody see the preposterous and perverse arrogance in thus reducing Africa to the role of props for the break-up of one petty European mind? But that is not even the point. The real question is the dehumanization of Africa and Africans which this age-long attitude has fostered and continues to foster in the world. And the question is whether a novel which celebrates this dehumanization, which depersonalizes a portion of the human race, can be called a great work of art. My answer is: No, it cannot.

Sherman Alexie

Sherman Alexie described his earliest response to books during his childhood on the Spokane Indian Reservation in eastern Washington State. His essay appeared in *The Most Wonderful Books* (1997), edited by Michael Dorris and Emilie Buchwald.

Superman and Me

1997

I learned to read with a *Superman* comic book. Simple enough, I suppose. I cannot recall which particular *Superman* comic book I read, nor can I remember which villain he fought in that issue. I cannot remember the plot, nor the means by which I obtained the comic book. What I can remember is this: I was three years old, a Spokane Indian boy living with his family on the Spokane Indian Reservation in eastern Washington state. We were poor by most standards, but one of my parents usually managed to find some minimum-wage job or another, which made us middle class by reservation standards. I had a brother and three sisters. We lived on a combination of irregular paychecks, hope, fear, and government-surplus food.

My father, who is one of the few Indians who went to Catholic school on purpose, was an avid reader of westerns, spy thrillers, murder mysteries, gangster epics, basketball-player biographies, and anything else he could find. He bought his books by the pound at Dutch's Pawn Shop, Goodwill, Salvation Army, and Value Village. When he had extra money, he bought new novels at supermarkets, convenience stores, and hospital gift shops. Our house was filled with books. They were stacked in crazy piles in the bathroom, bedrooms, and living room. In a fit of unemployment-inspired creative energy, my father built a set of bookshelves and soon filled them with a random assortment of books about the Kennedy assassination, Watergate, the Vietnam War, and the entire twenty-three-book series of the Apache westerns. My father loved books, and since I loved my father with an aching devotion, I decided to love books as well.

I can remember picking up my father's books before I could read. The words themselves were mostly foreign, but I still remember the exact moment when I first understood, with a sudden clarity, the purpose of a paragraph. I didn't have the vocabulary to say "paragraph," but I realized that a paragraph was a fence that held words. The words inside a paragraph worked together for a common purpose. They had some specific reason for being inside the same fence. This knowledge delighted me. I began to think of everything in terms of paragraphs. Our reservation was a small paragraph within the United States. My family's house was a paragraph, distinct from the other paragraphs of the LeBrets to the north, the Fords to our south, and the Tribal School to the west. Inside our house, each family member existed as a separate paragraph, but still had genetics and common experiences to link us. Now, using this logic, I can see my changed family as an essay of seven paragraphs: mother, father, older brother, the deceased sister, my younger twin sisters, and our adopted little brother.

At the same time I was seeing the world in paragraphs, I also picked up that *Superman* comic book. Each panel, complete with picture, dialogue, and narrative, was a three-dimensional paragraph. In one panel, Superman breaks through a door. His suit is red, blue, and yellow. The brown door shatters into many pieces. I look at the narrative above the picture. I cannot read the words, but I assume it tells me that Superman is breaking down the door. Aloud, I pretend to read the words and say "Superman is breaking down the door." Words, dialogue, also float out of Superman's mouth. Because he is breaking down the door, I assume he says, "I am breaking down the door." Once again, I pretend to read the words and say aloud, "I am breaking down the door." In this way, I learned to read.

This might be an interesting story all by itself. A little Indian boy teaches himself to read at an early age and advances quickly. He reads *Grapes of Wrath* in kindergarten when other children are struggling through Dick and Jane. If he'd been anything but an Indian boy living on the reservation, he might have been called a prodigy. But he is an Indian boy living on the reservation, and is simply an oddity. He grows into a man who often speaks of his childhood in the third-person, as if it will somehow dull the pain and make him sound more modest about his talents.

A smart Indian is a dangerous person, widely feared and ridiculed by Indians and non-Indians alike. I fought with my classmates on a daily basis. They wanted me to stay quiet when the non-Indian teacher asked for answers, for volunteers, for help. We were Indian children who were expected to be stupid. Most lived up to those expectations inside the classroom, but subverted them on the outside. They struggled with basic reading in school, but could remember how to sing a few dozen powwow songs. They were monosyllabic in front of their non-Indian teachers, but could tell complicated stories and jokes at the dinner table. They submissively ducked their heads when confronted by a non-Indian adult, but would slug it out with the Indian bully who was ten years older. As Indian children, we were expected to fail in the non-Indian world. Those who failed were ceremonially accepted by other Indians and appropriately pitied by non-Indians.

I refused to fail. I was smart. I was arrogant. I was lucky. I read books late into the night, until I could barely keep my eyes open. I read books at recess, then during lunch, and in the few minutes left after I had finished my classroom assignments. I read books in the car when my family traveled to powwows or basketball games. In shopping malls, I ran to the bookstores and read bits and pieces of as many books as I could. I read the books my father brought home from the pawnshops and secondhand stores. I read the books I borrowed from the library. I read the backs of cereal boxes. I read the newspaper. I read the bulletins posted on the walls of the school, the clinic, the tribal offices, the post office. I read junk mail. I read auto-repair manuals. I read magazines. I read anything that had words and paragraphs. I read with equal parts joy and desperation. I loved those books, but I also knew that love had only one purpose. I was trying to save my life.

Despite all the books I read, I am still surprised I became a writer. I was going to be a pediatrician. These days, I write novels, short stories, and poems. I visit schools and teach creative writing to Indian kids. In all my years in the reservation school system, I was never taught how to write poetry, short stories, or novels. I was certainly never taught that Indians wrote poetry, short stories, and novels. Writing was something beyond Indians. I cannot recall a single time that a guest teacher visited the reservation. There must have been visiting teachers. Who were they? Where are they now? Do they exist? I visit the schools as often as possible. The Indian kids crowd the classroom. Many are writing their own poems, short stories, and novels. They have read my books. They have read many other books. They look at me with bright eyes and arrogant wonder. They are trying to save their lives. Then there are the sullen and already defeated Indian kids who sit in the back rows and ignore me with theatrical precision. The pages of their notebooks are empty. They carry neither pencil nor pen. They stare out the window. They refuse and resist. "Books," I say to them. "Books," I say. I throw my weight against their locked doors. The door holds. I am smart. I am arrogant. I am lucky. I am trying to save our lives.

Paula Gunn Allen

Paula Gunn Allen was a poet and professor of literature. This story is from her book of Native American traditional tales, *Spider Woman's Granddaughters* (1989).

Whirlwind Man Steals Yellow Woman

1983

Kochinnenako, Yellow Woman, was grinding corn one day with her three sisters. They looked into the water jars and saw that they were empty. They said, "We need some water." Kochinnenako said she would go, and taking the jars made her way across the mesa and went down to the spring. She climbed the rockhewn stairs to the spring that lay in a deep pool of shade. As she knelt to dip the gourd dipper into the cool shadowed water, she heard someone coming down the steps. She looked up and saw Whirlwind Man. He said, "Gutwatzi, Kochinnenako. Are you here?"

"Da'waa'e," she said, dipping water calmly into the four jars beside her. She didn't look at him.

"Put down the dipper," he said. "I want you to come with me."

"I am filling these jars with water as you can see," she said. "My sisters and I are grinding corn, and they are waiting for me."

"No," Whirlwind Man said. "You must come and go with me. If you won't come, well, I'll have to kill you." He showed her his knife.

Kochinnenako put the dipper down carefully. "All right," she said. "I guess I'll go with you." She got up. She went with Whirlwind Man to the other side of the world where he lived with his mother, who greeted her like his wife.

The jars stayed, tall and fat and cool in the deep shade by the shadowed spring.

That was one story. She knew they laughed about Kochinnenako. Brought her up when some woman was missing for awhile. Said she ran off with a Navajo, or maybe with a mountain spirit, "Like Kochinnenako." Maybe the name had become synonymous with "whore" at Guadalupe. Ephanie knew that Yellow was the color of woman, ritual color of faces painted in death, or for some of the dances. But there was a tone of dismissal, or derision there that she couldn't quite pin down, there anyway. No one told how Kochinnenako went with Whirlwind Man because she was forced. Said, "Then Whirlwind Man raped Kochinnenako." Rather, the story was that his mother had greeted Yellow Woman, and made her at home in their way. And that when Kochinnenako wanted to return home, had agreed, asking only that she wait while the old woman prepared gifts for Kochinnenako's sisters. Ephanie wondered if Yellow Woman so long ago had known what was happening to her. If she could remember it or if she thought maybe she had dreamed it. If they laughed at her, or threw her out when she returned. She wondered if Kochinnenako cried.

Sherwood Anderson

Sherwood Anderson commented on his practice of writing short stories in his autobiography, *A Story Teller's Story*, published in 1924. This book was his first attempt to write his memoirs and authenticate his "legend" — an impoverished childhood, a revolt against business life, and an entrance into the avant-garde literary circles of Chicago, New Orleans, and New York. He was more concerned with the meaning than with the facts of his life. In his rejection of the "plot" story (a story emphasizing plot over character, setting, or theme), which he considered contrived fiction, he became a strong influence on many subsequent writers of short stories and revitalized the American short story tradition.

Form, Not Plot, in the Short Story

1924

For such men as myself you must understand there is always a great difficulty about telling the tale after the scent has been picked up. . . . Having, from a conversation overheard or in some other way, got the tone of a tale, I was like a woman who has just become impregnated. Something was growing inside me. At night when I lay in my bed I could feel the heels of the tale kicking against the walls of my body. Often as I lay thus every word of the tale came to me quite clearly but when I got out of bed to write it down the words would not come.

I had constantly to seek in roads new to me. Other men had felt what I had felt, had seen what I had seen — how had they met the difficulties I faced? My father when he told his tales walked up and down the room before his audience. He pushed out little experimental sentences and watched his audience narrowly. There was a dull-eyed old farmer sitting in a corner of the room. Father had his eyes on the fellow. "I'll get him," he said to himself. He watched the farmer's eyes. When the experimental sentence he had tried did not get anywhere he tried another and kept trying. Besides words he had — to help the telling of his tales — the advantage of being able to act out those parts for which he could find no words. He could frown, shake his fists, smile, let a look of pain or annoyance drift over his face.

These were his advantages that I had to give up if I was to write my tales rather than tell them and how often I had cursed my fate.

How significant words had become to me! At about this time an American woman living in Paris, Miss Gertrude Stein, had published a book called *Tender Buttons* and it had come into my hands. How it had excited me! Here was something purely experimental and dealing in words separated from sense — in the ordinary meaning of the word sense — an approach I was sure the poets must often be compelled to make. Was it an approach that would help me? I decided to try it.

A year or two before the time of which I am now writing an American painter, Mr. Felix Russman, had taken me one day into his workshop to show me his colors. He laid them out on a table before me and then his wife called him out of the room and he stayed for half an hour. It had been one of the most exciting moments of my life. I shifted the little pans of color about, laid one color against another. I walked away and came near. Suddenly there had flashed into my consciousness, for perhaps the first time in my life, the secret inner world of the painters. Before that time I had wondered often enough why certain paintings, done by the old masters, and hung in our Chicago Art Institute, had so strange an effect upon me. Now I thought I knew. The true painter revealed all of himself in every stroke of his brush. Titian made one feel so utterly the splendor of himself; from Fra Angelico and Sandro Botticelli there came such a deep human tenderness that on some days it fairly brought tears to the eyes; in a most dreadful way and in spite of all his skill Bouguereau gave away his own inner nastiness while Leonardo made one feel all of the grandeur of his mind just as Balzac[1] had made his readers feel the universality and wonder of his mind.

Very well then, the words used by the tale-teller were as the colors used by the painter. Form was another matter. It grew out of the materials of the tale and the teller's reaction to them. It was the tale trying to take form that kicked about inside the tale-teller at night when he wanted to sleep.

And words were something else. Words were the surfaces, the clothes of the tale. I thought I had begun to get something a little clearer now. I had smiled to myself a little at the sudden realization of how little native American words had been used by American story-writers. When most American writers wanted to be very American they went in for slang. Surely we American scribblers had paid long and hard for the English blood in our veins. The English had got their books into our schools, their ideas of correct forms of expression were firmly fixed in our minds. Words as commonly used in our writing were in reality an army that marched in a certain array and the generals in command of the army were still English. One saw the words as marching, always just so — in books — and came to think of them so — in books.

But when one told a tale to a group of advertising men sitting in a barroom in Chicago or to a group of laborers by a factory door in Indiana one instinctively disbanded the army. There were moments then for what have always been called by our correct writers "unprintable words." One got now and then a certain effect by a bit of profanity. One dropped instinctively into the vocabulary of the men about, was compelled to do so to get

---

[1] Honoré de Balzac (1799–1850), French novelist, one of the earliest realists.

the full effect sought for the tale. Was the tale he was telling not just the tale of a man named Smoky Pete and how he caught his foot in the trap set for himself? — or perhaps one was giving them the Mama Geigans story. The devil. What had the words of such a tale to do with Thackeray[2] or Fielding?[3] Did the men to whom one told the tale not know a dozen Smoky Petes and Mama Geigans? Had one ventured into the classic English models for tale-telling at that moment there would have been a roar. "What the devil! Don't you go high-toning us!"

And it was sure one did not always seek a laugh from his audience. Sometimes one wanted to move the audience, make them squirm with sympathy. Perhaps one wanted to throw an altogether new light on a tale the audience already knew.

Would the common words of our daily speech in shops and offices do the trick? Surely the Americans among whom one sat talking had felt everything the Greeks had felt, everything the English felt? Deaths came to them, the tricks of fate assailed their lives. I was certain none of them lived felt or talked as the average American novel made them live feel and talk and as for the plot short stories of the magazines — those bastard children of de Maupassant, Poe, and O. Henry[4] — it was certain there were no plot short stories ever lived in any life I had known anything about.

---

[2] William Makepeace Thackeray (1811–1863), English novelist.

[3] Henry Fielding (1707–1754), one of the first English novelists.

[4] O. Henry, pseudonym of William Sydney Porter (1862–1910), famous American author of short stories with elaborate plots and often "trick" endings.

Margaret Atwood

Margaret Atwood wrote "Reading Blind" as an introduction to *The Best American Short Stories 1989*, a volume she edited with Shannon Ravenel. *The Best American Short Stories* series was started in 1915, but since 1978 the publisher, Houghton Mifflin, has invited a different writer to edit it every year, hoping that a variety of viewpoints could be expressed in each book. Out of a total of two thousand stories published in 1989, Atwood's job was to pick twenty. She found herself asking some tough questions: "What would be my criteria, if any? How would I be able to tell the best from the merely better? How would I know?" This essay is her attempt to answer these questions.

Reading Blind

1989

Whenever I'm asked to talk about what constitutes a "good" story, or what makes one well-written story "better" than another, I begin to feel very uncomfortable. Once you start making lists or devising rules for stories, or for any other kind of writing, some writer will be sure to happen along and casually break every abstract rule you or anyone else has ever thought up, and take your breath away in the process. The word *should* is a dangerous one to use when speaking of writing. It's a kind of challenge to the deviousness and inventiveness and audacity and perversity of the creative spirit. Sooner or later, anyone who has been too free with it will be liable to end up wearing it like a dunce's cap. We don't judge good stories by the application to them of some set of external measurements, as we judge giant pumpkins at the Fall Fair. We judge them by the way they strike us. And that will depend on a great many subjective imponderables, which we lump together under the general heading of taste. . . .

I've spoken of "the voice of the story," which has become a sort of catch-all phrase; but by it I intend something more specific: a speaking voice, like the singing voice in music, that moves not across space, across the page, but through time. Surely every written story is, in the final analysis, a score for voice. Those little black marks on the page mean nothing without their retranslation into sound. Even when we read silently, we read with the ear, unless we are reading bank statements.

Perhaps, by abolishing the Victorian practice of family reading and by removing from our school curricula those old standbys, the set memory piece and the recitation, we've deprived both writers and readers of something essential to stories. We've led them to believe that prose comes in visual blocks, not in rhythms and cadences; that its texture should be flat because a page is flat; that written emotion should not be immediate, like a drumbeat, but more remote, like a painted landscape: something to be contemplated. But understatement can be overdone, plainsong can get too plain. When I asked a group of young writers, earlier this year, how many of them ever read their own work aloud, not one of them said she did.

I'm not arguing for the abolition of the eye, merely for the reinstatement of the voice, and for an appreciation of the way it carries the listener along with it at the pace of the story. (Incidentally, reading aloud disallows cheating; when you're reading aloud, you can't skip ahead.)

Our first stories come to us through the air. We hear voices.

Children in oral societies grow up within a web of stories; but so do all children. We listen before we can read. Some of our listening is more like listening in, to the calamitous or seductive voices of the adult world, on the radio or the television or in our daily lives. Often it's an overhearing of things we aren't supposed to hear, eavesdropping on scandalous gossip or family secrets. From all these scraps of voices, from the whispers and shouts that surround us, even from the ominous silences, the unfilled gaps in meaning, we patch together for ourselves an order of events, a plot or plots; these, then, are the things that happen, these are the people they happen to, this is the forbidden knowledge.

We have all been little pitchers with big ears, shooed out of the kitchen when the unspoken is being spoken, and we have probably all been tale-bearers, blurters at the dinner table, unwitting violators of adult rules of censorship. Perhaps this is what writers are: those who never kicked the habit. We remained tale-bearers. We learned to keep our eyes open, but not to keep our mouths shut.

If we're lucky, we may also be given stories meant for our ears, stories intended for us. These may be children's Bible stories, tidied up and simplified and with the vicious bits left out. They may be fairy tales, similarly sugared, although if we are very lucky it will be the straight stuff in both instances, with the slaughters, thunderbolts, and red-hot shoes left in. In any case, these tales will have deliberate, molded shapes, unlike the stories we have patched together for ourselves. They will contain mountains, deserts, talking donkeys, dragons; and, unlike the kitchen stories, they will have definite endings. We are likely to accept these stories as being on the same level of reality as the kitchen stories. It's only when we are older that we are taught to regard one kind of story as real and the other kind as mere invention. This is about the same time we're taught to believe that dentists are useful, and writers are not.

Traditionally, both the kitchen gossips and the readers-out-loud have been mothers or grandmothers, native languages have been mother tongues, and the kinds of stories that are told to children have been called nursery tales or old wives' tales. It struck me as no great coincidence when I learned recently that, when a great number of prominent writers were asked to write about the family member who had had the greatest influence on their literary careers, almost all of them, male as well as female, had picked their mothers. Perhaps this reflects the extent to which North American children have been deprived of their grandfathers, those other great repositories of story; perhaps it will come to change if men come to share in early child care, and we will have old husbands' tales. But as things are, language, including the language of our earliest-learned stories, is a verbal matrix, not a verbal patrix. . . .

Two kinds of stories we first encounter — the shaped tale, the overheard impromptu narrative we piece together — form our idea of what a story is and color the expectations we bring to stories later. Perhaps it's from the collisions between these two kinds of stories — what is often called "real life" (and which writers greedily think of as their "material") and what is sometimes dismissed as "mere literature" or "the kinds of things that happen only in stories" — that original and living writing is generated. A writer with nothing but a formal sense will produce dead work, but so will one whose only excuse for what is on the page is that it really happened. Anyone who has been trapped in a bus beside a nonstop talker graced with no narrative skill or sense of timing can testify to that. Or, as Raymond Chandler[1] says in "The Simple Art of Murder": "All language begins with speech, and the speech of common men at that, but when it develops to the point of becoming a literary medium it only looks like speech."

Expressing yourself is not nearly enough. You must express the story. . . .

Perhaps all I want from a good story is what children want when they listen to tales both told and overheard — which turns out to be a good deal.

They want their attention held, and so do I. I always read to the end, out of some puritanical, and adult, sense of duty owed; but if I start to fidget and skip pages, and wonder if conscience demands I go back and read the middle, it's a sign that the story has lost me, or I have lost it.

They want to feel they are in safe hands, that they can trust the teller. With children this may mean simply that they know the speaker will not betray them by closing the book in the middle, or mixing up the heroes and the villains. With adult readers it's more complicated than that, and involves many dimensions, but there's the same element of keeping faith. Faith must be kept with the language — even if the story is funny, its language must be taken seriously — with the concrete details of locale, mannerism, clothing; with the shape of the story itself. A good story may tease, as long as this activity is foreplay and not used as an end in itself. If there's a promise held out, it must be honored. Whatever is hidden behind the curtain must be revealed at last, and it must be at one and the same time completely unexpected and inevitable. It's in this last respect that the story (as distinct from the novel) comes closest to resembling two of its oral predecessors, the riddle and the joke. Both, or all three, require the same mystifying buildup, the same surprising twist, the same impeccable sense of timing. If we guess the riddle at once, or if we can't guess it because the answer makes no sense — if we see the joke coming, or if the point is lost because the teller gets it muddled — there is failure. Stories can fail in the same way.

But anyone who has ever told, or tried to tell, a story to children will know that there is one thing without which none of the rest is any good. Young children have little sense of dutifulness or of delaying anticipation. They are longing to hear a story, but only if you are longing to tell one. They will not put up with your lassitude or boredom: If you want their full attention, you must give them yours. You must hold them with your glittering eye or suffer the pinches and whispering. You need the Ancient Mariner[2] element, the Scheherazade[3] element: a sense of urgency. *This is the story I must tell; this is the story you must hear.*

---

[1] Raymond Chandler (1888–1959), American novelist and screenwriter whose work featured the popular fictional detective Philip Marlowe.

[2] In "The Rime of the Ancient Mariner," by Samuel Taylor Coleridge (1772–1834), the Ancient Mariner's "glittering eye" and supernatural tale enthrall his listener.

[3] Wily narrator of *Thousand and One Nights* who uses her stories to entertain her husband, the Sultan, to keep him from killing her.

Urgency does not mean frenzy. The story can be a quiet story, a story about dismay or missed chances or a wordless revelation. But it must be urgently told. It must be told with as much intentness as if the teller's life depended on it. And, if you are a writer, so it does, because your life as the writer of each particular story is only as long, and as good, as the story itself. Most of those who hear it or read it will never know you, but they will know the story. Their act of listening is its reincarnation. . . .

From listening to the stories of others, we learn to tell our own.

Matthew C. Brennan

Matthew C. Brennan made his comparison of Chekhov and Oates in "Plotting against Chekhov: Joyce Carol Oates and 'The Lady with the Dog'" from *Notes on Modern American Literature* (Winter 1985).

Plotting against Chekhov: Joyce Carol Oates and "The Lady with the Dog"

1985

In *Marriages and Infidelities*, Joyce Carol Oates has the main character of "The Dead," the writer Ilena Williams, describe her latest work as "a series of short stories in honor of certain dead writers." Here, in a story honoring James Joyce, Oates autobiographically describes *Marriages and Infidelities*. In another story in this collection, "The Lady with the Pet Dog," Oates honors Anton Chekhov, specifically, his story "The Lady with the Dog" (1899). Oates retains the same central characters — two lovers trapped in loveless marriages — and the same kinds of settings — resorts, small and large cities, hotels, concert halls. She even retains the same story line: a man and a woman, both away from their spouses, meet at a resort, make love, and return to their homes expecting never to meet again; however, strong feeling lingers in both lovers and, after the man reappears suddenly at a concert in the woman's home town, they resume the affair, finally realizing that they are truly husband and wife, even if legally married to other people.

Besides these elements, Oates also retains Chekhov's third-person point of view. But unlike Chekhov, who focuses on the male lover, Gurov, Oates makes Anna S., the female lover, the center of consciousness. Because Chekhov privileges Gurov, he represents Anna's feelings only when she speaks to Gurov. In fact, when Anna S. expresses her shame to Gurov, Chekhov says, "The solitary candle on the table scarcely lit up her face"; and rather than reveal her inner thoughts he merely tells us, "it was obvious that her heart was heavy." So, by subordinating Anna S. to Gurov, Chekhov gives readers no way to understand the feminine side of a masculine story. In contrast, Oates presents what Chekhov leaves out — the female's experience — and so relegates the male lover (who in her version is nameless) to the limited status Chekhov relegates Anna S.: Oates privileges the point of view of Anna. Furthermore, because Anna S. says she feels "like a madwoman," Oates fragments Chekhov's traditionally chronological plot, which becomes a subtext against which Oates can foreground Anna's confusion, doubt, and struggle to find an identity.

To record the brain of Gurov, the male lover, Chekhov develops a conventional, sequential plot. He spreads the five-step plot through the four formal divisions of his story. Part 1 consists of the exposition, during which Gurov and Anna S. meet at the resort, Yalta. Part 2 continues the exposition, as the characters become lovers, and it also introduces the rising action as they separate at the train station, Anna S. returning to her home in the town of S., Gurov to his in Moscow. Then, in part 3, the action continues to rise as Gurov misses Anna and eventually goes to the town of S. Here, at a concert, the two climactically meet again, and, as part 3 ends, Anna S. agrees to come to Moscow. Finally, in part 4, the action falls as Chekhov describes their affair and dramatizes it in a scene that forms the resolution, through which Gurov realizes, after looking in a mirror, that he is in love for the first time: he and Anna S. really are "as husband and wife," though separated by law.

Oates borrows all these events for her plot, but if Chekhov's is linear, hers is circular. Oates breaks her story into three parts. Part 1 depicts the climax, immediately giving her version the intensity that the high-strung center of consciousness, Anna, is experiencing. We are with her at the concert hall, where her lover appears and she faints, and then with her back home, where her husband clumsily makes love to her while she thinks of her lover. Part 2 opens with a flashback to the rising action — when the lover drives Anna to Albany where they separate, just as Chekhov's lovers separate at the train station; next, part 2 both repeats the climax (at the concert and in the bedroom) and relates, for the first time, the falling action in which the lovers continue their affair. Part 1, then, presents only the climax, and part 2 widens the plot to record not just the center, the climax, but also the rising and falling actions that surround it. Part 3, however, widens the circular plot still further. Expanding outward from the climactic center, first the plot regresses to embrace the exposition (in which the lovers meet and make love at the resort, in this version Nantucket); then it moves inward again, retracing chronologically the rising action, climax, and falling action; and finally, as part 3 concludes, the plot introduces the resolution, rounding out its pattern.

Before the resolution, however, as we witness the falling action (the resumption of the affairs) for the second time, Oates stresses the lack of development: Anna says, "'Everything is repeating itself. Everything is stuck.'" By having the plot repeat itself, and so fail to progress toward resolution, Oates conveys Anna's lack of identity: Anna is trapped between two relationships, two "husbands," and hence wavers throughout this version between feeling like "nothing" in her legal husband's house where "there was no boundary to her," "no precise limit," and feeling defined — as "recognizably Anna" — by her illicit lover, her true "husband," who has sketched her portrait, to which she continually refers as if grasping for a rope.

Here, then, with the climax repeated three times and the rising and falling actions twice, the plot finally progresses from this impasse to its resolution. And, appropriately, as the plot finally achieves its completion, so too does Anna, discovering as she symbolically looks into the mirror,

> this man was her husband, truly — they were truly married, here in this room — they had been married haphazardly and accidentally for a long time. In another part of the city she had another husband, a "husband," but she had not betrayed that man, not really. This man, whom she loved above any other person in the world . . . was her truest lover, her destiny.

Cleanth Brooks and
Robert Penn Warren

Cleanth Brooks and Robert Penn Warren utilized close reading when they wrote what they termed New Criticism in their analysis of "The Fall of the House of Usher." This excerpt is from their book *Understanding Fiction* (1943), where the two critics showed themselves unsympathetic to what they considered the excesses of Poe's romantic style.

A New Critical Reading of "The Fall of the House of Usher"

1943

This is a story of horror, and the author has used nearly every kind of device at his disposal in order to stimulate a sense of horror in the reader: not only is the action itself horrible but the descriptions of the decayed house, the gloomy landscape in which it is located, the furnishings of its shadowy interior, the ghastly and unnatural storm — all of these are used to build up in the reader the sense of something mysterious and unnatural. Within its limits, the story is rather successful in inducing in the reader the sense of nightmare; that is, if the reader allows himself to enter into the mood of the story, the mood infects him rather successfully.

But one usually does not find nightmares pleasant, and though there is an element of horror in many of the great works of literature — Dante's *Inferno*, Shakespeare's tragedies — still, we do not value the sense of horror for its own sake. What is the meaning, the justification of the horror in this story? Does the story have a meaning, or is the horror essentially meaningless, horror aroused for its own sake?

In the beginning of the story, the narrator says of the House of Usher that he experienced "a sense of insufferable gloom," a feeling which had nothing of that "half-pleasurable, because poetic, sentiment with which the mind usually receives even the sternest natural images of the desolate or terrible. . . . It was a mystery all insoluble. . . ." Does the reader feel, with regard to the story as a whole, what the narrator in the story feels toward the house in the story?

One point to determine is the quality of the horror — whether it is merely vague and nameless, or an effect of a much more precise and special imaginative perception. Here, the description which fills the story will be helpful: the horror apparently springs from a perception of decay, a decay which constitutes a kind of life-in-death, monstrous because it represents death and yet pulsates with a special vitality of its own. For example, the house itself gets its peculiar *atmosphere* . . . from its ability apparently to defy reality: to remain intact and yet seem to be completely decayed in every detail. By the same token, Roderick Usher has a wild vitality, a preternatural acuteness and sensitiveness which itself springs from the fact that he is sick unto death. Indeed, Roderick Usher is more than once in the story compared to the house, and by more subtle hints, by implications of descriptive detail, throughout the story, the house is identified with its heir and owner. For example, the house is twice described as having "vacant eye-like windows" — the house, it is suggested, is like a man. Or, again, the mad song, which Roderick Usher sings with evident reference to himself, describes a man under the *allegory* . . . of a house. To repeat, the action of the story, the description, and the symbolism, consistently insist upon the horror as that which springs from the unnatural and monstrous. One might reasonably conclude that the "meaning" of the story lies in its perception of the dangers of divorcement from reality and the attempt to live in an unreal world of the past, or in any private and abstract world of thought. Certainly, elements of such a critique are to be found in the story. But their mere presence there does not in itself justify the pertinacious and almost loving care with which Poe conjures up for us the sense of the horrors of the dying House of Usher.

One may penetrate perhaps further into the question by considering the relation of the horror to Roderick Usher himself. The story is obviously his story. It is not Madeline's — in the story she hardly exists for us as a human being — nor is it the narrator's story, though his relation to the occupants of the doomed House of Usher becomes most important when we attempt to judge the ultimate success or failure of the story.

Roderick Usher, it is important to notice, recognizes the morbidity of the life which he is leading. Indeed, he even calls his persistence in carrying on his mode of living in the house a deplorable "folly." And yet one has little or no sense in the story that Roderick Usher is actually making any attempt to get away from the haunting and oppressive gloom of the place. Actually, there is abundant evidence that he is in love with "the morbid acuteness of the senses" which he has cultivated in the gloomy mansion, and that in choosing between this and the honest daylight of the outside world, there is but one choice for him. But, in stating what might be called the moral issue of the story in such terms as these, we have perhaps already overstated it. The reader gets no sense of struggle, no sense of real choice at all. Rather, Roderick Usher impresses the reader as being as thoroughly doomed as the decaying house in which he lives.

One may go further with this point: we hardly take Roderick Usher seriously as a real human being at all. Even on the part of the narrator who tells us that Usher has been one of his intimate companions in boyhood, there is little imaginative identification of his interests and feelings with those of Usher. At the beginning of the story, the narrator admits that he "really knew little" of his friend. Even his interest in Usher's character tends to be what may be called a "clinical" interest. Now, baffled by the vague terrors and superstitions that beset Roderick Usher, he is able to furnish us, not so much a reading of his friends character as a list of symptoms and aberrations. Usher is a medical case, a fascinating case to be sure, a titillatingly horrible case, but merely another case after all.

In making these points, we are really raising questions that have to do with the limits of tragedy. The tragic protagonist must be a man who engages our own interests and hopes and fears as a Macbeth or a Lear, of superhuman stature though these be, engages them. We must not merely look on from without. . . .

In the case of Roderick Usher, then, there is on our part little imaginative sympathy and there is, on his own part, very little struggle. The story lacks tragic quality. One can go farther: the story lacks even pathos — that is, a feeling of pity, as for the misfortune of a weak person, or the death of a child. To sum up, Poe has narrowed the fate of his protagonist from a universal thing into something special and even peculiar, and he has played up the sense of gloom and monstrous derangement so heavily that free will and rational decision hardly exist in the nightmare world which he describes. The horror is relatively meaningless — it is generated for its own sake; and one is inclined to feel that Poe's own interest in the story was a morbid interest.

Ann Charters

Ann Charters studied German as an undergraduate and graduate student at Los Angeles City College, the University of California at Berkeley, and Columbia University.

Translating Kafka

2005

Why another translation of Franz Kafka's most famous story, "Die Verwandlung" (1915), from its original German into English? Several English translations of "The Metamorphosis" are available to the twenty-first century reader of Kafka's short fiction. In my translation I wanted to tell the story as well as I could in American English, not British English, the language used in the most widely available English versions by the early Kafka translators Willa Muir and Edwin Muir, who began to publish translations of Kafka's fiction only a few years after his death in 1924.

After years of reading Kafka's short fiction, I became dissatisfied with the older translations, especially when I considered them in the context of contemporary usage and literature. The Muirs' vocabulary seemed dated, especially their occasional use of old-fashioned terms in British English. In the second paragraph of their translation of "The Metamorphosis," for example, they call Gregor Samsa "a commercial traveler" instead of "a traveling salesman." In the middle of the first section, the Muirs use "chief clerk" as the title of the man from Gregor's office who visits the Samsa household to find out why Gregor hadn't shown up for work that morning. The modern equivalent of the job title is "office manager." In other stories, such as "A Hunger Artist," I felt it was possible to translate from German to English more closely than the Muirs' translations. In the final paragraph of that story, for example, they wrote, "The panther was all right." Closer to Kafka's intention are the words, "He lacked for nothing."

In the spring of 2002, I sat down with the German text of "Die Verwandlung" and *The New Cassell's German Dictionary* and attempted to create a fresh version of the story that I hoped would bring it more vividly to life for American readers. Right at the start, the story's title presented me with a challenge. Kafka's intent would be distorted for the casual reader if I translated it as "The Metamorphosis." The literal translation of "Die Verwandlung" is "The Transformation," a noun that doesn't imply the positive qualities associated with the experience of metamorphosis (for example, we say that a larva will metamorphose into a butterfly). As translator, I decided that Kafka wrote for the serious reader, who would appreciate the ironic implications in the choice of "The Metamorphosis," so I kept the famous English title for my version of his story.

Like all the other translators before me, I found that the opening sentence of "Die Verwandlung" posed the greatest difficulties. In the original German, Kafka wrote, "Als Gregor Samsa eines Morgens aus unruhigen Träumen erwachte, fand er sich in seinem Bett zu einem ungeheueren Ungeziefer verwandelt." English translators have no problem with the first seventeen words of the twenty-word sentence, usually translating them: "As Gregor Samsa awoke one morning from troubled dreams, he found himself transformed in his bed into . . ."

The Muirs translated "ungeheueren Ungeziefer" as "a gigantic insect." When I checked the definition of the two words in my German dictionary, I found that the adjective *ungeheueren* literally means "monstrous, gigantic, large," and the noun *Ungeziefer* means "vermin" or "verminous insect." Translators Stanley Corngold (1972), Joachim Neugroschel (1992), and Donna Freed (1996) translated the noun and adjective literally as "a monstrous vermin" in their versions of the story. Vladimir Nabokov (who translated parts of the story) and Malcolm Pasley (who translated it into British English in 1992) preferred "a monstrous insect"; Stanley Appelbaum (1996) chose the words "an enormous bug."

Working with Kafka's text, at first I couldn't accept the literal translation of "a monstrous vermin," because German and English usages are different for the word *vermin*. In English, *vermin* is rarely used as a singular noun. It means "small common harmful or objectionable animals (as lice or fleas) that are difficult to control." The plural implications of the word *vermin* bothered me. There had to be a better way in English to complete the most extraordinary opening sentence in short story literature.

Nowhere in the text does Kafka specify the type of insect that Gregor has become, so I couldn't consider translating "ungeheueren Ungeziefer" as "a monstrous louse" or "a monstrous cockroach." As Nabokov noted in his Cornell University lecture on Kafka's story, the vermin

> obviously belongs to the branch of "jointed leggers" (*Arthropoda*) to which insects, and spiders, and crustaceans belong. . . . Next question: what insect? Commentators say *cockroach*, which of course does not make sense. A cockroach is an insect that is flat in shape with large legs, and Gregor is anything but flat: he is convex on both sides, belly, and back, and his legs are small. He approaches a cockroach in only one aspect: his coloration is brown. That is all.

Initially when I completed my opening sentence of "The Metamorphosis," I chose the words "a giant insect." A giant was a monster, after all. I felt that as a one-syllable adjective, *giant* also possessed the palpable impact and solidity of a noun. On second thought, I realized that "a giant insect" seemed too simple a way to start the story, almost as if I were trying to turn Kafka's subtle, darkly humorous narrative into a comic monologue.

I rejected the words "an enormous bug" as being too colloquial. Born into an assimilated Jewish family in Prague, Kafka spoke Yiddish, German, and Czech. He chose to write in what is called "Prague German," a much blander version of the language found in Germany and Austria, lacking the

The Metamorphosis

just over 3 *feet long*

19

I

z z · *a troubled*

AS GREGOR SAMSA awoke one morning from uneasy dreams he found himself transformed in his bed into a *monstrous* gigantic insect. He was lying on his hard, as it were armor-plated, back and when he lifted his head a little he could see his dome-like brown belly divided into stiff *corrugated* arched segments on top of which the bed quilt could hardly keep in position and was about to slide off completely. His numerous legs, which were pitifully thin compared to the rest of his bulk, waved helplessly before his eyes. *flimmerten*

What has happened to me? he thought. It was no dream. His room, a regular human bedroom, only *though* rather too small, lay quiet between the *within its* four familiar walls. Above the table on which a collection of cloth samples was unpacked and spread out—Samsa was a commercial traveler—hung the picture which he had recently cut out of an illustrated magazine and put into a pretty gilt frame. It showed a lady, with a fur cap on *very straight* and a fur stole, sitting upright and holding out to the spectator a huge fur muff into which the whole of her forearm had vanished!

19

he had made the frame himself, of wood, coated with gold paint

The opening page of "The Metamorphosis" from Nabokov's teaching copy.

coloring of slang, colloquialisms, and dialectical influences found in High German. Kafka was aware that his Prague German was regarded as simple and "juiceless." Writing a letter to his friend Max Brod in June 1921, he said that he felt Prague German was "nothing but embers which can be brought to a semblance of life only when excessively lively Jewish hands rummage through them."

As I read and re-read the opening sentence of the German text of "Die Verwandlung," I couldn't disregard the troubling presence of the two syllables *unge* found in Kafka's selection of both the adjective and noun "ungeheueren Ungeziefer." His use of the double negative (*un*) strongly suggested that something unspecified had occurred in the past (*ge*) that was not a positive experience. The beginning syllables of both words tell me that Kafka *was* making a judgment: he was implying that something morally repugnant as well as physically unpleasant had happened to his protagonist. The words "giant insect" or "gigantic insect" just didn't carry enough emotional weight.

In my final version of the story, I decided to use "a monstrous insect" as being closer to Kafka's intentions. I still had a soft spot for the Muirs' translation. Though "a monstrous vermin" is the most literal translation in English (and perhaps comes the closest to expressing the author's dark intentions in his tale), the Muirs' choice of the word "insect" introduced millions of startled readers to the rich fantasy of Kafka's imagination. Around the time of creating "The Metamorphosis," he railed in his diary at "the impossibility of writing German," since it made him feel as if he "had to dance on the tightrope." Choosing between the words "vermin" and "insect" in the opening sentence of his most famous story made me feel as if I were dancing on Kafka's tightrope myself.

John Cheever

John Cheever wrote this article for the October 30, 1978, issue of *Newsweek*. He was newsworthy at that time because he had just published a collection of short fiction, *The Stories of John Cheever*, which had become a best-seller. Cheever humorously refers to his early financial struggles in the article, but in Susan Cheever's book about her father, she remembers that he was often deeply frustrated by how little he earned from *The New Yorker*: "The money they paid him just wasn't enough to live on — even in the years when we children were in public schools and the family in a rented house." The second part of the *Newsweek* article almost becomes a narrative about Cheever's suburban neighborhood. Evidently there was nothing in the contemporary scene that he couldn't turn into a short story.

Why I Write Short Stories

1978

To publish a definitive collection of short stories in one's late 60s seems to me, as an American writer, a traditional and a dignified occasion, eclipsed in no way by the fact that a great many of the stories in my current collection were written in my underwear.

This is not to say that I was ever a Bohemian. Hardly a man is now alive who can remember when Harold Ross edited *The New Yorker* magazine, but I am one of these. The Ross editorial queries were genuinely eccentric. In one short story of mine, I invented a character who returned home from work and changed his clothes before dinner. Ross wrote on the galley margin, "Eh? What's this? Cheever looks to me like a one-suiter." He was so right. At the space rates he paid, I could afford exactly one suit. In the mornings, I dressed in this and took the elevator to a windowless room in the basement where I worked. Here I hung my suit on a hanger, wrote until nightfall when I dressed and returned to our apartment. A great many of my stories were written in boxer shorts.

A collection of short stories appears like a lemon in the current fiction list, which is indeed a garden of love, erotic horseplay, and lewd and ancient family history; but so long as we are possessed by experience that is distinguished by its intensity and its episodic nature, we will have the short story in our literature, and without a literature we will, of course, perish. It was F. R. Leavis who said that literature is the first distinction of a civilized man.

Who reads short stories? one is asked, and I like to think that they are read by men and women in the dentist's office, waiting to be called to the chair; they are read on transcontinental plane trips instead of watching a banal and vulgar film spin out the time between our coasts; they are read by discerning and well-informed men and women who seem to feel that narrative fiction can contribute to our understanding of one another and the sometimes bewildering world around us.

The novel, in all its greatness, demands at least some passing notice of the classical unities, preserving that mysterious link between esthetics and moral fitness; but to have this unyielding antiquity exclude the newness in our ways of life would be regrettable. This newness is known to some of us through *Star Wars*, to some of us through the melancholy that follows a fielder's error in the late innings of a ball game. In the pursuit of this newness, contemporary painting seems to have lost the language of the landscape, the still-life, and — most important — the nude. Modern music has been separated from those rhythms and tonalities that are most deeply ingrained in our memories, but literature still possesses the narrative — the story — and one would defend this with one's life.

In the short stories of my esteemed colleagues — and in a few of my own — I find those rented summer houses, those one-night love affairs, and those lost key rings that confound traditional esthetics. We are not a nomadic people, but there is more than a hint of this spirit of our great country — and the short story is the literature of the nomad.

I like to think that the view of a suburban street that I imagine from my window would appeal to a wanderer or to someone familiar with loneliness. Here is a profoundly moving display of nostalgia, vision, and love, none of it more than 30 years old, including most of the trees. Here are white columns from the manorial South, brick and timber walls from Elizabethan England, saltbox houses from our great maritime past, and flat-roofed echoes of Frank Lloyd Wright and his vision of a day when we would all enjoy solar heating, serene and commodious interiors, and peace on earth.

The lots are 1½ acres, flowers and vegetables grow in the yards, and here and there one finds, instead of tomatoes, robust stands of cannabis with its feathery leaf. Here, in this victorious domesticity, the principal crop is a hazardous drug. And what do I see hanging in the Hartshores' clothes-yard but enough seasoning marijuana to stone a regiment.

Is forgetfulness some part of the mysteriousness of life? If I speak to Mr. Hartshore about his cannabis crop, will he tell me that the greatness of Chinese civilization stood foursquare on the fantasies of opium? But it is not I who will speak to Mr. Hartshore. It will be Charlie Dilworth, a very abstemious man who lives in the house next door. He has a No Smoking sign on his front lawn, and his passionate feelings about marijuana have been intelligently channeled into a sort of reverse blackmail.

I hear them litigating late one Saturday afternoon when I have come back from playing touch football with my sons. The light is going. It is autumn. Charlie's voice is loud and clear and can be heard by anyone interested. "You keep your dogs off my lawn, you cook your steaks in the house, you keep your record player down, you keep your swimming-pool filter off in the evenings, and you keep your window shades drawn. Otherwise, I'll report your drug crop to the police and with my wife's uncle sitting as judge this month you'll get at least six months in the can for criminal possession."

They part. Night falls. Here and there a housewife, apprehending the first frost, takes in her house plants while from an Elizabethan, a Nantucket, and a Frank Lloyd Wright chimney comes the marvelous fragrance of wood smoke. You can't put this scene in a novel.

Anton Chekhov

Anton Chekhov described his theories of literature and his practice as a storyteller in scores of letters to his family and friends. Here are excerpts from his letters to his older brother, his publisher, and a younger author whose work he admired. Chekhov was not a systematic critic, and he did not necessarily follow his own advice to other writers. Brevity and concentration on a few essentials of scene and character were the essence of his technique, but he was not always as drastically laconic in his stories as his letters suggest. What is consistently clear in his advice to other writers is his own untiring compassion and his desire to speak honestly in his efforts to help them. He wrote in his notebook, "Man will only become better when you make him see what he is like."

Technique in Writing the Short Story

1886–99 / Translated by Constance Garnett

From a Letter to Alexander P. Chekhov (1886)

In my opinion a true description of Nature should be very brief and have a character of relevance. Commonplaces such as "the setting sun bathing in the waves of the darkening sea, poured its purple gold, etc." — "the swallows flying over the surface of the water twittered merrily" — such commonplaces one ought to abandon. In descriptions of Nature one ought to seize upon the little particulars, grouping them in such a way that, in reading, when you shut your eyes, you get a picture.

For instance, you will get the full effect of a moonlight night if you write that on the mill-dam a little glowing star-point flashed from the neck of a broken bottle, and the round, black shadow of a dog, or a wolf, emerged and ran, etc. Nature becomes animated if you are not squeamish about employing comparisons of her phenomena with ordinary human activities, etc.

In the sphere of psychology, details are also the thing. God preserve us from commonplaces. Best of all is it to avoid depicting the hero's state of mind; you ought to try to make it clear from the hero's actions. It is not necessary to portray many characters. The center of gravity should be in two persons: him and her.

From a Letter to Aleksey S. Suvorin (1890)

You abuse me for objectivity, calling it indifference to good and evil, lack of ideals and ideas, and so on. You would have me, when I describe horse-thieves, say: "Stealing horses is an evil." But that has been known for ages without my saying so. Let the jury judge them; it's my job simply to show what sort of people they are. I write: You are dealing with horse-thieves, so let me tell you that they are not beggars but well-fed people, that they are people of a special cult, and that horse-stealing is not simply theft but a passion. Of course it would be pleasant to combine art with a sermon, but for me personally it is extremely difficult and almost impossible, owing to the conditions of technique. You see, to depict horse-thieves in seven hundred lines I must all the time speak and think in their tone and feel in their spirit, otherwise, if I introduce subjectivity, the image becomes blurred and the story will not be as compact as all short stories ought to be. When I write, I reckon entirely upon the reader to add for himself the subjective elements that are lacking in the story.

From a Letter to Maxim Gorky (1899)

More advice: when reading the proofs, cross out a host of terms qualifying nouns and verbs. You have so many such terms that the reader's mind finds it a task to concentrate on them, and he soon grows tired. You understand it at once when I say, "The man sat on the grass"; you understand it because it is clear and makes no demands on the attention. On the other hand, it is not easily understood, and it is difficult for the mind, if I write, "A tall, narrow-chested, middle-sized man, with a red beard, sat on the green grass, already trampled by pedestrians, sat silently, shyly, and timidly looked about him." That is not immediately grasped by the mind, whereas good writing should be grasped at once — in a second.

Kate Chopin

Kate Chopin made a number of translations, mostly of stories by Guy de Maupassant, and she published several essays on literature in St. Louis periodicals. She wrote about the influence of Maupassant on her fiction in response to an invitation from the editor of the *Atlantic Monthly* in 1896. He returned her first version of the essay, however, advising her to "set forth the matter directly." Her revised version was later included in the magazine with the title "In the Confidence of a Story-Teller," but the section describing how she first encountered Maupassant's tales and the impression they made on her was dropped, perhaps because she spoke so enthusiastically about the French writer's escape "from tradition and authority." This portion of the essay is reprinted from the original manuscript included in volume 2 of *The Complete Works of Kate Chopin* (1969).

How I Stumbled upon Maupassant

1896

About eight years ago there fell accidentally into my hands a volume of Maupassant's tales. These were new to me. I had been in the woods, in the fields, groping around; looking for something big, satisfying, convincing, and finding nothing but — myself; a something neither big nor satisfying but wholly convincing. It was at this period of my emerging from the vast solitude in which I had been making my own acquaintance, that I stumbled upon Maupassant. I read his stories and marvelled at them. Here was life, not fiction; for where were the plots, the old fashioned mechanism and stage trapping that in a vague, unthinking way I had fancied were essential to the art of story making? Here was a man who had escaped from tradition and authority, who had entered into himself and looked out upon life through his own being and with his own eyes; and who, in a direct and simple way, told us what he saw. When a man does this, he gives us the best that he can; something valuable for it is genuine and spontaneous. He gives us his impressions. Someone told me the other day that Maupassant had gone out of fashion. I was not grieved to hear it. He has never seemed to me to belong to the multitude, but rather to the individual. He is not one whom we gather in crowds to listen to — whom we follow in procession — with beating of brass instruments. He does not move us to throw ourselves into the throng — having the integral of an unthinking whole to shout his praise. I even like to think that he appeals to me alone. You probably like to think that he reaches you exclusively. A whole multitude may be secretly nourishing the belief in regard to him for all I know. Someway I like to cherish the delusion that he has spoken to no one else so directly, so intimately as he does to me. He did not say, as another might have done, "do you see these are charming stories of mine? take them into your closet — study them closely — mark their combination — observe the method, the manner of their putting together — and if ever you are moved to write stories you can do no better than to imitate."

Samuel Clemens (Mark Twain)

Samuel Clemens explained how he learned about the Greek origins of the story of "The Jumping Frog of Calaveras County" in 1894, nearly three decades after he had published his most popular tall tale.

Private History of the "Jumping Frog" Story

1894

Five or six years ago a lady from Finland asked me to tell her a story in our negro dialect, so that she could get an idea of what that variety of speech was like. I told her one of Hopkinson Smith's negro stories, and gave her a copy of *Harper's Monthly* containing it. She translated it for a Swedish newspaper, but by an oversight named me as the author of it instead of Smith. I was very sorry for that, because I got a good lashing in the Swedish press, which would have fallen to his share but for that mistake; for it was shown that Boccaccio had told that very story, in his curt and meager fashion, five hundred years before Smith took hold of it and made a good and tellable thing out of it.

I have always been sorry for Smith. But my own turn has come now. A few weeks ago Professor Van Dyke, of Princeton, asked this question:

"Do you know how old your Jumping Frog story is?"

And I answered:

"Yes — forty-five years. The thing happened in Calaveras County in the spring of 1849."

"No; it happened earlier — a couple of thousand years earlier; it is a Greek story."

I was astonished — and hurt. I said:

"I am willing to be a literary thief if it has been so ordained; I am even willing to be caught robbing the ancient dead alongside of Hopkinson Smith, for he is my friend and a good fellow, and I think would be as honest as any one if he could do it without occasioning remark; but I am not willing to antedate his crimes by fifteen hundred years. I must ask you to knock off part of that."

But the professor was not chaffing; he was in earnest, and could not abate a century. He named the Greek author, and offered to get the book and send it to me and the college text-book containing the English translation also. I thought I would like the translation best, because Greek makes me tired. January 30th he sent me the English version, and I will presently insert it in this article. It is my Jumping Frog tale in every essential. It is not strung out as I have strung it out, but it is all there.

To me this is very curious and interesting. Curious for several reasons. For instance:

I heard the story told by a man who was not telling it to his hearers as a thing new to them, but as a thing which *they had witnessed and would remember.* He was a dull person, and ignorant; he had no gift as a story-teller, and no invention; in his mouth this episode was merely history — history and statistics; and the gravest sort of history, too; he was entirely serious, for he was dealing with what to him were austere facts, and they interested him solely because they *were* facts; he was drawing on his memory, not his mind; he saw no humor in his tale, neither did his listeners; neither he nor they never smiled or laughed; in my time I have not attended a more solemn conference. To him and to his fellow gold-miners there were just two things in the story that were worth considering. One was the smartness of the stranger in taking in its hero, Jim Smiley, with a loaded frog; and the other was the stranger's deep knowledge of a frog's nature — for he knew (as the narrator asserted and the listeners conceded) that a frog *likes shot* and is always ready to eat it. Those men discussed those two points, and those only. They were hearty in their admiration of them, and none of the party was aware that a first-rate story had been told in a first-rate way, and that it was brimful of a quality whose presence they never suspected — humor.

Now, then, the interesting question is, *did* the frog episode happen in Angel's Camp in the spring of '49, as told in my hearing that day in the fall of 1865? I am perfectly sure that it did. I am also sure that its duplicate happened in Boeotia a couple of thousand years ago. I think it must be a case of history actually repeating itself, and not a case of a good story floating down the ages and surviving because too good to be allowed to perish.

I would now like to have the reader examine the Greek story and the story told by the dull and solemn Californian, and observe how exactly alike they are in essentials.

[Translation]

THE ATHENIAN AND THE FROG[1]

An Athenian once fell in with a Boeotian who was sitting by the roadside look-ing at a frog. Seeing the other approach, the Boeotian said his was a remark-able frog, and asked if he would agree to start a contest of frogs, on condition that he whose frog jumped farthest should receive a large sum of money. The Athenian replied that he would if the other would fetch him a frog, for the lake was near. To this he agreed, and when he was gone the Athenian took the frog, and, opening its mouth, poured some stones into its stomach, so that it did not indeed seem larger than before, but could not jump. The Boeotian soon returned with the other frog, and the contest began. The second frog first was pinched, and jumped moderately; then they pinched the Boeotian frog. And he gathered himself for a leap, and used the utmost effort, but he could not move his body the least. So the Athenian departed with the money. When he was gone the Boeotian, wondering what was the matter with the frog, lifted him up and examined him. And being turned upside down, he opened his mouth and vomited out the stones.

And here is the way it happened in California . . . [in] "The Celebrated Jumping Frog of Calaveras County" [see story, page 288]. . . .

The resemblances are deliciously exact. There you have the wily Boeo-tian and the wily Jim Smiley waiting — two thousand years apart — and wait-ing, each equipped with his frog and "laying" for the stranger. A contest is proposed — for money. The Athenian would take a chance "if the other would fetch him a frog"; the Yankee says: "I'm only a stranger here, and I ain't got no frog; but if I had a frog I'd bet you." The wily Boeotian and the wily Califor-nian, with that vast gulf of two thousand years between, retire eagerly and go frogging in the marsh; the Athenian and the Yankee remain behind and work a

---

[1] Sidgwick, *Greek Prose Composition*, page 116. [Clemens's footnote]

base advantage, the one with pebbles, the other with shot. Presently the contest began. In the one case "they pinched the Boeotian frog"; in the other, "him and the feller touched up the frogs from behind." The Boeotian frog "gathered himself for a leap" (you can just *see* him!), "but could not move his body in the least"; the Californian frog "give a heave, but it warn't no use — he couldn't budge." In both the ancient and the modern cases the strangers departed with the money. The Boeotian and the Californian wonder what is the matter with their frogs; they lift them and examine; they turn them upside down and out spills the informing ballast.

Yes, the resemblances are curiously exact. I used to tell the story of the Jumping Frog in San Francisco, and presently Artemus Ward came along and wanted it to help fill out a little book which he was about to publish; so I wrote it out and sent it to his publisher, Carleton; but Carleton thought the book had enough matter in it, so he gave the story to Henry Clapp as a present, and Clapp put it in his *Saturday Press*, and it killed that paper with a suddenness that was beyond praise. At least the paper died with that issue, and none but envious people have ever tried to rob me of the honor and credit of killing it. The "Jumping Frog" was the first piece of writing of mine that spread itself through the newspapers and brought me into public notice. Consequently, the *Saturday Press* was a cocoon and I the worm in it; also, I was the gay-colored literary moth which its death set free. This simile has been used before. . . .

So ends the private and public history of the Jumping Frog of Calaveras County, an incident which has this unique feature about it — that it is both old and new, a "chestnut" and not a "chestnut"; for it was original when it happened two thousand years ago, and was again original when it happened in California in our own time.

Stephen Crane

Stephen Crane wrote about the wreck of the *Commodore* in the article "Stephen Crane's Own Story" in the *New York Press* on January 7, 1897. At that time arms and provisions were being smuggled from Florida to Cuba to aid the insurrection against Spanish rule. Crane boarded the *Commodore* in Jacksonville on December 31, 1896. The ship was loaded with a cargo of rifles and ammunition. As the scholar Olov W. Fryckstedt explained, Crane "looked forward to a long period of unknown adventures and exciting dangers in the Cuban mountains. But during the night of January 1 the ship foundered fifteen miles off the coast of Florida after a mysterious explosion in the engine room." The first part of Crane's newspaper story describes the loading of the ship, the peril of sandbars, the explosion in the engine room, and the lowering of the lifeboats. Then, with the ship's "whistle of despair," it became clear to everyone on board that the situation was hopeless. The bustling action before the shipwreck is the substance of Crane's newspaper report; his thirty desperate hours afterward in the ten-foot dinghy became the story of "The Open Boat."

The Sinking of the *Commodore*

1897

A Whistle of Despair

Now the whistle of the *Commodore* had been turned loose, and if there ever was a voice of despair and death, it was in the voice of this whistle. It had gained a new tone. It was as if its throat was already choked by the water, and this cry on the sea at night, with a wind blowing the spray over the ship, and the waves roaring over the bow, and swirling white along the decks, was to each of us probably a song of man's end.

It was now that the first mate showed a sign of losing his grip. To us who were trying in all stages of competence and experience to launch the lifeboat he raged in all terms of fiery satire and hammerlike abuse. But the boat moved at last and swung down toward the water.

Afterward, when I went aft, I saw the captain standing, with his arm in a sling, holding on to a stay with his one good hand and directing the launching of the boat. He gave me a five-gallon jug of water to hold, and asked me what I was going to do. I told him what I thought was about the proper thing, and he told me then that the cook had the same idea, and ordered me to go forward and be ready to launch the ten-foot dinghy.

In the Ten-Foot Dinghy

I remember well that he turned then to swear at a colored stoker who was prowling around, done up in life preservers until he looked like a feather bed. I went forward with my five-gallon jug of water, and when the captain came we launched the dinghy, and they put me over the side to fend her off from the ship with an oar.

They handed me down the water jug, and then the cook came into the boat, and we sat there in the darkness, wondering why, by all our hopes of future happiness, the captain was so long in coming over to the side and ordering us away from the doomed ship.

The captain was waiting for the other boat to go. Finally he hailed in the darkness: "Are you all right, Mr. Graines?"

The first mate answered: "All right, sir."

"Shove off, then," cried the captain.

The captain was just about to swing over the rail when a dark form came forward and a voice said, "Captain, I go with you."

The captain answered: "Yes, Billy; get in."

Higgins Last to Leave Ship

It was Billy Higgins, the oiler. Billy dropped into the boat and a moment later the captain followed, bringing with him an end of about forty yards of lead line. The other end was attached to the rail of the ship.

As we swung back to leeward the captain said: "Boys, we will stay right near the ship till she goes down."

This cheerful information, of course, filled us all with glee. The line kept us headed properly into the wind, and as we rode over the monstrous waves we saw upon each rise the swaying lights of the dying *Commodore*.

When came the gray shade of dawn, the form of the *Commodore* grew slowly clear to us as our little ten-foot boat rose over each swell. She was floating with such an air of buoyancy that we laughed when we had time, and said, "What a gag it would be on those other fellows if she didn't sink at all."

But later we saw men aboard of her, and later still they began to hail us.

Helping Their Mates

I had forgot to mention that previously we had loosened the end of the lead line and dropped much further to leeward. The men on board were a mystery to us, of course, as we had seen all the boats leave the ship. We rowed back to the ship, but did not approach too near, because we were four men in a ten-foot boat, and we knew that the touch of a hand on our gunwale would assuredly swamp us.

The first mate cried out from the ship that the third boat had foundered alongside. He cried that they had made rafts, and wished us to tow them.

The captain said, "All right."

Their rafts were floating astern. "Jump in!" cried the captain, but there was a singular and most harrowing hesitation. There were five white men and two negroes. This scene in the gray light of morning impressed one as would a view into some place where ghosts move slowly. These seven men on the stern of the sinking *Commodore* were silent. Save the words of the mate to the captain there was no talk. Here was death, but here also was a most singular and indefinable kind of fortitude.

Four men, I remember, clambered over the railing and stood there watching the cold, steely sheen of the sweeping waves.

"Jump," cried the captain again.

The old chief engineer first obeyed the order. He landed on the outside raft and the captain told him how to grip the raft and he obeyed as promptly and as docilely as a scholar in riding school.

The Mate's Mad Plunge

A stoker followed him, and then the first mate threw his hands over his head and plunged into the sea. He had no life belt and for my part, even when he did this horrible thing, I somehow felt that I could see in the expression of his hands, and in the very toss of his head, as he leaped thus to death, that it was rage, rage, rage unspeakable that was in his heart at the time.

And then I saw Tom Smith, the man who was going to quit filibustering after this expedition, jump to a raft and turn his face toward us. On board the *Commodore* three men strode, still in silence and with their faces turned toward us. One man had his arms folded and was leaning against the deck-house. His feet were crossed, so that the toe of his left foot pointed downward. There they stood gazing at us, and neither from the deck nor from the rafts was a voice raised. Still was there this silence.

Tried to Tow the Rafts

The colored stoker on the first raft threw us a line and we began to tow. Of course, we perfectly understood the absolute impossibility of any such thing; our dinghy was within six inches of the water's edge, there was an enormous sea running, and I knew that under the circumstances a tugboat would have no light task in moving these rafts.

But we tried it, and would have continued to try it indefinitely, but that something critical came to pass. I was at an oar and so faced the rafts. The cook controlled the line. Suddenly the boat began to go backward and then we saw this negro on the first raft pulling on the line hand over hand and drawing us to him.

He had turned into a demon. He was wild—wild as a tiger. He was crouched on this raft and ready to spring. Every muscle of him seemed to be turned into an elastic spring. His eyes were almost white. His face was the face of a lost man reaching upward, and we knew that the weight of his hand on our gunwale doomed us.

The *Commodore* Sinks

The cook let go of the line. We rowed around to see if we could not get a line from the chief engineer, and all this time, mind you, there were no shrieks, no groans, but silence, silence and silence, and then the *Commodore* sank.

She lurched to windward, then swung afar back, righted and dove into the sea, and the rafts were suddenly swallowed by this frightful maw of the ocean. And then by the men on the ten-foot dinghy were words said that were still not words—something far beyond words.

The lighthouse of Mosquito Inlet stuck up above the horizon like the point of a pin. We turned our dinghy toward the shore.

The history of life in an open boat for thirty hours would no doubt be instructive for the young, but none is to be told here and now. For my part I would prefer to tell the story at once, because from it would shine the splendid manhood of Captain Edward Murphy and of William Higgins, the oiler, but let it suffice at this time to say that when we were swamped in the surf and making the best of our way toward the shore the captain gave orders amid the wildness of the breakers as clearly as if he had been on the quarter deck of a battleship.

John Kitchell of Daytona came running down the beach, and as he ran the air was filled with clothes. If he had pulled a single lever and undressed, even as the fire horses harness, he could not seem to me to have stripped with more speed. He dashed into the water and dragged the cook. Then he went after the captain, but the captain sent him to me, and then it was that he saw Billy Higgins lying with his forehead on sand that was clear of the water, and he was dead.

Ralph Ellison

Ralph Ellison gave an interview for the "Art of Fiction" series of the *Paris Review* that was reprinted in his volume of essays, *Shadow and Act* (1964). In the introduction to that book he said that what is basic to the fiction writer's confrontation with the world is "converting experience into symbolic action. Good fiction is made of that which is real, and reality is difficult to come by. So much of it depends upon the individual's willingness to discover his true self, upon his defining himself—for the time being at least—against his background."

The Influence of Folklore on "Battle Royal"

1964

Interviewer: Can you give us an example of the use of folklore in your own novel?

Ellison: Well, there are certain themes, symbols, and images which are based on folk material. For example, there is the old saying amongst Negroes: If you're black, stay back; if you're brown, stick around; if you're white, you're right. And there is the joke Negroes tell on themselves about their being so black they can't be seen in the dark. In my book this sort of thing was merged with the meanings which blackness and light have long had in Western mythology: evil and goodness, ignorance and knowledge, and so on. In my novel the narrator's development is one through blackness to light; that is, from ignorance to enlightenment: invisibility to visibility. He leaves the South and goes North; this, as you will notice in reading Negro folktales, is always the road to freedom—the movement upward. You have the same thing again when he leaves his underground cave for the open.

It took me a long time to learn how to adapt such examples of myth into my work — also ritual. The use of ritual is equally a vital part of the creative process. I learned a few things from Eliot, Joyce, and Hemingway, but not how to adapt them. When I started writing, I knew that in both *The Waste Land*[1] and *Ulysses*[2] ancient myth and ritual were used to give form and significance to the material; but it took me a few years to realize that the myths and rites which we find functioning in our everyday lives could be used in the same way. In my first attempt at a novel — which I was unable to complete — I began by trying to manipulate the simple structural unities of *beginning, middle,* and *end,* but when I attempted to deal with the psychological strata — the images, symbols, and emotional configurations — of the experience at hand, I discovered that the unities were simply cool points of stability on which one could suspend the narrative line — but beneath the surface of apparently rational human relationships there seethed a chaos before which I was helpless. People rationalize what they shun or are incapable of dealing with; these superstitions and their rationalizations become ritual as they govern behavior. The rituals become social forms, and it is one of the functions of the artist to recognize them and raise them to the level of art.

I don't know whether I'm getting this over or not. Let's put it this way: Take the "Battle Royal" passage in my novel, where the boys are blindfolded and forced to fight each other for the amusement of the white observers. This is a vital part of behavior pattern in the South, which both Negroes and whites thoughtlessly accept. It is a ritual in preservation of caste lines, a keeping of taboo to appease the gods and ward off bad luck. It is also the initiation ritual to which all greenhorns are subjected. This passage which states what Negroes will see I did not have to invent; the patterns were already there in society, so that all I had to do was present them in a broader context of meaning. In any society there are many rituals of situation which, for the most part, go unquestioned. They can be simple or elaborate, but they are the connective tissue between the work of art and the audience.

Interviewer: Do you think a reader unacquainted with this folklore can properly understand your work?

Ellison: Yes, I think so. It's like jazz; there's no inherent problem which prohibits understanding but the assumptions brought to it. We don't all dig Shakespeare uniformly, or even *Little Red Riding Hood.* The understanding of art depends finally upon one's willingness to extend one's humanity and one's knowledge of human life. I noticed, incidentally, that the Germans, having no special caste assumptions concerning American Negroes, dealt with my work simply as a novel. I think Americans will come to view it that way in twenty years — if it's around that long.

Interviewer: Don't you think it will be?

Ellison: I doubt it. It's not an important novel. I failed of eloquence, and many of the immediate issues are rapidly fading away. If it does last, it will be simply because there are things going on in its depth that are of more permanent interest than on its surface. I hope so, anyway.

---

[1] A long, extremely influential poem (1922) by T. S. Eliot (1888–1965).
[2] Experimental novel (1922) by James Joyce (1882–1941).

Richard Ellmann

Richard Ellmann was the author of prize-winning biographies of the Irish writers James Joyce and Oscar Wilde. As a biographer Ellmann seemed to have possessed an encyclopedic knowledge of his subject, yet his grasp of the facts of literary production was balanced by his brilliant use of these facts to suggest his sensitive perception of how the creative process functioned in an author's life. Instead of emphasizing biographical details in his discussion of "The Dead," Ellmann perceptively used the story to illuminate a stage of Joyce's development as an artist. This excerpt is from Ellmann's *James Joyce* (New and Revised Edition, 1982).

A Biographical Perspective on Joyce's "The Dead"

1982

And now Gabriel and Gretta go to the Hotel Gresham, Gabriel fired by his living wife and Gretta drained by the memory of her dead lover. He learns for the first time of the young man in Galway, whose name Joyce has deftly altered from Sonny or Michael Bodkin to Michael Furey. The new name implies, like the contrast of the militant Michael and the amiable Gabriel, that violent passion is in her Galway past, not in her Dublin present. Gabriel tries to cut Michael Furey down. "What was he?" he asks, confident that his own profession of language teacher (which of course he shared with Joyce) is superior; but she replies, "He was in the gasworks," as if this profession was as good as any other. Then Gabriel tries again, "And what did he die of so young, Gretta? Consumption, was it?" He hopes to register the usual expressions of pity, but Gretta silences and terrifies him by her answer, "I think he died for me."[1] Since Joyce has already made clear that Michael Furey was tubercular, this answer of Gretta has a fine ambiguity. It asserts the egoism of passion, and unconsciously defies Gabriel's reasonable question.

Now Gabriel begins to succumb to his wife's dead lover, and becomes a pilgrim to emotional intensities outside of his own experience. From a biographical point of view, these final pages compose one of Joyce's several

---

[1] Adaline Glasheen has discovered here an echo of Yeats's nationalistic play, *Cathleen ni Houlihan* (1902), where the old woman who symbolizes Ireland sings a song of "yellow-haired Donough that was hanged in Galway." When she is asked "What was it brought him to his death?" she replies, "He died for love of me; many a man has died for love of me." [Ellmann's note]

tributes to his wife's artless integrity. Nora Barnacle, in spite of her defects of education, was independent, unself-conscious, instinctively right. Gabriel acknowledges the same coherence in his own wife, and he recognizes in the west of Ireland, in Michael Furey, a passion he has himself always lacked. "Better pass boldly into the other world, in the full glory of some passion, than fade and wither dismally with age," Joyce makes Gabriel think. Then comes that strange sentence in the final paragraph: "The time had come for him to set out on his journey westward." The cliché runs that journeys westward are towards death, but the west has taken on a special meaning in the story. Gretta Conroy's west is the place where life has been lived simply and passionately. The context and phrasing of the sentence suggest that Gabriel is on the edge of sleep, and half-consciously accepts what he has hitherto scorned, the possibility of an actual trip to Connaught. What the sentence affirms, at last, on the level of feeling, is the west, the primitive, untutored, impulsive country from which Gabriel had felt himself alienated before; in the story, the west is paradoxically linked also with the past and the dead. It is like Aunt Julia Morkan who, though ignorant, old, grey-skinned, and stupefied, seizes in her song at the party "the excitement of swift and secure flight."

The tone of the sentence, "The time had come for him to set out on his journey westward," is somewhat resigned. It suggests a concession, a relinquishment, and Gabriel is conceding and relinquishing a good deal — his sense of the importance of civilized thinking, of continental tastes, of all those tepid but nice distinctions on which he has prided himself. The bubble of his self-possession is pricked; he no longer possesses himself, and not to possess oneself is in a way a kind of death. It is a self-abandonment not unlike Furey's, and through Gabriel's mind runs the imagery of Calvary. He imagines the snow on the cemetery at Oughterard, lying "thickly drifted on the crooked crosses and headstones, on the spears of the little gate, on the barren thorns." He thinks of Michael Furey who, Gretta has said, died for her, and envies him his sacrifice for another kind of love than Christ's. To some extent Gabriel too is dying for her, in giving up what he had most valued in himself, all that holds him apart from the simpler people at the party. He feels close to Gretta through sympathy if not through love; now they are both past youth, beauty, and passion; he feels close also to her dead lover, another lamb burnt on her altar, though she too is burnt now; he feels no resentment, only pity. In his own sacrifice of himself he is conscious of a melancholy unity between the living and the dead.

Gabriel, who has been sick of his own country, finds himself drawn inevitably into a silent tribute to it of much more consequence than his spoken tribute to the party. He has had illusions of the rightness of a way of life that should be outside of Ireland; but through this experience with his wife he grants a kind of bondage, of acceptance, even of admiration to a part of the country and a way of life that are most Irish. Ireland is shown to be stronger, more intense than he. At the end of A Portrait of the Artist, too, Stephen Dedalus, who has been so resolutely opposed to nationalism, makes a similar concession when he interprets his departure from Ireland as an attempt to forge a conscience for his race. . . .

———

That Joyce at the age of twenty-five and -six should have written this story ought not to seem odd. Young writers reach their greatest eloquence in dwelling upon the horrors of middle age and what follows it. But beyond this proclivity which he shared with others, Joyce had a special reason for writing the story of "The Dead" in 1906 and 1907. In his own mind he had thoroughly justified his flight from Ireland, but he had not decided the question of where he would fly *to*. In Trieste and Rome he had learned what he had unlearned in Dublin, to be a Dubliner. As he had written his brother from Rome with some astonishment, he felt humiliated when anyone attacked his "impoverished country." "The Dead" is his first song of exile.

William Faulkner

William Faulkner was writer-in-residence at the University of Virginia in 1957 and 1958. During that time he encouraged students to ask questions about his writing. He answered more than 2,000 queries on everything from spelling to the nature of man, including a series of questions about "A Rose for Emily" addressed to him at different interviews by students of Frederick Gwynn and Joseph Blotner. These professors later edited the book *Faulkner in the University* (1959), in which the following excerpt first appeared.

The Meaning of "A Rose for Emily"

1959

Interviewer: What is the meaning of the title "A Rose for Emily"?

Faulkner: Oh, it's simply the poor woman had had no life at all. Her father had kept her more or less locked up and then she had a lover who was about to quit her, she had to murder him. It was just "A Rose for Emily" — that's all.

Interviewer: I was wondering, one of your short stories, "A Rose for Emily," what ever inspired you to write this story . . . ?

Faulkner: That to me was another sad and tragic manifestation of man's condition in which he dreams and hopes, in which he is in conflict with himself or with his environment or with others. In this case there was the young girl with a young girl's normal aspirations to find love and then a husband and a family, who was brow-beaten and kept down by her father, a selfish man who didn't want her to leave home because he wanted a housekeeper, and it was a natural instinct of— repressed which— you can't repress it— you can mash it down but it comes up somewhere else and very likely in a tragic form, and that was simply another manifestation of man's injustice to man, of the poor tragic human being struggling with its own heart, with others, with its environment, for the simple things which all human beings want. In that case it was a young girl that just wanted to be loved and to love and to have a husband and a family.

Interviewer: And that purely came from your imagination?

Faulkner: Well, the story did but the condition is there. It exists. I didn't invent that condition, I didn't invent the fact that young girls dream of someone to love and children and a home, but the story of what her own particular tragedy was was invented, yes. . . .

Interviewer: Sir, it has been argued that "A Rose for Emily" is a criticism of the North, and others have argued saying that it is a criticism of the South. Now, could this story, shall we say, be more properly classified as a criticism of the times?

Faulkner: Now that I don't know, because I was simply trying to write about people. The writer uses environment— what he knows— and if there's a symbolism in which the lover represented the North and the woman who murdered him represents the South, I don't say that's not valid and not there, but it was no intention of the writer to say, Now let's see, I'm going to write a piece in which I will use a symbolism for the North and another symbol for the South, that he was simply writing about people, a story which he thought was tragic and true, because it came out of the human heart, the human aspiration, the human— the conflict of conscience with glands, with the Old Adam. It was a conflict not between the North and the South so much as between, well you might say, God and Satan.

Interviewer: Sir, just a little more on that thing. You say it's a conflict between God and Satan. Well, I don't quite understand what you mean. Who is— did one represent the——

Faulkner: The conflict was in Miss Emily, that she knew that you do not murder people. She had been trained that you do not take a lover. You marry, you don't take a lover. She had broken all the laws of her tradition, her background, and she had finally broken the law of God too, which says you do not take human life. And she knew she was doing wrong, and that's why her own life was wrecked. Instead of murdering one lover, and then to go and take another and when she used him up to murder him, she was expiating her crime.

Interviewer: Was the "Rose for Emily" an idea or a character? Just how did you go about it?

Faulkner: That came from a picture of the strand of hair on the pillow. It was a ghost story. Simply a picture of a strand of hair on the pillow in the abandoned house.

Richard Ford

Richard Ford edited *The Essential Tales of Chekhov* in 1998. He discussed his first encounter as a college student with the story "The Lady with the Little Dog" when he wrote "Why We Like Chekhov," his introduction to the volume.

Why We Like Chekhov

1998

As is true of many American readers who encountered Chekhov first in college, my experience with his stories was both abrupt and brief, and came too early. When I read him at age twenty, I had no idea of his prestige and importance or why I should be reading him — one of those gaps of ignorance for which a liberal education tries to be a bridge. But typical of my attentiveness then, I remember no one telling me anything more than that Chekhov was great, and that he was Russian.

And for all their surface plainness, their apparent accessibility and clarity, Chekhov's stories — especially the greatest ones — still do not seem so easily penetrable by the unexceptional young. Rather, Chekhov seems to me a writer for adults, his work becoming useful and also beautiful by attracting attention to mature feelings, to complicated human responses and small issues of moral choice within large, overarching dilemmas, any part of which, were we to encounter them in our complex, headlong life with others, might evade even sophisticated notice. Chekhov's wish is to complicate and compromise our view of characters we might mistakenly suppose we could understand with only a glance. He almost always approaches us with a great deal of focussed seriousness which he means to make irreducible and accessible, and by this concentration to insist that we take life to heart. Such instruction, of course, is not always easy to comply with when one is young.

My own college experience was to read the great anthology standard, "The Lady with the Dog" (published in 1899), and basically to be baffled by it, although the story's fundamental directness and authority made me highly respectful of something I can only describe as a profound-feeling gray light emanating from the story's austere interior.

"The Lady with the Dog" concerns the chance amorous meeting of two people married to two other people. One lover is a bored, middle-aged businessman from Moscow, and the other an idle young bride in her twenties — both on marital furlough in the Black Spa of Yalta. The two engage in a brief, fervid tryst that seems — at least to the story's principal character Dmitri Gurov, the Muscovite businessman — not very different from other trysts in his life. And after their short, breathless time together, their holiday predictably ends. The

1426

young wife, Anna Sergeyevna, departs for her home and husband in Petersburg, while Gurov, with no specific plans for Anna, travels back to his coolly intellectual wife and the tiresome business connections of Moscow.

But the effect of his affair and of Anna (the very lady with the dog — a Pomeranian) soon begin to infect and devil Gurov's daily life and torment him with desire, so that eventually he thinks up a lie, leaves home and travels to Petersburg where he reunites (more or less) with the pining Anna, whom he encounters between the acts of a play expressively titled *The Geisha*. In the weeks following this passionate lovers' meeting, Anna begins a routine of visiting Gurov in Moscow where, the omniscient narrator observes, they "loved each other like people very close and akin, like husband and wife, like tender friends; it seemed to them that fate itself had meant them for one another, and they could not understand why he had a wife and she a husband; and it was as though they were a pair of birds of passage, caught and forced to live in different cages."

Their union, while hot-burning, soon seems to them destined to stay furtive and intermittent. And in their secret lovers' room in the Slaviansky Bazaar, Anna cries bitterly over the predicament, while Gurov troubles himself in a slightly imperious manner to console her. The story ends with the narrator concluding with something of a knowing poker face, that . . . "it seemed as though in a little while the solution would be found, and then a new and splendid life would begin; and it was clear to both of them that they had still a long, long road before them, and that the most complicated and difficult part of it was only just beginning."

What I didn't understand back in 1964, when I was twenty, was: what made this drab set of nonevents a great short story — reputedly one of the greatest ever written. It was, I knew, a story about passion, and that passion was a capital subject; and that although Chekhov didn't describe any of it, sex took place, adulterous sex no less. I could also see that the effect of passion was calculated to be loss, loneliness, and indeterminacy, and that the institution of marriage came in for a beating. Clearly these were important matters.

But it seemed to me at the story's end, when Gurov and Anna meet in the hotel, away from spousal eyes, that far too little happened, or at least too little that *I* could detect. They make love (albeit offstage); Anna weeps; Gurov fussily says "Don't cry, my darling . . . that's enough. . . . Let us talk now, let us think of some plan." And then the story is over, with Gurov and Anna wandering off to who knows where — probably, I thought, no place very exciting were we to accompany them. Which we don't.

Back in 1964, I didn't dare to say, "I don't like this," because in truth I didn't *not* like "The Lady with the Dog." I merely didn't sense what in it was *so* to be liked. In class, much was made of its opening paragraph, containing the famously brief, complex, yet direct setting out of significant information, issues and strategies of telling which the story would eventually develop. For this reason — economy — it was deemed good. The ending was also said to be admirable *because* it wasn't very dramatic and wasn't conclusive. But beyond that, if anybody said something more specific about how the story

made itself excellent I don't remember it. Although I distinctly remember
thinking the story was over my head, and that Gurov and Anna were adults
(read: enigmatic, impenetrable) in a way I wasn't one, and what they did and
said to each other must reveal heretofore unheard of truths about love and
passion, only I wasn't a good enough reader or mature enough human to
recognize these truths. I'm certain that I eventually advertised actually *liking*
the story, though only because I thought I should. And not long afterward
I began maintaining the position that Chekhov was a story writer of near
mythical — and certainly mysterious — importance, one who seemed to tell
rather ordinary stories but who was really unearthing the most subtle, and
for that reason, unobvious and important truth. (It is of course still a useful habit of inquiry to wonder, when the surface of reputedly great literature — and life — seem plain and equable, if something important might not
be revealed upon closer notice; and also to realize that a story's ending may
not always be the place to locate that something.)

In 1998, what I would say is good about "The Lady with the Dog" (and
maybe you should stop here, read the story, then come back and compare
notes) and indeed why I like it is primarily that it concentrates its narrative
attentions *not* on the conventional hot spots — sex, deceit, and what happens
at the end — but rather, by its precision, pacing, and decisions about what to
tell, it directs our interest toward those flatter terrains of a love affair where
we, being conventional souls, might overlook something important. "The
Lady with the Dog" demonstrates by its scrupulous notice and detail that
ordinary goings-on contain moments of significant moral choice — willed
human acts judgeable as good or bad — and as such they have consequences
in life which we need to pay heed to, whereas before reading the story we
might've supposed they didn't. I'm referring specifically to Gurov's rather
prosaic feelings of "torment" at home in Moscow, followed by his decision
to visit Anna; his wife's reasonable dismissal of his suffering, the repetitive-
ness of trysts, the relative brevity of desire's satiation, and the necessity for
self-deception to keep a small passion inflamed. These are matters the story
wants us *not* to skip over, but to believe are important and that paying attention to them is good.

In a purely writerly way, I also find interest and take pleasure in Chekhov's
choosing *these* characters and this seemingly unspectacular liaison upon which
to stake a claim of significance and to treat with intelligence, amusement, and
some compassion. And superintending all there is Chekhov's surgical deploy-
ment of his probing narrator as inventor and mediator of Gurov's bland but
still provocative interior life with women: "It seemed to him," the narrator says
of the stolid Dmitri, "that he had been so schooled by bitter experience that
he might call them [women, of course] what he liked, and yet he could not
get on for two days together without 'the lower race.' In the society of men he
was bored and not himself, with them he was cool and uncommunicative; but
when he was in the company of women he felt free. . . ."

Finally, in "The Lady with the Dog," what seems good is Chekhov the fastidious and amused ironist who finds the right exalted language to accompany

staid Gurov and pliant Anna's most unexalted amours, and in so doing discloses their love's frothy mundaneness. High on a hill overlooking Yalta and the sea, the two lovers sit and moon off, while the narrator archly muses over the landscape.

> The leaves did not stir on the trees, grasshoppers chirruped, and the monotonous hollow sound of the sea rising up from below, spoke of peace, of the eternal sleep awaiting us. So it must have sounded when there was no Yalta, no Oreanda here; so it sounds now, and it will sound as indifferently and monotonously when we are all no more. And in this constancy, in this complete indifference to the life and death of each of us, there lies hid, perhaps, a pledge of our eternal salvation, of the unceasing movement of life upon earth, of unceasing progress towards perfection.

Over the years, "The Lady with the Dog" has come to stand high in my esteem as the story by whose subtleties I not only began to know how and why to like Chekhov, but also by its exemplary fullness I came to experience literature as F. R. Leavis portrays it in his famous essay on Lawrence, as the supreme means by which we "undergo a renewal of sensuous and emotional life, and learn a new awareness." Chekhov's representation of this minor-key love affair committed by respectable nonentities more than renewed, it helped give early form to my awareness of what the words "emotional life" might entail, but also conceal and importantly leave out. . . .

As readers of imaginative literature, we are always seeking clues, warnings: where in life to search more assiduously; what not to overlook; what's the origin of this sort of human calamity, that sort of joy and pleasure; how can we live nearer to the latter, further off from the former? And to such seekers as we are, Chekhov is guide, perhaps *the* guide.

To twentieth-century writers, of course, his presence has affected all of our assumptions about what's a fit subject for imaginative writing; about which moments in life are too crucial or precious to relegate to conventional language; about how stories should begin, and the variety of ways a writer may choose to end them; and importantly about how final life is, and therefore how tenacious must be our representations of it.

More than anything else, though, it is Chekhov's great sufficiency that moves us and makes us admire; our reader's awareness that story to story, degree by degree around the sphere of observable human existence, Chekhov's measure is perfect. Given the subjects, the characters, the actions he brings into play, we routinely feel that everything of importance is always there in Chekhov. And our imaginations are for that reason ignited to know exactly what that great sufficiency is a reply to; what is the underlying urgency such that almost any story of Chekhov's can cause us to feel, either joyfully or pitifully, confirmed in life? As adults, we usually like what makes us want to know more, and are flattered by an assertive authority which makes us trust and then provides good counsel. It is indeed as though Chekhov knew us.

Finally, the stories found here are never difficult but often demanding; always dense but never turgid; sometimes dour, but rarely hopeless. Yet occasionally, reading through the great body of Chekhov's stories (220 plus), I have experienced secret relief when a story, here or there, seemed somehow *lesser*, was possibly tossed off in a way that allows me to imagine this most humane of writers in a new light — as a man agreeably unburdened by some demonic masterpiece-only obsession, a man I could've known, as a writer indeed willing to take us unblinkingly into the musing consciousness of kittens(!) and offer us assurance that nothing very important goes on there: "The kitten lay awake thinking. Of what? . . . The soul of another is darkness, and a cat's soul more than most. . . . Fate had destined him to be the terror of cellars, storerooms and corn bins, and had it not been for education . . . we will not anticipate, however" ("Who Was to Blame").

And so, no more anticipation. Just read these wonderful stories for pleasure, first, and do not read them fast. The more you linger, the more you reread, the more you'll experience and feel addressed by this great genius who, surprisingly, in spite of distance and time, shared a world we know and saw as his great privilege the chance to redeem it with language.

Carlos Fuentes

Carlos Fuentes, the eminent Mexican writer, discussed "Mexico, the United States, and the Multicultural Future" in his nonfiction book *The Buried Mirror* (1992).

Mexico, the United States, and the Multicultural Future

1992

The two-thousand-mile border between Mexico and the U.S.A. is the only visible border between the developed and the developing worlds. It is also the border between Anglo-America and Latin America. But it is an unfinished border, made up of unfinished barriers, ditches, walls, barbed wire fences — the so-called Tortilla Curtain — which are hastily erected by North Americans to keep out the Hispanic immigrant and then abandoned, unfinished. . . .

The two cultures coexist, rubbing shoulders and questioning each other. We have too many common problems, which demand cooperation and understanding in a new world context, to clash as much as we do. We recognize each other more and more in challenges such as dealing with drugs, crime, the homeless, and the environment. But as the formerly homogenous society of the United States faces the immigration of vastly heterogeneous groups, Latin America faces the breakdown of the formerly homogenous spheres of political, military, and religious power through the movement of the urban dispossessed.

In this movement, which is taking place in all directions, we all give something to one another. The United States brings its own culture — the influence of its films, its music, its books, its ideas, its journalism, its politics, and its language — to each and every country in Latin America. We are not frightened by this, because we feel that our own culture is strong enough, and that in effect, the enchilada can coexist with the hamburger. Cultures only flourish in contact with others; they perish in isolation.

The culture of Spanish America also brings its own gifts. When asked, both new immigrants and long-established Hispanic Americans speak of religion — not only Catholicism, but something more like a deep sense of the sacred, a recognition that the world is holy, which is probably the oldest and deepest certitude of the Amerindian world. This is also a sensuous, tactile religion, a product of the meeting between the Mediterranean civilization and the Indian world of the Americas.

Then there is care and respect for elders, something called *respeto* — respect for experience and continuity, less than awe at change and novelty. This respect is not limited to old age in itself; in a basically oral culture, the old are the ones who remember stories, who have the store of memory. One could almost say that when an old man or an old woman dies in the Hispanic world, a whole library dies with that person.

And of course there is the family — family commitment, fighting to keep the family together, perhaps not avoiding poverty but certainly avoiding a *lonely* poverty. The family is regarded as the hearth, the sustaining warmth. It is almost a political party, the parliament of the social microcosm and the security net in times of trouble. And when have times not been troubled? The ancient stoic philosophy from Roman Iberia is deep indeed in the soul of Hispanics.

What else do Ibero-Americans bring to the U.S.A.? What would they like to retain? It is obvious that they would like to keep their language, the Spanish language. Some urge them to forget it, to integrate by using the dominant language, English. Others argue that they should use Spanish only to learn English and join the mainstream. More and more often, however, people are starting to understand that speaking more than one language does not harm anyone. There are automobile stickers in Texas that read MONOLINGUALISM IS A CURABLE DISEASE. Is monolingualism unifying and bilingualism disruptive? Or is monolingualism sterile and bilingualism fertile? The California state law decreeing that English is the official language of the state proves only one thing: that English is no longer the official language of California.

Multilingualism, then, appears as the harbinger of a multicultural world, of which Los Angeles is the prime example. A modern Byzantium, the City of the Angels receives each day, willy-nilly, the languages, the food, the mores not only of Spanish Americans but of Vietnamese, Koreans, Chinese, Japanese. This is the price — or the gift, depending on how you look at it — of global interdependence and communications.

So the cultural dilemma of the American of Mexican, Cuban, or Puerto Rican descent is suddenly universalized: to integrate or not? To maintain a personality and add to the diversity of North American society, or to fade away into anonymity in the name of the after all nonexistent "melting pot"? Well, perhaps the question is really, once more, to be or not to be? To be with others or to be alone? Isolation means death. Encounter means birth, even rebirth.

Janice H. Harris

Janice Hubbard Harris wrote *The Short Fiction of D. H. Lawrence* (1984) after the scholar Mark Spilka pointed out to her in the late 1960s that there was no critical literature on Lawrence's stories. "Where were the analyses of that lively body of fiction capable, as Julian Moynahan says, of bringing light back into the eyes of the reader exhausted by *The Plumed Serpent* or fainting amid the incremental repetitions of *The Rainbow*?" Her critical approach to the stories incorporates several modes — biographical, psychological, sociological, feminist. Comparing Lawrence with his contemporaries James Joyce, Katherine Mansfield, and Virginia Woolf, Harris concludes that "Lawrence is clearly the leader in range, sheer quantity of masterpieces, and, something harder to define, in stretching the conventions of the [short story] genre to include a variety of new possibilities."

Levels of Meaning in Lawrence's "The Rocking-Horse Winner"

1984

"The Rocking-Horse Winner" opens with the distant, singsong voice of a fairy tale: "There was a woman who was beautiful, who started with all the advantages, yet she had no luck." So begins an ancient tale. A brave young boy is challenged by his true love. He rides off into a dreamland where he struggles and succeeds at attaining secret knowledge. He brings the secret knowledge back and with it wins treasure houses of gold, giving all to his love. Undercutting this fairy tale, however, is another, which forms a grotesque shadow, a nightmare counter to the wish fulfillment narrative. The "true love" of the brave young boy is his cold-hearted mother. The quest he has embarked on is hopeless, for every success brings a new and greater trial. Like the exhausted and terrified daughter in Rumpelstiltskin, this son is perpetually set the task of spinning more gold. In this tale, no magical dwarf comes to the child's aid; the boy finally spins himself out, dropping dead on his journey, his eyes turned to stone. Like all good fairy tales, this one has several complementary levels of reference: social, familial, psychological.

On the social level, the tale reads as a satire on the equation of money, love, luck, and happiness. The target of the satire, the mother, cannot be happy without an unending flow of cold, sure cash. As she sees it, luck and lucre are the same thing. Yearning for some response and real affection from her, Paul adds the term "love," making a solid, tragic construction. Quite simply, the tale concludes that these equations are deadly. The mother, representing a society run on a money ethic, has given the younger generation a murderous education.

On a familial level, the tale dramatizes an idea implied as early as *Sons and Lovers* but overtly stated only in a late autobiographical fragment and these last tales. The idea is that mothers shape their sons into the desirable opposite of their husbands. Whatever they are powerless to prevent or alter in their mates, mothers will seek to prevent or alter in their sons. In "The Rocking-Horse Winner," the woman cannot alter her husband's ineffectuality. She herself tries to be effective in the world of commerce and money, but she fails, partly because of the lack of opportunities available to her. So she turns unconsciously to her son. In this reading, Paul's death owes less to the specific character of his mother's demands and more to the strength of those demands. He dies — cannot live, cannot grow and flourish — partly because he is too good a son, and she is a woman with unbounded desires and no way to work directly toward their gratification. In *Sons and Lovers*, the young son kills, literally and figuratively, the paralyzed and paralyzing mother. The alternative pattern, which Lawrence felt to be common among the men of his generation, is played out in "The Rocking-Horse Winner."

But the tale acts out still another nexus of meaning, one implied in both the satire on a society governed by a money ethic and in the dramatization of a mother devourer. On this level, the hobbyhorse comes more to the fore. . . . This lonely, preadolescent boy continually retreats to his own room where, in great secrecy, he mounts his play horse and rides himself into a trancelike ecstasy. His action and the result it brings powerfully echo Lawrence's description of masturbation, physical and psychic, in his essay "Pornography and Obscenity." Discussing censorship, Lawrence praises art that inspires genuine sexual arousal, that invites union with the other, whether the "other" is another person, an idea, a landscape, the sun. Obscene art is essentially solipsistic; it arouses the desire to turn inward, to chafe, to ride the self in an endless and futile circle of self-stimulation, analysis, gratification. In masturbation, there is no reciprocity, no exchange between self and other. Applying Lawrence's indictment of masturbation to Paul's situation, we see that Paul has been taught to ride himself, that is, his hobbyhorse or obsessions, obsessions he inherited from his mother. . . .

If one takes these three levels of reference and seeks out their complementarity, one sees the rich logic of the tale. The money ethic, the devouring of sons by mothers, and the preference for masturbation are parallel in cause and result. All develop and respect only the kind of knowledge that will increase one's capacity to control. For example, like any money-maker, Paul learns about the horses only to manipulate his earnings — money and love. Paul's mother, in a variation on the theme, does not bother to learn anything about her son because she does not perceive him as useful to her. Further, Paul mounts his hobby-horse, his surrogate sexual partner, only as a way of fulfilling his own narrowly defined program for success and happiness. In no case is the object that is to be known — horse, son, sexual partner — seen to have a life of its own, an otherness to be appreciated rather than manipulated, a furtherness that can give the knower a glimpse into all that is beyond him or her. In addition, the resolution of each nexus of meaning carries the same ironic denouement: The quest for absolute control leads to the loss of control. The mother's house, which she wants to be luxurious and proper, is haunted by crass whispers. She and her son, striving to control love and fortune, are compulsive, obsessed; Paul dies and thereby loses all chance for the very human love and contact he sought. The mother loses the very means by which her fortune was assured.

Zora Neale Hurston

Zora Neale Hurston often made what the critic Mary Helen Washington called "unorthodox and paradoxical assertions on racial issues." Often conveyed with great wit and style, Hurston's views were always passionately held, as in her 1928 essay "How It Feels to Be Colored Me."

How It Feels to Be Colored Me

1928

I am colored but I offer nothing in the way of extenuating circumstances except the fact that I am the only Negro in the United States whose grandfather on the mother's side was *not* an Indian chief.

I remember the very day that I became colored. Up to my thirteenth year I lived in the little Negro town of Eatonville, Florida. It is exclusively a colored town. The only white people I knew passed through the town going to or coming from Orlando. The native whites rode dusty horses, the Northern tourists chugged down the sandy village road in automobiles. The town knew the Southerners and never stopped cane chewing when they passed. But the

Zora Neale Hurston in Florida in the summer of 1935 while on the Lomax-Hurston-Barnicle recording expedition to Georgia, Florida, and the Bahamas.

Northerners were something else again. They were peered at cautiously from behind curtains by the timid. The more venturesome would come out on the porch to watch them go past and got just as much pleasure out of the tourists as the tourists got out of the village.

The front porch might seem a daring place for the rest of the town, but it was a gallery seat for me. My favorite place was atop the gate-post. Proscenium box for a born first-nighter. Not only did I enjoy the show, but I didn't mind the actors knowing that I liked it. I usually spoke to them in passing. I'd wave at them and when they returned my salute, I would say something like this: "Howdy-do-well-I-thank-you-where-you-goin'?" Usually automobile or the horse paused at this, and after a queer exchange of compliments, I would probably "go a piece of the way" with them, as we say in farthest Florida. If one of my family happened to come to the front in time to see me, of course negotiations would be rudely broken off. But even so, it is clear that I was the first "welcome-to-our-state" Floridian, and I hope the Miami Chamber of Commerce will please take notice.

During this period, white people differed from colored to me only in that they rode through town and never lived there. They liked to hear me "speak pieces" and sing and wanted to see me dance the parse-me-la, and gave me generously of their small silver for doing these things, which seemed strange to me for I wanted to do them so much that I needed bribing to stop. Only they didn't know it. The colored people gave no dimes. They deplored any joyful tendencies in me, but I was their Zora nevertheless. I belonged to them, to the nearby hotels, to the county — everybody's Zora.

But changes came in the family when I was thirteen, and I was sent to school in Jacksonville. I left Eatonville, the town of the oleanders, as Zora. When I disembarked from the river-boat at Jacksonville, she was no more. It seemed that I had suffered a sea change. I was not Zora of Orange County any more, I was now a little colored girl. I found it out in certain ways. In my heart as well as in the mirror, I became a fast brown — warranted not to rub nor run.

But I am not tragically colored. There is no great sorrow dammed up in my soul, nor lurking behind my eyes. I do not mind at all. I do not belong to the sobbing school of Negrohood who hold that nature somehow has given them a lowdown dirty deal and whose feelings are all hurt about it. Even in the helter-skelter skirmish that is my life, I have seen that the world is to the strong regardless of a little pigmentation more or less. No, I do not weep at the world — I am too busy sharpening my oyster knife.

Someone is always at my elbow reminding me that I am the granddaughter of slaves. It fails to register depression with me. Slavery is sixty years in the past. The operation was successful and the patient is doing well, thank you. The terrible struggle that made me an American out of a potential slave said "On the line!" The Reconstruction said "Get set!"; and the generation before said "Go!" I am off to a flying start and I must not halt in the stretch to look behind and weep. Slavery is the price I paid for civilization, and the choice was not with me. It is a bully adventure and worth all that I have paid through my ancestors for it. No one on earth ever had a greater chance for glory. The world to be won and nothing to be lost. It is thrilling to think — to know that for any act of mine, I shall get twice as much praise or twice as much blame. It is quite exciting to hold the center of the national stage, with the spectators not knowing whether to laugh or to weep.

The position of my white neighbor is much more difficult. No brown specter pulls up a chair beside me when I sit down to eat. No dark ghost thrusts its leg against mine in bed. The game of keeping what one has is never so exciting as the game of getting.

I do not always feel colored. Even now I often achieve the unconscious Zora of Eatonville before the Hegira. I feel most colored when I am thrown against a sharp white background.

For instance at Barnard. "Beside the waters of the Hudson" I feel my race. Among the thousand white persons, I am a dark rock surged upon, and over-swept, but through it all, I remain myself. When covered by the waters, I am; and the ebb but reveals me again.

Sometimes it is the other way around. A white person is set down in our midst, but the contrast is just as sharp for me. For instance, when I sit in the drafty basement that is The New World Cabaret with a white person, my color comes. We enter chatting about any little nothing that we have in common and are seated by the jazz waiters. In the abrupt way that jazz orchestras have, this one plunges into a number. It loses no time in circumlocutions, but gets right down to business. It constricts the thorax and splits the heart with its tempo and narcotic harmonies. This orchestra grows rambunctious, rears on its hind legs and attacks the tonal veil with primitive fury, rending it, clawing it until it breaks through to the jungle beyond. I follow those heathen — follow them exultingly. I dance wildly inside myself; I yell within, I whoop; I shake my assegai above my head, I hurl it true to the mark *yeeeeooww*! I am in the jungle and living in the jungle way. My face is painted red and yellow and my body is painted blue. My pulse is throbbing like a war drum. I want to slaughter some-thing — give pain, give death to what, I do not know. But the piece ends. The men of the orchestra wipe their lips and rest their fingers. I creep back slowly to the veneer we call civilization with the last tone and find the white friend sit-ting motionless in his seat, smoking calmly.

"Good music they have here," he remarks, drumming the table with his fingertips.

Music. The great blobs of purple and red emotion have not touched him. He has only heard what I felt. He is far away and I see him but dimly across the ocean and the continent that have fallen between us. He is so pale with his whiteness then and I am *so* colored.

At certain times I have no race, I am *me*. When I set my hat at a certain angle and saunter down Seventh Avenue, Harlem City, feeling as snooty as the lions in front of the Forty-Second Street Library, for instance. So far as my feelings are concerned, Peggy Hopkins Joyce on the Boule Mich with her gor-geous raiment, stately carriage, knees knocking together in a most aristocratic manner, has nothing on me. The cosmic Zora emerges. I belong to no race nor time. I am the eternal feminine with its string of beads.

I have no separate feeling about being an American citizen and colored. I am merely a fragment of the Great Soul that surges within the boundaries. My country, right or wrong.

Sometimes, I feel discriminated against, but it does not make me angry. It merely astonishes me. How *can* any deny themselves the pleasure of my company? It's beyond me.

But in the main, I feel like a brown bag of miscellany propped against a wall. Against a wall in company with other bags, white, red and yellow. Pour out the contents, and there is discovered a jumble of small things priceless and worthless. A first-water diamond, an empty spool, bits of broken glass, lengths of string, a key to a door long since crumbled away, a rusty knife-blade, old shoes saved for a road that never was and never will be, a nail bent under the weight of things too heavy for any nail, a dried flower or two still a little fragrant. In your hand is the brown bag. On the ground before you is the jumble it held — so much like the jumble in the bags, could they be emptied, that all might be dumped in a single heap and the bags refilled without altering the content of any greatly. A bit of colored glass more or less would not matter. Perhaps that is how the Great Stuffer of Bags filled them in the first place — who knows?

Zora Neale Hurston

One of Hurston's last essays, "What White Publishers Won't Print" appeared in the April 1950 issue of *Negro Digest*.

What White Publishers Won't Print

1950

I have been amazed by the Anglo-Saxon's lack of curiosity about the internal lives and emotions of the Negroes, and for that matter, any non-Anglo-Saxon peoples within our borders, above the class of unskilled labor.

This lack of interest is much more important than it seems at first glance. It is even more important at this time than it was in the past. The internal affairs of the nation have bearings on the international stress and strain, and this gap in the national literature now has tremendous weight in world affairs. National coherence and solidarity is implicit in a thorough understanding of the various groups within a nation, and this lack of knowledge about the internal emotions and behavior of the minorities cannot fail to bar our understanding. Man, like all the other animals, fears and is repelled by that which he does not understand, and mere difference is apt to connote something malign.

The fact that there is no demand for incisive and full-dress stories about Negroes above the servant class is indicative of something of vast importance to this nation. This blank is NOT filled by the fiction built around upper-class Negroes exploiting the race problem. Rather, it tends to point it up. A college-bred Negro still is not a person like other folks, but an interesting problem, more or less. It calls to mind a story of slavery time. In this story, a master with more intellectual curiosity than usual, set out to see how much he could teach a particularly bright slave of his. When he had gotten him up to higher mathematics and to be a fluent reader of Latin, he called in a neighbor to show off his brilliant slave, and to argue that Negroes had brains just like the slave-owners had, and given the same opportunities, would turn out the same.

The visiting master of slaves looked and listened, tried to trap the literate slave in Algebra and Latin, and failing to do so in both, turned to his neighbor and said:

"Yes, he certainly knows his higher mathematics, and he can read Latin better than many white men I know, but I cannot bring myself to believe that he understands a thing that he is doing. It is all an aping of our culture. All on the outside. You are crazy if you think that it has changed him inside in the least. Turn him loose, and he will revert at once to the jungle. He is still a savage, and no amount of translating Virgil and Ovid is going to change him. In fact, all you have done is to turn a useful savage into a dangerous beast."

That was in slavery time, yes, and we have come a long, long way since then, but the troubling thing is that there are still too many who refuse to believe in the ingestion and digestion of western culture as yet. Hence the lack of literature about the higher emotions and love life of upper-class Negroes and the minorities in general.

Publishers and producers are cool to the idea. Now, do not leap to the conclusion that editors and producers constitute a special class of unbelievers. That is far from true. Publishing houses and theatrical promoters are in business to make money. They will sponsor anything that they believe will sell. They shy away from romantic stories about Negroes and Jews because they feel that they know the public indifference to such works, unless the story or play involves racial tension. It can then be offered as a study in Sociology, with the romantic side subdued. They know the scepticism in general about the complicated emotions in the minorities. The average American just cannot conceive of it, and would be apt to reject the notion, and publishers and producers take the stand that they are not in business to educate, but to make money. Sympathetic as they might be, they cannot afford to be crusaders.

In proof of this, you can note various publishers and producers edging forward a little, and ready to go even further when the trial balloons show that the public is ready for it. This public lack of interest is the nut of the matter.

The question naturally arises as to the why of this indifference, not to say scepticism, to the internal life of educated minorities.

The answer lies in what we may call the AMERICAN MUSEUM OF UNNATURAL HISTORY. This is an intangible built on folk belief. It is assumed that all non-Anglo-Saxons are uncomplicated stereotypes. Everybody knows all about them. They are lay figures mounted in the museum where all may take them in at a glance. They are made of bent wires without insides at all. So how could anybody write a book about the nonexistent?

The American Indian is a contraption of copper wires in an eternal war-bonnet, with no equipment for laughter, expressionless face, and that says "How" when spoken to. His only activity is treachery leading us to massacres. Who is so dumb as not to know all about Indians, even if they have never seen one, nor talked with anyone who ever knew one?

The American Negro exhibit is a group of two. Both of these mechanical toys are built so that their feet eternally shuffle, and their eyes pop and roll. Shuffling feet and those popping, rolling eyes denote the Negro and no characterization is genuine without this monotony. One is seated on a stump picking away on his banjo and singing and laughing. The other is a most amoral character before a share-cropper's shack mumbling about injustice. Doing this makes him out to be a Negro "intellectual." It is as simple as all that.

The whole museum is dedicated to the convenient "typical." In there is the "typical" Oriental, Jew, Yankee, Westerner, Southerner, Latin, and even out-of-favor Nordics like the German. The Englishman "I say old chappie," and the gesticulating Frenchman. The least observant American can know all at a glance. However, the public willingly accepts the untypical in Nordics, but feels cheated if the untypical is portrayed in others. The author of *Scarlet Sister Mary*[1] complained to me that her neighbors objected to her book on the grounds that she had the characters thinking, "and everybody know that Nigras don't think."

But for the national welfare, it is urgent to realize that the minorities do think, and think about something other than the race problem. That they are very human and internally, according to natural endowment, are just like everybody else. So long as this is not conceived, there must remain that feeling of unsurmountable difference, and difference to the average man means something bad. If people were made right, they would be just like him.

The trouble with the purely problem arguments is that they leave too much unknown. Argue all you will or may about injustice, but as long as the majority cannot conceive of a Negro or a Jew feeling and reacting inside just as they do, the majority will keep right on believing that people who do not feel like them cannot possibly feel as they do, and conform to the established pattern. It is well known that there must be a body of waived matter, let us say, things accepted and taken for granted by all in a community before there can be that commonality of feeling. The usual phrase is having things in common. Until this is thoroughly established in respect to Negroes in America, as well as of other minorities, it will remain impossible for the majority to conceive of a Negro experiencing a deep and abiding love and not just the passion of sex. That a great mass of Negroes can be stirred by the pageants of Spring and Fall; the extravaganza of summer, and the majesty of winter. That they can and do

---

[1] The 1928 book by Julia Mood Peterkin (1880–1961).

experience discovery of the numerous subtle faces as a foundation for a great and selfless love, and the diverse nuances that go to destroy that love as with others. As it is now, this capacity, this evidence of high and complicated emotions, is ruled out. Hence the lack of interest in a romance uncomplicated by the race struggle has so little appeal.

This insistence on defeat in a story where upper-class Negroes are portrayed, perhaps says something from the subconscious of the majority. Involved in western culture, the hero or the heroine, or both, must appear frustrated and go down to defeat, somehow. Our literature reeks with it. Is it the same as saying, "You can translate Virgil, and fumble with the differential calculus, but can you really comprehend it? Can you cope with our subtleties?"

That brings us to the folklore of "reversion to type." This curious doctrine has such wide acceptance that it is tragic. One has only to examine the huge literature on it to be convinced. No matter how high we may *seem* to climb, put us under strain and we revert to type, that is, to the bush. Under a superficial layer of western culture, the jungle drums throb in our veins.

This ridiculous notion makes it possible for that majority who accept it to conceive of even a man like the suave and scholarly Dr. Charles S. Johnson[2] to hide a black cat's bone on his person, and indulge in a midnight voodoo ceremony, complete with leopard skin and drums if threatened with the loss of the presidency of Fisk University, or the love of his wife. "Under the skin . . . better to deal with them in business, etc., but otherwise keep them at a safe distance and under control. I tell you, Carl Van Vechten,[3] think as you like, but they are just not like us."

The extent and extravagance of this notion reaches the ultimate in nonsense in the widespread belief that the Chinese have bizarre genitals, because of that eye-fold that makes their eyes seem to slant. In spite of the fact that no biology has ever mentioned any such difference in reproductive organs makes no matter. Millions of people believe it. "Did you know that a Chinese has . . ." Consequently, their quiet contemplative manner is interpreted as a sign of slyness and a treacherous inclination.

But the opening wedge for better understanding has been thrust into the crack. Though many Negroes denounced Carl Van Vechten's *Nigger Heaven* because of the title, and without ever reading it, the book, written in the deepest sincerity, revealed Negroes of wealth and culture to the white public. It created curiosity even when it aroused scepticism. It made folks want to know. Worth Tuttle Hedden's *The Other Room* has definitely widened the opening. Neither of these well-written works takes a romance of upper-class Negro life as the central theme, but the atmosphere and the background is there. These works should be followed up by some incisive and intimate stories from the inside.

---

[2] Johnson (1893–1956) was the first African American president of Fisk University.
[3] Progressive white champion and patron of African American culture (1880–1964).

The realistic story around a Negro insurance official, dentist, general practitioner, undertaker, and the like would be most revealing. Thinly disguised fiction around the well-known Negro names is not the answer, either. The "exceptional" as well as the Ol' Man Rivers has been exploited all out of context already. Everybody is already resigned to the "exceptional" Negro, and willing to be entertained by the "quaint." To grasp the penetration of western civilization in a minority, it is necessary to know how the average behaves and lives. Books that deal with people like in Sinclair Lewis' *Main Street* is the necessary metier. For various reasons, the average, struggling, non-morbid Negro is the best-kept secret in America. His revelation to the public is the thing needed to do away with that feeling of difference which inspires fear and which ever expresses itself in dislike.

It is inevitable that this knowledge will destroy many illusions and romantic traditions which America probably likes to have around. But then, we have no record of anybody sinking into a lingering death on finding out that there was no Santa Claus. The old world will take it in its stride. The realization that Negroes are no better nor no worse, and at times just as boring as everybody else, will hardly kill off the population of the nation.

Outside of racial attitudes, there is still another reason why this literature should exist. Literature and other arts are supposed to hold up the mirror to nature. With only the fractional "exceptional" and the "quaint" portrayed, a true picture of Negro life in America cannot be. A great principle of national art has been violated.

These are the things that publishers and producers, as the accredited representatives of the American people, have not as yet taken into consideration sufficiently. Let there be light!

Shirley Jackson

Shirley Jackson wrote this "biography of a story" in 1960 as a lecture to be delivered before reading "The Lottery" to college audiences. After her death it was included in *Come Along with Me* (1968), edited by her husband, Stanley Edgar Hyman. The lecture also contained extensive quotations from letters she had received from readers who took the story literally. These so disgusted Jackson that she promised her listeners at the conclusion of her talk, "I am out of the lottery business for good."

The Morning of June 28, 1948, and "The Lottery"

1968

On the morning of June 28, 1948, I walked down to the post office in our little Vermont town to pick up the mail. I was quite casual about it, as I recall — I opened the box, took out a couple of bills and a letter or two, talked to the postmaster for a few minutes, and left, never supposing that it was the last time for months that I was to pick up the mail without an active feeling of panic. By the next week I had had to change my mailbox to the largest one in the post office, and casual conversation with the postmaster was out of the question, because he wasn't speaking to me. June 28, 1948, was the day *The New Yorker* came out with a story of mine in it. It was not my first published story, nor my last, but I have been assured over and over that if it had been the only story I ever wrote or published, there would be people who would not forget my name.

I had written the story three weeks before, on a bright June morning when summer seemed to have come at last, with blue skies and warm sun and no heavenly signs to warn me that my morning's work was anything but just another story. The idea had come to me while I was pushing my daughter up the hill in her stroller — it was, as I say, a warm morning, and the hill was steep, and beside my daughter the stroller held the day's groceries — and perhaps the effort of that last fifty yards up the hill put an edge to the story; at any rate, I had the idea fairly clearly in my mind when I put my daughter in her playpen and the frozen vegetables in the refrigerator, and, writing the story, I found that it went quickly and easily, moving from beginning to end without pause. As a matter of fact, when I read it over later I decided that except for one or two minor corrections, it needed no changes, and the story I finally typed up and sent off to my agent the next day was almost word for word the original draft. This, as any writer of stories can tell you, is not a usual thing. All I know is that when I came to read the story over I felt strongly that I didn't want to fuss with it. I didn't think it was perfect, but I didn't want to fuss with it. It was, I thought, a serious, straightforward story, and I was pleased and a little surprised at the ease with which it had been written; I was reasonably proud of it, and hoped that my agent would sell it to some magazine and I would have the gratification of seeing it in print.

My agent did not care for the story, but — as she said in her note at the time — her job was to sell it, not to like it. She sent it at once to *The New Yorker*, and about a week after the story had been written I received a telephone call from the fiction editor of *The New Yorker*; it was quite clear that he did not really care for the story, either, but *The New Yorker* was going to buy it. He asked for one change — that the date mentioned in the story be changed to coincide with the date of the issue of the magazine in which the story would appear, and I said of course. He then asked, hesitantly, if I had any particular interpretation of my own for the story; Mr. Harold Ross, then the editor of *The New Yorker*, was not altogether sure that he understood the story, and wondered if I cared to enlarge upon its meaning. I said no. Mr. Ross, he said, thought that the story might be puzzling to some people, and in case anyone telephoned the magazine, as sometimes happened, or wrote in asking about the story, was there anything in particular I wanted them to say? No, I said, nothing in particular; it was just a story I wrote.

I had no more preparation than that. I went on picking up the mail every morning, pushing my daughter up and down the hill in her stroller, anticipating pleasurably the check from *The New Yorker*, and shopping for groceries. The weather stayed nice and it looked as though it was going to be a good summer. Then, on June 28, *The New Yorker* came out with my story.

Things began mildly enough with a note from a friend at *The New Yorker*: "Your story has kicked up quite a fuss around the office," he wrote. I was flattered; it's nice to think that your friends notice what you write. Later that day there was a call from one of the magazine's editors; they had had a couple of people phone in about my story, he said, and was there anything I particularly wanted him to say if there were any more calls? No, I said, nothing particular; anything he chose to say was perfectly all right with me; it was just a story.

I was further puzzled by a cryptic note from another friend: "Heard a man talking about a story of yours on the bus this morning," she wrote. "Very exciting. I wanted to tell him I knew the author, but after I heard what he was saying I decided I'd better not."

One of the most terrifying aspects of publishing stories and books is the realization that they are going to be read, and read by strangers. I had never fully realized this before, although I had of course in my imagination dwelt lovingly upon the thought of the millions and millions of people who were going to be uplifted and enriched and delighted by the stories I wrote. It had simply never occurred to me that these millions and millions of people might be so far from being uplifted that they would sit down and write me letters I was downright scared to open; of the three-hundred-odd letters that I received that summer I can count only thirteen that spoke kindly to me, and they were mostly from friends. Even my mother scolded me: "Dad and I did not care at all for your story in *The New Yorker*," she wrote sternly, "it does seem, dear, that this gloomy kind of story is what all you young people think about these days. Why don't you write something to cheer people up?"

By mid-July I had begun to perceive that I was very lucky indeed to be safely in Vermont, where no one in our small town had ever heard of *The New Yorker*, much less read my story. Millions of people, and my mother, had taken a pronounced dislike to me.

The magazine kept no track of telephone calls, but all letters addressed to me care of the magazine were forwarded directly to me for answering, and all letters addressed to the magazine — some of them addressed to Harold Ross personally; these were the most vehement — were answered at the magazine and then the letters were sent me in great batches, along with carbons of the answers written at the magazine. I have all the letters still, and if they could be considered to give any accurate cross section of the reading public, or the reading public of *The New Yorker*, or even the reading public of one issue of *The New Yorker*, I would stop writing now.

Judging from these letters, people who read stories are gullible, rude, frequently illiterate, and horribly afraid of being laughed at. Many of the writers were positive that *The New Yorker* was going to ridicule them in print, and the most cautious letters were headed, in capital letters: NOT FOR PUBLICATION or PLEASE DO NOT PRINT THIS LETTER, or, at best, THIS LETTER MAY BE PUBLISHED AT YOUR USUAL RATES OF PAYMENT. Anonymous letters, of which there were a few, were destroyed. *The New Yorker* never published any comment of any kind about the story in the magazine, but did issue one publicity release saying that the story had received more mail than any piece of fiction they had ever published; this was after the newspapers had gotten into the act, in midsummer, with a front-page story in the San Francisco *Chronicle* begging to know what the story meant, and a series of columns in New York and Chicago papers pointing out that *New Yorker* subscriptions were being canceled right and left.

Curiously, there are three main themes which dominate the letters of that first summer — three themes which might be identified as bewilderment, speculation, and plain old-fashioned abuse. In the years since then, during which the story has been anthologized, dramatized, televised, and even — in one completely mystifying transformation — made into a ballet, the tenor of letters I receive has changed. I am addressed more politely, as a rule, and the letters largely confine themselves to questions like what does this story mean? The general tone of the early letters, however, was a kind of wide-eyed, shocked innocence. People at first were not so much concerned with what the story meant; what they wanted to know was where these lotteries were held, and whether they could go there and watch.

Henry James

Henry James described the origin of his story "The Real Thing" in his notebook entry for February 22, 1891. He kept a record of his works-in-progress for more than thirty years; his notes, often written hastily, were simply for his own eyes. In 1947 the scholars F. O. Matthiessen and Kenneth Murdock published *The Notebooks of Henry James*, a carefully edited volume that is invaluable for any study of James's fiction. It is also of interest to the aspiring writer, because it is full of James's insights into the process of literary creation.

The Genesis of "The Real Thing"

1891

In pursuance of my plan of writing some very short tales — things of from 7,000 to 10,000 words, the easiest length to "place," I began yesterday the little story that was suggested to me some time ago by an incident related to me by George du Maurier — the lady and gentleman who called upon him with a word from Frith, an oldish, faded, ruined pair — he an officer in the army — who unable to turn a penny in any other way, were trying to find employment as models. I was struck with the pathos, the oddity, and typicalness of the situation — the little tragedy of good-looking gentlefolk, who had been all their life stupid and well-dressed, living, on a fixed income, at country-houses, watering places, and clubs, like so many others of their class in England, and were now utterly unable to *do* anything, had no cleverness, no art nor craft to make use of as a *gagne-pain*[1] — could only *show* themselves, clumsily, for the fine, clean, well-groomed animals that they were, only hope to make a little money by — in this manner — just simply *being*. I thought I saw a subject for very brief treatment in this *donnée*[2] — and I think I do still; but to do anything worth while with it I must (as always, great Heavens!) be very clear as to what is in it and what I wish to get out of it. I tried a beginning yesterday, but I instantly became conscious that I must straighten out the little idea. It must be an idea — it can't be a "story" in the vulgar sense of the word. It must be a picture; it must illustrate something. God knows that's enough — if the thing *does* illustrate. To make little anecdotes of this kind real *morceaux de vie*[3] is a plan quite inspiring enough. *Voyons un peu,*[4] therefore, what one can put into this one — I mean how much of life. One must put a little action — not a stupid, mechanical, arbitrary action, but something that is of the real essence of the subject. I thought of representing the husband as jealous of the wife — that is, jealous of the artist employing her, from the moment that, in point of fact, she begins to sit. But this is vulgar and obvious — worth nothing. What I wish to represent is the baffled, ineffectual, incompetent character of their attempt, and how it illustrates once again the everlasting English amateurishness — the way superficial, untrained, unprofessional effort goes to the wall when confronted with trained, competitive, intelligent, *qualified* art — in whatever line it may be a question of. It is out of *that* element that my little action and movement must come; and now I begin to see just how — as one always *does* — Glory be to the Highest — when one begins to look at a thing hard and straight and seriously — to fix it — as I am so sadly lax and desultory about doing. What subjects I should find — for *everything* — if I could only achieve this more as a habit! Let my contrast and complication here come from the opposition — to my melancholy Major and

---

[1] A way to earn their bread.

[2] Literally, "given"; the situation or assumption with which one begins an argument.

[3] Slice of life.

[4] "Let us examine for a bit . . ."

his wife — of a couple of little vulgar professional people *who know*, with the consequent bewilderment, vagueness, depression of the former — their failure to understand how such people can be better than *they* — their failure, disappointment, disappearance — going forth into the vague again. *Il y a bien quelque chose à tirer de ça.*[5] They have no pictorial sense. They are only clean and stiff and stupid. The others are dirty, even — the melancholy Major and his wife remark on it, wondering. The artist is beginning a big illustrated book, a new edition of a famous novel — say *Tom Jones:*[6] and he is willing to try to work them in — for he takes an interest in their predicament, and feels — skeptically, but, with his flexible artistic sympathy — the appeal of their type. He is willing to give them a trial. Make it out that *he* himself is on trial — he is young and "rising," but he has still his golden spurs to win. He can't afford, *en somme,*[7] to make many mistakes. He has regular work in drawing every week for a serial novel in an illustrated paper; but the great project — that of a big house — of issuing an illustrated Fielding promises him a big lift. He has been intrusted with (say) *Joseph Andrews,*[8] experimentally; he will have to do this brilliantly in order to have the engagement for the rest confirmed. He has already two models in his service — the "complication" must come from *them.* One is a common, clever, London girl, of the smallest origin and without conventional beauty, but of aptitude, of perceptions — knowing thoroughly *how.* She says "lydy" and "plice" but she has the pictorial sense; and can look like anything he wants her to look like. She poses, in short, in perfection. So does her colleague, a professional Italian, a little fellow — ill dressed, smelling of garlic, but admirably serviceable, quite universal. They must be contrasted, confronted, *juxtaposed* with the others; whom they take for people who *pay,* themselves, till they learn the truth when they are overwhelmed with derisive amazement. The denouncement simply that the melancholy Major and his wife won't do — they're not "in it." Their surprise — their helpless, proud assent — without other prospects: yet at the same time *their* degree of more silent amazement at the success of the two inferior people — who are so much less nice-looking than themselves. Frankly, however, is this contrast enough of a *story*, by itself? It seems to me Yes — for it's an IDEA — and how the deuce should I get *more* into 7,000 words? It must be simply fifty pp. of my manuscript. The little tale of *The Servant (Brooksmith),* which I did the other day for *Black and White* and which I thought the same time as this, proved a very tight squeeze into the same tiny number of words, and I probably shall find that there is much more to be done with this than the compass will admit of. Make it tremendously succinct — with a very short pulse or rhythm — and the closest selection of detail — in other words *summarize* intensely and keep down the lateral development. It *should* be a little gem of bright, quick, vivid form. I shall get

---

[5] "There is indeed something to draw from that."

[6] Novel by Henry Fielding (1707–1754).

[7] In sum.

[8] Another, earlier novel by Fielding.

every grain of "action" that the space admits of if I make something, for the artist, hang in the balance — depend on the way he does this particular work. It's when he finds that he shall lose his great opportunity if he keeps on with them, that he has to tell the gentlemanly couple, that, frankly, they won't serve his turn — and make them wander forth into the cold world again. I must keep them the age I've made them — fifty and forty — because it's more touching; but I must bring up the age of the two real models to almost the same thing. That increases the incomprehensibility (to the amateurs) of their usefulness. Picture the immanence, in the latter, of the idle, provided-for, country-house habit — the blankness of their *manière d'être*.[9] But in how tremendously few words I must do it. This is a lesson — a *magnificent* lesson — if I'm to do a good many. Something as admirably compact and *selected* as Maupassant.

---

[9] Manner of being.

Gustav Janouch

Gustav Janouch published his recollections of Franz Kafka in *Conversations with Kafka* (1953). Janouch's father was employed by the Workers' Accident Insurance Institute with Kafka, and he introduced his son to Kafka in 1920 because they were both "scribblers." Janouch was only seventeen at the time, and very impressionable. Having read "The Metamorphosis," he was disappointed by his first sight of Kafka: "'So this is the creator of the mysterious bug, Samsa,' I said to myself, disillusioned to see before me a simple, well-mannered man." But when their conversation was over that day—after Kafka had told Janouch that he wrote at night because daytime was a "great enchantment . . . it distracts from the darkness within"—Janouch asked himself, "Is he not himself the unfortunate bug in 'The Metamorphosis'?" Their acquaintance ripened into a friendship, which lasted until Kafka's death in 1924.

Kafka's View of "The Metamorphosis"

1953 / Translated by Goronwy Rees

I spent my first week's wages on having Kafka's three stories — *The Metamorphosis*, *The Judgement*, and *The Stoker* — bound in a dark brown leather volume, with the name *Franz Kafka* elegantly tooled in gold lettering.

The book lay in the brief-case on my knee as I told Kafka about the warehouse-cinema. [Janouch was a pianist at the cinema.] Then I proudly took the volume out of the case and gave it across the desk to Kafka.

"What is this?" he asked in astonishment.

"It's my first week's wages."

"Isn't that a waste?"

Kafka's eyelids fluttered. His lips were sharply drawn in. For a few seconds he contemplated the name in the gold lettering, hastily thumbed through the pages of the book and — with obvious embarrassment — placed it before me on the desk. I was about to ask why the book offended him, when he began to cough. He took a handkerchief from his pocket, held it to his mouth, replaced it when the attack was over, stood up and went to the small washstand behind his desk and washed his hands, then said as he dried them: "You overrate me. Your trust oppresses me."

He sat himself at his desk and said, with his hands to his temples: "I am no burning bush. I am not a flame."

I interrupted him. "You shouldn't say that. It's not just. To me, for example, you are fire, warmth, and light."

"No, no!" he contradicted me, shaking his head. "You are wrong. My scribbling does not deserve a leather binding. It's only my own personal spectre of horror. It oughtn't to be printed at all. It should be burned and destroyed. It is without meaning."

I became furious. "Who told you that?" I was forced to contradict him — "How can you say such a thing? Can you see into the future? What you are saying to me is entirely your subjective feeling. Perhaps your scribbling, as you call it, will tomorrow represent a significant voice in the world. Who can tell today?"

I drew a deep breath.

Kafka stared at the desk. At the corners of his mouth were two short, sharp lines of shadow.

I was ashamed of my outburst, so I said quietly, in a low, explanatory tone: "Do you remember what you said to me about the Picasso exhibition?"

Kafka looked at me without understanding.

I continued: "You said that art is a mirror which — like a clock running fast — foretells the future. Perhaps your writing is, in today's *Cinema of the Blind*, only a mirror of tomorrow."

"Please, don't go on," said Kafka fretfully, and covered his eyes with both hands.

I apologized. "Please forgive me, I didn't mean to upset you. I'm stupid."

"No, no — you're not that!" Without removing his hands, he rocked his whole body to and fro. "You are right. You are certainly right. Probably that's why I can't finish anything. I am afraid of the truth. But can one do otherwise?" He took his hands away from his eyes, placed his clenched fists on the table, and said in a low, suppressed voice: "One must be silent, if one can't give any help. No one, through his own lack of hope, should make the condition of the patient worse. For that reason, all my scribbling is to be destroyed. I am no light. I have merely lost my way among my own thorns. I'm a dead end."

Kafka leaned backwards. His hands slipped lifelessly from the table. He closed his eyes.

"I don't believe it," I said with utter conviction, yet added appeasingly: "And even if it were true, it would be worthwhile to display the dead end to people."

Kafka merely shook his head slowly. "No, no . . . I am weak and tired."

"You should give up your work here," I said gently, to relax the tension which I felt between us.

Kafka nodded. "Yes, I should. I wanted to creep away behind this office desk, but it only increased my weakness. It's become — ," Kafka looked at me with an indescribably painful smile, " — a cinema of the blind."

Then he closed his eyes again.

I was glad at this moment there was a knock on the door behind me.

Sarah Orne Jewett

Sarah Orne Jewett wrote "Looking Back on Girlhood" for the *Youth's Companion* magazine. It was published in the issue of January 7, 1892, near the end of her long career as a writer (she published at least 146 stories between 1868 and 1904). Jewett's reminiscence of how she became a writer is marked by the same sympathy for others and love of her native landscape that permeates her local-color fiction. As the critic Richard Cary has noted, her lucid and unassuming prose style conveys her "marked regard for the significance of the ordinary."

Looking Back on Girlhood

1892

In giving this brief account of my childhood, or, to speak exactly, of the surroundings which have affected the course of my work as a writer, my first thought flies back to those who taught me to observe, and to know the deep pleasures of simple things; and to be interested in the lives of people about me.

With its high hills and pine forests, and all its ponds and brooks and distant mountain views, there are few such delightful country towns in New England as the one where I was born. Being one of the oldest colonial settlements, it is full of interesting traditions and relics of the early inhabitants, both Indians and Englishmen. Two large rivers join just below the village at the head of tidewater, and these, with the great inflow from the sea, make a magnificent stream, bordered on its seaward course now by high-wooded banks of dark pines and hemlocks, and again by lovely green fields that slope gently to long lines of willows at the water's edge.

Sarah Orne Jewett as a young girl near her home in South Berwick, Maine.

There is never-ending pleasure in making one's self familiar with such a region. One may travel at home in a most literal sense, and be always learning history, geography, botany, or biography — whatever one chooses.

I have had a good deal of journeying in my life, and taken great delight in it, but I have never taken greater delight than in my rides and drives and tramps and voyages within the borders of my native town. There is always something fresh, something to be traced or discovered, something particularly to be remembered. One grows rich in memories and associations.

I believe that we should know our native towns much better than most of us do, and never let ourselves be strangers at home. Particularly when one's native place is so really interesting as my own [Berwick, Maine]! . . .

My grandfather died in my eleventh year, and presently the Civil War began.

From that time the simple village life was at an end. Its provincial character was fading out; shipping was at a disadvantage, and there were no more bronzed sea-captains coming to dine and talk about their voyages, no more bags of filberts or oranges for the children, or great red jars of olives; but in these childish years I had come in contact with many delightful men and women of real individuality and breadth of character, who had fought the battle of life to good advantage, and sometimes against great odds.

In these days I was given to long, childish illnesses, and it must be honestly confessed, to instant drooping if ever I were shut up in school. I had apparently not the slightest desire for learning, but my father was always ready to let me be his companion in long drives about the country.

In my grandfather's business household, my father, unconscious of tonnage and timber measurement, of the markets of the Windward Islands or the Mediterranean ports, had taken to his book, as old people said, and gone to college and begun that devotion to the study of medicine which only ended with his life.

I have tried already to give some idea of my father's character in my story of *The Country Doctor*, but all that is inadequate to the gifts and character of the man himself. He gave me my first and best knowledge of books by his own delight and dependence upon them, and ruled my early attempts at writing by the severity and simplicity of his own good taste.

"Don't try to write *about* people and things, tell them just as they are!"

How often my young ears heard these words without comprehending them! But while I was too young and thoughtless to share in an enthusiasm for Sterne[1] or Fielding,[2] and Smollett[3] or Don Quixote,[4] my mother and grandmother were leading me into the pleasant ways of *Pride and Prejudice*,[5] and *The Scenes of Clerical Life*,[6] and the delightful stories of Mrs. Oliphant.[7]

---

[1] Laurence Sterne (1713–1768), English novelist best known for his humorous nine-volume series, *The Life and Opinions of Tristram Shandy*.

[2] Henry Fielding (1707–1754), English playwright and novelist known for his parodic style.

[3] Tobias George Smollett (1721–1771), Scottish novelist.

[4] Bewildered knight and main character of Miguel de Cervantes's satiric novel *Don Quixote* (1615).

[5] *Pride and Prejudice* (1813), novel by the English writer Jane Austen (1775–1817) that, by its treatment of an ordinary family with ordinary problems, influenced the modern English novel.

[6] *The Scenes of Clerical Life* (1885), book of fictional sketches by Victorian novelist George Eliot [Mary Ann Evans]. Eliot (1819–1880) developed the method of psychological analysis widely used in modern fiction.

[7] Margaret Oliphant (1828–1897), prolific Victorian novelist, historical writer, and biographer known for her sympathetic depictions of rural life.

The old house was well provided with leather-bound books of a deeply serious nature, but in my youthful appetite for knowledge, I could even in the driest find something vital, and in the more entertaining I was completely lost.

My father had inherited from his father an amazing knowledge of human nature, and from his mother's French ancestry, that peculiarly French trait, called *gaieté de cœur*.[8] Through all the heavy responsibilities and anxieties of his busy professional life, this kept him young at heart and cheerful. His visits to his patients were often made perfectly delightful and refreshing to them by his kind heart, and the charm of his personality.

I knew many of the patients whom he used to visit in lonely inland farms, or on the seacoast in York and Wells. I used to follow him about silently, like an undemanding little dog, content to follow at his heels.

I had no consciousness of watching or listening, or indeed of any special interest in the country interiors. In fact, when the time came that my own world of imaginations was more real to me than any other, I was sometimes perplexed at my father's directing my attention to certain points of interest in the character or surroundings of our acquaintances.

I cannot help believing that he recognized, long before I did myself, in what direction the current of purpose in my life was setting. Now, as I write my sketches of country life, I remember again and again the wise things he said, and the sights he made me see. He was only impatient with affectation and insincerity.

I may have inherited something of my father's and grandfather's knowledge of human nature, but my father never lost a chance of trying to teach me to observe. I owe a great deal to his patience with a heedless little girl given far more to dreams than to accuracy, and with perhaps too little natural sympathy for the dreams of others.

The quiet village life, the dull routine of farming or mill life, early became interesting to me. I was taught to find everything that an imaginative child could ask, in the simple scenes close at hand.

I say these things eagerly, because I long to impress upon every boy and girl this truth: that it is not one's surroundings that can help or hinder — it is having a growing purpose in one's life to make the most of whatever is in one's reach.

If you have but a few good books, learn those to the very heart of them. Don't for one moment believe that if you had different surroundings and opportunities you would find the upward path any easier to climb. One condition is like another, if you have not the determination and the power to grow in yourself.

I was still a child when I began to write down the things I was thinking about, but at first I always made rhymes and found prose so difficult that a school composition was a terror to me, and I do not remember ever writing one that was worth anything. But in course of time rhymes themselves became difficult and prose more and more enticing, and I began my work in life, most happy in finding that I was to write of those country characters and rural landscapes to which I myself belonged, and which I had been taught to love with all my heart.

---

[8] Lightheartedness (in French, literally, gaiety of heart).

I was between nineteen and twenty when my first sketch was accepted by Mr. Howells[9] for the *Atlantic*. I already counted myself as by no means a new contributor to one or two other magazines — *Young Folks* and *The Riverside* — but I had no literary friends "at court."

I was very shy about speaking of my work at home, and even sent it to the magazine under an assumed name, and then was timid about asking the postmistress for those mysterious and exciting editorial letters which she announced upon the post office list as if I were a stranger in the town.

---

[9] William Dean Howells (1837–1920), American novelist and editor.

Jamaica Kincaid

Jamaica Kincaid explained her symbolic interpretation of the theme of "Girl" to interviewer Allan Vorda. This excerpt appeared in *Face to Face: Interviews with Contemporary Novelists* (1993), edited by Allan Vorda.

On "Girl"

1993

AV: There is a litany of items in "Girl" from a mother to her daughter about what to do and what not to do regarding the elements of being "a nice young lady." Is this the way it was for you and other girls in Antigua?"

JK: In a word, yes.

AV: Was that good or bad?

JK: I don't think it's the way I would tell my daughter, but as a mother I would tell her what I think would be best for her to be like. This mother in "Girl" was really just giving the girl an idea about the things she would need to be a self-possessed woman in the world.

AV: But you didn't take your mother's advice?

JK: No, because I had other ideas on how to be a self-possessed woman in the world. I didn't know that at the time. I only remember these things. What the mother in the story sees as aids to living in the world, the girl might see as extraordinary oppression, which is one of the things I came to see.

AV: Almost like she's Mother England.

JK: I was just going to say that. I've come to see that I've worked through the relationship of the mother and the girl to a relationship between Europe and the place that I'm from, which is to say, a relationship between the powerful and the powerless. The girl is powerless and the mother is powerful. The mother shows her how to be in the world, but at the back of her mind she thinks she never will get it. She's deeply skeptical that this child could ever grow up to be a self-possessed woman and in the end she reveals her skepticism; yet even within the skepticism is, of course, dismissal and scorn. So it's not unlike the relationship between the conquered and the conqueror.

Anne Lamott

Anne Lamott wrote about "Finding Your Voice" in a chapter of her classic book about becoming a creative writer, *Bird by Bird* (1994).

Finding Your Voice

1994

I heard a tape once in which an actor talked about trying to find God in the modern world and how, left to our own devices, we seek instead all the worldly things — possessions, money, looks, and power — because we think they will bring us fulfillment. But this turns out to be a joke, because they are just props, and when we check out of this life, we have to give them all back to the great propmaster in the sky. "They're just on loan," he said. "They're not ours." This tape changed how I felt about my students emulating their favorite writers. It helped me see that it is natural to take on someone else's style, that it's a prop that you use for a while until you have to give it back. And it just might take you to the thing that is not on loan, the thing that is real and true: your own voice.

I often ask my students to scribble down in class the reason they want to write, why they are in my class, what is propelling them to do this sometimes-excruciating, sometimes-boring work. And over and over, they say in effect, "I will not be silenced again." They were good children, who often felt invisible and who saw some awful stuff. But at some point they stopped telling what they saw because when they did, they were punished. Now they want to look at their lives — at life — and they don't want to be sent to their rooms for doing so. But it is very hard to find their own voice and it is tempting to assume someone else's.

Every time Isabel Allende has a new book out, I'm happy because I will get to read it, and I'm unhappy because half of my students are going to start writing like her. Now, I love Ms. Allende's work, as I love a number of South and Central American writers. When I read their books, I feel like I'm sitting around a campfire at night where they are spinning their wild stories — these crazy Rube Goldberg clocks, with lots of birds and maidens and gongs and bells and whistles. I understand why this style is so attractive to my students: it's like primitive art. It's simple and decorative, with rich colors, satisfying old forms, and a lot of sophistication underneath that you feel but don't really see. I always feel like I'm watching a wild theater piece with lots of special effects — so many lives falling apart! But, more important, this style offers the nourishment of imagination and wonder. I love to enter into these fantastical worlds where we feel like we're looking through the wrong end of the binoculars, where everything is tiny and pretty and rich, because real life is so often big and messy and hurtful and drab. But when someone like Allende polishes and turns and twists her people and their lives and their families and their ghosts into universal curves and shapes, then the writing resonates in such a way that you think, Yes, yes, that's exactly what life is like.

I love for my students to want to have this effect. But their renditions never ring true, any more than they ring true a few months later when Ann Beattie's latest book arrives and my students start submitting stories about shiny bowls and windowpanes. We do live our lives on surfaces, and Beattie does surfaces beautifully, burnishing them, bringing out the details. But when my students do Beattie, their stories tend to be lukewarm, and I say to them, Life is lukewarm enough! Give us a little heat! If I'm going to read about a bunch of people who drive Volkswagens and seem to have mostly Volkswagen-sized problems, and the writer shows them driving around on top of the ice, I want a sense that there's a lot of very, very cold water down below. I eventually want for someone to crash through. I want people who write to crash or dive below the surface, where life is so cold and confusing and hard to see. I want writers to plunge through the holes — the holes we try to fill up with all the props. In those holes and in the spaces around them exist all sorts of possibility, including the chance to see who we are and to glimpse the mystery.

The great writers keep writing about the cold dark place within, the water under a frozen lake or the secluded, camouflaged hole. The light they shine on this hole, this pit, helps us cut away or step around the brush and brambles; then we can dance around the rim of the abyss, holler into it, measure it, throw rocks in it, and still not fall in. It can no longer swallow us up. And we can get on with things.

A sober friend once said to me, "When I was still drinking, I was a sedated monster. After I got sober, I was just a monster." He told me about his monster. His sounded just like mine without quite so much mascara. When people shine a little light on their monster, we find out how similar most of our monsters are. The secrecy, the obfuscation, the fact that these monsters can only be hinted at, gives us the sense that they must be very bad indeed. But when people let their monsters out for a little onstage interview, it turns out that we've all done or thought the same things, that this is our lot, our condition. We don't end up with a brand on our forehead. Instead, we compare notes.

We write to expose the unexposed. If there is one door in the castle you have been told not to go through, you must. Otherwise, you'll just be re-arranging furniture in rooms you've already been in. Most human beings are dedicated to keeping that one door shut. But the writer's job is to see what's behind it, to see the bleak unspeakable stuff, and to turn the unspeakable into words — not just into any words but if we can, into rhythm and blues.

You can't do this without discovering your own true voice, and you can't find your true voice and peer behind the door and report honestly and clearly to us if your parents are reading over your shoulder. They are probably the ones who told you not to open that door in the first place. You can tell if they're there because a small voice will say, "Oh, whoops, don't say that, that's a secret," or "That's a bad word," or "Don't tell anyone you jack off. They'll all start doing it." So you have to breathe or pray or do therapy to send them away. Write as if your parents are dead. As I've said, we will discuss libel later in this book.

"Why, though?" my students ask, staring at me intently. "Why are we sup-posed to open all these doors? Why are we supposed to tell the truth in our own voice?" And I stare back at them for a moment. I guess because it's our nature, I say. Also, I think that most of your characters believe, as children believe, that if the truth were known, they would be seen as good people. Truth seems to want expression. Unacknowledged truth saps your energy and keeps you and your characters wired and delusional. But when you open the closet door and let what was inside out, you can get a rush of liberation and even joy. If we can believe in the Gnostic gospel of Thomas, old Uncle Jesus said, "If you bring forth what is inside you, what you bring forth will save you. If you don't bring forth what is inside you, what you bring forth can destroy you."

And the truth of your experience can *only* come through in your own voice. If it is wrapped in someone else's voice, we readers will feel suspicious, as if you are dressed up in someone else's clothes. You cannot write out of some-one else's big dark place; you can only write out of your own. Sometimes wear-ing someone else's style is very comforting, warm and pretty and bright, and it can loosen you up, tune you into the joys of language and rhythm and con-cern. But what you say will be an abstraction because it will not have sprung from direct experience: when you try to capture the truth of your experience in some other person's voice or on that person's terms, you are removing your-self one step further from what you have seen and what you know.

Truth, or reality, or whatever you want to call it is the bedrock of life. A black man at my church who is nearing one hundred thundered last Sunday, "*God* is your home," and I pass this on mostly because all of the interesting characters I've ever worked with — including myself — have had at their center a feeling of oth-erness, of homesickness. And it's wonderful to watch someone finally open that forbidden door that has kept him or her away. What gets exposed is not people's baseness but their humanity. It turns out that the truth, or reality, is our home.

Look at the two extremes. Maybe you find truth in Samuel Beckett — that we're very much alone and it's all scary and annoying and it smells like dirty feet and the most you can hope for is that periodically someone will offer a hand or a rag or a tiny word of encouragement just when you're going under. The redemption in Beckett is so small: in the second act of *Waiting for Godot*, the barren dying twig of a tree has put out a leaf. Just one leaf. It's not much; still Beckett didn't commit suicide. He wrote.

Or maybe truth as you understand it is 180 degrees away — that God is everywhere and we are all where we're supposed to be and more will be revealed one day. Maybe you feel that Wordsworth was right, maybe Rumi, maybe Stephen Mitchell writing on Job: "The physical body is acknowledged as dust, the personal drama as delusion. It is as if the world we perceive through our senses, that whole gorgeous and terrible pageant, were the breath-thin surface of a bubble, and everything else, inside and outside, is pure radiance. Both suffering and joy come then like a brief reflection, and death like a pin."

But you can't get to any of these truths by sitting in a field smiling beatifically, avoiding your anger and damage and grief. Your anger and damage and grief are the way to the truth. We don't have much truth to express unless we have gone into those rooms and closets and woods and abysses that we were told not to go into. When we have gone in and looked around for a long while, just breathing and finally taking it in — then we will be able to speak in our own voice and to stay in the present moment. And that moment is home.

D. H. Lawrence

D. H. Lawrence was fascinated by Poe's genius in his tales and wrote an early form of psychological criticism of Poe's texts. This excerpt from Lawrence's writing on Poe is taken from the *English Review* of April 1919. It was later revised and reprinted in Lawrence's pioneering volume *Studies in Classic American Literature* (1923).

On "The Fall of the House of Usher" and "The Cask of Amontillado"

1919

[In "The Fall of the House of Usher,"] the love is between brother and sister. When the self is broken, and the mystery of the recognition of *otherness* falls, then the longing for identification with the beloved becomes a lust. And it is this longing for identification, utter merging, which is at the base of the incest problem. In psychoanalysis almost every trouble in the psyche is traced to an incest-desire. But this will not do. The incest-desire is only one of the manifestations of the self-less desire for merging. It is obvious that this desire for merging, or unification, or identification of the man with the woman, or the woman with the man, finds its gratification most readily in the merging of those things which are already near — mother with son, brother with sister, father with daughter. But it is not enough to say, as Jung does, that all life is a matter of lapsing towards, or struggling away from, mother-incest. It is necessary to see what lies at the back of this helpless craving for utter merging or identification with a beloved.

The motto to "The Fall of the House of Usher" is a couple of lines from De Béranger.

> "Son coeur est un luth suspendu;
> Sitôt qu'on le touche il résonne."

We have all the trappings of Poe's rather overdone vulgar fantasy. "I reined my horse to the precipitous brink of a black and lurid tarn that lay in unruffled lustre by the dwelling, and gazed down — but with a shudder even more thrilling than before — upon the remodelled and inverted images of the grey sedge, and the ghastly tree-stems, and the vacant and eye-like windows." The House of Usher, both dwelling and family, was very old. Minute fungi overspread the exterior of the house, hanging in festoons from the eaves. Gothic archways, a valet of stealthy step, sombre tapestries, ebon black floors, a profusion of tattered and antique furniture, feeble gleams of encrimsoned light through latticed panes, and over all "an air of stern, deep, irredeemable gloom" — this makes up the interior.

The inmates of the house, Roderick and Madeline Usher, are the last remnants of their incomparably ancient and decayed race. Roderick has the same large, luminous eye, the same slightly arched nose of delicate Hebrew model, as characterised Ligeia.[1] He is ill with the nervous malady of his family. It is he whose nerves are so strung that they vibrate to the unknown quiverings of the ether. He, too, has lost his self, his living soul, and become a sensitised instrument of the external influences; his nerves are verily like an aeollan harp which must vibrate. He lives in "some struggle with the grim phantasm, Fear," for he is only the physical, post-mortem reality of a living being.

It is a question how much, once the rich centrality of the self is broken, the instrumental consciousness of man can register. When man becomes self-less, wafting instrumental like a harp in an open window, how much can his elemental consciousness express? It is probable that even the blood as it runs has its own sympathies and responses to the material world, quite apart from seeing. And the nerves we know vibrate all the while to unseen presences, unseen forces. So Roderick Usher quivers on the edge of dissolution.

It is this mechanical consciousness which gives "the fervid facility of his impromptus." It is the same thing that gives Poe his extraordinary facility in

---

[1] A reference to the heroine of Poe's short story "Ligeia."

versification. The absence of real central or impulsive being in himself leaves him inordinately mechanically sensitive to sounds and effects, associations of sounds, association of rhyme, for example — mechanical, facile, having no root in any passion. It is all a secondary, meretricious process. So we get Roderick Ushers poem, "The Haunted Palace," with its swift yet mechanical subtleties of rhyme and rhythm, its vulgarity of epithet. It is all a sort of dream-process, where the association between parts is mechanical, accidental as far as passional meaning goes.

Usher thought that all vegetable things had sentience. Surely all material things have a form of sentience, even the inorganic: surely they all exist in some subtle and complicated tension of vibration which makes them sensitive to external influence and causes them to have an influence on other external objects, irrespective of contact. It is of this vibrational or inorganic consciousness that Poe is master: the sleep-consciousness. Thus Roderick Usher was convinced that his whole surroundings, the stones of the house, the fungi, the water in the tarn, the very reflected image of the whole, was woven into a physical oneness with the family, condensed, as it were, into one atmosphere — the special atmosphere in which alone the Ushers could live. And it was this atmosphere which had moulded the destinies of his family.

In the human realm, Roderick had one connection: his sister Madeline. She, too, was dying of a mysterious disorder, nervous, cataleptic. The brother and sister loved each other passionately and exclusively. They were twins, almost identical in looks. It was the same absorbing love between them, where human creatures are absorbed away from themselves, into a unification in death. So Madeline was gradually absorbed into her brother; the one life absorbed the other in a long anguish of love.

Madeline died and was carried down by her brother into the deep vaults of the house. But she was not dead. Her brother roamed about in incipient madness — a madness of unspeakable terror and guilt. After eight days they were suddenly startled by a clash of metal, then a distinct, hollow, metallic, and clangorous, yet apparently muffled, reverberation. Then Roderick Usher, gibbering, began to express himself: "*We have put her living into the tomb!* Said I not that my senses were acute? *I now* tell you that I heard her first feeble movements in the hollow coffin. I heard them — many, many days ago — yet I dared not — *I dared not speak.*"

It is again the old theme of "each man kills the thing he loves." He knew his love had killed her. He knew she died at last, like Ligeia, unwilling and unappeased. So, she rose again upon him. "But then without those doors there *did* stand the lofty and enshrouded figure of the Lady Madeline of Usher. There was blood upon her white robes, and the evidence of some bitter struggle upon every portion of her emaciated frame. For a moment she remained trembling and reeling to and fro upon the threshold, then, with a low moaning cry, fell heavily inward upon the person of her brother, and in her violent and now final death-agonies bore him to the floor a corpse, and a victim to the terrors he had anticipated."

It is lurid and melodramatic, but it really is a symbolic truth of what happens in the last stages of this inordinate love, which can recognise none of the sacred mystery of *otherness*, but must unite into unspeakable identification, oneness in death. Brother and sister go down together, made one in the unspeakable mystery of death. It is the world-long incest problem, arising inevitably when man, through insistence of his will in one passion or aspiration, breaks the polarity of himself.

The best tales all have the same burden. Hate is as inordinate as love, and as slowly consuming, as secret, as underground, as subtle. All this underground vault business in Poe only symbolises that which takes place *beneath* the consciousness. On top, all is fair-spoken. Beneath, there is the awful murderous extremity of burying alive. Fortunato, in "The Cask of Amontillado," is buried alive out of perfect hatred, as the Lady Madeline of Usher is buried alive out of love. The lust of hate is the inordinate desire to consume and unspeakably possess the soul of the hated one, just as the lust of love is the desire to possess, or to be possessed by the beloved, utterly. But in either case the result is the dissolution of both souls, each losing itself in transgressing its own bounds.

The lust of Montresor is to devour utterly the soul of Fortunato. It would be no use killing him outright. If a man is killed outright his soul remains integral, free to return into the bosom of some beloved, where it can enact itself. In walling-up his enemy in the vault, Montresor seeks to bring about the indescribable capitulation of the man's soul, so that he, the victor, can possess himself of the very being of the vanquished. Perhaps this can actually be done. Perhaps, in the attempt, the victor breaks the bounds of his own identity, and collapses into nothingness, or into the infinite.

What holds good for inordinate hate holds good for inordinate love. The motto, *Nemo me impune lacessit*,[2] might just as well be *Nemo me impune amat*.[3] . . .

As long as man lives he will be subject to the incalculable influence of love or of hate, which is only inverted love. The necessity to love is probably the source of all our unhappiness; but since it is the source of everything it is foolish to particularise. Probably even gravitation is only one of the lowest manifestations of the mystic force of love. But the triumph of love, which is the triumph of life and creation, does not lie in merging, mingling, in absolute identification of the lover with the beloved. It lies in the communion of beings, who, in the very perfection of communion, recognise and allow the mutual otherness. There is no desire to transgress the bounds of being. Each self remains utterly itself—becomes, indeed, most burningly and transcendently itself in the uttermost embrace or communion with the other. One self may yield honourable precedence to the other, may pledge itself to undying service, and in so doing become fulfilled in its own nature. For the highest achievement of some souls lies in perfect service. But the giving and the taking of service does not obliterate the mystery of otherness, the being-in-singleness, either in master or servant. On the other hand, slavery is an avowed obliteration of the singleness of being.

---

[2] No one hates me with impunity.
[3] No one loves me with impunity.

Ursula K. Le Guin

Ursula K. Le Guin published *The Wind's Twelve Quarters*, the collection of short fiction in which "The Ones Who Walk Away from Omelas" appeared, in 1975. The stories in this book form a disturbing group, posing questions that stay with the reader long after each story is finished. In her commentary Le Guin describes the source for the idea of her story.

The Scapegoat in Omelas

1975

The central idea of this psychomyth, the scapegoat, turns up in Dostoyevsky's *Brothers Karamazov*, and several people have asked me, rather suspiciously, why I gave the credit to William James. The fact is, I haven't been able to re-read Dostoyevsky, much as I loved him, since I was twenty-five, and I'd simply forgotten he used the idea. But when I met it in James's "The Moral Philosopher and the Moral Life," it was with a shock of recognition. Here is how James puts it:

> Or if the hypothesis were offered us of a world in which Messrs. Fourier's and Bellamy's and Morris's utopias should all be outdone, and millions kept permanently happy on the one simple condition that a certain lost soul on the far-off edge of things should lead a life of lonely torment, what except a specifical and independent sort of emotion can it be which would make us immediately feel, even though an impulse arose within us to clutch at the happiness so offered, how hideous a thing would be its enjoyment when deliberately accepted as the fruit of such a bargain?

The dilemma of the American conscience can hardly be better stated. Dostoyevsky was a great artist, and a radical one, but his early social radicalism reversed itself, leaving him a violent reactionary. Whereas the American James, who seems so mild, so naïvely gentlemanly — look how he says "us," assuming all his readers are so decent as himself — was, and remained, and remains, a genuinely radical thinker. Directly after the "lost soul" passage he goes on,

> All the higher, more penetrating ideals are revolutionary. They present themselves far less in the guise of effects of past experience than in that of probable causes of future experience, factors to which the environment and the lessons it has so far taught us must learn to bend.

The application of those two sentences to this story, and to science fiction, and to all thinking about the future, is quite direct. Ideals as "the probable causes of future experience" — that is a subtle and an exhilarating remark!

Of course I didn't read James and sit down and say, Now I'll write a story about that "lost soul." It seldom works that simply. I sat down and started a story, just because I felt like it, with nothing but the word "Omelas" in mind. It came from a road sign: Salem (Oregon) backwards. Don't you read road signs backwards? POTS, WOLS nerdlihc. Ocsicnarf Nas . . . Salem equals schelomo equals salaam equals Peace. Melas. O melas. Omelas. Homme hélas. "Where *do* you get your ideas from, Ms. Le Guin?" From forgetting Dostoyevsky and reading road signs backwards, naturally. Where else?

Simon Lewis

Simon Lewis analyzed Jhumpa Lahiri's story "Interpreter of Maladies" in the summer 2001 issue of the academic journal *Explicator*.

Lahiri's "Interpreter of Maladies"

2001

Jhumpa Lahiri's short story "Interpreter of Maladies," from her 1999 Pulitzer Prize–winning collection of the same name, is likely to become a classic of literature anthologies not just because of its great narrative and verbal craft, but also because it updates E. M. Forster's 1924 novel *A Passage to India*. The plots of both texts hinge on a misconceived tourist excursion — to the Marabar Caves in *A Passage to India*, to the monastic cells at Udayagiri and Khandagiri in "Interpreter of Maladies" — during which a male Indian guide and a female visitor misinterpret each other's verbal and nonverbal signals. In both cases the male guide's perceptions of the foreign visitor are at odds with those of the woman who, apparently prompted by her extraordinary and unfamiliar surroundings, tries to come to terms with pre-existing emotional dilemmas.

As one might expect in a postcolonial rewrite, Lahiri narrates her story from the point of view of the Indian host, the interpreter of maladies-cum-tourist guide Mr. Kapasi. What makes Lahiri's reworking of Forster so intriguing, however, is that the gulf of misunderstanding between Mr. Kapasi and the visiting Mrs. Das results from cultural rather than racial difference. Lahiri thus moves beyond Eurocentric or Oriental images of India to those of a contemporary postcolonial nation more concerned with dialogue with its own diaspora than with its former colonizers. The story may repeat the Forsterian theme of mutual human incomprehension, but the world of "Interpreter of Maladies" is an exclusively Indian one, in which Indians define notions of self and other, in which Indians move freely among countries and cultures, and in which India itself is an object of scrutiny by Indian eyes.

The Surya Temple in Konarak, India.

Although Mr. Kapasi and Mrs. Das are both Indian, the difference between them is just as gaping as that between Forster's Dr. Aziz and Adela Quested. With both Forster and Lahiri the question of misunderstanding is supposed to go even deeper than race and culture, representing something fundamental to the human condition. After fleeing from the first of the Marabar Caves, for instance, Forster's Mrs. Moore — so intuitively sympathetic to India and Indians up to this point — becomes exasperated with the emotional turmoil around her and formulates the thought that despite "centuries of carnal embracement, [. . .] man is no nearer to understanding man" (Forster 147–48). Likewise, in the novel's famous closing, the connection between Fielding and Aziz is denied by their material circumstances: the rocks between which they rode "didn't want it, they said in their hundred voices, 'No, not yet,' and the sky said, 'No, not there'" (Forster 316, original punctuation). In "Interpreter of Maladies" the material symbol of Kapasi's and Mrs. Das's non-connection, the "slip of paper with Mr. Kapasi's address on it" [788] flutters away unnoticed by anyone but Mr. Kapasi, who is left with a mental impression only of the Das family instead of the personal correspondence with Mrs. Das that he had anticipated.

Kapasi's final disappointment comes after he realizes how self-absorbed Mrs. Das is. After listening to her confession that her younger son Bobby had been fathered by an unnamed "Punjabi friend," Kapasi realizes that this confession is not the shared intimacy he had been hoping for, but that Mrs. Das had told him the story more or less to purge herself of it. When he fails to offer either absolution or a cure and instead quite reasonably asks, "'Is it really pain you feel, Mrs. Das, or is it guilt?'" [787], her withering glare "crushed him; he knew at that moment that he was not even important enough to be properly insulted" [787].

This moment has its analogue in *A Passage to India* when Adela's naive question to Aziz as to whether he has more than one wife irritates Aziz so much that he has to leave her and smoke a cigarette in order to regain his composure as host. Forster goes to some length to stress that there is absolutely no erotic charge in their encounter — the narrative records that Aziz "had never liked Miss Quested as much as Mrs. Moore" and that his mind was preoccupied with organizational details of the recent breakfast (Forster 162). Nonetheless, out of that encounter (or non-encounter) and Adela's subsequent hysterical experience come the accusation of rape and the raising of stereotypical issues of transracial desire that are so central to colonial fiction.

In "Interpreter of Maladies," by contrast, Kapasi's desire for Mrs. Das, though never physically expressed, is more frankly acknowledged. Right from the opening paragraph Lahiri shows Kapasi as intensely aware of Mrs. Das's physical presence: of "her shaved, largely bare legs" [774] and her clothes. Her "close-fitting blouse styled like a man's undershirt" and "decorated at chest level with a calico appliqué in the shape of a strawberry" [775] persistently draws his attention, and toward the end of the story he fantasizes about "complimenting her strawberry shirt, which he found irresistibly becoming" [784].

However whereas Kapasi, unlike Aziz, clearly finds his tourist-guest sexually attractive, his desire for her does not fit the stock transracial model of colonial fiction. Instead, part of her appeal seems to be his sense of Mrs. Das's similarity to him; she and her family all "looked Indian" even though they "dressed as foreigners did" [774]. Because it is almost impossible to ascribe exoticness or foreignness either to the Dases or to Mr. Kapasi, Lahiri's story here as elsewhere thoroughly confounds the Manichean sense of self and other that underlies the tension that Forster creates between the unmarried white woman visitor and her married Indian host. Each is partly familiar to the other, but neither is wholly representative of "Indianness."

Mr. Kapasi, for instance, in his crucial role as interpreter, refers easily to the television show *Dallas* (a reference the Das daughter does not recognize because it is so dated), and his English is more British than Indian or American. Indeed, unlike Aziz, whose idiosyncratically Indian English is the source of some humor in *A Passage to India*, Lahiri has Mr. Kapasi comment on the idiosyncrasies of Mrs. Das's American usage. At the height of his fantasy about Mrs. Das, for instance, Kapasi is rather perplexed by her casual use of "Neat" in response to his explanation of the significance of a bronze statue of Surya [783]. His hope that her noncommittal comment will allow him to continue his relationship with her, acting as an "interpreter between nations" [779] rather than of maladies, is finally quashed no less emphatically than Forster quashes the hope of Indian-British connection in *A Passage to India*.

Ultimately, although Lahiri's story reiterates Forster's elegant pessimism concerning human relations, it denies that the malady that comes between people has its origin in race or geographical location. To be sure, there is a Forsterian theme — that although Mr. Kapasi might be able to interpret both his own maladies (of thwarted ambitions, thwarted desire) and those of others, no one can bridge the communicative gaps that inevitably separate human beings. Yet in rendering this world in exclusively Indian terms, Lahiri's story tacitly exposes the outdated racialism of Forster's novel.

Works Cited

Forster, E. M. *A Passage to India*. Harmondsworth: Penguin, 1980. Print.
Lahiri, Jhumpa. *Interpreter of Maladies*, Boston: Houghton, 1999. Print. [Page citations in the text have been changed to refer to this anthology.]

Jack London

Jack London was asked several questions by the copyeditor of *Youth's Companion* in 1902 about "To Build a Fire," which was about to be published in the magazine. London, who wrote naturalistic stories, prided himself on the accuracy of his details, and he patiently clarified what he had written for his editor.

Letter to the Editor on
"To Build a Fire"

1902

Jack London
56 Bayo Vista Avenue
Oakland, Calif.
Feb. 5/02

Dear Mr. Revision Editor: —

In reply to questions will state (I) — At go off, Vincent[1] took matches from inside pocket. It does not matter what he does with matches during first several attempts to build fire — not until he leaves that place and starts along the trail. Then insert, page 6, after "The frost had beaten him. His hands were worthless," the following: "But he had the foresight to drop the bunch of matches into his wide-mouthed outside pocket. [*London's revision*] There, in dispair [*sic*], he slipped on his mittens and started to run up the trail," etc. etc. (II) Take my word for it, that a man simply cannot build a fire with heavy Klondike mittens on his hands. I have seen hundreds of such fires built in cold weather, and I never even saw a man attempt to build one fire with mittened hands. It is impossible. I have built a fire at 74° below zero, and I did it with my naked hands.

But the point with Vincent is that his wet feet are freezing. Had he not wet his feet, he could have simply kept right on traveling and never exposed his hands at all. But traveling or not, his feet *were* freezing all the time.

It is an old [*London's revision*] Alaskan tragedy, this fire-building. They have traced a man, from his first careful attempts at a fire to his last wild & feeble attempt, & then found his stiff body — and this has been done more than once.

You see, the time element must be considered. At such low temperature flesh freezes quickly. The fire also must be built quickly.

Why, I ran two hundred feet and back again, through the dead calm air at sixty-five below, and nipped my ear (exposed) so badly that it kept me awake that night, later turned black & peeled off all the skin.

In this connection, however, at the top of page 5, after "waited the match," you might insert: "It is impossible to build a fire with heavy Alaskan mittens on one's hands; so Vincent bared his, gathered a sufficient number of twigs, and knocking the snow, etc."

I do not know what kind of mittens you have in the East. Up north they are of fairly thick, pretty thick, moosehide (native-tanned) and they are warmly lined with flannel. It is impossible to strike a sulphur match & cherish the slow-growing flame therof [*sic*] with such mittens on one's hands. To [have] attempted it with

---

[1] The original name, dropped from the final version of the story, of the protagonist in "To Build a Fire."

a bunch would be to cause a healthy conflagration, wide-spread burns & much smoke — three things which would effectually put a quietus on the fire.

I hope I have explained.

By the way. The *Companion* has always been prompt in paying. "To Build a Fire" was sent about the middle of December. I now learn from you that the story is already in make-up. This leads me to fear that check for same has probably gone astray, as I have received no word from the Corresponding Editor. Will you please ask him to look into the matter? Also, last of December, I sent *Companion* another story: "Up the Slide." As with the other, I have had printed notice of its safe arrival, but nothing more.

Very truly yours,
Jack London

Katherine Mansfield

Katherine Mansfield reviewed Virginia Woolf's story "Kew Gardens" in the *Athenaeum* on June 13, 1919. As the literary historian Clare Hanson has noted, Mansfield might have suggested an idea for this story to Woolf in a letter two years before, describing a garden with people engaged in "conversation, their slow pacing—their glances as they pass one another—the pauses as the flowers 'come in' as it were." In her favorable review of Woolf's story, Mansfield stressed the elements she regarded most highly in short fiction: She preferred atmosphere to action, and she valued the language of the story as much as the subject of the narrative. She believed that atmosphere and language together give short fiction an ethical dimension. According to Hanson, Mansfield was following Anton Chekhov in this conviction: "While she did not suggest that the artist should in any crude sense set out to preach or prove a point, she did believe that the 'true' artist's work would make an ethical impression, and that it was the duty of the critic to register this impression and measure its depth and quality."

Review of Woolf's "Kew Gardens"

1919

If it were not a matter to sigh over, it would be almost amusing to remember how short a time has passed since Samuel Butler[1] advised the budding author to keep a note-book. What would be the author's reply to such counsel nowadays

---

[1] Samuel Butler (1835–1902), Victorian essayist and autobiographical novelist.

but an amused smile: "I keep nothing else!" True; but if we remember rightly, Samuel Butler goes a little further; he suggests that the note-book should be kept in the pocket, and that is what the budding author finds intolerably hard. Up till now he has been so busy growing and blowing that his masterpieces still are unwritten, but there are the public waiting, gaping. Hasn't he anything to offer before they wander elsewhere? Can't he startle their attention by sheer roughness and crudeness and general slapdashery? Out comes the note-book and the deed is done. And since they find its contents absolutely thrilling and satisfying, is it to be wondered at that the risk of producing anything bigger, more solid, and more positive — is not taken? The note-books of young writers are their laurels; they prefer to rest on them. It is here that one begins to sigh, for it is here that the young author begins to swell and to demand that, since he has chosen to make his note-books his All, they shall be regarded as of the first importance, read with a deadly seriousness and acclaimed as a kind of new Art — the art of not taking pains, of never wondering why it was one fell in love with this or that, but contenting oneself with the public's dreary interest in promiscuity.

Perhaps that is why one feels that Mrs Virginia Woolf's story belongs to another age. It is so far removed from the note-book literature of our day, so exquisite an example of love at second sight. She begins where the others leave off, entering Kew Gardens, as it were, alone and at her leisure when their little first screams of excitement have died away and they have rushed afield to some new brilliant joy. It is strange how conscious one is, from the first paragraph, of this sense of leisure: Her story is bathed in it as if it were a light, still and lovely, heightening the importance of everything, and filling all that is within her vision with that vivid, disturbing beauty that haunts the air the last moment before sunset or the first moment after dawn. Poise — yes, poise. Anything may happen; her world is on tiptoe.

This is her theme. In Kew Gardens there was a flower-bed full of red and blue and yellow flowers. Through the hot July afternoon men and women "straggled past the flower-bed with a curiously irregular movement not unlike that of the white and blue butterflies who crossed the turf in zig-zag flights from bed to bed," paused for a moment, were "caught" in its dazzling net, and then moved on again and were lost. The mysterious intricate life of the flower-bed goes on untouched by these odd creatures. A little wind moves, stirring the petals so that their colours shake on to the brown earth, grey of a pebble, shell of a snail, a rain-drop, a leaf, and for a moment the secret life is half-revealed; then a wind blows again, and the colours flash in the air and there are only leaves and flowers. . . .

It happens so often — or so seldom — in life, as we move among the trees, up and down the known and unknown paths, across the lawns and into the shade and out again, that something — for no reason that we can dis-cover — gives us pause. Why is it that, thinking back upon that July afternoon, we see so distinctly that flower-bed? We must have passed myriads of flowers that day; why do these particular ones return? It is true, we stopped in front of them, and talked a little and then moved on. But though we weren't conscious of it at the time, something was happening — something . . .

Kew Gardens, ca. 1930s.

But it would seem that the author, with her wise smile, is as indifferent as the flowers to these odd creatures and their ways. The tiny rich minute life of a snail — how she describes it! the angular high-stepping green insect — how passionate is her concern for him! Fascinated and credulous, we believe these things are all her concern until suddenly with a gesture she shows us the flower-bed, growing, expanding in the heat and light, filling a whole world.

Guy de Maupassant

Guy de Maupassant wrote an analysis of how he created fiction in the lengthy preface to his novel *Pierre and Jean* in 1888. In this excerpt he analyzes his intent as a writer and presents his view of realism. Maupassant wanted to clarify the point that no fiction can be called "realistic," if that term means a mirror image of life. Henry James later wrote that Maupassant's preface contains many insights into the nature of literature, including an important distinction between different kinds of fiction. James realized that Maupassant's

> readers must be grateful to him for such a passage as that in which he remarks that whereas the public at large very legitimately says to a writer, "Console me, amuse me, terrify me, make me cry, make me dream, or make me think," what the sincere critic says is, "Make me something fine in the form that shall suit you best, according to your temperament." This seems to me to put into a nutshell the whole question of the different classes of fiction. . . . There are simply as many different kinds as there are persons practising the art, for if a picture, a tale, or a novel be a direct impression of life (and that surely constitutes its interest and value), the impression will vary according to the plate [temperament] that takes it, the particular structure and mixture of the recipient.

The Writer's Goal

1888 / Translated by Mallay Charters

[The serious writer's] goal is not to tell us a story, to entertain or to move us, but to make us think and to make us understand the deep and hidden meaning of events. By virtue of having seen and meditated, he views the universe, objects, facts, and human beings in a certain way which is personal, the result of combining his observations and reflections. It is this personal view of the world that he tries to communicate to us by reproducing it in fiction. To move us, as he has been moved himself by the spectacle of life, he must reproduce it before our eyes with a scrupulous accuracy. He should compose his work so adroitly, and with such dissimulation and apparent simplicity, that it is impossible to uncover its plan or to perceive his intentions.

Instead of fabricating an adventure and spinning it out in a way that keeps it interesting until the end, the writer will pick up his characters at a certain point of their existence and carry them, by natural transitions, to the following period. He will show how minds are modified under the influence of environmental circumstances, and how sentiments and passions are developed. In this fashion, he will show our loves, our hates, our struggles in all kinds of social conditions; and how social interests, financial interests, political interests, and personal interests all compete with each other.

The writer's cleverness with his plot will thus consist not in the use of sentiment or charm, in an engaging beginning or an emotional catastrophe, but in the adroit grouping of small constant facts from which the reader will grasp a definitive sense of the work. . . . [The author] should know how to eliminate, among the minute and innumerable daily occurrences, all those which are useless to him. He must emphasize those which would have escaped the notice of less clear-sighted observers, which give the story its effect and value as fiction. . . .

A writer would find it impossible to describe everything in life, because he would need at least a volume a day to list the multitude of unimportant incidents filling up our hours.

Some selectivity is required — which is the first blow to the "entire truth" theory [of realistic literature].

Life, moreover, is composed of the most unpredictable, disparate, and contradictory elements. It is brutal, inconsequential, and disconnected, full of inexplicable, illogical catastrophes.

This is why the writer, having selected a theme, will take from this chaotic life, encumbered with hazards and trivialities, only the details useful to his subject and omit all the others.

One example out of a thousand: The number of people in the world who die every day in accidents is considerable. But can we drop a roof tile on a main character's head, or throw him under the wheels of a car, in the middle of a narrative, under the pretext that it is necessary to have an accident?

Life can leave everything the same as it was. Or it can speed up some events and drag out others. Literature, on the other hand, presents cleverly orchestrated events and concealed transitions, essential incidents high-lighted by the writer's skill alone. In giving every detail its exact degree of shading in accordance with its importance, the author produces the profound impression of the particular truth he wishes to point out.

To make things seem real on the page consists in giving the complete *illusion* of reality, following the logical order of facts, and not servilely transcribing the pell-mell succession of chronological events in life.

I conclude from this analysis that writers who call themselves realists should more accurately call themselves illusionists.

How childish, moreover, to believe in an absolute reality, since we each carry a personal one in our thoughts and in our senses. Our eyes, our ears, our sense of smell and taste create as many truths as there are individuals. Our minds, diversely impressed by the reception of the senses' information, comprehend, analyze, and judge as if each of us belonged to a separate race.

Thus each of us makes, individually, a personal illusion of the world. It may be a poetic, sentimental, joyful, melancholy, sordid, or dismal one, according to our nature. The writer's goal is to reproduce this illusion of life faithfully, using all the literary techniques at his disposal.

Herman Melville

Herman Melville wrote "Hawthorne and His Mosses," an eloquent essay on Nathaniel Hawthorne's volume of short stories, *Mosses from an Old Manse*, for the New York periodical the *Literary World* in August 1850. Unlike Edgar Allan Poe in his review of Hawthorne's short fiction, Melville did not use the opportunity to theorize about the form of the short story. Instead, he conveyed his enthusiasm for Hawthorne's tragic vision, what Melville saw as the "great power of blackness" in Hawthorne's writing. This was the aspect of Hawthorne's work that seemed most congenial to Melville's own genius while he continued work that summer on his novel-in-progress, *Moby-Dick*. As he wrote in his essay, "Great geniuses are parts of the times, they themselves are the times, and possess a corresponding coloring." In 1850 Melville exhorted America to "prize and cherish her writers," since they "are not so many in number as to exhaust her goodwill."

Blackness in Hawthorne's "Young Goodman Brown"

1850

It is curious, how a man may travel along a country road, and yet miss the grandest or sweetest of prospects, by reason of an intervening hedge so like all other hedges as in no way to hint of the wide landscape beyond. So has it been with me concerning the enchanting landscape in the soul of this Hawthorne, this most excellent Man of Mosses. His Old Manse has been written now four years, but I never read it till a day or two since. I had seen it in the bookstores — heard of it often — even had it recommended to me by a tasteful friend, as a rare, quiet book, perhaps too deserving of popularity to be popular. But there are so many books called "excellent" and so much unpopular merit, that amid the thick stir of other things, the hint of my tasteful friend was disregarded; and for four years the Mosses on the Old Manse never refreshed me with their perennial green. It may be, however, that all this while, the book, like wine, was only improving in flavor and body. . . .

At any rate, it so chanced that this long procrastination eventuated in a happy result. At breakfast the other day, a mountain girl, a cousin of mine, who for the last two weeks has every morning helped me to strawberries and raspberries, which, like the roses and pearls in the fairy tale, seemed to fall into the saucer from those strawberry beds, her cheeks — this delightful creature, this charming Cherry says to me — "I see you spend your mornings in the haymow; and yesterday I found there Dwight's *Travels in New England*. Now I have something far better than that; something more congenial to our summer on these hills. Take these raspberries, and then I will give you some moss." "Moss!" said I. "Yes, and you must take it to the barn with you, and good-by to Dwight."

With that she left me, and soon returned with a volume, verdantly bound, and garnished with a curious frontispiece in green; nothing less than a fragment of real moss, cunningly pressed to a fly-leaf. "Why, this," said I, spilling my raspberries, "this is the *Mosses from an Old Manse*." "Yes," said Cousin Cherry, "Yes, it is that flowery Hawthorne." "Hawthorne and Mosses," said I, "no more it is morning: it is July in the country: and I am off for the barn."

Stretched on that new-mown clover, the hillside breeze blowing over me through the wide barn door, and soothed by the hum of the bees in the meadows around, how magically stole over me this Mossy Man! and how amply, how bountifully, did he redeem that delicious promise to his guests in the Old Manse, of whom it is written: "Others could give them pleasure, or amusement, or instruction — these could be picked up anywhere; but it was for me to give them rest — rest, in a life of trouble! What better could be done for those weary and world-worn spirits? . . . what better could be done for anybody who came within our magic circle than to throw the spell of a tranquil spirit over him?" So all that day, half buried in the new clover, I watched this Hawthorne's "Assyrian dawn, and Paphian sunset and moonrise from the summit of our eastern hill."

The soft ravishments of the man spun me round about in a web of dreams, and when the book was closed, when the spell was over, this wizard "dismissed me with but misty reminiscences, as if I had been dreaming of him."

What a wild moonlight of contemplative humor bathes that Old Manse! — the rich and rare distillment of a spicy and slowly-oozing heart. No rollicking rudeness, no gross fun, fed on fat dinners, and bred in the lees of wine, — but a humor so spiritually gentle, so high, so deep, and yet so richly relishable, that it were hardly inappropriate in an angel. It is the very religion of mirth; for nothing so human but it may be advanced to that. The orchard of the Old Manse seems the visible type of the fine mind that has described it — those twisted and contorted old trees, "they stretch out their crooked branches, and take such hold of the imagination that we remember them as humorists and odd-fellows." And then, as surrounded by these grotesque forms, and hushed in the noonday repose of this Hawthorne's spell, how aptly might the still fall of his ruddy thoughts into your soul be symbolized by: "In the stillest afternoon, if I listened, the thump of a great apple was audible, falling without a breath of wind, from the mere necessity of perfect ripeness." For no less ripe than ruddy are the apples of the thoughts and fancies in this sweet Man of Mosses . . .

But it is the least part of genius that attracts admiration. Where Hawthorne is known, he seems to be deemed a pleasant writer, with a pleasant style — a sequestered, harmless man, from whom any deep and weighty thing would hardly be anticipated: a man who means no meanings. But there is no man, in whom humor and love, like mountain peaks, soar to such a rapt height, as to receive the irradiations of the upper skies; there is no man in whom humor and love are developed in that high form called genius — no such man can exist without also possessing, as the indispensable complement of these, a great, deep intellect, which drops down into the universe like a plummet. Or, love and humor are only the eyes, through which such an intellect views this world. The great beauty in such a mind is but the product of its strength. . . .

For spite of all the Indian-summer sunlight on the hither side of Hawthorne's soul, the other side — like the dark half of the physical sphere — is shrouded in a blackness, ten times black. But this darkness but gives more effect to the ever-moving dawn, that forever advances through it, and circumnavigates his world. Whether Hawthorne has simply availed himself of this mystical blackness as a means to the wondrous effects he makes it to produce in his lights and shades; or whether there really lurks in him, perhaps unknown to himself, a touch of Puritanic gloom — this I cannot altogether tell. Certain it is, however, that this great power of blackness in him derives its force from its appeals to that Calvinistic sense of Innate Depravity and Original Sin, from whose visitations, in some shape or other, no deeply thinking mind is always and wholly free. For, in certain moods, no man can weigh this world, without throwing in something, somehow like Original Sin, to strike the uneven balance.

At all events, perhaps no writer has ever wielded this terrific thought with greater terror than this same harmless Hawthorne. Still more: this black conceit pervades him through and through. You may be witched by his sunlight — transported by the bright gildings in the skies he builds over you; but there is the blackness of darkness beyond; and even his bright gildings but fringe and play upon the edges of thunder-clouds. In one word, the world is mistaken in this Nathaniel Hawthorne. He himself must often have smiled at its absurd misconception of him. He is immeasurably deeper than the plummet of the mere critic. For it is not the brain that can test such a man; it is only the heart. You cannot come to know greatness by inspecting it; there is no glimpse to be caught of it, except by intuition; you need not ring it, you but touch it, and you find it is gold.

Now, it is that blackness in Hawthorne, of which I have spoken, that so fixes and fascinates me. It may be, nevertheless, that it is too largely developed in him. Perhaps he does not give us a ray of light for every shade of his dark. But however this may be, this blackness it is that furnishes the infinite obscure of his background — that background against which Shakespeare plays his grandest conceits, the things that have made for Shakespeare his loftiest but most circumscribed renown, as the profoundest of thinkers. For by philosophers Shakespeare is not adored, as the great man of tragedy and comedy: "Off with his head; so much for Buckingham!" This sort of rant, interlined by another hand, brings down the house — those mistaken souls, who dream of Shakespeare as a mere man of Richard the Third humps and Macbeth daggers. But it is those deep, far-away things in him; those occasional flashings-forth of the intuitive Truth in him; those short, quick probings at the very axis of reality, — these are the things that make Shakespeare, Shakespeare. Through the mouths of the dark characters of Hamlet, Timon, Lear, and Iago, he craftily says, or sometimes insinuates the things which we feel to be so terrifically true that it were all but madness for any good man, in his own proper character, to utter, or even hint of them. Tormented into desperation, Lear, the frantic king, tears off the mask, and speaks the same madness of vital truth. But, as I before said, it is the least part of genius that attracts admiration. And so, much of the blind, unbridled admiration that has been heaped upon Shakespeare has been lavished upon the least part of him. And few of his endless commentators and critics seem to have remembered, or even perceived, that the immediate products of a great mind are not so great as that undeveloped and sometimes undevelopable yet dimly-discernible greatness to which those immediate products are but the infallible indices. In Shakespeare's tomb lies infinitely more than

Shakespeare ever wrote. And if I magnify Shakespeare, it is not so much for what he did do as for what he did not do, or refrained from doing. For in this world of lies, Truth is forced to fly like a sacred white doe in the woodlands; and only by cunning glimpses will she reveal herself, as in Shakespeare and other masters of the great Art of Telling the Truth, even though it be covertly and by snatches. . . .

And now, my countrymen, as an excellent author of your own flesh and blood — an unimitating, and, perhaps, in his way, an inimitable man — whom better can I commend to you, in the first place, than Nathaniel Hawthorne? He is one of the new, and far better generation of your writers. The smell of young beeches and hemlocks is upon him; your own broad prairies are in his soul; and if you travel away inland into his deep and noble nature, you will hear the far roar of his Niagara. Give not over to future generations the glad duty of acknowledging him for what he is. Take that joy to yourself, in your own generation; and so shall he feel those grateful impulses on him, that may possibly prompt him to the full flower of some still greater achievement in your eyes. And by confessing him you thereby confess others; you brace the whole brotherhood. For genius, all over the world, stands hand in hand, and one shock of recognition runs the whole circle round. . . .

But with whatever motive, playful or profound, Nathaniel Hawthorne has chosen to entitle his pieces in the manner he has, it is certain that some of them are directly calculated to deceive — egregiously deceive — the superficial skimmer of pages. To be downright and candid once more, let me cheerfully say that two of these titles did dolefully dupe no less an eagle-eyed reader than myself; and that, too, after I had been impressed with a sense of the great depth and breadth of this American man. "Who in the name of thunder" (as the country people say in this neighborhood), "who in the name of thunder," would anticipate any marvel in a piece entitled "Young Goodman Brown"? You would of course suppose that it was a simple little tale, intended as a supplement to "Goody Two-Shoes." Whereas it is deep as Dante; nor can you finish it, without addressing the author in his own words: "It is yours to penetrate, in every bosom, the deep mystery of sin." And with Young Goodman, too, in allegorical pursuit of his Puritan wife, you cry out in your anguish,

> "Faith!" shouted Goodman Brown, in a voice of agony and desperation; and the echoes of the forest mocked him, crying — "Faith! Faith!" as if bewildered wretches were seeking her, all through the wilderness.

Now this same piece, entitled "Young Goodman Brown," is one of the two that I had not at all read yesterday; and I allude to it now, because it is, in itself, such a strong positive illustration of that blackness in Hawthorne which I had assumed from the mere occasional shadows of it, as revealed in several of the other sketches. But had I previously perused "Young Goodman Brown," I should have been at no pains to draw the conclusion which I came to at a time when I was ignorant that the book contained one such direct and unqualified manifestation of it.

J. Hillis Miller

J. Hillis Miller analyzed the effect of what he called "Bartleby's celebrated immobility" in the critical study *Versions of Pygmalion* (1990). Miller was intent on examining "strange and unaccountable" versions of the Pygmalion myth in European literature; each story he discussed "contains a character who does something like falling in love with a statue."

A Deconstructive Reading of Melville's "Bartleby, the Scrivener"

1990

After the failure of all these strategies for getting rid of Bartleby, the narrator tries another. In part through charity but in part through the notion that it is his fate to have Bartleby permanently in his chambers, he decides to try to live with Bartleby, to take him as a permanent fixture in his office. The narrator looks into two quite different books that deny man free will in determining his life, "Edwards on the Will" and "Priestly on Necessity." For Jonathan Edwards man does not have free will because everything he does is predestined by God. For Joseph Priestly, on the other hand, man is bound within the chains of a universal material necessity. Everything happens through physical causality, and therefore everything happens as it must happen, as it has been certain through all time to happen. In either case Bartleby's presence in the narrator's rooms is something predestined:

> Gradually I slid into the persuasion that these troubles of mine touching the scrivener, had been all predestinated from eternity, and Bartleby was billeted upon me for some mysterious purpose of an all-wise Providence, which it was not for a mere mortal like me to fathom. Yes, Bartleby, stay there behind your screen, thought I; I shall persecute you no more; you are harmless and noiseless as any of these old chairs; in short, I never feel so private as when I know you are here. At last I see it, I feel it; I penetrate to the predestinated purpose of my life. I am content. Others may have loftier parts to enact; but my mission in this world, Bartleby, is to furnish you with office-room for such period as you may see fit to remain.

This strategy fails too, when the narrator's clients and associates let him know that Bartleby's presence in his offices is scandalizing his professional reputation. It is then that the narrator, who is nothing if not logical, conceives his strangest way of dealing with Bartleby. Since Bartleby will not budge, he himself will leave. The immobility of Bartleby turns the narrator into a nomad: "No more then. Since he will not quit me, I must quit him. I will change my offices; I will move elsewhere."

When the new tenants and the landlord of his old premises come to charge the narrator with responsibility for the nuisance Bartleby is causing, "haunting the building generally, sitting upon the banisters of the stairs by day, and sleeping in the entry by night," the narrator tries first a new strategy of saying he is in no way related to Bartleby or responsible for him. But it is no use: "I was the last person known to have anything to do with him, and they held me to the terrible account."

The narrator then meets Bartleby once more face to face. He offers to set him up in a respectable position, as a clerk in a dry-goods store, a bartender, a bill collector, or a companion for young gentlemen traveling to Europe. To all these ludicrous suggestions Bartleby replies that he is not particular, but he would prefer to remain "stationary." The narrator then, and finally, offers to take Bartleby home with him, like a stray cat, and give him refuge there. This meets with the same reply. The narrator flees the building and becomes truly a vagrant, wandering for days here and there in his rockaway.

The narrator's life and work seem to have been permanently broken by the irruption of Bartleby. It is not he but his old landlord who deals effectively with the situation. He has Bartleby "removed to the Tombs as a vagrant." This is just what the more intellectually consequent narrator has not been able to bring himself to do, not just because Bartleby is not, strictly speaking, a vagrant and not just because doing such violence to Bartleby would disobey the law of charity, but because he cannot respond with violence to a resistance that has been purely passive and has thereby "disarmed" or "unmanned" any decisive action: "Turn the man out by an actual thrusting I could not; to drive him away by calling him hard names would not do; calling in the police was an unpleasant idea. . . . You will not thrust him, the poor, pale, passive mortal, — you will not thrust such a helpless creature out of your door? you will not dishonor yourself by such cruelty? No, I will not, I cannot do that."

Even after the police have been called in and society has placed Bartleby where he belongs, the narrator continues to be haunted by a sense of unfulfilled responsibility. He visits him in the Tombs, the prison so called because it was in the Egyptian Revival style of architecture, but also no doubt in response to a deeper sense of kinship between incarceration and death: "The Egyptian character of the masonry weighed upon me with its gloom. But a soft imprisoned turf grew under foot. The heart of the eternal pyramids, it seemed, wherein, by some strange magic, through the clefts, grass-seed, dropped by birds, had sprung." Bartleby is appropriately placed in the Tombs since, if the prison courtyard where Bartleby dies is green life in the midst of death, Bartleby has been death in the midst of life. In the Tombs the narrator makes his last unsuccessful attempt to deal with Bartleby in a rational manner, to reincorporate him into ordinary life. He "narrates" to the prison authorities, as he says, "all I knew" about Bartleby, telling them Bartleby does not really belong there but must stay "till something less harsh might be done — though indeed I hardly knew what." He yields at last to the accounting for Bartleby that had been used by Ginger Nut: "I think, sir, he's a little *luny*." The narrator now tells the "grub-man" in the prison, Mr. Cutlets, "I think he is a little deranged." One powerful means society has for dealing with someone who does not fit any ordinary social category is to declare him insane.

Mr. Cutlets has his own curious and by no means insignificant way of placing Bartleby. He thinks Bartleby must be a forger. "Deranged? deranged is it? Well now, upon my word, I thought that friend of yourn was a gentleman forger; they are always pale and genteel-like, them forgers. I can't help pity 'em — can't help it, sir. Did you know Monroe Edwards?" To which the narrator answers, "No, I was never socially acquainted with any forgers." In a way Mr. Cutlets has got Bartleby right, since forgery involves the exact copying of someone else's handwriting in order to make a false document that functions performatively as if it were genuine. Bartleby is a species of forger in reverse. He copies documents all right, but he does this in such a way as to deprive them of their power to make anything happen. On the other hand, when the narrator has copied documents checked, corrected, and made functional, he is himself performing an act of forgery. He may not be socially acquainted with any forgers, but he is in a manner of speaking one himself.

The arrangement he makes with Mr. Cutlets to feed Bartleby in prison is the narrator's last attempt to reincorporate Bartleby into society. There is much emphasis on eating in the story, on what the narrator's different employees eat and drink and on how little Bartleby eats, apparently nothing at all in prison: "'I prefer not to dine to-day,' said Bartleby, turning away. 'It would disagree with me; I am unused to dinners.' So saying he slowly moved to the other side of the inclosure, and took up a position fronting the dead-wall." Eating is one of the basic ways to share our common humanity. This Bartleby refuses, or rather he says he would prefer not to share in the ritual of eating. To refuse that is in the end deadly. Bartleby's death makes him what he has been all along, a bit of death in the midst of life.

It is entirely appropriate that the narrator's account of Bartleby should end with Bartleby's death, not because any biography should end with the death of the biographee but because in death Bartleby becomes what he has always already been. As I have said, his "I would prefer not to" is strangely oriented toward the future. It opens the future, but a future of perpetual not-yet. It can only come as death, and death is that which can never be present. There, at the end, the narrator finds the corpse of Bartleby, "strangely huddled at the base of the wall, his knees drawn up, and lying on his side, his head touching the cold stones." In an earlier version, the "Bartleby" fragment in the Melville family papers in the Gansevoort-Lansing Collection at the New York Public Library, Bartleby is found by the narrator lying in a white-washed room with his head against a tombstone: "It was clean, well-lighted and scrupulously white washed. The head-stone was standing up against the wall, and stretched on a blanket at its base, his head touching the cold marble and his feet upon the threshold lay the wasted form of Bartleby."

The corpse of Bartleby is not the presence of Bartleby. It is his eternal absence. In death he becomes what he has always been, a cadaver who "lives without dining," as the narrator says to the grub-man. Bartleby returns at death, in the final version of the story, to a fetal position. He is the incursion into life of that unattainable realm somewhere before birth and after death. But the word "realm" is misleading. What Bartleby brings is not a realm in the sense of place we might go. It is the otherness that all along haunts or inhabits life from the inside. This otherness can by no method, such as the long series of techniques the narrator tries, be accounted for, narrated, rationalized, or in any other way reassimilated into ordinary life, though it is a permanent part of that ordinary life. Bartleby is the alien that may neither be thrust out the door nor domesticated, brought into the family, given citizenship papers. Bartleby is the invasion of death into life, but not death as something from outside life. He is death as the other side of life or the cohabitant with life. "Death," nevertheless, is not the proper name for this ghostly companion of life, as if it were an allegorical meaning identified at last. Nor is "Death" its generic or common name. "Death" is a catachresis for what can never be named properly.

The narrator's last method of attempting to deal with Bartleby is his narration, going all the way from "I am a rather elderly man" to "Ah Bartleby! Ah humanity!" This narration is explicitly said to be written down and addressed to a "reader." It repeats for a more indeterminate reader, that is, for whoever happens to read it, the quasi-legal deposition he has made before the proper officer of "the Tombs, or to speak more properly, the Halls of Justice." If the narrator can encompass Bartleby with words, if he can do justice to him, he may simultaneously have accounted for him, naturalized him after all, and freed himself from his unfulfilled obligation. He will have made an adequate response to the demand Bartleby has made on him. The narrator, that is, may have justified himself while doing justice to Bartleby.

This is impossible because Bartleby cannot be identified. His story cannot be told. But the reader at the end knows better just why this is so, since we have watched the narrator try one by one a whole series of strategies for accounting for someone and has seen them one by one fail. This failure leaves Bartleby still imperturbably bringing everything to a halt or indefinitely postponing everything with his "I would prefer not to." The narrator's account is not so much an account as an apology for his failure to give an adequate account.

The narrator's writing is also an attempt at a reading, a failed attempt to read Bartleby. In this sense it is the first in a long line of attempts to read Bartleby the scrivener, though the narrator's successors do this by trying to read the text written by Melville, "Bartleby, the Scrivener." Just as Bartleby by his immovable presence in the narrator's office has demanded to be read and accounted for by him, so Melville's strange story demands to be read and accounted for. Nor have readers failed to respond to the demand. A large secondary literature has grown up around "Bartleby," remarkable for its multiplicity and diversity. All claim in one way or another to have identified Bartleby and to have accounted for him, to have done him justice. They tend to exemplify that function of policing or putting things in their place which is entrusted by our society to literary studies as one realm among many of the academic forms of accounting or accounting for. In the case of the essays on "Bartleby" this accounting often takes one or the other of two main forms, as Warminski has observed. These forms could be put under the aegis of the two-pronged last paragraph of the story — "Ah Bartleby! Ah humanity!" — or they might be said to fly in the face either of Bartleby's "But I am not particular" or of the manifest failure of the narrator's attempt to draw close to Bartleby by way of "the bond of a common humanity." Many of the essays try to explain Bartleby either by making him an example of some universal type, for example "existential man," or by finding some particular original or explanatory context for him, for example one of Melville's acquaintances who worked in a law office, or some aspect of nineteenth-century capitalism in America. But Bartleby is neither general nor particular: he is neutral. As such, he disables reading by any of these strategies, any attempt to put "Bartleby, the Scrivener" in its place by answering the question, "In mercy's name, who is he?"

No doubt my own reading also claims to have identified Bartleby, in this case by defining him as the neutral in-between that haunts all thinking and living by dialectical opposition. All readings of the story, including my own, are more ways to call in the police. They are ways of trying to put Bartleby in his place, to convey him where we want to put him, to make sense of him, even if it is an accounting that defines him as the nonsense that inhabits all sense-making. All readings attempt in one way or another to fulfill what the narrator has tried and failed to do: to tell Bartleby's story in a way that will allow us to assimilate him and the story into the vast archives of rationalization that make up the secondary literature of our profession. We are institutionalized to do that work of policing for our society. None of these techniques of assimilation works any better than any of the narrator's methods, and we remain haunted by Bartleby, but haunted also by "Bartleby, the Scrivener: A Story of Wall-Street." I claim, however, that my accounting succeeds where the others fail by showing (though that is not quite the right word) why it is that "accounting for" in any of its usual senses cannot work, either for the story or for the character the story poses.

Alice Munro

Alice Munro revealed her unconventional way of structuring her stories by following her intuition in this excerpt from her essay "What Is Real?"

How I Write Short Stories

1982

What I would like to do here is what I can't do in two or three sentences at the end of a reading. I won't try to explain what fiction is, and what short stories are (assuming, which we can't, that there is any fixed thing that it is and they are), but what short stories are to me, and how I write them, and how I use things that are "real." I will start by explaining how I read stories written by other people. For one thing, I can start reading them anywhere; from beginning to end, from end to beginning, from any point in between in either direction. So obviously I don't take up a story and follow it as if it were a road, taking me somewhere, with views and neat diversions along the way. I go into it, and move back and forth and settle here and there, stay in it for a while. It's more like a house. Everybody knows what a house does, how it encloses space and makes connections between one enclosed space and another and presents what is outside in a new way. This is the nearest I can come to explaining what a story does for me, and what I want my stories to do for other people.

So when I write a story I want to make a certain kind of structure, and I know the feeling I want to get from being inside that structure. This is the hard part of the explanation, where I have to use a word like "feeling," which is not very precise, because if I attempt to be more intellectually respectable I will have to be dishonest. "Feeling" will have to do.

There is no blueprint for the structure. It's not a question of, "I'll make this kind of house because if I do it right it will have this effect." I've got to make, I've got to build up, a house, a story, to fit around the indescribable "feeling" that is like the soul of the story, and which I must insist upon in a dogged, embarrassed way, as being no more definable than that. And I don't know where it comes from. It seems to be already there, and some unlikely clue, such as a shop window or a bit of conversation, makes me aware of it. Then I start accumulating the material and putting it together. Some of the material I may have lying around already, in memories and observations, and some I invent, and some I have to go diligently look-ing for (factual details), while some is dumped in my lap (anecdotes, bits of speech). I see how this material might go together to make the shape I need, and I try it. I keep trying and seeing where I went wrong and trying again.

I suppose this is the place where I should talk about technical problems and how I solve them. The main reason I can't is that I'm never sure I do solve anything. Even when I say that I see where I went wrong, I'm being misleading. I never figure out how I'm going to change things, I never say to myself, "That page is heavy going, that paragraph's clumsy, I need some dialogue and shorter sentences." I feel a part that's wrong, like a soggy weight; then I pay attention to the story, as if it were really happening somewhere, not just in my head, and in its own way, not mine. As a result, the sentences may indeed get shorter, there may be more dialogue, and so on. But though I've tried to pay attention to the story, I may not have got it right; those shorter sentences may be an evasion, a mistake. Every final draft, every published story, is still only an attempt, an approach, to the story.

Vladimir Nabokov

Vladimir Nabokov delivered lectures on Russian literature to his classes at Cornell University from 1948 to 1958. Forced to leave his native country at the age of twenty to escape what he called "the bloated octopus of the state" after the Russian Revolution, he took with him a passionate love for his homeland and for the "fiery, fanciful, free" literature of prerevolutionary Russia. For Nabokov, the great Russian writers of the nineteenth century (he began his lecture series with Nikolai Gogol) were more than artists: They were the last free voices in Russia for whom the government did not dictate absolute limits of imagination.

Gogol's Genius in "The Overcoat"

1981

Gogol was a strange creature, but genius is always strange; it is only your healthy second-rater who seems to the grateful reader to be a wise old friend, nicely developing the reader's own notions of life. Great literature skirts the irrational. *Hamlet* is the wild dream of a neurotic scholar. Gogol's *The Overcoat* is a grotesque and grim nightmare making black holes in the dim pattern of life. The superficial reader of that story will merely see in it the heavy frolics of an extravagant buffoon; the solemn reader will take for granted that Gogol's prime intention was to denounce the horrors of Russian bureaucracy. But neither the person who wants a good laugh, nor the person who craves for books "that make one think" will understand what *The Overcoat* is really about. Give me the creative reader; this is a tale for him.

Steady Pushkin,[1] matter-of-fact Tolstoy, restrained Chekhov have all had their moments of irrational insight which simultaneously blurred the sentence and disclosed a secret meaning worth the sudden focal shift. But with Gogol this shifting is the very basis of his art, so that whenever he tried to write in the round hand of literary tradition and to treat rational ideas in a logical way, he lost all trace of talent. When, as in his immortal *The Overcoat*, he really let himself go and pottered happily on the brink of his private abyss, he became the greatest artist that Russia has yet produced.

The sudden slanting of the rational plane of life may be accomplished of course in many ways, and every great writer has his own method. With Gogol

---

[1] Aleksandr Pushkin (1799–1837), considered by many (including Nabokov) the greatest Russian poet. Nabokov translated his novel in verse, *Eugene Onegin*, into English. For headnotes to Anton Chekhov and Leo Tolstoy, see pages 261 and 1241.

it was a combination of two movements: a jerk and a glide. Imagine a trap-door that opens under your feet with absurd suddenness, and a lyrical gust that sweeps you up and then lets you fall with a bump into the next traphole. The absurd was Gogol's favorite muse — but when I say "the absurd," I do not mean the quaint or the comic. The absurd has as many shades and degrees as the tragic has, and moreover, in Gogol's case, it borders upon the latter. It would be wrong to assert that Gogol placed his characters in absurd situa-tions. You cannot place a man in an absurd situation if the whole world he lives in is absurd; you cannot do this if you mean by "absurd" something pro-voking a chuckle or a shrug. But if you mean the pathetic, the human condi-tion, if you mean all such things that in less weird worlds are linked up with the loftiest aspirations, the deepest sufferings, the strongest passions — then of course the necessary breach is there, and a pathetic human, lost in the midst of Gogol's nightmarish, irresponsible world would be "absurd," by a kind of secondary contrast.

On the lid of the tailor's snuff-box there was "the portrait of a General; I do not know what general because the tailor's thumb has made a hole in the general's face and a square of paper has been gummed over the hole." Thus with the absurdity of Akaky Akakievich Bashmachkin. We did not expect that, amid the whirling masks, one mask would turn out to be a real face, or at least the place where that face ought to be. The essence of mankind is irra-tionally derived from the chaos of fakes which form Gogol's world. Akaky Akakievich, the hero of *The Overcoat*, is absurd *because* he is pathetic, *because* he is human, and *because* he has been engendered by those very forces which seem to be in such contrast to him.

He is not merely human and pathetic. He is something more, just as the back-ground is not mere burlesque. Somewhere behind the obvious contrast there is a subtle genetic link. His being discloses the same quiver and shimmer as does the dream world to which he belongs. The allusions to something else behind the crudely painted screens, are so artistically combined with the superficial texture of the narration that civic-minded Russians have missed them completely. But a creative reading of Gogol's story reveals that here and there is the most innocent descriptive passage, this or that word, sometimes a mere adverb or a preposition, for instance the word "even" or "almost," is inserted in such a way as to make the harmless sentence explode in a wild display of nightmare fireworks; or else the passage that had started in a rambling colloquial manner all of a sudden leaves the tracks and swerves into the irrational where it really belongs; or again, quite as suddenly, a door bursts open and a mighty wave of foaming poetry rushes in only to dissolve in bathos,[2] or to turn into its own parody, or to be checked by the sentence breaking and reverting to a conjuror's patter, that patter which is such

---

[2] One source has defined *bathos* as "pathos [the evoking of sympathy, sorrow, or pity] so overdone that it evokes laughter rather than pity."

a feature of Gogol's style. It gives one the sensation of something ludicrous and at the same time stellar, lurking constantly around the corner — and one likes to recall that the difference between the comic side of things, and their cosmic side, depends upon one sibilant.

So what is that queer world, glimpses of which we keep catching through the gaps of the harmless looking sentences? It is in a way the *real* one but it looks wildly absurd to us, accustomed as we are to the stage setting that screens it. It is from these glimpses that the main character of *The Overcoat*, the meek little clerk, is formed, so that he embodies the spirit of that secret but real world which breaks through Gogol's style. He is, that meek little clerk, a ghost, a visitor from some tragic depths who by chance happened to assume the disguise of a petty official. Russian progressive critics sensed in him the image of the underdog and the whole story impressed them as a social protest. But it is something much more than that. The gaps and black holes in the texture of Gogol's style imply flaws in the texture of life itself. Something is very wrong and all men are mild lunatics engaged in pursuits that seem to them very important while an absurdly logical force keeps them at their futile jobs — this is the real "message" of the story. In this world of utter futility, of futile humility and futile domination, the highest degree that passion, desire, creative urge can attain is a new cloak which both tailors and customers adore on their knees. I am not speaking of the moral point or the moral lesson. There can be no moral lesson in such a world because there are no pupils and no teachers: this world *is* and it excludes everything that might destroy it, so that any improvement, any struggle, any moral purpose or endeavor, are as utterly impossible as changing the course of a star. It is Gogol's world and as such wholly different from Tolstoy's world, or Pushkin's, or Chekhov's, or my own. But after reading Gogol one's eyes may become gogolized and one is apt to see bits of his world in the most unexpected places. I have visited many countries, and something like Akaky Akakievich's overcoat has been the passionate dream of this or that chance acquaintance who never had heard about Gogol.

Vladimir Nabokov

Vladimir Nabokov, the Russian novelist, blended wit, irreverence, and critical insight in his analysis of "The Lady with the Little Dog" in his *Lectures on Russian Literature* (1981).

A Reading of Chekhov's "The Lady with the Little Dog"

1981

Chekhov comes into the story "The Lady with the Little Dog" without knocking. There is no dilly-dallying. The very first paragraph reveals the main character, the young fair-haired lady followed by her white Spitz dog on the waterfront of a Crimean resort, Yalta, on the Black Sea. And immediately after, the male character Gurov appears. His wife, whom he has left with the children in Moscow, is vividly depicted: her solid frame, her thick black eyebrows, and the way she has of calling herself "a woman who thinks." One notes the magic of the trifles the author collects — the wife's manner of dropping a certain mute letter in spelling and her calling her husband by the longest and fullest form of his name, both traits in combination with the impressive dignity of her beetle-browed face and rigid poise forming exactly the necessary impression. A hard woman with the strong feminist and social ideas of her time, but one whom her husband finds in his heart of hearts to be narrow, dull-minded, and devoid of grace. The natural transition is to Gurov's constant unfaithfulness to her, to his general attitude toward women — "that inferior race" is what he calls them, but without that inferior race he could not exist. It is hinted that these Russian romances were not altogether as light-winged as in the Paris of Maupassant. Complications and problems are unavoidable with those decent hesitating people of Moscow who are slow heavy starters but plunge into tedious difficulties when once they start going.

Then with the same neat and direct method of attack, with the bridging formula "and so . . ." (or perhaps still better rendered in English by that "Now" which begins a new paragraph in straightforward fairy tales), we slide back to the lady with the dog. Everything about her, even the way her hair was done, told him that she was bored. The spirit of adventure — though he realized perfectly well that his attitude toward a lone woman in a fashionable sea town was based on vulgar stories, generally false — this spirit of adventure prompts him to call the little dog, which thus becomes a link between her and him. They are both in a public restaurant.

> He beckoned invitingly to the Spitz, and when the dog approached him, shook his finger at it. The Spitz growled; Gurov threatened it again.
> The lady glanced at him and at once dropped her eyes.
> "He doesn't bite," she said and blushed.
> "May I give him a bone?" he asked; and when she nodded he inquired affably, "Have you been in Yalta long?"
> "About five days."

They talk. The author has hinted already that Gurov was witty in the company of women; and instead of having the reader take it for granted (you know the old method of describing the talk as "brilliant" but giving no samples of the conversation), Chekhov makes him joke in a really attractive, winning way. "Bored, are you? An average citizen lives in . . . (here Chekhov lists the names of beautifully chosen, super-provincial towns) and is not bored, but when he arrives here on his vacation it is all boredom and dust. One could think he came from Granada" (a name particularly appealing to the Russian imagination). The rest of their talk, for which this sidelight is richly sufficient, is conveyed indirectly. Now comes a first glimpse of Chekhov's own system of suggesting atmosphere by the most concise details of nature, "the sea was of a warm lilac hue with a golden path for the moon"; whoever has lived in Yalta knows how exactly this conveys the impression of a summer evening there. This first movement of the story ends with Gurov alone in his hotel room thinking of her as he goes to sleep and imagining her delicate weak-looking neck and her pretty gray eyes. It is to be noted that only now, through the medium of the hero's imagination, does Chekhov give a visible and definite form to the lady, features that fit perfectly with her listless manner and expression of boredom already known to us.

> Getting into bed he recalled that she had been a schoolgirl only recently, doing lessons like his own daughter; he thought how much timidity and angularity there was still in her laugh and her manner of talking with a stranger. It must have been the first time in her life that she was alone in a setting in which she was followed, looked at, and spoken to for one secret purpose alone, which she could hardly fail to guess. He thought of her slim, delicate throat, her lovely gray eyes.
> "There's something pathetic about her, though," he thought, and dropped off.

The next movement (each of the four diminutive chapters or movements of which the story is composed is not more than four or five pages long), the next movement starts a week later with Gurov going to the pavilion and bringing the lady iced lemonade on a hot windy day, with the dust flying; and then in the evening when the sirocco subsides, they go on the pier to watch the incoming steamer. "The lady lost her lorgnette in the crowd," Chekhov notes shortly, and this being so casually worded, without any direct influence on the story—just a passing statement—somehow fits in with that helpless pathos already alluded to.

Then in her hotel room her awkwardness and tender angularity are delicately conveyed. They have become lovers. She was now sitting with her long hair hanging down on both sides of her face in the dejected pose of a sinner in some old picture. There was a watermelon on the table. Gurov cut himself a piece and began to eat unhurriedly. This realistic touch is again a typical Chekhov device.

She tells him about her existence in the remote town she comes from and Gurov is slightly bored by her naiveté, confusion, and tears. It is only now that we learn her husband's name: von Dideritz—probably of German descent.

They roam about Yalta in the early morning mist.

> At Oreanda they sat on a bench not far from the church, looked down at the sea, and were silent. Yalta was barely visible through the morning mist; white clouds rested motionlessly on the mountaintops. The leaves did not

stir on the trees, the crickets chirped, and the monotonous muffled sound of the sea that rose from below spoke of the peace, the eternal sleep awaiting us. So it rumbled below when there was no Yalta, no Oreanda here; so it rumbles now, and it will rumble as indifferently and hollowly when we are no more. . . . Sitting beside a young woman who in the dawn seemed so lovely, Gurov, soothed and spellbound by these magical surroundings — the sea, the mountains, the clouds, the wide sky — thought how everything is really beautiful in this world when one reflects: everything except what we think or do ourselves when we forget the higher aims of life and our own human dignity.

A man strolled up to them — probably a watchman — looked at them and walked away. And this detail, too, seemed so mysterious and beautiful. They saw a steamer arrive from Feodosia, its lights extinguished in the glow of dawn.

"There is dew on the grass," said Anna Sergeievna, after a silence.

"Yes, it's time to go home."

Then several days pass and then she has to go back to her home town.

" 'Time for me, too, to go North,' thought Gurov as he returned after seeing her off." And there the chapter ends.

The third movement plunges us straight into Gurov's life in Moscow. The richness of a gay Russian winter, his family affairs, the dinners at clubs and restaurants, all this is swiftly and vividly suggested. Then a page is devoted to a queer thing that has happened to him: he cannot forget the lady with the little dog. He has many friends, but the curious longing he has for talking about his adventure finds no outlet. When he happens to speak in a very general way of love and women, nobody guesses what he means, and only his wife moves her dark eyebrows and says: "Stop that fatuous posing; it does not suit you."

And now comes what in Chekhov's quiet stories may be called the climax. There is something that your average citizen calls romance and something he calls prose — though both are the meat of poetry for the artist. Such a contrast has already been hinted at by the slice of watermelon which Gurov crunched in a Yalta hotel room at a most romantic moment, sitting heavily and munching away. This contrast is beautifully followed up when at last Gurov blurts out to a friend late at night as they come out of the club: If you knew what a delightful woman I met in Yalta! His friend, a bureaucratic civil servant, got into his sleigh, the horses moved, but suddenly he turned and called back to Gurov. Yes? asked Gurov, evidently expecting some reaction to what he had just mentioned. By the way, said the man, you were quite right. That fish at the club was decidedly smelly.

This is a natural transition to the description of Gurov's new mood, his feeling that he lives among savages where cards and food are life. His family, his bank, the whole trend of his existence, everything seems futile, dull, and senseless. About Christmas he tells his wife he is going on a business trip to St. Petersburg, instead of which he travels to the remote Volga town where the lady lives.

Critics of Chekhov in the good old days when the mania for the civic problem flourished in Russia were incensed with his way of describing what they considered to be trivial unnecessary matters instead of thoroughly examining and solving the problems of bourgeois marriage. For as soon as Gurov arrives in the early hours to that town and takes the best room at the local hotel, Chekhov, instead of describing his mood or intensifying his difficult moral position, gives what is artistic in the highest sense of the word: he notes the gray carpet, made of military cloth, and the inkstand, also gray with dust, with a horseman whose hand waves a hat and whose head is gone. That is all: it is nothing but it is everything in authentic literature. A feature in the same line is the phonetic transformation which the hotel porter imposes on the German name von Dideritz. Having learned the address Gurov goes there and looks at the house. Opposite was a long gray fence with nails sticking out. An unescapable fence, Gurov says to himself, and here we get the concluding note in the rhythm of drabness and grayness already suggested by the carpet, the inkstand, the illiterate accent of the porter. The unexpected little turns and the lightness of the touches are what places Chekhov, above all Russian writers of fiction, on the level of Gogol and Tolstoy.

Presently he saw an old servant coming out with the familiar little white dog. He wanted to call it (by a kind of conditional reflex), but suddenly his heart began beating fast and in his excitement he could not remember the dog's name — another delightful touch. Later on he decides to go to the local theatre, where for the first time the operetta *The Geisha* is being given. In sixty words Chekhov paints a complete picture of a provincial theatre, not forgetting the town-governor who modestly hid in his box behind a plush curtain so that only his hands were visible. Then the lady appeared. And he realized quite clearly that now in the whole world there was none nearer and dearer and more important to him than this slight woman, lost in a small-town crowd, a woman perfectly unremarkable, with a vulgar lorgnette in her hand. He saw her husband and remembered her qualifying him as a flunkey — he distinctly resembled one.

A remarkably fine scene follows when Gurov manages to talk to her, and then their mad swift walk up all kinds of staircases and corridors, and down again, and up again, amid people in the various uniforms of provincial officials. Neither does Chekhov forget "two schoolboys who smoked on the stairs and looked down at him and her."

> "You must leave," Anna Sergeievna went on in a whisper. "Do you hear, Dmitri Dmitrich? I will come and see you in Moscow. I have never been happy; I am unhappy now, and I never, never shall be happy, never! So don't make me suffer still more! I swear I'll come to Moscow. But now let us part. My dear, good, precious one, let us part!"
>
> She pressed his hand and walked rapidly downstairs, turning to look round at him, and from her eyes he could see that she really was unhappy. Gurov stood for a while, listening, then when all grew quiet, he found his coat and left the theatre.

The fourth and last little chapter gives the atmosphere of their secret meetings in Moscow. As soon as she would arrive she used to send a red-capped messenger to Gurov. One day he was on his way to her and his daughter was with him. She was going to school, in the same direction as he. Big damp snow-flakes were slowly coming down.

The thermometer, Gurov was saying to his daughter, shows a few degrees above freezing point (actually 37° above, Fahrenheit), but nevertheless snow is falling. The explanation is that this warmth applies only to the surface of the earth, while in the higher layers of the atmosphere the temperature is quite different.

And as he spoke and walked, he kept thinking that not a soul knew or would ever know about these secret meetings.

What puzzled him was that all the false part of his life, his bank, his club, his conversations, his social obligations — all this happened openly, while the real and interesting part was hidden.

> He had two lives, an open one, seen and known by all who needed to know of it, full of conventional truth and conventional falsehood, exactly like the lives of his friends and acquaintances; and another life that went on in secret. And through some strange, perhaps accidental, combination of circumstances, everything that was of interest and importance to him, everything that was essential to him, everything about which he felt sincerely and did not deceive himself, everything that constituted the core of his life, was going on concealed from others; while all that was false, the shell in which he hid to cover the truth — his work at the bank for instance, his discussions at the club, his references to the "inferior race," his appearances at anniversary celebrations with his wife — all that went on in the open. Judging others by himself, he did not believe what he saw, and always fancied that every man led his real, most interesting life under cover of secrecy as under cover of night. The personal life of every individual is based on secrecy, and perhaps it is partly for that reason that civilized man is so nervously anxious that personal privacy should be respected.

The final scene is full of that pathos which has been suggested in the very beginning. They meet, she sobs, they feel that they are the closest of couples, the tenderest of friends, and he sees that his hair is getting a little gray and knows that only death will end their love.

> The shoulders on which his hands rested were warm and quivering. He felt compassion for this life, still so warm and lovely, but probably already about to begin to fade and wither like his own. Why did she love him so much? He always seemed to women different from what he was, and they loved in him not himself, but the man whom their imagination had created and whom they had been eagerly seeking all their lives; and afterwards, when they saw their mistake, they loved him nevertheless. And not one of them had been happy with him. In the past he had met women, come together with them, parted from them, but he had never once loved; it was anything you please, but not love. And only now when his head was gray he had fallen in love, really, truly — for the first time in his life.

They talk, they discuss their position, how to get rid of the necessity of this sordid secrecy, how to be together always. They find no solution and in the typical Chekhov way the tale fades out with no definite full-stop but with the natural motion of life.

> And it seemed as though in a little while the solution would be found, and then a new and glorious life would begin; and it was clear to both of them that the end was still far off, and that what was to be most complicated and difficult for them was only just beginning.

All the traditional rules of story telling have been broken in this wonderful short story of twenty pages or so. There is no problem, no regular climax, no point at the end. And it is one of the greatest stories ever written.

J. C. C. Nachtigal

J. C. C. Nachtigal was a German folklorist who published under the pseudonym "Otmar" when *Folkssagen, Nacherzhaht von Otmar (Folktales, Transcribed by Otmar)*, his collection of folk narratives, appeared in Bremen in 1800. Many years later the American writer Washington Irving purchased a copy of this book in London when he began to teach himself German. In 1819 Irving made his own translation of the folktale "Peter Klaus the Goatherd" that he used as the source for his original story "Rip Van Winkle." This translation of the folktale is by Irving's English contemporary, Thomas Roscoe. Arthur Levine, president of Teachers' College at Columbia University, commented in *Daedalus* (Winter 1997) that Irving's version of the folktale became a classic for American readers because it was an allegory about the conditions of life in the United States: "It was more than a tale of a man who overslept; it was an account of the relentlessness of change in America, of an era of overwhelming demographic, economic, global, and technological changes called the Industrial Revolution. Rip Van Winkle was intended to be Everyman trying to orient himself to an unfamiliar world, which seemed to be changing radically overnight."

Peter Klaus the Goatherd

1800 / Translated by Thomas Roscoe (1820)

In the village of Littendorf at the foot of a mountain lived Peter Klaus, a goatherd, who was in the habit of pasturing his flock upon the Kyffhausen hills. Towards evening he generally let them browse upon a green plot not far off, surrounded with an old ruined wall from which he could take a muster of his whole flock.

For some days past he had observed that one of his prettiest goats, soon after its arrival at this spot, usually disappeared, nor joined the fold again until late in the evening. He watched her again and again, and at last found that she slipped through a gap in the old wall, whither he followed her. It led into a passage which widened as he went into a cavern; and here he saw the goat employed in picking up the oats that fell through some crevices in the place above. He looked up, shook his ears at this odd shower of oats, but could discover nothing. Where the deuce could it come from? At length he heard over his head the neighing and stamping of horses; he listened, and concluded that the oats must have fallen through the manger when they were fed. The poor goatherd was sadly puzzled what to think of these horses in this uninhabited part of the mountain, but so it was, for a groom making his appearance, without saying a word beckoned him to follow him. Peter obeyed, and followed him up some steps which brought him into an open court-yard surrounded by old walls. At the side of this was a still more spacious cavern, surrounded by rocky heights which only admitted a kind of twilight, through the overhanging trees and shrubs. He went on, and came to a smooth shaven green, where he saw twelve ancient knights none of whom spoke a word, engaged in playing at nine pins. His guide now beckoned to Peter in silence, to pick up the nine pins and went his way. Trembling in every joint Peter did not venture to disobey, and at times he cast a stolen glance at the players, whose long beards and slashed doublets were not at all in the present fashion. By degrees his looks grew bolder; he took particular notice of every thing around him; among other things observing a tankard near him filled with wine, whose odour was excellent, he took a good draught. It seemed to inspire him with life; and whenever he began to feel tired of running, he applied with fresh ardour to the tankard, which always renewed his strength. But finally it quite overpowered him, and he fell asleep.

When he next opened his eyes, he found himself on the grass-plot again, in the old spot where he was in the habit of feeding his goats. He rubbed his eyes, he looked round, but could see neither dog nor flock; he was surprised at the long rank grass that grew around him, and at trees and bushes which he had never before seen. He shook his head and walked a little farther, looking for the old sheep path and the hillocks and roads where he used daily to drive his flock; but he could find no traces of them left. Yet he saw the village just before him; it was the same Littendorf, and scratching his head he hastened at a quick pace down the hill to enquire after his flock.

All the people whom he met going into the place were strangers to him, were differently dressed, and even spoke in a different style to his old neighbors. When he asked about his goats, they only stared at him, and fixed their eyes upon his chin. He put his hand unconsciously to his mouth, and to his great surprise found that he had got a beard, at least a foot long. He now began to think that both he and all the world about him were in a dream; and yet he knew the mountain for that of the Kyffhausen (for he had just come down it) well enough. And there were the cottages, with their gardens and grass-plots, much as he had left them. Besides the lads who had all collected round him, answered to the enquiry of a passenger, what place it was: "Littendorf, sir."

Still shaking his head, he went farther into the village to look for his own house. He found it, but greatly altered for the worse; a strange goatherd in an old tattered frock lay before the door, and near him his old dog, which growled and showed its teeth at Peter when he called him. He went through the entrance which had once a door, but all within was empty and deserted; Peter staggered like a drunken man out of the house, and called for his wife and children by their names. But no one heard him, and no one gave him any answer.

Soon, however, a crowd of women and children got round the inquisitive stranger, with the long hoary beard; and asked him what it was he wanted. Now Peter thought it was such a strange kind of thing to stand before his own house, enquiring for his own wife and children, as well as about himself, that evading these inquiries he pronounced the first name that came into his head: "Kurt Steffen, the blacksmith?" Most of the spectators were silent, and only looked at him wistfully, till an old woman at last said, "Why, for these twelve years he has been at Sachsenburg, whence I suppose you are not come today." "Where is Valentine Meier, the tailor?" "The Lord rest his soul," cried another woman leaning on her crutch, "he has been lying more than fifteen years in a house he will never leave."

Peter recognized in the speakers, two of his young neighbours who seemed to have grown old very suddenly, but he had no inclination to enquire any farther. At this moment there appeared making her way through the crowd of spectators, a sprightly young woman with a year old baby in her arms, and a girl about four taking hold of her hand, all three as like his wife he was seeking for as possible. "What are your names?" he enquired in a tone of great surprise. "Mine is Maria." "And your father's?" continued Peter. "God rest his soul! Peter Klaus for sure. It's now twenty years ago since we were all looking for him day and night upon the Kyffhausen; for his flock came home without him, and I was then," continued the woman, "only seven years old."

The goatherd could no longer bear this. "I am Peter Klaus," he said. "Peter and no other," and he took his daughter's child and kissed it. The spectators appeared struck dumb with astonishment, until first one and then another began to say, "Yes, indeed, this is Peter Klaus! Welcome, good neighbour, after twenty years' absence, welcome home."

Tim O'Brien

Tim O'Brien described his platoon in "Alpha Company," a nonfiction account he wrote while serving in active duty as an infantryman in Vietnam in the early 1970s. It was included in his first book, *If I Die in a Combat Zone, Box Me Up and Ship Me Home* (1973).

Alpha Company

1973

The first month with Alpha Company was a peculiar time. It was mostly a vacation. We wandered up and down the beaches outside Chu Lai, pulling security patrols and a very few night ambushes. It was an infantryman's dream. There were no VC, no mines, sunny days, warm water to swim in, daily resupplies of milk and beer. We were a traveling circus. A caravan of local children and women followed us from one stretch of sand to the next, peddling Coke and dirty pictures, cleaning our weapons for a can of C rations. During the days we played football. Two or three lovers lounged under their ponchos with Vietnamese girls. They flirted, and there were some jealousies and hurt feelings. When we moved to a new position, our column stretched out for a quarter-mile, filled with soldiers and prostitutes and girls carrying bags of Coke and children carrying our packs and sometimes even our rifles. At dusk the children dug our foxholes. Each GI had his personal mascot, his valet. My own helper was a little guy called Champion. He was seven years old, perhaps even younger, but he knew how to disassemble and clean my rifle, and he knew how to give a back rub.

During the first month, I learned that FNG meant "fuckin' new guy," and that I would be one until the Combat Center's next shipment arrived. I learned that GI's in the field can be as lazy and careless and stupid as GI's anywhere. They don't wear helmets and armored vests unless an officer insists; they fall asleep on guard, and for the most part, no one really cares; they throw away or bury ammunition if it gets heavy and hot. I learned that REMF means "rear echelon motherfucker"; that a man is getting "Short" after his third or fourth month; that a hand grenade is really a "frag"; that one bullet is all it takes and that "you never hear the shot that gets you"; that no one in Alpha Company knows or cares about the cause or purpose of their war: it is about "dinks and slopes," and the idea is simply to kill them or avoid them. Except that in Alpha you don't kill a man, you "waste" him. You don't get mangled by a mine, you get fucked up. You don't call a man by his first name — he's the Kid or the Water Buffalo, Buddy Wolf or Buddy Barker or Buddy Barney, or if the fellow is bland or disliked, he's just Smith or Jones or Rodríguez. The NCO's who go through a crash two-month program to earn their stripes are called "instant NCO's"; hence the platoon's squad leaders were named Ready Whip, Nestle's Quick, and Shake and Bake. And when two of them — Tom and Arnold — were killed two months later, the tragedy was somehow mitigated and depersonalized by telling ourselves that ol' Ready Whip and Quick got themselves wasted by the slopes. There was Cop — an Irish fellow who wanted to join the police force in Danbury, Connecticut — and Reno and the Wop and the College Joe. You can go through a year in Vietnam and live with a platoon of sixty or seventy people, some going and some coming, and you can leave without knowing more than a dozen complete names, not that it matters.

Mad Mark was the platoon leader, a first lieutenant and a Green Beret. It was hard to tell if the name or the reason for the name came first. The madness in Mad Mark, at any rate, was not a hysterical, crazy, into-the-brink, to-the-fore madness. Rather, he was insanely calm. He never showed fear. He was a professional soldier, an ideal leader of men in the field. It was that kind of madness, the perfect guardian for the Platonic Republic. His attitude and manner seemed perfectly molded in the genre of the CIA or KGB operative.

This is not to say that Mad Mark ever did the work of the assassin. But it was his manner, and he cultivated it. He walked with a lanky, easy, silent, fearless stride. He wore tiger fatigues, not for their camouflage but for their look. He carried a shotgun — a weapon I'd thought was outlawed in international war — and the shotgun itself was a measure of his professionalism, for to use it effectively requires an exact blend of courage and skill and self-confidence. The weapon is neither accurate nor lethal at much over seventy yards. So it shows the skill of the carrier, a man who must work his way close enough to the prey to make a shot, close enough to see the enemy's retina and the tone of his skin. To get that close requires courage and self-confidence. The shotgun is not an automatic weapon. You must hit once, on the first shot, and the hit must kill. Mad Mark once said that after the war and in the absence of other U.S. wars he might try the mercenary's life in Africa.

Frank O'Connor

Frank O'Connor was a skilled teacher of the short story, and his comments on the literary form can be as irreverent as they are profound. In this interview in the *Paris Review*, reprinted from the first volume of *Writers at Work*, collections of interviews from that journal which appeared in 1958, O'Connor compared himself with Guy de Maupassant and then went on to discuss his own practice as a writer. His analysis of the history of the short story appeared in more extended form in his book *The Lonely Voice*, published in 1963.

The Nearest Thing to Lyric Poetry
Is the Short Story

1958

Interviewer: Why do you prefer the short story for your medium?

O'Connor: Because it's the nearest thing I know to lyric poetry — I wrote lyric poetry for a long time, then discovered that God had not intended me to be a lyric poet, and the nearest thing to that is the short story. A novel actually requires far more logic and far more knowledge of circumstances, whereas a short story can have the sort of detachment from circumstances that lyric poetry has. . . .

Interviewer: What about working habits? How do you start a story?

O'Connor: "Get black on white" used to be Maupassant's advice — that's what I always do. I don't give a hoot what the writing's like, I write any sort of rubbish which will cover the main outlines of the story, then I can begin to see it. When I write, when I draft a story, I never think of writing nice sentences about, "It was a nice August evening when Elizabeth Jane Moriarty was coming down the road." I just write roughly what happened, and then I'm able to see what the construction looks like. It's the design of the story which to me is most important, the thing that tells you there's a bad gap in the narrative here and you really ought to fill that up in some way or another. I'm always looking at the design of the story, not the treatment. Yesterday I was finishing off a piece about my friend A. E. Coppard, the greatest of all the English storytellers, who died about a fortnight ago. I was describing the way Coppard must have written these stories, going around with a notebook, recording what the lighting looked like, what that house looked like, and all the time using metaphor to suggest it to himself, "The road looked like a mad serpent going up the hill," or something of the kind, and "She said so-and-so, and the man in the pub said something else." After he had written them all out, he must have got the outline of his story, and he'd start working in all the details. Now, I could never do that at all. I've got to see what these people did, first of all, and *then* I start thinking of whether it was a nice August evening or a spring evening. I have to wait for the theme before I can do anything.

Interviewer: Do you rewrite?

O'Connor: Endlessly, endlessly, endlessly. And keep on rewriting, and after it's published, and then after it's published in book form, I usually rewrite it again. I've rewritten versions of most of my early stories and one of these days, God help, I'll publish these as well.

Interviewer: Do you keep notes as a source of supply for future stories?

O'Connor: Just notes of themes. If somebody tells me a good story, I'll write it down in my four lines; that is the secret of the theme. If you make the subject of a story twelve or fourteen lines, that's a treatment. You've already committed yourself to the sort of character, the sort of surroundings, and the moment you've committed yourself, the story is already written. It has ceased to be fluid, you can't design it any longer, you can't model it. So I always confine myself to my four lines. If it won't go into four, that means you haven't reduced it to its ultimate simplicity, reduced it to the fable.

Frank O'Connor

Frank O'Connor analyzed the stories in James Joyce's *Dubliners* in the chapter entitled "Work in Progress" in his 1963 study of the short story, *The Lonely Voice*. O'Connor addressed himself to the question of why Joyce gave up writing stories after *Dubliners*; he understood that "it is as difficult to think of a real storyteller, like Chekhov, who had experienced the thrill of the completed masterpiece, giving up short stories forever as it is to think of Keats giving up lyric poetry." The answer, for O'Connor, can be found by comparing the formal differences between the stories at the beginning of *Dubliners* and "The Dead" at the end. This is where his analysis begins.

Style and Form in Joyce's "The Dead"

1963

"The Dead," Joyce's last story, is entirely different from all the others. It is also immensely more complicated, and it is not always easy to see what any particular episode represents, though it is only too easy to see that it represents something. The scene is the annual dance of the Misses Morkan, old music teachers on Usher's Island, and ostensibly it is no more than a report of what happened at it, except at the end, when Gabriel Conroy and his wife Gretta return to their hotel room. There she breaks down and tells him of a youthful and innocent love affair between herself and a boy of seventeen in Galway, who had caught his death of cold from standing under her bedroom window. But this final scene is irrelevant only in appearance, for in effect it is the real story, and everything that has led up to it has been simply an enormously expanded introduction, a series of themes all of which find their climax in the hotel bedroom.

The setting of the story in a warm, vivacious lighted house in the midst of night and snow is an image of life itself, but every incident, almost every speech, has a crack in it through which we perceive the presence of death all about us, as when Gabriel says that Gretta "takes three *mortal* hours to dress herself," and the aunts say that she must be "perished alive" — an Irishism that ingeniously suggests both life and death. Several times the warmth and gaiety give rise to the idea of love and marriage, but each time it is knocked dead by phrase or incident. At the very opening of the story Gabriel suggests to the servant girl, Lily, that they will soon be attending her wedding, but she retorts savagely that "the men that is now is only all palaver and what they can get out of you," the major theme of the story, for all grace is with the dead: The younger generation have not the generosity of the two old sisters, the younger singers (Caruso, for instance!) cannot sing as well as some long dead English tenor. Gabriel's aunt actually sings "Arrayed for the Bridal," but she is only an old woman who has been dismissed from her position in the local church choir.

Gabriel himself is fired by passion for his wife, but when they return to their hotel bedroom the electric light has failed, and his passion is also extinguished when she tells him the story of her love for a dead boy. Whether it is Gabriel's quarrel with Miss Ivors, who wants him to spend his summer holiday patriotically in the West of Ireland (where his wife and the young man had met), the discussion of Cistercian monks who are supposed to sleep in their coffins, "to remind them of their last end," or the reminiscences of old singers and old relatives, everything pushes Gabriel toward the ultimate dissolution of identity in which real things disappear from about us, and we are as alone as we shall be on our deathbeds.

But it is easy enough to see from "The Dead" why Joyce gave up storytelling. One of his main passions — the elaboration of style and form — had taken control, and the short story is too tightly knit to permit expansion like this. And — what is much more important — it is quite clear from "The Dead" that he had already begun to lose sight of the submerged population that was his original subject. There are little touches of it here and there, as in the sketches of Freddy Malins and his mother — the old lady who finds everything "beautiful" — "beautiful crossing," "beautiful house," "beautiful scenery," "beautiful fish" — but Gabriel does not belong to it, nor does Gretta nor Miss Ivors. They are not characters but personalities, and Joyce would never again be able to deal with characters, people whose identity is determined by their circumstances. His own escape to Trieste, with its enlargement of his own sense of identity, had caused them to fade from his mind or — to put it more precisely — had caused them to reappear in entirely different guises. This is something that is always liable to happen to the provincial storyteller when you put him into a cosmopolitan atmosphere.

Daniel Orozco

Daniel Orozco explained what he admired about Steven Millhauser's literary technique in "Flying Carpets," one of Orozco's personal favorites. He was asked by The Paris Review to analyze what it took to write a great short story, and his response was included in Object Lessons (2012), edited by Lorin Stein and Sadie Stein.

Steven Millhauser's "Flying Carpets"

When I was a child, I spoke as a child, I understood as a child, I thought as a child: but when I became a man, I put away childish things.

—1 Corinthians 13:11

St. Paul's adage is the seed from which our dramas of nostalgia emerged. Stories of yearning for the irretrievable past are, I think, hard to write well, because they risk sentimentality — an excessive reaching for feeling that . . . well, feels contrived and false. The paradox is that stories of nostalgia are kind of *about* that excessive reaching, and so the writer is stymied by the Imitative Fallacy: how do you tell a story about sentimentality, while avoiding the excesses of sentimental prose?

"Flying Carpets" is told as memoir. The man doing the telling embodies the memory of the boy he was, and a childhood summer is evoked with sensory details as sharp as they are commonplace and quotidian — the flutter of sheets on clotheslines, the buzz of insects, the gleam of a bottle in the grass. It is sense memory that evokes the strongest emotions in us; that's *how* we remember. We experience the world through our senses, and in remembering we reach for sense memory in order to somehow feel what was, and is now gone. I feel lost love not by thinking *I loved Amanda*, but by recalling her laugh, smell of her hair, the tiny scar on her chin. Nostalgia is evoked by the precision and accumulation of concrete sensory detail — in other words, by heeding that writerly chestnut: *Show, Don't Tell.*

However commonplace the thing remembered, it is this precision and accumulation that makes the thing — and the emotions associated with it — profoundly *remembered*, and felt, and true. That goes for sheets and Coke bottles. And, oh yes, flying carpets. And this is what elevates this drama of nostalgia from the masterly to the sublime. Flying carpets are the diversion of the summer — ridden by neighborhood boys, skimming rooftops, drifting over fences from backyard to backyard — until one day the novelty wears off. Summer wanes, the earth turns, and the toys are put away. The fantastic is rendered commonplace, and the magic of a boy's childhood is recalled with the melancholy of the man who can never experience such again.

Cynthia Ozick

Cynthia Ozick urged the necessity of placing Isaac Babel beside Franz Kafka if readers wished to complete what she termed "the literary configuration of the twentieth century." Her essay appeared in her fifth collection of nonfiction, *The Din in the Head*, published in 2006 by Houghton Mifflin.

Isaac Babel: "Let Me Finish"

2006

On May 15, 1939, Isaac Babel, a writer whose distinction had earned him the Soviet privilege of a villa in the country, was arrested at Peredelkino and taken to Moscow's Lubyanka prison, headquarters of the secret police. His papers were confiscated and destroyed—among them half-completed stories, plays, film scripts, translations. Six months later, after three days and nights of hellish interrogation, he confessed to a false charge of espionage. The following year, a clandestine trial was briefly held in the dying hours of January 25; Babel recanted his confession, appealed to his innocence, and at 1:40 the next morning was summarily shot by a firing squad. He was forty-five. His final plea was not for himself, but for the power and truth of literature: "Let me finish my work."

What Kafka's art hallucinates—trial without cause, an inescapable predicament directed by an irrational force, a malignant social order—Babel is at last condemned to endure in the living flesh. Kafka and Babel can be said to be the twentieth century's European coordinates: they are separated by language, style, and temperament; but where their fevers intersect lies the point of infection. Each was an acutely conscious Jew. Each witnessed a pogrom while still very young, Kafka in enlightened Prague, Babel under a czarist regime that promoted harsh legal disabilities for Jews. Each invented a type of literary modernism, becoming a movement in himself, with no possibility of successors. To be influenced by Kafka is to end in parody; and because the wilderness of an astoundingly variegated experience is incised, unduplicatably, in the sinews of Babel's prose, no writer can effectively claim to be his disciple.

But of course they are opposites: Kafka ingrown, self-dissatisfied, indifferent to politics; hardly daring, despite genius, to feel entitlement to his own language; endlessly agonizing over a broken engagement; rarely leaving home. And here is Babel, insouciant, reckless, a womanizer, half a vagabond, a horseman, a propagandist, the father of three by three different women, only one of them legally his wife. Then why bring up Kafka when speaking of Babel? Kafka at least died in his bed. Babel was murdered by the criminal agency of a cynically criminal government. Kafka requested that his writing be destroyed, and was not obeyed. Babel's name and work were erased—as if he had never written at all—until 1954, when, during a "thaw," he was, in Soviet terminology, rehabilitated.

Yet taken together, they tell us what we in our time are obliged to know about the brutal tracings of force and deception, including self-deception. Kafka alone is not enough; his interiors are too circumscribed. Babel alone is not enough; his landscapes are too diffuse. Kafka supplies the grandly exegetical metaphor: the man who thinks but barely lives, the metaphysician who is ultimately consumed by a conflagration of lies. Babel, by contrast, lives, lives, lives! He lives robustly, inquisitively, hungrily; his appetite for unpredictable human impulse is gargantuan, inclusive, eccentric. He is trickster, rapscallion, ironist, wayward lover, imprudent impostor — and out of these hundred fiery selves insidious truths creep out, one by one, in a face, in the color of the sky, in a patch of mud, in a word. Violence, pity, comedy, illumination. It is as if he is an irritable membrane, subject to every creaturely vibration.

He was born in Odessa, a cosmopolitan and polyglot city that looked to the sea and beyond. It was, he wrote,

> the most charming city of the Russian Empire. If you think about it, it is a town in which you can live free and easy. Half the population is made up of Jews, and Jews are a people who have learned a few simple truths along the way. Jews get married so as not to be alone, love so as to live through the centuries, save money so they can buy houses and give their wives astrakhan jackets, love children because, let's face it, it is good and important to love one's children. The poor Odessa Jews get very confused when it comes to officials and regulations, but it isn't all that easy to get them to budge in their opinions, their very antiquated opinions. You might not be able to budge these Jews, but there's a whole lot you can learn from them. To a large extent it is because of them that Odessa has this light and easy atmosphere.

There is much of the affectionate and mirthful Babel in this paragraph: the honest yet ironic delight in people exactly as they are, the teasing sense of laughing entitlement ("so as to live through the centuries"), prosperity and poverty rubbing elbows, ordinary folk harried by officialdom, confusion and stubbornness, love and loneliness. As for poor Jews, Babel began as one of these, starting life in the Moldavanka, a mixed neighborhood with a sprinkling of mobsters. What he witnessed there, with a bright boy's perceptiveness, catapulted him early on into the capacious worldliness that burst out (he was twenty-nine) in the exuberant tales of Benya Krik and his gang — tough but honorable criminals with a Damon Runyonesque strain.

Lionel Trilling, among the first to write seriously about Babel in English, mistook him for "a Jew of the ghetto." If "ghetto" implies a narrow and inbred psyche, then Babel stands for the reverse. Though he was at home in Yiddish and Hebrew, and was familiar with the traditional tests and their demanding commentaries, he added to these a lifelong infatuation with Maupassant and Flaubert. His first stories were composed in fluent literary French. The breadth and scope of his social compass enabled him to see through the eyes of peasants, soldiers, priests, rabbis, children, artists, actors, women of all classes. He befriended whores, cab drivers, jockeys; he knew what it was to be penniless, to live on the edge and off the beaten track. He was at once a poet of the city — "the glass sun of Petersburg" — and a lyricist of the countryside: "the walls of sunset collapsing into the sky." He was drawn to spaciousness and elasticity, optimism and opportunity, and it was through these visionary seductions of societal freedom, expressed politically, that he welcomed the Revolution.

He not only welcomed it; he joined it. In order to be near Maxim Gorky, his literary hero, Babel had been living illegally in St. Petersburg, one of the cities prohibited to Jews under the hobbling restrictions of the czarist Pale of Settlement. With the advent of the Revolution the Pale dissolved, discriminatory quotas ceased, censorship vanished, promises multiplied, and Babel zealously attached himself to the Bolshevik cause. In 1920, as a war correspondent riding with the Red Cavalry to deliver Communist salvation to the reluctant Polish villages across the border, he fell into disenchantment. "They all say they're fighting for justice and they all loot," he wrote in his diary. "Murderers, it's unbearable, baseness and crime. . . . Carnage. The military commander and I ride along the tracks, begging the men not to butcher the prisoners." Six years later, Babel published his penetratingly authoritative *Red Cavalry* stories, coolly steeped in pity and blood, and found instant fame.

With Stalin's ascension in 1924, new tyrannies began to mimic the old. Postrevolutionary literary and artistic ferment, much of it experimental, ebbed or was suppressed. Censorship returned, sniffing after the subversive, favoring the coarse flatness of Socialist Realism. Babel's wife, Evgenia, whom he had married in 1919, emigrated to Paris, where his daughter Nathalie was born in 1929. His mother and sister, also disaffected, left for Brussels. Babel clung to Moscow, hotly wed to his truest bride, the Russian tongue, continuing his work on a cycle of childhood stories and venturing into writing for theater and film. The film scripts, especially those designed for silent movies, turned out to be remarkable: they took on, under the irresistible magnetism of the witnessing camera and the innovation of the present tense, all the surreal splendor of Babel's most plumaged prose. Several were produced and proved to be popular, but eventually they failed to meet Party guidelines, and the director of one of them, an adaptation of Turgenev, was compelled to apologize publicly.

Unable to conform to official prescriptiveness, Babel's publications grew fewer and fewer. He was charged with "silence" — the sin of Soviet unproductivity — and was denied the privilege of traveling abroad. His last journey to Paris occurred in 1935, when André Malraux intervened with the Soviet authorities to urge Babel's attendance at a Communist-sponsored International Congress of Writers for the Defense of Culture and Peace — after which Babel never again met with his wife and daughter. Later that year, back in Moscow, he set up a second household with Antonina Pirozhkova, with whom he fathered a second daughter; through an earlier liaison, he was already the father of a son. But if Babel's personal life was unpredictable, disorganized, and rash, his art was otherwise. He wrested his sentences out of a purifying immediacy. Like Pushkin, he said, he was in pursuit of "precision and brevity." His most pointed comment on literary style appears in "Guy de Maupassant," a cunning seriocomic sexual fable fixed on the weight and trajectory of language itself. The success of a phrase, the young narrator instructs, "rests in a crux that is barely discernible. One's fingertips must grasp the key, gently warming it. And then the key must be turned once, not twice." But even this is not the crux. The crux (Babel's severest literary dictum) is here: "No iron spike can pierce a human heart as icily as a period in the right place."

A writer's credo, and Babel's most intimate confession. Stand in awe of it, yes — but remember also that this same master of the white bone of truth, this artist of the delicately turned key, was once a shameless propagandist for the Revolution, capable of rabid rote exhortations: "Beat them, Red Fighters, clobber them to death, if it is the last thing you do! Right away! This minute! Now!" "Slaughter them, Red Army fighters! Stamp harder on the rising lids of their rancid coffins!" Such catchwords are locked cells for which there are no keys, and while it is a truism that every utopia contains the seeds of dystopia, Babel, after all, was granted skepticism almost from the start. Out of skepticism came disillusionment; out of disillusionment, revulsion. And in the end, as the tragic trope has it, the Revolution devoured its child.

Babel's art served as a way station to the devouring. He was devoured because he would not, could not, accommodate to falsehood; because he saw and he saw, with an eye as merciless as a klieg light; and because, like Kafka, he surrendered his stories to voices and passions tremulous with the unforeseen. If we wish to complete, and transmit, the literary configuration of the twentieth century — the image that will enduringly stain history's retina — now is the time (it is past time) to set Babel beside Kafka. Between them, they leave no nerve unshaken.

Grace Paley

Grace Paley talked with Ann Charters about her experiences as a short story writer during lunch in her Greenwich Village apartment on a snowy day in February 1986. On the wall above the kitchen table hung an oil painting, a still life of vegetables painted by her father after his retirement from medicine. Paley mentions her father's interest in art in her story "A Conversation with My Father."

A Conversation with Ann Charters

1986

Charters: Some literary critics think that short stories are more closely related to poetry than to the novel. Would you agree?

Paley: I would say that stories are closer to poetry than they are to the novel because first they are shorter, and second they are more concentrated, more economical, and that kind of economy, the pulling together of all the information and making leaps across the information, is really close to poetry. By leaps I mean thought leaps and feeling leaps. Also, when short stories are working right, you pay more attention to language than most novelists do.

Charters: Poe said unity was an essential factor of short stories. Do you have any ideas about this in your own work?

Paley: I suppose there has to be some kind of unity, but that's true in a novel too. It seems to me that unity is form. Form is really the vessel in which the story or poem or novel exists. The reason I don't have an answer for you is that there's really no telling — sometimes I like to start a story with one thing and end it with another. I don't know where the unity is in that case. I see the word *unity* meaning that something has to be whole, even if it ends in an open way.

Charters: You mean, as you wrote in "A Conversation with My Father," that "everyone, real or invented, deserves the open destiny of life."

Paley: Yes.

Charters: You started writing poetry before short stories, and the language of your fiction is often as compressed and metaphorical as the language of poetry. Can you describe the process of how you learned to write?

Paley: Let me put it this way: I went to school to poetry — that was where I learned how to write. People learn to write by doing various things. I suppose I also wrote a lot of letters, since it was the time of the Second World War. But apart from that I wrote poems, that's what I wrote. I thought about language a lot. That was important to me. That was my teacher. My fiction teacher was poetry.

Charters: What poets did you read when you were learning how to write?

Paley: I just read all the poets. If there was an anthology of poets, I read every single one. I knew all the Victorians. I read the Imagists. At a certain point I fell in love with the Englishmen who came to America — Christopher Isherwood, Stephen Spender, and W. H. Auden. I thought Auden was the greatest. And I loved the poetry of Dylan Thomas. Yeats meant a lot to me. I paid attention to all of them and listened to all of them. Some of them must have gotten into my ear. That's not up to me to say. That's for the reader to say. The reader of my stories will tell me, "This is whom you're influenced by," but I can't say that. I feel I was influenced by everybody.

Charters: Why did you stop writing poetry and start writing stories? What did the form of the short story offer you that the poem didn't?

Paley: First of all, I began to think of certain subject matter, women's lives specifically, and what was happening around me. I was in my thirties, which I guess is the time people start to notice these things, women's and men's lives and what their relationship is. I knew lots of women with small kids, and I was developing very close relationships with a variety of women. All sorts of things began to worry me, and I began to think about them a lot. I couldn't deal with any of this subject matter in poetry; I just didn't know how. I didn't have the technique. Other people can, but I didn't want to write poems saying "I feel this" and "I feel that." That was the last thing I wanted to do.

I can give you a definition that can be proven wrong in many ways, but for me it was that in writing poetry I wanted to talk to the world, I wanted to address the world, so to speak. But writing stories, I wanted to get the world to explain itself to me, to speak to me. And for me that was the essential difference between writing poetry and stories, and it still is, in many ways. So I had to get that world to talk to me. I had to reach out to it, a very different thing than writing poems. I had to reach out to the world and get it to tell me what it was all about, because I didn't understand it. I just didn't understand. Also, I'd always been very interested in people and told funny stories, and I didn't have any room for doing that in poems, again because of my own self. My poems were too literary, that's the real reason.

Charters: What do you mean, you had to get the world to tell you what it was all about?

Paley: In the first story I ever wrote, "The Contest," I did exactly what I just told you — I got this guy to talk. That's what I did. I had a certain guy in mind. In fact, I stuck pretty close to my notion of what he was, and the story was about a contest he had told me about. The second story I wrote was about Aunt Rose in "Goodbye and Good Luck." That began with my husband's aunt visiting us, and saying exactly the sentence I used to start the story: "I was popular in certain circles." But the rest has nothing to do with her life at all. She looked at us, this aunt of his, and she felt we didn't appreciate her, so she looked at us and she said to us, "Listen," she said. "I was popular in certain circles." That statement really began that particular story. That story was about lots of older women I knew who didn't get married, and I was thinking about them. These are two examples of how I began, how I got to my own voice by hearing and using all these other voices.

Charters: I suppose "A Conversation with My Father" isn't typical of your work, because the story you make up for him isn't what he wants, the old-fashioned Chekhov or Maupassant story, and it's not really one of your "voice" stories either, is it?

Paley: No. I'm just trying to oblige him.

Charters: So that may be one of the jokes of the story?

Paley: It could be, but I never thought of it that way. I think it's a good story. People have found it useful in literature classes, which I think is funny, but nice.

Charters: Did you make up the plot of "A Conversation with My Father," or did it actually happen when you were visiting him before he died?

Paley: My father was eighty-six years old and in bed. I spent a lot of time with him. He was an artist, and he painted pictures after he retired from being a doctor. I visited him at least once a week, and we were very close. We would have discussions. I never wrote a story for him about this neighbor, but he did say to me once, "Why can't you write a regular story, for God's sake?" something like that. So that particular story is both about literature and about that particular discussion, but it's also about generational differences, about different ways of looking at life. What my father thought could be done in the world was due to his own history. What I thought could be done in the world was different, not because I was a more open person, because he was also a very open person, but because I lived in a particularly open time, the late 1960s. The story I wrote for him was about all these druggies. It was made up, but it was certainly true. I could point out people on my block whose kids became junkies. Many of them have recovered from being junkies and are in good shape now.

Charters: Did you know any mothers in Greenwich Village who became junkies to keep their kids company?

Paley: Sure. It was a very open neighborhood then, with lots of freedom. But my father was born into a very different time. He was born in Czarist Russia and came over to America when he was twenty and worked hard and studied medicine and had a profession.

Charters: When you were growing up did you read the writers your father admired — Maupassant and Chekhov?

Paley: Actually, he had never mentioned Maupassant to me before. He did mention him in that conversation. He did read a lot, he loved Chekhov. And when he came to this country, he taught himself English by reading Dickens.

Charters: So the idea for the story came to you when he mentioned Maupassant?

Paley: Well, not really. He had just read my story "Faith in a Tree," and there are a lot of voices coming from all over in that story. And so he asked me, "What is this? All those voices? Voices from who knows where?" He wasn't actually that heavy. But when I wrote about our conversation it became a fiction, and it's different from what really happened.

Charters: It must have been fun for you to make up the two versions of the story about your neighbor in "A Conversation with My Father."

Paley: I enjoyed writing that story. Some stories you don't enjoy, because they're very hard. I didn't write it right off, but I enjoyed it.

Charters: How many days did it take you to write?

Paley: There's no such thing as days with me when I write a story. More like months. I write it and I write slow, and then I rewrite, and then I put it away, and then I take it out again. It's tedious in some respects. But that's the way it works.

Charters: When do you decide it's finished?

Paley: When I've gone over it and I can't think of another thing to change.

Charters: I was looking over your book *Enormous Changes at the Last Minute*, which is where "A Conversation with My Father" appears, and I noticed you've placed it between two very dark stories, "The Little Girl," about a runaway in the Village who commits suicide after she's raped, and "The Immigrant Story," about the starvation of the young children in a Jewish family in Poland before the mother emigrates to America. I assume you did this for a reason. When you put a collection of short fiction together, how do you order the stories?

Paley: I always have something in mind. I like to put one or two at the beginning that will be readable immediately, and then I just work it out. I like to mix the long and the short, and the serious and the funny ones. But I did put those two dark stories around "A Conversation with My Father" to show him I could look tragedy in the face. Remember he asks me at the end of the story, "When will you look it in the face?"

Charters: Was that one of the things he actually said to you when you visited him?

Paley: Well, he did tend to say that I wouldn't look things in the face. That things were hard, and I wasn't looking at it. I didn't see certain problems with my kids when they were small, and he was in some degree right. In "The Immigrant Story" a man tells me, "You have a rotten rosy temperament." But then she says, "Rosiness is not a worse windowpane than gloomy gray when viewing the world." They're both just prisms to look through.

Charters: Is that what you still believe?

Paley: Well, I do believe it, but I also believe that things are bad.

Charters: A theme that some students find when reading "A Conversation with My Father" is that one of the things you don't want to look in the face that your father is trying to prepare you for is his own death. Were you conscious of that when you wrote the story?

Paley: No.

Charters: Can you see that theme in it now?

Paley: No. But maybe you're right. As I said, that's not up to me to say. Maybe the reader of a particular story knows better than the writer what it means. But I know I wasn't thinking about that when I wrote it. I wasn't thinking of his death at all. I was thinking of him being sick and trying not to get him excited.

Jay Parini

Jay Parini analyzes John Steinbeck's debt to D. H. Lawrence's story "Odour of Chrysanthemums" in his 1995 biography of Steinbeck. The result was what Parini rates as perhaps Steinbeck's best story, "The Chrysanthemums."

Lawrence's and Steinbeck's "Chrysanthemums"

1995

The Long Valley had appeared when Steinbeck was just past the midpoint in writing *The Grapes of Wrath*. And while it did not sell quite on the same large scale as *Tortilla Flat* or *Of Mice and Men*, it made it onto the bestseller lists: an unusual thing, then and now, for a volume of stories. His movie agent, Annie Laurie Williams, wrote to Steinbeck on September 23: "*The Long Valley* is getting marvelous press."[1] Indeed, it was. Stanley Young, in the *New York Times Book Review* (September 25, 1938), predicted that Steinbeck would "become a genuinely great American writer." The next day, in *The New Yorker*, Clifton Fadiman called the book "a remarkable collection by a writer who has so far neither repeated himself nor allowed himself a single careless sentence."

The opening story, "The Chrysanthemums," sets the tone for the book.[2] It is a brilliant piece of writing, perhaps the best story Steinbeck ever wrote. In it we follow a brief period in the life of a woman, Elisa Allen, who is married to a dull but well-intentioned farmer. Steinbeck writes: "The high grey-flannel fog of winter closed off the Salinas Valley from the sky and from all the rest of the world." As in much of his fiction, this story opens with a personified landscape, a *paysage moralisé* in which the weather and geographical setting are deeply symbolic, gesturing in the direction of the story's ultimate meaning. Here, for instance, the claustrophobic world of Elisa Allen is signaled by the claustrophobic clouds pressing in on the valley. This frustrated woman will never break free.

The title of the story, as well as the theme, reflects again the author's interest in Lawrence (whose first published story was "Odour of Chrysanthemums"). For example, both writers seem to fasten intently on the idea that a new consciousness is growing under, or within, the old rotten one, and that the old must be sacrificed to the new; the apocalyptic flavor of Lawrence is rare in Steinbeck, who might be seen as a "cooler" writer, but they share an urgent belief that one version of civilization has come to an end, and that the artist must play a key role in developing the new one.

"The Chrysanthemums" is partly about the way Elisa's dreams are manipulated by a passing rogue — a man who repairs household goods. (Steinbeck's fiction is full of men like this one: there is Mac, for instance, from *In Dubious Battle*, who will do anything to win the migrant workers' confidence.) The repairman plays upon Elisa's feelings, pretending to sympathize with her love of flowers, which is all-consuming. Her passion for chrysanthemums in particular symbolizes her intimacy with the rhythms of the natural world and represents her most essential self. Only an author who was himself a gardener could have written about the process of gardening so eloquently:

---

[1] Unpublished letter from Williams to Steinbeck (September 23, 1928) in Rare Book and Manuscript Library, Columbia University.

[2] Two excellent articles that have influenced my view of this story are Mordecai Marcus's "The Lost Dream of Sex and Childbirth in 'The Chrysanthemums,'" *Modern Fiction Studies* II (Spring 1965), and Elizabeth E. McMahan's "'The Chrysanthemums': A Study of Woman's Sexuality," *Modern Fiction Studies* 14 (Winter 1968–69).

There was a little square sandy bed kept for rooting the chrysanthe-mums. With her trowel she turned the soil over and over, and smoothed it and patted it firm. Then she dug ten parallel trenches to receive the sets. Back at the chrysanthemum bed she pulled out the little crisp shoots, trimmed off the leaves of each one with her scissors and laid it on a small orderly pile.

Steinbeck understands the metaphor of gardening in a deeply symbolic way, using this knowledge to make his point. Elisa is finally hurt by the repair-man, who was merely toying with her, but she is not broken, as Charlotte Hadella notes: "Even though, in the end, she thinks of herself as a weak, old woman, the powerful imagery of the strong, new crop of chrysanthemums waiting for rain still dominates the story."[3] She compares Elisa's disappoint-ment to a kind of "pruning — the clipping back of the romantic 'shoots' of her imagination before they bud so that her energy can feed a strong reality and produce large, healthy blooms."

---

[3] Charlotte Hadella, "Steinbeck's Cloistered Women," in *The Steinbeck Question: New Essays in Criticism*, ed. Donald R. Noble (Troy, N.Y.: Whitston, 1993), p. 61.

Edgar Allan Poe

Edgar Allan Poe was one of the earliest writers to discuss the aesthetic qualities of the short story as a distinct prose narrative form. In his day literary criticism was still a new field, lacking a terminology and developed concepts. His two long reviews praising the tales of Nathaniel Hawthorne were published in *Graham's Magazine* in 1842 and *Godey's Lady's Book* in 1847; they are pioneering exam-ples of the analytic literary essay. The following excerpt is taken from the 1842 piece, in which Poe amplifies his theory of the short story and his views on the nature of originality in literature.

The Importance of the Single Effect in a Prose Tale

1842

But it is of [Hawthorne's] tales that we desire principally to speak. The tale proper, in our opinion, affords unquestionably the fairest field for the exer-cise of the loftiest talent, which can be afforded by the wide domains of mere prose. Were we bidden to say how the highest genius could be most

Courtesy of the Library of Congress

Edgar Allan Poe photographed less than one year before his death on October 7, 1849.

advantageously employed for the best display of its own powers, we should answer, without hesitation — in the composition of a rhymed poem, not to exceed in length what might be perused in an hour. Within this limit alone can the highest order of true poetry exist. We need only here say, upon this topic, that, in almost all classes of composition, the unity of effect or impression is a point of the greatest importance. It is clear, moreover, that this unity cannot be thoroughly preserved in productions whose perusal cannot be completed at one sitting. We may continue the reading of a prose composition, from the very nature of prose itself, much longer than we can persevere, to any good purpose, in the perusal of a poem. This latter, if truly fulfilling the demands of the poetic sentiment, induces an exaltation of the soul which cannot be long sustained. All high excitements are necessarily transient. Thus a long poem is a paradox. And, without unity of impression, the deepest effects cannot be brought about. Epics were the offspring of an imperfect sense of Art, and their reign is no more. A poem *too* brief may produce a vivid, but never an intense or enduring impression. Without a certain continuity of effort — without a certain duration or repetition of purpose — the soul is never deeply moved. There must be the dropping of the water upon the rock. . . .

Were we called upon, however, to designate that class of composition which, next to such a poem as we have suggested, should best fulfill the demands of high genius — should offer it the most advantageous field of exertion — we should unhesitatingly speak of the prose tale, as Mr. Hawthorne has here exemplified it. We allude to the short prose narrative, requiring from a half-hour to one or two hours in its perusal. The ordinary novel is objectionable, from its length, for reasons already stated in substance. As it cannot be read at one sitting, it deprives itself, of course, of the immense force derivable from *totality*. Worldly interests intervening during the pauses of perusal, modify, annul, or counteract, in a greater or less degree, the impressions of the book. But simple cessation in reading would, of itself, be sufficient to destroy the true unity. In the brief tale, however, the author is enabled to carry out the fullness of his intention, be it what it may. During the hour of perusal the soul of the reader is at the writer's control. There are no external or extrinsic influences — resulting from weariness or interruption.

A skillful literary artist has constructed a tale. If wise, he has not fashioned his thoughts to accommodate his incidents; but having conceived, with deliberate care, a certain unique or single *effect* to be wrought out, he then invents such incidents — he then combines such events as may best aid him in establishing this preconceived effect. If his very initial sentence tend not to the outbringing of this effect, then he has failed in his first step. In the whole composition there should be no word written, of which the tendency, direct or indirect, is not to the one pre-established design. And by such means, with such care and skill, a picture is at length painted which leaves in the mind of him who contemplates it with a kindred art, a sense of the fullest satisfaction. The idea of the tale has been presented unblemished, because undisturbed; and this is an end unattainable by the novel. Undue brevity is just as exceptionable here as in the poem; but undue length is yet more to be avoided.

We have said that the tale has a point of superiority even over the poem. In fact, while the *rhythm* of this latter is an essential aid in the development of the poem's highest idea — the idea of the Beautiful — the artificialities of this rhythm are an inseparable bar to the development of all points of thought or expression which have their basis in *Truth*. But Truth is often, and in very great degree, the aim of the tale. Some of the finest tales are tales of ratiocination. Thus the field of this species of composition, if not in so elevated a region of the mountain of Mind, is a tableland of far vaster extent than the domain of the mere poem. Its products are never so rich, but infinitely more numerous, and more appreciable by the mass of mankind. The writer of the prose tale, in short, may bring to his theme a vast variety of modes or reflections of thought and expression — (the ratiocinative, for example, the sarcastic, or the humorous) which are not only antagonistical to the nature of the poem, but absolutely forbidden by one of its most peculiar and indispensable adjuncts; we allude, of course, to rhythm. It may be added, here, *par parenthèse*, that the author who aims at the purely beautiful in a prose tale is laboring at a great disadvantage. For Beauty can be better treated in the poem. Not so with terror, or passion, or horror, or a multitude of such other points. . . .

Of Mr. Hawthorne's "Tales" we would say, emphatically, that they belong to the highest region of Art — an Art subservient to genius of a very lofty order. We have supposed, with good reason for so supposing, that he had been thrust into his present position by one of the impudent cliques which beset our literature, and whose pretensions it is our full purpose to expose at the earliest opportunity; but we have been most agreeably mistaken. We know of few compositions which the critic can more honestly commend than these "Twice-Told Tales." As Americans, we feel proud of the book.

Mr. Hawthorne's distinctive trait is invention, creation, imagination, originality — a trait which, in the literature of fiction, is positively worth all the rest. But the nature of the originality, so far as regards its manifestation in letters, is but imperfectly understood. The inventive or original mind as frequently displays itself in novelty of *tone* as in novelty of matter. Mr. Hawthorne is original in *all* points.

It would be a matter of some difficulty to designate the best of these tales; we repeat that, without exception, they are beautiful. . . . In the way of objection we have scarcely a word to say of these tales. There is, perhaps, a somewhat too general or prevalent *tone* — a tone of melancholy and mysticism. The subjects are insufficiently varied. There is not so much of *versatility* evinced as we might well be warranted in expecting from the high powers of Mr. Hawthorne. But beyond these trivial exceptions we have really none to make. The style is purity itself. Force abounds. High imagination gleams from every page. Mr. Hawthorne is a man of the truest genius.

Edward W. Said

Edward W. Said was one of the most eminent cultural critics in the United States. He wrote his doctoral thesis at Harvard University analyzing Joseph Conrad's method of writing fiction. Said's thesis was later published by Harvard University Press as his first book, *Joseph Conrad and the Fiction of Autobiography* (1966).

The Past and the Present: Joseph Conrad and the Fiction of Autobiography

1966

> Life as a reality is absolute presence: we cannot say that *there is* anything unless it be present, of this moment. If, then, *there is* a past, it must be as something present, something active in us now.
>
> — Ortega y Gasset

"Men," Conrad wrote to Mrs. Sanderson on March 17, 1900, "often act first and reflect afterwards." The implications of this simple remark take us directly into the rich and confusing world of Conrad's short fiction. There, action of any sort is either performed or witnessed without accompanying reflection or interpretation, as if the overriding and immediate sensation of action done to, by, or in front of one crowds out the informing work of the reason. The exotic settings that Conrad chose underline this: the action becomes even more foreign and inscrutable to the harried mind. But there is a place for retrospection after the fact. One thinks, for example, of the beleaguered Marlow, in command of his shabby Congo steamer, who watches his helmsman inexplicably and suddenly lie down; a few minutes later he is horrified to see a spear protruding from the man's body. Only then does he understand the direct malignancy that has caused what he saw. Further on he notes in a distracted moment the stakes surrounding Kurtz's compound, standing there with ball-like ends. In time he will realize that they are dried human heads, put there as a horrifying example to others. Indeed, the whole progress of Marlow's trip until he reaches Kurtz seems incredible as it happens. As he tells his experience to his audience, Marlow wishes it understood that the experience changed his life. But during the experience he is like Rilke's Malte, realizing that "nothing in the world can one imagine beforehand, not the least thing. Everything is made up of so many unique particulars that cannot be foreseen . . . But the realities are slow and indescribably detailed."[1] The details of reality, given only mute acknowledgment in action, are realized by the recollecting mind, which retraces — as Malte writes — the designs of experience.[2] And perhaps we can sense in the style itself the partial overtaking of action by thought. In a letter to F. N. Doubleday, T. E. Lawrence once wrote of Conrad's style as a manner of writing that "hungered" for a total capture of its subject, and that constantly applied itself to actions that appeared to refuse it.[3]

---

[1]Rainer Maria Rilke, *The Notebooks of Malte Laurids Brigge* (New York, 1964), p. 138.

[2]Ibid., p. 68.

[3]Lawrence's letter is dated March 20, 1920. The passage I refer to runs as follows: "You know, publishing Conrad must be a rare pleasure. He's absolutely the most haunting in prose that ever was; I wish I knew how every paragraph he writes (do you notice they are all paragraphs: he seldom writes a single sentence?) goes on sounding in waves, like the note of a tenor bell, after it stops. It's not built on the rhythm of ordinary prose, but on something existing only in his head, *and as he never says what it is he wants to say, all his things end in a kind of hunger*, a suggestion of something he can't say or do or think" (italics mine). *The Letters of T. E. Lawrence*, ed. David Garnett (London, 1938), pp. 301–02.

The retrospective mode of so many of Conrad's shorter works can be understood as the effort to interpret what, at the time of occurrence, would not permit reflection. And, most of the time, the action that has already occurred not only troubles the present, but also calls itself to immediate attention. Conrad's very first tale, "The Idiots," explicitly accounts for itself in this manner. The narrator is a traveler in Brittany who abruptly sees before him four idiot children. He then inquires after them and slowly the story of their birth pieces itself together in its pathetic sadness and terror. But the content of the tale, for all its sensational operatics, still seems somewhat "obscure" to the traveler. Between the recollecting narrator and the actual tale there is a barrier that is eternally closed. For a novelist, however, a barrier is not something merely to be ignored, and this hedge of mystery, as Conrad develops it in later tales, becomes an important fact in the story. . . .

Most of Conrad's short fiction, therefore, dramatizes the problematic relation between the past and the present, between then and now. It may be Conrad's own sense of the past conflicting with his sense of the present, or it may be a character's sense of the past disturbing his (the character's) sense of the present — the distinction is impossible to make. Of course there are some virtuosic variations on this simple motif, but the ground bass remains constant. Always the tale opens upon a scene of unnatural, ominous quiet. There is a story that needs to be told — and the inevitable analogy is the Ancient Mariner accosting the Wedding Guest, forcing the story upon him. In some cases the story does not involve the narrator himself: in "Falk" and *Heart of Darkness*, for example, the "I" of the story simply listens to a story told by someone else. In other instances — *The Nigger of the "Narcissus"* and "The Secret Sharer" are two — there is no specific audience and no specific occasion for the narrative, even though the tale is told in the first person. In still other works, Conrad dispenses with the first-person narrative as such, although he adheres to a "center-of-consciousness" technique similar to James's. But in each story Conrad's purpose is to consider not only the so-called plot (which has usually taken place in the past), but also the varying degrees of obscurity, difficulty, and loneliness that inevitably linger on into the present. For the past cannot, will not, be contained or circumscribed. We think we have passed out of it, but the mere thought of that reconfirms its powers over us. It is as if, to borrow an image from *The Waste Land*, each man in a prison thinks of the key that will free him and "Thinking of the key, each confirms a prison." The effect of the stories is to make solitude a universal.

According to one work on the generic characteristics of short fiction, this is exactly what should be true of stories. Frank O'Connor's *The Lonely Voice* describes short fiction as essentially the narrative of the eternal outcast, the lonely individual whose remoteness from society is made a center of intense awareness.[4] Beyond this, O'Connor discusses short fiction as a series

---

[4]Frank O'Connor, *The Lonely Voice* (Cleveland, 1963).

of individual voices (whether of Maupassant, Turgenev, or Chekhov) whose texture creates distinctive effects and delights for the reader. The conceptual scheme of Conrad's short fiction, however, is far more dramatic and subtle than a matter of delightful, if unique, effects. There is first of all the quality of attempted *intrusion*: the intrusion of the past into the present, and the intrusion of the present into the past. The real aim of the tale becomes that long, extended moment wherein past and present are brought together and allowed to interact. The past, requiring the illumination of slow reflection on former thoughtless impulses, is exposed to the present; the present, demanding that "desired unrest" without which it must remain mute and paralyzed, is exposed to the past. . . .

Furthermore, in the technical handling of the dominant plot, Conrad attempts to achieve a causal relation between the past and the present. When he wrote once that the truth of the story consisted in its presentation, he referred, I think, to the deliberate artistic manipulation that sought to bring the past into a causal relation with the present. We are thereby invited to consider how in *Heart of Darkness* the story of Marlow's "hankering after dark places" is not merely the result of an enforced wait on the Thames, but also a cause of it.[5] The characteristic, idiomatic twist in every Conrad story is that the attempt to see a direct relation between the past and the present, to see past and present as a continuous surface of interrelated events, is frustrated. Marlow, who wants his friends to see the outside and not the inner kernel of events (and Conrad in the famous 1897 preface to *The Nigger of the "Narcissus"* and in a letter of September 6, 1897, to Blackwood openly avowed this to be the aim of the prose writer), becomes quite invisible to his audience while, at the same time, the story he tells becomes increasingly obscure. Both story and teller seem to recede into an almost transcendent heart of darkness. This is the central and gripping paradox of Conrad's method: every attempt to establish a discipline of direct relation between events leads one further *into* the events themselves. And they yield up no single method or order by which they can be explained. Marlow quickly reminds the director of the Eldorado expedition that it is not a question of Kurtz's wrong method for getting ivory so expeditiously out of the jungle: rather, "no method at all." Nevertheless, the deep philosophical honesty of Conrad's artistic disposition preserves in each story the agonizing sense of being "a beginner in [its] own circumstances."[6] It is almost impossible not to remark that acting first and reflecting afterwards is always the problem, with reflection hopelessly far behind, hopelessly leading one further away from an inscrutable surface of action into a confusing "beyond."

---

[5]"One might go further and say that in the [short] story what precedes the crisis becomes a consequence of the crisis — this being what happened, that must necessarily be what preceded it." O'Connor, p. 105.

[6]Rilke, *Notebooks*, p. 67.

Leslie Marmon Silko

Leslie Marmon Silko discussed her view of her audience and her background growing up in a matriarchal society in a lecture titled "Language and Literature from a Pueblo Indian Perspective." It was originally published in *English Literature: Opening Up the Canon* (1979), where Silko added a footnote: "This 'essay' is an edited transcript of an oral presentation. The 'author' deliberately did not read from a prepared paper so that the audience could experience firsthand one dimension of the oral tradition — non-linear structure. Her remarks were intended to be heard, not read."

Language and Literature from a Pueblo Indian Perspective

1979

Where I come from, the words that are most highly valued are those which are spoken from the heart, unpremeditated and unrehearsed. Among the Pueblo people, a written speech or statement is highly suspect because the true feelings of the speaker remain hidden as he reads words that are detached from the occasion and the audience. I have intentionally not written a formal paper to read to this session because of this and because I want you to hear and to experience English in a nontraditional structure, a structure that follows patterns from the oral tradition. For those of you accustomed to a structure that moves from point A to point B to point C, this presentation may be somewhat difficult to follow because the structure of Pueblo expression resembles something like a spider's web — with many little threads radiating from a center, crisscrossing each other. As with the web, the structure will emerge as it is made and you must simply listen and trust, as the Pueblo people do, that meaning will be made.

I suppose the task that I have today is a formidable one because basically I come here to ask you, at least for a while, to set aside a number of basic approaches that you have been using and probably will continue to use in approaching the study of English or the study of language; first of all, I come to ask you to see language from the Pueblo perspective, which is a perspective that is very much concerned with including the whole of creation and the whole of history and time. And so we very seldom talk about breaking language down into words. As I will continue to relate to you, even the use of a specific language is less important than the one thing — which is the "telling," or the storytelling. And so, as Simon Ortiz has written, if you approach a Pueblo person and want to talk words or, worse than that, to break down an individual word into its components, ofttimes you will just get a blank stare, because we don't think of words as being isolated from the speaker, which, of course, is one element of the oral tradition. Moreover, we don't think of words as being alone: Words are always with other words, and the other words are almost always in a story of some sort.

Today I have brought a number of examples of stories in English because I would like to get around to the question that has been raised, or the topic that has come along here, which is what changes we Pueblo writers might make with English as a language for literature. But at the same time I would like to explain the importance of storytelling and how it relates to a Pueblo theory of language.

So first I would like to go back to the Pueblo Creation story. The reason I go back to that story is because it is an all-inclusive story of creation and how life began. Tséitsínako, Thought Woman, by thinking of her sisters, and together with her sisters, thought of everything which is, and this world was created. And the belief was that everything in this world was a part of the original creation, and that the people at home realized that far away there were others — other human beings. There is even a section of the story which is a prophesy — which describes the origin of the European race, the African, and also remembers the Asian origins.

Starting out with this story, with this attitude which includes all things, I would like to point out that the reason the people are more concerned with story and communication and less with a particular language is in part an outgrowth of the area [pointing to a map] where we find ourselves. Among the twenty Pueblos there are at least six distinct languages, and possibly seven. Some of the linguists argue — and I don't set myself up to be a linguist at all — about the number of distinct languages. But certainly Zuni is all alone, and Hopi is all alone, and from mesa to mesa there are subtle differences in language — very great differences. I think that this might be the reason that what particular language was being used wasn't as important as what a speaker was trying to say. And this, I think, is reflected and stems or grows out of a particular view of the story — that is, that language *is* story. At Laguna many words have stories which make them. So when one is telling a story, and one is using words to tell the story, each word that one is speaking has a story of its own too. Often the speakers or tellers go into the stories of the words they are using to tell one story so that you get stories within stories, so to speak. This structure becomes very apparent in the storytelling, and what I would like to show you later on by reading some pieces that I brought is that this structure also informs the writing and the stories which are currently coming from Pueblo people. I think what is essential is this sense of story, and story within story, and the idea that one story is only the beginning of many stories, and the sense that stories never truly end. I would like to propose that these views of structure and the dynamics of storytelling are some of the contributions which Native American cultures bring to the English language or at least to literature in the English language.

First of all, a lot of people think of storytelling as something that is done at bedtime — that it is something that is done for small children. When I use the term "storytelling," I include a far wider range of telling activity. I also do not limit storytelling to simply old stories, but to again go back to the original view of creation, which sees that it is all part of a whole; we do not differentiate or fragment stories and experiences. In the beginning, Tséitsínako, Thought Woman, thought of all these things, and all of these things are held together as one holds many things together in a single thought.

So in the telling (and today you will hear a few of the dimensions of this telling) first of all, as was pointed out earlier, the storytelling always includes the audience and the listeners, and, in fact, a great deal of the story is believed to be inside the listener, and the storyteller's role is to draw the story out of the listeners. This kind of shared experience grows out of a strong community base. The storytelling goes on and continues from generation to generation.

The Origin story functions basically as a maker of our identity—with the story we know who we are. We are the Lagunas. This is where we came from. We came this way. We came by this place. And so from the time you are very young, you hear these stories, so that when you go out into the wider world, when one asks who you are, or where are you from, you immediately know: We are the people who came down from the north. We are the people of these stories. It continues down into clans so that you are not just talking about Laguna Pueblo people, you are talking about your own clan. Within the clans there are stories which identify the clan.

In the Creation story, Antelope says that he will help knock a hole in the earth so that the people can come up, out into the next world. Antelope tries and tries, and he uses his hooves and is unable to break through; and it is then that Badger says, "Let me help you." And Badger very patiently uses his claws and digs a way through, bringing the people into the world. When the Badger clan people think of themselves, or when the Antelope people think of themselves, it is as people who are of *this* story, and this is *our* place, and we fit into the very beginning when the people first came, before we began our journey south.

So you can move, then, from the idea of one's identity as a tribal person into clan identity. Then we begin to get to the extended family, and this is where we begin to get a kind of story coming into play which some people might see as a different kind of story, though Pueblo people do not. Anthropologists and ethnologists have, for a long time, differentiated the types of oral language they find in the Pueblos. They tended to rule out all but the old and sacred and traditional stories and were not interested in family stories and the family's account of itself. But these family stories are just as important as the other stories—the older stories. These family stories are given equal recognition. There is no definite, pre-set pattern for the way one will hear the stories of one's own family, but it is a very critical part of one's childhood, and it continues on throughout one's life. You will hear stories of importance to the family—sometimes wonderful stories—stories about the time a maternal uncle got the biggest deer that was ever seen and brought back from the mountains. And so one's sense of who the family is, and who you are, will then extend from that—"I am from the family of my uncle who brought in this wonderful deer, and it was a wonderful hunt"—so you have this sort of building or sense of identity.

There are also other stories, stories about the time when another uncle, perhaps, did something that wasn't really acceptable. In other words, this process of keeping track, of telling, is an all-inclusive process which begins to create a total picture. So it is very important that you know all of the stories — both positive and not so positive — about one's own family. The reason that it is very important to keep track of all the stories in one's own family is because you are liable to hear a story from somebody else who is perhaps an enemy of the family, and you are liable to hear a version which has been changed, a version which makes your family sound disreputable — something that will taint the honor of the family. But if you have already heard the story, you know your family's version of what *really* happened that night, so when somebody else is mentioning it, you will have a version of the story to counterbalance it. Even when there is no way around it — old Uncle Pete did a terrible thing — by knowing the stories that come out of other families, by keeping very close watch, listening constantly to learn the stories about other families, one is in a sense able to deal with terrible sorts of things that might happen within one's own family. When a member of one's own family does something that cannot be excused, one always knows stories about similar things which happened in other families. And it is not done maliciously. I think it is very important to realize this. Keeping track of all the stories within the community gives a certain distance, a useful perspective which brings incidents down to a level we can deal with. If others have done it before, it cannot be so terrible. If others have endured, so can we.

The stories are always bringing us together, keeping this whole together, keeping this family together, keeping this clan together. "Don't go away, don't isolate yourself, but come here, because we have all had these kinds of experiences" — this is what the people are saying to you when they tell you these other stories. And so there is this constant pulling together to resist what seems to me to be a basic part of human nature: When some violent emotional experience takes place, people get the urge to run off and hide or separate themselves from others. And of course, if we do that, we are not only talking about endangering the group, we are also talking about the individual or the individual family never being able to recover or to survive. Inherent in this belief is the feeling that one does not recover or get well by one's self, but it is together that we look after each other and take care of each other.

In the storytelling, then, we see this process of bringing people together, and it works not only on the family level, but also on the level of the individual. Of course, the whole Pueblo concept of the individual is a little bit different from the usual Western concept of the individual. But one of the beauties of the storytelling is that when something happens to an individual, many people will come to you and take you aside, or maybe a couple of people will come and talk to you. These are occasions of storytelling. These occasions of storytelling are continuous; they are a way of life.

Storytelling lies at the heart of the Pueblo people, and so when someone comes in and says, "When did they tell the stories, or what time of day does the storytelling take place?" that is a ridiculous question. The storytelling goes on constantly—as some old grandmother puts on the shoes of a little child and tells the child the story of a little girl who didn't wear her shoes. At the same time somebody comes into the house for coffee to talk with an adolescent boy who has just been into a lot of trouble, to reassure him that *he* got into that kind of trouble, or somebody else's son got into that kind of trouble too. You have this constant ongoing process, working on many different levels.

One of the stories I like to bring up about helping the individual in crisis is a recent story, and I want to remind you that we make no distinctions between the stories—whether they are history, whether they are fact, whether they are gossip—these distinctions are not useful when we are talking about this particular experience with language. Anyway, there was a young man who, when he came back from the war in Vietnam, had saved up his Army pay and bought a beautiful red Volkswagen Beetle. He was very proud of it, and one night drove up to a place right across the reservation line. It is a very notorious place for many reasons, but one of the more notorious things about the place is a deep arroyo behind the place. This is the King's Bar. So he ran in to pick up a cold six-pack to take home, but he didn't put on his emergency brake. And his little red Volkswagen rolled back into the arroyo and was all smashed up. He felt very bad about it, but within a few days everybody had come to him and told him stories about other people who had lost cars to that arroyo. And probably the story that made him feel the best was about the time that George Day's station wagon, with his mother-in-law and kids in the back, rolled into that arroyo. So everybody was saying, "Well, at least your mother-in-law and kids weren't in the car when it rolled in," and you can't argue with that kind of story. He felt better then because he wasn't alone anymore. He and his smashed-up Volkswagen were now joined with all the other stories of cars that fell into that arroyo.

There are a great many parallels between Pueblo experiences and the remarks that have been made about South Africa and the Caribbean countries—similarities in experiences so far as language is concerned. More specifically, with the experience of English being imposed upon the people. The Pueblo people, of course, have seen intruders come and intruders go. The first they watched come were the Spaniards; while the Spaniards were there, things had to be conducted in Spanish. But as the old stories say, if you wait long enough, they'll go. And sure enough, they went. Then another bunch came in. And old stories say, well, if you wait around long enough, not so much that they'll go, but at least their ways will go. One wonders now, when you see what's happening to technocratic-industrial culture, now that we've used up most of the sources of energy, you think perhaps the old people are right.

But anyhow, our experience with English has been different because the Bureau of Indian Affairs schools were so terrible that we never heard of Shakespeare. There was Dick and Jane, and I can remember reading that the robins were heading south for winter, but I knew that all winter the robins were around Laguna. It took me a long time to figure out what was going on. I worried for quite a while about the robins because they didn't leave in the winter, not realizing that the textbooks were written in Boston. The big textbook companies are up here in Boston and *their* robins do go south in the winter.

But this freed us and encouraged us to stay with our narratives. Whatever literature we received at school (which was damn little), at home the storytelling, the special regard for telling and bringing together through the telling, was going on constantly. It has continued, and so we have a great body of classical oral literature, both in the narratives and in the chants and songs.

As the old people say, "If you can remember the stories, you will be all right. Just remember the stories." And, of course, usually when they say that to you, when you are young, you wonder what in the world they mean. But when I returned — I had been away from Laguna Pueblo for a couple of years, well more than a couple of years after college and so forth — I returned to Laguna and I went to Laguna-Acoma high school to visit an English class, and I was wondering how the telling was continuing, because Laguna Pueblo, as the anthropologists have said, is one of the more acculturated pueblos. So I walked into this high school English class and there they were sitting, these very beautiful Laguna and Acoma kids. But I knew that out in their lockers they had cassette tape recorders, and I knew that at home they had stereos, and they were listening to Kiss and Led Zeppelin and all those other things. I was almost afraid, but I had to ask — I had with me a book of short fiction (it's called *The Man to Send Rain Clouds* [New York: Viking Press, 1974]), and among the stories of other Native American writers, it has stories that I have written and Simon Ortiz has written. And there is one particular story in the book about the killing of a state policeman in New Mexico by three Acoma Pueblo men. It was an act that was committed in the early fifties. I was afraid to ask, but I had to. I looked at the class and I said, "How many of you heard this story before you read it in the book?" And I was prepared to hear this crushing truth that indeed the anthropologists were right about the old traditions dying out. But it was amazing, you know, almost all but one or two students raised their hands. They had heard that story, just as Simon and I had heard it, when we were young. That was my first indication that storytelling continues on. About half of them had heard it in English, about half of them had heard it in Laguna. I think again, getting back to one of the original statements, that if you begin to look at the core of the importance of the language and how it fits in with the culture, it is the *story* and the feeling of the story which matters more than what language it's told in.

Matt Steinglass

Matt Steinglass is the correspondent for the German news agency dpa [sic] in Hanoi, where he has lived since 2003. "Reading Tim O'Brien in Hanoi" was published in the *New York Times* on April 4, 2010.

Reading Tim O'Brien in Hanoi

2010

Last month, on a typically dull, gray late-winter Hanoi day, I stopped in at the city's sole respectable foreign-language bookstore, the Bookworm, for a conversation with a Vietnamese fan of Tim O'Brien. "The Things They Carried," O'Brien's celebrated collection of linked stories about the Vietnam War, has just been reissued in a 20th-anniversary edition, and I was interested in gathering a Vietnamese perspective on O'Brien's work. But it took me days of calls and e-mail messages to find anyone in Hanoi who had read any of it. Finally the manager of the Bookworm suggested I speak with Tran Ngoc Hieu, a lecturer at Hanoi's Pedagogical University. I needed a while to track him down, as he is perhaps the only person in the city who does not use a mobile phone. Hieu, 30, looks young for his age, and compensates by wearing a sport jacket and speaking a careful, deliberate English with an exceptionally rich vocabulary, interrupting himself frequently to apologize for not speaking English well.

"Vietnamese authors should learn to tell their war stories the way O'Brien does," Hieu said. "With parody, nonlinear plot exposition. The fusion of reality and dreams."

It shouldn't have been so hard to find Vietnamese who could talk about O'Brien. He is, after all, a seminal American novelist of the Vietnam War, and one would think his books — including "If I Die in a Combat Zone" (1973) and "Going After Cacciato" (1978) — would be reasonably well known to Vietnamese readers. They are not. In fact, almost none of the major American novels about the war are known to Vietnamese readers; they have not been translated and published here. You can buy photocopied English-language editions of Robert Stone's "Dog Soldiers," Denis Johnson's "Tree of Smoke" or many classic American works of nonfiction from wandering booksellers who ply the tourist neighborhoods in Hanoi and Ho Chi Minh City, but like most people around the world, few Vietnamese read in foreign languages for pleasure. A small group of the literary elite read unofficial translations of some American works on Vietnamese-language émigré literary Web sites, like Talawas. But for the most part, Vietnamese are simply unfamiliar with American fiction about the war.

To some extent, the lack of familiarity stems from censorship. Vietnam today is in many ways a rather open society; Vietnamese can surf the Internet (though writing blogs on political topics can get you arrested), foreign television streams in via satellite and cable, and pirated DVDs circulate freely. But when it comes to books, the old Communist machinery of censorship remains in place.

But censorship is only part of the story. Vietnamese also seem largely uninterested in foreign accounts of the war. For example, Graham Greene's "Quiet American" is available in translation, but most Vietnamese I've spoken to dislike it. They find the book's main Vietnamese character, the beautiful Phuong, demeaning in her passivity. The lack of interest extends to movies, too. You can purchase a copy of "Apocalypse Now" at any DVD store in Hanoi, but even the Vietnamese film buffs I've asked have not seen it. Last year, Vietnam's first chain of modern multiplexes showed two movies one would never have expected to make it past the censors: "Watchmen," which includes a sequence in which an American superhero ensures that Nixon wins the war, and "Tropic Thunder," a parody of serious Vietnam films like "Platoon." Audiences here yawned at both.

In the case of "Tropic Thunder," Vietnamese simply didn't recognize the themes it parodied. The film was essentially a burlesque of that central motif of Vietnam in American culture, the "heart of darkness" story: the descent of innocents into savagery, the dissolution of reason in a violent encounter with an incomprehensible alien society.

The Vietnamese, obviously, are that society. And they don't find themselves particularly incomprehensible. Nor do they find themselves silent and mysterious, like Greene's Phuong. Moreover, the current Vietnamese government is descended from the side that won the war, a condition much less conducive to irony than America's experience of quagmire and defeat.

A triumphant political narrative, enforced with deadening rigor in textbooks and museums, limits the kinds of stories that can be told in Vietnamese literature about the "American War."

As Hieu puts it, it's not just that censorship restricts the contents of most novels, but that it pushes even rebellious authors to concentrate on breaking the barriers of factual content, rather than on aesthetic innovations.

"Vietnamese writers are still focused on telling the 'true stories' that aren't taught in schools, the secret truths," Hieu said. Most forgo complex formal approaches. "If you watch Dang Nhat Minh's film of 'Don't Burn,' you'll see."

"Don't Burn" (published in the United States in 2007 as "Last Night I Dreamed of Peace") is the most important recent work of war literature in Vietnam. The diary of a young Vietcong doctor named Dang Thuy Tram who was killed in 1970, it sold hundreds of thousands of copies when it was published in Vietnam in 2005. Vietnamese found Tram's sincere, emotionally direct writing powerful and unexpected. Reviewers in the United States, though, mainly found it trite.

What Vietnamese literature seems to be missing, from an American perspective, is the kind of amoral chaos we have come to expect from war stories. Americans tend to embrace those Vietnamese works that do have a bit of the dark and the surreal. Bao Ninh's 1991 masterpiece "The Sorrow of War" (published in the United States in 1995) includes images of senseless death and waste on the Ho Chi Minh trail, presented in an ironic, nonchronological style that recalls O'Brien or Joseph Heller's "Catch-22." For the North Vietnamese soldiers in this novel, life in the mountains and jungles is every bit as alien and terrifying as it is for the Americans in O'Brien's.

In 1997, a fragment of "The Things They Carried" was published in the Vietnamese literary magazine *Foreign Literature*. The publishing house Nha Nam will publish the first full translation later this year, in a print run of a few thousand copies, typical for novels here. If O'Brien ends up translating better than other English language writers of the war, it may be because he explodes the expectations of readers, American and Vietnamese alike.

For example, in a startling chapter in the middle of "The Things They Carried," he depicts the telling of a story by Rat Kiley, the unit's medic and a narrator whose reliability is explicitly undermined from the start. In the story, a G.I. somehow manages to bring his gorgeous blond high-school sweetheart to his firebase. She gradually acclimates to the war, takes up with the Green Berets, and winds up padding through the jungle on weeklong ambushes and returning wearing a necklace of human tongues. We eventually realize we are reading an absurdist parody of the "heart of darkness" story.

In an earlier chapter called "How to Tell a True War Story," O'Brien tells us that if it matters whether it really happened, then the story isn't "true": "Without the grounding reality, it's just a trite bit of puffery, pure Hollywood, untrue in the way all such stories are untrue. Yet even if it did happen — and maybe it did, anything's possible — even then you know it can't be true, because a true war story doesn't depend on that kind of truth."

O'Brien is suggesting that what American soldiers discovered in Vietnam, amid the horrors, was a particular modern way of being that demanded a surrealistic kind of storytelling. And Vietnamese are interested in surrealism. (Haruki Murakami, for example, is hugely popular here.) They just aren't terribly interested in the war.

Amy Tan

Amy Tan discussed the subject of multicultural literature in an essay written for *The Threepenny Review* in 1996. There she admitted that she was proud to find her name on the reading lists for many college courses ("What writer wouldn't want her work to be read?") and then explained why she was "not altogether comfortable" about appearing on lists of required reading.

In the Canon, for All the Wrong Reasons

1996

Several years ago I learned that I had passed a new literary milestone. I had made it to the Halls of Education under the rubric of "Multicultural Literature," also known in many schools as "Required Reading."

Thanks to this development, I now meet students who proudly tell me they're doing their essays, term papers, or master's theses on me. By that they mean that they are analyzing not just my books but me — my grade-school achievements, youthful indiscretions, marital status, as well as the movies I watched as a child, the slings and arrows I suffered as a minority, and so forth — all of which, with the hindsight of classroom literary investigation, prove to contain many Chinese omens that made it inevitable that I would become a writer.

Once I read a master's thesis on feminist writings, which included examples from *The Joy Luck Club*. The student noted that I had often used the number four, something on the order of thirty-two or thirty-six times — in any case, a number divisible by four. She pointed out that there were four mothers, four daughters, four sections of the book, four stories per section. Furthermore, there were four sides to a mah jong table, four directions of the wind, four players. More important, she postulated, my use of the number four was a symbol for the four stages of psychological development, which corresponded in uncanny ways to the four stages of some type of Buddhist philosophy I had never heard of before. The student recalled that the story contained a character called Fourth Wife, symbolizing death, and a four-year-old girl with a feisty spirit, symbolizing regeneration.

In short, her literary sleuthing went on to reveal a mystical and rather Byzantine puzzle, which, once explained, proved to be completely brilliant and precisely logical. She wrote me a letter and asked if her analysis had been correct. How I longed to say "absolutely."

The truth is, if there are symbols in my work they exist largely by accident or through someone else's interpretive design. If I wrote of "an orange moon rising on a dark night," I would more likely ask myself later if the image was a cliché, not whether it was a symbol for the feminine force rising in anger, as one master's thesis postulated. To plant symbols like that, you need a plan, good organizational skills, and a prescient understanding of the story you are about to write. Sadly, I lack those traits.

All this is by way of saying that I don't claim my use of the number four to be a brilliant symbolic device. In fact, now that it's been pointed out to me in rather astonishing ways, I consider my overuse of the number to be a flaw.

Reviewers and students have enlightened me about not only how I write but why I write. Apparently, I am driven to capture the immigrant experience, to demystify Chinese culture, to point out the differences between Chinese and American culture, even to pave the way for other Asian American writers.

If only I were that noble. Contrary to what is assumed by some students, reporters, and community organizations wishing to bestow honors on me, I am not an expert on China, Chinese culture, mah jong, the psychology of mothers and daughters, generation gaps, immigration, illegal aliens, assimilation, acculturation, racial tension, Tiananmen Square, the Most Favored Nation trade agreements, human rights, Pacific Rim economics, the purported one million missing baby girls of China, the future of Hong Kong after 1997, or, I am sorry to say, Chinese cooking. Certainly I have personal opinions on many of these topics, but by no means do my sentiments and my world of make-believe make me an expert.

So I am alarmed when reviewers and educators assume that my very personal, specific, and fictional stories are meant to be representative down to the nth detail not just of Chinese Americans but, sometimes, of all Asian culture. Is Jane Smiley's *A Thousand Acres* supposed to be taken as representative of all of American culture? If so, in what ways? Are all American fathers tyrannical? Do all American sisters betray one another? Are all American conscientious objectors flaky in love relationships?

Over the years my editor has received hundreds of permissions requests from publishers of college textbooks and multicultural anthologies, all of them wishing to reprint my work for "educational purposes." One publisher wanted to include an excerpt from *The Joy Luck Club*, a scene in which a Chinese woman invites her non-Chinese boyfriend to her parents' house for dinner. The boyfriend brings a bottle of wine as a gift and commits a number of social gaffes at the dinner table. Students were supposed to read this excerpt, then answer the following question: "If you are invited to a Chinese family's house for dinner, should you bring a bottle of wine?"

———————

In many respects, I am proud to be on the reading lists for courses such as Ethnic Studies, Asian American Studies, Asian American Literature, Asian American History, Women's Literature, Feminist Studies, Feminist Writers of Color, and so forth. What writer wouldn't want her work to be read? I also take a certain perverse glee in imagining countless students, sleepless at three in the morning, trying to read *The Joy Luck Club* for the next day's midterm. Yet I'm also not altogether comfortable about my book's status as required reading.

Let me relate a conversation I had with a professor at a school in southern California. He told me he uses my books in his literature class but he makes it a point to lambast those passages that depict China as backward or unattractive. He objects to any descriptions that have to do with spitting, filth, poverty, or superstitions. I asked him if China in the 1930s and 1940s was free of these elements. He said, No, such descriptions are true; but he still believes it is "the obligation of the writer of ethnic literature to create positive, progressive images."

I secretly shuddered and thought, Oh well, that's southern California for you. But then, a short time later, I met a student from UC Berkeley, a school that I myself attended. The student was standing in line at a book signing. When his turn came, he swaggered up to me, then took two steps back and said in a loud voice, "Don't you think you have a responsibility to write about Chinese men as positive role models?"

In the past, I've tried to ignore the potshots. A *Washington Post* reporter once asked me what I thought of another Asian American writer calling me something on the order of "a running dog whore sucking on the tit of the imperialist white pigs."

"Well," I said, "You can't please everyone, can you?" I pointed out that readers are free to interpret a book as they please, and that they are free to appreciate or not appreciate the result. Besides, reacting to your critics makes a writer look defensive, petulant, and like an all-around bad sport.

But lately I've started thinking it's wrong to take such a laissez-faire attitude. Lately I've come to think that I must say something, not so much to defend myself and my work but to express my hopes for American literature, for what it has the potential to become in the twenty-first century—that is, a truly American literature, democratic in the way it includes many colorful voices.

Until recently, I didn't think it was important for writers to express their private intentions in order for their work to be appreciated; I believed that any analysis of my intentions belonged behind the closed doors of literature classes. But I've come to realize that the study of literature does have its effect on how books are being read, and thus on what might be read, published, and written in the future. For that reason, I do believe writers today must talk about their intentions — if for no other reason than to serve as an antidote to what others say our intentions should be.

For the record, I don't write to dig a hole and fill it with symbols. I don't write stories as ethnic themes. I don't write to represent life in general. And I certainly don't write because I have answers. If I knew everything there is to know about mothers and daughters, Chinese and Americans, I wouldn't have any stories left to imagine. If I had to write about only positive role models, I wouldn't have enough imagination left to finish the first story. If I knew what to do about immigration, I would be a sociologist or a politician and not a long-winded storyteller.

So why do I write?

Because my childhood disturbed me, pained me, made me ask foolish questions. And the questions still echo. Why does my mother always talk about killing herself? Why did my father and brother have to die? If I die, can I be reborn into a happy family? Those early obsessions led to a belief that writing could be my salvation, providing me with the sort of freedom and danger, satisfaction and discomfort, truth and contradiction I can't find in anything else in life.

I write to discover the past for myself. I don't write to change the future for others. And if others are moved by my work — if they love their mothers more, scold their daughters less, or divorce their husbands who were not positive role models — I'm often surprised, usually grateful to hear from kind readers. But I don't take either credit or blame for changing their lives for better or for worse.

Writing, for me, is an act of faith, a hope that I will discover what I mean by "truth." I also think of reading as an act of faith, a hope that I will discover something remarkable about ordinary life, about myself. And if the writer and the reader discover the same thing, if they have that connection, the act of faith has resulted in an act of magic. To me, that's the mystery and the wonder of both life and fiction — the connection between two individuals who discover in the end that they are more the same than they are different.

And if that doesn't happen, it's nobody's fault. There are still plenty of other books on the shelf. Choose what you like.

Leo Tolstoy

Leo Tolstoy wrote his commentary on "The Darling" in 1905, the year after his friend Anton Chekhov's death. The essay was a way of protesting what Tolstoy considered Chekhov's unfair caricature of a simple, good-hearted woman in the central character, Olenka. Tolstoy's argument is essentially based on his patriarchal point of view.

Chekhov's Intent in "The Darling"

1905 / Translated by Constance Garnett

There is a story of profound meaning in the Book of Numbers which tells how Balak, the King of the Moabites, sent for the prophet Balaam to curse the Israelites who were on his borders. Balak promised Balaam many gifts for this service, and Balaam, tempted, went to Balak, and went with him up the mountain, where an altar was prepared with calves and sheep sacrificed in readiness for the curse. Balak waited for the curse, but instead of cursing, Balaam blessed the people of Israel.

> And Balak said unto Balaam, What hast thou done unto me? I took thee to curse mine enemies, and, behold, thou hast blessed them altogether.
>
> And he answered and said, Must I not take heed to speak that which the Lord hath put in my mouth?
>
> And Balak said unto him, Come, I pray thee, with me into another place . . . and curse me them from thence.
>
> But again, instead of cursing, Balaam blessed. And so it was the third time also.
>
> And Balak's anger was kindled against Balaam, and he smote his hands together: And Balak said unto Balaam, I called thee to curse my enemies, and, behold, thou hast altogether blessed them these three times.
>
> Therefore now flee thee to thy place: I thought to promote thee unto great honour; but, lo, the Lord hast kept thee back from honour.
>
> And so Balaam departed without having received the gifts, because, instead of cursing, he had blessed the enemies of Balak. [Numbers 23:11–13; 24:10–11]

What happened to Balaam often happens to real poets and artists. Tempted by Balak's gifts, popularity, or by false preconceived ideas, the poet does not see the angel barring his way, though the ass sees him, and he means to curse, and yet, behold, he blesses.

This is just what happened to the true poet and artist Chekhov when he wrote this charming story "The Darling."

The author evidently means to mock at the pitiful creature — as he judges her with his intellect, but not with his heart — the Darling, who after first sharing Kukin's anxiety about his theater, then throwing herself into the interests of the timber trade, then under the influence of the veterinary surgeon regarding the campaign against the foot and mouth disease as the most important matter in the world, is finally engrossed in the grammatical questions and the interests of the little schoolboy in the big cap. Kukin's surname is absurd, even his illness and the telegram announcing his death, the timber merchant with his respectability, the veterinary surgeon, even the boy—all are absurd, but the soul of the Darling, with her faculty of devoting herself with her whole being to any one she loves, is not absurd, but marvelous and holy.

I believe that while he was writing "The Darling," the author had in his mind, though not in his heart, a vague image of a new woman; of her equality with man; of a woman mentally developed, learned, working independently for the good of society as well as, if not better than, a man; of the woman who has raised and upholds the woman question; and in writing "The Darling" he wanted to show what woman ought not to be. The Balak of public opinion bade Chekhov curse the weak, submissive undeveloped woman devoted to man; and Chekhov went up the mountain, and the calves and sheep were laid upon the altar, but when he began to speak, the poet blessed what he had come to curse. In spite of its exquisite gay humor, I at least cannot read without tears some passages of this wonderful story. I am touched by the description of her complete devotion and love for Kukin and all that he cares for, and for the timber merchant and for the veterinary surgeon, and even more of her sufferings when she is left alone and has no one to love; and finally the account of how with all the strength of womanly, motherly feelings (of which she has no experience in her own life) she devotes herself with boundless love to the future man, the schoolboy in the big cap.

The author makes her love the absurd Kukin, the insignificant timber merchant, and the unpleasant veterinary surgeon, but love is no less sacred whether its object is a Kukin or a Spinoza, a Pascal, or a Schiller,[1] and whether the objects of it change as rapidly as with the Darling, or whether the object of it remains the same throughout the whole life.

Some time ago I happened to read in the *Novoe Vremya* an excellent article upon woman. The author has in this article expressed a remarkably clever and profound idea about woman. "Women," he says, "are trying to show us they can do everything we men can do. I don't contest it; I am prepared to admit women can do everything men can do, and possibly better than men; but the trouble is that men cannot do anything faintly approaching to what women can do."

Yes, that is undoubtedly true, and it is true not only with regard to birth, nurture, and early education of children. Men cannot do that highest, best work which brings man nearest to God—the work of love, and complete devotion to the loved object, which good women have done, do, and will do so well and so naturally. What would become of the world, what would become of us men if women had not that faculty and did not exercise it? We could get on without women doctors, women telegraph clerks, women lawyers, women scientists, women writers, but life would be a sorry affair without mothers, helpers, friends, comforters, who love in men the best in them, and imperceptibly instill, evoke, and support it. There would have been no Magdalen

---

[1]Baruch Spinoza (1632–1677), Dutch philosopher; Blaise Pascal (1623–1662), French scientist and philosopher; Johann Christoph Friedrich von Schiller (1759–1805), German poet, playwright, and critic.

with Christ, no Claire with St. Francis; there would have been no wives of the Dekabrists[2] in Siberia; there would not have been among the Duhobors[3] those wives who, instead of holding their husbands back, supported them in their martyrdom for truth; there would not have been those thousands and thousands of unknown women — the best of all, as the unknown always are — the comforters of the drunken, the weak, and the dissolute, who, more than any, need the comfort of love. That love, whether devoted to a Kukin or to Christ, is the chief, grand, unique strength of woman.

What an amazing misunderstanding it is — all this so-called woman question, which, as every vulgar idea is bound to do, has taken possession of the majority of women, and even of men.

"Woman longs to improve herself" — what can be more legitimate and just than that?

But a woman's work is from her very vocation different from man's, and so the ideal of feminine perfection cannot be the same as the ideal of masculine perfection. Let us admit that we do not know what that ideal is; it is quite certain in any case that it is not the ideal of masculine perfection. And yet it is to the attainment of that masculine ideal that the whole and the absurd and evil activity of the fashionable woman movement, which is such a stumbling-block to woman, is directed.

I am afraid that Chekhov was under the influence of that misunderstanding when he wrote "The Darling."

He, like Balaam, intended to curse, but the god of poetry forbade him, and commanded him to bless. And he did bless, and unconsciously clothed this sweet creature in such an exquisite radiance that she will always remain a type of what a woman can be in order to be happy herself, and to make the happiness of those with whom destiny throws her.

What makes the story so excellent is that the effect is unintentional.

I learned to ride a bicycle in a hall large enough to drill a division of soldiers. At the other end of the hall a lady was learning. I thought I must be careful to avoid getting into her way, and began looking at her. And as I looked at her I began unconsciously getting nearer and nearer to her, and in spite of the fact that, noticing the danger, she hastened to retreat, I rode down upon her and knocked her down — that is, I did the very opposite of what I wanted to do, simply because I concentrated my attention upon her.

The same thing has happened to Chekhov, but in an inverse sense: He wanted to knock the Darling down, and concentrating upon her the close attention of the poet, he raised her up.

---

[2] Members of the unsuccessful December 1825 uprising against Czar Nicholas I.

[3] Members of the Christian sect that advocated following inner spirituality instead of church or government doctrine.

Leo Tolstoy

Leo Tolstoy first read the work of Guy de Maupassant in 1881. This excerpt is taken from Tolstoy's preface to a Russian edition of Maupassant's stories published in 1894. It was translated by Leo Wiener in 1905. Tolstoy was criticizing the French writer for lacking a moral point of view and for having an "insufficient comprehension of the lives and interests of the working classes," like the French clerk and his wife in "The Necklace."

"The Works of Guy de Maupassant"

1894

[Maupassant] was endowed with that particular gift, called talent, which consists in the author's ability to direct, according to his tastes, his intensified, strained attention to this or that subject. . . . Maupassant evidently possessed that gift of seeing in subjects something which others did not see. But, to judge from the small volume which I had read, he was devoid of the chief condition necessary, besides talent, for a truly artistic production.
Of the three conditions:

1. a correct, that is, a moral relation of the author to the subject,
2. the clearness of exposition, or the beauty of form, which is the same, and
3. sincerity, that is, an undisguised feeling of love or hatred for what the artist describes.

Maupassant possessed only the last two, and was entirely devoid of the first. He had no correct, that is, no moral relation to the subjects described [. . .]
People who are not very sensitive to art frequently imagine that an artistic production forms one whole, because the same persons act in it all the time, because everything is constructed on one plot, or because the life of one man is described. That is not true. That only seems to the superficial observer: the cement which binds every artistic production into one whole and so produces the illusion of a reflection of life is not the unity of persons and situations, but the unity of the original, moral relation of the author to his subject. In reality, when we read or contemplate an artistic production by a new author, the fundamental question which arises in our soul is always this: "Well, what kind of man are you? How do you differ from all other men whom I know, and what new thing can you tell me about the way we ought to look upon our life?"

No matter what the artist may represent — saints, robbers, kings, lackeys — we seek and see only the artist's soul. If he is an old, familiar artist, the question is no longer, "who are you?" but, "Well, what new thing can you tell me? From what new side will you now illumine my life for me?" And so an author who has no definite, clear, new view of the world, and still more so the one who does not consider this to be necessary, cannot give an artistic production. He can write beautifully, and a great deal, but there will be no artistic production.

Luis Alberto Urrea

Luis Alberto Urrea discussed the writing process that resulted in his story "Father Returns from the Mountain" in an interview with Margaret-Love Denman and Barbara Shoup. His explanation was included in their book *Story Matters: Contemporary Short Story Writers Share the Creative Process* (2006.)

On "Father Returns from the Mountain"

2006

Your story "Father Returns from the Mountain" has characteristics of fiction, poetry, and nonfiction. Would you talk about the occasion for writing the story and how you came to its very untraditional structure?

In 1977, January 10, my father was killed in a car accident. He didn't die immediately. He was left eight hours naked on a table in front of a broken window to die. I was in my senior year of college and he died bringing me a thousand dollars from his bank account, because I was the first one to get out of college. When he had his car wreck, he urinated on himself, so the money was soaked in urine and blood. So the police, who stole everything else, didn't steal it. Later on, when they brought me the body in a station wagon in a cardboard box, they made me pay bail. They said, "Even though he's dead, he's under arrest, and if you don't pay bail we'll just take him back with us." So they charged me seven hundred and fifty bucks to buy the corpse, which I paid with his wet money. They gave me the body, and I paid the rest of the money for the funeral. At one point, everybody was doing the Mexican wake and they took me to my dad at about two in the morning. Nobody came back, so I spent eighteen hours in a room with my father's corpse, just the two of us. There's a place in the story where it says I was sitting next to him, then laid down on the floor, and he started talking. Afterwards, when it was all over, I started having dreams where he was coming to me. I was, all that time, talking to people who were healer types to research this other book, and they were all saying that the dead speak to you in dreams. If they die violently, they don't know they're dead so you have to send them away. That's the first dream: He was lost and I sent him away. And at the end of them, he went away with his friends. It was very strange.

Anyway, Ursula LeGuin was coming to my college to do a workshop, and I wanted to get into this class very badly. You had to audition, so I actually typed that story out on a mimeograph master as my audition piece. She accepted me into the class, and we revised it. Then she accepted it for an anthology, so it was the first sale I ever made. She really started everything for me. It came out in this anthology in 1980 called *Edges*, which she edited. It's kicked around, and people have found it and have been really connected to it because of their experiences. When it came time to do this book, I wasn't going to put it in. Then I thought, no, I really should because it's been identified as a poem, a short story, and an essay–and it could be any of those.

In what ways do you think it works as a short story?

At the time, like many young, smart-ass males, I thought that experimental fiction was the answer to everything. I was going to be Robert Coover, Jr. I thought that sort of anti-story was really cool, so I used those techniques to tell it. I also took fictional elements that were the dream and reported them as reality. So, in that sense, I think it was a short story. There's a repetition of the red car, which I wanted to be a kind of funereal motif. The structure of it is all one long paragraph, with slashes breaking up pieces; some things are out of sequence and intermixed. I wanted it to represent the shattered glass and mirrors of the car. You're looking at broken glass and it's reflecting things, sometimes out of sequence; but, still, it's a mosaic that makes a whole. So it was fictional techniques, or at least anti-story techniques, that I used to tell the story. None of my experimentalist stories are in *Six Kinds of Sky*, except that one. I say in the afterward that it was a moment where I melded two things that worked together for my purposes.

What advice do you give to students who want to experiment with fictional technique?

I tell my students that before Picasso painted cubism, he learned how to draw and how to paint. You will find that a lot of writers in graduate school are stone cold experimentalists — mostly, I think, because they don't know how to tell a clear story. They do whatever trick they can do to avert your attention. I have met a few people who absolutely vibrate to that note. They are experimentalists all the way, and you can tell because it's their voice, their muse. I always want to make sure that people can actually communicate something first.

In what ways is the published story different from the draft you wrote for LeGuin?

Some of the language is refined. In the early draft, you can tell certain things are by a very young male. Stuff that I looked at later and thought, What are you *talking* about?

The lyricism in the story, the beautiful repetition — did that come in the revision?

That was always there. The revisions were more a technical thing, to make things clearer — just little tiny, tiny changes. I've always been interested in that kind of a voice, it's always been my voice. I wanted that sense of inevitability: You cannot escape this, *none* of us are going to escape it. We're all going to die. You're going to lose someone you love, there's no way out of it.

That's mirrored in the way that there's just no white space. There's literally no escaping the story itself. Were there other things that influenced you as a writer during that time?

I worked with a poet in college. I kept trying to write about my father's death, but I was so devastated and shocked by the horror of all that had happened I was out of control. I had never been confronted in a hard way before. I had made it my job to be better at writing than everybody else, so that I was always the cool guy in the workshop. But this guy called me in and sat me down and said, "Look, this is dreadful." I said, "What do you mean it's dreadful?" He said, "It's dreadful, it's dreadful. You're trying to hurt me. It's not my father who died, why should I care?" And I was like, "How *dare* you?" He said, "I'm sorry. But if you want me to care that your father died, get a little control of yourself and write it coldly and calmly. Don't be screaming at me, because I will just walk away from you." At the time, I was red-faced. I was twenty-one years old and I thought, my writing career is over. I learned a lesson, though, that has been good for me as a teacher. I can tell my students, "Just because you have something intense to say doesn't mean you have to write it that way." Why do you think all the hacks are writing true crime books? Because if a guy makes soup out of his grandma it's hard to go wrong with that material. But if you can have somebody kiss someone on the cheek and have your reader weep, then you're really writing."

Alice Walker

Alice Walker wrote about Zora Neale Hurston in her collection *In Search of Our Mothers' Gardens: Womanist Prose* (1983). There Walker also looked at Flannery O'Connor, Langston Hughes, Jean Toomer, and other writers from what she called her "womanist" perspective as a radical black woman. To clarify the meaning of her term, Walker added that "womanist is to feminist as purple is to lavender."

Zora Neale Hurston: A Cautionary Tale and a Partisan View

1979

During the early and middle years of her career Zora was a cultural revolutionary simply because she was always herself. Her work, so vigorous among the rather pallid productions of many of her contemporaries, comes from the essence of black folk life. During her later life she became frightened of the life she had always dared bravely before. Her work too became reactionary, static, shockingly misguided and timid. (This is especially true of her last novel, *Seraphs on the Sewannee*, which is not even about black people, which is no crime, but *is* about white people for whom it is impossible to care, which is.)

A series of misfortunes battered Zora's spirit and her health. And she was broke.

Being broke made all the difference.

Without money of one's own in a capitalist society, there is no such thing as independence. This is one of the clearest lessons of Zora's life, and why I consider the telling of her life "a cautionary tale." We must learn from it what we can.

Without money, an illness, even a simple one, can undermine the will. Without money, getting into a hospital is problematic and getting out without money to pay for the treatment is nearly impossible. Without money, one becomes dependent on other people, who are likely to be — even in their kindness — erratic in their support and despotic in their expectations of return. Zora was forced to rely, like Tennessee Williams's Blanche, "on the kindness of strangers." Can anything be more dangerous, if the strangers are forever in control? Zora, who worked so hard, was never able to make a living from her work.

She did not complain about not having money. She was not the type. (Several months ago I received a long letter from one of Zora's nieces, a bright ten-year-old, who explained to me that her aunt was so proud that the only way the family could guess she was ill or without funds was by realizing they had no idea where she was. Therefore, none of the family attended either Zora's sickbed or her funeral.) Those of us who have had "grants and fellowships from 'white folks'" know this aid is extended in precisely the way welfare is extended in Mississippi. One is asked, *curtly*, more often than not: How much do you need *just to survive*? Then one is — if fortunate — given a third of that. What is amazing is that Zora, who became an orphan at nine, a runaway at fourteen, a maid and manicurist (because of necessity and not from love of the work) before she was twenty — with one dress — managed to become Zora Neale Hurston, author and anthropologist, at all.

For me, the most unfortunate thing Zora ever wrote is her autobiography. After the first several chapters, it rings false. One begins to hear the voice of someone whose life required the assistance of too many transitory "friends." A Taoist proverb states that *to act sincerely with the insincere is dangerous.* (A mistake blacks as a group have tended to make in America.) And so we have Zora sincerely offering gratitude and kind words to people one knows she could not have respected. But this unctuousness, so out of character for Zora, is also a result of dependency, a sign of her powerlessness, her inability to pay back her debts with anything but words. They must have been bitter ones for her. In her dependency, it should be remembered, Zora was not alone — because it is quite true that America does not support or honor us as human beings, let alone as blacks, women, and artists. We have taken help where it was offered because we are committed to what we do and to the survival of our work. Zora was committed to the survival of her people's cultural heritage as well.

In my mind, Zora Neale Hurston, Billie Holiday,[1] and Bessie Smith[2] form a sort of unholy trinity. Zora *belongs* in the tradition of black women singers, rather than among "the literati," at least to me. There were the extreme highs and lows of her life, her undaunted pursuit of adventure, passionate emotional and sexual experience, and her love of freedom. Like Billie and Bessie she followed her own road, believed in her own gods, pursued her own dreams, and refused to separate herself from "common" people. It would have been nice if the three of them had had one another to turn to, in times of need. I close my eyes and imagine them: Bessie would be in charge of all the money; Zora would keep Billie's masochistic tendencies in check and prevent her from singing embarrassing anything-for-a-man songs, thereby preventing Billie's heroin addiction. In return, Billie could be, along with Bessie, the family that Zora felt she never had.

We are a people. A people do not throw their geniuses away. And if they are thrown away, it is our duty *as artists and as witnesses for the future* to collect them again for the sake of our children, and, if necessary, bone by bone.

---

[1] African American jazz singer (1915–1959).
[2] Prominent African American blues singer and songwriter (1898–1937).

Eudora Welty

Eudora Welty included this discussion of her story "The Worn Path" in her book *The Eye of the Story* (1977). It appeared in the section "On Writing," along with her most extensive essays on the art of short fiction — essays that take up general topics such as place and time in fiction, and the art of reading and writing stories. Her reviews of the work of Isak Dinesen, Ralph Ellison, William Faulkner, and Virginia Woolf from the *New York Times* are also included in this collection.

Is Phoenix Jackson's Grandson Really Dead?

1977

A story writer is more than happy to be read by students; the fact that these serious readers think and feel something in response to his work he finds life-giving. At the same time he may not always be able to reply to their specific questions in kind. I wondered if it might clarify something, for both the questioners and myself, if I set down a general reply to the question that comes to me most often in the mail, from both students and their teachers, after some classroom discussion. The unrivaled favorite is this: "Is Phoenix Jackson's grandson really *dead*?"

It refers to a short story I wrote years ago called "A Worn Path," which tells of a day's journey an old woman makes on foot from deep in the country into town and into a doctor's office on behalf of her little grandson; he is at home, periodically ill, and periodically she comes for his medicine; they give it to her as usual, she receives it and starts the journey back.

I had not meant to mystify readers by withholding any fact; it is not a writer's business to tease. The story is told through Phoenix's mind as she undertakes her errand. As the author at one with the character as I tell it, I must assume that the boy is alive. As the reader, you are free to think as you like, of course: The story invites you to believe that no matter what happens, Phoenix for as long as she is able to walk and can hold to her purpose will make her journey. The *possibility* that she would keep on even if he were dead is there in her devotion and its single-minded, single-track errand. Certainly the *artistic* truth, which should be good enough for the fact, lies in Phoenix's own answer to that question. When the nurse asks, "He isn't dead, is he?" she speaks for herself: "He still the same. He going to last."

The grandchild is the incentive. But it is the journey, the going of the errand, that is the story, and the question is not whether the grandchild is in reality alive or dead. It doesn't affect the outcome of the story or its meaning from start to finish. But it is not the question itself that has struck me as much as the idea, almost without exception implied in the asking, that for Phoenix's grandson to be dead would somehow make the story "better."

It's *all right*, I want to say to the students who write to me, for things to be what they appear to be, and for words to mean what they say. It's all right, too, for words and appearances to mean more than one thing — ambiguity is a fact of life. A fiction writer's responsibility covers not only what he presents as the facts of a given story but what he chooses to stir up as their implications; in the end, these implications, too, become facts, in the larger, fictional sense. But it is not all right, not in good faith, for things *not* to mean what they say.

The grandson's plight was real and it made the truth of the story, which is the story of an errand of love carried out. If the child no longer lived, the truth would persist in the "wornness" of the path. But his being dead can't increase the truth of the story, can't affect it one way or the other. I think I signal this, because the end of the story has been reached before old Phoenix gets home again: she simply starts back. To the question "Is the grandson really dead?" I could reply that it doesn't make any difference. I could also say that I did not make him up in order to let him play a trick on Phoenix. But my best answer would be: "*Phoenix is alive.*"

The origin of a story is sometimes a trustworthy clue to the author — or can provide him with the clue — to its key image; maybe in this case it will do the same for the reader. One day I saw a solitary old woman like Phoenix. She was walking; I saw her, at middle distance, in a winter country landscape, and watched her slowly make her way across my line of vision. That sight of her made me write the story. I invented an errand for her, but that only seemed a living part of the figure she was herself: What errand other than for someone else could be making her go? And her going was the first thing, her persisting in her landscape was the real thing, and the first and the real were what I wanted and worked to keep. I brought her up close enough, by imagination, to describe her face, make her present to the eyes, but the full-length figure moving across the winter fields was the indelible one and the image to keep, and the perspective extending into the vanishing distance the true one to hold in mind.

I invented for my character, as I wrote, some passing adventures — some dreams and harassments and a small triumph or two, some jolts to her pride, some flights of fancy to console her, one or two encounters to scare her, a moment that gave her cause to feel ashamed, a moment to dance and preen — for it had to be a *journey*, and all these things belonged to that, parts of life's uncertainty.

A narrative line is in its deeper sense, of course, the tracing out of a meaning, and the real continuity of a story lies in this probing forward. The real dramatic force of a story depends on the strength of the emotion that has set it going. The emotional value is the measure of the reach of the story. What gives any such content to "A Worn Path" is not its circumstances but its *subject*: the deep-grained habit of love.

What I hoped would come clear was that in the whole surround of this story, the world it threads through, the only certain thing at all is the worn path. The habit of love cuts through confusion and stumbles or contrives its way out of difficulty, it remembers the way even when it forgets, for a dumfounded moment, its reason for being. The path is the thing that matters.

Her victory — old Phoenix's — is when she sees the diploma in the doctor's office, when she finds "nailed up on the wall the document that had been stamped with the gold seal and framed in the gold frame, which matched the dream that was hung up in her head." The return with the medicine is just a matter of retracing her own footsteps. It is the part of the journey, and of the story, that can now go without saying.

In the matter of function, old Phoenix's way might even do as a sort of parallel to your way of work if you are a writer of stories. The way to get there is the all-important, all-absorbing problem, and this problem is your reason for undertaking the story. Your only guide, too, is your sureness about your subject, about what this subject is. Like Phoenix, you work all your life to find your way, through all the obstructions and the false appearances and the upsets you may have brought on yourself, to reach a meaning — using inventions of your imagination, perhaps helped out by your dreams and bits of good luck. And finally too, like Phoenix, you have to assume that what you are working in aid of is life, not death.

But you would make the trip anyway — wouldn't you? — just on hope.

PART THREE

CASEBOOKS

This part of the anthology assembles background material into seven casebooks for in-depth study of individual authors and stories. James Baldwin's "Sonny's Blues," Charlotte Perkins Gilman's "The Yellow Wallpaper," and Joyce Carol Oates's "Where Are You Going, Where Have You Been?" are the short stories, and Raymond Carver and Flannery O'Connor are the individual authors. Gathered here are commentaries on the two authors in different literary forms ranging from informal letters to formal essays, plus a variety of approaches to the stories taken by literary critics.

The next casebook explores the background of Magical Realism, a type of storytelling that came into its own in the mid-twentieth century. Statements by authors Jorge Luis Borges, Alejo Carpentier, Mario Vargas Llosa, William Gass, Ursula K. Le Guin, and the literary critic Luis Leal help to clarify what in Le Guin's opinion is perhaps "the kind of fiction most characteristic of our times."

A final casebook looks at graphic storytelling to help you understand this newly popular medium of telling stories. The excerpts include statements by the authors Alison Bechdel and Joe Sacco, as well as commentaries by the critics Charles Hatfield, Michael Kupperman, Sydney Plum, and Edward Said.

JAMES BALDWIN'S
"Sonny's Blues"

American author and civil rights activist James Baldwin listens to a reporter's question with a smile during an interview at the Whitehall Hotel in London in 1964.

James Baldwin presented "Autobiographical Notes" (p. 1544), his account of how he became a writer, in his book *Notes of a Native Son* (1955). There he admitted that "the most difficult (and most rewarding) thing in my life has been the fact that I was born a Negro and was forced, therefore, to effect some kind of truce with this reality." Also included in this casebook on "Sonny's Blues" is a commentary by Keith E. Byerman (p. 1548) on Baldwin's use of words and music to achieve narrative ambiguity. This article appeared in *Studies in Short Fiction 19* (1982). Kenneth A. McClane's personal essay on "Sonny's Blues" (p. 1553) was published in *You've Got to Read This: Contemporary American Writers Introduce Stories That Held Them in Awe* (1994), edited by Ron Hansen and Jim Shepard.

JAMES BALDWIN

Autobiographical Notes

1955

I was born in Harlem thirty-one years ago. I began plotting novels at about the time I learned to read. The story of my childhood is the usual bleak fantasy, and we can dismiss it with the unrestrained observation that I certainly would not consider living it again. In those days my mother was given to the exasperating and mysterious habit of having babies. As they were born, I took them over with one hand and held a book with the other. The children probably suffered, though they have since been kind enough to deny it, and in this way I read *Uncle Tom's Cabin* and *A Tale of Two Cities* over and over and over again; in this way, in fact, I read just about everything I could get my hands on — except the Bible, probably because it was the only book I was encouraged to read. I must also confess that I wrote — a great deal — and my first professional triumph, in any case, the first effort of mine to be seen in print, occurred at the age of twelve or thereabouts, when a short story I had written about the Spanish revolution won some sort of prize in an extremely short-lived church newspaper. I remember the story was censored by the lady editor, though I don't remember why, and I was outraged.

Also wrote plays, and songs, for one of which I received a letter of congratulations from Mayor La Guardia, and poetry, about which the less said, the better. My mother was delighted by all these goings-on, but my father wasn't; he wanted me to be a preacher. When I was fourteen I became a preacher, and when I was seventeen I stopped. Very shortly thereafter I left home. For God knows how long I struggled with the world of commerce and industry — I guess they would say they struggled with *me* — and when I was about twenty-one I had enough done of a novel to get a Saxton Fellowship. When I was twenty-two the fellowship was over, the novel turned out to be unsalable, and I started waiting on tables in a Village[1] restaurant and writing book reviews — mostly, as it turned out, about the Negro problem, concerning which the color of my skin made me automatically an expert. Did another book, in company with photographer Theodore Pelatowski, about the storefront churches in Harlem. This book met exactly the same fate as my first — fellowship, but no sale. (It was a Rosenwald Fellowship.) By the time I was twenty-four I had decided to stop reviewing books about the Negro problem — which, by this time, was only slightly less horrible in print than it was in life — and I packed my bags and went to France, where I finished, God knows how, *Go Tell It on the Mountain*.

---

[1] Greenwich Village, New York City.

Two boys and a man play ball in a vacant lot. Harlem, 1954. New York World-Telegram and the Sun Newspaper Photograph Collection.

    Any writer, I suppose, feels that the world into which he was born is nothing less than a conspiracy against the cultivation of his talent — which attitude certainly has a great deal to support it. On the other hand, it is only because the world looks on his talent with such a frightening indifference that the artist is compelled to make his talent important. So that any writer, looking back over even so short a span of time as I am here forced to assess, finds that the things which hurt him and the things which helped him cannot be divorced from each other; he could be helped in a certain way only because he was hurt in a certain way; and his help is simply to be enabled to move from one conundrum to the next — one is tempted to say that he moves from one disaster to the next. When one begins looking for influences one finds them by the score. I haven't thought much about my own, not enough anyway; I hazard that the King James Bible, the rhetoric of the store-front church, something ironic and violent and perpetually understated in Negro speech — and something of Dickens' love for bravura — have something to do with me today; but I wouldn't stake my life on it. Likewise, innumerable people have helped me in many ways; but finally, I suppose, the most difficult (and most rewarding) thing in my life has been the fact that I was born a Negro and was forced, therefore, to effect some kind of truce with this reality. (Truce, by the way, is the best one can hope for.)

One of the difficulties about being a Negro writer (and this is not special pleading, since I don't mean to suggest that he has it worse than anybody else) is that the Negro problem is written about so widely. The bookshelves groan under the weight of information, and everyone therefore considers himself informed. And this information, furthermore, operates usually (generally, popularly) to reinforce traditional attitudes. Of traditional attitudes there are only two — For or Against — and I, personally, find it difficult to say which attitude has caused me the most pain. I am perfectly aware that the change from ill-will to good-will, however motivated, however imperfect, however expressed, is better than no change at all.

But it is part of the business of the writer — as I see it — to examine attitudes, to go beneath the surface, to tap the source. From this point of view the Negro problem is nearly inaccessible. It is not only written about so widely; it is written about so badly. It is quite possible to say that the price a Negro pays for becoming articulate is to find himself, at length, with nothing to be articulate about. ("You taught me the language," says Caliban to Prospero,[2] "and my profit on't is I know how to curse.") Consider: The tremendous social activity that this problem generates imposes on whites and Negroes alike the necessity of looking forward, of working to bring about a better day. This is fine, it keeps the waters troubled; it is all, indeed, that has made possible the Negro's progress. Nevertheless, social affairs are not generally speaking the writer's prime concern, whether they ought to be or not; it is absolutely necessary that he establish between himself and these affairs a distance that will allow, at least, for clarity, so that before he can look forward in any meaningful sense, he must first be allowed to take a long look back. In the context of the Negro problem neither whites nor blacks, for excellent reasons of their own, have the faintest desire to look back; but I think that the past is all that makes the present coherent, and further, that the past will remain horrible for exactly as long as we refuse to assess it honestly.

I know, in any case, that the most crucial time in my own development came when I was forced to recognize that I was a kind of bastard of the West; when I followed the line of my past I did not find myself in Europe but in Africa. And this meant that in some subtle way, in a really profound way, I brought to Shakespeare, Bach, Rembrandt, to the stones of Paris, to the cathedral at Chartres, and to the Empire State Building, a special attitude. These were not really my creations, they did not contain my history; I might search in them in vain forever for any reflection of myself. I was an interloper; this was not my heritage. At the same time I had no other heritage which I could possibly hope to use — I had certainly been unfitted for the jungle or the tribe. I would have to appropriate these white centuries, I would have to make them mine — I would have to accept my special attitude, my special place in this scheme — otherwise I would have no place in *any* scheme. What was the most difficult was the fact that I was forced to admit something I had always hidden from myself, which the American Negro has had to hide from himself as

---

[2] In Shakespeare's *The Tempest*, the monster Caliban is a servant of the magician Prospero.

the price of his public progress; that I hated and feared white people. This did not mean that I loved black people; on the contrary, I despised them, possibly because they failed to produce Rembrandt. In effect, I hated and feared the world. And this meant, not only that I thus gave the world an altogether murderous power over me, but also that in such a self-destroying limbo I could never hope to write.

One writes out of one thing only — one's own experience. Everything depends on how relentlessly one forces from this experience the last drop, sweet or bitter, it can possibly give. This is the only real concern of the artist, to recreate out of the disorder of life that order which is art. The difficulty then, for me, of being a Negro writer was the fact that I was, in effect, prohibited from examining my own experience too closely by the tremendous demands and the very real dangers of my social situation.

I don't think the dilemma outlined above is uncommon. I do think, since writers work in the disastrously explicit medium of language, that it goes a little way towards explaining why, out of the enormous resources of Negro speech and life, and despite the example of Negro music, prose written by Negroes has been generally speaking so pallid and so harsh. I have not written about being a Negro at such length because I expect that to be my only subject, but only because it was the gate I had to unlock before I could hope to write about anything else. I don't think that the Negro problem in America can be even discussed coherently without bearing in mind its context; its context being the history, traditions, customs, the moral assumptions and preoccupations of the country; in short, the general social fabric. Appearances to the contrary, no one in America escapes its effects and everyone in America bears some responsibility for it. I believe this the more firmly because it is the overwhelming tendency to speak of this problem as though it were a thing apart. But in the work of Faulkner, in the general attitude and certain specific passages in Robert Penn Warren,[3] and, most significantly, in the advent of Ralph Ellison, one sees the beginnings — at least — of a more genuinely penetrating search. Mr. Ellison, by the way, is the first Negro novelist I have ever read to utilize in language, and brilliantly, some of the ambiguity and irony of Negro life.

About my interests: I don't know if I have any, unless the morbid desire to own a sixteen-millimeter camera and make experimental movies can be so classified. Otherwise, I love to eat and drink — it's my melancholy conviction that I've scarcely ever had enough to eat (this is because it's *impossible* to eat enough if you're worried about the next meal) — and I love to argue with people who do not disagree with me too profoundly, and I love to laugh. I do *not* like bohemia, or bohemians, I do not like people whose principal aim is pleasure, and I do not like people who are *earnest* about anything. I don't like people who like me because I'm a Negro; neither do I like people who find in the same accident grounds for contempt. I love America more than any other country in the world, and, exactly for this reason, I insist on the right to criticize her perpetually. I think all theories are suspect, that the finest principles

---

[3] Robert Penn Warren (1905–1989), American novelist, poet, and critic.

may have to be modified, or may even be pulverized by the demands of life, and that one must find, therefore, one's own moral center and move through the world hoping that this center will guide one aright. I consider that I have many responsibilities, but none greater than this: to last, as Hemingway says, and get my work done.

I want to be an honest man and a good writer.

KEITH E. BYERMAN
Words and Music: Narrative Ambiguity in "Sonny's Blues"

1982

"Sonny's Blues" has generally been accorded status as the best of James Baldwin's short stories. It tells of the developing relationship between Sonny, a musician and drug addict, and the narrator, his brother, who feels a conflict between the security of his middle-class life and the emotional risks of brotherhood with Sonny. The critics, who differ on whether the story is primarily Sonny's or the narrator's, generally agree that it resolves its central conflict.[1] If, however, resolution is not assumed but taken as problematical, then new thematic and structural possibilities are revealed. The story becomes a study of the nature and relationship of art and language. The commentary on the story has centered on the moral issue; the purpose of this essay is to focus on the underlying aesthetic question.

According to Jonathan Culler, resolution can be accomplished in a story when a message is received or a code deciphered.[2] In most cases the message is withheld in some manner—through deception, innocence, or ignorance—until a key moment in the narrative. In the case of "Sonny's Blues," however, the message is apparent from the beginning and is repeatedly made available to the narrator. The story, in part, is about his misreadings; more importantly, it is about his inability to read properly. The source of this inability is his reliance on a language that is at once rationalistic and

---

[1] See Stanley Macebuh, *James Baldwin: A Critical Study* (New York: Third World Press, 1973); Sherley Anne Williams, *Give Birth to Brightness* (New York: Dial, 1972), pp. 145–166; Harry L. Jones, "Style, Form and Content in the Short Fiction of James Baldwin," *James Baldwin: A Critical Evaluation*, ed. Therman O'Daniel (Washington, D.C.: Howard UP, 1977), pp. 143–150; Suzy Bernstein Goldman, "James Baldwin's 'Sonny's Blues': A Message in Music," *Negro American Literature Forum* 8 (1974), pp. 231–233; John Reilly, "'Sonny's Blues': James Baldwin's Image of Black Community," *Negro American Literature Forum* 4 (1970), pp. 56–60; and Donald C. Murray, "James Baldwin's 'Sonny's Blues': Complicated and Simple," *Studies in Short Fiction* 14 (1977), pp. 353–357. [All notes except note 4 are Byerman's.]

[2] *Structuralist Poetics: Structuralism, Linguistics, and the Study of Literature* (Ithaca: Cornell UP, 1975), pp. 202–238.

metaphoric. His sentences are always complete and balanced, and his figurative language puts on display his literary intelligence. Even in the description of his own emotional states, the verbal pattern overshadows the experience. Whenever the message is delivered, he evades it through language; he creates and then reads substitute texts, such as the messenger, or distorts the sense of the message by changing it to fit his preconceived ideas.

The message is first presented in the simplest, most straightforward manner, as a newspaper story: "I read about it in the paper, in the subway, on my way to work. I read it, and I couldn't believe it, and I read it again. Then perhaps I just stared at it, at the newsprint spelling out his name, spelling out the story."[3] The information is clearly there, "spelled out," a text that cannot be ignored. But the narrator's immediate action is to refract his emotions through metaphor: "I stared at it in the swinging lights of the subway car, and in the faces and bodies of the people, and in my own face, trapped in the darkness which roared outside" [p. 40]. This oblique allusion to the underground man is followed in the next paragraph by a reference to the ice at the center of his emotional Inferno. What is noteworthy is that these images call attention to themselves as images and not simply as natural expressions of emotional intensity. His response has built into it a strong sense of the need for proper verbal expression. This deflection from emotion to art is accompanied by repeated statements on the impossibility of believing the message.

The second scene dramatizes and verifies the information presented by the newspaper story. The narrator encounters an addict who had been a friend of Sonny's. In fact, "I saw this boy standing in the shadow of a doorway, looking just like Sonny" [p. 41]. Again there is a darkness and an explicit identification with Sonny. Again there is distancing through figurative language: "But now, abruptly, I hated him. I couldn't stand the way he looked at me, partly like a dog, partly like a cunning child" [p. 41]. Such language prepares us for, while guaranteeing, the failed communication of this episode. The narrator is offered knowledge, but he chooses to interpret the messenger rather than the message. He expresses a desire to know, and remorse when he does not listen, but he also repeats his unwillingness to understand.

A further complication occurs when, in the midst of this encounter, the narrator turns his attention from the addict to the music being played in a bar. The mark of his refusal to know is in his act of interpreting those associated with the music. "The juke box was blasting away with something black and bouncy and I half watched the barmaid as she danced her way from the juke box to her place behind the bar. And I watched her face as she laughingly responded to something someone said to her, still keeping time to the music. When she smiled one saw the little girl, one sensed the doomed, still-struggling woman beneath the battered face of the semi-whore" [p. 42]. Rather than listen to the conversation he is directly involved in, the narrator observes one he cannot possibly hear. In the process, he can distance himself by labeling the woman

---

[3] "Sonny's Blues," *Going to Meet the Man* (1965; rpt. New York: Dell, 1976), p. 86. [See p. 40; subsequent page citations in the text have been changed to refer to this anthology.]

he sees. He is thereby at once protected from and superior to the situation. The music, a motif repeated in subsequent scenes, here is part of what the narrator refuses to know; he substitutes his words for the non-verbal communication that music offers. In telling the incident, he suggests that he is listening to the music to avoid the addict-messenger; in fact, their messages are identical, and he avoids both by imposing his verbal pattern.

A similar evasion occurs in the next major scene, which is a flashback within a flashback. The narrator's mother, after hearing her son reassure her that nothing will happen to Sonny, tells him the story of his father and uncle, a story that parallels the one occurring in the present time of the narration. Her story, of the uncle's death and the father's inability to prevent it, is a parable of proper brotherly relationships. After telling the tale, she indicates its relevance: "'I ain't telling you all this,' she said, 'to make you scared or bitter or to make you hate nobody. I'm telling you this because you got a brother. And the world ain't changed'" [p. 49]. The narrator immediately offers his interpretation: "'Don't you worry, I won't forget. I won't let nothing happen to Sonny'" [p. 49]. His mother corrects his impression: "'You may not be able to stop nothing from happening. But you got to let him know you's *there*'" [p. 49].

No ambiguity can be found here. The message is clearly delivered, in transparent, non-metaphoric language. What prevents it from being received can only be the substitutions in the pattern. The musically talented uncle is Sonny's double and the helpless father is the narrator's. This parallel structure makes the point obvious to the reader, but the fact that it is *only* parallel justifies the continuation of the narrative. In his positivistic way, the narrator will not believe what does not occur to his immediate experience or what cannot be contained within his linguistic net. His mother's fatalistic message cannot be so contained. Thus, the story must continue until he has both evidence and the means of controlling it.

The final scene of the story, instead of validating the meaning, only deepens the ambiguity. The bar where Sonny plays and the people in it are presented as alien to the narrator's experience. The room is dark and narrow, suggestive not only of a birth passage, but also of the subway where the narrator first felt troubled by Sonny. The musicians tend to fit stereotypes of blacks: Creole, the band leader is "an enormous black man" and the drummer, "a coal-black, cheerful-looking man, built close to the ground . . . his teeth gleaming like a lighthouse and his laugh coming up out of him like the beginning of an earthquake" [p. 59]. The language grows more serious when the music itself begins: "All I know about music is that not many people ever really hear it. And even when on the rare occasion when something opens within, and the music enters, what we mainly hear, or hear corroborated, are personal, private, vanishing evocations. But the man who created the music is hearing something else, is dealing with the roar rising from the void and imposing order on it as it hits the air. What is evoked in him, then, is of another order, more terrible because it has no words, and triumphant, too, for that same reason" [p. 60]. Little preparation has been made for such a reaction to the music. The act of the musician seems a creative response to the impinging chaos described in

Charlie Parker (far right) playing the alto saxophone at the Birdland Restaurant in New York, 1949.

the opening subway scene. But this perception springs full-bodied from the brow of a man who has repeatedly indicated his antagonism to such music. One resolution of this apparent contradiction might be found in his comment about the terrible wordlessness of what he is hearing. A man committed to language, he finds himself confronted with a form whose power seems precisely its ability to create order without language.

In this context, it is highly significant that he immediately undertakes to explain the music through the metaphor of conversation. "The dry, low, black man said something awful on the drums, Creole answered, and the drums talked back. Then the horn insisted, sweet and high, slightly detached perhaps, and Creole listened, commenting now and then, dry, and driving, beautiful and calm and old" [p. 61]. If the terror of the music is its lack of words, then to explain it as language is to neutralize its power. By creating the metaphor, the narrator can control his experience and limit its effect. He can make the music fit the patterns that he chooses.

This is not readily apparent in what he calls the "tale" of Sonny's music. "For, while the tale of how we suffer, and how we are delighted, and how we may triumph is never new, it always must be heard. There isn't any other tale to tell, it's the only light we've got in all this darkness" [p. 61]. While music is changed to language, with the attendant change in meaning, and while the obsession is still with bringing light and thus reason, the narrator is opening up the meaning with reference to "we" and to the emotional conditions of suffering and delight. His language seems less logical and self-consciously artistic than before.

The specifics of the tale strengthen its emotional impact. The music frees the narrator and perhaps Sonny: "Freedom lurked around us and I understood, at last, that he could help us to be free if we would listen, that he would never be free until we did" [p. 62]. The narrator's freedom comes through his recapturing and acceptance of the past; the music conjures up his mother's face, his uncle's death, Grace's death accompanied by Isabel's tears "and I felt my own tears begin to rise" [p. 62]. Yet for all the emotional content, the form remains very logically, artistically structured. Sentences are very carefully balanced and arranged, the emotion is carried on such verbs as "saw" and "felt," and finally "we," after a series of generalizations, quickly becomes "I" again. This scene only has to be compared to the prologue of *Invisible Man* to demonstrate the extent of control. Both scenes deal with the emotional impact of the blues, but whereas Ellison's is surrealistic and high paradoxical, with its narrator barely living through the history of the vision, Baldwin's narrator remains firmly planted in the bar and firmly in control of the emotion he describes.

The story's underlying ambiguity has its richest expression in the final metaphor, a cocktail that the narrator sends to Sonny. As a symbolic representation of the message of the narrative, the scotch and milk transformed into the cup of trembling suggests the relief from suffering that YHWH[4] promised the children of Israel. Thus, Sonny's suffering will be made easier by the narrator's willingness to be involved in his life. But, as in earlier cases, this is not the only possible reading. First, the drink itself, scotch and milk, is an emblem of simultaneous destruction and nurture to the system; it cannot be reduced to one or the other. Sonny's acceptance of it indicates that his life will continue on the edge between the poison of his addiction and the nourishment of his music.

The narrator's reading of the drink as the cup of trembling offers a second ambiguity, which is not consistent with the first, for it implies clear alternatives. The cup of trembling was taken from Israel when YHWH chose to forgive the people for their transgressions. But it was YHWH who had given the cup of suffering to them in the first place.[5] Thus, it becomes important to the meaning of the story which verse is being alluded to in the metaphor. If the cup is given, then Sonny will continue to suffer and feel guilt; if the cup is taken away, then Sonny returns to a state of grace. There is no Biblical reference to the cup merely remaining.

The choice of image indicates the continuation of the narrator's practice of reading events through the vehicle of his own language. But the very limits of language itself raise problems as to the meaning of the narrative. The need to turn an act into a metaphor and thereby "enrich" the meaning depends upon

---

[4]Letters symbolizing the name of God in Hebrew.
[5]See Isaiah 51:17–23.

limitation in the use of language. The words, though, carry traces of meaning not intended. The result, as in this case, can be that the meaning can carry with it its very opposite. In such a situation, intended meaning is lost in the very richness of meaning.

"Sonny's Blues," then, is a story of a narrator caught in the "prison-house of language."[6] Both in describing experiences and explaining them, he is locked into a linguistic pattern that restricts his understanding. With the presentation of such a character, Baldwin offers an insight into the limits of language and the narrative art. In the very act of telling his story, the narrator falsifies (as do all storytellers) because he must use words to express what is beyond words. The irony is that much of Baldwin's own writing — essays, novels, stories — is premised on the transparency and sufficiency of language rather than on its duplicity.

Clearly a dialectic is at work. "Sonny's Blues" moves within the tension between its openly stated message of order and a community of understanding and its covert questioning, through form, allusion, and ambiguity, of the relationship between life and art. With the latter, the story suggests that literary art contributes to deceit and perhaps anarchy rather than understanding and order. What makes this tension dialectical is that the artifice of narration is necessary for the existence of the story and its overt message. The measure of Baldwin's success is his ability to keep this tension so well hidden, not his ability to resolve the conflict. What finally makes "Sonny's Blues" such a good story is its author's skill at concealing the fact that he must lie in order to tell the truth.

---

[6] The phrase comes from Frederic Jameson, *The Prison-House of Language: A Critical Account of Structuralism and Russian Formalism* (Princeton: Princeton UP, 1972).

KENNETH A. McCLANE

"Sonny's Blues" Saved My Life

1994

"Sonny's Blues" saved my life, and I am not being hyperbolic. In 1982, my brother Paul killed himself. He was an alcoholic, a brilliant jazz drummer, a tough, truculent kid, and an inspiration to his older brother, who, although not always understanding *who* Paul was, knew who Paul was not — and that was someone who was scared, timid, or obsequious. Paul did not talk much. If anything, he hated where we lived in Harlem; more precisely, he hated *how* we lived; and no one, in all my memory, ever made my brother cower. Life would lead him to more and more improbable scenarios — at first he was a college student, then a drifter, and all too soon he was on to drugs and alcohol. And yet Paul was strangely gentle and circumspect: his many girlfriends loved his characteristic good cheer — they knew him to be in their corner, and he had that ability (which is always the provender of the outwardly giving) to love those outside his immediate environs while dismissing those at his feet. If Paul was remote to his family, we were similarly distant. And yet he loved us and we him: one could glimpse it in the messiness of our interactions, the buoyancy which too often became icy. I vividly recall the many times when he walked up to his room, closed the door, and played his drums into the next morning, finally descending to have a bowl of cereal, sometimes providing a slight nod to one of us — and then, always returning to *that* room and its privacy. Paul would go to his drums, as he would travel through Harlem, with a saucy, ragged coolness. Those of you who know Baldwin's Sonny know my brother Paul.

Two years Paul's senior, I was, in every way, his absolute opposite. Where he was fearless and an inveterate street-blood, I was cautious, frightened, and retiring. Sometimes, he would push me to go out and I would beg off, suggesting that I wanted to see a movie or read a book. It was a lie, and Paul knew it. As he once said, half jokingly, "You live by not living."

When I began to teach at Cornell, Paul would often call me. We rarely talked about anything serious: Paul would hold court; I would pretend to be more in touch with life than I really was; the whole thing was rather comical. Then, one Friday, I received a call from my father telling me that Paul was dying. It was a surreal conversation, my father understandably uncontrollable, his son lying in a coma, his older son, hardly believing the inevitable: *Your brother is going to die.* Paul was in a New York hospital. I had best come immediately.

As luck would have it, I had been teaching summer school, and a student had suggested that we read James Baldwin's "Sonny's Blues" for our next class. Needing something to do and feigning to be the dutiful teacher, I read Baldwin's story on the plane ride to the hospital. It was a gift. The story involves an older unnamed man and his younger brother, Sonny, who is a jazz pianist and a heroin addict. The older brother is *safe* — that is, he has a job and a wonderful wife and has, at least temporarily, made peace with his existence. He is not rich, nor has he been able to truly escape Harlem — where he lives and where "dangers loom everywhere" — but he is a teacher. The younger brother, however, is menaced by his need to make life bearable.

The story, of course, is about much more, including love and how human beings cannot protect anyone, the reality that "sorrow never gets stopped," and the inexorable fact that the best among us may not survive — that life, sadly, often takes those whose dreams are greatest, whose voices are most needed. As the mother tells the far too cocky older brother when he protests that she needn't worry about Sonny, "It ain't only the bad ones, nor yet the dumb ones that gets sucked under." The older brother, at this early narrative moment, does not understand his mother; he is too caught in his own needful simplicity; reality is simply too costly. Yet as the story reminds, life is not interested in one's comfort, and the darkness — the terrors inside and outside — loom just above one's head.

"Sonny's Blues" saved my life. When my brother died, I felt terribly guilty. To my thinking I had not done all I could: I hadn't listened with enough passion; I had been too self-concerned, too self-infested. And yet the story admonishes that there is no ultimate safety, that a brother or a loved one may die (no matter what one does), and that, in the mother's wondrous and provident words, "You may not be able to stop nothing from happening. But you got to let him know you's *there*."

However tentatively and inappropriately, I did try to be my brother's witness. That I ultimately failed is certainly true: Paul is dead. But I am, at this hour, at this writing, *listening* to Sonny. *Deep water and drowning are not the same thing.* And yet they can be. And one can fall even further, farther. Baldwin does not lie about the landscape of suffering. Baldwin, quite simply, does not lie.

RAYMOND CARVER

Raymond Carver photographed in Paris, France in 1987.

Raymond Carver offers a clear example of how a contemporary author has responded to the work of earlier short story writers by following a line of thought that links him with his predecessors. In his essay "On Writing," Carver acknowledged the influence of Ernest Hemingway and Flannery O'Connor. He also described his class with the young novelist John Gardner at Chico State College in California in "Creative Writing 101" (p. 1560). "The Bath" (p. 1564) is an early version of "A Small, Good Thing" (p. 210) after the story was cut by 78 percent by editor Gordon Lish for publication in Carver's *What We Talk About When We Talk About Love* (1981). Carver's letters to Lish, protesting the cuts in his stories, are included in the notes on the texts in Carver's *Collected Stories,* published by the Library of America in 2009.

Also included in this casebook are essays by Tom Jenks ("The Origin of 'Cathedral,'" p. 1643), Arthur M. Saltzman ("A Reading of 'What We Talk About When We Talk About Love,'" p. 1570), and A. O. Scott ("Looking for Raymond Carver," p. 1572).

RAYMOND CARVER

On Writing

1981

Back in the mid-1960s, I found I was having trouble concentrating my attention on long narrative fiction. For a time I experienced difficulty in trying to read it as well as in attempting to write it. My attention span had gone out on me; I no longer had the patience to try to write novels. It's an involved story, too tedious to talk about here. But I know it has much to do now with why I write poems and short stories. Get in, get out. Don't linger. Go on. It could be that I lost any great ambitions at about the same time, in my late twenties. If I did, I think it was good it happened. Ambition and a little luck are good things for a writer to have going for him. Too much ambition and bad luck, or no luck at all, can be killing. There has to be talent.

Some writers have a bunch of talent; I don't know any writers who are without it. But a unique and exact way of looking at things, and finding the right context for expressing that way of looking, that's something else. *The World According to Garp* is, of course, the marvelous world according to John Irving. There is another world according to Flannery O'Connor, and others according to William Faulkner and Ernest Hemingway. There are worlds according to Cheever, Updike, Singer, Stanley Elkin, Ann Beattie, Cynthia Ozick, Donald Barthelme, Mary Robison, William Kittredge, Barry Hannah, Ursula K. Le Guin. Every great or even every very good writer makes the world over according to his own specifications.

It's akin to style, what I'm talking about, but it isn't style alone. It is the writer's particular and unmistakable signature on everything he writes. It is his world and no other. This is one of the things that distinguishes one writer from another. Not talent. There's plenty of that around. But a writer who has some special way of looking at things and who gives artistic expression to that way of looking: that writer may be around for a time.

Isak Dinesen said that she wrote a little every day, without hope and without despair. Someday I'll put that on a three-by-five card and tape it to the wall beside my desk. I have some three-by-five cards on the wall now. "Fundamental accuracy of statement is the ONE sole morality of writing." Ezra Pound. It is not everything by ANY means, but if a writer has "fundamental accuracy of statement" going for him, he's at least on the right track.

I have a three-by-five up there with this fragment of a sentence from a story by Chekhov: ". . . and suddenly everything became clear to him." I find these words filled with wonder and possibility. I love their simple clarity, and the hint of revelation that's implied. There is mystery, too. What has been unclear before? Why is it just now becoming clear? What's happened? Most of all — what now? There are consequences as a result of such sudden awakenings. I feel a sharp sense of relief — and anticipation.

I overheard the writer Geoffrey Wolff say "No cheap tricks" to a group of writing students. That should go on a three-by-five card. I'd amend it a little to "No tricks." Period. I hate tricks. At the first sign of a trick or a gimmick in a piece of fiction, a cheap trick or even an elaborate trick, I tend to look for cover. Tricks are ultimately boring, and I get bored easily, which may go along with my not having much of an attention span. But extremely clever chi-chi writing, or just plain tomfoolery writing, puts me to sleep. Writers don't need tricks or gimmicks or even necessarily need to be the smartest fellows on the block. At the risk of appearing foolish, a writer sometimes needs to be able to just stand and gape at this or that thing — a sunset or an old shoe — in absolute and simple amazement.

Some months back, in the *New York Times Book Review*, John Barth said that ten years ago most of the students in his fiction writing seminar were interested in "formal innovation," and this no longer seems to be the case. He's a little worried that writers are going to start writing mom-and-pop novels in the 1980s. He worries that experimentation may be on the way out, along with liberalism. I get a little nervous if I find myself within earshot of somber discussions about "formal innovation" in fiction writing. Too often "experimentation" is a license to be careless, silly, or imitative in the writing. Even worse, a license to try to brutalize or alienate the reader. Too often such writing gives us no news of the world, or else describes a desert landscape and that's all — a few dunes and lizards here and there, but no people; a place uninhabited by anything recognizably human, a place of interest only to a few scientific specialists.

It should be noted that real experiment in fiction is original, hard-earned and cause for rejoicing. But someone else's way of looking at things — Barthelme's, for instance — should not be chased after by other writers. It won't work. There is only one Barthelme, and for another writer to try to appropriate Barthelme's peculiar sensibility or mise en scène under the rubric of innovation is for that writer to mess around with chaos and disaster and, worse, self-deception. The real experimenters have to Make It New, as Pound urged, and in the process have to find things out for themselves. But if writers haven't taken leave of their senses, they also want to stay in touch with us, they want to carry news from their world to ours.

It's possible, in a poem or a short story, to write about commonplace things and objects using commonplace but precise language, and to endow those things — a chair, a window curtain, a fork, a stone, a woman's earring — with immense, even startling power. It is possible to write a line of seemingly innocuous dialogue and have it send a chill along the reader's spine — the source of artistic delight, as Nabokov would have it. That's the kind of writing that most interests me. I hate sloppy or haphazard writing whether it flies under the banner of experimentation or else is just clumsily rendered realism. In Isaac Babel's wonderful short story, "Guy de Maupassant," the narrator has this to say about the writing of fiction: "No iron can pierce the heart with such force as a period put just at the right place." This too ought to go on a three-by-five.

Evan Connell said once that he knew he was finished with a short story when he found himself going through it and taking out commas and then going through the story again and putting commas back in the same places. I like that way of working on something. I respect that kind of care for what is being done. That's all we have, finally, the words, and they had better be the right ones, with the punctuation in the right places so that they can best say what they are meant to say. If the words are heavy with the writer's own unbridled emotions, or if they are imprecise and inaccurate for some other reason — if the words are in any way blurred — the reader's eyes will slide right over them and nothing will be achieved. The reader's own artistic sense will simply not be engaged. Henry James called this sort of hapless writing "weak specification."

I have friends who've told me they had to hurry a book because they needed the money, their editor or their wife was leaning on them or leaving them — something, some apology for the writing not being very good. "It would have been better if I'd taken the time." I was dumbfounded when I heard a novelist friend say this. I still am, if I think about it, which I don't. It's none of my business. But if the writing can't be made as good as it is within us to make it, then why do it? In the end, the satisfaction of having done our best, and the proof of that labor, is the one thing we can take into the grave. I wanted to say to my friend, for heaven's sake go do something else. There have to be easier and maybe more honest ways to try and earn a living. Or else just do it to the best of your abilities, your talents, and then don't justify or make excuses. Don't complain, don't explain.

In an essay called, simply enough, "Writing Short Stories," Flannery O'Connor talks about writing as an act of discovery. O'Connor says she most often did not know where she was going when she sat down to work on a short story. She says she doubts that many writers know where they are going when they begin something. She uses "Good Country People" as an example of how she put together a short story whose ending she could not even guess at until she was nearly there:

> When I started writing that story, I didn't know there was going to be a Ph.D. with a wooden leg in it. I merely found myself one morning writing a description of two women I knew something about, and before I realized it, I had equipped one of them with a daughter with a wooden leg. I brought in the Bible salesman, but I had no idea what I was going to do with him. I didn't know he was going to steal that wooden leg until ten or twelve lines before he did it, but when I found out that this was what was going to happen, I realized it was inevitable.

When I read this some years ago it came as a shock that she, or anyone for that matter, wrote stories in this fashion. I thought this was my uncomfortable secret, and I was a little uneasy with it. For sure I thought this way of working on a short story somehow revealed my own shortcomings. I remember being tremendously heartened by reading what she had to say on the subject.

I once sat down to write what turned out to be a pretty good story, though only the first sentence of the story had offered itself to me when I began it. For several days I'd been going around with this sentence in my head: "He was running the vacuum cleaner when the telephone rang." I knew a story was there and that it wanted telling. I felt it in my bones, that a story belonged with that beginning, if I could just have the time to write it. I found the time, an entire day — twelve, fifteen hours even — if I wanted to make use of it. I did, and I sat down in the morning and wrote the first sentence, and other sentences promptly began to attach themselves. I made the story just as I'd make a poem; one line and then the next, and the next. Pretty soon I could see a story, and I knew it was my story, the one I'd been wanting to write.

I like it when there is some feeling of threat or sense of menace in short stories. I think a little menace is fine to have in a story. For one thing, it's good for the circulation. There has to be tension, a sense that something is imminent, that certain things are in relentless motion, or else, most often, there simply won't be a story. What creates tension in a piece of fiction is partly the way the concrete words are linked together to make up the visible action of the story. But it's also the things that are left out, that are implied, the landscape just under the smooth (but sometimes broken and unsettled) surface of things.

V. S. Pritchett's definition of a short story is "something glimpsed from the corner of the eye, in passing." Notice the "glimpse" part of this. First the glimpse. Then the glimpse given life, turned into something that illuminates the moment and may, if we're lucky — that word again — have even further-ranging consequences and meaning. The short story writer's task is to invest the glimpse with all that is in his power. He'll bring his intelligence and literary skill to bear (his talent), his sense of proportion and sense of the fitness of things: of how things out there really are and how he sees those things — like no one else sees them. And this is done through the use of clear and specific language, language used so as to bring to life the details that will light up the story for the reader. For the details to be concrete and convey meaning, the language must be accurate and precisely given. The words can be so precise they may even sound flat, but they can still carry; if used right, they can hit all the notes.

RAYMOND CARVER

Creative Writing 101

1983

A long time ago — it was the summer of 1958 — my wife and I and our two baby children moved from Yakima, Washington, to a little town outside of Chico, California. There we found an old house and paid twenty-five dollars a month rent. In order to finance this move, I'd had to borrow a hundred and twenty-five dollars from a druggist I'd delivered prescriptions for, a man named Bill Barton.

This is by way of saying that in those days my wife and I were stone broke. We had to eke out a living, but the plan was that I would take classes at what was then called Chico State College. But for as far back as I can remember, long before we moved to California in search of a different life and our slice of the American pie, I'd wanted to be a writer. I wanted to write, and I wanted to write anything — fiction, of course, but also poetry, plays, scripts, articles for *Sports Afield, True, Argosy*, and *Rogue* (some of the magazines I was then reading), pieces for the local newspaper — anything that involved putting words together to make something coherent and of interest to someone besides myself. But at the time of our move, I felt in my bones I had to get some education in order to go along with being a writer. I put a very high premium on education then — much higher in those days than now, I'm sure, but that's because I'm older and have an education. Understand that nobody in my family had ever gone to college or for that matter had got beyond the mandatory eighth grade in high school. I didn't know *anything*, but I knew I didn't know anything.

So along with this desire to get an education, I had this very strong desire to write; it was a desire so strong that, with the encouragement I was given in college, and the insight acquired, I kept on writing long after "good sense" and the "cold facts" — the "realities" of my life told me, time and again, that I ought to quit, stop the dreaming, quietly go ahead and do something else.

That fall at Chico State I enrolled in classes that most freshman students have to take, but I enrolled as well for something called Creative Writing 101. This course was going to be taught by a new faculty member named John Gardner, who was already surrounded by a bit of mystery and romance. It was said that he'd taught previously at Oberlin College but had left there for some reason that wasn't made clear. One student said Gardner had been fired — students, like everyone else, thrive on rumor and intrigue — and another student said Gardner had simply quit after some kind of flap. Someone else said his teaching load at Oberlin, four or five classes of freshman English each semester, had been too heavy and that he couldn't find time to write. For it was said that Gardner was a real, that is to say a practicing, writer — someone who had written novels and short stories. In any case, he was going to teach CW 101 at Chico State, and I signed up.

I was excited about taking a course from a real writer. I'd never laid eyes on a writer before, and I was in awe. But where were these novels and short stories, I wanted to know. Well, nothing had been published yet. It was said that he couldn't get his work published and that he carried it around with him in boxes. (After I became his student, I was to see those boxes of manuscript. Gardner had become aware of my difficulty in finding a place to work. He knew I had a young family and cramped quarters at home. He offered me the key to his office. I see that gift now as a turning point. It was a gift not made casually, and I took it, I think, as a kind of mandate — for that's what it was. I spent part of every Saturday and Sunday in his office, which is where he kept the boxes of manuscript. The boxes were stacked up on the floor beside the desk. *Nickel Mountain*, grease-pencilled on one of the boxes, is the only title I recall. But it was in his office, within sight of his unpublished books, that I undertook my first serious attempts at writing.) . . .

For short story writers in his class, the requirement was one story, ten to fifteen pages in length. For people who wanted to write a novel — I think there must have been one or two of these souls — a chapter of around twenty pages, along with an outline of the rest. The kicker was that this one short story, or the chapter of the novel, might have to be revised ten times in the course of the semester for Gardner to be satisfied with it. It was a basic tenet of his that a writer found what he wanted to say in the ongoing process of seeing what he'd said. And this seeing, or seeing more clearly, came about through revision. He *believed* in revision, endless revision; it was something very close to his heart and something he felt was vital for writers, at whatever stage of their development. And he never seemed to lose patience rereading a student story, even though he might have seen it in five previous incarnations.

I think his idea of a short story in 1958 was still pretty much his idea of a short story in 1982; it was something that had a recognizable beginning, middle, and an end to it. Once in a while he'd go to the blackboard and draw a diagram to illustrate a point he wanted to make about rising or falling emotion in a story — peaks, valleys, plateaus, resolution, *denouement,* things like that. Try as I might, I couldn't muster a great deal of interest or really understand this side of things, the stuff he put on the blackboard. But what I did understand was the way he would comment on a student story that was undergoing class discussion. Gardner might wonder aloud about the author's reasons for writing a story about a crippled person, say, and leaving out the fact of the character's crippledness until the very end of the story. "So you think it's a good idea not to let the reader know this man is crippled until the last sentence?" His tone of voice conveyed his disapproval, and it didn't take more than an instant for everyone in class, including the author of the story, to see that it wasn't a good strategy to use. Any strategy that kept important and necessary information away from the reader in the hope of overcoming him by surprise at the end of the story was cheating.

In class he was always referring to writers whose names I was not familiar with. Or if I knew their names, I'd never read the work. . . . He talked about James Joyce and Flaubert and Isak Dinesen as if they lived just down the road, in Yuba City. He said, "I'm here to tell you who to read as well as teach you how to write." I'd leave class in a daze and make straight for the library to find books by these writers he was talking about.

Hemingway and Faulkner were the reigning authors in those days. But altogether I'd probably read at the most two or three books by these fellows. Anyway, they were so well known and so much talked about, they couldn't be all that good, could they? I remember Gardner telling me, "Read all the Faulkner you can get your hands on, and then read all of Hemingway to clean the Faulkner out of your system."

He introduced us to the "little" or literary periodicals by bringing a box of these magazines to class one day and passing them around so that we could acquaint ourselves with their names, see what they looked like and what they felt like to hold in the hand. He told us that this was where most of the best fiction in the country and just about all of the poetry was appearing. Fiction, poetry, literary essays, book reviews of recent books, criticism of *living* authors *by* living authors. I felt wild with discovery in those days.

For the seven or eight of us who were in his class, he ordered heavy black binders and told us we should keep our written work in these. He kept his own work in such binders, he said, and of course that settled it for us. We carried our stories in those binders and felt we were special, exclusive, singled out from others. And so we were.

I don't know how Gardner might have been with other students when it came time to have conferences with them about their work. I suspect he gave everybody a good amount of attention. But it was and still is my impression that during that period he took my stories more seriously, read them closer and more carefully, than I had any right to expect. I was completely unprepared for the kind of criticism I received from him. Before our conference he would have marked up my story, crossing out unacceptable sentences, phrases, individual words, even some of the punctuation; and he gave me to understand that these deletions were not negotiable. In other cases he would bracket sentences, phrases, or individual words, and these were items we'd talk about, these cases were negotiable. And he wouldn't hesitate to add something to what I'd written — a word here and there, or else a few words, maybe a sentence that would make clear what I was trying to say. We'd discuss commas in my story as if nothing else in the world mattered more at that moment — and, indeed, it did not. He was always looking to find something to praise. When there was a sentence, a line of dialogue, or a narrative passage that he liked, something that he thought "worked" and moved the story along in some pleasant or unexpected way, he'd write "Nice" in the margin, or else "Good!" And seeing these comments, my heart would lift.

It was close, line-by-line criticism he was giving me, and the reasons behind the criticism, why something ought to be this way instead of that; and it was invaluable to me in my development as a writer. After this kind of detailed talk about the text, we'd talk about the larger concerns of the story, the "problem" it was trying to throw light on, the conflict it was trying to grapple with, and how the story might or might not fit into the grand scheme of story writing. It was his conviction that if the words in the story were blurred because of the author's insensitivity, carelessness, or sentimentality, then the story suffered from a tremendous handicap. But there was something even worse and something that must be avoided at all costs: if the words and the sentiments were dishonest, the author was faking it, writing about things he didn't care about or believe in, then nobody could ever care anything about it.

A writer's values and craft. This is what the man taught and what he stood for, and this is what I've kept by me in the years since that brief but all-important time.

The Bath

1981

Saturday afternoon the mother drove to the bakery in the shopping center. After looking through a loose-leaf binder with photographs of cakes taped onto the pages, she ordered chocolate, the child's favorite. The cake she chose was decorated with a spaceship and a launching pad under a sprinkling of white stars. The name SCOTTY would be iced on in green as if it were the name of the spaceship.

The baker listened thoughtfully when the mother told him Scotty would be eight years old. He was an older man, this baker, and he wore a curious apron, a heavy thing with loops that went under his arms and around his back and then crossed in front again where they were tied in a very thick knot. He kept wiping his hands on the front of the apron as he listened to the woman, his wet eyes examining her lips as she studied the samples and talked.

He let her take her time. He was in no hurry.

The mother decided on the spaceship cake, and then she gave the baker her name and her telephone number. The cake would be ready Monday morning, in plenty of time for the party Monday afternoon. This was all the baker was willing to say. No pleasantries, just this small exchange, the barest information, nothing that was not necessary.

Monday morning, the boy was walking to school. He was in the company of another boy, the two boys passing a bag of potato chips back and forth between them. The birthday boy was trying to trick the other boy into telling what he was going to give in the way of a present.

At an intersection, without looking, the birthday boy stepped off the curb, and was promptly knocked down by a car. He fell on his side, his head in the gutter, his legs in the road moving as if he were climbing a wall.

The other boy stood holding the potato chips. He was wondering if he should finish the rest or continue on to school.

The birthday boy did not cry. But neither did he wish to talk anymore. He would not answer when the other boy asked what it felt like to be hit by a car. The birthday boy got up and turned back for home, at which time the other boy waved good-bye and headed off for school.

The birthday boy told his mother what had happened. They sat together on the sofa. She held his hands in her lap. This is what she was doing when the boy pulled his hands away and lay down on his back.

Of course, the birthday party never happened. The birthday boy was in the hospital instead. The mother sat by the bed. She was waiting for the boy to wake up. The father hurried over from his office. He sat next to the mother. So now the both of them waited for the boy to wake up. They waited for hours, and then the father went home to take a bath.

The man drove home from the hospital. He drove the streets faster than he should. It had been a good life till now. There had been work, fatherhood, family. The man had been lucky and happy. But fear made him want a bath.

He pulled into the driveway. He sat in the car trying to make his legs work. The child had been hit by a car and he was in the hospital, but he was going to be all right. The man got out of the car and went up to the door. The dog was barking and the telephone was ringing. It kept ringing while the man unlocked the door and felt the wall for the light switch.

He picked up the receiver. He said, "I just got in the door!"

"There's a cake that wasn't picked up."

This is what the voice on the other end said.

"What are you saying?" the father said.

"The cake," the voice said. "Sixteen dollars."

The husband held the receiver against his ear, trying to understand. He said, "I don't know anything about it."

"Don't hand me that," the voice said.

The husband hung up the telephone. He went into the kitchen and poured himself some whiskey. He called the hospital.

The child's condition remained the same.

While the water ran into the tub, the man lathered his face and shaved. He was in the tub when he heard the telephone again. He got himself out and hurried through the house, saying, "Stupid, stupid," because he wouldn't be doing this if he'd stayed where he was in the hospital. He picked up the receiver and shouted, "Hello!"

The voice said, "It's ready."

The father got back to the hospital after midnight. The wife was sitting in the chair by the bed. She looked up at the husband and then she looked back at the child. From an apparatus over the bed hung a bottle with a tube running from the bottle to the child.

"What's this?" the father said.

"Glucose," the mother said.

The husband put his hand to the back of the woman's head.

"He's going to wake up," the man said.

"I know," the woman said.

In a little while the man said, "Go home and let me take over."

She shook her head. "No," she said.

"Really," he said. "Go home for a while. You don't have to worry. He's sleeping, is all."

A nurse pushed open the door. She nodded to them as she went to the bed. She took the left arm out from under the covers and put her fingers on the wrist. She put the arm back under the covers and wrote on the clipboard attached to the bed.

"How is he?" the mother said.

"Stable," the nurse said. Then she said, "Doctor will be in again shortly."

"I was saying maybe she'd want to go home and get a little rest," the man said. "After the doctor comes."

"She could do that," the nurse said.

The woman said, "We'll see what the doctor says." She brought her hand up to her eyes and leaned her head forward.

The nurse said, "Of course."

_____

The father gazed at his son, the small chest inflating and deflating under the covers. He felt more fear now. He began shaking his head. He talked to himself like this. The child is fine. Instead of sleeping at home, he's doing it here. Sleep is the same wherever you do it.

_____

The doctor came in. He shook hands with the man. The woman got up from the chair.

"Ann," the doctor said and nodded. The doctor said, "Let's just see how he's doing." He moved to the bed and touched the boy's wrist. He peeled back an eyelid and then the other. He turned back the covers and listened to the heart. He pressed his fingers here and there on the body. He went to the end of the bed and studied the chart. He noted the time, scribbled on the chart, and then he considered the mother and the father.

This doctor was a handsome man. His skin was moist and tan. He wore a three-piece suit, a vivid tie, and on his shirt were cufflinks.

The mother was talking to herself like this. He has just come from somewhere with an audience. They gave him a special medal.

The doctor said, "Nothing to shout about, but nothing to worry about. He should wake up pretty soon." The doctor looked at the boy again. "We'll know more after the tests are in."

"Oh, no," the mother said.

The doctor said, "Sometimes you see this."

The father said, "You wouldn't call this a coma, then?"

The father waited and looked at the doctor.

"No, I don't want to call it that," the doctor said. "He's sleeping. It's restorative. The body is doing what it has to do."

"It's a coma," the mother said. "A kind of coma."

The doctor said, "I wouldn't call it that."

He took the woman's hands and patted them. He shook hands with the husband.

_____

The woman put her fingers on the child's forehead and kept them there for a while. "At least he doesn't have a fever," she said. Then she said, "I don't know. Feel his head."

The man put his fingers on the boy's forehead. The man said, "I think he's supposed to feel this way."

The woman stood there awhile longer, working her lip with her teeth. Then she moved to her chair and sat down.

The husband sat in the chair beside her. He wanted to say something else. But there was no saying what it should be. He took her hand and put it in his lap. This made him feel better. It made him feel he was saying something. They sat like that for a while, watching the boy, not talking. From time to time he squeezed her hand until she took it away.

"I've been praying," she said.

"Me too," the father said. "I've been praying too."

A nurse came back in and checked the flow from the bottle.

A doctor came in and said what his name was. This doctor was wearing loafers.

"We're going to take him downstairs for more pictures," he said. "And we want to do a scan."

"A scan?" the mother said. She stood between this new doctor and the bed.

"It's nothing," he said.

"My God," she said.

Two orderlies came in. They wheeled a thing like a bed. They unhooked the boy from the tube and slid him over onto the thing with wheels.

It was after sunup when they brought the birthday boy back out. The mother and father followed the orderlies into the elevator and up to the room. Once more the parents took up their places next to the bed.

They waited all day. The boy did not wake up. The doctor came again and examined the boy again and left after saying the same things again. Nurses came in. Doctors came in. A technician came in and took blood.

"I don't understand this," the mother said to the technician.

"Doctor's orders," the technician said.

The mother went to the window and looked out at the parking lot. Cars with their lights on were driving in and out. She stood at the window with her hands on the sill. She was talking to herself like this. We're into something now, something hard.

She was afraid.

She saw a car stop and a woman in a long coat get into it. She made believe she was that woman. She made believe she was driving away from here to someplace else.

The doctor came in. He looked tanned and healthier than ever. He went to the bed and examined the boy. He said, "His signs are fine. Everything's good."

The mother said, "But he's sleeping."

"Yes," the doctor said.

The husband said, "She's tired. She's starved."

The doctor said, "She should rest. She should eat. Ann," the doctor said.

"Thank you," the husband said.

He shook hands with the doctor and the doctor patted their shoulders and left.

"I suppose one of us should go home and check on things," the man said. "The dog needs to be fed."

"Call the neighbors," the wife said. "Someone will feed him if you ask them to."

She tried to think who. She closed her eyes and tried to think anything at all. After a time she said, "Maybe I'll do it. Maybe if I'm not here watching, he'll wake up. Maybe it's because I'm watching that he won't."

"That could be it," the husband said.

"I'll go home and take a bath and put on something clean," the woman said.

"I think you should do that," the man said.

She picked up her purse. He helped her into her coat. She moved to the door, and looked back. She looked at the child, and then she looked at the father. The husband nodded and smiled.

She went past the nurses' station and down to the end of the corridor, where she turned and saw a little waiting room, a family in there, all sitting in wicker chairs, a man in a khaki shirt, a baseball cap pushed back on his head, a large woman wearing a housedress, slippers, a girl in jeans, hair in dozens of kinky braids, the table littered with flimsy wrappers and styrofoam and coffee sticks and packets of salt and pepper.

"Nelson," the woman said. "Is it about Nelson?"

The woman's eyes widened.

"Tell me now, lady," the woman said. "Is it about Nelson?"

The woman was trying to get up from her chair. But the man had his hand closed over her arm.

"Here, here," the man said.

"I'm sorry," the mother said. "I'm looking for the elevator. My son is in the hospital. I can't find the elevator."

"Elevator is down that way," the man said, and he aimed a finger in the right direction.

"My son was hit by a car," the mother said. "But he's going to be all right. He's in shock now, but it might be some kind of coma too. That's what worries us, the coma part, I'm going out for a little while. Maybe I'll take a bath. But my husband is with him. He's watching. There's a chance everything will change when I'm gone. My name is Ann Weiss."

The man shifted in his chair. He shook his head.

He said, "Our Nelson."

She pulled into the driveway. The dog ran out from behind the house. He ran in circles on the grass. She closed her eyes and leaned her head against the wheel. She listened to the ticking of the engine.

She got out of the car and went to the door. She turned on lights and put on water for tea. She opened a can and fed the dog. She sat down on the sofa with her tea.

The telephone rang.

"Yes!" she said. "Hello!" she said.

"Mrs. Weiss," a man's voice said.

"Yes," she said. "This is Mrs. Weiss. Is it about Scotty?" she said.

"Scotty," the voice said. "It is about Scotty," the voice said. "It has to do with Scotty, yes."

TOM JENKS

The Origin of "Cathedral"

1993

I first met Ray Carver in New York in early September 1984 at a publishing dinner to launch Gary Fisketjon's Vintage Contemporary paperback series. Many of the new VC authors and their friends were there: Richard Ford, Toby Wolff, Jay McInerney, Tom McGuane, Jim Crumley, and Ralph Beer — a distinctly male crowd, and what struck me most was that, as we geared up to move to a nightclub, Ray, amid teasing about running off somewhere to see a woman, put himself in a taxi and headed for his hotel room alone. By the ginger way he got himself into the cab and laughingly ducked the barbs all around him, there was no doubt he meant to keep himself out of trouble.

But he was fair game for the friendly taunts that followed him into the cab. We were witnessing the Good Ray, but we all knew about the Bad Ray, the one who used to be Lord Misrule himself.

Reformed, Ray was fast becoming the most famous short story writer in the world, and the facts of his life were well known, partly because they were often the stuff of his writing and because fame brings a peculiar public intimacy.

At the time, I was an editor of *Esquire* and had made Ray's acquaintance through the mail and on the phone. I had published some of his work and knew him somewhat, and as I watched him slip away in the cab, I imagined him going back to his hotel room (it was early yet — ten o'clock) and telephoning Tess Gallagher at their home in Syracuse. Each evening they set aside the hours beyond ten o'clock to spend with each other. He *was*, in a sense, running off to see a woman.

A year and a half later, I visited them in Syracuse. During the days, Ray and I read stories for a book we were working on and at night we watched TV. One night, we were watching a PBS version of *Wuthering Heights*, and Ray began to tell about another night of TV: the night the blind man for whom Tess once worked had come to visit. Tess told her side, too — how Ray was uneasy about the man's visit, uncomfortable with his blindness and his familiarity with Tess, a mild jealousy rising in Ray. Their evening was slow and tedious, and ended with the three of them watching PBS, just as we were. But on the night the blind man was visiting, Tess had fallen asleep, and then a program about cathedrals came on. The blind man had no idea what a cathedral looked like, and, in the end, Ray sat on the floor with him, holding his hands, drawing a cathedral so the blind man could sense the miracle of the shape.

Ray had written this story and titled it "Cathedral." Tess, who with Ray's encouragement had recently begun writing stories, had her own version, titled "The Harvest."[1] She gave me a copy, humorously telling Ray, "Watch out, I'm nipping at your heels." Their good-natured competition and openness was rare in my experience of writers, many of whom are cagey about the intimate, personal connections in their work. . . .

---

[1] Gallagher later retitled her story "Rain Flooding Your Campfire."

ARTHUR M. SALTZMAN

A Reading of "What We Talk About When We Talk About Love"

1988

The volume's title story extends the theme of the heart's perpetual commotion by updating and burlesquing Plato's *Symposium*. "What We Talk About When We Talk About Love" also features the most expansive conversationalists in this collection: Mel and Terri, both of whom are married for the second time and both sporting scars from their first marriages, and Nick (the narrator) and Laura, newlyweds who are still in the throes of a mutual romantic trance. Mel and Terri carry on the bulk of the gin-induced discussion of love, whereas Nick and Laura are more equivocal and seem content to placate their friends or to reassure one another with intimate gestures.

Mel and Terri propose divergent definitions of "real love." A cardiologist who once spent five years studying in a seminary, Mel contends that love is a spiritual phenomenon whose pinnacle was and continues to be the chivalric code. Terri, on the other hand, argues that the brutality of her first husband, Ed, displayed the formidableness of his passion for her. As the conversation gains momentum, contradictions surface in their testimonies. Mel, the self-proclaimed spiritual scientist, confesses his daydreams about murdering his first wife that parallel Terri's grotesque tales of her relationship with Ed. Meanwhile, Terri grows increasingly anxious about redeeming her volatile past, even at the expense of offending her present husband: "'He did love me though, Mel. Grant me that,' Terri said. 'That's all I'm asking. He didn't love me the way you love me. I'm not saying that. But he loved me. You can grant me that, can't you?'"

The greatest obstacle to any ideal of love turns out to be the transitoriness of love. After all, both Mel and Terri had vowed allegiance to their original partners, so what is there to prevent the same deterioration from happening again? Ironically, the "saving grace" of love is its elasticity — one can move on from divorce or tragedy and love anew — but this is further evidence against love's absolute status and hollows out current protestations of devotion. In other words, love's transient nature could be either its vindication or its vanquishment — the source of its preciousness or its untrustworthiness. Consequently, the very situation that the four friends occupy as they conduct their leisurely talking and drinking around the dinner table is shown to have the same fragile charms as the subject at hand:

> The afternoon sun was like a presence in this room, the spacious light of ease and generosity. We could have been anywhere, somewhere enchanted. We raised our glasses again and grinned at each other like children who had agreed on something forbidden.

The relative articulateness of these characters by no means enables them to reach a satisfactory conclusion, and as a result Mel suggests that "it ought to make us feel ashamed when we talk like we know what we're talking about when we talk about love." In this way, Mel echoes Pausanias' declaration in *The Symposium*: "I do not think, Phaidros, that the rules were properly laid down, I mean that we should just simply belaud Love. For if Love were one, that would do, but really he is not one; since he is not one, it is more proper to say first which we are to praise."

Mel's crowning point regarding the spiritual core of love recalls Holly's envious vision of the dignified intimacy of the old people she encountered in "Gazebo." Mel relates how, after a terrible automobile accident, an old man and woman lay barely alive in their hospital beds; they were completely covered by casts and bandages. However, despite his horrible injuries, the husband was primarily depressed because he could not see his wife through the tiny eyeholes in his bandages. By this time Mel has grown rather drunk and profane, and his testiness toward Terri belies his argument. So, too, is his chivalric hero, the medieval knight, tarnished by the admission that he often suffocated in his armor; moreover, his protective gear was also a measure of his inaccessibility. Finally, when Mel fantasizes about arriving in the guise of a beekeeper (helmeted, anonymous, and padded from head to toe) at the house of his first wife in order to release a swarm of bees, he modernizes and disqualifies the knight's noble image.

Nick and Laura come close to embodying a simple yet profound enjoyment of one another's company, but when Nick ostentatiously kisses Laura's hand, Mel and Terri find it more amusing than tender. They all toast to "true love," but Terri's gentle admonishment to Laura — "Wait awhile" — suggests that time misses no one in its assault on affection. Rating the quality of the consolation that remains at the end of the story depends upon to what extent the elusive, unpredictable, hazardous process of love compensates for the skewering of the romantic ideal (upon which the discussants cannot agree anyway). In the darkened room, silent save for "the human noise we sat there making," perhaps these moments together, deeply imbued with shared sensibilities, make up for the antagonisms, the regrets, the flirtations, the spilled gin.

A. O. SCOTT

Looking for Raymond Carver

1999

"And did you get what
you wanted from this life, even so?
I did.
And what did you want?
To call myself beloved, to feel myself
beloved on the earth."

Plenty of writers are admired, celebrated, imitated, and hyped. Very few writers can, as Raymond Carver does in his poem "Late Fragment," call themselves beloved. In the years since his death in 1988, at fifty, from lung cancer, Carver's reputation has blossomed. He has gone from being an influential — and controversial — member of a briefly fashionable school of experimental fiction to being an international icon of traditional American literary values. His genius — but more his honesty, his decency, his commitment to the exigencies of craft — is praised by an extraordinarily diverse cross section of his peers. . . .

Through the ministrations of his friends and the tireless efforts of his widow, the poet and short-story writer Tess Gallagher, to keep his memory alive, Carver has begun to approach something like literary sainthood. Certain facts about his life and death — his stoicism in the face of terminal illness, his generosity as a friend and teacher, his successful battle with alcoholism, the happy and productive life he made in Port Angeles, Washington, with Gallagher after the collapse of his first marriage — have added luster to his image. The best of Carver's writing now seems, in retrospect, to be suffused with the best of his personality — affable, humble, battered, wise. But to say this may also be to note that the adversities and triumphs of Carver's life have obscured his work, that we now read that work through the screen of biography, and that his identity as a writer is, in consequence, blurred. What kind of a writer was he, and how are we to assess his achievement? Was he a hard-boiled cynic or an open-hearted sentimentalist? A regionalist rooted in his native Pacific Northwest or the chronicler of an America whose trailer parks and subdivisions had become indistinguishable? Did he help to revive American fiction or contribute to its ruin? Is he, as the London *Times* once declared, "America's Chekhov," or merely the O. Henry of America's graduate writing programs?

If anything, the current state of Carver's published work makes these questions, which have lingered for some time, more difficult than ever to address. More than a decade after his death, Carver's *oeuvre* is still taking shape. Last autumn Knopf brought out his collected poems, and the Atlantic Monthly Press issued a tenth-anniversary hardcover edition of *Where I'm Calling From*, which Carver viewed as the definitive collection of his stories. Around the same time, a *New York Times Magazine* article raised questions about the extent to which Carver was the sole, or even the primary, begetter of his own work, pointing to evidence that Gordon Lish, the editor of Carver's first two books, had drastically cut, rearranged, and even rewritten many of the stories which established Carver's fame.[1] And then there is the question of Gallagher's role, which seems to have been that of soulmate, sounding board, first reader — and collaborator. The journal *Philosophy and Literature* recently printed some short plays Carver and Gallagher wrote together. The journal also ran a photograph of the manuscript of the final page of "Errand," Carver's last published story; the concluding paragraph is in Gallagher's handwriting. . . .

———

To his admirers, Carver's taciturnity becomes its own kind of eloquence. But critics, especially those who are bothered by Carver's disproportionate influence on other writers, have complained about how much he leaves out. For Sven Birkerts, writing in 1986, the fiction of Carver and his followers is marked by "a total refusal of any vision of larger social connection." And it is true that the inhabitants of Carver's world appear to exist not only in states of isolation and impermanence, but, to borrow a phrase from George W. S. Trow, in a context of no context, without geographical, social, or historical coordinates. We seldom learn the name of the town, or even the state, in which a given story takes place. The stories tend to be devoid of the cultural and commercial references — popular songs, brand names, movies — that so many contemporary writers use to fix their narratives in time and space. And though Carver began writing in the early 1960s, and came to prominence over the next two decades, his stories, at first glance, take no notice of the social and political tumult of the era. We never know who the president is, or whether men have walked on the moon; the characters never read newspapers; and nobody expresses any political interests or opinions. As far as I can tell, Vietnam is mentioned exactly once: in "Vitamins" the leering, predatory behavior of a black man named Nelson — one of the very few nonwhite characters who appear in Carver's work — is ascribed to the fact that he is a veteran just returned from combat in Southeast Asia.

Carver's people often exist not only outside history and politics, but beyond psychology, unless the psychology in question is Skinnerian behaviorism. Their thoughts are typically left unreported; they are creatures of simple speech and sudden action:

---

[1] D. T. Max, "The Carver Chronicles," *The New York Times Magazine*, August 9, 1998. [Scott's note]

She unbuttoned her coat and put her purse down on the counter. She looked at L.D. and said, "L.D., I've had it. So has Rae. So has everyone who knows you. I've been thinking it over. I want you out of here. Tonight. This minute. Now. Get the hell out of here right now."

L.D. had no intention of going anywhere. He looked from Maxine to the jar of pickles that had been on the table since lunch. He picked up the jar and pitched it through the kitchen window.

The jaggedness, the deadpan narration, the rigorous refusal of any inflection of language that would suggest interpretation, judgment, or inwardness — these are the aspects of Carver's style that inspired people to think of him as a minimalist. The passage above is from "One More Thing," which, like "Why Don't You Dance?," appears both in *What We Talk About When We Talk About Love* and in *Where I'm Calling From.* The earlier book, which did a great deal to solidify Carver's reputation as an important voice in American fiction in the 1980s, has also done him lasting damage. It was on this book that the editorial hand of Gordon Lish fell most heavily, as Lish cut, rearranged, and rewrote freely, without regard for Carver's wishes or feelings. According to Tess Gallagher, "Ray felt the book, even at the time of its publication, did not represent the main thrust of his writing, nor his true pulse and instinct in the work. He had, in fact, even begged Gordon Lish, to no avail, not to publish the book in this misbegotten version."

Carver, it seems to me, was well within his rights. He was also, as a matter of literary judgment, right. There has been much discussion of the changes Lish imposed on two stories in particular, "The Bath" (which Carver had originally and would subsequently title "A Small, Good Thing") and "So Much Water So Close to Home." The Lish versions are jarring and, briefly, horrifying: the stories, like the people who inhabit them, seem violently discombobulated. In "The Bath," events happen almost at random, and crucial information — for instance, whether a child is alive or dead — is cruelly, capriciously, withheld. . . .

For Lish, the paring of a story down to its verbal and narrative skeleton was a mode of formal experimentation — a trick, if you will. The kind of writing he championed in the 1980s was not an antidote to the antirealist, avant-garde impulse of the 1960s and 1970s, of writers like John Barth and Donald Barthelme, but rather its most extreme expression. The refusal of explanation, the resistance to psychology, and the deliberate impoverishment of language reflect, on Lish's part, an aesthetic choice, and it is clear that he saw affinities between Carver's plain manner and his own stark vision. But the aesthetic principles that Carver discovered in the course of his literary education — from his readings in the modernist tradition, from his first teacher, the novelist John Gardner, and from Lish himself — were ultimately less important than the ethical commitments that are the deepest source of his work. . . .

To read *Where I'm Calling From* from beginning to end, supplemented by some of the stories from earlier collections that Carver chose not to reprint, is to discover that a great deal of what is supposed to be missing — in particular, the changing social landscape of the United States — has been there all along, but that it has been witnessed from a perspective almost without precedent in American literature. Stories like "What Do You Do in San Francisco?" and "After the Denim" record the curious, suspicious, and disgusted reactions of the small-town working class to interlopers from the urban, well-to-do counterculture. "Jerry and Molly and Sam," "Nobody Said Anything," and "Bicycles, Muscles, Cigarettes," among others, are ultimately about how the spread of the suburbs transformed family life, and about the crisis of masculinity that resulted. Carver's work, read closely and in the aggregate, also carries a lot of news about feminism, working conditions, and substance abuse in late-twentieth-century provincial America.

To generalize in this way is, of course, to engage in a kind of analytical discourse Carver resolutely mistrusted. More often than not, the big talkers in Carver's stories are in possession of a degree of class privilege. "My friend Mel McGinnis was talking," goes the famous opening of "What We Talk About When We Talk About Love." "Mel McGinnis is a cardiologist, and sometimes that gives him the right." The imperious homeowner in "Put Yourself in My Shoes" and the jealous college teacher in "Will You Please Be Quiet, Please?" also come to mind. People who carry on as if they know what they're talking about are regarded with suspicion. Carver's greatest sympathy is reserved for those characters who struggle to use language to make sense of things, but who founder or fail in the attempt.

It is striking how many of his stories turn on the inability or refusal of people to say what happened. Think of the girl at the end of "Why Don't You Dance?," unable to convey the fullness of what she has seen on the strange man's lawn, or the narrator of "Where Is Everyone?," clamming up at his AA meetings. And there are many more examples. "Why, Honey?" is a mother's desperate, almost incoherent, and yet strangely formal effort ("Dear Sir," it begins) to explain to a nameless, prying stranger how her darling son went wrong. In "Distance" (also published as "Everything Stuck to Him"), a father, asked by his grown daughter to tell her "what it was like when she was a kid," produces a fairy tale of young parenthood (the main characters in which are referred to only as "the boy" and "the girl") that leaves both teller and listener unsettled, unenlightened, and remote from each other.

And then there is "Cathedral," one of Carver's most beloved stories and the closest thing he produced to an allegory of his own method. The narrator is visited by a garrulous blind man, an old friend of his wife's, whose arrival he anticipates with apprehension. The two men end up smoking marijuana together, while the television airs a documentary about the cathedrals of Europe. It starts to bother the narrator that his new acquaintance, while he knows something about the history of church-building, has no idea of what cathedrals really are, and he tries to tell him about them:

> "They're really big," I said. "They're massive. They're built of stone. Marble, too, sometimes. In those olden days, when they built cathedrals, men wanted to be close to God. In those olden days, God was an important part of everyone's life. You could tell this from their cathedral-building. I'm

sorry," I said, "but it looks like that's the best I can do for you. I'm just no good at it."

The blind man proposes that they draw a cathedral instead, and they do — the narrator's eyes closed, the blind man's hand guiding his. The narrator undergoes an epiphany: "It was like nothing else in my life up to now."

The reader is left out: the men's shared experience, visual and tactile, is beyond the reach of words. But the frustrating vicariousness of the story is also the source of its power. Art, according to Carver, is a matter of the blind leading the tongue-tied. Carver was an artist of a rare and valuable kind: he told simple stories, and made it look hard.

CHARLOTTE PERKINS GILMAN'S
"The Yellow Wallpaper"

Charlotte Perkins Gilman photographed by
C. F. Lummis in 1900.

Courtesy of the Library of Congress.

Charlotte Perkins Gilman was a prolific author who wrote several articles on the medical treatment of women's nervous disorders, urging reforms throughout her lifetime. In the October 1913 issue of *The Forerunner* she spoke frankly about her own breakdown and explained how she used her experience to write "The Yellow Wallpaper" (p. 1578). "Undergoing the Cure for Nervous Prostration" (p. 1579) is an excerpt from her autobiography, *The Living of Charlotte Perkins Gilman* (1935), written in the last years of her career as an eminent American feminist. Sandra M. Gilbert and Susan Gubar (p. 1581) gave a feminist reading of "The Yellow Wallpaper" in their groundbreaking book *The Madwoman in the Attic: The Woman Writer and the Nineteenth-Century Literary Imagination* (1979). They read Gilman's story as belonging to a tradition of the "literature of confinement," in which a woman writer, trapped by the patriarchal society, struggles to break free "through strategic redefinitions of self, art, and society." Elaine Showalter (p. 1583) described the importance of Gilman's "Feminist Nightmares" in Showalter's recent history of literature by American women, *A Jury of Her Peers* (2009).

CHARLOTTE PERKINS GILMAN

Why I Wrote "The Yellow Wallpaper"

1913

Many and many a reader has asked that. When the story first came out, in the *New England Magazine* about 1891, a Boston physician made protest in *The Transcript.* Such a story ought not to be written, he said; it was enough to drive anyone mad to read it.

Another physician, in Kansas I think, wrote to say that it was the best description of incipient insanity he had ever seen, and — begging my pardon — had I been there?

Now the story of the story is this: For many years I suffered from a severe and continuous nervous breakdown tending to melancholia — and beyond. During about the third year of this trouble I went, in devout faith and some faint stir of hope, to a noted specialist in nervous diseases, the best known in the country. This wise man put me to bed and applied the rest cure, to which a still-good physique responded so promptly that he concluded there was nothing much the matter with me, and sent me home with solemn advice to "live as domestic a life as far as possible," to "have but two hours' intellectual life a day," and "never to touch pen, brush, or pencil again" as long as I lived. This was in 1887.

I went home and obeyed those directions for some three months, and came so near the borderline of utter mental ruin that I could see over.

Then, using the remnants of intelligence that remained, and helped by a wise friend, I cast the noted specialist's advice to the winds and went to work again — work, the normal life of every human being; work, in which is joy and growth and service, without which one is a pauper and a parasite — ultimately recovering some measure of power.

Being naturally moved to rejoicing by this narrow escape, I wrote "The Yellow Wallpaper," with its embellishments and additions, to carry out the ideal (I never had hallucinations or objections to my mural decorations) and sent a copy to the physician who so nearly drove me mad. He never acknowledged it.

The little book is valued by alienists and as a good specimen of one kind of literature. It has, to my knowledge, saved one woman from a similar fate — so terrifying her family that they let her out into normal activity and she recovered.

But the best result is this. Many years later I was told that the great specialist had admitted to friends of his that he had altered his treatment of neurasthenia since reading "The Yellow Wallpaper." [This is apparently Gilman's wishful thinking, according to literary historian Julie Bates Dock in a 1996 *PMLA* article.]

It was not intended to drive people crazy, but to save people from being driven crazy, and it worked.

CHARLOTTE PERKINS GILMAN

Undergoing the Cure for Nervous Prostration

1935

This was a worse horror than before, for now I saw the stark fact — that I was well while away and sick while at home — a heartening prospect! Soon ensued the same utter prostration, the unbearable inner misery, the ceaseless tears. A new tonic had been invented, Essence of Oats, which was given me, and did some good for a time. I pulled up enough to do a little painting that fall, but soon slipped down again and stayed down. An old friend of my mother's, dear Mrs. Diman, was so grieved at this condition that she gave me a hundred dollars and urged me to go away somewhere and get cured.

Doctor S. Weir Mitchell in consultation, c. 1890.

© The Library of College of Physicians of Philadelphia.

At that time the greatest nerve specialist in the country was Dr. S. W. Mitchell of Philadelphia. Through the kindness of a friend of Mr. Stetson's living in that city, I went to him and took "the rest cure"; went with the utmost confidence, prefacing the visit with a long letter giving "the history of the case" in a way a modern psychologist would have appreciated. Dr. Mitchell only thought it proved self-conceit. He had a prejudice against the Beechers. "I've had two women of your blood here already," he told me scornfully. This eminent physician was well versed in two kinds of nervous prostration; that of the business man exhausted from too much work, and the society woman exhausted from too much play. The kind I had was evidently behind him. But he did reassure me on one point — there was no dementia, he said, only hysteria.

I was put to bed and kept there. I was fed, bathed, rubbed, and responded with the vigorous body of twenty-six. As far as he could see there was nothing the matter with me, so after a month of this agreeable treatment he sent me home, with this prescription:

> Live as domestic a life as possible. Have your child with you all the time. (Be it remarked that if I did but dress the baby it left me shaking and crying — certainly far from a healthy companionship for her, to say nothing of the effect on me.) Lie down an hour after each meal. Have but two hours' intellectual life a day. And never touch pen, brush, or pencil as long as you live.

I went home, followed those directions rigidly for months, and came perilously near to losing my mind. The mental agony grew so unbearable that I would sit blankly moving my head from side to side — to get out from under the pain. Not physical pain, not the least "headache" even, just mental torment, and so heavy in its nightmare gloom that it seemed real enough to dodge.

I made a rag baby, hung it on a doorknob, and played with it. I would crawl into remote closets and under beds — to hide from the grinding pressure of that profound distress. . . .

Finally, in the fall of '87, in a moment of clear vision, we agreed to separate, to get a divorce. There was no quarrel, no blame for either one, never an unkind word between us, unbroken mutual affection — but it seemed plain that if I went crazy, it would do my husband no good, and be a deadly injury to my child.

What this meant to the young artist, the devoted husband, the loving father, was so bitter a grief and loss that nothing would have justified breaking the marriage save this worse loss which threatened. It was not a choice between going and staying, but between going, sane, and staying, insane. If I had been of the slightest use to him or to the child, I would have "stuck it," as the English say. But this progressive weakening of the mind made a horror unnecessary to face; better for that dear child to have separated parents than a lunatic mother.

We had been married four years and more. This miserable condition of mind, this darkness, feebleness, and gloom, had begun in those difficult years of courtship, had grown rapidly worse after marriage, and was now threatening utter loss; whereas I had repeated proof that the moment I left home I began to recover. It seemed right to give up a mistaken marriage.

Our mistake was mutual. If I had been stronger and wiser I should never have been persuaded into it. Our suffering was mutual too, his unbroken devotion, his manifold cares and labors in tending a sick wife, his adoring pride in the best of babies, all coming to naught, ending in utter failure — we sympathized with each other but faced a bitter necessity. The separation must come as soon as possible, the divorce must wait for conditions.

If this decision could have been reached sooner it would have been much better for me, the lasting mental injury would have been less. Such recovery as I have made in forty years, and the work accomplished, seem to show that the fear of insanity was not fulfilled, but the effects of nerve bankruptcy remain to this day. So much of my many failures, of misplay and misunderstanding and "queerness" is due to this lasting weakness, and kind friends so unfailingly refuse to allow for it, to believe it, that I am now going to some length in stating the case.

SANDRA M. GILBERT

AND SUSAN GUBAR

A Feminist Reading of Gilman's "The Yellow Wallpaper"

1979

As if to comment on the unity of all these points — on, that is, the anxiety-inducing connections between what women writers tend to see as their parallel confinements in texts, houses, and maternal female bodies — Charlotte Perkins Gilman brought them all together in 1890 in a striking story of female confinement and escape, a paradigmatic tale which (like *Jane Eyre*) seems to tell *the* story that all literary women would tell if they could speak their "speechless woe." "The Yellow Wallpaper," which Gilman herself called "a description of a case of nervous breakdown," recounts in the first person the experiences of a woman who is evidently suffering from a severe postpartum psychosis. Her husband, a censorious and paternalistic physician, is treating her according to methods by which S. Weir Mitchell, a famous "nerve specialist," treated Gilman herself for a similar problem. He has confined her to a large garret room in an "ancestral hall" he has rented, and he has forbidden her to touch pen to paper until she is well again, for he feels, says the narrator, "that with my imaginative power and habit of story-making, a nervous weakness like mine is sure to lead to all manner of excited fancies, and that I ought to use my will and good sense to check the tendency."

The cure, of course, is worse than the disease, for the sick woman's mental condition deteriorates rapidly. "I think sometimes that if I were only well enough to write a little it would relieve the press of ideas and rest me," she remarks, but literally confined in a room she thinks is a one-time nursery because it has "rings and things" in the walls, she is literally locked away from creativity. The "rings and things," although reminiscent of children's gymnastic equipment, are really the paraphernalia of confinement, like the gate at the head of the stairs, instruments that definitively indicate her imprisonment. Even more tormenting, however, is the room's wallpaper: a sulphurous yellow paper, torn off in spots, and patterned with "lame uncertain curves" that "plunge off at outrageous angles" and "destroy themselves in unheard of contradictions." Ancient, smoldering, "unclean" as the oppressive structures of the society in which she finds herself, this paper surrounds the narrator like an inexplicable text, censorious and overwhelming as her physician husband, haunting as the "hereditary estate" in which she is trying to survive. Inevitably she studies its suicidal implications — and inevitably, because of her "imaginative power and habit of story-making," she revises it, projecting her own passion for escape into its otherwise incomprehensible hieroglyphics. "This wallpaper," she decides, at a key point in her story,

> has a kind of sub-pattern in a different shade, a particularly irritating one, for you can only see it in certain lights, and not clearly then.
> But in the places where it isn't faded and where the sun is just so — I can see a strange, provoking, formless sort of figure, that seems to skulk about behind that silly and conspicuous front design.

As time passes, this figure concealed behind what corresponds (in terms of what we have been discussing) to the facade of the patriarchal text becomes clearer and clearer. By moonlight the pattern of the wallpaper "becomes bars! The outside pattern I mean, and the woman behind it is as plain as can be." And eventually, as the narrator sinks more deeply into what the world calls madness, the terrifying implications of both the paper and the figure imprisoned behind the paper begin to permeate — that is, to *haunt* — the rented ancestral mansion in which she and her husband are immured. The "yellow smell" of the paper "creeps all over the house," drenching every room in its subtle aroma of decay. And the woman creeps too — through the house, in the house, and out of the house, in the garden and "on that long road under the trees." Sometimes, indeed, the narrator confesses, "I think there are a great many women" both behind the paper and creeping in the garden, "and sometimes only one, and she crawls around fast, and her crawling shakes [the paper] all over. . . . And she is all the time trying to climb through. But nobody could climb through that pattern — it strangles so; I think that is why it has so many heads."

Eventually it becomes obvious to both reader and narrator that the figure creeping through and behind the wallpaper is both the narrator and the narrator's double. By the end of the story, moreover, the narrator has enabled this double to escape from her textual/architectural confinement: "I pulled and she shook, I shook and she pulled, and before morning we had peeled off yards of that paper." Is the message of the tale's conclusion mere madness? Certainly the righteous Doctor John — whose name links him to the anti-hero of Charlotte Brontë's *Villette* — has been temporarily defeated, or at least momentarily stunned. "Now why should that man have fainted?" the narrator ironically asks as she creeps around her attic. But John's unmasculine swoon of surprise is the least of the triumphs Gilman imagines for her madwoman. More significant are the madwoman's own imaginings and creations, mirages of health and freedom with which her author endows her like a fairy godmother showering gold on a sleeping heroine. The woman from behind the wallpaper creeps away, for instance, creeps fast and far on the long road, in broad daylight. "I have watched her sometimes away off in the open country," says the narrator, "creeping as fast as a cloud shadow in a high wind."

Indistinct and yet rapid, barely perceptible but inexorable, the progress of that cloud shadow is not unlike the progress of nineteenth-century literary women out of the texts defined by patriarchal poetics into the open spaces of their own authority. That such an escape from the numb world behind the patterned walls of the text was a flight from disease into health was quite clear to Gilman herself. When "The Yellow Wallpaper" was published she sent it to Weir Mitchell whose strictures had kept her from attempting the pen during her own breakdown, thereby aggravating her illness, and she was delighted to learn, years later, that "he had changed his treatment of nervous prostration since reading" her story. "If that is a fact," she declared, "I have not lived in vain." Because she was a rebellious feminist besides being a medical iconoclast, we can be sure that Gilman did not think of this triumph of hers in narrowly therapeutic terms. Because she knew, with Emily Dickinson, that "Infection in the sentence breeds," she knew that the cure for female despair must be spiritual as well as physical, aesthetic as well as social. What "The Yellow Wallpaper" shows she knew, too, is that even when a supposedly "mad" woman has been sentenced to imprisonment in the "infected" house of her own body, she may discover that, as Sylvia Plath[1] was to put it seventy years later, she has "a self to recover, a queen."

---

[1] Sylvia Plath (1932–1963), American poet.

ELAINE SHOWALTER

On "The Yellow Wallpaper"

2009

Charlotte Perkins Gilman (1860–1935), the leading American feminist theoretician and New Woman writer to come out of the 1890s, also experimented with utopian writing, and with the idea that writing itself could be a separate country for women. Her father, Frederick Beecher Perkins, was related to the great Beecher family, but he abandoned his wife and children a year after Charlotte was born in Hartford, Connecticut, and the couple were divorced in 1873. Through the rest of her life, Charlotte's father was absent as a source of love and support. As she wrote in her autobiography, *The Living of Charlotte Perkins Gilman* (1935), "The word 'Father,' in the sense of love, care, one to go to when in trouble, means nothing to me, save indeed in advice about books and the care of them — which seems more the librarian than the father." In fact, her father was a professional librarian who eventually became head of the San Francisco Public Library, and despite his remoteness, she maintained an irregular correspondence with him and consulted him about her reading. Thus, like many of her precursors, she was educated in her father's library.

Charlotte's mother, Mary Westcott Perkins, raised her son and daughter in Providence, Rhode Island, living with various relatives and struggling to support the family. Because she had been so betrayed and hurt herself, she tried to train Charlotte to do without affection: "She would not let me caress her, and would not caress me, unless I was asleep," Gilman sadly recalled. Her mother also tried, unsuccessfully, to curb her imagination and ambition; she was forbidden to read novels, write poetry, or go to the theater. Nevertheless, at eighteen, Charlotte went to study art at the Rhode Island School of Design, and was soon able to support herself as a commercial artist.

In her girlhood years, her most intense relationship was with a girlfriend, Martha Luther, and when Martha married, she was heartbroken and resolved always to live alone and independent: "I am fonder of freedom than anything else . . . I like to have my own unaided will in all my surroundings — in dress, diet, hours, behaviors, speech, and thought." Yet soon after, she met and married a young painter, Charles Walter Stetson. Their daughter Katherine was born in 1885, and Charlotte suffered a severe bout of postpartum depression. At first, she tried going away to visit a friend, Grace Channing, in California, but the symptoms came back when she returned home.

Dr. Silas Weir Mitchell (1829–1914), who had treated Rebecca Harding Davis in the 1860s, was the leading American specialist on female depression and neurasthenia, and had developed a famous "rest cure" for its treatment. Believing that neurasthenic New Women were suffering from a deep resistance to the female role, he attempted to induce a therapeutic state of dependence, weight gain, and inertia. He removed the exhausted and often anorexic patient from the family setting to a clinic, where she was confined to bed for several weeks, forbidden to do any intellectual work, and treated with a rich diet, massage, and electric stimulation. As Mitchell understood, the boredom and isolation of the treatment was "rather a bitter medicine" that made many women "glad enough to accept the order to rise and go about when the doctor issues a mandate." For depressed, anxious, and exhausted men, however, he recommended the "West cure" — a vacation on the frontier, or in the country, with physical labor and wholesome outdoor living replacing their stressful urban lives and repetitive jobs.

Gilman turned to Weir Mitchell in desperation, writing a letter about her family genealogy and her emotional torment after her daughter's birth: "This agony of mind set in with the child's coming. I nursed her in slow tears. All that summer I did nothing but cry, save for times when the pain was unbearable and I grew almost hysterical, almost imbecile at times." In the spring of 1887, Gilman went to Weir Mitchell's clinic in Philadelphia for a last-chance rest cure. Ordered to "live as domestic a life as possible" and "have your child with you all the time," and never "to touch pen, brush, or pencil as long as you live," Gilman had a complete breakdown. She saved herself by determining on a separation from her husband: "It seemed plain that if I went crazy it would do my husband no good and be a deadly injury to my child." In October 1888, she decided that what she really needed was the "West cure." Moving to Pasadena, California, with her little daughter, Gilman lectured, tutored, acted in community theater, and wrote stories, poems, articles, and satirical pieces.

As Gilman's biographer Mary A. Hill points out, "California in the early 1890s was an ideal training ground for rebels. It was a vital center of contemporary protest thought, a relatively supportive community for radicals and nonconformists, an engaging political environment in which Charlotte could broaden and intensify her sense of alliance with nationally based currents of reform." Gilman realized that the change of environment and lifestyle was a rebirth: "With Pasadena begins my professional 'living.' Before that, there was no assurance of serious work." She reveled in "the vivid beauty of the land, its tumultuous growth of flowers and fruit, the shining glory of the days and nights, [which] gave me happiness and health."

On a June day in Pasadena, with the "thermometer at one hundred and three," Gilman wrote her most important short story, "The Yellow Wall-paper." Told in a series of brief paragraphs of one or two sentences, "The Yellow Wall-paper" is a first-person narrative, a secret journal covering three months from approximately June 1 to the end of August. Its author is an unnamed woman who has been taken by her physician-husband, John, to a secluded house in the country, a "colonial mansion, a hereditary estate," in order to cure a nervous illness, a "slight hysterical tendency," she has developed after the birth of a son. The house is isolated, three miles from the nearest village. On its extensive grounds there are high hedges and locked gates, and inside the house, at the top, a large room with barred windows, rings on the walls, and an iron bed nailed down to the floor, which is "gouged and splintered," while the room's yellow wallpaper has been ripped and torn. This is the bedroom the narrator and her husband share at night, although she is alone in it during the long summer days when she secretly writes in her diary.

The realistic subtext of the story is that she is suffering a postpartum depression so severe that her husband and relatives are afraid she may harm herself or the baby or both. The remote house sounds like an abandoned private mental hospital, where the barred windows and nailed-down bed are signs of former patients who have been incarcerated. Like the "dead paper" of her journal, to which she confides her thoughts, the narrator also projects her suicidal feelings and violent obsessions onto the art nouveau wallpaper, which has a maddening pattern, a "florid arabesque." "It is dull enough to confuse the eye in following, pronounced enough to constantly irritate and provoke study, and when you follow the lame uncertain curves for a little distance they suddenly commit suicide — plunge off at outrageous angles, destroy themselves in unheard of contradictions." The pattern of the wallpaper takes on elements of a human face, which reminds her of a strangled baby: "there is a recurrent spot where the pattern lolls like a broken neck and two bulbous eyes stare at you upside down."

"I am sitting by the Window in this Atrocious Nursery."

THE YELLOW WALL-PAPER.

By Charlotte Perkins Stetson.

Illustration by J. H. Hatfield from the *New England Magazine* edition of "The Yellow Wallpaper" (1892), while Gilman was still married to her first husband, Charles Walter Stetson.

The color of the wallpaper also begins to prey upon her mind: "The color is repellent, almost revolting: a smoldering unclean yellow, strangely faded by the slow-turning sunlight. It is dull yet lurid orange in some places, a sickly sulphur tint in others." Later the narrator has olfactory hallucinations about the paper as well: "There is something else about that paper — the smell! . . . It creeps all over the house." She even thinks of burning down the house to destroy the "yellow smell." Although never stated directly, the odor suggests urine and soiled diapers.

In contrast to the disgusting paper inside the room is the "delicious" garden she can see from her window, a garden that suggests another traditional imagery of femininity and the maternal body much celebrated by American women writers, full of "mysterious deepshaded arbors, . . . riotous old-fashioned flowers, and bushes and gnarly trees." Soon she sees another woman — her double — trapped behind the paper and trying to get through, "but nobody could get through that pattern — it strangles so"; she also sees women creeping around in the garden, perhaps the ghosts of former mental patients. By the end, the narrator is completely mad, and contemplating murder and suicide. When her husband breaks into the room where she has locked herself, she has ripped off all the paper, and is creeping around the walls. "I've got out in spite of you," she tells him triumphantly, and he faints in shock. Gilman constructed an impossible narrative, for the narrator is apparently still writing in her diary in the present tense while she is mad. She expresses her anger toward men and medicine in self-destructive illness.

Gilman, however, did not destroy herself but used her writing to fight back against confinement. She sent the story to the *Atlantic Monthly,* but it was rejected by the editor Horace Elisha Scudder. She then sent it to a literary agent, Henry Austin. Austin told her he had got it published and then absconded with her forty-dollar fee, but probably William Dean Howells intervened to get it published in the *New England Magazine* in 1892. There it was well received; Henry B. Blackwell wrote: "Nothing more graphic and suggestive has ever been written to show why so many women go crazy, especially farmers' wives, who live lonely, monotonous lives." Gilman said that she had also sent the story to Weir Mitchell, who never acknowledged it, but that she had been told by friends "that the great specialist . . . had altered his treatment of neurasthenia." There is, alas, no evidence of this. He continued to use the rest cure for other women, including Edith Wharton, and in 1908, he was still defending it before the American Neurological Association. . . .

Charlotte divorced Charles Walter Stetson in 1894, and they formed a new arrangement that scandalized their friends: he married Grace Channing, and nine-year-old Katherine was sent to live with her father and stepmother. For several years, Charlotte also had a passionate friendship with a woman journalist, Adeline Knapp. But in 1900 she was happily remarried to her cousin George Houghton Gilman, by whose name she was known thereafter. In a rapid series of books and articles, Gilman outlined her Darwinian agenda of sexual evolution and equality. Some of her most progressive ideas were about the differences between masculine and feminine literature. Men, she wrote, have written about adventure, hunting, war, crime, and punishment. But New Women's literature promised something different, with the familiar male bee of nineteenth-century American women's writing reduced to the level of a drone, and the queen bee and her servants, the feminist symbols of the twentieth century, taking over their power. . . .

In April 1891, Gilman read "The Yellow Wall-paper" to a friend in California, and recorded in her diary, "she likes it." The friend was Gertrude Atherton

(1857–1948), a widowed young novelist who soon left the country and went to seek her literary fortune in London. Her real feelings about "The Yellow Wall-paper" were quite different from the impression she gave Gilman. In her autobiography, *Adventures of a Novelist,* she describes hosting an unnamed visitor — "the most able and intellectual woman in California" and "an EMI- NENT FEMINIST" — at a soiree at her San Francisco home. The guest announced that she "had written a wonderful ghost story," and would read it aloud. Sitting in the dark, by the light of a single candle, she read and read and read. "That was probably the worst story ever written," Atherton opined, "ghost or other- wise. It went on and on and on. In the author's nasal monotonous voice. An atmosphere of depression settled over the room. Sighs. Rustlings. Everyone I knew, cursing me in his or her heart." She assured Gilman, however, that she had been vastly impressed. As Atherton's biographer writes, "Although she wrote one frankly suffragist novel, another in which women stage a revolution against men, and many others with spirited, bright, and assertive heroines, Atherton was the kind of feminist who complains about how ugly most other feminists are."

FLANNERY O'CONNOR

Flannery O'Connor in the summer of 1962 at Andalusia, her family farm and home outside Milledgeville, Georgia.

Flannery O'Connor is unusual among writers in that she shared with readers her own interpretations of her stories. While acknowledging that there is usually more than one way to read a story, she also stated that there was only one way she could possibly have written it. O'Connor's discussion of "A Good Man Is Hard to Find" in her letters (p. 1590) can be read alongside the interpretations of "Good Country People" (p. 1611) and "Everything That Rises Must Converge" (p. 1608) by academic critics Dorothy Tuck McFarland and Wayne C. Booth, respectively. Joyce Carol Oates (p. 1600) gave her view of "The Parables of Flannery O'Connor" in *The New York Review of Books,* April 9, 2009, on the occasion of the publication of Brad Gooch's biography, *Flannery: A Life of Flannery O'Connor.*

From Letters, 1954–55

1955

To Sally Fitzgerald

26 Dec 54

... I have finally got off the ms. for my collection [*A Good Man Is Hard to Find*] and it is scheduled to appear in May. Without yr kind permission I have taken the liberty of dedicating (grand verb) it to you and Robert. This is because you all are my adopted kin and if I dedicated it to any of my blood kin they would think they had to go into hiding. Nine stories about original sin, with my compliments.

I have been invited to go to Greensboro to the Women's College in March to be on an arts panel. That is where Brother Randall Jarrell holds forth. I accepted but I am not looking forward to it. Can you fancy me hung in conversation with the likes of him?

When I had lunch with Giroux [O'Connor's editor] in Atlanta he told me about Cal's escapade in Cincinnati. It seems [Cal] convinced everybody it was Elizabeth who was going crazy.[1] ... Toward the end he gave a lecture at the university that was almost pure gibberish. I guess nobody noticed, thinking it was the new criticism. ...

I just got a check for $200 for the 2nd prize in the O. Henry book this year. My ex-mentor Paul Engle does the selecting. Jean Stafford got the first one.

I am walking with a cane these days which gives me a great air of distinction. The scientist tells me this has nothing to do with the lupus but is rheumatism. I would not believe it except that the dose of ACTH has not been increased. Besides which I now feel it makes very little difference what you call it. As the niggers say, I have the misery.

I am reading everything I can of Romano Guardini's [Italian priest and theologian]. Have you become acquainted with his work? A book called *The Lord* of his is very fine.

To Elizabeth McKee

13 January 1955

The carbon of "An Exile in the East" is enclosed, but I don't know if you realize or not that this is a rewritten version of "The Geranium" originally printed in *Accent*. *Accent* didn't pay me for it and it is rather much changed, but I enclose both stories so [the editor] can see what she's doing. I don't want to go to the penitentiary for selling a story twice (but if I do I would like to get a good price for the story).

---

[1] Cal and Elizabeth are the poet Robert Lowell (1917–1977) and writer Elizabeth Hardwick (1916–2007), who were married at the time.

To Robert Giroux

22 January 55

Nothing has been said about a picture for the jacket of this collection *but if you have to have one*, I would be much obliged if you could use the enclosed so that I won't have to have a new picture made. This is a self-portrait with a pheasant cock, that I painted in 1953; however, I think it will do justice to the subject for some time to come.

26 February 55

I have just written a story called "Good Country People" that Allen and Caroline [Tate?] both say is the best thing I have written and should be in this collection. I told them I thought it was too late, but anyhow I am writing now to ask if it is. It is really a story that would set the whole collection on its feet. It is 27 pages and if you can eliminate the one called "A Stroke of Good Fortune," and the other called "An Afternoon in the Woods," this one would fit the available space nicely. Also I remember you said it would be good to have one that had never been published before. I could send it to you at once *on being wired*. Please let me know.

[Giroux wired O'Connor that every effort would be made to include the story. After he had read it, he wrote suggesting that an appearance by the mother and Mrs. Freeman at the end might improve it. Flannery recognized the value of the suggestion and added the sentences that are now a part of the story.]

7 March 55

I like the suggestion about the ending of "Good Country People" and enclose a dozen or so lines that can be added on to *the present end*. I enclose them in case you can get them put on before I get the proofs. I am mighty wary of making changes on proofs. . . .

To Sally and Robert Fitzgerald

1 April 55

We are wondering if #6 is here yet or due to arrive momentarily. Let us hear and if you need any names, I'll be glad to cable you a rich collection. I have just got back from Greensboro where I said nothing intelligent the whole time, but enjoyed myself. Mr. Randall Jarrell, wife and stepdaughters I met and et dinner with. I must say I was shocked at what a very kind man he is — that is the last impression I expected to have of him. I also met Peter Taylor, who is more like folks. Mrs. Jarrell is writing a novel. You get the impression the two stepdaughters may be at it too and maybe the dog. Mr. Jarrell has a beard and looks like Mephistopheles (sp?) only fatter. Mrs. Jarrell is very friendly & sunkist.

The Easter rabbit is bringing my mother a three-quarter ton truck.

I trust Giroux will be sending you a copy of the book soon. I wrote a very hot story at the last minute called "Good Country People": so now there are ten.

While I was in NC I heard somebody recite a barroom ballad. I don't remember anything but the end but beinst you all are poets I will give it to you as it is mighty deathless:

"They stacked the stiffs outside the door.
They made, I reckon, a cord or more."

I call that real poetry.

I have put the cane up and am walking on my own very well. Let us hear. Regards to children.

FLANNERY O'CONNOR

Writing Short Stories

1961

. . . Perhaps the central question to be considered in any discussion of the short story is what do we mean by short. Being short does not mean being slight. A short story should be long in depth and should give us an experience of meaning. I have an aunt who thinks that nothing happens in a story unless somebody gets married or shot at the end of it. I wrote a story about a tramp who marries an old woman's idiot daughter in order to acquire the old woman's automobile. After the marriage, he takes the daughter off on a wedding trip in the automobile and abandons her in an eating place and drives on by himself. Now that is a complete story. There is nothing more relating to the mystery of that man's personality that could be shown through that particular dramatization. But I've never been able to convince my aunt that it's a complete story. She wants to know what happened to the idiot daughter after that.

Not long ago that story was adapted for a television play, and the adapter, knowing his business, had the tramp have a change of heart and go back and pick up the idiot daughter and the two of them ride away, grinning madly. My aunt believes that the story is complete at last, but I have other sentiments about it — which are not suitable for public utterance. When you write a story, you only have to write one story, but there will always be people who will refuse to read the story you have written.

And this naturally brings up the awful question of what kind of a reader you are writing for when you write fiction. Perhaps we each think we have a personal solution for this problem. For my own part, I have a very high opinion of the art of fiction and a very low opinion of what is called the "average" reader. I tell myself that I can't escape him, that this is the personality I am supposed to keep awake, but that at the same time, I am also supposed to provide the intelligent reader with the deeper experience that he looks for in fiction. Now actually, both of these readers are just aspects of the writer's own personality, and in the last analysis, the only reader he can know anything about is himself. We all write at our own level of understanding, but it is the peculiar characteristic of fiction that its literal surface can be made to yield entertainment on an obvious physical plane to one sort of reader while the selfsame surface can be made to yield meaning to the person equipped to experience it there.

Meaning is what keeps the short story from being short. I prefer to talk about the meaning in a story rather than the theme of a story. People talk about the theme of a story as if the theme were like the string that a sack of chicken feed is tied with. They think that if you can pick out the theme, the way you pick the right thread in the chicken-feed sack, you can rip the story open and feed the chickens. But this is not the way meaning works in fiction.

When you can state the theme of a story, when you can separate it from the story itself, then you can be sure the story is not a very good one. The meaning of a story has to be embodied in it, has to be made concrete in it. A story is a way to say something that can't be said any other way, and it takes every word in the story to say what the meaning is. You tell a story because a statement would be inadequate. When anybody asks what a story is about, the only proper thing is to tell him to read the story. The meaning of fiction is not abstract meaning but experienced meaning, and the purpose of making statements about the meaning of a story is only to help you to experience that meaning more fully.

Fiction is an art that calls for the strictest attention to the real — whether the writer is writing a naturalistic story or a fantasy. I mean that we always begin with what is or with what has an eminent possibility of truth about it. Even when one writes a fantasy, reality is the proper basis of it. A thing is fantastic because it is so real, so real that it is fantastic. Graham Greene has said that he can't write, "I stood over a bottomless pit," because that couldn't be true, or "Running down the stairs I jumped into a taxi," because that couldn't be true either. But Elizabeth Bowen can write about one of her characters that "she snatched at her hair as if she heard something in it," because that is eminently possible.

I would even go so far as to say that the person writing a fantasy has to be even more strictly attentive to the concrete detail than someone writing in a naturalistic vein — because the greater the story's strain on the credulity, the more convincing the properties in it have to be.

A good example of this is a story called "The Metamorphosis" by Franz Kafka. This is a story about a man who wakes up one morning to find that he has turned into a cockroach overnight, while not discarding his human nature. The rest of the story concerns his life and feelings and eventual death as an insect with human nature, and this situation is accepted by the reader because the concrete detail of the story is absolutely convincing. The fact is that this story describes the dual nature of man in such a realistic fashion that it is almost unbearable. The truth is not distorted here, but rather, a certain distortion is used to get at the truth. If we admit, as we must, that appearance is not the same thing as reality, then we must give the artist the liberty to make certain rearrangements of nature if these will lead to greater depths of vision. The artist himself always has to remember that what he is rearranging *is* nature, and that he has to know it and be able to describe it accurately in order to have the authority to rearrange it at all.

The peculiar problem of the short-story writer is how to make the action he describes reveal as much of the mystery of existence as possible. He has only a short space to do it in and he can't do it by statement. He has to do it by showing, not by saying, and by showing the concrete — so that his problem is really how to make the concrete work double time for him.

In good fiction, certain of the details will tend to accumulate meaning from the action of the story itself, and when this happens they become symbolic in the way they work. I once wrote a story called "Good Country People," in which a lady Ph.D. has her wooden leg stolen by a Bible salesman whom she has tried to seduce. Now I'll admit that, paraphrased in this way, the situation is simply a low joke. The average reader is pleased to observe anybody's wooden leg being stolen. But without ceasing to appeal to him and without making any statements of high intention, this story does manage to operate at another level of experience, by letting the wooden leg accumulate meaning. Early in the story, we're presented with the fact that the Ph.D. is spiritually as well as physically crippled. She believes in nothing but her own belief in nothing, and we perceive that there is a wooden part of her soul that corresponds to her wooden leg. Now of course this is never stated. The fiction writer states as little as possible. The reader makes this connection from things he is shown. He may not even know that he makes the connection, but the connection is there nevertheless and it has its effect on him. As the story goes on, the wooden leg continues to accumulate meaning. The reader learns how the girl feels about her leg, how her mother feels about it, and how the country woman on the place feels about it; and finally, by the time the Bible salesman comes along, the leg has accumulated so much meaning that it is, as the saying goes, loaded. And when the Bible salesman steals it, the reader realizes that he has taken away part of the girl's personality and has revealed her deeper affliction to her for the first time.

If you want to say that the wooden leg is a symbol, you can say that. But it is a wooden leg first, and as a wooden leg it is absolutely necessary to the story. It has its place on the literal level of the story, but it operates in depth as well as on the surface. It increases the story in every direction, and this is essentially the way a story escapes being short.

Now a little might be said about the way in which this happens. I wouldn't want you to think that in that story I sat down and said, "I am now going to write a story about a Ph.D. with a wooden leg, using the wooden leg as a symbol for another kind of affliction." I doubt myself if many writers know what they are going to do when they start out. When I started writing that story, I didn't know there was going to be a Ph.D. with a wooden leg in it. I merely found myself one morning writing a description of two women that I knew something about, and before I realized it, I had equipped one of them with a daughter with a wooden leg. As the story progressed, I brought in the Bible salesman, but I had no idea what I was going to do with him. I didn't know he was going to steal that wooden leg until ten or twelve lines before he did it, but when I found out that this was what was going to happen, I realized that it was inevitable. This is a story that produces a shock for the reader, and I think one reason for this is that it produced a shock for the writer.

Now despite the fact that this story came about in this seemingly mindless fashion, it is a story that almost no rewriting was done on. It is a story that was under control throughout the writing of it, and it might be asked how this kind of control comes about, since it is not entirely conscious.

I think the answer to this is what Maritain[1] calls "the habit of art." It is a fact that fiction writing is something in which the whole personality takes part — the conscious as well as the unconscious mind. Art is the habit of the artist; and habits have to be rooted deep in the whole personality. They have to be cultivated like any other habit, over a long period of time, by experience; and teaching any kind of writing is largely a matter of helping the student develop the habit of art. I think this is more than just a discipline, although it is that; I think it is a way of looking at the created world and of using the senses so as to make them find as much meaning as possible in things.

Now I am not so naïve as to suppose that most people come to writers' conferences in order to hear what kind of vision is necessary to write stories that will become a permanent part of our literature. Even if you do wish to hear this, your greatest concerns are immediately practical. You want to know how you can actually write a good story, and further, how you can tell when you've done it; and so you want to know what the form of a short story is, as if the form were something that existed outside of each story and could be applied or imposed on the material. Of course, the more you write, the more you will realize that the form is organic, that it is something that grows out of the material, that the form of each story is unique. A story that is any good can't be reduced, it can only be expanded. A story is good when you continue to see more and more in it, and when it continues to escape you. In fiction two and two is always more than four.

The only way, I think, to learn to write short stories is to write them, and then to try to discover what you have done. The time to think of technique is when you've actually got the story in front of you. The teacher can help the student by looking at his individual work and trying to help him decide if he has written a complete story, one in which the action fully illuminates the meaning.

Perhaps the most profitable thing I can do is to tell you about some of the general observations I made about these seven stories I read of yours. All of these observations will not fit any one of the stories exactly, but they are points nevertheless that it won't hurt anyone interested in writing to think about.

The first thing that any professional writer is conscious of in reading anything is, naturally, the use of language. Now the use of language in these stories was such that, with one exception, it would be difficult to distinguish one story from another. While I can recall running into several clichés, I can't remember one image or one metaphor from the seven stories. I don't mean there weren't

---

[1]Jacques Maritain (1882–1973), French philosopher and critic.

images in them; I just mean that there weren't any that were effective enough to take away with you.

In connection with this, I made another observation that startled me considerably. With the exception of one story, there was practically no use made of the local idiom. Now this is a Southern Writers' Conference. All the addresses on these stories were from Georgia or Tennessee, yet there was no distinctive sense of Southern life in them. A few place-names were dropped, Savannah or Atlanta or Jacksonville, but these could just as easily have been changed to Pittsburgh or Passaic without calling for any other alteration in the story. The characters spoke as if they had never heard any kind of language except what came out of a television set. This indicates that something is way out of focus.

There are two qualities that make fiction. One is the sense of mystery and the other is the sense of manners. You get the manners from the texture of existence that surrounds you. The great advantage of being a Southern writer is that we don't have to go anywhere to look for manners; bad or good, we've got them in abundance. We in the South live in a society that is rich in contradiction, rich in irony, rich in contrast, and particularly rich in its speech. And yet here are six stories by Southerners in which almost no use is made of the gifts of the region.

Of course the reason for this may be that you have seen these gifts abused so often that you have become self-conscious about using them. There is nothing worse than the writer who doesn't *use* the gifts of the region, but wallows in them. Everything becomes so Southern that it's sickening, so local that it is unintelligible, so literally reproduced that it conveys nothing. The general gets lost in the particular instead of being shown through it.

However, when the life that actually surrounds us is totally ignored, when our patterns of speech are absolutely overlooked, then something is out of kilter. The writer should then ask himself if he is not reaching out for a kind of life that is artificial to him.

An idiom characterizes a society, and when you ignore the idiom, you are very likely ignoring the whole social fabric that could make a meaningful character. You can't cut characters off from their society and say much about them as individuals. You can't say anything meaningful about the mystery of a personality unless you put that personality in a believable and significant social context. And the best way to do this is through the character's own language. When the old lady in one of Andrew Lytle's stories says contemptuously that she has a mule that is older than Birmingham, we get in that one sentence a sense of a society and its history. A great deal of the Southern writers' work is done for him before he begins, because our history lives in our talk. In one of Eudora Welty's stories a character says, "Where I come from, we use fox for yard dogs and owls for chickens, but we sing true." Now there is a whole book in that one sentence; and when the people of your section can talk like that, and you ignore it, you're just not taking advantage of what's yours. The sound of our talk is too definite to be discarded with impunity, and if the writer tries to get rid of it, he is liable to destroy the better part of his creative power.

Another thing I observed about these stories is that most of them don't go very far inside a character, don't reveal very much of the character. I don't mean that they don't enter the character's mind, but they simply don't show that he has a personality. Again this goes back partly to speech. These characters have no distinctive speech to reveal themselves with; and sometimes they have no really distinctive features. You feel in the end that no personality is revealed because no personality is there. In most good stories it is the character's personality that creates the action of the story. In most of these stories, I feel that the writer has thought of some action and then scrounged up a character to perform it. You will usually be more successful if you start the other way around. If you start with a real personality, a real character, then something is bound to happen; and you don't have to know what before you begin. In fact it may be better if you don't know what before you begin. You ought to be able to discover something from your stories. If you don't, probably nobody else will.

FLANNERY O'CONNOR

A Reasonable Use of the Unreasonable

1969

A story really isn't any good unless it successfully resists paraphrase, unless it hangs on and expands in the mind. Properly, you analyze to enjoy, but it's equally true that to analyze with any discrimination, you have to have enjoyed already, and I think that the best reason to hear a story read is that it should stimulate that primary enjoyment.

I don't have any pretensions to being an Aeschylus or Sophocles and providing you in this story with a cathartic experience out of your mythic background, though this story I'm going to read certainly calls up a good deal of the South's mythic background, and it should elicit from you a degree of pity and terror, even though its way of being serious is a comic one. I do think, though, that like the Greeks you should know what is going to happen in this story so that any element of suspense in it will be transferred from its surface to its interior.

I would be most happy if you had already read it, happier still if you knew it well, but since experience has taught me to keep my expectations along these lines modest, I'll tell you that this is the story of a family of six which, on its way driving to Florida, gets wiped out by an escaped convict who calls himself the Misfit. The family is made up of the Grandmother and her son, Bailey, and his children, John Wesley and June Star and the baby, and there is also the cat and the children's mother. The cat is named Pitty Sing, and the Grandmother is taking him with them, hidden in a basket.

Now I think it behooves me to try to establish with you the basis on which reason operates in this story. Much of my fiction takes its character from a reasonable use of the unreasonable, though the reasonableness of my use of it may not always be apparent. The assumptions that underlie this use of it, however, are those of the central Christian mysteries. These are assumptions to which a large part of the modern audience takes exception. About this I can only say that there are perhaps other ways than my own in which this story could be read, but none other by which it could have been written. Belief, in my own case anyway, is the engine that makes perception operate.

The heroine of this story, the Grandmother, is in the most significant position life offers the Christian. She is facing death. And to all appearances she, like the rest of us, is not too well prepared for it. She would like to see the event postponed. Indefinitely.

I've talked to a number of teachers who use this story in class and who tell their students that the Grandmother is evil, that in fact, she's a witch, even down to the cat. One of these teachers told me that his students, and particularly his southern students, resisted this interpretation with a certain bemused vigor, and he didn't understand why. I had to tell him that they resisted it because they all had grandmothers or great-aunts just like her at home, and they knew, from personal experience, that the old lady lacked comprehension, but that she had a good heart. The southerner is usually tolerant of those weaknesses that proceed from innocence, and he knows that a taste for self-preservation can be readily combined with the missionary spirit.

This same teacher was telling his students that morally the Misfit was several cuts above the Grandmother. He had a really sentimental attachment to the Misfit. But then a prophet gone wrong is almost always more interesting than your grandmother, and you have to let people take their pleasures where they find them.

It is true that the old lady is a hypocritical old soul; her wits are no match for the Misfit's, nor is her capacity for grace equal to his; yet I think the unprejudiced reader will feel that the Grandmother has a special kind of triumph in this story which instinctively we do not allow to someone altogether bad.

I often ask myself what makes a story work, and what makes it hold up as a story, and I have decided that it is probably some action, some gesture of a character that is unlike any other in the story, one which indicates where the real heart of the story lies. This would have to be an action or a gesture which was both totally right and totally unexpected; it would have to be one that was both in character and beyond character; it would have to suggest both the world and eternity. The action or gesture I'm talking about would have to be on the anagogical level, that is, the level which has to do with the Divine life and our participation in it. It would be a gesture that transcended any neat allegory that might have been intended or any pat moral categories a reader could make. It would be a gesture which somehow made contact with mystery.

There is a point in this story where such a gesture occurs. The Grandmother is at last alone, facing the Misfit. Her head clears for an instant and she realizes, even in her limited way, that she is responsible for the man before her and joined to him by ties of kinship which have their roots deep in the mystery she has been merely prattling about so far. And at this point, she does the right thing, she makes the right gesture.

I find that students are often puzzled by what she says and does here, but I think myself that if I took out this gesture and what she says with it, I would have no story. What was left would not be worth your attention. Our age not only does not have a very sharp eye for the almost imperceptible intrusions of grace, it no longer has much feeling for the nature of the violences which precede and follow them. The devil's greatest wile, Baudelaire has said, is to convince us that he does not exist.

I suppose the reasons for the use of so much violence in modern fiction will differ with each writer who uses it, but in my own stories I have found that violence is strangely capable of returning my characters to reality and preparing them to accept their moment of grace. Their heads are so hard that almost nothing else will do the work. This idea, that reality is something to which we must be returned at considerable cost, is one which is seldom understood by the casual reader, but it is one which is implicit in the Christian view of the world.

I don't want to equate the Misfit with the devil. I prefer to think that, however unlikely this may seem, the old lady's gesture, like the mustard-seed, will grow to be a great crow-filled tree in the Misfit's heart, and will be enough of a pain to him there to turn him into the prophet he was meant to become. But that's another story.

This story has been called grotesque, but I prefer to call it literal. A good story is literal in the same sense that a child's drawing is literal. When a child draws, he doesn't intend to distort but to set down exactly what he sees, and as his gaze is direct, he sees the lines that create motion. Now the lines of motion that interest the writer are usually invisible. They are lines of spiritual motion. And in this story you should be on the lookout for such things as the action of grace in the Grandmother's soul, and not for the dead bodies.

We hear many complaints about the prevalence of violence in modern fiction, and it is always assumed that this violence is a bad thing and meant to be an end in itself. With the serious writer, violence is never an end in itself. It is the extreme situation that best reveals what we are essentially, and I believe these are times when writers are more interested in what we are essentially than in the tenor of our daily lives. Violence is a force which can be used for good or evil, and among other things taken by it is the kingdom of heaven. But regardless of what can be taken by it, the man in the violent situation reveals those qualities least dispensable in his personality, those qualities which are all he will have to take into eternity with him; and since the characters in this story are all on the verge of eternity, it is appropriate to think of what they take with them. In any case, I hope that if you consider these points in connection with the story, you will come to see it as something more than an account of a family murdered on the way to Florida.

JOYCE CAROL OATES

The Parables of Flannery O'Connor

2009

Writers who see by the light of their Christian faith will have, in these times, the
sharpest eye for the grotesque, for the perverse, and for the unacceptable. . . .
To the hard of hearing you shout, and for the almost-blind you draw large and
startling figures.

— Flannery O'Connor, "The Fiction Writer and His Country"

Whenever I'm asked why Southern writers particularly have a penchant for
writing about freaks, I say it is because we are still able to recognize one.

— Flannery O'Connor, "Some Aspects of the Grotesque in Southern Fiction"

Short stories, for all the dazzling diversity of the genre, are of two general types:
those that yield their meanings subtly, quietly, and are as nuanced and delicate
and without melodrama as the unfolding of miniature blossoms in Japanese
chrysanthemum tea, and those that explode in the reader's face. Flannery
O'Connor (1925–1964) came of age in a time when subtlety and "atmosphere"
in short stories were fashionable — as in the finely wrought, understated stories of such classic predecessors as Anton Chekhov, Henry James, and James
Joyce, and such American contemporaries as Katherine Anne Porter, Eudora
Welty, Peter Taylor, and Jean Stafford.

But O'Connor's plainspoken, blunt, comic-cartoonish, and flagrantly
melodramatic short stories were anything but fashionable. The novelty of her
"acidly comic tales with moral and religious messages" — as Brad Gooch puts
it in his new life of O'Connor — lay in their frontal assault upon the reader's
sensibility: these were not refined *New Yorker* stories of the era in which nothing happens except inside characters' minds, but stories in which something
happens of irreversible magnitude, often death by violent means.

An escaped convict called the Misfit offhandedly slaughters a Southern
family in backcountry Georgia ("A Good Man Is Hard to Find"). A conniv-
ing old woman marries off her retarded daughter to a sinister one-armed
tramp named Shiftlet, who immediately abandons the girl and drives off
with the old woman's car ("The Life You Save May Be Your Own"). An
embittered young woman, crippled by the loss of a leg (in a "hunting accident" when she was ten), who has changed her name from Joy to Hulga, is
seduced by a hypocritical young Bible salesman who steals her wooden leg
("Good Country People"). Boy arsonists set fire to a wooded property out
of pure meanness, like latter-day prophets "dancing in the fiery furnace"
("A Circle in the Fire"). A widowed property owner who imagines herself superior to her tenant farmers is gored to death by their runaway bull
("Greenleaf"). A mentally disturbed girl reading a textbook called *Human
Development* in a doctor's waiting room suddenly throws the book at the

head of a garrulous middle-class woman who holds herself above "poor-white trash" ("Revelation").

In the novella-length *Wise Blood* (1952), O'Connor's first published book, the fanatic Hazel Motes proclaims himself a prophet of the "Church without Christ" and does penance for his sins by gouging out an eye. In O'Connor's second, kindred novel, *The Violent Bear It Away* (1960), the young Francis Marion Tarwater drowns an idiot cousin while baptizing him, is drugged and raped by a sexual predator, and revives and lurches off, like Yeats's rough beast awakened, "toward the dark city, where the children of God lay sleeping."

In the 1950s, when Flannery O'Connor first began to publish such idiosyncratic and mordantly comic fiction as *Wise Blood* and the story collection *A Good Man Is Hard to Find* (1955), the seemingly reclusive young writer from Milledgeville, Georgia — in Brad Gooch's description a "sleepy community at the dead center of Georgia" of which O'Connor said dryly, "We have a girls' college here, but the lacy atmosphere is fortunately destroyed by a reformatory, an insane asylum, and a military school" — was perceived as a younger cousin of such showier, more renowned, and best-selling Southern Gothic contemporaries as Carson McCullers and Truman Capote.[1] How ironic that during their turbulent, highly publicized lifetimes McCullers and Capote were far more famous than Flannery O'Connor, of whose invalided private life little was known, or might be said to be worth knowing; as O'Connor observed to a friend, "As for biographies, there won't be any biographies of me because, for only one reason, lives spent between the house and the chicken yard do not make exciting copy."

Throughout her radically truncated career, O'Connor's outwardly sensational, quirkily "Christian" fiction aroused mixed critical responses and modest sales; yet though she was to die of lupus at the young age of thirty-nine, leaving behind a relatively small body of work, her reputation has steadily increased in the intervening years, while those of McCullers and Capote have dramatically shrunk. Having long exhausted his talent by the time of his alcohol- and drug-related death in 1984, at the age of fifty-nine, Capote is now most regarded for his "nonfiction novel" *In Cold Blood*, atypical of his work.

McCullers may be remembered as a precocious but unevenly gifted writer of fiction for young adults whose work has failed to transcend its time and place. In such anthologies as *The Best American Short Stories of the Century*, edited by John Updike, Flannery O'Connor is included with one of her most frequently reprinted stories, "Greenleaf," while McCullers and Capote are missing altogether. Indeed, no postwar and posthumous literary reputation of the

---

[1] In "Some Aspects of the Grotesque in Southern Fiction," O'Connor remarks bemusedly, "When I first began to write, my own particular *bête noire* was that mythical entity, The School of Southern Degeneracy. Every time I heard about The School of Southern Degeneracy, I felt like Br'er Rabbit stuck on the Tarbaby." [All notes are Oates's.]

twentieth century, with the notable exception of Sylvia Plath, has grown more rapidly and dramatically than that of O'Connor, whose work has acquired a canonical status since her death in 1964.[2]

All this, in the face of O'Connor's unfashionable religious sensibility, in a mid-twentieth-century secular, materialist literary culture largely indifferent to conservative Christian belief of the kind that seems to have shaped every aspect of her life. It's instructive to learn, for instance, in Gooch's meticulously detailed account of O'Connor's parochial school background in Savannah, Georgia, and her similarly circumscribed girlhood in Milledgeville, that she was born to an "Old Catholic" family with social pretensions on her mother Regina's side. A life-long tug-of-war seems to have been enacted between the (quietly, slyly) rebellious Flannery and the stubborn, self-righteous, and unflagging Regina, whose efforts to mold her daughter into "the perfect Southern little girl" were doomed to failure. Instructive, too, to learn that the precociously gifted O'Connor thought of herself as "ancient" while still a child; the great trauma of her girlhood was her father Edward's death, from lupus, when O'Connor was fifteen, an event perceived by the stricken girl as a sign of God's grace equivalent to "a bullet in the side." "I can with one eye squinting take it all as a blessing."

By temperament and training puritanical, if not virulently antisexual, O'Connor was drawn to the writings of the eminent French Catholic novelist François Mauriac, whose books addressed "the irreconcilability of sexual passion with the world of pure spirit"; in her early twenties, as a graduate writing student in the Iowa Writers' Workshop, O'Connor was so timid about sexual matters that she worried that an obscure "seduction" passage in one of her workshop stories was "liable to corrupt anybody that read it and me too." (Her solution was to seek advice from an Iowa City priest who told her, commendably, that she "didn't need to write for fifteen-year-old girls" — though there is no evidence in O'Connor's fiction that she ever did write about anything remotely sexual, let alone salacious or obscene. The closest is the implied pederast rape scene at the end of *The Violent Bear It Away*.)

---

[2]In 2008, the Modern Language Association catalogued 1,340 entries under "Flannery O'Connor," including 195 doctoral dissertations and several book-length studies in addition to such meritorious earlier books as *Conversations with Flannery O'Connor*, edited by Rosemary M. Magee (U P of Mississippi, 1987); *The Art and Vision of Flannery O'Connor*, by Robert H. Brinkmeyer Jr. (Louisiana State U P, 1989); *Flannery O'Connor: A Life*, by Jean W. Cash (U of Tennessee P, 2002); *Flannery O'Connor: A Biography*, by Melissa Simpson (Greenwood, 2005); and the closely argued and refreshingly unhagiographic *Flannery O'Connor's South*, by Robert Coles (U of Georgia P, 1993).

Gooch notes — surprisingly, given the greater ambition, achievement, and international acclaim of the work of William Faulkner — that the 1988 Library of America edition of O'Connor's work "widely outsold" Faulkner's volume published three years earlier. (See O'Connor's misplaced dread of the magisterial Faulkner in an essay of 1960: "The presence alone of Faulkner in our [Southern literary] midst makes a great difference in what the writer can and cannot permit himself to do. Nobody wants his mule and wagon stalled on the same track the Dixie Limited is roaring down.")

Religious belief seems to be irrevocably fused, in O'Connor's imagination, with extreme sexual repression characteristic of the 1950s — like one of her fanatic adolescent preachers, O'Connor was given to denouncing the "fornication" of New York City. She impressed Elizabeth Hardwick, in 1949, when they'd met at Yaddo, as being

> like some quiet, puritanical convent girl from the harsh provinces of Canada. . . . A plain sort of young, unmarried girl, a little bit sickly. And she had a very small-town Southern accent . . . whiney. She whined. She was amusing. She was so gifted, immensely gifted.

Gooch includes a somewhat caddish account by a Harcourt, Brace textbook salesman named Erik Langkjaer who in 1953 forged a romantic sort of friendship with O'Connor that seems to have involved mostly long, intimate drives into the Georgia countryside:

> "I may not have been in love [Langkjaer recounts in an interview], but I was very much aware that she was a woman, and so I felt that I'd like to kiss her. . . . She may have been surprised that I suggested the kiss, but she was certainly prepared to accept it."
>
> Yet, for [Langkjaer], the kiss felt odd. Remarkably inexperienced for a woman of her age [near thirty], Flannery's passivity alarmed him. "As our lips touched I had a feeling that her mouth lacked resilience, as if she had no real muscle tension in her mouth, a result being that my own lips touched her teeth rather than lips, and this gave me an unhappy feeling of a sort of memento mori, and so the kissing stopped. . . ."

As O'Connor's earlier infatuation with the young, attractive, charismatic poet Robert Lowell, whom she'd encountered in a manic state at the Yaddo writers' colony in 1948, remained unrequited, so her relationship with Langkjaer must have been disappointing to her, if not devastating, when, not long after this clumsy encounter, Langkjaer fell in love with a Danish woman whom he eventually married. O'Connor's reaction to Langkjaer's abrupt departure from her life — the writer's inspired revenge on her erstwhile "material" — can be gauged by the brilliantly acidulous short story "Good Country People," clearly modeled after O'Connor's thwarted romance, in which a crudely manipulative Bible salesman kisses the one-legged philosophy Ph.D. Joy/Hulga prior to running off with her wooden leg:

> . . . He put his hand on her back again and drew her against him without a word and kissed her heavily.
>
> The kiss, which had more pressure than feeling behind it, produced that extra surge of adrenalin in the girl that enables one to carry a packed trunk out of a burning house, but in her, the power went at once to the brain. Even before he released her, her mind, clear and detached and ironic anyway, was regarding him from a great distance, with amusement but with pity. She had never been kissed before and she was pleased to discover that it was an unexceptional experience and all a matter of the mind's control.

As Nietzsche tersely observed: "A joke is an epitaph on the death of a feeling." So sorrow in love might be transformed, through the corrosive alchemy of art, into something that, if a sour sort of compensation, can lay claim at least to a kind of quasi permanence.

More touching than O'Connor's relationship with Langkjaer, and far more crucial to her emotional life, was her close friendship of many years with an ardent admirer of her fiction named Betty Hester who'd been "dishonorably discharged" from the military for something called "sexual indiscretion"; Gooch is gentlemanly and tactful in suggesting that O'Connor herself may have been attracted to Hester, as to another intimate friend of this period, the "irrepressible" Maryat Lee, in ways other than merely Platonic. To the Atlanta novelist and critic Greg Johnson, to whom Betty Hester wrote more than several decades after O'Connor's death, Hester said, "As you must sense, I did love her very, *very* much — and, God knows, *do*."

In his engaging, sympathetic, and yet intellectually scrupulous biography of O'Connor, Brad Gooch provides the ideal biographical commentary: his voice is never obtrusive, yet we feel his judgment throughout; his allegiance to his subject is never in doubt, yet we sense his critical detachment, especially in his tracing of the ways in which "Flannery" — as Gooch calls O'Connor — seems to have mapped out a strategy of survival for herself. The most poignant sections of *Flannery* are the later chapters when, trapped by her illness in her mother's house in the backcountry Georgia she'd once hoped to flee, O'Connor bravely strove to redeem her situation through her art and through every outward gesture of her intractable faith — including even a visit to Lourdes in 1958. (Though many visit Lourdes with the implicit hope of experiencing a miracle, O'Connor cast herself as something of an "accidental pilgrim" who joked that she was "one of those people who could die for his religion sooner than take a bath for it" — meaning an immersion in "holy water.")

As her lupus steadily worsened, O'Connor remained an unfailingly devout Catholic waking each morning, "as soon as the first chicken cackles," with a ritual reading of prayers from a breviary before being driven into Milledgeville by Regina to attend 7:00 AM mass at Sacred Heart Church; her writing life was compressed into just a few hours, but these hours were precious to her, under the protection of her mother. On her very deathbed O'Connor was determined to work — "My my I do like to work. . . . I et up that one hour like it was filet mignon." O'Connor had a childlike dependence upon her formidable mother, who was the model, as Gooch suggests, for a striking number of older, garrulous, smugly self-centered and self-righteous Southern women in O'Connor's fiction, several of whom come to rudely abrupt, violent ends.[3] She strictly

---

[3] Poor Regina O'Connor! We have only fleeting glimpses in Gooch's biography of this pretentious "hide-bound Southern lady [who] always wore hat and gloves in public." In *A Jury of Her Peers: American Women Writers from Anne Bradstreet to Annie Proulx*, Elaine Showalter has provocatively suggested that Flannery O'Connor was "among the American women writers of the fifties who confronted matrophobia, or the fear of becoming one's mother. Hating one's mother was the prefeminist enlightenment" of the era.

adhered to religious ritual and custom, and had an unswerving faith in the literal — i.e., not merely "symbolic" — Eucharist, believed by Catholics at the moment of transubstantiation to be the actual blood and body of their savior Jesus Christ. To believe in this transformation of bread and wine is the test of a Catholic's faith, characterized by O'Connor as submission to the mystery at the core of our spiritual beings:

> If the writer believes that our life is and will remain essentially mysterious, if he looks upon us as beings existing in a created order to whose laws we freely respond, then what he sees on the surface will be of interest to him only as he can go through it into an experience of mystery itself. His kind of fiction will always be pushing its own limits outward toward the limits of mystery. . . .

Only in the final years of her life did O'Connor come to feel dissatisfaction with her "large and startling figures" as a mode of artistic expression, as Gooch poignantly draws a parallel between the physical exhaustion caused by her worsening lupus and her sense of the limitations of her art. In a letter to a Catholic nun, O'Connor asks for the woman's prayers:

> I've been writing eighteen years and I've reached the point where I can't do again what I know I can do well, and the larger things that I need to do now, I doubt my capacity for doing.

Rarely did O'Connor complain, still less protest her fate: "I expect anything that happens." If she claims, with what sounds like commingled wonder and rage, "I have never been anywhere but sick," quickly she modifies her statement by adding, aphoristically:

> In a sense sickness is a place more instructive than a long trip to Europe, and it's a place where there's no company, where nobody can follow. . . . Success is almost as isolating and nothing points out vanity as well.

Like many invalids with a predilection for the "spiritual" — the "mystical" — O'Connor seems to have made a connection, as Gooch suggests a kind of "magical thinking," between her lupus and her writing:

> I was five years writing [*Wise Blood*] and up to the last was sure it was a failure and didn't work. When it was almost finished I came down with [lupus] and began to take cortisone in large doses and cortisone makes you think night and day until I suppose the mind dies of exhaustion if you are not rescued. . . . The large doses of ACTH send you off in a rocket and are scarcely less disagreeable than the disease. . . .

Writing of the fanatic preacher Hazel Motes, under the spell of her medication, O'Connor conceived the notion that

> I would eventually become paralyzed and was going blind and . . . in the book I had spelled out my own course, or that in the illness I had spelled out the book.

In the fall of such physical dissolution, how comforting the promises of the Holy Roman Catholic Church:

> As I understand it, the Church teaches that our resurrected bodies will be intact as to personality, that is, intact with all the contradictions beautiful to you, except the contradiction of sin . . . for when all you see will be God, all you will want will be God.

O'Connor managed a brave public persona, when addressing mostly Southern college audiences by way of "talks" about fiction writing, and in her interviews and essays; it was her habit to assume a defensive pride in what others might define as limitations — "I am a Catholic peculiarly possessed of the modern consciousness, that thing Jung describes as unhistorical, solitary, and guilty." She was unapologetic in her allegiance to her place of birth and her parochial upbringing: "I'm pleased to be a member of my particular family and to live in Baldwin County in the sovereign State of Georgia, and to see what I can see from here." (As Brad Gooch notes, at this time in the early 1950s Georgia was ranked highest in the nation "in the rate of lynchings and other murders.")

At times O'Connor seemed dismissive of the civil rights movement in the South — "I say a plague on everybody's house as far as the race business goes." Yet in 1963, before the passage of the Civil Rights Act of 1964, she also said in a letter:

> I feel very good about those changes in the South that have been long overdue — the whole racial picture. I think it is improving by the minute, particularly in Georgia, and I don't see how anybody could feel otherwise than good about that.

Several of her later stories — "The Displaced Person," "Everything That Rises Must Converge," and "The Enduring Chill" — contain striking portraits of black, i.e., "Negro," characters presented with as much, or more, sympathy than their white neighbors; and in the fragment "Why Do the Heathen Rage?" a black servant named Roosevelt is the only person who responds sensitively, with tears, to the spectacle of his employer crippled by a stroke. Like William Faulkner — who famously said (in a "feverish" moment, according to Gooch) that, if need be, he would take up arms and fight on the side of his (white, racist) Mississippi neighbors against the threat of integration imposed by the federal government in the 1950s — O'Connor seems, as Gooch puts it, to have been something of a "cultural racist" in her private life but in her "incarnational" art, she was a writer who transcended the limitations of her time, her place, and her being.[4]

Is the art of caricature a lesser or secondary art, set beside what we might call the art of complexity or subtlety? Is "cartoon" art invariably inferior to

---

[4]O'Connor's favorite among her stories, "The Artificial Nigger," has become virtually unteachable as a consequence of its blunt pseudo-racist title. Ironically, O'Connor had intended the "artificial nigger" — a crude blackface lawn ornament observed in a Southern town by the backcountry Mr. Head and his grandson Nelson — to be a simulacrum of Jesus Christ and the

While O'Connor attended Georgia State College for Women,
her cartoons were published in the yearbook, newspaper,
and literary magazine. The original caption for this image
reads, "'I don't enjoy looking at these old pictures either, but
it doesn't hurt my reputation for people to think I'm a lover of
fine arts.'"

"realist" art? The caricaturist has the advantage of being cruel, crude, reductive,
and often very funny; as the "realist" struggles to establish the *trompe l'oeil* of
verisimilitude, without which the art of realism has little power to persuade, the
caricaturist wields a hammer, or an ax, or sprays the target with machine-gun
fire, transmuting what might be rage — the savage indignation of Jonathan Swift,
for instance — into devastating humor. Satire is the weapon of rectitude, a way
of meting out punishment. Satire regrets nothing, and revels in unfairness in its
depiction of what Flannery O'Connor called "large and startling figures."

story to evoke a tender sort of redemption unexpected in O'Connor's *oeuvre*: "[Mr. Head and
Nelson] stood gazing at the artificial Negro as if they were faced with some great mystery, some
monument to another's victory that brought them together in their common defeat. They could
both feel it dissolving their differences like an action of mercy."

It isn't surprising to learn that O'Connor began her career as a creative artist by drawing cartoons in mockery of human fatuousness and frailty or that her earliest efforts were satirical pieces; her first "book," written at the age of ten and assembled by her proud father Edward, was titled "My Relitives." O'Connor observed with typical acerbic insight: "I come from a family where the only emotion respectable to show is irritation. In some this tendency produces hives, in others literature, in me both."

Not the shimmering multidimensionality of modernism but the two-dimensionality of cartoon art is at the heart of the work of O'Connor, whose unshakable absolutist faith provided her with a rationale with which to mock both her secular and bigoted Christian contemporaries in a succession of brilliantly orchestrated short stories that read like parables of human folly confronted by mortality: "She would of been a good woman" — the murderous Misfit says of an annoyingly chatty Southern woman at the conclusion of O'Connor's "A Good Man Is Hard to Find" — "if it had been somebody there to shoot her every minute of her life."

WAYNE C. BOOTH

A Rhetorical Reading of O'Connor's "Everything That Rises Must Converge"

1974

This is an extremely complex story, not only in its ironic undercuttings but in its affirmations. No reading of it can be considered adequate unless it somehow relates the curious title to the various attempts to "rise" and to the failures to "converge." In the web of inference that we must create to see the story whole, our running translation of Julian's judgments into alternative judgments is only one strand. But once we have discerned that strand clearly, the rest of the story gives few difficulties.

Since Julian's is the only mind offering us opinions (except for a few observations and metaphors from the narrator, most notably the final sentence), we must sooner or later decide how far we can trust him. It is not hard to see that he is unreliable about many things. "He never spoke of it without contempt or thought of it without longing" — what kind of man is it, we ask, who always belies his true feelings? His life is full of such contradictions, showing that in his own way he is as far out of touch with reality as he takes his mother to be. His radical self-deception is perhaps clearest in the long fantasy that begins when he "withdraws into the inner compartment of his mind where he spent most of his time." No one could misread his own character more thoroughly than Julian does in thinking that he has "turned out so well," that he has a "first rate education," that he has a "large" mind, that he is "free of prejudice and unafraid to face facts" — remember, this is the boy who "did not like to consider all she did for him" and who can take pride in having "cut himself emotionally free of her." The closer we look at the disharmonies among his various opinions and actions, the more vigorously we must work in reconstructing the terrible lost young man we see behind his self-defensive rhetoric. His childish efforts to hurt his mother begin in a comic light, as he poses like a martyr and does everything he possibly can to spoil her one pleasant time of the week. But the comedy slowly gives place to pathos and horror as he runs over in his mind the possible tortures he might subject her to, then enjoys her humiliation about the duplicate hat, and finally — so wrapped up in his own petty bitterness and futility that he cannot see what is in front of his eyes — shouts irony-laden insults at the stricken woman. "You aren't who you think you are," he says, summarizing himself as much as his mother. "You've got to live in the new world and face a few realities for a change. Buck up, it won't kill you." It *is* killing her, and *he* is the one who must now begin to "face a few realities for a change."

These disharmonies are simple and clear. But the reconstruction of what "the realities" are — of what Julian must face — is not so easy. It is obviously not to be found in the "unreal," absurdly "innocent" world of the class-bound mother, nor in the equally unreal and absurd but vicious world of Julian. One kind of unmistakable reality is found in the irreducible, often harsh details of the life that Julian and his mother encounter but cannot see because of the abstractions that blur their vision. The mother does not see real "Negroes," for example, only the stereotypes that her childhood has provided her with. But Julian does not see real people either; instead he sees only the stereotypes that his liberal opinions dictate. Similarly, neither of them can see the other: Julian cannot see his mother for what she is; she cannot see what a miserable failure she has helped to create in him.

Our question then becomes: is there some ordering of values that for this story constitutes an alternative reality, one that in a sense judges everything the characters do? Our knowledge that Flannery O'Connor was known as a devout Catholic, or even that she herself talked about her stories in religious terms, can only alert us to one possible direction of interpretation. She might, after all, write one story that was entirely different from the others; for all I know, independently of my reading, she could have written this one before being converted, or after losing her faith. Even the most detailed knowledge about the author's life and statements of purpose can only alert me to certain possibilities; I must finally ask what kinds of clues the story itself provides to aid in the task of reconstructing a world of values that contrast with Julian's inanities.

The curious title is itself a kind of warning that seems to be spoken, as it were, in a special tone of voice. It simply does not harmonize easily with most of the surface, and indeed at first hardly makes sense at all. Does everything that "rises" in the story "converge"? Hardly. The black characters are "rising," but in spite of the liberal platitudes of Julian, there is no sign in the story that in their rising they will converge with the whites or with each other; one must thus ask whether or in what limited sense they are rising at all. Julian's liberal abstractions lead him to expect all Negroes to want his sympathy and interest, and to conform to his stereotyped demand that they "rise" to "talk on subjects that would be *above* the comprehension of those around him." But they insist on dwelling in a totally inaccessible world.

Julian has been "rising," too, as he obtains what he likes to think was a "first-class education." But his sense of elevation has, obviously, separated him not only from his mother but from all of his roots, without providing him with any other allegiances that could possibly support the claim of the title. What, then, can the title mean? It does not help us much to learn that it comes from the works of Teilhard de Chardin, the Catholic priest whose scientific and theological speculations earned him the accusation of heresy.

Is there any genuine change in the story that could be considered a "rising"? There is one, indeed, if we take seriously the change in Julian produced by the catastrophe. Julian is not just nasty and petty throughout the story; he is totally absorbed in his own ego. In contrast to his mother, who is "innocent," he is corrupt. Her desire is not to do ill in the world, but good, and only the limitations of what Julian calls her "fantasy world" betray her. But Julian, as we discover him behind his rationalizations, is actually malevolent, totally incapable of "converging" with the interests of any other person. His thoughts run constantly on his hatred of the world and his desire to "justify" himself in ways that he knows will hurt his mother deeply. "He would be entirely justified [in bringing home a Negro wife] but her blood pressure would rise to 300. He could not push her to the extent of making her have a stroke, and moreover, he had never been successful at making any Negro friends."

Throughout his absurd but vicious fantasies there thus run clues that prepare us for his discovery at the end. "For a moment he had an uncomfortable sense of her *innocence*, but it lasted only a second before *principle* rescued him. *Justice* entitled him to laugh." Dimly aware of her "innocence," passionately devoted to proving his own "principles" and obtaining "justice," he can be touched only by the greatest of disasters. Having never once been genuinely touched by any trouble, having in fact used his mother and her innocence as a shield against knowledge of himself, he is at last "stricken," "stunned." The change in him is as startling as the physical change produced in her by the stroke which he has helped to induce: "Darling, sweetheart, wait!" He is "crumpled," crushed into letting his defenses down and trying, too late, to call to his mother in love.

It would probably be a mistake to see anything strongly affirmative in this final dropping of all his egotistical defenses and crying "Mamma, mamma." He has not risen very far, but as he watches her destruction, falls at her side, and then runs for help, there has been, at last, a "convergence," a meeting of two human wills, that *might* presage his genuine "entry into the world of guilt and sorrow." For the Julian we have known throughout the story to experience either genuine guilt or sorrow would be a "rise" indeed, a rise based on the final convergence. The honest nightmare of his nothingness moving into "nowhere" in the final paragraph is thus a great improvement — in the light of this view of reality we now share with the implied author — over the "mental bubble" in which he established himself, where "he was safe from any kind of penetration from without." In his bubble he had been able to "see her with absolute clarity," or so he thought. Now, at the end, his bubble has been penetrated; he is swept by a "tide of darkness," and we are led to feel that he is for the first time in a position from which some sort of genuine human life is conceivable.

Whether this interpretation is sound or not, it certainly is never stated. Except for the ending, most of the words report Julian's misguided thoughts without open correction, and they must consequently be reconstructed. But they are not translated into a message.

There is perhaps no absolute need to go further than this. Readers of many different faiths and anti-faiths can presumably participate in this story of punishment and discovery, without pushing toward any special meaning for words like sin, innocence, faith, realities, guilt, and sorrow. But those of us who have read many of Flannery O'Connor's stories and studied her life will be unable to resist seeing Julian's final problematic redemption as presented in a religious light, even a specifically Roman Catholic light. Once the story is reread from this point of view, many additional ironies accumulate, ranging from Julian's name and his saintly posings at the beginning to the gratuitousness of grace at the end. But Flannery O'Connor was eager to write stories that were not mere allegories; as she intended, this story can be experienced by anyone who catches the essential contrast among the three systems of norms, Julian's, his mother's, and the cluster of traditional, conventional values we share with the author. Though it may seem thinner to those for whom Julian's self-absorption and cruelty are judged in secular terms than for a Catholic who sees him as in mortal sin, the structure of experience will be the same for both: Everyone will be forced to reject all or most of what the words seem to say. At every point we must decide on one out of many possible reconstructions, on the basis of a set of unshakable but silent beliefs that we are expected to share (however fleetingly) with the author. No one who fails to discern and feel some sympathy for these beliefs — only a few of them specifically Roman Catholic — is likely to make very much of the story.

For readers who do see behind Julian's absurd and egotistical words, the energy devoted to the act of seeing will of course increase the emotional effect and thus their estimate of the story's worth. This will not necessarily lead them to agree with me that it is a first-class story. But if they like it at all, the force of their liking will have been strengthened by the active engagement with the ironies.

DOROTHY TUCK McFARLAND
On "Good Country People"

1976

"Good Country People," the penultimate story in the collection, is something of a comic variation on "A Good Man Is Hard to Find." As the grandmother of the title story thinks of herself as a good Christian woman who believes in all the conventional platitudes, Hulga Hopewell, the Ph.D. in philosophy who is the protagonist of "Good Country People," thinks of herself as a good nihilist who energetically disbelieves in all the conventional platitudes. In their titles both stories implicitly ask the reader to consider what are good men or good people. And in both stories O'Connor uses conventional language for comic and ironic purposes, emphasizing the meaninglessness of the platitudes in the mouths of her characters, and at the same time using their words to sound the main themes of the story. For instance, Hulga's mother, Mrs. Hopewell, characteristically strings together remarks like "Everybody is different. . . . It takes all kinds to make the world. . . . Nothing is perfect." Nevertheless, she actually tolerates differences and imperfections very poorly. Two of the themes in the story grow out of the characters' attitudes toward uniqueness ("everybody is different") and imperfection.

Mrs. Hopewell and her tenant's wife, Mrs. Freeman, embody contrasting ways of looking at the world that provide the frame for the story. Whereas Mrs. Hopewell is determined always to put a smiling face on things and never look beneath the surface, the gimlet-eyed Mrs. Freeman has a fondness for hidden things: "the details of secret infections, hidden deformities, assaults upon children." She is obsessed with the physical demands and ills of the body, and in her conversation about her two daughters she dwells on the details of two major aspects of their physical being: their sexuality and their ailments. One daughter, Glynese, is being courted by several admirers, one of whom is going to chiropractor school and who cures her of a sty by popping her neck. The other daughter, Carramae, is pregnant and unable to "keep anything on her stomach."

Mrs. Hopewell's daughter, Hulga, is antagonized by her mother's platitudinous optimism to the extent that her face has come to wear a look of constant outrage that "obliterated every other expression." She finds Mrs. Freeman tolerable only on the ground that Mrs. Freeman diverts some of her mother's attention from her; otherwise, she is uncomfortable with Mrs. Freeman's fascination with the secrets of the body.

Hulga has rejected the physical world and the life of the body in preference for the life of the mind: "She didn't like dogs or cats or birds or flowers or nature or nice young men. She looked at nice young men as if she could smell their stupidity." Her rejection of the physical world stems from her awareness of its liability to imperfection. Hulga's own imperfection is gross — she lost a leg when she was ten — but O'Connor obviously intended her to be a figure of all mankind, which suffers from the imperfections of the human condition. Hulga insists on calling attention to her physical imperfection and refuses to try to improve her appearance. However, this defensive insistence that she be accepted "LIKE I AM" does not indicate that *she* has really accepted what she is; rather, it suggests that she is trying to insulate herself against the pain of difference and imperfection.

Hulga's choice of her name reflects her response to her condition. Named Joy by her mother, she could not tolerate the incongruity between the idea of joy and her knowledge that she was "dust." She therefore chose to emphasize her deformity and ugliness by assuming an ugly name — Hulga — and a rude manner, and closed herself to joy for the sake of affirming the truth about herself. The persona she creates with the name Hulga is a blind, stony, armored creature. To her mother, the name Hulga suggests the "broad blank hull of a battleship."

Hulga herself is described as being "square and rigid-shouldered," and as standing "blank and solid and silent." Her face is characteristically expressionless, and her "icy blue" eyes have the "look of someone who has achieved blindness by an act of will and means to keep it." Though she believes the self she has created is her true self, this imagery suggests that her willful blindness prevents her from seeing the true nature of the human condition as much as does her mother's insistence on always looking "at the bright side of things."

Though she has rejected joy for herself, Hulga has not given up on the possibility of love, and this secret desire is her one area of vulnerability. However, she thinks the persona she has created through her name is a means of making herself invulnerable, so that she can command and control love from a position of strength. She envisions her name working "like the ugly sweating Vulcan who stayed in the furnace and to whom the goddess [of love] had to come when called."

When an apparently naive country boy appears selling Bibles, Hulga feels that he offers no threat to her and allows herself to respond to his open admiration. Despite her utter inexperience (she has never been kissed) she decides to demonstrate her command of love by seducing him. She reinforces her image of herself as a woman of intellectual superiority and worldly wisdom by imagining that the simple Bible salesman, once seduced, will suffer from remorse, whereupon she will take away his shame and "transform it into something useful."

However, the Bible salesman's simplicity seduces her. Having climbed with her into the loft of an isolated barn, the Bible salesman gets Hulga to declare (with some reservations) that she loves him. He then demands that she prove it by showing him where her wooden leg joins on. At first shocked by his proposal, Hulga resists until he tells her why: "because [the wooden leg is] what makes you different." She feels that the Bible salesman, "with an instinct that came from beyond wisdom, had touched the truth about her." She comes to the conclusion that for the first time in her life she has encountered true innocence. She is so moved by her perception of his innocence that she lets down her defenses and allows her hidden vulnerability to emerge.

This area of vulnerability O'Connor equates with Hulga's soul and symbolizes it by her wooden leg: "she was as sensitive about the artificial leg as a peacock about his tail. No one ever touched it but her. She took care of it as someone else would his soul, in private and almost with her own eyes turned away." The leg is also, as the Bible salesman cannily recognized, what makes her different — a difference which, up to now, she has worn defensively and defiantly. Now, for the first time in the story, she accepts her difference, and allows herself to be touched in what is symbolically her soul. Accepting herself, she can surrender herself, and having surrendered herself she finds herself again, in the classic progression of love. When she allows the Bible salesman to remove her leg, "it was like surrendering to him completely. It was like losing her own life and finding it again, miraculously, in his."

Significantly, she surrenders to love in a scene in which her physical grotesqueness is not only emphasized but becomes the very means of love's expression and fulfillment. Though this scene of the Bible salesman removing Hulga's wooden leg is objectively ludicrous (and O'Connor's handling of it is full of irony), Hulga herself is, for the first time, completely without irony. The boy seems to her to be "entirely reverent" as he approaches the leg, and his removal of it is clearly the psychological and emotional equivalent to Hulga of the act of love: "She was thinking that she would run away with him and that every night he would take the leg off and every morning put it back on again."

Hulga's surrender to love also makes her vulnerable to a revelation of her own blindness. She had been convinced that she can see and that others cannot, and that she knows the truth. "Woman!" she had once shouted at her mother, enraged at Mrs. Hopewell's habit of blandly papering over ugliness with smiles. "Do you ever look inside . . . and see what you are *not*?" As a philosopher, Hulga is professionally concerned with truth. She is convinced that she has no illusions, that she has seen through appearances to the nothing that is beneath. "Some of us," she informs the Bible salesman, "have taken off our blindfolds and see that there's nothing to see." And she is utterly convinced of the truth of her assessment of the Bible salesman's innocence.

The Bible salesman, however, is anything but an innocent. Having put Hulga's leg out of her reach, he takes out of his suitcase a hollowed-out Bible containing a flask of whiskey, a deck of pornographic playing cards, and a packet of contraceptives. In response to Hulga's evident dismay, he replies, "What's the matter with you all of a sudden? . . . You just a while ago said you didn't believe in nothing. I thought you was some girl!" When he sees that he will get no farther with her, he snatches up her wooden leg, thrusts it into his suitcase, and disappears down the ladder of the barn loft.

The Bible salesman's thoroughgoing nihilism shows up Hulga's claim to believe in nothing as a superficial intellectual posture. Both his actions and his words devastate her assumption of intellectual superiority: "he turned and regarded her with a look that no longer had any admiration in it. . . . 'And I'll tell you another thing, Hulga,' he said, using the name as if he didn't think much of it, 'you ain't so smart. I been believing in nothing ever since I was born!'"

Hulga is left stranded, her previously stony face "churning" with emotion. But the Bible salesman's destruction of her illusions and her defenses (like the destruction of conventional order that resulted from the grandmother's encounter with The Misfit) may be, for Hulga, the means of her salvation. That the Bible salesman might be a kind of savior is suggested in the description of Hulga's final glimpse of him. Looking out the window of the barn loft, she sees him making his way across the pasture. O'Connor implicitly compares him to Christ walking on the water; to Hulga's blurred vision (the Bible salesman has also taken her glasses), he seems to be "struggling successfully over the green speckled lake."

The actual or implied references to Christ in *A Good Man Is Hard to Find* are numerous. The climactic moment in the title story comes about after The Misfit expresses his intense concern over the question of whether or not Jesus raised the dead. . . . The Bible salesman in "Good Country People" is implicitly compared to Christ.

Christ, as Simeon prophesied in St. Luke's gospel, is a "sign that will be contradicted," a sign of the presence of God in the world that, to many, will not seem to be a sign of God at all — will seem, rather, its opposite. The unexpected and often grotesque and incongruous ways in which O'Connor felt Christ to be present in the world is, I think, the real subject of this collection. Not only is the image of Christ suggested in unlikely places or associated with unlikely characters; but in style as well the stories embody contradiction and incongruity — in the double point of view, in the mixture of comedy and horror, in the pervasive tone of emotional flatness and irony, on the one hand, and the intimations of depth and serious meaning on the other. Thematically and stylistically, the centrality of Christ — of that which we experience as contradictory — provides *A Good Man Is Hard to Find* with a unity that makes it more than simply a random collection of stories. . . . I would add another gloss on the meaning of the title: the good man is so hard to find because he appears in such unlikely guises, because he is hidden in irony and contradiction.

JOYCE CAROL OATES'S
"Where Are You Going,
Where Have You Been?"

Portrait of Joyce Carol Oates, 1978.

Joyce Carol Oates is probably the most prolific author of literary fiction in the United States, writing a multitude of stories and novels in a variety of genres and aesthetic approaches. Creating narratives out of hundreds of thousands of words each year, she told an interviewer from the *New York Times* that "I am not conscious of working especially hard, or of 'working' at all. Writing and teaching [at Princeton University] have always been, for me, so richly rewarding that I don't think of them as work in the usual sense of the word." In her National Book Award acceptance speech for her novel *them* (1975), Oates stated her belief that

> the writer of prose is committed to recreating the world through language, and she should not be distracted from this task by even the most attractive of temptations. The opposite of language is silence; silence for human beings

is death. . . . I have tried to give a shape to certain obsessions of Americans: a confusion of love and money, of the categories of public and private experience, of a demonic urge I sense all around me, an urge to violence as the answer to all problems, an urge to self-annihilation, suicide, the ultimate experience, and the ultimate surrender. The use of language is all we have to pit against death and silence.

In this casebook, Oates recalls her earliest fascination with storytelling in "Stories That Define Me: The Making of a Writer," an essay that first appeared in the *New York Times Book Review* on July 11, 1982. *"Smooth Talk:* Short Story into Film" (p. 1619) is her response to the film version of her story "Where Are You Going, Where Have You Been?" It was published in her book *(Woman) Writer: Occasions and Opportunities* in 1989.

Oates has stated that she wrote "Where Are You Going, Where Have You Been?" after reading an article in the March 4, 1966, issue of *Life* magazine, "The Pied Piper of Tucson: He Cruised in a Golden Car, Looking for the Action." In the article the journalist Don Moser described a psychopathic young man in his early twenties named Charles Howard Schmid Jr. who wore elaborate face makeup, stuffed rags in his boots to make himself taller, and was impervious to feelings of guilt or remorse. Schmid, nicknamed "Smitty," was suspected of murdering three teenage girls.

Oates was intrigued by the idea of girls from "good families" who fell under the spell of a serial killer. She has stated, "I do recall deliberately not reading the full article because I didn't want to be distracted by too much detail." Reprinted here (p. 1622) is the first part of Moser's long article from 1966 that inspired Oates's story. Later at his trial, "Smitty" was found guilty of the murder of two of the girls and sentenced to death by lethal injection. After the state of Arizona temporarily abolished the death penalty, he was sentenced to prison for fifty years. In 1975, he was beaten and stabbed by two other prisoners, and he died in the prison hospital.

Oates has described "Where Are You Going, Where Have You Been?" as a modern tale, "Hawthornean, romantic, shading into parable" about the American obsession with violence. She has also remarked that "for the writer, the serial killer is, abstractly, an analogue of the imagination's caprices and amorality; the sense that, no matter the dictates and even the wishes of the conscious social self, the life or will or purpose of the imagination is incomprehensible, unpredictable."

JOYCE CAROL OATES

Stories That Define Me:
The Making of a Writer

1982

Telling stories, I discovered at the age of three or four, is a way of being told stories. One picture yields another; one set of words, another set of words. Like our dreams, the stories we tell are also the stories we are told. If I say that I write with the enormous hope of altering the world — and why write without that hope? — I should first say that I write to discover what it is *I will have written*. A love of reading stimulates the wish to write — so that one can read, as a reader, the words one has written. Storytellers may be finite in number but stories appear to be inexhaustible. . . .

Those stories I told to myself, and eventually to others in the family, as a child were tirelessly executed in pictures, in pencil or crayon, because I couldn't yet write. (I simulated handwriting at the bottom of pages, being eager to enter adulthood. Wasn't handwriting what adults did?) My adult self, examining these aged and yellowed notebooks, judges the effort somewhat odd — the human and animal figures too detailed to be cartoon figures, yet not skillful enough to be drawings. The tablets were filled with these characters acting out complicated narratives — surprises, chase scenes, mistaken identities, happy endings — in the unconscious pursuit of (as I couldn't have known then) the novel.

Eventually, at about the age of five, like everyone else I learned to write. . . . For some years my child-novels contained both drawings and prose, inspired, frequently, by the first great book of my life, the handsome 1946 edition of Grosset & Dunlap's *Alice in Wonderland* and *Through the Looking Glass*, with the Tenniel illustrations. I might have wished to be Alice, that prototypical heroine of our race, but I knew myself too shy, too readily frightened of both the unknown and the known (Alice, never succumbing to terror, is not a real child), and too mischievous. Alice is a character in a story and must embody, throughout, a modicum of good manners and common sense. Though a child like me, she wasn't telling her own story: That godly privilege resided with someone named, in gilt letters on the book's spine, "Lewis Carroll." Being Lewis Carroll was infinitely more exciting than being Alice, so I became Lewis Carroll. One part of Joyce Carol Oates lodges there — but to what degree, to what depth, I am unable to say. (How curious that thirty-six long years passed before I finally wrote a formal essay on Alice. But not on Alice; in fact, on Lewis Carroll.)

As for telling or writing stories, short stories in place of novels, I seem to have been unaware of the form until many years had passed and I had written several thousands of pages of prose (on tablets dutifully supplied by my parents), eventually on sheets of real paper by way of first a toy typewriter — marvelous zany invention — and then on a real typewriter, given to me at the age of fourteen. As a sophomore in high school, though my discovery had nothing to do with school, I accidentally opened a copy of Hemingway's *In Our Time* in the public library one day and saw how chapters in an ongoing narrative might be self-contained units, both in the service of the larger structure and detachable, in a manner of speaking, from it. So I apprenticed myself, with my usual zeal, to this beautiful and elusive new form. I wrote several novels in imitation of Hemingway's book, though not his prose style (that ironic burnt-out voice being merely monotonous to my adolescent ear), and eventually — though why it took so long I don't know — I worked my way back to, or into, the short story as a prose work complete in itself.

JOYCE CAROL OATES

Smooth Talk: Short Story into Film

1989

Some years ago in the American Southwest there surfaced a tabloid psychopath known as "The Pied Piper of Tucson." I have forgotten his name, but his
specialty was the seduction and occasional murder of teen-aged girls. He may
or may not have had actual accomplices, but his bizarre activities were known
among a circle of teenagers in the Tucson area; for some reason they kept his
secret, deliberately did not inform parents or police. It was this fact, not the
fact of the mass murderer himself, that struck me at the time. And this was a
pre-Manson time, early or mid-1960s.

The Pied Piper mimicked teenagers in their talk, dress, and behavior,
but he was not a teenager — he was a man in his early thirties. Rather short,
he stuffed rags in his leather boots to give himself height. (And sometimes
walked unsteadily as a consequence: did none among his admiring constitu-
ency notice?) He charmed his victims as charismatic psychopaths have always
charmed their victims, to the bewilderment of others who fancy themselves
free of all lunatic attractions. The Pied Piper of Tucson: a trashy dream, a
tabloid archetype, sheer artifice, comedy, cartoon — surrounded, however
improbably, and finally tragically, by real people. You think that, if you look
twice, he won't be there. But there he is.

I don't remember any longer where I first read about this Pied Piper — very
likely in *Life* Magazine. I do recall deliberately not reading the full article
because I didn't want to be distracted by too much detail. It was not after all
the mass murderer himself who intrigued me, but the disturbing fact that a
number of teenagers — from "good" families — aided and abetted his crimes.
This is the sort of thing authorities and responsible citizens invariably call
"inexplicable" because they can't find explanations for it. *They* would not have
fallen under this maniac's spell, after all.

An early draft of my short story "Where Are You Going, Where Have You
Been?" — from which the film *Smooth Talk* was adapted by Joyce Chopra and
Tom Cole — had the rather too explicit title "Death and the Maiden." It was cast
in a mode of fiction to which I am still partial — indeed, every third or fourth
story of mine is probably in this mode — "realistic allegory," it might be called.
It is Hawthornean, romantic, shading into parable. Like the medieval German
engraving from which my title was taken, the story was minutely detailed yet
clearly an allegory of the fatal attractions of death (or the devil). An innocent
young girl is seduced by way of her own vanity; she mistakes death for erotic
romance of a particularly American/trashy sort.

In subsequent drafts the story changed its tone, its focus, its language, its
title. It became "Where Are You Going, Where Have You Been?" Written at a
time when the author was intrigued by the music of Bob Dylan, particularly
the hauntingly elegiac song "It's All Over Now, Baby Blue," it was dedicated to
Bob Dylan. The charismatic mass murderer drops into the background and his

Laura Dern and Treat Williams in *Smooth Talk* (1985), directed by Joyce Chopra. Screenplay by Tom Cole, with music by James Taylor.

innocent victim, a fifteen-year-old, moves into the foreground. She becomes the true protagonist of the tale, courting and being courted by her fate, a self-styled 1950s pop figure, alternately absurd and winning. There is no suggestion in the published story that "Arnold Friend" has seduced and murdered other young girls, or even that he necessarily intends to murder Connie. Is his interest "merely" sexual? (Nor is there anything about the complicity of other teen-agers. I saved that yet more provocative note for a current story, "Testimony.") Connie is shallow, vain, silly, hopeful, doomed — but capable nonetheless of an unexpected gesture of heroism at the story's end. Her smooth-talking seducer, who cannot lie, promises her that her family will be unharmed if she gives herself to him; and so she does. The story ends abruptly at the point of her "crossing over." We don't know the nature of her sacrifice, only that she is generous enough to make it.

———

In adapting a narrative so spare and thematically foreshortened as "Where Are You Going, Where Have You Been?" film director Joyce Chopra and screenwriter Tom Cole were required to do a good deal of filling in, expanding, inventing. Connie's story becomes lavishly, and lovingly, textured; she is not an allegorical figure so much as a "typical" teen-aged girl (if Laura Dern, spectacularly good-looking, can be so defined). Joyce Chopra, who has done documentary films on contemporary teenage culture and, yet more authoritatively, has an adolescent daughter of her own, creates in *Smooth Talk* a vivid and absolutely believable world for Connie to inhabit. Or worlds: as in the original story there is Connie-at-home, and there is Connie-with-her-friends.

Two fifteen-year-old girls, two finely honed styles, two voices, sometimes but not often overlapping. It is one of the marvelous visual features of the film that we *see* Connie and her friends transform themselves, once they are safely free of parental observation. The girls claim their true identities in the neighborhood shopping mall. What freedom, what joy!

Smooth Talk is, in a way, as much Connie's mother's story as it is Connie's; its center of gravity, its emotional nexus, is frequently with the mother — warmly and convincingly played by Mary Kay Place. (Though the mother's sexual jealousy of her daughter is slighted in the film.) Connie's ambiguous relationship with her affable, somewhat mysterious father (well played by Levon Helm) is an excellent touch: I had thought, subsequent to the story's publication, that I should have built up the father, suggesting, as subtly as I could, an attraction there paralleling the attraction Connie feels for her seducer, Arnold Friend. And Arnold Friend himself — "A. Friend" as he says — is played with appropriately overdone sexual swagger by Treat Williams, who is perfect for the part; and just the right age. We see that Arnold Friend isn't a teenager even as Connie, mesmerized by his presumed charm, does not seem to *see* him at all. What is so difficult to accomplish in prose — nudging the reader to look over the protagonist's shoulder, so to speak — is accomplished with enviable ease in film.

Treat Williams as Arnold Friend is supreme in his very awfulness, as, surely, the original Pied Piper of Tucson must have been. (Though no one involved in the film knew about the original source.) Mr. Williams flawlessly impersonates Arnold Friend as Arnold Friend impersonates — is it James Dean? James Dean regarding himself in mirrors, doing James Dean impersonations? That Connie's fate is so trashy is in fact her fate.

What is outstanding in Joyce Chopra's *Smooth Talk* is its visual freshness, its sense of motion and life; the attentive intelligence the director has brought to the semi-secret world of the American adolescent — shopping mall flirtations, drive-in restaurant romances, highway hitchhiking, the fascination of rock music played very, very loud. (James Taylor's music for the film is wonderfully appropriate. We hear it as Connie hears it; it is the music of her spiritual being.) Also outstanding, as I have indicated, and numerous critics have noted, are the acting performances. Laura Dern is so dazzlingly right as "my" Connie that I may come to think I modeled the fictitious girl on her, in the way that writers frequently delude themselves about motions of causality.

My difficulties with *Smooth Talk* have primarily to do with my chronic hesitation — about seeing/hearing work of mine abstracted from its contexture of language. All writers know that language is their subject; quirky word choices, patterns of rhythm, enigmatic pauses, punctuation marks. Where the quick scanner sees "quick" writing, the writer conceals nine tenths of the iceberg. Of course we all have "real" subjects, and we will fight to the death to defend those subjects, but beneath the tale-telling it is the tale-telling that grips us so very fiercely. The writer works in a single dimension, the director works in three. I assume they are professionals to their fingertips; authorities in their

medium as I am an authority (if I am) in mine. I would fiercely defend the placement of a semicolon in one of my novels but I would probably have deferred in
the end to Joyce Chopra's decision to reverse the story's conclusion, turn it upside
down, in a sense, so that the film ends not with death, not with a sleepwalker's
crossing over to her fate, but upon a scene of reconciliation, rejuvenation.

A girl's loss of virginity, bittersweet but not necessarily tragic. Not today. A
girl's coming-of-age that involves her succumbing to, but then rejecting, the
"trashy dreams" of her pop teenage culture. "Where Are You Going, Where
Have You Been?" defines itself as allegorical in its conclusion: Death and
Death's chariot (a funky souped-up convertible) have come for the Maiden.
Awakening is, in the story's final lines, moving out into the sunlight where
Arnold Friend waits:

> "My sweet little blue-eyed girl," he said in a half-sung sigh that had nothing
> to do with [Connie's] brown eyes but was taken up just the same by the vast
> sunlit reaches of the land behind him and on all sides of him — so much
> land that Connie had never seen before and did not recognize except to
> know that she was going to it.

— a conclusion impossible to transfigure into film.

DON MOSER

The Pied Piper of Tucson: He Cruised in a Golden Car, Looking for the Action

1966

At dusk in Tucson, as the stark, yellow-flared mountains begin to blur against
the sky, the golden car slowly cruises Speedway. Smoothly it rolls down the
long, divided avenue, past the supermarkets, the gas stations and the motels;
past the twist joints, the sprawling drive-in restaurants. The car slows for
an intersection, stops, then pulls away again. The exhaust mutters against
the pavement as the young man driving takes the machine swiftly, expertly
through the gears. A car pulls even with him; the teenage girls in the front
seat laugh, wave and call his name. The young man glances toward the rearview mirror, turned always so that he can look at his own reflection, and he
appraises himself.

The face is his own creation: the hair dyed a raven black, the skin darkened to a deep tan with pancake make-up, the lips whitened, the whole effect

heightened by a mole he has painted on one cheek. But the deep-set blue eyes are all his own. Beautiful eyes, the girls say.

Approaching the Hi-Ho, the teenagers' nightclub, he backs off on the accelerator, then slowly cruises on past Johnie's Drive-in. There the cars are beginning to orbit and accumulate in the parking lot—neat sharp cars with deep throated mufflers and Maltese-cross decals on the windows. But it's early yet. Not much going on. The driver shifts up again through the gears, and the golden car slides away along the glitter and gimcrack of Speedway. Smitty keeps looking for the action.

Whether the juries in the two trials decide that Charles Howard Schmid Jr. did or did not brutally murder Alleen Rowe, Gretchen Fritz, and Wendy Fritz has from the beginning seemed of almost secondary importance to the people of Tucson. They are not indifferent. But what disturbs them far beyond the question of Smitty's guilt or innocence are the revelations about Tucson itself that have followed on the disclosure of the crimes. Starting with the bizarre circumstances of the killings and on through the ugly fragments of the plot—which in turn hint at other murders as yet undiscovered, at teenage sex, blackmail, even connections with the *Cosa Nostra*—they have had to view their city in a new and unpleasant light. The fact is that Charles Schmid—who cannot be dismissed as a freak, an aberrant of no consequence—had for years functioned successfully as a member, even a leader of the yeastiest stratum of Tucson's teenage society.

As a high school student Smitty had been, as classmates remember, an outsider—but not that far outside. He was small but he was a fine athlete, and

Charles Schmid Jr., around the time of his arrest in 1966.

in his last year — 1960 — he was a state gymnastics champion. His grades were poor, but he was in no trouble to speak of until his senior year, when he was suspended for stealing tools from a welding class.

But Smitty never really left the school. After his suspension he hung around waiting to pick up kids in a succession of sharp cars which he drove fast and well. He haunted all the teenage hangouts along Speedway, including the bowling alleys and the public swimming pool — and he put on spectacular diving exhibitions for girls far younger than he.

At the time of his arrest last November, Charles Schmid was twenty-three years old. He wore face make-up and dyed his hair. He habitually stuffed three or four inches of old rags and tin cans into the bottoms of his high-topped boots to make himself taller than his five-foot-three and stumbled about so awkwardly while walking that some people thought he had wooden feet. He pursed his lips and let his eyelids droop in order to emulate his idol, Elvis Presley. He bragged to girls he knew a hundred ways to make love, that he ran dope, that he was a Hell's Angel. He talked about being a rough customer in a fight (he was, though he was rarely in one), and he always carried in his pocket tiny bottles of salt and pepper, which he said he used to blind his opponents. He liked to use highfalutin language and had a favorite saying, "I can manifest my neurotical emotions, emancipate an epicureal instinct, and elaborate on my heterosexual tendencies."

He occasionally shocked even those who thought they knew him well. A friend says he once saw Smitty tie a string to a tail of his pet cat, swing it around his head and beat it bloody against a wall. Then he turned calmly and asked, "You feel compassion — why?"

Yet even while Smitty tried to create an exalted, heroic image of himself, he had worked on a pitiable one. "He thrived on feeling sorry for himself," recalls a friend, "and making others feel sorry for him." At various times Smitty told intimates that he had leukemia and didn't have long to live. He claimed that he was adopted, that his real name was Angel Rodriguez, that his father was a "bean" (local slang for Mexican, an inferior race in Smitty's view), and that his mother was a famous lawyer who would have nothing to do with him.

———————

He had a nice car. He had plenty of money from his parents, who ran a nursing home, and he was always glad to spend it on anyone who'd listen to him. He had a pad of his own where he threw parties and he had impeccable manners. He was always willing to help a friend and he would send flowers to girls who were ill. He was older and more mature than most of his friends. He knew where the action was, and if he wore make-up — well, at least he was *different*.

Some of the older kids — those who worked, who had something else to do — thought Smitty was a creep. But to the youngsters — to the bored and the lonely, to the dropout and the delinquent, to the young girls with beehive hair-dos and tight pants they didn't quite fill out, and to the boys with acne and no jobs — to these people, Smitty was a kind of folk hero. Nutty maybe, but at least more dramatic, more theatrical, more *interesting* than anyone else in their lives: a semi-ludicrous, sexy-eyed pied-piper who, stumbling along in his rag-stuffed boots, led them up and down Speedway.

On the evening of May 31, 1964, Alleen Rowe prepared to go to bed early. She had to be in class by six A.M. and she had an examination the next day. Alleen was a pretty girl of fifteen, a better-than-average student who talked about going to college and becoming an oceanographer. She was also a sensitive child — given to reading romantic novels and taking long walks in the desert at night. Recently she had been going through a period of adolescent melancholia, often talking with her mother, a nurse, about death. She would, she hoped, be some day reincarnated as a cat.

On this evening, dressed in a black bathing suit and thongs, her usual costume around the house, she had watched the Beatles on TV and had tried to teach her mother to dance the Frug. Then she took her bath, washed her hair, and came out to kiss her mother good night. Norma Rowe, an attractive, womanly divorcée, was somehow moved by the girl's clean fragrance and said, "You smell so good — are you wearing perfume?"

"No, Mom," the girl answered, laughing, "it's just me."

A little later Mrs. Rowe looked in on her daughter, found her apparently sleeping peacefully, and then left for her job as a night nurse in a Tucson hospital. She had no premonition of danger, but she had lately been concerned about Alleen's friendship with a neighbor girl named Mary French.

Mary and Alleen had been spending a good deal of time together, smoking and giggling and talking girl talk in the Rowe backyard. Norma Rowe did not approve. She particularly did not approve of Mary French's friends, a tall, gangling boy of nineteen named John Saunders and another named Charles Schmid. She had seen Smitty racing up and down the street in his car and once, when he came to call on Alleen and found her not at home, he had looked at Norma so menacingly with his "pinpoint eyes" that she had been frightened.

Her daughter, on the other hand, seemed to have mixed feelings about Smitty. "He's creepy," she once told her mother, "he just makes me crawl. But he can be nice when he wants to."

At any rate, later that night — according to Mary French's sworn testimony — three friends arrived at Alleen Rowe's house: Smitty, Mary French, and Saunders. Smitty had frequently talked with Mary French about killing the Rowe girl by hitting her over the head with a rock. Mary French tapped on Alleen's window and asked her to come out and drink beer with them. Wearing a shift over her bathing suit, she came willingly enough.

Schmid's two accomplices were strange and pitiable creatures. Each of them was afraid of Smitty, yet each was drawn to him. As a baby, John Saunders had been so afflicted with allergies that scabs encrusted his entire body. To keep him from scratching himself his parents had tied his hands and feet to the crib each night, and when eventually he was cured he was so conditioned that he could not go to sleep without being bound hand and foot.

Later, a scrawny boy with poor eyesight ("Just a skinny little body with a big head on it"), he was taunted and bullied by larger children; in turn he bullied those who were smaller. He also suffered badly from asthma and he had few friends. In high school he was a poor student and constantly in minor trouble.

Mary French, nineteen, was — to put it straight — a frump. Her face, which might have been pretty, seemed somehow lumpy, her body shapeless. She was not dull but she was always a poor student, and she finally had simply stopped going to high school. She was, a friend remembers, "fantastically in love with Smitty. She just sat home and waited while he went out with other girls."

Now, with Smitty at the wheel, the four teen-agers headed for the desert, which begins out Golf Links Road. It is spooky country, dry and empty, the yellow sand clotted with cholla and mesquite and stunted, strangely green palo verde trees, and the great humanoid saguaro that hulk against the sky. Out there at night you can hear the yip and ki-yi of coyotes, the piercing screams of wild creatures — cats, perhaps.

According to Mary French, they got out of the car and walked down into a wash, where they sat on the sand and talked for a while, the four of them. Schmid and Mary then started back to the car. Before they got there, they heard a cry and Schmid turned back toward the wash. Mary went on to the car and sat in it alone. After forty-five minutes, Saunders appeared and said Smitty wanted her to come back down. She refused, and Saunders went away. Five or ten minutes later, Smitty showed up. "He got into the car," says Mary, "and he said, 'We killed her. I love you very much.' He kissed me. He was breathing real hard and seemed excited." Then Schmid got a shovel from the trunk of the car and they returned to the wash. "She was lying on her back and there was blood on her face and head," Mary French testified. Then the three of them dug a shallow grave and put the body in it and covered it up. Afterwards, they wiped Schmid's car clean of Alleen's fingerprints.

More than a year passed. Norma Rowe had reported her daughter missing and the police searched for her — after a fashion. At Mrs. Rowe's insistence they picked up Schmid, but they had no reason to hold him. The police, in fact, assumed that Alleen was just one more of Tucson's runaways.

Norma Rowe, however, had become convinced that Alleen had been killed by Schmid, although she left her kitchen light on every night in case Alleen did come home. She badgered the police and she badgered the sheriff until the authorities began to dismiss her as a crank. She began to imagine a high-level conspiracy against her. She wrote the state attorney general, the FBI, the U.S. Department of Health, Education and Welfare. She even contacted a New Jersey mystic, who said she could see Alleen's body out in the desert under a big tree.

Ultimately Norma Rowe started her own investigation, questioning Alleen's friends, poking around, dictating her findings to a tape recorder; she even tailed Smitty at night, following him in her car, scared stiff that he might spot her.

Schmid, during this time, acquired a little house of his own. There he held frequent parties, where people sat around amid his stacks of *Playboy* magazines, playing Elvis Presley records and drinking beer. . . .

MAGICAL REALISM

Argentine writer Julio Cortázar (left) and Colombian writer Gabriel García Márquez (right).

When you look up the literary term "magical realism" in the glossary of this textbook, you will discover it defined as fiction often associated with Latin America "that interweaves realistic and fantastic details, juxtaposing the marvelous with the ordinary."

This definition mentions Latin America as often being associated with magical realism, which suggests that the term possesses a special history. It is this history that concerns us here. Today the term is used casually to describe just about any work of fantasy fiction, but a half century ago magical realism in Latin America had more specific associations. The background of the term will help you to understand what the Latin American magical realists in this anthology were attempting to create in their short stories. Writers such as the Argentines Jorge Luis Borges and Julio

Cortázar, the Cuban Alejo Carpentier, the Colombian Gabriel García Márquez, and the Chilean Isabel Allende, whose narratives, originally written in Spanish, can be read as magical realist fiction.

Borges is generally credited as the chief mover and creator behind the literary genre of magical realist fiction. Before him Latin American writers tended to be strongly nationalistic, but in 1967 they attracted readers world-wide and caused a "boom" of attention after the publication of Gabriel García Márquez's bestselling novel *One Hundred Years of Solitude*. This casebook opens with Borges's philosophical reflection "Borges and I," published in English six years earlier.

Borges never called himself a magical realist, though he brushed against the term. His surreal imagination shaped his narratives about human situations and characters until they extended far beyond his Argentine tradition into universal statements. In his 1932 essay "Narrative Art and Magic," Borges suggested that causality, the idea behind realistic narrative, is in itself an illusion, a form of magic, since causality can only be inferred and never proven. In 1966 he told his *Paris Review* interviewer that he agreed with the writer Joseph Conrad, "that when one wrote, even in a realistic way, about the world, one was writing a fantastic story, because the world itself is fantastic and unfathomable and mysterious." The relation of cause and effect is the rational force propelling the development of plot and character in most stories, but Borges urged authors to be open to everything, to all possibilities, not only realism, in their fiction. They should try to evoke what the critic Luis Leal described as "the mystery that breathes behind things."

As Leal explained in 1967, the term "magical realism" was first used in reference to postexpressionist art by the German historian Franz Roh around 1925. The writer Alejo Carpentier is credited with the creation of the term "marvelous real," the progenitor of magical realism in Latin America in the 1940s. This casebook contains excerpts from two of his articles, "On the Marvelous Real in America" (1949, 1967) and "The Baroque and the Marvelous Real" (1975). In "On the Marvelous Real in America" Carpentier suggested a useful kind of litmus test to determine if a text belonged in the magical realist genre when he defined it as originating as "an unaccustomed insight that is singularly favored by the unexpected richness of reality or an amplification of the scale and categories of reality, perceived with particular intensity by virtue of an exaltation of the spirit that leads it to a kind of extreme state."

In "The Baroque and the Marvelous Real," Carpentier defined "baroque" as "art in motion, a pulsating art, an art that moves outward and away from the center, that somehow breaks through its own borders." Carpentier felt the need to develop a special literary genre that went beyond realism in order to express what he envisioned as the mythical greatness of America, a continent viewed by its early European explorers and settlers as "marvelous" in suggesting the manifestation of the Promised Land.

Carlos Fuentes understood how Carpentier "took the language of the Spanish baroque and made it imagine a world where literature does not imitate reality but, rather, adds to reality. We are all his descendants." In 1982, accepting the Nobel Prize for literature, García Márquez referred to Carpentier's vision when he said, "I dare to think that it is this outsized reality, and not only its literary expression, that has deserved the attention of the Swedish Academy of Letters. Poets and beggars, musicians and prophets, warriors and scoundrels, all creatures of that unbridled reality, we have had to ask but little of imagination, for our crucial problem [in Latin America] has been a lack of conventional means to render our lives believable."

William Gass's article appeared in the 1987 issue of *Latin American Literary Review*, which was devoted to "The Boom in Retrospect." Gass is writing a personal essay, and he is sensitive to "the malice of the [gringo] critics" hidden in their words of welcome to the widely heralded Latin American authors in the 1960s. "No one would accuse Europe of a boom. The French might arrogate the noise for themselves while refusing the name; the Italians slip in wearing another country's coat; but booms reverberate only from unexpected places, sudden and sonically, as if from empty air. Nothing was there before, and then BOOM!"

This casebook concludes with Mario Vargas Llosa's comparison of the literary styles of Borges and García Márquez, preceded by Ursula K. Le Guin's 1987 introduction to the first English translation of *The Book of Fantasy*. First published in Spanish in 1940, it contains short stories selected by Borges, Silvina Ocampo, and A. Bioy Casares. This anthology includes the famous allegorical short story by the Chinese Taoist philosopher Chuang Tzu (369–286 B.C.), "The Dream of the Butterfly." Here it is in its one-sentence entirety: "The philosopher Chuang Tzu dreamed he was a butterfly, and when he woke up he said he did not know whether he was Chuang Tzu who had dreamed he was a butterfly, or a butterfly now dreaming that it was Chuang Tzu." This was one of Borges' favorite stories, illustrating his belief in the mysterious nature of our existence.

As Le Guin recognized, in recent decades our increasingly complex "global, multilingual, enormously irrational" society has given many readers the sense that realistic stories can hardly do justice any more to our everyday reality. She understood that "the 'magical realists' of South America are read for their entire truthfulness to the way things are, and have lent their name as perhaps the most fitting to the kind of fiction most characteristic of our times."

Works Cited

Borges, Jorge Luis. "Borges and I." Translated by Anthony Kerrigan. *A Personal Anthology*. New York: Grove Press, 1967. Print.

Borges, Jorge Luis. Excerpt from "Narrative Art and Magic." *Magical Realism and the Postcolonial Novel.* Ed. Christopher Warnes. New York: Palgrave Macmillan/St. Martin's Press. 2009. 45. Print.

Borges, Jorge Luis. Interview. *The Paris Review Latin American Writers At Work.* Ed. George Plimpton. New York: Modern Library, 2003. 30. Print.

Carpentier. Alejo. "On the Marvelous Real in America" and "The Baroque and the Marvelous Real"; also Luis Leal, "Magical Realism in Spanish American Literature." *Magical Realism: Theory, History, Community.* Ed. Lois Parkinson Zamore and Wendy B. Faris. Durham: Duke UP 1995. 86, 93, 120–21. Print.

García Márquez, Gabriel. "Nobel Prize Acceptance Speech." *Garcia Marquez for Beginners.*
    Ed. Mariana Solanet. New York: Writers and Readers Publishing, 2001. 133. Print.
Gass, William H. "The First Seven Pages of the Boom." *Latin American Literary Review.* XV:29.
    January-June 1987. Pittsburgh: University of Pittsburgh. 33–35. Print.
Le Guin, Ursula K. "Introduction." *The Book of Fantasy.* Ed. Jorge Luis Borges, Silvina Ocampo,
    and A. Bioy Casares. New York: Carroll and Graf Publishers, 1990. 9–12. Chuang Tzu's story
    is on p. 95. Print.
Vargas Llosa, Mario. *Letters to a Young Novelist.* Translated by Natasha Wimmer. New York:
    Farrar, Straus and Giroux, 2002. 36–38, 79. Print.

JORGE LUIS BORGES

Portrait of Argentine writer Jorge Luis Borges, 1980.

Borges and I

1961 / Translated by Anthony Kerrigan

Things happen to him, the other one, to Borges. I stroll about Buenos Aires and stop, almost mechanically now perhaps, to look at the arch of an entrance-way and the ironwork gate; news of Borges reaches me in the mail and I see his name on an academic ballot or in a biographical dictionary. I like hour-glasses, maps, eighteenth-century typography, etymologies, the taste of coffee, and Robert Louis Stevenson's prose; he shares these preferences, but with a vanity that turns them into the attributes of an actor. It would be an exaggera-tion to say that our relationship is a hostile one; I live, I go on living, so that Borges may contrive his literature; and that literature justifies me. I do not find it hard to admit that he has achieved some valid pages, but these pages can not save me, perhaps because what is good no longer belongs to anyone, not even to him, the other one, but to the language or to tradition. In any case, I am destined to perish, definitively, and only some instant of me may live on in him. Little by little, I yield him ground, the whole terrain, though I am quite aware of his perverse habit of magnifying and falsifying. Spinoza realized that all things strive to persist in their own nature: the stone eternally wishes to be stone and the tiger a tiger. I shall subsist in Borges, not in myself (assuming I am someone), and yet I recognize myself less in his books than in many another, or than in the intricate flourishes played on a guitar. Years ago I tried to free myself from him, and I went from the mythologies of the city suburbs to games with time and infinity, but now those games belong to Borges, and I will have to think up something else. Thus is my life a flight, and I lose everything, and everything belongs to oblivion, or to him.

I don't know which one of the two of us is writing this page.

ALEJO CARPENTIER

Alejo Carpentier photographed by Swiss photographer, Luc Chessex.

On the Marvelous Real in America

1949 / Translated by Tanya Huntington and Lois Parkinson Zamora

I will say that my first inkling of the marvelous real [*lo real maravilloso*] came
to me when, near the end of 1943, I was lucky enough to visit Henri Christophe's kingdom[1] — such poetic ruins, Sans-Souci and the bulk of the Citadel
of La Ferrière, imposingly intact in spite of lightning and earthquakes; and I

---

[1] Henri Christophe (1767–1820) was a former slave and key figure in the Haitian Revolution. In a power struggle following the revolution, the country was divided and Christophe
declared himself king of the North. He is know for constructing the military fort, the Citadel
of La Ferrière, as well as the opulent Sans-Souci Palace. Alejo Carpentier's novel *The Kingdom of This World* (*El reino de este mundo*, 1949) tells the story of the Haitian Revolution.

saw the still-Norman Cape Town, the Cap Français of the former colony, where a house with great long balconies leads to the palace of hewn stone inhabited years ago by Pauline Bonaparte.[2] My encounter with Pauline Bonaparte there, so far from Corsica, was a revelation to me. I saw the possibility of establishing certain synchronisms, American, recurrent, timeless, relating this to that, yesterday to today. I saw the possibility of bringing to our own latitudes certain European truths, reversing those who travel against the sun and would take our truths to a place where, just thirty years ago, there was no capacity to understand or measure those truths in their real dimensions. . . .

After having felt the undeniable spell[3] of the lands of Haiti, after having found magical warnings along the red roads of the Central Meseta, after having heard the drums of the Petro and the Rada,[4] I was moved to set this recently experienced marvelous reality beside the tiresome pretension of creating the marvelous that has characterized certain European literatures over the past thirty years. The marvelous, sought in the old clichés of the Brocelianda jungle, the Knights of the Round Table, Merlin the sorcerer and the Arthurian legend.

The problem here is that many [authors] disguise themselves cheaply as magicians, forgetting that the marvelous begins to be unmistakably marvelous when it arises from an unexpected alteration of reality (the miracle), from a privileged revelation of reality, an unaccustomed insight that is singularly favored by the unexpected richness of reality or an amplification of the scale and categories of reality, perceived with particular intensity by virtue of an exaltation of the spirit that leads it to a kind of extreme state [*estado limíte*]. To begin with, the phenomenon of the marvelous presupposes faith. Those who do not believe in saints cannot cure themselves with the miracles of saints. . . .

. . . .For Van Gogh, his faith in the sunflower was enough to fix his revelation upon the canvas. Therefore, it seems that the marvelous invoked in disbelief — the case of the Surrealists for so many years — was never anything more than a literary ruse, just as boring in the end as the literature that is oneiric "by arrangement" or those praises of folly that are now back in style. (This does not mean that I agree with those who support a return to realism — a term that now implies a slavishly political agenda.) All they do is to substitute the tricks of the magician for the worn-out phrases of academics or the eschatological glee of certain existentialists. . . .

. . . .Because of the virginity of the land, our upbringing, our ontology, the Faustian presence of the Indian and the black man, the revelation constituted

---

[2] Pauline Bonaparte (1780–1825) was the sister of Napoleon, Emperor of France; she was married to the French General Charles Leclerc who was appointed governor-general of the French colony of Saint-Domingue (Haiti) in 1801.

[3] I turn here to the text of the prologue for the first edition of my novel *The Kingdom of this World* (1949), which did not appear in later editions, even though I still consider it to be, except for certain details, as pertinent now as it was then. Surrealism no longer constitutes for us a process of erroneously directed imitation, as it did so acutely even fifteen years ago. However, we are left with a very different sort of *marvelous real*, which is growing more palpable and discernible and is beginning to proliferate in the fiction of some young novelists on our continent. [Carpentier's note]

[4] Petro and Rada refer to "nanchons," or families of spirits in Haitian Voodoo.

by its recent discovery, its fecund racial mixing [*mestizaje*], America is far from using up its wealth of mythologies. After all, what is the entire history of America if not a chronicle of the marvelous real?

ALEJO CARPENTIER

The Baroque and the Marvelous Real

1975 / Translated by Tanya Huntington and Lois Parkinson Zamora

. . . The marvelous real that I defend and that is our own marvelous real is encountered in its raw state, latent and omnipresent, in all that is Latin American. Here the strange is commonplace, and always was commonplace. The stories of knighthood were written in Europe but they were acted out in America because even though the adventures of Amadis of Gaul were written in Europe, it is Bernal Díaz del Castillo, who in *The True History of the Conquest of New Spain* gives us the first authentic chivalric romance.[1] And constantly — we must not forget this — the conquerors saw very clearly aspects of the marvelous real in America; here I want to recall Bernal Díaz's phrase as he contemplates Tenochtitlán/Mexico City for the first time and exclaims, in the middle of a page written in an absolutely baroque prose: "We were all amazed and we said that these lands, temples and lakes were like the enchantments in the book of Amadís." Here we have the European man in contact with the American marvelous real.

How could America be anything other marvelously real, if we recognize certain very interesting factors that must be taken into account? The conquest of Mexico occurs in 1521, when François I ruled France. Do you know how big the urban area of Paris was under François I? Thirteen square kilometers. In Garnier's *Universal Atlas*, published less than one hundred years ago, we are told that the metropolitan area of Madrid was twenty kilometers in 1889 and that the area of Paris, capital of capitals, was eighty kilometers. When Bernal Díaz del Castillo laid eyes for the first time on the panorama of the city of Tenochtitlán, the capital of Mexico, the empire of Montezuma, it had an urban area of one hundred square kilometers — at a time when Paris had only thirteen. And marveling at the sight, the conquerors encountered a dilemma that

---

[1] *Amadis de Gaula* is a notable literary work of the knight-errant tradition written in fifteenth-century Spain by an unknown author. Bernal Díaz del Castillo (1498–1585) was a Spanish conquistador who participated in the conquest of Mexico under the leadership of Hernán Cortés. He wrote an account of the conquest in 1568.

we, the writers of America, would confront centuries later: the search for the vocabulary we need in order to translate it all. I find that there is something beautifully dramatic, almost tragic, in a sentence written by Hernán Cortés in his *Cartas de Relación* [Letters from Mexico] addressed to Charles V. After attempting to tell the king what he has seen in Mexico, he acknowledges that the Spanish language is too narrow to identify so many new things and says to Charles V: "As I do not know what to call these things, I cannot express them." And of the native culture, he says. "There is no human tongue that can explain its grandeurs and peculiarities." In order to understand and interpret this new world, a new vocabulary was needed, not to mention — because you can't have one without the other — a new optic. . . .

The baroque that you are familiar with in the contemporary Latin American novel, which is often called the "new novel," or the "boom" — and the "boom," as I have said before, is not a concrete thing nor does it define anything — is the result of a generation of novelists still alive today who are producing works that translate the scope of America from its cities to its jungles and fields in a wholly baroque fashion.

As far as the marvelous real is concerned, we have only to reach out our hand to grasp it. Our contemporary history presents us with strange occurrences every day. The mere fact that the first socialist revolution on the continent should occur in the country [Cuba] least likely to sustain a revolution — I say "least likely" in the *geographical* sense — is a strange event in contemporary history, a strange event added to many strange events that, to our credit, have occurred in American history from the Conquest to the present, and with magnificent results. But faced with strange events that await us in that world of the marvelous real, we must not give up and say as Hernán Cortés said to this monarch: "As I do not know what to call these things, I cannot express them." Today, we know the names of these things, the forms of these things, the texture of these things; we know where our internal and external enemies are. We have forged a language appropriate to the expression of our realities, and the events that await us will find that we, the novelists of Latin America, are the witnesses, historians, and interpreters of our great Latin American reality. We have prepared ourselves for this, we have studied our classics, our authors, and our history. In order to express our moment in America, we have sought and found our maturity. We will be the classics of an enormous baroque world that still holds the most extraordinary surprises for us and for the world.

LUIS LEAL

Magical Realism in Spanish American Literature

1967 / Translated by Wendy B. Faris

The term "magical realism" was first used by the art critic Franz Roh to designate the pictorial output of the Postexpressionist period, beginning around 1925. Roh explains the origin of the term by saying that with the word "magical," as opposed to "mystical," he wished to emphasize that "the mystery does not descend to the represented world but rather hides and palpitates behind it."[1] In Hispanic America, it seems to have been Arturo Uslar Pietri who first used the term in his book *Letras y hombres de Venezuela* [The Literature and Men of Venezuela] (1948), where he says: "What became prominent in the short story and left an indelible mark there was the consideration of man as a mystery surrounded by realistic facts. A poetic prediction or a poetic denial of reality. What for lack of another name could be called a magical realism."[2] After Uslar Pietri, Alejo Carpentier has paid this phenomenon the most attention. In the prologue to his magical realist novel *The Kingdom of this World* [*El reino de este mundo*] (1949), he makes this interesting observation: "the marvelous" — he says — "begins to be unmistakably marvelous when it arises from an unexpected alteration of reality (the miracle), from a privileged revelation of reality, an unusual insight that particularly favors the unexpected richness of reality or an amplification of the scale and categories of reality, a reality thus perceived with special intensity by virtue of an exaltation of the spirit that leads it to a kind of extreme state [*estado límite*]."[3]

So we see that magical realism cannot be identified either with fantastic literature or with psychological literature, or with the surrealist or hermetic literature. . . . Unlike superrealism, magical realism does not use dream motifs; neither does it distort reality or create imagined worlds, as writers of fantastic literature or science fiction do; nor does it emphasize psychological analysis of characters, since it doesn't try to find reasons for their actions or their inability to express themselves. Magical realism is not an aesthetic movement either, as was modernism, which was interested in creating works dominated by a refined style; neither is it interested in the creation of complex structures per se.[4]

Magical realism is not magic literature either. Its aim, unlike that of magic, is to express emotions, not to evoke them. Magical realism is, more than

---

[1] Cited by Juan Eduardo Cirlot, *Diccianario de los ismos* 2nd ed. (Barcelona, 1956), p. 365. [Franz Roh, "Magical Realism: Postexpressionism," trans. Faris.] Roh's book was translated into Spanish by Fernando Vela and published by the Revista de Occidente: *Realismo mágico* (Madrid, 1927). Review by Antonio Espina in the *Revista de Occidente*, XVI (1927), pp. 110–113.

[2] Trans. note: See Arturo Uslar Pietri, *Letras y hombres de Venezuela* (1948; Mexico City: Fondo de Cultura Económica, 1949), pp. 161–62.

[3] Alejo Carpentier, "On the Marvelous Real in America," trans. Huntington and Zamora.

[4] Leal refers here to the Hispanic American movement of "Modernismo," to be distinguished from European and North American modernism, and closer to symbolism.

anything else, an attitude toward reality that can be expressed in popular or cultured forms, in elaborate or rustic styles, in closed or open structures. What is the attitude of the magical realist toward reality? I have already said that he doesn't create imaginary worlds in which we can hide from everyday reality. In magical realism the writer confronts reality and tries to untangle it, to discover what is mysterious in things, in life, in human acts. . . .

Magical realism does not derive, as Professor Flores[5] claims, from Kafka's work. In the prologue to *The Metamorphosis* Borges makes the astute observation that the basic characteristic of Kafka's stories is "the invention of intolerable situations." And we might add: if, as Professor Flores notices, in Kafka's story the characters accept the transformation of a man into a cockroach, their attitude toward reality is not magic; they find the situation intolerable and they don't accept it. In the stories of Borges himself, as in those by other writers of fantastic literature, the principal trait is the creation of infinite hierarchies. Neither of those two tendencies permeates works of magical realism, where the principal thing is not the creation of imaginary beings or worlds but the discovery of the mysterious relationship between man and his circumstances. The existence of the marvelous real is what started magical realist literature, which some critics claim is *the* truly American literature. . . .[6]

In magical realism key events have no logical or psychological explanation. The magical realist does not try to copy the surrounding reality (as the realists did) or to wound it (as the Surrealists did) but to seize the mystery that breathes behind things. In Carpentier's "Journey to the Seed" time flows backward at the exact moment when the old black gardener twirls his staff; in Carpentier's *The Lost Steps*, the protagonist, returning to the jungle, is unable to find the arm of the river through which he had gone from the present to the past, from modern civilization, where life has lost its meaning, to a primitive American paradise. Let us keep in mind that in these magical realist works the author does not need to justify the mystery of events, as the fantastic writer has to. In fantastic literature the supernatural invades a world ruled by reason. In magical realism "the mystery does not descend to the represented world, but rather hides and palpitates behind it."[7] In order to seize reality's mysteries the magical realist writer heightens his senses until he reaches an extreme state [*estado límite*] that allows him to intuit the imperceptible subtleties of the external world, the multifarious world in which we live.

Originally published as "El realismo mágico en la literatura hispanoamericana," *Cuadernos americanos* 43.4 (1967): 230–35.

---

[5] See Angel Flores, "Magical Realism in Spanish American Fiction." *Hispania* 38.2 (1955): 187–192.

[6] Arturo Uslar Pietri, Angel Flores, Alejo Carpentier. See the essay by the latter: "De lo real maravillosamente americano," *Tintosy diferencias* (México, 1946), pp. 115–35. Trans. Huntington and Zamora.

[7] Franz Roh, cited by Juan Eduardo Cirlot in his *Diccionario de los ismos*, 2nd edition (Barcelona, 1956), p. 365.

WILLIAM GASS

The First Seven Pages of the Boom

1987

The critics have called it "the boom." As in "business is booming." As in "What a loud racket!" As in a cannon shot sent North. As in "blow-up," an enlargement of image which uncovers a crime. Boom as in "Big Bang," and the first milliseconds of creation.

The malice of the critics is ill-concealed.

It is boom as in "bust." It is boom as in land rush, oil strike, a wow Dow. It is the boom in any boomtown: opportunists, gamblers, whores, mud. It is not the boom that sleeves the sail or extends the wind, but the boom in "fall down and go bump."

> . . .some of the authors of the "boom" — such as García Márquez — are beginning to repeat themselves, even to rewrite themselves, and not necessarily because their imaginations are failing them, but rather because they have found the formula for success, that enemy most dangerous to artists.
>
> Mempo Giardinelli, "Known Virtues and Vices," paper presented at Faculty Seminar in the Humanities, April, 1986.

One must mistrust a word which begins as a hobo from the Bronx: but one must trust a word which middles with amazement and ends on *om* — the birth button of the world.

It is boom as in booster, as in a deep exuberant uprush, as in increase, growth, wild overflow. It connotes vulgarity, excess, hoopla. Boom as in Baroque.

> . . .it turns out that now we, the Latin American novelists, have to name everything, everything that defines us, that surrounds and encircle us: everything that operates with an energy of context — in order to place it in the universal. [The prose that will give the named objects life] is a baroque prose, of necessity baroque, as is all prose that encircles detail, that describes it fully, coloring it, making it stand out in order to emphasize it and to define it.
>
> Alejo Carpentier. *Tientos y diferencias*, as quoted by M. Ian Adams, *Three Authors of Alienation: Bombal, Onetti, Carpentier*, Austin: U. of Texas Press, 1975, pp. 82–3.

This boom is not a floating timber, then but it may well be a motion picture camera's elongated arm. It is not boom as in "lower the boom," but as in advertise or plug-persistently. It is related to the bee's buzz. It goes tah-rah-rah-*boom*-tah-ray over and over again.

As if it were sudden in coming . . . and not long in lasting. As if it were the sound of a beaten drum. The renaissance of Irish writing, for both the Orange sex and the Green, was not called a boom, nor was the surprising efflorescence of Greek poetry recently marvelled at in those terms. After all, these were peninsular or island people, whereas the noise we have most immediately heard and named comes from many countries and from one of the larger land masses in the world.

The word "boom" is an American word; the idea "boom" is an American idea; the attitude "boom" is an American attitude. Most of the principals of the boom went away to Europe and to the USA to grow their decibels, and they brought back the boom and the word "boom" and the thought "boom." It's our word, right enough, but in whose mouth, like a slow sweet, does it now dissolve?

And if these South American nations had not been previously despised by a North American commercial culture which had continuously exploited them; and if they weren't so carelessly differentiated and indiscriminately lumped (Brazilians and Bolivians are simply Latins, Central America is the same as South; in fact, in the mind of most Americans, Mexico falls like a full skirt all the way to Patagonia); if they hadn't been thought to be Spaniards gone native, mostly asleep beneath their sombreros, and of slowly mixing blood, although when awake also of mean bandito intentions; then where would the boom have come from — this boom as if from one gun? Are these people peninsular after all, Iberians spread out like butter on toast? For no one would accuse Europe of a boom. The French might arrogate the noise for themselves while refusing the name; the Italians slip in wearing another country's coat: but booms reverberate only from unexpected places, suddenly and sonically, as if from empty air. Nothing was there before, and then BOOM!

It may not matter terribly that we Nords think "boom" about the Boom, but the Latin American novelists think "boom," enjoy "boom," suffer "boom," and, because they do, the Boom may come from a weapon they have aimed at their own foot.

It is because we have not been paying proper attention that everything seems to be going off at once. And because we gesture grandly and cry out "boom!" we do not have to distinguish between the books that merely make noise and the books that really knock something down.

The poets had already loaded the cannon, lit the fuse. Neruda, Parra, Mistral, Vallejo, Borges.[1] They were men and women of the world, most of them — diplomats, politicians, critics, linguists, travelers-although the long journey from Santiago del Chuco to Paris, which Vallejo had to make, was not the norm. Nevertheless, we must notice that poets, however, popular and important, do not go boom.

Then Asturias, Onetti, Carpentier, and Rulfo all came into prominence in the fifties, when the youthful work of those writers most closely associated with the explosion (like Fuentes, Cortázar, Donoso, and García Márquez)[2] was also beginning to appear. However, as everyone but our own *el señor presidente* knows, it is a long way up here from down there, and sound doesn't travel well in low air. . . .

---

[1] Chilean poet Pablo Neruda (1904-1973), Chilean poet Nicanor Parra Sandoval (b. 1914), Chilean poet Gabriela Mistral (1889-1957), Peruvian poet César Vallejo (1892–1938), and Argentinian poet and author Jorge Luis Borges (1899–1986).

[2] Refers to Guatemalan poet and writer Miguel Angel Asturias (1899–1974), Uruguayan author Juan Carlos Onetti (1909–1994), Cuban novelist Alejo Carpentier (1904–1980), Mexican writer Juan Rulfo (1917–1986), Mexican novelist Carlos Fuentes (1928-2005), Argentinian author Julio Cortázar (1914–1984), Chilean writer José Donoso (1924–1996), and Colombian writer Gabriel García Márquez (b. 1927).

URSULA K. LE GUIN

The Kind of Fiction Most Characteristic of Our Times

1987

There are two books which I look upon as esteemed and cherished great-aunts or grandmothers, wise and mild though sometimes rather dark of counsel, to be turned to when the judgment hesitates for want of material to form itself upon. One of these books provides facts, of a peculiar sort. The other does not. The *I Ching* or *Book of Changes*[1] is the visionary elder who has outlived fact, the Ancestor so old she speaks a different tongue. Her counsel in sometimes appallingly clear, sometimes very obscure indeed. "The little fox crossing the river wets its tail," she says, smiling faintly, or, "A dragon appears in the field," or, "Biting upon dried gristly meat . . . " One retires to ponder long upon such advice. The other Auntie is younger, and speaks English — indeed, she speaks more English than anybody else. She offers fewer dragons and much more dried gristly meat. And yet the *Oxford English Dictionary*, or *A New English Dictionary on Historical Principles*, is also a Book of Changes. Most wonderful in its transmutations, it is not a Book of Sand, yet is inexhaustible; not an Aleph,[2] yet all we can ever say is there, if we can but find it.

"Auntie!" I say (magnifying glass in hand, because my edition, the Compact Auntie, is compressed into two volumes of terrifyingly small print) — "Auntie! please tell me about *fantasy*, because I want to talk about *The Book of Fantasy*, but I am not sure what I am talking about."

"Fantasy, or Phantasy," replies Auntie, clearing her throat, "is from the Greek *øαvrala*, lit. 'a making visible.'" She explains that *øαvraola*, is related to *øαvrdζav*, "to make visible," or in Late Greek, "to imagine, have visions," and to *øαvralv*, "to show." And she summarizes the older uses of the word in English: an appearance, a phantom, the mental process of sensuous perception, the faculty of imagination, a false notion, caprice, or whim. Then, though she eschews the casting of yarrow stalks or coins polished with sweet oil, being after all an Englishwoman, she begins to tell the Changes: the mutations of a word moving through the minds of people moving through the centuries. She shows how a word that to the Schoolmen of the late Middle Ages meant "the mental apprehension of an objective perception," that is, the mind's very act of linking itself to the phenomenal world, came in time to signify just the reverse — an hallucination, or a phantasm, or the habit of deluding oneself. After which, doubling back on its tracks like a hare, the word *fantasy* was used to mean the imagination, "the process, the faculty, or the result of forming mental

---

[1] The *I Ching* or *Book of Changes* is an ancient Chinese text dating to the 2nd millennium B.C. and containing a divination system.

[2] Refers to two short stories by Jorge Luis Borges: "The Book of Sand" in which a mysterious book appears to be infinite, and "The Aleph" in which an aleph is a point in space which contains all other points in space.

representations of things not actually present." This definition seems very close to the Scholastic sense of *fantasy*, but leads, of course, in quite the opposite direction — going so far in that direction, these days, as often to imply that the representation is extravagant, or visionary, or merely fanciful. (*Fancy* is *fantasy's* own daughter, via elision of the penult; while *fantastic* is a sister-word with a family of her own.)

So *fantasy* remains ambiguous; it stands between the false, the foolish, the delusory, the shallows of he mind, and the mind's deep connection with the real. On this threshold sometimes it faces one way, masked and beribboned, frivolous, an escapist; then it turns, and we glimpse as it turns the face of an angel, bright truthful messenger, arisen Urizen.

Since the *Oxford English Dictionary* was compiled, the tracks of the word *fantasy* have been complicated still further by the comings and goings of psychologists. The technical uses in psychology of *fantasy* and *phantasy* have deeply influenced our sense and use of the word; and they have also given us the handy verb *to fantasize*. But Auntie does not acknowledge the existence of that word. Into the Supplement, through the back door, she admits only *fantasist*; and she defines the newcomer, politely but with, I think, a faint curl of the lip, as "one who 'weaves' fantasies." One might think that a fantasist was one who fantasizes, but it is not so. Currently, one who fantasizes is understood either to be daydreaming, or to be using the imagination therapeutically as a means of discovering reasons Reason does not know, discovering oneself to oneself. A fantasist is one who writes a fantasy for others. But the element of discovery is there, too.

Auntie's use of "weave" may be taken as either patronizing or quaint, for writers don't often say nowadays that they "weave" their works, but bluntly that they write them. Fantasists earlier in the century, in the days of victorious Realism, were often apologetic about what they did, offering it as something less than "real" fiction — mere fancywork, bobble-fringing to literature. More fantasists are rightly less modest now that what they do is generally recognized as literature, or at least as a genre of subliterature, or at least as a commercial product. For *fantasies* are rife and many-colored on the bookstalls. The head of the fabled Unicorn is laid upon the lap of Mammon, and the offering is acceptable to Mammon.[3] Fantasy, in fact, has become quite a business.

But when one night in Buenos Aires in 1937 three friends sat talking together about fantastic literature, it was not yet a business. Nor was it even known as fantastic literature, when one night in a villa in Geneva in 1818 three friends sat talking together, telling one another ghost stories. They were Mary Shelley, her husband Percy, and Lord Byron — and Claire Clairmont was probably with them, and the strange young Dr Polidori — and they told awful tales, and Mary Shelley was frightened. "We will each," cried Byron, "write a ghost story!" So Mary went away and thought about it, fruitlessly, until a few nights later she dreamed a nightmare in which a "pale student" used strange arts and

---

[3] In the New Testament, Mammon is personified as a deity representing wealth and greed.

machineries to arouse from unlife the "hideous phantasm of a man." And so, alone of the friends, she wrote her ghost story, *Frankenstein: or, A Modern Prometheus*, which I think is the first great modern fantasy. There are no ghosts in it; but fantasy as the Dictionary showed us, is often seen as ghoulie-mongering. Because ghosts inhabit, or haunt, one part of the vast domain of fantastic literature, both oral and written, people familiar with that corner of it call the whole thing Ghost Stories, or Horror Tales; just as others call it Fairyland after the part of it they know or love best, and others call it Science Fiction, and other call it Stuff and Nonsense. But the nameless being given life by Dr Frankestein's, or Mary Shelley's, arts and machineries is neither ghost nor fairy, and science-fictional only in intent; stuff and nonsense he is not. He is a creature of fantasy, archetypal, deathless. Once raised he will not sleep again, for his pain will not let him sleep, the unanswered moral questions that woke with him will not let him rest in peace. When there began to be money in the fantasy business, plenty of money was made out of him in Hollywood, but even that did not kill him. If his story were not too long for this anthology, it might well be here; very likely it was mentioned on that night in 1937 in Buenos Aires, when Jorge Luis Borges, Adolfo Bioy Casares, and Silvina Ocampo fell to talking — so Casares tells us — "about fantastic literature . . . discussing the stories which seemed best to us. One of us suggested that if we put together the fragments of the same type we had listed in our notebooks, we would have a good book. As a result we drew up this book . . . simply a compilation of stories from fantastic literature which seemed to us to be the best."

So that, charmingly, is how *The Book of Fantasy* came to be, fifty years ago. Three friends talking. No plans, no definitions, no business, except the intention of "having a good book." Of course, in the making of such a book by such makers, certain definitions were implied by inclusion, and by exclusion other definitions were ignored; so one will find, perhaps for the first time, horror and ghosts and fairy and science-fiction stories all together within the covers of *The Book of Fantasy*; while any bigot wishing to certify himself as such by dismissing it as all stuff and nonsense is tacitly permitted to do so. The four lines in the book by Chuang Tzu should suffice to make him think twice, permanently.

It is an idiosyncratic selection, and completely eclectic. Some of the stories will be familiar to anyone who reads, others are exotic discoveries. A very well-known piece such as "The Cask of Amontillado" seems less predictable, set among works and fragments from the Orient and South America and distant centuries, by Kafka, Swedenborg, Cortázar, Agutagawa, Niu Chiao; its own essential strangeness is restored to it. There is some weighting towards writers, especially English writers, of the late nineteenth and early twentieth centuries, which reflects, I imagine, the taste of the anthologizers and perhaps particularly that of Borges, who was himself a member and direct inheritor of the international tradition of fantasy which included Kipling and Chesterton.

Perhaps I should not say "tradition," since it has no name as such and little recognition in critical circles, and is distinguished in college English departments mainly by being ignored; but I believe that there is a company of fantasists that Borges belonged to even as he transcended it, and which he honored even as he transformed it. As he included these older writers in *The Book of Fantasy*, it may be read truly as his "notebook" of sources and affiliations and elective affinities. . . .

If in the 1890s fantasy appeared to be a kind of literary fungus-growth, if in the 1920s it was still perceived as secondary, if in the 1980s it has been degraded by commercial exploitation, it may well seem quite safe and proper to the critics to ignore it. And yet I think that our narrative fiction has been going slowly and vaguely and massively, not in the wash and slap of fad and fashion but as a deep current, for years, in one direction, and that that direction is the way of fantasy.

An American fiction writer now may yearn toward the pure veracity of Sarah Orne Jewett or Dreiser's *Sister Carrie*, as an English writer, such as Margaret Drabble, may look back with longing to the fine solidities of Bennett; but the limited and rationally perceived societies in which those books were written, and their shared language, are lost. Our society — global, multilingual, enormously irrational — can perhaps describe itself only in the global, intuitional language of fantasy.

So it may be that the central ethical dilemma of our age, the use or non-use of annihilating power, was posed most cogently in fictional terms by the purest of fantasists. Tolkien began *The Lord of the Rings* in 1937 and finished it about ten years later. During those years, Frodo withheld his hand from the Ring of Power, but the nations did not.

So it is that Italo Calvino's *Invisible Cities* serves many of us as a better guidebook to our world than any Michelin or Fodor's.

So it is that the most revealing and accurate descriptions of our daily life in contemporary fiction may be shot through with strangeness, or displaced in time, or set upon imaginary planets, or dissolved into the phantasmagoria of drugs or of psychosis, or may rise from the mundane suddenly into the visionary and as simply descend from it again.

So it is that the "magical realists" of South America are read for their entire truthfulness to the way things are, and have lent their name as perhaps the most fitting to the kind of fiction most characteristic of our times.

And so it is that Jorge Luis Borges's own poems and stories, his reflections, his libraries, labyrinths, forking paths, and amphisbaenae, his books of tigers, of rivers, of sand, of mysteries, of changes, have been and will be honored by so many readers for so long: because they are beautiful, because they are nourishing, because they do supremely well what poems and stories do, fulfilling the most ancient, urgent function of words, just as the *I Ching* and the *Dictionary* do: to form for us "mental representations of things not actually present," so that we can form a judgment of what world we live in and where we might be going in it.

MARIO VARGAS LLOSA

The Prose Style of Jorge Luis Borges
and Gabriel García Márquez

2002 / Translated by Natasha Wimmer

Borges is one of the most original prose stylists of the Spanish language, and perhaps the greatest Spanish stylist of the twentieth century. For that very reason, he has exerted a great influence and, if I may say so, an unfortunate one. Borges's style is unmistakable and functions extraordinarily well, giving life and credibility to a world of sophisticated intellectual and abstract ideas and curiosities. In this world, philosophical systems, theological disquisitions, myths and literary symbols, reflection and speculation, and universal history (contemplated from an eminently literary perspective) are the raw material of invention. Borges's style adapts itself to its subject matter and merges with it in a powerful alloy, and the reader feels from the first sentences of his stories and of many of his essays that these works have the inventive and sovereign quality of true fictions, that they could only have been told in this way, in this intelligent, ironic, and mathematically precise language — not a word too few, not a word too many — with its cold elegance and aristocratic defiance, privileging intellect and knowledge over sensation and emotion, playing with erudition, making a technique of presumption, eluding all forms of sentimentality, and ignoring the body and sensuality (or noting them at a great distance, as lower manifestations of existence). His stories are humanized thanks to their subtle irony, a fresh breeze that lightens the complexity of the arguments, intellectual labyrinths, and baroque constructions that are almost always their subject matter. The color and grace of Borges's style lies first and foremost in his use of adjectives, which shake the reader with their audacity and eccentricity ("No one saw him disembark in the *unanimous* night"), and in his violent and unexpected metaphors, whose adjectives and adverbs, besides fleshing out an idea or highlighting a physical or psychological trait, often serve to foster a Borgesian atmosphere. Precisely because it is essential, Borges's style is inimitable. When his admirers or literary followers copy his way of using adjectives, his irreverent sallies, his witticisms and poses, their stylings are as out of place as badly made wigs that fail to pass as real hair, proclaiming their falseness and bringing ridicule down on the unhappy heads they cover. Jorge Luis Borges was a formidable creator, and there is nothing more irritating or bothersome than the "mini-Borges" imitators whose imitations lack the essentiality of the prose they mimic, making what was original, authentic, beautiful, and stimulating something caricaturish, ugly, and insincere. (The question of sincerity or lack of sincerity in literature is not an ethical issue but an aesthetic one.)

Something similar has happened around another great prose stylist, Gabriel García Márquez. Unlike Borges's style, his is not sober but exuberant and not intellectualized at all; rather, it is sensory and sensual. Its clarity and correctness reveal its classical origins, but it is not stiff or old-fashioned — it is open to the assimilation of sayings and popular expressions and to neologisms and foreign words, and it possesses a rich musicality and conceptual purity free of complications or intellectual wordplay. Heat, taste, music, all the textures of perception and the appetites of the body are expressed naturally and without fuss, and fantasy draws breath with the same freedom, casting itself toward the extraordinary. Reading [García Márquez] we are overwhelmed by the certainty that only in these words, with this grace and rhythm, would these stories be believable, convincing, fascinating, moving; that separated from these words they would not have been able to enchant us as they have: his stories *are* the words in which they are told.

And the truth is that words are also the stories they tell. As a result, when a writer borrows a style, the literature that is produced sounds false, like mere parody. After Borges, García Márquez is the most imitated writer is the language, and although some of his disciples have been successful — that is to say, they've attracted many readers — the work, no matter how diligent the disciple, fails to take on a life of its own, and its secondary, forced character is immediately evident. Literature is pure artifice, but great literature is able to hide the fact while mediocre literature gives itself away.

GRAPHIC STORYTELLING

If one picture is worth a thousand words, then what's it worth when pages of pictures and words are juxtaposed to tell a story? Cartoon stories or *graphic novels*, substantial single volumes of pictorial images arranged in a sequence to narrate a story with or without words, have begun to be taken seriously. As the critic Charles McGrath explained in an article in the *New York Times Magazine* on July 11, 2004, "Comics are also enjoying a renaissance and a newfound respectability right now. . . . There is something like a critical mass of artists, young and old, uncovering new possibilities in this once-marginal form."

This casebook includes commentaries by graphic artists Alison Bechdel ("What the Little Old Ladies Feel," below), Joe Sacco ("Some Reflections on *Palestine*," p. 1655), and Michael Kupperman ("Are Comics Serious Literature?" p. 1652). There are also interpretive essays by Charles Hatfield (from his book *Alternative Comics*, p. 1649), Sydney Plum ("Reading 'The Veil' by Marjane Satrapi," p. 1653), and Edward W. Said ("Homage to Joe Sacco," p. 1658).

ALISON BECHDEL

What the Little Old Ladies Feel

2007

I knew I would have to tell my mother that I was writing a memoir about my father. But I didn't do it until I'd been working on the book, *Fun Home*, for a year. I wanted to make sure I had enough of a purchase on the material so that no matter what kind of reaction she had, I wouldn't lose my grasp.

I decided to tell her in person, when I went to visit for Christmas. I was quite anxious about how to broach the topic, and on the nine-hour drive to her house, I rehearsed what I would say. I pretty much had my lines nailed down by the time I hit Scranton, not far from where she lives. The driving on this particular stretch of I–81 is always hairy, and all of a sudden a truck pulled into my lane just in front of me — I must have been in his blind spot. I had to swerve onto the median so I didn't get clipped.

I was pissed off. After I recovered, I sped up to the truck to get its license number. That's when I saw the logo on the side: It was a Stroehmann's Sunbeam Bread truck. My father had died after being hit by — and probably intentionally jumping in front of — a Stroehmann's Sunbeam Bread truck.

After that synchronistic little brush with death, the prospect of telling my mom about the book loomed rather smaller. And indeed, she took the news

Alison Bechdel photographed for *Out Magazine* in December 2012.

quite well. She didn't quite understand why I wanted to reveal all our sordid family secrets to the general public, but she never tried to talk me out of it.

I know I hurt her by writing this book. She made that clear, but she also let me know that she grasped the complexity of the situation. At one point after *Fun Home* came out, she sent me a review from a local newspaper. It cited the William Faulkner quote, "The writer's only responsibility is to his art. . . . If a writer has to rob his mother, he will not hesitate; the 'Ode on a Grecian Urn' is worth any number of old ladies." Then the reviewer went on to say, "Rarely are the old ladies asked how they felt about it." Mom liked that — that someone was considering her side of the story.

I do feel that I robbed my mother in writing this book. I thought I had her tacit permission to tell the story, but in fact I never asked for it, and she never gave it to me. Now I know that no matter how responsible you try to be in writing about another person, there's something inherently hostile in the act. You're violating their subjectivity. I thought I could write about my family without hurting anyone, but I was wrong. I probably will do it again. And that's just an uncomfortable fact about myself that I have to live with.

CHARLES HATFIELD

From *Alternative Comics*

Toward the Habit of Questioning

2005

Comics *are* complex objects . . . the experience of reading them would seem to call for negotiation among various possible meanings. Despite the codification of techniques designed to ease this negotiation — for example, the use of overdetermined transitions (*Meanwhile . . .*), rigid gridlines, and various pictographic conventions — there is no one "right" way to read the comics page, nor any stable, Platonic conception of that page. There is simply no consistent formula for resolving the tensions intrinsic to the experience. In fact awareness of these tensions, an awareness expected of the prepared or "sophisticated" reader, may multiply the number of choices available to the reader and can result in an even more intensive questioning of the page (as the above discussion of timing, for instance, makes clear). The foregoing analysis, then, cannot tell us How to Read Comics; it can only suggest certain heretofore neglected aspects of the experience.

Some may yet object that the form needs no instruction manual, no "how to" book to get between readers and their pleasure. Admittedly, there is much in comics that seems intuitive, much that seems naively pleasurable; the form's reliance on pictures can make it (or certain aspects of it) immediately accessible, even to many readers who have not mastered all the disciplines that formal literacy demands. I have seen evidence of this among the children in my own life. Yet, as the above discussion shows, the form uses diverse means to solicit and guide reader participation and always involves *choosing* among different options — different strategies of interpretation, different ways of understanding. There may be much more going on than mere "picture reading": comic art is characterized by plurality, instability, and tension, so much so that no single formula for interpreting the page can reliably unlock *every* comic. Far from being too simple to warrant analysis, comic art is complex enough to frustrate any attempt at an airtight analytical scheme.

In fact comic art is growing more complex all the time. The form is in flux, becoming more self-conscious in its explorations as creators increasingly recognize the knowledge and sophistication of readers. Ploys once deemed necessary to relieve formal tensions and to settle ambiguities (overdetermined transitions, word/image redundancy, predictable layouts, and so forth) have become less common, as authors have come to expect readers who are experienced, playful, and tolerant of discontinuity. This vision of a knowing readership has changed the art form, for an author's imagining of her audience profoundly influences her sense of form and her willingness to take chances, just as, conversely, the reader's awareness of form enables her to become the kind of audience the author envisions. As comics readers have become more experienced, comics have traced an arc of development similar to other cultural forms, such as the novel and cinema: away from presentational devices designed to ease audience adjustment and toward a more confident and thorough exploration of the form's peculiar tensions, potentialities, and limits.

This is not to say that today's comics are uniformly more sophisticated than the comics of yesteryear. Indeed, one would be hard-pressed to find a more thoroughgoing exploration of the comics page than the Sundays in George Herriman's *Krazy Kat* (1916–44), which playfully poke at every convention without ever compromising the strip's blend of wry lyricism and thematic depth. Likewise, in the work of the form's pioneers — for example, in Rodolphe Töpffer's epochal series of comics albums (c. 1827–46) — we find continual, and ever-surprising, experimentation. But the interrogation of comics form has recently become more widespread, intensive, and self-conscious. This is true even in the tightly controlled precincts of American newspaper strips, where, for example, Bill Watterson's use of breakdown to juxtapose reality and fantasy (in *Calvin and Hobbes*) has led to comparable moves in many other strips. Yet it is especially true of alternative comics and graphic novels in the wake of Spiegelman's *Maus*. In the alternative comics avant-garde, we find radical reexaminations of form from such respected cartoonists as Chris Ware, whose *ACME Novelty Library* brings a post-Spiegelman rigor to the manipulation of design and color, and France's Marc-Antoine Mathieu (*Julius Corentin Acquefacques, prisonnier des rêves*), who has experimented, dizzyingly, with the design and material packaging of comics-as-books (see Beaty, "Compelling Experimentation"[1]). All of these works point to a growing awareness of "the audience" as experienced, knowledgeable, and eager to recognize its own role in making meaning.

We cannot acknowledge the scope and sophistication of that role as long as we insist on the ease and simplicity of comics. The notion of *ease*, so often mobilized in criticism (even appreciative criticism) of the form, overlooks the complexity and complicity involved in reading comics, reducing this interactive process to the passive registration of a few highly-charged impressions. This is why criticism in English, until very recently, has been unable to distinguish between *skimming* comics and *reading* comics, with the result that critical discussion of the form has been generally impoverished and, at times, irresponsible. My hope is that the above discussion, though it stops short of trying to construct a universal critical scheme, will inspire readers to ask probing questions of the comics they read, questions such as:

- What can I glean from the different codes (images, words, symbols) invoked here? What can I learn from their interaction? How do words and images relate to or approach each other?

---

[1] Bart Beaty, "The Compelling Experimentation of Marc-Antoine Mathieu," in *The Comics Journal* 196 (June 1997): 29–34.

- Does the appearance of the written text seem to influence or inflect my reading of it, and if so, how?
- Does there seem to be one unified "message" here, reinforced by the over-lapping of codes, or instead a conflict and contradiction between messages?
- How am I to understand this sequence of images, based on what I have to do to connect one image to the next? What is included, and what excluded, from the sequence? How do words and symbols assist, or complicate, my efforts to read this sequence as such?
- How does the layout of this page or surface — the relative size, shape, and positioning of its images — inflect my understanding of the narrative? When I look at this page, am I conscious of its overall design, or of the way I move from one design element to the next? Are there moments at which it helps to be aware of both? How are the boundaries, or margins, of the page used? How are the successive images delimited and juxtaposed?
- What relationship does this page create between time and space? Am I ever in doubt about that relationship?
- How does the design of this publication reinforce or work against its content? Does reading this text feel like witnessing a story, or handling an object, or both?

Such questions, while perhaps impressionistic, provide lenses through which we can more fully appreciate, and more pointedly critique, the comics text.

In fact addressing such questions is a must, not only for the discussion of comics as literature but also for sociological and ideological analyses of comics as artifacts of mass culture. For it is the reader's effort to resolve such questions that positions her vis-à-vis the text, indeed that defines her as "the reader," calling on her to assume a particular role. If reading is an act of reimagining oneself in response to the demands of a text, then we need to consider how comics present their "demands," that is, how they reach out to their readers and urge them to fulfill certain tasks. Comics demand a different order of literacy: they are never transparent, but beckon their readers in specific, often complex ways, by generating tension among their formal elements. Recognition of this complex relationship is prerequisite to grappling with the literary, sociohistorical and ideological aspects of the form. . . .

Are Comics Serious Literature?

2009

Reading "The Veil" by Marjane Satrapi

2009

The opening chapter of Marjane Satrapi's graphic memoir *Persepolis*, "The Veil," begins a coming-of-age story in which conventions are redrawn to describe the impact of the Islamic Revolution on Satrapi's friends and family. *Persepolis* was first published in France in serial form — one reason why "The Veil" may be read as a self-contained short story. In language and iconography, it introduces a girl who is on the verge of a difficult, complicated journey into adulthood and has the story-telling ability, imagination, and humor to take us with her. It makes you want to turn the page.

"The Veil" introduces ten-year-old Marjane, who faces dramatic changes in her society that will leave her, as well as her friends and family, trying to come to terms with a disjuncture between their inner lives and the faces they now have to present. Satrapi uses graphic literature to expose the conflict between

Marjane Satrapi, 2008.

Kevin Winter/Getty Images.

the veil she is required to wear and the individual hidden behind it. She uses humor to soften any antagonism. In the first panel of "The Veil" her solemn pose underscores her sincerity, but belies the humor of the second panel, which infuses her story.

Although practices vary about when a Muslim girl must begin wearing the veil, or hijab, as an expression of female modesty, the symbolism of passage into womanhood is clear. However, in this narrative, the veil is represented by the young Marjane as one aspect of the repression that closes down her bilingual school and separates the boys from the girls. It suppresses the individuality even of ten-year-olds, as shown by the difference between Golnaz, Mahshid, Narine, and Minna in the second panel of the story and the playful, individuated girls of the fifth panel. The Revolution causes her mother to change her appearance and attitude, confusing a young girl proud of her mother's stance and confused about female role models (suggested by the repetition of framed images). She must consider not only what it is to be a woman, but also what it is to be a woman veiled.

The precocious Marjane is also confused about the religious nature of this suppression of identity, as she has experienced religion as fostering her childlike sense of her own importance in her family and beyond. How could a religious belief require her to hide her light behind a veil?

This bemusement is the impetus for the second half of the chapter — a flashback to her younger life — in which she depicts herself as a prophet in the making, with her own holy book and a personal relationship with God. It might seem odd that a ten-year-old would need to look back on her life so far, yet isn't it the case that when we look back on our early childhood, we see ourselves as children in that lost world, rather than re-experiencing childhood subjectivity? In the forty-five panels of "The Veil," the narrative moves back and forth in time both subtly and abruptly. These movements are coherent because of the nature of graphic literature. As Scott McCloud explains in *Understanding Comics: The Invisible Art*, graphic literature is a sequential art that depends upon the reader/viewer's mind to complete what is missing, close gaps in time and space, and construct narratives, or at least relationships, from a static iconography enclosed in separate panels.

Consider the connections among the following images. An isolated Marjane in the first panel lets us know it is her story and that she sees herself set apart from her classmates. However, the solid, black tabletop of the first two panels joins her to her classmates in the next panel. A solid, black background unifies the sequence, in panels eight through eleven, embodying the Cultural Revolution in forbidding, apparently omniscient eyes set in a bearded face from an Assyrian relief. The same background is used toward the end of the chapter to signal nighttime, when Marjane has her conversations with God — as distinct from daytime confrontations with classmates and parents. The presence of these iconographically straightforward sequences makes it possible to take in slightly jarring synapses, which is as it should be — as Marjane's world has been severely fractured.

Throughout *Persepolis*, Satrapi's iconography shows us a figure struggling to find reason and meaning in a world captured in bold blocks of black and white. Sometimes the drawings seem to simplify Marjane's world into opposing forces, but much of the time the contrasts suggest connections between figures and ideas that complicate rather than simplify — as when Marjane's mother dyes her hair blond and wears dark glasses. Or when Marjane confesses to God that she has betrayed His choice of her as a prophet, and her white nightdress is suddenly figured with black and white flowers — and then she becomes a trinity.

All the sequences and asides are in the service of revealing to us the temperament, interests, and family background of a quite complicated protagonist. In the second panel, Satrapi draws the row of girls such that we can only see her elbow and fingers, describing the drawing as a class photo — from which she has been mysteriously cropped. She portrays herself as "the Last Prophet" looking like something from a kindergarten play, with a cardboard sunburst around her face. And the God with whom she converses from her bed looks amazingly like Albert Einstein. All of these images — some playful, others thought-provoking — lead us into a better understanding of and connection with this bright girl from another culture. Through the character of Marjane, we are drawn into a world that might otherwise not have interested us, eager to follow the engaging, amusing, often perplexed figure at its center.

JOE SACCO

Some Reflections on *Palestine*

2007

I have often been asked why I stuck my nose in the Israeli-Palestinian conflict. In fact, I have answered the question so many times that long ago my response began to seem stale even to me, but I will repeat it here because it is true: I went to the Occupied Territories because I felt compelled to. That is, I had begun to understand something of the oppression of the Palestinians, I was appalled, and I was overwhelmed with an almost physical need to act.

Yes, as I've been told, there are worse injustices in the world and greater mounds of bodies elsewhere. But two things ate at me besides the vague obligation to pay attention to a distant people's suffering: I was a U.S. taxpayer whose money — *my* money — was being spent to perpetuate the occupation; and I was a graduate of the University of Oregon's School of Journalism, aghast at how poorly — should I say awfully? — American journalists were presenting the issue.

As far as the former point goes, Israel, as you probably know, gets more U.S. financial aid than any other nation, and I didn't (and don't) like the idea of directly or indirectly funding its land-grabbing settlement projects or any other aspect of its brutal occupation.

Joe Sacco, author of *Palestine*.

But the latter point — about American journalists — was even more galling because I had strived so hard to be cast in their mold only to find their work on this subject so utterly wanting and shameful. They had not informed me at all. Up until I was out of university, despite all my newspaper reading and television news-watching, I never had the vaguest clue who the Palestinians were or what their struggle was about. In fact, as I detail in this book, I simply associated Palestinians with terrorism. My future archivists may well come across a comic strip I started in high school called "Meet The Asshole" featuring Yassir Arafat as the first guest. I knew nothing about him except what I was learning through the mainstream media, which is why I was so easily able to demonize him.

I first began to question my received notions about Israel as an innocent and beleaguered underdog awash in a sea of mad Arabs during its air bombardment of Beirut (using certain bombs provided by the U.S. supposedly for "defensive" purposes only) and its subsequent invasion of Lebanon in the early 1980s. The massacres at the Sabra and Shatila refugee camps, in which hundreds of defenseless Palestinians were killed by a Christian militia allied to the Israeli invasion forces in an area cordoned off by the Israelis, gave me the first inkling that the power dynamics in that part of the world were not quite what I had been made to understand. So I began to read something other than American newspapers. I credit *Blaming the Victims*, edited by Christopher Hitchens and Edward Said, *The Question of Palestine*, by Said, and *The Fateful Triangle*, by Noam Chomsky, for moving my education along at a rapid clip. Other books filled in the gaps, but these are the ones that lifted the wool from over my eyes. And here's the thing: Until I read them I thought I was a smart and relatively well informed person. I was very shaken up by what I hadn't known and what I didn't know.

Later, I abandoned regular print journalism as a career though not out of skepticism: I simply couldn't find a journalism job that was remotely gratifying. I fell back on cartooning — a lifelong passion — and tried to make a living that way. I moved to Berlin where I worked on comic books and posters for rock bands. But my interest in the Palestinian issue remained, and I toyed with the idea of using the comics medium to address the subject, perhaps to tell stories of the occupation. I contemplated illustrating human rights reports, but they read like courtroom testimony and would have made for unrelentingly grim (and dull) words and pictures.

At some point I decided I should go to the Occupied Territories myself. I could do comics about my experiences, a sort of illustrated travelogue of my journey through the ebbing days of the First Intifada. I would interview people, jot down facts, keep a daily journal. Beyond that, I didn't develop an exact notion of what I was going to do or how. I had not developed a theory of what I would later call — without much forethought — "comics journalism."

I made my arrangements and traveled to Israel and the Occupied Territories for about two and a half months in the winter of 1991–92. I returned to Berlin, finished up some other comics projects, and moved back to the United States a few months later.

I thought finding a publisher for *Palestine* would be difficult, but Fantagraphics Books, which had already published a series of low-selling comics of mine called *Yahoo*, committed itself to the project without hesitation. *Palestine* was originally issued as 24- and 32-page comic books which came out every few months from early 1993 to late 1995.

Perhaps it is inevitable that *Palestine* will be considered my defining work, the book that set me on my "comics journalism" path. As a comic book artist — (I am loathe to use the unfortunate marketing term "graphic novelist") — I think I have since written more fully rounded works of nonfiction, but, for me, *Palestine* retains a sort of propulsive vitality I could probably never duplicate. My work has become more self-conscious. I am more aware of what I am doing. I am not as loose.

For one thing, my approach to drawing has evolved. The first few dozen pages of *Palestine* are in (what we in the comics community call) the "bigfoot" style. My depictions were not meant as disrespect for the Arabs and Jews I was drawing; I simply drew people that way back then; I was never formally trained to draw people representationally; in fact, I was never formally trained to draw at all. It is no wonder that I heard, for example, that a Palestinian-American playwright took one look at the first issue and tore it to pieces. I realized that the drawings had to reflect the weight of the material I was presenting, and slowly but surely I forced more realism out of my pen though I could never shake — nor did I desire to lose — my "cartoony" line.

The more serious criticism of *Palestine* has been that it tells only one side of the Palestinian-Israeli conflict. That is a correct assessment of the book, but it doesn't move me. My contention was and remains that the Israeli government's point of view is very well represented in the mainstream American media and is trumpeted loudly, even competitively, by almost every person holding an important elected office in the United States. *Palestine* was an effort to show something of the Palestinian experience under the occupation during the First Intifada. Since then there has been a Second Intifada in which the conflict has escalated terribly, with hundreds of Israelis and thousands of Palestinians killed. Israel started building what it calls a security fence — but what is in reality a wall — not *on* its 1967 border with the West Bank but *in* what Palestinians hope to be their future state. Israel unilaterally withdrew its settlers and military forces from Gaza, but continued to assert control over its borders and airspace and attacked it with impunity. In 2007, murderous Palestinian in-fighting, partly attributable to the attempts by Israel, the United States, and their European allies to isolate and break a democratically elected Hamas government, led to a fissure in the Palestinian movement and two separately ruled Palestinian entities, one in Gaza and one in the West Bank. It was another low-point in recent Palestinian history, but, sadly, it may not yet be the nadir.

The conflict between Israelis and Palestinians will continue as long as the occupation — in any of its shapes and forms — continues, and this book, though it presents material that must seem mild in comparison with today's violence and dramatic turns, touches on the essence of that occupation. It is not an objective work if by objectivity we take the American approach which lets each side have its say and doesn't mind if reality is not revealed. My idea was not to present an objective book but an honest one.

EDWARD W. SAID

Homage to Joe Sacco

2007

Comic books are a universal phenomenon associated with adolescence. They seem to exist in all languages and cultures, from East to West. In subject matter they go the whole range from inspired and fantastic to sentimental and silly; all of them, however, are easy to read, to pass around, store, and throw away. Many comics are like *Asterix* and *Tin-Tin*, a continuing serial adventure for the young people who read them faithfully month after month; over time, like the two I mentioned, they seem to acquire a life of their own, with recurring characters, plot situations, and phrases that turn their readers, whether in Egypt, India or Canada, into a sort of club in which every member knows and can refer to a whole set of common assumptions and names. Most adults, I think, tend to connect comics with what is frivolous or ephemeral, and there is an assumption that as one grows older they are put aside for more serious pursuits, except very occasionally (as is the case with Art Spiegelman's *Maus*) when a forbiddingly grim subject is treated by a serious comic book artist. But, as we shall soon see, these are very rare occasions indeed, since what is first of all required is a first-rate talent.

I don't remember when exactly I read my first comic book, but I do remember exactly how liberated and subversive I felt as a result. Everything about the enticing book of colored pictures, but specially its untidy, sprawling format, the colorful, riotous extravagance of its pictures, the unrestrained passage between what the characters thought and said, the exotic creatures and adventures reported and depicted: all this made up for a hugely wonderful thrill, entirely unlike anything I had hitherto known or experienced.

My incongruously Arab Protestant family and education in the colonial post World War Two Middle East were very bookish and academically very demanding. An unremitting sobriety governed all things. These were certainly not the days either of television, or of numerous easily available entertainments. Radio was our link to the outside world, and because Hollywood films were considered both inevitable and somehow morally risky, we were kept to a regimen of one per week, each carefully vetted by my parents, certified by some unrevealed (to us) standard of judgment as acceptable and therefore not *bad* for children.

Not quite thirteen, I entered high school just after the fall of Palestine in 1948. Like all the members of my family, male and female, I was enrolled in British schools, which seemed to be modeled after their story-book equivalents in *Tom Brown's Schooldays* and the various accounts of Eton, Harrow, Rugby that I had gleaned from my omnivorous reading of almost exclusively English books. In that late imperial setting of a highly conflicted world of mostly Arab and Levantine children, British teachers, in largely Muslim Arab countries themselves undergoing turbulent change, where the curriculum was based on the Oxford and Cambridge School Certificate (as the standardized English high school diploma was called in those days), the sudden intrusion of American comic books — which were instantly banned by parents and school authorities — burst like a small typhoon. In a matter of hours I was illicitly awash in a flood of Superman, Tarzan, Captain Marvel and Wonder Woman adventures that boggled and certainly diverted my mind from the stricter and grayer things I should have been addressing.

Trying to reason why the ban against this pleasurable new world was so strict and seemed so rigidly enforced at home got me absolutely nowhere with my adamant parents except for the explanation that comics interfered with one's schoolwork. I have spent years trying to reconstruct the logic of the ban and have concluded over time that the prohibition very accurately grasped (certainly more than I did at the time) what it is that comics did so well and so uniquely. There were first of all such things as slang and violence which ruffled the pretended calm of the learning process. Second, and perhaps more important though never stated, there was the release provided to my sexually repressed young life by outrageous characters (some of them like Sheena of the Jungle, dressed far too skimpily and sexily) who did and said things that could not be admitted either for reasons of probability and logic or, perhaps more crucially, because they violated conventional norms — norms of behavior, thought, accepted social forms. Comics played havoc with the logic of a+b+c+d and they certainly encouraged one not to think in terms of what the teacher expected or what a subject like history demanded. I vividly remember the elation I felt as I surreptitiously smuggled a copy of *Captain Marvel* in my briefcase and read it furtively on the bus or under the covers or in the back of the class. Besides, comics provided one with a directness of approach (the attractively and literally overstated combination of pictures and words) that seemed unassailably true on the one hand, and marvelously close, impinging, familiar on the other. In ways that I still find fascinating to decode, comics in their relentless foregrounding — far more, say, than film cartoons or funnies, neither of which mattered much to me — seemed to say what couldn't otherwise be said, perhaps what wasn't permitted to be said or imagined, defying the ordinary processes of thought, which are policed, shaped and re-shaped by all sorts of pedagogical as well as ideological pressures. I knew nothing of this then, but I felt that comics freed me to think and imagine and see differently.

Cut now to the final decade of the twentieth century. As an American of Palestinian origin, I have found myself necessarily involved in the battle for Palestinian self-determination and human rights. Sidelined by distance, illness, and exile, my role has been to defend this most difficult cause, to defend and attempt to portray its complicated and often suppressed dimensions in writing and speaking in public, all the while trying to keep up with the unfolding of our history as a people in places like Amman, Beirut, and then finally, when I was able to return to Palestine in 1992 for the first time since my family and I left Jerusalem in 1947, on the actual West Bank and Gaza.

When I began this effort just after the June 1967 War even the word "Palestine" was next to impossible to use in public discourse. I recall signs carried outside teach-ins and lectures on Palestine in that period blaring "there is no Palestine," and in 1969 Golda Meir made her famous statement saying that the Palestinians did not exist. Much of my work as a writer and lecturer was concerned with refuting the misrepresentations and dehumanizations of our history, trying at the same time to give the Palestinian narrative — so effectively blotted out by the media and legions of antagonistic polemicists — a presence and a human shape.

Without any warning or preparation, about ten years ago my young son brought home Joe Sacco's first comic book on Palestine. Cut off as I was from the world of active comic reading, trading and bartering, I had no idea at all that Sacco or his gripping work existed. I was plunged directly back into the world of the first great intifada (1987–92) and, with even greater effect, back into the animated, enlivening world of the comics I had read so long ago. The shock of recognition was therefore a double one, and the more I read compulsively in Sacco's *Palestine* comic books, of which there are about ten, all of them now collected into one volume which I hope will make them widely available not only to American readers but all over the world, the more convinced I was that here was a political and aesthetic work of extraordinary originality, quite unlike any other in the long, often turgid and hopelessly twisted debates that had occupied Palestinians, Israelis, and their respective supporters.

As we also live in a media-saturated world in which a huge preponderance of the world's news images are controlled and diffused by a handful of men sitting in places like London and New York, a stream of comic book images and words, assertively etched, at times grotesquely emphatic and distended to match the extreme situations they depict, provide a remarkable antidote. In Joe Sacco's world there are no smooth-talking announcers and presenters, no unctuous narrative of Israeli triumphs, democracy, achievements, no assumed and re-confirmed representations — all of them disconnected from any historical or social source, from any lived reality — of Palestinians as rock-throwing, rejectionist, and fundamentalist villains whose main purpose is to make life difficult for the peace-loving, persecuted Israelis. What we get instead is seen through the eyes and persona of a modest-looking ubiquitous crew-cut young American man who appears to have wandered into an unfamiliar, inhospitable world of military occupation, arbitrary arrest, harrowing experiences of houses demolished and land expropriated, torture ("moderate physical pressure") and sheer brute force generously, if cruelly, applied (e.g., an Israeli soldier refusing to let people through a roadblock on the West Bank because, he says, revealing an enormous, threatening set of teeth, of THIS, the M-16 rifle he brandishes) at whose mercy Palestinians live on a daily, indeed hourly basis.

There's no obvious spin, no easily discernible line of doctrine in Joe Sacco's often ironic encounters with Palestinians under occupation, no attempt to smooth out what is for the most part a meager, anxious existence of uncertainty, collective unhappiness, and deprivation, and, especially in the Gaza comics, a life of aimless wandering within the place's inhospitable confines, wandering and mostly waiting, waiting, waiting. With the exception of one or two novelists and poets, no one has ever rendered this terrible state of affairs better than Joe Sacco. Certainly his images are more graphic than anything you can either read or see on television. With his friend, the Japanese photographer Saburo (who seems to get lost at one point), Joe is a listening, watchful presence, sometimes skeptical, sometimes fed up, but mostly sympathetic and funny, as he notes that a cup of Palestinian tea is often drowned in sugar, or how perhaps involuntarily they congregate in order to exchange tales of woe and suffering, the way fishermen compare the size of their catch or hunters the stealth of their prey.

The cast of characters in the many episodes collected here is wondrously varied and, with the comic draughtsman's uncanny ability to catch the telling detail, a carefully sculpted mustache here, overly large teeth there, a drab suit here, Sacco manages to keep it all going with almost careless virtuosity. The unhurried pace and the absence of a goal in his wanderings emphasizes that he is neither a journalist in search of a story nor an expert trying to nail down the facts in order to produce a policy. Joe is there to be in Palestine, and only that — in effect to spend as much time as he can sharing, if not finally living the life that Palestinians are condemned to lead. Given the realities of power and his identification with the underdog, Sacco's Israelis are depicted with an unmistakable skepticism, if not always distrust. Mostly they are figures of unjust power and dubious authority. I am not referring only to obviously unattractive personages like the

many soldiers and settlers who keep popping up to make life for Palestinians difficult and deliberately unbearable but, especially in one telling episode, even the
so-called peaceniks whose support for Palestinian rights appears so hedged, so
timid, and finally ineffective as to make them also objects of disappointed scorn.

Joe is there to find out why things are the way they are and why there seems
to have been an impasse for so long. He is drawn to the place partly because
(we learn from an exceptionally weird earlier comic *War Junkie*[1]) of his Mal-
tese family background during World War Two, partly because the post-mod-
ern world is so accessible to the young and curious American, partly because
like Joseph Conrad's Marlow he is tugged at by the forgotten places and people
of the world, those who don't make it on to our television screens, or if they
do, who are regularly portrayed as marginal, unimportant, perhaps even neg-
ligible were it not for their nuisance value which, like the Palestinians, seems
impossible to get rid of. Without losing the comics' unique capacity for delivering a kind of surreal world as animated and in its own way as arrestingly
violent as a poet's vision of things, Joe Sacco can also unostentatiously transmit a great deal of information, the human context and historical events that
have reduced Palestinians to their present sense of stagnating powerlessness,
despite the peace process and despite the sticky gloss put on things by basically
hypocritical leaders, policy-makers and media pundits.

Nowhere does Sacco come closer to the existential lived reality of the average Palestinian than in his depiction of life in Gaza, the national Inferno. The
vacancy of time, the drabness not to say sordidness of everyday life in the
refugee camps, the network of relief workers, bereaved mothers, unemployed
young men, teachers, police, hangers-on, the ubiquitous tea or coffee circle,
the sense of confinement, permanent muddiness and ugliness conveyed by the
refugee camp which is so iconic to the whole Palestinian experience: these are
rendered with almost terrifying accuracy and, paradoxically enough, gentleness at the same time. Joe the character is there sympathetically to understand
and to try to experience not only why Gaza is so representative a place in its
hopelessly overcrowded and yet rootless spaces of Palestinian dispossession,
but also to affirm that it is there, and must somehow be accounted for in
human terms, in the narrative sequences with which any reader can identify.

If you pay attention therefore you will note the scrupulous rendering of the
generations, how children and adults make their choices and live their meager
lives, how some speak and some remain silent, how they are dressed in the drab
sweaters, miscellaneous jackets, and warm *hattas* of an improvised life, on the
fringes of their homeland in which they have become that saddest and most
powerless and contradictory of creatures, the unwelcome alien. You can see
this all in a sense through Joe's own eyes as he moves and tarries among them,
attentive, unaggressive, caring, ironic, and so his visual testimony becomes
himself, himself so to speak in his own comics, in an act of the profoundest
solidarity. Above all, his Gaza series animates and confirms what three other

---

[1] Reissued in expanded form as *Notes from a Defeatist* in 2003.

remarkable witnesses before him, all of them women, have written about (one of them Israeli, another one American-Jewish, a third one an American with no previous connection with the Middle East) so unforgettably: Amira Hass, the brave Israeli *Ha'aretz* correspondent who lived in and wrote about Gaza for four years, Sara Roy, who wrote the definitive study of how Gaza's economy was de-developed, and Gloria Emerson, prize-winning journalist and novelist who gave a year of her time to live among the people of Gaza.

But what finally makes Sacco so unusual a portrayer of life in the Occupied Palestinian Territories is that his true concern is finally history's victims. Recall that most of the comics we read almost routinely conclude with someone's victory, the triumph of good over evil, or the routing of the unjust by the just, or even the marriage of two young lovers. Superman's villains get thrown out and we hear of and see them no more. Tarzan foils the plans of evil white men and they are shipped out of Africa in disgrace. Sacco's *Palestine* is not at all like that. The people he lives among are history's losers, banished to the fringes where they seem so despondently to loiter, without much hope or organization, except for their sheer indomitability, their mostly unspoken will to go on, and their willingness to cling to their story, to retell it, and to resist designs to sweep them away altogether. Astutely, Sacco seems to distrust militancy, particularly of the collective sort that bursts out in slogans or verbal flag-waving. Neither does he try to provide *solutions* of the kind that have made such a mockery of the Oslo peace process. But his comics about Palestine furnish his readers with a long enough sojourn among a people whose suffering and unjust fate have been scanted for far too long and with too little humanitarian and political attention. Sacco's art has the power to detain us, to keep us from impatiently wandering off in order to follow a catch-phrase or a lamentably predictable narrative of triumph and fulfillment. And this is perhaps the greatest of his achievements.

PART FOUR

APPENDICES

Reading Short Stories

> Fiction is like the spider's web, attached ever so slightly perhaps, but still attached to life at all four corners.
>
> — Virginia Woolf, *A Room of One's Own*

People have told stories to each other since before the dawn of history, but the literary genre that we call the **short story** is a relatively recent phenomenon, much younger than the genres of poetry and drama. The terms *story* and *short story* do not necessarily mean the same thing. The word *story* itself has two meanings. It can refer to a literary text (for example, we can say that Grace Paley wrote a story titled "Samuel"), or it can refer to the events themselves that are represented in the text (we can say that the story of "Samuel" is about an accident on a New York subway in which a young boy is killed). In contrast, the term *short story* always means the name of a particular literary genre. It refers to a short fictional prose narrative, usually involving one unified episode, and it is often applied to any work of narrative prose fiction shorter than a novel.

Most of us have spent our lives listening to, telling, watching, and reading stories, and we think we can recognize them. But what are the essential qualities of a short story such as Paley's "Samuel"?

GRACE PALEY

Samuel

1968

Some boys are very tough. They're afraid of nothing. They are the ones who climb a wall and take a bow at the top. Not only are they brave on the roof, but they make a lot of noise in the darkest part of the cellar where even the super hates to go. They also jiggle and hop on the platform between the locked doors of the subway cars.

Four boys are jiggling on the swaying platform. Their names are Alfred, Calvin, Samuel, and Tom. The men and the women in the cars on either side watch them. They don't like them to jiggle or jump but don't want to interfere. Of course some of the men in the cars were once brave boys like these. One of them had ridden the tail of a speeding truck from New York to Rockaway

Beach without getting off, without his sore fingers losing hold. Nothing happened to him then or later. He had made a compact with other boys who preferred to watch: Starting at Eighth Avenue and Fifteenth Street, he would get to some specified place, maybe Twenty-third and the river, by hopping the tops of the moving trucks. This was hard to do when one truck turned a corner in the wrong direction and the nearest truck was a couple of feet too high. He made three or four starts before succeeding. He had gotten his idea from a film at school called *The Romance of Logging*. He had finished high school, married a good friend, was in a responsible job and going to night school.

These two men and others looked at the four boys jumping and jiggling on the platform and thought, It must be fun to ride that way, especially now the weather is nice and we're out of the tunnel and way high over the Bronx. Then they thought, These kids do seem to be acting sort of stupid. They *are* little. Then they thought of some of the brave things they had done when they were boys and jiggling didn't seem so risky.

The ladies in the car became very angry when they looked at the four boys. Most of them brought their brows together and hoped the boys could see their extreme disapproval. One of the ladies wanted to get up and say, Be careful, you dumb kids, get off that platform or I'll call a cop. But three of the boys were Negroes and the fourth was something else she couldn't tell for sure. She was afraid they'd be fresh and laugh at her and embarrass her. She wasn't afraid they'd hit her, but she was afraid of embarrassment. Another lady thought, Their mothers never know where they are. It wasn't true in this particular case. Their mothers all knew that they had gone to see the missile exhibit on Fourteenth Street.

Out on the platform, whenever the train accelerated, the boys would raise their hands and point them up to the sky to act like rockets going off, then they rat-tat-tatted the shatterproof glass pane like machine guns, although no machine guns had been exhibited.

For some reason known only to the motorman, the train began a sudden slowdown. The lady who was afraid of embarrassment saw the boys jerk forward and backward and grab the swinging guard chains. She had her own boy at home. She stood up with determination and went to the door. She slid it open and said, "You boys will be hurt. You'll be killed. I'm going to call the conductor if you don't just go into the next car and sit down and be quiet."

Two of the boys said, "Yes'm," and acted as though they were about to go. Two of them blinked their eyes a couple of times and pressed their lips together. The train resumed its speed. The door slid shut, parting the lady and the boys. She leaned against the side door because she had to get off at the next stop.

The boys opened their eyes wide at each other and laughed. The lady blushed. The boys looked at her and laughed harder. They began to pound each other's back. Samuel laughed the hardest and pounded Alfred's back until Alfred coughed and the tears came. Alfred held tight to the chain hook. Samuel pounded him even harder when he saw the tears. He said, "Why you bawling? You a baby, huh?" and laughed. One of the men whose boyhood had been more watchful than brave became angry. He stood up straight and looked at the boys for a couple of seconds. Then he walked in a citizenly way to the end of the car, where he pulled the emergency cord. Almost at once, with a terrible hiss, the pressure of air abandoned the brakes and the wheels were caught and held.

People standing in the most secure places fell forward, then backward. Samuel had let go of his hold on the chain so he could pound Tom as well as Alfred. All the passengers in the cars whipped back and forth, but he pitched only forward and fell head first to be crushed and killed between the cars.

The train had stopped hard, halfway into the station, and the conductor called at once for the trainmen who knew about this kind of death and how to take the body from the wheels and brakes. There was silence except for passengers from other cars who asked, What happened! What happened! The ladies waited around wondering if he might be an only child. The men recalled other afternoons with very bad endings. The little boys stayed close to each other, leaning and touching shoulders and arms and legs.

When the policeman knocked at the door and told her about it, Samuel's mother began to scream. She screamed all day and moaned all night, though the doctors tried to quiet her with pills.

Oh, oh, she hopelessly cried. She did not know how she could ever find another boy like that one. However, she was a young woman and she became pregnant. Then for a few months she was hopeful. The child born to her was a boy. They brought him to be seen and nursed. She smiled. But immediately she saw that this baby wasn't Samuel. She and her husband together have had other children, but never again will a boy exactly like Samuel be known.

When you finished reading "Samuel," you probably sensed that it was a short story, different from a newspaper account, but how did you know this? For one thing, the story wasn't simply reporting the facts of a particular subway accident that had occurred recently. Paley begins and ends her narrative with her subjective response to the death of a young boy. Her first sentence "Some boys are very tough" is not the way a newspaper reporter would open a story, unless perhaps it was meant for the editorial page. Also by the second paragraph of "Samuel," Paley is describing the antics of a group of boys on the swaying platform between two subway cars as they stunt for each other. As a short story writer, she is *showing* you their antics, not *telling* you about their presumed toughness any more. She is making the events she describes come alive in your imagination as you read the page.

The way that the writer uses language to show the events of a narrative, not merely to tell about it, is the most important difference between a short story author and a newspaper reporter. In an interview, Paley explained that her decision to write stories was her attempt to "get the world to explain itself to me, to speak to me." She regarded her decision to dramatize the events of her stories as an effort "to reach out to the world and get it to tell me what it was all about." To accomplish this dramatization, this ability to suggest a living world on the page, writers of short fiction have various means at their disposal, including plot, characterization, setting, point of view, style, and theme.

With these elements of short fiction, skillful writers such as Paley can create stories that communicate their own unique sense of the mystery of life, the realization that "never again will a boy exactly like Samuel be known." Paley's story is very short, because she wanted to attempt a literary style that was close to poetry. As she described it in an interview,

> I would say that stories are closer to poetry than they are to the novel because first they are shorter, and second they are more concentrated, more economical, and that kind of economy, the pulling together of all the information and making leaps across the information, is really close to poetry. By leaps I mean thought leaps and feeling leaps. Also, when short stories are working right, you pay more attention to language than most novelists do.

The length of "Samuel" is of less importance than what the author succeeds in accomplishing with her few words. Paley believes that the form of the story is very flexible. "It can be just telling a little tale, or writing a complicated philosophical story. It can be a song, almost."

Like poetry, the short story is a concentrated use of language dependent for its success on feeling and suggestion. Edgar Allan Poe was one of the first to attempt an analysis of the short story's aesthetic properties. He stressed unity of *effect* as the story's most characteristic feature. All successful art gives an impression of unity, but for over a hundred years readers of short fiction have pondered what Poe could have meant by the word *effect*. The critic Louis Menand has analyzed it cogently in his essay "True Story: The Art of Short Fiction."

> A short story is not as restrictive as a sonnet, but, of all the literary forms, it is possibly the most single-minded. Its aim, as it was identified by the modern genre's first theorist, Edgar Allan Poe, is to create "an effect" — by which Poe meant something almost physical, like a sensation or (the term is appropriate, since Poe's reputation was always greater in France than in his own country), a *frisson*. Every word in a story, Poe said, is in the service of this effect. . . . [A]t the end there has to be the literary equivalent of the magician's puff of smoke, an outcome that is both startling and anticipated. . . .
>
> The difficulty of putting into words the effect a story produces is part of the point. The story is words; the effect is wordless. . . . James Joyce called the effect an "epiphany," a term whose theological connotations have led, over the years, to a lot of critical misunderstanding. What Joyce meant by an epiphany was, he said, just "a revelation of the whatness of a thing" — a sudden apprehension of the way the world unmediatedly is. Language being one of the principal means by which the world is mediated, the epiphany is an experience beyond (or after, or without) words. "Snow was general all over Ireland." The sentence is as banal and literal as a weather report. (In fact, in the story it *is* a weather report.) But if "The Dead" works, then that sentence, when it comes, triggers the exact shiver of recognition that Joyce wants you to have.

Paley wrote her story to set you up for the "shiver of recognition" in her final sentence. When you understand the intricate way she used language to create her fictional world, the story's effect has an even greater emotional impact. As the writer Annie Proulx told a *Paris Review* interviewer, "The short story deserves more honor and attention than it gets." She believed that "in a rough way the short story writer is to the novelist as a cabinetmaker is to a house carpenter. . . . Short stories are often very difficult and demanding, drawing on deep knowledge of human nature and the particulars of pivotal events." Though stories are short, "every single word counts heavily. The punctuation is critical. Finding the right words and making honorable sentences takes time." Proulx felt that the "general reading public has no idea of what goes into a short story because it is literally short and can give the impression that the writer sat down and rattled the thing out in an hour or two."

Paley created her harrowing story "Samuel" nearly a half century ago, but it seems timeless because it comes alive again in our imagination every time we read it carefully. Each reader creates it anew. When we read a story, savoring the details of the fictional narrative adds to our enjoyment of the storyteller's achievement. The writer Angela Carter even argued that "The limited trajectory of the short narrative concentrates its meaning. Sign and sense can fuse to an extent impossible to achieve among the multiplying ambiguities of an extended narrative."

Writers of short fiction must forgo the comprehensiveness of the novel, but they often gain a striking compression by using language with the force of poetry. Like poets, short story writers can impress on us the unity of their vision of life by focusing on a single effect.

Close Reading Short Fiction

In your reading you will find that all writers create their short stories by using the elements of fiction: plot, character, setting, point of view, style, and theme. When you read a story for the first time, you may find it relatively easy to see how the elements of plot, character, and setting interact on the page. They stand out because they seem to make the story happen, and — at least for the casual reader — they appear to be what the story is about. Point of view, style, and theme, on the other hand, are less visible elements. Many insecure readers regard them with dread as part of what they call the "hidden meaning" of a story. While it is true that you may have to look for these particular elements deliberately, you will find that this hunt is worth the treasure. The more attentively you read, the easier it will be to appreciate how all the elements operate in short fiction. Your close reading will help you to understand more clearly that *how* a story is written is an essential part of *what* it is saying.

Stories are shorter than novels, but they're not necessarily easier to read. The editor Charles McGrath cautions that

> stories aren't just *brief*, they're *different*, and they require of the reader something like the degree of concentration they require of the writer. . . .
> You can't skim or coast or leap ahead, and if you have to put a story down, it's not always easy to pick up — emotionally, that is — where you left off.

You have to backtrack a little, or even start over. It's not enough to read a story the way you read a book or a newspaper. Stories ask of us that we surrender ourselves to them.

Guidelines for Close Reading Short Fiction

1. Read the story with a pen or pencil in hand, asking questions and making observations as you go or highlighting if the text is electronic. Don't be afraid to write in the margins of the text. (On the following pages you can see how you might annotate the opening of Paley's "Samuel.") Questions to consider as you read: What do you notice about the title? What's happening in the narrative? Are there words you should look up in a dictionary? Are there puzzling passages you'll want to reconsider once you've finished reading? How are the elements of fiction at work? Notice that simply highlighting sentences will not help you think as you go. You could also write your comments in a notebook.

2. Make an entry in your notebook for each story assigned in class, writing down the author's name and the story's title and date. As you begin to read your assignments, remember T. S. Eliot's advice in his essay "Tradition and the Individual Talent." This important poet believed that "criticism is as inevitable as breathing, and that we should be none the worse for articulating what passes in our minds when we read a book and feel an emotion about it, for criticizing our own minds in their work of criticism."

3. Use a dictionary to look up any words in the story and its headnote that you do not understand.

4. After you have read the story, take notes about the way the author has used the elements of fiction; this will help you remember when you review the story later. Note, for example, the names of the characters, the geographical setting, the author's choice of a point of view, and the literary style in which it is written. Try summing up the story's theme in a sentence.

5. If you have difficulty understanding the story's meaning or how any of the elements of fiction work within it, write down your questions so you can ask them in class. The related commentaries may also throw light on the stories.

6. In class, take notes on the important material about the story that you learn from lectures and discussions, and ask any questions you have about the assignment. Later your notes may suggest new ideas to develop in your papers.

7. Review technical words about short fiction used in class in the glossary of literary terms (p. 1736). This will help you to understand them better and to use them more confidently in your writing.

8. If you have particularly enjoyed a story, go online or to the library to check out other works by its writer. Reading on your own will enrich the class assignments.

Sample Close Reading

Grace Paley

Samuel 1968

Some boys are very tough. They're afraid of nothing. They are the ones who climb a wall and take a bow at the top. Not only are they brave on the roof, but they make a lot of noise in the darkest part of the cellar where even the super hates to go. They also jiggle and hop on the platform between the locked doors of the subway cars.

Four boys are jiggling on the swaying platform. Their names are Alfred, Calvin, Samuel, and Tom. The men and the women in the cars on either side watch them. They don't like them to jiggle or jump but don't want to interfere. Of course some of the men in the cars were once brave boys like these. One of them had ridden the tail of a speeding truck from New York to Rockaway Beach without getting off, without his sore fingers losing hold. Nothing happened to him then or later. He had made a compact with other boys who preferred to watch: Starting at Eighth Avenue and Fifteenth Street, he would get to some specified place, maybe Twenty-third and the river, by hopping the tops of the moving trucks. This was hard to do when one truck turned a corner in the wrong direction and the nearest truck was a couple of feet too high. He made three or four starts before succeeding. He had gotten his idea from a film at school called *The Romance of Logging*. He had finished high school, married a good friend, was in a responsible job and going to night school.

These two men and others looked at the four boys jumping and jiggling on the platform and thought, It must be fun to ride that way, especially now the weather is nice and we're out of the tunnel and way high over the Bronx. Then they thought, These kids do seem to be acting sort of stupid. They *are* little. Then they thought of some of the brave things they had done when they were boys and jiggling didn't seem so risky.

The ladies in the car became very angry when they looked at the four boys. Most of them brought their brows together and hoped the boys could see their extreme disapproval. One of the ladies wanted to get up and say, Be careful, you dumb kids, get off that platform or I'll call a cop. But three of the boys were Negroes and the fourth was something else she couldn't tell for sure. She was afraid they'd be fresh and laugh at her and embarrass her. She wasn't afraid they'd hit her, but she was afraid of embarrassment. Another lady thought, Their mothers never know where they are. It wasn't true in this particular case. Their mothers all knew that they had gone to see the missile exhibit on Fourteenth Street . . .

In the title, Paley uses a full name, not nickname — serious tone

Introduction — Setting is a subway in New York City

Rising action — 4 boys are riding between the cars. Dangerous.

The men watching them are sympathetic.

Details about a minor character suggest that many boys take risks.

Hint of foreshadowing — they're really very young.

The women are angry and judgmental.

Actually the boys have responsible mothers.

Critical Thinking About Short Fiction

You will find that reading a story carefully for the first time is only part of the process of understanding it. Usually your thinking about a story begins with interpreting it, clarifying what the author is saying in the action of the plot, and making sure you understand the characters and have a clear idea of the theme of the story. Critical thinking goes a step beyond interpretation when you consider how the form of the story is related to its content or when you analyze the story's significance, how it relates to your own experience.

Reading a commentary about a story can help you to think critically. Always read the story a second time to feel that you thoroughly understand it as a whole. When you read it again, notice the passages that strike you with particular force. Underline the words and sentences you consider significant — or, even better, make a list in your notebook of what seems important while you are rereading the story. These can be outstanding descriptions of the characters or settings, passages of meaningful dialogue, details showing the way the author builds toward the story's climax, or hints that foreshadow the conclusion. You may want to jot down answers to the following questions about the elements of the story as you reread it.

Plot. Does the plot depend on chance, or coincidence? Or does it grow out of the personalities of the characters? Are any later incidents foreshadowed early in the story? Are the events presented in chronological order? If not, why is this so? Does the climax indicate a change in a situation or a change in a character? How dramatic is this change? Or is there no change at all?

Point of View. How does the point of view shape the story? Would the story change if told from a different viewpoint? In first-person narration, can you trust the narrator?

Characterization. Are the characters believable? Are they stereotypes? Are they sympathetic or unsympathetic? Do they suggest real people or abstract qualities? Is there one protagonist, or are there several? Does the story have an antagonist? How does the author tell you about the main character: through description of physical appearance, actions, thoughts, and emotions, or through contrast with a minor character? Does the main character change in the course of the story? If so, how? Why?

Setting. How does the setting influence the plot and the characters? Does it help to suggest or develop the meaning of the story or to heighten the drama of the story?

Style. Is the story realistic or a fantasy? If dialect or colloquial speech is used, what is its effect? Does the author call attention to the way he or she uses words, or is the literary style inconspicuous? What is the tone of the story? Can you find evidence of any objects used as symbols in the narrative? If so, what do they symbolize?

Theme. Does the story's title help explain its meaning? Can you find a sugges-tion of the theme in specific passages of dialogue or description? Are certain symbols or repetitions of images important in revealing the author's intent in the story, what Edgar Allan Poe would call "the single effect"?

Close reading and critical thinking about the stories will help you to understand the author's creation of design and pattern in the text. If you make the effort, you will find that reading literature is an activity that offers a worthy challenge. After finishing a short story for the first time, you may feel con-tradictory responses to it, uncertain how to interpret what you have read. A second reading may help clarify your impressions, or you may find you have to close your book and think about the story if it doesn't fit easily into your pre-conceptions about human behavior.

The effort is worthwhile. As the critic Ray Carey has explained, the differ-ent forms of storytelling can "point a way out of some of the traps of received forms of thinking and feeling. Every artist makes a fresh effort of awareness.... He [or she] can help us to new and potentially revolutionary understandings of our lives." Reading a good story can be an enlightening experience. You will discover that analyzing the means available to the storyteller will often help you to reach a deeper understanding of what you have read.

RELATED COMMENTARIES
Grace Paley, "A Conversation with Ann Charters," page 1503; Edgar Allan Poe, "The Importance of the Single Effect in a Prose Tale," page 1509.

APPENDIX TWO

The Elements of Fiction

I had a teacher I liked who used to say good fiction's job was to comfort the disturbed and disturb the comfortable. I guess a big part of serious fiction's purpose is to give the reader, who like all of us is sort of marooned in her own skull, to give her imaginative access to other selves. Since an ineluctable part of being a human self is suffering, part of what we humans come to art for is an experience of suffering, necessarily a vicarious experience, more like a sort of "generalization" of suffering. Does this make sense? We all suffer alone in the real world; true empathy's impossible. But if a piece of fiction can allow us imaginatively to identify with a character's pain, we might then also more easily conceive of others identifying with our own. This is nourishing, redemptive; we become less alone inside. It might just be that simple. But now realize that TV and popular film and most kinds of "low" art — which just means art whose primary aim is to make money — is lucrative precisely because it recognizes that audiences prefer 100 percent pleasure to the reality that tends to be 49 percent pleasure and 51 percent pain. Whereas "serious" art, which is not primarily about getting money out of you, is more apt to make you uncomfortable, or to force you to work hard to access its pleasures, the same way that in real life true pleasure is usually a by-product of hard work and discomfort. So it's hard for an art audience, especially a young one that's been raised to expect art to be 100 percent pleasurable and to make that pleasure effortless, to read and appreciate serious fiction. That's not good. The problem isn't that today's readership is "dumb," I don't think. Just that TV and the commercial-art culture's trained it to be sort of lazy and childish in its expectations. But it makes trying to engage today's readers both imaginatively and intellectually unprecedentedly hard.

—David Foster Wallace, *1993 interview*

Most of us read casually for the pleasure it gives us, but how do we read more attentively and imaginatively so we can enjoy what David Foster Wallace called "serious" art, a term that encompasses the short fiction in this anthology? Understanding the different elements of fiction available during the writing process to every storyteller can enhance our reading.

Plot

Since the short story is defined as a prose narrative involving one unified episode or a sequence of related events, plot is basic to this literary form. It determines the way we experience the story. **Plot** is the sequence of events in a story and their relation to one another as they develop and often resolve a conflict. Usually, writers present the events of the plot in a coherent time frame that the reader can follow easily. When we read, we sense that the events are related by causation, and their meaning lies in this relation. To the casual reader, causation (or why something in the plot happened next) seems to result only from the writer's organization of the events into a chronological sequence. A more thoughtful reader understands that causation in the plot of a memorable short story reveals a good deal about the author's use of the other elements of fiction as well, especially characterization.

As the English novelist E. M. Forster realized, plot not only answers *what* happened next, but it also suggests *why*. The psychologist James Hillman has explained that plot reveals "human intentions. Plot shows how it all hangs together and makes sense. Only when a narrative receives inner coherence in terms of the depths of human nature do we have fiction, and for this fiction we have to have plot. . . . To plot is to move from asking the question *And then what happened?* to the question *Why did it happen?*"

A short story can dramatize the events of a brief episode or compress a longer period of time. Analyzing why a short story is short, the critic Norman Friedman suggests that it "may be short not because its action is inherently small, but rather because the author has chosen — in working with an episode or plot — to omit certain of its parts. In other words, an action may be large in size and still be short in the telling because not all of it is there." A short story can describe something that happens in a few minutes or encompass action that takes years to conclude. The narrative possibilities are endless, as the writer may omit or condense complex episodes to intensify their dramatic effect or expand a single incident to make a relatively long story.

Regardless of length, the plot of a short story usually has what critics term an *end orientation* — the outcome of the action or the conclusion of the plot — inherent in its opening paragraphs. As Mark Twain humorously observed, "Fiction is obliged to stick to possibilities. Truth isn't." The novelist may conclude a single episode long before the end of a novel and then pick up the thread of another narrative, or interpret an event from another angle in a different character's point of view, linking episode to episode and character to character so that each illuminates the others. But a story stops earlier. As Edgar Allan Poe recognized in 1842, its narrative dramatizes a single effect complete unto itself.

The events in the plot of a short story usually involve a conflict or struggle between opposing forces. When you analyze a plot, you can often (but not always) see it develop in a pattern during the course of the narration. Typically you find that the first paragraphs of the story or **exposition** give the background or setting of the conflict. The **rising action** dramatizes the specific events that set the conflict in motion. Often there is a **turning point** in the story midway before further complications prolong the suspense of the conflict's resolution. The **climax** is the emotional high point of the narration. In the **falling action**, the events begin to wind down and point the reader toward the **conclusion** or dénouement at the end of the story, which resolves the conflict to a greater or lesser degree. Sometimes the conclusion introduces an unexpected turn of events or a surprise ending.

The plot of Grace Paley's short story "Samuel" is easily summarized. It relates a sequence of events about four young boys who are fooling around on the platform between two cars of a moving subway train. A woman watching them tells them they'll get hurt, but the boys only laugh at her. Witnessing their response, a man gets angry and pulls the emergency cord. The train lurches to a stop, causing one of the boys to fall and be crushed to death. The mother of the dead boy grieves, then becomes hopeful after she becomes pregnant again. But after the birth of her baby she realizes that the new child can never replace the son she has lost.

The first part of the plot, or exposition, of "Samuel" is the opening paragraph. It introduces the idea that motivates the main characters of Paley's little drama, the idea that boys like to show off for each other. The rising action dramatizes the conflict of interest between the young boys and the adults watching them in the subway car. Some of the men in the car sympathize with the kids, remembering the dangerous stunts they pulled when they were young. Most of the women in the car are angry at the boys and want them to behave more responsibly, to take seats and calm down.

The turning point is when one of the women, with a son at home, summons her courage and admonishes the boys. They make fun of her, and this raises the tension of the story by adding a complicating factor of defiance to their behavior. The climax of "Samuel" is when the self-righteous male passenger pulls the emergency cord and Samuel is killed. In the falling action, Paley describes the result of the accident. Traffic on the subway is stopped, the passengers who saw the accident are in shock, the others riding the train are curious, and a policeman notifies Samuel's mother of his death. The conclusion is the final paragraph of the story, more than a year later, when Samuel's parents understand the full dimension of their loss.

A short story can cover the events of a brief episode, as does Grace Paley's "Samuel," or encompass action that takes years to conclude, as in Leo Tolstoy's "The Death of Ivan Ilych." Usually stories that are static, where little change occurs, are relatively short (as Paley's), while more dynamic actions, covering a longer time and involving the characters' changes from one state to another, are longer (as Tolstoy's). Yet the narrative possibilities are endless. The writer may omit or condense complex episodes to intensify their dramatic effect (Nathaniel Hawthorne's "Young Goodman Brown") or expand a single incident to make a relatively long story (Charlotte Perkins Gilman's "The Yellow Wallpaper").

The plot of a short story usually involves a conflict or struggle between opposing forces. The discerning reader can see it develop in a pattern during the course of the narration, whether its events proceed chronologically, as in "Samuel," or are rearranged with flashbacks, as in Ambrose Bierce's "An Occurrence at Owl Creek Bridge." Even if a plot lacks a momentous peak in the action, it always includes the basic pattern of a beginning, a middle, and an end.

In most stories the beginning sets up the problem or conflict; the middle is where the author introduces various complications that prolong suspense and make the struggle more meaningful; and the end resolves the conflict to a greater or lesser degree. In successful stories the writer shapes these stages into a complex structure that impresses the reader with its balance and proportion, often suggesting a fresh aspect of a familiar human situation.

The particular pattern varies from story to story, of course, and from author to author. Nathaniel Hawthorne began "Young Goodman Brown," for example, with only a few short paragraphs of exposition, the leave-taking between Goodman Brown and his young wife, Faith. Herman Melville devoted pages to exposition in his much longer story "Bartleby, the Scrivener," describing the lawyer, his two eccentric copyists, and his office boy before introducing the title character.

Plot can work in several ways. It can be an outgrowth of a character's personality or will, as in Young Goodman Brown's insistence on his meeting with the devil, or in Bartleby's refusal to participate in the lawyer's office routines, or in Montresor's insane scheme of revenge against Fortunato in Edgar Allan Poe's "The Cask of Amontillado." It can be propelled by an apparent accident of fate, as when two mustachioed thieves appear out of nowhere on a winter night in Nikolai Gogol's "The Overcoat" and steal Akaky Akakievich's new overcoat right off his back. It can be controlled by the setting, as in Stephen Crane's "The Open Boat." Most often the plots of stories can be understood as the interaction of character with circumstances: for example, in Sarah Orne Jewett's "A White Heron."

Plot does not emerge just through the description of events in the story. It can also be carried forward in dialogue, as when Hawthorne introduced the characters, the time, and the situation through the conversation between Goodman Brown and his wife in the beginning of the story. Readers also respond to **foreshadowing** and **dramatic irony** as the plot moves along, anticipating a turn of events which may or may not go along with our expectations. In the opening of Flannery O'Connor's "A Good Man Is Hard to Find," we can visualize the grandmother beginning the car trip dressed in navy blue trimmed with white organdy and lace and a sachet of cloth violets so that "in case of an accident, anyone seeing her dead on the highway would know at once that she was a lady." Later in the story we learn that although she survives the car accident, being dressed so neatly doesn't save her from being killed by the Misfit after she pleads with him, "I know you wouldn't shoot a lady!"

Paley's story is very short, more of a sketch than a fully developed narrative. The only dialogue is between the lady who warns the boys that they might get hurt and the boys themselves, who find her warning hilarious. Samuel pounds his buddy Alfred's back until the tears come, saying "You a baby, huh?" Paley gives a hint of foreshadowing in the opening paragraphs of her story, suggesting the action to come, when some of the men watching the boys think, "These kids do seem to be acting sort of stupid. They *are* little."

These words anticipate a turn of events that may or may not go along with our expectations, but when we reread the story, we see that Paley's plot runs along as solidly as a subway train. Not for her are the tricky surprise endings favored in short stories by earlier writers such as Guy de Maupassant, Kate Chopin, and Ambrose Bierce. We sense Paley's emotional involvement in her characters as she chronicles the tragedy of a small boy's senseless death.

Along with her choice of a title, Paley sets up an expectation in the reader early on with her hint of foreshadowing — the story will be about Samuel, and its "single effect" will be the shock of his accidental, senseless death on the people around him. Paley doesn't go on to tell us about the lives of the three boys who survive the accident, or about the guilty feelings (and subsequent nervous breakdown?) of the man who pulls the emergency cord. These would be other stories.

Regardless of the author's method of developing the plot, the goal is the same: The writer of short stories must *show* the reader something about human nature through the dramatic action of the plot and the other elements of the story, and not just *tell* the reader what to think. A good plot arouses our curiosity, engages our emotions, and keeps us in suspense.

As the contemporary American writer Eudora Welty understood, "A narrative line is in its deeper sense, of course, the tracing out of a meaning, and the real continuity of a story lies in this probing forward." A storyteller must sustain the illusion of reality until the end of the story, unfolding events with the continuing revelation of an apparently endless silk handkerchief drawn from a skillful magician's coat sleeve.

Character

If you are like most people, plot is what keeps you going when you first read a story, and character is what stays with you after you have finished reading it. The title of Paley's short narrative is "Samuel," the name of the foolish young boy (he lacked prudence) who is the **protagonist** or central character in the story.

Characters are usually the people who are involved in what happens in a story. Writers can use animals as characters, or giant insects such as Gregor Samsa, the protagonist of Franz Kafka's "The Metamorphosis," or even such inanimate objects as houses, trees, chairs, and shoes. But by the term *character* we usually mean a human being with emotions whose mind works something like our own.

With a plot we do not just ask, What next? We also ask, Why? The answer is usually found in the characters, who are plausible if we can understand their actions. The characters themselves don't always have a conscious awareness of why they act the way they do, or — if they have an awareness — it isn't always accurate. Yet there always *are* reasons, and the reader may discover them before the characters do. The reader instinctively wants to connect the events of a story by more than their simple chronological sequence. Assuming a relation between the events and the characters makes the story seem coherent.

Paley chooses to keep her story so short that she doesn't give her characters any time to develop. They are *static*, not *dynamic*. We are told their names, but we don't see them change during the narrative or after Samuel's death. They are **flat**, not **round** characters. For characters to emerge as round, the reader must feel the play and pull of their actions and responses to situations. Yet Paley's character types are familiar to all of us. Samuel is a schoolboy clowning for his buddies, and we understand why he acts as he does. The man who pulls the emergency cord in the subway car is a little more complex. We aren't told much about him, except that his "boyhood had been more watchful than brave." Unlike some of the other male spectators, he has no sense of empathy with the boys who are fooling around on the moving platform.

Perhaps part of the anger the man feels toward the boys is prompted by their mockery of the lady who issues the reprimand. Paley tells us only that "he walked in a citizenly way" when he went to pull the emergency cord. Considering the dire results of the man's action, Paley is using **verbal irony** here, meaning the opposite of the literal meaning of the words *good citizen*. No one acting like a good citizen wants to cause a small boy's death. As readers, we instinctively strive to connect the events of a story by more than their simple chronological sequence, because assuming connections between the events and the inner life of the characters makes the story seem coherent.

How are the characters in a short story to be understood? Any discussion of character tends to drift into a value judgment, as our principles of definition and evaluation for fictional characters are based on the ones we use for real people, tentative and unfocused as they may be. We must remember that we are reading about *fictional* characters in a short story, not real ones. The only evidence we have about characters is what the author puts into the story.

We are on firmer ground in literary discussions when we analyze the writer's method of characterization as well as the character's personality. Paley's method is one of economy; the extremely short length of her story mirrors Samuel's brief lifetime. Writing a realistic story, she might be suggesting that characters from modest economic backgrounds have little control over their fates in the big city, underscoring the tragedy of the loss of a young boy who never had the chance to grow up.

Other authors, such as Poe, create a fantasy world in their stories, imagining situations in which their characters have total control. We know that Poe's protagonist Montresor gets away with murder in "The Cask of Amontillado." Pigeonholing his character does not bring us close to understanding the sense of horror that Poe evokes in the story.

We can appreciate it more readily by relishing the language Poe uses in dialogue and description to show us Montresor's thoughts and responses as he acts out his obsessive plan to avenge his honor and lure Fortunato to his death. As the literary critic David Reynolds has realized, the two characters in this classic short story, although limited, are not flat.

They come swiftly alive before our eyes because Poe describes them with acute psychological realism. Montresor is a complex Machiavellian criminal, exhibiting a full range of traits from clever ingratiation to stark sadism. Fortunato, the dupe whose pride leads to his own downfall, nevertheless exhibits . . . admirable qualities. . . . The drama of the story lies in the carefully orchestrated interaction between the two. Poe directs our attention away from the merely sensational and toward the psychological. . . .

In all successful fiction the characters come alive as individuals. They must materialize on the page through the accumulation of details about their appearance, actions, and responses as seen, heard, and felt physical realities. Hawthorne told us little about the physical appearance of Goodman Brown except that he is young and newly married. We do not even know his first name — "Goodman" was used by the Puritans as a title of respect for men in the community who owned land. We know more about his wife — her name is Faith, she is pretty and affectionate, and she wears pink ribbons on her cap.

The lack of physical details about him makes Goodman Brown less than flesh and blood to most readers. He remains an abstraction in a moral allegory. Thus Hawthorne was able to reveal more clearly the figure of a man on trial for his belief in good and evil. As we are caught up in reading the story, Goodman Brown's actions as a fictional "person" provoke our curiosity and his responses arouse our alarm. If he continues to interest us after we have finished reading the story, it is because we are fascinated, as Hawthorne was, with the moral dilemma that the narrative dramatizes.

Each writer of short fiction puts his or her own emphasis on character. An attentive reader can perceive that Anton Chekhov and Jorge Luis Borges, for example, did not develop characters in the same way. Chekhov, a great nineteenth-century realist, placed highest emphasis on character, believing that it determines our fate. Borges, a contemporary teller of philosophical tales, believed that our subjective nature makes it impossible for us to understand the essential riddle of human existence, so he made plot more important than character.

Different fictional worlds make different demands on the reader's imagination. What is most important to the reader's enjoyment of the tale is the emotional truth conveyed by the characters, whether they are flat or round, dynamic or static. To avoid **sentimentality** (emotional overindulgence) and **stereotyping** (oversimplified judgment) in creating characters, the writer must be able to suggest enough complexity to engage the reader's emotions, or the story will not succeed.

Setting

Setting is the place and time of the story. To set the scene and suggest a mood or atmosphere for the events to follow, the writer attempts to create in the reader's visual imagination the illusion of a solid world in which the story takes place. Paley uses only a few words to describe the subway setting of her story, but they create an image of power and danger. The doors are "locked." The platform is "swaying." The cars on either side are full of people, who are watching the boys uneasily. When the cars unexpectedly slow down suddenly for the first time, the boys "grab the swinging guard chains," nearly falling down. Paley's description of the second slowdown, after the man pulls the emergency cord, is more shocking, relying on strong active verbs such as *abandoned, caught, held, fell, whipped, pitched, crushed,* and *killed*:

> Almost at once, with a terrible hiss, the pressure of air abandoned the brakes and the wheels were caught and held.
>
> People standing in the most secure places fell forward, then backward. Samuel had let go of his hold on the chain so he could pound Tom as well as Alfred. All the passengers in the cars whipped back and forth, but he pitched only forward and fell head first to be crushed and killed between the cars.

When the writer locates the narrative in a physical setting, the reader is moved step by step toward acceptance of the fiction. The *external* reality of the setting is always an illusion, our mental images stimulated by the words that the writer has put on paper. Yet this invented setting is essential if we are to share the *internal* emotional life of the characters involved in the plot. A sense of place engages us in the fictional characters' situations.

In Nathaniel Hawthorne's story "Young Goodman Brown," for example, when the protagonist Goodman Brown enters the dark, tangled world of the forest surrounding the colonial village of Salem to keep his appointment with the devil, the attentive reader may perceive that Brown really enters the troubled world of his own mind. Exercising his own free will, he voluntarily exchanges the companionship of his pretty young wife and her pink ribbons for the attractions of Satan.

The setting of a story furnishes the location for its world of feeling, the different emotional associations awakened in the reader's mind by a gloomy New England forest in a Hawthorne story, a dank burial crypt in a Poe story, or a crowded Manhattan subway train in a Paley story. A sense of place is essential for us to imagine the fictional characters' situations as the author creates the story.

Place helps the characters seem real, but, to be most effective, the setting must also have a dramatic use. It must be shown, or at least felt, to affect character or plot. The emergency brake in the subway car precipitates the disaster of Samuel's death. Exchanging the windy street in Salem village for the dreary, solitary path through the tangled forest leads Young Goodman Brown straight to the devil. The mound of bones piled outside the damp niche where Montresor has planned to entomb his victim Fortunato foreshadows the evil deed to come. Imagining the details of setting in the creation of stories, writers must exert their talents to make the reader see only the fictional world that emerges on the printed page, under the illusion that while the story unfolds, it is the real world itself.

Point of View

Point of view refers to the author's choice of a narrator for the story. At the start, the writer must decide whether to employ **first-person narration**, using the pronoun *I*, or **third-person narration**, using the pronouns *he*, *she*, and *they*. (Second-person narration, *you*, is less common, although the dramatic intimacy of second-person narrative address is often used in poetry and song lyrics.) The writer's choice of a point of view to narrate stories usually falls into two major categories:

> *First-Person Narration (narrator apparently a participant in the story)*
> 1. A major character
> 2. A minor character
>
> *Third-Person Narration (narrator a nonparticipant in the story)*
> 1. Omniscient — seeing into the minds of all characters
> 2. Limited omniscient — seeing into one or, sometimes, two characters' minds
> 3. Objective — seeing into none of the characters' minds

First-Person Narration

Samuel is the protagonist, but telling his side of the story in a first-person narration by a major character isn't Paley's objective as a writer in "Samuel." The young boy dies before the conclusion of events, before Paley reaches the point she wants to make as the storyteller. Perhaps we can imagine Samuel telling his story in the first person from his vantage point in heaven, but then Paley is a realistic writer.

If the chosen point of view is not right for the complete dramatic ordering of the subject, the narrative will not reveal all its possibilities to the writer, and the pattern of the story will be incomplete. If Hawthorne had chosen to tell his story from the point of view of Goodman Brown, for example, using the first-person narrator to describe how an evening in the forest with the devil ruined his life forever, it is likely that the story would have struck the reader as the gloomy ruminations of a religious fanatic. It would also necessarily have ended with Goodman Brown's death, and its larger meaning would not have emerged so explicitly.

There is little surprise in finding Goodman Brown "a distrustful, if not a desperate man" after his fearful night in the forest, but Hawthorne gave the story a final unexpected twist in the last sentence describing the funeral. Goodman Brown's survivors "carved no hopeful verse upon his tombstone, for his dying hour was gloom." In this conclusion Hawthorne's continuation of the narrative to a point in time beyond his main character's death places the individual conflict dramatized in the story in a larger moral context. The author reveals to the reader a deeper perception of the situation, a more subtle reflection of what life is like.

The first-person narrator can move freely within the fictional world, and he or she can approach other fictional characters as closely as one human being can approach another, but the narrator has no way of understanding these characters except by observation of what they say and do. By making his first-person narrator a major character in the action in "The Cask of Amontillado," Poe intensified the impact of Montresor's insane behavior, showing us his apparent imperviousness to the horror of what he is doing.

Paley might have considered presenting the narrative through the voice of a minor character as a first-person speaker. For example, Samuel's mother, who understands that there will never be another boy like Samuel, could have told the tale, but she wasn't present when the accident on the subway occurred, so she couldn't have described it in close detail. All the women and men in the subway car who witnessed Samuel's death were minor characters in the drama. They could have gone home to their families or friends that evening and told the story of the accident as eyewitnesses, using first-person narration. No doubt their stories would have been highly emotional — "I can't believe what happened on the Lexington Avenue express today. I've been riding the subway all my life, and I've never seen anything like it" — but their personal accounts, while dramatic, would lack Paley's compassionate insight into what the loss of the young boy's life really means.

The first-person narrator, whether a major or a minor character, can be reliable or unreliable, making us aware as we read his or her story that the account is skewed and that we can't quite trust the point of view. In a story such as Herman Melville's "Bartleby, the Scrivener," the garrulous lawyer telling us about his difficult relationship with his eccentric scrivener is actually a minor character in Bartleby's life. Despite his obvious concern for Bartleby and attempts to help him, the lawyer inadvertently serves as a screen between the reader and the protagonist of the story, making it impossible for us to understand Bartleby's point of view. At the beginning of Charlotte Perkins Gilman's "The Yellow Wallpaper," the first-person narrator, who is the major character in the story, says that she is trying to regain her health after a mental breakdown. While she tells her story, an attentive reader notices that her disorientation from the so-called real world becomes much more acute. Poe, Melville, and Gilman choose first-person narrators to heighten the emotional effect of their stories.

The biased report of the first-person narrator must have a dramatic significance in the story, since there is often a discrepancy between the way he or she sees characters and events and the reader's sense of what really happened. At the end of "The Cask of Amontillado," Montresor says that his heart "grew sick — on account of the dampness of the catacombs." The reader may perceive the truth differently and feel that Montresor has at least subconsciously realized the horror of what he has just done to Fortunato.

In "Bartleby, the Scrivener," Melville's first-person narrator tells us he is sympathetic to Bartleby. But the lawyer's incessant self-congratulation in his description of his tolerant treatment of the scrivener may cause some readers to mistrust him. The lawyer's suggestions to Bartleby that he seek other employment by working as a bartender or entertaining a young gentleman with his conversation are ludicrously inappropriate. Bartleby's four quiet words "I prefer not to" reverberate against the constant stream of the narrator's well-intentioned but self-important explanations. The story would read very differently if Melville had let Bartleby tell it.

Third-Person Narration

Third-person narration means that the author tells the story using the pronouns *he* or *she* instead of the presumably more subjective *I*. Paley uses third-person narration in "Samuel." The narrator isn't a person who participates in the story, but she knows everything about it. She is an **omniscient** narrator, aware that the boys' mothers gave them permission to take the subway downtown and see the missile exhibit on Fourteenth Street in Manhattan. Despite the short length of her tale, Paley communicates her authority as the storyteller because she is so knowledgeable about the incident. We trust her to get the story right and to help us understand what happened. Most people enjoy reading stories told by omniscient narrators, anticipating that they will usually find meaning in the events that they describe.

The omniscient point of view of third-person narration is most clearly apparent in fairy tales beginning "Once upon a time," when the teller knows everything there is to know about all the characters, both inside and out — what they think and feel as well as what they do. In the hands of a master such as Hawthorne, a feeling for the complexity of human life emerges through the controlling authority of the omniscient narrator. This is achieved by a continual shifting of focus from the close view to a larger perspective. When this type of narration is used by a writer who is also a genius at the realistic rendering of experience, as is Tolstoy in "The Death of Ivan Ilych," the powerful combination of the author's great imaginative ability and moral authority invests the various characters and scenes with such reality that we accept them without question.

There can be significant differences in the way authors handle third-person narration. Like Paley, Sherwood Anderson is highly sympathetic to his characters in "Hands," but he uses **limited-omniscient** narration, confining himself to revealing the thoughts of only one character, his protagonist Wing Biddlebaum. Anderson is making an effort to engage our sympathies for this sad character.

Limited-omniscient narration was brilliantly developed in short fiction by Gustave Flaubert, who exchanged the distancing of "once upon a time" (with its implied moral view) for an interior, more subjective view of characters and events. F. Scott Fitzgerald's "Winter Dreams" is an example of limited-omniscient narration. Its narrator also sticks to **impartial** (not judgmental) **omniscience**; he tells the story without really evaluating or commenting on the actions, which speak for themselves.

Henry James developed another way to use limited-omniscient narration. He referred to certain characters in his stories as the **central intelligence**. Stories told by this method of narration involve a character, placed at the center of the story's action, through whose "intelligence" the author registers and evaluates everything that happens, including what happens to and within the character.

In this kind of story, such as James Joyce's "The Dead," this central character's psyche is the stage for the drama. Having established this single evaluating intelligence, the writer may range over the whole cast of characters and dramatize their views of the action. These will, however, always be perceived through or measured against the thoughts and feelings of the central intelligence, who may not understand what is going on at the time but will finally perceive the truth. In "The Dead" the central character, Gabriel Conroy, sees himself as a very different man at the end of the story from the man he imagined himself at the beginning. The actual drama of the story is not the events described but rather Gabriel's growth in moral awareness.

The stories of Stephen Crane are another variant of the limited-omniscient point of view. The narration may at any given moment in a Crane story reveal a different character's perceptions and feelings. In "The Open Boat" Crane rendered the sensations of the various participants in the shipwreck, subtly changing his perspective to borrow the eyes, ears, and tactile senses of all four men in the boat. If the war correspondent has the last word, it is because the author found him the best person to say what the pattern of the story required at that point.

Objective narration presents what appears to be a detached perspective on the characters and the plot of a story. Setting, action, and dialogue are laid out on the page without the narrator's comments or the characters' reflection. When Conrad said that Maupassant was interested in using only *facts* to tell his story, Conrad was implying that Maupassant was attempting objective narration. Maupassant himself insisted on his "personal view" as a writer and his selectivity presenting "the illusion of reality." For example, Maupassant's "personal view" included a snobbish disdain for the social-climbing wife from a modest background in "The Necklace," apparent in his choice of words in the first page of the story.

Hemingway is an example of an author attempting a more rigorous use of objective narration. In "Hills Like White Elephants," the reader must supply the interpretation for the characters' tense dialogue. This technique often forces the reader to read between the lines and participate more fully in the story in order to make sense of what the fictional characters cannot allow themselves to feel or say about their situation.

Narration can be classified into further subcategories — for example, stream-of-consciousness first- or third-person narrator — but the different ways of telling stories available to writers are always more flexible than rigid categories imply. Franz Kafka, who used Gregor Samsa as his central intelligence through most of "The Metamorphosis," continued the story well beyond Gregor's death. There is also the editorial point of view, when the third-person narrator adds his or her own comments, which may or may not reflect the author's opinions. Washington Irving used the editorial point of view in "Rip Van Winkle." Awareness of the point of view helps the reader become sensitive to the construct of language that is the story. Good readers understand that the way the story is written is an essential part of what it is saying.

Style

Style is the characteristic way an author uses language to create literature. Style is the result of the writer's habitual use of certain rhetorical patterns, including sentence length and complexity, word choice and placement, and punctuation. Paley's style in "Samuel" is informal, even colloquial in her choice of language. In her story she uses mostly one-syllable words, even slang occasionally (*super* in the first paragraph refers to the superintendent or caretaker of an apartment building).

You might think of the author's prose style as a projection of her or his **voice** as a writer, as if you were hearing the story instead of reading it. Voice, as the Canadian writer Margaret Atwood described it, is "a speaking voice, like the singing voice in music, that moves not across a space, across the page, but through time. Surely every written story is, in the final analysis, a score for voice. These little black marks on the page mean nothing without their retranslation into sound."

Suggested by the verbal patterns of literary style, voice is an essential element of all good fiction. Voice is the total effect of the author's rhetorical and stylistic choices. It can be flat, as in Atwood's "Happy Endings," to suggest the narrator's psychological exhaustion. Or voice can be exuberant, as in Toni Cade Bambara's "The Lesson," suggesting the naiveté of the young narrator. As a creation of the writer, the narrative voice is always part of the "lie" of fiction, not always identical with the voice of the writer telling the story. Good readers remember D. H. Lawrence's dictum: Trust the tale, not the teller.

The way that authors use language to tell a story conveys the quality of their mind to the reader. As we follow the story on the page we seem to hear the narration as well as see it in our imaginations. Eudora Welty once said that "my own words, when I am at work on a story, I hear too as they go, in the same voice that I hear when I read in books. When I write and the sound of it comes back to my ears, then I act to make my changes. I have always trusted this voice." From the reader's initial encounter with the first words on the page, the voice of the storyteller is the agent that evokes the imaginary landscape of fiction and conveys part of the story's meaning. For example, Lawrence's fairytale tone at the beginning of "The Rocking-Horse Winner" prepares the reader for the strange, otherworldly events as the story progresses.

An author's choice of **tone** in a narrative conveys his or her unstated attitudes toward the story. Paley's tone is serious in "Samuel," despite her use of colloquial language. The dry restraint in Hawthorne's comment about Goodman Brown's "excellent resolve" as he turns the corner by the meetinghouse and enters the forest is an example of the way tone contributes to Hawthorne's dignified, lofty prose style. A subtle **irony**, drawing attention to the differences between what is said in the omniscient point of view of the storyteller and what Hawthorne really thought, helped him keep an emotional distance from his characters suitable to the level of abstraction he created in the narrative. In contrast, Sherwood Anderson used everyday speech and more understated irony to set up a feeling of intimacy with the reader. This narrative voice suggests a sympathy for the characters in his realistic stories about frustrated, small-town lives.

Be careful in judging the tone of stories that have been translated from foreign languages. It is nearly impossible for a translation to capture the exact tone of the original language, even if it renders most other details of the story accurately.

Irony is another aspect of style. Irony makes the reader aware of a reality that differs from the reality the characters perceive (**dramatic irony**) or from the literal meaning of the author's words (**verbal irony**). Paley uses verbal irony when she says that the man who pulls the emergency cord "walked in a citizenly way." Earlier in the story, Samuel pounds his buddy Alfred's back until the tears come, saying "You a baby, huh?" This is an example of dramatic irony. In only a few minutes Samuel will be crushed between the wheels of the subway car and his life will end while he is still, comparatively, a baby.

Symbolism and allegory can also be aspects of the author's style. A literary **symbol** can be anything in a story's setting, plot, or characterization that suggests an abstract meaning to the reader in addition to its literal significance. Consider the pink ribbons on Faith's cap in Hawthorne's "Young Goodman Brown." They may be interpreted as an abstract symbol of the awakening sexuality of the young wife in the story, suggesting her innocence and purity.

The total context of a story often suggests a symbolic as well as literal reading of the narrative. After closing the anthology and thinking about a story you've just read, you may be struck by the way some elements of the story suggest deeper meaning by eliciting your emotional responses. Charlotte Perkins Gilman used the claustrophobic setting of her story "The Yellow Wallpaper" to help her reverse and subvert her readers' traditional associations about marriage. Instead of being a conventional symbol of home — safety, comfort, and refuge — the house in the story becomes a symbol of the wife's imprisonment and deterioration.

Symbols are not always interpreted the same way by different readers. Faith's pink ribbons in "Young Goodman Brown" may symbolize her youth and innocence to one reader, and her femininity and coquettishness to another. Faith is such an abstract character that either interpretation is possible. Regardless of how the symbol of the pink ribbons is interpreted, they are experienced as a dominant image in the somber landscape of Hawthorne's fiction. Some readers may even see them as an example of Hawthorne's exploration of the ambiguous nature of signs, similar to the ambiguous nature of Goodman Brown's night in the forest. Symbols are more eloquent as specific images — visual ideas — than any paraphrase, unifying the story and suggesting infinitely more than they state.

A story becomes an **allegory** when all the characters, places, things, and events represent symbolic qualities, and their interactions are meant to reveal a moral truth. Whereas symbolism results from the multiple meanings inherent in a good story, allegory tends to have a fixed meaning. Hawthorne's "Young Goodman Brown" and Shirley Jackson's "The Lottery" seem to exist more on the abstract, symbolic level of moral allegory than as realistic fiction in most readers' imaginations. Kafka's genius in describing Gregor's internal state in "The Metamorphosis" is so extraordinary that we read the details of the fantasy story quite literally; to many readers its allegorical meaning as a fable of alienation seems more restrictive and less compelling than Kafka's painful dramatization of Gregor's waking nightmare after he finds himself transformed into a monstrous creature.

All of these aspects of style work together to create a distinctive literary voice. As the writer Vladimir Nabokov once said in a lecture, "Style is not a tool, it is not a method, it is not a choice of words alone. Being much more than all this, style constitutes an intrinsic component or characteristic of the author's personality."

Theme

Theme is a generalization about the meaning of a story. It is more than the *subject* of the story, which is what the narrative is generally about. While the subject can be expressed in a word or two ("'Young Goodman Brown' is about religious fanaticism"), the theme requires a phrase or a sentence. The theme of a story is also different from the plot. Whereas the plot of Hawthorne's story can be summarized by stating what happened in the action (a young Puritan husband loses his faith in God and humankind after attending a witches' coven), the theme is an abstract statement of the meaning of the story (losing religious faith can destroy a person's life).

The theme of a story abstracts its meaning from the concrete details of its plot, characterization, setting, point of view, and style. Theme is the implied meaning of all the details of a story. It need not always be stated as a moral judgment. The story's meaning can and often does suggest principles of right and wrong behavior, but the impulse to tell a story can arise from several universal urges of the human spirit — to communicate, to create, to raise ultimate questions and not just pragmatic ones; in short, to provide a personal expression in narrative form of our sense of what life is like. As the writer Steven Millhauser has remarked, "When I write I have the sense that what compels me isn't the promotion of certain values, but something else — the working out of a harmony, the completion of a necessary design. This may be just another way of insisting that the values that belong to art are aesthetic. Exactly how moral values fit in is for a trained philosopher to say."

To paraphrase the writer Milan Kundera, great storytellers refuse to give explicit moral judgment a place in their fiction. Their stories usually aren't simple parables in which good triumphs over evil. To create a complex fictional world reflecting actual human experience, writers are rarely led by the desire to give a simple sermon. Instead, they provide multiple viewpoints within their stories through their dramatizations of the conflicting points of view of the various characters. They leave it to readers to come up with their own moral judgments in the statement of the story's theme.

A gifted storyteller says, "Let me tell you how it is," and our interest as readers is always in what the whole story can show us about human experience. Your statement of the theme suggests your understanding of the author's vision of the meaning of life. For example, if you realize that Anton Chekhov deliberately created sympathetic characterizations of Gurov and Anna in "The Lady with the Little Dog," you will probably decide that the author's theme is better rendered as a statement of a deep truth (love is a serious business) than as a moral injunction (do not commit adultery).

Theme comes last in a discussion of the elements of fiction because it is a consequence of all the other elements in a story. The structure and theme of a story are fused like the body and soul of a reader; their interaction creates a living pattern. Authors work hard to breathe life into their fiction. Most do not like to abstract the meaning of their stories to explain what they are "about." Even when they do, as the southern writer Flannery O'Connor did in her explanation of the theme of "A Good Man Is Hard to Find" or as William Faulkner did in discussing "A Rose for Emily," some readers agree intellectually but not emotionally with the writer's interpretation. O'Connor said she understood that her story might be read in different ways by different people, but she could have written it only with the one meaning she had in mind.

To say that a story can have more than a single meaning doesn't imply that it can mean anything at all. You have to be able to find sufficient important details that support your interpretation. Often readers find it difficult to formulate a single sentence that captures their impression of what a story means. After many futile minutes of trying to "boil it down" to a one-sentence essence, they may find words coming irresistibly to mind from another context, written by the American poet Archibald MacLeish: "A poem should not mean / But be."

The way the author creates the narrative by using all the elements of fiction to embody the theme is, of course, the most important achievement of the story. To appreciate the fact that the story itself is always more complex than its bare-bones meaning, try this experiment: Write a sentence summarizing what you believe to be the theme of "Samuel" and then close your anthology and try to re-create Paley's story.

Though the summary of a writer's theme is no substitute for the story in its entirety, your attempt to state it can help you to understand the story better. Flannery O'Connor insisted that a story is not its abstract meaning but rather what she called its "experienced" meaning: "A story is a way to say something that can't be said any other way, and it takes every word in the story to say what the meaning is. . . . When anybody asks what a story is about, the only proper thing is to tell him to read the story."

A Brief History
of the Short Story

The history of storytelling extends far back to a time long before the invention of the alphabet and the printing press. Stories have such a long history, and their forms are so diverse, that anyone attempting to investigate their earliest development in close detail would be taking on a herculean task. A brief chronological survey, however, may help readers gain a perspective on the human miracle that is the modern literary form.

In their broadest categories, stories can be intended and accepted as *factual* — examples include histories or narratives of real battles, victories, happenings, and so forth — or *fictional*, stories made up to instruct or entertain the listener. Early fictional narratives are what interest us here. The first tales we know of are those in the oral tradition, the creation myths of tribal peoples who were trying to explain how things got started and various legends about national heroes that evolved into epic narratives.

The development of written stories awaited the invention of an easily accessible alphabet, one of humankind's most original and important intellectual discoveries in the development of civilization, as well as durable material for scribes to write on. Nearly four thousand years ago *The Epic of Gilgamesh*, about the legendary Mesopotamian hero, was the earliest story to survive in the written word, on twelve cuneiform clay tablets.

The first experiments with an alphabet appear to be the work of Semitic people living in Egypt west of the Nile between 1900 and 1800 B.C. The first complete alphabet tablet (Semitic) dates from around 1400 B.C. in northern Syria. By 1100 B.C. an early Hebrew alphabet also existed. A century later the Phoenician alphabet (like Hebrew, of Semitic origin) dominated the Mediterranean. Through the Greeks it was the foundation for all Western alphabetic literature, beginning with the great poet Homer's tales about the Trojan War in the *Iliad* and about Odysseus's ten-year journey home to Ithaca after the war in the *Odyssey*, written down between 725 and 675 B.C.

Literary scholars believe that an important stage in the evolution of storytelling was the period of the beast fables, stories in which animals are shown acting like humans in order to teach a moral lesson. The fables of the Greek slave Aesop (620?–560? B.C.) are still well known, and the beast fable form is even used occasionally by modern writers.

Another very early form of the story is the religious parable, a short and pithy story with a moral twist, such as the parable of the wise and foolish virgins in the New Testament. These stories, as well as passages of narrative in the

Old Testament such as the description of the creation of the universe in Genesis or the story of Samson in Judges, were not intended as fiction, which is a word derived from Latin that means "something shaped, molded, or devised."

In the classical and postclassical literature of Greece and Rome, brief tales were often included in larger narrative collections, such as the *Satyricon* of Petronius in the first century A.D. and the *Metamorphoses* of Apuleius in the second century. These stories, along with fiction from Asian cultures, which was brought to Europe from the East by various means, became part of the reservoir of traditional material for later storytellers. An example of the tortuous path taken by such works is the *Panchatantra*. Its original Sanskrit form dates back at least to the early sixth century. In a variety of translations it spread through Europe in the Middle Ages. Finally, according to the editor Frank Edgerton, it was translated by Thomas North into English in 1570 from "an Italian version of a Latin version of a Hebrew version of an Arabic version of a [lost] Pahlavi [middle Iranian] version of some [lost] Sanskrit version of the original *Panchatantra*."

In the medieval period in Europe, short narratives were most commonly written in verse, whether they were heroic episodes such as the *Battle of Maldon* or low-life comic tales of French origin called *fabliaux*. Prose was usually reserved for devotional and instructive pieces until the fourteenth century. Around that time paper was introduced instead of parchment, and then secular tales in both prose and verse became popular, most notably the short prose tales of the Italian writer Giovanni Boccaccio (1313–1375). His best-known book is the *Decameron*, a series of one hundred tales told by seven ladies and three gentlemen who fled the plague that devastated Florence in 1348. In the same century, the Englishman Geoffrey Chaucer (d. 1400) wrote the *Canterbury Tales*, a collection of religious and secular tales, some derived from Boccaccio. Most of Chaucer's stories were narrated in verse.

The *Canterbury Tales* include several different short fictional genres such as the religious parable, the romance, and the fabliau. While Chaucer's collection exhibits remarkable stylistic polish and variety, a common theme is the unresolved relation between art and morality. The medieval distrust of purely imaginative literature extends far back in European culture, appearing in Plato's philosophy as well as in many other sources.

Boccaccio and Chaucer took great care to assure their readers that their stories would give both pleasure and moral instruction. The "moral behind the story" was a guarantee that the tales were more than mere entertainment. In the thirteenth century, the Christian theologian St. Thomas Aquinas cautioned against what he called "secular eloquence." Aquinas said, "He who strives principally after eloquence does not intend that men should admire what he says, but strives rather to gain their admiration for himself. Eloquence, however, is commendable when the speaker has no desire to display himself but wishes only to benefit his listeners." Imaginative stories were distrusted because they could be too entertaining. Five hundred years ago the first book ever printed in Europe was a collection of *exempla*, short prose narratives meant to serve as the basis for instruction by clergy, illustrating what an early writer called "excellent Lessons of Morality." The earliest surviving Korean book, a collection of Buddhist sermons and prayers, was printed with metal type in 1377.

The medieval distrust of stories as entertainment took hundreds of years to overcome. Most of the Renaissance storytellers in Italy, England, France, and Spain continued the Boccaccian tradition and included explicit moral and religious passages in their narratives. Through the centuries writers in different countries drew from the tales of preceding collections, so that by 1795, according to the scholar Roger Paulin, "the claim of a given story to be unusual or extraordinary, original or authentic, often did not stand up to very close scrutiny."

It wasn't until the eighteenth century, after secularization had gathered force in Europe, that fictional narratives were given the opportunity to evolve into forms we recognize as closer relations of modern stories and novels. These prose forms developed in periodicals that became popular with readers from Europe's emerging middle class, who had the education and the leisure time to enjoy them. The new periodicals printed a variety of prose — character sketches, satires, gothic tales, rogue stories, simple adventure stories, and sentimental sketches with predictable moral outcomes in which the hero or heroine is rewarded and the villain is punished. In France, Voltaire also composed his philosophical tales in the mid-eighteenth century, and his contemporaries Denis Diderot and the Marquis de Sade wrote stories to illustrate their theories of morality and psychology. These authors used satire to convey their views of the debasement of morality in conventional fiction, and the falsification of reality in many traditional tales. The older tradition had played itself out, and a new era of storytelling was about to begin.

The periodicals, with a rapidly growing number of readers, became a new market for professional writers. Their prose narratives were shaped and given vitality by the spirit of the age, the romantic period in European literature. At that time originality and imagination were valued above all other qualities in writing. This was in contrast to the emphasis on tradition and reason that had shaped the attitude of eighteenth-century neoclassical writers. In short fiction from the early years of the new periodicals, there is also a fascination with psychology and with unusual or eccentric behavior. Horror stories and criminal stories became popular, and gradually narratives opened up, as Paulin has stated, "to take in more moral and social awareness, satire, and the realm of the fancy and romantic imagination."

The mostly anonymous early writers for periodicals are not credited with inventing what is known today as the short story, even if their writing prepared the way for it. Most historians of this genre agree that the short story did not appear until the nineteenth century, almost a hundred years after the novel began to flourish as a literary form. Then a different kind of short fictional narrative emerged, an original prose work in which every word chosen in the structure of the plot, and every detail of description and characterization, contributed to a unified impression. Until the second half of the nineteenth century, the word *tale* referred to a self-contained narrative sequence as often found in poetry as in prose, not at all what we consider a short story today. For example, the English poet John Keats wrote a friend in 1819 that he was composing "two Tales, one from Boccaccio call'd the Pot of Basil; and another call'd St. Agnes Eve on a popular superstition."

In the early nineteenth century, German writers were the first to develop original, imaginative prose narratives that resemble what we call short stories. Johann Wolfgang von Goethe (1749–1832) wrote some short prose fiction, but he composed his stories in collections or included them in his novels. His contemporary Ludwig Tieck (1773–1853), a reader of English Gothic tales and the fantastic novels of Laurence Sterne (1713–1768), was more of an innovator. Tieck was a slick popular writer for magazines, and he experimented with stories he called "novelle," which blend fantasy and reality in ways that influenced his contemporaries, especially the German writers E. T. A. Hoffmann (1776–1822) and Heinrich von Kleist (1777–1811).

Kleist presented events as more logically connected than in Tieck's and Hoffmann's stories, but even Kleist's fiction plays with the notion that a tale doesn't always have to follow a rational pattern or allow for a moral explanation. Probably the most famous German writers of prose tales from the early nineteenth century are Jakob and Wilhelm Grimm. They assembled a collection of "Childhood and Household Tales" from folk material; it was soon translated throughout the world, along with the original stories of the later Danish writer Hans Christian Andersen. The early German and French fairy tales have such a strong hold on our imagination that they have been reimagined as gothic fiction by Angela Carter; the Italian folktales have also been edited by Italo Calvino. As Carter realized, "Each century tends to create or re-create fairy tales after its own taste."

Most literary historians agree that the first successful American short story was created by Washington Irving. While living in London in 1818, he translated a German folktale titled "Peter Klaus the Goatherd," collected by the pioneering folklorist J. C. C. Nachtigal and originally published in Bremen in 1800 as part of a collection titled *Folkssagen, Nacherzhaht von Otmar* (*Folktales, Transcribed by Otmar* [Nachtigal's pseudonym]). Irving was inspired to create "Rip Van Winkle," his own humorous version of this pithy tale with a newly imagined setting in upstate New York. Irving's *Sketch Book* (1819–1820) contains "Rip Van Winkle" and "The Legend of Sleepy Hollow," two of the earliest American short stories based on European folklore.

Irving was challenged by the new literary form. He understood that "there is a constant activity of thought and a nicety of execution required in writings of this kind. . . . [In a novel] the mere interest of the story [permits] pages of careless writing . . . but in these short writings every page must have its merit." In 1827 Irving's contemporary Walter Scott (1771–1832), who suggested that he begin to study German, followed Irving's example and published the first modern short story in England, "The Two Drovers." Irving's tales had an enormous influence on the next generation of writers in America. He handled fictional narrative in a relaxed, predominantly descriptive and discursive manner, saying, "I consider a story merely as a frame on which to sketch my materials."

Shortly afterward, the young American writers Nathaniel Hawthorne and Edgar Allan Poe began contributing fiction to magazines. They chose typically romantic subjects, writing about colorful or extraordinary individuals living in remote times and places, but they structured their narratives differently than did Irving. They used more dramatic compression in developing their plots and revealing their characters. Most literary historians credit them as the first American writers to create a considerable number of successful short stories.

Hawthorne never explained fully how he wrote his stories, but Poe published his theories about short fiction in his book reviews. He did not insist that a short story be written any certain way. Instead, he stressed the concept that power and unity could be achieved in works of short fiction. As Poe stated, he believed that the prose tale was the type of writing that, after the poem, "should best fulfill the demands of high genius." This idea was a novelty in Poe's time, when the short story was not a highly regarded literary form.

Most critics regard Edgar Allan Poe and the Russian author Nikolai Gogol as the two greatest and most influential writers of short fiction during the romantic era. Their stories, together with the moral fiction of Hawthorne, are more properly called "tales," the label the writers themselves gave to their work. The tale, according to the scholar Northrop Frye's definition, is closer to the prose romance than to the novel. In the tale the author makes no attempt to delineate the characters as real people. Instead, they are stylized figures who "expand into psychological archetypes."

Herman Melville's "Bartleby, the Scrivener," by contrast, is more of a story. Melville subtitled it "A Story of Wall Street." He was acutely aware of the fickle literary tastes of his readers, and in "Bartleby, the Scrivener," his first published story, which appeared in 1853, he consciously created a humorous surface that he hoped would have popular appeal while concealing the serious meanings. The attorney who narrates the story of Bartleby is not a psychological abstraction, as is Hawthorne's Goodman Brown or Poe's Montresor. Melville gave us so many realistic details about the lawyer's life that we get a strong sense of his perplexity in the face of his mysterious scrivener's stubborn will.

Bartleby is also one of the "little men" who Frank O'Connor theorized is the true subject of the short story, a character originating in a "submerged population group." O'Connor argued that Melville's scrivener, and Gogol's even earlier Russian clerk in "The Overcoat," were the progenitors of fictional offspring who would later emerge in scores of stories by important writers of short fiction, including Sherwood Anderson, Anton Chekhov, and James Joyce. They would also create, in O'Connor's words, "outlawed figures wandering about the fringes of society, superimposed sometimes on symbolic figures whom they caricature and echo — Christ, Socrates, Moses."

The mid-nineteenth century was a time of great transition in literature as the earlier mode of romanticism slowly gave way to realism. If the tale is a close relation of the early prose romance, then the short story is akin to the later realist novel. Instead of being, as Frye has said, "idealized by revery" as in a romance, characters in a novel (and in short stories) wear recognizable social masks and reflect an everyday reality.

Leo Tolstoy's fiction illustrates this realist mode. In his stories the characters are products of a highly developed society, and his fictive world is a mirror of the actual world of men and women at the time. Realist authors usually refrain from commenting at great length on their characters' psychology. Instead, their psychology is manifested in things said and done by the characters themselves. While romantic writers are interested in subjective states of awareness per se, realist writers are likely to be more concerned with the social causes and consequences of those states. They put greater emphasis on the particular physical circumstances in which they place their characters.

In America around the time of the Civil War, the popular magazine tale slowly gave way to the more realistic story. This is when local-color stories, set in particular regions (for example, New England or the South) emerged. Sarah Orne Jewett and Kate Chopin are two of the important writers of stories in this idiom.

In the 1890s Ambrose Bierce developed the macabre world of Poe's fantasy vision, writing short stories with a realistic surface that explore the workings of the protagonist's mind. Sometimes — as in "An Occurrence at Owl Creek Bridge" — Bierce ventured close to the stream-of-consciousness technique developed by later modernist writers. Bierce's fiction combines elements of romanticism, realism, and modernism. Trying to fit his stories into a neat historical category illustrates the impossibility of presenting the history of the short story as a smooth, linear evolution.

The realists Jack London, Willa Cather, Stephen Crane, Henry James, and Edith Wharton were America's most distinguished short story authors at the end of the century. But European influences were also strong. In 1893, in his introduction to Hamlin Garland's story collection *Main-Travelled Roads*, William Dean Howells wrote that magazine fiction was so popular in America that finally "the hour of the short story in book form has struck." To account for what he called the "material prosperity" of short fiction, Howells credited — among other factors — "the vogue that Maupassant's tales in the original or in versions have enjoyed."

Two Europeans, the French writer Guy de Maupassant and the Russian Anton Chekhov, were the most influential creators of short fiction at the end of the nineteenth century. They brought remarkable innovations to the content and form of the short story. Both wrote realistic fiction, and both are considered modern writers because of the content of their stories. They insisted on focusing on the particular here-and-now quality of ordinary human existence rather than proselytizing for any particular religious, philosophical, or political system of belief.

As Kate Chopin realized, Maupassant was a writer "who had escaped from tradition and authority, who had entered into himself and looked out upon life through his own being and with his own eyes; and who, in a direct and simple way, told us what he saw." This is reminiscent of Chekhov's statement about his own difficult process of squeezing "the slave out of himself" in order to become a decent human being and an honest writer.

In Maupassant's short stories, plots are tightly organized and usually conclude with a decisive action. Details of the characters' appearance and behavior are sharply etched into the narrative, as if their physicality were especially important to the skeptical materialist Maupassant. In Chekhov's stories, by contrast, plots include less decisive action. They are subordinate to sympathetic dramatization of the characters' psychology and mood. The writer Sean O'Faolain has labeled Maupassant "the relentless realist" and Chekhov "the persistent moralist" to distinguish further between them.

Maupassant's stories were translated and published in the United States as early as 1891, sometimes with the warning that the material might shock a fastidious reader. They were so popular that in 1903 an enterprising New York publisher invested in a seventeen-volume set of Maupassant's writing featuring a frontispiece drawing of a nearly naked woman holding a skull in one hand and, in the other, a glass of champagne out of which a winged cupid was sipping. At this time, using the pen name "O. Henry," the American writer William S. Porter began to create short stories featuring the ironic coincidences and surprise endings favored by Maupassant. Porter's role in popularizing the short story in the United States is commemorated by the annual *O. Henry Memorial Award Prize Stories*, an anthology of the best works of short fiction published in the United States and Canada each year.

Later experimental writers of short fiction were more influenced by Chekhov than by Maupassant, developing the Russian author's less sharply detailed, more subtly impressionistic atmosphere in their work. These were the modernist writers in the early years of the twentieth century, who challenged the conventions of the dominant literature and culture. In Europe this group included Joseph Conrad, James Joyce, Franz Kafka, D. H. Lawrence, Katherine Mansfield, and Virginia Woolf. Influenced profoundly by both Chekhov and Maupassant were the American modernists, including Sherwood Anderson, William Faulkner, Ernest Hemingway, Katherine Anne Porter, and Richard Wright.

These great modernists are all masters of realism, but they questioned the validity of the *status quo*, creating a new kind of short fiction that undermined it, transcended it, and helped to transform it. To do this, many modernist writers explored the concept of an interiorized plot. As Mansfield said, "If we are not to look for [external] facts and events . . . we must be sure of finding these central points of significance transferred to the endeavors and emotions of the characters portrayed." Joyce's *Dubliners*, fifteen stories begun in 1904 and published in 1916, was one of the landmarks of this period.

Rather than constructing his stories around a dramatic climax in the action, Joyce heightened the climactic moment of self-realization that he found in Chekhov's stories. He coined a special literary term, *epiphany* (a "showing forth"), for this inner revelation. Such often painful flashes of recognition illuminate Joyce's fluid narratives, for instance, the boy's realization at the end of "Araby": "Gazing up into the darkness I saw myself as a creature driven and derided by vanity; and my eyes burned with anguish and anger." The critic Ian Reid has pointed out that the significant revelation in modernist stories may sometimes be only for perceptive readers, not for the fictional character. Gregor Samsa's consciousness is but a dimly flickering spark at the conclusion of Kafka's "The Metamorphosis," and he expires still trapped inside his suffocating transformation.

Since the end of the modernist period, authors have explored a variety of patterns of short narrative fiction. Most writers of popular magazine fiction favor old-fashioned closed plots, dramatizing a single, unified incident with a decisive conclusion. But we now enjoy a great diversity of periodicals — mass-circulation specialty magazines, little magazines, highbrow magazines, and regional magazines. Authors of "quality fiction" for these periodicals, such as Alice Munro and Steven Millhauser in *The New Yorker*, for example, often favor stories dramatizing less conclusive action, which does not rise to any momentous peak. These writers invite close thematic scrutiny from attentive readers because their stories seem to lack both the certain meaning of earlier realist stories and the consistent subjective point of view of the nineteenth-century romantic tales.

Literary critics distinguish between two types of stories being written today: "traditional stories," descending from Poe and Maupassant, which are plotted and closed (like the work of Ha Jin and Alice Walker, among many others in this anthology), and "modern stories," descending from Chekhov and Joyce, which are less plotted and more open (like the work of Denis Johnson and Jamaica Kincaid, among others). The same writer may use either traditional or modern structures in different works, depending on the material. The short story is so flexible that it may well be ideally suited, as Nadine Gordimer has said, to "convey the quality of human life, where contact is more like the flash of fireflies, in and out, now here, now there, in darkness. Short story writers see by the light of the flash; theirs is the art of the only thing one can be sure of — the present moment."

Fiction by contemporary writers is so close to us that it is better examined on a thematic or aesthetic spectrum, as the critic Susan Lohafer has suggested in her book *Coming to Terms with the Short Story*. She even pokes fun at the conventional historical survey of the short story in introductory literature courses at American colleges and universities:

> As the result of undergraduate survey courses, there are many people who can tell you how the form developed; how it emerged from the sleepy hollows of Washington Irving; took on the moral and arabesque shapes of Hawthorne and Poe; how it stretched socially and regionally to James and Jewett; how it spoke the vernacular in Calaveras County, turned naturalistic in an open boat, reached deep into the psyche in Winesburg, in Babylon, and, of course, In Our Time; how it branched out southern and suburban and ethnic and far.

In one great sweep, Lohafer surveys the contribution of our earliest writers and then alludes to well-known stories by Mark Twain ("Calaveras County") and Stephen Crane ("open boat"). Next comes a reference to three great short story writers publishing after World War I who "reached deep into the psyche" — Sherwood Anderson ("Winesburg"), F. Scott Fitzgerald ("Babylon"), and Ernest Hemingway (his earliest story collection, *In Our Time*). These authors revitalized the American short story by writing in what Anderson called "the

common words of our daily speech" to tell stories that often featured characters outside mainstream society. In their best work the three authors suggested
implicitly more than they stated explicitly.

After these American modernist writers redefined the possibilities of the
short story, there was a proliferation of short story writers during and after
the 1930s who developed the literary form even further. "How it branched
out southern" refers to the fiction of William Faulkner, Flannery O'Connor,
Katherine Anne Porter, Eudora Welty, and Richard Wright; "suburban" refers
to the stories from the 1940s and 1950s by John Cheever and Shirley Jackson
as well as to more recent "suburban" fiction by Ann Beattie, Joyce Carol
Oates, and John Updike. "Ethnic" refers to the stories from the 1960s to the
present by James Baldwin, Philip Roth, Alice Walker, and Julie Otsuka, among
many others who write from the perspective of minority cultures in the United
States. "And far" refers to writers such as George Saunders, Donald Barthelme,
and Art Spiegelman, inventors of ironic parodies, self-reflexive metafictions,
collages, and other language and graphic narrative experiments that offer a
sometimes difficult but often dazzling postmodernist spectrum of contemporary short fiction. However brief Lohafer's summary, her conclusion is helpful:
Once readers have a solid context for the evolution of the short story form, the
guideline of its historical development may be less important than the quality
of the individual voices of contemporary authors.

In the 1970s and 1980s, the development of feminist literary criticism and
the sophistication of structuralist, poststructuralist, and new historical theory
offered new perspectives on the traditional academic literary canon. American feminists emphasized the importance of earlier short story writers such
as Charlotte Perkins Gilman, Zora Neale Hurston, and Tillie Olsen, among
others. Literary theorists refined the definition and categories of traditional
and experimental narrative. Traditional storytellers such as Raymond Carver
still tried to make their fiction appear to be a mirror of reality, whereas experimental authors such as Lydia Davis challenge the linguistic conventions of
narrative to the point at which communication ceases. Then the storyteller
forces the reader to become an equal participant in the creation of the story.
Thus narrative sequence appears to be the most fundamental element in storytelling, since experimental writers often rely on their readers' imaginations to
provide coherence and closure for their works of short fiction.

With the proliferation of creative writing courses in colleges and universities, the short story is such a popular form in the United States that it serves
as a reflection of the country's national consciousness. Many recent contemporary American writers are exploring their multicultural heritage, as in the
stories of Sherman Alexie, Sandra Cisneros, Junot Díaz, Louise Erdrich, Leslie
Marmon Silko, Amy Tan, and Helena María Viramontes.

The twentieth century witnessed many accomplished writers of short
fiction throughout the world, from Jorge Luis Borges and Gabriel García
Márquez in Latin America; to Margaret Atwood and Alice Munro in Canada;
Albert Camus in France; Chinua Achebe in Africa; and Haruki Murakami
in Japan. The tradition continues with a rich diversity of literary forms and

styles as new generations of writers come of age. The significant differences among contemporary short stories are in the attitudes toward life that govern an author's sense of reality and the literary techniques of expression that these attitudes call forth.

As John Cheever realized, "So long as we are possessed by experience that is distinguished by its intensity and its episodic nature, we will have the short story in our literature." The history of the short story is open-ended, as befits a mature and vigorous literary form. The ideal reader is also open to new writing, ready to be enchanted by the magic of each writer's imagination, revealed in his or her engagement with the short story.

For reference and further reading, see Walter Allen, *The Short Story in English* (1981); W. M. Aycock, ed., *The Teller and the Tale* (1982); H. E. Bates, *The Modern Short Story* (1972); John Bayley, *The Short Story: Henry James to Elizabeth Bowen* (1988); Peter Brooks, *Reading for the Plot* (1984); Daniel Burke, *Beyond Interpretation: Studies in the Modern Short Story* (1991); Joseph Campbell, *The Flight of the Wild Gander* (1969); Eugene Current-Garcia (with W. R. Patrick), *What Is the Short Story?* (1961); Geoffrey Day, *From Fiction to the Novel* (1987); Margaret Anne Doody, *The True Story of the Novel* (1996); Frank Edgerton, *The Panchatantra* (1965); Hans Eichner, *Four German Writers* (1964); Norman Friedman, *Form and Meaning in Fiction* (1975); Clare Hanson, *Short Stories and Short Fictions* (1985); Dominic Head, *The Modernist Short Story* (1992); M. J. Hoffman and P. D. Murphy, eds., *Essentials of the Theory of Fiction* (1988); Susan Lohafer, *Coming to Terms with the Short Story* (1985); Susan Lohafer and J. E. Clarey, eds., *Short Story Theory at a Crossroads* (1989); John Man, *Alpha Beta: How Twenty-Six Letters Shaped the Western World* (2000); Charles E. May, ed., *Short Story Theories* (1976) and *Edgar Allan Poe* (1991); Heather McClave, ed., *Women Writers of the Short Story* (1980); Elizabeth Minchin, *Homer and the Resources of Memory* (2001); A. C. Moorhouse, *Writing and the Alphabet* (1946); Frank O'Connor, *The Lonely Voice* (1963); Sean O'Faolain, *The Short Story* (1951); Viorica Patea (ed.), *Short Story Theories: A Twenty-First-Century Perspective* (2012); Roger Paulin, *The Brief Compass: The Nineteenth-Century German Novelle* (1985); T. G. Pavel, *Fictional Worlds* (1986); Anne Pellowski, *The World of Storytelling* (1977); Ian Reid, *The Short Story* (1977); Danforth Ross, *The American Short Story* (1961); Robert Scholes and Robert Kellogg, *The Nature of Narrative* (1966); Valerie Shaw, *The Short Story* (1983); Michael Stephens, *The Dramaturgy of Style: Voice in Short Fiction* (1986); Peter O. Stummer, ed., *The Story Must Be Told: Short Narrative Prose* (1986); Gordon Weaver, ed., *The American Short Story, 1945–1980* (1983); and Alfred Weber and Walter F. Greiner, *Short-Story-Theorien 1573–1973* (1977).

Writing About Short Stories

In writing about literature, you clarify your relationship to what you have read. This relationship goes beyond a basic emotional response to the story, whether you enjoyed it or not. You write to reveal what Ernest Hemingway referred to as "the measure of what you brought to the reading." As soon as you ask the smallest question about the meaning or structure of a story and try to answer it, you are beginning a critical inquiry that involves your intellect as well as your emotions. This activity is called the interpretation of the text. What makes it valuable is that it reveals to you and to others how you respond to the stories after they have entertained, instructed, and perhaps enchanted you. Now it is your turn to explain their effect on you, and to analyze how they did it. Once you have asked yourself what there is about a story that gives you pleasure — the style, the form, the meaning — you have begun to discover "the measure of what you brought to the reading." Keeping a journal in which you record your responses to the stories you read is often the first stage of the process of writing about short fiction. The next stage is to communicate your ideas to someone else. Turning yourself from a reader into a writer takes time, but if you understand the various steps involved, the process becomes much easier.

Keeping a Short Story Journal

In her essay "On Keeping a Notebook," Joan Didion put her finger on the reason why writers keep a record of their experience: "We forget all too soon the things we thought we could never forget. . . . Keeping in touch is what notebooks are all about." If you keep a section of your notebook for recording your impressions after reading the stories assigned in class, you will find that writing down your responses soon after you've finished a story helps you to remember what you thought about it. This journal also ensures that you will set aside the time necessary to put your reactions into words, which always involves gathering your thoughts and finding the language to express them adequately. Your journal is a relatively painless first step in the journey of transforming yourself from a reader into a writer.

Some students prefer to record their responses systematically, taking each of the different elements of fiction as separate categories and recording separate impressions of the story's characterization, setting, plot, style, point of view, and theme. Other students proceed less analytically and write a running commentary of observations and comments as they read the story. Regardless of how you proceed, you should jot down quotations from the story to illustrate your observations and include queries if something in the story puzzled you in your first reading. You can go back to these questions and answer them after you've read the story a second time or discussed them in class. These reading notes can help you review for an exam, but they are also a primary resource when you begin to write an assigned essay about what you have read.

Using the Commentaries and Casebooks

Reading commentaries can help you feel more confident when you begin to think critically about short fiction. Commentaries by authors and critics often introduce you to important aspects of the significance of a story that you might have missed on your own. You may agree or disagree with the commentaries, but they will stimulate your critical thinking.

Writing the Paper

An essay about literature can take various forms and be various lengths, depending on the nature of the assignment. Whether you are writing an essay of only a few paragraphs or a research paper of several thousand words, the basic requirement is always the same. You must keep in mind that an essay on short stories (or on any subject, for that matter) is a type of expository writing, and *expository* means "serving to clarify, set forth, or explain in detail" an idea about the subject. Writing about literature helps you clarify your ideas. If you want your essay to communicate these ideas clearly to a reader, you must understand that it always requires two things to be effective: a strong thesis sentence or central idea about your topic and an adequate development of your thesis sentence. How you organize your paper will depend on the way you choose to develop your central idea. The three principal ways of organizing essays about short stories — explication, analysis, and comparison and contrast — will be taken up after a discussion of ways to find a thesis sentence.

Getting Ideas for Your Topic and Thesis Sentence

Most effective short papers (about 500 words) usually treat one aspect of the story: its theme, characterization, setting, point of view, or literary style. These are some of the possible *topics* for your paper, the general subject you are going to write about. Usually your first response to a story is a jumble of impressions that do not separate themselves into neat categories of topics and thesis sentences. You must sort through these impressions to select a topic on which to concentrate in order to get ideas for your thesis sentence.

Before you can start your essay, you should feel that you understand the story thoroughly as a whole. Read it again to remind yourself of the passages that strike you with particular force. Underline the words and sentences you consider significant — or, even better, make a list in your notebook of what seems important while you are rereading the story.

Now put the text aside and look over the notes in your journal. Can you see any pattern in them? You may find that you have been most impressed by the way the author developed characterizations, for example. Then you will have a possible topic for your paper. Certainly if you have a choice, you should pick whatever appeals to you the most in the story and concentrate on it.

If you still cannot come up with a topic, ask for help in your next class. Perhaps your instructor will suggest something: "Why don't you discuss the way Hawthorne used irony in 'Young Goodman Brown'?" Often the class will be assigned one topic to write about. Some students think assigned topics make writing more difficult; others find they make it easier to begin to write.

A topic, however, is not the same as a thesis sentence. A topic is a general subject (for example, the character of Goodman Brown). A thesis sentence, by contrast, makes a statement about a topic; it is usually the result of thinking about the topic and narrowing it down to focus on some relationship of the topic to the story as a whole. A good thesis sentence has two important functions. First, it suggests a way for you to write about the story. Second, it makes clear to your reader the approach you have taken toward the topic. To *write* critically about short fiction, you must *think* critically about it. You start with an interpretation of the entire story and then show how some particular aspect of it contributes to what you think is its overall pattern and meaning.

Narrowing Ideas to a Thesis

A thesis sentence states the central idea you will develop in your paper. It should be easy for the reader of your essay to recognize — even if it takes some time for you to formulate. A thesis sentence is a complete sentence that points the way you will take to clarify your interpretation of the story. In Hawthorne's story, for example, you might decide to write about the character of Goodman Brown (*topic*). You interpret the story to be a warning about the danger of losing religious faith (*theme*). If you think about the way your topic relates to the theme of the story, your analysis might lead you to the idea that Goodman Brown lost his religious faith through the sin of pride. This thought process narrows the topic into a thesis, which you can state as the sentence "The story 'Young Goodman Brown' shows how a man can lose his religious faith through the sin of pride."

The test of a good thesis sentence is whether your *subject* ("The story 'Young Goodman Brown'") is followed by a clearly focused *predicate* ("shows how a man can lose his religious faith through the sin of pride"). What you want is a statement of an idea that you can then develop in your essay.

Finding a thesis sentence is often the biggest stumbling block for writers of expository prose. How do you know if your idea is worth developing in a paper? Generally speaking, a thesis will work if it expresses a specific idea about the story that you *want* to develop. If you are not interested to begin with, or do not like the story you are writing about, you probably will find it hard to get started, but you will always write better about an idea if it is sharply focused.

Sometimes the thesis sentence occurs to you while you are thinking about the story; then you can jot it down as a fully formed idea right away. Other times you may find that you are unable to formulate any definite idea about the story until you start to write. No single procedure works for all writers at all times. You might begin writing with a trial thesis in mind, putting down rough ideas or a string of sentences as you think about the general topic you have chosen. Or you might decide to go back to the notes you took in your journal while reading the story and try to organize them into a simple outline about your topic, looking for connections between things that might suggest a direction to take in a trial essay and then hoping a thesis sentence will emerge while you free-associate with paper and pencil in hand. You might also get an idea for a thesis sentence by brainstorming about the story with a friend and noticing the ideas that surface in your conversation.

Whatever way you start, do not settle for anything quick and facile. "Hawthorne's use of irony in 'Young Goodman Brown' is interesting" is much too general to be helpful to you in writing a good essay. Keep thinking or scribbling away at your first rough draft until you find an idea that gives you a specific direction to take in your paper. "Hawthorne's use of irony in 'Young Goodman Brown' suggests his judgment of the Puritan moral code" is a thesis sentence that has a clearly focused predicate. It states a definite relationship of the topic to the implications of the thesis you want to explore. Then you know you are on your way to writing a good essay.

Writing and Revising

If you begin the first paragraph of your essay with a strong thesis sentence, your ideas will usually flow in writing and revising the paper. You will often discover further possibilities for refining your thesis while using it to interpret the text. That is one reason you should allow plenty of time to complete a writing assignment. It's an unusual first draft in which the central idea is developed coherently and fully enough to be turned in as a finished paper. Revision often stimulates further thought, sharpening and strengthening the development of your thesis. In the process of writing, you will come to understand the story more fully as your thesis takes you closer to its meaning.

Try not to become discouraged about writing by visualizing some distant final product — a well-organized essay, neatly printed on clean, white paper, shimmering on the page in what looks like pristine perfection. Remember that it took time to get that way. Your essay originated in half-formed, often confused thoughts that had to be coaxed to arrange themselves into coherent paragraphs linked by what only much later appear to be inevitable transitions. More often than not, the 500 words you might think are a perfect essay when you turn in your final paper will be the end result — if you took enough time in writing — of winnowing down 1,000 or more words from your rough drafts. You must amplify and clarify your thesis, editing your sentences and paragraphs so that each one relates coherently to your central idea. Then your essay will express your insights about the story so clearly that they can be understood as you intended.

At the beginning, it is best to forget about the end result and give all your thought and effort to the *process* of writing. If you find it useful, make an outline and try to follow it, but this practice varies with different writers. Some find it valuable to organize their notes about the story into a formal outline, whereas others prefer to make a rough sketch of the steps they plan to follow in developing their central idea. You may find that you do not want to use an outline at all, although in general it can help to keep you from straying too far from the point you are trying to make. Remember, too, that there is no fixed rule about the number of drafts or the amount of revision necessary before you have a finished essay. Every essay changes from the first rough draft through various revisions; an essay is often gone over several times in the days or weeks between getting the assignment and bringing the finished paper to class. In the various stages of writing, different aspects of the central idea often reveal themselves and are integrated into the paper, depending on your degree of concentration and involvement in the assignment. Even if you scrap sentences or whole paragraphs that do not relate to your final discussion, you have not wasted your time, because your early efforts to put your thoughts down on paper bring you to the point where you have better insights.

You will probably have to rewrite your opening paragraph many times to tailor your thesis sentence to the final shape your ideas have taken. Some writers just sketch in the first paragraph and go back to polish it when the rest of the essay is finished. Often you will want to amplify and refine your thesis sentence, dividing it into several sentences in your introductory remarks. Then it becomes a *thesis statement*, rather than a single sentence.

Developing the Thesis

While it is possible to write many different kinds of papers about short fiction, most college instructors assign students the task of interpreting the text. The literary terms used in the headnotes on each writer in this anthology and defined in the Glossary (p. 1736–1745) can help you find a vocabulary to express your ideas. You cannot write intelligently about any subject without using the special terminology of that subject, whether it is English, economics, psychology, or engineering. At the same time, dropping the terms in your paper the way a person might drop names at a party will not impress your readers. Understand what the terms mean so you can use them to think and write critically about the elements of a story when you begin to interpret the text in the light of your central idea.

You will usually develop your thesis statement in the body of your essay by following one or more of the three common methods of writing about literature: *explication, analysis,* and *comparison and contrast.*

Types of Literary Papers

Explication

The word *explication* is derived from a Latin word that means "unfolding." When you explicate a text, you unfold its meaning in an essay, proceeding carefully to interpret it passage by passage, sometimes even line by line or word by word. A good explication concentrates on details, quoting the text of the story to bring them to the attention of a reader who might have missed them approaching the story from a different perspective. An entire story is usually too long to explicate completely — the explication would be far longer than the story — so you will usually select a short passage or section that relates to the idea you are developing. Often this short section is a key scene, a crucial conversation, or an opening or closing paragraph in which the implications of the text can be revealed to develop the central idea of your essay.

Although explication does not concern itself with the author's life or times, his or her historical period may determine the definitions of words or the meaning of concepts that appear in the passage being interpreted. If the story is a decade or more old, the meanings of some words may have changed. The explication is supposed to reveal what the author might have meant when he or she wrote the story, not assuming conscious intentions, but explicating possibilities. For some older stories, you will have to do a little research if the narrative chosen for explication contains words such as "gay" whose meanings may have changed. The *Oxford English Dictionary*, available in the reference section of your college library, will give you the meaning of a word in a particular era. The philosophical, religious, scientific, or political beliefs of the author, or the story's specific historical period may also be relevant to your interpretation of the text. The main emphasis in explication, however, is on the meaning of the words — both *denotative* and *connotative* — and the way those words affect the reader.

The following student paper on Hawthorne's "Young Goodman Brown" is an example of how explication is used to develop a central idea in an essay. Whether you accept the student's interpretation of the scene with the pink ribbon or not, it is a good example of the use of explication to show a way to read the text that develops the central idea of an essay. The thesis statement is clearly presented in the opening paragraph, so the reader knows what the essay will be about. At first the student approached the explication with the idea that Goodman Brown's essential weakness was his pride in trusting his senses more than his faith in God. The student felt from the start that the entire scene with the ribbon was a trick played on the protagonist. Rereading the story, he found evidence in Hawthorne's words to support this interpretation. Then, in writing the essay, he developed this thesis a step further, concluding the paper with two sentences about the "short step from believing in the devil to being taken in by him." This is an example of how the writing process itself can clarify and develop ideas. Just be sure the ideas are closely related, so your reader can follow you. Do not get sidetracked or introduce a new topic.

Quoting passages from the story to support your interpretation is always more effective than giving a summary of events. Summarizing the plot is a common error of inexperienced essay writers. Most stories are so short that the reader remembers them without a summary. Some instructors assign plot summaries as writing exercises, but they should not be confused with interpretive essays. An essay develops your interpretation of the story and is organized according to logic as you give evidence to develop your thesis sentence by quoting from the text. Explication — at its simplest, a quotation followed by your interpretation of the words — should develop an *idea* about the story, which is the reason you were asked to write your interpretation in the first place.

Student Essay: Explication

The Devil's Tricks in Hawthorne's
"Young Goodman Brown"

Hawthorne's "Young Goodman Brown" is the story of a man whose life is ruined because of the sin of pride, which makes him lose his faith in God. Goodman Brown agrees to meet the devil in the forest, and his faith is destroyed when he sees a pink ribbon fluttering to earth. He believes this ribbon could only have fallen from his beloved wife's cap. It is this scene in the story that reveals his weakness. His pride makes him trust the evidence of his own senses more than his faith in God.

Hawthorne begins the scene in which Goodman Brown loses his faith by leaving him without other characters around him for the first time in the story. Alone with his soul, he has only himself to depend on. The devil has abandoned him in the middle of the dark woods with the maple staff that became a witch's broomstick when it was borrowed by Goody Cloyse earlier in the evening. Thus the reader has already seen the devil's tricks.

Other black magic is in store for Goodman Brown. Gazing upward "into the deep arch of the firmament," he lifts his hands to pray. The word "firmament," with its biblical connotations, suggests that Goodman Brown has set his mind on God. He has scarcely begun his prayer, however, when his concentration is broken: "a cloud, though no wind was stirring, hurried across the zenith and hid the brightening stars" (582–583). The devil's magic show has begun, although Goodman Brown is not aware of it.

He accepts the appearance of the "black mass" of the cloud overhead and forgets his prayer, listening instead to a "*confused* and *doubtful* sound of voices. . . . The next moment, so *indistinct* were the sounds, he doubted whether he had heard aught . . ." (583). The adjectives and verbs I have italicized in Hawthorne's description suggest the lack of substance in what Goodman Brown hears and sees; he is, after all, standing under a dark cloud. The next moment he believes he hears the voice "of a young woman, uttering lamentations, yet with an *uncertain* sorrow, and entreating for some favor, which, *perhaps*, it would grieve her to obtain; and all the *unseen* multitude, both saints and sinners, *seemed* to encourage her onward" (583) [my emphasis].

At this point Goodman Brown believes not only that he hears the voice of a young woman, but also that the woman is his wife, Faith. By now he is completely deluded. When he shouts his wife's name he is mocked by the ghosts he senses around him: "the *echoes* of the forest mocked him crying, 'Faith! Faith!' *as if*

Use quotation marks for titles of stories.

Start with general thesis sentence.

Narrow the thesis to show specific direction your paper will take.

Transition: Repeat key words of thesis.

Suggest background of scene before you begin explication.

Start to quote from the story. Do not set off short quotation.

Main section of the explication: Text quoted in the order it appears.

OK to use "I"; emphasis added by writer.

Good active verbs.

bewildered wretches were seeking her all through the wilderness" (583). Here Hawthorne has built his description out of thin air. The echoes of Goodman Brown's voice sound *as if* bewildered, which is certainly ironic, since he himself is *truly* bewildered here.

Paragraph concludes with a strong idea about Hawthorne's use of irony in the scene.

Goodman Brown's temptation leads to his fall in the next paragraph, when "the dark cloud swept away, leaving the clear and silent sky above Goodman Brown. But something fluttered lightly down through the air and caught on the branch of a tree. The young man seized it, and *beheld* a pink ribbon" (583). Hawthorne's language has changed, becoming simple and stark. It suggests the physicality of what it describes. Goodman Brown might have doubted the evidence of his eyes and ears if he stopped to reflect on what he had been shown in the "clear and silent sky" above his head, but before he could reflect, the devil gave him what he took to be something tangible to hold onto, something that looks like a pink ribbon.

Good insight into change in language.

Thoughtful analysis of character's motivation.

On the evidence of what he sees as a ribbon, Goodman Brown jumps to the conclusion that Faith has joined in the worship of the devil. He surrenders his trust in God forever. He becomes a victim of his own pride, believing in the evidence of his own senses more than in God. As a Puritan, Goodman Brown believes in the devil as much as he believes in God. Hawthorne might be suggesting that Goodman Brown's belief contributed to his downfall. The story shows that it is but a short step from believing in the devil to being taken in by him.

End explication; start conclusion, tying back to thesis.

Conclusion goes one step further, to a wider implication of the thesis (logically connected).

WORK CITED

Hawthorne, Nathaniel. "Young Goodman Brown." *The Story and Its Writer*, edited by Ann Charters, 9th ed., Bedford/St. Martin's, 2015, pp. 578–587.

Analysis

An *analysis* of a story is the result of the process of separating it into its parts in order to study the whole. Analysis is commonly applied in thinking about almost any complex subject. When you are asked to analyze a story, you must break it down into various parts and then usually select a single aspect for close study. If you are writing a short essay, try to keep the topic small enough to handle in a few paragraphs. Often what you are analyzing is one of the elements of fiction or an aspect of style, such as symbolism, for example.

While explication deals with a specific section of the text, analysis can range further, discussing details throughout the narrative that are related to your thesis. It is not possible to analyze every word of an entire story, any more than you would attempt to explicate an entire work. You may begin with a general idea, or arrive at one by thinking about some smaller detail in the story that catches your attention.

Perhaps you begin by noticing the path through the forest as you read "Young Goodman Brown." When you stop to think about it later, you realize that Hawthorne's various descriptions of this path contribute to the pattern of the story. You sense a connection of the path with the effect of "blackness" or darkness you feel building up in the narrative. This single detail of the setting can suggest a central idea that you might want to investigate. You could write, for example, about the path the protagonist takes on his walk through the forest and analyze the way its use in the different sections of the narrative develops what Melville called Hawthorne's "power of blackness."

Regardless of where you start to think analytically — with the whole or with one of its parts — you will usually begin to write an essay that is developed by analysis by moving from a general thesis statement to the particular part of the story being analyzed. The essay "The Path toward Evil" is an example of how a student has analyzed "Young Goodman Brown" by following Hawthorne's references to the path through the forest.

Here the thesis sentence opens the essay, and the analysis follows from it. The student separated the story into various parts, analyzing the way the path figured in it at each stage of narration. You will notice that explication also plays a role in this essay. Even when analysis is your chosen method of developing your central idea, you should quote examples from the story to support your main points. Each time you use a quotation, comment on it to integrate it smoothly into your discussion.

Student Essay: Analysis

The Path toward Evil

The path's purpose in "Young Goodman Brown" is to show that "evil is the nature of mankind" (586), which is the dominant theme of Nathaniel Hawthorne's story. It is a very dark theme, as Herman Melville realized in his 1850 review of Hawthorne's *Mosses from an Old Manse*. Satan has been with the Puritans since they came to America. The "dreary . . . narrow" path (578) Goodman Brown follows through the gloomy forest is proof that human beings have frequently walked with the devil in the new land. Goodman Brown's journey on the path makes him realize that there are two kinds of evil: social and personal. He meets social evil first, and is confused by it. Then he meets the "blackness" that is the evil within himself, and he is totally destroyed.

Thesis sentence, supported by evidence from supplementary reading.

When he begins to walk on the path with the devil, Goodman Brown is too innocent to understand what he hears. He does not realize that the religious intolerance of the early Puritan settlers is wrong. So his companion, the devil, enlightens him further,

Analysis narrows thesis and points to direction of paper's development.

Analysis is coherent — organized from beginning of story to end.

telling him about present-day corruption in the community. The church deacons have drunk the communion wine, and the lawyers "are firm supporters of my interest" (580). Now Goodman Brown is horrified because he understands the meaning of the devil's remarks. He takes the first step along the path from innocence to disillusionment when he recognizes hypocrisy in the respected village elders.

Specific quote from story to illustrate general idea.

He proceeds a step further when he sees his own catechism teacher, the deacon, and the minister on the forest path, too. He does not understand what they are doing there. He asks himself, "Whither, then, could these holy men be journeying so deep into the heathen wilderness?" (582). While Goodman Brown now recognizes social evil, he does not understand it. He must go further along the path to discover his own evil nature.

Good transition: One step leads to another.

Quote evidence for assertion.

End of first part (social evil).

Goodman Brown finds the answer to his question in the story's climax. The path takes him and the "holy men" to the same destination. After he has come to believe that his wife is about to become one of the devil's accomplices, he runs desperately down the path, which "grew wilder and drearier and more faintly traced, and vanished at length, leaving him in the heart of the dark wilderness, still rushing onward with the instinct that guides mortal man to evil" (583). Although the trail is a path toward evil, it is, paradoxically, his last connection with the familiar Puritan life that has sustained him. When it stops, he is lost.

Begin second part (personal evil).

Good comment on the quotation — relates it to central idea.

The path terminates in the forest clearing, with its altar dedicated to the worship of Satan. Here he learns "to behold the whole earth one stain of guilt, one mighty blood spot" (585). There are no paths out of the wilderness now for Goodman Brown. The whole earth is bathed in blood, with no firm ground upon which to fix a path that will lead him safely home. Overwhelmed by his visions in the forest, he is a lost soul. He has realized his own evil nature.

Evidence to support the analysis of the personal evil in Goodman Brown.

As Hawthorne knew, the Puritan settlers of Salem felt the forest was evil. They had to make paths in order to live in it. They would have died of exposure if left alone in the woods, and they needed paths to walk to other nearby settlements. To journey alone in the forest was, as Goodman Brown learned, to leave the clearly defined, if hypocritical, moral path of the established religious community and so to invite damnation. Hawthorne dramatized his dark theme of man's essentially evil nature by showing Goodman Brown's fate. He leaves the apparently straight and narrow path of the religious settlement for the twisting, crooked path of the forest. It is a dark journey of his soul to meet "the deep mystery" (585) of original sin.

Begin conclusion: Historical background relates to particular details of the story.

Restatement of thesis.

WORK CITED

Hawthorne, Nathaniel. "Young Goodman Brown." *The Story and Its Writer*, edited by Ann Charters, 9th ed., Bedford/St. Martin's, 2015, pp. 578–587.

Comparison and Contrast

If you were to write about the two Hawthorne stories in this anthology, or to develop an idea about any two stories, you would probably use comparison and contrast. When using the technique of comparison, you place the two stories side by side and comment on their similarities. In contrasting two stories, you point out their differences. Most of the time you will use both methods, since no two stories are exactly the same. It is always more meaningful to compare and contrast two stories that have something in common than two that are completely unrelated. As you work on your essay you will find that if there are no important similarities in the stories, your discussion will be as strained and pointless as an attempt to link closely any two dissimilar objects, whether mismatched stories or apples and crankcases.

You can also compare and contrast two or more elements within a single story. For example, in Poe's "The Cask of Amontillado," you could discuss the character of Montresor as he sees himself and as he is viewed by the reader, or the differences between the two characters, Fortunato and Montresor. If your topic calls for you to use the method of comparison and contrast to elucidate your central idea, it is usually smoother to mingle your treatment of the two stories or elements as you go along than to write the first half of your paper about one and the second half about the other. The result of such a fifty-fifty split is rarely a unified essay; rather, it tends to give the impression of two separate discussions flimsily linked together.

In the example of a paper about "Peter Klaus the Goatherd" and Washington Irving's "Rip Van Winkle," in which the thesis is developed by the method of comparison and contrast of the oral folktale and the written story, the student shaped the first paragraph to conclude with the central idea, serving as an introduction to the comparison and contrast of the two stories. Throughout, elements of both stories were compared and contrasted side by side, sometimes with general analytic comments, at other times with explication and interpretation of the text. The technique of comparison and contrast is also a way to analyze stories. Specific quotations from the texts always help the reader get a clearer idea of the general points you are making in your analysis.

Student Essay: Comparison and Contrast

Bringing Fiction to Life:

From Folktale to Short Story in "Peter

Klaus the Goatherd" and "Rip Van Winkle"

Short stories are carefully crafted works of fiction that captivate readers in ways that the simple transcription of an oral folktale cannot. What separates the short story from oral storytelling? Irving's intentions are illustrated in his story "Rip Van Winkle," a rendition of the German folktale "Peter Klaus the Goatherd." Irving uses the plot of the traditional tale, but he retells the story in such a skillful way that he enchants his readers into considering it the first successful American short story. Irving's detailed characterization of Rip Van Winkle helps us understand the power of the short story.

General background information on topic.

Topic narrowed to thesis sentence.

In J. C. C. Nachtigal's transcription, Peter Klaus is briefly described in two words as "a goatherd," and then the events of the story proceed. Perhaps the original storyteller who narrated the tale in front of an audience of rapt German peasants went into more detail, but today's reader does not have an opportunity to step into Peter's shoes or to form an imaginative connection with him. The words in the transcribed folktale make the reader focus on the plot action of the story and not think twice about how or why its events took place.

Specific examples.

As Irving understood, the author of a short story can take an entirely different approach. This type of narrative is primarily meant to be read by an individual, not enacted by a storyteller. The conclusion of the plot becomes secondary to the "how" and "why" of the characters' actions. When an author reveals the thoughts of the protagonist and gives colorful details to describe his behavior, the reader can identify with the fictional character. The reader has the time to focus on every detail or to turn the pages back to reconsider something he might have missed earlier in the story. This permits a much more complex way of writing than a literal transcription of a folktale, and it explains why the short story has become so popular.

Begin analyzing differences.

"Peter Klaus the Goatherd" tells a tale of a man who falls asleep one day while hunting squirrels, wakes up twenty years later to find his circumstances greatly altered, and is eventually reconciled with his daughter and her family. The folk legend shows us how much we take life for granted; it suggests that we never know what we have until we lose it. The story of "Rip Van Winkle," on the other hand, does not have such a clear-cut theme.

Plot summary relevant to theme of story.

Contrast with Irving's treatment.

Details about Rip's lackadaisical character as a man who "would rather starve on a penny than work for a pound" (614)--his avoidance of his demanding "termagant" wife (615), his pleasure in hunting squirrels in the wild Catskill mountains with his dog Wolf ("as much hen-pecked as his master" [614]), and his sleeping away the momentous events of the Revolutionary War--add humor to his characterization and suggest several different themes. What the story says to one reader may differ from another reader's response to it. By getting imaginatively involved in Rip's situation, each reader can take an active role in enjoying the story. Perhaps this is the strongest appeal of the short story: It brings fiction to life by inventing a world and inviting you to make something of it.

Specific quotations give evidence of differences.

Concluding summary clear, if a little brief.

WORKS CITED

Irving, Washington. "Rip Van Winkle." *The Story and Its Writer*, edited by Ann Charters, 9th ed., Bedford/St. Martin's, 2015, pp. 612–623.

Nachtigal, J.C.C. "Peter Klaus the Goatherd." *The Story and Its Writer*, edited by Ann Charters, 9th ed., Bedford/St. Martin's, 2015, pp. 1491–1493.

Writing about the Context and the Stories

In addition to developing an idea about short fiction by explication, analysis, or comparison and contrast — all methods primarily involving a close reading of the text — there are other ways to write about short stories. The *context* of short fiction is important as well as the text, as the headnotes to each author's work in this anthology have stressed. The context of literature is usually defined as the biographical and historical background of the work. Literature does not exist in a vacuum. Created by an individual at some particular time in history, it is intended to speak to other human beings about ideas that have human relevance. Any critical method that clarifies the meaning and the pattern of a short story is valuable, and often literary critics use more than one method in their approach to a text.

A paper on the context of a story is also an expository essay based on the development of a central idea or thesis statement. Usually this kind of critical essay develops the thesis of the paper by suggesting the connection of *cause and effect*. That is to say, you maintain that the story has characteristics that originate from causes or sources in the author's background — personal life, historical period, or literary influences. For example, you can use Kate Chopin's statement on her discovery of Maupassant's stories (on p. 1412) to show something about her own method of writing short fiction. To establish this connection between the life and work of a writer, you could also analyze or explicate a Chopin story, or compare one of her stories with one of Maupassant's.

The amount of time you spend on the context or the text of the story will depend on the emphasis you wish to make in your paper. You have already read a student essay (p. 1710) that briefly mentions the context of the stories, referring to Melville's recognition of the power of blackness in Hawthorne's short fiction (p. 1473).

You have probably written papers about literature in a biographical context. A favorite high school term paper project is to assign the student an author to write about, requiring research into his or her life or historical period. If you wrote this kind of a paper, you may have organized your material chronologically, tracing the life of your author and briefly describing his or her most important literary works, often with no clearly defined thesis in mind. In writing an essay based on a unified central idea, by contrast, you must ask yourself how knowing the facts of an author's life can help you understand that author's story. You should never assume a connection between a writer's life and the literary work. A story can reflect the life of the man or woman who wrote it, but there are often disparities between the work of fiction and the realities of the life that are as important as the connections you can draw between them. If you plan to give a biographical analysis of Melville's "Bartleby, the Scrivener," for example, showing how it illustrates Melville's own decision to stop earning his living as a writer, you must remember that he wrote the story in 1853, several years before he decided to give up writing fiction for a popular audience. In 1853, Bartleby's "I would prefer not to" was not yet Melville's conscious choice. This particular biographical reading of the story will not take you very far in your interpretation of its psychological, sociological, or philosophical complexities.

A biographical approach to literature requires at least as much care as textual criticism of the story, care in discovering and presenting the facts of an author's life and in using a sensitive interpretation of them to show relevant connections between a writer and a story. Richard Ellmann's biographical perspective on James Joyce's "The Dead" in the Commentaries section (p. 1422) is a masterful example of the application of this particular critical strategy.

You will usually be proceeding on firmer ground when you combine biographical facts with a discussion of an author's thematic or aesthetic intentions in writing fiction, and then relate this material to specific stories. Here again, be cautious. Statements by writers about how and why they created short stories are not necessarily the same as what a given story may show. Use your judgment carefully. Poe wrote model stories based on his theory of the "single effect," but Anton Chekhov did not always follow his own advice about how to write fiction. In "The Lady with the Little Dog" (p. 271) he wrote beautifully about the physical setting of Yalta, instead of restricting himself to the barest description, as he advised another writer to do in his letters (p. 1411).

The contexts supplied by the writers themselves in the commentaries on the short story form and on particular stories included in this anthology are meant to stimulate ideas for your essays. They give the historical and biographical backgrounds of some of the stories. These excerpts can furnish a perspective from which you may view the individual stories, as did the student who quoted Melville in one of the sample essays here. Or you can write about the commentaries as a subject in themselves, part of the wider context of short story literature. You can report on the entire books they came from (Frank O'Connor's study of the short story form, for example, or Eudora Welty's *The Eye of the Story*), if they are available to you.

Other Perspectives

Material from other classes can also be used in papers about short stories. If you major in history or psychology, for example, you can investigate the way stories are sometimes read to give valuable historical or psychological information about the world they describe. You are not limited to writing about remote times when considering essays that take this approach. Joyce Carol Oates's story "Where Are You Going, Where Have You Been?" is about modern teenage life. A paper about it could investigate the connection between Oates's fiction and psychological theories about adolescence in contemporary America. Characters in literature are often used in psychological and sociological textbooks to illustrate pathological symptoms or complexes. Sociology textbooks, for example, cite Oates's fictional characters as representing current tendencies toward *anomie*, a condition in which normative standards of conduct have weakened or disappeared. It is possible in writing about literature to illustrate philosophical, historical, sociological, or psychological material you are familiar with through your work in other college courses.

Finally, you can argue a particular ideological point of view in writing about literature. Being aware of different critical approaches may lead you to think about stories in ways you might never have considered. If you look up critical articles on the stories in the Commentaries section of this anthology or in your college library, you will find that academic critics usually write about literature using particular strategies. The more traditional approaches before 1970 tended to be formalist or biographical and historical (and occasionally Marxist). In recent years more innovative contemporary theory has developed.

At times the background of the author can suggest an ideological approach: Richard Wright was a communist, Tillie Olsen was a feminist, Flannery O'Connor was a Catholic, and so forth. At other times an ideology held by the student but not necessarily by the author can lead to a fresh reading of a story. Depending on what you as a reader bring to "The Metamorphosis," for example, there is a "Freudian Kafka, an existentialist Kafka, a Catholic Kafka, a Marxist Kafka, a Zionist Kafka," and so forth, as suggested by the critic Hans Eichner.

Proceed with your literary analysis according to your ideology with great care, realizing that you might become insensitive to nuances of meaning other than those you are predisposed to find in a doctrinaire interpretation of the text. (This anthology includes examples of many different critical approaches, including deconstructionist, historical, folkloric, rhetorical, biographical, feminist, psychological, and gender criticism.) An ideological approach can illuminate aspects of a story that are valid and relevant for contemporary readers. A feminist interpretation of "Young Goodman Brown," for example, must not take the story literally, because Hawthorne wrote it as a moral allegory, but a feminist could use the story to argue provocatively about implied sexual stereotyping in Hawthorne's characterization of women.

Arguments about the interpretation of literature are acceptable so long as they are supported by evidence from the text. Writers do not intend their readers to worship literature like priests at an altar. Take courage, and try to express your own point of view. Leo Tolstoy's attempt to read his own philosophy into Anton Chekhov's "The Darling" (p. 1528) and Chinua Achebe's spirited critique of Joseph Conrad's "Heart of Darkness" (p. 1385) are two examples of iconoclastic but well-presented interpretations of great short stories. Literary critics and scholars are now examining and revising the canon of accepted masterpieces as changes in society alter our expectations of what we look for in literature. Interpretations of great works change, as we enlarge and redefine the canon to reflect our hopes for a more enlightened community of readers.

You misread stories if you think of them as absolute, perfect, final statements far removed from the commonplaces of life. They need the reader's involvement to come alive as imaginative literature. As Raymond Carver said, "Good fiction is partly a bringing of the news from one world to another. That end is good in and of itself, I think. . . . [Reading] just has to be there for the fierce pleasure we take in doing it, and the different kind of pleasure that's taken in reading something that's durable and made to last, as well as beautiful in and of itself." Through their aesthetic patterns, stories show us what life is like. What they are ultimately saying, in their affirmation of life and human creativity, is — in the words of Henry James — "Live! Live!"

If you possess fluency in a foreign language, you can also bring your own special knowledge to your papers about literature. One student who could read Russian went back to the original version of Anton Chekhov's "The Darling." She read the story in Russian and compared the English translation with the original text. In the opening paragraph of her essay, she wrote personally as a reader-response critic, but in the next paragraph she gave a detailed analysis of the Russian words she found in the story.

Student Essay

Anton Chekhov's "The Darling"
in Russian and English Translation

The Russian version of Anton Chekhov's "The Darling" was clearer to me than the translated version. Because I grew up in Russia before emigrating to the United States, I could relate to the description of the streets and the house in the provincial town where Olenka lived. This was clear in both the English and the Russian versions of the story. But the original version gave me a better understanding of the character of Olenka. She appeared as a genuinely religious person in the Russian version, not only because she went to church and used expressions like "May the Mother of God give you health," but also because Chekhov's choice of words for the title of the story made you understand how religious Olenka truly is.

In the Russian version, the title of the story is "Duschechka," a word that comes from the word *soul*—*duscha*. The direct translation would be "the dear little soul," meaning a spiritual person with a good heart. This description perfectly suits Olenka. She is affectionate but naive in her relationships with men, falling in love with each of her two husbands out of pity. Introducing her in the first paragraph, Chekhov calls her by her nickname "Olenka" instead of her Christian name "Olga" to suggest that her character is childish and foolish: "Olenka, daughter of the retired collegiate assessor, Plemy-anniakov, was sitting on the back porch in her courtyard, deep in thought."

Later in the story we learn that Olenka completely identifies with all of the men in her life, including her lover the veterinary surgeon and his young son, Sasha. She thinks like each of them and talks about what they talk about. She does not have her own opinion about anything; just like a child she needs to depend upon someone. Chekhov successfully emphasized her complete emotional dependency on others throughout the story. Just as the soul needs the body for completion, so Olenka needs to be in love to feel alive. Chekhov wrote realistic stories, not religious parables, but as Tolstoy once noted in an essay about this story (p. 1528), there seems to be a religious subtext here. I believe I came closer to understanding Chekhov's narrative about "The Dear Little Soul" when I read it in Russian.

WORKS CITED

Chekhov, Anton. "The Darling." Translated by Contance Garnett. *The Story and Its Writer*, edited by Ann Charters, 9th ed., Bedford/St. Martin's, 2015, pp. 262–270.

Tolstoy, Leo. "Chekhov's Intent in 'The Darling.'" *The Story and Its Writer*, edited by Ann Charters, 9th ed., Bedford/St. Martin's, 2015, pp. 1528–1530.

Writing the Research Paper

The main difference between research papers and other literary papers is that you will draw on secondary sources, such as literary criticism, biography, or other works, in addition to the story you are asked to write about. It is possible to enjoy research if you have a topic of interest and look forward to the opportunity of expanding your knowledge about the subject. It also gives you the chance to refine and strengthen your own interpretations of literature by citing authorities who bolster your argument. In writing a research paper, you will continue to use the skills that you developed composing shorter essays. As before, you will need a strong thesis or central idea about your topic, and you will need to organize your essay effectively so that you demonstrate your original approach to the assignment, using comparison and contrast, for example. Don't procrastinate until the last moment to begin the research and writing. You will probably need extra editing and proofreading time to make sure you get the details of citation and documentation just right.

Finding and Using Sources

Library Research. Your research will most likely require you to use a combination of electronic and print resources. The best way to begin your search for material to support the thesis of your paper is by conducting a search of your library's holdings on your author and story. You can access your library's catalog by visiting the library or its Web site. For the sample research paper on page 1721, the writer searched under "Wright, Richard" and "Man Who Was Almost a Man." You can also investigate related contexts for your story such as "film adaptation."

After you check the catalog, you should check the *MLA International Bibliography*, published by the Modern Language Association. This guide is the most complete listing of publications in the field of literature. Published annually and available at many libraries in a print or an electronic Web-based format, this bibliography can provide the most thorough list of sources if you are looking for scholarly books and articles about writers and their work. It also covers linguistics, folklore, and film criticism.

The reference section of your library is a rich source of background and factual information. A series such as *Contemporary Literary Criticism* or *American Writers* can provide a quick overview of a writer's life and work. Your library may also subscribe to full-text journal collections such as Project Muse or JSTOR, which reproduce the contents of hundreds of scholarly journals in Web format. Your library may afford access to general resources such as Lexis Nexis Universe, which provides newspaper and magazine coverage as well as political and legal information. These sites are not part of the "free" Web and are not indexed by general search engines. They are generally available to a campus community either through the campus network or by modem.

Using the Web for Research. The World Wide Web is the most popular place to conduct research. For some topics, such as public affairs, politics, and popular culture, it is an excellent source of information; for others, including many topics in literature, it is less useful. However, you might find many sites devoted to the culture of a period or digitized primary-source collections, such as the Electronic Text Center at the University of Virginia or the American Memory project at the Library of Congress, where you can find old film clips, recordings of speeches, and other treasures.

General search engines are of limited use for the literary scholar. Search engines work by mining the Web mechanically, pulling together sites based on words used on pages and in URLs, regardless of quality or depth. If you use a search engine, such as Google Scholar, try to focus your search with several key search terms. An alternative to using general search engines is to use subject-oriented selective Web directories such as Argus Clearinghouse or Scout Signpost. These have been compiled by researchers who have attempted to find and organize by subject the best sites on the Web. Finally, be sure to check out bedfordstmartins.com/rewritinglit, where annotated Author Links direct you to some of the most informative Web sites for a particular author.

Evaluating Your Sources

Just because an item has found its way into print (or has a place on a flashy Web site), you should not necessarily believe it. You should evaluate every potential source in at least two ways before you include it in your paper. First, find out whether the source is respectable (that is, likely to be accurate), and second, determine if it is really appropriate to your purpose.

Dates are also worth noting. Not all literary research needs to be absolutely up to date; sometimes historical research is the key to a successful paper. But as a general rule, use the most recent printed sources. Not only will the recent work utilize recently discovered information, but it is also likely to incorporate the ideas of earlier researchers as well. Check the bibliographies of the books and articles you read. Often they will be crucial to your research because they will provide authors and titles you may not have encountered in your own search for relevant information on your topic.

Special caution is needed when evaluating online sources. The Internet is a vast and largely uncensored place, and much of the information available on it is incomplete, misleading, or just plain wrong. If you can't tell whether a Richard Wright Web page was posted by a professor of American literature or by a middle-school student doing a project for English class, be sure to confirm any doubtful information. Sometimes the author of a Web site will include a link to a personal home page at the bottom of the page, where you might learn more about the author's credentials. If an organization has sponsored a Web project, look for links to information about the purpose and nature of the organization. Apply to Web sites the same criteria of accuracy and relevance that you use in evaluating printed information.

Documenting Sources

If you like to work on a computer and have a laptop or tablet model you can take to the library with you, you can keep your working bibliography this way.

The traditional method is to use 3" × 5" note cards, one reference to a card. Complete instructions on turning your working bibliography into a list of works cited at the end of your research paper can be found in the *MLA Handbook*, 8th edition (Modern Language Association, 2016). This handbook will also give you good advice about how to integrate quotations into your essay.

Here are some examples of the most frequently used documentation in research papers as well as a short research paper about the film adaptation of Wright's "The Man Who Was Almost a Man" that concludes with a works cited page.

A Book by a Single Author

McKee, Robert. *Story: Substance, Structure, Style, and the Principles of Screenwriting.* HarperCollins, 1997.

A Signed Article in a Reference Book

Clark, Edward D. "Richard Wright." *Afro-American Writers, 1940–1955.* Edited by Trudier Harris and Thadious M. Davis, Gale Research, 1988, pp. 199–221.

A Signed Article in a Magazine, Journal, or Newspaper

O'Brien, Geoffrey. "What Does the Audience Want?" *New York Times Magazine* 16 Nov. 1997, sec. 6, pp. 110–11.

Book in an Online Database

Goldsmith, Oliver. *The Vicar of Wakefield: A Tale.* Philadelphia, 1801. *America's Historical Imprints,* infoweb.newsbank.com.ezproxy.bpl.org/.

Film

Scott, Ridley, director. *The Martian.* Performances by Matt Damon, Jessica Chastain, Kristen Wiig, and Kate Mara, Twentieth Century Fox, 2015.

Student Essay: Research

Making Mental Things Physical:
Wright's "The Man Who Was Almost a Man"
and the Film *Almos' a Man*

The widespread popularity of television and motion pictures in recent decades has made fiction accessible to the average person on a level unprecedented in history. Many critics have argued that this proliferation of commercial entertainment has made people less inclined to read and appreciate classic literature. A recent survey conducted by *USA Today* revealed that "twenty-four hours in the life of American culture contained twenty-three references to television, six to film, six to popular music, three to radio, and one to fiction (*The Bridges of Madison County*)" (Franzen 41).

Use relevant background research to introduce topic.

Still, some Americans continue to read serious fiction in this country, even after they leave college. The social scientist Shirley Brice Heath has studied this population. She has found that adult readers are usually people who have grown up in households where one or both of the parents read literature and encouraged their children to do so. Frequently these young readers are what Heath calls "social isolates," children who felt different from others around them. Heath theorizes that

> What happens is you take that sense of being different into an imaginary world. But that world, then, is a world you can't share with the people around you -- because it's imaginary. And so the important dialogue in your life is with the *authors* of the books you read. Though they aren't present, they become your community. (Qtd. in Franzen 46)

Indent long quotation by a noted authority.

This total immersion in an imaginary "community" is also one of the attractions of film, of course. In a good film treatment of a story, all the viewers in the audience can share a sense of community as they lose themselves in the imaginary world projected by the actors on the screen. This sense of shared experience watching a film is intense, but it doesn't last very long. The popularity of cinema in the twentieth century, according to critic Geoffrey O'Brien, has resulted in a "glut of product and a pervasive loss of surprise" (110). It is no wonder that many recent filmmakers have adapted classic short stories in order to keep the audience "coming back, hoping to see something different *this* time" (O'Brien 110).

Work short quotations into your sentences.

Movie and television versions of literature have brought the works of great writers to a large audience. These adaptations, if done well, can enhance the viewer's understanding and appreciation of the author's intent. Unfortunately, some film versions sacrifice characterization and theme in favor of a fast-moving plot with a broad appeal. Leslie Lee's film version of Richard Wright's "The Man Who Was Almost a Man" retains much of the sensitive characterization present in the short story. The screenwriter also does an excellent job of presenting Dave's generational conflict with the adults in the story. In fact, this theme is more fully dramatized in the movie than on the page.

The frustration felt by an adolescent growing up in an adult-dominated society is the theme emphasized in *Almos' a Man*. The film opens with Dave, played sympathetically by actor LeVar Burton as a high-spirited teenage boy from a poor black family, plowing fields for Mr. Hawkins, the white farmer for whom he works. When adapting Wright's story into a film, Lee invented

No need to cite source of general information.

new scenes to strengthen the motivation of the protagonist. This is apparently a common practice when screenwriters develop a work of short fiction into a screenplay. Since drama is based on action, screenwriters try to invent dramatic action that suggests the emotional states of the characters described by the author of a story.

Paraphrase words of an authority.

In the first new scene at the beginning of *Almos' a Man,* Dave sees Mr. Hawkins in the fields hunting birds with a rifle. The boy stops his plowing to imitate his employer's actions, pretending like a small child that he also has a gun. This brief scene serves to clarify the connection Dave makes between owning a gun and having power and helps explain how Dave becomes fixated on owning a gun.

The movie proceeds to show Dave plotting to get a gun and his frustration at the lack of respect and trust he is shown by adults. When Dave comes home after talking to the manipulative storekeeper who is willing to sell him an old gun, his parents treat him as an inferior. After supper his mother washes his hair as if he were still a little boy (another scene added by Leslie Lee). This treatment makes the viewer sympathetic toward Dave, although here the teenager shows the same unmistakable lack of maturity as when he playfully skipped along and made gunshot noises pretending to shoot imaginary targets.

Lee's film dramatizes Dave's actions, but in the story Wright takes us into Dave's thoughts as he fantasizes about owning a gun. "He could almost feel the slickness of the weapon with his fingers. If he had a gun like that he would polish it and keep it shining so it would never rust. N Ah'd keep it loaded, by Gawd!" ("The Man" 1372). The film version is less subtle, showing Dave playing out his fantasies. The screenwriter Robert McKee has noted that "we cannot drive a camera lens through an actor's forehead and photograph his thoughts, although there are those who would try. Somehow we must lead the audience to interpret the inner life from outer behavior without loading the soundtrack with expositional narration" (McKee 43–44). Lee's skillful adaptation illustrates the fact that "movies are about making mental things physical" (McKee 44).

Compare film with story.

No need to indent short quotation.

When we have access to Dave's thoughts in Wright's story, the racial theme becomes much clearer. Dave thinks, "Could kill a man with a gun like this. Kill anybody, black or white" ("The Man" 1373). It is clear that some of his frustration is a result of his perception of racial inequality, although the pressures in Dave's world "must often be *teased*, rather than cited, from the story" (Coonfield). Dave's anger is particularly evident in his

Use quotations from story to support your interpretation.

feelings toward Mr. Hawkins. At the end of the story Dave states
that "they treat me like a mule" (1378), referring not only to
his parents but also to white men like Mr. Hawkins. Dave then
resolves to go after his gun, reasoning, "Ef other men kin shoota
gun, by Gawd, Ah kin!" (1378).

　　After he recovers the gun, Dave walks to within sight of
Hawkins's house and thinks, "ef Ah had just one mo bullet Ah'd
taka shot at tha house. Ah'd like t scare ol man Hawkins jusa
little. . . . Jusa enough t let im know Dave Saunders is a man"
(1378). Thoughts like these, which the reader can access readily
in the original story, indicate that Dave sees his gun as a way
to escape being treated as inferior by white people. Since we
are usually not privy to a character's thoughts in a film, Wright's
message of racial inequality is less strong in the adaptation for
the screen.

Contrast story with film.

　　Almos' a Man shows that a dramatization of a story can
enhance the experience of reading it. Taj Mahal's background
music of blues guitar and harmonica eloquently suggests an adolescent's mood swings between elation and despair. The visual
images of Dave's childlike behavior pretending to shoot his gun
at the beginning of the story, and the additional scene suggesting his tender feelings about his mother when she washes his
hair, deepen his characterization and make him a more sympathetic protagonist.

　　However, Wright's theme of racial inequality is central to his
work. In his essay "The Ethics of Living Jim Crow," Wright pointed
out that white people refused to discuss "any topic calling for positive knowledge or manly self-assertion on the part of the Negro"
(276). As a young man like Dave growing up in a poor share-
cropper's family, Wright himself "experienced some of the most
severe abuses of racial oppression in Mississippi" (Clark 201).

Conclude with quotations from Wright and two leading scholars to strengthen your argument.

　　Wright also wrote fiction to dramatize his feelings of alienation. This philosophical dimension to his writing is easier
to access in interior monologues on the page than in action
sequences on the screen. The critic Fred Stocking noted that
Wright's "most persistent interests" were "the dramatizing
of psychological states, particularly of blacks who have been
treated with scorn, and the lonely search of any man, of any
race, for an authentic identity in an alien universe" (280).

　　The strength of film as a medium is the presentation of visual
images. While this can enhance any story, to appreciate Wright's
achievement to its fullest extent, the reader must have access to
the words on the page that express Dave's thoughts.

WORKS CITED

Clark, Edward D. "Richard Wright." *Afro-American Writers, 1940–1955*, edited by Trudier Harris and Thadious M. Davis, Gale Research, 1988, pp. 199–221.

Coonfield, Gordon. "Community and Coming of Age in 'The Man Who Was Almost a Man.'" Instructor home page, Fall 1997. Michigan Technological University, Dept. of Humanities. Accessed 8 Sept. 1997, http://www.mtu.edu/humanities/people/faculty/gordon-coonfield/.

Franzen, Jonathan. "Perchance to Dream: In the Age of Images, a Reason to Write Novels." *Harper's Magazine*, Apr. 1996, pp. 41–46.

Lee, Leslie, writer. *Almos' a Man*. Directed by Stan Lathan, Perspective Films, 1977.

McKee, Robert. *Story: Substance, Structure, Style, and the Principles of Screenwriting*. HarperCollins, 1997.

O'Brien, Geoffrey. "What Does the Audience Want?" *New York Times Magazine*, 16 Nov. 1997, sec. 6, pp. 110–11.

Stocking, Fred. "On Richard Wright." *The American Short Story I*, edited by Calvin Skaggs, Dell, 1977, pp. 275–80.

Wright, Richard. "The Ethics of Living Jim Crow." Quoted in *The American Short Story I*, Dell, 1977, pp. 276.

---. "The Man Who Was Almost a Man." *The Story and its Writer*, edited by Ann Charters. 9th ed., Bedford/St. Martin's, 2015, pp. 1370–79.

Revising Your Research Paper

The smooth flow of a completed research paper is usually the result of many revisions. Once you have completely drafted your paper, with all sources fully integrated and documented, you should leave ample time to revise it, just as you would any other paper. The following checklist provides a systematic method for approaching revision. You might also ask a classmate, or even your instructor, to look over the draft and offer advice.

1. **First, look again at your tentative thesis statement.** Now that you have written the paper, does the thesis still seem exactly right? It is possible, even likely, that in the process of writing you may have refined or changed your ideas about your topic. If so, reword the thesis to accurately reflect your new thinking.

2. **Now look again at the supporting evidence you offer in each body paragraph.** Do all of the ideas directly relate to and uphold the thesis? If any of them do not, you should cut these sections from your paper, regardless of the intrinsic interest of the ideas or the strength of the writing. Cutting

out something you have labored on is one of the most difficult things a writer can do. Remember, though, that your paper will be stronger in the long run if it stays on track and all the parts are clearly related.

3. **Are there any portions of the paper where you worry that the argument may be thin or underdeveloped or where the connection to your thesis may not be entirely clear?** If so, you should try to explain your ideas more fully. You may even need to do a bit of additional research to fill in the gaps.

4. **After any necessary cuts and additions have been made, you may need to slightly reorganize the paper.** Is your argument presented in the most logical order and are all related ideas kept together? Rearrange and revise any awkwardly placed paragraphs or sentences.

5. **Does the style and voice sound at all like your usual writing?** It is easy when reading the thoughts and words of other authors to begin adopting the style of these authors and losing your own voice. Check to make sure that the vocabulary and tone reflect your personality and your attitude toward the subject. By writing in your own voice, you make the material and the project your own. Many students believe that research papers must be solemn in tone, but as long as the subject allows for it, there is no reason you cannot bring to your research paper the same sorts of creative techniques, and even humor, that you would to any other paper. Most instructors do not mind if you write in the first person or include occasional personal anecdotes and comments — provided, of course, that these support the main point of your paper. If you are uncertain how your instructor feels about this, be sure to ask.

6. **Finally, carefully review the assignment and make sure that your essay conforms to your instructor's guidelines in all respects.** Some teachers, for instance, ask you to include a cover sheet or an outline; some might want you to underline your thesis or to format the works cited page in a particular manner. Whatever your instructor asks, remember that in the event of disagreement, his or her guidelines should always take precedence over those offered here or anywhere else.

7. **Unless your teacher calls for some other format (such as a cover page), you should begin in the upper left corner of page 1 with your name, your instructor's name, the course for which you are writing the paper, and the date you turn it in.** Double-space and center the title of your paper in capital and lowercase letters without underlining or quotation marks (unless, of course, a quotation or title appears within your own title). Then begin the paper itself with regular one-inch margins and double-spacing throughout (including quotations and the list of works cited). A running head with your last name and the page number should appear in the upper right corner of each page.

8. **Your essay should now be ready for the final polish before you turn it in.** Print out a clean copy and review it twice more. The first time, edit and proofread for word choice, grammar, spelling, and punctuation as well as any other small changes that will improve style and readability. If you are

in doubt about anything, look it up. Even small mistakes can have a large negative effect on a reader, and after spending so much time and effort on your paper, it would be a shame to let careless errors ruin your credibility as a writer. The second time, go over the format of all quotations, parenthetical references, and your works cited page to make sure that they are consistent and conform exactly to guidelines. You are now ready to make your last changes, print out a final copy, and turn in a research paper you can be proud of.

9. **Read your essay over one last time for typographical errors.** Make corrections. Have you put quotation marks around titles of short stories and underlined the titles of films and books? Have you placed commas and periods within quotation marks in the titles and quotations that appear in your essay? Have you inadvertently left out any words or sentences when you went from the rough draft to the final version of your essay?

10. **Finally, make a copy of your paper — a duplicate printout or a photocopy — before you hand it in, and keep it.** It is a good idea to save your notes and rough drafts as well, in case the accuracy of a quotation or the originality of your work is called into question.

What do you do after you hand in your paper? You have probably spent so much time on it, thinking, organizing, writing, and rewriting, that you feel you may never want to read it again. The act of writing will have clarified your thinking about the story, so you carry with you the intangible benefit of something learned in the writing process. Returning to your paper in the future might have one final benefit: It will refresh your memory, reminding you of what you did not know you knew, about both yourself and the short story.

Literary Theory and Critical Perspectives

Literature is what gets taught.

—Roland Barthes

In the opening pages of his book *Literary Theory*, the contemporary English critic Terry Eagleton wrote that "hostility to theory usually means an opposition to other people's theories and an oblivion of one's own." You may feel that literary theory is formidable, but as you begin to explore the various commentaries by short story writers and critics in this anthology, you will discover that they make available many different approaches to the study of literature. For example, Sandra M. Gilbert and Susan Gubar give a feminist reading of Charlotte Perkins Gilman's "The Yellow Wallpaper" (p. 1581), and J. Hillis Miller develops a deconstructive reading of Herman Melville's "Bartleby, the Scrivener" (p. 1477), to list only two selections in the anthology. Reading different critical interpretations may also make you become more aware of the assumptions that underlie your own thoughts about literature.

Literary theory is the term used in academic criticism to characterize particular methods of inquiry into the nature and value of literature. Formulating general critical principles — rather than analyzing particular literary texts — is the job of theorists like Terry Eagleton, whereas your assignment is usually to analyze a specific story, poem, or play. The following critical approaches to literary texts are the ones you will encounter most frequently in your reading of the commentaries or secondary sources. They offer some useful perspectives to consider in your critical thinking and writing about literature.

Formalist Criticism

Formalist criticism is probably the most basic approach to the analysis of literature. Along with other theoretical perspectives, critics often use it to develop their interpretation of literary texts. René Wellek and Austin Warren, the pioneering practitioners of formalism in the United States, wrote in their *Theory of Literature* (1942) that "the natural and sensible starting point for work in literary scholarship is the interpretation and analysis of the works of literature themselves."

Formalists regard a work of literature as a world in itself that can be understood by its intrinsic nature — focusing on form over content. A pure formalist would approve of the chapter on the elements of fiction, but he or she would not include headnotes about the authors, considering facts about the author's life and historical times irrelevant to the appreciation of a text. Instead, a formalist would concentrate on analyzing how the various elements of a literary work are integrated into the complex and unique structure of a self-contained aesthetic work.

For example, the academic critic Cleanth Brooks and the poet Robert Penn Warren give a formalist analysis of Poe's "The Fall of the House of Usher" on page 1402. Their discussion was included in *Understanding Fiction* (1943), a college textbook that introduced generations of teachers and students to the formalist techniques of what was then called "New Criticism" based on a close reading of the text. In Brooks and Warren's discussion of Poe's tale, they looked for the presence of irony in the text. Their critical approach worked best when explicating the complexity of an author's linguistic and cultural erudition.

Biographical Criticism

In "The Formalist Critic," Cleanth Brooks stated that

> the formalist critic is concerned primarily with the work itself. Speculation on the mental processes of the author takes the critic away from the work into biography and psychology. There is no reason, of course, why he should not turn away into biography and psychology. Such explorations are very much worth making. But they should not be confused with an account of the work. Such studies describe the process of composition, not the structure of the thing composed. . . .

Unlike formalist criticism, **biographical criticism** starts with the premise that stories, poems, and plays are written by human beings, and that important facts about the life of an author can shed light on literary texts. Usually this kind of critical approach develops the thesis of an essay by suggesting the connection of *cause and effect*. That is, you maintain that the imaginative world of the text has characteristics that originate from causes or sources in the author's background.

A biographical approach to literature requires at least as much care as formalist criticism — care in presenting only the relevant facts of an author's life and in using a sensitive interpretation of them to show clear connections between the writer's experience or personality and the work. Richard Ellmann gives a biographical perspective on James Joyce's story "The Dead" on page 1422 of the Commentaries section, analyzing how the creative process functioned in an author's life.

Psychological Criticism

Psychological criticism is indebted to modern psychology, which began with the psychoanalytic theories of its founder, the Austrian psychoanalyst

Sigmund Freud (1856–1939). Freud wrote that he learned nearly as much about psychology from reading authors such as Sophocles and Shakespeare as he did from his clinical work with his patients in Vienna as an analyst and physician. Freud's writing about psychology, along with books by his disciples including Carl Jung, Marie Bonaparte, and Bruno Bettelheim, modified our understanding of human behavior, introducing such concepts as the unconscious forces of the id and the superego active within every individual.

Three approaches are most often taken by critics interested in exploring the psychological aspect of literature. First is the investigation of the creative process and the nature of literary genius. This field of investigation can also include other forms of genius — musical, mathematical, and so forth. The second is the study of an individual writer (or artist or musician or scientist), particularly appropriate if the individual was deeply involved in psychological therapy or analysis. The third is the analysis of fictional characters, which began with Freud's study of the character of Oedipus when he analyzed Sophocles' play in his book *The Interpretation of Dreams* (1900). Moving from literary analysis to psychological generalizations, Freud used literature to formulate universal theories about human psychology that have continued to influence our ideas for over a century.

D. H. Lawrence's approach in 1919 to his discussion of "The Fall of the House of Usher" and "The Cask of Amontillado" (p. 1458) is an early form of psychological criticism.

Historical Criticism

Historical criticism approaches a literary work through its historical context, the events that were occurring in the world during the time the author wrote a particular story, poem, or play. This method is often combined with the biographical approach, if the historical events contributed to the author's thought process and resulted in the creation of a work of literature. Historical critics may also explain the meaning that the work had for its original readers, especially if the text includes words that had different connotations in the past.

Chinua Achebe introduces a historical context into his commentary "An Image of Africa: Racism in Conrad's 'Heart of Darkness'" when Achebe refers to what he calls Marlow's "bleeding-heart sentiments" and attributes them to "the kind of liberalism" that "touched all the best minds of the age in England, Europe, and America" (p. 1385). Achebe then compares Conrad's "liberalism" with that of the missionary Albert Schweitzer, and concludes that Conrad was, even more than Schweitzer, "a thoroughgoing racist."

Reader-Response Criticism

For much of the twentieth century, the formalist approach to "close reading" of stories, poems, and plays was the most popular method of analysis in American college classrooms. After the turbulent social changes of the 1960s, literary critics in the United States became receptive to many new approaches to the text. The critic Ross Murfin has summarized the reaction against the "New Critical" practices:

> About 1970, the New Criticism came under attack by reader-response critics (who believe that the meaning of a work is not inherent in its internal form but rather is cooperatively produced by the reader and the text) and poststructuralists (who, following the philosophy of Jacques Derrida, argue that texts are inevitably self-contradictory and that we can find form in them only by ignoring or suppressing conflicting details or elements). In retrospect it is clear that, in their outspoken opposition to the New Criticism notwithstanding, the reader-response critics and poststructuralists of the 1970s were very much *like* their formalist predecessors in two important respects: for the most part, they ignored the world beyond the text and its reader, and, for the most part, they ignored the historical contexts within which literary works are written and read.

Reader-response criticism postulates that reading is as much a creative act as the writing of a text, because both involve the play of imagination and intelligence. Some reader-response critics even go so far as to say that a literary text has no existence outside of a reader's mind. Recognizing that different readers can find different meaning in works of literature, reader-response critics also emphasize the fact that the same reader can, at different periods of his or her life, find the experience of reading a book changes with maturity. If you keep the notes you take on reading *Hamlet* as a college freshman, for example, you will probably find that in twenty years or so, your interpretation of the play will change if you read it again or see a new production in the theater.

On page 1553 of this anthology, the literary critic Kenneth A. McClane gives a reader-response interpretation of James Baldwin's "Sonny's Blues" in the essay " 'Sonny's Blues' Saved My Life."

Poststructuralist and Deconstructionist Criticism

Poststructuralist and **deconstructionist criticism** are two modern approaches to critical theory that, like reader-response criticism, focus on the multiple, sometimes self-contradictory meanings that exist in a literary work — meanings that resist a final interpretation. Critics who practice these approaches believe in a basic logical syllogism:

A. Human language is fundamentally unstable, as its meaning is dependent on changing but omnipresent social and historical factors.

B. Literary texts are composed of human language.

C. Therefore, literary texts are fundamentally unstable. Q.E.D.

Arguing that the literary text is unstable, deconstructionist critics like the French authorities Roland Barthes and Michel Foucault have called for "the

death of literature" and "the death of the author." In 1968 Barthes explained in
his essay "The Death of the Author" that

> Once the Author is removed, the claim to decipher a text becomes quite
> futile. To give a text an Author is to impose a limit on that text, to furnish it
> with a final signified, to close the writing. Such a conception suits criticism
> very well, the latter then allotting itself the important task of discovering
> the Author (or its hypostases: society, history, psyche, liberty) beneath the
> work: when the Author has been found, the text is "explained" — victory
> to the critic. . . . In the multiplicity of writing, everything is to be *dis-
> entangled,* nothing *deciphered*; the structure can be followed, "run" (like
> the thread of a stocking) at every point and at every level, but there is nothing
> beneath. . . . writing ceaselessly posits meaning ceaselessly to evaporate it,
> carrying out a systematic exemption of meaning.

While formalists find coherence in the different elements of a text, decon-
structionists show how the author's language can be broken or "deconstructed"
into irreconcilable meanings. Their efforts have influenced many contemporary critics, and their theories are worth investigating if you continue your
study of literature in upper-division courses and graduate school.

You can sample their approach in the books listed at the end of this
appendix on page 1733, as well as in J. Hillis Miller's deconstructive reading of
Herman Melville's "Bartleby, the Scrivener" on page 1477 of this anthology.
Miller takes a mythological approach (analyzing versions of the Pygmalion
myth) in his deconstruction of Melville's text. The critic illuminates how Melville
"disables reading" any one particular interpretation into the story by selecting
the lawyer, Bartleby's employer, as his narrator.

Gender Criticism

Gender criticism emerged in the wake of the development of feminist criticism on American college campuses in the 1970s, gradually evolving into gender criticism with the inclusion of gay and lesbian critics. This branch of critical
theory is indebted to early works such as the French critic Simone de Beau-
voir's *The Second Sex* (1949) as well as the American feminists Betty Friedan's
The Feminine Mystique (1963) and Kate Millett's *Sexual Politics* (1970).

Gender critics are concerned with the gender and sexual orientation of
both writers and readers of literature. They argue that our patriarchal culture
is so imbued with assumptions of heterosexual male superiority that we must
continuously correct the imbalance by identifying and analyzing its components and negative influences. Explaining how gender has influenced both
an author's work and a reader's response to a literary text, this approach often
contains aspects of reader-response criticism.

On page 1581 of this anthology you can read the feminist commentary of
the eminent critics Sandra M. Gilbert and Susan Gubar on Charlotte Perkins
Gilman's "The Yellow Wallpaper." This excerpt is taken from their book, *The

Madwoman in the Attic: The Woman Writer and the Nineteenth-Century Literary Imagination (1979). Gilbert and Gubar place the story within the context of what they call the "literature of confinement," where a woman trapped by the patriarchal society attempts to free herself "through strategic re-definitions of self, art, and society."

Cultural Criticism

Cultural criticism, like gender criticism, can be viewed as an important contemporary development in literary studies erected upon the sturdy but limited foundation of formalist practice. Cultural critics, including New Historicists, do not advocate any one particular approach to literary study. Frequently they participate in interdisciplinary approaches, combining more than one field of academic study due to their assumption that individual works of literature should be approached as part of a larger cultural context. For example, if you investigated the changes in 1960s popular music as reflected in Joyce Carol Oates's "Where Are You Going, Where Have You Been?" (p. 977), incorporating musical history into your essay, you have been practicing cultural criticism.

As the poet X. J. Kennedy realizes,

> In theory, a cultural studies critic might employ any methodology. In practice, however, he or she will most often borrow concepts from deconstruction, Marxism analysis, gender criticism, race theory, and psychology. . . . Whereas traditional critical approaches often sought to demonstrate the unity of a literary work, cultural studies often seeks to portray social, political, and psychological conflicts it masks.

Leslie Marmon Silko uses the methodology of a cultural critic in her essay analyzing "Language and Literature from a Pueblo Indian Perspective" on page 1516 of this anthology.

Selected Bibliography

General Overview

Eagleton, Terry. *After Theory*. New York: Basic Books, 2003. Print.

Eagleton, Terry. *Literary Theory: An Introduction*. 2nd ed. Minneapolis: U of Minnesota P, 1996. Print.

Selden, Raman. *The Theory of Criticism from Plato to the Present*. New York: Longman, 1988. Print.

The Changing Literary Canon

Lauter, Paul. *Canons and Contexts*. New York: Oxford UP, 1991. Print.

Formalist Criticism

Ransom, John Crowe. *The New Criticism*. Norfolk, CT: New Directions, 1941. Print.

Wellek, René, and Austin Warren. *Theory of Literature*. New York: Harcourt, Brace and World, 1949. Print.

Biographical and Psychological Criticism

Bloom, Harold. *The Anxiety of Influence*. 2nd ed. New York: Oxford UP, 1997.

Crews, Frederick. *Out of My System: Psychoanalysis, Ideology, and Critical Method*. New York: Oxford UP, 1975. Print.

Freud, Sigmund. *The Standard Edition of the Complete Psychological Works*. Ed. James Strachey. 24 vols. London: Hogarth Press and the Institute of Psychoanalysis, 1940–68. Print.

Lesser, Simon O. *Fiction and the Unconscious*. Chicago: U of Chicago P, 1957. Print.

Skura, Meredith Anne. *The Literary Use of the Psychoanalytic Process*. New Haven: Yale UP, 1981. Print.

Historical Criticism

Lindenberger, Herbert. *Historical Drama: The Relation of Literature and Reality*. Chicago: U of Chicago P, 1975. Print.

Reader-Response Criticism

Booth, Wayne C. *The Rhetoric of Fiction*. 2nd ed. Chicago: U of Chicago P, 1983. Print.

Eco, Umberto. *The Role of the Reader: Explorations in the Semiotics of Texts*. Bloomington: Indiana UP, 1979. Print.

Fish, Stanley. *Is There a Text in This Class? The Authority of Interpretive Communities*. Cambridge, MA: Harvard UP, 1980. Print.

Freund, Elizabeth. *The Return of the Reader: Reader-Response Criticism*. London: Methuen, 1987. Print.

Tompkins, Jane P., ed. *Reader-Response Criticism: From Formalism to Post-Structuralism*. Baltimore: Johns Hopkins UP, 1980. Print.

Poststructuralist and Deconstructionist Criticism

Barthes, Roland. *The Rustle of Language*. New York: Hill and Wang, 1986. Print.

Culler, Jonathan. *On Deconstruction: Theory and Criticism after Structuralism*. Ithaca: Cornell UP, 1982. Print.

Derrida, Jacques. *Of Grammatology*. Baltimore: Johns Hopkins UP, 1976. Print.

Foucault, Michel. *Language, Counter-Memory, Practice*. Ithaca: Cornell UP, 1977. Print.

Smith, Barbara Herrnstein. *On the Margins of Discourse: The Relation of Literature to Language*. Chicago: U of Chicago P, 1979. Print.

Gender Criticism

Baym, Nina. *Feminism and American Literary History*. New Brunswick: Rutgers UP, 1992. Print.

Edelman, Lee. *Homographesis: Essays in Gay Literary and Cultural Theory*. New York: Routledge, 1994. Print.

Fetterley, Judith. *The Resisting Reader: A Feminist Approach to American Fiction*. Bloomington: Indiana UP, 1978. Print.

Jagose, Annamarie. *Queer Theory*. Victoria: Melbourne UP, 1996. Print.

Sedgwick, Eve Kosofsky. *Between Men: English Literature and Male Homosocial Desire*. New York: Columbia UP, 1985. Print.

Showalter, Elaine. *A Literature of Their Own*. Princeton: Princeton UP, 1977. Print.

Smith, Barbara. *Toward a Black Feminist Criticism*. New York: Out and Out, 1977. Print.

Cultural Criticism

Clayton, Jay, and Eric Rothstein, eds. *Influence and Intertextuality in Literary History.* Madison: U of Wisconsin P, 1991. Print.

Cox, Jeffrey N., and Larry J. Reynolds. *New Historical Literary Study: Essays on Reproducing Texts, Representing History.* Princeton: Princeton UP, 1993. Print.

Geertz, Clifford. *The Interpretation of Cultures.* New York: Basic Books, 1973. Print.

Storey, John, ed. *What Is Cultural Studies?* New York: St. Martin's, 1996. Print.

White, Hayden. *Tropics of Discourse: Essays in Cultural Criticism.* Baltimore: Johns Hopkins UP, 1978. Print.

Glossary of Literary Terms

Abstract language Language that describes ideas or qualities rather than specific, observable people, places, and things, which are described in CONCRETE LANGUAGE.

Action At its simplest, the thing or things that happen in a story's PLOT — what the CHARACTERS do and what is done to them. A story may have more than one action (a plot and one or more SUB-PLOTS), but a successful short story usually has one identifiable central action.

Allegory A narrative in which CHARACTERS, places, things, and events represent general qualities and their interactions are meant to reveal a general or abstract truth. Such characters, places, things, and events thus often function as SYMBOLS of the concepts or ideas referred to.

Allusion An implied or indirect reference to something with which the reader is supposed to be familiar.

Ambiguity A situation expressed in such a way as to admit more than one possible interpretation; also, the way of expressing such a situation. Many short story writers intend some element of their work to be ambiguous, but careless or sloppy writing often creates unintentional ambiguity, or *vagueness*.

Analysis A separation of a STORY into its component parts, as a means of understanding its meaning or structure.

Anecdote A brief, unified NARRATION of one incident or EPISODE, often humorous and often based on an actual event. Some very good short stories may consist of nothing more than an anecdote; others may be made up of several anecdotes strung together, or may use one or more anecdotes as a way of advancing the PLOT or developing a CHARACTER.

Antagonist A CHARACTER in some stories who is in real or imagined opposition to the PROTAGONIST or HERO. The CONFLICT between these characters makes up the ACTION, or PLOT, of the story. It is usually resolved in some way, but it need not be.

Anticlimax An unexpected, insignificant RESOLUTION to a NARRATIVE, sometimes appearing in the place of a CLIMAX, sometimes after a true climax. Many anticlimaxes are the unintended result of inept writing, but often — especially in modern works — they are used intentionally to indicate the randomness, futility, or boredom of human life and action.

Antihero A PROTAGONIST who lacks the conventional qualities of a HERO. Generally the antihero is considered a modern form of characterization, a commentary on traditional portrayals of idealized heroes. Franz Kafka's protagonist Gregor Samsa is one example.

Anti-story An experimental short story that attempts to convey OBJECTIVE reality by avoiding what its authors consider the false CONVENTIONS of PLOT, CHARACTER, and THEME, relying instead on seemingly uninterpreted and unarranged fragments of direct experience and language.

Atmosphere The MOOD, feeling, or quality of life in a story as conveyed by the author's choices of language and organization in describing the SETTING in which the speech and activity of the CHARACTERS takes place. The atmosphere in which an author makes characters appear and events occur is often important in determining the TONE of the work.

Authorial intrusion See EDITORIAL POINT OF VIEW.

Central intelligence A CHARACTER (often but not always the NARRATOR) through whose perception the author observes the ACTION of a story and whose perspective thus shapes the reader's view of that action. The term was coined by Henry James, who felt, essentially, that the true subject matter of FICTION is the effect of the action on the understanding of this central intelligence.

Character Any person who plays a part in a narrative. Characters may be FLAT — simple, one-dimensional, unsurprising, and usually unchanging or *static* — or ROUND — complex, full, described in detail, often contradictory, and usually *dynamic*, i.e., changing in some way during the story. The main character in the story can usually be labeled the PROTAGONIST or HERO; he or she is often in CONFLICT with some other character, an ANTAGONIST. Other characters who affect the ACTION slightly or only indirectly may be called *minor* characters; but, depending on the intention or the skill of the author, the main characters need not be round, nor the minor characters flat. Minor characters can sometimes be complex and dynamic also.

Climax The turning point or point of highest interest in a narrative; the point at which the most important part of the ACTION takes place and the final outcome or RESOLUTION of the PLOT becomes inevitable. Leading up to the climax is the RISING ACTION of the story; after the climax, the FALLING ACTION takes the reader to the DENOUEMENT or CONCLUSION, in which the results of the climactic action are presented.

Closed ending The conclusion of a STORY in which the ACTION ends in unambiguous success or failure (or death) for the PROTAGONIST.

Close reading A method of analyzing literature using careful step-by-step EXPLICATION of the text.

Coincidence An event or situation that arises for no apparent reason and with little or no preparation and then has a significant effect on the working out of the PLOT or the lives of one or more of the CHARACTERS in a work; a chance happening that has an important consequence or result; an accident of fate.

Colloquial English The correct but informal and casual language of ordinary native speakers, including slang and contractions.

Coming-of-age story See INITIATION STORY.

Complication The introduction and development of a CONFLICT between CHARACTERS or between a character and his or her situation. A complication moves the PLOT forward by exciting the reader's expectation that the conflict so introduced must lead to a CLIMAX and reach some ultimate RESOLUTION as a result.

Compression The use of few or short words, sentences, or paragraphs, or of very brief descriptions of CHARACTERS and SETTINGS and NARRATIONS of incidents, to tell a story as clearly and simply as possible; in general, an economical use of language.

Conclusion The outcome or RESOLUTION of a PLOT at the end of a STORY. Also called DENOUEMENT, as it may untie or resolve the plot complications encountered during the RISING ACTION. See also CLOSED ENDING, O. HENRY ENDING, and OPEN ENDING.

Concrete language Language that describes or portrays specific, observable persons, places, and things rather than general ideas or qualities, which are described in ABSTRACT LANGUAGE.

Conflict The opposition presented to the main CHARACTER (or PROTAGONIST) of a narrative by another character (an ANTAGONIST), by events or situations, by fate, or by some aspect of the protagonist's own personality or nature. The conflict is introduced by means of a COMPLICATION that sets in motion the RISING ACTION, usually toward a CLIMAX and eventual RESOLUTION.

Connotation The meaning of a word (or words) that is implied or suggested by the specific associations the word calls to mind and by the TONE in which it is used, as opposed to its literal meaning or denotation.

Convention A traditional or commonly accepted technique of writing or device used in writing, often an unbelievable device that the reader agrees to believe — such as, for example, the fact that a FIRST-PERSON NARRATOR is addressing the reader in a friendly and intimate manner.

Conventional Following or observing CONVENTIONS; often used in a derogatory manner to indicate a certain overreliance on such conventions and thus a lack of originality or failure of imagination on the part of the writer.

Crisis The turning point in a NARRATIVE; the point at which the ACTION reaches its CLIMAX and its RESOLUTION becomes inevitable.

Deconstruction A critical approach investigating the unstable properties of language, especially the destabilization of single definitions of meaning and the defamiliarization of literary CONVENTIONS. In the words of one critic, deconstruction is "not a dismantling of the structure of a text, but a demonstration that it has already dismantled itself."

Denouement The conclusion of an ACTION or PLOT, in which the FALLING ACTION is brought to a close and the outcome or outcomes of the CLIMAX are presented to the reader; from a French word meaning "the untying of a knot."

Description The use of language to present the features of a person, place, or thing.

Dialect A particular variety of language spoken in a specific region, usually by a poorly educated person. Authors can use dialect to suggest significant differences or similarities in class or background between fictional CHARACTERS.

Dialogue The written presentation of words spoken by CHARACTERS in a NARRATIVE; used to introduce the CONFLICT, give some impressions of the lives and personalities of the characters who are speaking, and advance the ACTION to its CLIMAX and RESOLUTION.

Diction The choice and arrangement of specific words and types of words to tell a story. A writer's diction is an important element of STYLE, and has a significant effect on the meaning of a story: The same ACTION will leave a different impression on the reader when it is narrated in street slang, in the clear, precise language of an old schoolteacher, or in the professional jargon of a lawyer or a social scientist.

Didactic A term used to describe a NARRATIVE or other work of art that is presented in order to teach a specific lesson, convey a MORAL, or inspire and provide a model for proper behavior.

Distance An author's or a NARRATOR's spatial or temporal — and hence emotional — removal or aloofness from the ACTION of a NARRATIVE, and from its CHARACTERS.

Dramatic irony The reader's awareness of a discrepancy between a CHARACTER's perception of his or her own situation or activities, or of their consequences, and the true nature of that situation or those consequences.

Editorial point of view The occasion in a text in THIRD-PERSON NARRATION when the narrator adds his or her own comments, which may or may not be the opinions of the author.

Epigraph A quotation an author places at the beginning of a literary work that often suggests its THEME.

Epiphany A "showing forth" or sudden revelation of the true nature of a CHARACTER or situation through a specific event — a word, gesture, or other action — that causes the reader to see the significance of that character or situation in a new light. The term was first popularized in modern literature by James Joyce.

Episode A specific, usually very brief incident, often complete in itself and usually narrated at once and as a whole (as in an

ANECDOTE). A story may consist of the NARRATION of one episode or of several episodes strung together and united by a common SETTING or common CHARACTERS or proceeding toward a single CLIMAX and RESOLUTION; the latter kind of story is referred to as an *episodic* narrative.

Explication The act of explaining or interpreting the meaning of a text.

Exposition The presentation of background information that a reader must be aware of, especially of situations that exist and events that have occurred before the ACTION of a story begins.

Fable A very short, often humorous NARRATIVE told to present a MORAL. A fable's CHARACTERS are often animals, and particular animals have CONVENTIONAL associations with specific abstract qualities or values — the fox represents wiliness, the ant industry, and the lion nobility, for example. Leo Tolstoy said that "the bad fable has a moral, while the good fable is a moral."

Fairy tale A story or FANTASY that appeals to our sense of the marvelous, in which we suspend disbelief and let our subconscious patterns of wish fulfillment express themselves through magical occurrences, characters, or objects.

Falling action The events of a NARRATIVE that follow the CLIMAX and resolve the CONFLICT that reached its highest point in that climax before bringing the story to its conclusion or DENOUEMENT.

Fantasy A NARRATIVE or events in a narrative that have no possible existence in reality and could not have occurred in a real world; used sometimes to amuse or delight readers, sometimes to comment on or illustrate by contrast some aspect of reality, and sometimes, as in a FABLE, to present a clear MORAL that will not be complicated or diminished by the untidiness or inconsistency of reality, or as in a FAIRY TALE, to express patterns of wish fulfillment.

Fiction A NARRATIVE drawn from an author's imagination, made up of a PLOT of imagined events involving imagined CHARACTERS in imagined or imaginatively reconstructed SETTINGS; lies told with the tolerance, consent, and even complicity of the listener or reader. The word *fiction* comes from the Latin *ficio*, "an act of fashioning, a shaping, a making."

Figurative language The use of a word or a group of words that is literally inaccurate to describe or define a person, event, or thing vividly by calling forth the sensations or responses that person, event, or thing evokes. Such language often takes the form of METAPHORS, in which one thing is equated with another, or of SIMILES, in which one thing is compared to another by using *like, as,* or some other such connecting word.

First-person narration The telling of a story by a person who was involved in or directly observed the ACTION narrated. Such a NARRATOR refers to himself or herself as *I* and becomes a CHARACTER in the story, with his or her understanding shaping the reader's perception of the events and CHARACTERS.

Flashback A technique of EXPOSITION in which the flow of events in a NARRATIVE is interrupted to present to the reader an earlier incident or situation that has a bearing on the story or film or its CHARACTERS.

Flat character A simple, one-dimensional, usually unchanging CHARACTER who shows none of the human depth, complexity, and contrariness of a ROUND CHARACTER or of most real people.

Folktale A NARRATIVE that comes out of the tradition — usually the oral tradition — of a specific culture and is used to communicate that culture's beliefs, values, and history from generation to generation. See also LEGEND and MYTH.

Foreshadowing The introduction of specific words, IMAGES, or events into a NARRATIVE to suggest or anticipate later events that are central to the ACTION and its RESOLUTION.

Formal English The heightened language of educated users, usually written, although spoken on dignified and ceremonial occasions.

Formalism A critical approach that stresses the self-contained and self-referential nature of a work of art. Formalism took root in the 1920s and 1930s, flourished in the "New Criticism" of the 1940s and 1950s, and is still influential today. Formalists promote close reading, focusing on internal patterns of language and meaning within a text and excluding "external" considerations such as the author's biography, social history, or the reader's personal idiosyncratic response.

Frame story A story within a story; a NARRATIVE told within the framework of another fictional SETTING and situation. In film, the term *frame* refers to an individual photograph on a strip of film.

General English The ordinary speech of educated speakers.

Genre A type of literary work, such as SHORT STORY, NOVEL, essay, play, or poem. The term may also be used to classify literature within a type, such as science-fiction stories or detective novels. In film, the term refers to a recognizable type of movie, such as a western or a thriller, that follows familiar NARRATIVE and visual CONVENTIONS.

Graphic storytelling Substantial single volumes of pictorial images arranged in a sequence to narrate a story with or without words.

Hero/Heroine The PROTAGONIST of a story or other NARRATIVE; the main CHARACTER, whose CONFLICT is presented and resolved in the ACTION OR PLOT. Traditionally, *heroine* has been used to refer to a female hero, but *hero* may be (and is more and more being) used to refer to a protagonist of either sex.

Image A word or group of words used to give a CONCRETE representation, either literal or FIGURATIVE, of a sensory experience or an object that is perceived by the senses.

Imagery The use of IMAGES, especially of a consistent pattern of related images — often FIGURATIVE ones — to convey an overall sensory impression.

Impartial omniscience The telling of a story by a THIRD-PERSON NARRATOR whose OMNISCIENCE does not allow for any evaluation or judgment of the CHARACTERS and their activities.

Impressionism A way of writing in which an author presents CHARACTERS and events in a highly subjective and personal light, freely admitting an authorial POINT OF VIEW and effectively denying any claim to OBJECTIVITY or disinterestedness; after the style of the French impressionist painters of the late years of the nineteenth century, who sought to free painting from the REALISTIC, representational CONVENTIONS of the day.

Initiation story Also called a COMING-OF-AGE STORY, this type of narrative confronts a PROTAGONIST, often a child or adolescent, with a difficult experience or rite of passage that prepares him or her for adult life.

Innocent or naive narrator A FIRST-PERSON NARRATION told from the POINT OF VIEW of a young, inexperienced, uneducated, or unintelligent NARRATOR who doesn't understand the implications of the story. This approach is used by the author to generate IRONY or sympathy in the reader.

Irony The reader's or audience's awareness of a reality that differs from the reality the CHARACTERS perceive (DRAMATIC IRONY) or the literal meaning of the author's words (VERBAL IRONY).

Legend A STORY transmitted by popular oral tradition about a famous person or an important event. Unlike other FOLKTALES, legends take place in real locations and are about genuine historical figures.

Levels of diction In English, the four levels of formality in word choice are classified as vulgate (DIALECT speech), COLLOQUIAL ENGLISH, GENERAL ENGLISH, and FORMAL ENGLISH.

Limited omniscience The ability of a THIRD-PERSON NARRATOR to tell the reader directly about any events that have occurred, are occurring, or will occur in the PLOT of a story, and about the thoughts and feelings of one particular CHARACTER, or a few characters; distinguished from simple OMNISCIENCE, whereby such a NARRATOR can tell the reader directly about the thoughts and feelings of any character.

Magical realism Fiction often associated with Latin America that interweaves REALISTIC and FANTASTIC details, juxtaposing the marvelous with the ordinary, as in the stories of Jorge Luis Borges and Gabriel García Márquez.

Metafiction Stories about language and the process of writing, exemplified by the work of Julio Cortázar among many others.

Metaphor An implied comparison of two different things that is achieved by a FIGURATIVE verbal equation of those things. "Love is a rose," "War is hell," and "The exam was a killer" are all metaphors, intended not to define the first terms mentioned but to attribute certain qualities to the thing being discussed.

Minimalism A literary style exemplifying economy and restraint, as seen in the stories of Donald Barthelme and Raymond Carver. Some of Ernest Hemingway's stories, such as "Hills Like White Elephants," could be considered pioneering works of minimalism in American literature.

Mise en scène (*mee zahn SEN*) A French term meaning "putting into the scene," it refers to the arrangement or design of visual elements such as props, lighting, costume, and actors on the stage of a theater or in the FRAME of a film. In film, the term also refers to the POINT OF VIEW from which a scene is photographed.

Modernism A label loosely applied to the work of certain writers of the late nineteenth and early twentieth centuries who investigated the structure and texture of literature and challenged its CONVENTIONS.

Montage (*mahn TAHZH*) The art of editing a film. More specifically, the term refers to an approach to editing developed by Russian filmmakers in the 1920s that aims to create emotional impact and visual meaning through a rapid sequence of brief, and often juxtaposed, shots.

Mood The ATMOSPHERE that is created by the author's choice of details and the words with which to present them.

Moral The lesson to be drawn from a story, especially from a FABLE or (in this sense the word is often used disparagingly) from a heavily DIDACTIC story.

Motivation The external forces (SETTING, circumstance) and internal forces (personality, temperament, morality, intelligence) that compel a CHARACTER to act as he or she does in a NARRATIVE.

Myth A symbolic NARRATIVE, often a FOLKTALE arising out of a culture's oral tradition and involving gods or superhumanly heroic figures, that is used to explain the way things are and the way things happen and to transmit the culture's values and beliefs from generation to generation.

Narration The dramatic telling of the events that make up the ACTION or PLOT of a story. FIRST-PERSON NARRATION is the telling of a story by a NARRATOR who participated in or directly observed the events being recounted and who is thus a CHARACTER in the story, identifying himself or herself as *I*. THIRD-PERSON NARRATION is the telling of a story by a detached, almost always anonymous voice who refers to the characters as *he, she,* and *they*. A THIRD-PERSON NARRATOR may or may not be OMNISCIENT.

Narrative A sequence of events, often (but not always) unified and connected in storytelling.

Narrator The teller of a story; usually either a CHARACTER who participates in the story's ACTION (see FIRST-PERSON NARRATION) or a detached, anonymous observer who may or may not present himself or herself as OMNISCIENT of the story's action from the beginning (see THIRD-PERSON NARRATION).

Naturalism An extreme form of REALISM in which authors present their work as a scientific observation of a world in which people's acts are strictly determined by their nature and the nature of their surroundings.

Novel A long fictional prose NARRATIVE.

Novella A short novel; a work of prose FICTION whose length falls somewhere between that of a SHORT STORY and that of a NOVEL; sometimes (though infrequently today) referred to as a *novelette*. Different critics have attempted to specify different standards of length for a novella or short novel — some saying 15,000 to 50,000 words, others 50 to 125 ordinary book pages — but there is no universal agreement on such a standard.

Objectivity An attempt by an author to remove himself or herself from any personal involvement with the CHARACTERS and ACTIONS of a story, to tell the story without bias and without expressing any personal opinions or making any personal judgments of the characters.

O. Henry ending A surprising CONCLUSION that reverses the reader's expectations of the way a NARRATIVE will end, often affected by an unexpected source or by withholding information at an earlier stage of the STORY. This type of ending in works of short fiction was made popular by O. Henry (William Sydney Porter) in the early twentieth century.

Omniscience Literally, "all-knowingness"; the ability of an author or a NARRATOR (usually a THIRD-PERSON NARRATOR) to tell the reader directly about any events that have occurred, are occurring, or will occur in the PLOT of a story and about the thoughts and feelings of any CHARACTER.

Open ending An ambiguous CONCLUSION to a STORY, which suggests there might be different possibilities in the future of the PROTAGONIST.

Pace The rate at which the ACTION of a story progresses. Pace may be affected by varying the lengths of words, sentences, and paragraphs, by COMPRESSING or expanding the NARRATION of certain incidents or EPISODES, or by introducing and repeating certain key words and formulaic phrases.

Parable A NARRATIVE, usually short, that is told to answer a difficult moral question or teach a moral truth; often a form of ALLEGORY, because each person, event, or thing in the parable represents a literally unrelated person, event, thing, or quality that is involved in the moral dilemma being examined.

Parody A humorous imitation of another, usually serious, work or type of work, in which the parodist adopts the quirks of STYLE or the CONVENTIONS of the work or works being imitated and uses them in extreme and ridiculous ways or applies them to a comically inappropriate subject matter.

Pathos The quality in a work that evokes sorrow or pity. Inappropriate pathos, or a too-frequent resorting to pathetic effects, can reduce a work to SENTIMENTALITY, or *bathos*.

Persona The fictional mask or voice an author may adopt to tell a story.

Plot The series of events in a NARRATIVE that form the ACTION, in which a CHARACTER or characters face an internal or external CONFLICT that propels the STORY to a CLIMAX and an ultimate RESOLUTION. Plot determines the way the reader experiences the story. It is an aesthetic pattern created in the different stages of the narrative, encompassing the EXPOSITION, RISING ACTION, CLIMAX, FALLING ACTION, and CONCLUSION.

Point of view The perspective from which an author lets the reader view the ACTION of a narrative; thus, the choice of who tells the story. In FIRST-PERSON NARRATION the NARRATOR tells a story he or she took part in or observed directly; such a narrator usually knows only what has been explicitly revealed or what he or she has been able to deduce from that. In THIRD-PERSON NARRATION the narrator is not directly involved in the story and so views it from a certain DISTANCE. Such a narrator may be OMNISCIENT about the CHARACTERS and their actions and MOTIVATIONS, or his or her knowledge may be LIMITED to what one or a few characters know or even to the plainly observable speeches and acts of the characters.

Protagonist The main CHARACTER of a narrative; its HERO. The ACTION of the story is usually the presentation and RESOLUTION of some internal or external CONFLICT of the protagonist; if the conflict is with another major character, that character may be called the ANTAGONIST.

Realism The telling of a story in a manner that is faithful to the reader's experience of real life, limiting events in the PLOT to things that might actually happen and CHARACTERS to people who might actually exist.

Resolution The FALLING ACTION of a NARRATIVE, in which the CONFLICT, set in motion during the RISING ACTION and reaching its high point in the CLIMAX, is settled, or at least significantly altered, and the story moves swiftly toward its conclusion or DENOUEMENT.

Reversal Any turnabout in the fortunes of a CHARACTER, especially of the PROTAGONIST.

Rising action The event or events that present and develop the CONFLICT whose dramatization is the story's ACTION; the COMPLICATION (or set of complications) that leads up to the CLIMAX.

Romanticism A literary movement that flourished in the nineteenth century, valuing individuality, imagination, and the truth revealed in nature.

Round character A full, complex, multidimensional CHARACTER whose personality reveals some of the richness and contradictoriness we are accustomed to observing in actual people, rather than

the transparent obviousness of a FLAT CHARACTER.

Satire A work that ridicules some aspect of human behavior by portraying it at its most extreme; distinguished from PARODY, which burlesques the STYLE or content of a particular work or type of work.

Screenplay A script for a film containing all of the scenes, DIALOGUE, ACTION, and often camera position and angle.

Sentimentality An overreliance on emotional effect or PATHOS so great as to strain the reader's willingness to believe; also referred to as *bathos*.

Setting The place and time in which a story's ACTION takes place; also, in a broader sense, the culture and the ways of life of the CHARACTERS and the shared beliefs and assumptions that guide their lives.

Short story A short fictional prose NARRATIVE, often including the YARN, the SKETCH, the FABLE, and the TALE. The term is often applied to any work of narrative prose FICTION shorter than a NOVEL. Edgar Allan Poe said the story's distinguishing factors were that it possesses aesthetic UNITY and can be read in one sitting. The trouble with that definition, as the writer William Saroyan once pointed out, is that some people can sit longer than others. See the discussion of this term in the Introduction and in the Elements of Fiction.

Simile A FIGURATIVE comparison of one thing to another, especially to one that is not usually thought of as similar. The comparison is achieved by using connecting words such as *like* or *as*. An old country song says, "Life is like a mountain railway," and then goes on to describe the narrow, tortuous paths people must follow in dealing with life's moral dilemmas, and the steep fall that awaits those who are not careful. The simile makes possible this figurative comparison of two such dissimilar things as *life*, a very large abstraction, and *mountain railway*, a very specific and seemingly unrelated object.

Sketch A relaxed, static, predominantly descriptive prose composition that may include action but no PLOT or causally related actions that develop and resolve a CONFLICT.

Step-outline A story told in one- or two-sentence steps for a film TREATMENT.

Stereotype A generalized, oversimplified CHARACTER (often a STOCK CHARACTER) whose thoughts and actions are excessively predictable because they are used so frequently that they have become CONVENTIONAL.

Stock characters CONVENTIONAL CHARACTERS who appear in numerous works, especially in works of the same type, and behave in predictable ways. Examples include the cruel stepmother in fairy tales and the hard-boiled detective in certain mystery stories.

Story An account of an incident or a series of events, either factual or invented. See SHORT STORY.

Stream of consciousness The NARRATIVE technique by which an author attempts to capture the flow of a CHARACTER's thoughts, often in a series of separate and apparently unrelated passages that unite to give an IMPRESSIONISTIC view of reality as seen by that character.

Structuralism A critical approach that developed contemporaneously with FORMALISM, similarly stressing attention to the formal elements of texts but regarding them as manifestations of a larger series of cultural codes and CONVENTIONS that govern responses to works of art (and indeed all other human artifacts). Structuralist criticism studies categories of thought and finds them embedded in language itself — or, more precisely, in the relations among the constituent parts of language.

Style The habitual manner of expression of an author. An author's style is the product of choices, made consciously or unconsciously, about elements such as vocabulary, organization, DICTION, IMAGERY, PACE, and even certain recurring THEMES or subjects.

Subplot A minor PLOT, often involving one or more secondary CHARACTERS, that may add a COMPLICATION to the ACTION of a NARRATIVE or may reinforce that action or provide an enlightening contrast to it or a welcome relief from its tension.

Surrealism A way of writing that involves the presentation of a super-real, dreamlike world where CONVENTIONS are upended and rationality is dispensed with. The spontaneous creations of the unconscious are depicted in a surrealistic work through FANTASY and incongruous IMAGERY.

Suspense The anxious uncertainty an author creates in a reader about the outcome of a story's ACTION. Suspense is often resolved when the action reaches a CLIMAX, after which the RESOLUTION is more or less inevitable.

Symbol A person, event, or thing that stands for or represents by association some other, usually broader, idea or range of ideas, in addition to maintaining its own literal meaning.

Tale An early form of the SHORT STORY, usually involving remote places and times, and events leading to a dramatic, conclusive ending.

Tall tale A TALE or SHORT STORY based on a consciously ludicrous distortion.

Theme The central, unifying point or idea that is made concrete, developed, and explored in the ACTION and the IMAGERY of a work of fiction.

Third-person narration The telling of a story by a detached, usually anonymous NARRATOR, a voice who refers to all the CHARACTERS as *he, she,* and *they.* Such a narrator may view the story with full OMNISCIENCE, which may or may not be IMPARTIAL OMNISCIENCE; or he or she may have only LIMITED OMNISCIENCE, seeing through the eyes of only one or a few characters.

Tone The expression of the author's attitude toward his or her subject matter — the CHARACTERS, their SETTING, and the ACTION they undertake or undergo. Tone is revealed in the author's DICTION,

IMAGERY, organization, vocabulary, and various other choices that contribute to the making of a STYLE.

Treatment The expansion of a film's step-outline from one or two sentences to paragraphs of present-tense, moment-by-moment description.

Unity The relation of all parts of a work to one central or organizing principle that forms them into a complete and coherent whole.

Unreliable narrator A fictional CHARACTER telling the story whose knowledge or judgment about events and other characters is so flawed or limited as to make him or her a misleading guide to the reader.

Verbal irony The reader's awareness of a discrepancy between the real meaning of the situation being presented and the literal meaning of the author's words in presenting it.

Verisimilitude The use of certain lifelike details to give an imaginative NARRATIVE work the semblance of reality or actuality.

Voice A term referring to the specific manner chosen by the author to tell the story. Voice encompasses elements of POINT OF VIEW and literary STYLE (TONE, DICTION, etc.).

Yarn An elaborated ANECDOTE or series of anecdotes narrated in colloquial language.

Chronological Listing
of Authors and Stories

Washington Irving (1783–1859)
Rip Van Winkle (1819–20)

Nathaniel Hawthorne (1804–1864)
Young Goodman Brown (1835)
The Minister's Black Veil (1836)

Nikolai Gogol (1809–1852)
The Overcoat (1840)

Edgar Allan Poe (1809–1849)
The Fall of the House of Usher (1839)
The Tell-Tale Heart (1843)
The Cask of Amontillado (1846)

Herman Melville (1819–1891)
Bartleby, the Scrivener (1853)

Leo Tolstoy (1828–1910)
The Death of Ivan Ilych (1886)

Samuel Clemens (Mark Twain)
(1835–1910)
The Celebrated Jumping Frog of Calaveras
County (1865)

Ambrose Bierce (1842–1914?)
An Occurrence at Owl Creek Bridge (1891)

Henry James (1843–1916)
The Real Thing (1891)

Sarah Orne Jewett (1849–1909)
A White Heron (1886)

Guy de Maupassant (1850–1893)
The Necklace (1884)

Kate Chopin (1851–1904)
Désirée's Baby (1892)
The Story of an Hour (1894)

Joseph Conrad (1857–1924)
Heart of Darkness (1899)

Anton Chekhov (1860–1904)
The Darling (1899)
The Lady with the Little Dog (1899)

Charlotte Perkins Gilman (1860–1935)
The Yellow Wallpaper (1892)

William Sydney Porter (O. Henry)
(1862–1910)
The Gift of the Magi (1906)

Edith Wharton (1862–1937)
The Other Two (1904)

Edith Maud Eaton (Sui Sin Far)
(1865–1914)
The Story of One White Woman Who
Married a Chinese (1910)
Her Chinese Husband (1910)

Stephen Crane (1871–1900)
The Open Boat (1897)

Willa Cather (1873–1947)
Paul's Case (1905)

Sherwood Anderson (1876–1941)
Hands (1919)

Jack London (1876–1916)
To Build a Fire (1908)

James Joyce (1882–1941)
Araby (1914)
The Dead (1914)

Virginia Woolf (1882–1941)
Kew Gardens (1919)

Franz Kafka (1883–1924)
The Metamorphosis (1915)
A Hunger Artist (1924)

William Carlos Williams (1883–1963)
The Use of Force (1938)

D. H. Lawrence (1885–1930)
Odour of Chrysanthemums (1909)
The Rocking-Horse Winner (1926)

Katherine Mansfield (1888–1923)
Miss Brill (1920)

Donald Barthelme (1931–1989)
At the Tolstoy Museum (1969)

Alice Munro (b. 1931)
Age of Faith (1971)

John Updike (1932–2009)
A & P (1961)

Philip Roth (b. 1933)
The Conversion of the Jews (1959)

Annie Proulx (b. 1935)
Job History (1999)

Raymond Carver (1938–1988)
Cathedral (1981)
What We Talk About When We Talk About
    Love (1981)
A Small, Good Thing (1983)

Joyce Carol Oates (b. 1938)
Where Are You Going, Where Have You
    Been? (1966)
The Lady with the Pet Dog (1972)

Margaret Atwood (b. 1939)
Happy Endings (1983)

Toni Cade Bambara (1939–1995)
The Lesson (1972)

Russell Banks (b. 1940)
Black Man and White Woman in Dark
    Green Rowboat (1981)

Angela Carter (1940–1992)
The Kiss (1985)

John Edgar Wideman (b. 1941)
newborn thrown in trash and
    dies (1992)

Isabel Allende (b. 1942)
An Act of Vengeance (1990)

Bobbie Ann Mason (b. 1942)
Shiloh (1982)

Steven Millhauser (b. 1943)
Flying Carpets (1998)

Alice Walker (b. 1944)
Everyday Use (1973)

Tobias Wolff (b. 1945)
Say Yes (1985)
Bullet in the Brain (1995)

Tim O'Brien (b. 1946)
The Things They Carried (1986)

Ann Beattie (b. 1947)
Janus (1985)

Lydia Davis (b. 1947)
Blind Date (1999)

T. Coraghessan Boyle (b. 1948)
Birnam Wood (2012)

Leslie Marmon Silko (b. 1948)
Yellow Woman (1974)

Art Spiegelman (b. 1948)
Prisoner on the Hell Planet: A Case
    History (1972)

Denis Johnson (b. 1949)
Work (1992)

Jamaica Kincaid (b. 1949)
Girl (1978)

Haruki Murakami (b. 1949)
UFO in Kushiro (1995)

Dagoberto Gilb (b. 1950)
Love in L.A. (1993)

Amy Tan (b. 1952)
Two Kinds (1989)

Roberto Bolano (1953–2003)
Jim (2003)

Sandra Cisneros (b. 1954)
Barbie-Q (1991)

Louise Erdrich (b. 1954)
The Red Convertible (1984)

Mary Gaitskill (b. 1954)
The Other Place (2011)

Helena María Viramontes (b. 1954)
Miss Clairol (1988)

Luis Alberto Urrea (b. 1955)
Father Returns from the Mountain (1980)

Lynda Barry (b. 1956)
San Francisco (2002)

Ha Jin (b. 1956)
Saboteur (2000)

Lorrie Moore (b. 1957)
Referential (2012)

Daniel Orozco (b. 1958)
Orientation (1994)

George Saunders (b. 1958)
Sticks (1994)

Thematic Index to the Stories and Guide to the Commentaries

Thematic Index to the Stories

Related Stories

Babel, *My First Goose*, Keret, *Not Human Beings*, and Frank O'Connor, *Guests of the Nation*

Bambara, *The Lesson* **and** Packer, *Brownies*

Carver **and** Englander, *What We Talk About…*

Chekhov, *The Lady with the Little Dog* **and** Oates, *The Lady with the Pet Dog*

Cortázar, *Axolotl* **and** Nazarian, *Fish Spine*

Gilman, *The Yellow Wallpaper* **and** Lessing, *To Room 19*

Hemingway, *Hills Like White Elephants* **and** Banks, *Black Man and White Woman in Dark Green Rowboat*

Irving, *Rip Van Winkle* **and** Nachtigal, *Peter Klaus the Goatherd*

Joyce, *Araby* **and** Updike, *A & P*

Lawrence, *Odour of Chrysanthemums* **and** Steinbeck, *The Chrysanthemums*

Melville, *Bartleby, the Scrivener* **and** Orozco, *Orientation*

Nabokov, *Signs and Symbols* **and** Moore, *Referential*

Roth, *The Conversion of the Jews* **and** Munro, *Age of Faith*

Tolstoy, *The Death of Ivan Ilych* **and** Barthelme, *At the Tolstoy Museum*

Welty, *A Worn Path* **and** Quatro, *I.7 to Tennessee*

On Writing

Atwood, *Happy Endings*

Barthelme, *At the Tolstoy Museum*

Carpentier, *Journey to the Seed*

Eigner, *Act*

Fuentes, *Pain*

Gass, *A Fugue*

Gogol, *The Overcoat*

James, *The Real Thing*

Paley, *A Conversation with My Father*

Woolf, *Kew Gardens*

Fantasy and the Supernatural

Barthelme, *At the Tolstoy Museum*

Borges, *The South*

Bradbury, *August 2026: There Will Come Soft Rains*

Carpentier, *Journey to the Seed*

Carter, *The Kiss*

Cheever, *The Swimmer*

Clemens, *The Celebrated Jumping Frog of Calaveras County*

Cortázar, *Axolotl*

Fitzgerald, *Winter Dreams*

Gaitskill, *The Other Place*

García Márquez, *A Very Old Man with Enormous Wings*

Gilman, *The Yellow Wallpaper*

Gogol, *The Overcoat*

Hawthorne, *Young Goodman Brown*

Irving, *Rip Van Winkle*

Jackson, *The Lottery*

Kafka, *A Hunger Artist*

Kafka, *The Metamorphosis*

Lawrence, *The Rocking-Horse Winner*

Le Guin, *The Ones Who Walk Away from Omelas*

Lispector, *The Smallest Woman in the World*

Millhauser, *Flying Carpets*

Murakami, *UFO in Kushiro*

Paz, *My Life with the Wave*

Poe, *The Fall of the House of Usher*

Silko, *Yellow Woman*

Urrea, *Father Returns from the Mountain*

Vonnegut, *Harrison Bergeron*

Wideman, *newborn thrown in trash and dies*

Wolff, *Bullet in the Brain*

Chopin, *Désirée's Baby*
Chopin, *The Story of an Hour*
Eaton, *The Story of One White Woman Who Married a Chinese*
Eaton, *My Chinese Husband*
Faulkner, *A Rose for Emily*
Fitzgerald, *Winter Dreams*
Fuentes, *Pain*
Gilb, *Love in L.A.*
Gilman, *The Yellow Wallpaper*
Hawthorne, *Young Goodman Brown*
Hemingway, *Hills Like White Elephants*
Hurston, *The Gilded Six-Bits*
Hurston, *Sweat*
Joyce, *The Dead*
Lahiri, *Interpreter of Maladies*
Lawrence, *Odour of Chrysanthemums*
Lessing, *To Room 19*
Mason, *Shiloh*
Maupassant, *The Necklace*
Murakami, *UFO in Kushiro*
Nazarian, *Fish Spine*
Oates, *The Lady with the Pet Dog*
Paz, *My Life with the Wave*
Porter (O. Henry), *The Gift of the Magi*
K.A. Porter, *Maria Concepcíon*
Silko, *Yellow Woman*
Steinbeck, *The Chrysanthemums*
Wallace, *Everything is Green*
Wharton, *The Other Two*
Wolff, *Say Yes*

Parents and Children

Bechdel, *From* Fun Home: *Old Father, Old Artificer*
Cather, *Paul's Case*
Carver, *A Small, Good Thing*
Cisneros, *Barbie-Q*
Danticat, *Night Women*
Faulkner, *That Evening Sun*
Gaitskill, *The Other Place*
Gass, *A Fugue*
Kafka, *The Metamorphosis*
Kincaid, *Girl*
Lawrence, *The Rocking-Horse Winner*
Moore, *Referential*
Munro, *Age of Faith*

Nabokov, *Signs and Symbols*
Flannery O'Connor, *Everything That Rises Must Converge*
Olsen, *I Stand Here Ironing*
Otsuka, *The Children*
Ozick, *The Shawl*
Paley, *A Conversation with My Father*
Paley, *Mother*
Quarto, *1.7 to Tennessee*
Roth, *The Conversion of the Jews*
Saunders, *Sticks*
Spiegelman, *Prisoner on the Hell Planet: A Case History*
Tan, *Two Kinds*
Urrea, *Father Returns from the Mountain*
Viramontes, *Miss Clairol*
Vonnegut, *Harrison Bergeron*
Walker, *Everyday Use*
Wideman, *newborn thrown in trash and dies*
Wright, *The Man Who Was Almost a Man*

Work

Anderson, *Hands*
Babel, *My First Goose*
Baldwin, *Sonny's Blues*
Beattie, *Janus*
Borowski, *This Way for the Gas, Ladies and Gentlemen*
Boyle, *Birnam Wood*
Camus, *The Guest*
Carver, *A Small, Good Thing*
Carver, *What We Talk About When We Talk About Love*
Conrad, *Heart of Darkness*
Crane, *The Open Boat*
Ellison, *Battle Royal*
Faulkner, *That Evening Sun*
Hurston, *Sweat*
Irving, *Rip Van Winkle*
Jewett, *A White Heron*
Jin, *Saboteur*
Johnson, *Work*
Kafka, *A Hunger Artist*
Keret, *Not Human Beings*
Lahiri, *Interpreter of Maladies*
Lawrence, *Odour of Chrysanthemums*
Melville, *Bartleby, the Scrivener*
Nazarian, *Fish Spine*

Poe, *The Fall of the House of Usher*
Poe, *The Tell-Tale Heart*
Proulx, *Job History*
Quatro, *I.7 to Tennessee*
Roth, *The Conversion of the Jews*
Sacco, *From* Palestine: *Refugeeland*
Saunders, *Sticks*
Spiegelman, *Prisoner on the Hell Planet: A Case History*
Sayrafiezadeh, *Brief Encounter with the Enemy*
Tolstoy, *The Death of Ivan Ilych*
Toomer, *Blood-Burning Moon*
Urrea, *Father Returns from the Mountain*
Vonnegut, *Harrison Bergeron*
Wideman, *newborn thrown in trash and dies*
Williams, *The Use of Force*
Wolff, *Bullet in the Brain*

Guide to the Commentaries

Writers on Writing

Alexie, *Superman and Me*
Anderson, *Form, Not Plot, in the Short Story*
Atwood, *Reading Blind*
Baldwin, *Autobiographical Notes*
Bechdel, *What the Little Old Ladies Feel*
Borges, *Borges and I*
Carver, *On Writing; Creative Writing; The Bath*
Cheever, *Why I Write Short Stories*
Chekhov, *Technique in Writing the Short Story*
Clemens (Mark Twain), *Private History of the "Jumping Frog" Story*
Ellison, *The Influence of Folklore on "Battle Royal"*
Faulkner, *The Meaning of "A Rose for Emily"*
Gilman, *Why I Wrote "The Yellow Wallpaper"*
Jackson, *The Morning of June 28, 1948, and "The Lottery"*
James, *The Genesis of "The Real Thing"*
Jewett, *Looking Back on Girlhood*
Kincaid, *On "Girl"*
Lamott, *Finding Your Voice*
Le Guin, *The Scapegoat in Omelas*

London, *Letter to the Editor on "To Build a Fire"*
Maupassant, *The Writer's Goal*
Munro, *How I Write Short Stories*
Oates, *Stories That Define Me: The Making of a Writer; Smooth Talk: Short Story into Film*
Flannery O'Connor, *Writing Short Stories; A Reasonable Use of the Unreasonable*
Frank O'Connor, *The Nearest Thing to Lyric Poetry Is the Short Story*
Paley, *A Conversation with Ann Charters*
Poe, *The Importance of the Single Effect in a Prose Tale*
Sacco, *Some Reflections on Palestine*
Silko, *Language and Literature from a Pueblo Indian Perspective*
Tan, *In the Canon, for All the Wrong Reasons*
Urrea, *On "Father Returns from the Mountain"*
Welty, *Is Phoenix Jackson's Grandson Really Dead?*

Writers on Other Writers

Achebe, *An Image of Africa: Racism in Conrad's "Heart of Darkness"*
Chopin, *How I Stumbled upon Maupassant*
Ford, *Why We Like Chekhov*
Lawrence, *On "The Fall of the House of Usher" and "The Cask of Amontillado"*
Mansfield, *Review of Woolf's "Kew Gardens"*
Melville, *Blackness in Hawthorne's "Young Goodman Brown"*
Nabokov, *Gogol's Genius in "The Overcoat"; A Reading of Chekhov's "The Lady with the Little Dog"*
Oates, *The Parables of Flannery O'Connor*
Frank O'Connor, *Style and Form in Joyce's "The Dead"*
Orozco, *On Millhauser's "Flying Carpets"*
Ozick, *Isaac Babel: "Let Me Finish"*
Tolstoy, *Chekhov's Intent in "The Darling"*

Acknowledgments (continued from p. iv)

Chinua Achebe: "Civil Peace" from *Girls at War and Other Stories* by Chinua Achebe, copyright ©
1972, 1973 by Chinua Achebe. "An Image of Africa: Racism in Conrad's Heart of Darkness"
copyright © 1988 by Chinua Achebe, from *Hopes and Impediments* by Chinua Achebe. Both used
by permission of Doubleday, an imprint of the Knopf Doubleday Publishing Group, a division
of Random House LLC, and The Wylie Agency LLC. All rights reserved. Any third-party use of
this material, outside of this publication, is prohibited. Interested parties must apply directly to
Random House LLC for permission.

Sherman Alexie: "The Lone Ranger and Tonto Fistfight in Heaven" from *The Lone Ranger and Tonto
Fistfight in Heaven*, copyright © 1993, 2005 by Sherman Alexie. Used by permission of Grove/
Atlantic, Inc. and Nancy Stauffer Associates Literary Agency. Any third-party use of this mate-
rial, outside of this publication, is prohibited. "Superman and Me" by Sherman Alexie, published
in *The Most Wonderful Books*, edited by Michael Dorris and Emilie Buchwald. Milkweed
Editions, 1997. Copyright © Sherman Alexie. Used by permission of Nancy Stauffer Associates
Literary Agents.

Paula Gunn Allen: "Whirlwind Man Steals Yellow Woman" from *Spider Woman's Granddaughters*
by Paula Gunn Allen. Introduction and notes copyright © 1989 by Paula Gunn Allen. Reprinted
by permission of Beacon Press, Boston.

Isabel Allende: "An Act of Vengeance" from *Short Stories by Latin American Women* by Isabel
Allende is reprinted with permission from the publisher (© 1990 Arte Publico Press — University
of Houston).

Sherwood Anderson: "Form, Not Plot, in the Short Story" copyright 1924 by Sherwood Anderson.
Copyright renewed 1952 by Eleanor Coppenhaver Anderson. Reprinted from *A Story Teller's
Story* by Sherwood Anderson (Ann Arbor: The University of Michigan Press 2005) by permis-
sion of the publisher.

Margaret Atwood: "Happy Endings" from *Good Bones and Simple Murders* by Margaret Atwood,
copyright © 1983, 1992, 1994, by O. W. Toad Ltd. Used by permission of Random House Canada
and Nan A. Talese, an imprint of the Knopf Doubleday Publishing Group, a division of Random
House LLC. All rights reserved. Any third-party use of this material, outside of this publication, is
prohibited. Interested parties must apply directly to Random House LLC for permission. "Reading
Blind" from *Writing with Intent: Essays, Reviews, Personal Prose 1983–2005* by Margaret Atwood.
Copyright © 2004, 2005 by O.W. Toad, Ltd. Appears by permission of the publisher, Carroll & Graf
Publishers, a member of Perseus Books Group via Copyright Clearance Center.

Isaac Babel: "My First Goose" translated by Walter Morison. From *The Collected Stories of Isaac
Babel*, copyright © 1955 by S. G. Phillips. Reprinted by permission of Writer's House.

James Baldwin: "Sonny's Blues" © 1957 by James Baldwin was originally published in *Partisan
Review*. Copyright renewed. Collected in *Going to Meet the Man*, published by Vintage Books.
Reprinted by arrangement with the James Baldwin Estate. "Autobiographical Notes" from *Notes
of a Native Son* by James Baldwin. Copyright © 1955, renewed 1983 by James Baldwin. Reprinted
by permission of Beacon Press, Boston. Permission conveyed through Copyright Clearance
Center.

Toni Cade Bambara: "The Lesson" copyright © 1972 by Toni Cade Bambara, from *Gorilla, My
Love* by Toni Cade Bambara. Used by permission of Random House, an imprint and division
of Random House LLC. All rights reserved. Any third-party use of this material, outside of this
publication, is prohibited. Interested parties must apply directly to Random House LLC for
permission.

Russell Banks: "Black Man and White Woman in Dark Green Rowboat" from *The Angel on the
Roof: Stories* by Russell Banks. Copyright © 2000 by Russell Banks. Reprinted by permission of
HarperCollins Publishers.

Lynda Barry: "San Francisco" from *One! Hundred! Demons!* By Lynda Barry (Sasquatch Books, 2002) copyright © 2002 by Lynda Barry. All rights reserved. Used by permission.

Donald Barthelme: "At the Tolstoy Museum" by Donald Barthelme. Copyright © 1987 by Donald Barthelme, originally published in the *New Yorker*, currently collected in *Forty Stories*, used by permission of The Wylie Agency LLC.

Ann Beattie: "Janus" is reprinted with the permission of Scribner Publishing Group from *Where You'll Find Me: And Other Stories* by Ann Beattie. Copyright © 1986 by Iron and Pity, Inc. All rights reserved.

Alison Bechdel: "Old Father, Old Artificer" from *Fun Home: A Family Tragicomic* by Alison Bechdel. Copyright © 2006 by Alison Bechdel. Reprinted by permission of Houghton Mifflin Harcourt Publishing Company. All rights reserved. "What the Little Old Ladies Feel" by Alison Bechdel from *Slate*, posted March 27, 2007 (www.slate.com/id/2162410). Reprinted by permission of the author.

Roberto Bolaño: "Jim" by Roberto Bolaño, translated by Chris Andrews, from *The Insufferable Gaucho*, copyright © 2003 by The Heirs of Roberto Bolaño, translation copyright © 2010 by Chris Andrews. Reprinted by permission of New Directions Publishing Corp.

Wayne C. Booth: "A Rhetorical Reading of O'Connor's 'Everything That Rises Must Converge'" from *A Rhetoric of Irony*, by Wayne C. Booth. Copyright © 1974 by the University of Chicago Press. Reprinted by permission of the author and the University of Chicago Press.

Jorge Luis Borges: "The South" from *Collected Fictions* by Jorge Luis Borges, translated by Andrew Hurley, copyright © 1998 by Maria Kodama. Translation copyright © 1998 by Penguin Putnam Inc. Used by permission of Viking Penguin, a division of Penguin Group (USA) LLC, Penguin Canada Books, Inc. and The Wylie Agency LLC. "Borges and I" from *A Personal Anthology*, copyright © 1967 by Grove Press. Used by permission of Grove/Atlantic, Inc. Any third-party use of this material, outside of this publication, is prohibited.

Tadeusz Borowski: "This Way for the Gas, Ladies and Gentlemen" from *This Way for the Gas, Ladies and Gentlemen* by Tadeusz Borowski, translated by Barbara Vedder, copyright © 1959 by Maria Borowski. Translation copyright © 1967 by Penguin Books Ltd. Used by permission of Viking Penguin, a division of Penguin Group (USA) Inc. and Penguin Group (UK).

T. Coraghessan Boyle: "Birnam Wood" from *T.C. Boyle Stories II: The Collected Stories of T. Coraghessan Boyle* by T. Coraghessan Boyle, copyright © 2013 by T. Coraghessan Boyle. Used by permission of Viking Penguin, a division of Penguin Group (USA) LLC.

Ray Bradbury: "There Will Come Soft Rains" published in *Collier's* May 6, 1950. Copyright © 1950 by the Crowell Collier Publishing Company, renewed 1977 by Ray Bradbury. Reprinted by permission of Don Congdon Associates, Inc.

Matthew C. Brennan: "Plotting Against Chekhov: Joyce Carol Oates and 'The Lady with the Dog'" from *Notes on Modern American Literature*, Winter 1985. Item 13. Copyright © 1985 Matthew C. Brennan. Reprinted by permission of the author.

Cleanth Brooks and Robert Penn Warren: Excerpt from *Understanding Fiction* 3rd Edition, © 1943, pp. 202–205. Reprinted by permission of Pearson Education, Inc., Upper Saddle River, NJ.

Keith E. Byerman: "Words and Music: Narrative Ambiguity in 'Sonny's Blues'" from *Studies in Short Fiction* 19 (1982: 367–72). Reprinted by permission of the author.

Albert Camus: "The Guest" from *Exile and the Kingdom* by Albert Camus, translated by Justin O'Brien, copyright © 1957, 1958 by Alfred A. Knopf, a division of Random House, LLC. Used by permission of Alfred A. Knopf, an imprint of the Knopf Doubleday Publishing Group, a division of Random House LLC. All rights reserved. Any third-party use of this material, outside of this publication, is prohibited. Interested parties must apply directly to Random House LLC for permission.

Alejo Carpentier: "Journey to the Seed" by Alejo Carpentier, translated by Jean Franco, reprinted by permission of Fundación Alejo Carpentier. "On the Marvelous Real in America" by Alejo Carpentier, (pages 77–88) and "The Baroque and the Marvelous Real" (pages 89–108) translated by Tanya Huntington and Lois Parkinson Zamora, in *Magical Realism*, edited by Lois Parkinson Zamora and Wendy B. Farris, Copyright, 1995, Duke University Press. All rights reserved. Republished by permission of the copyright holder. www.dukeupress.edu.

Angela Carter: "The Kiss" from *Saints and Strangers* by Angela Carter, copyright © 1985, 1986 by Angela Carter. Used by permission of Viking Penguin, a division of Penguin Group (USA) LLC and The Estate of Angela Carter c/o Rogers, Coleridge & White Ltd., 20 Powis Mews, London W11 1JN.

Raymond Carver: "A Small, Good Thing" and "Cathedral" from *Cathedral* by Raymond Carver, copyright © 1981, 1982, 1983 by Raymond Carver. "What We Talk About When We Talk About Love" from *What We Talk About When We Talk About Love: Stories* by Raymond Carver, copyright © 1974, 1976, 1978, 1980, 1981 by Raymond Carver. "The Bath," copyright © 1981 by Raymond Carver; from *What We Talk About When We Talk About Love: Stories* by Raymond Carver. All used by permission of Alfred A. Knopf, an imprint of the Knopf Doubleday Publishing Group, a division of Random House LLC. All rights reserved. Any third-party use of this material, outside of this publication, is prohibited. Interested parties must apply directly to Random House LLC for permission. Electronic permission granted by The Wylie Agency LLC. "On Writing" from *Fires: Essays, Poems, Stories* by Raymond Carver. Copyright © 1968, 1969, 1970, 1971, 1972, 1973, 1974, 1975, 1976, 1977, 1978, 1979, 1980, 1981, 1982, 1983 by Raymond Carver. Copyright © 1983, 1984 by the Estate of Raymond Carver. Used by permission of The Wylie Agency LLC. Foreword by Raymond Carver to *On Becoming a Novelist* by John Gardner copyright © 1983 by Raymond Carver. Reprinted by permission of HarperCollins Publishers.

Ann Charters: "Translating Kafka" from *Literature and Its Writers: A Compact Introduction, Third Edition* by Ann Charters. Reprinted by permission from Bedford/St. Martin's.

John Cheever: "The Swimmer" from *The Stories of John Cheever* by John Cheever, copyright © 1978 by John Cheever. Used by permission of Alfred A. Knopf, an imprint of the Knopf Doubleday Publishing Group, a division of Random House LLC. All rights reserved. Any third-party use of this material, outside of this publication, is prohibited. Interested parties must apply directly to Random House LLC for permission. "Why I Write Short Stories" by John Cheever, originally appeared in *Newsweek*. Copyright © 1978 by John Cheever, renewed in 2000 by Mary W. Cheever, used by permission of The Wylie Agency LLC.

Anton Chekhov: "The Lady with the Little Dog" translation copyright © 2000 by Richard Pevear and Larissa Volokhonsky, from *The Selected Short Stories of Anton Chekhov* by Anton Chekhov. Used by permission of Bantam Books, an imprint of The Random House Publishing Company, a division of Random House LLC. All rights reserved. Any third-party use of this material, outside of this publication, is prohibited. Interested parties must apply directly to Random House LLC for permission.

Sandra Cisneros: "Barbie-Q" from *Woman Hollering Creek* by Sandra Cisneros. Copyright © 1991 by Sandra Cisneros. Published by Vintage Books, a division of Random House Inc. and originally in hardcover by Random House Inc. By permission of Susan Bergholz Literary Services, New York, NY and Lamy, NM. All rights reserved.

Julio Cortázar: "Axolotl" copyright © 1967 by Random House LLC; from *End of the Game and Other Stories* by Julio Cortázar. Used by permission of Pantheon Books, an imprint of the Knopf Doubleday Publishing Group, a division of Random House LLC. All rights reserved. Any third-party use of this material, outside of this publication, is prohibited. Interested parties must apply directly to Random House LLC for permission.

Edwidge Danticat: "Night Women" from *Krik? Krak!*, copyright © 1991, 1995 by Edwidge Danticat. Reprinted by permission of Soho Press. All rights reserved.

Lydia Davis: "Blind Date" from *The Collected Stories of Lydia Davis*, copyright © 2009 by Lydia Davis. Reprinted by permission of Farrar, Straus & Giroux, LLC.

Junot Díaz: "How to Date a Browngirl, Blackgirl, Whitegirl, or Halfie" from *Drown* by Junot Díaz, copyright © 1996 by Junot Díaz. Used by permission of Riverhead Books, an imprint of Penguin Group (USA) LLC.

Larry Eigner: "Act" from *Country/Harbor/Quite/Act/Around: Selected Prose* by Larry Eigner. © 1978 by Larry Eigner. Published by This Press. Reprinted by permission of the Estate of Larry Eigner.

Ralph Ellison: "Battle Royal" copyright © 1948 and renewed 1976 by Ralph Ellison; from *Invisible Man* by Ralph Ellison. "The Influence of Folklore on 'Battle Royal'" from *Shadow and Act* by Ralph Ellison, copyright © 1953, 1964 and renewed 1981, 1992 by Ralph Ellison. Both used by permission of Random House, an imprint and division of Random House LLC. All rights reserved. Any third-party use of this material, outside of this publication, is prohibited. Interested parties must apply directly to Random House LLC for permission.

Richard Ellmann: "A Biographical Perspective on Joyce's 'The Dead'" from *James Joyce: New and Revised Edition* by Richard Ellmann. Copyright © 1982 by Richard Ellmann. Used by permission of Oxford University Press.

Nathan Englander: "What We Talk About When We Talk About Anne Frank" from *What We Talk About When We Talk About Anne Frank: Stories* by Nathan Englander, copyright © 2012 by Nathan Englander. Used by permission of Alfred A. Knopf, an imprint of the Knopf Doubleday Publishing Group, a division of Random House LLC. All rights reserved. Any third-party use of this material, outside of this publication, is prohibited. Interested parties must apply directly to Random House LLC for permission.

Louise Erdrich: "The Red Convertible" from *The Red Convertible: Selected and New Stories, 1978–2008* by Louise Erdrich. Copyright © 2009 by Louise Erdrich. Reprinted by permission of HarperCollins Publishers.

William Faulkner: "A Rose for Emily" copyright © 1930 and renewed 1958 by William Faulkner, "That Evening Sun" copyright © 1931 and renewed 1959 by William Faulkner, from *Collected Stories of William Faulkner* by William Faulkner. Used by permission of Random House, an imprint and division of Random House LLC. All rights reserved. Any third-party use of this material, outside of this publication, is prohibited. Interested parties must apply directly to Random House LLC for permission. Electronic rights to "That Evening Sun" granted by permission of W. W. Norton & Company. Excerpt from *Faulkner in the University*, Frederick L. Gwynn and Joseph L. Blotner, editors © 1995 by the Rector and Visitors of the University of Virginia. Reprinted by permission of the University of Virginia Press.

Richard Ford: Excerpt from the Introduction "Why We Like Chekhov" from *The Essential Tales of Chekhov*, edited and with an Introduction by Richard Ford. Introduction copyright © 1998 by Richard Ford. Reprinted by permission of HarperCollins Publishers. Translations by Constance Garnett. Copyright 1919, © 1972 Macmillan Company.

Janet Frame: "Two Sheep" from *Prizes* by Janet Frame. Copyright © 2009 by Janet Frame Literary Trust. Originally appeared in *Snowman: Fables and Fantasies*, currently collected in *Prizes*. Used by permission of The Wylie Agency LLC.

Carlos Fuentes: "Pain" from *The Crystal Frontier* by Carlos Fuentes. Copyright © 1995 by Carlos Fuentes. Translation copyright © 1997 by Alfred J. MacAdam. Reprinted by permission of Farrar, Straus and Giroux, LLC. Excerpt from *The Buried Mirror* by Carlos Fuentes. Copyright © 1992 by Carlos Fuentes. Reprinted by permission of Houghton Mifflin Harcourt Publishing Company. All rights reserved.

Mary Gaitskill: "The Other Place" by Mary Gaitskill. Copyright © 2011 by Mary Gaitskill. Originally appeared in the *New Yorker*, used by permission of The Wylie Agency LLC.

Gabriel García Márquez: "A Very Old Man with Enormous Wings" from *Leaf Storm and Other Stories* by Gabriel García Márquez. Translated by Gregory Rabassa. Copyright © 1971 by Gabriel García Márquez. Reprinted by permission of HarperCollins Publishers. "Un señor muy viejo con unas alas enormes," *La increíble y triste historia de la cándida Eréndira y de su abuela desalmada* © Gabriel García Márquez, 1972. Reprinted by permission of Agencia Literaria Carmen Balcells S.A., Barcelona.

William H. Gass: "Excerpt from *The Tunnel*" by William H. Gass, copyright © 1995 by William H. Gass. Used by permission of Alfred A. Knopf, an imprint of the Knopf Doubleday Publishing

Group, a division of Random House LLC. All rights reserved. Any third-party use of this material, outside of this publication, is prohibited. Interested parties must apply directly to Random House LLC for permission. "The First Seven Years of the Boom" from *Latin American Literary Review*, XV: 29, January–June 1987. Reprinted by permission of *Latin American Literary Review*.

Dagoberto Gilb: "Love in L. A." from *The Magic of Blood* by Dagoberto Gilb is reprinted by permission of the author.

Sandra Gilbert and Susan Gubar: "A Feminist Reading of Gilman's 'The Yellow Wallpaper'" from *The Madwoman in the Attic*. Copyright © 1979. Reprinted by permission of Yale University Press.

Janice H. Harris: "Levels of Meaning in Lawrence's 'The Rocking-Horse Winner'" from *The Short Fiction of D.H. Lawrence* by Janice H. Harris. Copyright © 1984 by Rutgers, the State University. Reprinted by permission of Rutgers University Press.

Charles Hatfield: "Alternative Comics: Towards the Habit of Questioning" from *Alternative Comics: An Emerging Literature* by Charles Hatfield. Copyright © 2005. Reprinted by permission of the University Press of Mississippi.

Ernest Hemingway: "Hills Like White Elephants" reprinted with the permission of Scribner Publishing Group from *Men Without Women* by Ernest Hemingway. Copyright © 1927 by Charles Scribner's Sons. Copyright renewed 1955 by Ernest Hemingway. All rights reserved.

Shirley Jackson: "The Lottery" from *The Lottery and Other Stories* by Shirley Jackson. Copyright © 1948, 1949 by Shirley Jackson. Copyright renewed 1976, 1977 by Laurence Hyman, Barry Hyman, Mrs. Sarah Webster, and Mrs. Joanne Schnurer. Reprinted by permission of Farrar, Straus and Giroux, LLC. "Biography of a Story" copyright © 1968 by Stanley Edgar Hyman, from *Come Along With Me* by Shirley Jackson, edited by Stanley Edgar Hyman. Used by permission of Viking Penguin, a division of Penguin Group (USA) LLC.

Gustav Janouch: "Kafka's View of 'The Metamorphosis'" by Gustav Janouch, translated by Goronwy Rees, from *Conversations with Kafka*, copyright © 1968 by S. Fischer Verlag GMBH, translation copyright © 1971 S. Fischer Verlag GMBH. Reprinted by permission of New Directions Publishing Corp.

Tom Jenks: Excerpt from "The Origin of 'Cathedral'" by Tom Jenks from *Remembering Ray: A Composite Biography of Raymond Carver*, edited by William L. Stull and Maureen P. Carroll. Copyright © Tom Jenks. Reprinted by permission of Tom Jenks.

Ha Jin: "Saboteur" from *The Bridegroom: Stories* by Ha Jin, copyright © 2000 by Ha Jin. Used by permission of Pantheon Books, an imprint of the Knopf Doubleday Publishing Group, a division of Random House LLC. All rights reserved. Any third-party use of this material, outside of this publication, is prohibited. Interested parties must apply directly to Random House LLC for permission.

Denis Johnson: "Work" from *Jesus' Son* by Denis Johnson. Copyright © 1992 by Denis Johnson. Reprinted by permission of Farrar, Straus and Giroux, LLC.

Franz Kafka: "The Metamorphosis" and "A Hunger Artist" by Franz Kafka, translated by Ann Charters. Copyright © 2002 by Ann Charters. Reprinted by permission of the translator.

Etgar Keret: "Not Human Beings" from *The Girl on the Fridge* by Etgar Keret. Copyright © 1992, 1994 by Etgar Keret. English translation copyright © by Etgar Keret. Reprinted by permission of Farrar, Straus and Giroux, LLC.

Jamaica Kincaid: "Girl" from *At the Bottom of the River* by Jamaica Kincaid. Copyright © 1983 by Jamaica Kincaid. Reprinted by permission of Farrar, Straus and Giroux, LLC. "On 'Girl'" from "An Interview with Jamaica Kincaid" in *Face to Face: Interviews with Contemporary Novelists*, edited by Allan Vorda. Reprinted by permission of Texas A&M University Press.

Nora Krug: "Kamikaze" from *A Public Space* by Nora Krug. Reprinted by permission of the author.

Michael Kupperman: "Are Comics Serious Literature?" from *Tales Designed to Thrizzle, Volume One*. Reprinted by permission of Fantagraphics Books Inc.

Jhumpa Lahiri: "Interpreter of Maladies" from *Interpreter of Maladies* by Jhumpa Lahiri. Copyright © 1999 by Jhumpa Lahiri. Reproduced by permission of Houghton Mifflin Harcourt Publishing Company. All rights reserved.

Anne Lamott: "Finding Your Voice" from *Bird by Bird: Some Instructions on Writing and Life* by Anne Lamott, copyright © 1994 by Anne Lamott. Used by permission of Pantheon Books, an imprint of the Knopf Doubleday Publishing Group, a division of Random House LLC. All rights reserved. Any third-party use of this material, outside of this publication, is prohibited. Interested parties must apply directly to Random House LLC for permission.

D. H. Lawrence: "The Rocking-Horse Winner," copyright © 1933 by the Estate of D. H. Lawrence, renewed © 1961 by Angelo Ravagli and C. Montague Weekley, Executors of the Estate of Frieda Lawrence Ravagli, from *The Complete Short Stories of D. H. Lawrence* by D. H. Lawrence. Used by permission of Viking Penguin, a division of Penguin Group (USA) LLC.

Ursula K. Le Guin: "The Ones Who Walk Away from Omelas" copyright © 1973 by Ursula K. Le Guin. First appeared in *New Dimension* 3 in 1973 and then in *The Wind's Twelve Quarters*, published by HarperCollins in 1975. "The Scapegoat in Omelas" copyright © 1975 by Ursula K. Le Guin. First appeared in *The Wind's Twelve Quarters*, published by HarperCollins in 1975. Both reprinted by permission of Curtis Brown, Ltd. "Introduction" by Ursula K. Le Guin, copyright © 1989 by Ursula K. Le Guin, from *The Book of Fantasy* by Jorge Luis Borges, Silvina Ocampo, and Adolfo Bioy Casares (editors). Used by permission of Viking Penguin, a division of Penguin Group (USA) LLC, and Curtis Brown Ltd.

Louis Leal: "Magical Realism in Spanish American Literature," by Louis Leal, translated by Wendy Faris, in *Magical Realism*, Lois Parkinson Zamora and Wendy B. Faris, eds., pp. 119–24. Copyright 1995, Duke University Press. All rights reserved. Republished by permission of the copyright holder. www.dukeupress.edu.

Doris Lessing: "To Room 19" © Doris Lessing 1963. Reprinted by permission of Jonathan Clowes Ltd.

Simon Lewis: "Lahiri's Interpreter of Maladies" from *The Explicator*, Summer 2001 Vol 59 Issue 4, p. 219, by the University of South Carolina; Virginia Commonwealth University. Reproduced with permission of Heldref Publications, in the format republish in a book/textbook via Copyright Clearance.

Clarice Lispector: Elizabeth Bishop's translation of "The Smallest Woman in the World" by Clarice Lispector first appeared in *The Kenyon Review*, Summer 1964, Volume XXVI, Number 3. Copyright 1964 by Kenyon College. Translation copyright © 1964 by Elizabeth Bishop. Reprinted by permission of Farrar, Straus & Giroux, LLC. The story first appeared in book form in Clarice Lispector's collection *Laços De Familia*, copyright © 1960, which was published in the translation by Giovanni Pontiero under the title *Family Ties*, copyright © 1970 by the University of Texas Press. Reprinted by permission of the University of Texas Press. "The Smallest Woman in the World" by Clarice Lispector, translated by Elizabeth Bishop from *Prose* by Elizabeth Bishop. Copyright © 2011 by The Alice H. Methfessel Trust. Editor's Note and compilation copyright © 2011 by Lloyd Schwartz. Reprinted by permission of Farrar, Straus and Giroux, LLC.

Mario Vargas Llosa: Excerpt from *Letters to a Young Novelist* by Mario Vargas Llosa, translated by Natasha Wimmer. Translation copyright © 2002 by Natasha Wimmer. Reprinted by permission of Farrar, Straus and Giroux, LLC.

Bobbie Ann Mason: "Shiloh" from *Shiloh and Other Stories* by Bobbie Ann Mason. Copyright © 1982 by Bobbie Ann Mason. Reprinted by permission of International Creative Management, Inc.

Kenneth McClane: Introduction by Kenneth McClane to *You've Got to Read This: Contemporary American Writers Introduce Stories that Held Them in Awe*, edited by Ron Hansen and Jim Shepard, reprinted by permission of Kenneth McClane.

Dorothy Tuck McFarland: "On 'Good Country People'" from *Flannery O'Connor* by Dorothy Tuck McFarland. Reproduced with permission of Frederick Ungar via Copyright Clearance Center.

J. Hillis Miller: Excerpt from "Who is He? Melville's Bartleby the Scrivener" in *Versions of Pygmalion* by J. Hillis Miller, Cambridge, Mass: Harvard University Press, Copyright © 1990 by the President and Fellows of Harvard College. Reprinted by permission of the publisher.

Steven Millhauser: "Flying Carpets" from *The Knife Thrower and Other Stories* by Steven Millhauser, copyright © 1998 by Steven Millhauser. Used by permission of Crown Books, an imprint of the

Flannery O'Connor by Flannery O'Connor, edited by Sally Fitzgerald. Copyright © 1979 by Regina O'Connor. Excerpts from "A Reasonable Use of the Unreasonable" and "Writing Short Stories" from *Mystery and Manners* by Flannery O'Connor, edited by Sally and Robert Fitzgerald. Copyright © 1969 by the Estate of Mary Flannery O'Connor. All reprinted by permission of Farrar, Straus and Giroux, LLC. "Good Country People" and "A Good Man Is Hard to Find" from *A Good Man Is Hard to Find and Other Stories*, copyright © 1955 by Flannery O'Connor and renewed 1983 by Regina O'Connor. Both reprinted by permission of Houghton Mifflin Harcourt Publishing Company.

Frank O'Connor: "Guests of the Nation" from *Collected Stories* by Frank O'Connor, copyright © 1981 by Harriet O'Donovan Sheehy, Executrix of the Estate of Frank O'Connor. Used by permission of Alfred A. Knopf, an imprint of the Knopf Doubleday Publishing Group, a division of Random House LLC. All rights reserved. Any third-party use of this material, outside of this publication, is prohibited. Interested parties must apply directly to Random House LLC for permission. Permission for Canada granted by The Jennifer Lyons Literary Agency, LLC for the Estate of Frank O'Connor. Excerpts from *The Lonely Voice: A Study of the Short Story* (Cleveland: World Publishing Company, 1963). Copyright © 1963 by Frank O'Connor. Reprinted with the permission of The Jennifer Lyons Literary Agency, LLC for the Estate of Frank O'Connor.

Tillie Olsen: "I Stand Here Ironing" is reprinted from *Tell Me a Riddle, Requa I, and Other Works* by Tillie Olsen by permission of the University of Nebraska Press. Copyright © 1961 by Tillie Olsen.

Daniel Orozco: "Orientation" from *Orientation* by Daniel Orozco. Copyright © 2011 by Daniel Orozco. Reprinted by permission of Farrar, Straus and Giroux, LLC. "On Steven Millhauser's 'Flying Carpets'" by Daniel Orozco from *Object Lessons: The Paris Review Presents the Art of the Short Story*, edited by Lorin Stein, Sadie Stein. Reprinted by permission of The Gernert Company.

Julie Otsuka: "The Children" from *The Buddha in the Attic* by Julie Otsuka, copyright © 2011 by Julie Otsuka, Inc. Used by permission of Alfred A. Knopf, an imprint of the Knopf Doubleday Publishing Group, a division of Random House LLC. All rights reserved. Any third-party use of this material, outside of this publication, is prohibited. Interested parties must apply directly to Random House LLC for permission.

Cynthia Ozick: "Let Me Finish" from *The Din in the Head: Essays* by Cynthia Ozick. Copyright © 2006 by Cynthia Ozick. Reprinted by permission of Houghton Mifflin Harcourt Publishing Company. All rights reserved. "The Shawl" from *The Shawl* by Cynthia Ozick, copyright © 1980, 1983 by Cynthia Ozick. Used by permission of Alfred A. Knopf, an imprint of the Knopf Doubleday Publishing Group, a division of Random House LLC. All rights reserved. Any third-party use of this material, outside of this publication, is prohibited. Interested parties must apply directly to Random House LLC for permission.

ZZ Packer: "Brownies" from *Drinking Coffee Elsewhere* by ZZ Packer, copyright © 2003 by ZZ Packer. Used by permission of Riverhead Books, an imprint of Penguin Group (USA) LLC.

Grace Paley: "Mother" from *Later the Same Day* by Grace Paley. Copyright © 1985 by Grace Paley. "A Conversation with My Father" and "Samuel" from *Enormous Changes at the Last Minute* by Grace Paley. Copyright © 1971, 1974 by Grace Paley. Both reprinted by permission of Farrar, Straus and Giroux, LLC. "A Conversation with Ann Charters" is reprinted by permission of Bedford/St. Martin's.

Jay Parini: "Lawrence and Steinbeck's 'Chrysanthemums'" from *John Steinbeck* by Jay Parini. Copyright © 1995 by Jay Parini. Reprinted by arrangement with Henry Holt and Company,

Octavio Paz: "My Life with the Wave" by Octavio Paz, translated by Eliot Weinberger, from *Eagle or Sun?*, copyright © 1976 by Octavio Paz and Eliot Weinberger. Reprinted by permission of New Directions Publishing Corp.

Sydney Plum: "Reading Marjane Satrapi's 'The Veil'" is reprinted by permission of the author.

Annie Proulx: "Job History" reprinted with the permission of Scribner, a Division of Simon & Schuster, Inc., from *Close Range: Wyoming Stories* by Annie Proulx. Copyright © 1999 by Dead Line Ltd. All rights reserved.

Jamie Quatro: "I.7 to Tennessee" from *I Want to Show You More*, copyright © 2013 by Jamie Quatro. Used by permission of Grove/Atlantic, Inc. Any third-party use of this material, outside of this publication, is prohibited.

Philip Roth: "The Conversion of the Jews" from *Goodbye Columbus* by Philip Roth. Copyright © 1959, and renewed 1987 by Philip Roth. Reprinted by permission of Houghton Mifflin Harcourt Publishing Company. All rights reserved.

Joe Sacco: "Some Reflections on Palestine" Fantagraphic Books, July 2007. Reprinted by permission of Fantagraphics Books, Inc. "Refugeeland" from *Palestine*, reprinted by permission of Fantagraphics Books, Inc.

Edward Said: "The Past and Present: Joseph Conrad and the Fiction of Autobiography" from *Joseph Conrad and the Fiction of Autobiography* by Edward W. Said. Copyright © 1966 by Edward W. Said. Reprinted by permission of Columbia University Press. "Introduction from *Palestine* entitled 'Homage to Joe Sacco'" by Edward Said. Copyright © 2002 by Edward Said. Used by permission of The Wylie Agency LLC.

Arthur M. Saltzmann: "A Reading of 'What We Talk About When We Talk About Love'" from *Understanding Raymond Carver* by Arthur M. Saltzmann. 1988. Reprinted by permission of the University of South Carolina Press.

Marjane Satrapi: Graphic novel excerpt from *Persepolis: The Story of a Childhood* by Marjane Satrapi, translation copyright © 2003 by L'Association, Paris, France. Used by permission of Pantheon Books, an imprint of the Knopf Doubleday Publishing Group, a division of Random House LLC. All rights reserved. Any third-party use of this material, outside of this publication, is prohibited. Interested parties must apply directly to Random House LLC for permission.

George Saunders: "Sticks" from *Tenth of December: Stories* by George Saunders, copyright © 2013 by George Saunders. Used by permission of Random House, an imprint and division of Random House LLC. All rights reserved. Any third party-use of this material, outside of this publication, is prohibited. Interested parties must apply directly to Random House LLC for permission.

Saïd Sayrafiezadeh: "A Brief Encounter with the Enemy" by Saïd Sayrafiezadeh was originally published in the *New Yorker*, January 16, 2012. Reprinted by permission of The Zoë Pagnamenta Agency.

A. O. Scott: "Looking for Raymond Carver" reprinted with permission from *The New York Review of Books*. Copyright © 1999 NYREV, Inc.

Elaine Showalter: Excerpt from *A Jury of Her Peers: American Women Writers from Anne Bradstreet to Annie Proulx* by Elaine Showalter, copyright © 2009 by Elaine Showalter. Used by permission of Alfred A. Knopf, an imprint of the Knopf Doubleday Publishing Group, a division of Random House LLC. All rights reserved. Any third-party use of this material, outside of this publication, is prohibited. Interested parties must apply directly to Random House LLC for permission.

Leslie Marmon Silko: "Yellow Woman" from *Storyteller* by Leslie Marmon Silko. Copyright © 1981, 2012 by Leslie Marmon Silko. Used by permission of Viking Penguin, a division of Penguin Group (USA) LLC. "Language and Literature from a Pueblo Indian Perspective" from *English Literature: Opening Up to Canon, Selected Papers from the English Institute* edited by Leslie A. Fiedler and Houston A. Baker, Jr. Reprinted by permission of The English Institute.

Art Spiegelman: "Prisoner on the Hell Planet: A Case History" copyright © 1972 by Art Spiegelman; from *The Complete Maus: A Survivor's Tale* by Art Spiegelman. Used by permission of Pantheon Books, an imprint of the Knopf Doubleday Publishing Group, a division of Random House, LLC. All rights reserved. Any third-party use of this material, outside of this publication, is prohibited. Interested parties must apply directly to Random House LLC for permission. Copyright (c) 1973, 1980, 1981, 1982, 1983, 1984, 1985, 1986 by Art Spiegelman, used by permission of The Wylie Agency LLC.

John Steinbeck: "The Chrysanthemums" copyright © 1937, renewed 1965 by John Steinbeck, from *The Long Valley* by John Steinbeck. Used by permission of Viking Penguin, a division of Penguin Group (USA) Inc.

1766   ACKNOWLEDGMENTS

Matt Steinglass: "Letter From Vietnam: Reading Tim O'Brien in Hanoi" from the *New York Times,*
April 4, 2010. Reprinted by permission of the author. Matt Steinglass, a correspondent for the
Financial Times, The Economist, and other publications, lives in the Netherlands.

Amy Tan: "Two Kinds" from *The Joy Luck Club* by Amy Tan, copyright © 1989 by Amy Tan. Used
by permission of G. P. Putnam's Sons, a division of Penguin Group (USA) LLC. "In the Canon,
for All the Wrong Reasons" copyright © 1996 by Amy Tan. First appeared in *The Threepenny
Review*. Reprinted by permission of the author and the Sandra Dijkstra Literary Agency.

Jean Toomer: "Blood-Burning Moon" from *Cane* by Jean Toomer. Copyright © 1923 by Boni & Liveright, renewed 1951 by Jean Toomer. Used by permission of Liveright Publishing Corporation.

John Updike: "A & P" from *Pigeon Feathers and Other Stories* by John Updike, copyright © 1962 and
renewed 1990 by John Updike. Used by permission of Alfred A. Knopf, a division of Random
House, Inc.

Luis Alberto Urrea: "Father Returns from the Mountain" from *Six Kinds of Sky* by Luis Alberto
Urrea. © 2002. "A Conversation with Luis Alberto Urrea" conducted by Margaret-Love Denman
and Barbara Shoup from *Story Matters: Contemporary Short Story Writers Share the Creative
Process* (Houghton Mifflin 2006). All reprinted by permission of Luis Alberto Urrea.

Helena María Viramontes: "Miss Clairol" by Helena Maria Viramontes. Reprinted from *Chicana
Creativity and Criticism*, edited by Maria Herrera-Sobek and Helena Viramontes. Copyright ©
1996 University of New Mexico Press, 1996.

Kurt Vonnegut, Jr.: "Harrison Bergeron" from *Welcome to the Monkey House* by Kurt Vonnegut, Jr.,
copyright © 1961 by Kurt Vonnegut Jr. Used by permission of Dell Publishing, an imprint of The
Random House Publishing Group, a division of Random House LLC. All rights reserved. Any
third-party use of this material, outside of this publication, is prohibited. Interested parties must
apply directly to Random House LLC for permission.

Alice Walker: "Everyday Use" from *In Love & Trouble: Stories of Black Women*, copyright © 1973 by
Alice Walker. Reprinted by permission of Houghton Mifflin Harcourt Publishing Company and
the Joy Harris Literary Agency, Inc. Foreword: "Zora Neale Hurston — A Cautionary Tale and
a Partisan View" by Alice Walker from *Zora Neale Hurston: A Literary Biography* by Robert E.
Hemenway. Copyright © 1977 by the Board of Trustees of the University of Illinois. Used with
permission of the author and the University of Illinois Press.

David Foster Wallace: "Everything Is Green" from *The Girl with Curious Hair* by David Foster
Wallace. Copyright © 1989 by David Foster Wallace. Used by permission of W. W. Norton &
Company, Inc.

Eudora Welty: "A Worn Path" from *A Curtain of Green and Other Stories*, copyright © 1941 and
renewed 1969 by Eudora Welty. Reprinted by permission of Houghton Mifflin Harcourt Publishing Company. "Is Phoenix Jackson's Grandson Really Dead?" from *The Eye of the Story* by
Eudora Welty. Copyright © 1978 by Eudora Welty. Used by permission of Random House, Inc.,
an imprint and a division of Random House LLC. All rights reserved. Any third-party use of this
material, outside of this publication, is prohibited. Interested parties must apply directly to Random House LLC for permission.

John Edgar Wideman: "newborn thrown in trash and dies" from *All Stories Are True* by John Edgar
Wideman, copyright © 1992 by John Edgar Wideman. Used by permission of Pantheon Books,
an imprint of the Knopf Doubleday Publishing Group, a division of Random House LLC. All
rights reserved. Any third-party use of this material, outside of this publication, is prohibited.
Interested parties must apply directly to Random House LLC for permission.

William Carlos Williams: "The Use of Force" from *The Collected Stories of William Carlos Williams*.
Copyright © 1938 by William Carlos Williams. Reprinted by permission of New Directions
Publishing Corp.

Tobias Wolff: "Say Yes" from *Back in the World* by Tobias Wolff. Copyright © 1981 by Tobias
Wolff. Used by permission of International Creative Management, Inc. All rights reserved.
"Bullet in the Brain" from *The Night in Question* by Tobias Wolff, copyright © 1996 by
Tobias Wolff. Used by permission of Alfred A. Knopf, an imprint of the Knopf Doubleday

Publishing Group, a division of Random House LLC. All rights reserved. Any third-party use of this material, outside of this publication, is prohibited. Interested parties must apply directly to Random House LLC for permission.

Richard Wright: "The Man Who Was Almost a Man" from *Eight Men* by Richard Wright. Copyright © 1940, 1961 by Richard Wright; renewed © 1989 by Ellen Wright. Introduction © by Paul Gilroy. Reprinted by permission of HarperCollins Publishers. Excerpt from *Black Boy* by Richard Wright. Copyright © 1937, 1942, 1944, 1945 by Richard Wright; renewed © 1973 by Ellen Wright. Reprinted by permission of HarperCollins Publishers, John Hawkins & Associates, Inc., and the Estate of Richard Wright.

Index of Authors and Titles